Robert Hayden, 1913–1980
Tillie Olsen, b. 1913
Muriel Rukeyser, 1913–1980
Karl Shapiro, b. 1913
Randall Jarrell, 1914–1965
Dudley Randall, b. 1914
Henry Reed, 1914–1986
William Stafford, 1914–1993
Dylan Thomas, 1914–1953
Tom Whitecloud, 1914–1972
Arthur Miller, b. 1915
P. K. Page, b. 1916
Gwendolyn Brooks, b. 1917
Al Purdy, b. 1918
Shirley Jackson, 1919–1965
May Swenson, 1919–1989
Amy Clampitt, 1920–1994
Richard Wilbur, b. 1921
James Dickey, 1923–1997
Denise Levertov, b. 1923
Edward Field, b. 1924
Brian W. Aldiss, b. 1925
Donald Justice, b. 1925
Maxine Kumin, b. 1925
Flannery O'Connor, 1925–1964
Gerald Stern, b. 1925
Allen Ginsberg, b. 1926
Margaret Laurence, 1926–1987
Frank O'Hara, 1926–1966
W. D. Snodgrass, b. 1926
David Wagoner, b. 1926
W. S. Merwin, b. 1927
Phyllis Webb, b. 1927
James Wright, 1927–1980
Maya Angelou, b. 1928
Donald Hall, b. 1928
Philip Levine, b. 1928
Cynthia Ozick, b. 1928
Anne Sexton, 1928–1974
X. J. Kennedy, b. 1929
Adrienne Rich, b. 1929
Etheridge Knight, 1931–1991
Alice Munro, b. 1931
Judith Viorst, b. 1931
Joanne Greenberg, b. 1932
Linda Pastan, b. 1932
Sylvia Plath, 1932–1963
John Updike, b. 1932
Imamu Amiri Baraka (LeRoi Jones), b. 1934
Leonard Cohen, b. 1934
Audre Lorde, 1934-1992
Marge Piercy, b. 1934
Sonia Sanchez, b. 1934
Mark Strand, b. 1934

Paul Zimmer, b. 1934
Betty Keller, b. 1935
Mary Oliver, b. 1935
Lucille Clifton, b. 1936
Andre Dubus, b. 1936
H. S. (Sam) Hamod, b. 1936
C. K. Williams, b. 1936
Marvin Bell, b. 1937
Michael S. Harper, b. 1938
Jack Hodgins, b. 1938
Virginia Scott, b. 1938
Margaret Atwood, b. 1939
Raymond Carver, 1939–1989
Seamus Heaney, b. 1939
Joseph Brodsky, 1940–1996
William Heyen, b. 1940
Billy Collins, b. 1941
Robert Hass, b. 1941
Gwendolyn MacEwen, 1941–1987
Simon Ortiz, b. 1941
Marilyn Hacker, b. 1942
Sharon Olds, b. 1942
Dave Smith, b. 1942
Michel Tremblay, b. 1942
Nikki Giovanni, b. 1943
Jim Northrup, b. 1943
Michael Ondaatje, b. 1943
James Tate, b. 1943
Peter Ulisse, b. 1944
Alice Walker, b. 1944
Joy Williams, b. 1944
Robert Olen Butler, b. 1945
Daniel Halpern, b. 1945
Carol Muske, b. 1945
Tim O'Brien, b. 1946
Maura Stanton, b. 1946
Jane Kenyon, 1947–1995
Alan Lightman, b. 1948
Leslie Marmon Silko, b. 1948
Gary Soto, b. 1948
Shelly Wagner, b. 1948
Katha Pollitt, b. 1949
Bruce Weigl, b. 1949
Carolyn Forché, b. 1950
Jorie Graham, b. 1951
Joy Harjo, b. 1951
Beth Henley, b. 1952
Amy Tan, b. 1952
Charles H. Webb, b. 1952
David Wojahn, b. 1953
Irene Zabytko, b. 1954
Cathy Song, b. 1955
Li-Young Lee, b. 1957
Lorrie Moore, b. 1957

LITERATURE

COMPACT
EDITION

LITERATURE

An Introduction to Reading and Writing

Edgar V. Roberts
Lehman College
The City University of New York

Henry E. Jacobs

PRENTICE HALL, Upper Saddle River, New Jersey 07458

The Library of Congress has catalogued the full edition of this work as follows:

Library of Congress Cataloging-in-Publication Data

Roberts, Edgar V.
   Literature : an introduction to reading and writing / Edgar
V. Roberts, Henry E. Jacobs. — 5th ed.
     p.   cm.
   Includes index.
   ISBN 0-13-263773-1 (case cover: alk. paper)
    1. Literature. 2. Exposition (Rhetoric) 3. Literature—
Collections. 4. College readers. 5. Report writing. I. Jacobs,
Henry E. II. Title.
   PN45.R575 1998
808´.0668—DC21   97-19366
                                        CIP

Editorial Director: Charlyce Jones Owen
Acquisitions Editor: Carrie Brandon
Development Editor-in-Chief: Susanna Lesan
Development Editor: Marlane Miriello
Director of Production and Manufacturing: Barbara Kittle
Senior Managing Editor: Bonnie Biller
Production Editor: Joan E. Foley
Copyeditor: Kathryn Graehl
Permissions Specialists: DK Research, Inc., and Yvonne Thrower
Editorial Assistant: Darla Landau
Manufacturing Manager: Nick Sklitsis
Prepress and Manufacturing Buyer: Mary Ann Gloriande
Marketing Director: Gina Sluss
Marketing Manager: Robert Mejia
Art Director: Jayne Conte
Cover Design: Bruce Kenselaar
Cover Art: Michael Busselle/Tony Stone Images
Photo Research: Eloise Donnelly and Carolyn Gauntt

This book was set in 10/12 Baskerville by Lithokraft II
and was printed and bound by the Courier Companies, Inc.
The cover was printed by Phoenix Color Corp.

 © 1998 by Prentice-Hall, Inc.
Simon & Schuster / A Viacom Company
Upper Saddle River, New Jersey 07458

For permission to use copyrighted material, grateful
acknowledgment is made to the copyright holders listed
on pages 1451–1459, which is considered an extension
of this copyright page.

Printed in the United States of America
10 9 8 7 6 5 4 3 2

ISBN   0-13-012123-1

Prentice-Hall International (UK) Limited, *London*
Prentice-Hall of Australia Pty. Limited, *Sydney*
Prentice-Hall Canada Inc., *Toronto*
Prentice-Hall Hispanoamerica, S.A., *Mexico*
Prentice-Hall of India Private Limited, *New Delhi*
Prentice-Hall of Japan, Inc., *Tokyo*
Simon & Schuster Asia Pte. Ltd., *Singapore*
Editora Prentice-Hall do Brasil, Ltda., *Rio de Janeiro*

Contents

READING AND WRITING ABOUT FICTION

7   TONE AND STYLE: THE WORDS THAT CONVEY ATTITUDES IN FICTION   268

8   SYMBOLISM AND ALLEGORY: KEYS TO EXTENDED MEANING   318

12   **WORDS: THE BUILDING BLOCKS OF POETRY**   **468**

15   TONE: THE CREATION OF ATTITUDE IN POETRY   543

17   FORM: THE SHAPE OF THE POEM   619

18   SYMBOLISM AND ALLUSION: WINDOWS TO A WIDE EXPANSE OF MEANING   657

READING AND WRITING ABOUT DRAMA

SPECIAL WRITING TOPICS ABOUT LITERATURE

Thematic
Table of Contents

For analytical purposes, the following alternative table of contents groups the selections into twenty-one separate thematic categories. The subject headings are advisory at best; they are *not* meant to dictate approaches or interpretations. Although many works belong naturally and easily within the niches we have provided, some of the works defy exclusive classification. We have accordingly assigned such works to two or more categories.

Because this table of contents is to be as brief as possible, we use only the last names of authors, eliminate most beginning definite and indefinite articles, and shorten most of the titles. Thus we refer to "*Thomas*, **Refusal to Mourn**," and to "*Shakespeare*, **That Time of Year**," and so on, using recognizable short titles whenever possible rather than the full titles that appear in the regular table of contents, the text itself, and the index. For authors with the same last name (e.g., Phyllis Webb, Charles H. Webb; C.K. Williams, Joy Williams, Tennessee Williams, William Carlos Williams), we supply the complete name.

CONFORMITY AND REBELLION

Stories

Poems

Plays

ENDINGS AND BEGINNINGS

Stories

Poems

Plays

FAITH AND DOUBT

Stories

Poems

Play

GOD AND HUMANITY

Stories

PARENTS AND CHILDREN

Stories

Poems

Plays

PAST AND PRESENT

Stories

Poems

Plays

RACE, ETHNICITY, AND NATIONALITY

Stories

Poems

YOUTH AND AGE

Preface to the Compact Edition

The compact edition of *Literature: An Introduction to Reading and Writing* is derived from the fifth edition. As in the full edition, the anthologized works are by American, British, and Canadian authors, but classical writers from ancient Greece and Rome are also represented, along with more recent writers who lived in or came from Norway, Belgium, Ceylon, Indonesia, and Russia. In total, 211 authors are represented, including anonymous writers. One hundred twenty-nine of the authors—roughly sixty-two per cent—were born after 1900. Interestingly, of the writers born since 1935, twenty-six are women and twenty-seven are men—a nearly equal number that dramatizes the contribution of women to modern literature. The book includes a total of 342 separate works. There are forty-two stories, 288 poems, and twelve plays. Each work is suitable for discussion either alone or in comparison. Fifty-three works are entirely new in the compact edition, including eleven stories and forty-two poems.

Readers will note that the eleven new stories are drawn exclusively from American and Canadian authors. Some are classic, like Poe, Bierce, and Cather, and some, such as Carver, O'Brien, Butler, Hodgins, and Laurence, are well on their way to becoming classic. The new stories by authors like these complement the thirty-one stories, such as those by Atwood, Faulkner, Crane, Hawthorne, Joyce, Gilman, Porter, and Welty, that were included in the regular fourth edition.

The forty-two new poems represent a wide variety of American, British, and Canadian poets. Most of these poets are widely recognized. Browning (Elizabeth Barrett), Herrick, Spender, and Whitman come readily to mind (there are five newly added poems by Whitman). More recent poets, most of them with multiple prizes and awards to their credit, are Clampitt, Graham, Hass, Heaney, Levertov, Levine, Olds, Oliver, Rich, Updike, and Wagoner. A poet new to the compact edition is Michael Ondaatje, who achieved wide recognition because of the many Academy awards received by the film version of his novel *The English Patient.* Even with these many new poems in the compact edition of *Literature: An Introduction to Reading and Writing*, the book still retains 246 poems that were in the regular fourth edition. Thus the anthology includes representative poems from late medieval times to our own day, including poets such as Shakespeare, Gray, Keats, Byron, Tennyson, Rossetti, Pound, and Eliot.

Although this is a compact edition that contains 100 fewer poems than the regular fifth edition, we include a poetic careers chapter featuring two poets—Dickinson and Frost. The compact edition contains twenty-five Dickinson poems and thirteen Frost poems—enough to enable students to gain a concentrated understanding of these two major poets.

A Brief Overview of the Compact Edition

The compact edition reaffirms a principle to which the book is dedicated—flexibility. Earlier editions have been used for introduction-to-literature courses, genre courses, and both composition and composition-and-literature courses. Adaptability and flexibility have been the keys to this variety. Instructors can use the book for classroom discussions, panel discussions, essay or paragraph-length assignments, and special topics not covered in class. Students will find incentives for understanding and writing about literature through questions, study and writing guides, and also through many suggestions for strengthening their own writing—both on essays and examinations.

FICTION.   The fiction section consists of nine chapters. Chapter 2 is a general introduction to fiction while Chapters 3–9,—the "topical" chapters—introduce students to such important topics as structure, character, point of view, and theme. Chapter 10 consists of seven stories for additional study.

POETRY.   The eleven poetry chapters are arranged similarly to the fiction chapters. Chapter 11 is introductory. Chapters 12–19 deal with topics such as symbolism, imagery, and myth. Chapter 20 is the poetic careers chapter, consisting of selections by Dickinson and Frost, and Chapter 21 contains 104 poems for additional study. In the appendix we include the biographies of each of the anthologized poets to make the poetry section parallel with the drama and fiction sections.

DRAMA.   In the drama section Chapter 22 is introductory. Chapters 23 and 24 concern tragedy and comedy. Concluding the drama section is Chapter 25, which contains three full-length plays for additional study (*A Dollhouse, Death of a Salesman,* and *The Glass Menagerie*).

Seven of the longer plays from the regular fifth edition have been kept in the compact edition because they are important in an introductory study of drama (*Oedipus the King, Hamlet, A Midsummer Night's Dream, Death of a Salesman, The Glass Menagerie, Mulatto, A Dollhouse*). In an anthology of this scope, the five short plays (*Am I Blue, The Bear, Before Breakfast, Tea Party,* and *Trifles*) are valuable because they may be covered in no more than one or two classroom hours, and also because they may be enlivened by having parts acted out by students. Indeed, Keller's *Tea Party* is brief enough to permit both reading and discussion in a single classroom period.

Additional Features

SPECIAL WRITING TOPICS.   In the fifth edition we have included a new section, titled "Special Writing Topics about Literature," which follows the drama section. This new section contains four chapters. These chapters were formerly appendices, but on the advice of many readers they are now an integral feature of the book. The chapters, which contain general literary assignments, are newly arranged to place emphasis on research and recent critical theories.

THE GLOSSARY.   In the introductory discussions to the various chapters, key terms and concepts are **boldfaced,** and these are gathered alphabetically and explained briefly, with relevant page numbers in the text, in the comprehensive glossary following the appendix. The terms in the glossary are also listed, with page number references, in the inside back cover. Because *Literature: An Introduction to Reading and Writing* may sometimes be used for reference, the glossary is intended not only for use within the book, but also for general use.

QUESTIONS.   Following each anthologized selection in the detailed chapters are study questions designed to help students in their exploration and understanding of literature. Some questions are factual and may be answered quickly. Others provoke extended thought and classroom discussion and may also serve for both in-class and out-of-class writing assignments. At the ends of twenty-two chapters we include a number of more general "Special Writing Topics for Studying" (Character, Symbolism, Tragedy, etc.). Many of these are comparison-contrast topics, and a number of them—at least one in each chapter—are assignments requiring creative writing (for example, "Write a poem" or "Compose a short scene"). What is unique about these topics is that students are asked not only to write creatively, but also to analyze their own creative processes. As already indicated, the compact edition, like the regular fifth edition, adds entirely new questions designed to add a research component to the study of the chapter topics.

DATES.   To place the various works in historical context, we include the life dates for all authors. For reference at a glance, all the authors are listed chronologically on the inside front cover (except for the three anonymous authors). Along with the title of each anthologized work we list the year of publication.

NUMBERING.   For convenient reference, we have adopted a regular style of numbering the selections by fives:

Stories: every fifth *paragraph*.

Poems: every fifth *line*.

Poetic plays: every fifth *line*, starting at *1* with each new scene and act.

Prose plays: every fifth *speech*, starting at *1* with each new scene and act.

GLOSSES.   For the poetry and poetic plays, we provide brief marginal glosses wherever they are needed. For all works, including poetry, we supply explanatory footnotes when necessary. Words and phrases that are glossed or footnoted are highlighted by a small degree sign (°). Footnotes are located according to line, paragraph, or speech numbers.

BOXED DISCUSSIONS WITHIN THE CHAPTERS.   In some of the chapters, particularly Chapters 1, 16, and 23, separately boxed sections contain brief discussions of a number of important and related matters. The topics chosen for this treatment—such as the use of tenses in discussing a work, the use of authorial names, the concept of decorum, and brief summaries of previous material—were based on the recommendations of instructors and students.

THEMATIC TABLE OF CONTENTS.   To make the compact edition of *Literature: An Introduction to Reading and Writing* as flexible as possible, we have continued the thematic table of contents that was first added in the regular fourth edition. In this listing, which is located immediately following the organizational contents, twenty-one thematic topics are provided, such as *Women and Men; Conformity and Rebellion; Women and Their Roles; Race, Ethnicity, and Nationality; Endings and Beginnings;* and *Innocence and Experience.* Under these topics, generous numbers of stories, poems, and plays are listed (many in a number of categories), so that entire thematic units may be created should instructors wish to use them.

FICTION AND DRAMATIZATION.   To strengthen the connection between fiction and dramatization, a number of stories are included that are available on videocassettes, which can be used as teaching tools for support and interpretation. A discussion of the videocassettes is included in the *Instructor's Manual.* In addition, we include two versions of the same subject matter for comparison—a short story and a one-act play by the same author—Susan Glaspell's "A Jury of Her Peers" (in the fiction section) and *Trifles* (in the drama section).

Revisions

There is little in this edition that has not been reexamined, revised, or rewritten. All the chapter introductions have been reorganized and strengthened. Particularly noteworthy are the introductions to the first two chapters on drama, which have been reworked significantly enough to justify calling them new. In all the chapters, the sections marked "Questions for Discovering Ideas" and "Strategies for Organizing Ideas" have also been revised and refocused with the goal of helping students concentrate on their writing assignments.

Writing and Reading

The compact edition of *Literature: An Introduction to Reading and Writing*, like all the previous editions, is dedicated throughout to the interlocking processes of writing and reading. There is no chapter in the book that does not contain essential information and guides for writing. Moreover, we do not simply say what *can* be done with a topic of literary study, but we also show ways in which it *might* be done. In most chapters a sample student essay exemplifies the strategies and methods brought out in the chapter. Following each essay is an analytical commentary showing how the writing principles of the discussion have been carried out. The emphasis throughout these sections is the openness of the writing process along with the unique nature of writing for each topic—while fully acknowledging the need to produce more polished drafts.

Because writing is a major mode of thinking, it is an essential reinforcement of reading. Students who write about what they read learn their assignments well. As they plan and develop their writing they necessarily grow as thinkers. Such a combined approach is the essential quality of the compact edition of *Literature: An Introduction to Reading and Writing*.

Reading and Writing Now and in the Future

The premise of this book is that the techniques students acquire in approaching literature as a reading-writing undertaking will help them in every course they may ever take, and in whatever profession they follow. Students will always *read*—if not the authors contained here, then other authors, and certainly newspapers, legal documents, magazine articles, technical reports, business proposals, and much more. Although students may never again be required to write about topics like setting, structure, or poetic rhythm, they will certainly find a future need to *write*.

Indeed, the more effectively students learn to write about literature when taking their literature courses, the better they will be able to write later on—no matter what the topic. It is undeniable that the power to analyze problems and make convincing written and oral presentations is a major quality of leadership and success in all fields. To acquire the skills of disciplined reading and strong writing is therefore the best possible preparation that students can make for the future, whatever it may hold.

While we stress the value of our book as a teaching tool, we also emphasize that literature is to be enjoyed and loved. Sometimes we neglect the truth that study and delight are complementary, and that intellectual stimulation and emotional enjoyment develop not only from the immediate responses of pleasure, involvement, and sympathy, but also from the understanding, contemplation, and confidence generated by knowledge and developing skill. We therefore hope that the selections in the compact edition of *Literature: An Introduction to Reading and Writing* will teach students about humanity, about their own perceptions, feelings, and lives, and about the timeless patterns of human existence. We hope they will take satisfaction in such discoveries and grow as they make them. We see the book as a steppingstone to lifelong understanding and joy in great literature.

ACKNOWLEDGMENTS

As the book goes into the compact edition, I wish to acknowledge the many people who have offered helpful advice, information, and suggestions. To name them, as Dryden says in *Absalom and Achitophel*, is to praise them. They are Professors Eileen Allman, David Bady, Rex Butt, Nancy Ellis, Alice Griffin, Robert Halli, Karen Holt, Claudia Johnson, Matthew Marino, Evan Matthews, Ruth Milberg-Kaye, Nancy Miller, Michael Paull, Dan Rubey, Scott Westrem, Mardi Valgemae, Matthew Winston, and Ruth Zerner, and also Christel Bell, Linda Bridgers, Catherine Davis, Jim Freund, Edward Hoeppner, Anna F. Jacobs, Eleanor Tubbs, Nanette Roberts, April Roberts, David Roberts, and Eve Zarin. The skilled assistance of Jonathan Roberts has been essential and invaluable at every stage of all the editions.

A number of other people have provided sterling guidance for the preparation of the compact edition. They are Professors Stanley Coberly, West Virginia University; Betty L. Dixon, Rancho Santiago College; Elizabeth Keats Flores, College of Lake County; Rebecca Heintz, Polk Community College; JoAnna Stephens Mink, Mankato State University; Ervin Nieves, Rutgers University, Newark; Bonnie Ronson, Hillsborough Community College; Margaret Ellen Sherwood, Devry Institute of Technology; Beverly J. Slaughter, Brevard Community College; Keith Walters, Lehman College; and Chloe Warner, Polk Community College.

I wish especially to thank Carrie Brandon, English Editor at Prentice Hall, and Maggie Barbieri and Nancy Perry, former Editors of this book. Their understanding, creativity, and cheerfulness have made working with them the greatest of pleasures. I also thank Phil Miller, President, Humanities, and Alison Reeves, Kate Morgan Jackson, Bill Oliver, and Paul O'Connell, earlier Prentice Hall English Editors, for their imagination and foresight, and also for their patience with me and support of me over the years. Of major importance was the work of Ray Mullaney, Editor-in-Chief, Development, for his pioneering work with the text and for his continued interest and support. I am deeply grateful to Marlane Miriello, development editor of the compact edition, for the insight and intelligence of her many suggestions for improvement, chapter by chapter. In addition I thank Viqi Wagner and Kathryn Graehl, both of whom leave me in awe because of their combination of knowledge, insight, and care; and Mary Comstock and Becky Rolfe. I am also deeply indebted to Anne Marie Welsh, Arts Critic of the San Diego *Union-Tribune*, for her thoughtful and constructive reading of chapters in the drama section. Special words of thanks are reserved for Joan Foley of Prentice Hall, our production editor, who has devoted her knowledge, intelligence, diligence, and skill to the many tasks needed to bring a book of this size to fruition. Additional thanks are due to Diane Kraut for her work on securing permissions. I also extend my gratitude to Rob Mejia, Senior Marketing Manager, and to Bonnie Biller, Senior Managing Editor. I give final thanks to Gina Sluss of Prentice Hall for her constant support and enthusiasm.

My sorrow is undiminished for the loss of my associate, Professor Henry E. Jacobs (1946–1986) of the University of Alabama. His energy and creativity were essential in planning and writing the first edition. All later editions are in effect extended collaborations, even though the current volume is different in many details from what we would have presented together.

EDGAR V. ROBERTS

LITERATURE

Introduction: Reading, Responding to, and Writing about Literature

WHAT IS LITERATURE, AND WHY DO WE STUDY IT?

Although the word **literature** broadly includes just about everything written, we use the word more specifically to refer to compositions that tell stories, dramatize situations, express emotions, and analyze and advocate ideas. Before the invention of writing thousands of years ago, literary works were necessarily spoken or sung, and were retained only as long as living people continued to repeat them. In some societies, the oral tradition of literature still exists, with many poems and stories designed exclusively for spoken delivery. Even in our modern age of writing and printing, much literature is still heard aloud rather than read silently. Parents delight their children with stories and poems; poets and story writers read their works directly before live audiences; plays and scripts are interpreted on stages and before moving-picture cameras for the benefit of a vast public.

No matter how we assimilate literature, we gain much from it. In truth, readers often cannot explain why they enjoy reading, for goals and ideals are not easily articulated. There are, however, areas of general agreement about the value of systematic and extensive reading.

Literature helps us grow, both personally and intellectually. It provides an objective base for knowledge and understanding. It links us with the cultural, philosophic, and religious world of which we are a part. It enables us to recognize human dreams and struggles in different places and times we otherwise would never know existed. It helps us develop mature sensibility and compassion for the condition of *all* living things—human, animal, and vegetable. It gives us the knowledge and perception to appreciate the beauty of order and arrangement, just as a well-structured song or a beautifully painted canvas can. It provides the comparative basis from which to see worthiness in the aims of all people, and it therefore helps us see beauty in the world around us. It exercises our emotions through interest, concern, sympathy, tension, excitement, regret, fear, laughter, and hope. It encourages us to assist creative and talented people who need recognition and support. Through our cumulative experience in reading, literature shapes our goals and values by clarifying our own identities—both positively, through acceptance of the admirable in human beings, and negatively, through rejection of the sinister. It enables us to develop perspectives on events occurring locally and globally, and thereby it gives us understanding and control. It is one of the shaping influences of life. It makes us human.

TYPES OF LITERATURE: THE GENRES

Literature may be classified into four categories or **genres:** (1) prose fiction, (2) poetry, (3) drama, and (4) nonfiction prose. Usually the first three are classed as **imaginative literature.**

The genres of imaginative literature have much in common, but they also have distinguishing characteristics. **Prose fiction,** or **narrative fiction,** includes **myths, parables, romances**, **novels**, and **short stories**. Originally, *fiction* meant anything made up, crafted, or shaped, but today the word refers to prose stories based in the author's imagination. The essence of fiction is **narration,** the relating or recounting of a sequence of events or actions. Works of fiction usually focus on one or a few major characters who change and grow (in their ability to make decisions, awareness and insight, attitude toward others, sensitivity, and moral capacity) as a result of how they deal with other characters and how they attempt to solve their problems. While fiction, like all imaginative literature, may introduce true historical details, it is not real history. Its main purpose is to interest, stimulate, instruct, and divert, not to create a precise historical record.

Poetry expresses a monologue or a conversation grounded in the most deeply felt experiences of human beings. It exists in many formal and informal shapes, from the brief **haiku** to the extensive **epic.** More economical than prose fiction in its use of words, poetry relies heavily on **imagery, figurative language,** and **sound.**

Drama is literature designed to be performed by actors for the benefit and delight of an audience. Like fiction, drama may focus on a single character or a small number of characters; and it enacts fictional events as if they were happening in the present. The audience therefore becomes a direct witness to the events as they occur, from start to finish. Although most modern plays use prose dialogue, on the principle that the language of drama should resemble the language of ordinary persons as much as possible, many plays from the past, such as those of ancient Greece and Renaissance England, are in poetic form.

Nonfiction prose consists of news reports, feature articles, essays, editorials, textbooks, historical and biographical works, and the like, all of which describe or interpret facts and present judgments and opinions. In nonfiction prose the goal is to present truths and conclusions about the factual world of history, science, and current events. Imaginative literature, while also grounded in facts, is less concerned with the factual record than with the revelation of truths about life and human nature.

READING LITERATURE
AND RESPONDING TO IT ACTIVELY

Regrettably, our first readings do not provide us with full understanding. After we complete a work, we may find it embarrassingly difficult to answer pointed questions or to say anything intelligent about it. But more active and thoughtful readings give us the understanding to develop well-considered answers. Obviously, we need to follow the work and understand its details, but just as importantly, we need to respond to the words, get at the ideas, and understand the implications of what is happening. We rely on our own fund of knowledge and experience to verify the accuracy and truth of situations and incidents, and we try to articulate our own emotional responses to the characters.

To illustrate such active responding, the following story, "The Necklace" (1884), by the French writer Guy de Maupassant,[1] is printed with marginal annotations like those that any reader might make during original and follow-up readings. Many observations, particularly at the beginning, are *assimilative;* that is, they do little more than record details about the action. But as the story progresses, the comments reflect conclusions about the story's meaning. Toward the end, the comments are full rather than minimal; they result not only from first responses, but also from considered thought. Here, then, is Maupassant's "The Necklace."

GUY DE MAUPASSANT   (1850–1893)

The Necklace ———————————————————————— *1884*

Translated by Edgar V. Roberts

She was one of those pretty and charming women, born, as if by an error of destiny, into a family of clerks and copyists. She had no dowry, no prospects, no way of getting known, courted, loved, married by a rich and distinguished man. She finally settled for a marriage with a minor clerk in the Ministry of Education.

> "She" is pretty but poor. Apparently there is no other life for her than marriage. Without connections, she has no entry into high society, and she marries an insignificant clerk.

---

[1] Maupassant, an apostle of Gustave Flaubert, was one of the major nineteenth-century French naturalists. He was an especially careful writer, devoting great attention to reality and economy of detail. His stories focus on the difficulties and ironies of existence among not only the Parisian middle class, as in "The Necklace," but also among both peasants and higher society. Two of his better-known novels are *A Life* (1883) and *A Good Friend* (1885). Among his other famous stories are "The Rendezvous" and "The Umbrella." "The Necklace" is notable for its concluding ironic twist, and for this reason it is perhaps the best known of his stories.

She was a simple person, without the money to dress well, but she was as unhappy as if she had gone through bankruptcy, for women have neither rank nor race. In place of high birth or important family connections, they can rely only on their beauty, their grace, and their charm. Their inborn finesse, their elegant taste, their engaging personalities, which are their only power, make working-class women the equals of the grandest ladies.

She is unhappy.

A view of women that excludes the possibility of a career. In 1884, women had little else than their personalities to get ahead.

She suffered constantly, feeling herself destined for all delicacies and luxuries. She suffered because of her grim apartment with its drab walls, threadbare furniture, ugly curtains. All such things, which most other women in her situation would not even have noticed, tortured her and filled her with despair. The sight of the young country girl who did her simple housework awakened in her only a sense of desolation and lost hopes. She daydreamed of large, silent anterooms, decorated with oriental tapestries and lighted by high bronze floor lamps, with two elegant valets in short culottes dozing in large armchairs under the effects of forced-air heaters. She imagined large drawing rooms draped in the most expensive silks, with fine end tables on which were placed knickknacks of inestimable value. She dreamed of the perfume of dainty private rooms, which were designed only for intimate tête-à-têtes with the closest friends, who because of their achievements and fame would make her the envy of all other women.

She suffers because of her cheap belongings, wanting expensive things. She dreams of wealth and of how other women would envy her if she had all these fine things. But these luxuries are unrealistic and unattainable for her.

When she sat down to dinner at her round little table covered with a cloth that had not been washed for three days, in front of her husband who opened the kettle while declaring ecstatically, "Ah, good old boiled beef! I don't know anything better," she dreamed of expensive banquets with shining place settings, and wall hangings portraying ancient heroes and exotic birds in an enchanted forest. She imagined a gourmet-prepared main course carried on the most exquisite trays and served on the most beautiful dishes, with whispered gallantries which she would hear with a sphinxlike smile as she dined on the pink meat of a trout or the delicate wing of a quail.

Her husband's taste is for plain things, while she dreams of expensive gourmet food. He has adjusted to his status. She has not.

5   She had no decent dresses, no jewels, nothing. And she loved nothing but these; she believed herself born only for these. She burned with the desire to please, to be envied, to be attractive and sought after.

She lives for her unrealistic dreams, and these increase her frustration.

She had a rich friend, a comrade from convent days, whom she did not want to see anymore because she suffered so much when she returned home. She would weep for the entire day afterward with sorrow, regret, despair, and misery.

She even thinks of giving up a rich friend because she is so depressed after visiting her.

Well, one evening, her husband came home glowing and carrying a large envelope.

"Here," he said, "this is something for you."

A new section in the story.

She quickly tore open the envelope and took out a card
engraved with these words:

> The CHANCELLOR OF EDUCATION *and*
> MRS. GEORGE RAMPONNEAU
> *request that*
> MR. AND MRS. LOISEL
> *do them the honor of coming to dinner*
> *at the Ministry of Education*
> *on the evening of January 8.*

An invitation to dinner at
the Ministry of Education.
A big plum.

10   Instead of being delighted, as her husband had hoped,
she threw the invitation spitefully on the table, muttering:
"What do you expect me to do with this?"

It only upsets her.

"But honey, I thought you'd be glad. You never get to go
out, and this is a special occasion! I had a lot of trouble getting
the invitation. Everyone wants one. The demand is high and
not many clerks get invited. Everyone important will be there."
She looked at him angrily and stated impatiently:
"What do you expect me to wear to go there?"

She declares that she
hasn't anything to wear.

15   He had not thought of that. He stammered:
"But your theater dress. That seems nice to me . . ."

He tries to persuade her
that her theater dress
might do for the occasion.

He stopped, amazed and bewildered, as his wife began
to cry. Large tears fell slowly from the corners of her eyes to
her mouth. He said falteringly:
"What's wrong? What's the matter?"
But with a strong effort she had recovered, and she
answered calmly as she wiped her damp cheeks:
20   "Nothing, except that I have nothing to wear and therefore can't go to the party. Give your invitation to someone else
at the office whose wife will have nicer clothes than mine."
Distressed, he responded:
"Well, all right, Mathilde. How much would a new dress
cost, something you could use at other times, but not anything
fancy?"

Her name is Mathilde.

He volunteers to pay for a
new dress.

She thought for a few moments, adding things up and
thinking also of an amount that she could ask without getting
an immediate refusal and a frightened outcry from the frugal
clerk.

She is manipulating him.

Finally she responded tentatively:
25   "I don't know exactly, but it seems to me that I could get
by on four hundred francs."
He blanched slightly at this, because he had set aside just
that amount to buy a shotgun for Sunday lark-hunts the next
summer with a few friends in the Plain of Nanterre.

The dress will cost him his
next summer's vacation.
(He doesn't seem to have
included her in his plans.)

However, he said:

"All right, you've got four hundred francs, but make it a pretty dress."

As the day of the party drew near, Mrs. Loisel seemed sad, uneasy, anxious, even though her gown was all ready. One evening her husband said to her:

30   "What's the matter? You've been acting funny for several days."

She answered:

"It's awful, but I don't have any jewels to wear, not a single gem, nothing to dress up my outfit. I'll look like a beggar. I'd almost rather not go to the party."

He responded:

"You can wear a corsage of cut flowers. This year it's all the rage. For only ten francs you can get two or three gorgeous roses."

35   She was not convinced.

"No . . . there's nothing more humiliating than looking shabby in the company of rich women."

But her husband exclaimed:

"God, but you're silly! Go to your friend Mrs. Forrestier, and ask her to lend you some jewelry. You know her well enough to do that."

She uttered a cry of joy:

40   "That's right. I hadn't thought of that."

The next day she went to her friend's house and described her problem.

Mrs. Forrestier went to her mirrored wardrobe, took out a large jewel box, opened it, and said to Mrs. Loisel:

"Choose, my dear."

She saw bracelets, then a pearl necklace, then a Venetian cross of finely worked gold and gems. She tried on the jewelry in front of a mirror, and hesitated, unable to make up her mind about each one. She kept asking:

45   "Do you have anything else?"

"Certainly. Look to your heart's content. I don't know what you'd like best."

Suddenly she found a superb diamond necklace in a black satin box, and her heart throbbed with desire for it. Her hands shook as she picked it up. She fastened it around her neck, watched it gleam at her throat, and looked at herself ecstatically.

Then she asked, haltingly and anxiously:

"Could you lend me this, nothing but this?"

50   "Why yes, certainly."

She jumped up, hugged her friend joyfully, then hurried away with her treasure.

Marginal notes:

A new section, the third in the story. The day of the party is near.

Now she complains that she doesn't have any nice jewelry. She is manipulating him again.

She has a good point, but there seems to be no way out.

He proposes a solution: borrow jewelry from Mrs. Forrestier, who is apparently the rich friend mentioned earlier.

Mathilde will have her choice of jewels.

A "superb" diamond necklace.

This is what she wants, just this.

She leaves with the "treasure."

The day of the party came. Mrs. Loisel was a success. She was prettier than anyone else, stylish, graceful, smiling and wild with joy. All the men saw her, asked her name, sought to be introduced. All the important administrators stood in line to waltz with her. The Chancellor himself eyed her.

She danced joyfully, passionately, intoxicated with pleasure, thinking of nothing but the moment, in the triumph of her beauty, in the glory of her success, on cloud nine with happiness made up of all the admiration, of all the aroused desire, of this victory so complete and so sweet to the heart of any woman.

She did not leave until four o'clock in the morning. Her husband, since midnight, had been sleeping in a little empty room with three other men whose wives had also been enjoying themselves.

55 He threw, over her shoulders, the shawl that he had brought for the trip home—a modest everyday wrap, the poverty of which contrasted sharply with the elegance of her evening gown. She felt it and hurried away to avoid being noticed by the other women who luxuriated in rich furs.

Loisel tried to hold her back:

"Wait a minute. You'll catch cold outdoors. I'll call a cab."

But she paid no attention and hurried down the stairs. When they reached the street they found no carriages. They began to look for one, shouting at cabmen passing by at a distance.

They walked toward the Seine, desperate, shivering. Finally, on a quay, they found one of those old night-going buggies that are seen in Paris only after dark, as if they were ashamed of their wretched appearance in daylight.

60 It took them to their door, on the Street of Martyrs, and they sadly climbed the stairs to their flat. For her, it was finished. As for him, he could think only that he had to begin work at the Ministry of Education at ten o'clock.

She took the shawl off her shoulders, in front of the mirror, to see herself once more in her glory. But suddenly she cried out. The necklace was no longer around her neck!

Her husband, already half undressed, asked:

"What's wrong?"

She turned toward him frantically:

65 "I . . . I . . . I no longer have Mrs. Forrestier's necklace."

He stood up, bewildered:

"What? . . . How? . . . It's not possible!"

And they looked in the folds of the gown, in the folds of the shawl, in the pockets, everywhere. They found nothing.

He asked:

70 "You're sure you still had it when you left the party?"

A new section.

The Party. Mathilde is a huge success.

Another judgment about women. Does the author mean that only women want to be admired? Don't men want admiration, too?

Loisel, with other husbands, is bored, while the wives are having a ball.

Ashamed of her shabby wrap, she rushes away to avoid being seen.

A comedown after the nice evening. They take a wretched-looking buggy home.

"Street of Martyrs." Is this name significant?

Loisel is down-to-earth.

She has lost the necklace!

They can't find it.

"Yes. I checked it in the vestibule of the Ministry."

"But if you'd lost it in the street, we would've heard it fall. It must be in the cab."

"Yes, probably. Did you notice the number?"

"No. Did you see it?"

75   "No."

Overwhelmed, they looked at each other. Finally, Loisel got dressed again:

"I'm going out to retrace all our steps," he said, "to see if I can find the necklace that way."

And he went out. She stayed in her evening dress, without the energy to get ready for bed, stretched out in a chair, drained of strength and thought.

> He goes out to search for the necklace.

Her husband came back at about seven o'clock. He had found nothing.

> But is unsuccessful.

80   He went to Police Headquarters and to the newspapers to announce a reward. He went to the small cab companies, and finally he followed up even the slightest hopeful lead.

> He really tries. He's doing his best.

She waited the entire day, in the same enervated state, in the face of this frightful disaster.

Loisel came back in the evening, his face pale and haggard. He had found nothing.

"You'll have to write to your friend," he said, "that you broke a clasp on her necklace and that you're having it fixed. That'll give us time to look around."

> Loisel's plan to explain delaying the return. He takes charge, is resourceful.

She wrote as he dictated.

85   At the end of a week they had lost all hope.

> Things are hopeless.

And Loisel, looking five years older, declared:

"We'll have to see about replacing the jewels."

The next day they took the case which had contained the necklace and went to the jeweler whose name was inside. He looked at his books:

> They hunt for a replacement.

"I wasn't the one, Madam, who sold the necklace. I only made the case."

90   Then they went from jeweler to jeweler, searching for a necklace like the other one, racking their memories, both of them sick with worry and anguish.

In a shop in the Palais-Royal, they found a necklace of diamonds that seemed to them exactly like the one they were looking for. It was priced at forty thousand francs. They could buy it for thirty-six thousand.

> A new diamond necklace will cost 36,000 francs, a monumental amount.

They got the jeweler to promise not to sell it for three days. And they made an agreement that he would buy it back for thirty-four thousand francs if the original was recovered before the end of February.

> They make a deal with the jeweler. (Is Maupassant hinting that things might work out for them?)

Loisel had saved eighteen thousand francs that his father had left him. He would have to borrow the rest.

> It will take all of Loisel's inheritance plus another

He borrowed, asking a thousand francs from one, five hundred from another, five louis° here, three louis there. He wrote promissory notes, undertook ruinous obligations, did business with finance companies and the whole tribe of loan sharks. He compromised himself for the remainder of his days, risked his signature without knowing whether he would be able to honor it, and, terrified by anguish over the future, by the black misery that was about to descend on him, by the prospect of all kinds of physical deprivations and moral tortures, he went to get the new necklace, and put down thirty-six thousand francs on the jeweler's counter.

> 18,000 francs that must be borrowed at enormous rates of interest.

95 Mrs. Loisel took the necklace back to Mrs. Forrestier, who said with an offended tone:

"You should have brought it back sooner; I might have needed it."

> Mrs. Forrestier complains about the delay.

She did not open the case, as her friend feared she might. If she had noticed the substitution, what would she have thought? What would she have said? Would she not have taken her for a thief?

> Is this enough justification for not telling the truth? It seems to be for the Loisels.

Mrs. Loisel soon discovered the horrible life of the needy. She did her share, however, completely, heroically. That horrifying debt had to be paid. She would pay. They dismissed the maid; they changed their address; they rented an attic flat.

> A new section, the fifth.

She learned to do the heavy housework, dirty kitchen jobs. She washed the dishes, wearing away her manicured fingernails on greasy pots and encrusted baking dishes. She hand-washed dirty linen, shirts, and dish towels that she hung out on the line to dry. Each morning, she took the garbage down to the street, and she carried up water, stopping at each floor to catch her breath. And, dressed in cheap house dresses, she went to the fruit dealer, the grocer, the butchers, with her basket under her arms, haggling, insulting, defending her measly cash penny by penny.

> They suffer to repay their debts. Loisel works late at night. Mathilde accepts a cheap attic flat, and does all the heavy housework herself to save on domestic help.
>
> She pinches pennies, and haggles with the local tradesmen.

100 They had to make installment payments every month, and, to buy more time, to refinance loans.

> They struggle to meet payments.

The husband worked evenings to make fair copies of tradesmen's accounts, and late into the night he made copies at five cents a page.

> Mr. Loisel moonlights to make extra money.

And this life lasted ten years.

> For ten years they struggle, but they endure.

At the end of ten years, they had paid back everything—everything—including the extra charges imposed by loan sharks and the accumulation of compound interest.

> The last section. They have finally paid back the entire debt.

° *louis:* a gold coin worth twenty francs.

Mrs. Loisel looked old now. She had become the strong, hard, and rude woman of poor households. Her hair unkempt, with uneven skirts and rough, red hands, she spoke loudly, washed floors with large buckets of water. But sometimes, when her husband was at work, she sat down near the window, and she dreamed of that evening so long ago, of that party, where she had been so beautiful and so admired.

Mrs. Loisel (how come the narrator does not say "Mathilde"?) is roughened and aged by the work. But she has behaved "heroically" (¶ 98), and has shown her mettle.

105   What would life have been like if she had not lost that necklace? Who knows? Who knows? Life is so peculiar, so uncertain. How little a thing it takes to destroy you or to save you!

A moral? Our lives are shaped by small, uncertain things; we hang by a thread.

Well, one Sunday, when she had gone for a stroll along the Champs-Elysées to relax from the cares of the week, she suddenly noticed a woman walking with a child. It was Mrs. Forrestier, still youthful, still beautiful, still attractive.

A scene on the Champs-Elysées. She sees Jeanne Forrestier, after ten years.

Mrs. Loisel felt moved. Would she speak to her? Yes, certainly. And now that she had paid, she could tell all. Why not?

She walked closer.

"Hello, Jeanne."

110   The other gave no sign of recognition and was astonished to be addressed so familiarly by this working-class woman. She stammered:

They seem to have lost contact with each other totally during the last ten years. Would this have happened in real life?

"But . . . Madam! . . . I don't know . . . You must have made a mistake."

"No. I'm Mathilde Loisel."

Her friend cried out:

"Oh! . . . My poor Mathilde, you've changed so much."

Jeanne notes Mathilde's changed appearance.

115   "Yes. I've had some tough times since I saw you last; in fact, hardships . . . and all because of you! . . ."

"Of me . . . how so?"

"You remember the diamond necklace that you lent me to go to the party at the Ministry of Education?"

"Yes. What then?"

"Well, I lost it."

120   "How, since you gave it back to me?"

"I returned another exactly like it. And for ten years we've been paying for it. You understand that this wasn't easy for us, who have nothing. . . . Finally it's over, and I'm damned glad."

Mathilde tells Jeanne everything.

Mrs. Forrestier stopped her.

"You say that you bought a diamond necklace to replace mine?"

"Yes, you didn't notice it, eh? It was exactly like yours."

125   And she smiled with proud and childish joy.

Mrs. Forrestier, deeply moved, took both her hands.

"Oh, my poor Mathilde! But mine was only costume jewelry. At most, it was worth only five hundred francs! . . ."

*SURPRISE! The lost necklace was **not** real diamonds, and the Loisels slaved for no reason at all. But hard work and sacrifice probably brought out better qualities in Mathilde than she otherwise might have shown. Is this the moral of the story?*

READING AND RESPONDING IN A JOURNAL

The comments included alongside the story demonstrate the active reading-responding process you should apply to everything you read. Use the margins in your text to record your comments and questions, but, in addition, plan to keep a **journal** for lengthier responses. Your journal, which may consist of a notebook, notecards, separate sheets of paper, or a computer file, will be immeasurably useful to you as you move from your initial impressions toward more carefully considered thought.

In keeping your journal, your objective should be to learn assigned works inside and out and then to say perceptive things about them. To achieve this goal, you need to read the work more than once. You will need a good note-taking system so that as you read you can develop a "memory bank" of your own knowledge about a work. You can draw from this fund of ideas when you begin to write. As an aid in developing your own procedures for reading and "depositing" your ideas, you may wish to begin with the following *Guidelines for Reading*. Of course, you will want to modify these suggestions, and add to them, as you become a more experienced, disciplined reader.

GUIDELINES FOR READING

1. **Observations for Basic Understanding**
   a. Explain words, situations, and concepts. Write down words that are new to you or not immediately clear. If you find a passage that you do not quickly understand, try to discover whether the problem arises from unknown words. Use your dictionary and record the relevant meanings in your journal, and be sure that these meanings clarify your understanding. Make note of special difficulties so that you may ask your instructor about them.
   b. Determine what is happening. For a story or play, where do the actions take place? What do they show? Who is involved? Who is the major figure? Why is he or she major? What relationships do the characters have with one another? What concerns do the characters have? What do they do? Who says what to whom? How do the speeches advance the action and reveal the characters? For a poem, what is the situation? Who is talking, and to whom? What does the speaker say about the situation? Why does the poem end as it does and where it does?

2. **Notes on First Impressions**
   a. Make a record of your reactions and responses, which you may derive from your marginal notations. What did you think was memorable, noteworthy, funny, or otherwise striking? Did you worry, get scared, laugh, smile, feel a thrill, learn a great deal, feel proud, find a lot to think about? In your journal, record these responses and explain them more fully.
   b. Describe interesting characterizations, events, techniques, and ideas. If you like a character or idea, explain what you like, and do the same for

characters and ideas you don't like. Is there anything else in the work that you especially like or dislike? Are parts easy or difficult to understand? Why? Are there any surprises? What was your reaction to them? Be sure to use *your own* words when writing your explanations.

3. **Development of Ideas and Enlargement of Responses**

   a. Trace developing patterns. Make an outline or scheme: What conflicts appear? Do these conflicts exist between people, groups, or ideas? How does the author resolve them? Is one force, idea, or side the winner? Why? How do you respond to the winner, or loser?

   b. Write expanded notes about characters, situations, and actions. What explanations need to be made about the characters? Which actions, scenes, and situations invite interpretation? What assumptions do the characters and speakers reveal about life and humanity generally; about themselves, the people around them, their families, their friends; and about work, the economy, religion, politics, philosophy, and the state of the world and the universe? What manners or customs do they exhibit? What sort of language do they use? What literary conventions and devices have you noticed, and what do these contribute to the action and ideas of the story?

   c. Write a paragraph or several paragraphs describing your reactions and thoughts. If you have an assignment, your paragraphs may be useful later because you might transfer them directly as early drafts. Even if you are making only a general preparation, however, always write down your thoughts.

   d. Memorize interesting, well-written, and important passages. Use note cards to write them out in full, and keep them in your pocket or purse. When walking to class, riding public transportation, or otherwise not occupying your time, learn them by heart.

   e. Always write down questions that arise as you read. You may raise these in class, and they may also aid your own study.

Specimen Journal Entries

The following entries illustrate how you can use the guidelines in your first writing attempts. You should try to develop enough observations and responses to be useful later, both for additional study and for developing essays. Notice that the entries are not only comments, but also questions.

JOURNAL ENTRIES ON MAUPASSANT'S
"THE NECKLACE"

Early in the story, Mathilde seems spoiled. She is poor, or at least lower middle class, but is unable to face her own situation.

She is a dreamer and seems harmless. Her daydreams about a fancy home, with all the expensive belongings, are not unusual. Most people dream about being well off.

She is embarrassed by her husband's taste for plain food. The story contrasts her taste for trout and quail with Loisel's cheaper favorites.

When the Loisels get the invitation, Mathilde becomes especially difficult. Her wish for an expensive dress (the cost of Loisel's summer hunting weekends), and then her wanting the jewelry, are problems.

Her success at the party shows that she has the charm the storyteller talks about in paragraph 2. She seems never to have had any other chance to exert her power.

The worst part of her personality is shown when she hurries away from the party because she is ashamed of her everyday shawl. It is Mathilde's unhappiness and unwillingness to adjust to her modest means that cause the financial downfall of the Loisels. This disaster is her fault.

Borrowing the money to replace the necklace shows that both Loisel and Mathilde have a strong sense of honor. Making up for the loss is good, even if it destroys them financially.

There are some nice touches, like Loisel's seeming to be five years older (paragraph 86) and his staying with the other husbands of women enjoying themselves (paragraph 54). These are well done.

It's too bad that Loisel and Mathilde don't confess to Jeanne that the jewels are lost. Their pride or their honor stops them—or perhaps their fear of being accused of theft.

Their ten years of slavish work (paragraphs 98–102) show how they have come down in life. Mathilde does all her work by hand, so she really does pitch in and is, as the narrator says, heroic.

Mathilde becomes loud and frumpy when living in the attic flat (paragraph 99), but she also develops strength. She does what she has to. The earlier apartment and the elegance of her imaginary rooms had brought out her limitations.

The setting of the Champs-Elysées also reflects her character, for she feels free there to tell Jeanne about the disastrous loss and sacrifice (paragraph 121), producing the surprise ending.

The narrator's thought about "how little a thing it takes to destroy you or to save you" (paragraph 105) is full of thought. The necklace is little, but it makes a huge problem. This creates the story's irony.

Questions: Is this story more about the surprise ending or about the character of Mathilde? Is she to be condemned or admired? Does the outcome stem from the little things that make us or break us, as the narrator suggests; or from the difficulty of rising above one's economic class, which seems true; or both? What do the speaker's remarks about women's status mean? (Remember, the story was published in 1884.) This probably isn't relevant, but wouldn't Jeanne, after hearing about the substitution, give the full value of the necklace to the Loisels, and wouldn't they then be pretty well off?

These are reasonable, if fairly full, remarks and observations about "The Necklace." Use your journal similarly for *all* reading assignments. If your assignment is simply to learn about a work, general notes like these should be enough. If you are preparing for a test, you might write pointed observations more in line with what is happening in your class, and also write and answer your own questions (see Chapter 28, *Taking Examinations on Literature*). If you have a writing assignment, these entries can help you focus more closely on your topic—such as character, idea, or setting. Whatever your purpose, always use a journal when you read, and put into it as many details and responses as you can. Your journal will then be invaluable in helping you develop your ideas and refresh your memory.

WRITING ESSAYS ON LITERARY TOPICS

Writing is the sharpened, focused expression of thought and study. It begins with the search for something to say—an idea. Not all ideas are equal; some are better than others, and getting good ideas is an ability that you will develop the more you think and write. As you discover ideas and write them down, you will also improve your perceptions and increase your critical faculties.

In addition, because literature itself contains the subject material, though not in a systematic way, of philosophy, religion, psychology, sociology, and politics, learning to analyze literature and to write about it will also improve your capacity to deal with these and other disciplines.

At the outset, it is important to realize that writing is a process that begins in uncertainty and hesitation, and that becomes certain and confident only as a result of diligent thought and considerable care. When you read a complete, polished, well-formed piece of writing, you might believe at first that the writer wrote this perfect version in only one draft and never needed to make any changes and improvements in it at all. Nothing could be further from the truth.

If you could see the early drafts of writing you admire, you would be surprised and startled—and also encouraged—to see that good writers are also human, and that what they first write is often uncertain, vague, tangential, tentative, incomplete, and messy. Usually, they do not like these first drafts, but nevertheless they work with their efforts and build upon them: They discard some details, add others, chop paragraphs in half, reassemble the parts elsewhere, throw out much (and then maybe recover some of it), revise or completely rewrite sentences, change words, correct misspellings, and add new material to tie all the parts together and make them flow smoothly.

Three Major Stages of Thinking and Writing

For good and not-so-good writers alike, the writing task follows three basic stages. (1) The first—*discovering ideas*—shares many of the qualities of ordinary conversation. Usually, conversation is random and disorganized. It shifts from topic to topic, often without any apparent cause, and it is repetitive. In discovering ideas for writing, your process is much the same, for you jump from idea to idea and do not necessarily identify the connections or bridges between them. (2) By the second step—*creating an early, rough draft of a critical paper*—your thought should be less like ordinary conversation and more like classroom discussion. Such discussions generally stick to a point, but they are also free and spontaneous, and digressions often occur. (3) At the third stage—*preparing a finished essay*—your thinking must be sharply focused, and your writing must be organized, definite, concise, and connected.

If you find that trying to write an essay gets you into difficulties like false starts, dead ends, total cessation of thought, digressions, despair, hopelessness, and other such frustrations, remember that *it is important just to start.* Just write anything at all—no matter how unacceptable your first efforts may seem—and force yourself to come to grips with the material. Beginning to write does not commit you to your first ideas. They are not untouchable and holy just because they are on paper or on your computer screen. You may throw them out in favor of new ideas. You may also cross out words or move sections around, as you wish, but if you keep your first thoughts buried in your mind, you will have nothing to work with. It is essential to accept the uncertainties in the writing process and make them work *for* you rather than *against* you.

DISCOVERING IDEAS

You cannot know your own ideas fully until you write them down. Thus, the first thing to do in the writing process is to dig deeply into your mind and drag out all your responses and ideas about the story. Write anything and everything that occurs to you. Don't be embarrassed if your work does not look great at first; keep working toward improvement. If you have questions you can't answer, write them down and plan on answering them later. In your attempts to discover ideas, use the following prewriting techniques.

Brainstorming or Freewriting

Brainstorming or **freewriting** is an informal way to describe your own written but private no-holds-barred conversation with yourself. It is your first step in writing. When you begin freewriting you do not know what is going to happen, so you let your mind play over all the possibilities you generate as you consider the work, or a particular element of the work, or your own early responses to it. In effect, you are talking to yourself and writing down all your thoughts, whether they fall into patterns or seem disjointed, beside the point, or even foolish. At this time, do not try to organize or criticize your thoughts. Later you can decide which ideas to keep and which to throw out. For now, *the goal is to get all your ideas on paper or on the computer screen.* As you are developing your essay later on, you may, *at any time,* return to the brainstorming or freewriting process to initiate and develop new ideas.

Focusing on Specific Topics

DEVELOPING SUBJECTS FROM BRAINSTORMING AND NOTE TAKING.   Although the goal of brainstorming is to be totally free about the topics, you should recognize that you are trying to think creatively. You will therefore need to start directing your mind into specific channels. Once you start focusing on definite topics, your thinking, as we have noted, is analogous to classroom discussion. Let us assume that in freewriting you produce a topic that you find especially interesting. You might then start to focus on this topic and write as much as you can about it. The following examples from early thoughts about Maupassant's "The Necklace" show how a writer can zero in on such a topic—in this case, honor—once the word comes up in freewriting:

> Mathilde could have gone to her friend and told her she lost the necklace. But she didn't. Was she overcome with shame? Would she have felt a loss of honor by confessing the loss of the necklace?

> What is honor? Doing what you think you should even if you don't want to, or if it's hard? Or is it pride? Was Mathilde too proud or too honorable to tell her friend? Does having honor mean going a harder way, when either would probably be okay? Do you have to suffer to be honorable? Does pride or honor produce a choice for suffering?

> Mathilde wants others to envy her, to find her attractive. Later she tells Loisel that she would feel humiliated at the party with rich women unless she wore jewelry. Maybe she is more concerned about being admired than about the necklace. Having high self-esteem has something to do with honor, but more with pride.

> Duty. Is it the same as honor? Is it Mathilde's duty to work so hard? Certainly her pride causes her to do her duty and behave honorably, and therefore pride is a step toward honor.

> Honor is a major part of life, I think. It seems bigger than any one life or person. Honor is just an idea or feeling—can an idea of honor be larger than a life, take over someone's life? Should it?

These paragraphs do not represent finished writing, but they do demonstrate how a writer may attempt to define a term and determine the degree to which it applies to a major character or circumstance. Although the last item departs from the story, this digression is perfectly acceptable because in the freewriting stage, writers treat ideas as they arise. If the ideas amount to something, they may be used in the developing essay; and if they don't, they can be thrown away. The important principle in brainstorming is to record *all* ideas, with no initial concern about how they might seem to a reader. The results of freewriting are for the eyes of the writer only.

BUILDING ON YOUR ORIGINAL NOTES.   An essential way to focus your mind is to mine your journal notes for relevant topics. For example, let us assume that you have made an original note on "The Necklace" about the importance of the attic flat to which Mathilde and her husband move in order to save money. With this note as a start, you can develop a number of ideas, as in the following:

> The attic flat is important. Before, in her apartment, Mathilde was dreamy and impractical. She was delicate, but after losing the necklace, no way. She becomes a worker when in the flat. She can do a lot more now.
>
> M. gives up her servant, climbs stairs carrying buckets of water, washes greasy pots, throws water around to clean floors, does all the wash by hand.
>
> While she gets stronger, she also gets loud and frumpy—argues with shop-keepers to get the lowest prices. She stops caring for herself. A reversal here, from incapable and well groomed to coarse but capable. All this change happens in the attic flat.

Notice that even a brief original note can help you discover thoughts that you did not originally have. This act of stretching your mind leads you to put elements of the story together in ways that create support for ideas that you can use to build good essays. Even in an assertion as basic as "The attic flat is important," the process itself, which is a form of concentrated thought, leads you creatively forward.

RAISING AND ANSWERING QUESTIONS.   A major way to discover ideas about a work is to raise and answer questions as you read. The *Guidelines for Reading* (p. 11) will help you formulate questions, but you may also raise specific questions like these (assuming that you are considering a story):

- What explanations are needed for the characters? Which actions, scenes, and situations invite interpretation? Why?
- What assumptions do the characters and speakers reveal about life and humanity generally, about themselves, the people around them, their families, their friends; and about work, the economy, religion, politics, and the state of the world?
- What are their manners or customs?
- What kinds of words do they use: formal or informal words, slang or profanity?
- What literary conventions and devices have you discovered, and how do these add to the work? (When an author addresses readers directly, for example, that is a **convention;** when a comparison is used, that is a **device,** which might be either a **metaphor** or a **simile.**)

Of course you may raise other questions as you reread the piece, or you may be left with one or two major questions that you decide to pursue.

USING THE PLUS-MINUS, PRO-CON, OR EITHER-OR METHOD.   A common method of discovering ideas is to develop a set of contrasts: plus-minus, pro-con, either-or. Let us use a plus-minus method of considering the character of Mathilde in "The Necklace": Should she be admired (plus) or condemned (minus)?

PLUS: ADMIRED?

MINUS: CONDEMNED?

PLUS: ADMIRED?	MINUS: CONDEMNED?
After she cries when they get the invitation, she recovers with a "strong effort"—maybe she doesn't want her husband to feel bad.	She wants to be envied and admired only for being attractive (end of first part), not for more important qualities.
She really scores a great victory at the dance. She does have the power to charm and captivate.	She wastes her time in daydreaming about things she can't have and whines because she is unhappy.
Once she loses the necklace, she and her husband become impoverished. But she does "her share . . . completely, heroically" (paragraph 98) to make up for the loss.	She manipulates her husband into giving her a lot of money for a party dress, but they live poorly.
Even when she is poor, she still dreams about that marvelous, shining moment. She gets worse than she deserves.	She assumes that her friend would think she was a thief if she knew she was returning a different necklace. Shouldn't she have had more confidence in the friend?
At the end, she confesses the loss to her friend.	She becomes loud and coarse and haggles about pennies, thus undergoing a total cheapening of her character.

Once you begin putting contrasting ideas side by side, new discoveries will occur to you. Filling the columns almost demands that you list as many contrasting positions as you can, and that you think about how material in the work supports each position. It is in this way that true, genuine thinking takes place.

Your notes will therefore be useful regardless of how you finally organize your essay. You may develop either column in a full essay, or you might use your notes to support the idea that Mathilde is too complex to be wholly admired or condemned. You might even introduce an entirely new idea, such as that Mathilde should be pitied rather than condemned or admired. In short, arranging materials in the plus-minus pattern is a powerful way to discover ideas you can develop in directions that you might not otherwise find.

TRACING DEVELOPING PATTERNS.   You can also discover ideas by making a list or scheme for the story or main idea. What conflicts appear? Do these conflicts exist between people, groups, or ideas? How does the author resolve them? Is one force, idea, or side the winner? Why? How do you respond to the winner, or loser?

Using this method, you might make a list similar to this one:

Beginning: M. is a fish out of water. She dreams of wealth, but her life is drab and her husband is ordinary.

Fantasies make her even more dissatisfied—punishes herself by thinking of a wealthy life.

Her character relates to the places in the story: the Street of Martyrs, the dinner party scene, the attic flat. Also the places she dreams of—she fills them with the most expensive things she can imagine.

They get the dinner invitation—she pouts and whines. Her husband feels discomfort, but she doesn't really harm him. She manipulates him into buying her an expensive party dress, though.

Her dream world hurts her real life when her desire for wealth causes her to borrow the necklace. Losing the necklace is just plain bad luck.

The attic flat brings out her potential coarseness. But she also develops a spirit of sacrifice and cooperation. She loses, but she's really a winner.

These observations all focus on Mathilde's character, but you may wish to trace other patterns you find in the story. If you start planning an essay about another pattern, be sure to account for all the actions and scenes that relate to your topic. Otherwise, you may miss a piece of evidence that can lead you to new conclusions.

THINKING BY WRITING. No matter what method of discovering ideas you use, it is important to realize that *unwritten thought is incomplete thought.* Make a practice of writing notes about your reactions and any questions that occur to you. Very likely they will lead you to the most startling discoveries you will make about a work.

DRAFTING YOUR ESSAY

As you use the brainstorming and focusing techniques for discovering ideas, you are also beginning to draft your essay. You will need to revise your ideas as connections among them become more clear, and as you reexamine the work for support for the ideas you are developing, but you already have many of the raw materials you need for developing your topic.

Creating a Central Idea

By definition, an essay is *a fully developed and organized set of paragraphs that develop and enlarge a central idea.* All parts of an essay should contribute to the reader's understanding of the idea. To achieve unity and completeness, each paragraph refers to the central idea and demonstrates how selected details from the work relate to it and support it. The central idea will help you control and shape your essay, and it will provide guidance for your reader.

A successful essay about literature is a brief but thorough (not exhaustive) examination of a literary work in light of a particular element, such as *character, point of view,* or *symbolism.* Typical central ideas might be (1) that a character is strong and tenacious, or (2) that the point of view makes the action seem "distant and objective," or (3) that a major symbol governs the actions and thoughts of the major characters. In essays on these topics, all points must be tied to such central ideas. Thus, it is a fact that Mathilde Loisel in "The Necklace" endures ten years of slavish work and sacrifice. This fact is not relevant to an essay on her character, however, unless you connect it by showing how it demonstrates one of her major traits—in this case, her growing strength or her perseverance.

Look through all of your ideas for one or two that catch your eye for development. If you have used more than one prewriting technique, the chances are that you have already discovered at least a few ideas that are more thought-provoking or more important than the others.

WRITING BY HAND, TYPEWRITER, OR WORD PROCESSOR

It is important for you to realize that writing is an inseparable part of thinking and that unwritten thought is incomplete thought.

Because thinking and writing are so interdependent, it is essential to get ideas into a visible form so that you may develop them further. For many students, it is psychologically necessary to carry out this process by writing down ideas by hand or by typewriter. If you are one of these students, make your written or typed responses on only one side of your paper or note cards. This will enable you to spread your materials out and get a physical overview of them when you begin writing. Everything will be open to you; none of your ideas will be hidden on the back of the paper.

Today, word processing is thoroughly established as an indispensable tool for writers. The word processor can help you develop ideas, for it enables you to eliminate unworkable thoughts and replace them with others. You can move sentences and paragraphs tentatively into new contexts, test how they look, and move them somewhere else if you choose.

In addition, with the rapid printers available today, you can print drafts even in the initial and tentative stages of writing. Using your printed draft, you can make notes, marginal corrections, and suggestions for further development. With the marked-up draft for guidance, you can go back to your word processor and fill in your changes and improvements, and you can repeat this procedure as often as you like. This facility makes the machine an additional incentive for improvement, right up to your final draft.

Word processing also helps you in the final preparation of your essays. Studies have shown that errors and awkward sentences are frequently found at the bottoms of pages prepared by hand or with a conventional typewriter. The reason is that writers hesitate to make improvements when they get near the end of a page because they shun the dreariness of starting the page over. Word processors eliminate this difficulty completely. Changes can be made anywhere in the draft, at any time, without damage to the appearance of the final draft.

Regardless of your writing method, it is important to realize that *unwritten thought is incomplete thought.* Even with the word processor's screen, you cannot lay everything out at once. You can see only a small part of what you are writing. Therefore, somewhere in your writing process, you need to prepare a complete draft of what you have written. A clean, readable draft permits you to gather everything together and to make even more improvements through the act of revision.

Once you choose an idea that you think you can work with, write it as a complete sentence. A *complete sentence* is important: A simple phrase, such as "setting and character," does not focus thought the way a sentence does. A sentence moves the topic toward new exploration and discovery because it combines a topic with an outcome, such as "The setting of 'The Necklace' reflects Mathilde's character." You may choose to be even more specific: "Mathilde's strengths and weaknesses are reflected in the real and imaginary places in 'The Necklace.'"

With a single, central idea for your essay, you have a standard for accepting, rejecting, rearranging, and changing the ideas you have been developing. You may now draft a few paragraphs to see whether your idea seems valid, or you may decide that it would be more helpful to make an outline or list before you attempt to support your ideas in a rough draft. In either case, you should use your notes for evidence to connect to your central idea. If you need more ideas, use any of the brainstorming-prewriting techniques to discover them. If you need to bolster your argument by including more details that are relevant, jot them down as you reread the work.

Using the central idea that *changes in the story's settings reflect Mathilde's character* might produce a discovery paragraph like the following, which stresses Mathilde's negative qualities:

> The original apartment in the Street of Martyrs and the dream world of wealthy places both show negative sides of Mathilde's character. The real-life apartment, though livable, is shabby. The furnishings all bring out her discontent. The shabbiness makes her think only of luxury, and her one servant girl causes her to dream of having many servants. The luxury of her dream life heightens her unhappiness with what she actually has.

Even in such a discovery draft, however, where the purpose is to write initial thoughts about the central idea, many details from the story are used in support. In the final draft, this kind of support is absolutely essential.

Creating a Thesis Sentence

With your central idea as a guide, you can now decide which of your earlier observations and ideas to develop further. Your goal is to establish a number of major topics to support the central idea, and to express them in a **thesis sentence**—an organizing sentence that plans or forecasts the major topics you will treat in your essay. Suppose you choose three ideas from your discovery stage of development. If you put the central idea at the left and the list of topics at the right, you have the shape of the thesis sentence. Note that the first two topics have been taken from the discovery paragraph.

CENTRAL IDEA	*TOPICS*
The setting of "The Necklace" reflects Mathilde's character.	1. Real-life apartment
	2. Dream surroundings
	3. Attic flat

This arrangement leads to the following thesis statement:

> Mathilde's character growth is related to her first apartment, her dream-life mansion rooms, and her attic flat.

You can revise the thesis statement at any stage of the writing process if you find you do not have enough evidence from the work to support it. Perhaps a new topic will occur to you, and you can include it, appropriately, as a part of your thesis sentence.

As we have seen, the central idea is the glue of the essay. The thesis sentence *lists the parts to be fastened together*—that is, the topics in which the central idea is to be demonstrated and argued. To alert your readers to your essay's structure, you will usually place the thesis sentence at the end of the introductory paragraph, just before the body of the essay begins.

WRITING A FIRST DRAFT

To write a first draft, you support the points of your thesis statement with your notes and discovery materials. You may alter, reject, and rearrange ideas and details as you wish, as long as you also alter your thesis sentence to account for the changes (a major reason why most writers write their introductions last). The thesis statement above contains three topics (it could be two, or four, or more) to be used in forming the body of the essay.

BEGIN WITH YOUR TOPIC SENTENCE.   Just as the organization of the entire essay is based on the thesis, the form of each paragraph is based on its **topic sentence.** A topic sentence is an assertion about how a topic from the predicate of the thesis statement supports the central idea. The first topic in our example is the relationship of Mathilde's character to her first apartment, and the resulting paragraph should emphasize this relationship. If you choose to discuss the coarsening of her character during the ten-year travail, you can then form a topic sentence by connecting the trait with the location, as follows:

> The attic flat reflects the coarsening of Mathilde's character.

Beginning with this sentence, the paragraph can show how Mathilde's rough, heavy housework has a direct effect on her behavior, appearance, and general outlook.

DEVELOP NO MORE THAN ONE TOPIC IN EACH PARAGRAPH.   Usually you should treat each separate topic in a single paragraph. However, if a topic seems especially difficult, long, or heavily detailed, you may divide it into two or more subtopics, each receiving a separate paragraph of its own. Should you make this division, your topic then is really a section, and each paragraph in the section should have its own topic sentence.

USING THE PRESENT TENSE OF VERBS
WHEN REFERRING TO ACTIONS AND IDEAS

Literary works spring into life with each and every reading. Thus, when writing about literature you may assume that everything happening takes place in the present, and you should use the *present tense of verbs*. It is correct to say, "Mathilde and her husband *work* and *economize* (not *worked* and *economized*) for ten years to pay off the 18,000-franc debt they *undertake* [not *undertook*] to pay for the lost necklace."

When you consider an author's ideas, the present tense is also proper, on the principle that the words of an author are just as alive and current today (and tomorrow) as they were at the moment of writing, even if the author has been dead for hundreds or even thousands of years.

Because it is incorrect to shift tenses inappropriately, you may encounter problems when you want to refer to actions that occurred prior to the time of the main action. An instance is Hemingway's "Soldier's Home," in which the main character is discontented and unsettled as a result of his combat experiences in Europe during World War I. In such a situation it is important to keep details in order, and thus you may use the past tense as long as you make the relationship clear between past and present, as in this example: "Krebs *cannot settle down* [present tense] because he *is always thinking* [present tense] about the actions he *went through* [past tense] during the fighting in Europe." This use of the past and present tenses is acceptable because it corresponds to the cause-and-effect relationship brought out in the story.

A problem also arises when you introduce historical or biographical details about a work or an author. It is appropriate to use the *past tense* for such details as long as they actually do belong to the past. Thus it is correct to state, "Shakespeare *lived* from 1564 to 1616," or "Shakespeare *wrote Hamlet* in about 1599–1600." It is also permissible to mix past and present tenses when you are treating historical facts about a literary work and also considering it as a living text. Of prime importance is to keep things straight. Here is an example showing how past and present tenses can be used appropriately:

> Because *Hamlet was* first *performed* in about 1600, Shakespeare most probably *wrote* it shortly before this time. In the play, a tragedy, Shakespeare *treats* an act of vengeance, but more importantly he *demonstrates* the difficulty of ever learning the exact truth. The hero, Prince Hamlet, *is* the focus of this difficulty, for the task of revenge *is assigned* to him by the Ghost of his father. Though the Ghost *claims* that his brother, Claudius, *is* his murderer, Hamlet *is* not able to verify this claim.

Here, the historical details are in the past tense, while all details about the play *Hamlet*, including Shakespeare as the creating author whose ideas and words are still alive, are in the present.

As a general principle, you will be right most of the time if you use the present tense exclusively for literary details and the past tense for historical details. When in doubt, however, *consult your instructor*.

USE THE TOPIC SENTENCE TO DEVELOP A PARAGRAPH. Once you choose your thesis sentence, you can use it to focus your observations and conclusions.

Let us see how our topic about the attic flat can be developed as a paragraph:

The attic flat reflects the coarsening of Mathilde's character. Maupassant empha-sizes the burdens Mathilde endures to save money, such as mopping floors, clean-ing greasy and encrusted pots and pans, taking out the garbage, and handwashing clothes and dishes. This work makes her rough and coarse, an effect that is height-ened by her giving up care of her hair and hands, wearing the cheapest dresses possible, and becoming loud and penny-pinching in haggling with the local shop-keepers. If at the beginning she is delicate and attractive, at the end she is unpleas-ant and coarse.

Notice that details from the story are introduced to provide support for the topic sentence. All the subjects—the hard work, the lack of personal care, the wearing of cheap dresses, and the haggling with the shopkeepers—are intro-duced not to retell the story but rather to exemplify the claim the writer is making about the coarsening of Mathilde's character.

Developing an Outline

So far we have been developing an *outline*—that is, a skeletal plan of organization for your essay. Some writers never use formal outlines at all, pre-ferring to make informal lists of ideas, while others rely on them constantly. Still other writers insist that they cannot make outlines until they have finished their essays. Regardless of your preference, *your finished essay should have a tight structure.* Therefore, you should create a guiding outline to develop or to shape your essay.

The outline we have been developing here is an **analytical sentence out-line.** This type is easier to create than it sounds. It consists of (1) an *introduc-tion,* including the central idea and the thesis sentence, together with (2) *topic sentences* that are to be used in each paragraph of the body, followed by (3) a *conclusion.*

When applied to the subject we have been developing, such an outline looks like this:

Title: *How Setting in "The Necklace" Is Related to the Character of Mathilde*

1. **Introduction**
   a. *Central idea:* Maupassant uses his setting to show Mathilde's character.
   b. *Thesis statement:* Her character growth is related to her first apartment, her daydreams about elegant rooms in a mansion, and her attic flat.
2. **Body:** *Topic sentences* a, b, and c (and d, e, f, if necessary)
   a. Details about her first apartment explain her dissatisfaction and depression.
   b. Her daydreams about mansion rooms are like the apartment because they too make her unhappy.
   c. The attic flat reflects the coarsening of her character.

3. **Conclusion**

> *Topic sentence:* All details in the story, particularly the setting, are focused on the character of Mathilde.

The *conclusion* may be a summary of the body; it may evaluate the main idea; it may briefly suggest further points of discussion; or it may be a reflection on the details of the body.

Using the Outline

The sample essays included throughout this book are organized according to the principles of the analytical sentence outline. To emphasize the shaping effect of these outlines, all central ideas, thesis sentences, and topic sentences are underlined. In your own writing, you may underline or italicize these "skeletal" sentences as a check on your organization. Unless your instructor requires such markings, however, remove them in your final drafts.

SAMPLE STUDENT ESSAY, FIRST DRAFT

The following sample essay is a first draft of the topic we have been developing. It follows the outline presented above and includes details from the story in support of the various topics. It is by no means, however, as good a piece of writing as it could be. The draft omits a topic, some additional details, and some new insights that are included in the final draft (pp. 35–36). It therefore reveals that the writer needs to make improvements through additional brainstorming and discovery-prewriting techniques.

How Setting in "The Necklace" Is Related to the Character of Mathilde°

[1]   In "The Necklace" Guy de Maupassant does not give much detail about the setting. He does not even describe the necklace itself, which is the central object in his plot, but he says only that it is "superb" (paragraph 47). Rather, he uses the setting to reflect the character of the central figure, Mathilde Loisel.* All his details are presented to bring out her traits. Her character growth is related to her first apartment, her daydreams about mansion rooms, and her attic flat.†

[2]   Details about her first apartment explain her dissatisfaction and depression. The walls are "drab," the furniture "threadbare," and the curtains "ugly" (paragraph 3). There is only a simple country girl to do the housework. The tablecloth is not changed daily, and the best dinner dish is boiled beef. Mathilde has no evening clothes, only a theater dress that she does not like. These details show her dissatisfaction about her life with her low-salaried husband.

° See pp. 3–10 for this story.
* Central idea.
† Thesis sentence.

[3]   Her dream-life images of wealth are like the apartment because they too make her unhappy. In her daydreams about life in a mansion, the rooms are large, filled with expensive furniture and bric-a-brac, and draped in silk. She imagines private rooms for intimate talks, and big dinners with delicacies like trout and quail. With dreams of such a rich home, she feels even more despair about her modest apartment on the Street of Martyrs in Paris.

[4]   The attic flat reflects the coarsening of Mathilde's character. Maupassant emphasizes the burdens Mathilde endures to save money, such as mopping floors, cleaning greasy and encrusted pots and pans, taking out the garbage, and handwashing clothes and dishes. This work makes her rough and coarse, a fact also shown by her giving up care of her hair and hands, wearing the cheapest dresses possible, haggling with local shopkeepers, and becoming loud and penny-pinching. If at the beginning she is delicate and attractive, at the end she is unpleasant and coarse.

[5]   Maupassant focuses everything in the story, including the setting, on the character of Mathilde. Anything extra is not needed, and he does not include it. Thus he says little about the big party scene, but emphasizes the necessary detail that Mathilde was a "success" (paragraph 52). It is this detail that brings out some of her early attractiveness and charm (despite her more usual unhappiness). Thus in "The Necklace," Maupassant uses setting as a means to his end--the story of Mathilde and her needless sacrifice.

DEVELOPING AND STRENGTHENING YOUR ESSAY: REVISION

After finishing a first draft like this one, you may wonder what more you can do. You have read the work several times, discovered ideas to write about through brainstorming techniques, made an outline of your ideas, and written a full draft. How can you do better?

The best way to begin is to observe that *a major mistake writers make when writing about literature is to do no more than retell a story or reword an idea.* Retelling a story shows only that you have read it, not that you have thought about it. Writing a good essay requires you to arrange your thoughts into a pattern that can be followed by a perceptive reader.

Using Your Own Order of References

There are many ways to escape the trap of summarizing stories and to set up your own pattern of development. One is to stress *your own* order when referring to parts of a work. Do not treat details as they happen, but rearrange them to suit your own thematic plans. Rarely, if ever, should you begin by talking about a work's opening; it is better to talk first about the conclusion or middle. As you examine your first draft, if you find that you have followed the chronological order of the work instead of stressing your own order, you may use one of the prewriting techniques to figure out new ways to connect your materials. The principle is that you should introduce references to the work to support the points you wish to make, and only these points.

Using Literary Material as Evidence

Whenever you write, your position is like that of a detective using clues as evidence for building a case or a lawyer using evidence as support for an **argument.** Your goal should be to convince your readers of your own knowledge and the reasonableness of your conclusions.

It is vital to use evidence convincingly so that your readers can follow your ideas. Let us look briefly at two drafts of a new example to see how writing can be improved by the pointed use of details. These are from a longer essay on the character of Mathilde.

PARAGRAPH 1

The major extenuating detail about Mathilde is that she seems to be isolated, locked away from other people. She and her husband do not talk to each other much, except about external things. He speaks about his liking for boiled beef, and she states that she cannot accept the party invitation because she has no nice dresses. Once she gets the dress, she complains because she has no jewelry. Even when borrowing the necklace from Jeanne Forrestier, she does not say much. When she and her husband discover that the necklace is lost, they simply go over the details, and Loisel dictates a letter of explanation, which she writes in her own hand. Even when she meets Jeanne on the Champs-Elysées, she does not say a great deal about her life but only goes through enough details about the loss and replacement of the necklace to make Jeanne exclaim about the needlessness of the ten-year sacrifice.

PARAGRAPH 2

The major flaw of Mathilde's character is that she is withdrawn and uncommunicative, apparently unwilling or unable to form an intimate relationship. For example, she and her husband do not talk to each other much, except about external things such as his taste for boiled beef and her lack of a party dress and jewelry. With such an uncommunicative marriage, one might suppose that she would be more open with her close friend, Jeanne Forrestier, but Mathilde does not say much even to her. This flaw hurts her greatly, because if she were more open she might have explained the loss and avoided the horrible sacrifice. This lack of openness, along with her self-indulgent dreaminess, is her biggest defect.

A comparison of these paragraphs shows that although the first has more words than the second (158 to 120), it is more appropriate for a rough than a final draft because the writer does little more than retell the story. The paragraph is cluttered with details that do not support any conclusions. If you examine it for what you might learn about Maupassant's actual use of Mathilde's solitary traits in "The Necklace," you will find that it gives you little help. The writer needs to consider why these details should be shared, and to revise the paragraph according to the central idea.

On the other hand, the details in the right-hand paragraph all support the declared topic. Phrases such as "for example," "even to her," and "this lack" show that the writer of paragraph 2 has assumed that the audience knows the story and now wants help in interpretation. Paragraph 2 therefore guides readers *by connecting the details to the topic*. It uses these details *as evidence*, not as a retelling of actions. By contrast, paragraph 1 recounts a number of relevant actions but does not *connect* them to the topic. More details, of course, could have been added to paragraph 2, but they are unnecessary because the paragraph demonstrates the point with the details used. There are many qualities that make good writing good, but one of the most important is shown in a comparison of the two paragraphs: *In good writing, no details are included unless they serve as evidence in an original pattern of thought.*

Keeping to Your Point

To show another distinction between first- and second-draft writing, let us consider a third example. The following paragraph, in which the writer assumes an audience that is interested in the relationship of economics and politics to literature, is drawn from an essay titled "The Idea of Economic Determinism in 'The Necklace.'" In this paragraph the writer shows how economics are related to a number of incidents from the story. The idea is to assert that Mathilde's difficulties result not from character but rather from financial restrictions:

> More important than chance in governing life is the idea that people are controlled by economic circumstances. Mathilde, as is shown at the story's opening, is born poor. Therefore she doesn't get the right doors opened for her, and her marriage is to a minor clerk. With a vivid imagination and a burning desire for luxury, seeming to be born only for the wealthy life, she finds that her poor home brings out her daydreams of expensive surroundings. She taunts her husband, Loisel, when he brings the party invitation, because she does not have a suitable (read "expensive") dress. Once she gets the dress it is jewelry that she lacks, and she borrows that and loses it. The loss of the necklace is the greatest trouble because it forces the Loisels to borrow deeply and to lead an impoverished life for ten years.

This paragraph begins with an effective topic sentence, indicating that the writer has a good plan. The remaining part, however, shows how easily writers can stray from their objective. The flaw is that the material of the paragraph, while accurate, *is not tied to the topic*. Once the second sentence is under way, the paragraph gets lost in a retelling of events, and the fine opening sentence is left behind. The paragraph therefore shows that writers cannot assume that detail alone will make an intended meaning clear. They must do the connecting themselves, to make sure that all relationships are explicitly clear. *This point cannot be overstressed.*

Let us see how the problem can be treated. If the ideal paragraph can be schematized with line drawings, we might say that the paragraph's topic should be a straight line, moving toward and reaching a specific goal (explicit meaning), with an exemplifying line moving away from the straight line briefly to bring in evidence, but returning to the line after each new fact to demonstrate the relevance of the fact. Thus, the ideal scheme looks like this, with a straight line touched a number of times by an undulating line:

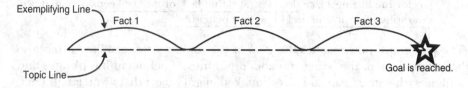

Notice that the exemplifying line, waving to illustrate how documentation or exemplification is to be used, always returns to the topic line. A scheme for the faulty paragraph on "The Necklace," however, would look like this, with the line never returning, but flying out into space:

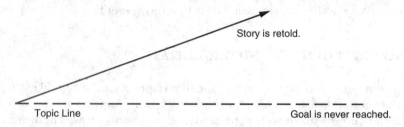

How might the faulty paragraph be improved? The best way is to remind the reader again and again of the topic, and to use examples from the text in support.

As our model diagram indicates, each time a topic is mentioned, the undulating line merges with the straight topic line that sets out the central idea. This relationship of topic to illustrative examples should prevail no matter what subject you write about. If you are analyzing *point of view*, for example, you should keep connecting your material to the speaker or narrator, and the same applies to topics like character, theme, or setting. According to this principle, we might revise the paragraph on economic determinism in "The Necklace" as follows. (Underlined words stress the relationship of the examples to the topic of the paragraph.)

> More important than chance in governing life is the idea that people are controlled by economic circumstances. <u>As illustration,</u> the speaker begins by emphasizing that Mathilde, the main character, is born poor. Therefore she doesn't get the right doors opened for her, and her marriage is to a minor clerk. <u>In keeping with the idea,</u> her vivid imagination and burning desire for luxury (she seems to

have been born only for the wealthy life) feed on her weakness of character as she feels deep unhappiness and depression because of the contrast between her daydreams of expensive surroundings and the poor home she actually has. These straitened economic circumstances inhibit her relationship with her husband, and she taunts him when he brings the big invitation because she does not have a suitable (read "expensive") dress. As a merging of her unrealistic dream life with actual reality, her borrowing of the necklace suggests the impossibility of overcoming economic restrictions. In the context of the idea, the ten-year sacrifice to pay for the lost necklace demonstrates that lack of money keeps people down, destroying their dreams and hopes of a better life.

The paragraph now reaches the goal of the topic sentence. While it has also been lengthened, the writer has added not inessential detail but phrases and sentences that give form and direction. You might object that if you lengthened all your paragraphs in this way, your essays would grow too bulky. The answer is to reduce the number of major points and paragraphs, on the theory that *it is better to develop a few topics pointedly than to develop many pointlessly.* Revising for the purpose of strengthening central and topic ideas requires that you either throw out some topics or else incorporate them as subpoints in the topics you keep. To control your writing in this way can result only in improvement.

CHECKING DEVELOPMENT AND ORGANIZATION

It bears repeating over and over again that the first requirement of a good essay is to introduce a point or main idea and then stick to it. Another major step toward excellence is to make your central idea expand and grow. The word *growth* is a metaphor describing the creation of new insights, the disclosure of ideas that were not at first noticeable, and the expression of original, new, and fresh interpretations.

BEING ORIGINAL.   An argument against this idea might be that you cannot be original when you are writing about someone else's work. "The author has said everything," might go the argument, "and therefore I can do little more than follow the story." This claim presupposes that you have no choice in selecting material and no opportunity to express individual thoughts and make original contributions.

But you do have choices and opportunities to be original. One obvious area of originality is the *development and formulation of your central idea.* For example, a natural first response to "The Necklace" is "The story is about a woman who loses a borrowed necklace and endures hardship to help pay for it." Because this response refers only to events in the story and not to any idea, an area of thought might be introduced if the hardship is called "needless." The use of this word alone demands that you explain the differences between *needed* and *unneeded* hardships, and your application of these differences to the heroine's plight would produce an original essay. Even better and more original insights could result if the topic of the budding essay were to connect the dreamy, withdrawn traits of the main character to her misfortunes and also to general misfortunes. A resulting central idea might be "People themselves create their own difficulties." Such an idea would require you to define not only the personal but also the representative nature of Mathilde's experiences, an avenue of exploration that could produce much in the way of a fresh, original essay about "The Necklace."

You can also develop your ability to treat your subject freshly and originally if you plan the body of the essay *to build up to what you think is your most important and incisive idea.* The following brief outline suggests how a central idea can be widened and expanded:

Subject: *Mathilde as a growing character*

1. Mathilde has normal daydreams about a better life.

2. She takes a risk, and loses, in trying to make her daydreams seem real.

3. She develops by facing her mistake and working hard to correct it.

The list shows how a subject can be enlarged if the exemplifying topic is treated in an increasing order of importance. In this case, the order moves from Mathilde's habit of daydreaming to the development of her character strength. The pattern shows how two primary standards of excellence in writing— organization and growth—can be met.

Clearly, you should always try to develop your central idea. Constantly adhere to your topic and constantly develop it. Nurture it and make it grow. Admittedly, in a short essay you will be able to move only a short distance with an idea, but *you should never be satisfied to leave the idea exactly where you found it.* To the degree that you can learn to develop your ideas, you will receive recognition for increasingly original writing.

Write with Your Readers in Mind

Whenever you write, you must decide how much detail to discuss. Usually you base this decision on your judgment of your readers. For example, if you assume that they have not read the work you are writing about, you will need to include a short summary as background. Otherwise, they may not understand your argument.

Consider, too, whether your readers have any special interests or concerns. If they are particularly interested in politics, sociology, religion, or psychology, for example, you may need to select and develop your materials accordingly.

Your instructor will let you know who your audience is. Usually, it will be your instructor or your fellow students. They will be familiar with the work and will not expect you to retell a story or summarize an argument. Rather they will look to you as an *explainer* or *interpreter.* Thus, you may omit details from the work that do not exemplify and support your central idea, even if the details are important parts of the work. What you write should always be based on your developing idea together with your assessment of your readers.

USING EXACT, COMPREHENSIVE, AND FORCEFUL LANGUAGE

In addition to being organized and well developed, the best writing is expressed in *exact, comprehensive*, and *forceful* language. At every stage of the composition process, you should try to correct your earliest sentences and paragraphs, which usually need to be rethought, reworded, and rearranged.

First of all, ask yourself whether your sentences really *mean* what you intend, or whether you can make them more exact and therefore stronger. For example, consider these two sentences from essays about "The Necklace":

> It seems as though the main character's dreams of luxury cause her to respond as she does in the story.
>
> This incident, although it may seem trivial or unimportant, has substantial significance in the creation of the story; by this I mean the incident which occurred is essentially what the story is all about.

These sentences are inexact and vague, and therefore unhelpful; neither of them goes anywhere. The first is satisfactory up to the verb *cause*, but then it falls apart because the writer has lost sight of the meaning. It is best to describe *what* that response is, rather than to be satisfied with nothing more than that there *is* a response. The following revision makes the sentence more exact:

> Mathilde's dreams of luxury make it impossible for her to accept her own possessions, and therefore she goes beyond her means to attend the party.

With this revision, the writer could consider the meaning of the story's early passages and could contrast the ideas there with those in the latter part. Without the revision, it is not clear where the writer might go.

The second sentence is vague because again the writer has lost sight of the topic. If we adopt the principle of trying to be exact, however, we can bring the dead sentence to life:

> The accidental loss of the necklace, which is trivial though costly, supports the narrator's claim that major turns in life are produced not by earthshaking events, but rather by minor ones.

In addition to working for exactness, writers strive to make sentences—all sentences, but particularly thesis and topic sentences—complete and comprehensive. Consider the following sentence:

> The idea in "The Necklace" is that Mathilde and her husband work hard to pay for the lost necklace.

This sentence does not offer us any ideas about the story. It needs additional rethinking and rephrasing to make it more comprehensive, as in these two revisions:

> In "The Necklace" Maupassant shows that hard work and responsibility are basic and necessary in life.
>
> Maupassant's surprise ending in "The Necklace" symbolizes the need for always being truthful.

Both new sentences are connected to "Mathilde and her husband work hard to pay for the lost necklace," although they point toward differing treatments. The first concerns the virtue shown by the Loisels in their sacrifice. Because the second sentence includes the word *symbolizes*, an essay stemming from it would stress the Loisels' mistake in not confessing the loss. In dealing with the symbolic meaning of their failure, an essay developed along the lines of the sentence would focus on the negative aspects of their characters, and an essay developed from the first sentence would stress their positive aspects. Either of the revised sentences, therefore, is more comprehensive than the original sentence and would help a writer get on the track toward an accurate and thoughtful essay.

Of course it is never easy to create fine sentences, but as a mode of improvement, you might create some self-testing mechanisms:

- *For treating story materials.* Always relate the materials to an idea or point. Do not say simply, "Mathilde works constantly for ten years to help pay off the debt." Instead, blend the material into a point, like this: "Mathilde's ten-year effort *shows the horror of indebtedness*," or "Mathilde's ten-year effort *demonstrates the emergence of her strength of character.*"

- *For responses and impressions.* Do not say simply, "The story's ending left me with a definite impression," but *state* what the impression is: "The story's ending surprised me and also made me sympathetic to the major character."

- *For ideas.* Try to make the idea clear and direct. Do not say, "Mathilde is living in a poor household," but rather get at an idea like this one: "The story of Mathilde shows that poor circumstances reduce the quality of life."

- *For critical commentary.* Do not rest with a statement such as "I found 'The Necklace' interesting," but try to describe *what* was interesting and *why* it was interesting: "I found 'The Necklace' interesting because it shows how chance can either make or destroy people's lives."

Good writing begins with attempts, like these, to rephrase sentences to make them really say something. If you always name and pin down descriptions, responses, and judgments, no matter how difficult the task seems, your sentences can be strong because you will be making them exact.

USING THE NAMES OF AUTHORS

For both men and women writers, you should typically include the author's *full name* in the *first sentence* of your essay. Here are two model first sentences:

Shirley Jackson's "The Lottery" is a story featuring both suspense and horror.

"The Lottery," by Shirley Jackson, is a story featuring both suspense and horror.

For all later references, use only last names, such as *Jackson, Steinbeck, Munro, Crane,* or *Porter.* However, for the "giants" of literature, you should use the last names exclusively. In referring to writers like Shakespeare and Milton, for example, there is no need to include *William* or *John.*

In spite of today's informal standards, do not use an author's first name, as in "*Shirley* skillfully creates suspense and horror in 'The Lottery.'" Also, do not use a familiar title before the names of dead authors, such as "*Ms.* Jackson's 'The Lottery' is a suspenseful horror story," or "*Mr.* Shakespeare's idea is that information is uncertain." Use the last names alone.

As with all conventions, of course, there are exceptions. If you are referring to a childhood work of a writer, the first name is appropriate, but you should shift to the last name when referring to the writer's mature works. If your writer has a professional or a noble title, such as "*Judge* O'Connor," "*Governor* Cross," "*Lord* Byron," or "*Lady* Winchelsea," it is not improper to use the title. Even then, however, the titles are commonly omitted for males, so that most references to Lord Byron and Lord Tennyson should be simply to "Byron" and "Tennyson."

Referring to living authors is somewhat problematical. Some journals and newspapers, like the *New York Times,* use the respectful titles *Mr.* and *Ms.* in their reviews. However, scholarly journals, which are likely to remain on library shelves for many decades, follow the general principle of beginning with the entire name and then using only the last name for subsequent references.

SAMPLE STUDENT ESSAY, FINAL DRAFT

If you refer again to the first draft of the essay about Maupassant's use of setting to illustrate Mathilde's character (pp. 25–26), you will notice that several parts of the draft need extensive reworking and revising. For example, paragraph 2 contains a series of short, unconnected comments, and its last sentence implies that Mathilde's dissatisfaction relates mainly to her husband rather than to her general circumstances. Paragraph 4 focuses too much on Mathilde's coarseness and not enough on her sacrifice and cooperation. The draft also ignores the fact that the story ends in another location, the Champs-Elysées, where Maupassant continues to demonstrate the nature of Mathilde's character. Finally, there is not enough support in this draft for the contention (in paragraph 5) that *everything* in the story is related to the character of Mathilde.

To discover how these issues can be more fully considered, the following revision of the earlier draft creates more introductory detail, includes an additional paragraph, and reshapes each of the paragraphs to stress the relationship of central idea to topic. Within the limits of a short assignment, the essay illustrates all the principles of organization and unity we have been discussing.

Maupassant's Use of Setting in "The Necklace" to Show the Character of Mathilde°

[1]
In "The Necklace" Guy de Maupassant uses setting to reflect the character and development of the main character, Mathilde Loisel.* As a result, his setting is not particularly vivid or detailed. He does not even describe the ill-fated necklace—the central object in the story—but states only that it is "superb" (paragraph 47). In fact, however, he includes descriptions of setting only if they illuminate qualities about Mathilde. Her changing character may be related to the first apartment, the dream-life mansion rooms, the attic flat, and the public street.†

[2]
Details about the modest apartment of the Loisels on the Street of Martyrs indicate Mathilde's peevish lack of adjustment to life. Though everything is serviceable, she is unhappy with the "drab" walls, "threadbare" furniture, and "ugly" curtains (paragraph 3). She has domestic help, but she wants more servants than the simple country girl who does the household chores in the apartment. Her embarrassment and dissatisfaction are shown by details of her irregularly cleaned tablecloth and the plain and inelegant boiled beef that her husband adores. Even her best theater dress, which is appropriate for her ordinary life but inappropriate for more wealthy surroundings, makes her unhappy. All these details of the apartment establish that Mathilde's dominant character trait at the story's beginning is maladjustment. She therefore seems unpleasant and unsympathetic.

Like the real-life apartment, the impossibly expensive setting of her daydreams about living in a mansion strengthens her unhappiness and her avoidance of reality. All the rooms of her fantasies are large and expensive, draped in silk and filled with nothing but the best furniture and bric-a-brac. Maupassant gives us the following description of her dream world:

[3]
She imagined a gourmet-prepared main course carried on the most exquisite trays and served on the most beautiful dishes, with whispered gallantries which she would hear with a sphinxlike smile as she dined on the pink meat of a trout or the delicate wing of a quail. (paragraph 4)

With impossible dreams like this one, her despair is complete. Ironically, this despair, together with her inability to live with reality, brings about her undoing. It makes her agree to borrow the necklace (which is just as unreal as her

---

° See pp. 3–10 for this story.
* Central idea.
† Thesis sentence.

daydreams of wealth), and losing the necklace drives her into the reality of giving up her apartment and moving into the attic flat.

[4]   Also ironically, the attic flat is related to the coarsening of her character while at the same time it brings out her best qualities of cooperativeness and honesty. Maupassant emphasizes the drudgery of the work Mathilde endures to maintain the flat, such as walking up many stairs, washing floors with large buckets of water, cleaning greasy and encrusted pots and pans, taking out the garbage, handwashing clothes, and haggling loudly with local tradespeople. All this reflects her coarsening and loss of sensibility, also shown by her giving up care of her hair and hands, and wearing the cheapest dresses. The work she performs, however, makes her heroic (paragraph 98). As she cooperates to help her husband pay back the loans, her dreams of a mansion fade, and all she has left is the memory of her triumphant appearance at the Minister of Education's party. Thus the attic flat brings out her physical change for the worse at the same time as it also brings out her psychological and moral change for the better.

[5]   Her walk on the Champs-Elysées illustrates another combination of traits--self-indulgence and frankness. The Champs-Elysées is the most fashionable street in Paris, and her walk to it is similar to her earlier indulgences in her day-dreams of upper-class wealth. But it is on this street where she meets Jeanne, and it is Mathilde's frankness in confessing the loss and replacement to Jeanne that makes Mathilde completely honest. While the walk thus serves as the occasion for the story's concluding surprise and irony, Mathilde's being on the Champs-Elysées is totally in character, in keeping with her earlier reveries about luxury.

[6]   Other details in the story also have a similar bearing on Mathilde's character. For example, the story presents little detail about the party scene beyond the statement that Mathilde is a great "success" (paragraph 52)--a judgment that shows her ability to shine if given the chance. After she and Loisel accept the fact that the necklace cannot be found, Maupassant includes details about the Parisian streets, the visits to loan sharks, and the jewelry shops in order to bring out Mathilde's sense of honesty and pride as she "heroically" prepares to live her new life of poverty. Thus, in "The Necklace," Maupassant uses setting to highlight Mathilde's maladjustment, her needless misfortune, her loss of youth and beauty, and finally her growth as a responsible human being.

Commentary on the Essay

Several improvements to the first draft are seen here. The language of paragraph 2 has been revised to show more clearly the inappropriateness of Mathilde's dissatisfaction. In paragraph 3, the irony of the story is brought out, and the writer has connected the details to the central idea in a richer pattern of ideas, showing the effects of Mathilde's despair. Paragraph 5—new in this revision—includes additional details about how Mathilde's walk on the Champs-Elysées is related to her character. In paragraph 6, the fact that Mathilde is able to "shine" at the dinner party is interpreted according to the central idea. Finally, the conclusion is now much more specific, summarizing the change in Mathilde's character rather than saying simply that the setting reveals her "needless sacrifice." In short, the second draft reflects the complexity of "The Necklace" better than the first draft. Because the writer has revised the first-draft ideas about the story, the final essay is tightly structured, insightful, and forceful.

ESSAY COMMENTARIES

Throughout this book, the sample student essays are followed by short commentaries that show how the essays embody the chapter's instruction and guidelines. For each essay that has a number of possible approaches, the commentary points out which one is employed, and when a sample essay uses two or more approaches, the commentary makes this fact clear. In addition, each commentary singles out one of the paragraphs for detailed analysis of its strategy and use of detail. The commentaries will help you develop the insight necessary to use the essays as aids in your own study and writing.

Follow these guidelines whenever you write about a story or any kind of literature:

- Never just retell the story. Use story materials only to support your central idea or argument.
- Throughout your essay, keep reminding your reader of your central idea. Keep returning to your points.
- Within each paragraph, make sure that you stress your topic idea.
- Develop your topic. Make it bigger than it was when you began.
- Always make your statements exact, comprehensive, and forceful.
- *And remember, never just retell the story!*

SPECIAL WRITING TOPICS FOR STUDYING THE WRITING PROCESS

1. Write a brainstorming paragraph on the topic of anything in a literary work that you find especially good or interesting. Write as the thoughts occur to you; do not slow yourself down in an effort to make your writing seem perfect. You can make corrections and improvements later.

2. Using marginal and journal notations, together with any additional thoughts, describe the way in which the author of a particular work has resolved particularly important ideas and difficulties.

3. Create a plus-minus table to list your responses about a character or ideas in a work.

4. Raise questions about the actions of characters in a story or play in order to determine the various customs and manners of the society out of which the work is derived.

5. Analyze and explain the way in which the conflicts in a story or play are developed. What pattern or patterns seem to develop? How does the work grow out of the conflicts?

6. Basing your ideas on your marginal and journal notations, select an idea and develop a thesis sentence from it, using your idea and a list of possible topics for the development of an essay.

7. Using the thesis sentence you write for exercise 6, develop a brief topical outline for an essay.

RESPONDING TO LITERATURE: LIKES AND DISLIKES

People read literature because they like it. Even if they don't like everything they read, they nevertheless enjoy reading, and people usually pick out authors and types of literature that they think they might enjoy. It is therefore worth considering those qualities that at the simplest level produce responses of pleasure or displeasure. You either like or dislike a story, poem, or play. If you say no more than this, however, you have not said much. Analyzing and explaining your likes and dislikes requires you to describe the reasons for your responses. The goal should be to form your responses as judgments, which are usually *informed* and *informative*, rather than as simple reactions, which may be *uninformed* and *unexplained*.

Sometimes a reader's first responses are that a story is either "okay" or "boring." These reactions usually mask an incomplete and superficial first reading. They are neither informative nor informed. As you study most stories, however, you will be drawn into them and become *interested* and *involved*. To be interested in a story is to be taken into it emotionally; to be involved suggests that your emotions become almost wrapped up in your story's characters, problems, and outcomes. Both interest and involvement describe genuine responses to reading. Once you get interested and involved, your reading ceases to be a task or assignment and grows into a pleasure.

Using Your Journal to Record Responses

No one can tell you what you should or should not like; liking is your own concern. While your experience of reading is still fresh, therefore, you should use your journal to record not only your observations about a work but also your responses. Be frank in your judgment. Write down what you like or dislike, and try to explain the reasons for your responses, even if these are brief and incomplete. If, after later thought and fuller understanding, you change or modify your first impressions, record these changes too. Here is a journal entry that explains a favorable response to Guy de Maupassant's "The Necklace":

I like "The Necklace" because of the surprise ending. It isn't that I like Mathilde's bad luck, but I like the way Maupassant hides the most important fact in the story until the end. Mathilde does all that work and makes sacrifices for no reason at all, and the surprise ending makes this point strongly.

This paragraph could be expanded. It is a clear statement of liking, followed by references to likable things in the work. This response pattern, which can be simply phrased as "I like [dislike] this work because . . .," is a useful way to begin journal entries because it always requires that a response be followed with an explanation. If at first you cannot write any full sentences detailing the causes of your responses, at least make a brief list of the things you like or dislike. If you write nothing, you will probably forget your reactions. Recovering them later, either for discussion or writing, will be difficult.

RESPONDING FAVORABLY

Usually you can equate your interest in a work with liking it. You can be more specific about favorable responses by citing one or more of the following:

- You like and admire the characters and what they do and stand for. You get involved with them. When they are in danger you are concerned; when they succeed you are happy; when they speak you like what they say.
- When you read the last word in a story or play, you are sorry to part with these characters and wish that there were more to read about them and their activities.
- Even if you do not particularly like a character or characters, you are nevertheless interested in the reasons and outcomes of their actions.
- You get so interested and involved in what happens in the work that you do not want to put the work down until you have finished it.
- You learn something new—something you had never known or thought before about human beings and their ways of handling their problems.
- You gain new insights into aspects of life that you thought you already understood.
- You learn about customs and ways of life in different places and times.
- You feel happy or thrilled because of reading the work.
- You are amused and laugh often as you read.
- You like the author's ways of describing scenes and actions.
- You find that many of the ideas and expressions are beautiful and worth remembering.

RESPONDING UNFAVORABLY

Although so far we have dismissed *"okay"* and "boring" and stressed *interest, involvement,* and *liking,* it is important to know that disliking all or part of a work is normal and acceptable. You do not need to hide this response.

Here, for example, are two short journal responses expressing dislike for Maupassant's "The Necklace":

1. I do not like "The Necklace" because Mathilde seems spoiled, and I don't think she is worth reading about.
2. "The Necklace" is not an adventure story, and I like reading only adventure stories.

These are both legitimate responses because they are based on a clear standard of judgment. The first stems from a distaste for one of the main character's unlikable traits, the second from a preference for rapidly moving stories that evoke interest in the dangers that main characters face and overcome.

Here is a paragraph-length journal entry that might be developed from the first response. Notice that the reasons for dislike are explained. They would need only slightly more development for use in an essay.

> I don't like "The Necklace" because Mathilde seems spoiled and I don't think she is worth reading about. She is a phony. She nags her husband because he is not rich. She never tells the truth. I dislike her for hurrying away from the party because she is afraid of being seen in her shabby shawl. She is foolish and dishonest for not telling Jeanne Forrestier about losing the necklace. It's true that she works hard to pay the debt, but she also puts her husband through ten years of hardship. If Mathilde had faced facts, she might have had a better life. I do not like her and cannot like the story because of her.

As long as you include reasons for your dislike, as in the list and the paragraph, you can use them again in considering the story more fully, when you will surely also expand thoughts, include new details, pick new topics for development as paragraphs, and otherwise modify your journal entry. You might even change your mind. However, even if you do not, it is better to record your original responses and reasons honestly than to force yourself to say you like a story that you do not like.

Putting Dislikes into a Larger Context

While it is important to be honest about disliking a work, it is more important to broaden your perspective and expand your taste. For example, a dislike based on the preference for only mystery or adventure stories, if generally applied, would cause a person to dislike most works of literature. This attitude seems unnecessarily self-limiting.

If negative responses are put in a larger context, it is possible to expand the capacity to like and appreciate good literature. For instance, some readers might be preoccupied with their own concerns and therefore be uninterested in remote or "irrelevant" literary figures. However, if by reading about literary characters they can gain insight into general problems of life, and therefore their own concerns, they can find something to like in just about any work.

Other readers might like sports and therefore not read anything but the daily sports pages. What probably interests them about sports is competition, however, so if they can follow the competition or conflict in a literary work, they will have discovered something to like in that work.

As an example, let us consider again the dislike of "The Necklace" based on a preference for adventure stories and see if this preference can be widened. Here are some reasons for liking adventures:

1. Adventure has fast action.
2. It has danger and tension and therefore interest.
3. It has daring, active, and successful characters.
4. It has obstacles that the characters work hard to overcome.

No one could claim that the first three points apply to "The Necklace," but the fourth point is promising. Mathilde, the major character, works hard to overcome an obstacle: She pitches in to help her husband pay the large debt. If you like adventures because the characters try to attain worthy goals, then you can also like "The Necklace" for the same reason. The principle here is clear: If a reason for liking a favorite work or type of work can be found in another work, then there is reason to like that new work.

The following paragraph shows a possible application of this "bridging" process of extending preferences. (The sample student essay on pp. 43–44 is also developed along these lines.)

> I usually like only adventure stories, and therefore I disliked "The Necklace" at first because it is not adventure. But one of my reasons for liking adventure is that the characters work hard to overcome difficult obstacles, like finding buried treasure or exploring new places. Mathilde, Maupassant's main character in "The Necklace," also works hard to overcome an obstacle—helping to pay back the money and interest for the borrowed 18,000 francs used as part of the payment for the replacement necklace. I like adventure characters because they stick to things and win out. I see the same toughness in Mathilde. Her problems get more interesting as the story moves on after a slow beginning. I came to like the story.

The principle of "bridging" from like to like is clear: *If a reason for liking a favorite work or type of work can be found in another work, then there is reason to like that new work.* A person who adapts to new reading in this open-minded way can redefine dislikes, no matter how slowly, and may consequently expand the ability to like and appreciate many kinds of literature.

An equally open-minded way to develop understanding and widen taste is to put dislikes in the following light: An author's creation of an *unlikable* character, situation, attitude, or expression may be deliberate. Your dislike might then result from the author's *intentions*. A first task of study is therefore to understand and explain the intention or plan. As you put the plan into your own words, you may find that you can like a work with unlikable things in it.

Here is paragraph that traces this pattern of thinking, based again on "The Necklace":

> Maupassant apparently wants the reader to dislike Mathilde, and I do. At first, he shows her being unrealistic and spoiled. She lies to everyone and nags her husband. Her rushing away from the party so that no one can see her shabby shawl is a form of lying. But I like the story itself because Maupassant makes another kind of point. He does not hide her bad qualities, but makes it clear that she herself is the cause of her trouble. If people like Mathilde never face the truth, they will get into bad situations. This is a good point, and I like the way Maupassant makes it. The entire story is therefore worth liking even though I still do not like Mathilde.

Both of these paragraphs are honest, true to the writer's original negative reactions. In the first paragraph, the writer applies one of his principles of liking to include "The Necklace." In the second, the writer considers her initial dislike in the context of the work, and she discovers a basis for liking the story as a whole while still disliking the main character. The main concern in both responses is to keep an open mind despite initial dislike, and then to see if the unfavorable response can be more fully and broadly considered.

However, if you decide that your dislike overbalances any reasons you can find for liking, then you should explain your dislike. As long as you relate your response to the work accurately, and measure it by a clear standard of judgment, your dislike of even a commonly liked work is not unacceptable. The important issue is not so much that you like or dislike a particular work but that you *develop your own abilities to analyze and express your ideas*.

WRITING ABOUT RESPONSES: LIKES AND DISLIKES

Earlier in this chapter we looked briefly at the process of writing, with two drafts of the same essay for illustration. You are now ready to apply the principles of the writing process to your own writing. The first application will be an essay about how you like or dislike a particular work of literature. Because at least a little time will have elapsed between your first reading and your gathering of materials to begin writing, you will need your journal observations to guide you in your prewriting as you reconstruct your initial informed reactions to the work. Develop your essay by stressing those characters, incidents, and ideas that interest (or do not interest) you.

As with many essays, you will be challenged to connect details from the work to your central idea. That is, once you have begun by stating that you like (or dislike) the story, you might forget to highlight this response as you enumerate details. Therefore you need to stress your involvement in the work. You can show your attitudes by indicating approval (or disapproval), by commenting favorably (or unfavorably) on the details, by indicating ideas that seem new (or shopworn) and particularly instructive (or wrong), and by giving assent to (or explaining dissent from) ideas or expressions of feeling.

Strategies for Organizing Ideas

In your essay, briefly describe the conditions that influence your response. Your central idea should be why you like or dislike the work. Your thesis sentence should include the major causes of your response, which are to be developed in the body of the essay.

The most common approach is to consider specific details that you like or dislike. The list on page 39 may help you articulate your responses. For example, maybe you admired a particular character, or maybe you got so interested in the story that you could not put it down. Also, you may wish to develop a major idea, a fresh insight, or a particular outcome, as in the sample paragraph on page 38, which shows a surprise ending as the cause of a favorable response.

A second approach (see p. 40) is to explain any changes in your responses about the work (i.e., negative to positive and vice versa). This approach requires that you isolate the causes of the change, but it does *not* require you to retell the story from beginning to end. There are two ways to explain such changes:

1. You can use the "bridge" method of transferring preference from one type of work to another, shown in the sample student essay on pages 43–44.
2. You can explain a change in terms of a new awareness or understanding that you did not have on a first reading. Thus, for example, your first response to Poe's "The Cask of Amontillado" (Chapter 6) might be unfavorable or neutral because the story seems unnecessarily sensational and lurid. But further consideration might lead you to discover new insights that change your mind, like the causes leading to evil, or the danger of being deceived by flattery. Your essay would then explain how these new insights have caused you to like the story.

In your conclusion you might summarize the reasons for your major response. You might also face any issues brought up by a change or modification of your first reactions. For example, if you have always held certain assumptions about your taste in literature but like the work despite these assumptions, you may wish to talk about your own change or development. This topic is personal, but in an essay about likes or dislikes, discovery about yourself is legitimate and worthy.

SAMPLE STUDENT ESSAY

Some Reasons for Liking Maupassant's "The Necklace"°

[1] To me, the most likable kind of reading is adventure. There are many reasons for my preference, but an important one is that adventure characters work hard to overcome obstacles. Because Guy de Maupassant's "The Necklace" is not adventure, I did not like it at first. But in one respect the story is like adventure: The major character, Mathilde Loisel, works hard with her husband for ten

° See pp. 3–10 for this story.

years to overcome a difficult obstacle. Thus, because Mathilde does what adventure characters also do, the story is likable.* Mathilde's appeal results from her hard work, strong character, and sad fate, and also from the way our view of her changes.†

[2] Mathilde's hard work makes her seem good. Once she and her husband are faced with the huge debt of 18,000 francs, she works hard to pay it back. She gives up her servant and moves to a cheaper place. She does the household drudgery, wears cheap clothes, and haggles with shopkeepers. Just like the characters in adventure stories who do difficult and unpleasant things, she does what she has to, and this makes her admirable.

[3] Her strong character shows her endurance, a likable trait. At first she is nagging and fussy, and she always dreams about wealth and tells lies, but she changes and gets better. She recognizes her blame in losing the necklace, and she has the toughness to help her husband redeem the debt. She sacrifices "heroically" (paragraph 98) by giving up her comfortable way of life, even though in the process she also loses her youth and beauty. Her jobs are not the exotic and glamorous ones of adventure stories, but her force of character makes her as likable as an adventure heroine.

[4] Her sad fate also makes her likable. In adventure stories the characters often suffer as they do their jobs. Mathilde also suffers, but in a different way, because her suffering is permanent while the hardships of adventure characters are temporary. This fact makes her especially pitiable because all her sacrifices are not necessary. This unfairness invites the reader to take her side.

[5] The most important quality promoting admiration is the way in which Maupassant shifts our view of Mathilde. As she goes deeper into her hard life, Maupassant stresses her work and not the innermost thoughts he reveals at the beginning. In other words, the view into her character at the start, when she dreams about wealth, invites dislike; but the focus at the end is on her achievements, with never a complaint--even though she still has golden memories, as the narrator tells us:

> But sometimes, when her husband was at work, she sat down near the window, and she dreamed of that evening so long ago, of that party, where she had been so beautiful and so admired. (paragraph 104)

A major quality of Maupassant's changed emphasis is that Mathilde's fond memories do not lead to anything unfortunate. His shift in focus, from Mathilde's dissatisfaction to her sharing of responsibility and sacrifice, encourages the reader to like her.

[6] "The Necklace" is not an adventure story, but Mathilde has some of the good qualities of adventure characters. Also, the surprise revelation that the lost necklace was false is an unforgettable twist, and this makes her more deserving than she seems at first. Maupassant has arranged the story so that the reader finally admires Mathilde. "The Necklace" is a skillful and likable story.

---

* Central idea.
† Thesis sentence.

Commentary on the Essay

This essay demonstrates how a reader may develop appreciation by transferring a preference for one type of work to a work that does not belong to the type. In the essay, the "bridge" is an already established taste for adventure stories, and the grounds for liking "The Necklace" are that Mathilde, the main character, shares the admirable qualities of adventure heroes and heroines.

Paragraph 1, the introduction, establishes the grounds for transferring preferences. Paragraph 2 deals with Mathilde's capacity to work hard, and paragraph 3 considers the equally admirable quality of endurance. Paragraph 4 describes how Mathilde's condition evokes sympathy and pity. These paragraphs thus explain the story's appeal by asserting that the main character is similar to admirable characters from works of adventure.

Paragraph 5 shows that as the story unfolds, Maupassant alters the reader's perceptions of Mathilde from bad to good. For this reason paragraph 5 marks a new direction from paragraphs 2, 3, and 4: It moves away from the topic material itself—Mathilde's character—to Maupassant's *technique* in handling the topic material.

Paragraph 6, the conclusion, restates the comparison and also introduces the surprise ending as an additional reason for liking "The Necklace." With the body and conclusion together, therefore, the essay establishes five separate reasons for approval. Three of these, derived directly from the main character, constitute the major grounds for liking the story, and two are related to Maupassant's techniques as an author.

Throughout the essay, the central idea is brought out in words and expressions such as "likable," "Mathilde's appeal," "strong character," "she does what she has to," "pitiable," and "take her side." Many of these expressions were first made in the writer's journal; and, mixed as they are with details from the story, they make for continuity. It is this thematic development, together with details from the story as supporting evidence, that shows how an essay on the responses of liking and disliking can be both informed and informative.

SPECIAL WRITING TOPICS FOR RESPONDING TO LITERATURE

1. In the last six months, what literary works did you read which you liked or disliked? Write a brief essay explaining your reasons for your positive or negative responses. To illustrate your points you may make liberal references to these works, and, in addition, you may refer to films or TV shows that you have recently seen.

2. Consider the sample student essay on Maupassant's "The Necklace" on pages 43–44. Do you accept the arguments in the essay? What other details and arguments can you think of for either liking or disliking the story?

3. Write contrasting paragraphs about a character, either someone you know or someone you have read about. In the first, try to make your reader like the character. In the second, try to create a hostile response to the character. Write an additional paragraph explaining the ways in which you tried to create these opposite responses. How fair would it be for a reader to dislike your negative paragraph even though your hostile portrait is successful?

READING
AND
WRITING
ABOUT

FICTION

2
Fiction:
An Overview

Fiction originally meant anything made up or shaped. As we understand the word now, it refers to prose stories, short or long—a meaning it has retained since its first recorded use in this sense in 1599. Fiction is distinguished from the works it imitates, such as *historical accounts, reports, biographies, autobiographies, letters,* and *personal memoirs* and *meditations.* While fiction often resembles these forms, it has a separate identity because it originates not in historical facts but in the imaginative and creative powers of the author. Writers of fiction may include historically accurate details, but their primary goal is to tell a story and say something significant about life.

The essence of fiction, as opposed to drama, is **narration,** the recounting or telling of a sequence of events or actions. The earliest works of fiction relied almost exclusively on narration, with speeches or dialogue being reported rather than quoted directly. Much recent fiction includes extended passages of dialogue, thereby becoming more *dramatic* even though narration is still the primary mode.

Fiction is rooted in ancient legends and myths. Local priests narrated stories about their gods and heroes, as shown in some of the narratives of ancient Egypt. In the course of history, traveling storytellers would appear in a court or village to entertain listeners with tales of adventure in faraway countries. Although many of these were fictionalized accounts of events and people who may not ever have existed, they were largely accepted as fact or history. An especially long tale, an **epic,** was recited over a period of days. To aid their memories and to impress and entertain their listeners, the storytellers chanted their tales in poetry, often accompanying themselves on a stringed instrument.

Legends and epics also reinforced the local religions and power structures. Myths of gods like Zeus and Athena (Greece), Jupiter and Minerva (Rome), and Baal and Ishtar (Mesopotamia) abounded, together with stories of famous men and women like Oedipus, Helen of Troy, Hercules, Achilles, Odysseus, Penelope, Utu-Napishtim, Joseph, David, and Ruth. The ancient Macedonian king and general Alexander the Great (356–323 B.C.E.) developed many of his ideas about nobility and valor from *The Iliad,* Homer's epic about the Trojan War—and, we might add, from discussing the epic with his tutor, Aristotle.

Perhaps nowhere is the moralistic-argumentative aspect of ancient storytelling better illustrated than in the **fables** of Aesop, a Greek who wrote in the sixth century B.C.E., and in the **parables** of Jesus as told in the Gospels of the New Testament. In these works, a short narrative provides an illustration of a religious, philosophic, or psychological conclusion. A Roman story of the first century C.E., "The Widow of Ephesus" by Gaius Petronius, illustrates this type of persuasive intention, in which the use of narrative events for a rhetorical and persuasive purpose is made clear right at the beginning.

Starting about eight hundred years ago, storytelling in Western civilization was developed to a fine art by writers such as Marie de France, a Frenchwoman who wrote in England near the end of the twelfth century; Giovanni Boccaccio (Italian, 1313–1375); and Geoffrey Chaucer (English, ca. 1340–1400). William Shakespeare (1564–1616) drew heavily on history and legend for the stories and characters in his plays.

MODERN FICTION

Fiction in the modern sense of the word did not begin to flourish until the seventeenth and eighteenth centuries, when human beings of all social stations and ways of life became important literary topics. As one writer put it in 1709, human nature was not simple, and it could be explained only with reference to many complex motives, such as "passion, humor, caprice, zeal, faction, and a thousand other springs."[1] Thus began the individual and psychological concerns that characterize fiction today. Indeed, fiction is strong because it is so real and personal. Most characters have both first and last names; the countries and cities in which they live are modeled on real places; and their actions and interactions are like those which readers themselves have experienced, could experience, or could easily imagine themselves experiencing.

Along with attention to character, fiction is also concerned with the place of individuals in their environments. In the simplest sense, environment is a backdrop or setting within which characters speak, move, and act. But more broadly, environment comprises the social, economic, and political conditions that affect the outcomes of people's lives. Fiction is usually about the interactions among people, but it also involves these larger interactions—either

---

[1] Anthony Ashley Cooper, Third Earl of Shaftesbury, *Sensus Communis,* Part III, Section iii.

directly or indirectly. Indeed, in a typical work of fiction there are always many forces, both small and large, that influence the ways in which characters meet and deal with their problems.

The first true works of fiction in Europe, however, were less concerned with society or politics than adventure. These were the lengthy Spanish and French **romances** of the sixteenth and seventeenth centuries. (The French word for "novel" is still *roman*.) In English the word **novel** was borrowed from French and Italian to describe these works and to distinguish them from medieval and classical romances as something that was *new* (the meaning of *novel*). The word **story** was used along with *novel* in reference to the new literary form.

The increased levels of education and literacy in the eighteenth century facilitated the development of fiction. During the times of Shakespeare (1564–1616) and Dryden (1631–1700), the only way a writer could make a living from writing was either to be a member of the nobility or to have a subsidy from a member of the nobility, or to have a play accepted at a theater, and then receive either a direct payment or the proceeds of an "author's benefit." The paying audiences, however, were limited to people who lived within a short distance of the theater or who had the leisure and money to stay in town during the theater season.

Once great numbers of people could read for themselves, the paying audience for literature expanded. A writer could write a novel and receive money for it from a publisher, who could then profit from a wide sale. Readers could pick up the book when they wished and finish it when they chose. Reading a novel could even be a social event, for people would read to each other as a means of sharing the experience. With this wider audience, authors could make a career out of writing. Fiction had arrived as a major genre of literature.

THE SHORT STORY

Because novels were long, they took a long time to read—hours, days, even weeks. The American writer Edgar Allan Poe (1809–1849) addressed this problem and developed a theory of the **short story,** which he described in a review of Nathaniel Hawthorne's *Twice-Told Tales.* Poe was convinced that "worldly interests" prevented people from gaining the "totality" of comprehension and response that he believed reading should provide. A short, concentrated story (he called it "a brief prose tale" which could be read at a single sitting) was ideal for producing such a strong impression.

In the wake of the taste for short fiction after Poe, many writers have worked in the form. Today, innumerable stories are printed in periodicals, such as *Story* magazine, and collections, such as *American Short Story Masterpieces.* Some of the better-established writers, such as William Faulkner, Ernest Hemingway,

Shirley Jackson, Guy de Maupassant, Flannery O'Connor, Alice Walker, and Eudora Welty, to name only a small number, have collected their works and published them in single volumes.

ELEMENTS OF FICTION I:
VERISIMILITUDE AND *DONNÉE*

Fiction, along with drama, has a basis in **realism** or **verisimilitude.** That is, the situations or characters, though they are the **invention** of writers, are similar to those that many human beings experience, know, or think. Even **fantasy,** the creation of events that are dreamlike or fantastic, is anchored in the real world, however remotely. This connection of art and life has led some critics to label fiction, and also drama, as an art of **imitation.** Shakespeare's Hamlet states that an actor attempts to portray real human beings in realistic situations ("to hold . . . a mirror up to Nature").

The same may also be said about writers of fiction, with the provisos that reality is not easily defined and that authors can follow many paths in imitating it. What counts in fiction is the way in which authors establish the *ground rules* for their works, whether with realistic or nonrealistic characters, places, actions, and physical and chemical laws. The assumption that authors make about the nature of their story material is called a **postulate** or a **premise**—what Henry James called a *donnée* (something given). The *donnée* of some stories is to resemble the everyday world as much as possible. Welty's "A Worn Path" is such a story. It tells of a woman's walking journey through a wooded area to the streets of a town, and then to the interior of a building. The events of the story are common; they could happen in life just as Welty presents them.

Once a *donnée* is established, it governs the directions in which the story moves. Jackson's "The Lottery," for example, contains a premise or *donnée* that can be phrased like this: "Suppose that a small, ordinary town held a lottery in which the prize was not money but a ritual punishment." Everything in Jackson's story follows from this premise. At first we seem to be reading about innocent actions in a rural American community. By the end, however, in accord with the premise, the story departs from ordinary matters and enters the realms of nightmare.

In such ways authors can lead us into remote, fanciful, and symbolic levels of reality, as in Tremblay's "The Thimble," which stems from the *donnée* that the entire universe may be squeezed into an ordinary thimble. In Poe's "The Fall of the House of Usher," the phantasmagoric *donnée* is that the collapse and disappearance of a large mansion accompanies the psychological deterioration and actual deaths of the people who live there. Scenes and actions such as these, which do not conform to everyday reality, are normal in stories *as long as they follow the author's own stated or implied ground rules.* You may always judge a work by the standard of whether it is consistent with its *donnée* or major premise. As long as the author makes the *donnée* clear, literally nothing is out of bounds.

In addition to referring to various levels of reality, the word *donnée* may also be taken more broadly. In *futuristic* and *science fiction,* for example, there is an assumption or *donnée* of certain situations and technological developments (e.g., interstellar space travel) that are not presently in existence. In a *love story,* the *donnée* is that two people meet and overcome an obstacle of some sort (usually not a serious one) on the way to fulfilling their love. Interesting variations of this type are seen in Lawrence's "The Horse Dealer's Daughter," Munro's "The Found Boat," Dixon's "All Gone," and Joyce's "Araby."

There are of course other types. An *apprenticeship* or *growth story,* for example, is about the growth of a major character, such as Jackie in "First Confession," Sarty in "Barn Burning," and Emily in "I Stand Here Ironing." In the *detective story,* a mysterious event is posited, and then the detective draws conclusions from the available evidence. A variation on the detective story is seen in Glaspell's "A Jury of Her Peers," in which the correct detective work is done by two women, not by the legally sanctioned police investigator.

In addition to setting levels of reality and fictional types, authors can use other controls or springboards as their *données.* Sometimes an initial situation is the occasion from which the story develops (such as the social worker calling the mother to express concern about the daughter in Olsen's "I Stand Here Ironing"). Or the key may be a pattern of behavior (the boy's reactions to the people around him in O'Connor's "First Confession") or a lunchtime conversation (as in Atwood's "Rape Fantasies"). There is always a shaping force, or a *donnée,* that guides the actions, and often a number of such controls operate at the same time.

ELEMENTS OF FICTION II:
CHARACTER, PLOT, STRUCTURE, AND THEME

Works of fiction share a number of common elements, which we discuss in detail in subsequent chapters. The more significant ones are *character, plot, structure,* and *idea* or *theme.*

Character

Stories, like plays, are about characters—characters who are *not* real people but who are nevertheless *like* real people. A **character,** discussed in detail in Chapter 4, may be defined as a reasonable facsimile of a human being, with all the good and bad traits of being human. Most stories are concerned with characters who are facing a major problem, which may involve interactions with other characters, with difficult situations, or with an idea or general circumstances that force action. The characters may win, lose, or tie.

They may learn and be the better for the experience or may miss the point and be unchanged.

Earlier we mentioned that modern fiction has accompanied the development of a psychological interest in human beings. Psychology itself has grown out of the philosophical and religious idea that people are not evil by nature, but rather that they have many inborn capacities—some for good and others for bad. People are not free of problems, and they make many mistakes in their lives, but they nevertheless are important and interesting and are therefore worth writing about, whether male or female, young or old, of any race or any occupation.

The range of fictional characters is vast. A married couple struggling to repay an enormous debt, a woman meditating about her daughter's growth, a young man learning about sin and forgiveness, a young woman struggling to overcome the bitter memory of early sexual abuse, a man regretting that he cannot admit a lie, a woman living amid her insensitive and self-seeking brothers, a man preserving love in the face of overwhelming difficulties, a woman learning to cope with her son's handicap—all these, and more, are found in fiction. Because as human beings all of us share the same capacities for concern, involvement, sympathy, happiness, sorrow, exhilaration, and disappointment, we are able to find endless interest in such characters and their ways of responding to their circumstances.

Plot

Fictional characters, who are drawn from life, go through a series of lifelike **actions** or **incidents,** which make up the story. In a well-done story, all the actions or incidents, speeches, thoughts, and observations are linked together to make up an entirety, sometimes called an **organic unity.** The essence of this unity is the development and resolution of a **conflict**—or conflicts—in which the **protagonist,** or central character, is engaged. The interactions of causes and effects as they develop **sequentially** or **chronologically** make up the story's **plot.** That is, a story's actions follow one another in time as the protagonist meets and tries to overcome opposing forces. Sometimes plot has been compared to a story's map, scheme, or blueprint.

Often the protagonist's struggle is directed against another character—an **antagonist.** Just as often, however, the struggle occurs between the protagonist and opposing groups, forces, ideas, and choices—all of which make up a collective antagonist. The conflict may be carried out wherever human beings spend time, such as a kitchen, a bedroom, a restaurant, a town square, a farm, an estate, a workshop, or a battlefield. The conflict may also take place internally, within the mind of the protagonist.

Structure

Structure refers to the way a story is assembled. Chronologically, all stories are similar because they move from beginning to end in accord with the time needed for *causes* to produce *effects*. But authors choose many different ways to put their stories together. Some stories are told in straightforward sequential order, and a description of the plot of such stories is identical to a description of the structure. Other stories, however, are pieced together through out-of-sequence and widely separated episodes, speeches, secondhand reports, remembrances, dreams, nightmares, periods of delirium, fragments of letters, overheard conversations, and the like. In such stories, the plot and the structure diverge widely. Therefore, in dealing with the structure of stories, we emphasize not chronological order but the actual *arrangement* and *development* of the stories as they unfold, part by part. Usually we study an entire story, but we may also direct our attention toward a smaller aspect of arrangement such as an episode or passage of dialogue.

Idea or Theme

The word **idea** refers to the result or results of general and abstract thinking. In literary study the consideration of ideas relates to meaning, interpretation, explanation, and significance. Fiction necessarily embodies issues and ideas. Even stories written for entertainment alone are based in an idea or position. Thus, writers of comic works are committed to the idea that human difficulties can be treated with humor. More serious works may force characters to make difficult moral choices—the thought being that in a losing situation the only winners are those who maintain honor and self-respect. Mystery and suspense stories rest on the belief that problems have solutions, even if they are not at first apparent. Writers may deal with the triumphs and defeats of life, the admirable and the despicable, the humorous and the pathetic, but whatever their goal, writers are always expressing ideas about human experience. We therefore raise questions such as these as we look for ideas in fiction: *What does this mean? Why does the author include it? What idea or ideas does it show? Why is it significant?*

Fictional ideas can also be considered as major **themes** that tie individual works together. Often an author makes the theme obvious, as in the Aesop fable in which a man uses an ax to kill a fly on his son's forehead. The theme of this fable might loosely be expressed in a sentence like "The cure should not be worse than the disease." A major theme in Maupassant's "The Necklace" (see pp. 3–10) is that people may be destroyed or saved by unlucky and unforeseeable events. The accidental loss of the borrowed necklace is just such an event, for this misfortune ruins the lives of both Mathilde and her husband.

The process of determining and describing the themes or ideas in stories is never complete; there is always another theme that we could discuss. Thus in "The Necklace," we might note the additional themes that adversity brings out worth, that telling the truth is better than concealing it, that envy often produces ill fortune, and that good fortune is never recognized until it is lost. Indeed, one of the ways in which we may judge stories is to determine the degree to which they embody a number of valid and important ideas.

ELEMENTS OF FICTION III:
THE WRITER'S TOOLS

Narration

Writers have a number of modes of presentation, or "tools," which they may use in writing their stories. The principal tool (and the heart of fiction) is **narration,** the reporting of actions in sequential order. The object of narration is to render the story, to make it clear, and to bring it alive to the reader's imagination through the movement of sentences through time. Unlike works of painting and sculpture, the reading and comprehension of a narration cannot be done in a single view. In one of the best-known of all works of art, for example, Michelangelo's paintings on the ceiling and walls of the Sistine Chapel in Rome, a central picture shows God delivering life, through His extended hand, to Adam, who receives life through his own extended hand. This moment of the creation of human life is one of the most significant in Biblical literature, but it is *only* this moment that Michelangelo is able to capture in this single painting. In contrast, writers of narrative may include all the events leading up to and following such a moment, for narrations move in continuous lines from word to word, scene to scene, action to action, and speech to speech. As a result of this chronological movement, the reader's comprehension must necessarily also be chronological.

Style

The medium of fiction and of all literature is language, and the manipulation of language—the **style**—is a primary skill of the writer (see Chapter 7 on style and tone). A mark of a good style is the use of *active verbs* and nouns that are **specific** and **concrete.** Even with the most active and graphic diction possible, writers can never render their incidents and scenes exactly, but they can be judged on how vividly they tell their stories.

Point of View

One of the most important ways in which writers knit their stories together, and also an important way in which they try to interest and engage readers, is the careful control of **point of view** (see Chapter 5). Point of view is the **voice** of the story, the speaker who does the narrating. It is the way the reality of a story is made to seem authentic. It can be regarded as the story's *focus,* the *angle of vision* from which things are not only seen and reported but also judged.

Basically, there are two kinds of points of view, but there are many variations, sometimes obvious and sometimes subtle. In the **first-person point of view,** a fictitious observer tells us what he or she saw, heard, concluded, and thought. This viewpoint is characterized by the use of the pronoun *I* as the speaker refers to his or her position as an observer or commentator. The

speaker, or **narrator**—terms that are interchangeable—may sometimes seem to be the author speaking directly using an **authorial voice,** but more often the speaker is an independent character—a **persona** with characteristics that separate her or him from the author.

In common with all narrators, the first-person narrator establishes a clearly defined relationship to the story's events. Some narrators are deeply engaged in the action; others are only minor participants or observers; still others are not involved at all but are transmitting the reports of others more deeply involved. Sometimes the narrator uses the pronoun *we* if he or she is represented as part of a group that has witnessed the action or participated in it. Often, too, the narrator might use *we* when referring to ideas and interpretations shared with the reader or listener—the idea being to draw readers into the story as much as possible.

The **third-person point of view** uses third-person pronouns (*she, he, it, they, her, him, them,* etc.).[2] The third-person point of view may be (1) **limited,** with the focus being on one particular character and what he or she does, says, hears, thinks, and otherwise experiences; (2) **omniscient,** with the possibility that the activities and thoughts of all the characters are open and fully known by the speaker; or (3) **dramatic,** or **objective,** in which the story is confined *only* to the reporting of actions and speeches, with no commentary and no revelation of the thoughts of any of the characters unless the characters themselves reveal their thoughts dramatically.

Understanding point of view usually requires subtlety of perception—indeed, it may be one of the most difficult concepts in the study of fiction. In fuller perspective, therefore, we can think of it as the *total position* from which things are viewed, understood, and communicated. The position might be simply physical: *Where was the speaker located when the events occurred,* or *Does the speaker give us a close or distant view of the events?* The position might also be personal or philosophical: *Do the events illustrate a personal opinion* (Maupassant's "The Necklace"), *embody a philosophical judgment* (Hawthorne's "Young Goodman Brown"), or *argue for a theological viewpoint* ("The Parable of the Prodigal Son")?

Point of view is one of the major ways by which authors make fiction vital. By controlling point of view, authors raise some of the same questions in their fiction that perplex us in life, and they help us make reasonable inferences about fictional actions. As we do with what real people tell us, we need to evaluate what fictional narrators say, for their words are affected by their interests, limitations, attitudes, opinions, and degree of candidness. An instance is the narrator of Walker's "Everyday Use," who clearly considers her visiting daughter, Dee (Wangero) presumptuous and also a bit foolish because Dee does not respect the utility ("everyday use") of the objects of the family home. Her feelings are plain, but one might also question whether the narrator gives Dee's thoughts sufficient consideration. In other words, are Dee's attitudes quite as

---

[2] The possibilities of a second-person point of view are discussed in Chapter 5.

silly as the narrator makes them seem? For readers, the perception of a fictional point of view can be as complex as life itself, for it may be as difficult—in fiction as in life—to evaluate our sources of information.

Description

Together with narration, a vital aspect of fiction is **description,** which is intended to cause readers to imagine or re-create the scenes and actions of the story. Description can be both physical (places and persons) and psychological (an emotion or set of emotions). Excessive description sometimes interrupts or postpones a story's actions, so many writers include only as much as is necessary to keep the action moving along.

Mood and **atmosphere** are important aspects of descriptive writing, and to the degree that descriptions are evocative, they may reach the level of **metaphor** and **symbolism.** These characteristics of fiction are a property of all literature, and you will also encounter them whenever you read poems and plays.

Dialogue

Another major tool of the writer of fiction is **dialogue.** By definition, dialogue is the conversation of two people, but more than two characters may also participate. It is of course the major medium of the playwright, and it is one of the means by which the fiction writer makes a story vivid and dramatic. Straight narration and description can do no more than make a secondhand ("hearsay") assertion that a character's thoughts and responses exist, but dialogue makes everything firsthand and real.

Dialogue is hence a means of *showing* rather than *reporting*. If characters feel pain or declare love, their own words can be taken as the expression of what is on their minds. Some dialogue is terse and minimal; other dialogue is expanded, depending on the situation, the personalities of the characters, and the author's intent. Dialogue can concern any topic, including personal feelings, reactions to the past, future plans, changing ideas, sudden realizations, and political, social, philosophic, or religious ideas.

The language of dialogue can indicate the intelligence, articulateness, educational level, or emotional state of the speakers. Hence the author might use *grammatical mistakes, faulty pronunciation,* or *slang* to show a character of limited or disadvantaged background or a character who is trying to be seen in that light. *Dialect* shows the region from which the speaker comes, just as an *accent* indicates a place of national origin. *Jargon* and *cliché* suggest self-inflation or intellectual limitations—usually reasons for laughter. The use of *private, intimate expressions* might show people who are close to each other emotionally. Speech that is interrupted by *voiced pauses* (e.g., "er," "ah," "um," "you know") or speech characterized by *inappropriate words* might show a character who is unsure or not in control. There are many possibilities in dialogue, but no matter what qualities you find, writers include dialogue to enable you to know their characters better.

Tone and Irony

In every story we can consider **tone,** that is, the ways in which authors convey attitudes toward readers and also toward the story material. **Irony,** one of the major components of tone, refers to language and situations that seem to reverse normal expectations. *Word choice* is the characteristic of **verbal irony,** in which what is meant is usually the opposite of what is said, as when we *mean* that people are doing badly even though we *say* that they are doing well (see Chapter 7, pp. 273–74). Broader forms of irony are *situational* and *dramatic:* **Situational irony** refers to circumstances in which bad things happen to good people, or in which rewards are not earned because forces beyond human comprehension seem to be in total control. In **dramatic irony** characters have only a nonexistent, partial, incorrect, or misguided understanding of what is happening to them, while both readers and other characters understand the situation more fully. Readers hence become concerned about the characters and hope that they will develop understanding quickly enough to avoid the problems bedeviling them and the pitfalls endangering them.

Symbolism and Allegory

In literature, even apparently ordinary things may acquire symbolic value; that is, everyday objects may be understood to have meanings that are beyond themselves, bigger than themselves. In fiction, many functional and essential incidents, objects, speeches, and characters may also be construed as symbols (see Chapter 8). Some symbols are widely recognized and therefore are considered **cultural** or **universal symbols.** Water, flowers, jewels, the sun, certain stars, the flag, altars, and minarets are examples of cultural symbols. Others are **contextual symbols;** that is, they take on symbolic meaning only in their individual works, as when in Maupassant's "The Necklace" Mathilde and her husband move into an attic flat to save money that they need to repay their enormous debt. These new quarters may be taken to symbolize the hardship experienced by the poor.

When a complete story can be applied point by point to a parallel set of situations, in addition to maintaining its own narrative integrity, it is an **allegory.** Many stories are not complete allegories, however, even though they contain sections having allegorical parallels. Thus, the Loisels' long servitude in Maupassant's "The Necklace" calls to mind the lives and activities of many people who perform tasks for mistaken or meaningless reasons. "The Necklace" is therefore allegorical even though it is not an allegory.

Commentary

Writers may also include **commentary, analysis,** or **interpretation,** in the expectation that readers need insight into the characters and actions. When fiction was new, authors often expressed such commentary directly. Henry Fielding (1707–1754) divided his novels into "books" and included a chapter of personal and philosophic commentary at the beginning of each of these. In the next century, George Eliot (1819–1880) included many extensive passages of commentary in her novels.

Later writers have kept commentary at a minimum, preferring instead to concentrate on direct action and dialogue, and allowing readers to draw their own conclusions about meaning. In first-person narrations, however, you can expect the narrators to make their own personal comments, as in Olsen's "I Stand Here Ironing" and Zabytko's "Home Soil." Observations made by dramatic speakers in works like these may be accepted at face value, but you should recognize that anything the speakers say is also a mode of character disclosure. Such commentary is therefore just as much a part of the story as the narrative incidents.

The Elements Together

These, then, are the major tools of writers of fiction. For analytical purposes, one or another of them may be considered separately so that the artistic achievement of a particular author can be recognized. It is also important to realize that authors may use all the tools simultaneously. The story may be told by a character who is a witness, and thus it has a **first-person point of view.** The major **character,** the **protagonist,** goes through a series of **actions** as a result of a carefully arranged **plot.** Because of this plot, together with the author's chosen method of **narration,** the story will follow a certain kind of arrangement, or **structure,** such as a straightforward **sequence** or a disjointed series of **episodes.** One thing that the action may demonstrate is the **theme** or **central idea.** The writer's **style** may be manifested in **ironic** expressions. The description of the character's actions may reveal **irony of situation,** while at the same time this situation is made vivid through **dialogue** in which the character is a participant. Because the plight of the character is like the plight of many persons in the world, it is an **allegory,** and the character herself or himself may be considered as a **symbol.**

Throughout each story we read, no matter what characteristics we are considering, it is most important to realize that a work of fiction is an entirety, a unity. Any reading of a story should be undertaken not to break things down into parts, but to understand and assimilate the work *as a whole.* The separate analysis of various topics, to which this book is committed, is thus a *means* to that end, *not* the end itself. The study of fiction, like the study of all literature, is designed to foster our growth and to increase our understanding of the human condition.

 ## STORIES FOR STUDY

TIM O'BRIEN   (b. 1946)

William Timothy O'Brien was born in Minnesota and attended Macalester College in St. Paul. Drafted during the Vietnam war, he was wounded in combat. After returning home he did graduate study, worked as a reporter, and became a writer. Among the works he has regularly published since the 1970s are If I Die in a Combat Zone, Box Me Up and Ship Me Home *(1973);* Northern Lights *(1974);* Going After Cacciato *(1978); and* The Things They Carried *(1990). In his stories, which interweave fiction and autobiography, he realistically treats both the horrors of the Vietnam war and the ways in which returning veterans and their loved ones adjust to life after returning home. Because he portrays the lives and feelings of combat soldiers so well, he has been called one of the best American writers about war.*

The Things They Carried _____ *1990*

First Lieutenant Jimmy Cross carried letters from a girl named Martha, a junior at Mount Sebastian College in New Jersey. They were not love letters, but Lieutenant Cross was hoping, so he kept them folded in plastic at the bottom of his rucksack. In the late afternoon, after a day's march, he would dig his foxhole, wash his hands under a canteen, unwrap the letters, hold them with the tips of his fingers, and spend the last hour of light pretending. He would imagine romantic camping trips into the White Mountains in New Hampshire. He would sometimes taste the envelope flaps, knowing her tongue had been there. More than anything, he wanted Martha to love him as he loved her, but the letters were mostly chatty, elusive on the matter of love. She was a virgin, he was almost sure. She was an English major at Mount Sebastian, and she wrote beautifully about her professors and roommates and midterm exams, about her respect for Chaucer and her great affection for Virginia Woolf. She often quoted lines of poetry; she never mentioned the war, except to say, Jimmy, take care of yourself. The letters weighed 10 ounces. They were signed Love, Martha, but Lieutenant Cross understood that Love was only a way of signing and did not mean what he sometimes pretended it meant. At dusk, he would carefully return the letters to his rucksack. Slowly, a bit distracted, he would get up and move among his men, checking the perimeter, then at full dark he would return to his hole and watch the night and wonder if Martha was a virgin.

The things they carried were largely determined by necessity. Among the necessities or near-necessities were P-38 can openers, pocket knives, heat tabs, wristwatches, dog tags, mosquito repellent, chewing gum, candy, cigarettes, salt tablets, packets of Kool-Aid, lighters, matches, sewing kits, Military Payment Certificates, C rations, and two or three canteens of water. Together, these items weighed between 15 and 20 pounds, depending upon a man's habits or rate of metabolism. Henry Dobbins, who was a big man, carried extra rations; he was especially fond of canned peaches in heavy syrup over pound cake. Dave Jensen, who practiced field hygiene, carried a toothbrush, dental floss, and several hotel-sized bars of soap he'd stolen on R&R in Sydney, Australia. Ted Lavender, who was scared, carried tranquilizers until he was shot in the head outside the village of Than Khe in mid-April. By necessity, and because it was SOP, they all carried steel helmets that weighed 5 pounds including the liner and camouflage cover. They carried the standard fatigue jackets and trousers. Very few carried underwear. On their feet they carried jungle boots—2.1 pounds—and Dave Jensen carried three pairs of socks and a can of Dr. Scholl's foot powder as a precaution against trench foot. Until he was shot, Ted Lavender carried six or seven ounces of premium dope, which for him was a necessity. Mitchell Sanders, the RTO, carried condoms. Norman Bowker carried a diary. Rat Kiley carried comic books. Kiowa, a devout Baptist, carried an illustrated New Testament that had been presented to him by his father, who taught Sunday school in Oklahoma City, Oklahoma. As a hedge against bad times, however, Kiowa also carried his grandmother's distrust of the white man, his grandfather's old hunting hatchet. Necessity dictated. Because the land was mined and booby-trapped, it was SOP for each man to carry a steel-centered, nylon-covered flak jacket, which weighed 6.7 pounds, but which on hot days seemed much heavier. Because you could die so quickly, each man carried at least one large compress bandage, usually in the helmet band for easy access. Because the nights were cold, and because the monsoons were wet, each carried a green plastic poncho that could be used as a raincoat or groundsheet or makeshift tent. With its quilted liner, the poncho weighed almost two pounds, but it was worth every ounce. In April, for instance, when Ted Lavender was shot, they used his poncho to wrap him up, then to carry him across the paddy, then to lift him into the chopper that took him away.

They were called legs or grunts.

To carry something was to hump it, as when Lieutenant Jimmy Cross humped his love for Martha up the hills and through the swamps. In its intransitive form, to hump meant to walk, or to march, but it implied burdens far beyond the intransitive.

Almost everyone humped photographs. In his wallet, Lieutenant Cross carried   5
two photographs of Martha. The first was a Kodacolor snapshot signed Love, though he knew better. She stood against a brick wall. Her eyes were gray and neutral, her lips slightly open as she stared straight-on at the camera. At night, sometimes, Lieutenant Cross wondered who had taken the picture, because he knew she had boyfriends, because he loved her so much, and because he could see the shadow of the picture-taker spreading out against the brick wall. The second photograph had been clipped from the 1968 Mount Sebastian yearbook. It was an action shot—women's volleyball—and Martha was bent horizontal to the floor, reaching, the palms of her hands in sharp focus, the tongue taut, the expression frank and competitive. There was no visible sweat. She wore white gym shorts. Her legs, he thought, were almost certainly the legs of a virgin, dry and without hair, the left knee cocked and carrying her entire weight, which was just over one hundred pounds. Lieutenant Cross remembered touching that left knee. A dark theater, he remembered, and the movie was *Bonnie and Clyde,* and Martha wore a tweed skirt, and during the final scene, when he touched her knee, she turned and looked at him in a sad, sober way that made him pull his hand back, but he would always remember the feel of the tweed skirt and the knee beneath it and the sound of the gunfire that killed Bonnie and Clyde, how embarrassing it was, how slow and oppressive. He remembered kissing her good night at the dorm door. Right then, he thought, he should've done something brave. He should've carried her up the stairs to her room and tied her to the bed and touched that left knee all night long. He should've risked it. Whenever he looked at the photographs, he thought of new things he should've done.

What they carried was partly a function of rank, partly of field specialty.

As a first lieutenant and platoon leader, Jimmy Cross carried a compass, maps, code books, binoculars, and a .45-caliber pistol that weighed 2.9 pounds fully loaded. He carried a strobe light and the responsibility for the lives of his men.

As an RTO, Mitchell Sanders carried the PRC-25 radio, a killer, 26 pounds with its battery.

As a medic, Rat Kiley carried a canvas satchel filled with morphine and plasma and malaria tablets and surgical tape and comic books and all the things a medic must carry, including M&M's for especially bad wounds, for a total weight of nearly 20 pounds.

As a big man, therefore a machine gunner, Henry Dobbins carried the M-60,   10
which weighed 23 pounds unloaded, but which was almost always loaded. In addition, Dobbins carried between 10 and 15 pounds of ammunition draped in belts across his chest and shoulders.

As PFCs or Spec 4s, most of them were common grunts and carried the standard M-16 gas-operated assault rifle. The weapon weighed 7.5 pounds unloaded, 8.2 pounds with its full 20-round magazine. Depending on numerous factors, such as topography and psychology, the riflemen carried anywhere from 12 to 20 magazines, usually in cloth bandoliers, adding on another 8.4 pounds at minimum, 14 pounds at maximum. When it was available, they also carried M-16 maintenance gear—rods and steel brushes and swabs and tubes of LSA oil—all of which weighed about a pound. Among the grunts, some carried the M-79 grenade launcher, 5.9 pounds unloaded, a reasonably light weapon except for the ammunition, which was heavy. A single round weighed 10 ounces. The typical load was 25 rounds. But Ted Lavender, who was scared, carried 34 rounds when he was shot and killed outside Than Khe, and he went down under an exceptional burden, more than 20 pounds of ammunition, plus the flak jacket and helmet and rations and water and toilet paper and tranquilizers and all the rest, plus the unweighed fear. He was dead weight. There was no twitching or flopping. Kiowa, who saw it happen, said it was like watching a rock fall, or a big sandbag or something— just boom, then down—not like the movies where the dead guy rolls around and does fancy spins and goes ass over teakettle—not like that, Kiowa said, the poor bastard just flat-fuck fell. Boom. Down. Nothing else. It was a bright morning in mid-April. Lieutenant Cross felt the pain. He blamed himself. They stripped off Lavender's canteens and ammo, all the heavy things, and Rat Kiley said the obvious, the guy's dead, and Mitchell Sanders used his radio to report one U.S. KIA and to request a chopper. Then they wrapped Lavender in his poncho. They carried him out to a dry paddy, established security, and sat smoking the dead man's dope until the chopper came. Lieutenant Cross kept to himself. He pictured Martha's smooth young face, thinking he loved her more than anything, more than his men, and now Ted Lavender was dead because he loved her so much and could not stop thinking about her. When the dustoff arrived, they carried Lavender aboard. Afterward they burned Than Khe. They marched until dusk, then dug their holes, and that night Kiowa kept explaining how you had to be there, how fast it was, how the poor guy just dropped like so much concrete. Boom-down, he said. Like cement.

In addition to the three standard weapons—the M-60, M-16, and M-79—they carried whatever presented itself, or whatever seemed appropriate as a means of killing or staying alive. They carried catch-as-catch-can. At various times, in various situations, they carried M-14s and CAR-15s and Swedish Ks and grease guns and captured AK-47s and Chi-Coms and RPGs and Simonov carbines and black market Uzis and .38-caliber Smith & Wesson handguns and 66 mm LAWs and shotguns and silencers and blackjacks and bayonets and C-4 plastic explosives. Lee Strunk carried a slingshot; a weapon of last resort, he called it. Mitchell Sanders carried brass knuckles. Kiowa carried his grand-father's feathered hatchet. Every third or fourth man carried a Claymore antipersonnel mine—3.5 pounds with its firing device. They all carried fragmentation grenades—14 ounces each. They all carried at least one M-18 colored smoke grenade—24 ounces. Some carried CS or tear gas grenades. Some carried white phosphorus grenades. They carried all they could bear, and then some, including a silent awe for the terrible power of the things they carried.

In the first week of April, before Lavender died, Lieutenant Jimmy Cross received a good-luck charm from Martha. It was a simple pebble, an ounce at most. Smooth to the touch, it was a milky white color with flecks of orange and violet, oval-shaped, like a miniature egg. In the accompanying letter, Martha wrote that she had found the pebble on the Jersey shoreline, precisely where the land touched water at high tide, where things came together but also separated. It was this separate-but-together quality, she wrote, that had inspired her to pick up the pebble and to carry it in her breast pocket for several days, where it seemed weightless, and then to send it through the mail, by air, as a token of her truest feelings for him. Lieutenant Cross found this romantic. But he wondered what her truest feelings were, exactly, and what she meant by separate-but-together. He wondered how the tides and waves had come into play on that afternoon along the Jersey shoreline when Martha saw the pebble and bent down to rescue it from geology. He imagined bare feet. Martha was a poet, with the poet's sensibilities, and her feet would be brown and bare, the toenails unpainted, the eyes chilly and somber like the ocean in March, and though it was painful, he wondered who had been with her that afternoon. He imagined a pair of shadows moving along the strip of sand where things came together but also separated. It was phantom jealousy, he knew, but he couldn't help himself. He loved her so much. On the march, through the hot days of early April, he carried the pebble in his mouth, turning it with his tongue, tasting sea salt and moisture. His mind wandered. He had difficulty keeping his attention on the war. On occasion he would yell at his men to spread out the column, to keep their eyes open, but then he would slip away into daydreams, just pretending, walking barefoot along the Jersey shore, with Martha, carrying nothing. He would feel himself rising. Sun and waves and gentle winds, all love and lightness.

What they carried varied by mission.

When a mission took them to the mountains, they carried mosquito netting, machetes, canvas tarps, and extra bug juice.   15

If a mission seemed especially hazardous, or if it involved a place they knew to be bad, they carried everything they could. In certain heavily mined AOs, where the land was dense with Toe Poppers and Bouncing Betties, they took turns humping a 28-pound mine detector. With its headphones and big sensing plate, the equipment was a stress on the lower back and shoulders, awkward to handle, often useless because of the shrapnel in the earth, but they carried it anyway, partly for safety, partly for the illusion of safety.

On ambush, or other night missions, they carried peculiar little odds and ends. Kiowa always took along his New Testament and a pair of moccasins for silence. Dave Jensen carried night-sight vitamins high in carotene. Lee Strunk carried his slingshot; ammo, he claimed, would never be a problem. Rat Kiley carried brandy and M&M's candy. Until he was shot, Ted Lavender carried the starlight scope, which weighed

6.3 pounds with its aluminum carrying case. Henry Dobbins carried his girlfriend's pantyhose wrapped around his neck as a comforter. They all carried ghosts. When dark came, they would move out single file across the meadows and paddies to their ambush coordinates, where they would quietly set up the Claymores and lie down and spend the night waiting.

Other missions were more complicated and required special equipment. In mid-April, it was their mission to search out and destroy the elaborate tunnel complexes in the Than Khe area south of Chu Lai. To blow the tunnels, they carried one-pound blocks of pentrite high explosives, four blocks to a man, 68 pounds in all. They carried wiring, detonators, and battery-powered clackers. Dave Jensen carried earplugs. Most often, before blowing the tunnels, they were ordered by higher command to search them, which was considered bad news, but by and large they just shrugged and carried out orders. Because he was a big man, Henry Dobbins was excused from tunnel duty. The others would draw numbers. Before Lavender died there were 17 men in the platoon, and whoever drew the number 17 would strip off his gear and crawl in headfirst with a flashlight and Lieutenant Cross's .45-caliber pistol. The rest of them would fan out as security. They would sit down or kneel, not facing the hole, listening to the ground beneath them, imagining cobwebs and ghosts, whatever was down there—the tunnel walls squeezing in—how the flashlight seemed impossibly heavy in the hand and how it was tunnel vision in the very strictest sense, compression in all ways, even time, and how you had to wiggle in—ass and elbows—a swallowed-up feeling—and how you found yourself worrying about odd things: Will your flashlight go dead? Do rats carry rabies? If you screamed, how far would the sound carry? Would your buddies hear it? Would they have the courage to drag you out? In some respects, though not many, the waiting was worse than the tunnel itself. Imagination was a killer.

On April 16, when Lee Strunk drew the number 17, he laughed and muttered something and went down quickly. The morning was hot and very still. Not good, Kiowa said. He looked at the tunnel opening, then out across a dry paddy toward the village of Than Khe. Nothing moved. No clouds or birds or people. As they waited, the men smoked and drank Kool-Aid, not talking much, feeling sympathy for Lee Strunk but also feeling the luck of the draw. You win some, you lose some, said Mitchell Sanders, and sometimes you settle for a rain check. It was a tired line and no one laughed.

Henry Dobbins ate a tropical chocolate bar. Ted Lavender popped a tranquilizer and went off to pee.   20

After five minutes, Lieutenant Jimmy Cross moved to the tunnel, leaned down, and examined the darkness. Trouble, he thought—a cave-in maybe. And then suddenly, without willing it, he was thinking about Martha. The stresses and fractures, the quick collapse, the two of them buried alive under all that weight. Dense, crushing love. Kneeling, watching the hole, he tried to concentrate on Lee Strunk and the war, all the dangers, but his love was too much for him, he felt paralyzed, he wanted to sleep inside her lungs and breathe her blood and be smothered. He wanted her to be a virgin and not a virgin, all at once. He wanted to know her. Intimate secrets: Why poetry? Why so sad? Why that grayness in her eyes? Why so alone? Not lonely, just alone—riding her bike across campus or sitting off by herself in the cafeteria—even dancing, she danced alone—and it was the aloneness that filled him with love. He remembered telling her that one evening. How she nodded and looked away. And how, later, when he kissed her, she received the kiss without returning it, her eyes wide open, not afraid, not a virgin's eyes, just flat and uninvolved.

Lieutenant Cross gazed at the tunnel. But he was not there. He was buried with Martha under the white sand at the Jersey shore. They were pressed together, and the pebble in his mouth was her tongue. He was smiling. Vaguely, he was aware of how quiet the day was, the sullen paddies, yet he could not bring himself to worry about matters of security. He was beyond that. He was just a kid at war, in love. He was twenty-four years old. He couldn't help it.

A few moments later Lee Strunk crawled out of the tunnel. He came up grinning, filthy but alive. Lieutenant Cross nodded and closed his eyes while the others clapped Strunk on the back and made jokes about rising from the dead.

Worms, Rat Kiley said. Right out of the grave. Fuckin' zombie.

The men laughed. They all felt great relief.   25

Spook city, said Mitchell Sanders.

Lee Strunk made a funny ghost sound, a kind of moaning, yet very happy, and right then, when Strunk made that high happy moaning sound, when he went *Ahhooooo*, right then Ted Lavender was shot in the head on his way back from peeing. He lay with his mouth open. The teeth were broken. There was a swollen black bruise under his left eye. The cheekbone was gone. Oh shit, Rat Kiley said, the guy's dead. The guy's dead, he kept saying, which seemed profound—the guy's dead. I mean really.

The things they carried were determined to some extent by superstition. Lieutenant Cross carried his good-luck pebble. Dave Jensen carried a rabbit's foot. Norman Bowker, otherwise a very gentle person, carried a thumb that had been pre-sented to him as a gift by Mitchell Sanders. The thumb was dark brown, rubbery to the touch, and weighed four ounces at most. It had been cut from a VC corpse, a boy of fifteen or sixteen. They'd found him at the bottom of an irrigation ditch, badly burned, flies in his mouth and eyes. The boy wore black shorts and sandals. At the time of his death he had been carrying a pouch of rice, a rifle and three magazines of ammunition.

You want my opinion, Mitchell Sanders said, there's a definite moral here.

He put his hand on the dead boy's wrist. He was quiet for a time, as if counting a   30
pulse, then he patted the stomach, almost affectionately, and used Kiowa's hunting hatchet to remove the thumb.

Henry Dobbins asked what the moral was.

Moral?

You know. *Moral.*

Sanders wrapped the thumb in toilet paper and handed it across to Norman Bowker. There was no blood. Smiling, he kicked the boy's head, watched the flies scatter, and said, It's like with that old TV show—Paladin. Have gun, will travel.

Henry Dobbins thought about it.   35

Yeah, well, he finally said. I don't see no moral.

There it *is*, man.

Fuck off.

They carried USO stationery and pencils and pens. They carried Sterno, safety pins, trip flares, signal flares, spools of wire, razor blades, chewing tobacco, liberated joss sticks and statuettes of the smiling Buddha, candles, grease pencils, *The Stars and Stripes,* fingernail clippers, Psy Ops leaflets, bush hats, bolos, and much more. Twice a week, when the resupply choppers came in, they carried hot chow in green mermite cans and large canvas bags filled with iced beer and soda pop. They carried plastic water containers, each with a two-gallon capacity. Mitchell Sanders carried a set of starched tiger fatigues for special occasions. Henry Dobbins carried Black Flag insecticide. Dave Jensen carried empty sandbags that could be filled at night for added protection. Lee Strunk carried tanning lotion. Some things they carried in common. Taking turns, they carried the big PRC-77 scrambler radio, which weighed 30 pounds with its battery. They shared the weight of memory. They took up what others could no longer bear. Often, they carried each other, the wounded or weak. They carried infections. They carried chess sets, basketballs, Vietnamese-English dictionaries, insignia of rank, Bronze Stars and Purple Hearts, plastic cards imprinted with the Code of Conduct. They carried diseases, among them malaria and dysentery. They carried lice and ringworm and leeches and paddy algae and various rots and molds. They carried the land itself—Vietnam, the place, the soil—a powdery orange-red dust that covered their boots and fatigues and faces. They carried the sky. The whole atmosphere, they carried it, the humidity, the monsoons, the stink of fungus and decay, all of it, they carried gravity. They moved like mules. By daylight they took sniper fire, at night they were mortared, but it was not battle, it was just the endless march, village to village, without purpose, nothing won or lost. They marched for the sake of the march. They plodded along slowly, dumbly, leaning forward against the heat, unthinking, all blood and bone, simple grunts, soldiering with their legs, toiling up the hills and down into the paddies and across the rivers and up again and down, just humping, one step and then the next and then another, but no volition, no will, because it was automatic, it was anatomy, and the war was entirely a matter of posture and carriage, the hump was everything, a kind of inertia, a kind of emptiness, a dullness of desire and intellect and conscience and hope and human sensibility. Their principles were in their feet. Their calculations were biological. They had no sense of strategy or mission. They searched the villages without knowing what to look for, not caring, kicking over jars of rice, frisking children and old men, blowing tunnels, sometimes setting fires and sometimes not, then forming up and moving on to the next village, then other villages, where it would always be the same. They carried their own lives. The pressures were enormous. In the heat of early afternoon, they would remove their helmets and flak jackets, walking bare, which was dangerous but which helped ease the strain. They would often discard things along the route of march. Purely for comfort, they would throw away rations, blow their Claymores and grenades, no matter, because by nightfall the resupply choppers would arrive with more of the same, then a day or two later still more, fresh watermelons and crates of ammunition and sunglasses and woolen sweaters—the resources were stunning—sparklers for the Fourth of July, colored eggs for Easter—it was the great American war chest—the fruits of science, the smokestacks, the canneries, the arsenals at Hartford, the Minnesota forests, the machine shops, the vast fields of corn and wheat—they carried like freight trains; they carried it on their backs and shoulders—and for all the ambiguities of Vietnam, all the mysteries and unknowns, there was at least the single abiding certainty that they would never be at a loss for things to carry.

     After the chopper took Lavender away. Lieutenant Jimmy Cross led his men into the village of Than Khe. They burned everything. They shot chickens and dogs, they trashed the village well, they called in artillery and watched the wreckage, then they marched for several hours through the hot afternoon, and then at dusk, while Kiowa explained how Lavender died, Lieutenant Cross found himself trembling.

     He tried not to cry. With his entrenching tool, which weighed five pounds, he began digging a hole in the earth.

40

He felt shame. He hated himself. He had loved Martha more than his men, and as a consequence Lavender was now dead, and this was something he would have to carry like a stone in his stomach for the rest of the war.

All he could do was dig. He used his entrenching tool like an ax, slashing, feeling both love and hate, and then later, when it was full dark, he sat at the bottom of his foxhole and wept. It went on for a long while. In part, he was grieving for Ted Lavender, but mostly it was for Martha, and for himself, because she belonged to another world, which was not quite real, and because she was a junior at Mount Sebastian College in New Jersey, a poet and a virgin and uninvolved, and because he realized she did not love him and never would.

Like cement, Kiowa whispered in the dark. I swear to God—boom, down. Not a word.

I've heard this, said Norman Bowker.   45

A pisser, you know? Still zipping himself up. Zapped while zipping.

All right, fine. That's enough.

Yeah, but you had to see it, the guy just—

I *heard*, man. Cement. So why not shut the fuck *up?*

Kiowa shook his head sadly and glanced over at the hole where Lieutenant Jimmy   50
Cross sat watching the night. The air was thick and wet. A warm dense fog had settled over the paddies and there was the stillness that precedes rain.

After a time Kiowa sighed.

One thing for sure, he said. The lieutenant's in some deep hurt. I mean that crying jag—the way he was carrying on—it wasn't fake or anything, it was real heavy-duty hurt. The man cares.

Sure, Norman Bowker said.

Say what you want, the man does care.

We all got problems.   55

Not Lavender.

No, I guess not, Bowker said. Do me a favor, though.

Shut up?

That's a smart Indian. Shut up.

Shrugging, Kiowa pulled off his boots. He wanted to say more, just to lighten up   60
his sleep, but instead he opened his New Testament and arranged it beneath his head as a pillow. The fog made things seem hollow and unattached. He tried not to think about Ted Lavender, but then he was thinking how fast it was, no drama, down and dead, and how it was hard to feel anything except surprise. It seemed unchristian. He wished he could find some great sadness, or even anger, but the emotion wasn't there and he couldn't make it happen. Mostly he felt pleased to be alive. He liked the smell of the New Testament under his cheek, the leather and ink and paper and glue, whatever the chemicals were. He liked hearing the sounds of night. Even his fatigue, it felt fine, the stiff muscles and the prickly awareness of his own body, a floating feeling. He enjoyed not being dead. Lying there, Kiowa admired Lieutenant Jimmy Cross's capacity for grief. He wanted to share the man's pain, he wanted to care as Jimmy Cross cared. And yet when he closed his eyes, all he could think was Boom-down, and all he could feel was the pleasure of having his boots off and the fog curling in around him and the damp soil and the Bible smells and the plush comfort of night.

After a moment Norman Bowker sat up in the dark.

What the hell, he said. You want to talk, *talk*. Tell it to me.

Forget it.

No, man, go on. One thing I hate, it's a silent Indian.

For the most part they carried themselves with poise, a kind of dignity. Now and   65
then, however, there were times of panic, when they squealed or wanted to squeal but
couldn't, when they twitched and made moaning sounds and covered their heads and
said Dear Jesus and flopped around on the earth and fired their weapons blindly and
cringed and sobbed and begged for the noise to stop and went wild and made stupid
promises to themselves and to God and to their mothers and fathers, hoping not to die.
In different ways, it happened to all of them. Afterward, when the firing ended, they
would blink and peek up. They would touch their bodies, feeling shame, then quickly
hiding it. They would force themselves to stand. As if in slow motion, frame by frame, the
world would take on the old logic—absolute silence, then the wind, then sunlight, then
voices. It was the burden of being alive. Awkwardly, the men would reassemble themselves, first in private, then in groups, becoming soldiers again. They would repair the
leaks in their eyes. They would check for casualties, call in dust-offs, light cigarettes, try
to smile, clear their throats and spit and begin cleaning their weapons. After a time
someone would shake his head and say, No lie, I almost shit my pants, and someone else
would laugh, which meant it was bad, yes, but the guy had obviously not shit his pants, it
wasn't that bad, and in any case nobody would ever do such a thing and then go ahead
and talk about it. They would squint into the dense, oppressive sunlight. For a few
moments, perhaps, they would fall silent, lighting a joint and tracking its passage from
man to man, inhaling, holding in the humiliation. Scary stuff, one of them might say.
But then someone else would grin or flick his eyebrows and say, Roger-dodger, almost
cut me a new asshole, *almost*.

There were numerous such poses. Some carried themselves with a sort of wistful
resignation, others with pride or stiff soldierly discipline or good humor or macho zeal.
They were afraid of dying but they were even more afraid to show it.

They found jokes to tell.

They used a hard vocabulary to contain the terrible softness. *Greased* they'd say.
Offed, lit up, zapped while zipping. It wasn't cruelty, just stage presence. They were actors.
When someone died, it wasn't quite dying, because in a curious way it seemed scripted,
and because they had their lines mostly memorized, irony mixed with tragedy, and
because they called it by other names, as if to encyst and destroy the reality of death
itself. They kicked corpses. They cut off thumbs. They talked grunt lingo. They told stories about Ted Lavender's supply of tranquilizers, how the poor guy didn't feel a thing,
how incredibly tranquil he was.

There's a moral here, said Mitchell Sanders.

They were waiting for Lavender's chopper, smoking the dead man's dope.   70

The moral's pretty obvious, Sanders said, and winked. Stay away from drugs. No
joke, they'll ruin your day every time.

Cute, said Henry Dobbins.

Mind blower, get it? Talk about wiggy. Nothing left, just blood and brains.

They made themselves laugh.

There it is, they'd say. Over and over—there it is, my friend, there it is—as if the   75
repetition itself were an act of poise, a balance between crazy and almost crazy, knowing
without going, there it is, which meant be cool, let it ride, because Oh yeah, man, you

can't change what can't be changed, there it is, there it absolutely and positively and fucking well *is*.

They were tough.

They carried all the emotional baggage of men who might die. Grief, terror, love, longing—these were intangibles, but the intangibles had their own mass and specific gravity, they had tangible weight. They carried shameful memories. They carried the common secret of cowardice barely restrained, the instinct to run or freeze or hide, and in many respects this was the heaviest burden of all, for it could never be put down, it required perfect balance and perfect posture. They carried their reputations. They carried the soldier's greatest fear, which was the fear of blushing. Men killed, and died, because they were embarrassed not to. It was what had brought them to the war in the first place, nothing positive, no dreams of glory or honor, just to avoid the blush of dishonor. They died so as not to die of embarrassment. They crawled into tunnels and walked point and advanced under fire. Each morning, despite the unknowns, they made their legs move. They endured. They kept humping. They did not submit to the obvious alternative, which was simply to close the eyes and fall. So easy, really. Go limp and tumble to the ground and let the muscles unwind and not speak and not budge until your buddies picked you up and lifted you into the chopper that would roar and dip its nose and carry you off to the world. A mere matter of falling, yet no one ever fell. It was not courage, exactly; the object was not valor. Rather, they were too frightened to be cowards.

By and large they carried these things inside, maintaining the masks of composure. They sneered at sick call. They spoke bitterly about guys who had found release by shooting off their own toes or fingers. Pussies, they'd say. Candy-asses. It was fierce, mocking talk, with only a trace of envy or awe, but even so the image played itself out behind their eyes.

They imagined the muzzle against flesh. So easy: squeeze the trigger and blow away a toe. They imagined it. They imagined the quick, sweet pain, then the evacuation to Japan, then a hospital with warm beds and cute geisha nurses.

And they dreamed of freedom birds.

At night, on guard, staring into the dark, they were carried away by jumbo jets. They felt the rush of takeoff. *Gone!* they yelled. And then velocity—wings and engines—a smiling stewardess—but it was more than a plane, it was a real bird, a big sleek silver bird with feathers and talons and high screeching. They were flying. The weights fell off; there was nothing to bear. They laughed and held on tight, feeling the cold slap of wind and altitude, soaring, thinking *It's over, I'm gone!*—they were naked, they were light and free—it was all lightness, bright and fast and buoyant, light as light, a helium buzz in the brain, a giddy bubbling in the lungs as they were taken up over the clouds and the war, beyond duty, beyond gravity and mortification and global entanglements—*Sin loi!* they yelled. *I'm sorry, motherfuckers, but I'm out of it, I'm goofed, I'm on a space cruise, I'm gone!*—and it was a restful, unencumbered sensation, just riding the light waves, sailing that big silver freedom bird over the mountains and oceans, over America, over the farms and great sleeping cities and cemeteries and highways and the golden arches of McDonald's, it was flight, a kind of fleeing, a kind of falling, falling higher and higher, spinning off the edge of the earth and beyond the sun and through the vast, silent vacuum where there were no burdens and where everything weighed exactly nothing— *Gone!* they screamed. *I'm sorry but I'm gone!*—and so at night, not quite dreaming, they gave themselves over to lightness, they were carried, they were purely borne.

80

On the morning after Ted Lavender died, First Lieutenant Jimmy Cross crouched at the bottom of his foxhole and burned Martha's letters. Then he burned the two photographs. There was a steady rain falling, which made it difficult, but he used heat tabs and Sterno to build a small fire, screening it with his body, holding the photographs over the tight blue flame with the tips of his fingers.

He realized it was only a gesture. Stupid, he thought. Sentimental, too, but mostly just stupid.

Lavender was dead. You couldn't burn the blame.

Besides, the letters were in his head. And even now, without photographs, Lieutenant Cross could see Martha playing volleyball in her white gym shorts and yellow T-shirt. He could see her moving in the rain.

When the fire died out, Lieutenant Cross pulled his poncho over his shoulders and ate breakfast from a can.

There was no great mystery, he decided.

In those burned letters Martha had never mentioned the war, except to say, Jimmy, take care of yourself. She wasn't involved. She signed the letters Love, but it wasn't love, and all the fine lines and technicalities did not matter. Virginity was no longer an issue. He hated her. Yes, he did. He hated her. Love, too, but it was a hard, hating kind of love.

The morning came up wet and blurry. Everything seemed part of everything else, the fog and Martha and the deepening rain.

He was a soldier, after all.

Half smiling, Lieutenant Jimmy Cross took out his maps. He shook his head hard, as if to clear it, then bent forward and began planning the day's march. In ten minutes, or maybe twenty, he would rouse the men and they would pack up and head west, where the maps showed the country to be green and inviting. They would do what they had always done. The rain might add some weight, but otherwise it would be one more day layered upon all the other days.

He was realistic about it. There was that new hardness in his stomach. He loved her but he hated her.

No more fantasies, he told himself.

Henceforth, when he thought about Martha, it would be only to think that she belonged elsewhere. He would shut down the daydreams. This was not Mount Sebastian, it was another world, where there were no pretty poems or midterm exams, a place where men died because of carelessness and gross stupidity. Kiowa was right. Boom-down, and you were dead, never partly dead.

Briefly, in the rain, Lieutenant Cross saw Martha's gray eyes gazing back at him.

He understood.

It was very sad, he thought. The things men carried inside. The things men did or felt they had to do.

He almost nodded at her, but didn't.

Instead he went back to his maps. He was now determined to perform his duties firmly and without negligence. It wouldn't help Lavender, he knew that, but from this point on he would comport himself as an officer. He would dispose of his good-luck pebble. Swallow it, maybe, or use Lee Strunk's slingshot, or just drop it along the trail. On the march he would impose strict field discipline. He would be careful to send out flank security, to prevent straggling or bunching up, to keep his troops moving at the proper pace and at the proper interval. He would insist on clean weapons. He would confiscate the remainder of Lavender's dope. Later in the day, perhaps, he would call the men together and speak to them plainly. He would accept the blame for what had happened to Ted Lavender. He would be a man about it. He would look them in the eyes, keeping his chin level, and he would issue the new SOPs in a calm, impersonal tone of voice, a lieutenant's voice, leaving no room for argument or discussion. Commencing immediately, he'd tell them, they would no longer abandon equipment along the route of march. They would police up their acts. They would get their shit together, and keep it together, and maintain it neatly and in good working order.

He would not tolerate laxity. He would show strength, distancing himself.   100

Among the men there would be grumbling, of course, and maybe worse, because their days would seem longer and their loads heavier, but Lieutenant Jimmy Cross reminded himself that his obligation was not to be loved but to lead. He would dispense with love; it was not now a factor. And if anyone quarreled or complained, he would simply tighten his lips and arrange his shoulders in the correct command posture. He might give a curt little nod. Or he might not. He might just shrug and say, Carry on, then they would saddle up and form into a column and move out toward the villages west of Than Khe.

QUESTIONS

1. What do we learn about Lieutenant Jimmy Cross? How do we learn about him? Why does he blame himself for Lavender's death? How does Kiowa misinterpret his emotions? How do his concerns unify the story? What other unifying elements does the story contain?

2. What is the effect of the repetitions in the story (the constant descriptions of how much things weigh, the regular need to carry things, the way in which Lavender died)?

3. Why is Mitchell Sanders unable to put into words the moral of the dead man's thumb? How would you describe the moral?

4. Analyze paragraph 39. Discuss the various burdens the men of the platoon must carry. What bearing does this paragraph have upon other parts of the story?

ALICE WALKER   (b. 1944)

Walker was born in Georgia and attended Sarah Lawrence College, graduating in 1965. In addition to teaching at Yale, Wellesley, and other schools, she has edited and published fiction, poetry, and biography, and she received a Guggenheim Fellowship in 1977. Her main hobby is gardening. For her collection of poems Revolutionary Petunias *(1973), she received a Wall Book Award nomination. Her best-known novel,* The Color Purple *(1982), was made into a movie that won an Academy Award for 1985.*

Everyday Use ───────────────────────────── *1973*

for your grandmama

I will wait for her in the yard that Maggie and I made so clean and wavy yesterday after-noon. A yard like this is more comfortable than most people know. It is not just a yard. It is like an extended living room. When the hard clay is swept clean as a floor and the fine sand around the edges lined with tiny, irregular grooves, anyone can come and sit and look up into the elm tree and wait for the breezes that never come inside the house.

Maggie will be nervous until after her sister goes: she will stand hopelessly in cor-ners, homely and ashamed of the burn scars down her arms and legs, eying her sister with a mixture of envy and awe. She thinks her sister has held life always in the palm of one hand, that "no" is a word the world never learned to say to her.

You've no doubt seen those TV shows° where the child who has "made it" is con-fronted, as a surprise, by her own mother and father, tottering in weakly from backstage. (A pleasant surprise, of course: What would they do if parent and child came on the show only to curse out and insult each other?) On TV mother and child embrace and smile into each other's faces. Sometimes the mother and father weep, the child wraps them in her arms and leans across the table to tell how she would not have made it with-out their help. I have seen these programs.

Sometimes I dream a dream in which Dee and I are suddenly brought together on a TV program of this sort. Out of a dark and soft-seated limousine I am ushered into a bright room filled with many people. There I meet a smiling, gray, sporty man like Johnny Carson who shakes my hand and tells me what a fine girl I have. Then we are on the stage and Dee is embracing me with tears in her eyes. She pins on my dress a large orchid, even though she has told me once that she thinks orchids are tacky flowers.

In real life I am a large, big-boned woman with rough, man-working hands. In the winter I wear flannel nightgowns to bed and overalls during the day. I can kill and clean a hog as mercilessly as a man. My fat keeps me hot in zero weather. I can work outside all day, breaking ice to get water for washing; I can eat pork liver cooked over the open fire minutes after it comes steaming from the hog. One winter I knocked a bull calf straight in the brain between the eyes with a sledge hammer and had the meat hung up to chill before nightfall. But of course all this does not show on television. I am the way my daughter would want me to be: a hundred pounds lighter, my skin like an uncooked barley pancake. My hair glistens in the hot bright lights. Johnny Carson has much to do to keep up with my quick and witty tongue. 5

But that is a mistake, I know even before I wake up. Who ever knew a Johnson with a quick tongue? Who can even imagine me looking a strange white man in the eye? It seems to me I have talked to them always with one foot raised in flight, with my head turned in whichever way is farthest from them. Dee, though. She would always look anyone in the eye. Hesitation was no part of her nature.

"How do I look, Mama?" Maggie says, showing just enough of her thin body enveloped in pink skirt and red blouse for me to know she's there, hidden by the door.

"Come out into the yard," I say.

TV shows: In the early days of television, a popular show was "This Is Your Life," which the narrator describes exactly here.

Have you ever seen a lame animal, perhaps a dog run over by some careless person rich enough to own a car, sidle up to someone who is ignorant enough to be kind to him? That is the way my Maggie walks. She has been like this, chin on chest, eyes on ground, feet in shuffle, ever since the fire that burned the other house to the ground.

Dee is lighter than Maggie, with nicer hair and a fuller figure. She's a woman now, though sometimes I forget. How long ago was it that the other house burned? Ten, twelve years? Sometimes I can still hear the flames and feel Maggie's arms sticking to me, her hair smoking and her dress falling off her in little black papery flakes. Her eyes seemed stretched open, blazed open by the flames reflected in them. And Dee, I see her standing off under the sweet gum tree she used to dig gum out of; a look of concentration on her face as she watched the last dingy gray board of the house fall in toward the red-hot brick chimney. Why don't you do a dance around the ashes? I'd wanted to ask her. She had hated the house that much.

I used to think she hated Maggie, too. But that was before we raised the money, the church and me, to send her to Augusta° to school. She used to read to us without pity; forcing words, lies, other folks' habits, whole lives upon us two, sitting trapped and ignorant underneath her voice. She washed us in a river of make-believe, burned us with a lot of knowledge we didn't necessarily need to know. Pressed us to her with the serious way she read, to shove us away at just the moment, like dimwits, we seemed about to understand.

Dee wanted nice things. A yellow organdy dress to wear to her graduation from high school; black pumps to match a green suit she'd made from an old suit somebody gave me. She was determined to stare down any disaster in her efforts. Her eyelids would not flicker for minutes at a time. Often I fought off the temptation to shake her. At sixteen she had a style of her own: and knew what style was.

I never had an education myself. After second grade the school was closed down. Don't ask me why: in 1927 colored asked fewer questions than they do now. Sometimes Maggie reads to me. She stumbles along good-naturedly, but can't see well. She knows she is not bright. Like good looks and money, quickness passed her by. She will marry John Thomas (who has mossy teeth in an earnest face) and then I'll be free to sit here and I guess just sing church songs to myself. Although I never was a good singer. Never could carry a tune. I was always better at a man's job. I used to love to milk till I was hooked in the side° in '49. Cows are soothing and slow and don't bother you, unless you try to milk them the wrong way.

I have deliberately turned my back on the house. It is three rooms, just like the one that burned, except the roof is tin; they don't make shingle roofs any more. There are no real windows, just some holes cut in the sides, like the portholes on a ship, but not round and not square, with rawhide holding the shutters up on the outside. This house is in a pasture, too, like the other one. No doubt when Dee sees it she will want to tear it down. She wrote me once that no matter where we "choose" to live, she will manage to come see us. But she will never bring her friends. Maggie and I thought about this and Maggie asked me, "Mama, when did Dee ever *have* any friends?"

She has a few. Furtive boys in pink shirts hanging about on washday after school. Nervous girls who never laughed. Impressed with her they worshiped the well-turned

Augusta: city in eastern Georgia, the location of Paine College.
hooked in the side: kicked by a cow.

phrase, the cute shape, the scalding humor that erupted like bubbles in lye. She read to them.

When she was courting Jimmy T she didn't have much time to pay to us, but turned all her faultfinding power on him. He *flew* to marry a cheap city girl from a family of ignorant flashy people. She hardly had time to recompose herself.

When she comes I will meet—but there they are!

Maggie attempts to make a dash for the house, in her shuffling way, but I stay her with my hand. "Come back here," I say. And she stops and tries to dig a well in the sand with her toe.

It is hard to see them clearly through the strong sun. But even the first glimpse of leg out of the car tells me it is Dee. Her feet were always neat-looking, as if God himself had shaped them with a certain style. From the other side of the car comes a short, stocky man. Hair is all over his head a foot long and hanging from his chin like a kinky mule tail. I hear Maggie suck in her breath. "Uhnnnh," is what it sounds like. Like when you see the wriggling end of a snake just in front of your foot on the road. "Uhnnnh."

Dee next. A dress down to the ground, in this hot weather. A dress so loud it hurts my eyes. There are yellows and oranges enough to throw back the light of the sun. I feel my whole face warming from the heat waves it throws out. Earrings gold, too, and hanging down to her shoulders. Bracelets dangling and making noises when she moves her arm up to shake the folds of the dress out of her armpits. The dress is loose and flows, and as she walks closer, I like it. I hear Maggie go "Uhnnnh" again. It is her sister's hair. It stands straight up like the wool on a sheep. It is black as night and around the edges are two long pigtails that rope about like small lizards disappearing behind her ears.

"Wa-su-zo-Tean-o!"° she says, coming on in that gliding way the dress makes her move. The short stocky yellow with the hair to his navel is all grinning and he follows up with "Asalamalakim,° my mother and my sister!" He moves to hug Maggie but she falls back, tight up against the back of my chair. I feel her trembling there and when I look up I see the perspiration falling off her chin.

"Don't get up," says Dee. Since I am stout it takes something of a push. You can see me trying to move a second or two before I make it. She turns, showing white heels through her sandals, and goes back to the car. Out she peeks next with a Polaroid. She stoops down quickly and lines up picture after picture of me sitting there in front of the house with Maggie cowering behind me. She never takes a shot without making sure the house is included. When a cow comes nibbling around the edge of the yard she snaps it and me and Maggie *and* the house. Then she puts the Polaroid in the back seat of the car, and comes up and kisses me on the forehead.

Meanwhile Asalamalakim is going through motions with Maggie's hand. Maggie's hand is as limp as a fish, and probably as cold, despite the sweat, and she keeps trying to pull it back. It looks like Asalamalakim wants to shake hands but wants to do it fancy. Or maybe he don't know how people shake hands. Anyhow, he soon gives up on Maggie.

"Well," I say, "Dee."

"No, Mama," she says. "Not 'Dee,' Wangero Leewanika Kemanjo!"

"What happened to 'Dee'?" I wanted to know.

Wa-su-zo-Tean-o: greeting used by black Muslims.
Asalamalakim: Muslim salutation meaning "Peace be with you."

20

25

"She's dead," Wangero said. "I couldn't bear it any longer, being named after the people who oppress me."

"You know as well as me you was named after your aunt Dicie," I said. Dicie is my sister. She named Dee. We called her "Big Dee" after Dee was born.

"But who was *she* named after?" asked Wangero.

"I guess after Grandma Dee," I said.   30

"And who was she named after?" asked Wangero.

"Her mother," I said, and saw Wangero was getting tired. "That's about as far back as I can trace it," I said. Though, in fact, I probably could have carried it back beyond the Civil War through the branches.

"Well," said Asalamalakim, "there you are."

"Uhnnnh," I heard Maggie say.

"There I was not," I said, "before 'Dicie' cropped up in our family, so why should   35
I try to trace it that far back?"

He just stood there grinning, looking down on me like somebody inspecting a Model A car.° Every once in a while he and Wangero sent eye signals over my head.

"How do you pronounce this name?" I asked.

"You don't have to call me by it if you don't want to," said Wangero.

"Why shouldn't I?" I asked. "If that's what you want us to call you, we'll call you."

"I know it might sound awkward at first," said Wangero.   40

"I'll get used to it," I said. "Ream it out again."

Well, soon we got the name out of the way. Asalamalakim had a name twice as long and three times as hard. After I tripped over it two or three times he told me to just call him Hakim-a-barber. I wanted to ask him was he a barber, but I didn't really think he was, so I didn't ask.

"You must belong to those beef-cattle peoples down the road," I said. They said "Asalamalakim" when they met you, too, but they didn't shake hands. Always too busy: feeding the cattle, fixing the fences, putting up salt-lick shelters,° throwing down hay. When the white folks poisoned some of the herd the men stayed up all night with rifles in their hands. I walked a mile and a half just to see the sight.

Hakim-a-barber said, "I accept some of their doctrines, but farming and raising cattle is not my style." (They didn't tell me, and I didn't ask, whether Wangero (Dee) had really gone and married him.)

We sat down to eat and right away he said he didn't eat collards and pork was   45
unclean. Wangero, though, went on through the chitlins and corn bread, the greens and everything else. She talked a blue streak over the sweet potatoes. Everything delighted her. Even the fact that we still used the benches her daddy made for the table when we couldn't afford to buy chairs.

"Oh, Mama!" she cried. Then turned to Hakim-a-barber. "I never knew how lovely these benches are. You can feel the rump prints," she said, running her hands underneath her and along the bench. Then she gave a sigh and her hand closed over Grandma Dee's butter dish. "That's it!" she said. "I knew there was something I wanted to ask you if I could have." She jumped up from the table and went over in the corner where the churn stood, the milk in it clabber° by now. She looked at the churn and looked at it.

Model A car: The Ford car that replaced the Model T in the late 1920s. The Model A was proverbial for its quality and durability.

   salt-lick shelters: shelters built to prevent rain from dissolving large blocks of rock salt set up on poles for cattle.

   clabber: curdled, turned sour.

"This churn top is what I need," she said. "Didn't Uncle Buddy whittle it out of a tree you all used to have?"

"Yes," I said.

"Uh huh," she said happily. "And I want the dasher, too."

"Uncle Buddy whittle that, too?" asked the barber.

Dee (Wangero) looked up at me.

"Aunt Dee's first husband whittled the dash," said Maggie so low you almost couldn't hear her. "His name was Henry, but they called him Stash."

"Maggie's brain is like an elephant's," Wangero said, laughing. "I can use the churn top as a centerpiece for the alcove table," she said, sliding a plate over the churn, "and I'll think of something artistic to do with the dasher."

When she finished wrapping the dasher the handle stuck out. I took it for a moment in my hands. You didn't even have to look close to see where hands pushing the dasher up and down to make butter had left a kind of sink in the wood. In fact, there were a lot of small sinks; you could see where thumbs and fingers had sunk into the wood. It was beautiful light yellow wood, from a tree that grew in the yard where Big Dee and Stash had lived.

After dinner Dee (Wangero) went to the trunk at the foot of my bed and started rifling through it. Maggie hung back in the kitchen over the dishpan. Out came Wangero with two quilts. They had been pieced by Grandma Dee and then Big Dee and me had hung them on the quilt frames on the front porch and quilted them. One was in the Lone Star pattern. The other was Walk Around the Mountain. In both of them were scraps of dresses Grandma Dee had worn fifty and more years ago. Bits and pieces of Grandpa Jarrell's Paisley shirts. And one teeny faded blue piece, about the size of a penny matchbox, that was from Great Grandpa Ezra's uniform that he wore in the Civil War.

"Mama," Wangero said sweet as a bird. "Can I have these old quilts?"

I heard something fall in the kitchen, and a minute later the kitchen door slammed.

"Why don't you take one or two of the others?" I asked. "These old things was just done by me and Big Dee from some tops your grandma pieced before she died."

"No," said Wangero. "I don't want those. They are stitched around the borders by machine."

"That'll make them last better," I said.

"That's not the point," said Wangero. "These are all pieces of dresses Grandma used to wear. She did all this stitching by hand. Imagine!" She held the quilts securely in her arms, stroking them.

"Some of the pieces, like those lavender ones, come from old clothes her mother handed down to her," I said, moving up to touch the quilts. Dee (Wangero) moved back just enough so that I couldn't reach the quilts. They already belonged to her.

"Imagine!" she breathed again, clutching them closely to her bosom.

"The truth is," I said, "I promised to give them quilts to Maggie, for when she marries John Thomas."

She gasped like a bee had stung her.

"Maggie can't appreciate these quilts!" she said. "She'd probably be backward enough to put them to everyday use."

"I reckon she would," I said. "God knows I been saving 'em for long enough with nobody using 'em. I hope she will!" I didn't want to bring up how I had offered Dee (Wangero) a quilt when she went away to college. Then she had told me they were old-fashioned, out of style.

"But they're *priceless!*" she was saying now, furiously; for she has a temper. "Maggie would put them on the bed and in five years they'd be in rags. Less than that!"

"She can always make some more," I said. "Maggie knows how to quilt."

Dee (Wangero) looked at me with hatred. "You just will not understand. The point is these quilts, *these* quilts!"   70

"Well," I said, stumped. "What would *you* do with them?"

"Hang them," she said. As if that was the only thing you *could* do with quilts.

Maggie by now was standing in the door. I could almost hear the sound her feet made as they scraped over each other.

"She can have them, Mama," she said, like somebody used to never winning anything, or having anything reserved for her. "I can 'member Grandma Dee without the quilts."

I looked at her hard. She had filled her bottom lip with checkerberry snuff and it   75
gave her face a kind of dopey, hangdog look. It was Grandma Dee and Big Dee who taught her how to quilt herself. She stood there with her scarred hands hidden in the folds of her skirt. She looked at her sister with something like fear but she wasn't mad at her. This was Maggie's portion. This was the way she knew God to work.

When I looked at her like that something hit me in the top of my head and ran down to the soles of my feet. Just like when I'm in church and the spirit of God touches me and I get happy and shout. I did something I never had done before: hugged Maggie to me, then dragged her on into the room, snatched the quilts out of Miss Wangero's hands and dumped them into Maggie's lap. Maggie just sat there on my bed with her mouth open.

"Take one or two of the others," I said to Dee.

But she turned without a word and went out to Hakim-a-barber.

"You just don't understand," she said, as Maggie and I came out to the car.

"What don't I understand?" I wanted to know.   80

"Your heritage," she said. And then she turned to Maggie, kissed her, and said, "You ought to try to make something of yourself, too, Maggie. It's really a new day for us. But from the way you and Mama still live you'd never know it."

She put on some sunglasses that hid everything above the tip of her nose and her chin.

Maggie smiled; maybe at the sunglasses. But a real smile, not scared. After we watched the car dust settle I asked Maggie to bring me a dip of snuff. And then the two of us sat there just enjoying, until it was time to go in the house and go to bed.

QUESTIONS

1. Describe the narrator. Who is she? What is she like? Where and how does she live? What kind of life has she had? How does the story bring out her judgments about her two daughters?

2. Describe the narrator's daughters. How are they different physically and mentally? How have their lives been different?

3. Why did Dee change her name to "Wangero"? How is this change important, and how is it reflected in her attitude toward the family artifacts?

4. Describe the importance of the phrase "everyday use" (paragraph 66). How does this phrase highlight the conflicting values in the story?

JOY WILLIAMS (b. 1944)

Williams was born in Massachusetts and graduated from Marietta College and the University of Iowa. While still in her twenties she published her first stories. Among her novels are State of Grace *(1973),* The Changeling *(1978), and* Breaking and Entering *(1988). Her story collection* Taking Care, *including the title story, appeared in 1982. Her varied interests are shown by the fact that she has published a history and guide to the Keys of Florida, her adopted home state. Among her distinctions are a judgeship of the PEN/Faulkner Award for Fiction, a Wallace Stegner Fellowship, and a Guggenheim Fellowship.*

Taking Care ────────────────────────────── *1982*

Jones, the preacher, has been in love all his life. He is baffled by this because as far as he can see, it has never helped anyone, even when they have acknowledged it, which is not often. Jones's love is much too apparent and arouses neglect. He is like an animal in a traveling show who, through some aberration, wears a vital organ outside the skin, awkward and unfortunate, something that shouldn't be seen, certainly something that shouldn't be watched working. Now he sits on a bed beside his wife in the self-care unit of a hospital fifteen miles from their home. She has been committed here for tests. She is so weak, so tired. There is something wrong with her blood. Her arms are covered with bruises where they have gone into the veins. Her hip, too, is blue and swollen where they have drawn out samples of bone marrow. All of this is frightening. The doctors are severe and wise, answering Jones's questions in a way that makes him feel hopelessly deaf. They have told him that there really is no such thing as a disease of the blood, for the blood is not a living tissue but a passive vehicle for the transportation of food, oxygen and waste. They have told him that abnormalities in the blood corpuscles, which his wife seems to have, must be regarded as symptoms of disease elsewhere in the body. They have shown him, upon request, slides and charts of normal and pathological blood cells which look to Jones like canapés. They speak (for he insists) of leukocytosis,° myelocytes° and megaloblasts.° None of this takes into account the love he has for his wife! Jones sits beside her in this dim pleasant room, wearing a grey suit and his clerical collar, for when he leaves her he must visit other parishioners who are patients here. This part of the hospital is like a motel. One may wear one's regular clothes. The rooms have ice-buckets, rugs and colorful bedspreads. How he wishes that they were traveling and staying overnight, this night, in a motel. A nurse comes in with a tiny paper cup full of pills. There are three pills, or rather, capsules, and they are not for his wife but for her blood. The cup is the smallest of its type that Jones has ever seen. All perspective, all sense of time and scale seem abandoned in this hospital. For example, when Jones turns to kiss his wife's hair, he nicks the air instead.

Jones and his wife have one child, a daughter, who, in turn, has a single child, a girl, born one-half year ago. Jones's daughter has fallen in with the stars and is using the heavens, as Jones would be the first to admit, more than he ever has. It has, however,

leukocytosis: elevated number of white blood cells.
myelocytes: nuclei of nerve cells.
megaloblasts: damaged red blood cells characteristic of anemia and leukemia.

brought her only grief and confusion. She has left her husband and brought the baby to Jones. She has also given him her dog. She is going to Mexico where soon, in the mountains, she will have a nervous breakdown. Jones does not know this, but his daughter has seen it in the stars and is going out to meet it. Jones quickly agrees to care for both the baby and the dog, as this seems to be the only thing his daughter needs from him. The day of the baby's birth is secondary to the position of the planets and the terms of houses, quadrants and gradients.° Her symbol is a bareback rider. To Jones, this is a graceful thought. It signifies audacity. It also means luck. Jones slips a twenty dollar bill in the pocket of his daughter's suitcase and drives her to the airport. The plane taxis down the runway and Jones waves, holding all their luck in his arms.

One afternoon, Jones had come home and found his wife sitting in the garden, weeping. She had been transplanting flowers, putting them in pots before the first frost came. There was dirt on her forehead and around her mouth. Her light clothes felt so heavy. Their weight made her body ache. Each breath was a stone she had to swallow. She cried and cried in the weak autumn sunshine. Jones could see the veins throbbing in her neck. "I'm dying," she said. "It's taking me months to die." But after he had brought her inside, she insisted that she felt better and made them both a cup of tea while Jones potted the rest of the plants and carried them down cellar. She lay on the sofa and Jones sat beside her. They talked quietly with one another. Indeed, they were almost whispering, as though they were in a public place surrounded by strangers instead of in their own house with no one present but themselves. "It's the season," Jones said. "In fall everything slows down, retreats. I'm feeling tired myself. We need iron. I'll go to the druggist right now and buy some iron tablets." His wife agreed. She wanted to go with him, for the ride. Together they ride, through the towns, for miles and miles, even into the next state. She does not want to stop driving. They buy sandwiches and milkshakes and eat in the car. Jones drives. They have to buy more gasoline. His wife sits close to him, her eyes closed, her head tipped back against the seat. He can see the veins beating on in her neck. Somewhere there is a dreadful sound, almost audible. "First I thought it was my imagination," his wife said. "I couldn't sleep. All night I would stay awake, dreaming. But it's not in my head. It's in my ears, my eyes. They ache. Everything. My tongue. My hair. The tips of my fingers are dead." Jones pressed her cold hand to his lips. He thinks of something mad and loving better than he—running out of control, deeply in the darkness of his wife. "Just don't make me go to the hospital," she pleaded. Of course she will go there. The moment has already occurred.

Jones is writing to his daughter. He received a brief letter from her this morning, telling him where she could be reached. The foreign postmark was so large that it almost obliterated Jones's address. She did not mention either her mother or the baby, which makes Jones feel peculiar. His life seems increate as his God's life, perhaps even imaginary. His daughter tells him about the town in which she lives. She does not plan to stay there long. She wants to travel. She will find out exactly what she wants to do and then she will come home again. The town is poor but interesting and there are many Americans there her own age. There is a zoo right on the beach. Almost all the towns, no matter how small, have little zoos. There are primarily eagles and hawks in cages. And what can Jones reply to that? He writes *Everything is fine here. We are burning wood from the old apple tree in the fire place and it smells wonderful. Has the baby had her full series of polio shots? Take care.* Jones uses this expression constantly, usually in totally unwarranted situations, as when he purchases pipe cleaners or drives through toll booths. Distracted,

---

planets . . . gradients: terms used by believers in astrology to determine the future.

Jones writes off the edge of the paper and onto the blotter. He must begin again. He will mail this on the way to the hospital. They have been taking X-rays for three days now but the pictures are cloudy. They cannot read them. His wife is now in a real sickbed with high metal sides. He sits with her while she eats her dinner. She asks him to take her good nightgown home and wash it with a bar of Ivory. They won't let her do anything now, not even wash out a few things. *You must take care.*

Jones is driving down a country road. It is the first snowfall of the season and he   5 wants to show it to the baby who rides beside him in a small cushioned car seat all her own. Her head is almost on a level with his and she looks earnestly at the landscape, sometimes smiling. They follow the road that winds tightly between fields and deep pine woods. Everything is white and clean. It has been snowing all afternoon and is doing so still, but very very lightly. Fat snowflakes fall solitary against the windshield. Sometimes the baby reaches out for them. Sometimes she gives a brief kick and cry of joy. They have done their errands. Jones has bought milk and groceries and two yellow roses which lie wrapped in tissue and newspaper in the trunk, in the cold. He must buy two on Saturday as the florist is closed on Sunday. He does not like to do this but there is no alternative. The roses do not keep well. Tonight he will give one to his wife. The other he will pack in sugar water and store in the refrigerator. He can only hope that the bud will remain tight until Sunday when he brings it into the terrible heat of the hospital. The baby rocks against the straps of her small carrier. Her lips are pursed as she watches intently the fields, the grey stalks of crops growing out of the snow, the trees. She is warmly dressed and she wears a knitted orange cap. The cap is twenty-three years old, the age of her mother. Jones found it just the other day. It has faded almost to pink on one side. At one time, it must have been stored in the sun. Jones, driving, feels almost gay. The snow is so beautiful. Everything is white. Jones is an educated man. He has read Melville, who said that white is the colorless all-color of atheism from which we shrink.° Jones does not believe this. He sees a holiness in snow, a promise. He hopes that his wife will know that it is snowing even though she is separated from the window by a curtain. Jones sees something moving across the snow, a part of the snow itself running. Although he is going slowly, he takes his foot completely off the accelerator. "Look, darling, a snowshoe rabbit." At the sound of his voice, the baby stretches open her mouth and narrows her eyes in soundless glee. The hare is splendid. So fast! It flows around invisible obstructions, something out of a kind dream. It flies across the ditch, its paws like paddles, faintly yellow, the color of raw wood. "Look, sweet," cries Jones, "How big he is!" But suddenly the hare is curved and falling, round as a ball, its feet and head tucked closely against its body. It strikes the road and skids upside down for several yards. The car passes around it, avoids it. Jones brakes and stops, amazed. He opens the door and trots back to the animal. The baby twists about in her seat as well as she can and peers after him. It is as though the animal had never been alive at all. Its head is broken in several places. Jones bends to touch its fur, but straightens again, not doing so. A man emerges from the woods, swinging a shotgun. He nods at Jones and picks the hare up by the ears. As he walks away, the hare's legs rub across the ground. There are small crystal stains on the snow. Jones returns to the car. He wants to apologize but he does not know to whom or for what. His life has been devoted to apologetics.° It is his profession. He is concerned with both justification and remorse. He has always acted rightly, but nothing

colorless . . . shrink: quotation from Chapter 42, "The Whiteness of the Whale." of *Moby-Dick* (1851) by Herman Melville (1819–1891).

apologetics: the explanation and defense of religion, here, specifically, of Christianity.

has ever come of it. He gets in the car, starts the engine. "Oh, sweet," he says to the baby. She smiles at him, exposing her tooth. At home that night, after the baby's supper, Jones reads a story to her. She is asleep, panting in her sleep, but Jones tells her the story of al-Boraq,° the milk-white steed of Mohammed, who could stride out of the sight of mankind with a single step.

Jones sorts through a collection of records, none of which have been opened. They are still wrapped in cellophane. The jacket designs are subdued, epic. Names, instruments and orchestras are mentioned confidently. He would like to agree with their importance, for he knows that they have worth, but he is not familiar with the references. His daughter brought these records with her. They had been given to her by an older man, a professor she had been having an affair with. Naturally, this pains Jones. His daughter speaks about the men she has been involved with but no longer cares about. Where did these men come from? Where were they waiting and why have they gone? Jones remembers his daughter when she was a little girl, helping him rake leaves. What can he say? For years on April Fool's Day, she would take tobacco out of his humidor and fill it with corn flakes. Jones is full of remorse and astonishment. When he saw his daughter only a few weeks ago, she was thin and nervous. She had torn out almost all her eyebrows with her fingers from this nervousness. And her lashes. The roots of her eyes were white, like the bulbs of flowers. Her fingernails were crudely bitten, some bleeding below the quick. She was tough and remote, wanting only to go on a trip for which she had a ticket. What can he do? He seeks her in the face of the baby but she is not there. All is being both continued and resumed, but the dream is different. The dream cannot be revived. Jones breaks into one of the albums, blows the dust from the needle, plays a record. Outside it is dark. The parsonage is remote and the only buildings nearby are barns. The river cannot be seen. The music is Bruckner's *Te Deum.*° Very nice, Dedicated to God. He plays the other side. A woman, Kathleen Ferrier,° is singing in German. Jones cannot understand the words but the music stuns him. *Kindertotenlieder.*° It is devastating. In college he had studied only scientific German, The vocabulary of submarines, dirigibles and steam engines. Jones plays the record again and again, searching for his old grammar. At last he finds it. The wings of insects are between some of the pages. There are notes in pencil, written in his own young hand.

RENDER:

A. WAS THE TEACHER SATISFIED WITH YOU TODAY?

B. NO. HE IS NOT. MY ESSAY WAS GOOD BUT IT WAS NOT COPIED WELL.

C. I AM SORRY YOU WERE NOT INDUSTRIOUS THIS TIME FOR YOU GENERALLY ARE.

---

al-Boraq: According to the Koran, the angel Gabriel brought the prophet Mohammed to the Islamic Seventh Heaven (made up of divine light) on the mystical horse Borak or al-Borak ("lightning").

Bruckner: Anton Bruckner (1824–1896), Austrian composer and organist. His *Te Deum* for chorus, soloists, and orchestra was completed in 1884. The long-play record is Columbia ML 4980.

Kathleen Ferrier: celebrated English contralto (1912–1953), who died of cancer.

Kindertotenlieder: "Songs on the Death of Children" (1902–1904), a cycle of five songs for voice and orchestra by Gustav Mahler (1860–1911), Austrian composer and conductor. Mahler's elder daughter died three years after he completed the work.

These lessons are neither of life or death. Why was he instructed in them? In the hospital, his wife waits to be translated, no longer a woman, the woman whom he loves, but a situation. Her blood moves mysteriously as constellations. She is under scrutiny and attack and she has abandoned Jones. She is a swimmer waiting to get on with the drowning. Jones is on the shore. In Mexico, his daughter walks along the beach with two men. She is acting out a play that has become her life. Jones is on the mountaintop. The baby cries and Jones takes her from the crib to change her. The dog paws the door. Jones lets him out. He settles down with the baby and listens to the record. He still cannot make out many of the words. The baby wiggles restlessly on his lap. Her eyes are a foal's eyes, navy-blue. She has grown in a few weeks to expect everything from Jones. He props her on one edge of the couch and goes to her small toy box where he keeps a bear, a few rattles and balls. On the way, he opens the door and the dog immediately enters. His heavy coat is cold, fragrant with ice. He noses the baby and she squeals.

> Oft denk' ich, sie sind nur ausgegangen:
> Bald werden sie wieder nach Hause gelangen!°

Jones selects a bright ball and pushes it gently in her direction.

It is Sunday morning and Jones is in the pulpit. The church is very old but the walls of the sanctuary have recently been painted a pale blue. In the cemetery adjoining, some of the graves are three hundred years old. It has become a historical landmark and no one has been buried there since World War I. There is a new place, not far away, which the families now use. Plots are marked not with stones but with small tablets, and immediately after any burial, workmen roll grassed sod over the new graves so that there is no blemish on the grounds, not even for a little while. Present for today's service are seventy-eight adults, eleven children and the junior choir. Jones counts them as the offertory is received. The church rolls say that there are three hundred fifty members but as far as Jones can see, everyone is here today. This is the day he baptizes the baby. He has made arrangements with one of the ladies to hold her and bring her up to the font at the end of the first hymn. The baby looks charming in a lacy white dress. Jones has combed her fine hair carefully, slicking it in a curl with water, but now it has dried and it sticks up awkwardly like the crest of a kingfisher. Jones bought the dress in Mammoth Mart, an enormous store which has a large metal elephant dressed in overalls dancing on the roof. He feels foolish at buying it there but he had gone to several stores and that is where he saw the prettiest dress. He blesses the baby with water from the silver bowl. He says, *We are saved not because we are worthy. We are saved because we are loved.* It is a brief ceremony. The baby, looking curiously at Jones, is taken out to the nursery. Jones begins his sermon. He can't remember when he wrote it, but here it is, typed, in front of him. *There is nothing wrong in what one does but there is something wrong in what one becomes.* He finds this questionable but goes on speaking. He has been preaching for thirty-four years. He is gaunt with belief. But his wife has a red cell count of only 2.3 millions. It is not enough! She is not getting enough oxygen! Jones is giving his sermon. Somewhere he has lost what he was looking for. He must have known once, surely. The congregation sways, like the wings of a ray in water. It is Sunday and for patients it is a holiday. The doctors don't visit. There are no tests or diagnoses. Jones would like to leave, to walk

---

Oft . . . gelangen: opening two lines of the fourth song in Mahler's *Kindertotenlieder,* from a poem by Friedrich Rückert (1788–1866): "Often I think they've just gone outside:/They'll get back home again soon!"

down the aisle and out into the winter, where he would read his words into the ground. Why can't he remember his life! He finishes, sits down, stands up to present communion. Tiny cubes of bread lie in a slumped pyramid. They are offered and received. Jones takes his morsel, hacked earlier from a sliced enriched loaf with his own hand. It is so dry, almost wicked. The very thought now sickens him. He chews it over and over again, but it lies unconsumed, like a mussel in his mouth.

Jones is waiting in the lobby for the results of his wife's operation. Has there ever been a time before dread? He would be grateful even to have dread back, but it has been lost, for a long time, in rapid possibility, probability and fact. The baby sits on his knees and plays with his tie. She woke very early this morning for her orange juice and then gravely, immediately, spit it all up. She seems fine now, however, her fingers exploring Jones's tie. Whenever he looks at her, she gives him a dazzling smile. He has spent most of the day fiercely cleaning the house, changing the bed-sheets and the pages of the many calendars that hang in the rooms, things he should have done a week ago. He has dusted and vacuumed and pressed all his shirts. He has laundered all the baby's clothes, soft small sacks and gowns and sleepers which froze in his hands the moment he stepped outside. And now he is waiting and watching his wristwatch. The tumor is precisely this size, they tell him, the size of his clock's face.

Jones has the baby on his lap and he is feeding her. The evening meal is lengthy and complex. First he must give her vitamins, then, because she has a cold, a dropper of liquid aspirin. This is followed by a bottle of milk, eight ounces, and a portion of strained vegetables. He gives her a rest now so that the food can settle. On his hip, she rides through the rooms of the huge house as Jones turns lights off and on. He comes back to the table and gives her a little more milk, a half jar of strained chicken and a few spoonfuls of dessert, usually cobbler, buckle° or pudding. The baby enjoys all equally. She is good. She eats rapidly and neatly. Sometimes she grasps the spoon, turns it around and thrusts the wrong end into her mouth. Of course there is nothing that cannot be done incorrectly. Jones adores the baby. He sniffs her warm head. Her birth is a deep error, an abstraction. Born in wedlock but out of love. He puts her in the playpen and tends to the dog. He fills one dish with water and one with horsemeat. He rinses out the empty can before putting it in the wastebasket. The dog eats with great civility. He eats a little meat and then takes some water, then meat, then water. When the dog has finished, the dishes are as clean as though they'd been washed. Jones now thinks about his own dinner. He opens the refrigerator. The ladies of the church have brought brownies, venison, cheese and apple sauce. There are turkey pies, pork chops, steak, haddock and sausage patties. A brilliant light exposes all this food. There is so much of it. It must be used. A crust has formed around the punctures in a can of Pet. There is a clear bag of chicken livers stapled shut. There are large brown eggs in a bowl. Jones stares unhappily at the beads of moisture on cartons and bottles, at the pearls of fat on the cold cooked stew. He sits down. The room is full of lamps and cords. He thinks of his wife, her breathing body deranged in tubes, and begins to shake. All objects here are perplexed by such grief.

Now it is almost Christmas and Jones is walking down by the river, around an abandoned house. The dog wades heavily through the snow, biting it. There are petals of ice on the tree limbs and when Jones lingers under them, the baby puts out her hand and her mouth starts working because she would like to have it, the ice, the branch, everything. His wife will be coming home in a few days, in time for Christmas. Jones has

buckle: blueberry buckle, a sweet quickbread filled with blueberries.

already put up the tree and brought the ornaments down from the attic. He will not trim it until she comes home. He wants very much to make a fine occasion out of opening the boxes of old decorations. The two of them have always enjoyed this greatly in the past. Jones will doubtlessly drop and smash a bauble, for he does every year. He tramps through the snow with his small voyager. She dangles in a shoulder sling, her legs wedged around his hip. They regard the rotting house seriously. Once it was a doctor's home and offices but long before Jones's time, the doctor, who was very respected, had been driven away because a town girl accused him of fathering her child. The story goes that all the doctor said was, "Is that so?" This incensed the town and the girl's parents, who insisted that he take the child as soon as it was born. He did and he cared for the child very well even though his practice was ruined and no one had anything to do with him. A year later the girl told the truth—that the actual father was a young college boy whom she was now going to marry. They wanted the child back, and the doctor willingly returned the infant to them. Of course it is a very old, important story. Jones has always appreciated it, but now he is annoyed at the man's passivity. His wife's sickness has changed everything for Jones. He will continue to accept but he will no longer surrender. Surely things are different for Jones now.

For insurance purposes, Jones's wife is brought out to the car in a wheelchair. She is thin and beautiful. Jones is grateful and confused. He has a mad wish to tip the orderly. Have so many years really passed? Is this not his wife, his love, fresh from giving birth? Isn't everything about to begin? In Mexico, his daughter wanders disinterestedly through a jewelry shop where she picks up a small silver egg. It opens on a hinge and inside are two figures, a bride and groom. Jones puts the baby in his wife's arms. At first the baby is alarmed because she cannot remember this person very well and she reaches for Jones, whimpering. But soon she is soothed by his wife's soft voice and she falls asleep in her arms as they drive. Jones has readied everything carefully for his wife's homecoming. The house is clean and orderly. For days he has restricted himself to only one part of the house so that his clutter will be minimal. Jones helps his wife up the steps to the door. Together they enter the shining rooms.

QUESTIONS

1. Describe the character of Jones. What is his major trait? How do you learn about it? Why does he continue to practice his profession and care for his family?

2. On the basis of this story, what can you say about the use of tenses in a narration? Why is the story told mainly in the present tense? What is the relationship here between past and present tense?

3. Explain why there are so few paragraphs in the story and why they are rather long. Why do you think Williams does not use more dialogue?

4. Explore the sad or depressing references and situations in the story (e.g., the ill wife, the dead rabbit, the daughter abandoning her child, the songs on the death of children). In the light of such references, how does the story make you think and feel?

THE PRÉCIS OR ABRIDGMENT

A **précis** (*pray-SEE*) is a concise summary, in your own words, of a written work. The closely related word *precise* helps to explain that a précis emphasizes just the most significant details. Other words for *précis* are *abridgment, paraphrase,* *abstract, condensation,* and *epitome. Epitome* (*ee-PIT-uh-mee*), from the Greek for a "cutting away" so that only the essential parts remain, is a particularly helpful explanation of the objective of a précis.

Uses of the Précis

Beyond enabling you to follow a story with accuracy, the précis is important in study, research, and speaking and writing. One of the best ways to study any work is to write a précis of it, for the process forces you to grasp each of the parts. Précis writing can be used in taking notes, preparing for exams, establishing and clarifying facts, studying for classroom discussion, and reinforcing details and ideas learned in the past. The object of a précis should be to retell not all a story's details, but only enough to give the highlights, so that any reader will know the main sections of the work. Although you may sometimes need to condense an entire plot or epitomize an entire argument, most often you will refer to no more than parts of works, because your arguments will depend on a number of separate interpretations for these portions.

GUIDELINES FOR PRÉCIS WRITING

The following guidelines will help you in developing a précis.

1. SELECTION. Only essential details belong in a précis. For example, at the opening of the story "Everyday Use," Walker's narrator describes herself as a large woman who has lived a very hard life. We learn that she can kill animals for food. She is fully capable of taking care of herself and her family. Including all these details would needlessly lengthen a précis of "Everyday Use." Instead it is sufficient to say "Mrs. Johnson is a strong woman," because this fact is the most vital one about her. Concentrating on the essentials enables the shortening required of a précis. Thus a 5,000-word story might be epitomized in 100, 300, or 600 words, with the amount of detail being governed by the desired length. Regardless of the length of your précis, however, base your selection of detail on your judgment of its importance.

2. ACCURACY. All details in a précis should be both correct and accurate. Avoid misstatement, and avoid using words that give a misleading impression of the original. In Maupassant's story "The Necklace," for example, Mathilde cooperates with her husband for ten years to repay their 18,000-franc debt. In a précis it would be possible to say no more than she "works" during this time. The word *works* is misleading, however, for it could be interpreted to mean that Mathilde gets paid for outside employment. In fact she does not. What Maupassant tells us is that Mathilde gives up her servant girl and then does all the heavy housework herself as part of her general economizing in her *own* household, not in the houses of others.

As important as the need to condense long sections of a story accurately is the need to be comprehensive. In Walker's "Everyday Use," there is a concluding dispute between the mother (the narrator) and her visiting daughter about the daughter's request for two homemade quilts. Wangero (Dee), the daughter, wants to use the quilts to adorn a wall, but the mother refuses on the grounds that she has promised them to her other daughter for "everyday use" during her approaching marriage. These details are complex, and they represent the climax of the major conflict in the story. In a précis it is important not only to explain the claims but also to present enough language to highlight the conflict. Thus, accurate and comprehensive language might be: "Mrs. Johnson hesitates, having already promised the quilts to Maggie for use when she gets married. Though Maggie offers to give Wangero the quilts, Mrs. Johnson insists on her original promise. Wangero then objects, claiming that the quilts will be spoiled by 'everyday use' and that her mother misunderstands the value of the family heritage." This language explains the details accurately and comprehensively—the goal of précis writing.

3. DICTION. A précis should be an original essay, and therefore it should be written *in your own words*, not those of the work you are abridging. The best way to ensure original wording is to read the work, take note of the major actions and situations, and then put the work out of reach as you write. In that way you can avoid the temptation to borrow words.

However, if a number of words from the text find their way into the précis even after you have tried to keep them out, then you must use quotation marks to set them off. As long as direct quotations are kept to a minimum, they are permissible. Too many quoted words, however, indicate that your précis is not original.

4. OBJECTIVITY. A précis should be scrupulously factual. Avoid explanatory or introductory material unless it is a true part of the story. Just as you need to *include* judgments and interpretations in other kinds of writing about literature, you need to *avoid* them in a précis. Here is a comparative example of what to do and what to avoid in a précis:

WHAT TO DO

Mrs. Johnson, a strong black woman living on her southern farm with her younger daughter, Maggie, is waiting for a visit by her elder daughter, Dee. Dee is returning from her home in the city, and the mother has cleaned and swept the house and yard in order to make a good impression.

WHAT TO AVOID

Walker opens the story by building up the contrast that will soon be made apparent. Her narrator, Mrs. Johnson, is a plain, down-to-earth woman who has worked hard all her life and whose basic value is her home and possessions. The contrast is her daughter Dee, whose visit she is waiting for. Dee has left home and lives a sophisticated life in the city. Mrs. Johnson takes pride in her home, while Dee will regard the home and her mother's belongings as being of no more use than to be put on display.

The right-hand column starts with a topic sentence, to which the sentences that follow adhere. Such writing is commendable elsewhere, but not in a précis. The left-hand paragraph is better writing *as a précis*, for it presents a selection of details only as they appear in the story, without introductory sentences. In the story there are no such introductions.

5. SENTENCES.   Because a précis should be concise and factual, it is tempting to write sentences that are like short bursts of machine-gun fire. Sentences of this kind are often called "choppy," or "bumpy." Here is an example of choppy sentences:

> Dee comes in a car. She is dressed flamboyantly. She is with a strange man. He is short and bearded. She greets her mother and sister in foreign phrases. The man does, too. She immediately begins taking pictures. She snaps her mother with her sister in the background. She also takes pictures of wandering cows. She makes sure to get the house in all the shots. She kisses her mother then, on the forehead.

An entire essay consisting of sentences like these might make readers feel as though they have been machine-gunned. Although you should include details, you also need to shape and organize your sentences. Here is a more acceptable set of sentences revised to contain the same information:

> When Dee comes, she is flamboyantly dressed, and she gets out of the car with a strange, short, and bearded man. Both Dee and the man greet Mrs. Johnson and Maggie in foreign phrases. Before embracing her mother, Dee gets her Polaroid camera and takes pictures of her mother, her sister, and wandering cows, taking care to include the house in all her shots. Only then does she kiss her mother, and then only on the forehead.

This revision blends the shorter sentences together while still attempting to cover the essential details from the story. The phrase "only then" beginning the last sentence gets at Dee's ridiculous behavior without calling it ridiculous. Even though sentences in a précis must be almost rigidly factual, you should try to make them as graceful as possible.

WRITING A PRÉCIS

Your writing task is to condense the original work with the least possible distortion. Thus it is necessary to keep intact the arrangement and sequence of the original. Let us suppose that a work has a surprise ending, like that in "The Necklace." In a précis, it is important to keep the same order and withhold the conclusion until the very end. It is appropriate, however, to introduce essential details of circumstance, such as names and places, at the beginning of the précis, even if these details are not brought out immediately in the story. For example,

Maupassant does not name Mathilde right away, and he never says that she is French, but a précis of "The Necklace" would be obscure without these details.

If your assignment is a very short précis, say 100 to 150 words, you might confine everything to only one paragraph. For a longer précis, the normal principle of devoting a separate paragraph to each topic applies. If each major division, episode, scene, action, or section of the story (or play) is considered a topic, then the précis may be divided into paragraphs devoted to each of the divisions.

SAMPLE STUDENT ESSAY

A Précis of Alice Walker's "Everyday Use"°

[1] Mrs. Johnson, a strong black woman living on her southern farm with her younger daughter, Maggie, is waiting for a visit by her elder daughter, Dee. Dee is returning from her home in the city, and the mother has cleaned and swept the house and yard in order to make a good impression.

[2] As she waits, she thinks of how independent Dee has been in the past, and of how self-confident and sophisticated she may be now. She contrasts Dee with Maggie, who is awkward, homely, and burn-scarred, and who has never left home. She also contrasts Dee with herself, thinking of Dee's many opportunities for self-improvement while she herself has never had any opportunities at all.

[3] When Dee comes, she is flamboyantly dressed, and she gets out of the car with a strange, short, and bearded man. Both Dee and the man greet Mrs. Johnson in foreign phrases. Before embracing her mother, Dee gets her Polaroid camera and takes pictures of her mother, her sister, and wandering cows, taking care to get the house in all her shots. Only then does she kiss her mother, and then only on the forehead.

[4] Dee soon explains that she no longer wishes to be called "Dee," but that she has taken a new name, "Wangero Leewanika Kemanjo," which she regards as her own, and not the name that previous oppressors had given her. The man she is with has an incomprehensible name, which the family understands as "Hakim-a-Barber," which he has also taken in keeping with his present philosophy.

[5] Once greetings are past, the family sits down to eat. Wangero (Dee) is impressed with the artistic qualities of the homemade furniture, and she asks for the lid to the family butter churn and the churn's dasher for display in her present home. After dinner, Wangero also asks for two homemade quilts that have been in the family for years. Mrs. Johnson hesitates, having already promised the quilts to Maggie for use when she gets married. Though Maggie offers to give Wangero the quilts, Mrs. Johnson insists on her original promise. Wangero then objects, claiming that the quilts will be spoiled by "everyday use" and that her mother misunderstands the value of the family heritage. Wangero hurriedly leaves with Hakim, while Mrs. Johnson and Maggie remain together, enjoying their snuff, until bedtime.

° See pp. 73–78 for this story.

Commentary on the Essay

This précis, about four hundred words long, illustrates the selection of major actions and the omission of interesting but inessential detail. Thus, the phrase "a strong black woman" contains four words, and it condenses more than one hundred fifty words of detailed description in paragraph 5 of the story. By contrast, paragraph 3 of the sample student essay deals with a relatively short paragraph of the story (paragraph 22). This amount of detail, however, is important because it indicates, right at Dee's entrance, her confused attitudes about her mother and the farm; the farm seems to her more like something for a scrapbook or for a wall than for real living. It is this confusion on Dee's part that underlies the major conflict of the story.

To demonstrate omissions, some materials that disclose things about Hakim's character and philosophy, to be found in paragraphs 42 through 45 of the story, are left out entirely from the précis because they are not essential to the main characters—namely, the three women.

Each of the five paragraphs in the précis is devoted to comparable sections of "Everyday Use." Paragraphs 1 and 2 describe the story up to the appearance of Dee and her man. Paragraph 3 details Dee's activity at her entrance. Paragraph 4 treats the conversation and narrative from paragraphs 24 through 44 of the story. Paragraph 5 condenses the dinner and post-dinner scene, featuring Dee's requests to take away family heirlooms, including the vitally important quilts.

The paragraphs of the précis require not only fidelity to the narrative development of the story, but also unity of subject matter. Thus, paragraph 1 is unified by the speaker's expectations, while paragraph 2 is unified by her contrast of her two daughters and also her contrast of herself with her returning daughter. Each of the other paragraphs is similarly unified—paragraph 3 by Dee's photography, paragraph 4 by the use of new names, and paragraph 5 by the conflicting attitudes about the disposal of family heirlooms. In any précis, similar attempts should be made to unify paragraphs.

SPECIAL WRITING TOPICS FOR STUDYING FICTION

1. Consider Williams's "Taking Care" as a narrative. To what extent is the author's concern more to reveal a character than to tell a story? If the major quality of a fully developed character in short fiction is adaptation to change, how does the story make Jones's adaptation apparent?

2. Describe the mixture of narration and dialogue in Walker's "Everyday Use." Why is there is a great deal of dialogue from paragraph 24 to the end? On the basis of the mixture of dialogue and narration, what conclusions can you draw about the use that fiction makes of these elements?

3. Suppose that someone has told you that "The Things They Carried" is too detailed and realistic to be considered a story. Explain to this person why the assertion should be considered wrong. What elements of narrative, character, plot, point of view, idea, and description justify calling "The Things They Carried" a story?

4. Write a brief episode or story that takes place in a historical period you believe you know well, being as factually accurate as you can. Introduce your own fictional characters as important "movers and shakers," and deal with their public or personal affairs, or both. You may model your characters and episodes on historical persons, but you are free to exercise your imagination completely and construct your own characters.

5. Using standard library reference works (e.g., encyclopedias; biographies of contemporary authors; comprehensive histories of classical, English, or American literature), gather biographical material about one of the writers included in this chapter. Using this material, write a brief biography of the writer, including references to some of the writer's major works.

3

Plot and Structure: The Development and Organization of Stories

Stories and plays are made up mostly of **actions** or **incidents** that follow one after another in chronological order. Finding a sequential or narrative order, however, is only the first step toward the more important consideration—the **plot**, or the controls governing the development of the actions.

PLOT, THE MOTIVATION AND CAUSATION OF FICTION

The English novelist E. M. Forster, in *Aspects of the Novel*, presents a memorable illustration of plot. To show a bare set of actions, he uses the following: "The king died, and then the queen died." He points out, however, that this sequence does not form a plot because it lacks *motivation* and *causation*. These he introduces in his next example: "The king died, and then the queen died of grief." The phrase "of grief" shows that one thing (grief) controls or overcomes another (the normal desire to live), and motivation and causation enter the sequence to form a plot. In a well-plotted story or play, a thing precedes or follows another not simply because time ticks away, but more importantly because *effects* follow *causes*. In a good work nothing is irrelevant or accidental; everything is related and causative.

Conflict

The controlling impulse in a connected pattern of causes and effects is **conflict,** which refers to people or circumstances a character must face and try to overcome. Conflict brings out the extremes of human energy, causing characters to engage in the decisions, actions, responses, and interactions that make up stories.

In its most elemental form, a conflict is the opposition of two people. Their conflict may take the shape of envy, hatred, anger, argument, avoidance, gossip, lies, fighting, and many other forms and actions. Conflicts may also exist between groups, although conflicts between individuals are more identifiable and therefore more suitable for stories. Conflicts may also be abstract, as when an individual opposes larger forces such as natural objects, ideas, modes of behavior, or public opinion. A difficult or even impossible choice—a **dilemma**—is a natural conflict for an individual person. A conflict may also be brought out in ideas and opinions that clash. In short, conflict shows itself in many ways.

CONFLICT, DOUBT, TENSION, AND INTEREST. Conflict is the major element of plot because opposing forces arouse *curiosity*, cause *doubt*, create *tension*, and produce *interest*. The same responses are the lifeblood of athletic competition. Consider which kind of game is more interesting: (1) One team gets so far ahead that the winner is no longer in doubt, or (2) Both teams are so evenly matched that the winner is in doubt even in the final seconds. Obviously, games are uninteresting—as games—unless they are contests between teams of comparable strength. The same applies to conflicts in stories and dramas. There should be uncertainty about a protagonist's success: Unless there is doubt there is no tension, and without tension there is no interest.

PLOT IN OPERATION. To see a plot in operation, let us build on Forster's description. Here is a simple plot for a story of our own: "John and Jane meet, fall in love, and get married." This is a plot because it shows cause and effect (they get married *because* they fall in love), but with no conflict the plot is not interesting. However, let us introduce conflicting elements in this common "boy meets girl" story:

> John and Jane meet at school and fall in love. They go together for two years and plan to marry, but a problem arises. Jane wants a career first, and after marriage she wants to be an equal contributor to the family. John understands Jane's wishes, but he wants to get married and have children first and says Jane can finish her studies and have her career later. Jane believes that John's plan is not for her because it constitutes a trap from which she will never escape. This conflict interrupts their plans, and they part in anger and regret even though they still love each other. Both marry other people, and they build separate lives and careers. They are not happy even though they like and respect their spouses. The years pass, and, after children and grandchildren, Jane and John meet again. He is now divorced and she is a widow. Because their earlier conflict is no longer a barrier, they marry and try to make up for the past. Even their new happiness, however, is tinged with regret and reproach because of their earlier conflict, their unhappy solution, their lost years, and their increasing age.

Here we have a true plot because our "boy meets girl" story outline contains a major conflict from which a number of related conflicts develop. These conflicts lead to attitudes, choices, and outcomes that make the story interesting. The situation is lifelike; the conflicts rise out of realistic aims and hopes; the outcome is true to life.

THE STRUCTURE OF FICTION

Structure describes how writers arrange materials in accord with the general ideas and purposes of their works. Unlike plot, which is concerned with conflict or conflicts, structure defines the layouts of fictional works—the ways the story, play, or narrative poem is shaped. Structure is about matters such as placement, balance, recurring themes, true and misleading conclusions, suspense, and the imitation of models or forms like reports, letters, conversations, or confessions. A story might be divided into numbered sections or parts, or it might begin in a countryside (or one state) and conclude in a city (or in another state), or it might develop a relationship between two people from their first introduction to their falling in love. To study structure is to study such arrangements and the purposes for which they are made.

Formal Categories of Structure

Many aspects of structure are common to all genres of literature. Particularly for stories and plays, however, the following aspects form a skeleton, a pattern of development.

EXPOSITION.   **Exposition** is the laying out, the putting forth, of the materials in the story—the main characters, their backgrounds, and their characteristics, interests, goals, limitations, potentials, and basic assumptions. It may not be limited to the beginning of the work, where it is most expected, but may be found anywhere. Thus, intricacies, twists, turns, false leads, blind alleys, surprises, and other quirks may be introduced to interest, perplex, intrigue, and otherwise please readers. Whenever something new arises, to the degree that it is new it is a part of exposition.

COMPLICATION.   The **complication** is the *onset* of the major conflict—the plot. The major participants are the protagonist and antagonist, together with whatever ideas and values they represent, such as good or evil, freedom or oppression, independence or dependence, love or hate, intelligence or stupidity, or knowledge or ignorance.

CRISIS.   The **crisis** (Greek for "turning point") is the separation between what has gone before and what will come after, usually a decision or action undertaken to resolve the conflict. The crisis is that point at which curiosity, uncertainty, and tension are greatest. Usually the crisis is followed closely by the next stage, the climax. Often, in fact, the two occur so closely together that they are considered the same.

CLIMAX. Because the **climax** (Greek for "ladder") is a consequence of the crisis, it is the story's high point. It may take the shape of a decision, an action, an affirmation or denial, or an illumination or realization. The climax is the logical conclusion of the preceding actions; no new major developments follow it. In most stories, the climax occurs at the end or close to it. For example, in Crane's "The Blue Hotel," the climax is the Swede's verbal and physical encounter with the gambler. Everything that happens prior to this confrontation leads to it: the Swede's nervousness and suspicion, his odd behavior at the card table, his drunkenness, his pugnaciousness, his exultation after beating Johnnie, and his defiant exit from the Blue Hotel. The primitive power he thinks he has gained at the hotel causes him to antagonize the gambler—the story's climax—and thus to bring his existence to its sudden end.

RESOLUTION OR DÉNOUEMENT. The **resolution** (a releasing or untying) or **dénouement** (untying) is the completing of the story after the climax, for once the climax has occurred, the story's tension and uncertainty are finished, and most authors conclude quickly to avoid losing their readers' interest. For instance, the dénouement of "The Blue Hotel" comprises a few short details about the gambler's departure, the appearance of the dead Swede, the news of the gambler's sentence, and the concluding chat between the cowboy and the Easterner. Some authors provide even fewer details. Welty, for example, ends "A Worn Path" with the main character beginning her long walk home. In a similarly brief way, Whitecloud ends "Blue Winds Dancing" with the narrator's brief statement that he is home. In other words, after the story's major conflicts are finished, the job of the dénouement is to bring things to a satisfying and rapid ending.

Formal and Actual Structure

The structure just described is a *formal* one, an ideal pattern that moves directly from beginning to end. Few narratives and dramas follow this pattern exactly, however. A mystery story, for example, holds back crucial details of exposition (because the goal is to mystify); a suspense story keeps the protagonist ignorant but provides readers with abundant details in order to maximize concern and tension about the outcome.

More realistic, less "artificial" stories might also contain structural variations. For example, Welty's "A Worn Path" produces a *double take* because of unique structuring. During most of the story, Phoenix's conflicts are against age, poverty, and environment. At the end, however, we are introduced to an additional difficulty—a new conflict—which enlarges our responses to include not just concern but also heartfelt anguish. "A Worn Path" is just one example of how a structural variation maximizes the impact of a work.

There are many other possible variants in structure. One of these is the **flashback,** in which present circumstances are explained by the selective introduction of past events. The moment at which the flashback is introduced may be a part of the resolution of the plot, and the flashback might lead you into a moment of climax but then go from there to develop the details that are more properly part of the exposition. Let us again consider our brief plot about John and Jane and use the flashback method of structuring the story.

> Jane is now old, and a noise outside causes her to remember the argument that forced her to part with John many years before. They were deeply in love, but their disagreement about her wishes for a career split them apart. Then she pictures in her mind the years she and John have spent happily together after they married. She then contrasts her present happiness with her memory of her earlier, less happy, marriage, and from there she recalls her youthful years of courtship with John before their disastrous conflict developed. Then she looks over at John, reading in a chair, and smiles. John smiles back, and the two embrace. Even then, Jane has tears on her face.

In this structure the action begins and remains in the present. Important parts of the past flood the protagonist's memory in flashback, though not in the order in which they happened. Memory might be used structurally in other ways. An example is Tillie Olsen's "I Stand Here Ironing," which is a narrative spoken (or thought silently) by a mother at her ironing board. The events of the story itself, however, develop through flashbacks—memories of her daughter's growth. In short, a technique like flashback creates a unique story that departs significantly from a strictly formal and chronological structural pattern.

Each narrative or drama has a unique structure. Some stories may be structured according to simple geography, as in Whitecloud's "Blue Winds Dancing" (a trip from California to Wisconsin), Munro's "The Found Boat" (from a spring flood to an exploration on and beside a river), and Welty's "A Worn Path" (a walk from the country to town). Parts or scenes might be carried on through conversations, as in "The Blue Hotel" and "Everyday Use," or through a ceremony witnessed by a major character, as in "Young Goodman Brown." A story may unfold in an apparently accidental way, with the characters making vital discoveries about the major characters, as in Glaspell's "A Jury of Her Peers." Additionally, parts of a work may be set out as fragments of conversation, as in "A Worn Path," or as an announcement of a party, as in "The Necklace." The possible means of structuring stories are extensive.

 ## STORIES FOR STUDY

STEPHEN CRANE   (1871–1900)

Born in New Jersey, Crane began writing stories at the age of eight, and by the time he was sixteen he was helping his brothers write for newspapers. He attended a number of colleges but did not graduate. While at Syracuse University he completed his first novel, Maggie: A Girl of the Streets, *which he published with borrowed money in 1893. During the remainder of his brief and turbulent life he worked as a writer and war correspondent. He spent a year in the West, and two of his better-known stories, "The Bride Comes to Yellow Sky" and "The Blue Hotel," came out of this experience. His best-known novel,* The Red Badge of Courage, *was published in 1895. "The Blue Hotel" was included in* The Monster and Other Stories *in 1899.*

The Blue Hotel _____ *1899*

I

The Palace Hotel at Fort Romper was painted a light blue, a shade that is on the legs of a kind of heron, causing the bird to declare its position against any background. The Palace Hotel, then, was always screaming and howling in a way that made the dazzling winter landscape of Nebraska seem only a grey swampish hush. It stood alone on the prairie, and when the snow was falling the town two hundred yards away was not visible. But when the traveller alighted at the railway station he was obliged to pass the Palace Hotel before he could come upon the company of low clapboard houses which composed Fort Romper, and it was not to be thought that any traveller could pass the Palace Hotel without looking at it. Pat Scully, the proprietor, had proved himself a master of strategy when he chose his paints. It is true that on clear days, when the great transcontinental expresses, long lines of swaying Pullmans, swept through Fort Romper, passengers were overcome at the sight, and the cult that knows the brown-reds and the subdivisions of the dark greens of the East expressed shame, pity, horror, in a laugh. But to the citizens of this prairie town and to the people who would naturally stop there, Pat Scully had performed a feat. With this opulence and splendour, these creeds, classes, egotisms, that streamed through Romper on the rails day after day, they had no colour in common.

As if the displayed delights of such a blue hotel were not sufficiently enticing, it was Scully's habit to go every morning and evening to meet the leisurely trains that stopped at Romper and work his seductions upon any man that he might see wavering, gripsack in hand.

One morning, when a snow-crusted engine dragged its long string of freight cars and its one passenger coach to the station, Scully performed the marvel of catching three men. One was a shaky and quick-eyed Swede, with a great shining cheap valise; one was a tall bronzed cowboy, who was on his way to a ranch near the Dakota line; one was a little silent man from the East, who didn't look it, and didn't announce it. Scully practically made them prisoners. He was so nimble and merry and kindly that each probably felt it would be the height of brutality to try to escape. They trudged off over the creaking board sidewalks in the wake of the eager little Irishman. He wore a heavy fur cap squeezed tightly down on his head. It caused his two red ears to stick out stiffly, as if they were made of tin.

At last, Scully, elaborately, with boisterous hospitality, conducted them through the portals of the blue hotel. The room which they entered was small. It seemed to be merely a proper temple for an enormous stove, which, in the centre, was humming with godlike violence. At various points on its surface the iron had become luminous and glowed yellow from the heat. Beside the stove Scully's son Johnnie was playing High-Five° with an old farmer who had whiskers both grey and sandy. They were quarreling. Frequently the old farmer turned his face toward a box of sawdust—coloured brown from tobacco juice—that was behind the stove, and spat with an air of great impatience and irritation. With a loud flourish of words Scully destroyed the game of cards, and bustled his son upstairs with part of the baggage of the new guests. He himself conducted them to three basins of the coldest water in the world. The cowboy and the Easterner burnished themselves fiery red with this water, until it seemed to be some kind of metal-polish. The Swede, however, merely dipped his fingers gingerly and with trepidation. It was notable that throughout this series of small ceremonies the three travellers were made to feel that Scully was very benevolent. He was conferring great favours upon them. He handed the towel from one to another with an air of philanthropic impulse.

Afterward they went to the first room, and, sitting about the stove, listened to   5
Scully's officious clamour at his daughters, who were preparing the midday meal. They reflected in the silence of experienced men who tread carefully amid new people. Nevertheless, the old farmer, stationary, invincible in his chair near the warmest part of the stove, turned his face from the sawdust-box frequently and addressed a glowing commonplace to the strangers. Usually he was answered in short but adequate sentences by either the cowboy or the Easterner. The Swede said nothing. He seemed to be occupied in making furtive estimates of each man in the room. One might have thought that he had the sense of silly suspicion which comes to guilt. He resembled a badly frightened man.

Later, at dinner, he spoke a little, addressing his conversation entirely to Scully. He volunteered that he had come from New York, where for ten years he had worked as a tailor. These facts seemed to strike Scully as fascinating, and afterward he volunteered that he had lived at Romper for fourteen years. The Swede asked about the crops and the price of labour. He seemed barely to listen to Scully's extended replies. His eyes continued to rove from man to man.

Finally, with a laugh and a wink, he said that some of these Western communities were very dangerous; and after his statement he straightened his legs under the table, tilted his head, and laughed again, loudly. It was plain that the demonstration had no meaning to the others. They looked at him wondering and in silence.

II

As the men trooped heavily back into the front room, the two little windows presented views of a turmoiling sea of snow. The huge arms of the wind were making attempts—mighty, circular, futile—to embrace the flakes as they sped. A gate-post like a still man with a blanched face stood aghast amid this profligate fury. In a hearty voice Scully announced the presence of a blizzard. The guests of the blue hotel, lighting their

---

High-Five: the most commonly played card game in the United States before it was replaced in popularity by poker.

pipes, assented with grunts of lazy masculine contentment. No island of the sea could be exempt in the degree of this little room with its humming stove. Johnnie, son of Scully, in a tone which defined his opinion of his ability as a card-player, challenged the old farmer of both grey and sandy whiskers to a game of High-Five. The farmer agreed with a contemptuous and bitter scoff. They sat close to the stove, and squared their knees under a wide board. The cowboy and the Easterner watched the game with interest. The Swede remained near the window, aloof, but with a countenance that showed signs of an inexplicable excitement.

The play of Johnnie and the grey-beard was suddenly ended by another quarrel. The old man arose while casting a look of heated scorn at his adversary. He slowly buttoned his coat, and then stalked with fabulous dignity from the room. In the discreet silence of all other men the Swede laughed. His laughter rang somehow childish. Men by this time had begun to look at him askance, as if they wished to inquire what ailed him.

A new game was formed jocosely. The cowboy volunteered to become the part-   10
ner of Johnnie, and they all then turned to ask the Swede to throw in his lot with the little Easterner. He asked some questions about the game, and, learning that it wore many names, and that he had played it when it was under an alias, he accepted the invitation. He strode toward the men nervously, as if he expected to be assaulted. Finally, seated, he gazed from face to face and laughed shrilly. This laugh was so strange that the Easterner looked up quickly, the cowboy sat intent and with his mouth open, and Johnnie paused, holding the cards with still fingers.

Afterward there was a short silence. Then Johnnie said, "Well, let's get at it. Come on now!" They pulled their chairs forward until their knees were bunched under the board. They began to play, and their interest in the game caused the others to forget the manner of the Swede.

The cowboy was a board-whacker. Each time that he held superior cards he whanged them, one by one, with exceeding force, down upon the improvised table, and took the tricks with a glowing air of prowess and pride that sent thrills of indignation into the hearts of his opponents. A game with a board-whacker in it is sure to become intense. The countenances of the Easterner and the Swede were miserable whenever the cowboy thundered down his aces and kings, while Johnnie, his eyes gleaming with joy, chuckled and chuckled.

Because of the absorbing play none considered the strange ways of the Swede. They paid strict heed to the game. Finally, during a lull caused by a new deal, the Swede suddenly addressed Johnnie: "I suppose there have been a good many men killed in this room." The jaws of the others dropped and they looked at him.

"What in hell are you talking about?" said Johnnie.

The Swede laughed again his blatant laugh, full of a kind of false courage and   15
defiance. "Oh, you know what I mean all right," he answered.

"I'm a liar if I do!" Johnnie protested. The card was halted, and the men stared at the Swede. Johnnie evidently felt that as the son of the proprietor he should make a direct inquiry. "Now, what might you be drivin' at, mister?" he asked. The Swede winked at him. It was a wink full of cunning. His fingers shook on the edge of the board. "Oh, maybe you think I have been to nowheres. Maybe you think I'm a tenderfoot?"

"I don't know nothin' about you," answered Johnnie, "and I don't give a damn where you've been. All I got to say is that I don't know what you're driving at. There hain't never been nobody killed in this room."

The cowboy, who had been steadily gazing at the Swede, then spoke. "What's wrong with you, mister?"

Apparently it seemed to the Swede that he was formidably menaced. He shivered and turned white near the corners of his mouth. He sent an appealing glance in the direction of the little Easterner. During these moments he did not forget to wear his air of advanced pot-valour. "They say they don't know what I mean," he remarked mockingly to the Easterner.

The latter answered after prolonged and cautious reflection. "I don't understand   20 you," he said, impassively.

The Swede made a movement then which announced that he thought he had encountered treachery from the only quarter where he had expected sympathy, if not help. "Oh, I see you are all against me. I see—"

The cowboy was in a state of deep stupefaction. "Say," he cried, as he tumbled the deck violently down upon the board, "say, what are you gittin' at, hey?"

The Swede sprang up with the celerity of a man escaping from a snake on the floor. "I don't want to fight!" he shouted, "I don't want to fight!"

The cowboy stretched his long legs indolently and deliberately. His hands were in his pockets. He spat into the sawdust-box. "Well, who the hell thought you did?" he inquired.

The Swede backed rapidly toward a corner of the room. His hands were out pro-   25 tectingly in front of his chest, but he was making an obvious struggle to control his fright. "Gentlemen," he quavered. "I suppose I am going to be killed before I can leave this house! I suppose I am going to be killed before I can leave this house!" In his eyes was the dying-swan° look. Through the windows could be seen the snow turning blue in the shadow of dusk. The wind tore at the house, and some loose thing beat regularly against the clapboards like a spirit tapping.

A door opened, and Scully himself entered. He paused in surprise as he noted the tragic attitude of the Swede. Then he said. "What's the matter here?"

The Swede answered him swiftly and eagerly: "These men are going to kill me."

"Kill you!" ejaculated Scully. "Kill you! What are you talkin'?"

The Swede made the gesture of a martyr.

Scully wheeled sternly upon his son. "What is this, Johnnie?"   30

The lad had grown sullen. "Damned if I know," he answered. "I can't make no sense of it." He began to shuffle the cards, fluttering them together with an angry snap. "He says a good many men have been killed in this room, or something like that. And he says he's goin' to be killed here too. I don't know what ails him. He's crazy, I shouldn't wonder."

Scully then looked for explanation to the cowboy, but the cowboy simply shrugged his shoulders.

"Kill you?" said Scully again to the Swede. "Kill you? Man, you're off your nut."

"Oh, I know," burst out the Swede. "I know what will happen. Yes, I'm crazy—yes. Yes, of course, I'm crazy—yes. But I know one thing—" There was a sort of sweat of misery and terror upon his face. "I know I won't get out of here alive."

The cowboy drew a deep breath, as if his mind was passing into the last stages of   35 dissolution. "Well, I'm doggoned," he whispered to himself.

Scully wheeled suddenly and faced his son. "You've been troublin' this man!"

---

dying swan: Proverbially, a swan sings its most beautiful notes when it is about to die.

Johnnie's voice was loud with its burden of grievance. "Why, good Gawd, I ain't done nothin' to 'im."

The Swede broke in. "Gentlemen, do not disturb yourselves. I will leave this house. I will go away, because"—he accused them dramatically with his glance—"because I do not want to be killed."

Scully was furious with his son. "Will you tell me what is the matter, you young divil? What's the matter, anyhow? Speak out!"

"Blame it!" cried Johnnie in despair, "don't I tell you I don't know? He—he says   40
we want to kill him, and that's all I know. I can't tell what ails him."

The Swede continued to repeat: "Never mind, Mr. Scully; never mind. I will leave this house. I will go away, because I do not wish to be killed. Yes, of course, I am crazy— yes. But I know one thing! I will go away. I will leave this house. Never mind, Mr. Scully; never mind, I will go away."

"You will not go 'way," said Scully. "You will not go 'way until I hear the reason of this business. If anybody has troubled you I will take care of him. This is my house. You are under my roof, and I will not allow any peaceable man to be troubled here." He cast a terrible eye upon Johnnie, the cowboy, and the Easterner.

"Never mind, Mr. Scully; never mind. I will go away. I do not wish to be killed." The Swede moved toward the door which opened upon the stairs. It was evidently his intention to go at once for his baggage.

"No, no," shouted Scully peremptorily; but the white-faced man slid by him and disappeared. "Now," said Scully severely, "what does this mane?"°

Johnnie and the cowboy cried together: "Why, we didn't do nothin' to 'im!"   45

Scully's eyes were cold. "No," he said, "you didn't?"

Johnnie swore a deep oath. "Why, this is the wildest loon I ever see. We didn't do nothin' at all. We were just sittin' here playin cards, and he—"

The father suddenly spoke to the Easterner. "Mr. Blanc," he asked, "what has these boys been doin'?"

The Easterner reflected again. "I didn't see anything wrong at all," he said at last, slowly.

Scully began to howl, "But what does it mane?" He stared ferociously at his son. "I   50
have a mind to lather you for this, me boy."

Johnnie was frantic. "Well, what have I done?" he bawled at his father.

III

"I think you are tongue-tied," said Scully finally to his son, the cowboy, and the Easterner; and at the end of this scornful sentence he left the room.

Upstairs the Swede was swiftly fastening the straps of his great valise. Once his back happened to be half turned toward the door, and, hearing a noise there, he wheeled and sprang up, uttering a loud cry. Scully's wrinkled visage showed grimly in the light of the small lamp he carried. This yellow effulgence, streaming upward, coloured only his prominent features, and left his eyes, for instance, in mysterious shadow. He resembled a murderer.

"Man! man!" he exclaimed, "have you gone daffy?"

mane: mean. Scully speaks with a slight Irish brogue (see, for example, paragraphs 58, 70, and 114).

"Oh, no! Oh, no!" rejoined the other. "There are people in this world who know   55
pretty nearly as much as you do—understand?"

For a moment they stood gazing at each other. Upon the Swede's deathly pale
cheeks were two spots brightly crimson and sharply edged, as if they had been carefully
painted. Scully placed the light on the table and sat himself on the edge of the bed. He
spoke ruminatively. "By cracky, I never heard of such a thing in my life. It's a complete
muddle. I can't, for the soul of me, think how you ever got this idea into your head."
Presently he lifted his eyes and asked: "And did you sure think they were going to kill you?"

The Swede scanned the old man as if he wished to see into his mind. "I did," he
said at last. He obviously suspected that this answer might precipitate an outbreak. As
he pulled on a strap his whole arm shook, the elbow wavering like a bit of paper.

Scully banged his hand impressively on the footboard of the bed. "Why, man,
we're goin' to have a line of ilictric street-cars in this town next spring."

"'A line of electric street-cars,'" repeated the Swede, stupidly.

"And," said Scully, "there's a new railroad goin' to be built down from Bro-   60
ken Arm to here. Not to mintion the four churches and the smashin' big brick
schoolhouse. Then there's the big factory, too. Why, in two years Romper'll be a
met-tro-*pol*-is."

Having finished the preparation of his baggage, the Swede straightened himself.
"Mr. Scully," he said, with sudden hardihood, "how much do I owe you?"

"You don't owe me anythin'," said the old man, angrily.

"Yes, I do," retorted the Swede. He took seventy-five cents from his pocket and
tendered it to Scully; but the latter snapped his fingers in disdainful refusal. However, it
happened that they both stood gazing in a strange fashion at three silver pieces on the
Swede's open palm.

"I'll not take your money," said Scully at last. "Not after what's been goin' on
here." Then a plan seemed to strike him. "Here," he cried, picking up his lamp and
moving toward the door. "Here! Come with me a minute."

"No," said the Swede, in overwhelming alarm.   65

"Yes," urged the old man. "Come on! I want you to come and see a picter—just
across the hall—in my room."

The Swede must have concluded that his hour was come. His jaw dropped and
his teeth showed like a dead man's. He ultimately followed Scully across the corridor,
but he had the step of one hung in chains.

Scully flashed the light high on the wall of his own chamber. There was revealed a
ridiculous photograph of a little girl. She was leaning against a balustrade of gorgeous
decoration, and the formidable bang to her hair was prominent. The figure was as
graceful as an upright sled-stake, and, withal, it was of the hue of lead. "There," said
Scully, tenderly, "that's the picter of my little girl that died. Her name was Carrie. She
had the purtiest hair you even saw! I was that fond of her, she—"

Turning then, he saw that the Swede was not contemplating the picture at all, but,
instead, was keeping keen watch on the gloom in the rear.

"Look, man!" cried Scully, heartily. "That's the picter of my little gal that died.   70
Her name was Carrie. And then here's the picter of my oldest boy, Michael. He's a
lawyer in Lincoln, an' doin' well. I gave that boy a grand eddication, and I'm glad for it
now. He's a fine boy. Look at 'im now. Ain't he bold as blazes, him there in Lincoln, an
honoured an' respicted gintleman! An honoured and respicted gintleman," concluded
Scully with a flourish. And, so saying, he smote the Swede jovially on the back.

The Swede faintly smiled.

"Now," said the old man, "there's only one more thing." He dropped suddenly to the floor and thrust his head beneath the bed. The Swede could hear his muffled voice. "I'd keep it under me piller if it wasn't for that boy Johnnie. Then there's the old woman—Where is it now? I never put it twice in the same place. Ah, now come out with you!"

Presently he backed clumsily from under the bed, dragging with him an old coat rolled into a bundle. "I've fetched him," he muttered. Kneeling on the floor, he unrolled the coat and extracted from its heart a large yellow-brown whiskey-bottle.

His first maneuver was to hold the bottle up to the light. Reassured, apparently, that nobody had been tampering with it, he thrust it with a generous movement toward the Swede.

The weak-kneed Swede was about to eagerly clutch this element of strength, but   75
he suddenly jerked his hand away and cast a look of horror upon Scully.

"Drink," said the old man affectionately. He had risen to his feet, and now stood facing the Swede.

There was a silence. Then again Scully said: "Drink!"

The Swede laughed wildly. He grabbed the bottle, put it to his mouth; and as his lips curled absurdly around the opening and his throat worked, he kept his glance, burning with hatred, upon the old man's face.

IV

After the departure of Scully the three men, with the card-board still upon their knees, preserved for a long time an astounded silence. Then Johnnie said: "That's the dod-dangedest Swede I ever see."

"He ain't no Swede," said the cowboy, scornfully.   80

"Well, what is he then?" cried Johnnie. "What is he then?"

"It's my opinion," replied the cowboy deliberately, "he's some kind of a Dutchman." It was a venerable custom of the country to entitle as Swedes all light-haired men who spoke with a heavy tongue. In consequence the idea of the cowboy was not without its daring. "Yes, sir," he repeated. "It's my opinion this feller is some kind of Dutchman."

"Well, he says he's a Swede, anyhow," muttered Johnnie, sulkily. He turned to the Easterner: "What do you think, Mr. Blanc?"

"Oh, I don't know," replied the Easterner.

"Well, what do you think makes him act that way?" asked the cowboy.   85

"Why, he's frightened." The Easterner knocked his pipe against the rim of the stove. "He's clear frightened out of his boots."

"What at?" cried Johnnie, and the cowboy together.

The Easterner reflected over his answer.

"What at?" cried the others again.

"Oh, I don't know, but it seems to me this man has been reading dime novels,   90
and he thinks he's right out in the middle of it—the shootin' and stabbin' and all."

"But," said the cowboy, deeply scandalized, "this ain't Wyoming, ner none of them places. This is Nebrasker."

"Yes," added Johnnie, "an' why don't he wait till he gits *out West?*"

The travelled Easterner laughed. "It isn't different there even—not in these days. But he thinks he's right in the middle of hell."

Johnnie and the cowboy mused long.

"It's awful funny," remarked Johnnie at last.

"Yes," said the cowboy. "This is a queer game. I hope we don't git snowed in, because then we'd have to stand this here man bein' around with us all the time. That wouldn't be no good."

"I wish pop would throw him out," said Johnnie.

Presently they heard a loud stamping on the stairs, accompanied by ringing jokes in the voice of old Scully, and laughter, evidently from the Swede. The men around the stove stared vacantly at each other. "Gosh!" said the cowboy. The door flew open, and old Scully, flushed and anecdotal, came into the room. He was jabbering at the Swede, who followed him, laughing bravely. It was the entry of two roisterers from a banquet hall.

"Come now," said Scully sharply to the three seated men, "move up and give us a chance at the stove." The cowboy and the Easterner obediently sidled their chairs to make room for the new-comers. Johnnie, however, simply arranged himself in a more indolent attitude, and then remained motionless.

"Come! Git over, there," said Scully.

"Plenty of room on the other side of the stove," said Johnnie.

"Do you think we want to sit in the draught?" roared the father.

But the Swede here interposed with a grandeur of confidence. "No, no. Let the boy sit where he likes," he cried in a bullying voice to the father.

"All right! All right!" said Scully, deferentially. The cowboy and the Easterner exchanged glances of wonder.

The five chairs were formed in a crescent about one side of the stove. The Swede
began to talk; he talked arrogantly, profanely, angrily. Johnnie, the cowboy, and the Easterner maintained a morose silence, while old Scully appeared to be receptive and eager, breaking in constantly with sympathetic ejaculations.

Finally the Swede announced that he was thirsty. He moved in his chair, and said that he would go for a drink of water.

"I'll git it for you," cried Scully at once.

"No," said the Swede contemptuously. "I'll get it for myself." He arose and stalked with the air of an owner off into the executive parts of the hotel.

As soon as the Swede was out of hearing Scully sprang to his feet and whispered intensely to the others: "Upstairs he thought I was tryin' to poison 'im."

"Say," said Johnnie, "this makes me sick. Why don't you throw 'im out in the
snow?"

"Why, he's all right now," declared Scully. "It was only that he was from the East, and he thought this was a tough place. That's all. He's all right now."

The cowboy looked with admiration upon the Easterner. "You were straight," he said. "You were on to that there Dutchman."

"Well," said Johnnie to his father, "he may be all right now, but I don't see it. Other time he was scared, but now he's too fresh."

Scully's speech was always a combination of Irish brogue and idiom, Western twang and idiom, and scraps of curiously formal diction taken from the storybooks and newspapers. He now hurled a strange mass of language at the head of his son. "What do I keep? What do I keep? What do I keep?" he demanded, in a voice of thunder. He slapped his knee impressively, to indicate that he himself was going to make reply, and that all should heed. "I keep a hotel," he shouted. "A hotel, do you mind? A guest under my roof has sacred privileges. He is to be intimidated by none. Not one word shall he hear that would prijudice him in favor of goin' away. I'll not have it. There's no place in this here town where they can say they iver took in a guest of mine because he was afraid to stay here." He wheeled suddenly upon the cowboy and the Easterner. "Am I right?"

"Yes, Mr. Scully," said the cowboy, "I think you're right."   115

"Yes, Mr. Scully," said the Easterner, "I think you're right."

V

At six-o'clock supper, the Swede fizzed like a fire-wheel. He sometimes seemed on the point of bursting into riotous song, and in all his madness he was encouraged by old Scully. The Easterner was encased in reserve; the cowboy sat in wide-mouthed amazement, forgetting to eat, while Johnnie wrathily demolished great plates of food. The daughters of the house, when they were obliged to replenish the biscuits, approached as warily as Indians, and, having succeeded in their purpose, fled with ill-concealed trepidation. The Swede domineered the whole feast, and he gave it the appearance of a cruel bacchanal. He seemed to have grown suddenly taller; he gazed, brutally disdainful, into every face. His voice rang through the room. Once when he jabbed out harpoon-fashion with his fork to pinion a biscuit, the weapon nearly impaled the hand of the Easterner, which had been stretched quietly out for the same biscuit.

After supper, as the men filed toward the other room, the Swede smote Scully ruthlessly on the shoulder. "Well, old boy, that was a good, square meal." Johnnie looked hopefully at his father; he knew that shoulder was tender from an old fall; and, indeed, it appeared for a moment as if Scully was going to flame out over the matter, but in the end he smiled a sickly smile and remained silent. The others understood from his manner that he was admitting his responsibility for the Swede's new viewpoint.

Johnnie, however, addressed his parent in an aside. "Why don't you license somebody to kick you downstairs?" Scully scowled darkly by way of reply.

When they were gathered about the stove, the Swede insisted on another game   120
of High-Five. Scully gently deprecated the plan at first, but the Swede turned a wolfish glare upon him. The old man subsided, and the Swede canvassed the others. In his tone there was always a great threat. The cowboy and the Easterner both remarked indifferently that they would play. Scully said that he would presently have to go to meet the 6:58 train, and so the Swede turned menacingly upon Johnnie. For a moment their glances crossed like blades, and then Johnnie smiled and said, "Yes, I'll play."

They formed a square, with the little board on their knees. The Easterner and the Swede were again partners. As the play went on, it was noticeable that the cowboy was not board-whacking as usual. Meanwhile, Scully, near the lamp, had put on his spectacles and, with an appearance curiously like an old priest, was reading a newspaper. In time he went out to meet the 6:58 train, and, despite his precautions, a gust of polar wind whirled into the room as he opened the door. Besides scattering the cards, it chilled the players to the marrow. The Swede cursed frightfully. When Scully returned, his entrance disturbed a cosy and friendly scene. The Swede again cursed. But presently they were once more intent, their heads bent forward and their hands moving swiftly. The Swede had adopted the fashion of board-whacking.

Scully took up his paper and for a long time remained immersed in matters which were extraordinarily remote from him. The lamp burned badly, and once he stopped to adjust the wick. The newspaper, as he turned from page to page, rustled with a slow and comfortable sound. Then suddenly he heard three terrible words: "You are cheatin'!"

Such scenes often prove that there can be little of dramatic import in environment. Any room can present a tragic front: any room can be comic. This little den was now hideous as a torture-chamber. The new faces of the men themselves had changed it upon the instant. The Swede held a huge fist in front of Johnnie's face, while the latter looked steadily over it into the blazing orbs of his accuser. The Easterner had grown pallid: the cowboy's jaw had dropped in that expression of bovine amazement which was one of his important mannerisms. After the three words, the first sound in the room was made by Scully's paper as it floated forgotten to his feet. His spectacles had also fallen from his nose, but by a clutch he had saved them in air. His hand, grasping the spectacles, now remained poised awkwardly and near his shoulder. He stared at the card-players.

Probably the silence was while a second elapsed. Then, if the floor had been suddenly twitched out from under the men they could not have moved quicker. The five had projected themselves headlong toward a common point. It happened that Johnnie, in rising to hurl himself upon the Swede, had stumbled slightly because of his curiously instinctive care for the cards and the board. The loss of the moment allowed time for the arrival of Scully, and also allowed the cowboy time to give the Swede a great push which sent him staggering back. The men found tongue together, and hoarse shouts of rage, appeal, or fear burst from every throat. The cowboy pushed and jostled feverishly at the Swede, and the Easterner and Scully clung wildly to Johnnie; but through the smoky air, above the swaying bodies of the peace-compellers, the eyes of the two warriors ever sought each other in glances of challenge that were at once hot and steely.

Of course the board had been overturned, and now the whole company of cards   125
was scattered over the floor, where the boots of the men trampled the fat and painted kings and queens as they gazed with their silly eyes at the war that was waging above them.

Scully's voice was dominating the yells. "Stop now! Stop, I say! Stop, now—" Johnnie, as he struggled to burst through the rank formed by Scully and the Easterner, was crying. "Well, he says I cheated! He says I cheated! I won't allow no man to say I cheated! If he says I cheated, he's a —— ——!"

The cowboy was telling the Swede, "Quit, now! Quit, d'ye hear—"

The screams of the Swede never ceased: "He did cheat! I saw him! I saw him—"

As for the Easterner, he was importuning in a voice that was not heeded: "Wait a moment, can't you? Oh, wait a moment. What's the good of a fight over a game of cards? Wait a moment—"

In this tumult no complete sentences were clear. "Cheat"—"Quit"—"He says"—   130
these fragments pierced the uproar and rang out sharply. It was remarkable that, whereas Scully undoubtedly made the most noise, he was the least heard of any of the riotous band.

Then suddenly there was a great cessation. It was as if each man had paused for breath; and although the room was still lighted with the anger of men, it could be seen that there was no danger of immediate conflict, and at once Johnnie, shouldering his way forward, almost succeeded in confronting the Swede. "What did you say I cheated for? What did you say I cheated for? I don't cheat, and I won't let no man say I do!"

The Swede said, "I saw you! I saw you!"

"Well," cried Johnnie, "I'll fight any man what says I cheat!"

"No, you won't," said the cowboy. "Not here."

"Ah, be still, can't you?" said Scully, coming between them.   135

The quiet was sufficient to allow the Easterner's voice to be heard. He was repeating, "Oh, wait a moment, can't you? What's the good of a fight over a game of cards? Wait a moment!"

Johnnie, his red face appearing above his father's shoulder, hailed the Swede again. "Did you say I cheated?"

The Swede showed his teeth. "Yes."

"Then," said Johnnie, "we must fight."

"Yes, fight," roared the Swede. He was like a demoniac. "Yes, fight! I'll show you   140
what kind of a man I am! I'll show you who you want to fight! Maybe you think I can't fight! Maybe you think I can't! I'll show you, you skin, you card-sharp! Yes, you cheated! You cheated! You cheated!"

"Well, let's go at it, then, mister," said Johnnie coolly.

The cowboy's brow was beaded with sweat from his efforts in intercepting all sorts of raids. He turned in despair to Scully. "What are you goin' to do now?"

A change had come over the Celtic visage of the old man. He now seemed all eagerness; his eyes glowed.

"We'll let them fight," he answered stalwartly. "I can't put up with it any longer. I've stood this damned Swede till I'm sick. We'll let them fight."

VI

The men prepared to go out of doors. The Easterner was so nervous that he had   145
great difficulty in getting his arms into the sleeves of his new leather coat. As the cowboy drew his fur cap down over his ears his hands trembled. In fact, Johnnie and old Scully were the only ones who displayed no agitation. These preliminaries were conducted without words.

Scully threw open the door. "Well, come on," he said. Instantly a terrific wind caused the flame of the lamp to struggle at its wick, while a puff of black smoke sprang from the chimney-top. The stove was in mid-current of the blast, and its voice swelled to equal the roar of the storm. Some of the scarred and bedabbled cards were caught up from the floor and dashed helplessly against the farther wall. The men lowered their heads and plunged into the tempest as into a sea.

No snow was falling, but great whirls and clouds of flakes, swept up from the ground by the frantic winds, were streaming southward with the speed of bullets. The covered land was blue with the sheen of an unearthly satin, and there was no other hue save where, at the low, black railway station—which seemed incredibly distant—one light gleamed like a tiny jewel. As the men floundered into a thigh-deep drift, it was known that the Swede was bawling out something. Scully went to him, put a hand on his shoulder, and projected an ear. "What's that you say?" he shouted.

"I say," bawled the Swede again. "I won't stand much show against this gang, I know you'll all pitch on me."

Scully smote him reproachfully on the arm. "Tut, man!" he yelled. The wind tore the words from Scully's lips and scattered them far alee.

"You are all a gang of—" boomed the Swede, but the storm also seized the remain-   150
der of this sentence.

Immediately turning their backs upon the wind, the men had swung around a corner to the sheltered side of the hotel. It was the function of the little house to

preserve here, amid this great devastation of snow, an irregular V-shape of heavily
encrusted grass, which crackled beneath the feet. One could imagine the great drifts
piled against the windward side. When the party reached the comparative peace of this
spot it was found that the Swede was still bellowing.

"Oh, I know what kind of a thing this is! I know you'll all pitch on me. I can't lick
you all!"

Scully turned upon him panther-fashion. "You'll not have to whip all of us. You'll
have to whip my son Johnnie. An' the man what troubles you durin' that time will have
me to dale with."

The arrangements were swiftly made. The two men faced each other, obedient to
the harsh commands of Scully, whose face, in the subtly luminous gloom, could be seen
set in the austere impersonal lines that are pictured on the countenances of the Roman
veterans. The Easterner's teeth were chattering, and he was hopping up and down like a
mechanical toy. The cowboy stood rock-like.

The contestants had not stripped off any clothing. Each was in his ordinary attire.   155
Their fists were up, and they eyed each other in a calm that had the elements of leo-
nine cruelty in it.

During this pause, the Easterner's mind, like a film, took lasting impressions of
three men—the iron-nerved master of the ceremony; the Swede, pale, motionless, terrible; and Johnnie, serene yet ferocious, brutish yet heroic. The entire prelude had in it
a tragedy greater than the tragedy of action, and this aspect was accentuated by the long,
mellow cry of the blizzard, as it sped the tumbling and wailing flakes into the black abyss
of the south.

"Now!" said Scully.

The two combatants leaped forward and crashed together like bullocks. There
was heard the cushioned sound of blows, and of a curse squeezing out from between
the tight teeth of one.

As for the spectators, the Easterner's pent-up breath exploded from him with a
pop of relief, absolute relief from the tension of the preliminaries. The cowboy bounded
into the air with a yowl. Scully was immovable as from supreme amazement and fear at
the fury of the fight which he himself had permitted and arranged.

For a time the encounter in the darkness was such a perplexity of flying arms that   160
it presented no more detail than would a swiftly revolving wheel. Occasionally a face, as
if illumined by a flash of light, would shine out, ghastly and marked with pink spots. A
moment later, the men might have been known as shadows, if it were not for the involuntary utterance of oaths that came from them in whispers.

Suddenly a holocaust of warlike desire caught the cowboy, and he bolted forward
with the speed of a broncho. "Go it, Johnnie! go it! Kill him! Kill him!"

Scully confronted him. "Kape back," he said; and by his glance the cowboy could
tell that this man was Johnnie's father.

To the Easterner there was a monotony of unchangeable fighting that was an
abomination. This confused mingling was eternal to his sense, which was concentrated
in a longing for the end, the priceless end. Once the fighters lurched near him, and as
he scrambled hastily backward he heard them breathe like men on the rack.

"Kill him, Johnnie! Kill him! Kill him! Kill him!" The cowboy's face was contorted
like one of those agony masks in museums.

"Keep still," said Scully, icily.   165

Then there was a sudden loud grunt, incomplete, cut short, and Johnnie's body
swung away from the Swede and fell with sickening heaviness to the grass. The cowboy

was barely in time to prevent the mad Swede from flinging himself upon his prone adversary. "No, you don't," said the cowboy, interposing an arm. "Wait a second."

Scully was at his son's side. "Johnnie! Johnnie, me boy!" His voice had a quality of melancholy tenderness. "Johnnie! Can you go on with it?" He looked anxiously down into the bloody, pulpy face of his son.

There was a moment of silence, and then Johnnie answered in his ordinary voice, "Yes, I—it—yes."

Assisted by his father he struggled to his feet. "Wait a bit now till you git your wind," said the old man.

A few paces away the cowboy was lecturing the Swede. "No, you don't! Wait a   170
second!"

The Easterner was plucking at Scully's sleeve. "Oh, this is enough," he pleaded. "This is enough! Let it go as it stands. This is enough!"

"Bill," said Scully, "git out of the road." The cowboy stepped aside. "Now." The combatants were actuated by a new caution as they advanced toward collision. They glared at each other, and then the Swede aimed a lightning blow that carried with it his entire weight. Johnnie was evidently half stupid from weakness, but he miraculously dodged, and his fist sent the over-balanced Swede sprawling.

The cowboy, Scully, and the Easterner burst into a cheer that was like a chorus of triumphant soldiery, but before its conclusion the Swede has scuffed agilely to his feet and come in berserk abandon at his foe. There was another perplexity of flying arms, and Johnnie's body again swung away and fell, even as a bundle might fall from a roof. The Swede instantly staggered to a little wind-waved tree and leaned upon it, breathing like an engine, while his savage and flamelit eyes roamed from face to face as the men bent over Johnnie. There was a splendour of isolation in his situation at this time which the Easterner felt once when, lifting his eyes from the man on the ground, he beheld that mysterious and lonely figure, waiting.

"Are you any good yet, Johnnie?" asked Scully in a broken voice.

The son gasped and opened his eyes languidly. After a moment he answered,   175
"No—I ain't—any good—any—more." Then, from shame, and bodily ill, he began to weep, the tears furrowing down through the blood-stains on his face. "He was too—too—too heavy for me."

Scully straightened and addressed the waiting figure.

"Stranger," he said, evenly, "it's all up with our side." Then his voice changed into that vibrant huskiness which is commonly the tone of the most simple and deadly announcements. "Johnnie is whipped."

Without replying, the victor moved off on the route to the front door of the hotel.

The cowboy was formulating new and unspellable blasphemies. The Easterner was startled to find that they were out in a wind that seemed to come direct from the shadowed arctic floes. He heard again the wail of the snow as it was flung to its grave in the south. He knew now that all this time the cold had been sinking into him deeper and deeper, and he wondered that he had not perished. He felt indifferent to the condition of the vanquished man.

"Johnnie, can you walk?" asked Scully.   180

"Did I hurt—hurt him any?" asked the son.

"Can you walk, boy? Can you walk?"

Johnnie's voice was suddenly strong. There was a robust impatience in it. "I asked you whether I hurt him any!"

"Yes, yes, Johnnie," answered the cowboy, consolingly; "he's hurt a good deal."

They raised him from the ground, and as soon as he was on his feet he went   185
tottering off, rebuffing all attempts at assistance. When the party rounded the corner
they were fairly blinded by the pelting of the snow. It burned their faces like fire. The
cowboy carried Johnnie through the drift to the door. As they entered, some cards again
rose from the floor and beat against the wall.

The Easterner rushed to the stove. He was so profoundly chilled that he almost
dared to embrace the glowing iron. The Swede was not in the room. Johnnie sank into a
chair and, folding his arms on his knees, buried his face in them. Scully, warming one
foot and then the other at a rim of the stove, muttered to himself with Celtic mournful-
ness. The cowboy had removed his fur cap, and with a dazed and rueful air he was running one hand through his tousled locks. From overhead they could hear the creaking
of boards, as the Swede tramped here and there in his room.

The sad quiet was broken by the sudden flinging open of a door that led toward
the kitchen. It was instantly followed by an inrush of women. They precipitated themselves upon Johnnie amid a chorus of lamentation. Before they carried their prey off to
the kitchen, there to be bathed and harangued with that mixture of sympathy and abuse
which is a feat of their sex, the mother straightened herself and fixed old Scully with an
eye of stern reproach, "Shame be upon you, Patrick Scully!" she cried. "Your own son,
too. Shame be upon you!"

"There, now! Be quiet, now!" said the old man, weakly.

"Shame be upon you, Patrick Scully!" The girls, rallying to this slogan, sniffed disdainfully in the direction of those trembling accomplices, the cowboy and the Easterner.
Presently they bore Johnnie away, and left the three men to dismal reflection.

VII

"I'd like to fight this here Dutchman myself," said the cowboy, breaking a long   190
silence.

Scully wagged his head sadly. "No, that wouldn't do. It wouldn't be right. It would-
n't be right."

"Well, why wouldn't it?" argued the cowboy. "I don't see no harm in it."

"No," answered Scully, with mournful heroism. "It wouldn't be right. It was
Johnnie's fight, and now we mustn't whip the man just because he whipped Johnnie."

"Yes, that's true enough," said the cowboy; "but—he better not get fresh with me,
because I couldn't stand no more of it."

"You'll not say a word to him," commanded Scully, and even then they heard the   195
tread of the Swede on the stairs. His entrance was made theatric. He swept the door
back with a bang and swaggered to the middle of the room. No one looked at him.
"Well," he cried, insolently, at Scully, "I s'pose you'll tell me now how much I owe you?"

The old man remained stolid. "You don't owe me nothin'."

"Huh!" said the Swede, "huh! Don't owe 'im nothin'."

The cowboy addressed the Swede. "Stranger, I don't see how you come to be so
gay around here."

Old Scully was instantly alert. "Stop!" he shouted, holding his hand forth, fingers
upward. "Bill, you shut up!"

The cowboy spat carelessly into the sawdust-box. "I didn't say a word, did I?"   200
he asked.

"Mr. Scully," called the Swede, "how much do I owe you?" It was seen that he was attired for departure, and that he had his valise in his hand.

"You don't owe me nothin'," repeated Scully in the same imperturbable way.

"Huh!" said the Swede. "I guess you're right. I guess if it was any way at all, you'd owe me somethin'. That's what I guess." He turned to the cowboy. "'Kill him! Kill him! Kill him!'" he mimicked, and then guffawed victoriously. "'Kill him!'" He was convulsed with ironical humour.

But he might have been jeering the dead. The three men were immovable and silent, staring with glassy eyes at the stove.

The Swede opened the door and passed into the storm, giving one derisive glance   205
backward at the still group.

As soon as the door was closed, Scully and the cowboy leaped to their feet and began to curse. They trampled to and fro, waving their arms and smashing into the air with their fists. "Oh, but that was a hard minute!" wailed Scully. "That was a hard minute! Him there leerin' and scoffin'! One bang at his nose was worth forty dollars to me that minute! How did you stand it, Bill?"

"How did I stand it?" cried the cowboy in a quivering voice. "How did I stand it? Oh!"

The old man burst into sudden brogue. "I'd loike to take that Swade," he wailed, "and hould 'im down on a shtone flure and bate 'im to a jelly wid a shtick!"

The cowboy groaned in sympathy. "I'd like to git him by the neck and hammer him"—he brought his hand down on a chair with a noise like a pistol-shot— "hammer that there Dutchman until he couldn't tell himself from a dead coyote!"

"I'd bate 'im until he—"   210

"I'd show *him* some things—"

And then together they raised a yearning, fanatic cry—"Oh-o-oh! if we only could—"

"Yes!"

"Yes!"

"And then I'd—"   215

"O-o-oh!"

VIII

The Swede, tightly gripping his valise, tacked across the face of the storm as if he carried sails. He was following a line of little naked, gasping trees which, he knew, must mark the way of the road. His face, fresh from the pounding of Johnnie's fists, felt more pleasure than pain in the wind and the driving snow. A number of square shapes loomed upon him finally, and he knew them as the houses of the main body of the town. He found a street and made travel along it, leaning heavily upon the wind whenever, at a corner, a terrific blast caught him.

He might have been in a deserted village. We picture the world as thick with conquering and elate humanity, but here, with the bugles of the tempest pealing, it was hard to imagine a peopled earth. One viewed the existence of man then as marvel, and conceded a glamour of wonder to these lice which were caused to cling to a whirling, fire-smitten, ice-locked, disease-stricken, space-lost bulb. The conceit of man was explained by this storm to be the very engine of life. One was a coxcomb not to die in it. However, the Swede found a saloon.

In front of it an indomitable red light was burning, and the snowflakes were made blood-colour as they flew through the circumscribed territory of the lamp's shining. The Swede pushed open the door of the saloon and entered. A sanded expanse was before him, and at the end of it four men sat about a table drinking. Down one side of the room extended a radiant bar, and its guardian was leaning upon his elbows listening to the talk of the men at the table. The Swede dropped his valise upon the floor and, smiling fraternally upon the barkeeper, said, "Gimme some whisky, will you?" The man placed a bottle, a whisky-glass, and a glass of ice-thick water upon the bar. The Swede poured himself an abnormal portion of whisky and drank it in three gulps. "Pretty bad night," remarked the bartender, indifferently. He was making the pretension of blindness which is usually a distinction of his class; but it could have been seen that he was furtively studying the half-erased blood-stains on the face of the Swede. "Bad night," he said again.

"Oh, it's good enough for me," replied the Swede, hardily, as he poured himself some more whisky. The barkeeper took his coin and manoeuvred it through its reception by the highly nickelled cash-machine. A bell rang; a card labelled "20 cts." had appeared.

"No," continued the Swede, "this isn't too bad weather. It's good enough for me."

"So?" murmured the barkeeper, languidly.

The copious drams made the Swede's eyes swim, and he breathed a trifle heavier. "Yes, I like this weather. I like it. It suits me." It was apparently his design to impart a deep significance to these words.

"So?" murmured the bartender again. He turned to gaze dreamily at the scroll-like birds and bird-like scrolls which had been drawn with soap upon the mirrors in back of the bar.

"Well, I guess I'll take another drink," said the Swede, presently. "Have something?"

"No, thanks; I'm not drinkin'," answered the bartender. Afterward he asked, "How did you hurt your face?"

The Swede immediately began to boast loudly. "Why, in a fight. I thumped the soul out of a man down here at Scully's hotel."

The interest of the four men at the table was at last aroused.

"Who was it?" said one.

"Johnnie Scully," blustered the Swede. "Son of the man what runs it. He will be pretty near dead for some weeks, I can tell you. I made a nice thing of him. I did. He couldn't get up. They carried him in the house. Have a drink?"

Instantly the men in some subtle way encased themselves in reserve. "No, thanks," said one. The group was of curious formation. Two were prominent local business men; one was the district attorney; and one was a professional gambler of the kind known as "square." But a scrutiny of the group would not have enabled an observer to pick the gambler from the men of more reputable pursuits. He was, in fact, a man so delicate in manner, when among people of fair class, and so judicious in his choice of victims, that in the strictly masculine part of the town's life he had come to be explicitly trusted and admired. People called him a thoroughbred. The fear and contempt with which his craft was regarded were undoubtedly the reason why his quiet dignity shone conspicuous above the quiet dignity of men who might be merely hatters, billiard-markers, or grocery clerks. Beyond an occasional unwary traveller who came by rail, this gambler was supposed to prey solely upon reckless and senile farmers, who, when flush with good crops, drove into town in all the pride and confidence of an absolutely invulnerable stupidity. Hearing at times in circuitous fashion of the despoilment of such a farmer, the important men of Romper invariably laughed in contempt of the victim, and if they thought of the wolf at all, it was with a kind of pride at the knowledge that he would never dare think of attacking their wisdom and courage. Besides, it was popular that this gambler had a real wife and two real children in a neat cottage in a suburb, where he led an exemplary home life; and when any one even suggested a discrepancy in his character, the crowd immediately vociferated descriptions of this virtuous family circle. Then men who led exemplary home lives, and men who did not lead exemplary home lives, all subsided in a bunch, remarking that there was nothing more to be said.

However, when a restriction was placed upon him—as, for instance, when a strong clique of members of the new Pollywog Club refused to permit him, even as a spectator, to appear in the rooms of the organization—the candour and gentleness with which he accepted the judgment disarmed many of his foes and made his friends more desperately partisan. He invariably distinguished between himself and a respectable Romper man so quickly and frankly that his manner actually appeared to be a continual broadcast compliment.

And one must not forget to declare the fundamental fact of his entire position in Romper. It is irrefutable that in all affairs outside his business, in all matters that occur eternally and commonly between man and man, this thieving cardplayer was so generous, so just, so moral, that, in a contest, he could have put to flight the consciences of nine tenths of the citizens of Romper.

And so it happened that he was seated in this saloon with the two prominent local merchants and the district attorney.

The Swede continued to drink raw whisky, meanwhile babbling at the barkeeper   235
and trying to induce him to indulge in potations. "Come on. Have a drink. Come on. What—no? Well, have a little one, then. By gawd, I've whipped a man tonight, and I want to celebrate. I whipped him good, too. Gentlemen," the Swede cried to the men at the table, "have a drink?"

"Ssh!" said the barkeeper.

The group at the table, although furtively attentive, had been pretending to be deep in talk, but now a man lifted his eyes toward the Swede and said, shortly, "Thanks. We don't want any more."

At this reply the Swede ruffled out his chest like a rooster. "Well," he exploded, "it seems I can't get anybody to drink with me in this town. Seems so, don't it? Well!"

"Ssh!" said the barkeeper.

"Say," snarled the Swede, "don't you try to shut me up. I won't have it. I'm a   240
gentleman, and I want people to drink with me. And I want 'em to drink with me now. *Now*—do you understand?" He rapped the bar with his knuckles.

Years of experience had calloused the bartender. He merely grew sulky. "I hear you," he answered.

"Well," cried the Swede, "listen hard then. See those men over there? Well, they're going to drink with me, and don't you forget it. Now you watch."

"Hi!" yelled the barkeeper, "this won't do!"

"Why won't it?" demanded the Swede. He stalked over to the table, and by chance laid his hand upon the shoulder of the gambler. "How about this?" he asked wrathfully. "I asked you to drink with me."

The gambler simply twisted his head and spoke over his shoulder. "My friend, I   245
don't know you."

"Oh, hell!" answered the Swede, "come and have a drink."

"Now, my boy," advised the gambler, kindly, "take your hand off my shoulder and go 'way and mind your own business." He was a little, slim man, and it seemed strange to hear him use this tone of heroic patronage to the burly Swede. The other men at the table said nothing.

"What! You won't drink with me, you little dude? I'll make you, then! I'll make you!" The Swede had grasped the gambler frenziedly at the throat, and was dragging him from his chair. The other men sprang up. The barkeeper dashed around the corner of his bar. There was a great tumult, and then was seen a long blade in the hand of the gambler. It shot forward, and a human body, this citadel of virtue, wisdom, power, was pierced as easily as if it had been a melon. The Swede fell with a cry of supreme astonishment.

The prominent merchants and the district attorney must have at once tumbled out of the place backward. The bartender found himself hanging limply to the arm of a chair and gazing into the eyes of a murderer.

"Henry," said the latter, as he wiped his knife on one of the towels that hung   250
beneath the bar rail, "you tell 'em where to find me. I'll be home, waiting for 'em." Then he vanished. A moment afterward the barkeeper was in the street dinning through the storm for help and, moreover, companionship.

The corpse of the Swede, alone in the saloon, had its eyes fixed upon a dreadful legend that dwelt atop the cash-machine: "This registers the amount of your purchase."

IX

Months later, the cowboy was frying pork over the stove of a little ranch near the Dakota line, when there was a quick thud of hoofs outside, and presently the Easterner entered with the letters and the papers.

"Well," said the Easterner at once, "the chap that killed the Swede has got three years. Wasn't much, was it?"

"He has? Three years?" The cowboy poised his pan of pork, while he ruminated upon the news. "Three years. That ain't much."

"No. It was a light sentence," replied the Easterner as he unbuckled his spurs.   255
"Seems there was a good deal of sympathy for him in Romper."

"If the bartender had been any good," observed the cowboy, thoughtfully, "he would have gone in and cracked that there Dutchman on the head with a bottle in the beginnin' of it and stopped all this here murderin'."

"Yes, a thousand things might have happened," said the Easterner, tartly.

The cowboy returned his pan of pork to the fire, but his philosophy continued. "It's funny, ain't it? If he hadn't said Johnnie was cheatin' he'd be alive this minute. He was an awful fool. Game played for fun, too. Not for money. I believe he was crazy."

"I feel sorry for that gambler," said the Easterner.

"Oh, so do I," said the cowboy. "He don't deserve none of it for killin' who he did."   260

"The Swede might not have been killed if everything had been square."

"Might not have been killed?" exclaimed the cowboy. "Everythin' square? Why, when he said that Johnnie was cheatin' and acted like such a jackass? And then in the saloon he fairly walked up to git hurt?" With these arguments the cowboy browbeat the Easterner and reduced him to rage.

"You're a fool!" cried the Easterner, viciously. "You're a bigger jackass than the Swede by a million majority. Now let me tell you one thing. Let me tell you something. Listen! Johnnie *was* cheating!"

"'Johnnie,'" said the cowboy, blankly. There was a minute of silence, and then he said, robustly, "Why, no. The game was only for fun."

"Fun or not," said the Easterner, "Johnnie was cheating. I saw him. I know it. I saw him. And I refused to stand up and be a man. I let the Swede fight it out alone. And you—you were simply puffing around the place wanting to fight. And then old Scully himself! We are all in it! This poor gambler isn't even a noun. He is a kind of an adverb. Every sin is the result of collaboration. We, five of us, have collaborated in the murder of this Swede. Usually there are from a dozen to forty women really involved in every murder, but in this case it seems to be only five men—you, I, Johnnie, old Scully; and that fool of an unfortunate gambler came merely as a culmination, the apex of a human movement, and gets all the punishment." 265

The cowboy, injured and rebellious, cried out blindly into this fog of mysterious theory: "Well, I didn't do anythin', did I?"

QUESTIONS

1. Describe the conflict in the story. Why is the Swede the major antagonist? How could he be seen as protagonist, instead of antagonist? Why do the others stress his identity as a Swede, and why is he never named?

2. Consider the Easterner's analysis (paragraph 90) as a plausible explanation of the Swede's behavior before the fight. How fully does this analysis explain these actions? How could the analysis be used in an argument that "The Blue Hotel" is a critique of conventional, dime-store-novel views of the wild west?

3. Analyze the structure of the story. What relationship do the parts of abstract formal structure (described on pp. 94–95) have to the part divisions marked by Crane himself? Why is most of the story about events at the Blue Hotel, and why do events at the saloon, where the murder occurs, occupy only a small section? Explain, in relation to the story's structure, why we do not learn until the very end that Johnny actually *was* cheating.

4. How adequately does the Easterner's "noun-adverb" analysis in the concluding paragraphs explain the events of the story? Could such events be stopped at a certain point, or are they inevitable regardless of the Easterner's theory about collaborative control and responsibility?

EUDORA WELTY   (b. 1909)

One of the major southern writers, Welty was born in Jackson, Mississippi. She attended the Mississippi State College for Women and the University of Wisconsin, and she began her writing career during the Great Depression. By 1943 she had published two major story collections, Curtain of Green *(1941, including "A Worn Path") and* The Wide Net *(1943). She is the author of many stories and was awarded the Pulitzer Prize in 1973 for her short novel* The Optimist's Daughter *(1972). "A Worn Path" received an O. Henry Award in 1941.*

A Worn Path _____ *1941*

It was December—a bright frozen day in the early morning. Far out in the country there was an old Negro woman with her head tied in a red rag, coming along a path through the pinewoods. Her name was Phoenix Jackson. She was very old and small and she walked slowly in the dark pine shadows, moving a little from side to side in her steps, with the balanced heaviness and lightness of a pendulum in a grandfather clock. She carried a thin, small cane made from an umbrella, and with this she kept tapping the frozen earth in front of her. This made a grave and persistent noise in the still air, that seemed meditative like the chirping of a solitary little bird.

She wore a dark striped dress reaching down to her shoe tops, and an equally long apron of bleached sugar sacks, with a full pocket: all neat and tidy, but every time she took a step she might have fallen over her shoelaces, which dragged from her unlaced shoes. She looked straight ahead. Her eyes were blue with age. Her skin had a pattern all its own of numberless branching wrinkles and as though a whole little tree stood in the middle of her forehead, but a golden color ran underneath, and the two knobs of her cheeks were illuminated by a yellow burning under the dark. Under the rag her hair came down on her neck in the frailest of ringlets, still black, and with an odor like copper.

Now and then there was a quivering in the thicket. Old Phoenix said, "Out of my way, all you foxes, owls, beetles, jack rabbits, coons and wild animals! . . . Keep out from under these feet, little bob-whites. . . . Keep the big wild hogs out of my path. Don't let none of those come running my direction. I got a long way." Under her small black-freckled hand her cane, limber as a buggy whip, would switch at the brush as if to rouse up any hiding things.

On she went. The woods were deep and still. The sun made the pine needles almost too bright to look at, up where the wind rocked. The cones dropped as light as feathers. Down in the hollow was the mourning dove—it was not too late for him.

The path ran up a hill. "Seem like there is chains about my feet, time I get this far," she said, in the voice of argument old people keep to use with themselves. "Something always take a hold of me on this hill—pleads I should stay."

After she got to the top she turned and gave a full, severe look behind her where she had come. "Up through pines," she said at length. "Now down through oaks."

Her eyes opened their widest, and she started down gently. But before she got to the bottom of the hill a bush caught her dress.

Her fingers were busy and intent, but her skirts were full and long, so that before she could pull them free in one place they were caught in another. It was not possible to allow the dress to tear. "I in the thorny bush," she said. "Thorns, you doing your appointed work. Never want to let folks pass, no sir. Old eyes thought you was a pretty little *green* bush."

Finally, trembling all over, she stood free, and after a moment dared to stoop for her cane.

"Sun so high!" she cried, leaning back and looking, while the thick tears went over her eyes. "The time getting all gone here."

At the foot of this hill was a place where a log was laid across the creek.

"Now comes the trial," said Phoenix.

Putting her right foot out, she mounted the log and shut her eyes. Lifting her skirt, leveling her cane fiercely before her, like a festival figure in some parade, she began to march across. Then she opened her eyes and she was safe on the other side.

"I wasn't as old as I thought," she said.

But she sat down to rest. She spread her skirts on the bank around her and folded   15
her hands over her knees. Up above her was a tree in a pearly cloud of mistletoe. She did
not dare to close her eyes, and when a little boy brought her a plate with a slice of
marble-cake on it she spoke to him. "That would be acceptable," she said. But when she
went to take it there was just her own hand in the air.

So she left that tree, and had to go through a barbed-wire fence. There she had
to creep and crawl, spreading her knees and stretching her fingers like a baby trying to
climb the steps. But she talked loudly to herself: she could not let her dress be torn now,
so late in the day, and she could not pay for having her arm or leg sawed off if she got
caught fast where she was.

At last she was safe through the fence and risen up out in the clearing. Big dead
trees, like black men with one arm, were standing in the purple stalks of the withered
cotton field. There sat a buzzard.

"Who you watching?"

In the furrow she made her way along.

"Glad this is not the season for bulls," she said, looking sideways, "and the good   20
Lord made his snakes to curl up and sleep in the winter. A pleasure I don't see no two-
headed snake coming around that tree, where it come once. It took a while to get by
him, back in the summer."

She passed through the old cotton and went into a field of dead corn. It whispered and shook and was taller than her head. "Through the maze now," she said, for
there was no path.

Then there was something tall, black, and skinny there, moving before her.

At first she took it for a man. It could have been a man dancing in the field. But
she stood still and listened, and it did not make a sound. It was as silent as a ghost.

"'Ghost," she said sharply, "who be you the ghost of? For I have heard of nary
death close by."

But there was no answer—only the ragged dancing in the wind.   25

She shut her eyes, reached out her hand, and touched a sleeve. She found a coat
and inside that an emptiness, cold as ice.

"You scarecrow," she said. Her face lighted. "I ought to be shut up for good," she
said with laughter. "My senses is gone. I too old, I the oldest people I ever know. Dance,
old scarecrow," she said, "while I dancing with you."

She kicked her foot over the furrow, and with mouth drawn down, shook her head
once or twice in a little strutting way. Some husks blew down and whirled in steamers
about her skirts.

Then she went on, parting her way from side to side with the cane, through the
whispering field. At last she came to the end, to a wagon track where the silver grass
blew between the red ruts. The quail were walking around like pullets, seeming all dainty
and unseen.

"Walk pretty," she said. "This is the easy place. This the easy going."   30

She followed the track, swaying through the quiet bare fields, through the little
strings of trees silver in their dead leaves, past cabins silver from weather, with the doors
and windows boarded shut, all like old women under a spell sitting there. "I walking in
their sleep," she said, nodding her head vigorously.

In a ravine she went where a spring was silently flowing through a hollow log. Old
Phoenix bent and drank. "Sweet-gum makes the water sweet," she said, and drank more.
"Nobody know who made this well, for it was here when I was born."

The track crossed a swampy part where the moss hung as white as lace from every limb. "Sleep on, alligators, and blow your bubbles." Then the track went into the road.

Deep, deep the road went down between the high green-colored banks. Overhead the live-oaks met, and it was as dark as a cave.

A black dog with a lolling tongue came up out of the weeds by the ditch. She was   35
meditating, and not ready, and when he came at her she only hit him a little with her cane. Over she went in the ditch, like a little puff of milkweed.

Down there, her sense drifted away. A dream visited her, and she reached her hand up, but nothing reached down and gave her a pull. So she lay there and presently went to talking. "Old woman," she said to herself, "that black dog come up out of the weeds to stall you off, and now there he sitting on his fine tail smiling at you."

A white man finally came along and found her—a hunter, a young man, with his dog on a chain.

"Well, Granny!" he laughed. "What are you doing there?"

"Lying on my back like a June-bug waiting to be turned over, mister," she said, reaching up her hand.

He lifted her up, gave her a swing in the air, and set her down. "Anything broken,   40
Granny?"

"No sir, them old dead weeds is springy enough," said Phoenix, when she had got her breath. "I thank you for your trouble."

"Where do you live, Granny?" he asked, while the two dogs were growling at each other.

"Away back yonder, sir, behind the ridge. You can't even see it from here."

"On your way home?"

"No sir, I goin to town."   45

"Why, that's too far! That's as far as I walk when I come out myself, and I get something for my trouble." He patted the stuffed bag he carried, and there hung down a little closed claw. It was one of the bob-whites, with its beak hooked bitterly to show it was dead. "Now you go on home, Granny!"

"I bound to go to town, mister," said Phoenix. "The time come around."

He gave another laugh, filling the whole landscape. "I know you old colored people! Wouldn't miss going to town to see Santa Claus!"

But something held old Phoenix very still. The deep lines in her face went into a fierce and different radiation. Without warning, she had seen with her own eyes a flashing nickel fall out of the man's pocket onto the ground.

"How old are you, Granny?" he was saying.   50

"There is no telling, mister," she said, "no telling."

Then she gave a little cry and clapped her hands and said, "Git on away from here, dog! Look! Look at that dog!" She laughed as if in admiration. "He ain't scared of nobody. He a big black dog." She whispered, "Sic him!"

"Watch me get rid of that cur," said the man. "Sic him, Pete! Sic him!"

Phoenix heard the dogs fighting, and heard the man running and throwing sticks. She even heard a gunshot. But she was slowly bending forward by that time, further and further forward, the lids stretched down over her eyes, as if she were doing this in her sleep. Her chin was lowered almost to her knees. The yellow palm of her hand came out from the fold of her apron. Her fingers slid down and along the ground under the piece of money with the grace and care they would have in lifting an egg from under a setting hen. Then she slowly straightened up, she stood erect, and the nickel was in her apron pocket. A bird flew by. Her lips moved. "God watching me the whole time. I come to stealing."

The man came back, and his own dog panted about them. "Well, I scared him off that time," he said, and then he laughed and lifted his gun and pointed it at Phoenix.   55

She stood straight and faced him.

"Doesn't the gun scare you?" he said, still pointing it.

"No, sir. I seen plenty go off closer by, in my day, and for less than what I done," she said, holding utterly still.

He smiled, and shouldered the gun. "Well, Granny," he said, "you must be a hundred years old, and scared of nothing. I'd give you a dime if I had any money with me. But you take my advice and stay home, and nothing will happen to you."

"I bound to go on my way, mister," said Phoenix. She inclined her head in the red   60 rag. Then they went in different directions, but she could hear the gun shooting again and again over the hill.

She walked on. The shadows hung from the oak trees to the road like curtains. Then she smelled wood-smoke, and smelled the river, and she saw a steeple and the cabins on their steep steps. Dozens of little black children whirled around her. There ahead was Natchez shining. Bells were ringing. She walked on.

In the paved city it was Christmas time. There were red and green electric lights strung and crisscrossed everywhere, and all turned on in the daytime. Old Phoenix would have been lost if she had not distrusted her eyesight and depended on her feet to know where to take her.

She paused quietly on the sidewalk where people were passing by. A lady came along in the crowd, carrying an armful of red-, green-, and silver-wrapped presents; she gave off perfume like the red roses in hot summer, and Phoenix stopped her.

"Please, missy, will you lace up my shoe?" She held up her foot.

"What do you want, Grandma?"   65

"See my shoe," said Phoenix. "Do all right for out in the country, but wouldn't look right to go in a big building."

"Stand still then, Grandma," said the lady. She put her packages down on the sidewalk beside her and laced and tied both shoes tightly.

"Can't lace 'em with a cane," said Phoenix. "Thank you, missy. I doesn't mind asking a nice lady to tie up my shoe, when I gets out on the street."

Moving slowly and from side to side, she went into the big building, and into a tower of steps, where she walked up and around and around until her feet knew to stop.

She entered a door, and there she saw nailed up on the wall the document that   70 had been stamped with the gold seal and framed in the gold frame, which matched the dream that was hung up in her head.

"Here I be," she said. There was a fixed and ceremonial stiffness over her body.

"A charity case, I suppose," said an attendant who sat at the desk before her.

But Phoenix only looked above her head. There was sweat on her face, the wrinkles in her skin shone like a bright net.

"Speak up, Grandma," the woman said, "What's your name? We must have your history, you know. Have you been here before? What seems to be the trouble with you?"

Old Phoenix only gave a twitch to her face as if a fly were bothering her.   75

"Are you deaf?" cried the attendant.

But then the nurse came in.

"Oh, that's just old Aunt Phoenix," she said. "She doesn't come for herself—she has a little grandson. She makes these trips just as regular as clockwork. She lives away back off the Old Natchez Trace." She bent down. "Well, Aunt Phoenix, why don't you just take a seat? We won't keep you standing after your long trip." She pointed.

The old woman sat down, bolt upright in the chair.

"Now, how is the boy?" asked the nurse.

Old Phoenix did not speak.

"I said, how is the boy?"

But Phoenix only waited and stared straight ahead, her face very solemn and withdrawn into rigidity.

"Is his throat any better?" asked the nurse. "Aunt Phoenix, don't you hear me? Is your grandson's throat any better since the last time you came for the medicine?"

With her hands on her knees, the old woman waited, silent, erect, and motionless, just as if she were in armor.

"You mustn't take up our time this way, Aunt Phoenix," the nurse said. "Tell us quickly about your grandson, and get it over. He isn't dead, is he?"

At last there came a flicker and then a flame of comprehension across her face, and she spoke.

"My grandson. It was my memory had left me. There I sat and forgot why I made my long trip."

"Forgot?" the nurse frowned. "After you came so far?"

Then Phoenix was like an old woman begging a dignified forgiveness for waking up frightened in the night. "I never did go to school, I was too old at the Surrender," she said in a soft voice. "I'm an old woman without an education. It was my memory fail me. My little grandson, he is just the same, and I forgot it in the coming."

"Throat never heals, does it?" said the nurse, speaking in a loud, sure voice to old Phoenix. By now she had a card with something written on it, a little list. "Yes. Swallowed lye. When was it—January—two, three years ago—"

Phoenix spoke unasked now. "No missy, he not dead, he just the same. Every little while his throat begin to close up again, and he not able to swallow. He not get his breath. He not able to help himself. So the time come around, and I go on another trip for the soothing medicine."

"All right. The doctor said as long as you came to get it, you could have it," said the nurse. "But it's an obstinate case."

"My little grandson, he sit up there in the house all wrapped up, waiting by himself," Phoenix went on. "We is the only two left in the world. He suffer and it don't seem to put him back at all. He got a sweet look. He going to last. He wear a little patch quilt and peep out holding his mouth open like a little bird. I remembers so plain now. I not going to forget him again, no, the whole enduring time. I could tell him from all the others in creation."

"All right." The nurse was trying to hush her now. She brought her a bottle of medicine. "Charity," she said, making a check mark in a book.

Old Phoenix held the bottle close to her eyes, and then carefully put it into her pocket.

"I thank you," she said.

"It's Christmas time, Grandma," said the attendant. "Could I give you a few pennies out of my purse?"

"Five pennies is a nickel," said Phoenix stiffly.

"Here's a nickel," said the attendant.   100

Phoenix rose carefully and held out her hand. She received the nickel and then fished the other nickel out of her pocket and laid it beside the new one. She stared at her palm closely, with her head on one side.

Then she gave a tap with her cane on the floor.

"This is what come to me to do," she said, "I going to the store and buy my child a little windmill they sells, made out of paper. He going to find it hard to believe there such a thing in the world. I'll march myself back where he waiting, holding it straight up in this hand."

She lifted her free hand, gave a little nod, turned around, and walked out of the doctor's office. Then her slow step began on the stairs, going down.

QUESTIONS

1. From the description of Phoenix, what do you conclude about her economic condition? How do you know that she has taken the path through the woods before? Is she accustomed to being alone? What do you make of her speaking to animals, and of her imagining a boy offering her a piece of cake? What does her speech show about her education and background?

2. Describe the plot of the story. With Phoenix as the protagonist, what are the obstacles ranged against her? How might Phoenix be considered to be in the grip of large and indifferent social and political forces?

3. Comment on the meaning of this dialogue between Phoenix and the hunter:

    "Doesn't the gun scare you?" he said, still pointing it.
    "No, sir. I seen plenty go off closer by, in my day, and for less than what I done," she said, holding utterly still.

4. A number of responses might be made to this story, among them admiration for Phoenix, pity for her and her grandson and for the downtrodden generally, anger at her impoverished condition, and apprehension about her approaching senility. Do you share in any of these responses? Do you have any others?

TOM WHITECLOUD   (1914–1972)

Thomas St. Germain Whitecloud was born in New York City. However, he spent much of his youth on the Lac du Flambeau Indian Reservation near Woodruff, Wisconsin, the town mentioned in paragraph 20 of "Blue Winds Dancing." After attending colleges in New Mexico and California, he received his degree in medicine from Tulane University. He lived in Louisiana and Texas throughout his medical career, and at the time of his death he was a consultant for the Texas Commission on Alcoholism and Drug Abuse for Indians. "Blue Winds Dancing," which can be considered as either a story or a fictionalized autobiographical fragment, received a prize in 1938 from both Scribner's Magazine, *in which it was published, and the Phi Beta Kappa National Honor Society.*

Blue Winds Dancing _____ 1938

There is a moon out tonight. Moon and stars and clouds tipped with moonlight. And there is a fall wind blowing in my heart. Ever since this evening, when against a fading sky I saw geese wedge southward. They were going home. . . . Now I try to study, but against the pages I see them again, driving southward. Going home.

Across the valley there are heavy mountains holding up the night sky, and beyond the mountains there is home. Home, and peace, and the beat of drums, and blue winds dancing over snowfields. The Indian lodge will fill with my people, and our gods will come and sit among them. I should be there then. I should be at home.

But home is beyond the mountains, and I am here. Here where fall hides in the valleys, and winter never comes down from the mountains. Here where all the trees grow in rows; the palms stand stiffly by the roadsides, and in the groves the orange trees line in military rows, and endlessly bear fruit. Beautiful, yes; there is always beauty in order, in rows of growing things! But it is the beauty of captivity. A pine fighting for existence on a windy knoll is much more beautiful.

In my Wisconsin, the leaves change before the snows come. In the air there is the smell of wild rice and venison cooking; and when the winds come whispering through the forests, they carry the smell of rotting leaves. In the evenings, the loon calls, lonely; and birds sing their last songs before leaving. Bears dig roots and eat late fall berries, fattening for their long winter sleep. Later, when the first snows fall, one awakens in the morning to find the world white and beautiful and clean. Then one can look back over his trail and see the tracks following. In the woods there are tracks of deer and snow-shoe rabbits, and long streaks where partridges slide to alight. Chipmunks make tiny footprints on the limbs and one can hear squirrels busy in hollow trees, sorting acorns. Soft lake waves wash the shores, and sunsets burst each evening over the lakes, and make them look as if they were afire.

That land which is my home! Beautiful, calm—where there is no hurry to get anywhere, no driving to keep up in a race that knows no ending and no goal. No classes where men talk and talk and then stop now and then to hear their own words come back to them from the students. No constant peering into the maelstrom of one's mind; no worries about grades and honors; no hysterical preparing for life until that life is half over; no anxiety about one's place in the thing they call Society.

I hear again the ring of axes in deep woods, the crunch of snow beneath my feet. I feel again the smooth velvet of ghost-birch bark. I hear the rhythm of the drums. . . . I am tired. I am weary of trying to keep up this bluff of being civilized. Being civilized means trying to do everything you don't want to, never doing anything you want to. It means dancing to the strings of custom and tradition; it means living in houses and never knowing or caring who is next door. These civilized white men want us to be like them—always dissatisfied—getting a hill and wanting a mountain.

Then again, maybe I am not tired. Maybe I'm licked. Maybe I am just not smart enough to grasp these things that go to make up civilization. Maybe I am just too lazy to think hard enough to keep up.

Still, I know my people have many things that civilization has taken from the whites. They know how to give; how to tear one's piece of meat in two and share it with one's brother. They know how to sing—how to make each man his own songs and sing them; for their music they do not have to listen to other men singing over a radio. They know how to make things with their hands, how to shape beads into design and make a thing of beauty from a piece of birch bark.

But we are inferior. It is terrible to have to feel inferior; to have to read reports of intelligence tests, and learn that one's race is behind. It is terrible to sit in classes and hear men tell you that your people worship sticks of wood—that your gods are all false, that the Manitou forgot your people and did not write them a book.

I am tired. I want to walk again among the ghost-birches. I want to see the leaves turn in autumn, the smoke rise from the lodgehouses, and to feel the blue winds. I want to hear the drums; I want to hear the drums and feel the blue whispering winds. **10**

There is a train wailing into the night. The trains go across the mountains. It would be easy to catch a freight. They will say he has gone back to the blanket; I don't care. The dance at Christmas. . . .

A bunch of bums warming at a tiny fire talk politics and women and joke about the Relief and the WPA and smoke cigarettes. These men in caps and overcoats and dirty overalls living on the outskirts of civilization are free, but they pay the price of being free in civilization. They are outcasts. I remember a sociology professor lecturing on adjustment to society; hobos and prostitutes and criminals are individuals who never adjusted, he said. He could learn a lot if he came and listened to a bunch of bums talk. He would learn that work and a woman and a place to hang his hat are all the ordinary man wants. These are all he wants, but other men are not content to let him want only these. He must be taught to want radios and automobiles and a new suit every spring. Progress would stop if he did not want these things. I listen to hear if there is any talk of communism or socialism in the hobo jungles. There is none. At best there is a sort of disgusted philosophy about life. They seem to think there should be a better distribution of wealth, or more work, or something. But they are not rabid about it. The radicals live in the cities.

I find a fellow headed for Albuquerque, and talk road-talk with him. "It is hard to ride fruit cars. Bums break in. Better to wait for a cattle car going back to the Middle West, and ride that." We catch the next east-bound and walk the tops until we find a cattle car. Inside, we crouch near the forward wall, huddle, and try to sleep. I feel peaceful and content at last. I am going home. The cattle car rocks. I sleep.

Morning and the desert. Noon and the Salton Sea, lying more lifeless than a mirage under a somber sun in a pale sky. Skeleton mountains rearing on the skyline, thrusting out of the desert floor, all rock and shadow and edges. Desert. Good country for an Indian reservation. . . .

Yuma and the muddy Colorado. Night again, and I wait shivering for the dawn. **15**

Phoenix. Pima country. Mountains that look like cardboard sets on a forgotten stage. Tucson, Papago country. Giant cacti that look like petrified hitchhikers along the highways. Apache country. At El Paso my road-buddy decides to go on to Houston. I leave him, and head north to the mesa country. Las Cruces and the terrible Organ Mountains, jagged peaks that instill fear and wondering. Albuquerque. Pueblos along the Rio Grande. On the boardwalk there are some Indian women in colored sashes selling bits of pottery. The stone age offering its art to the twentieth century. They hold up a piece and fix the tourist with black eyes until, embarrassed, he buys or turns away. I feel suddenly angry that my people should have to do such things for a living. . . .

Santa Fe trains are fast, and they keep them pretty clean of bums. I decide to hurry and ride passenger coaltenders. Hide in the dark, judge the speed of the train as it leaves, and then dash out, and catch it. I hug the cold steel wall of the tender and think of the roaring fire in the engine ahead, and of the passengers back in the dining car reading their papers over hot coffee. Beneath me there is a blur of rails. Death would come quick if my hands should freeze and I fall. Up over the Sangre De Cristo range, around cliffs and through canyons to Denver. Bitter cold here, and I must watch out for Denver Bob. He is a railroad bull who has thrown bums from fast freights. I miss him. It is too cold, I suppose. On north to the Sioux country.

Small towns lit for the coming Christmas. On the streets of one I see a beam-shouldered young farmer gazing into a window filled with shining silver toasters. He is tall and wears a blue shirt buttoned, with no tie. His young wife by his side looks at him hopefully. He wants decorations for his place to hang his hat to please his woman. . . .

Northward again. Minnesota, and great white fields of snow; frozen lakes, and dawn running into dusk without noon. Long forests wearing white. Bitter cold, and one night the northern lights. I am nearing home.

I reach Woodruff at midnight. Suddenly I am afraid, now that I am but twenty miles from home. Afraid of what my father will say, afraid of being looked on as a stranger by my own people. I sit by a fire and think about myself and all other young Indians. We just don't seem to fit in anywhere—certainly not among the whites, and not among the older people. I think again about the learned sociology professor and his professing. So many things seem to be clear now that I am away from school and do not have to worry about some man's opinion of my ideas. It is easy to think while looking at dancing flames.

Morning, I spend the day cleaning up, and buying some presents for my family with what is left of my money. Nothing much, but a gift is a gift, if a man buys it with his last quarter. I wait until evening, then start up the track toward home.

Christmas Eve comes in on a north wind. Snow clouds hang over the pines, and the night comes early. Walking along the railroad bed, I feel the calm peace of snow-bound forests on either side of me. I take my time; I am back in a world where time does not mean so much now. I am alone; alone but not nearly so lonely as I was back on the campus at school. Those are never lonely who love the snow and the pines; never lonely when the pines are wearing white shawls and snow crunches coldly underfoot. In the woods I know there are the tracks of deer and rabbit; I know that if I leave the rails and go into the woods I shall find them. I walk along feeling glad because my legs are light and my feet seem to know that they are home. A deer comes out of the woods ahead of me, and stands silhouetted on the rails. The North, I feel, has welcomed me home. I watch him and am glad that I do not wish for a gun. He goes into the woods quietly, leaving only the design of his tracks in the snow. I walk on. Now and then I pass a field, white under the night sky, with houses at the far end. Smoke comes from the chimneys of the houses, and I try to tell what sort of wood each is burning by the smoke; some burn pine, others aspen, others tamarack. There is one from which comes black coal smoke that rises lazily and drifts out over the tops of the trees. I like to watch houses and try to imagine what might be happening in them.

Just as a light snow begins to fall I cross the reservation boundary; somehow it seems as though I have stepped into another world. Deep woods in a white-and-black winter night. A faint trail leading to the village.

The railroad on which I stand comes from a city sprawled by a lake—a city with a million people who walk around without seeing one another; a city sucking the life from all the country around; a city with stores and police and intellectuals and criminals and movies and apartment houses; a city with its politics and libraries and zoos.

Laughing, I go into the woods. As I cross a frozen lake I begin to hear the drums. Soft in the night the drums beat. It is like the pulse beat of the world. The white line of the lake ends at a black forest, and above the trees the blue winds are dancing.

I come to the outlying houses of the village. Simple box houses, etched black in the night. From one or two windows soft lamplight falls on the snow. Christmas here, too, but it does not mean much; not much in the way of parties and presents. Joe Sky will get drunk. Alex Bodidash will buy his children red mittens and a new sled. Alex is a Carlisle man, and tries to keep his home up to white standards. White standards. Funny that my people should be ever falling farther behind. The more they try to imitate whites the more tragic the result. Yet they want us to be imitation white men. About all we imitate well are their vices.

The village is not a sight to instill pride, yet I am not ashamed; one can never be ashamed of his own people when he knows they have dreams as beautiful as white snow on a tall pine.

Father and my brother and sister are seated around the table as I walk in. Father stares at me for a moment, then I am in his arms, crying on his shoulder. I give them the presents I have brought, and my throat tightens as I watch my sister save carefully bits of red string from the packages. I hide my feelings by wrestling with my brother when he strikes my shoulder in token of affection. Father looks at me, and I know he has many questions, but he seems to know why I have come. He tells me to go alone to the lodge, and he will follow.

I walk along the trail to the lodge, watching the northern lights forming in the heavens. White waving ribbons that seem to pulsate with the rhythm of the drums. Clean snow creaks beneath my feet, and a soft wind sighs through the trees, singing to me. Everything seems to say, "Be happy! You are home now—you are free. You are among friends—we are your friends; we, the trees, and the snow, and the lights." I follow the trail to the lodge. My feet are light, my heart seems to sing to the music, and I hold my head high. Across white snow fields blue winds are dancing.

Before the lodge door I stop, afraid, I wonder if my people will remember me. I wonder—"Am I Indian, or am I white?" I stand before the door a long time. I hear the ice groan on the lake, and remember the story of the old woman under the ice, trying to get out, so she can punish some runaway lovers. I think to myself, "If I am white I will not believe that story; If I am Indian, I will know that there is an old woman under the ice." I listen for a while, and I know that there is an old woman under the ice. I look again at the lights, and go in.

Inside the lodge there are many Indians. Some sit on benches around the walls, others dance in the center of the floor around a drum. Nobody seems to notice me. It seems as though I were among a people I have never seen before. Heavy women with long hair. Women with children on their knees—small children that watch with intent black eyes the movements of the dancers, whose small faces are solemn and serene. The faces of the old people are serene, too, and their eyes are merry and bright. I look at the old men. Straight, dressed in dark trousers and beaded velvet vests, wearing soft moccasins. Dark, lined faces intent on the music. I wonder if I am at all like them. They dance on, lifting their feet to the rhythm of the drums swaying lightly, looking upward. I look at their eyes, and am startled at the rapt attention to the rhythm of the music.

The dance stops. The men walk back to the walls, and talk in low tones or with their hands. There is little conversation, yet everyone seems to be sharing some secret. A woman looks at a small boy wandering away, and he comes back to her.

Strange, I think and then remember. These people are not sharing words—they are sharing a mood. Everyone is happy. I am so used to white people that it seems strange so many people could be together without someone talking. These Indians are happy because they are together, and because the night is beautiful outside, and the

30

music is beautiful. I try hard to forget school and white people, and be one of these—my people. I try to forget everything but the night, and it is a part of me that I am one with my people and we are all a part of something universal. I watch eyes, and see now that the old people are speaking to me. They nod slightly, imperceptibly, and their eyes laugh into mine. I look around the room. All the eyes are friendly; they all laugh. No one questions my being here. The drums begin to beat again, and I catch the invitation in the eyes of the old men. My feet begin to lift to the rhythm, and I look out beyond the walls into the night and see the lights. I am happy. It is beautiful. I am home.

QUESTIONS

1. Describe the first section of the story in terms of the structure. Could a case be made that this first section contains its own crisis and climax and that the rest of the story is really a resolution?

2. What do you learn in the first section about the conflict in the attitudes of the narrator? What is his attitude about "civilization"? What values make him think this way? If he is the protagonist, who or what is the antagonist?

3. What does the narrator mean by saying, "I am alone; alone but not nearly so lonely as I was back on the campus at school" (paragraph 22)?

4. What is meant by the dancing of the blue winds—what kind of wisdom? What is the place for such wisdom in a computerized, industrialized society?

WRITING ABOUT THE PLOT OF A STORY

An essay about plot is an analysis of the conflict and its developments. The organization of the essay should not be modeled on sequential sections and principal events, however, because these invite only a retelling of the story. Instead, the organization is to be developed from the important elements of conflict. Ask yourself the following questions as you look for ideas about plot.

Questions for Discovering Ideas

*   Who are the protagonist and antagonist, and how do their characteristics put them in conflict? How would you describe the conflict?
*   How does the action develop from the conflict?
*   If the conflict stems from contrasting ideas or values, what are these, and how are they brought out?
*   Does the major character face a dilemma? What is the dilemma? How does the character deal with it?
*   How do the major characters achieve (or not achieve) their major goal(s)? What obstacles do they overcome? What obstacles overcome them?
*   At the end, are the characters happy or unhappy, satisfied or dissatisfied, changed or about the same, enlightened or ignorant? How has the resolution of the major conflict produced these results?

Strategies for Organizing Ideas

To keep your essay brief, you need to be selective. Rather than detailing every-thing a major character does, for example, stress the major elements in his or her con-flict. Such an essay on Welty's "A Worn Path" might emphasize Phoenix as she encounters the various obstacles both in the woods and in town. When there is a conflict between two major characters, the obvious approach is to focus equally on both. For brevity, however, emphasis might be placed on just one. Thus, an essay on the plot of "The Blue Hotel" might stress the things we learn about the Swede that are important to his being a major participant in the conflict.

In addition, the plot may be analyzed more broadly in terms of impulses, goals, values, issues, and historical perspectives. Thus, you might emphasize the elements of chance working against Mathilde in Maupassant's "The Necklace" as a contrast to her dreams about wealth. A discussion of the plot of Poe's "The Fall of the House of Usher" might stress the nervousness and deterioration of Roderick Usher, the major character, because the plot depends on how these qualities undermine his sanity and also his life.

The conclusion may contain a brief summary of the points you have made. It is also a fitting location for a brief consideration of the effect or *impact* produced by the conflict. Additional ideas might focus on whether the author has arranged actions and dialogue to direct your favor toward one side or the other, or whether the plot is possible or impossible, serious or comic, fair or unfair, or powerful or weak.

SAMPLE STUDENT ESSAY

The Plot of Eudora Welty's "A Worn Path"°

[1]   At first, the complexity of Eudora Welty's plot in "A Worn Path" is not clear. The main character is Phoenix Jackson, an old, poor, and frail woman; the story seems to be no more than a record of her walk to Natchez through the woods from her rural home. By the story's end, however, the plot is clear: It consists of the brave attempts of a courageous, valiant woman to carry on against overwhelming forces.* Her determination despite the great odds against her gives the story its impact. The powers ranged against her are old age, poverty, environment, and illness.†

[2]   Old age as a silent but overpowering antagonist is shown in signs of Phoenix's increasing senility. Not her mind but her feet tell her where to find the medical office in Natchez. Despite her inner strength, she is unable to explain her errand when the nursing attendant asks her. Instead she sits dumbly and unknowingly for a time, until "a flame of comprehension" comes across her face (paragraph 87). Against the power of advancing age, Phoenix is slowly losing. The implication is that she soon will lose entirely.

° See p. 116 for this story.
* Central idea.
† Thesis sentence.

[3]   An equally crushing opponent is her poverty. She cannot afford to ride to town, but must walk. She has no money and acquires her ten cents for the paper windmill by stealing and begging. The "soothing medicine" she gets for her grandson (paragraph 92) is given to her out of charity. Despite the boy's need for advanced medical care, she has no money to provide it, and the story therefore shows that her guardianship is doomed.

[4]   Closely connected to her poverty is the way through the woods, which during her walk seems to be an almost active opponent. The long hill tires her, the thornbush catches her clothes, the log endangers her balance as she crosses the creek, and the barbed-wire fence threatens to puncture her skin. Another danger on her way is the stray dog, which topples her over. Apparently not afraid, however, Phoenix carries on a cheerful monologue:

> "Out of my way, all you foxes, owls, beetles, jack rabbits, coons and wild animals! . . . Keep out from under these feet, little bob-whites. . . . Keep the big wild hogs out of my path. Don't let none of those come running my direction. I got a long way." (paragraph 3)

She prevails for the moment as she enters Natchez, but all the hazards of her walk are still there, waiting for her to return.

[5]   The force against Phoenix which shows her plight most clearly and pathetically is her grandson's incurable illness. His condition highlights her helplessness, for she is his only support. Her difficulties would be enough for one person alone, but with the grandson the odds against her are doubled. Despite her care, there is nothing anyone can do for the grandson but take the long worn path to get something to help him endure his pain.

[6]   This brief description of the conflicts in "A Worn Path" only hints at the story's power. Welty layers the details to bring out the full range of the conditions against Phoenix, who cannot win despite her determination and devotion. The most hopeless fact, the condition of the invalid grandson, is not revealed until she reaches the medical office, and this delayed final revelation makes one's heart go out to her. The plot is strong because it is so real, and Phoenix is a pathetic but memorable protagonist struggling against overwhelming odds.

Commentary on the Essay

The strategy of this essay is to explain the elements of plot in "A Worn Path" selectively, without duplicating the story's narrative order. Thus the third aspect of conflict, the woods, might be introduced first if the story's narrative order were to be followed, but it is deferred while the more personal elements of old age and poverty are considered first. It is important to note that the essay does not consider other characters as part of Phoenix's conflict; rather, Phoenix's antagonist takes the shape of impersonal and unconquerable forces, such as the grandson's illness.

Paragraph 1 briefly describes how the reader's first impressions are changed by the story's ending. The thesis sentence anticipates the body by listing the four topics about to be treated. Paragraph 2 concerns Phoenix's old age; paragraph 3, her poverty; paragraph 4, the woods; and paragraph 5, her grandson's illness. The concluding paragraph (6) points out that in this set of conflicts the protagonist cannot win except as she lives out her duty and her devotion to help her grandson. Continuing the idea in the introduction, the last paragraph also accounts for the power of the plot: By building up to Phoenix's personal strength against unbeatable forces, the story evokes sympathy and admiration.

WRITING ABOUT STRUCTURE IN A STORY

Your essay should concern arrangement and shape. In form, the essay should not follow the part-by-part unfolding of the narrative or argument. Rather it should explain why things are where they are: "Why is this here and not there?" is the fundamental question you need to answer. Thus it is possible to begin with a consideration of a work's crisis, and then to consider how the exposition and complication have built up to it. A vital piece of information, for example, might have been withheld in the earlier exposition (as in Bierce's "An Occurrence at Owl Creek Bridge" and Welty's "A Worn Path"), and introduced only at or near the conclusion; thus the crisis might be heightened because there would have been less suspense if the detail had been introduced earlier. Consider the following questions as you examine the story's structure.

Questions for Discovering Ideas

- If spaces or numbers divide the story into sections or parts, what structural importance do these parts have?
- If there are no marked divisions, what major sections can you discover? (You might make divisions according to places where actions occur, various times of day, changing weather, or increasingly important events.)
- If the story departs in major ways from the formal structure of exposition, complication, crisis, climax, and resolution, what purpose do these departures have?
- What variations in chronological order, if any, appear in the story (e.g., gaps in the time sequence, flashbacks)? What effects are achieved by these variations?
- Does the story delay any crucial details of exposition? Why? What effect is achieved by the delay?
- Where does an important action or major section (such as the climax) begin? End? How is it related to the other formal structural elements, such as the crisis? Is the climax an action, a realization, or a decision? To what degree does it relieve the work's tension? What is the effect of the climax on your understanding of the characters involved in it? How is this effect related to the arrangement of the climax?

Strategies for Organizing Ideas

Your essay should discuss why an entire story is arranged the way it is—perhaps to reveal the nature of a character's situation, to create surprise, or to bring out maximum humor. You might also, however, discuss the structure of no more than a part of the story, such as the climax or the complication.

The essay is best developed in concert or agreement with what the work contains. The location of scenes is an obvious organizing element. Thus, an essay on the structure of "A Worn Path" might be based on the countryside, the town, and the medical building, where the actions of the story occur. Hawthorne's "Young Goodman Brown" and Mansfield's "Miss Brill" both take place outside (a dark forest for one and a sunny public park for the other). Maupassant's "The Necklace" begins in interiors and concludes outdoors. The locations of Updike's "A & P" are the aisles and the checkout counter of a supermarket. A structural study of any of these works might be based on these locations and their effect on the plot.

Other ways to consider structure can be derived from a work's notable aspects, such as the growing suspense and horrible conclusion of Poe's "The Cask of Amontillado" or the revelation about the father's sinister past in Zabytko's "Home Soil."

The conclusion should highlight the main parts of your essay. You may also deal briefly with the relationship of structure to the plot. If the work you have analyzed departs from chronological order, you might stress the effects of this departure. Your aim should be to focus on the success of the work as it has been brought about by the author's choices in development.

SAMPLE STUDENT ESSAY

The Structure of Eudora Welty's "A Worn Path"°

[1]   The narrative of Eudora Welty's "A Worn Path" is not difficult to follow. Events occur in sequence. The main character is Phoenix Jackson, an old and poor woman. She walks from her rural home in Mississippi through the woods to Natchez to get a free bottle of medicine for her grandson, who is a hopeless invalid. Everything takes place in just a few hours. This action is only the frame, however, for a skillfully and powerfully structured plot.* The masterly control of structure is shown in the story's locations and in the way in which the delayed revelation produces both mystery and complexity.†

° See p. 116 for this story.
* Central idea.
† Thesis sentence.

[2] The locations in the story coincide with the increasing difficulties that Phoenix encounters. The first and most obvious worn path is the rural woods with all its natural difficulties. For most people the obstacles would not be challenging, but for an old woman they are formidable. In Natchez, the location of the next part of the story, Phoenix's inability to bend over to tie her shoe demonstrates the lack of flexibility of old age. In the medical office, where the final scene takes place, two major difficulties of the plot are brought out. One is Phoenix's increasing senility, and the other is the disclosure that her grandson is an incurable invalid. This set of oppositions, the major conflicts in the plot, thus coincide with locations or scenes and show the powerful forces opposing Phoenix.

[3] The strongest of these forces, the revelation about the grandson, makes the story something like a mystery. Because detail about the boy is delayed until the end, the reader wonders for most of the story what bad thing might happen next. In fact, some parts of the story are false leads. For example, the episode with the hunter's dog is threatening, but it leads nowhere: Phoenix, with the aid of the hunter, is unharmed. That she picks up and keeps the nickel dropped by the hunter might seem at first to be cause for punishment. In fact, she thinks it does, as this scene with the hunter shows:

> [H]e laughed and lifted his gun and pointed it at Phoenix.
> She stood straight and faced him.
> "Doesn't the gun scare you?" he said, still pointing it.
> "No, sir. I seen plenty go off closer by, in my day, and for less than what I done," she said, holding utterly still. (paragraphs 55–58)

But the young hunter does not notice that the coin is missing, and he does not accuse her. Right up to the moment of her entering the medical building, the reader is still wondering what might happen.

[4] Therefore, the details about the grandson, carefully concealed until the end, make the story more complex than it at first seems. Because of this concluding revelation, the reader must do a double take and reconsider what has gone on before. Phoenix's difficult walk into town must be seen not as an ordinary errand but as a hopeless mission of mercy. Her character also bears reevaluation: She is not just a funny old woman who speaks to the woods and animals, but she is also a brave and pathetic woman carrying on against crushing odds. These conclusions are not apparent for most of the story, and the late emergence of the carefully concealed details makes "A Worn Path" both forceful and powerful.

[5] Thus the parts of "A Worn Path," while appearing simple at first, are skillfully arranged. The key to the double take and reevaluation is Welty's withholding of the crucial detail of exposition until the very end. The result is that parts of the exposition and complication, through the speeches of the attendant and the nurse, merge with the climax near the story's end. In some respects, the detail makes it seem as though Phoenix's entire existence is a crisis, although she is not aware of this condition as she leaves the office to buy the paper windmill. It is this complex buildup and emotional peak that make the structure of "A Worn Path" the creation of a master writer.

Commentary on the Essay

To highlight the differences between essays on plot and structure, the topic of this sample student essay on structure—Welty's "A Worn Path"—is also analyzed in the sample student essay on plot (p. 127). Both essays are concerned with the conflicts of the story, but the essay on plot concentrates on the opposing forces while the essay on structure focuses on the placement and arrangement of the story's details. Notice that neither essay retells the story event by event. Instead, these are analytical essays that explain the *conflict* (for plot) and the *arrangement and layout* (for structure). In both essays, the assumption is that the reader has read "A Worn Path"; hence there is no need in the essay to tell the story again.

The introductory paragraph points out that the masterly structure accounts for the story's power. Paragraph 2 develops the topic that the geographical locations are arranged climactically to demonstrate the forces against the major character. Paragraph 3 considers how the early exposition creates uncertainty about the issues and direction of the story. As supporting evidence, the paragraph cites two important details—the danger from the hunter's dog and the theft of his nickel—as structural false leads about Phoenix's troubles. Paragraph 4 deals with the complexity brought about by the delayed information about the grandson: the necessary reevaluation of Phoenix's character and her mission to town. The concluding paragraph also considers this complexity, accounting for the story's power by showing how a number of plot elements merge near the end to bring the narrative to a climax swiftly and powerfully.

SPECIAL WRITING TOPICS FOR STUDYING PLOT AND STRUCTURE

1. What kind of story might "A Worn Path" be, structurally, if the detail about the invalid grandson were introduced at the start, before Phoenix begins her walk to town?

2. Compare the structuring of the interior scenes in "The Blue Hotel," "A Worn Path," and "Blue Winds Dancing." How do these scenes bring out the various conflicts of the stories? How do characters in the interiors contribute to plot developments? What is the relationship of these characters to the major themes of the stories?

3. Compare "Everyday Use" (Chapter 2) and "Blue Winds Dancing" as stories developing plots about clashing social and cultural values. In what ways are the plots similar and different?

4. Consider those aspects of "A Worn Path" that seem socially and politically significant. You might consider questions such as whether elderly women like Phoenix are living in such remote areas today, whether her grandson should be left entirely in her care, or whether she should be near public transportation so that she would not need to walk great distances to attend to her needs. You might also consider her as a representative of a group suffering discrimination and treat her as an example of the need for legislation that would improve her condition.

5. Select a circumstance in your life that caused you doubt, difficulty, and conflict. Making yourself anonymous (give yourself a fictitious name and put yourself in a fictitious location), write a brief story about the occasion, stressing how your conflict began, how it affected you, and how you resolved it. You might choose to describe the details in chronological order, or you might begin the story in the present tense and introduce details in flashback.

6. Eudora Welty is considered one of the major contemporary southern writers. How valid is this assertion? Use books and articles that you obtain from your library to substantiate your arguments. What is particularly southern about her work? What is less regional and more general about what she is saying? (You may use "A Worn Path" as representative of her writing.)

4

Characters:
The People
in Fiction

Writers of fiction create narratives that enhance and deepen our understanding of human character and human life. In our own day, under the influences of pioneers like Freud, Jung, and Skinner, the flourishing science of psychology has affected both the creation and the study of literature. It is well known that Freud buttressed some of his psychological conclusions by referring to literary works, especially plays by Shakespeare; well-known films such as *Spellbound, The Snake Pit,* and *Final Analysis* have popularized the relationships between literary character and psychology. Without doubt, the presentation and understanding of character is a major aim of fiction (and literature generally).

In literature, a **character** can be defined as a verbal representation of a human being. Through action, speech, description, and commentary, authors portray characters who are worth caring about, rooting for, and even loving, although there are also characters you may laugh at, dislike, or even hate.

In a story emphasizing a major character, you may expect that each action or speech, no matter how small, is part of a total presentation of that complex combination of both the inner and outer self that constitutes a human being. Whereas in life things may "just happen," in stories all actions, interactions, speeches, and observations are deliberate. Thus, you read about important actions such as a long period of work and sacrifice (Maupassant's "The Necklace"), the taking of a regular journey of mercy (Welty's "A Worn Path"), an act of vengeance (Poe's "The Cask of Amontillado"), or a man's dream of freedom (Bierce's "An Occurrence at Owl Creek Bridge"). By making such actions interesting, authors help you understand and appreciate their major characters and life itself.

CHARACTER TRAITS

In studying a literary character, you should try to determine the character's outstanding traits. A **trait** is a quality of mind or habitual mode of behavior, such as never repaying borrowed money, avoiding eye contact, or always thinking oneself the center of attention. Sometimes, of course, the traits we encounter are minor and therefore negligible, but often a trait is a person's *primary* distinguishing characteristic (not only in fiction but also in life). Thus, characters may be ambitious or lazy, serene or anxious, aggressive or fearful, thoughtful or inconsiderate, open or secretive, confident or self-doubting, kind or cruel, quiet or noisy, visionary or practical, careful or careless, impartial or biased, straightforward or underhanded, "winners" or "losers," and so on.

With this sort of list, to which you may add at will, you can analyze and develop conclusions about character. For example, Mathilde in Maupassant's "The Necklace" indulges in dreams of unattainable wealth and comfort, and she is so swept up in her visions that she scorns her comparatively good life with her reliable but dull husband. It is fair to say that this aversion to reality is her major trait. It is also a major weakness, because Maupassant shows how her dream life harms her real life. By contrast, the narrator of Tan's "Two Kinds" describes her childhood anger at being forced by her mother to learn how to play the piano. In her adult judgment she clearly regrets this anger and the embarrassment she caused her mother, and by this recognition she shows character strength. By similarly analyzing the actions, speeches, and thoughts in the characters you encounter, you can draw conclusions about their qualities and strengths.

DISTINGUISHING BETWEEN
CIRCUMSTANCES AND TRAITS

When you study a fictional person, you need to distinguish between circumstances and character, for circumstances have value *only if they demonstrate important traits.* Thus, if Sam wins a lottery, let us congratulate him on his luck; but the win does not say much about his *character*—not much, that is, unless we also learn that he has been spending hundreds of dollars each week for lottery tickets. In other words, making the effort to win a lottery *is* a character trait, but winning (or losing) *is not.*

Or, let us suppose that an author stresses the neatness of one character and the sloppiness of another. If you accept the premise that people care for their appearance according to choice—and that choices develop from character—you can use these details to make conclusions about a person's self-esteem or the lack of it. In short, when reading about fictional characters, you should look beyond circumstances, actions, and appearances and *determine what these things show about character.* Always try to get from the outside to the inside, for it is the *internal* quality that determines the *external* behavior.

TYPES OF CHARACTERS: ROUND AND FLAT

No writer can present an entire life history of a protagonist; nor can each character in a story get "equal time" for development. Accordingly, some characters grow to be full and alive while others remain shadowy. The British novelist and critic E. M. Forster, in his critical work *Aspects of the Novel,* calls the two major types "round" and "flat."

ROUND CHARACTERS.   The basic trait of **round characters** is that authors present enough detail about them to render them full, lifelike, and memorable. Their roundness is characterized by both individuality and unpredictability. A complementary quality about round characters is therefore that they are **dynamic.** That is, they *recognize, change with,* or *adjust to* circumstances. Such changes may be shown in (1) an action or actions, (2) the realization of new strength and therefore the affirmation of previous decisions, (3) the acceptance of a new condition and the need for making changes, or (4) the discovery of unrecognized truths. For example, Minnie Wright, in Glaspell's "A Jury of Her Peers," is dynamic. We learn that as a young woman she was happy and musical, but she has been deprived and blighted by her twenty-year marriage. Finally, however, a particularly cruel action by her husband so enrages her that she breaks out of her subservient role and commits an act of violence. In short, her action shows her as a dynamic character capable of radical change.

Because a round character usually plays a major role in a story, he or she is often called the **hero** or **heroine.** Some round characters are not particularly heroic, however, so it is sometimes preferable to use the more neutral word **protagonist** (the "first actor"). The protagonist is central to the action, moves against an **antagonist** (the "opposing actor"), and exhibits the ability to adapt to new circumstances.

FLAT CHARACTERS.   In contrast, **flat characters** do not grow. They remain the same because they are stupid or insensitive or because they lack knowledge or insight. They end where they begin and are **static,** not dynamic. Flat characters are not worthless, however, for they highlight the development of the round characters, as with the lawmen in Glaspell's "A Jury of Her Peers." Usually, flat characters are minor (e.g., relatives, acquaintances, functionaries), although not all minor characters are necessarily flat.

Sometimes flat characters are prominent in certain types of literature, such as cowboy, police, and detective stories, in which the focus is less on character than on performance. Such characters might be lively and engaging, even though they do not develop or change. They must be strong, tough, and clever enough to perform recurring tasks such as solving a crime, overcoming a villain, or finding a treasure. The term **stock character** refers to characters in these repeating situations. To the degree that stock characters have many common traits, they are **representative** of their class or group. Such characters, with variations in names, ages, and sexes, have been constant in literature since the ancient Greeks. Some regular stock characters are the insensitive father, the interfering mother, the sassy younger sister or brother, the greedy politician, the resourceful cowboy or detective, the overbearing or henpecked husband, the submissive or nagging wife, the angry police captain, the lovable drunk, and the town do-gooder.

Stock characters stay flat as long as they do no more than perform their roles and exhibit conventional and unindividual traits. When they possess no attitudes except those of their class, they are called **stereotype** characters, because they all seem to be cast from the same mold.

Characters that are brought into focus, however, no matter what roles they perform, emerge from flatness and move into roundness. For example, though most of us would expect grocery-store checkout clerks to be flat, the clerk Sammy in Updike's "A & P" is round, not flat, because he grows quickly under the special circumstances in the store where he works. Similarly, Sarty of Faulkner's "Barn Burning" is just a little boy, but he grows morally in opposition to his father's criminal acts. In sum, the ability to grow and develop and to be altered by circumstances makes characters round and dynamic; absence of these traits makes characters flat and static.

HOW IS CHARACTER DISCLOSED IN FICTION?

Authors use five ways to make their characters live. Remember that you must use your own knowledge and experience to make judgments about the qualities of the characters being revealed.

1. *Actions.* What characters *do* is our best clue to understanding what they *are.* For example, walking in the woods is recreation for most people, and it shows little about their characters. But Phoenix's walk through the woods (Welty's "A Worn Path") is difficult and dangerous for her. Her walk, seen within the context of her age and her mission, may be taken as an expression of a loving, responsible character. Similar strength may be seen when a character faces psychological difficulties, as in Joy Williams's "Taking Care." For Jones, the central character who is also a minister, all aspects of life are going badly—with his wife, his daughter, and his own religious faith. Despite these incentives to despair, however, he preserves his caring and loving role, thus showing a character of great devotion and determination.

Like ordinary human beings, fictional characters do not necessarily understand how they may be changing or why they do the things they do. Nevertheless, their actions express their characters. Sarty of Faulkner's "Barn Burning" is such a character; he is developing a sense of rightness and responsibility, but he does not show the knowledge that is causing his growth. Actions may also signal qualities such as naiveté, weakness, deceit, a scheming person-ality, strong inner conflicts, a realization, or other growth or change. The actions of Abner Snopes in Faulkner's "Barn Burning" indicate a character of suspicion and resentment. Similarly, a strong inner conflict is seen in the two women in Glaspell's "A Jury of Her Peers." They have a theoretical obligation to the law, but they recognize a stronger personal obligation to the accused killer, Minnie. Hence their silence about the incriminating evidence they uncover is an action showing their roundness and dynamism.

2. *Descriptions, both personal and environmental.* Appearance and environ-ment reveal much about a character's social and economic status, of course, but they also tell us more about character traits. A desire for elegance is a trait of Mathilde in Maupassant's "The Necklace." Although her unrealizable taste is destructive, it also brings out her strength of character. In Walker's "Everyday Use," the mother and younger daughter devote great care to the appearance of their poor and unpretentious house, and their self-esteem is shown in this care.

3. *Dramatic statements and thoughts.* Although the speeches of most charac-ters are functional—essential to keep the action moving along—they provide material from which you may draw conclusions. When the second traveler of "Young Goodman Brown" speaks, for example, he reveals his devious and deceptive nature even though ostensibly he is friendly. The lawmen in "A Jury of Her Peers" speak straightforwardly and directly, and these speeches suggest that their characters are similarly orderly. Their constant ridicule of the two women, however, indicates the men's limitations.

Often, characters use speech to hide their motives, though we as readers should see through such a ploy. The narrator Montresor in Poe's "The Cask of Amontillado," for example, is a vengeful schemer, and we conclude this much from his indirect and manipulative language to the equally unpleasant but gullible Fortunato. To Fortunato, Montresor seems friendly and sociable, but to us he is lurid and cynical.

4. *Statements by other characters.* By studying what characters say about each other, you may enhance your understanding of the character being discussed. Thus the two medical attendants talking about Phoenix's condition in "A Worn Path" tell us much about her difficult life, but more importantly they provide a basis for conclusions about Phoenix's great strength.

Ironically, speeches often indicate something other than what the speakers intend, perhaps because of prejudice, stupidity, or foolishness. Lengel's dispar-agement of the girls in bathing suits in "A & P," for example, reveals to us not his wisdom but his rigidity and limited judgment.

5. *Statements by the author speaking as storyteller or observer.* What the author, speaking with the authorial voice, says about a character is usually accurate, and the authorial voice can be accepted factually. However, when the authorial voice *interprets* actions and characteristics, as in Hawthorne's "Young Goodman Brown," the author himself or herself assumes the role of a reader or critic, and any opinions may be questioned. For this reason, authors frequently avoid

interpretations and devote their skill to arranging events and speeches so that readers may draw their own conclusions.

REALITY AND PROBABILITY: VERISIMILITUDE

Characters in fiction should be true to life. That is, their actions, statements, and thoughts must all be what human beings are *likely* to do, say, and think under the conditions presented in the story. This is the standard of **verisimilitude, probability,** or **plausibility.** That is, there may be persons *in life* who perform tasks or exhibit characteristics that are difficult or seemingly impossible (such as always throwing the touchdown pass, getting A+'s on every test, always being cheerful and helpful, or always understanding the needs of others). Such characters *in fiction* would not be true to life, however, because they do not fit within *normal* or *usual* behavior.

One should therefore distinguish between what characters may *possibly* do and what they *most frequently* or *most usually* do. Thus, in "The Necklace," it is possible that Mathilde could be truthful and tell her friend Jeanne Forrestier about the lost necklace. In light of her pride, honor, and respectability, however, it is more in character for her and her husband to hide the loss, borrow money for a replacement, and endure the consequences for ten years. Granted the possibilities of the story (either self-sacrifice or the admission of a fault), the decision she makes with her husband is the more *probable* one.

Nevertheless, probability does not rule out surprise or even exaggeration. It is unusual that young Sarty tries to inform on his father in Faulkner's "Barn Burning," but it is not improbable because he has been developing a sense of morality throughout the story. Likewise, in Porter's "The Jilting of Granny Weatherall," the accomplishments of Granny—such as having fenced 100 acres of farmland all by herself—do not seem impossible even if they do seem unlikely. But we learn that when she was young she became compulsively determined to overcome the betrayal of her unfaithful lover. It is therefore probable that she would be capable of a monumental achievement like doing the fence.

There are many ways of rendering probability in character. Works that attempt to mirror life—realistic, naturalistic, or "slice of life" stories like Welty's "A Worn Path"—set up a pattern of everyday probability. Less realistic conditions establish different frameworks of probability, in which characters are *expected* to be unusual. Such an example is Hawthorne's "Young Goodman Brown." Because a major way of explaining this story is that Brown is having a nightmarish psychotic trance, his bizarre and unnatural responses are probable, just as Phoenix Jackson's speeches, influenced as they are by her approaching senility, are probable in "A Worn Path."

You might also encounter works containing *supernatural* figures such as the second traveler in "Young Goodman Brown." You may wonder whether such characters are probable or improbable. Usually, gods and goddesses embody qualities of the best and most moral human beings, and devils like Hawthorne's guide take on attributes of the worst. However, you might remember that the devil is often given dashing and engaging qualities so that he may deceive gullible sinners and lead them into hell. The friendliness of Brown's guide is therefore not improbable. In judging characters of this or any type, your best criteria are probability, consistency, and believability.

 ## STORIES FOR STUDY

WILLA CATHER   (1873–1947)

Willa Cather is acknowledged as one of America's foremost writers. Her life spanned the period from the decade after the Civil War to the conclusion of World War II. She was born in Virginia and as a girl was taken to Nebraska during the mass migrations of homesteaders into the midwest in the decades after the Civil War. She received a degree from the University of Nebraska in 1895 and spent time after that as a teacher in both Pittsburgh and New York. In 1911 she decided to become a writer, ultimately living in New York. During her career she published twelve novels and fifty-eight short stories. Her best-known novels are O Pioneers! *(1913),* My Antonía *(1918),* A Lost Lady *(1923), and* Death Comes for the Archbishop *(1927). She was the recipient of the Pulitzer Prize for 1923 for her novel* One of Ours. *"Paul's Case" was one of her earliest stories, appearing in her collection* The Troll Garden *(1905).*

Paul's Case ——————————————————————————————— 1905

A Study in Temperament

It was Paul's afternoon to appear before the faculty of the Pittsburgh High School to account for his various misdemeanors. He had been suspended a week ago, and his father had called at the Principal's office and confessed his perplexity about his son. Paul entered the faculty room suave and smiling. His clothes were a trifle outgrown, and the tan velvet on the collar of his open overcoat was frayed and worn; but for all that there was something of the dandy about him, and he wore an opal pin in his neatly knotted black four-in-hand, and a red carnation in his buttonhole. This latter adornment the faculty somehow felt was not properly significant of the contrite spirit befitting a boy under the ban of suspension.

Paul was tall for his age and very thin, with high, cramped shoulders and a narrow chest. His eyes were remarkable for a certain hysterical brilliancy, and he continually used them in a conscious, theatrical sort of way, peculiarity offensive in a boy. The pupils were abnormally large, as though he were addicted to belladonna, but there was a glassy glitter about them which that drug does not produce.

When questioned by the Principal as to why he was there, Paul stated, politely enough, that he wanted to come back to school. This was a lie, but Paul was quite accustomed to lying; found it, indeed, indispensable for overcoming friction. His teachers were asked to state their respective charges against him, which they did with such a rancor and aggrievedness as evinced that this was not a usual case. Disorder and impertinence were among the offenses named, yet each of his instructors felt that it was scarcely possible to put into words the real cause of the trouble, which lay in a sort of hysterically defiant manner of the boy's; in the contempt which they all knew he felt for them, and which he seemingly made not the least effort to conceal. Once, when he had been making a synopsis of a paragraph at the blackboard, his English teacher had stepped to his side and attempted to guide his hand. Paul had started back with a shudder and thrust his hands violently behind him. The astonished woman could scarcely have been more hurt and embarrassed had he struck at her. The insult was so involuntary and definitely personal as to be unforgettable. In one way and another, he had made all his teachers, men and women alike, conscious of the same feeling of physical aversion. In one class he habitually sat with his hand shading his eyes; in another he always looked out of the window during the recitation; in another he made a running commentary on the lecture, with humorous intent.

His teachers felt this afternoon that his whole attitude was symbolized by his shrug and his flippantly red carnation flower, and they fell upon him without mercy, his English teacher leading the pack. He stood through it smiling, his pale lips parted over his white teeth. (His lips were continually twitching, and he had a habit of raising his eyebrows that was contemptuous and irritating to the last degree.) Older boys than Paul had broken down and shed tears under that ordeal, but his set smile did not once desert him, and his only sign of discomfort was the nervous trembling of the fingers that toyed with the buttons of his overcoat, and an occasional jerking of the other hand which held his hat. Paul was always smiling, always glancing about him, seeming to feel that people might be watching him and trying to detect something. This conscious expression, since it was as far as possible from boyish mirthfulness, was usually attributed to insolence or "smartness."

As the inquisition proceeded, one of his instructors repeated an impertinent remark of the boy's, and the Principal asked him whether he thought that a courteous speech to make to a woman. Paul shrugged his shoulders slightly and his eyebrows twitched.

"I don't know," he replied, "I didn't mean to be polite or impolite, either. I guess it's a sort of way I have, of saying things regardless."

The Principal asked him whether he didn't think that a way it would be well to get rid of. Paul grinned and said he guessed so. When he was told that he could go, he bowed gracefully and went out. His bow was like a repetition of the scandalous red carnation.

His teachers were in despair, and his drawing master voiced the feeling of them all when he declared there was something about the boy which none of them understood.

5

He added, "I don't really believe that smile of his comes altogether from insolence; there's something sort of haunted about it. The boy is not strong, for one thing. There is something wrong about the fellow."

The drawing master had come to realize that, in looking at Paul, one saw only his white teeth and the forced animation of his eyes. One warm afternoon the boy had gone to sleep at his drawing board, and his master had noted with amazement what a white, blue-veined face it was; drawn and wrinkled like an old man's about the eyes, the lips twitching even in his sleep.

His teachers left the building dissatisfied and unhappy; humiliated to have felt so   10 vindictive toward a mere boy, to have uttered this feeling in cutting terms, and to have set each other on, as it were, in the gruesome game of intemperate reproach. One of them remembered having seen a miserable street cat set at bay by a ring of tormentors.

As for Paul, he ran down the hill whistling the Soldiers' Chorus from *Faust*,° looking wildly behind him now and then to see whether some of his teachers were not there to witness his light-heartedness. As it was now late in the afternoon and Paul was on duty that evening as usher at Carnegie Hall,° he decided that he would not go home to supper.

When he reached the concert hall the doors were not yet open. It was chilly outside, and he decided to go up into the picture gallery—always deserted at this hour—where there were some of Raffaëlli's° gay studies of Paris streets and an airy blue Venetian scene or two that always exhilarated him. He was delighted to find no one in the gallery but the old guard, who sat in the corner, a newspaper on his knee, a black patch over one eye and the other closed. Paul possessed himself of the place and walked confidently up and down, whistling under his breath. After a while he sat down before a blue Rico° and lost himself. When he bethought him to look at his watch, it was after seven o'clock, and he rose with a start and ran downstairs, making a face at Augustus Caesar,° peering out from the cast-room, and an evil gesture at the Venus of Milo° as he passed her on the stairway.

When Paul reached the ushers' dressing-room half a dozen boys were there already, and he began excitedly to tumble into his uniform. It was one of the few that at all approached fitting, and Paul thought it very becoming—though he knew the tight, straight coat accentuated his narrow chest, about which he was exceedingly sensitive. He was always excited while he dressed, twanging all over to the tuning of the strings and preliminary flourishes of the horns in the music-room; but tonight he seemed quite beside himself, and he teased and plagued the boys until, telling him that he was crazy, they put him down on the floor and sat on him.

Somewhat calmed by his suppression, Paul dashed out to the front of the house to seat the early comers. He was a model usher. Gracious and smiling he ran up and down the aisles. Nothing was too much trouble for him; he carried messages and brought programs as though it were his greatest pleasure in life, and all the people in his section thought him a charming boy, feeling that he remembered and admired them. As the house filled, he grew more and more vivacious and animated, and the

Faust: the most popular opera of Charles Gounod (1818–1893), first produced in 1859.
Carnegie Hall: in Pittsburgh, not the more famous one in New York.
Raffaëlli: Jean-François Rafaëlli (1850–1924), impressionist painter, sculptor, and engraver, known for his scenes of Parisian life.
Rico: Martin Rico (1833–1908). Spanish painter, known for his landscapes.
Caesar . . . Milo: copies of the famous statues of Augustus in the Vatican Museum and the Venus de Milo in the Louvre.

color came to his cheeks and lips. It was very much as though this were a great reception and Paul were the host. Just as the musicians came out to take their places, his English teacher arrived with checks for the seat which a prominent manufacturer had taken for the season. She betrayed some embarrassment when she handed Paul the tickets, and a *hauteur* which subsequently made her feel very foolish. Paul was startled for a moment and had the feeling of wanting to put her out; what business had she here among all these fine people and gay colors? He looked her over and decided that she was not appropriately dressed and must be a fool to sit downstairs in such togs. The tickets had probably been sent her out of kindness, he reflected, as he put down a seat for her, and she had about as much right to sit there as he had.

When the symphony began Paul sank into one of the rear seats with a long sigh of relief, and lost himself as he had done before the Rico. It was not that symphonies, as such, meant anything in particular to Paul, but the first sigh of the instruments seemed to free some hilarious spirit within him; something that struggled there like the Genius in the bottle found by the Arab fisherman.° He felt a sudden zest of life; the lights danced before his eyes and the concert hall blazed into unimaginable splendor. When the soprano soloist came on, Paul forgot even the nastiness of his teacher's being there, and gave himself up to the peculiar intoxication such personages always had for him. The soloist chanced to be a German woman, by no means in her first youth, and the mother of many children; but she wore a satin gown and a tiara, and she had that inde-finable air of achievement, that world-shine upon her, which always blinded Paul to any possible defects.

15

After a concert was over, Paul was often irritable and wretched until he got to sleep—and tonight he was even more than usually restless. He had the feeling of not being able to let down; of its being impossible to give up this delicious excitement which was the only thing that could be called living at all. During the last number he withdrew and, after hastily changing his clothes in the dressing-room, slipped out to the side door where the singer's carriage stood. Here he began pacing rapidly up and down the walk, waiting to see her come out.

Over yonder the Schenley, in its vacant stretch, loomed big and square through the fine rain, the windows of its twelve stories glowing like those of a lighted cardboard house under a Christmas tree. All the actors and singers of any importance stayed there when they were in the city, and a number of the big manufacturers of the place lived there in the winter. Paul had often hung about the hotel, watching the people go in and out, longing to enter and leave schoolmasters and dull care° behind him forever.

As last the singer came out, accompanied by the conductor, who helped her into her carriage and closed the door with a cordial *auf Wiedersehen*° — which set Paul to won-dering whether she were not an old sweetheart of his. Paul followed the carriage over to the hotel, walking so rapidly as not to be far from the entrance when the singer alighted and disappeared behind the swinging glass doors which were opened by a Negro in a tall hat and a long coat. In the moment that the door was ajar, it seemed to Paul that he, too, entered. He seemed to feel himself go after her up the steps, into the warm, lighted building, into an exotic, a tropical world of shiny, glistening surfaces and basking ease. He reflected upon the mysterious dishes that were brought into the dining-room, the green bottles in buckets of ice, as he had seen them in the supper party pictures of

---

Arab fisherman: reference to the tale of "The Fisherman and the Jinni" from *The Arabian Nights*.

dull care: phrase from the popular seventeenth-century song "Begone, Dull Care."

auf Wiedersehen: German for "goodbye" (literally "until the seeing again").

the Sunday supplement. A quick gust of wind brought the rain down with sudden vehemence, and Paul was startled to find that he was still outside in the slush of the gravel driveway; that his boots were letting in the water and his scanty overcoat was clinging wet about him; that the lights in front of the concert hall were out, and that the rain was driving in sheets between him and the orange glow of the windows above him. There it was, what he wanted—tangibly before him, like the fairy world of Christmas pantomime; as the rain beat in his face, Paul wondered whether he were destined always to shiver in the black night outside looking up at it.

He turned and walked reluctantly toward the car° tracks. The end had to come some time; his father in his night-clothes at the top of the stairs, explanations that did not explain, hastily improvised fictions that were forever tripping him up, his upstairs room and its horrible yellow wallpaper, the creaking bureau with the greasy plush collarbox, and over his painted wooden bed the pictures of George Washington and John Calvin,° and the framed motto, "Feed my Lambs,"° which had been worked in red worsted by his mother, whom Paul could not remember.

Half an hour later, Paul alighted from the Negley Avenue car and went slowly   20 down one of the side streets off the main thoroughfare. It was a highly respectable street, where all the houses were exactly alike, and where business men of moderate means begot and reared large families of children, all of whom went to Sabbath-school and learned the shorter catechism, and were interested in arithmetic; all of whom were as exactly alike as their homes, and of a piece with the monotony in which they lived. Paul never went up Cordelia Street without a shudder of loathing. His home was next to the house of the Cumberland° minister. He approached it tonight with the nerveless sense of defeat, the hopeless feeling of sinking back forever into ugliness and commonness that he had always had when he came home. The moment he turned into Cordelia Street he felt the waters close above his head. After each of these orgies of living, he experienced all the physical depression which follows a debauch; the loathing of respectable beds, of common food, of a house permeated by kitchen odors; a shuddering repulsion for the flavorless, colorless mass of everyday existence; a morbid desire for cool things and soft lights and fresh flowers.

The nearer he approached the house, the more absolutely unequal Paul felt to the sight of it all; his ugly sleeping chamber, the cold bathroom with the grimy zinc tub, the cracked mirror, the dripping spigots; his father, at the top of the stairs, his hairy legs sticking out from his nightshirt, his feet thrust into carpet slippers. He was so much later than usual that there would certainly be inquiries and reproaches. Paul stopped short before the door. He felt that he could not be accosted by his father tonight; that he could not toss again on that miserable bed. He would not go in. He would tell his father that he had no car fare, and it was raining so hard he had gone home with one of the boys and stayed all night.

Meanwhile, he was wet and cold. He went around to the back of the house and tried one of the basement windows, found it open, raised it cautiously, and scrambled down the cellar wall to the floor. There he stood, holding his breath, terrified by the noise he had made; but the floor above him was silent, and there was no creak on

---

car: streetcar.
John Calvin: John Calvin (1509–1564), a major theologian of the early Reformation in Switzerland.
"Feed my Lambs:" See John 21:15–17.
Cumberland: an independent, Evangelical branch of the Presbyterian Church, established in 1810.

the stairs. He found a soap-box and carried it over to the soft ring of light that streamed from the furnace door, and sat down. He was horribly afraid of rats, so he did not try to sleep, but sat looking distrustfully at the dark, still terrified lest he might have awakened his father. In such reactions, after one of the experiences which made days and nights out of the dreary blanks of the calendar, when his senses were deadened, Paul's head was always singularly clear. Suppose his father had heard him getting in at the window and had come down and shot him for a burglar? Then, again, suppose his father had come down, pistol in hand, and he had cried out in time to save himself, and his father had been horrified to think how nearly he had killed him? Then, again, suppose a day should come when his father would remember that night, and wish there had been no warning cry to stay his hand? With this last supposition Paul entertained himself until daybreak.

The following Sunday was fine; the sodden November chill was broken by the last flash of autumnal summer. In the morning Paul had to go to church and Sabbath-school, as always. On seasonable Sunday afternoons the burghers of Cordelia Street usually sat out on their front "stoops," and talked to their neighbors on the next stoop, or called to those across the street in neighborly fashion. The men sat placidly on gay cushions placed upon the steps that led down to the sidewalk, while the women, in their Sunday "waists,"° sat in rockers on the cramped porches, pretending to be greatly at their ease. The children played in the streets; there were so many of them that the place resembled the recreation grounds of a kindergarten. The men on the steps—all in their shirt sleeves, their vests unbuttoned—sat with their legs well apart, their stomachs comfortably protruding, and talked of the prices of things, or told anecdotes of the sagacity of their various chiefs and overlords. They occasionally looked over the multitude of squabbling children, listened affectionately to their high-pitched, nasal voices, smiling to see their own proclivities reproduced in their offspring, and interspersed their legends of the iron kings with remarks about their son's progress at school, their grades in arithmetic, and the amounts they had saved in their toy banks. On this last Sunday of November, Paul sat all the afternoon on the lowest step of his "stoop," staring into the street, while his sisters, in their rockers, were talking to the minister's daughters next door about how many shirtwaists they had made in the last week, and how many waffles someone had eaten at the last church supper. When the weather was warm, and his father was in a particularly jovial frame of mind, the girls made lemonade, which was always brought out in a red-glass pitcher, ornamented with forget-me-nots in blue enamel. This the girls thought very fine, and the neighbors joked about the suspicious color of the pitcher.

Today Paul's father, on the top step, was talking to a young man who shifted a restless baby from knee to knee. He happened to be the young man who was daily held up to Paul as a model, and after whom it was his father's dearest hope that he would pattern. This young man was of a ruddy complexion, with a compressed, red mouth, and faded, near-sighted eyes, over which he wore thick spectacles, with gold bows that curved about his ears. He was clerk to one of the magnates of a great steel corporation, and was looked upon in Cordelia Street as a young man with a future. There was a story that, come five years ago—he was now barely twenty-six—he had been a trifle 'dissipated,' but in order to curb his appetites and save the loss of time and strength that a sowing of wild oats might have entailed, he had taken his chief's advice, oft reiterated to his employees, and at twenty-one had married the first woman whom he could persuade to

---

waists: laced, close-fitting vests or jackets.

share his fortunes. She happened to be an angular school mistress, much older than he, who also wore thick glasses, and who had now borne him four children, all nearsighted, like herself.

The young man was relating how his chief, now cruising in the Mediterranean, 25 kept in touch with all the details of the business, arranging his office hours on his yacht just as though he were at home, and "knocking off work enough to keep two stenographers busy." His father told, in turn, the plan his corporation was considering, of putting in an electric railway plant at Cairo. Paul snapped his teeth; he had an awful apprehension that they might spoil it all before he got there. Yet he rather liked to hear these legends of the iron kings, that were told and retold on Sundays and holidays; these stories of palaces in Venice, yachts on the Mediterranean, and high play at Monte Carlo appealed to his fancy, and he was interested in the triumphs of cash boys° who had become famous, though he had no mind for the cash-boy stage.

After supper was over, and he had helped to dry the dishes, Paul nervously asked his father whether he could go to George's to get some help in his geometry, and still more nervously asked for car fare. This latter request he had to repeat, as his father, on principle, did not like to hear requests for money, whether much or little. He asked Paul whether he could not go to some boy who lived nearer, and told him that he ought not to leave his school work until Sunday; but he gave him the dime. He was not a poor man, but he had a worthy ambition to come up in the world. His only reason for allowing Paul to usher was that he thought a boy ought to be earning a little.

Paul bounded upstairs, scrubbed the greasy odor of the dishwater from his hands with the ill-smelling soap he hated, and then shook over his fingers a few drops of violet water from the bottle he kept hidden in his drawer. He left the house with his geometry conspicuously under his arm, and the moment he got out of Cordelia Street and boarded a downtown car, he shook off the lethargy of two deadening days, and began to live again.

The leading juvenile of the permanent stock company which played at one of the downtown theaters was an acquaintance of Paul's, and the boy had been invited to drop in at the Sunday night rehearsals whenever he could. For more than a year Paul had spent every available moment loitering about Charley Edwards's dressing-room. He had won a place among Edwards's following not only because the young actor, who could not afford to employ a dresser, often found him useful, but because he recognized in Paul something akin to what churchmen term "vocation."

It was at the theater and at Carnegie Hall that Paul really lived; the rest was but a sleep and a forgetting.° This was Paul's fairy tale, and it had for him all the allurement of a secret love. The moment he inhaled the gassy, painty, dusty odor behind the scenes, he breathed like a prisoner set free, and felt within him the possibility of doing or saying splendid, brilliant things. The moment the cracked orchestra beat out the overture for *Martha,*° or jerked at the serenade from *Rigoletto,*° all stupid and ugly things slid from him, and his senses were deliciously, yet delicately fired.

---

    cash boys: The Cash Boy, a novel by Horatio Alger (1832–1899), tells about the progress of a young boy from a $156 a year "cash boy" position to the inheritance of a million dollars.
    a sleep and a forgetting: from "Intimations of Immortality," an ode by William Wordsworth (1770–1850), published in 1807.
    Martha: opera by Friedrich von Flotow (1812–1883), first performed in 1847, the source of "The Last Rose of Summer."
    Rigoletto: one of the best-known operas of Giuseppe Verdi (1813–1901), first performed in 1851.

Perhaps it was because, in Paul's world, the natural nearly always wore the guise of
ugliness, that a certain element of artificiality seemed to him necessary in beauty.
Perhaps it was because his experience of life elsewhere was so full of Sabbath-school
picnics, petty economies, wholesome advice as to how to succeed in life, and the
unescapable odors of cooking, that he found this existence so alluring, these smartly-
clad men and women so attractive, that he was so moved by these starry apple orchards
that bloomed perennially under the limelight.

It would be difficult to put it strongly enough how convincingly the stage entrance
of that theater was for Paul the actual portal of Romance. Certainly none of the company ever suspected it, least of all Charley Edwards. It was very like the old stories that
used to float about London of fabulously rich Jews, who had subterranean halls, with
palms, and fountains, and soft lamps and richly apparelled women who never saw the
disenchanting light of London day. So, in the midst of that smoke-palled city, enamored
of figures and grimy toil, Paul had his secret temple, his wishing-carpet, his bit of blue-
and-white Mediterranean shore bathed in perpetual sunshine.

Several of Paul's teachers had a theory that his imagination had been perverted
by garish fiction; but the truth was, he scarcely ever read at all. The books at home were
not such as would either tempt or corrupt a youthful mind, and as for reading the
novels that some of his friends urged upon him—well, he got what he wanted much
more quickly from music; any sort of music, from an orchestra to a barrel organ. He
needed only the spark, the indescribable thrill that made his imagination master of his
senses, and he could make plots and pictures enough of his own. It was equally true
that he was not stage-struck—not at any rate, in the usual acceptation of that expression. He had no desire to become an actor, any more than he had to become a musician. He felt no necessity to do any of these things; what he wanted was to see, to be in
the atmosphere, float on the wave of it, to be carried out, blue league after blue league,
away from everything.

After a night behind the scenes, Paul found the school-room more than ever
repulsive; the bare floors and naked walls; the prosy men who never wore frock coats, or
violets in their buttonholes; the women with their dull gowns, shrill voices, and pitiful
seriousness about prepositions that govern the dative. He could not bear to have the
other pupils think, for a moment, that he took these people seriously; he must convey to
them that he considered it all trivial, and was there only by way of a joke, anyway. He
had autograph pictures of all the members of the stock company which he showed to
classmates, telling them the most incredible stories of his familiarity with these people, of
his acquaintance with the soloists who came to Carnegie Hall, his suppers with them
and the flowers he sent them. When these stories lost their effect, and his audience grew
listless, he would bid all the boys good-by, announcing that he was going to travel for a
while; going to Naples, to California, to Egypt. Then, next Monday, he would slip back,
conscious and nervously smiling; his sister was ill, and he would have to defer his voyage
until spring.

Matters went steadily worse with Paul at school. In the itch to let his instructors
know how heartily he despised them, and how thoroughly he was appreciated elsewhere,
he mentioned once or twice that he had no time to fool with theorems; adding—with
a twitch of the eyebrows and a touch of that nervous bravado which so perplexed
them—that he was helping the people down at the stock company; they were old friends
of his.

The upshot of the matter was, that the Principal went to Paul's father, and Paul
was taken out of school and put to work. The manager at Carnegie Hall was told to get

another usher in his stead; the door-keeper at the theater was warned not to admit him to the house; and Charley Edwards remorsefully promised the boy's father not to see him again.

The members of the stock company were vastly amused when some of Paul's stories reached them—especially the women. They were hard-working women, most of them supporting indolent husbands or brothers, and they laughed rather bitterly at having stirred the boy to such fervid and florid inventions. They agreed with the faculty and with his father, that Paul's was a bad case.

The east-bound train was plowing through a January snowstorm; the dull dawn was beginning to show gray when the engine whistled a mile out of Newark.° Paul started up from the seat where he had lain curled in uneasy slumber, rubbed the breath-misted window glass with his hand, and peered out. The snow was whirling in curling eddies above the white bottom lands, and the drifts lay already deep in the fields and along the fences, while here and there the long dead grass and dried weed stalks protruded black above it. Lights shone from the scattered houses, and a gang of laborers who stood beside the track waved their lanterns.

Paul had slept very little, and he felt grimy and uncomfortable. He had made the all-night journey in a day coach because he was afraid if he took a Pullman he might be seen by some Pittsburgh business man who had noticed him in Denny & Carson's office. When the whistle woke him, he clutched quickly at his breast pocket, glancing about him with an uncertain smile. But the little, clay-bespattered Italians were still sleeping, the slatternly women across the aisle were in open-mouthed oblivion, and even the crumby, crying babies were for the nonce stilled. Paul settled back to struggle with his impatience as best he could.

When he arrived at the Jersey City° station, he hurried through his breakfast, manifestly ill at ease and keeping a sharp eye about him. After he reached the Twenty-third Street station° he consulted a cabman, and had himself driven to a men's furnishing establishment which was just opening for the day. He spent upward of two hours there, buying with endless reconsidering and great care. His new street suit he put on in the fitting-room; the frock coat and dress clothes he had bundled into the cab with his new shirts. Then he drove to a hatter's and a shoe house. His next errand was at Tiffany's, where he selected silver-mounted brushes° and a scarf-pin. He would not wait to have his silver marked, he said. Lastly, he stopped at a trunk shop on Broadway, and had his purchases packed into various traveling bags.

It was a little after one o'clock when he drove up to the Waldorf, and, after settling with the cabman, went into the office. He registered from Washington; said his mother and father had been abroad, and that he had come down to await the arrival of their steamer. He told his story plausibly and had no trouble, since he offered to pay for them in advance, in engaging his rooms; a sleeping-room, sitting room and bath.

Not once, but a hundred times Paul had planned this entry into New York. He had gone over every detail of it with Charley Edwards, and in his scrap book at home there were pages of description about New York hotels, cut from the Sunday papers.

Newark: New Jersey city within twenty miles of New York.
Jersey City: New Jersey city on the Hudson River, directly across from the southern tip of Manhattan.
Twenty-third Street station: Paul's final destination in Manhattan.
brushes: hairbrushes.

When he was shown to his sitting room on the eighth floor, he saw at a glance that everything was as it should be; there was but one detail in his mental picture that the place did not realize, so he rang for the bell boy and sent him down for flowers. He moved about nervously until the boy returned, putting away his new linen and fingering it delightedly as he did so. When the flowers came, he put them hastily into water, and then tumbled into a hot bath. Presently he came out of his white bathroom, resplendent in his new silk underwear, and playing with the tassels of his red robe. The snow was whirling so fiercely outside his windows that he could scarcely see across the street; but within, the air was deliciously soft and fragrant. He put the violets and jonquils on the tabouret beside the couch, and threw himself down with a long sigh, covering himself with a Roman blanket. He was thoroughly tired; he had been in such haste, he had stood up to such a strain, covered so much ground in the last twenty-four hours, that he wanted to think how it had all come about. Lulled by the sound of the wind, the warm air, and the cool fragrance of the flowers, he sank into deep, drowsy retrospection.

It had been wonderfully simple; when they had shut him out of the theater and concert hall, when they had taken away his bone, the whole thing was virtually determined. The rest was a mere matter of opportunity. The only thing that at all surprised him was his own courage—for he realized well enough that he had always been tormented by fear, a sort of apprehensive dread that, of late years, as the meshes of the lies he had told closed about him, had been pulling the muscles of his body tighter and tighter. Until now, he could not remember a time when he had not been dreading something. Even when he was a little boy, it was always there—behind him or before, or on either side. There had always been the shadowed corner, the dark place into which he dared not look, but from which something seemed always to be watching him—and Paul had done things that were not pretty to watch, he knew.

But now he had a curious sense of relief, as though he had at least thrown down the gauntlet to the thing in the corner.

Yet it was but a day since he had been sulking in the traces; but yesterday afternoon that he had been sent to the bank with Denny & Carson's deposit, as usual—but this time he was instructed to leave the book to be balanced. There was above two thousand dollars in checks, and nearly a thousand in the bank notes which he had taken from the book and quietly transferred to his pocket. At the bank he had made out a new deposit slip. His nerves had been steady enough to permit of his returning to the office, where he had finished his work and asked for a full day's holiday tomorrow, Saturday, giving a perfectly reasonable pretext. The bank book, he knew, would not be returned before Monday or Tuesday, and his father would be out of town for the next week. From the time he slipped the bank notes into his pocket until he boarded the night train for New York, he had not known a moment's hesitation.

45

How astonishingly easy it had all been; here he was, the thing done; and this time there would be no awakening, no figure at the top of the stairs. He watched the snowflakes whirling by his window until he fell asleep.

When he awoke, it was four o'clock in the afternoon. He bounded up with a start; one of his precious days gone already! He spent nearly an hour in dressing, watching every stage of his toilet carefully in the mirror. Everything was quite perfect; he was exactly the kind of boy he had always wanted to be.

When he went downstairs, Paul took a carriage and drive up Fifth Avenue toward the Park.° The snow had somewhat abated; carriages and tradesmen's wagons were

the Park: Central Park.

hurrying soundlessly to and fro in the winter twilight; boys in woolen mufflers were shoveling off the doorsteps; the avenue stages° made fine spots of color against the white street. Here and there on the corners whole flower gardens blooming behind glass windows, against which the snow flakes stuck and melted; violets, roses, carnations, lilies of the valley—somehow vastly more lovely and alluring that they blossomed thus unnaturally in the snow. The Park itself was a wonderful stage winter-piece.

When he returned, the pause of the twilight had ceased, and the tune of the streets had changed. The snow was falling faster, lights streamed from the hotels that reared their many stories fearlessly up into the storm, defying the raging Atlantic winds. A long, black stream of carriages poured down the avenue, intersected here and there by other streams, tending horizontally. There were a score of cabs about the entrance of his hotel, and his driver had to wait. Boys in livery were running in and out of the awning stretched across the sidewalk, up and down the red velvet carpet laid from the door to the street. Above, about, within it all, was the rumble and roar, the hurry and toss of thousands of human beings as hot for pleasure as himself, and on every side of him towered the glaring affirmation of the omnipotence of wealth.

The boy set his teeth and drew his shoulders together in a spasm of realization;   5 the plot of all dramas, the text of all romances, the nerve-stuff of all sensations was whirling about him like the snowflakes. He burnt like a faggot in a tempest.

When Paul came down to dinner, the music of the orchestra floated up the elevator shaft to greet him. As he stepped into the thronged corridor, he sank back into one of the chairs against the wall to get his breath. The lights, the chatter, the perfumes, the bewildering medley of color—he had, for a moment, the feeling of not being able to stand it. But only for a moment; these were his own people, he told himself. He went slowly about the corridors, through the writing-rooms, smoking-rooms, reception-rooms, as though he were exploring the chambers of an enchanted palace, built and peopled for him alone.

When he reached the dining room he sat down at a table near a window. The flowers, the white linen, the many-colored wine glasses, the gay toilettes of the women, the low popping of corks, the undulating repetitions of the *Blue Danube*° from the orchestra, all flooded Paul's dream with bewildering radiance. When the roseate tinge of his champagne was added—that cold, precious, bubbling stuff that creamed and foamed in his glass—Paul wondered that there were honest men in the world at all. This was what all the world was fighting for, he reflected; this was what all the struggle was about. He doubted the reality of his past. Had he ever known a place called Cordelia Street, a place where fagged-looking business men boarded the early car? Mere rivets in a machine they seemed to Paul—sickening men, with combings of children's hair always hanging to their coats, and the smell of cooking in their clothes. Cordelia Street—Ah, that belonged to another time and country! Had he not always been thus, had he not sat here night after night, from as far back as he could remember, looking pensively over just such shimmering textures, and slowly twirling the stem of a glass like this one between his thumb and middle finger? He rather thought he had.

He was not in the least abashed or lonely. He had no special desire to meet or to know any of these people; all he demanded was the right to look on and conjecture, to

---

avenue stages: display windows.
Blue Danube: Composed in 1866, "The Blue Danube" is perhaps the best-known waltz of Johann Strauss (1825–1899).

watch the pageant. The mere stage properties were all he contended for. Nor was he lonely later in the evening, in his loge at the Opera. He was entirely rid of his nervous misgivings, of his forced aggressiveness, of the imperative desire to show himself different from his surroundings. He felt now that his surroundings explained him. Nobody questioned the purple;° he had only to wear it passively. He had only to glance down at his dress coat to reassure himself that here it would be impossible for anyone to humiliate him.

He found it hard to leave his beautiful sitting room to go to bed that night, and sat long watching the raging storm from his turret window. When he went to sleep, it was with the lights turned on in his bedroom; partly because of his old timidity, and partly so that, if he should wake in the night, there would be no wretched moment of doubt, no horrible suspicion of yellow wall-paper, or of Washington and Calvin above his bed.

On Sunday morning the city was practically snow-bound. Paul breakfasted late, and in the afternoon he fell in with a wild San Francisco boy, a freshman at Yale, who said he had run down for a "little flyer" over Sunday. The young man offered to show Paul the night side of the town, and the two boys went off together after dinner, not returning to the hotel until seven o'clock the next morning. They had started out in the confiding warmth of a champagne friendship, but their parting in the elevator was singularly cool. The freshman pulled himself together to make his train, and Paul went to bed. He woke at two o'clock in the afternoon, very thirsty and dizzy, and rang for ice water, coffee, and the Pittsburgh papers. 55

On the part of the hotel management, Paul excited no suspicion. There was this to be said for him, that he wore his spoils with dignity and in no way made himself conspicuous. His chief greediness lay in his ears and eyes, and his excesses were not offensive ones. His dearest pleasures were the gray winter twilights in his sitting room; his quiet enjoyment of his flowers, his clothes, his wide divan, his cigarette and his sense of power. He could not remember a time when he had felt so at peace with himself. The mere release from the necessity of petty lying, lying every day and every day, restored his self-respect. He had never lied for pleasure, even at school; but to make himself noticed and admired, to assert his difference from other Cordelia Street boys; and he felt a good deal more manly, more honest, even, now that he had no need for boastful pretensions, now that he could, as his actor friends used to say, "dress the part." It was characteristic that remorse did not occur to him. His golden days went by without a shadow, and he made each as perfect as he could.

On the eighth day after his arrival in New York, he found the whole affair exploited in the Pittsburgh papers, exploited with a wealth of detail which indicated that local news of a sensational nature was at a low ebb. The firm of Denny & Carson announced that the boy's father had refunded the full amount of his theft, and that they had no intention of prosecuting. The Cumberland minister had been interviewed, and expressed his hope of yet reclaiming the motherless lad, and Paul's Sabbath-school teacher declared that she would spare no effort to that end. The rumor had reached Pittsburgh that the boy had been seen in a New York hotel, and his father had gone East to find him and bring him home.

Paul had just come in to dress for dinner; he sank into a chair, weak in the knees, and clasped his head in his hands. It was to be worse than jail, even; the tepid waters of

purple: that is, clothing fit for royalty.

Cordelia Street were to close over him finally and forever. The gray monotony stretched before him in hopeless, unrelieved years; Sabbath-school, Young People's Meeting, the yellow-papered room, the damp dish-towels; it all rushed back upon him with sickening vividness. He had the old feeling that the orchestra had suddenly stopped, the sinking sensation that the play was over. The sweat broke out on his face, and he sprang to his feet, looked about him with his white, conscious smile, and winked at himself in the mirror. With something of the childish belief in miracles with which he had so often gone to class, all his lessons unlearned, Paul dressed and dashed whistling down the corridor to the elevator.

He had no sooner entered the dining room and caught the measure of the music, than his remembrance was lightened by his old elastic power of claiming the moment, mounting with it, and finding it all sufficient. The glare and glitter about him, the mere scenic accessories had again, and for the last time, their old potency. He would show himself that he was game, he would finish the thing splendidly. He doubted, more than ever, the existence of Cordelia Street, and for the first time he drank his wine recklessly. Was he not, after all, one of these fortunate beings? Was he not still himself, and in his own place? He drummed a nervous accompaniment to the music and looked about him, telling himself over and over that it had paid.

He reflected drowsily, to the swell of the violin and the chill sweetness of his wine,   60
that he might have done it more wisely. He might have caught an outbound steamer and been well out of their clutches before now. But the other side of the world had seemed too far away and too uncertain then; he could not have waited for it; his need had been too sharp. If he had to choose over again, he would do the same thing tomorrow. He looked affectionately about the dining room, now gilded with a soft mist. Ah, it has paid indeed!

Paul was awakened the next morning by a painful throbbing in his head and feet. He had thrown himself across the bed without undressing, and had slept with his shoes on. His limbs and hands were lead heavy, and his tongue and throat were parched. There came upon him one of those fateful attacks of clear-headedness that never occurred except when he was physically exhausted and his nerves hung loose. He lay still and closed his eyes and let the tide of realities wash over him.

His father was in New York: "stopping at some joint or other," he told himself. The memory of successive summers on the front stoop fell upon him like a weight of black water. He had not a hundred dollars left, and he knew now, more than ever, that money was everything, the wall that stood between all he loathed and all he wanted. The thing was winding itself up; he had thought of that on his first glorious day in New York, and had even provided a way to snap the threat. It lay on his dressing-table now; he had got it out last night when he came blindly up from dinner—but the shiny metal hurt his eyes, and he disliked the look of it, anyway.

He rose and moved about with a painful effort, succumbing now and again to attacks of nausea. It was the old depression exaggerated; all the world had become Cordelia Street. Yet somehow he was not afraid of anything, was absolutely calm; perhaps because he had looked into the dark corner at last, and knew. It was bad enough, what he saw there, but somehow not so bad as his long fear of it had been. He saw everything clearly now. He had a feeling that he had made the best of it, that he had lived the sort of life he was meant to live, and for half an hour he sat staring at the revolver. But he told himself that was not the way, so he went downstairs and took a cab to the ferry.

When Paul arrived at Newark, he got off the train and took another cab, directing the driver to follow the Pennsylvania tracks out of town. The snow lay heavy on the road-ways and had drifted deep in the open fields. Only here and there the dead grass or dried weed stalks projected, singularly black, above it. Once well into the country, Paul dismissed the carriage and walked, floundering along the tracks, his mind a medley of irrelevant things. He seemed to hold in his brain an actual picture of everything he had seen that morning. He remembered every feature of both his drivers, the toothless old woman from whom he had bought the red flowers in his coat, the agent from whom he had got his ticket, and all of his fellow-passengers on the ferry. His mind, unable to cope with vital matters near at hand, worked feverishly and deftly at sorting and grouping these images. They made for him a part of the ugliness of the world, of the ache in his head, and the bitter burning on his tongue. He stopped and put a handful of snow into his mouth as he walked, but that, too, seemed hot. When he reached a little hillside, where the tracks ran through a cut some twenty feet below him, he stopped and sat down.

The carnations in his coat were drooping with the cold, he noticed; all their red   65
glory over. It occurred to him that all the flowers he had seen in the show windows that first night must have gone the same way, long before this. It was only one splendid breath they had, in spite of their brave mockery at the winter outside the glass. It was a losing game in the end, it seemed, this revolt against the homilies by which the world is run. Paul took one of the blossoms carefully from his coat and scooped a little hole in the snow, where he covered it up. Then he dozed a while, from his weak condition, seeming insensible to the cold.

The sound of an approaching train woke him, and he started to his feet, remem-bering only his resolution, and afraid lest he should be too late. He stood watching the approaching locomotive, his teeth chattering, his lips drawn away from them in a fright-ened smile; once or twice he glanced nervously sidewise, as though he were being watched. When the right moment came, he jumped. As he fell, the folly of his haste occurred to him with merciless clearness, the vastness of what he had left undone. There flashed through his brain, clearer than ever before, the blue of Adriatic water, the yellow of Algerian sands.

He felt something strike his chest—his body was being thrown swiftly through the air, on and on, immeasurably far and fast, while his limbs gently relaxed. Then, because the picture-making mechanism was crushed, the disturbing visions flashed into black, and Paul dropped back into the immense design of things.

QUESTIONS

1. Describe Paul as a character. How does he grow, or change? What are his strengths? Weaknesses? What do his preferences and annoyances show about him? What is shown by his meeting with the college boy in New York? Why is the story called "Paul's Case"?

2. Describe the speaker. How does the speaker describe Paul? The other charac-ters? When does the speaker shift attention exclusively to Paul? Why?

3. What future does Paul see for himself? To what degree is his dislike of the life on Cordelia Street justified? Why does he think that forgiveness and correction would be worse for him than imprisonment? How can the story be seen as a criticism not of Paul but of early twentieth-century society?

WILLIAM FAULKNER   (1897–1962)

Faulkner spent his childhood in Mississippi and became one of the foremost American novelists of the twentieth century. He twice received the Pulitzer Prize (in 1955 and 1963), and he also received the Nobel Prize in literature in 1949. Throughout his extensive fiction about the special world he called "Yoknapatawpha County," he treats life in the southern United States as a symbol of humankind generally, emphasizing the decline of civilization and culture in the wake of the Civil War. Often he deals with degraded, sullen, and degenerate characters, and in this respect Abner Snopes of "Barn Burning" is typical. The loyalty he tries to exact from his son Sarty is one that excludes any allegiance to morality. Faulkner also uses the Snopes family as subjects in The Hamlet *(1940),* The Town *(1957), and* The Mansion *(1960).*

Barn Burning _____ 1939

The store in which the Justice of the Peace's court was sitting smelled of cheese. The boy, crouched on his nail keg at the back of the crowded room, knew he smelled cheese, and more; from where he sat he could see the ranked shelves close-packed with the solid, squat, dynamic shapes of tin cans whose labels his stomach read, not from the lettering which meant nothing to his mind but from the scarlet devils and the silver curve of fish—this, the cheese which he knew he smelled and the hermetic meat° which his intestines believed he smelled coming in intermittent gusts momentary and brief between the other constant one, the smell and sense just a little of fear because mostly of despair and grief, the old fierce pull of blood. He could not see the table where the Justice sat and before which his father and his father's enemy (*our enemy* he thought in that despair; *ourn! mine and his both! He's my father!*) stood, but he could hear them, the two of them that is, because his father had said no word yet:

"But what proof have you, Mr. Harris?"

"I told you. The hog got into my corn. I caught it up and sent it back to him. He had no fence that would hold it. I told him so, warned him. The next time I put the hog in my pen. When he came to get it I gave him enough wire to patch up his pen. The next time I put the hog up and kept it. I rode down to his house and saw the wire I gave him still rolled on to the spool in his yard. I told him he could have the hog when he paid me a dollar pound fee. That evening a nigger came with the dollar and got the hog. He was a strange nigger. He said, 'He say to tell you wood and hay kin burn.' I said, 'What?' 'That what he say to tell you,' the nigger said. 'Wood and hay kin burn.' That night my barn burned. I got the stock out but I lost the barn."

"Where is the nigger? Have you got him?"

"He was a strange nigger, I tell you. I don't know what became of him."

"But that's not proof. Don't you see that's not proof?"

"Get that boy up here. He knows." For a moment the boy thought too that the man meant his older brother until Harris said. "Not him. The little one. The boy," and, crouching, small for his age, small and wiry like his father, in patched and faded jeans

5

---

hermetic meat: canned meat.

even too small for him, with straight, uncombed, brown hair and eyes gray and wild as storm scud, he saw the men between himself and the table part and become a lane of grim faces, at the end of which he saw the Justice, a shabby, collarless, graying man in spectacles, beckoning him. He felt no floor under his bare feet; he seemed to walk beneath the palpable weight of the grim turning faces. His father, stiff in his black Sunday coat donned not for the trial but for the moving, did not even look at him. *He aims for me to lie,* he thought, again with that frantic grief and despair. *And I will have to do hit.*

"What's your name, boy?" the Justice said.

"Colonel Sartoris Snopes," the boy whispered.

"Hey?" the Justice said. "Talk louder. Colonel Sartoris? I reckon anybody named   10
for Colonel Sartoris in this country can't help but tell the truth, can they?" The boy said nothing. *Enemy! Enemy!* he thought; for a moment he could not even see, could not see that the Justice's face was kindly nor discern that his voice was troubled when he spoke to the man named Harris: "Do you want me to question this boy?" But he could hear, and during those subsequent long seconds there was absolutely no sound in the crowded little room save that of quiet and intent breathing it was as if he had swung outward at the end of a grape vine, over a ravine, and at the top of the swing had been caught in a prolonged instant of mesmerized gravity, weightless in time.

"No!" Harris said violently, explosively. "Damnation! Send him out of here!" Now time, the fluid world, rushed beneath him again, the voices coming to him again through the smell of cheese and sealed meat, the fear and despair and the old grief of blood:

"This case is closed. I can't find against you, Snopes, but I can give you advice. Leave this country and don't come back to it."

His father spoke for the first time, his voice cold and harsh, level, without emphasis: "I aim to. I don't figure to stay in a country among people who . . ." he said something unprintable and vile, addressed to no one.

"That'll do," the Justice said, "Take your wagon and get out of this country before dark. Case dismissed."

His father turned, and he followed the stiff black coat, the wiry figure walking a   15
little stiffly, from where a Confederate provost's man's musket ball had taken him in the heel on a stolen horse thirty years ago, followed the two backs now, since his older brother had appeared from somewhere in the crowd, no taller than the father but thicker, chewing tobacco steadily, between the two lines of grim-faced men and out of the store and across the worn gallery and down the sagging steps and among the dogs and half-grown boys in the mild May dust, where as he passed a voice hissed:

"Barn burner!"

Again he could not see, whirling; there was a face in a red haze, moonlike, bigger than the full moon, the owner of it half again his size, he leaping in the red haze toward the face, feeling no blow, feeling no shock when his head struck the earth, scrabbling up and leaping again, feeling no blow this time either and tasting no blood, scrabbling up to see the other boy in full flight and himself already leaping into pursuit as his father's hand jerked him back, the harsh, cold voice speaking above him: "Go get in the wagon."

It stood in a grove of locusts and mulberries across the road. His two hulking sisters in their Sunday dresses and his mother and her sister in calico and sunbonnets were already in it, sitting on and among the sorry residue of the dozen and more movings which even the boy could remember—the battered stove, the broken beds and chairs, the clock inlaid with mother-of-pearl, which would not run, stopped at some fourteen minutes past two o'clock of a dead and forgotten day and time, which had been his mother's dowry. She was crying, though when she saw him she drew her sleeve across her face and began to descend from the wagon. "Get back," the father said.

"He's hurt, I got to get some water and wash his . . ."

"Get back in the wagon." his father said. He got in too, over the tail-gate. His   20
father mounted to the seat where the older brother already sat and struck the gaunt mules two savage blows with the peeled willow, but without heat. It was not even sadistic; it was exactly that same quality which in later years would cause his descendants to over-run the engine before putting a motor car into motion, striking and reining back in the same movement. The wagon went on, the store with its quiet crowd of grimly watching men dropped behind; a curve in the road hid it. *Forever* he thought. *Maybe he's done satisfied now, now that he has* . . . stopping himself, not to say it aloud even to himself. His mother's hand touched his shoulder.

"Does hit hurt?" she said.

"Naw," he said. "Hit don't hurt. Lemme be."

"Can't you wipe some of the blood off before hit dries?"

"I'll wash tonight," he said. "Lemme be, I tell you."

The wagon went on. He did not know where they were going. None of them ever   25
did or ever asked, because it was always somewhere, always a house of sorts waiting for them a day or two days or even three days away. Likely his father had already arranged to make a crop on another farm before he. . . . Again he had to stop himself. He (the father) always did. There was something about his wolflike independence and even courage when the advantage was at least neutral which impressed strangers, as if they got from his latent ravening ferocity not so much a sense of dependability as a feeling that his ferocious conviction in the rightness of his own actions would be of advantage to all whose interest lay with his.

That night they camped, in a grove of oaks and beeches where a spring ran. The nights were still cool and they had a fire against it, of a rail lifted from a nearby fence and cut into lengths—a small fire, neat, niggard almost, a shrewd fire; such fires were his father's habit and custom always, even in freezing weather. Older, the boy might have remarked this and wondered why not a big one; why should not a man who had not only seen the waste and extravagance of war, but who had in his blood an inherent prodigality with material not his own, have burned everything in sight? Then he might have gone a step farther and thought that that was the reason; that niggard blaze was the living fruits of nights passed during those four years in the woods hiding from all men, blue or grey, with his strings of horses (captured horses, he called them). And older still, he might have divined the true reason: that the element of fire spoke to some deep mainspring of his father's being, as the element of steel or of powder spoke to other men, as the one weapon for the preservation of integrity, else breath were not worth the breathing, and hence to be regarded with respect and used with discretion.

But he did not think this now and he had seen those same niggard blazes all his life. He merely ate his supper beside it and was already half asleep over his iron plate when his father called him, and once more he followed the stiff back, the stiff and ruthless limp, up the slope and on to the starlit road where, turning, he could see his father against the stars but without face or depth—a shape black, flat, and bloodless as though cut from tin in the iron folds of the frockcoat which had not been made for him, the voice harsh like tin and without heat like tin:

"You were fixing to tell them. You would have told him." He didn't answer. His father struck him with the flat of his hand on the side of the head, hard but without heat, exactly as he had struck the two mules at the store, exactly as he would strike either of them with any stick in order to kill a horse fly, his voice still without heat or anger: "You're getting to be a man. You got to learn. You got to learn to stick to your own blood or you ain't going to have any blood to stick to you. Do you think either of them, any man there this morning, would? Don't you know all they wanted was a chance to get at me because they knew I had them beat? Eh?" Later, twenty years later, he was to tell himself, "If I had said they wanted only truth, justice, he would have hit me again." But now he said nothing. He was not crying. He just stood there. "Answer me," his father said.

"Yes," he whispered. His father turned.

"Get on to bed. We'll be there tomorrow." 30

Tomorrow they were there. In the early afternoon the wagon stopped before a paintless two-room house identical almost with the dozen others it had stopped before even in the boy's ten years, and again, as on the other dozen occasions, his mother and aunt got down and began to unload the wagon, although his two sisters and his father and brother had not moved.

"Likely hit ain't fitten for hawgs," one of the sisters said.

"Nevertheless, fit it will and you'll hog it and like it," his father said. "Get out of them chairs and help your Ma unload."

The two sisters got down, big, bovine, in a flutter of cheap ribbons; one of them drew from the jumbled wagon bed a battered lantern, the other a worn broom. His father handed the reins to the older son and began to climb stiffly over the wheel. "When they get unloaded, take the team to the barn and feed them." Then he said, and at first the boy thought he was still speaking to his brother: "Come with me."

"Me?" he said. 35

"Yes," his father said. "You."

"Abner," his mother said. His father paused and looked back—the harsh level stare beneath the shaggy, graying, irascible brows.

"I reckon I'll have a word with the man that aims to begin tomorrow owning me body and soul for the next eight months."

They went back up the road. A week ago—or before last night, that is—he would have asked where they were going, but not now. His father had struck him before last night but never before had he paused afterward to explain why; it was as if the blow and the following calm, outrageous voice still rang, repercussed, divulging nothing to him save the terrible handicap of being young, the light weight of his few years, just heavy enough to prevent his soaring free of the world as it seemed to be ordered but not heavy enough to keep footed solid in it, to resist it and try to chance the course of its events.

Presently he could see the grove of oaks and cedars and the other flowering trees 40 and shrubs where the house would be, though not the house yet. They walked beside a fence massed with honeysuckle and Cherokee roses and came to a gate swinging open between two brick pillars, and now, beyond a sweep of drive, he saw the house for the first time and at that instant he forgot his father and the terror and despair both, and even when he remembered his father again (who had stopped) the terror and despair did not return. Because, for all the twelve movings, they had sojourned until now in a poor country, a land of small farms and fields and houses, and he had never seen a house like this before. *Hit's big as a courthouse* he thought quietly, with a surge of peace and joy whose reason he could not have thought into words, being too young for that: *They are safe from him. People whose lives are a part of this peace and dignity are beyond his touch, he no more to them than a buzzing wasp: capable of stinging for a little moment but that's all; the spell of this peace and dignity rendering even the barns and stable and cribs which belong to it* *impervious to the puny flames he might contrive* . . . this, the peace and joy, ebbing for an instant as he looked again at the stiff black back, the stiff and implacable limp of the figure which was not dwarfed by the house, for the reason that it had never looked big anywhere and which now, against the serene columned backdrop, had more than ever that impervious quality of something cut ruthlessly from tin, depthless, as though, side-wise to the sun, it would cast no shadow. Watching him, the boy remarked the absolutely undeviating course which his father held and saw the stiff foot come squarely down in a pile of fresh droppings where a horse had stood in the drive and which his father could have avoided by a simple change of stride. But it ebbed only for a moment, though he could not have thought this into words either, walking on in the spell of the house, which he could even want but without envy, without sorrow, certainly never with that ravening and jealous rage which unknown to him walked in the ironlike black coat before him: *Maybe he will feel it too. Maybe it will even change him now from what maybe he* *couldn't help but be.*

They crossed the portico. Now he could hear his father's stiff foot as it came down on the boards with clocklike finality, a sound out of all proportion to the dis-placement of the body it bore and which was not dwarfed either by the white door before it, as though it had attained to a sort of vicious and ravening minimum not to be dwarfed by anything—the flat, wide, black hat, the formal coat of broadcloth which had once been black but which had now that friction-glazed greenish cast of the bodies of old house flies, the lifted sleeve which was too large, the lifted hand like a curled claw. The door opened so promptly that the boy knew the Negro must have been watching them all the time, an old man with neat grizzled hair, in a linen jacket, who stood barring the door with his body, saying "Wipe yo foots, white man, fo you come in here. Major ain't home nohow."

"Get out of my way, nigger," his father said, without heat too, flinging the door back and the Negro also and entering, his hat still on his head. And now the boy saw the prints of the stiff foot on the doorsill and saw them appear on the pale rug behind the machinelike deliberation of the foot which seemed to bear (or transmit) twice the weight which the body compassed. The Negro was shouting "Miss Lula! Miss Lula!" somewhere behind them, then the boy, deluged as though by a warm wave by a suave turn of carpeted stair and a pendant glitter of chandeliers and a mute gleam of gold frames, heard the swift feet and saw her too, a lady—perhaps he had never seen her like before either—in a gray, smooth gown with lace at the throat and an apron tied at the waist and the sleeves turned back, wiping cake or biscuit dough from her hands with a towel as she came up the hall, looking not at his father at all but at the tracks on the blond rug with an expression of incredulous amazement.

"I tried," the Negro cried. "I tole him to . . ."

"Will you please go away?" she said in a shaking voice. "Major de Spain is not at home. Will you please go away?"

His father had not spoken again. He did not speak again. He did not even look at   45 her. He just stood stiff in the center of the rug, in his hat, the shaggy iron-gray brows twitching slightly above the pebble-colored eyes as he appeared to examine the house with brief deliberation. Then with the same deliberation he turned; the boy watched him pivot on the good leg and saw the stiff foot drag round the arc of the turning, leav-ing a final long and fading smear. His father never looked at it, he never once looked down at the rug. The Negro held the door. It closed behind them, upon the hysteric and indistinguishable woman-wail. His father stopped at the top of the steps and scraped his boot clean on the edge of it. At the gate he stopped again. He stood for a moment, planted stiffly on the stiff foot, looking back at the house. "Pretty and white, ain't it?" he said. "That's sweat. Nigger sweat. Maybe it ain't white enough yet to suit him. Maybe he wants to mix some white sweat with it."

Two hours later the boy was chopping wood behind the house within which his mother and aunt and the two sisters (the mother and aunt, not the two girls, he knew that; even at this distance and muffled by walls the flat loud voices of the two girls emanated an incorrigible idle inertia) were setting up the stove to prepare a meal, when he heard the hooves and saw the linen-clad man on a fine sorrel mare, whom he recognized even before he saw the rolled rug in front of the Negro youth following on a fat bay carriage horse—a suffused, angry face vanishing, still at full gallop, beyond the corner of the house where his father and brother were sitting in the two tilted chairs; and a moment later, almost before he could have put the axe down, he heard the hooves again and watched the sorrel mare go back out of the yard, already galloping again. Then his father began to shout one of the sisters' names, who presently emerged backward from the kitchen door dragging the rolled rug along the ground by one end while the other sister walked behind it.

"If you ain't going to tote, go on and set up the wash pot," the first said.

"You, Sarty!" the second shouted. "Set up the wash pot!" His father appeared at the door, framed against that shabbiness, as he had been against that other bland perfection, impervious to either, the mother's anxious face at his shoulder.

"Go on," the father said. "Pick it up." The two sisters stooped, broad, lethargic; stooping, they presented an incredible expanse of pale cloth and a flutter of tawdry ribbons.

"If I thought enough of a rug to have to git hit all the way from France I wouldn't keep hit where folks coming in would have to tromp on hit," the first said. They raised the rug.   50

"Abner," the mother said. "Let me do it."

"You go back and git dinner," his father said. "I'll tend to this."

From the woodpile through the rest of the afternoon the boy watched them, the rug spread flat in the dust beside the bubbling wash pot, the two sisters stooping over it with that profound and lethargic reluctance, while the father stood over them in turn, implacable and grim, driving them though never raising his voice again. He could smell the harsh homemade lye they were using; he saw his mother come to the door once and look toward them with an expression not anxious now but very like despair; he saw his father turn, and he fell to with the axe and saw from the corner of his eye his father raise from the ground a flattish fragment of field stone and examine it and return to the pot, and this time his mother actually spoke: "Abner. Abner. Please don't. Please, Abner."

Then he was done too. It was dusk; the whippoorwills had already begun. He could smell coffee from the room where they would presently eat the cold food remaining from the mid-afternoon meal, though when he entered the house he realized they were having coffee again because there was a fire on the hearth, before which the rug now lay spread over the backs of the two chairs. The tracks of his father's foot were gone. Where they had been were now long, water-cloudy scoriations resembling the sporadic course of a Lilliputian mowing machine.

It still hung there while they ate the cold food and then went to bed, scattered   55
without order or claim up and down the two rooms, his mother in one bed, where his

father would later lie, the older brother in the other, himself, the aunt, and the two sisters on pallets on the floor. But his father was not in bed yet. The last thing the boy remembered was the depthless, harsh silhouette of the hat and coat bending over the rug and it seemed to him that he had not even closed his eyes when the silhouette was standing over him, the fire almost dead behind it, the stiff foot prodding him awake. "Catch up the mule," his father said.

When he returned with the mule his father was standing in the black door, the rolled rug over his shoulder. "Ain't you going to ride?" he said.

"No. Give me your foot."

He bent his knee into his father's hand, the wiry, surprising power flowed smoothly, rising, he rising with it, on to the mule's bare back (they had owned a saddle once; the boy could remember it though not when or where) and with the same effortlessness his father swung the rug up in front of him. Now in the starlight they retraced the afternoon's path, up the dusty road rife with honeysuckle, through the gate and up the black tunnel of the drive to the lightless house, where he sat on the mule and felt the rough warp of the rug drag across his thighs and vanish.

"Don't you want me to help?" he whispered. His father did not answer and now he heard again that stiff foot striking the hollow portico with that wooden and clocklike deliberation, that outrageous overstatement of the weight it carried. The rug, hunched, not flung (the boy could tell that even in the darkness) from his father's shoulder, struck the angle of wall and floor with a sound unbelievably loud, thunderous, then the foot again, unhurried and enormous; a light came on in the house and the boy sat, tense, breathing steadily and quietly and just a little fast, though the foot itself did not increase its beat at all, descending the steps now; now the boy could see him.

"Don't you want to ride now?" he whispered. "We kin both ride now," the light within the house altering now, flaring up and sinking. *He's coming down the stairs now,* he thought. He had already ridden the mule up beside the horse block; presently his father was up behind him and he doubled the reins over and slashed the mule across the neck, but before the animal could begin to trot the hard, thin arm came round him, the hard, knotted hand jerking the mule back to a walk.

In the first red rays of the sun they were in the lot, putting plow gear on the mules. This time the sorrel mare was in the lot before he heard it at all, the rider collarless and even bareheaded, trembling, speaking in a shaking voice as the woman in the house had done, his father merely looking up once before stooping again to the hame he was buckling, so that the man on the mare spoke to his stooping back:

"You must realize you have ruined that rug. Wasn't there anybody here, any of your women . . ." He ceased, shaking, the boy watching him, the older brother leaning now in the stable door, chewing, blinking slowly and steadily at nothing apparently. "It cost a hundred dollars. But you never had a hundred dollars. You never will. So I'm going to charge you twenty bushels of corn against your crop. I'll add it in your contract and when you come to the commissary you can sign it. That won't keep Mrs. de Spain quiet but maybe it will teach you to wipe your feet off before you enter her house again."

Then he was gone. The boy looked at his father, who still had not spoken or even looked up again, who was now adjusting the logger-head in the hame.

"Pap," he said. His father looked at him—the inscrutable face, the shaggy brows beneath which the gray eyes glinted coldly. Suddenly the boy went toward him, fast, stopping as suddenly. "You done the best you could!" he cried. "If he wanted hit done different why didn't he wait and tell you how? He won't git no twenty bushels! He won't git none! We'll get hit and hide hit! I kin watch . . ."

"Did you put the cutter back in that straight stock like I told you?" 65
"No, sir," he said.
"Then go do it."

That was Wednesday. During the rest of that week he worked steadily, at what was within his scope and some which was beyond it, with an industry that did not need to be driven nor even commanded twice; he had this from his mother, with the difference that some at least of what he did he liked to do, such as splitting wood with the half-size axe which his mother and aunt had earned, or saved money somehow, to present him with at Christmas. In company with the two older women (and on one afternoon even one of the sisters), he built pens for the shoat and the cow which were a part of his father's contract with the landlord, and one afternoon, his father being absent, gone somewhere on one of the mules, he went to the field.

They were running a middle buster now, his brother holding the plow straight while he handled the reins, and walking beside the straining mule, the rich black soil shearing cool and damp against his bare ankles, he thought *Maybe this is the end of it. Maybe even that twenty bushels that seems hard to have to pay for just a rug will be a cheap price for him to stop forever and always from being what he used to be;* thinking, dreaming now, so that his brother had to speak sharply to him to mind the mule: *Maybe he even won't collect the twenty bushels. Maybe it will all add up and balance and vanish—corn, rug, fire; the terror and grief, the being pulled two ways like between two teams of horses—gone, done with forever and ever.*

Then it was Saturday; he looked up from beneath the mule he was harnessing 70
and saw his father in the black coat and hat. "Not that," his father said. "The wagon gear." And then, two hours later, sitting in the wagon bed behind his father and brother on the seat, the wagon accomplished a final curve, and he saw the weathered paintless store with its tattered tobacco- and patent-medicine posters and the tethered wagons and saddle animals below the gallery. He mounted the gnawed steps behind his father and brother, and there again was the lane of quiet, watching faces for the three of them to walk through. He saw the man in spectacles sitting at the plank table and he did not need to be told this was a Justice of the Peace; he sent one glare of fierce, exultant, partisan defiance at the man in collar and cravat now, whom he had seen but twice in his life, and that on a galloping horse, who now wore on his face an expression not of rage but of amazed unbelief which the boy could not have known was at the incredible circumstance of being sued by one of his own tenants, and came and stood against his father and cried at the Justice: "He ain't done it! He ain't burnt . . ."

"Go back to the wagon," his father said.

"Burnt?" the Justice said. "Do I understand this rug was burned too?"

"Does anybody here claim it was?" his father said. "Go back to the wagon." But he did not, he merely retreated to the rear of the room, crowded as that other had been, but not to sit down this time, instead, to stand pressing among the motionless bodies, listening to the voices:

"And you claim twenty bushels of corn is too high for the damage you did to the rug?"

"He brought the rug to me and said he wanted the tracks washed out of it. I 75
washed the tracks out and took the rug back to him."

"But you didn't carry the rug back to him in the same condition it was in before you made the tracks on it."

His father did not answer, and now for perhaps half a minute there was no sound at all save that of breathing, the faint, steady suspiration of complete and intent listening.

"You decline to answer that, Mr. Snopes?" Again his father did not answer. "I'm going to find against you, Mr. Snopes. I'm going to find that you were responsible for the injury to Major de Spain's rug and hold you liable for it. But twenty bushels of corn seems a little high for a man in your circumstances to have to pay. Major de Spain claims it cost a hundred dollars. October corn will be worth about fifty cents. I figure that if Major de Spain can stand a ninety-five-dollar loss on something he paid cash for, you can stand a five-dollar loss you haven't earned yet. I hold you in damages to Major de Spain to the amount of ten bushels of corn over and above your contract with him, to be paid to him out of your crop at gathering time. Court adjourned."

It had taken no time hardly, the morning was but half begun. He thought they would return home and perhaps back to the field, since they were late, far behind all other farmers. But instead his father passed on behind the wagon, merely indicating with his hand for the older brother to follow with it, and crossed the road toward the blacksmith shop opposite, pressing on after his father, overtaking him, speaking, whispering up at the harsh, calm face beneath the weathered hat: "He won't git no ten bushels neither. He won't git one. We'll . . ." until his father glanced for an instant down on him, the face absolutely calm, the grizzled eyebrows tangled above the cold eyes, the voice almost pleasant, almost gentle:

"You think so? Well, we'll wait till October anyway."

The matter of the wagon—the setting of a spoke or two and the tightening of the tires—did not take long either, the business of the tires accomplished by driving the wagon into the spring branch behind the shop and letting it stand there, the mules nuzzling into the water from time to time, and the boy on the seat with the idle reins, looking up the slope and through the sooty tunnel of the shed where the slow hammer rang and where his father sat on an upended cypress bolt, easily, either talking or listening, still sitting there when the boy brought the dripping wagon up out of the branch and halted it before the door.

"Take them on to the shade and hitch," his father said. He did so and returned. His father and the smith and a third man squatting on his heels inside the door were talking, about crops and animals; the boy, squatting too in the ammoniac dust and hoofparings and scales of rust, heard his father tell a long and unhurried story out of the time before the birth of the older brother even when he had been a professional horsetrader. And then his father came up beside him where he stood before a tattered last year's circus poster on the other side of the store, gazing rapt and quiet at the scarlet horses, the incredible poisings and convolutions of tulle and tights and the painted leers of comedians, and said, "It's time to eat."

But not at home. Squatting beside his brother against the front wall, he watched his father emerge from the store and produce from a paper sack a segment of cheese and divided it carefully and deliberately into three with his pocket knife and produce crackers from the same sack. They all three squatted on the gallery and ate slowly, without talking; then in the store again, they drank from a tin dipper tepid water smelling of the cedar bucket and of living beech trees. And still they did not go home. It was a horse lot this time, a tall rail fence upon and along which men stood and sat and out of which one by one horses were led, to be walked and trotted and then cantered back and forth along the road while the slow swapping and buying went on and the sun began to slant westward, they—the three of them—watching and listening, the older brother with his muddy eyes and his steady inevitable tobacco, the father commenting now and then on certain of the animals, to no one in particular.

80

It was after sundown when they reached home. They ate supper by lamplight, then, sitting on the doorstep, the boy watched the night fully accomplish, listening to the whippoorwills and the frogs, when he heard his mother's voice: "Abner! No! No! Oh, God, Oh, God, Abner!" and he rose, whirled, and saw the altered light through the door where a candle stub now burned in a bottle neck on the table and his father, still in the hat and coat, at once formal and burlesque as though dressed carefully for some shabby and ceremonial violence, emptying the reservoir of the lamp back into the five-gallon kerosene can from which it had been filled, while the mother tugged at his arm until he shifted the lamp to the other hand and flung her back, not savagely or viciously, just hard, into the wall, her hands flung out against the wall for balance, her mouth open and in her face the same quality of hopeless despair as had been in her voice. Then his father saw him standing in the door.

"Go to the barn and get that can of oil we were oiling the wagon with," he said.   85
The boy did not move. Then he could speak.

"What . . ." he cried. "What are you . . ."

"Go get that oil," his father said. "Go."

Then he was moving, running, outside the house, toward the stable: this the old habit, the old blood which he had not been permitted to choose for himself, which had been bequeathed him willy nilly and which had run for so long (and who knew where, battening on what of outrage and savagery and lust) before it came to him. *I could keep on,* he thought. *I could run on and on and never look back, never need to see his face again. Only I can't. I can't,* the rusted can in his hand now, the liquid sloshing in it as he ran back to the house and into it, into the sound of his mother's weeping in the next room, and handed the can to his father.

"Ain't you going to even send a nigger?" he cried. "At least you sent a nigger before!"

This time his father didn't strike him. The hand came even faster than the blow   90
had, the same hand which had set the can on the table with almost excruciating care flashing from the can toward him too quick for him to follow it, gripping him by the back of his shirt and on to tiptoe before he had seen it quit the can, the face stooping at him in breathless and frozen ferocity, the cold, dead voice speaking over him to the older brother who leaned against the table, chewing with that steady, curious, sidewise motion of cows:

"Empty the can into the big one and go on. I'll catch up with you."

"Better tie him up to the bedpost," the brother said.

"Do like I told you," the father said. Then the boy was moving, his bunched shirt and the hard, bony hand between his shoulder-blades, his toes just touching the floor, across the room and into the other one, past the sisters sitting with spread heavy thighs in the two chairs over the cold hearth, and to where his mother and aunt sat side by side on the bed, the aunt's arms about the mother's shoulders.

"Hold him," the father said. The aunt made a startled movement. "Not you," the father said. "Lennie. Take hold of him. I want to see you do it." His mother took him by the wrist. "You'll hold him better than that. If he gets loose don't you know what he is going to do? He will go up yonder." He jerked his head toward the road. "Maybe I'd better tie him."

"I'll hold him," his mother whispered.   95

"See you do then." Then his father was gone, the stiff foot heavy and measured upon the boards, ceasing at last.

Then he began to struggle. His mother caught him in both arms, he jerking and wrenching at them. He would be stronger in the end, he knew that. But he had not time to wait for it. "Lemme go!" he cried. "I don't want to have to hit you!"

"Let him go!" the aunt said. "If he don't go, before God, I am going up there myself!"

"Don't you see I can't?" his mother cried. "Sarty! Sarty! No! No! Help me, Lizzie!"

Then he was free. His aunt grasped at him but it was too late. He whirled, run-   100
ning, his mother stumbled forward on to her knees behind him, crying to the nearer sister: "Catch him, Net! Catch him!" But that was too late too, the sister (the sisters were twins, born at the same time, yet either of them now gave the impression of being, encompassing as much living meat and volume and weight as any other two of the family) not yet having begun to rise from the chair, her head, face, alone merely turned, presenting to him in the flying instant an astonishing expanse of young female features untroubled by any surprise even, wearing only an expression of bovine interest. Then he was out of the room, out of the house, in the mild dust of the starlit road and the heavy rifeness of honeysuckle, the pale ribbon unspooling with terrific slowness under his running feet, reaching the gate at last and turning in, running, his heart and lungs drumming, on up the drive toward the lighted house, the lighted door. He did not knock, he burst in, sobbing for breath, incapable for the moment of speech; he saw the astonished face of the Negro in the linen jacket without knowing when the Negro had appeared.

"De Spain!" he cried, panted. "Where's . . ." then he saw the white man too emerging from a white door down the hall. "Barn!" he cried. "Barn!"

"What?" the white man said. "Barn?"

"Yes!" the boy cried. "Barn!"

"Catch him!" the white man shouted.

But it was too late this time too. The Negro grasped his shirt, but the entire sleeve,   105
rotten with washing, carried away, and he was out that door too and in the drive again, and had actually never ceased to run even while he was screaming into the white man's face.

Behind him the white man was shouting. "My horse! Fetch my horse!" and he thought for an instant of cutting across the park and climbing the fence into the road, but he did not know the park nor how high the vine-massed fence might be and he dared not risk it. So he ran on down the drive, blood and breath roaring; presently he was in the road again though he could not see it. He could not hear either: the galloping mare was almost upon him before he heard her, and even then he held his course, as if the very urgency of his wild grief and need must in a moment more find him wings, waiting until the ultimate instant to hurl himself aside and into the weed-choked road-side ditch as the horse thundered past and on, for an instant in furious silhouette against the stars, the tranquil early summer night sky which, even before the shape of the horse and rider vanished, strained abruptly and violently upward: a long, swirling roar incredible and soundless, blotting the stars, and he springing up and into the road again, running again, knowing it was too late yet still running even after he heard the shot and, an instant later, two shots, pausing now without knowing he had ceased to run, crying "Pap! Pap!," running again before he knew he had begun to run, stumbling, tripping over something and scrabbling up again without ceasing to run, looking backward over his shoulder at the glare as he got up, running on among the invisible trees, panting, sobbing, "Father! Father!"

At midnight he was sitting on the crest of a hill. He did not know it was midnight and he did not know how far he had come. But there was no glare behind him now and he sat now, his back toward what he had called home for four days anyhow, his face toward the dark woods which he would enter when breath was strong again, small, shaking steadily in the chill darkness, hugging himself into the remainder of his thin, rotten shirt, the grief and despair now no longer terror and fear but just grief and despair. *Father. My father*, he thought. "He was brave!" he cried suddenly, aloud but not loud, no more than a whisper: "He was! He was in the war! He was in Colonel Sartoris' cav'ry!" not knowing that his father had gone to that war a private in the fine old European sense, wearing no uniform, admitting the authority of and giving fidelity to no man or army or flag, going to war as Malbrouck° himself did: for booty—it meant nothing and less than nothing to him if it were enemy booty or his own.

The slow constellations wheeled on. It would be dawn and then sun-up after a while and he would be hungry. But that would be tomorrow and now he was only cold, and walking would cure that. His breathing was easier now and he decided to get up and go on, and then he found that he had been asleep because he knew it was almost dawn, the night almost over. He could tell that from the whippoorwills. They were everywhere now among the dark trees below him, constant and inflectioned and ceaseless, so that, as the instant for giving over to the day birds drew nearer and nearer, there was no interval at all between them. He got up. He was a little stiff, but walking would cure that too as it would the cold, and soon there would be the sun. He went on down the hill, toward the dark woods within which the liquid silver voices of the birds called unceasing—the rapid and urgent beating of the urgent and quiring heart of the late spring night. He did not look back.

QUESTIONS

1. Explain why Sarty's character is round rather than flat. In what ways does he change and grow? What conflicts does he face? What does he learn? How does he feel about the things his father does? Why does he leave and "not look back" at the end?

2. In the Bible, 2 Samuel, Chapters 2 and 3, Abner, the cousin of King Saul, is a powerful commander, warrior, and king maker. He is loyal to the son of King Saul and fights against the supporters of King David. Abner's death makes it possible for David to become uncontested ruler. Why do you think that Faulkner chose the name Abner for the father of the Snopes family? What actions of Abner Snopes make him seem heroic? Antiheroic? Why?

3. When and where is the story occurring? How does Faulkner convey this information to you?

4. Describe the characters of Sarty's mother and sisters. What do you learn about them? To what extent do any of them exhibit growth or development?

5. At the story's end, who is the rider of the horse? Who fires the three shots? Why does Faulkner not tell us the result of the shooting? (In Book I of *The Hamlet*, Faulkner explains that Abner and his other son, Flem, escape.)

Malbrouck: hero of an old French ballad ("Malbrouck s'en va-t-en guerre"). The original Malbrouck, the English Duke of Marlborough (1650–1722) had been accused of profiteering during the War of the Spanish Succession (1702–13).

SUSAN GLASPELL   (1882–1948)

For a brief biography, please see Chapter 22.

A Jury of Her Peers° _____ *1917*

When Martha Hale opened the storm-door and got a cut of the north wind, she ran back for her big woolen scarf. As she hurriedly wound that round her head her eye made a scandalized sweep of her kitchen. It was no ordinary thing that called her away— it was probably further from ordinary than anything that had ever happened in Dickson County. But what her eye took in was that her kitchen was in no shape for leaving: her bread all ready for mixing, half the flour sifted and half unsifted.

She hated to see things half done; but she had been at that when the team from town stopped to get Mr. Hale, and then the sheriff came running in to say his wife wished Mrs. Hale would come too—adding, with a grin, that he guessed she was getting scary and wanted another woman along. So she had dropped everything right where it was.

"Martha!" now came her husband's impatient voice. "Don't keep folks waiting out here in the cold."

She again opened the storm-door, and this time joined the three men and the one woman waiting for her in the big two-seated buggy.

After she had the robes tucked around her she took another look at the woman who sat beside her on the back seat. She had met Mrs. Peters the year before at the county fair, and the thing she remembered about her was that she didn't seem like a sheriff's wife. She was small and thin and didn't have a strong voice. Mrs. Gorman, sheriff's wife before Gorman went out and Peters came in, had a voice that somehow seemed to be backing up the law with every word. But if Mrs. Peters didn't look like a sheriff's wife, Peters made it up in looking like a sheriff. He was to a dot the kind of man who could get himself elected sheriff—a heavy man with a big voice, who was particularly genial with the law-abiding, as if to make it plain that he knew the difference between criminals and non-criminals. And right there it came into Mrs. Hale's mind, with a stab, that this man who was so pleasant and lively with all of them was going to the Wrights' now as a sheriff.

"The country's not very pleasant this time of year," Mrs. Peters at last ventured, as if she felt they ought to be talking as well as the men.

Mrs. Hale scarcely finished her reply, for they had gone up a little hill and could see the Wright place now, and seeing it did not make her feel like talking. It looked very lonesome this cold March morning. It had always been a lonesome-looking place. It was down in a hollow, and the poplar trees around it were lonesome-looking trees. The men were looking at it and talking about what had happened. The county attorney was bending to one side of the buggy, and kept looking steadily at the place as they drew up to it.

"I'm glad you came with me," Mrs. Peters said nervously, as the two women were about to follow the men in through the kitchen door.

Even after she had her foot on the door-step, her hand on the knob, Martha Hale had a moment of feeling she could not cross that threshold. And the reason it seemed

5

Glaspell's play *Trifles*, with which this story may be compared, appears in Chapter 22.

she couldn't cross it now was simply because she hadn't crossed it before. Time and time again it had been in her mind, "I ought to go over and see Minnie Foster"—she still thought of her as Minnie Foster, though for twenty years she had been Mrs. Wright. And then there was always something to do and Minnie Foster would go from her mind. But *now* she could come.

The men went over to the stove. The women stood close together by the door. Young Henderson, the county attorney, turned around and said, "Come up to the fire, ladies."   10

Mrs. Peters took a step forward, then stopped. "I'm not—cold," she said.

And so the two women stood by the door, at first not even so much as looking around the kitchen.

The men talked for a minute about what a good thing it was the sheriff had sent his deputy out that morning to make a fire for them, and then Sheriff Peters stepped back from the stove, unbuttoned his outer coat, and leaned his hands on the kitchen table in a way that seemed to mark the beginning of official business. "Now, Mr. Hale," he said in a sort of semi-official voice, "before we move things about, you tell Mr. Henderson just what it was you saw when you came here yesterday morning."

The county attorney was looking around the kitchen.

"By the way," he said, "has anything been moved?" He turned to the sheriff. "Are   15
things just as you left them yesterday?"

Peters looked from cupboard to sink; from that to a small worn rocker a little to one side of the kitchen table.

"It's just the same."

"Somebody should have been left here yesterday," said the county attorney.

"Oh—yesterday," returned the sheriff, with a little gesture as of yesterday having been more than he could bear to think of. "When I had to send Frank to Morris Center for that man who went crazy—let me tell you. I had my hands full *yesterday*. I knew you could get back from Omaha by today, George, and as long as I went over everything here myself—"

"Well, Mr. Hale," said the county attorney, in a way of letting what was past and   20
gone go, "tell just what happened when you came here yesterday morning."

Mrs. Hale, still leaning against the door, had that sinking feeling of the mother whose child is about to speak a piece. Lewis often wandered along and got things mixed up in a story. She hoped he would tell this straight and plain, and not say unnecessary things that would just make things harder for Minnie Foster. He didn't begin at once, and she noticed that he looked queer—as if standing in that kitchen and having to tell what he had seen there yesterday morning made him almost sick.

"Yes, Mr. Hale?" the county attorney reminded.

"Harry and I had started to town with a load of potatoes," Mrs. Hale's husband began.

Harry was Mrs. Hale's oldest boy. He wasn't with them now, for the very good reason that those potatoes never got to town yesterday and he was taking them this morning, so he hadn't been home when the sheriff stopped to say he wanted Mr. Hale to come over to the Wright place and tell the county attorney his story there, where he could point it all out. With all Mrs. Hale's other emotions came the fear now that maybe Harry wasn't dressed warm enough—they hadn't any of them realized how that north wind did bite.

"We come along this road," Hale was going on, with a motion of his hand to the 2:
road over which they had just come, "and as we got in sight of the house I says to Harry,
'I'm goin' to see if I can't get John Wright to take a telephone.' You see," he explained to
Henderson, "unless I can get somebody to go in with me they won't come out this
branch road except for a price *I* can't pay. I'd spoke to Wright about it once before; but
he put me off, saying folks talked too much anyway, and all he asked was peace and
quiet—guess you know about how much he talked himself. But I thought maybe if I
went to the house and talked about it before his wife, and said all the women-folks liked
the telephones, and that in this lonesome stretch of road it would be a good thing—
well, I said to Harry that that was what I was going to say—though I said at the same
time that I didn't know as what his wife wanted made much difference to John—"

Now there he was!—saying things he didn't need to say. Mrs. Hale tried to catch
her husband's eye, but fortunately the county attorney interrupted with:

"Let's talk about that a little later, Mr. Hale. I do want to talk about that, but I'm
anxious now to get along to just what happened when you got here."

When he began this time, it was very deliberately and carefully:

"I didn't see or hear anything. I knocked at the door. And still it was all quiet
inside. I knew they must be up—it was past eight o'clock. So I knocked again, louder,
and I thought I heard somebody say, 'Come in.' I wasn't sure—I'm not sure yet. But I
opened the door—this door," jerking a hand toward the door by which the two women
stood, "and there, in that rocker"—pointing to it—"sat Mrs. Wright."

Everyone in the kitchen looked at the rocker. It came into Mrs. Hale's mind that 3(
that rocker didn't look in the least like Minnie Foster—the Minnie Foster of twenty years
before. It was a dingy red, with wooden rungs up the back, and the middle rung was
gone, and the chair sagged to one side.

"How did she—look?" the county attorney was inquiring.

"Well," said Hale, "she looked—queer."

"How do you mean—queer?"

As he asked it he took out a note-book and pencil. Mrs. Hale did not like the sight
of that pencil. She kept her eye fixed on her husband, as if to keep him from saying
unnecessary things that would go into that note-book and make trouble.

Hale did speak guardedly, as if the pencil had affected him too. 3.

"Well, as if she didn't know what she was going to do next. And kind of—
done up."

"How did she seem to feel about your coming?"

"Why, I don't think she minded—one way or other. She didn't pay much attention. I said, 'Ho' do, Mrs. Wright? It's cold, ain't it?' And she said. 'Is it?'—and went on
pleatin' at her apron.

"Well, I was surprised. She didn't ask me to come up to the stove, or to sit down,
but just set there, not even lookin' at me. And so I said: 'I want to see John.'

"And then she—laughed. I guess you would call it a laugh. 4(

"I thought of Harry and the team outside, so I said, a little sharp, 'Can I see John?'
'No,' says she—kind of dull like. 'Ain't he home?' says I. Then she looked at me. 'Yes,'
says she, 'he's home.' 'Then why can't I see him?' I asked her, out of patience with her
now. 'Cause he's dead' says she, just as quiet and dull—and fell to pleatin' her apron.
'Dead?' says I, like you do when you can't take in what you've heard.

"She just nodded her head, not getting a bit excited, but rockin' back and forth.

"'Why—where is he?' says I, not knowing *what* to say.

"She just pointed upstairs—like this"—pointing to the room above.

"I got up, with the idea of going up there myself. By this time I—didn't know what   45
to do. I walked from there to here; then I says: 'Why, what did he die of?'

"'He died of a rope around his neck,' says she; and just went on pleatin' at her
apron."

Hale stopped speaking, and stood staring at the rocker, as if he were still seeing
the woman who had sat there the morning before. Nobody spoke; it was as if every one
were seeing the woman who had sat there the morning before.

"And what did you do then?" the county attorney at last broke the silence.

"I went out and called Harry. I thought I might—need help. I got Harry in,
and we went upstairs." His voice fell almost to a whisper. "There he was—lying over
the—"

"I think I'd rather have you go into that upstairs," the county attorney interrupted,   50
"where you can point it all out. Just go on now with the rest of the story."

"Well, my first thought was to get that rope off. It looked—"

He stopped, his face twitching.

"But Harry, he went up to him, and he said. 'No, he's dead all right, and we'd
better not touch anything.' So we went downstairs.

"She was still sitting that same way. 'Has anybody been notified?' I asked. 'No,'
says she, unconcerned.

"'Who did this, Mrs. Wright?' said Harry. He said it businesslike, and she stopped   55
pleatin' at her apron. 'I don't know,' she says. 'You don't *know*?' says Harry. 'Weren't
you sleepin' in the bed with him?' 'Yes,' says she, 'but I was on the inside.' 'Somebody
slipped a rope round his neck and strangled him, and you didn't wake up?' says Harry.
'I didn't wake up,' she said after him.

"We may have looked as if we didn't see how that could be, for after a minute she
said, 'I sleep sound.'

"Harry was going to ask her more questions, but I said maybe that weren't our
business; maybe we ought to let her tell her story first to the coroner or the sheriff.
So Harry went fast as he could over to High Road—the Rivers' place, where there's a
telephone."

"And what did she do when she knew you had gone for the coroner?" The attorney got his pencil in his hand all ready for writing.

"She moved from that chair to this one over here"—Hale pointed to a small chair
in the corner—"and just sat there with her hands held together and looking down. I
got a feeling that I ought to make some conversation, so I said I had come in to see if
John wanted to put in a telephone; and at that she started to laugh, and then she
stopped and looked at me—scared."

At the sound of a moving pencil the man who was telling the story looked up.   60

"I dunno—maybe it wasn't scared," he hastened: "I wouldn't like to say it was.
Soon Harry got back, and then Dr. Lloyd came, and you, Mr. Peters, and so I guess that's
all I know that you don't."

He said that last with relief, and moved a little, as if relaxing. Everyone moved a
little. The county attorney walked toward the stair door.

"I guess we'll go upstairs first—then out to the barn and around there."

He paused and looked around the kitchen.

"You're convinced there was nothing important here?" he asked the sheriff.   65
"Nothing that would—point to any motive?"

The sheriff too looked all around, as if to re-convince himself.

"Nothing here but kitchen things," he said, with a little laugh for the insignificance of kitchen things.

The county attorney was looking at the cupboard—a peculiar, ungainly structure, half closet and half cupboard, the upper part of it being built in the wall, and the lower part just the old-fashioned kitchen cupboard. As if its queerness attracted him, he got a chair and opened the upper part and looked in. After a moment he drew his hand away sticky.

"Here's a nice mess," he said resentfully.

The two women had drawn nearer, and now the sheriff's wife spoke.   70

"Oh—her fruit," she said, looking to Mrs. Hale for sympathetic understanding. She turned back to the county attorney and explained: "She worried about that when it turned so cold last night. She said the fire would go out and her jars might burst."

Mrs. Peters' husband broke into a laugh.

"Well, can you beat the woman! Held for murder, and worrying about her preserves!"

The young attorney set his lips.

"I guess before we're through with her she may have something more serious than   75
preserves to worry about."

"Oh, well," said Mrs. Hale's husband, with good-natured superiority, "women are used to worrying over trifles."

The two women moved a little closer together. Neither of them spoke. The county attorney seemed suddenly to remember his manners—and think of his future.

"And yet," said he, with the gallantry of a young politician. "for all their worries, what would we do without the ladies?"

The women did not speak, did not unbend. He went to the sink and began washing his hands. He turned to wipe them on the roller towel—whirled it for a cleaner place.

"Dirty towels! Not much of a housekeeper, would you say, ladies?"   80
He kicked his foot against some dirty pans under the sink.

"There's a great deal of work to be done on a farm," said Mrs. Hale stiffly.

"To be sure. And yet"—with a little bow to her—"I know there are some Dickson County farm-houses that do not have such roller towels." He gave it a pull to expose its full length again.

"Those towels get dirty awful quick. Men's hands aren't always as clean as they might be."

"Ah, loyal to your sex, I see," he laughed. He stopped and gave her a keen look.   85
"But you and Mrs. Wright were neighbors. I suppose you were friends, too."

Martha Hale shook her head.

"I've seen little enough of her of late years. I've not been in this house—it's more than a year."

"And why was that? You didn't like her?"

"I liked her well enough," she replied with spirit. "Farmers' wives have their hands full, Mr. Henderson. And then—" She looked around the kitchen.

"Yes?" he encouraged.   90

"It never seemed a very cheerful place," said she, more to herself than to him.

"No," he agreed; "I don't think anyone would call it cheerful. I shouldn't say she had the home-making instinct."

"Well, I don't know as Wright had, either," she muttered.

"You mean they didn't get on very well?" he was quick to ask.

"No; I don't mean anything," she answered, with decision. As she turned a little   95
away from him, she added: "But I don't think a place would be any the cheerfuller for
John Wright's bein' in it."

"I'd like to talk to you about that a little later, Mrs. Hale," he said. "I'm anxious to
get the lay of things upstairs now."

He moved toward the stair door, followed by the two men.

"I suppose anything Mrs. Peters does'll be all right?" the sheriff inquired. "She
was to take in some clothes for her, you know—and a few little things. We left in such a
hurry yesterday."

The county attorney looked at the two women whom they were leaving alone
there among the kitchen things.

"Yes—Mrs. Peters," he said, his glance resting on the woman who was not Mrs.   100
Peters, the big farmer woman who stood behind the sheriff's wife. "Of course Mrs. Peters
is one of us," he said, in a manner of entrusting responsibility. "And keep your eye out,
Mrs. Peters, for anything that might be of use. No telling; you women might come upon
a clue to the motive—and that's the thing we need."

Mr. Hale rubbed his face after the fashion of a showman getting ready for a
pleasantry.

"But would the women know a clue if they did come upon it?" he said; and, having
delivered himself of this, he followed the others through the stair door.

The women stood motionless and silent, listening to the footsteps, first upon the
stairs, then in the room above them.

Then, as if releasing herself from something strange, Mrs. Hale began to arrange
the dirty pans under the sink, which the county attorney's disdainful push of the foot
had deranged.

"I'd hate to have men comin' into my kitchen," she said testily—"snoopin' round   105
and criticizin'."

"Of course it's no more than their duty," said the sheriff's wife, in her manner of
timid acquiescence.

"Duty's all right," replied Mrs. Hale bluffly; "but I guess that deputy sheriff that
come out to make the fire might have got a little of this on." She gave the roller towel a
pull. "Wish I'd thought of that sooner! Seems mean to talk about her for not having
things slicked up, when she had to come away in such a hurry."

She looked around the kitchen. Certainly it was not "slicked up." Her eye was held
by a bucket of sugar on a low shelf. The cover was off the wooden bucket, and beside it
was a paper bag—half full.

Mrs. Hale moved toward it.

"She was putting this in there," she said to herself—slowly.   110

She thought of the flour in her kitchen at home—half sifted, half not sifted. She
had been interrupted, and had left things half done. What had interrupted Minnie
Foster? Why had that work been left half done? She made a move as if to finish it,—
unfinished things always bothered her,—and then she glanced around and saw that Mrs.
Peters was watching her—and she didn't want Mrs. Peters to get that feeling she had
got of work begun and then—for some reason—not finished.

"It's a shame about her fruit," she said, and walked toward the cupboard that the
county attorney had opened, and got on the chair, murmuring: "I wonder if it's all gone."

It was a sorry enough looking sight, but "Here's one that's all right," she said at last. She held it toward the light. "This is cherries, too." She looked again. "I declare I believe that's the only one."

With a sigh, she got down from the chair, went to the sink, and wiped off the bottle.

"She'll feel awful bad, after all her hard work in the hot weather. I remember the   115 afternoon I put up my cherries last summer."

She set the bottle on the table, and, with another sigh, started to sit down in the rocker. But she did not sit down. Something kept her from sitting down in that chair. She straightened—stepped back, and, half turned away, stood looking at it, seeing the woman who had sat there "pleatin' at her apron."

The thin voice of the sheriff's wife broke in upon her: "I must be getting those things from the front-room closet." She opened the door into the other room, started in, stepped back. "You coming with me, Mrs. Hale?" she asked nervously. "You—you could help me get them."

They were soon back—the stark coldness of that shut-up room was not a thing to linger in.

"My!" said Mrs. Peters, dropping the things on the table and hurrying to the stove.

Mrs. Hale stood examining the clothes the woman who was being detained in   120 town had said she wanted.

"Wright was close!"° she exclaimed, holding up a shabby black skirt that bore the marks of much making over. "I think maybe that's why she kept so much to herself. I s'pose she felt she couldn't do her part; and then, you don't enjoy things when you feel shabby. She used to wear pretty clothes and be lively—when she was Minnie Foster, one of the town girls, singing in the choir. But that—oh, that was twenty years ago."

With a carefulness in which there was something tender, she folded the shabby clothes and piled them at one corner of the table. She looked up at Mrs. Peters, and there was something in the other woman's look that irritated her.

"She don't care," she said to herself. "Much difference it makes to her whether Minnie Foster had pretty clothes when she was a girl."

Then she looked again, and she wasn't so sure; in fact, she hadn't at any time been perfectly sure about Mrs. Peters. She had that shrinking manner, and yet her eyes looked as if they could see a long way into things.

"This all you was to take in?" asked Mrs. Hale.   125

"No," said the sheriff's wife; "she said she wanted an apron. Funny thing to want," she ventured in her nervous little way, "for there's not much to get you dirty in jail, good-ness knows. But I suppose just to make her feel more natural. If you're used to wearing an apron—. She said they were in the bottom drawer of this cupboard. Yes—here they are. And then her little shawl that always hung on the stair door."

She took the small gray shawl from behind the door leading upstairs, and stood a minute looking at it.

Suddenly Mrs. Hale took a quick step toward the other woman.

"Mrs. Peters!"

"Yes, Mrs. Hale?"   130

"Do you think she—did it?"

A frightened look blurred the other thing in Mrs. Peters' eyes.

---

close: that is, frugal, tightfisted.

"Oh, I don't know," she said, in a voice that seemed to shrink away from the subject.

"Well, I don't think she did," affirmed Mrs. Hale stoutly. "Asking for an apron, and her little shawl. Worryin' about her fruit."

"Mr. Peters says——." Footsteps were heard in the room above; she stopped, looked   135
up, then went on in a lowered voice: "Mr. Peters says—it looks bad for her. Mr. Henderson is awful sarcastic in a speech, and he's going to make fun of her saying she didn't—wake up."

For a moment Mrs. Hale had no answer. Then, "Well, I guess John Wright didn't wake up—when they was slippin' that rope under his neck," she muttered.

"No, it's *strange*," breathed Mrs. Peters. "They think it was such a—funny way to kill a man."

She began to laugh; at sound of the laugh, abruptly stopped.

"That's just what Mr. Hale said," said Mrs. Hale, in a resolutely natural voice. "There was a gun in the house. He says that's what he can't understand."

"Mr. Henderson said, coming out, that what was needed for the case was a motive.   140
Something to show anger—or sudden feeling."

"Well, I don't see any signs of anger around here," said Mrs. Hale, "I don't—" She stopped. It was as if her mind tripped on something. Her eye was caught by a dish-towel in the middle of the kitchen table. Slowly she moved toward the table. One half of it was wiped clean, the other half messy. Her eyes made a slow, almost unwilling turn to the bucket of sugar and the half empty bag beside it. Things begun—and not finished.

After a moment she stepped back, and said, in that manner of releasing herself:

"Wonder how they're finding things upstairs? I hope she had it a little more red up° up there. You know,"—she paused, and feeling gathered,—"it seems kind of *sneaking*: locking her up in town and coming out here to get her own house to turn against her!"

"But, Mrs. Hale," said the sheriff's wife, "the law is the law."

"I s'pose 'tis," answered Mrs. Hale shortly.   145

She turned to the stove, saying something about that fire not being much to brag of. She worked with it a minute, and when she straightened up she said aggressively:

"The law is the law—and a bad stove is a bad stove. How'd you like to cook on this?"—pointing with the poker to the broken lining. She opened the oven door and started to express her opinion of the oven; but she was swept into her own thoughts, thinking of what it would mean, year after year, to have that stove to wrestle with. The thought of Minnie Foster trying to bake in that oven—and the thought of her never going over to see Minnie Foster—.

She was startled by hearing Mrs. Peters say: "A person gets discouraged—and loses heart."

The sheriff's wife had looked from the stove to the sink—to the pail of water which had been carried in from outside. The two women stood there silent, above them the footsteps of the men who were looking for evidence against the woman who had worked in that kitchen. That look of seeing into things, of seeing through a thing to something else, was in the eyes of the sheriff's wife now. When Mrs. Hale next spoke to her, it was gently:

"Better loosen up your things, Mrs. Peters. We'll not feel them when we go out."   150

red up: neat.

Mrs. Peters went to the back of the room to hang up the fur tippet she was wearing. A moment later she exclaimed, "Why, she was piecing a quilt," and held up a large sewing basket piled high with quilt pieces.

Mrs. Hale spread some of the blocks on the table.

"It's a log-cabin pattern," she said, putting several of them together, "Pretty, isn't it?"

They were so engaged with the quilt that they did not hear the footsteps on the stairs. Just as the stair door opened Mrs. Hale was saying:

"Do you suppose she was going to quilt it or just knot it?"   15

The sheriff threw up his hands.

"They wonder whether she was going to quilt it or just knot it!"

There was a laugh for the ways of women, a warming of hands over the stove, and then the county attorney said briskly:

"Well, let's go right out to the barn and get that cleared up."

"I don't see as there's anything so strange," Mrs. Hale said resentfully, after the outside door had closed on the three men—"our taking up our time with little things while we're waiting for them to get the evidence. I don't see as it's anything to laugh about."   16

"Of course they've got awful important things on their minds," said the sheriff's wife apologetically.

They returned to an inspection of the block for the quilt. Mrs. Hale was looking at the fine, even sewing, and preoccupied with thoughts of the woman who had done that sewing, when she heard the sheriff's wife say, in a queer tone:

"Why, look at this one."

She turned to take the block held out to her.

"The sewing," said Mrs. Peters, in a troubled way, "All the rest of them have been so nice and even—but—this one. Why, it looks as if she didn't know what she was about!"   16

Their eyes met—something flashed to life, passed between them; then, as if with an effort, they seemed to pull away from each other. A moment Mrs. Hale sat there, her hands folded over that sewing which was so unlike all the rest of the sewing. Then she had pulled a knot and drawn the threads.

"Oh, what are you doing, Mrs. Hale?" asked the sheriff's wife, startled.

"Just pulling out a stitch or two that's not sewed very good," said Mrs. Hale mildly.

"I don't think we ought to touch things," Mrs. Peters said, a little helplessly.

"I'll just finish up this end," answered Mrs. Hale, still in that mild, matter-of-fact fashion.   17

She threaded a needle and started to replace bad sewing with good. For a little while she sewed in silence. Then, in that thin, timid voice, she heard:

"Mrs. Hale!"

"Yes, Mrs. Peters?"

"What do you suppose she was so—nervous about?"

"Oh, *I* don't know," said Mrs. Hale, as if dismissing a thing not important enough to spend much time on. "I don't know as she was—nervous. I sew awful queer sometimes when I'm just tired."   17

She cut a thread, and out of the corner of her eye looked up at Mrs. Peters. The small, lean face of the sheriff's wife seemed to have tightened up. Her eyes had that look of peering into something. But next moment she moved, and said in her thin, indecisive way:

"Well, I must get those clothes wrapped. They may be through sooner than we think. I wonder where I could find a piece of paper—and string."

"In that cupboard, maybe," suggested to Mrs. Hale, after a glance around.

One piece of the crazy sewing remained unripped. Mrs. Peter's back turned, Martha Hale now scrutinized that piece, compared it with the dainty, accurate sewing of the other blocks. The difference was startling. Holding this block made her feel queer, as if the distracted thoughts of the woman who had perhaps turned to it to try and quiet herself were communicating themselves to her.

Mrs. Peters' voice roused her. 180

"Here's a bird-cage," she said. "Did she have a bird, Mrs. Hale?"

"Why, I don't know whether she did or not." She turned to look at the cage Mrs. Peters was holding up. "I've not been here in so long." She sighed. "There was a man round last year selling canaries cheap—but I don't know as she took one. Maybe she did. She used to sing real pretty herself."

Mrs. Peters looked around the kitchen.

"Seems kind of funny to think of a bird here." She half laughed—an attempt to put up a barrier. "But she must have had one—or why would she have a cage? I wonder what happened to it."

"I suppose maybe the cat got it," suggested Mrs. Hale, resuming her sewing. 185

"No; she didn't have a cat. She's got that feeling some people have about cats—being afraid of them. When they brought her to our house yesterday, my cat got in the room, and she was real upset and asked me to take it out."

"My sister Bessie was like that," laughed Mrs. Hale.

The sheriff's wife did not reply. The silence made Mrs. Hale turn round. Mrs. Peters was examining the bird-cage.

"Look at this door," she said slowly. "It's broke. One hinge has been pulled apart."

Mrs. Hale came nearer. 190

"Looks as if someone must have been—rough with it."

Again their eyes met—startled, questioning, apprehensive. For a moment neither spoke nor stirred. Then Mrs. Hale, turning away, said brusquely:

"If they're going to find any evidence, I wish they'd be about it. I don't like this place."

"But I'm awful glad you came with me, Mrs. Hale." Mrs. Peters put the bird-cage on the table and sat down. "It would be lonesome for me—sitting here alone."

"Yes, it would, wouldn't it?" agreed Mrs. Hale, a certain determined naturalness in 195 her voice. She had picked up the sewing, but now it dropped in her lap, and she murmured in a different voice: "But I tell you what I *do* wish, Mrs. Peters. I wish I had come over sometimes when she was here. I wish—I had."

"But of course you were awful busy, Mrs. Hale. Your house—and your children."

"I could've come," retorted Mrs. Hale shortly. "I stayed away because it weren't cheerful—and that's why I ought to have come. I"—she looked around—"I've never liked this place. Maybe because it's down in a hollow and you don't see the road. I don't know what it is, but it's a lonesome place, and always was. I wish I had come over to see Minnie Foster sometimes. I can see now—" She did not put it into words.

"Well, you mustn't reproach yourself," counseled Mrs. Peters. "Somehow, we just don't see how it is with other folks till—something comes up."

"Not having children makes less work," mused Mrs. Hale, after a silence, "but it makes a quiet house—and Wright out to work all day—and no company when he did come in. Did you know John Wright, Mrs. Peters?"

"Not to know him. I've seen him in town. They say he was a good man." 200

"Yes—good," conceded John Wright's neighbor grimly. "He didn't drink, and kept his word as well as most, I guess, and paid his debts. But he was a hard man, Mrs. Peters. Just to pass the time of day with him—." She stopped, shivered a little. "Like a raw wind that gets to the bone." Her eye fell upon the cage on the table before her, and she added, almost bitterly: "I should think she would've wanted a bird!"

Suddenly she leaned forward, looking intently at the cage. "But what do you s'pose went wrong with it?"

"I don't know," returned Mrs. Peters; "unless it got sick and died."

But after she said it she reached over and swung the broken door. Both women watched it as if somehow held by it.

"You didn't know—her?" Mrs. Hale asked, a gentler note in her voice.   205

"Not till they brought her yesterday," said the sheriff's wife.

"She—come to think of it, she was kind of like a bird herself. Real sweet and pretty, but kind of timid and—fluttery. How—she—did—change."

That held her for a long time. Finally, as if struck with a happy thought and relieved to get back to everyday things, she exclaimed:

"Tell you what, Mrs. Peters, why don't you take the quilt in with you? It might take up her mind."

"Why, I think that's a real nice idea, Mrs. Hale," agreed the sheriff's wife, as if she   210
too were glad to come into the atmosphere of a simple kindness. "There couldn't possibly be any objection to that, could there? Now, just what will I take? I wonder if her patches are in here—and her things?"

They turned to the sewing basket.

"Here's some red," said Mrs. Hale, bringing out a roll of cloth. Underneath that was a box. "Here, maybe her scissors are in here—and her things." She held it up. "What a pretty box! I'll warrant that was something she had a long time ago—when she was a girl."

She held it in her hand a moment; then, with a little sigh, opened it.

Instantly her hand went to her nose.

"Why—!"   215

Mrs. Peters drew nearer—then turned away.

"There's something wrapped up in this piece of silk," faltered Mrs. Hale.

"This isn't her scissors," said Mrs. Peters, in a shrinking voice.

Her hand not steady, Mrs. Hale raised the piece of silk. "Oh, Mrs. Peters!" she cried. "It's—"

Mrs. Peters bent closer.   220

"It's the bird," she whispered.

"But, Mrs. Peters!" cried Mrs. Hale. "*Look* at it! Its *neck*—look at its neck! It's all—other side *to*."

She held the box away from her.

The sheriff's wife again bent closer.

"Somebody wrung its neck," said she, in a voice that was slow and deep.   225

And then again the eyes of the two women met—this time clung together in a look of dawning comprehension, of growing horror. Mrs. Peters looked from the dead bird to the broken door of the cage. Again their eyes met. And just then there was a sound at the outside door.

Mrs. Hale slipped the box under the quilt pieces in the basket, and sank into the chair before it. Mrs. Peters stood holding to the table. The county attorney and the sheriff came in from outside.

"Well, ladies," said the county attorney, as one turning from serious things to little pleasantries, "have you decided whether she was going to quilt it or knot it?"

"We think," began the sheriff's wife in a flurried voice, "that she was going to— knot it."

He was too preoccupied to notice the change that came in her voice on that last. 230

"Well, that's very interesting, I'm sure," he said tolerantly. He caught sight of the bird-cage. "Has the bird flown?"

"We think the cat got it," said Mrs. Hale in a voice curiously even.

He was walking up and down, as if thinking something out.

"Is there a cat?" he asked absently.

Mrs. Hale shot a look up at the sheriff's wife. 235

"Well, not *now*," said Mrs. Peters. "They're superstitious, you know; they leave."

She sank into her chair.

The county attorney did not heed her. "No sign at all of anyone having come in from the outside," he said to Peters, in the manner of continuing an interrupted conversation. "Their own rope. Now let's go upstairs again and go over it, piece by piece. It would have to have been someone who knew just the—"

The stair door closed behind them and their voices were lost.

The two women sat motionless, not looking at each other, but as if peering into 240 something and at the same time holding back. When they spoke now it was as if they were afraid of what they were saying, but as if they could not help saying it.

"She liked the bird," said Martha Hale, low and slowly. "She was going to bury it in that pretty box."

"When I was a girl," said Mrs. Peters, under her breath, "my kitten—there was a boy took a hatchet, and before my eyes—before I could get there—" She covered her face an instant. "If they hadn't held me back I would have"—she caught herself, looked upstairs where footsteps were heard, and finished weakly—"hurt him."

Then they sat without speaking or moving.

"I wonder how it would seem," Mrs. Hale at last began, as if feeling her way over strange ground—"never to have had any children around?" Her eyes made a slow sweep of the kitchen, as if seeing what that kitchen had meant through all the years. "No, Wright wouldn't like the bird," she said after that—"a thing that sang. She used to sing. He killed that too." Her voice tightened.

Mrs. Peters moved uneasily. 245

"Of course we don't know who killed the bird."

"I knew John Wright," was Mrs. Hale's answer.

"It was an awful thing was done in this house that night, Mrs. Hale," said the sheriff's wife. "Killing a man while he slept—slipping a thing round his neck that choked the life out of him."

Mrs. Hale's hand went out to the bird cage.

"His neck. Choked the life out of him." 250

"We don't *know* who killed him," whispered Mrs. Peters wildly. "We don't *know*."

Mrs. Hale had not moved. "If there had been years and years of—nothing, then a bird to sing to you, it would be awful—still—after the bird was still."

It was as if something within her not herself had spoken, and it found in Mrs. Peters something she did not know as herself.

"I know what stillness is," she said, in a queer, monotonous voice. "When we homesteaded in Dakota, and my first baby died—after he was two years old—and me with no other then—"

Mrs. Hale stirred.   255

"How soon do you suppose they'll be through looking for the evidence?"

"I know what stillness is," repeated Mrs. Peters, in just that same way. Then she too pulled back. "The law has got to punish crime, Mrs. Hale," she said in her tight little way.

"I wish you'd seen Minnie Foster," was the answer, "when she wore a white dress with blue ribbons, and stood up there in the choir and sang."

The picture of that girl, the fact that she had lived neighbor to that girl for twenty years, and had let her die for lack of life, was suddenly more than she could bear.

"Oh, I *wish* I'd come over here once in a while!" she cried. "That was a crime!   260
Who's going to punish that?"

"We mustn't take on," said Mrs. Peters, with a frightened look toward the stairs.

"I might 'a' *known* she needed help! I tell you, it's *queer*, Mrs. Peters. We live close together, and we live far apart. We all go through the same things—it's all just a different kind of the same thing! If it weren't—why do you and I *understand*? Why do we *know*—what we know this minute?"

She dashed her hand across her eyes. Then, seeing the jar of fruit on the table, she reached for it and choked out:

"If I was you I wouldn't *tell* her her fruit was gone! Tell her it *ain't*. Tell her it's all right—all of it. Here—take this in to prove it to her! She—she may never know whether it was broke or not."

She turned away.   265

Mrs. Peters reached out for the bottle of fruit as if she were glad to take it—as if touching a familiar thing, having something to do, could keep her from something else. She got up, looked about for something to wrap the fruit in, took a petticoat from the pile of clothes she had brought from the front room, and nervously started winding that round the bottle.

"My!" she began, in a high, false voice, "it's a good thing the men couldn't hear us! Getting all stirred up over a little thing like a—dead canary." She hurried over that. "As if that could have anything to do with—with—My, wouldn't they *laugh*?"

Footsteps were heard on the stairs.

"Maybe they would," muttered Mrs. Hale—"maybe they wouldn't."

"No, Peters," said the county attorney incisively; "it's all perfectly clear, except the   270
reason for doing it. But you know juries when it comes to women. If there was some definite thing—something to show. Something to make a story about. A thing that would connect up with this clumsy way of doing it."

In a covert way Mrs. Hale looked at Mrs. Peters. Mrs. Peters was looking at her. Quickly they looked away from each other. The outer door opened and Mr. Hale came in.

"I've got the team° round now," he said. "Pretty cold out there."

"I'm going to stay here awhile by myself," the county attorney suddenly announced. "You can send Frank out for me, can't you?" he asked the sheriff. "I want to go over everything. I'm not satisfied we can't do better."

Again, for one brief moment, the two women's eyes found one another.

The sheriff came up to the table.   275

"Did you want to see what Mrs. Peters was going to take in?"

team: team of horses pulling the buggy or sleigh in which the group had come.

The county attorney picked up the apron. He laughed.

"Oh, I guess they're not very dangerous things the ladies have picked out."

Mrs. Hale's hand was on the sewing basket in which the box was concealed. She felt that she ought to take her hand off the basket. She did not seem able to. He picked up one of the quilt blocks which she had piled on to cover the box. Her eyes felt like fire. She had a feeling that if he took up the basket she would snatch it from him.

But he did not take it up. With another little laugh, he turned away, saying: 280

"No; Mrs. Peters doesn't need supervising. For that matter, a sheriff's wife is married to the law. Ever think of it that way, Mrs. Peters?"

Mrs. Peters was standing beside the table. Mrs. Hale shot a look up at her; but she could not see her face. Mrs. Peters had turned away. When she spoke, her voice was muffled.

"Not—just that way," she said.

"Married to the law!" chuckled Mrs. Peters' husband. He moved toward the door into the front room, and said to the county attorney:

"I just want you to come in here a minute, George. We ought to take a look at 285 these windows."

"Oh—windows," said the county attorney scoffingly.

"We'll be right out, Mr. Hale," said the sheriff to the farmer, who was still waiting by the door.

Hale went to look after the horses. The sheriff followed the county attorney into the other room. Again—for one final moment—the two women were alone in that kitchen.

Martha Hale sprang up, her hands tight together, looking at that other woman, with whom it rested. At first she could not see her eyes, for the sheriff's wife had not turned back since she turned away at that suggestion of being married to the law. But now Mrs. Hale made her turn back. Her eyes made her turn back. Slowly, unwillingly, Mrs. Peters turned her head until her eyes met the eyes of the other woman. There was a moment when they held each other in a steady, burning look in which there was no evasion nor flinching. Then Martha Hale's eyes pointed the way to the basket in which was hidden the thing that would make certain the conviction of the other woman—that woman who was not there and yet who had been there with them all through that hour.

For a moment Mrs. Peters did not move. And then she did it. With a rush for- 290 ward, she threw back the quilt pieces, got the box, tried to put it in her handbag. It was too big. Desperately she opened it, started to take the bird out. But there she broke—she could not touch the bird. She stood there helpless, foolish.

There was the sound of a knob turning in the inner door. Martha Hale snatched the box from the sheriff's wife, and got it in the pocket of her big coat just as the sheriff and the county attorney came back into the kitchen.

"Well, Henry," said the county attorney facetiously, "at least we found out that she was not going to quilt it. She was going to—what is it you call it, ladies?"

Mrs. Hale's hand was against the pocket of her coat.

"We call it—knot it, Mr. Henderson."

QUESTIONS

1. Who is the central character? That is, on whom does the story focus?

2. Describe the differences between Mrs. Hale and Mrs. Peters, in terms of their status, backgrounds, and comparative strengths of character.

3. Why do the two women not voice their conclusions about the murderer? How does Glaspell show that they both know the murderer's identity, the reasons, and the method? Why do they both "cover up" at the story's conclusion?

AMY TAN   (b. 1952)

Tan was born almost three years after her parents left China during the Maoist revolution in that country. They settled in California and moved frequently within that state when Tan was a child. She attended schools in California and in Switzerland and received an M.A. at Berkeley. In addition to working as a freelance writer, she has been on many committees and boards serving the interests of minorities. As an imaginative writer she has drawn upon her own experiences as a Chinese-American growing up in the United States. Her most successful work to date is The Joy Luck Club *(1989), which was made into a movie (1993) and from which "Two Kinds" is excerpted. She has also published two other novels,* The Kitchen God's Wife *(1991) and* The Hundred Secret Senses *(1995), in addition to children's books.*

Two Kinds _____ 1989

My mother believed you could be anything you wanted to be in America. You could open a restaurant. You could work for the government and get good retirement. You could buy a house with almost no money down. You could become rich. You could become instantly famous.

"Of course you can be prodigy, too," my mother told me when I was nine. "You can be best anything. What does Auntie Lindo know? Her daughter, she is only best tricky."

America was where all my mother's hopes lay. She had come here in 1949 after losing everything in China: her mother and father, her family home, her first husband, and two daughters, twin baby girls. But she never looked back with regret. There were so many ways for things to get better.

We didn't immediately pick the right kind of prodigy. At first my mother thought I could be a Chinese Shirley Temple. We'd watch Shirley's old movies on TV as though they were training films. My mother would poke my arm and say, *"Ni kan"*—You watch. And I would see Shirley tapping her feet, or singing a sailor song, or pursing her lips into a very round O while saying, "Oh my goodness."

"Ni kan," said my mother as Shirley's eyes flooded with tears. "You already know how. Don't need talent for crying!"   5

Soon after my mother got this idea about Shirley Temple, she took me to a beauty training school in the Mission district and put me in the hands of a student who could barely hold the scissors without shaking. Instead of getting big fat curls, I emerged with an uneven mass of crinkly black fuzz. My mother dragged me off to the bathroom and tried to wet down my hair.

"You look like Negro Chinese," she lamented, as if I had done this on purpose.

The instructor of the beauty training school had to lop off these soggy clumps to make my hair even again. "Peter Pan is very popular these days," the instructor assured my mother. I now had hair the length of a boy's, with straight-across bangs that hung at a slant two inches above my eyebrows. I liked the haircut and it made me actually look forward to my future fame.

In fact, in the beginning, I was just as excited as my mother, maybe even more so. I pictured this prodigy part of me as many different images, trying each one on for size. I was a dainty ballerina girl standing by the curtains, waiting to hear the right music that would send me floating on my tiptoes. I was like the Christ child lifted out of the straw manger, crying with holy indignity. I was Cinderella stepping from her pumpkin carriage with sparkly cartoon music filling the air.

In all of my imaginings, I was filled with a sense that I would soon become *perfect*.   10
My mother and father would adore me. I would be beyond reproach. I would never feel the need to sulk for anything.

But sometimes the prodigy in me became impatient. "If you don't hurry up and get me out of here, I'm disappearing for good," it warned. "And then you'll always be nothing."

Every night after dinner, my mother and I would sit at the Formica kitchen table. She would present new tests, taking her examples from stories of amazing children she had read in *Ripley's Believe It or Not,* or *Good Housekeeping, Reader's Digest,* and a dozen other magazines she kept in a pile in our bathroom. My mother got these magazines from people whose houses she cleaned. And since she cleaned many houses each week, we had a great assortment. She would look through them all, searching for stories about remarkable children.

The first night she brought out a story about a three-year-old boy who knew the capitals of all the states and even most of the European countries. A teacher was quoted as saying the little boy could also pronounce the names of the foreign cities correctly.

"What's the capital of Finland?" my mother asked me, looking at the magazine story.

All I knew was the capital of California, because Sacramento was the name of the   15
street we lived on in Chinatown. "Nairobi!" I guessed, saying the most foreign word I could think of. She checked to see if that was possibly one way to pronounce "Helsinki" before showing me the answer.

The tests got harder—multiplying numbers in my head, finding the queen of hearts in a deck of cards, trying to stand on my head without using my hands, predicting the daily temperatures in Los Angeles, New York, and London.

One night I had to look at a page from the Bible for three minutes and then report everything I could remember. "Now Jehoshaphat had riches° and honor in abundance and . . . that's all I remember, Ma," I said.

And after seeing my mother's disappointed face once again, something inside of me began to die. I hated the tests, the raised hopes and failed expectations. Before going

---

Now Jehoshaphat had riches: Jing-Mei had been told to report on the Hebrew monarch Jehoshaphat as narrated in the eighteenth chapter of II Chronicles.

to bed that night, I looked in the mirror above the bathroom sink and when I saw only my face staring back—and that it would always be this ordinary face—I began to cry. Such a sad, ugly girl! I made high-pitched noises like a crazed animal, trying to scratch out the face in the mirror.

And then I saw what seemed to be the prodigy side of me—because I had never seen that face before. I looked at my reflection, blinking so I could see more clearly. The girl staring back at me was angry, powerful. This girl and I were the same. I had new thoughts, willful thoughts, or rather thoughts filled with lots of won'ts. I won't let her change me, I promised myself. I won't be what I'm not.

So now on nights when my mother presented her tests, I performed listlessly, my   20
head propped on one arm. I pretended to be bored. And I was. I got so bored I started counting the bellows of the foghorns out on the bay while my mother drilled me in other areas. The sound was comforting and reminded me of the cow jumping over the moon. And the next day, I played a game with myself, seeing if my mother would give up on me before eight bellows. After a while I usually counted only one, maybe two bellows at most. At last she was beginning to give up hope.

Two or three months had gone by without any mention of my being a prodigy again. And then one day my mother was watching *The Ed Sullivan Show* ° on TV. The TV was old and the sound kept shorting out. Every time my mother got halfway up from the sofa to adjust the set, the sound would go back on and Ed would be talking. As soon as she sat down, Ed would go silent again. She got up, the TV broke into loud piano music. She sat down. Silence. Up and down, back and forth, quiet and loud. It was like a stiff embraceless dance between her and the TV set. Finally she stood by the set with her hand on the sound dial.

She seemed entranced by the music, a little frenzied piano piece with this mesmerizing quality, sort of quick passages and then teasing lilting ones before it returned to the quick playful parts.

"*Ni kan,*" my mother said, calling me over with hurried hand gestures, "Look here."

I could see why my mother was fascinated by the music. It was being pounded out by a little Chinese girl, about nine years old, with a Peter Pan haircut. The girl had the sauciness of a Shirley Temple. She was proudly modest like a proper Chinese child. And she also did this fancy sweep of a curtsy, so that the fluffy skirt of her white dress cascaded slowly to the floor like the petals of a large carnation.

In spite of these warning signs, I wasn't worried. Our family had no piano and we   25
couldn't afford to buy one, let alone reams of sheet music and piano lessons. So I could be generous in my comments when my mother bad-mouthed the little girl on TV.

"Play note right, but doesn't sound good! No singing sound," complained my mother.

"What are you picking on her for?" I said carelessly. "She's pretty good. Maybe she's not the best, but she's trying hard." I knew almost immediately I would be sorry I said that.

"Just like you," she said. "Not the best. Because you not trying." She gave a little huff as she let go of the sound dial and sat down on the sofa.

Ed Sullivan Show: Ed Sullivan (1902–1974), originally a newspaper columnist, hosted this popular variety television show from 1948 to 1971.

The little Chinese girl sat down also to play an encore of "Anitra's Dance" by Grieg.° I remember the song, because later on I had to learn how to play it.

Three days after watching *The Ed Sullivan Show,* my mother told me what my   30
schedule would be for piano lessons and piano practice. She had talked to Mr. Chong, who lived on the first floor of our apartment building. Mr. Chong was a retired piano teacher and my mother had traded housecleaning services for weekly lessons and a piano for me to practice on every day, two hours a day, from four until six.

When my mother told me this, I felt as though I had been sent to hell. I whined and then kicked my foot a little when I couldn't stand it anymore.

"Why don't you like me the way I am? I'm *not* a genius! I can't play the piano. And even if I could, I wouldn't go on TV if you paid me a million dollars!" I cried.

My mother slapped me. "Who ask you be genius?" she shouted. "Only ask you be your best. For you sake. You think I want you be genius? Hnnh! What for! Who ask you!"

"So ungrateful," I heard her mutter in Chinese. "If she had as much talent as she has temper, she would be famous now."

Mr. Chong, whom I secretly nicknamed Old Chong, was very strange, always tap-   35
ping his fingers to the silent music of an invisible orchestra. He looked ancient in my eyes. He had lost most of the hair on top of his head and he wore thick glasses and had eyes that always looked tired and sleepy. But he must have been younger than I thought, since he lived with his mother and was not yet married.

I met Old Lady Chong once and that was enough. She had this peculiar smell like a baby that had done something in its pants. And her fingers felt like a dead person's, like an old peach I once found in the back of the refrigerator; the skin just slid off the meat when I picked it up.

I soon found out why Old Chong had retired from teaching piano. He was deaf. "Like Beethoven!" he shouted to me. "We're both listening only in our head!" And he would start to conduct his frantic silent sonatas.

Our lessons went like this. He would open the book and point to different things, explaining their purpose: "Key! Treble! Bass! No sharps or flats! So this is C major! Listen now and play after me!"

And then he would play the C scale a few times, a simple chord, and then, as if inspired by an old, unreachable itch, he gradually added more notes and running trills and a pounding bass until the music was really something quite grand.

I would play after him, the simple scale, the simple chord, and then I just played   40
some nonsense that sounded like a cat running up and down on top of garbage cans. Old Chong smiled and applauded and then said, "Very good! But now you must learn to keep time!"

So that's how I discovered that Old Chong's eyes were too slow to keep up with the wrong notes I was playing. He went through the motions in half-time. To help me keep rhythm, he stood behind me, pushing down on my right shoulder for every beat. He balanced pennies on top of my wrists so I would keep them still as I slowly played scales and arpeggios. He had me curve my hand around an apple and keep that shape when playing chords. He marched stiffly to show me how to make each finger dance up and down, staccato like an obedient little soldier.

"Anitra's Dance" by Grieg: A portion of the suite composed for Ibsen's *Peer Gynt* by Norwegian composer Edvard Grieg (1843–1907).

He taught me all these things, and that was how I also learned I could be lazy and get away with mistakes, lots of mistakes. If I hit the wrong notes because I hadn't practiced enough, I never corrected myself. I just kept playing in rhythm. And Old Chong kept conducting his own private reverie.

So maybe I never really gave myself a fair chance. I did pick up the basics pretty quickly, and I might have become a good pianist at that young age. But I was so determined not to try, not to be anybody different that I learned to play only the most ear-splitting preludes, the most discordant hymns.

Over the next year, I practiced like this, dutifully in my own way. And then one day I heard my mother and her friend Lindo Jong both talking in a loud bragging tone of voice so others could hear. It was after church, and I was leaning against the brick wall wearing a dress with stiff white petticoats. Auntie Lindo's daughter, Waverly, who was about my age, was standing farther down the wall about five feet away. We had grown up together and shared all the closeness of two sisters squabbling over crayons and dolls. In other words, for the most part, we hated each other. I thought she was snotty. Waverly Jong had gained a certain amount of fame as "Chinatown's Littlest Chinese Chess Champion."

"She bring home too many trophy," lamented Auntie Lindo that Sunday. "All day   45
she play chess. All day I have no time do nothing but dust off her winnings." She threw a scolding look at Waverly, who pretended not to see her.

"You lucky you don't have this problem," said Auntie Lindo with a sigh to my mother.

And my mother squared her shoulders and bragged: "Our problem worser than yours. If we ask Jing-Mei wash dish, she hear nothing but music. It's like you can't stop this natural talent."

And right then, I was determined to put a stop to her foolish pride.

A few weeks later, Old Chong and my mother conspired to have me play in a talent show which would be held in the church hall. By then, my parents had saved up enough to buy me a secondhand piano, a black Wurlitzer spinet with a scarred bench. It was the showpiece of our living room.

For the talent show, I was to play a piece called "Pleading Child" from Schumann's   50
Scenes from Childhood.° It was a simple, moody piece that sounded more difficult than it was. I was supposed to memorize the whole thing, playing the repeat parts twice to make the piece sound longer. But I dawdled over it, playing a few bars and then cheating, looking up to see what notes followed. I never really listened to what I was playing. I daydreamed about being somewhere else, about being someone else.

The part I liked to practice best was the fancy curtsy: right foot out, touch the rose on the carpet with a pointed foot, sweep to the side, left leg bends, look up and smile.

My parents invited all the couples from the Joy Luck Club to witness my debut. Auntie Lindo and Uncle Tin were there. Waverly and her two older brothers had also come. The first two rows were filled with children both younger and older than I was. The littlest ones got to go first. They recited simple nursery rhymes, squawked out tunes on miniature violins, twirled Hula Hoops, pranced in pink ballet tutus, and when they bowed or curtsied, the audience would sigh in unison, "Awww," and then clap enthusiastically.

Scenes from Childhood: Scenes from Childhood, or *Kinderszenen* (1836), is one of the best-known works for piano by Robert Schumann (1810–1856).

When my turn came, I was very confident. I remember my childish excitement. It was as if I knew, without a doubt, that the prodigy side of me really did exist. I had no fear whatsoever, no nervousness. I remember thinking to myself, This is it! This is it! I looked out over the audience, at my mother's blank face, my father's yawn, Auntie Lindo's stiff-lipped smile, Waverly's sulky expression. I had on a white dress layered with sheets of lace, and a pink bow in my Peter Pan haircut. As I sat down I envisioned people jumping to their feet and Ed Sullivan rushing up to introduce me to everyone on TV.

And I started to play. It was so beautiful. I was so caught up in how lovely I looked that at first I didn't worry how I would sound. So it was a surprise to me when I hit the first wrong note and I realized something didn't sound quite right. And then I hit another and another followed that. A chill started at the top of my head and began to trickle down. Yet I couldn't stop playing, as though my hands were bewitched. I kept thinking my fingers would adjust themselves back, like a train switching to the right track. I played this strange jumble through two repeats, the sour notes staying with me all the way to the end.

When I stood up, I discovered my legs were shaking. Maybe I had just been nervous and the audience, like Old Chong, had seen me go through the right motions and had not heard anything wrong at all. I swept my right foot out, went down on my knee, looked up and smiled. The room was quiet, except for Old Chong, who was beaming and shouting, "Bravo! Bravo! Well done!" But then I saw my mother's face, her stricken face. The audience clapped weakly, and as I walked back to my chair, with my whole face quivering as I tried not to cry, I heard a little boy whisper loudly to his mother, "That was awful," and the mother whispered back, "Well, she certainly tried."

And now I realized how many people were in the audience, the whole world it seemed. I was aware of eyes burning into my back. I felt the shame of my mother and father as they sat stiffly throughout the rest of the show.

We could have escaped during intermission. Pride and some strange sense of honor must have anchored my parents to their chairs. And so we watched it all: the eighteen-year-old boy with a fake mustache who did a magic show and juggled flaming hoops while riding a unicycle. The breasted girl with white makeup who sang from *Madama Butterfly*° and got honorable mention. And the eleven-year-old boy who won first prize playing a tricky violin song that sounded like a busy bee.°

After the show, the Hsus, the Jongs, and the St. Clairs from the Joy Luck Club came up to my mother and father.

"Lots of talented kids," Auntie Lindo said vaguely, smiling broadly.

"That was somethin' else," said my father, and I wondered if he was referring to me in a humorous way, or whether he even remembered what I had done.

Waverly looked at me and shrugged her shoulders. "You aren't a genius like me," she said matter-of-factly. And if I hadn't felt so bad, I would have pulled her braids and punched her stomach.

But my mother's expression was what devastated me: a quiet, blank look that said she had lost everything. I felt the same way, and it seemed as if everybody were now coming up, like gawkers at the scene of an accident, to see what parts were actually missing. When we got on the bus to go home, my father was humming the busy-bee tune and my mother was silent. I kept thinking she wanted to wait until we got home before

55

60

Madama Butterfly: The girl probably sang "Un Bel Di," the signature soprano aria from the opera *Madama Butterfly* by Giacomo Puccini (1858–1924).

busy bee: Probably the well-known "Flight of the Bumblebee" by Nikolay Rimsky-Korsakov (1844–1908).

shouting at me. But when my father unlocked the door to our apartment, my mother walked in and then went to the back, into the bedroom. No accusations. No blame. And in a way, I felt disappointed. I had been waiting for her to start shouting, so I could shout back and cry and blame her for all my misery.

I assumed my talent-show fiasco meant I never had to play the piano again. But two days later, after school, my mother came out of the kitchen and saw me watching TV.

"Four clock," she reminded me as if it were any other day. I was stunned, as though she were asking me to go through the talent-show torture again. I wedged myself more tightly in front of the TV.

"Turn off TV," she called from the kitchen five minutes later.   65

I didn't budge. And then I decided. I didn't have to do what my mother said anymore. I wasn't her slave. This wasn't China. I had listened to her before and look what happened. She was the stupid one.

She came out from the kitchen and stood in the arched entryway of the living room. "Four clock," she said once again, louder.

"I'm not going to play anymore," I said nonchalantly. "Why should I? I'm not a genius."

She walked over and stood in front of the TV. I saw her chest was heaving up and down in an angry way.

"No!" I said, and I now felt stronger, as if my true self had finally emerged. So this   70
was what had been inside me all along.

"No! I won't!" I screamed.

She yanked me by the arm, pulled me off the floor, snapped off the TV. She was frighteningly strong, half pulling, half carrying me toward the piano as I kicked the throw rugs under my feet. She lifted me up and onto the hard bench. I was sobbing by now, looking at her bitterly. Her chest was heaving even more and her mouth was open, smiling crazily as if she were pleased I was crying.

"You want me to be someone that I'm not!" I sobbed. "I'll never be the kind of daughter you want me to be!"

"Only two kinds of daughters," she shouted in Chinese. "Those who are obedient and those who follow their own mind! Only one kind of daughter can live in this house. Obedient daughter!"

"Then I wish I wasn't your daughter. I wish you weren't my mother," I shouted.   75
As I said these things I got scared. It felt like worms and toads and slimy things crawling out of my chest, but it also felt good, as if this awful side of me had surfaced, at last.

"Too late change this," said my mother shrilly.

And I could sense her anger rising to its breaking point. I wanted to see it spill over. And that's when I remembered the babies she had lost in China, the ones we never talked about. "Then I wish I'd never been born!" I shouted. "I wish I were dead! Like them."

It was as if I had said the magic words. Alakazam!—and her face went blank, her mouth closed, her arms went slack, and she backed out of the room, stunned, as if she were blowing away like a small brown leaf, thin, brittle, lifeless.

It was not the only disappointment my mother felt in me. In the years that followed, I failed her so many times, each time asserting my own will, my right to fall short of expectations. I didn't get straight As. I didn't become class president. I didn't get into Stanford. I dropped out of college.

For unlike my mother, I did not believe I could be anything I wanted to be. I could only be me. 80

And for all those years, we never talked about the disaster at the recital or my terrible accusations afterward at the piano bench. All that remained unchecked, like a betrayal that was now unspeakable. So I never found a way to ask her why she had hoped for something so large that failure was inevitable.

And even worse, I never asked her what frightened me the most: Why had she given up hope?

For after our struggle at the piano, she never mentioned my playing again. The lessons stopped. The lid to the piano was closed, shutting out the dust, my misery, and her dreams.

So she surprised me. A few years ago, she offered to give me the piano, for my thirtieth birthday. I had not played in all those years. I saw the offer as a sign of forgiveness, a tremendous burden removed.

"Are you sure?" I asked shyly. "I mean, won't you and Dad miss it?" 85

"No, this your piano," she said firmly. "Always your piano. You only one can play."

"Well, I probably can't play anymore," I said. "It's been years."

"You pick up fast," said my mother, as if she knew this was certain. "You have natural talent. You could been genius if you want to."

"No I couldn't."

"You just not trying," said my mother. And she was neither angry nor sad. She 90 said it as if to announce a fact that could never be disproved. "Take it," she said.

But I didn't at first. It was enough that she had offered it to me. And after that, every time I saw it in my parents' living room, standing in front of the bay windows, it made me feel proud, as if it were a shiny trophy I had won back.

Last week I sent a tuner over to my parents' apartment and had the piano reconditioned, for purely sentimental reasons. My mother had died a few months before and I had been getting things in order for my father, a little bit at a time. I put the jewelry in special silk pouches. The sweaters she had knitted in yellow, pink, bright orange—all the colors I hated—I put those in moth-proof boxes. I found some old Chinese silk dresses, the kind with little slits up the sides. I rubbed the old silk against my skin, then wrapped them in tissue and decided to take them home with me.

After I had the piano tuned, I opened the lid and touched the keys. It sounded even richer than I remembered. Really, it was a very good piano. Inside the bench were the same exercise notes with handwritten scales, the same secondhand music books with their covers held together with yellow tape.

I opened up the Schumann book to the dark little piece I had played at the recital. It was on the left-hand side of the page, "Pleading Child." It looked more difficult than I remembered. I played a few bars, surprised at how easily the notes came back to me.

And for the first time, or so it seemed, I noticed the piece on the right-hand side. 95 It was called "Perfectly Contented." I tried to play this one as well. It had a lighter melody but the same flowing rhythm and turned out to be quite easy. "Pleading Child" was shorter but slower; "Perfectly Contented" was longer, but faster. And after I played them both a few times, I realized they were two halves of the same song.

QUESTIONS

1. What major characteristics about the narrator, Jing-Mei, are brought out in the story?
2. Describe the relationship between Jing-Mei and her mother. Why does Jing-Mei resist all efforts to develop her talents?
3. Characterize the mother. To what degree is she sympathetic? Unsympathetic? At the story's end, how does Jing-Mei feel about her mother?
4. What general details about the nature of first- or second-generation immigrants are presented in the story? (For a broader comparison, you might relate "Two Kinds" to Zabytko's "Home Soil" and Butler's "Snow.")

WRITING ABOUT CHARACTERS

Usually your topic will be a major character, although you might also study a minor character or characters. After your customary overview, begin taking notes. List as many traits as you can, and also determine how the author presents details about the character through actions, appearance, speeches, comments by others, or authorial explanations. If you discover unusual traits, determine what they show. The following suggestions and questions will help you get started.

Questions for Discovering Ideas

- Describe the importance of a character to the story's principal action. Is the character the protagonist or antagonist?
- How do the protagonist and antagonist interact? What changes do their interactions bring about?
- What actions bring out important traits of the character? To what degree is the character creating or just responding to events?
- Characterize the protagonist's actions: Are they good or bad, intelligent or stupid, deliberate or spontaneous? How do they help you understand the protagonist?
- Describe and explain the character's traits, both major and minor. To what extent do the traits permit you to judge the character? What is your judgment?
- What descriptions (if any) of the character's appearance do you discover in the story? What does the appearance demonstrate about the character?
- In what ways is the character's major trait a strength—or a weakness? As the story progresses, to what degree does the trait become more (or less) prominent?
- Is the character round and dynamic? How does the character recognize, change with, or adjust to circumstances?
- If the character is minor (flat or static), what function does he or she perform in the story (for example, by doing a task or by bringing out qualities of the major character)?
- If the character is a stereotype, to what type does he or she belong? To what degree does the character stay in the stereotypical role or rise above it? How?

- What do any of the other characters do, say, or think to give you insight into the character? What does the character say or think about himself or herself? What does the storyteller or narrator say? How valid are their comments and insights? How helpful in providing insights into the character?

- Is the character lifelike or unreal? Consistent or inconsistent? Believable or not believable?

Strategies for Organizing Ideas

Consider one of the following approaches to organize your ideas and form the basis for your essay.

1. *Organization around central traits or major characteristics,* such as "unquestioning devotion and service" (Phoenix of "A Worn Path") or "the habit of seeing the world only in one's own terms" (Miss Brill of "Miss Brill"). This kind of structure would show how the work embodies the trait. For example, in one part of the story a trait may be brought out through comments that characters make about the major character (as at the end of Mansfield's "Miss Brill"), and in another part through that character's own speeches and actions. Studying the trait thus enables you to focus on the differing ways in which the author presents the character, and it also enables you to focus on separate parts of the work.

2. *Organization around a character's growth or change.* This type of essay describes a character's traits at the story's opening and then analyzes changes or developments. *It is important to stress the actual alterations as they emerge, but at the same time to avoid retelling the story.* Additionally, you should not only describe the changing traits but also analyze how they are brought out within the work (such as the childhood stubbornness of Jing-Mei, or Minnie Wright's long ordeal).

3. *Organization around central actions, objects, or quotations that reveal primary characteristics.* Key incidents may stand out, along with objects closely associated with the character being analyzed. There may be important quotations spoken by the character or by someone else in the work. Show how such elements serve as signposts or guides to understanding the character. (See the following sample student essay for an illustration of this type of development.)

4. *Organization around qualities of a flat character or characters.* If the character is flat (such as the sisters in "Barn Burning" or the Cowboy in "The Blue Hotel"), you might develop topics such as the function and relative significance of the character, the group the character represents, the relationship of the flat character to the round ones, the importance of this relationship, and any additional qualities or traits. For a flat character, you should explain the circumstances or defects that keep the character from being round and the importance of these shortcomings in the author's presentation of character.

In your conclusion, show how the character's traits are related to the work as a whole. If the person is good but comes to a bad end, does this misfortune make him or her seem especially worthy? If the person suffers, does this fact suggest any attitudes about the class or type of which he or she is a part? Or does it illustrate the author's general view of human life? Or both? Do the characteristics explain why the person helps or hinders other characters? How does your essay help in clearing up first-reading misunderstandings? These and similar questions are appropriate for your conclusion.

SAMPLE STUDENT ESSAY

The Character of Minnie Wright in Glaspell's "A Jury of Her Peers"°

[1]   Minnie Wright is Susan Glaspell's major character in "A Jury of Her Peers." We learn about her, however, not from seeing and hearing her, for she does not act or speak, but rather from the secondhand evidence provided by the major characters. Lewis Hale, the neighboring farmer, tells about Minnie's behavior on the morning when her husband, John, was found strangled in his bed. Martha Hale, Hale's wife, tells about Minnie's young womanhood and about how she became alienated from her nearest neighbors because of John's stingy and unfriendly ways. Both Martha and Mrs. Peters, the Sheriff's wife, make observations about Minnie based on the condition of her kitchen. From this information we get a full portrait of Minnie, who has changed from passivity to destructive assertiveness.* Her change in character is indicated by her clothing, her dead canary, and her unfinished patchwork quilt.†

[2]   The clothes that Minnie has worn in the past and in the present indicate her character as a person of charm who has withered under neglect and contempt. Martha mentions Minnie's attractive and colorful dresses as a young woman, even recalling a white dress with blue ribbons (paragraph 258). Martha also recalls that Minnie, when young, was "sweet and pretty, but kind of timid and--fluttery" (paragraph 207). In the light of these recollections, Martha observes that Minnie had changed, and changed for the worse, during her twenty years of marriage with John Wright, who is characterized as "a raw wind that gets to the bone" (paragraph 201). As more evidence for Minnie's acceptance of her drab life, Mrs. Peters says that Minnie asks for no more than an apron and shawl when under arrest in the sheriff's home. This modest clothing, as contrasted with the colorful dresses of her youth, suggests her suppression of spirit.

[3]   Minnie's dead canary, however, while indicating her love of music, also shows the end of her suppression and the emergence of her rage. For nineteen years of marriage Minnie endures her cheerless farm home, the contempt of her husband, her life of solitude, the abandonment of her early enjoyment of singing, a general lack of pretty things, and the recognition that she could not share the social life of the local farm women as an equal. But her buying the canary (paragraph 182) suggests the reemergence of her love of song, just as it also suggests her growth toward self-assertion. That her husband wrings the bird's neck may thus be seen as the cause not only of immediate grief (shown by the dead bird in a "pretty box" [paragraphs 212–225]) but also of the anger that marks her change from a stock, obedient wife to a person angry enough to kill.

° See pp. 166–79 for this story.
* Central idea.
† Thesis sentence.

[4] Like her love of song, her unfinished quilt indicates her creativity. In twenty years on the farm, never having had children, she has nothing creative to do except for needlework like the quilt. Mrs. Hale comments on the beauty of Minnie's log-cabin design (paragraph 153), and observes the colorful patches of cloth in her sewing basket (paragraph 212). The inference is that even though Minnie's life has been bleak, she has been able to indulge her characteristic love of color and form--and also of warmth, granted the purpose of a quilt.

[5] Ironically, the quilt also shows Minnie's creativity in the murder of her husband. Both Mrs. Hale and Mrs. Peters interpret the breakdown of Minnie's stitching on the quilt as signs of distress about the dead canary and also of her nervousness in planning revenge (paragraph 166). Further, even though nowhere in the story is it said that John is strangled with a quilting knot, no other conclusion is possible. Both Mrs. Hale and Mrs. Peters agree that Minnie probably intended to knot the quilt rather than sew it in a quilt stitch, and Glaspell pointedly causes the men to learn this detail also, even though they scoff at it and ignore it. In other words, we learn that Minnie's only outlet for creativity--needlework--has enabled her to perform the murder in the only way she can, by strangling John with a slip-proof quilting knot. Even though her plan for the murder is deliberate (Mrs. Peters reports that the arrangement of the rope was a "funny way to kill" [paragraph 137]), Minnie is not cold or remorseless. Her passivity after the crime demonstrates that planning to evade guilt, beyond simple denial, is not in her character. She is not so diabolically creative that she plans or even understands the irony of strangling her husband just as he killed the bird by wringing its neck. Glaspell, however, has made the irony plain.

[6] It is important to emphasize again that we learn about Minnie from others. Indeed, Glaspell describes her as "that woman who was not there and yet who had been there with them all through that hour" (paragraph 289). Undeniably, then, Minnie is fully realized, round, and poignant. For the greater part of her adult life, she has been representative of women whose capacities for growth and expression are stunted by the grind of life and the cruelty and insensitivity of others. She patiently accepts her drab and colorless marriage that is so different from her youthful expectations. Amid the dreary farm surroundings, she suppresses her grudges, just as she suppresses her prettiness, colorfulness, and creativity. In short, she has been nothing more than a flat character. But the killing of the canary causes her to change and to destroy her husband in an assertive rejection of her stock role as the suffering wife. She is a patient woman whose patience finally reaches the breaking point.

Commentary on the Essay

The strategy of this essay is to use details from the story to support the central idea that Minnie Wright is a round, developing character. Hence the essay illustrates one of the types in strategy 3 for organizing ideas about characters, described on page 189. Other plans of organization could also have been chosen, such as the qualities of acquiescence, fortitude, and potential for anger (strategy 1); the change in Minnie from submission to vengefulness (strategy 2); or the reported actions of Minnie's singing, knotting quilts, and sitting in the kitchen on the morning after the murder (another way of using strategy 3).

Because Minnie does not appear in the story, but is described only in the words of the major characters, the introductory paragraph deals with the way we learn about her. The essay thus highlights how Glaspell uses methods 1, 3, and 4 (see pp. 137–38) as the ways of rendering the story's main character, while omitting methods 2 and 5.

The body is developed through inferences made from details in the story, namely, Minnie's clothing (paragraph 2), her canary (paragraph 3), and her quilt (paragraphs 4 and 5). The last paragraph summarizes a number of these details, and it also considers how Minnie transcends the stock qualities of her role as a farm wife and gains roundness as a result of this outbreak.

As a study in composition, paragraph 3 demonstrates how a specific character trait, together with related details, can contribute to the essay's central idea. The trait is Minnie's love of music (shown by her canary). The connecting details, selected from study notes, are the loss of music in her life, her isolation, her lack of pretty clothing, the contemptibility of her husband, and her grief when putting the dead bird into the box. In short, the paragraph weaves together enough material to show the relationship between Minnie's trait of loving music and the crisis of her developing anger—a change that marks her as a round character.

SPECIAL WRITING TOPICS FOR STUDYING CHARACTER

1. Compare the ways in which actions (or speeches, or the comments of others) are used to bring out the character traits of Sarty of "Barn Burning," Jing-Mei's mother of "Two Kinds," and Paul of "Paul's Case."

2. Write a brief essay comparing the changes or developments of two major or *round* characters in stories included in this chapter. You might deal with issues such as what the characters are like at the beginning; what conflicts they confront, deal with, or avoid; what qualities are brought out that signal the changes or developments; and so on.

3. Compare the qualities and functions of two or more *flat* characters (e.g., Paul's father, Paul's teachers, one of the men in "A Jury of Her Peers" [including John Wright], the twins in "Barn Burning"). How do they bring out qualities of the major characters? What do you discover about their own character traits?

4. Topics for brief essays:

   a. Why does Abner Snopes burn barns? What qualities of character do these actions reveal? In the light of your assessment of his character, how might Abner justify to himself his role as an arsonist?

   b. Consider this proposition: *To good friends, we are round characters, but to minor acquaintances, we are flat.*

5. Using Sarty, Minnie Wright, and Jing-Mei as examples, describe the effects of circumstance on character. Under the rubric "circumstance" you may

consider elements such as education, family, economic and social status, wartime conditions, and geographic isolation.

6. Write a brief story about an important decision you have made (e.g., picking a school, beginning or leaving a job, declaring a major, starting or ending a friendship, etc.). Show how your own qualities of character (to the extent that you understand them), together with your own experiences, have gone into the decision. You may write more comfortably if you give yourself another name and describe your actions in the third person.

7. Using the card catalogue or computer catalogue in your library, find two critical studies of William Faulkner published by university presses. How fully do these studies describe and explain the characters living in Yoknapatawpha County, the imaginary place where Faulkner locates much of his fiction? Referring to these studies, write a short research-based essay on the characters and activities of the Snopes family.

5

Point of View: The Position or Stance of the Narrator or Speaker

The term **point of view** refers to the **speaker, narrator, persona,** or **voice** created by authors to tell stories, present arguments, and express attitudes and judgments. Point of view involves not only the speaker's physical position as an observer and recorder, but also the ways in which the speaker's social, political, and mental circumstances affect the narrative. For this reason, point of view is one of the most complex and subtle aspects of literary study.

Bear in mind that authors try not only to make their works vital and interesting but also to bring their *presentations* alive. The presentation is similar to a dramatic performance: In a play, the actors are always themselves, but in their roles they *impersonate* and temporarily *become* the characters they act. In fictional narratives, authors not only impersonate or pretend to be characters who do the talking, but they also *create* these characters. One such character is Sammy of Updike's "A & P"; another is the unnamed speaker of Hawthorne's "Young Goodman Brown." Updike's Sammy is visualized as a real person describing an important event in his own life. We read Sammy's words, and we know that Sammy is a distinct though fictional character; but because Updike is the author we know that he is the one putting the words in Sammy's mouth. Unlike Sammy, Hawthorne's speaker is telling a story about someone else and is uninvolved and distant from the action. Because of this distance the speaker is not easily separated from the author, even though the words we read may be different from those that Hawthorne himself might have chosen if speaking in his own person. In other words, the speaker is Hawthorne's authorial creation— his assumed voice which tells us the story of "Young Goodman Brown."

Because of the ramifications of creating a narrative voice, point of view can also be considered as the centralizing or guiding intelligence in a work— the mind that filters the fictional experience and presents only the most important details to create the maximum impact. Thus in Moore's "How to Become a Writer" we constantly hear the speaker's voice and are influenced not only by her narration but also by her attitudes, and we are similarly affected by the narrator, the mother, of Olsen's "I Stand Here Ironing." In other words, the way reality is presented in stories—the point of view or guiding intelligence created by the author—determines how we read, understand, and respond.

AN EXERCISE IN POINT OF VIEW: REPORTING AN ACCIDENT

As an exercise to show that point of view is derived from lifelike situations, let us imagine that there has been an auto accident: Two cars, driven by Alice and Bill, have collided, and the scene is as we see it in the drawing on page 196. How might this accident be reported by a number of people? What would Alice say? What would Bill say?

Now assume that Frank, who is Bill's best friend, and Mary, who knows neither Bill nor Alice, were witnesses. What might Frank say about who was responsible? What might Mary say? Additionally, assume that you are a reporter for a local newspaper and are sent to report on the accident. You know none of the people involved. How will your report differ from the other reports? Finally, to what degree are all the statements designed to persuade listeners and readers of the correctness of the details and claims made in the respective reports?

The likely differences in the various reports can be explained by reference to point of view. Obviously, because both Alice and Bill are deeply involved—each of them is a major participant or what may be called a *major mover*—they will probably arrange their words to make themselves seem blameless. Frank, because he is Bill's best friend, will likely report things in Bill's favor. Mary will favor neither Alice nor Bill, but let us assume that she did not look up to see the colliding cars until she heard the crash. Thus she did not see the accident happening but only the immediate aftereffects. Amid all this mixture of partial and impartial views of the action, to whom should we attribute the greatest reliability?

It seems clear that each person's report will have the "hidden agenda" of making herself or himself seem honest, objective, intelligent, impartial, and thorough. Thus, although both Alice and Bill may be truthful in their own eyes, it is unlikely that their reports will be reliable because they both have something to gain from avoiding responsibility for the accident. Also, Frank may not be reliable because he is Bill's friend and may report things to Bill's advantage. Mary could be reliable, but she did not see everything; therefore she is unreliable not because of motivation but rather because of her position as a witness. Most likely, *your* account as an impartial reporter will be the most reliable and objective of all, because your major interest is to learn all the details and report the truth accurately, with no concern about the personal interests of either Alice or Bill.

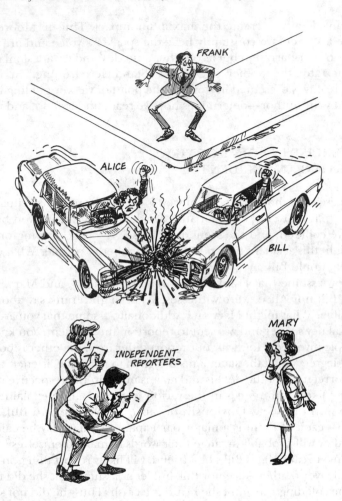

As you can see, the ramifications of describing actions are far-reaching, and the consideration of the various interests and situations is subtle. Indeed, of all the aspects of literature, point of view is the most complex because it is so much like life itself. On the one hand, point of view is intertwined with the many interests and wishes of humanity at large; on the other hand, it is linked to the enormous difficulty of uncovering and determining truth.

CONDITIONS THAT AFFECT POINT OF VIEW

As this exercise in observation and expression demonstrates, point of view depends on two major factors. First is *the physical situation of the narrator as an observer.* How close to the action is the speaker? Is she a major participant or no more than a witness, either close or distant? How much is he privileged to know? How accurate and complete are her reports? How do his characteristics emerge from the narration? What are her qualifications or limitations as an observer? Second is *the speaker's intellectual and emotional position:* How might the speaker gain or lose from what takes place in the story? Are the speaker's observations and words colored by these interests? Does she have any persuasive purpose beyond being a straightforward recorder or observer? What values does he impart to the action?

In a story, as in many poems using narrative, authors take into account all these subtleties. For example, Olsen's narrator in "I Stand Here Ironing" is a mother who regrets the adversities that beset her when her daughter was growing up. Joyce's speaker in "Araby" tells about his boyhood infatuation with a friend's sister, but does not understand the beauty and charm of his youthful feelings. For these reasons, the narrators reveal their involvement and concern in the events they describe. By contrast, the narrator of Jackson's "The Lottery" is not an involved observer. This narrator listens, sees, and reports but expresses no immediate concern about events in the unnamed country village. As readers, we need to determine how such differing modes of presentation determine the effects of these and all stories.

Distinguishing Point of View from Opinion

Sometimes people mistakenly equate point of view with *opinions* or *beliefs.* It must be stressed that point of view is not synonymous with ideas. Rather, point of view refers to a work's mode of narration, comprising narrator, language, audience, and perceptions of events and characters. Opinions and beliefs are thoughts and ideas that may have nothing to do with a narration. A discussion of point of view should therefore emphasize how the dramatic situation of a work actually *shapes* and *creates* the work. If ideas seem to be a particularly important matter in a story, your objective should not be to analyze and discuss the ideas *as ideas,* but rather to consider *whether and how these ideas affect what the narrator concludes and says about the story's actions and situations.*

KINDS OF POINTS OF VIEW

In your reading you will encounter a wide variety of points of view. To begin your analysis, first determine the work's grammatical voice. Then, study the ways in which the subject, characterization, dialogue, and form interact with the point of view.

First-Person Point of View

If the voice of the work is an "I," the author is using the **first-person point of view**—the impersonation of a fictional narrator or speaker who may be named or unnamed. In our hypothetical accident reports, both Alice and Bill are first-person speakers who are named. In stories, the narrators of Olsen's "I Stand Here Ironing" and Poe's "The Fall of the House of Usher" are unnamed first-person speakers. In Moore's "How to Become a Writer," Poe's "The Cask of Amontillado," and Updike's "A & P" the narrators are named.

First-person speakers might report events as though they have acquired their knowledge in a number of ways:

- What they themselves have done, said, heard, and thought (firsthand experience).
- What they have observed others do and say (firsthand witness).
- What others have said to them or otherwise communicated to them (secondhand testimony and hearsay).
- What they are able to infer or deduce from the information they have found (inferential information).
- What they are able to conjecture about how a character or characters might think and act, given their knowledge of a situation (conjectural, imaginative, or intuitive information).

Of all the points of view, the first person is the most independent of the author, because the first-person speaker may have a unique identity, with name, job, and economic and social position. Often, however, the author creates a more anonymous but still independent first-person speaker, as with the unnamed narrator of Poe's "The Fall of the House of Usher." There are also situations in which an "I" narrative is pluralized by "we" when the first person includes other characters. Such a first-person plural point of view lends reliability to the narrative, as in Hodgins's "The Concert Stages of Europe" and Zabytko's "Home Soil," because the characters included as "we" can be considered additional witnesses.

RELIABLE AND UNRELIABLE NARRATORS. When you encounter a first-person narrative (whether a story or poem), you need to determine the narrator's position and ability, prejudices or self-interest, and judgment of the readers or listeners. Most first-person speakers describing their own experiences are to be accepted as *reliable* and authoritative. But sometimes first-person speakers are *unreliable* because they may have interests or limitations that lead them to mislead, distort, or even lie. There is reason to question the entire truth of the narrator's confession in Zabytko's "Home Soil," for example, even though this speaker seems quite honest in most of his narration. A more clearly unreliable narrator is the speaker of Gilman's "Yellow Wallpaper," for her descriptions become increasingly delusional as the story progresses. Whether first-person speakers are reliable or unreliable, however, they are one of the means by which authors confer an authentic, lifelike aura to their works.

Second-Person Point of View

The **second-person point of view,** the least common of the points of view, offers the writer two major possibilities. In the first, a narrator (almost necessarily a first-person speaker) tells a present and involved listener what he or she has done and said at a past time. The actions might be a simple retelling of events, as when a parent tells an older child about something the child did during infancy, or when a doctor tells a patient with amnesia about events before the causative injury. The actions might also be subject to dispute and interpretation, as when a prosecuting attorney describes a crime for which a defendant is on trial or when a spouse lists grievances against an alienated spouse in a custody or divorce case.

The second possibility is more complex. Some narrators seem to be addressing a "you" but are instead referring mainly to themselves—and to listeners only tangentially—in preference to an "I." In addition, some narrators follow the usage—common in colloquial speech—of the indefinite "you," as in Updike's "A & P." In this kind of narration, speakers use *you* to refer not to a specific listener but rather to anyone at all—in this way avoiding the more formal use of words like *one, a person,* or *people.* (Incidentally, the selection of *you* is non–gender-specific, because it eliminates the need for pronouns such as *he, she,* or *he or she.*). A clever variation of the "you" point of view is seen in Lorrie Moore's "How to Become a Writer" (p. 219), in which the narrator is apparently describing her own experiences under the guise of giving directions to a listener interested in developing a writing career.

Third-Person Point of View

If events in the work are described in the third person (*he, she, it, they*), the author is using the **third-person point of view.** It is not always easy to characterize the voice in this point of view. Sometimes the speaker may use an "I" (as in Laurence's "The Loons") and be seemingly identical with the author, but at other times the author may create a distinct **authorial voice,** as in Faulkner's "Barn Burning." There are three variants of the third-person point of view: *dramatic* or *objective, omniscient,* and *limited omniscient.*

DRAMATIC OR OBJECTIVE. The most direct presentation of action and dialogue is the **dramatic** or **objective point of view** (also called **third-person objective**). It is the basic method of rendering action and speech, and all the points of view use it. The narrator of the dramatic point of view is an unidentified speaker who reports things in a way that is analogous to a hovering or tracking motion-picture camera or to what some critics have called "a fly on the wall (or tree)." Somehow, the narrator is always on the spot—within rooms, forests, village squares, or moving vehicles or even in outer space—to tell us what is happening and what is being said.

The dramatic presentation is limited only to what is said and what happens. There is no attempt to draw conclusions or make interpretations, because the premise of the dramatic point of view is that readers, like a jury, can form their own interpretations if they are given the right evidence. Thus Jackson's "The Lottery"—a powerful example of the dramatic point of view—is an objective story about a bizarre small-town lottery. We the readers draw many conclusions about this story (such as that people are tradition bound, insensitive, cruel, and so on), but because of the dramatic point of view, Jackson does not *state* any of these conclusions for us.

OMNISCIENT.   The third-person point of view is **omniscient** (all-knowing) when the speaker not only presents action and dialogue, but also is able to report what goes on in the minds of the characters. In our everyday real world we can never know *absolutely* what other people are thinking. However, we always make assumptions about the thoughts of others, and these assumptions are the basis of the omniscient point of view. Authors use it freely but judiciously to explain responses, thoughts, feelings, and plans—an additional dimension that aids in the development of character. For example, in Maupassant's "The Necklace," the speaker assumes omniscience to explain the responses and thoughts of the major character and also, though to a lesser degree, of her husband.

LIMITED, OR LIMITED OMNISCIENT.   More common than the omniscient point of view is the *limited third person* or **limited omniscient third-person point of view,** in which the author confines or *limits* the narration to the actions and thoughts of a major character. In our accident case, Frank, being Bill's friend, would be sympathetic to Bill; thus his report of the collision would likely be third-person limited, with Bill as the center of interest. Depending on whether a narration focuses on action or motivation, the narrative may explore the mentalities of the characters either lightly or in depth. The name given to the central figure on whom the third-person omniscient point of view is focused is the **point-of-view character.** Thus, Miss Brill in "Miss Brill," Peyton Farquhar in "An Occurrence at Owl Creek Bridge," and Goodman Brown in "Young Goodman Brown" are all point-of-view characters. Virtually everything in these stories is there because the point-of-view characters see it, hear it, respond to it, think about it, imagine it entirely, do it or share in it, try to control it, or are controlled by it.

MINGLING POINTS OF VIEW

In some works, authors mingle points of view in order to imitate reality. For example, many first-person narrators use various types of the third-person point of view during much of their narration. Authors may also vary points of view to sustain interest, create suspense, or put the burden of response entirely upon readers. For example, Mansfield in "Miss Brill" interrupts the limited omniscient focus on Miss Brill's thoughts and reactions immediately after she has been insulted by the young couple on the bench. The last paragraphs are objective until the last sentence, when the limited omniscient point of view is resumed.

The result is that Miss Brill is made totally alone in her grief, cut off; readers can no longer share her sorrow as they earlier shared her observations about the characters in the park. A similar shift occurs at the end of Hawthorne's "Young Goodman Brown," where the narrator objectively and almost brutally summarizes Brown's morose and loveless life after his nightmare about evil.

POINT OF VIEW AND VERB TENSE

Usually *point of view* refers to the ways narrators and speakers perceive and report actions and speeches, but in the broadest sense, point of view may be considered as a total way of rendering truth, and for this reason the *tense* chosen by the narrators is important. Most narratives rely on the past tense: The actions happened in the past, and they are now over. The introduction of dialogue, however, even in a past-tense narration, is a dramatic means of bringing the story into the present. The dialogue concluding Maupassant's "The Necklace," for example, emphasizes the immediacy of Mathilde's problems. In addition, the narrator of a past-tense narrative may introduce present-tense commentary during the narration—a strong means of signifying the importance of past events. Such narrators occur in Olsen's "I Stand Here Ironing," in which the past tense story is begun and ended in the present tense, and Updike's "A & P," in which Sammy the narrator shifts freely from past tense to present tense both to express past action and also to make general comments. In addition, as noted in Chapter 8, the narrators of *parables* and *fables* use past-tense narratives as vehicles for teaching current lessons in philosophy and religion.

In recent years, many writers have used the present tense as their principal time reference. With the present tense, the narrative story or poem is rendered as a virtual drama that is unfolded moment by moment. In Whitecloud's "Blue Winds Dancing," for instance, Whitecloud employs the present tense to emphasize the immediate experience of the narrator's return home. Williams uses the present tense in Williams's "Taking Care" as a means not only of emphasizing the immediacy of the main character's situation, but also of demonstrating his future challenges.

Some writers intermingle tenses to show how time itself may be merged with the human consciousness and to show the fusion of past, present, and future within a character's mind. For example, toward the end of Bierce's "An Occurrence at Owl Creek Bridge" the past tense narration shifts into the present tense to demonstrate the vividness of the main character's perception that he had actually cheated the hangman.

GUIDELINES FOR POINTS OF VIEW

The following guidelines summarize and further classify the types of points of view. Use them to distinguish differences and shades of variation in stories and poems.

1. **First person (*I, my, me; we, our, us*).** First-person speakers are involved to at least some degree in the actions of the work. Such narrators may have (1) complete understanding, (2) partial or incorrect understanding, (3) no understanding at all, or (4) complete understanding with the motive to

mislead or lie. Although narrators 2 through 4 usually are *reliable* and tell the truth, they may also sometimes be *unreliable*.

a.   *Major participant*

   i.   Tells his or her own story and thoughts as a major mover.

   ii. Tells a story about others and also about herself or himself as one of the major movers.

   iii. Tells a story mainly about others, and about himself or herself only tangentially.

b.   *Minor participant* tells a story about events experienced and witnessed.

c.   *Nonparticipating but identifiable speaker* learns about events in other ways (e.g., listening to participants, examining documents, hearing news reports, imagining what might have occurred). The narrative of such a speaker is a combination of fact and conjectural reconstruction.

2. **Second person** *(you)*. Occurs (1) when the speaker (e.g., parent, psychologist) knows more about a character's actions than the character himself or herself; or (2) when the speaker (e.g., lawyer, spouse, friend, sports umpire) is explaining to another person (the "you") that person's disputable actions and statements. The speaker may also use "you" to mean (3) himself or herself or (4) anyone at all.

3. **Third person** *(she, he, it, they)*. The speaker is outside the action and is mainly a reporter of actions and speeches. Some speakers may have unique and distinguishing traits even though no separate identity is claimed for them ("the unnamed third-person narrator"). Other third-person speakers who are not separately identifiable may represent the words and views of the authors themselves ("the authorial voice").

a.   *Dramatic or third-person objective.* The narrator reports only what can be seen and heard. The thoughts of characters are included only if they are spoken or written (dialogue, reported or overheard conversation, letters, reports, etc.).

b.   *Omniscient.* The omniscient speaker sees all, reports all, knows all, and explains the inner workings of the minds of any or all characters (when necessary).

c.   *Limited, or limited omniscient.* The focus is on the actions, responses, thoughts, and feelings of a single major character. The narration may involve primarily what the character does, and it may also probe deeply within the consciousness of the character.

 STORIES FOR STUDY

AMBROSE BIERCE   (1842—1914?)

Bierce was a native of Ohio, the youngest of nine children in the highly religious family of a poor farmer. When the Civil War began he enlisted in the Union army as a drummer boy and rose to the rank of major by the war's end. After the war he went to San Francisco to begin a career in journalism. At various times he reported, edited, and wrote reviews for papers such as the San Francisco Examiner *and the* San Francisco News-Letter. *After he married he and his wife spent five years in England, but eventually she left him and their two children died—events that had an embittering effect on him. In 1913 he traveled to Mexico, and nothing further is known about him; he is presumed to have died in revolutionary fighting there in 1914. Bierce published his first story in 1871 and later published two volumes of stories:* In the Midst of Life *(1892, originally published in 1891 as* Tales of Soldiers and Civilians, *which included "An Occurrence at Owl Creek Bridge"), and* Can Such Things Be? *(1893). He is perhaps best known for his sometimes cynical* The Devil's Dictionary *(1911). He favored the short story as a form over the novel on much the same grounds as Poe, namely that the story could be designed to produce a single effect. He believed that fiction should be realistic and should build to concluding twists and surprises—goals that are seen in "An Occurrence at Owl Creek Bridge." His complete works, which he edited himself, appeared in twelve volumes from 1909 to 1912.*

An Occurrence at Owl Creek Bridge _____ *1891*

A man stood upon a railroad bridge in northern Alabama, looking down into the swift water twenty feet below. The man's hands were behind his back, the wrists bound with a cord. A rope closely encircled his neck. It was attached to a stout cross-timber above his head and the slack fell to the level of his knees. Some loose boards laid upon the sleepers supporting the metals of the railway supplied a footing for him and his executioners—two private soldiers of the Federal army, directed by a sergeant who in civil life may have been a deputy sheriff. At a short remove upon the same temporary platform was an officer in the uniform of his rank, armed. He was a captain. A sentinel at each end of the bridge stood with his rifle in the position known as "support," that is to say, vertical in front of the left shoulder, the hammer resting on the forearm thrown straight across the chest—a formal and unnatural position, enforcing an erect carriage of the body. It did not appear to be the duty of these two men to know what was occurring at the center of the bridge; they merely blockaded the two ends of the foot planking that traversed it.

Beyond one of the sentinels nobody was in sight; the railroad ran straight away into a forest for a hundred yards, then, curving, was lost to view. Doubtless there was an outpost farther along. The other bank of the stream was open ground—a gentle acclivity topped with a stockade of vertical tree trunks, loopholed for rifles, with a single embrasure through which protruded the muzzle of a brass cannon commanding the bridge. Midway of the slope between the bridge and fort were the spectators—a single company of infantry in line, at "parade rest," the butts of the rifles on the ground, the barrels inclining slightly backward against the right shoulder, the hands crossed upon the stock. A lieutenant stood at the right of the line, the point of his sword upon the ground, his left hand resting upon his right. Excepting the group of four at the center of the bridge, not a man moved. The company faced the bridge, staring stonily, motionless. The sentinels, facing the banks of the stream, might have been statues to adorn the bridge. The captain stood with folded arms, silent, observing the work of his subordinates, but making no sign. Death is a dignitary who when he comes announced is to be received with formal manifestations of respect, even by those most familiar with him. In the code of military etiquette silence and fixity are forms of deference.

The man who was engaged in being hanged was apparently about thirty-five years of age. He was a civilian, if one might judge from his habit, which was that of a planter. His features were good—a straight nose, firm mouth, broad forehead, from which his long, dark hair was combed straight back, falling behind his ears to the collar of his well-fitting frock coat. He wore a mustache and pointed beard, but no whiskers; his eyes were large and dark gray, and had a kindly expression which one would hardly have expected in one whose neck was in the hemp. Evidently this was no vulgar assassin. The liberal military code makes provision for hanging many kinds of persons, and gentlemen are not excluded.

The preparations being complete, the two private soldiers stepped aside and each drew away the plank upon which he had been standing. The sergeant turned to the captain, saluted and placed himself immediately behind that officer, who in turn moved apart one pace. These movements left the condemned man and the sergeant standing on the two ends of the same plank, which spanned three of the cross-ties of the bridge. The end upon which the civilian stood almost, but not quite, reached a fourth. This plank had been held in place by the weight of the captain; it was now held by that of the sergeant. At a signal from the former the latter would step aside, the plank would tilt and the condemned man go down between two ties. The arrangement commended itself to his judgment as simple and effective. His face had not been covered nor his eyes bandaged. He looked a moment at his "unsteadfast footing," then let his gaze wander to the swirling water of the stream racing madly beneath his feet. A piece of dancing driftwood caught his attention and his eyes followed it down the current. How slowly it appeared to move! What a sluggish stream!

He closed his eyes in order to fix his last thoughts upon his wife and children. The water, touched to gold by the early sun, the brooding mists under the banks at some distance down the stream, the fort, the soldiers, the piece of driftwood—all had distracted him. And now he became conscious of a new disturbance. Striking through the thought of his dear ones was a sound which he could neither ignore nor understand, a sharp, distinct, metallic percussion like the stroke of a blacksmith's hammer upon the anvil; it had the same ringing quality. He wondered what it was, and whether immeasurably distant or near by—it seemed both. Its recurrence was regular, but as slow as the tolling of a death knell. He awaited each stroke with impatience and—he knew not why—apprehension. The intervals of silence grew progressively longer; the delays became maddening. With their greater infrequency the sounds increased in strength and sharpness. They hurt his ear like the thrust of a knife; he feared he would shriek. What he heard was the ticking of his watch.

He unclosed his eyes and saw again the water below him. "If I could free my hands," he thought, "I might throw off the noose and spring into the stream. By diving I could evade the bullets and, swimming vigorously, reach the bank, take to the woods and get away home. My home, thank God, is as yet outside their lines; my wife and little ones are still beyond the invader's farthest advance."

As these thoughts, which have here to be set down in words, were flashed into the doomed man's brain rather than evolved from it the captain nodded to the sergeant. The sergeant stepped aside.

5

II

Peyton Farquhar was a well-to-do planter, of an old and highly respected Alabama family. Being a slave owner and like other slave owners a politician he was naturally an original secessionist and ardently devoted to the Southern cause. Circumstances of an imperious nature, which it is unnecessary to relate here, had prevented him from taking service with the gallant army that had fought the disastrous campaigns ending with the fall of Corinth,° and he chafed under the inglorious restraint, longing for the release of his energies, the larger life of the soldier, the opportunity for distinction. That opportunity, he felt, would come, as it comes to all in war time. Meanwhile he did what he could. No service was too humble for him to perform in aid of the South, no adventure too perilous for him to undertake if consistent with the character of a civilian who was at heart a soldier, and who in good faith and without too much qualification assented to at least a part of the frankly villainous dictum that all is fair in love and war.

One evening while Farquhar and his wife were sitting on a rustic bench near the entrance to his grounds, a gray-clad soldier rode up to the gate and asked for a drink of water. Mrs. Farquhar was only too happy to serve him with her own white hands. While she was fetching the water her husband approached the dusty horseman and inquired eagerly for news from the front.

"The Yanks are repairing the railroads," said the man, "and are getting ready for   10
another advance. They have reached the Owl Creek bridge, put it in order and built a stockade on the north bank. The commandant has issued an order, which is posted everywhere, declaring that any civilian caught interfering with the railroad, its bridges, tunnels or trains will be summarily hanged. I saw the order."

"How far is it to the Owl Creek bridge?" Farquhar asked.

"About thirty miles."

"Is there no force on this side of the creek?"

"Only a picket post half a mile out, on the railroad, and a single sentinel at this end of the bridge."

"Suppose a man—a civilian and student of hanging—should elude the picket post   15
and perhaps get the better of the sentinel," said Farquhar, smiling, "what could he accomplish?"

The soldier reflected. "I was there a month ago," he replied. "I observed that the flood of last winter had lodged a great quantity of driftwood against the wooden pier at this end of the bridge. It is now dry and would burn like tow."

The lady had now brought the water, which the soldier drank. He thanked her ceremoniously, bowed to her husband and rode away. An hour later, after nightfall, he repassed the plantation, going northward in the direction from which he had come. He was a Federal scout.

III

As Peyton Farquhar fell straight downward through the bridge he lost consciousness and was as one already dead. From this state he was awakened—ages later, it seemed to him—by the pain of a sharp pressure upon his throat, followed by a sense of suffocation. Keen, poignant agonies seemed to shoot from his neck downward through every

---

Corinth: In the northeast corner of Mississippi, near the Alabama state line, Corinth was the site of a battle in 1862 won by the Union army.

fiber of his body and limbs. These pains appeared to flash along well-defined lines of ramification and to beat with an inconceivably rapid periodicity. They seemed like streams of pulsating fire heating him to an intolerable temperature. As to his head, he was conscious of nothing but a feeling of fulness—of congestion. These sensations were unaccompanied by thought. The intellectual part of his nature was already effaced; he had power only to feel, and feeling was torment. He was conscious of motion. Encompassed in a luminous cloud, of which he was now merely the fiery heart, without material substance, he swung through unthinkable arcs of oscillation, like a vast pendulum. Then all at once, with terrible suddenness, the light about him shot upward with the noise of a loud plash; a frightful roaring was in his ears, and all was cold and dark. The power of thought was restored; he knew that the rope had broken and he had fallen into the stream. There was no additional strangulation; the noose about his neck was already suffocating him and kept the water from his lungs. To die of hanging at the bottom of a river!—the idea seemed to him ludicrous. He opened his eyes in the darkness and saw above him a gleam of light, but how distant, how inaccessible! He was still sinking, for the light became fainter and fainter until it was a mere glimmer. Then it began to grow and brighten, and he knew that he was rising toward the surface—knew it with reluctance, for he was now very comfortable. "To be hanged and drowned," he thought, "that is not so bad; but I do not wish to be shot. No; I will not be shot; that is not fair."

He was not conscious of an effort, but a sharp pain in his wrist apprised him that he was trying to free his hands. He gave the struggle his attention, as an idler might observe the feat of a juggler, without interest in the outcome. What splendid effort—what magnificent, what superhuman strength! Ah, that was a fine endeavor! Bravo! The cord fell away; his arms parted and floated upward; the hands dimly seen on each side in the growing light. He watched them with a new interest as first one and then the other pounced upon the noose at his neck. They tore it away and thrust it fiercely aside, its undulations resembling those of a water snake. "Put it back, put it back!" He thought he shouted these words to his hands, for the undoing of the noose had been succeeded by the direst pang that he had yet experienced. His neck ached horribly; his brain was on fire; his heart, which had been fluttering faintly, gave a great leap, trying to force itself out at his mouth. His whole body was racked and wrenched with an insupportable anguish! But his disobedient hands gave no heed to the command. They beat the water vigorously with quick, downward strokes, forcing him to the surface. He felt his head emerge; his eyes were blinded by the sunlight; his chest expanded convulsively, and with a supreme and crowning agony his lungs engulfed a great draught of air, which instantly he expelled in a shriek!

He was now in full possession of his physical senses. They were indeed, preternaturally keen and alert. Something in the awful disturbance of his organic system had so exalted and refined them that they made record of things never before perceived. He felt the ripples upon his face and heard their separate sounds as they struck. He looked at the forest on the bank of the stream, saw the individual trees, the leaves and the veining of each leaf—saw the very insects upon them: the locusts, the brilliant-bodied flies, the gray spiders stretching their webs from twig to twig. He noted the prismatic colors in all the dewdrops upon a million blades of grass. The humming of the gnats that danced above the eddies of the stream, the beating of the dragon flies' wings, the strokes of the water-spiders' legs, like oars which had lifted their boat—all these made audible music. A fish slid along beneath his eyes and he heard the rush of its body parting the water.

He had come to the surface facing down the stream; in a moment the visible world seemed to wheel slowly round, himself the pivotal point, and he saw the bridge, the fort, the soldiers upon the bridge, the captain, the sergeant, the two privates, his executioners. They were in silhouette against the blue sky. They shouted and gesticulated, pointing at him. The captain had drawn his pistol, but did not fire; the others were unarmed. Their movements were grotesque and horrible, their forms gigantic.

Suddenly he heard a sharp report and something struck the water smartly within a few inches of his head, spattering his face with spray. He heard a second report, and saw one of the sentinels with his rifle at his shoulder, a light cloud of blue smoke rising from the muzzle. The man in the water saw the eye of the man on the bridge gazing into his own through the sights of the rifle. He observed that it was a gray eye and remembered having read that gray eyes were keenest, and that all famous marksmen had them. Nevertheless, this one had missed.

A counter-swirl had caught Farquhar and turned him half round; he was again looking into the forest on the bank opposite the fort. The sound of a clear, high voice in a monotonous singsong now rang out behind him and came across the water with a distinctness that pierced and subdued all other sounds, even the beating of the ripples in his ears. Although no soldier, he had frequented camps enough to know the dread significance of that deliberate, drawling, aspirated chant; the lieutenant on shore was taking a part in the morning's work. How coldly and pitilessly—with what an even, calm intonation, presaging, and enforcing tranquility in the men—with what accurately measured intervals fell those cruel words:

"Attention, company! . . . Shoulder arms! . . . Ready! . . . Aim! . . . Fire!"

Farquhar dived—dived as deeply as he could. The water roared in his ears like the voice of Niagara, yet he heard the dulled thunder of the volley and, rising again toward the surface, met shining bits of metal, singularly flattened, oscillating slowly downward. Some of them touched him on the face and hands, then fell away, continuing their descent. One lodged between his collar and neck; it was uncomfortably warm and he snatched it out.

As he rose to the surface, gasping for breath, he saw that he had been a long time under water; he was perceptibly farther down stream—nearer to safety. The soldiers had almost finished reloading; the metal ramrods flashed all at once in the sunshine as they were drawn from the barrels, turned in the air, and thrust into their sockets. The two sentinels fired again, independently and ineffectually.

The hunted man saw all this over his shoulder; he was now swimming vigorously with the current. His brain was as energetic as his arms and legs; he thought with the rapidity of lightning.

"The officer," he reasoned, "will not make that martinet's error a second time. It is as easy to dodge a volley as a single shot. He has probably already given the command to fire at will. God help me, I cannot dodge them all!"

An appalling plash within two yards of him was followed by a loud, rushing sound, *diminuendo,* which seemed to travel back through the air to the fort and died in an explosion which stirred the very river to its deeps! A rising sheet of water curved over him, fell down upon him, blinded him, strangled him! The cannon had taken a hand in the game. As he shook his head free from the commotion of the smitten water he heard

25

the deflected shot humming through the air ahead, and in an instant it was cracking and smashing the branches in the forest beyond.

"They will not do that again," he thought; "the next time they will use a charge of grape. I must keep my eye upon the gun; the smoke will apprise me—the report arrives too late; it lags behind the missile. That is a good gun."

Suddenly he felt himself whirled round and round—spinning like a top. The water, the banks, the forests, the now distant bridge, fort and men—all were commingled and blurred. Objects were represented by their colors only; circular horizontal streaks of color—that was all he saw. He had been caught in a vortex and was being whirled on with a velocity of advance and gyration that made him giddy and sick. In a few moments he was flung upon the gravel at the foot of the left bank of the stream— the southern bank—and behind a projecting point which concealed him from his enemies. The sudden arrest of his motion, the abrasion of one of his hands on the gravel, restored him, and he wept with delight. He dug his fingers into the sand, threw it over himself in handfuls and audibly blessed it. It looked like diamonds, rubies, emeralds; he could think of nothing beautiful which it did not resemble. The trees upon the bank were giant garden plants; he noted a definite order in their arrangement, inhaled the fragrance of their blooms. A strange, roseate light shone through the spaces among their trunks and the wind made in their branches the music of Æolian harps. He had no wish to perfect his escape—was content to remain in that enchanting spot until retaken.

A whiz and rattle of grapeshot among the branches high above his head roused him from his dream. The baffled cannoneer had fired him a random farewell. He sprang to his feet, rushed up the sloping bank, and plunged into the forest.

All that day he traveled, laying his course by the rounding sun. The forest seemed interminable; nowhere did he discover a break in it, not even a woodman's road. He had not known that he lived in so wild a region. There was something uncanny in the revelation.

By nightfall he was fatigued, footsore, famishing. The thought of his wife and children urged him on. At last he found a road which led him in what he knew to be the right direction. It was as wide and straight as a city street, yet it seem untraveled. No fields bordered it, no dwelling anywhere. Not so much as the barking of a dog suggested human habitation. The black bodies of the trees formed a straight wall on both sides, terminating on the horizon in a point, like a diagram in a lesson in perspective. Overhead, as he looked up through this rift in the wood, shone great golden stars looking unfamiliar and grouped in strange constellations. He was sure they were arranged in some order which had a secret and malign significance. The wood on either side was full of singular noises, among which—once, twice, and again—he distinctly heard whispers in an unknown tongue.

His neck was in pain and lifting his hand to it found it horribly swollen. He knew that it had a circle of black where the rope had bruised it. His eyes felt congested; he could no longer close them. His tongue was swollen with thirst; he relieved its fever by thrusting it forward from between his teeth into the cold air. How softly the turf had carpeted the untraveled avenue—he could no longer feel the roadway beneath his feet!

Doubtless, despite his suffering, he had fallen asleep while walking, for now he sees another scene—perhaps he has merely recovered from a delirium. He stands at the gate of his own home. All is as he left it, and all bright and beautiful in the morning sunshine. He must have traveled the entire night. As he pushes open the gate and passes up the wide white walk, he sees a flutter of female garments; his wife, looking fresh and cool and sweet, steps down from the veranda to meet him. At the bottom of the steps she stands waiting, with a smile of ineffable joy, an attitude of matchless grace and dignity. Ah, how beautiful she is! He springs forward with extended arms. As he is about to clasp her he feels a stunning blow upon the back of the neck; a blinding white light blazes all about him with a sound like the shock of a cannon—then all is darkness and silence!

Peyton Farquhar was dead; his body, with a broken neck, swung gently from side to side beneath the timbers of the Owl Creek bridge.

QUESTIONS

1. What is the situation in the story? What did Farquhar do to deserve his execution?

2. Describe the various shifts in the story's point of view, particularly as indicated in paragraphs 5 and 37. How does Bierce make you aware of Farquhar's heightened consciousness?

3. According to Farquhar's perception of time, how long does it take him to get home after his escape (see paragraphs 33 and 36)?

4. What evidence can you find to indicate that Farquhar is experiencing great pain, despite his feelings that he is escaping?

5. What is the effect of the shift into the present tense in paragraph 36?

SHIRLEY JACKSON   (1919–1965)

Jackson was a native of California. She graduated from Syracuse University in New York and lived much of her life in Vermont. Although her life was short, she was a successful writer of novels, short stories, biographies, and children's fiction. Her stories often depict unusual, unreal, or bizarre events in common settings, of which "The Lottery" is a major example. She wrote the story in only two hours and submitted it to the New Yorker *without major revisions. When it was published many readers raised questions about how to interpret the conclusion. Jackson steadfastly refused to explain, leaving readers to decide for themselves.*

The Lottery ———————————————————— *1948*

The morning of June 27th was clear and sunny, with the fresh warmth of a full summer day; the flowers were blossoming profusely and the grass was richly green. The people of the village began to gather in the square, between the post office and the bank, around ten o'clock; in some towns there were so many people that the lottery took two days and had to be started on June 26th, but in this village, where there were only about three hundred people, the whole lottery took less than two hours, so it could begin at ten o'clock in the morning and still be through in time to allow the villagers to get home for noon dinner.

The children assembled first, of course. School was recently over for the summer, and the feeling of liberty sat uneasily on most of them; they tended to gather together quietly for a while before they broke into boisterous play, and their talk was still of the classroom and the teacher, of books and reprimands. Bobby Martin had already stuffed his pockets full of stones, and the other boys soon followed his example, selecting the smoothest and roundest stones; Bobby and Harry Jones and Dickie Delacroix—the villagers pronounced this name "Dellacroy"—eventually made a great pile of stones in one corner of the square and guarded it against the raids of the other boys. The girls stood aside, talking among themselves, looking over their shoulders at the boys, and the very small children rolled in the dust or clung to the hands of their older brothers or sisters.

Soon the men began to gather, surveying their own children, speaking of planting and rain, tractors and taxes. They stood together, away from the pile of stones in the corner, and their jokes were quiet and they smiled rather than laughed. The women, wearing faded house dresses and sweaters, came shortly after their menfolk. They greeted one another and exchanged bits of gossip as they went to join their husbands. Soon the women, standing by their husbands, began to call to their children, and the children came reluctantly, having to be called four or five times. Bobby Martin ducked under his mother's grasping hand and ran, laughing, back to the pile of stones. His father spoke up sharply, and Bobby came quickly and took his place between his father and his oldest brother.

The lottery was conducted—as were the square dances, the teen-age club, the Halloween program—by Mr. Summers, who had time and energy to devote to civic activities. He was a round-faced, jovial man and he ran the coal business, and people were sorry for him, because he had no children and his wife was a scold. When he arrived in the square, carrying the black wooden box, there was a murmur of conversation among the villagers, and he waved and called, "Little late today, folks." The postmaster, Mr. Graves, followed him, carrying a three-legged stool, and the stool was put in the center of the square and Mr. Summers set the black box down on it. The villagers kept their distance, leaving a space between themselves and the stool, and when Mr. Summers said, "Some of you fellows want to give me a hand?" there was a hesitation before two men, Mr. Martin and his oldest son, Baxter, came forward to hold the box steady on the stool while Mr. Summers stirred up the papers inside it.

The original paraphernalia for the lottery had been lost long ago, and the black box now resting on the stool had been put into use even before Old Man Warner, the oldest man in town, was born. Mr. Summers spoke frequently to the villagers about making a new box, but no one liked to upset even as much tradition as was represented by the black box. There was a story that the present box had been made with some pieces of the box that had preceded it, the one that had been constructed when the first people settled down to make a village here. Every year, after the lottery, Mr. Summers began talking again about a new box, but every year the subject was allowed to fade off without anything's being done. The black box grew shabbier each year; by now it was no longer completely black but splintered badly along one side to show the original wood color, and in some places faded or stained.

Mr. Martin and his oldest son, Baxter, held the black box securely on the stool until Mr. Summers had stirred the papers thoroughly with his hand. Because so much of the ritual had been forgotten or discarded, Mr. Summers had been successful in having slips of paper substituted for the chips of wood that had been used for generations. Chips of wood, Mr. Summers had argued, had been all very well when the village was tiny, but now that the population was more than three hundred and likely to keep on growing, it was necessary to use something that would fit more easily into the black box. The night before the lottery, Mr. Summers and Mr. Graves made up the slips of paper and put them in the box, and it was then taken to the safe of Mr. Summers' coal company and locked up until Mr. Summers was ready to take it to the square next morning. The rest of the year, the box was put away, sometimes one place, sometimes another; it had spent one year in Mr. Graves's barn and another year underfoot in the post office, and sometimes it was set on a shelf in the Martin grocery and left there.

There was a great deal of fussing to be done before Mr. Summers declared the lottery open. There were the lists to make up—of heads of families, heads of households in each family, members of each household in each family. There was the proper swearing-in of Mr. Summers by the postmaster, as the official of the lottery; at one time, some people remembered, there had been a recital of some sort, performed by the official of the lottery, a perfunctory, tuneless chant that had been rattled off duly each year; some people believed that the official of the lottery used to stand just so when he said or sang it, others believed that he was supposed to walk among the people, but years and years ago this part of the ritual had been allowed to lapse. There had been, also, a ritual salute, which the official of the lottery had had to use in addressing each person who came up to draw from the box, but this also had changed with time, until now it was felt necessary only for the official to speak to each person approaching. Mr. Summers was very good at all this; in his clean white shirt and blue jeans, with one hand resting carelessly on the black box, he seemed very proper and important as he talked interminably to Mr. Graves and the Martins.

Just as Mr. Summers finally left off talking and turned to the assembled villagers, Mrs. Hutchinson came hurriedly along the path to the square, her sweater thrown over her shoulders, and slid into place in the back of the crowd. "Clean forgot what day it was," she said to Mrs. Delacroix, who stood next to her, and they both laughed softly. "Thought my old man was out back stacking wood," Mrs. Hutchinson went on, "and then I looked out the window and the kids was gone, and then I remembered it was the twenty-seventh and came a-running." She dried her hands on her apron, and Mrs. Delacroix said, "You're in time, though. They're still talking away up there."

Mrs. Hutchinson craned her neck to see through the crowd and found her husband and children standing near the front. She tapped Mrs. Delacroix on the arm as a farewell and began to make her way through the crowd. The people separated good-humoredly to let her through; two or three people said, in voices just loud enough to be heard across the crowd, "Here comes your Missus, Hutchinson," and "Bill, she made it after all." Mrs. Hutchinson reached her husband, and Mr. Summers, who had been waiting, said cheerfully, "Thought we were going to have to get on without you, Tessie." Mrs. Hutchinson said, grinning, "Wouldn't have me leave m'dishes in the sink, now, would you, Joe?," and soft laughter ran through the crowd as the people stirred back into position after Mrs. Hutchinson's arrival.

"Well, now," Mr. Summers said soberly, "guess we better get started, get this over with, so's we can go back to work. Anybody ain't here?"   10

"Dunbar," several people said. "Dunbar, Dunbar."

Mr. Summers consulted his list. "Clyde Dunbar," he said. "That's right. He's broke his leg, hasn't he? Who's drawing for him?"

"Me, I guess," a woman said, and Mr. Summers turned to look at her. "Wife draws for her husband," Mr. Summers said. "Don't you have a grown boy to do it for you, Janey?" Although Mr. Summers and everyone else in the village knew the answer perfectly well, it was the business of the official of the lottery to ask such questions formally. Mr. Summers waited with an expression of polite interest while Mrs. Dunbar answered.

"Horace's not but sixteen yet," Mrs. Dunbar said regretfully. "Guess I gotta fill in for the old man this year."

"Right," Mr. Summers said. He made a note on the list he was holding. Then he asked, "Watson boy drawing this year?"

A tall boy in the crowd raised his hand. "Here," he said. "I'm drawing for m'mother and me." He blinked his eyes nervously and ducked his head as several voices in the crowd said things like "Good fellow, Jack," and "Glad to see your mother's got a man to do it."

"Well," Mr. Summers said, "guess that's everyone. Old Man Warner make it?"

"Here," a voice said, and Mr. Summers nodded.

A sudden hush fell on the crowd as Mr. Summers cleared his throat and looked at the list. "All ready?" he called. "Now, I'll read the names—heads of families first—and the men come up and take a paper out of the box. Keep the paper folded in your hand without looking at it until everyone has had a turn. Everything clear?"

The people had done it so many times that they only half listened to the directions; most of them were quiet, wetting their lips, not looking around. Then Mr. Summers raised one hand high and said, "Adams." A man disengaged himself from the crowd and came forward. "Hi, Steve," Mr. Summers said, and Mr. Adams said, "Hi, Joe." They grinned at one another humorlessly and nervously. Then Mr. Adams reached into the black box and took out a folded paper. He held it firmly by one corner as he turned and went hastily back to his place in the crowd, where he stood a little apart from his family, not looking down at his hand.

"Allen," Mr. Summers said. "Anderson. . . . Bentham."

"Seems like there's no time at all between lotteries any more," Mrs. Delacroix said to Mrs. Graves in the back row. "Seems like we got through with the last one only last week."

"Time sure goes fast," Mrs. Graves said.

"Clark. . . . Delacroix."

"There goes my old man," Mrs. Delacroix said. She held her breath while her husband went forward.

"Dunbar," Mr. Summers said, and Mrs. Dunbar went steadily to the box while one of the women said, "Go on, Janey," and another said, "There she goes."

"We're next," Mrs. Graves said. She watched while Mr. Graves came around from the side of the box, greeted Mr. Summers gravely, and selected a slip of paper from the box. By now, all through the crowd there were men holding the small folded papers in their large hands, turning them over and over nervously. Mrs. Dunbar and her two sons stood together, Mrs. Dunbar holding the slip of paper.

"Harburt. . . . Hutchinson."

"Get up there, Bill," Mrs. Hutchinson said, and the people near her laughed.

"Jones."

"They do say," Mr. Adams said to Old Man Warner, who stood next to him, "that over in the north village they're talking of giving up the lottery."

Old Man Warner snorted. "Pack of crazy fools," he said. "Listening to the young folks, nothing's good enough for *them*. Next thing you know, they'll be wanting to go back to living in caves, nobody work any more, live *that* way for a while. Used to be a saying about 'Lottery in June, corn be heavy soon.' First thing you know, we'd all be eating stewed chickweed and acorns. There's *always* been a lottery," he added petulantly. "Bad enough to see young Joe Summers up there joking with everybody."

"Some places have already quit lotteries," Mrs. Adams said.

"Nothing but trouble in *that*," Old Man Warner said stoutly. "Pack of young fools."

"Martin." And Bobby Martin watched his father go forward. "Overdyke. . . .   35
Percy."

"I wish they'd hurry," Mrs. Dunbar said to her older son. "I wish they'd hurry."

"They're almost through," her son said.

"You get ready to run tell Dad," Mrs. Dunbar said.

Mr. Summers called his own name and then stepped forward precisely and selected a slip from the box. Then he called, "Warner."

"Seventy-seventh year I been in the lottery," Old Man Warner said as he went   40
through the crowd. "Seventy-seventh time."

"Watson." The tall boy came awkwardly through the crowd. Someone said, "Don't be nervous, Jack," and Mr. Summers said, "Take your time, son."

"Zanini."

After that, there was a long pause, a breathless pause, until Mr. Summers, holding his slip of paper in the air, said, "All right, fellows." For a minute, no one moved, and then all the slips of paper were opened. Suddenly, all the women began to speak at once, saying, "Who is it?" "Who's got it?" "Is it the Dunbars?" "Is it the Watsons?" Then the voices began to say, "It's Hutchinson. It's Bill," "Bill Hutchinson's got it."

"Go tell your father," Mrs. Dunbar said to her older son.

People began to look around to see the Hutchinsons. Bill Hutchinson was stand-   45
ing quiet, staring down at the paper in his hand. Suddenly, Tessie Hutchinson shouted to Mr. Summers, "You didn't give him time enough to take any paper he wanted. I saw you. It wasn't fair!"

"Be a good sport, Tessie," Mrs. Delacroix called, and Mrs. Graves said, "All of us took the same chance."

"Shut up, Tessie," Bill Hutchinson said.

"Well, everyone," Mr. Summers said, "that was done pretty fast, and now we've got to be hurrying a little more to get done in time." He consulted his next list. "Bill," he said, "you draw for the Hutchinson family. You got any other households in the Hutchinsons?"

"There's Don and Eva," Mrs. Hutchinson yelled. "Make *them* take their chance!"

"Daughters draw with their husbands' families, Tessie," Mr. Summers said   50
gently. "You know that as well as anyone else."

"It wasn't *fair*," Tessie said.

"I guess not, Joe," Bill Hutchinson said regretfully. "My daughter draws with her husband's family, that's only fair. And I've got no other family except the kids."

"Then, as far as drawing for families is concerned, it's you," Mr. Summers said in explanation, "and as far as drawing for households is concerned, that's you, too. Right?"

"Right," Bill Hutchinson said.

"How many kids, Bill?" Mr. Summers asked formally.   55

"Three," Bill Hutchinson said. "There's Bill, Jr., and Nancy, and little Dave. And Tessie and me."

"All right, then," Mr. Summers said. "Harry, you got their tickets back?"

Mr. Graves nodded and held up the slips of paper. "Put them in the box, then," Mr. Summers directed. "Take Bill's and put it in."

"I think we ought to start over," Mrs. Hutchinson said, as quietly as she could. "I tell you it wasn't *fair*. You didn't give him time enough to choose. *Every*body saw that."

Mr. Graves had selected the five slips and put them in the box, and he dropped all   60
the papers but those onto the ground, where the breeze caught them and lifted them off.

"Listen, everybody," Mrs. Hutchinson was saying to the people around her.

"Ready, Bill?" Mr. Summers asked, and Bill Hutchinson, with one quick glance around at his wife and children, nodded.

"Remember," Mr. Summers said, "take the slips and keep them folded until each person has taken one. Harry, you help little Dave." Mr. Graves took the hand of the little boy, who came willingly with him up to the box. "Take a paper out of the box, Davy," Mr. Summers said. Davy put his hand into the box and laughed. "Take just *one* paper," Mr. Summers said. "Harry, you hold it for him." Mr. Graves took the child's hand and removed the folded paper from the tight fist and held it while little Dave stood next to him and looked up at him wonderingly.

"Nancy next," Mr. Summers said. Nancy was twelve, and her school friends breathed heavily as she went forward, switching her skirt, and took a slip daintily from the box. "Bill, Jr.," Mr. Summers said, and Billy, his face red and his feet over-large, nearly knocked the box over as he got a paper out. "Tessie," Mr. Summers said. She hesitated for a minute, looking around defiantly, and then set her lips and went up to the box. She snatched a paper out and held it behind her.

"Bill," Mr. Summers said, and Bill Hutchinson reached into the box and felt   65
around, bringing his hand out at last with the slip of paper in it.

The crowd was quiet. A girl whispered, "I hope it's not Nancy," and the sound of the whisper reached the edges of the crowd.

"It's not the way it used to be," Old Man Warner said clearly. "People ain't they way they used to be."

"All right," Mr. Summers said. "Open the papers. Harry, you open little Dave's."

Mr. Graves opened the slip of paper and there was a general sigh through the crowd as he held it up and everyone could see that it was blank. Nancy and Bill, Jr., opened theirs at the same time, and both beamed and laughed, turning around to the crowd and holding their slips of paper above their heads.

"Tessie," Mr. Summers said. There was a pause, and then Mr. Summers looked at   70
Bill Hutchinson, and Bill unfolded his paper and showed it. It was blank.

"It's Tessie," Mr. Summers said, and his voice was hushed. "Show us her paper, Bill."

Bill Hutchinson went over to his wife and forced the slip of paper out of her hand. It had a black spot on it, the black spot Mr. Summers had made the night before with the heavy pencil in the coal-company office. Bill Hutchinson held it up, and there was a stir in the crowd.

"All right, folks," Mr. Summers said. "Let's finish quickly."

Although the villagers had forgotten the ritual and lost the original black box, they still remembered to use stones. The pile of stones the boys had made earlier was ready; there were stones on the ground with the blowing scraps of paper that had come out of the box. Mrs. Delacroix selected a stone so large she had to pick it up with both hands and turned to Mrs. Dunbar. "Come on," she said. "Hurry up."

Mrs. Dunbar had small stones in both hands, and she said, gasping for breath, "I   75
can't run at all. You'll have to go ahead and I'll catch up with you."

The children had stones already, and someone gave little Davy Hutchinson a few pebbles.

Tessie Hutchinson was in the center of a cleared space by now, and she held her hands out desperately as the villagers moved in on her. "It isn't fair," she said. A stone hit her on the side of the head.

Old Man Warner was saying, "Come on, come on, everyone." Steve Adams was in the front of the crowd of villagers with Mrs. Graves beside him.

"It isn't fair, it isn't right," Mrs. Hutchinson screamed, and then they were upon her.

QUESTIONS

1. Describe the point of view of the story. What seems to be the position from which the narrator sees and describes the events? How much extra information does the narrator provide?

2. What would the story be like if it were done with an omniscient point of view? With the first person? Could the story be as suspenseful as it is? In what other ways might the story be different with another point of view?

3. Does the conclusion of "The Lottery" seem to come as a surprise? In retrospect, what hints earlier in the story tell about what is to come?

4. A scapegoat, in the ritual of purification described in the Old Testament, was an actual goat that was released into the wilderness after having been ceremonially heaped with the "iniquities" of the people (Leviticus 16:22). What traces of such a ritual are suggested in "The Lottery"? Can you think of any other kinds of rituals that are retained today even though their purpose is now remote or even nonexistent?

5. Is "The Lottery" a horror story or a surprise story, or neither or both? Explain.

KATHERINE MANSFIELD   (1888–1923)

Mansfield was born in New Zealand but spent most of her brief adult life in England, where her stories earned a reputation for originality and experimentation. She treats topics of crucial importance in the lives of individuals, such as those in the stories "Bliss" and "The Garden Party." In "Miss Brill," an insignificant woman, who sustains herself with fancies and daydreams, is subjected to the crisis of shattering, callously cruel words. Mansfield's artistry is pointed and skillful, and the ending quizzically leaves readers wondering how the heroine will deal with her grief.

Miss Brill° _____ *1920*

Although it was so brilliantly fine—the blue sky powdered with gold and great spots of light like white wine splashed over the Jardins Publiques°—Miss Brill was glad that she

---

Miss Brill: Brill is the name of a common deep-sea flatfish.
Jardins Publiques: public gardens or park. The setting of the story is apparently a French seaside town.

had decided on her fur. The air was motionless, but when you opened your mouth there was just a faint chill, like a chill from a glass of iced water before you sip, and now and again a leaf came drifting—from nowhere, from the sky. Miss Brill put up her hand and touched her fur. Dear little thing! It was nice to feel it again. She had taken it out of its box that afternoon, shaken out the moth-powder, given it a good brush, and rubbed the life back into the dim little eyes. "What has been happening to me?" said the sad little eyes. Oh, how sweet it was to see them snap at her again from the red eider-down! . . . But the nose, which was of some black composition, wasn't at all firm. It must have had a knock, somehow. Never mind—a little dab of black sealing-wax when the time came—when it was absolutely necessary. . . . Little rogue! Yes, she really felt like that about it. Little rogue biting its tail just by her left ear. She could have taken it off and laid it on her lap and stroked it. She felt a tingling in her hands and arms, but that came from walking, she supposed. And when she breathed, something light and sad— no, not sad, exactly—something gentle seemed to move in her bosom.

There were a number of people out this afternoon, far more than last Sunday. And the band sounded louder and gayer. That was because the Season had begun. For although the band played all the year round on Sundays, out of season it was never the same. It was like some one playing with only the family to listen; it didn't care how it played if there weren't any strangers present. Wasn't the conductor wearing a new coat, too? She was sure it was new. He scraped with his foot and flapped his arms like a rooster about to crow, and the bandsmen sitting in the green rotunda blew out their cheeks and glared at the music. Now there came a little "flutey" bit—very pretty!—a little chain of bright drops. She was sure it would be repeated. It was; she lifted her head and smiled.

Only two people shared her "special" seat: a fine old man in a velvet coat, his hands clasped over a huge carved walking-stick, and a big old woman, sitting upright, with a roll of knitting on her embroidered apron. They did not speak. This was disap-pointing, for Miss Brill always looked forward to the conversation. She had become really quite expert, she thought, at listening as though she didn't listen, at sitting in other people's lives just for a minute while they talked round her.

She glanced, sideways, at the old couple. Perhaps they would go soon. Last Sunday, too, hadn't been as interesting as usual. An Englishman and his wife, he wearing a dreadful Panama hat and she button boots. And she'd gone on the whole time about how she ought to wear spectacles; she knew she needed them; but that it was no good getting any; they'd be sure to break and they'd never keep on. And he'd been so patient. He'd suggested everything—gold rims, the kind that curved round your ears, little pads inside the bridge. No, nothing would please her. "They'll always be sliding down my nose!" Miss Brill had wanted to shake her.

The old people sat on the bench, still as statues. Never mind, there was always the crowd to watch. To and fro, in front of the flower-beds and the band rotunda, the couples and groups paraded, stopped to talk, to greet, to buy a handful of flowers from the old beggar who had his tray fixed to the railings. Little children ran among them, swooping and laughing; little boys with big white silk bows under their chins, little girls, little French dolls, dressed up in velvet and lace. And sometimes a tiny staggerer came suddenly rocking into the open from under the trees, stopped, stared, as suddenly sat down "flop," until its small high-stepping mother, like a young hen, rushed scolding to its rescue. Other people sat on the benches and green chairs, but they were nearly always the same, Sunday after Sunday, and—Miss Brill had often noticed—there was something funny about nearly all of them. They were odd, silent, nearly all old, and

5

from the way they stared they looked as though they'd just come from dark little rooms or even—even cupboards!

Behind the rotunda the slender trees with yellow leaves down drooping, and through them just a line of sea, and beyond the blue sky with gold-veined clouds.

Tum-tum-tum tiddle-um! tiddle-um! tum tiddle-um tum ta! blew the band.

Two young girls in red came by and two young soldiers in blue met them, and they laughed and paired and went off arm-in-arm. Two peasant women with funny straw hats passed, gravely, leading beautiful smoke-coloured donkeys. A cold, pale nun hurried by. A beautiful woman came along and dropped her bunch of violets, and a little boy ran after to hand them to her, and she took them and threw them away as if they'd been poisoned. Dear me! Miss Brill didn't know whether to admire that or not! And now an ermine toque° and a gentleman in grey met just in front of her. He was tall, stiff, digni-fied, and she was wearing the ermine toque she'd bought when her hair was yellow. Now everything, her hair, her face, even her eyes, was the same colour as the shabby ermine, and her hand, in its cleaned glove, lifted to dab her lips, was a tiny yellowish paw. Oh, she was so pleased to see him—delighted! She rather thought they were going to meet that afternoon. She described where she'd been—everywhere, here, there, along by the sea. The day was so charming—didn't he agree? And wouldn't he, perhaps? . . . But he shook his head, lighted a cigarette, slowly breathed a great deep puff into her face, and, even while she was still talking and laughing, flicked the match away and walked on. The ermine toque was alone; she smiled more brightly than ever. But even the band seemed to know what she was feeling and played more softly, played tenderly, and the drum beat, "The Brute! The Brute!" over and over. What would she do? What was going to happen now? But as Miss Brill wondered, the ermine toque turned, raised her hand as though she'd seen some one else, much nicer, just over there, and pattered away. And the band changed again and played more quickly, more gaily than ever, and the old couple on Miss Brill's seat got up and marched away, and such a funny old man with long whiskers hobbled along in time to the music and was nearly knocked over by four girls walking abreast.

Oh, how fascinating it was! How she enjoyed it! How she loved sitting here, watching it all! It was like a play. It was exactly like a play. Who could believe the sky at the back wasn't painted? But it wasn't till a little brown dog trotted on solemn and then slowly trotted off, like a little "theatre" dog, a little dog that had been drugged, that Miss Brill discovered what it was that made it so exciting. They were all on the stage. They weren't only the audience, not only looking on; they were act-ing. Even she had a part and came every Sunday. No doubt somebody would have noticed if she hadn't been there; she was part of the performance after all. How strange she'd never thought of it like that before! And yet it explained why she made such a point of starting from home at just the same time each week—so as not to be late for the performance—and it also explained why she had quite a queer, shy feeling at telling her English pupils how she spent her Sunday afternoons. No wonder! Miss Brill nearly laughed out loud. She was on the stage. She thought of the old invalid gentleman to whom she read the newspaper four afternoons a week while he slept in the garden. She had got quite used to the frail head on the cotton pillow, the hollowed eyes, the open mouth and the high pinched nose. If he'd been dead

---

ermine toque: close-fitting hat made of the white fur of an ermine; here the phrase stands for the woman wearing the hat.

she mightn't have noticed for weeks; she wouldn't have minded. But suddenly he knew he was having the paper read to him by an actress! "An actress!" The old head lifted; two points of light quivered in the old eyes. "An actress—are ye?" And Miss Brill smoothed the newspaper as though it were the manuscript of her part and said gently: "Yes, I have been an actress for a long time."

The band had been having a rest. Now they started again. And what they played was warm, sunny, yet there was just a faint chill—a something, what was it?—not sadness—no, not sadness—a something that made you want to sing. The tune lifted, lifted, the light shone; and it seemed to Miss Brill that in another moment all of them, all the whole company, would begin singing. The young ones, the laughing ones who were moving together, they would begin, and the men's voices, very resolute and brave, would join them. And then she too, she too, and the others on the benches—they would come in with a kind of accompaniment—something low, that scarcely rose or fell, something so beautiful—moving. . . . And Miss Brill's eyes filled with tears and she looked smiling at all the other members of the company. Yes, we understand, we understand, she thought—though what they understood she didn't know.

Just at that moment a boy and girl came and sat down where the old couple had been. They were beautifully dressed; they were in love. The hero and heroine, of course, just arrived from his father's yacht. And still soundlessly singing, still with that trembling smile, Miss Brill prepared to listen.

"No, not now," said the girl, "Not here, I can't."

"But why? Because of that stupid old thing at the end there?" asked the boy. "Why does she come here at all—who wants her? Why doesn't she keep her silly old mug at home?"

"It's her fu-fur which is so funny," giggled the girl. "It's exactly like a fried whiting."

"Ah, be off with you!" said the boy in an angry whisper. Then: "Tell me, ma petite chérie—"

"No, not here," said the girl. "Not *yet.*"

On her way home she usually bought a slice of honeycake at the baker's. It was her Sunday treat. Sometimes there was an almond in her slice, sometimes not. It made a great difference. If there was an almond it was like carrying home a tiny present— a surprise—something that might very well not have been there. She hurried on the almond Sundays and struck the match for the kettle in quite a dashing way.

But to-day she passed the baker's by, climbed the stairs, went into the little dark room—her room like a cupboard—and sat down on the red eiderdown. She sat there for a long time. The box that the fur came out of was on the bed. She unclasped the necklet quickly; quickly, without looking, laid it inside. But when she put the lid on she thought she heard something crying.

QUESTIONS

1.   Describe the point of view of "Miss Brill." Who says, in paragraph 1, "Dear little thing!" about the fur? How do you justify your conclusion about the source of this and similar insights that appear throughout the story?

2.   Would this story be possible if told in the first person by Miss Brill herself? What might it have been like if told by a walker in the park who observed Miss Brill and overheard the conversation about her by the boy and girl?

3. A shift in the point of view occurs when the boy and girl sit down and Miss Brill overhears them. Describe the nature of this shift. Why do you think Mansfield made the change at this point?

4. In relation to the point of view, explain the last sentence of the story: "But when she put the lid on she thought she heard something crying."

LORRIE MOORE   (b. 1957)

One of the youngest writers represented in this book, Lorrie Moore teaches at the University of Wisconsin. She was born in upstate New York and received a master of fine arts degree from Cornell. Following her first collection of stories, Self-Help *(1985), from which "How to Become a Writer" is taken, she published her first novel,* Anagrams, *in 1986. A recent work is* Like Life *(1991), a collection of eight stories taking its title from the last story, a grim portrait of life in a polluted, deteriorating future. She has received awards from the National Endowment for the Humanities and the Rockefeller Foundation. Her fiction has been heralded for its combination of wry humor, deep feeling, and impending tragedy.*

How to Become a Writer _____ 1985

First, try to be something, anything, else. A movie star/astronaut. A movie star/missionary. A movie star/kindergarten teacher. President of the World. Fail miserably. It is best if you fail at an early age—say, fourteen. Early, critical disillusionment is necessary so that at fifteen you can write long haiku sequences about thwarted desire. It is a pond, a cherry blossom, a wind brushing against sparrow wing leaving for mountain. Count the syllables. Show it to your mom. She is tough and practical. She has a son in Vietnam and a husband who may be having an affair. She believes in wearing brown because it hides spots. She'll look briefly at your writing, then back up at you with a face blank as a donut. She'll say: "How about emptying the dishwasher?" Look away. Shove the forks in the fork drawer. Accidentally break one of the freebie gas station glasses. This is the required pain and suffering. This is only for starters.

In your high school English class look only at Mr. Killian's face. Decide faces are important. Write a villanelle about pores. Struggle. Write a sonnet. Count the syllables: nine, ten, eleven, thirteen. Decide to experiment with fiction. Here you don't have to count syllables. Write a short story about an elderly man and woman who accidentally shoot each other in the head, the result of an inexplicable malfunction of a shotgun which appears mysteriously in their living room one night. Give it to Mr. Killian as your final project. When you get it back, he has written on it: "Some of your images are quite nice, but you have no sense of plot." When you are home, in the privacy of your own room, faintly scrawl in pencil beneath his black-inked comments: "Plots are for dead people, pore-face."

Take all the babysitting jobs you can get. You are great with kids. They love you. You tell them stories about old people who die idiot deaths. You sing them songs like

"Blue Bells of Scotland," which is their favorite. And when they are in their pajamas and have finally stopped pinching each other, when they are fast asleep, you read every sex manual in the house, and wonder how on earth anyone could ever do those things with someone they truly loved. Fall asleep in a chair reading Mr. McMurphy's *Playboy.* When the McMurphys come home, they will tap you on the shoulder, look at the magazine in your lap, and grin. You will want to die. They will ask you if Tracey took her medicine all right. Explain, yes, she did, that you promised her a story if she would take it like a big girl and that seemed to work out just fine. "Oh, marvelous," they will exclaim.

Try to smile proudly.

Apply to college as a child psychology major.

As a child psychology major, you have some electives. You've always liked birds. Sign up for something called "The Ornithological Field Trip." It meets Tuesdays and Thursdays at two. When you arrive at Room 134 on the first day of class, everyone is sitting around a seminar table talking about metaphors. You've heard of these. After a short, excruciating while, raise your hand and say diffidently, "Excuse me, isn't this Bird-watching One-oh-one?" The class stops and turns to look at you. They seem to all have one face—giant and blank as a vandalized clock. Someone with a beard booms out, "No, this is Creative Writing." Say: "Oh—right," as if perhaps you knew all along. Look down at your schedule. Wonder how the hell you ended up here. The computer, apparently, has made an error. You start to get up to leave and then don't. The lines at the registrar this week are huge. Perhaps you should stick with this mistake. Perhaps your creative writing isn't all that bad. Perhaps it is fate. Perhaps this is what your dad meant when he said, "It's the age of computers, Francie, it's the age of computers."

Decide that you like college life. In your dorm you meet many nice people. Some are smarter than you. And some, you notice, are dumber than you. You will continue, unfortunately, to view the world in exactly these terms for the rest of your life.

The assignment this week in creative writing is to narrate a violent happening. Turn in a story about driving with your Uncle Gordon and another one about two old people who are accidentally electrocuted when they go to turn on a badly wired desk lamp. The teacher will hand them back to you with comments: "Much of your writing is smooth and energetic. You have, however, a ludicrous notion of plot." Write another story about a man and a woman who, in the very first paragraph, have their lower torsos accidentally blitzed away by dynamite. In the second paragraph, with the insurance money, they buy a frozen yogurt stand together. There are six more paragraphs. You read the whole thing out loud in class. No one likes it. They say your sense of plot is outrageous and incompetent. After class someone asks you if you are crazy.

Decide that perhaps you should stick to comedies. Start dating someone who is funny, someone who has what in high school you called a "really great sense of humor" and what now your creative writing class calls "self-contempt giving rise to comic form." Write down all of his jokes, but don't tell him you are doing this. Make up anagrams of his old girlfriend's name and name all of your socially handicapped characters with them. Tell him his old girlfriend is in all of your stories and then watch how funny he can be, see what a really great sense of humor he can have.

Your child psychology advisor tells you you are neglecting courses in your major.   10
What you spend the most time on should be what you're majoring in. Say yes, you
understand.

In creative writing seminars over the next two years, everyone continues to smoke
cigarettes and ask the same things: "But does it work?" "Why should we care about this
character?" "Have you earned this cliché?" These seem like important questions.

On days when it is your turn, you look at the class hopefully as they scour your
mimeographs for a plot. They look back up at you, drag deeply, and then smile in a
sweet sort of way.

You spend too much time slouched and demoralized. Your boyfriend suggests
bicycling. Your roommate suggests a new boyfriend. You are said to be self-mutilating
and losing weight, but you continue writing. The only happiness you have is writing
something new, in the middle of the night, armpits damp, heart pounding, something no one has yet seen. You have only those brief, fragile, untested moments of
exhilaration when you know: you are a genius. Understand what you must do. Switch
majors. The kids in your nursery project will be disappointed, but you have a calling, an
urge, a delusion, an unfortunate habit. You have, as your mother would say, fallen in
with a bad crowd.

Why write? Where does writing come from? These are questions to ask yourself.
They are like: Where does dust come from? Or: Why is there war? Or: If there's a God,
then why is my brother now a cripple?

These are questions that you keep in your wallet, like calling cards. These are   15
questions, your creative writing teacher says, that are good to address in your journals
but rarely in your fiction.

The writing professor this fall is stressing the Power of the Imagination. Which
means he doesn't want long descriptive stories about your camping trip last July. He
wants you to start in a realistic context but then to alter it. Like recombinant DNA.
He wants you to let your imagination sail, to let it grow big-bellied in the wind. This is a
quote from Shakespeare.

Tell your roommate your great idea, your great exercise of imaginative power: a
transformation of Melville to contemporary life. It will be about monomania and the
fish-eat-fish world of life insurance in Rochester, New York. The first line will be "Call
me Fishmeal," and it will feature a menopausal suburban husband named Richard, who
because he is so depressed all the time is called "Mopey Dick" by his witty wife Elaine. Say
to your roommate: "Mopey Dick, get it?" Your roommate looks at you, like a buddy, and
puts an arm around your burdened shoulders. "Listen, Francie," she says, slow as speech
therapy. "Let's go out and get a big beer."

The seminar doesn't like this one either. You suspect they are beginning to feel sorry
for you. They say: "You have to think about what is happening. Where is the story here?"

The next semester the writing professor is obsessed with writing from personal experience. You must write from what you know, from what has happened to

you. He wants deaths, he wants camping trips. Think about what has happened to you. In three years there have been three things: you lost your virginity; your parents got divorced; and your brother came home from a forest ten miles from the Cambodian border with only half a thigh, a permanent smirk nestled into one corner of his mouth.

About the first you write: "It created a new space, which hurt and cried in a voice   20
that wasn't mine, 'I'm not the same anymore, but I'll be okay.'"

About the second you write an elaborate story of an old married couple who stumble upon an unknown land mine in their kitchen and accidentally blow themselves up. You call it: "For Better or for Liverwurst."

About the last you write nothing. There are no words for this. Your typewriter hums. You can find no words.

At undergraduate cocktail parties, people say, "Oh, you write? What do you write about?" Your roommate, who has consumed too much wine, too little cheese, and no crackers at all, blurts: "Oh, my god, she always writes about her dumb boyfriend."

Later on in life you will learn that writers are merely open, helpless texts with no real understanding of what they have written and therefore must half-believe anything and everything that is said of them. You, however, have not yet reached this stage of literary criticism. You stiffen and say, "I do not," the same way you said it when someone in the fourth grade accused you of really liking oboe lessons and your parents really weren't just making you take them.

Insist you are not very interested in any one subject at all, that you are interested   25
in the music of language, that you are interested in—in—syllables, because they are the atoms of poetry, the cells of the mind, the breath of the soul. Begin to feel woozy. Stare into your plastic wine cup.

"Syllables?" you will hear someone ask, voice trailing off, as they glide slowly toward the reassuring white of the dip.

Begin to wonder what you do write about. Or if you have anything to say. Or if there even is such a thing as a thing to say. Limit these thoughts to no more than ten minutes a day; like sit-ups, they can make you thin.

You will read somewhere that all writing has to do with one's genitals. Don't dwell on this. It will make you nervous.

Your mother will come visit you. She will look at the circles under your eyes and hand you a brown book with a brown briefcase on the cover. It is entitled: *How to Become a Business Executive.* She has also brought the *Names for Baby* encyclopedia you asked for; one of your characters, the aging clown–school teacher, needs a new name. You mother will shake her head and say: "Francie, Francie, remember when you were going to be a child psychology major?"

Say: "Mom, I like to write."   30

She'll say: "Sure you like to write. Of course. Sure you like to write."

Write a story about a confused music student and title it: "Schubert Was the One with the Glasses, Right?" It's not a big hit, although your roommate likes the part where the two violinists accidentally blow themselves up in a recital room. "I went out with a violinist once," she says, snapping her gum.

Thank god you are taking other courses. You can find sanctuary in nineteenth-century ontological snags and invertebrate courting rituals. Certain globular mollusks have what is called "Sex by the Arm." The male octopus, for instance, loses the end of one arm when placing it inside the female body during intercourse. Marine biologists call it "Seven Heaven." Be glad you know these things. Be glad you are not just a writer. Apply to law school.

From here on in, many things can happen. But the main one will be this: you decide not to go to law school after all, and, instead, you spend a good, big chunk of your adult life telling people how you decided not to go to law school after all. Somehow you end up writing again. Perhaps you go to graduate school. Perhaps you work odd jobs and take writing courses at night. Perhaps you are working on a novel and writing down all the clever remarks and intimate personal confessions you hear during the day. Perhaps you are losing your pals, your acquaintances, your balance.

You have broken up with your boyfriend. You now go out with men who, instead   35
of whispering "I love you," shout: "Do it to me, baby." This is good for your writing.

Sooner or later you have a finished manuscript more or less. People look at it in a vaguely troubled sort of way and say, "I'll bet becoming a writer was always a fantasy of yours, wasn't it?" Your lips dry to salt. Say that of all the fantasies possible in the world, you can't imagine being a writer even making the top twenty. Tell them you were going to be a child psychology major. "I bet," they always sigh, "you'd be great with kids." Scowl fiercely. Tell them you're a walking blade.

Quit classes. Quit jobs. Cash in old savings bonds. Now you have time like warts on your hands. Slowly copy all of your friends' addresses into a new address book.

Vacuum. Chew cough drops. Keep a folder full of fragments.

An eyelid darkening sideways.
World as conspiracy.
Possible plot? A woman gets on a bus.
Suppose you threw a love affair and nobody came.

At home drink a lot of coffee. At Howard Johnson's order the cole slaw. Consider   40
how it looks like the soggy confetti of a map: where you've been, where you're going—
"You Are Here," says the red star on the back of the menu.

Occasionally a date with a face blank as a sheet of paper asks you whether writers often become discouraged. Say that sometimes they do and sometimes they do. Say it's a lot like having polio.

"Interesting," smiles your date, and then he looks down at his arm hairs and starts to smooth them, all, always, in the same direction.

QUESTIONS

1. To whom does the "you" in the story refer? How strong a case may be made that the "you" refers really to "I," and that Francie is actually telling a story about herself?

2. In light of the title, how adequate are Francie's "directions" for becoming a writer?

3. Describe some of the comic elements of the story. What serious ideas about the development of a writer's profession undergird the story's humor?

TILLIE OLSEN   (b. 1913)

Olsen was born in 1913 in Nebraska. Early in her life she performed domestic service, but then she married and had four daughters. She began writing early, fictionalizing many of her own experiences, but her work has been deliberate, careful, and slow. She began her major novel, Yonnondio, *while in her late teens, but did not complete and publish the work until fifty years later, in 1974. She has been a staunch advocate of feminism and minorities and has lectured frequently at colleges and universities. "I Stand Here Ironing" is from her 1956 collection* Tell Me a Riddle. *If one judges the story as being related to Olsen's own experience, it is visualized as happening in about 1951, when Emily is 19 and the mother is 38.*

I Stand Here Ironing ————————————————— *1953–1954*

I stand here ironing, and what you asked me moves tormented back and forth with the iron.

"I wish you would manage the time to come in and talk with me about your daughter. I'm sure you can help me understand her. She's a youngster who needs help and whom I'm deeply interested in helping."

"Who needs help." . . . Even if I came, what good would it do? You think because I am her mother I have a key, or that in some way you could use me as a key? She has lived for nineteen years. There is all that life that has happened outside of me, beyond me.

And when is there time to remember, to sift, to weigh, to estimate, to total? I will start and there will be an interruption and I will have to gather it all together again. Or I will become engulfed with all I did or did not do, with what should have been and what cannot be helped.

She was a beautiful baby. The first and only one of our five that was beautiful at   5
birth. You do not guess how new and uneasy her tenancy in her now-loveliness. You did not know her all those years she was thought homely, or see her poring over her baby pictures, making me tell her over and over how beautiful she had been—and would be, I would tell her—and was now, to the seeing eye. But the seeing eyes were few or nonexistent. Including mine.

I nursed her. They feel that's important nowadays. I nursed all the children, but with her, with all the fierce rigidity of first motherhood, I did like the books then said. Though her cries battered me to trembling and my breasts ached with swollenness, I waited till the clock decreed.

Why do I put that first? I do not even know if it matters, or if it explains anything.

She was a beautiful baby. She blew shining bubbles of sound. She loved motion, loved light, loved color and music and textures. She would lie on the floor in her blue overalls patting the surface so hard in ecstasy her hands and feet would blur. She was a miracle to me, but when she was eight months old I had to leave her daytimes with the woman downstairs to whom she was no miracle at all, for I worked or looked for work and for Emily's father, who "could no longer endure" (he wrote in his good-bye note) "sharing want with us."

I was nineteen. It was the pre-relief, pre-WPA world of the depression. I would start running as soon as I got off the streetcar, running up the stairs, the place smelling sour, and awake or asleep to startle awake, when she saw me she would break into a clogged weeping that could not be comforted, a weeping I can hear yet.

After a while I found a job hashing at night so I could be with her days, and it was better. But it came to where I had to bring her to his family and leave her. 10

It took a long time to raise the money for her fare back. Then she got chicken pox and I had to wait longer. When she finally came, I hardly knew her, walking quick and nervous like her father, looking like her father, thin, and dressed in a shoddy red that yellowed her skin and glared at the pockmarks. All the baby loveliness gone.

She was two. Old enough for nursery school they said, and I did not know then what I know now—the fatigue of the long day, and the lacerations of group life in the kinds of nurseries that are only parking places for children.

Except that it would have made no difference if I had known. It was the only place there was. It was the only way we could be together, the only way I could hold a job.

And even without knowing, I knew. I knew the teacher that was evil because all these years it has curdled into my memory, the little boy hunched in the corner, her rasp, "why aren't you outside, because Alvin hits you? that's no reason, go out, scaredy." I knew Emily hated it even if she did not clutch and implore "don't go Mommy" like the other children, mornings.

She always had a reason why we should stay home. Momma, you look sick. 15 Momma, I feel sick. Momma, the teachers aren't there today, they're sick. Momma, we can't go, there was a fire there last night. Momma, it's a holiday today, no school, they told me.

But never a direct protest, never rebellion. I think of our others in their three-, four-year-oldness—the explosions, the tempers, the denunciations, the demands—and I feel suddenly ill. I put the iron down. What in me demanded that goodness in her? And what was the cost, the cost to her of such goodness?

The old man living in the back once said in his gentle way: "You should smile at Emily more when you look at her." What *was* in my face when I looked at her? I loved her. There were all the acts of love.

It was only with the others I remembered what he said, and it was the face of joy, and not of care or tightness or worry I turned to them—too late for Emily. She does not smile easily, let alone almost always as her brothers and sisters do. Her face is closed and sombre, but when she wants, how fluid. You must have seen it in her pantomimes, you spoke of her rare gift for comedy on the stage that rouses a laughter out of the audience so dear they applaud and applaud and do not want to let her go.

Where does it come from, that comedy? There was none of it in her when she came back to me that second time, after I had had to send her away again. She had a new daddy now to learn to love, and I think perhaps it was a better time.

Except when we left her alone nights, telling ourselves she was old enough. 20

"Can't you go some other time, Mommy, like tomorrow?" she would ask. "Will it be just a little while you'll be gone? Do you promise?"

The time we came back, the front door open, the clock on the floor in the hall. She rigid awake. "It wasn't just a little while. I didn't cry. Three times I called you, just three times, and then I ran downstairs to open the door so you could come faster. The clock talked loud. I threw it away, it scared me what it talked."

She said the clock talked loud again that night I went to the hospital to have Susan. She was delirious with the fever that comes before red measles, but she was fully conscious all the week I was gone and the week after we were home when she could not come near the new baby or me.

She did not get well. She stayed skeleton thin, not wanting to eat, and night after night she had nightmares. She would call for me, and I would rouse from exhaustion to sleepily call back: "You're all right, darling, go to sleep, it's just a dream," and if she still called, in a sterner voice, "now go to sleep, Emily, there's nothing to hurt you." Twice, only twice, when I had to get up for Susan anyhow, I went in to sit with her.

Now when it is too late (as if she would let me hold and comfort her like I do the   25 others) I get up and go to her at once at her moan or restless stirring. "Are you awake, Emily? Can I get you something?" And the answer is always the same: "No, I'm all right, go back to sleep, Mother."

They persuaded me at the clinic to send her away to a convalescent home in the country where "she can have the kind of food and care you can't manage for her, and you'll be free to concentrate on the new baby." They still send children to that place. I see pictures on the society page of sleek young women planning affairs to raise money for it, or dancing at the affairs, or decorating Easter eggs or filling Christmas stockings for the children.

They never have a picture of the children so I do not know if the girls still wear those gigantic red bows and the ravaged looks on the every other Sunday when parents can come to visit "unless otherwise notified"—as we were notified the first six weeks.

Oh it is a handsome place, green lawns and tall trees and fluted flower beds. High up on the balconies of each cottage the children stand, the girls in their red bows and white dresses, the boys in white suits and giant red ties. The parents stand below shrieking up to be heard and the children shriek down to be heard, and between them the invisible wall "Not To Be Contaminated by Parental Germs or Physical Affection."

There was a tiny girl who always stood hand in hand with Emily. Her parents never came. One visit she was gone. "They moved her to Rose Cottage" Emily shouted in explanation. "They don't like you to love anybody here."

She wrote once a week, the labored writing of a seven-year-old. "I am fine. How is   30 the baby. If I write my leter nicly I will have a star. Love." There never was a star. We wrote every other day, letters she could never hold or keep but only hear read—once. "We simply do not have room for children to keep any personal possessions," they patiently explained when we pieced one Sunday's shrieking together to plead how much it would mean to Emily, who loved so to keep things, to be allowed to keep her letters and cards.

Each visit she looked frailer. "She isn't eating," they told us.

(They had runny eggs for breakfast or mush with lumps, Emily said later, I'd hold it in my mouth and not swallow. Nothing ever tasted good, just when they had chicken.)

It took us eight months to get her released home, and only the fact that she gained back so little of her seven lost pounds convinced the social worker.

I used to try to hold and love her after she came back, but her body would stay stiff, and after a while she'd push away. She ate little. Food sickened her, and I think much of life too. Oh she had physical lightness and brightness, twinkling by on skates, bouncing like a ball up and down up and down over the jump rope, skimming over the hill; but these were momentary.

She fretted about her appearance, thin and dark and foreign-looking at a time   35 when every little girl was supposed to look or thought she should look a chubby blonde replica of Shirley Temple. The doorbell sometimes rang for her, but no one seemed to come and play in the house or be a best friend. Maybe because we moved so much.

There was a boy she loved painfully through two school semesters. Months later she told me how she had taken pennies from my purse to buy him candy. "Licorice was his favorite and I brought him some every day, but he still liked Jennifer better'n me. Why, Mommy?" The kind of question for which there is no answer.

School was a worry to her. She was not glib or quick in a world where glibness and quickness were easily confused with ability to learn. To her overworked and exasperated teachers she was an overconscientious "slow learner" who kept trying to catch up and was absent entirely too often.

I let her be absent, though sometimes the illness was imaginary. How different from my now-strictness about attendance with the others. I wasn't working. We had a new baby, I was home anyhow. Sometimes, after Susan grew old enough, I would keep her home from school, too, to have them all together.

Mostly Emily had asthma, and her breathing, harsh and labored, would fill the house with a curiously tranquil sound. I would bring the two old dresser mirrors and her boxes of collections to her bed. She would select beads and single earrings, bottle tops and shells, dried flowers and pebbles, old postcards and scraps, all sorts of odd-ments; then she and Susan would play Kingdom, setting up landscapes and furniture, peopling them with action.

Those were the only times of peaceful companionship between her and Susan. I have edged away from it, that poisonous feeling between them, that terrible balancing of hurts and needs I had to do between the two, and did so badly, those earlier years. 40

Oh there are conflicts between the others too, each one human, needing, demanding, hurting, taking—but only between Emily and Susan, no, Emily toward Susan that corroding resentment. It seems so obvious on the surface, yet it is not obvi-ous. Susan, the second child, Susan, golden- and curly-haired and chubby, quick and articulate and assured, everything in appearance and manner Emily was not; Susan, not able to resist Emily's precious things, losing or sometimes clumsily breaking them; Susan telling jokes and riddles to company for applause while Emily sat silent (to say to me later; that was *my* riddle, Mother, I told it to Susan); Susan, who for all the five years' dif-ference in age was just a year behind Emily in developing physically.

I am glad for that slow physical development that widened the difference between her and her contemporaries, though she suffered over it. She was too vulnerable for that terrible world of youthful competition, of preening and parading, of constant mea-suring of yourself against every other, of envy, "If I had that copper hair," "If I had that skin. . . ." She tormented herself enough about not looking like the others, there was enough of the unsureness, the having to be conscious of words before you speak, the constant caring—what are they thinking of me? without having it all magnified by the merciless physical drives.

Ronnie is calling. He is wet and I change him. It is rare there is such a cry now. That time of motherhood is almost behind me when the ear is not one's own but must always be racked and listening for the child cry, the child call. We sit for a while and I hold him, looking out over the city spread in charcoal with its soft aisles of light, "*Shoogily*," he breathes and curls closer. I carry him back to bed, asleep. *Shoogily*. A funny word, a family word, inherited from Emily, invented by her to say: *comfort*.

In this and other ways she leaves her seal, I say aloud. And startle at my saying it. What do I mean? What did I start to gather together, to try and make coherent? I was at the terrible, growing years. War years. I do not remember them well. I was working, there were four smaller ones now, there was not time for her. She had to help be a mother, a housekeeper, and shopper. She had to set her seal. Mornings of crisis and near hysteria trying to get lunches packed, hair combed, coats and shoes found, everyone to school or Child Care on time, the baby ready for transportation. And always the paper scribbled on by a smaller one, the book looked at by Susan then mislaid, the homework not done. Running out to that huge school where she was one, she was lost, she was a drop; suffering over the unpreparedness, stammering and unsure in her classes.

There was so little time left at night after the kids were bedded down. She would   45
struggle over books, always eating (it was in those years she developed her enormous appetite that is legendary in our family) and I would be ironing, or preparing food for the next day, or writing V-mail to Bill, or tending the baby. Sometimes, to make me laugh, or out of her despair, she would imitate happenings or types at school.

I think I said once: "Why don't you do something like this in the school amateur show?" One morning she phoned me at work, hardly understandable through the weeping: "Mother, I did it. I won, I won; they gave me first prize; they clapped and clapped and wouldn't let me go."

Now suddenly she was Somebody, and as imprisoned in her difference as she had been in anonymity.

She began to be asked to perform at other high schools, even in colleges, then at city and statewide affairs. The first one we went to, I only recognized her that first moment when thin, shy, she almost drowned herself into the curtains. Then: Was this Emily? The control, the command, the convulsing and deadly clowning, the spell, then the roaring, stamping audience, unwilling to let this rare and precious laughter out of their lives.

Afterwards: You ought to do something about her with a gift like that—but without money or knowing how, what does one do? We have left it all to her, and the gift has as often eddied inside, clogged and clotted, as been used and growing.

She is coming. She runs up the stairs two at a time with her light graceful step,   50
and I know she is happy tonight. Whatever it was that occasioned your call did not happen today.

"Aren't you ever going to finish the ironing, Mother? Whistler painted his mother in a rocker. I'd have to paint mine standing over an ironing board." This is one of her communicative nights and she tells me everything and nothing as she fixes herself a plate of food out of the icebox.

She is so lovely. Why did you want me to come in at all? Why were you concerned? She will find her way.

She starts up the stairs to bed. "Don't get me up with the rest in the morning." "But I thought you were having midterms." "Oh, those," she comes back in, kisses me, and says quite lightly, "in a couple of years when we'll all be atom-dead they won't matter a bit."

She has said it before. She *believes* it. But because I have been dredging the past, and all that compounds a human being is so heavy and meaningful in me, I cannot endure it tonight.

I will never total it all. I will never come in to say: She was a child seldom smiled at. Her father left me before she was a year old. I had to work her first six years when there was work, or I sent her home and to his relatives. There were years she had care she hated. She was dark and thin and foreign-looking in a world where the prestige went to blondeness and curly hair and dimples, she was slow where glibness was prized.

She was a child of anxious, not proud, love. We were poor and could not afford for her the soil of easy growth. I was a young mother, I was a distracted mother. There were the other children pushing up, demanding. Her younger sister seemed all that she was not. There were years she did not want me to touch her. She kept too much in herself, her life was such she had to keep too much in herself. My wisdom came too late. She has much to her and probably little will come of it. She is a child of her age, of depression, of war, of fear.

Let her be. So all that is in her will not bloom—but in how many does it? There is still enough left to live by. Only help her to know—help make it so there is cause for her to know—that she is more than this dress on the ironing board, helpless before the iron.

QUESTIONS

1.   Describe the story's point of view. Who is the narrator? What is she doing as she narrates the story? What prompts her to begin and continue her narration?

2.   What has the mother's life been like? How have the adversities she has undergone affected her bringing up Emily? How does she feel about her experiences?

3.   What is Emily like? What previously unrecognized talent has she discovered?

JOHN UPDIKE   (b. 1932)

Updike was born and reared in Pennsylvania during the Great Depression. His parents were diligent about his education, and in 1950 he received a scholarship for study at Harvard, graduating in 1954. He worked for the New Yorker *for two years before deciding to devote himself exclusively to his own writing, but since then he has remained a frequent contributor of stories and poems to that magazine. In 1959, he published his first story collection,* The Same Door, *and his first novel,* The Poorhouse Fair. *In 1960, with* Rabbit, Run, *he began his extensive* Rabbit *chronicles. In 1981 he received the Pulitzer Prize for* Rabbit Is Rich. *His collected poems were published in 1993, and he is continually productive in writing new stories and poems. Today he is considered one of the best of America's major writers of fiction and poetry.*

A & P° _____ *1961*

In walks these three girls in nothing but bathing suits. I'm in the third checkout slot, with my back to the door, so I don't see them until they're over by the bread. The one that caught my eye first was the one in the plaid green two-piece. She was a chunky kid, with a good tan and a sweet broad soft-looking can with those two crescents of white just under it, where the sun never seems to hit, at the top of the backs of her legs. I stood there with my hand on a box of HiHo crackers trying to remember if I rang it

---

A & P: The Great Atlantic and Pacific Tea Company, the large grocery chain established in 1859 and still flourishing in 21 states, with more than 800 stores in the United States and 213 in Canada.

up or not. I ring it up again and the customer starts giving me hell. She's one of these cash-register-watchers, a witch about fifty with rouge on her cheekbones and no eyebrows, and I know it made her day to trip me up. She'd been watching cash registers for fifty years and probably never seen a mistake before.

By the time I got her feathers smoothed and her goodies into a bag—she gives me a little snort in passing, if she'd been born at the right time they would have burned her over in Salem—by the time I get her on her way the girls had circled around the bread and were coming back, without a pushcart, back my way along the counters, in the aisle between the checkouts and the Special bins. They didn't even have shoes on. There was this chunky one, with the two-piece—it was bright green and the seams on the bra were still sharp and her belly was still pretty pale so I guessed she just got it (the suit)—there was this one, with one of those chubby berry-faces, the lips all bunched together under her nose, this one, and a tall one, with black hair that hadn't quite frizzed right, and one of these sunburns right across under the eyes, and a chin that was too long—you know, the kind of girl other girls think is very "striking" and "attractive" but never quite makes it, as they very well know, which is why they like her so much—and then the third one, that wasn't quite so tall. She was the queen. She kind of led them, the other two peeking around and making their shoulders round. She didn't look around, not this queen, she just walked straight on slowly, on these long white prima-donna legs. She came down a little hard on her heels, as if she didn't walk in her bare feet that much, putting down her heels and then letting the weight move along to her toes as if she was testing the floor with every step, putting a little deliberate extra action into it. You never know for sure how girls' minds work (do you really think it's a mind in there or just a little buzz like a bee in a glass jar?) but you got the idea she had talked the other two into coming in here with her, and now she was showing them how to do it, walk slow and hold yourself straight.

She had on a kind of dirty-pink—beige, maybe, I don't know—bathing suit with a little nubble all over it and, what got me, the straps were down. They were off her shoulders looped loose around the cool tops of her arms, and I guess as a result the suit had slipped a little on her, so all around the top of the cloth there was this shining rim. If it hadn't been there you wouldn't have known there could have been anything whiter than those shoulders. With the straps pushed off, there was nothing between the top of the suit and the top of her head except just *her*, this clean bare plane of the top of her chest down from the shoulder bones like a dented sheet of metal tilted in the light. I mean, it was more than pretty.

She had sort of oaky hair that the sun and salt had bleached, done up in a bun that was unraveling, and a kind of prim face. Walking into the A & P with your straps down, I suppose it's the only kind of face you *can* have. She held her head so high her neck, coming up out of those white shoulders, looked kind of stretched, but I didn't mind. The longer her neck was, the more of her there was.

She must have felt in the corner of her eye me and over my shoulder Stokesie in the second slot watching, but she didn't tip. Not this queen. She kept her eyes moving across the racks, and stopped, and turned so slow it made my stomach rub the inside of my apron, and buzzed to the other two, who kind of huddled against her for relief, and then they all three of them went up the cat-and-dog-food-breakfast-cereal-macaroni-rice-raisins-seasonings-spreads-spaghetti-soft-drinks-crackers-and-cookies aisle. From the third slot I look straight up this aisle to the meat counter, and I watched them all the way. The fat one with the tan sort of fumbled with the cookies, but on second thought she put the package back. The sheep pushing their carts down the aisle—the

5

girls were walking against the usual traffic (not that we have one-way signs or anything)—were pretty hilarious. You could see them, when Queenie's white shoulders dawned on them, kind of jerk, or hop, or hiccup, but their eyes snapped back to their own baskets and on they pushed. I bet you could set off dynamite in an A & P and the people would by and large keep reaching and checking oatmeal off their lists and muttering "Let me see, there was a third thing, began with A, asparagus, no ah, yes, applesauce!" or whatever it is they do mutter. But there was no doubt, this jiggled them. A few houseslaves in pin curlers even looked around after pushing their carts past to make sure what they had seen was correct.

You know, it's one thing to have a girl in a bathing suit down on the beach, where what with the glare nobody can look at each other much anyway, and another thing in the cool of the A & P, under the fluorescent lights, against all those stacked packages, with her feet paddling along naked over our checkerboard green-and-cream rubber-tile floor.

"Oh Daddy," Stokesie said beside me. "I feel so faint."

"Darling," I said. "Hold me tight." Stokesie's married, with two babies chalked up on his fuselage already, but as far as I can tell that's the only difference. He's twenty-two, and I was nineteen this April.

"Is it done?" he asks, the responsible married man finding his voice. I forgot to say he thinks he's going to be manager some sunny day, maybe in 1990 when it's called the Great Alexandrov and Petrooshki° Tea Company or something.

What he meant was, our town is five miles from the beach, with a big summer   10
colony out on the Point, but we're right in the middle of town, and the women generally put on a shirt or shorts or something before they get out of the car into the street. And anyway these are usually women with six children and varicose veins mapping their legs and nobody, including them, could care less. As I say, we're right in the middle of town, and if you stand at our front doors you can see two banks and the Congregational church and the newspaper store and three real-estate offices and about twenty-seven old freeloaders tearing up Central Street because the sewer broke again. It's not as if we're on the Cape,° we're north of Boston and there's people in this town haven't seen the ocean for twenty years.

The girls had reached the meat counter and were asking McMahon something. He pointed, they pointed, and they shuffled out of sight behind a pyramid of Diet Delight peaches. All that was left for us to see was old McMahon patting his mouth and looking after them sizing up their joints. Poor kids, I began to feel sorry for them, they couldn't help it.

Now here comes the sad part of the story, at least my family says it's sad, but I don't think it's so sad myself. The store's pretty empty, it being Thursday afternoon, so there was nothing much to do except lean on the register and wait for the girls to show up again. The whole store was like a pinball machine and I didn't know which tunnel they'd come out of. After a while they come around out of the far aisle, around the light bulbs, records at discount of the Caribbean Six or Tony Martin Sings or some such gunk you wonder they waste the wax on, sixpacks of candy bars, and plastic toys done up in

Great Alexandrov and Petrooshki: apparently a reference to the possibility that someday Russia might rule the United States.

the Cape: Cape Cod, the southeastern area of Massachusetts, a place of many resorts and beaches.

cellophane that fall apart when a kid looks at them anyway. Around they come, Queenie still leading the way, and holding a little gray jar in her hand. Slots Three through Seven are unmanned and I could see her wondering between Stokes and me, but Stokesie with his usual luck draws an old party in baggy gray pants who stumbles up with four giant cans of pineapple juice (what do these bums *do* with all that pineapple juice? I've often asked myself) so the girls come to me. Queenie puts down the jar and I take it into my fingers icy cold. Kingfish Fancy Herring Snacks in Pure Sour Cream: 49¢. Now her hands are empty, not a ring or a bracelet, bare as God made them, and I wonder where the money's coming from. Still with that prim look she lifts a folded dollar bill out of the hollow at the center of her nubbed pink top. The jar went heavy in my hand. Really, I thought that was so cute.

Then everybody's luck begins to run out. Lengel comes in from haggling with a truck full of cabbages on the lot and is about to scuttle into that door marked MANAGER behind which he hides all day when the girls touch his eye. Lengel's pretty dreary, teaches Sunday school and the rest, but he doesn't miss that much. He comes over and says, "Girls, this isn't the beach."

Queenie blushes, though maybe it's just a brush of sunburn I was noticing for the first time, now that she was so close. "My mother asked me to pick up a jar of herring snacks." Her voice kind of startled me, the way voices do when you see the people first, coming out so flat and dumb yet kind of tony, too, the way it ticked over "pick up" and "snacks." All of a sudden I slid right down her voice into her living room. Her father and the other men were standing around in ice-cream coats and bow ties and the women were in sandals picking up herring snacks on toothpicks off a big glass plate and they were all holding drinks the color of water with olives and sprigs of mint in them. When my parents have somebody over they get lemonade and if it's a real racy affair Schlitz in tall glasses with "They'll Do It Every Time"° cartoons stenciled on.

"That's all right," Lengel said. "But this isn't the beach." His repeating this struck me as funny, as if it had just occurred to him, and he had been thinking all these years the A & P was a great big dune and he was the head lifeguard. He didn't like my smiling—as I say he doesn't miss much—but he concentrates on giving the girls that sad Sunday-school-superintendent stare.   15

Queenie's blush is no sunburn now, and the plump one in plaid, that I liked better from the back—a really sweet can—pipes up, "We weren't doing any shopping. We just came in for the one thing."

"That makes no difference," Lengel tells her, and I could see from the way his eyes went that he hadn't noticed she was wearing a two-piece before. "We want you decently dressed when you come in here."

"We *are* decent," Queenie says suddenly, her lower lip pushing, getting sore now that she remembers her place, a place from which the crowd that runs the A & P must look pretty crummy. Fancy Herring Snacks flashed in her very blue eyes.

"Girls, I don't want to argue with you. After this come in here with your shoulders covered. It's our policy." He turns his back. That's policy for you. Policy is what the king-pins want. What the others want is juvenile delinquency.

All this while, the customers had been showing up with their carts but, you know, sheep, seeing a scene, they had all bunched up on Stokesie, who shook open a paper bag as gently as peeling a peach, not wanting to miss a word. I could feel in the silence   20

"They'll Do It Every Time": syndicated daily and Sunday cartoon created by Jimmy Hatlo.

everybody getting nervous, most of all Lengel, who asks me, "Sammy, have you rung up their purchase?"

I thought and said "No" but it wasn't about that I was thinking. I go through the punches, 4, 9, GROC, TOT—it's more complicated than you think, and after you do it often enough, it begins to make a little song, that you hear words to, in my case "Hello (*bing*) there, you (*gung*) hap-py *pee*-pul (*splat*)!"—the *splat* being the drawer flying out. I uncrease the bill, tenderly as you may imagine, it just having come from between the two smoothest scoops of vanilla I had ever known were there, and pass a half and a penny into her narrow pink palm, and nestle the herrings in a bag and twist its neck and hand it over, all the time thinking.

The girls, and who'd blame them, are in a hurry to get out, so I say "I quit" to Lengel quick enough for them to hear, hoping they'll stop and watch me, their unsuspected hero. They keep right on going, into the electric eye; the door flies open and they flicker across the lot to their car, Queenie and Plaid and Big Tall Goony-Goony (not that as raw material she was so bad), leaving me with Lengel and a kink in his eyebrow.

"Did you say something, Sammy?"

"I said I quit."

"I thought you did."   25

"You didn't have to embarrass them."

"It was they who were embarrassing us."

I started to say something that came out "Fiddle-de-doo." It's a saying of my grandmother's, and I know she would have been pleased.

"I don't think you know what you're saying," Lengel said.

"I know you don't," I said. "But I do." I pull the bow at the back of my apron and   30
start shrugging it off my shoulders. A couple customers that had been heading for my slot begin to knock against each other, like scared pigs in a chute.

Lengel sighs and begins to look very patient and old and gray. He's been a friend of my parents for years. "Sammy, you don't want to do this to your Mom and Dad," he tells me. It's true, I don't. But it seems to me that once you begin a gesture it's fatal not to go through with it. I fold the apron, "Sammy" stitched in red on the pocket, and put it on the counter, and drop the bow tie on top of it. The bow tie is theirs, if you've ever wondered. "You'll feel this for the rest of your life," Lengel says, and I know that's true, too, but remembering how he made that pretty girl blush makes me so scrunchy inside I punch the No Sale tab and the machine whirs "pee-pul" and the drawer splats out. One advantage to this scene taking place in summer, I can follow this up with a clean exit, there's no fumbling around getting your coat and galoshes, I just saunter into the electric eye in my white shirt that my mother ironed the night before, and the door heaves itself open, and outside the sunshine is skating around on the asphalt.

I look around for my girls, but they're gone, of course. There wasn't anybody but some young married screaming with her children about some candy they didn't get by the door of a powder-blue Falcon° station wagon. Looking back in the big windows, over the bags of peat moss and aluminum lawn furniture stacked on the pavement, I could see Lengel in my place in the slot, checking the sheep through. His face was dark gray and his back stiff, as if he'd just had an injection of iron, and my stomach kind of fell as I felt how hard the world was going to be to me hereafter.

Falcon: small car that had recently been introduced by the Ford Motor Company.

QUESTIONS

1. From Sammy's language, what do you learn about his view of himself? About his educational and class level? The first sentence, for example, is grammatically incorrect in standard English but not uncommon in colloquial English. Point out and explain similar passages.

2. Consider the first eleven paragraphs as exposition, in which you learn about the location, the issues, and the participants in the story's conflict. Is there anything inessential in this section? Do you learn enough to understand the story? How might someone other than Sammy present the material?

3. How do you learn that Sammy is an experienced "girl watcher"? What does *he think* he thinks about most girls? To what degree is this estimate inconsistent with what he finally does after the girls leave?

4. Why does Sammy say "I quit" so abruptly? What does he mean when he says that the world is going to be hard to him after his experience at the A & P?

WRITING ABOUT POINT OF VIEW

Your goal is to explain how point of view contributes to making the work exactly as it is. In prewriting, therefore, consider language, authority and opportunity for observation, the involvement or detachment of the speaker, the selection of detail, interpretive commentaries, and narrative development. The following questions will help you get started.

Questions for Discovering Ideas

• How is the narration made to seem real or probable? Are the actions and speeches reported authentically, as they might be seen and reported in life? Is the narrator identifiable? What are the narrator's qualifications as an observer? How much of the story seems to result from the imaginative or creative powers of the narrator?

• How does the narrator perceive the time of the actions? If the predominant tense is the past, what relationship, if any, does the speaker establish between the past and the present (e.g., drawing conclusions, providing explanations)? If the tense is present, what effect does this tense have on your understanding of the story?

• To what extent does the point of view make the work interesting and effective, or uninteresting and ineffective?

FIRST-PERSON POINT OF VIEW

• What is the speaker's background? What situation prompts her to tell the story?

• Is the speaker talking to the reader, a listener, or himself? How does his audience affect what he says? Is the level of language appropriate to him and the situation? How much does he tell about himself?

• To what degree is the narrator involved in the action (i.e., as a major participant, minor participant, or nonparticipating observer)? Does she make herself the center of humor or admiration? How? Does she seem aware of changes she undergoes?

- Does the speaker criticize other characters? Why? Does he seem to report fairly and accurately what others have told him?
- How reliable is the speaker? Does the speaker seem to have anything to hide? Does it seem that she may be using the story for self-justification or exoneration? What effect does this complexity have on the story?

SECOND-PERSON POINT OF VIEW

- What is the situation that prompts the use of the second person? How does the speaker acquire the authority to explain things to the listener? How directly involved is the listener? If the listeners are indefinite, why does the speaker choose to use the "you" as the basis of the narration?

THIRD-PERSON POINT OF VIEW

- Does the author seem to be speaking in an authorial voice, or has the author adopted a special but unnamed voice for the work?
- What is the speaker's level of language? Are actions, speeches, and explanations made fully or sparsely?
- From what apparent vantage point does the speaker report action and speeches? Does this vantage point make the characters seem distant or close? How much sympathy does the speaker express for the characters?
- To what degree is your interest centered on a particular character? Does the speaker give you thoughts and responses of this character (limited third person)?
- If the work is third-person omniscient, how extensive is this omniscience (e.g., does this point of view extend to all the characters or just a few)? Generally, what limitations or freedoms can be attributed to this point of view?
- What special kinds of knowledge does the narrator assume that the listeners or readers possess (e.g., art, religion, history, navigation, music)?

Strategies for Organizing Ideas

Throughout your essay, your object should be to develop your analysis of how the point of view determines such aspects as situation, form, general content, and language. The questions in the preceding section will help you decide how the point of view interacts with these other elements.

Begin by briefly stating the major influence of the point of view on the work. (Examples: "The omniscient point of view permits many insights into the major character," or "The first-person point of view permits the work to resemble an exposé of back-room political deals.") How does the point of view make the work interesting and effective? How will your analysis support your central idea?

An excellent way to build your argument is to explore how some other point of view might affect the work you are considering. Updike's "A & P," for example, uses a first-person narrator—a young man telling about an unpleasant incident in his life. You might consider whether this story could work with a third-person narration. A third-person limited narration would certainly state that the protagonist is self-critical, but the first-person point of view is superior because we learn, firsthand, about the narrator's actual feelings. Indeed, the story seems totally dependent on the use of the first-person narrator. Conversely, Mansfield's "Miss Brill" employs the third-person limited point of view, with the speaker presenting an intimate portrait of the major character but also preserving an objective and ironic distance. If Miss Brill herself were the narrator, we would get the intimacy that encourages us to sympathize with her, but we would lose the distance that permits us to see her objectively.

You can see that this approach requires creative imagination, for you must speculate about a point of view that is not present. Considering alternative points of view deeply, however, will greatly enhance your analytical and critical abilities.

In your conclusion, evaluate the success of the point of view: Is it consistent, effective, truthful? What (if anything) does the writer gain or lose with the selection of this point of view?

SAMPLE STUDENT ESSAY

Ambrose Bierce's Control over Point of View in "An Occurrence at Owl Creek Bridge"[°]

[1]   Ambrose Bierce's control over point of view in "An Occurrence at Owl Creek Bridge" is essential to his success in showing the human mental capacity to register an immense length of perceived time and action in no more than an instant of real time.[*] The story is based on the idea that it is an individual's mind, not the actual passage of time, that governs time perception. Ordinarily, time seems steady and unvarying, like the ticking of a clock (see paragraph 5 of the story); but at certain heightened moments of perception--in the story, the instant just before death--a person may fully imagine experiences that take much longer than the measurable, real time. Bierce brings this idea to life by using a narrative in the dramatic point of view as the frame of a narrative in the third-person limited omniscient point of view.[†]

[2]   The story is framed, at both the opening and closing, by materials narrated from the dramatic point of view. The opening is an objective account of the story's basic circumstances: During the Civil War, Peyton Farquhar, a southern loyalist, is about to be hanged by the Union army, apparently for the attempted sabotage of the railroad bridge spanning Owl Creek, a stream in northern Alabama. Bierce changes from the objective point of view in paragraph 4, and he then centers on Farquhar through the limited omniscient point of view. The second section of the story, which views Farquhar objectively, explains how Farquhar got to the point of hanging. Almost the entire third section--twenty descriptive paragraphs--focuses exclusively on Farquhar's last moments of life. Beginning with the reality of his drop, he perceives that the rope breaks and that he falls into the water, avoids the rifle and cannon fire of the Union soldiers, swims to shore, walks home, and is greeted by his wife. This dream of happiness is ended in paragraph 37, the last, which marks an abrupt and brutal return to the dramatic point of view with which the story opens:

[°] See pp. 203–209 for this story.
[*] Central idea.
[†] Thesis sentence.

Peyton Farquhar was dead; his body, with a broken neck, swung gently from side to side beneath the timbers of the Owl Creek bridge.

[3] The best part of the story, the "framed" part, is Bierce's use of a limited third-person narration to render Farquhar's mental perceptions. We first encounter this method in the narrator's ironic statement about Farquhar: "The arrangement [i.e., the apparatus for hanging] commended itself to his judgment as simple and effective" (paragraph 4). Bierce carefully explains how the rest of the story is to be told. First, he states that Farquhar's "thoughts, which have here to be set down in words, were flashed into the doomed man's brain" (paragraph 7). He also states that the hanging man's agony heightens his understanding: "something in the awful disturbance of his organic system" exalts and refines his physical senses so that they record things *"never before perceived"* (paragraph 20, italics added). On this principle of narration, Bierce's narrator plumbs the depths of Farquhar's dying consciousness--an entire narrative of escape that "flashes" through Farquhar's mind during his last moments.

[4] The escape, which forms the narrative of the third section, seems to be happening plausibly and realistically in just the way that the reader, naturally sympathetic to Farquhar, wants it to happen. The power of the story results from this tension between desire and actuality. Bierce's limited omniscient narrator is careful in the very second sentence of the third section to fuse together the two elements of time and perception so vital to the story's development: "ages later, it seemed to him" (paragraph 18). All the details about Farquhar's dreams of escape stem out of the words *ages* and *seemed*. Under special circumstances, in other words, human perception can fit almost a lifetime of detail into no more than fractions of a second.

[5] Therefore the dying man's perception of detail is the story's major emphasis. At first, the narrator's descriptions indicate that Farquhar's imagination is sharp enough even to record the eye color of one of the Union soldiers. Farquhar's mind soon gets weaker, however, and his perceptions become more dreamlike and impressionistic. By describing the road bordered by "black bodies" of trees forming "a straight wall on both sides, terminating on the horizon in a point," Bierce's narrator demonstrates Farquhar's dimming consciousness and increasing distortion of reality (paragraph 34). Paragraph 36, which changes the narrative from the past to the present tense, contains Farquhar's vision during the last split second of his life. His final mental image is that his wife "*steps* down from the veranda to meet him" and "*stands* waiting" for him (present tenses italicized). It is then that his life is ended forever by the very realistic "blow upon the back of the neck."

[6] Even though the events are told through Farquhar's hopeful vision of escape, however, this realistic blow reminds us that the narrative constantly reveals his physical agony. A number of times we are told that Farquhar is feeling "pain," that he is "suffocating," that he feels a "sharp pain in his wrist" and that "his neck ached horribly; his brain was on fire" (paragraphs 18, 19). We may take as equally real Farquhar's sensation that his "visible world" seems to be wheeling "slowly round" (paragraph 21), for this perception is consistent with the sensations of a hanging, dying man. In other words, just as the narrative concentrates on Farquhar's understanding of reality, it also demonstrates the true reality of his final death pangs.

[7]   Without doubt, the merging of Bierce's narrative voice with the consciousness of the dying man makes the story unique. No other method could give the story its credibility and power, which depend on the disclosure of what is happening in the protagonist's mind. For example, the use of the dramatic point of view, with which the story opens and closes, does not permit access to the internal thoughts of a character. In much the same way, the first-person point of view—focusing on an unconscious and dying man—does not permit any recording of what is happening. It is therefore clear that Bierce's limited omniscient point of view is absolutely right. The method permits him to make the events seem both realistic and convincing and also to create sympathy for Farquhar because of his poignant hopes and dreams.

[8]   Such masterly control over point of view is a major cause of Bierce's success in "An Occurrence at Owl Creek Bridge." His narrative method is to establish a frame of normal reality and normal time and then to render contrasting interior perceptions of reality and time. He is so successful that a casual reader might at first conclude that Farquhar's escape is real. The reality is not in the events, however, but in the perceptions. Without Bierce's mingling of the dramatic and the limited points of view, it would not be possible to claim such success for the story.

Commentary on the Essay

The strategy of this essay is to explain how Bierce's use of the limited omniscient point of view is fundamental to his success in demonstrating how time may be compressed in heightened moments of awareness. Words of tribute throughout the essay are "success," "control," "right," and "masterly."

The introductory paragraph sets out two major areas of investigation for the essay: first, the use of the dramatic point of view as a frame, and second, the limited omniscient point of view as the center of concentration.

The first part of the essay (paragraph 2) is relatively brief. Only enough is brought out about the dramatic point of view to establish that Bierce uses it as a beginning and ending frame for the deep examination of the narration happening in the protagonist's mind.

The second part of the body (paragraphs 3–7) emphasizes how Bierce delves into the dying protagonist's mind. The goal of paragraphs 3–5 is to show how the narrator's point of view virtually merges with that of Farquhar. Paragraph 6 is designed as a defense of the narrative method because throughout the narration, Bierce always reports the immense pain that Farquhar is feeling. In other words, the story faithfully and truthfully renders the perception of both agony and extended time. Continuing the thread of the argument, paragraph 7 examines other narrative possibilities for presenting Farquhar's vision and concludes that Bierce's actual choices are the best that could have been made.

The conclusion, paragraph 8, emphasizes again how Bierce's success is attributable to his use of both the dramatic and the limited omniscient points of view.

SPECIAL WRITING TOPICS FOR STUDYING POINT OF VIEW

1. Write a short narrative from the point of view of one of these characters:
   a. Mathilde Loisel in "The Necklace": *How I ruined ten years of my life by not telling the truth.*
   b. The baker in "Miss Brill": *My favorite customer.*
   c. Old Man Warner in "The Lottery": *People ain't the way they used to be.*
   d. Lengel in "A & P": *What could possibly have gotten into Sammy?*

2. How would the story "Young Goodman Brown" (Chapter 8) be affected if told by a narrator with a different point of view (different knowledge, different interests, different purposes for telling the story), such as the narrators of "A Worn Path" or "An Occurrence at Owl Creek Bridge"?

3. Recall a childhood occasion on which you were punished. Write an explanation of the punishment as though you were the adult who was in the position of punishing you. Be sure to consider your childhood self objectively, in the third person. Present things from the viewpoint of the adult, and try to determine how the adult would have learned about your action, judged it, and decided on your punishment.

4. Write an essay about the proposition that people often have something to gain when they speak, and that therefore we need to be critical about what others tell us. Are they trying to change our judgments and opinions? Are they telling the truth? Are they leaving out any important details? Are they trying to sell us something? In your discussion you may strengthen your ideas by referring to stories that you have been reading.

5. In the reference section of your library, find two books on literary terms and concepts. How completely and clearly do these works explain the concept of point of view? With the aid of these books, together with the materials in this chapter, describe the interests and views of the narrators in "How to Become a Writer," "I Stand Here Ironing," or another story of your choice.

6
Setting:
The Background
of Place, Objects,
and Culture in Stories

Like all human beings, literary characters do not exist in isolation. Just as they become human by interacting with other characters, they gain identity because of their possessions, their jobs, their homes, and their cultural and political allegiances. Plays, stories, and narrative poems must therefore necessarily include descriptions of objects, places, and backgrounds—the **setting.**

WHAT IS SETTING?

Setting is a work's natural, manufactured, political, cultural, and temporal environment, including everything that characters know and own. Characters may be either helped or hurt by their surroundings, and they may fight about possessions and goals. Further, as characters speak with each other, they reveal the degree to which they share the customs and ideas of their times.

Types of Settings

NATURE AND THE OUTDOORS.   The natural world is an obvious location for the action of many narratives (and plays). It is therefore important to note natural surroundings (hills, shorelines, valleys, mountains, meadows, fields, trees, lakes, streams), living creatures (birds, dogs, horses, snakes), and also the times, seasons, and conditions in which things happen (day or night, summer or winter, sunlight or darkness, wind or stillness, rain or snow, day or night, fogginess or clarity, heat or cold, dryness or humidity, storminess or calmness)—any or all of which may influence character and action.

OBJECTS OF HUMAN MANUFACTURE AND CONSTRUCTION.   To reveal or highlight qualities of character, and also to make narratives lifelike, authors include many details about objects of human manufacture and construction. Houses, both interiors and exteriors, are common, as are possessions, such as walking sticks, fences, park benches, toys, necklaces, hair ribbons, and cash registers. In Maupassant's "The Necklace," the loss of a comfortable home brings out the best in a character by causing her to adjust to her economic reversal, whereas in Lawrence's "The Horse Dealer's Daughter," such a loss leads a character to suicidal depression. In Walker's "Everyday Use," a shabby but neat house reveals strength of character. In Greenberg's "And Sarah Laughed," the major character's life within the solitude of a farm setting influences her to reach out for a new form of communication.

Objects also enter directly into fictional action and character. The wearing of bathing suits is a major cause of conflict in "A & P"; a broken birdcage reveals the pathetic husband–wife relationship in "A Jury of Her Peers"; a fur piece leads to heartbreak in "Miss Brill." Welty uses a bottle of medicine to represent the beauty of a character's love as well as the goal of her journey in "A Worn Path."

CULTURAL CONDITIONS AND ASSUMPTIONS.   Just as physical setting influences characters, so do historical and cultural conditions and assumptions. The broad cultural setting of Jackson's "The Lottery" is built on the persistence of a primitive belief in our modern and scientific age. In Chopin's "The Story of an Hour" we see how the major character, a wife, is destroyed by the traditional value that the husband should be master in the home.

THE LITERARY USES OF SETTING

Painters render ideas through the use of backgrounds and objects; in much the same way, authors render ideas through the manipulation of settings. Such uses of setting are seen in Welty's "A Worn Path" and Hawthorne's "Young Goodman Brown," where major topographical features are many obstacles and ill-defined woodland paths. Although such difficulties are normal granted the location, time, and circumstances of the stories, they succeed in conveying the idea that life is difficult and uncertain. Similarly, in Glaspell's "A Jury of Her Peers," the fixtures and utensils in the kitchen of the Wright farm indicate the bleakness and oppressiveness of midwestern homesteads early in the twentieth century.

Important Purposes of Setting

To study the setting in a narrative (or play), you need to discover the important details and then try to explain their function. Depending on the author's purpose, the amount of detail may vary. Poe provides many graphic and also impressionistic details in "The Cask of Amontillado," so that we can follow, almost visually, the bizarre action at the story's end. In some works the setting is so intensely present, like the woods in Welty's "A Worn Path," that it is almost literally an additional participant in the action.

SETTING AND CREDIBILITY.   One of the major purposes of literary setting is to establish **realism** or **verisimilitude.** As the description of location and objects becomes particular and detailed, the events of the work become more believable. In "The Story of an Hour" Chopin gives us details about the inside of the Mallard household, particularly Louise's room and the stairway landing leading to the front door. These are essential aspects of setting for the story's major scenes. Even futuristic, symbolic, and fantastic stories, as well as ghost stories, seem more believable if they include places and objects from the real world. Hawthorne's "Young Goodman Brown" and Poe's "The Fall of the House of Usher" are such stories. Though they make no pretenses to everyday realism, their credibility is enhanced because their settings are so realistic.

SETTING AND CHARACTER.   Setting may intersect with character as a means by which authors underscore the importance of place, circumstance, and time in human growth and change. Glaspell's setting in "A Jury of Her Peers" is the kitchen of the lonely, dreary Wright farm. The kitchen is a place of such hard work, oppression, and unrelieved joylessness that it explains the extinguishing of Minnie's early brightness and promise, and also helps us understand her angry action. (A blending of setting and character as seen in Maupassant's "The Necklace" is explored in the two drafts of the sample student essay in Chapter 1.)

The way characters respond and adjust to setting can reveal their strength or weakness. Peyton Farquhar's scheme to make an escape from his fate, even when it is almost literally hanging before him, suggests his character strength ("An Occurrence at Owl Creek Bridge"). In contrast, Goodman Brown's Calvinistic religious conviction that human beings are totally depraved, which not reality but his nightmarish encounter confirms, indicates the weakness of his character because it alienates him from family and community ("Young Goodman Brown").

SETTING AND ORGANIZATION.   An author may often use setting to organize a story, as in Maupassant's "The Necklace" where Mathilde and her husband move from a respectable apartment to a cheap attic flat. The story's final scene is believable because Mathilde takes a nostalgic walk on the Champs-Elysées, the most fashionable street in Paris. Without this shift of setting, she would not have encountered Jeanne Forrestier again, for their ways of life no longer bring them together.

Another organizational application of place, time, and object is the **framing** or **enclosing setting,** whereby a work begins and ends with descriptions of the same scene, thus forming a frame or enclosure. An example is Welty's "A Worn Path," which begins with the major character walking toward Natchez and ends with her leaving the clinic. The use of objects as a frame is seen in Mansfield's "Miss Brill," which opens and closes with references to the heroine's shabby fur piece. In such ways, framing creates a formal completeness, just as it may underscore the author's ideas about the human condition.

SETTING AND SYMBOL.   If the scenes and materials of setting are high-lighted or emphasized, they also may be taken as symbols through which the author expresses ideas. Such an emphasis is made in Ozick's "The Shawl," in which the shawl has the ordinary function of providing cover and warmth for the baby. Because it is so prominent, however, the shawl also suggests or sym-bolizes the attempt to preserve future generations, and because its loss also produces a human loss, it symbolizes the helplessness of the Nazi extermina-tion camp victims during World War II. In Updike's "A & P" (Chapter 5), the reference to the local Congregational church symbolizes the decorum and restraint that the people of the town—including those shopping at the A & P—are expected to exercise.

SETTING AND ATMOSPHERE.   Setting also helps to create **atmosphere** or **mood,** which refers to an enveloping or permeating emotional texture within a work. Most actions *require* no more than a functional description of setting. Thus, taking a walk in a forest needs just the statement that there are trees. However, if a story includes descriptions of shapes, light and shadow, animals, wind, and sounds, you can be sure that the author is creating an atmosphere or mood for the action (as in Hawthorne's "Young Goodman Brown"). There are many ways to develop moods. Descriptions of bright colors (red, orange, yellow) may contribute to a mood of happiness. Darkness and dark colors, like those in Poe's "The Fall of the House of Usher," may invoke gloom or augment hysteria. References to smells and sounds further bring the setting to life by asking additional sensory responses from the reader. The setting of a story in a small town or large city, in green or snow-covered fields, or in middle-class or lower-class residences may evoke responses to these places that contribute to the work's atmosphere.

SETTING AND IRONY.   Just as setting may reinforce character and theme, so it may establish expectations that are the opposite of what occurs. At the beginning of "The Lottery," for example, Jackson describes the folksiness of the assembling townspeople—details that make the conclusion ironic, for it is just these real, everyday folks who participate in the final horror. A bizarre irony is created by Poe in "The Cask of Amontillado," when Montresor repeats Fortunato's appeal "For the love of God" as he puts in place the final bricks of Fortunato's living tomb.

 # STORIES FOR STUDY

KATE CHOPIN   (1851–1904)

*Born in St. Louis, Chopin lived in Louisiana from the time
of her marriage until 1882. After her husband's death she
returned to St. Louis and began to write. She published two
collections of stories based on the life she had known back
in Louisiana:* Bayou Folk *(1894) and* A Night in
Acadie *(1897). However, she became best known for her
major novel,* The Awakening *(1899), which aroused negative reactions because it mentioned taboo subjects like adul-
tery and miscegenation. Indeed, the critical disapproval was
so intense that Chopin published no further works, even
though she was at the height of her literary power and lived
five years after the controversy.*

The Story of an Hour _____ *1894*

Knowing that Mrs. Mallard was afflicted with a heart trouble, great care was taken to
break to her as gently as possible the news of her husband's death.

It was her sister Josephine who told her, in broken sentences: veiled hints that
revealed in half concealing. Her husband's friend Richards was there, too, near her. It
was he who had been in the newspaper office when intelligence of the railroad disaster
was received, with Brently Mallard's name leading the list of "killed." He had only taken
the time to assure himself of its truth by a second telegram, and had hastened to forestall
any less careful, less tender friend in bearing the sad message.

She did not hear the story as many women have heard the same, with a paralyzed
inability to accept its significance. She wept at once, with sudden, wild abandonment,
in her sister's arms. When the storm of grief had spent itself she went away to her room
alone. She would have no one follow her.

There stood, facing the open window, a comfortable, roomy armchair. Into this
she sank, pressed down by a physical exhaustion that haunted her body and seemed to
reach into her soul.

She could see in the open square before her house the tops of trees that were all
aquiver with the new spring life. The delicious breath of rain was in the air. In the street
below a peddler was crying his wares. The notes of a distant song which some one was
singing reached her faintly, and countless sparrows were twittering in the eaves.

There were patches of blue sky showing here and there through the clouds that
had met and piled one above the other in the west facing her window.

She sat with her head thrown back upon the cushion of the chair, quite motionless, except when a sob came up into her throat and shook her, as a child who has cried
itself to sleep continues to sob in its dreams.

She was young, with a fair, calm face, whose lines bespoke repression and even a
certain strength. But now there was a dull stare in her eyes, whose gaze was fixed away off
yonder on one of those patches of blue sky. It was not a glance of reflection, but rather
indicated a suspension of intelligent thought.

There was something coming to her and she was waiting for it, fearfully. What
was it? She did not know; it was too subtle and elusive to name. But she felt it, creeping
out of the sky, reaching toward her through the sounds, the scents, the color that filled
the air.

Now her bosom rose and fell tumultuously. She was beginning to recognize this   10
thing that was approaching to possess her, and she was striving to beat it back with her
will—as powerless as her two white slender hands would have been.

When she abandoned herself a little whispered word escaped her slightly parted
lips. She said it over and over under her breath: "free, free, free!" The vacant stare and
the look of terror that had followed it went from her eyes. They stayed keen and bright.
Her pulses beat fast, and the coursing blood warmed and relaxed every inch of her body.

She did not stop to ask if it were or were not a monstrous joy that held her. A clear
and exalted perception enabled her to dismiss the suggestion as trivial.

She knew that she would weep again when she saw the kind, tender hands folded
in death; the face that had never looked save with love upon her, fixed and gray and
dead. But she saw beyond that bitter moment a long procession of years to come that
would belong to her absolutely. And she opened and spread her arms out to them in
welcome.

There would be no one to live for during those coming years; she would live for
herself. There would be no powerful will bending hers in that blind persistence with
which men and women believe they have a right to impose a private will upon a
fellow-creature. A kind intention or a cruel intention made the act seem no less a crime
as she looked upon it in that brief moment of illumination.

And yet she had loved him—sometimes. Often she had not. What did it matter!   15
What could love, the unsolved mystery, count for in face of this possession of self-
assertion which she suddenly recognized as the strongest impulse of her being!

"Free! Body and soul free!" she kept whispering.

Josephine was kneeling before the closed door with her lips to the keyhole,
imploring for admission. "Louise, open the door! I beg; open the door—you will make
yourself ill. What are you doing, Louise? For heaven's sake open the door."

"Go away. I am not making myself ill." No; she was drinking in a very elixir of life
through that open window.

Her fancy was running riot along those days ahead of her. Spring days, and
summer days, and all sorts of days that would be her own. She breathed a quick prayer
that life might be long. It was only yesterday she had thought with a shudder that life
might be long.

She arose at length and opened the door to her sister's importunities. There was a   20
feverish triumph in her eyes, and she carried herself unwittingly like a goddess of
Victory. She clasped her sister's waist, and together they descended the stairs. Richards
stood waiting for them at the bottom.

Some one was opening the front door with a latchkey. It was Brently Mallard who
entered, a little travel-stained, composedly carrying his grip-sack and umbrella. He had
been far from the scene of accident, and did not even know there had been one. He
stood amazed at Josephine's piercing cry: at Richards' quick motion to screen him from
the view of his wife.

But Richards was too late.

When the doctors came they said she had died of heart disease—of joy that kills.

QUESTIONS

1.   What do we learn about Louise's husband? How has he justified her responses?
     How are your judgments about him controlled by the context of the story?

2. How does the information about Brently Mallard's "accident" reach Louise? How is this information verified?

3. How does Louise react to the news of the accident? How do the details of her room make her reactions and thoughts possible?

4. How are the locations of the stairs and the front landing in the Mallard house essential to Louise's response at seeing her returning husband?

5. What is the apparent attitude of the narrator toward the institution of marriage? What descriptions and statements bring out this attitude?

JOANNE GREENBERG   (b. 1932)

Greenberg, a resident of Colorado, graduated from American University in Washington and also attended the University of London. Under the pseudonym "Hannah Green," she achieved wide recognition in 1964 with the novel I Never Promised You a Rose Garden, *which describes the struggles of a teenage girl against schizophrenia. In 1977, the story was made into a successful film, featuring Kathleen Quinlan. Greenberg's fiction reflects her deep concern for "problems of the less fortunate." She is a member of the National Association for the Deaf and has taught sign language. As a writer she has been prolific, producing nearly a dozen novels. "And Sarah Laughed" is taken from her collection* Rites of Passage *(1972). Recent works are* With the Snow Queen *(1991) and* No Reck'ning Made *(1993).*

And Sarah Laughed° _____ *1972*

She went to the window every fifteen minutes to see if they were coming. They would be taking the new highway cutoff; it would bring them past the south side of the farm; past the unused, dilapidated outbuildings instead of the orchards and fields that were now full and green. It would look like a poor place to the new bride. Her first impression of their farm would be of age and bleached-out, dried-out buildings on which the doors hung open like a row of gaping mouths that said nothing.

All day, Sarah had gone about her work clumsy with eagerness and hesitant with dread, picking up utensils to forget them in holding, finding them two minutes later a surprise in her hand. She had been planning and working ever since Abel wrote to them from Chicago that he was coming home with a wife. Everything should have been clean and orderly. She wanted the bride to know as soon as she walked inside what kind of woman Abel's mother was—to feel, without a word having to be said, the house's dignity, honesty, simplicity, and love. But the spring cleaning had been late, and Alma Yoder had gotten sick—Sarah had had to go over to the Yoders and help out.

Now she looked around and saw that it was no use trying to have everything ready in time. Abel and his bride would be coming any minute. If she didn't want to get caught shedding tears of frustration, she'd better get herself under control. She stepped over the pile of clothes still unsorted for the laundry and went out on the back porch.

And Sarah Laughed: See Genesis 18:12.

The sky was blue and silent, but as she watched, a bird passed over the fields crying. The garden spread out before her, displaying its varying greens. Beyond it, along the creek, there was a row of poplars. It always calmed her to look at them. She looked today. She and Matthew had planted those trees. They stood thirty feet high now, stately as figures in a procession. Once—only once and many years ago—she had tried to describe in words the sounds that the wind made as it combed those trees on its way west. The little boy to whom she had spoken was a grown man now, and he was bringing home a wife. Married. . . .

Ever since he had written to tell them he was coming with his bride, Sarah had been going back in her mind to the days when she and Matthew were bride and groom and then mother and father. Until now, it hadn't seemed so long ago. Her life had flowed on past her, blurring the early days with Matthew when this farm was strange and new to her and when the silence of it was sharp and bitter like pain, not dulled and familiar like an echo of old age.

Matthew hadn't changed much. He was a tall, lean man, but he had had a boy's spareness then. She remembered how his smile came, wavered and went uncertainly, but how his eyes had never left her. He followed everything with his eyes. Matthew had always been a silent man; his face was expressionless and his body stiff with reticence, but his eyes had sought her out eagerly and held her and she had been warm in his look.

Sarah and Matthew had always known each other—their families had been neighbors. Sarah was a plain girl, a serious "decent" girl. Not many of the young men asked her out, and when Matthew did and did again, her parents had been pleased. Her father told her that Matthew was a good man, as steady as any woman could want. He came from honest, hardworking people and he would prosper any farm he had. Her mother spoke shyly of how his eyes woke when Sarah came into the room, and how they followed her. If she married him, her life would be full of the things she knew and loved, an easy, familiar world with her parents' farm not two miles down the road. But no one wanted to mention the one thing that worried Sarah: the fact that Matthew was deaf. It was what stopped her from saying yes right away; she loved him, but she was worried about his deafness. The things she feared about it were the practical things: a fall or a fire when he wouldn't hear her cry for help. Only long after she had put those fears aside and moved the scant two miles into his different world, did she realize that the things she had feared were the wrong things.

Now they had been married for twenty-five years. It was a good marriage—good enough. Matthew was generous, strong, and loving. The farm prospered. His silence made him seem more patient, and because she became more silent also, their neighbors saw in them the dignity and strength of two people who do not rail against misfortune, who were beyond trivial talk and gossip; whose lives needed no words. Over the years of help given and meetings attended, people noticed how little they needed to say. Only Sarah's friend Luita knew that in the beginning, when they were first married, they had written yearning notes to each other. But Luita didn't know that the notes also were mute. Sarah had never shown them to anyone, although she kept them all, and sometimes she would go up and get the box out of her closet and read them over. She had saved every scrap, from questions about the eggs to the tattered note he had left beside his plate on their first anniversary. He had written it when she was busy at the stove and then he'd gone out and she hadn't seen it until she cleared the table.

The note said: "I love you derest wife Sarah. I pray you have happy day all day your life."

5

When she wanted to tell him something, she spoke to him slowly, facing him, and   10
he took the words as they formed on her lips. His speaking voice was thick and hard to
understand and he perceived that it was unpleasant. He didn't like to use it. When he
had to say something, he used his odd, grunting tone, and she came to understand what
he said. If she ever hungered for laughter from him or the little meaningless talk that
confirms existence and affection, she told herself angrily that Matthew talked through
his work. Words die in the air; they can be turned one way or another, but Matthew's
work prayed and laughed for him. He took good care of her and the boys, and they idolized him. Surely that counted more than all the words—words that meant and didn't
mean—behind which people could hide.

Over the years she seldom noticed her own increasing silence, and there were
times when his tenderness, which was always given without words, seemed to her to make
his silence beautiful.

She thought of the morning she had come downstairs feeling heavy and off balance with her first pregnancy—with Abel. She had gone to the kitchen to begin the
day, taking the coffeepot down and beginning to fill it when her eye caught something
on the kitchen table. For a minute she looked around in confusion. They had already
laid away what the baby would need: diapers, little shirts and bedding, all folded away in
the drawer upstairs, but here on the table was a bounty of cloth, all planned and
scrimped for and bought from careful, careful study of the catalogue—yards of patterned flannel and plissé, coat wool and bright red corduroy. Sixteen yards of yellow
ribbon for bindings. Under the coat wool was cloth Matthew had chosen for her; blue
with a little gray figure. It was silk, and there was a card on which was rolled precisely
enough lace edging for her collar and sleeves. All the long studying and careful planning, all in silence.

She had run upstairs and thanked him and hugged him, but it was no use showing
delight with words, making plans, matching cloth and figuring which pieces would be
for the jacket and which for sleepers. Most wives used such fussing to tell their husbands
how much they thought of their gifts. But Matthew's silence was her silence too.

When he had left to go to the orchard after breakfast that morning, she had gone
to their room and stuffed her ears with cotton, trying to understand the world as it must
be to him, with no sound. The cotton dulled the outside noises a little, but it only magnified all the noises in her head. Scratching her cheek caused a roar like a downpour of
rain; her own voice was like thunder. She knew Matthew could not hear his own voice in
his head. She could not be deaf as he was deaf. She could not know such silence ever.

So she found herself talking to the baby inside her, telling it the things she would   15
have told Matthew, the idle daily things: Didn't Margaret Amson look peaked in town?
Wasn't it a shame the drugstore had stopped stocking lump alum—her pickles wouldn't
be the same.

Abel was a good baby. He had Matthew's great eyes and gentle ways. She chattered
to him all day, looking forward to his growing up, when there would be confidences
between them. She looked to the time when he would have his own picture of the world,
and with that keen hunger and hope she had a kind of late blooming into a beauty that
made people in town turn to look at her when she passed in the street holding the baby
in the fine clothes she had made for him. She took Abel everywhere, and came to know
a pride that was very new to her, a plain girl from a modest family who had married a
neighbor boy. When they went to town, they always stopped over to see Matthew's parents and her mother.

Mama had moved to town after Pa died. Of course they had offered to have Mama come and live with them, but Sarah was glad she had gone to a little place in town, living where there were people she knew and things happening right outside her door. Sarah remembered them visiting on a certain spring day, all sitting in Mama's new front room. They sat uncomfortably in the genteel chairs, and Abel crawled around on the floor as the women talked, looking up every now and then for his father's nod of approval. After a while he went to catch the sunlight that was glancing off a crystal nut dish and scattering rainbow bands on the floor. Sarah smiled down at him. She too had a radiance, and, for the first time in her life, she knew it. She was wearing the dress she had made from Matthew's cloth—it became her and she knew that too, so she gave her joy freely as she traded news with Mama.

Suddenly they heard the fire bell ringing up on the hill. She caught Matthew's eye and mouthed, "Fire engines," pointing uphill to the firehouse. He nodded.

In the next minutes there was the strident, off-key blare as every single one of Arcadia's volunteer firemen—his car horn plugged with a matchstick and his duty before him—drove hellbent for the firehouse in an ecstasy of bell and siren. In a minute the ding-ding-ding-ding careened in deafening, happy privilege through every red light in town.

"Big bunch of boys!" Mama laughed. "You can count two Saturdays in good weather when they don't have a fire, and that's during the hunting season!"   20

They laughed. Then Sarah looked down at Abel, who was still trying to catch the wonderful colors. A madhouse of bells, horns, screaming sirens had gone right past them and he hadn't cried, he hadn't looked, he hadn't turned. Sarah twisted her head sharply away and screamed to the china cats on the whatnot shelf as loud as she could, but Abel's eyes only flickered to the movement and then went back to the sun and its colors.

Mama whispered, "Oh, my dear God!"

Sarah began to cry bitterly, uncontrollably, while her husband and son looked on, confused, embarrassed, unknowing.

The silence drew itself over the season and the seasons layered into years. Abel was a good boy; Matthew was a good man.

Later, Rutherford, Lindsay, and Franklin Delano came. They too were silent.   25
Hereditary nerve deafness was rare, the doctors all said. The boys might marry and produce deaf children, but it was not likely. When they started to school, the administrators and teachers told her that the boys would be taught specially to read lips and to speak. They would not be "abnormal," she was told. Nothing would show their handicap, and with training no one need know that they were deaf. But the boys seldom used their lifeless voices to call to their friends; they seldom joined games unless they were forced to join. No one but their mother understood their speech. No teacher could stop all the jumping, turning, gum-chewing schoolboys, or remember herself to face front from the blackboard to the sound-closed boys. The lip-reading exercises never seemed to make plain differences—"man," "pan," "began."

But the boys had work and pride in the farm. The seasons varied their silence with colors—crows flocked in the snowy fields in winter, and tones of golden wheat darkened across acres of summer wind. If the boys couldn't hear the bedsheets flapping on the washline, they could see and feel the autumn day. There were chores and holidays and the wheel of birth and planting, hunting, fishing, and harvest. The boys were familiar in town; nobody ever laughed at them, and when Sarah met neighbors at the store, they praised her sons with exaggerated praise, well meant, saying that no one could tell, no one could really tell unless they knew, about the boys not hearing.

Sarah wanted to cry to these kindly women that the simple orders the boys obeyed by reading her lips were not a miracle. If she could ever hear in their long-practiced robot voices a question that had to do with feelings and not facts, and answer it in words that rose beyond the daily, tangible things done or not done, *that* would be a miracle.

Her neighbors didn't know that they themselves confided to one another from a universe of hopes, a world they wanted half lost in the world that was; how often they spoke pitting inflection against meaning to soften it, harden it, make a joke of it, curse by it, bless by it. They didn't realize how they wrapped the bare words of love in gentle humor or wild insults that the loved ones knew were ways of keeping the secret of love between the speaker and the hearer. Mothers lovingly called their children crow-bait, mouse-meat, devils. They predicted dark ends for them, and the children heard the secrets beneath the words, heard them and smiled and knew, and let the love said-unsaid caress their souls. With her own bitter knowledge Sarah could only thank them for well-meaning and return to silence.

Standing on the back porch now, Sarah heard the wind in the poplars and she sighed. It was getting on to noon. Warm air was beginning to ripple the fields. Matthew would be ready for lunch soon, but she wished she could stand out under the warm sky forever and listen to birds stitching sounds into the endless silence. She found herself thinking about Abel again, and the bride. She wondered what Janice would be like. Abel had gone all the way to Chicago to be trained in drafting. He had met her there, in the school. Sarah was afraid of a girl like that. They had been married quickly, without family or friends or toasts or gifts or questions. It hinted at some kind of secret shame. It frightened her. That kind of girl was independent and she might be scornful of a dowdy mother-in-law. And the house was still a mess.

From down the road, dust was rising. Matthew must have seen it too. He came over the rise and toward the house walking faster than usual. He'd want to slick his hair down and wash up to meet the stranger his son had become. She ran inside and bundled up the unsorted laundry, ran upstairs and pulled a comb through her hair, put on a crooked dab of lipstick, banged her shin, took off her apron and saw a spot on her dress, put the apron on again and shouted a curse to all the disorder she suddenly saw around her.

Now the car was crunching up the thin gravel of the driveway. She heard Matthew downstairs washing up, not realizing that the bride and groom were already at the house. Protect your own, she thought, and ran down to tell him. Together they went to the door and opened it, hoping that at least Abel's familiar face would comfort them.

They didn't recognize him at first, and he didn't see them. He and the tiny bride might have been alone in the world. He was walking around to open the door for her, helping her out, bringing her up the path to the house, and all the time their fingers and hands moved and spun meanings at which they smiled and laughed; they were talking somehow, painting thoughts in the air so fast with their fingers that Sarah couldn't see where one began and the other ended. She stared. The school people had always told her that such finger-talk set the deaf apart. It was abnormal; it made freaks of them. . . . How soon Abel had accepted someone else's strangeness and bad ways. She felt so dizzy she thought she was going to fall, and she was more bitterly jealous than she had ever been before.

The little bride stopped before them appealingly and in her dead, deaf-rote voice, said, "Ah-am pliizd to meet'ou." Sarah put out her hand dumbly and it was taken and the

30

girl's eyes shone. Matthew smiled, and this time the girl spoke and waved her hands in time to her words, and then gave Matthew her hand. So Abel had told that girl about Matthew's deafness. It had never been a secret, but Sarah felt somehow betrayed.

They had lunch, saw the farm, the other boys came home from their summer school and met Janice. Sarah put out cake and tea and showed Abel and Janice up to the room she had made ready for them, and all the time the two of them went on with love-talk in their fingers; the jokes and secrets knitted silently between them, fears told and calmed, hopes spoken and echoed in the silence of a kitchen where twenty-five years of silence had imprisoned her. Always they would stop and pull themselves back to their good manners, speaking or writing polite questions and answers for the family; but in a moment or two, the talk would flag, the urgent hunger would overcome them and they would fight it, resolutely turning their eyes to Sarah's mouth. Then the signs would creep into their fingers, and the joy of talk into their faces, and they would fall before the conquering need of their communion.

Sarah's friend Luita came the next day, in the afternoon. They sat over tea with the kitchen window open for the cool breeze and Sarah was relieved and grateful to hold to a familiar thing now that her life had suddenly become so strange to her. Luita hadn't changed at all, thank God—not the hand that waved her tea cool or the high giggle that broke into generous laughter.

"She's darling!" Luita said after Janice had been introduced, and, thankfully, had left them. Sarah didn't want to talk about her, so she agreed without enthusiasm.

Luita only smiled back. "Sarah, you'll never pass for pleased with a face like that."

"It's just—just her ways," Sarah said. "She never even wrote to us before the wedding, and now she comes in and—and changes everything. I'll be honest, Luita, I didn't want Abel to marry someone who was deaf. What did we train him for, all those special classes? . . . *not* to marry another deaf person. And she hangs on him like a wood tick all day. . ." She didn't mention the signs. She couldn't.

Luita said, "It's just somebody new in the house, that's all. She's important to you, but a stranger. Addie Purkhard felt the same way and you know what a lovely girl Velma turned out to be. It just took time. . . . She's going to have a baby, did she tell you?"

"Baby? Who?" Sarah cried, feeling cold and terrified.

"Why, *Velma*. A baby due about a month after my Dolores'."

It had never occurred to Sarah that Janice and Abel could have a baby. She wanted to stop thinking about it and she looked back at Luita whose eyes were glowing with something joyful that had to be said. Luita hadn't been able to see beyond it to the anguish of her friend.

Luita said, "You know, Sarah, things haven't been so good between Sam and me. . . ." She cleared her throat. "You know how stubborn he is. The last few weeks, it's been like a whole new start for us. I came over to tell you about it because I'm so happy, and I had to share it with you."

She looked away shyly, and Sarah pulled herself together and leaned forward, putting her hand on her friend's arm. "I'm so happy for you. What happened?"

"It started about three weeks ago—a night that neither of us could get to sleep. We hadn't been arguing; there was just that awful coldness, as if we'd both been frozen stiff. One of us started talking—just lying there in the dark. I don't even know who started, but pretty soon we were telling each other the most secret things—things we never could have said in the light. He finally told me that Dolores having a baby makes him feel old and scared. He's afraid of it, Sarah, and I never knew it, and it explains why he hates to go over and see them, and why he argues with Ken all the time. Right there beside me

35

40

45

he told me so many things I'd forgotten or misunderstood. In the dark it's like thinking out loud—like being alone and yet together at the same time. I love him so and I came so close to forgetting it. . . ."

Sarah lay in bed and thought about Luita and Sam sharing their secrets in the dark. Maybe even now they were talking in their flower-papered upstairs room, moving against the engulfing seas of silence as if in little boats, finding each other and touching and then looking out in awe at the vastness all around them where they might have rowed alone and mute forever. She wondered if Janice and Abel fingered those signs in the dark on each other's body. She began to cry. There was that freedom, at least; other wives had to strangle their weeping.

When she was cried out, she lay in bed and counted all the good things she had: children, possessions, acres of land, respect of neighbors, the years of certainty and success. Then she conjured the little bride, and saw her standing in front of Abel's old car as she had at first—with nothing; all her virtues still unproven, all her fears still forming, and her bed in another woman's house. Against the new gold ring on the bride's finger, Sarah threw all the substance of her years to weigh for her. The balance went with the bride. It wasn't fair! The balance went with the bride because she had put that communion in the scales as well, and all the thoughts that must have been given and taken between them. It outweighed Sarah's twenty-five years of muteness; outweighed the house and barn and well-tended land, and the sleeping family keeping their silent thoughts.

The days went by. Sarah tortured herself with elaborate courtesy to Janice and politeness to the accomplice son, but she couldn't guard her own envy from herself and she found fault wherever she looked. Now the silence of her house was throbbing with her anger. Every morning Janice would come and ask to help, but Sarah was too restless to teach her, so Janice would sit for a while waiting and then get up and go outside to look for Abel. Then Sarah would decide to make coleslaw and sit with the chopping bowl in her lap, smashing the chopper against the wood with a vindictive joy that she alone could hear the sounds she was making, that she alone knew how savage they were and how satisfying.

At church she would see the younger boys all clean and handsome, Matthew greeting friends, Janice demure and fragile, and Abel proud and loving, and she would feel a terrible guilt for her unreasonable anger; but back from town afterwards, and after Sunday dinner, she noticed as never before how disheveled the boys looked, how ugly their hollow voices sounded. Had Matthew always been so patient and unruffled? He was like one of his own stock, an animal, a dumb animal.

Janice kept asking to help and Sarah kept saying there wasn't time to teach her.   50
She was amazed when Matthew, who was very fussy about his fruit, suggested to her that Janice might be able to take care of the grapes and, later, work in the orchard.

"I haven't time to teach her!"

"Ah owill teeech Ja-nuss," Abel said, and they left right after dinner in too much of a hurry.

Matthew stopped Sarah when she was clearing the table and asked why she didn't like Janice. Now it was Sarah's turn to be silent, and when Matthew insisted, Sarah finally turned on him. "You don't understand," she shouted. "You don't understand a thing!" And she saw on his face the same look of confusion she had seen that day in Mama's fussy front room when she had suddenly begun to cry and could not stop. She turned away with the plates, but suddenly his hand shot out and he struck them to the floor, and the voice he couldn't hear or control rose to an awful cry, "Ah ahm dehf! Ah ahm dehf!" Then he went out, slamming the door without the satisfaction of its sound.

If a leaf fell or a stalk sprouted in the grape arbor, Janice told it over like a set of prayers. One night at supper, Sarah saw the younger boys framing those dumb-signs of hers, and she took them outside and slapped their hands. "*We* don't do that!" she shouted at them, and to Janice later she said, "Those . . . signs you make—I know they must have taught you to do that, but out here . . . well, it isn't our way."

Janice looked back at her in a confusion for which there were no words.   55

It was no use raging at Janice. Before she had come there had never been anything for Sarah to be angry about. . . . What did they all expect of her? Wasn't it enough that she was left out of a world that heard and laughed without being humiliated by the love-madness they made with their hands? It was like watching them undressing.

The wind cannot be caught. Poplars may sift it, a rising bird can breast it, but it will pass by and no one can stop it. She saw the boys coming home at a dead run now, and they couldn't keep their hands from taking letters, words, and pictures from the fingers of the lovers. If they saw an eagle, caught a fish, or got scolded, they ran to their brother or his wife, and Sarah had to stand in the background and demand to be told.

One day Matthew came up to her and smiled and said, "Look." He put out his two index fingers and hooked the right down on the left, then the left down gently on the right. "Fwren," he said, "Ja-nuss say, fwren."

To Sarah there was something obscene about all those gestures, and she said, "I don't like people waving their hands around like monkeys in a zoo!" She said it very clearly so that he couldn't mistake it.

He shook his head violently and gestured as he spoke. "Mouth eat; mouth kiss,   60
mouth tawk! Fin-ger wohk; fin-ger tawk. E-ah" (and he grabbed his ear, violently), "e-ah dehf. *Mihn*," (and he rapped his head, violently, as if turning a terrible impatience against himself so as to spare her) "*mihn not* dehf!"

Later she went to the barn after something and she ran into Lindsay and Franklin Delano standing guilty, and when she caught them in her eye as she turned, she saw their hands framing signs. They didn't come into the house until it was nearly dark. Was their hunger for those signs so great that only darkness could bring them home? They weren't bad boys, the kind who would do a thing just because you told them not to. Did their days have a hunger too, or was it only the spell of the lovers, honey-honeying to shut out a world of moving mouths and silence?

At supper she looked around the table and was reassured. It could have been any farm family sitting there, respectable and quiet. A glance from the father was all that was needed to keep order or summon another helping. Their eyes were lowered, their faces composed. The hands were quiet. She smiled and went to the kitchen to fix the shortcake she had made as a surprise.

When she came back, they did not notice her immediately. They were all busy talking. Janice was telling them something and they all had their mouths ridiculously pursed with the word. Janice smiled in assent and each one showed her his sign and she smiled at each one and nodded, and the signers turned to one another in their joy, accepting and begging acceptance. Then they saw Sarah standing there; the hands came down, the faces faded.

She took the dinner plates away and brought in the dessert things, and when she went back to the kitchen for the cake, she began to cry. It was beyond envy now; it was too late for measuring or weighing. She had lost. In the country of the blind, Mama used to say, the one-eyed man is king. Having been a citizen of such a country, she knew better. In the country of the deaf, the hearing man is lonely. Into that country a girl had come who, with a wave of her hand, had given the deaf ears for one another, and had made Sarah the deaf one.

Sarah stood, staring at her cake and feeling for that moment the profundity of the silence which she had once tried to match by stuffing cotton in her ears. Everyone she loved was in the other room, talking, sharing, standing before the awful, impersonal heaven and the unhearing earth with pictures of his thoughts, and she was the deaf one now. It wasn't "any farm family," silent in its strength. It was a yearning family, silent in its hunger, and a demure little bride had shown them all how deep the hunger was. She had shown Sarah that her youth had been sold into silence. She was too old to change now.

An anger rose in her as she stared at the cake. Why should they be free to move and gesture and look different while she was kept in bondage to their silence? Then she remembered Matthew's mute notes, his pride in Abel's training, his face when he had cried, "I am deaf!" over and over. She had actually fought that terrible yearning, that hunger they all must have had for their own words. If they could all speak somehow, what would the boys tell her?

She knew what she wanted to tell them. That the wind sounds through the poplar trees, and people have a hard time speaking to one another even if they aren't deaf. Luita and Sam had to have a night to hide their faces while they spoke. It suddenly occurred to her that if Matthew made one of those signs with his hands and she could learn that sign, she could put her hands against his in the darkness, and read the meaning—that if she learned those signs she could hear him. . . .

She dried her eyes hurriedly and took in the cake. They saw her and the hands stopped, drooping lifelessly again; the faces waited mutely. Silence. It was a silence she could no longer bear. She looked from face to face. What was behind those eyes she loved? Didn't everyone's world go deeper than chores and bread and sleep?

"I want to talk to you," she said. "I want to talk, to know what you think." She put her hands out before her, offering them.

Six pairs of eyes watched her.

Janice said, "Mo-ther."

Eyes snapped away to Janice; thumb was under lip: the Sign.

Sarah followed them. "Wife," she said, showing her ring.

"Wife," Janice echoed, thumb under lip to the clasp of hands.

Sarah said, "I love. . . ."

Janice showed her and she followed hesitantly and then turned to Matthew to give and to be received in that sign.

QUESTIONS

1. Characterize Sarah. What do we learn about her character from the way she cares for her surroundings and tends to her tasks?

2. What kinds of detail about the appearance and circumstances of the farm appear in the story? Why are these details included?

3. Why does Greenberg not disclose right away that Matthew is deaf? Why does she withhold the same detail about Abel? How does Sarah respond when she learns that Abel is deaf?

4. What attitudes toward deafness and communication does Janice, with her mastery of sign language, bring out in Sarah? To what degree may her attitudes be considered a crisis? How does Sarah respond to the crisis? Why?

CYNTHIA OZICK   (b. 1928)

Ozick has published three novels, Trust *(1966),* The Cannibal Galaxy *(1983), and* The Messiah of Stockholm *(1987); three short-story collections,* The Pagan Rabbi *(1971),* Bloodshed *(1976), and* Levitation *(1982); and frequent essays and reviews, among which is the recent collection* Fame and Folly *(1996). Among her many recognitions and awards, she serves on the Board of Advisers of the* American Poetry Review. *Her 1990 novella "Puttermesser Paired" was the first story featured in* Prize Stories 1992: The O. Henry Awards, *edited by William Abrahams. "The Shawl," first published in the* New Yorker *in 1980, was republished in* The Shawl *in 1989, with a companion story describing the heroine's experiences in the United States after surviving the death camp.*

The Shawl _____ *1980*

Stella, cold, cold the coldness of hell. How they walked on the roads together, Rosa with Magda curled up between sore breasts, Magda wound up in the shawl. Sometimes Stella carried Magda. But she was jealous of Magda. A thin girl of fourteen, too small, with thin breasts of her own, Stella wanted to be wrapped in a shawl, hidden away, asleep, rocked by the march, a baby, a round infant in arms. Magda took Rosa's nipple, and Rosa never stopped walking, a walking cradle. There was not enough milk; sometimes Magda sucked air; then she screamed. Stella was ravenous. Her knees were tumors on sticks, her elbows chicken bones.

Rosa did not feel hunger; she felt light, not like someone walking but like someone in a faint, in trance, arrested in a fit, someone who is already a floating angel, alert and seeing everything, but in the air, not there, not touching the road. As if teetering on the tips of her fingernails. She looked into Magda's face through a gap in the shawl: a squirrel in a nest, safe, no one could reach her inside the little house of the shawl's windings. The face, very round, a pocket mirror of a face: but it was not Rosa's bleak complexion, dark like cholera, it was another kind of face altogether, eyes blue as air, smooth feathers of hair nearly as yellow as the Star sewn into Rosa's coat. You could think she was one of *their* babies.

Rosa, floating, dreamed of giving Magda away in one of the villages. She could leave the line for a minute and push Magda into the hands of any woman on the side of the road. But if she moved out of line they might shoot. And even if she fled the line for half a second and pushed the shawl-bundle at a stranger, would the woman take it? She might be surprised, or afraid; she might drop the shawl, and Magda would fall out and strike her head and die. The little round head. Such a good child, she gave up screaming, and sucked now only for the taste of the drying nipple itself. The neat grip of the tiny gums. One mite of a tooth tip sticking up in the bottom gum, how shining, an elfin tombstone of white marble gleaming there. Without complaining, Magda relinquished

Rosa's teats, first the left, then the right; both were cracked, not a sniff of milk. The duct crevice extinct, a dead volcano, blind eye, chill hole, so Magda took the corner of the shawl and milked it instead. She sucked and sucked, flooding the threads with wetness. The shawl's good flavor, milk of linen.

It was a magic shawl, it could nourish an infant for three days and three nights. Magda did not die, she stayed alive, although very quiet. A peculiar smell, of cinnamon and almonds, lifted out of her mouth. She held her eyes open every moment, forgetting how to blink or nap, and Rosa and sometimes Stella studied their blueness. On the road they raised one burden of a leg after another and studied Magda's face. "Aryan," Stella said, in a voice grown as thin as a string; and Rosa thought how Stella gazed at Magda like a young cannibal. And the time that Stella said "Aryan," it sounded to Rosa as if Stella had really said "Let us devour her."

But Magda lived to walk. She lived that long, but she did not walk very well, partly because she was only fifteen months old, and partly because the spindles of her legs could not hold up her fat belly. It was fat with air, full and round. Rosa gave almost all her food to Magda, Stella gave nothing; Stella was ravenous, a growing child herself, but not growing much. Stella did not menstruate. Rosa did not menstruate. Rosa was ravenous, but also not; she learned from Magda how to drink the taste of a finger in one's mouth. They were in a place without pity, all pity was annihilated in Rosa, she looked at Stella's bones without pity. She was sure that Stella was waiting for Magda to die so she could put her teeth into the little thighs.

Rosa knew Magda was going to die very soon; she should have been dead already, but she had been buried away deep inside the magic shawl, mistaken there for the shivering mound of Rosa's breasts; Rosa clung to the shawl as if it covered only herself. No one took it away from her. Magda was mute. She never cried. Rosa hid her in the barracks, under the shawl, but she knew that one day someone would inform; or one day someone, not even Stella, would steal Magda to eat her. When Magda began to walk Rosa knew that Magda was going to die very soon, something would happen. She was afraid to fall asleep; she slept with the weight of her thigh on Magda's body; she was afraid she would smother Magda under her thigh. The weight of Rosa was becoming less and less; Rosa and Stella were slowly turning into air.

Magda was quiet, but her eyes were horribly alive, like blue tigers. She watched. Sometimes she laughed—it seemed a laugh, but how could it be? Magda had never seen anyone laugh. Still, Magda laughed at her shawl when the wind blew its corners, the bad wind with pieces of black in it, that made Stella's and Rosa's eyes tear. Magda's eyes were always clear and tearless. She watched like a tiger. She guarded her shawl. No one could touch it; only Rosa could touch it. Stella was not allowed. The shawl was Magda's own baby, her pet, her little sister. She tangled herself up in it and sucked on one of the corners when she wanted to be very still.

Then Stella took the shawl away and made Magda die.

Afterward Stella said: "I was cold."

And afterward she was always cold, always. The cold went into her heart: Rosa saw that Stella's heart was cold. Magda flopped onward with her little pencil legs scribbling this way and that, in search of the shawl; the pencils faltered at the barracks opening, where the light began. Rosa saw and pursued. But already Magda was in the square outside the barracks, in the jolly light. It was the roll-call arena. Every morning Rosa had to conceal Magda under the shawl against a wall of the barracks and go out and stand in the arena with Stella and hundreds of others, sometimes for hours, and Magda, deserted, was quiet under the shawl, sucking on her corner. Every day Magda was silent,

5

10

and so she did not die. Rosa saw that today Magda was going to die, and at the same time a fearful joy ran into Rosa's two palms, her fingers were on fire, she was astonished, febrile: Magda, in the sunlight, swaying on her pencil legs, was howling. Ever since the drying up of Rosa's nipples, ever since Magda's last scream on the road, Magda had been devoid of any syllable; Magda was a mute. Rosa believed that something had gone wrong with her vocal cords, with her windpipe, with the cave of her larynx; Magda was defective, without a voice; perhaps she was deaf; there might be something amiss with her intelligence; Magda was dumb. Even the laugh that came when the ash-stippled wind made a clown out of Magda's shawl was only the air-blown showing of her teeth. Even when the lice, head lice and body lice, crazed her so that she became as wild as one of the big rats that plundered the barracks at daybreak looking for carrion, she rubbed and scratched and kicked and bit and rolled without a whimper. But now Magda's mouth was spilling a long viscous rope of clamor.

"Maaaa—"

It was the first noise Magda had ever sent out from her throat since the drying up of Rosa's nipples.

"Maaaa . . . aaa!"

Again! Magda was wavering in the perilous sunlight of the arena, scrabbling on such pitiful little bent shins. Rosa saw. She saw that Magda was grieving for the loss of her shawl, she saw that Magda was going to die. A tide of commands hammered in Rosa's nipples: Fetch, get, bring! But she did not know which to go after first, Magda or the shawl. If she jumped out into the arena to snatch Magda up, the howling would not stop, because Magda would still not have the shawl; but if she ran back into the barracks to find the shawl, and if she found it, and if she came after Magda holding it and shaking it, then she would get Magda back, Magda would put the shawl in her mouth and turn dumb again.

Rosa entered the dark. It was easy to discover the shawl. Stella was heaped under it, asleep in her thin bones. Rosa tore the shawl free and flew—she could fly, she was only air—into the arena. The sunheat murmured of another life, of butterflies in summer. The light was placid, mellow. On the other side of the steel fence, far away, there were green meadows speckled with dandelions and deep-colored violets; beyond them, even farther, innocent tiger lilies, tall, lifting their orange bonnets. In the barracks they spoke of "flowers," of "rain": excrement, thick turd-braids, and the slow stinking maroon waterfall that slunk down from the upper bunks, the stink mixed with a bitter fatty floating smoke that greased Rosa's skin. She stood for an instant at the margin of the arena. Sometimes the electricity inside the fence would seem to hum; even Stella said it was only an imagining, but Rosa heard real sounds in the wire: grainy sad voices. The farther she was from the fence, the more clearly the voices crowded at her. The lamenting voices strummed so convincingly, so passionately, it was impossible to suspect them of being phantoms. The voices told her to hold up the shawl, high; the voices told her to shake it, to whip with it, to unfurl it like a flag. Rosa lifted, shook, whipped, unfurled. Far off, very far, Magda leaned across her air-fed belly, reaching out with the rods of her arms. She was high up, elevated, riding someone's shoulder. But the shoulder that carried Magda was not coming toward Rosa and the shawl, it was drifting away, the speck of Magda was moving more and more into the smoky distance. Above the shoulder a helmet glinted. The light tapped the helmet and sparkled it into a goblet. Below the helmet a black body like a domino and a pair of black boots hurled themselves in the direction of the electrified fence. The electric voices began to chatter wildly. "Maa-maa, maaamaaa," they all hummed together. How far Magda was from Rosa

15

now, across the whole square, past a dozen barracks, all the way on the other side! She was no bigger than a moth.

All at once Magda was swimming through the air. The whole of Magda traveled through loftiness. She looked like a butterfly touching a silver vine. And the moment Magda's feathered round head and her pencil legs and balloonish belly and zigzag arms splashed against the fence, the steel voices went mad in their growling, urging Rosa to run and run to the spot where Magda had fallen from her flight against the electrified fence; but of course Rosa did not obey them. She only stood, because if she ran they would shoot, and if she tried to pick up the sticks of Magda's body they would shoot, and if she let the wolf's screech ascending now through the ladder of her skeleton break out, they would shoot; so she took Magda's shawl and filled her own mouth with it, stuffed it in and stuffed it in, until she was swallowing up the wolf's screech and tasting the cinnamon and almond depth of Magda's saliva; and Rosa drank Magda's shawl until it dried.

QUESTIONS

1. Describe how Ozick presents the setting. Why do you not receive a clear picture of how things look? Why does Ozick present the details as she does?

2. In paragraph 15, what is on the other side of the fence? Explain Ozick's description here. Why does Ozick include these details so close to the story's end?

3. What character is the center of interest in "The Shawl"? Why is she being treated as she is? What are her impressions of the conditions and circumstances around her? What are her responses to her hunger and deprivation?

4. Explain the function of the more unpleasant and brutal details. What do you need to know about the circumstances of the story to respond to these details?

EDGAR ALLAN POE   (1809–1849)

Orphaned as an infant, Poe was brought up in the household of John Allan, a prospering Virginia merchant. He entered West Point in 1830, but was expelled in 1831. He then took up his literary career—poet, fiction writer, essayist, critic, and lecturer—which kept him fed but never secure. As a fiction writer he created the genres of detective story, murder story, horror story, and psychological story (sometimes overlapping in the same work). His fictional topics are uncanny and often weird, consisting of intricate punishments, live burials, mysterious substitutions of personality, journeys into unknown regions, trips to the moon, physical and psychological collapse, and strange and sometimes comic resurrections of the dead. In the decades after his death Poe was not highly regarded, but today, of all nineteenth-century American writers, he is the most widely read. His stature was fully acknowledged in 1986, when his name was placed in the Hall of Fame of American Authors.

The Cask of Amontillado _____ 1846

The thousand injuries of Fortunato I had borne as I best could; but when he ventured upon insult, I vowed revenge. You, who so well know the nature of my soul, will not suppose, however, that I gave utterance to a threat. *At length* I would be avenged: this was a point definitively settled—but the very definitiveness with which it was resolved, precluded the idea of risk. I must not only punish, but punish with impunity. A wrong is unredressed when retribution overtakes its redresser. It is equally unredressed when the avenger fails to make himself felt as such to him who has done the wrong.

It must be understood, that neither by word nor deed had I given Fortunato cause to doubt my good-will. I continued. as was my wont, to smile in his face, and he did not perceive that my smile *now* was at the thought of his immolation.

He had a weak point—this Fortunato—although in other regards he was a man to be respected and even feared. He prided himself on his connoisseurship in wine. Few Italians have the true virtuoso spirit. For the most part their enthusiasm is adopted to suit the time and opportunity—to practice imposture upon the British and Austrian millionaires. In painting and gemmary Fortunato, like his countrymen, was a quack— but in the matter of old wines he was sincere. In this respect I did not differ from him materially: I was skilful in the Italian vintages myself, and bought largely whenever I could.

It was about dusk, one evening during the supreme madness of the carnival season, that I encountered my friend. He accosted me with excessive warmth, for he had been drinking much. The man wore motley. He had on a tight-fitting parti-striped dress, and his head was surmounted by the conical cap and bells. I was so pleased to see him, that I thought I should never have done wringing his hand.

I said to him: "My dear Fortunato, you are luckily met. How remarkably well you are looking today! But I have received a pipe of what passes for Amontillado, and I have my doubts."   5

"How?" said he. "Amontillado? A pipe? Impossible! And in the middle of the carnival!"

"I have my doubts," I replied; "and I was silly enough to pay the full Amontillado price without consulting you in the matter. You were not to be found, and I was fearful of losing a bargain."

"Amontillado!"

"I have my doubts."

"Amontillado!"   10

"And I must satisfy them."

"Amontillado!"

"As you are engaged, I am on my way to Luchesi. If anyone has a critical turn, it is he: He will tell me—"

"Luchesi cannot tell Amontillado from Sherry."

"And yet some fools will have it that his taste is a match for your own."   15

"Come, let us go."

"Whither?"

"To your vaults."

"My friend, no; I will not impose upon your good nature. I perceive you have an engagement. Luchesi—"

"I have no engagement;—come."   20

"My friend, no. It is not the engagement, but the severe cold with which I perceive you are afflicted. The vaults are insufferably damp. They are encrusted with nitre."

"Let us go, nevertheless. The cold is merely nothing. Amontillado! You have been imposed upon. And as for Luchesi, he cannot distinguish Sherry from Amontillado."

Thus speaking, Fortunato possessed himself of my arm. Putting on a mask of black silk, and drawing a *roquelaure*° about my person, I suffered him to hurry me to my palazzo.

There were no attendants at home; they had absconded to make merry in honor of the time. I had told them that I should not return until the morning, and had given them explicit orders not to stir from the house. These orders were sufficient, I well knew, to insure their immediate disappearance, one and all, as soon as my back was turned.

I took from their sconces two flambeaux, and giving one to Fortunato, bowed him   25
through several suites of rooms to the archway that led into the vaults. I passed down a long and winding staircase, requesting him be cautious as he followed. We came at length to the foot of the descent, and stood together on the damp ground of the catacombs of the Montresors.

The gait of my friend was unsteady, and the bells upon his cap jingled as he strode.

"The pipe?" said he.

"It is farther on," said I; "but observe the white webwork which gleams from these cavern walls."

He turned toward me, and looked into my eyes with two filmy orbs that distilled the rheum of intoxication.

"Nitre?" he asked, at length.   30

"Nitre," I replied. "How long have you had that cough?"

"Ugh! ugh! ugh!—ugh! ugh! ugh!—ugh! ugh! ugh!—ugh! ugh! ugh!—ugh! ugh! ugh!"

My poor friend found it impossible to reply for many minutes.

"It is nothing," he said at last.

"Come," I said, with decision, "we will go back; your health is precious. You are   35
rich, respected, admired, beloved; you are happy, as once I was. You are a man to be missed. For me it is no matter. We will go back; you will be ill, and I cannot be responsible. Besides, there is Luchesi—"

"Enough," he said; "the cough is a mere nothing; it will not kill me. I shall not die of a cough."

"True—true," I replied; "and, indeed, I had no intention of alarming you unnecessarily; but you should use all proper caution. A draught of this Medoc will defend us from the damps."

Here I knocked off the neck of a bottle which I drew from a long row of its fellows that lay upon the mould.

"Drink," I said, presenting him the wine.

He raised it to his lips with a leer. He paused and nodded to me familiarly, while   40
his bells jingled.

"I drink," he said, "to the buried that repose around us."

"And I to your long life."

He again took my arm, and we proceeded.

"These vaults," he said, "are extensive."

"The Montresors," I replied, "were a great and numerous family."   45

"I forget your arms."

"A huge human foot *d'or*, in a field azure; the foot crushes a serpent rampant whose fangs are imbedded in the heel."

roquelaure: a type of cloak.

"And the motto?"

"Nemo me impune lacessit."°

"Good!" he said.   50

The wine sparkled in his eyes and the bells jingled. My own fancy grew warm with the Medoc. We had passed through walls of piled bones, with casks and puncheons intermingling, into the inmost recesses of the catacombs. I paused again, and this time I made bold to seize Fortunato by an arm above the elbow.

"The nitre!" I said; "see, it increases. It hangs like moss upon the vaults. We are below the river's bed. The drops of moisture trickle among the bones. Come, we will go back ere it is too late. Your cough—"

"It is nothing," he said; "let us go on. But first, another draught of the Medoc."

I broke and reached him a flagon of De Grâve. He emptied it at a breath. His eyes flashed with a fierce light. He laughed and threw the bottle upward with a gesticulation I did not understand.

I looked at him in surprise. He repeated the movement—a grotesque one.   55

"You do not comprehend?" he said.

"Not I," I replied.

"Then you are not of the brotherhood."

"How?"

"You are not of the Masons."   60

"Yes, yes," I said; "yes, yes."

"You? Impossible! A Mason?"

"A Mason," I replied.

"A sign," he said.

"It is this," I answered, producing a trowel from beneath the folds of my *roquelaure*.   65

"You jest," he exclaimed, recoiling a few paces. "But let us proceed to the Amontillado."

"Be it so," I said, replacing the tool beneath the cloak, and again offering him my arm. He leaned upon it heavily. We continued our route in search of the Amontillado. We passed through a range of low arches, descended, passed on, and descending again, arrived at a deep crypt, in which the foulness of the air caused our flambeaux rather to glow than flame.

At the most remote end of the crypt there appeared another less spacious. Its walls had been lined with human remains, piled to the vault overhead, in the fashion of the great catacombs of Paris. Three sides of this interior crypt were still ornamented in this manner. From the fourth the bones had been thrown down, and lay promiscuously upon the earth, forming at one point a mound of some size. Within the wall thus exposed by the displacing of the bones, we perceived a still interior recess, in depth about four feet, in width three, in height six or seven. It seemed to have been constructed for no especial use within itself, but formed merely the interval between two of the colossal supports of the roof of the catacombs, and was backed by one of their circumscribing walls of solid granite.

It was in vain that Fortunato, uplifting his dull torch, endeavored to pry into the depth of the recess. Its termination the feeble light did not enable us to see.

"Proceed," I said; "herein is the Amontillado. As for Luchesi—"   70

"He is an ignoramus," interrupted my friend, as he stepped unsteadily forward, while I followed immediately at his heels. In an instant he had reached the extremity of

Nemo me impune lacessit: No one attacks me with impunity.

the niche, and finding his progress arrested by the rock, stood stupidly bewildered. A moment more and I had fettered him to the granite. In its surface were two iron staples, distant from each other about two feet, horizontally. From one of these depended a short chain, from the other a padlock. Throwing the links about his waist, it was but the work of a few seconds to secure it. He was too much astounded to resist. Withdrawing the key I stepped back from the recess.

"Pass your hand," I said, "over the wall; you cannot help feeling the nitre. Indeed it is *very* damp. Once more let me *implore* you to return. No? Then I must positively leave you. But I must first render you all the little attentions in my power."

"The Amontillado!" ejaculated my friend, not yet recovered from his astonishment.

"True," I replied; "the Amontillado."

As I said these words I busied myself among the pile of bones of which I have before spoken. Throwing them aside, I soon uncovered a quantity of building stone and mortar. With these materials and with the aid of my trowel, I began vigorously to wall up the entrance of the niche.

I had scarcely laid the first tier of the masonry when I discovered that the intoxication of Fortunato had in a great measure worn off. The earliest indication I had of this was a low moaning cry from the depth of the recess. It was *not* the cry of a drunken man. There was then a long and obstinate silence. I laid the second tier, and the third, and the fourth; and then I heard the furious vibrations of the chain. The noise lasted for several minutes, during which, that I might hearken to it with the more satisfaction, I ceased my labors and sat down upon the bones. When at last the clanking subsided, I resumed the trowel, and finished without interruption the fifth, the sixth, and the seventh tier. The wall was now nearly upon a level with my breast. I again paused, and holding the flambeaux over the mason-work, threw a few feeble rays upon the figure within.

A succession of loud and shrill screams, bursting suddenly from the throat of the chained form, seemed to thrust me violently back. For a brief moment I hesitated— I trembled. Unsheathing my rapier, I began to grope with it about the recess; but the thought of an instant reassured me. I placed my hand upon the solid fabric of the catacombs, and felt satisfied. I reapproached the wall. I replied to the yells of him who clamored. I reechoed—I aided—I surpassed them in volume and in strength. I did this, and the clamorer grew still.

It was now midnight, and my task was drawing to a close. I had completed the eighth, the ninth, and the tenth tier. I had finished a portion of the last and the eleventh; there remained but a single stone to be fitted and plastered in. I struggled with its weight; I placed it partially in its destined position. But now there came from out the niche a low laugh that erected the hairs upon my head. It was succeeded by a sad voice, which I had difficulty in recognizing as that of the noble Fortunato. The voice said—

"Ha! ha! ha!—he! he!—a very good joke indeed—an excellent jest. We will have many a rich laugh about it at the palazzo—he! he! he!—over our wine—he! he! he!"

"The Amontillado!" I said.

"He! he! he!—he! he! he!—yes, the Amontillado. But is it not getting late? Will not they be awaiting us at the palazzo, the Lady Fortunato and the rest? Let us be gone."

"Yes," I said, "let us be gone."

"For the love of God, Montresor!"

"Yes," I said, "for the love of God!"

But to these words I hearkened in vain for a reply. I grew impatient. I called aloud:

"Fortunato!"

No answer. I called again:

"Fortunato!"

No answer still. I thrust a torch through the remaining aperture and let it fall within. There came forth in return only a jingling of the bells. My heart grew sick—on account of the dampness of the catacombs. I hastened to make an end of my labor. I forced the last stone into its position. I plastered it up. Against the new masonry I reerected the old rampart of bones. For the half of a century no mortal has disturbed them. *In pace requiescat!*°

QUESTIONS

1. What is the nature of the narration? Who is speaking? To whom is he speaking? What is the purpose of the narrator's "May he rest in peace" at the end? Why is the nature of Fortunato's insult against Montresor not explained?

2. What do you learn about revenge from Montresor? What do you learn about Montresor from his analysis of revenge and from his family's coat of arms?

3. How does Montresor manipulate Fortunato so that Fortunato seems to be the originator of the trip to examine the Amontillado? Who is Luchesi? What does Fortunato think of Luchesi?

4. Describe Poe's use of setting in "The Cask of Amontillado" (e.g., the cap and bells, Montresor's clothing, the interior recess in which Fortunato is pinioned, etc.).

In pace requiescat: May he rest in peace.

WRITING ABOUT SETTING

In preparing to write about setting, determine the number and importance of locations, artifacts, and customs. Ask questions such as those in the following section.

Questions for Discovering Ideas

- How fully are objects described? How vital are they to the action? How important are they in the development of the plot or idea? How are they connected to the mental states of the characters?

- What connections, if any, are apparent between locations and characters? Do the locations bring characters together, separate them, facilitate their privacy, make intimacy and conversation difficult?

- How well done are the visual descriptions? Does the author provide such vivid and carefully arranged details about surroundings that you might even be able to draw a map or plan? Or is the scenery vague and difficult to imagine?

- How important to plot and character are shapes, colors, times of day, clouds, storms, light and sun, seasons of the year, and conditions of vegetation?

- Are the characters poor, moderately well-off, or rich? How does their economic lot determine what happens to them? How does their economic condition affect their actions and attitudes?

- What cultural, religious, and political conditions are displayed and acted upon in the story? How do the characters accept and adjust to these conditions? How do the conditions affect the characters' judgments and actions?

- What is the state of houses, furniture, and objects (e.g., new and polished, old and worn)? What connections can you find between this condition and the outlook and behavior of the characters?

- How important are sounds or silences? To what degree is music or other sound important in the development of character and action?

- Do characters respect or mistreat the environment? If there is an environmental connection, how central is it to the story?

- What conclusions do you think the author expects you to draw as a result of the neighborhood, culture, and larger world of the story?

Strategies for Organizing Ideas

Following are five possible approaches to essays on setting. Choose one that seems appropriate, bearing in mind that some works invite one approach rather than others. As you develop your essay, however, you may find it necessary to introduce one or more of the other approaches. Whatever approach you use, be sure to consider setting not as an end in itself, but rather as illustration and evidence.

1. *Setting and action.* Explore the importance of setting in the work. How extensively is the setting described? Are locations essential or incidental to the actions? Does the setting serve as part of the action (e.g., places of flight or concealment; public places where people meet openly, or hidden places where they meet privately; natural or environmental conditions; seasonal conditions such as searing heat or numbing cold; customs and conventions)? Do any objects cause inspiration, difficulty, or conflict (for example, a bridge, a cellar, a fur piece, a walking stick, a necklace, a nickel, a hair ribbon, a toy windmill, a dead bird)? How directly do these objects influence the action?

2. *Setting and organization.* How is the setting connected to the various parts of the work? Does it undergo any changes as the action develops? Why are some parts of the setting more important than others? Is the setting used as a structural frame or enclosure for the story? How do objects, such as money or property, affect the motivation of the characters? How do descriptions made at the start become important in the action later on?

3. *Setting and character.* (For examples of this approach, see the two drafts of the sample student essay in Chapter 1, pp. 25 and 35.) Analyze the degree to which setting influences and interacts with character. Are the characters happy or unhappy where they live? Do they get into discussions or arguments about their home environments? Do they want to stay or leave? Do the economic, philosophical, religious, or ethnic aspects of the setting make the characters undergo changes? What jobs do the characters perform because of their ways of life? What freedoms or restraints do these jobs cause? How does the setting influence their decisions, transportation, speech habits, eating habits, attitudes about love and honor, and general behavior?

4. *Setting and atmosphere.* To what extent does setting contribute to the atmosphere of the story? Does the setting go beyond the minimum needed for action or character? How do descriptive words paint verbal pictures and evoke moods through references to colors, shapes, sounds, smells, or tastes? Does the setting establish a feeling, say, of joy or hopelessness, plenty or scarcity? Do events happen in daylight or at night? Do the movements and locations of the characters suggest permanence or impermanence (like the return to a darkened room, the creation of a brick wall, or the purchase of a fragile toy)? Are things warm and pleasant, or cold and harsh? What connection do you find between the story's atmosphere and the author's apparent thoughts about existence?

5. *Setting and other aspects.* Does setting reinforce the story's credibility and meaning? Does it establish irony about the circumstances and ideas in the story? If you choose this approach, consult the section earlier in this chapter titled "Important Purposes of Setting." If you want to write about the symbolic implications of a setting, consult the discussions of symbolism in Chapter 8.

To conclude, summarize your major points or write about related aspects of setting that you have not considered. Thus, if your essay treats the relationship of setting and action, your conclusion could mention connections of the setting with character or atmosphere. You might also point out whether your central idea about setting also applies to other major aspects of the story.

SAMPLE STUDENT ESSAY

Edgar Allan Poe's Use of Setting to Create a Mood of Horror and Repulsion in "The Cask of Amontillado"°

[1]

In "The Cask of Amontillado," Poe uses many details of setting to create a mood of horror and repulsion.* The story is a detailed narration of an act of premeditated and ghastly vengeance. Poe's character Montresor is both the narrator and the principal creator of the twisted act of murder. He believes that his vengeance must be known by the victim, Fortunato, and that it must be threatening and irrevocable. At the end he is successful, and the reader is both fascinated and repulsed by the story's mood of ghastliness and heartlessness. The mood is established through Poe's descriptions of underground rooms, space, and sound.†

[2]

The height of Poe's graphic description is the story's evocation of gloomy and threatening vaults. The journey into the hellish "catacombs of the Montresors" (paragraph 25), which are also the area for the storage of Montresor's wine collection, ends with a room "lined with human remains, piled to the vault overhead" (paragraph 68). The walls in the rooms leading to this last, horrible room are dark and damp, and they drip moisture from the river above;

° See pp. 258–63 for this story.
* Central idea.
† Thesis sentence.

they also become increasingly airless and suffocating. The bones on the walls and floors are evidence of generations of death. In addition, Montresor uses the bones first to hide his bricks and mortar and then to disguise the wall within which he entombs Fortunato. The mood is further fixed by the narrator's observations that each of the catacomb rooms is progressively more covered and shrouded by spiderlike white and ghostly films of nitre, which gloomily suggest increasing death and decay.

[3]   The most disturbing of the catacomb rooms is the last one, the "interior recess" which is to be Fortunato's vertical grave. It is an inauspicious area, which Poe indicates was built "for no especial use within itself" (paragraph 68), but its measurements are ominous. It is no accident that Poe gives us the dimensions of the recess. It is four feet deep, three feet wide, and 6 or 7 feet high--exactly the size of a large coffin standing on end. The failure of the faltering torches to illuminate the area suggests the ending of breath and light, and the beginning of death. What could be more appropriately sinister, distressing, and ghostly?

[4]   The rooms not only provoke horror, but they are spatially arranged to complement Montresor's horrible act of vengeance. To reach these increasingly dark areas, the characters must continually walk downward. A circular staircase begins the descent, followed by a first and then a second set of stairs that end in the last deep crypt. The downward direction is like an inevitable journey toward the grave, and it also suggests a journey into a bleak, cold, dark, and damp hell.

[5]   Within this interior of death, Poe adds the eeriness of fearsome sound. Fortunato has a terrible rasping cough, to which Poe devotes an entire paragraph (paragraph 32). The jingling of the bells on Fortunato's carnival cap appear at first ordinary (paragraph 26), then bizarre (paragraph 40), and finally sepulchral (paragraph 89). Fortunato's attempt to get free of the chains results in desperate clanking (paragraph 76). He also moans (paragraph 76), laughs in fear and disbelief (paragraph 78), speaks weakly and sadly (paragraph 78), and at the end is silent (paragraph 89). Perhaps the most grisly sounds described by Poe are those of Fortunato's screams of protest, which Montresor cruelly stifles by screaming even louder and longer (paragraph 77)--an action that was duplicated for the insane man in the film The Silence of the Lambs. These described sounds, having their source in Montresor's diabolical action, create a mood of uneasiness, anxiety, repulsion, and horror.

[6]   Thus Poe's setting within the eerie catacombs is both descriptive and evocative. The major action takes place in the last room, in the gravelike recess, leading to the climax of the story's movement into darkness and the very walls of death. In this way, Poe uses his setting to show the horror of a twisted mind prompting a diseased individual to create a cruel and pitiless act of revenge. The events of the story, the sustained mood, and the narrator's compulsion with vengeance are all tied together by Poe's skillful control of setting.

Commentary on the Essay

Because it treats the relationship of setting to mood or atmosphere, this essay illustrates approach 4 described on page 265. The essay considers those aspects of setting needed for the story and then stresses how Poe's descriptions create the story's dominant mood of horror and repulsion.

In the body, paragraphs 2 and 3 form a unit describing the physical layout of the deathly catacombs, and also pointing out the exactness and evocativeness of Poe's descriptions. Paragraph 4 concentrates on Poe's description of downward movement, suggesting that this use of space is a visual accompaniment of the story's conclusion in Fortunato's death.

Paragraph 5 treats Poe's use of sound as an accompaniment to the descriptions of the deadly catacombs. The paragraph's topic idea is that the sounds move progressively toward silence, in keeping with Montresor's creation of death. References to sound are therefore one of Poe's major means of achieving an atmosphere complementary to the repulsive and horrible action.

The conclusion summarizes the central idea, stressing once again that Poe goes beyond simple description to heighten the twisted, macabre mood of his story.

SPECIAL WRITING TOPICS FOR STUDYING SETTING

1. Compare and contrast how details of setting establish qualities and traits of the following female characters: Sarah of "And Sarah Laughed," Stella of "The Shawl," Mrs. Johnson of "Everyday Use" (Chapter 2), and Miss Brill of "Miss Brill" (Chapter 5). For suggestions about how to proceed with a comparison-contrast essay, see Chapter 29.

2. In what ways might we say that both "The Story of an Hour" and "The Cask of Amontillado" are inseparable from their settings? To answer this question, consider the relationship of character to place and circumstance? How could the actions of the stories happen without the locations in which they occur?

3. Choose a story included in this chapter and rewrite a page or two, taking the characters out of their setting and placing them in an entirely new setting, or in the setting of another story (you choose). Then write a brief analysis dealing with these questions: How were your characters affected by their new settings? Did you make them change slowly or rapidly? Why? As a result of your rewriting, what can you conclude about the uses of setting in fiction?

4. Write a short narrative as though it is part of a story (which you may also wish to write for the assignment), using option *a* and/or *b*.

    a. Relate a natural setting or type of day to a mood—for example, a nice day to happiness and satisfaction or a cold, cloudy, rainy day to sadness. Or create irony by relating the nice day to sadness or the rainy day to happiness.

    b. Indicate how an object or circumstance becomes the cause of conflict or reconciliation (such as the shawl in "The Shawl," the sign language in "And Sarah Laughed," or the wine in "The Cask of Amontillado."

5. In your library locate two books on the career of Edgar Allan Poe. Based on information you find in these sources, write a brief account of Poe's uses of setting and place to evoke atmosphere and to bring out qualities of human character.

7

Tone and Style:
The Words That Convey
Attitudes in Fiction

Tone refers to the methods by which writers and speakers reveal attitudes or feelings—toward the material, toward their readers, and toward the general situation they are describing or analyzing. It is an aspect of all spoken and written statements, whether earnest declarations of love, requests to pass a dinner dish, letters from students asking parents for money, or official government notices threatening penalties if taxes and fines are not paid. Because tone is often equated with *attitude,* it is important to realize that tone refers not to attitude as such but rather to those modes of expression that reveal or create attitude.

Although tone is a vast subject that can involve large matters of action and situation, in this chapter we will treat the interconnectedness of tone and style. **Style** is usually understood to refer to the ways in which writers assemble words to tell the story, to develop the argument, to dramatize the play, or to compose the poem. Sometimes style is distinguished from content, but actually style is best considered as the choice of words in the *service* of content. The written expression of an action or scene, in other words, cannot be separated from the action or scene itself, nor can it be separated from the impressions and attitudes it creates.

By reading a story carefully, we may deduce the author's attitude or attitudes toward the subject matter and toward readers. In "The Story of an Hour," for example (Chapter 6), Kate Chopin sympathetically portrays a young wife's secret wishes for freedom, just as she also sardonically reveals the unwitting smugness that sometimes pervades men's relationships with women.

Words and subject matter may also indicate the writer's assessment of readers. When Hawthorne's woodland guide in "Young Goodman Brown" refers to "King Philip's War," for example, Hawthorne assumes that his readers know that this war was cruel and inhumane. In this way he indicates respect for the knowledge of his readers, and he also supposes their agreement with his interpretation. Authors always make such considerations about readers by implicitly complimenting them on their capacity to recognize and understand the ways in which materials are presented.

DICTION: WORD CHOICES

Control over style and tone is highly individual, because all authors put words uniquely together to fit the specific conditions in specific works. We may therefore speak of the *style* of Ernest Hemingway and the *style* of Margaret Atwood, even though both writers adapt words to situations. Thus an author may have a distinct style for narrative and descriptive passages, but a very different style for dialogue.

The essential aspect of style is **diction,** the writer's selection of words. Words must foremost be accurate and comprehensive, so that all actions, scenes, and ideas are clear. If a writer's work is effective—if it portrays an action graphically and clearly, explains ideas accurately, and indicates the conditions of human relationships among the major characters—we may confidently say that the words are right. Additionally, right words bear the burden of controlling the ways in which readers respond to the material. Thus, a passage of action should verbally create the action and the place or places in which things happen, and it should also cause readers to be interested and involved. Similarly, explanatory or reflective passages should be clear but should also pique the curiosity and satisfy the understanding of readers. In short, the writer should make all efforts to control the work's tone.

Formal, Neutral, and Informal Diction

As a guide to the types of words authors use to control tone, a major classification of words can be made according to degrees of formality or informality. The choices of diction are **formal** or *high*, **neutral** or *middle*, and **informal** or *low*. *Formal* or *high* diction is designed to confer major importance to the characters and actions being described. It consists of standard and also "elegant" words (frequently polysyllabic), correct word order, and the absence of contractions. The sentence "It is I," for example, is formal, for this expression is more "elegant" than most people normally now use. An example of formal diction may be seen in the narrative sections of Hawthorne's "Young Goodman Brown" (Chapter 8).

Neutral or *middle* diction is ordinary, everyday standard vocabulary, shunning longer words but using contractions when necessary. The sentence "It's me," is an example of what many people naturally say in preference to the formal "It is I." Neutral diction is appropriate for stories about everyday, ordinary people going through situations they encounter or can imagine encountering in their lives. Generally, today's writers favor neutral diction as a means of putting their characters in a light that is normal and appropriate but also respectful. Thus Hodgins's "The Concert Stages of Europe" is about a major event in the life of a young boy living in a small town in the west of Canada during World War II, and the language describing the situation is, appropriately, middle rather than high. In Alice Munro's "The Found Boat" we see neutral, middle diction:

> Nobody said a word this time, they all bent and stripped themselves. Eva, naked first, started running across the field, and then all the others ran, all five of them running bare through the knee-high hot grass, running towards the river. Not caring now about being caught but in fact leaping and yelling to call attention to themselves, if there was anybody to hear or see. They felt as if they were going to jump off a cliff and fly. They felt that something was happening to them different from anything that had happened before, and it had to do with the boat, the water, the sunlight, the dark ruined station, and each other. They thought of each other now hardly as names or people, but as echoing shrieks, reflections, all bold and white and loud and scandalous, and as fast as arrows. They went running without a break into the cold water and when it came almost to the tops of their legs they fell on it and swam. It stopped their noise. Silence, amazement, came over them in a rush. They dipped and floated and separated, sleek as mink. (paragraph 87)

The words of this passage are ordinary and easy. They are centered directly on the subject and do not draw attention to themselves. In an almost ritualistic way, the paragraph describes young people running impetuously toward a river and diving in. This action can be construed as sexually symbolic, but Munro's diction focuses on the experience itself, and the words are not analytical. If her intention had been to create searching psychological scrutiny, she might have used formal or high words from the language of psychology (*libido, urge, sublimation,* and so on). Instead, she uses words that could have been in the vocabularies of the characters and that they themselves might have used to express their sensations. Hence they feel "as if they were going to jump off a cliff and fly" and in their excitement they think "that something was happening to them different from anything that had happened before." These middle, neutral words enable us to focus on the excitement of the situation rather than on hidden psychological significance. Munro therefore does not instruct us so much as she causes us to be amused and happy about the young people cavorting on the field and in the water.

Informal or *low* diction may range from *colloquial*—the language of relaxed, common activities—to the level of *substandard* or *slang* expressions. A person speaking to a close friend uses diction that would not be appropriate in public and formal situations and even in some social situations. Informal or low diction is thus appropriate for some narrative dialogue, depending, of course, on individual speakers. It is also a natural choice for stories told in the first-person point of view as though the speaker is talking directly to sympathetic and relaxed close friends—"pals." In Updike's "A & P" (Chapter 5) Sammy's first sentence illustrates informal, low diction:

In walks these three girls in nothing but bathing suits.

Note the idiomatic and ungrammatical "In walks these three girls," a singular verb followed by a plural subject. Note also the colloquial use of "these" as a demonstrative adjective with no antecedent. The idea underlying these expressions is to set us at ease, to encourage us to listen attentively to the story that the young speaker is about to tell us.

SPECIFIC-GENERAL AND CONCRETE-ABSTRACT LANGUAGE

Another aspect of language is its degree of explicitness. **Specific** refers to words that bring to mind images from the real world. "My dog Woofie is barking" is specific. **General** statements refer to broad classes, such as "All people like pets" and "Dogs make good pets." There is an ascending order of generality from (1) very specific, to (2) less specific, to (3) general, as though the words themselves climb a stairway. Thus *peach* is a specific fruit. *Fruit* is specific but more general because it may also include apples, oranges, and all other fruits. *Dessert* is a still more general word, which can include all sweets, including fruits and peaches, and also other confections, like ice cream.

While *specific-general* refers to categories, *concrete-abstract* refers to qualities or conditions. **Concrete** words describe qualities of immediate perception. If you say "Ice cream is cold," the word *cold* is concrete because it describes a condition that you can feel, just as you can taste ice cream's *sweetness* and feel its *creamy* texture in your mouth. **Abstract** words refer to broader, less palpable qualities; they may therefore apply to many separate things. If we describe ice cream as *good*, our word is abstract because *good* is far removed from ice cream itself and conveys no descriptive information about it. A vast number of things may be *good*, just as they may be *bad*, *fine*, *"cool,"* *excellent*, and so on.

Usually, narrative and descriptive writing features specific and concrete words that are intended to help us visualize actions, scenes, and objects, for with more specificity and concreteness there is less ambiguity. Because exactness and vividness are goals of most fiction, specific and concrete words are the fiction writer's basic tools, with general and abstract words being used sparingly.

The point, however, is not that abstract and general words have no place at all, but rather that *words should be appropriate in the context*. Good writers control style in the interests of tone as well as description. Observe, for example, Hemingway's diction in "Soldier's Home," a story about a young veteran who has just come back home to Oklahoma after serving in World War I and who is uneasy about going back to the life he knew before the war. By combining specific and abstract language to convey this situation, Hemingway appropriately fits style to subject. In paragraph 6, for example, he uses abstract terms to describe the mental state of Krebs, the young veteran. We read that Krebs feels "nausea in regard to experience that is the result of untruth or exaggeration," that he goes into the "easy pose of the old soldier" when he meets another veteran, and that he "lost everything" during his time abroad. Because the words are mainly abstract and general, and also vague, they accurately show Krebs's disassociation from the world around him.

Hemingway also conveys this same disconnection through his specific descriptions of Krebs's daily activities: getting out of bed, walking to the library, eating lunch, reading on the front porch, and drifting down to the local pool hall. These details show that Krebs's actions are repetitive and meaningless. Thus the two paragraphs form a pair, with the specificity of paragraph 7 complementing the abstraction of paragraph 6. In short, Hemingway skillfully combines abstract and specific words to build his portrait of a young man caught between two worlds—foreign warfare and peaceful life at home—and because of changing circumstances having no place in either. Through these passages, and others in the story, Hemingway controls the tone in such a way that readers share something of his major character's discomfort.

Denotation and Connotation

Another way to understand the connection of style and tone is to study the author's management of *denotation* and *connotation*. **Denotation** refers to what a word means, and **connotation** to what the word suggests. For example, if a person in a social situation behaves in ways that are *friendly, warm, polite,* or *cordial,* these words all suggest slight differences in tone because they have different connotations. Similarly, both *cat* and *kitten* are close to each other denotatively, but *kitten* connotes more playfulness and cuteness than *cat.* Consider the connotations of words describing physical appearance. For example, what attitudes are conveyed by calling a person *thin,* and what contrasting tone is conveyed by *skinny, gaunt,* and *skeletal,* or *slim, slender, fit, trim,* and *shapely?*

Through the careful choice of words, not only for denotation but also for connotation, writers control tone even though they might be describing similar or even identical situations. Let us look briefly at Eudora Welty's description of Phoenix, the main character in "A Worn Path" (Chapter 3):

> Her eyes were blue with age. Her skin had a pattern all its own of numberless branching wrinkles and as though a whole little tree stood in the middle of her forehead, but a golden color ran underneath, and the two knobs of her cheeks were illumined by a yellow burning under the dark. Under the rag her hair came down on her neck in the frailest of ringlets, still black, and with an odor like copper. (paragraph 2)

The description conveys a compelling attitude of admiration. Specifically, the words *golden color* and *illumined* would be appropriate in the description of delicate and lovely medieval book paintings; *frailest of ringlets, still black* suggests girlishness and personal care, despite Phoenix's advancing age and weakness.

Comparably, in "A & P," Sammy's words describing the "queen" (paragraphs 2–4) suggest his admiration of both her sexual beauty and her grace. These examples demonstrate the ways in which an author's control over connotation governs the tone of individual passages and entire works.

TONE, IRONY, AND STYLE

The capacity to have more than one attitude toward someone or something is a uniquely human trait. We know that people are not perfect, but we love a number of them anyway. Therefore we speak to them not only with love and praise, but also with banter and criticism. On occasion, you may have given mildly insulting greeting cards to your loved ones, not to affront them but to amuse them. You share smiles and laughs at the words you send them, but at the same time you remind them of your affection.

The word **irony,** specifically **verbal irony,** describes such contradictory statements, in which one thing is said and the opposite is meant. There are important types of verbal irony. In **understatement** the expression does not fully describe the importance of a situation, and therefore makes its point by implication. For example, in Bierce's "An Occurrence at Owl Creek Bridge" (Chapter 5) the condemned man, Farquhar, contemplates the apparatus designed by the Soldiers to hang him. After considering the method, Farquhar's response is described by the narrator: "The arrangement commended itself to his judgment as simple and effective" (paragraph 4). These words would be appropriate for ordinary machinery, perhaps, but because the apparatus will cause Farquhar's death, the understated observation is ironic.

By contrast, in **overstatement** or **hyperbole,** the words are far in excess of the situation, and readers or listeners therefore understand that the true meaning is considerably less than what is said. An example is the priest's exaggerated dialogue with Jackie in "First Confession" (paragraphs 38–50). Though the priest makes incongruously hyperbolic comments on Jackie's plans for slaughtering his grandmother, readers automatically know he means no such thing. The gulf between what is said and what is meant creates smiles and chuckles.

Often verbal irony is ambiguous, having double meaning or **double entendre.** Midway through "Young Goodman Brown," for example, the woodland guide leaves Brown alone while stating, "when you feel like moving again, there is my staff to help you along" (paragraph 40). The word "staff" is ambiguous, for it refers to the staff that resembles a serpent (paragraph 13). The word therefore suggests that the devilish guide is leaving Brown not only with a real staff but also with the spirit of evil (unlike the divine "staff" of Psalm 23 that gives comfort). Ambiguity of course may be used in relation to any topic. Quite often *double-entendre* is used in statements about sexuality, usually for the amusement of listeners or readers.

TONE, HUMOR, AND STYLE

A major aspect of tone is humor. Everyone likes to laugh, and shared laughter is part of good human relationships; but not everyone can explain why things are funny. Laughter resists close analysis; it is unplanned, personal, idiosyncratic, and usually unpredictable. Laughter depends on seeing something new or unique, or on experiencing something familiar in a new light.

A first ingredient in humor is something to laugh at—a person, thing, situation, custom, habit of speech or dialect, or arrangement of words. But once we have this ingredient we must also have *incongruity;* that is, something happens or is said that violates what we normally expect. The language itself may be exploited for incongruity. A well-known example is the stand-up comedian's statement that one day, when he was walking on a sidewalk, he turned into a drugstore. Here the comedian causes laughter through the ambiguous meaning of "turned into," thus verbally changing an ordinary walk into a miraculous event. Another verbal incongruity is this: "Barking loudly, I was awakened by my dog." Here the humor depends on the misplacement of the modifier "barking loudly," which makes the sentence seem to say that the speaker, and not the dog, is barking. A student once stated that he had trouble with the "*congregation* of verbs." The same student also described the grammatical parts of speech as "nouns, verbs, and *proverbs.*" The student meant the *conjugation* of verbs, of course, and also (maybe) either *adverbs* or *pronouns*, but somehow his understanding slipped and he created a comic incongruity. If such inadvertent verbal errors are included in a story, the author is controlling tone by directing humor against the speaker, for the amusement of both readers and author alike.

It is important to recognize that laughter is spontaneous because it is prompted by flashes of insight or sudden revelations. Indeed, the task of the writer is to develop ordinary materials to that point when spontaneity frees us to laugh. This is not to say that works that you already know are not spontaneous or new. You can read and reread Frank O'Connor's "First Confession" and laugh each time because, even though you know what happens, the story shapes your acceptance of how the passage of time penetrates a wall of anger and guilt. Young Jackie's experience is and always will be comic because it is so incongruous and spontaneous.

 STORIES FOR STUDY

MARGARET ATWOOD   (b. 1939)

Atwood is one of Canada's premier writers, having published many books of poetry, a number of novels and stories, and much criticism. In addition, she is editor of The Oxford Book of Canadian Verse *(1982). One of her most widely recognized works is the anti-utopian novel,* The Handmaid's Tale *(1986), which describes a futuristic nightmare society of fear and repression for women. This story was adapted as a movie in 1990. The stories in a collection,* Wilderness Tips *(1992), reflect regret and diminished hopes, unlike the more comic topics of her story "Rape Fantasies" and her poem "Siren Song." The scope of her work may be inferred from recent publications:* The Robber Bride *(1993),* Good Bones and Simple Murders *(1994),* Poems *(1994),* Princess Prunella and the Purple Peanut *(1995), and* Morning in the Burned House *(1995).*

Rape Fantasies _____ *1977*

The way they're going on about it in the magazines you'd think it was just invented, and not only that but it's something terrific, like a vaccine for cancer. They put it in capital letters on the front cover, and inside they have these questionnaires like the ones they used to have about whether you were a good enough wife or an endomorph or an ectomorph, remember that? with the scoring upside down on page 73, and then these numbered do-it-yourself dealies, you know? RAPE, TEN THINGS TO DO ABOUT IT, like it was ten new hairdos or something. I mean, what's so new about it?

So at work they all have to talk about it because no matter what magazine you open, there it is, staring you right between the eyes, and they're beginning to have it on the television, too. Personally I'd prefer a June Allyson° movie anytime but they don't make them any more and they don't even have them that much on the Late Show. For instance, day before yesterday, that would be Wednesday, thank god it's Friday as they say, we were sitting around in the women's lunch room—the *lunch* room, I mean you'd think you could get some peace and quiet in there—and Chrissy closes up the magazine she's been reading and says, "How about it, girls, do you have rape fantasies?"

The four of us were having our game of bridge the way we always do, and I had a bare twelve points counting the singleton with not that much of a bid in anything. So I said one club, hoping Sondra would remember about the one club convention, because the time before when I used that she thought I really meant clubs and she bid us up to three, and all I had was four little ones with nothing higher than a six, and we went down two and on top of that we were vulnerable. She is not the world's best bridge player. I mean, neither am I but there's a limit.

Darlene passed but the damage was done, Sondra's head went round like it was on ball bearings and she said, "*What* fantasies?"

June Allyson: actress (b. 1917) known for her bright smile and scratchy voice. She specialized in "sweet" movie and musical roles, 1943–1959, and still appears regularly in TV commercials.

"Rape fantasies," Chrissy said. She's a receptionist and she looks like one; she's   5
pretty but cool as a cucumber, like she's been painted all over with nail polish, if you
know what I mean. Varnished. "It says here all women have rape fantasies."

"For Chrissake, I'm eating an egg sandwich," I said, "and I bid one club and
Darlene passed."

"You mean, like some guy jumping you in an alley or something," Sondra said.
She was eating her lunch, we all eat our lunches during the game, and she bit into a
piece of that celery she always brings and started to chew away on it with this thoughtful
expression in her eyes and I knew we might as well pack it in as far as the game was
concerned.

"Yeah, sort of like that," Chrissy said. She was blushing a little, you could see it
even under her makeup.

"I don't think you should go out alone at night," Darlene said, "you put yourself in
a position," and I may have been mistaken but she was looking at me. She's the oldest,
she's forty-one though you wouldn't know it and neither does she, but I looked it up in
the employees' file. I like to guess a person's age and then look it up to see if I'm right.
I let myself have an extra pack of cigarettes if I am, though I'm trying to cut down. I
figure it's harmless as long as you don't tell. I mean, not everyone has access to that file,
it's more or less confidential. But it's all right if I tell you, I don't expect you'll ever meet
her, though you never know, it's a small world. Anyway.

"For *heaven's* sake, it's only *Toronto*," Greta said. She worked in Detroit for three   10
years and she never lets you forget it, it's like she thinks she's a war hero or something,
we should all admire her just for the fact that she's still walking this earth, though she
was really living in Windsor° the whole time, she just worked in Detroit. Which for me
doesn't really count. It's where you sleep, right?

"Well, do you?" Chrissy said. She was obviously trying to tell us about hers but she
wasn't about to go first, she's cautious, that one.

"I certainly don't," Darlene said, and she wrinkled up her nose, like this, and I
had to laugh. "I think it's disgusting." She's divorced, I read that in the file too, she never
talks about it. It must've been years ago anyway. She got up and went over to the coffee
machine and turned her back on us as though she wasn't going to have anything more
to do with it.

"Well," Greta said. I could see it was going to be between her and Chrissy. They're
both blondes, I don't mean that in a bitchy way but they do try to outdress each other.
Greta would like to get out of Filing, she'd like to be a receptionist too so she could
meet more people. You don't meet much of anyone in Filing except other people in
Filing. Me, I don't mind it so much, I have outside interests.

"Well," Greta said, "I sometimes think about, you know my apartment? It's got
this little balcony, I like to sit out there in the summer and I have a few plants out there.
I never bother that much about locking the door to the balcony, it's one of those sliding
glass ones, I'm on the eighteenth floor for heaven's sake, I've got a good view of the
lake and the CN Tower and all. But I'm sitting around one night in my housecoat,
watching TV with my shoes off, you know how you do, and I see this guy's feet, coming
down past the window, and the next thing you know he's standing on the balcony, he's
let himself down by a rope with a hook on the end of it from the floor above, that's the
nineteenth, and before I can even get up off the chesterfield he's inside the apartment.

Windsor: city south of Detroit, noted as the only place where any portion of Canada is south
of the United States.

He's all dressed in black with black gloves on"—I knew right away what show she got the black gloves off because I saw the same one—"and then he, well, you know."

"You know what?" Chrissy said, but Greta said, "And afterwards he tells me that he goes all over the outside of the apartment building like that, from one floor to another, with his rope and his hook . . . and then he goes out to the balcony and tosses his rope, and he climbs up it and disappears."

"Just like Tarzan," I said, but nobody laughed.

"Is that all?" Chrissy said. "Don't you ever think about, well, I think about being in the bathtub, with no clothes on . . ."

"So who takes a bath in their clothes?" I said, you have to admit it's stupid when you come to think of it, but she just went on, ". . . with lots of bubbles, what I use is Vitabath, it's more expensive but it's so relaxing, and my hair pinned up, and the door opens and this fellow's standing there. . . ."

"How'd he get in?" Greta said.

"Oh, I don't know, through a window or something. Well, I can't very well get out of the bathtub, the bathroom's too small and besides he's blocking the doorway, so I just *lie* there, and he starts to very slowly take his own clothes off, and then he gets into the bathtub with me."

"Don't you scream or anything?" said Darlene. She'd come back with her cup of coffee, she was getting really interested. "I'd scream like bloody murder."

"Who'd hear me?" Chrissy said. "Besides, all the articles say it's better not to resist, that way you don't get hurt."

"Anyway you might get bubbles up your nose," I said, "from the deep breathing," and I swear all four of them looked at me like I was in bad taste, like I'd insulted the Virgin Mary or something. I mean, I don't see what's wrong with a little joke now and then. Life's too short, right?

"Listen," I said, "those aren't *rape* fantasies. I mean, you aren't getting *raped*, it's just some guy you haven't met formally who happens to be more attractive than Derek Cummins"—he's the Assistant Manager, he wears elevator shoes or at any rate they have these thick soles and he has this funny way of talking, we call him Derek Duck—"and you have a good time. Rape is when they've got a knife or something and you don't want to."

"So what about you, Estelle," Chrissy said, she was miffed because I laughed at her fantasy, she thought I was putting her down. Sondra was miffed too, by this time she'd finished her celery and she wanted to tell about hers, but she hadn't got in fast enough.

"All right, let me tell you one," I said. "I'm walking down this dark street at night and this fellow comes up and grabs my arm. Now it so happens that I have a plastic lemon in my purse, you know how it always says you should carry a plastic lemon in your purse? I don't really do it, I tried it once but the darn thing leaked all over my cheque-book, but in this fantasy I have one, and I say to him, "You're intending to rape me, right?" and he nods, so I open my purse to get the plastic lemon, and I can't find it! My purse is full of all this junk, Kleenex and cigarettes and my change purse and my lip-stick and my driver's licence, you know the kind of stuff: so I ask him to hold out his hands, like this, and I pile all this junk into them and down at the bottom there's the plastic lemon, and I can't get the top off. So I hand it to him and he's very obliging, he twists the top off and hands it back to me, and I squirt him in the eye."

I hope you don't think that's too vicious. Come to think of it, it is a bit mean, especially when he was so polite and all.

"*That's* your rape fantasy?" Chrissy says, "I don't believe it."

"She's a card," Darlene says, she and I are the ones that've been here the longest and she never will forget the time I got drunk at the office party and insisted I was going to dance under the table instead of on top of it, I did a sort of Cossack number° but then I hit my head on the bottom of the table—actually it was a desk—when I went to get up, and I knocked myself out cold. She's decided that's the mark of an original mind and she tells everyone new about it and I'm not sure that's fair. Though I did do it.

"I'm being totally honest," I say. I always am and they know it. There's no point in being anything else, is the way I look at it, and sooner or later the truth will out so you might as well not waste the time, right? "You should hear the one about the Easy-Off Cleaner."   30

But that was the end of the lunch hour, with one bridge game shot to hell, and the next day we spent most of the time arguing over whether to start a new game or play out the hands we had left over from the day before, so Sondra never did get a chance to tell about her rape fantasy.

It started me thinking though, about my own rape fantasies. Maybe I'm abnormal or something, I mean I have fantasies about handsome strangers coming in through the window too, like Mr. Clean, I wish one would, please god somebody without flat feet and big sweat marks on his shirt, and over five feet five, believe me being tall is a handicap though it's getting better, tall guys are starting to like someone whose nose reaches higher than their belly button. But if you're being totally honest you can't count those as rape fantasies. In a real rape fantasy, what you should feel is this anxiety, like when you think about your apartment building catching on fire and whether you should use the elevator or the stairs or maybe just stick your head under a wet towel, and you try to remember everything you've read about what to do but you can't decide.

For instance, I'm walking along this dark street at night and this short, ugly fellow comes up and grabs my arm, and not only is he ugly, you know, with a sort of puffy nothing face, like those fellows you have to talk to in the bank when your account's overdrawn—of course I don't mean they're all like that—but he's absolutely covered in pimples. So he gets me pinned against the wall, he's short but he's heavy, and he starts to undo himself and the zipper gets stuck. I mean, one of the most significant moments in a girl's life, it's almost like getting married or having a baby or something, and he sticks the zipper.

So I say, kind of disgusted, "Oh for Chrissake," and he starts to cry. He tells me he's never been able to get anything right in his entire life, and this is the last straw, he's going to go jump off a bridge.

"Look," I say, I feel so sorry for him, in my rape fantasies I always end up feeling sorry for the guy, I mean there has to be something *wrong* with them, if it was Clint Eastwood° it'd be different but worse luck it never is. I was the kind of little girl who buried dead robins, know what I mean? It used to drive my mother nuts, she didn't like me touching them, because of the germs I guess. So I say, "Listen, I know how you feel. You really should do something about those pimples, if you got rid of them you'd be quite good looking, honest; then you wouldn't have to go around doing stuff like this. I had them myself once," I say, to comfort him, but in fact I did, and it ends up I give him the name of my old dermatologist, the one I had in high school, that was back in   35

Cossack number: a Ukrainian folk dance movement performed in a squatting position, with much hand clapping.

Clint Eastwood: born 1930, star of many tough-guy detective and western movies; most famous as "Dirty Harry" (1971).

Leamington,° except I used to go to St. Catharine's for the dermatologist. I'm telling you, I was really lonely when I first came here; I thought it was going to be such a big adventure and all, but it's a lot harder to meet people in a city. But I guess it's different for a guy.

Or I'm lying in bed with this terrible cold, my face is all swollen up, my eyes are red and my nose is dripping like a leaky tap, and this fellow comes in through the window and *he* has a terrible cold too, it's a new kind of flu that's been going around. So he says, "I'b goig do rabe you"—I hope you don't mind me holding my nose like this but that's the way I imagine it—and he lets out this terrific sneeze, which slows him down a bit, also I'm no object of beauty myself, you'd have to be some kind of pervert to want to rape someone with a cold like mine, it'd be like raping a bottle of LePages mucilage the way my nose is running. He's looking wildly around the room, and I realize it's because he doesn't have a piece of Kleenex! "Id's ride here," I say, and I pass him the Kleenex, god knows why he even bothered to get out of bed, you'd think if you were going to go around climbing in windows you'd wait till you were healthier, right? I mean, that takes a certain amount of energy. So I ask him why doesn't he let me fix him a NeoCitran and scotch, that's what I always take, you still have the cold but you don't feel it, so I do and we end up watching the Late Show together. I mean, they aren't all sex maniacs, the rest of the time they must lead a normal life. I figure they enjoy watching the Late Show just like anybody else.

I do have a scarier one though . . . where the fellow says he's hearing angel voices that're telling him he's got to kill me, you know, you read about things like that all the time in the papers. In this one I'm not in the apartment where I live now, I'm back in my mother's house in Leamington and the fellow's been hiding in the cellar, he grabs my arm when I go downstairs to get a jar of jam and he's got hold of the axe too, out of the garage, that one is really scary. I mean, what do you say to a nut like that?

So I start to shake but after a minute I get control of myself and I say, is he sure the angel voices have got the right person, because I hear the same angel voices and they've been telling me for some time that I'm going to give birth to the reincarnation of St. Anne who in turn has the Virgin Mary and right after that comes Jesus Christ and the end of the world, and he wouldn't want to interfere with that, would he? So he gets confused and listens some more, and then he asks for a sign and I show him my vaccination mark, you can see it's sort of an odd-shaped one, it got infected because I scratched the top off, and that does it, he apologizes and climbs out the coal chute° again, which is how he got in in the first place, and I say to myself there's some advantage in having been brought up a Catholic even though I haven't been to church since they changed the service into English,° it just isn't the same, you might as well be a Protestant. I must write to Mother and tell her to nail up that coal chute, it always has bothered me. Funny, I couldn't tell you at all what this man looks like but I know exactly what kind of shoes he's wearing, because that's the last I see of him, his shoes going up the coal chute, and they're the old-fashioned kind that lace up the ankles, even though he's a young fellow. That's strange, isn't it?

Leamington: in Ontario on the north shore of Lake Erie, southeast of Windsor.

coal chute: trough for delivering coal from a truck into a basement coal bin. Estelle's remark indicates that the chute was not fastened over the opening to the bin, thus permitting an illegal entry.

into English: In accord with the Second Vatican Council (1962–1965), the latin Mass was replaced by vernacular languages in the late 1960s.

Let me tell you though I really sweat until I see him safely out of there and I go upstairs right away and make myself a cup of tea. I don't think about that one much. My mother always said you shouldn't dwell on unpleasant things and I generally agree with that, I mean, dwelling on them doesn't make them go away. Though not dwelling on them doesn't make them go away either, when you come to think of it.

Sometimes I have these short ones where the fellow grabs my arm but I'm really a Kung-Fu° expert, can you believe it, in real life I'm sure it would just be a conk on the head and that's that, like getting your tonsils out, you'd wake up and it would be all over except for the sore places, and you'd be lucky if your neck wasn't broken or something, I could never even hit the volleyball in gym and a volleyball is fairly large, you know?— and I just go *zap* with my fingers into his eyes and that's it, he falls over, or I flip him against a wall or something. But I could never really stick my fingers in anyone's eyes, could you? It would feel like hot jello and I don't even like cold jello, just thinking about it gives me the creeps. I feel a bit guilty about that one, I mean how would you like walking around knowing someone's been blinded for life because of you?   40

But maybe it's different for a guy.

The most touching one I have is when the fellow grabs my arm and I say, sad and kind of dignified, "You'd be raping a corpse." That pulls him up short and I explain that I've just found out I have leukaemia and the doctors have only given me a few months to live. That's why I'm out pacing the streets alone at night, I need to think, you know, come to terms with myself. I don't really have leukaemia but in the fantasy I do, I guess I chose that particular disease because a girl in my grade four class died of it, the whole class sent her flowers when she was in the hospital. I didn't understand then that she was going to die and I wanted to have leukaemia too so I could get flowers. Kids are funny, aren't they? Well, it turns out that he has leukaemia himself, and *he* only has a few months to live, that's why he's going around raping people, he's very bitter because he's so young and his life is being taken from him before he's really lived it. So we walk along gently under the street lights, it's spring and sort of misty, and we end up going for coffee, we're happy we've found the only other person in the world who can understand what we're going through, it's almost like fate, and after a while we just sort of look at each other and our hands touch, and he comes back with me and moves into my apartment and we spend our last months together before we die, we just sort of don't wake up in the morning, though I've never decided which one of us gets to die first. If it's him I have to go on and fantasize about the funeral, if it's me I don't have to worry about that, so it just about depends on how tired I am at the time. You may not believe this but sometimes I even start crying. I cry at the end of movies, even the ones that aren't all that sad, so I guess it's the same thing. My mother's like that too.

The funny thing about these fantasies is that the man is always someone I don't know, and the statistics in the magazines, well, most of them anyway, they say it's often someone you do know, at least a little bit, like your boss or something—I mean, it wouldn't be *my* boss, he's over sixty and I'm sure he couldn't rape his way out of a paper bag, poor old thing, but it might be someone like Derek Duck, in his elevator shoes, perish the thought—or someone you just met, who invites you up for a drink, it's getting so you can hardly be sociable any more, and how are you supposed to meet people if you can't trust them even that basic amount? You can't spend your whole life in the

---

Kung-Fu: elaborate self-defense system developed in China, similar to karate.

Filing Department or cooped up in your own apartment with all the doors and windows locked and the shades down. I'm not what you would call a drinker but I like to go out now and then for a drink or two in a nice place, even if I am by myself, I'm with Women's Lib on that even though I can't agree with a lot of the other things they say. Like here for instance, the waiters all know me and if anyone, you know, bothers me . . . I don't know why I'm telling you all this, except I think it helps you get to know a person, especially at first, hearing some of the things they think about. At work they call me the office worry wart, but it isn't so much like worrying, it's more like figuring out what you should do in an emergency, like I said before.

Anyway, another thing about it is that there's a lot of conversation, in fact I spend most of my time, in the fantasy that is, wondering what I'm going to say and what he's going to say, I think it would be better if you could get a conversation going. Like, how could a fellow do that to a person he's just had a long conversation with, once you let them know you're human, you have a life too, I don't see how they could go ahead with it, right? I mean, I know it happens but I just don't understand it, that's the part I really don't understand.

QUESTIONS

1. What elements of the various rape fantasies are comic? How is the comedy brought out (e.g., through subject matter, circumstances of description, attitudes and understanding of the characters, comments by the narrator)?

2. What do the various fantasies of Estelle have in common, and what do they show about her? How does Atwood control the tone so as to keep Estelle from considering rape as a problem in psychology or criminology?

3. Describe the story's tone. How does tone affect your perception of Estelle?

4. Consider the tone of the very last paragraph. What is Atwood's apparent attitude toward the subject? How is it tempered by her attitude toward Estelle?

5. Studies point out that rape is an act of violence. What do the women in the story do to deflect the seriousness of the potential violence involved?

ERNEST HEMINGWAY   (1899–1961)

Hemingway was born in Illinois. During World War I he served in the Ambulance Corps in France, where he was wounded. In the 1920s he published The Sun Also Rises *(1926) and* A Farewell to Arms *(1929), and the resulting critical fame made him a major literary celebrity. He developed a sparse style in keeping with the elemental, stark lives of many of the characters he depicted. "Soldier's Home," from the collection* In Our Time *(1925), typifies that pared, annealed style. Notice the ambiguity and irony of the title. It may mean either "The soldier is home" or "The home of the soldier," but, ironically, the soldier's home no longer seems to be home.*

Soldier's Home _____ *1925*

Krebs went to the war from a Methodist college in Kansas. There is a picture which shows him among his fraternity brothers, all of them wearing exactly the same height and style collar. He enlisted in the Marines in 1917 and did not return to the United States until the second division returned from the Rhine in the summer of 1919.

There is a picture which shows him on the Rhine with two German girls and another corporal. Krebs and the corporal look too big for their uniforms. The German girls are not beautiful. The Rhine does not show in the picture.

By the time Krebs returned to his home town in Oklahoma the greeting of heroes was over. He came back much too late. The men from the town who had been drafted had all been welcomed elaborately on their return. There had been a great deal of hysteria. Now the reaction had set in. People seemed to think it was rather ridiculous for Krebs to be getting back so late, years after the war was over.

At first Krebs, who had been at Belleau Wood, Soissons, the Champagne, St. Mihiel and in the Argonne, did not want to talk about the war at all. Later he felt the need to talk but no one wanted to hear about it. His town had heard too many atrocity stories to be thrilled by actualities. Krebs found that to be listened to at all he had to lie, and after he had done this twice he, too, had a reaction against the war and against talking about it. A distaste for everything that had happened to him in the war set in because of the lies he had told. All of the times that had been able to make him feel cool and clean inside himself when he thought of them; the times so long back when he had done the one thing, the only thing for a man to do, easily and naturally, when he might have done something else, now lost their cool, valuable quality and then were lost themselves.

His lies were quite unimportant lies and consisted in attributing to himself things other men had seen, done or heard of, and stating as facts certain apocryphal incidents familiar to all soldiers. Even his lies were not sensational at the pool room. His acquaintances, who had heard detailed accounts of German women found chained to machine guns in the Argonne forest and who could not comprehend, or were barred by their patriotism from interest in, any German machine gunners who were not chained, were not thrilled by his stories.

Krebs acquired the nausea in regard to experience that is the result of untruth or exaggeration, and when he occasionally met another man who had really been a soldier and they talked a few minutes in the dressing room at a dance he fell into the easy pose of the old soldier among other soldiers: that he had been badly, sickeningly frightened all the time. In this way he lost everything.

During this time, it was late summer, he was sleeping late in bed, getting up to walk down town to the library to get a book, eating lunch at home, reading on the front porch until he became bored and then walking down through the town to spend the hottest hours of the day in the cool dark of the pool room. He loved to play pool.

In the evening he practised on his clarinet, strolled down town, read and went to bed. He was still a hero to his two young sisters. His mother would have given him breakfast in bed if he had wanted it. She often came in when he was in bed and asked him to tell her about the war, but her attention always wandered. His father was non-committal.

Before Krebs went away to the war he had never been allowed to drive the family motor car. His father was in the real estate business and always wanted the car to be at

5

his command when he required it to take clients out into the country to show them a piece of farm property. The car always stood outside the First National Bank building where his father had an office on the second floor. Now, after the war, it was still the same car.

Nothing was changed in the town except that the young girls had grown up. But they lived in such a complicated world of already defined alliances and shifting feuds that Krebs did not feel the energy or the courage to break into it. He liked to look at them, though. There were so many good-looking young girls. Most of them had their hair cut short. When he went away only little girls wore their hair like that or girls that were fast. They all wore sweaters and shirt waists with round Dutch collars. It was a pattern. He liked to look at them from the front porch as they walked on the other side of the street. He liked to watch them walking under the shade of the trees. He liked the round Dutch collars above their sweaters. He liked their silk stockings and flat shoes. He liked their bobbed hair and the way they walked.

When he was in town their appeal to him was not very strong. He did not like them when he saw them in the Greek's ice cream parlor. He did not want them themselves really. They were too complicated. There was something else. Vaguely he wanted a girl but he did not want to have to work to get her. He would have liked to have a girl but he did not want to have to spend a long time getting her. He did not want to get into the intrigue and the politics. He did not want to have to do any courting. He did not want to tell any more lies. It wasn't worth it.

He did not want any consequences. He did not want any consequences ever again. He wanted to live along without consequences. Besides he did not really need a girl. The army had taught him that. It was all right to pose as though you had to have a girl. Nearly everybody did that. But it wasn't true. You did not need a girl. That was the funny thing. First a fellow boasted how girls mean nothing to him, that he never thought of them, that they could not touch him. Then a fellow boasted that he could not get along without girls, that he had to have them all the time, that he could not go to sleep without them.

That was all a lie. It was all a lie both ways. You did not need a girl unless you thought about them. He learned that in the army. Then sooner or later you always got one. When you were really ripe for a girl you always got one. You did not have to think about it. Sooner or later it would come. He had learned that in the army.

Now he would have liked a girl if she had come to him and not wanted to talk. But here at home it was all too complicated. He knew he could never get through it all again. It was not worth the trouble. That was the thing about French girls and German girls. There was not all this talking. You couldn't talk much and you did not need to talk. It was simple and you were friends. He thought about France and then he began to think about Germany. On the whole he had liked Germany better. He did not want to leave Germany. He did not want to come home. Still, he had come home. He sat on the front porch.

He liked the girls that were walking along the other side of the street. He liked the look of them much better than the French girls or the German girls. But the world they were in was not the world he was in. He would like to have one of them. But it was not worth it. They were such a nice pattern. He liked the pattern. It was exciting. But he would not go through all the talking. He did not want one badly enough. He liked to look at them all, though. It was not worth it. Not now when things were getting good again.

He sat there on the porch reading a book on the war. It was a history and he was reading about all the engagements he had been in. It was the most interesting reading he had ever done. He wished there were more maps. He looked forward with a good feeling to reading all the really good histories when they would come out with good detail maps. Now he was really learning about the war. He had been a good soldier. That made a difference.

One morning after he had been home about a month his mother came into his bedroom and sat on the bed. She smoothed her apron.

"I had a talk with your father last night, Harold," she said, "and he is willing for you to take the car out in the evenings."

"Yeah?" said Krebs, who was not fully awake. "Take the car out? Yeah?"

"Yes. Your father has felt for some time that you should be able to take the car   20
out in the evenings whenever you wished but we only talked it over last night."

"I'll bet you made him," Krebs said.

"No. It was your father's suggestion that we talk the matter over."

"Yeah. I'll bet you made him," Krebs sat up in bed.

"Will you come down to breakfast, Harold?" his mother said.

"As soon as I get my clothes on," Krebs said.   25

His mother went out of the room and he could hear her frying something downstairs while he washed, shaved and dressed to go down into the dining-room for breakfast. While he was eating breakfast his sister brought in the mail.

"Well, Hare," she said. "You old sleepy-head. What do you ever get up for?"

Krebs looked at her. He liked her. She was his best sister.

"Have you got the paper?" he asked.

She handed him *The Kansas City Star* and he shucked off its brown wrapper and   30
opened it to the sporting page. He folded *The Star* open and propped it against the water pitcher with his cereal dish to steady it, so he could read while he ate.

"Harold," his mother stood in the kitchen doorway, "Harold, please don't muss up the paper. You father can't read his *Star* if it's been mussed."

"I won't muss it," Krebs said.

His sister sat down at the table and watched him while he read.

"We're playing indoor° over at school this afternoon," she said. "I'm going to pitch."

"Good," said Krebs. "How's the old wing?"   35

"I can pitch better than lots of the boys. I tell them all you taught me. The other girls aren't much good."

"Yeah?" said Krebs.

"I tell them all you're my beau. Aren't you my beau, Hare?"

"You bet."

"Couldn't your brother really be your beau just because he's your brother?"   40

"I don't know."

"Sure you know. Couldn't you be my beau, Hare, if I was old enough and if you wanted to?"

"Sure. You're my girl now."

"Am I really your girl?"

"Sure."   45

"Do you love me?"

---

indoor: that is, a softball game.

"Uh, huh."

"Will you love me always?"

"Sure."

"Will you come over and watch me play indoor?"

"Maybe."

"Aw, Hare, you don't love me. If you loved me, you'd want to come over and watch me play indoor."

Krebs's mother came into the dining-room from the kitchen. She carried a plate with two fried eggs and some crisp bacon on it and a plate of buckwheat cakes.

"You run along, Helen," she said. "I want to talk to Harold."

She put eggs and bacon down in front of him and brought in a jug of maple syrup for the buckwheat cakes. Then she sat down across the table from Krebs.

"I wish you'd put down the paper a minute, Harold," she said.

Krebs took down the paper and folded it.

"Have you decided what you are going to do yet, Harold?" his mother said, taking off her glasses.

"No," said Krebs.

"Don't you think it's about time?" His mother did not say this in a mean way. She seemed worried.

"I hadn't thought about it," Krebs said.

"God has some work for every one to do," his mother said. "There can be no idle hands in His Kingdom."

"I'm not in His Kingdom," Krebs said.

"We are all of us in His Kingdom."

Krebs felt embarrassed and resentful as always.

"I've worried about you so much, Harold," his mother went on. "I know the temptations you must have been exposed to. I know how weak men are. I know what your own dear grandfather, my own father, told us about the Civil War and I have prayed for you. I pray for you all day long, Harold."

Krebs looked at the bacon fat hardening on his plate.

"Your father is worried, too," his mother went on. "He thinks you have lost your ambition, that you haven't got a definite aim in life. Charley Simmons, who is just your age, has a good job and is going to be married. The boys are all settling down; they're all determined to get somewhere; you can see that boys like Charley Simmons are on their way to being really a credit to the community."

Krebs said nothing.

"Don't look that way, Harold," his mother said. "You know we love you and I want to tell you for your own good how matters stand. Your father does not want to hamper your freedom. He thinks you should be allowed to drive the car. If you want to take some of the nice girls out riding with you, we are only too pleased. We want you to enjoy yourself. But you are going to have to settle down to work, Harold. Your father doesn't care what you start in at. All work is honorable as he says. But you've got to make a start at something. He asked me to speak to you this morning and then you can stop in and see him at his office."

"Is that all?" Krebs said.

"Yes. Don't you love your mother, dear boy?"

"No," Krebs said.

His mother looked at him across the table. Her eyes were shiny. She started crying.

"I don't love anybody," Krebs said.

It wasn't any good. He couldn't tell her, he couldn't make her see it. It was silly to have said it. He had only hurt her. He went over and took hold of her arm. She was crying with her head in her hands.

"I didn't mean it," he said. "I was just angry at something. I didn't mean I didn't love you."

His mother went on crying. Krebs put his arm on her shoulder.

"Can't you believe me, mother?"

His mother shook her head.   80

"Please, please, mother. Please believe me."

"All right," his mother said chokily. She looked up at him. "I believe you, Harold."

Krebs kissed her hair. She put her face up to him.

"I'm your mother," she said. "I held you next to my heart when you were a tiny baby."

Krebs felt sick and vaguely nauseated.   85

"I know, Mummy," he said. "I'll try and be a good boy for you."

"Would you kneel and pray with me, Harold?" his mother asked.

They knelt down beside the dining-room table and Krebs's mother prayed.

"Now, you pray, Harold," she said.

"I can't," Krebs said.   90

"Try, Harold."

"I can't."

"Do you want me to pray for you?"

"Yes."

So his mother prayed for him and then they stood up and Krebs kissed his mother   95
and went out of the house. He had tried so to keep his life from being complicated. Still, none of it had touched him. He had felt sorry for his mother and she had made him lie. He would go to Kansas City and get a job and she would feel all right about it. There would be one more scene maybe before he got away. He would not go down to his father's office. He would miss that one. He wanted his life to go smoothly. It had just gotten going that way. Well, that was all over now, anyway. He would go over to the schoolyard and watch Helen play indoor baseball.

QUESTIONS

1. Describe Harold Krebs. How do we learn about him? What does his relationship with his sister show about him? How does he change in the story? What is his attitude toward his home town? What is his feeling about the war? Girls? His parents? What does he want to do with his life? Why?

2. Why does Krebs seem to have no ideals? What judgment do you think Hemingway wants you to make of him? What in the story causes you to form this judgment?

3. Analyze the last paragraph. How long are the sentences? Why are they no longer or shorter? How specific are the words in the paragraph? Is anything not clear? How might a certain lack of clarity in the diction be complimentary to Krebs's attitudes? What does the phrase "before he got away" mean in reference to Krebs's thoughts about life in his home town, and in the United States?

4. Consider the meaning or meanings of the title, "Soldier's Home." Do you think that Hemingway intends any irony in the title? How? Why?

JACK HODGINS   (b. 1938)

Both a novelist and short-story writer, Hodgins is a native of British Columbia. His works, some quite realistic and others tinged with the aura of "magic realism," are derived from his knowledge of the people and the countryside of this area. Among his novels are The Invention of the Word *(1977),* The Resurrection of Joseph Bourne *(1979),* The Honorary Patron *(1987), and* The Macken Charm *(1995). He has also written works for children, and is the editor of three anthologies. His ideas about writing fiction are the substance of* A Passion for Narrative, *which was published in 1993. His story collections are* Spit Delaney's Island *(1977) and* The Barclay Family Theater *(1981), in which Hodgins included "The Concert Stages of Europe."*

The Concert Stages of Europe  *1978*

Now I know Cornelia Horncastle would say I'm blaming the wrong person. I know that. I know too that she would say thirty years is a long time to hold a grudge, and that if I needed someone to blame for the fact that I made a fool of myself in front of the whole district and ruined my life in the process, then I ought to look around for the person who gave me my high-flown ideas in the first place. But she would be wrong; because there is no doubt I'd have led a different sort of life if it weren't for her, if it weren't for that piano keyboard her parents presented her with on her eleventh birthday. And everything—everything would have been different if that piano keyboard hadn't been the kind made out of stiff paper that you unfolded and laid out across the kitchen table in order to do your practising.

I don't suppose there would have been all that much harm in her having the silly thing, if only my mother hadn't got wind of it. What a fantastic idea, she said. You could learn to play without even making a sound! You could practise your scales without having to hear that awful racket when you hit a wrong note! A genius must have thought of it, she said. Certainly someone who'd read his Keats: *Heard melodies are sweet, but those unheard are sweeter.* "And don't laugh," she said, "because Cornelia Horncastle is learning to play the piano and her mother doesn't even have to miss an episode of *Ma Perkins* while she does it."

That girl, people had told her, would be giving concerts in Europe some day, command performances before royalty, and her parents hadn't even had to fork out the price of a piano. It was obvious proof, if you needed it, that a person didn't have to be rich to get somewhere in this world.

In fact, Cornelia's parents hadn't needed to put out even the small amount that paper keyboard would have cost. A piano teacher named Mrs. Humphries had moved onto the old Dendoff place and, discovering that almost no one in the district owned a piano, gave the keyboard to the Horncastles along with a year's free lessons. It was her idea, apparently, that when everyone heard how quickly Cornelia was learning they'd be lining up to send her their children for lessons. She wanted to make the point that having no piano needn't stop anyone from becoming a pianist. No doubt she had a vision of paper keyboards in every house in Waterville, of children everywhere thumping their scales out on the kitchen table without offending anyone's ears, of a whole generation turning silently into Paderewskis without ever having played a note.

They would, I suppose, have to play a real piano when they went to her house   5
for lessons once a week, but I was never able to find out for myself, because all that talk
of Cornelia's marvellous career on the concert stages of Europe did not prompt my parents to buy one of those fake keyboards or sign me up for lessons with Mrs. Humphries.
My mother was born a Barclay, which meant she had a few ideas of her own, and
Cornelia's glorious future prompted her to go one better. We would buy a *real* piano,
she announced. And I would be sent to a teacher we could trust, not to that newcomer.
If those concert stages of Europe were ever going to hear the talent of someone from the
stump ranches of Waterville, it wouldn't be Cornelia Horncastle, it would be Barclay
Desmond. Me.

My father nearly choked on his coffee. "But Clay's a boy!"

"So what?" my mother said. *All* those famous players used to be boys. What did
he think Chopin was? Or Tchaikovsky?

My father was so embarrassed that his throat began to turn a dark pink. Some
things were too unnatural even to think about.

But eventually she won him over. "Think how terrible you'd feel," she said, "if he
ended up in the bush, like you. If Mozart's father had worked for the Comox Logging
Company and thought piano-playing was for sissies, where would the world be today?"

My father had no answer to that. He'd known since before his marriage that   10
though my mother would put up with being married to a logger, expecting every day
to be made a widow, she wouldn't tolerate for one minute the notion that a child of hers
would follow him up into those hills. The children of Lenora Barclay would enter the
professions.

She was right, he had to agree; working in the woods was the last thing in the
world he wanted for his sons. He'd rather they take up ditch-digging or begging than
have to work for that miserable logging company, or take their orders from a son-of-a-
bitch like Tiny Beechman, or get their skulls cracked open like Stanley Kirck. It was a
rotten way to make a living, and if he'd only had a decent education he could have made
something of himself.

Of course, I knew he was saying all this just for my mother's benefit. He didn't
really believe it for a minute. My father loved his work. I could tell by the way he was
always talking about Ab Jennings and Shorty Cresswell, the men he worked with. I could
tell by the excitement that mounted in him every year as the time grew near for the
annual festival of loggers' sports where he usually won the bucking contest. It was obvious, I thought, that the man really wanted nothing more in this world than that one of
his sons should follow in his footsteps. And much as I disliked the idea, I was sure that
I was the one he'd set his hopes on. Kenny was good in school. Laurel was a girl. I was
the obvious choice. I even decided that what he'd pegged me for was high-rigger. I was
going to be one of those men who risked their necks climbing hundreds of feet up the
bare lonely spar tree to hang the rigging from the top. Of course I would fall and
kill myself the first time I tried it, I knew that, but there was no way I could convey my
hesitation to my father since he would never openly admit that this was really his goal
for me.

And playing the piano on the concert stages of Europe was every bit as unattrac-
tive. "Why not Kenny?" I said, when the piano had arrived, by barge, from Vancouver.

"He's too busy already with his school work," my mother said. Kenny was hoping
for a scholarship, which meant he got out of just about everything unpleasant.

"What about Laurel?"   15

"With her short fat fingers?"

In the meantime, she said, though she was no piano-player herself (a great sigh here for what might have been), she had no trouble at all identifying which of those ivory keys was the all-important Middle C and would show it to me, to memorize, so that I wouldn't look like a total know-nothing when I showed up tomorrow for my first lesson. She'd had one piano lesson herself as a girl, she told me, and had learned all about Mister Middle C, but she'd never had a second lesson because her time was needed by her father, outside, helping with the chores. Seven daughters altogether, no sons, and she was the one who was the most often expected to fill the role of a boy. The rest of them had found the time to learn chords and chromatic scales and all those magic things she'd heard them practising while she was scrubbing out the dairy and cutting the runners off strawberry plants. They'd all become regular show-offs in one way or another, learning other instruments as well, putting on their own concerts and playing in dance bands and earning a reputation all over the district as entertaining livewires— The Barclay Sisters. And no one ever guessed that all the while she was dreaming about herself at that keyboard, tinkling away, playing beautiful music before huge audiences in elegant theatres.

"Then it isn't me that should be taking lessons," I said. "It's you."

"Don't be silly." But she walked to the new piano and pressed down one key, a black one, and looked as if I'd tempted her there for a minute. "It's too late now," she said. And then she sealed my fate: "But I just know that you're going to be a great pianist."

When my mother "just knew" something, that was as good as guaranteeing it   20 already completed. It was her way of controlling the future and, incidentally, the rest of us. By "just knowing" things, she went through life commanding the future to fit into certain patterns she desired while we scurried around making sure that it worked out that way so she'd never have to be disappointed. She'd had one great disappointment as a girl—we were never quite sure what it was, since it was only alluded to in whispers with far-off looks—and it was important that it never happen again. I was trapped.

People were always asking what you were going to be when you grew up. As if your wishes counted. In the first six years of my life the country had convinced me it wanted me to grow up and get killed fighting Germans and Japanese. I'd seen the coils of barbed wire along the beach and knew they were there just to slow down the enemy while I went looking for my gun. The teachers at school obviously wanted me to grow up and become a teacher just like them, because as far as I could see nothing they ever taught me could be of any use or interest to a single adult in the world except someone getting paid to teach it to someone else. My mother was counting on my becoming a pianist with a swallow-tail coat and standing ovations. And my father, despite all his noises to the contrary, badly wanted me to climb into the crummy every morning with him and ride out those gravelly roads into mountains and risk my life destroying forests.

I did not want to be a logger. I did not want to be a teacher. I did not want to be a soldier. And I certainly did not want to be a pianist. If anyone had ever asked me what I did want to be when I grew up, in a way that meant they expected the truth, I'd have said quite simply that what I wanted was to be a Finn.

Our new neighbours, the Korhonens, were Finns. And being a Finn, I'd been told, meant something very specific. A Finn would give you the shirt off his back, a Finn was as honest as the day is long, a Finn could drink anybody under the table and beat up half a dozen Germans and Irishmen without trying, a Finn was not afraid of work, a Finn kept a house so clean you could eat off the floors. I knew all these things before ever meeting our neighbours, but as soon as I had met them I was able to add a couple more generalizations of my own to the catalogue: Finnish girls were blonde and beautiful and flirtatious, and Finnish boys were strong, brave, and incredibly intelligent. These conclusions were reached immediately after meeting Lilja Korhonen, whose turned-up nose and blue eyes fascinated me from the beginning, and Larry Korhonen, who was already a teenager and told me for starters that he was actually Superman, having learned to fly after long hours of practice off their barn roof. Mr. and Mrs. Korhonen, of course, fitted exactly all the things my parents had told me about Finns in general. And so I decided my ambition in life was to be just like them.

I walked over to their house every Saturday afternoon and pretended to read their coloured funnies. I got in on the weekly steam-bath with Larry and his father in the sauna down by the barn. Mr. Korhonen, a patient man whose eyes sparkled at my eager attempts, taught me to count to ten—*yksi, kaksi, kolme, nelja, viisi, kuusi, seitseman, kahdeksan, yhdeksan, kymmenen.* I helped Mrs. Korhonen scrub her linoleum floors and put down newspapers so no one could walk on them, then I gorged myself on cinnamon cookies and *kala loota* and coffee sucked through a sugar cube. If there was something to be caught from just being around them, I wanted to catch it. And since being a Finn seemed to be a full-time occupation, I didn't have much patience with my parents, who behaved as if there were other things you had to prepare yourself for.

The first piano teacher they sent me to was Aunt Jessie, who lived in a narrow, cramped house up a gravel road that led to the mountains. She'd learned to play as a girl in Toronto, but she had no pretensions about being a real teacher, she was only doing this as a favour to my parents so they wouldn't have to send me to that Mrs. Humphries, an outsider. But one of the problems was that Aunt Jessie—who was no aunt of mine at all, simply one of those family friends who somehow get saddled with an honorary family title—was exceptionally beautiful. She was so attractive, in fact, that even at the age of ten I had difficulty keeping my eyes or my mind on the lessons. She exuded a dreamy sort of delicate femininity; her soft, intimate voice made the hair on the back of my neck stand on end. Besides that, her own playing was so much more pleasant to listen to than my own stumbling clangs and clunks that she would often begin to show me how to do something and become so carried away with the sound of her own music that she just kept right on playing through the rest of my half-hour. It was a simple matter to persuade her to dismiss me early every week so that I'd have a little time to play in the creek that ran past the back of her house, poling a homemade raft up and down the length of her property while her daughters paid me nickels and candies for a ride. At the end of a year my parents suspected I wasn't progressing as fast as I should. They found out why on the day I fell in the creek and nearly drowned, had to be revived by a distraught Aunt Jessie, and was driven home soaked and shivering in the back seat of her old Hudson.

Mr. Korhonen and my father were huddled over the taken-apart cream separator on the verandah when Aunt Jessie brought me up to the door. My father, when he saw me, had that peculiar look on his face that was halfway between amusement and concern, but Mr. Korhonen laughed openly. "That boy lookit like a drowny rat."

I felt like a drowned rat too, but I joined his laughter. I was sure this would be the end of my piano career, and could hardly wait to see my mother roll her eyes to the ceiling, throw out her arms, and say, "I give up."

She did nothing of the sort. She tightened her lips and told Aunt Jessie how disappointed she was. "No wonder the boy still stumbles around on that keyboard like a blindfolded rabbit; he's not going to learn the piano while he's out risking his life on the *river!*"

When I came downstairs in dry clothes Aunt Jessie had gone, no doubt wishing she'd left me to drown in the creek, and my parents and the Korhonens were all in the

25

kitchen drinking coffee. The Korhonens sat at either side of the table, smoking hand-rolled cigarettes and squinting at me through the smoke. Mrs. Korhonen could blow beautiful white streams down her nostrils. They'd left their gumboots on the piece of newspaper just inside the door, of course, and wore the same kind of grey work-socks on their feet that my father always wore on his. My father was leaning against the wall with both arms folded across his chest inside his wide elastic braces, as he sometimes did, swishing his mug gently as if he were trying to bring something up from the bottom. My mother, however, was unable to alight anywhere. She slammed wood down into the firebox of the stove, she rattled dishes in the sink water, she slammed cupboard doors, she went around the room with the coffee pot, refilling mugs, and all the while she sang the song of her betrayal, cursing her own stupidity for sending me to a friend instead of to a professional teacher, and suddenly in a flash of inspiration dumping all the blame on my father: "If you hadn't made me feel it was somehow pointless I wouldn't have felt guilty about spending more money!"

From behind the drifting shreds of smoke Mr. Korhonen grinned at me. Sucked   30
laughter between his teeth. "Yust *teenk*, boy, looks like-it you're saved!"

Mrs. Korhonen stabbed out her cigarette in an ashtray, picked a piece of tobacco off her tongue, and composed her face into the most serious and ladylike expression she could muster. "Yeh! Better he learn to drive the tractor." And swung me a conspirator's grin.

"Not on your life," my mother said. Driving a machine may have been a good enough ambition for some people, she believed, but the Barclays had been in this country for four generations and she knew there were a few things higher. "What we'll do is send him to a real teacher. Mrs. Greensborough."

Mrs. Greensborough was well known for putting on a public recital in town once a year, climaxing the program with her own rendition of Grieg's Piano Concerto—so beautiful that all went home, it was said, with tears in their eyes. The problem with Mrs. Greensborough had nothing to do with her teaching. She was, as far as I could see, an excellent piano teacher. And besides, there was something rather exciting about playing on her piano, which was surrounded and nearly buried by a thousand tropical plants and dozens of cages full of squawking birds. Every week's lesson was rather like putting on a concert in the midst of the Amazon jungle. There was even a monkey that swung through the branches and sat on the top of the piano with the metronome between its paws. And Mrs. Greensborough was at the same time warm and demanding, complimentary and hard to please—though given a little, like Aunt Jessie, to taking off on long passages of her own playing, as if she'd forgotten I was there.

It took a good hour's hard bicycling on uphill gravel roads before I could present myself for the lesson—past a dairy farm, a pig farm, a turkey farm, a dump, and a good long stretch of bush—then more washboard road through heavy timber where driveways disappeared into the trees and one dog after another lay in wait for its weekly battle with my right foot. Two spaniels, one Irish setter, and a bulldog. But it wasn't a spaniel or a setter or even a bulldog that met me on the driveway of the Greensborough's chicken farm, it was a huge German shepherd that came barking down the slope the second I had got the gate shut, and stuck its nose into my crotch. And kept it there, growling menacingly, the whole time it took me to back him up to the door of the house. There was no doubt in my mind that I would come home from piano lesson one Saturday minus a few parts. Once I had got to the house, I tried to get inside quickly and shut the door in his face, leaving him out there in the din of cackling hens; but he always got his nose between the door and the jamb, growled horribly and pushed himself inside so that he could lie on the floor at my feet and watch me hungrily the whole time I sat at the kitchen table waiting for Ginny Stamp to finish off her lesson and get out of there. By the time my turn came around my nerves were too frayed for me to get much benefit out of the lesson.

Still, somehow I learned. That Mrs. Greensborough was a marvellous teacher, my   35
mother said. The woman really knew her stuff. And I was such a fast-learning student that it took less than two years for my mother to begin thinking it was time the world heard from me.

"Richy Ryder," she said, "is coming to town."

"What?"

"Richy Ryder, CJMT. *The Talent Show.*"

I'd heard the program. Every Saturday night Richy Ryder was in a different town somewhere in the province, hosting his one-hour talent contest from the stage of a local theatre and giving away free trips to Hawaii.

Something rolled over in my stomach.   40

"And here's the application form right here," she said, whipping two sheets of paper out of her purse to slap down on the table.

"No thank you," I said. If she thought I was going in it, she was crazy.

"Don't be silly. What harm is there in trying?" My mother always answered objections with great cheerfulness, as if they were hardly worth considering.

"I'll make a fool of myself."

"You play beautifully," she said. "It's amazing how far you've come in only two   45
years. And besides, even if you don't win, the experience would be good for you."

"You have to go door-to-door ahead of time, begging for pledges, for money."

"Not begging," she said. She plunged her hands into the sink, peeling carrots so fast I couldn't see the blade of the vegetable peeler. "Just giving people a chance to vote for you. A dollar a vote." The carrot dropped, skinned naked, another one was picked up. She looked out the window now toward the barn and, still smiling, delivered the argument that never failed. "I just know you'd win it if you went in, I can feel it in my bones."

"Not this time!" I shouted, nearly turning myself inside out with the terror. "Not this time. I just can't do it."

Yet somehow I found myself riding my bicycle up and down all the roads around Waterville, knocking at people's doors, explaining the contest, and asking for their money and their votes. I don't know why I did it. Perhaps I was doing it for the same reason I was tripping over everything, knocking things off tables, slamming my shoulder into doorjambs; I just couldn't help it, everything had gone out of control. I'd wakened one morning that year and found myself six feet two inches tall and as narrow as a fence stake. My feet were so far away they seemed to have nothing to do with me. My hands flopped around on the ends of those lanky arms like fish, something alive. My legs had grown so fast the bones in my knees parted and I had to wear elastic bandages to keep from falling apart. When I turned a corner on my bicycle, one knee would bump the handlebar, throwing me into the ditch. I was the same person as before, apparently, saddled with this new body I didn't know what to do with. Everything had gone out of control. I seemed to have nothing to do with the direction of my own life. It was perfectly logical that I should end up playing the piano on the radio, selling myself to the countryside for a chance to fly off to Hawaii and lie on the sand under the whispering palms.

There were actually two prizes offered. The all-expense, ten-day trip to Hawaii   50
would go to the person who brought in the most votes for himself, a dollar a vote. But

lest someone accuse the radio station of getting its values confused, there was also a prize for the person judged by a panel of experts to have the most talent. This prize, which was donated by Nelson's Hardware, was a leatherette footstool.

"It's not the prize that's important," people told me. "It's the chance to be heard by all those people."

I preferred not to think of all those people. It seemed to me that if I were cut out to be a concert pianist it would be my teacher and not my parents encouraging me in this thing. Mrs. Greensborough, once she'd forked over her two dollars for two votes, said nothing at all. No doubt she was hoping I'd keep her name out of it.

But it had taken no imagination on my part to figure out that if I were to win the only prize worth trying for, the important thing was not to spend long hours at the keyboard, practising, but to get out on the road hammering at doors, on the telephone calling relatives, down at the General Store approaching strangers who stopped for gas. Daily piano practice shrank to one or two quick run-throughs of "The Robin's Return," school homework shrank to nothing at all, and home chores just got ignored. My brother and sister filled in for me, once in a while, so the chickens wouldn't starve to death and the woodbox would never be entirely empty, but they did it gracelessly. It was amazing, they said, how much time a great pianist had to spend out on the road, meeting his public. Becoming famous, they said, was more work than it was worth.

And becoming famous, I discovered, was what people assumed I was after. "You'll go places," they told me. "You'll put this place on the old map." I was a perfect combination of my father's down-to-earth get-up-and-go and my mother's finer sensitivity, they said. How wonderful to see a young person with such high ambition!

"I always knew this old place wouldn't be good enough to hold you," my grandmother said as she fished out a five-dollar bill from her purse. But my mother's sisters, who appeared from all parts of the old farmhouse in order to contribute a single collective vote, had some reservations to express. Eleanor, the youngest, said she doubted I'd be able to carry it off, I'd probably freeze when I was faced with a microphone, I'd forget what a piano was for. Christina announced she was betting I'd faint, or have to run out to the bathroom right in the middle of my piece. And Mabel, red-headed Mabel who'd played accordion once in an amateur show, said she remembered a boy who made such a fool of himself in one of these things that he went home and blew off his head. "Don't be so morbid," my grandmother said. "The boy probably had no talent. Clay here is destined for higher things."

From behind her my grandfather winked. He seldom had a chance to contribute more than that to a conversation. He waited until we were alone to stuff a five-dollar bill in my pocket and squeeze my arm.

I preferred my grandmother's opinion of me to the aunts'. I began to feed people lies so they'd think that about me—that I was destined for dizzying heights. I wanted to be a great pianist, I said, and if I won that trip to Hawaii I'd trade it in for the money so that I could go off and study at the Toronto Conservatory. I'd heard of the Toronto Conservatory only because it was printed in big black letters on the front cover of all those yellow books of finger exercises I was expected to practise.

I don't know why people gave me their money. Pity, perhaps. Maybe it was impossible to say no to a six-foot-two-inch thirteen-year-old who trips over his own bike in front of your house, falls up your bottom step, blushes red with embarrassment when you open the door, and tells you he wants your money for a talent contest so he can become a Great Artist. At any rate, by the day of the contest I'd collected enough money to put me in the third spot. I would have to rely on pledges from the studio audience and

55

phone-in pledges from the radio audience to rocket me up to first place. The person in second place when I walked into that theatre to take my seat down front with the rest of the contestants was Cornelia Horncastle.

I don't know how she managed it so secretly. I don't know where she found the people to give her money, living in the same community as I did, unless all those people who gave me their dollar bills when I knocked on their doors had just given her two the day before. Maybe she'd gone into town, canvassing street after street, something my parents wouldn't let me do on the grounds that town people already had enough strangers banging on their doors every day. Once I'd got outside the vague boundaries of Waterville I was to approach only friends or relatives or people who worked in the woods with my dad, or stores that had—as my mother put it—done a good business out of us over the years. Cornelia Horncastle, in order to get herself secretly into that second place, must have gone wild in town. Either that or discovered a rich relative.

She sat at the other end of the front row of contestants, frowning over the sheets of music in her hands. A short nod and a quick smile were all she gave me. Like the other contestants, I was kept busy licking my dry lips, rubbing my sweaty palms together, wondering if I should whip out to the bathroom one last time, and rubbernecking to get a look at people as they filled up the theatre behind us. Mrs. Greensborough, wearing dark glasses and a big floppy hat, was jammed into the far corner at the rear, studying her program. Mr. and Mrs. Korhonen and Lilja came partway down the aisle and found seats near the middle. Mr. Korhonen winked at me. Larry, who was not quite the hero he had once been, despite the fact that he'd recently beat up one of the teachers and set fire to the bus shelter, came in with my brother Kenny—both of them looking uncomfortable—and slid into a back seat. My parents came all the way down front, so they could look back up the slope and pick out the seats they wanted. My mother smiled as she always did in public, as if she expected the most delightful surprise at any moment. They took seats near the front. Laurel was with them, reading a book.

My mother's sisters—with husbands, boyfriends, a few of my cousins—filled up the entire middle section of the back row. Eleanor, who was just a few years older than myself, crossed her eyes and stuck out her tongue when she saw that I'd turned to look. Mabel pulled in her chin and held up her hands, which she caused to tremble and shake. Time to be nervous, she was suggesting, in case I forgot. Bella, Christina, Gladdy, Frieda—all sat puffed up like members of a royal family, or the owners of this theatre, looking down over the crowd as if they believed every one of these people had come here expressly to watch their nephew and for no other reason. "Look, it's the Barclay girls," I heard someone behind me say. And someone else: "Oh, *them.*" The owner of the first voice giggled. "It's a wonder they aren't all entered in this thing, you know how they like to perform." A snort. "They *are* performing, just watch them." I could tell by the muffled "Shhh" and the rustling of clothing that one of them was nudging the other and pointing at me, at the back of my neck. "One of them's son." When I turned again, Eleanor stood up in the aisle by her seat, did a few steps of a tap dance, and quickly sat down. In case I was tempted to take myself seriously.

When my mother caught my eye, she mouthed a silent message: stop gawking at the audience, I was letting people see how unusual all this was to me, instead of taking it in my stride like a born performer. She indicated with her head that I should notice the stage.

As if I hadn't already absorbed every detail. It was exactly as she must have hoped. A great black concert grand with the lid lifted sat out near the front of the stage, against a painted backdrop of palm trees along a sandy beach, and—in great scrawled letters—

60

the words "Richy Ryder's CJMT Talent Festival." A long blackboard leaned against one end of the proscenium arch, with all the contestants' names on it and the rank order of each. Someone named Brenda Roper was in first place. On the opposite side of the stage, a microphone seemed to have grown up out of a heap of pineapples. I felt sick.

Eventually Richy Ryder came out of whatever backstage room he'd been hiding in and passed down the row of contestants, identifying us and telling us to get up onto the stage when our turns came without breaking our necks on those steps. "You won't be nervous, when you get up there," he said. "I'll make you feel at ease." He was looking off somewhere else as he said it, and I could see his jaw muscles straining to hold back a yawn. And he wasn't fooling me with his "you won't be nervous" either, because I knew without a doubt that the minute I got up on that stage I would throw up all over the piano.

Under the spotlight, Richy Ryder acted like a different person. He did not look the least bit like yawning while he told the audience the best way of holding their hands to get the most out of applause, cautioned them against whistling or yelling obscenities, painted a glorious picture of the life ahead for the talented winner of this contest, complimented the audience on the number of happy, shiny faces he could see out there in the seats, and told them how lucky they were to have this opportunity of showing off the fine young talent of the valley to all the rest of the province. I slid down in my seat, sure that I would rather die than go through with this thing.

The first contestant was a fourteen-year-old girl dressed up like a gypsy, singing something in a foreign language. According to the blackboard she was way down in ninth place, so I didn't pay much attention until her voice cracked open in the middle of a high note and she clutched at her throat with both hands, a look of incredulous surprise on her face. She stopped right there, face a brilliant red, and after giving the audience a quick curtsey hurried off the stage. A great beginning, I thought. If people were going to fall to pieces like that through the whole show no one would even notice my upchucking on the Heintzman. I had a vision of myself dry-heaving the whole way through "The Robin's Return."

Number two stepped up to the microphone and answered all of Richy Ryder's questions as if they were some kind of test he had to pass in order to be allowed to perform. Yes sir, his name was Roger Casey, he said with a face drawn long and narrow with seriousness, and in case that wasn't enough he added that his father was born in Digby, Nova Scotia, and his mother was born Esther Romaine in a little house just a couple of blocks up the street from the theatre, close to the Native Sons' Hall, and had gone to school with the mayor though she'd dropped out of Grade Eight to get a job at the Safeway cutting meat. And yes sir, he was going to play the saxophone because he'd taken lessons for four years from Mr. D. P. Rowbottom on Seventh Street though he'd actually started out on the trumpet until he decided he didn't like it all that much. He came right out to the edge of the stage, toes sticking over, leaned back like a rooster about to crow, and blasted out "Softly As in a Morning Sunrise" so loud and hard that I thought his bulging eyes would pop right out of his head and his straining lungs would blast holes through that red-and-white shirt. Everyone moved forward, tense and straining, waiting for something terrible to happen—for him to fall off the stage or explode or go sailing off into the air from the force of his own fantastic intensity—but he stopped suddenly and everyone fell back exhausted and sweaty to clap for him.

The third contestant was less reassuring. A kid with talent. A smart-aleck ten-year-old with red hair, who told the audience he was going into show business when he grew up, started out playing "Swanee River" on his banjo, switched in the middle of a bar to a

65

mouth organ, tap-danced across the stage to play a few bars on the piano, and finished off on a trombone he'd had stashed away behind the palm tree. He bowed, grinned, flung himself around the stage as if he'd spent his whole life on it, and looked as if he'd do his whole act again quite happily if the audience wanted him to. By the time the tremendous applause had died down my jaw was aching from the way I'd been grinding my teeth the whole time he was up there. The audience would not have gone quite so wild over him, I thought, if he hadn't been wearing a hearing aid and a leg brace.

Then it was my turn. A strange calm fell over me when my name was called, the kind of calm that I imagine comes over a person about to be executed when his mind finally buckles under the horror it has been faced with, something too terrible to believe in. I wondered for a moment if I had died. But no, my body at least hadn't died, for it transported me unbidden across the front of the audience, up the staircase (with only a slight stumble on the second step, hardly noticeable), and across the great wide stage of the theatre to stand facing Richy Ryder's enormous expanse of white smiling teeth, beside the microphone.

"And you are Barclay Philip Desmond," he said.

"Yes," I said.

And again "yes," because I realized that not only had my voice come out as thin and high as the squeal of a dry buzz-saw, but the microphone was at least a foot too low. I had to bend my knees to speak into it.

"You don't live in town, do you?" he said. He had no intention of adjusting that microphone. "You come from a place called . . . Waterville. A logging and farming settlement?"

"Yes," I said.

And again "yes" because while he was speaking my legs had straightened up, I'd returned to my full height and had to duck again for the microphone.

He was speaking to me but his eyes, I could see, were busy keeping all that audience gathered together, while his voice and his mind were obviously concentrated on the thousands of invisible people who were crouched inside that microphone, listening, the thousands of people who—I imagined now—were pulled up close to their sets all over the province, wondering if I was actually a pair of twins or if my high voice had some peculiar way of echoing itself, a few tones lower.

"Does living in the country like that mean you have to milk the cows every morning before you go to school?"

"Yes."

And again "yes."

I could see Mrs. Greensborough cowering in the back corner. I promise not to mention you, I thought. And the Korhonens, grinning. I had clearly passed over into another world they couldn't believe in.

"If you've got a lot of farm chores to do, when do you find the time to practise the piano?"

He had me this time. A "yes" wouldn't be good enough. "Right after school," I said, and ducked to repeat. "Right after school. As soon as I get home. For an hour."

"And I just bet," he said, throwing the audience an enormous wink, "that like every other red-blooded country kid you hate every minute of it. You'd rather be outside playing baseball."

The audience laughed. I could see my mother straining forward; she still had the all-purpose waiting-for-the-surprise smile on her lips but her eyes were frowning at the master of ceremonies. She did not approve of the comment. And behind that face she was no doubt thinking to herself "I just know he's going to win" over and over so hard that she was getting pains in the back of her neck. Beside her, my father had a tight grin on his face. He was chuckling to himself, and sliding a look around the room to see how the others were taking this.

Up at the back, most of my aunts—and their husbands, their boyfriends—had tilted their chins down to their chests, offering me only the tops of their heads. Eleanor, however, had both hands behind her neck. She was laughing harder than anyone else.

Apparently I was not expected to respond to the last comment, for he had another question as soon as the laughter had died. "How old are you, son?"

"Thirteen."

For once I remembered to duck the first time.

"Thirteen. Does your wife like the idea of your going on the radio like this?"

Again the audience laughed. My face burned. I felt tears in my eyes. I had no control over my face. I tried to laugh like everyone else but realized I probably looked like an idiot. Instead, I frowned and looked embarrassed and kicked at one shoe with the toe of the other.

"Just a joke," he said, "just a joke." The jerk knew he'd gone too far. "And now seriously, one last question before I turn you loose on those ivories over there."

My heart had started to thump so noisily I could hardly hear him. My hands, I realized, had gone numb. There was no feeling at all in my fingers. How was I ever going to play the piano?

"What are you going to be when you grow up?"

The thumping stopped. My heart stopped. A strange, cold silence settled over the world. I was going to die right in front of all those people. What I was going to be was a corpse, dead of humiliation, killed in a trap I hadn't seen being set. What must have been only a few seconds crawled by while something crashed around in my head, trying to get out. I sensed the audience, hoping for some help from them. My mother had settled back in her seat and for the first time that surprise-me smile had gone. Rather, she looked confident, sure of what I was about to say.

And suddenly, I was aware of familiar faces all over that theatre. Neighbours. Friends of the family. My aunts. People who had heard me answer that question at their doors, people who thought they knew what I wanted.

There was nothing left of Mrs. Greensborough but the top of her big hat. My father, too, was looking down at the floor between his feet. I saw myself falling from that spar tree, high in the mountains.

"Going to be?" I said, turning so fast that I bumped the microphone with my hand, which turned out after all not to be numb.

I ducked.

"Nothing," I said. "I don't know. Maybe . . . maybe nothing at all."

I don't know who it was that snorted when I screwed up the stool, sat down, and stood up to screw it down again. I don't know how well I played, I wasn't listening. I don't know how loud the audience clapped, I was in a hurry to get back to my seat. I don't know what the other contestants did, I wasn't paying any attention except when Cornelia Horncastle got up on the stage, told the whole world she was going to be a professional pianist, and sat down to rattle off Rachmaninoff's Rhapsody on a Theme of Paganini as if she'd been playing for fifty years. As far as I know it may have been the first time she'd ever heard herself play it. She had a faint look of surprise on her face the whole time, as if she couldn't quite get over the way the keys went down when you touched them.

As soon as Cornelia came down off the stage, smiling modestly, and got back into her seat, Richy Ryder announced a fifteen-minute intermission while the talent judges made their decision and the studio audience went out into the lobby to pledge their money and their votes. Now that the talent had been displayed, people could spend their money according to what they'd heard rather than according to who happened to come knocking on their door. Most of the contestants got up to stretch their legs but I figured I'd stood up once too often that night and stayed in my seat. The lower exit was not far away; I contemplated using it; I could hitch-hike home and be in bed before any of the others got out of there.

I was stopped, though, by my father, who sat down in the seat next to mine and put a greasy carton of popcorn in my lap.

"Well," he said, "that's that."

His neck was flushed. This must have been a terrible evening for him. He had a carton of popcorn himself and tipped it up to gather a huge mouthful. I had never before in my life, I realized, seen my father eat popcorn. It must have been worse for him than I thought.

Not one of the aunts was anywhere in sight! I could see my mother standing in   105
the far aisle, talking to Mrs. Korhonen. Still smiling. She would never let herself fall apart in public, no matter what happened. My insides ached with the knowledge of what it must have been like right then to be her. I felt as if I had just betrayed her in front of the whole world. Betrayed everyone.

"Let's go home," I said.

"Not yet. Wait a while. Might as well see this thing to the end."

True, I thought. Wring every last drop of torture out of it.

He looked hard at me a moment, as if he were trying to guess what was going on in my head. And he did, he did, he always knew. "My old man wanted me to be a doctor," he said. "My mother wanted me to be a florist. She liked flowers. She thought if I was a florist I'd be able to send her a bouquet every week. But what does any of that matter now?"

Being part of a family was too complicated. And right then I decided I'd be a   110
loner. No family for me. Nobody whose hearts could be broken every time I opened my mouth. Nobody expecting anything of me. Nobody to get me all tangled up in knots trying to guess who means what and what is it that's really going on inside anyone else. No temptations to presume I knew what someone else was thinking or feeling or hoping for.

When the lights had flickered and dimmed, and people had gone back to their seats, a young man with a beard came out onto the stage and changed the numbers behind the contestants' names. I'd dropped to fifth place, and Cornelia Horncastle had moved up to first. She had also, Richy Ryder announced, been awarded the judges' footstool for talent. The winner of the holiday in sunny Hawaii would not be announced until the next week, he said, when the radio audience had enough time to mail in their votes.

"And that," my mother said when she came down the aisle with her coat on, "is the end of a long and tiring day." I could find no disappointment showing in her eyes, or in the set of her mouth. Just relief. The same kind of relief that I felt myself. "You did a good job," she said, "and thank goodness it's over."

As soon as we got in the house I shut myself in the bedroom and announced I was never coming out. Lying on my bed, I tried to read my comic books but my mind passed from face to face all through the community, imagining everyone having a good laugh at the way my puffed-up ambition had got its reward. My face burned. Relatives, the aunts, would be ashamed of me. Eleanor would never let me forget. Mabel would remind me of the boy who'd done the only honourable thing, blown off his head. Why wasn't I doing the same? I lay awake the whole night, torturing myself with these thoughts. But when morning came and the hunger pains tempted me out of the bedroom as far as the breakfast table, I decided the whole wretched experience had brought one benefit with it: freedom from ambition. I wouldn't worry any more about becoming a pianist for my mother. Nor would I worry any more about becoming a high-rigger for my father. I was free at last to concentrate on pursuing the only goal that ever really mattered to me: becoming a Finn.

Of course I failed at that too. But then neither did Cornelia Horncastle become a great pianist on the concert stages of Europe. In fact, I understand that once she got back from her holiday on the beaches of Hawaii she announced to her parents that she was never going to touch a piano again as long as she lived, ivory, or cardboard, or any other kind. She had already, she said, accomplished all she'd ever wanted from it. And as far as I know, she's kept her word to this day.

QUESTIONS

1. Describe the attitude of Barclay Desmond toward his own experience as a young pianist and recitalist. Why does the story devote so much attention to Richy Ryder's introductory questions to Clay? Might Clay's experience have been different if he could have had a different kind of introduction?

2. How does Hodgins make the story comic? Describe the uses of farce, verbal humor, and fancifulness. Even though Clay makes himself the object of much humor, what is your attitude toward him at the story's end?

3. In what ways is the story serious? How seriously do you treat Clay's statements about his own ambitions (see paragraphs 22, 94–99, 113)?

4. Why do you think Clay begins and ends by referring to Cornelia Hardcastle? In what ways do you think Clay is similar to Cornelia, and also different from her?

ALICE MUNRO   (b. 1931)

Munro, one of Canada's premier story writers, grew up in Western Ontario, twenty miles east of Lake Huron—the locale of the town of Jubilee explored in the story collection Something I've Been Meaning to Tell You *(1974), from which "The Found Boat" is selected. She received her higher education at the University of Western Ontario, married, and moved to British Columbia, where she began her writing career. Her first Collection was* Dance of the Happy Shades *(1968), followed three years later by the novelistic* Lives of Girls and Women. *Later volumes are* The Beggar Maid *(1978),* The Moons of Jupiter *(1982),* The Progress of Love *(1986),* Friend of My Youth *(1990), and* Open Secrets *(1995). Her stories are mainly regional and have a realistic basis in her own experiences. The stories are not autobiographical, however; her characters and their actions develop out of her powerful imagination and strong sympathy and compassion. Recipient of Canada's Governor-General's Award for her very first work, she has merited additional honors throughout her distinguished career.*

The Found Boat _____ *1974*

At the end of Bell Street, McKay Street, Mayo Street, there was the Flood. It was the Wawanash River, which every spring overflowed its banks. Some springs, say one in every five, it covered the roads on that side of town and washed over the fields, creating a shallow choppy lake. Light reflected off the water made everything bright and cold, as it is in a lakeside town, and woke or revived in people certain vague hopes of disaster. Mostly during the late afternoon and early evening, there were people straggling out to look at it, and discuss whether it was still rising, and whether this time it might invade the town. In general, those under fifteen and over sixty-five were most certain that it would.

Eva and Carol rode out on their bicycles. They left the road—it was the end of Mayo Street, past any houses—and rode right into a field, over a wire fence entirely flattened by the weight of the winter's snow. They coasted a little way before the long grass stopped them, then left their bicycles lying down and went to the water.

"We have to find a log and ride on it," Eva said.

"Jesus, we'll freeze our legs off."

"Jesus, we'll freeze our legs off!" said one of the boys who were there too at the   5
water's edge. He spoke in a sour whine, the way boys imitated girls although it was nothing like the way girls talked. These boys—there were three of them—were all in the same class as Eva and Carol at school and were known to them by name (their names being Frank, Bud and Clayton), but Eva and Carol, who had seen and recognized them from the road, had not spoken to them or looked at them or, even yet, given any sign of knowing they were there. The boys seemed to be trying to make a raft, from lumber they had salvaged from the water.

Eva and Carol took off their shoes and socks and waded in. The water was so cold it sent pain up their legs, like blue electric sparks shooting through their veins, but they went on, pulling their skirts high, tight behind and bunched so they could hold them in front.

"Look at the fat-assed ducks in wading."

"Fat-assed fucks."

Eva and Carol, of course, gave no sign of hearing this. They laid hold of a log and climbed on, taking a couple of boards floating in the water for paddles. There were always things floating around in the Flood—branches, fence-rails, logs, road signs, old lumber; sometimes boilers, washtubs, pots and pans, or even a car seat or stuffed chair, as if somewhere the Flood had got into a dump.

They paddled away from shore, heading out into the cold lake. The water was per-   10
fectly clear, they could see the brown grass swimming along the bottom. Suppose it was the sea, thought Eva. She thought of drowned cities and countries. Atlantis. Suppose they were riding in a Viking boat—Viking boats on the Atlantic were more frail and narrow than this log on the Flood—and they had miles of clear sea beneath them, then a spired city, intact as a jewel irretrievable on the ocean floor.

"This is a Viking boat," she said. "I am the carving on the front." She stuck her chest out and stretched her neck, trying to make a curve, and she made a face, putting out her tongue. Then she turned and for the first time took notice of the boys.

"Hey, you sucks!" she yelled at them. "You'd be scared to come out here, this water is ten feet deep!"

"Liar," they answered without interest, and she was.

They steered the log around a row of trees, avoiding floating barbed wire, and got into a little bay created by a natural hollow of the land. Where the bay was now, there would be a pond full of frogs later in the spring, and by the middle of summer there would be no water visible at all, just a low tangle of reeds and bushes, green, to show that mud was still wet around their roots. Larger bushes, willows, grew around the steep bank of this pond and were still partly out of the water. Eva and Carol let the log ride in. They saw a place where something was caught.

It was a boat, or part of one. An old rowboat with most of one side ripped out,   15
the board that had been the seat just dangling. It was pushed up among the branches, lying on what would have been its side, if it had a side, the prow caught high.

Their idea came to them without consultation, at the same time:

"You guys! Hey, you guys!"

"We found you a boat!"

"Stop building your stupid raft and come and look at the boat!"

What surprised them in the first place was that the boys really did come, scram-   20
bling overland, half running, half sliding down the bank, wanting to see.

"Hey, where?"

"Where is it. I don't see no boat."

What surprised them in the second place was that when the boys did actually see what boat was meant, this old flood-smashed wreck held up in the branches, they did not understand that they had been fooled, that a joke had been played on them. They did not show a moment's disappointment, but seemed as pleased at the discovery as if the boat had been whole and new. They were already barefoot, because they had been wading in the water to get lumber, and they waded in here without a stop, surrounding the boat and appraising it and paying no attention even of an insulting kind to Eva and Carol who bobbed up and down on their log. Eva and Carol had to call to them.

"How do you think you're going to get it off?"

"It won't float anyway."   25

"What makes you think it will float?"

"It'll sink. Glub-blub-blub, you'll all be drownded."

The boys did not answer, because they were too busy walking around the boat, pulling at it in a testing way to see how it could be got off with the least possible damage. Frank, who was the most literate, talkative and inept of the three, began referring to the boat as *she*, an affectation which Eva and Carol acknowledged with fish-mouths of contempt.

"She's caught two places. You got to be careful not to tear a hole in her bottom. She's heavier than you'd think."

It was Clayton who climbed up and freed the boat, and Bud, a tall fat boy, who   30
got the weight of it on his back to turn it into the water so that they could half float, half carry it to shore. All this took some time. Eva and Carol abandoned their log and waded out of the water. They walked overland to get their shoes and socks and bicycles. They did not need to come back this way but they came. They stood at the top of the hill, leaning on their bicycles. They did not go on home, but they did not sit down and frankly watch, either. They stood more or less facing each other, but glancing down at the water and at the boys struggling with the boat, as if they had just halted for a moment out of curiosity, and staying longer than they intended, to see what came of this unpromising project.

About nine o'clock, or when it was nearly dark—dark to people inside the houses, but not quite dark outside—they all returned to town, going along Mayo Street in a sort of procession. Frank and Bud and Clayton came carrying the boat, upside-down, and Eva and Carol walked behind, wheeling their bicycles. The boys' heads were almost hidden in the darkness of the overturned boat, with its smell of soaked wood, cold swampy water. The girls could look ahead and see the street lights in their tin reflectors, a necklace of lights climbing Mayo Street, reaching all the way up to the standpipe. They turned onto Burns Street heading for Clayton's house, the nearest house belonging to any of them. This was not the way home for Eva or for Carol either, but they followed along. The boys were perhaps too busy carrying the boat to tell them to go away. Some younger children were still out playing, playing hopscotch on the sidewalk though they could hardly see. At this time of year the bare sidewalk was still such a novelty and delight. These children cleared out of the way and watched the boat go by with unwilling respect; they shouted questions after it, wanting to know where it came from and what was going to be done with it. No one answered them. Eva and Carol as well as the boys refused to answer or even look at them.

The five of them entered Clayton's yard. The boys shifted weight, as if they were going to put the boat down.

"You better take it round to the back where nobody can see it," Carol said. That was the first thing any of them had said since they came into town.

The boys said nothing but went on, following a mud path between Clayton's house and a leaning board fence. They let the boat down in the back yard.

"It's a stolen boat, you know," said Eva, mainly for the effect. "It must've belonged to somebody. You stole it."   35

"You was the ones who stole it then," Bud said, short of breath. "It was you seen it first."

"It was you took it."

"It was all of us then. If one of us gets in trouble then all of us does."

"Are you going to tell anybody on them?" said Carol as she and Eva rode home, along the streets which were dark between the lights now and potholed from winter.

"It's up to you, I won't if you won't."   40

"I won't if you won't."

They rode in silence, relinquishing something, but not discontented.

The board fence in Clayton's back yard had every so often a post which supported it, or tried to, and it was on these posts that Eva and Carol spent several evenings sitting, jauntily but not very comfortably. Or else they just leaned against the fence while the boys worked on the boat. During the first couple of evenings neighborhood children attracted by the sound of hammering tried to get into the yard to see what was going on, but Eva and Carol blocked their way.

"Who said you could come in here?"

"Just us can come in this yard."   45

These evenings were getting longer, the air milder. Skipping was starting on the sidewalks. Further along the street there was a row of hard maples that had been tapped. Children drank the sap as fast as it could drip into the buckets. The old man and woman who owned the trees, and who hoped to make syrup, came running out of the house making noises as if they were trying to scare away crows. Finally, every spring, the old man would come out on his porch and fire his shotgun into the air, and then the thieving would stop.

None of those working on the boat bothered about stealing sap, though all had done so last year.

The lumber to repair the boat was picked up here and there, along back lanes. At this time of year things were lying around—old boards and branches, sodden mitts, spoons flung out with the dishwater, lids of pudding pots that had been set in the snow to cool, all the debris that can sift through and survive winter. The tools came from Clayton's cellar—left over, presumably, from the time when his father was alive—and though they had nobody to advise them the boys seemed to figure out more or less the manner in which boats are built, or rebuilt. Frank was the one who showed up with diagrams from books and *Popular Mechanics* magazines. Clayton looked at these diagrams and listened to Frank read the instructions and then went ahead and decided in his own way what was to be done. Bud was best at sawing. Eva and Carol watched everything from the fence and offered criticism and thought up names. The names for the boat that they thought of were: Water Lily, Sea Horse, Flood Queen, and Caro-Eve, after them because they had found it. The boys did not say which, if any, of these names they found satisfactory.

The boat had to be tarred. Clayton heated up a pot of tar on the kitchen stove and brought it out and painted slowly, his thorough way, sitting astride the overturned boat. The other boys were sawing a board to make a new seat. As Clayton worked, the tar cooled and thickened so that finally he could not move the brush any more. He turned to Eva and held out the pot and said, "You can go in and heat this on the stove."

Eva took the pot and went up the back steps. The kitchen seemed black after out-   50
side, but it must be light enough to see in, because there was Clayton's mother standing at the ironing board, ironing. She did that for a living, took in wash and ironing.

"Please may I put the tar pot on the stove?" said Eva, who had been brought up to talk politely to parents, even wash-and-iron ladies, and who for some reason especially wanted to make a good impression on Clayton's mother.

"You'll have to poke up the fire then," said Clayton's mother, as if she doubted whether Eva would know how to do that. But Eva could see now, and she picked up the lid with the stove-lifter, and took the poker and poked up a flame. She stirred the tar as it softened. She felt privileged. Then and later. Before she went to sleep a picture of Clayton came to her mind; she saw him sitting astride the boat, tar-painting, with such concentration, delicacy, absorption. She thought of him speaking to her, out of his isolation, in such an ordinary peaceful taking-for-granted voice.

On the twenty-fourth of May, a school holiday in the middle of the week, the boat was carried out of town, a long way now, off the road over fields and fences that had been repaired, to where the river flowed between its normal banks. Eva and Carol, as well as the boys, took turns carrying it. It was launched in the water from a cow-trampled spot between willow bushes that were fresh out in leaf. The boys went first. They yelled with triumph when the boat did float, when it rode amazingly down the river current. The boat was painted black, and green inside, with yellow seats, and a strip of yellow all the way around the outside. There was no name on it, after all. The boys could not imagine that it needed any name to keep it separate from the other boats in the world.

Eva and Carol ran along the bank, carrying bags full of peanut butter-and-jam sandwiches, pickles, bananas, chocolate cake, potato chips, graham crackers stuck together with corn syrup and five bottles of pop to be cooled in the river water. The bottles bumped against their legs. They yelled for a turn.

"If they don't let us they're bastards," Carol said, and they yelled together. "We   55
found it! We found it!"

The boys did not answer, but after a while they brought the boat in, and Carol and Eva came crashing, panting down the bank.

"Does it leak?"

"It don't leak yet."

"We forgot a bailing can," wailed Carol, but nevertheless she got in, with Eva, and Frank pushed them off, crying. "Here's to a Watery Grave!"

And the thing about being in a boat was that it was not solidly bobbing, like a log, but was cupped in the water, so that riding in it was not like being on something in the water, but like being in the water itself. Soon they were all going out in the boat in mixed-up turns, two boys and a girl, two girls and a boy, a girl and a boy, until things were so confused it was impossible to tell whose turn came next, and nobody cared anyway. They went down the river—those who weren't riding, running along the bank to keep up. They passed under two bridges, one iron, one cement. Once they saw a big carp just resting, it seemed to smile at them, in the bridge-shaded water. They did not know how far they had gone on the river, but things had changed—the water had got shallower, and the land flatter. Across an open field they saw a building that looked like a house, abandoned. They dragged the boat up on the bank and tied it and set out across the field.

"That's the old station," Frank said. "That's Pedder Station." The others had heard this name but he was the one who knew, because his father was the station agent in town. He said that this was a station on a branch line that had been torn up, and that there had been a sawmill here, but a long time ago.

Inside the station it was dark, cool. All the windows were broken. Glass lay in shards and in fairly big pieces on the floor. They walked around finding the larger pieces of glass and tramping on them, smashing them, it was like cracking ice on puddles. Some partitions were still in place, you could see where the ticket window had been. There was a bench lying on its side. People had been here, it looked as if people came here all the time, though it was so far from anywhere. Beer bottles and pop bottles were lying around, also cigarette packages, gum and candy wrappers, the paper from a loaf of bread. The walls were covered with dim and fresh pencil and chalk writings and carved with knives.

    I LOVE RONNIE COLES

    I WANT TO FUCK

    KILROY WAS HERE

    RONNIE COLES IS AN ASS-HOLE

    WHAT ARE YOU DOING HERE?

    WAITING FOR A TRAIN

    DAWNA MARY-LOU BARBARA JOANNE

It was exciting to be inside this large, dark, empty place, with the loud noise of breaking glass and their voices ringing back from the underside of the roof. They tipped the old beer bottles against their mouths. That reminded them that they were hungry and thirsty and they cleared a place in the middle of the floor and sat down and ate the lunch. They drank the pop just as it was, lukewarm. They ate everything there was and licked the smears of peanut butter and jam off the bread-paper in which the sandwiches had been wrapped.

They played Truth or Dare.

"I dare you to write on the wall, I am a Stupid Ass, and sign your name."

"Tell the truth—what is the worst lie you ever told?"

"Did you ever wet the bed?"

"Did you ever dream you were walking down the street without any clothes on?"

"I dare you to go outside and pee on the railway sign."

It was Frank who had to do that. They could not see him, even his back, but they knew he did it, they heard the hissing sound of his pee. They all sat still, amazed, unable to think of what the next dare would be.

"I dare everybody," said Frank from the doorway. "I dare—Everybody."

"What?"

"Take off all our clothes."

Eva and Carol screamed.

"Anybody who won't do it has to walk—has to *crawl*—around this floor on their   75
hands and knees."

They were all quiet, till Eva said, almost complacently, "What first?"

"Shoes and socks."

"Then we have to go outside, there's too much glass here."

They pulled off their shoes and socks in the doorway, in the sudden blinding sun.
The field before them was bright as water. They ran across where the tracks used to go.

"That's enough, that's enough," said Carol. "Watch out for thistles!"   80

"Tops! Everybody take off their tops!"

"I won't! We won't, will we, Eva?"

But Eva was whirling round and round in the sun where the track used to be.
"I don't care, I don't care! Truth or Dare! Truth or Dare!"

She unbuttoned her blouse as she whirled, as if she didn't know what her hand
was doing, she flung it off.

Carol took off hers. "I wouldn't have done it, if you hadn't!"   85

"Bottoms!"

Nobody said a word this time, they all bent and stripped themselves. Eva, naked
first, started running across the field, and then all the others ran, all five of them running bare through the knee-high hot grass, running towards the river. Not caring now
about being caught but in fact leaping and yelling to call attention to themselves, if
there was anybody to hear or see. They felt as if they were going to jump off a cliff and
fly. They felt that something was happening to them different from anything that had
happened before, and it had to do with the boat, the water, the sunlight, the dark
ruined station, and each other. They thought of each other now hardly as names or
people, but as echoing shrieks, reflections, all bold and white and loud and scandalous,
and as fast as arrows. They went running without a break into the cold water and when
it came almost to the tops of their legs they fell on it and swam. It stopped their noise.
Silence, amazement, came over them in a rush. They dipped and floated and separated, sleek as mink.

Eva stood up in the water her hair dripping, water running down her face. She
was waist deep. She stood on smooth stones, her feet fairly wide apart, water flowing
between her legs. About a yard away from her Clayton also stood up, and they were
blinking the water out of their eyes, looking at each other. Eva did not turn or try to
hide; she was quivering from the cold of the water, but also with pride, shame, boldness,
and exhilaration.

Clayton shook his head violently, as if he wanted to bang something out of it, then
bent over and took a mouthful of river water. He stood up with his cheeks full and made
a tight hole of his mouth and shot the water at her as if it was coming out of a hose, hitting her exactly, first one breast and then the other. Water from his mouth ran down
her body. He hooted to see it, a loud self-conscious sound that nobody would have
expected, from him. The others looked up from wherever they were in the water and
closed in to see.

Eva crouched down and slid into the water, letting her head go right under. She   90
swam, and when she let her head out, downstream, Carol was coming after her and the
boys were already on the bank, already running into the grass, showing their skinny

backs, their white, flat buttocks. They were laughing and saying things to each other but she couldn't hear, for the water in her ears.

"What did he do?" said Carol.

"Nothing."

They crept in to shore. "Let's stay in the bushes till they go," said Eva. "I hate them anyway. I really do. Don't you hate them?"

"Sure," said Carol, and they waited, not very long, until they heard the boys still noisy and excited coming down to the place a bit upriver where they had left the boat. They heard them jump in and start rowing.

"They've got all the hard part, going back," said Eva, hugging herself and shivering violently. "Who cares? Anyway. It never was our boat."

"What if they tell?" said Carol.

"We'll say it's all a lie."

Eva hadn't thought of this solution until she said it, but as soon as she did she felt almost light-hearted again. The ease and scornfulness of it did make them both giggle, and slapping themselves and splashing out of the water they set about developing one of those fits of laughter in which, as soon as one showed signs of exhaustion, the other would snort and start up again, and they would make helpless—soon genuinely helpless—faces at each other and bend over and grab themselves as if they had the worst pain.

QUESTIONS

1. Consider the details used in passages of description in the story. What kinds of details are included?

2. What is the level of diction in the dialogue of the story? From the dialogue, what do you learn about the various speakers?

3. Study paragraph 10. What does the paragraph tell you about Eva as a limited-point-of-view center of interest? How?

4. Consider the last paragraph in the story as a paragraph of action. What verbs are used, and how well do they help you visualize and imagine the sounds of the scene? What is the effect of the verb "snort"?

5. From the lifestyle and artifacts mentioned, what do you learn about the time of the events and the economic level of the town? What is the effect of the facts that it is early springtime, that the water is still cold, but that in May the water is swimmable? What are the implications for summer?

FRANK O'CONNOR   (1903–1966)

Frank O'Connor, the nom de plume *of Michael O'Donovan, was an only child of poor parents in County Cork, Ireland. He began writing when young, and for a time he was a director of Ireland's national theater. His output as a writer was considerable, with sixty-seven stories appearing in the posthumous* Collected Stories *of 1981. A meticulous writer, he was constantly revising his work. "First Confession," for example, went through a number of stages before the final version included here.*

First Confession ———————————————————————— *1951*

All the trouble began when my grandfather died and my grandmother—my father's mother—came to live with us. Relations in the one house are a strain at the best of times, but, to make matters worse, my grandmother was a real old countrywoman and quite unsuited to the life in town. She had a fat, wrinkled old face, and, to Mother's great indignation, went round the house in bare feet—the boots had her crippled, she said. For dinner she had a jug of porter° and a pot of potatoes with—sometimes—a bit of salt fish, and she poured out the potatoes on the table and ate them slowly, with great relish, using her fingers by way of a fork.

Now, girls are supposed to be fastidious, but I was the one who suffered most from this. Nora, my sister, just sucked up to the old woman for the penny she got every Friday out of the old-age pension, a thing I could not do. I was too honest, that was my trouble; and when I was playing with Bill Connell, the sergeant-major's son, and saw my grandmother steering up the path with the jug of porter sticking out from beneath her shawl I was mortified. I made excuses not to let him come into the house, because I could never be sure what she would be up to when we went in.

When Mother was at work and my grandmother made the dinner I wouldn't touch it. Nora once tried to make me, but I hid under the table from her and took the bread-knife with me for protection. Nora let on to be very indignant (she wasn't, of course, but she knew Mother saw through her, so she sided with Gran) and came after me. I lashed out at her with the bread-knife, and after that she left me alone. I stayed there till Mother came in from work and made my dinner, but when Father came in later Nora said in a shocked voice: "Oh, Dadda, do you know what Jackie did at dinner-time?" Then, of course, it all came out; Father gave me a flaking; Mother interfered, and for days after that he didn't speak to me and Mother barely spoke to Nora. And all because of that old woman! God knows, I was heart-scalded.

Then, to crown my misfortune, I had to make my first confession and communion. It was an old woman called Ryan who prepared us for these. She was about the one age with Gran; she was well-to-do, lived in a big house on Montenotte, wore a black cloak and bonnet, and came every day to school at three o'clock when we should have been going home, and talked to us of hell. She may have mentioned the other place as well, but that could only have been by accident, for hell had the first place in her heart.

She lit a candle, took out a new half-crown, and offered it to the first boy who would hold one finger—only one finger!—in the flame for five minutes by the school clock. Being always very ambitious I was tempted to volunteer, but I thought it might look greedy. Then she asked were we afraid of holding one finger—only one finger!—in a little candle flame for five minutes and not afraid of burning all over in roasting hot furnaces for all eternity. "All eternity! Just think of that! A whole lifetime goes by and it's nothing, not even a drop in the ocean of your sufferings." The woman was really interesting about hell, but my attention was all fixed on the half-crown. At the end of the lesson she put it back in her purse. It was a great disappointment; a religious woman like that, you wouldn't think she'd bother about a thing like a half-crown.

Another day she said she knew a priest who woke one night to find a fellow he didn't recognize leaning over the end of his bed. The priest was a bit frightened—naturally enough—but he asked the fellow what he wanted, and the fellow said in a deep, husky voice that he wanted to go to confession. The priest said it was an awkward time

5

---

porter: a dark-brown beer.

and wouldn't it do in the morning, but the fellow said that last time he went to confession, there was one sin he kept back, being ashamed to mention it, and now it was always on his mind. Then the priest knew it was a bad case, because the fellow was after making a bad confession and committing a mortal sin. He got up to dress, and just then the cock crew in the yard outside, and—lo and behold!—when the priest looked round there was no sign of the fellow, only a smell of burning timber, and when the priest looked at his bed didn't he see the print of two hands burned in it? That was because the fellow had made a bad confession. This story made a shocking impression on me.

But the worst of all was when she showed us how to examine our conscience. Did we take the name of the Lord, our God, in vain? Did we honour our father and our mother? (I asked her did this include grandmothers and she said it did.) Did we love our neighbours as ourselves? Did we covet our neighbour's goods? (I thought of the way I felt about the penny that Nora got every Friday.) I decided that, between one thing and another, I must have broken the whole ten commandments, all on account of that old woman, and so far as I could see, so long as she remained in the house I had no hope of ever doing anything else.

I was scared to death of confession. The day the whole class went I let on to have a toothache, hoping my absence wouldn't be noticed; but at three o'clock, just as I was feeling safe, along comes a chap with a message from Mrs. Ryan that I was to go to confession myself on Saturday and be at the chapel for communion with the rest. To make it worse, Mother couldn't come with me and sent Nora instead.

Now, that girl had ways of tormenting me that Mother never knew of. She held my hand as we went down the hill, smiling sadly and saying how sorry she was for me, as if she were bringing me to the hospital for an operation.

"Oh, God help us!" she moaned. "Isn't it a terrible pity you weren't a good boy?   10
Oh, Jackie, my heart bleeds for you! How will you ever think of all your sins? Don't forget you have to tell him about the time you kicked Gran on the shin."

"Lemme go!" I said, trying to drag myself free of her. "I don't want to go to confession at all."

"But sure, you'll have to go to confession, Jackie," she replied in the same regretful tone. "Sure, if you didn't the parish priest would be up to the house, looking for you. 'Tisn't, God knows, that I'm not sorry for you. Do you remember the time you tried to kill me with the bread-knife under the table? And the language you used to me? I don't know what he'll do with you at all, Jackie. He might have to send you up to the bishop."

I remember thinking bitterly that she didn't know the half of what I had to tell— if I told it. I knew I couldn't tell it, and understood perfectly why the fellow in Mrs. Ryan's story made a bad confession; it seemed to me a great shame that people wouldn't stop criticizing him. I remember that steep hill down to the church, and the sunlit hillsides beyond the valley of the river, which I saw in the gaps between the houses like Adam's last glimpse of Paradise.°

Then, when she had manœuvered me down the long flight of steps to the chapel yard, Nora suddenly changed her tone. She became the raging malicious devil she really was.

"There you are!" she said with a yelp of triumph, hurling me through the church   15
door. "And I hope he'll give you the penitential psalms, you dirty little caffler."

I knew then I was lost, given up to eternal justice. The door with the coloured-glass panels swung shut behind me, the sunlight went out and gave place to deep

Adam's last glimpse of Paradise: Genesis 3:23–24.

shadow, and the wind whistled outside so that the silence within seemed to crackle like ice under my feet. Nora sat in front of me by the confession box. There were a couple of old women ahead of her, and then a miserable-looking poor devil came and wedged me in at the other side, so that I couldn't escape even if I had the courage. He joined his hands and rolled his eyes in the direction of the roof, muttering aspirations in an anguished tone, and I wondered had he a grandmother too. Only a grandmother could account for a fellow behaving in that heartbroken way, but he was better off than I, for he at least could go and confess his sins; while I would make a bad confession and then die in the night and be continually coming back and burning people's furniture.

Nora's turn came, and I heard the sound of something slamming, and then her voice as if butter wouldn't melt in her mouth, and then another slam, and out she came. God, the hypocrisy of women! Her eyes were lowered, her head was bowed, and her hands were joined very low down on her stomach, and she walked up the aisle to the side altar looking like a saint. You never saw such an exhibition of devotion, and I remembered the devilish malice with which she had tormented me all the way from our door, and wondered were all religious people like that, really. It was my turn now. With the fear of damnation in my soul I went in, and the confessional door closed of itself behind me.

It was pitch-dark and I couldn't see priest or anything else. Then I really began to be frightened. In the darkness it was a matter between God and me, and He had all the odds. He knew what my intentions were before I even started; I had no chance. All I had ever been told about confession got mixed up in my mind, and I knelt to one wall and said: "Bless me, father, for I have sinned; this is my first confession." I waited for a few minutes, but nothing happened, so I tried it on the other wall. Nothing happened there either. He had me spotted all right.

It must have been then that I noticed the shelf at about one height with my head. It was really a place for grown-up people to rest their elbows, but in my distracted state I thought it was probably the place you were supposed to kneel. Of course, it was on the high side and not very deep, but I was always good at climbing and managed to get up all right. Staying up was the trouble. There was room only for my knees, and nothing you could get a grip on but a sort of wooden moulding a bit above it. I held on to the moulding and repeated the words a little louder, and this time something happened all right. A slide was slammed back; a little light entered the box, and a man's voice said: "Who's there?"

"'Tis me, father," I said for fear he mightn't see me and go away again. I couldn't see him at all. The place the voice came from was under the moulding, about level with my knees, so I took a good grip of the moulding and swung myself down till I saw the astonished face of a young priest looking up at me. He had to put his head on one side to see me, and I had to put mine on one side to see him, so we were more or less talking to one another upside-down. It struck me as a queer way of hearing confessions, but I didn't feel it my place to criticize.

"Bless me, father, for I have sinned; this is my first confession," I rattled off all in one breath, and swung myself down the least shade more to make it easier for him.

"What are you doing up there?" he shouted in an angry voice, and the strain the politeness was putting on my hold of the moulding, and the shock of being addressed in such an uncivil tone, were too much for me. I lost my grip, tumbled, and hit the door an unmerciful wallop before I found myself flat on my back in the middle of the aisle. The people who had been waiting stood up with their mouths open. The priest opened the door of the middle box and came out, pushing his biretta back from his forehead; he looked something terrible. Then Nora came scampering down the aisle.

20

"Oh, you dirty little caffler!" she said. "I might have known you'd do it. I might have known you'd disgrace me. I can't leave you out of my sight for one minute."

Before I could even get to my feet to defend myself she bent down and gave me a clip across the ear. This reminded me that I was so stunned I had even forgotten to cry, so that people might think I wasn't hurt at all, when in fact I was probably maimed for life. I gave a roar out of me.

"What's all this about?" the priest hissed, getting angrier than ever and pushing Nora off me. "How dare you hit the child like that, you little vixen?"

"But I can't do my penance with him, father," Nora cried, cocking an outraged eye up to him.

"Well, go and do it, or I'll give you some more to do," he said, giving me a hand up. "Was it coming to confession you were, my poor man?" he asked me.

"'Twas, father," said I with a sob.

"Oh," he said respectfully, "a big hefty fellow like you must have terrible sins. Is this your first?"

"'Tis, father," said I.

"Worse and worse," he said gloomily. "The crimes of a lifetime. I don't know will I get rid of you at all today. You'd better wait now till I'm finished with these old ones. You can see by the looks of them they haven't much to tell."

"I will, father," I said with something approaching joy.

The relief of it was really enormous. Nora stuck out her tongue at me from behind his back, but I couldn't even be bothered retorting. I knew from the very moment that man opened his mouth that he was intelligent above the ordinary. When I had time to think, I saw how right I was. It only stood to reason that a fellow confessing after seven years would have more to tell than people that went every week. The crimes of a lifetime, exactly as he said. It was only what he expected, and the rest was the cackle of old women and girls with their talk of hell, the bishop, and the penitential psalms. That was all they knew. I started to make my examination of conscience, and barring the one bad business of my grandmother it didn't seem so bad.

The next time, the priest steered me into the confession box himself and left the shutter back the way I could see him get in and sit down at the further side of the grille from me.

"Well, now," he said, "what do they call you?"

"Jackie, father," said I.

"And what's a-trouble to you, Jackie?"

"Father," I said, feeling I might as well get it over while I had him in good humour, "I had it all arranged to kill my grandmother."

He seemed a bit shaken by that, all right, because he said nothing for quite a while.

"My goodness," he said at last, "that'd be a shocking thing to do. What put that into your head?"

"Father," I said, feeling very sorry for myself, "she's an awful woman."

"Is she?" he asked. "What way is she awful?"

"She takes porter, father," I said, knowing well from the way Mother talked of it that this was a mortal sin, and hoping it would make the priest take a more favourable view of my case.

"Oh, my!" he said, and I could see he was impressed.

"And snuff, father," said I.

"That's a bad case, sure enough, Jackie," he said.

"And she goes round in her bare feet, father," I went on in a rush of self-pity, "and she knows I don't like her, and she gives pennies to Nora and none to me, and my da sides with her and flakes me, and one night I was so heartscalded I made up my mind I'd have to kill her."

"And what would you do with the body?" he asked with great interest.

"I was thinking I could chop that up and carry it away in a barrow I have," I said.

"Begor, Jackie," he said, "do you know you're a terrible child?"

"I know, father," I said, for I was just thinking the same thing myself. "I tried to kill Nora too with a bread-knife under the table, only I missed her."

"Is that the little girl that was beating you just now?" he asked.

"'Tis, father."

"Someone will go for her with a bread-knife one day, and he won't miss her," he said rather cryptically. "You must have great courage. Between ourselves, there's a lot of people I'd like to do the same to but I'd never have the nerve. Hanging is an awful death."

"Is it, father?" I asked with the deepest interest—I was always very keen on hanging. "Did you ever see a fellow hanged?"

"Dozens of them," he said solemnly. "And they all died roaring."

"Jay!" I said.

"Oh, a horrible death!" he said with great satisfaction. "Lots of fellows I saw killed their grandmothers too, but they all said 'twas never worth it."

He had me there for a full ten minutes talking, and then walked out the chapel yard with me. I was genuinely sorry to part with him, because he was the most entertaining character I'd ever met in the religious line. Outside, after the shadow of the church, the sunlight was like the roaring of waves on a beach; it dazzled me; and when the frozen silence melted and I heard the screech of trams on the road my heart soared. I knew now I wouldn't die in the night and come back, leaving marks on my mother's furniture. It would be a great worry to her, and the poor soul had enough.

Nora was sitting on the railing, waiting for me, and she put on a very sour puss when she saw the priest with me. She was made jealous because a priest had never come out of the church with her.

"Well," she asked coldly, after he left me, "what did he give you?"

"Three Hail Marys," I said.

"Three Hail Marys," she repeated incredulously. "You mustn't have told him anything."

"I told him everything," I said confidently.

"About Gran and all?"

"About Gran and all."

(All she wanted was to be able to go home and say I'd made a bad confession.)

"Did you tell him you went for me with the bread-knife?" she asked with a frown.

"I did to be sure."

"And he only gave you three Hail Marys?"

"That's all."

She slowly got down from the railing with a baffled air. Clearly, this was beyond her. As we mounted the steps back to the main road she looked at me suspiciously.

"What are you sucking?" she asked.

"Bullseyes."

"Was it the priest gave them to you?"

"'Twas."

"Lord God," she wailed bitterly, "some people have all the luck! 'Tis no advantage to anybody trying to be good. I might just as well be a sinner like you."

QUESTIONS

1. Describe Jackie as a narrator. What is the level of his language? To whom does he seem to be speaking or writing? What elements of language do you find in the story that seem characteristically Irish?

2. Describe Jackie's character. How old do you think he is at the time of the narration? Is there evidence that he has grown as a person since the time of the story's events? Do you think his attitudes have changed about his grandmother? His parents? His sister? Mrs. Ryan? The priest?

3. Is Jackie's confession a "good" one? Whose religion seems more appealing, Mrs. Ryan's or the priest's?

4. To what degree are the relationships within Jackie's family either ordinary or unusual?

5. "First Confession" is a funny story. What contributions are made to the humor by the situations? The language?

WRITING ABOUT TONE AND STYLE

The task of writing about tone is to identify attitudes that you find in the work and then to explain how attitudes are made obvious by the author's style. How do words describing characters, scenes, thoughts, and actions indicate attitude? In Poe's "The Cask of Amontillado," for example (Chapter 6), do the descriptions of the gloomy catacombs evoke fear or tension, or do they seem exaggerated? Depending on the story, your devising and answering such questions will help you understand an author's control over tone.

Questions for Discovering Ideas

• Use a dictionary to discover the meaning of any words you do not immediately know. Are there any unusual words? Any especially difficult or uncommon ones? Do any of the words distract you as you read?

• How strongly do you respond to the story? What words bring out your interest, concern, indignation, fearfulness, anguish, amusement, or sense of affirmation?

• Does the diction seem unusual or noteworthy, such as words in dialect, polysyllabic words, or foreign words or phrases that the author assumes you know? Are there any especially connotative or emotive words? What do these words suggest about the author's apparent assumptions about the readers?

• Can you easily visualize and imagine the situations described by the words? If you find it easy, or hard, to what degree does your success or difficulty stem from the level of diction?

• For passages describing *action*, how vivid are the words? How do they help you picture the action? How do they hold your attention?

• For passages describing *exterior* or *interior scenes*, how specific are the words? How much detail does the writer provide? Should there be more or fewer words?

How vivid are the descriptions? How successfully does the author locate scenes spatially? How many words are devoted to colors, shapes, sizes, and so on? What is the effect of such passages?

* For passages of dialogue, what does the level of speech indicate about the characters? How do a person's speeches help to establish her or his character? For what purposes does the author use formal or informal diction? How much slang (low or informal language) do you find? Why is it there? How does dialogue shape your responses to the characters and to the actions?

* What role does the narrator/speaker play in your attitudes toward the story material? Does the speaker seem intelligent/stupid, friendly/unfriendly, sane/insane, or idealistic/pragmatic?

* What verbal irony do you find in the story? How is the irony connected to philosophies of marriage, family, society, politics, religion, or morality? How do you think you are expected to respond to the irony?

* Did anything in the story make you laugh? What placement of words brought out the humor? Try to explain how the word arrangement caused your laughter.

Strategies for Organizing Ideas

Begin with a careful reading, noting particularly those elements of language that convey attitudes. How does the author establish the dominant moods of the story (e.g., the humor of "Rape Fantasies" and "First Confession," the uneasiness in "Soldier's Home")? Some possibilities are the use or misuse of language, the exposé of a pretentious speaker, the use of exact and specific descriptions, the isolation of a major character, the failure of plans, and the continuance of naiveté in a disillusioned world.

Some of the things to discuss are these:

1. *Audience, situation, and characters.* Is any person or group directly addressed by the speaker? What attitude is expressed (love, respect, condescension, confidentiality, confidence, etc.)? What is the basic situation in the story? Do you find instances of verbal irony? What do these show (optimism or pessimism, for example)? How is the situation of the story controlled to shape your responses? That is, can actions, situations, or characters be seen as expressions of attitude, or as embodiments of certain favorable or unfavorable ideas or positions? What is the nature of the narrator or persona? Why does the narrator speak exactly as he or she does? How is the narrator's character manipulated to show apparent authorial attitude and to elicit reader response? Does the story promote respect, admiration, dislike, or other feelings about character or situation? How?

2. *Descriptions, diction.* Your concern here is not to analyze descriptions or diction for themselves alone, but to relate these matters to attitude. *For descriptions:* Do descriptions of natural scenery and conditions (snowstorms, cold, rain, ice, intense sunlight) complement or oppose the circumstances of the characters? Are there any systematic references to colors, sounds, or noises that collectively reflect an attitude? *For diction:* Do connotative meanings of words control response in any way? Does the diction require readers to have a

large or technical vocabulary? Do speech patterns or the use of dialect evoke attitudes about speakers or their condition of life? Is the level of diction formal, middle, or informal? Do you find any substandard or slang expressions? What effect do these create? Are there unusual or particularly noteworthy expressions? If so, what attitudes do these show?

3. *Humor.* Is the story funny? How funny, how intense? How is the humor achieved? How does the language bring out the incongruity of funny situations? Are the objects of laughter still respected or even loved even though the story's treatment of them causes amusement?

4. *Ideas.* Are any ideas advocated, defended mildly, or attacked? How does the author clarify his or her attitude toward these ideas—directly, by statement, or indirectly, through understatement, overstatement, or a character's speeches? In what ways does the story assume agreement between author and readers? What religious views can you find? Political views? Moral and behavioral standards, etc.?

In concluding, first summarize your main points and then go on to redefinitions, explanations, or afterthoughts, together with ideas reinforcing earlier points. To what extent has your analysis increased or reinforced your appreciation of the author's technique? Does the passage take on added importance as a result of your study? Is there anything else in the work comparable to the content, words, or ideas you have discussed in the passage?

Numbers for Easy Reference

To focus this assignment on specifics of style and tone, the assignment visualized here is to analyze a passage—either short or long—from a story. After you have selected a passage, include a copy at the beginning of your essay, as in the example. For your reader's convenience, number the sentences in the passage, and use these numbers when you refer to them. To focus your essay, either single out one aspect of style and tone, or discuss everything, depending on the length of the assignment. Be sure to consider relationships that you can discover between tone and *levels of diction, specific and general words, concrete and abstract words, denotation and connotation, irony,* and *humor.*

SAMPLE STUDENT ESSAY

O'Connor's Control of Tone and Style in "First Confession"°

[1] Nora's turn came, and I heard the sound of something slamming, and then her voice as if butter wouldn't melt in her mouth, and then another slam, and out she came. [2] God, the hypocrisy of women! [3] Her eyes were lowered, her head was bowed, and her hands were joined very low down on her stomach, and she walked up the aisle to the side altar looking like a saint. [4] You never saw such an exhibition

°For this story, see pp. 307–12.

of devotion, and I remembered the devilish malice with which she had tormented me all the way from our door, and wondered were all religious people like that, really. [5] It was my turn now. [6] With the fear of damnation in my soul I went in, and the confessional door closed of itself behind me.

[1] This paragraph from Frank O'Connor's "First Confession" appears midway in the story. It is transitional, coming between Jackie's "heartscalded" memories of family troubles and his happier memory of the confession itself. Though mainly narrative, the passage is punctuated by Jackie's recollections of disgust with his sister and fear of eternal punishment for his childhood "sins." It is the controlled contrast of these attitudes that creates the humor of the passage.* In all respects--brevity, word level, concreteness, and grammatical control--the passage is typical of the story's humor.†

[2] The actions and responses of the paragraph are described briefly and accurately. The first four sentences convey Jackie's exaggerated reactions to Nora's confession. Sentence 1 describes his recollections of her voice in the confessional, and the tone of sentence 3 makes his judgment clear about the hypocrisy of her pious appearance when she leaves for the altar. Each of these descriptive sentences is followed by Jackie's angry reactions, at which readers smile if not laugh. This depth of feeling is transformed to "fear of damnation" at the beginning of sentence 6, which describes Jackie's own entry into the confessional, with the closing door suggesting that he is being shut off from the world and thrown into hell. In other words, the paragraph succinctly presents the sounds, reactions, sights, and confusion of the scene itself, all of which furnish readers with a brief and comic family drama.

[3] The humorous action of the passage is augmented by O'Connor's neutral level of diction, which enables readers to concentrate fully on Jackie's responses. Jackie is recalling unpleasant childhood memories, and the neutral, middle diction enables readers both to sympathize with him and to be amused by him. His words are neither unusual nor difficult. What could be more ordinary, for example, than *butter, slam, out, hands, joined, low, people,* and *closed*? Even Jackie's moral and religious words fall within the vocabulary of ordinary discussions about sin and punishment: *hypocrisy, exhibition, devilish malice, tormented,* and *damnation*. In the passage, therefore, the diction accurately conveys Jackie's vision of the oppressive religious forces which he dislikes and fears, and which he also exaggerates. Readers follow these words easily and with amusement.

[4] Additionally, the words of the paragraph are appropriate to Jackie's boyhood anger because they are specific and concrete. When he tells about Nora going into the confessional, he says specifically that "something slammed," followed by the sound of Nora's "voice," "another slam," and then her appearance as "she came" out of the confessional. Equally specific, and equally comic, is his description of Nora's appearance as she leaves. Readers can easily visualize her bowed head, her lowered eyes, and her prayerful hands, and are amused by the scene just as Jackie was angered by it. In addition to these specific descriptions, sentences 2 and 4 contain Jackie's angry responses, which also

* Central idea.
† Thesis sentence.

provoke amusement. Sentence 4 presents the greater number of connotative abstractions—first the "exhibition of devotion," and second the "devilish malice with which she had tormented me." But these define Jackie's childhood conclusions about his sister, not his adult ones, and their incongruity furnishes readers with a realistic basis for laughter.

[5]

A major element contributing to Jackie's remembrance of his boyhood attitudes is the control over grammar that O'Connor gives to him. At the time of the narrative Jackie is presumably no longer angry, even though as a child he felt misunderstood and unfairly treated. He therefore does not need to recall his story in angry outbursts, despite his exclamation about the "hypocrisy of women," but rather he presents details in correct and grammatical--controlled--sentences. The very first sentence, for example, contains three parallel grammatical direct objects (*sound, voice, slam*), thereby using a minimal number of words while still detailing the major sounds of Nora's confession. The grammar of the third sentence illustrates the swiftness and spareness of O'Connor's (and Jackie's) narrative style. The first three parallel clauses are each made up of four words ("her eyes were lowered," "her head was bowed," and "her hands were joined"). These clauses give Jackie the opportunity to introduce his sarcastic and amusing phrase "looking like a saint" at the end to express his disgust over his sister's hypocrisy. This control shapes the developing comedy of the paragraph.

[6]

In all respects, the passage is a model of how the right use of words can create a story's tone. Jackie's accurate descriptions are mixed with his expressions of childhood emotions--all to the effect of O'Connor's general good humor. In retrospect, Jackie's anger and disgust were unnecessary, but they were important to him as a child--so much so that his exaggerations make him the center of the story's comedy. The words that O'Connor skillfully puts in Jackie's mouth (or on his page) enable readers to share this particular experience of a first confession but to do so while smiling. Jackie's bittersweet memories are successfully rendered and made comic through O'Connor's control over style.

Commentary on the Essay

Paragraph 1 demonstrates how a passage being studied may be related to the entire work of which it is a part. The central idea connects the story's comic tone to O'Connor's control over situation and diction. Throughout the essay, the connection of style and humor are emphasized. The thesis sentence presents four topics that the essay will develop. Any one of these topics, if necessary, could also be treated separately.

In the body of the essay, the writer stresses the way O'Connor creates the story's tone by the careful manipulation of words and expressions. Paragraph 2 indicates O'Connor's verbal economy in describing the actions and reactions of the passage. Paragraph 3 deals with the level of diction, noting that the words are appropriate both to the action and to Jackie's anger when recollecting it. In paragraph 4 the topic is O'Connor's use of specific and concrete diction, a quality which makes for easy visualization of the details. This paragraph also considers the small number of abstract and general words that appear in O'Connor's sentences 2 and 4.

Paragraph 5 connects O'Connor's grammatical control with the speaker's recollected anger and disgust. Examples of parallelism are three direct objects in sentence 1 and the first three clauses in sentence 3. Paragraph 6, the conclusion of the essay, summarizes the means by which O'Connor uses style to spread an aura of comedy over the characterization of Jackie and his recollected feelings.

SPECIAL WRITING TOPICS FOR STUDYING TONE AND STYLE

1. In "First Confession" the adult narrator is describing events that happened to him as a child. To what degree has this narrator, Jackie, separated himself from his childish emotions? What does he say that might be considered residual childhood responses? What effect, if any, do such comments create? For an additional dimension to this topic you might compare Jackie as a narrator with the unnamed narrator of Joyce's "Araby" (Chapter 9)

2. Describe the attitude of Estelle, the narrator in "Rape Fantasies," toward sexual molestation. How does her speech (e.g., treating the subject of rape in an amusing, uncomprehending, or serious manner) influence your responses?

3. Munro's "The Found Boat," and Gilman's "The Yellow Wallpaper" (Chapter 10) probe the psychological makeup of the major characters. Write an essay about the nature and effect of the language of character depiction in these stories.

4. In "Soldier's Home," how does Hemingway's descriptive and narrative style shape your responses to the main character, Krebs? How much does Hemingway disclose about what happened to Krebs in Europe during the war? What are Krebs's apparent feelings about his family, particularly his mother? How do you respond to what Krebs says to her? What responses do you think Hemingway wants you to have about Krebs and his situation?

5. Consider a short story in which the narrator is the central character (for example, "The Concert Stages of Europe" [Chapter 7], "A & P" [Chapter 5], "First Confession" [Chapter 7], "Everyday Use" [Chapter 2], and "Blue Winds Dancing" [Chapter 3]). Write an essay showing how the language of the narrator affects your attitudes toward him or her (that is, your sympathy for the narrator, your interest in the narrative, your feelings toward the other characters and what they do). Be sure to emphasize the relationship between the narrator's language and the attitudes they demonstrate and elicit.

6. Write two brief character sketches, or a description of an action, to be included in a longer story. Make the first favorable, and the second negative. Analyze your word choices in the contrasting accounts: What kinds of words do you select, and on what principles do you select them? What kinds of words might you select if you wanted to create a neutral account? On the basis of your answers, what can you conclude about the development of a fiction writer's style?

7. In your school library, consult the most recent copy of the *MLA International Bibliography of Books and Articles on the Modern Languages and Literatures,* and make a short list of books and articles on Atwood, Chopin, Hodgins, or O'Connor. Consult at least three of the works, and with these, together with your own insights, write a short description of the writer's irony (comic or serious) and social criticism.

8

Symbolism and Allegory: Keys to Extended Meaning

Symbolism and **allegory** are modes that expand meaning. They are literary devices developed from the connections that real-life people make between their own existence and particular objects, places, or occurrences—either through experience or reading. One person might remember making a vital realization about his moral being during a rowboat ride. Another might associate her belief in freedom with catching large fish and then letting it go. The significance of details like these can be meaningful not just at the time they occur, but throughout an entire lifetime. Merely bringing them to mind or speaking about them unlocks all their meanings, implications, and consequences. It is as though the reference alone can be the same as pages upon pages of explanation and analysis.

It is from this principle that both symbolism and allegory are derived. By highlighting details as *symbols* and stories or parts of stories as *allegories*, writers expand their meaning while keeping their works within reasonable lengths.

SYMBOLISM

The words **symbol** and **symbolism** are derived from the Greek word meaning "to throw together" (*syn*, together, and *ballein*, to throw). A symbol creates a direct meaningful equation between (1) a specific object, scene, character, or action and (2) ideas, values, persons, or ways of life. In effect, a symbol is a *substitute* for the elements being signified, much as the flag stands for the ideals of the nation.

When we first encounter a symbol in a story or in any literary work, it may seem to carry no more weight than its surface or obvious meaning. It may be a description of a character, object, place, action, or situation, and may function perfectly well in this capacity. What makes a symbol symbolic, however, is its capacity to signify additional levels of meaning—major ideas, simple or complex emotions, or philosophical or religious qualities or values. There are two types of symbols—*universal* and *contextual.*

Cultural Symbols

Many symbols are generally or universally recognized and are therefore **cultural** (also called **universal**). They embody ideas and emotions that writers and readers share as heirs of the same historical and cultural tradition. When using these symbols, a writer assumes that readers already know what the symbols represent. An example is the character Sisyphus of ancient Greek myth. As a punishment for trying to overcome death not just once but twice, the underworld gods doomed him forever to roll a large boulder up a high hill. Just as he got it to the top, it rolled down, and then he was fated to roll it up again—and again—and again—because the rock always rolled back. The plight of Sisyphus has been interpreted as a symbol of the human condition: In spite of constant struggle, a person rarely if ever completes anything. Work must always be done over and over from day to day and from generation to generation, and the same problems confront humanity throughout all time. Because of such fruitless effort, life seems to have little or no meaning. Nevertheless, there is hope: People who confront their tasks, as Sisyphus does, stay involved and active, and their work makes their lives meaningful. A writer referring to Sisyphus would expect us to understand that this ancient mythological figure symbolizes these conditions.

Similarly, ordinary water, because living creatures cannot live without it, is recognized as a symbol of life. It has this meaning in the ceremony of baptism, and it may convey this meaning and dimension in a variety of literary contexts. Thus, a spouting fountain may symbolize optimism (as upwelling, bubbling life), and a stagnant pool may symbolize the pollution and diminution of life. Water is also a universal symbol of sexuality, and its condition or state may symbolize various romantic relationships. For instance, stories in which lovers meet near a turbulent stream, a roaring waterfall, a wide river, a stormy sea, a mud puddle, or a calm lake symbolically represent love relationships that range from uncertainty to serenity.

Contextual Symbols

Objects and descriptions that are not universal symbols can be symbols *only if they are made so within individual works.* These are **contextual, private,** or **authorial** symbols. Unlike cultural symbols, these gain symbolic meaning within their *context.* For example, the Usher mansion in "The Fall of the House of Usher" is a magnificent but melancholy and deteriorating residence that becomes symbolic of the decaying and dying condition of its principal inhabitants, Roderick and Madeline Usher. Another contextual symbol is Elisa's chrysanthemums in Steinbeck's "The Chrysanthemums." At first her flowers seem like nothing more or less than prized flowers, but they soon gain symbolic significance. The traveling tinsmith's expression of interest in them is the wedge he uses to get a small mending job from Elisa. Her description of the care needed in planting and tending them suggests that they signify her kindness, love, orderliness, femininity, and motherliness.

Like the Usher mansion, Steinbeck's chrysanthemums are a major *contextual* symbol. But there is no carryover: In other stories, houses and flowers are not symbolic unless the authors of these stories deliberately give them symbolic meaning. Further, if such objects are symbols, they may be given different meanings than in the Poe and Steinbeck stories.

Determining What Is Symbolic

In determining whether a particular object, action, or character is a symbol, you need to judge the importance the author gives to it. If the element is prominent and also maintains a constancy of meaning, you may justify interpreting it as a symbol. For example, Miss Brill's fur piece in Mansfield's "Miss Brill" is shabby and moth-eaten. It has no value; but because Mansfield makes it especially important at both the beginning and ending of the story, it contextually symbolizes Miss Brill's poverty and isolation. At the end of Welty's "A Worn Path," Phoenix, the major character, plans to spend all her money for a toy windmill for her sick grandson. Readers will note that the windmill is small and fragile, like her life and that of her grandson, but that Phoenix wants to give the boy a little pleasure despite their poverty and hopelessness. For these reasons the windmill is a contextual or authorial symbol of Phoenix's strong character, generous nature, and pathetic existence.

ALLEGORY

An **allegory** is like a symbol because it transfers and broadens meaning. The term is derived from the Greek word *allegorein*, which means "to speak so as to imply other than what is said." Allegory, however, is more sustained than symbolism. An allegory is to a symbol as a motion picture is to a still picture. In form, an allegory is a complete and self-sufficient narrative, but it also signifies another series of events or conditions. While some stories are allegories from beginning to end, many stories that are not allegories may nevertheless contain brief sections or episodes that are allegorical.

The Uses of Allegory

Allegories and the allegorical method are more than literary exercises. Without question, readers and listeners learn and memorize stories more easily than moral lessons, and therefore allegory is a favorite method of teaching morality. In addition, thought and expression have not always been free. The threat of censorship and the danger of reprisal have sometimes caused authors to express their views indirectly in the form of allegory rather than to write openly, name names, and risk political reprisal or accusations of libel. Hence, the double meaning of many allegories is based in both need and reality.

In studying allegory, determine whether all or part of a story may have an extended, allegorical meaning. The popularity of George Lucas's film *Star Wars* and its sequels, for example, (in videotape and newly refurbished re-releases) is attributable at least partly to its being an allegory about the conflict between good and evil. Obi Wan Kenobi (intelligence) enlists the aid of Luke Skywalker (heroism, boldness), and instructs him in "the force" (moral or religious faith). Thus armed and guided, Skywalker opposes the powers of Darth Vader (evil) to rescue the Princess Leia (purity and goodness) with the aid of the latest spaceships and weaponry (technology). The story is an exciting adventure film, accompanied by dramatic music and ingenious visual and sound effects. With the obvious allegorical overtones, however, it stands for any person's quest for self-fulfillment.

To apply a part of the allegory more specifically, consider that for a time the evil Vader imprisons Skywalker, who must exert all his skill and strength to get free and overcome Vader. In the allegorical application of the episode, this temporary imprisonment signifies those moments of doubt, discouragement, and depression that people experience while trying to better themselves through education, work, self-improvement, friendship, marriage, and so on.

Almost from the beginning of recorded literature, similar heroic deeds have been represented in allegorical forms. From ancient Greece, the allegorical hero Jason sails on the *Argo* to distant lands to gain the Golden Fleece (those who take risks are rewarded). From Anglo-Saxon England, the hero Beowulf saves King Hrothgar's throne by killing Grendel and his monstrous mother (victory comes to those who rely on the forces of good). From seventeenth-century England, Bunyan's *The Pilgrim's Progress* tells how the hero Christian overcomes difficulties and temptations while traveling from this world to the next (belief, perseverance, and resistance to temptation save the faithful). As long as the parallel connections are close and consistent, like those mentioned here, an allegorical interpretation is valid.

FABLE, PARABLE, AND MYTH

Closely related to symbolism and allegory in the ability to extend and expand meaning are three additional forms—*fable, parable,* and *myth.*

FABLE.   The **fable** (from Latin *fabula,* a story or narration) is an old, brief, and popular form. Often but not always, fables are about animals that possess human traits (such fables are called **beast fables**). Past collectors and editors of fables have attached "morals" or explanations to the brief stories, as is the case with Aesop, the most enduringly popular of fable writers. Tradition has it that Aesop was a slave who composed fables in ancient Greece. His fable "The Fox and the Grapes" signifies the trait of belittling things we cannot have. More recent contributions to the fable tradition include Walt Disney's "Mickey Mouse," Walt Kelly's "Pogo," and Berke Breathed's "Bloom County." The adjective *fabulous* refers to the collective body of fables of all sorts, even though the word is often used as little more than a vague term of approval.

PARABLE.   A **parable** (from Greek *parabolé*, a "setting beside" or comparison) is a short, simple allegory with a moral or religious bent. Parables are most often associated with Jesus, who used them to embody unique religious insights and truths. His parables "The Good Samaritan" and "The Prodigal Son," for example, are interpreted to show God's love, concern, understanding, and forgiveness.

MYTH.   A **myth** (from Greek *muthos*, a story or plot) is a traditional story that embodies and codifies the religious, philosophical, and cultural values of the civilization in which it is composed. Usually the central figures of mythical stories are heroes, Gods, and demigods, such as Zeus, Hera, Prometheus, Athena, Sisyphus, Oedipus, or Atalanta from ancient Greece. Most myths are of course fictional, but some have a basis in historical truth. They are by no means confined to the past, for the word *myth* may also refer to abstractions and ideas that people today hold collectively, such as the concept of never-ending economic growth, or the idea that all problems may be solved by science. Sometimes the words *myth* and *mythical* are used with the meaning "fanciful" or "untrue." Such disparagement is misleading because the truths of mythology are not to be found literally in the myths themselves but rather in their symbolic and allegorical interpretations.

ALLUSION IN SYMBOLISM AND ALLEGORY

Cultural or universal symbols and allegories often **allude** to other works from our cultural heritage, such as the Bible, ancient history and literature, and works of the British and American traditions. Sometimes understanding a story may require knowledge of politics and current events.

If the meaning of a symbol is not immediately clear to you, you will need a dictionary or other reference work. The scope of your college dictionary will surprise you. If you cannot find an entry there, however, try one of the major encyclopedias or ask your reference librarian, who can direct you to shelves loaded with helpful books. A few excellent guides are *The Oxford Companion to Classical Literature* (ed. M. C. Howatson and I. Chilvers), *The Oxford Companion to English Literature* (ed. Margaret Drabble), William Rose Benét's *The Reader's Encyclopedia*, Timothy Gantz's *Early Greek Myth: A Guide to Literary and Artistic Sources,* and Richmond Y. Hathorn's *Greek Mythology.* Useful aids in finding biblical references are *Cruden's Complete Concordance,* which in various editions has been used since 1737, or *Strong's Exhaustive Concordance,* which has been revised and expanded regularly since it first appeared in the nineteenth century. These concordances list all the major words used in the Bible, so you can easily locate the chapter and verse of any and all biblical passages. If you still have trouble after using sources like these, see your instructor.

 ## STORIES FOR STUDY

AESOP   (ca. 6th c. B.C.E.)

Not much is known about the ancient fabulist Aesop. According to tradition, he was a freed slave who lived from ca. 620 to 560 B.C.E. Aristotle claimed that he had been a public defender, but there is no other evidence that he existed at all. In fact, versions of some of the fables were known a millennium before his time. Aesop might therefore be considered as much a collector as a creator of fables.

The Fox and the Grapes _____ *(ca. 6th c. B.C.E.)*

A hungry Fox came into a vineyard where there hung delicious clusters of ripe Grapes; his mouth watered to be at them; but they were nailed up to a trellis so high, that with all his springing and leaping he could not reach a single bunch. At last, growing tired and disappointed, "Let who will take them!" says he, "they are but green and sour; so I'll e'en let them alone."

QUESTIONS

1. How much do you learn about the characteristics of the fox? How are these characteristics related to the moral or message of the fable?
2. What is the conflict in the fable? What is the resolution?
3. In your own words, explain the meaning of the fable. Is the "sour grapes" explanation a satisfactory excuse, or is it a rationalization for failure?
4. From your reading of "The Fox and the Grapes," explain the characteristics of the fable as a type of literature.

NATHANIEL HAWTHORNE   (1804–1864)

Hawthorne, a friend and associate of the fourteenth president of the United States, Franklin Pierce, is one of the great American writers of the nineteenth century. His most famous work is The Scarlet Letter *(1850), the sale of which gave him a degree of independence. During the administration of President Pierce (1853–1857), Hawthorne served as American consul in Liverpool, England, and this opportunity enabled him to travel extensively in Europe. Throughout his writing there runs a conflict between freedom and conventionality, with those choosing freedom sometimes suffering from the guilt that their choice brings. "Young Goodman Brown," which is one of the early stories that he included in* Twice-Told Tales *(1837, 1842), embodies this conflict.*

Young Goodman Brown _____ 1835

Young Goodman Brown came forth at sunset, into the street of Salem village,° but put his head back, after crossing the threshold, to exchange a parting kiss with his young wife. And Faith, as the wife was aptly named, thrust her own pretty head into the street, letting the wind play with the pink ribbons of her cap, while she called to Goodman Brown.

"Dearest heart," whispered she, softly and rather sadly, when her lips were close to his ear, "prithee, put off your journey until sunrise, and sleep in your own bed tonight. A lone woman is troubled with such dreams and such thoughts, that she's afeared of herself, sometimes. Pray, tarry with me this night, dear husband, of all nights in the year!"

"My love and my Faith," replied young Goodman Brown, "of all nights in the year, this one night must I tarry away from thee. My journey, as thou callest it, forth and back again, must needs be done 'twixt now and sunrise. What, my sweet, pretty wife, dost thou doubt me already, and we but three months married!"

"Then God bless you!" said Faith with the pink ribbons, "and may you find all well, when you come back."

"Amen!" cried Goodman Brown. "Say thy prayers, dear Faith, and go to bed at dusk, and no harm will come to thee."   5

So they parted; and the young man pursued his way, until, being about to turn the corner by the meeting-house, he looked back and saw the head of Faith still peeping after him, with a melancholy air, in spite of her pink ribbons.

"Poor little Faith!" thought he, for his heart smote him. "What a wretch am I, to leave her on such an errand! She talks of dreams, too. Methought, as she spoke, there was trouble in her face, as if a dream had warned her what work is to be done tonight. But no, no! 't would kill her to think it. Well; she's a blessed angel on earth; and after this one night, I'll cling to her skirts and follow her to Heaven."

With this excellent resolve for the future, Goodman Brown felt himself justified in making more haste on his present evil purpose. He had taken a dreary road, darkened by all the gloomiest trees of the forest, which barely stood aside to let the narrow path

Salem village: in Massachusetts, about fifteen miles north of Boston. The time of the story is the late seventeenth or early eighteenth century.

creep through, and closed immediately behind. It was all as lonely as could be; and there is this peculiarity in such a solitude, that the traveller knows not who may be concealed by the innumerable trunks and the thick boughs overhead; so that, with lonely footsteps, he may yet be passing through an unseen multitude.

"There may be a devilish Indian behind every tree," said Goodman Brown to himself; and he glanced fearfully behind him, as he added, "What if the devil himself should be at my very elbow!"

His head being turned back, he passed a crook of the road, and looking forward again, beheld the figure of a man, in grave and decent attire, seated at the foot of an old tree. He arose at Goodman Brown's approach, and walked onward, side by side with him.

"You are late, Goodman Brown," said he. "The clock of the Old South° was striking, as I came through Boston; and that is full fifteen minutes agone."

"Faith kept me back awhile," replied the young man, with a tremor in his voice, caused by the sudden appearance of his companion, though not wholly unexpected.

It was now deep dusk in the forest, and deepest in that part of it where these two were journeying. As nearly as could be discerned, the second traveller was about fifty years old, apparently in the same rank of life as Goodman Brown, and bearing a considerable resemblance to him, though perhaps more in expression than features. Still, they might have been taken for father and son. And yet, though the elder person was as simply clad as the younger, and as simple in manner too, he had an indescribable air of one who knew the world, and would not have felt abashed at the governor's dinner-table, or in King William's° court, were it possible that his affairs should call him thither. But the only thing about him that could be fixed upon as remarkable, was his staff, which bore the likeness of a great black snake, so curiously wrought, that it might almost be seen to twist and wriggle itself like a living serpent. This, of course, must have been an ocular deception, assisted by the uncertain light.

"Come, Goodman Brown!" cried his fellow-traveller, "this is a dull pace for the beginning of a journey. Take my staff, if you are so soon weary."

"Friend," said the other, exchanging his slow pace for a full stop, "having kept covenant by meeting thee here, it is my purpose now to return whence I came. I have scruples, touching the matter thou wot'st of."°

"Sayest thou so?" replied he of the serpent, smiling apart. "Let us walk on, nevertheless, reasoning as we go, and if I convince thee not, thou shalt turn back. We are but a little way in the forest, yet."

"Too far, too far!" exclaimed the goodman, unconsciously resuming his walk. "My father never went into the woods on such an errand, nor his father before him. We have been a race of honest men and good Christians, since the days of the martyrs.° And shall I be the first of the name of Brown that ever took this path and kept—"

"Such company, thou wouldst say," observed the elder person, interrupting his pause. "Well said, Goodman Brown! I have been as well acquainted with your family as ever a one among the Puritans; and that's no trifle to say. I helped your grandfather, the constable, when he lashed the Quaker woman so smartly through the streets of Salem. And it was I that brought your father a pitch-pine knot, kindled at my own hearth, to

10

15

Old South: The Old South Church, in Boston, is still there.

King William: William III was king of England from 1688 to 1701 (the time of the story). William IV was king from 1830 to 1837 (the period when Hawthorne wrote the story).

thou wot'st: you know.

days of the martyrs: the martyrdoms of Protestants in England during the reign of Queen Mary (1553–1558).

set fire to an Indian village, in King Philip's war.° They were my good friends, both; and many a pleasant walk have we had along this path, and returned merrily after midnight. I would fain be friends with you, for their sake."

"If it be as thou sayest," replied Goodman Brown, "I marvel they never spoke of these matters. Or, verily, I marvel not, seeing that the least rumor of the sort would have driven them from New England. We are a people of prayer, and good works to boot, and abide no such wickedness."

"Wickedness or not," said the traveller with twisted staff, "I have a very general   20 acquaintance here in New England. The deacons of many a church have drunk the communion wine with me; the selectmen, of divers towns, make me their chairman; and a majority of the Great and General Court are firm supporters of my interest. The governor and I, too—but these are state secrets."

"Can this be so!" cried Goodman Brown, with a stare of amazement at his undisturbed companion. "Howbeit, I have nothing to do with the governor and council; they have their own ways, and are no rule for a simple husbandman like me. But, were I to go on with thee, how should I meet the eye of that good old man, our minister, at Salem village? Oh, his voice would make me tremble, both Sabbath-day and lecture-day!"

Thus far, the elder traveller had listened with due gravity, but now burst into a fit of irrepressible mirth, shaking himself so violently, that his snakelike staff actually seemed to wriggle in sympathy.

"Ha! ha! ha!" shouted he, again and again; then composing himself, "Well, go on, Goodman Brown, go on; but, prithee, don't kill me with laughing!"

"Well, then, to end the matter at once," said Goodman Brown, considerably nettled, "there is my wife, Faith. It would break her dear little heart; and I'd rather break my own!"

"Nay, if that be the case," answered the other, "e'en go thy ways, Goodman Brown.   25 I would not, for twenty old women like the one hobbling before us, that Faith should come to any harm."

As he spoke, he pointed his staff at a female figure on the path, in whom Goodman Brown recognized a very pious and exemplary dame, who had taught him his catechism in youth, and was still his moral and spiritual adviser, jointly with the minister and Deacon Gookin.

"A marvel, truly, that Goody° Cloyse should be so far in the wilderness, at night-fall!" said he. "But, with your leave, friend, I shall take a cut through the woods, until we have left this Christian woman behind. Being a stranger to you, she might ask whom I was consorting with, and whither I was going."

"Be it so," said his fellow-traveller. "Betake you to the woods, and let me keep the path."

Accordingly, the young man turned aside, but took care to watch his companion, who advanced softly along the road, until he had come within a staff's length of the old dame. She, meanwhile, was making the best of her way, with singular speed for so aged a woman, and mumbling some indistinct words, a prayer, doubtless, as she went. The

King Philip's war: This war (1675–1676), infamous for the atrocities committed by the New England settlers, resulted in the suppression of Indian tribal life and prepared the way for unlimited settlement of New England by European immigrants. "Philip" was the English name of Chief Metacomet of the Wampanoag tribe.

Goody: shortened form of "goodwife," a respectful name for a married woman of low rank. A "Goody Cloyse" was one of the women sentenced to execution by Hawthorne's great-grandfather, Judge John Hathorne.

traveller put forth his staff, and touched her withered neck with what seemed the serpent's tail.

"The devil!" screamed the pious old lady.   30

"Then Goody Cloyse knows her old friend?" observed the traveller, confronting her, and leaning on his writhing stick.

"Ah, forsooth, and is it your worship, indeed?" cried the good dame. "Yea, truly is it, and in the very image of my old gossip,° Goodman Brown, the grandfather of the silly fellow that now is. But, would your worship believe it? My broomstick hath strangely disappeared, stolen, as I suspect, by that unhanged witch, Goody Cory,° and that, too, when I was all anointed with the juice of smallage and cinquefoil and wolf's-bane—"°

"Mingled with fine wheat and the fat of a new-born babe," said the shape of old Goodman Brown.

"Ah, your worship knows the recipe," cried the old lady, cackling aloud. "So, as I was saying, being all ready for the meeting, and no horse to ride on, I made up my mind to foot it; for they tell me there is a nice young man to be taken into communion to-night. But now your good worship will lend me your arm, and we shall be there in a twinkling."

"That can hardly be," answered her friend. "I will not spare you my arm, Goody   35
Cloyse, but here is my staff, if you will."

So saying, he threw it down at her feet, where, perhaps, it assumed life, being one of the rods which its owner had formerly lent to the Egyptian Magi.° Of this fact, however, Goodman Brown could not take cognizance. He had cast up his eyes in astonishment, and looking down again, beheld neither Goody Cloyse nor the serpentine staff, but his fellow-traveller alone, who waited for him as calmly as if nothing had happened.

"That old woman taught me my catechism!" said the young man; and there was a world of meaning in this simple comment.

They continued to walk onward, while the elder traveller exhorted his companion to make good speed and persevere in the path, discoursing so aptly, that his arguments seemed rather to spring up in the bosom of his auditor, than to be suggested by himself. As they went he plucked a branch of maple, to serve for a walking-stick, and began to strip it of the twigs and little boughs, which were wet with evening dew. The moment his fingers touched them, they became strangely withered and dried up, as with a week's sunshine. Thus the pair proceeded, at a good free pace, until suddenly, in a gloomy hollow of the road, Goodman Brown sat himself down on the stump of a tree, and refused to go any farther.

"Friend," said he, stubbornly, "my mind is made up. Not another step will I budge on this errand. What if a wretched old woman do choose to go to the devil, when I thought she was going to Heaven! Is that any reason why I should quit my dear Faith, and go after her?"

"You will think better of this by and by," said his acquaintance, composedly. "Sit   40
here and rest yourself a while; and when you feel like moving again, there is my staff to help you along."

Without more words, he threw his companion the maple stick, and was as speedily out of sight as if he had vanished into the deepening gloom. The young man sat a few moments by the roadside, applauding himself greatly, and thinking with how clear

---

gossip: from "good sib" or "good relative."
Goody Cory: name of a woman who was also sent to execution by Judge Hathorne.
smallage and cinquefoil and wolf's-bane: plants commonly used by witches in making ointments.
lent to the Egyptian Magi: See Exodus 7:10–12.

a conscience he should meet the minister, in his morning walk, nor shrink from the eye of good old Deacon Gookin. And what calm sleep would be his, that very night, which was to have been spent so wickedly, but purely and sweetly now, in the arms of Faith! Amidst these pleasant and praiseworthy meditations, Goodman Brown heard the tramp of horses along the road, and deemed it advisable to conceal himself within the verge of the forest, conscious of the guilty purpose that had brought him thither, though now so happily turned from it.

On came the hoof-tramps and the voices of the riders, two grave old voices, conversing soberly as they drew near. These mingled sounds appeared to pass along the road, within a few yards of the young man's hiding-place; but owing, doubtless, to the depth of the gloom, at that particular spot, neither the travellers nor their steeds were visible. Though their figures brushed the small boughs by the wayside, it could not be seen that they intercepted, even for a moment, the faint gleam from the strip of bright sky, athwart which they must have passed. Goodman Brown alternately crouched and stood on tiptoe, pulling aside the branches, and thrusting forth his head as far as he durst, without discerning so much as a shadow. It vexed him the more, because he could have sworn, were such a thing possible, that he recognized the voices of the minister and Deacon Gookin, jogging° along quietly, as they were wont to do, when bound to some ordination or ecclesiastical council. While yet within hearing, one of the riders stopped to pluck a switch.

"Of the two, reverend Sir," said the voice like the deacon's, "I had rather miss an ordination dinner than to-night's meeting. They tell me that some of our community are to be here from Falmouth and beyond, and others from Connecticut and Rhode Island; besides several of the Indian powwows,° who, after their fashion, know almost as much deviltry as the best of us. Moreover, there is a goodly young woman to be taken into communion."

"Mighty well, Deacon Gookin!" replied the solemn old tones of the minister. "Spur up, or we shall be late. Nothing can be done, you know, until I get on the ground."

The hoofs clattered again, and the voices, talking so strangely in the empty air,   45 passed on through the forest, where no church had ever been gathered, nor solitary Christian prayed. Whither, then, could these holy men be journeying, so deep into the heathen wilderness? Young Goodman Brown caught hold of a tree, for support, being ready to sink down on the ground, faint and over-burthened with the heavy sickness of his heart. He looked up to the sky, doubting whether there really was a Heaven above him. Yet, there was the blue arch, and the stars brightening in it.

"With Heaven above, and Faith below, I will yet stand firm against the devil!" cried Goodman Brown.

While he still gazed upward, into the deep arch of the firmament, and had lifted his hands to pray, a cloud, though no wind was stirring, hurried across the zenith, and hid the brightening stars. The blue sky was still visible, except directly overhead, where this black mass of cloud was sweeping swiftly northward. Aloft in the air, as if from the depths of the cloud, came a confused and doubtful sound of voices. Once, the listener fancied that he could distinguish the accents of town's people of his own, men and women, both pious and ungodly, many of whom he had met at the communion-table, and had seen others rioting at the tavern. The next moment, so indistinct were the

---

jogging: riding a horse at a slow trot.
powwow: a Narragansett Indian word describing a ritual ceremony of dancing, incantation, and magic.

sounds, he doubted whether he had heard aught but the murmur of the old forest, whispering without a wind. Then came a stronger swell of those familiar tones, heard daily in the sunshine, at Salem village, but never, until now, from a cloud at night. There was one voice, of a young woman, uttering lamentations, yet with an uncertain sorrow, and entreating for some favor, which, perhaps, it would grieve her to obtain. And all the unseen multitude, both saints and sinners, seemed to encourage her onward.

"Faith!" shouted Goodman Brown, in a voice of agony and desperation; and the echoes of the forest mocked him, crying—"Faith! Faith!" as if bewildered wretches were seeking her, all through the wilderness.

The cry of grief, rage, and terror was yet piercing the night, when the unhappy husband held his breath for a response. There was a scream, drowned immediately in a louder murmur of voices fading into far-off laughter, as the dark cloud swept away, leaving the clear and silent sky above Goodman Brown. But something fluttered lightly down through the air, and caught on the branch of a tree. The young man seized it and beheld a pink ribbon.

"My Faith is gone!" cried he, after one stupefied moment. "There is no good on earth, and sin is but a name. Come, devil! for to thee is this world given."   50

And maddened with despair, so that he laughed loud and long, did Goodman Brown grasp his staff and set forth again, at such a rate, that he seemed to fly along the forest path, rather than to walk or run. The road grew wilder and drearier, and more faintly traced, and vanished at length, leaving him in the heart of the dark wilderness, still rushing onward, with the instinct that guides mortal man to evil. The whole forest was peopled with frightful sounds; the creaking of the trees, the howling of wild beasts, and the yell of Indians; while, sometimes, the wind tolled like a distant church bell, and sometimes gave a broad roar around the traveller, as if all Nature were laughing him to scorn. But he was himself the chief horror of the scene, and shrank not from its other horrors.

"Ha! ha! ha!" roared Goodman Brown, when the wind laughed at him. "Let us hear which will laugh loudest! Think not to frighten me with your deviltry! Come witch, come wizard, come Indian powwow, come devil himself! and here comes Goodman Brown. You may as well fear him as he fear you!"

In truth, all through the haunted forest, there could be nothing more frightful than the figure of Goodman Brown. On he flew, among the black pines, brandishing his staff with frenzied gestures, now giving vent to an inspiration of horrid blasphemy, and now shouting forth such laughter, as set all the echoes of the forest laughing like demons around him. The fiend in his own shape is less hideous than when he rages in the breast of man. Thus sped the demoniac on his course, until, quivering among the trees, he saw a red light before him, as when the felled trunks and branches of a clearing have been set on fire, and throw up their lurid blaze against the sky, at the hour of midnight. He paused, in a lull of the tempest that had driven him onward, and heard the swell of what seemed a hymn, rolling solemnly from a distance, with the weight of many voices. He knew the tune. It was a familiar one in the choir of the village meeting-house. The verse died heavily away, and was lengthened by a chorus, not of human voices, but of all the sounds of the benighted wilderness, pealing in awful harmony together. Goodman Brown cried out; and his cry was lost to his own ear, by its unison with the cry of the desert.

In the interval of silence, he stole forward, until the light glared full upon his eyes. At one extremity of an open space, hemmed in by the dark wall of the forest, arose a rock, bearing some rude, natural resemblance either to an altar or a pulpit, and surrounded by four blazing pines, their tops aflame, their stems untouched, like candles at an evening meeting. The mass of foliage, that had overgrown the summit of the rock, was all on fire, blazing high into the night, and fitfully illuminating the whole field. Each pendent twig and leafy festoon was in a blaze. As the red light arose and fell, a numerous congregation alternately shone forth, then disappeared in shadow, and again grew, as it were, out of the darkness, peopling the heart of the solitary woods at once.

"A grave and dark-clad company!" quoth Goodman Brown.   55

In truth, they were such. Among them, quivering to-and-fro, between gloom and splendor, appeared faces that would be seen, next day, at the council-board of the province, and others which, Sabbath after Sabbath, looked devoutly heavenward, and benignantly over the crowded pews, from the holiest pulpits in the land. Some affirm that the lady of the governor was there. At least, there were high dames well known to her, and wives of honored husbands, and widows a great multitude, and ancient maidens, all of excellent repute, and fair young girls, who trembled lest their mothers should espy them. Either the sudden gleams of light, flashing over the obscure field, bedazzled Goodman Brown, or he recognized a score of the church members of Salem village, famous for their especial sanctity. Good old Deacon Gookin had arrived, and waited at the skirts of that venerable saint, his reverend pastor. But, irreverently consorting with these grave, reputable, and pious people, these elders of the church, these chaste dames and dewy virgins, there were men of dissolute lives and women of spotted fame, wretches given over to all mean and filthy vice, and suspected even of horrid crimes. It was strange to see, that the good shrank not from the wicked, nor were the sinners abashed by the saints. Scattered, also, among their pale-faced enemies, were the Indian priests, or powwows, who had often scared their native forest with more hideous incantations than any known to English witchcraft.

"But, where is Faith?" thought Goodman Brown; and, as hope came into his heart, he trembled.

Another verse of the hymn arose, a slow and mournful strain, such as the pious love, but joined to words which expressed all that our nature can conceive of sin, and darkly hinted at far more. Unfathomable to mere mortals is the lore of fiends. Verse after verse was sung, and still the chorus of the desert swelled between, like the deepest tone of a mighty organ. And, with the final peal of that dreadful anthem, there came a sound, as if the roaring wind, the rushing streams, the howling beasts, and every other voice of the unconverted wilderness were mingling and according with the voice of guilty man, in homage to the prince of all. The four blazing pines threw up a loftier flame, and obscurely discovered shapes and visages of horror on the smoke-wreaths, above the impious assembly. At the same moment, the fire on the rock shot redly forth, and formed a glowing arch above its base, where now appeared a figure. With reverence be it spoken, the apparition bore no slight similitude, both in garb and manner, to some grave divine of the New England churches.

"Bring forth the converts!" cried a voice, that echoed through the field and rolled into the forest.

At the word, Goodman Brown stepped forth from the shadow of the trees, and   60
approached the congregation, with whom he felt a loathful brotherhood, by the sympathy of all that was wicked in his heart. He could have well-nigh sworn, that the shape of his own dead father beckoned him to advance, looking downward from a smoke-wreath, while a woman, with dim features of despair, threw out her hand to warn him back. Was it his mother? But he had no power to retreat one step, nor to resist, even in thought, when the minister and good old Deacon Gookin seized his arms, and led him to the

blazing rock. Thither came also the slender form of a veiled female, led between Goody Cloyse, that pious teacher of the catechism, and Martha Carrier, who had received the devil's promise to be queen of hell. A rampant hag was she! And there stood the proselytes, beneath the canopy of fire.

"Welcome, my children," said the dark figure, "to the communion of your race! Ye have found, thus young, your nature and your destiny. My children, look behind you!"

They turned; and flashing forth, as it were, in a sheet of flame, the fiend-worshippers were seen; the smile of welcome gleamed darkly on every visage.

"There," resumed the sable form, "are all whom ye have reverenced from youth. Ye deemed them holier than yourselves, and shrank from your own sin, contrasting it with their lives of righteousness and prayerful aspirations heavenward. Yet, here are they all, in my worshipping assembly! This night it shall be granted you to know their secret deeds; how hoary-bearded elders of the church have whispered wanton words to the young maids of their households; how many a woman, eager for widow's weeds, has given her husband a drink at bedtime, and let him sleep his last sleep in her bosom; how beardless youths have made haste to inherit their father's wealth; and how fair damsels—blush not, sweet ones!—have dug little graves in the garden, and bidden me, the sole guest, to an infant's funeral. By the sympathy of your human hearts for sin, ye shall scent out all the places—whether in church, bed-chamber, street, field, or forest—where crime has been committed, and shall exult to behold the whole earth one stain of guilt, one mighty blood-spot. Far more than this! It shall be yours to penetrate, in every bosom, the deep mystery of sin, the fountain of all wicked arts, and which inexhaustibly supplies more evil impulses than human power—than my power, at its utmost!—can make manifest in deeds. And now, my children, look upon each other."

They did so; and, by the blaze of the hell-kindled torches, the wretched man beheld his Faith, and the wife her husband, trembling before that unhallowed altar.

"Lo! there ye stand, my children," said the figure, in a deep and solemn tone, almost sad, with its despairing awfulness, as if his once angelic nature° could yet mourn for our miserable race. "Depending upon one another's hearts, ye had still hoped that virtue were not all a dream! Now are ye undeceived!—Evil is the nature of mankind. Evil must be your only happiness. Welcome, again, my children, to the communion of your race!"

"Welcome!" repeated the fiend-worshippers, in one cry of despair and triumph.

And there they stood, the only pair, as it seemed, who were yet hesitating on the verge of wickedness, in this dark world. A basin was hollowed, naturally, in the rock. Did it contain water, reddened by the lurid light? or was it blood? or, perchance, a liquid flame? Herein did the Shape of Evil dip his hand, and prepare to lay the mark of baptism upon their foreheads, that they might be partakers of the mystery of sin, more conscious of the secret guilt of others, both in deed and thought, than they could now be of their own. The husband cast one look at his pale wife, and Faith at him. What polluted wretches would the next glance show them to each other, shuddering alike at what they disclosed and what they saw!

"Faith! Faith!" cried the husband. "Look up to Heaven, and resist the Wicked One!"

Whether Faith obeyed, he knew not. Hardly had he spoken, when he found himself amid calm night and solitude, listening to a roar of the wind, which died heavily

65

---

once angelic nature: Lucifer ("light bearer"), another name for the Devil, led the traditional revolt of the angels and was thrown into hell as his punishment. See Isaiah 14:12–15.

away through the forest. He staggered against the rock, and felt it chill and damp, while a hanging twig, that had been all on fire, besprinkled his cheek with the coldest dew.

The next morning, young Goodman Brown came slowly into the street of Salem   70
village staring around him like a bewildered man. The good old minister was taking a walk along the grave-yard, to get an appetite for breakfast and meditate his sermon, and bestowed a blessing, as he passed, on Goodman Brown. He shrank from the venerable saint, as if to avoid an anathema. Old Deacon Gookin was at domestic worship, and the holy words of his prayer were heard through the open window. "What God doth the wizard pray to?" quoth Goodman Brown. Goody Cloyse, that excellent old Christian, stood in the early sunshine, at her own lattice, catechising a little girl, who had brought her a pint of morning's milk. Goodman Brown snatched away the child, as from the grasp of the fiend himself. Turning the corner by the meetinghouse, he spied the head of Faith, with the pink ribbons, gazing anxiously forth, and bursting into such joy at the sight of him that she skipt along the street, and almost kissed her husband before the whole village. But Goodman Brown looked sternly and sadly into her face, and passed on without a greeting.

Had Goodman Brown fallen asleep in the forest, and only dreamed a wild dream of a witch-meeting?

Be it so, if you will. But, alas! it was a dream of evil omen for young Goodman Brown. A stern, a sad, a darkly meditative, a distrustful, if not a desperate man did he become, from the night of that fearful dream. On the Sabbath day, when the congregation were singing a holy psalm, he could not listen, because an anthem of sin rushed loudly upon his ear, and drowned all the blessed strain. When the minister spoke from the pulpit, with power and fervid eloquence, and with his hand on the open Bible, of the sacred truths of our religion, and of saint-like lives and triumphant deaths, and of future bliss or misery unutterable, then did Goodman Brown turn pale, dreading lest the roof should thunder down upon the gray blasphemer and his hearers. Often, awaking suddenly at midnight, he shrank from the bosom of Faith, and at morning or eventide, when the family knelt down in prayer, he scowled, and muttered to himself, and gazed sternly at his wife, and turned away. And when he had lived long, and was borne to his grave, a hoary corpse, followed by Faith, an aged woman, and children and grandchildren, a goodly procession, besides neighbors not a few, they carved no hopeful verse upon his tombstone; for his dying hour was gloom.

QUESTIONS

1. Near the end of the story the narrator asks the following: "Had Goodman Brown fallen asleep in the forest, and only dreamed a wild dream of a witch-meeting?" What is the answer? If Goodman Brown's visions come out of his own dreams (mind, subconscious), what do they tell us about him?

2. Is Goodman Brown round or flat? To what extent is he a symbolic "everyman" or representative of humankind?

3. Consider Hawthorne's use of symbolism, such as sunset and night, the walking stick, the witches' sabbath, the marriage to Faith, and the vague shadows amid the darkness, together with other symbols that you may find.

4. What details establish the two settings? What characterizes Salem? The woods? Why might we be justified in seeing the forest as a symbolic setting?

5. To what extent are the people, objects, and events in Goodman Brown's adventure invested with enough *consistent* symbolic resonance to justify calling his

episode in the woods an allegory? Consider Brown's wife, Faith, as an allegorical figure. What do you make of Brown's statements that "I'll cling to her skirts and follow her to Heaven" (paragraph 7) and "Faith kept me back awhile" (paragraph 12). In this same light, consider the other characters Brown meets in the forest, the sunset, the walk into the forest, and the staff "which bore the likeness of a great black snake" (paragraph 13).

ST. LUKE (1st c. C.E.)

Although little is known about St. Luke, evidence in Colossians, Philemon, and 2 Timothy indicates that a man named Luke was the "beloved physician" and traveling companion of the apostle Paul, who journeyed in the Mediterranean area during the middle of the first century C.E. Scholars indicate that Luke built his gospel from the Gospel of St. Mark and also from written sources known as "Q," some of which were also used by St. Matthew. Luke also relied on other sources that were available only to him. In addition to his gospel, Luke is also accepted as the author of the Acts of the Apostles.

The Parable of the Prodigal Son (Luke 15:11–32) _____ *(ca. 90 C.E.)*

11 And he [Jesus] said, A certain man had two sons:

12 And the younger of them said to *his* father, Father, give me the portion of goods that falleth *to me.* And he divided unto them *his* living.°

13 And not many days after the younger son gathered all together, and took his journey into a far country,° and there wasted his substance with riotous living.

14 And when he had spent all, there arose a mighty famine in that land; and he began to be in want.

15 And he went and joined himself to a citizen of that country; and he sent him into his fields to feed swine.°

16 And he would fain have filled his belly with the husks° that the swine did eat: and no man gave unto him.

17 And when he came to himself, he said, How many hired servants of my father's have bread enough and to spare, and I perish with hunger!

18 I will arise and go to my father, and will say unto him, Father, I have sinned against heaven, and before thee.

19 And am no more worthy to be called thy son: make me as one of thy hired servants.

20 And he arose, and came to his father. But when he was yet a great way off, his father saw him, and had compassion, and ran, and fell on his neck, and kissed him.

21 And the son said unto him, Father, I have sinned against heaven, and in thy sight, and am no more worthy to be called thy son.

22 But the father said to his servants, Bring forth the best robe, and put *it* on him; and put a ring on his hand, and shoes on *his* feet:

---

divided . . . his living: one-third of the father's estate; the son had to renounce all further claim.

far country: countries of the Jewish dispersal, or diaspora, in the areas bordering the Mediterranean Sea.

feed swine: In Jewish custom, pigs were unclean.

husks: pods of the carob tree, the eating of which was thought to be penitential.

23 And bring hither the fatted calf,° and kill *it;* and let us eat, and be merry:

24 For this my son was dead, and is alive again; he was lost, and is found. And they began to be merry.

25 Now his elder son was in the field: and as he came and drew nigh to the house, he heard music and dancing.

26 And he called one of the servants, and asked what these things meant.

27 And he said unto him, Thy brother is come; and thy father hath killed the fatted calf, because he hath received him safe and sound.°

28 And he was angry, and would not go in: therefore came his father out, and intreated him.

29 And he answering said to *his* father, Lo, these many years do I serve thee, neither transgressed I at any time thy commandment: and yet thou never gavest me a kid, that I might make merry with my friends:

30 But as soon as this thy son was come, which hath devoured thy living with harlots, thou hast killed for him the fatted calf.

31 And he said unto him, Son, thou art ever with me, and all that I have is thine.

32 It was meet° that we should make merry, and be glad: for this thy brother was dead, and is alive again: and was lost, and is found.

fatted calf: grain-fed calf.
meet: appropriate.

QUESTIONS

1. Describe the character of the Prodigal Son. Is he flat or round, representative or individual? Why is it necessary that the character be considered representatively, even though he has individual characteristics?

2. What is the plot? What is the antagonism against which the Prodigal Son contends? Why is it necessary that the brother resent the brother's return?

3. What is the resolution of the parable? Why is there no "they lived happily ever after" ending?

4. Using verse numbers, analyze the structure of the parable. What determines your division of the parts? Do these parts coincide with the development of the plot? Describe the relationship of plot to structure in the parable.

5. What is the point of view here? How does the emphasis shift with verse 22?

6. On the basis of the fact that there are many characteristics here of many stories you have read, write a description of the parable as a type of literature.

EDGAR ALLAN POE   (1809–1849)

For a brief biography, please see page 258.

The Fall of the House of Usher _____ 1839

> *Son cœur est un luth suspendu;*
> *Sitôt qu'on le touche il resonne.*
> *—De Béranger.°*

Son coeur . . . De Béranger: a passage of a poem by Pierre-Jean de Béranger (1780–1857): "His heart is a tightly strung lute;/It rings as soon as it is touched."

During the whole of a dull, dark, and soundless day in the autumn of the year, when the clouds hung oppressively low in the heavens, I had been passing alone, on horseback, through a singularly dreary tract of country; and at length found myself, as the shades of the evening drew on, within view of the melancholy House of Usher. I know not how it was—but, with the first glimpse of the building, a sense of insufferable gloom pervaded my spirit. I say insufferable; for the feeling was unrelieved by any of that half-pleasurable, because poetic, sentiment, with which the mind usually receives even the sternest natural images of the desolate or terrible. I looked upon the scene before me—upon the mere house, and the simple landscape features of the domain—upon the bleak walls—upon the vacant eye-like windows—upon a few rank sedges—and upon a few white trunks of decayed trees—with an utter depression of soul which I can compare to no earthly sensation more properly than to the afterdream of the reveller upon opium—the bitter lapse into everyday life—the hideous dropping off of the veil. There was an iciness, a sinking, a sickening of the heart—an unredeemed dreariness of thought which no goading of the imagination could torture into aught of the sublime. What was it—I paused to think—what was it that so unnerved me in the contemplation of the House of Usher? It was a mystery all insoluble; nor could I grapple with the shadowy fancies that crowded upon me as I pondered. I was forced to fall back upon the unsatisfactory conclusion, that while, beyond doubt, there *are* combinations of very simple natural objects which have the power of thus affecting us, still the analysis of this power lies among considerations beyond our depth. It was possible, I reflected, that a mere different arrangement of the particulars of the scene, of the details of the picture, would be sufficient to modify, or perhaps to annihilate its capacity for sorrowful impression; and, acting upon this idea, I reined my horse to the precipitous brink of a black and lurid tarn that lay in unruffled lustre by the dwelling, and gazed down—but with a shudder even more thrilling than before—upon the remodelled and inverted images of the gray sedge, and the ghastly tree-stems, and the vacant and eye-like windows.

Nevertheless, in this mansion of gloom I now proposed to myself a sojourn of some weeks. Its proprietor, Roderick Usher, had been one of my boon companions in boyhood; but many years had elapsed since our last meeting. A letter, however, had lately reached me in a distant part of the country—a letter from him—which, in its wildly importunate nature, had admitted of no other than a personal reply. The MS. gave evidence of nervous agitation. The writer spoke of acute bodily illness—of a mental disorder which oppressed him—and of an earnest desire to see me, as his best, and indeed his only personal friend, with a view of attempting, by the cheerfulness of my society, some alleviation of his malady. It was the manner in which all this, and much more, was said—it was the apparent *heart* that went with his request—which allowed me no room for hesitation; and I accordingly obeyed forthwith what I still considered a very singular summons.

Although, as boys, we had been even intimate associates, yet I really knew little of my friend. His reserve had been always excessive and habitual. I was aware, however, that his very ancient family had been noted, time out of mind, for a peculiar sensibility of temperament, displaying itself, through long ages, in many works of exalted art, and manifested, of late, in repeated deeds of munificent yet unobtrusive charity, as well as in a passionate devotion to the intricacies, perhaps even more than to the orthodox and easily recognisable beauties, of musical science. I had learned, too, the very remarkable fact, that the stem of the Usher race, all time-honored as it was, had put forth, at no period, any enduring branch; in other words, that the entire family lay in the direct line of descent, and had always, with very trifling and very temporary variation, so lain. It was this deficiency, I considered, while running over in thought the perfect keeping of the character of the premises with the accredited character of the people, and while speculating upon the possible influence which the one, in the long lapse of centuries, might have exercised upon the other—it was this deficiency, perhaps, of collateral issue, and the consequent undeviating transmission, from sire to son, of the patrimony with the name, which had, at length, so identified the two as to merge the original title of the estate in the quaint and equivocal appellation of the "House of Usher"—an appellation which seemed to include, in the minds of the peasantry who used it, both the family and the family mansion.

I have said that the sole effect of my somewhat childish experiment—that of looking down within the tarn—had been to deepen the first singular impression. There can be no doubt that the consciousness of the rapid increase of my superstition—for why should I not so term it?—served mainly to accelerate the increase itself. Such, I have long known, is the paradoxical law of all sentiments having terror as a basis. And it might have been for this reason only, that, when I again uplifted my eyes to the house itself, from its image in the pool, there grew in my mind a strange fancy—a fancy so ridiculous, indeed, that I but mention it to show the vivid force of the sensations which oppressed me. I had so worked upon my imagination as really to believe that about the whole mansion and domain there hung an atmosphere peculiar to themselves and their immediate vicinity—an atmosphere which had no affinity with the air of heaven, but which had reeked up from the decayed trees, and the gray wall, and the silent tarn—pestilent and mystic vapor, dull, sluggish, faintly discernible, and leaden-hued.

Shaking off from my spirit what *must* have been a dream, I scanned more narrowly the real aspect of the building. Its principal feature seemed to be that of an excessive antiquity. The discoloration of ages had been great. Minute fungi overspread the whole exterior, hanging in a fine tangled web-work from the eaves. Yet all this was apart from any extraordinary dilapidation. No portion of the masonry had fallen; and there appeared to be a wild inconsistency between its still perfect adaptation of parts, and the crumbling condition of the individual stones. In this there was much that reminded me of the specious totality of old wood-work which has rotted for long years in some neglected vault, with no disturbance from the breath of the external air. Beyond this indication of extensive decay, however, the fabric gave little token of instability. Perhaps the eye of a scrutinizing observer might have discovered a barely perceptible fissure, which, extending from the roof of the building in front, made its way down the wall in a zigzag direction, until it became lost in the sullen waters of the tarn.

Noticing these things, I rode over a short causeway to the house. A servant in waiting took my horse, and I entered the Gothic archway of the hall. A valet, of stealthy step, thence conducted me, in silence, through many dark and intricate passages in my progress to the *studio* of his master. Much that I encountered on the way contributed, I know not how, to heighten the vague sentiments of which I have already spoken. While the objects around me—while the carvings of the ceilings, the sombre tapestries of the walls, the ebon blackness of the floors, and the phantasmagoric armorial trophies which rattled as I strode, were but matters to which, or to such as which, I had been accustomed from my infancy—while I hesitated not to acknowledge how familiar was all this—I still wondered to find how unfamiliar were the fancies which ordinary images were stirring up. On one of the staircases, I met the physician of the family. His countenance, I thought, wore a mingled expression of low cunning and perplexity. He accosted me with trepidation and passed on. The valet now threw open a door and ushered me into the presence of his master.

The room in which I found myself was very large and lofty. The windows were long, narrow, and pointed, and at so vast a distance from the black oaken floor as to be altogether inaccessible from within. Feeble gleams of encrimsoned light made their way through the trellissed panes, and served to render sufficiently distinct the more prominent objects around; the eye, however, struggled in vain to reach the remoter angles of the chamber, or the recesses of the vaulted and fretted ceiling. Dark draperies hung upon the walls. The general furniture was profuse, comfortless, antique, and tattered. Many books and musical instruments lay scattered about, but failed to give any vitality to the scene. I felt that I breathed an atmosphere of sorrow. An air of stern, deep, and irredeemable gloom hung over and pervaded all.

Upon my entrance, Usher arose from a sofa on which he had been lying at full length, and greeted me with a vivacious warmth which had much in it, I at first thought, of an overdone cordiality—of the constrained effort of the *ennuyé* man of the world. A glance, however, at his countenance, convinced me of his perfect sincerity. We sat down; and for some moments, while he spoke not, I gazed upon him with a feeling half of pity, half of awe. Surely, man had never before so terribly altered, in so brief a period, as had Roderick Usher! It was with difficulty that I could bring myself to admit the identity of the wan being before me with the companion of my early boyhood. Yet the character of his face had been at all times remarkable. A cadaverousness of complexion; an eye large, liquid, and luminous beyond comparison; lips somewhat thin and very pallid, but of a surpassingly beautiful curve; a nose of a delicate Hebrew model, but with a breadth of nostril unusual in similar formations; a finely moulded chin, speaking, in its want of prominence, of a want of moral energy; hair of a more than web-like softness and tenuity; these features, with an inordinate expansion above the regions of the temple, made up altogether a countenance not easily to be forgotten. And now in the mere exaggeration of the prevailing character of these features, and of the expression they were wont to convey, lay so much of change that I doubted to whom I spoke. The now ghastly pallor of the skin, and the now miraculous lustre of the eye, above all things startled and even awed me. The silken hair, too, had been suffered to grow all unheeded, and as, in its wild gossamer texture, it floated rather than fell about the face, I could not, even with effort, connect its Arabesque expression with any idea of simple humanity.

In the manner of my friend I was at once struck with an incoherence—an inconsistency; and I soon found this to arise from a series of feeble and futile struggles to overcome an habitual trepidancy—an excessive nervous agitation. For something of this nature I had indeed been prepared, no less by his letter, than by reminiscences of certain boyish traits, and by conclusions deduced from his peculiar physical conformation and temperament. His action was alternately vivacious and sullen. His voice varied rapidly from a tremulous indecision (when the animal spirits seemed utterly in abeyance) to that species of energetic concision—that abrupt, weighty, unhurried, and hollow-sounding enunciation—that leaden, self-balanced and perfectly modulated guttural utterance, which may be observed in the lost drunkard, or the irreclaimable eater of opium, during the periods of his most intense excitement.

It was thus that he spoke of the object of my visit, of his earnest desire to see me,   10
and of the solace he expected me to afford him. He entered, at some length, into what he conceived to be the nature of his malady. It was, he said, a constitutional and a family evil, and one for which he despaired to find a remedy—a mere nervous affection, he immediately added, which would undoubtedly soon pass off. It displayed itself in a host of unnatural sensations. Some of these, as he detailed them, interested and bewildered me; although, perhaps, the terms, and the general manner of the narration had their

weight. He suffered much from a morbid acuteness of the senses; the most insipid food was alone endurable; he could wear only garments of certain texture; the odors of all flowers were oppressive; his eyes were tortured by even a faint light; and there were but peculiar sounds, and these from stringed instruments, which did not inspire him with horror.

To an anomalous species of terror I found him a bounden slave. "I shall perish," said he, "I *must* perish in this deplorable folly. Thus, thus, and not otherwise, shall I be lost. I dread the events of the future, not in themselves, but in their results. I shudder at the thought of any, even the most trivial, incident, which may operate upon this intolerable agitation of soul. I have, indeed, no abhorrence of danger, except in its absolute effect—in terror. In this unnerved—in this pitiable condition—I feel that the period will sooner or later arrive when I must abandon life and reason together, in some struggle with the grim phantasm, FEAR."

I learned, moreover, at intervals, and through broken and equivocal hints, another singular feature of his mental condition. He was enchained by certain superstitious impressions in regard to the dwelling which he tenanted, and whence, for many years, he had never ventured forth—in regard to an influence whose supposititious force was conveyed in terms too shadowy here to be re-stated—an influence which some peculiarities in the mere form and substance of his family mansion, had, by dint of long sufferance, he said, obtained over his spirit—an effect which the *physique* of the gray walls and turrets, and of the dim tarn into which they all looked down, had, at length, brought about upon the *morale* of his existence.

He admitted, however, although with hesitation, that much of the peculiar gloom which thus afflicted him could be traced to a more natural and far more palpable origin—to the severe and long-continued illness—indeed to the evidently approaching dissolution—of a tenderly beloved sister—his sole companion for long years—his last and only relative on earth. "Her decease," he said, with a bitterness which I can never forget, "would leave him (him the hopeless and the frail) the last of the ancient race of the Ushers." While he spoke, the lady Madeline (for so was she called) passed slowly through a remote portion of the apartment, and, without having noticed my presence, disappeared. I regarded her with an utter astonishment not unmingled with dread—and yet I found it impossible to account for such feelings. A sensation of stupor oppressed me, as my eyes followed her retreating steps. When a door, at length, closed upon her, my glance sought instinctively and eagerly the countenance of the brother—but he had buried his face in his hands, and I could only perceive that a far more than ordinary wanness had overspread the emaciated fingers through which trickled many passionate tears.

The disease of the lady Madeline had long baffled the skill of her physicians. A settled apathy, a gradual wasting away of the person, and frequent although transient affections of a partially cataleptical character, were the unusual diagnosis. Hitherto she had steadily borne up against the pressure of her malady, and had not betaken herself finally to bed; but, on the closing in of the evening of my arrival at the house, she succumbed (as her brother told me at night with inexpressible agitation) to the prostrating power of the destroyer; and I learned that the glimpse I had obtained of her person would thus probably be the last I should obtain—that the lady, at least while living, would be seen by me no more.

For several days ensuing, her name was unmentioned by either Usher or myself: and during this period I was busied in earnest endeavors to alleviate the melancholy of   15 my friend. We painted and read together; or I listened, as if in a dream, to the wild improvisations of his speaking guitar. And thus, as a closer and still closer intimacy admitted me more unreservedly into the recesses of his spirit, the more bitterly did I perceive the futility of all attempt at cheering a mind from which darkness, as if an inherent positive quality, poured forth upon all objects of the moral and physical universe, in one unceasing radiation of gloom.

I shall ever bear about me a memory of the many solemn hours I thus spent alone with the master of the House of Usher. Yet I should fail in any attempt to convey an idea of the exact character of the studies, or of the occupations, in which he involved me, or led me the way. An excited and highly distempered ideality threw a sulphureous lustre over all. His long improvised dirges will ring forever in my ears. Among other things, I hold painfully in mind a certain singular perversion and amplification of the wild air of the last waltz of Von Weber.° From the paintings over which his elaborate fancy brooded, and which grew, touch by touch, into vaguenesses at which I shuddered the more thrillingly, because I shuddered knowing not why;—from these paintings (vivid as their images now are before me) I would in vain endeavor to educe more than a small portion which should lie within the compass of merely written words. By the utter simplicity, by the nakedness of his designs, he arrested and overawed attention. If ever mortal painted an idea, that mortal was Roderick Usher. For me at least—in the circumstances then surrounding me—there arose out of the pure abstractions which the hypochondriac contrived to throw upon his canvass, an intensity of intolerable awe, no shadow of which felt I ever yet in the contemplation of the certainly glowing yet too concrete reveries of Fuseli.

One of the phantasmagoric conceptions of my friend, partaking not so rigidly of the spirit of abstraction, may be shadowed forth, although feebly, in words. A small picture presented the interior of an immensely long and rectangular vault or tunnel, with low walls, smooth, white, and without interruption or device. Certain accessory points of the design served well to convey the idea that this excavation lay at an exceeding depth below the surface of the earth. No outlet was observed in any portion of its vast extent, and no torch, or other artificial source of light was discernible; yet a flood of intense rays rolled throughout, and bathed the whole in a ghastly and inappropriate splendor.

I have just spoken of that morbid condition of the auditory nerve which rendered all music intolerable to the sufferer, with the exception of certain effects of stringed instruments. It was, perhaps, the narrow limits to which he thus confined himself upon the guitar, which gave birth, in great measure, to the fantastic character of his performances. But the fervid *facility* of his *impromptus* could not be so accounted for. They must have been, and were, in the notes, as well as in the words of his wild fantasias (for he not unfrequently accompanied himself with rhymed verbal improvisations), the result of that intense mental collectedness and concentration to which I have previously alluded as observable only in particular moments of the highest artificial excitement. The words of one of these rhapsodies I have easily remembered. I was, perhaps, the more forcibly impressed with it, as he gave it, because, in the under or mystic current of its meaning, I fancied that I perceived, and for the first time, a full consciousness on the part of Usher, of the tottering of his lofty reason upon her throne. The verses, which were entitled "The Haunted Palace," ran very nearly, if not accurately, thus:

Von Weber: Carl Maria Von Weber (1786–1826), German composer.

I

In the greenest of our valleys,
    By good angels tenanted,
Once a fair and stately palace—
    Radiant palace—reared its head.
In the monarch Thought's dominion—
    It stood there!
Never seraph spread a pinion
    Over fabric half so fair.

II

Banners yellow, glorious, golden,
    On its roof did float and flow;   20
(This—all this—was in the olden
    Time long ago)
And every gentle air that dallied,
    In that sweet day,
Along the ramparts plumed and pallid,
    A winged odor went away.

III

Wanderers in that happy valley
    Through two luminous windows saw
Spirits moving musically
    To a lute's well-tunéd law,
Round about a throne, where sitting
    (Porphyrogene!)°
In state his glory well befitting,
    The ruler of the realm was seen.

IV

And all with pearl and ruby glowing
    Was the fair palace door,
Through which came flowing, flowing, flowing,
    And sparkling evermore,
A troop of Echoes whose sweet duty
    Was but to sing,
In voices of surpassing beauty,
    The wit and wisdom of their king.

V

But evil things, in robes of sorrow,
    Assailed the monarch's high estate;
(Ah, let us mourn, for never morrow
    Shall dawn upon him, desolate!)

Porphyrogene: i.e., made of porphyry, a red stone that takes a high-gloss finish.

And, round about his home, the glory
    That blushed and bloomed
Is but a dim-remembered story
    Of the old time entombed.

                            VI
And travellers now within that valley,
    Through the red-litten windows, see
Vast forms that move fantastically
    To a discordant melody;
While, like a rapid ghastly river,
    Through the pale door,
A hideous throng rush out forever,
    And laugh—but smile no more.

I well remember that suggestions arising from this ballad, led us into a train of   25
thought wherein there became manifest an opinion of Usher's which I mention not so
much on account of its novelty, (for other men* have thought thus,) as on account of
the pertinacity with which he maintained it. This opinion, in its general form, was that
of the sentience of all vegetable things. But, in his disordered fancy, the idea had
assumed a more daring character, and trespassed, under certain conditions, upon the
kingdom of inorganization. I lack words to express the full extent, or the earnest *abandon* of his persuasion. The belief, however, was connected (as I have previously hinted)
with the gray stones of the home of his forefathers. The conditions of the sentience had
been here, he imagined, fulfilled in the method of collocation of these stones—in the
order of their arrangement, as well as in that of the many *fungi* which overspread them,
and of the decayed trees which stood around—above all, in the long undisturbed
endurance of this arrangement, and in its reduplication in the still waters of the tarn. Its
evidence—the evidence of the sentience—was to be seen, he said, (and I here started as
he spoke,) in the gradual yet certain condensation of an atmosphere of their own about
the waters and the walls. The result was discoverable, he added, in that silent, yet importunate and terrible influence which for centuries had moulded the destinies of his
family, and which made *him* what I now saw him—what he was. Such opinions need no
comment, and I will make none.

Our books—the books which, for years, had formed no small portion of the
mental existence of the invalid—were, as might be supposed, in strict keeping with this
character of phantasm. We pored together over such works as the Ververt et Chartreuse
of Gresset; the Belphegor of Machiavelli; the Heaven and Hell of Swedenborg; the
Subterranean Voyage of Nicholas Klimm by Holberg; the Chiromancy of Robert Flud, of
Jean D'Indaginé, and of De la Chambre; the Journey into the Blue Distance of Tieck;
and the City of the Sun of Campanella. One favorite volume was a small octavo edition
of the *Directorium Inquisitorium,* by the Dominican Eymeric de Gironne; and there were
passages in Pomponius Mela, about the old African Satyrs and Œgipans, over which
Usher would sit dreaming for hours. His chief delight, however, was found in the perusal

---

* Watson, Dr. Percival, Spallanzani, and especially the Bishop of Landaff.—See "Chemical
Essays," vol. v. [Poe's own note. He is citing these scientific and historical writers as support for his
assertions.]

of an exceedingly rare and curious book in quarto Gothic—the manual of a forgotten church—the *Vigiliae Mortuorum secundum Chorum Ecclesiae Maguntinae.*°

I could not help thinking of the wild ritual of this work, and of its probable influence upon the hypochondriac, when, one evening, having informed me abruptly that the lady Madeline was no more, he stated his intention of preserving her corpse for a fortnight, (previously to its final internment,) in one of the numerous vaults within the main walls of the building. The worldly reason, however, assigned for this singular proceeding, was one which I did not feel at liberty to dispute. The brother had been led to his resolution (so he told me) by consideration of the unusual character of the malady of the deceased, of certain obtrusive and eager inquiries on the part of her medical men, and of the remote and exposed situation of the burial-ground of the family. I will not deny that when I called to mind the sinister countenance of the person whom I met upon the staircase, on the day of my arrival at the house, I had no desire to oppose what I regarded as at best but a harmless, and by no means an unnatural, precaution.

At the request of Usher, I personally aided him in the arrangements for the temporary entombment. The body having been encoffined, we two alone bore it to its rest. The vault in which we placed it (and which had been so long unopened that our torches, half smothered in its oppressive atmosphere, gave us little opportunity for investigation) was small, damp, and entirely without means of admission for light; lying, at great depth, immediately beneath that portion of the building in which was my own sleeping apartment. It had been used, apparently, in remote feudal times, for the worst purposes of a donjon-keep and, in later days, as a place of deposit for powder, or some other highly combustible substance, as a portion of its floor, and the whole interior of a long archway through which we reached it, were carefully sheathed with copper. The door, of massive iron, had been, also, similarly protected. Its immense weight caused an unusually sharp grating sound, as it moved upon its hinges.

Having deposited our mournful burden upon tressels within this region of horror, we partially turned aside the yet unscrewed lid of the coffin, and looked upon the face of the tenant. A striking similitude between the brother and sister now first arrested my attention; and Usher, divining, perhaps, my thoughts, murmured out some few words from which I learned that the deceased and himself had been twins, and that sympathies of a scarcely intelligible nature had always existed between them. Our glances, however, rested not long upon the dead—for we could not regard her unawed. The disease which had thus entombed the lady in the maturity of youth, had left, as usual in all maladies of a strictly cataleptical character, the mockery of a faint blush upon the bosom and the face, and that suspiciously lingering smile upon the lip which is so terrible in death. We replaced and screwed down the lid, and, having secured the door of iron, made our way, with toil, into the scarcely less gloomy apartments of the upper portion of the house.

And now, some days of bitter grief having elapsed, an observable change came over the features of the mental disorder of my friend. His ordinary manner had vanished. His ordinary occupations were neglected or forgotten. He roamed from chamber to chamber with hurried, unequal, and objectless step. The pallor of his countenance

30

Our books . . . Maguntinae (paragraph 27): Poe's speaker characterizes the works of the writers contained in the paragraph as being "in keeping with this character of phantasm." This judgment is right; the works are about mysticism, utopias, travels to fantastic underworld countries, palmistry, and forest deities such as Pan. The concluding reference is to a 1500 publication describing ceremonies and prayers for the dead.

had assumed, if possible, a more ghastly hue—but the luminousness of his eye had utterly gone out. The once occasional huskiness of his tone was heard no more; and a tremulous quaver, as if of extreme terror, habitually characterized his utterance. There were times, indeed, when I thought his unceasingly agitated mind was laboring with some oppressive secret, to divulge which he struggled for the necessary courage. At times, again, I was obliged to resolve all into the mere inexplicable vagaries of madness, for I beheld him gazing upon vacancy for long hours, in an attitude of the profoundest attention, as if listening to some imaginary sound. It was no wonder that condition terrified—that it infected me. I felt creeping upon me, by slow yet certain degrees, the wild influences of his own fantastic yet impressive superstitions.

It was, especially, upon retiring to bed late in the night of the seventh or eighth day after the placing of the lady Madeline within the donjon, that I experienced the full power of such feelings. Sleep came not near my couch—while the hours waned and waned away. I struggled to reason off the nervousness which had dominion over me. I endeavored to believe that much, if not all of what I felt, was due to the bewildering influence of the gloomy furniture of the room—of the dark and tattered draperies, which, tortured into motion by the breath of a rising tempest, swayed fitfully to and fro upon the walls, and rustled uneasily about the decorations of the bed. But my efforts were fruitless. An irrepressible tremor gradually pervaded my frame; and, at length, there sat upon my very heart an incubus of utterly causeless alarm. Shaking this off with a gasp and a struggle, I uplifted myself upon the pillows, and, peering earnestly within the intense darkness of the chamber, harkened—I know not why, except that an instinctive spirit prompted me—to certain low and indefinite sounds which came, through the pauses of the storm, at long intervals, I knew not whence. Overpowered by an intense sentiment of horror, unaccountable yet unendurable, I threw on my clothes with haste (for I felt that I should sleep no more during the night), and endeavored to arouse myself from the pitiable condition into which I had fallen, by pacing rapidly to and fro through the apartment.

I had taken but few turns in this manner, when a light step on an adjoining staircase arrested my attention. I presently recognised it as that of Usher. In an instant afterward he rapped, with a gentle touch, at my door, and entered, bearing a lamp. His countenance was, as usual, cadaverously wan—but, moreover, there was a species of mad hilarity in his eyes—an evidently restrained *hysteria* in his whole demeanor. His air appalled me—but anything was preferable to the solitude which I had so long endured, and I even welcomed his presence as a relief.

"And you have not seen it?" he said abruptly, after having stared about him for some moments in silence—"you have not then seen it?—but, stay! you shall." Thus speaking, and having carefully shaded his lamp, he hurried to one of the casements, and threw it freely open to the storm.

The impetuous fury of the entering gust nearly lifted us from our feet. It was, indeed, a tempestuous yet sternly beautiful night, and one wildly singular in its terror and its beauty. A whirlwind had apparently collected its force in our vicinity; for there were frequent and violent alterations in the direction of the wind; and the exceeding density of the clouds (which hung so low as to press upon the turrets of the house) did not prevent our perceiving the life-like velocity with which they flew careering from all points against each other, without passing away into the distance. I say that even their exceeding density did not prevent our perceiving this—yet we had no glimpse of the moon or stars—nor was there any flashing forth of the lightning. But the under surfaces of the huge masses of agitated vapor, as well as all terrestrial objects immediately around us, were glowing in the unnatural light of a faintly luminous and distinctly visible gaseous exhalation which hung about and enshrouded the mansion.

"You must not—you shall not behold this!" said I, shudderingly, to Usher, as I led him, with a gentle violence, from the window to a seat. "These appearances, which bewilder you, are merely electrical phenomena not uncommon—or it may be that they have their ghastly origin in the rank miasma of the tarn. Let us close this casement;—the air is chilling and dangerous to your frame. Here is one of your favorite romances. I will read, and you shall listen;—and so we will pass away this terrible night together."

The antique volume which I had taken up was the "Mad Trist" of Sir Launcelot Canning;° but I had called it a favorite of Usher's more in sad jest than in earnest; for, in truth, there is little in its uncouth and unimaginative prolixity which could have had interest for the lofty and spiritual ideality of my friend. It was, however, the only book immediately at hand; and I indulged a vague hope that the excitement which now agitated the hypochondriac, might find relief (for the history of mental disorder is full of similar anomalies) even in the extremeness of the folly which I should read. Could I have judged, indeed, by the wild overstrained air of vivacity with which he harkened, or apparently harkened, to the words of the tale, I might well have congratulated myself upon the success of my design.

I had arrived at that well-known portion of the story where Ethelred, the hero of the Trist, having sought in vain for peaceable admission into the dwelling of the hermit, proceeds to make good an entrance by force. Here, it will be remembered, the words of the narrative run thus:

"And Ethelred, who was by nature of a doughty heart, and who was now mighty withal, on account of the powerfulness of the wine which he had drunken, waited no longer to hold parley with the hermit, who, in sooth, was of an obstinate and maliceful turn, but, feeling the rain upon his shoulders, and fearing the rising of the tempest, uplifted his mace outright, and, with blows, made quickly room in the plankings of the door for his gauntleted hand; and now pulling therewith sturdily, he so cracked, and ripped, and tore all asunder, that the noise of the dry and hollow-sounding wood alarummed and reverberated throughout the forest."

At the termination of this sentence I started, and for a moment, paused; for it appeared to me (although I at once concluded that my excited fancy had deceived me)—it appeared to me that, from some very remote portion of the mansion, there came, indistinctly, to my ears, what might have been, in its exact similarity of character, the echo (but a stifled and dull one certainly) of the very cracking and ripping sound which Sir Launcelot had so particularly described. It was, beyond doubt, the coincidence alone which had arrested my attention; for, amid the rattling of the sashes of the casements, and the ordinary commingled noises of the still increasing storm, the sound, in itself, had nothing, surely, which should have interested or disturbed me. I continued the story:

"But the good champion Ethelred, now entering within the door, was sore enraged and amazed to perceive no signal of the maliceful hermit; but, in the stead thereof, a dragon of a scaly and prodigious demeanor, and of a fiery tongue, which sate in guard

35

40

---

the "Mad Trist" of Sir Launcelot Canning: There was no Sir Launcelot Canning, unlike the authors cited in paragraph 27. The "passages" from "Canning" read by the narrator to Usher were all written by Poe.

before a palace of gold, with a floor of silver; and upon the wall there hung a shield of shining brass with this legend enwritten—

> Who entereth herein, a conqueror hath bin;
> Who slayeth the dragon, the shield he shall win;

And Ethelred uplifted his mace, and struck upon the head of the dragon, which fell before him, and gave up his pesty breath, with a shriek so horrid and harsh, and withal so piercing, that Ethelred had fain to close his ears with his hands against the dreadful noise of it, the like whereof was never before heard."

Here again I paused abruptly and now with a feeling of wild amazement—for there could be no doubt whatever that, in this instance, I did actually hear (although from what direction it proceeded I found it impossible to say) a low and apparently distant, but harsh, protracted, and most unusual screaming or grating sound—the exact counterpart of what my fancy had already conjured up for the dragon's unnatural shriek as described by the romancer.

Oppressed, as I certainly was, upon the occurrence of this second and most extraordinary coincidence, by a thousand conflicting sensations, in which wonder and extreme terror were predominant, I still retained sufficient presence of mind to avoid exciting, by any observation, the sensitive nervousness of my companion. I was by no means certain that he had noticed the sounds in question; although, assuredly, a strange alteration had, during the last few minutes, taken place in his demeanor. From a position fronting my own, he had gradually brought round his chair, so as to sit with his face to the door of the chamber; and thus I could but partially perceive his features, although I saw that his lips trembled as if he were murmuring inaudibly. His head had dropped upon his breast—yet I knew that he was not asleep, from the wide and rigid opening of the eye as I caught a glance of it in profile. The motion of his body, too, was at variance with this idea—for he rocked from side to side with a gentle yet constant and uniform sway. Having rapidly taken notice of all this, I resumed the narrative of Sir Launcelot, which thus proceeded:

"And now, the champion, having escaped from the terrible fury of the dragon, bethinking himself of the brazen shield, and of the breaking up of the enchantment which was upon it, removed the carcass from out of the way before him, and approached valorously over the silver pavement of the castle to where the shield was upon the wall; which in sooth tarried not for his full coming, but fell down at his feet upon the silver floor, with a mighty great and terrible ringing sound."

No sooner had these syllables passed my lips, than—as if a shield of brass had indeed, at the moment, fallen heavily upon a floor of silver—I became aware of a distinct, hollow, metallic, and clangorous, yet apparently muffled reverberation. Completely unnerved, I leaped to my feet; but the measured rocking movement of Usher was undisturbed. I rushed to the chair in which he sat. His eyes were bent fixedly before him, and throughout his whole countenance there reigned a stony rigidity. But, as I placed my hand upon his shoulder, there came a strong shudder over his whole person; a sickly smile quivered about his lips; and I saw that he spoke in a low, hurried, and gibbering murmur, as if unconscious of my presence. Bending closely over him, I at length drank in the hideous import of his words.

"Not hear it?—yes, I hear it, and *have* heard it. Long—long—long—many minutes, many hours, many days, have I heard it—yet I dared not—oh, pity me, miserable

45

wretch that I am!—I dared not—*I dared* not speak! *We have put her living in the tomb!* Said I not that my senses were acute? I *now* tell you that I heard her first feeble movements in the hollow coffin I heard them—many, many days ago—yet I dared not—I *dared not speak!* And now—to-night—Ethelred—ha! ha!—the breaking of the hermit's door, and the death-cry of the dragon, and the clangor of the shield!—say, rather, the rending of her coffin, and the grating of the iron hinges of her prison, and her struggles within the coppered archway of the vault! Oh whither shall I fly? Will she not be here anon? Is she not hurrying to upbraid me for my haste? Have I not heard her footstep on the stair? Do I not distinguish that heavy and horrible beating of her heart? Madman!"— here he sprang furiously to his feet, and shrieked out his syllables, as if in the effort he were giving up his soul— *"Madman! I tell you that she now stands without the door!"*

As if in the superhuman energy of his utterance there had been found the potency of a spell—the huge antique pannels to which the speaker pointed, threw slowly back, upon the instant, their ponderous and ebony jaws. It was the work of the rushing gust—but then without those doors there *did* stand the lofty and enshrouded figure of the lady Madeline of Usher. There was blood upon her white robes, and the evidence of some bitter struggle upon every portion of her emaciated frame. For a moment she remained trembling and reeling to and fro upon the threshold—then, with a low moaning cry, fell heavily inward upon the person of her brother, and in her violent and now final death-agonies, bore him to the floor a corpse, and victim to the terrors he had anticipated.

From that chamber, and from that mansion, I fled aghast. The storm was still abroad in all its wrath as I found myself crossing the old causeway. Suddenly there shot along the path a wild light, and I turned to see whence a gleam so unusual could have issued; for the vast house and its shadows were alone behind me. The radiance was that of the full, setting, and blood-red moon, which now shone vividly through that once barely-discernible fissure, of which I have before spoken as extending from the roof of the building, in a zigzag direction, to the base. While I gazed, this fissure rapidly widened—there came a fierce breath of the whirlwind—the entire orb of the satellite burst at once upon my sight—my brain reeled as I saw the mighty walls rushing asunder—there was a long tumultuous shouting sound like the voice of a thousand waters— and the deep and dank tarn at my feet closed sullenly and silently over the fragments of the *"House of Usher."*

QUESTIONS

1. Consider Poe's use of setting in "The Fall of the House of Usher." What details (e.g., landscape, weather) seem realistic? What is the condition of the house, both outside and inside? What is the relationship between the house and the Usher family?

2. Should Poe's descriptions be taken literally or symbolically, or both? Explain.

3. What is the relationship between the narrator and Usher? Why is the narrator not named? Is he as involved in the events as the named narrator of "The Cask of Amontillado"?

4. In what ways is Madeline a double of Usher himself? Why is Usher unwilling or unable to rescue her from the burial vault? What is the meaning of her falling on him and bringing about his death?

5. Why is Usher's poem included as part of the story? How does the poem explain the condition of the Usher household?

JOHN STEINBECK   (1902–1968)

*Steinbeck was born in Salinas, California, and for a time
attended Stanford University. In the 1920s, while working
at jobs such as surveying, picking fruit, and hatching trout,
he began his writing career. A number of stories and novels
preceded his best-known novel,* The Grapes of Wrath
*(1939), for which he was awarded the Pulitzer Prize in
1940. He received the Nobel Prize in literature in 1962. His
fiction, often set in rural areas, features a realistic and pessimistic view of life. A number of his novels have been made
into films, the best known of which is* The Grapes of
Wrath. *His home in Salinas is open to the visiting public.*

The Chrysanthemums ———————————————————— *1937*

The high grey-flannel fog of winter closed off the Salinas Valley° from the sky and from
all the rest of the world. On every side it sat like a lid on the mountains and made of the
great valley a closed pot. On the broad, level land floor the gang plows bit deep and left
the black earth shining like metal where the shares had cut. On the foothill ranches
across the Salinas River, the yellow stubble fields seemed to be bathed in pale cold sunshine, but there was no sunshine in the valley now in December. The thick willow scrub
along the river flamed with sharp and positive yellow leaves.

It was a time of quiet and of waiting. The air was cold and tender. A light wind
blew up from the southwest so that the farmers were mildly hopeful of a good rain
before long; but fog and rain do not go together.

Across the river, on Henry Allen's foothill ranch there was little work to be done,
for the hay was cut and stored and the orchards were plowed up to receive the rain
deeply when it should come. The cattle on the higher slopes were becoming shaggy and
rough-coated.

Elisa Allen, working in her flower garden, looked down across the yard and saw
Henry, her husband, talking to two men in business suits. The three of them stood by
the tractor shed, each man with one foot on the side of the little Fordson.° They smoked
cigarettes and studied the machines as they talked.

Elisa watched them for a moment and then went back to her work. She was thirty-
five. Her face was lean and strong and her eyes were as clear as water. Her figure looked
blocked and heavy in her gardening costume, a man's black hat pulled low down over
her eyes, clodhopper shoes, a figured print dress almost completely covered by a big
corduroy apron with four big pockets to hold the snips, the trowel and scratcher, the
seeds and the knife she worked with. She wore heavy leather gloves to protect her hands
while she worked.

She was cutting down the old year's chrysanthemum stalks with a pair of short
and powerful scissors. She looked down toward the men by the tractor shed now and
then. Her face was eager and mature and handsome; even her work with the scissors
was over-eager, over-powerful. The chrysanthemum stems seemed too small and easy for
her energy.

5

Salinas Valley: in Monterey County, California, about 50 miles south of San Jose.
Fordson: a tractor manufactured by the Ford Motor Company, with large steel-lugged
rear wheels.

She brushed a cloud of hair out of her eyes with the back of her glove, and left a smudge of earth on the cheek in doing it. Behind her stood the neat white farm house with red geraniums close-banked around it as high as the windows. It was a hard-swept looking little house, with hard-polished windows, and a clean mud-mat on the front steps.

Elisa cast another glance toward the tractor shed. The strangers were getting into their Ford coupe. She took off a glove and put her strong fingers down into the forest of new green chrysanthemum sprouts that were growing around the old roots. She spread the leaves and looked down among the close-growing stems. No aphids were there, no sowbugs or snails or cutworms. Her terrier fingers destroyed such pests before they could get started.

Elisa started at the sound of her husband's voice. He had come near quietly, and he leaned over the wire fence that protected her flower garden from cattle and dogs and chickens.

"At it again," he said. "You've got a strong new crop coming."   10

Elisa straightened her back and pulled on the gardening glove again. "Yes. They'll be strong this coming year." In her tone and on her face there was a little smugness.

"You've got a gift with things," Henry observed. "Some of those yellow chrysanthemums you had this year were ten inches across. I wish you'd work out in the orchard and raise some apples that big."

Her eyes sharpened. "Maybe I could do it, too. I've a gift with things, all right. My mother had it. She could stick anything in the ground and make it grow. She said it was having planters' hands that knew how to do it."

"Well, it sure works with flowers," he said.

"Henry, who were those men you were talking to?"   15

"Why, sure, that's what I came to tell you. They were from the Western Meat Company. I sold those thirty head of three-year-old steers. Got nearly my own price, too."

"Good," she said. "Good for you."

"And I thought," he continued, "I thought how it's Saturday afternoon, and we might go to Salinas for dinner at a restaurant, and then to a picture show—to celebrate, you see."

"Good," she repeated. "Oh, yes. That will be good."

Henry put on his joking tone. "There's fights tonight. How'd you like to go to the   20 fights?"

"Oh, no," she said breathlessly. "No, I wouldn't like fights."

"Just fooling, Elisa. We'll go to a movie. Let's see. It's two now. I'm going to take Scotty and bring down those steers from the hill. It'll take us maybe two hours. We'll go in town about five and have dinner at the Cominos Hotel. Like that?"

"Of course I'll like it. It's good to eat away from home."

"All right, then. I'll go get up a couple of horses."

She said, "I'll have plenty of time to transplant some of these sets, I guess."   25

She heard her husband calling Scotty down by the barn. And a little later she saw the two men ride up the pale yellow hillside in search of the steers.

There was a little square sandy bed kept for rooting the chrysanthemums. With her trowel she turned the soil over and over, and smoothed it and patted it firm. Then she dug ten parallel trenches to receive the sets. Back at the chrysanthemum bed she pulled out the little crisp shoots, trimmed off the leaves of each one with her scissors and laid it on a small orderly pile.

A squeak of wheels and plod of hoofs came from the road. Elisa looked up. The country road ran along the dense bank of willows and cottonwoods that bordered the river, and up this road came a curious vehicle, curiously drawn. It was an old spring-wagon, with a round canvas top on it like the cover of a prairie schooner. It was drawn by an old bay horse and a little grey-and-white burro. A big stubble-bearded man sat between the cover flaps and drove the crawling team. Underneath the wagon, between the hind wheels, a lean and rangy mongrel dog walked sedately. Words were painted on the canvas in clumsy, crooked letters. "Pots, pans, knives, sisors, lawn mores. Fixed." Two rows of articles and the triumphantly definitive "Fixed" below. The black paint had run down in little sharp points beneath each letter.

Elisa, squatting on the ground, watched to see the crazy, loose-jointed wagon pass by. But it didn't pass. It turned into the farm road in front of her house, crooked old wheels skirling and squeaking. The rangy dog darted from between the wheels and ran ahead. Instantly the two ranch shepherds flew out at him. Then all three stopped, and with stiff and quivering tails, with taut straight legs, with ambassadorial dignity, they slowly circled, sniffing daintily. The caravan pulled up to Elisa's wire fence and stopped. Now the newcomer dog, feeling outnumbered, lowered his tail and retired under the wagon with raised hackles and bared teeth.

The man on the wagon seat called out. "That's a bad dog in a fight when he gets started."   30

Elisa laughed. "I see he is. How soon does he generally get started?"

The man caught up her laughter and echoed it heartily. "Sometimes not for weeks and weeks," he said. He climbed stiffly down, over the wheel. The horse and the donkey dropped like unwatered flowers.

Elisa saw that he was a very big man. Although his hair and beard were greying, he did not look old. His worn black suit was wrinkled and spotted with grease. The laughter had disappeared from his face and eyes the moment his laughing voice ceased. His eyes were dark and they were full of the brooding that gets in the eyes of teamsters and of sailors. The calloused hands he rested on the wire fence were cracked, and every crack was a black line. He took off his battered hat.

"I'm off my general road, ma'am," he said. "Does this dirt road cut over across the river to the Los Angeles highway?"

Elisa stood up and shoved the thick scissors in her apron pocket. "Well, yes, it   35
does, but it winds around and then fords the river. I don't think your team could pull through the sand."

He replied with some asperity, "It might surprise you what them beasts can pull through."

"When they get started?" she asked.

He smiled for a second. "Yes. When they get started."

"Well," said Elisa, "I think you'll save time if you go back to the Salinas road and pick up the highway there."

He drew a big finger down the chicken wire and made it sing. "I ain't in any hurry,   40
ma'am. I go from Seattle to San Diego and back every year. Takes all my time. About six months each way. I aim to follow nice weather."

Elisa took off her gloves and stuffed them in the apron pocket with the scissors. She touched the under edge of her man's hat, searching for fugitive hairs. "That sounds like a nice kind of a way to live," she said.

He leaned confidentially over the fence. "Maybe you noticed the writing on my wagon. I mend pots and sharpen knives and scissors. You got any of them things to do?"

"Oh, no," she said quickly. "Nothing like that." Her eyes hardened with resistance.

"Scissors is the worst thing," he explained. "Most people just ruin scissors trying to sharpen 'em, but I know how. I got a special tool. It's a little bobbit kind of thing, and patented. But it sure does the trick."

"No. My scissors are all sharp."   45

"All right, then. Take a pot," he continued earnestly, "a bent pot, or a pot with a hole. I can make it like new so you don't have to buy no new ones. That's a saving for you."

"No," she said shortly. "I tell you I have nothing like that for you to do."

His face fell to an exaggerated sadness. His voice took on a whining undertone. "I ain't had a thing to do today. Maybe I won't have no supper tonight. You see I'm off my regular road. I know folks on the highway clear from Seattle to San Diego. They save their things for me to sharpen up because they know I do it so good and save them money."

"I'm sorry," Elisa said irritably. "I haven't anything for you to do."

His eyes left her face and fell to searching the ground. They roamed about until   50 they came to the chrysanthemum bed where she had been working. "What's them plants, ma'am?"

The irritation and resistance melted from Elisa's face. "Oh, those are chrysanthemums, giant whites and yellows. I raise them every year, bigger than anybody around here."

"Kind of a long-stemmed flower? Looks like a quick puff of colored smoke?" he asked.

"That's it. What a nice way to describe them."

"They smell kind of nasty till you get used to them," he said.

"It's a good bitter smell," she retorted, "not nasty at all."   55

He changed his tone quickly. "I like the smell myself."

"I had ten-inch blooms this year," she said.

The man leaned farther over the fence. "Look. I know a lady down the road a piece, has got the nicest garden you ever seen. Got nearly every kind of flower but no chrysantheums. Last time I was mending a copper-bottom washtub for her (that's a hard job but I do it good), she said to me, 'If you ever run acrost some nice chrysantheums I wish you'd try to get me a few seeds.' That's what she told me."

Elisa's eyes grew alert and eager. "She couldn't have known much about chrysanthemums. You can raise them from seed, but it's much easier to root the little sprouts you see there."

"Oh," he said. "I s'pose I can't take none to her, then."   60

"Why yes you can," Elisa cried. "I can put some in damp sand, and you can carry them right along with you. They'll take root in the pot if you keep them damp. And then she can transplant them."

"She'd sure like to have some, ma'am. You say they're nice ones?"

"Beautiful," she said. "Oh, beautiful." Her eyes shone. She tore off the battered hat and shook out her dark pretty hair. "I'll put them in a flower pot, and you can take them right with you. Come into the yard."

While the man came through the picket gate Elisa ran excitedly along the geranium-bordered path to the back of the house. And she returned carrying a big red flower pot. The gloves were forgotten now. She kneeled on the ground by the starting bed and dug up the sandy soil with her fingers and scooped it into the bright new flower pot. Then she picked up the little pile of shoots she had prepared. With her strong fingers she pressed them into the sand and tamped around them with her knuckles.

The man stood over her. "I'll tell you what to do," she said. "You remember so you can tell the lady."

"Yes, I'll try to remember."

"Well, look. These will take root in about a month. Then she must set them out, about a foot apart in good rich earth like this, see?" She lifted a handful of dark soil for him to look at. "They'll grow fast and tall. Now remember this. In July tell her to cut them down, about eight inches from the ground."

"Before they bloom?" he asked.

"Yes, before they bloom." Her face was tight with eagerness. "They'll grow right up again. About the last of September the buds will start."

She stopped and seemed perplexed. "It's the budding that takes the most care," she said hesitantly. "I don't know how to tell you." She looked deep into his eyes, searchingly. Her mouth opened a little, and she seemed to be listening. "I'll try to tell you," she said. "Did you ever hear of planting hands?"

"Can't say I have, ma'am."

"Well, I can only tell you what it feels like. It's when you're picking off the buds you don't want. Everything goes right down into your fingertips. You watch your fingers work. They do it themselves. You can feel how it is. They pick and pick the buds. They never make a mistake. They're with the plant. Do you see? Your fingers and the plant. You can feel that, right up your arm. They know. They never make a mistake. You can feel it. When you're like that you can't do anything wrong. Do you see that? Can you understand that?"

She was kneeling on the ground looking up at him. Her breast swelled passionately.

The man's eyes narrowed. He looked away self-consciously. "Maybe I know," he said. "Sometimes in the night in the wagon there—"

Elisa's voice grew husky. She broke in on him. "I've never lived as you do, but I know what you mean. When the night is dark—why, the stars are sharp-pointed, and there's quiet. Why, you rise up and up! Every pointed star gets driven into your body. It's like that. Hot and sharp and—lovely."

Kneeling there, her hand went out toward his legs in the greasy black trousers. Her hesitant fingers almost touched the cloth. Then her hand dropped to the ground. She crouched low like a fawning dog.

He said, "It's nice, just like you say. Only when you don't have no dinner, it ain't."

She stood up then, very straight, and her face was ashamed. She held the flower pot out to him and placed it gently in his arms. "Here. Put it in your wagon, on the seat, where you can watch it. Maybe I can find something for you to do."

At the back of the house she dug in the can pile and found two old and battered aluminum saucepans. She carried them back and gave them to him. "Here, maybe you can fix these."

His manner changed. He became professional. "Good as new I can fix them." At the back of his wagon he set a little anvil, and out of an oily tool box dug a small machine hammer. Elisa came through the gate to watch him while he pounded out the dents in the kettles. His mouth grew sure and knowing. At a difficult part of the work he sucked his under-lip.

"You sleep right in the wagon?" Elisa asked.

"Right in the wagon, ma'am. Rain or shine. I'm dry as a cow in there."

"It must be nice," she said. "It must be very nice. I wish women could do such things."

"It ain't the right kind of a life for a woman."

Her upper lip raised a little, showing her teeth. "How do you know? How can you tell?" she said.

"I don't know ma'am," he protested. "Of course I don't know. Now here's your   85
kettles, done. You don't have to buy no new ones."

"How much?"

"Oh, fifty cents'll do. I keep my prices down and my work good. That's why I have all them satisfied customers up and down the highway."

Elisa brought him a fifty-cent piece from the house and dropped it in his hand. "You might be surprised to have a rival some time. I can sharpen scissors, too. And I can beat the dents out of little pots. I could show you what a woman might do."

He put his hammer back in the oily box and shoved the little anvil out of sight. "It would be a lonely life for a woman, ma'am, and a scarey life, too, with animals creeping under the wagon all night." He climbed over the single-tree, steadying himself with a hand on the burro's white rump. He settled himself in the seat, picked up the lines. "Thank you kindly, ma'am," he said. "I'll do like you told me; I'll go back and catch the Salinas road."

"Mind," she called, "if you're long in getting there, keep the sand damp."   90

"Sand, ma'am? . . . Sand? Oh, sure. You mean round the chrysantheums. Sure I will." He clucked his tongue. The beasts leaned luxuriously into their collars. The mongrel dog took his place between the back wheels. The wagon turned and crawled out the entrance road and back the way it had come, along the river.

Elisa stood in front of her wire fence watching the slow progress of the caravan. Her shoulders were straight, her head thrown back, her eyes half-closed, so that the scene came vaguely into them. Her lips moved silently, forming the words "Good-bye—good-bye." Then she whispered, "That's a bright direction. There's a glowing there." The sound of her whisper startled her. She shook herself free and looked about to see whether anyone had been listening. Only the dogs had heard. They lifted their heads toward her from their sleeping in the dust, and then stretched out their chins and settled asleep again. Elisa turned and ran hurriedly into the house.

In the kitchen she reached behind the stove and felt the water tank. It was full of hot water from the noonday cooking. In the bathroom she tore off her soiled clothes and flung them into the corner. And then she scrubbed herself with a little block of pumice, legs and thighs, loins and chest and arms, until her skin was scratched and red. When she had dried herself she stood in front of a mirror in her bedroom and looked at her body. She tightened her stomach and threw out her chest. She turned and looked over her shoulder at her back.

After a while she began to dress, slowly. She put on her newest under-clothing and her nicest stockings and the dress which was the symbol of her prettiness. She worked carefully on her hair, pencilled her eyebrows and rouged her lips.

Before she was finished she heard the little thunder of hoofs and the shouts of   95
Henry and his helper as they drove the red steers into the corral. She heard the gate bang shut and set herself for Henry's arrival.

His step sounded on the porch. He entered the house calling "Elisa, where are you?"

"In my room, dressing. I'm not ready. There's hot water for your bath. Hurry up. It's getting late."

When she heard him splashing in the tub, Elisa laid his dark suit on the bed, and shirt and socks and tie beside it. She stood his polished shoes on the floor beside the bed. Then she went to the porch and sat primly and stiffly down. She looked toward the river road where the willow-line was still yellow with frosted leaves so that under the high grey fog they seemed a thin band of sunshine. This was the only color in the grey afternoon. She sat unmoving for a long time. Her eyes blinked rarely.

Henry came banging out of the door, shoving his tie inside his vest as he came. Elisa stiffened and her face grew tight. Henry stopped short and looked at her. "Why—why, Elisa. You look so nice!"

"Nice? You think I look nice? What do you mean by 'nice'?"   100

Henry blundered on. "I don't know. I mean you look different, strong and happy."

"I am strong? Yes, strong. What do you mean 'strong'?"

He looked bewildered. "You're playing some kind of a game," he said helplessly. "It's a kind of a play. You look strong enough to break a calf over your knee, happy enough to eat it like watermelon."

For a second she lost her rigidity. "Henry! Don't talk like that. You didn't know what you said." She grew complete again. "I'm strong," she boasted. "I never knew before how strong."

Henry looked down toward the tractor shed, and when he brought his eyes back   105
to her, they were his own again. "I'll get out the car. You can put on your coat while I'm starting."

Elisa went into the house. She heard him drive to the gate and idle down his motor, and then she took a long time to put on her hat. She pulled it here and pressed it there. When Henry turned the motor off she slipped into her coat and went out.

The little roadster bounced along on the dirt road by the river, raising the birds and driving the rabbits into the brush. Two cranes flapped heavily over the willow-line and dropped into the river-bed.

Far ahead on the road Elisa saw a dark speck. She knew.

She tried not to look as they passed it, but her eyes would not obey. She whispered to herself sadly. "He might have thrown them off the road. That wouldn't have been much trouble, not very much. But he kept the pot," she explained. "He had to keep the pot. That's why he couldn't get them off the road."

The roadster turned a bend and she saw the caravan ahead. She swung full   110
around toward her husband so she could not see the little covered wagon and the mis-matched team as the car passed them.

In a moment it was over. The thing was done. She did not look back. She said loudly, to be heard above the motor, "It will be good, tonight, a good dinner."

"Now you're changed again," Henry complained. He took one hand from the wheel and patted her knee. "I ought to take you in to dinner oftener. It would be good for both of us. We get so heavy out on the ranch."

"Henry," she asked, "could we have wine at dinner?"

"Sure we could. Say! That will be fine."

She was silent for a little while; then she said, "Henry, at those prize fights, do the   115
men hurt each other very much?"

"Sometimes a little, not often. Why?"

"Well, I've read how they break noses, and blood runs down their chests. I've read how the fighting gloves get heavy and soggy with blood."

He looked around at her. "What's the matter, Elisa? I didn't know you read things like that." He brought the car to a stop, then turned to the right over the Salinas River bridge.

"Do any women ever go to the fights?" she asked.

"Oh, sure, some. What's the matter, Elisa? Do you want to go? I don't think you'd like it, but I'll take you if you really want to go."   120

She relaxed limply in the seat. "Oh, no. No. I don't want to go. I'm sure I don't." Her face was turned away from him. "It will be enough if we can have wine. It will be plenty." She turned up her coat collar so he could not see that she was crying weakly—like an old woman.

QUESTIONS

1. What point of view is used in the story? What are the advantages of this point of view?

2. Consider the symbolism of the setting in this story with respect to the Salinas Valley, the time of year, and the description of the Allen house. What do these things tell us about Elisa Allen and her world?

3. To what extent is Steinbeck's description of Elisa in paragraphs 5 and 6 symbolic? What is she wearing? What do her clothes hide or suppress?

4. What do the chrysanthemums symbolize for Elisa? What do they symbolize *about* her? What role do these flowers play in her life?

5. How does Elisa's character or sense of self change during the episode in which she washes and dresses for dinner? To what extent is this washing-dressing episode symbolic? How would you explain the symbolism?

6. Consider the symbolic impact of Elisa's seeing the chrysanthemum sprouts at the roadside. What does her reaction tell us about her values?

MICHEL TREMBLAY   (b. 1942)

Tremblay, a French-Canadian native of Montreal, is both a dramatist and writer of fiction. He is known as an experimental and avant-garde writer. In one of his plays, for example (Albertine, en cinq temps *[1984]*), *five actresses play one character at various times of life. His innovativeness and boldness extend to his treating subjects such as incest, transvestitism, and prostitution. His works are strongly symbolic and, as with "The Thimble," allegorical. He has written a number of novels, including the autobiographical* The Fat Woman Next Door Is Pregnant *(1981). His collection of stories* Contes pour buveurs attardés *(1966; translated as* Stories for Late-Night Drinkers, *1974) included "The Thimble."*

The Thimble _____ *1966*

Translated by Jay Bochner

If Bobby Stone had known what was to happen that day, he probably would never have got out of bed. And . . . well, the catastrophe might have been avoided.

Bobby Stone wasn't a bad fellow. He worked in an office, drank in moderation, went to mass every Sunday, and had a weakness for plump women. He was neither old nor young, though he wore a hat to cover an expanding bald spot.

Bobby Stone had not the slightest inkling that he was going to be the cause of the catastrophe.

"Now, now, my dear lady, please stop this silly game. People are looking at us!" He was right. A throng of loafers had gathered around them and some were beginning to eye Bobby Stone reproachfully, because this woman was weeping and wailing. "Sir, I beg of you," she cried, "take it! Take it! I give it to you. It's yours!" But Bobby Stone didn't want it; he didn't want to have anything to do with it. "What do you expect me to do with it?" he said. "And besides, it's a . . . thing that belongs to women." More and more people gathered on the sidewalk and Bobby Stone began to sweat. He took out his handkerchief to wipe his forehead, but he didn't remove his hat. *She's crazy. That's it, she's crazy. And all those people looking at us. But I don't want to have her thimble!*

A man emerged from the crowd and grabbed Bobby Stone by the collar. "So," he said, breathing a rotten smell into his face, "we make women cry in the middle of the street?" Bobby Stone was trembling. "But Mister, I don't know this woman! She wants to give me her thimble, and I don't want her thimble, I don't. . . . " Really, Bobby Stone had had enough. In an abrupt surge of courage—or was it cowardice?—he slammed his fist into the face of the man who was threatening him and took off, knocking over two or three people who tried to stop him.

As you might have expected, he worked very poorly that day. The columns of figures swayed on the page, and when he closed his eyes Bobby Stone saw the strange woman offering him the thimble. "It is yours."

The five o'clock bell rang. Bobby Stone slumped in his desk chair, his tie undone and one hand on his chest. *I never would have believed such a stupid incident. . . . Oh, no that's too much, following me to my office!* But it was no vision this time; his eyes were wide open. She was sitting in the chair directly in front of him on the other side of his desk. "If you do not take it immediately," said the woman, "I will have to forbid you from taking it, and then you'll run after me to steal it from me. I'm telling you, you'll steal it from me." Bobby Stone, mad with fear, jumped up and ran towards the door. "Very well then," the woman cried out, "I forbid you to take my thimble!" Bobby Stone stopped short. Oh, what a fine thimble, such a fine beautiful thimble! Made out of plastic with tiny dimples in it. A fine thimble! He must have this thimble. Nothing else in the world existed outside of this pink and yellow thimble. He ran after the woman, who pretended to flee but was careful to lose ground all the while. . . .

Smack! And another! You bitch! So, you wanted to keep it all to yourself, did you? The thimble for you and nothing for me! This is for you. Some good kicks, you see, and the back of my hand, and a few with the knee. . . .

When he left the building his clothes were all mussed and there was some blood on his fingernails, but he had the thimble. It was his and no one—but no one, do you hear?—would ever be able to take it from him. He knew the secret of the thimble now. Before she died the woman had whispered, "In the thimble . . . in the thimble . . . I have locked the universe."

When he awoke the next morning Bobby Stone remembered nothing. He found a pink and yellow thimble on his night-table. What an ugly thimble! He threw it in the garbage. But before he left for the office Bobby Stone tore a loose button from his overcoat. He found some thread and a needle and thought of the thimble at the bottom of the garbage pail. He went and got it. And so as not to prick himself while he sewed on his coat button, Bobby Stone pushed his little finger into the little thimble. He squashed the entire universe.

QUESTIONS

1. Why does the story begin with a premonition of "catastrophe"? What is the catastrophe? To what degree is the narrative realistic or unrealistic?

2. What does the woman say is the significance of the thimble? What does Bobby do with the thimble after he takes it from her? Might some other object have worked as well, for purposes of the story?

3. Explain the story as an allegory of desire, denial, and the consequences of these emotions. What happens when Bobby puts his finger into the thimble? Is there a scientific basis for this happening, and if so, what is it? What is the allegorical meaning?

4. What elements of "The Thimble" may be compared with Aesop's "The Fox and the Grapes"?

WRITING ABOUT SYMBOLISM OR ALLEGORY

To discover possible parallels that determine the presence of symbolism or allegory, consider the following questions:

Questions for Discovering Ideas

A. SYMBOLISM

- What cultural or universal symbols can you discover in names, objects, places, situations, or actions in a work (e.g., the character Faith and the walking stick in "Young Goodman Brown,"Abner in "Barn Burning," the woods in either "Young Goodman Brown" or "A Worn Path")?

- What contextual symbolism can be found in a work? What makes you think it is symbolic? What is being symbolized? How definite or direct is the symbolism? How systematically is it used? How necessary to the work is it? To what degree does it strengthen the work? How strongly does the work stand on its own without the reading for symbolism?

- Is it possible to make parallel lists to show how qualities of a particular symbol match the qualities of a character or action? Here is such a list for the toy windmill in Welty's "A Worn Path":

QUALITIES OF THE WINDMILL	COMPARABLE QUALITIES IN PHOENIX
1. Cheap	1. Poor, but she gives all she has for the windmill
2. Breakable	2. Old, and not far from death
3. A gift	3. Generous
4. Not practical	4. Needs relief from reality and practicality
5. Colorful	5. Needs something new and cheerful

B. ALLEGORY

- How clearly does the author point you toward an allegorical reading (i.e., through names and allusions, consistency of narrative, literary context)?
- How consistent is the allegorical application? Does the entire work, or only a part, embody the allegory? On what basis do you draw these conclusions?
- How complete is the allegorical reading? How might the allegory yield to a diagram such as the following, which shows how characters, actions, objects, or ideas correspond to an allegorical meaning?

Star Wars	Luke Skywalker	Obi-Wan Kenobi	Darth Vader	Princess Leia	Capture	Escape; defeat of Vader
Allegorical Application to Morality and Faith	Forces of good	Education and faith	Forces of evil	Object to be saved; ideals to be rescued and restored	Doubt, spiritual negligence	Restoration of faith
Allegorical Application to Personal and General Concerns	Individual in pursuit of goals	The means by which goals may be reached	Obstacles to be overcome	Occupation, happiness, goals	Temporary failure, depression, discouragement, disappointment	Success

C. OTHER FORMS

- What enables you to identify the story as a parable or fable? What lesson or moral is either clearly stated or implicit?
- What mythological identification is established in the work? What do you find in the story (names, situations, etc.) that enables you to determine its mythological significance? How is the myth to be understood? What symbolic value does the myth have? What current and timeless application does it have?

Strategies for Organizing Ideas

Relate the central idea of your essay to the meaning of the major symbols or allegorical thrust of the story. An idea about "Young Goodman Brown," for example, is that fanaticism darkens and limits the human soul. An early incident in the story provides symbolic support for this idea. Specifically, Goodman Brown enters the woods, resolving to "stand firm against the devil" (paragraph 46), and he looks up toward "Heaven above him." As he looks, a "black mass of cloud" appears to hide the "brightening stars" (paragraph 47). Within the limits of our central idea, the cloud can be seen as a symbol, just like the widening path or the night walk itself. Look for ways to make solid connections like this in your symbolic ascriptions.

Also, your essay will need to include justifications for your symbols or allegorical parallels. If you treat the Usher mansion in Poe's "The Fall of the House of Usher" as a symbol of deterioration and death, for example, it is important to draw attention to its perilous state in the tarn and also to the immense crack that is endangering its stability. These defects justify the mansion's symbolism. In the same way, in treating the allegorical elements in "Young Goodman Brown," you need to establish a comprehensive statement such as the following: People lose ideals and forsake principles not because they are evil, but because they misunderstand the people around them.

There are a number of other strategies for discussing symbolism and allegory. You might use one exclusively, or a combination. If you want to write about symbolism, you might consider the following:

1. *The meaning of a major symbol.* Identify the symbol and what it stands for. Then answer questions such as these: Is the symbol cultural or contextual? How do you decide? How do you derive your interpretation of the symbolic meaning? What is the extent of the meaning? Does the symbol undergo modification or new applications if it reappears? How does the symbol affect your understanding of the story? Does the symbol bring out any ironies? How does the symbol add strength and depth to the story?

2. *The development and relationship of symbols.* For two or more symbols, consider issues such as these: How do the symbols connect with each other (like night and the cloud in "Young Goodman Brown" as symbols of a darkening mind)? What additional meanings do the symbols provide? Are they complementary, contradictory, or ironic? (The windmill and the medicine in "A Worn Path," for example, are ironic because the windmill suggests cheer while the medicine suggests hopelessness.) Do the symbols control the form of the work? How? (For example, at the beginning of Steinbeck's "The Chrysanthemums" the barren wintry countryside is compared to a "closed pot," and at the ending Elisa learns that the tinsmith has dumped the earth out of the pot which she had given to him as a gift. In a similar vein, Joyce's "Araby" [Chapter 9] begins with the "blind" or dead-end street, and ends with the darkness of the closed bazaar.) Can these comparable objects and conditions be viewed symbolically in relationship to the development of the two stories? Other issues are whether the symbols fit naturally or artificially into the context of the story, or whether and how the writer's symbols create unique qualities or excellences.

When writing about allegory, you might use one of the following approaches:

1. *The application and meaning of the allegory.* What is the subject of the story (allegory, fable, parable, myth)? How can it be more generally applied to ideas or to qualities of human character, not only of its own time but also of our own? What other versions of the story do you know, if any? Does it illustrate, either closely or loosely, particular philosophies or religious views? If so, what are these? How do you know?

2. *The consistency of the allegory.* Is the allegory used consistently throughout the story, or is it used intermittently? Explain and illustrate this use. Would it be correct to call your story *allegorical* rather than an *allegory*? Can you determine how parts of the story are introduced for their allegorical importance?

Examples are the natural obstacles in the woods in Welty's "A Worn Path" (Chapter 3) which are allegorical equivalents of life's difficulties, and the Usher mansion in "The Fall of the House of Usher," which corresponds to the tenuous nature of life and sanity.

In concluding you might summarize main points, describe general impressions, explain the impact of the symbolic or allegorical methods, indicate personal responses, or suggest further lines of thought and application. You might also assess the quality and appropriateness of the symbolism or allegory (such as the opening of "Young Goodman Brown" being in darkness, with the closing in gloom).

SAMPLE STUDENT ESSAY

Allegory and Symbolism in Hawthorne's "Young Goodman Brown"°

[1] It is hard to read beyond the third paragraph of Nathaniel Hawthorne's "Young Goodman Brown" without recognizing the story's allegory and symbolism. The opening at first seems realistic. Goodman Brown, a young Puritan, leaves his home in colonial Salem to take an overnight trip. His wife's name, "Faith," however, suggests a symbolic reading, and as soon as Brown goes into the forest, his ordinary walk changes into an allegorical trip into evil. The idea that Hawthorne shows by this trip is that rigid belief destroys even the best human qualities.* He develops this thought in the allegory and in many symbols, particularly the sunset, the walking stick, and the path.†

[2] The allegory of the story concerns the ways in which people develop destructive ideas. Most of the story is dreamlike and unreal, and the ideas that Brown gains are also unreal. At the weird "witch meeting," he concludes that everyone he knows is sinful, and he then permits mistrust and loathing to distort his previous love for his wife and neighbors. As a result, he becomes harsh and gloomy for the rest of his life. The location of the story in colonial Salem indicates that Hawthorne's allegorical target is the zealous pursuit of religious principles that exclude love while dwelling on sinfulness. However, modern readers can also apply the allegory to the ways in which people uncritically accept *any* ideal (most often political loyalties or racial or national prejudices) and thereby reject the integrity and rights of others. If people like Brown apply a rigid standard and if they never try to understand those they condemn, they can condemn anyone. In this way, Hawthorne's allegory applies to any narrow-minded acceptance of ideals or systems that exclude the importance of love, understanding, and tolerance.

° See pp. 324–32 for this story.
* Central idea.
† Thesis sentence.

[3]   Hawthorne's attack on such dehumanizing belief is found not just in the allegory but also in his many symbols. For example, the seventh word in the story, "sunset," can be taken as a symbol. In reality, sunset merely indicates the end of day. Coming at the beginning of the story, however, it suggests that Goodman Brown is beginning his long night of hatred, his spiritual death. For him the night will never end because his final days are shrouded in "gloom" (paragraph 72).

The next symbol, the guide's walking stick or staff, suggests the arbitrariness of the standard by which Brown judges his neighbors. Hawthorne's description indicates the symbolic nature of this staff:

[4]   . . . the only thing about him [the guide] that could be fixed upon as remarkable, was his staff, which bore the likeness of a great black snake, so curiously wrought, that it might almost be seen to twist and wriggle itself like a living serpent. This, of course, must have been an ocular deception, assisted by the uncertain light. (paragraph 13)

The serpent symbolically suggests Satan, who in Genesis (3:1–7) is the originator of all evil, but the phrase "ocular deception" creates an interesting and realistic ambiguity about the symbol. Since the perception of the snake may depend on nothing more than the "uncertain" light, the staff may be less symbolic of evil than of the tendency to find evil where it does not exist (and could the uncertain light symbolize the uncertainty of human understanding?).

[5]   In the same vein, the path through the forest is a major symbol of the destructive mental confusion that overcomes Brown. As he walks, the path grows "wilder and drearier, and more faintly traced," and "at length" it vanishes (paragraph 51). This is like the biblical description of the "broad" way that leads "to Destruction" (Matthew 7:13). As a symbol, the path shows that most human acts are bad, and a small number, like the "narrow" way to life (Matthew 7:14), are good. Goodman Brown's path is at first clear, as though sin is at first unique and unusual. Soon, however, the path is so indistinct that he can see only sin wherever he turns. The symbol suggests that when people follow evil, their moral vision becomes blurred and they soon fall prey to "the instinct that guides mortal man to evil" (paragraph 51).

[6]   Through Hawthorne's allegory and symbols, "Young Goodman Brown" presents the paradox of how noble beliefs can backfire. Goodman Brown dies in gloom because he believes that his wrong vision is true. This form of evil is the hardest to stop, because wrongdoers who are convinced of their own goodness are beyond reach. In view of such self-righteous evil, whether cloaked in the apparent virtues of Puritanism or of some other blindly rigorous doctrine (political as well as religious), Hawthorne writes, "The fiend in his own shape is less hideous than when he rages in the breast of man" (paragraph 53). Young Goodman Brown thus is the central symbol of the story. He is one of those who think they walk in light but who really create their own darkness.

Commentary on the Essay

The introduction justifies the treatment of allegory and symbolism on the grounds that Hawthorne early in the story invites such a reading. The central idea relates Hawthorne's method to the idea that rigid belief destroys the best human qualities.

Paragraph 2 considers the allegory as a criticism of rigid Puritan morality. The major thread running through the paragraph is the hurtful effect of mono-maniacal views like those of Brown. Paragraphs 3, 4, and 5 deal with three major symbols: sunset, the staff, and the path. The aim of this discussion is to show how the symbols apply to Hawthorne's attack on unquestioning belief. Throughout these three paragraphs the central idea—the relationship of rigid-ity to destructiveness—is stressed. Hawthorne's allusions to both the Old and New Testaments are pointed out in paragraphs 4 and 5. The last paragraph builds to the conclusion that Brown symbolizes the idea that the primary cause of evil is the inability to separate reality from unreality.

If you write exclusively about allegory, you can use paragraph 2 of the sample essay as a guide either for a single paragraph or, when expanded, for an entire essay. If the allegory of "Young Goodman Brown," for example, were to be expanded, additional topics might be Brown's gullibility, the meaning of faith and the requirements for maintaining it, and the causes for preferring to think evil rather than good of other people. Such points are sufficiently impor-tant to sustain an entire essay on the topic of allegory.

SPECIAL WRITING TOPICS FOR STUDYING SYMBOLISM AND ALLEGORY

1. Compare and contrast the symbolism in Steinbeck's "The Chrysanthemums," Tremblay's "The Thimble," and Munro's "The Found Boat" (Chapter 7). To what degree do the stories rely on contextual symbols? On universal symbols? On the basis of your comparison, what is the case for asserting that realism and fantasy are directly related to the nature of the symbolism employed by the writer? (Consult Chapter 29 for a discussion of comparison and contrast essays.)

2. Why do you think writers interested in morality and religion rely heavily on sym-bolism and allegory? In discussing this question, you might introduce refer-ences from "The Parable of the Prodigal Son," "The Thimble," and "Young Goodman Brown."

3. Write an essay on the allegorical method of one or more of the allegories included in the Gospel of St. Luke, such as "The Bridegroom" (5:34–35), "The Garments and the Wineskins" (5:36–39), "The Sower" (8:4–15), "The Good Samaritan" (10:25–37), "The Prodigal Son" (15:11-32), "The Ox in the Well" (14:5–6), "The Watering of Animals on the Sabbath" (13:15–17), "The Rich Fool" (12:16–21), "Lazarus" (16:19–31), "The Widow and the Judge" (18:1–8), and "The Pharisee and the Publican" (18:9–14).

4. Write a brief story using a widely recognized cultural symbol such as the flag (patriotism, love of country, a certain type of politics), water (life, sexuality, regeneration), or the population explosion (the end of life on earth). By arranging actions and dialogue, make clear the issues conveyed by your symbol, and also try to resolve the conflicts that the symbol might raise among your characters.

5. Write a brief story in which you develop your own contextual symbol. You might, for example, demonstrate how holding a job brings out character strengths that are not at first apparent, or how neglecting to care for the inside or outside of a house indicates a character's decline. The principle is to take something that may at first seem normal and ordinary, and then to make that thing symbolic as you develop your story.

6. Using the card or computer catalogue of your library, discover a recent critical-biographical book or books about Hawthorne. Explain what the book says about Hawthorne's uses of symbolism. To what extent does the book relate Hawthorne's symbolism to his religious and family heritage?

9
Idea or Theme:
The Meaning and the
Message in Fiction

The word **idea** refers to the result or results of general and abstract thinking. Synonymous words are *concept, thought, opinion*, and *principle*. In literary study the consideration of ideas relates to *meaning, interpretation, explanation*, and *significance*. Although ideas are usually extensive and complex, separate ideas may be named by single words, such as *justice, right, good, love, piety, causation*, and, not unsurprisingly, *idea* itself.

IDEAS AND ASSERTIONS

While single words alone may thus name ideas, we must put these words into operation in *sentences* or *assertions* before they can advance our understanding. Good operational sentences about ideas are not the same as ordinary conversational statements such as "It's a nice day." An observation of this sort may be true (depending on the weather), but it gives us no ideas and does not stimulate our minds. Rather, a sentence asserting an idea should initiate *thought* about the day's quality, such as "A nice day requires light breezes, blue sky, a warm sun, and relaxation." Because this sentence makes an assertion about "nice," it allows us to consider and develop the idea of a nice day.

In studying literature, you should always express ideas as assertions. For example, you might state that an idea in Lawrence's "The Horse Dealer's Daughter" is "love," but it would be difficult to discuss anything more unless you make an assertion such as "This story demonstrates the idea that love is irresistible and irrational." This assertion would lead you to explain the unlikely love that bursts out in the story. Similarly, for Eudora Welty's "A Worn Path" an assertion like the following would help advance further thinking: "Phoenix embodies the idea that caring for others gives no reward but the continuation of the duty itself."

Although we have noted only one idea in these two stories, most stories contain many ideas. When one of the ideas seems to be the major one, it is called the **theme**. In practice, the *theme* and the *major idea* are the same.

IDEAS AND VALUES

Literature embodies **values** along with ideas. This means that ideas imply that certain conditions and standards should be—or should not be—highly esteemed. For example, the *idea of justice* may be considered abstractly and broadly, as Plato does in his *Republic* when developing his concept of a just government. In comparison, justice is also a subject in Margaret Laurence's story "The Loons" (Chapter 10). While Plato uses analysis and comparison to explain justice as a condition of equal balance in society, however, Laurence uses narrative fiction to tell the story of an impoverished Indian girl who is brought up in neglect and who is killed when still young in a house fire. Laurence's idea is that if justice is a prized value in society, then all people deserve equal treatment and opportunity. The young woman's death symbolizes graphically the injustice of denying rights and opportunities to people because of race and low social condition. In short, to talk about Laurence's ideas is also to talk about her values.

THE PLACE OF IDEAS IN LITERATURE

Because writers of poems, plays, and stories are usually not systematic philosophers, it would be a mistake to go "message hunting" as though their works contained nothing but ideas. Indeed, there is great benefit and pleasure to be derived from just savoring a work—following the patterns of narrative and conflict, getting to like the characters, understanding the work's implications and suggestions, and listening to the sounds of the author's words—to name only a few of the reasons for which literature is treasured.

Nevertheless, ideas are vital to understanding and appreciating literature: Writers have ideas and want to communicate them. For example, in "The Horse Dealer's Daughter," Lawrence tells us about two unlikely characters who fall suddenly and unpredictably in love. This love is unusual, and the story is therefore effective, but the story is also provocative because it raises the idea that love pushes aside other decisions that people make. Zabytko's story "Home Soil" in part describes a father's problems in relating to his son, who has just returned from the Vietnamese war, but the story's *ideas* concern the need for family ties, the difficulty of post-war adjustment, the pain of remembered wrongdoing, and the moral ambiguity of war.

Distinguishing between Ideas and Actions

As you analyze works for ideas, it is important to avoid the trap of confusing ideas and actions. Such a trap is contained in the following sentence about Updike's story "A & P" (Chapter 5): "The major character, Sammy, quits his job to protest the way his boss mistreats three girls." This sentence successfully describes the story's major action, but it does not express an *idea* that connects characters and events, and for this reason it obstructs understanding. Some possible connections might be achieved with sentences like these: "'A & P' illustrates the idea that making a protest also makes life hard," or "'A & P' shows that individual rights are more important than arbitrary regulations." A study based on these connecting formulations could be focused on ideas and would not be sidetracked into doing no more than retelling Updike's story.

Distinguishing between Ideas and Situations

You should also distinguish between ideas and situations. For example, in Joyce's "Araby," the narrator describes his frustration and embarrassment at the "Araby" bazaar in Dublin. This is a *situation,* but it is not the *idea* brought out by the situation. Joyce's idea here is rather that immature love causes unreal dreams and hopes that produce disappointment and self-reproach. If you are able to distinguish a story's various situations from the writer's major idea or ideas, as we have done here, you will be able to focus on ideas and therefore sharpen your own thinking.

HOW TO FIND IDEAS

Ideas are not as obvious as characters or setting. To determine an idea, you need to consider the meaning of what you read and then develop explanatory and comprehensive assertions. Your assertions need not be the same as those that others might make. People notice different things, and individual formulations vary. In Joyce's "Araby," for example, an initial expression of some of the story's ideas might take any of the following forms: (1) The force of sexual attraction is strong and begins early in life. (2) Sexual attraction leads some individuals to the idealization of the loved one. (3) Sexual feelings are private and may therefore cause embarrassment and shame. Although any one of these choices could be a basic idea for studying "Araby," they all have in common the narrator's idealization of his friend's sister. In discovering ideas, you should follow a similar process—making a number of formulations for an idea, and then selecting one for further development.

As you read, be alert to the different ways in which authors convey ideas. One author might prefer an indirect way through a character's speeches while another may prefer direct statement. In practice, authors may employ any or all of the following methods.

Direct Statements by the Authorial Voice

Although authors mainly render action, dialogue, and situation, they sometimes state ideas to guide us and deepen our understanding. In the second paragraph of "The Necklace," for example, Maupassant's authorial voice presents the idea that women have only charm and beauty to get on in the world. Ironically, Maupassant uses the story to show that for the major character Mathilde, nothing is effective, for her charm cannot prevent disaster. Hawthorne, in "Young Goodman Brown," expresses a powerful idea that "The fiend in his own shape is less hideous than when he rages in the breast of man" (paragraph 53). This statement is made as authorial commentary just when the major character, Goodman Brown, is speeding through the "benighted wilderness" on his way to the satanic meeting. Although the idea is complex and will bear extensive discussion, its essential aspect is that the causes of evil originate within human beings themselves, with the implication that we alone are responsible for all our actions, whether good or evil.

Direct Statements by the First-Person Speaker

First-person narrators or speakers frequently express ideas along with their depiction of actions and situations. (See also Chapter 5.) Because their ideas are part of a dramatic presentation, they may be right or wrong, well considered or thoughtless, or brilliant or half-baked, depending on the speaker. The narrator of Atwood's "Rape Fantasies," for example, is not noteworthy for her intelligence, yet she voices penetrating ideas about the relationships of men and women. In Zabytko's "Home Soil," the narrator considers the idea that war always causes regret and guilt, no matter when it is fought or who fights in it. A half-baked speaker, yet an interesting one, is Sammy, the narrator of Updike's "A & P," who seems engulfed in intellectual commonplaces, particularly in his insinuation about the intelligence of women (paragraph 2). In his defense, however, Sammy *acts* on the worthy idea that people generally have the freedom and right to wear any clothes they please.

Dramatic Statements Made by Characters

In many stories, characters express their own views, which may be right or wrong, admirable or contemptible. When you consider such dramatic speeches, you must do considerable interpreting and evaluating yourself. For example, Krebs's mother in Hemingway's "Soldier's Home" (Chapter 8) expresses the idea that all work is honorable, and therefore asks Krebs to give up his idleness and get a job, any job (paragraph 70). By stressing this idea it is clear that she sees him in conventional terms and also that she cannot understand the causes of his deep uneasiness. In Jackson's "The Lottery," Old Man Warner states that the lottery is valuable even though we learn from the narrator that the beliefs underlying it have long been forgotten. Because Warner is a zealous and noisy person, however, his words show that outdated ideas continue to do harm even when there is strong reason to throw them out and adopt new ones.

Figurative Language

Figurative language is one of the major components of poetry, but it also abounds in fiction. In Joyce's "Araby," for example, the narrator uses a beautiful figure of speech to describe his youthful admiration for his friend's sister. He says that his body "was like a harp and her words and gestures were like fingers running upon the wires." Another notable figure occurs at the opening of Mansfield's "Miss Brill," when the narrator likens a sunny day to gold and white wine—a lovely comparison conveying the idea that the world is a place of beauty and happiness. This idea contrasts ironically with the indifference and cruelty that Miss Brill experiences.

Characters Who Stand for Ideas

Characters and their actions can often be equated with certain ideas and values. The power of "The Necklace," for example, justifies the claim that the main character, Mathilde, embodies the idea that unrealizable dreams can invade and damage the real world. Two diverse or opposed characters may embody contrasting ideas, as with Sammy and Lengel of Updike's "A & P," who stand for opposing views about rights of expression.

In effect, characters who stand for ideas may assume symbolic status, as in Hawthorne's "Young Goodman Brown," where the protagonist symbolizes the alienation accompanying zealousness, or in "The Shawl," where the small child Magda embodies the vulnerability and helplessness of human beings in the face of dehumanizing state brutality. Such characters can be equated directly with particular ideas, and to talk about them is a shorthand way of talking about the ideas.

The Work Itself as It Represents Ideas

One of the most important ways in which authors express ideas is to interlock them within all parts and aspects of the work, as in "Araby," where Joyce dramatizes the idea that the urgency of youthful affection conflicts with conventional inhibitions, or in "Home Soil," where Zabytko demonstrates that warfare forces people to perform actions that they will always hide publicly but forever remember privately. Although Joyce and Zabytko do not use these exact words, their stories powerfully embody these ideas. The conclusion of Whitecloud's "Blue Winds Dancing" drives the point home that human beings will not accept anything new when they truly believe that their own way of life is of equal or superior value. Most stories represent ideas in a similar way. Even "escape literature," which ostensibly enables readers to forget their immediate concerns, contains conflicts between good and evil, love and hate, good spies and bad, earthlings and aliens, and so on. Thereby, such stories *do* embody ideas, even though their avowed intention is not to make readers think but rather to help them forget.

 ## STORIES FOR STUDY

JAMES JOYCE   (1882–1941)

Joyce, one of the greatest twentieth-century writers, was born in Ireland and received a vigorous and thorough education there. He left Ireland in 1902 and spent most of the rest of his life in Switzerland and France. His best-known works are Dubliners *(1914),* A Portrait of the Artist as a Young Man *(1914–1915),* Ulysses *(1922), and* Finnegans Wake *(1939). Much of his work has been called "fictionalized autobiography," a quality shown in "Araby," which is selected from* Dubliners. *As a young child, Joyce had lived on North Richmond Street, just like the narrator of the story. The bazaar that the narrator visits actually did take place in Dublin, from May 14 to 19, 1894, when Joyce was the same age as the narrator. It was called "Araby in Dublin" and was advertised as a "Grand Oriental Fete."*

Araby _____ 1914

North Richmond Street,° being blind,° was a quiet street except at the hour when the Christian Brothers' School set the boys free. An uninhabited house of two storeys stood at the blind end, detached from its neighbours in a square ground. The other houses of the street, conscious of decent lives within them, gazed at one another with brown imperturbable faces.

The former tenant of our house, a priest, had died in the back drawing room. Air, musty from having long been enclosed, hung in all the rooms, and the waste room behind the kitchen was littered with old useless papers. Among these I found a few paper-covered books, the pages of which were curled and damp: *The Abbott*, by Walter Scott, *The Devout Communicant*° and *The Memoirs of Vidocq*.° I liked the last best because its leaves were yellow. The wild garden behind the house contained a central apple-tree and a few straggling bushes under one of which I found the late tenant's rusty bicycle-pump. He had been a very charitable priest; in his will he had left all his money to institutions and the furniture of his house to his sister.

When the short days of winter came dusk fell before we had well eaten our dinners. When we met in the street the houses had grown sombre. The space of sky above us was the colour of ever-changing violet and towards it the lamps of the street lifted their feeble lanterns. The cold air stung us and we played till our bodies glowed. Our shouts echoed in the silent street. The career of our play brought us through the dark muddy lanes behind the houses where we ran the gauntlet of the rough tribes from the cottages, to the back doors of the dark dripping gardens where odours arose from the ashpits, to the dark odorous stables where a coachman smoothed and combed the horse or shook music from the buckled harness. When we returned to the street light from the kitchen windows had filled the areas. If my uncle was seen turning the corner we hid in the shadow until we had seen him safely housed. Or if Mangan's sister came

---

North Richmond Street: name of a real street in Dublin on which Joyce lived as a boy.
blind: dead-end street.
The Devout Communicant: a book of meditations by Pacificus Baker, published 1873.
The Memoirs of Vidocq: published 1829, the story of François Vidocq, a Parisian chief of detectives.

out on the doorstep to call her brother in to his tea we watched her from our shadow peer up and down the street. We waited to see whether she would remain or go in and, if she remained, we left our shadow and walked up to Mangan's steps resignedly. She was waiting for us, her figure defined by the light from the half-opened door. Her brother always teased her before he obeyed and I stood by the railings looking at her. Her dress swung as she moved her body and the soft rope of her hair tossed from side to side.

Every morning I lay on the floor in the front parlor watching her door. The blind was pulled down within an inch of the sash so that I could not be seen. When she came out on the doorstep my heart leaped. I ran to the hall, seized my books and followed her. I kept her brown figure always in my eye and, when we came near the point at which our ways diverged, I quickened my pace and passed her. This happened morning after morning. I had never spoken to her, except for a few casual words, and yet her name was like a summons to all my foolish blood.

Her image accompanied me even in places the most hostile to romance. On   5
Saturday evenings when my aunt went marketing I had to go to carry some of the parcels. We walked through the flaring street, jostled by drunken men and bargaining women, amid the curses of labourers, the shrill litanies of shop-boys who stood on guard by the barrels of pigs' cheeks, the nasal chanting of street singers, who sang a *come-all-you* about O'Donovan Rossa,° or a ballad about the troubles in our native land. These noises converged in a single sensation of life for me: I imagined that I bore my chalice safely through the throng of foes. Her name sprang to my lips at moments in strange prayers and praises which I myself did not understand. My eyes were often full of tears (I could not tell why) and at times a flood from my heart seemed to pour itself out into my bosom. I thought little of the future. I did not know whether I would ever speak to her or not or, if I spoke to her, how I could tell her of my confused adoration. But my body was like a harp and her words and gestures were like fingers running upon the wires.

One evening I went into the back drawing-room in which the priest had died. It was a dark rainy evening and there was no sound in the house. Through one of the broken panes I heard the rain impinge upon the earth, the fine incessant needles of water playing in the sodden beds. Some distant lamp or lighted window gleamed below me. I was thankful that I could see so little. All my senses seemed to desire to veil themselves and, feeling that I was about to slip from them, I pressed the palms of my hands together until they trembled, murmuring: *O love! O love!* many times.

At last she spoke to me. When she addressed the first words to me I was so confused that I did not know what to answer. She asked me was I going to *Araby.*° I forget whether I answered yes or no. It would be a splendid bazaar, she said; she would love to go.

—And why can't you? I asked.

While she spoke she turned a silver bracelet round and round her wrist. She could not go, she said, because there would be a retreat° that week in her convent. Her brother and two other boys were fighting for their caps and I was alone at the railings. She held one of the spikes, bowing her head towards me. The light from the lamp opposite our door caught the white curve of her neck, lit up her hair that rested there and, falling, lit up the hand upon the railing. It fell over one side of her dress and caught the white border of a petticoat, just visible as she stood at ease.

O'Donovan Rossa: popular ballad about Jeremiah O'Donovan (1831–1915), a leader in the movement to free Ireland from English control. He was called "Dynamite Rossa."
Araby: the bazaar held in Dublin from May 14–19, 1894.
retreat: a special time set aside for concentrated religious instruction, discussion, and prayer.

—It's well for you, she said.   10

—If I go, I said, I will bring you something.

What innumerable follies laid waste my waking and sleeping thoughts after that evening! I wished to annihilate the tedious intervening days. I chafed against the work of school. At night in my bedroom and by day in the classroom her image came between me and the page I strove to read. The syllables of the word *Araby* were called to me through the silence in which my soul luxuriated and cast an Eastern enchantment over me. I asked for leave to go to the bazaar on Saturday night. My aunt was surprised and hoped it was not some Freemason° affair. I answered few questions in class. I watched my master's face pass from amiability to sternness; he hoped I was not beginning to idle. I could not call my wandering thoughts together. I had hardly any patience with the serious work of life which, now that it stood between me and my desire, seemed to me child's play, ugly monotonous child's play.

On Saturday morning I reminded my uncle that I wished to go to the bazaar in the evening. He was fussing at the hall-stand, looking for the hatbrush, and answered me curtly:

—Yes, boy, I know.

As he was in the hall I could not go into the front parlour and lie at the window. I   15
left the house in bad humour and walked slowly towards the school. The air was pitilessly raw and already my heart misgave me.

When I came home to dinner my uncle had not yet been home. Still, it was early. I sat staring at the clock for some time and, when its ticking began to irritate me, I left the room. I mounted the staircase and gained the upper part of the house. The high cold empty gloomy rooms liberated me and I went from room to room singing. From the front window I saw my companions playing below in the street. Their cries reached me weakened and indistinct and, leaning my forehead against the cool glass, I looked over at the dark house where she lived. I may have stood there for an hour, seeing nothing but the brown-clad figure cast by my imagination, touched discreetly by the lamplight at the curved neck, at the hand upon the railing and at the border below the dress.

When I came downstairs again I found Mrs. Mercer sitting at the fire. She was an old garrulous woman, a pawnbroker's widow, who collected used stamps for some pious purpose. I had to endure the gossip of the tea-table. The meal was prolonged beyond an hour and still my uncle did not come. Mrs. Mercer stood up to go: she was sorry she couldn't wait any longer, but it was after eight o'clock and she did not like to be out late, as the night air was bad for her. When she had gone I began to walk up and down the room, clenching my fists. My aunt said:

—I'm afraid you may put off your bazaar for this night of Our Lord.

At nine o'clock I heard my uncle's latchkey in the halldoor. I heard him talking to himself and heard the hall-stand rocking when it had received the weight of his overcoat. I could interpret these signs. When he was midway through his dinner I asked him to give me the money to go to the bazaar. He had forgotten.

—The people are in bed and after their first sleep now, he said.   20

I did not smile. My aunt said to him energetically:

—Can't you give him the money and let him go? You've kept him late enough as it is.

My uncle said he was very sorry he had forgotten. He said he believed in the old saying: *All work and no play makes Jack a dull boy.* He asked me where I was going and,

Freemason: and therefore Protestant.

when I had told him a second time he asked me did I know *The Arab's Farewell to his Steed.*°
When I left the kitchen he was about to recite the opening lines of the piece to my aunt.

   I held a florin° tightly in my hand as I strode down Buckingham Street towards
the station. The sight of the streets thronged with buyers and glaring with gas recalled to
me the purpose of my journey. I took my seat in a third-class carriage of a deserted train.
After an intolerable delay the train moved out of the station slowly. It crept onward
among ruinous houses and over the twinkling river. At Westland Row Station a crowd of
people pressed to the carriage doors; but the porters moved them back, saying that it
was a special train for the bazaar. I remained alone in the bare carriage. In a few minutes
the train drew up beside an improvised wooden platform. I passed out on to the road
and saw by the lighted dial of a clock that it was ten minutes to ten. In front of me was a
large building which displayed the magical name.

   I could not find any sixpenny entrance and, fearing that the bazaar would be   25
closed, I passed in quickly through a turnstile, handing a shilling to a weary-looking
man. I found myself in a big hall girdled at half its height by a gallery. Nearly all the
stalls were closed and the greater part of the hall was in darkness. I recognized a silence
like that which pervades a church after a service. I walked into the centre of the bazaar
timidly. A few people were gathered about the stalls which were still open. Before a curtain, over which the words *Café Chantant* were written in coloured lamps, two men were
counting money on a salver. I listened to the fall of the coins.

   Remembering with difficulty why I had come I went over to one of the stalls and
examined porcelain vases and flowered tea-sets. At the door of the stall a young lady was
talking and laughing with two young gentlemen. I remarked their English accents and
listened vaguely to their conversation.

   —O, I never said such a thing!

   —O, but you did!

   —O, but I didn't!

   —Didn't she say that?   30

   —Yes I heard her.

   —O, there's a . . . fib!

   Observing me the young lady came over and asked me did I wish to buy anything.
The tone in her voice was not encouraging; she seemed to have spoken to me out of a
sense of duty. I looked humbly at the great jars that stood like eastern guards at either
side of the dark entrance to the stall and murmured:

   —No, thank you.

   The young lady changed the position of one of the vases and went back to the   35
two young men. They began to talk of the same subject. Once or twice the young lady
glanced at me over her shoulder.

   I lingered before her stall, though I knew my stay was useless, to make my interest
in her wares seem the more real. Then I turned away slowly and walked down the middle
of the bazaar. I allowed the two pennies to fall against the sixpence in my pocket. I heard
a voice call from one end of the gallery that the light was out. The upper part of the
hall was now completely dark.

   Gazing up into the darkness I saw myself as a creature driven and derided by
vanity; and my eyes burned with anguish and anger.

The Arab's Farewell to his Steed: poem by Caroline Norton (1808–1877).
   florin: a two-shilling coin in the 1890s (when the story takes place), worth perhaps ten dollars in today's money.

QUESTIONS

1. Describe what you consider to be the story's major idea.
2. How might the bazaar, "Araby," be considered symbolically in the story? To what extent does this symbol embody the story's central idea?
3. Consider the attitude of the speaker toward his home as indicated in the first paragraph. Why do you think the speaker uses the word *blind* to describe the dead-end street? What relationship exists between the speaker's pain at the end of the story to the ideas in the first paragraph?
4. Who is the narrator? About how old is he at the time of the story? About how old when he tells the story? What effect is produced by this difference in age between narrator-as-character and narrator-as-storyteller?

D. H. LAWRENCE   (1885–1930)

Lawrence was born in an English mining community, but he received a sufficient education to enable him to become a teacher and writer. He fictionalized the early years of his life in the novel Sons and Lovers *(1913). His most controversial work,* Lady Chatterley's Lover, *was printed privately in Italy in 1928, but was not published in an uncut version in the United States until the 1960s. He shocked his contemporaries with his emphasis on the importance of sexuality, an idea that is central to "The Horse Dealer's Daughter." He was afflicted with tuberculosis and lived in a number of warm, sunny places, including Italy, New Zealand, and New Mexico, in an attempt to restore his health. Nevertheless, his illness claimed him in 1930, when he was only forty-five years old.*

The Horse Dealer's Daughter _____ 1922

"Well, Mabel, and what are you going to do with yourself?" asked Joe, with foolish flippancy. He felt quite safe himself. Without listening for an answer, he turned aside, worked a grain of tobacco to the tip of his tongue, and spat it out. He did not care about anything, since he felt safe himself.

The three brothers and the sister sat round the desolate breakfast table, attempting some sort of desultory consultation. The morning's post had given the final tap to the family fortunes, and all was over. The dreary dining-room itself, with its heavy mahogany furniture, looked as if it were waiting to be done away with.

But the consultation amounted to nothing. There was a strange air of ineffectuality about the three men, as they sprawled at table, smoking and reflecting vaguely on their own condition. The girl was alone, a rather short, sullen-looking young woman of twenty-seven. She did not share the same life as her brothers. She would have been good-looking, save for the impassive fixity of her face, "bulldog," as her brothers called it.

There was a confused tramping of horses' feet outside. The three men all sprawled round in their chairs to watch. Beyond the dark holly-bushes that separated the strip of lawn from the high-road, they could see a cavalcade of shire horses swinging out of their own yard, being taken for exercise. This was the last time. These were the last horses that would go through their hands. The young men watched with critical, callous look. They were all frightened at the collapse of their lives, and the sense of disaster in which they were involved left them no inner freedom.

Yet they were three fine, well-set fellows enough. Joe, the eldest, was a man of   5 thirty-three, broad and handsome in a hot, flushed way. His face was red, he twisted his black moustache over a thick finger, his eyes were shallow and restless. He had a sensual way of uncovering his teeth when he laughed, and his bearing was stupid. Now he watched the horses with a glazed look of helplessness in his eyes, a certain stupor of downfall.

The great draught-horses swung past. They were tied head to tail, four of them, and they heaved along to where a lane branched off from the highroad, planting their great hoofs floutingly in the fine black mud, swinging their great rounded haunches sumptuously, and trotting a few sudden steps as they were led into the lane, round the corner. Every movement showed a massive, slumbrous strength, and a stupidity which held them in subjection. The groom at the head looked back, jerking the leading rope. And the cavalcade moved out of sight up the lane, the tail of the last horse, bobbed up tight and stiff, held out taut from the swinging great haunches as they rocked behind the hedges in a motionlike sleep.

Joe watched with glazed hopeless eyes. The horses were almost like his own body to him. He felt he was done for now. Luckily, he was engaged to a woman as old as himself, and therefore her father, who was steward of a neighbouring estate, would provide him with a job. He would marry and go into harness. His life was over, he would be a subject animal now.

He turned uneasily aside, the retreating steps of the horses echoing in his ears. Then, with foolish restlessness, he reached for the scraps of bacon-rind from the plates, and making a faint whistling sound, flung them to the terrier that lay against the fender. He watched the dog swallow them, and waited till the creature looked into his eyes. Then a faint grin came on his face, and in a high, foolish voice he said:

"You won't get much more bacon, shall you, you little b———?"

The dog faintly and dismally wagged its tail, then lowered its haunches, circled   10 round, and lay down again.

There was another helpless silence at the table. Joe sprawled uneasily in his seat, not willing to go till the family conclave was dissolved. Fred Henry, the second brother, was erect, clean-limbed, alert. He had watched the passing of the horses with more *sang-froid*.° If he was an animal, like Joe, he was an animal which controls, not one which is controlled. He was master of any horse, and he carried himself with a well-tempered air of mastery. But he was not master of the situations of life. He pushed his coarse brown moustache upwards, off his lip, and glanced irritably at his sister, who sat impassive and inscrutable.

"You'll go and stop with Lucy for a bit, shan't you?" he asked. The girl did not answer.

"I don't see what else you can do," persisted Fred Henry.

"Go as a skivvy,"° Joe interpolated laconically.

The girl did not move a muscle.   15

sang-froid: unconcern (literally, cold blood).
skivvy: British slang for housemaid.

"If I was her, I should go in for training for a nurse," said Malcolm, the youngest of them all. He was the baby of the family, a young man of twenty-two, with a fresh, jaunty *museau.*°

But Mabel did not take any notice of him. They had talked at her and round her for so many years, that she hardly heard them at all.

The marble clock on the mantel-piece softly chimed the half-hour, the dog rose uneasily from the hearthrug and looked at the party at the breakfast table. But still they sat on in ineffectual conclave.

"Oh, all right," said Joe suddenly, *à propos* of nothing. "I'll get a move on."

He pushed back his chair, straddled his knees with a downward jerk, to get them   20
free, in horsey fashion, and went to the fire. Still he did not go out of the room; he was curious to know what the others would do or say. He began to charge his pipe, looking down at the dog and saying, in a high, affected voice:

"Going wi' me? Going wi' me are ter? Tha'rt goin' further than tha counts on just now, dost hear?"

The dog faintly wagged its tail, the man stuck out his jaw and covered his pipe with his hands, and puffed intently, losing himself in the tobacco, looking down all the while at the dog, with an absent brown eye. The dog looked up at him in mournful distrust. Joe stood with his knees stuck out, in real horsey fashion.

"Have you had a letter from Lucy?" Fred Henry asked of his sister.

"Last week," came the neutral reply.

"And what does she say?"   25

There was no answer.

"Does she *ask* you to go and stop there?" persisted Fred Henry.

"She says I can if I like."

"Well, then, you'd better. Tell her you'll come on Monday."

This was received in silence.   30

"That's what you'll do then, is it?" said Fred Henry, in some exasperation.

But she made no answer. There was a silence of futility and irritation in the room. Malcolm grinned fatuously.

"You'll have to make up your mind between now and next Wednesday," said Joe loudly, "or else find yourself lodgings on the kerbstone."

The face of the young woman darkened, but she sat on immutable.

"Here's Jack Fergusson!" exclaimed Malcolm, who was looking aimlessly out of   35
the window.

"Where?" exclaimed Joe, loudly.

"Just gone past."

"Coming in?"

Malcolm craned his neck to see the gate.

"Yes," he said.   40

There was a silence. Mabel sat on like one condemned, at the head of the table. Then a whistle was heard from the kitchen. The dog got up and barked sharply. Joe opened the door and shouted:

"Come on."

After a moment, a young man entered. He was muffled up in overcoat and a purple woolen scarf, and his tweed cap, which he did not remove, was pulled down on his head. He was of medium height, his face was rather long and pale, his eyes looked tired.

museau: French for nose, snout.

"Hello, Jack! Well, Jack!" exclaimed Malcolm and Joe. Fred Henry merely said "Jack!"

"What's doing?" asked the newcomer, evidently addressing Fred Henry.   45

"Same. We've got to be out by Wednesday—Got a cold?"

"I have—got it bad, too."

"Why don't you stop in?"

"*Me* stop in? When I can't stand on my legs, perhaps I shall have a chance." The young man spoke huskily. He had a slight Scotch accent.

"It's a knock-out, isn't it," said Joe boisterously, "if a doctor goes round croaking   50
with a cold. Looks bad for the patients, doesn't it?"

The young doctor looked at him slowly.

"Anything the matter with *you*, then?" he asked, sarcastically.

"Not as I know of. Damn your eyes, I hope not. Why?"

"I thought you were very concerned about the patients, wondered if you might be one yourself."

"Damn it, no, I've never been patient to no flaming doctor, and hope I never shall   55
be," returned Joe.

At this point Mabel rose from the table, and they all seemed to become aware of her existence. She began putting the dishes together. The young doctor looked at her, but did not address her. He had not greeted her. She went out of the room with the tray, her face impassive and unchanged.

"When are you off then, all of you?" asked the doctor.

"I'm catching the eleven-forty," replied Malcolm. "Are you goin' down wi' th' trap,° Joe?"

"Yes, I've told you I'm going down wi' th' trap, haven't I?"

"We'd better be getting her in then.—So long, Jack, if I don't see you before I   60
go," said Malcolm, shaking hands.

He went out, followed by Joe, who seemed to have his tail between his legs.

"Well, this is the devil's own," exclaimed the doctor, when he was left alone with Fred Henry. "Going before Wednesday, are you?"

"That's the orders," replied the other.

"Where, to Northampton?"

"That's it."   65

"The devil!" exclaimed Fergusson, with quiet chagrin.

And there was silence between the two.

"All settled up, are you?" asked Fergusson.

"About."

There was another pause.   70

"Well, I shall miss yer, Freddy boy," said the young doctor.

"And I shall miss thee, Jack," returned the other.

"Miss you like hell," mused the doctor.

Fred Henry turned aside. There was nothing to say. Mabel came in again, to finish clearing the table.

"What are *you* going to do then, Miss Pervin?" asked Fergusson. "Going to your   75
sister's, are you?"

Mabel looked at him with her steady, dangerous eyes, that always made him uncomfortable, unsettling his superficial ease.

trap: small wagon.

"No," she said.

"Well, what in the name of fortune *are* you going to do? Say what you *mean* to do," cried Fred Henry, with futile intensity.

But she only averted her head, and continued her work. She folded the white table-cloth, and put on the chenille cloth.

"The sulkiest bitch that ever trod!" muttered her brother.   80

But she finished her task with perfectly impassive face, the young doctor watching her interestedly all the while. Then she went out.

Fred Henry stared after her, clenching his lips, his blue eyes fixing in sharp antagonism, as he made a grimace of sour exasperation.

"You could bray her into bits, and that's all you'd get out of her," he said, in a small, narrowed tone.

The doctor smiled faintly.

"What's she *going* to do then?" he asked.   85

"Strike me if *I* know!" returned the other.

There was a pause. Then the doctor stirred.

"I'll be seeing you to-night, shall I?" he said to his friend.

"Ay—where's it to be? Are we going over to Jessdale?"

"I don't know. I've got such a cold on me. I'll come round to the Moon and Stars,   90
anyway."

"Let Lizzie and May miss their night for once, eh?"

"That's it—if I feel as I do now."

"All's one—"

The two young men went through the passage and down to the back door together. The house was large, but it was servantless now, and desolate. At the back was a small bricked house-yard, and beyond that a big square, gravelled fine and red, and having stables on two sides. Sloping, dank, winter-dark fields stretched away on the open sides.

But the stables were empty. Joseph Pervin, the father of the family, had been a   95
man of no education, who had become a fairly large horse dealer. The stables had been full of horses, there was a great turmoil and come-and-go of horses and of dealers and grooms. Then the kitchen was full of servants. But of late things had declined. The old man had married a second time, to retrieve his fortunes. Now he was dead and everything was gone to the dogs, there was nothing but debt and threatening.

For months, Mabel had been servantless in the big house, keeping the home together in penury for her ineffectual brothers. She had kept house for ten years. But previously, it was with unstinted means. Then, however brutal and coarse everything was, the sense of money had kept her proud, confident. The men might be foul-mouthed, the women in the kitchen might have bad reputations, her brothers might have illegitimate children. But so long as there was money, the girl felt herself established, and brutally proud, reserved.

No company came to the house, save dealers and coarse men. Mabel had no associates of her own sex, after her sister went away. But she did not mind. She went regularly to church, she attended to her father. And she lived in the memory of her mother, who had died when she was fourteen, and whom she had loved. She had loved her father, too, in a different way, depending upon him, and feeling secure in him, until at the age of fifty-four he married again. And then she had set hard against him. Now he had died and left them all hopelessly in debt.

She had suffered badly during the period of poverty. Nothing, however, could shake the curious sullen, animal pride that dominated each member of the family. Now, for Mabel, the end had come. Still she would not cast about her. She would follow her own way just the same. She would always hold the keys of her own situation. Mindless and persistent, she endured from day to day. Why should she think? Why should she answer anybody? It was enough that this was the end, and there was no way out. She need not pass any more darkly along the main street of the small town, avoiding every eye. She need not demean herself any more, going into the shops and buying the cheapest food. This was at an end. She thought of nobody, not even of herself. Mindless and persistent, she seemed in a sort of ecstasy to be coming nearer to her fulfilment, her own glorification, approaching her dead mother, who was glorified.°

In the afternoon she took a little bag, with shears and sponge and a small scrubbing brush, and went out. It was a grey, wintry day, with saddened, dark-green fields and an atmosphere blackened by the smoke of foundries not far off. She went quickly, darkly along the causeway, heeding nobody, through the town to the churchyard.

There she always felt secure, as if no one could see her, although as a matter of   100
fact she was exposed to the stare of everyone who passed along under the churchyard wall. Nevertheless, once under the shadow of the great looming church, among the graves, she felt immune from the world, reserved within the thick churchyard wall as in another country.

Carefully she clipped the grass from the grave, and arranged the pinky-white, small chrysanthemums in the tin cross. When this was done, she took an empty jar from a neighbouring grave, brought water, and carefully, most scrupulously sponged the marble headstone and the coping-stone.

It gave her sincere satisfaction to do this. She felt in immediate contact with the world of her mother. She took minute pains, went through the park in a state bordering on pure happiness, as if in performing this task she came into a subtle, intimate connection with her mother. For the life she followed here in the world was far less real than the world of death she inherited from her mother.

The doctor's house was just by the church. Fergusson, being a mere hired assistant, was slave to the countryside. As he hurried now to attend to the outpatients in the surgery, glancing across the graveyard with his quick eye, he saw the girl at her task at the grave. She seemed so intent and remote, it was like looking into another world. Some mystical element was touched in him. He slowed down as he walked, watching her as if spell-bound.

She lifted her eyes, feeling him looking. Their eyes met. And each looked again at once, each feeling, in some way, found out by the other. He lifted his cap and passed on down the road. There remained distinct in his consciousness, like a vision, the memory of her face, lifted from the tombstone in the churchyard, and looking at him with slow, large, portentous eyes. It *was* portentous, her face. It seemed to mesmerise him. There was a heavy power in her eyes which laid hold of his whole being, as if he had drunk some powerful drug. He had been feeling weak and done before. Now the life came back into him, he felt delivered from his own fretted, daily self.

He finished his duties at the surgery as quickly as might be, hastily filling up the   105
bottles of the waiting people with cheap drugs. Then, in perpetual haste, he set off again to visit several cases in another part of his round, before teatime. At all times he preferred to walk, if he could, but particularly when he was not well. He fancied the motion restored him.

who was glorified: See Romans 8:17, 30.

The afternoon was falling. It was grey, deadened, and wintry, with a slow, moist, heavy coldness sinking in and deadening all the faculties. But why should he think or notice? He hastily climbed the hill and turned across the dark-green fields, following the black cinder-track. In the distance, across a shallow dip in the country, the small town was clustered like smouldering ash, a tower, a spire, a heap of low, raw, extinct houses. And on the nearest fringe of the town, sloping into the dip, was Oldmeadow, the Pervins' house. He could see the stables and the outbuildings distinctly, as they lay towards him on the slope. Well, he would not go there many more times! Another resource would be lost to him, another place gone: the only company he cared for in the alien, ugly little town he was losing. Nothing but work, drudgery, constant hastening from dwelling to dwelling among the colliers and the iron-workers. It wore him out, but at the same time he had a craving for it. It was a stimulant to him to be in the homes of the working people, moving as it were through the innermost body of their life. His nerves were excited and gratified. He could come so near, into the very lives of the rough, inarticulate, powerfully emotional men and women. He grumbled, he said he hated the hellish hole. But as a matter of fact it excited him, the contact with the rough, strongly-feeling people was a stimulant applied direct to his nerves.

Below Oldmeadow, in the green, shallow, soddened hollow of fields, lay a square, deep pond. Roving across the landscape, the doctor's quick eye detected a figure in black passing through the gate of the field, down towards the pond. He looked again. It would be Mabel Pervin. His mind suddenly became alive and attentive.

Why was she going down there? He pulled up on the path on the slope above, and stood staring. He could just make sure of the small black figure moving in the hollow of the failing day. He seemed to see her in the midst of such obscurity, that he was like a clairvoyant, seeing rather with the mind's eye than with ordinary sight. Yet he could see her positively enough, whilst he kept his eye attentive. He felt, if he looked away from her, in the thick, ugly falling dusk, he would lose her altogether.

He followed her minutely as she moved, direct and intent, like something transmitted rather than stirring in voluntary activity, straight down the field towards the pond. There she stood on the bank for a moment. She never raised her head. Then she waded slowly into the water.

He stood motionless as the small black figure walked slowly and deliberately   110 towards the centre of the pond, very slowly, gradually moving deeper into the motionless water, and still moving forward as the water got up to her breast. Then he could see her no more in the dusk of the dead afternoon.

"There!" he exclaimed. "Would you believe it?"

And he hastened straight down, running over the wet, soddened fields, pushing through the hedges, down into the depression of callous wintry obscurity. It took him several minutes to come to the pond. He stood on the bank, breathing heavily. He could see nothing. His eyes seemed to penetrate the dead water. Yes, perhaps that was the dark shadow of her black clothing beneath the surface of the water.

He slowly ventured into the pond. The bottom was deep, soft clay, he sank in, and the water clasped dead cold round his legs. As he stirred he could smell the cold, rotten clay that fouled up into the water. It was objectionable in his lungs. Still, repelled and yet not heeding, he moved deeper into the pond. The cold water rose over his thighs, over his loins, upon his abdomen. The lower part of his body was all sunk in the hideous cold element. And the bottom was so deeply soft and uncertain, he was afraid of pitching with his mouth underneath. He could not swim, and was afraid.

He crouched a little, spreading his hands under the water and moving them round, trying to feel for her. The dead cold pond swayed upon his chest. He moved again, a little deeper, and again, with his hands underneath, he felt all around under the water. And he touched her clothing. But it evaded his fingers. He made a desperate effort to grasp it.

And so doing he lost his balance and went under, horribly, suffocating in the foul earthy water, struggling madly for a few moments. At last, after what seemed an eternity, he got his footing, rose again into the air and looked around. He gasped, and knew he was in the world. Then he looked at the water. She had risen near him. He grasped her clothing, and drawing her nearer, turned to take his way to land again.

115

He went very slowly, carefully, absorbed in the slow progress. He rose higher, climbing out of the pond. The water was not only about his legs; he was thankful, full of relief to be out of the clutches of the pond. He lifted her and staggered on to the bank, out of the horror of wet, grey clay.

He laid her down on the bank. She was quite unconscious and running with water. He made the water come from her mouth, he worked to restore her. He did not have to work very long before he could feel the breathing begin again in her; she was breathing naturally. He worked a little longer. He could feel her live beneath his hands; she was coming back. He wiped her face, wrapped her in his overcoat, looked round into the dim, dark-grey world, then lifted her and staggered down the bank and across the fields.

It seemed an unthinkably long way, and his burden so heavy he felt he would never get to the house. But at last he was in the stable-yard, and then in the house-yard. He opened the door and went into the house. In the kitchen he laid her down on the hearthrug, and called. The house was empty. But the fire was burning in the grate.

Then again he kneeled to attend to her. She was breathing regularly, her eyes were wide open as if conscious, but there seemed something missing in her look. She was conscious in herself, but unconscious of her surroundings.

He ran upstairs, took blankets from a bed, and put them before the fire to warm. Then he removed her saturated, earthy-smelling clothing, rubbed her dry with a towel, and wrapped her naked in the blankets. Then he went into the dining-room, to look for spirits. There was a little whiskey. He drank a gulp himself, and put some into her mouth.

120

The effect was instantaneous. She looked full into his face, as if she had been seeing him for some time, and yet had only just become conscious of him.

"Dr. Fergusson?" she said.

"What?" he answered.

He was divesting himself of his coat, intending to find some dry clothing upstairs. He could not bear the smell of the dead, clayey water, and he was mortally afraid for his own health.

"What did I do?" she asked.

125

"Walked into the pond," he replied. He had begun to shudder like one sick, and could hardly attend to her. Her eyes remained full on him, he seemed to be going dark in his mind, looking back at her helplessly. The shuddering became quieter in him, his life came back in him, dark and unknowing, but strong again.

"Was I out of my mind?" she asked, while her eyes were fixed on him all the time.

"Maybe, for the moment," he replied. He felt quiet, because his strength had come back. The strange fretful strain had left him.

"Am I out of my mind now?" she asked.

"Are you?" he reflected a moment. "No," he answered truthfully, "I don't see that   130
you are." He turned his face aside. He was afraid, now, because he felt dazed, and felt
dimly that her power was stronger than his, in this issue. And she continued to look at
him fixedly all the time. "Can you tell me where I shall find some dry things to put on?"
he asked.

"Did you dive into the pond for me?" she asked.

"No," he answered. "I walked in. But I went in overhead as well."

There was silence for a moment. He hesitated. He very much wanted to go upstairs
to get into dry clothing. But there was another desire in him. And she seemed to hold
him. His will seemed to have gone to sleep, and left him, standing there slack before her.
But he felt warm inside himself. He did not shudder at all, though his clothes were
sodden on him.

"Why did you?" she asked.

"Because I didn't want you to do such a foolish thing," he said.   135

"It wasn't foolish," she said, still gazing at him as she lay on the floor, with a sofa
cushion under her head. "It was the right thing to do. *I* knew best, then."

"I'll go and shift these wet things," he said. But still he had not the power to move
out of her presence, until she sent him. It was as if she had the life of his body in her
hands, and he could not extricate himself. Or perhaps he did not want to.

Suddenly she sat up. Then she became aware of her own immediate condition.
She felt the blankets about her, she knew her own limbs. For a moment it seemed as if
her reason were going. She looked round, with wild eye, as if seeking something. He
stood still with fear. She saw her clothing lying scattered.

"Who undressed me?" she asked, her eyes resting full and inevitable on his face.

"I did," he replied, "to bring you round."   140

For some moments she sat and gazed at him awfully, her lips parted.

"Do you love me then?" she asked.

He only stood and stared at her, fascinated. His soul seemed to melt.

She shuffled forward on her knees, and put her arms round him, round his legs,
as he stood there, pressing her breasts against his knees and thighs, clutching him with
strange, convulsive certainty, pressing his thighs against her, drawing him to her face,
her throat, as she looked up at him with flaring, humble eyes of transfiguration, triumphant in first possession.

"You love me," she murmured, in strange transport, yearning and triumphant and   145
confident. "You love me. I know you love me, I know."

And she was passionately kissing his knees, through the wet clothing, passionately
and indiscriminately kissing his knees, his legs, as if unaware of everything.

He looked down at the tangled wet hair, the wild, bare, animal shoulders. He was
amazed, bewildered, and afraid. He had never thought of loving her. He had never
wanted to love her. When he rescued her and restored her, he was a doctor, and she was
a patient. He had had no single personal thought of her. Nay, this introduction of the
personal element was very distasteful to him, a violation of his professional honour. It
was horrible to have her there embracing his knees. It was horrible. He revolted from it,
violently. And yet—and yet—he had not the power to break away.

She looked at him again, with the same supplication of powerful love, and that
same transcendent, frightening light of triumph. In view of the delicate flame which
seemed to come from her face like a light, he was powerless. And yet he had never
intended to love her. He had never intended. And something stubborn in him could
not give way.

"You love me," she repeated, in a murmur of deep, rhapsodic assurance. "You love me."

Her hands were drawing him, drawing him down to her. He was afraid, even a   150
little horrified. For he had, really, no intention of loving her. Yet her hands were drawing him towards her. He put out his hand quickly to steady himself, and grasped her bare shoulder. A flame seemed to burn the hand that grasped her soft shoulder. He had no intention of loving her: his whole will was against his yielding. It was horrible—And yet wonderful was the touch of her shoulder, beautiful the shining of her face. Was she perhaps mad? He had a horror of yielding to her. Yet something in him ached also.

He had been staring away at the door, away from her. But his hand remained on her shoulder. She had gone suddenly very still. He looked down at her. Her eyes were now wide with fear, with doubt, the light was dying from her face, a shadow of terrible greyness was returning. He could not bear the touch of her eyes' question upon him, and the look of death behind the question.

With an inward groan he gave way, and let his heart yield towards her. A sudden gentle smile came on his face. And her eyes, which never left his face, slowly, slowly filled with tears. He watched the strange water rise in her eyes, like some slow fountain coming up. And his heart seemed to burn and melt away in his breast.

He could not bear to look at her any more. He dropped on his knees and caught her head with his arms and pressed her face against his throat. She was very still. His heart, which seemed to have broken, was burning with a kind of agony in his breast. And he felt her slow, hot tears wetting his throat. But he could not move.

He felt the hot tears wet his neck and the hollows of his neck, and he remained motionless, suspended through one of man's eternities. Only now it had become indispensable to him to have her face pressed close to him; he could never let her go again. He could never let her head go away from the close clutch of his arm. He wanted to remain like that for ever, with his heart hurting him in a pain that was also life to him. Without knowing, he was looking down on her damp, soft brown hair.

Then, as it were suddenly, he smelt the horrid stagnant smell of the water. And at   155
the same moment she drew away from him and looked at him. Her eyes were wistful and unfathomable. He was afraid of them, and he fell to kissing her, not knowing what he was doing. He wanted her eyes not to have that terrible, wistful, unfathomable look.

When she turned her face to him again, a faint delicate flush was glowing, and there was again dawning that terrible shining of joy in her eyes, which really terrified him, and yet which he now wanted to see, because he feared the look of doubt still more.

"You love me?" she said, rather faltering.

"Yes." The word cost him a painful effort. Not because it wasn't true. But because it was too newly true, the *saying* seemed to tear open again his newly-torn heart. And he hardly wanted it to be true, even now.

She lifted her face to him, and he bent forward and kissed her on the mouth gently, with the one kiss that is an eternal pledge. And as he kissed her his heart strained again in his breast. He never intended to love her. But now it was over. He had crossed over the gulf to her, and all that he had left behind had shrivelled and become void.

After the kiss, her eyes again slowly filled with tears. She sat still, away from him,   160
with her face drooped aside, and her hands folded in her lap. The tears fell very slowly. There was complete silence. He too sat there motionless and silent on the hearthrug. The strange pain of his heart that was broken seemed to consume him. That he should love her? That this was love! That he should be ripped open in this way!—Him, a

doctor!—How they would all jeer if they knew!—It was agony to him to think they might know.

In the curious naked pain of the thought he looked again to her. She was sitting there drooped into a muse. He saw a tear fall, and his heart flared hot. He saw for the first time that one of her shoulders was quite uncovered, one arm bare, he could see one of her small breasts; dimly, because it had become almost dark in the room.

"Why are you crying?" he asked, in an altered voice.

She looked up at him, and behind her tears the consciousness of her situation for the first time brought a dark look of shame to her eyes.

"I'm not crying, really," she said, watching him half frightened.

He reached his hand, and softly closed it on her bare arm.   165

"I love you! I love you!" he said in a soft, low vibrating voice, unlike himself.

She shrank, and dropped her head. The soft, penetrating grip of his hand on her arm distressed her. She looked up at him.

"I want to go," she said. "I want to go and get you some dry things."

"Why?" he said. "I'm all right."

"But I want to go," she said. "And I want you to change your things."   170

He released her arm, and she wrapped herself in the blanket, looking at him rather frightened. And still she did not rise.

"Kiss me," she said wistfully.

He kissed her, but briefly, half in anger.

Then, after a second, she rose nervously, all mixed up in the blanket. He watched her in her confusion, as she tried to extricate herself and wrap herself up so that she could walk. He watched her relentlessly, as she knew.

And as she went, the blanket trailing, and as he saw a glimpse of her feet and her   175
white leg, he tried to remember her as she was when he had wrapped her in the blanket. But then he didn't want to remember, because she had been nothing to him then, and his nature revolted from remembering her as she was when she was nothing to him.

A tumbling muffled noise from within the dark house startled him. Then he heard her voice:—"There are clothes." He rose and went to the foot of the stairs, and gathered up the garments she had thrown down. Then he came back to the fire, to rub himself down and dress. He grinned at his own appearance, when he had finished.

The fire was sinking, so he put on coal. The house was now quite dark, save for the light of a street-lamp that shone in faintly from beyond the holly trees. He lit the gas with matches he found on the mantel-piece. Then he emptied the pockets of his own clothes, and threw all his wet things in a heap into the scullery. After which he gathered up her sodden clothes, gently, and put them in a separate heap on the copper-top in the scullery.

It was six o'clock on the clock. His own watch had stopped. He ought to be back to the surgery. He waited, and still she did not come down. So he went to the foot of the stairs and called:

"I shall have to go."

Almost immediately he heard her coming down. She had on her best dress of   180
black voile, and her hair was tidy, but still damp. She looked at him—and in spite of herself, smiled.

"I don't like you in those clothes," she said.

"Do I look a sight?" he answered.

They were shy of one another.

"I'll make you some tea," she said.

"No, I must go."   185

"Must you?" And she looked at him again with the wide, strained, doubtful eyes. And again, from the pain of his breast, he knew how he loved her. He went and bent to kiss her, gently, passionately, with his heart's painful kiss.

"And my hair smells so horrible," she murmured in distraction. "And I'm so awful, I'm so awful! Oh, no, I'm too awful." And she broke into bitter, heartbroken sobbing. "You can't want to love me, I'm horrible."

"Don't be silly, don't be silly," he said, trying to comfort her, kissing her, holding her in his arms. "I want you, I want to marry you, we're going to be married, quickly, quickly—to-morrow if I can."

But she only sobbed terribly, and cried.

"I feel awful. I feel awful. I feel I'm horrible to you."   190

"No, I want you, I want you," was all he answered blindly, with that terrible intonation which frightened her almost more than her horror lest he should *not* want her.

QUESTIONS

1. What idea is Lawrence illustrating by the breakup of the Pervin household?

2. What does the comparison of Joe Pervin and the draft horses mean with regard specifically to Joe, and generally to people without love?

3. What kind of person is Mabel? How do her brothers treat her? How does she feel about her brothers? What dilemma does she face as the story begins?

4. What effect does Mabel have on Fergusson as he watches her in her home, in the churchyard, and at the pond? What does this effect contribute to Lawrence's ideas about love?

5. What do Mabel and Fergusson realize as he revives and warms her? How do their responses signify their growth as characters?

6. Why does the narrator tell us at the story's end that Fergusson "had no intention of loving" Mabel? What idea does this repeated assertion convey?

7. In this story, there is an extensive exploration of the ambiguous feelings of both Fergusson and Mabel after they realize their love. Why does Lawrence explore these feelings so extensively?

IRENE ZABYTKO   (b. 1954)

Zabytko was born in Chicago's Ukrainian neighborhood and did her undergraduate and graduate study at Vermont College. A proficient speaker of Ukrainian, she has lived in Ukraine and taught English language courses there. She is a past winner of the PEN Syndicated Fiction Project and has held fellowships at the Helene Wurlitzer Foundation, the Hambidge Center, and the Virginia Center for the Creative Arts and Sciences. She is the founder/publisher of OdessaPressa Productions. Her fiction has appeared in Catholic Girls *(1992) and* Earth Tones *(1994). Recently she published* Don't Call Me Fluffy: Radical Feline Poetry, *poems "written" by her cat. She has also been heard on "The Sound of Writing" program of National Public Radio. Currently she is completing a novel based on the Chernobyl nuclear accident.*

Home Soil _____ *1992*

I watch my son crack his knuckles, oblivious to the somber sounds of the Old Slavonic hymns the choir behind us is singing.

We are in the church where Bohdan, my son, was baptized nineteen years ago. It is Sunday. The pungent smell of frankincense permeates the darkened atmosphere of this cathedral. Soft sun rays illuminate the stained-glass windows. I sit near the one that shows Jesus on the cross looking down on some unidentifiable Apostles who are kneeling beneath His nailed feet. In the background, a tiny desperate Judas swings from a rope, the thirty pieces of silver thrown on the ground.

There is plenty of room in my pew, but my son chooses not to sit with me. I see him staring at the round carapace of a ceiling, stoic icons staring directly back at him. For the remainder of the Mass, he lightly drums his nervous fingers on top of the cover of *My Divine Friend,* the Americanized prayer book of the Ukrainian service. He took bongo lessons before he graduated high school, and learned the basic rolls from off a record, "Let's Swing with Bongos." I think it was supposed to make him popular with the girls at parties. I also think he joined the army because he wanted the virile image men in uniforms have that the bongos never delivered. When he returned from Nam, he mentioned after one of our many conversational silences that he lost the bongos, and the record is cracked, with the pieces buried somewhere deep inside the duffel bag he still hasn't unpacked.

Bohdan, my son, who calls himself Bob, has been back for three weeks. He looks so "American" in his green tailored uniform: his spit-shined vinyl dress shoes tap against the red-cushioned kneelers. It was his idea to go to church with me. He has not been anywhere since he came home. He won't even visit my garden.

Luba, my daughter, warned me he would be moody. She works for the Voice of   5
America and saw him when he landed from Nam in San Francisco. "Just don't worry, *tato,*"° she said to me on the telephone. "He's acting weird. Culture shock."

"Explain what you mean."

"Just, you know, strange." For a disc jockey, and a bilingual one at that, she is so inarticulate. She plays American jazz and tapes concerts for broadcasts for her anonymous compatriots in Ukraine. That's what she was doing when she was in San Francisco, taping some jazz concert. Pure American music for the huddled gold-toothed youths who risk their *komsomol* privileges and maybe their lives listening to these clandestine broadcasts and to my daughter's sweet voice. She will never be able to visit our relatives back there because American security won't allow it, and she would lose her job. But it doesn't matter. After my wife died, I have not bothered to keep up with anyone there, and I don't care if they have forgotten all about me. It's just as well.

I noticed how much my son resembled my wife when I first saw him again at the airport. He was alone, near the baggage claim ramp. He was taller than ever, and his golden hair was bleached white from the jungle sun. He inherited his mother's high cheekbones, but he lost his baby fat, causing his cheeks to jut out from his lean face as sharp as the arrowheads he used to scavenge for when he was a kid.

We hugged briefly. I felt his medals pinch through my thin shirt. "You look good, son," I lied. I avoided his eyes and concentrated on a pin shaped like an open parachute that he wore over his heart.

tato: "Father" or "Dad."

"Hi, *tato*," he murmured. We spoke briefly about his flight home from San   10
Francisco, how he'd seen Luba. We stood apart, unlike the other soldiers with their families who were hugging and crying on each other's shoulders in a euphoric delirium.

He grabbed his duffle bag from the revolving ramp and I walked behind him to
see if he limped or showed any signs of pain. He showed nothing.

"Want to drive?" I asked, handing him the keys to my new Plymouth.

"Nah," he said. He looked around at the cars crowding the parking lot, and I
thought he seemed afraid. "I don't remember how the streets go anymore."

An usher in his best borscht-red polyester suit waits for me to drop some money
into the basket. It is old Pan° Medved, toothless except for the prominent gold ones he
flashes at me as he pokes me with his basket.

"*Nu*, give," he whispers hoarsely, but loud enough for a well-dressed woman with   15
lacquered hair who sits in front of me to turn around and stare in mute accusation.

I take out the gray and white snakeskin wallet Bohdan brought back for me, and
transfer out a ten dollar bill. I want the woman to see it before it disappears into the
basket. She smiles at me and nods.

Women always smile at me like that. Especially after they see my money and find
out that I own a restaurant in the neighborhood. None of the Ukies° go there; they
don't eat fries and burgers much. But the "jackees"—the Americans—do when they're
sick of eating in the cafeteria at the plastics factory. My English is pretty good for a D.P.,
and no one has threatened to bomb my business because they accuse me of being a no-
god bohunk commie. Not yet anyway.

But the women are always impressed. I usually end up with the emigrés—some of
them Ukrainians. The Polish women are the greediest for gawdy trinkets and for a man
to give them money so that they can return to their husbands and children in Warsaw. I
like them the best anyway because they laugh more than the other women I see, and
they know how to have a good time.

Bohdan knows nothing about my lecherous life. I told the women to stay clear
after my son arrived. He is so lost with women. I think he was a virgin when he joined the
army, but I'm sure he isn't now. I can't ask him.

After mass ends, I lose Bohdan in the tight clusters of people leaving their pews   20
and genuflecting toward the iconostasis. He waits for me by the holy water font. It looks
like a regular porcelain water fountain but without a spout. There is a sponge in the
basin that is moistened with the holy water blessed by the priests here. Bohdan stands
towering over the font, dabs his fingers into the sponge, but doesn't cross himself the
way he was taught to do as a boy.

"What's the matter?" I ask in English. I hope he will talk to me if I speak to him in
his language.

But Bohdan ignores me and watches an elderly woman gingerly entering the door
of the confessional. "What she got to say? Why is she going in there?"

"Everyone has sins."

"Yeah, but who forgives?"

"God forgives," I say. I regret it because it makes me feel like a hypocrite when-   25
ever I parrot words I still find difficult to believe.

Pan: a term of respect for adult males, the equivalent of *Mr.*
Ukies: Ukrainian Americans.

We walk together in the neighborhood; graffiti visible in the alley-ways despite the well-trimmed lawns with flowers and "bathtub" statues of the Blessed Mary smiling benevolently at us as we pass by the small bungalows. I could afford to move out of here, out of Chicago and into some nearby cushy suburb, Skokie or something. But what for? Some smart Jewish lawyer or doctor would be my next door neighbor and find out that I'm a Ukie and complain to me about how his grandmother was raped by Petliura.° I've heard it before. Anyway, I like where I am. I bought a three-flat apartment building after my wife died and I live in one of the apartments rent-free. I can walk to my business, and see the past—old women in babushkas sweeping the sidewalks in front of their cherished gardens; men in Italian-made venetian-slat sandals and woolen socks rushing to a chess match at the Soyuiez, a local meeting place where the D.P.s sit for hours rehashing the war over beers and chess.

Bohdan walks like a soldier. Not exactly a march, but a stiff gait that a good posture in a rigid uniform demands. He looks masculine, but tired and worn. Two pimples are sprouting above his lip where a faint moustache is starting.

"Want a cigarette?" I ask. Soldiers like to smoke. During the forties, I smoked that horrible cheap tobacco, *mahorka*. I watch my son puff heavily on the cigarette I've given him, with his eyes partially closed, delicately cupping his hands to protect it from the wind. In my life, I have seen so many soldiers in that exact pose; they all look the same. When their faces are contorted from sucking the cigarette, there is an unmistakable shadow of vulnerability and fear of living. That gesture and stance are more eloquent than the blood and guts war stories men spew over their beers.

Pan Medved, the battered gold-toothed relic in the church, has that look. Pan Holewski, one of my tenants, has it too. I would have known it even if he never openly displayed his old underground soldier's cap that sits on a bookshelf in the living room between small Ukrainian and American flags. I see it every time I collect the rent.

I wish Bohdan could tell me what happened to him in Vietnam. What did he do?   30
What was done to him? Maybe now isn't the time to tell me. He may never tell me. I never told anyone either.

I was exactly his age when I became a soldier. At nineteen, I was a student at the university in L'vov, which the Poles occupied. I was going to be a poet, to study poetry and write it, but the war broke out, and my family could not live on the romantic epics I tried to publish, so I was paid very well by the Nazis to write propaganda pamphlets. "Freedom for Ukrainians" I wrote—"Freedom for our people. Fight the Poles and Russians alongside our German brothers" and other such dreck. I even wrote light verse that glorified Hitler as the protector of the free Ukrainian nation that the Germans promised us. My writing was as naïve as my political ideas.

My new career began in a butcher shop, commandeered after the Polish owner was arrested and shot. I set my battered Underwood typewriter atop an oily wooden table where crescents of chicken feathers still clung between the cracks. Meat hooks that once held huge sides of pork hung naked in a back room, and creaked ominously like a deserted gallows whenever anyone slammed the front door. Every shred of meat had been stolen by looters after the Germans came into the city. Even the little bell that shopkeepers kept at the entrance was taken. But I was very comfortable in my surroundings. I thought only about how I was to play a part in a historical destiny that my valiant words

Petliura: Simeon Petliura (1879–1926), an anti-Bolshevik Ukrainian leader who was accused of responsibility for Jewish pogroms during World War I. When his forces were defeated by the Russians he went into exile in Paris, where he was ultimately assassinated by a Jewish nationalist.

would help bring about. That delusion lasted only about a week or so until three burly Nazis came in. *"Schnell!"* they said to me, pushing me out of my chair and pointing to the windows where I saw crowds chaotically swarming about. Before I could question the soldiers, one of them shoved a gun into my hands and pushed me out into the streets. I felt so bewildered until the moment I pointed my rifle at a man who was about—I thought—to hit me with a club of some sort. Suddenly, I felt such an intense charge of power, more so than I had ever felt writing some of my best poems. I was no longer dealing with abstract words and ideas for a mythological cause; I was responsible for life and death.

I enjoyed that power, until it seeped into my veins and poisoned my soul. It was only an instant, a brief interlude, a matter of hours until that transformation occurred. I still replay that scene in my mind almost forty years after it happened, no matter what I am doing, or who I am with.

I think she was a village girl. Probably a Jew, because on that particular day, the Jews were the ones chosen to be rounded up and sent away in cattle cars. Her hair was golden red, short and wavy as was the style, and her neck was awash in freckles. It was a crowded station in the center of the town, not far from the butcher shop. There were Germans shouting and women crying and church bells ringing. I stood with that German regulation rifle I hardly knew how to handle, frozen because I was too light-headed and excited. I too began to yell at people and held the rifle against my chest, and I was very much aware of how everyone responded to my authority.

Then, this girl appeared in my direct line of vision. Her back was straight, her shoulders tensed; she stopped in the middle of all the chaos. Simply stopped. I ran up and pushed her. I pushed her hard, she almost fell. I kept pushing her, feeling the thin material of her cheap wool jacket against my chapped eager hand; her thin muscles forced forward by my shoves. Once, twice, until she toppled into the open door of a train and fell toward a heap of other people moving deeper into the tiny confines of the stinking cattle car. She never turned around.

I should have shot her. I should have spared her from whatever she had to go through. I doubt she survived. I should have tried to find out what her name was, so I could track down her relatives and confess to them. At least in that way, they could have spat at me in justice and I would have finally received the absolution I will probably never find in this life.

* * *

I don't die. Instead, I go to the garden. It is Sunday evening. I am weeding the crop of beets and cabbages I planted in the patch in my backyard. The sun is lower, a breeze kicks up around me, but my forehead sweats. I breathe in the thick deep earth smells as the dirt crumbles and rotates against the blade of my hoe. I should destroy the honeysuckle vine that is slowly choking my plants, but the scent is so sweet, and its intoxicating perfume reminds me of a woman's gentleness.

I hoe for a while, but not for long, because out of the corner of my eye, I see Bohdan sitting on the grass tearing the firm green blades with his clenched hands. He is still wearing his uniform, all except the jacket, tie, and cap. He sits with his legs apart, his head down, ignoring the black flies that nip at his ears.

I wipe my face with a bright red bandana, which I brought with me to tie up the stalks of my drooping sunflowers. "Bohdan," I say to my son. "Why don't we go into the house and have a beer. I can finish this another time." I look at the orange sun. "It's humid and there's too many flies—means rain will be coming."

35

My son is quietly crying to himself.   40

"*Tato*, I didn't know anything," he cries out. "You know, I just wanted to jump out from planes with my parachute. I just wanted to fly . . ."

"I should have stopped you," I say more to myself than to him. Bohdan lets me stroke the thin spikes of his army regulation crew-cut which is soft and warm and I am afraid of how easily my hand can crush his skull.

I rock him in my arms the way I saw his mother embrace him when he was afraid to sleep alone.

There is not much more I can do right now except to hold him. I will hold him until he pulls away.

QUESTIONS

1. Where does the narrator live now, and what does he do? What do you learn about his past? What event remains fixed in his memory? Why?

2. What ideas about the exercise of power during warfare are brought out by the narrator's speaking of "the absolution I will probably never find in this life" (paragraph 36)?

3. Why is the narrator's son Bohdan in tears (paragraph 40)? How are Bohdan's experiences parallel with the narrator's? What ideas underlie this paralleling of experience?

4. What is the significance of the narrator's saying "I am afraid of how easily my hand can crush his skull" (paragraph 42)?

WRITING ABOUT MEANING IN FICTION

Most likely you will write about a major idea or theme, but you may also get interested in one of your story's other ideas. As you begin brainstorming and developing your first drafts, consider questions such as those below.

Questions for Discovering Ideas

IDEAS IN GENERAL

- What ideas do you discover in the work? How do you discover them (through action, character depiction, scenes, language)?

- To what do the ideas pertain? To individuals and themselves? To individuals and society? To religion? To social, political, or economic justice?

- How balanced are the ideas? If a particular idea is strongly presented, what conditions and qualifications are also presented (if any)? What contradictory ideas are presented?

- Are the ideas limited to members of any groups represented by the characters (age, race, nationality, personal status)? Or are they applicable to general conditions of life? Explain.

- Which characters in their own right represent or embody ideas? How do their actions and speeches bring these ideas out?

- If characters state ideas directly, how persuasive is their expression, how intelligent and well considered? How germane to the story? How germane to more general conditions?
- With children, young adults, or the old, how do the circumstances express or embody an idea?

A SPECIFIC IDEA

- What idea seems most important in the story? Why? Is it asserted directly, indirectly, dramatically, ironically? Does any one method predominate? Why?
- How pervasive in the story is the idea (throughout or intermittent)? To what degree is it associated with a major character or action? How does the structure of the story affect or shape your understanding of the idea?
- What value or values are embodied in the idea? Of what importance are the values to the story's meaning?
- How compelling is the idea? How could the work be appreciated without reference to any idea at all?

Strategies for Organizing Ideas

Remember that in well-written stories, poems, and plays, narrative and dramatic elements have a strong bearing on ideas. In this sense, an idea is like a key in music or like a continuous thread tying together actions, characters, statements, symbols, and dialogue. As readers, we can trace such threads throughout the entire fabric of the work.

As you write about ideas, you may find yourself relying most heavily on the direct statements of the authorial voice, or on a combination of these and your interpretation of characters and action, or you might focus exclusively on a first-person speaker and use his or her ideas to develop your analysis. Always make clear the sources of your details and distinguish the sources from your own commentary.

In your essay, your general goal is to describe an idea and show its importance in the story. Each separate work will invite its own approach, but here are a number of strategies you might use to organize your essay:

1. *Analyzing the idea as it applies to character.* Example: "Minnie Wright embodies the idea that living with cruelty and insensitivity leads to alienation, unhappiness, despair, and maybe to violence."
2. *Showing how actions bring out the idea.* Example: "That Mabel and Dr. Fergusson fall in love rather than go their separate ways indicates Lawrence's idea that love literally rescues human lives."
3. *Showing how dialogue and separate speeches bring out the idea.* Example: "The priest's responses to Jackie's confession embody the idea that kindness and understanding are the best means to encourage religious and philosophical commitment."
4. *Showing how the story's structure is determined by the idea.* Example: "The idea that horror may exist in ordinary things leads to a structure in which Jackson (in 'The

Lottery') introduces seemingly commonplace people, builds suspense about an impending misfortune, and develops a conclusion of mob destructiveness."

5. *Treating variations or differing manifestations of the idea.* Example: "The idea that zealousness leads to harm is shown in Goodman Brown's nightmarish distortion of reality, his rejection of others, and his dying gloom."

6. *Dealing with a combination of these (together with any other significant aspect).* Example: "The idea in 'Araby' that devotion is complex and contradictory is shown in the narrator's romantic mission as a carrier of parcels, his outcries to love in the back room of his house, and his self-reproach and shame at the story's end." (Here the idea is traced through both speech and action.)

Your conclusion might begin with a summary, together with your evaluation of the validity or force of the idea. If you have been convinced by the author's ideas, you might say that the author has expressed the idea forcefully and convincingly, or else you might show the relevance of the idea to current conditions. If you are not persuaded by the idea, you should demonstrate the idea's shortcomings or limitations. If you wish to mention a related idea, whether in the story you have studied or in some other story, you might introduce that here, but be sure to stress the connections.

SAMPLE STUDENT ESSAY

The Idea in D. H. Lawrence's "The Horse Dealer's Daughter" That Human Destiny Is to Love°

[1]
There are many ideas in "The Horse Dealer's Daughter" about the love between men and women. The story suggests that love is uncontrollable, and also that love must have a physical basis. It also suggests that love transforms life into something new, that love gives security, that only love gives meaning to life, and that love is not only something to live for but something to be feared. The idea that takes in all these is that loving is an essential part of human nature and that it is human destiny to love.* This idea is embodied negatively in characters who are without love and positively in characters who find love.†

[2]
In the first part of the story, loveless characters are negative and incomplete. Their lack of love causes them to be sullen, argumentative, and even cruel. Their lives are similar to those of the draught-horses on the Pervin farm, who move with a "massive, slumbrous strength, and a stupidity which [holds] them in subjection" (paragraph 6). The idea is brought across with force, for the story implies that time is running out for people in this condition, and unless they find love they are doomed to misery. The love they find must be real; the underlying theme is that anything short of that is an evasion and will hasten their doom. Joe, the eldest of the Pervin brothers, is the major example of what can happen

---

° See pp. 372–83 for this story.
* Central idea.
† Thesis sentence.

without love--he is planning a loveless marriage. His motives are thus destroying him. As the narrator says, in emphasizing the story's major idea, Joe's "life was over, he would be a subject animal" like the horses (paragraph 7).

[3] The idea that life is impossible without love is exemplified most fully in Mabel Pervin, the "horse dealer's daughter." Just as her father's death is breaking up the way of life she knew with her brothers, so is it forcing her toward drastic action. She assumes that the loss of both parents has deprived her of all love. Therefore her attempt to drown herself, which she undertakes quickly after caring for her mother's grave, demonstrates the idea that a life without love, and therefore a life with no constructive purpose, is a kind of death.

[4] Rather than ending life, however, the mucky pond illustrates the idea that love begins life. Dr. Jack Fergusson, who rescues Mabel, is her destiny, despite the fact that the two have never thought about loving each other before. Jack has been introduced as an amiable but rudderless person. His common cold, which is mentioned when he first appears, is compatible with the idea that the soul without love is sick. When Jack leaves the Pervin house, his route is aimless, and it is only accidental that he sees Mabel trying to drown herself. His heroic entry into the pond is unplanned, but it also is a first step in establishing a new direction for both his life and Mabel's. The rescue thus underscores the idea that once love is found, it restores life.

[5] But love is also complex, and when it comes it creates unforeseen problems--certainly an idea that is compatible with human destiny. As Lawrence shows his characters finding each other, he also shows that love brings out new and strange emotions and that it upsets lifelong habits and attitudes. Indeed, there is a strong element of fear in love; it changes life so completely that no one can ever be the same after experiencing it. We see this kind of fearful change in Jack. The narrator tells us that Jack has "no intention of loving" Mabel, (paragraph 150) but that destiny drives him into this state. The final paragraph of the story indicates the mixture of desire and terror that love and change can produce:

> "No, I want you, I want you," was all he answered blindly, with that terrible intonation which frightened her almost more than her horror lest he should *not* want her. (paragraph 191)

Thus, the story forcefully makes the point that the human destiny that drives people toward love is both exhilarating and fearsome at the same time.

[6] This realistic presentation of human emotions raises Lawrence's treatment of his idea above the popular and romantic conception of love. Love creates problems as great as those it solves, but it also builds a platform of emotional strength from which these new problems can be attacked. This strength can be achieved only when men and women know love, because only then, in keeping with Lawrence's idea, are they living life as it was destined to be lived. The problems facing them then are the real ones that men and women should face, since such problems are a natural result of destiny. By contrast, the problems of men and women without love, like those at the beginning of the story, are irrelevant to life as it should be lived. The entire story of Mabel and Jack is an illustration of the idea that it is the destiny of men and women to love.

Commentary on the Essay

This essay follows strategy 6 for organizing ideas about meaning (p. 390) by showing how separate components from the story exhibit the theme's pervasiveness. Throughout, citations of actions, speeches, circumstances, and narrator's observations are used as evidence for the various conclusions. Transitions between paragraphs are effected by phrases like "The idea that . . ." (3), "Rather than" (4), "But" (5), and "This" (6), all of which emphasize the continuity of the topic.

The introductory paragraph first illustrates a number of ideas about love that the story suggests, then produces a comprehensive statement of the theme which is made the central idea. This assertion is developed as it applies (1) to characters without love and (2) to those who find it. In the body of the essay, paragraphs 2 and 3 emphasize the emptiness of the lives of the characters without love. The relationship of these two paragraphs to the main idea is that if the characters are not living in accord with human destiny, they are cut off from life. Thus Joe is dismissed in the story as a "subject animal," and Mabel, his sister, attempts suicide. These details are brought out in support of the essay's central idea. Paragraphs 4 and 5 treat the positive aspects of the main idea, focusing on the renewing effect of love on both Mabel and Jack and also on the complexity of their emotional responses to their newly realized love. The last paragraph evaluates the idea or theme of the story and concludes that the story is realistic and well-balanced.

SPECIAL WRITING TOPICS FOR STUDYING IDEAS

1. Compare two stories containing similar events and themes (examples: Butler's "Snow" and Lawrence's "The Horse Dealer's Daughter"; Zabytko's "Home Soil" and Hemingway's "Soldier's Home"; Faulkner's "Barn Burning" and Munro's "The Found Boat"; Chopin's "The Story of an Hour" and Gilman's "The Yellow Wallpaper"). For help in developing your essay, consult Chapter 29 on the technique of comparison-contrast.

2. Consider "The Horse Dealer's Daughter" in terms of the idea of economic determinism (see also Chapter 27). That is, to what degree are the circumstances and traits of the characters, particularly Mabel and Dr. Fergusson, controlled and limited by their economic status? According to the idea, how likely is it that the characters can ever rise above their circumstances?

3. Write an essay criticizing the ideas in a story in this anthology that you dislike or to which you are indifferent. With what statements in the story do you disagree? What actions? What characters? How do your own beliefs and values cause you to dislike the story's ideas? How might the story be changed to illustrate ideas with which you would agree?

4. Select an idea that particularly interests you, and write a brief story showing how characters may or may not live up to the idea. If you have difficulty getting started, try one of these possible ideas:

    a. Interest and enthusiasm are hard to maintain for long.

    b. People always want more than they have or need.

    c. The concerns of adults are different from those of children.

    d. It is awkward to confront another person about a grievance.

    e. Making a decision is hard because it requires a complete change in life's directions.

5. Using books that you discover in the card or computer catalogue in your college or local library, search for discussions of only one of the following topics, and write a brief report on what you find.

    a. D. H. Lawrence on the power of the working classes.

    b. James Joyce on the significance of religion.

    c. Cynthia Ozick on the effects of the Holocaust.

    d. Ernest Hemingway on individualism and self-realization.

    e. Stephen Crane on the power of chance in life.

10

Stories for Additional Study

ROBERT OLEN BUTLER (b. 1945)

Butler was born in Granite City, Illinois, and was educated at Northwestern and Iowa (M.A., 1969). He served in Army Intelligence in Vietnam from 1969–1972 and became proficient in the Vietnamese language. After his discharge he worked in a steel mill, drove a cab, and taught high school. At the present time he lives in Louisiana, where he teaches at McNeese State University. He has been prolific as a novelist and story writer ever since the first of his seven novels, The Alleys of Eden, *was published in 1981 after it had been rejected by twenty-one publishers. He has had many honors, including a Guggenheim Fellowship in fiction and a grant from the National Endowment for the Arts. For* A Good Scent from a Strange Mountain *(1993), a collection of stories about Vietnam and its aftermath, he received the Pulitzer Prize in fiction for 1993. He has written for movies and television, and his most recent collection of stories,* Tabloid Dreams *(1996), is being readied as a film to be produced on the Home Box Office network. The story "Snow" is taken from* A Good Scent from a Strange Mountain.

Snow _____ *1992*

I wonder how long he watched me sleeping. I still wonder that. He sat and he did not wake me to ask about his carry-out order. Did he watch my eyes move as I dreamed? When I finally knew he was there and I turned to look at him, I could not make out his whole face at once. His head was turned a little to the side. His beard was neatly trimmed, but the jaw it covered was long and its curve was like a sampan sail and it held my eyes the way a sail always did when I saw one on the sea. Then I raised my eyes and looked at his nose. I am Vietnamese, you know, and we have a different sense of these proportions. Our noses are small and his was long and it also curved, gently, a reminder of his jaw, which I looked at again. His beard was dark gray, like he'd crawled out of a charcoal kiln. I make these comparisons to things from my country and village, but it is only to clearly say what this face was like. It is not that he reminded me of home. That was the farthest thing from my mind when I first saw Mr. Cohen. And I must have stared at him in those first moments with a strange look because when his face turned full to me and I could finally lift my gaze to his eyes, his eyebrows made a little jump like he was asking me, What is it? What's wrong?

I was at this same table before the big window at the front of the restaurant. The Plantation Hunan does not look like a restaurant, though. No one would give it a name like that unless it really was an old plantation house. It's very large and full of antiques. It's quiet right now. Not even five, and I can hear the big clock—I had never seen one till I came here. No one in Vietnam has a clock as tall as a man. Time isn't as important as that in Vietnam. But the clock here is very tall and they call it Grandfather, which I like, and Grandfather is ticking very slowly right now, and he wants me to fall asleep again. But I won't.

This plantation house must feel like a refugee. It is full of foreign smells, ginger and Chinese pepper and fried shells for wonton, and there's a motel on one side and a gas station on the other, not like the life the house once knew, though there are very large oak trees surrounding it, trees that must have been here when this was still a plantation. The house sits on a busy street and the Chinese family who owns it changed it from Plantation Seafood into a place that could hire a Vietnamese woman like me to be a waitress. They are very kind, this family, though we know we are different from each other. They are Chinese and I am Vietnamese and they are very kind, but we are both here in Louisiana and they go somewhere with the other Chinese in town—there are four restaurants and two laundries and some people, I think, who work as engineers at the oil refinery. They go off to themselves and they don't seem to even notice where they are.

I was sleeping that day he came in here. It was late afternoon of the day before Christmas. Almost Christmas Eve. I am not a Christian. My mother and I are Buddhist. I live with my mother and she is very sad for me because I am thirty-four years old and I am not married. There are other Vietnamese here in Lake Charles, Louisiana, but we are not a community. We are all too sad, perhaps, or too tired. But maybe not. Maybe that's just me saying that. Maybe the others are real Americans already. My mother has two Vietnamese friends, old women like her, and her two friends look at me with the same sadness in their faces because of what they see as my life. They know that once I might have been married, but the fiancé I had in my town in Vietnam went away in the Army and though he is still alive in Vietnam, the last I heard, he is driving a cab in Hô Chí Minh City and he is married to someone else. I never really knew him, and I don't feel any loss. It's just that he's the only boy my mother ever speaks of when she gets frightened for me.

I get frightened for me, too, sometimes, but it's not because I have no husband.   5
That Christmas Eve afternoon I woke slowly. The front tables are for cocktails and for waiting for carry-out, so the chairs are large and stuffed so that they are soft. My head was very comfortable against one of the high wings of the chair and I opened my eyes without moving. The rest of me was still sleeping, but my eyes opened and the sky was still blue, though the shreds of cloud were turning pink. It looked like a warm sky. And it was. I felt sweat on my throat and I let my eyes move just a little and the live oak in front of the restaurant was quivering—all its leaves were shaking and you might think that it would look cold doing that, but it was a warm wind, I knew. The air was thick and wet, and cutting through the ginger and pepper smell was the fuzzy smell of mildew.

Perhaps it was from my dream but I remembered my first Christmas Eve in America. I slept and woke just like this, in a Chinese restaurant. I was working there. But it was in a distant place, in St. Louis. And I woke to snow. The first snow I had ever seen. It scared me. Many Vietnamese love to see their first snow, but it frightened me in some very deep way that I could not explain, and even remembering that moment—especially as I woke from sleep at the front of another restaurant—frightened me. So I turned my face sharply from the window in the Plantation Hunan and that's when I saw Mr. Cohen.

I stared at those parts of his face, like I said, and maybe this was a way for me to hide from the snow, maybe the strangeness that he saw in my face had to do with the snow. But when his eyebrows jumped and I did not say anything to explain what was going on inside me, I could see him wondering what to do. I could feel him thinking: Should I ask her what is wrong or should I just ask her for my carry-out? I am not an especially shy person, but I hoped he would choose to ask for the carry-out. I came to myself with a little jolt and I stood up and faced him—he was sitting in one of the stuffed chairs at the next table. "I'm sorry," I said, trying to turn us both from my dreaming. "Do you have an order?"

He hesitated, his eyes holding fast on my face. These were very dark eyes, as dark as the eyes of any Vietnamese, but turned up to me like this, his face seemed so large that I had trouble taking it in. Then he said, "Yes. For Cohen." His voice was deep, like a movie actor who is playing a grandfather, the kind of voice that if he asked what it was that I had been dreaming, I would tell him at once.

But he did not ask anything more. I went off to the kitchen and the order was not ready. I wanted to complain to them. There was no one else in the restaurant, and everyone in the kitchen seemed like they were just hanging around. But I don't make any trouble for anybody. So I just went back out to Mr. Cohen. He rose when he saw me, even though he surely also saw that I had no carry-out with me.

"It's not ready yet," I said. "I'm sorry."   10

"That's okay," he said, and he smiled at me, his gray beard opening and showing teeth that were very white.

"I wanted to scold them," I said. "You should not have to wait for a long time on Christmas Eve."

"It's okay," he said. "This is not my holiday."

I tilted my head, not understanding. He tilted his own head just like mine, like he wanted to keep looking straight into my eyes. Then he said, "I am Jewish."

I straightened my head again, and I felt a little pleasure at knowing that his   15
straightening his own head was caused by me. I still didn't understand, exactly, and he clearly read that in my face. He said, "A Jew doesn't celebrate Christmas."

"I thought all Americans celebrated Christmas," I said.

"Not all. Not exactly." He did a little shrug with his shoulders, and his eyebrows rose like the shrug, as he tilted his head to the side once more, for just a second. It all seemed to say, What is there to do, it's the way the world is and I know it and it all makes me just a little bit weary. He said, "We all stay home, but we don't all celebrate."

He said no more, but he looked at me and I was surprised to find that I had no words either on my tongue or in my head. It felt a little strange to see this very American man who was not celebrating the holiday. In Vietnam we never miss a holiday and it did not make a difference if we were Buddhist or Cao Đài or Catholic. I thought of this Mr. Cohen sitting in his room tonight alone while all the other Americans celebrated Christmas Eve. But I had nothing to say and he didn't either and he kept looking at me and I glanced down at my hands twisting at my order book and I didn't even remember taking the book out. So I said, "I'll check on your order again," and I turned and went off to the kitchen and I waited there till the order was done, though I stood over next to the door away from the chatter of the cook and the head waiter and the mother of the owner.

Carrying the white paper bag out to the front, I could not help but look inside to see how much food there was. There was enough for two people. So I did not look into Mr. Cohen's eyes as I gave him the food and rang up the order and took his money. I was counting his change into his palm—his hand, too, was very large—and he said, "You're not Chinese, are you?"

I said, "No. I am Vietnamese," but I did not raise my face to him, and he went away.   20

Two days later, it was even earlier in the day when Mr. Cohen came in. About four-thirty. The grandfather had just chimed the half hour like a man who is really crazy about one subject and talks of it at any chance he gets. I was sitting in my chair at the front once again and my first thought when I saw Mr. Cohen coming through the door was that he would think I am a lazy girl. I started to jump up, but he saw me and he motioned with his hand for me to stay where I was, a single heavy pat in the air, like he'd just laid this large hand of his on the shoulder of an invisible child before him. He said, "I'm early again."

"I am not a lazy girl," I said.

"I know you're not," he said and he sat down in the chair across from me.

"How do you know I'm not?" This question just jumped out of me. I can be a cheeky girl sometimes. My mother says that this was one reason I am not married, that this is why she always talks about the boy I was once going to marry in Vietnam, because he was a shy boy, a weak boy, who would take whatever his wife said and not complain. I myself think this is why he is driving a taxi in Hô Chí Minh City. But as soon as this cheeky thing came out of my mouth to Mr. Cohen, I found that I was afraid. I did not want Mr. Cohen to hate me.

But he was smiling. I could even see his white teeth in this smile. He said, "You're right. I have no proof."   25

"I am always sitting here when you come in," I said, even as I asked myself, Why are you rubbing on this subject?

I saw still more teeth in his smile, then he said, "And the last time you were even sleeping."

I think at this I must have looked upset, because his smile went away fast. He did not have to help me seem a fool before him. "It's all right," he said. "This is a slow time of day. I have trouble staying awake myself. Even in court."

I looked at him more closely, leaving his face. He seemed very prosperous. He was wearing a suit as gray as his beard and it had thin blue stripes, almost invisible, running through it. "You are a judge?"

"A lawyer," he said.   30

"You will defend me when the owner fires me for sleeping."

This made Mr. Cohen laugh, but when he stopped, his face was very solemn. He seemed to lean nearer to me, though I was sure he did not move. "You had a bad dream the last time," he said.

How did I know he would finally come to ask about my dream? I had known it from the first time I'd heard his voice. "Yes," I said. "I think I was dreaming about the first Christmas Eve I spent in America. I fell asleep before a window in a restaurant in St. Louis, Missouri. When I woke, there was snow on the ground. It was the first snow I'd ever seen. I went to sleep and there was still only a gray afternoon, a thin little rain, like a mist. I had no idea things could change like that. I woke and everything was covered and I was terrified."

I suddenly sounded to myself like a crazy person. Mr. Cohen would think I was lazy and crazy both. I stopped speaking and I looked out the window. A jogger went by in the street, a man in shorts and a T-shirt, and his body glistened with sweat. I felt beads of sweat on my own forehead like little insects crouching there and I kept my eyes outside, wishing now that Mr. Cohen would go away.

"Why did it terrify you?" he said.   35

"I don't know," I said, though this wasn't really true. I'd thought about it now and then, and though I'd never spoken them, I could imagine reasons.

Mr. Cohen said, "Snow frightened me, too, when I was a child. I'd seen it all my life, but it still frightened me."

I turned to him and now he was looking out the window.

"Why did it frighten you?" I asked, expecting no answer.

But he turned from the window and looked at me and smiled just a little bit, like   40
he was saying that since he had asked this question of me, I could ask him, too. He answered, "It's rather a long story. Are you sure you want to hear it?"

"Yes," I said. Of course I did.

"It was far away from here," he said. "My first home and my second one. Poland and then England. My father was a professor in Warsaw. It was early in 1939. I was eight years old and my father knew something was going wrong. All the talk about the corridor to the sea was just the beginning. He had ears. He knew. So he sent me and my mother to England. He had good friends there. I left that February and there was snow everywhere and I had my own instincts, even at eight. I cried in the courtyard of our apartment building. I threw myself into the snow there and I would not move. I cried like he was sending us away from him forever. He and my mother said it was only for some months, but I didn't believe it. And I was right. They had to lift me bodily and carry me to the taxi. But the snow was in my clothes and as we pulled away and I scrambled up to look out the back window at my father, the snow was melting against my skin and I began to shake. It was as much from my fear as from the cold. The snow was telling me he would die. And he did. He waved at me in the street and he grew smaller and we turned a corner and that was the last I saw of him."

Maybe it was foolish of me, but I thought not so much of Mr. Cohen losing his father. I had lost a father, too, and I knew that it was something that a child lives through. In Vietnam we believe that our ancestors are always close to us, and I could tell that about Mr. Cohen, that his father was still close to him. But what I thought about was Mr. Cohen going to another place, another country, and living with his mother. I live with my mother, just like that. Even still.

He said, "So the snow was something I was afraid of. Every time it snowed in England I knew that my father was dead. It took a few years for us to learn this from others, but I knew it whenever it snowed."

"You lived with your mother?" I said.   45

"Yes. In England until after the war and then we came to America. The others from Poland and Hungary and Russia that we traveled with all came in through New York City and stayed there. My mother loved trains and she'd read a book once about New Orleans, and so we stayed on the train and we came to the South. I was glad to be in a place where it almost never snowed."

I was thinking how he was a foreigner, too. Not an American, really. But all the talk about the snow made this little chill behind my thoughts. Maybe I was ready to talk about that. Mr. Cohen had spoken many words to me about his childhood and I didn't want him to think I was a girl who takes things without giving something back. He was looking out the window again, and his lips pinched together so that his mouth disappeared in his beard. He seemed sad to me. So I said, "You know why the snow scared me in St. Louis?"

He turned at once with a little humph sound and a crease on his forehead between his eyes and then a very strong voice saying, "Tell me," and it felt like he was scolding himself inside for not paying attention to me. I am not a vain girl, always thinking that men pay such serious attention to me that they get mad at themselves for ignoring me even for a few moments. This is what it really felt like and it surprised me. If I was a vain girl, it wouldn't have surprised me. He said it again: "Tell me why it scared you."

I said, "I think it's because the snow came so quietly and everything was underneath it, like this white surface was the real earth and everything had died—all the trees and the grass and the streets and the houses—everything had died and was buried. It was all lost. I knew there was snow above me, on the roof, and I was dead, too."

"Your own country was very different," Mr. Cohen said.   50

It pleased me that he thought just the way I once did. You could tell that he wished there was an easy way to make me feel better, make the dream go away. But I said to him, "This is what I also thought. If I could just go to a warm climate, more like home. So I came down to New Orleans, with my mother, just like you, and then we came over to Lake Charles. And it is something like Vietnam here. The rice fields and the heat and the way the storms come in. But it makes no difference. There's no snow to scare me here, but I still sit alone in this chair in the middle of the afternoon and I sleep and I listen to the grandfather over there ticking."

I stopped talking and I felt like I was making no sense at all, so I said, "I should check on your order."

Mr. Cohen's hand came out over the table. "May I ask your name?"

"I'm Miss Giàu," I said.

"Miss Giàu?" he asked, and when he did that, he made a different word, since   55
Vietnamese words change with the way your voice sings them.

I laughed. "My name is Giàu, with the voice falling. It means 'wealthy' in Vietnamese. When you say the word like a question, you say something very different. You say I am Miss Pout."

Mr. Cohen laughed and there was something in the laugh that made me shiver just a little, like a nice little thing, like maybe stepping into the shower when you are covered with dust and feeling the water expose you. But in the back of my mind was his carry-out and there was a bad little feeling there, something I wasn't thinking about, but it made me go off now with heavy feet to the kitchen. I got the bag and it was feeling different as I carried it back to the front of the restaurant. I went behind the counter and I put it down and I wished I'd done this a few moments before, but even with his eyes on me, I looked into the bag. There was one main dish and one portion of soup.

Then Mr. Cohen said, "Is this a *giau* I see on your face?" And he pronounced the word exactly right, with the curling tone that made it "pout."

I looked up at him and I wanted to smile at how good he said the word, but even wanting to do that made the pout worse. I said, "I was just thinking that your wife must be sick. She is not eating tonight."

He could have laughed at this. But he did not. He laid his hand for a moment   60
on his beard, he smoothed it down. He said, "The second dinner on Christmas Eve was for my son passing through town. My wife died some years ago and I am not remarried."

I am not a hard-hearted girl because I knew that a child gets over the loss of a father and because I also knew that a man gets over the loss of a wife. I am a good girl, but I did not feel sad for Mr. Cohen. I felt very happy. Because he laid his hand on mine and he asked if he could call me. I said yes, and as it turns out, New Year's Eve seems to be a Jewish holiday. Vietnamese New Year comes at a different time, but people in Vietnam know to celebrate whatever holiday comes along. So tonight Mr. Cohen and I will go to some restaurant that is not Chinese, and all I have to do now is sit here and listen very carefully to Grandfather as he talks to me about time.

RAYMOND CARVER   (1938–1988)

Originally from Oregon, Carver lived in Washington and spent much of his adult life in California. He studied at Chico State and at the Iowa Writers Workshop. After doing blue-collar jobs for a time, he worked as an editor and then, finally, as a teacher. Some of his collections are Will You Please Be Quiet, Please? *(1976) and* Cathedral *(1983).* Where I'm Calling From *(1988) collects earlier stories and adds a number of new ones.* Short Cuts *(1993) is a selection of ten stories that were woven together into a film (1993) by Robert Altman. Carver is considered a master of minimalism, that is, fiction that stresses only the essentials of action and description. Generally, his writing is economical, stripped to the bone. Many of his characters seem unusual if not odd or even cruel. For example, one of his brief stories, "Popular Mechanics," takes little more than a single page to depict how a couple breaking up is also about to break up (literally) their child. "Neighbors" is taken from* Where I'm Calling From.

Neighbors _____ *1988*

Bill and Arlene Miller were a happy couple. But now and then they felt they alone among their circle had been passed by somehow, leaving Bill to attend to his bookkeeping duties and Arlene occupied with secretarial chores. They talked about it sometimes, mostly in comparison with the lives of their neighbors, Harriet and Jim Stone. It seemed to the Millers that the Stones lived a fuller and brighter life. The Stones were always going out for dinner, or entertaining at home, or traveling about the country somewhere in connection with Jim's work.

The Stones lived across the hall from the Millers. Jim was a salesman for a machine-parts firm and often managed to combine business with pleasure trips, and on this occasion the Stones would be away for ten days, first to Cheyenne, then on to St. Louis to visit relatives. In their absence, the Millers would look after the Stones' apartment, feed Kitty, and water the plants.

Bill and Jim shook hands beside the car. Harriet and Arlene held each other by the elbows and kissed lightly on the lips.

"Have fun," Bill said to Harriet.

"We will," said Harriet. "You kids have fun too."   5

Arlene nodded.

Jim winked at her. "Bye, Arlene. Take good care of the old man."

"I will," Arlene said.

"Have fun," Bill said.

"You bet," Jim said, clipping Bill lightly on the arm. "And thanks again, you guys."   10

The Stones waved as they drove away, and the Millers waved too.

"Well, I wish it was us," Bill said.

"God knows, we could use a vacation," Arlene said. She took his arm and put it around her waist as they climbed the stairs to their apartment.

After dinner Arlene said, "Don't forget. Kitty gets liver flavor the first night." She stood in the kitchen doorway folding the handmade tablecloth that Harriet had bought for her last year in Santa Fe.

Bill took a deep breath as he entered the Stones' apartment. The air was already   15
heavy and it was vaguely sweet. The sunburst clock over the television said half past eight. He remembered when Harriet had come home with the clock, how she had crossed the hall to show it to Arlene, cradling the brass case in her arms and talking to it through the tissue paper as if it were an infant.

Kitty rubbed her face against his slippers and then turned onto her side, but jumped up quickly as Bill moved to the kitchen and selected one of the stacked cans from the gleaming drainboard. Leaving the cat to pick at her food, he headed for the bathroom. He looked at himself in the mirror and then closed his eyes and then looked again. He opened the medicine chest. He found a container of pills and read the label —*Harriet Stone. One each day as directed*—and slipped it into his pocket. He went back to the kitchen, drew a pitcher of water, and returned to the living room. He finished watering, set the pitcher on the rug, and opened the liquor cabinet. He reached in back for the bottle of Chivas Regal. He took two drinks from the bottle, wiped his lips on his sleeve, and replaced the bottle in the cabinet.

Kitty was on the couch sleeping. He switched off the lights, slowly closing and checking the door. He had the feeling he had left something.

"What kept you?" Arlene said. She sat with her legs turned under her, watching television.

"Nothing. Playing with Kitty," he said, and went over to her and touched her breasts.

"Let's go to bed, honey," he said.   20

The next day Bill took only ten minutes of the twenty-minute break allotted for the afternoon and left at fifteen minutes before five. He parked the car in the lot just as

Arlene hopped down from the bus. He waited until she entered the building, then ran up the stairs to catch her as she stepped out of the elevator.

"Bill! God, you scared me. You're early," she said.

He shrugged. "Nothing to do at work," he said.

She let him use her key to open the door. He looked at the door across the hall before following her inside.

"Let's go to bed," he said.   25

"Now?" She laughed. "What's gotten into you?"

"Nothing. Take your dress off." He grabbed for her awkwardly, and she said, "Good God, Bill."

He unfastened his belt.

Later they sent out for Chinese food, and when it arrived they ate hungrily, without speaking, and listened to records.

"Let's not forget to feed Kitty," she said.   30

"I was just thinking about that," he said. "I'll go right over."

* * *

He selected a can of fish flavor for the cat, then filled the pitcher and went to water. When he returned to the kitchen, the cat was scratching in her box. She looked at him steadily before she turned back to the litter. He opened all the cupboards and examined the canned goods, the cereals, the packaged foods, the cocktail and wine glasses, the china, the pots and pans. He opened the refrigerator. He sniffed some celery, took two bites of cheddar cheese, and chewed on an apple as he walked into the bedroom. The bed seemed enormous, with a fluffy white bedspread draped to the floor. He pulled out a nightstand drawer, found a half-empty package of cigarettes and stuffed them into his pocket. Then he stepped to the closet and was opening it when the knock sounded at the front door.

He stopped by the bathroom and flushed the toilet on his way.

"What's been keeping you?" Arlene said. "You've been over here more than an hour."

"Have I really?" he said.   35

"Yes, you have," she said.

"I had to go to the toilet," he said.

"You have your own toilet," she said.

"I couldn't wait," he said.

That night they made love again.   40

In the morning he had Arlene call in for him. He showered, dressed, and made a light breakfast. He tried to start a book. He went out for a walk and felt better. But after a while, hands still in his pockets, he returned to the apartment. He stopped at the Stones' door on the chance he might hear the cat moving about. Then he let himself in at his own door and went to the kitchen for the key.

Inside it seemed cooler than his apartment, and darker too. He wondered if the plants had something to do with the temperature of the air. He looked out the window, and then he moved slowly through each room considering everything that fell under his gaze, carefully, one object at a time. He saw ashtrays, items of furniture, kitchen utensils, the clock. He saw everything. At last he entered the bedroom, and the cat appeared at his feet. He stroked her once, carried her into the bathroom, and shut the door.

He lay down on the bed and stared at the ceiling. He lay for a while with his eyes closed, and then he moved his hand under his belt. He tried to recall what day it was. He tried to remember when the Stones were due back, and then he wondered if they would ever return. He could not remember their faces or the way they talked and dressed. He sighed and with effort rolled off the bed to lean over the dresser and look at himself in the mirror.

He opened the closet and selected a Hawaiian shirt. He looked until he found Bermudas, neatly pressed and hanging over a pair of brown twill slacks. He shed his own clothes and slipped into the shorts and the shirt. He looked in the mirror again. He went to the living room and poured himself a drink and sipped it on his way back to the bedroom. He put on a blue shirt, a dark suit, a blue and white tie, black wing-tip shoes. The glass was empty and he went for another drink.

In the bedroom again, he sat on a chair, crossed his legs, and smiled, observing himself in the mirror. The telephone rang twice and fell silent. He finished the drink and took off the suit. He rummaged through the top drawers until he found a pair of panties and a brassiere. He stepped into the panties and fastened the brassiere, then looked through the closet for an outfit. He put on a black and white checkered skirt and tried to zip it up. He put on a burgundy blouse that buttoned up the front. He considered her shoes, but understood they would not fit. For a long time he looked out the living-room window from behind the curtain. Then he returned to the bedroom and put everything away.   45

He was not hungry. She did not eat much, either. They looked at each other shyly and smiled. She got up from the table and checked that the key was on the shelf and then she quickly cleared the dishes.

He stood in the kitchen doorway and smoked a cigarette and watched her pick up the key.

"Make yourself comfortable while I go across the hall," she said. "Read the paper or something." She closed her fingers over the key. He was, she said, looking tired.

He tried to concentrate on the news. He read the paper and turned on the television. Finally he went across the hall. The door was locked.

"It's me. Are you still there, honey?" he called.   50

After a time the lock released and Arlene stepped outside and shut the door. "Was I gone so long?" she said.

"Well, you were," he said.

"Was I?" she said. "I guess I must have been playing with Kitty."

He studied her, and she looked away, her hand still resting on the doorknob.

"It's funny," she said. "You know—to go in someone's place like that."   55

He nodded, took her hand from the knob, and guided her toward their own door. He let them into their apartment.

"It *is* funny," he said.

He noticed white lint clinging to the back of her sweater, and the color was high in her cheeks. He began kissing her on the neck and hair and she turned and kissed him back.

"Oh, damn," she said. "Damn, damn," she sang, girlishly clapping her hands. "I just remembered. I really and truly forgot to do what I went over there to do. I didn't feed Kitty or do any watering." She looked at him. "Isn't that stupid?"

"I don't think so," he said. "Just a minute. I'll get my cigarettes and go back with   60
you."

She waited until he had closed and locked their door, and then she took his arm
at the muscle and said. "I guess I should tell you. I found some pictures."

He stopped in the middle of the hall. "What kind of pictures?"

"You can see for yourself," she said, and she watched him.

"No kidding." He grinned. "Where?"

"In a drawer," she said.   65

"No kidding," he said.

And then she said, "Maybe they won't come back," and was at once astonished at
her words.

"It could happen," he said. "Anything could happen."

"Or maybe they'll come back and . . ." but she did not finish.

They held hands for the short walk across the hall, and when he spoke she could   70
barely hear his voice.

"The key," he said. "Give it to me."

"What?" she said. She gazed at the door.

"The key," he said. "You have the key."

"My God," she said, "I left the key inside."

He tried the knob. It was locked. Then she tried the knob. It would not turn. Her   75
lips were parted, and her breathing was hard, expectant. He opened his arms and she
moved into them.

"Don't worry," he said into her ear. "For God's sake, don't worry."

They stayed there. They held each other. They leaned into the door as if against a
wind, and braced themselves.

ANDRE DUBUS   (b. 1936)

*Dubus was born in Louisiana and received degrees from McNeese State College and the
University of Iowa. He taught at Bradford College in Massachusetts before he was struck and
disabled by a speeding automobile. Currently he lives northwest of Boston near the Merrimack
River, an area he often employs as the setting in his fiction. The stories in his* Selected Stories
*(1988), from which "The Curse" is taken, touch the darker areas of human existence, but
nevertheless have a compelling force. In "They Now Live in Texas," for example, a woman
sees a horror ghost movie on her VCR and then awaits her own demons. In another story,
"Townies," a drifting, purposeless young man kills his girlfriend and then achieves a curious
serenity as he waits for the police. Dubus's most recent short story collection is* Dancing After
Hours *(1996). He has also worked in the longer form of the novella and published several
novellas in* We Don't Live Here Anymore *(1984). He gained many honors, among which
are a Guggenheim Fellowship and a MacArthur Fellowship.*

The Curse ——————————————————————— *1988*

Mitchell Hayes was forty-nine years old, but when the cops left him in the bar with Bob,
the manager, he felt much older. He did not know what it was like to be very old, a
shrunken and wrinkled man, but he assumed it was like this: fatigue beyond relieving
by rest, by sleep. He also was not a small man: his weight moved up and down in the
hundred and seventies and he was five feet, ten inches tall. But now his body seemed
short and thin. Both stood at one end of the bar; he was a large blackhaired man, and

there was nothing in front of him but an ash tray he was using. He looked at Mitchell at the cash register and said: "Forget it. You heard what Smitty said."

Mitchell looked away, at the front door. He had put the chairs upside down on the table. He looked from the door past Bob to the empty space of floor at the rear; sometimes people danced there, to the jukebox. Opposite Bob, on the wall behind the bar, was a telephone; Mitchell looked at it. He had told Smitty there were five guys and when he moved to the phone one of them stepped around the corner of the bar and shoved him: one hand against Mitchell's chest, and it pushed him backward; he nearly fell. That was when they were getting rough with her at the bar. When they took her to the floor Mitchell looked once at her sounds, then looked down at the duckboard he stood on, or at the belly or chest of a young man in front of him.

He knew they were not drunk. They had been drinking before they came to his place, a loud popping of motorcycles outside, then walking into the empty bar, young and sunburned and carrying helmets and wearing thick leather jackets in August. They stood in front of Mitchell and drank drafts. When he took their first order he thought they were on drugs and later, watching them, he was certain. They were not relaxed, in the way of most drinkers near closing time. Their eyes were quick, alert as wary animals, and they spoke loudly, with passion, but their passion was strange and disturbing, because they were only chatting, bantering. Mitchell knew nothing of the effects of drugs, so could not guess what was in their blood. He feared and hated drugs because of his work and because he was the stepfather of teenagers: a boy and a girl. He gave last call and served them and leaned against the counter behind him.

Then the door opened and the girl walked in from the night, a girl he had never seen, and she crossed the floor toward Mitchell. He stepped forward to tell her she had missed last call, but before he spoke she asked for change for the cigarette machine. She was young, he guessed nineteen to twenty-one, and deeply tanned and had dark hair. She was sober and wore jeans and a dark blue tee shirt. He gave her the quarters but she was standing between two of the men and she did not get to the machine.

When it was over and she lay crying on the cleared circle of floor, he left the bar and picked up the jeans and tee shirt beside her and crouched and handed them to her. She did not look at him. She lay the clothes across her breasts and what Mitchell thought of now as her wound. He left her and dialed 911, then Bob's number. He woke up Bob. Then he picked up her sneakers from the floor and placed them beside her and squatted near her face, her crying. He wanted to speak to her and touch her, hold a hand or press her brow, but he could not.

The cruiser was there quickly, the siren coming east from town, then slowing and deepening as the car stopped outside. He was glad Smitty was one of them; he had gone to high school with Smitty. The other was Dave, and Mitchell knew him because it was a small town. When they saw the girl Dave went out to the cruiser to call for an ambulance, and when he came back he said two other cruisers had those scumbags and were taking them in. The girl was still crying and could not talk to Smitty and Dave. She was crying when a man and woman lifted her onto a stretcher and rolled her out the door and she vanished forever in a siren.

Bob came in while Smitty and Dave were sitting at the bar drinking coffee and Smitty was writing his report; Mitchell stood behind the bar. Bob sat next to Dave as Mitchell said: "I could have stopped them, Smitty."

"That's our job," Smitty said. "You want to be in the hospital now?"

Mitchell did not answer. When Smitty and Dave left, he got a glass of Coke from the cobra and had a cigarette with Bob. They did not talk. Then Mitchell washed his

5

glass and Bob's cup and they left, turning off the lights. Outside Mitchell locked the front door, feeling the sudden night air after almost ten hours of air conditioning. When he had come to work the day had been very hot, and now he thought it would not have happened in winter. They had stopped for a beer on their way somewhere from the beach; he had heard them say that. But the beach was not the reason. He did not know the reason, but he knew it would not have happened in winter. The night was cool and now he could smell trees. He turned and looked at the road in front of the bar. Bob stood beside him on the small porch.

"If the regulars had been here," Bob said.   10

He turned and with his hand resting on the wooden rail he walked down the ramp to the ground. At his car he stopped and looked over its roof at Mitchell.

"You take it easy," he said.

Mitchell nodded. When Bob got in his car and left, he went down the ramp and drove home to his house on a street that he thought was neither good nor bad. The houses were small and there were old large houses used now as apartments for families. Most of the people had work, most of the mothers cared for their children, and most of the children were clean and looked like they lived in homes, not caves like some he saw in town. He worried about the older kids, one group of them anyway. They were idle. When he was a boy in a town farther up the Merrimack River, he and his friends committed every mischievous act he could recall on afternoons and nights when they were idle. His stepchildren were not part of that group. They had friends from the high school. The front porch light was on for him and one in the kitchen at the rear of the house. He went in the front door and switched off the porch light and walked through the living and dining rooms to the kitchen. He got a can of beer from the refrigerator, turned out the light, and sat at the table. When he could see, he took a cigarette from Susan's pack in front of him.

Down the hall he heard Susan move on the bed then get up and he hoped it wasn't for the bathroom but for him. He had met her eight years ago when he had given up on ever marrying and having kids, then one night she came into the bar with two of her girl friends from work. She made six dollars an hour going to homes of invalids, mostly what she called her little old ladies, and bathing them. She got the house from her marriage, and child support the guy paid for a few months till he left town and went south. She came barefoot down the hall and stood in the kitchen doorway and said: "Are you all right?"

"No."   15

She sat across from him, and he told her. Very soon she held his hand. She was good. He knew if he had fought all five of them and was lying in pieces in a hospital bed she would tell him he had done the right thing, as she was telling him now. He liked her strong hand on his. It was a professional hand and he wanted from her something he had never wanted before: to lie in bed while she bathed him. When they went to bed he did not think he would be able to sleep, but she kneeled beside him and massaged his shoulders and rubbed his temples and pressed her hands on his forehead. He woke to the voices of Marty and Joyce in the kitchen. They had summer jobs, and always when they woke him he went back to sleep till noon, but now he got up and dressed and went to the kitchen door. Susan was at the stove, her back to him, and Marty and Joyce were talking and smoking. He said good morning, and stepped into the room.

"What are you doing up?" Joyce said.

She was a pretty girl with her mother's wide cheekbones and Marty was a tall good-looking boy, and Mitchell felt as old as he had before he slept. Susan was watching him.

Then she poured him a cup of coffee and put it at his place and he sat. Marty said: "You getting up for the day?"

"Something happened last night. At the bar." They tried to conceal their excitement, but he saw it in their eyes. "I should have stopped it. I think I *could* have stopped it. That's the point. There were these five guys. They were on motorcycles but they weren't bikers. Just punks. They came in late, when everybody else had gone home. It was a slow night anyway. Everybody was at the beach."

"They rob you?" Marty said.

"No. A girl came in. Young. Nice looking. You know: just a girl, minding her business."

They nodded, and their eyes were apprehensive.

"She wanted cigarette change, that's all. Those guys were on dope. Coke or something. You know: they were flying in place."

"Did they rape her?" Joyce said.

"Yes, honey."

"The *fuckers*."

Susan opened her mouth then closed it and Joyce reached quickly for Susan's pack of cigarettes. Mitchell held his lighter for her and said: "When they started getting rough with her at the bar I went for the phone. One of them stopped me. He shoved me, that's all. I should have hit him with a bottle."

Marty reached over the table with his big hand and held Mitchell's shoulder.

"No, Mitch. Five guys that mean. And coked up or whatever. No way. You wouldn't be here this morning."

"I don't know. There was always a guy with me. But just one guy, taking turns."

"Great," Joyce said. Marty's hand was on Mitchell's left shoulder; she put hers on his right hand.

"They took her to the hospital," he said. "The guys are in jail."

"They are?" Joyce said.

"I called the cops. When they left."

"You'll be a good witness," Joyce said.

He looked at her proud face.

"At the trial," she said.

The day was hot but that night most of the regulars came to the bar. Some of the younger ones came on motorcycles. They were a good crowd: they all worked, except the retired ones and no one ever bothered the women, not even the young ones with their summer tans. Everyone talked about it: some had read the newspaper story, some had heard the story in town, and they wanted to hear it from Mitchell. He told it as often as they asked but he did not finish it because he was working hard and could not stay with any group of customers long enough.

He watched their faces. Not one of them, even the women, looked at him as if he had not cared enough for the girl, or was a coward. Many of them even appeared sympathetic, making him feel for moments that he was a survivor of something horrible, and when that feeling left him he was ashamed. He felt tired and old, making drinks and change, moving and talking up and down the bar. At the stool at the far end Bob drank coffee and whenever Mitchell looked at him he smiled or nodded and once raised his right fist, with the thumb up.

Reggie was drinking too much. He did that two or three times a month and Mitchell had to shut him off and Reggie always took it humbly. He was a big gentle man with a long brown beard. But tonight shutting off Reggie demanded from Mitchell an

20

25

30

35

40

act of will, and when the eleven o'clock news came on the television and Reggie ordered another shot and a draft, Mitchell pretended not to hear him. He served the customers at the other end of the bar, where Bob was. He could hear Reggie calling: Hey Mitch; shot and a draft, Mitch. Mitchell was close to Bob now. Bob said softly: "He's had enough."

Mitchell nodded and went to Reggie, leaned closer to him so he could speak quietly, and said: "Sorry, Reggie. Time for coffee. I don't want you dead out there."

Reggie blinked at him.

"Okay, Mitch." He pulled some bills from his pocket and put them on the bar. Mitchell glanced at them and saw at least a ten dollar tip. When he rang up Reggie's tab the change was sixteen dollars and fifty cents, and he dropped the coins and shoved the bills into the beer mug beside the cash register. The mug was full of bills, as it was on most nights, and he kept his hand in there, pressing Reggie's into the others, and saw the sunburned young men holding her down on the floor and one kneeling between her legs, spread and held, and he heard their cheering voices and her screaming and groaning and finally weeping and weeping and weeping, until she was the siren crying then fading into the night. From the floor behind him, far across the room, he felt her pain and terror and grief, then her curse upon him. The curse moved into his back and spread down and up his spine, into his stomach and legs and arms and shoulders until he quivered with it. He wished he were alone so he could kneel to receive it.

CHARLOTTE PERKINS GILMAN (1860–1938)

Born in 1860, Gilman did not begin writing seriously until after the birth of her daughter in the 1880s, which was followed by her "nervous breakdown." Attempting to establish her own independence, she left her husband in 1890 and went to California, where she launched what was to become a distinguished career as an advocate for women's rights. For many decades she lectured and wrote extensively, her touchstone work being Women and Economics *(1898), in which she championed the need for women's financial independence. Among her many writings were* Concerning Children *(1900),* Human Work *(1904), and* His Religion and Hers *(1923). In the 1930s she became incurably ill, and with death facing her, she took her own life in 1938.*

The Yellow Wallpaper° _____ *1892*

It is very seldom that mere ordinary people like John and myself secure ancestral halls for the summer.

A colonial mansion, a hereditary estate, I would say a haunted house and reach the height of romantic felicity—but that would be asking too much of fate!

The Yellow Wallpaper: The story is based on the "rest cure" developed after the Civil War by the famous Philadelphia physician S. Weir Mitchell (1829–1914); see paragraph 83. The Mitchell treatment required confining the patient to a hospital, hotel, or some other remote residence. Once isolated, the patient was to have complete bed rest, increased food intake, iron supplements, exercise, and sometimes massage and electric shock therapy. Gilman had experienced Mitchell's "cure," and sent a copy of this story to him as criticism. After receiving the story Mitchell modified his methods.

Still I will proudly declare that there is something queer about it.

Else, why should it be let so cheaply? And why have stood so long untenanted?

John laughs at me, of course, but one expects that.   5

John is practical in the extreme. He has no patience with faith, an intense horror of superstition, and he scoffs openly at any talk of things not to be felt and seen and put down in figures.

John is a physician, and *perhaps*—(I would not say it to a living soul, of course, but this is dead paper and a great relief to my mind)—*perhaps* that is one reason I do not get well faster.

You see, he does not believe I am sick! And what can one do?

If a physician of high standing, and one's own husband, assures friends and relatives that there is really nothing the matter with one but temporary nervous depression—a slight hysterical tendency—what is one to do?

My brother is also a physician, and also of high standing, and he says the same   10
thing.

So I take phosphates or phosphites—whichever it is—and tonics, and air and exercise, and journeys, and am absolutely forbidden to "work" until I am well again.

Personally, I disagree with their ideas.

Personally, I believe that congenial work, with excitement and change, would do me good.

But what is one to do?

I did write for a while in spite of them; but it *does* exhaust me a good deal—having   15
to be so sly about it, or else meet with heavy opposition.

I sometimes fancy that in my condition, if I had less opposition and more society and stimulus—but John says the very worst thing I can do is to think about my condition, and I confess it always makes me feel bad.

So I will let it alone and talk about the house.

The most beautiful place! It is quite alone, standing well back from the road, quite three miles from the village. It makes me think of English places that you read about, for there are hedges and walls and gates that lock, and lots of separate little houses for the gardeners and people.

There is a *delicious* garden! I never saw such a garden—large and shady, full of box-bordered paths, and lined with long grape-covered arbors with seats under them.

There were greenhouses, but they are all broken now.   20

There was some legal trouble, I believe, something about the heirs and co-heirs; anyhow, the place has been empty for years.

That spoils my ghostliness, I am afraid, but I don't care—there is something strange about the house—I can feel it.

I even said so to John one moonlight evening, but he said what I felt was a draught, and shut the window.

I get unreasonably angry with John sometimes. I'm sure I never used to be so sensitive. I think it is due to this nervous condition.

But John says if I feel so I shall neglect proper self-control; so I take pains to control myself—before him, at least, and that makes me very tired.   25

I don't like our room a bit. I wanted one downstairs that opened onto the piazza and had roses all over the window, and such pretty old-fashioned chintz hangings! But John would not hear of it.

He said there was only one window and not room for two beds, and no near room for him if he took another.

He is very careful and loving, and hardly lets me stir without special direction.

I have a schedule prescription for each hour in the day; he takes all care from me, and so I feel basely ungrateful not to value it more.

He said he came here solely on my account, that I was to have perfect rest and all   30
the air I could get. "Your exercise depends on your strength, my dear," said he, "and your food somewhat on your appetite; but air you can absorb all the time." So we took the nursery at the top of the house.

It is a big, airy room, the whole floor nearly, with windows that look all ways, and air and sunshine galore. It was nursery first, and then playroom and gymnasium, I should judge, for the windows are barred for little children, and there are rings and things in the walls.

The paint and paper look as if a boys' school had used it. It is stripped off—the paper—in great patches all around the head of my bed, about as far as I can reach, and in a great place on the other side of the room low down. I never saw a worse paper in my life. One of those sprawling, flamboyant patterns committing every artistic sin.

It is dull enough to confuse the eye in following, pronounced enough constantly to irritate and provoke study, and when you follow the lame uncertain curves for a little distance they suddenly commit suicide—plunge off at outrageous angles, destroy themselves in unheard-of contradictions.

The color is repellent, almost revolting: a smouldering unclean yellow, strangely faded by the slow-turning sunlight. It is a dull yet lurid orange in some places, a sickly sulphur tint in others.

No wonder the children hated it! I should hate it myself if I had to live in this   35
room long.

There comes John, and I must put this away—he hates to have me write a word.

We have been here two weeks, and I haven't felt like writing before, since that first day.

I am sitting by the window now, up in this atrocious nursery, and there is nothing to hinder my writing as much as I please, save lack of strength.

John is away all day, and even some nights when his cases are serious.

I am glad my case is not serious!   40

But these nervous troubles are dreadfully depressing.

John does not know how much I really suffer. He knows there is no reason to suffer, and that satisfies him.

Of course it is only nervousness. It does weigh on me so not to do my duty in any way!

I meant to be such a help to John, such a real rest and comfort, and here I am a comparative burden already!

Nobody would believe what an effort it is to do what little I am able—to dress and   45
entertain, and order things.

It is fortunate Mary is so good with the baby. Such a dear baby!

And yet I *cannot* be with him, it makes me so nervous.

I suppose John never was nervous in his life. He laughs at me so about this wallpaper!

At first he meant to repaper the room, but afterward he said that I was letting it get the better of me, and that nothing was worse for a nervous patient than to give way to such fancies.

He said that after the wallpaper was changed it would be the heavy bedstead, and   50
then the barred windows, and then that gate at the head of the stairs, and so on.

"You know the place is doing you good," he said, "and really, dear, I don't care to
renovate the house just for a three months' rental."

"Then do let us go downstairs," I said. "There are such pretty rooms there."

Then he took me in his arms and called me a blessed little goose, and said he
would go down cellar, if I wished, and have it whitewashed into the bargain.

But he is right enough about the beds and windows and things.

It is as airy and comfortable a room as anyone need wish, and, of course, I would   55
not be so silly as to make him uncomfortable just for a whim.

I'm really getting quite fond of the big room, all but that horrid paper.

Out of one window I can see the garden—those mysterious deep-shaded arbors,
the riotous old-fashioned flowers, and bushes and gnarly trees.

Out of another I get a lovely view of the bay and a little private wharf belonging to
the estate. There is a beautiful shaded lane that runs down there from the house. I
always fancy I see people walking in these numerous paths and arbors, but John has cautioned me not to give way to fancy in the least. He says that with my imaginative power
and habit of story-making, a nervous weakness like mine is sure to lead to all manner of
excited fancies, and that I ought to use my will and good sense to check the tendency. So
I try.

I think sometimes that if I were only well enough to write a little it would relieve
the press of ideas and rest me.

But I find I get pretty tired when I try.   60

It is so discouraging not to have any advice and companionship about my work.
When I get really well, John says we will ask Cousin Henry and Julia down for a long
visit; but he says he would as soon put fireworks in my pillow-case as to let me have those
stimulating people about now.

I wish I could get well faster.

But I must not think about that. This paper looks to me as if it *knew* what a vicious
influence it had!

There is a recurrent spot where the pattern lolls like a broken neck and two bulbous eyes stare at you upside down.

I get positively angry with the impertinence of it and the everlastingness. Up and   65
down and sideways they crawl, and those absurd unblinking eyes are everywhere. There
is one place where two breadths didn't match, and the eyes go all up and down the line,
one a little higher than the other.

I never saw so much expression in an inanimate thing before, and we all know
how much expression they have! I used to lie awake as a child and get more entertainment and terror out of blank walls and plain furniture than most children could find in
a toy-store.

I remember what a kindly wink the knobs of our big old bureau used to have, and
there was one chair that always seemed like a strong friend.

I used to feel that if any of the other things looked too fierce I could always hop
into that chair and be safe.

The furniture in this room is no worse than inharmonious, however, for we had to
bring it all from downstairs. I suppose when this was used as a playroom they had to take
the nursery things out, and no wonder! I never saw such ravages as the children have
made here.

The wallpaper, as I said before, is torn off in spots, and it sticketh closer than a   70
brother°—they must have had perseverance as well as hatred.

Then the floor is scratched and gouged and splintered, the plaster itself is dug
out here and there, and this great heavy bed, which is all we found in the room, looks as
if it had been through the wars.

But I don't mind it a bit—only the paper.

There comes John's sister. Such a dear girl as she is, and so careful of me! I must
not let her find me writing.

She is a perfect and enthusiastic housekeeper, and hopes for no better profession.
I verily believe she thinks it is the writing which made me sick!

But I can write when she is out, and see her a long way off from these windows.   75

There is one that commands the road, a lovely shaded winding road, and one
that just looks off over the country. A lovely country, too, full of great elms and velvet
meadows.

This wallpaper has a kind of sub-pattern in a different shade, a particularly irritating one, for you can only see it in certain lights, and not clearly then.

But in the places where it isn't faded and where the sun is just so—I can see a
strange, provoking, formless sort of figure that seems to skulk about behind that silly
and conspicuous front design.

There's sister on the stairs!

Well, the Fourth of July is over! The people are all gone, and I am tired out. John   80
thought it might do me good to see a little company, so we just had Mother and Nellie
and the children down for a week.

Of course I didn't do a thing. Jennie sees to everything now.

But it tired me all the same.

John says if I don't pick up faster he shall send me to Weir Mitchell° in the fall.

But I don't want to go there at all. I had a friend who was in his hands once, and
she says he is just like John and my brother, only more so!

Besides, it is such an undertaking to go so far.   85

I don't feel as if it was worthwhile to turn my hand over for anything, and I'm getting dreadfully fretful and querulous.

I cry at nothing, and cry most of the time.

Of course I don't when John is here, or anybody else, but when I am alone.

And I am alone a good deal just now. John is kept in town very often by serious
cases, and Jennie is good and lets me alone when I want her to.

So I walk a little in the garden or down that lovely lane, sit on the porch under the   90
roses, and lie down up here a good deal.

I'm getting really fond of the room in spite of the wallpaper. Perhaps *because* of
the wallpaper.

It dwells in my mind so!

I lie here on this great immovable bed—it is nailed down, I believe—and follow
that pattern about by the hour. It is as good as gymnastics, I assure you. I start, we'll
say, at the bottom, down in the corner over there where it has not been touched, and I

---

sticketh closer than a brother: Proverbs: 18:24.
Weir Mitchell: See note on p. 408.

determine for the thousandth time that I *will* follow that pointless pattern to some sort of a conclusion.

I know a little of the principle of design, and I know this thing was not arranged on any laws of radiation, or alternation, or repetition, or symmetry, or anything else that I ever heard of.

It is repeated, of course, by the breadths, but not otherwise.   95

Looked at in one way, each breadth stands alone; the bloated curves and flourishes—a kind of "debased Romanesque" with delirium tremens—go waddling up and down in isolated columns of fatuity.

But, on the other hand, they connect diagonally, and the sprawling outlines run off in great slanting waves of optic horror, like a lot of wallowing sea-weeds in full chase.

The whole thing goes horizontally, too, at least it seems so, and I exhaust myself trying to distinguish the order of its going in that direction.

They have used a horizontal breadth for a frieze, and that adds wonderfully to the confusion.

There is one end of the room where it is almost intact, and there, when the   100
crosslights fade and the low sun shines directly upon it, I can almost fancy radiation after all—the interminable grotesque seems to form around a common center and rush off in headlong plunges of equal distraction.

It makes me tired to follow it. I will take a nap, I guess.

I don't know why I should write this.

I don't want to.

I don't feel able.

And I know John would think it absurd. But I *must* say what I feel and think in   105
some way—it is such a relief!

But the effort is getting to be greater than the relief.

Half the time now I am awfully lazy, and lie down ever so much. John says I mustn't lose my strength, and has me take cod liver oil and lots of tonics and things, to say nothing of ale and wine and rare meat.

Dear John! He loves me very dearly, and hates to have me sick. I tried to have a real earnest reasonable talk with him the other day, and tell him how I wish he would let me go and make a visit to Cousin Henry and Julia.

But he said I wasn't able to go, nor able to stand it after I got there; and I did not make out a very good case for myself, for I was crying before I had finished.

It is getting to be a great effort for me to think straight. Just this nervous weak-   110
ness, I suppose.

And dear John gathered me up in his arms, and just carried me upstairs and laid me on the bed, and sat by me and read to me till it tired my head.

He said I was his darling and his comfort and all he had, and that I must take care of myself for his sake, and keep well.

He says no one but myself can help me out of it, that I must use my will and self-control and not let any silly fancies run away with me.

There's one comfort—the baby is well and happy, and does not have to occupy this nursery with the horrid wallpaper.

If we had not used it, that blessed child would have! What a fortunate escape!   115
Why, I wouldn't have a child of mine, an impressionable little thing, live in such a room for worlds.

I never thought of it before, but it is lucky that John kept me here after all; I can stand it so much easier than a baby, you see.

Of course I never mention it to them any more—I am too wise—but I keep watch for it all the same.

There are things in that wallpaper that nobody knows about but me, or ever will.

Behind that outside pattern the dim shapes get clearer every day.

It is always the same shape, only very numerous.   120

And it is like a woman stooping down and creeping about behind that pattern. I don't like it a bit. I wonder—I begin to think—I wish John would take me away from here!

It is so hard to talk with John about my case, because he is so wise, and because he loves me so.

But I tried it last night.

It was moonlight. The moon shines in all around just as the sun does.

I hate to see it sometimes, it creeps so slowly, and always comes in by one window   125
or another.

John was asleep and I hated to waken him, so I kept still and watched the moon-light on that undulating wallpaper till I felt creepy.

The faint figure behind seemed to shake the pattern, just as if she wanted to get out.

I got up softly and went to feel and see if the paper *did* move, and when I came back John was awake.

"What is it, little girl?" he said. "Don't go walking about like that—you'll get cold."

I thought it was a good time to talk, so I told him that I really was not gaining   130
here, and that I wished he would take me away.

"Why, darling!" said he. "Our lease will be up in three weeks, and I can't see how to leave before.

"The repairs are not done at home, and I cannot possibly leave town just now. Of course, if you were in any danger, I could and would, but you really are better, dear, whether you can see it or not. I am a doctor, dear, and I know. You are gaining flesh and color, your appetite is better, I feel really much easier about you."

"I don't weigh a bit more," said I, "nor as much; and my appetite may be better in the evening when you are here but it is worse in the morning when you are away!"

"Bless her little heart!" said he with a big hug. "She shall be as sick as she pleases! But now let's improve the shining hours by going to sleep, and talk about it in the morning!"

"And you won't go away?" I asked gloomily.   135

"Why, how can I, dear? It is only three weeks more and then we will take a nice little trip of a few days while Jennie is getting the house ready. Really, dear, you are better!"

"Better in body perhaps—" I began, and stopped short, for he sat up straight and looked at me with such a stern, reproachful look that I could not say another word.

"My darling," said he, "I beg of you, for my sake and for our child's sake, as well as for your own, that you will never for one instant let that idea enter your mind! There is nothing so dangerous, so fascinating, to a temperament like yours. It is a false and fool-ish fancy. Can you not trust me as a physician when I tell you so?"

So of course I said no more on that score, and we went to sleep before long. He thought I was asleep first, but I wasn't, and lay there for hours trying to decide whether that front pattern and the back pattern really did move together or separately.

On a pattern like this, by daylight, there is a lack of sequence, a defiance of law,   140
that is a constant irritant to a normal mind.

The color is hideous enough, and unreliable enough, and infuriating enough,
but the pattern is torturing.

You think you have mastered it, but just as you get well under way in following, it
turns a back-somersault and there you are. It slaps you in the face, knocks you down,
and tramples upon you. It is like a bad dream.

The outside pattern is a florid arabesque, reminding one of a fungus. If you can
imagine a toadstool in joints, an interminable string of toadstools, budding and sprouting in endless convolutions—why, that is something like it.

That is, sometimes!

There is one marked peculiarity about this paper, a thing nobody seems to notice   145
but myself, and that is that it changes as the light changes.

When the sun shoots in through the east window—I always watch for that first
long, straight ray—it changes so quickly than I never can quite believe it.

That is why I watch it always.

By moonlight—the moon shines in all night when there is a moon—I wouldn't
know it was the same paper.

At night in any kind of light, in twilight, candlelight, lamplight, and worst of all by
moonlight, it becomes bars! The outside pattern, I mean, and the woman behind it is as
plain as can be.

I didn't realize for a long time what the thing was that showed behind, that dim   150
sub-pattern, but now I am quite sure it is a woman.

By daylight she is subdued, quiet. I fancy it is the pattern that keeps her so still. It
is so puzzling. It keeps me quiet by the hour.

I lie down ever so much now. John says it is good for me, and to sleep all I can.

Indeed he started the habit by making me lie down for an hour after each meal.

It is a very bad habit, I am convinced, for you see, I don't sleep.

And that cultivates deceit, for I don't tell them I'm awake—oh, no!   155

The fact is I am getting a little afraid of John.

He seems very queer sometimes, and even Jennie has an inexplicable look.

It strikes me occasionally, just as a scientific hypothesis, that perhaps it is the paper!

I have watched John when he did not know I was looking, and come into the
room suddenly on the most innocent excuses, and I've caught him several times *looking
at the paper!* And Jennie too. I caught Jennie with her hand on it once.

She didn't know I was in the room, and when I asked her in a quiet, a very quiet   160
voice, with the most restrained manner possible, what she was doing with the paper, she
turned around as if she had been caught stealing, and looked quite angry—asked me
why I should frighten her so!

Then she said that the paper stained everything it touched, that she had found
yellow smooches on all my clothes and John's and she wished we would be more careful!

Did not that sound innocent? But I know she was studying that pattern, and I am
determined that nobody shall find it out but myself.

Life is very much more exciting now than it used to be. You see, I have something
more to expect, to look forward to, to watch. I really do eat better, and am more quiet
than I was.

John is so pleased to see me improve! He laughed a little the other day, and said I
seemed to be flourishing in spite of my wallpaper.

I turned it off with a laugh. I had no intention of telling him it was *because* of the   165
wallpaper—he would make fun of me. He might even want to take me away.

I don't want to leave now until I have found it out. There is a week more, and I
think that will be enough.

I'm feeling so much better!

I don't sleep much at night, for it is so interesting to watch developments; but
sleep a good deal during the daytime.

In the daytime it is tiresome and perplexing.

There are always new shoots on the fungus, and new shades of yellow all over it. I   170
cannot keep count of them, though I have tried conscientiously.

It is the strangest yellow, that wallpaper! It makes me think of all the yellow things
I ever saw—not beautiful ones like buttercups, but old, foul, bad yellow things.

But there is something else about that paper—the smell! I noticed it the moment
we came into the room, but with so much air and sun it was not bad. Now we have had a
week of fog and rain, and whether the windows are open or not, the smell is here.

It creeps all over the house.

I find it hovering in the dining-room, skulking in the parlor, hiding in the hall,
lying in wait for me on the stairs.

It gets into my hair.   175

Even when I go to ride, if I turn my head suddenly and surprise it—there is that
smell!

Such a peculiar odor, too! I have spent hours in trying to analyze it, to find what it
smelled like.

It is not bad—at first—and very gentle, but quite the subtlest, most enduring odor
I ever met.

In this damp weather it is awful. I wake up in the night and find it hanging
over me.

It used to disturb me at first. I thought seriously of burning the house—to reach   180
the smell.

But now I am used to it. The only thing I can think of that it is like is the *color* of
the paper! A yellow smell.

There is a very funny mark on this wall, low down, near the mopboard. A streak
that runs round the room. It goes behind every piece of furniture, except the bed, a
long, straight, even *smooch*, as if it had been rubbed over and over.

I wonder how it was done and who did it, and what they did it for. Round and
round and round—round and round and round—it makes me dizzy!

I really have discovered something at last.

Through watching so much at night, when it changes so, I have finally found out.   185

The front pattern *does* move—and no wonder! The woman behind shakes it!

Sometimes I think there are a great many women behind, and sometimes only
one, and she crawls around fast, and her crawling shakes it all over.

Then in the very bright spots she keeps still, and in the very shady spots she just
takes hold of the bars and shakes them hard.

And she is all the time trying to climb through. But nobody could climb through
that pattern—it strangles so; I think that is why it has so many heads.

They get through and then the pattern strangles them off and turns them upside   190
down, and makes their eyes white!

If those heads were covered or taken off it would not be half so bad.

I think that woman gets out in the daytime!

And I'll tell you why—privately—I've seen her!

I can see her out of every one of my windows!

It is the same woman, I know, for she is always creeping, and most women do not   195
creep by daylight.

I see her in that long shaded lane, creeping up and down. I see her in those dark
grape arbors, creeping all around the garden.

I see her on that long road under the trees, creeping along, and when a carriage
comes she hides under the blackberry vines.

I don't blame her a bit. It must be very humiliating to be caught creeping by
daylight!

I always lock the door when I creep by daylight. I can't do it at night, for I know
John would suspect something at once.

And John is so queer now that I don't want to irritate him. I wish he would take   200
another room! Besides, I don't want anybody to get that woman out at night but myself.

I often wonder if I could see her out of all the windows at once.

But, turn as fast as I can, I can only see out of one at a time.

And though I always see her, she *may* be able to creep faster than I can turn! I
have watched her sometimes away off in the open country, creeping as fast as a cloud
shadow in a wind.

If only that top pattern could be gotten off from the under one! I mean to try it,
little by little.

I have found out another funny thing, but I shan't tell it this time! It does not do   205
to trust people too much.

There are only two more days to get this paper off, and I believe John is beginning to notice. I don't like the look in his eyes.

And I heard him ask Jennie a lot of professional questions about me. She had a
very good report to give.

She said I slept a good deal in the daytime.

John knows I don't sleep very well at night, for all I'm so quiet!

He asked me all sorts of questions, too, and pretended to be very loving and kind.   210

As if I couldn't see through him!

Still, I don't wonder he acts so, sleeping under this paper for three months.

It only interests me, but I feel sure John and Jennie are affected by it.

Hurrah! This is the last day, but it is enough. John is to stay in town over night,
and won't be out until this evening.

Jennie wanted to sleep with me—the sly thing; but I told her I should undoubtedly   215
rest better for a night all alone.

That was clever, for really I wasn't alone a bit! As soon as it was moonlight and
that poor thing began to crawl and shake the pattern, I got up and ran to help her.

I pulled and she shook. I shook and she pulled, and before morning we had
peeled off yards of that paper.

A strip about as high as my head and half around the room.

And then when the sun came and that awful pattern began to laugh at me, I
declared I would finish it today!

We go away tomorrow, and they are moving all my furniture down again to leave   220
things as they were before.

Jennie looked at the wall in amazement, but I told her merrily that I did it out of
pure spite at the vicious thing.

She laughed and said she wouldn't mind doing it herself, but I must not get tired.
How she betrayed herself that time!

But I am here, and no person touches this paper but Me—not *alive!*

She tried to get me out of the room—it was too patent! But I said it was so quiet   225
and empty and clean now that I believed I would lie down again and sleep all I could,
and not to wake me even for dinner—I would call when I woke.

So now she is gone, and the servants are gone, and the things are gone, and
there is nothing left but that great bedstead nailed down, with the canvas mattress we
found on it.

We shall sleep downstairs tonight, and take the boat home tomorrow.

I quite enjoy the room, now it is bare again.

How those children did tear about here!

This bedstead is fairly gnawed!   230

But I must get to work.

I have locked the door and thrown the key down into the front path.

I don't want to go out, and I don't want to have anybody come in, till John comes.

I want to astonish him.

I've got a rope up here that even Jennie did not find. If that woman does get out,   235
and tries to get away, I can tie her!

But I forgot I could not reach far without anything to stand on!

This bed will *not* move!

I tried to lift and push it until I was lame, and then I got so angry I bit off a little
piece at one corner—but it hurt my teeth.

Then I peeled off all the paper I could reach standing on the floor. It sticks horribly and the pattern just enjoys it! All those strangled heads and bulbous eyes and waddling fungus growths just shriek with derision!

I am getting angry enough to do something desperate. To jump out of the window   240
would be admirable exercise, but the bars are too strong even to try.

Besides I wouldn't do it. Of course not. I know well enough that a step like that is
improper and might be misconstrued.

I don't like to *look* out of the windows even—there are so many of those creeping
women, and they creep so fast.

I wonder if they all came out of that wallpaper as I did?

But I am securely fastened now by my well-hidden rope—you don't get *me* out in
the road there!

I suppose I shall have to get back behind the pattern when it comes night, and   245
that is hard!

It is so pleasant to be out in this great room and creep around as I please!

I don't want to go outside. I won't, even if Jennie asks me to.

For outside you have to creep on the ground, and everything is green instead of
yellow.

But here I can creep smoothly on the floor, and my shoulder just fits in that long
smooch around the wall, so I cannot lose my way.

Why, there's John at the door!   250

It is no use, young man, you can't open it!

How he does call and pound!

Now he's crying to Jennie for an axe.

It would be a shame to break down that beautiful door!

"John, dear!" said I in the gentlest voice. "The key is down by the front steps,   255
under a plantain leaf!"

That silenced him for a few moments.

Then he said, very quietly indeed, "Open the door, my darling!"

"I can't," said I. "The key is down by the front door under a plantain leaf!" And
then I said it again, several times, very gently and slowly, and said it so often that he had
to go and see, and he got it of course, and came in. He stopped short by the door.

"What is the matter?" he cried. "For God's sake, what are you doing!"

I kept on creeping just the same, but I looked at him over my shoulder.   260

"I've got out at last," said I, "in spite of you and Jane. And I've pulled off most of
the paper, so you can't put me back!"

Now why should that man have fainted? But he did, and right across my path by
the wall, so that I had to creep over him every time!

MARGARET LAURENCE   (1926–1987)

*Laurence wss born in Neepawa, Manitoba, and was edu-
cated in Winnipeg, the provincial capital. She spent her
twenties in Somalia and Ghana, and one of her earliest
writing efforts was to make translations from the Somali
language. Eventually she lived in both England and
Canada. Afer publication of her first novel,* This Side
Jordan *(1960), and her first collection of stories,* The
Tomorrow-Tamer *(1964), she wrote prolifically, her most
acclaimed work being her novels and stories dramatizing
the lives of women in Manawaka, her fictionalized name for
Neepawa. The best known of the Manawaka novels is* The
Diviners *(1974). Laurence also wrote travel books, collec-
tions of essays, and children's stories; her autobiographical memoir* Dance on the Earth *was
published in 1989, two years after her death. "The Loons" is taken from* A Bird in the House
(1970), her collection of eight Manawaka stories.

The Loons _____ *1970*

Just below Manawaka, where the Wachakwa River ran brown and noisy over the pebbles, the scrub oak and grey-green willow and chokecherry bushes grew in a dense
thicket. In a clearing at the centre of the thicket stood the Tonnerre family's shack.
The basis of this dwelling was a small square cabin made of poplar poles and chinked
with mud, which had been built by Jules Tonnerres some fifty years before, when he
came back from Batoche with a bullet in his thigh, the year that Riel was hung and the
voices of the Metis entered their long silence. Jules had only intended to stay the winter
in the Wachakwa Valley, but the family was still there in the thirties, when I was a child.
As the Tonnerres had increased, their settlement had been added to, until the clearing
at the foot of the town hill was a chaos of lean-tos, wooden packing cases, warped
lumber, discarded car tyres, ramshackle chicken coops, tangled strands of barbed wire
and rusty tin cans.

The Tonnerres were French halfbreeds, and among themselves they spoke a *patois* that was neither Cree nor French. Their English was broken and full of obscenities. They did not belong among the Cree of the Galloping Mountain reservation, further north, and they did not belong among the Scots-Irish and Ukrainians of Manawaka, either. They were, as my Grandmother MacLeod would have put it, neither flesh, fowl, nor good salt herring. When their men were not working at odd jobs or as section hands on the C.P.R.,° they lived on relief. In the summers, one of the Tonnerre youngsters, with a face that seemed totally unfamiliar with laughter, would knock at the doors of the town's brick houses and offer for sale a lard-pail full of bruised wild strawberries, and if he got as much as a quarter he would grab the coin and run before the customer had time to change her mind. Sometimes old Jules, or his son Lazarus, would get mixed up in a Saturday-night brawl, and would hit out at whoever was nearest, or howl drunkenly among the offended shoppers on Main Street, and then the Mountie would put them for the night in the barred cell underneath the Court House, and the next morning they would be quiet again.

Piquette Tonnerre, the daughter of Lazarus, was in my class at school. She was older than I, but she had failed several grades, perhaps because her attendance had always been sporadic and her interest in schoolwork negligible. Part of the reason she had missed a lot of school was that she had had tuberculosis of the bone, and had once spent many months in hospital. I knew this because my father was the doctor who had looked after her. Her sickness was almost the only thing I knew about her, however. Otherwise, she existed for me only as a vaguely embarrassing presence, with her hoarse voice and her clumsy limping walk and her grimy cotton dresses that were always miles too long. I was neither friendly nor unfriendly towards her. She dwelt and moved somewhere within my scope of vision, but I did not actually notice her very much until that peculiar summer when I was eleven.

"I don't know what to do about that kid," my father said at dinner one evening. "Piquette Tonnerre, I mean. The damn bone's flared up again. I've had her in hospital for quite a while now, and it's under control all right, but I hate like the dickens to send her home again."

"Couldn't you explain to her mother that she has to rest a lot?" my mother said.   5

"The mother's not there," my father replied. "She took off a few years back. Can't say I blame her. Piquette cooks for them, and she says Lazarus would never do anything for himself as long as she's there. Anyway, I don't think she'd take much care of herself, once she got back. She's only thirteen, after all. Beth, I was thinking—what about taking her up to Diamond Lake with us this summer? A couple of months rest would give that bone a much better chance."

My mother looked stunned.

"But Ewen—what about Roddie and Vanessa?"

"She's not contagious," my father said. "And it would be company for Vanessa."

"Oh dear," my mother said in distress, "I'll bet anything she has nits in her hair."   10

"For Pete's sake," my father said crossly, "do you think Matron would let her stay in the hospital for all this time like that? Don't be silly, Beth."

Grandmother MacLeod, her delicately featured face as rigid as a cameo, now brought her mauve-veined hands together as though she were about to begin a prayer.

C.P.R.: Canadian Pacific Railway.

"Ewen, if that half-breed youngster comes along to Diamond Lake, I'm not going," she announced. "I'll go to Morag's for the summer."

I had trouble in stifling my urge to laugh, for my mother brightened visibly and quickly tried to hide it. If it came to a choice between Grandmother MacLeod and Piquette, Piquette would win hands down, nits or not.

"It might be quite nice for you, at that," she mused. "You haven't seen Morag for   15
over a year, and you might enjoy being in the city for a while. Well, Ewen dear, you do what you think best. If you think it would do Piquette some good, then we'll be glad to have her, as long as she behaves herself."

So it happened that several weeks later, when we all piled into my father's old Nash, surrounded by suitcases and boxes of provisions and toys for my ten-month-old brother, Piquette was with us and Grandmother MacLeod, miraculously, was not. My father would only be staying at the cottage for a couple of weeks, for he had to get back to his practice, but the rest of us would stay at Diamond Lake until the end of August.

Our cottage was not named, as many were, "Dew Drop Inn," or "Bide-a-Wee," or "Bonnie Doon." The sign on the roadway bore in austere letters only our name, MacLeod. It was not a large cottage, but it was on the lakefront. You could look out the windows and see, through the filigree of the spruce trees, the water glistening greatly as the sun caught it. All around the cottage were ferns, and sharp-branched raspberry bushes, and moss that had grown over fallen tree trunks. If you looked carefully among the weeds and grass, you could find wild strawberry plants which were in white flower now and in another month would bear fruit, the fragrant globes hanging like miniature scarlet lanterns on the thin hairy stems. The two gray squirrels were still there, gossiping at us from the tall spruce beside the cottage, and by the end of the summer they would again be tame enough to take pieces of crust from my hands. The broad moose antlers that hung above the back door were a little more bleached and fissured after the winter, but otherwise everything was the same. I raced joyfully around my kingdom, greeting all the places I had not seen for a year. My brother, Roderick, who had not been born when we were here last summer, sat on the car rug in the sunshine and examined a brown spruce cone, meticulously turning it round and round in his small and curious hands. My mother and father toted the luggage from car to cottage, exclaiming over how well the place had wintered, no broken windows, thank goodness, no apparent damage from storm-felled branches or snow.

Only after I had finished looking around did I notice Piquette. She was sitting on the swing, her lame leg held stiffly out, and her other foot scuffing the ground as she swung slowly back and forth. Her long hair hung black and straight around her shoulders, and her broad coarse-featured face bore no expression—it was blank, as though she no longer dwelt within her own skull, as though she had gone elsewhere. I approached her very hesitantly.

"Want to come and play?"

Piquette looked at me with a sudden flash of scorn.   20

"I ain't a kid," she said.

Wounded, I stamped angrily away, swearing I would not speak to her for the rest of the summer. In the days that followed, however, Piquette began to interest me, and I began to want to interest her. My reasons did not appear bizarre to me. Unlikely as it may seem, I had only just realised that the Tonnerre family, whom I had always heard called half-breeds, were actually Indians, or as near as made no difference. My acquaintance with Indians was not extensive. I did not remember ever having seen a real Indian, and my new awareness that Piquette sprang from the people of Big Bear and Poundmaker, of Tecumseh, of the Iroquois who had eaten Father Brebeuf's heart—all this gave her an instant attraction in my eyes. I was a devoted reader of Pauline Johnson at this age, and sometimes would orate aloud and in an exalted voice, *West Wind, blow from your prairie nest; Blow from the mountains, blow from the west*—and so on. It seemed to me that Piquette must be in some way a daughter of the forest, a kind of junior prophetess of the wilds, who might impart to me, if I took the right approach, some of the secrets which she undoubtedly knew—where the whippoorwill made her nest, how the coyote reared her young, or whatever it was that it said in Hiawatha.

I set about gaining Piquette's trust. She was not allowed to go swimming, with her bad leg, but I managed to lure her down to the beach—or rather, she came because there was nothing else to do. The water was always icy, for the lake was fed by springs, but I swam like a dog, thrashing my arms and legs around at such speed and with such an output of energy that I never grew cold. Finally, when I had had enough, I came out and sat beside Piquette on the sand. When she saw me approaching, her hand squashed flat the sand castle she had been building, and she looked at me sullenly, without speaking.

"Do you like this place?" I asked, after a while, intending to lead on from there into the question of forest lore.

Piquette shrugged. "It's okay. Good as anywhere."   25

"I love it," I said. "We come here every summer."

"So what?" Her voice was distant, and I glanced at her uncertainly, wondering what I could have said wrong.

"Do you want to come for a walk?" I asked her. "We wouldn't need to go far. If you walk just around the point, you come to a bay where great big reeds grow in the water, and all kinds of fish hang around there. Want to? Come on."

She shook her head.

"Your dad said I ain't supposed to do no more walking than I got to."   30

I tried another line.

"I bet you know a lot about the woods and all that, eh ?" I began respectfully.

Piquette looked at me from her large dark unsmiling eyes.

"I don't know what in hell you're talkin' about," she replied. "You nuts or somethin'? If you mean where my old man, and me, and all them live, you better shut up, by Jesus, you hear?"

I was startled and my feelings were hurt, but I had a kind of dogged perseverance.   35
I ignored her rebuff.

"'You know something, Piquette? There's loons here, on this lake. You can see their nests just up the shore there, behind those logs. At night, you can hear them even from the cottage, but it's better to listen from the beach. My dad says we should listen and try to remember how they sound, because in a few years when more cottages are built at Diamond Lake and more people come in, the loons will go away."

Piquette was picking up stones and snail shells and then dropping them again.

"Who gives a good goddamn?" she said.

It became increasingly obvious that, as an Indian, Piquette was a dead loss. That evening I went out by myself, scrambling through the bushes that overhung the steep path, my feet slipping on the fallen spruce needles that covered the ground. When I reached the shore, I walked along the firm damp sand to the small pier that my father had built, and sat down there. I heard someone else crashing through the undergrowth and the bracken, and for a moment I thought Piquette had changed her mind, but it turned out to be my father. He sat beside me on the pier and we waited, without speaking.

At night the lake was like black glass with a streak of amber which was the path of the moon. All around, the spruce trees grew tall and close-set, branches blackly sharp against the sky, which was lightened by a cold flickering of stars. Then the loons began their calling. They rose like phantom birds from the nests on the shore, and flew out onto the dark still surface of the water.

No one can ever describe that ululating sound, the crying of the loons, and no one who has heard it can ever forget it. Plaintive, and yet with a quality of chilling mockery, those voices belonged to a world separated by aeons from our neat world of summer cottages and the lighted lamps of home.

"They must have sounded just like that," my father remarked, "before any person ever set foot here."

Then he laughed. "You could say the same, of course, about sparrows, or chipmunks, but somehow it only strikes you that way with the loons."

"I know," I said.

Neither of us suspected that this would be the last time we would ever sit here together on the shore, listening. We stayed for perhaps half an hour, and then we went back to the cottage. My mother was reading beside the fireplace. Piquette was looking at the burning birch log, and not doing anything.

"You should have come along," I said, although in fact I was glad she had not.

"Not me," Piquette said. "You wouldn' catch me walkin' way down there jus' for a bunch of squawkin' birds."

Piquette and I remained ill at ease with one another. I felt I had somehow failed my father, but I did not know what was the matter, nor why she would not or could not respond when I suggested exploring the woods or playing house. I thought it was probably her slow and difficult walking that held her back. She stayed most of the time in the cottage with my mother, helping her with the dishes or with Roddie, but hardly ever talking. Then the Duncans arrived at their cottage, and I spent my days with Mavis, who was my best friend. I could not reach Piquette at all, and I soon lost interest in trying. But all that summer she remained as both a reproach and a mystery to me.

That winter my father died of pneumonia, after less than a week's illness. For some time I saw nothing around me, being completely immersed in my own pain and my mother's. When I looked outward once more, I scarcely noticed that Piquette Tonnerre was no longer at school. I do not remember seeing her at all until four years later, one Saturday night when Mavis and I were having Cokes in the Regal Café. The jukebox was booming like tuneful thunder, and beside it, leaning lightly on its chrome and its rainbow glass, was a girl.

Piquette must have been seventeen then, although she looked about twenty. I stared at her, astounded that anyone could have changed so much. Her face, so stolid and expressionless before, was animated now with a gaiety that was almost violent. She laughed and talked very loudly with the boys around her. Her lipstick was bright carmine, and her hair was cut short and frizzily permed. She had not been pretty as a child, and she was not pretty now, for her features were still heavy and blunt. But her dark and slightly slanted eyes were beautiful, and her skin-tight skirt and orange sweater displayed to enviable advantage a soft and slender body.

She saw me, and walked over. She teetered a little, but it was not due to her once-tubercular leg, for her limp was almost gone.

"Hi, Vanessa." Her voice still had the same hoarseness. "Long time no see, eh?"

40

45

50

"Hi," I said. "Where've you been keeping yourself, Piquette?"

"Oh, I been around," she said. "I been away almost two years now. Been all over the place—Winnipeg, Regina, Saskatoon. Jesus, what I could tell you! I come back this summer, but I ain't stayin'. You kids goin' to the dance?"

"No," I said abruptly, for this was a sore point with me. I was fifteen, and thought I 55 was old enough to go to the Saturday-night dances at the Flamingo. My mother, however, thought otherwise.

"Y'oughta come," Piquette said. "I never miss one. It's just about the on'y thing in this jerkwater town that's any fun. Boy, you couldn' catch me stayin' here. I don' give a shit about this place. It stinks."

She sat down beside me, and I caught the harsh over-sweetness of her perfume.

"Listen, you wanna know something, Vanessa?" she confided, her voice only slightly blurred. "Your dad was the only person in Manawaka that ever done anything good to me."

I nodded speechlessly. I was certain she was speaking the truth. I knew a little more than I had that summer at Diamond Lake, but I could not reach her now any more than I had then. I was ashamed, ashamed of my own timidity, the frightened tendency to look the other way. Yet I felt no real warmth towards her—I only felt that I ought to, because of that distant summer and because my father had hoped she would be company for me, or perhaps that I would be for her, but it had not happened that way. At this moment, meeting her again, I had to admit that she repelled and embarrassed me, and I could not help despising the self-pity in her voice. I wished she would go away. I did not want to see her. I did not know what to say to her. It seemed that we had nothing to say to one another.

"I'll tell you something else," Piquette went on. "All the old bitches an' biddies in 60 this town will sure be surprised. I'm gettin' married this fall—my boyfriend, he's an English fella, works in the stockyards in the city there, a very tall guy, got blond wavy hair. Gee, is he ever handsome. Got this real classy name. Alvin Gerald Cummings— some handle, eh? They call him Al."

For the merest instant, then, I saw her. I really did see her, for the first and only time in all the years we had both lived in the same town. Her defiant face, momentarily, became unguarded and unmasked, and in her eyes there was a terrifying hope.

"Gee, Piquette—" I burst out awkwardly, "that's swell. That's really wonderful. Congratulations—good luck—I hope you'll be happy—"

As I mouthed the conventional phrases, I could only guess how great her need must have been, that she had been forced to seek the very things she so bitterly rejected.

When I was eighteen, I left Manawaka and went away to college. At the end of my first year, I came back home for the summer. I spent the first few days in talking nonstop with my mother, as we exchanged all the news that somehow had not found its way into letters—what had happened in my life and what had happened here in Manawaka while I was away. My mother searched her memory for events that concerned people I knew.

"Did I ever write you about Piquette Tonnerre, Vanessa?" she asked one morning. 65

"No, I don't think so," I replied. "Last I heard of her, she was going to marry some guy in the city. Is she still there?"

My mother looked perturbed, and it was a moment before she spoke, as though she did not know how to express what she had to tell and wished she did not need to try.

"She's dead," she said at last. Then, as I stared at her, "Oh, Vanessa, when it happened, I couldn't help thinking of her as she was that summer—so sullen and gauche and badly dressed. I couldn't help wondering if we could have done something more at that time—but what could we do? She used to be around in the cottage there with me all day, and honestly, it was all I could do to get a word out of her. She didn't even talk to your father very much, although I think she liked him, in her way."

"What happened?" I asked.

'"Either her husband left her, or she left him," my mother said. "I don't know which. Anyway, she came back here with two youngsters, both only babies—they must have been born very close together. She kept house, I guess, for Lazarus and her brothers, down in the valley there, in the old Tonnerre place. I used to see her on the street sometimes, but she never spoke to me. She'd put on an awful lot of weight, and she looked a mess, to tell you the truth, a real slattern, dressed any old how. She was up in court a couple of times—drunk and disorderly, of course. One Saturday night last winter, during the coldest weather, Piquette was alone in the shack with the children. The Tonnerres made home brew all the time, so I've heard, and Lazarus said later she'd been drinking most of the day when he and the boys went out that evening. They had an old woodstove there—you know the kind, with exposed pipes. The shack caught fire. Piquette didn't get out, and neither did the children."

I did not say anything. As so often with Piquette, there did not seem to be anything to say. There was a kind of silence around the image in my mind of the fire and the snow, and I wished I could put from my memory the look that I had seen once in Piquette's eyes.

I went up to Diamond Lake for a few days that summer, with Mavis and her family. The MacLeod cottage had been sold after my father's death, and I did not even go to look at it, not wanting to witness my long-ago kingdom possessed now by strangers. But one evening I went down to the shore by myself.

The small pier which my father had built was gone, and in its place there was a large and solid pier built by the government, for Galloping Mountain was now a national park, and Diamond Lake had been re-named Lake Wapakata, for it was felt that an Indian name would have a greater appeal to tourists. The one store had become several dozen, and the settlement had all the attributes of a flourishing resort—hotels, a dancehall, cafés with neon signs, the penetrating odours of potato chips and hot dogs.

I sat on the government pier and looked out across the water. At night the lake at least was the same as it had always been, darkly shining and bearing within its black glass the streak of amber that was the path of the moon. There was no wind that evening, and everything was quiet all around me. It seemed too quiet, and then I realized that the loons were no longer here. I listened for some time, to make sure, but never once did I hear that long-drawn call, half mocking and half plaintive, spearing through the stillness across the lake.

I did not know what had happened to the birds. Perhaps they had gone away to some far place of belonging. Perhaps they had been unable to find such a place, and had simply died out, having ceased to care any longer whether they lived or not.

I remembered how Piquette had scorned to come along, when my father and I sat there and listened to the lake birds. It seemed to me now that in some unconscious and totally unrecognised way, Piquette might have been the only one, after all, who had heard the crying of the loons.

70

75

FLANNERY O'CONNOR   (1925–1964)

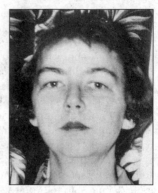

Mary Flannery O'Connor, a Georgia native, graduated from the Women's College of Georgia and received a master of fine arts degree from the University of Iowa in 1947. She contracted lupus, a disorder of the immune system, and was an invalid for the last ten years of her life. Despite her illness, she wrote extensively, publishing two novels and many short stories. Her first collection was A Good Man Is Hard to Find, *in 1955. A posthumous collection,* Everything That Rises Must Converge, *was published in 1965, and* Complete Stories *appeared in 1971. Her works combine flat realism with grotesque situations; violence occurs without apparent reason or preparation. Many of her characters are odd, eccentic, and bizarre. Others, such as the Misfit in* "A Good Man Is Hard to Find," *are gratuitously cruel. Ironically, however, their cold and depraved actions highlight the need for religious awakening because they enable some of the characters, such as the grandmother in the following story, to achieve spiritual elevation.*

A Good Man Is Hard to Find ——————————————— 1955

The grandmother didn't want to go to Florida. She wanted to visit some of her connections in east Tennessee and she was seizing at every chance to change Bailey's mind. Bailey was the son she lived with, her only son. He was sitting on the edge of his chair at the table, bent over the orange sports section of the *Journal.* "Now look here, Bailey," she said, "see here, read this," and she stood with one hand on her thin hip and the other rattling the newspaper at his bald head. "Here this fellow that calls himself The Misfit is aloose from the Federal Pen and headed toward Florida and you read here what it says he did to these people. Just you read it. I wouldn't take my children in any direction with a criminal like that aloose in it. I couldn't answer to my conscience if I did."

Bailey didn't look up from his reading so she wheeled around then and faced the children's mother, a young woman in slacks, whose face was as broad and innocent as a cabbage and was tied round with a green head-kerchief that had two points on the top like rabbit's ears. She was sitting on the sofa, feeding the baby his apricots out of a jar. "The children have been to Florida before," the old lady said. "You all ought to take them somewhere else for a change so they would see different parts of the world and be broad. They never have been to east Tennessee."

The children's mother didn't seem to hear her but the eight-year-old boy, John Wesley, a stocky child with glasses, said, "If you don't want to go to Florida, why dontcha stay at home?" He and the little girl, June Star, were reading the funny papers on the floor.

"She wouldn't stay at home to be queen for a day," June Star said without raising her yellow head.

"Yes and what would you do if this fellow, The Misfit, caught you?" the grand-   5
mother asked.

"I'd smack his face," John Wesley said.

"She wouldn't stay at home for a million bucks," June Star said. "Afraid she'd miss something. She has to go everywhere we go."

"All right, Miss," the grandmother said. "Just remember that the next time you want me to curl your hair."

June Star said her hair was naturally curly.

The next morning the grandmother was the first one in the car, ready to go. She   10
had her big black valise that looked like the head of a hippopotamus in one corner, and
underneath it she was hiding a basket with Pitty Sing, the cat, in it. She
didn't intend for the cat to be left alone in the house for three days because he would
miss her too much and she was afraid he might brush against one of the gas burners
and accidentally asphyxiate himself. Her son, Bailey, didn't like to arrive at a motel with
a cat.

She sat in the middle of the back seat with John Wesley and June Star on either
side of her. Bailey and the children's mother and the baby sat in the front and they left
Atlanta at eight forty-five with the mileage on the car at 55890. The grandmother wrote
this down because she thought it would be interesting to say how many miles they had
been when they got back. It took them twenty minutes to reach the outskirts of the city.

The old lady settled herself comfortably, removing her white cotton gloves and
putting them up with her purse on the shelf in front of the back window. The children's mother still had on slacks and still had her head tied up in a green kerchief, but
the grandmother had on a navy blue straw sailor hat with a bunch of white violets on
the brim and a navy blue dress with a small white dot in the print. Her collar and cuffs
were white organdy trimmed with lace and at her neckline she had pinned a purple
spray of cloth violets containing a sachet. In case of an accident, anyone seeing her
dead on the highway would know at once that she was a lady.

She said she thought it was going to be a good day for driving, neither too hot
nor too cold, and she cautioned Bailey that the speed limit was fifty-five miles an hour
and that the patrolmen hid themselves behind billboards and small clumps of trees and
sped out after you before you had a chance to slow down. She pointed out interesting
details of the scenery: Stone Mountain; the blue granite that in some places came up to
both sides of the highway; the brilliant red clay banks slightly streaked with purple; and
the various crops that made rows of green lacework on the ground. The trees were full of
silver-white sunlight and the meanest of them sparkled. The children were reading
comic magazines and their mother had gone back to sleep.

"Let's go through Georgia fast so we won't have to look at it much," John Wesley
said.

"If I were a little boy," said the grandmother, "I wouldn't talk about my native state   15
that way. Tennessee has the mountains and Georgia has the hills."

"Tennessee is just a hillbilly dumping ground," John Wesley said, "and Georgia is
a lousy state too."

"You said it," June Star said.

"In my time," said the grandmother, folding her thin veined fingers, "children
were more respectful of their native states and their parents and everything else. People
did right then. Oh look at the cute little pickaninny!" she said and pointed to a Negro
child standing in the door of a shack. "Wouldn't that make a picture, now?" she asked
and they all turned and looked at the little Negro out of the back window. He waved.

"He didn't have any britches on," June said.

"He probably didn't have any," the grandmother explained. "Little niggers in the   20
country don't have things like we do. If I could paint, I'd paint that picture," she said.

The children exchanged comic books.

The grandmother offered to hold the baby and the children's mother passed him
over the front seat to her. She set him on her knee and bounced him and told him about
the things they were passing. She rolled her eyes and screwed up her mouth and stuck

her leathery thin face into his smooth bland one. Occasionally he gave her a faraway smile. They passed a large cotton field with five or six graves fenced in the middle of it, like a small island. "Look at the graveyard!" the grandmother said, pointing it out. "That was the old family burying ground. That belonged to the plantation."

"Where's the plantation?" John Wesley asked.

"Gone With the Wind," said the grandmother. "Ha. Ha."

When the children finished all the comic books they had brought, they opened   25 the lunch and ate it. The grandmother ate a peanut butter sandwich and an olive and would not let the children throw the box and the paper napkins out the window. When there was nothing else to do they played a game by choosing a cloud and making the other two guess what shape it suggested. John Wesley took one the shape of a cow and June Star guessed a cow and John Wesley said, no, an automobile, and June Star said he didn't play fair, and they began to slap each other over the grandmother.

The grandmother said she would tell them a story if they would keep quiet. When she told a story, she rolled her eyes and waved her head and was very dramatic. She said once when she was a maiden lady she had been courted by a Mr. Edgar Atkins Teagarden from Jasper, Georgia. She said he was a very good-looking man and a gentleman and that he brought her a watermelon every Saturday afternoon with his initials cut in it, E. A. T. Well, one Saturday, she said, Mr. Teagarden brought the watermelon and there was nobody at home and he left it on the front porch and returned in his buggy to Jasper, but she never got the watermelon, she said, because a nigger boy ate it when he saw the initials, E. A. T.! This story tickled John Wesley's funny bone and he giggled and giggled but June Star didn't think it was any good. She said she wouldn't marry a man that just brought her a watermelon on Saturday. The grandmother said she would have done well to marry Mr. Teagarden because he was a gentleman and had bought Coca-Cola stock when it first came out and that he had died only a few years ago, a very wealthy man.

They stopped at The Tower for barbecued sandwiches. The Tower was a part stucco and part wood filling station and dance hall set in a clearing outside of Timothy. A fat man named Red Sammy Butts ran it and there were signs stuck here and there on the building and for miles up and down the highway saying, TRY RED SAMMY'S FAMOUS BARBECUE. NONE LIKE FAMOUS RED SAMMY'S! RED SAM! THE FAT BOY WITH THE HAPPY LAUGH. A VETERAN! SAMMY'S YOUR MAN!

Red Sammy was lying on the bare ground outside The Tower with his head under a truck while a gray monkey about a foot high, chained to a small chinaberry tree, chattered nearby. The monkey sprang back into the tree and got on the highest limb as soon as he saw the children jump out of the car and run toward him.

Inside, The Tower was a long dark room with a counter at one end and tables at the other and dancing space in the middle. They all sat down at a broad table next to the nickelodeon and Red Sam's wife, a tall burnt-brown woman with hair and eyes lighter than her skin, came and took their order. The children's mother put a dime in the machine and played "The Tennessee Waltz," and the grandmother said the tune always made her want to dance. She asked Bailey if he would like to dance but he only glared at her. He didn't have a naturally sunny disposition like she did and trips made him nervous. The grandmother's brown eyes were very bright. She swayed her head from side to side and pretended she was dancing in her chair. June Star said play something she could tap to so the children's mother put in another dime and played a fast number and June Star stepped out onto the dance floor and did her tap routine.

"Ain't she cute?" Red Sam's wife said, leaning over the counter. "Would you like to come be my little girl?" 30

"No I certainly wouldn't," June Star said. "I wouldn't live in a broken-down place like this for a million bucks!" and she ran back to the table.

"Ain't she cute?" the woman repeated, stretching her mouth politely.

"Aren't you ashamed?" hissed her grandmother.

Red Sam came in and told his wife to quit lounging on the counter and hurry with these people's order. His khaki trousers reached just to his hip bones and his stomach hung over them like a sack of meal swaying under his shirt. He came over and sat down at a table nearby and let out a combination sigh and yodel. "You can't win," he said. "You can't win," and he wiped his sweating red face with a gray handkerchief. "These days you don't know who to trust," he said. "Ain't that the truth?"

"People are certainly not nice like they used to be," said the grandmother. 35

"Two fellers come in here last week," Red Sammy said, "driving a Chrysler. It was a old beat-up car but it was a good one and these boys looked all right to me. Said they worked at the mill and you know I let them fellers charge the gas they bought? Now why did I do that?"

"Because you're a good man!" the grandmother said at once.

"Yes'm, I suppose so," Red Sam said as if he were struck with the answer.

His wife brought the orders, carrying the five plates all at once without a tray, two in each hand and one balanced on her arm. "It isn't a soul in this green world of God's that you can trust," she said. "And I don't count anybody out of that, not nobody," she repeated, looking at Red Sammy.

"Did you read about that criminal, The Misfit, that's escaped?" asked the grandmother. 40

"I wouldn't be a bit surprised if he didn't attack this place right here," said the woman. "If he hears about it being here, I wouldn't be none surprised to see him. If he hears it's two cent in the cash register, I wouldn't be a tall surprised if he . . ."

"That'll do," Red Sam said. "Go bring these people their Co'Colas," and the woman went off to get the rest of the order.

"A good man is hard to find," Red Sammy said. "Everything is getting terrible. I remember the day you could go off and leave your screen door unlatched. Not no more."

He and the grandmother discussed better times. The old lady said that in her opinion Europe was entirely to blame for the way things were now. She said the way Europe acted you would think we were made of money and Red Sam said it was no use talking about it, she was exactly right. The children ran outside into the white sunlight and looked at the monkey in the lacy chinaberry tree. He was busy catching fleas on himself and biting each one carefully between his teeth as if it were a delicacy.

They drove off again into the hot afternoon. The grandmother took cat naps and woke up every few minutes with her own snoring. Outside of Toombsboro she woke up and recalled an old plantation that she had visited in this neighborhood once when she was a young lady. She said the house had six white columns across the front and that there was an avenue of oaks leading up to it and two little wooden trellis arbors on either side in front where you sat down with your suitor after a stroll in the garden. She recalled exactly which road to turn off to get to it. She knew that Bailey would not be willing to lose any time looking at an old house, but the more she talked about it, the more she wanted to see it once again and find out if the little twin arbors were still standing. "There was a secret panel in this house," she said craftily, not telling the truth but wishing 45 that she were, "and the story went that all the family silver was hidden in it when Sherman° came through but it was never found . . ."

"Hey!" John Wesley said, "Let's go see it! We'll find it! We'll poke all the woodwork and find it! Who lives there? Where do you turn off at? Hey Pop, can't we turn off there?"

"We never have seen a house with a secret panel!" June Star shrieked. "Let's go to the house with the secret panel! Hey, Pop, can't we go see the house with the secret panel!"

"It's not far from here, I know," the grandmother said. "It wouldn't take over twenty minutes."

Bailey was looking straight ahead. His jaw was as rigid as a horseshoe. "No," he said.

The children began to yell and scream that they wanted to see the house with the   50 secret panel. John Wesley kicked the back of the front seat and June Star hung over her mother's shoulder and whined desperately into her ear that they never had any fun even on their vacation, and that they could never do what THEY wanted to do. The baby began to scream and John Wesley kicked the back of the seat so hard that his father could feel the blows in his kidney.

"All right!" he shouted, and drew the car to a stop at the side of the road. "Will you all shut up? Will you all just shut up for one second? If you don't shut up, we won't go anywhere."

"It would be very educational for them," the grandmother murmured.

"All right," Bailey said, "but get this: this is the only time we're going to stop for anything like this. This is the one and only time."

"The dirt road that you have to turn down is about a mile back," the grandmother directed. "I marked it when we passed."

"A dirt road," Bailey groaned.   55

After they had turned around and were headed toward the dirt road, the grandmother recalled other points about the house, the beautiful glass over the front doorway and the candle-lamp in the hall. John Wesley said that the secret panel was probably in the fireplace.

"You can't go inside this house," Bailey said. "You don't know who lives there."

"While you all talk to the people in front, I'll run around behind and get in a window," John Wesley suggested.

"We'll all stay in the car," his mother said.

They turned onto the dirt road and the car raced roughly along in swirl of pink   60 dust. The grandmother recalled the times when there were no paved roads and thirty miles was a day's journey. The dirt road was hilly and there were sudden washes in it and sharp curves on dangerous embankments. All at once they would be on a hill, looking down over the blue tops of trees for miles around, then the next minute, they would be in a red depression with the dust-coated trees looking down on them.

"This place had better turn up in a minute," Bailey said, "or I'm going to turn around."

The road looked as if no one had traveled on it in months.

"It's not much farther," the grandmother said and just as she said it, a horrible thought came to her. The thought was so embarrassing that she turned red in the face and her eyes dilated and her feet jumped up, upsetting her valise in the corner. The instant the valise moved, the newspaper top she had over the basket under it rose with a snarl and Pitty Sing, the cat, sprang onto Bailey's shoulder.

Sherman: William Tecumseh Sherman (1820–1892), Union general during the Civil War.

The children were thrown to the floor and their mother, clutching the baby, was thrown out the door onto the ground; the old lady was thrown into the front seat. The car turned over once and landed right-side-up in a gulch on the side of the road. Bailey remained in the driver's seat with the cat—gray-striped with a broad white face and an orange nose—clinging to his neck like a caterpillar.

As soon as the children saw they could move their arms and legs, they scrambled   65
out of the car, shouting, "We've had an ACCIDENT!" The grandmother was curled up under the dashboard, hoping she was injured so that Bailey's wrath would not come down on her all at once. The horrible thought she had had before the accident was that the house she had remembered so vividly was not in Georgia but in Tennessee.

Bailey removed the cat from his neck with both hands and flung it out the window against the side of a pine tree. Then he got out of the car and started looking for the children's mother. She was sitting against the side of the red gutted ditch, holding the screaming baby, but she only had a cut down her face and a broken shoulder. "We've had an ACCIDENT!" the children screamed in a frenzy of delight.

"But nobody's killed," June Star said with disappointment as the grandmother limped out of the car, her hat still pinned to her head but the broken front brim standing up at a jaunty angle and the violet spray hanging off the side. They all sat down in the ditch, except the children, to recover from the shock. They were all shaking.

"Maybe a car will come along," said the children's mother hoarsely.

"I believe I have injured an organ," said the grandmother, pressing her side, but no one answered her. Bailey's teeth were clattering. He had on a yellow sport shirt with bright blue parrots designed in it and his face was as yellow as the shirt. The grandmother decided that she would not mention that the house was in Tennessee.

The road was about ten feet above and they could see only the tops of the trees on   70
the other side of it. Behind the ditch they were sitting in there were more woods, tall and dark and deep. In a few minutes they saw a car some distance away on top of a hill, coming slowly as if the occupants were watching them. The grandmother stood up and waved both arms dramatically to attract their attention. The car continued to come on slowly, disappeared around a bend and appeared again, moving even slower, on top of the hill they had gone over. It was a big black battered hearse-like automobile. There were three men in it.

It came to a stop just over them and for some minutes, the driver looked down with a steady expressionless gaze to where they were sitting, and didn't speak. Then he turned his head and muttered something to the other two and they got out. One was a fat boy in black trousers and a red sweat shirt with a silver stallion embossed on the front of it. He moved around on the right side of them and stood staring, his mouth partly open in a kind of loose grin. The other had on khaki pants and a blue striped coat and a gray hat pulled down very low, hiding most of his face. He came around slowly on the left side. Neither spoke.

The driver got out of the car and stood by the side of it, looking down at them. He was an older man than the other two. His hair was just beginning to gray and he wore silver-rimmed spectacles that gave him a scholarly look. He had a long creased face and didn't have on any shirt or undershirt. He had on blue jeans that were too tight for him and was holding a black hat and a gun. The two boys also had guns.

"We've had an ACCIDENT!" the children screamed.

The grandmother had the peculiar feeling that the bespectacled man was some-one she knew. His face was as familiar to her as if she had known him all her life but she could not recall who he was. He moved away from the car and began to come down the embankment, placing his feet carefully so that he wouldn't slip. He had on tan and white shoes and no socks, and his ankles were red and thin. "Good afternoon," he said. "I see you all had a little spill."

"We turned over twice!" said the grandmother.   75

"Oncet," he corrected. "We seen it happen. Try their car and see will it run, Hiram," he said quietly to the boy with the gray hat.

"What you got that gun for?" John Wesley asked, "Whatcha gonna do with that gun?"

"Lady," the man said to the children's mother, "would you mind calling them children to sit down by you? Children make me nervous. I want all you all to set down right together there where you're at."

"What are you telling us what to do for?" June Star asked.

Behind them the line of woods gaped like a dark open mouth. "Come here," said   80
their mother.

"Look here now," Bailey began suddenly, "we're in a predicament! We're in . . ."

The grandmother shrieked. She scrambled to her feet and stood staring. "You're The Misfit!" she said. "I recognized you at once."

"Yes'm" the man said, smiling slightly as if he were pleased in spite of himself to be known, "but it would have been better for all of you, lady, if you hadn't reckernized me."

Bailey turned his head sharply and said something to his mother that shocked even the children. The old lady began to cry and The Misfit reddened.

"Lady," he said, "don't you get upset: Sometimes a man says things he don't mean.   85
I don't reckon he meant to talk to you thataway."

"You wouldn't shoot a lady, would you?" the grandmother said and removed a clean handkerchief from her cuff and began to slap at her eyes with it.

The Misfit pointed the toe of his shoe into the ground and made a little hole and then covered it up again. "I would hate to have to," he said.

"Listen," the grandmother almost screamed, "I know you're a good man. You don't look a bit like you have common blood. I know you must come from nice people!"

"Yes mam," he said, "finest people in the world." When he smiled he showed a row of strong white teeth. "God never made a finer woman than my mother and my daddy's heart was pure gold," he said. The boy with the red sweat shirt had come around behind them and was standing with his gun at his hip. The Misfit squatted down on the ground. "Watch them children, Bobby Lee," he said. "You know they make me nervous." He looked at the six of them huddled together in front of him and he seemed to be embarrassed as if he couldn't think if anything to say. "Ain't a cloud in the sky," he remarked, looking up at it. "Don't see no sun but don't see no cloud neither."

"Yes, it's a beautiful day," said the grandmother. "Listen," she said, "you   90
shouldn't call yourself The Misfit because I know you're a good man at heart. I can just look at you and tell."

"Hush!" Bailey yelled. "Hush! Everybody shut up and let me handle this!" He was squatting in the position of a runner about to sprint forward but he didn't move.

"I pre-chate that, lady," The Misfit said and drew a little circle in the ground with the butt of his gun.

"It'll take a half a hour to fix this here car," Hiram called, looking over the raised hood of it.

"Well, first you and Bobby Lee get him and that little boy to step over yonder with you," The Misfit said, pointing to Bailey and John Wesley. "The boys want to ask you something," he said to Bailey. "Would you mind stepping back in them woods there with them?"

"Listen," Bailey began, "we're in a terrible predicament. Nobody realizes what this is," and his voice cracked. His eyes were as blue and intense as the parrots in his shirt and he remained perfectly still.

The grandmother reached up to adjust her hat brim as if she were going to the woods with him but it came off in her hand. She stood staring at it and after a second she let it fall to the ground. Hiram pulled Bailey up by the arm as if he were assisting an old man. John Wesley caught hold of his father's hand and Bobby Lee followed. They went off toward the woods and just as they reached the dark edge, Bailey turned and supporting himself against a gray naked pine trunk, he shouted, "I'll be back in a minute, Mamma, wait on me!"

"Come back this instant!" his mother shrilled but they all disappeared into the woods.

"Bailey Boy!" the grandmother called in a tragic voice but she found she was looking at The Misfit squatting on the ground in front of her. "I just know you're a good man," she said desperately. "You're not a bit common!"

"Nome, I ain't a good man," The Misfit said after a second as if he had considered her statement carefully, "but I ain't the worst in the world neither. My daddy said I was different breed of dog from my brothers and sisters. 'You know,' Daddy said, 'it's some that can live their whole life out without asking about it and it's others has to know why it is, and this boy is one of the latters. He's going to be into everything!'" He put on his black hat and looked up suddenly and then away deep into the woods as if he were embarrassed again. "I'm sorry I don't have on a shirt before you ladies," he said, hunching his shoulders slightly. "We buried our clothes that we had on when we escaped and we're just making do until we can get better. We borrowed these from some folks we met," he explained.

"That's perfectly all right," the grandmother said. "Maybe Bailey has an extra shirt in his suitcase."

"I'll look and see terrectly," the Misfit said.

"Where are they taking him?" the children's mother screamed.

"Daddy was a card himself," the Misfit said. "You couldn't put anything over on him. He never got in trouble with the Authorities though. Just had the knack of handling them."

"You could be honest too if you'd only try," said the grandmother. "Think how wonderful it would be to settle down and live a comfortable life and not have to think about somebody chasing you all the time."

The Misfit kept scratching in the ground with the butt of his gun as if he were thinking about it. "Yes'm, somebody is always after you," he murmured.

The grandmother noticed how thin his shoulder blades were just behind his hat because she was standing up looking down on him. "Do you ever pray?" she asked.

He shook his head. All she saw was the black hat wiggle between his shoulder blades. "Nome," he said.

There was a pistol shot from the woods, followed closely by another. Then silence. The old lady's head jerked around. She could hear the wind move through the tree tops like a long satisfied insuck of breath. "Bailey Boy!" she called.

"I was a gospel singer for a while," The Misfit said. "I been most everything. Been in the arm service, both land and sea, at home and abroad, been twict married, been an undertaker, been with the railroads, plowed Mother Earth, been in a tornado, seen a man burnt alive oncet," and he looked up at the children's mother and the little girl who were sitting close together, their faces white and their eyes glassy; "I even seen a woman flogged," he said.

"Pray, pray," the grandmother began, "pray, pray . . ." 110

"I never was a bad boy that I remember of," The Misfit said in an almost dreamy voice, "but somewheres along the line I done something wrong and got sent to the penitentiary. I was buried alive," and he looked up and held her attention to him by a steady stare.

"That's when you should have started to pray," she said. "What did you do to get sent to the penitentiary that first time?"

"Turn to the right, it was a wall," The Misfit said, looking up again at the cloudless sky. "Turn to the left, it was a wall. Look up it was a ceiling, look down it was a floor. I forgot what I done, lady. I set there and set there, trying to remember what it was I done and I ain't recalled it to this day. Oncet in a while, I would think it was coming to me, but it never come."

"Maybe they put you in by mistake," the old lady said vaguely.

"Nome," he said. "It wasn't no mistake. They had the papers on me." 115

"You must have stolen something," she said.

The Misfit sneered slightly. "Nobody had nothing I wanted," he said. "It was a head-doctor at the penitentiary said what I had done was kill my daddy but I know that for a lie. My daddy died in nineteen ought nineteen of the epidemic flu and I never had a thing to do with it. He was buried in the Mount Hopewell Baptist churchyard and you can go there and see for yourself."

"If you would pray," the old lady said, "Jesus would help you."

"That's right," The Misfit said.

"Well then, why don't you pray?" she asked trembling with delight suddenly. 120

"I don't want no hep," he said. "I'm doing all right by myself."

Bobby Lee and Hiram came ambling back from the woods. Bobby Lee was dragging a yellow shirt with bright blue parrots in it.

"Throw me that shirt, Bobby Lee," The Misfit said. The shirt came flying at him and landed on his shoulder and he put it on. The grandmother couldn't name what the shirt reminded her of. "No, lady," The Misfit said while he was buttoning it up. "I found out the crime don't matter. You can do one thing or you can do another, kill a man or take a tire off his car, because sooner or later you're going to forget what it was you done and just be punished for it."

The children's mother had begun to make heaving noises as if she couldn't get her breath. "Lady," he asked, "would you and that little girl like to step off yonder with Bobby Lee and Hiram and join your husband?"

"Yes, thank you," the mother said faintly. Her left arm dangled helplessly and she 125 was holding the baby, who had gone to sleep, in the other. "Hep that lady up, Hiram," The Misfit said as she struggled to climb out of the ditch, "and Bobby Lee, you hold onto that little girl's hand."

"I don't want to hold hands with him," June Star said. "He reminds me of a pig."

The fat boy blushed and laughed and caught her by the arm and pulled her off into the woods after Hiram and her mother.

Alone with The Misfit, the grandmother found that she had lost her voice. There was not a cloud in the sky nor any sun. There was nothing around her but woods. She wanted to tell him that he must pray. She opened and closed her mouth several times before anything came out. Finally she found herself saying, "Jesus, Jesus," meaning Jesus will help you, but the way she was saying it, it sounded as if she might be cursing.

"Yes'm," The Misfit said as if he agreed. "Jesus thown everything off balance. It was the same case with Him as with me except He hadn't committed any crime and they could prove I had committed one because they had the papers on me. Of course," he said, "they never shown me any papers. That's why I sign myself now. I said long ago, you get you a signature and sign everything you do and keep a copy of it. Then you'll know what you done and you can hold up the crime to the punishment and see do they match and in the end you'll have something to prove you ain't been treated right. I call myself The Misfit," he said, "because I can't make what all I done wrong fit what all I gone through in punishment."

There was a piercing scream from the woods, followed closely by a pistol report. 130 "Does it seem right to you, lady, that one is punished a heap and another ain't punished at all?"

"Jesus!" the old lady cried. "You've got good blood! I know you wouldn't shoot a lady! I know you come from nice people! Pray! Jesus, you ought not to shoot a lady: I'll give you all the money I've got!"

"Lady," The Misfit said, looking beyond her far into the woods, "there never was a body that give the undertaker a tip."

There were two more pistol reports and the grandmother raised her head like a parched old turkey hen crying for water and called, "Bailey Boy, Bailey Boy!" as if her heart would break.

"Jesus was the only One that ever raised the dead," The Misfit continued, "and He shouldn't have done it. He thown everything off balance. If He did what He said then it's nothing for you to do but thow away everything and follow Him, and if He didn't, then it's nothing for you to do but enjoy the few minutes you got left the best way you can—by killing somebody or burning down his house or doing some other meanness to him. No pleasure but meanness," he said and his voice had become almost a snarl.

"Maybe He didn't raise the dead," the old lady mumbled, not knowing what she 135 was saying and feeling so dizzy that she sank down in the ditch with her legs twisted under her.

"I wasn't there so I can't say He didn't." The Misfit said, "I wisht I had of been there," he said, hitting the ground with his fist. "It ain't right I wasn't there because if I had of been there I would of known. Listen lady," he said in a high voice, "if I had of been there I would of known and I wouldn't be like I am now." His voice seemed about to crack and the grandmother's head cleared for an instant. She saw the man's face twisted close to her own as if he were going to cry and she murmured, "Why you're one of my babies. You're one of my own children!" She reached out and touched him on the shoulder. The Misfit sprang back as if a snake had bitten him and shot her three times through the chest. Then he put his gun down on the ground and took off his glasses and began to clean them.

Hiram and Bobby Lee returned from the woods and stood over the ditch, looking down at the grandmother who half sat and half lay in a puddle of blood with her legs crossed under her like a child's and her face smiling up at the cloudless sky.

Without his glasses, The Misfit's eyes were red-rimmed and pale and defenseless-looking. "Take her off and thow her where you thown the others," he said, picking up the cat that was rubbing itself against his leg.

"She was a talker, wasn't she?" Bobby Lee said, sliding down the ditch with a yodel.

"She would of been a good woman," The Misfit said, "if it had been somebody   140
there to shoot her every minute of her life."

"Some fun!" Bobby Lee said.

"Shut up, Bobby Lee," The Misfit said. "It's no real pleasure in life."

KATHERINE ANNE PORTER   (1894–1980)

Porter, born Callie Russell Porter, was a native of Texas but made her home in many places during her life, spending considerable time in Mexico and Germany. She established her reputation with her early collections Flowering Judas *(1930) and* Pale Horse, Pale Rider *(1939), for which she was praised for her analyses and insights into human character. A later collection of stories was* The Leaning Tower *(1944). Her major novel,* Ship of Fools, *appeared in 1962 and was made into a motion picture. She was awarded the Pulitzer Prize for fiction and also the National Book Award in 1966 for her* The Collected Stories. *"The Jilting of Granny Weatherall" first appeared in* Flowering Judas.

The Jilting of Granny Weatherall _____ 1930

She flicked her wrist neatly out of Doctor Harry's pudgy careful fingers and pulled the sheet up to her chin. The brat ought to be in knee breeches. Doctoring around the country with spectacles on his nose! "Get along now, take your schoolbooks and go. There's nothing wrong with me."

Doctor Harry spread a warm paw like a cushion on her forehead where the forked green vein danced and made her eyelids twitch. "Now, now, be a good girl, and we'll have you up in no time."

"That's no way to speak to a woman nearly eighty years old just because she's down. I'd have you respect your elders, young man."

"Well, Missy, excuse me." Doctor Harry patted her cheek. "But I've got to warn you, haven't I? You're a marvel, but you must be careful or you're going to be good and sorry."

"Don't tell me what I'm going to be. I'm on my feet now, morally speaking. It's   5
Cornelia. I had to go to bed to get rid of her."

Her bones felt loose, and floated around in her skin, and Doctor Harry floated like a balloon around the foot of the bed. He floated and pulled down his waistcoat and swung his glasses on a cord. "Well, stay where you are, it certainly can't hurt you."

"Get along and doctor your sick," said Granny Weatherall. "Leave a well woman alone. I'll call for you when I want you. . . . Where were you forty years ago when I pulled through milk-leg and double pneumonia? You weren't even born. Don't let Cornelia lead you on," she shouted, because Doctor Harry appeared to float up to the ceiling and out. "I pay my own bills, and I don't throw my money away on nonsense!"

She meant to wave good-by, but it was too much trouble. Her eyes closed of themselves, it was like a dark curtain drawn around the bed. The pillow rose and floated under her, pleasant as a hammock in a light wind. She listened to the leaves rustling outside the window. No, somebody was swishing newspapers: no, Cornelia and Doctor Harry were whispering together. She leaped broad awake, thinking they whispered in her ear.

"She was never like this, *never* like this!" "Well, what can we expect?" "Yes, eighty years old. . . . "

Well, and what if she was? She still had ears. It was like Cornelia to whisper around doors. She always kept things secret in such a public way. She was always being tactful and kind. Cornelia was dutiful; that was the trouble with her. Dutiful and good: "So good and dutiful," said Granny, "that I'd like to spank her." She saw herself spanking Cornelia and making a fine job of it.

"What'd you say, Mother?"

Granny felt her face tying up in hard knots.

"Can't a body think, I'd like to know?"

"I thought you might want something."

"I do. I want a lot of things. First off, go away and don't whisper."

She lay and drowsed, hoping in her sleep that the children would keep out and let her rest a minute. It had been a long day. Not that she was tired. It was always pleasant to snatch a minute now and then. There was always so much to be done, let me see: tomorrow.

Tomorrow was far away and there was nothing to trouble about. Things were finished somehow when the time came; thank God there was always a little margin over for peace: then a person could spread out the plan of life and tuck in the edges orderly. It was good to have everything clean and folded away, with the hair brushes and tonic bottles sitting straight on the white embroidered linen: the day started without fuss and the pantry shelves laid out with rows of jelly glasses and brown jugs and white stone-china jars with blue whirligigs and words painted on them: coffee, tea, sugar, ginger, cinnamon, allspice: and the bronze clock with the lion on top nicely dusted off. The dust that lion could collect in twenty-four hours! The box in the attic with all those letters tied up, well she'd have to go through that tomorrow. All those letters—George's letters and John's letters and her letters to them both—lying around for the children to find afterwards made her uneasy. Yes, that would be tomorrow's business. No use to let them know how silly she had been once.

While she was rummaging around she found death in her mind and it felt clammy and unfamiliar. She had spent so much time preparing for death there was no need for bringing it up again. Let it take care of itself now. When she was sixty she had felt very old, finished, and went around making farewell trips to see her children and grandchildren, with a secret in her mind: This is the very last of your mother, children! Then she made her will and came down with a long fever. That was all just a notion like a lot of other things, but it was lucky too, for she had once for all got over the idea of dying for a long time. Now she couldn't be worried. She hoped she had better sense now. Her father had lived to be one hundred and two years old and had drunk a noggin of strong hot toddy on his last birthday. He told the reporters it was his daily habit, and he owed his long life to that. He had made quite a scandal and was very pleased about it. She believed she'd just plague Cornelia a little.

"Cornelia! Cornelia!" No footsteps, but a sudden hand on her cheek. "Bless you, where have you been?"

"Here, mother."

"Well, Cornelia, I want a noggin of hot toddy."

"Are you cold, darling?"

"I'm chilly, Cornelia. Lying in bed stops the circulation. I must have told you that a thousand times."

Well, she could just hear Cornelia telling her husband that Mother was getting childish and they'd have to humor her. The thing that most annoyed her was that Cornelia thought she was deaf, dumb, and blind. Little hasty glances and tiny gestures tossed around her and over her head saying. "Don't cross her, let her have her way, she's eighty years old," and she sitting there as if she lived in a thin glass cage. Sometimes Granny almost made up her mind to pack up and move back to her own house where nobody could remind her every minute that she was old. Wait, wait, Cornelia, till your own children whisper behind your back!

In her day she had kept a better house and had got more work done. She   25 wasn't too old yet for Lydia to be driving eighty miles for advice when one of the children jumped the track, and Jimmy still dropped in and talked things over: "Now, Mammy, you've a good business head, I want to know what you think of this? . . ." Old Cornelia couldn't change the furniture around without asking. Little things, little things! They had been so sweet when they were little. Granny wished the old days were back again with the children young and everything to be done over. It had been a hard pull, but not too much for her. When she thought of all the food she had cooked, and all the clothes she had cut and sewed, and all the gardens she had made—well, the children showed it. There they were, made out of her, and they couldn't get away from that. Sometimes she wanted to see John again and point to them and say, Well, I didn't do so badly, did I? But that would have to wait. That was for tomorrow. She used to think of him as a man, but now all the children were older than their father, and he would be a child beside her if she saw him now. It seemed strange and there was something wrong in the idea. Why, he couldn't possibly recognize her. She had fenced in a hundred acres once, digging the post holes herself and clamping the wires with just a negro boy to help. That changed a woman. John would be looking for a young woman with the peaked Spanish comb in her hair and the painted fan. Digging post holes changed a woman. Riding country roads in the winter when women had their babies was another thing: sitting up nights with sick horses and sick negroes and sick children and hardly ever losing one. John, I hardly ever lost one of them! John would see that in a minute, that would be something he could understand, she wouldn't have to explain anything!

It made her feel like rolling up her sleeves and putting the whole place to rights again. No matter if Cornelia was determined to be everywhere at once, there were a great many things left undone on this place. She would start tomorrow and do them. It was good to be strong enough for everything, even if all you made melted and changed and slipped under your hands, so that by the time you finished you almost forgot what you were working for. What was it I set out to do? she asked herself intently, but she could not remember. A fog rose over the valley, she saw it marching across the creek swallowing the trees and moving up the hill like an army of ghosts. Soon it would be at the near edge of the orchard, and then it was time to go in and light the lamps. Come in children, don't stay out in the night air.

Lighting the lamps had been beautiful. The children huddled up to her and breathed like little calves waiting at the bars in the twilight. Their eyes followed the match and watched the flame rise and settle in a blue curve, then they moved away from her. The lamp was lit, they didn't have to be scared and hang on to mother any more.

Never, never, never more. God, for all my life I thank Thee. Without Thee, my God, I could never have done it. Hail, Mary, full of grace.

I want you to pick all the fruit this year and see that nothing is wasted. There's always someone who can use it. Don't let good things rot for want of using. You waste life when you waste good food. Don't let things get lost. It's bitter to lose things. Now, don't let me get to thinking, not when I am tired and taking a little nap before supper. . . .

The pillow rose about her shoulders and pressed against her heart and the memory was being squeezed out of it: oh, push down the pillow, somebody: it would smother her if she tried to hold it. Such a fresh breeze blowing and such a green day with no threats in it. But he had not come, just the same. What does a woman do when she has put on the white veil and set out the white cake for a man and he doesn't come? She tried to remember. No, I swear he never harmed me but in that. He never harmed me but in that . . . and what if he did? There was the day, the day, but a whirl of dark smoke rose and covered it, crept up and over into the bright field where everything was planted so carefully in orderly rows. That was hell, she knew hell when she saw it. For sixty years she had prayed against remembering him and against losing her soul in the deep pit of hell, and now the two things were mingled in one and the thought of him was a smoky cloud from hell that moved and crept in her head when she had just got rid of Doctor Harry and was trying to rest a minute. Wounded vanity, Ellen, said a sharp voice in the top of her mind. Don't let your wounded vanity get the upper hand of you. Plenty of girls get jilted. You were jilted, weren't you. Then stand up to it. Her eyelids wavered and let in streamers of blue-gray light like tissue paper over her eyes. She must get up and pull the shades down or she'd never sleep. She was in bed again and the shades were not down. How could that happen? Better turn over, hide from the light, sleeping in the light gave you nightmares. "Mother, how do you feel now?" and a stinging wetness on her forehead. But I don't like having my face washed in cold water!

Hapsy? George? Lydia? Jimmy? No, Cornelia, and her features were swollen and full of little puddles. "They're coming, darling, they'll all be here soon." Go wash your face, child, you look funny.   30

Instead of obeying, Cornelia knelt down and put her head on the pillow. She seemed to be talking but there was no sound. "Well, are you tongue-tied? Whose birthday is it? Are you going to give a party?"

Cornelia's mouth moved urgently in strange shapes. "Don't do that, you bother me, daughter."

"Oh, no, Mother, Oh, no . . ."

Nonsense. It was strange about children. They disputed your every word. "No what, Cornelia?"

"Here's Doctor Harry."   35

"I won't see that boy again. He just left five minutes ago."

"That was this morning, Mother. It's night now. Here's the nurse."

"This is Doctor Harry, Mrs. Weatherall. I never saw you look so young and happy!"

"Ah, I'll never be young again—but I'd be happy if they'd let me lie in peace and get rested."

She thought she spoke up loudly, but no one answered. A warm weight on her forehead, a warm bracelet on her wrist, and a breeze went on whispering, trying to tell her something. A shuffle of leaves in the everlasting hand of God. He blew on them and they danced and rattled. "Mother, don't mind, we're going to give you a little   40 hypodermic." "Look here, daughter, how do ants get in this bed? I saw sugar ants yesterday." Did you send for Hapsy too?

It was Hapsy she really wanted. She had to go a long way back through a great many rooms to find Hapsy standing with a baby on her arm. She seemed to herself to be Hapsy also, and the baby on Hapsy's arm was Hapsy and himself and herself, all at once, and there was no surprise in the meeting. Then Hapsy melted from within and turned flimsy as gray gauze and the baby was a gauzy shadow, and Hapsy came up close and said, "I thought you'd never come," and looked at her very searchingly and said, "You haven't changed a bit!" They leaned forward to kiss, when Cornelia began whispering from a long way off, "Oh, is there anything you want to tell me? Is there anything I can do for you?"

Yes, she had changed her mind after sixty years and she would like to see George. I want you to find George. Find him and be sure to tell him I forgot him. I want him to know I had my husband just the same and my children and my house like any other woman. A good house too and a good husband that I loved and fine children out of him. Better than I hoped for even. Tell him I was given back everything he took away and more. Oh, no, oh, God, no, there was something else besides the house and the man and the children. Oh, surely they were not all? What was it? Something not given back. . . . Her breath crowded down under her ribs and grew into a monstrous frightening shape with cutting edges; it bored up into her head, and the agony was unbelievable: Yes, John, get the doctor now, no more talk, my time has come.

When this one was born it should be the last. The last. It should have been born first, for it was the one she had truly wanted. Everything came in good time. Nothing left out, left over. She was strong, in three days she would be as well as ever. Better. A woman needed milk in her to have her full health.

"Mother, do you hear me?"

"I've been telling you—" 45

"Mother, Father Connolly's here."

"I went to Holy Communion only last week. Tell him I'm not so sinful as all that."

"Father just wants to speak to you."

He could speak as much as he pleased. It was like him to drop in and inquire about her soul as if it were a teething baby, and then stay on for a cup of tea and a round of cards and gossip. He always had a funny story of some sort, usually about an Irishman who made his little mistakes and confessed them, and the point lay in some absurd thing he would blurt out in the confessional showing his struggles between native piety and original sin. Granny felt easy about her soul. Cornelia, where are your manners? Give Father Connolly a chair. She had her secret comfortable understanding with a few favorite saints who cleared a straight road to God for her. All as surely signed and sealed as the papers for the new Forty Acres. Forever . . . heirs and assigns forever. Since the day the wedding cake was not cut, but thrown out and wasted. The whole bottom dropped out of the world, and there she was blind and sweating with nothing under her feet and the walls falling away. His hand had caught her under the breast, she had not fallen, there was the freshly polished floor with the green rug on it, just as before. He had cursed like a sailor's parrot and said. "I'll kill him for you." Don't lay a hand on him, for my sake leave something to God. "Now, Ellen, you must believe what I tell you. . . ."

So there was nothing, nothing to worry about any more, except sometimes in the 50 night one of the children screamed in a nightmare, and they both hustled out shaking and hunting for the matches and calling, "There, wait a minute, here we are!" John, get the doctor now. Hapsy's time has come. But there was Hapsy standing by the bed in a white cap. "Cornelia, tell Hapsy to take off her cap. I can't see her plain."

Her eyes opened very wide and the room stood out like a picture she had seen somewhere. Dark colors with the shadow rising towards the ceiling in long angles. The tall black dresser gleamed with nothing on it but John's picture, enlarged from a little one, with John's eyes very black when they should have been blue. You never saw him, so how do you know how he looked? But the man insisted the copy was perfect, it was very rich and handsome. For a picture, yes, but it's not my husband. The table by the bed had a linen cover and a candle and a crucifix. The light was blue from Cornelia's silk lampshades. No sort of light at all, just frippery. You had to live forty years with kerosene lamps to appreciate honest electricity. She felt very strong and she saw Doctor Harry with a rosy nimbus around him.

"You look like a saint, Doctor Harry, and I vow that's as near as you'll ever come to it."

"She's saying something."

"I heard you, Cornelia. What's all this carrying-on?"

"Father Connolly's saying—"

Cornelia's voice staggered and bumped like a cart in a bad road. It rounded corners and turned back again and arrived nowhere. Granny stepped up in the cart very lightly and reached for the reins, but a man sat beside her and she knew him by his hands, driving the cart. She did not look in his face, for she knew without seeing, but looked instead down the road where the trees leaned over and bowed to each other and a thousand birds were singing a Mass. She felt like singing too, but she put her hand in the bosom of her dress and pulled out a rosary, and Father Connolly murmured Latin in a very solemn voice and tickled her feet. My God, will you stop that nonsense? I'm a married woman. What if he did run away and leave me to face the priest by myself? I found another a whole world better. I wouldn't have exchanged my husband for anybody except St. Michael himself, and you may tell him that for me with a thank you in the bargain.

Light flashed on her closed eyelids, and a deep roaring shook her. Cornelia, is that lightning? I hear thunder. There's going to be a storm. Close all the windows. Call the children in . . . "Mother, here we are, all of us." "Is that you, Hapsy?" "Oh, no, I'm Lydia. We drove as fast as we could." Their faces drifted above her, drifted away. The rosary fell out of her hands and Lydia put it back. Jimmy tried to help, their hands fumbled together, and Granny closed two fingers around Jimmy's thumb. Beads wouldn't do, it must be something alive. She was so amazed her thoughts ran round and round. So, my dear Lord, this is my death and I wasn't even thinking about it. My children have come to see me die. But I can't, it's not time. Oh, I always hated surprises. I wanted to give Cornelia the amethyst set—Cornelia, you're to have the amethyst set, but Hapsy's to wear it when she wants, and, Doctor Harry, do shut up. Nobody sent for you. Oh, my dear Lord, do wait a minute. I meant to do something about the Forty Acres, Jimmy doesn't need it and Lydia will later on with that worthless husband of hers. I meant to finish the altar cloth and send six bottles of wine to Sister Borgia for her dyspepsia. I want to send six bottles of wine to Sister Borgia, Father Connolly, now don't let me forget.

Cornelia's voice made short turns and tilted over and crashed. "Oh, Mother, oh, Mother, oh, Mother. . . ."

"I'm not going, Cornelia. I'm taken by surprise. I can't go."

55

You'll see Hapsy again. What about her? "I thought you'd never come." Granny   60
made a long journey outward, looking for Hapsy. What if I don't find her? What then?
Her heart sank down and down, there was no bottom to death, she couldn't come to
the end of it. The blue light from Cornelia's lampshade drew into a tiny point in the
center of her brain, it flickered and winked like an eye, quietly it fluttered and dwin-
dled. Granny lay curled down within herself, amazed and watchful, staring at the point
of light that was herself; her body was now only a deeper mass of shadow in an endless
darkness and this darkness would curl around the light and swallow it up. God, give
a sign!

For the second time there was no sign. Again no bridegroom and the priest in
the house. She could not remember any other sorrow because this grief wiped them all
away. Oh, no, there's nothing more cruel than this—I'll never forgive it. She stretched
herself with a deep breath and blew out the light.

READING
AND
WRITING
ABOUT

POETRY

11
Meeting Poetry: An Overview

Poetry and **poem** describe a wide variety of spoken and written forms, styles, and patterns, and also a wide variety of subjects. Because of the variety, it is not possible to make a single, comprehensive definition. The origin of the word is the Greek word *poiema,* that is, "something made or fashioned [in words]"—a meaning that applies to both poetry and to poems. Naturally, a **poet** was, and is, a person who writes or speaks poems. Rather than trying to understand poetry by defining it, we believe the best way to understand it is to read it, learn it, savor it, and enjoy it. As your understanding of poetry deepens, you will develop your own ideas and definitions.

THE NATURE OF POETRY

We begin with a poem based in the life of students and teachers alike.

BILLY COLLINS   (b. 1941)

Schoolsville ————————————————————————— *1985*

Glancing over my shoulder at the past,
I realize the number of students I have taught
is enough to populate a small town.

I can see it nestled in a paper landscape,
chalk dust flurrying down in winter,   5
nights dark as a blackboard.

The population ages but never graduates.
On hot afternoons they sweat the final in the park

and when it's cold they shiver around stoves
reading disorganized essays out loud.   10
A bell rings on the hour and everybody zigzags
in the streets with their books.

I forgot all their last names first and their
first names last in alphabetical order.
But the boy who always had his hand up   15
is an alderman and owns the haberdashery.
The girl who signed her papers in lipstick
leans against the drugstore, smoking,
brushing her hair like a machine.

Their grades are sewn into their clothes   20
like references to Hawthorne.°   i.e., *The Scarlet Letter*
The A's stroll along with other A's.
The D's honk whenever they pass another D.

All the creative writing students recline
on the courthouse lawn and play the lute.   25
Wherever they go, they form a big circle.

Needless to say, I am the mayor.
I live in the white colonial at Maple and Main.
I rarely leave the house. The car deflates
in the driveway. Vines twirl around the porchswing.   30

Once in a while a student knocks on the door
with a term paper fifteen years late
or a question about Yeats or double-spacing.
And sometimes one will appear in a window pane
to watch me lecturing the wall paper,   35
quizzing the chandelier, reprimanding the air.

QUESTIONS

1. What recognizable school experiences does the poem mention? Why is "Schoolsville" the title?

2. Describe the speaker. How does he indicate affection for students?

3. What details indicate that the poem is fantasy and not reality? To what degree is the poem humorous?

4. Compare the details of this poem with those in Roethke's "Dolor" (p. 485). What similarities do you find in the choice and appropriateness of detail? What differences?

5. Each poem you read may help you understand, and therefore define, poetry. How might this poem help you begin making a definition?

"Schoolsville" reveals the variety and freedom of poetry. Unlike poems that are set out in strict line lengths, rhythms, and rhymes, "Schoolsville," though arranged in lines, does not follow measured rhythmical or rhyming patterns. The language is not difficult, the descriptions are straightforward, and the scenes seem both real and amusing. Many details—such as the "chalk dust flurrying down" like snow, the girl who signs her name in lipstick, and the students forming a circle when they meet—are outrightly funny. But the poem moves from apparent reality to something beyond reality. Unifying the poem is the fanciful idea that school life is, like life generally, at once comical, serious, and poignant. It is therefore clear that this poem describing a school community is designed primarily to elicit our responses with its underlying insight and power.

We should always recognize that good poems, regardless of their topic, have similar power. To see this, let us look at another poem, by the seventeenth-century English poet Robert Herrick.

ROBERT HERRICK (1591–1664)

Here a Pretty Baby Lies ———————————————————— *1648*

Here a pretty baby lies
Sung asleep with lullabies:
Pray be silent, and not stir
Th'easy earth that covers her.

QUESTIONS

1. What is the apparent situation described in this poem? To what degree is this situation either ordinary or unusual?
2. How does the final line change your perception of the first three lines? How does it change your response to the poem?
3. Consider the double meanings of the following words and phrases: "Here . . . lies"; "sung asleep"; "lullabies"; "stir."

The first three lines of this short poem seem quite ordinary. A scene is described that takes place over and over again everywhere in the world: A baby is sleeping quietly, and we are told to make no sounds that would awaken her. But the last line strikes us unexpectedly and powerfully, making us realize that nothing in the poem is what we understood at first. We immediately change our initial impressions and realize that the baby is not just sleeping but dead, lying not in a cradle but in a coffin; the lullabies are not only lullabies sung by a grieving mother but religious songs sung at a funeral ceremony; and the stirring is not just making noise but disturbing the still-loose earth that newly covers the baby's grave. The effect of this poem has legitimately been called overwhelming.

The two poems have much in common; they are both serious, engaging, original, and powerful. One, however, is amusing and slightly perplexing while the other is sad and deeply moving. There are no other poems like them. Once we understand them, we will never forget them. Even if we never read them again, they will echo in our minds as time passes, sometimes with great vividness and power, sometimes with less. Actually to read them again may cause us to rediscover our original feelings, and often we will experience entirely new feelings about them. In short, like all good poetry, these poems live, and as long as we too live, they will be a permanent part of our thoughts.

Some Brief Descriptive Statements about Poetry

As "Schoolsville" and "Here a Pretty Baby Lies" demonstrate, all good poems are unique. Because this is so, we cannot formulate a single definition of poetry. We can nevertheless offer a number of descriptive statements about poetry that may be helpful. To begin with, poems are imaginative works expressed in words that are used with the utmost compression, force, and economy. Unlike prose, which is expansive if not exhaustive, most poems are brief but also comprehensive, offering us high points of thought, feeling, reflection, and resolution. Poems may be formed in just about any coherent and developed shape, from a line of a single word to lines of twenty, thirty, or more words; and these lines may be organized into any number of repeating or nonrepeating patterns. Some poems make us think, give us new and unexpected insights, and generally instruct us. Other poems arouse our emotions, surprise us, amuse us, and inspire us. Ideally, reading and understanding poetry should prompt us to reexamine, reinforce, and reshape our ideas, our attitudes, our feelings, and our lives.

POETRY OF THE ENGLISH LANGUAGE

Today, most nations with their own languages have their own literatures, including poetry, with their own unique histories and characteristics. In this anthology, however, we are concerned primarily, but not exclusively, with poetry in our own language by American, British, and Canadian poets.

The earliest poems in English date back to late in the period of *Old English* (450–1100). Many of these early English poems reflect the influence of Christianity. Indeed, the most famous poem, the epic *Beowulf*, was probably interpreted as a Christian allegory even though it concerns the secular themes of adventure, courage, and war. Ever since the *Middle English* period (1100–1500), poets have written about many other subjects, although religious themes have remained important. Today, we find poetry on virtually all topics, including sexuality, love, society, individuality, warfare, strong drink, government and politics, worship, and music; some poems treat such special and unusual topics as fishing, computers, exotic birds, and car crashes.

In short, poetry is alive and flourishing. Some people read it aloud in front of audiences, friends, and families; others read it silently in private. A poem set to music and sung aloud is especially powerful. Francis Scott Key's

"The Star-Spangled Banner," for example, which he wrote about events in a battle in the War of 1812, has become our national anthem. More recently, musical groups like the Beatles, U2, and Smashing Pumpkins, along with singer Bruce Springsteen, have given poetic expression to ideas that huge masses of people have taken to heart. Ever since the 1960s, people devoted to civil rights have been unified and strengthened by the simple poetic lyrics of "We Shall Overcome," not only in the United States but throughout the world. The strength and vitality of poetry could be similarly documented time and time again.

HOW TO READ A POEM

With poetry, as with any other literary form, the more effort we put into understanding, the greater will be our reward. Poems are often about subjects that we have never experienced directly. We have never met the poet, never had his or her exact experiences, and never thought about things in exactly the same way. To recapture the experience of the poem, we need to understand the language, ideas, attitudes, and frames of reference that will make the poem come alive.

We must therefore read all poems carefully, thoughtfully, and sympathetically—words that sum up the best approach to reading poetry. The economy and compression of poetry mean that every part of the poem must carry some of the impact and meaning, and thus every part repays careful attention. Try to interact with the poem. Do not expect the poem (or the poet) to do all the work. The poem contributes its language, imagery, rhythms, ideas, and all the other aspects that make it poetry, but you, the reader, will need to open your mind to the poem's impact.

There is no single technique for reading, absorbing, and appreciating poetry. In Chapter 1 we offer a number of guidelines for studying any work of literature (pp. 11–12). In addition to following the guidelines, read each poem more than once, and keep in mind these objectives:

1. *Read straight through to get a general sense of the poem.* In this first reading, do not stop to puzzle out hard passages or obscure words; just read through from beginning to end.

2. *Try to understand the poem's meaning and organization.* As you read and reread the poem, study these elements:

- **The title.** The title is almost always informative. The title "Schoolsville" suggests that the poem will contain a somewhat flippant treatment of school life. The title of Robert Frost's "Stopping by Woods on a Snowy Evening" suggests that the poem will present ideas derived from the natural world in cold and darkness.
- **The speaker.** Poems are dramatic, having points of view just like prose fiction. First-person speakers talk from the "inside" because they are directly involved in the action (like the speaker in "Schoolsville"). Other speakers are "outside"

observers demonstrating the third-person limited and omniscient points of view, as in "Sir Patrick Spens" (see also Chapter 5).

- **The meanings of all words, whether familiar or unfamiliar.** The words in many poems are immediately clear, as in "Here a Pretty Baby Lies," but other poems may contain unfamiliar words and references that need looking up. You will need to consult dictionaries, encyclopedias, and other sources until you gain a fairly clear grasp of the poem's content. If you have difficulty with meanings even after using your sources, speak to your instructor.

- **The poem's setting and situation.** Some poems establish their settings and circumstances vividly. "Stopping by Woods on a Snowy Evening," for example, describes an evening scene in which the speaker stops his sleigh by a woods so that he can watch snow falling amid the trees. Although not all poems are so clear, you should learn as much as you can about setting and situation in every poem you read.

- **The poem's basic form and development.** Some poems, like "Sir Patrick Spens," are narratives; others, like Northrup's "Ogichidag," are personal statements; still others may be speeches to another person, like "Here a Pretty Baby Lies." The poems can be laid out in a sonnet form or may develop in two-line sequences (couplets). They may contain stanzas, each unified by a particular action or thought. Try to determine the form and trace the way in which the poem unfolds, part by part.

- **The poem's subject and theme.** The **subject** indicates the general or specific topic, while the **theme** refers to the idea or ideas that the poem explores. Jarrell's "The Death of the Ball Turret Gunner" announces its subject in the title. However, you must usually infer the theme. This poem's theme is the repulsive ugliness of war, the poignancy of untimely death, the callousness of the living toward the dead, and the suddenness with which war forces young people to face cruelty and horror.

3. *Read the poem aloud, sounding each word clearly.* Although this step may seem unnecessary, reading aloud will enable you to judge the effect of sound, rhythm, and rhyme. If you read "The Death of the Ball Turret Gunner" aloud, for example, you will notice the impact of rhyming *froze* with *hose* and the suggestion of the percussive sounds of cannon fire in the repeated and rhyming *l*, *a*, and *k* sounds of *black flak*. (For further discussion of sounds in poetry, see Chapter 16.)

4. *Prepare a paraphrase of the poem, and make an explication of the ideas and themes.* A paraphrase (discussed later in this chapter) is a restatement of the poem in your own words which helps crystallize your understanding (see also Chapter 2, pp. 86–90). An explication, which is both explanation and interpretation, goes beyond paraphrase to consider significance—either of brief passages or of the entire poem.

STUDYING POETRY

Let us now look in detail at a poem, in this case one that tells a story. It was composed orally as a song sometime during the late Middle Ages or early

Renaissance, when most people got information about the outside world from strolling balladeers who sang the news to them (there were no newspapers, and besides, few people could read). It tells a story that is probably true, or at least based on a real event.

ANONYMOUS

Sir Patrick Spens ——————————————————— *Fifteenth century*

The king sits in Dumferline° town,		
Drinking the blood-red wine:		
"O where will I get a good sailor		
To sail this ship of mine?"		

Up and spoke an eldern° knight   *old, elderly*   5
    Sat° at the king's right knee: *who sat*
"Sir Patrick Spens is the best sailor
    That sails upon the sea."

The king has written a braid° letter   *large, commanding*
    And signed it wi'° his hand,   *with*   10
And sent it to Sir Patrick Spens,
    Was° walking on the sand.   *who was*

The first line that Sir Patrick read,
    A loud laugh laughèd he;
The next line that Sir Patrick read,   15
    A tear blinded his eye.

"O who is this has° done this deed,   *who has*
    This ill deed done to me,
To send me out this time o'° the year,   *of*
    To sail upon the sea?   20

"Make haste, make haste, my merry men all,
    Our good ship sails the morn."°   *in the morning*
"O say not so, my master dear,
    For I fear a deadly storm.

Late late yestere'en° I saw the new moon   *yesterday evening*   25
    With the old moon in her arm,
And I fear, I fear, my dear master,
    That we will come to harm."

O our Scots nobles were right loath
    To wet their cork-heeled shoon,°   *shoes*   30
But long ere a'° the play were played   *all*
    Their hats they swam aboon.°   *about (in the water)*

SIR PATRICK SPENS.   1 *Dumferline:* a town on the Firth of Forth, in Scotland.

O long, long may their ladies sit
   Wi' their fans into their hand,
Or e'er they see Sir Patrick Spens   35
   Come sailing to the land.

O long, long may the ladies stand,
   Wi' their gold combs in their hair,
Waiting for their own dear lords,
   For they'll see them no more.   40

Half o'er, half o'er to Aberdour°
   It's fifty fathom deep,
And there lies good Sir Patrick Spens,
   Wi' the Scots lords at his feet.

SIR PATRICK SPENS.   41 *Aberdour:* Aberdeen, on the east coast of Scotland on the North Sea, about eighty miles north of Dumferline.

QUESTIONS

1.   What action does the poem describe? Who are the principal individual figures? What groups of people are involved with and concerned about the action?

2.   What do you learn about the principal figure, Sir Patrick Spens? Why does he follow the king's orders rather than his own judgment?

3.   What conflicts do you find in the poem? Do they seem personal or political?

4.   What emotions are conveyed in the last two stanzas? Since the poem does not explain why the king sends Sir Patrick and his men to sea, how might the emotions have been expressed more strongly?

5.   Describe the poem's use of dialogue. How many people speak? How do the speeches assist in conveying the poem's action?

   "Sir Patrick Spens" is a **narrative ballad.** A narrative tells a story, and the term *ballad* defines the poem's shape or form. The first two stanzas set up the situation: The king needs a sailor to undertake a vital mission, and an old knight—one of the king's close advisers—suggests choosing Sir Patrick Spens. The rest of the poem focuses on the feelings and eventual death of Sir Patrick and his men. The third stanza provides a transition from the king to Sir Patrick. The king orders Sir Patrick to sea, and Sir Patrick reads the order. At first he laughs—maybe because the king begins by flattering him, or maybe because Sir Patrick at first believes that an order to go to sea at an obvious time of danger is nothing more than a grim joke. But when he realizes that the order is real, he foresees disaster. Our sense of impending calamity is increased when we learn that Sir Patrick's crew is also frightened (lines 23–28).

   The shipwreck, described in the eighth stanza, is presented with ironic understatement. There is no description of the storm or of the crew's panic, nor does the speaker describe the masts splitting or the ship sinking under the waves. Although these horrors are omitted, the floating hats are grim evidence of destruction and death. The remainder of the poem continues in this vein of understatement. In the ninth and tenth stanzas the focus shifts back to the land, and to the ladies who will wait a "long, long" time (forever) for Sir Patrick and his men to return. The poem ends with a vision of Sir Patrick and the "Scots lords" lying "fifty fathom deep."

On first reflection, "Sir Patrick Spens" tells a sad tale without complications. The subject seems to describe no more than Sir Patrick's unfortunate drowning, along with his crew and the Scots noblemen. One might therefore claim that the poem does not have a clear theme. Even the understated irony of the floating hats and the waiting ladies is straightforward and unambiguous.

However, you might consider what the poem suggests about the contradictions and conflicts between authority and individuals. Sir Patrick knows the danger, yet he still obeys the king. In addition, there is a suggestion in lines 5, 17 to 20, and 32 of political infighting. The "eldern knight" is in effect responsible for dooming the ship. Moreover, the "play" being "played" suggests that a political game is taking place over and beyond the grim game of the men caught in the deadly storm (if Sir Patrick knows the danger, would not the knight also know it, and would not this knight also know the consequences of choosing Sir Patrick?). These political motives are not spelled out, but they are implied. Thus the poem is not only a sad tale, but also a poignant dramatization of how power operates, of how a loyal person responds to a tragic dilemma, and of the pitiful consequences of that response.

In reading poetry, then, let the poem be your guide. Get all the words, try to understand dramatic situations, follow the emotional cues the poet gives you, and try to explain everything that is happening. If you find implications that you believe are important (as with the political overtones of "Sir Patrick Spens"), use specific details from the poem to support your observations. Resist the temptation to "uncover" unusual or far-fetched elements in the poem (as a student once did by claiming that Frost's "Stopping by Woods on a Snowy Evening" is a celebration of Santa Claus, stopping on Christmas Eve for a brief rest before carrying out his mission to deliver presents throughout the world). Draw only those conclusions that the poem itself will support.

❀ POEMS FOR STUDY

ROBERT BROWNING   (1812–1889)

My Last Duchess° _____ *1842*

FERRARA

That's my last Duchess painted on the wall,
Looking as if she were alive. I call
That piece a wonder, now: Frà Pandolf's° hands
Worked busily a day, and there she stands.
Will't please you sit and look at her? I said   5
"Frà Pandolf" by design, for never read
Strangers like you that pictured countenance,
The depth and passion of its earnest glance,
But to myself they turned (since none puts by
The curtain I have drawn for you, but I)   10
And seemed as they would ask me, if they durst,°   *dared*
How such a glance came there; so, not the first
Are you to turn and ask thus. Sir, 'twas not
Her husband's presence only, called that spot
Of joy into the Duchess' cheek: perhaps   15
Frà Pandolf chanced to say "Her mantle laps
Over my lady's wrist too much," or "Paint
Must never hope to reproduce the faint
Half-flush that dies along her throat": such stuff
Was courtesy, she thought, and cause enough   20
For calling up that spot of joy. She had
A heart—how shall I say?—too soon made glad,
Too easily impressed; she liked whate'er
She looked on, and her looks went everywhere.
Sir, 'twas all one! My favor at her breast,   25
The dropping of the daylight in the West,
The bough of cherries some officious fool
Broke in the orchard for her, the white mule
She rode with round the terrace—all and each
Would draw from her alike the approving speech,   30
Or blush, at least. She thanked men—good! but thanked
Somehow—I know not how—as if she ranked
My gift of a nine-hundred-years-old name
With anybody's gift. Who'd stoop to blame
This sort of trifling? Even had you skill   35
In speech—(which I have not)—to make your will
Quite clear to such a one, and say, "Just this
Or that in you disgusts me; here you miss,
Or there exceed the mark"—and if she let
Herself be lessoned so, nor plainly set   40

MY LAST DUCHESS.   The poem is based on incidents in the life of Alfonso II, duke of Ferrara, whose first wife died in 1561. Some claimed she was poisoned. The duke negotiated his second marriage to the daughter of the count of Tyrol through an agent.   3 *Frà Pandolf:* an imaginary painter who is also a monk.

Her wits to yours, forsooth, and made excuse
—E'en then would be some stooping; and I choose
Never to stoop. Oh sir, she smiled, no doubt,
Whene'er I passed her; but who passed without
Much the same smile? This grew; I gave commands;   45
Then all smiles stopped together. There she stands
As if alive. Will't please you rise? We'll meet
The company below, then. I repeat,
The Count your master's known munificence
Is ample warrant that no just pretense   50
Of mine for dowry will be disallowed;
Though his fair daughter's self, as I avowed
At starting, is my object. Nay, we'll go
Together down, sir. Notice Neptune,° though,
Taming a sea horse, thought a rarity,   55
Which Claus of Innsbruck° cast in bronze for me!

54 *Neptune:* Roman god of the sea.   56 *Claus of Innsbruck:* an imaginary sculptor.

QUESTIONS

1. Who dominates the conversation in this poem? Who is the listener? Why does the main speaker avoid the obvious purpose of the conversation until near the poem's end?

2. What third character does the speaker describe? In what ways are his descriptions accurate or innacurate? What judgment do you think Browning wants you to make of the speaker? Why?

3. How does the poem illustrate the speaker's misuse of power?

EMILY DICKINSON   (1830–1886)

Because I Could Not Stop for Death _____ *1890 (ca. 1863)*

Because I could not stop for Death—
He kindly stopped for me—
The Carriage held but just Ourselves—
And Immortality.

We slowly drove—He knew no haste   5
And I had put away
My labor and my leisure too,
For His Civility—

We passed the School, where Children strove
At Recess—in the Ring—   10
We passed the Fields of Gazing Grain—
We passed the Setting Sun—

Or rather—He passed Us—
The Dews drew quivering and chill—

For only Gossamer,° my Gown—   *thin fabric*   15
My Tippet°—only Tulle°—   *cape, scarf; thin silk*

We passed before a House that seemed
A Swelling of the Ground—
The Roof was scarcely visible—
The Cornice—in the Ground—   20

Since then—'tis Centuries—and yet
Feels shorter than the Day
I first surmised the Horses' Heads
Were toward Eternity—

QUESTIONS

1. Who is the speaker, and what is she like? Why couldn't she stop for death? What perspective does her present position give the poem?

2. In what unusual ways does the poem characterize death?

3. What does the carriage represent? Where is it headed? Who are the riders? What is meant by the things the carriage passes?

4. What is represented by the house in line 17? Why does the poet use the word "house" in preference to some other word?

ROBERT FROST   (1874–1963)

Stopping by Woods on a Snowy Evening _____ 1923

Whose woods these are I think I know.
His house is in the village though;
He will not see me stopping here
To watch his woods fill up with snow.

My little horse must think it queer   5
To stop without a farmhouse near
Between the woods and frozen lake
The darkest evening of the year.

He gives his harness bells a shake
To ask if there is some mistake.   10
The only other sound's the sweep
Of easy wind and downy flake.

The woods are lovely, dark and deep,
But I have promises to keep,
And miles to go before I sleep,   15
And miles to go before I sleep.

QUESTIONS

1. What do we learn about the speaker? Where is he? What is he doing?

2. What is the setting (place, weather, time) of this poem?

3. Why does the speaker want to watch the "woods fill up with snow"?

4. What evidence suggests that the speaker is embarrassed or self-conscious about stopping? Consider the words "though" in line 2 and "must" in line 5.

5. The last stanza offers two alternative attitudes and courses of action. What are they? Which does the speaker choose?

6. To what extent do the sound and rhyme of this poem contribute to its impact? Note especially the *s* sounds in line 11 and the *w* sounds in line 12.

THOMAS HARDY   (1840–1928)

The Man He Killed _____ *1902*

"Had he and I but met
  By some old ancient inn,
We should have sat us down to wet
  Right many a nipperkin!°   *half-pint cup*

"But ranged as infantry,   5
  And staring face to face,
I shot at him as he at me,
  And killed him in his place.

"I shot him dead because—
  Because he was my foe.   10
Just so: my foe of course he was;
  That's clear enough; although

"He thought he'd 'list,° perhaps,   *enlist*
  Off-hand like—just as I—
Was out of work—had sold his traps°—   *possessions*   15
  No other reason why.

"Yes; quaint and curious war is!
  You shoot a fellow down
You'd treat if met where any bar is,
  Or help to half-a-crown."°   20

THE MAN HE KILLED.   20 *half a crown:* today about 40 cents, but at the time, the equivalent of $10 or $20.

QUESTIONS

1. Who and what is the speaker? What do you learn about him from his language?

2. What situation and event is the speaker recalling and relating?

3. What is the effect produced by repeating the word "because" in lines 9 and 10 and using the word "although" in line 12?

4. What is the speaker's attitude toward his "foe" and toward what he has done?

5. What point, if any, does this poem make about war? How are this poem and Jarrell's "The Death of the Ball Turret Gunner" similar and different?

JOY HARJO   (b. 1951)

Eagle Poem ——————————————————————————— *1990*

To pray you open your whole self
To sky, to earth, to sun, to moon
To one whole voice that is you.
And know there is more
That you can't see, can't hear,   5
Can't know except in moments
Steadily growing, and in languages
That aren't always sound but other
Circles of motion.
Like eagle that Sunday morning   10
Over Salt River. Circled in blue sky
In wind, swept our hearts clean
With sacred wings.
We see you, see ourselves and know
That we must take the utmost care   15
And kindness in all things.
Breathe in, knowing we are made of
All this, and breathe, knowing
We are truly blessed because we
Were born, and die soon within a   20
True circle of motion,
Like eagle rounding out the morning
Inside us.
We pray that it will be done
In beauty.   25
In beauty.

QUESTIONS

1. What is meant by the requirement that "to pray you open your whole self/To sky, to earth, to sun, to moon"? What is the meaning of lines 4–9?

2. Why is the eagle significant to the speaker? Of what importance is the figure that the eagle makes?

3. Why does the poet repeat the phrase "In beauty" at the poem's end? (For comparison, see the Navajo Healing Prayer from the Beautyway Chant, Chapter 12.)

A. E. HOUSMAN   (1859–1936)

Loveliest of Trees, the Cherry Now ——————————————— *1896*

Loveliest of trees, the cherry now
Is hung with bloom along the bough,

And stands about the woodland ride°   *path*   5
Wearing white for Eastertide.

Now, of my threescore years and ten,
Twenty will not come again,
And take from seventy springs a score,
It only leaves me fifty more.   10

And since to look at things in bloom
Fifty springs are little room,
About the woodland I will go
To see the cherry hung with snow.

QUESTIONS

1. How old is the speaker? How can you tell? Why does he assume he will live seventy years ("threescore years and ten")?

2. How would you describe the speaker's perception or sense of time? What is the effect of the words "only" (line 8) and "little" (line 10)?

3. What ideas about time, beauty, and life does this poem explore? What does it suggest about the way we should live?

RANDALL JARRELL   (1914–1965)

The Death of the Ball Turret Gunner° _____ *1945*

From my mother's sleep I fell into the State
And I hunched in its belly till my wet fur froze.°
Six miles from earth, loosed from its dream of life,
I woke to black flak° and the nightmare fighters.
When I died they washed me out of the turret with a hose.   5

THE DEATH OF THE BALL TURRET GUNNER.   *Ball Turret Gunner:* High-altitude bombers in World War II (1941–1945) contained a revolvable gun turret both at the top and at the bottom, from which a machine-gunner could shoot at attacking fighter planes. Gunners in these turrets were sometimes mutilated by the gunfire of attacking planes.   2 *froze:* The stratospheric below-zero temperatures caused the moisture in the gunner's breath to freeze as it contacted the collar of his flight jacket.   4 *flak:* The round, black explosions of antiaircraft shells fired at bombers from the ground, an acronym of the German word *Fliegerabwehrkanone.*

QUESTIONS

1. Who is the speaker? Where has he been, and what has he been doing? What has happened to him?

2. In the first line, what is the poet saying about the age of the speaker and the opportunities he had for living before he was killed? How may this line be read politically and polemically?

3. What is a turret? What is your response to the last line?

JIM NORTHRUP   (b. 1943)

Ogichidag° _____ *1993*

I was born in war, WW Two.
Listened as the old men told stories
of getting gassed in the trenches, WW One.
Saw my uncles come back from
Guadalcanal, North Africa,   5
and the Battle of the Bulge.
Memorized the war stories
my cousins told of Korea.
Felt the fear in their voices.
Finally it was my turn,   10
my brothers too.
Joined the marines in time
for the Cuban Missile Crisis.
Heard the crack of rifles
in the rice paddies south of Da Nang.   15
Watched my friends die there
then tasted the bitterness of
the only war America ever lost.
My son is now a warrior.
Will I listen to his war stories   20
or cry into his open grave?

OGICHIDAG.   The title is the Ojibway word for "warriors."

QUESTIONS

1. What battles are mentioned in the poem, and over what period of time do these battles extend?

2. How does the speaker state that he learned about the battles? Why is this method of gaining knowledge important? What experience has the speaker had with war?

3. Why does the speaker finish the poem by referring to his son? In relationship to the poem's structure, why is the concluding question important?

WILLIAM SHAKESPEARE   (1564–1616)

Sonnet 55:
Not Marble, Nor the Gilded Monuments _____ *1609*

Not marble, nor the gilded monuments
Of princes, shall outlive this powerful rhyme;
But you shall shine more bright in these contents
Than unswept stone, besmeared with sluttish time.

When wasteful war shall statues overturn,   5
And broils root out the work of masonry,
Nor° Mars his° sword nor war's quick fire shall burn   *Neither; Mars's*
The living record of your memory.
'Gainst death and all-oblivious enmity
Shall you pace forth; your praise shall still find room   10
Even in the eyes of all posterity
That wear this world out to the ending doom.°   *Judgment Day*
So, till the judgment that yourself arise,
You live in this, and dwell in lovers' eyes.

QUESTIONS

1. Who is the speaker of the poem, and who is being addressed?

2. What powers of destruction does the speaker mention? What, according to the speaker, will survive these powers?

3. What does "the living record of your memory" (line 8) mean?

4. What is the poem's subject? Theme?

WRITING A PARAPHRASE OF A POEM

Paraphrasing is especially useful in the study of poetry. It fixes both the general shape and the details of a poem in your mind, and it also reveals the poetic devices at work. A comparison of the original poem with the paraphrase highlights the techniques and the language that make the poem effective.

To paraphrase a poem, rewrite it in prose, in your own words. Decide what details to include—a number that you determine partly by the length of the poem and partly by the total length of your paraphrase. When you deal with lyrics, sonnets, and other short poems, you may include all the details, and thus your paraphrase may be as long as the work, or longer. Paraphrases of long poems, however, will be shorter than the originals because some details must be summarized briefly while others may be cut entirely.

It is vital to make your paraphrase accurate, and also to use *only your own words*. To make sure that your words are all your own, read through the poem several times. Then, put the poem out of sight and write your paraphrase. Once you've finished, check yourself both for accuracy and vocabulary. If you find that you've borrowed too many of the poem's words, choose other words that mean the same thing, or else use quotation marks to set off the original words (but do not overuse quotations).

Above all, remain faithful to the poem, but *avoid drawing conclusions and giving unnecessary explanations*. It would be wrong in a paraphrase of "The Death of the Ball Turret Gunner," for example, to state, "This poem makes a forceful argument against the brutal and wasteful deaths caused by war." This assertion states the poem's *theme*, but it *does not* describe the poem's actual *content*.

Organizing Your Paraphrase

The organization of your paraphrase should reflect the poem's form or development. Include material in the order in which it occurs. With short poems, organize your paraphrase to reflect the poem's development line by line or stanza by stanza. In paraphrasing Shakespeare's "Not Marble, Nor the Gilded Monuments," for example, you should deal with each quatrain in sequence and then consider the final couplet. With longer poems, look for natural divisions such as groups of related stanzas, verse paragraphs, or other possible organizational units. In every situation, the poem's shape should determine the form of your paraphrase.

SAMPLE STUDENT ESSAY

A Paraphrase of Thomas Hardy's "The Man He Killed"

[1]   If the man I killed had met me in an inn, we would have sat down together and had many drinks. Because we belonged to armies of warring foot soldiers lined up on a battlefield, however, we shot at each other, and my shot killed him.

[2]   The reason I killed him, I think, was that he and I were enemies--just that. But as I think of it, I realize that he had enlisted in just the way I did. Perhaps he did it on a whim, or perhaps he had lost his job and sold everything he owned. There was no other reason to enlist.

[3]   Being at war is unusual and strange. Instead of buying a man a drink or helping him out with a little money, you have to kill him.

Commentary on the Essay

Because Hardy's poem is short, the paraphrase attempts to include all its details. The organization closely follows the poem's development. Paragraph 1, for example, restates the contents of the first two stanzas. Paragraph 2 restates the third and fourth stanzas. Finally, the last paragraph separately paraphrases the last stanza, which contains the reflections made by the poem's "I" speaker. This paragraph concludes the paraphrase just as the last stanza concludes the poem.

Notice that the essay does not abstract details from the poem, such as "The dead man might have become a good friend in peacetime" for stanza 5; nor does it extend details, such as "We would have gotten acquainted, had drinks together, told many stories, and done quite a bit of laughing" for stanza 1 (even though both stanzas suggest these details). Although the paraphrase reflects the poem's strong antiwar sentiments, an interpretive sentence like "By his very directness, the narrator brings out the senselessness and brutality of warfare" would be out of place. What is needed is a short restatement of the poem to demonstrate the essay writer's understanding of the poem's content, and no more.

WRITING AN EXPLICATION OF A POEM

Explication goes beyond the assimilation required for a paraphrase and thus provides you with the opportunity to show your understanding. There is no need, however, to explain everything in the poem. A complete, or total, explication would theoretically require you to explain the meaning and implications of each word and every line—a technique that obviously would be exhaustive (and exhausting). It would also be self-defeating, for explicating everything would prohibit you from using your judgment and deciding what is important.

A more manageable and desirable technique is therefore the **general explication,** which devotes attention to the meaning of individual parts in relationship to the entire work, as in the discussion of "Sir Patrick Spens" (p. 452). You might think of a *general explication* as your explanation or "reading" of the poem. Because it does not require you to go into exhaustive detail, you will need to be selective and to consider only those details that are significant in themselves and vital to your own thematic development.

Questions for Discovering Ideas

- What does the title contribute to the reader's understanding?
- Who is speaking? Where is the speaker when the poem is happening?
- What is the situation? What has happened in the past, or what is happening in the present, that has brought about the speech?
- What difficult, special, or unusual words does the poem contain? What references need explaining? How does an explanation assist in the understanding of the poem?
- How does the poem develop? Is it a personal statement? Is it a story?
- What is the main idea of the poem? What details make possible the formulation of the main idea?

Strategies for Organizing Ideas

Your general explication demonstrates your ability to (1) follow the essential details of the poem (the same as in a paraphrase), (2) understand the issues and the meaning the poem reveals, (3) explain some of the relationships of content to technique, and (4) note and discuss especially important or unique aspects of the poem.

In your introduction, use your central idea to express a general view of the poem, which your essay will bear out. The discussion of "Sir Patrick Spens" (p. 452) suggests some possible central ideas, namely that (1) the poem highlights a conflict between self-preservation and obedience to authority, and (2) innocent people may be caught in political infighting. In the sample student essay explicating Hardy's "The Man He Killed" (p. 462), the central idea is that war is senseless.

In the body of your essay, first explain the poem's content—not with a paraphrase, but with a description of the poem's major organizing elements.

Hence, if the speaker of the poem is "inside" the poem as a first-person involved "I," you do not need to reproduce this voice yourself in your description, as with the sample student essay paraphrasing "The Man He Killed." Instead, *describe* the poem in your own words, with whatever brief introductory phrases you find necessary, as in the second paragraph of the following sample student essay.

Next, explicate the poem in relationship to your central idea. *You* choose *your own* order of discussion, depending on your topics. You should, however, keep stressing your central idea with each new topic. Thus, you may wish to follow your description by discussing the poem's meaning, or even by presenting two or more possible interpretations. You might also wish to refer to significant techniques. For example, in "Sir Patrick Spens" a noteworthy technique is the unintroduced quotations (i.e., quotations appearing without any "he said" or "quoth he" phrases) as the ballad writer's means of dramatizing the commands and responses of Sir Patrick and his doomed crew.

You might also introduce special topics, such as the crewman who explains that there will be bad luck because the new moon has "the old moon in her arm" (line 26). Such a reference to superstition might include the explanation of the crewman's assumptions, the relationship of his uneasiness to the remainder of the poem, and also how the ballad writer keeps the narrative brief. In short, discuss those aspects of meaning and technique that bear upon your central idea.

In your conclusion, you may repeat your major idea to reinforce your essay's thematic structure. Because your essay is a general explication, there will be parts of the poem that you will not have discussed. You might therefore mention what might be gained from an exhaustive discussion of various parts of the poem (do not, however, begin to exhaust any subject in the conclusion of your essay). The last stanza of Hardy's "The Man He Killed," for example, contains the words "quaint and curious" in reference to war. These words are unusual, particularly because the speaker might have chosen *hateful, senseless, destructive,* or other similarly descriptive words. Why did Hardy have his speaker make such a choice? With brief attention to such a problem, you may conclude.

SAMPLE STUDENT ESSAY

An Explication of Hardy's "The Man He Killed"°

Thomas Hardy's "The Man He Killed" exposes the senselessness of war.* It does this through a silent contrast between the needs of ordinary people, as represented by a young man--the speaker--who has killed an enemy soldier in battle, and the antihuman and unnatural deaths of war. Of major note in this

---

° See p. 457 for this poem.
* Central idea.

contrast are the speaker's circumstances, his language, his sense of identity with the dead man, and his concerns and wishes.†

[2] The speaker begins by contrasting the circumstances of warfare with those of peace. He does not identify himself, but his speech reveals that he is an ordinary sort--a person, one of "the people"--who enjoys drinking in a bar and who prefers friendship and helpfulness to violence. If he and the man he killed had met in an inn, he says, they would have shared many drinks, but because they met on a battlefield they shot at each other, and he killed the other man. The speaker tries to justify the killing, but he can produce no stronger reason than that the dead man was his "foe." Once he states this reason, he again thinks of the similarities between himself and the dead man, and he then concludes that warfare is "quaint and curious" (line 17) because it forces a man to kill another man whom he would have befriended if they had met during peacetime.

[3] To make the irony of warfare clear, the poem uses easy, colloquial language to bring out the speaker's ordinary qualities. His manner of speech is conversational, as in "We should have sat us down" (line 3), and "list" (for "enlist," line 13), and his use of "you" in the last stanza. Also, his word choices, shown in words like "nipperkin," "traps," and "fellow" (lines 4, 15, and 18), are common and informal, at least in British usage. This language is important because it establishes that the speaker is an ordinary man whom war has thrown into an unnatural role.

[4] As another means of stressing the stupidity of war, the poem makes clear that the two men--the live soldier who killed and the dead soldier who was killed --were so alike that they could have been brothers or even twins. They had similar ways of life, similar economic troubles, similar wishes to help other people, and similar motives in doing things like enlisting in the army. Symbolically, at least, the "man he killed" is the speaker himself, and hence the killing is a form of suicide. The poem thus raises the question of why two people who are almost identical should be shoved into opposing battle lines in order to kill each other. This question is rhetorical, for the obvious answer is that there is no good reason.

[5] Because the speaker (and also, very likely, the dead man) is shown as a person embodying the virtues of friendliness and helpfulness, Hardy's poem is a strong disapproval of war. Clearly, political reasons for violence as policy are irrelevant to the characters and concerns of the men who fight. They, like the speaker, would prefer to follow their own needs rather than remote and meaningless ideals. The failure of complex but irrelevant political explanations is brought out most clearly in the third stanza, in which the speaker tries to give a reason for shooting the other man. Hardy's use of punctuation--the dashes-- stresses the fact that the speaker has no commitment to the cause he served when killing. Thus the speaker stops at the word "because--" and gropes for a reason (line 9). Not being articulate, he can say only "Because he was my foe. / Just so: my foe of course he was; / That's clear enough" (lines 10–12). These short bursts of words indicate that he cannot explain things to himself or to anyone else except in the most obvious and trite terms, and in apparent embarrassment he inserts "of course" as a way of emphasizing hostility even though he felt none toward the man he killed.

† Thesis sentence.

[6]   A reading thus shows the power of the poem's dramatic argument. Hardy does not establish closely detailed reasons against war as a policy, but rather dramatizes the idea that all political arguments are unimportant in view of the central and glaring brutality of war--killing. Hardy's speaker is not able to express deep feelings; rather he is confused because he is an average sort who wants only to live and let live and to enjoy a drink in a bar with friends. But this very commonness stresses the point that everyone is victimized by war--both those who die and those who kill. The poem is a powerful argument for peace and reconciliation.

Commentary on the Essay

This explication begins by stating a central idea about "The Man He Killed," and then indicates the topics to follow that will develop the idea. Although nowhere does the speaker state that war is senseless, the essay takes the position that the poem embodies this idea. A more detailed examination of the poem's themes might develop the idea by discussing the ways in which individuals are caught up in social and political forces, or the contrast between individuality and the state. In this essay, however, the simple statement of the idea is enough.

Paragraph 2 describes the major details of the poem, with guiding phrases like "The speaker begins," "he says," and "he again thinks." Thus the paragraph goes over the poem, like a paraphrase, but explains how things occur, as is appropriate for an explication. Paragraph 3 is devoted to the speaker's words and idioms, with the idea that his conversational manner is part of the poem's contrasting method of argument. If these brief references to style were more detailed, this topic could be more fully developed as an aspect of Hardy's implied argument against war.

Paragraph 4 extends paragraph 3 inasmuch as it points out the similarities of the speaker and the man he killed. If the situation were reversed, the dead man might say exactly the same things about the present speaker. This affinity underscores the suicidal nature of war. Paragraph 5 treats the style of the poem's third stanza. In this context, the treatment is brief. The last paragraph reiterates the main idea and concludes with a tribute to the poem as an argument.

The entire essay therefore represents a reading and explanation of the poem's high points. It stresses a particular interpretation and briefly shows how various aspects of the poem bear it out.

SPECIAL WRITING TOPICS FOR STUDYING THE NATURE OF POETRY

1. Skim the titles of poems listed in the table of contents of this book. Judging by the subjects of these poems, describe and discuss the possible range of subject matter for poetry. What topics seem most suitable? Why? Do any topics seem to be ruled out? Why? What additional subject matter would you suggest as possible topics for poems?

2. How accurate is the proposition that poetry is a particularly compressed form of expression? To support your position, you might refer to poems such as "The Man He Killed," "Here a Pretty Baby Lies," and "Stopping by Woods on a Snowy Evening."

3. Consider the subject of war as brought out in "The Death of the Ball Turret Gunner," "The Man He Killed," and "Ogichidag." What ideas are common to all these poems? What ideas are distinct and unique? On the basis of your comparison, consider the use of poetry as a vehicle for the expression of moral and political ideas.

4. Write two poems of your own about your future plans. In one, assume that the world is stable and will go on forever. In the other, assume that a large asteroid is out of orbit and is hurtling toward earth at great speed, and a collision six months from now will bring untold destruction and may even end life on earth. After composing your poems, write a brief explanation of how and why they differ in terms of language; references; attitudes toward friends, family, country, and religion; and so on.

5. Consult the brief section on reader-response criticism in Chapter 27. Then write an essay about your responses to one poem, or a number of poems, in this chapter. Assume that your own experiences are valuable guides for your judgment. In the poems that you have read, what has had a bearing on your experiences? What in your own experiences has given you insights into the poems? Try to avoid being anecdotal; instead, try to find a relationship between your experiences and the poetry.

6. In the reference section of your library, find two books (anthologies, encyclopedias, introductions, dictionaries of literary terms) about the general subject of poetry. On the basis of how these two sources define and explain poetry, write a brief essay telling a person younger than you what to expect from the reading of poems.

12
Words:
The Building Blocks
of Poetry

Words are the recognized and accepted *signifiers* of thoughts, objects, and actions. They are also the building blocks of both poetry and prose, but poetry is unique because by its nature it uses words with the utmost economy. The words of poetry create rhythm, rhyme, meter, and form. They define the speaker, the characters, the setting, and the situation. They also carry the ideas and the emotions. For this reason, each poet searches for perfect and indispensable words, words that convey all the compressed meanings, overtones, and emotions that each poem requires, and also the words that look right and sound right.

Life—and poetry—might be simpler (but less interesting) if there were an exact one-to-one correspondence between words and the objects or ideas they signify. Such close correspondence exists in artificial language systems such as chemical equations and computer languages. This identical correlation, however, is not characteristic of English or any other natural language. Instead, words have the independent and glorious habit of acquiring a vast array of different meanings.

Even if we have not thought much about language, most of us recognize that words are sometimes ambiguous, and much literature is built on ambiguity. For instance, in Shakespeare's *Romeo and Juliet*, when Mercutio says, "Seek for me tomorrow and you shall find me a grave man," the joke works because *grave* has two separate meanings, both of which come into play. In reading poetry, we recognize that poets rejoice in this shifting and elusive but also rich nature of language.

CHOICE OF DICTION: SPECIFIC AND CONCRETE
VS. GENERAL AND ABSTRACT

Because poets always try to use only the exactly right words, they constantly make conscious and subconscious decisions about diction. One of the major categories of their choice is diction that is either *specific* and *concrete* or *general* and *abstract*.

Specific language refers to objects or conditions that can be perceived or imagined; **general** language signifies broad classes of persons, objects, and phenomena. **Concrete** diction describes conditions or qualities that are exact and particular; **abstract** diction refers to qualities that are rarefied and theoretical. In practice, poems using specific and concrete words tend to be visual, familiar, and compelling. By contrast, poems using general and abstract words tend to be detached and cerebral, frequently dealing with universal questions or emotions.

These distinctions become clear when we compare Housman's "Loveliest of Trees" (p. 458) and Richard Eberhart's "The Fury of Aerial Bombardment." Many of the terms and images that Housman uses, such as "three score years and ten" and "cherry . . . hung with bloom," are specific and concrete; they evoke exact time and clear visualization. By contrast, Eberhart's terms, such as "infinite spaces" and "eternal truth," are general and abstract. It is hard to envision them with clarity and exactness. This contrast, which by no means implies that Housman is superior to Eberhart, reflects differences in word choices for different objectives.

Most poets employ mixtures of words in these categories because in many poems they draw general observations and abstract conclusions from specific situations and concrete responses. They therefore interweave their words to fit their situations and ideas, as in Theodore Roethke's "Dolor," which uses specific and concrete words to define a series of abstract emotional states.

LEVELS OF DICTION

Like ordinary speakers and writers of prose, poets choose words from the category of the three levels of diction: *high or formal, middle or neutral,* and *low or informal* (see also Chapter 7).

High or Formal Diction

High or **formal diction** is elevated and elaborate; it follows the rules of syntax exactly, and it avoids idioms, colloquialisms, contractions, and slang. Beyond "correctness," formal language is characterized by complex words and a lofty tone. Graves uses formal diction in "The Naked and the Nude" when the speaker asserts that the terms in the title are "By lexicographers construed/As synonyms that should express/The same deficiency of dress." These Latinate words stiffen and generalize the passage. We find *lexicographers* instead of *dictionary writers, construed* (from Latin) instead of *thought* (native English), *express* (from Latin) instead of *say* or *show* (native English), and *deficiency* (Latin) instead of *lack* (English).

Middle or Neutral Diction

Middle or **neutral diction** maintains the correct language and word order of formal diction but avoids elaborate words and elevated tone. For example, Emily Dickinson's "Because I Could Not Stop for Death" (p. 455) is almost entirely in middle diction.

Low or Informal Diction

Low or **informal diction** is the language of everyday use; it is relaxed and conversational. Poems using informal diction often include common and simple words, idiomatic expressions, slang, and contractions. Informal diction is seen in Thomas Hardy's "The Man He Killed" (p. 457), where the speaker uses words and phrases like "many a nipperkin," "He thought he'd 'list," and "off-hand like." In general, formal diction uses longer words of French, Latin, and Greek derivation, while informal diction uses words of native English, most of which are short (together with many short words that were originally taken from French, such as *use, common, delight, tender,* and *trace*). A good college-level dictionary includes etymologies; as an exercise, you might trace the origins of a number of words in a poem.

SPECIAL TYPES OF DICTION

Depending on their subjects and purposes, poets (and writers of prose) may wish to introduce four special types of diction into their poems: *idiom, dialect, slang,* and *jargon.*

Idiom

The words *idiom* and *idioms* refer to words and phrases that are common and acceptable in a given level of language, even though they might, upon analysis, seem peculiar. Standard idioms are so ingrained into our language that we hardly notice them. Poems automatically reflect these idioms. Thus, for example, a poet may "think *of*" an idea, speak of "living *in*" a house, talk of "going *out* to play," or describe a woman "lovely *as* chandeliers." Poets hardly have choices about such idioms as long as they are using standard English. Real choice occurs when poets select idioms that are unusual or even ungrammatical, as in phrases like "had he and I but met," "we was happy," and "except that You than He." Idioms like these enable poets to achieve levels of ordinary and colloquial diction, depending on their purposes.

Dialect

Dialect refers to the words and pronunciation of a particular region or group. In addition to "general American," we can recognize many common dialects such as Brooklynese, American Black English, Yiddish English, Texan, Southern, and Scottish English. Dialect is concerned with whether we refer to a *pail* (general American) or a *bucket* (southern); or sit down on a *sofa* (eastern) or a *couch* (general American) or *davenport* (midwestern); or drink *soda* (eastern), *pop* (midwestern), *soda pop* (a confused midwesterner living in the east, or a confused easterner living in the midwest), or *tonic* (Bostonian). Hardy's "The Man He Killed" (p. 457) and Burns's "Green Grow the Rashes, O" illustrate the poetic use of dialect.

Slang

Slang refers to informal and substandard vocabulary and idiom. It is made up of spontaneous words and phrases that may exist for a time and then vanish. Recently, for example, the word *bad* has been slang for "good." Slang has a way of persisting, as may be seen in the many phrases that Americans have developed to describe dying, such as *kick the bucket, croak, be wasted, be disappeared,* and *be offed.* A non-native speaker of English would have difficulty understanding that a person who "kicked the bucket" or was "offed" had actually died.

Even when slang is widely accepted, it usually goes no further than colloquial or conversational levels. If it is introduced into a standard context it will stand out, as in cummings's "Buffalo Bill's Defunct" (p. 630) where the speaker refers to Buffalo Bill as the "blueeyed boy" of "Mister Death." Because the poem deals with the universality of death, the phrase, which usually means a young man on the way to success, ironically underscores this intention.

Jargon

Jargon refers to words and idioms developed by a particular group to fit their special needs. Without some kind of initiation (including intensive study), people not in the group cannot understand the jargon. Usually such groups are members of specific professions or trades, such as lawyers, plumbers, astronauts, doctors, and football players. Although jargon at its worst befuddles rather than informs, it is interesting when it becomes part of mainstream English or is used in literature. Poets may introduce jargon for special effects. For example, Zimmer, in "The Day Zimmer Lost Religion" (Chapter 21), wryly uses the phrase "ready for Him now," a boxing expression that describes a fighter in top condition. Linda Pastan uses "gives me an A" and "I'm dropping out," both phrases from school life, to create comic effects in "Marks" (Chapter 21). Poems in this chapter employing jargon are Reed's "Naming of Parts" and Eberhart's "The Fury of Aerial Bombardment." Both poems use technical terms about firearms to establish the authenticity of their references and therefore to reinforce their judgments about warfare.

DECORUM

A vital literary concept is **decorum;** that is, words and subjects should be exactly appropriate—formal words for serious subjects, informal words for low subjects and comedy. In Shakespeare's *A Midsummer Night's Dream,* for example, the nobles usually speak poetry and the "mechanicals" speak prose. When the nobility are relaxed and in the forest, however, they speak prose. *Decorum* governs such choices of language.

In the eighteenth century, writers aimed to make the English language as dignified as ancient Latin, which was the international language of discourse. They therefore asserted that only formal diction was appropriate for poetry; common life and colloquial language were excluded except in drama and popular ballads. These rules of decorum required standard and elevated language rather than common words and phrases. The development of scientific terminology during the eighteenth century also influenced language. In the scientific mode, poets of the time used genus-species phrases like "lowing herd" for cattle (Gray) and "finny prey" for fish (Pope). In this vein, Thomas Gray observed the dependence of color on light in the line "cheerful fields resume their green attire" from the "Sonnet on the Death of Richard West" (p. 481).

Alexander Pope, one of the greatest eighteenth-century poets, maintained these rules of decorum—and also made fun of them—in his mock-epic poem *The Rape of the Lock,* and more fully in the mock-critical work *The Art of Sinking in Poetry.* In *The Rape of the Lock,* he refers to a scissors as a "glittering forfex." Similarly, in the following couplet he elevates the simple act of pouring coffee:

> From silver spouts the grateful liquors glide,
> While China's earth receives the smoking tide.

After William Wordsworth transformed poetic diction early in the nineteenth century, the topics and language of people of all classes, with a special stress on common folk, have become a feature of poetry (see Chapter 20). Poets have continued to follow rules of decorum, however, inasmuch as the use of colloquial diction and even slang is a necessary consequence of popular subject matter.

SYNTAX

Syntax refers to word order and sentence structure. Normal English word order is firmly fixed in a *subject-verb-object* sequence. At the simplest level, we say, "A dog (*subject*) bites (*verb*) a man (*object*)." This order is so central to our communication that any change significantly affects meaning: "A dog bites a man" is not the same as "A man bites a dog."

Much of the time, poets follow normal word order. In "The Lamb," for example, Blake creates a simple, easy order in keeping with the poem's purpose of presenting a childlike praise of God. Many modern poets such as James Wright (p. 488) go out of their way to create ordinary, everyday syntax, on the theory that a poem's sentence structures should not get in the way of the reader's perceptions.

Yet, just as good poets always explore the limits of ideas, so also do they sometimes explore the many possibilities of syntax. In Donne's "Batter My Heart," for example, line 7 is "Reason, Your viceroy in me, me should defend." In prose, this sentence would read "Reason, which is Your viceroy in me, should defend me." But note that Donne drops out the "which is," thus making an appositive instead of a relative clause. In the predicate, he places the direct object "me" before and not after the verb. The resulting emphasis on the pronoun "me" is appropriate to the personal-divine relationship that is the topic of the sonnet. The alteration also meets the demand of the poem's rhyme scheme. A set of particularly noteworthy syntactic variations occurs in Roethke's "Dolor." The poet uses an irregular and idiosyncratic combination of direct objects, prepositional phrases, and appositives to create ambiguity and uncertainty that reflects the poem's meaning—that school and office routines produce aimlessness and depression.

In addition to these techniques used by Blake, Wright, Donne, and Roethke, there are many other ways in which poets shape word order to create emphasis. Rhetoric, for example, has an important influence on sentence structures. A fundamental and easily recognized device is **parallelism,** the duplication of forms and word order. The simplest form of parallelism is the **repetition** of the same words and phrases, seen in Blake's "The Lamb." Through the use of the same *forms* of *different* words, parallelism produces lines or portions of lines that impress our minds strongly, as in this passage from Robinson's "Richard Cory," in which there are four parallel past-tense verbs (italicized here):

So on we *worked*, and *waited* for the light,
And *went* without the meat, and *cursed* the bread;

The final two lines of this poem demonstrate how parallelism may embody **antithesis**—a contrasting situation or idea that effects the strength of surprise and climax:

And Richard Cory, one calm summer night,
Went home and *put* a bullet through his head.

A major quality of parallelism is the packing of words (the *economy* and *compression* of poetry), for by using a parallel structure the poet makes a single word or phrase function a number of times, with no need for repetition. The opening verb phrase "have known" in Roethke's "Dolor," though used once, controls six parallel direct objects. At the end of Donne's "Batter My Heart," parallelism permits Donne to omit the italicized words added and bracketed in the last line here:

for I,
Except You enthrall me, never shall be free,
Nor *[shall I]* ever *[be]* chaste, except° You ravish me.   *unless*

Note also that parallelism and antithesis make possible the unique *abba* ordering of these two lines, with the pattern "enthrall" (verb), "free" (adjective), "chaste" (adjective), "ravish" (verb). This pattern is called **chiasmus** or **antimetabole** and is a common means by which poets create emphasis.

DENOTATION AND CONNOTATION

The control over denotation and connotation (also discussed in Chapter 7) is so important in poetry that it has been called the very soul of the poet's art. **Denotation** refers to the standard dictionary meaning of a word. It indicates conventional correspondences between a sign (the word) and an object or idea. We might expect denotation to be fairly straightforward. However, most English words have multiple denotations. The word *house*, for example, can refer to a *building*, a *family*, a *chamber of congress*, a *theater*, a *theater audience*, a *sorority* or *fraternity*, an *astrological classification*, or a *brothel*. Although context usually makes the denotation of *house* more specific, the various meanings confer a built-in ambiguity to this simple word.

Denotation presents problems because with the passing of time new meanings emerge and old ones are shed. In poems written in the eighteenth century and earlier, there are many words that have changed so completely that a modern dictionary is not much help. In Andrew Marvell's "To His Coy Mistress," for example (Chapter 17), the speaker asserts that his "vegetable love should grow/Vaster than empires, and more slow." At first, some readers may imagine that "vegetable" refers to something like a giant, loving cabbage. When we turn to a current dictionary, we discover that *vegetable* is an adjective meaning "plantlike," but *plantlike love* does not get us much beyond *vegetable love*. A reference to the *Oxford English Dictionary (OED)*, however, tells us that *vegetable* was used as an adjective in the seventeenth century to mean "living or growing like a plant." Thus we find out that "vegetable love" means love that grows slowly but steadily larger.

Connotation refers to the emotional, psychological, or social overtones that words carry beyond their denotations. According to the dictionary, the words *childish* and *childlike* denote the state of being like a child. Nevertheless, they connote or imply different sets of characteristics. *Childish* suggests a person who is bratty, stubborn, immature, silly, and petulant, whereas *childlike* describes a person who is innocent, charming, and unaffected. These different meanings are based entirely on connotation, for the denotations make little distinction.

We constantly encounter the manipulation of connotation. Advertising, for example, depends on the skillful management of connotation. This manipulation may be as simple as calling a *used* car *pre-owned* to avoid the negative connotations of *used*. On the other hand, the manipulation may be as sophisticated as the current use of the words *lite* or *light* to describe foods and drinks. In all such products, *lite* means dietetic, low-calorie, or even weak. The distinction—and the selling point—is found in connotation. Imagine how difficult it would be to sell a drink called "dietetic beer" or "weak beer." *Light* and *lite*, however, carry none of the negative connotations. Instead, *lite* suggests a product that is pleasant, sparkling, bright, and healthy.

Poets always try to make individual words carry as many appropriate and effective denotations and connotations as possible. Put another way, poets use *packed* or *loaded* words that carry a broad range of meaning and association. With this in mind, read the following poem by Robert Graves.

ROBERT GRAVES (1895–1985)

The Naked and the Nude ————————————————————————— *1957*

For me, the naked and the nude
(By lexicographers° construed
As synonyms that should express
The same deficiency of dress
Or shelter) stand as wide apart   5
As love from lies, or truth from art.

Lovers without reproach will gaze
On bodies naked and ablaze;
The Hippocratic° eye will see
In nakedness, anatomy;   10
And naked shines the Goddess when
She mounts her lion among men.

The nude are bold, the nude are sly
To hold each treasonable eye.
While draping by a showman's trick   15
Their dishabille° in rhetoric,
They grin a mock-religious grin
Of scorn at those of naked skin.

The naked, therefore, who compete
Against the nude may know defeat;   20
Yet when they both together tread
The briary pastures of the dead,
By Gorgons° with long whips pursued,
How naked go the sometime nude!

THE NAKED AND THE NUDE. 2 *lexicographers:* writers of dictionaries. 9 *Hippocratic:* medical; the adjective derives from Hippocrates (ca. 460–377 B.C.E.), the ancient Greek who is considered the "father of medicine." 16 *dishabille:* being carelessly or partly dressed. 23 *Gorgons:* mythological female monsters with snakes for hair.

QUESTIONS

1. How does the speaker explain the denotations and connotations of "naked" and "nude" in the first stanza? What is indicated by the fact that the word *naked* is derived from Old English *nacod* while *nude* comes from Latin *nudus*?

2. What examples of "the naked" and "the nude" do the second and third stanzas provide? What do the examples have in common?
3. How do the connotations of words like "sly," "draping," "dishabille," "rhetoric," and "grin" contribute to the poem's ideas about "the nude"?
4. What does "briary pastures of the dead" mean in line 22?

This poem explores the connotative distinctions between the title words, *naked* and *nude*, which share a common denotation. The title also suggests that the poem is about human customs, for if the speaker were considering the words alone, he would say "naked" and "nude" instead of "*the* naked and *the* nude." The speaker's use of *the* signifies a double focus on both language and human perspectives. In the first five lines the poem establishes that the two key words should be "synonyms that should express/The same deficiency of dress" (lines 3–4). By introducing elevated and complex words such as "lexicographers" and "construed," however, Graves implies that the connection between "the naked" and "the nude" is highly sophisticated and artificial.

In the rest of the poem, Graves develops this distinction, linking the word *naked* to virtues of love, truth, innocence, and honesty, while connecting *nude* to artifice, hypocrisy, and deceit. At the end, he visualizes a classical underworld in which all pretentiousness will disappear, and the nude will lose their sophistication and become merged with the naked. The implication is that artifice will vanish in the face of eternal reality. A thorough study of the words in the poem bears out the consistency of Graves's idea, not only about the two title words, but also about the accumulated layers of history, usage, and philosophy that weigh upon human life and thought.

POEMS FOR STUDY

WILLIAM BLAKE   (1757–1827)

The Lamb _____ *1789*

Little Lamb, who made thee?
Dost thou know who made thee?
Gave thee life & bid thee feed,
By the stream & o'er the mead;
Gave thee clothing of delight,   5
Softest clothing wooly bright;
Gave thee such a tender voice,
Making all the vales rejoice!
Little Lamb who made thee?
Dost thou know who made thee?   10

Little Lamb I'll tell thee,
Little Lamb I'll tell thee!
He is called by thy name,
For he calls himself a Lamb:
He is meek & he is mild,   15
He became a little child:
I a child & thou a lamb,
We are callèd by his name.
Little Lamb God bless thee.
Little Lamb God bless thee.   20

QUESTIONS

1. Who or what is the speaker in this poem? The listener? How are they related?
2. What is the effect of repetition in the poem?
3. How would you characterize the diction in this poem? High, middle, or low? Abstract or concrete? How is it consistent with the speaker?
4. What are the connotations of "softest," "bright," "tender," "meek," and "mild"? What do these words imply about the Creator?
5. Describe the characteristics of God imagined in this poem. Contrast the image here with the image of God in Donne's "Batter My Heart."

ROBERT BURNS   (1756–1796)

Green Grow the Rashes, O _____ *1787*

1

There's naught but care on ev'ry han',°   *hand*
   In every hour that passes, O;
What signifies the life o'° man   *of*
   An' 'twere na° for the lasses, O?   *if it were not*

Chorus:
Green grow the rashes,° O;   rushes   5
Green grow the rashes, O;
The sweetest hours that e'er I spend
    Are spent among the lasses, O!

                    2
The war'ly° race may riches chase,   worldly
    An' riches still may fly them, O;   10
An' tho' at last they catch them fast,
    Their hearts can ne'er enjoy them, O.
Chorus.

                    3
But gie me a cannie° hour at e'en,°   give me a happy; evening
    My arms about my dearie, O,
An' war'ly cares an' war'ly men   15
    May a' gae tapsalteerie,° O!   all go topsy-turvy
Chorus.

                    4
For you sae douce° ye sneer at this,   so sober, so straitlaced
    Ye're naught but senseless asses, O:
The wisest man the warl' e'er° saw,   world ever
    He dearly loved the lasses, O.   20
Chorus.

                    5
Auld Nature swears the lovely dears
    Her noblest work she classes, O;
Her prentice han'° she tried on man,   apprentice hand
    An' then she made the lasses, O.
Chorus.

QUESTIONS

1. Who is the speaker? What is he like? What is his highest value? How seriously do you take his pronouncements?

2. How does the speaker justify his feelings? How does he compare his interests with those of other people?

3. What is the speaker's explanation of the origins of men and women? How might this explanation have been received in 1787, the year of publication, when most people accepted the creation story as told in Genesis?

e. e. cummings   (1894–1962)

next to of course god america i ————————————————— *1926*

"next to of course god america i
love you land of the pilgrims' and so forth oh
say can you see by the dawn's early my
country 'tis of centuries come and go
and are no more what of it we should worry   5
in every language even deafanddumb
thy sons acclaim your glorious name by gorry
by jingo by gee by gosh by gum
why talk of beauty what could be more beaut-
iful than these heroic happy dead   10
who rushed like lions to the roaring slaughter
they did not stop to think they died instead
then shall the voice of liberty be mute?"

He spoke. And drank rapidly a glass of water.

QUESTIONS

1. What is the form of the poem? What is the rhyme scheme? What does cum-
    mings achieve by not using capitalization and punctuation?
2. Who is the speaker? What characteristics and capacities does he show? How do
    you respond to him?
3. What ideas does the poem bring out? In what ways does the speaker parody the
    speakers that one is likely to hear on the Fourth of July throughout the United
    States? What is cummings saying not only about the speakers but also about the
    crowds that listen to such speeches?

JOHN DONNE   (1572–1631)

Holy Sonnet 14: Batter My Heart, Three-Personed God ——————— *1633*

Batter my heart, three-personed God; for You
As yet but knock, breathe, shine, and seek to mend;
That I may rise and stand, o'erthrow me, and bend
Your force to break, blow, burn and make me new.
I, like an usurped° town, to another due,   *conquered*   5
Labor to admit You, but Oh, to no end;
Reason, Your viceroy in me, me should defend,
But is captived, and proves weak or untrue.
Yet dearly I love You, and would be loved fain,°   *gladly*
But am betrothed unto Your enemy.   10
Divorce me, untie or break that knot again;
Take me to You, imprison me, for I,
Except You enthrall me, never shall be free,
Nor ever chaste, except you ravish me.

QUESTIONS

1. What kind of God is suggested by the words "batter," "knock," "overthrow," and "break"? What does "three-personed God" mean?
2. With which person of God might the verbs "knock" and "break" be associated? The verbs "breathe" and "blow"? The verbs "shine" and "burn"?
3. What is the effect of the altered word order at the ends of lines 7 and 9?
4. Explain the words "enthrall" (line 13) and "ravish" (line 14) to resolve the apparent paradox or contradiction in the last two lines.

RICHARD EBERHART   (b. 1904)

The Fury of Aerial Bombardment _____ 1947

You would think the fury of aerial bombardment
Would rouse God to relent; the infinite spaces
Are still silent. He looks on shock-pried faces.
History, even, does not know what is meant.

You would feel that after so many centuries   5
God would give man to repent; yet he can kill
As Cain could, but with multitudinous will,
No farther advanced than in his ancient furies.

Was man made stupid to see his own stupidity?
Is God by definition indifferent, beyond us all?   10
Is the eternal truth man's fighting soul
Wherein the Beast ravens in its own avidity?

Of Van Wettering I speak, and Averill,
Names on a list, whose faces I do not recall
But they are gone to early death, who late in school   15
Distinguished the belt feed lever from the belt holding pawl.

QUESTIONS

1. Who or what is the speaker in this poem? What does the last stanza tell you about him? (Eberhart was a gunnery instructor during World War II.)
2. What type and level of diction predominates in lines 1–12? What observations about God are made in these lines? Compare the image of God presented here with the one found in Donne's "Batter My Heart, Three-Personed God" and Blake's "The Lamb." What similarities or differences do you find?
3. How does the level and type of diction change in the last stanza? What is the effect of these changes? How is jargon used here?
4. Compare this poem with Wilfred Owen's "Anthem for Doomed Youth" (p. 497). How are the ideas in the poems similar?

THOMAS GRAY   (1716–1771)

Sonnet on the Death of Richard West _____ *(1742) 1775*

In vain to me the smiling mornings shine,
   And redd'ning Phoebus° lifts his golden fire;
The birds in vain their amorous descant° join,   *love songs*
   Or cheerful fields resume their green attire:°
These ears, alas! for other notes repine;   5
   A different object do these eyes require.
My lonely anguish melts no heart but mine,
   And in my breast the imperfect joys expire.
Yet morning smiles the busy race to cheer,
   And new-born pleasure brings to happier men;   10
The fields to all their wonted tribute bear;°
   To warm their little loves the birds complain:°
I fruitless mourn to him that cannot hear,
   And weep the more because I weep in vain.

SONNET ON THE DEATH OF RICHARD WEST.   2 *Phoebus:* Apollo, the Sun God   4 *resume their green attire:* During the darkness of night, the "cheerful fields" have no color, but in the light of the morning sun they become green again.   11 *The fields: . . . bear:* The fields contribute their customary harvest to benefit all creation.   12 *complain:* sing love songs

QUESTIONS

  1. What is the poem's subject, the speaker or the dead friend? How effective is the poem as a lament or dirge?

  2. Describe the poem's level of diction. Why does the speaker use phrases like "smiling mornings" (line 1), "redd'ning Phoebus" (2), "golden fire" (2), "resume their green attire" (4), and "notes" (5)? How common are these phrases? What is their effect?

  3. Consider the syntax in lines 5, 6, 9, 10, 11, and 12. What is unusual about the word order in these lines? What is the effect of this word order?

  4. In the 1800 *Preface* to *Lyrical Ballads*, William Wordsworth printed this poem. He italicized lines 6–8 and 13 and 14, and wrote, "It will easily be perceived, that the only part of this Sonnet which is of any value is the lines printed in Italics; it is equally obvious, that . . . the language of these lines does in no respect differ from that of prose." What does Wordsworth's criticism mean? To what degree is it justified?

MAXINE KUMIN   (b. 1925)

Hello, Hello Henry _____ *1982*

My neighbor in the country, Henry Manley,
with a washpot warming on his woodstove,
with a heifer and two goats and yearly chickens,

has outlasted Stalin, Roosevelt and Churchill
but something's stirring in him in his dotage.   5

Last fall he dug a hole and moved his privy
and a year ago in April reamed his well out.
When the county sent a truck and poles and cable,
his daddy ran the linemen off with birdshot
and swore he'd die by oil lamp, and did.   10

Now you tell me that all yesterday in Boston
you set your city phone at mine, and had it ringing
inside a dead apartment for three hours
room after empty room, to keep yours busy.
I hear it in my head, that ranting summons.   15

That must have been about the time that Henry
walked up two miles, shy as a girl come calling,
to tell me he has a phone now, 264, ring two.
It rang one time last week—wrong number.
He'd be pleased if one day I would think to call him.   20

Hello, hello Henry? Is that you?

QUESTIONS

1. What is the poem's level of diction? What does this level contribute to your
    response to the poem?
2. What words in this poem are appropriate for a country location? What do the
    words show about Henry Manley, and about the conditions on his farm?
3. Who is the speaker? What does the selection of words indicate about the
    speaker's character and state of mind?
4. How does the listener enter into the poem's action in the third stanza? What is
    the meaning of the listener's action?

LINDA PASTAN   (b. 1932)

Ethics _____ *1980*

In ethics class so many years ago
our teacher asked this question every fall:
if there were a fire in a museum
which would you save, a Rembrandt painting
or an old woman who hadn't many   5
years left anyhow? Restless on hard chairs
caring little for pictures or old age
we'd opt one year for life, the next for art
and always half-heartedly. Sometimes
the woman borrowed my grandmother's face   10

leaving her usual kitchen to wander
some drafty, half-imagined museum.
One year, feeling clever, I replied
why not let the woman decide herself?
Linda, the teacher would report, eschews   15
the burdens of responsibility.
This fall in a real museum I stand
before a real Rembrandt, old woman,
or nearly so, myself. The colors
within this frame are darker than autumn,   20
darker even than winter—the browns of earth,
though earth's most radiant elements burn
through the canvas. I know now that woman
and painting and season are almost one
and all beyond saving by children.   25

QUESTIONS

1. What can we surmise about the speaker in this poem? How does this knowledge contribute to our understanding of theme?

2. What are the two settings, situations, and actions presented here? How are they related? How much time has passed between them? How does the contrast between them help create meaning?

3. How has the passage of time changed the speaker's attitudes? What does she now realize about "woman / and painting and season" (lines 23–24)? About children?

4. What is the subject of this poem? The theme? What point does it make about art, life, time, and values?

HENRY REED (1914–1986)

Naming of Parts _____ *1946*

To-day we have naming of parts. Yesterday,
We had daily cleaning. And to-morrow morning,
We shall have what to do after firing. But to-day,
To-day we have naming of parts. Japonica
Glistens like coral in all of the neighboring gardens,   5
    And to-day we have naming of parts.

This is the lower sling swivel. And this
Is the upper sling swivel, whose use you will see,
When you are given your slings. And this is the piling swivel,
Which in your case you have not got. The branches   10
Hold in the gardens their silent, eloquent gestures,
    Which in our case we have not got.

This is the safety-catch, which is always released
With an easy flick of the thumb. And please do not let me
See anyone using his finger. You can do it quite easy   15
If you have any strength in your thumb. The blossoms
Are fragile and motionless, never letting anyone see
   Any of them using their finger.

And this you can see is the bolt. The purpose of this
Is to open the breech, as you see. We can slide it   20
Rapidly backwards and forwards: we call this
Easing the spring. And rapidly backwards and forwards
The early bees are assaulting and fumbling the flowers:
   They call it easing the Spring.

They call it easing the Spring: it is perfectly easy   25
If you have any strength in your thumb: like the bolt,
And the breech, and the cocking-piece, and the point of balance,
Which in our case we have not got; and the almond-blossom
Silent in all of the gardens and the bees going backwards and forwards,
   For to-day we have naming of parts.   30

QUESTIONS

1. There may be two speakers in this poem, or one speaker repeating the words of another and adding his own thoughts. What two voices do you hear?
2. What is the setting? The situation? How do these affect the speaker?
3. How and why is jargon used in the poem? With what set of "parts" is the jargon initially associated? How does this change?
4. How are phrases like "easing the spring" (lines 22, 24, 25) and "point of balance" (27) used ambiguously? What is the effect of repetition?

EDWIN ARLINGTON ROBINSON   (1869–1935)

Richard Cory —————————————————————————— *1897*

Whenever Richard Cory went down town,
We people on the pavement looked at him:
He was a gentleman from sole to crown,
Clean favored, and imperially slim.

And he was always quietly arrayed,   5
And he was always human when he talked;
But still he fluttered pulses when he said,
'Good-morning,' and he glittered when he walked.

And he was rich—yes, richer than a king—
And admirably schooled in every grace: 10
In fine, we thought that he was everything
To make us wish that we were in his place.

So on we worked, and waited for the light,
And went without the meat, and cursed the bread;
And Richard Cory, one calm summer night,   15
Went home and put a bullet through his head.

QUESTIONS

1. What is the effect of using "down town," "pavement," "meat," and "bread" in connection with the people who admire Richard Cory?
2. What are the connotations and implications of the name "Richard Cory"? Of the word "gentleman"?
3. Why does the poet use "sole to crown" instead of "head to toe" and "imperially slim" instead of "very thin" to describe Cory?
4. What effect does repetition produce in this poem? Consider especially the six lines that begin with "And."
5. What positive characteristic does Richard Cory possess (at least from the perspective of the speaker) besides wealth?

THEODORE ROETHKE   (1907–1963)

Dolor _____ *1943*

I have known the inexorable sadness of pencils,
Neat in their boxes, dolor of pad and paper-weight,
All the misery of manila folders and mucilage,
Desolation in immaculate public places,
Lonely reception room, lavatory, switchboard,   5
The unalterable pathos of basin and pitcher,
Ritual of multigraph, paper-clip, comma,
Endless duplication of lives and objects.
And I have seen dust from the walls of institutions,
Finer than flour, alive, more dangerous than silica,   10
Sift, almost invisible, through long afternoons of tedium,
Dropping a fine film on nails and delicate eyebrows,
Glazing the pale hair, the duplicate grey standard faces.

QUESTIONS

1. What does "dolor" mean? What words objectify the concept?
2. Why does "Dolor" not contain the fourteen lines usual in a sonnet?
3. What institutions, conditions, and places does the speaker associate with "dolor"? What do these have in common?
4. Describe the relationships of sentence structures and lines in "Dolor."

STEPHEN SPENDER   (1909–1995)

I Think Continually of Those Who Were Truly Great _____ *1934*

I think continually of those who were truly great.
Who, from the womb, remembered the soul's history
Through corridors of light where the hours are suns,
Endless and singing. Whose lovely ambition
Was that their lips, still touched with fire,   5
Should tell of the spirit clothed from head to foot in song.
And who hoarded from the spring branches
The desires falling across their bodies like blossoms.

What is precious is never to forget
The delight of the blood drawn from ageless springs   10
Breaking through rocks in worlds before our earth;
Never to deny its pleasure in the simple morning light,
Nor its grave evening demand for love;
Never to allow gradually the traffic to smother
With noise and fog the flowering of the spirit.   15

QUESTIONS

1. How does this poem cause you to reconsider what is usually understood by the word "great"? What are the principal characteristics of people "who were truly great"?

2. Why does Spender use the words "were great" rather than "are great"? What difference, if any, does this distinction make to Spender's definition of greatness?

3. What is the meaning of phrases like "delight of the blood," "in worlds before our earth," "hours are suns," "still touched with fire"? What other phrases need similar thought and explanation?

4. How practical is the advice of the poem in the light of its definitions of "great" and "precious"? Why should the practicality or impracticality of these definitions probably not be considered in your judgment of the poem?

WALLACE STEVENS   (1879–1955)

Disillusionment of Ten O'Clock _____ *1923*

The houses are haunted
By white night-gowns.
None are green,
Or purple with green rings,
Or green with yellow rings,   5
Or yellow with blue rings.
None of them are strange,
With socks of lace

And beaded ceintures.°   *belts*
People are not going   10
To dream of baboons and periwinkles.
Only, here and there, an old sailor,
Drunk and asleep in his boots,
Catches tigers
In red weather.   15

QUESTIONS

1. Is the "Ten O'Clock" here morning or night? How can you tell?

2. What do "haunted" and "white night-gowns" suggest about the people who live in the houses? What do the negative images in lines 3–9 suggest?

3. To whom are these people contrasted in lines 12–15?

4. What are the connotations of "socks with lace" and "beaded ceintures"? With which character in the poem would you associate these things?

5. What is the effect of using words and images like "baboons," "periwinkles," "tigers," and "red weather" in lines 11–15? Who will dream of these things?

6. Explain the term "disillusionment" and explore its relation to the point that this poem makes about dreams, images, and imagination.

MARK STRAND   (b. 1934)

Eating Poetry ———————————————————————— *1968*

Ink runs from the corners of my mouth.
There is no happiness like mine.
I have been eating poetry.

The librarian does not believe what she sees.
Her eyes are sad   5
and she walks with her hands in her dress.

The poems are gone.
The light is dim.
The dogs are on the basement stairs and coming up.

Their eyeballs roll,   10
their blond legs burn like brush.
The poor librarian begins to stamp her feet and weep.

She does not understand.
When I get on my knees and lick her hand,
She screams.   15

I am a new man.
I snarl at her and bark.
I romp with joy in the bookish dark.

QUESTIONS

1. In the first three lines, which words tell you that the poem is not to be taken literally?
2. What is the serious topic of the poem? What words indicate that the poem has a serious intent?
3. What is the comic topic? Which words tell you that the poem's action is comic?

JAMES WRIGHT   (1927–1980)

A Blessing —————————————————————————— 1963

Just off the highway to Rochester, Minnesota,
Twilight bounds softly forth on the grass.
And the eyes of those two Indian ponies
Darken with kindness.
They have come gladly out of the willows   5
To welcome my friend and me.
We step over the barbed wire into the pasture
Where they have been grazing all day, alone.
They ripple tensely, they can hardly contain their happiness
That we have come.   10
They bow shyly as wet swans. They love each other.
There is no loneliness like theirs.
At home once more,
They begin munching the young tufts of spring in the darkness.
I would like to hold the slenderer one in my arms.   15
For she has walked over to me
And nuzzled my left hand.
She is black and white,
Her mane falls wild on her forehead,
And the light breeze moves me to caress her long ear   20
That is delicate as the skin over a girl's wrist.
Suddenly I realize
That if I stepped out of my body I would break
Into blossom.

QUESTIONS

1. What has happened just before the poem opens? Account for the poet's use of the present tense in his descriptions.
2. Is the setting specific or general? What happens as the poem progresses?
3. What realization overtakes the speaker? How does this realization constitute a "blessing," and what does it show about his character?
4. To what degree is it necessary for the poet to include all the detail of the first twenty-one lines before the realization of the last three?

WRITING ABOUT DICTION
AND SYNTAX IN POETRY

Study your poem carefully, line by line, to gain a general sense of its meaning. Try to establish how diction and syntax may be connected to elements such as tone, character, and idea. As you develop your ideas, look for effective and consistent patterns of word choice, connotation, repetition, and syntactic patterns that help create and reinforce the conclusions you have already reached about the poem. Ask questions like those below.

Questions for Discovering Ideas

* Who is the speaker? What is the speaker's profession or way of life? How does the speaker's background affect his or her powers of observation? How does the background affect his or her level of speech?
* Who is the listener? How does the listener affect what the speaker says?
* What other characters are in the poem? How are their actions described? How accurate and fair do you think these descriptions are?
* Is the level of diction in the poem elevated, neutral, or informal, and how does this level affect your perception of the speaker, subject, and main idea or ideas?
* What patterns of diction or syntax do you discover in the poem? (Example: Consider words related to situation, action, setting, or particular characters.) How ordinary or unusual are these words? Which, if any, are unusual enough to warrant further examination?
* Does the poem contain many "loaded" or connotative words in connection with any single element, such as setting, speaker, or theme?
* Does the poem contain a large number of general and abstract or specific and concrete words? What is the effect of these choices?
* Does the poem contain dialect? Colloquialisms? Jargon? If so, how does this special diction shape your response to the poem?
* What is the nature of the poem's syntax? Is there any unusual word order? What seems to be the purpose or effect of syntactic variations?
* Has the poet used any striking patterns of sentence structure such as parallelism or repetition? If so, what is the effect?

Strategies for Organizing Ideas

When you narrow your examination to one or two specific areas of diction or syntax, you should list important words, phrases, and sentences, and investigate the full range of meaning and effect that the examples produce. Begin grouping examples that work in similar ways or produce similar effects. Eventually you may be able to develop the related examples as potential units or sections for your essay.

Your central idea should emerge from your investigation of the specific diction or syntax that you find most fruitful and interesting. Let the poem be your guide. Since diction and syntax contribute to the poem's impact and meaning, try to connect your thesis and examples to your other conclusions. If you are writing about Stevens's "Disillusionment of Ten O'Clock," for example, your central idea might assert that Stevens uses words describing colors (i.e., "white," "green," "purple," "yellow," "blue," "red") to contrast life's visual reality with the psychological "disillusionment" of the "houses," "People," and "old sailor." Such a formulation makes a clear connection between diction and meaning.

There are many different ways to organize your material. If you choose to deal with only one aspect of diction, such as connotative words, you might treat these in the order in which they appear in the poem. When you deal with two or three different aspects of diction and syntax, however, you might devote a series of paragraphs to related examples of multiple denotation, then connotation, and finally jargon (assuming the presence of jargon in the poem). In such an instance, your organization would be controlled by the types of material under consideration rather than by the order in which the words occur.

Alternatively, you might deal with the impact of diction or syntax on a series of other elements, such as character, setting, or situation. Such an essay would focus on a single type of lexical or syntactic device as it relates to these different elements in sequence. Thus, you might discuss the link between connotation and character, then setting, and finally situation. Whatever organization you select, keep in mind that each poem will suggest its own avenues of exploration and strategies of organization.

In your conclusion summarize your ideas about the impact of the poem's diction or syntax. You might also consider the larger implications of your ideas in connection with the thoughts and emotions evoked by your reading.

SAMPLE STUDENT ESSAY

Extraordinary Definitions in Sir Stephen Spender's "I Think Continually of Those Who Were Truly Great"°

[1]   In the two-stanza poem "I Think Continually of Those Who Were Truly Great," Sir Stephen Spender considers the meaning of true greatness. He begins the poem as though the speaker has been talking to an unnamed person who has spoken about greatness as the word is usually understood. The poem itself might then be considered a one-sided response by the speaker in which he presents his own definition of greatness, with particular emphasis on the *truly* in "truly great." The poem creates a different and new concept of greatness.* Spender develops his argument in two parts, each of which is knitted together by particular attitudes and grammatical structures.†

° See p. 486 for this poem.
* Central idea.
† Thesis sentence.

Because the poem concentrates on new definitions, it is important to discuss what Spender does with the understanding that readers might have about greatness. Usually the type of person most readers think of as great is a leader of some sort--a king, a president, an emperor, a general, or a financial mogul. It is presumably this understanding that Spender is contradicting in the poem. Readers find that he says nothing about leadership, nor are there any references at all to specific great persons. Instead, Spender goes beyond usual definitions and asks readers to consider the meaning of greatness in a deeply individual and personal way. His first line is designed to catch the interest of readers, just as the rest of the poem is designed to surprise and lead them. Something unusual is being said, something new, something extraordinary.

[2]

The first stanza presents a set of positive qualities that define true greatness. Spender carries out his definitions within three relative clauses that modify and therefore define the word "great" ("who . . . remembered," "whose . . . ambition . . . was," and "who hoarded"). Interestingly, the speaker's reference to "history" (line 2) immediately puts readers on guard because it does not refer to history as a record of human accomplishments. Rather the history of greatness is the "soul's history," which has no written record but which is composed of "corridors of light . . . endless and singing." The unusual idea here is that song, not business, gives form to the world by persons who become great by connecting themselves with the very origins of life. Going on, Spender provides a new definition of "tell" (line 6). Usually people telling about greatness describe politics, economics, or world domination, but in this poem the telling is about the "spirit." Spender introduces readers to the concept of hoarding, but, as with telling, readers discover that the truly great do not hoard wealth, but rather accept and hoard "desires" (lines 7, 8).

[3]

The key words in Spender's first stanza, in short, go beyond their commonly used economic and political meanings and refer instead to basic human feelings and human spirituality. Readers thus consider the poem's references as being not to documented history, but rather to a deeper remembrance of a preexisting condition of glory. Spender's redefined meaning of greatness means that those who are great can tune themselves into the basic song of the human spirit. The words redefining "great" therefore enable readers to expand their understanding of greatness into new and unexamined areas of thought.

[4]

The second stanza is unified by three negatives, which are cast within infinitive phrases ("never to forget," "never to deny," and "never to allow") which define the word "precious" in line 9. As in the first stanza, Spender uses a common definition as a starting point: What is precious--a necessary part of greatness--is not a large bank account but rather the connection with ageless springs of human delight. Of highest value is the quality of joy that has been in our human blood long before our world was created, existing in unknown worlds going back to the moment of divine creation. Preciousness also consists of accepting the pleasure of "morning light" (line 12) and the more sober ("grave") needs of "evening . . . love" (line 13). Spender's third definition of what is precious (lines 14, 15) is the insistence that people should allow their spirits to flower despite the smothering grind of daily business ("the traffic"). In all these thoughts about what is precious, readers are faced with new definitions and new ways of seeing.

[5]

It is clear that the poem presents readers with the possibility of greatness in accord with Spender's unique definitions. Such greatness asks readers to

[6]

forge a new being for themselves. From the poem, readers can conclude that this new being is a free spirit who achieves greatness through song, who finds joy in the morning light of endless and rhythmical sunshine, and who willingly accepts pleasure in desires and love. Greatness, in short, is the ability to reconnect oneself with the very springs of existence.

[7]   "I Think Continually of Those Who Were Truly Great," then, is a defining and also a guiding poem. It presents readers with a set of ordinary words defined in a completely new way. Readers find no advice to abandon the needs of ordinary living, but rather are told of a need to re-analyze and freshen their assumptions of what life is about. The poem suggests to readers that everyone can become great by resisting the grind of daily living ("the traffic") and reconnecting with the ages-old sources of human strength. Even if people are never in positions of political or military leadership--the usual avenue of greatness--they can reestablish such connections. Thus Spender's poem reaffirms life by offering new ways for readers to think about becoming "truly great."

Commentary on the Essay

This essay considers how Spender redefines the two major words within the poem, "great" and "precious," and also how he redefines other words (e.g., "history," "tell"). In addition, it deals with how Spender's syntax unifies the poem's two major parts (through adjective or relative clauses and through infinitive phrases). Finally, it attempts to treat the subject matter of the poem in the light of reader responses (see Chapter 27). Note that throughout the essay there are references to readers, their expectations, and their responses. A major element of the essay is that Spender leads readers to new understanding along the pathway of usual or commonly accepted understanding.

The opening paragraph makes assertions about the poem's dramatic situation and also about Spender's goal of redefining the key word "great." The body of the essay, in five paragraphs, deals with definition and redefinition. Because the poem is concerned with redefinition, paragraph 2 describes how the word "great" is usually understood. On this basis, paragraphs 3 and 4 move ahead to consider how the poem redefines this word.

The next two paragraphs (5 and 6) focus on the meaning of "precious" which Spender uses as an equivalent to greatness. The examples are examined here in the order in which they appear in the poem. Thus, paragraph 5 shows how Spender establishes three areas of life that are particularly precious, unlike the large bank account that is usually considered precious. Paragraph 6 extends this idea by considering the implications of a reevaluated existence in the light of Spender's redefinition.

The conclusion in paragraph 7 reasserts that Spender's definitions are designed to show readers the ways to personal, not public, greatness, and that therefore everyone and not just a few may become great. In this way, the words examined in the essay are linked to the poem's reaffirmation of life.

SPECIAL WRITING TOPICS FOR STUDYING THE WORDS OF POETRY

1. Using the poems of Reed and Eberhart in this chapter, together with poems by Jarrell (p. 459) and Owen (p. 546), study the words that these poets use to indicate the weapons and actions of warfare. In an essay, consider these questions: What shared details make the poems similar? What separate details make them different? How do the poets use word choices to make their points about war as action, tragedy, and horror?

2. Compare Wright's "A Blessing," Blake's "The Lamb," and Donne's "Batter My Heart" as devotional poems. Among the topics you might consider are these: How does the language in each poem contribute to the poem's devotional spirit? In what ways is word selection appropriate to the subject and thought of the poems? How does the language set each poem apart from the others?

3. Write an essay on the choices of words in "Eating Poetry" by Mark Strand, "Hello, Hello Henry" by Maxine Kumin, or "Green Grow the Rashes, O" by Robert Burns (just one). What ideas do the poets convey? What especially noticeable words do the poets use to get these ideas across? What level of diction do the poems exhibit?

4. Write a short poem describing a violent crime and commenting on it. Then, assume that you are the "perpetrator" of the crime, and write another poem on the same topic. Even though you describe the same situation, how do your words differ, and why have you made these different choices? Explain the other different word choices you have made. You might also discuss words that you first used but later rejected.

5. Find a book or books in your library about the works of Robinson, Blake, Stevens, or another poet in this chapter. How fully do these sources discuss the style of any of these poets? Write a brief report explaining how the writers of the book or books deal with poetic diction.

13

Imagery:
The Poem's Link
to the Senses

In literature, **imagery** refers to words that trigger your imagination to recall and recombine **images**—memories or mental pictures of sights, sounds, tastes, smells, sensations of touch, and motions. The process is active and even vigorous, for when words or descriptions produce images, you are using your personal experiences with life and language to help you understand the poems you are reading. In effect, you are re-creating the work *in your own way* through the controlled stimulation produced by the poet's words. Imagery is therefore one of the strongest modes of literary expression because it provides a channel to your active imagination, and along this channel, poets, like all writers, bring their works directly to you and into your consciousness.

For example, reading the word *lake* may bring to your mind your literal memory of a particular lake. Your mental picture—or image—may be a distant view of calm waters reflecting blue sky, a nearby view of gentle waves rippling in the wind, a close-up view of the sandy lake bottom from a boat, or an overhead view of a sun-drenched shoreline. Similarly, the words *rose, apple, hot dog, malted milk,* and *pizza* all cause you to recollect these objects, and, in addition, may cause you to recall their smells and tastes. Active and graphic words like *row, swim,* and *dive* stimulate you to picture moving images of someone performing these actions.

RESPONSES AND THE WRITER'S USE OF DETAIL

In studying imagery we try to comprehend and explain our imaginative reconstruction of the pictures and impressions evoked by the work's images. We let the poet's words simmer and percolate in our minds. To get our imaginations stirring, we might follow Coleridge in this description from "Kubla Khan":

A damsel with a dulcimer
In a vision once I saw:
It was an Abyssinian maid,
And on her dulcimer she played
Singing of Mount Abora.   (lines 37–41)

We do not read about the color of the young woman's clothing or anything else about her appearance except that she is playing a stringed instrument, a dulcimer, and that she is singing a song about a mountain in a foreign, remote land. But Coleridge's image is enough. From it we can imagine a vivid, exotic picture of a young woman from a distant land singing, together with the loveliness of her song (even though we never hear it or understand it). The image lives.

IMAGERY, IDEAS, AND ATTITUDES

Images do more than elicit impressions. By the *authenticating* effects of the vision and perceptions underlying them, they give you new ways of seeing the world and strengthen your old ways of seeing it. Langston Hughes, in "Theme for English B," for example (p. 556), develops the idea that human beings are equal. Rather than stating the idea directly, he uses a number of images of everyday, ordinary activities that his speaker shares in common with most human beings:

Well, I like to eat, sleep, drink, and be in love.   (line 21)

These literal action images form an equalizing link that is not only true, but unarguable. Such uses of imagery are one of the strongest means by which literature reinforces ideas.

In addition, as you form mental pictures from a poet's images, you also respond with appropriate attitudes and feelings. Thus the phrase "Beside the lake, beneath the trees," from Wordsworth's poem "Daffodils" (Chapter 16) prompts both the visualization of a wooded lakeshore and also the related pleasantness of outdoor relaxation and happiness (p. 603). Imagery used in a negative is seen in Page's "Photos of a Salt Mine," which offers grim images of a mine in such a way that it seems to be hell itself:

But hoses douse the brilliance of these jewels,
melt fire to brine.
Salt's bitter water trickles thin and forms,
slow fathoms down,
a lake within a cave,
lacquered with jet—
white's opposite. (lines 30–36)

By using such imagery, artists and poets not only create sensory vividness, but also influence and control the attitudes of their readers.

CLASSIFICATION OF IMAGERY

SIGHT.   Sight is the most significant of our senses, for it is the key to our remembrance of other impressions. Therefore, the most frequently occurring literary imagery is to things we can visualize either exactly or approximately—**visual images.** In "Cargoes" (the subject of the sample student essay on p. 512), Masefield asks us to re-create mental pictures or images of oceangoing merchant vessels from three periods of human history.

JOHN MASEFIELD   (1878–1967)

Cargoes ———————————————————————————— *1902*

Quinquereme° of Nineveh° from distant Ophir,°
Rowing home to haven in sunny Palestine,
With a cargo of ivory,
And apes and peacocks,°
Sandalwood, cedarwood,° and sweet white wine.   5

Stately Spanish galleon coming from the Isthmus,°
Dipping through the Tropics by the palm-green shores,
With a cargo of diamonds,
Emeralds, amethysts,
Topazes, and cinnamon, and gold moidores.°   10

Dirty British coaster with a salt-caked smoke-stack,
Butting through the Channel in the mad March days,
With a cargo of Tyne coal,°
Road-rails, pig-lead,
Firewood, iron-ware, and cheap tin trays.   15

CARGOES.   1 *quinquereme:* the largest of the ancient ships. It was powered by three tiers of oars and was named "quinquereme" because five men operated each vertical oar station. The top two oars were each taken by two men, while one man alone took the bottom oar.   1 *Nineveh:* capital of ancient Assyria, an "exceeding great city" (Jonah 3:3).   *Ophir:* Ophir probably was in Africa and was known for its gold (1 Kings 10:22; 1 Chron. 29:4). Masefield echoes some of the biblical verses in his first stanza.   4 *apes and peacocks:* see 1 Kings 10:22 and 2 Chron. 9:21.   5 *cedarwood:* see 1 Kings 9:11.   6 *Isthmus:* the Isthmus of Panama. 10 *moidores:* coins used in Portugal and Brazil at the time the New World was being explored.   13 *Tyne coal:* coal from Newcastle upon Tyne, in northern England, renowned for its coal production.

QUESTIONS

1. Consider the images of life during three periods of history: Ancient Israel at the time of Solomon (ca. 950 B.C.E.), sixteenth-century Spain, and modern England. What do these images tell you about Masefield's interpretation of modern commercial life?

2. To what senses do most of the images refer (e.g., sight, taste, etc.)?

3. The poem contains no complete sentences. Why do you think that Masefield included only verbals ("rowing," "dipping," "butting") to begin the second line of each stanza, rather than finite verbs?

4. In historical reality, the quinquereme was likely rowed by slaves, and the Spanish galleon likely carried riches stolen from Central American natives. How might these unpleasant details affect the impressions otherwise achieved in the first two stanzas?

Masefield's images in "Cargoes" are vivid as they stand and need no further amplification. In order to reconstruct them imaginatively, we do not need ever to have seen the ancient biblical lands or waters, or ever to have seen or handled the cheap commodities on a modern merchant ship. We have seen enough in our lives both in reality and in pictures to *imagine* places and objects like these, and hence Masefield is successful in fixing his visual images into our minds.

SOUND. **Auditory images** trigger our experiences with sound. For such images, let us consider Wilfred Owen's "Anthem for Doomed Youth."

WILFRED OWEN   (1893–1918)

Anthem for Doomed Youth _____ *1920*

What passing-bells° for these who die as cattle?
Only the monstrous anger of the guns.
Only the stuttering rifles' rapid rattle
Can patter out their hasty orisons.°   *prayers*
No mockeries for them from prayers or bells,   5
Nor any voice of mourning save the choirs—
The shrill, demented choirs of wailing shells;
And bugles calling for them from sad shires.°

What candles may be held to speed them all?
Not in the hands of boys, but in their eyes   10
Shall shine the holy glimmers of good-byes.
The pallor of girls' brows shall be their pall;
Their flowers the tenderness of patient minds,
And each slow dusk a drawing-down of blinds.

ANTHEM FOR DOOMED YOUTH.   1 *passing-bells:* church bells that are tolled at the entry of a funeral cortege into a church cemetery.   8 *shires:* British counties.

QUESTIONS

1. What type of imagery predominates in the first eight lines? How does the imagery change in the last six lines?
2. Contrast the images of death at home and death on the battlefield. How does this contrast affect your experience and understanding of the poem?
3. Consider these images: "holy glimmers of good-byes," "pallor of girls' brows," "patient minds," "drawing-down of blinds." What relationship do the people imagined in these images have to the doomed youth?

In asking what "passing-bells" may be tolled for "these who die as cattle," Owen's speaker is referring to the traditional tolling of a parish church bell to announce the burial of a parishioner. Such a ceremony suggests a period of peace and order, when there is time to pay respect to the dead. But the poem then points out that the only sound for those who have fallen in battle is the "rapid rattle" of "stuttering" rifles—in other words, not the solemn, dignified sounds of peace, but the horrifying noises of war. Owen's auditory images evoke corresponding sounds in our imaginations and help us experience the poem and hate the uncivilized depravity of war.

SMELL, TASTE, AND TOUCH.   In addition to sight and sound, you will also find images from the other senses. An **olfactory image** refers to smell, a **gustatory image** to taste, and a **tactile image** to touch. A great deal of love poetry, for example, includes olfactory images about the fragrances of flowers. As a twist on this common olfactory imagery, Shakespeare's speaker in Sonnet 130, "My Mistress' Eyes," candidly admits that the breath of his woman friend is not the same as the scent of perfume (lines 7–8).

Images derived from and referring to taste—gustatory images—are also common, though less frequent than those referring to sight and sound. In lines 5 and 10 of Masefield's "Cargoes," for example, there are references to "sweet white wine" and "cinnamon." Although the poem refers to these commodities as cargoes, the words themselves also register in our minds as gustatory images because they evoke our sense of taste.

Tactile images of touch and texture are not as common because touch is difficult to render except in terms of effects. The speaker of Lowell's "Patterns," for example (Chapter 21), uses tactile imagery when imagining a never-to-happen embrace with her fiancé, who we learn has been killed on a wartime battlefield. Her imagery records the effect of the embrace ("bruised"), while her internalized feelings are expressed in metaphors ("aching, melting"):

And the buttons of his waistcoat bruised my body as he clasped me,
Aching, melting, unafraid. (lines 51–52)

Tactile images are not uncommon in love poetry, where references to touch and feeling are natural. Usually, however, love poetry deals with yearning and hope rather than sexual fulfillment (as in Keats's "Bright Star," Chapter 14).

MOTION AND ACTIVITY.   References to movement are also images. Images of general motion are **kinetic** (remember that *motion pictures* are also called "cinema"), while the term **kinesthetic** is applied to human or animal movement. Imagery of motion is closely related to visual images, for motion is most often seen. Masefield's "British coaster," for example, is a visual image, but when it goes "Butting through the Channel," the motion makes it also kinetic. When the speaker of Levertov's "A Time Past" stands to tell the listener of her love (p. 506), the image is kinesthetic, as is the action of Amy Lowell's speaker walking in the garden after hearing about her fiancé's death (Chapter 21). Both types are seen at the conclusion of the following poem, Elizabeth Bishop's "The Fish."

ELIZABETH BISHOP   (1911–1979)

The Fish ———————————————————————— *1946*

I caught a tremendous fish
and held him beside the boat
half out of water, with my hook
fast in a corner of his mouth.
He didn't fight.   5
He hadn't fought at all.
He hung a grunting weight,
battered and venerable
and homely. Here and there
his brown skin hung in strips   10
like ancient wallpaper,
and its pattern of darker brown
was like wallpaper:
shapes like full-blown roses
stained and lost through age.   15
He was speckled with barnacles,
fine rosettes of lime,
and infested
with tiny white sea-lice,
and underneath two or three   20
rags of green weed hung down.
While his gills were breathing in
the terrible oxygen
—the frightening gills,
fresh and crisp with blood,   25
that can cut so badly—
I thought of the coarse white flesh
packed in like feathers,
the big bones and the little bones,
the dramatic reds and blacks   30
of his shiny entrails,
and the pink swim-bladder
like a big peony.
I looked into his eyes
which were far larger than mine   35
but shallower, and yellowed,
the irises backed and packed
with tarnished tinfoil
seen through the lenses
of old scratched isinglass.°   40
They shifted a little, but not
to return my stare.
—It was more like the tipping

THE FISH.   40 *isinglass:* mica.   45

of an object toward the light.
I admired his sullen face,
the mechanism of his jaw,
and then I saw
that from his lower lip   50
—if you could call it a lip—
grim, wet, and weaponlike,
hung five old pieces of fish-line,
or four and a wire leader
with the swivel still attached,   55
with all their five big hooks
grown firmly in his mouth.
A green line, frayed at the end
where he broke it, two heavier lines,
and a fine black thread   60
still crimped from the strain and snap
when it broke and he got away.
Like medals with their ribbons
frayed and wavering,
a five-haired beard of wisdom   65
trailing from his aching jaw.
I stared and stared
and victory filled up
the little rented boat,
from the pool of bilge   70
where oil had spread a rainbow
around the rusted engine
to the bailer rusted orange,
the sun-cracked thwarts,
the oarlocks on their strings,
the gunnels—until everything
was rainbow, rainbow, rainbow!
And I let the fish go.

QUESTIONS

1. Describe the poem's images of action. What is unusual about them?
2. What impression does the fish make upon the speaker? Is the fish beautiful? Ugly? Why is the fish described in such detail?
3. What do the "five old pieces of fish-line" indicate?
4. How is the rainbow formed around the boat's engine? What does the rainbow mean to the speaker?
5. What right does the speaker have to keep the fish? Why does she choose to relinquish this right?

The kinetic images at the end of "The Fish" are those of victory filling the boat (difficult to visualize) and the oil spreading to make a rainbow (easier to visualize). The kinesthetic images are readily imagined—the speaker's staring, observing, and letting the fish go—and they are vivid and real. The final gesture is the necessary outcome of the observed contrast between the deteriorating artifacts of human beings and the natural world of the fish, and it is a vivid expression of the right of the natural world to exist without human intervention. In short, Bishop's kinetic and kinesthetic images are designed to objectivize the need for freedom not only for human beings but for all the earth and animated Nature.

The areas from which kinetic and kinesthetic imagery can be derived are almost too varied and unpredictable to describe. Occupations, trades, professions, businesses, recreational activities—all these might furnish images. One poet introduces references from gardening, another from money and banking, another from modern real estate developments, another from life in the jungle. The freshness, newness, and surprise of much poetry result from the many and varied areas from which poets draw their images.

 ## POEMS FOR STUDY

WILLIAM BLAKE   (1757–1827)

The Tyger° _____ *1794*

Tyger! Tyger! burning bright
In the forests of the night,
What immortal hand or eye
Could frame thy fearful symmetry?

In what distant deeps or skies   5
Burnt the fire of thine eyes?
On what wings dare he aspire?
What the hand, dare seize the fire?

THE TYGER.   The title refers not only to a tiger but to any large, wild, ferocious cat.

And what shoulder, & what art,
Could twist the sinews of thy heart?   10
And when thy heart began to beat,
What dread hand? & what dread feet?

What the hammer? what the chain?
In what furnace was thy brain?
What the anvil? what dread grasp   15
Dare its deadly terrors clasp?

When the stars threw down their spears,
And water'd heaven with their tears,
Did he smile his work to see?
Did he who made the Lamb make thee?   20

Tyger! Tyger! burning bright
In the forests of the night,
What immortal hand or eye
Dare frame thy fearful symmetry?

QUESTIONS

1. What do the associations of the image of "burning" suggest? Why is the burning
    done at night rather than day? What does night suggest?
2. Describe the kinesthetic images of lines 5–20. What ideas is Blake's speaker rep-
    resenting by these images? What attributes does the speaker suggest may belong
    to the blacksmith-type initiator of these actions?
3. Line 20 presents the kinesthetic image of a creator. What is implied about the
    mixture of good and evil in the world? What answer does the poem offer? Why
    does Blake phrase this line as a question rather than an assertion?
4. The sixth stanza repeats the first stanza with only one change of imagery of
    action. Contrast these stanzas, stressing the difference between "could" (line 4)
    and "dare" (24).

ELIZABETH BARRETT BROWNING   (1806–1861)

Sonnets from the Portuguese: Number 14 _____ *1850*

If thou must love me, let it be for nought
Except for love's sake only. Do not say
"I love her for her smile—her look—her way
Of speaking gently,—for a trick of thought
That falls in well with mine, and certes° brought   *certainly*   5
A sense of pleasant ease on such a day"—
For these things in themselves, Belovèd, may
Be changed, or change for thee,—and love, so wrought,°   *created*
May be unwrought so. Neither love me for
Thine own dear pity's wiping my cheeks dry,—   10

A creature might forget to weep, who bore
Thy comfort long, and lose thy love thereby!
But love me for love's sake, that evermore
Thou mayst love on, through love's eternity.

QUESTIONS

1. Who is the speaker of this poem? Why might you conclude that the speaker is female?
2. What images does the speaker use to indicate possible causes for loving? What kinds of images are they? How does the speaker explain why they should be rejected?
3. How does the idea of lines 1, 13, and 14 build upon the ideas in the rest of the poem?

SAMUEL TAYLOR COLERIDGE   (1772–1834)

Kubla Khan _____ *1816*

In Xanadu did Kubla Khan
A stately pleasure dome decree:
Where Alph,° the sacred river, ran
Through caverns measureless to man
   Down to a sunless sea.   5
So twice five miles of fertile ground
With walls and towers were girdled round:
And there were gardens bright with sinuous rills,
Where blossomed many an incense-bearing tree;
And here were forest ancient as the hills,   10
Enfolding sunny spots of greenery.

But oh! that deep romantic chasm which slanted
Down the green hill athwart a cedarn cover!
A savage place! as holy and enchanted
As e'er beneath a waning moon was haunted   15
By woman wailing for her demon lover!
And from this chasm, with ceaseless turmoil seething,
As if this earth in fast thick pants were breathing,
A mighty fountain momently was forced:
Amid whose swift half-intermitted burst   20
Huge fragments vaulted like rebounding hail,
Or chaffy grain beneath the thresher's flail:
And 'mid these dancing rocks at once and ever
It flung up momently the sacred river.

KUBLA KHAN.   3 *Alph:* possibly a reference to the river Alpheus in Greece, as described by the ancient writers Virgil and Pausanias.

Five miles meandering with a mazy motion   25
Through wood and dale the sacred river ran,
Then reached the caverns measureless to man,
And sank in tumult to a lifeless ocean:
And 'mid this tumult Kubla heard from far
Ancestral voices prophesying war!   30
    The shadow of the dome of pleasure
    Floated midway on the waves;
    Where was heard the mingled measure
    From the fountain and the caves.
It was a miracle of rare device,   35
A sunny pleasure dome with caves of ice!

    A damsel with a dulcimer
    In a vision once I saw:
    It was an Abyssinian maid,
    And on her dulcimer she played   40
    Singing of Mount Abora.°
Could I revive within me
Her symphony and song,
To such a deep delight 'twould win me,
That with music loud and long,   45
I would build that dome in air,
That sunny dome! those caves of ice!
And all who heard should see them there,
And all should cry, Beware! Beware!
His flashing eyes, his floating hair!   50
Weave a circle round him thrice,
And close your eyes with holy dread,
For he on honeydew hath fed,
And drunk the milk of Paradise.

41 *Mount Abora:* a mountain of Coleridge's imagination. But see John Milton's *Paradise Lost,* IV,
lines 268–284.

QUESTIONS

1. How many of the poem's images might be sketched or visualized? Which ones
    would be panoramic landscapes? Which might be close-ups?

2. What is the effect of auditory images such as "wailing," "fast thick pants,"
    "tumult," "ancestral voices prophesying war," and "mingled measure"?

3. When Coleridge was writing this poem, he was recalling it from a dream. At
    line 54 he was interrupted, and when he resumed he could write no more. How
    might an argument be made that the poem is finished?

4. How do lines 35–36 establish the pleasure dome as a place of mysterious oddity?
    What is the effect of the words "miracle" and "rare"? The effect of combining
    the images "sunny" and "caves of ice"?

5. Why does the speaker yearn for the power of the singing Abyssinian maid? What
    kinesthetic images end the poem? How are these images important in the
    speaker's desire to reconstruct the vision of the pleasure dome?

GEORGE HERBERT   (1593–1633)

The Pulley ———————————————————————— *1633*

When God at first made man,
Having a glass of blessings standing by,
   "Let us," said he, "pour on him all we can.
Let the world's riches, which dispersed lie,
     Contract into a span."°   5

So strength first made a way;
Then beauty flowed, then wisdom, honor, pleasure.
   When almost all was out, God made a stay,
Perceiving that, alone of all his treasure,
     Rest° in the bottom lay.   10

   "For if I should," said he,
"Bestow this jewel also on my creature,
   He would adore my gifts instead of me.
And rest in Nature, not the God of Nature;
     So both should losers be.   15

   "Yet let him keep the rest,
But keep them with repining restlessness.
   Let him be rich and weary, that at least,
If goodness lead him not, yet weariness
     May toss him to my breast."   20

THE PULLEY.   5 *into a span:* that is, within the control of human beings.   10 *rest:* (1) repose, security; (2) all that remains.

QUESTIONS

1. Describe the dramatic scene of the poem. Who is doing what?
2. What are the particular "blessings" that God confers on humanity, according to the speaker? Why should these be considered blessings?
3. Consider the image of the pulley as the means, or device (through "repining restlessness"), by which God compels people to become worshipful.
4. Analyze and discuss the meaning of the kinetic images signified by the words "pour," "flowed," "rest," and "toss."

GERARD MANLEY HOPKINS   (1844–1889)

Spring ———————————————————————— *1877*

Nothing is so beautiful as Spring—
   When weeds, in wheels, shoot long and lovely and lush;
   Thrush's eggs look little low heavens, and thrush
Through the echoing timber does so rinse and wring

The ear, it strikes like lightnings to hear him sing;   5
   The glassy peartree leaves and blooms, they brush
   The descending blue; that blue is all in a rush
With richness; the racing lambs too have fair their fling.

What is all this juice and all this joy?
   A strain of the earth's sweet being in the beginning   10
In Eden garden.—Have, get, before it cloy,
   Before it cloud, Christ, lord, and sour with sinning,
Innocent mind and Mayday in girl and boy,
   Most, O maid's child, thy choice and worthy the winning.

QUESTIONS

1. What images does the speaker mention as support for his first line, "Nothing is so beautiful as Spring"? Are these images those that you would normally expect? To what degree do they seem to be new or unusual?

2. What images of motion and activity do you find in the poem? Are these mainly static or dynamic? What do these suggest about the speaker's view of spring?

3. What is the relationship between "Eden garden" in line 11 and the scene described in lines 1–8? To what extent are spring and "Innocent mind and Mayday" a glimpse of the Garden of Eden?

4. Christ is mentioned in lines 12 and 14 (as "maid's child"). Do these references seal the poem off from readers who are not Christian? Why or why not?

DENISE LEVERTOV   (b. 1923)

A Time Past _____ *1975*

The old wooden steps to the front door
where I was sitting that fall morning
when you came downstairs, just awake,
and my joy at sight of you (emerging
into golden day—   5
                     the dew almost frost)
pulled me to my feet to tell you
how much I loved you:

those wooden steps
are gone now, decayed   10
replaced with granite,
hard, gray, and handsome.
The old steps live
only in me:
my feet and thighs   15
remember them, and my hands
still feel their splinters.

Everything else about and around that house
brings memories of others—of marriage,
of my son. And the steps do too: I recall   20
sitting there with my friend and her little son who died,
or was it the second one who lives and thrives?
And sitting there 'in my life,' often, alone or with my husband.
Yet that one instant,
your cheerful, unafraid, youthful, 'I love you too,'   25
the quiet broken by no bird, no cricket, gold leaves
spinning in silence down without
any breeze to blow them,
                    is what twines itself
in my head and body across those slabs of wood   30
that were warm, ancient, and now
wait somewhere to be burnt.

QUESTIONS

1. Describe the visual imagery of the poem. What tactile imagery is associated with
    the steps? What other images are part of the speaker's memory?

2. How is the image of the "old wooden steps" developed in the poem? What has
    happened to the wooden steps? What meaning may be derived from their
    having been replaced by the granite steps? How are these steps tied to the
    speaker's "time past"?

3. Why do you think the speaker expressly denies the recollection of any sounds of
    bird or cricket?

P. K. PAGE   (b. 1916)

Photos of a Salt Mine _____ *1954*

How innocent their lives look,
how like a child's
dream of caves and winter, both combined;
the steep descent to whiteness
and the stope°   5
with its striated walls
their folds all leaning as if pointing to
the greater whiteness still,
that great white bank
with its decisive front,   10
that seam upon a slope,
salt's lovely ice.

And wonderful underfoot the snow of salt
the fine

PHOTOS OF A SALT MINE.   5 *stope:* a mining excavation taking the form of huge steps.

particles a broom could sweep,   15
one thinks
muckers might make angels in its drifts
as children do in snow,
lovers in sheets,
lie down and leave imprinted where they lay   20
a feathered creature holier than they.

And in the outworked stopes
with lamps and ropes
up miniature matterhorns
the miners climb   25
probe with their lights
the ancient folds of rock—
syncline and anticline°—
and scoop from darkness an Aladdin's cave:
rubies and opals glitter from its walls.   30

But hoses douse the brilliance of these jewels,
melt fire to brine.
Salt's bitter water trickles thin and forms,
slow fathoms down,
a lake within a cave,   35
lacquered with jet—
white's opposite.
There grey on black the boating miners float
to mend the stays and struts of that old stope
and deeply underground   40
their words resound,
are multiplied by echo, swell and grow
and make a climate of a miner's voice.

So all the photographs like children's wishes
are filled with caves or winter,   45
innocence
has acted as a filter,
selected only beauty from the mine.
Except in the last picture,
it is shot   50
from an acute high angle. In a pit
figures the size of pins are strangely lit
and might be dancing but you know they're not.
Like Dante's vision of the nether hell
men struggle with the bright cold fires of salt,   55
locked in the black inferno of the rock:
the filter here, not innocence but guilt.

PHOTOS OF A SALT MINE.   28 *syncline and anticline:* A syncline is a U-shaped formation of rock
strata; an anticline is a formation bending down from a high point.

QUESTIONS

1. What "filter" conditions the images in the first 47 lines? What characterizes the images in this section of the poem?

2. What beauties does the poet bring out through such images? What impressions does she convey with images like "miniature matterhorns," "brilliance of these jewels," "lacquered with jet," and "striated walls"?

3. What "filter" conditions the images in the last nine lines? What significance should be placed on the "figures the size of pins" (line 52)? How do the images of "pit," "nether hell," and "black inferno" suggest the poet's view of the lives imposed on the people working in such a mine?

4. What images of motion and activity do you find in the poem? What ideas do these images convey?

EZRA POUND (1885–1972)

In a Station of the Metro° _____ *1916*

The apparition of these faces in the crowd;
Petals on a wet, black bough.

IN A STATION OF THE METRO.   *Metro:* the Paris subway.

QUESTIONS

1. Is the image of the wet, black bough happy or sad? If the petals were on a tree in the sunlight, what would be the effect?

2. What is the meaning of the image suggested by "apparition"? Does it suggest a positive or negative view of human life?

3. This poem contains only two lines. Is it proper to consider it as a poem nevertheless? If it is not a poem, what is it?

WILLIAM SHAKESPEARE (1564–1616)

Sonnet 130: My Mistress' Eyes Are Nothing Like the Sun _____ *1609*

My mistress' eyes are nothing like the sun;
Coral is far more red than her lips' red;
If snow be white, why then her breasts are dun;
If hairs be wires, black wires grow on her head.
I have seen roses damasked,° red and white,   *set in an elaborate bouquet*   5
But no such roses see I in her cheeks;
And in some perfumes is there more delight
Than in the breath that from my mistress reeks.

I love to hear her speak, yet well I know
That music hath a far more pleasing sound;   10
I grant I never saw a goddess go;
My mistress, when she walks, treads on the ground.
And yet, by heaven, I think my love as rare
As any she belied with false compare.

QUESTIONS

1. To what does the speaker negatively compare his mistress's eyes? Lips? Breasts? Hair? Cheeks? Breath? Voice? Walk? What kinds of images are created in these negative comparisons?

2. What conventional images does this poem ridicule? What sort of poem is Shakespeare mocking by using the negative images in lines 1–12?

3. In the light of the last two lines, do you think the speaker intends the images as insults? If not as insults, how should they be taken?

4. Are most of the images auditory, olfactory, visual, or kinesthetic? Explain.

5. What point does this poem make about love poetry? About human relationships? How does the imagery contribute to the development of both points?

DAVID WOJAHN   (b. 1953)

"*It's Only Rock and Roll, but I Like It*": *The Fall of Saigon* _____ 1975

The guttural stammer of the chopper blades
Raising arabesques of dust, tearing leaves
From the orange trees lining the Embassy compound:
One chopper left, and a CBS cameraman leans
From inside its door, exploiting the artful   5
Mayhem. Somewhere a radio blares the Stones,
"I like it, like it, yes indeed. . . ." Carts full
Of files blaze in the yard. Flak-jacketed marines
Gunpoint the crowd away. The overloaded chopper strains
And blunders from the roof. An ice-cream-suited   10
Saigonese drops his briefcase; both hands
Now cling to the airborne skis. The camera gets
It all: the marine leaning out the copter bay,
His fists beating time. Then the hands giving way.

QUESTIONS

1. What actions take place in this poem? Why does the Saigonese "cling to the airborne skis"? What happens to him?

2. Describe the poem's images of sound. How many such images does the poem contain? What is their effect? What images of sight do you find? What other types of images?

3. Contrast the poem's title with its content.
4. Cumulatively, what is the relationship of the poem's images to the phrase "artful/Mayhem" in lines 5 and 6 and also to the poem's judgment about the American presence in Vietnam?

WRITING ABOUT IMAGERY

Questions for Discovering Ideas

In preparing to write, you should develop a set of thoughtful notes dealing with issues such as the following:

- What type or types of images prevail in the work? Visual (shapes, colors)? Auditory (sounds)? Olfactory (smells)? Tactile (touch and texture)? Gustatory (taste)? Kinetic or kinesthetic (motion)? Or is the imagery a combination of these?
- To what degree do the images reflect the poet's actual observation or the poet's reading and knowledge of fields such as science or history?
- How well do the images stand out? How vivid are they? How is this vividness achieved?
- Within a group of images, say visual or auditory, do the images pertain to one location or area rather than another (e.g., natural scenes rather than interiors, snowy scenes rather than grassy ones, loud and harsh sounds rather than quiet and civilized ones)?
- What explanation is needed for the images? (Images might be derived from the classics or the Bible, the Revolutionary War or World War II, the behaviors of four-footed creatures or birds, and so on.)
- What effect do the circumstances described in the poem (e.g., conditions of brightness or darkness, warmth or cold, etc.) have upon your responses to the images? What poetic purpose do you think the poet achieves by controlling these responses?
- How well are the images integrated within the poem's argument or development?

Answering questions like these should provide you with a sizable body of ready-made material that you can convert directly to the body of your essay.

Strategies for Organizing Ideas

Connect a brief overview of the poem to your plan for the body of your essay, such as that the writer uses images to strengthen ideas about war, character, or love, or that the writer relies predominantly on images of sight, sound, and action. You might deal exclusively with one of the following aspects, or, equally likely, you may combine your approaches, as you wish.

1. *Images suggesting ideas and/or moods.* Such an essay should emphasize the effects of the imagery. What ideas or moods are evoked by the images? (The auditory images beginning Owen's "Anthem for Doomed Youth," for example, all point toward a condemnation of war's brutal cruelty. The visual images of

Levertov's "A Time Past," which are accompanied by words like "old," "decayed," and "died," point toward a loss of happiness and the anticipation of death.) Do the images promote approval or disapproval? Cheerfulness? Melancholy? Are the images drab, exciting, vivid? How? Why? Are they conducive to humor or surprise? How does the writer achieve these effects? Are the images consistent, or are they ambiguous? (For example, the images in Masefield's "Cargoes" indicate first approval and then disapproval, with no ambiguity. By contrast, Shakespeare's images in "My Mistress' Eyes" might be construed as insults, but in context, they can be seen as compliments.)

2. *The types of images.* Here the emphasis is on the categories of images themselves. Is there a predominance of a particular type of image (e.g., visual or auditory images), or is there a blending? Is there a bunching of types at particular points in the poem or story? If so, why? Is there any shifting as the work develops (as, for example, in Owen's "Anthem for Doomed Youth" (p. 497), where the auditory images first suggest loudness and harshness, but later images describe quietness and sorrow)? Are the images appropriate, granted the nature and apparent intent of the work? Do they assist in making the ideas seem convincing? If there seems to be any inappropriateness, what is its effect?

3. *Systems of images.* Here the emphasis should be on the areas from which the images are drawn. This is another way of considering the appropriateness of the imagery. Is there a pattern of similar or consistent images, such as color and activity (Hopkins's "Spring")? Do all the images adhere consistently to a particular frame of reference, such as a sunlit garden (Lowell's "Patterns" [Chapter 21]), an extensive recreational forest and garden (Coleridge's "Kubla Khan"), a front stair (Levertov's "A Time Past"), or a darkened forest (Blake's "The Tyger")? What is unusual or unique about the set of images? What unexpected or new responses do they produce?

Your conclusion, in addition to recapitulating your major points, is the place for additional insights. It would not be proper to go too far in new directions here, but you might briefly take up one or more of the ideas that you have not developed in the body. In short, what have you learned from your study of imagery in your poem?

SAMPLE STUDENT ESSAY

The Images of Masefield's "Cargoes"°

[1]   In the three-stanza poem "Cargoes," John Masefield develops imagery to create a negative impression of modern commercial life.* There is a contrast between the first two stanzas and the third, with the first two idealizing the romantic, distant past and the third demeaning the modern, gritty, grimy present.

° See p. 496 for this poem.
* Central idea.

Masefield's images are thus both positive and lush, on the one hand, and negative and stark, on the other.[†]

The most evocative and pleasant images in the poem are in the first stanza. The speaker asks that we imagine a "Quinquereme of Nineveh from distant Ophir" (line 1), an oceangoing, many-oared vessel loaded with treasure for the biblical King Solomon. As Masefield identifies the cargo, the visual images are rich and romantic (lines 3–5):

[2]

> With a cargo of ivory,
> And apes and peacocks,
> Sandalwood, cedarwood, and sweet white wine.

Ivory suggests richness, which is augmented by the exotic "apes and peacocks" in all their exciting strangeness. The "sandalwood, cedarwood, and sweet white wine" evoke pungent smells and tastes. The "sunny" light of ancient Palestine (line 2) not only illuminates the imaginative scene (visual), but invites readers to imagine the sun's warming touch (tactile). The references to animals and birds also suggest the sounds that these creatures would make (auditory). Thus, in this lush first stanza, images derived from all the senses are introduced to create impressions of a glorious past.

[3]

Almost equally lush are the images of the second stanza, which completes the poem's first part. Here the visual imagery evokes the royal splendor of a tall-masted, full-sailed galleon (line 6) at the height of Spain's commercial power in the sixteenth century. The galleon's cargo suggests wealth, with sparkling diamonds and amethysts, and Portuguese "gold moidores" gleaming in open chests (line 10). With cinnamon in the second stanza's bill of lading (line 10), Masefield includes the image of a pleasant-tasting spice.

[4]

The negative imagery of the third stanza is in stark contrast to the first two stanzas. The visual image is a modern "Dirty British coaster" (line 11), which draws attention to the griminess and suffocation of modern civilization. This spray-swept ship is loaded with materials that pollute the earth with noise and smoke. The smoke-stack of the coaster (line 11) and the firewood it is carrying suggest choking smog. The "Tyne coal" (line 13) and "road-rails" (line 14) suggest the noise and smoke of puffing railroad engines. As if this were not enough, the "pig-lead" (line 14) to be used in various industrial processes indicates not just more unpleasantness, but also something poisonous and deadly. In contrast to the lush and stately imagery of the first two stanzas, the images in the third stanza invite the conclusion that people now, when the "Dirty British coaster" butts through the English Channel, are surrounded and threatened by visual, olfactory, and auditory pollution.

[5]

The poem thus establishes a romantic past and ugly present through images of sight, smell, and sound. The images of motion also emphasize this view: In the first two stanzas the quinquereme is "rowing" and the galleon is "dipping." These kinetic images suggest dignity and lightness. The British coaster, however, is "butting," an image indicating bull-like hostility and stupid force. These, together with all the other images, focus the poem's negative views of modern life. The facts that existence for both the ancient Palestinians and the

[†] Thesis sentence.

Renaissance Spaniards included slavery (of those men rowing the quinquereme) and piracy (by those Spanish "explorers" who robbed and killed the natives of the Isthmus) should probably not be emphasized as a protest against Masefield's otherwise valid contrasts in images. His final commentary may hence be thought of as the banging of his "cheap tin trays" (line 15), which makes a percussive climax of the oppressive images filling too large a portion of modern lives.

Commentary on the Essay

This essay illustrates the first strategy for writing about imagery (p. 511), using images to develop ideas and moods. All the examples—derived directly from the poem—emphasize the qualities of Masefield's images. This method permits the introduction of imagery drawn from all the senses in order to demonstrate Masefield's ideas about the past and the present. Other approaches might have concentrated exclusively on Masefield's visual images, or upon his images drawn from trade and commerce. Because Masefield uses auditory and gustatory images but does not develop them extensively, sound or taste might be appropriately treated in short, paragraph-length essays.

The introductory paragraph of the essay presents the central idea that Masefield uses his images climactically to lead to his negative view of modern commercialism. The thesis sentence indicates that the topics to be developed are those of (1) lushness and (2) starkness.

Paragraphs 2 and 3 form a unit stressing the lushness and exoticism of the first stanza and the wealth and colorfulness of the second stanza. In particular, paragraph 2 uses words like "lush," "evocative," "rich," "exotic," "pungent," and "romantic" to characterize the pleasing mental pictures the images invoke. Although the paragraph indicates enthusiastic responses to the images, it does not go beyond the limits of the images themselves.

Paragraph 4 stresses the contrast of Masefield's images in the third stanza with those of the first two stanzas. To this end the paragraph illustrates the imaginative reconstruction needed to develop an understanding of this contrast. The unpleasantness, annoyance, and even the danger of the cargoes mentioned in the third stanza are therefore emphasized as the qualities evoked by the images.

The last paragraph demonstrates that the imagery of motion—not much stressed in the poem—is in agreement with the rest of Masefield's imagery. As a demonstration of the need for fair, impartial judgment, the conclusion introduces the possible objection that Masefield may be slanting his images by including not a full but rather a partial view of their respective historical periods. Thus the concluding paragraph adds balance to the analysis illustrated in paragraphs 2, 3, and 4.

SPECIAL WRITING TOPICS FOR STUDYING IMAGERY IN POETRY

1. Compare the images of home in Owen's "Anthem for Doomed Youth" (p. 497) and Seeger's "I Have a Rendezvous with Death" (p. 796). Describe the differing

effects of the images. How are the images used? How effectively do these images aid in the development of the attitudes toward war expressed in each poem? How is your reading of the poems affected by the knowledge that both Owen and Seeger were killed in war?

2. Based on the poems in this chapter by Blake, Coleridge, and Hopkins, write an essay discussing the poetic use of images drawn from the natural world. What sorts of references do the poets make? What attitudes do they express about the details they select? What is the relationship between the images and religious views? What judgments about God and nature do the poets show by their images?

3. Considering the imagery of Levertov's "A Time Past," Wojahn's "It's Only Rock and Roll, but I Like It," or Blake's "The Tyger," write an essay explaining the power of imagery. As you develop your thoughts, be sure to consider the dramatic nature of the images in the poem you choose, and to account for the impressions and ideas that they create. You may also wish to introduce references to images from other poems that are relevant to your points.

4. Write a poem describing one of these:

   a. Athletes who have just completed an exhausting run.

   b. Children getting out of school for the day.

   c. Your recollection of having been lost as a child.

   d. A cat that always sits down on your school work.

   e. A particularly good meal you had recently.

   f. The best concert you ever attended.

   g. Driving to work/school on a rainy/snowy day.

   Then, write an analysis of the images you selected for your poem, and explain your choices. What details stand out in your mind? What do you recall best—sight, smell, sound, action? What is the relationship between your images and the ideas you express in your poem?

5. Write an essay considering the graphic or pictorial nature of the imagery in Coleridge's "Kubla Khan," Herbert's "The Pulley," Pound's "In a Station of the Metro," and Wojahn's "It's Only Rock and Roll, but I Like It," along with other poems that you may wish to include. What similarities and differences do you find in subject matter, treatment, arrangement, and general idea? On the basis of your comparison, what relationships do you perceive between sight and poetic imagery?

6. Use the retrieval system (computer or card catalogue) in your library to research the topic of imagery in Shakespeare (see *imagery* or *style and imagery*). How many titles do you find? Over how many years have these works been published? Take one of the books out, and write a brief report on one of the chapters. What topics are discussed? What types of imagery are introduced? What relationship does the author make between imagery and content?

14

Rhetorical Figures: A Source of Depth and Range in Poetry

Figurative language refers to expressions that conform to regularized arrangements of words and thought. These patterns, called **rhetorical figures** or **rhetorical devices,** are the tools that help make literary works effective, persuasive, and forceful. It would be difficult to find any piece of good writing that does not use figurative language to some degree. Such language is most vital, however, in imaginative writing, particularly poetry, where it compresses thought, promotes understanding, and shapes response.

The two most important figures are *metaphor* and *simile.* Others are *paradox, anaphora, apostrophe, personification, synecdoche* and *metonymy, synesthesia, pun* (or *paronomasia*), *overstatement,* and *understatement.* All these figures are modes of comparison, and they may be expressed in single words, phrases, clauses, and entire structures. The use of figures enables poets to extend and deepen their range of subject matter just as symbolism does. Indeed, the words *metaphor* and *metaphorical* are often broadly applied to most rhetorical figures, including symbols.

METAPHOR AND SIMILE: THE MAJOR RHETORICAL FIGURES

Metaphor

A **metaphor** (a "carrying out a change") describes something as though it were actually something else. One of Shakespeare's best-known metaphors is "All the world's a stage, / And all the men and women merely players," in which Shakespeare's character Jacques (jay´-queez) from Act II, scene 7 of *As You Like It*, explains human life in terms of stage life. It is important to recognize that the comparison, as a metaphor, does not state that the world is *like* a stage, but that it literally *is* a stage.

Simile

Whereas a metaphor merges identities, a **simile** (the "showing of similarity or oneness") utilizes *similarity* to carry out the explanation. A simile is distinguishable from a metaphor because it is introduced by *like* with nouns and *as* (also *as if* and *as though*) with clauses. Consider this stanza from Donne's "A Valediction: Forbidding Mourning":

Our two souls therefore, which are one,
    Though I must go, endure not yet
A breach, but an expansion
    Like gold to airy thinness beat.

The concluding simile invites the comparison of the souls of the speaker and his sweetheart with the malleability of gold, the point being that the speaker's impending departure will not be a separation but rather a thinning out, so that the speaker and his sweetheart will still be together even though the distance between them will expand. Because the simile is introduced by *like*, the emphasis of the figure is on the similarity of the lovers' departure to malleable gold, not on the *identification* of the two.

IMAGERY AND THE LANGUAGE OF METAPHOR AND SIMILE.   In Chapter 13, we saw how imagery stimulates the imagination and recalls memories (*images*) of sights, sounds, tastes, smells, sensations of touch, and motions. Metaphors and similes go beyond literal imagery to introduce perceptions and comparisons that can be unusual, unpredictable, and surprising, as in Donne's classic simile, just discussed, comparing the lovers' relationship to gold. How many people have ever perceived such a metaphorical connection—between the malleability of metal and the constancy of lovers? But is it not true that the comparison emphasizes the bond between two lovers, and also that gold shows how valuable the bond is? Metaphorical language extends knowledge and awareness by introducing perceptions that otherwise would not come to light. In Kenyon's "Portrait of a Figure Near Water," for example, anger is metaphorically called "the inner arsonist." Such perceptions as these connect the thing or things to be communicated—such as qualities of love or the excitement of unexpected discovery—with a new insight that is made objective through the comparison of a simile or the equation of a metaphor. First and foremost, then, the use of metaphors and similes is one of the ways in which great literature leads us to see the world in fresh and original ways.

Let us take a commonly expressed idea, for example—the notion of happiness. To communicate a character's joy and excitement, the sentence "She was happy" is accurate but not interesting. A more vivid way of saying the same thing is to use an image of an action, such as "She jumped for joy." This image gives us a literal picture of an action demonstrating happiness. But an even better way of communicating a happy state is the following simile: "She felt as if she had just inherited fifty million tax-free dollars." Because readers easily understand the excitement, disbelief, exhilaration, and joy that such an event would bring, they also understand—and feel—the character's happiness. It is the *simile* that evokes this perception, for no simple description could help a reader comprehend the same degree of emotion.

As a parallel poetic example, let us refer to Keats's "On First Looking into Chapman's Homer," which Keats wrote soon after reading the translation of Homer's *Iliad* and *Odyssey* by the Renaissance poet George Chapman. Keats's main idea is that Chapman not only translated Homer's words but also transmitted Homer's greatness.

JOHN KEATS   (1795–1821)

On First Looking into Chapman's Homer° _____ *1816*

Much have I travell'd in the realms of gold,
    And many goodly states and kingdoms seen:
    Round many western islands have I been
Which bards in fealty to Apollo° hold.
Oft of one wide expanse had I been told   5
    That deep-brow'd Homer ruled as his demesne;°   *realm, estate*
    Yet did I never breathe its pure serene°
Till I heard Chapman speak out loud and bold:
Then felt I like some watcher of the skies
    When a new planet swims into his ken;°   *field of sight*   10
Or like stout Cortez° when with eagle eyes
    He star'd at the Pacific—and all his men
Look'd at each other with a wild surmise—
    Silent, upon a peak in Darien.

ON FIRST LOOKING INTO CHAPMAN'S HOMER.   George Chapman (c. 1560–1634) published his translations of Homer's *Iliad* in 1612 and *Odyssey* in 1614–15.   4 *bards . . . Apollo:* writers who are sworn subjects of Apollo, the Greek god of light, music, poetry, prophecy, and the sun.   7 *serene:* a clear expanse of air; also grandeur, clarity; rulers were also sometimes called "serene majesty."   11 *Cortez:* Hernando Cortez (1485–1547), a Spanish general and the conqueror of Mexico. Keats confuses him with Vasco de Balboa (c. 1475–1519), the first European to see the Pacific Ocean (in 1510) from Darien, an old name for the Isthmus of Panama.

QUESTIONS

1.   What is being discovered in this poem? To what extent is such discovery a universal experience?

2.   Explain the metaphor of land and travel that Keats develops in lines 1–6. Be careful to consider the words "realms," "states," "kingdoms," "islands," "expanse," and "demesne."

3   How successfully does Keats convey excitement through the similes in lines 9–10 and 11–14? Create a simile of your own to express a feeling about discovery. How does yours compare with Keats's?

4.   Describe the metaphor of "swims" in line 10. What might have been the impact if Keats had used words such as *drifts, floats, flows,* or *wanders?*

To illustrate the power of metaphorical language, we can first briefly paraphrase the sonnet's content:

> I have enjoyed much art and read much European literature, and I have been told that Homer is the best writer of all. However, because I do not know Greek, I could not really appreciate his works until I discovered them in Chapman's translation. To me, this experience was exciting and awe-inspiring.

If all Keats had written were a paragraph like this one, we would pay no attention to it, for it carries no sense of excitement or stimulation. But the last six lines of the sonnet as Keats wrote them contain two memorable similes ("like some watcher of the skies" and "like stout Cortez"). They stand out and demand a special effort of imagination. When we mull them over, we might suppose that we actually *are* astronomers just discovering a new planet, and that we actually *are* the first explorers to see the Pacific. As we imagine ourselves in these roles, we come to understand the amazement, wonder, excitement, exhilaration, anticipation, joy, and feeling of accomplishment that would accompany such discoveries. If we imagine these feelings, then Keats has unlocked experiences that the relatively unpromising title does not suggest. He has given us something new. He has enlarged us.

VEHICLE AND TENOR.   To describe the relationship between a writer's ideas and the metaphorical figures objectifying them, two useful terms have been coined by I. A. Richards (in *The Philosophy of Rhetoric*). First is the **vehicle,** or the literal details of the figures. Second is the **tenor,** which is the totality of ideas and attitudes borne by the vehicle. The vehicle of the fifty-million-dollar simile is the description of the inheritance, while the tenor is joy. Similarly, the tenor of Keats's similes in the last lines of the Chapman sonnet is awe and wonder; the vehicle is the imagery of astronomical and geographical discovery.

OTHER RHETORICAL FIGURES

Paradox

A **paradox** ("a thought beyond a thought") is a device in which a seeming contradiction is revealed to be truthful and non-contradictory. The phrase "I, a child, very old" in Whitman's "Facing West from California's Shores" is a paradox. The obvious contradiction is that no one can be old and young at the same time, but this contradiction can be reconciled if we realize that even as people get older they still retain childlike qualities (such as enthusiasm and hope). Thus Whitman's contradiction is not contradictory (is this clause a paradox?), and the speaker may genuinely be "a child, very old." The second line of Wyatt's sonnet "I Find No Peace" embodies two paradoxes. One opposes fear with hope, the other fire with ice: "I fear and hope, I burn and freeze like ice." These paradoxes genuinely reflect the contradictory states of people in love—

wanting love ("hope," "burn"), but also being uncertain and unsure about the relationship ("fear," "freeze"). The paradoxes thus highlight the truth that love is a complex and sometimes unsettling emotion.

Anaphora

Anaphora ("to carry again or repeat") is the repetition of the same word or phrase throughout a work or a section of a work. The effect is to lend weight and emphasis. In "The Bells," for example, Poe repeats the word *bells* many times, both for emphasis and also to suggest tolling bells. In Blake's "The Tyger" (p. 501), the interrogative word *what* is used five times to emphasize the mystery of evil (italics added):

What the hammer? *what* the chain?
In *what* furnace was thy brain?
What the anvil? *what* dread grasp
Dare its deadly terrors clasp?

Anaphora is the most obvious feature of Rukeyser's "Looking at Each Other," where the word *yes* begins each of the poem's twenty-five lines.

Apostrophe

In an **apostrophe** (a "turning away," or redirection of attention) a speaker addresses a real or imagined listener who is not present. It is like a public speech, with readers as audience. Apostrophe enables the speaker to develop ideas that might arise naturally on a public occasion, as in Wordsworth's sonnet "London, 1802," which is addressed to the long dead English poet Milton. In Keats's sonnet "Bright Star," the speaker addresses a distant and inanimate star, yet through apostrophe he proceeds as though the star has human understanding and divine power.

JOHN KEATS   (1795–1822)

Bright Star _____ *1838 (1819)*

Bright star! would I were steadfast as thou art—
    Not in lone splendor hung aloft the night,
And watching, with eternal lids apart,
    Like Nature's patient, sleepless eremite,°   *hermit*
The moving waters at their priestlike task   5
    Of pure ablution round earth's human shores,
Or gazing on the new soft-fallen mask
    Of snow upon the mountains and the moors;
No—yet still steadfast, still unchangeable,
    Pillowed upon my fair love's ripening breast,   10

To feel forever its soft fall and swell,
  Awake forever in a sweet unrest,
    Still, still to hear her tender-taken breath,
    And so live ever—or else swoon to death.

QUESTIONS

1. With what topic is the speaker concerned in this sonnet? How does he compare himself with the distant star?

2. What qualities does the speaker attribute specifically to the star? What sort of role does he seem to assign to it? In light of this role, and the qualities needed to serve in it, how might the star be compared to a divine and benign presence?

3. In light of the stress made on the words "forever" and "ever" in lines 11–14, how appropriate is the choice of the star as the subject of the apostrophe in the poem?

In this sonnet the speaker addresses the star as though it is a person or god, an object of adoration, and the poem is therefore like a petitional prayer. The star is idealized with qualities that the speaker wishes to establish in himself, namely, steadfastness, eternal watchfulness, and fidelity. The point of the apostrophe is thus to dramatize the speaker's yearning and to stress the permanence of space and eternity as contrasted with earthly impermanence.

Personification

A close neighbor of apostrophe is **personification**—the attribution of human characteristics to either nonhuman objects or abstractions. Poets introduce personification to explore relationships to environment, ideals, and inner lives. In "Bright Star," as we have just seen, Keats personifies the star addressed by the speaker. Shakespeare, in Sonnet 146, "Poor Soul, the Center of My Sinful Earth" (p. 798), personifies his own soul so that he can deal with earthly versus heavenly concerns. Other major examples of personification are Keats's "To Autumn" and "Ode on a Grecian Urn" and Shelley's "Ode to the West Wind" (pp. 527, 675, 598).

Synecdoche and Metonymy

These figures are close in purpose and effect. **Synecdoche** ("taking one thing out of another") is a device in which a part stands for the whole, or a whole for a part, like the expression "All hands aboard" to signify that a ship's crew should return to ship. **Metonymy** (a "transfer of name") substitutes one thing for another with which it is closely identified, as when "the White House" signifies the policies and activities of the U.S. president. The purpose of both devices is the creation of new insights and ideas, just like metaphors and similes.

Synecdoche is seen in Keats's "To Autumn," where the gourd and hazel shells in lines 7–8, which are single instances of ripe produce, stand for the entire autumnal harvest. In Wordsworth's "London, 1802," the phrase "thy heart" (line 13) is a synecdoche in which a part—the heart—refers to the complete person. Metonymy is seen again in Keats's "To Autumn" when the "granary floor" (line 14), the place where grain is stored, bears the transferred meaning of the entire harvest stored there. In "Exit, Pursued by a Bear," Ogden Nash metonymically uses brand names, the names of artists, and the names of cities to mean objects, artworks, and places.

Synesthesia

In **synesthesia** (the "bringing together of feelings") a poet describes one feeling or perception with words that are usually used for a totally different or even opposite feeling or perception, as in darkness that is visible, a thought that is green, or a soul that claps its hands. Keats makes great use of synesthesia, as, for example, in the "Ode to a Nightingale" (p. 636), where a plot of ground is "melodious," a draught of wine tastes of "Dance, and Provençal song, and sunburnt mirth," and beaded bubbles of wine are "winking at the brim" of a glass.

Pun, or Paronomasia

Another transferring figure is the **pun** ("a point or a puncture"), or **paronomasia** ("something beside a name"). A pun is wordplay which reveals that words with different meanings have similar or even identical sounds. Because puns can be outrageous and often require a little bit of thinking, people may groan when they hear them (even while they enjoy them). Also, because many puns seem to play only with sound, they have not always enjoyed critical acclaim, but good puns can always be relished because they work with sounds to *reveal* ideas. John Gay, for example, utilizes clever and complex puns in the following song, sung by the gang of thieves in *The Beggar's Opera* (1728), a play which, incidentally, marked the beginning of the musical comedy tradition.

JOHN GAY   (1685–1732)

Let Us Take the Road _____ *1728*

Let us take the road.
    Hark! I hear the sound of coaches!
    The hour of attack approaches,
To your arms, brave boys, and load.
    See the ball I hold! [*holding up a bullet*]   5
Let the chymists° toil like asses,   *alchemists*
Our fire their fire surpasses,°   *Our fire surpasses their fire*
    And turns all our lead to gold.

QUESTIONS

    1.   What traits are shown by the singers of this poem? Why do they not seem frightening, despite their "profession" of theft?

2. Describe the puns in the poem. What kind of knowledge is needed to explain them fully? How many puns are there? How are they connected? Why do the puns seem particularly witty and also outrageous?

Here "fire," "lead," and "gold" are puns. *Lead* was the "base" or "low" metal that the medieval alchemists ("chymists") tried to transform into *gold*, using the heat from their *fires*. The puns develop because the gang of cutthroats singing the song is about to go out to rob people riding in horse-drawn coaches. Hence their "lead" is in the form of bullets, which will be transformed into the "gold" coins they steal. Their "fire" is not the fire of alchemists, but rather the firing of pistols. Through these puns, Gay's villains charm us by their wit, even though in real life they would scare us to death.

Overstatement and Understatement

Two important devices creating emphasis are **overstatement,** or **hyperbole,** and **understatement.** Overstatement, also called the *overreacher,* is exaggeration for effect. In "London, 1802," for example, Wordsworth declares that England "is a fen / of stagnant waters." That is, the country and its people make up collectively a stinking, smelly, polluted marsh, a muddy dump. What Wordsworth establishes by this overstatement is his judgment that England in 1802 needed a writer like Milton to unite the people around noble moral and political ideas.

In contrast with overstatement, *understatement* is the deliberate underplaying or undervaluing of a thing for purposes of emphasis. One of the most famous poetic understatements is in Andrew Marvell's "To His Coy Mistress" (p. 639):

The grave's a fine and private place,
But none, I think, do there embrace.

Here the understatement grimly emphasizes the eternity of death by contrasting the permanent privacy of the grave with the temporary privacy of a trysting place sought by lovers. Another ironic use of understatement is in lines 17–20 of Ogden Nash's "Exit, Pursued by a Bear," where the speaker indicates that the "lion and the lizard" cannot hear "heavenly harmonies." In this figure Nash emphasizes that the people have been killed who once inhabited the rooms where such melodies were played, and therefore he emphasizes the ignorance and horror of war.

 POEMS FOR STUDY

ELIZABETH BISHOP   (1911–1979)

Rain Towards Morning ――――――――――――――――――――――― *1947*

The great light cage has broken up in the air,
freeing, I think, about a million birds
whose wild ascending shadows will not be back,
and all the wires come falling down.
No cage, no frightening birds; the rain   5
is brightening now. The face is pale
that tried the puzzle of their prison
and solved it with an unexpected kiss,
whose freckled unsuspected hands alit.

QUESTIONS

1. What sort of personal situation is being described in the poem? How much does
    the poet allow you to learn about the situation? Do you discover enough to
    determine the general pattern of what is happening?

2. Describe the effect of the overstatement in lines 1–4. In light of the "kiss," which
    is more powerful: understatement or overstatement?

3. What is the meaning of the "great light cage" in lines 1–4? What is the "puzzle"
    of the birds' prison in line 7?

4. How can the "face" of line 6 and the "kiss" in line 8 be explained, through the
    figure of synecdoche, to have "hands" in line 9? What do these figures suggest
    about the nature of the experience being described?

5. Explain the paradox of how rain can be brightening (line 6).

ROBERT BURNS   (1759–1796)

A Red, Red Rose _____ *1796*

O my Luve's like a red, red rose,
   That's newly sprung in June:
O my Luve's like the melodie
   That's sweetly play'd in tune.

As fair art thou, my bonnie lass,   5
   So deep in luve am I;
And I will luve thee still, my Dear,
   Till a'° the seas gang° dry.   *all; go*

Till a' the seas gang dry, my Dear,
   And the rocks melt wi'° the sun: *with* 10
And I will luve thee still, my Dear,
   While the sands o'° life shall run.   *of*

And fare thee weel, my only Luve!
   And fare thee weel, awhile!
And I will come again, my Luve,   15
   Tho' it were ten thousand mile!

QUESTIONS

1. In light of the character and background of the speaker, do the two opening similes seem common or unusual? If they are just ordinary, does that fact diminish their value? How and why?

2. Describe the shift of listener envisioned after the first stanza. How are the last three stanzas related to the first?

3. Consider the metaphors concerning time and travel. How do the metaphors assist you in comprehending the speaker's character?

JOHN DONNE   (1572–1631)

A Valediction: Forbidding Mourning _____ *1633*

As virtuous men pass mildly away,
   And whisper to their souls to go,
Whilst some of their sad friends do say
   The breath goes now, and some say, No;

So let us melt, and make no noise,   5
   No tear-floods, nor sigh-tempests move,
'Twere profanation of our joys
   To tell the laity° our love.

A VALEDICTION: FORBIDDING MOURNING.   7, 8 *profanation . . . laity:* as though the lovers are priests of love, whose love is a mystery.

Moving of th'earth° brings harm and fears,   *earthquakes*
   Men reckon what it did and meant: 10
But trepidation° of the spheres,
   Though greater far, is innocent.

Dull sublunary lovers' love
   (Whose soul is sense°) cannot admit
Absence, because it doth remove   15
   Those things which elemented it.

But we by a love so much refined
   That our selves know not what it is,
Inter-assured of the mind,
   Care less, eyes, lips, and hands to miss.   20

Our two souls therefore, which are one,
   Though I must go, endure not yet
A breach, but an expansion
   Like gold to airy thinness beat.°

If they be two, they are two so   25
   As stiff twin compasses° are two;
Thy soul, the fixt foot, makes no show
   To move, but doth, if th'other do.

And though it in the center sit,
   Yet when the other far doth roam,   30
It leans and harkens after it,
   And grows erect, as that comes home.

Such wilt thou be to me, who must
   Like th'other foot, obliquely run;
Thy firmness draws my circle just,°   35
   And makes me end where I begun.

11 *trepidation:* Before Sir Isaac Newton explained the precession of the equinoxes, it was assumed that the positions of heavenly bodies should be constant and perfectly circular. The clearly observable irregularities (caused by the slow wobbling of the earth's axis) were explained by the concept of *trepidation,* or a trembling or oscillation that occurred in the outermost of the spheres surrounding the earth.   14 *soul is sense:* lovers whose attraction is totally physical.   24 *gold to airy thinness beat:* a reference to the malleability of gold.   26 *compasses:* a compass used for drawing circles.   35 *just:* perfectly round.

QUESTIONS

1. What is the situation envisioned as the occasion for the poem? Who is talking to whom? What is their relationship?

2. What is the intention of the first two stanzas? What is the effect of the phrases "tear-floods" and "sigh-tempests"?

3. Describe the effect of the opening simile about men on their deathbeds.

4. What is the metaphor of the third stanza (lines 9–12)? In what sense might the "trepidation of the spheres" be less harmful than the parting of the lovers?

5. In lines 13–20 there is a comparison making the love of the speaker and his sweetheart superior to the love of average lovers. What is the basis for the speaker's claim?

6. What is the comparison begun by the word "refined" in line 17 and continued by the simile in line 24?

LANGSTON HUGHES   (1902–1967)

Harlem _____ *1951*

What happens to a dream deferred?

Does it dry up
like a raisin in the sun?
Or fester like a sore—
And then run?   5
Does it stink like rotten meat?
Or crust and sugar over—
like a syrupy sweet?

Maybe it just sags
like a heavy load.   10

Or does it explode?

QUESTIONS

1. In the light of the black experience with the "American Dream," what do you think is meant by the phrase "dream deferred"?

2. Explain the structure of the poem in terms of the speaker's questions and answers. How is the structure here similar to the one in Blake's "The Tyger" (p. 501)?

3. Explain the similes in lines 3, 4, 6, 8, and 10. Why are these apt comparisons? What sorts of human actions are implied in these figures?

4. What is the meaning of the metaphor in line 11? Why do you think Hughes shifted from similes to a metaphor in this line?

JOHN KEATS   (1795–1821)

To Autumn _____ *1820*

Season of mists and mellow fruitfulness!
   Close bosom-friend of the maturing sun;
Conspiring with him how to load and bless
   With fruit the vines that round the thatch-eaves run;
To bend with apples the mossed cottage-trees,   5
   And fill all fruit with ripeness to the core;
      To swell the gourd, and plump the hazel shells

With a sweet kernel; to set budding more,
  And still more, later flowers for the bees,
  Until they think warm days will never cease,   10
    For Summer has o'erbrimmed their clammy cells.

Who hath not seen thee oft amid thy store?
  Sometimes whoever seeks abroad may find
Thee sitting careless on a granary floor,
  Thy hair soft-lifted by the winnowing wind,   15
Or on a half-reaped furrow sound asleep,
Drowsed with the fume of poppies, while thy hook
  Spares the next swath and all its twinèd flowers;
And sometimes like a gleaner thou dost keep
  Steady thy laden head across a brook;   20
  Or by a cider-press, with patient look,
  Thou watchest the last oozings hours by hours.

Where are the songs of Spring? Ay, where are they?
  Think not of them, thou hast thy music too,—
While barrèd clouds bloom the soft-dying day,   25
  And touch the stubble-plains with rosy hue;
Then in a wailful choir the small gnats mourn
  Among the river sallows, borne aloft
  Or sinking as the light wind lives or dies;
And full-grown lambs loud bleat from hilly bourn;   30
  Hedge-crickets sing; and now with treble soft
  The redbreast whistles from a garden-croft;
    And gathering swallows twitter in the skies.

QUESTIONS

1. How is personification used in the first stanza? How does it change in the
    second? What is the effect of such personification?

2. How does Keats structure the poem to accord with his apostrophe to autumn?
    That is, in what ways can the stanzas be distinguished by the type of discourse
    addressed to the season?

3. Analyze Keats's metonymy in the first stanza and synecdoche in the second.
    What effects does he achieve with these devices?

4. How, through the use of images, does Keats develop his idea that autumn is a
    season of "mellow fruitfulness"?

JANE KENYON   (1947–1995)

Portrait of a Figure Near Water _____ *1996*

Rebuked, she turned and ran
uphill to the barn. Anger, the inner
arsonist, held a match to her brain.
She observed her life: against her will
it survived the unwavering flame.   5

The barn was empty of animals.
Only a swallow tilted
near the beams, and bats
hung from the rafters
the roof sagged between.   10

Her breath became steady
where, years past, the farmer cooled
the big tin amphorae of milk.
The stone trough was still
filled with water: she watched it   15
and received its calm.

So it is when we retreat in anger
we think we burn alone
and there is no balm.
Then water enters, though it makes   20
no sound.

QUESTIONS

1. What do you think has happened before the poem opens? What sort of rebuke has the woman received? What does it lead her to do?

2. What is the effect of "tilted" (line 7), and why does the speaker draw attention to the roof sagging between the rafters (line 10)? Why does the writer call the large milk cans "amphorae" (line 13)? How do these word choices affect the poem's context?

3. What is the metaphorical sense of anger as "the inner / arsonist" (lines 2–3)? In what way is the water in the stone trough for animals metaphorical? What metaphorical meanings should be attributed to water?

OGDEN NASH   (1902–1970)

Exit, Pursued by a Bear° _____ 1954

Chipmunk chewing the Chippendale,°
Mice on the Meissen° shelf,
Pigeon stains on the Aubusson,°
Spider lace on the delf.°

Squirrel climbing the Sheraton,°   5
Skunk on the Duncan Phyfe,°

EXIT, PURSUED BY A BEAR.   The title is a stage direction in Shakespeare's *The Winter's Tale* (Act III, scene 3, line 58). The character is torn apart by the bear. When this poem was first published, the atomic bomb had existed for nine years, and the hydrogen bomb for two. In late 1953, Russia, which is sometimes symbolized by a bear, announced that it possessed the hydrogen bomb.   1 *Chippendale:* ornate furniture made by Thomas Chippendale (1718–1779).   2 *Meissen:* expensive chinaware made in Meissen, Germany. Also called "Dresden China."   3 *Aubusson:* carpet imported from France.   4 *delf:* expensive pottery made in Delft, The Netherlands.   5 *Sheraton:* furniture made by Thomas Sheraton (1751–1806).   6 *Duncan Phyfe:* furniture made by Duncan Phyfe (1768–1854), a Scotsman who came to America in 1783.

Silverfish in the Gobelins°
And the calfbound volumes of *Life*.

Pocks on the pink Picasso,
Dust on the four Cézannes,   5
Kit on the keys of the Steinway,
Cat on the Louis Quinze.°

Rings on the Adam° mantel
From a thousand bygone thirsts,
Mold on the Henry Millers°   10
And the Ronald Firbank° firsts.

The lion and the lizard°
No heavenly harmonies hear
From the high-fidelity speaker
Concealed behind the Vermeer.   15

Jamshid° squats in a cavern
Screened by a waterfall,
Catered by Heinz and Campbell,
And awaits the fireball.

7 *Gobelins:* rare and exquisitely crafted tapestries made by Gobelin of Paris.   12 *Louis Quinze:* furniture made in France during the reign of Louis XV (1710–1774).   13 *Adam:*   Robert Adam
(1728–1792) was one of the most famous English architects.   15 *Henry Miller:* American author
(1891–1980).   16 *Ronald Firbank:* Arthur Ainsley Ronald Firbank (1886–1926), British
author.   17 *The lion and the lizard:* See Edward Fitzgerald's (1809–1883) version of *The Rubáiyát of
Omar Khayyám,* stanza 18, particularly in reference to Nash's last stanza.   21 *Jamshid:* a reference to
the legendary Persian hero Jamshid, who found a cup containing the elixir of life and lived for 700
years. At one point in the story Jamshid remained hidden for a hundred years. Note also the reference to Fitzgerald's *Rubáiyát,* stanza 18.

QUESTIONS

1. In relationship to the serious subject matter of the poem, what is the effect of
    the title? What is the possible pun on the word "bear"?

2. What location is the speaker describing? How is metonymy used to suggest the
    wealth of the collections of household items and art? What sort of lifestyle is
    suggested by the metonymy?

3. Why is it that animals rather than people are living with the expensive artifacts?
    Judging from line 14, how long has this situation existed?

4. How might the situation presented in the poem be considered a paradox?

MARGE PIERCY   (b. 1934)

A Work of Artifice _____ *1973*

The bonsai tree
in the attractive pot
could have grown eighty feet tall

on the side of a mountain
till split by lightning.   5
But a gardener
carefully pruned it.
It is nine inches high.
Every day as he
whittles back the branches   10
the gardener croons,
It is your nature
to be small and cozy
domestic and weak;
how lucky, little tree,   15
to have a pot to grow in.
With living creatures
one must begin very early
to dwarf their growth:
the bound feet,   20
the crippled brain,
the hair in curlers,
the hands you
love to touch.

QUESTIONS

1. What is a bonsai tree? In what ways is it an apt metaphor for women? The tree
   "could have grown eighty feet tall." What would be the comparable growth and
   development of a woman?

2. What do you make of the gardener's song (lines 12–16)? If the bonsai tree were
   able to respond, would it accept the gardener's consolation? What conclusions
   about women's lives are implied by the metaphor of the tree?

3. How does the poem shift at line 17? To what extent do the next images (lines
   20–24) embody women's lives? How are the images metaphorical?

SYLVIA PLATH   (1932–1963)

Metaphors _____ *1960*

I'm a riddle in nine syllables,
An elephant, a ponderous house,
A melon strolling on two tendrils.
O red fruit, ivory, fine timbers!
This loaf's big with its yeasty rising.   5
Money's new-minted in this fat purse.
I'm a means, a stage, a cow in calf.
I've eaten a bag of green apples,
Boarded the train there's no getting off.

QUESTIONS

1. What evidence can you find in the poem that the speaker is a woman?

2. The speaker calls herself a "riddle in nine syllables." What is the answer to the riddle? Why nine syllables (as opposed to eight or ten)? In what sense is the poem also a riddle? How are the answers to both riddles related?

3. Which of the metaphors do you find amusing, shocking, or demeaning? What do these suggest about the speaker's attitude toward herself?

4. What aspect of the speaker's condition is captured in the "bag of green apples" metaphor (line 8)? What two meanings are suggested by the "stage" metaphor (line 7)? Why is the "train" metaphor (line 9) appropriate to the speaker's condition and the results of that condition?

MURIEL RUKEYSER   (1913–1980)

Looking at Each Other _____ *1978*

Yes, we were looking at each other
Yes, we knew each other very well
Yes, we had made love with each other many times
Yes, we had heard music together
Yes, we had gone to the sea together   5
Yes, we had cooked and eaten together
Yes, we had laughed often day and night
Yes, we fought violence and knew violence
Yes, we hated the inner and outer oppression
Yes, that day we were looking at each other   10
Yes, we saw the sunlight pouring down
Yes, the corner of the table was between us
Yes, bread and flowers were on the table
Yes, our eyes saw each other's eyes
Yes, our mouths saw each other's mouth   15
Yes, our breasts saw each other's breasts
Yes, our bodies entire saw each other
Yes, it was beginning in each
Yes, it threw waves across our lives
Yes, the pulses were becoming very strong   20
Yes, the beating became very delicate
Yes, the calling   the arousal
Yes, the arriving   the coming
Yes, there it was for both entire
Yes, we were looking at each other   25

QUESTIONS

1. What is the dramatic situation of the poem? What sort of listener is the speaker addressing?

2. Describe the rhetorical device at work here. How many different words are being repeated?

3. What is the effect of the repetitions? What is their relationship to the emotions and experiences that the speaker is describing?

WILLIAM SHAKESPEARE   (1564–1616)

Sonnet 18: Shall I Compare Thee to a Summer's Day? _____ *1609*

Shall I compare thee to a summer's day?	
Thou art more lovely and more temperate:	
Rough winds do shake the darling° buds of May,	*dear, cherished*
And summer's lease hath all too short a date:	
Sometime too hot the eye of heaven° shines	*the sun* 5
And often is his° gold complexion dimmed;	*its*
And every fair from fair sometime declines,	
By chance, or nature's changing course, untrimmed;	
But thy eternal summer shall not fade,	
Nor lose possession of that fair thou owest;°	*own, possess* 10
Nor shall Death brag thou wander'st in his shade,	
When in eternal lines to time thou growest:	
So long as men can breathe, or eyes can see,	
So long lives this, and this gives life to thee.	

QUESTIONS

1. What is the dramatic situation of the poem? Who is speaking to whom?

2. What do the metaphors in lines 1–8 assert? Why does the speaker emphasize life's brevity?

3. Describe the shift in topic beginning in line 9. How do these lines both deny and echo the subject of lines 1–8?

4. What relationship do the last two lines have to the rest of the poem? What is the meaning of "this" (line 14)? What sort of immortality does Shakespeare exalt in the sonnet?

WILLIAM SHAKESPEARE   (1564–1616)

Sonnet 30: When to the Sessions of Sweet Silent Thought _____ *1609*

When to the sessions° of sweet silent thought	*holding of court*
I summon° up remembrance of things past,	
I sigh the lack of many a thing I sought,	
And with old woes new wail my dear time's waste:°	
Then can I drown an eye (un-used to flow)	5
For precious friends hid in death's dateless° night,	*endless*

SONNET 30.   2 *summon:* to issue a summons to appear at a legal hearing.   4 *old woes . . . waste:* revive old sorrows about lost opportunities and express sorrow for them again.

And weep afresh love's long since canceled° woe,   *paid in full*
And moan th'expense° of many a vanished sight.   *cost, loss*
Then can I grieve at grievances foregone,
And heavily° from woe to woe tell° o'er   *sadly; count*   5
The sad account of fore-bemoanèd moan,
Which I new pay, as if not paid before.
   But if the while I think on thee (dear friend)
   All losses are restored, and sorrows end.

QUESTIONS

1. Explain the metaphor of "sessions" and "summon" in lines 1–2. Where are the "sessions" being held? What is a "summons" for remembrance?

2. What is the metaphor brought out by the word "canceled" in line 7? In what sense might a "woe" of love be canceled? Explain the metaphor of "expense" in line 8.

3. What type of transaction does Shakespeare refer to in the metaphor of lines 9–12? What understanding does the metaphor provide about the sadness and regret that a person feels about past mistakes and sorrows?

4. What role does the speaker assign to the "dear friend" of line 13 in relation to the metaphors of the poem?

WALT WHITMAN   (1819–1892)

Facing West from California's Shores ———————————————— *1860*

Facing west from California's shores,
Inquiring, tireless, seeking what is yet unfound,
I, a child, very old, over waves, towards the house of maternity,°
   the land of migrations, look afar,
Look off the shores of my Western sea, the circle almost circled;   5
For starting westward from Hindustan,° from the vales of Kashmir,
From Asia, from the north, from the God, the sage, and the hero,
From the south, from the flowery peninsulas° and the spice islands,°
Long having wandered since, round the earth having wandered
Now I face home again, very pleased and joyous.   10
(But where is what I started for so long ago?
And why is it yet unfound?)

FACING WEST FROM CALIFORNIA'S SHORES.   3 *house of maternity:* Asia, then considered the cradle of human civilization.   5 *Hindustan:* India.   7 *flowery peninsulas:* south India, south Burma, and the Malay peninsula.   7 *spice islands:* the Molucca Islands of Indonesia.

QUESTIONS

1. What major paradox, or apparently contradictory situation, is described in this poem? How does the poet bring out this paradox? What has the speaker been seeking? Where has he looked for it?

2.   Describe the meaning of the phrase "a child, very old"; "where is what I started for"; "the circle almost circled." In what ways are these phrases paradoxical?

3.   Why does the speaker twice use the word "unfound" (lines 2, 11)? How might the word be considered a theme of the poem?

WILLIAM WORDSWORTH   (1770–1850)

London, 1802 _____ *1807 (1802)*

Milton! thou should'st be living at this hour:
England hath need of thee: she is a fen°   *bog, marsh*
Of stagnant waters: altar, sword, and pen,
Fireside, the heroic wealth of hall and bower,
Have forfeited their ancient English dower°   *widow's inheritance*   5
Of inward happiness. We are selfish men;
Oh! raise us up, return to us again;
And give us manners,° virtue, freedom, power.
Thy soul was like a star, and dwelt apart:
Thou hadst a voice whose sound was like the sea: 10
Pure as the naked heavens, majestic, free,
So didst thou travel on life's common way,
In cheerful godliness; and yet thy heart
The lowliest duties on herself did lay.

LONDON, 1802.   8 *manners:* customs, moral modes of social and political conduct.

QUESTIONS

1.   What is the effect of Wordworth's apostrophe to Milton? What elements of Milton's career as a writer does Wordsworth emphasize?

2.   In lines 3 and 4, the device of metonymy is used. How does Wordsworth judge the respective institutions represented by the details?

3.   Consider the use of overstatement, or hyperbole, from lines 2–6. What effect does Wordsworth achieve by using the device as extensively as he does here?

4.   What effect does Wordsworth make through his use of overstatement in his praise of Milton in lines 9–14? What does he mean by the metonymic references to "soul" (line 9) and "heart" (line 13)?

SIR THOMAS WYATT   (1503–1542)

I Find No Peace _____ *1557*

I find no peace, and all my war is done,
   I fear and hope, I burn and freeze like ice;
   I fly above the wind yet can I not arise;
   And naught I have and all the world I season.

That looseth nor locketh holdeth me in prison,°   5
   And holdeth me not, yet I can scape° nowise;   *escape*
   Nor letteth me live nor die at my devise,°   *choice*
And yet of death it giveth none occasion.
Without eyen° I see, and without tongue I plain;°   *eyes*
   I desire to perish, and yet I ask health;   10
   I love another, and thus I hate myself;
I feed me in sorrow, and laugh in all my pain.
   Likewise displeaseth me both death and life°
   And my delight is causer of this strife.

I FIND NO PEACE.   5 *that . . . prison:* that is, "that which neither lets me go nor contains me holds me in prison." At the time of Wyatt, *-eth* was used for the third person singular present tense.   9 *plain:* express desires about love.   13 *likewise . . . life:* literally, "it is displeasing to me, in the same way, both death and life." That is, "both death and life are equally distasteful to me."

QUESTIONS

1.   What situation is the speaker reflecting upon? What metaphors and similes express his feelings? How successful are these figures?

2.   How many paradoxes are in the poem? What is their cumulative effect? What is the topic of the paradoxes in lines 1–4? In lines 5–8? Why does the speaker declare that hating himself is a consequence of loving another? Why is it ironic that his "delight" is the "causer of this strife"?

3.   To what extent do you think the paradoxes express the feelings of a person in love, particularly because in the sixteenth century, the free and unchaperoned meetings of lovers were not easily arranged?

WRITING ABOUT RHETORICAL FIGURES

Begin by determining the use, line by line, of metaphors, similes, or other rhetorical figures. Obviously, similes are the easiest figures to recognize because they introduce comparisons with the words *like* or *as.* Metaphors can be recognized because the topics are discussed not as themselves but as other topics. If the poems speak of falling leaves or law courts, for example, but the subjects are memory or increasing age, you are looking at metaphors. Similarly, if the poet is addressing an absent person or a natural object, or if you find clear double meanings in words, you may have apostrophe, personification, or puns.

Questions for Discovering Ideas

•   What figures does the work contain? Where do they occur? Under what circumstances? How extensive are they?

•   How do you recognize them? Are they signaled by a word or a few words, like "lead to gold " in Gay's "Let Us Take the Road," like "bows" in Campion's "Cherry Ripe," or are they more extensively detailed, as in Shakespeare's Sonnet 30, "When to the Sessions of Sweet Silent Thought"?

- How vivid are the figures? How obvious? How unusual? What kind of effort is needed to understand them in context?

- Structurally, how are the figures developed? How do they rise out of the situation? To what degree are the figures integrated into the poem's development of ideas? How do they relate to other aspects of the poem?

- Is one type of figure used in a particular section while another predominates in another? Why?

- If you have discovered a number of figures, what relationships can you find among them (such as the judicial and financial connections in Shakespeare's Sonnet 30)?

- How do they broaden, deepen, or otherwise assist in making the ideas in the poem forceful?

- In general, how appropriate and meaningful are the figures in the poem? What effect do the figures have on the poem's tone? On your understanding and appreciation of the poem?

Strategies for Organizing Ideas

For this essay, two types of compositions are possible. One is a full-scale essay. The other, because some rhetorical figures may occupy only a small part of the poem, is a single paragraph. Let us consider the single paragraph first.

1. *A paragraph.* For a single paragraph you need only one topic, such as the paradoxes of Wyatt's "I Find No Peace." The goal is to deal with the single figure and its relationship to the poem's main idea. Thus the essay should describe the figure and discuss its meaning and implications. It is important to begin with a comprehensive topic sentence, such as one that explains the cleverness of the puns in Gay's "Let Us Take the Road," or the use of synesthesia in Keats's "Ode to a Nightingale" (p. 636).

2. *A full-length essay.* One type of essay might examine just one figure, if the figure is pervasive enough in the poem to justify a full treatment. Most often, the poet's use of metaphors and similes is suitable for extensive discussion. This second type of essay might explore the meaning and effect of two or more figures, with the various parts of the body of the essay being taken up with each figure. The unity of this second kind of essay is achieved by the linking of a series of two or three different rhetorical devices to a single idea or emotion.

In the introduction, relate the quality of the figures to the general nature of the work. Thus, metaphors and similes of suffering might be appropriate to a religious, redemptive work, while those of sunshine and cheer might be right for a romantic one. If there is any discrepancy between the metaphorical language and the topic, you could consider that contrast as a possible central idea, for it would clearly indicate the writer's ironic perspective. Suppose that the topic of the poem is love, but the figures put you in mind of darkness and cold: What would the writer be saying about the quality of love? You should also try to justify any claims that you make about the figures. For example, one of the similes in Coleridge's "Kubla Khan" (p. 503) compares the sounds of a "mighty fountain" to the breathing of the earth in "fast thick pants." How is this simile to be taken? As a reference to the animality of the earth? As a suggestion that the fountain, and the earth, are dangerous? Or simply as a comparison suggesting immense, forceful noise? How do you explain your answer or answers? Your introduction is the place to establish ideas and justifications of this sort.

The following approaches for discussing rhetorical figures are not mutually exclusive, and you may combine them as you wish. Most likely, your essay will bring in most of the following classifications.

1. *Interpret the meaning and effect of the figures.* Here you explain how the figures enable you to make an interpretation. In the second stanza of "A Valediction: Forbidding Mourning," for example, the following metaphor equates love with hierarchical nomenclature of the church:

'Twere profanation of our joys
To tell the laity our love.

Here Donne emphasizes the mystical relationship of two lovers, drawing the metaphor from the religious tradition whereby any explanation of religious mysteries is considered a desecration. This interpretive approach is a direct one, requiring that metaphors, similes, or other figures be expanded and interpreted, including the explanation of necessary references and allusions.

2. *Analyze the frames of reference and their appropriateness to the subject matter.* Here you classify and locate the sources and types of the references and determine the appropriateness of these to the poem's subject matter. Ask questions similar to those you might ask in a study of imagery: Does the writer refer extensively to nature, science, warfare, politics, business, reading (e.g., Shakespeare's metaphor equating personal reverie with courtroom proceedings)? Does the metaphor seem appropriate? How? Why?

3. *Focus on the interests and sensibilities of the poet.* In a way this approach is like strategy 2, but the emphasis here is on what the selectivity of the writer might show about his or her vision and interests. You might begin by listing the figures in the poem and then determining the sources, just as you would do in discussing the sources of images generally. But then you should raise questions like the following: Does the writer use figures derived from one sense rather than another (i.e., sight, hearing, taste, smell, touch)? Does he or she record color, brightness, shadow, shape, depth, height, number, size, slowness, speed, emptiness, fullness, richness, drabness? Has the writer relied on the associations of figures of sense? Do metaphors and similes referring to green plants and trees, to red roses, or to rich fabrics, for example, suggest that life is full and beautiful, or do references to touch suggest amorous warmth? This approach is designed to help you draw conclusions about the author's taste or sensibility.

4. *Examine the effect of one figure on the other figures and ideas of the poem.* The assumption of this approach is that each literary work is unified and organically whole, so that each part is closely related and inseparable from everything else. Usually it is best to pick a figure that occurs at the beginning of the poem and then determine how this figure influences your perception of the rest of

the poem. Your aim is to consider the relationship of part to parts and part to whole. The beginning of Donne's "A Valediction: Forbidding Mourning," for example, contains a simile comparing the parting of the speaker and his listener to the quiet dying of "virtuous men." What is the effect of this comparison upon the poem? To help you with questions like this, you might substitute a totally different detail, such as, here, the violent death of a condemned criminal, or the slaughter of a domestic animal, rather than the deaths of "virtuous men." Such suppositions, which would clearly be out of place, may help you to understand and then explain the poet's rhetorical figures.

In your conclusion, summarize your main points, describe your general impressions, try to describe the impact of the figures, indicate your personal responses, or show what might further be done along the lines you have been developing. If you know other works by the same writer, or other works by other writers who use comparable or contrasting figures, you might explain the relationship of the other work or works to your present analysis.

SAMPLE STUDENT ESSAY

Wordsworth's Use of Overstatement in "London, 1802"°

Through overstatement in "London, 1802," William Wordsworth emphasizes his tribute to Milton as a master of idealistic thought. The speaker's claim that England is "a fen/Of stagnant waters" (lines 2–3) is overstated, as is the implication that people ("we") in England have no "manners, virtue, freedom, [or] power" (line 8). With the overstatements, however, Wordsworth implies that the nation's well-being depends on the constant flow of creative thoughts by persons of great ideas. Because Milton was clearly the greatest of these, in the view of Wordsworth's speaker, the overstatements stress the need for leadership. Milton is the model, and the overstated criticism lays the foundation in the real political and moral world for the rebirth of another Milton. Thus, through overstatement, Wordsworth emphasizes Milton's importance and in this way pays tribute to him.

Commentary on the Paragraph

This essay shows how a short paragraph can deal with a single rhetorical figure, in this case Wordsworth's overstatements in "London, 1802." Although most often the figure will be prominent, as this one is, prominence is not a requirement. In addition, there is no need to write an excessively long paragraph. The goal here is not to describe all the details of Wordsworth's overstatement, but to show how the figure affects his tribute to Milton. For this reason the paragraph shows the need for clear and direct support of the major point.

° See p. 535 for this poem.

SAMPLE STUDENT ESSAY

A Study of Shakespeare's Metaphors in Sonnet 30: "When to the Sessions of Sweet Silent Thought"°

[1]   In this sonnet Shakespeare's speaker stresses the sadness and regret of remembered experience, but he states that a person with these feelings may be cheered by the thought of a friend. His metaphors, cleverly used, create new and fresh ways of seeing personal life in this perspective.* He presents metaphors drawn from the public and business world of law courts, money, and banking or money-handling.†

[2]   The courtroom metaphor of the first four lines shows that memories of past experience are constantly present and influential. Like a judge commanding defendants to appear in court, the speaker "summon[s]" his memory of "things past" to appear on trial before him. This metaphor suggests that people are their own judges and that their ideals and morals are like laws by which they measure themselves. The speaker finds himself guilty of wasting his time in the past. Removing himself, however, from the strict punishment that a real judge might require, he does not condemn himself for his "dear time's waste," but instead laments it (line 4). The metaphor is thus used to indicate that a person's consciousness is made up just as much of self-doubt and reproach as of more positive qualities.

[3]   With the closely related reference of money in the next group of four lines, Shakespeare shows that living is a lifelong investment and is valuable for this reason. According to the money metaphor, living requires the spending of emotions and commitment to others. When friends move away and loved ones die, it is as though this expenditure has been lost. Thus, the speaker's dead friends are "precious" because he invested time and love in them, and the "sights" that have "vanished" from his eyes make him "moan" because he went to great "expense" for them (lines 6–8).

[4]   Like the money metaphor, the metaphor of banking or money-handling in the next four lines emphasizes that memory is a bank in which life's experiences are deposited. The full emotions surrounding experience are recorded there, and they can be withdrawn in moments of "sweet silent thought" just as a depositor can withdraw money. Thus the speaker states that he counts out the sad parts of his experience--his woe--just as a merchant or banker counts money: "And heavily from woe to woe *tell* o'er" (line 10). Because strong emotions still accompany his memories of past mistakes, the metaphor extends to borrowing and the payment of interest. The speaker thus says that he pays again with "new" woe the accounts that he had already paid with old woe. The metaphor suggests that the past is so much a part of the present that a person never stops feeling pain and regret.

[5]   The legal, financial, and money-handling metaphors combine in the last two lines to show how a healthy present life can overcome past regrets. The

---

° See p. 533 for this poem.
* Central idea.
† Thesis sentence.

"dear friend" being addressed in these lines has the resources (financial) to settle all the emotional judgments that the speaker as a self-judge has made against himself (legal). It is as though the friend is a rich patron who rescues him from emotional bankruptcy (legal and financial) and the possible doom resulting from the potential sentence of emotional misery and depression (legal).

[6]
In these metaphors, therefore, Shakespeare's references are drawn from everyday public and business actions, but his use of them is creative and unusual. In particular, the idea of line 8 ("And moan th'expense of many a vanished sight") stresses that people spend much emotional energy on others. Without such personal commitment, one cannot have precious friends and loved ones. In keeping with this metaphor of money and investment, one could measure life not in months or years, but in the spending of emotion and involvement in personal relationships. Shakespeare, by inviting readers to explore the values brought out by his metaphors, gives new insights into the nature and value of life.

Commentary on the Essay

This essay treats the three classes of metaphors that Shakespeare introduces in Sonnet 30. It thus illustrates strategy 2 described on page 538. But the aim of the discussion is not to explore the extent and nature of the comparison between the metaphors and the personal situations described in the sonnet. Instead the goal is to explain how the metaphors develop Shakespeare's meaning. This essay therefore also illustrates strategy 1 described on page 538.

In addition to providing a brief description of the sonnet, the introduction brings out the central idea and the thesis sentence. Paragraph 2 deals with the meaning of Shakespeare's courtroom metaphor. His money metaphor is explained in paragraph 3. Paragraph 4 considers the banking or money-handling figure. Paragraph 5 shows how Shakespeare's last two lines bring together the three strands of metaphor. The conclusion comments generally on the creativity of Shakespeare's metaphors, and it also amplifies the way in which the money metaphor leads toward an increased understanding of life.

Throughout the essay, transitions are brought about by the linking words in the topic sentences. In paragraph 3, for example, the words "closely related" and "next group" move the reader from paragraph 2 to the new content. In paragraph 4, the words effecting the transition are "like the money metaphor" and "the next four lines." The opening sentence of paragraph 5 refers collectively to the subjects of paragraphs 2, 3, and 4, thereby focusing them on the new topic of paragraph 5.

SPECIAL WRITING TOPICS FOR STUDYING RHETORICAL FIGURES IN POETRY

1. Study the similarity of the "stiff twin compasses" in Donne's "A Valediction: Forbidding Mourning." Using such a compass or a drawing of one, write an essay that demonstrates the accuracy of Donne's descriptions. What light does

the simile shed on the relationship of two lovers? How does it emphasize any or all of these aspects of love: closeness, immediacy, extent, importance, duration, intensity?

2. Consider some of the metaphors and similes in the poems included in this chapter. Write an essay that answers the following questions. How effective are the figures you select? (Examples: the bonsai tree [Piercy], the explosive [Hughes], the summer's day [Shakespeare].) What insights do the figures provide within the contexts of their respective poems? How appropriate are they? Might they be expanded more fully, and if they were, what would be the effect?

3. Consider some of the other rhetorical figures in the poems of this chapter. Write an essay describing the importance of figures in creating emphasis and in extending and deepening the ideas of poetry. A few topics might be
    *   Paradox in Wyatt's "I Find No Peace" or Whitman's "Facing West from California's Shores"
    *   The simile of the compass in Donne's "Valediction"
    *   Metaphor in Minty's "Conjoined" or Piercy's "A Work of Artifice."
    *   Anaphora in Rukeyser's "Yes, We Were Looking at Each Other"
    *   Similes in King's "Sic Vita" or Hughes's "Harlem"
    *   Personification in Wordsworth or Keats
    *   Metonymy in Keats's "To Autumn" or Nash's "Exit, Pursued by a Bear"

4. Write a poem in which you create a governing metaphor or simile. An example might be "My girl/boy friend is like (a) an opening flower, (b) a difficult book, (c) an insoluble mathematical problem, (d) a bill that cannot be paid, (e) a slow-moving chess game." Another example: "Teaching a person how to do a particular job is like (a) shoveling heavy snow, (b) climbing a mountain during a landslide, (c) having someone force you underwater when you're gasping for breath." When you finish, describe the relationship between your comparison and the development and structure of your poem.

5. In your library's reference section, find the third edition of J. A. Cuddon's *A Dictionary of Literary Terms and Literary Theory* (1991) or some other dictionary of literary terms. Study the entries for *metaphysical* and *conceit*, and write a brief report on these sections. You might attempt to answer questions like these: What is meant by *conceit?* What are some of the kinds of conceit the reference work discusses? What is a metaphysical conceit? Who are some of the writers considered metaphysical? Of what importance is John Donne in the *metaphysical* entry?

15

Tone:
The Creation of Attitude
in Poetry

Tone (see also Chapter 7), a term describing the shaping of attitudes in poetry, is borrowed from the phrase *tone of voice* that is often applied to the ways people speak in ordinary conversations (often as "I don't like your tone of voice"). In poetry, therefore, it is important to determine the speaker and the attitudes he or she expresses. How much self-awareness does the speaker show? What is his or her background? What relationship does the speaker establish with listeners and readers? What does the speaker assume about readers and about their knowledge? How do these assumptions affect the ideas and the choices of words?

Through the speaker, the poet shapes responses by controlling denotation and connotation, seriousness or humor, irony, metaphors, similes, understatement, overstatement, and other rhetorical figures. In a poem written in a conversational style there should be no formal words, just as in a more formal poem there should be no slang, no rollicking rhythms, and no frivolous rhymes—that is, unless the poet deliberately intends that readers be startled or shocked. The sentences must be just long enough to achieve the poet's intended effect—no shorter and no longer. In all the features that contribute to a poem's tone, the poet's consistency of intention is primary. Any unintentional deviations will cause the poem to sink and the poet to fail.

TONE, CHOICE, AND RESPONSE

Remember that a major objective of poets is to inform, enrich, inspire, and generally affect readers. Poets may begin their poems with a brief idea, a vague feeling, or a fleeting impression. Then, in the light of their developing design, they *choose* what to say—the form of their material and the words and phrases to express their ideas. The poem "Theme for English B" by Langston Hughes illustrates this process in almost outline form. Hughes's speaker lays out many interests that he shares with his intended reader, his English teacher. In this way Hughes enables all readers to accept his ideas of human equality.

In the long run, readers might not accept all the ideas in any poem, but the successful poem will have gained the reader's agreement—at least for a time—because the poet's control over tone will have been right. Each poem attempts to evoke *total* responses, which lapses in tone might destroy. Let us look at a poem in which the tone misses, and misses badly.

CORNELIUS WHUR   (1782–1853)

The First-Rate Wife _____ 1837

This brief effusion I indite,
    And my vast wishes send,
That thou mayst be directed right,
And have ere long within thy sight
    A most *enchanting* friend!   5

The *maiden* should have *lovely face*,
    And be of *genteel mien;*
If not, within thy dwelling place,
There may be vestige of disgrace,
    Not much admired—when seen.   10

Nor will thy dearest be complete
    Without *domestic* care;
If otherwise, howe'er discreet,
Thine eyes will very often meet
    What none desire to share!   15

And further still—thy future *dear*,
    Should have some *mental* ray;
If not, thou mayest drop a tear,
Because no *real sense* is there
    To charm life's dreary day!   20

QUESTIONS

1. What kind of person is the poem's speaker? The listener? What is the situation? What requirements does the speaker create for the "first-rate wife"?

2. Describe the poem's tone. How does the speaker's character influence the tone? In light of the tone, to what degree may the poem be considered insulting?

3. How might lines 14 and 15 be interpreted as a possible threat if the woman as a wife does not take care of the house?

In this poem the speaker is talking to a friend or associate and is explaining his requirements for a "first-rate wife." From his tone, he clearly regards getting married as little more than hiring a pretty housekeeper. In the phrase "some *mental* ray," for example, the word *some* does not mean "a great deal," but is more like "*at least* some," as though nothing more could be expected of a woman. Even allowing for the fact that the poem was written in the nineteenth century and represents a benighted view of women and marriage, "The First-Rate Wife" offends most readers. Do you wonder why you've never heard of Cornelius Whur before?

TONE IN CONVERSATION AND POETRY

Many readers think that tone is a subtle and difficult subject, but it is nevertheless true that in ordinary situations we master tone easily and expertly. We constantly use standard questions and statements that deal with tone, such as "What do you mean by that?" "What I'm saying is this . . . ," and "Did I hear you correctly?," together with other comments that extend to humor and, sometimes, to hostility. In poetry we do not have everyday speech situations; we have only the poems themselves and are guided by the materials they provide us. Some poems are straightforward and unambiguous, but in other poems feeling and mood are essential to our understanding. In Hardy's "The Workbox" (p. 548), for example, the husband's gift to his wife indicates not love but suspicion. Also, the husband's relentless linking of the dead man's coffin to the gift reveals his underlying anger. Pope, in the passage from the "Epilogue to the Satires" included in this chapter (p. 560), satirically describes deplorable habits and customs of his English contemporaries in the 1730s. His concluding lines (of the passage and also of the poem) punctuate his disapproval:

> Yet may this verse (if such a verse remain)
> Show there was one who held it in disdain.

The speaker on Ondaatje's "Late Movies with Skyler" (p. 558) describes how Skyler and he watch the late show. The activities described in the poem clearly establish a friendly and companionable bond between the two men. Poems of course may also reveal respect and wonder, as shown in the last six lines of Keats's "On First Looking into Chapman's Homer" (p. 518). By attending carefully to the details of such poems, you can draw conclusions about poetic tone that are as accurate as those you draw in normal speech situations.

TONE AND THE NEED FOR CONTROL

"The First-Rate Wife" demonstrates the need for the poet to be in control over all facets of the poem. The speaker must be aware of his or her situation and should not, like Whur's speaker, demonstrate any smugness or insensitivity, unless the poet is deliberately revealing the shortcomings of the speaker by dramatizing them for the reader's amusement, as e. e. cummings does in the poem "next to of course god america i" (p. 479). In a poem with well-controlled tone, details and situations should be factually correct; observations should be both logical and fair, within the poem's structure, and also comprehensive and generally applicable. The following poem illustrates a masterly control over tone.

WILFRED OWEN   (1893–1918)

Dulce et Decorum Est° _____ *1920*

Bent double, like old beggars under sacks,
Knock-kneed, coughing like hags, we cursed through sludge,
Till on the haunting flares we turned our backs
And towards our distant rest began to trudge.
Men marched asleep. Many had lost their boots   5
But limped on, blood-shod. All went lame; all blind;
Drunk with fatigue; deaf even to the hoots
Of tired, outstripped Five-Nines° that dropped behind.

Gas!° GAS! Quick, boys!—An ecstasy of fumbling,
Fitting the clumsy helmets° just in time;   10
But someone still was yelling out and stumbling
And flound'ring like a man in fire or lime . . .
Dim, through the misty panes and thick green° light,
As under a green sea, I saw him drowning.

In all my dreams, before my helpless sight,   15
He plunges at me, guttering, choking, drowning.

If in some smothering dreams you too could pace
Behind the wagon that we flung him in.
And watch the white eyes writhing in his face,
His hanging face, like a devil's sick of sin;   20
If you could hear, at every jolt, the blood
Come gargling from the froth-corrupted lungs,
Obscene as cancer, bitter as the cud
Of vile, incurable sores on innocent tongues.—
My friend, you would not tell with such high zest   25
To children ardent for some desperate glory,
The old Lie: Dulce et decorum est
Pro patria mori.

DULCE ET DECORUM EST.   The Latin title comes from Horace's *Odes*, book 3, line 13: *Dulce et decorum est pro patria mori* ("It is sweet and honorable to die for the fatherland").   8 *Five-Nines:* artillery shells that made a hooting sound just before landing.   9 *Gas:* Chlorine gas was used as an antipersonnel weapon in 1915 by the Germans at Ypres, in Belgium.   10 *helmets:* Soldiers carried gas masks as normal battle equipment.   13 *thick green:* The chlorine gas used in gas attacks has a greenish-yellow color.

QUESTIONS

1.   What is the scene described in lines 1–8? What expressions does the speaker use to indicate his attitude toward the conditions?

2.   What does the title of the poem mean? What attitude or conviction does it embody?

3. Does the speaker really mean "my friend" in line 25? In what tone of voice might this phrase be spoken?
4. What is the tonal relationship between the patriotic fervor of the Latin phrase and the images of the poem? How does the tonal contrast create the dominant tone of the poem?

The tone of "Dulce et Decorum Est" never lapses. The poet intends the description to evoke a response of horror, for he contrasts the strategic goals of warfare with the speaker's up-close experience of terror in battle. The speaker's language skillfully emphasizes first the dreariness and fatigue of warfare (with words like "sludge," "trudge," "lame," and "blind") and second the agony of violent death from chlorine gas (embodied in the participles "guttering," "choking," "drowning," "smothering," and "writhing"). With these details established, the concluding attack against the "glory" of war is difficult to refute, even if warfare is undertaken to defend or preserve one's country. Although the details about the agonized death may distress or discomfort a sensitive reader, they are not designed to do that alone, but instead are integral to the poem's argument. Ultimately, it is the contrast between the high ideals of the Latin phrase and the ugliness of battlefield death that creates the dominant tone of the poem. The Latin phrase treats war and death in the abstract; the poem makes images of battle and death vividly real. The resultant tone is that of controlled bitterness and irony.

TONE AND COMMON GROUNDS OF ASSENT

Not all those reading Owen's poem will deny that war is ever necessary. The issues of politics and warfare are far too complex for that. But the poem does show another important aspect of tone—namely, the degree to which the poet judges and tries to control responses through the establishment of a *common ground of assent.* An appeal to a bond of commonly held interests, concerns, and assumptions is essential if a poet is to maintain an effective tone. Owen, for example, does not create arguments against the necessity of a just war. Instead, he bases the poem upon realistic details about the writhing, spastic death suffered by the speaker's comrade, and he appeals to emotions that everyone, pacifist and militarist alike, would commonly feel—horror at the contemplation of violent death. Even assuming a widely divergent audience, in other words, the *tone* of the poem is successful because it is based on commonly acknowledged facts and commonly felt emotions. Knowing a poem like this one, even advocates of a strong military would need to defend their ideas on the grounds of *preventing* just such needless, ugly deaths. Owen wisely and carefully considers the responses of his readers, and he regulates speaker, situation, detail, and argument in order to make the poem acceptable for the broadest possible spectrum of opinion.

TONE AND IRONY

Irony is a mode of indirection, a means of making a point by emphasizing a discrepancy or opposite. Thus Owen uses the title "Dulce et Decorum Est" to emphasize that death in warfare is not sweet and honorable, but rather demeaning and horrible. The title ironically reminds us of eloquent holiday speeches at the tombs of unknown soldiers, but as we have seen, it also reminds us of the reality of the agonized death of Owen's soldier. As an aspect of tone, therefore, irony is a powerful way of conveying attitudes, for it draws your attention to at least two ways of seeing a situation, enabling you not only to *understand* but also to *feel.*

Situational Irony

Poetry shares with fiction and drama the various kinds of ironies that poets believe may afflict human life. "The Workbox," by Thomas Hardy, illustrates a skillful manipulation of irony.

THOMAS HARDY   (1840–1928)

The Workbox _____ *1914*

"See, here's the workbox, little wife,
    That I made of polished oak."
He was a joiner,° of village° life;   *cabinetmaker*
    She came of borough° folk.

He holds the present up to her   5
    As with a smile she nears
And answers to the profferer,
    "'Twill last all my sewing years!"

"I warrant it will. And longer too.
    'Tis a scantling° that I got   10
Off poor John Wayward's coffin, who
    Died of they knew not what.

"The shingled pattern that seems to cease
    Against your box's rim
Continues right on in the piece   15
    That's underground with him.

"And while I worked it made me think
    Of timber's varied doom:
One inch where people eat and drink,
    The next inch in a tomb.   20

THE WORKBOX.   4, 5 *village, borough:* A village was small and rustic; a borough was larger and more sophisticated.   10 *scantling:* a small leftover piece of wood.

"But why do you look so white, my dear,
    And turn aside your face?
You knew not that good lad, I fear,
    Though he came from your native place?"

"How could I know that good young man,   25
    Though he came from my native town,
When he must have left far earlier than
    I was a woman grown?"

"Ah, no. I should have understood!
    It shocked you that I gave   30
To you one end of a piece of wood
    Whose other is in a grave?"

"Don't, dear, despise my intellect.
    Mere accidental things
Of that sort never have effect   35
    On my imaginings."

Yet still her lips were limp and wan,
    Her face still held aside,
As if she had known not only John,
    But known of what he died.   40

QUESTIONS

1. Who does most of the speaking here? What does the speaker's tone show about
    the characters of the man and the wife? What does the tone indicate about the
    poet's attitude toward them?
2. What do lines 21–40 indicate about the wife's knowledge of John and about her
    earlier relationship with him? Why does she deny such knowledge? What does
    the last stanza show about her? Why is John's death kept a mystery?
3. In lines 17–20, what irony is suggested by the fact that the wood was used both
    for John's coffin and the workbox?
4. Why is the husband's irony more complex than he realizes? What do his words
    and actions show about his character?
5. The narrator, or poet, speaks only in lines 3–7 and 37–40. How much of his
    explanation is essential? How much shows his attitude? How might the poem
    have been more effectively concluded?

"The Workbox" is a domestic drama of deception, cruelty, and sadness.
The complex details are evidence of situational irony, that is, an awareness that
human beings do not control their lives but are rather controlled by powerful
forces—in this case by both death and earlier feelings and commitments.
Beyond this irony evolving out of the domestic scene, Hardy also emphasizes
symbolically the direct connection that death has with the living. As a result of
the husband's gift made of the wood with which he has also made a coffin for
the dead man, the wife will never escape being reminded of this man. Within

the life imagined in the poem, she will have to live with regret and the endless need to deny her true emotions.

Dramatic Irony

In addition to situational irony, the wife's deception reveals that the husband is in a situation of **dramatic irony.** The character understands one set of circumstances while the readers understand, in greater perspective, something completely different. In this poem, the husband does not know that the wife is not being truthful or open about her earlier relationship with the dead man. The tone of "The Workbox," however, suggests that the husband may be suspicious. By emphasizing the wood, he is apparently trying to draw her out. But he does not actually *know* the true circumstances, and hence he is unsure of his wife's attitude toward him. Because of this mixture of dramatic and situational irony, Hardy has created a poem of great complexity.

Verbal Irony

Poetry often contains **verbal irony,** that is, ambiguous language. For example, "she being Brand / -new" by e. e. cummings is filled with double meanings that develop from the terms used for the breaking in of a new car. Indeed, the entire poem is a virtuoso piece of double entendre. Another example of verbal irony is seen in Roethke's "My Papa's Waltz," in which the speaker uses the name of this orderly, stately dance to describe his childhood memories of his father's whirling him around the kitchen in wild, boisterous drunkenness.

TONE AND SATIRE

Satire, an important genre in the study of tone, is designed to expose human follies and vices. In method, a satiric poem may be bitter and vituperative, but often it employs humor and irony, on the grounds that anger turns readers away while a comic tone more easily wins agreement. The speaker of a satiric poem either may attack folly and vice *directly* or may dramatically *embody* the folly or vice, and thus serve as an illustration of the subject of satire. An example of the first type is the following short poem by Alexander Pope, in which the speaker directly attacks a listener who has claimed to be a poet, but whom the speaker considers a fool. The speaker cleverly uses insult as the tone of attack.

ALEXANDER POPE   (1688–1744)

Epigram from the French _____ *1732*

Sir, I admit your general rule
That every poet is a fool:
But you yourself may serve to show it,
That every fool is not a poet.

QUESTIONS

1. What has the listener said before the poem begins? How does the speaker build on the listener's previous comment?

2. Considering this poem as a brief satire, describe the nature of satiric attack and the corresponding tone of attack.

3. Look at the pattern "poet," "fool," "fool," "poet." This is a pattern (*a, b, b, a*) called *chiasmus* or *antimetabole*. What does the pattern contribute to the poem's effectiveness?

An example of the second type of satiric poem is another of Pope's epigrams, in which the speaker is an actual embodiment of the subject being attacked.

ALEXANDER POPE　(1688–1744)

Epigram. Engraved on the Collar of a Dog
which I Gave to His Royal Highness _____ *1738 (1737)*

I am his Highness' dog at Kew:°　　　　　　　　　　　　　*a royal palace near London*
Pray tell me sir, whose dog are you?

QUESTIONS

1. Who or what is the subject of the satiric attack?
2. What attitude is expressed in this poem toward class pretensions?

Here the speaker is the king's dog, and the listener an unknown dog. Pope's satire is directed not against canines, however, but against human pretentiousness based on class. The first line ridicules those who claim derived, not earned, status. The second implies an unwillingness to recognize the listener until the question of rank is resolved. Pope, by using the dog as a speaker, reduces such snobbishness to an absurdity. A similar satiric poem attacking pretentiousness is "next to of course god america i" by e. e. cummings (p. 479), where the speaker voices a set of patriotic platitudes, and in doing so illustrates cummings's satiric point that most speeches of this sort are empty-headed. Satiric tone may thus range widely, being sometimes objective, comic, and distant; sometimes deeply concerned and scornful; and sometimes dramatic, ingenuous, and revelatory. Always, however, the satiric mode aims toward confrontation and exposé.

 POEMS FOR STUDY

WILLIAM BLAKE   (1757–1827)

London _____ *1794*

I wander thro' each charter'd° street,
Near where the charter'd Thames does flow,
And mark in every face I meet
Marks of weakness, marks of woe.

In every cry of every Man,   5
In every Infant's cry of fear,
In every voice, in every ban,°   *public pronouncement*
The mind-forg'd manacles I hear.

How the Chimney-sweeper's cry
Every blackning Church appalls;°   10
And the hapless Soldier's sigh
Runs in blood down Palace walls.

But most thro' midnight streets I hear
How the youthful Harlot's curse
Blasts the new-born Infant's tear,   15
And blights with plagues the Marriage hearse.

LONDON.   1 *charter'd:* privileged, licensed, authorized.   10 *appalls:* weakens, makes pale,
shocks.

QUESTIONS

1. What does London represent to the speaker? How do the persons who live
    there contribute to the poem's ideas about the state of humanity?

2. What sounds does the speaker mention as a part of the London scene?
    Characterize these sounds in relation to the poem's main idea.

3. Because of the tension in the poem between civilized activity (as represented in the chartering of the street and the river) and free human impulses, explain how the poem might be considered revolutionary.

4. The poem appeared in *Songs of Experience*, published in 1794. Explain the appropriateness of Blake's including the poem in a collection so named.

ANNE BRADSTREET   (1612–1672)

The Author to Her Book _____ *1678*

Thou ill-formed offspring of my feeble brain,
Who after birth did'st by my side remain,
Till snatched from thence by friends, less wise than true,
Who thee abroad exposed to public view;
Made thee in rags, halting, to the press to trudge,   5
Where errors were not lessened, all may judge.
At thy return my blushing was not small,
My rambling brat° (in print) should mother call;
I cast thee by as one unfit for light,
Thy visage was so irksome in my sight;   10
Yet being mine own, at length affection would
Thy blemishes amend, if so I could:
I washed thy face, but more defects I saw,
And rubbing off a spot, still made a flaw.
I stretched thy joints to make thee even feet,°   *regular poetic meter*   15
Yet still thou run'st more hobbling than is meet;
In better dress to trim thee was my mind,
But nought save homespun cloth, in the house I find.
In this array, 'mongst vulgars may'st thou roam;
In critics' hands beware thou dost not come;   20
And take thy way where yet thou art not known.
If for thy Father asked, say thou had'st none;
And for thy Mother, she alas is poor,
Which caused her thus to send thee out of door.

THE AUTHOR TO HER BOOK.   8 *brat:* The word here emphasizes the insignificance rather than the unpleasant aspects of a child.

QUESTIONS

1. What is the tone of the speaker's references to those friends who "exposed" her book to "public view" (that is, circulated it without her consent)? How does this tone indicate her ambiguous feelings about them?

2. How does the speaker excuse the fact that she is issuing her book of poetry on her own initiative? How does the tone produce humor? How does the tone of the concluding metaphor encourage you to smile, or even to laugh?

3. What attitude toward herself does the speaker express? How do you react to this attitude? How do you think you are expected by the poet to react?

4. What is the tone of the extended metaphor of the child in lines 11–18?

LUCILLE CLIFTON   (b. 1936)

homage to my hips _____ *1987*

these hips are big hips
they need space to
move around in.
they don't fit into little
petty places. these hips   5
are free hips.
they don't like to be held back.
these hips have never been enslaved.
they go where they want to go.
they do what they want to do.   10
these hips are mighty hips.
these hips are magic hips.
i have known them
to put a spell on a man and
spin him like a top!   15

QUESTIONS

1. What is unusual about the subject matter? Considering that some people are embarrassed to mention their hips, what attitudes does the speaker express here?

2. How do the words "enslaved," "want to go," "want to do," "mighty," and "spell" define the poem's ideas about the relationship between mentality and physicality?

3. To what degree is this a comic poem? What about the subject and the diction makes the poem funny?

e. e. cummings   (1894–1962)

she being Brand / -new _____ *1926*

she being Brand

-new;and you
know consequently a
little stiff i was
careful of her and(having   5
thoroughly oiled the universal

joint tested my gas felt of
her radiator made sure her springs were O.
K.)i went right to it flooded-the-carburetor cranked her

up,slipped the   10
clutch(and then somehow got into reverse she
kicked what
the hell)next
minute i was back in neutral tried and

again slo-wly;bare,ly nudg. ing(my   15

lev-er Right-
oh and her gears being in

A 1 shape passed
from low through
second-in-to-high like   20
greasedlightning) just as we turned the corner of Divinity

avenue i touched the accelerator and give

her the juice,good

        (it
was the first ride and believe i we was   25
happy to see how nice she acted right up to
the last minute coming back down by the Public
Gardens i slammed on
the

internalexpanding   30
&
externalcontracting
brakes Bothatonce and

brought allofher tremB
-ling   35
to a:dead.

stand-
;Still)

QUESTIONS

1. How extensive is the verbal irony, the double entendre, in this poem? This
   poem is considered comic. Do you agree? Why or why not?

2. How do the spacing and alignment affect your reading of the poem? How does
   the unexpected and sometimes absent punctuation—such as in line 15, "again
   slo-wly;bare,ly nudg. ing(my"—contribute to the humor?

3. Can this poem in any respect be called off-color or bawdy? How might you
   refute such charges in light of the tone the speaker uses to equate a first sexual
   experience with the breaking in of a new car?

LANGSTON HUGHES   (1902–1967)

Theme for English B ————————————————————— *1959*

The instructor said,

> Go home and write
> a page tonight.
> And let that page come out of you—
> Then, it will be true.   5

I wonder if it's that simple?

I am twenty-two, colored, born in Winston-Salem.
I went to school there, then Durham, then here
to this college on the hill above Harlem.°
I am the only colored student in my class.   10
The steps from the hill lead down to Harlem,
through a park, then I cross St. Nicholas,
Eighth Avenue, Seventh, and I come to the Y,
the Harlem Branch Y, where I take the elevator
up to my room, sit down, and write this page: 15

It's not easy to know what is true for you or me
at twenty-two, my age. But I guess I'm what
I feel and see and hear. Harlem, I hear you:
hear you, hear me—we two—you, me talk on this page.
(I hear New York, too.) Me—who?   20

Well, I like to eat, sleep, drink, and be in love.
I like to work, read, learn, and understand life.
I like a pipe for a Christmas present,
or records—Bessie,° bop,° or Bach.°

I guess being colored doesn't make me not like   25
the same things other folks like who are other races.
So will my page be colored that I write?
Being me, it will not be white.
But it will be
a part of you, instructor.   30
You are white—
yet a part of me, as I am a part of you.
That's American.

Sometimes perhaps you don't want to be a part of me.
Nor do I often want to be a part of you.   35

THEME FOR ENGLISH B.   9 *college . . . Harlem:* a reference to Columbia University in the
Columbia Heights section of New York City. The other streets and buildings mentioned in lines
11–14 refer to specific places in the same vicinity.   24 *Bessie:* Bessie Smith (ca. 1898–1937),
American jazz singer, famed as the "Empress of the Blues."   *bop:* a type of popular music that
was in vogue in the 1940s through the 1960s.   *Bach:* Johann Sebastian Bach (1685–1750),
German composer, considered the master of the baroque style of music.

But we are, that's true!
As I learn from you,
I guess you learn from me—
although you're older—and white—
and somewhat more free.   40

This is my page for English B.

QUESTIONS

1.   What is the tone of the speaker's self-assessment? What does the tone indicate
     about his feelings toward the situation in the class and at the Y?

2.   What tone is implicit in the fact that the speaker, in response to a theme assign-
     ment, has composed a poem rather than a prose essay?

3.   What is the tone of lines 21–24, where the speaker indicates his likes? In what
     way can the characteristics brought out in these lines serve as an argument for
     social and political equality?

4.   How does the tone in lines 27–40, particularly lines 34–36, prevent the state-
     ments of the speaker from becoming overly assertive or strident?

X. J. KENNEDY   (b. 1929)

John while swimming in the ocean _____ *1986*

John while swimming in the ocean
Rubbed sharks' backs with suntan lotion.
Now those sharks have skin of bronze
In their bellies—namely, John's.

QUESTIONS

1.   What is the "action" of the poem? Why is it ludicrous?

2.   What do the rhymes contribute to the poem's comic tone?

3.   Describe the poem's attitude toward beach and ocean culture.

SHARON OLDS   (b. 1942)

The Planned Child _____ *1996*

I hated the fact that they had planned me, she had taken
a cardboard out of his shirt from the laundry
as if sliding the backbone up out of his body,
and made a chart of the month and put
her temperature on it, rising and falling   5

to know the day to make me—I would have
liked to have been conceived in heat,
in haste, by mistake, in love, in sex,
not on cardboard, the little x on the
rising line that did not fall again.   10

But when a friend was pouring wine
and said that I seem to have been a child who had been wanted,
I took the wine against my lips
as if my mouth were moving along
that valved wall in my mother's body, she was   15
bearing down, and then breathing from the mask, and then
bearing down, pressing me out into
the world that was not enough for her without me in it,
not the moon, the sun, Orion
cartwheeling across the dark, not   20
the earth, the sea—none of it
was enough, for her, without me.

QUESTIONS

1. Who is the speaker? What is she like? What is she talking about? Why does she
    begin the poem talking about something she hated?

2. What change of attitudes is described by the poem? Why does the poem seem
    to require such a change?

3. What attitude is expressed in the concluding global, planetary, solar, and stellar
    refrences? Why does the speaker state that, to her mother, she has more value
    than this image?

4. What unique qualities of perception and expression does the speaker exhibit?
    Have you ever read a poem before in which details about conception and child-
    birth have been so prominent? Why are these details included in this poem?

MICHAEL ONDAATJE   (b. 1943)

Late Movies with Skyler _____ *1979*

All week since he's been home
he has watched late movies alone
terrible one star films and then staggering
through the dark house to his bed
waking at noon to work on the broken car   5
he has come home to fix.

21 years old and restless
back from logging on Vancouver Island
with men who get rid of crabs with Raid

2 minutes bending over in agony   10
and then into the showers!

Last night I joined him for *The Prisoner of Zenda*
a film I saw three times in my youth
and which no doubt influenced me morally.
Hot coffee bananas and cheese   15
we are ready at 11.30 for adventure.

At each commercial Sky
breaks into midnight guitar practice
head down playing loud and intensely
till the movie comes on and the music suddenly stops.   20
Skyler's favourite hour's when he's usually alone
cooking huge meals of anything in the frying pan
thumbing through *Advanced Guitar* like a bible.
We talk during the film
and break into privacy during commercials   25
or get more coffee or push
the screen door open and urinate under the trees.

Laughing at the dilemmas of 1920 heroes
suggestive lines, cutaways to court officials
who raise their eyebrows at least 4 inches   30
when the lovers kiss . . .
only the anarchy of the evil Rupert of Hentzau°
is appreciated.
                    And still somehow
by 1.30 we are moved   35
as Stewart Granger° girl-less and countryless
rides into the sunset with his morals and his horse.
The perfect world is over. Banana peels
orange peels ashtrays guitar books.
2 a.m. We stagger through   40
into the slow black rooms of the house.

I lie in bed fully awake. The darkness
breathes to the pace of a dog's snoring.
The film is replayed to sounds
of an intricate blues guitar.   45
Skyler is Rupert then the hero.
He will leave in a couple of days
for Montreal or the Maritimes.
In the movies of my childhood the heroes
after skilled swordplay and moral victories   50
leave with absolutely nothing
to do for the rest of their lives.

LATE MOVIES WITH SKYLER.   32 *Rupert of Hentzau:* evil character in the *Prisoner of Zenda* (1952).
35 *Stewart Granger:* British actor (1913–1993) who appeared as the king in *The Prisoner of Zenda*.

QUESTIONS

1. What value does the speaker place on old movies? What details does he introduce to contrast the world of movies with the world around him? What effect do the activities during the commercials have on the value of the film to Skyler and the speaker?

2. Who is Skyler? Where has he been? What has he been doing? What will he be doing in the future? What is the speaker's attitude toward Skyler and his activities?

3. What comic details can you discover in the poem? What makes them comic? How does this humor affect the speaker's sympathy for Skyler and for himself?

4. Describe the tone of the last four lines. In what way are the lines relevant to Skyler and to the speaker? To what degree are these lines integral to the poem?

ALEXANDER POPE   (1685–1744)

From *Epilogue to the Satires, Dialogue I*
Lines 137–172 _____ *1738*

Virtue may choose the high or low degree,
'Tis just alike to Virtue, and to me;
Dwell in a monk, or light upon a king,
She's still the same, beloved, contented thing.   140
Vice is undone, if she forgets her birth,
And stoops from angels to the dregs of earth:
But 'tis the Fall degrades her to a whore;
Let Greatness own her, and she's mean no more:°
Her birth, her beauty, crowds and courts confess,°   145
Chaste matrons praise her, and grave bishops bless:
In golden chains the willing world she draws,
And hers the gospel is, and hers the laws:
Mounts the tribunal, lifts her scarlet head,
And sees pale Virtue carted° in her stead!   150
Lo! at the wheels of her triumphal car,°   *carriage*
Old England's genius, rough with many a scar,
Dragged in the dust! his arms hang idly round,
His flag inverted trails along the ground!°
Our youth, all liveried o'er with foreign gold,   155
Before her dance; behind her crawl the old!

EPILOGUE TO THE SATIRES, DIALOGUE I.   144 *mean no more:* i.e., if the rich and powerful follow vice, vice is no longer low, but fashionable.   145 *Her birth . . . confess:* i.e., Under the dictates of fashion, both crowds and courts claim that Vice is both high-born and beautiful. 150 *carted:* It was an eighteenth-century punishment to display prostitutes in a cart; in addition, condemned criminals were carried in a cart from prison to Tyburn, in London, where they were hanged.   152–4 *Old England's genius . . . along the ground:* i.e., the spirit of England is humiliated by being tied to Vice's triumphal carriage and then dragged along the ground. The idea is that corrupt politicians have sacrificed England's defensive power for their own gain.

See thronging millions to the pagod° run,
And offer country, parent, wife, or son!
Hear her black trumpet through the land proclaim,
That "not to be corrupted is the shame."   160
In soldier, churchman, patriot, man in power,
'Tis avarice all, ambition is no more!
See, all our nobles begging to be slaves!
See all our fools aspiring to be knaves!
The wit of cheats, the courage of a whore,   165
Are what ten thousand envy and adore.
All, all look up, with reverential awe,
On crimes that scape,° or triumph o'er the law: *escape*
While truth, worth, wisdom, daily they decry—
"Nothing is sacred now but villainy."   170
    Yet may this verse (if such a verse remain)
Show there was one who held it in disdain.

---

157 *pagod:* i.e., a pagoda, a symbol of how people have forsaken their own religion and adopted foreign religions.

QUESTIONS

1. The entire poem is in the form of a dialogue, in which these concluding lines are identified as being spoken by "P" (Pope). Should readers therefore take these lines as an expression of Pope's own ideas? In your answer, pay special attention to the final couplet.

2. Explain this poem as social satire. What is attacked? What evidence does the speaker advance to support his case that society has deserted virtue and religion?

3. Describe the poem's tone. What specific charges does the speaker make against the prevailing social-political structure?

4. How timely is the poem? To what degree might such charges be advanced in our society today?

AL PURDY   (b. 1918)

Poem _____ *1971*

You are ill and so I lead you away
and put you to bed in the dark room
—you lie breathing softly and I hold your hand
feeling the fingertips relax as sleep comes

You will not sleep more than a few hours   5
and the illness is less serious than my anger or cruelty
and the dark bedroom is like a foretaste of other darknesses
to come later which all of us must endure alone
but here I am permitted to be with you

After a while in sleep your fingers clutch tightly   10
and I know that whatever may be happening
the fear coiled in dreams or the bright trespass of pain
there is nothing at all I can do except hold your hand
and not go away

QUESTIONS

1. What is the dramatic situation of this poem? Who is speaking to whom? What is their relationship?

2. What is the condition of the speaker? Of the listener? What traits of character does the speaker exhibit?

3. Compare this poem to Hardy's "The Walk." In what ways are the situations similar? Different?

THEODORE ROETHKE   (1907–1963)

My Papa's Waltz _____ *1942*

The whiskey on your breath
Could make a small boy dizzy;
But I hung on like death:
Such waltzing was not easy.

We romped until the pans   5
Slid from the kitchen shelf;
My mother's countenance
Could not unfrown itself.

The hand that held my wrist
Was battered on one knuckle;   10
At every step you missed
My right ear scraped a buckle.

You beat time on my head
With a palm caked hard by dirt,
Then waltzed me off to bed   15
Still clinging to your shirt.

QUESTIONS

1. What is the tone of the speaker's opening description of his father? What is the tone of the phrases "like death" and "such waltzing"?

2. What is the "waltz" the speaker describes? What is the tone of his words describing it in lines 5–15?

3. What does the reference to his "mother's countenance" contribute to the tone? What situation is suggested by the selection of the word "unfrown"?

4. What does the tone of the physical descriptions of the father contribute to your understanding of the speaker's attitude toward his childhood experiences as his father's dancing partner?

JUDITH VIORST   (b. 1931)

True Love° _____ *1968*

It is true love because
I put on eyeliner and a concerto and make pungent observations about the great
    issues of the day
Even when there's no one here but him,
And because
I do not resent watching the Green Bay Packers   5
Even though I am philosophically opposed to football,
And because
When he is late for dinner and I know he must be either having an affair or lying dead
    in the middle of the street,
I always hope he's dead.

It's true love because   10
If he said quit drinking martinis but I kept drinking them and the next morning I
    couldn't get out of bed,
He wouldn't tell me he told me,
And because
He is willing to wear unironed undershorts
Out of respect for the fact that I am philosophically opposed to ironing,   15
And because
If his mother was drowning and I was drowning and he had to choose one of us to
    save,
He says he'd save me.

It's true love because
When he went to San Francisco on business while I had to stay home with the painters
    and the exterminator and the baby who was getting the chicken pox,   20
He understood why I hated him,
And because
When I said that playing the stock market was juvenile and irresponsible and then the
    stock I wouldn't let him buy went up twenty-six points,
I understood why he hated me,
And because   25
Despite cigarette cough, tooth decay, acid indigestion, dandruff, and other features of
    married life that tend to dampen the fires of passion,
We still feel something
We can call
True love.

TRUE LOVE.   See Shakespeare's *A Midsummer Night's Dream*, Act I, scene 1, line 132: "The course
of true love never did run smooth."

QUESTIONS

1. What does the poet mean by "true love"?
2. What situations described here are antiromantic? What importance do they
   have in the speaker's idea of the wife-husband relationship?

3.   What comic situations and statements does the poem contain? How do these elements contribute to the poem's tone and meaning?

4.   Explain why lines 2, 8, 11, 17, 20, 23, and 26 are the poem's longest lines. In what ways is the meaning of these lines contrasted with the meaning of the shorter lines?

DAVID WAGONER   (b. 1926)

My Physics Teacher _____ *1981*

He tried to convince us, but his billiard ball
Fell faster than his pingpong ball and thumped
To the floor first, in spite of Galileo.°
The rainbows from his prism skidded off-screen
Before we could tell an infra from an ultra.   5
His hand-cranked generator refused to spit
Sparks and settled for smoke. The dangling pith
Ignored the attractions of his amber wand,
No matter how much static he rubbed and dubbed
From the seat of his pants, and the housebrick
He lowered into a tub of water weighed   10
(Eureka!) more than the overflow.°

He believed in a World of Laws, where problems had answers,
Where tangible objects and intangible forces
Acting thereon could be lettered, numbered, and crammed
Through our tough skulls for lifetimes of homework.   15
But his only uncontestable demonstration
Came with our last class: he broke his chalk
On a formula, stooped to catch it, knocked his forehead
On the eraser-gutter, staggered slewfoot, and stuck
One foot forever into the wastebasket.   20

MY PHYSICS TEACHER.   3–12 *Galileo . . . overflow:* These lines describe classic classroom demonstrations in physics. Galileo first formulated the law of uniform falling bodies. Newton explained that a prism will divide light into the colors of the rainbow. ("Infra" refers to infrared light; "ultra" to ultraviolet.) Sparks leaping across the space between two wires graphically demonstrate electrical generation and power. The motion of dried pith toward a charged piece of amber demonstrates the magnetic power of static electricity. Archimedes explained how the weight of a floating object is the same as the weight of water it displaces, and also how the volume of an immersed object (not the weight) is the same as the volume of displaced water. The physics teacher did not understand this distinction. (According to legend, Archimedes made this discovery when taking a bath, and then shouted *"Eureka!"* ["I have found it"].)

QUESTIONS

1.   What idea underlies the physics teacher's use of classroom demonstrations? What is the speaker's apparent response to this idea?

2.   What happens to these demonstrations? Why are these failures comic and farcical? What effect do the poem's farcical actions have upon the validity of the teacher's ideas?

C.K. WILLIAMS   (b. 1936)

Dimensions _____ *1969*

There is a world somewhere else that is unendurable.
Those who live in it are helpless in the hands of the elements,
they are like branches in the deep woods in wind
that whip their leaves off and slice the heart of the night
and sob. They are like boats bleating wearily in fog.   5

But here, no matter what, we know where we stand.
We know more or less what comes next. We hold out.
Sometimes a dream will shake us like little dogs, a fever
hang on so we're not ourselves or love wring us out,
but we prevail, we certify and make sure, we go on.   10

There is a world that uses its soldiers and widows
for flour, its orphans for building stone, its legs for pens.
In that place, eyes are softened and harmless like God's
and all blend in the traffic of their tragedy and pass by
like people. And sometimes one of us, losing the way,   15
will drift over the border and see them there, dying,
laughing, being revived. When we come home, we are half way.
Our screams heal the torn silence. We are like scars.

QUESTIONS

  1. Why should this poem be called ironic? Should the irony be called situational?
      Cosmic? Why?
  2. What is intended by the poem's title? What is the implication of the first line?
      What irony does the line bring out? Describe the irony of the second stanza
      (lines 6–10).
  3. What is meant by "losing the way" and drifting " over the border" (lines 15–16)?
      What is the meaning and the irony of the last three lines? What does it mean to
      be "like scars" (line 18)?

WILLIAM WORDSWORTH   (1770–1850)

Composed upon Westminster Bridge, September 3, 1802 _____ *1807*

Earth has not any thing to show more fair:
Dull would he be of soul who could pass by
A Sight so touching in its majesty:
This City now doth, like a garment, wear
The beauty of the morning; silent, bare,   5
Ships, towers, domes, theatres, and temples lie
Open unto the fields, and to the sky;
All bright and glittering in the smokeless air.
Never did sun more beautifully steep

In his first splendour, valley, rock, or hill;
Ne'er saw I, never felt, a calm so deep!
The river glideth at his own sweet will:
Dear God! the very houses seem asleep;
And All that mighty heart is lying still!

QUESTIONS

1. What is the situation of the poem? Where is the speaker? What is he describing?
2. How is the poem organized?
3. What conclusions does the poem make about the London morning scene? How does the speaker make his attitudes clear?

WRITING ABOUT TONE IN POETRY

Be careful to note those elements of the work that touch particularly on attitudes or authorial consideration. Thus, for example, you may be studying Hughes's "Theme for English B," where it is necessary to consider the force of the poet's claim for equality. How serious is the claim? Does the speaker's apparent matter-of-factness make him seem less than enthusiastic? Or does this tone indicate that equality is so fundamental a right that its realization should be an everyday part of life? Devising and answering such questions can help you understand the degree to which authors show control of tone.

Similar questions apply when you study internal qualities such as style and characterization.

Questions for Discovering Ideas

- What is the speaker like? Is he or she intelligent, observant, friendly, idealistic, realistic, trustworthy? How do you think you should respond to the speaker's characteristics?

- Do all the speeches seem right for the speaker and situation? Are all descriptions appropriate, all actions believable?

- If the work is comic, at what is the comedy directed? At situations? At characters? At the speaker himself or herself? What is the poet's apparent attitude toward the comic objects?

- Does the writer ask you to (1) sympathize with those in misfortune, (2) rejoice with those who have found happiness, (3) lament the human condition, (4) become angry against unfairness and inequality, (5) admire examples of noble human behavior, (6) have another appropriate emotional response?

- Do any words seem unusual or especially noteworthy, such as dialect, polysyllabic words, foreign words or phrases that the author assumes you know, or especially connotative words? What is the effect of such words on the poem's tone?

Strategies for Organizing Ideas

The goal of your essay is to examine all aspects bearing on the tone. Some of the things to cover might be these:

1. *The audience, situation, and characters.* Is any person or group directly addressed by the speaker? What attitude is expressed (love, respect, condescension, confidentiality, confidence, etc.)? What is the basic situation in the work? What is the nature of the speaker or persona? What is the relationship of the speaker to the material? What is the speaker's authority? Does the speaker give you the whole truth? Is he or she trying to withhold anything? Why? How is the speaker's character manipulated to show apparent authorial attitude and to stimulate responses? Do you find any of the various sorts of irony? If so, what does the irony show (optimism or pessimism, for example)? How is the situation controlled to shape your responses? That is, can actions, situations, or characters be seen as expressions of attitude, or as embodiments of certain favorable or unfavorable ideas or positions? How does the work promote respect, admiration, dislike, or other feelings about character or situation?

2. *Descriptions, diction.* Your concern here is to relate style to attitude. Are there any systematic references, such as to colors, sounds, noises, natural scenes, and so on, that collectively reflect an attitude? Do connotative meanings of words control response in any way? Is any special knowledge of references or unusual words expected of readers? What is the extent of this knowledge? Do speech or dialect patterns indicate attitudes about speakers or their condition of life? Are speech patterns normal and standard, or slang or substandard? What is the effect of these patterns? Are there unusual or particularly noteworthy expressions? If so, what attitudes do these show? Does the author use verbal irony? To what effect?

3. *Humor.* Is the work funny? How funny, how intense? How is the humor achieved? Does the humor develop out of incongruous situations or language, or both? Is there an underlying basis of attack in the humor, or are the objects of laughter still respected or even loved despite having humor directed against them?

4. *Ideas.* Ideas may be advocated, defended mildly, or attacked. Which is present in the work you have been studying? How does the author make his or her attitude clear—directly, by statement, or indirectly, through understatement, overstatement, or the language of a character? In what ways does the work assume a common ground of assent between author and reader? That is, are there apparently common assumptions about religious views, political ideas, moral and behavioral standards, and so on? Are these common ideas readily acceptable, or is any concession needed by the reader to approach the work? (For example, a major subject of "Dover Beach" is that absolute belief in the truth of Christianity has been lost. This subject may not be important to everyone, but even an irreligious reader, or a follower of another faith, may find common ground in the poem's psychological situation, or in the desire to learn

as much as possible about so important a phenomenon of modern Western society.)

5. *Unique characteristics.* Each work has unique properties that contribute to the tone. Anne Bradstreet, for example, in "The Author to Her Book," introduces the metaphor that her work is like an unwanted child whom she is sending out into the world. Her apology hence introduces a tone of amused but sincere self-effacement that the reader must consider. Theodore Roethke's "My Papa's Waltz" is a brief narrative in which the speaker's recollected feelings about his father's boisterously drunken behavior must be inferred from understatement like "waltz." Hardy's "Channel Firing" develops from the comic idea that the firing of guns at sea is so loud it could awaken the dead. Be alert for such special circumstances in your poem, and as you plan and develop your essay, take them into account.

Your conclusion may summarize your main points and from there go on to any needed definitions, explanations, or afterthoughts, together with ideas reinforcing earlier points. If you have changed your mind or have made new realizations, briefly explain these. Finally, you might mention some other major aspect of the work's tone that you did not develop in the body.

SAMPLE STUDENT ESSAY

The Shifting Attitudes of Sharon Olds's Speaker in "The Planned Child"°

[1]   "The Planned Child" is a striking and unusual poem because in it Sharon Olds deals so frankly with her speaker's concern about the circumstances of her conception and birth. Few people ever learn about how they were conceived, and even fewer ever think about it enough to criticize it, and yet the poem's details concern this topic. As unusual as such details are, however, the poem's power results from the way the speaker traces the development of her attitudes toward her origins--from hate, to uncertainty, to acceptance.* These attitudes can be traced in the poem's two stanzas, its ordinary diction, and the way its use of the first-person pronoun indicates the speaker's importance.†

[2]   Olds's first stanza contrasts the speaker's hatred for planning and organization with a preference for disorganization. The stanza is arresting, if not shocking, because in it the speaker goes into the past to describe her feelings about how her mother calculated ovulation times to ensure conception. Rather than finding it humorous that she owes her existence to the chart her mother made on a laundry cardboard, the speaker says she hated this planned record keeping. She explains this attitude because the planning, to her way of thinking, reduced her to little more than an *X* on a rising graph line and by implication, therefore, it seemed cold and impersonal. From the description the speaker makes of conception in lines 7 and 8, it would seem that spontaneous and disorganized love

° See p. 557 for this poem.
* Central idea.
† Thesis sentence.

by her parents would have created a warmer, more welcoming reason for her existence.

[3] The second stanza is continuous with the first because it stems out of feelings occasioned by an unplanned but significant moment. A friend serves wine to the speaker and tells her that she seems to have been "a child who had been *wanted*" (line 12, italics added). This casual social event is symbolic (is it a kind of communion experience?) because it gives the speaker a life-giving insight into her existence. The conclusion of the poem is then devoted to the speaker's newly created feelings of involvement with her mother. She finds affection for her mother in the details of childbirth--bearing down, breathing, pressing, and the creation of the speaker herself. The poem's climax is the speaker's apparently amazed realization that she herself was actually *wanted*. The *X* on the graph therefore was a means of achieving a far greater goal, for her mother valued her more than the world or the galaxy. As the speaker imagines her mother's life-giving act, she imagines how loving it was, and therefore she senses how vitally important she is.

[4] With such an unusual topic, one might expect a fair amount of abstract and medical diction, but such is not the case. Most of the words are flat and ordinary (e.g., "a friend was pouring wine"). Despite their simplicity, however, the diction confronts readers with direct physical details of planned conception and the labor of childbirth. The speaker refers matter-of-factly to a temperature chart, the birth canal, and breathing into a mask and bearing down during labor. Of major note is the intensity that Olds achieves through the selection of simple but strong verbs and verbals ("hated," "planned," "had taken," "sliding," "make," "pouring," "were moving," "bearing down," "breathing," "pressing," and "cartwheeling"). All these words fit the poet's aim to connect with one of life's most basic facts--being conceived and delivered.

[5] As this basic detail indicates, the central figure of the poem is the speaker and her attitudes. This centrality is emphasized by the frequent use of the first-person pronoun throughout the poem. A form of the pronoun appears twelve times, and the poem begins with "I" and concludes with "me." This number may not seem high in a personal poem of twenty-two lines, but it is high enough to support the idea that the poem is about attitudes toward self-realization. The poem explores some vital personal questions: Could the speaker love herself knowing that she was planned and not spontaneous? Not when these calculations seemed to result from nothing more than cold science. But could she love herself after learning that the calculations were preceded by love for her? Yes, and as a result the speaker makes inferences from this new information. She imagines that nothing in the world was more important to her mother than she. She therefore has more value than the earth and stars themselves, and this vision closes the poem on a strongly positive and affirmative note:

> not the moon, the sun, Orion
> cartwheeling across the dark, not
> the earth, the sea--none of it
> was enough, for her, without me. (lines 20-22)

[6] Thus, an examination of "The Planned Child" reveals both the need and difficulty of self-understanding. The poem is a confession of changing attitudes in

the light of a growing sense of personal origin. Olds makes this point through the commonness and universality of details about birth. Yet the poem is not personal or egocentric because it is about the need of discovering who one is. Without this knowledge the poem's speaker is uncertain and hostile. But once she can see that she is part of a pattern of love and creativity, she becomes positive and assertive. "The Planned Child" shows the growth of confidence resulting from increased knowledge and awareness.

Commentary on the Essay

Because this essay embodies a number of approaches by which tone may be studied in any work (situation, diction, special characteristics), it is typical of many essays that use a combined approach. The central idea, expressed in the first paragraph, is that the dominant attitudes in "The Planned Child" are the speaker's change from hostility to certainty.

Paragraph 2 considers the poem's first section, in which the speaker explains why a preference for spontaneity caused her initial hatred of how she came into being (see strategy 4, p. 567). Paragraph 3 shows how the explanation of a unique situation can be seen as a feature of tone (strategy 5). The paragraph pursues the speaker's thoughts that develop from an unexpected comment from a friend. In this sense, a casual moment explains how the speaker's relative confusion shifts to the greater self-confidence and acceptance of her mother's labors to bring her into the world.

Paragraph 4 concerns the poem's treatment of the unusual subject matter through comparatively simple diction (strategy 1). Words in the paragraph that indicate attitudes are "confronts," "matter-of-factly," "intensity," and "desire." Paragraph 5 considers how Olds's use of the first-person pronoun fits into the poem's recognition of the speaker's importance (strategy 2). The paragraph asserts that the poem's positive conclusion is augmented by images on a planetary, solar, galactic, geographic, and marine scale (strategy 5).

The concluding paragraph points out that the speaker's concern with her origins is not simply a matter of egocentrism, but rather results from her need to connect with an attitude that is more human and loving than the act of planning might seem to convey.

SPECIAL WRITING TOPICS FOR STUDYING TONE IN POETRY

1. Consider "homage to my hips," "she being Brand / -new," "The Workbox," and "The First-Rate Wife" as poems about love. What similarities do you find? That is, do the poets state that love creates joy, satisfaction, distress, embarrassment, trouble? How does the tone of each of the poems enable you to draw your conclusions? What differences do you find in the ways the poets either control or do not control tone?

2. Consider these same poems from a feminist viewpoint (see Chapter 27). What importance and value do the poems give to women? How do they view women's actions? Generally, what praise or blame do the poems deserve because of their treatment of women?

3. a. Consider the tone of "My Papa's Waltz." Some readers have concluded that the speaker is expressing fond memories of his childhood experiences with his father. Others believe that the speaker is ambiguous about the father, and that he blocks out remembered pain as he describes the father's boisterousness in the kitchen. Basing your conclusion from the tone of the poem alone, how should the poem be interpreted?

    b. In your library, find two critical biographies about Theodore Roethke published by university presses. What do these books disclose about Roethke's childhood and his family, particularly his father? On the basis of what you learn, should your interpretation of the tone of "My Papa's Waltz" be changed or unchanged? Why?

4. Write a poem about a person or occasion that has made you either glad or angry. Try to create the same feelings in your reader, but create these feelings through your rendering of situation and your choices of the right words. (Possible topics: a social injustice, an unfair grade, a compliment you have received on a task well done, the landing of a good job, the winning of a game, a rise in the price of gasoline, a good book or movie, and so on.)

5. Consider the judgments about city life that you find in Blake's "London" (p. 552), Field's "Icarus" (p. 699), Sandburg's "Chicago" (p. 794), and Wordsworth's "Earth Hath Not Anything to Show More Fair" (p. 565)— together with any other poems you wish to include. What details do the poets include to demonstrate their attitudes? What levels of diction do they presesnt? How are attitudes controlled through word choices?

6. Describe the relationship between idea and tone in Williams's "Dimensions." What is the poem's major idea? Of what importance is irony in the development of the poem? If one grants that there may be ambiguity in the poem, how does Williams make his ideas clear?

16

Prosody: Sound, Rhythm,
and Rhyme in Poetry

Prosody (the pronunciation of a song or poem) is the general word describing the study of poetic sounds and rhythms. Common alternative words are **metrics, versification, mechanics of verse,** and **music of poetry.** Most readers, when reading poetry aloud, interpret the lines and develop an appropriate speed and expressiveness of delivery—a proper *rhythm.* Indeed, some people think that rhythm and sound are the *music* of poetry because they convey musical rhythms and tempos. Like music, poetry often requires a regular beat. The tempo and loudness may vary freely, however, and a reader may stop at any time to repeat the sounds and to think about the words and ideas.

It is important to recognize that poets, being especially attuned to language, blend words and ideas together so that "the sound" becomes "an echo to the sense" (Pope). Readers may therefore accept as a rule that *prosodic technique cannot be separated from a poem's content.* For this reason, the study of prosody aims at determining how poets have controlled their words so that the sound of a poem complements its expression of emotions and ideas.

IMPORTANT DEFINITIONS FOR STUDYING PROSODY

To study prosody you need a few basic linguistic facts. Individual sounds in combination make up syllables and words, and separate words in combination make up lines of poetry. Syllables and words are made up of **segments,** or individually meaningful sounds (*segmental phonemes*). In the word *top* there are three segments: *t, o,* and *p.* When you hear these three sounds in order, you recognize the word *top.* It takes three alphabetical letters—*t, o,* and *p*—to spell (or *graph*) *top,* because each letter is identical with a segment. Sometimes, however, it takes more than one letter to spell a segment. For example, in the word *enough* there are four segments (*e, n, u, f*), although six letters are required for the correct spelling: *e, n, ou,* and *gh.* The last two segments (*u* and *f*) require two letters each (two letters forming one segment are called a *digraph*). In the word *through* there are three segments but *seven* letters. To be correctly spelled in this word, the *oo* segment must have four letters (*ough*). Note, however, that in the word *flute* the *oo* segment requires only one letter, *u.* When we study the effects of various segments in relationship to the poetic rhythm, we deal with **sound;** usually our concern is with prosodic devices such as **alliteration, assonance,** and **rhyme.**

When segments are meaningfully combined, they make up syllables and words. A **syllable,** in both prose and poetry, consists of a single meaningful strand of sound such as the article *a* in "*a* table," *lin* in "*lin*en," and *flounce* in "the little girls *flounce* into the room." (The article *a,* which is both a syllable and a word, has only one segment; *lin,* the first syllable of a two-syllable word (*lin* never occurs alone—it is always used in combinations such as *lingerie* and *linoleum*), contains three segments; *flounce* is a word of one syllable consisting of six segments: *f, l, ow, n, t,* and *s*). The understanding of what constitutes syllables is important because the rhythm of most poetry is determined by the measured relationship of heavily stressed to less heavily stressed syllables.

SOUND AND SPELLING

It is important—vital—to distinguish between spelling, or **graphics,** and pronunciation, or **phonetics.** Not all English sounds are spelled and pronounced in the same way, as with *top.* Thus the letter *s* has three very different sounds in the words *sweet, sugar,* and *flows: s, sh* (*sh*arp), and *z.* On the other hand, the words *shape, ocean, nation, sure, fissure, Eschscholtzia,* and *machine* use different letters or combinations of letters to spell the same *sh* sound.

Vowel sounds may also be spelled in different ways. The *e* sound, for example, can be spelled *i* in *machine, ee* in *speed, ea* in *eat, e* in *even,* and *y* in *funny,* yet the vowel sounds in *eat, break,* and *bear* are not the same even though they are spelled the same. Remember this: With both consonants and vowel sounds, *do not confuse spellings with sounds.*

RHYTHM

Rhythm in speech is a combination of vocal speeds, rises and falls, starts and stops, vigor and slackness, and relaxation and tension. In ordinary speech and in prose, rhythm is not as important as the flow of ideas. In poetry, rhythm is significant because poetry is so emotionally charged, compact, and intense. Poets invite us to change speeds while reading—to slow down and linger over some words and sounds, and to pass rapidly over others. They also invite us to give more-than-ordinary vocal stress or emphasis to certain syllables and less stress to others. The more intense syllables are called **heavy stress** syllables, and it is the heavy stresses that determine the **accent** or **beat** of a poetic line. The less intense syllables receive **light stress.** In traditional verse, poets select patterns called **feet,** which consist of a regularized relationship of heavy stresses to light stresses.

Rhythm and Scansion

To study the patterns of versification in any poem, you **scan** the poem. The act of scanning—**scansion**—enables you to discover how the poem establishes a prevailing metrical pattern, and also how and why there are variations in the pattern.

RECORDING STRESSES OR BEATS.   In scansion, it is important to use a commonly recognized notational system to record stresses or accents. A *heavy* or *primary* stress (also called an **accented syllable**) is commonly indicated by a prime mark or acute accent (´). A *light* stress (also called an **unaccented syllable**) is indicated by a bowl-like half circle called a **breve** (˘) or sometimes by a raised circle or degree sign (°). To separate one foot from another, a **virgule** or slash (/) is used. Thus, the following line, from Coleridge's "The Rime of the Ancient Mariner," is schematized formally in this way:

Wă - tĕr, / wă - tĕr, / ĕv - erў whére, /

Here the virgules show that the line contains two two-syllable feet followed by a three-syllable foot.

RECORDING THE METER OR MEASURE.   Another important part of scansion is the determination of a poem's **meter,** or the number of feet in its lines. Lines containing five feet are **pentameter,** four are **tetrameter,** three are **trimeter,** two are **dimeter,** and one is **monometer.** (To these may be added the less common line lengths **hexameter,** a six-foot line; **heptameter** or **the septenary,** seven feet; and **octameter,** eight feet.) In terms of accent or beat, a trimeter line has three beats (heavy stresses), a pentameter line five beats, and so on.

Metrical Feet

Equipped with this knowledge, you are ready to scan poems and determine the rhythmical patterns of feet. The most important ones, the specific names of which are derived from Greek poetry, are the two-syllable foot, the three-syllable foot, and the one-syllable (or imperfect) foot.

THE TWO-SYLLABLE FOOT.
1. **The iamb.** The most important two-syllable foot in English is the **iamb,** which contains a light stress followed by a heavy stress:

thĕ winds

The iamb is the most common foot in English poetry because it most nearly duplicates natural speech while also elevating speech to poetry. It is the most versatile of English poetic feet, and it is capable of great variation. Even within the same line, iambic feet may vary in intensity, so that they may support or undergird the shades of meaning designed by the poet. For example, in this line of iambic pentameter from Wordsworth ("The World Is Too Much with Us"), each foot is unique:

The winds / that will / be howl- / ing at / all hours, /

Even though "will" and "at" receive the heavy stress in their individual iambic feet, they are not as strongly emphasized as "winds," "howl-," and "hours" (indeed, they are also less strong than "all," which is in the light-stress position in the concluding iamb). Such variability, approximating the stresses and rhythms of actual speech, makes the iamb suitable for both serious and light verse, and it therefore helps poets focus attention on ideas and emotions. If they use it with skill, it never becomes monotonous, for it does not distract readers by drawing attention to its own rhythm.

    2. **The trochee.** The trochee consists of a heavy accent followed by a light:

flow - er

Rhythmically, most English words are trochaic, like *water, snowfall, author, willow, morning, early, follow, singing, window,* and *something.* A major exception is seen in two-syllable words beginning with prefixes, such as *sublime, because,* and *impel.* Another exception is found in two-syllable words that are borrowed from another language but are still pronounced as in the original language, as with *machine, technique, garage,* and *chemise,* all of which are French importations. To see the strength of the trochaic tendency in English, French words borrowed six hundred or more years ago have lost their original iambic structure and have become trochaic, as with *language, very, nation,* and *cherry.*

    Because trochaic rhythm has often been called *falling, dying, light,* or *anticlimactic,* while iambic rhythm is *rising, elevating, serious,* and *climactic,* poets have preferred the iambic foot. They therefore have arranged various placements of single and multiple-syllable words, and have used a variety of other means, so that the heavy-stress syllable is at the end of the foot, as in Shakespeare's

With-in / his bend - / ing sick - /le's com - / pass come; /

in which three successive trochaic words are arranged to match the iambic meter.

    3. **The spondee.** The **spondee**—also called a **hovering accent**—consists of two successive, equally heavy accents, as in "men's eyes" in Shakespeare's line:

When, in / dis -grace / with For - / tune and / men's eyes, /

The spondee is mainly a substitute foot in English verse because successive spondees usually become iambs or trochees. An entire poem written in spondees would be unlikely within traditional metrical patterns and ordinary

English syntax (but see Brooks's poem "We Real Cool," p. 586). As a substitute, however, the spondee creates emphasis. The usual way to indicate the spondaic foot is to link the two syllables together with chevronlike marks ( ), like this:

$$\bigwedge$$
men's eyes

4. The pyrrhic. The pyrrhic foot consists of two unstressed syllables (even though one of them may be in a normally stressed position), as in "on their" in Pope's line:

Now sleep - / ing flocks / on their / soft fleec - /es lie. /

The pyrrhic is made up of weakly accented words such as prepositions (e.g., *on, to*) and articles (*the, a*). Like the spondee, it is usually substituted for an iamb or trochee, and therefore a complete poem cannot be in pyrrhics. As a substitute foot, however, the pyrrhic acts as a rhythmic catapult to move the reader swiftly to the next heavy-stress syllable, and therefore it undergirds the ideas conveyed by more important words.

THE THREE-SYLLABLE FOOT.
1. **The anapest.** The anapest consists of two light accents followed by a heavy accent:

by the dawn's / ear-ly light.   (Key)

2. **The dactyl.** The dactylic foot has a heavy stress followed by two lights:

green as our / hope in it, / white as our/ faith in it. /   (Swinburne)

THE IMPERFECT FOOT.   The imperfect foot consists of a single stressed syllable (´) by itself or an unstressed syllable (˘) by itself. This foot is a variant or substitute occurring in a poem in which one of the major feet forms the metrical pattern. The second line of Key's "The Star-Spangled Banner," for example, is anapestic, but it contains an imperfect foot at the end:

What so proud -/ly we hailed/at the twi-/light's last gleam-/ing. /

SPECIAL METERS

In many poems you will find meters other than those described above. Poets like Browning, Tennyson, Poe, and Swinburne introduce special or unusual meters. Other poets manipulate pauses or **caesurae** (discussed later) to create the effects of unusual meters. For these reasons, you should know about metrical feet such as the following:

continued

1. **Amphibrach.** A light, heavy, and light:

    Ah feed me / and fill me / with pleas - sure. (Swinburne)

2. **Amphimacer or Cretic.** A heavy, light, and heavy:

    Love is best. (Browning)

3. **Bacchius or Bacchic.** A light stress followed by two heavy stresses:

    Some late lark / [sing -ing]. (Henley)

4. **Dipodic measure, or Syzygy.** Dipodic measure (literally, "two feet" combining to make one) develops in longer lines when a poet submerges two regular feet under a stronger beat, so that a "galloping" or "rollicking" rhythm results. The following line from Masefield's "Cargoes," for example, can be scanned as trochaic hexameter, with the concluding foot being an iamb:

    Quin-que- / reme of / Nin-e- / veh from / dis-tant / O-phir,

    In reading, however, a stronger beat is superimposed, which makes one foot out of two—dipodic measure or syzygy:

    Quin-que-reme of / Nin-e veh from / dis-tant Ophir,

Other Rhythmic Devices

ACCENTUAL, STRONG-STRESS, AND "SPRUNG" RHYTHMS.   Accentual or strong-stress lines are historically derived from the poetry of Old English (see p. 447). At that time, each line was divided in two, with two major stresses, also alliterated, occurring in each half. In the nineteenth century, Gerard Manley Hopkins (1844–1889) developed what he called "sprung" rhythm, a rhythm in which the major stresses would be released or "sprung" from the line. The method is complex, but one characteristic is the juxtaposing of one-syllable stressed words, as in this line from "Pied Beauty":

With swift, slow; sweet, sour; adazzle, dim;

Here a number of elements combine to create six major stresses. Many of Hopkins's lines combine alliteration and strong stresses in this way to create the same effect of heavy emphasis.

A parallel instance of strongly stressed lines is seen in "We Real Cool" by Brooks. In this poem the effect is achieved by the exclusive use of monosyllabic stressed words combined with internal rhyme, repetition, and alliteration.

THE CAESURA, OR PAUSE.   Whenever we speak, we run our words together rapidly, without pause. We do, however, stop briefly and almost unnoticeably between significant units or phrases. These significant units, both grammatically and rhythmically, are **cadence groups.** In poetry that emphasizes a regular meter, the cadence groups operate just as they do in prose to make the ideas intelligible. Although we are following the poetic rhythm, we also pause briefly at the ends of phrases and make longer pauses at the ends of sentences. In scansion, the name of these pauses, which linguists call *junctures,* is **caesura** (plural **caesurae**). When scanning a line, we note a caesura with two diagonal lines or virgules (//) so that the caesura can be distinguished from the single virgule separating feet. Sometimes the caesura coincides with the end of a foot, as at the end of the second iamb in this line by William Blake ("To Mrs. Anna Flaxman"):

With hands / di- vine // he mov'd / the gen - / tle Sod. /

The caesura, however, may fall within a foot, and there may be more than one in a line, as within the second and third iambs in this line by Ben Jonson:

Thou art / not, // Pens - / hurst, // built / to en - / vious show. /

When a caesura ends a line, usually marked by a comma, semicolon, or period, that line is **end-stopped,** as in this line which opens Keats's "Endymion":

A thing / of beau - / ty // is / a joy / for - ev - er. /

If a line has no punctuation at the end and runs over to the next line, it is called **run-on.** A term also used to indicate run-on lines is **enjambement.** The following passage, a continuation of the line from Keats, contains three run-on lines:

> Its loveliness increases; // it will never
> Pass into nothingness; // but still will keep
> A bower quiet for us, // and a sleep
> Full of sweet dreams, // . . .

FORMAL SUBSTITUTION.   Most regular poems follow a formal pattern that can be analyzed according to the feet we have been describing here. For interest and emphasis, however (and also perhaps because of the natural rhythms of English speech), poets may **substitute** other feet for the regular feet of the poem. For example, the following line is from the "January" Eclogue of Edmund Spenser's *Shepherd's Calendar.* Although the pattern of the poem is iambic pentameter (i.e., five iambs per line), Spenser includes two substitute feet in this line:

All in / a sun - / shine day, / as did / be - fall./

In the first foot, "All in" is a trochee, and "shine day" is a spondee. These are *formal substitutions;* that is, Spenser uses separate, formally structured feet in place of the normal iambic feet. The effect is to move rapidly from "All" to "sunshine day" in order to allow the reader to delight in the sound of the words and also to savor the idea of unexpectedly nice weather during the middle of winter.

RHETORICAL SUBSTITUTION. By manipulating the caesura, poets can achieve the effects that are provided by formal substitution. If the pauses are placed within feet, they may cause us actually to *hear* trochees, amphibrachs, and other variant feet even though the line may scan regularly in the established meter. This type of *de facto* variation is **rhetorical substitution.** A noteworthy example in an iambic pentameter line is this one from Pope's *Essay on Man:*

His ăc-/tĭons', // păs-/sĭons', // bĕ-/ĭng's, // use/and end.

The theory of this type of line is that there should be a caesura after the fourth syllable, but in this one Pope has made three, each producing a strong pause. The line is regularly iambic, but the effect is different in actual reading or speaking. Because of the caesurae after the third, fifth, and seventh syllables, the rhythm produces an amphibrach, a trochee, another trochee, and an amphimacer, thus:

His ăc-/tĭons', // păs-/sĭons', // bĕ-/ĭng's, // use/and end.

AMPHIBRACH   TROCHEE   TROCHEE   AMPHIMACER

The spoken substitutions produced by the caesurae in this regular line produce the effect of substitution and therefore tension and interest.

When studying rhythm, your main concern in noting substitutions is to determine the formal metrical pattern, and then to analyze the formal and rhetorical variations on this pattern and their principal techniques and effects. Always try to show how these variations have enabled the poet to get points across and to achieve emphasis.

SEGMENTAL POETIC DEVICES

Once you have completed your analysis of rhythms, you can go on to consider the segmental poetic devices in the poem. Usually these devices are used to create emphasis, but sometimes in context they may echo or imitate actions and objects. The segmental devices most common in poetry are *assonance, alliteration, onomatopoeia,* and *euphony* and *cacophony.*

Assonance

Assonance is the repetition of identical *vowel* sounds in different words—for example, the short *ĭ* in "swĭft Camĭlla skĭms." It is a strong means of emphasis, as in the following line, where the *ŭ* sound connects the two words *lull* and *slumber,* and the short *ĭ* connects *him, in,* and *his:*

And more, to lŭll hĭm ĭn hĭs slŭmber soft (Spenser)

In some cases, poets use assonance elaborately, as in the first line of Pope's *An Essay on Criticism:*

'Tĭs härd to sāy, ĭf grēater wänt of skĭll

Here the line is framed and balanced with the short *ĭ* in "'Tis," "if," and "skill." The *ä* in "hard" and "want" forms another, internal frame, and the *ā* in "say" and "greater" creates still another frame. Such a balanced use of vowels is unusual, however, for in most lines assonance occurs simply as a means of highlighting important words, without such elaborate patterning.

Alliteration

Like assonance, **alliteration** is a means of highlighting ideas with words containing the same **consonant** sound—for example, the repeated *m* in Spenser's "*M*ixed with a *m*urmuring wind," or the *s* sound in Waller's praise of Cromwell, "Your never-failing *s*word made war to *c*ease," which emphasizes the connection between the words "sword" and "cease."

There are two kinds of alliteration. Most commonly, alliteration is regarded as the repetition of identical consonant sounds that begin syllables in close patterns—for example, in Pope's lines "La*b*orious, heavy, *b*usy, *b*old, and *b*lind," and "While *p*ensive *p*oets *p*ainful vigils keep." Used judiciously, alliteration gives strength to ideas by emphasizing key words, but too much *c*an *c*ause *c*omic and *c*atastrophic *c*onse*q*uences. The second form of alliteration occurs when a poet repeats identical or similar consonant sounds that do not begin syllables but nevertheless create a pattern—for example, the z segment in the line "In the*s*e place*s* freezing bree*z*es ea*s*ily cau*s*e snee*z*es," or the *m, b,* and *p* segments (all of which are made *bilabially,* that is, with both lips) in "The *m*is-era*b*ly *m*u*mb*ling and *m*o*m*entously *m*ur*m*uring *b*eggar *p*ro*p*els *p*egs and *p*e*bb*les in the *b*u*bb*ling *p*ool." Such clearly designed patterns are hard to overlook.

Onomatopoeia

Onomatopoeia is a blend of consonant and vowel sounds designed to *imitate* or *suggest* a situation or action. It is made possible in poetry because many English words are **echoic** in origin; that is, they are verbal echoes of the actions they describe, such as *buzz, bump, slap,* and so on. Poe used such words to create onomatopoeia in "The Bells," where through the combined use of assonance and alliteration he imitates the kinds of bells he celebrates. Thus, wedding bells sound softly with "m*o*lten g*o*lden n*o*tes" (*o*), while alarm bells "*cl*ang and *cl*ash and roar" (*kl*). David Wagoner includes imitative words like "tweedledy," "thump," and "wheeze" to suggest the sounds of the music produced by the protagonist of his "March for a One-Man Band."

Euphony and Cacophony

Words describing smooth or jarring sounds, particularly those resulting from consonants, are **euphony** and **cacophony**. Euphony ("good sound") refers to words containing consonants that permit an easy and smooth flow of spoken sound. Although there is no rule that some consonants are inherently more pleasant than others, students of poetry often cite sounds like *m, n, ng, l, v,* and *z,* together with *w* and *y,* as being especially easy on the ears. The opposite of euphony is cacophony ("bad sound"), in which percussive and choppy sounds make for vigorous and noisy pronunciation, as in tongue twisters like "black bug's blood" and "shuffling shellfish fashioned by a selfish sushi chef." Obviously, unintentional cacophony is a mark of imperfect control. When a poet deliberately creates it for effect, however, as in Tennyson's line "The bare black cliff clang'd round him," Pope's "The hoarse, rough verse should like the torrent roar," and Coleridge's "Huge fragments vaulted like rebounding hail, / Or chaffy grain beneath the thresher's flail," cacophony is a mark of poetic skill. Although poets generally aim at easily flowing, euphonious lines, cacophony does have a place, always depending on the poet's intention and subject matter.

RHYME

Rhyme refers to words containing identical final syllables. One type of rhyme involves words with identical concluding vowel sounds, or assonance, as in *day, weigh, grey, bouquet, fiancé,* and *matinee.* A second type of rhyme is created by assonance combined with identical consonant sounds, as in *ache, bake, break,* and *opaque;* or *turn, yearn, fern, spurn,* and *adjourn;* or *apple* and *dapple;* or *slippery* and *frippery.* Rhymes like these, because their rhyming sounds are identical, are called **exact rhymes.** It is important to note that rhymes result from *sound* rather than spelling; words do not have to be spelled the same way or look alike to rhyme. All the words rhyming with *day,* for example, are spelled differently, but because they all contain the same *ā* sound, they rhyme.

The Nature and Function of Rhyme

Rhyme, above all, gives delight. It also strengthens a poem's psychological impact. Through its network of similar sounds that echo and resonate in our minds, it promotes memory by clinching feelings and ideas. It has been an important aspect of poetry for hundreds of years, and, although many poets have shunned it because they find it restrictive and artificial, it is closely connected with how well given poems move us or leave us flat.

Most often, rhymes are placed at the ends of lines. Two successive lines may rhyme, for example, and rhymes may appear in alternating lines. It is also possible to introduce rhyming words at intervals of four, five, or more lines. A problem, however, is that if rhyming sounds are too far away from each other, they lose their immediacy and therefore their effectiveness.

Poets who are skillful and original rhymers are able to create fresh, unusual, and surprising turns of thought. We can therefore judge poets on their use of rhyme. Often poets become quite creative rhymers, putting together words like *bent 'em* and *Tarentum* or *masterly* and *dastardly*. Some rhymers, whom an anonymous sixteenth-century critic called a "rakehelly route of ragged rhymers," are satisfied with easy rhymes, or **cliché rhymes,** like *trees* and *breeze* (a rhyme that Alexander Pope criticized in 1711). But good rhymes and good poets go together, in creative cooperation. The seventeenth-century poet John Dryden, who wrote volumes of rhyming couplets, acknowledged that the need to find rhyming words inspired ideas that he had not anticipated. In this sense, rhyme has been—and still is—a vital element of poetic creativity.

There are few restrictions on English rhymes. Poets may rhyme nouns with other nouns, or with verbs and adjectives, or with any other rhyming word, regardless of part of speech. Of course, exact rhymes are to be preferred, but the shortage of exact rhymes in English has enabled poets to be creative, rhyming words that almost rhyme but don't exactly (*slant rhyme*) or words that look alike but sound different (*eye rhyme*). Some poets use the same words to complete a rhyming pattern (*identical rhyme*), although this repetition eliminates some of the surprise and interest that good rhymes should produce.

Rhyme and Meter

HEAVY-STRESS RHYME.   The effects of rhyme are closely connected with those of rhythm and meter. Rhymes that are produced with one-syllable words—like *moon, June, tune,* and *soon*—or with multisyllabic words in which the accent falls on the last syllable—like *combine, decline, supine,* and *refine*—are called **heavy-stress rhyme, accented rhyme,** or **rising rhyme.** In general, rising rhyme lends itself to serious effects. The accenting of heavy-stress rhyme appears in the opening lines of Robert Frost's "Stopping by Woods on a Snowy Evening" (p. 456, italics added):

Whose woods / these are / I think / I *know.*
His house / is in / the vil - / lage *though;*

Here, the rhyming sounds are produced by one-syllable words—*know* and *though*—that occur in the final heavy-stress positions of the lines.

TROCHAIC AND DACTYLIC RHYME.   Rhymes using words of two or more syllables in which the heavy stress falls on any syllable other than the last are called *trochaic* or *double rhyme* for rhymes of two syllables, and *dactylic* or *triple rhyme* for rhymes of three syllables. Less technically, these types of rhymes are also called

falling or **dying rhymes;** this is probably because the intensity of pronunciation decreases on the light accent or accents following the heavy accent.

In general, **trochaic** or **double rhymes** are appropriate to light, amusing, and satiric poetry, as seen in lines 2 and 4 of the first stanza of "Miniver Cheevy" by Edwin Arlington Robinson (italics added):

Miniver Cheevy, child of scorn,
   Grew lean while he assailed the *seasons;*
He wept that he was ever born,
   And he had *reasons.*

In this poem the effect of the double rhyme is humorous, thus helping to make Miniver Cheevy seem ridiculous and pathetic.

Double rhymes can also be a means of emphasizing or underscoring irony or anticlimax in serious poems, as in "A-flying" and "dying" in the first stanza of Herrick's "To the Virgins, to Make Much of Time":

Gather ye rosebuds while ye may,
   Old time is still a-flying;
And this same flower that smiles today
   Tomorrow will be dying.

Herrick uses falling rhymes in the second and fourth lines of every stanza of this poem. The result is a poignant contrast between pleasures of everyday life and the eternal truths of mortality.

Dactylic or **triple rhyme** is often light or humorous because it tends to divert attention from the subject to the words, as in these lines from Browning's "The Pied Piper of Hamelin" (italics added):

Small feet were *pattering,* wooden shoes *clattering,*
Little hands clapping and little tongues *chattering.*
And, like fowls in a farm-yard where barley is *scattering,*

Here, the ending words "*clattering,*" "*chattering,*" and "*scattering*" are all instances of triple rhyme. The poem indeed does make a serious point (about the failure to keep a pledge), but in this stanza, which deals with the children following the Pied Piper, the triple rhyme is appropriate to the sounds of running children.

Variations in Rhyme

INTERNAL RHYME.   In the stanza from Browning, the fourth word in the first line, "pattering," rhymes with the line-ending rhymes. This is an example of **internal rhyme**—the presence of a rhyming word within a line of verse. It is not a common variation, but you should be alert for it and make note of it when it occurs.

INEXACT RHYME.   Writers of English poetry have often felt limited in selecting rhymes because our language is short in identical word terminations.

Italian, by contrast, in which most words end in vowel sounds, offers virtually endless rhyming possibilities. A tradition has therefore grown in English that words may be rhymed even though they are not exact.

Rhymes may often be created out of words with similar but not identical sounds. In most of these instances, either the vowel segments are different while the consonants are the same, or vice versa. This type of rhyme is variously called **slant rhyme, near rhyme, half rhyme, off rhyme, analyzed rhyme,** or **suspended rhyme.** In employing slant rhyme, a poet can pair *bleak* with *broke* or *could* with *solitude.* Emily Dickinson uses slant rhyme extensively in "To Hear an Oriole Sing" (p. 586); in the second stanza of the poem she rhymes "Bird," "unheard," and "Crowd." "Bird" and "unheard" make up an exact rhyme, but the vowel and consonant shift in "Crowd" produces a slant rhyme.

Another common variation is **eye rhyme** or **sight rhyme.** In eye rhyme, the sounds to be eye-rhymed are *identical in spelling* but *different in pronunciation.* Entire words may be eye-rhymed, so that *wind* (verb) may be joined to *wind* (noun), and *cóntest* (noun) may be used with *contést* (verb). In most eye rhymes, however, it is only the relevant parts of words that must be spelled identically. Thus *stove* may pair with *prove* and *above,* and *bough* may match *cough, dough, enough,* and *through,* despite all the differing pronunciations. The following anonymous lines contain eye rhyme:

Although his claim was not to praise but *bury,*
His speech for Caesar roused the crowd to *fury.*

The different pronunciations of "bury" and "fury" make clear the contrast between exact rhyme and eye rhyme. In exact rhyme identical sound is crucial; spelling is usually the same but may be different as long as the sounds remain identical. In eye rhyme, the eye-rhyming patterns must be spelled identically but the sounds must be different.

ADDITIONAL VARIATIONS.   Poets sometimes use **identical rhyme** (noted earlier), that is, the same words in rhyming positions, such as *veil* and *veil* or *stone* and *stone.* **Vowel rhyme** is the use of any vowels in rhyming positions, as in *day* and *sky* or *key* and *play.*

Rhyme Schemes

A **rhyme scheme** refers to a poem's pattern of rhyming sounds, which are indicated by alphabetical letters. The first rhyming sounds, such as *love* and *dove,* are marked with an *a;* the next rhyming sounds, such as *swell* and *fell,* receive a *b;* the next sounds, such as *first* and *burst,* receive a *c,* and so on. Thus, a pattern of lines ending with the words *love, moon, thicket; dove, June, picket;* and *above, croon,* and *wicket* can be schematized as *a b c; a b c; a b c.*

To formulate a rhyme scheme or pattern, you include the meter and the number of feet in each line as well as the letters indicating rhymes. Here is such a formulation:

Iambic pentameter: *a b a b, c d c d, e f e f*

This scheme shows that all the lines in the poem are iambic, with five feet in each. Commas separating the units indicate a stanzaic pattern of three 4-line units, or **quatrains,** with the rhymes falling on the first and third, and the second and fourth, lines of each quatrain.

Should the number of feet in the lines of a poem or **stanza** vary, you show this fact by using a number in front of each letter:

Iambic: *4a 3b 4a 3b 5a 5a 4b*

This formulation shows an intricate pattern of rhymes and line-lengths in a stanza of seven lines. The first, third, fifth, and sixth lines rhyme, and vary from four to five feet. The second, fourth, and seventh lines also rhyme, and vary from three to four feet.

The absence of a rhyme sound is indicated by an *x*. Thus, you formulate the rhyme scheme of **ballad measure** like this:

Iambic: *4x 3a 4x 3a*

The formulation shows that the quatrain alternates iambic tetrameter with trimeter. In this ballad quatrain, only lines 2 and 4 rhyme; there is no end rhyme in lines 1 and 3.

POEMS FOR STUDY

GWENDOLYN BROOKS   (b. 1917)

We Real Cool _____ *1959*

> The Pool Players.
> *Seven at the Golden Shovel.*

We real cool. We
Left school. We

Lurk late. We
Strike straight. We

Sing sin. We   5
Thin gin. We

Jazz June. We
Die soon.

QUESTIONS

1. What is the major idea of the poem? Who is the speaker? How is the last sentence a climax? How is this sentence consistent with the declarations in lines 1–7? How is the poet's attitude made clear?
2. Describe the patterning of stresses in the poem. Explain the absence of light stresses. What method is employed to achieve the constant strong stresses?

EMILY DICKINSON   (1830–1886)

To Hear an Oriole Sing _____ *1891 (ca. 1862)*

To hear an Oriole sing
May be a common thing—
Or only a divine.

It is not of the Bird
Who sings the same, unheard,   5
As unto Crowd—

The Fashion of the Ear
Attireth that it hear
In Dun, or fair—

So whether it be Rune,   10
Or whether it be none
Is of within.

The "Tune is in the Tree—"
The Skeptic–showeth me—
"No Sir! In Thee!"   15

QUESTIONS

1. What can you deduce about the speaker? The listener? Who speaks in line 13? To whom is line 15 addressed?

2. Formulate the rhyme scheme of this poem. How does it help subdivide the poem into cohesive units of thought? To what extent does it unify the poem?

3. Locate all the slant rhymes in this poem. What effect do these have on your reading and perception? How is the rhyme here like the oriole's song?

4. To what degree does rhyme reinforce meaning? Note especially the rhyme words in the final stanza.

JOHN DONNE   (1572–1631)

The Sun Rising _____ *1633*

     Busy old fool, unruly Sun,
      Why dost thou thus,
Through windows, and through curtains call on us?
Must to thy motions lovers'seasons run?
      Saucy pedantic wretch, go chide   5
      Late school boys and sour prentices,°   *apprentices*
    Go tell Court-huntsmen, that the King will ride,
    Call country ants to harvest offices;°
Love, all alike, no season knows, nor clime,°   *climate*
Nor hours, days, months, which are the rags of time.   10

     Thy beams, so reverend, and strong
      Why shouldst thou think?°
I could eclipse and cloud them with a wink,
But that I would not lose her sight so long;
      If her eyes have not blinded thine,   15
      Look, and tomorrow late, tell me,
    Whether both the Indias of spice and Mine°
    Be where thou leftst them, or lie here with me.
Ask for those kings whom thou saw'st yesterday,
And thou shalt hear, All here in one bed lay.   20

     She'is° all States, and all Princes, I,
      Nothing else is.
Princes do but play us; compared to this,
All honor's mimic; all wealth alchemy.°
      Thou, sun, art half as happy'as° we,   25

THE SUN RISING.   8 *Call . . . offices:* i.e., notify the country's ants to carry out the duty of eating the harvest of grain and produce.   11, 12 *Thy beams . . . think?:* i.e., Why shouldst thou think that thy beams are so reverend and strong?   17 *Indias of spice and Mine:* The India of "spice" is the East Indies; the India of "Mine" (gold) is the West Indies.   21 *She'is:* For scansion, these two words are to be considered one syllable ("shé's").   24 *all wealth alchemy:* i.e., all wealth is false because it has been created by alchemists.   25 *happy'as:* to be scanned as a trochee ("hápp-yằz")

In that the world's contracted thus;
  Thine age asks ease, and since thy duties be
  To warm the world, that's done in warming us.
Shine here to us, and thou art everywhere;
This bed thy center° is, these walls, thy sphere.   30

30 *center:* the earth, around which the sun revolves (according the the Ptolemaic view of the solar system).

QUESTIONS

1. What is the speaker like? How deeply does he seem to be in love? How does he feel about love? What evidence do you find that the speaker has a good sesnse of humor?

2. To whom is the poem addressed? What is the speaker's attitude toward this listener?

3. What solar, seasonal, geographical, and political metaphors are developed in the poem?

4. What is the poem's rhyme scheme? What is the metrical norm of the lines? What variations on this norm do you find in the poem?

T. S. ELIOT   (1888–1965)

Macavity: The Mystery Cat ———————————————————— *1939*

Macavity's a Mystery Cat: he's called the Hidden Paw—
For he's the master criminal who can defy the Law.
He's the bafflement of Scotland Yard, the Flying Squad's despair:
For when they reach the scene of the crime—*Macavity's not there!*

  Macavity, Macavity, there's no one like Macavity,   5
He's broken every human law, he breaks the law of gravity.
His powers of levitation would make a fakir stare,
And when you reach the scene of crime—*Macavity's not there!*
You may seek him in the basement, you may look up in the air—
But I tell you once and once again, *Macavity's not there!*   10

  Macavity's a ginger cat, he's very tall and thin;
You would know him if you saw him, for his eyes are sunken in.
His brow is deeply lined with thought, his head is highly domed;
His coat is dusty from neglect, his whiskers are uncombed.
He sways his head from side to side, with movements like a snake;   15
And when you think he's half asleep, he's always wide awake.

  Macavity, Macavity, there's no one like Macavity,
For he's a fiend in feline shape, a monster of depravity.
You may meet him in a by-street, you may see him in the square—
But when a crime's discovered, then *Macavity's not there!*   20

He's outwardly respectable. (They say he cheats at cards.)
And his footprints are not found in any file of Scotland Yard's.
And when the larder's looted, or the jewel-case is rifled,
Or when the milk is missing, or another Peke's been stifled,°
Or the greenhouse glass is broken, and the trellis past repair—   25
Ay, there's the wonder of the thing! *Macavity's not there!*

And when the Foreign Office find a Treaty's gone astray,
Or the Admiralty lose some plans and drawings by the way,
There may be a scrap of paper in the hall or on the stair—
But it's useless to investigate—*Macavity's not there!*   30
And when the loss has been disclosed, the Secret Service say:
"It *must* have been Macavity!"—but he's a mile away.
You'll be sure to find him resting, or a-licking of his thumbs,
Or engaging in doing complicated long division sums.

Macavity, Macavity, there's no one like Macavity,   35
There never was a Cat of such deceitfulness and suavity.
He always has an alibi, and one or two to spare:
At whatever time the deed took place—MACAVITY WASN'T THERE!
And they say that all the Cats whose wicked deeds are widely known
(I might mention Mungojerrie, I might mention Griddlebone)   40
Are nothing more than agents for the Cat who all the time
Just controls their operations: the Napoleon of Crime!

MACAVITY: THE MYSTERY CAT.   24 *Peke's been stifled:* A Pekinese dog (a small animal, with silky hair) has been found dead.

QUESTIONS

1. What are some of Macavity's major "crimes" as a master criminal and "mystery cat"? How, if the "crimes" had been attributed to a human being, would they be grievous wrongs? Since they are attributed to a cat, how do they add to the comic qualities of the poem?

2. What is the basic metrical foot of the poem? How many feet are contained in each of the lines? What is the norm?

3. Once you begin reading and getting into the lines, what new kind of pattern emerges? How many major stresses appear in each line? In light of the nature of the poem, how is the dipodic rhythm appropriate?

ROBERT HERRICK   (1591–1674)

Upon Julia's Voice _____ *1648*

So smooth, so sweet, so silv'ry is thy voice,
As, could they hear, the damned would make no noise,
But listen to thee (walking in thy chamber)
Melting melodious words, to lutes of amber.

QUESTIONS

1. How do the words "silv'ry" and "amber" contribute to the praise of Julia's voice? How powerful does the speaker claim her voice is?

2. What is the "joke" of the poem? How can the praise of Julia's voice be interpreted as general praise for Julia herself?

3. How and where is alliteration used in the poem? Which of the alliterative sounds best complement the words praising the sweetness of Julia's voice?

GERARD MANLEY HOPKINS   (1844–1889)

God's Grandeur _____ *1877*

The world is charged with the grandeur of God.
    It will flame out, like shining from shook foil;
    It gathers to a greatness, like the ooze of oil
Crushed. Why do men then now not reck his rod?°
Generations have trod, have trod, have trod;   5
    And all is seared with trade; bleared, smeared with toil;
    And wears man's smudge and shares man's smell: the soil
Is bare now, nor can foot feel, being shod.
And for all this, nature is never spent;
    There lives the dearest freshness deep down things;   10
And though the last lights off the black West went
    Oh, morning, at the brown brink eastward, springs—
Because the Holy Ghost over the bent
    World broods with warm breast and with ah! bright wings.

GOD'S GRANDEUR.   4 *reck his rod:* God as king holds a scepter, making official laws through scriptures which people ("men") disobey.

QUESTIONS

1. What is the contrast between the assertions in lines 1–4 and 5–8? How do lines 9–14 develop out of this contrast?

2. Analyze Hopkins's use of alliteration. What alliterative patterns occur? How do these affect meter and emphasis? On the basis of your analysis, describe "sprung rhythm" as used by Hopkins.

3. What instances of assonance, repetitions, and internal rhyme do you find?

LANGSTON HUGHES   (1902–1967)

Let America Be America Again _____ *1936*

Let America be America again.
Let it be the dream it used to be.
Let it be the pioneer on the plain
Seeking a home where he himself is free.

(America never was America to me.)   5

Let America be the dream the dreamers dreamed—
Let it be that great strong land of love
Where never kings connive nor tyrants scheme
That any man be crushed by one above.

(It never was America to me.)   10

O, let my land be a land where Liberty
Is crowned with no false patriotic wreath,
But opportunity is real, and life is free,
Equality is in the air we breathe.

(There's never been equality for me,   15
Nor freedom in this "homeland of the free.")

Say who are you that mumbles in the dark?
And who are you that draws your veil across the stars?
I am the poor white, fooled and pushed apart,
I am the Negro bearing slavery's scars.   20
I am the red man driven from the land,
I am the immigrant clutching the hope I seek—
And finding only the same old stupid plan
Of dog eat dog, of mighty crush the weak.

I am the young man, full of strength and hope,   25
Tangled in that ancient endless chain
Of profit, power, gain, of grab the land!
Of grab the gold! Of grab the ways of satisfying need!
Of work the men! Of take the pay!
Of owning everything for one's own greed!   30

I am the farmer, bondsman to the soil.
I am the worker sold to the machine.
I am the Negro, servant to you all.
I am the people, worried, hungry, mean—
Hungry yet today despite the dream.   35
Beaten yet today—O, Pioneers!
I am the man who never got ahead,
The poorest worker bartered through the years.

Yet I'm the one who dreamt our basic dream
In the Old World while still a serf of kings,   40
Who dreamt a dream so strong, so brave, so true,
That even yet its mighty daring sings
In every brick and stone, in every furrow turned
That's made America the land it has become.
O, I'm the man who sailed those early seas   45
In search of what I meant to be my home—
For I'm the one who left dark Ireland's shore,
And Poland's plain, and England's grassy lea,
And torn from Black Africa's strand I came

To build a "homeland of the free."   50
The free?

A dream—
Still beckoning to me!

O, let America be America again—
The land that never has been yet—   55
And yet must be—
The land where *every* man is free.
The land that's mine—
The poor man's, Indian's, Negro's, ME—
Who made America,   60
Whose sweat and blood, whose faith and pain,
Whose hand at the foundry, whose plow in the rain,
Must bring back our mighty dream again.

Sure, call me any ugly name you choose—
The steel of freedom does not stain.   65
From those who live like leeches on the people's lives,
We must take back our land again,
America!

O, yes,
I say it plain,   70
America never was America to me,
And yet I swear this oath—
America will be!
An ever-living seed,
Its dream   75
Lies deep in the heart of me.

We, the people, must redeem
Our land, the mines, the plants, the rivers,
The mountains and the endless plain—
All, all the stretch of these great green states—   80
And make America again!

QUESTIONS

1. In light of the poet's ideas, what is the effect of the changing stanzaic patterns? After the opening, fairly regular quatrains, why do the groupings become irregular?

2. What is the effect of the refrains in lines 5, 10, and 15–16? Why does the poet stop using the refrain after the third quatrain and not bring it out again until line 71?

3. Describe the use of alliteration. In phrases like "pushed apart" and "slavery's scars," together with other phrases, how does the alliteration emphasize the poet's ideas?

4. Describe the use of assonance, rhyme, and slant rhyme. What is gained by the slant rhymes?

PHILIP LEVINE   (b. 1928)

A Theory of Prosody ————————————————————— *1988*

When Nellie, my old pussy
cat, was still in her prime,
she would sit behind me
as I wrote, and when the line
got too long she'd reach   5
one sudden black foreleg down
and paw at the moving hand,
the offensive one. The first
time she drew blood I learned
it was poetic to end   10
a line anywhere to keep her
quiet. After all, many mornings she'd gotten to the chair
long before I was even up.
Those nights I couldn't sleep   15
she'd come and sit in my lap
to calm me. So I figured
I owed her the short cat line.
She's dead now almost nine years,
and before that there was one   20
during which she faked attention
and I faked obedience.
Isn't that what it's about—
pretending there's an alert cat
who leaves nothing to chance.   25

QUESTIONS

1. Why is this poem comic? How effective a "theory of prosody" is contained in
    the poem? What is suggested by the syllable break in line 12? How seriously are
    we to take the final lines?

2. What is the relationship between the speaker and his cat, Nellie? How true is it
    that cats sitting at a table with their masters and mistresses sometimes take a
    swipe at what they are writing?

3. Compare this poem with Robert Frost's "A Considerable Speck" (p. 739). In
    what ways do the poets seem to be having a good time? Nevertheless, what
    truths about writing are they advancing in the poems?

EDGAR ALLAN POE   (1809–1849)

The Bells ——————————————————————————— *1849*

                    I
Hear the sledges with the bells—
        Silver bells!

What a world of merriment their melody foretells!
How they tinkle, tinkle, tinkle,
   In the icy air of night!   5
While the stars that oversprinkle
All the heavens, seem to twinkle
   With a crystalline delight;
      Keeping time, time, time,
      In a sort of Runic rhyme,   10
To the tintinnabulation that so musically wells
      From the bells, bells, bells, bells,
         Bells, bells, bells—
From the jingling and the tinkling of the bells.

                    II
   Hear the mellow wedding bells—   15
         Golden bells!
What a world of happiness their harmony foretells!
   Through the balmy air of night
   How they ring out their delight!—
      From the molten-golden notes,   20
      And all in tune,
   What a liquid ditty floats
To the turtle-dove that listens, while she gloats
         On the moon!
      Oh, from out the sounding cells,   25
What a gush of euphony voluminously wells!
      How it swells!
      How it dwells
   On the Future!—how it tells
   Of the rapture that impels   30
   To the swinging and the ringing
      Of the bells, bells, bells—
Of the bells, bells, bells, bells,
      Bells, bells, bells—
To the rhyming and the chiming of the bells!   35

                    III
   Hear the loud alarum bells—
         Brazen bells!
What a tale of terror, now, their turbulency tells!
   In the startled ear of night
   How they scream out their affright!   40
      Too much horrified to speak,
      They can only shriek, shriek,
         Out of tune,
In a clamorous appealing to the mercy of the fire,
In a mad expostulation with the deaf and frantic fire,   45
      Leaping higher, higher, higher,
      With a desperate desire,

And a resolute endeavor
 Now—now to sit, or never,
By the side of the pale-faced moon,
  Oh, the bells, bells, bells!
  What a tale their terror tells
   Of Despair!
 How they clang, and clash, and roar!
 What a horror they outpour
On the bosom of the palpitating air!
  Yet the ear, it fully knows,
   By the twanging
   And the clanging,
  How the danger ebbs and flows;
  Yet the ear distinctly tells,
   In the jangling
   And the wrangling,
 How the danger sinks and swells,
By the sinking or the swelling in the anger of the bells—
   Of the bells,—
 Of the bells, bells, bells, bells,
   Bells, bells, bells—
In the clamor and the clangor of the bells!

    IV
Hear the tolling of the bells—
   Iron bells!
What a world of solemn thought their monody compels!
 In the silence of the night,
 How we shiver with affright
At the melancholy menace of their tone!
 For every sound that floats
 From the rust within their throats
   Is a groan.
  And the people—ah, the people—
  They that dwell up in the steeple,
   All alone,
 And who tolling, tolling, tolling,
 In that muffled monotone,
Feel a glory in so rolling
  On the human heart a stone—
They are neither man nor woman—
They are neither brute nor human—
   They are Ghouls:—
 And their king it is who tolls:—
 And he rolls, rolls, rolls,
   Rolls
  A paean from the bells!
And his merry bosom swells
  With the paean of the bells!

50

55

60

65

70

75

80

85

90

And he dances, and he yells;   95
Keeping time, time, time,
In a sort of Runic rhyme,
    To the paean of the bells—
     Of the bells:
Keeping time, time, time,   100
In a sort of Runic rhyme,
    To the throbbing of the bells—
  Of the bells, bells, bells—
    To the sobbing of the bells;
Keeping time, time, time,   105
  As he knells, knells, knells,
In a happy Runic rhyme,
    To the rolling of the bells—
  Of the bells, bells, bells:—
    To the tolling of the bells—   110
Of the bells, bells, bells, bells,
    Bells, bells, bells—
To the moaning and the groaning of the bells.

QUESTIONS

1. What kinds of bells does Poe extol in each of the stanzas? What metals and images does he associate with each type of bell? How appropriate are these? Why do you think the stanzas become progressively longer?

2. What segmental sounds does Poe utilize as imitative of the various bells? What differences in vowels are observable between the silver sledge bells, for example, and the brass ("brazen") alarum bells? Between the vowels describing the iron bells and the golden bells?

3. What is the effect of the repetition of the word "bells" throughout? What onomatopoeic effect is created by these repetitions?

4. Describe the pattern of rhymes in this poem.

5. How effectively does Poe use spondees? What relationship do the spondees have to the poem's subject?

EDWIN ARLINGTON ROBINSON (1869–1935)

Miniver Cheevy ———————————————————————— *1910*

Miniver Cheevy, child of scorn,
  Grew lean while he assailed the seasons;
He wept that he was ever born,   5
  And he had reasons.

Miniver loved the days of old
  When swords were bright and steeds were prancing;
The vision of a warrior bold
  Would set him dancing.

Miniver sighed for what was not,
   And dreamed, and rested from his labors;   10
He dreamed of Thebes° and Camelot,°
   And Priam's° neighbors.

Miniver mourned the ripe renown
   That made so many a name so fragrant;
He mourned Romance, now on the town,   15
   And Art, a vagrant.

Miniver loved the Medici,°
   Albeit he had never seen one;
He would have sinned incessantly
   Could he have been one.   20

Miniver cursed the commonplace
   And eyed a khaki suit with loathing;
He missed the medieval grace
   Of iron clothing.°   *i.e., armor*

Miniver scorned the gold he sought,   25
   But sore annoyed was he without it;
Miniver thought, and thought, and thought,
   And thought about it.

Miniver Cheevy, born too late,
   Scratched his head and kept on thinking;   30
Miniver coughed, and called it fate,
   And kept on drinking.

MINIVER CHEEVY.   11 *Thebes:* a city in Greece prominent in Greek legend and mythology in connection with Cadmus and Oedipus.   *Camelot:* legendary seat of the Round Table and capital of Britain during the reign of King Arthur.   12 *Priam's:* Priam was the king of Troy during the Trojan War.   17 *Medici:* wealthy Italian family that ruled Florence from the fifteenth to the eighteenth century. During the Renaissance, Lorenzo de'Medici was an important patron of the arts.

QUESTIONS

1. What is the speaker's attitude toward the central character? How does rhyme help define this attitude?

2. How does repetition reinforce the image of the central character and the speaker's attitude? Consider the beginning of each stanza and lines 27–28.

3. What rhyme predominates in lines 2 and 4 of each stanza? How does this rhyme help make sound echo sense?

WILLIAM SHAKESPEARE   (1564–1616)

Sonnet 73: That Time of Year Thou Mayst in Me Behold _____ *1609*

That time of year thou mayst in me behold
When yellow leaves, or none, or few, do hang

Upon those boughs which shake against the cold,
Bare ruined choirs,° where late the sweet birds sang.
In me thou see'st the twilight of such day   5
As after sunset fadeth in the west;
Which by and by black night doth take away,
Death's second self,° that seals up all in rest.
In me thou see'st the glowing of such fire,
That on the ashes of his° youth doth lie,   *its*   10
As the death-bed whereon it must expire,
Consumed with that which it was nourished by,°
    This thou perceivest, which makes thy love more strong,
    To love that well which thou must leave ere long.

SONNET 73.   4 *choirs:* the part of a church just in front of the altar.   8 *Death's . . . self:* That is,
night is a mirror image of death inasmuch as it brings the sleep of rest just as death brings the
sleep of actual death.   12 *Consumed . . . by:* That is, the ashes of the fuel burned at the fire's
height now prevent the fire from continuing, and in fact extinguish it.

QUESTIONS

1. Describe the content of lines 1–4, 5–8, and 9–12. What connects these three
    sections? How does the concluding couplet relate to the first twelve lines?

2. Analyze the iambic pentameter of the poem. Consider the spondees in lines 2
    ("do hang"), 4 ("bare ru-" and "birds sang"), 5 ("such day"), 7 ("black night"), 8
    ("death's sec-"), 9 ("such fire"), 10 ("doth lie"), 11 ("death-bed"), 13 ("more
    strong"), and 14 ("ere long"). What is the effect of these substitutions on the
    poem's ideas?

3. How does the enjambement of lines 1–3 and 5–6 permit these lines to seem to
    conclude *as lines* even though grammatically they carry over to form sentences?

4. In lines 2, 5, 6, and 9, where does Shakespeare place the caesurae? What rela-
    tionship is there between the rhythms produced by these caesurae and the con-
    tent of lines 1–12? In lines 13 and 14, how do the rising stressed caesurae relate
    to the content?

PERCY BYSSHE SHELLEY   (1792–1822)

Ode to the West Wind _____ *1820*

                                        I
O wild West Wind, thou breath of Autumn's being,
Thou, from whose unseen presence the leaves dead
Are driven, like ghosts from an enchanter fleeing,

Yellow, and black, and pale, and hectic° red,
Pestilence-stricken multitudes: O Thou,   5
Who chariotest to their dark wintry bed

ODE TO THE WEST WIND.   4 *hectic:* a tubercular fever that produced flushed cheeks.

The winged seeds, where they lie cold and low,
Each like a corpse within its grave, until
Thine azure sister of the Spring° shall blow

Her clarion o'er the dreaming earth, and fill   10
(Driving sweet buds like flocks to feed in air)
With living hues and odours plain and hill:

Wild Spirit, which art moving everywhere;
Destroyer and Preserver; hear, O hear!

                              II
Thou on whose stream, 'mid the steep sky's commotion,   15
Loose clouds like Earth's decaying leaves are shed,
Shook from the tangled boughs of Heaven and Ocean,

Angels of rain and lightning: there are spread
On the blue surface of thine aery surge,
Like the bright hair uplifted from the head   20

Of some fierce Maenad,° even from the dim verge
Of the horizon to the zenith's height,
The locks of the approaching storm. Thou Dirge

Of the dying year, to which this closing night
Will be the dome of a vast sepulchre,   25
Vaulted with all thy congregated might

Of vapours,° from whose solid atmosphere   *clouds*
Black rain and fire and hail will burst: O hear!

                              III
Thou who didst waken from his summer dreams
The blue Mediterranean, where he lay,   30
Lulled by the coil of his crystalline streams,

Beside a pumice isle in Baiae's bay,°
And saw in sleep old palaces and towers
Quivering within the wave's intenser day,

All overgrown with azure moss and flowers   35
So sweet, the sense faints picturing them! Thou
For whose path the Atlantic's level powers

9 *Spring:* the wind that will blow in the spring.   21 *Maenad:* a frenzied female worshipper of
Dionysus, the god of wine and fertility in Greek mythology.   32 *Baiae's bay:* a bay of the
Mediterranean Sea west of Naples, famous for the elaborate villas built on the shore by Roman
emperors.

Cleave themselves into chasms, while far below
The sea-blooms and the oozy woods which wear
The sapless foliage of the ocean, know   40

Thy voice, and suddenly grow grey with fear,
And tremble and despoil themselves: O hear!

IV

If I were a dead leaf thou mightest bear;
If I were a swift cloud to fly with thee;
A wave to pant beneath thy power, and share   45

The impulse of thy strength, only less free
Than thou, O Uncontrollable! If even
I were as in my boyhood, and could be

The comrade of thy wanderings over Heaven,
As then, when to outstrip thy skiey speed   50
Scarce seemed a vision; I would ne'er have striven

As thus with thee in prayer in my sore need,
Oh! lift me as a wave, a leaf, a cloud!
I fall upon the thorns of life! I bleed!

A heavy weight of hours has chained and bowed   55
One too like thee: tameless, and swift, and proud.

V

Make me thy lyre,° even as the forest is:
What if my leaves are falling like its own!
The tumult of thy mighty harmonies

Will take from both a deep, autumnal tone,   60
Sweet though in sadness. Be thou, Spirit fierce,
My spirit! Be thou me, impetuous one!

Drive my dead thoughts over the universe
Like withered leaves to quicken a new birth!
And, by the incantation of this verse,   65

Scatter, as from an unextinguished hearth
Ashes and sparks, my words among mankind!
Be through my lips to unawakened Earth

The trumpet of a prophecy! O Wind,
If Winter comes, can Spring be far behind?   70

57 *Lyre:* an Aeolian harp, a musical device which is sounded by the wind blowing across strings.

QUESTIONS

1. Formulate the structure (meter of each line and rhyme scheme) of the stanzas.

2. How many times (and where) is the *e* rhyme of the first stanza repeated as a rhyme sound throughout the poem? What is the effect of this repetition?

3. What aspect of the natural world does the wind affect in the first section of the poem? The second section? The third?

4. What does the speaker assert (in section IV) that time has done to him? What does he want from the West Wind? What does he want to become?

5. To what extent are the speaker's thoughts and feelings organized by the poem's five sections? What is the logical progression from section to section?

6. What does the West Wind symbolize? Compare this poem to Keats's "Ode to a Nightingale." How are the nightingale's song and the West Wind related to each other as symbols?

ALFRED, LORD TENNYSON   (1809–1892)

From *Idylls of the King: The Passing of Arthur*
Lines 344–393 _____ 1869 (1842)

But, as he walked, King Arthur panted hard,
Like one that feels a nightmare on his bed   345
When all the house is mute. So sighed the King,
Muttering and murmuring at his ear, "Quick, quick!
I fear it is too late, and I shall die."
But the other swiftly strode from ridge to ridge,
Clothed with his breath, and looking, as he walked,   350
Larger than human on the frozen hills.
He heard the deep behind him, and a cry
Before. His own thought drove him like a goad.
Dry clashed his harness in the icy caves
And barren chasms, and all to left and right   355
The bare black cliff clanged round him, as he based
His feet on juts of slippery crag that rang
Sharp-smitten with the dint of armèd heels—
And on a sudden, lo! the level lake,
And the long glories of the winter moon.   360

Then saw they how there hove a dusky barge,
Dark as a funeral scarf from stem to stern,
Beneath them; and descending they were ware°   *aware*
That all the decks were dense with stately forms,
Black-stoled, black-hooded, like a dream—by these   365
Three Queens with crowns of gold: and from them rose
A cry that shivered to the tingling stars,

And, as it were one voice, an agony
Of lamentation, like a wind that shrills
All night in a waste land, where no one comes,   370
Or hath come, since the making of the world.

Then murmured Arthur, "Place me in the barge."
So to the barge they came. There those three Queens
Put forth their hands, and took the King, and wept.
But she, that rose the tallest of them all   375
And fairest, laid his head upon her lap,
And loosed the shattered casque,° and chafed his hands,   *helmet*
And called him by his name, complaining loud,
And dropping bitter tears against a brow
Striped with dark blood: for all his face was white   380
And colorless, and like the withered moon
Smote by the fresh beam of the springing east;
And all his greaves and cuisses° dashed with drops   *pieces of armor*
Of onset;° and the light and lustrous curls—   *blood*
That made his forehead like a rising sun   385
High from the dais-throne—were parched with dust:
Or, clotted into points and hanging loose,
Mixed with the knightly growth that fringed his lips.
So like a shattered column lay the King:
Not like that Arthur who, with lance in rest,   390
From spur to plume a star of tournament,
Shot through the lists at Camelot, and charged
Before the eyes of ladies and of kings.

QUESTIONS

1. How does Tennyson develop the mood of depression and loss associated with the dying of Arthur? What is the effect of the concluding simile?

2. Analyze the patterns of assonance and alliteration in the passage. What patterns are developed most extensively? What effects are thus achieved?

3. Describe Tennyson's use of onomatopoeia in lines 349–360, 369–371, and 380–383. What segments contribute to this effect?

DAVID WAGONER   (b. 1926)

March for a One-Man Band _____ *1983*

He's *a boom a blat* in the uniform
Of an army *tweedledy* band *a toot*
Complete with medals *a honk* cornet
Against *a thump* one side of his lips
And the other stuck with *a sloop a tweet*   5
A whistle *a crash* on top of *a crash*
A helmet *a crash* a cymbal a drum

At his *bumbledy* knee and a *rimshot* flag
A click he stands at attention *a wheeze*
And plays the Irrational Anthem *bang*.   10

QUESTIONS

1. What attitude does the speaker convey about the one-man band? Why is the Anthem "Irrational" rather than "National"?

2. Describe the onomatopoeic effect of the italicized percussive words. What is the purpose of the rhythms that these words cause?

3. What ambiguity is suggested by the *bang* of line 10? How does this ambiguity make the poem seem more than simply an entertaining display of sounds?

WILLIAM WORDSWORTH   (1770–1850)

Daffodils (I Wandered Lonely as a Cloud)° _____ *1807 (1804)*

I wandered lonely as a cloud
That floats on high o'er vales and hills,
When all at once I saw a crowd,
A host, of golden daffodils;
Beside the lake, beneath the trees,   5
Fluttering and dancing in the breeze.

Continuous as the stars that shine
And twinkle on the milky way,
They stretched in never-ending line
Along the margin of a bay: 10
Ten thousand saw I at a glance,
Tossing their heads in sprightly dance.

The waves beside them danced; but they
Out-did the sparkling waves in glee:
A poet could not but be gay,   15
In such a jocund° company: *cheerful, merry*
I gazed—and gazed—but little thought
What wealth the show to me had brought:

For oft, when on my couch I lie
In vacant or in pensive mood,   20
They flash upon that inward eye
Which is the bliss of solitude;
And then my heart with pleasure fills,
And dances with the daffodils.

Wordsworth's note: "Written at Town-end, Grasmere. Daffodils grew and still grow on the margin of Ullswater, and probably may be seen to this day as beautiful in the month of March, nodding their golden heads beside the dancing and foaming waves." Wordsworth also pointed out that lines 21 and 22, the "best lines," were by his wife, Mary.

QUESTIONS

1. Describe the occasion that prompts the poem. Why does the speaker specify that he was alone? How has the scene affected the speaker? What general conclusion about human beings and Nature does the speaker draw, and invite us to draw?
2. What is the significance of the verbs and verbals describing the flowers? What idea about Nature is suggested by these words?
3. Describe the basic metrical pattern of the poem? What is the effect of the trochees beginning lines 6 and 12?
4. Describe the poem's rhyme scheme. What kinds of words are rhymed (e.g., nouns, verbs, etc)? Consider the rhyming of hills, daffodils, and fills. What is the effect of this rhyming sound on the poem's structure?

WRITING ABOUT PROSODY

Because studying prosody requires a good deal of specific detail and description, it is best to limit your study to a short poem or to a short passage from a long poem. A sonnet, a stanza of a lyric poem, or fragment from a long poem will usually be sufficient. If you choose a fragment, it should be self-contained, such as an entire speech or short episode or scene (as in the example from Tennyson chosen for the sample student essay on pp. 608–10).

The analysis of even a short poem, however, can grow long because of the need to describe word positions and stresses, and also to determine the various effects. For this reason you do not have to exhaust your topic. Try to make your discussion representative of the prosody of your poem or passage.

Your first reading in preparation for your essay should be for comprehension. On second and third readings, make notes of sounds, accents, and rhymes by reading the poem aloud. To perceive sounds, one student helped herself by reading aloud in an exaggerated way in front of a mirror. If you have privacy, or are not self-conscious, you might do the same. Let yourself go a bit. As you dramatize your reading (maybe even in front of fellow students), you will find that heightened levels of reading also accompany the poet's expression of important ideas. Mark these spots for later analysis, so that you will be able to make strong assertions about the relationship of sound to sense.

In planning, it is vital to prepare study sheets, so that your observations will be correct, for if your factual analysis is wrong, your writing will also be wrong. Experience has shown that it is best to make four triple-spaced copies of the poem or passage (with photocopy or, if necessary, carbon paper). These will be for the separate analysis of rhythm, assonance, alliteration, and rhyme. If you have been assigned just one of these, of course, only one copy will be necessary. Leave spaces between syllables and words for marking out the various feet of the poem. Ultimately, this duplication of the passage, with your markings, should be included as a first page, as in the sample student essays in this chapter.

Carry out your study of the passage in the following way:

Strategies for Discovering Ideas

- Number each line of the passage, regardless of length, beginning with 1, so that you can use these numbers as location references in your essay.
- Determine the formal pattern of feet, using the short acute accent or stress mark for heavily stressed syllables (´) and the breve for unaccented or lightly stressed syllables (˘). Use chevrons to mark spondees (/\ ).
- Indicate the separate feet by a diagonal slash or virgule (/). Indicate caesurae and end-of-line pauses by double virgules (//).
- Use colored pencils to underline, circle, make boxes, or otherwise mark the formal and rhetorical substitutions that you discover. Because such substitutions may occur throughout the poem, develop a numbering system for each type (e.g., 1 = anapest, 6 = trochee, etc., as in the sample worksheet on p. 608). Provide a key to your numbers at the bottom of the page.
- Do the same for alliteration, assonance, onomatopoeia, and rhyme. It has proved particularly effective to draw lines to connect the repeating sounds, for these effects will be close together in the poem, and your connections will dramatize this closeness. The use of a separate color for each separate effect is helpful, for different colors make prosodic distinctions stand out clearly.
- Use your worksheets as a reference for your reader's benefit. In writing your essay, however, you make your examples specific by including brief illustrative quotations, as in the examples (i.e., words, phrases, and entire lines, with proper marks and accents). Do not rely on line numbers alone.

Once you have analyzed the various effects in your poem, and you have recorded these on your worksheets and in your notes, you will be ready to formulate a central idea and organization. The focus of your essay should reflect the most significant features of prosody in relationship to some other element of the poem, such as speaker, tone, or ideas. Thus, in planning an essay about Eliot's "Macavity," you might argue that the dipodic rhythm contributes to the humor of the poem, and makes the "Napoleon of Crime" seem comic.

Strategies for Organizing Ideas

Depending on your assignment, you might wish to discuss all aspects of rhythm or sound, or perhaps just one, such as the poet's use of regular meter, a particular substitution, alliteration, or assonance. It would be possible, for example, to devote an entire essay to (1) regular meter; (2) one particular variation in meter, such as the anapest or spondee; (3) the caesura; (4) assonance; (5) alliteration; (6) onomatopoeia; or (7) rhyme. For brevity, we here treat rhythm and segments together in one essay, and rhyme in a separate essay.

After a brief description of the poem (such as that it is a sonnet, a two-stanza lyric, a dipodic burlesque poem, and so on), establish the scope of your essay. Your central idea will outline the thought you wish to carry out through your prosodic analysis, such as that regularity of meter is consistent with a happy, firm vision of love or life, or that frequent spondees emphasize the solidity of the speaker's wish to love, or that particular sounds echo some of the poem's actions.

1. *Rhythm.* Establish the formal metrical pattern. What are the dominant metrical foot and line length? Are some lines shorter than the pattern? What relationship do the variable lengths have with the subject matter? If the poem is a lyric, or a sonnet, are important words and syllables successfully placed in stressed positions in order to achieve emphasis? Try to relate line lengths to exposition, development of ideas, and rising or falling emotions. It is also important to look for either repeating or varying metrical patterns as the subject matter reaches peaks or climaxes. Generally, deal with the relationship between the formal rhythmical pattern and the poet's ideas and attitudes.

When noting substitutions, analyze the formal variations and the principal effects of these. If you concentrate on only one substitution, describe any apparent pattern in its use, that is, its locations, recurrences, and effects on meaning.

For caesurae, treat the effectiveness of the poet's control. Can you see any pattern of use? Are the pauses regular or random? Describe noticeable principles of placement, such as (1) the creation of rhythmical similarities in various parts of the poem, (2) the development of particular rhetorical effects, or (3) the creation of interest through rhythmical variety. Do the caesurae lead to important ideas and attitudes? Are the lines all end-stopped, or do you discover enjambement? How do these rhythmical characteristics aid in descriptions and in the expressions of ideas?

2. *Segmental effects.* Here you might be discussing, collectively or separately, the use and effects of assonance, alliteration, onomatopoeia, and cacophony and euphony. Be sure to establish that the instances you choose have really occurred systematically enough within the poem to form a pattern. Illustrate sounds by including relevant words within parentheses. You might make separate paragraphs on alliteration, assonance, and any other seemingly important pattern. Also, because space is always at a premium, you might concentrate on only one noteworthy effect, such as a certain pattern of assonance, rather than on everything. Throughout your discussion, always keep foremost the relationship between content and sound.

Note: To make illustrations clear, emphasize the sounds to which you are calling attention. If you use an entire word to illustrate a sound, underline or italicize only the sound, not the entire word, and put the word within quotation marks (for example: The poet uses a t ["tip," "top," and "terrific"]).

3. *Rhyme.* An essay on rhyme should describe the major features of the poem's rhymes, specifically the scheme and variants, the lengths and rhythms of

the rhyming words, and noteworthy segmental characteristics. In discussing the grammar of the rhymes, note the kinds of words (i.e., verbs, nouns, etc.) used for rhymes: Are they all the same? Does one form predominate? Is there variety? Can you determine the grammatical positions of the rhyming words? How may these characteristics be related to the idea or theme of the poem?

You might also discuss the qualities of the rhyming words. Are the words specific? Concrete? Abstract? Are there any striking rhymes? Any surprises? Any rhymes that are particularly clever and witty? Do any rhymes give unique comparisons or contrasts? How?

Generally, note striking or unique rhyming effects. Without becoming overly subtle or far-fetched, you can make valid and interesting conclusions. Do any sounds in the rhyming words appear in patterns of assonance or alliteration elsewhere in the poem? Do the rhymes enter into any onomatopoeic effects? Broadly, what aspects of rhyme are uniquely effective because they blend so fully with the poem's thought and mood?

In your conclusion, try to develop a short evaluation of the poet's prosodic performance. If we accept the premise that poetry is designed not only to stimulate emotions, but also to provide information and transfer attitudes, to what degree do the prosodic techniques of your poem contribute to these goals? Without going into excessive detail (and writing another essay), what more can say here? What has been the value of your study to your understanding and appreciating the poem? If you think your analysis has helped you to develop new awareness of the poet's craft, it would be appropriate to state what you have learned.

SAMPLE STUDENT ESSAY

A Study of Tennyson's Rhythm and Segments in "The Passing of Arthur," 349–360*

* For illustration, this essay analyzes a passage from Tennyson's "The Passing of Arthur," which is part of **Idylls of the King.** *Containing 469 lines, "The Passing of Arthur" describes the last battle and death of Arthur, legendary king of early Britain. After the fight, in which Arthur has been mortally wounded by the traitor Mordred, only Arthur and his follower Sir Bedivere remain alive. Arthur commands Bedivere to throw the royal sword Excalibur into the lake from which Arthur had originally received it. After great hesitation and some false claims, Bedivere does throw the sword into the lake, and a hand rises out of the water to catch it. Bedivere then carries Arthur to the lake shore, where the dying king is taken aboard a mysterious funeral barge. In the passage selected for discussion (lines 349–360), Tennyson describes Bedivere carrying Arthur down the hills and cliffs from the battlefield to the lake below.*

1. RHYTHMICAL ANALYSIS*

But the ŏ -/ thĕr swíft -/ lў stróde // from rídge / tŏ rídge, //   1

Clóthed wĭth / hĭs bréath, // ănd loók - / ĭng, // ăs / hĕ waĺk'd, //   2

Laŕ - gĕr / thăn hŭ -/ măn // ŏn / thĕ fró - / zĕn hílls //   3

Hĕ heárd / thĕ deép / bĕ - hínd / hĭm, // ănd / ă crý   4

Bĕ - fóre. // Hĭs ówn / thought drove / hĭm // líke / ă góad. //   5

Drў clash'd / hĭs haŕ - / nĕss // ĭn / thĕ í / cy cáves   6

Ănd baŕ - rĕn / chásms, // ănd aĺl / tŏ léft / ănd ríght   7

Thĕ báre / black clíff / clang'd round / hĭm, // ăs / hĕ básed   8

Hĭs feét / ŏn júts / ŏf slíp - / pĕ-rў crág // thăt ráng   9

Sharp - smít - / tĕn // wíth / thĕ / dínt / ŏf aŕ - / mĕd heéls— //   10

Ănd ón / ă súd -/ dĕn, // lŏ! // thĕ lév - / eĭ láke, //   11

Ănd thĕ / long glór - / ĭes // ŏf / thĕ wín - / tĕr moón. //   12

1 = Anapaest, or effect of anapaest.
2 = Amphibrach, or the effect of amphibrach.
3 = Spondee.

4 = Effect of imperfect foot.
5 = Pyrrhic.
6 = Trochee, or the effect of trochee.

* Pronunciation symbols as in *Webster's New World Dictionary,* 2nd ed.

2. *ALLITERATION*

But the other ⓢwiftly ⓢtrode from ridge to ridge.   1

Clothed with his breath, and looking, as ⓗe walked,   2

Larger than ⓗuman on the frozen ⓗills.   3

Ⓗe ⓗeard the deep be ⓗind ⓗim, and a cry   4

Before. Ⓗis own thought drove him like a goad.   5

Dry ⓒlash'd ⓗis ⓗarness in the icy ⓒaves   6

And ⓑarren ⓒhasms, and all to left and right   7

The ⓑare ⓑⓁack ⓒⓁiff ⓒⓁang'd round him, as he ⓑased   8

His feet on juts of sⓁippery ⓒrag that rang   9

Sharp-smitten with the dint of armed heels—   10

And on a sudden, Ⓛo! the Ⓛevel, Ⓛake,   11

And Ⓛong gⓁories of the winter moon.   12

⌇⌇⌇⌇ = s   ———— = b

- - - - - - = h   ⌇⌇⌇⌇ = l as second consonant
                                          sound in words

············ = k   — · — · — · — = l

3. ASSONANCE

But the other sw(i)ftly str(o)de from r(i)dge to r(i)dge,   1

Cl(o)thed w(i)th h(i)s breath, and looking, as he walked,   2

Larger than human on the fr(o)zen hills.   3

He heard the deep beh(i)nd him, and a cr(y)   4

Before. His (ow)n thought dr(o)ve him l(i)ke a g(oa)d.   5

Dr(y) clash'd his harness in the (i)cy caves   6

And barren ch(a)sms, and all to left and r(i)ght   7

The bare bl(a)ck cliff cl(a)ng'd round him, as he based   8

H(i)s feet on juts of sl(i)ppery cr(a)g that r(a)ng   9

Sh(ar)p-sm(i)tten w(i)th the d(i)nt of (ar)med heels—   10

And on a sudden, lo! the level lake,   11

And the long glories of the winter moon!   12

————————— = ō   •—·—·—•· = ä

- - - - - - - - - - = ī   ⌣⌣⌣⌣⌣ = ĭ

· · · · · · · · · · = a

[1]

In these twelve lines, Tennyson describes the ordeal of Sir Bedivere as he carries King Arthur, who is dying, from the mountainous heights, where he was wounded, down to the lake, where he will be sent to his final rest. Tennyson emphasizes the bleakness and hostility of this ghostly and deserted landscape. The metrical pattern he uses is unrhymed iambic pentameter--blank verse--which is suitable for descriptions of actions and scenes. Appropriately, the verse augments the natural descriptions and echoes first Bedivere's tenseness and then his relaxation.* Tennyson's control enables a true blending of sound and sense, as seen in his use of rhythm and in his manipulation of segmental devices, including onomatopoeia.†

[2]

Tennyson controls his meter to emphasize exertions and moods. In line 1 the meter is regular, except for an anapest in the first foot. This regularity can be interpreted as emphasizing the swiftness and surefootedness of Bedivere. But he is about to undergo a severe test, and the rhythm quickly becomes irregular, as though to strain the pentameter verse in illustration of Bedivere's exertions. Tennyson therefore uses variations to highlight key words. For example, he uses the effect of anapests in a number of lines. In line 2 he emphasizes the chill air and Bedivere's vitality in the following way:

Clothed with / his breath, //

The image is one of being surrounded by one's own breath that vaporizes on hitting the cold air, and the rhythmical variation--a trochaic substitution in the first foot--enables the voice to build up to the word "breath," a most effective internal climax.

[3]

Tennyson uses the same kind of rhythmical effect in line 3. He emphasizes the "frozen hills" by creating a caesura in the middle of the third foot, and then by making the heavy stress of the third foot fall on the preposition "on," which with "the" creates the effect of an anapest consisting of two unstressed syllables leading up to the first, stressed, syllable of "frozen." The effect is that the voice builds up to the word and thus emphasizes the extreme conditions in which Bedivere is walking:

// on / the fro - / zen hills. //

Tennyson uses this rhythmical effect eleven times in the passage. It is one of his major means of rhetorical emphasis.

[4]

Tennyson's most effective metrical variation is the spondee, which appears in lines 5, 6, 8 (twice), 10, and 12. These substitutions, occurring mainly in the section describing how Bedivere forces his way down the frozen hills, permits the descriptive lines to ring out, as in:

The bare / black cliff / clanged round /

* Central idea.
† Thesis sentence.

and

    ⋀

Dry clash'd / his har - / ness //

These substitutions are so strong that they are almost literally like the actual
[4] sounds of Bedivere's exertions. In addition to this use of the spondee as a sound
effect, a remarkable use of the spondee for psychological effect occurs in line 5.
Here, the stresses internalize Bedivere's distress, reaching a climax on the word
"drove":

    ⋀

His own / thought drove / him //

 There is other substitution, too, both formal and rhetorical, and the tension
these variations create keeps the responsive reader aware of Bedivere's tasks.
One type of variation is the appearance of amphibrachic rhythm, which is produced in lines 2, 3, 4, 6, 7, and 11. The effect is achieved by a pattern that complements the rhetorical anapests. A caesura in the middle of a foot leaves the
three preceding syllables as a light, heavy, and light, the rhythmical form of the
[5] amphibrach. In line 2, for example, it appears thus:

// and look - / ing, //

In line 6 it takes this form:

/ his har - / ness //

 Still another related variation is that of the apparently imperfect feet in lines
5, 8, 11, and 12. These imperfect feet are produced by a caesura, which isolates
the syllable, as "him" is in line 8:

    ⋀   ⋀

The bare / black cliff / clang'd round / him, //

[6] In line 11 the syllable (on the word "lo!") is surrounded by two caesurae and is
therefore thrust into a position of great stress:

And on / a sud - / den, // lo! // the lev - / el lake,

Other, less significant substitutions are the trochees in lines 3 and 7 and the
pyrrhic in line 12. All the described variations suggest the energy that Bedivere
expends during his heroic action.

 Many of the variations are produced by Tennyson's sentence structure,
which results in a free placement of the caesurae and in a free use of end-
[7] stopping and enjambement. Four of the first five lines are end-stopped (two by
commas, two by periods). Bedivere is exerting himself during these lines and he
is making short tests to gather strength. His dangerous descent is described

during the next four lines, and none of these lines is end-stopped. Bedivere is disturbed (being goaded by "his own thought"), but he must keep going, and the free sentence structure and free metrical variation underscore his physical and mental difficulties. But in the last two lines, when he has reached the lake, the lines "relax" with falling caesurae exactly at the fifth syllable. In other words, the sentence structure of the last two lines is regular, an effect suggesting the return to order and beauty after the previous, rugged chaos.

[8] This rhythmical virtuosity is accompanied by a similarly brilliant control over segmental devices. Alliteration is the most obvious, permitting Tennyson to tie key words and their signifying actions together, as in the *s*'s in "*s*wiftly *s*trode" in line 1, or the *b*'s in "*b*arren," "*b*are," "*b*lack," and "*b*ased" in lines 7 and 8. Other notable examples are the aspirated *h*'s in lines 2–6 ("*h*e," "*h*uman," "*h*ills," "*h*eard," "*b*e*h*ind," "*h*im," "*h*is," "*h*arness"); the *k*'s in lines 6–9 ("*c*lash'd," "*c*aves," "*c*hasms," "*c*liff," "*c*langed," "*c*rag"); and the *l*'s in lines 11 and 12 ("*l*o," "*l*evel," "*l*ake," "*l*ong," "g*l*ories"). One might compare these *l*'s with the *l*'s in the more anguished context of lines 8 and 9, where the sounds appear as the second seg-ment in the heavy, ringing words there ("b*l*ack," "c*l*iff," "c*l*anged," "s*l*ippery"). The sounds are the same, and the emphasis is similar, but the effects are different.

Assonance is also present throughout the passage. In the first five lines, for example, the *o* appears in six words. The first three *ō*'s are in descriptive or metaphoric words ("strōde," "clōthed," "frōzen"), while the last three are in words describing Bedivere's pain and anguish ("*o*wn," "dr*o*ve," "g*o*ad"). The *ō* there-fore ties the physical to the psychological. Other patterns of assonance are the *ă* in lines 7, 8, and 9 ("chăsms," "clăng'd," "blăck," "crăg," "răng"), the *ä* of line 10 ("shärp," "ärmed"), the *ī* of lines 4–7 ("behīnd," "crȳ," "līke," "drȳ," "īcy," "rīght"),

[9] and the short *ĭ* of lines 1, 2, 9, and 10 ("swĭftly," "rĭdge," "wĭth," "hĭs," "slĭppery," "smĭtten," "wĭth," "dĭnt"). One might remark also that in the last two lines, which describe the level lake and the moon, Tennyson introduces a number of relaxed *o* and *oo* and similar vowel sounds:

> And *o*n a s*u*dden, l*o*! the level lake,
>
> And the l*o*ng gl*o*ries of the winter m*oo*n.

[10] The last two lines are, in fact, onomatopoeic, since the liquid *l* sounds suggest the gentle lapping of waves on a lake shore. There are other exam-ples of onomatopoeia, too. In line 2 Tennyson describes Bedivere in the cold air as being "Clothed with his breath," and in the following five lines Tennyson employs many words with the aspirated *h* (e.g., "*h*is *h*arness"). In the context, these sounds enable readers to see and hear sights and sounds just like those of Bedivere as he carries his royal burden. Similarly, the explosive stops *b, k, d,* and *t* in lines 6–10 suggest the sounds of Sir Bedivere's feet striking the "juts of slippery crag."

[11] This short passage is filled with many examples of poetic excellence. Tennyson's sounds and rhythms actually speak along with the meaning. They emphasize the grandeur of Arthur and his faithful follower, and for one brief moment they bear out the magic that Tennyson associated with the fading past.

Commentary on the Essay

This essay presents a full treatment of the prosody of the passage from Tennyson. Paragraphs 2 through 7 deal with the relationship of the rhythm to the content. Note that prosody is not discussed in isolation, but as it augments Tennyson's descriptions of action and scenes. Thus, paragraph 4 refers to the use of the spondee as a substitute foot to reinforce ideas. Also in this paragraph, there is a short comparison of alternative ways of saying what Tennyson says so well. While such a speculative comparison should not be attempted often, it is effective here in bringing out the quality of Tennyson's use of the spondee as a means of emphasis.

Paragraphs 8 and 9 present a discussion of the alliteration and assonance of the passage, and paragraph 10 considers onomatopoeia.

Of greatest importance for the clarity of the essay, there are many supporting examples, spaced, centered and accurately marked, and numbered by line. In any essay about prosody, readers are likely to be unsure of the validity of the writer's observation unless such examples are provided and are located within the poem.

SAMPLE STUDENT ESSAY

The Rhymes in Christina Rossetti's "Echo"

                                  n

1   Come to me in the silence of the night;   5a

                          n

2   Come in the speaking silence of a dream;   5b

                                      adj

3   Come with soft rounded cheeks and eyes as bright   5a

                    n

4   As sunlight on a stream;   3b

                    n

5   Come back in tears,   2c

                        n

6   O memory, hope, love of finished years.   5c

                              adj

7   O dream how sweet, too sweet, too bitter sweet,   5d

                                 n

8   Whose wakening should have been in paradise,   5e

                         v

9   Where souls brimful of love abide and meet;   5d

	n	
10	Where thirsty longing eyes	3e

	n	
11	Watch the slow door	2f

	adv	
12	That opening, letting in, lets out no more.	5f

	v	
13	Yet come to me in dreams, that I may live	5g

	n	
14	My very life again though cold in death;	5h

	v	
15	Come back to me in dreams, that I may give	5g

	n	
16	Pulse for pulse, breath for breath:	3h

	adv	
17	Speak low, lean low,	2i

	adj	
18	As long ago, my love, how long ago!	5i

Repeated words		n = noun
~~	dream, dreams	v = verb
———	sweet	adj = adjective
- · - · -	breath	adv = adverb
······	low	
- - - - -	long ago	
~~	come	

[1]

      In the three-stanza lyric poem "Echo," Christina Rossetti uses rhyme as a way of saying that one might regain in dreams a love that is lost in reality.* As the real love is to the dream of love, so is an original sound to an echo. This connection underlies the poem's title and also Rossetti's unique use of rhyme. Aspects of her rhyme are the lyric pattern, the forms and qualities of the rhyming words, and the special use of repetition.†

---

* Central idea.
† Thesis sentence.

The rhyme pattern is simple, and, like rhyme generally, it may be thought of as a pattern of echoes. Each stanza contains four lines of alternating rhymes concluded by a couplet, as follows:

Iambic: 5a, 5b, 5a, 3b, 2c, 5c

[2]

There are nine separate rhymes throughout the poem, three in each stanza. Only two words are used for each rhyme, and no rhyme is used twice. Of the eighteen rhyming words, sixteen are one syllable long--almost all the rhymes. The remaining two words consist of two and three syllables. With such a great number of single-syllable words, the rhymes are all rising ones, on the accented halves of iambic feet, and the end-of-line emphasis is on simple words.

The grammatical forms and positions of the rhyming words lend support to the introspective subject matter. Although there is variety, more than half the rhyming words are nouns. There are ten in all, and eight are placed as the objects of prepositions (e.g., "of a dream," "on a stream," "of finished years"). The nouns that are not the objects of prepositions are the subject and object of the same subordinate clause (lines 10 and 11). It seems clear that much of the poem's verbal energy occurs in the first parts of the lines, leaving the rhymes to occur in modifying elements, as in these lines:

[3]

Come to me in the silence of the night; (1)

Yet come to me in dreams, that I may live (13)

My very life again though cold in death: (14)

Most of the other rhymes are also in such internalized positions. This careful arrangement is consistent with the speaker's emphasis on her yearning to relive her love within dreams.

The qualities of the words are also consistent with the poem's emphasis on the speaker's internal life. Most of the rhyming words are impressionistic. Even the specific words--"stream," "tears," "eyes," "door," and "breath"--reflect the speaker's mental condition. In this regard, the rhyming words of lines 1 and 3 are effective. These are "night" and "bright," which contrast the bleakness of the speaker's solitary condition with the vitality of her inner life. Another effective contrast is in lines 14 and 16, where "death" and "breath" are rhymed. This rhyme underscores the sad fact that even though the speaker's love has vanished, it lives in present memory just as an echo continues after the original sound is gone.

[4]

It is in emphasizing how memory echoes experience that Rossetti creates her special use of rhyming words. She creates an ingenious repetition of a number of words; these are the poem's echoes. The major echoing word is the verb "come," which appears six times at the beginnings of lines in stanzas 1 and 3. But some of the rhyming words are also repeated. The most notable is "dream," the rhyming word in line 2. Rossetti repeats the word in line 7 and uses the plural, "dreams," in lines 13 and 15. In line 7 the rhyming word "sweet" is the third use of that word, a climax of "how *sweet*, too *sweet*, too bitter *sweet*." Concluding the poem, Rossetti repeats "breath" (16), "low" (17), and the phrase

[5]

"long ago" (18). These repeating words justify the title "Echo," and they also stress the major idea that it is only in memory that experience has reality, even if dreams are no more than echoes.

[6]

Thus rhyme is not just ornamental in "Echo," but integral. The ease of Rossetti's rhymes, like the poem's diction generally, keeps the focus on regret and yearning rather than self-indulgence. As in all rhyming poems, Rossetti's rhymes emphasize the line endings. The rhymes go beyond this effect, however, because of the internal repetition--echoes--of the rhyming words. "Echo" is a poem in which rhyme is inseparable from meaning.

Commentary on the Essay

Throughout, illustrative words are highlighted, and numbers are used to indicate the lines from which the illustrations are drawn. The introductory paragraph asserts that rhyme is vital in Rossetti's poem. It also attempts to explain the title "Echo." The thesis statement indicates the four topics to be developed in the body.

Paragraph 2 deals with the mechanical, mathematical aspects of the poem's rhymes. The high number of monosyllabic rhyming words is used to explain the rising, heavy-stress rhyme.

Paragraph 3 treats the grammar of the rhymes. For example, an analysis and count reveal that there are ten rhyming nouns and three rhyming verbs. The verb of command "come" is mentioned to show that most of the rhyming words exist within groups modifying this word. The grammatical analysis is thus related to the internalized nature of the poem's subject.

Paragraph 4 emphasizes the impressionistic nature of the rhyming words and also points out two instances in which rhymes stress the contrast between real life and the speaker's introspective life. Paragraph 5 deals with how Rossetti repeats five of the poem's rhyming words. This repetition creates a pattern of echoes, in keeping with the poem's title.

The concluding paragraph summarizes that Rossetti uses rhyme integrally within "Echo," not ornamentally. In addition, the point is emphasized that the internal rhymes or echoes are an additional facet of Rossetti's rhyming skill.

SPECIAL WRITING TOPICS FOR STUDYING PROSODY

1. For Shakespeare's Sonnet 73, "That Time of Year Thou Mayst in Me Behold," analyze the ways in which Shakespeare creates his iambics. That is, what is the relationship of lightly accented syllables to the heavily accented ones? Where does Shakespeare use articles (*the*), pronouns (*this, his*), prepositions (*upon, against, of*), relative clause markers (*which, that*) and adverb clause markers (*as, when*) in relation to syllables of heavy stress? On the basis of this study, how would you characterize Shakespeare's control of the iambic foot?

2. Compare the sounds used in Poe's "The Bells" with those of Wagoner's "March for a One-Man Band." What effects are achieved by each poet? What is the relationship in each poem between sound and content? Which poem do you prefer on the basis of sound? Why?

3. The poems "Miniver Cheevy," "The Bells," "Ode to the West Wind," and "Upon Julia's Voice" all use falling, or trochaic rhyme. What is the effect of this rhyming pattern in the four poems? How do the poems achieve seriousness, despite the fact that trochaic rhyme is often used generally to complement humorous and light verse?

4. Analyze the rhymes in one of Shakespeare's sonnets, or else the rhymes in Coleridge's "Kubla Khan" or Arnold's "Dover Beach" (or another poem of your choice). What is interesting or unique about the various rhyming words? What relationships can you discover between the rhymes and the topics of the poems?

5. Compare one of the rhyming poems with one of the nonrhyming poems included in this book. What differences in reading and sound can you discover as a result of the use or nonuse of rhyme? What benefits does rhyme give to the poem? What benefits does nonrhyme give?

6. Write a short poem of your own using double or triple rhymes, with words such as *computer, emetic, scholastic, remarkable, along with me, inedible, moron, anxiously, emotion, fishing,* and so on. If you have trouble with exact rhymes, see what you can do with slant rhymes and eye rhymes. The idea is to use your ingenuity.

7. Using the topical index in your library, take out a book on prosody, such as Harvey Gross's *Sound and Form in Modern Poetry* (1968) or *The Structure of Verse* (1966), or Gay Wilson Allen's *American Prosody* (1935, rpt. 1966). Select a topic (e.g., formal or experimental prosody) or poet (e.g., Frost, Thomas, Poe, Whitman), and write a summary of the ideas and observations the writers make on your subject. What relationship do the writers make about prosody and the poet's ideas? How does prosody enter into the writer's thought? Into the ways in which the poets emphasize ideas and images?

17

Form: The Shape of the Poem

Because poetry is tightly compressed and highly rhythmical, it always exists under self-imposed restrictions, or conventions, some of which are examined in Chapter 16. Traditionally, many poets have chosen a variety of clearly recognizable shapes or forms—**closed-form poetry.** Since the middle of the nineteenth century, however, many poets have rejected the more regular patterns in favor of poems that appear more free and spontaneous—**open-form poetry.** Bear in mind that these terms refer to the structure and technique of the poems, not to content or ideas.

CLOSED-FORM POETRY

Closed-form poetry is written in specific and traditional patterns of lines produced through *rhyme, meter, line length,* and *line groupings.* In the closed form (and also in the open form), the **stanza** is the poetic analogue of the prose paragraph. It consists of lines connected by subject or theme and often grouped or separated both topically and visually. Examples of closed forms that have been used for hundreds of years are *ballads, sonnets, couplets, blank verse, limericks, hymns, odes,* and *lyrics.*

The Building Blocks of Closed-Form Poetry

The basic building block of closed-form poetry is the single line of verse. Various numbers of lines may be grouped together through rhyme to form stanzas or sections of poems, which in turn are assembled to create the many *traditional* closed forms.

BLANK VERSE. One of the most common types of English poetry is **blank verse,** or *unrhymed iambic pentameter* (see p. 573). Shakespeare uses blank verse extensively in his plays, and Milton's long epic, *Paradise Lost,* uses it exclusively. An example of Shakespeare's blank verse is this speech from the first act of *Hamlet,* where the prince tells his mother that his sorrow over his father's death is real and not superficial:

Seems, madam? nay it is, I know not "seems."
'Tis not alone my inky cloak good mother,
Nor customary suits of solemn black,
Nor windy suspiration of forced breath,
No, nor the fruitful river in the eye,°   *tears*
Nor the dejected havior° of the visage,°   *appearance; face*
Together with all forms, moods, shapes of grief,
That can denote me truly: these indeed seem,
For they are actions that a man might play,
But I have that within which passes show,
These but the trappings and the suits of woe.

                                                        (Act I, scene 2, lines 77–86)

While these lines are linked together to make up the entire speech, each one creates an identifiable unit of thought and grammatical coherence. (The rhyming lines mark the conclusion, not a new form.) In the footsteps of Shakespeare, poets of English have used blank verse again and again, for without forsaking its poetic identity, it sounds like normal speech.

THE COUPLET.   The basic two-line poetic form is the **couplet.** The two lines often rhyme and usually are of equal length, although biblical poetry contains couplets unified by parallel ideas, not by meter and rhyme. Some couplets are short; even monometric lines like "Some play/All day" comprise a couplet. However, couplets are most often in iambic pentameter and iambic tetrameter. They have been a regular feature of English poetry ever since Chaucer used them in the fourteenth century. In the seventeenth and eighteenth centuries, the five-stress couplet was considered particularly appropriate for epic, or heroic, poetry. For this reason it is called a **heroic couplet.** Because the period is considered the "neoclassic" age of literature, the form is also called the **neoclassic couplet.** It was used with consummate skill by John Dryden (1631–1700) and also by Alexander Pope (1685–1744).

　　Usually, the heroic couplet expresses a complete idea and is grammatically self-sufficient. It thrives on the rhetorical strategies of **parallelism** and **antithesis.** Look, for example, at these lines from "The Rape of the Lock," Pope's great mock-epic poem (1711):

Here Britain's statesmen oft the fall foredoom
Of foreign tyrants, and of nymphs at home;
Here thou, great Anna! whom three realms obey,
Dost sometimes counsel take—and sometimes tea.

These lines describe activities at Hampton Court, the royal palace and residence of Queen Anne (reigned 1701–1714). Notice that the first couplet allows

Pope to link "*Britain's* Statesmen" with two related but antithetical events: the fall of nations and the fall of young women. Similarly, the second heroic couplet allows for the parallel and comic linking of royal meetings of state (*counsel*) and teatime (in the early eighteenth century, *tea* was pronounced "tay"). The example thus demonstrates how the heroic couplet may place contrasting actions and situations in amusing and ironic parallels.

THE TERCET OR TRIPLET. A three-line stanza is called a **tercet** or **triplet.** Tercets may be written in any uniform line length or meter; they most commonly contain three rhymes (*a a a, b b b,* and so on), which are, in effect, short stanzas. The following poem is in iambic tetrameter triplets.

ALFRED, LORD TENNYSON (1809–1892)

The Eagle _____ *1851*

He clasps the crag with crooked hands;
Close to the sun in lonely lands,
Ring'd with the azure world, he stands.

The wrinkled sea beneath him crawls;
He watches from his mountain walls,   5
And like a thunderbolt he falls.

In the first tercet, we view the eagle as though at a distance. In the second, the perspective shifts, and we see through the eagle's eyes and follow his actions. In this tercet the verbs are active: the sea "crawls" and the eagle "falls." While the two tercets and the shift in perspective divide the poem, alliteration pulls things back together. This is especially true of the *k* sound in "clasps," "crag," "crooked," "close," and "crawls" and the *w* sound in "with," "world," "watches," and "walls."

There are two important variations on the tercet pattern, each requiring a high degree of ingenuity and control. The first tercet variation is **terza rima,** in which stanzas are interlocked through a pattern that requires the center termination in one tercet to be rhymed twice in the next: *a b a, b c b, c d c, d e d,* and so on. You can see an example of terza rima in Shelley's "Ode to the West Wind" (p. 598).

The most complex variation of the tercet pattern is the **villanelle,** in which every triplet in the poem is rhymed *a b a,* and the first and third lines of the first tercet are repeated alternately in subsequent stanzas as a refrain and also are used as the concluding lines (for examples, see Thomas's "Do Not Go Gentle into That Good Night," p. 646, and Roethke's "The Waking," p. 793).

THE QUATRAIN. The most common and adaptable stanzaic building block in English and American poetry is the four-line **quatrain.** This stanza has been popular for hundreds of years and has lent itself to a great many variations. Like couplets and triplets, quatrains may be written in any line length and meter; even the line lengths *within* a quatrain may vary. The determining factor is the rhyme scheme, and even that is variable, depending on the form and the poet's aims. Quatrains may be rhymed *a a a a*, but they can also be rhymed *a b a b, a b b a, a a b a*, or even *a b c b*. All these variations are determined, at least in part, by the larger patterns or forms in which quatrains are used. Quatrains are basic components of many traditional closed forms, most notably ballads and sonnets.

Common Types of Closed-Form Poetry

Over the centuries English and American poetry has evolved or appropriated many traditional closed forms, all of them determined by combinations of meter, rhyme scheme, line length, and stanza, and embodying couplets, tercets, and quatrains. The following are the more common forms.

THE ITALIAN OR PETRARCHAN SONNET.   The **sonnet** is one of the most popular and durable forms. All sonnets are fourteen lines long. Initially, they were an Italian poetic form (*sonnetto* means "little song") popularized by Petrarch (1304–1374), who wrote long collections or *cycles* of sonnets. The form and style of Petrarch's sonnets were adapted to English poetry in the early sixteenth century and with variations have been used ever since. The **Italian** or **Petrarchan sonnet** is in iambic pentameter and contains two quatrains (the **octave**) and two tercets (the **sestet**). In terms of structure and meaning, the octave presents a problem or situation that is resolved in the sestet, as in Milton's "When I Consider How My Light Is Spent." The rhyme scheme of the Petrarchan octave is fixed in an *a b b a, a b b a* pattern. The sestet offers a number of different rhyming possibilities, including *c d c, c d c* and *c d e, c d e*.

THE SHAKESPEAREAN OR ENGLISH SONNET.   Shakespeare recognized that there are fewer rhyming words in English than in Italian. He therefore based his **Shakespearean** or **English sonnet** on seven rhymes (in the pattern *a b a b, c d c d, e f e f, g g*) rather than the five rhymes of the Italian sonnet. As indicated by the rhyme scheme, the Shakespearean sonnet contains three quatrains and a concluding couplet. The pattern of thought therefore shifts from the octave-sestet organization of the Italian sonnet to a four-part argument on a single thought or emotion. Each Shakespearean quatrain contains a separate development of the sonnet's central idea or problem, and the couplet provides a climax and resolution. Shakespeare's Sonnet 116, "Let Me Not to the Marriage of True Minds," is an example of the Shakespearean sonnet.

THE BALLAD.   The **ballad,** which fuses narrative description with much dramatic dialogue, originated in folk literature and is the oldest closed form in English poetry. Ballads consist of a long series of quatrains in which lines of iambic tetrameter alternate with iambic trimeter. Normally, only the second and fourth lines of each stanza rhyme, in the pattern *x a x a, x b x b, x c x c*, and so on. The ballad was designed for singing, like the anonymous ballad "Sir

Patrick Spens" (p. 451). Popular ballad tunes were used over and over again by later balladeers, often as many as forty and fifty times, and many of the tunes have survived to the present day.

COMMON MEASURE OR HYMNAL STANZA.   **Common measure** is similar to the ballad stanza. It shares with the ballad the alternation of four-beat and three-beat iambic lines but adds a second rhyme to each quatrain: *a b a b, c d c d,* and so on. As with the ballad, the building block of common measure is the quatrain. Because the measure is often used in hymns, it is sometimes called the **hymnal stanza.** Many of Emily Dickinson's poems, including "Because I Could Not Stop for Death" (p. 455), are written in common measure.

THE SONG OR LYRIC.   The **song** or **lyric** is a stanzaic form originally designed to be sung to a repeating melody. The structure and rhyme scheme of the first stanza are therefore duplicated in all subsequent stanzas. Next to the ballad, it is one of the oldest traditional poetic forms. The individual stanzas of a lyric may be built from any combination of single lines, couplets, triplets, and quatrains. The line lengths may shift, and a great deal of metrical variation is common.

There is theoretically no limit to the number of stanzas in a lyric, although there are usually no more than five or six. There is much variation in the structure. A. E. Housman's "Loveliest of Trees" (p. 458), for example, is made up of three quatrains containing two couplets each. It is in iambic tetrameter and rhymes *a a b b.* The second and third stanzas repeat the same pattern. Christina Rossetti's "Echo" (p. 614) is also a lyric, but its structure is different from that of Housman's poem. Here, the structural formulation of each stanza is iambic: *5a 5b 5a 3b 2c 5c.* Lyrics can have very complex and ingenious stanzaic structures. John Donne's "The Canonization" (p. 667), for instance, contains five stanzas that reflect the following pattern: *iambic: 5a 4b 5b 5a 4c 4c 4c 4a 3a.* The nine-line stanza contains three different rhymes and three different line lengths. Nevertheless, the same intricate pattern is repeated in each of the five stanzas.

THE ODE.   The **ode** is a more variable stanzaic form than the lyric, with varying line lengths and intricate rhyme schemes. Some odes have repeating patterns, while others offer no duplication and introduce a new structure in each stanza. There is no set form for the ode. Poets have developed their own structure according to their needs. John Keats's great odes were particularly congenial to his ideas, as in the "Ode to a Nightingale," which consists of ten stanzas in iambic pentameter with the repeating form *a b a b c d e 3c d e.* Although some odes have been set to music, most do not fit repeating melodies.

THE HAIKU.   The **haiku** originated in Japan, where it has been a favorite genre for hundreds of years. It traditionally imposes strict rules on the writer: (1) The topic should be derived from nature. (2) There should be three lines of *five, seven,* and *five* syllables per line, for a total of seventeen syllables. Today English-language poets have adapted the haiku but have taken liberties with the subject matter and precise syllable count. Whether the haiku is traditional or more free, however, all haiku must be short, simple, objective, clear, and often symbolic. The following anonymous haiku illustrates some of these qualities.

Spun in high, dark clouds

Spun in high, dark clouds,
Snow forms vast webs of white flakes
And drifts lightly down

In the tradition of haiku, the subject is derived from nature, and the line pattern is 5-7-5. The central metaphor equates gathering snow with the webs of silk-worms or spiders. To supply tension, the lines contrast "high" with "down" and "dark" with "white." Because of the enforced brevity, the diction is simple and, except for the word "forms," is of English derivation (the word *form* was originally French). In addition, the words are mainly monosyllabic, and the poem therefore crowds sixteen words to fulfill the seventeen-syllable requirement.

Closed Form and Meaning

Although closed forms seem restrictive to many contemporary poets, they have always provided both a framework and a challenge for poets to express new and fresh ideas, attitudes, and feelings. Let us look at the way Shakespeare uses a specific closed form—the sonnet—to shape thoughts and emotions.

WILLIAM SHAKESPEARE   (1564–1616)

Sonnet 116: Let Me Not to the Marriage of True Minds _____ *1609*

Let me not to the marriage of true minds
Admit impediments.° Love is not love
Which alters when it alteration finds,
Or bends with the remover to remove:
Oh, no! it is an ever-fixéd mark,   5
That looks on tempests and is never shaken;
It is the star to every wandering bark,
Whose worth's unknown, although his height° be taken   *altitude*
Love's not Time's fool,° though rosy lips and cheeks   *slave*
Within his° bending sickle's compass come;   *Time's*   10
Love alters not with his brief hours and weeks,
But bears it out even to the edge of doom.°   *the Last Judgment*

SONNET 116.   2 *impediments:* a reference to "The Order of Solemnization of Matrimony" in the Anglican *Book of Common Prayer:* "I require that if either of you know of any impediment why ye may not be lawfully joined together in Matrimony, ye do now confess it."

If this be error and upon me proved,
I never writ, nor no man ever loved.

QUESTIONS

    1.   Describe the restrictions of this closed form. How is the poem's argument structured by the form?

    2.   What is the poem's meter? Rhyme scheme? Structure?

    3.   Describe the varying ideas about love explored in the three quatrains.

    4.   What does the concluding couplet contribute to the poem's argument about love?

Even if we didn't know that the poem is Shakespeare's, we would instantly know that it is a Shakespearean sonnet. It is in iambic pentameter and contains three quatrains and a concluding couplet, rhyming *a b a b, c d c d, e f e f, g g*. The sonnet form provides the organization for the poem's argument—that real love is a "marriage of true minds" existing independent of earthly time and change. Each quatrain advances a new perspective on this idea.

This is not to say that Shakespeare exhausts the subject or that he wants to. The ideas in the third quatrain, for example, about how love transcends time, could be greatly expanded. A philosophical analysis of the topic would need to deal extensively with Platonic ideas about reality—whether it exists in *particulars* or *universals*. Similarly, the poem's very last line, if it became the topic of a prose inquiry, might require the introduction of evidence about the poet's own writing, and also about many examples of human love. But the two lines are enough, granted the restrictions of the form, and more would be superfluous. One might add that most readers find Shakespeare's poem interesting and vital, while extensive philosophical discourses often drop into laps as readers fall asleep.

The closed poetic form therefore may be viewed as a complex consequence of poetic compression. No matter what form a poet chooses—couplet, sonnet, song, ballad, ode—that form imposes restrictions, and it therefore challenges and shapes the poet's thought. The poet of the closed form shares with all writers the need to make ideas seem logical and well supported, but the challenge of the form is to make all this happen *within the form itself.* The thought must be developed clearly and also fully, and there should be no lingering doubts once the poem is completed. The words must be the most fitting and exact ones that could be selected. When we look at good poems in the closed form, in short, we may be sure that they represent the ultimate degree of poetic thought, discipline, and skill.

OPEN-FORM POETRY

Open-form poetry avoids traditional patterns of organization to produce order. Poetry of this type was once termed **free verse** (from the French *vers* *libre*) to signify its liberation from regular metrics and its embrace of spoken rhythms. But open-form poetry is not therefore disorganized or chaotic. Open-form poets have instead sought new ways to arrange words and lines, new ways to express thoughts and feelings, and new ways to order poetic experience.

The Building Blocks of Open-Form Poetry

Poets of the open form attempt to fuse form and content by stressing speechlike rhythms, creating a natural and easy-flowing word order, altering and varying line lengths according to the importance of ideas, and creating emphasis through the control of shorter and longer pauses. They often isolate individual words, phrases, and clauses into single lines; freely emphasize their ideas through the manipulation of spaces separating words and sentences; and sometimes even break up individual words to highlight their importance. Sometimes they create poems that look exactly like prose and that are printed in blocks and paragraphs instead of stanzas or lines, as with "Museum" by Robert Hass. Such **prose poems** rely on a progression of images and the cadences of language.

Open Form and Meaning

We can see an early instance of open-form poetry in Walt Whitman's "Reconciliation," a poem that was written as part of *Drum Taps*, a collection of fifty-three poems about the poet's reactions to Civil War battles in Virginia.

WALT WHITMAN   (1819–1892)

Reconciliation ———————————————————————— *1865, 1881*

Word over all, beautiful as the sky,
Beautiful that war and all its deeds of carnage must in time be utterly lost,
That the hands of the sisters Death and Night incessantly softly wash again, and ever
  again, this soiled world;
For my enemy is dead, a man divine as myself is dead,
I look where he lies white-faced and still in the coffin—I draw near,   5
Bend down and touch lightly with my lips the white face in the coffin.

QUESTIONS

1. How do individual lines, varying line lengths, punctuation, pauses, and cadences create rhythm and organize the images and ideas in this poem?

2. How do alliteration, assonance, and the repetition of words unify the poem and reinforce its content?

3. What is the "word" referred to in line 1? What does the speaker find "beautiful" about this "word" and the passage of time?

4. What instances of personification can you find? What do these personified figures do? What does the speaker do in lines 5–6? Why does he do this?

Whitman's "Reconciliation" shows the power of open-form poetry. There is no dominant meter, rhyme scheme, or stanza pattern. Instead, the poet uses individual lines and varying line lengths to organize and emphasize the images, ideas, and emotions. He also uses repetition, alliteration, and assonance to make internal line connections.

Without going into every aspect of the poem, one may note the unifying elements in the first few lines. The "word over all" (i.e., reconciliation, peace) is linked to the second line by the repetition of the words "beautiful" and "all," while "beautiful" is grammatically complemented by the clauses "that . . . lost" (line 2) and "That . . . world" (line 3). The reconciling word is thus connected to the image of the two personified figures, Death and Night, who "wash" war and carnage (bloodshed) out of "this soiled world."

In line 3, unity and emphasis are created through the repetition of "again" and the alliteration on the *ly* sound of "incessant*ly*" and "soft*ly*," the *s* sound in "*s*isters," "in*ce*ssantly," "*s*oftly," and "*s*oil'd," and the *d* sound in "han*ds*, "*D*eath," "soil'*d*," and "Worl*d*." One may also note the unifying assonance patterns of *ĭ* in "*i*ts," "*i*n," "s*i*sters," "*i*ncessantly," and "th*i*s," and *ī* in "sky," "t*i*me," and "N*i*ght." The pauses, or junctures, of the line create remarkable internal rhythms that coincide with the thought "That the hands // of the sisters // Death and Night // incessantly softly // wash again, and ever again, // this soiled world."

This selective analysis demonstrates that open-form poetry creates its own unity. While some of the unifying elements, such as alliteration and assonance, are also a property of closed-form poetry, many are unique to poetry of the open form, such as the repetitions, the reliance on grammatical structures, and the careful control of rhythms. The concept of the open form is that the topic itself shapes the number of lines, the line lengths, and the physical appearance on the page. Unity is there—development is there—but the open form demands that there be as many shapes and forms as there are topics.

VISUAL AND CONCRETE POETRY

In **visual poetry** poets not only emphasize the idea and emotion of their subject, but also fashion the poem into a recognizable shape on the page, as with the figure of a cone in Charles H. Webb's "The Shape of History." Some visual poetry seeks to balance the pleasures of seeing with those of hearing. Other visual poetry, however, abandons sound completely and invests all its impact in our perception of the visual image or picture.

Visual poetry is not a recent development. The Chinese have been producing it for thousands of years, and there are surviving examples from ancient Greece. In the seventeenth century, traditional English poets were manipulating the lines of their poems to represent wings, altars, squares, triangles, stars, and the like. This type of poetry, also called **shaped verse,** was often more ingenious than significant. Exceptional poets, however, produced shaped verse in which the visual image and the meaning strikingly echo each other.

After World War II, picture poems experienced a revival when visual poetry reentered the literary landscape with the birth of a new movement called **concrete poetry.** Poets in this tradition focus almost completely on the medium from which the poem is created. With printed work, this means that the poets pay far more attention to the visual arrangement of letters, words, lines, and white spaces than they do to content. Concrete poetry represents a fusion of writing with painting or graphic design, and the emphasis is on the visual.

Form and Meaning in Visual Concrete Poetry

In reading visual and concrete poetry, you should seek correspondences between the image and the words. In your consideration, describe the shape of the poem and the figures it resembles, the varying line lengths, the placement of individual words and phrases, and the use of space. A superb example of seventeenth-century visual poetry is George Herbert's "Easter Wings," a religious poem that offers two differing but related shapes.

GEORGE HERBERT   (1593–1633)

Easter Wings ——————————————————————————— *1633*

Lord, who createdst man in wealth and store,°   *abundance*
   Though foolishly he lost the same,
      Decaying more and more
         Till he became
           Most poor: 5
          With thee
         O let me rise
      As larks, harmoniously,
   And sing this day thy victories:
Then shall the fall° further the flight in me.   10

My tender age in sorrow did I begin:
   And still with sicknesses and shame
      Thou didst so punish sin,
         That I became
           Most thin.   15
          With thee
         Let me combine,
      And feel this day thy victory;°
   For, if I imp° my wing on thine,
Affliction shall advance the flight in me.   20

EASTER WINGS.   10 *fall:* the biblical account of how sin and death were introduced as a punishment for humankind after Adam and Eve disobeyed God. See also line 2.   18 *victory:* 1 Corinthians 15:54–57.   19 *imp:* to repair a falcon's wing or tail by grafting on feathers.

QUESTIONS

1. What does the poem look like when viewed straight on? When viewed sideways, with the left side at the top? How do these two images echo and emphasize the poem's content?
2. How does the typographical arrangement echo the sense? In lines 5 and 15, for example, how are typography, shape, and meaning fused?
3. What do lines 1–5 tell you about humanity's spiritual history, according to Herbert? What do lines 11–15 tell you about the speaker's spiritual state? How are these parallel?

This poem is an admission of sin and a prayer for redemption. It compares humanity's loss of Eden ("wealth and store") to the speaker's spiritual state as a petitioner seeking salvation. When viewed straight on, each stanza resembles an altar. Sideways, the stanzas resemble the wings of two angels. The images are thus linked with the title of the poem, and they connote contrition, prayer, grace, and angelic reward.

The correspondence between shape and meaning goes even further. Herbert reinforces the ideas by the careful manipulation of line lengths. Thus, in discussing humanity's spiritual history, the original "wealth and store" of Eden are described in the poem's longest line (line 1). As the fall from grace is described, the lines get progressively shorter (narrower), until humanity's fallen state is described in the narrowest line, "Most poor" (line 5). This same pattern is repeated in lines 11–15 to portray the "sickness and shame" that have made the speaker spiritually "Most thin." In the second half of both stanzas, this pattern is reversed; the lines expand to complement the speaker's prayers for grace and salvation. The full lengths of lines 10 and 20 depict the speaker's hope of a victorious redemption—in effect the restoration of the divine favor described in line 1.

 POEMS FOR STUDY

e.e. cummings   (1874–1963)

Buffalo Bill's Defunct° _____ *1923*

Buffalo Bill's
defunct
    who used to
    ride a watersmooth-silver
            stallion   5
and break onetwothreefourfive pigeonsjustlikethat
                       Jesus

he was a handsome man
            and what i want to know is
how do you like your blueeyed boy   10
Mister Death

BUFFALO BILL'S DEFUNCT.   The poem has no title; it is usually referred to as "Portrait" or by its first two lines. Buffalo Bill (William F. Cody, 1846–1917) was an American plainsman, hunter, army scout, sharpshooter, and showman whose Wild West show began touring the world in 1883; he became a symbol of the Wild West.

QUESTIONS

1. What is the effect of devoting a whole line to "Buffalo Bill's" (line 1), "defunct" (line 2), "stallion" (line 5), "Jesus" (line 7), and "Mister Death" (line 11)? How does this technique reflect and emphasize the content of the poem?

2. How does the typographical arrangement of line 6 contribute to the fusion of sound and sense? What other examples of this technique do you find?

3. Explain the denotations and connotations of *defunct*. What would be lost (or gained) by using the term *dead* or *deceased* instead?

4. To what extent is this poem a "portrait" of Buffalo Bill? What do we learn about him? Is the portrait respectful, mocking, or something in between?

JOHN DRYDEN   (1631–1700)

To the Memory of Mr. Oldham° _____ *1684*

Farewell, too little and too lately known,
Whom I began to think and call my own:
For sure our souls were near allied, and thine

Cast in the same poetic mold with mine.
One common note on either lyre did strike,   5
And knaves and fools we both abhorred alike.
To the same goal did both our studies drive;
The last set out the soonest did arrive.
Thus Nisus° fell upon the slipp'ry place,
While his young friend performed and won the race.   10
O early ripe! to thy abundant store
What could advancing age have added more?
It might (what nature never gives the young)
Have taught the numbers of thy native tongue.
But satire needs not those, and wit will shine   15
Through the harsh cadence of a rugged line;
A noble error, and but seldom made,
When poets are by too much force betrayed.
Thy gen'rous fruits, though gathered ere their prime,
Still showed a quickness; and maturing time   20
But mellows what we write to the dull sweets of rhyme.
Once more, hail and farewell;° farewell, thou young.
But ah too short, Marcellus° of our tongue;
Thy brows with ivy and with laurels° bound;
But fate and gloomy night encompass thee around.   25

TO THE MEMORY OF MR. OLDHAM.   John Oldham (1653–1683) was a young poet whom
Dryden admired.   9 *Nisus:* a character in Vergil's *Aeneid* who slipped in a pool of blood while
running a race, thus allowing his best friend to win.   22 *hail and farewell:* an echo of the Latin
phrase "ave atque vale" spoken by gladiators about to fight.   23 *Marcellus:* a Roman general
who was adopted by the Emperor Augustus as his successor but died at the age of twenty.
24 *laurels:* a plant sacred to Apollo, the Greek god of poetry; the traditional prize given to poets is
a wreath of laurel.

QUESTIONS

1. What is the meter of this poem? Rhyme scheme? Closed form? How does the
   form control the tempo? Why is this tempo appropriate?

2. What does the speaker reveal about himself in lines 1–10? About Oldham?
   About his relationship with Oldham? What did the two have in common?

3. What is the effect of Dryden's frequent classical allusions? What pairs of
   rhyming words most effectively clinch ideas?

ROBERT FROST   (1874–1963)

Desert Places _____ *1936*

Snow falling and night falling fast, oh, fast
In a field I looked into going past,
And the ground almost covered smooth in snow,
But a few weeds and stubble showing last.

The woods around it have it—it is theirs.   5
All animals are smothered in their lairs.
I am too absent-spirited to count;
The loneliness includes me unawares.

And lonely as it is that loneliness
Will be more lonely ere it will be less—   10
A blanker whiteness of benighted snow
With no expression, nothing to express.

They cannot scare me with their empty spaces
Between stars—on stars where no human race is.
I have it in me so much nearer home   15
To scare myself with my own desert places.

QUESTIONS

1. What is the meter? The rhyme scheme? The form?

2. What setting and situation are established in lines 1–4? What does the snow affect here? What does it affect in lines 5–8? In lines 9–12?

3. What different kinds of "desert places" is this poem about? Which kind is the most important? Most frightening?

4. How does the type of rhyme (rising or falling) change in the last stanza? How does this change affect the tone and impact of the poem?

5. How does the stanzaic pattern of this poem organize the progression of the speaker's thoughts, feelings, and conclusions?

ALLEN GINSBERG   (1926–1997)

A Supermarket in California _____ *1955*

What thoughts I have of you tonight, Walt Whitman,° for
I walked down the sidestreets under the trees with a headache
self-conscious looking at the full moon.
    In my hungry fatigue, and shopping for images, I went
into the neon fruit supermarket, dreaming of your enumerations!°   5
    What peaches and what penumbras! Whole families
shopping at night! Aisles full of husbands! Wives in the
avocados, babies in the tomatoes!—and you, Garcia Lorca,° what
were you doing down by the watermelons?

    I saw you, Walt Whitman, childless, lonely old grubber,   10
poking among the meats in the refrigerator and eyeing the
grocery boys.

A SUPERMARKET IN CALIFORNIA.   1 *Walt Whitman:* American poet (1819–1892) who experimented with open forms and significantly influenced the development of twentieth-century
poetry.   5 *enumerations:* Many of Whitman's poems contain long lists.   9 *Garcia Lorca:*
Spanish surrealist poet and playwright (1896–1936) whose later poetry became progressively more
like prose.

I heard you asking questions of each: Who killed the pork
chops? What price bananas? Are you my Angel?
I wandered in and out of the brilliant stacks of cans   15
following you, and followed in my imagination by the store
detective.
We strode down the open corridors together in our solitary
fancy tasting artichokes, possessing every frozen delicacy, and
never passing the cashier.   20

Where are we going, Walt Whitman? The doors close in
an hour. Which way does your beard point tonight?
(I touch your book and dream of our odyssey in the supermarket
and feel absurd.)
Will we walk all night through solitary streets? The trees   25
add shade to shade, lights out in the houses, we'll both be
lonely.

Will we stroll dreaming of the lost America of love past blue
automobiles in driveways, home to our silent cottage?
Ah, dear father, graybeard, lonely old courage-teacher,   30
what America did you have when Charon° quit poling his ferry
and you got out on a smoking bank and stood watching the
boat disappear on the black waters of Lethe?°

32 *Charon:* boatman in Greek mythology who ferried the souls of the dead across the river Styx
into Hades, the underworld.   34 *Lethe:* the river of forgetfulness in Hades. The dead drank
from this river and forgot their former lives.

QUESTIONS

1. Where is the speaker? What is he doing? What is his condition?
2. What effect is produced by placing Whitman and Lorca in the market?
3. To what extent do we find Whitman-like enumerations in this work? What is
   the effect of such enumerations?
4. Why is this a poem? What poetic devices are employed here? To what extent
   might it make more sense to consider this prose rather than poetry?

NIKKI GIOVANNI (b. 1943)

Nikki-Rosa _____ *1968*

childhood remembrances are always a drag
if you're Black
you always remember things like living in Woodlawn°
with no inside toilet
and if you become famous or something   5
they never talk about how happy you were to have your mother
all to yourself and
how good the water felt when you got your bath from one of those

NIKKI-ROSA.   3 *Woodlawn:* a predominantly black suburb of Cincinnati, Ohio.

big tubs that folk in chicago barbecue in
and somehow when you talk about home   10
it never gets across how much you
understood their feelings
as the whole family attended meetings about Hollydale
and even though you remember
your biographers never understand   15
your father's pain as he sells his stock
and another dream goes
and though you're poor it isn't poverty that
concerns you
and though they fought a lot   20
it isn't your father's drinking that makes any difference
but only that everybody is together and you
and your sister have happy birthdays and very good christmasses
and I really hope no white person ever has cause to write about me
because they never understand Black love is Black wealth and they'll   25
probably talk about my hard childhood and never understand that
all the while I was quite happy

QUESTIONS

1. To what extent do individual lines, caesurae, and cadences create a rhythm and
   reinforce the sense of this poem?
2. What points does the speaker make about childhood in general, the childhoods
   of blacks, and her own childhood?
3. What ideas about the ways in which whites understand or misunderstand blacks
   does this poem explore?

ROBERT HASS   (b. 1941)

Museum ————————————————————————————————— *1989*

On the morning of the Käthe Kollwitz° exhibit, a young man and woman come into
the museum restaurant. She is carrying a baby; he carries the air-freight edition of the
Sunday *New York Times.* She sits in a high-backed wicker chair, cradling the infant in
her arms. He fills a tray with fresh fruit, rolls, and coffee in white cups and brings it to
the table. His hair is tousled, her eyes are puffy. They look like they were thrown down
into sleep and then yanked out of it like divers coming up for air. He holds the baby.
She drinks coffee, scans the front page, butters a roll and eats it in their little corner in
the sun. After a while, she holds the baby. He reads the *Book Review* and eats some fruit.
Then he holds the baby while she finds the section of the paper she wants and eats
fruit and smokes. They've hardly exchanged a look. Meanwhile, I have fallen in love with
this equitable arrangement, and with the baby who cooperates by sleeping. All around
them are faces Käthe Kollwitz carved in wood of people with no talent or capacity for suffering who are suffering the numbest kinds of pain: hunger, helpless terror. But this

MUSEUM.   1 *Käthe Kollwitz:* Kollwitz (1867–1945) was a German artist well known for her sculptures and engravings portraying the misery of poverty and war.

young couple is reading the Sunday paper in the sun, the baby is sleeping, the green has begun to emerge from the rind of the cantaloupe, and everything seems possible.

QUESTIONS

1. Does this poem contain material that you ordinarily think of as poetic? What seems "poetic"? "Unpoetic"? Why?

2. Why does Hass not present the poem in lines? On what principle (topical, grammatical) might you set it up in line form? How might its being in lines change the way you read it as well as see it?

3. How does the poem contrast the young couple and their baby with the art of Käthe Kollwitz?

4. In the light of this poem, how seriously should we take the final statement ("and everything seems possible")?

GEORGE HERBERT   (1593–1633)

Virtue° _____ *1633*

Sweet day, so cool, so calm, so bright,		
The bridal of the earth and sky:		
The dew shall weep thy fall tonight;		
For thou must die.		
Sweet rose, whose hue, angry° and brave,°	*red; splendid*	5
Bids the rash° gazer wipe his eye:		
Thy root is ever in its grave,		
And thou must die.		
Sweet spring, full of sweet days and roses,		
A box where sweets° compacted lie:	*perfumes*	10
My music shows ye have your closes,°		
And all must die.		
Only a sweet and virtuous soul,		
Like seasoned timber, never gives;°		
But though the whole world turn to coal,°		15
Then chiefly lives.		

VIRTUE.   The title can allude to (*a*) divine Power operating both outside and inside an individual; (*b*) a characteristic quality or property; (*c*) conformity to divine and moral laws.   6 *rash:* eager or sympathetic.   11 *closes:* A *close* is the conclusion of a musical composition.   14 *never gives:* i.e., never gives in, never deteriorates and collapses (like rotted timber). 15 *turn to coal:* the burned-out residue of the earth and universe after the universal fire on Judgment Day.

QUESTIONS

1. What is the rhyme scheme of this poem? The meter? The form?

2. What points does the speaker make about the day, the rose, spring, and the "sweet and virtuous soul"?

WILLIAM HEYEN   (b. 1940)

Mantle° _____ *1980*

Mantle ran so hard, they said,
    he tore his legs to pieces.
        What is this but spirit?

52 homers in '56, the triple crown.
I was a high school junior, batting   5
    fourth behind him in a dream.

I prayed for him to quit, before
his lifetime dropped below .300.
    But he didn't, and it did.

He makes Brylcreem commercials now,   10
models with open mouths draped around him
    as they never were in Commerce, Oklahoma,

        where the sandy-haired, wide-shouldered boy
            stood up against his barn,
                lefty for an hour (Ruth, Gehrig),   15

                    then righty (DiMaggio),
                as his father winged them in,
                    and the future blew toward him,

                        now a fastball, now a slow
                            curve hanging   20
                        like a model's smile.

MANTLE.   Mickey Mantle (1931–1995) a Yankee outfielder from 1951–1968. A switch hitter, he hit eighteen world series home runs (a record) and 536 career home runs. He was the American League's most valuable player in 1956, the year he won the triple crown (line 4).

QUESTIONS

1.   Describe the shape of the poem, being careful to study the last stanza. Why is this shape appropriate for a famous baseball player?
2.   How does the poet use Mantle as a symbol in this poem?
3.   Who are Ruth, Gehrig, and DiMaggio? In what ways are they like Mantle?

JOHN KEATS   (1795–1821)

Ode to a Nightingale _____ *1819*

                            1
My heart aches, and a drowsy numbness pains
    My sense, as though of hemlock° I had drunk,   *a poisonous herb*
Or emptied some dull opiate to the drains

One minute past, and Lethe-wards° had sunk:
'Tis not through envy of thy happy lot,   5
   But being too happy in thine happiness,—
      That thou, light-winged Dryad° of the trees,
         In some melodious plot
Of beechen green, and shadows numberless,
      Singest of summer in full-throated ease.   10

2

O, for a draught of vintage! that hath been
   Cool'd a long age in the deep-delved earth,
Tasting of Flora° and the country green,
Dance, and Provençal song, and sunburnt mirth!
O for a beaker full of the warm South,   15
   Full of the true, the blushful Hippocrene,°
      With beaded bubbles winking at the brim,
         And purple-stainèd mouth;
That I might drink, and leave the world unseen,
      And with thee fade away into the forest dim: 20

3

Fade far away, dissolve, and quite forget
   What thou among the leaves hast never known,
The weariness, the fever, and the fret
Here, where men sit and hear each other groan;
Where palsy shakes a few, sad, last gray hairs,   25
   Where youth grows pale, and spectre-thin, and dies;
      Where but to think is to be full of sorrow
         And leaden-eyed despairs,
   Where Beauty cannot keep her lustrous eyes,
      Or new Love pine at them beyond to-morrow.   30

4

Away! away! for I will fly to thee,
   Not charioted by Bacchus° and his pards,°   leopards
But on the viewless wings of Poesy,°   poetry
   Though the dull brain perplexes and retards:
Already with thee! tender is the night,   35
   And haply the Queen-Moon is on her throne,
      Cluster'd around by all her starry Fays;°   fairies
         But here there is no light,

ODE TO A NIGHTINGALE.   4 *Lethe-wards:* toward the river of forgetfulness in Hades, the underworld of Greek mythology.   7 *Dryad:* in Greek mythology, a semidivine tree spirit.   13 *Flora:*
the Roman goddess of flowers.   16 *Hippocrene:* the fountain of the Muses on Mt. Helicon in
Greek mythology; the phrase thus refers to both the waters of poetic inspiration and a cup of wine.
32 *Bacchus:* the Greek god of wine. See p. 890.

Save what from heaven is with the breezes blown
Through verdurous glooms and winding mossy ways.   40

5

I cannot see what flowers are at my feet,
  Nor what soft incense hangs upon the boughs,
But, in embalmed° darkness, guess each sweet   *fragrant*
  Wherewith the seasonable month endows
The grass, the thicket, and the fruit-tree wild;   45
  White hawthorn, and the pastoral eglantine;°   *honeysuckle*
    Fast fading violets cover'd up in leaves;
      And mid-May's eldest child,
  The coming musk-rose, full of dewy wine,
    The murmurous haunt of flies on summer eves.   50

6

Darkling° I listen; and, for many a time   *in the dark*
  I have been half in love with easeful Death,
Call'd him soft names in many a musèd rhyme,
  To take into the air my quiet breath;
Now more than ever seems it rich to die,   55
  To cease upon the midnight with no pain,
    While thou art pouring forth thy soul abroad
      In such an ecstasy!
  Still wouldst thou sing, and I have ears in vain—
    To thy high requiem become a sod.   60

7

Thou wast not born for death, immortal Bird!
  No hungry generations tread thee down;
The voice I hear this passing night was heard
  In ancient days by emperor and clown:
Perhaps the self-same song that found a path   65
  Through the sad heart of Ruth,° when, sick for home,
    She stood in tears amid the alien corn;°   *wheat, grain*
      The same that oft-times hath
  Charm'd magic casements, opening on the foam
    Of perilous seas, in faery lands forlorn.   70

8

Forlorn! the very word is like a bell
  To toll me back from thee to my sole self!

66 *Ruth:* the widow of Boaz in the biblical Book of Ruth.

Adieu! the fancy° cannot cheat so well   *imagination*
    As she is fam'd to do, deceiving elf.
Adieu! adieu! thy plaintive anthem fades   75
    Past the near meadows, over the still stream,
       Up the hill-side; and now 'tis buried deep
          In the next valley-glades:
    Was it a vision, or a waking dream?
       Fled is that music:—Do I wake or sleep?   80

QUESTIONS

1. Formulate the structure (meter of each line and rhyme scheme) of the stanzas. What traditional form is employed here?

2. What is the speaker's mental and emotional state in stanza 1? What similes are employed to describe this condition?

3. What does the speaker want in stanza 2? Whom does he want to join? Why? From what aspects of the world (stanza 3) does he want to escape?

4. How do the speaker's mood and perspective change in stanza 4? How does he achieve this transition? What characterizes the world that the speaker enters in stanza 5? What senses are employed to describe this world?

5. What does the speaker establish about the nightingale's song in stanza 7? What does the song come to symbolize?

ANDREW MARVELL   (1621–1678)

To His Coy Mistress _____ *1681*

    Had we but world enough, and time,
This coyness, lady, were no crime.
We would sit down, and think which way
To walk, and pass our long love's day.

Thou by the Indian Ganges° side   5
Shouldst rubies find; I by the tide
Of Humber° would complain. I would
Love you ten years before the flood,°   *Noah's flood*
And you should, if you please, refuse
Till the conversion of the Jews.°   10
My vegetable love should grow
Vaster than empires and more slow;

TO HIS COY MISTRESS.   5 *Ganges:* a large river that runs across most of India.   7 *Humber:* a small river that runs through the north of England to the North Sea.   10 *Jews:* Traditionally, this conversion is supposed to occur just before the Last Judgment.

An hundred years should go to praise
Thine eyes, and on thy forehead gaze;
Two hundred to adore each breast,   15
But thirty thousand to the rest;
An age at least to every part,
And the last age should show your heart.
For, lady, you deserve this state,
Nor would I love at lower rate.   20
   But at my back I always hear
Time's wingèd chariot hurrying near;
And yonder all before us lie
Deserts of vast eternity.
Thy beauty shall no more be found,   25
Nor, in thy marble vault, shall sound
My echoing song; then worms shall try
That long-preserved virginity,
And your quaint honor turn to dust,
And into ashes all my lust: 30
The grave's a fine and private place,
But none, I think, do there embrace.
   Now therefore, while the youthful hue
Sits on thy skin like morning dew,
And while thy willing soul transpires   35
At every pore with instant fires,
Now let us sport us while we may,
And now, like amorous birds of prey,
Rather at once our time devour
Than languish in his slow-chapped° power.   *slow-jawed*   40
Let us roll all our strength and all
Our sweetness up into one ball,
And tear our pleasures with rough strife
Thorough° the iron gates of life: *through*
Thus, though we cannot make our sun   45
Stand still, yet we will make him run.

QUESTIONS

1. In lines 1 through 20 the speaker sets up a hypothetical situation and the first
    part of a pseudo-logical proof: If *A* then *B*. What specific words indicate the
    logic of this section? What hypothetical situation is established?

2. How do geographic and biblical allusions affect our sense of time and place?

3. In lines 21 through 32 the speaker refutes the hypothetical condition set up in
    the first twenty lines. What word indicates that this is a refutation? How does
    imagery help create and reinforce meaning here?

4. The last part of the poem (lines 33–46) presents the speaker's "logical" conclu-
    sion. What words indicate that this is a conclusion? What is the conclusion?

JOHN MILTON   (1608–1674)

When I Consider How My Light Is Spent° _____ *1655*

When I consider how my light is spent
  Ere half my days, in this dark world and wide,
  And that one talent° which is death to hide,
  Lodged with me useless, though my soul more bent
To serve therewith my Maker, and present   5
  My true account, lest he returning chide;
  "Doth God exact day-labor, light denied?"
  I fondly° ask; but Patience to prevent°   *foolishly; forestall*
That murmur, soon replies, "God doth not need
  Either man's work or his own gifts; who best   10
  Bear his mild yoke, they serve him best. His state
Is kingly. Thousands at his bidding speed
  And post o'er land and ocean without rest;
  They also serve who only stand and wait."

WHEN I CONSIDER HOW MY LIGHT IS SPENT.   Milton began to go blind in the late 1640s and was completely blind by 1651.   3 *talent:* both a skill and a reference to the talents discussed in the parable in Matthew 25:14–30.

QUESTIONS

1. What is the meter of this poem? The rhyme scheme? The closed form?
2. To what extent do the two major divisions of this form organize the poem's ideas?
3. What problem is raised in the octave? What are the speaker's complaints? Who is the speaker in the sestet? How are the earlier conflicts resolved?
4. Explore the word *talent* and relate its various meanings to the poem as a whole.

DUDLEY RANDALL   (b. 1914)

Ballad of Birmingham° _____ *1966*

(On the bombing of a church in Birmingham, Alabama, 1963)

"Mother dear, may I go downtown
Instead of out to play,
And march the streets of Birmingham
In a Freedom March today?"

BALLAD OF BIRMINGHAM.   Four black children were killed when the 16th Street Baptist Church in Birmingham, Alabama, was bombed in 1963. A man was finally indicted for the murders in 1977 and convicted in 1982. A film on the topic (1998) was directed by Spike Lee.

"No, baby, no, you may not go,   5
For the dogs are fierce and wild,
And clubs and hoses, guns and jails
Aren't good for a little child."

"But, mother, I won't be alone.
Other children will go with me,   10
And march the streets of Birmingham
To make our country free."

"No, baby, no, you may not go,
For I fear those guns will fire.
But you may go to church instead   15
And sing in the children's choir."

She has combed and brushed her night-dark hair,
And bathed rose petal sweet,
And drawn white gloves on her small brown hands,
And white shoes on her feet.   20

The mother smiled to know her child
Was in the sacred place,
But that smile was the last smile
To come upon her face.

For when she heard the explosion,   25
Her eyes grew wet and wild.
She raced through the streets of Birmingham
Calling for her child.

She clawed through bits of glass and brick,
Then lifted out a shoe   30
"Oh, here's the shoe my baby wore,
But, baby, where are you?"

QUESTIONS

1. Formulate the structure (meter, rhyme scheme, stanza form) of this poem. What traditional closed form is employed here?

2. Who is the speaker in stanzas 1 and 3? In stanzas 2 and 4? How are quotation and repetition employed to create tension?

3. What ironies do you find in the mother's assumptions? In the poem as a whole? In the society pictured in the poem?

4. Compare the poem to "Sir Patrick Spens" (p. 451) and to Keats's "La Belle Dame Sans Merci" (p. 673). How are the structures of all three alike? To what extent do all three deal with the same type of subject matter?

CHRISTINA ROSSETTI   (1830–1894)

A Christmas Carol _____ *1872*

In the bleak mid-winter
   Frosty wind made moan,
Earth stood hard as iron,
   Water like a stone;
Snow had fallen, snow on snow,   5
   Snow on snow,
In the bleak mid-winter
   Long ago.

Our God, Heaven cannot hold Him
   Nor earth sustain;   10
Heaven and earth shall flee away
   When He comes to reign:
In the bleak mid-winter
   A stable-place sufficed°   *see Luke 2:7*
The Lord God Almighty   15
   Jesus Christ.

Enough for Him whom cherubim
   Worship night and day,
A breastful of milk
   And a mangerful of hay;   20
Enough for Him whom angels
   Fall down before,
The ox and ass and camel
   Which adore.

Angels and archangels   25
   May have gathered there,
Cherubim and seraphim
   Throng'd the air,
But only His mother
   In her maiden bliss   30
Worshipped the Beloved
   With a kiss.

What can I give Him,
   Poor as I am?
If I were a shepherd°   *see Luke 2:8–20*   35
   I would bring a lamb,
If I were a wise man°   *see Matthew 2:1–12*
   I would do my part,—
Yet what I can I give Him,
   Give my heart.   40

QUESTIONS

1. Why does Rossetti stress the bitterness and bleakness of the winter setting in this poem?

2. Why does the speaker stress the simplicity of the birthplace of "The Lord God Almighty"? What is the origin and tradition of this setting?

3. How does the fourth stanza prepare you for the speaker's description of her own condition in the fifth stanza?

4. How are the objects considered gifts by the speaker a part of the setting traditionally associated with the birth of Jesus? How does the speaker's gift reveal her character and condition?

PERCY BYSSHE SHELLEY   (1792–1822)

Ozymandias _____ 1818

I met a traveller from an antique land,
Who said—"Two vast and trunkless legs of stone
Stand in the desert. . . . Near them, on the sand,
Half sunk, a shattered visage lies, whose frown,
And wrinkled lip, and sneer of cold command,   5
Tell that its sculptor well those passions read
Which yet survive, stamped on these lifeless things,
The hand that mocked them, and the heart that fed;
And on the pedestal, these words appear;
'My name is Ozymandias, King of Kings,   10
Look on my Works, ye Mighty, and despair!'
Nothing beside remains. Round the decay
Of that colossal Wreck, boundless and bare
The lone and level sands stretch far away."

QUESTIONS

1. What is the meter of this poem? The rhyme scheme? What traditional closed form is modified here? How do the modifications affect the poem?

2. To what extent are content and meaning shaped by the closed form? What is described in the octave? In the sestet?

3. Characterize Ozymandias (thought to be Ramses II, pharaoh of Egypt, who died in 1225 B.C.E.) from the way he is portrayed in this poem.

MAY SWENSON   (1919–1989)

Women _____ *1968*

Women
  should be
    pedestals
     moving
      pedestals
     moving
    to the
     motions
    of men

```
Women                 Or they
  should be             should be
    pedestals            little horses
     moving               those wooden
      pedestals            sweet                          5
       moving              oldfashioned
      to the               painted
       motions             rocking
        of men             horses

              the gladdest things in the toyroom         10

        The                  feelingly
        pegs                 and then
        of their             unfeelingly
        ears                 To be
        so familiar          joyfully                     15
        and dear             ridden
        to the trusting      rockingly
        fists                ridden until
To be chafed            the restored

egos dismount and the legs stride away                    20

Immobile               willing
  sweetlipped            to be set
    sturdy                 into motion
      and smiling           Women
        women               should be                     25
          should always      pedestals
            be waiting        to men
```

QUESTIONS

1. Is this poem an instance of closed-form, open-form, or visual poetry? In what different ways or sequences can it be read? How do the different sequences change the meaning?

2. How well does the image of the poem reinforce its meaning? Would the effect be different if the columns of words were straight instead of undulating?

3. To what extent do repetition and alliteration help to organize the poem and underscore its sense? Note especially *w, m, f, r,* and *s* sounds.

4. What does this poem *say* that women should be? Does it mean what it says? How are men characterized? In what way is this poem ironic?

DYLAN THOMAS   (1914–1953)

Do Not Go Gentle into That Good Night —————————————— *1951*

Do not go gentle into that good night,
Old age should burn and rave at close of day;
Rage, rage against the dying of the light.

Though wise men at their end know dark is right,
Because their words had forked no lightning they   5
Do not go gentle into that good night.

Good men, the last wave by, crying how bright
Their frail deeds might have danced in a green bay,
Rage, rage against the dying of the light.

Wild men who caught and sang the sun in flight,   10
And learn, too late, they grieved it on its way,
Do not go gentle into that good night.

Grave men, near death, who see with blinding sight
Blind eyes could blaze like meteors and be gay,
Rage, rage against the dying of the light.   15

And you, my father, there on the sad height,
Curse, bless, me now with your fierce tears, I pray.
Do not go gentle into that good night.
Rage, rage against the dying of the light.

QUESTIONS

1. This poem is written in a traditional closed form called the villanelle, which was
    developed in France during the Middle Ages. A villanelle is nineteen lines long.
    There are additional rules governing the length and structure of stanzas, the
    rhyme scheme, and the repetition of complete lines. Try to formulate these
    rules. To look at another example, see Roethke's "The Waking" (p. 793).

2. What do you conclude about the speaker, listener, and situation here?

3. What four different kinds of men does the speaker discuss in lines 4–15? What
    do they have in common?

4. What puns and connotative words can you find in this poem? Consider the
    "good" of "good night" and the word "grave" (line 13).

JEAN TOOMER   (1894–1967)

Reapers ———————————————————————— *1923*

Black reapers with the sound of steel on stones
Are sharpening scythes. I see them place the hones
In their hip-pockets as a thing that's done,
And start their silent swinging, one by one.

Black horses drive a mower through the weeds,   5
And there, a field rat, startled, squealing bleeds,
His belly close to ground. I see the blade,
Blood-stained, continue cutting weeds and shade.

QUESTIONS

1. What is the poem's meter? The rhyme scheme? The form? What is the difference between Toomer's use of the form and Dryden's?

2. How do the images of this poem relate to each other? How does the image of the bleeding field rat and the "blood-stained" blade heighten the impact?

3. How does alliteration unify this poem and make sound echo sense? Note especially the *s* and *b* sounds, and the phrase "silent swinging."

CHARLES H. WEBB   (b. 1952)

The Shape of History —————————————————————————— *1995*

> *Turning and turning in the widening gyre . . .°*

Today's paper is crammed full of news: pages and pages on the Somalia
Famine, the Balkan Wars, Gays in the Military. On this date a year ago,
only 1/365 of "The Year's Top Stories" happened. *Time* magazine fits a
decade into one thin retrospective. Barely enough occurred a century
    ago to fill one sub-chapter in a high school text. 500 years ago, one   5
      or two things happened every 50 years. 5000 years ago, a city
        was founded, a grain cultivated, a civilization toppled every
         other century. Still farther back, the years march by in
          groups like graduates at a big state university: 10,000 to
           20,000 BC; 50,000 – 100,000 BC; 1 – 10 million BC.   10
            Before that, things happened once an Era: Mam-
             mals in the Cenozoic, Dinosaurs in the Meso-
             zoic, Forests in the Paleozoic, Protozoans in
              the Pre-Cambrian. Below that, at the
               very base of time's twisting gyre, its   15
                cornucopia, its ram's-horn trum-
                 pet, its tornado tracking across
                  eternity, came what Chris-
                  tians call Creation, astro-
                   physicists call the Big   20
                   Bang. Then, for tril-
                   lions of years,
                   nothing at
                   all.

THE SHAPE OF HISTORY.   *Turning . . . gyre:* See line 1 of Yeats's "The Second Coming," p. 680.

QUESTIONS

1. What shape does the poet give to history? How accurate is this shape?

2. How do the lengths of the first and final two lines graphically show how civilization has grown? What "top stories" are mentioned in the first few lines? How representative of modern news are these stories? How long will it take for such stories to be replaced by new, similar stories?

3. In the light of the epigraph by Yeats, what does the speaker apparently think will happen in the future?

4. Considering the content and the diminishing shape of the poem's twenty-four lines, what do you think is meant by "nothing at/all"?

PHYLLIS WEBB   (b. 1927)

Poetics Against the Angel of Death° _____ *1962*

I am sorry to speak of death again
(some say I'll have a long life)
but last night Wordsworth's 'Prelude'°
suddenly made sense—I mean the measure,
the elevated tone, the attitude   5
of private Man speaking to public men.
Last night I thought I would not wake again
but now with this June morning I run ragged to elude
the Great Iambic Pentameter
who is the Hound of Heaven° in our stress   10
because I want to die
writing Haiku
or, better,
long lines, clean and syllabic as knotted bamboo. Yes!

POETICS AGAINST THE ANGEL OF DEATH.   *Angel of Death:* See Byron's "The Destruction of Sennacherib," stanza 3 (p. 750).   3 *Wordsworth's 'Prelude':* A long autobiographical poem (1805–1850) by Wordsworth.   10 *Hound of Heaven (The):* A long poem (1893) by Francis Thompson (1859–1907) about attempting to evade God's love.

QUESTIONS

1. In the poem itself, what is meant by the "Angel of Death"?

2. What attitude does the speaker express about iambic pentameter? How does the speaker explain this attitude? How defensible is the attitude?

3. For what poetic forms does the speaker express a preference? Why? How does the form of this poem bear out the preference?

Pieter Brueghel the Elder, *The Peasant Dance (The Kermess)*. Kunsthistorisches Museum, Vienna, Austria. Foto Marburg/Art Resource, New York, NY.

WILLIAM CARLOS WILLIAMS   (1883–1963)

The Dance _____ *1944*

In Brueghel's° great picture, The Kermess,
the dancers go round, they go round and
around, the squeal and the blare and the
tweedle of bagpipes, a bugle and fiddles
tipping their bellies (round as the thick-
sided glasses whose wash they impound)   5
their hips and their bellies off balance
to turn them. Kicking and rolling about
the Fair Grounds, swinging their butts, those
shanks must be sound to bear up under such
rollicking measures, prance as the dance   10
in Breughel's great picture, The Kermess.

THE DANCE.   1 *Brueghel's:* Pieter Brueghel (ca. 1525–1569), a Flemish painter. *The Kermess* (reproduced above) shows peasants dancing in celebration of the anniversary of the founding of a church (*church mass*).

QUESTIONS

1. What effect is produced by repeating the first line as the last line?
2. How do repetition, alliteration, assonance, onomatopoeia, and internal rhyme affect the tempo, feeling, and meaning of the poem? How do the numerous participles (like "tipping," "kicking," "rolling") make sound echo sense?
3. What words are capitalized? What effect is produced by omitting the capital letters at the beginning of each line? How does this typographical choice reinforce the sound and the sense of the poem?
4. Most of the lines of this poem are run-on rather than end-stopped, and many of them end with fairly weak words such as *and, the, about,* and *such.* What effect is produced through these techniques?
5. How successful is Williams in making the words and sentence rhythms echo the visual rhythms in Breughel's painting? Why is this open form more appropriate to the images of the poem than any closed form could be?

WILLIAM WORDSWORTH   (1770–1850)

The Solitary Reaper —————————————————— *1807*

Behold her, single in the field,
Yon solitary Highland Lass!
Reaping and singing by herself;
Stop here, or gently pass!

Alone she cuts and binds the grain,   5
And sings a melancholy strain;
O listen! for the Vale profound
Is overflowing with the sound.

No Nightingale did ever chaunt
More welcome notes to weary bands   10
Of travelers in some shady haunt,
Among Arabian sands;
A voice so thrilling ne'er was heard
In springtime from the Cuckoo bird,
Breaking the silence of the seas   15
Among the farthest Hebrides.°

Will no one tell me what she sings?°
Perhaps the plaintive numbers flow
For old, unhappy, far-off things,
And battles long ago;   20

THE SOLITARY REAPER.   16 *Hebrides:* a group of islands off the west coast of Scotland.
17 *Will . . . sings:* The speaker does not understand Scots Gaelic, the language in which the woman
sings.

Or is it some more humble lay,
Familiar matter of today?
Some natural sorrow, loss, or pain,
That has been, and may be again?

Whate'er the theme, the Maiden sang   25
As if her song could have no ending;
I saw her singing at her work,
And o'er the sickle bending—

I listened, motionless and still;
And, as I mounted up the hill,   30
The music in my heart I bore,
Long after it was heard no more.

QUESTIONS

1. What is the subject of stanzas 1, 2, and 5? What are the concerns of stanzas 3
    and 4? How does the last stanza, 6, summarize the poet's concerns in this
    poem?
2. In stanza 4, what speculation does the speaker make about the meaning of the
    woman's song?
3. Why does the poet shift from present to past tense at line 25? What is gained by
    this shift?
4. Even though stanzas 3 and 4 contain eight lines each, why is it possible to state
    that, in form, the poem is really a song containing eight stanzas?

WRITING ABOUT FORM IN POETRY

An essay about form in poetry should demonstrate a relationship between a
poem's sense and its form. Do not discuss form or shape in isolation, for such
an essay would be no more than a detailed description. The first thing to do in
prewriting is to examine the poem's main ideas. Consider the various elements
that contribute to the poem's impact and effectiveness: the speaker, listener,
setting, situation, diction, imagery, and rhetorical devices. Once you understand
these, it will be easier to establish a connection between form and content.

It will be helpful to prepare a worksheet much like the ones for writing
about prosody (pp. 607, 608, and 609). In this case the worksheet will highlight
structural elements. For closed forms, these will include the rhyme scheme,
meter, line lengths, and stanzaic pattern. They may also include significant
words and phrases that connect stanzas. The worksheet for an open-form poem
should indicate variables such as rhythm and phrases, pauses and enjambe-
ments, significant words that are isolated or emphasized through typography,
and patterns of repeated sounds, words, phrases, and images.

Questions for Discovering Ideas

CLOSED FORM

- What is the predominant meter? Line length? Rhyme scheme? To what extent do these establish and/or reinforce the form?
- What is the form of each stanza or unit? What building blocks does the poet use? How many stanzas or divisions does the poem contain? How does the poem establish a pattern? How is the pattern repeated?
- What is the form of the poem (e.g., a ballad or a sonnet)? In what ways is the poem traditional, and what variations does it introduce? What is the effect of the variations?
- How effectively does the structure create or reinforce the poem's internal logic? What topical, logical, or thematic progressions can unite the various parts of the poem?
- To what extent does the form organize the images of the poem? Are key images developed within single units or stanzas? Do images recur in several units?
- To what extent does the form organize and bring out the ideas or emotions of the poem?

OPEN FORM

- What does the poem look like on the page? What is the relationship of its shape to its meaning?
- How does the poet use variable line lengths, spaces, punctuation, capitalization, and the like to shape the poem? How do these variables contribute to the poem's sense and impact?
- What rhythms are built into the poem through language or typography? How are these relevant to the poem's content?
- What is the poem's progression of ideas, images, and/or emotions? How is the logic created, and what does it contribute?
- How does form or typography isolate or group, and thus emphasize, various words and phrases? What is the effect of such emphasis?
- What patterns do you discover of words and sounds? To what degree do the patterns create order and structure? How are they related to the sense of the poem?

Strategies for Organizing Ideas

In developing your central idea, you should illustrate the connections between form and meaning. For example, in planning an essay on Randall's "Ballad of Birmingham" you might develop your ideas according to the speeches that are a normal feature of the ballad form. The poem's first part is a dialogue between mother and child about the hazard of the local streets and the safety of the local church. In the second part, after the explosion, the mother runs toward the church and calls for her child, who, ironically, will never again engage with her in further dialogue. Another plan is needed for an essay on Williams's "The Dance"; such a plan might link the lively, bustling movement of the dancers pictured in Brueghel's painting (p. 649) to the rhythms, repetitions, and run-on lines of the poem. Another plan is needed for a discussion of Heyen's "Mantle," the form of which requires enough stanzas of approximately equal length to make up the pattern of a pitched ball (what is this pattern?).

Your introduction may contain general remarks about the poem, but it should focus on the connection between form and substance. Describe the ways in which structure and content interact together, with a brief listing of your specific topics.

Early in the body, describe the formal characteristics of your poem, using schemes and numbers (as in paragraph 2 of the sample student essay that follows). With closed forms, your description should detail such standard features as the traditional form, meter, rhyme scheme, stanzaic structure, and number of stanzas. With open-form poetry, you should focus on the most striking and significant features of the verse (as in the brief discussion of Whitman's "Reconciliation" on p. 627).

Be sure to integrate your discussion of both form and content. It may be that you have uncovered a good deal of information about technical features such as alliteration or rhyme, or you may wish to stress how words, phrases, and clauses develop a pattern of ideas. Remember that you are not making a paraphrase or a general explication, but instead are showing how the poet uses form—either an open or a closed one—in the service of meaning. The order in which you deal with your topics is entirely your call.

The conclusion of your essay might contain additional relevant observations about shape or structure. It might also summarize your argument. Here, as in all essays about literature, make sure to reach an actual conclusion rather than simply a stopping point.

SAMPLE STUDENT ESSAY

Form and Meaning in Herbert's "Virtue"°

[1] George Herbert's devotional four-stanza poem "Virtue" (1633) contrasts the mortality of worldly things with the immortality of the "virtuous soul." This is not an uncommon topic in religious poetry and hymns, and there is nothing unusual about this contrast. What is unusual, however, is the simplicity and directness of Herbert's expressions and the way in which he integrates his ideas within his stanzaic song pattern. Each part of the poem organizes the images logically and underscores the supremacy of life over death.* Through control

---

° See p. 635 for this poem.
* Central idea.

over line and stanza groupings, rhyme scheme, and repeated sounds and words, Herbert's stanzas create a structural and visual distinction between the "sweet" soul and the rest of creation.†

[2] Herbert's control over lines within the stanzas is particularly strong. Each stanza follows the same basic *a b a b* rhyme scheme. Since some rhyme sounds and words are repeated throughout the first three stanzas, however, the structure of the poem can be formulated as *4a 4b 4a 2b, 4c 4b 4c 2b, 4d 4b 4d 2b, 4e 4f 4e 2f*. Each stanza thus contains three lines of iambic tetrameter with a final line of iambic dimeter--an unusual pattern that creates a unique emphasis. In the first three stanzas, the dimeter lines repeat the phrase "must die," while in the last stanza the contrast is made on the words "Then chiefly lives." These rhythms require a sensitive reading, and they powerfully underscore Herbert's idea that death is conquered by eternal life.

[3] Like individual lines, Herbert's stanzaic structure provides the poem's pattern of organization and logic. The first stanza focuses on the image of the "Sweet day," comparing the day to "The bridal of the earth and sky" (line 2) and asserting that the day inevitably "must die." Similarly, the second stanza focuses on the image of a "Sweet rose" and asserts that it too "must die." The third stanza shifts to the image of "Sweet spring." Here the poet blends the images of the first two stanzas into the third by noting that the "Sweet spring" is "full of sweet days and roses" (line 9). The stanza concludes with the summarizing claim that "all must die." In this way, the third stanza is the climax of Herbert's imagery of beauty and mortality. The last stanza introduces a new image--"a sweet and virtuous soul"--and an assertion that is the opposite of the ideas expressed in the previous three stanzas. Although the day, the rose, and the spring "must die," the soul "never" deteriorates, but "chiefly lives" even "though the whole world turn to coal" (line 15). With its key image of the "virtuous soul," this last stanza marks the logical conclusion of Herbert's argument. His pattern of organization allows this key image of permanence to be separated structurally from the images of impermanence.

[4] This structural organization of images and ideas is repeated and reinforced by other techniques. Herbert's rhyme scheme, for example, links the first three stanzas while isolating the fourth. That the *b* rhyme is repeated at the ends of the second and fourth lines of each of the first three stanzas makes these stanzas into a complete unit. The fourth stanza, however, is different, both in content and rhyme. The stanza introduces the concept of immortality, and it also introduces entirely new rhymes, replacing the *b* rhyme with an *f* rhyme. Thus the rhyme scheme, by sound alone, parallels the poem's imagery and logic.

[5] As a complement to the rhyming sounds, the poem also demonstrates organizing patterns of assonance. Most notable is the *oo* sound, which is repeated throughout the first three stanzas in the words "cool," "dew," "whose," "hue," "root," and "music." In Herbert's time, the sound might still have been prominent in the word "thou," so that in the first three stanzas the *oo*, which is not unlike a moan (certainly appropriate to things that die), is repeated eight times. In the last stanza there is a stress on the *o* sound, in "only," "soul," "though,"

† Thesis sentence.

"whole," and "coal." While *oh* may also be a moan, in this context it is more like an exclamation, in keeping with the triumph contained in the final line.

[6] Herbert's repetition of key words and phrases also distinguishes the first three stanzas from the last stanza. Each of the first three stanzas begins with "sweet" and ends with "must die." These repetitions stress both the beauty and the mortality of worldly things. In the last stanza, however, this repetition is abandoned, just as the stress on immortality transcends mortality. The "sweet" that begins each of the first three stanzas is replaced by "Only" (line 13). Similarly, "must die" is replaced with "chiefly lives." Both substitutions separate this final stanza from the three previous stanzas. More important, the shift in the verbal pattern emphasizes the conceptual transition from death to the virtuous soul's immortality.

[7] It is therefore clear that the lyric form of Herbert's "Virtue" provides an organizational pattern for the poem's images and ideas. At the same time, the pattern of stanzas and the rhyme scheme allow the poet to draw a valid structural distinction between the corruptible world and the immortal soul. The closed form of his poem is not arbitrary or incidental; it is an integral way of asserting the singularity of the key image, the "sweet and virtuous soul."

Commentary on the Essay

The introductory paragraph establishes the groundwork of the essay—the treatment of form in relationship to content. The main idea is that each part of the poem represents a complete blending of image, logic, and meaning.

Paragraph 2, the first in the body, demonstrates how the poem's schematic formulation is integrated into Herbert's contrast of death and life. In this respect the paragraph demonstrates how a formal enumeration can be integrated within an essay's thematic development.

The focus of paragraph 3 is the organization of both images and ideas from stanza to stanza. Paragraph 4 begins with a transitional sentence that repeats part of the essay's central idea and, at the same time, connects it to paragraph 3. In the same way, paragraph 4 is closely tied to both paragraphs 1 and 3. The main topic here, the rhyme scheme of "Virtue," is introduced in the second sentence, which asserts that rhythm also reinforces the division between mortality and immortality. On much the same topic, paragraph 5 introduces Herbert's use of assonance, which can be seen as integral in the poem's blending of form and content.

Paragraph 6 takes up the last structural element mentioned in the introduction—the repetition of key words and phrases. The paragraph asserts that repeated words and phrases underscore the poem's division between mortality and immortality.

Paragraph 7, the conclusion, provides a brief overview and summation of the essay's argument. In addition, it concludes that form in "Virtue" is neither arbitrary nor incidental, but rather an integral part of the poem's meaning.

SPECIAL WRITING TOPICS FOR STUDYING POETIC FORM

1. Describe the use of the ode form as exemplified by Shelley's "Ode to the West Wind" (p. 598) and Keats's "Ode to a Nightingale." What patterns of regularity do you find? What differences do you find in the form and content of the poems? How do you account for these differences?

2. How do Cummings, Thomas, Randall, and Dryden use different forms to consider the subject of death (in "Buffalo Bill's Defunct," "Do Not Go Gentle into that Good Night," "Ballad of Birmingham," and "To the Memory of Mr. Oldham")? What differences in form and treatment do you find? What similarities do you find, despite these differences?

3. Consider the structural arrangement and shaping of the following works: Ginsberg's "A Supermarket in California," Hass's "Museum," Heyen's "Mantle," Herbert's "Easter Wings," Wagoner's "March for a One-Man Band" (p. 602), Webb's "The Shape of History," and Williams's "The Dance." How do the poets utilize topic, arrangement, shape, and space to draw attention to their main ideas? How do the shaped and prose poems (Hass, Herbert, Heyen, and Webb) blend poetic and artistic techniques?

4. Write a visual poem, and explain the principles on which you develop your lines. Here are some possible topics (just to get you started): a "boom box," a duck, a car, a football, a snow shovel, a giraffe. After finishing your poem, write a short essay that considers these questions: What are the strengths and limitations of the visual form, according to your experience? How does the form help make your poem serious or comic? How does it encourage creative language and original development of ideas?

5. Write a haiku. Be sure to fit your poem to the 5-7-5 pattern of syllables. What challenges and problems do you encounter in this form? Once you have completed your haiku (which, to be traditional, should be on a topic concerned with nature), try to cut the number of syllables to 4-5-4. Explain how you establish the first haiku pattern, and also explain how you go about cutting the total number of syllables. Be sure to explain what kinds of words you use (length, choice of diction, etc.).

6. Using a computer reference system or card catalogue, look up one of the following topics: "ballads, England"; "concrete poetry"; or "blank verse." How many references are included under these listings? What sorts of topics are included under the basic topic?

18

Symbolism and Allusion: Windows to a Wide Expanse of Meaning

As we note in Chapter 8, a **symbol** has meaning in and of itself, but it also stands for something else, like the flag for the country or the school song for the school. Symbols occur in stories as well as in poems, but poetry relies more heavily on symbols because it is more concise and because it comprises more forms than fiction, which is confined to a narrative structure.

Words are symbols, for they stand for various objects without actually being those objects. When we say *horse*, for example, or *tree*, these words are not horses or trees, but are only symbols of horses and trees. They direct our minds to real horses and real trees in the real world that we have seen and can therefore easily imagine. In literature, however, symbolism implies a special relationship that expands our ordinary understanding of words, descriptions, and arguments.

SYMBOLISM AND MEANING IN POETRY

Symbolism goes beyond the close referral of word to thing; it is more like a window through which one can get a glimpse at the extensive world outside. Because poetry is compact, its descriptions and portrayals of experience are brief. Symbolism is therefore one of its primary characteristics. It is a shorthand way of referring to extensive ideas or attitudes that otherwise would be impossible to state in the brief format of a poem. Thus William Butler Yeats, who believed that the city of Constantinople, or Byzantium, represented a pinnacle of human civilization, used the city as a symbol of human achievement in peace, politics, and particularly art and literature. His poem "Sailing to Byzantium" (Chapter 21) does not expand upon the full meaning and interpretation of this idea, for it would take a long history and a detailed analysis of Byzantine art and literature to do that. But the poem does use Byzantium as a symbol of excellence—a standard by which Yeats measures what he states is the declining state of twentieth-century civilization. In short, the use of symbols is a means of encapsulating or crystallizing information—a means of saying a great deal within a short space.

Symbolism in Operation

Symbolism expands meaning beyond the normal connotation of words. For example, at the time of William Blake (1757–1827), the word *tiger* meant both a large, wild cat and also the specific animal we know today as a tiger. The word's connotation therefore links it with wildness and predation. As a symbol in "The Tyger," however, Blake uses the animal as a stand-in for the negativism and evil in the world—the savage, wild forces that prompt human beings to evil actions. Thus the tiger as a symbol is more meaningful than either the denotation or the connotation of the word would indicate.

CULTURAL OR UNIVERSAL SYMBOLS.   In poetry, some symbols possess a ready-made, clearly agreed-upon meaning. These are **cultural** or **universal symbols** (also described in Chapter 8). Many such symbols, like the tiger, are drawn directly from nature. Springtime and morning are universal symbols signifying beginnings, growth, hope, optimism, and love. A reference to spring is normal and appropriate in a love poem. If the topic were death, however, the symbol of spring would still be appropriate as the basis of ironic observations about the untimeliness with which death claims its victims.

Cultural symbols are drawn from history and custom, such as the many Judeo-Christian religious symbols that appear in poetry. References to the lamb, Eden, Egyptian bondage, shepherds, exile, the temple, blood, water, bread, the cross, and wine—all Jewish and/or Christian symbols—occur over and over again. Sometimes these symbols are prominent in a purely devotional context. In other contexts, however, they may be contrasted with symbols of warfare and corruption to show how extensively people neglect their moral and religious obligations.

CONTEXTUAL, PRIVATE, OR AUTHORIAL SYMBOLS.   Symbols that are not widely or universally recognized are termed **contextual, private,** or **authorial symbols** (also discussed in Chapter 8). Some of these have a natural relationship with the objects and ideas being symbolized. Snow, for example, is cold and white, and when it falls it covers everything. A poet can thus exploit this quality and make snow a symbol. At the beginning of the long poem "The Waste Land," for example, T. S. Eliot ironically uses snow to symbolize a retreat from life, an intellectual and moral hibernation. Another poem utilizing snow as a symbol linking the living and the dead both literally and figuratively is the following one.

VIRGINIA SCOTT (b. 1938)

Snow _____ *1977*

A doe stands at the roadside,
spirit of those who have lived here
and passed known through our memory.
The doe stands at the edge of the icy road,
then darts back into the woods.   5

Snow falling,
mother-spirit hovering,
white on the drops in the road and fields,
light from the windows
of the old house   10
brightening the snow.

Presences: mother,
grandmother,
here in their place
at the foot of *ben lomond,*   15
green trees black in the hemlock night.

The doe stands at the edge of the icy road,
then darts back into the woods.

Golden Grove, New Brunswick, Canada
January 5, 1977

QUESTIONS

1. How is snow described in the poem? How and where is it seen? As a symbol, what does it signify in relationship to the doe, the memory of persons, the mother-spirit, the old house, the light, the presences, the mountains, and the trees?

2. Explain the structural purpose for which the doe is mentioned three times in the poem, with lines 17 and 18 repeating 4 and 5. As a symbol, what might the doe signify?

3. What are the relationships described in the poem between memory of the past and existence in the present? What does the symbolism contribute to your understanding of these relationships?

    This poem describes a real circumstance at a real place at a real time; the poet has even provided an actual location and date, just as we do when writing a letter. We can therefore presume that the snow is real snow, falling at a time in the evening when lights go on in the nearby houses. This detail by itself would be sufficient as a realistic image, but as Scott develops the poem, the snow symbolizes the link between the speaker's memory of the past and perception of the present. The reality of the moment is suffused with the memory of the people—"mother,/grandmother"—who "lived here." The poet is meditating on the idea that individuals, though they may often be alone like the speaker, are never alone as long as they have a vivid memory of the past. Symbolically, the past and present are always connected, just as the snow covers the scene.

At the poem's conclusion, the doe darting into the woods suggests a linking of present and future (i.e., as long as there are woods, there will be does darting into them). Both the snow and the deer are private and contextual symbols, for they are established and developed within the poem, and they do not necessarily have symbolic value elsewhere. Through the symbolism, therefore, the poet has converted a private moment into an idea of general significance.

Similarly, references to other ordinary materials may be symbolic if the poet emphasizes them sufficiently. Keats's "La Belle Dame Sans Merci," for example, opens and closes with the image of withered sedge, or grass. What might seem like an appropriate detail therefore becomes symbolic of the loss and bewilderment felt by people when the persons they love seem to be unreal, faithless, and destructive rather than genuine, loyal, and supportive.

The Integration of Symbols into Poetry

Poets may integrate symbols into their poems through the use of single words, the introduction of various actions, the description of settings, the development of characters and character traits, and the control of situations.

SINGLE WORDS.   With general and universal symbols, a single word is often sufficient, as with references to the lamb, shepherd, cross, blood, bread, and wine; or to summer and winter; or to drought and flood, morning and night, heat and shade, storm and calm, or feast and famine. The nightingale is an example of how a single word may become instantly symbolic. Because the bird has such a beautiful song, it frequently symbolizes natural, unspoiled beauty as contrasted with the contrived attempts by human beings to create beauty. Keats refers to the bird in this way in his "Ode to a Nightingale," and he compares the virtually eternal beauty of this singer with his own mortality.

Another word also referring to a bird as a symbol is *geese*. Because geese migrate south in the fall, they symbolize the loss of summer abundance, seasonal change, alteration, and loss, with accompanying feelings of regret and sorrow. Because they return north in the spring, however, they also symbolize regeneration, newness, anticipation, and hope. These contrasting symbolic values are important in Jorie Graham's "The Geese" and Mary Oliver's "Wild Geese." Graham emphasizes that the geese are "crossing" overhead but nevertheless that human affairs of "the everyday" continue despite the changes the geese symbolize. In contrast, Oliver emphasizes geese as symbols of renewal, for the returning geese suggest that "the world offers itself to your imagination."

ACTIONS.   Not only words but also actions may be presented as symbols. In Scott's "Snow," as we have just observed, the doe darting into the darkening woods symbolizes both the renewal and the mystery of life. In Jeffers's "The Purse Seine" the drawing of the seine symbolizes how modern technology has virtually entrapped and doomed all people within a net of industrialism and pollution.

SETTINGS. Sometimes, a setting or natural scene may be symbolic. For example, Randall Jarrell's brief poem "The Death of the Ball Turret Gunner" (p. 459) unites the ball turret of a World War II high-altitude bomber with a mother's womb, symbolically suggesting that war and brutal death are the human lot from the very beginning of life. Similarly, the "elfin grot" (grotto) of the "lady in the meads" in Keats's "La Belle Dame Sans Merci" is an unreal and magical womblike location symbolizing both the allure and the disappointment that sometimes characterize sexual attraction.

CHARACTERS. Poets also devise characters or people as symbols representing ideas or values. In e. e. cummings's "in just-," for example, the balloonman is such a figure. Although the balloonman is not fully visualized, cummings includes enough detail about him to indicate that he symbolizes the primitive vitality, joy, and sexuality that calls children out of childhood. The "fairy's child" of "La Belle Dame Sans Merci" is a symbol of the mystery of love. The speaker of Arnold's "Dover Beach" is a symbol of thinking people who find that the world no longer offers religious answers that are satisfying and convenient, and who therefore seek satisfaction in human relationships.

SITUATIONS. Situations, circumstances, and conditions can also be used symbolically. Jarrell's ball turret gunner, vulnerable and helpless six miles in the air, symbolizes the condition of humankind in the age of fear and anxiety, under the threat of global war and technological annihilation. In "she being Brand/-new," e. e. cummings cleverly uses the situation of the speaker's breaking in a new automobile as the symbol of another kind of encounter involving the speaker (p. 554).

The Qualities of Symbols

The meanings of symbols can be placed on a continuum of qualities from good to bad, high to low, favorable to unfavorable. For example, cummings's old balloonman of "in just-" is on the positive end, symbolizing the irresistible and joyful call of growth and sexuality. Outright horror is suggested by the symbol of the rough beast slouching toward Bethlehem in Yeats's "The Second Coming." While the beast shares the same birthplace with Jesus, the commonality is ironic because the beast represents the extremes of anger, hatred, and brutality that in Yeats's judgment are dominant in twentieth-century politics.

ALLUSION AND MEANING IN POETRY

Just as symbolism enriches meaning, so also does **allusion** (see Chapter 8), which is the adaptation and assimilation of (1) unacknowledged brief quotations from other works and (2) references to historical events and any aspect of human culture—art, music, literature, and so on. It is a means of recognizing both the literary tradition and the broader cultural environment of which the poem is a part. In addition it assumes a common bond of knowledge between the poet and the reader. On the one hand, allusion compliments the past, and on the other, it salutes the reader who is able to recognize it and find its new meaning in its new context.

Allusions may be seen in no more than a single word, provided that the word is unusual enough or associative enough to bear the weight of the reference. Virginia Scott's "Snow," for example, speaks of "green trees black in the hemlock night." *Hemlock,* of course, refers to a type of evergreen tree observed by the speaker, but hemlock was also the poison drunk by Socrates when the ancient Athenians executed him. Just about any reference to hemlock calls to mind the death of Socrates and also the idea that death is oblivion and the common end of all life. At the beginning of "Ode to a Nightingale" (p. 636), Keats's speaker describes a numbness that might come "as though of hemlock [he] had drunk." Here the allusion is placed in the context of a wish to be connected and united to the universal spirit not of oblivion but of creative power.

Allusions may also be longer, consisting of extensive phrases or also of descriptions or situations. When these are made, they add their own interest and power before the poet moves on to other ideas. Line 6 of Scott's "Snow," for example, is simply "Snow falling." This phrase is descriptive and accurate, but it also is a direct quotation from the first line of Robert Frost's poem "Desert Places" (p. 631). The contexts are of course different. Frost's line introduces the topic of the speaker's fear of bleakness, unconcern, coldness—his "desert places"—while in "Snow," as we stated earlier, Scott is referring to the continuity of the past and the present. By making the allusion, Scott emphasizes the difference between her idea and Frost's.

The Sources of Allusions

Allusions may be drawn from just about any area of life, history, and art. Sometimes symbols are allusions as well as symbols. In "The Second Coming," Yeats's "lion body and the head of a man" is a descriptive allusion to the Sphinx, which was an ancient mythical monster that destroyed those who could not solve its riddle. As Yeats uses the description, he therefore symbolizes the mystery, coldness, brutality, and horror that often infest human political institutions.

Once works become well known, they become a source of allusions for subsequent writers, as with Frost's famous line that concludes "Stopping by Woods on a Snowy Evening": "And miles to go before I sleep." This line is so often quoted that it has become a metaphor for having a task to complete and responsibilities to fulfill. Interestingly, Frost's line itself alludes to a line in Keats's sonnet "Keen Fitful Gusts," where Keats says "The stars are very cold about the sky,/And I have many miles on foot to fare." Any allusion to Frost is therefore also an indirect allusion to Keats's lines.

The Original Context of Allusions

If an allusion is made to a literary work, it carries with it the entire context of the work from which it is drawn. Perhaps the richest storehouses of such ready-made stories and quotations are the plays of Shakespeare and the King James Bible. In "Ode to a Nightingale," Keats alludes to the biblical story of Ruth who, he says, was "sick for home," standing "in tears amid the alien corn." This allusion is particularly rich because Ruth became the mother of Jesse. According to the Gospel of Matthew, it was from the line of Jesse that King David was born, and it was from the house of David that Jesus was born. Thus Keats's nightingale is not only a symbol of natural beauty, but through this Biblical allusion it symbolizes regeneration and redemption, much in keeping with Keats's assertion that the bird is "not born for death." In Yeats's "The Second Coming," the reference to the "blood-dimmed tide" suggests Macbeth's soliloquy in the second act of Shakespeare's *Macbeth*. Macbeth, after murdering Duncan, asks if there is enough water in Neptune's ocean to wash the blood from his hands. His immediate, guilt-ridden response is that Duncan's blood will instead stain the ocean, turning the green of the water to red. This image of crime being bloody enough to stain the ocean's water is thus the allusion of Yeats's "blood-dimmed tide."

Allusions are an important means by which poets broaden the context and deepen the meaning of their poems. The issues a poet raises in a new poem, in other words, are not important only there, but are linked through allusion to issues raised earlier by other thinkers or brought out by previous events, places, or persons. With connections made through allusions, poets clarify their own ideas. Allusion is hence not literary "theft" but is rather a means of enrichment.

STUDYING FOR SYMBOLS AND ALLUSIONS

As you study poetry for its symbols and allusions, remember that these devices do not come ready marked with special notice and fanfare. A decision to call a feature of the poem *symbolic* is based on qualities within the poem. Perhaps a major item of importance is introduced at a climactic part of the poem, or a description has something noteworthy or unusual about it, such as the connection between "stony sleep" and the "rough beast" in Yeats's "The Second Coming." When such a connection occurs, the element may no longer be taken just literally, but should be read as a symbol.

Even after you have found a hint such as this, however, you will have to discover its symbolic value. For instance, in the context of Yeats's "The Second Coming," the phrase "rough beast" might refer to the person or persons hinted at in traditional interpretations of the New Testament as the "Antichrist." In a secular frame of reference, the associations of blankness and pitilessness suggest brutality and suppression. Still further, however, if the last hundred years had not been a period in which millions of people were persecuted and exterminated in military and secret police operations, even these associations might make the "rough beast" quizzical but not necessarily symbolic. But because of the rightness of the application, together with the traditional Biblical associations, the figure clearly should be construed as a symbol of heartless persecution and brutality.

As you can see, the interpretation of a symbol requires that you identify and objectivize the person, object, situation, or action. If the element can be seen as general and representative—characteristic of the condition of a large number of human beings—it assumes symbolic significance. As a rule, the more ideas that you can associate with the element, the more likely it is to be a symbol.

As for allusions, the identification of an allusion is often quite simple. A word, situation, or phrase either is an allusion or it is not, and hence the matter is easily settled once a source is located. The problem comes in determining how the allusion affects the context of the poem you are reading. Thus we understand that in the poem "Snow," Virginia Scott alludes to Robert Frost's "Desert Places" by borrowing Frost's phrase "Snow falling." Once this allusion is established, its purpose must still be learned. Thus, on the one hand, the allusion might mean that the situation in "Snow" is the same as in Frost's poem, namely that the authorial speaker is making observations about interior blankness—the "desert places" of the mind, or soul. On the other hand, the poet may be using the allusion in a new sense, and this indeed seems to be the case. Whereas Frost uses the falling snow to suggest coldness of spirit, Scott uses it, more warmly, to connect the natural scene to the memory of family. In other words, once the presence of an allusion is established, the challenge of reading and understanding still continues.

 ## POEMS FOR STUDY

MATTHEW ARNOLD   (1822–1888)

Dover Beach _____ *1867 (1849)*

The sea is calm tonight.
The tide is full, the moon lies fair
Upon the straits—on the French coast the light
Gleams and is gone; the cliffs of England stand,
Glimmering and vast, out in the tranquil bay.   5
Come to the window, sweet is the night air!
Only, from the long line of spray
Where the sea meets the moon-blanched land,
Listen! you hear the grating roar
Of pebbles which the waves draw back, and fling,   10
At their return, up the high strand,
Begin, and cease, and then again begin,
With tremulous cadence slow, and bring
The eternal note of sadness in.

Sophocles long ago   15
Heard it on the Aegean, and it brought
Into his mind the turbid ebb and flow
Of human misery; we
Find also in the sound a thought,
Hearing it by this distant northern sea.   20

The Sea of Faith
Was once, too, at the full, and round earth's shore
Lay like the folds of a bright girdle furled.
But now I only hear
Its melancholy, long, withdrawing roar,   25
Retreating, to the breath
Of the night wind, down the vast edges drear
And naked shingles° of the world.   *beaches*

Ah, love, let us be true
To one another! for the world, which seems   30
To lie before us like a land of dreams,
So various, so beautiful, so new,
Hath really neither joy, nor love, nor light,
Nor certitude, nor peace, nor help for pain;
And we are here as on a darkling plain   35
Swept with confused alarms of struggle and flight,
Where ignorant armies clash by night.

QUESTIONS

1. What words and details establish the setting?
2. Where are the speaker and listener? What can they see? Hear?

3. What sort of movement may be topographically traced in the first six lines of the poem, so that the scene finally focuses on the speaker and the listener?

4. What is meant by comparing the English Channel to the Aegean Sea, and relating the Aegean surf to the thought of Sophocles?

5. What faith remains after the loss of religious faith? Defend the claim that being true to one another is the speaker's commitment to personal fidelity rather than love.

e. e. cummings   (1894–1962)

in just- _____ 1923

in Just-
spring   when the world is mud-
luscious the little
lame balloonman

whistles   far   and wee   5

and eddieandbill come
running from marbles and
piracies and it's
spring

when the world is puddle-wonderful   10

the queer
old balloonman whistles
far   and   wee
and bettyandisbel come dancing

from hop-scotch and jump-rope and   15
it's
spring
and
      the
          goat-footed°   20

balloonMan   whistles
far
and
wee

IN JUST-.   20 *goat-footed:* The mythological Greek god Pan, a free-spirited and lascivious god who presides over fields, forests, and herds, was portrayed with the body of a man and the legs of a goat.

QUESTIONS

1. Explain the following as symbols: "spring," "mud-luscious," "marbles," "puddle-wonderful," "hop-scotch." What does the whistle of the balloonman symbolize?

2. In what way is the balloonman symbolic?

3. Besides the balloonman, there are four other characters in the poem. Who are they? Why does cummings run their names together? What impulses do these characters represent symbolically?

4. Read the poem aloud. Taking into account the spacing and alignment, how does the physical arrangement on the page influence your perception?

JOHN DONNE   (1572–1731)

The Canonization° _____ *1633*°

For Godsake hold your tongue, and let me love,
    Or chide my palsy, or my gout,
My five gray hairs, or ruin'd fortune flout,
      With wealth your state, your mind with Arts improve,°
         Take you a course,° get you a place,°   5
         Observe His Honor,° or his grace,°
Or the King's real, or his stampèd face
      Contemplate,° what you will, approve,°
    So you will let me love.

Alas, alas, who's injured by my love?   10
    What merchant's ships have my sighs drown'd?
Who says my tears have overflow'd his ground?
      When did my colds a forward spring° remove?
         When did the heats which my veins fill°
         Add one more to the plaguy Bill?°   15
Soldiers find wars, and Lawyers find out still
      Litigious men, which quarrels move,
    Though she and I do love.

Call us what you will, we are made such by love;
    Call her one, me another fly,°   20
We'are Tapers° too, and at our own cost die,°   *candles*
      And we in us find the'Eagle and the Dove.°
         The Phoenix riddle° hath more wit
         By us, we two, being one, are it.
So, to one neutral thing both sexes fit,   25

THE CANONIZATION.   *The Canonization:* the making of saints.   4 *With wealth . . . improve:* i.e., Improve your state with wealth and your mind with arts.   5 *Take you a course:* take up a career.   *place:* a political appointment.   6 *His Honor:* any important courtier.   *his grace:* a person of greatest eminence, such as a bishop or the king.   7, 8 *Or . . . contemplate:* i.e., Or contemplate either the king's real face (at court) or stamped face (on coins).   8 *What . . . approve:* Try anything you like (i.e., "Mind your own business").   13 *a forward spring:* an early spring (season).   14 *the heats . . . fill:* i.e., "the heats (fevers) that fill my veins." Donne apparently wrote this line before the discovery of blood circulation was announced by William Harvey in 1616. 15 *plaguy Bill:* a regularly published list of deaths caused by the plague.   20 *fly:* a butterfly or moth (and apparently superficial and light-headed).   21 *at . . . die:* It was supposed that sexual climax shortened life.   22 *the'Eagle and the Dove:* masculine and feminine symbols. 23 *Phoenix riddle:* In ancient times the Phoenix, a mythical bird that lived for a thousand years, was supposed to die and rise five hundred years later from its own ashes; hence the Phoenix symbolized immortality and the renewal of life and desire.

We die and rise the same, and prove
Mysterious° by this love.

We can die by it, if not live by love,
    And if unfit for tombs and hearse
Our legend be, it will be fit for verse;   30
    And if no piece of Chronicle we prove,
        We'll build in sonnets pretty rooms;
        As well a well wrought urn becomes
The greatest ashes, as half-acre tombs,
    And by these hymns, all shall approve   35
    Us *Canoniz'd* for love:°

And thus invoke° us; "You whom reverend love   *pray to saints*
    Made one another's hermitage;°
You, to whom love was peace, that now is rage;
    Who did the whole world's soul extract, and drove   40
        Into the glasses of your eyes
        So made such mirrors, and such spies,
That they did all to you epitomize,°
    Countries, towns, courts: Beg from above
    A pattern of your love!"   45

27 *Mysterious:* unknowable to anyone but God, and therefore quintessentially holy.   35, 36 *by these hymns . . . Canoniz'd for love:* The idea is that later generations will remember the lovers and elevate them to the sainthood of a religion of love. Because the lovers' love is recorded so powerfully in the speaker's poems ("sonnets" in line 33), these later generations will use the poems as hymns in their worship of love.   38 *Made . . . hermitage:* made a religious retreat for each other.   40–43 *Who did . . . epitomize:* An allusion to reputed alchemical processes, and therefore to be understood approximately like this: "Who extracted the whole world's soul and, through your eyes, assimilated this soul into yours, so that you, whose eyes saw and reflected each other, embodied the love and desire felt by all human beings."

QUESTIONS

1.   What is the situation of the poem? Whom is the speaker addressing? Why does he begin as he does? How does he defend his love?

2.   What symbols do you find in the poem? What are the symbols? What is being symbolized?

3.   What mythic and religious mysteries are linked with sexual love in the third stanza? What does "canonization" mean? What canonizes and immortalizes the lovers? How does the "canonization" symbolize the poem's idea about the nature of love?

4.   What will future lovers ask of these saints of love? Of what use will the speaker's poem be at that time? What do you think of the speaker's claim about love?

JORIE GRAHAM   (b. 1954)

The Geese ———————————————————————— *1980*

Today as I hang out the wash I see them again, a code
as urgent as elegant,

tapering with goals.
For days they have been crossing. We live beneath these geese

as if beneath the passage of time, or a most perfect heading.   5
Sometime I fear their relevance.
Closest at hand,
between the lines,

the spiders imitate the paths the geese won't stray from,
imitate them endlessly to no avail: 10
things will not remain connected,
will not heal,

and the world thickens with texture instead of history,
texture instead of place.
Yet the small fear of the spiders   15
binds and binds

the pins to the lines, the lines to the eaves, to the pincushion bush,
as if, at any time, things could fall further apart
and nothing could help them
recover their meaning. And if these spiders had their way,   20

chainlink over the visible world,
would we be in or out? I turn to go back in.
There is a feeling the body gives the mind
of having missed something, a bedrock poverty, like falling

without the sense that you are passing through one world,   25
that you could reach another
anytime. Instead the real
is crossing you,

your body an arrival
you know is false but can't outrun. And somewhere in between   30
these geese forever entering and
these spiders turning back

this astonishing delay, the everyday, takes place.

QUESTIONS

1. What is the dominant tense of the poem? What effect does this tense have on
   the speaker's conclusions?

2. What action does the speaker perform in the course of the poem? What is the
   relationship between this action and the final lines?

3. What do the geese symbolize? What do the spiders symbolize? How are these
   symbols contrasted?

4. The first half of this poem, particularly lines 11 and 18, is reminiscent of Yeats's
   "The Second Coming" (p. 680). In your judgment, what use does Graham
   make of this allusion?

GEORGE HERBERT   (1593–1633)

The Collar° _____ *1633*

I struck the board, and cry'd, "No more;
    I will abroad!
What? shall I ever sigh and pine?
My lines and life are free; free as the road,
  Loose as the wind, as large as store,   5
    Shall I be still in suit?°
  Have I no harvest but a thorn°
  To let me blood, and not restore
What I have lost with cordial fruit?
    Sure there was wine   10
  Before my sighs did dry it: there was corn
    Before my tears did drown it.
  Is the year only lost to me?
    Have I no bays° to crown it?
No flowers, no garlands gay? all blasted?   15
    All wasted?
  Not so, my heart: but there is fruit,
    And thou hast hands.
  Recover all thy sigh-blown age
On double pleasures: leave thy cold dispute   20
Of what is fit, and not; forsake thy cage;
    Thy rope of sands,
Which petty thoughts have made, and made to thee
  Good cable, to enforce and draw,
    And be thy law,   25
While thou didst wink and wouldst not see.
    Away; take heed:
    I will abroad.
Call in thy death's head there: tie up thy fears.
    He that forbears   30
To suit° and serve his need,   *follow*
    Deserves his load."
But as I rav'd and grew more fierce and wild
    At every word,
  Me thought I heard one calling, "Child:"   35
    And I replied, "*My Lord.*"

THE COLLAR.   *collar:* (a) the collar worn by a member of the clergy; (b) the collar of the harness of a draft animal such as a horse; (c) a restraint placed on prisoners; (d) a pun on *choler* (yellow bile), a bodily substance that was thought to cause quick rages.   6 *in suit:* waiting upon a person of power to gain favor or position.   7 *thorn:* See Mark 15:17.   14 *bays:* laurel crowns to signify victory and honor.

QUESTIONS

    1.   What is the opening situation? Why is the speaker angry? Against what role in life is he complaining?

2. In light of the many possible meanings of *collar* (see note), explain the title as a symbol in the poem.

3. Explain the symbolism of the thorn (line 7), blood (line 8), wine (line 10), bays (line 14), flowers and garlands (line 15), cage (line 21), rope of sands (line 22), death's head (line 29), and the dialogue in lines 35 and 36.

ROBERT HERRICK   (1591–1674)

To the Virgins, to Make Much of Time _____ *1648*

Gather ye rosebuds while ye may,
  Old time is still a-flying;
And this same flower that smiles today
  Tomorrow will be dying.

The glorious lamp of heaven, the sun,   5
  The higher he's a-getting,
The sooner will his race be run,
  And nearer he's to setting.

That age is best which is the first,
  When youth and blood are warmer;   10
But being spent, the worse, and worst
  Times still succeed the former.

Then be not coy, but use your time,
  And, while ye may, go marry;
For, having lost but once your prime,   15
  You may forever tarry.

QUESTIONS

1. What does the title of this poem tell us? What can we deduce about the speaker? To whom is the poem addressed?

2. What point does this poem make about time? Life? Love?

3. How does symbolism help shape the message and meaning of the poem? Consider especially "rosebuds," "flower," and "the sun."

4. How do rhyme and tone help create and focus the meaning of this poem?

5. This type of poem is called *carpe diem* (Latin for "seize the day" or "enjoy the present"). Compare this poem with Jonson's "To Celia" and Marvell's "To His Coy Mistress," which are also *carpe diem* poems. How are the tone and message of this poem similar to and different from those in the poems by Jonson and Marvell?

ROBINSON JEFFERS   (1887–1962)

The Purse-Seine _____ *1937*

1

Our sardine fishermen work at night in the dark of the moon; daylight or
  moonlight

They could not tell where to spread the net, unable to see the phosphorescence
   of the shoals of fish.
They work northward from Monterey, coasting Santa Cruz; off New Year's Point
   or off Pigeon Point
The look-out man will see some lakes of milk-color light on the seas's night-purple;
   he points, and the helmsman
Turns the dark prow, the motorboat circles the gleaming shoal and drifts out   5
   her seine-net. They close the circle
And purse the bottom of the net, then with great labor haul it in.

                                        2
                                                   I cannot tell you
How beautiful the scene is, and a little terrible, then, when the crowded fish
Know they are caught, and wildly beat from one wall to the other of their closing
   destiny the phosphorescent
Water to a pool of flame, each beautiful slender body sheeted with flame, like a   10
   live rocket
A comet's tail wake of clear yellow flame; while outside the narrowing
Floats and cordage of the net great sea-lions come up to watch, sighing in the
   dark; the vast walls of night
Stand erect to the stars.

                                        3
                        Lately I was looking from a night mountain-top
On a wide city, the colored splendor, galaxies of light: how could I help but recall 15
   the seine-net
Gathering the luminous fish? I cannot tell you how beautiful the city appeared,
   and a little terrible.
I thought, We have geared the machines and locked all together into
   interdependence; we have built the great cities; now
There is no escape. We have gathered vast populations incapable of free survival,
   insulated
From the strong earth, each person in himself helpless, on all dependent. The
   circle is closed, and the net
Is being hauled in. They hardly feel the cords drawing, yet they shine already.   20
   The inevitable mass-disasters
Will not come in our time nor in our children's, but we and our children
Must watch the net draw narrower, government take all powers—or revolution,
   and the new government
Take more than all, add to kept bodies kept souls—or anarchy, the mass-disasters.

                                        4
                        These things are Progress;
Do you marvel our verse is troubled or frowning, while it keeps its reason? Or it   25
   lets go, lets the mood flow
In the manner of the recent young men into mere hysteria, splintered gleams,
   crackled laughter. But they are quite wrong.
There is no reason for amazement: surely one always knew that cultures decay,
   and life's end is death.

QUESTIONS

1. Describe how the purse-seine is used to haul in the sardines. What is the speaker's reaction to the scene as described in stanza 2?

2. How does the speaker explain that the purse-seine is a symbol? What does it symbolize? What do the sardines symbolize?

3. Compare the ideas of Jeffers with those of Yeats in "The Second Coming." Are the ideas of Jeffers less or more methodical?

4. Is the statement at the end to be taken as a fact or as a resigned acceptance of that fact? Does the poem offer any solution to the problem?

5. How can the sea-lions of line 12, and their sighs, be construed as a symbol?

JOHN KEATS   (1795–1821)

La Belle Dame Sans Merci: A Ballad° _____ *1820 (1819)*

1

O what can ail thee, knight at arms,
  Alone and palely loitering?
The sedge has wither'd from the lake,
  And no birds sing.

2

O what can ail thee, knight at arms,   5
  So haggard and so woe-begone?
The squirrel's granary is full,
  And the harvest's done.

3

I see a lily on thy brow
  With anguish moist and fever dew,   10
And on thy cheeks a fading rose
  Fast withereth too.

4

I met a lady in the meads,°   *meadows*
  Full beautiful, a fairy's child;
Her hair was long, her foot was light,   15
  And her eyes were wild.

5

I made a garland for her head,
  And bracelets too, and fragrant zone;°   *belt*

LA BELLE DAME SANS MERCI: French for "The beautiful lady without pity" (that is, "The heartless woman"). "La Belle Dame Sans Merci" is the title of a medieval poem by Alain Chartier; Keats's poem bears no other relationship to the medieval poem, which was thought at the time to have been by Chaucer.

She look'd at me as she did love,
   And made sweet moan.   20

6

I set her on my pacing steed,
   And nothing else saw all day long,
For sidelong would she bend, and sing
   A fairy's song.

7

She found me roots of relish° sweet,   *magical potion*   25
   And honey wild, and manna° dew,   *see Exodus 16:14–36*
And sure in language strange she said—
   I love thee true.

8

She took me to her elfin grot,°   *grotto*
   And there she wept, and sigh'd full sore,   30
And there I shut her wild wild eyes
   With kisses four.

9

And there she lullèd me asleep,
   And there I dream'd—Ah! woe betide!
The latest° dream I ever dream'd   *last*   35
   On the cold hill's side.

10

I saw pale kings, and princes too,
   Pale warriors, death pale were they all;
They cried—"La belle dame sans merci
   Hath thee in thrall!"°   *slavery*   40

11

I saw their starv'd lips in the gloam
   With horrid warning gapèd wide,
And I awoke and found me here
   On the cold hill's side.

12

And this is why I sojourn here,   45
   Alone and palely loitering,
Though the sedge is wither'd from the lake,
   And no birds sing.

QUESTIONS

   1. Who is the speaker of stanzas 1–3? Who speaks after that?
   2. In light of the dreamlike content of the poem, how can the knight's experience
      be viewed as symbolic? What is being symbolized?

3. Consider "relish" (line 25), "honey" (line 26), and "manna" (line 26) as symbols. Are they realistic or mythical? What does the allusion to manna signify? What is symbolized by the "pale kings, and princes too" and "Pale warriors" (lines 37–38)?

4. Consider the poem's setting as symbols of the knight's state of mind.

JOHN KEATS (1795–1821)

*Ode on a Grecian Urn°*_____ *1820 (1819)*

1

Thou still unravish'd bride of quietness,
  Thou foster-child of silence and slow time,
Sylvan historian, who canst thus express
A flowery tale more sweetly than our rhyme:
What leaf-fring'd legend° haunts about thy shape   *border and tale*   5
  Of deities or mortals, or of both,
    In Tempe° or the dales of Arcady?°
  What men or gods are these? What maidens loth?
What mad pursuit? What struggle to escape?
    What pipes and timbrels? What wild ecstasy?   10

2

Heard melodies are sweet, but those unheard
  Are sweeter; therefore, ye soft pipes, play on;
Not to the sensual ear, but, more endear'd,
  Pipe to the spirit ditties of no tone:
Fair youth, beneath the trees, thou canst not leave   15
  Thy song, nor ever can those trees be bare;
    Bold lover, never, never canst thou kiss,
Though winning near the goal—yet, do not grieve;
    She cannot fade, though thou hast not thy bliss,
  For ever wilt thou love, and she be fair!   20

3

Ah, happy, happy boughs! that cannot shed
  Your leaves, nor ever bid the spring adieu;
And, happy melodist, unwearied,
  For ever piping songs for ever new;
More happy love! more happy, happy love!   25
  For ever warm and still to be enjoy'd,
    For ever panting, and for ever young;
All breathing human passion far above,

ODE ON A GRECIAN URN.   The imaginary Grecian urn to which the poem is addressed combines design motifs from many different existing urns. This imaginary one is decorated with a border of leaves and trees, men (or gods) chasing women, a young musician sitting under a tree, lovers, and a priest and congregation leading a heifer to sacrifice.   7 *Tempe:* a beautiful rustic valley in Greece.   *Arcady:* refers to the valleys of Arcadia, a state in ancient Greece known for its beauty and peacefulness.

That leaves a heart high-sorrowful and cloy'd,
  A burning forehead, and a parching tongue.   30

                              4
Who are these coming to the sacrifice?
  To what green altar, O mysterious priest,
Lead'st thou that heifer lowing at the skies,
  And all her silken flanks with garlands drest?
What little town by river or sea shore,   35
  Or mountain-built° with peaceful citadel,   *built on a mountain*
    Is emptied of this folk, this pious morn?
And, little town, thy streets for evermore
  Will silent be; and not a soul to tell
    Why thou art desolate, can e'er return.   40

                              5
O Attic shape! Fair attitude! with brede°   *braid, pattern*
  Of marble men and maidens overwrought,°   *ornamented*
With forest branches and the trodden weed;
  Thou, silent form, dost tease us out of thought
As doth eternity: Cold Pastoral!   45
  When old age shall this generation waste,
    Thou shalt remain, in midst of other woe
Than ours, a friend to man, to whom thou say'st,
"Beauty is truth, truth beauty,"—that is all
  Ye know on earth, and all ye need to know.   50

QUESTIONS

1. What is the dramatic situation? What does the speaker see and do?
2. What does the speaker call the urn in the first stanza? What is suggested in these lines about the urn's relationship to time and change? To poetry?
3. What are "unheard" melodies (line 11) and "ditties of no tone" (line 14)? Why are these "sweeter" than songs heard by "the sensual ear" (line 13)? What central contrast is created through this comparison?
4. What do the trees, the musician, and the lovers have in common? How are they all related to the real world of time and change?

CAROL MUSKE   (b. 1945)

Real Estate _____ *1981*

You think you earned this space on earth,
but look at the gold face of the teen-age
pharaoh,° smug as a Shriner, in his box

REAL ESTATE.   3 *teen-age pharaoh:* Tutankhamen, the Egyptian "boy king" of the fourteenth century B.C. The discovery of his tomb in 1922, when hundreds of precious household objects were found with the sarcophagus, showed the lavishness of Egyptian royal burials. The mummy of King Tut was covered with a mask of gold and colored metals.

with no diploma, a plot flashy enough
for Manhattan.° Early death, then what.   5
a task dragging a sofa into the grave,
a couple of floor lamps, the alarm set

for another century. Someday we'll heed
the testament of that paid escort watching
himself in all the ballroom mirrors: slide   10

with each slide of the old trombone,
be good to the bald, press up against
the ugly duck-like.° Time is never old,

never lies. What a past you'd have
if you'd only admit to it: the real estate   15
your family dabbled in for generations,
the vacant lots° developed like the clan

overbite—through years of sudden
foreclosure. Who knows what it costs?
First you stand for the national anthem,   20

then you start waltzing around without
strings, reminding yourself of yourself,
expecting to live in that big city
against daddy's admonition: buy land°

get some roots down under those spike   25
heels, let the river bow and scrape as
it enters the big front door of your property.

5 *Manhattan:* In 1981 a large number of treasures from Tutankhamen's tomb were displayed at
the Metropolitan Museum of Art in Manhattan.   13 *ugly duck-like:* "The Ugly Duckling" is a
children's story by Hans Christian Andersen.   17 *vacant lots:* See T. S. Eliot, "Preludes," concluding lines.   24 *buy land:* See Robert Frost's poem "Build Soil" (1932).

QUESTIONS

1. Who is speaking? Who is being addressed? What sort of person is the speaker?
    What does she think of old age? Of sex? What advice does she offer?

2. What does "the teen-age pharaoh" symbolize? Why does the poet mention
    modern objects that might be found in a comparable tomb of a person of the
    twentieth century? What might these things symbolize?

3. What does the "paid escort" (line 9) symbolize? What does the "old trombone"
    symbolize? What does the choice of these symbolize about the traditional role of
    women with regard to men? What attitude is conveyed by this choice?

4. Consider the ambiguity of lines 25–27. What might "roots" and "property" sig-
    nify as the means of causing the "river" to "bow and scrape"? Why is it difficult
    to understand these lines without symbolic explanations?

5. Consider the allusion in line 24 to Robert Frost's "Build Soil" (1932). Frost delivered his poem at Columbia University just before the party conventions of 1932. The United States was in its worst economic depression. Frost spoke about agriculture, world politics, and the need for developing the nation's resources. In comparison, what does Muske achieve by the allusion?

MARY OLIVER   (b. 1935)

Wild Geese _____ *1986*

You do not have to be good.
You do not have to walk on your knees
for a hundred miles through the desert, repenting.
You only have to let the soft animal of your body
    love what it loves.
Tell me about despair, yours, and I will tell you mine.   5
Meanwhile the world goes on.
Meanwhile the sun and the clear pebbles of the rain
are moving across the landscapes,
over the prairies and the deep trees,
the mountains and the rivers.   10
Meanwhile the wild geese, high in the clean blue air,
are heading home again.
Whoever you are, no matter how lonely,
the world offers itself to your imagination,
calls to you like the wild geese, harsh and exciting—   15
over and over announcing your place
in the family of things.

QUESTIONS

1. What idea is contained in the first five lines? What ideas are expressed in lines 6–12? In what ways are lines 13–17 a climax of the poem? How does this last section build on the poem's earlier parts?
2. What is symbolized by the references to "the sun and the clear pebbles of the rain," etc., in lines 7–10? Do these symbols suggest futility or hope?
3. What do the wild geese symbolize (lines 11–12, 15)? How is the symbol of the geese a response to the poem's first six lines? How well would the words "acceptance," "self-knowledge," or "adjustment" describe the poem's ideas? What other words would be better or more suitable? Why?

WALT WHITMAN   (1819–1892)

A Noiseless Patient Spider _____ *1868*

A noiseless patient spider,
I marked where on a little promontory it stood isolated,

Marked how to explore the vacant vast surrounding,
It launched forth filament, filament, filament out of itself,
Ever unreeling them, ever tirelessly speeding them.   5

And you O my soul where you stand,
Surrounded, detached, in measureless oceans of space,
Ceaselessly musing, venturing, throwing, seeking the spheres
    to connect them,
Till the bridge you will need be formed, till the ductile anchor hold,
Till the gossamer thread you fling catch somewhere, O my soul.   10

QUESTIONS

1. The subject of the second stanza is seemingly unrelated to the subject of the first. How are these stanzas related?

2. In what way does the spider's web symbolize the soul and the poet's view of the isolation of human beings? How does the web symbolize the soul's ceaseless "musing . . . seeking" and the attempt "to connect"?

3. Explain why the second stanza is not a complete sentence. How might this grammatical feature be related to the spider's web? To the poet's idea that life requires striving but does not offer completeness?

WILLIAM WORDSWORTH   (1770–1850)

Lines Written in Early Spring ———————————————— *1798*

I heard a thousand blended notes,
While in a grove I sate° reclined,   *sat*
In that sweet mood when pleasant thoughts
Bring sad thoughts to the mind.

To her fair works did Nature link   5
The human soul that through me ran;
And much it grieved my heart to think
What man has made of man.

Through primrose tufts, in that green bower,
The periwinkle° trailed its wreaths;   10
And 'tis my faith that every flower
Enjoys the air it breathes.

The birds around me hopped and played,
Their thoughts I cannot measure—
But the least motion which they made,   15
It seemed a thrill of pleasure.

LINES WRITTEN IN EARLY SPRING.   10 *periwinkle:* a trailing evergreen plant with blue or white flowers.

The budding twigs spread out their fan,
To catch the breezy air;
And I must think, do all I can,
That there was pleasure there.   20

If this belief from heaven be sent,
If such be Nature's holy plan,
Have I not reason to lament
What man has made of man?

QUESTIONS

1. What is the situation of the poem? What sounds does the speaker hear? How may these sounds be considered symbolic? What is symbolic about the birds and the twigs in stanzas 4 and 5?

2 . What experience is described in stanza 2? What faith does the speaker proclaim?

3 . How does his faith prompt him to meditate on the human mistreatment of human beings?

WILLIAM BUTLER YEATS   (1865–1939)

The Second Coming° _____ *1920 (1919)*

Turning and turning in the widening gyre°
The falcon cannot hear the falconer;
Things fall apart; the center cannot hold;
Mere anarchy is loosed upon the world,

THE SECOND COMING.   The phrase "second coming" has been traditionally used to refer to expectations of the return of Jesus for the salvation of believers, as described in the New Testament. The prophecies foretold that Christ's return would be preceded by famine, epidemics, wars between nations, and general civil disturbance. Yeats believed that human history could be measured in cycles of approximately 2,000 years (see line 19, "twenty centuries"). According to this system, the birth of Jesus ended the Greco-Roman cycle and in 1919, when Yeats wrote "The Second Coming," it appeared to him that the Christian period was ending and a new era was about to take its place. The New Testament expectation was that Jesus would reappear. Yeats, by contrast, holds that the disruptions of the twentieth century were preceding a takeover by the forces of evil.   1 *gyre:* a radiating spiral, cone, or vortex. Yeats used the intersecting of two of these shapes as a visual symbol of his cyclic theory. As one gyre spiraled and widened out, to become dissipated, one period of history would end; at the same time a new gyre, closer to the center, would begin and spiral in a reverse direction to the starting point of the old gyre. A drawing of this plan looks like this:

The falcon of line 2 is at the broadest, centrifugal point of one gyre, symbolically illustrating the end of a cycle. The "indignant desert birds" of line 17 "reel" in a tighter circle, symbolizing the beginning of the new age in the new gyre.

The blood-dimmed tide° is loosed, and everywhere   5
The ceremony of innocence is drowned;
The best lack all conviction, while the worst
Are full of passionate intensity.

Surely some revelation is at hand;
Surely the Second Coming is at hand.   10
The Second Coming! Hardly are those words out
When a vast image out of *Spiritus Mundi*°
Troubles my sight; somewhere in sands of the desert
A shape with lion body and the head of a man,°
A gaze blank and pitiless as the sun,   15
Is moving its slow thighs, while all about it
Reel shadows of the indignant desert birds.
The darkness drops again; but now I know
That twenty centuries of stony sleep
Were vexed to nightmare by a rocking cradle,   20
And what rough beast, its hour come round at last,
Slouches towards Bethlehem to be born?

5 *blood-dimmed tide:* quotation from Shakespeare's *Macbeth*, Act II, scene 2, lines 60–63.   12
Spiritus Mundi: literally, the spirit of the world, a collective human consciousness that furnished
writers and thinkers with a common fund of images and symbols. Yeats referred to this collective
repository as "a great memory passing on from generation to generation."   14 *lion body and
the head of a man:* that is, the Sphinx, which in ancient Egypt symbolized the pharaoh as a spirit of
the sun. Because of this pre-Christian origin, the reincarnation of a sphinx could therefore represent qualities associated in New Testament books like Revelation (11, 13, 17), Mark (13:14–20),
and 2 Thessalonians (2:1–12) with a monstrous, superhuman, satanic figure. For a picture of the
Sphinx, see p. 705.

QUESTIONS

1. Consider the following as symbols: the "gyre," the "falcon," the "blood-dimmed
   tide," the "ceremony of innocence," the "worst" who are "full of passionate
   intensity." What ideas and values do these symbolize in the poem?

2. Why does Yeats capitalize the phrase "Second Coming"? To what does this
   phrase refer? Explain the irony of Yeats's use of the phrase in this poem.

3. Contrast the symbols of the falcon of line 2 and the desert birds of line 17.
   Considering that these are realistically presented, how does the realism contribute to their identity as symbols?

4. What is symbolized by the sphinx being revealed as a "rough beast"? What is
   the significance of the beast's going "towards Bethlehem to be born"?

WRITING ABOUT SYMBOLISM
AND ALLUSION IN POETRY

As you read your poem, take notes and make all the observations you can about
the presence of symbols or allusions or both. Explanatory notes will help you

establish basic information, but you also need to explain meanings and create interpretations in your own words. Use a dictionary for understanding words or phrases that require further study. For allusions, you might check out original sources to determine original contexts. Try to determine the ways in which your poem is similar to, or different from, the original work or source, and then determine the purpose served by the allusion.

Questions for Discovering Ideas

CULTURAL OR UNIVERSAL SYMBOLS

- What symbols that you can characterize as cultural or universal can you discover in names, objects, places, situations, or actions in the poem (e.g., nightingales, hemlock, a thorn, two lovers, Bethlehem)?
- How are these symbols used? What do they mean, both specifically, in the poem, and universally, in a broader context? What would the poem be like without the symbolic meaning?

CONTEXTUAL SYMBOLS

- What contextual symbols can you locate in the poem (e.g., withered sedge, a spiraling gyre, a doe running into a woods)? How are these symbols used specifically in the poem? What would the poem be like if the contextual symbol were not taken to be symbolic?
- What causes you to conclude that the symbols are truly symbolic? What is being symbolized? What do the symbols mean? How definite or direct is the symbolism?
- Is the symbolism used systematically throughout the poem, or is it used only once? How does the symbolism affect the ideas or emotions expressed in the poem?

ALLUSIONS

- Granted your knowledge of literature, science, geography, television, the Bible, film, popular culture, and other fields of knowledge, what kinds of allusion are you likely to recognize immediately?
- Do you find any references that fit into any of these or other categories? What do these allusions mean in their original context? What do they mean in the context of the poem?
- Do you see any possible allusions that you are not sure about? What help do you find in the explanatory notes in the text you are using? Consult a dictionary or other reference work (ask your reference librarian) to discover the nature of these allusions.

Strategies for Organizing Ideas

Begin with a brief description of the poem and of the symbolism or allusions in it. A symbol might be central to the poem, or an allusion might be introduced at a particularly important point. Your central idea might take you in a number of directions, such as that the symbolism is based on objects like flowers and natural scenes, or that it stems out of an action or set of actions, or that it is developed from an initial situation. The symbols may be universal, or they may be contextual; they may be applicable particularly to personal life or to political or social life. Allusions may emphasize the differences between your poem and the work or event being alluded to, or they may highlight the circumstances of your poem. Also, you might make a point that the symbols and/or allusions make your poem seem optimistic, or pessimistic, and so on.

Some possible approaches for your essay, which may be combined as need arises, are discussed below.

1. *The meaning of symbols or allusions.* This approach is the most natural one to take for an essay on symbolism or allusion. If you have discovered a symbol or symbols, or allusions, explain the meaning as best you can. Thus you will need to answer questions like these: What is the poem's major idea? How do you know that your interpretation is valid? How do the poem's symbols and allusions contribute to your interpretation? How pervasive, how applicable, are these devices? If you have discovered many symbols and allusions, which ones predominate? What do they mean? Why are some more important than others? What connects them with each other and with the poem's main idea? How are you able to make conclusions about all this?

2. *The effect of symbols or allusions on the poem's form.* Here the goal is to determine how symbolism or allusion is related to the poetic structure. Where does the symbol occur in the poem? If it is early, how do the subsequent parts relate to the ideas of the symbol? What logical or chronological function does the symbol serve in the poem's development? Is the symbol repeated, and if so, to what effect? If the symbol is introduced later, has it been anticipated earlier? How do you know? Can the symbol be considered climactic? What might the structure of the poem have been like if the symbolism had not been used? (Answering this question can help you judge how the symbol influences the poem's structure.) Many of these same questions might also be applied to an allusion or allusions. In addition, for an allusion, it is important to compare the contexts of the work you are studying and the original to determine how the poet has used the allusion as a part of the poem's form or structure.

3. *The relationship between the literal and the symbolic.* The object here is to describe the literal nature of the symbols, and then to determine their appropriateness to the poem's context. If the symbol is part of a narrative, what is its literal function? If the symbol is a person, object, or setting, what physical aspects are described? Are colors included? Shapes? Sizes? Sounds? In the light of this description, how applicable is the symbol to the ideas it embodies? How appropriate is the literal condition to the symbolic? The answers to questions like these should lead not so much to a detailed account of the meaning of the symbols, but rather to an account of their appropriateness to the topics and ideas of the poem.

4. *The implications and resonances of symbols and allusions.* This type of essay is more personal than the others, for it is devoted to the suggestions and associations—the "implications and resonances"—that the poem's symbols and allusions bring out. The object of the essay is to describe your own process or chain of thinking that the poem sets in motion. You are therefore free to move in your own direction as long as you base your discussion in the symbols and allusions you find in the poem. If the poet is speaking in general terms about the end of an era, for example, as with the symbol of the "rough beast" in Yeats's "The Second Coming" and the giant fishnets in Jeffers's "The Purse-Seine," then you could apply these symbols to your own thinking. It is not easy to summon the knowledge and authority to contradict the work of any poet, but if you can point out shortcomings in the thought of the symbols or allusions, you should do so.

Your conclusion might contain a summary of your main points. If your poem is particularly rich in symbols or allusions, you might also briefly consider some of the elements that you have not considered fully in the body and try to tie these together with those you have already discussed. It would also be appropriate to introduce any responses or new ideas you developed as a result of your study.

SAMPLE STUDENT ESSAY

Symbolism and Allusion in Yeats's "The Second Coming"°

[1] William Butler Yeats's "The Second Coming" is a prophetic poem that lays out reasons for being scared about the future. The poem's symbolism and allusiveness combine traditional materials from ancient history and literature together with Yeats's own scheme for visualizing the rise and fall of civilizations. These devices are arranged to explain both the disruption of our present but old culture and also the installation of a fearsome new one.* To make his prophecies clear, Yeats includes major symbols and allusions separately and combines them as a reflection of horror.†

[2] Yeats's first symbol, the gyre, or rather two interconnecting gyres, pervades the poem, for it outlines the cyclical nature of political changes. Flying outward at the widest point of the gyre--symbolizing our present era--a falcon is used by Yeats to introduce the idea that "the center cannot hold." The "desert birds," hovering around the "lion body and the head of a man" (the Sphinx-like figure), show a tighter circle in a second gyre, symbolizing a new stage of human existence. Thus the widening symbolic gyre in line 1 is interpenetrating with the narrowing gyre pointing at the "rough beast." This intersecting and blending

---

° See p. 680 for this poem.
* Central idea.
† Thesis sentence.

show that new things both emerge and separate from old things. The spatial and geometrical symbolism thus illustrates that the past is breaking up while the future is about to take the shape of the past--but at its worst, not at its best.

[3] Embodying this horror-to-be, the second major symbol is the Sphinx-like creature "moving its slow thighs" "in sands of the desert." The attributes of the monstrous creature are blankness and pitilessness. Yeats describes it as a "rough beast," with the "indignant desert birds" flying in circles above it like vultures. This description symbolizes the brutal nature of the new age. Yeats wrote the poem in 1919, right after the conclusion of World War I, which had seen particularly mindless and vicious trench warfare. The disruption of life caused by this war was a disturbing indicator that the new period would become repressive and brutal.

It is this forthcoming brutality that makes ironic the poem's major allusion-- the "Second Coming." Yeats alludes to the Second Coming in the poem's title and also in lines 9 and 10:

Surely some revelation is at hand;
Surely the Second Coming is at hand.

[4] The allusion is to the usual understanding of New Testament prophecies about the return of Christ at the end of historical time, when the Kingdom of God will come on earth. In the Bible, war and rumors of war are claimed as being the signs indicating that the return, or "Second Coming," is near. Thus far, both the biblical signs and the observations of Yeats coincide. The twist, however, is that Yeats is suggesting in the allusion that after the breakup of the present age, the new age will be marked not by God's Kingdom but by the "rough beast." Because Yeats describes the beast as a Sphinx, his model is the kind of despotism known in ancient Egypt, when power was held absolutely by the pharaoh, and when few people were granted any freedom or civil rights.

[5] A unique aspect of Yeats's symbolism and allusiveness is that he fuses the two together. The "ceremony of innocence," for example (line 6), refers to the ritual of communion and also to its symbolic value of regeneration. By indicating that it is being "drowned," he doubles the impact of his assertion that tradition is being lost and brutalized. The *"Spiritus Mundi"* is an abstract allusion to a common human bond of images and characteristics, but because of the image of brutality it produces, as a symbol it demonstrates that horror is a normal condition of human life. In addition, the "blood-dimmed tide" is an allusion to Shakespeare's Macbeth, who symbolically has stained the ocean red with King Duncan's blood. The "blood-dimmed tide" therefore both allusively and symbolically indicates the global scope of the evil age being born.

[6] "The Second Coming" is therefore rich in symbols that are both traditional and also personal with Yeats, but there are additional symbols and allusions. The most easily visualized of these is the falcon out of control, flying higher and higher and farther away from "the falconer," to symbolize the anarchy that Yeats mentions in line 4 as being "loosed" in the world. An example of a symbol being used ironically is the reference to Bethlehem where, according to Matthew and Luke, Jesus, who is called the Prince of Peace, was born. In "The Second Coming," Yeats asserts that the new birth will not lead to peace, but instead will

bring about a future age of repression and brutality. <u>The poem thus offers a
complex and disturbing fabric of symbol and allusion.</u>

Commentary on the Essay

This essay combines the topics of symbolism and allusion and illustrates
how each can be treated. The introduction briefly characterizes the poem and
asserts that the arguments are made through the use of symbols and allusions.
The central idea is about the replacement of the old by the new, and the thesis
sentence states that Yeats combines major symbols and allusions to achieve an
effect of horror. Paragraph 2 describes the shape of the symbol, thus illustrating
strategy 2 as described on page 683, and also explains it, illustrating strategy 1
(p. 683). Paragraph 3 considers the "rough beast" as a symbol of emerging brutality. Paragraph 4 treats the title's allusion to New Testament prophetic tradition, showing that Yeats makes his point by reversing the outcome that that
tradition had predicted. Paragraph 5 demonstrates the complexity of Yeats's
poem by stressing how he fuses symbolism and allusion as a common topic. The
sixth and last paragraph summarizes and characterizes the body briefly and proceeds to illustrate the richness of "The Second Coming" with brief references to
additional symbols and allusions.

SPECIAL WRITING TOPICS FOR STUDYING
SYMBOLISM AND ALLUSION IN POETRY

1. Analyze the ways in which Keats, Herbert, and Jeffers use symbols to convey the
    fact and idea of capture and thralldom ("La Belle Dame Sans Merci," "The
    Collar," and "The Purse-Seine"). What major symbols do the three poets use?
    How appropriate is each symbol in its respective poem? How do the poets use
    the symbols to focus on the problems they present in their poems?

2. Describe the differences in the ways in which e. e. cummings, Jorie Graham,
    and W. B. Yeats use allusions in "in just-," "The Geese," and "The Second
    Coming." How completely can we understand these poems without an expla-
    nation of the allusions? How extensive should explanations be? To what extent
    does the allusiveness make the poems difficult? Challenging? Interesting?
    Enriching?

3. Write a poem in which you develop a major symbol, as Jeffers does in "The
    Purse-Seine" and Herbert does in "The Collar." Some symbols you might con-
    sider are these:

    Atomic waste or nuclear weapons

    Foreign-made cars

    A superstar athlete

    A computer

    A dog staring out a window as children leave for school

Write an essay describing the process of your creation. How do you begin? How much detail is necessary? How many conclusions do you need to bring out about your symbol? When do you think you have said enough? Too much? How do you know?

4. Write a poem in which you make your own allusions to your own experiences, such as school, an activity, a team, a book, a movie character, or a recent artistic or political event. What assumptions do you make about your reader when you bring out your allusions? How do you make the allusion (i.e., by a quotation, a name, a title, an indirect reference)? How does your allusion deepen your meaning? How does your allusion increase your own power of expression?

5. From your library, take out a critical study of Yeats or Jeffers published by a university press. How much detail is devoted in the study to either poet's use of symbols? How pervasively is symbolism employed by the poet? How does the poet use symbolism to express ideas about science or nationalism? What other use or uses does the poet make of symbolism?

19
Myth: Systems of Symbolic Allusion in Poetry

Our word *myth* is derived from the Greek word *muthos* or *mythos,* meaning a story, narrative, or plot. Primarily, a **myth** is a story that deals with the relationships of gods to humanity (the *myths* of Oedipus or Odysseus) or with battles among heroes (the *myths* of Hercules or Achilles). A myth may also be a set of beliefs or assumptions among societies. **Mythology** refers collectively to all the stories and beliefs, either of a group (*Greek mythology*) or of a number of groups (*mythology of the Ancient Near East*). A system of beliefs and religious or historical doctrine is a **mythos** (the *Islamic mythos* or the *Buddhist mythos*).

MYTHOLOGY AS AN EXPLANATION
OF HOW THINGS ARE

Throughout the ages, people have developed myths because they want to know who they are, where they have been, where they are going, how the world got the way it is, and whether anyone up there cares. Mythical stories and characters answer these questions. They comprise narrative systems that explain the history, culture, religion, and collective psychology of individual societies and civilizations. They also satisfy the human need to understand and humanize conditions that are otherwise mysterious and frightening.

Although many myths originated in primitive times, they still provide a wealth of material and allusion in literature and art. The world around us seems more rich, awesome, and divine when we know that many events, places, creatures, trees, and flowers are important in the beautiful stories and legends that we have inherited from the past.

Myth, Science, and Belief

Myth and science overlap, since both attempt to provide explanations for the universe. At the beginning of civilization, almost all the vital questions were answered by myths, such those about gods, the creation of the earth and humanity, lightning and thunder, earthquakes and volcanoes, sexuality, birth, good, evil, and death.

As Western civilization became progressively more educated and sophisticated, particularly after the time of Copernicus (1473–1543), scientific discoveries replaced myths as the means of explaining the "how's" of life and existence. Thus we understand today that lightning and thunder are produced by electrically charged clouds, not by the great and powerful gods Zeus and Thor hurling lightning bolts from the sky (but lightning is still not a thoroughly understood phenomenon). Wherever volcanoes erupt, we know that the cause is molten rock deep within the earth's crust being vented violently through fissures in the volcanoes.

Even though myths are not scientific, they should not be dismissed. While we know an immense amount scientifically about *how* things happen, we do not really know *why* they happen. For instance, although cosmogonists tell us a great deal about the early stages of the universe and the development of galaxies, stars, the solar system, and our earth, they do not even approach answering the imponderable religious and philosophical questions about causes that myths attempt to explain.

The Power of Symbolic Mythical Truth

Myths are ingrained in our minds and in our speech. For example, we *know* with scientific certainty that we have daylight when we are turned into the sun's direct light, and that we have night when we are turned away from the sun and are in the earth's shadow. Nevertheless, we continue to use the phrases "the sun rises" and "the sun sets" to explain day and night, as though we still believed the mythical story about a flat earth with the sun circling around it. Such mythically originated language is inseparable from our minds. Even the belief that science and technology can solve all earthly problems may be seen as a myth. Human beings, in short, are **mythopoeic**—that is, not only do we live with myths, but we habitually create them.

It is therefore important to realize that myths express truth symbolically even if mythical heroes and stories themselves are scientifically or historically inadmissible. The truths are not to be found in the actual lore itself but rather in what they show about our earthly existence. Thus, when we read about the problems of the ancient Theban king Oedipus, we can safely assume that the specific details of his life (if he actually ever did live) did not happen just as Sophocles dramatizes them in *Oedipus the King*. But we find in the play a powerful rendering of how human beings make mistakes and how they must pay for them. In short, the truth of the Oedipus myth is psychological, not literal and historical.

Myth as Concept and Perspective

We can broaden our consideration by adding that myths also imply a special perspective about how people see their place and purpose in the world. This kind of myth may be constructive and generative. Thus, at one time most North Americans accepted the myth that Nature was limitless and wild and in need of being conquered. With this concept in mind, settlers moved into every available corner of the land—to build, farm, create industries, and establish new ways of life. Without such an inspiring myth, people would have stayed put, and the nation would never have achieved its current prominence.

This is not to say that all myths are positive; indeed, some myths may be destructive. Thus, the once-positive myth of limitless and inexhaustible nature has led us into the massive problems we face today with environmental exploitation and degradation. A new attitude is in the process of coming into existence—that the earth is no longer inimical, in need of taming, but is beautiful, tender, and fragile, in need of conservation. While the reasons for the changing attitude are largely scientific, the attitude itself marks a new myth—that of a caring relationship for nature, with all the consequent approaches to preserving wild animals, the land, and natural resources.

Mythological Themes or Motifs

Since myths address our human need to know, it is not surprising to find that many civilizations, separated by time and space, have parallel myths, such as the many stories accounting for the creation of the universe. The details of these myths are different, but the *patterns* are similar inasmuch as they all posit both an original time and action of creation, and a creator god or gods who also take part in human history. The principal god is perceived as a shaper, a modeler, a divine artisan, who has fashioned the orderly systems we find in the world, such as life, daylight, ecological dependence, tides, warmth, fertility, harvests, morality, and social stability.

One of the most crucial of all myths involves sin, disobedience, and evil, which are usually blamed for winter, natural calamities, and death. A corollary of the myth is that a god-hero or goddess-heroine must undergo a sacrifice to atone for sin and to ensure the renewed vitality of spring. In *The Golden Bough*, a massive collection and analysis of mythic stories, Sir James Frazer (1854–1941) compares a series of mythical death-renewal motifs. Among such sacrificed and reborn gods are Thammuz (Babylonia), Attis (Phrygia), Osiris (Egypt), and Adonis, Dionysus, and Persephone (Greece). Again, the specific myths take different forms, but they reflect the same mysteries, fears, and hopes.

Scholars and anthropologists like Frazer were among the first to observe the interrelationships among myths produced by diverse cultures. The Swiss psychoanalyst Carl Gustav Jung (1875–1961) offered an explanation for this duplication. He noticed that images, characters, and events similar to those in literature, mythology, and religion also occurred in the dreams of his patients. He termed these recurring images **archetypes** (from the Greek word meaning "model" or "first mold") and developed a theory that all human beings share in a universal or collective unconscious mind. Even if Jung's theory is ignored, the fact remains that types of mythic creatures such as dragons and centaurs, archetypal mother-daughter and father-son stories, and narratives involving sacrifices, heroic quests, and trips to the underworld recur throughout various mythologies and pervade our literature.[1]

MYTHOLOGY AND LITERATURE

When writing was invented, the first written works recorded mythologies that already existed. The ancient Greek poet Homer, for example (perhaps a mythical figure himself), told about the mythical gods and heroes of the Trojan War. Homer did not actually write (tradition says he was blind), but other writers recorded and transmitted his epics. The Latin writer Ovid (43 B.C.E.–17 C.E.) knew a large body of mythology and wrote poetic stories based on it. The result of this assimilation of myth into poetry was a combination of literature and religion that served the double purpose of teaching and entertaining. In this way, poets throughout antiquity used mythology as a mine for ideas, images, and symbols.

Although almost two thousand years have passed since Ovid lived, writers and artists still rely on mythology. In every generation since the earliest Anglo-Saxon poems and legends, poets of English have retold and updated mythological stories. Indeed, many of the poems in this chapter are from the twentieth century. Modern poetry utilizing mythology, however, is no longer designed to reinforce the dominant religion. Instead, it uses mythology to link past and present, to dramatize important concerns, and to symbolize universal patterns of thought.

Most Western poets who use mythological material in their verse turn to long-standing bodies of myth, particularly those of Greco-Roman, Norse-Teutonic, and Judeo-Christian origin. These systems of mythology are **universal** or **public,** since they are part of a vast common heritage. Like universal symbols, they make up a reservoir of material that all writers are free to employ.

Mythological References in Poetry

When poets make references to a myth, as in poems like Tennyson's "Ulysses" and Parker's "Penelope," both of which refer to the myth of Odysseus (Ulysses), they assume that readers already understand something about the stories and characters. With these poems, readers are expected to know enough of Homer's *Odyssey* to recall that this hero fought in the Trojan War for ten years and then was forced to spend ten years returning home. In other words, during most of his reign as king of Ithaca he was a warrior and

---

[1] See also Chapter 27 for a further discussion of archetypes.

adventurer—an absentee ruler—but at the same time his queen, Penelope, stayed at home.

While you may often have enough background in mythology to understand all the poet's references, you may sometimes need to fill in or reinforce your knowledge. A good place to start is a dictionary or general encyclopedia, where you will find brief identifications of mythic figures and a key to further reading. Eventually you will want access to more detailed information. Excellent books that retell the stories of Greco-Roman mythology are Richmond Hathorn's *Greek Mythology*, M. C. Howatson's *The Oxford Companion to Classical Literature*, and Timothy Gantz's *Early Greek Myth: A Guide to Literary and Artistic Sources*. Bulfinch's *The Age of Fable* and Edith Hamilton's *Mythology* are respected traditional books. There are also many classical dictionaries, such as the *Oxford Classical Dictionary*, that are immensely useful. John Keats learned much of his mythology from John Lemprière's *Classical Dictionary*. Many libraries have this book on their reference shelves, and your use of it will both inform you and impress you with a sense of historical scholarship. Not all allusions are classical. Should you want to understand allusions to the myths of Paul Bunyan and Johnny Appleseed, for example, you would want a collection of American folk tales. References to Odin, Thor, the Valkyries, or Asgard should lead you to a collection of Norse-Teutonic mythology.

Studying Mythology in Poetry

We are now ready to look at a poem that is built upon a myth. The poem is by William Butler Yeats, and it draws on Greco-Roman mythology.

WILLIAM BUTLER YEATS   (1865–1939)

Leda and the Swan _____ *1924 (1923)*

A sudden blow: the great wings beating still
Above the staggering girl, her thighs caressed
By the dark webs, her nape caught in his bill,
He holds her helpless breast upon his breast.

How can those terrified vague fingers push   5
The feathered glory from her loosening thighs?
And how can body, laid in that white rush,
But feel the strange heart beating where it lies?

A shudder in the loins engenders there
The broken wall, the burning roof and tower   10
And Agamemnon dead.
                        Being so caught up,
So mastered by the brute blood of the air,
Did she put on his knowledge with his power
Before the indifferent beak could let her drop?

QUESTIONS

1. What mythic event does the poem retell? Who was Leda? The swan? Who were Leda's children? What events are alluded to in lines 10 and 11?

2. How is Leda described? What words suggest her helplessness? What phrases suggest the swan's mystery and divinity?

3. What question is raised in the last two lines? To what extent does the poem provide an answer to this question?

Yeats's sonnet focuses on a specific event of ancient Greek mythology: Zeus, king of the gods, having taken the form of a swan, raped Leda, a Spartan queen. According to the myth, this violent event was a starting point not only of Greek civilization, but also of humanity's angers and troubles. One of the children born of the rape was Helen of Troy, whose abduction by Paris precipitated the Trojan War. Yeats's phrase "The broken wall, the burning roof and tower" refers to the destruction of Troy. Another child was Clytemnestra, married to Agamemnon, king of Mycenae and leader of the allied Greek forces. Because Agamemnon had sacrificed their daughter Iphigeneia as a part of the war effort, Clytemnestra vowed revenge and had him murdered when he returned home from the Trojan War.

After a graphic recounting of the swan's attack on Leda, and a brief reference to the sack of Troy and Agamemnon's death, Yeats's concluding lines raise a central issue stemming from the myth. While Leda took on some of Zeus's divine power with the rape (through the process of childbearing), the poem asks whether she also "put on" some of his divine knowledge—whether she acquired Zeus's foreknowledge of the fall of Troy, the murder of Agamemnon, and, by extension, the subsequent events in history. Of course, the question is rhetorical and the answer is negative.

If all the poem did were to question the ancient myth in this way, it would be of limited interest for modern readers. But it does more than that; it directs our attention to concerns of today. Thus, we may conclude from Yeats's use of the myth that human beings, like Leda, do not have foreknowledge, but have only their own culture, experience, and intelligence as their guides. If divine beings exist, they have no interest in human affairs, but are rather uninvolved and "indifferent" (line 14). By extension the myth suggests that the burden of civilization is on human beings themselves, and that if knowledge and power are ever to be combined for constructive goals, that blending must be a human achievement.

Yeats thus employs mythic material in this sonnet to raise a searching question about the nature of existence, knowledge, and power. The historical process is embodied in the rape, the children born out of it, and their troubles. As the central figure of the myth, Leda is the focal point of circumstances and concerns that have extended from the distant past to the present, and that will likely extend into the future.

Because most myths similarly embody recurring issues, they have great value for modern readers. Muriel Rukeyser's "Myth," for example, uses the ancient myth about Oedipus to shed light amusingly on misperceptions about male-female relationships. Edward Field's "Icarus" (one of a number of Icarus poems we include here) uses the ancient Icarus myth to decry the impact of modern society upon individuals. In these and in other poems based in mythology, you may look for such original ways in which poets receive something old and make it new. Myths do not belong only to the past but are alive and well in the present.

The poems in this chapter feature mythical material about Odysseus, Icarus, the Phoenix, and Oedipus. Although all the poems delve into ancient mythology for their subjects, they are remarkably different; each offers its own meaning, impact, and poetic experience. The poets shape their mythic material to illustrate and symbolize ideas about pride, daring, disillusionment, suffering, indignation, creativity, idealism, and indifference to the plights of others, and therefore the poems demonstrate how myths can be used for original effects in new poetic contexts. As you study the poems, consider the following general questions along with the questions following the poems:

1. How completely does the poem deal with the myth? What is included? What is excluded? What does the poet expect that you should know about the myth? How does the poet create a variation on the myth beyond the original?

2. Why do modern poets treat mythical subjects? Are they simply interpreting or reinterpreting ancient stories, or are they using the ancient stories to shed light on modern circumstances? Why? How?

FOUR POEMS RELATED TO HOMER'S *ODYSSEY*

Odysseus ruled the island realm of Ithaca and was one of the major Greek generals during the ten-year siege and destruction of Troy. When he tried to return home he was opposed by the Sea-God Poseidon because he, Odysseus, had blinded Polyphemus the Cyclops, the god's son. However, Odysseus was a favorite of Athena, the Goddess of Wisdom, who always kept him alive through the dangers and delays Poseidon created. For example, when Odysseus sailed near the Sirens, who lured sailors to death with their songs of heavenly beauty, he resisted their attractions by having himself lashed to the mast of his ship. Odysseus was also endangered by Circe, an enchantress, who turned men to swine. He escaped this transformation by taking a magical herb, but he was then confined by Circe on Aeaea, her island kingdom, for a year. After leaving Circe he was kept for eight years by Calypso, a nymph who treated him with love, but at the end of this time the gods allowed him to leave for home, mainly because of the intercession of Athena. During his absence, he had entrusted his kingdom to his wife and queen, Penelope. She was faithful but was besieged by crowds of suitors, each of whom sought to take over the Ithacan kingdom by marrying her. She promised to accept one of the suitors when she finished making a shroud for her father-in-law. During the day she wove the shroud, but at night she unraveled her day's work. The suitors discovered her ruse, but by this time Odysseus, after a twenty-year absence, had returned to Ithaca and, with help, killed all the suitors, restored himself as king, and made peace with the relatives of the suitors.

POEMS FOR STUDY

MARGARET ATWOOD   (b. 1939)

Siren Song _____ *1974*

This is the one song everyone
would like to learn: the song
that is irresistible:

the song that forces men
to leap overboard in squadrons   5
even though they see the beached skulls

the song nobody knows
because anyone who has heard it
is dead, and the others can't remember.

Shall I tell you the secret   10
and if I do, will you get me
out of this bird suit?

I don't enjoy it here
squatting on this island
looking picturesque and mythical   15

with these two feathery maniacs,
I don't enjoy singing
this trio, fatal and valuable.

I will tell the secret to you,
to you, only to you.   20
Come closer. This song

is a cry for help: Help me!
Only you, only you can,
you are unique

at last, Alas   25
it is a boring song
but it works every time.

QUESTIONS

1. Who were the Sirens in Greek mythology? What effect did their song have?
2. Who is the speaker in this poem? What is the effect of her colloquial diction? What does she tell you about her song?
3. Who is the "you" referred to in lines 10–24? What does the speaker say about her life? What "works every time"? To what extent is the conclusion amusing?

W. S. MERWIN   (b. 1927)

Odysseus _____ *1960*

Always the setting forth was the same,
Same sea, same dangers waiting for him
As though he had got nowhere but older.
Behind him on the receding shore
The identical reproaches, and somewhere   5
Out before him, the unravelling patience
He was wedded to. There were the islands
Each with its woman and twining welcome
To be navigated, and one to call "home."
The knowledge of all that he betrayed   10
Grew till it was the same whether he stayed
Or went. Therefore he went. And what wonder
If sometimes he could not remember
Which was the one who wished on his departure
Perils that he could never sail through,   15
And which, improbable, remote, and true,
Was the one he kept sailing home to?

QUESTIONS

1. What aspects of the Odysseus myth are evoked in this poem? What point does the poem make about Odysseus's experiences?
2. To what extent is Odysseus symbolic of a specific kind of life and attitude toward life? How does our knowledge of Odysseus contribute to the impact and meaning of the poem?
3. Compare this poem with Parker's "Penelope." How is the same mythic material used toward different ends in these poems?

DOROTHY PARKER   (1893–1967)

Penelope _____ *1936*

In the pathway of the sun,
   In the footsteps of the breeze,
Where the world and sky are one,

He shall ride the silver seas,
  He shall cut the glittering wave.   5
I shall sit at home, and rock;
Rise, to heed a neighbor's knock;
Brew my tea, and snip my thread;
Bleach the linen for my bed.
  They will call him brave.   10

QUESTIONS

1. How does the speaker describe her life? How is her life different from that of the male figure described in lines 1–5?

2. To what extent is Penelope a symbol? What does she symbolize? How does our knowledge of the myth deepen our response to this symbolism?

PETER ULISSE   (b. 1944)

Odyssey: 20 Years Later _____ *1995*

I battled Trojans with Odysseus.
Bludgeoning the eye of Polyphemus
I meandered past Scylla and Charybdis,
descended into Hades, outwitted Calypso.   5
I ate of the lotus, and forgot.
Twenty years I roamed—

Wandering Jew, Prodigal Son, opener
of doors in empty streets I
embraced strangers like a lover's quest,   10
searched for the beautiful which
alone
could make a life complete.
I released hands in bedrooms,
turned to St. Augustine   15

It is only now I feel the pull
of salmon swimming up current,
turtles drawn to Galapagos,
fowls finding a path through
a thousand mile sky,   20
only now I understand
Odyssey not as Cyclops, Sirens,
or unfavorable winds but

simply as
coming home.

QUESTIONS

1. Who is the "I" of line 1? How does this line reveal the identity of the "I"? What do the final lines tell you about the speaker's and Odysseus's journeys?

2. Consider the speaker's description of having duplicated the actions performed by Odysseus and other ancient figures. What ideas does the speaker present about the repetitive or cyclical nature of human experience?

3. What autobiographical or confessional details are contained in lines 13–19? What educational experiences are alluded to in these lines?

FOUR POEMS ABOUT THE STORY OF ICARUS

Icarus was the son of Daedalus, the greatest master of applied science in ancient Greek myth. The story begins with Minos, king of Crete, who ruled Athens and the rest of the Greek world. Each year (or, according to other versions of the story, every nine years) Minos compelled the Athenians to make a tribute of seven young people to be sacrificed to the Minotaur, an enormously powerful monster who was half man and half bull. Needing to control the monster, Minos hired Daedalus, who was in exile from Athens, to build an enclosure—a labyrinth. Daedalus was so skillful that Minos kept him on Crete, confining both him and his son Icarus in the labyrinth. Additionally, Daedalus may have aided the Athenian hero, Theseus, in killing the Minotaur, thereby freeing Athens from the burden of the living tribute. Wishing to be free, Daedalus exerted his great skills to carry out an aerial escape; he made two pairs of wings out of wax and feathers—one for himself and one for Icarus. Daedalus flew safely away and eventually made his home in Sicily. Icarus, however, flew too close to the sun: The wax melted and the wings fell apart; Icarus fell into the Icarian Sea (named after him), and he drowned.

❧ POEMS FOR STUDY

BRIAN W. ALDISS   (b. 1925)

Flight 063 _____ *1994*

Why always speak of Icarus' fall?—
That legendary plunge
Amid a shower of tallow
And feathers and the poor lad's
Sweat? And that little splash   5

Which caught the eye of Brueghel°
While the sun remained
Aloof within its private zone?

    That fall remains
Suspended in the corporate mind.   10
Yet as our Boeing flies
High above the Arctic Circle
Into the sun's eye, think—
Before the fall the flight was.
(So with Adam—just before   15
The Edenic Fall, he had
That first taste of Eve.)

Dinner is served aboard Flight 063.
We eat from plastic trays, oblivious
To the stratosphere.   20

But Icarus—his cliff-top jump,
The leap of heart, the blue air scaled—
His glorious sense of life
Imperiled. Time
Fell far below, the everyday   25
Was lost in his ascent.

Up, up, he sailed, unheeding
Such silly limitations as
The melting point of wax.

FLIGHT 063   6 Brueghel: Pieter Brueghel or Breughel (ca. 1525–1569) was a Flemish painter whose subjects include the Nativity, the Crucifixion, reapers in the fields, and the fall of Icarus. His *Landscape with the Fall of Icarus* is one of his best known paintings, which exists in a number of versions.

QUESTIONS

1. What attitude toward Icarus does the speaker present (see lines 21–26)? What emotions does he attribute to Icarus during the beginning of the flight? What is the significance of line 14 ("Before the fall the flight was")?

2. What do the words "dinner" and "oblivious" suggest about modern attitudes toward flight?

3. Why does the speaker emphasize the word "think" (line 13)? Why is the melting point of wax a "silly" limitation?

EDWARD FIELD   (b. 1924)

Icarus _____ *1963*

Only the feathers floating around the hat
Showed that anything more spectacular had occurred
Than the usual drowning. The police preferred to ignore
The confusing aspects of the case,

And the witnesses ran off to a gang war.   5
So the report filed and forgotten in the archives read simply
"Drowned," but it was wrong: Icarus
Had swum away, coming at last to the city
Where he rented a house and tended the garden.

"That nice Mr. Hicks" the neighbors called him,   10
Never dreaming that the gray, respectable suit
Concealed arms that had controlled huge wings
Nor that those sad, defeated eyes had once
Compelled the sun. And had he told them
They would have answered with a shocked, uncomprehending stare.   15
No, he could not disturb their neat front yards;
Yet all his books insisted that this was a horrible mistake:
What was he doing aging in a suburb?
Can the genius of the hero fall
To the middling stature of the merely talented?   20

And nightly Icarus probes his wound
And daily in his workshop, curtains carefully drawn,
Constructs small wings and tries to fly
To the lighting fixture on the ceiling:
Fails every time and hates himself for trying.   25

He had thought himself a hero, had acted heroically,
And dreamt of his fall, the tragic fall of the hero;
But now rides commuter trains,
Serves on various committees,
And wishes he had drowned.   30

QUESTIONS

   1.   What twist on the Icarus myth occurs in this poem?
   2.   How does Field undercut the heroic myth of Icarus? What happens to Icarus
        after he rents a house and tends his garden? What does Icarus, the daily subur-
        ban commuter with "sad, defeated eyes," wish at the poem's end?
   3.   What level of language does Field use in this poem? How does this language
        complement the poem's antiheroic view of Icarus?

MURIEL RUKEYSER   (1913–1980)

Waiting for Icarus ————————————————————————— *1973*

He said he would be back and we'd drink wine together
He said that everything would be better than before
He said we were on the edge of a new relation
He said he would never again cringe before his father

He said that he was going to invent full-time   5
He said he loved me that going into me
He said was going into the world and the sky
He said all the buckles were very firm
He said the wax was the best wax
He said Wait for me here on the beach   10
He said Just don't cry

I remember the gulls and the waves
I remember the islands going dark on the sea
I remember the girls laughing
I remember they said he only wanted to get away from me   15
I remember mother saying: Inventors are like poets,
                              a trashy lot
I remember she told me those who try out inventions are worse
I remember she added: Women who love such are the worst of all
I have been waiting all day, or perhaps longer.   20
I would have liked to try those wings myself.
It would have been been better than this.

QUESTIONS

1. Who is speaking? How long has she been waiting for Icarus? When is she speak-
    ing? Does she know what has happened to Icarus?

2. In what ways is the speaker's narration a complaint? What does she complain
    about? How do the things she says bring ancient and modern circumstances to
    a common level?

3. To what degree is this poem humorous? What effect does Rukeyser's use of
    anaphora (see p. 520) have on the development of the poem?

WILLIAM CARLOS WILLIAMS   (1883–1963)

Landscape with the Fall of Icarus _____ *1962*

According to Brueghel°
when Icarus fell
it was spring

a farmer was ploughing
his field   5
the whole pageantry

of the year was
awake tingling
near

LANDSCAPE WITH THE FALL OF ICARUS.   1 *Brueghel:* See the note for line 6 of Aldiss's
"Flight 063," p. 699.

the edge of the sea   10
concerned
with itself

sweating in the sun
that melted
the wings' wax   15

unsignificantly
off the coast
there was

a splash quite unnoticed
this was   20
Icarus drowning

QUESTIONS

1. The poem is in tercets (three-line groups), and no line has more than four
    words. What is the effect of these sparse lines on the seriousness of Icarus's sit-
    uation? Why does the poem not contain more detail?

2. Why does the speaker mention other things, specifically, the season, the farmer,
    the act of ploughing, the "tingling" pageant "of the year," and the shoreline—
    before he describes the splash in the last three lines?

3. Compare the view of ancient myth in this poem with the views of Aldiss, Field,
    and Rukeyser.

TWO POEMS RELATED TO THE PHOENIX

In ancient myth, the Phoenix was a gold-and-red Arabian bird resembling an
eagle. At the end of a long period, perhaps five hundred years, perhaps fifteen
hundred, the Phoenix would be mysteriously consumed by fire. A new Phoenix
would then be constituted from the ashes of the old, and a new life cycle would
begin—a process that continued indefinitely. Because of this constant renewal,
many religions have considered the Phoenix story as a symbol of life overcoming death.

 **POEMS FOR STUDY**

AMY CLAMPITT   (1920–1994)

Berceuse° _____ *1982*

Listen to Gieseking° playing a Berceuse
of Chopin°—the mothwing flutter
light as ash, perishable as burnt paper—

and sleep, now the furnaces of Auschwitz°
are all out, and tourists go there.   5
The purest art has slept with turpitude,

we all pay taxes. Sleep. The day of waking
waits, cloned from the phoenix—
a thousand replicas in upright silos,

nurseries of the ultimate enterprise.   10
Decay will undo what it can, the rotten
fabric of our repose connives with doomsday.

Sleep on, scathed felicity. Sleep, rare
and perishable relic. Imagining's no shutter
against the absolute, incorrigible sunrise.   15

BERCEUSE.   *Berceuse:* A lullaby or cradle song.   1 *Gieseking:* Walter Gieseking (1895–1956),
famous French pianist.   2 *Chopin:* Frédéric Chopin (1810–1849), Polish composer and pianist.
4 *Auschwitz:* World War II Nazi death camp near Kraków, Poland.

QUESTIONS

1. In what ways is this poem pessimistic? How does the speaker contrast the best
   and worst aspects of human life?
2. What is meant by line 6? What irony is contained in the image of the Phoenix
   (stanza 3)? What objects are replicated in the "upright silos"?
3. What are the "felicity" and "relic" of lines 13 and 14? Why should these "sleep"
   (see also line 7)? What is meant by the "absolute, incorrigible sunrise" of line 15?

MAY SARTON   (b. 1912)

The Phoenix° Again _____ *1988*

On the ashes of this nest
Love wove with deathly fire
The phoenix takes its rest
Forgetting all desire.

THE PHOENIX AGAIN.   *Phoenix:* See the note to line 23 of John Donne's "The Canonization,"
(p. 667).

After the flame, a pause,   5
After the pain, rebirth.
Obeying nature's laws
The phoenix goes to earth.

You cannot call it old
You cannot call it young.   10
No phoenix can be told,
This is the end of song.

It struggles now alone
Against death and self-doubt,
But underneath the bone   15
The wings are pushing out.

And one cold starry night
Whatever your belief
The phoenix will take flight
Over the seas of grief   20

To hear her thrilling song
To stars and waves and sky
For neither old nor young
The phoenix does not die.

QUESTIONS

1. What is the Phoenix? What does it signify?
2. What significance does the Phoenix have for the speaker? What personal situa-
    tion does the speaker seem to be describing? Why does the speaker invoke the
    details of the Phoenix's return to life after death?
3. Compare Sarton's use of the Phoenix with the uses by Donne in "The
    Canonization" (p. 667) and Clampitt in "Berceuse" (p. 703).

A POEM ABOUT OEDIPUS

For the story of Oedipus, see the introduction to *Oedipus the King* by Sophocles
(p. 906).

POEM FOR STUDY

MURIEL RUKEYSER (1913–1980)

Myth _____ *1978*

Long afterward, Oedipus, old and blinded, walked the
roads.   He smelled a familiar smell.   It was
the Sphinx.°   Oedipus said, "I want to ask one question.
Why didn't I recognize my mother?"   "You gave the
wrong answer," said the Sphinx.   "But that was what   5
made everything possible," said Oedipus.   "No," she said.
"When I asked, What walks on four legs in the morning,
two at noon, and three in the evening, you answered,
Man.   You didn't say anything about woman."
"When you say Man," said Oedipus, "you include women   10
too. Everyone knows that."   She said, "That's what
you think."

MYTH.   3 *Sphinx:* The photograph below shows the Sphinx at Gîza in Egypt.

QUESTIONS

1. Who was Oedipus? The Sphinx? According to this poem, what was wrong with
    Oedipus's answer to the Riddle of the Sphinx?
2. What elements and techniques in this work allow you to consider it a poem?
3. What two myths and meanings of *myth* are embodied in the title?
4. To what extent does the poem's colloquial language revitalize the mythic
    material?

The Great Sphinx, Gîza, Egypt. Foto Marburg/Art Resource, New York, NY.

WRITING ABOUT MYTH IN POETRY

An essay on myth in poetry will normally connect the mythic material in a poem to some other consideration, such as speaker, character, action, tone, setting, situation, imagery, form, and meaning. This suggests a two-part exploration of the poem: one concerned with its general sense, and the other with the ways in which myth shapes and controls that sense.

As you reexamine the poem, look for the ways in which myth enriches the poem and focuses its meaning. The following questions should help.

Questions for Discovering Ideas

- To what extent does the title identify the mythic content of the poem and thus provide a key for understanding?

- How much of the poem's action, setting, and situation are borrowed from mythology? What is the significance of the action in the myth? What does this action symbolize? How does the poet reshape the action and its significance?

- To what extent does our understanding of the myth explain the poem's speaker, characters, situations, and ideas? What characters, including the speaker, are drawn from mythology?

- In what ways are these characters symbolic? What aspects of this symbolism are carried into the poem? How does the poem either maintain or change the symbolism?

- How do the various formal elements of the poem, such as diction, rhyme, meter, and form, reshape the mythic material and affect the meaning and impact of the myth?

- Do specific words and phrases, for instance, undercut or reinforce the ideas and implications that we find in the myth itself?

- Does the rhyme (if any) lead us to deal with the mythic content seriously or humorously?

- Does the tone of the poem support or undercut the implications of the myth?

- Generally, how does the mythic content help develop and clarify the poem?

Strategies for Organizing Ideas

As with most other essays, the main challenge in writing about myths is developing a focus or central idea. If, for example, you find that the poem retells a myth in order to make a point about history or society, you should fashion your central idea to reflect that connection. Similarly, if the poem employs a mythical speaker or character to convey ideas about war or heroism, your essay will focus on the linkage of myth, character, and those ideas.

When you formulate a central idea, draft it as a complete sentence that conveys the full scope of your ideas. It is not enough merely to assert that a given poem contains a great deal of mythic material. If you are writing about Yeats's "Leda and the Swan," for example, you might be tempted to form a central idea that argues, "William Butler Yeats's 'Leda and the Swan' retells the myth of Leda's rape by Zeus and the consequences of that event." That sentence does not tell the reader anything about the *way* the Leda myth works in the poem. Nor does it provide a basis for moving beyond summary and paraphrase. A more effective formulation would be the following: "In Yeats's 'Leda and the Swan,' the myth of Leda's rape by Zeus and the consequences of that rape illustrate the process of history and question the connection between knowledge and power." This sentence points to a specific connection between mythological content and the poem's effect, and it gives a clear direction to the essay.

In your introductory paragraph or paragraphs, you should briefly summarize the significant parts of your poem's mythical elements, together with any noteworthy details about the poem's form or circumstances of composition. Your aim should be to focus on the poem (and the mythic material within the poem) rather than on the myth itself. Thus, you should link the mythical elements with other aspects of the poem and make assertions about the effects of this connection.

You can employ various strategies to organize the body of your essay.

1. You might decide to echo the organization of the poem, and shape the central paragraphs so as to reflect the poem's line-by-line or stanza-by-stanza logic.

2. You might choose an organization based on a series of different mythic elements or figures. For instance, if a poem alludes to Odysseus; his wife, Penelope; and his son, Telemachus, you might devote paragraphs to the way each figure shapes the poem's impact and meaning.

3. You might use the relevant elements of poetry as the focal points of organization. Thus, if you argue that diction, rhyme, and tone shape the mythological material to produce significant effects, you would deal with each element in turn.

To bring your essay to a convincing and assertive close, you might summarize your major points. At the same time, you might draw your reader's attention to the significance of your observations and to any further implications of the ways in which the myth is integrated into the poem you have considered.

SAMPLE STUDENT ESSAY

Myth and Meaning in Dorothy Parker's "Penelope"°

[1] Dorothy Parker's short lyric poem "Penelope" uses mythic allusion and symbolism to criticize conventional ideas about the roles of women and men. Her speaker is the mythic figure Penelope, the wife of King Odysseus of the ancient realm of Ithaca. Not only is Penelope the speaker, but she is also the poem's major figure. Parker uses her to assert that society has consistently misjudged and undervalued women's lives.* Her assertions are brought out

° See p. 696 for this poem.
* Central idea.

through the poem's title, its mythic resonance, its diction, and its view of the representative lives of both Odysseus and Penelope.†

[2]   The key to the poem's use of myth is the title, "Penelope." As the only place where the poem's mythological speaker is named, the title alludes to Homer's *Odyssey,* which tells that Penelope waits at home in Ithaca for twenty years while her husband adventures in the Trojan War and struggles to return home despite the enmity of the sea god, Poseidon. Penelope's seemingly interminable wait is filled with trouble. Her palace is occupied by boorish suitors who assume that Odysseus is dead and that his kingship is vacant. They therefore demand that Penelope choose a new husband. Only Penelope and Telemachus, her son, cling to the hope that Odysseus is still alive. She keeps the arrogant suitors at bay by promising to marry one of them after she finishes weaving a shroud for Odysseus's father. To delay this event, she works at the loom by day and unravels the work by night.

[3]   Although the title refers directly to Penelope, the poem itself also deals with Odysseus. Lines 1–5 evoke the King's adventures in the phrases "He shall ride the silver seas" (line 4) and "He shall cut the glittering wave" (line 5). Because Odysseus is not identified by name, but only by the pronoun "he," readers might see this male figure as a symbol of all men who leave home to pursue adventure. The adjectives "silver" and "glittering" connote splendor and glory, while the verbs "ride" and "cut" suggest resoluteness and boldness. In addition, the phrases "pathway of the sun" (line 1) and "footsteps of the breeze" (line 2) add romance and mystery. In the same lines, however, one may perceive a subtle undercutting of the heroic figure. The phrase "ride the silver seas," for example, suggests that some of the Homeric lines are clichés. The implication is that an overglorified image of active heroes like Odysseus is both exaggerated and inaccurate.

[4]   Just as this language has general implications for men, the language about Penelope is significant for women. In lines 6–9 she, as the speaker, contrasts her restricted life with the freedom of males. Here we find no adjectives at all; the woman's existence is thus rendered drab and tedious. In addition, the verbs represent passive and domestic activities: "sit," "rock," "rise," "brew," "snip," and "bleach." These last two verbs are especially effective. The phrase "snip my thread" (line 8) is the only allusion to Penelope's unhappy existence. It refers to her daring deception of the suitors through her nightly unraveling of the shroud. At the same time, "snip" is contrasted with the verb "cut" used earlier in the poem. While the words are synonyms, their connotations are different, for "cut" implies a degree of violence while "snip" suggests careful and delicate activity. "Bleach" is equally connotative; although it refers directly to "the linen for my bed," it is consistent with the view that Penelope's life is faded and colorless.

[5]   The poem's final line ironically clarifies Penelope's attitude toward the different roles of men and women. Penelope asserts that "They will call him brave." "They" refers to society, to the world at large, and to generations of readers who have admired Odysseus in Homer's *Iliad* and *Odyssey.* The meter of the line--a concluding spondee--places a great emphasis on the word "him," thus

† Thesis sentence.

demonstrating the speaker's realization, and the poet's assertion, that society ignores or dismisses the quiet bravery of women. In myth and in life, the woman's role often demands just as much courage and conviction as the man's.

"Penelope" thus employs mythic figures and events to criticize the historical perception of the roles of men and women. Odysseus, the mythical and typical male, is presented as a heroic figure, but he too is human, and his adventures are tinged with overdramatization. Parker's point is not to demean him, however, but rather to emphasize that women, too, have their own heroism. Biology and destiny may have traditionally confined women to stay at home, [6] weave tapestries, and keep house while men are granted the freedom to find adventure in far-off lands. But waiting at home while meeting domestic challenges takes courage too. Penelope and Odysseus lived at a time of the old ways, but if Parker's poem is understood properly, it is time for new ways to begin. Penelope is right to express annoyance and irony when considering the judgment of history. Our knowledge of her courageous survival in Ithaca during the absence of Odysseus adds significantly to the truth and depth of her feelings.

Commentary on the Essay

This essay's major rhetorical purpose is to show how the poet uses the Penelope-Odysseus myth to shed new light on conventional attitudes about men and women. As a guide for your own writing aims, therefore, the essay illustrates how the mythological material can lead to ideas for development.

The body of the essay follows the organization of the poem itself. Thus, paragraph 2 focuses on the title, paragraph 3 on lines 1–5, paragraph 4 on lines 6–9, and paragraph 5 on the last line. Each of the paragraphs also advances a specific aspect of the essay's central idea. In paragraph 2 Penelope is identified and the relevant mythic material is reviewed. Logically, the information in this paragraph is essential for the remainder of the essay.

In paragraph 3, the title and its mythic importance introduce Odysseus and the symbol of the heroic male. Here, the point is that Parker's diction undercuts the active male image while seeming to glorify it. The first sentence of paragraph 4 provides a transition from Odysseus and heroic males to Penelope and the perceived passiveness of women. Again, the essay explores the way diction and mythic allusion in the poem demonstrate that there is more to the lives of women than usually is claimed. Paragraph 5 looks at the poem's final line in relation to the contrasted lives of "heroic" men and "passive" women. Here, the essay shows how tone and meter reveal the speaker's attitude toward these contrasting lives and society's misperception of them.

The conclusion goes quickly over the essay's basic points, and it emphasizes how the poem, with its ancient myth, brings new light to a traditional problem. The writer has ended with a brief personal essay that considers the poem's ideas and their current importance.

SPECIAL WRITING TOPICS FOR STUDYING MYTH IN POETRY

1. In Atwood's "Siren Song," Merwin's "Odysseus," Parker's "Penelope," and Ulisse's "Odyssey: 20 Years Later," the poets evoke the same myth but for different purposes. What are these purposes? What views do you find about adventure, domesticity, and sexuality? What attitudes toward figures in the myth (Odysseus, Penelope, the Siren) do the poets bring out? How do word choice, selection of detail, and point of view influence each poet's conclusions?

2. The myth of Icarus is used by Aldiss, Field, Rukeyser, and Williams. Basing your conclusions on two or more of the poems by these poets, what similarities and differences can you describe? How do the poets present the myth? How do they use the myth to create unusual or surprising endings, and to comment on contemporary but also permanent attitudes about life and the sufferings of others?

3. What point does Muriel Rukeyser's "Myth" make about both men and women and their attitudes toward each other? How does our knowledge of the Oedipus myth (see Sophocles's play *Oedipus the King*, Chapter 23) help clarify these aspects of the poem? In what respects is the poem contemporary?

4. In your library, choose a book on myths, such as Kenneth McLeish, *Myth: Myths and Legends of the World Explored* (1996), or Richard Erdoes and Alfonso Ortiz, *American Indian Myths and Legends* (1984). Select a story from among the many myths described there (e.g., Oedipus, Jason, Prometheus, Antigone, Sisyphus, Beaver stealing fire from the Pines, Coyote placing the stars, Elder Brother). To these you might add biblical stories (e.g., the fight between God and Satan, Noah, Leviathan, Joseph and his brothers, the Hebrew captivity in Egypt, the Exodus, the Babylonian captivity) and other legends and actual historical stories (Robin Hood, Paul Bunyan, Davy Crockett, the Amistad event, the forty-niners, the Civil War, the Lone Ranger, the log cabin, the Rough Riders, etc.). Write a poem based on the story you choose. Try to present your own view about the importance, timeliness, intelligence, and truth of your story. What kinds of detail do you select? How do you give the figures mythic status? How do you make your own attitudes apparent by your arrangement of detail and your word choice?

20

Two Poetic Careers: Emily Dickinson and Robert Frost

In Chapters 11–19 we consider poetry in terms of its elements and effects. In this chapter we examine collections of poems by two major poets: Emily Dickinson (1830–1886) and Robert Frost (1874–1963). Dickinson and Frost are both American poets and New Englanders. Dickinson is one of the most prominent poetic voices of the nineteenth century, and Frost is recognized as a poetic giant of the twentieth century. Although the poems included here cannot encompass their entire poetic careers, they do provide an opportunity to consider a substantial representative body of their work. We have chosen poems that illustrate the central concerns and major characteristics of each poet.

EMILY DICKINSON   (1830–1886)

Life and Work

Emily Elizabeth Dickinson, who is acknowledged as one of America's greatest poets, was born on December 10, 1830. She was raised in Amherst, Massachusetts, which in the nineteenth century was a small and tradition-bound town. Dominating the Dickinson family was Emily's father Edward, a lawyer, a legislator, and also a rigorous Calvinist, whose concept of life was stern religious observance and obedience to God's laws as expressed in the Bible and lyricized in the Protestant hymnal. Emily was taken to Sunday school, but late in her teens she declined to pronounce herself a believing Christian. She spent a number of years at primary school and eventually studied classics at Amherst Academy. She also enrolled at the South Hadley Seminary for Women (now Mount Holyoke College), but her parents withdrew her after a year because of ill health. At about this time she sat for a photograph, a daguerreotype showing her as a slender young woman. It is the only reliable likeness.*

During these years of childood and youth, she led a normally active life. She saw many people, liked school and her teachers, wrote essays, acquired a number of good friends, sang at the piano to her own accompaniment, treasured spring flowers, amused her friends with impromptu stories, studied theology, read Pope's *Essay on Man*, and planned to become the "Belle of Amherst" at the age of seventeen. She also began writing poetry, mostly occasional verses and valentines.

After leaving school she returned home and spent the rest of her life there, sharing in family and household duties. In 1856 she won a second prize at the local fair for her recipe for rye and Indian bread. She took occasional trips, including long stays in Boston in 1864 and 1865 to be treated for an undisclosed eye ailment. Eventually, however, she stopped traveling altogether.

She included a number of men among her friends and correspondents. One was Benjamin Newton, a law student whom she met in 1848 and who undertook to guide her reading. This guidance was cut short, however, because Newton married, moved away, and died of tuberculosis in 1853. The second man was Reverend Charles Wadsworth, a Philadelphia minister whom she met in 1854. She regarded him as an intellectual adviser and her "dearest earthly friend." Her poetic activity increased considerably during the time she knew and corresponded with him, particularly after he left for San Francisco in 1862 to accept a ministerial call. The two saw each other only once more, in 1880, when he returned for a visit.

After Wadsworth's departure, Dickinson began corresponding with Thomas Higginson, a literary critic and Civil War hero who had written an article encouraging young writers. She sent him some of her poetry and asked if her verses "breathed" enough to warrant publication. She may have viewed Higginson as another mentor, but she soon discovered that his literary judgments were stultifying. Indeed, some critics consider his inability to understand her poetic methods to be a major reason she did not publish collections of her poems during her lifetime. He visited her in August 1870 and noted her nervousness and her girlish energy (she was thirty-nine at the time). He listened more than he spoke, believing that to interrupt her would cause her to withdraw from conversation. Later he wrote that she exhibited a unique capacity to drain his "nerve power" and that he was therefore glad he did not live near her. Ironically, Higginson became one of the first editors of her work after her death in 1886.

Still another man of importance to her, to whom she wrote often, was Otis Lord, a judge who had been her father's closest friend (her father died in 1874).

*Richard B. Sewall, however, includes a photograph of a young woman as the frontispiece of the second volume of his *The Life of Emily Dickinson* (1974). On the back of this photograph is written "Emily Dickinson 1860" in an unknown hand, and the features of the portrayed woman are consistent with those in the daguerreotype of Dickinson at seventeen. If genuine, this photograph would show how Dickinson looked as a woman of thirty, approximately thirteen years after the authenticated photograph.

Emily Dickinson

Lord regularly visited the Dickinson household, and he proposed marriage to her in 1878. She declined his offer but always remained on good terms with him.

Dickinson wrote the great bulk of her poetry during the decade of the 1860s. At this same time she was also becoming increasingly reclusive. She took to wearing only white dresses, and she generally removed herself from much of life's business. Naturally, such behavior created much interest and speculation. One of the stories about her was that her reclusiveness was so extreme that even when she gave gingerbread to local children she stayed at an upper window and lowered the sweets in a basket so that she might not be seen. Another was that she concealed herself behind doors when speaking to visitors. She was not totally housebound, however, for she shared both outside and inside household work, and she visited friends occasionally in Amherst. But her clear preference was to remain at home. By the time she was forty she refused invitations to leave home, spending the remainder of her life taking care of her parents until they died. She herself became an invalid during her last year of life. Her younger sister Lavinia, who was her lifelong companion, nursed her until her death in May 1886.

Poetic Characteristics

Although Dickinson had written poems since her school days, she did not fully devote herself to poetry until her late twenties—in about 1858. After this time her poetic output expanded, almost miraculously. Many of her poems are quite short, consisting of no more than a single stanza, but some are much longer. Only a few of them, however, were actually published during her lifetime. Instead, her "publication" consisted of making fair copies of the poems in long-hand (her writing is not easy to read). In the privacy of her own room she put numbers of poems together in "fascicles," which consisted of folded sheets of stationery bound with thread. The poems she didn't put into fascicles were kept in little packets. She locked everything away, to be discovered only after her death.

In all 1,775 of her poems have been recovered. This is the number included in Thomas H. Johnson's 1955 edition of *The Complete Poems of Emily Dickinson*. In addition, a number of brief poems have been recently mined from the prose of her letters and published as 498 new poems, on the theory that her prose frequently reaches a succinctness and rhythm more characteristic of poetry than prose. These poems are short, some being no more than two lines long. If one accepts these as additional Dickinson poems, they bring the total count to 2,273. Her most productive years were between 1862 and 1865, when she wrote at least 760 poems. This amazingly high number is hard to account for on biographical grounds. As much as one can say is that, by her thirties, she had matured as an observer, thinker, and poet, and that she compulsively turned to verse as the expression of her thought and meditation.

What Dickinson sought in poetry—both what she read and what she wrote—was intensity more than form. When Thomas Higginson visited her in 1870 she declared her views quite clearly. She said that if she was reading a book and found that

> . . . it makes my whole body so cold no fire ever can warm me I know *that* is poetry. If I feel physically as if the top of my head were taken off, I know *that* is poetry. These are the only way I know it. Is there any other way.

In her poetry she successfully achieves such intensity. Her poems are energetic, imaginative, astoundingly creative, and also economical. Within a small number of lines she covers vast distances. Who but Dickinson, for example, could conceive the first line of "I Heard a Fly Buzz—When I Died," and even more, who could progress from this opening to the concluding sentence, "I could not see to see"? Because she covers so much territory, her style is often elliptical and obscure, producing a rapid interplay of thoughts and images. Her diction is dominantly neutral, but she frequently introduces formal words. Her sentences are regularly broken by interjections and sentence fragments. She uses these grammatical irregularities deliberately, just as she employs capital letters to emphasize words. In addition, she indulges in eccentricities of punctuation: Because her poems are mostly private monologues, she usually ignores periods and commas, instead adopting the dash and the exclamation point to mark rhythm and vocal modulations. To suggest varying degrees of expressiveness, she uses dashes of differing lengths, although printed texts obscure this subtlety.

The poetic forms that Dickinson most often uses are common measure and the ballad stanza (see p. 622), but many of her stanzaic forms are irregular.

Her earliest poetic experiences would have been with the quatrain form, which abounds in the Protestant hymnal, a major text of her youth. She is no metronomic follower of the form, however, for she achieves great flexibility and originality by shortening many lines, varying many of the meters, and freely inserting midline *caesurae*. She uses rhyme with great skill, preferring exact rhymes but also using slant rhymes, eye rhymes, vowel rhymes, and repeated-word rhymes (*identical rhyme*). These irregularities confounded Dickinson's first editors, but they have since been recognized as important and effective elements of her poetic craft.

Everywhere in her poems one finds evidence of her reading and general knowledge. In her desire for accuracy she regularly referred to Webster's *Dictionary,* one of the books she kept at her side. This fact has caused critics to observe that reading her poetry often requires the aid of a dictionary.

Poetic Subjects

Although, as we have seen, a surprising amount of biographical information is available about Dickinson, the key details are missing—the connections between events in her life and her poems. Nevertheless, the outward occasions inspiring some of her poems are specific and clear. The world she lived in was small, and she found subjects in her surroundings: house, garden, yard, and village. She even wrote a poem about the railroad locomotives servicing Amherst. A lowly snake is the topic of one of her poems—one of the few published when she was alive—as are butterflies, a singing oriole, and a vibrating hummingbird.

Sometimes no more than a recollection, a single word, a concept, or a paradox that arose from her own interior monologue enabled her to originate poems (a memory, a haunted mind, the condition of solitude, the state of self-reliance, the angle of winter light, the condition of dying), but we can only guess about the specific situations that prompted her responses. The conclusion of "I Died for Beauty," for example, is poignantly, crushingly sad—and it is also ironic—but biography is silent about the cause or causes of the sadness. Even the poems on death must have occasional sources, albeit these sources may be far removed from the specific times and circumstances of the poems. For instance, one of Dickinson's dearest childhood friends was Sophia Holland, who died in 1844. Perhaps the loss of Sophia was one of her memories when she wrote "I Never Lost as Much But Twice" and "This World Is Not Conclusion," together with her other poems on death. It is a fact that death was a regular visitor in her town, and Dickinson's concerns led her to consider death's finality and eternal silence, the littleness of human beings, the effects of death on a household, and the hope and expectation of eternal life.

Much of her other poetry may have a similar if remote occasional origin. She wrote poems about love and the psychology of personal relationships, even though she never married or had a love affair that we know about. We may therefore wonder about the internal necessity that caused her to write poems like "Wild Nights—Wild Nights!" and "I Cannot Live with You," which portray alternating states of sexual ecstasy and final renunciation. And what sorts of personal experience and introspection underlay such poems as "After Great Pain, a Formal Feeling Comes," "The Soul Selects Her Own Society," and "One Need Not Be a Chamber—To Be Haunted"?

In the absence of specific details linking her life to her poetry, therefore, the occasions of her poems must remain no more than peripherally relevant— themselves unseen, though in the effects they remain. We are left to conclude that her inspiration rose from within herself. She is a personal, contemplative, confessional poet, whether she herself is the omnipresent "I" of her poems or whether the "I" is an objective speaker to whom she assigns all the strength of her imagination and her dreams. This speaker possesses bright wit, clever and engaging playfulness, acute powers of observation, deep sensitivity, and tender responsiveness. She is alive, quick, and inventive. She enjoys riddles. She leads readers into new and unexplored regions of thought and feeling.

She expresses a vital joy and delirious energy in "I Taste a Liquor Never Brewed," a witty bluffness in "I'm Nobody! Who Are You?," inner terror in "One Need Not Be a Chamber—To Be Haunted," and immense tenderness and regret at the end of "The Bustle in a House." In the last stanza of "I Cannot Live with You" she captures the deep anguish of a relationship that is ending:

So We must meet apart—
You there—I—here—
With just the Door ajar
That Oceans are—and Prayer—
And that White Sustenance—
Despair—

She is also reverent, and a number of poems introduce the topics of God, immortality, and the final judgment. But she can also be saucy and flippant about religion. Going to church on Sunday, for example, was expected of the dutiful Christian, but she explains why she prefers staying home with "a Bobo-link for a Chorister":

So instead of getting to Heaven, at last—
I'm going, all along.

Dickinson was at the height of her poetic power during the Civil War, a pro-tracted conflict that was remote for her. She was not oblivious to the horrors of war, however, for she wrote in "My Triumph Lasted Till the Drums" that "A Bayonet's contrition/Is nothing to the Dead." It is not possible to read poems like these without revering the poet.

Undeniably, Dickinson's external daily life was uneventful. Her inner life was anything but uneventful, however, for she was always reflecting and thinking. What we know about her is that her inquiring and restless mind was the source of her compulsive poetic strength, and that her poetry expresses the vital personal feelings and psychological insights that emerged from her thoughts about life, love, death, Nature, and God.

Bibliographic Sources

After Dickinson died, her sister, Lavinia, was astonished to find the many fascicles and packets of poems that she had left. Lavinia recognized the significance of this work and eventually turned much of it over to Thomas Higginson and Mabel L. Todd for editing and publication. They published three separate volumes of Dickinson's verse (in 1890, 1891, and 1896), each containing about a hundred poems. In these volumes, the editors eliminated slant rhymes, smoothed out the meter, revised those metaphors that struck them as outrageous, and regularized the punctuation. In short, they removed the poetry from Dickinson's poems.

The well-intentioned but destructive editorial adjustments remained intact until 1955, when Harvard University Press published Thomas H. Johnson's three-volume complete edition. Johnson went back to the manuscripts to establish the original texts, with variants. He also published a single-volume edition of the poems in 1961 and, in addition, a paperback selection titled *Final Harvest: Emily Dickinson's Poems* (1961). The poems that have been extracted from her letters, which we have already mentioned, were edited by William Shurr, with Anna Dunlap and Emily Shurr, as *New Poems of Emily Dickinson* (Chapel Hill: North Carolina UP, 1993). Because only a few of Dickinson's poems were published during her lifetime, the handwritten copies were for her eyes only, except for those she included in her letters. The versions in her manuscripts must therefore be considered as her final wishes for publication. These will be the basis for a new variorum edition of her poetry (*The Poems of Emily Dickinson*), which is now in progress under the editorship of Ralph W. Franklin, the editor of the facsimile edition of the handwritten poems, *The Manuscript Books of Emily Dickinson* (Cambridge: Harvard, 1981).

Definitive biographies of Dickinson are Richard B. Sewall, *The Life of Emily Dickinson* (New York: Farrar, 1974) and Cynthia Griffin Wolff, *Emily Dickinson* (New York: Knopf, 1986). There is no shortage of important critical studies. Some of these are Albert J. Gelpi, *Emily Dickinson: The Mind of the Poet* (Cambridge: Harvard UP, 1966); Joanne F. Diehl, *Dickinson and the Romantic Imagination* (Princeton: Princeton UP, 1981); David Porter, *Dickinson, the Modern Idiom* (Cambridge: Harvard UP, 1981); Susan Juhasz, *The Undiscovered Continent: Emily Dickinson and the Space of the Mind* (Bloomington: Indiana UP, 1983); E. Miller Budick, *Emily Dickinson and the Life of Language: A Study in Symbolic Poetics* (Baton Rouge: Louisiana State UP, 1985); Donna Dickenson, *Emily Dickinson* (Leamington Spa, UK: Berg, 1985); Sharon Leder and Andrea Abbott, *The Language of Exclusion: The Poetry of Emily Dickinson and Christina Rossetti* (New York: Greenwood, 1987); Cristanne Miller, *Emily Dickinson: A Poet's Grammar* (Cambridge: Harvard UP, 1987); Elizabeth Phillips, *Emily Dickinson: Personae and Performance* (University Park: Pennsylvania State UP, 1988); Joanne Dobson, *Dickinson and the Strategies of Reticence: The Woman Writer in Nineteenth-Century America* (Bloomington: Indiana UP, 1989); Paula Bennett, *Emily Dickinson: Woman Poet* (Iowa City: U of Iowa P, 1990); Gary Lee Stonum, *The Dickinson Sublime* (Madison: U of Wisconsin P, 1990); Joan Kirkby, *Emily Dickinson* (New York: St. Martin's, 1991); Judith Farr, *The Passion of Emily Dickinson* (Cambridge: Harvard UP, 1992); Claudia Ottlinger, *The Death-Motif in the Poetry of Emily Dickinson and Christina Rossetti* (Frankfurt: Lang, 1996); and Paul Crumbley, *Inflections of the Pen: Dash and Voice in Emily Dickinson* (Lexington: UP of Kentucky, 1996). Collections of essays on Dickinson are Paul J. Ferlazzo, ed., *Critical Essays on Emily Dickinson* (Boston: Hall, 1958), an historical collection; Richard B. Sewall, ed., *Emily Dickinson: A Collection of Critical Essays* (Englewood Cliffs: Prentice Hall, 1963); and Judith Farr, ed., *Emily Dickinson: A Collection of Critical Essays* (Upper Saddle River: Prentice Hall, 1996). One of the hour-long programs in the PBS *Voices and Visions* series (1987) features Dickinson's work.

WRITING TOPICS FOR DICKINSON

1. Dickinson's characteristic brevity in the explanation of situations and the expression of ideas.
2. Dickinson's use of personal but not totally disclosed subject matter.
3. Dickinson's use of imagery and symbolism: sources, types, meanings.
4. Dickinson's ideas about love, separation, personal pain, war, death, faith, religion, science, the soul.
5. Dickinson's humor and irony.
6. Dickinson's poems as they appear on the page: the relationship of meaning to lines, stanzas, capitalization, punctuation, the use of the dash.
7. The structuring of a number of Dickinson's poems: subject, development, conclusions.
8. The character of the speaker in a number of Dickinson's poems: personality, things noticed, accuracy of conclusions. If there appears to be a listener in the poems, what effect does this listener have on the speaker?
9. Dickinson's verse forms and use of rhymes.
10. Themes of exhilaration, sorrow, pity, triumph, and regret in Dickinson.

POEMS BY EMILY DICKINSON*

After Great Pain, a Formal Feeling Comes (Poem 341), 719
The Bustle in a House (Poem 1078), 719
"Faith" Is a Fine Invention (Poem 185), 720

*See also two additional Dickinson poems in this anthology: "Because I Could Not Stop for Death" (Poem 712), p. 455, and "To Hear an Oriole Sing" (Poem 526), p. 586. The selections here are arranged alphabetically by first lines; poem numbers following the titles refer to the numbers in Thomas H. Johnson's *The Complete Poems of Emily Dickinson*.

After Great Pain, a Formal Feeling Comes (Poem 341) _____ 1929 (ca. 1862)

After great pain, a formal feeling comes—
The Nerves sit ceremonious, like Tombs—
The Stiff Heart questions was it He, that bore,
And Yesterday, or Centuries before?

The Feet, mechanical, go round—   5
Of Ground, or Air, or Ought°—   *anything, nothing*
A Wooden way
Regardless grown.
A Quartz contentment, like a stone—

This is the Hour of Lead—   10
Remembered, if outlived,
As Freezing persons, recollect the Snow—
First—Chill—then Stupor—then the letting go—

The Bustle in a House (Poem 1078) _____ 1890 (ca. 1866)

The Bustle in a House
The Morning after Death
Is solemnest of industries
Enacted upon Earth—

The Sweeping up the Heart   5
And putting Love away
We shall not want to use again
Until Eternity.

"Faith" Is a Fine Invention (Poem 185) _____ *1891 (ca. 1860)*

"Faith" is a fine invention
When Gentlemen can *see*—
But *Microscopes* are prudent
In an Emergency.

The Heart Is the Capital of the Mind (Poem 1354) _____ *1929 (ca. 1876)*

The Heart is the Capital of the Mind—
The Mind is a single State—
The Heart and the Mind together make
A single Continent—

One—is the Population—   5
Numerous enough—
This ecstatic Nation
Seek—it is Yourself.

I Cannot Live with You (Poem 640) _____ *1890 (ca. 1862)*

I cannot live with You—
It would be Life—
And Life is over there—
Behind the Shelf

The Sexton keeps the Key to—   5
Putting up
Our Life—His Porcelain—
Like a Cup—

Discarded of the Housewife—
Quaint—or Broke—   10
A newer Sevres° pleases—   *a fine French porcelain*
Old Ones crack—

I could not die—with You—
For One must wait
To shut the Other's Gaze down—   15
You—could not—

And I—Could I stand by
And see You—freeze—

Without my Right of Frost—
Death's privilege? 20

Nor could I rise—with You—
Because Your Face
Would put out Jesus'—
That New Grace

Glow plain—and foreign 25
On my homesick Eye—
Except that You than He
Shone closer by—

They'd judge Us—How—
For You—served Heaven—You know, 30
Or sought to—
I could not—

Because You saturated Sight—
And I had no more Eyes
For sordid excellence 35
As Paradise

And were You lost, I would be—
Though My Name
Rang loudest
On the Heavenly fame— 40

And were You—saved—
And I—condemned to be
Where You were not—
That self—were Hell to Me—

So We must meet apart— 45
You there—I—here—
With just the Door ajar
That Oceans are—and Prayer—
And that White Sustenance—
Despair— 50

I Died for Beauty—but Was Scarce (Poem 449) _____ *1890 (ca. 1862)*

I died for Beauty—but was scarce
Adjusted in the tomb
When One who died for Truth, was lain
In an adjoining Room—

He questioned softly "Why I failed"? 5
"For Beauty", I replied—
"And I—for Truth—Themself are One—
We Brethren, are", He said—

And so, as Kinsmen, met a Night—
We talked between the Rooms—   10
Until the Moss had reached our lips—
And covered up—our names—

I Heard a Fly Buzz—When I Died (Poem 465) _____ 1896 (ca. 1862)

I heard a Fly buzz—when I died—
The Stillness in the Room
Was like the Stillness in the Air—
Between the Heaves of Storm—

The Eyes around—had wrung them dry—   5
And Breaths were gathering firm
For that last Onset—when the King
Be witnessed—in the Room—

I willed my Keepsakes—Signed away
What portion of me be   10
Assignable—and then it was
There interposed a Fly—

With Blue—uncertain stumbling Buzz—
Between the Light—and me—
And then the Windows failed—and then   15
I could not see to see—

I Like to See It Lap the Miles (Poem 585) _____ 1891 (ca. 1862)

I like to see it lap the Miles—
And lick the Valleys up—
And stop to feed itself at Tanks—
And then—prodigious step

Around a Pile of Mountains—   5
And supercilious peer
In Shanties—by the sides of Roads—
And then a Quarry pare

To fit its sides
And crawl between   10
Complaining all the while
In horrid—hooting stanza—
Then chase itself down Hill—

And neigh like Boanerges°—
Then—prompter than a Star   15
Stop—docile and omnipotent
At its own stable door—

I LIKE TO SEE IT LAP THE MILES.   14 *Boanerges:* a surname meaning "the sons of thunder"
that appears in Mark 3:17.

I'm Nobody! Who Are You? (Poem 288) _____ *1891 (ca. 1861)*

I'm Nobody! Who are you?
Are you—Nobody—Too?
Then there's a pair of us?
Don't tell! they'd advertise—you know!

How dreary—to be—Somebody!   5
How public—like a Frog—
To tell one's name—the livelong June—
To an admiring Bog!

I Never Felt at Home—Below—(Poem 413) _____ *1929 (ca. 1862)*

I never felt at Home—Below—
And in the Handsome Skies
I shall not feel at Home—I know—
I don't like Paradise—

Because it's Sunday—all the time—   5
And Recess—never comes—
And Eden'll be so lonesome
Bright Wednesday Afternoons—

If God could make a visit—
Or ever took a Nap—   10
So not to see us—but they say
Himself—a Telescope

Perennial beholds us—
Myself would run away
From Him—and Holy Ghost—and All—   15
But there's the "Judgment Day"!

I Never Lost as Much But Twice (Poem 49) _____ *1890 (ca. 1858)*

I never lost as much but twice,
And that was in the sod.
Twice have I stood a beggar
Before the door of God!

Angels—twice descending   5
Reimbursed my store—
Burglar! Banker—Father!
I am poor once more!

I Taste a Liquor Never Brewed (Poem 214) _____ *1861, 1891 (ca. 1860)*

I taste a liquor never brewed—
From Tankards scooped in Pearl—

Not all the Frankfort Berries°   *grapes*
Yield such an Alcohol!

Inebriate of Air—am I—   5
And Debauchee of Dew—
Reeling—thro endless summer days—
From inns of Molten Blue—

When "Landlords" turn the drunken Bee
Out of the Foxglove's door—   10
When Butterflies—renounce their "drams"—
I shall but drink the more!

Till Seraphs swing their Snowy Hats—
And Saints—to windows run—
To see the little Tippler   15
From Manzanilla° come!

I TASTE A LIQUOR NEVER BREWED.   16 *Manzanilla:* a pale sherry from Spain. Dickinson may
also have been thinking of Manzanillo, a Cuban city often associated with rum.

Much Madness Is Divinest Sense (Poem 435) ———————— 1890 (ca. 1862)

Much Madness is divinest Sense—
To a discerning Eye—
Much Sense—the starkest Madness—
'Tis the Majority

In this, as All, prevail—   5
Assent—and you are sane—
Demur—you're straightway dangerous—
And handled with a Chain—

My Life Closed Twice Before Its Close (Poem 1732) ———————— 1896

My life closed twice before its close;
It yet remains to see
If Immortality unveil
A third event to me,

So huge, so hopeless to conceive   5
As these that twice befel.
Parting is all we know of heaven,
And all we need of hell.

My Triumph Lasted Till the Drums (Poem 1227) ———————— 1935 (ca. 1872)

My Triumph lasted till the Drums
Had left the Dead alone
And then I dropped my Victory

And chastened stole along
To where the finished Faces   5
Conclusion turned on me
And then I hated Glory
And wished myself were They.
What is to be is best descried
When it has also been—   10
Could Prospect taste of Retrospect
The tyrannies of Men
Were Tenderer—diviner
The Transitive toward.
A Bayonet's contrition   15
Is nothing to the Dead.

One Need Not Be a Chamber—To Be Haunted (Poem 670) ___ 1891 (ca. 1863)

One need not be a Chamber—to be Haunted—
One need not be a House—
The Brain has Corridors—surpassing
Material Place—

Far safer, of a Midnight Meeting   5
External Ghost
Than its interior Confronting—
That Cooler Host.

Far safer, through an Abbey gallop,
The Stones a'chase—   10
Than Unarmed, one's a'self encounter—
In lonesome Place—

Ourself behind ourself, concealed—
Should startle most—
Assassin hid in our Apartment   15
Be Horror's least.

The Body—borrows a Revolver—
He bolts the Door—
O'erlooking a superior spectre—
Or More—   20

Safe in Their Alabaster Chambers (Poem 216) _____ 1862, 1890 (1861)

Safe in their Alabaster Chambers—
Untouched by Morning—
And untouched by Noon—
Lie the meek members of the Resurrection—
Rafter of Satin—and Roof of Stone!   5

Grand go the Years—in the Crescent—above them—
Worlds scoop their Arcs—
And Firmaments—row—
Diadems—drop—and Doges°—surrender—
Soundless as dots—on a Disc of Snow—   10

SAFE IN THEIR ALABASTER CHAMBERS.   9 *Doges:* Renaissance rulers of the Italian city-states
of Venice and Genoa.

Some Keep the Sabbath Going to Church (Poem 324) _____ *1864 (ca. 1862)*

Some keep the Sabbath going to Church—
I keep it, staying at Home—
With a Bobolink for a Chorister—
And an Orchard, for a Dome—

Some keep the Sabbath in Surplice—   5
I just wear my Wings—
And instead of tolling the Bell, for Church,
Our little Sexton—sings.

God preaches, a noted Clergyman—
And the sermon is never long.   10
So instead of getting to Heaven, at last—
I'm going, all along.

The Soul Selects Her Own Society (Poem 303) _____ *1890 (ca. 1862)*

The Soul selects her own Society—
Then—shuts the Door—
To her divine Majority—
Present no more—

Unmoved—she notes the Chariots—pausing—   5
At her low Gate—
Unmoved—an Emperor be kneeling
Upon her Mat—

I've known her—from an ample nation—
Choose One—   10
Then—close the Valves of her attention—
Like Stone—

Success Is Counted Sweetest (Poem 67) _____ *1878, 1890 (ca. 1859)*

Success is counted sweetest
By those who ne'er succeed.
To comprehend a nectar
Requires sorest need.

Not one of all the purple Host   5
Who took the Flag today
Can tell the definition
So clear of Victory

As he defeated—dying—
On whose forbidden ear   10
The distant strains of triumph
Burst agonized and clear!

There's a Certain Slant of Light (Poem 258) _____ *1890 (ca. 1861)*

There's a certain Slant of light,
Winter Afternoons—
That oppresses, like the Heft
Of Cathedral Tunes—

Heavenly Hurt, it gives us—   5
We can find no scar,
But internal difference,
Where the Meanings, are—

None may teach it—Any—
'Tis the Seal Despair—   10
An imperial affliction
Sent us of the Air—

When it comes, the Landscape listens—
Shadows—hold their breath—
When it goes, 'tis like the Distance   15
On the look of Death—

This World Is Not Conclusion (Poem 501) _____ *1896 (ca. 1862)*

This World is not Conclusion.
A Species stands beyond—
Invisible, as Music—
But—positive, as Sound—
It beckons, and it baffles—   5
Philosophy—don't know—
And through a Riddle, at the last—
Sagacity, must go—
To guess it, puzzles scholars—
To gain it, Men have borne   10
Contempt of Generations
And Crucifixion, shown—
Faith slips—and laughs, and rallies—
Blushes, if any see—
Plucks at a twig of Evidence—   15

And asks a Vane, the way—
Much Gesture, from the Pulpit—
Strong Hallelujahs roll—
Narcotics cannot still the Tooth
That nibbles at the soul—   20

Wild Nights—Wild Nights! (Poem 249) _____ *1890 (ca. 1861)*

Wild Nights—Wild Nights!
Were I with thee
Wild Nights should be
Our luxury!

Futile—the Winds—   5
To a Heart in port—
Done with the Compass—
Done with the Chart!

Rowing in Eden—
Ah, the Sea!   10
Might I but moor—Tonight—
In Thee!

ROBERT FROST   (1874–1963)

Life and Work

Robert Lee Frost (1874–1963) published his first book of poems, *A Boy's Will*, in England in 1913. At that time he was virtually unknown in the United States. Ezra Pound wrote that "it is a sinister thing that so American . . . a talent . . . should have to be exported before it can find due encouragement and recognition." Time, of course, made Frost the most visible and admired American poet of his day. He eventually received over twenty honorary degrees and four Pulitzer Prizes. Although there was no officially recognized national poet until the 1980s (when the annual poet laureateships were established), he came as close as possible to being America's official poet when he read "The Gift Outright" at the inauguration of President John F. Kennedy in 1961. His collected poetic works continue to earn him that recognition.

Although he presented himself as the quintessential New Englander in person and in his poetry, he was born in San Francisco on March 26, 1874. His father had moved the family west so that he could take a job with the *San Francisco Bulletin*. When his father died in 1885, Frost's mother brought the family back to Lawrence, Massachusetts, where Frost attended high school, studied classics, and began writing poetry. He graduated in 1892 as co-valedictorian with Elinor White, whom he married in 1895. After high school he attended

Robert Frost

Dartmouth College for seven weeks and then turned to newspaper work and teaching school. He continued to write poetry, little of which was published. Two years after his marriage, he began attending classes at Harvard (1897–1899), but he left without a degree.

In 1900 Frost's grandfather gave him a farm in Derry, New Hampshire, and for the next twelve years he farmed, wrote poetry, and taught English at Pinkerton Academy. His life was hard and his poetry was mostly ignored. In 1912 he sold the farm to devote himself to writing. He moved to England, where he met a number of emerging and established poets, including Ezra Pound and William Butler Yeats. His first two books of poetry were published in England and received favorable reviews. These books, *A Boy's Will* (1913) and *North of Boston* (1914), were published in the United States in 1915, and Frost then began to receive recognition at home.

That same year Frost and his family returned to the United States and took up residence on a farm near Franconia, New Hampshire. More books of poetry and greater acclaim followed quickly. In 1916 he published *Mountain Interval*, a book containing "The Road Not Taken," "Birches," and "Out, Out—." He also became poet-in-residence at Amherst College, a relationship that would continue sporadically for much of his life.

More books of poetry and more recognition followed throughout Frost's life. In 1923 he published *Selected Poems* and *New Hampshire*. The latter book, for which he won a Pulitzer Prize, contains some of his best-known work: "Stopping by Woods on a Snowy Evening," "Fire and Ice," and "Nothing Gold Can Stay." These were followed by *West-Running Brook* (1928), *Collected Poems* (1930), *A Further Range* (1936), *A Witness Tree* (1942), *Steeple Bush* (1947), *Complete Poems* (1949), *Aforesaid* (1954), and *In the Clearing* (1962).

Poetic Characteristics

Early in his career and throughout his long public experience as a speaker and lecturer, Frost cultivated his persona as a philosophical, wry, and wise country poet. This is the friendly, almost avuncular voice we usually hear, the one that expresses knowledge and concern for the land, history, and human nature. Even with this point of view, however, there are complicated undertones of wit and irony. There is also what Randall Jarrell called "The Other Frost," the often agonized and troubled spirit whose voice is heard in poems like "Acquainted with the Night" and "Fire and Ice."

Regardless of the voice we hear, Frost's poetic style is consistent. His diction is informal, plain, and conversational, and his phrases are simple and direct. More often than not, he uses and refines the natural speech patterns and rhythms of New England, polishing the language that people actually speak, and fashioning it into a compact and terse poetic texture.

Structurally, Frost's poems typically move in a smooth, uninterrupted flow from an event or an object, through a metaphor, to an idea. Within this pattern, he usually describes a complete event rather than a single vision. The heart of the process is the image or metaphor. Frost's metaphors are sparse and careful; they are brought sharply into focus and skillfully interwoven within each poem. Frost himself saw metaphors as the beginning of the process. In *Education by Poetry* (1931) he wrote that "poetry begins in trivial metaphors, pretty metaphors, 'grace' metaphors, and goes on to the profoundest thinking that we have. Poetry provides the one permissible way of saying one thing and meaning another."

Frost preferred traditional poetic forms and rhythms, and he was so disapproving of free verse that he once asserted that writing it was like playing tennis without a net. We therefore find conventional rhyme schemes and clear meters (with traditional metrical substitutions) in much of his work, together with closed forms such as couplets, sonnets (with interesting varying rhyme patterns), terza rima (see p. 621), quatrains, stanzas, and blank verse.

Poetic Subjects

Frost's poems are usually based in everyday life and rural settings. Poems are occasioned by flowers, stone fences, woodcutting, picking apples, sleigh riding, falling leaves, rain, snow, birch trees, insects, birds, hired men, and children, to name just a few of the topics. However, the Frostian poetic structure always moves from such subjects toward philosophical generalizations about life and death, survival and responsibility, and nature and humanity.

One of Frost's major appeals is that his poems are easily accessible. They are by no means simplistic, however, but run deep, as seen, for example, in "The Road Not Taken" and "Misgiving." They also may be complex and ambiguous. In "Mending Wall," for example, the philosophies of the speaker and his fence-repairing neighbor are well presented and contrasted. Readers often conclude that the speaker's wish to remove barriers is the major idea, but the neighbor's argument for maintaining them is equally strong. In "Desert Places" we are presented with a chilling view of the infinite desert within the human mind. In "Acquainted with the Night," Frost's sophisticated urban speaker tells us of the night of the city and also presents hints about the dark night of the soul.

Bibliographic Sources

The new standard edition of Frost's work is by Richard Poirier and Mark Richardson, eds., *Robert Frost: Collected Poems, Prose, & Plays* (New York: Library of America, 1995). During his later years, Frost was much in demand as a speaker, and he was the first American poet to appear frequently before the television camera. Twelve of his lectures are published in Reginald Cook, *Robert Frost, A Living Voice* (Amherst: U of Massachusetts P, 1974). The standard biography is by Lawrance S. Thompson, in three volumes: *Robert Frost: The Early Years*; *The Years of Triumph;* and *The Later Years* (New York: Holt Rinehart, 1966–1977). The last volume was completed after Thompson's death by Roy H. Winnick. Useful criticism includes George Nitchie, *Human Values in the Poetry of Robert Frost* (Durham: Duke UP, 1960); Reuben Brower, *The Poetry of Robert Frost: Constellations of Intention* (New York: Oxford UP, 1963); Philip L. Gerber, *Robert Frost* (Boston: Twayne, 1966); Richard Poirier, *Robert Frost: The Work of Knowing* (New York: Oxford UP, 1977); John Kemp, *Robert Frost and New England: The Poet as Regionalist* (Princeton: Princeton UP, 1979); Richard Wakefield, *Robert Frost and the Opposing Lights of the Hour* (New York: Lang, 1985); James Potter, *A Robert Frost Handbook* (University Park: Pennsylvania State UP, 1980); Harold Bloom, ed., *Robert Frost* (New York: Chelsea House, 1986), a collection of critical essays; George Monteiro, *Robert Frost and the New England Renaissance* (Lexington: U of Kentucky P, 1988); Judith Oster, *Toward Robert Frost: The Reader and the Poet* (Athens: U of Georgia P, 1991); George F. Bagby, *Frost and the Book of Nature* (Knoxville: U of Tennessee P, 1993); and Katherine Kearns, *Robert Frost and a Poetics of Appetite* (New York: Cambridge UP, 1994). One of the hour-long programs in the PBS *Voices and Visions* series (1987) features his work.

WRITING TOPICS FOR FROST

1. The nature of Frost's topics (situations, scenes, actions) and his use of them for observation, narration, and metaphor.
2. Frost's assessment of the human situation: work, love, death, choices, diminution of life, Stoicism, keeping or not keeping boundaries.

3. Frost's speaker: character, experiences, recollections, and reflections. In developing his subjects, to what degree does the speaker take a possible listener into account?
4. Frost as a poet of ideas. His vision of the way things are or should be.
5. Frost as a "confessional" poet: misgivings, the admission of personal error and personal fears.
6. Frost's use of narration and description in his poetry.
7. The structuring of Frost's poems: situation, observation, and generalization.
8. Frost's poetic diction: level and relationship to topic; conversational style.
9. Poetic forms in Frost: rhythm, meter, rhyme, and line and stanza patterns.
10. Frost's wry humor.

 # POEMS BY ROBERT FROST*

*See also two additional poems by Frost in this anthology: "Desert Places," p. 631, and "Stopping by Woods on a Snowy Evening," p. 456. The Frost poems in this chapter are arranged chronologically.

A Line-Storm Song _____ *1913*

The line-storm clouds fly tattered and swift.
   The road is forlorn all day,
Where a myriad snowy quartz stones lift,
   And the hoof-prints vanish away.
The roadside flowers, too wet for the bee,   5
   Expend their bloom in vain.
Come over the hills and far with me,
   And be my love in the rain.

The birds have less to say for themselves
   In the wood-world's torn despair   10

Than now these numberless years the elves,
  Although they are no less there:
All song of the woods is crushed like some
  Wild, easily shattered rose.
Come, be my love in the wet woods, come,   15
  Where the boughs rain when it blows.

There is the gale to urge behind
  And bruit our singing down,
And the shallow waters aflutter with wind
  From which to gather your gown.   20
What matter if we go clear to the west,
  And come not through dry-shod?
For wilding brooch shall wet your breast
  The rain-fresh goldenrod.

Oh, never this whelming east wind swells   25
  But it seems like the sea's return
To the ancient lands where it left the shells
  Before the age of the fern;
And it seems like the time when after doubt
  Our love came back amain.   30
Oh, come forth into the storm and rout
  And be my love in the rain.

Mending Wall _____ *1914*

Something there is that doesn't love a wall,
That sends the frozen-ground-swell under it,
And spills the upper boulders in the sun;
And makes gaps even two can pass abreast.
The work of hunters is another thing: 5
I have come after them and made repair
Where they have left not one stone on a stone,
But they would have the rabbit out of hiding,
To please the yelping dogs. The gaps I mean,
No one has seen them made or heard them made,   10
But at spring mending-time we find them there.
I let my neighbor know beyond the hill;
And on a day we meet to walk the line
And set the wall between us once again.
We keep the wall between us as we go.   15
To each the boulders that have fallen to each.
And some are loaves and some so nearly balls
We have to use a spell to make them balance:
'Stay where you are until our backs are turned!'
We wear our fingers rough with handling them.   20
Oh, just another kind of outdoor game,

One on a side. It comes to little more:
There where it is we do not need the wall:
He is all pine and I am apple orchard.
My apple trees will never get across   25
And eat the cones under his pines, I tell him.
He only says, 'Good fences make good neighbors.'
Spring is the mischief in me, and I wonder
If I could put a notion in his head:
'*Why* do they make good neighbors? Isn't it   30
Where there are cows? But here there are no cows.
Before I built a wall I'd ask to know
What I was walling in or walling out,
And to whom I was like to give offense.
Something there is that doesn't love a wall,   35
That wants it down.' I could say 'Elves' to him,
But it's not elves exactly, and I'd rather
He said it for himself. I see him there
Bringing a stone grasped firmly by the top
In each hand, like an old-stone savage armed.   40
He moves in darkness as it seems to me,
Not of woods only and the shade of trees.
He will not go behind his father's saying,
And he likes having thought of it so well
He says again, 'Good fences make good neighbors.'   45

Birches _____ *1915*

When I see birches bend to left and right
Across the lines of straighter darker trees,
I like to think some boy's been swinging them.
But swinging doesn't bend them down to stay
As ice-storms do. Often you must have seen them   5
Loaded with ice a sunny winter morning
After a rain. They click upon themselves
As the breeze rises, and turn many-colored
As the stir cracks and crazes their enamel.
Soon the sun's warmth makes them shed crystal shells   10
Shattering and avalanching on the snow-crust—
Such heaps of broken glass to sweep away
You'd think the inner dome of heaven had fallen.
They are dragged to the withered bracken by the load,
And they seem not to break; though once they are bowed   15
So low for long, they never right themselves:
You may see their trunks arching in the woods
Years afterwards, trailing their leaves on the ground
Like girls on hands and knees that throw their hair
Before them over their heads to dry in the sun.   20

But I was going to say when Truth broke in
With all her matter-of-fact about the ice-storm
I should prefer to have some boy bend them
As he went out and in to fetch the cows—
Some boy too far from town to learn baseball,   25
Whose only play was what he found himself,
Summer or winter, and could play alone.
One by one he subdued his father's trees
By riding them down over and over again
Until he took the stiffness out of them,   30
And not one but hung limp, not one was left
For him to conquer. He learned all there was
To learn about not launching out too soon
And so not carrying the tree away
Clear to the ground. He always kept his poise   35
To the top branches, climbing carefully
With the same pains you use to fill a cup
Up to the brim, and even above the brim.
Then he flung outward, feet first, with a swish,
Kicking his way down through the air to the ground.   40
So was I once myself a swinger of birches.
And so I dream of going back to be.
It's when I'm weary of considerations,
And life is too much like a pathless wood
Where your face burns and tickles with the cobwebs   45
Broken across it, and one eye is weeping
From a twig's having lashed across it open.
I'd like to get away from earth awhile
And then come back to it and begin over.
May no fate willfully misunderstand me   50
And half grant what I wish and snatch me away
Not to return. Earth's the right place for love:
I don't know where it's likely to go better.
I'd like to go by climbing a birch tree,
And climb black branches up a snow-white trunk   55
Toward Heaven, till the tree could bear no more,
But dipped its top and set me down again.
That would be good both going and coming back.
One could do worse than be a swinger of birches.

The Road Not Taken ————————————————— *1915*

Two roads diverged in a yellow wood,
And sorry I could not travel both
And be one traveler, long I stood
And looked down one as far as I could
To where it bent in the undergrowth;   5

Then took the other, as just as fair,
And having perhaps the better claim,
Because it was grassy and wanted wear;
Though as for that the passing there
Had worn them really about the same,   10
And both that morning equally lay
In leaves no step had trodden black.
Oh, I kept the first for another day!
Yet knowing how way leads on to way,
I doubted if I should ever come back.   15

I shall be telling this with a sigh
Somewhere ages and ages hence:
Two roads diverged in a wood, and I—
I took the one less traveled by,
And that has made all the difference.   20

'Out, Out—' _____ 1916

The buzz saw snarled and rattled in the yard
And made dust and dropped stove-length sticks of wood,
Sweet-scented stuff when the breeze drew across it.
And from there those that lifted eyes could count
Five mountain ranges one behind the other   5
Under the sunset far into Vermont.
And the saw snarled and rattled, snarled and rattled,
As it ran light, or had to bear a load.
And nothing happened: day was all but done.
Call it a day, I wish they might have said   10
To please the boy by giving him the half hour
That a boy counts so much when saved from work.
His sister stood beside them in her apron
To tell them 'Supper.' At the word, the saw,
As if to prove saws knew what supper meant,   15
Leaped out at the boy's hand, or seemed to leap—
He must have given the hand. However it was,
Neither refused the meeting. But the hand!
The boy's first outcry was rueful laugh,
As he swung toward them holding up the hand   20
Half in appeal, but half as if to keep
The life from spilling. Then the boy saw all—
Since he was old enough to know, big boy
Doing a man's work, though a child at heart—
He saw all spoiled. 'Don't let him cut my hand off—   25
The doctor, when he comes. Don't let him, sister!'
So. But the hand was gone already.
The doctor put him in the dark of ether.
He lay and puffed his lips out with his breath.

And then—the watcher at his pulse took fright.   30
No one believed. They listened at his heart.
Little–less–nothing!–and that ended it.
No more to build on there. And they, since they
Were not the one dead, turned to their affairs.

The Oven Bird —————————————————————— 1916

There is a singer everyone has heard,
Loud, a mid-summer and a mid-wood bird,
Who makes the solid tree trunks sound again.
He says that leaves are old and that for flowers
Mid-summer is to spring as one to ten.   5
He says the early petal-fall is past
When pear and cherry bloom went down in showers
On sunny days a moment overcast;
And comes that other fall we name the fall.
He says the highway dust is over all.   10
The bird would cease and be as other birds
But that he knows in singing not to sing.
The question that he frames in all but words
Is what to make of a diminished thing.

Fire and Ice ————————————————————————— 1920

Some say the world will end in fire,
Some say in ice.
From what I've tasted of desire
I hold with those who favor fire.
But if it had to perish twice,   5
I think I know enough of hate
To say that for destruction ice
Is also great
And would suffice.

Nothing Gold Can Stay ————————————————— 1923

Nature's first green is gold,
Her hardest hue to hold.
Her early leaf's a flower;
But only so an hour.
Then leaf subsides to leaf.   5
So Eden sank to grief,
So dawn goes down to day.
Nothing gold can stay.

Misgiving _____ *1923*

All crying, 'We will go with you, O Wind!'
The foliage follow him, leaf and stem;
But a sleep oppresses them as they go,
And they end by bidding him stay with them.

Since ever they flung abroad in spring   5
The leaves had promised themselves this flight,
Who now would fain seek sheltering wall,
Or thicket, or hollow place for the night.

And now they answer his summoning blast
With an ever vaguer and vaguer stir,   10
Or at utmost a little reluctant whirl
That drops them no further than where they were.

I only hope that when I am free
As they are free to go in quest
Of the knowledge beyond the bounds of life   15
It may not seem better to me to rest.

Acquainted with the Night _____ *1928*

I have been one acquainted with the night.
I have walked out in rain—and back in rain.
I have outwalked the furthest city light.

I have looked down the saddest city lane.
I have passed by the watchman on his beat   5
And dropped my eyes, unwilling to explain.

I have stood still and stopped the sound of feet
When far away an interrupted cry
Came over houses from another street,

But not to call me back or say good-by;   10
And further still at an unearthly height,
One luminary clock against the sky

Proclaimed the time was neither wrong nor right.
I have been one acquainted with the night.

Design _____ *1936*

I found a dimpled spider, fat and white,
On a white heal-all,° holding up a moth
Like a white piece of rigid satin cloth—
Assorted characters of death and blight

DESIGN   2 *heal-all:* a flower, usually blue, thought to have healing powers.

Mixed ready to begin the morning right, 5
Like the ingredients of a witches' broth—
A snow-drop spider, a flower like a froth,
And dead wings carried like a paper kite.

What had that flower to do with being white,
The wayside blue and innocent heal-all? 10
What brought the kindred spider to that height,
Then steered the white moth thither in the night?
What but design of darkness to appall?—
If design govern in a thing so small.

A Considerable Speck ———————————————— *1942*

(Microscopic)

A speck that would have been beneath my sight
On any but a paper sheet so white
Set off across what I had written there.
And I had idly poised my pen in air
To stop it with a period of ink 5
When something strange about it made me think.
This was no dust speck by my breathing blown,
But unmistakably a living mite
With inclinations it could call its own.
It paused as with suspicion of my pen, 10
And then came racing wildly on again
To where my manuscript was not yet dry;
Then paused again and either drank or smelt—
With loathing, for again it turned to fly.
Plainly with an intelligence I dealt. 15
It seemed too tiny to have room for feet,
Yet must have had a set of them complete
To express how much it didn't want to die.
It ran with terror and with cunning crept.
It faltered: I could see it hesitate; 20
Then in the middle of the open sheet
Cower down in desperation to accept
Whatever I accorded it of fate.
I have none of the tenderer-than-thou
Collectivistic regimenting love 25
With which the modern world is being swept
But this poor microscopic item now!
Since it was nothing I knew evil of
I let it lie there till I hope it slept.
I have a mind myself and recognize 30
Mind when I meet with it in any guise.
No one can know how glad I am to find
On any sheet the least display of mind.

21
Poems for
Additional Study

MAYA ANGELOU   (b. 1928)

My Arkansas _____ *1978*

There is a deep brooding
in Arkansas.
Old crimes like moss pend
from poplar trees.
The sullen earth   5
is much too
red for comfort.

Sunrise seems to hesitate
and in that second
lose its   10
incandescent aim, and
dusk no more shadows
than the noon.
The past is brighter yet.

Old hates and   15
ante-bellum° lace, are rent
but not discarded.
Today is yet to come
in Arkansas.
It writhes. It writhes in awful   20
waves of brooding.

MY ARKANSAS.   16 *ante-bellum:* before the U.S. Civil War (1861–1865).

ANONYMOUS (NAVAJO)

Healing Prayer from the Beautyway Chant ⸻ *Traditional*

Out of the East, Beauty has come home,
Out of the South, Beauty has come home,
Out of the West, Beauty has come home,
Out of the North, Beauty has come home,
Out of the highest heavens and the lowest lands,   5
    Beauty has come home.
    Everywhere around us, Beauty has come home.
As we live each day, everything evil will leave us.
    We will be entirely healed,
    Our bodies will exult in the fresh winds,   10
    Our steps will be firm.
As we live each day,
    Everything before us will be Beautiful;
    Everything behind us will be Beautiful;
    Everything above us will be Beautiful;   15
    Everything below us will be Beautiful;
    Everything around us will be Beautiful;
    All our thoughts will be Beautiful;
    All our words will be Beautiful;
    All our dreams will be Beautiful.   20
We will be forever restored, forever whole.
All things will be Beautiful forever.

MARGARET ATWOOD (b. 1939)

Variation on the Word Sleep ⸻ *1981*

I would like to watch you sleeping,
which may not happen.
I would like to watch you,
sleeping. I would like to sleep
with you, to enter   5
your sleep as its smooth dark wave
slides over my head

and walk with you through that lucent
wavering forest of bluegreen leaves
with its watery sun & three moons   10
towards the cave where you must descend,
towards your worst fear

I would like to give you the silver
branch, the small white flower, the one
word that will protect you   15

from the grief at the center
of your dream, from the grief
at the center. I would like to follow
you up the long stairway
again & become   20
the boat that would row you back
carefully, a flame
in two cupped hands
to where your body lies
beside me, and you enter   25
it as easily as breathing in

I would like to be the air
that inhabits you for a moment
only. I would like to be that unnoticed
& that necessary.   30

W. H. AUDEN   (1907–1973)

The Unknown Citizen _____ *1940*

(To JS/07/M/378
This Marble Monument
Is Erected by the State)

He was found by the Bureau of Statistics to be
One against whom there was no official complaint,
And all the reports on his conduct agree
That, in the modern sense of an old-fashioned word, he was a saint,
For in everything he did he served the Greater Community.   5

Except for the War till the day he retired
He worked in a factory and never got fired,
But satisfied his employers, Fudge Motors Inc.
Yet he wasn't a scab° or odd in his views.   *strikebreaker*
For his Union reports that he paid his dues,   10
(Our report on his Union shows it was sound)
And our Social Psychology workers found
That he was popular with his mates° and liked a drink.   *co-workers*
The Press are convinced that he bought a paper every day
And that his reactions to advertisements were normal in every way. 15
Policies taken out in his name prove that he was fully insured,
And his Health-card shows he was once in hospital but left it cured.
Both Producers Research and High-Grade Living declare
He was fully sensible to the advantages of the Installment Plan
And had everything necessary to the Modern Man,   20
A phonograph, a radio, a car and a frigidaire.
Our reseachers into Public Opinion are content
That he held the proper opinions for the time of year;

When there was peace, he was for peace; when there was war, he went.
He was married and added five children to the population, 25
Which our Eugenist says was the right number for a parent of his generation,
And our teachers report that he never interfered with their education.
Was he free? Was he happy? The question is absurd:
Had anything been wrong, we should certainly have heard.

IMAMU AMIRI BARAKA (LEROI JONES)   (b. 1934)

Ka 'Ba _____ *1969*

A closed window looks down
on a dirty courtyard, and black people
call across or scream across or walk across
defying physics in the stream of their will

Our world is full of sound 5
Our world is more lovely than anyone's
tho we suffer, and kill each other
and sometimes fail to walk the air

We are beautiful people
with african imaginations 10
full of masks and dances and swelling chants
with african eyes, and noses, and arms,
though we sprawl in grey chains in a place
full of winters, when what we want is sun.

We have been captured, 15
brothers. And we labor
to make our getaway, into
the ancient image, into a new

correspondence with ourselves
and our black family. We need magic 20
now we need the spells, to raise up
return, destroy, and create. What will be

the sacred words?

MARVIN BELL   (b. 1937)

Things We Dreamt We Died For _____ *1969*

Flags of all sorts.
The literary life.
Each time we dreamt we'd done
the gentlemanly thing,
covering our causes 5

in closets full of bones
to remove ourselves forever
from dearest possibilities,
the old weapons re-injured us,
the old armies conscripted us,   10
and we gave in to getting even,
a little less like us
if a lot less like others.
Many, thus, gained fame
in the way of great plunderers,   15
retiring to the university
to cultivate grand plunder-gardens
in the service of literature,
the young and no more wars.
Their continuing tributes   20
make them our greatest saviours,
whose many fortunes are followed
by the many who have not one.

EARLE BIRNEY   (b. 1904)

Can. Lit.° _____ 1962

(or them able leave her ever)

since we'd always sky about
when we had eagles they flew out
leaving no shadow bigger than wren's
to trouble even our broodiest hens
too busy bridging loneliness   5
to be alone
we hacked in railway ties
what Emily° etched in bone

we French & English never lost
our civil war   10
endure it still
a bloody civil bore

the wounded sirened off
no Whitman° wanted
it's only by our lack of ghosts   15
we're haunted

CAN. LIT.   The title is an abbreviation for "Canadian Literature."   8 *Emily:* Emily Dickinson
(1830–1886), American poet (see pp. 711–28).   14 *Whitman:* Walt Whitman (1819–1892),
American poet.

ARNA BONTEMPS   (1902–1973)

A Black Man Talks of Reaping _____ *1940*

I have sown beside all waters in my day.
I planted deep, within my heart the fear
that wind or fowl would take the grain away.
I planted safe against this stark, lean year.

I scattered seed enough to plant the land   5
in rows from Canada to Mexico
but for my reaping only what the hand
can hold at once is all that I can show.

Yet what I sowed and what the orchard yields
my brother's sons are gathering stalk and root;   10
small wonder then my children glean in fields
they have not sown, and feed on bitter fruit.

ANNE BRADSTREET   (1612–1672)

To My Dear and Loving Husband _____ *1678*

If ever two were one, then surely we.
If ever man were loved by wife, then thee;
If ever wife was happy in a man,
Compare with me ye women if you can.
I prize thy love more than whole mines of gold,   5
Or all the riches that the East doth hold.
My love is such that rivers cannot quench,
Nor ought but love from thee give recompense.
Thy love is such I can no way repay;
The heavens reward thee manifold, I pray.   10
Then while we live, in love let's so persever,
That when we live no more we may live ever.

JOSEPH BRODSKY   (1940–1996)

In Memory of My Father: Australia _____ *1990*

You arose—I dreamt so last night—and left for
Australia. The voice, with a triple echo,
ebbed and flowed, complaining about climate,
grime, that the deal with the flat is stymied,
pity it's not downtown, though near the ocean,   5
no elevator but the bathtub's indeed an option,
ankles keep swelling. "Looks like I've lost my slippers"
came through rapt yet clear via satellite.

And at once the receiver burst into howling "*Adelaida!Adelaida!*"—
into rattling and crackling, as if a shutter,   10
ripped off its hinges, were pounding the wall with inhuman power.

Still, better this than the silky powder
canned by the crematorium, than the voucher—
better these snatches of voice, this patchwork
monologue of a recluse trying to play a genie   15

for the first time since you formed a cloud above a chimney.

GWENDOLYN BROOKS   (b. 1917)

Primer for Blacks _____ *1980*

Blackness
is a title,
is a preoccupation,
is a commitment Blacks
are to comprehend—   5
and in which you are
to perceive your Glory.

The conscious shout
of all that is white is
"It's Great to be white."   10
The conscious shout
of the slack in Black is
"It's Great to be white."
Thus all that is white
has white strength and yours.   15

The word Black
has geographic power,
pulls everybody in:
Blacks here—
Blacks there—   20
Blacks wherever they may be.
And remember, you Blacks, what they told you—
remember your Education:
"one Drop—one Drop
maketh a brand new Black."   25
        Oh mighty Drop.
——And because they have given us kindly
so many more of our people

Blackness
stretches over the land.   30
Blackness—
the Black of it,
the rust-red of it,

the milk and cream of it,
the tan and yellow-tan of it,   35
the deep-brown middle-brown high-brown of it,
the "olive" and ochre of it—
Blackness
marches on.

The huge, the pungent object of our prime out-ride   40
is to Comprehend,
to salute and to Love the fact that we are Black,
which *is* our "ultimate Reality,"
which is the lone ground
from which our meaningful metamorphosis,   45
from which our prosperous staccato,
group of individual, can rise.

Self-shriveled Blacks.
Begin with gaunt and marvelous concession:
YOU are our costume and our fundamental bone.   50

    All of you—
    You COLORED ones,
    you NEGRO ones,
those of you who proudly cry
    "I'm half INDian"—   55
    those of you who proudly screech
    "I'VE got the blood of George WASHington in
      MY veins"—

ALL of you—
    you proper Blacks,   60
you half-Blacks,
you wish-I-weren't Blacks,
Niggeroes and Niggerenes.

You.

ELIZABETH BARRETT BROWNING   (1806–1861)

Sonnets from the Portuguese: Number 43 _____ *1850*

How do I love thee? Let me count the ways.
I love thee to the depth and breadth and height
My soul can reach, when feeling out of sight
For the ends of Being and ideal Grace.
I love thee to the level of every day's   5
Most quiet need, by sun and candlelight.
I love thee freely, as men strive for Right;
I love thee purely, as they turn from Praise.
I love thee with the passion put to use

In my old griefs, and with my childhood's faith.   10
I love thee with a love I seemed to lose
With my lost saints,—I love thee with the breath,
Smiles, tears, of all my life!—and, if God choose,
I shall but love thee better after death.

ROBERT BROWNING   (1812–1889)

Soliloquy of the Spanish Cloister _____ *1842*

1

Gr-r-r—there go, my heart's abhorrence!
    Water your damned flowerpots, do!
If hate killed men, Brother Lawrence,
    God's blood, would not mine kill you!
What? your myrtle bush wants trimming?   5
    Oh, that rose has prior claims—
Needs its leaden vase filled brimming?
    Hell dry you up with its flames!

2

At the meal we sit together:
    Salve tibi!° I must hear   *Hail to thee!*   10
Wise talk of the kind of weather,
    Sort of season, time of year:
Not a plenteous cork crop: scarcely
    Dare we hope oak-galls, I doubt:
What's the Latin name for "parsley"?   15
    What's the Greek name for Swine's Snout?

3

Whew! We'll have our platter burnished,
    Laid with care on our own shelf!
With a fire-new spoon we're furnished,
    And a goblet for ourself,   20
Rinsed like something sacrificial
    Ere 'tis fit to touch our chaps°   *jaws*
Marked with L. for our initial!
    (He-he! There his lily snaps!)

4

Saint, forsooth! While brown Dolores   25
    Squats outside the Convent bank
With Sanchicha, telling stories,
    Steeping tresses in the tank,
Blue-black, lustrous, thick like horsehairs,
    —Can't I see his dead eye glow,   30
Bright as 'twere a Barbary corsair's?°   *pirate's*
    (That is, if he'd let it show!)

5

When he finishes refection,°   *dinner*
    Knife and fork he never lays
Cross-wise, to my recollection,   35
    As do I, in Jesu's praise.
I the Trinity illustrate,
    Drinking watered orange-pulp—
In three sips the Arian° frustrate;   *Anti-Trinitarian (a heretic)*
    While he drains his at one gulp.   40

6

Oh, those melons? If he's able
    We're to have a feast! so nice!
One goes to the Abbot's table,
    All of us get each a slice.
How go on your flowers? None double?   45
    Not one fruit-sort can you spy?
Strange!—And I, too, at such trouble,
    Keep them close-nipped on the sly!

7

There's a great text in Galatians,°   *perhaps 3:10 or 5:19–21*
    Once you trip on it, entails   50
Twenty-nine distinct damnations,
    One sure, if another fails:
If I trip him just a-dying,
    Sure of heaven as sure can be,
Spin him round and send him flying   55
    Off to hell, a Manichee?°   *heretic*

8

Or, my scrofulous° French novel   *pornographic*
    On gray paper with blunt type!
Simply glance at it, you grovel
    Hand and foot in Belial's° gripe: *the Devil*   60
If I double down its pages
    At the woeful sixteenth print,
When he gathers his greengages,
    Ope a sieve and slip it in't?

9

Or, there's Satan!—one might venture   65
    Pledge one's soul to him, yet leave
Such a flaw in the indenture°   *contract*
    As he'd miss till, past retrieve,
Blasted lay that rose-acacia
    We're so proud of! *Hy, Zy, Hine . . .*   70
'St, there's Vespers! *Plena gratiâ*°   *full of grace*
    Ave, Virgo!° Gr-r-r—you swine!   *Hail, Virgin!*

GEORGE GORDON, LORD BYRON (1788–1824)

The Destruction of Sennacherib° _____ *1815*

The Assyrian came down like the wolf on the fold,
And his cohorts were gleaming in purple and gold;
And the sheen of their spears was like stars on the sea,
When the blue wave rolls nightly on deep Galilee.

Like the leaves of the forest when summer is green,   5
That host with their banners at sunset were seen:
Like the leaves of the forest when autumn hath blown,
That host on the morrow lay withered and strown.

For the Angel of Death spread his wings on the blast,
And breathed in the face of the foe as he passed;   10
And the eyes of the sleepers waxed deadly and chill,
And their hearts but once heaved—and for ever grew still!

And there lay the steed with his nostril all wide,
But through it there rolled not the breath of his pride;
And the foam of his gasping lay white on the turf,   15
And cold as the spray of the rock-beating surf.

And there lay the rider distorted and pale,
With the dew on his brow, and the rust on his mail;
And the tents were all silent, the banners alone,
The lances unlifted, the trumpet unblown.   20

And the widows of Ashur° are loud in their wail,
And the idols are broke in the temple of Baal;°
And the might of the Gentile, unsmote by the sword,
Hath melted like snow in the glance of the Lord!

THE DESTRUTION OF SENNACHERIB.   Sennacherib was king of the ancient Near Eastern
empire of Assyria from 705 to 681 B.C.E. He laid seige to Jerusalem in about 702 B.C.E., even though
King Hezekiah had already rendered tribute to Assyria. According to 2 Kings 19:35–36, a miracle
occurred to save the besieged Hebrews: "the angel of the Lord went out and smote . . . [185,000
Assyrian soldiers]; and when they [the Hebrews] arose early in the morning, behold, they [the
Assyrians] were all dead corpses."   21 *Ashur:* the land of the Assyrians.   22 *Baal:* a god who
supposedly controlled weather and storms.

LUCILLE CLIFTON (b. 1936)

this morning
(for the girls of eastern high school) _____ *1987*

this morning
this morning
       i met myself

coming in

a bright   5
jungle girl
shining
quick as a snake
a tall
tree girl a   10
me girl

       i met myself
this morning
coming in

and all day   15
i have been
a black bell
ringing
i survive

      survive   20

survive

LUCILLE CLIFTON   (b. 1936)

the poet ——————————————————————— *1987*

i beg my bones to be good but
they keep clicking music and
i spin in the center of myself
a foolish frightful woman
moving my skin against the wind and   5
tap dancing for my life.

LEONARD COHEN   (b. 1934)

'The killers that run . . .' ——————————————————— *1972*

The killers that run
      the other countries
are trying to get us
to overthrow the killers
      that run our own   5
I for one
prefer the rule
      of our native killers
I am convinced
      the foreign killer   10

will kill more of us
than the old familiar killer does
        Frankly I don't believe
anyone out there
really wants us to solve   15
our social problems
        I base this all on how I feel
about the man next door
I just hope he doesn't
        get any uglier   20
Therefore I am a patriot
I don't like to see
        a burning flag
because it excites
the killers on either side   25
to unfortunate excess
which goes on gaily
        quite unchecked
until everyone is dead

STEPHEN CRANE   (1871–1900)

Do Not Weep, Maiden, for War Is Kind —————————— *1896, 1899 (1895)*

Do not weep, maiden, for war is kind.
Because your lover threw wild hands toward the sky
And the affrighted steed ran on alone,
Do not weep.
War is kind.   5

    Hoarse, booming drums of the regiment
    Little souls who thirst for fight,
    These men were born to drill and die
    The unexplained glory flies above them
    Great is the battle-god, great, and his kingdom—   10
    A field where a thousand corpses lie.

Do not weep, babe, for war is kind.
Because your father tumbled in the yellow trenches,
Raged at his breast, gulped and died,
Do not weep.   15
War is kind.

    Swift, blazing flag of the regiment
    Eagle with crest of red and gold,
    These men were born to drill and die
    Point for them the virtue of slaughter   20
    Make plain to them the excellence of killing
    And a field where a thousand corpses lie.

Mother whose head hung humble as a button
On the bright splendid shroud of your son,
Do not weep.   25
War is kind.

COUNTÉE CULLEN   (1903–1946)

Yet Do I Marvel _____ *1925*

I doubt not God is good, well-meaning, kind,
And did He stoop to quibble could tell why
The little buried mole continues blind,
Why flesh that mirrors Him must some day die.
Make plain the reason tortured Tantalus°   5
Is baited by the fickle fruit, declare
If merely brute caprice dooms Sisyphus°
To struggle up a never-ending stair.
Inscrutable His ways are, and immune
To catechism by a mind too strewn   10
With petty cares to slightly understand
What awful brain compels His awful hand.
Yet do I marvel at this curious thing:
To make a poet black, and bid him sing!

YET I DO MARVEL.   5 *Tantalus:* a figure in Greek mythology condemned to eternal hunger and thirst. He stood in Hades chin deep in water with a fruit-laden branch just above his head, but could never eat or drink.   7 *Sisyphus:* a figure in Greek mythology condemned to eternally useless labor. He was fated to roll a huge boulder up a hill in the underworld, but each time he neared the top, the stone slipped and he had to begin anew. See also p. 319.

e. e. cummings   (1894–1962)

if there are any heavens _____ *1931*

if there are any heavens my mother will(all by herself)have
one.   It will not be a pansy heaven nor
a fragile heaven of lilies-of-the-valley but
it will be a heaven of blackred roses

my father will be(deep like a rose   5
tall like a rose)

standing near my

swaying over her
(silent)
with eyes which are really petals and see   10

nothing with the face of a poet really which
is a flower and not a face with
hands

which whisper
This is my beloved my   15

                    (suddenly in sunlight

he will bow,

& the whole garden will bow)

JAMES DICKEY   (1923–1997)

The Lifeguard ————————————————————— *1962*

In a stable of boats I lie still,
From all sleeping children hidden.
The leap of a fish from its shadow
Makes the whole lake instantly tremble.
With my foot on the water, I feel   5
The moon outside

Take on the utmost of its power.
I rise and go out through the boats.
I set my broad sole upon silver,
On the skin of the sky, on the moonlight,   10
Stepping outward from earth onto water
In quest of the miracle

This village of children believed
That I could perform as I dived
For one who had sunk from my sight.   15
I saw his cropped haircut go under.
I leapt, and my steep body flashed
Once, in the sun.

Dark drew all the light from my eyes.
Like a man who explores his death   20
By the pull of his slow-moving shoulders,
I hung head down in the cold,
Wide-eyed, contained, and alone
Among the weeds,

And my fingertips turned into stone   25
From clutching immovable blackness.
Time after time I leapt upward
Exploding in breath, and fell back
From the change in the children's faces
At my defeat.   30

Beneath them I swam to the boathouse
With only my life in my arms
To wait for the lake to shine back
At the risen moon with such power

That my steps on the light of the ripples   35
Might be sustained.

Beneath me is nothing but brightness
Like the ghost of a snowfield in summer.
As I moved toward the center of the lake,
Which is also the center of the moon,   40
I am thinking of how I may be
The saviour of one

Who has already died in my care.
The dark trees fade from around me.
The moon's dust hovers together.   45
I call softly out, and the child's
Voice answers through blinding water.
Patiently, slowly,

He rises, dilating to break
The surface of stone with his forehead.   50
He is one I do not remember
Having ever seen in his life.
The ground I stand on is trembling
Upon his smile.

I wash the black mud from my hands.   55
On a light given off by the grave
I kneel in the quick of the moon
At the heart of a distant forest
And hold in my arms a child
Of water, water, water.   60

JOHN DONNE   (1572–1631)

Holy Sonnet 6: This Is My Play's Last Scene _____ *1633*

This is my play's last scene; here heavens appoint
My pilgrimage's last mile; and my race
Idly, yet quickly run, hath this last pace,
My span's last inch, my minute's last point,
And gluttonous Death will instantly unjoint   5
My body, and soul, and I shall sleep a space,
But my ever-waking part° shall see that face,   *the soul*
Whose fear already shakes my every joint.
Then, as my soul, t'heaven her first seat, takes flight,
And earth-borne body, in the earth shall dwell,   10
So, fall my sins, that all may have their right,
To where they are bred, and would press me, to hell.
Impute me righteous, thus purged of evil,
For thus I leave the world, the flesh, and devil.

JOHN DONNE   (1572–1631)

Holy Sonnet 7: At the Round Earth's Imagined Corners ——————— *1633*

At the round earth's imagined corners, blow
Your trumpets, angels,° and arise, arise
From death, you numberless infinities
Of souls, and to your scattered bodies go,
All whom the flood did, and fire shall o'erthrow,   5
All whom war, dearth, age, agues, tyrannies,
Despair, law, chance, hath slain, and you whose eyes
Shall behold God, and never taste death's woe.°
But let them sleep, Lord, and me mourn a space,
For, if above all these, my sins abound,   10
'Tis late to ask abundance of Thy grace,
When we are there. Here on this lowly ground,
Teach me how to repent; for that's as good
As if Thou hadst sealed my pardon with Thy blood.

AT THE ROUND EARTH'S IMAGINED CORNERS.   1–2 *At . . . angels:* The lines combine the
image of the angels or winds drawn at the four corners of old maps with an allusion to the four
angels mentioned in Revelations 7:1.   7–8 *you whose eyes . . . woe:* a reference to those people
who are still living on the day at the Last Judgment and thus move directly from life to judgment
without experiencing death.

JOHN DONNE   (1572–1631)

Holy Sonnet 10: Death Be Not Proud ——————————— *1633*

Death, be not proud, though some have callèd thee
Mighty and dreadful, for thou art not so;
For those whom thou think'st thou dost overthrow
Die not, poor Death, nor yet canst thou kill me.
From rest and sleep, which but thy pictures° be,   *imitations*   5
Much pleasure; then from thee much more must flow,
And soonest our best men with thee do go,
Rest of their bones, and soul's delivery.
Thou art slave to fate, chance, kings, and desperate men,
And dost with poison, war, and sickness dwell,   10
And poppy° or charms can make us sleep as well   *opium*
And better than thy stroke; why swell'st° thou then?   *puff up with pride*
One short sleep past, we wake eternally°   *on Judgment Day*
And death shall be no more; Death, thou shalt die.

JOHN DONNE   (1572–1631)

A Hymn to God the Father ————————————— *1633 (1623?)*

Wilt Thou forgive that sin where I begun,
  Which is my sin, though it were done before?

Wilt Thou forgive those sins through which I run,
  And do them still, though still I do deplore?
    When Thou hast done, Thou hast not done,   5
      For I have more.

Wilt Thou forgive that sin by which I won
  Others to sin and made my sin their door?
Wilt Thou forgive that sin which I did shun
  A year or two, but wallowed in a score?   10
    When Thou hast done, Thou hast not done,
      For I have more.

I have a sin of fear, that when I have spun
  My last thread, I shall perish on the shore;
Swear by Thy Self, that at my death Thy sun   15
  Shall shine as it shines now and heretofore;
    And, having done that, Thou hast done,
      I have no more.

JOHN DONNE   (1572–1631)

Song (Go, and Catch a Falling Star) ———————————— *1633*

Go, and catch a falling star,
  Get with child a mandrake root,°
Tell me where all past years are,
  Or who cleft the Devil's foot,
Teach me to hear mermaids singing,
Or to keep off envy's stinging,   5
    And find
    What wind
Serves to advance an honest mind.

If thou beest born to strange sights,
  Things invisible to see,   10
Ride ten thousand days and nights
  Till age snow white hairs on thee,
Thou, when thou return'st, wilt tell me
All strange wonders that befell thee
    And swear   15
    Nowhere
Lives a woman true, and fair.

If thou findst one, let me know,
  Such a Pilgrimage were sweet;
Yet do not, I would not go,   20
  Though at next door we might meet;

SONG.   2 *mandrake root:* The mandrake, or mandragora, is a European narcotic herb once considered an aphrodisiac because the two-pronged root was thought to resemble a woman's torso and legs.

Though she were true when you met her,
And last till you write your letter,
  Yet she   25
  Will be
False, ere I come, to two, or three.

MICHAEL DRAYTON   (1563–1631)

Since There's No Help —————————————————————— *1619*

Since there's no help, come let us kiss and part;
Nay, I have done, you get no more of me,
And I am glad, yea glad with all my heart
That thus so cleanly I myself can free;
Shake hands forever, cancel all our vows,
And when we meet at any time again,
Be it not seen in either of our brows   5
That we one jot of former love retain.
Now at the last gasp of love's latest breath,
When, his pulse failing, passion speechless lies,
When faith is kneeling by his bed of death,
And innocence is closing up his eyes;   10
Now if thou wouldst, when all have given him over,
From death to life thou mightst him yet recover.

PAUL LAURENCE DUNBAR   (1872–1906)

Sympathy ————————————————————————————— *1895*

I know what the caged bird feels, alas!
When the sun is bright on the upland slopes;
When the wind stirs soft through the springing grass
And the river flows like a stream of glass;
When the first bird sings and the first bud opes,
And the faint perfume from its chalice steals—   5
I know what the caged bird feels!

I know why the caged bird beats his wing
Till its blood is red on the cruel bars;
For he must fly back to his perch and cling
When he fain would be on the bough a-swing;   10
And a pain still throbs in the old, old scars
And they pulse again with a keener sting—
I know why he beats his wing!

I know why the caged bird sings, ah me,
When his wing is bruised and his bosom sore,   15

When he beats his bars and would be free;
It is not a carol of joy or glee,
But a prayer that he sends from his heart's deep core,
But a plea, that upward to Heaven he flings—   20
I know why the caged bird sings!

T. S. ELIOT   (1888–1965)

The Love Song of J. Alfred Prufrock° _____ *1915 (1910–1911)*

> *S'io credesse che mia risposta fosse°*
> *A persona che mai tornasse al mondo,*
> *Questa fiamma staria senza piu scosse.*
> *Ma perciocche giammai di questo fondo*
> *Non torno vivo alcun, s'i'odo il vero,*
> *Senza tema d'infamia ti rispondo.*

Let us go then, you and I
When the evening is spread out against the sky
Like a patient etherized upon a table;
Let us go, through certain half-deserted streets,
The muttering retreats   5
Of restless nights in one-night cheap hotels
And sawdust restaurants with oyster shells;
Streets that follow like a tedious argument
Of insidious intent
To lead you to an overwhelming question . . .   10

Oh, do not ask, "What is it?"
Let us go and make our visit.

In the room the women come and go
Talking of Michelangelo.°

The yellow fog that rubs its back upon the windowpanes,   15
The yellow smoke that rubs its muzzle on the windowpanes
Licked its tongue into the corners of the evening,
Lingered upon the pools that stand in drains,
Let fall upon its back the soot that falls from chimneys,
Slipped by the terrace, made a sudden leap,   20
And seeing that it was a soft October night,
Curled once about the house, and fell asleep.

THE LOVE SONG OF J. ALFRED PRUFROCK.   The poem is a monologue spoken by Prufrock;
the name is invented but suggests a businessman.   EPIGRAPH: The Italian epigraph is quoted
from Dante's *Inferno* (Canto 27, lines 61–66) and is spoken by a man who relates his evil deeds to
Dante because he assumes that Dante will never return to the world: "If I believed that my
response were made to a person who would ever revisit the world, this flame would stand motionless. But since none has ever returned from this depth alive, if I hear the truth, I answer you without fear of infamy."   14 *Michelangelo:* one of the greatest Italian Renaissance painters and sculp-
tors (1475–1564). The name suggests that the women are cultured, or at least pretending to be so.

And indeed there will be time
For the yellow smoke that slides along the street,
Rubbing its back upon the windowpanes;   25
There will be time, there will be time°
To prepare a face to meet the faces that you meet;
There will be time to murder and create,
And time for all the works and days° of hands
That lift and drop a question on your plate;   30
Time for you and time for me,
And time yet for a hundred indecisions,
And for a hundred visions and revisions,
Before the taking of a toast and tea.

In the room the women come and go   35
Talking of Michelangelo.

And indeed there will be time
To wonder, "Do I dare?" and, "Do I dare?"
Time to turn back and descend the stair,
With a bald spot in the middle of my hair—   40
(They will say: "How his hair is growing thin!")
My morning coat, my collar mounting firmly to the chin,
My necktie rich and modest, but asserted by a simple pin—
(They will say: "But how his arms and legs are thin!")
Do I dare   45
Disturb the universe?
In a minute there is time
For decisions and revisions which a minute will reverse.

For I have known them all already, known them all—
Have known the evenings, mornings, afternoons,   50
I have measured out my life with coffee spoons;
I know the voices dying with a dying fall°
Beneath the music from a farther room.
    So how should I presume?

And I have known the eyes already, known them all—   55
The eyes that fix you in a formulated phrase,
And when I am formulated, sprawling on a pin,
When I am pinned and wriggling on the wall,
Then how should I begin
To spit out all the butt-ends of my days and ways?   60
And how should I presume?

And I have known the arms already, known them all—
Arms that are braceleted and white and bare
(But in the lamplight, downed with light brown hair!)

26 *time:* a possible allusion to Andrew Marvell's "To His Coy Mistress" (p. 639).   29 *works and days:* the title of a poem about farming by the Greek poet Hesiod. Here the phrase ironically refers to social gestures.   52 *dying fall:* an allusion to a speech by Orsino in Shakespeare's *Twelfth Night* (Act I, scene 1, line 4).

Is it perfume from a dress   65
That makes me so digress?
Arms that lie along a table, or wrap about a shawl.
    And should I then presume?
    And how should I begin?

Shall I say, I have gone at dusk through narrow streets   70
And watched the smoke that rises from the pipes
Of lonely men in shirt-sleeves, leaning out of windows? . . .

I should have been a pair of ragged claws
Scuttling across the floors of silent seas.

And the afternoon, the evening, sleeps so peacefully!   75
Smoothed by long fingers,
Asleep . . . tired . . . or it malingers,°
Stretched on the floor, here beside you and me.
Should I, after tea and cakes and ices,
Have the strength to force the moment to its crisis?   80

But though I have wept and fasted, wept and prayed,
Though I have seen my head (grown slightly bald) brought in upon a platter,°
I am no prophet—and here's no great matter;
I have seen the moment of my greatness flicker,
And I have seen the eternal Footman hold my coat, and snicker,   85
And in short, I was afraid.

And would it have been worth it, after all,
After the cups, the marmalade, the tea,
Among the porcelain, among some talk of you and me,
Would it have been worth while,   90
To have bitten off the matter with a smile,
To have squeezed the universe into a ball°
To roll it toward some overwhelming question,
To say: "I am Lazarus,° come from the dead,
Come back to tell you all, I shall tell you all"—   95
If one, setting a pillow by her head,
    Should say: "That is not what I meant at all.
    That is not it, at all."

And would it have been worth it, after all,
Would it have been worth while,   100
After the sunsets and the dooryards and the sprinkled streets,
After the novels, after the teacups, after the skirts that trail along the floor—
And this, and so much more?—
It is impossible to say just what I mean!
But as if a magic lantern threw the nerves in patterns on a screen: 105

77 *malingers:* pretends to be ill.   82 *platter:* as was the head of John the Baptist; see Mark
6:17–28 and Matthew 14:3–11.   92 *ball:* another allusion to Marvell's "Coy Mistress" (p.639).
94 *Lazarus:* See John 11:1–44.

Would it have been worth while
If one, setting a pillow or throwing off a shawl,
And turning toward the window, should say:
   "That is not it at all,
   That is not what I meant, at all."   110

No! I am not Prince Hamlet,° nor was meant to be;
Am an attendant lord, one that will do
To swell a progress,° start a scene or two,
Advise the prince; no doubt, an easy tool,
Deferential, glad to be of use,   115
Politic, cautious, and meticulous;
Full of high sentence,° but a bit obtuse;
At times, indeed, almost ridiculous—
Almost, at times, the Fool.

I grow old . . . I grow old . . .   120
I shall wear the bottoms of my trousers rolled.°

Shall I part my hair behind? Do I dare to eat a peach?
I shall wear white flannel trousers, and walk upon the beach.
I have heard the mermaids singing, each to each.

I do not think that they will sing to me.   125

I have seen them riding seaward on the waves
Combing the white hair of the waves blown back
When the wind blows the water white and black.

We have lingered in the chambers of the sea
By sea-girls wreathed with seaweed red and brown   130
Till human voices wake us, and we drown.

111 *Prince Hamlet:* the hero of Shakespeare's play *Hamlet.*   113 *swell a progress:* enlarge a royal
procession.   117 *sentence:* ideals, opinions, sentiment.   121 *rolled:* a possible reference to
cuffs, which were becoming fashionable in 1910.

CAROLYN FORCHÉ   (b. 1950)

Because One Is Always Forgotten _____ *1981*

IN MEMORIAM, JOSÉ RUDOLFO VIERA
1939–1981: EL SALVADOR

When Viera was buried we knew it had come to an end,
his coffin rocking into the ground like a boat or a cradle.

I could take my heart, he said, and give it to a *campesino*°   *peasant*   5
and he would cut it up and give it back:

you can't eat heart in those four dark
chambers where a man can be kept years.

A boy soldier in the bone-hot sun works his knife
to peel the face from a dead man   10

and hang it from the branch of a tree
flowering with such faces.

The heart is the toughest part of the body.
Tenderness is in the hands.

NIKKI GIOVANNI   (b. 1943)

Woman _____ *1978*

she wanted to be a blade
of grass amid the fields
but he wouldn't agree
to be the dandelion

she wanted to be a robin singing   5
through the leaves
but he refused to be
her tree

she spun herself into a web
    and looking for a place to rest   10
turned to him
but he stood straight
declining to be her corner

she tried to be a book
but he wouldn't read   15
she turned herself into a bulb
but he wouldn't let her grow

she decided to become
a woman
and though he still refused   20
to be a man
she decided it was all
right

MARILYN HACKER   (b. 1942)

Sonnet Ending with a Film Subtitle _____ *1979*

For Judith Landry

Life has its nauseating ironies:
The good die young, as often has been shown;
Chaste spouses catch Venereal Disease;

And feminists sit by the telephone.
Last night was rather bleak, tonight is starker.   5
I may stare at the wall till half-past-one.
My friends are all convinced Dorothy Parker
Lives, but is not well, in Marylebone.°   *a district in London*
I wish that I could imitate my betters
And fortify my rhetoric with guns.   10
Some day we women all will break our fetters
And raise our daughters to be Lesbians.
(I wonder if the bastard kept my letters?)
Here follow untranslatable French puns.

DANIEL HALPERN   (b. 1945)

Snapshot of Hué _____ *1982*

For Robert Stone

They are riding bicycles on the other side
of the Perfume River.

A few months ago the bridges were down
and there was no one on the streets.

There were the telling piles on corners,   5
debris that contained a little of everything.

There was nothing not under cover—
even the sky remained impenetrable

day after day. And if you were seen
on the riverbank you were knocked down.   10

It is clear today. The litter in the streets
has been swept away. It couldn't have been

that bad, one of us said, the river barely moving,
the bicycles barely moving, the sun posted above.

H. S. (SAM) HAMOD   (b. 1936)

Leaves _____ *1973*

(for Sally)

Tonight, Sally and I are making stuffed
grapeleaves, we get out a package, it's
drying out, I've been saving it in the freezer, it's
one of the last things my father ever picked in this
life—they're over five years old   5

and up to now
we just kept finding packages of them in the
freezer, as if he were still picking them
somewhere packing them
carefully to send to us   10
making sure they didn't break into pieces.

***

"To my Dar Garnchildn
Davd and Lura
from Thr Jido"
twisted on tablet paper   15
between the lines
in this English lettering
hard for him even to print,
I keep this small torn record,
this piece of paper stays in the upstairs storage,   20
one of the few pieces of American
my father ever wrote. We find his Arabic letters
all over the place, even in the files we find
letters to him in English, one I found from Charles Atlas
telling him, in 1932,   25
"Of course, Mr. Hamod, you too can build
your muscles like mine . . ."

***

Last week my mother told me, when I was
asking why I became a poet, "But don't you remember,
your father made up poems, don't you remember him   30
singing in the car as we drove—those were poems."
Even now, at night, I sometimes
get out the Arabic grammar book
though it seems so late.

FRANCES E. W. HARPER   (1825–1911)

She's Free! _____ *1854*

How say that by law we may torture and chase
A woman whose crime is the hue of her face?—
With her step on the ice, and her arm on her child,
The danger was fearful, the pathway was wild. . . .
But she's free! yes, free from the land where the slave,   5
From the hand of oppression, must rest in the grave;
Where bondage and blood, where scourges and chains,
Have placed on our banner indelible stains. . . .

The bloodhounds have miss'd the scent of her way,
The hunter is rifled and foiled of his prey,   10
The cursing of men and clanking of chains
Make sounds of strange discord on Liberty's plains. . . .
Oh! poverty, danger and death she can brave,
For the child of her love is no longer a slave.

MICHAEL S. HARPER   (b. 1938)

Called ————————————————————————— *1975*

Digging the grave
through black dirt,
gravel and rocks
that will hold her down,
we speak of her heat   5
which has driven her out
over the highway
in her first year.

A fly glides from her mouth
as we take her four legs,   10
and the great white neck
muddled at the lakeside
bends gracefully into the arc
of her tongue, colorless, now,
and we set her in the bed   15
of earth and rock
which will hold her as the sun
sets over her shoulders.

You had spoken of her brother,
100 lbs or more,   20
and her slight frame
from the diet of chain
she had broken;
on her back
as the spade cools her brow   25
with black dirt, rocks,
sand, white tongue,
what pups does she hold
that are seeds unspayed
in her broken body;   30
what does her brother say
to the seed gone out over
the prairie, on the hunt
of the unreturned:
and what do we say   35
to the master of the dog dead,

heat, highway, this bed
on the shoulder
of the road west
where her brother called, calls   40

ROBERT HASS   (b. 1941)

Spring Rain _____ *1989*

Now the rain is falling, freshly, in the intervals between sunlight,

a Pacific squall started no one knows where, drawn east as the drifts of
warm air make a channel;

it moves its own way, like water or the mind,

and spills this rain passing over. The Sierras will catch it as last snow   5
flurries before summer, observed only by the wakened marmots at ten
thousand feet,

and we will come across it again as larkspur and penstemon sprouting
along a creek above Sonora Pass next August,

where the snowmelt will have trickled into Dead Man's Creek and the   10
creek spilled into the Stanislaus and the Stanislaus into the San Joaquin
and the San Joaquin into the slow salt marshes of the bay.

That's not the end of it: the gray jays of the mountains eat larkspur seeds,
which cannot propagate otherwise.

To simulate the process, you have to soak gathered seeds all night in the   15
acids of coffee

and then score them gently with a very sharp knife before you plant them
in the garden.

ROBERT HAYDEN   (1913–1980)

Those Winter Sundays _____ *1962*

Sundays too my father got up early
and put his clothes on in the blueblack cold,
then with cracked hands that ached
from labor in the weekday weather made
banked fires blaze. No one ever thanked him.   5
I'd wake and hear the cold splintering, breaking,
When the rooms were warm, he'd call,
and slowly I would rise and dress,
fearing the chronic angers of that house,

Speaking indifferently to him,   10
who had driven out the cold

and polished my good shoes as well.
What did I know, what did I know
of love's austere and lonely offices?

SEAMUS HEANEY   (b. 1939)

The Otter _____ 1979

When you plunged
The light of Tuscany wavered
And swung through the pool
From top to bottom.

I loved your wet head and smashing crawl,   5
Your fine swimmer's back and shoulders
Surfacing and surfacing again
This year and every year since.

I sat dry-throated on the warm stones.
You were beyond me.   10
The mellowed clarities, the grape-deep air
Thinned and disappointed.

Thank God for the slow loadening,
When I hold you now
We are closed and deep   15
As the atmosphere on water.

My two hands are plumbed water.
You are my palpable, lithe
Otter of memory
In the pool of the moment,   20

Turning to swim on your back,
Each silent, thigh-shaking kick
Re-tilting the light,
Heaving the cool at your neck.

And suddenly you're out,   25
Back again, intent as ever,
Heavy and frisky in your freshened pelt,
Printing the stones.

WILLIAM HEYEN   (b. 1940)

The Hair: Jacob Korman's Story _____ 1980

Ten kilometers from Warsaw,
I arrived in Rembertow where

hundreds of Jews had lived
until the wheel turned: *Judenrein.*°   *cleansed; rid of Jews*

You think they let themselves be taken?   5
They would not fill the trucks.
Men were shot trying to pull guns
from the guards' hands.

and hands of dead women   10
clutched hair, hair of SS guards
blood-patched hair everywhere,
a *velt mit hor,* a field of hair.

A. D. HOPE   (b. 1907)

Advice to Young Ladies ——————————————————— *1970*

A.U.C.° 334: about this date
For a sexual misdemeanor, which she denied,
The vestal virgin Postumia was tried.
Livy records it among affairs of state.

They let her off: it seems she was perfectly pure;   5
The charge arose because some thought her talk
Too witty for a young girl, her ways, her walk
Too lively, her clothes too smart to be demure.

The Pontifex Maximus, summing up the case,
Warned her in future to abstain from jokes,   10
To wear less modish and more pious frocks.
She left the court reprieved, but in disgrace.

What then? With her the annalist is less
Concerned than what the men achieved that year;
Plots, quarrels, crimes, with oratory to spare!   15
I see Postumia with her dowdy dress,

Stiff mouth and listless step; I see her strive
To give dull answers. She had to knuckle down.
A vestal virgin who scandalized that town
Had fair trial, then they buried her alive.   20

Alive, bricked up in suffocating dark,
A ration of bread, a pitcher if she was dry
Preserved the body they did not wish to die
Until her mind was quenched to the last spark.

A.U.C.   *A.U.C.* stands for *ab urbe condita,* "from the founding of the city." A.U.C. 334 therefore means
334 years after the founding of ancient Rome.

How many the black maw has swallowed in its time!   25
Spirited girls who would not know their place.
Talented girls who found that the disgrace
Of being a woman made genius a crime;

How many others, who would not kiss the rod
Domestic bullying broke, or public shame?   30
Pagan or Christian, it was much the same:
Husbands, Saint Paul declared, rank next to God.

Livy and Paul, it may be, never knew
That Rome was doomed; each spoke of her with pride.
Tacitus, writing after both had died,   35
Showed that whole fabric rotten through and through.

Historians spend their lives and lavish ink
Explaining how great commonwealths collapse
From great defects of policy—perhaps
The cause is sometimes simpler than they think.   40

It may not seem so grave an act to break
Postumia's spirit as Galileo's, to gag
Hypatia as crush Socrates, or drag
Joan as Giordano Bruno to the stake.

Can we be sure: Have more states perished, then,   45
For having shackled the enquiring mind,
Than those who, in their folly not less blind,
Trusted the servile womb to breed free men?

GERARD MANLEY HOPKINS   (1844–1889)

Pied Beauty ———————————————————————————— *(1918) 1877*

Glory be to God for dappled things—
    For skies of couple-colour as a brinded° cow;
        For rose-moles all in stipple upon trout that swim;
Fresh-firecoal chestnut-falls;° finches' wings;
    Landscape plotted and pieced°—fold,° fallow,° and plough;   5
        And áll trádes, their gear and tackle and trim.

All things counter,° original, spare,° strange;
    Whatever is fickle, freckled (who knows how?)
        With swift, slow; sweet, sour; adazzle, dim;
He fathers-forth whose beauty is past change: 10
Praise him.

PIED BEAUTY.   2 *brinded:* brindled, that is, grey with dark spots.   4 *chestnut-falls:* the meat
of a roasted chestnut.   5 *pieced:* divided into fields of different colors, depending on the crops
or use.   *fold:* an enclosed field for animals.   *fallow:* a plowed but unplanted field.
7 *counter:* opposed, as in contrasting patterns.   *spare:* rare.

LANGSTON HUGHES   (1902–1967)

Negro ———————————————————————— *1958*

I am a Negro:
 Black as the night is black,
 Black like the depths of my Africa.

I've been a slave:
 Caesar told me to keep his door-steps clean.   5
 I brushed the boots of Washington.

I've been a worker:
 Under my hand the pyramids arose.
 I made mortar for the Woolworth Building.

I've been a singer: 10
 All the way from Africa to Georgia
 I carried my sorrow songs.
 I made ragtime.

I've been a victim:
 The Belgians cut off my hands in the Congo.   15
 They lynch me still in Mississippi.

I am a Negro:
 Black as the night is black,
 Black like the depths of my Africa.

ROBINSON JEFFERS   (1887–1962)

The Answer ———————————————————————— *1937*

Then what is the answer?—Not to be deluded by dreams.
To know that great civilizations have broken down into violence, and their tyrants
 come, many times before.
When open violence appears, to avoid it with honor or choose the least ugly faction;
 these evils are essential.
To keep one's own integrity, be merciful and uncorrupted and not wish for evil;
 and not be duped
By dreams of universal justice or happiness. These dreams will not be fulfilled. 5
To know this, and know that however ugly the parts appear the whole remains
 beautiful. A severed hand
Is an ugly thing, and man dissevered from the earth and stars and his history . . . for
 contemplation or in fact . . .

Often appears atrociously ugly. Integrity is wholeness, the greatest beauty is
Organic wholeness, the wholeness of life and things, the divine beauty of the universe.
 Love that, not man
Apart from that, or else you will share man's pitiful confusions, or drown in despair
 when his days darken.   10

ETHERIDGE KNIGHT   (1931–1991)

Haiku° _____ *1968*

1

Eastern guard tower
glints in sunset; convicts rest
like lizards on rocks.

2

The piano man
is sitting at 3 am
his songs drop like plum.

3

Morning sun slants cell.
Drunks stagger like cripple flies
On the Jailhouse floor.

4

To write a blues song
is to regiment riots
and pluck gems from graves.

5

A bare pecan tree
slips a pencil shadow down
a moonlit snow slope.

6

The falling snow flakes
Can not blunt the hard aches nor
Match the steel stillness.

7

Under moon shadows
A tall boy flashes knife and
Slices star bright ice.

8

In the August grass
Struck by the last rays of sun
The cracked teacup screams.

9

Making jazz swing in
Seventeen syllables AIN'T
No square poet's job.

HAIKU.   The haiku is a Japanese lyric verse form consisting of three lines that total seventeen syllables, divided 5-7-5. See the discussion on p. 623.

MAXINE KUMIN   (b. 1925)

Woodchucks _____ *1972*

Gassing the woodchucks didn't turn out right.
The knockout bomb from the Feed and Grain Exchange
was featured as merciful, quick at the bone
and the case we had against them was airtight,
both exits shoehorned shut with puddingstone,   5
but they had a sub-sub-basement out of range.

Next morning they turned up again, no worse
for the cyanide than we for our cigarettes
and state-store Scotch, all of us up to scratch.
They brought down the marigolds as a matter of course   10
and then took over the vegetable patch
nipping the broccoli shoots, beheading the carrots.

The food from our mouths, I said, righteously thrilling
to the feel of the .22, the bullet's neat noses.
I, a lapsed pacifist fallen from grace   15
puffed with Darwinian pieties° for killing,
now drew a bead on the littlest woodchuck's face.
He died down in the everbearing roses.

Ten minutes later I dropped the mother. She
flipflopped in the air and fell, her needle teeth   20
still hooked in a leaf of early Swiss chard.
Another baby next. O one-two-three
the murderer inside me rose up hard,
the hawkeye killer came on stage forthwith.

There's one chuck left. Old wily fellow, he keeps   25
me cocked and ready day after day after day.
All night I hunt his humped-up form. I dream
I sight along the barrel in my sleep.
If only they'd all consented to die unseen
gassed underground the quiet Nazi way.°   30

WOODCHUCKS.   16 *Darwinian pieties:* Charles Darwin (1809–1892) was a British naturalist who
formulated the theory of evolution; the piety is "survival of the fittest."   30 *gassed . . . way:* a reference to the extermination of millions of people in gas chambers by the Nazis during World War II.

IRVING LAYTON   (b. 1912)

Rhine Boat Trip° _____ *1977*

The castles on the Rhine
are all haunted

RHINE BOAT TRIP: The title refers to the Rhine River, which flows through Germany.

by the ghosts of Jewish mothers
looking for their ghostly children

And the clusters of grapes   5
in the sloping vineyards
are myriads of blinded eyes
staring at the blind sun

The tireless Lorelei°
can never comb from their hair   10
the crimson beards
of murdered rabbis

However sweetly they sing
one hears only
the low wailing of cattle-cars°   15
moving invisibly across the land

9 *Lorelei:* legendary seductive nymphs who lived in the cliffs overlooking the Rhine, and whose singing lured sailors to shipwreck.   15 *cattle-cars:* railroad cars designed to transport cattle but used by the Nazis to transport Jews from the cities of Europe to extermination camps.

LI-YOUNG LEE   (b. 1957)

A Final Thing _____ *1990*

I am that last, that
final thing, the body
in a white sheet listening,

the whole of me trained,
curled like one great ear on   5
a sound, a noise I know, a

woman talking
in another room,
the woman I love; and

though I can't hear   10
her words, by their voicing
I can guess

she is telling a story,

using a voice which speaks to another,
weighted with that other's attention,   15
and avowing it
by deepening in intention.

Rich with the fullness of what's declared,
this voice points
away from itself   20
to some place

in the hearer,
sends the hearer back
to himself
to find what he knows.   25

A saying full of hearing,
a murmuring full of telling
and compassion for the listener
and for what's told,

now interrupted by a second voice,   30

thinner, higher, uncertain.
Querying, it seems
an invitation to be met,
stirring anticipation, embodying
incompletion of time and the day.   35

My son, my first-born, and his mother
are involved in a story no longer only theirs,
for I am implicated,
all three of us now
clinging to expectancy, riding sound and air.   40

Will my first morning of heaven be this?
No. And this is not
my last morning on earth.
I am simply last
in my house   45

to waken, and the first
sound I hear
is the voice of one I love
speaking to one we love.
I hear it through the bedroom wall;   50

something, someday, I'll close my eyes to recall.

ALAN P. LIGHTMAN   (b. 1948)

In Computers ──────────────────────────────────── *1982 (1981)*

In the magnets of computers will
    be stored

Blend of sunset over wheat
    fields.
Low thunder of gazelle.   5
Light, sweet wind on high
    ground.
Vacuum stillness spreading from
    a thick snowfall.

Men will sit in rooms   10
upon the smooth, scrubbed earth
or stand in tunnels on the moon
and instruct themselves in how it
    was.
Nothing will be lost.   15
Nothing will be lost.

AUDRE LORDE   (1934–1992)

Every Traveler Has One Vermont Poem ———————————— *(1986)*

Spikes of lavender aster under Route 91
hide a longing or confession
"I remember when air was invisible"
from Chamberlin Hill down to Lord's Creek
tree mosses point the way home.   5

Two nights of frost
and already the hills are turning
curved green against the astonished morning
sneeze-weed and ox-eye daisies
nor caring   I am a stranger   10
making a living choice.

Tanned boys I do not know
on their first proud harvest
wave from their father's tractor
one smiles as we drive past   15
the other hollers
nigger
into cropped and fragrant air.

RICHARD LOVELACE   (1618–1657)

To Lucasta, Going to the Wars ———————————————— *1649*

Tell me not, Sweet, I am unkind
That from the nunnery
Of thy chaste breast and quiet mind,
To war and arms I fly.

True, a new mistress now I chase,   5
The first foe in the field;
And with a stronger faith embrace
A sword, a horse, a shield.

Yet this inconstancy is such
As you too shall adore;   10
I could not love thee, Dear, so much,
Loved I not honor more.

AMY LOWELL   (1874–1925)

Patterns ————————————————————————— *1916*

I walk down the garden paths,
And all the daffodils
Are blowing, and the bright blue squills.
I walk down the patterned garden-paths
In my stiff, brocaded gown.   5
With my powdered hair and jewelled fan,
I too am a rare
Pattern. As I wander down
The garden paths.
My dress is richly figured,   10
And the train
Makes a pink and silver stain
On the gravel, and the thrift
Of the borders.
Just a plate of current fashion   15
Tripping by in high-heeled, ribboned shoes.
Not a softness anywhere about me,
Only whalebone° and brocade.
And I sink on a seat in the shade
Of a lime tree. For my passion   20
Wars against the stiff brocade.
The daffodils and squills
Flutter in the breeze
As they please.
And I weep;   25
For the lime-tree is in blossom
And one small flower has dropped upon my bosom.

And the plashing of waterdrops
In the marble fountain
Comes down the garden-paths.   30
The dripping never stops.

Underneath my stiffened gown
Is the softness of a woman bathing in a marble basin,
A basin in the midst of hedges grown
So thick, she cannot see her lover hiding,   35
But she guesses he is near,
And the sliding of the water
Seems the stroking of a dear
Hand upon her.
What is Summer in a fine brocaded gown!   40

PATTERNS.   18 *whalebone:* Baleen from whales was used to make corsets for women because it
was strong and flexible, like an early plastic.

I should like to see it lying in a heap upon the ground.
All the pink and silver crumpled up on the ground.

I would be the pink and silver as I ran along the paths,
And he would stumble after,
Bewildered by my laughter.   45
I should see the sun flashing from his sword-hilt and buckles on his shoes.
I would choose
To lead him in a maze along the patterned paths,
A bright and laughing maze for my heavy-booted lover.
Till he caught me in the shade,   50
And the buttons of his waistcoat bruised my body as he clasped me,
Aching, melting, unafraid.
With the shadows of the leaves and the sundrops,
And the plopping of the waterdrops,
All about us in the open afternoon—   55
I am very like to swoon
With the weight of this brocade,
For the sun sifts through the shade.

Underneath the fallen blossom
In my bosom,   60
Is a letter I have hid.
It was brought to me this morning by a rider from the Duke.
Madam, we regret to inform you that Lord Hartwell
Died in action Thursday se'nnight.°
As I read it in the white, morning sunlight,   65
The letters squirmed like snakes.
"Any answer, Madam," said my footman.
"No," I told him.
"See that the messenger takes some refreshment.

No, no answer."   70
And I walked into the garden,
Up and down the patterned paths,
In my stiff, correct brocade.
The blue and yellow flowers stood up proudly in the sun,
Each one.   75
I stood upright too,
Held rigid to the pattern
By the stiffness of my gown.
Up and down I walked.
Up and down.   80

In a month he would have been my husband.
In a month, here, underneath this lime,
We would have broken the pattern;
He for me, and I for him,

64 *se'nnight:* seven nights, hence a week ago.

He as Colonel, I as Lady,   85
On this shady seat.
He had a whim
That sunlight carried blessing.
And I answered, "It shall be as you have said."
Now he is dead.   90

In Summer and In Winter I shall walk
Up and down
The patterned garden-paths
In my stiff, brocaded gown.
The squills and daffodils   95
Will give place to pillared roses, and to asters, and to snow.
I shall go
Up and down,
In my gown.
Gorgeously arrayed,   100
Boned and stayed.
And the softness of my body will be guarded from embrace
By each button, hook, and lace.
For the man who should loose me is dead,
Fighting with the Duke in Flanders,°   105
In a pattern called a war.
Christ! What are patterns for?

105 *Flanders:* a place of frequent warfare in Belgium. The speaker's clothing (lines 5, 6) suggests
the time of the duke of Marlborough's Flanders campaigns of 1702–1710. The Battle of Waterloo
(1815) was also fought nearby under the duke of Wellington. During World War I, fierce fighting
against the Germans occurred in Flanders in 1914 and 1915, with great loss of life.

GWENDOLYN MacEWEN   (b. 1941)

Dark Pines under Water ———————————————————— *1969*

This land like a mirror turns you inward
And you become a forest in a furtive lake;
The dark pines of your mind reach downward,
You dream in the green of your time,
Your memory is a row of sinking pines.   5

Explorer, you tell yourself this is not what you came for
Although it is good here, and green;
You had meant to move with a kind of largeness,
You had planned a heavy grace, an anguished dream.

But the dark pines of your mind dip deeper   10
And you are sinking, sinking, sleeper
In an elementary world;
There is something down there and you want it told.

CLAUDE McKAY   (1890–1948)

The White City _____ *1922*

I will not toy with it nor bend an inch.
Deep in the secret chambers of my heart
I muse my life-long hate, and without flinch
I bear it nobly as I live my part.
My being would be a skeleton, a shell,   5
If this dark Passion that fills my every mood,
And makes my heaven in the white world's hell,
Did not forever feed me vital blood.
I see the mighty city through a mist—
The strident trains that speed the goaded mass,   10
The poles and spires and towers vapor-kissed,
The fortressed port through which the great ships pass,
The tides, the wharves, the dens I contemplate,
Are sweet like wanton loves because I hate.

EDNA ST. VINCENT MILLAY   (1892–1950)

What Lips My Lips Have Kissed, and Where, and Why _____ *1923*

What lips my lips have kissed, and where, and why,
I have forgotten, and what arms have lain
Under my head till morning; but the rain
Is full of ghosts tonight, that tap and sigh
Upon the glass and listen for reply,   5
And in my heart there stirs a quiet pain
For unremembered lads that not again
Will turn to me at midnight with a cry.
Thus in the winter stands the lonely tree,
Nor knows what birds have vanished one by one,   10
Yet knows it boughs more silent than before:
I cannot say what loves have come and gone,
I only know that summer sang in me
A little while, that in me sings no more.

OGDEN NASH   (1902–1971)

Very Like a Whale° _____ *1934*

One thing that literature would be greatly the better for
Would be a more restricted employment by authors of simile and metaphor.
Authors of all races, be they Greeks, Romans, Teutons or Celts,

VERY LIKE A WHALE.   See *Hamlet*, Act III, scene 2, line 358.

Can't seem just to say that anything is the thing it is but have to go out of their
    way to say that it is like something else.
What does it mean when we are told   5
That the Assyrian came down like a wolf on the fold?
In the first place, George Gordon Byron° had had enough experience
To know that it probably wasn't just one Assyrian, it was a lot of Assyrians.
However, as too many arguments are apt to induce apoplexy and thus hinder
    longevity,
We'll let it pass as one Assyrian for the sake of brevity.   10
Now then, this particular Assyrian; the one whose cohorts were gleaming in purple
    and gold,
Just what does the poet mean when he says he came down like a wolf on the
    fold?
In heaven and earth more than is dreamed of in our philosophy there are a great
    many things,
But I don't imagine that among them there is a wolf with purple and gold cohorts
    or purple and gold anythings.
No, no, Lord Byron, before I'll believe that this Assyrian was actually like a wolf   15
    I must have some kind of proof;
Did he run on all fours and did he have a hairy tail and a big red mouth and big
    white teeth and did he say Woof woof woof?
Frankly I think it very unlikely, and all you were entitled to say, at the very most,
Was that the Assyrian cohorts came down like a lot of Assyrian cohorts about to
    destroy the Hebrew host.
But that wasn't fancy enough for Lord Byron, oh dear me no, he had to invent a
    lot of figures of speech and then interpolate them.
With the result that whenever you mention Old Testament soldiers to people they   20
    say Oh yes, they're the ones that a lot of wolves dressed up in gold and purple
    ate them.
That's the kind of thing that's being done all the time by poets, from Homer to
    Tennyson;
They're always comparing ladies to lilies° and veal to venison.
How about the man who wrote,
Her little feet stole in and out like mice beneath her petticoat?°
Wouldn't anybody but a poet think twice   25
Before stating that his girl's feet were mice?
Then they always say things like that after a winter storm
The snow is a white blanket. Oh it is, is it, all right then, you sleep under a six-
    inch blanket of snow and I'll sleep under a half-inch blanket of unpoetical
    blanket material and we'll see which one keeps warm.
And after that maybe you'll begin to comprehend dimly
What I meant by too much metaphor and simile.   30

7 *George Gordon Byron:* See Byron, "The Destruction of Sennacherib," (p. 750), which Nash is
satirizing in this poem.   22 *ladies to lilies:* See Burns, "A Red, Red Rose."   24 *little feet . . .
petticoat:* In Sir John Suckling's "A Ballad upon a Wedding" (1641), the following lines appear:
"Her feet beneath her petticoat / Like little mice stole in and out." Also in a poem by Robert
Herrick complimenting the feet of Susanna Southwell (1648), he wrote: "Her pretty feet / Like
snails did creep."

JIM NORTHRUP   (b. 1943)

wahbegan° ————————————————————————— *1993*

Didja ever hear a sound
smell something
taste something
that brought you back
to Vietnam, instantly?   5
Didja ever wonder
when it would end?
It ended for my brother.
He died in the war
but didn't fall down   10
for fifteen tortured years.
His flashbacks are over,
another casualty whose name
will never be on the Wall.
Some can find peace   15
only in death.
The sound of his
family crying hurt.
The smell of the flowers
didn't comfort us.   20
The bitter taste
in my mouth
still sours me.
How about a memorial
for those who made it   25
through the war
but still died
before their time?

WAHBEGAN.   The title is an Ojibway name.

FRANK O'HARA   (1926–1966)

Poem ————————————————————————————— *1952*

The eager note on my door said "Call me,
call when you get in!" so I quickly threw
a few tangerines into my overnight bag,
straightened my eyelids and shoulders, and
headed straight for the door. It was autumn   5
by the time I got around the corner, oh all
unwilling to be either pertinent or bemused, but
the leaves were brighter than grass on the sidewalk!

Funny, I thought, that the lights are on this late
and the hall door open; still up at this hour, a   10
champion jai-alai player like himself? Oh fie!
for shame! What a host, so zealous! And he was

there in the hall, flat on a sheet of blood that
ran down the stairs. I did appreciate it. There are few
hosts who so thoroughly prepare to greet a guest   15
only casually invited, and that several months ago.

MARY OLIVER   (b. 1935)

Ghosts ───────────────────────────────────── *1983*

    1
Have you noticed?

    2
Where so many millions of powerful bawling beasts
lay down on the earth and died
it's hard to tell now
what's bone, and what merely   5
was once.

The golden eagle, for instance,
has a bit of heaviness in him;
moreover the huge barns
seem ready, sometimes, to ramble off   10
toward deeper grass.

    3
1805
near the Bitterroot Mountains:
a man named Lewis kneels down
on the prairie watching   15

a sparrow's nest cleverly concealed in the wild hyssop
and lined with buffalo hair. The chicks,
not more than a day hatched, lean
quietly into the thick wool as if
content, after all,   20
to have left the perfect world and fallen,
helpless and blind
into the flowered fields and the perils
of this one.

    4
In the book of the earth it is written: 25
nothing can die.

In the book of the Sioux it is written:
they have gone away into the earth to hide.
Nothing will coax them out again
but the people dancing.   30

            5

Said the old-timers:
the tongue
is the sweetest meat.

Passengers shooting from train windows
could hardly miss, they were   35
that many.

Afterward the carcasses
stank unbelievably, and sang with flies, ribboned
with slopes of white fat,
black ropes of blood—hellhunks   40
in the prairie heat.

            6

Have you noticed? how the rain
falls soft as the fall
of moccasins. *Have you noticed?*
how the immense circles still,   45
stubbornly, after a hundred years,
mark the grass where the rich droppings
from the roaring bulls
fell to the earth as the herd stood
day after day, moon after moon   50
in their tribal circle, outwaiting
the packs of yellow-eyed wolves that are also
have you noticed? gone now.

            7

Once only, and then in a dream,
I watched while, secretly   55
and with the tenderness of any caring woman,
a cow gave birth
to a red calf, tongued him dry and nursed him
in a warm corner
of the clear night   60
in the fragrant grass
in the wild domains
of the prairie spring, and I asked them,
in my dream I knelt down and asked them
to make room for me.   65

SIMON ORTIZ   (b. 1941)

A Story of How a Wall Stands _____ *1976*

> *At Aacqu there is a wall almost 400 years old which*
> *supports hundreds of tons of dirt and bones—it's a*
> *graveyard built on a steep incline—and it looks like*
> *it's about to fall down the incline but will not for a long time.*

My father, who works with stone,
says, "That's just the part you see,
the stones which seem to be
just packed in on the outside,"
and with his hands put the stone and mud   5
in place. "Underneath
what looks like loose stone,
there is stone woven together."
He ties one hand over the other,
fitting like the bones of his hands   10
and fingers. "That's what is
holding it together."

"It is built that carefully,"
he says, "the mud mixed
to a certain texture," patiently   15
"with the fingers," worked
in the palm of his hand. "So that
placed between the stones, they hold
together for a long, long time."

He tells me those things,   20
the story of them worked
with his fingers, in the palm
of his hands, working the stone
and the mud until they become
the wall that stands a long, long time.   25

DOROTHY PARKER   (1893–1967)

Résumé _____ *1936*

Razors pain you;
Rivers are damp;
Acids stain you;
And drugs cause cramp.
Guns aren't lawful;   5
Nooses give;
Gas smells awful;
You might as well live.

LINDA PASTAN   (b. 1932)

Marks _____ *1978*

My husband gives me an A
for last night's supper,
an incomplete for my ironing,
a B plus in bed.
My son says I am average,   5
an average mother, but if
I put my mind to it
I could improve.
My daughter believes
in Pass/Fail and tells me   10
I pass. Wait 'til they learn
I'm dropping out.

MARGE PIERCY   (b. 1936)

The Secretary Chant _____ *1973*

My hips are a desk.
From my ears hang
chains of paper clips.
Rubber bands form my hair.
My breasts are wells of mimeograph ink.   5
My feet bear casters.
Buzz. Click.
My head is a badly organized file.
My head is a switchboard
where crossed lines crackle.   10
Press my fingers
and in my eyes appear
credit and debit.
Zing. Tinkle.
My navel is a reject button.   15
From my mouth issue canceled reams.
Swollen, heavy, rectangular
I am about to be delivered
of a baby
Xerox machine.   20
File me under W
because I wonce
was
a woman.

SYLVIA PLATH   (1932–1963)

Last Words ———————————————————————— *1971 (1961)*

I do not want a plain box, I want a sarcophagus
With tigery stripes, and a face on it
Round as the moon, to stare up.
I want to be looking at them when they° come
Picking among the dumb minerals, the roots,   5
I see them already—the pale, star-distance faces.
Now they are nothing, they are not even babies.
I imagine them without fathers or mothers, like the first gods.
They will wonder if I was important.
I should sugar and preserve my days like fruit!   10
My mirror is clouding over—
A few more breaths, and it will reflect nothing at all.
The flowers and the faces whiten to a sheet.

I do not trust the spirit. It escapes like steam
In dreams, through mouth-hole or eye-hole. I can't stop it.   15
One day it won't come back. Things aren't like that.
They stay, their little particular lusters
Warmed by much handling. They almost purr.
When the soles of my feet grow cold,
The blue eye of my turquoise will comfort me.   20
Let me have my copper cooking pots, let my rouge pots
Bloom about me like night flowers, with a good smell.
They will roll me up in bandages, they will store my heart
Under my feet in a neat parcel.°
I shall hardly know myself. It will be dark,   25
And the shine of these small things sweeter than the face of Ishtar.°

LAST WORDS.   4 *they:* possibly archeologists exploring the speaker's tomb or stone coffin ("sarcophagus").   19–24 *When . . . parcel:* The objects and procedures here refer to the household goods normally entombed with a body in ancient Egypt and to the preparation of a mummy.   27 *Ishtar:* Ancient Babylonian goddess of fertility, love, and war.

SYLVIA PLATH   (1932–1963)

Mirror ———————————————————————————— *1965 (1961)*

I am silver and exact. I have no preconceptions.
Whatever I see I swallow immediately
Just as it is, unmisted by love or dislike.
I am not cruel, only truthful—
The eye of a little god, four-cornered.   5
Most of the time I meditate on the opposite wall.
It is pink, with speckles. I have looked at it so long

I think it is a part of my heart. But it flickers.
Faces and darkness separate us over and over.

Now I am a lake. A woman bends over me,   10
Searching my reaches for what she really is.
Then she turns to those liars, the candles or the moon.
I see her back, and reflect it faithfully.
She rewards me with tears and an agitation of hands.
I am important to her. She comes and goes.   15
Each morning it is her face that replaces the darkness.
In me she has drowned a young girl, and in me an old woman
Rises toward her day after day, like a terrible fish.

EDGAR ALLAN POE   (1809–1849)

Annabel Lee _____ *1848*

It was many and many a year ago,
    In a kingdom by the sea,
That a maiden there lived whom you may know
    By the name of Annabel Lee;
And this maiden she lived with no other thought   5
    Than to love and be loved by me.

She was a child and *I* was a child,
    In this kingdom by the sea,
But we loved with a love that was more than love—
    I and my Annabel Lee—   10
With a love that the wingèd seraphs of Heaven
    Coveted her and me.

And this was the reason that, long ago,
    In this kingdom by the sea,
A wind blew out of a cloud by night   15
    Chilling my Annabel Lee;
So that her high-born kinsmen came
    And bore her away from me,
To shut her up in a sepulchre
    In this kingdom by the sea.   20

The angels, not half so happy in Heaven,
    Went envying her and me:—
Yes! that was the reason (as all men know,
    In this kingdom by the sea)
That the wind came out of the cloud chilling   25
    And killing my Annabel Lee.

But our love it was stronger by far than the love
    Of those who were older than we—
    Of many far wiser than we—
And neither the angels in Heaven above   30

Nor the demons down under the sea
Can ever dissever my soul from the soul
   Of the beautiful Annabel Lee:—

For the moon never beams without bringing me dreams
   Of the beautiful Annabel Lee;   35
And the stars never rise but I feel the bright eyes
   Of the beautiful Annabel Lee:
And so all the night-tide, I lie down by the side
Of my darling, my darling, my life and my bride
   In her sepulchre there by the sea—   40
   In her tomb by the side of the sea.

KATHA POLLITT   (b. 1949)

Archaeology ———————————————————————— *1981*

> "Our real poems are already in us
> and all we can do is dig."
>   —Jonathan Galassi

You knew the odds on failure from the start,
that morning you first saw, or thought you saw,
beneath the heartstruck plains of a second-rate country
the outline of buried cities. A thousand to one
you'd turn up nothing more than the rubbish heap   5
of a poor Near Eastern backwater:
a few chipped beads,
splinters of glass and pottery, broken tablets
whose secret lore, laboriously deciphered,
would prove to be only a collection of ancient grocery lists.   10
Still, the train moved away from the station without you.

How many lives ago
was that? How many choices?
Now that you've got your bushelful of shards
do you say, *give me back my years*   15
or wrap yourself in the distant
glitter of desert stars,
telling yourself it was foolish after all
to have dreamed of uncovering
some fluent vessel, the bronze head of a god?   20
Pack up your fragments. Let the simoom°   *a desert sandstorm*
flatten the digging site. Now come
the passionate midnights in the museum basement
when out of that random rubble you'll invent
the dusty market smelling of sheep and spices,   25
streets, palmy gardens, courtyards set with wells
to which, in the blue of evening, one by one
come strong veiled women, bearing their perfect jars.

EZRA POUND   (1885–1972)

The River-Merchant's Wife: A Letter° _____ *1926 (1915)*

While my hair was still cut straight across my forehead
I played about the front gate, pulling flowers.
You came by on bamboo stilts, playing horse,
You walked about my seat, playing with blue plums.
And we went on living in the village of Chokan:°   5
Two small people, without dislike or suspicion.

At fourteen I married My Lord you.
I never laughed, being bashful.
Lowering my head, I looked at the wall.
Called to, a thousand times, I never looked back.   10

At fifteen I stopped scowling,
I desired my dust to be mingled with yours
Forever and forever and forever.
Why should I climb the look out?

At sixteen you departed,   15
You went into far Ku-tō-en,° by the river of swirling eddies,
And you have been gone five months.
The monkeys make sorrowful noise overhead.

You dragged your feet when you went out.
By the gate now, the moss is grown, the different mosses,   20
Too deep to clear them away!
The leaves fall early this autumn, in wind.
The paired butterflies are already yellow with August

Over the grass in the West garden;
They hurt me, I grow older.   25
If you are coming down through the narrows of the river Kiang,
Please let me know beforehand,
And I will come out to meet you
As far as Chō-fŭ-sa.°

THE RIVER-MERCHANTS WIFE: A LETTER.   Freely translated from the Chinese of Li Po
(701–762).   5 *Chokan:* a suburb of Nanking, China.   16 *Ku-tō-en:* an island several hundred
miles up the Kiang River from Nanking.   29 *Chō-fŭ-sa:* a beach near Ku-tō-en.

JOHN CROWE RANSOM   (1888–1974)

Bells for John Whiteside's Daughter _____ *1924*

There was such speed in her little body,
And such lightness in her footfall,
It is no wonder her brown study
Astonishes us all.

Her wars were bruited in our high window.   5
We looked among orchard trees and beyond
Where she took arms against her shadow,
Or harried unto the pond.

The lazy geese, like a snow cloud
Dripping their snow on the green grass,   10
Tricking and stopping, sleepy and proud,
Who cried in goose, Alas,

For the tireless heart within the little
Lady with rod that made them rise
From their noon apple-dreams and scuttle   15
Goose-fashion under the skies!

But now go the bells, and we are ready,
In one house we are sternly stopped
To say we are vexed at her brown study,
Lying so primly propped.   20

ADRIENNE RICH   (b. 1929)

Diving into the Wreck _____ *1973*

First having read the book of myths,
and loaded the camera,
and checked the edge of the knife-blade,
I put on
the body armor of black rubber   5
the absurd flippers
the grave and awkward mask.
I am having to do this
not like Cousteau with his
assiduous team   10
aboard the sun-flooded schooner
but here alone.

There is a ladder.
The ladder is always there
hanging innocently   15
close to the side of the schooner.
We know what it is for,
we who have used it.
otherwise
it is a piece of maritime floss   20
some sundry equipment.

I go down.
Rung after rung and still

the oxygen immerses me
the blue light
the clear atoms   25
of our human air.
I go down.
My flippers cripple me,
I crawl like an insect down the ladder   30
and there is no one
to tell me when the ocean
will begin.

First the air is blue and then
it is bluer and then green and then   35
black I am blacking out and yet
my mask is powerful
it pumps my blood with power
the sea is another story
the sea is not a question of power   40
I have to learn alone
to turn my body without force
in the deep element.

And now: it is easy to forget
what I came for   45
among so many who have always
lived here
swaying their crenellated fans
between the reefs
and besides   50
you breathe differently down here.

I came to explore the wreck.
The words are purposes.
The words are maps.
I came to see the damage that was done   55
and the treasures that prevail.
I stroke the beam of my lamp
slowly along the flank
of something more permanent
than fish or weed   60

the thing I came for:
the wreck and not the story of the wreck
the thing itself and not the myth
the drowned face always staring
toward the sun   65
the evidence of damage
worn by salt and sway into this threadbare beauty
the ribs of the disaster
curving their assertion
among the tentative haunters.   70

This is the place.
And I am here, the mermaid whose dark hair
streams black, the merman in his armored body.
We circle silently
about the wreck   75
we dive into the hold.
I am she: I am he

whose drowned face sleeps with open eyes
whose breasts still bear the stress
whose silver, copper, vermeil cargo lies   80
obscurely inside barrels
half-wedged and left to rot
we are the half-destroyed instruments
that once held to a course
the water-eaten log   85
the fouled compass

We are, I am, you are
by cowardice or courage
the one who find our way
back to this scene   90
carrying a knife, a camera
a book of myths
in which
our names do not appear.

THEODORE ROETHKE   (1908–1963)

The Waking ———————————————————— *1953*

I wake to sleep, and take my waking slow.
I feel my fate in what I cannot fear.
I learn by going where I have to go.

We think by feeling. What is there to know?
I hear my being dance from ear to ear.   5
I wake to sleep, and take my waking slow.

Of those so close beside me, which are you?
God bless the Ground! I shall walk softly there,
And learn by going where I have to go.

Light takes the Tree; but who can tell us how?   10
The lowly worm climbs up a winding stair;
I wake to sleep, and take my waking slow.

Great Nature has another thing to do
To you and me; so take the lively air,
And, lovely, learn by going where to go.   15

This shaking keeps me steady. I should know.
What falls away is always. And is near.
I wake to sleep, and take my waking slow.
I learn by going where I have to go.

SONIA SANCHEZ   (b. 1934)

right on: white america _____ *1970*

this country might have
been a pio
   neer land
once.
   but.   there ain't   5
no mo
     indians   blowing
custer's° mind
      with a different
image of america.   10
              this country
might have
        needed shoot/
outs/ daily/
      once.   15
     but. there ain't
no mo real/ white/   allamerican
             bad/guys.
just
   u & me.   20
      blk/ and un/armed.
this country might have
been a pion
      eer land.   once.
             and it still is.   25
check out
    the falling
gun/shells   on our blk/tomorrows.

RIGHT ON: WHITE AMERICA.   8 *custer's:* General George Armstrong Custer (1839–1876) was
killed in his "last stand" at the Little Bighorn in Montana during a battle with Sioux Indians.

CARL SANDBURG   (1878–1967)

Chicago _____ *1916*

   Hog Butcher for the World,
   Tool Maker, Stacker of Wheat,

Player with Railroads and the Nation's Freight Handler;
    Stormy, husky, brawling,
    City of the Big Shoulders: 5

They tell me you are wicked and I believe them, for I have seen your painted
    women under the gas lamps luring the farm boys.
And they tell me you are crooked and I answer: Yes, it is true I have seen the
    gunman kill and go free to kill again.
And they tell me you are brutal and my reply is: On the faces of women and
    children I have seen the marks of wanton hunger.
And having answered so I turn once more to those who sneer at this my city,
    and I give them back the sneer and say to them:
Come and show me another city with lifted head singing so proud to be alive   10
    and coarse and strong and cunning.
Flinging magnetic curses amid the toil of piling job on job, here is a tall bold
    slugger set vivid against the little soft cities;
Fierce as a dog with tongue lapping for action, cunning as a savage pitted against
    the wilderness,
    Bareheaded,
    Shoveling,
    Wrecking,   15
    Planning,
    Building, breaking, rebuilding,
Under the smoke, dust all over his mouth, laughing with white teeth,
Under the terrible burden of destiny laughing as a young man laughs,
Laughing even as an ignorant fighter laughs who has never lost a battle,   20
Bragging and laughing that under his wrist is the pulse, and under his ribs the
    heart of the people,
            Laughing!
Laughing the stormy, husky, brawling laughter of Youth, half-naked, sweating,
    proud to be Hog Butcher, Tool Maker, Stacker of Wheat, Player with Railroads
    and Freight Handler to the Nation.

SIEGFRIED SASSOON   (1886–1967)

Dreamers ——————————————————————— *1918*

Soldiers are citizens of death's grey land,
    Drawing no dividend from time's to-morrows.
In the great hour of destiny they stand,
    Each with his feuds, and jealousies, and sorrows.

    Soldiers are sworn to action; they must win   5
    Some flaming, fatal climax with their lives.
Soldiers are dreamers; when the guns begin
    They think of firelit homes, clean beds, and wives.

I see them in foul dug-outs, gnawed by rats,
    And in the ruined trenches, lashed with rain,   10
Dreaming of things they did with balls and bats,
    And mocked by hopeless longing to regain
Bank-holidays,° and picture shows, and spats,
    And going to the office in the train.

DREAMERS.   13 *Bank-holidays:* legal holidays in Great Britain.

ALAN SEEGER   (1886–1916)

I Have a Rendezvous with Death _____ *1916*

I have a rendezvous with Death
At some disputed barricade,
When Spring comes back with rustling shade
And apple blossoms fill the air—
I have a rendezvous with Death   5
When Spring brings back blue days and fair.

It may be he shall take my hand
And lead me into his dark land
And close my eyes and quench my breath—
It may be I shall pass him still.   10

I have a rendezvous with Death
On some scarred slope of battered hill,
When Spring comes round again this year
And the first meadow flowers appear.

God knows 'twere better to be deep   15
Pillowed in silk and scented down,
Where Love throbs out in blissful sleep,
Pulse nigh to pulse and breath to breath,
Where hushed awakenings are dear. . . .
But I've a rendezvous with Death   20
At midnight in some flaming town,
When Spring trips north again this year,
And I to my pledged word am true,
I shall not fail that rendezvous.

WILLIAM SHAKESPEARE   (1564–1616)

Fear No More the Heat o' the Sun° _____ *1623 (ca. 1609)*

Fear no more the heat o' the sun,
    Nor the furious winter's rages;
Thou thy worldly task hast done,

Home art gone, and ta'en° thy wages: *taken*
Golden lads and girls all must,   5
As° chimney-sweepers, come to dust.   *like*

Fear no more the frown o' the great;
   Thou art past the tyrant's stroke;
Care no more to clothe and eat;
   To thee the reed is as the oak;   10
The scepter, learning, physic, must
All follow this, and come to dust.

Fear no more the lightning flash,
   Nor the all-dreaded thunder stone;°
Fear not slander, censure rash;   15
   Thou hast finished joy and moan:°
                                    sadness
All lovers young, all lovers must
Consign to thee, and come to dust.

No exorciser harm thee!
Nor no witchcraft charm thee!   20
Ghost unlaid forbear thee!
Nothing ill come near thee!
Quiet consummation have;
And renownéd be thy grave!

FEAR NO MORE THE HEAT O' THE SUN.   A dirge or lament sung over the supposedly dead body of Imogen in Act IV of Shakespeare's *Cymbeline*.   14 *thunder stone:* The sound of thunder was believed to be caused by stones falling from the sky.

WILLIAM SHAKESPEARE   (1564–1616)

Sonnet 29: When in Disgrace with Fortune and Men's Eyes ——————— *1609*

When, in disgrace with Fortune and men's eyes,
I all alone beweep my outcast state,
And trouble deaf heaven with my bootless° cries,   *futile, useless*
And look upon myself and curse my fate,
Wishing me like to one more rich in hope,   5
Featured like him, like him with friends possessed,
Desiring this man's art and that man's scope,
With what I most enjoy contented least;
Yet in these thoughts myself almost despising,
Haply I think on thee, and then my state,   10
(Like to the lark at break of day arising)
From sullen earth sings hymns at heaven's gate,
For thy sweet love remembered such wealth brings
That then I scorn to change my state with kings.

WILLIAM SHAKESPEARE   (1564–1616)

Sonnet 146: Poor Soul, The Center of My Sinful Earth _____ *1609*

Poor soul, the center of my sinful earth,
Thrall° to these rebel powers that thee array,°   captive
Why dost thou pine within and suffer dearth
Painting thy outward walls so costly gay?
Why so large cost having so short a lease,   5
Dost thou upon thy fading mansion spend?
Shall worms, inheritors of this excess,
Eat up thy charge? Is this thy body's end?
Then, soul, live thou upon thy servant's loss,°
And let that pine to aggravate thy store;°   10
Buy terms° divine in selling hours of dross°   *i.e., eternal life; refuse*
Within be fed, without be rich no more:
So shalt thou feed on Death, that feeds on men,
And Death once dead, there's no more dying then.

POOR SOUL.   2 *array:* surround or dress out, as in a military formation.   9 *thy servant's loss:*
the loss of the body.   10 *let . . . store:* let the body ("that") dwindle ("pine") to increase ("aggravate") the riches ("store") of the soul.

KARL SHAPIRO   (b. 1913)

Auto Wreck _____ *1941*

Its quick soft silver bell beating, beating,
And down the dark one ruby flare
Pulsing out red light like an artery,
The ambulance at top speed floating down
Past beacons and illuminated clocks   5
Wings in a heavy curve, dips down,
And brakes speed, entering the crowd.
The doors leap open, emptying light;
Stretchers are laid out, the mangled lifted
And stowed into the little hospital.   10
Then the bell, breaking the hush, tolls once,
And the ambulance with its terrible cargo
Rocking, slightly rocking, moves away,
As the doors, an afterthought, are closed.

We are deranged, walking among the cops   15
Who sweep glass and are large and composed.
One is still making notes under the light.
One with a bucket douches ponds of blood
Into the street and gutter.

One hangs lanterns on the wrecks that cling,   20
Empty husks of locusts, to iron poles.
Our throats were tight as tourniquets,
Our feet were bound with splints, but now,
Like convalescents intimate and gauche,
We speak through sickly smiles and warn   25
With the stubborn saw of common sense,
The grim joke and the banal resolution.
The traffic moves around with care,
But we remain, touching a wound
That opens to our richest horror.   30
Already old, the question Who shall die?
Becomes unspoken Who is innocent?
For death in war is done by hands;
Suicide has cause and stillbirth, logic;
And cancer, simple as a flower, blooms.   35
But this invites the occult mind,
Cancels our physics with a sneer,
And spatters all we knew of dénouement
Across the expedient and wicked stones.

LESLIE MARMON SILKO   (b. 1948)

Where Mountain Lion Lay Down with Deer _____ *1974*

I climb the black rock mountain
    stepping from day to day
                        silently.
I smell the wind for my ancestors
    pale blue leaves   5
        crushed wild mountain smell.
Returning
    up the gray stone cliff
    where I descended
                a thousand years ago.   10

Returning to faded black stone
    where mountain lion lay down with deer.
It is better to stay up here
                watching wind's reflection
                in tall yellow flowers.   15
The old ones who remember me are gone
                the old songs are all forgotten
and the story of my birth.
How I danced in snow-frost moonlight
        distant stars to the end of the Earth,   20

How I swam away
         in freezing mountain water
         narrow mossy canyon tumbling down
             out of the mountain
                out of the deep canyon stone   25
      down
         the memory
             spilling out
             into the world.

DAVE SMITH   (b. 1942)

Bluejays ———————————————————————— *1981*

She tries to call them down,
quicknesses of air.
They bitch and scorn,
they roost away from her.

It isn't that she's brutal.   5
She's just a girl. Worse,
her touch is total.
Her play is dangerous.

Darkly they spit each at each,
from tops of pine and spruce.   10
Her words are shy and sweet,
but it's no use.

Ragged, blue, shrill,
they dart around like boys.
They fear the beautiful   15
but do not fly away.

STEVIE SMITH   (1902–1971)

Not Waving But Drowning ———————————————— *1957*

Nobody heard him, the dead man,
But still he lay moaning:
I was much further out than you thought
And not waving but drowning.

Poor chap, he always loved larking   5
And now he's dead
It must have been too cold for him his heart gave way,
They said.

Oh, no no no, it was too cold always
(Still the dead one lay moaning)   10
I was much too far out all my life
And not waving but drowning.

W. D. SNODGRASS   (b. 1926)

These Trees Stand . . . _____ *1960*

These trees stand very tall under the heavens.
While *they* stand, if I walk, all stars traverse
This steep celestial gulf their branches chart.
Though lovers stand at sixes and at sevens
While civilizations come down with the curse,   5
Snodgrass is walking through the universe.

I can't make any world go around *your* house.
But note this moon. Recall how the night nurse
Goes ward-rounds, by the mild, reflective art
Of focusing her flashlight on her blouse.   10
Your name's safe conduct into love or verse;
Snodgrass is walking through the universe.

Your name's absurd, miraculous as sperm
And as decisive. If you can't coerce
One thing outside yourself, why you're the poet!   15
What irrefrangible atoms whirl, affirm
Their destiny and form Lucinda's skirts!
She can't make up your mind. Soon as you know it,
Your firmament grows touchable and firm.
If all this world runs battlefield or worse,   20
Come, let us wipe our glasses on our shirts:
Snodgrass is walking through the universe.

CATHY SONG   (b. 1955)

Lost Sister _____ *1983*

                        1
In China,
even the peasants
named their first daughters
Jade—°
the stone that in the far fields   5

LOST SISTER.   4 *Jade:* Both the mineral and the name are considered signs of good fortune and health in China.

could moisten the dry season,
could make men move mountains
for the healing green of the inner hills
glistening like slices of winter melon.
And the daughters were grateful: 10
they never left home.
To move freely was a luxury
stolen from them at birth.
Instead, they gathered patience,
learning to walk in shoes   15
the size of teacups,°
without breaking—
the arc of their movements
as dormant as the rooted willow,
as redundant as the farmyard hens.   20
But they traveled far
in surviving,
learning to stretch the family rice,
to quiet the demons,
the noisy stomachs.   25

                                    2
There is a sister
across the ocean,
who relinquished her name,
diluting jade green
with the blue of the Pacific.   30
Rising with a tide of locusts,
she swarmed with others
to inundate another shore.
In America,
there are many roads   35
and women can stride along with men.

But in another wilderness,
the possibilities,
the loneliness,
can strangulate like jungle vines.   40
The meager provisions and sentiments
of once belonging—
fermented roots, Mah-Jongg° tiles and firecrackers—
set but a flimsy household
in a forest of nightless cities.   45
A giant snake rattles above,
spewing black clouds into your kitchen.

16 *teacups:* Traditionally, girls' feet were bound at the age of seven in China because minuscule feet were considered beautiful and aristocratic. The binding inhibited the natural growth of the feet and made it painful and difficult to walk.   43 *Mah-Jongg:* a Chinese game played with 144 domino-like tiles marked in suits, counters, and dice.

Dough-faced landlords
slip in and out of your keyholes,
making claims you don't understand,   50
tapping into your communication systems
of laundry lines and restaurant chains.

You find you need China:
your one fragile identification,
a jade link   55
handcuffed to your wrist.
You remember your mother
who walked for centuries,
footless—
and like her,   60
you have left no footprints,
but only because
there is an ocean in between,
the unremitting space of your rebellion.

GARY SOTO   (b. 1952)

Oranges ————————————————————————— *1984*

The first time I walked
With a girl, I was twelve,
Cold, and weighted down
With two oranges in my jacket.
December. Frost cracking   5
Beneath my steps, my breath
Before me, then gone,
As I walked toward
Her house, the one whose
Porch light burned yellow   10
Night and day, in any weather.
A dog barked at me, until
She came out pulling
At her gloves, face bright
With rouge. I smiled,   15
Touched her shoulder, and led
Her down the street, across
A used car lot and a line
Of newly planted trees,
Until we were breathing   20
Before a drugstore. We
Entered, the tiny bell
Bringing a saleslady
Down a narrow aisle of goods.
I turned to the candies   25

Tiered like bleachers,
And asked what she wanted—
Light in her eyes, a smile
Starting at the corners
Of her mouth. I fingered   30
A nickel in my pocket,
And when she lifted a chocolate
That cost a dime,
I didn't say anything.
I took the nickel from   35
My pocket, then an orange,
And set them quietly on
The counter. When I looked up,
The lady's eyes met mine,
And held them, knowing   40
Very well what it was all
About.
　　　Outside,
A few cars hissing past,
Fog hanging like old   45
Coats between the trees.
I took my girl's hand
In mine for two blocks,
Then released it to let
Her unwrap the chocolate.   50
I peeled my orange
That was so bright against
The gray of December
That, from some distance,
Someone might have thought   55
I was making a fire in my hands.

WILLIAM STAFFORD   (1914–1993)

Traveling Through the Dark ————————————————————— *1960*

Traveling through the dark I found a deer
dead on the edge of the Wilson River road.
It is usually best to roll them into the canyon:
that road is narrow; to swerve might make more dead.

By glow of the tail-light I stumbled back of the car   5
and stood by the heap, a doe, a recent killing;
she had stiffened already, almost cold.
I dragged her off; she was large in the belly.

My fingers touching her side brought me the reason—
her side was warm; her fawn lay there waiting,   10
alive, still, never to be born.
Beside that mountain road I hesitated.

The car aimed ahead its lowered parking lights;
under the hood purred the steady engine.
I stood in the glare of the warm exhaust turning red;   15
around our group I could hear the wilderness listen.
I thought hard for us all—my only swerving—,
then pushed her over the edge into the river.

GERALD STERN   (b. 1925)

Burying an Animal on the Way to New York _____ *1977*

Don't flinch when you come across a dead animal lying on the road;
you are being shown the secret of life.
Drive slowly over the brown flesh;
you are helping to bury it.
If you are the last mourner there will be no caress   5
at all from the crushed limbs
and you will have to slide over the dark spot imagining
the first suffering all by yourself
Shreds of spirit and little ghost fragments will be spread out
for two miles above the white highway.   10
Slow down with your radio off and your window open
to hear the twittering as you go by.

WALLACE STEVENS   (1879–1955)

The Emperor of Ice-Cream _____ *1923*

Call the roller of big cigars,
The muscular one, and bid him whip
In kitchen cups concupiscent curds.
Let the wenches dawdle in such dress
As they are used to wear, and let the boys   5
Bring flowers in last month's newspapers.
Let be be finale° of seem.
The only emperor is the emperor of ice-cream.
Take from the dresser of deal,°
Lacking the three glass knobs, that sheet   10
On which she embroidered fantails° once
And spread it so as to cover her face.
If her horny feet protrude, they come
To show how cold she is, and dumb.
Let the lamp affix its beam.   15
The only emperor is the emperor of ice-cream.

THE EMPEROR OF ICE-CREAM. 7 *finale:* the grand conclusion.   9 *deal:* unfinished pine
or fir used to make cheap furniture.   11 *fantails:* fantail pigeons.

JAMES TATE (b. 1943)

The Blue Booby _____ *1969*

The blue booby lives
on the bare rocks
of Galápagos°
and fears nothing.
It is a simple life: 5
they live on fish,
and there are few predators.
Also, the males do not
make fools of themselves
chasing after the young   10
ladies. Rather,
they gather the blue
objects of the world
and construct from them
a nest—an occasional   15
Gaulois° package,
a string of beads,
a piece of cloth from
a sailor's suit. This
replaces the need for   20
dazzling plumage;
in fact, in the past
fifty million years
the male has grown
considerably duller,   25
nor can he sing well.
The female, though,

asks little of him—
the blue satisfies her
completely, has   30
a magical effect
on her. When she returns
from her day of
gossip and shopping,
she sees he has found her   35
a new shred of blue foil:
for this she rewards him
with her dark body,
the stars turn slowly
in the blue foil beside them   40
like the eyes of a mild savior.

THE BLUE BOOBY.   3 *Galápagos:* islands in the Pacific Ocean on the equator about six hundred miles west of Ecuador where many unique species of animals live.   16 *Gaulois:* a brand of
French cigarettes with a blue package.

DYLAN THOMAS   (1914–1953)

A Refusal to Mourn the Death, by Fire, of a Child in London ———— *1946*

Never until the mankind making
Bird beast and flower
Fathering and all humbling darkness
Tells with silence the last light breaking
And the still hour   5
Is come of the sea tumbling in harness

And I must enter again the round
Zion of the water bead
And the synagogue of the ear of corn
Shall I let pray the shadow of a sound   10
Or sow my salt seed
In the least valley of sackcloth to mourn

The majesty and burning of the child's death.
I shall not murder
The mankind of her going with a grave truth   15
Nor blaspheme down the stations of the breath
With any further
Elegy of innocence and youth.

Deep with the first dead lies London's daughter,
Robed in the long friends,   20
The grains beyond age, the dark veins of her mother,
Secret by the unmourning water
Of the riding Thames.°
After the first death, there is no other.

A REFUSAL TO MOURN.   23 *Thames:* the River Thames, which flows through London.

JOHN UPDIKE   (b. 1932)

Perfection Wasted ———————————————————— *1990*

And another regrettable thing about death
is the ceasing of your own brand of magic,
which took a whole life to develop and market—
the quips, the witticisms, the slant
adjusted to a few, those loved ones nearest   5
the lip of the stage, their soft faces blanched
in the footlight glow, their laughter close to tears,
their tears confused with their diamond earrings,
their warm pooled breath in and out with your heartbeat,
their response and your performance twinned.   10
The jokes over the phone. The memories packed

in the rapid-access file. The whole act.
Who will do it again? That's it: no one;
imitators and descendants aren't the same.

SHELLY WAGNER   (b. ca. 1950)

The Boxes ——————————————————————————— *1991*

When I told the police I couldn't find you,
they began a search that included everything—
even the boxes in the house:
the footlockers of clothes in the attic,
the hamper in the bathroom,   5
and the Chinese lacquered trunk by the sofa.
They made me raise every lid.
I told them you would never stay in a box,
not with all the commotion.
You would have jumped out,   10
found your flashlight
and joined the search.

Poor Thomas, taking these men
who don't know us
through our neighbors' garages   15
where you never played,
hoping they were right
and we were wrong
and he would find you and
snatch you home by the hand   20

so the police cars could
get out of our driveway
and the divers would
get out of our river
because it was certainly   25
past our bedtime.
We would double-bolt our doors
like always,
say longer prayers than usual
and go to bed. But during the night   30
I would have sat till morning
beside my sleeping boys.

But that's not what happened.
Thomas is still here, now older.
I still go to his room   35
when he is sleeping
just to look at him.
I still visit the cemetery,
not as often,

but the urge is the same: 40
to lie down on the grass,
put my arm around the hump of ground
and tell you, "Get out of this box!
Put a stop to this commotion. Come home.
You should be in bed."   45

ALICE WALKER   (b. 1944)

Revolutionary Petunias ———————————————————————— *1972*

Sammy Lou of Rue
sent to his reward
the exact creature who
murdered her husband,
using a cultivator's hoe   5
with verve and skill;
and laughed fit to kill
in disbelief
at the angry, militant
pictures of herself   10
the Sonneteers quickly drew:
not any of them people that
she knew.
A backwoods woman
her house was papered with   15
funeral home calendars and
faces appropriate for a Mississippi
Sunday School. She raised a George,
a Martha, a Jackie and a Kennedy. Also
a John Wesley Junior.°   20
"Always respect the word of God,"
she said on her way to she didn't
know where, except it would be by
electric chair, and she continued
"Don't yall forget to *water*   25
my purple petunias."

REVOLUTIONARY PETUNIAS.   18–20 *George . . . Junior:* The children are named after George
and Martha Washington, Jackie and John Fitzgerald Kennedy (1917–1963, thirty-fifth U.S. president), and John Wesley (1703–1791), English evangelical preacher who founded Methodism.

EDMUND WALLER   (1606–1687)

Go, Lovely Rose ———————————————————————————— *1645*

   Go, lovely rose!
Tell her that wastes her time and me
   That now she knows,

When I resemble° her to thee,   *compare*
How sweet and fair she seems to be.   5

   Tell her that's young,
And shuns to have her graces spied,
   That hadst thou sprung
In deserts, where no men abide,
Thou must have uncommended died.   10

   Small is the worth
Of beauty from the light retired;
   Bid her come forth,
Suffer herself to be desired,
And not blush so to be admired.   15

   Then die! that she
The common fate of all things rare
   May read in thee;
How small a part of time they share
That are so wondrous sweet and fair.   20

ROBERT PENN WARREN (1905–1989)

Heart of Autumn _____ *1978*

Wind finds the northwest gap, fall comes.
Today, under gray cloud-scud and over gray
Wind-flicker of forest, in perfect formation, wild geese
Head for a land of warm water, the *boom*, the lead pellet.

Some crumple in air, fall. Some stagger, recover control,   5
Then take the last glide for a far glint of water. None
Knows what has happened. Now, today, watching
How tirelessly *V* upon *V* arrows the season's logic,

Do I know my own story? At least, they know
When the hour comes for the great wing-beat. Sky-strider,   10
Star-strider—they rise, and the imperial utterance,
Which cries out for distance, quivers in the wheeling sky.

That much they know, and in their nature know
The path of pathlessness, with all the joy
Of destiny fulfilling its own name.   15
I have known time and distance, but not why I am here.

Path of logic, path of folly, all
The same—and I stand, my face lifted now skyward,
Hearing the high beat, my arms outstretched in the tingling
Process of transformation, and soon tough legs,   20

With folded feet, trail in the sounding vacuum of passage,
And my heart is impacted with a fierce impulse

To unwordable utterance—
Toward sunset, at a great height.

BRUCE WEIGL   (b. 1949)

Song of Napalm ————————————————————— *1985*

For My Wife

After the storm, after the rain stopped pounding,
We stood in the doorway watching horses
Walk off lazily across the pasture's hill.
We stared through the black screen,
Our vision altered by the distance   5
So I thought I saw a mist
Kicked up around their hooves when they faded
Like cut-out horses
Away from us.
The grass was never more blue in that light, more   10
Scarlet; beyond the pasture
Trees scraped their voices in the wind, branches
Criss-crossed the sky like barbed-wire
But you said they were only branches.

Okay. The storm stopped pounding.   15
I am trying to say this straight: for once
I was sane enough to pause and breathe
Outside my wild plans and after the hard rain
I turned my back on the old curses, I believed
They swung finally away from me . . .   20

But still the branches are wire
And thunder is the pounding mortar,
Still I close my eyes and see the girl
Running from her village, napalm
Stuck to her dress like jelly,   25
Her hands reaching for the no one
Who waits in waves of heat before her.

So I can keep on living,
So I can stay here beside you,
I try to imagine she runs down the road and wings   30
Beat inside her until she rises
Above the stinking jungle and her pain
Eases, and your pain, and mine.
But the lie swings back again.
The lie works only as long as it takes to speak   35
And the girl runs only so far
As the napalm allows
Until her burning tendons and crackling

Muscles draw her up
Into that final position   40
Burning bodies so perfectly assume. Nothing
Can change that; she is burned behind my eyes
And not your good love and not the rain-swept air
And not the jungle green
Pasture unfolding before us can deny it.   45

PHILLIS WHEATLEY   (1754–1784)

On Being Brought from Africa to America _____ *1773*

'Twas mercy brought me from my *Pagan* land,
Taught my benighted soul to understand
That there's a God, that there's a *Saviour* too:
Once I redemption neither sought nor knew.
Some view our sable race with scornful eye,   5
"Their colour is a diabolic die."
Remember, *Christians, Negroes*, black as *Cain*,
May be refin'd, and join th' angelic train.

WALT WHITMAN   (1819–1892)

Full of Life Now _____ *1857*

Full of life now, compact, visible,
I, forty years old the eighty-third year of the States,
To one a century hence or any number of centuries hence,
To you yet unborn these, seeking you.

When you read these I that was visible am become invisible,   5
Now it is you, compact, visible, realizing my poems, seeking me,
Fancying how happy you were if I could be with you and become your comrade;
Be it as if I were with you. (Be not too certain but I am now with you.)

WALT WHITMAN   (1819–1892)

Beat! Beat! Drums! _____ *1861*

Beat! beat! drums!—blow! bugles! blow!
Through the windows—through doors—burst like a ruthless force,
Into the solemn church, and scatter the congregation,
Into the school where the scholar is studying;
Leave not the bridegroom quiet—no happiness must he have now with his bride,   5
Nor the peaceful farmer any peace, plowing his field or gathering his grain,
So fierce you whir and pound you drums—so shrill you bugles blow.

Beat! beat! drums!—blow! bugles! blow!

Over the traffic of cities—over the rumble of wheels in the streets;
Are beds prepared for sleepers at night in the houses? no sleepers must sleep in
    those beds,   10
No bargainers' bargains by day—no brokers or speculators—would they continue?
Would the talkers be talking? would the singer attempt to sing?
Would the lawyer rise in the court to state his case before the judge?
Beat! beat! drums—blow! bugles! blow!
Then rattle quicker, heavier drums—you bugles wilder blow.   15
Make no parley—stop for no expostulation,
Mind not the timid—mind not the weeper or prayer,
Mind not the old man beseeching the young man,
Let not the child's voice be heard, nor the mother's entreaties,
Make even the trestles to shake the dead where they lie awaiting the hearses,   20
So strong you thump O terrible drums—so loud you bugles blow.

WALT WHITMAN   (1819–1892)

Dirge for Two Veterans —————————————————————— *1865*

   The last sunbeam
Lightly falls from the finished Sabbath,
On the pavement here, and there beyond it is looking,
   Down a new-made double grave.

   Lo, the moon ascending,   5
Up from the east the silvery round moon,
Beautiful over the house-tops, ghastly, phantom moon,
   Immense and silent moon.

   I see a sad procession,
And I hear the sound of coming full-keyed bugles,   10
All the channels of the city streets they're flooding,
   As with voices and with tears.

   I hear the great drums pounding
And the small drums steady whirring,
And every blow of the great convulsive drums,   15
   Strikes me through and through.

   For the son is brought with the father,
(In the foremost ranks of the fierce assault they fell,
Two veterans son and father dropped together,
   And the double grave awaits them.)   20

   Now nearer blow the bugles,
And the drums strike more convulsive,
And the daylight o'er the pavement quite has faded,
   And the strong dead-march enwraps me.

   In the eastern sky up-buoying,   25
The sorrowful vast phantom moves illumined,

('Tis some mother's large transparent face,
  In heaven brighter growing.)

  O strong dead-march you please me!
O moon immense with your silvery face you soothe me!   30
O my soldiers twain! O my veterans passing to burial!
  What I have I also give you.

  The moon gives you light,
And the bugles and the drums give you music,
And my heart, O my soldiers, my veterans,   35
  My heart gives you love.

RICHARD WILBUR   (b.\ 1921)

The Sirens _____ *1950*

I never knew the road
From which the whole earth didn't call away,
With wild birds rounding the hill crowns,
Haling out of the heart an old dismay,
Or the shore somewhere pounding its slow code,   5
Or low-lighted towns
Seeming to tell me, stay.

Lands I have never seen
And shall not see, loves I will not forget,
All I have missed, or slighted, or foregone   10
Call to me now. And weaken me. And yet
I would not walk a road without a scene.
I listen going on,
The richer for regret.

WILLIAM CARLOS WILLIAMS   (1883–1963)

The Red Wheelbarrow _____ *1923*

      so much depends
      upon

      a red wheel
      barrow

      glazed with rain   5
      water

      beside the white
      chickens.

WILLIAM BUTLER YEATS   (1865–1939)

Sailing to Byzantium° _____ *1927*

1

That is no country for old men. The young
In one another's arms, birds in the trees
—Those dying generations—at their song,
The salmon-falls, the mackerel-crowded seas,
Fish, flesh, or fowl, commend all summer long   5
Whatever is begotten, born, and dies.
Caught in that sensual music all neglect
Monuments of unaging intellect.

2

An aged man is but a paltry thing.
A tattered coat upon a stick, unless   10
Soul clap its hands and sing, and louder sing
For every tatter in its mortal dress,
Nor is there singing school but studying
Monuments of its own magnificence;
And therefore I have sailed the seas and come   15
To the holy city of Byzantium.

3

O sages standing in God's holy fire
As in the gold mosaic of a wall,
Come from the holy fire, perne in a gyre,°
And be the singing-masters of my soul.   20
Consume my heart away; sick with desire
And fastened to a dying animal
It knows not what it is; and gather me
Into the artifice of eternity.

4

Once out of nature I shall never take   25
My bodily form from any natural thing,
But such a form as Grecian goldsmiths make
Of hammered gold and gold enameling
To keep a drowsy Emperor awake;
Or set upon a golden bough to sing   30
To lords and ladies of Byzantium
Of what is past, or passing, or to come.

SAILING TO BYZANTIUM.   In Yeat's private mythology, Byzantium (called Constantinople in Roman times and Istanbul today) symbolizes art, artifice, sophistication, and eternity as opposed to the natural world and physicality.   19 *perne in a gyre:* turning about in a spiral motion. See the diagram on p. 683.

PAUL ZIMMER   (b. 1934)

The Day Zimmer Lost Religion _____ *1973*

The first Sunday I missed Mass on purpose
I waited all day for Christ to climb down
Like a wiry flyweight° from the cross and
Club me on my irreverent teeth, to wade into
My blasphemous gut and drop me like a   5
Red hot thurible,° the devil roaring in
Reserved seats until he got the hiccups.

It was a long cold way from the old days
When cassocked and surpliced° I mumbled Latin
At the old priest and rang his obscure bell.   10
A long way from the dirty wind that blew
The soot like venial sins° across the schoolyard
Where God reigned as a threatening,
One-eyed triangle high in the fleecy sky.

The first Sunday I missed Mass on purpose   15
I waited all day for Christ to climb down
Like the playground bully, the cuts and mice
Upon his face agleam, and pound me
Till my irreligious tongue hung out.
But of course He never came, knowing that   20
I was grown up and ready for Him now.

THE DAY ZIMMER LOST RELIGION.   3 *flyweight:* a boxer weighing a maximum of 112
pounds.   6 *thurible:* a censer, a container in which incense is burned.   9 *cassocked and
surpliced:* wearing the traditional garb of an altar boy during Mass.   12 *venial sins:* minor inadvertent sins.

READING
AND
WRITING
ABOUT

DRAMA

22
The Dramatic Vision:
An Overview

Drama has much in common with the other genres of literature: Both drama and fiction, for example, focus on one or a few major characters who enjoy success or endure failure in facing challenges and in dealing with other characters. Many plays are written in prose, as is fiction, on the principle that the language of drama should resemble the language of life as much as possible.

Drama is also like poetry in that both genres can develop situations through speech and action. Indeed, a great number of plays, particularly those of past ages, exist as poetry. For example, the plays of ancient Athens were composed in intricate poetic forms. Many European plays from the Renaissance through the nineteenth century were written in blank verse or rhymed couplets, a tradition of poetic drama preserved by twentieth-century dramatists such as T. S. Eliot and Christopher Fry.

As separate genres, however, there are necessarily major differences among drama, fiction, and poetry. Fiction is distinguished from drama because the essence of fiction is narration—the relating or recounting of a sequence of events or actions, the actual telling of a story. Poetry is unlike both drama and fiction because it exists in many formal and informal shapes, and it is usually the shortest of the genres. Although we frequently read poetry silently and alone, it can be profitably read aloud by a single person to a group. Unlike both fiction and poetry, drama is literature designed for impersonation by people—actors—for the benefit and delight of other people—an audience.

DRAMA AS LITERATURE
AND DRAMA AS PERFORMANCE

Drama as Literature

Drama is special because it can be presented and discussed both as *litera-ture*—drama itself—and as *performance*—the production of plays in the theater. The major literary aspects of drama are the *text, character, plot, structure, language, tone,* and *theme* or *meaning.* All these elements have remained constant through-out the history of drama. In addition, drama written in poetic forms, such as Shakespeare's *Hamlet* and *A Midsummer Night's Dream,* includes elements such as *meter* and *rhyme.*

THE TEXT.   The text of a play is in effect a plan for bringing the play into action on the stage. The most notable features of the text are *dialogue, monologue,* and *stage directions.* **Dialogue** is the conversation of two or more characters. A **monologue** is spoken by a single character who is usually alone onstage. **Stage directions** are the playwright's instructions about facial and vocal expression, movement and action, gesture and "body language," stage appearance, lighting, and similar matters. In addition, some dramatists, like Tennessee Williams, pro-vide introductions and explanations for their plays. Such material can be con-sidered as additional directions for interpretation and staging.

CHARACTER.   Drama necessarily focuses on its **characters,** who are persons the playwright creates to embody the play's actions, ideas, and attitudes. Of course characters are characters, no matter where we find them, and many of the character types that populate drama are also found in fiction. The major quality of characters in drama, however, is that they become alive through speech and action. To understand them we must listen to their words and watch and interpret how they react both to their circumstances and to the characters around them. They are also sometimes described and discussed by other char-acters, but primarily they are rendered dramatically.

Drama is not designed to present the full life stories of its characters. Rather, the plots of drama bring out intense and highly focused oppositions or conflicts in which the characters are engaged. In accord with such conflicts, most major dramatic characters are considered as *protagonists* and *antagonists.* The **protagonist,** usually the central character, is opposed by the **antagonist.** A classic conflict is seen in Shakespeare's *Hamlet,* in which Prince Hamlet, the protago-nist, tries first to confirm and then to punish the crime of his uncle, King Claud-ius, the antagonist.

Just as in fiction, drama presents us with both *round* and *flat* characters. A **round, dynamic, developing,** and **growing character,** like Shakespeare's Hamlet and Ibsen's Nora, profits from experience and undergoes a development in awareness, insight, understanding, moral capacity, and the ability to make decisions. A **flat, static, fixed,** and **unchanging character,** like the men in Glaspell's *Trifles*, does not undergo any change or growth. There is no rule, however, that flat characters must be dull. They can be charming, vibrant, entertaining, and funny, but even if they are memorable in these ways, they remain fixed and static.

Throughout the ages, drama and other types of literature have relied on **stereotype** or **stock characters,** that is, unindividualized characters whose actions and speeches make them seem to have been taken from a mold. The general types developed in the comedy of ancient Athens and Rome, and in the drama of the Renaissance, are the *stubborn father,* the *romantic hero* and *heroine,* the *clever male servant,* the *saucy maidservant,* the *braggart soldier,* the *bumpkin,* the *trickster,* the *victim,* the *insensitive husband,* the *shrewish wife,* and the *lusty youth.* Modern drama continues these stereotypes, and it has also invented many of its own, such as the *private eye,* the *stupid bureaucrat,* the *corrupt politician,* the *independent pioneer,* the *sensitive prostitute,* the *loner cowboy,* and the *town sheriff who never loses the draw in a showdown.*

There are also **ancillary characters** who set off or highlight the protagonist and who provide insight into the action. The first type, the **foil,** has been a feature of drama since its beginnings in ancient Athens. The foil is a character who is to be compared and contrasted with the protagonist. Laertes and Fortinbras are foils in *Hamlet.* Because of the play's circumstances, Laertes is swept into destruction along with Hamlet, whereas Fortinbras picks up the pieces and gets life moving again after the final death scene. The second type is the **choric figure,** who is loosely connected to the choruses of ancient drama. Usually the choric figure is a single character, often a confidant of the protagonist, such as Hamlet's friend Horatio. When the choric figure expresses ideas about the play's major issues and actions, he or she is called a **raisonneur** (the French word meaning "reasoner") or **commentator.**

Any of the foregoing types of characters can also be **symbolic** in the context of individual plays. They can symbolize ideas, moral values, religious concepts, ways of life, or some other abstraction. For instance, Linda in *Death of a Salesman* symbolizes helplessness before destructive forces, while Fred Higgins in *Mulatto* symbolizes the cynicism, indifference, cruelty, and misuse of responsibility that accompany the concept of racial supremacy.

ACTION, CONFLICT, AND PLOT.   Plays are made up of a series of sequential and related **actions** or **incidents.** The actions are connected by **chronology**—the logic of time—and the term given to the principles underlying this ordered chain of actions and reactions is **plot,** which is a connected plan or pattern of causation. The impulse controlling the connections is **conflict,** which refers to people or circumstances—the antagonist—that the protagonist tries to overcome. Most dramatic conflicts are vividly apparent because the clashes of wills and characters take place onstage, right in front of our eyes. Conflicts can also exist between groups, although conflicts between individuals are more identifiable and therefore more suitable for plays.

Although dramatic plots can be simplified and schematized, most of them are as complicated as life itself. Special complications result from a **double** or **multiple plot**—two or more different but related lines of action. Usually one of these plots is the **main plot,** but the **subplot** can be independently important and sometimes even more interesting. Such a situation occurs in *A Midsummer Night's Dream,* where the exploits of Bottom and the "mechanicals," which form just one of the four strands of plot, are so funny that they usually steal the show.

STRUCTURE.   The term describing a play's pattern of organization is **structure.** With variations, many traditional plays contain elements that constitute a *five-stage* structure: (1) *exposition* or *introduction,* (2) *complication* and *development,* (3) *crisis* or *climax,* (4) *falling action,* and (5) *dénouement, resolution,* or *catastrophe.* In the nineteenth century, the German novelist and critic Gustav Freytag (1816–1895) visualized this pattern as a pyramid (though he used six elements rather than five). In the so-called Freytag pyramid, the exposition and complication lead up to a high point of tension—the crisis or climax—followed by the falling action and the catastrophe.

The Freytag Pyramid

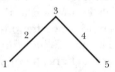

1. Exposition or Introduction
2. Complication and Development
3. Crisis or Climax
4. Falling Action
5. Dénouement, Resolution, or Catastrophe

This pyramidal pattern of organization can be observed to greater or lesser degrees throughout many plays. Some plays follow the pattern closely, but often there is uncertainty about when one phase of the structure ends and the next one begins. In addition, words defining some of the stages are variable. Even though students of drama agree about the meaning of the first two stages, the terms for the final three are not used with precision. With these reservations, the Freytag pyramid is valuable in the analysis of dramatic plot structure.

1. Exposition or introduction. In the first part of a drama, the dramatist introduces the play's background, characters, situations, and conflicts. Although exposition is occasionally presented through direct statements to the audience, the better method is to render it dramatically. Both major and minor characters thus perform the task of exposition through dramatic dialogue—describing situations, actions, and plans, and also explaining the traits and motives of other characters. In such a way, Sophocles in *Oedipus the King* provides expository material in the prologue featuring Oedipus, the Priest, and Creon; and Glaspell in *Trifles* presents exposition in the early conversations of the two farm women. In *Hamlet*, Horatio's explanations to Barnardo and Marcellus provide vital information about circumstances at the Danish court.

2. Complication and development. In this second stage, also called the **rising action,** we see the onset of difficulties that seem overwhelming and insoluble, as in both *Hamlet* and *Trifles*, where we learn in the exposition that a death has occurred before the play opens. Complication develops as the characters try to learn answers to some of the following perplexing questions: Was the death a murder? If so, who did it? How was it done? How can the murderer be identified? Is the murderer truly guilty? What should be done about the murder? What punishment should there be? In *A Midsummer Night's Dream*, less serious complications result from attempts to resolve issues like these: Can young lovers overcome parental opposition? Can a bumbling group of amateur actors successfully perform a play before the highest social group in the nation? Can a squabble among supernatural beings be brought to a peaceful conclusion?

3. Crisis or climax. The uncertainty and anxiety of the complication lead to the third stage, the crisis ("turning point") or climax ("high point"). In this third stage, all the converging circumstances compel the hero or heroine to recognize what needs to be done to resolve the play's major conflict. Another way of considering the crisis or climax is to define it as that point in the play when uncertainty ends and inevitability begins, as when Hamlet vows vengeance after drawing conclusions about the king's reaction to the player scene.

4. Falling action. The downward slope of the pyramid is the falling action, which contains complicating elements deferring the play's conclusion. In *Hamlet*, for example, a number of scenes make up the falling action: Hamlet's decision not to kill Claudius at prayer, Hamlet's departure for England, the gravediggers' scene and the conflicts at Ophelia's grave, and the murderous conspiracy of Claudius and Laertes. In *Oedipus the King*, Oedipus continues to seek confirming evidence about the death of his father, although by the end of Episode 3—the climax—he has all the information he needs to determine that he himself is the murderer.

5. Dénouement. The final stage is the **dénouement** ("unraveling") or **resolution** ("untying"), also called the **catastrophe** ("overturning"), in which all tragic protagonists undergo suffering or death, all mysteries are explained, all conflicts are resolved, all mistakes are corrected, all dastardly schemes are defeated, all long-lost children are identified, all obstacles to love are overcome, all deserving characters are rewarded, and the play ends. In short, the function of the dénouement is to end complications and conflicts, not to create new ones. It is important to observe that the word *catastrophe* for the final dramatic stage should not necessarily be construed in the sense of a calamity, even though most tragic catastrophes are calamitous. It is probably best, however, to use the words *dénouement* and *resolution* as general descriptions of a play's final stage and to reserve *catastrophe* for tragedies.

Of great significance is that the various points of the pyramid define an abstract model that is applicable to most plays—tragedy, comedy, and tragicomedy alike. Since the time of Shakespeare, however, most dramatists writing in English have been concerned less with dramatic *form* than with dramatic *effect*. As a result, many plays in English do not perfectly follow the pattern charted in the Freytag pyramid. You should therefore be prepared for plays that conceal or delay essential parts of the exposition; create a number of separate crises and climaxes; crowd the climax, falling action, and dénouement into a short space at the play's end; or modify the formal pattern in other significant ways.

DICTION, IMAGERY, STYLE, AND LANGUAGE.   What we learn about characters, relationships, and conflicts is conveyed in dramatic language. Through dialogue, and sometimes through soliloquy and aside, characters use language to reveal intimate details about their lives and their deepest thoughts—their loves, hatreds, plans, and hopes.

To bring such revelations before the audience, dramatists employ words that have wide-ranging connotations and that acquire many layers of meaning. Such is the case with the words *trifle* and *knot* in Glaspell's *Trifles*. Similarly, playwrights can have their characters speak in similes or metaphors that contribute significantly to the play's meaning and impact. Again in *Trifles*, the major (but offstage) character is compared to a bird, and this simile becomes one of the play's central symbols.

Dramatists also make sure that the words of their characters fit the circumstances, the time, and the place of the play. Thus, Miller's Willy Loman uses the language of modern America, and Shakespeare's Hamlet uses Elizabethan blank verse, almost academic prose, and "one-liner" remarks. In addition, dramatists employ accents, dialects, idiom, jargon, and clichés to indicate character traits. The gravediggers in *Hamlet* speak in a Renaissance English lower-class dialect that distinguishes them from the aristocratic characters in the play. Some of the characters in *The Glass Menagerie* speak in dialect, complete with slang expressions, that fits their southern locale.

TONE AND ATMOSPHERE.   Tone in drama, as in fiction and poetry, signifies the way moods and attitudes are created and presented. In plays, tone can be controlled through voice and stage gestures, such as rolling one's eyes, throwing up one's hands, holding one's forehead in despair, jumping for joy, and staggering in grief. Even silence can be an effective device for creating certain moods.

Whereas voice and movement establish mood on stage, we do not have these guides in reading. Nevertheless, there are guides to dramatic tone: Sometimes a playwright uses stage directions as an indication of tone, as Ibsen does in *A Dollhouse*, directing the inflections of a speaker's voice with the stage direction that she is shaking her head when speaking. Similarly, Hughes suggests the mood of one of his characters in *Mulatto* with the direction that he "runs" to his mother and hugs her "teasingly."

One of the most common methods playwrights employ to control the tone of the play is **dramatic irony.** This type of **situational** (as opposed to **verbal**) **irony** refers to circumstances in which characters have only a partial, incorrect, or misguided understanding of what is happening, while both readers and other characters understand the situation completely. Readers hence become concerned about the characters and hope that they will develop understanding quickly enough to avoid the problems bedeviling them and the threats endangering them. The classic example of dramatic irony occurs in Sophocles's *Oedipus the King:* As Oedipus condemns the murderer of his father, he also unwittingly condemns himself. Another example of dramatic irony occurs in Glaspell's *Trifles,* when the male characters mockingly dismiss the women's concerns by noting that "women are used to worrying about such trifles." The line acquires vast dramatic irony as we watch Mrs. Hale and Mrs. Peters achieve understanding through careful attention to the "trifles" that the men ignore.

SUBJECT AND THEME.   Most playwrights do not aim to propagandize their audience, but nevertheless they do embody ideas in their plays. The aspects of humanity a playwright explores constitute the play's **subject.** Plays can be *about* love, religion, hatred, war, ambition, death, envy, or anything else that is part of the human condition.

The ideas that the play dramatizes make up the play's **theme** or meaning. A play might explore the idea that love will always find a way or that marriage can be destructive, that pride always leads to disaster, or that grief can be conquered through strength and a commitment to life. Full, evening-long plays can contain many thematic strands. Ibsen creates such complexity in *A Dollhouse,* where he deals with themes of selfless devotion, egotism, pompousness, hypocrisy, betrayal, and women's self-determination. Even short plays can have complex themes, as in O'Neill's *Before Breakfast,* which explores the themes that anger can be stronger than love, that deceit is a consequence of alienation, and that despair and fear can conquer the normal wish to live.

Drama as Performance

As we read and talk about drama, we should always remind ourselves that plays are meant to be acted. It is **performance** that makes a play immediate, exciting, and powerful. The elements of performance are the *actors;* the *director* and the *producer;* the *stage; sets* or *scenery; lighting; costumes* and *makeup;* and the *audience.*

THE ACTORS.   Good actors have the training and experience to bring a play to life, exerting their intelligence, emotions, imaginations, voices, and bodies in their roles. Actors speak as they imagine the characters might speak—eagerly, calmly, excitedly, prayerfully, exultantly, sorrowfully, or angrily. When they respond, they respond as they imagine the characters might respond—with surprise, expectation, approval, happiness, irony, acceptance, rejection, resignation, or resolution. When they move about the stage according to patterns called **blocking,** they move as they imagine the characters might move—slowly, swiftly, smoothly, hesitatingly, furtively, stealthily, or clumsily, and gesturing broadly or subtly. Actors also frequently engage in **stage business**—gestures or movements that make the play dynamic, spontaneous, and often funny.

THE DIRECTOR AND THE PRODUCER.   In the theater, all aspects of performance are controlled by the **producer** and the **director.** The producer, the one with the money, is responsible for financing and arranging the production. Working closely with the producer is the director, who cooperates closely with the actors and guides them in speaking, responding, standing, and moving in ways that are consistent with his or her vision of the play. When a play calls for special effects (for example, the Ghost in *Hamlet*) both the producer and the director work with specialists such as musicians, choreographers, and sound and lighting technicians to enhance and enliven the performance.

THE STAGE.   Most modern theaters feature an interior **proscenium stage**—a picture-frame stage that is like a room with one wall missing so that the audience can look in on the action. In most proscenium stages, a large curtain representing that missing wall is usually opened and closed to indicate the beginning and ending of acts. Members of the audience seated directly before the stage are close to the action, but people seated at the sides, to the rear, behind a tall person, or in the balcony are to greater or lesser degrees removed from the vital and up-close involvement that is desirable in good theater. There is no question that such remoteness is a built-in disadvantage of many proscenium stages.

Modern theater designers have therefore experimented with stage designs inspired by theaters of the past. One notable success has been to revive the shape of the ancient Greek amphitheater (with seats rising from the stage in an expanding half-circle), a structure employed in theaters like the Tyrone Guthrie in Minneapolis and the Shakespeare Festival Theatre in Ashland, Oregon. Because seats for the audience ascend in semicircular tiers around three sides of the stage, most of the audience is closer to the action—and better able to see—than in a theater with a proscenium stage. The audience is also, therefore, more closely involved in the dramatic action.

Like many other modern theaters, these theaters feature a **thrust stage** or **apron stage** (like the **platform stage** used in the time of Shakespeare), which enlarges the proscenium stage with an acting area projecting into the audience by twenty or more feet. It is on this apron that a good deal of the acting occurs. Closely related to the apron stage is **theater-in-the-round,** a stage open on all sides like a boxing ring, surrounded by the audience. Productions for both types of stages are especially lively because the actors usually enter and leave through the same doorways and aisles used by the audience.

SETS OR SCENERY.   Most productions use **sets** (derived from the phrase "set scenes" i.e., fixed scenes) or **scenery** to establish the action in place and time, to underscore the ideas of the director, and to determine the level of reality of the production. Sets are constructed and decorated to indicate a specific place (a living room, a kitchen, a throne room, a forest, a graveyard) or a detached and indeterminate place with a specific atmosphere (an open plain, a heavenly or hellish location, a nightmarish future). When we first see the stage at the beginning of a performance, it is the scenery that we see, bringing the play to life through walls, windows, stairways, furniture, furnishings, and painted locations.

In most proscenium stages, the sets establish a permanent location or **scene** resembling a framed picture. All characters enter this setting, and they leave once they have achieved their immediate purpose. Such a fixed scene is established in *Oedipus the King*, which is set entirely in front of the royal palace of ancient Thebes, and in *Before Breakfast*, set in an apartment kitchen. Generally, one-act plays rely on a single setting and a short imagined time of action. Many full-length plays also confine the action to a single setting despite the longer imagined time during which the action takes place.

Because sets are often elaborate and costly, many producers use single-fixed-scene sets that are flexible and easily changed. Some productions employ a single, neutral set throughout the play and then mark scene changes with the physical introduction of movable **properties** (or **props**)—chairs, tables, beds, flower vases, trees, shovels, skulls, and so on. The use of props to mark separate scenes is a necessity in modern productions of plays that require constant scene changes, like *Hamlet*. Interestingly, many productions make scene changes an integral part of the drama by having costumed stagehands, or even the actors themselves, carry props on and off the stage. In a 1995 New York production of *Hamlet*, for example, Hamlet himself (actor Ralph Fiennes) carried in the chairs needed for the spectators of the player scene.

The constant changing of scenery is sometimes avoided by the use of a **unit set**—a series of platforms, rooms, stairs, and exits that form the locations for all the play's actions, as in *Death of a Salesman*. The movement of the characters from place to place within the unit set marks the shifting of scenes and the changing of topics.

Like characters, the setting can be realistic or nonrealistic. A **realistic setting,** sometimes called a **naturalistic setting,** requires extensive construction and properties, for the object is to create as lifelike a stage as possible. In *Trifles*, for example, the setting is a realistic copy of an early-twentieth-century midwestern farm kitchen. A **nonrealistic setting** is nonrepresentational and often symbolic. Sometimes a realistic play can be made suggestive and expressive through the use of a nonrealistic setting.

LIGHTING.   In ancient and medieval times, plays were performed in daylight, and hence no artificial light was required. With the advent of indoor theaters and evening performances, **lighting** became a necessity. At first, artificial illumination was provided by lanterns, candelabras, sconces, and torches (yes, some theaters burned down), and indirect lighting was achieved by reflectors and valances—all of which were used with great ingenuity and effect. Later, gaslight and limelight lamps replaced the earlier open flames.

The evolution of theater lighting reached its climax with the development of electric lights in the nineteenth century. Today, dramatic performances are enhanced by virtually all the technical features of our electronic age, including specialized lamps, color filters, spotlights, dimmers, and simulated fires. This dazzling technology, which employs hundreds or even thousands of lights of varying intensity in unlimited combination, is used to highlight individual characters, to isolate and emphasize various parts of the stage, to establish times, and generally to shape the moods of individual scenes. Lighting can also divide the stage or a unit set into different acting areas simply through the illumination of one section and the darkening of the rest, as in productions of plays like *The Glass Menagerie* and *Death of a Salesman*. The result is that lighting has become an integral element of set design, especially when the dramatist uses a *scrim* (a curtain that becomes transparent when illuminated from behind), which permits great variety in the portrayal of scenes and great rapidity in scene changes. In our day it is a rare stage indeed that does not contain an elaborate, computerized, and complicated (and expensive) lighting system.

COSTUMES AND MAKEUP.   Actors make plays vivid by wearing **costumes** and using **makeup,** which help the audience understand a play's time period together with the occupations, mental outlooks, and socioeconomic conditions of the characters. Costumes, which include not only dress but items such as jewelry, good-luck charms, swords, firearms, and canes, can be used realistically (farm women in plain clothes, a salesman in a business suit, a king in rich robes) or symbolically (a depressed character wearing black). Makeup usually enhances an actor's facial features, just as it can fix the illusion of youth or age or emphasize a character's joy or sorrow.

THE AUDIENCE.   To be complete, plays require an interaction of actors and **audience.** Drama enacts fictional or historical events as if they were happening in the present, and members of the audience—whether spectators or readers—are direct witnesses to the dramatic action from start to finish. The audience most definitely has a creative impact upon theatrical performances. Although audiences are made up of people who otherwise do not know each other, they have a common bond of interest in the play. Therefore, even though they are isolated by the darkness of the theater in which they sit, they create communal responses. Their reactions to the onstage action (e.g., laughter, gasps, applause) provide instant feedback to the actors and thus continually influence the delivery and pace of the performance. For this reason, drama *in the theater* is the most immediate and accessible of the literary arts. There is no intermediary between the audience and the stage action—no narrator, as in prose fiction, and no speaker, as in poetry.

TYPES OF DRAMA: TRAGEDY, COMEDY, AND OTHER FORMS

Today, people interested in drama have more options than at any other time in human history. There is professional live theater in many major cities, and touring theatrical troupes reach areas with smaller populations. Many cities and towns have amateur community theaters that put on plays regularly. Movie theaters and multiplexes are flourishing. Television of course has brought film versions of plays to the home screen, together with virtually infinite numbers of situation comedies ("sitcoms"), continuous narrative dramas (including soap operas), made-for-TV films, documentary dramas ("docudramas"), short skits on comedy shows, and many other types. All these different genres ultimately spring from the drama that was developed twenty-six hundred years ago in Athens, the leading ancient Greek city-state. Although the centuries have produced many variations, the types the Athenians created are still as important today as they were then. They are *tragedy* and *comedy*.[1]

The Development of Tragedy and Comedy in Ancient Greece

During the sixth century B.C.E., drama first arose from choral presentations the Athenians held during religious festivals celebrating Dionysus, the god of wine, conviviality, sexual vitality, ecstasy, and freedom. The choruses comprised young men who sang or chanted lengthy songs that the Athenians called **dithyrambs;** the choruses may also have performed dance movements during the presentations. The dithyrambs were not dramatizations but rather recitations, which became dramatic when a member of the chorus was designated to step forward and impersonate—act—one of the heroes. Soon, additional men from the choruses took acting roles, and the focus of the performances shifted from the choral group to individual actors: Greek tragedy as we know it had come into being. It was this pattern of drama that during the fifth century B.C.E. produced a golden age of tragedy. Most of the tragedies have been lost, and only a small number of plays by the three great Athenian dramatists—Aeschylus, Sophocles, and Euripides—have survived.

Not long after the emergence of tragedy, comedy became an additional feature of the festivals. Because the ancient Athenians encouraged free speech, at least for males, the comedy writers created a boisterous, lewd, and freely critical type of burlesque comedy that later critics called Old Comedy. The eleven

[1] Fuller discussions of tragedy and comedy are presented in Chapters 23 and 24.

surviving plays of Aristophanes represent this tradition. In the fourth century B.C.E., after Athenian power and freedom had declined because of the debilitating Peloponnesian Wars at the end of the fifth century, this type of comedy was replaced by Middle Comedy, a more social, discreet, and international drama; and then by New Comedy, a type of play featuring the development of situation, plot, and character. The best-known writer of New Comedy was Menander, whose plays were long thought to be totally lost; in the last hundred years, however, a number of fragments of his work have been discovered, including one play in its entirety.

Both of these Greek dramatic types have proved long-lasting. The introduction of subject matter about loss in the earliest tragedies has led to today's common understanding that tragedy dramatizes an individual's fall from a secure and elevated position to social or personal defeat. Likewise, what we usually consider typical comedies are directly linked to the pattern of ancient New Comedy: plays that dramatize the regeneration of individuals who begin in insecurity and end with their troubles over and happiness before them.

Tragedy and Comedy in Ancient Rome

The two Athenian dramatic forms were adopted by the Romans during the periods of the Republic (before 29 B.C.E.) and the Empire (after 29 B.C.E.). Although Republican Rome produced writers of note who created comedies (Plautus, ca. 254–184 B.C.E., and Terence, ca. 185–159 B.C.E.), the only significant playwright of imperial times was the tragedian Seneca (4 B.C.E.–65 C.E.), who wrote "closet dramas"—that is, plays designed to be read but not performed.

Medieval Religious Drama: A New Tradition

After the fall of the western Roman Empire in the fifth century C.E., organized drama was all but forgotten. When it reemerged it had little to do with the Greek and Roman dramatic tradition because it was a creation of the Christian church. Beginning in the eleventh and twelfth centuries, special short dramatizations were performed during Easter and Christmas masses. By the end of the thirteenth century, these religious spectacles had taken on an independent character and had also grown too long to be performed as part of normal services. Accordingly, they were moved outdoors and were performed during early summer or late spring as a part of the post-Easter celebrations of Corpus Christi Day. These religiously inspired plays, later called **Corpus Christi plays** or **mystery plays,** were collections or cycles of plays dramatizing biblical stories such as Adam and Eve, Cain and Abel, Noah, Abraham and Isaac, Herod, the Shepherds Abiding in the Field (of which *The Second Shepherds' Play* is an example), the Trial of Jesus, the Crucifixion, and the Resurrection. Later, another type of play developed—the **morality play,** which consisted almost literally of dramatized instructions for living a devout and holy life.

The Fusion of Ancient and Medieval Traditions in the Renaissance

In the sixteenth century, drama became liberated from its religious foundations and began rendering the twists and turns of more secular human conflicts. It was also at this time that the culture and drama of ancient Greece and Rome were rediscovered. Therefore, the performing tradition growing out of the medieval church was combined with the surviving ancient tragedies and comedies to create an entirely new drama that quickly reached its highest point in the plays of Shakespeare. In this way, tragedy and comedy, the forms originated by the Athenians, had a revival during the Renaissance in Europe.[2]

Other Types of Drama Since the Renaissance

Renaissance drama was by no means a copy of ancient forms, however, even though a number of sixteenth- and seventeenth-century playwrights, including Shakespeare, reworked many of the ancient plays. The plays of Renaissance England, and later the plays of the United States, offered mixtures of tragedy and comedy. For example, some of Shakespeare's comedies treat disturbing and potentially destructive topics, just as many of his tragedies include scenes that are farcical, witty, and ironic. When the patterns and emotions are truly mixed, the play is called a **tragicomedy,** a term first used by the Roman playwright Plautus. In many ways tragicomedy is the dominant form of twentieth-century drama.

Additional types of drama that evolved from tragedy and comedy include *farce, melodrama,* and *social drama.* The major purpose of **farce,** which was also a strong element in the Athenian Old Comedy, is to make audiences laugh. Typically, it is crammed full of extravagant dialogue, stage business, and slapstick, with exaggerated emotions and rapid extremes of action. The "mechanicals" in Shakespeare's *A Midsummer Night's Dream* offer us a good example of farce.

Resembling tragedy but stepping back from tragic outcomes is **melodrama,** a form in which most situations and characters are so exaggerated that they seem ridiculous. In its pure form, melodrama brings characters to the brink of ruin but saves them through the superhuman resources of a hero who always arrives just in time to pay the mortgage, save the business, and rescue

[2] The Renaissance revival of drama also transformed the theater into a business. Earlier drama had been a product of the church and religious life, but during the Renaissance, actors and theater people found that they could make a living in the theater. Although at first there was little money in acting and in writing plays, the theater managers were often able to do quite well. Shakespeare, for example, was a theater manager as well as a dramatist and minor actor. He earned enough from his shares in the Globe Theatre to retire in 1611 and leave London to spend his remaining days in his native Stratford-upon-Avon.

the heroine, while the grumbling villain flees the stage, muttering "Curses, foiled again!"

The nineteenth century saw the creation of a form of topical drama known as **social drama,** (sometimes called *problem drama*), a type that still exists as serious drama today. This type of play explores social problems and the individual's place in society. The plays can be tragic, comic, or mixed. Examples of social drama are Ibsen's *A Dollhouse,* Glaspell's *Trifles,* and Miller's *Death of a Salesman.*

Despite all these terms and types, keep in mind that classification is not the goal of reading or seeing plays. It is less important to identify the melodramatic elements in *Before Breakfast* or the farcical elements in *The Bear* than it is to understand and share the experiences and ideas that each play offers.

READING PLAYS

As we have noted, drama relies heavily on actors and directors to bring it to life. You might therefore ask why we bother to read plays without seeing them performed. The most obvious answer is that we may never get the chance actually to *see* a professional or amateur performance of a particular play, but we also read plays to familiarize ourselves with important literature. Plays are not simply maps to theatrical production; they are a significant and valuable part of our literary heritage. Dramas like *Oedipus the King, Hamlet, Death of a Salesman,* and *The Glass Menagerie* have become cultural touchstones. Finally, we read plays in order to have the time to study and understand them. Only through reading do we have the opportunity to look at the parts that make up the whole, and to determine how they fit together to create a moving and meaningful experience.

Reading a play, as opposed to watching a performance, carries both advantages and disadvantages. The major disadvantage is that we lack the immediacy of live theater. We do not see a majestic palace or a run-down living room, the rich robes of a king or the pathetic rags of a beggar, a vital and smiling young person or a tired and tearful old person. We do not hear the lovers flirting, the servants complaining, the soldiers boasting, the opponents threatening, the conspirators plotting, nor do we hear fanfares of trumpets or the sounds of a wedding procession or a funeral march.

The major advantage of reading is that we can consider each element in the play at length, and we can "stage" the play in our imaginations. In the theater, the action proceeds at the director's pace. There is no opportunity to turn back to an interesting scene or to reconsider an important speech. In addition, a performance always represents someone else's interpretation. The director and the actors have already made choices that emphasize certain avenues of exploration and cut off others. Reading a play lets us avoid these drawbacks—

provided that we read attentively and with understanding. We can read at our own tempo, turn back and reread a particular speech or scene, or explore those implications or ideas that strike us as interesting.

Try to use the advantages of reading and study to compensate for the disadvantages. You have time and freedom to read carefully, reflect deeply, and follow your thoughts. Rely on your experiences in watching theatrical productions, movies, and television to enhance your reading. Use your imagination. Stage the play as fully as you can in the theater of your mind. Become the director, set designer, lighting technician, costume designer, and all the actors. Build whatever mental sets you like, dress your actors as you see fit, and move the characters across the stage of your mind. Enjoy.

 ## PLAYS FOR STUDY

SUSAN GLASPELL, *TRIFLES*

Susan Glaspell, a writer of both plays and fiction, was a native of Iowa. She was educated at Drake University and the University of Chicago. In her thirties she moved to the northeast and became interested in theater. Along with her husband, George Cook, she was a founder and director of the Provincetown Players of Cape Cod in 1914. The organization encouraged lesser-known young dramatists and was often experimental, but nevertheless became successful enough to justify the opening of a second theater in New York. The first offerings of the theater were many one-act plays, featuring the earlier works of Glaspell herself, Eugene O'Neill, Edna Ferber, Edmund Wilson, and Edna St. Vincent Millay.

Glaspell wrote or coauthored over ten plays for the Provincetown Players, including *Suppressed Desires* (1914), *Close the Book* (1917), *Women's Honor* (1918), *Tickless Time* (1918), *Bernice* (1919, her first full-length play), *The Inheritors* (1921), and *The Verge* (1921). After 1922, however, she gave up the theater and turned almost exclusively to fiction. The exception was *Alison's House* (1930), a play loosely based on the life and family of Emily Dickinson, for which she won a Pulitzer Prize.

Glaspell deals with diverse topics in her drama, including misunderstood parentage, the effects of psychoanalysis, rejection of the machine age, the function and importance of honor, the tensions between political conservatives and liberals, and the onset of psychosis. Running through much of her work are strongly feminist ideas, based on a critique of the power—personal, social, and political—that men possess and that women are denied. Usually, Glaspell focuses on the negative and destructive effects that male-female relationships have on women, but she also stresses the ways in which women cope with their circumstances: To maintain character integrity and to preserve their domestic strength, women are forced into roles that are characterized not by direct but by indirect action.

Trifles, Glaspell's best-known drama, displays these characteristics. She wrote it in ten days for the Provincetown Players, who produced the play in 1916. Its inspiration was a murder trial she had covered while working as a reporter for a Des Moines newspaper before moving to the northeast. In 1917 she refashioned the material for the short story "A Jury of Her Peers," with which *Trifles* can be compared (see p. 166). Although Glaspell preserves a considerable amount of dramatic dialogue in the story, the additions and changes she makes are indicative of the differences between drama and fiction.

Trifles concerns a murder investigation, but the play is not a mystery. Soon after the characters enter and go about their business, the two women characters begin to uncover the circumstances that reveal the killer and the nature of the crime. Once the facts are established, however, the action focuses on the significant details of motive. Indeed, the heart of the play consists of the contrasting ways in which the men and the women attempt to uncover and understand the motive. The men—the county attorney and the sheriff—look for signs of violent rage, and they move onstage and offstage throughout the house in their search. The women—Mrs. Hale and Mrs. Peters—stay onstage and draw their conclusions from the ordinary, everyday details of a farm woman's kitchen. It is finally the women, not the men, who realize the true power that comes from understanding. Their realization—as well as their strength—leads them to their final decisions about how to judge the killer and treat the evidence.

The language that Glaspell gives to her characters is in keeping with the plain and simple lives the characters lead: simple, specific, and unadorned. Of the two groups, the women are more direct in the expression of their ideas. Once they realize the gravity of the situation they are exploring, however, they become indirect, but only because they fear to speak the words that describe the truths they have discovered. By contrast, the men usually talk convivially and smugly about the crime and their own roles in life, patronizingly among themselves about the women, and almost scornfully to the women about womanly concerns.

SUSAN GLASPELL (1882–1948)

Trifles _____ *1916*

CAST OF CHARACTERS

George Henderson, *county attorney*
Henry Peters, *sheriff*
Lewis Hale, *a neighboring farmer*
Mrs. Peters
Mrs. Hale

SCENE. *The kitchen in the now abandoned farmhouse of* JOHN WRIGHT, *a gloomy kitchen, and left without having been put in order—unwashed pans under the sink, a loaf of bread outside the bread-box, a dish-towel on the table—other signs of incompleted work. At the rear the outer door opens and the* SHERIFF *comes in followed by the* COUNTY ATTORNEY *and* HALE. *The* SHERIFF *and* HALE *are men in middle life, the* COUNTY ATTORNEY *is a young man; all are much bundled up and go at once to the stove. They are followed by the two women—the* SHERIFF'S *wife first; she is a slight wiry woman, a thin nervous face.* MRS. HALE *is larger and would ordinarily be called more comfortable looking, but she is disturbed now and looks fearfully about as she enters. The women have come in slowly, and stand close together near the door.*

COUNTY ATTORNEY. [*Rubbing his hands.*] This feels good. Come up to the fire, ladies.

MRS. PETERS. [*After taking a step forward.*] I'm not—cold.

SHERIFF. [*Unbuttoning his overcoat and stepping away from the stove as if to mark the beginning of official business.*] Now, Mr. Hale, before we move things about, you explain to Mr. Henderson just what you saw when you came here yesterday morning.

COUNTY ATTORNEY. By the way, has anything been moved? Are things just as you left them yesterday?

SHERIFF. [*Looking about.*] It's just the same. When it dropped below zero last night   5
I thought I'd better send Frank out this morning to make a fire for us—no use getting pneumonia with a big case on, but I told him not to touch anything except the stove— and you know Frank.

COUNTY ATTORNEY. Somebody should have been left here yesterday.

SHERIFF. Oh—yesterday. When I had to send Frank to Morris Center for that man who went crazy—I want you to know I had my hands full yesterday. I knew you could get back from Omaha by today and as long as I went over everything here myself—

COUNTY ATTORNEY. Well, Mr. Hale, tell just what happened when you came here yesterday morning.

HALE. Harry and I had started to town with a load of potatoes. We came along the road from my place and as I got here I said, "I'm going to see if I can't get John Wright to go in with me on a party telephone." I spoke to Wright about it once before and he put me off, saying folks talked too much anyway, and all he asked was peace and quiet—I guess you know about how much he talked himself; but I thought maybe if I went to the house and talked about it before his wife, though I said to Harry that I didn't know as what his wife wanted made much difference to John—

COUNTY ATTORNEY.   Let's talk about that later, Mr. Hale. I do want to talk about   10
that, but tell now just what happened when you got to the house.

HALE.   I didn't hear or see anything; I knocked at the door, and still it was all
quiet inside. I knew they must be up, it was past eight o'clock. So I knocked again, and I
thought I heard somebody say, "Come in." I wasn't sure, I'm not sure yet, but I opened
the door—this door [*Indicating the door by which the two women are still standing.*] and there
in that rocker—[*Pointing to it.*] sat Mrs. Wright.

[*They all look at the rocker.*]

COUNTY ATTORNEY.   What—was she doing?

HALE.   She was rockin' back and forth. She had her apron in her hand and was
kind of—pleating it.

COUNTY ATTORNEY.   And how did she—look?

HALE.   Well, she looked queer.   15

COUNTY ATTORNEY.   How do you mean—queer?

HALE.   Well, as if she didn't know what she was going to do next. And kind of
done up.

COUNTY ATTORNEY.   How did she seem to feel about your coming?

HALE.   Why, I don't think she minded—one way or other. She didn't pay much
attention. I said, "How do, Mrs. Wright, it's cold, ain't it?" And she said, "Is it?"—and
went on kind of pleating at her apron. Well, I was surprised; she didn't ask me to come
up to the stove, or to set down, but just sat there, not even looking at me, so I said, "I
want to see John." And then she—laughed. I guess you would call it a laugh. I thought of
Harry and the team outside, so I said a little sharp: "Can't I see John?" "No," she says,
kind o' dull like. "Ain't he home?" says I. "Yes," says she, "he's home." "Then why can't I
see him?" I asked her, out of patience. "'Cause he's dead," says she. "*Dead?*" says I. She
just nodded her head, not getting a bit excited, but rockin' back and forth. "Why—
where is he?" says I, not knowing what to say. She just pointed upstairs—like that.
[*Himself pointing to the room above.*] I got up, with the idea of going up there. I walked
from there to here—then I says, "Why, what did he die of?" "He died of a rope round his
neck," says she, and just went on pleatin' at her apron. Well, I went out and called Harry.
I thought I might—need help. We went upstairs and there he was lyin'—

COUNTY ATTORNEY.   I think I'd rather have you go into that upstairs, where you   20
can point it all out. Just go on now with the rest of the story.

HALE.   Well, my first thought was to get that rope off. It looked . . . [*Stops, his face
twitches.*] . . . but Harry, he went up to him, and he said, "No, he's dead all right, and
we'd better not touch anything." So we went back downstairs. She was still sitting that
same way. "Has anybody been notified?" I asked. "No," says she, unconcerned. "Who
did this, Mrs. Wright?" said Harry. He said it businesslike—and she stopped pleatin' of
her apron. "I don't know," she says. "You don't *know?*" says Harry. "No," says she.
"Weren't you sleepin' in the bed with him?" says Harry. "Yes," says she, "but I was on the
inside." "Somebody slipped a rope round his neck and strangled him and you didn't
wake up?" says Harry. "I didn't wake up," she said after him. We must 'a looked as if we
didn't see how that could be, for after a minute she said, "I sleep sound." Harry was
going to ask her more questions but I said maybe we ought to let her tell her story first to
the coroner, or the sheriff, so Harry went fast as he could to Rivers' place, where there's
a telephone.

COUNTY ATTORNEY.   And what did Mrs. Wright do when she knew that you had
gone for the coroner?

HALE.   She moved from that chair to this one over here [*Pointing to a small chair in the corner.*] and just sat there with her hands held together and looking down. I got a feeling that I ought to make some conversation, so I said I had come in to see if John wanted to put in a telephone, and at that she started to laugh, and then she stopped and looked at me—scared. [*The COUNTY ATTORNEY, who has had his notebook out, makes a note.*] I dunno, maybe it wasn't scared. I wouldn't like to say it was. Soon Harry got back, and then Dr. Lloyd came, and you, Mr. Peters, and so I guess that's all I know that you don't.

COUNTY ATTORNEY.   [*Looking around.*] I guess we'll go upstairs first—and then out to the barn and around there. [*To the SHERIFF.*] You're convinced that there was nothing important here—nothing that would point to any motive.

SHERIFF.   Nothing here but kitchen things.   25

[*The COUNTY ATTORNEY, after again looking around the kitchen, opens the door of a cupboard closet. He gets up on a chair and looks on a shelf. Pulls his hand away, sticky.*]

COUNTY ATTORNEY.   Here's a nice mess.

[*The women draw nearer.*]

MRS. PETERS.   [*To the other woman.*] Oh, her fruit; it did freeze. [*To the LAWYER.*] She worried about that when it turned so cold. She said the fire'd go out and her jars would break.

SHERIFF.   Well, can you beat the women! Held for murder and worryin' about her preserves.

COUNTY ATTORNEY.   I guess before we're through she may have something more serious than preserves to worry about.

HALE.   Well, women are used to worrying over trifles.   30

[*The two women move a little closer together.*]

COUNTY ATTORNEY.   [*With the gallantry of a young politician.*] And yet, for all their worries, what would we do without the ladies? [*The women do not unbend. He goes to the sink, takes a dipperful of water from the pail and pouring it into a basin, washes his hands. Starts to wipe them on the roller-towel, turns it for a cleaner place.*] Dirty towels! [*Kicks his foot against the pans under the sink.*] Not much of a housekeeper, would you say, ladies?

MRS. HALE.   [*Stiffly.*] There's a great deal of work to be done on a farm.

COUNTY ATTORNEY.   To be sure. And yet [*With a little bow to her.*] I know there are some Dickson county farmhouses which do not have such roller towels.

[*He gives it a pull to expose its full length again.*]

MRS. HALE.   Those towels get dirty awful quick. Men's hands aren't always as clean as they might be.

COUNTY ATTORNEY.   Ah, loyal to your sex, I see. But you and Mrs. Wright were   35
neighbors. I suppose you were friends, too.

MRS. HALE.   [*Shaking her head.*] I've not seen much of her of late years. I've not been in this house—it's more than a year.

COUNTY ATTORNEY.   And why was that? You didn't like her?

MRS. HALE.   I liked her all well enough. Farmers' wives have their hands full, Mr. Henderson. And then—

COUNTY ATTORNEY.   Yes—?

MRS. HALE.   [*Looking about.*] It never seemed a very cheerful place.   40

COUNTY ATTORNEY.   No—it's not cheerful. I shouldn't say she had the homemaking instinct.

MRS. HALE.   Well, I don't know as Wright had, either.

COUNTY ATTORNEY.   You mean that they didn't get on very well?

MRS. HALE.   No, I don't mean anything. But I don't think a place'd be any cheerfuller for John Wright's being in it.

COUNTY ATTORNEY.   I'd like to talk more of that a little later. I want to get the lay   45
of things upstairs now.

[*He goes to the left, where three steps lead to a stair door.*]

SHERIFF.   I suppose anything Mrs. Peters does'll be all right. She was to take in some clothes for her, you know, and a few little things. We left in such a hurry yesterday.

COUNTY ATTORNEY.   Yes, but I would like to see what you take, Mrs. Peters, and keep an eye out for anything that might be of use to us.

MRS. PETERS.   Yes, Mr. Henderson.

[*The women listen to the men's steps on the stairs, then look about the kitchen.*]

MRS. HALE.   I'd hate to have men coming into my kitchen, snooping around and criticising.

[*She arranges the pans under the sink which the* LAWYER *had shoved out of place.*]

MRS. PETERS.   Of course it's no more than their duty.   50

MRS. HALE.   Duty's all right, but I guess that deputy sheriff that came out to make the fire might have got a little of this on. [*Gives the roller towel a pull.*] Wish I'd thought of that sooner. Seems mean to talk about her for not having things slicked up when she had to come away in such a hurry.

MRS. PETERS.   [*Who had gone to a small table in the left rear corner of the room, and lifted one end of a towel that covers a pan.*] She had bread set.

[*Stands still.*]

MRS. HALE.   [*Eyes fixed on a loaf of bread beside the breadbox, which is on a low shelf at the other side of the room. Moves slowly toward it.*] She was going to put this in there. [*Picks up loaf, then abruptly drops it. In a manner of returning to familiar things.*] It's a shame about her fruit. I wonder if it's all gone. [*Gets up on the chair and looks.*] I think there's some here that's all right, Mrs. Peters. Yes—here; [*Holding it toward the window.*] this is cherries, too. [*Looking again.*] I declare I believe that's the only one. [*Gets down, bottle in her hand. Goes to the sink and wipes it off on the outside.*] She'll feel awful bad after all her hard work in the hot weather. I remember the afternoon I put up my cherries last summer.

[*She puts the bottle on the big kitchen table, center of the room. With a sigh, is about to sit down in the rocking-chair. Before she is seated realizes what chair it is; with a slow look at it, steps back. The chair which she has touched rocks back and forth.*]

MRS. PETERS.   Well, I must get those things from the front room closet. [*She goes to the door at the right, but after looking into the other room, steps back.*] You coming with me, Mrs. Hale? You could help me carry them.

[*They go in the other room; reappear,* MRS. PETERS *carrying a dress and skirt,* MRS. HALE *following with a pair of shoes.*]

MRS. PETERS.   My, it's cold in there.   55

[*She puts the clothes on the big table and hurries to the stove.*]

MRS. HALE.   [*Examining the skirt.*] Wright was close. I think maybe that's why she kept so much to herself. She didn't even belong to the Ladies Aid. I suppose she felt she couldn't do her part, and then you don't enjoy things when you feel shabby. She used to wear pretty clothes and be lively, when she was Minnie Foster, one of the town girls singing in the choir. But that—oh, that was thirty years ago. This all you was to take in?

MRS. PETERS.   She said she wanted an apron. Funny thing to want, for there isn't much to get you dirty in jail, goodness knows. But I suppose just to make her feel more natural. She said they was in the top drawer in this cupboard. Yes, here. And then her little shawl that always hung behind the door. [*Opens stair door and looks.*] Yes, here it is.

[*Quickly shuts door leading upstairs.*]

MRS. HALE.   [*Abruptly moving toward her.*] Mrs. Peters?
MRS. PETERS.   Yes, Mrs. Hale?
MRS. HALE.   Do you think she did it?   60
MRS. PETERS.   [*In a frightened voice.*] Oh, I don't know.
MRS. HALE.   Well, I don't think she did. Asking for an apron and her little shawl. Worrying about her fruit.
MRS. PETERS.   [*Starts to speak, glances up, where footsteps are heard in the room above. In a low voice.*] Mr. Peters says it looks bad for her. Mr. Henderson is awful sarcastic in a speech and he'll make fun of her sayin' she didn't wake up.
MRS. HALE.   Well, I guess John Wright didn't wake when they was slipping that rope under his neck.
MRS. PETERS.   No, it's strange. It must have been done awful crafty and still. They   65
say it was such a—funny way to kill a man, rigging it all up like that.
MRS. HALE.   That's just what Mr. Hale said. There was a gun in the house. He says that's what he can't understand.
MRS. PETERS.   Mr. Henderson said coming out that what was needed for the case was a motive; something to show anger, or—sudden feeling.
MRS. HALE.   [*Who is standing by the table.*] Well, I don't see any signs of anger around here. [*She puts her hand on the dish towel which lies on the table, stands looking down at table, one half of which is clean, the other half messy.*] It's wiped to here. [*Makes a move as if to finish work, then turns and looks at loaf of bread outside the breadbox. Drops towel. In that voice of coming back to familiar things.*] Wonder how they are finding things upstairs. I hope she had it a little more red-up° up there. You know, it seems kind of *sneaking*. Locking her up in town and then coming out here and trying to get her own house to turn against her!
MRS. PETERS.   But Mrs. Hale, the law is the law.
MRS. HALE.   I s'pose 'tis. [*Unbuttoning her coat.*] Better loosen up your things, Mrs.   70
Peters. You won't feel them when you go out.

[*MRS. PETERS takes off her fur tippet,° goes to hang it on hook at back of room, stands looking at the under part of the small corner table.*]

---

red-up: neat, arranged in order.   *tippet:* scarf-like garment of fur or wool for the neck and shoulders.

MRS. PETERS.   She was piecing a quilt.

[*She brings the large sewing basket and they look at the bright pieces.*]

MRS. HALE.   It's log cabin pattern. Pretty, isn't it? I wonder if she was goin' to quilt it or just knot it?

[*Footsteps have been heard coming down the stairs. The* SHERIFF *enters followed by* HALE *and the* COUNTY ATTORNEY.]

SHERIFF.   They wonder if she was going to quilt it or just knot it!

[*The men laugh; the women look abashed.*]

COUNTY ATTORNEY.   [*Rubbing his hands over the stove.*] Frank's fire didn't do much up there, did it? Well, let's go out to the barn and get that cleared up.

[*The men go outside.*]

MRS. HALE.   [*Resentfully.*] I don't know as there's anything so strange, our takin'   75
up our time with little things while we're waiting for them to get the evidence. [*She sits down at the big table smoothing out a block with decision.*] I don't see as it's anything to laugh about.

MRS. PETERS.   [*Apologetically.*] Of course they've got awful important things on their minds.

[*Pulls up a chair and joins* MRS. HALE *at the table.*]

MRS. HALE.   [*Examining another block.*] Mrs. Peters, look at this one. Here, this is the one she was working on, and look at the sewing! All the rest of it has been so nice and even. And look at this! It's all over the place! Why, it looks as if she didn't know what she was about!

[*After she has said this they look at each other, then start to glance back at the door. After an instant* MRS. HALE *has pulled at a knot and ripped the sewing.*]

MRS. PETERS.   Oh, what are you doing, Mrs. Hale?

MRS. HALE.   [*Mildly.*] Just pulling out a stitch or two that's not sewed very good. [*Threading a needle.*] Bad sewing always made me fidgety.

MRS. PETERS.   [*Nervously.*] I don't think we ought to touch things.   80

MRS. HALE.   I'll just finish up this end. [*Suddenly stopping and leaning forward.*] Mrs. Peters?

MRS. PETERS.   Yes, Mrs. Hale?

MRS. HALE.   What do you suppose she was so nervous about?

MRS. PETERS.   Oh—I don't know. I don't know as she was nervous. I sometimes sew awful queer when I'm just tired. [*MRS. HALE starts to say something, looks at* MRS. PETERS, *then goes on sewing.*] Well I must get these things wrapped up. They may be through sooner than we think. [*Putting apron and other things together.*] I wonder where I can find a piece of paper, and string.

MRS. HALE.   In that cupboard, maybe.   85

MRS. PETERS.   [*Looking in cupboard.*] Why, here's a bird-cage. [*Holds it up.*] Did she have a bird, Mrs. Hale?

MRS. HALE.   Why, I don't know whether she did or not—I've not been here for so long. There was a man around last year selling canaries cheap, but I don't know as she took one; maybe she did. She used to sing real pretty herself.

MRS. PETERS.   [*Glancing around.*] Seems funny to think of a bird here. But she must have had one, or why would she have a cage? I wonder what happened to it?

MRS. HALE.   I s'pose maybe the cat got it.

MRS. PETERS.   No, she didn't have a cat. She's got that feeling some people have   90
about cats—being afraid of them. My cat got in her room and she was real upset and asked me to take it out.

MRS. HALE.   My sister Bessie was like that. Queer, ain't it?

MRS. PETERS.   [*Examining the cage.*] Why, look at this door. It's broke. One hinge is pulled apart.

MRS. HALE.   [*Looking too.*] Looks as if someone must have been rough with it.

MRS. PETERS.   Why, yes.

[*She brings the cage forward and puts it on the table.*]

MRS. HALE.   I wish if they're going to find any evidence they'd be about it. I don't   95
like this place.

MRS. PETERS.   But I'm awful glad you came with me, Mrs. Hale. It would be lonesome for me sitting here alone.

MRS. HALE.   It would, wouldn't it? [*Dropping her sewing.*] But I tell you what I do wish, Mrs. Peters. I wish I had come over sometimes when *she* was here. I—[*Looking around the room.*]—wish I had.

MRS. PETERS.   But of course you were awful busy, Mrs. Hale—your house and your children.

MRS. HALE.   I could've come. I stayed away because it weren't cheerful—and that's why I ought to have come. I—I've never liked this place. Maybe because it's down in a hollow and you don't see the road. I dunno what it is, but it's a lonesome place and always was. I wish I had come over to see Minnie Foster sometimes. I can see now—

[*Shakes her head.*]

MRS. PETERS.   Well, you mustn't reproach yourself, Mrs. Hale. Somehow we just   100
don't see how it is with other folks until—something comes up.

MRS. HALE.   Not having children makes less work—but it makes a quiet house, and Wright out to work all day, and no company when he did come in. Did you know John Wright, Mrs. Peters?

MRS. PETERS.   Not to know him; I've seen him in town. They say he was a good man.

MRS. HALE.   Yes—good; he didn't drink, and kept his word as well as most, I guess, and paid his debts. But he was a hard man, Mrs. Peters. Just to pass the time of day with him—[*Shivers.*] Like a raw wind that gets to the bone. [*Pauses, her eye falling on the cage.*] I should think she would 'a wanted a bird. But what do you suppose went with it?

MRS. PETERS.   I don't know, unless it got sick and died.

[*She reaches over and swings the broken door, swings it again, both women watch it.*]

MRS. HALE.   You weren't raised round here, were you? [*MRS. PETERS shakes her   105
head.*] You didn't know—her?

MRS. PETERS.   Not till they brought her yesterday.

MRS. HALE.   She—come to think of it, she was kind of like a bird herself—real sweet and pretty, but kind of timid and—fluttery. How—she—did—change. [*Silence; then as if struck by a happy thought and relieved to get back to everyday things.*] Tell you what, Mrs. Peters, why don't you take the quilt in with you? It might take up her mind.

MRS. PETERS.   Why, I think that's a real nice idea, Mrs. Hale. There couldn't possibly be any objection to it, could there? Now, just what would I take? I wonder if her patches are in here—and her things.

[*They look in the sewing basket.*]

MRS. HALE.   Here's some red. I expect this has got sewing things in it. [*Brings out a fancy box.*] What a pretty box. Looks like something somebody would give you. Maybe her scissors are in here. [*Opens box. Suddenly puts her hand to her nose.*] Why— [*MRS. PETERS bends nearer, then turns her face away.*] There's something wrapped up in this piece of silk.

MRS. PETERS.   Why, this isn't her scissors.   110

MRS. HALE.   [*Lifting the silk.*] Oh, Mrs. Peters—it's—

[*MRS. PETERS bends closer.*]

MRS. PETERS.   It's the bird.

MRS. HALE.   [*Jumping up.*] But, Mrs. Peters—look at it! Its neck! Look at its neck! It's all—other side *to*.

MRS. PETERS.   Somebody—wrung—its—neck.

[*Their eyes meet. A look of growing comprehension, of horror. Steps are heard outside. MRS. HALE slips box under quilt pieces, and sinks into her chair. Enter SHERIFF and COUNTY ATTORNEY. MRS. PETERS rises.*]

COUNTY ATTORNEY.   [*As one turning from serious things to little pleasantries.*] Well,   115
ladies, have you decided whether she was going to quilt it or knot it?

MRS. PETERS.   We think she was going to—knot it.

COUNTY ATTORNEY.   Well, that's interesting, I'm sure. [*Seeing the bird-cage.*] Has the bird flown?

MRS. HALE.   [*Putting more quilt pieces over the box.*] We think the—cat got it.

COUNTY ATTORNEY.   [*Preoccupied.*] Is there a cat?

[*MRS. HALE glances in a quick covert way at MRS. PETERS.*]

MRS. PETERS.   Well, not *now*. They're superstitious, you know. They leave.   120

COUNTY ATTORNEY.   [*To SHERIFF PETERS, continuing an interrupted conversation.*] No sign at all of anyone having come from the outside. Their own rope. Now let's go up again and go over it piece by piece. [*They start upstairs.*] It would have to have been someone who knew just the—

[*MRS. PETERS sits down. The two women sit there not looking at one another, but as if peering into something and at the same time holding back. When they talk now it is in the manner of feeling their way over strange ground, as if afraid of what they are saying, but as if they cannot help saying it.*]

MRS. HALE.   She liked the bird. She was going to bury it in that pretty box.

MRS. PETERS.   [*In a whisper.*] When I was a girl—my kitten—there was a boy took a hatchet, and before my eyes—and before I could get there—[*Covers her face an instant.*] If they hadn't held me back I would have—[*Catches herself, looks upstairs where steps are heard, falters weakly.*]—hurt him.

MRS. HALE.   [*With a slow look around her.*] I wonder how it would seem never to have had any children around. [*Pause.*] No, Wright wouldn't like the bird—a thing that sang. She used to sing. He killed that, too.

MRS. PETERS. [*Moving uneasily.*] We don't know who killed the bird. 125

MRS. HALE. I knew John Wright.

MRS. PETERS. It was an awful thing was done in this house that night, Mrs. Hale. Killing a man while he slept, slipping a rope around his neck that choked the life out of him.

MRS. HALE. His neck. Choked the life out of him.

[*Her hand goes out and rests on the bird-cage.*]

MRS. PETERS. [*With rising voice.*] We don't know who killed him. We don't know.

MRS. HALE. [*Her own feeling not interrupted.*] If there'd been years and 130 years of nothing, then a bird to sing to you, it would be awful—still, after the bird was still.

MRS. PETERS. [*Something within her speaking.*] I know what stillness is. When we homesteaded in Dakota, and my first baby died—after he was two years old, and me with no other then—

MRS. HALE. [*Moving.*] How soon do you suppose they'll be through, looking for the evidence?

MRS. PETERS. I know what stillness is. [*Pulling herself back.*] The law has got to punish crime, Mrs. Hale.

MRS. HALE. [*Not as if answering that.*] I wish you'd seen Minnie Foster when she wore a white dress with blue ribbons and stood up there in the choir and sang. [*A look around the room.*] Oh, I *wish* I'd come over here once in a while! That was a crime! That was a crime! Who's going to punish that?

MRS. PETERS. [*Looking upstairs.*] We mustn't—take on. 135

MRS. HALE. I might have known she needed help! I know how things can be— for women. I tell you, it's queer, Mrs. Peters. We live close together and we live far apart. We all go through the same things—it's all just a different kind of the same thing. [*Brushes her eyes, noticing the bottle of fruit, reaches out for it.*] If I was you I wouldn't tell her her fruit was gone. Tell her it *ain't.* Tell her it's all right. Take this in to prove it to her. She—she may never know whether it was broke or not.

MRS. PETERS. [*Takes the bottle, looks about for something to wrap it in; takes petticoat from the clothes brought from the other room, very nervously begins winding this around the bottle. In a false voice.*] My, it's a good thing the men couldn't hear us. Wouldn't they just laugh! Getting all stirred up over a little thing like a—dead canary. As if that could have anything to do with—with—wouldn't they *laugh!*

[*The men are heard coming down stairs.*]

MRS. HALE. [*Under her breath.*] Maybe they would—maybe they wouldn't.

COUNTY ATTORNEY. No, Peters, it's all perfectly clear except a reason for doing it. But you know juries when it comes to women. If there was some definite thing. Something to show—something to make a story about—a thing that would connect up with this strange way of doing it—

[*The women's eyes meet for an instant. Enter HALE from outer door.*]

HALE. Well, I've got the team° around. Pretty cold out there. 140

---

team: team of horses drawing a wagon or sleigh.

COUNTY ATTORNEY.   I'm going to stay here a while by myself. [*To the* SHERIFF.] You can send Frank out for me, can't you? I want to go over everything. I'm not satisfied that we can't do better.

SHERIFF.   Do you want to see what Mrs. Peters is going to take in?

[*The* COUNTY ATTORNEY *goes to the table, picks up the apron, laughs.*]

COUNTY ATTORNEY.   Oh, I guess they're not very dangerous things the ladies have picked out. [*Moves a few things about, disturbing the quilt pieces which cover the box. Steps back.*] No, Mrs. Peters doesn't need supervising. For that matter, a sheriff's wife is married to the law. Ever think of it that way, Mrs. Peters?

MRS. PETERS.   Not—just that way.

SHERIFF.   [*Chuckling.*] Married to the law. [*Moves toward the other room.*] I just want   145
you to come in here a minute, George. We ought to take a look at these windows.

COUNTY ATTORNEY.   [*Scoffingly.*] Oh, windows!

SHERIFF.   We'll be right out, Mr. Hale.

[HALE *goes outside. The* SHERIFF *follows the* COUNTY ATTORNEY *into the other room. Then* MRS. HALE *rises, hands tight together, looking intensely at* MRS. PETERS, *whose eyes make a slow turn, finally meeting* MRS. HALE'S. *A moment* MRS. HALE *holds her, then her own eyes point the way to where the box is concealed. Suddenly* MRS. PETERS *throws back quilt pieces and tries to put the box in the bag she is wearing. It is too big. She opens box, starts to take bird out, cannot touch it, goes to pieces, stands there helpless. Sound of a knob turning in the other room.* MRS. HALE *snatches the box and puts it in the pocket of her big coat. Enter* COUNTY ATTORNEY *and* SHERIFF.]

COUNTY ATTORNEY.   [*Facetiously.*] Well, Henry, at least we found out that she was not going to quilt it. She was going to—what is it you call it, ladies?

MRS. HALE.   [*Her hand against her pocket.*] We call it—knot it, Mr. Henderson.

CURTAIN

QUESTIONS

1.   How does the first entrance of the characters establish a distinction between the men and women in the play? What is suggested by the different reactions of the men and women to the frozen preserves?

2.   What does Mr. Hale report to the County Attorney in his extended narrative? How observant is he? How accurate?

3.   What is needed for a strong legal case against Minnie? What does the Sheriff conclude about the kitchen? What do his conclusions tell you about the men?

4.   What are the women's conclusions about the bad sewing? What does Mrs. Hale do about it? At this point, what might she be thinking about the murder?

5.   Of what importance are Mrs. Hale's descriptions (a) of Minnie as a young woman and (b) of the Wrights' marriage?

6.   What do the women deduce from the broken birdcage and the dead bird? How are these symbolic, and what do they symbolize?

7.   How did Minnie Wright murder her husband? What hints lead you to this solution? What information permits the women to make the right inferences about the crime and the method of strangulation?

8. What does Mrs. Hale do with the "trifles" of evidence? Why? How is her reaction to the evidence different from that of Mrs. Peters? What conflict develops between these women? How is it resolved?

9. Why does Mrs. Hale feel guilty about her relationship with Minnie Wright? To what degree does her guilt shape her decisions and actions?

GENERAL QUESTIONS

1. To what does the title of this play refer? How does this irony of the word *trifles* help shape the play's meaning?

2. What are the men like? Are they round characters or flat? How observant are they? What is their attitude toward their jobs? Toward their own importance? Toward the women and "kitchen things"?

3. What is Mrs. Hale like? How observant is she? What is her attitude toward the men and their work, and toward herself?

4. Some critics argue that Minnie is the play's most important character, even though she never appears onstage. Do you agree? Why do you think Glaspell did not make Minnie a speaking character?

5. How is symbolism employed to establish and underscore the play's meaning? Consider especially the birdcage, the dead bird, and the repeated assertion that Mrs. Wright was going to "knot" (tie) rather than "quilt" (sew) the quilt.

LANGSTON HUGHES, *MULATTO*

James Mercer Langston Hughes was born in Missouri in 1902 and reared in Kansas and Ohio. After living for a year in Mexico he attended Columbia University, but he left after one year. He received a B.A. from Lincoln University in Pennsylvania in 1929, and when he came to New York he soon became one of the leading figures in the Harlem Renaissance, an energetic burst of African-American literary creativity that also included Countée Cullen and Claude McKay (see pp. 753 and 780). Over the next forty-five years, Hughes was to write in every major literary genre, including  translations, regular columns for a weekly newspaper, and reports on the Spanish Civil War. His earliest works were poems that he published in the *Crisis*, the official journal of the National Association for the Advancement of Colored People. Eventually he published fourteen books of poems and two novels, together with a number of short-story collections and many plays and texts for musical plays.

The Great Depression, which began with the New York stock market crash in 1929, destroyed the economic underpinnings of the Harlem Renaissance. It was during the Depression that Hughes became radicalized. After visiting Haiti and Cuba he attacked what he considered American imperialist interventions in those countries. He then spent a year in Soviet Russia, assisting in the preparation of a film on American race relations. When he returned he published his first collection of stories, *The Ways of White Folks* (1934), in which he fictionalized his disaffection with the condition of both southern and northern African-Americans. One of the stories included in this collection was "Father and Son," a version of the material that he turned into the two-act play *Mulatto*, which was produced at the Vanderbilt Theater in New York in October 1935. The play had a run of 373 performances, the record at that time for a Broadway play by an African-American dramatist.

At that time, the growing African-American theater was dominated by two major themes, the first being the customs and problems of southern blacks. The most pressing problem was of course the cruelty and injustice of lynching. Angelina Weld Grimké's *Rachel* (1920) and James Miller's *Never No More* (1932) openly condemned the practice. Dennis Donaghue's *Legal Murder* (1934) was an attack on the false conviction for rape of nine young black men from Scottsboro, Alabama, a topic that Hughes also treated in his early drama *Scottsboro Limited: Four Poems and a Play in Verse* (1932). The second major theme concerned the adjustments that blacks needed to make after they left the south and migrated to cities in the north. Frank Wilson's *Meek Mose* was perhaps the most optimistic of these plays, in which dispossessed blacks discover oil on their new property. More typical were Garland Anderson's *Appearances* (1925), about how a black bellhop overcomes false charges of rape, and Wallace Thurman's *Harlem* (1929), about the difficulties of a black family living in Chicago. This theme also dominates Lorraine Hansberry's *A Raisin in the Sun* (1959), the classic drama that marked the coming of age of post-World War II African-American playwrights.

Although Langston Hughes is not thought of principally as a dramatist, he wrote plays throughout his career. In addition to the plays already mentioned, he wrote *Little Ham* (1936) and *Soul Gone Home* (1937), a short fantasy play. As the first production for the radical Suitcase Theater, which he founded after returning as a correspondent from the Spanish Civil War, he wrote *Don't You Want to Be Free* (1938). He collaborated with Arna Bontemps in *When the Jack Hollers* (1936) and with Zora Neale Hurston in *Mule Bone* (reissued in 1991). In 1948 he wrote the lyrics for the Kurt Weill and Elmer Rice musical *Street Scene*, perhaps the best-known of the plays in which he was involved. In 1951 he produced a libretto, *Just Around the Corner*, and in 1957 he wrote *Simply Heavenly*, a blues-musical play featuring the character Jesse Semple, whom he had created as a character in his weekly columns for the *Chicago Defender*. Although *Simply Heavenly* (which is a musical version of an earlier play, *Simple Takes a Wife*) concludes optimistically, one can find within it the serious theme of frustration resulting from the difficulties that African-Americans experience in seeking identity and recognition. Semple says, at one point:

I'm broke, busted, and disgusted. And just spent mighty near my last nickel for a paper—and there ain't no news in it about colored folks. Unless we commit murder, robbery or rape, or are being chased by a mob, do we get on the front page, or hardly on the back. (Act I, scene 5)

Hughes's interests in the last decades of his life were in the musical theater, particularly the introduction of gospel-related music and jazz. Three of his major efforts were *Black Nativity* (1961), *The Gospel Glory* (1962), and *Jericho-Jim Crow* (1964). His output as a dramatist was indeed great, even if it is overshadowed by his preeminence as a poet and fiction writer.

Hughes's *Mulatto* is one of his plays dealing with life in the south during the 1930s, a time when the system of white control over blacks was absolute and uncompromisingly harsh. Hughes's first conception of the play, as one dealing with "father and son," is a perennial one. Colonel Tom Norwood and Robert Lewis, his mulatto son, recognize their relationship but also hate and reject each other. In *Mulatto* the realistic cause of conflict is the "color line"—the symbolic line that people must cross in order to accept each other as human beings. This is an ideal goal, just as it is also an insurmountable obstacle, in the society that the play depicts. The lack of ability or will to cross the line governs the pattern of action and also the violent outcome. Colonel Norwood has lived in the same house with Cora Lewis for many years, and they do well together as long as he is not confronted with the issues of his paternity and his control over the plantation. There is no way he can recognize the four "yard blacks" on his plantation as his legitimate children, however, unless he is willing to forsake his identity as a white.

There are many other marks of dramatic realism, particularly the exploitation of black women (described in Act I, speech 61), the front entrance of the Norwood house, Robert's complaints about Miss Gray, and his speeding with the Ford. All of Robert's so-called "uppity" actions would not be unacceptable to white society if he were white, but because he is black they indicate a state of revolt. In addition, Robert's identity as half white, half black—he is called "yellow" by Colonel Tom—leaves him in an anomalous position, for he is not "white" enough to be equal or "black" enough to be subservient. The reality of his situation leads him to hate both whites and blacks alike, and the sudden eruption of his seething anger leads to his uncontrolled violence.

It is important to note that *Mulatto* reflects the reality of language in the south of the 1930s. Hughes's blacks, except for Robert and Sallie, use southern black vernacular (called "darky talk" by Hughes). The introduction of such speech in literature was controversial at the time. Many black intellectuals who had also been a part of the Harlem Renaissance believed that dialect should be shunned, on the principle that it reinforced negative African-American stereotypes. However, Hughes believed that using the vernacular was above all truthful and realistic, enabling writers to demonstrate that blacks are not stereotypes, that they face human problems just like everyone else, and that they succeed and fail just like everyone else. Moreover, there were precedents for the realistic use of dialect that had been set by Mark Twain in *Tom Sawyer* and *Huckleberry Finn*, both of which were acknowledged classics of American literature.

Mulatto is one of Hughes's most important plays. In 1950 he refashioned it as a libretto, titled *The Barrier*, that was set to music by the composer Jan Meyerowitz. In addition, the play was translated into Spanish and published in South America in 1954.

LANGSTON HUGHES   (1902–1967)

Mulatto _____ *1935*

CHARACTERS

> Colonel Thomas Norwood. *Plantation owner, a still vigorous man of about sixty, nervous, refined, quick-tempered, and commanding; a widower who is the father of four living mulatto children by his Negro housekeeper.*
>
> Cora Lewis. *A brown woman in her forties who has kept the house and been the mistress of Colonel Norwood for some thirty years.*
>
> William Lewis. *The oldest son of Cora Lewis and the Colonel; a fat, easy-going, soft looking mulatto of twenty-eight; married.*
>
> Sallie Lewis. *The seventeen-year-old daughter, very light with sandy hair and freckles, who could pass for white.*
>
> Robert Lewis [Bert]. *Eighteen, the youngest boy; strong and well-built; a light mulatto with ivory-yellow skin and proud thin features like his father's; as tall as the Colonel, with the same gray-blue eyes, but with curly black hair instead of brown; of a fiery, impetuous temper—immature and willful—resenting his blood and the circumstances of his birth.*
>
> Fred Higgins. *A close friend of Colonel Norwood; a county politician; fat and elderly, conventionally Southern.*
>
> Sam. *An old Negro retainer, a personal servant of the Colonel.*
>
> Billy. *The small son of William Lewis; a chubby brown kid about five.*
>
> Talbot. *The overseer.*
>
> Mose. *An elderly Negro, chauffeur for Mr. Higgins.*
>
> A Storekeeper.
>
> An Undertaker.
>
> Undertaker's Helper. *Voice offstage only.*
>
> The Mob.

ACT I

> TIME.   *An afternoon in early fall.*
>
> THE SETTING.   *The living room of the Big House on a plantation in Georgia. Rear center of the room, a vestibule with double doors leading to the porch; at each side of the doors, a large window with lace curtains and green shades; at left a broad flight of stairs leading to the second floor; near the stairs, downstage, a doorway leading to the dining room and kitchen; opposite at right of stage, a door to the library. The room is furnished in the long outdated horsehair and*

walnut style of the nineties; a crystal chandelier, a large old-fashioned rug, a marble-topped table, upholstered chairs. At the right there is a small cabinet. It is a very clean, but somewhat shabby and rather depressing room, dominated by a large oil painting of NORWOOD's *wife of his youth on the center wall. The windows are raised. The afternoon sunlight streams in.*

ACTION.   *As the curtain rises, the stage is empty. The door at the right opens and* COLONEL NORWOOD *enters, crossing the stage toward the stairs, his watch in his hand. Looking up, he shouts:*

NORWOOD.   Cora! Oh Cora!

CORA.   [*Heard above*] Yes, sir, Colonel Tom.

NORWOOD.   I want to know if that child of yours means to leave here this afternoon?

CORA.   [*At head of steps now*] Yes, sir, she's goin' directly. I's gettin' her ready now, packin' up an' all. 'Course, she wants to tell you goodbye 'fore she leaves.

NORWOOD.   Well, send her down here. Who's going to drive her to the railroad?   5
The train leaves at three—and it's after two now. You ought to know you can't drive ten miles in no time.

CORA.   [*Above*] Her brother's gonna drive her. Bert. He ought to be back here most any time now with the Ford.

NORWOOD.   [*Stopping on his way back to the library*] Ought to be *back* here? Where's he gone?

CORA.   [*Coming downstairs nervously*] Why, he driv in town 'fore noon, Colonel Tom. Said he were lookin' for some tubes or somethin' 'nother by de mornin' mail for de radio he's been riggin' up out in de shed.

NORWOOD.   Who gave him permission to be driving off in the middle of the morning? I bought that Ford to be used when I gave orders for it to be used, not . . .

CORA. Yes, sir, Colonel Tom, but . . .   10

NORWOOD.   But what? [*Pausing. Then deliberately*] Cora, if you want that hard-headed yellow son of yours to get along around here, he'd better listen to me. He's no more than any other black buck on this plantation—due to work like the rest of 'em. I don't take such a performance from nobody under me—driving off in the middle of the day to town, after I've told him to bend his back in that cotton. How's Talbot going to keep the rest of those darkies working right if that boy's allowed to set that kind of an example? Just because Bert's your son, and I've been damn fool enough to send him off to school for five or six years, he thinks he has a right to privileges, acting as if he owned this place since he's been back here this summer.

CORA.   But, Colonel Tom . . .

NORWOOD.   Yes, I know what you're going to say. I don't give a damn about him! There's no nigger-child of mine, yours, ours—no darkie—going to disobey me. I put him in that field to work, and he'll stay on this plantation till I get ready to let him go. I'll tell Talbot to use the whip on him, too, if he needs it. If it hadn't been that he's yours, he'd-a had a taste of it the other day. Talbot's a damn good overseer, and no saucy, lazy Nigras stay on this plantation and get away with it. [*To* CORA] Go on back upstairs and see about getting Sallie out of here. Another word from you and I won't send your [*Sarcastically*] pretty little half-white daughter anywhere, either. Schools for darkies! Huh! If you take that boy of yours for an example, they do 'em more harm than good. He's learned nothing in college but impudence, and he'll stay here on this place and work for me awhile before he gets back to any more schools. [*He starts across the room.*]

CORA.   Yes, sir, Colonel Tom. [*Hesitating*] But he's just young, sir. And he was mighty broke up when you said last week he couldn't go back to de campus. [COLONEL

NORWOOD *turns and looks at* CORA *commandingly. Understanding, she murmurs*] Yes, sir. [*She starts upstairs, but turns back.*] Can't I run and fix you a cool drink, Colonel Tom?

NORWOOD.   No, damn you! Sam'll do it.   15

CORA.   [*Sweetly*] Go set down in de cool, then, Colonel. 'Taint good for you to be going' on this way in de heat. I'll talk to Robert maself soon's he comes in. He don't mean nothing—just smart and young and kinder careless, Colonel Tom, like ma mother said you used to be when you was eighteen.

NORWOOD.   Get on upstairs, Cora. Do I have to speak again? Get on! [*He pulls the cord of the servants' bell.*]

CORA.   [*On the steps*] Does you still be in the mind to tell Sallie good-bye?

NORWOOD.   Send her down here as I told you. [*Impatiently*] Where's Sam? Send him here first. [*Fuming*] Looks like he takes his time to answer that bell. You colored folks are running the house to suit yourself nowadays.

CORA.   [*Coming downstairs again and going toward door under the steps*] I'll get Sam   20
for you.

[CORA *exits left.* NORWOOD *paces nervously across the floor. Goes to the window and looks out down the road. Takes a cigar from his pocket, sits in a chair with it unlighted, scowling. Rises, goes toward servants' bell and rings it again violently as* SAM *enters, out of breath.*]

NORWOOD.   What the hell kind of a tortoise race is this? I suppose you were out in the sun somewhere sleeping?

SAM.   No, sah, Colonel Norwood. Just tryin' to get Miss Sallie's valises down to de yard so's we can put 'em in de Ford, sah.

NORWOOD.   [*Out of patience*] Huh! Darkies waiting on darkies! I can't get service in my own house. Very well. [*Loudly*] Bring me some whiskey and soda, and ice in a glass. Is that damn Frigidaire working right? Or is Livonia still too thickheaded to know how to run it? Any ice cubes in the thing?

SAM.   Yes, sah, Colonel, yes, sah. [*Backing toward door left*] 'Scuse me, please sah, but [*as* NORWOOD *turns toward library*] Cora say for me to ask you is it all right to bring that big old trunk what you give Sallie down by de front steps. We ain't been able to tote it down them narrer little back steps, sah. Cora, say, can we bring it down de front way through here?

NORWOOD.   No other way? [SAM *shakes his head*] Then pack it on through the back,   25
quick. Don't let me catch you carrying any of Sallie's baggage out of that front door here. You-all'll be wanting to go in and out the front way next. [*Turning away, complaining to himself*] Darkies have been getting mighty fresh in this part of the country since the war. The damn Germans should've . . . [*To* SAM] Don't take that trunk out that front door.

SAM.   [*Evilly, in a cunning voice*] I's seen Robert usin' de front door—when you ain't here, and he comes up from de cabin to see his mammy. [SALLIE, *the daughter, appears at the top of the stairs, but hesitates about coming down.*]

NORWOOD.   Oh, you have, have you? Let me catch him and I'll break his young neck for him. [*Yelling at* SAM] Didn't I tell you some whiskey and soda an hour ago?

[SAM *exits left.* SALLIE *comes shyly down the stairs and approaches her father. She is dressed in a little country-style coat-suit ready for traveling. Her features are Negroid, although her skin is very fair.* COLONEL NORWOOD *gazes down at her without saying a word as she comes meekly toward him, half-frightened.*]

SALLIE.   I just wanted to tell you goodbye, Colonel Norwood, and thank you for letting me go back to school another year, and for letting me work here in the house all summer where mama is. [*NORWOOD says nothing. The girl continues in a strained voice as if making a speech*] You mighty nice to us colored folks certainly, and mama says you the best white man in Georgia. [*Still NORWOOD says nothing. The girl continues.*] You been mighty nice to your—I mean to us colored children, letting my sister and me go off to school. The principal says I'm doing pretty well and next year I can go to Normal and learn to be a teacher. [*Raising her eyes*] You reckon I can, Colonel Tom?

NORWOOD.   Stand up straight and let me see how you look. [*Backing away*] Humm-m-m! Getting kinder grown, ain't you? Do they teach you in that school to have good manners, and not be afraid of work, *and to respect white folks?*

SALLIE.   Yes, sir, I been taking up cooking and sewing, too.   30

NORWOOD.   Well, that's good. As I recall it, that school turned your sister out a right smart cook. Cora tells me she's got a good job in some big hotel in Chicago. I'm thinking about you going on up North there with her in a year or two. You're getting too old to be around here, and too womanish. [*He puts his hands on her arms as if feeling her flesh*]

SALLIE.   [*Drawing back slightly*] But I want to live down here with mama. I want to teach school in that there empty school house by the Cross Roads what hasn't had a teacher for five years.

[*SAM has been standing with the door cracked, overhearing the conversation. He enters with the drink and places it on the table, right. NORWOOD sits down, leaving the girl standing, as SAM pours out a drink.*]

NORWOOD.   Don't get that into your head, now. There's been no teacher there for years—and there won't be any teacher there, either. Cotton teaches these pickaninnies enough around here. Some of 'em's too smart as it is. The only reason I did have a teacher there once was to get you young ones o' Cora's educated. I gave you all a chance and I hope you appreciate it. [*He takes a long drink.*] Don't know why I did it. No other white man in these parts ever did it, as I know of. [*To SAM*] Get out of here! [*SAM exits left*] Guess I couldn't stand to see Cora's kids working around here dumb as the rest of these no good darkies—need a dozen of 'em to chop one row of cotton, or to keep a house clean. Or maybe I didn't want Talbot eyeing you gals. [*Taking another drink*] Anyhow, I'm glad you and Bertha turned out right well. Yes, hum-m-m! [*Straightening up*] You know I tried to do something for those brothers of yours, too, but William's stupid as an ox—good for work, though—and that Robert's just an impudent, hardheaded, yellow young fool. I'm gonna break his damn neck for him if he don't watch out. Or else put Talbot on him.

SALLIE.   [*Suddenly frightened*] Please, sir, don't put the overseer on Bert, Colonel Tom. He was the smartest boy at school, Bert was. On the football team, too. Please, sir, Colonel Tom. Let brother work here in the house, or somewhere else where Talbot can't mistreat him. He ain't used . . .

NORWOOD.   [*Rising*] Telling me what to do, heh? [*Staring at her sternly*] I'll use   35 the back of my hand across your face if you don't hush. [*He takes another drink. The noise of a Ford is heard outside.*] That's Bert now, I reckon. He's to take you to the railroad line, and while you're riding with him, you better put some sense into his head. And tell him I want to see him as soon as he gets back here. [*CORA enters left with a bundle and an umbrella. SAM and WILLIAM come downstairs with a big square trunk, and exit hurriedly, left.*]

SALLIE.   Yes, sir, I'll tell him.

CORA.   Colonel Tom, Sallie ain't got much time now. [*To the girl*] Come on, chile. Bert's here. Yo' big brother and Sam and Livonia and everybody's all waiting at de back door to say goodbye. And your baggage is being packed in. [*Noise of another car is heard outside.*] Who else is that there coming up de drive? [*CORA looks out the window.*] Mr. Higgins' car, Colonel Tom. Reckon he's coming to see you . . . Hurry up out o' this front room, Sallie. Here, take these things of your'n [*Hands her the bundle and parasol*] while I opens de door for Mr. Higgins. [*In a whisper*] Hurry up, chile! Get out! [*NORWOOD turns toward the front door as CORA goes to open it*]

SALLIE.   [*Shyly to her father*] Goodbye, Colonel Tom.

NORWOOD.   [*His eyes on the front door, scarcely noticing the departing SALLIE, he motions.*] Yes, yes goodbye! Get on now! [*CORA opens the front door as her daughter exits left.*] Well, well! Howdy do, Fred. Come in, come in! [*CORA holds the outer door of the vestibule wide as FRED HIGGINS enters with rheumatic dignity, supported on the arm of his chauffeur, MOSE, a very black Negro in a slouchy uniform. CORA closes the door and exits left hurriedly, following SALLIE.*]

NORWOOD.   [*Smiling*] How's the rheumatiz today? Women or licker or heat   40
must've made it worse—from the looks of your speed!

HIGGINS   [*Testily, sitting down puffing and blowing in a big chair*] I'm in no mood for fooling, Tom, not now. [*To MOSE*] All right. [*The CHAUFFEUR exits front. HIGGINS continues angrily.*] Norwood, that damned yellow nigger buck of yours that drives that new Ford tried his best just now to push my car off the road, then got in front of me and blew dust in my face for the last mile coming down to your gate, trying to beat me in here—which he did. Such a deliberate piece of impudence I don't know if I've ever seen out of a nigger before in all the sixty years I've lived in this country. [*The noise of the Ford is heard going out the drive, and the cries of the NEGROES shouting farewells to SALLIE. HIGGINS listens indignantly.*] What kind of crazy coons have you got on your place, anyhow? Sounds like a black Baptist picnic to me. [*Pointing to the window with his cane*] Tom, listen to that.

NORWOOD.   [*Flushing*] I apologize to you, Fred, for each and every one of my darkies. [*SAM enters with more ice and another glass.*] Permit me to offer you a drink. I realize I've got to tighten down here.

HIGGINS.   Mose tells me that was Cora's boy in that Ford—and that young black fool is what I was coming here to talk to you about today. That boy! He's not gonna be around here long—not the way he's acting. The white folks in town'll see to that. Knowing he's one of your yard niggers, Norwood, I thought I ought to come and tell you. The white folks at the Junction aren't intending to put up with him much longer. And I don't know what good the jail would do him once he got in there.

NORWOOD.   [*Tensely*] What do you mean, Fred—jail? Don't I always take care of the folks on my plantation without any help from the Junction's police force? Talbot can do more with an unruly black buck than your marshal.

HIGGINS.   Warn't lookin' at it that way, Tom. I was thinking how weak the doors   45
to that jail is. They've broke 'em down and lynched four niggers to my memory since it's been built. After what happened this morning, you better keep that yellow young fool out o' town from now on. It might not be safe for him around there—today, or no other time.

NORWOOD.   What the hell? [*Perturbed*] He went in just now to take his sister to the depot. Damn it, I hope no ruffians'll break up my new Ford. What was it, Fred, about this morning?

HIGGINS.   You haven't heard? Why, it's all over town already. He sassed out Miss Gray in the post office over a box of radio tubes that come by mail.

NORWOOD.   He did, heh?

HIGGINS.   Seems like the stuff was sent C.O.D. and got here all smashed up, so he wouldn't take it. Paid his money first before he saw the box was broke. Then wanted the money order back. Seems like the post office can't give money orders back—rule against it. Your nigger started to argue, and the girl at the window—Miss Gray—got scared and yelled for some of the mail clerks. They threw Bert out of the office that's all. But that's enough. Lucky nothing more didn't happen. [*Indignantly*] That Bert needs a damn good beating—talking back to a white woman—and I'd like to give it to him myself, the way he kicked the dust up in my eyes all the way down the road coming out here. He was mad, I reckon. That's one yellow buck don't know his place, Tom, and it's your fault he don't—sending 'em off to be educated.

NORWOOD.   Well, by God, I'll show him. I wish I'd have known it before he left   50
here just now.

HIGGINS.   Well, he's sure got mighty aggravating ways for a buck his color to have. Drives down the main street and don't stop for nobody, white or black. Comes in my store and if he ain't waited on as quick as the white folks are, he walks out and tells the clerk his money's as good as a white man's any day. Said last week standing out on my store front that he wasn't *all* nigger no how; said his name was Norwood—not Lewis, like the rest of his family—and part of your plantation here would be his when you passed out—and all that kind of stuff, boasting to the walleyed coons listening to him.

NORWOOD.   [*Astounded*] Well, I'll be damned!

HIGGINS.   Now, Tom, you know that don't go 'round these parts 'o Georgia, nor nowhere else in the South. A darkie's got to keep in his place down here. Ruinous to other niggers hearing that talk, too. All this postwar propaganda on the radio about freedom and democracy—why the niggers think it's meant for them! And that Eleanor Roosevelt,° she ought to been muzzled. She's driving our niggers crazy—your boy included! Crazy! Talking about civil rights. Ain't been no race trouble in our country for three years—since the Deekin's lynching—but I'm telling you, Norwood, you better see that that buck of yours goes away from here. I'm speaking on the quiet, but I can see ahead. And what happened this morning about them radio tubes wasn't none too good.

NORWOOD.   [*Beside himself with rage*] A black ape! I——I . . .

HIGGINS.   You been too decent to your darkies, Norwood. That's what's the   55
matter with you. And then the whole country suffers from a lot of impudent bucks who take lessons from your crowd. Folks been kicking about that, too. Guess you know it. Maybe that's the reason you didn't get that nomination for committeeman a few years back.

NORWOOD.   Maybe 'tis, Higgins. [*Rising and pacing the room*] God damn niggers! [*Furiously*] Everything turns on niggers, niggers, niggers! No wonder Yankees call this the Black Belt! [*He pours a large drink of whiskey.*]

HIGGINS.   [*Soothingly*] Well, let's change the subject. Hand me my glass, there, too.

NORWOOD.   Pardon me, Fred. [*He puts ice in his friend's glass and passes him the bottle.*]

HIGGINS.   Tom, you get excited too easy for warm weather . . . Don't ever show black folks they got you going, though. I think sometimes that's where you make your mistake. Keep calm, keep calm—and then you command. Best plantation manager I ever had never raised his voice to a nigger—and they were scared to death of him.

---

53 *Eleanor Roosevelt:* Eleanor Roosevelt [1884–1962], the wife of President Franklin D. Roosevelt, was an outspoken champion of minority causes.

NORWOOD.   Have a smoke. [*Pushes cigars toward HIGGINS*]   60

HIGGINS.   You ought've married again, Tom—brought a white woman out here on this damn place o' yours. A woman could help you run things. Women have soft ways, but they can keep things humming. Nothing but blacks in the house—a man gets soft like niggers are inside. [*Puffing at cigar*] And living with a colored woman! Of course, I know we all have 'em—I didn't know you could make use of a white girl till I was past twenty. Thought too much o' white women for that—but I've given many a yellow gal a baby in my time. [*Long puff at cigar*] But for a man's own house you need a wife, not a black woman.

NORWOOD.   Reckon you're right, Fred, but it's too late to marry again now. [*Shrugging his shoulders*] Let's get off of darkies and women for awhile. How's crops? [*Sitting down*] How's politics going?

HIGGINS.   Well, I guess you know the Republicans is trying to stir up trouble for us in Washington. I wish the South had more men like Bilbo and Rankin° there. But, say, by the way, Lawyer Hotchkiss wants to see us both about that budget money next week. He's got some real Canadian stuff at his office, in his filing case, too—brought back from his vacation last summer. Taste better'n this old mountain juice we get around here. Not meaning to insult your drinks, Tom, but just remarking. I serve the same as you myself, label and all.

NORWOOD.   [*Laughing*] I'll have you know, sir, that this is prewar licker, sir!

HIGGINS.   Hum-m-m! Well, it's got me feelin' better'n I did when I come in   65
here—whatever it is. [*Puffs at his cigar*] Say, how's your cotton this year?

NORWOOD.   Doin' right well, specially down in the south field. Why not drive out that road when you leave and take a look at it? I'll ride down with you. I want to see Talbot, anyhow.

HIGGINS.   Well, let's be starting. I got to be back at the Junction by four o'clock. Promised to let that boy of mine have the car to drive over to Thomasville for a dance tonight.

NORWOOD.   One more shot before we go. [*He pours out drinks.*] The young ones must have their fling, I reckon. When you and I grew up down here it used to be a carriage and the best pair of black horses when you took the ladies out—now it's an automobile. That's a good lookin' new car of yours, too.

HIGGINS.   Right nice.

NORWOOD.   Been thinking about getting a new one myself, but money's been   70
kinder tight this year, and conditions are none too good yet, either. Reckon that's why everybody's so restless. [*He walks toward stairs calling.*] Cora! Oh, Cora! . . . If I didn't have a few thousand put away, I'd feel the pinch myself. [*As CORA appears on the stairs.*] Bring me my glasses up there by the side of my bed . . . Better whistle for Mose, hadn't I, Higgins? He's probably 'round back with some of his women. [*Winking*] You know I got some nice black women in this yard.

HIGGINS.   Oh, no, not Mose. I got my servants trained to stay in their places— right where I want 'em—while they're working for me. Just open the door and tell him to come in here and help me out. [*NORWOOD goes to the door and calls the CHAUFFEUR. MOSE enters and assists his master out to the car. CORA appears with the glasses, goes to the vestibule and gets the COLONEL'S hat and cane which she hands him.*]

63 *Bilbo, Rankin:* Theodore Bilbo [1877–1947], senator from Mississippi from 1935 to 1947, and John Eliot Rankin [1882–1960], Mississippi Representative to the House from 1921 to 1953, were both noted advocates of white supremacy.

NORWOOD.   [*To* CORA] I want to see that boy o' yours soon as I get back. That won't be long, either. And tell him to put up that Ford of mine and don't touch it again.

CORA.   Yes, sir, I'll have him waiting here. [*In a whisper*] It's hot weather, Colonel Tom. Too much of this licker makes your heart upset. It ain't good for you, you know. [NORWOOD *pays her no attention as he exits toward the car. The noise of the departing motor is heard. Cora begins to tidy up the room. She takes a glass from a side table. She picks up a doily that was beneath the glass and looks at it long and lovingly. Suddenly she goes to the door left and calls toward the kitchen.*] William, you William! Com'ere, I want to show you something. Make haste, son. [*As* CORA *goes back toward the table, her eldest son,* WILLIAM *enters carrying a five-year-old boy.*] Look here at this purty doily yo' sister made this summer while she been here. She done learned all about sewing and making purty things at school. Ain't it nice, son?

WILLIAM.   Sho' is. Sallie takes after you, I reckon. She's a smart little crittur, ma. [*Sighs*] De Lawd knows, I was dumb at school. [*To his child*] Get down, Billy, you's too heavy. [*He puts the boy on the floor*] This here sewin's really fine.

BILLY.   [*Running toward the big upholstered chair and jumping up and down on the spring seat*] Gityap! I's a mule driver. Haw! Gee!   75

CORA.   You Billy, get out of that chair 'fore I skins you alive. Get on into de kitchen, sah.

BILLY.   I'm playin' horsie, grandma. [*Jumps up in the chair*] Horsie! Horsie!

CORA.   Get! That's de Colonel's favorite chair. If he knows any little darkie's been jumpin' on it, he raise sand. Get on, now.

BILLY.   Ole Colonel's ma grandpa, ain't he? Ain' he ma white grandpa?

WILLIAM.   [*Snatching the child out of the chair*] Boy, I'm gonna fan your hide if you   80
don't hush!

CORA.   Shs-ss-s! You Billy, hush yo' mouth! Chile, where you hear that? [*To her son*] Some o' you all been talking too much in front o' this chile. [*To the boy*] Honey, go on in de kitchen till yo' daddy come. Get a cookie from 'Vonia and set down on de back porch. [*Little* BILLY *exits left*]

WILLIAM.   Ma, you know it 'twarn't me told him. Bert's the one been goin' all over de plantation since he come back from Atlanta remindin' folks right out we's Colonel Norwood's chilluns.

CORA.   [*Catching her breath*] Huh!

WILLIAM.   He comes down to my shack tellin' Billy and Marybell they got a white man for grandpa. He's gonna get my chilluns in trouble sho'—like he got himself in trouble when Colonel Tom whipped him.

CORA.   Ten or 'leven years ago, warn't it?   85

WILLIAM.   And Bert's *sho'* in trouble now. Can't go back to that college like he could-a if he'd-a had any sense. You can't fool with white folks—an de Colonel ain't never really liked Bert since that there first time he beat him, either.

CORA.   No, he ain't. Leastwise, he ain't understood him. [*Musing sadly in a low voice*] Time Bert was 'bout seven, warn't it? Just a little bigger'n yo' Billy.

WILLIAM.   Yes.

CORA.   Went runnin' up to Colonel Tom out in de horse stables when de Colonel was showin' off his horses—I 'members so well—to fine white company from town. Lawd, that boy's always been foolish! He went runnin' up and grabbed a-holt de Colonel and yelled right in front o' de white folks' faces, "O, papa, Cora say de dinner's ready, papa!" Ain't never called him papa before, and I don't know where he got it from. And Colonel Tom knocked him right backwards under de horse's feet.

WILLIAM.   And when de company were gone, he beat that boy unmerciful.   90

CORA.   I thought sho' he were gonna kill ma chile that day. And he were mad at me, too, for months. Said I was teaching you chilluns who they pappy were. Up till then Bert had been his favorite little colored child round here.

WILLIAM.   Sho' had.

CORA.   But he never like him no more. That's why he sent him off to school so soon to stay, winter and summer, all these years. I had to beg and plead to have him home this summer—but I's sorry now I ever got that boy back here again.

WILLIAM.   He's sho' growed more like de Colonel all de time, ain't he? Bert thinks he's a real white man hisself now. Look at de first thing he did when he come home, he ain't seen de Colonel in six years—and Bert sticks out his hand fo' to shake hands with him!

CORA.   Lawd! That chile!   95

WILLIAM.   Just like white folks! And de Colonel turns his back and walks off. Can't blame him. He ain't used to such doings from colored folks. God knows what's got into Bert since he come back. He's acting like a fool—just like he was a boss man round here. Won't even say "Yes, sir" and "No, sir" no more to de white folks. Talbot asked him warn't he gonna work in de field this mornin'. Bert say "No!" and turn and walk away. White man so mad, I could see him nearly foam at de mouth. If he warn't yo' chile, ma, he'd been knocked in de head fo' now.

CORA.   You's right.

WILLIAM.   And you can't talk to him. I tried to tell him something the other day, but he just laughed at me, and said we's all just scared niggers on this plantation. Says he ain't no nigger, no how. He's a Norwood. He's half-white, and he's gonna act like it. [*In amazement at his brother's daring*] And this is Georgia, too!

CORA.   I's scared to death for de boy, William. I don't know what to do. De Colonel says he won't send him off to school no mo'. Says he's mo' sassy and impudent now than any nigger he ever seed. Bert never has been like you was, and de girls, quiet and sensible like you knowed you had to be. [*She sits down*] De Colonel say he's gonna make Bert stay here now and work on this plantation like de rest of his niggers. He's gonna show him what color he is. Like that time when he beat him for callin' him "papa." He say he's gwine to teach him his place and make de boy know where he belongs. Seems like me or you can't show him. Colonel Tom has to take him in hand, or these white folks'll kill him around here and then—oh, My God!

WILLIAM.   A nigger's just got to know his place in de South, that's all, ain't   100 he, ma?

CORA.   Yes, son. That's all, I reckon.

WILLIAM.   And ma brother's one damn fool nigger. Don't seems like he knows nothin'. He's gonna ruin us all round here. Makin' it bad for everybody.

CORA.   Oh, Lawd, have mercy! [*Beginning to cry*] I don't know what to do. De way he's acting up can't go on. Way he's acting to de Colonel can't last. Somethin's gonna happen to ma chile. I had a bad dream last night, too, and I looked out and seed de moon all red with blood. I seed a path o' living blood across this house, I tell you, in my sleep. Oh, Lawd, have mercy! [*Sobbing*] Oh, Lawd, help me in ma troubles. [*The noise of the returning Ford is heard outside.* CORA *looks up, rises, and goes to the window.*] There's de chile now, William. Run out to de back door and tell him I wants to see him. Bring him in here where Sam and Livonia and de rest of 'em won't hear ever'thing we's sayin'. I got to talk to ma boy. He's ma baby boy, and he don't know de way.

[*Exit* WILLIAM *through the door left.* CORA *is wiping her eyes and pulling herself together when the front door is flung open with a bang and* ROBERT *enters.*]

ROBERT.   [*Running to his mother and hugging her teasingly*] Hello, ma! Your daughter got off, and I've come back to keep you company in the parlor! Bring out the cookies and lemonade. *Mister* Norwood's here!

CORA.   [*Beginning to sob anew*] Take yo' hands off me, boy! Why don't you mind?   105
Why don't you mind me?

ROBERT.   [*Suddenly serious, backing away*] Why, mamma, what's the matter? Did I scare you? Your eyes are all wet! Has somebody been telling you 'bout this morning?

CORA.   [*Not heeding his words*] Why don't you mind me, son? Ain't I told you and told you not to come in that front door, never? [*Suddenly angry*] Will somebody have to beat it into you? What's got wrong with you when you was away at that school? What am I gonna do?

ROBERT.   [*Carelessly*] Oh, I knew that the Colonel wasn't here. I passed him and old man Higgins on the road down by the south patch. He wouldn't even look at me when I waved at him. [*Half playfully*] Anyhow, isn't this my old man's house? Ain't I his son and heir? [*Grandly, strutting around*] Am I not Mr. Norwood, Junior?

CORA.   [*Utterly serious*] I believe you goin' crazy, Bert. I believes you wants to get us all killed or run away or something awful like that. I believes . . . [WILLIAM *enters left*]

WILLIAM.   Where's Bert? He ain't come round back—[*Seeing his brother in the room*]   110
How'd you get in here?

ROBERT.   [*Grinning*] Houses have front doors.

WILLIAM.   Oh, usin' de front door like de white folks, heh? You gwine do that once too much.

ROBERT.   Yes, like de white folks. What's a front door for, you rabbit-hearted coon?

WILLIAM.   Rabbit-hearted coon's better'n a dead coon any day.

ROBERT.   I wouldn't say so. Besides you and me's only half-coons, anyhow, big   115
boy. And I'm gonna act like my white half, not my black half. Get me, kid?

WILLIAM.   Well, you ain't gonna act like it long here in de middle o' Georgy. And you ain't gonna act like it when de Colonel's around, either.

ROBERT.   Oh, no? My stay down here'll be short and sweet, boy, short and sweet. The old man won't send me away to college no more—so you think I'm gonna stick around and work in the fields? Like fun? I might stay here awhile and teach some o' you darkies to think like men, maybe—till it gets too much for the old Colonel—but no more bowing down to white folks for me—not Robert Norwood.

CORA.   Hush, son!

ROBERT.   Certainly not right on my own old man's plantation—Georgia or no Georgia.

WILLIAM.   [*Scornfully*] I hears you.   120

ROBERT.   *You* can do it if you want to, but I'm ashamed of you. I've been away from here six years. [*Boasting*] I've learned something, seen people in Atlanta, and Richmond, and Washington where the football team went—real colored people who don't have to take off their hats to white folks or let 'em go to bed with their sisters—like that young Higgins boy, asking me what night Sallie was comin' to town. A damn cracker! [*To* CORA] 'Scuse me, ma. [*Continuing*] Back here in these woods maybe Sam and Livonia and you and mama and everybody's got their places fixed for 'em, but not me. [*Seriously*] Nobody's gonna fix a place for me. I'm old man Norwood's son. Nobody fixed a place for him. [*Playfully again*] Look at me. I'm a 'fay boy. [*Pretends to shake his hair back*] See these gray eyes? I got the right to everything everybody else has. [*Punching his brother in the belly*], Don't talk to me, old slavery-time Uncle Tom.

WILLIAM.   [*Resentfully*] I ain't playin', boy. [*Pushes younger brother back with some force*] I ain't playin' a-tall.

CORA.   All right, chilluns, stop. Stop! And William, you take Billy and go on home. 'Vonia's got to get supper and she don't like no young-uns under her feet in de kitchen. I wants to talk to Bert in here now 'fore Colonel Tom gets back. [*Exit WILLIAM left. CORA continues to BERT*] Sit down, child, right here a minute and listen.

ROBERT.   [*Sitting down*] All right, ma.

CORA.   Hard as I's worked and begged and humbled maself to get de Colonel to   125
keep you chilluns in school, you comes home wid yo' head full o' stubbornness and yo' mouth full o' sass for me an' de white folks an' everybody. You know can't no colored boy here talk like you's been doin' to no white folks, let alone to de Colonel and that old devil of a Talbot. They ain't gonna stand fo' yo' sass. Not only you, but I 'spects we's all gwine to pay fo' it, every colored soul on this place. I was scared to death today fo' yo' sister, Sallie, scared de Colonel warn't gwine to let her go back to school, neither, 'count o' yo' doins, but he did, thank Gawd—and then you come near makin' her miss de train. Did she have time to get her ticket and all?

ROBERT.   Sure! Had to drive like sin to get there with her, though. I didn't mean to be late getting back here for her, ma, but I had a little run-in about them radio tubes in town.

CORA.   [*Worried*] What's that?

ROBERT.   The tubes was smashed when I got 'em, and I had already made out my money order, so the woman in the post office wouldn't give the three dollars back to me. All I did was explain to her that we could send the tubes back—but she got hot because there were two or three white folks waiting behind me to get stamps, I guess. So she yells at me to move on and not give her any of my "educated nigger talk." So I said, "I'm going to finish showing you these tubes before I move on"—and then she screamed and called the mail clerk working in the back, and told him to throw me out. [*Boasting*] He didn't do it by himself, though. Had to call all the white loafers out in the square to get me through that door.

CORA.   [*Fearfully*] Lawd have mercy!

ROBERT.   Guess if I hadn't-a had the Ford then, they'd've beat me half-to-death,   130
but when I saw how many crackers there was, I jumped in the car and beat it on away.

CORA.   Thank God for that!

ROBERT.   Not even a football man [*Half-boasting*] like me could tackle the whole junction. 'Bout a dozen colored guys standing around, too, and not one of 'em would help me—the dumb jiggaboos! They been telling me ever since I been here, [*Imitating darky talk*] "You can't argue wid whut folks, man. You better stay out o' this Junction. You must ain't got no sense, nigger! You's a fool" . . . Maybe I am a fool, ma—but I didn't want to come back here nohow.

CORA.   I's sorry I sent for you.

ROBERT.   Besides you, there ain't nobody in this country but a lot of evil white folks and cowardly niggers. [*Earnstly*] I'm no nigger, anyhow, am I, ma? I'm half-white. The Colonel's my father—the richest man in the county—and I'm not going to take a lot of stuff from nobody if I do have to stay here, not from the old man either. He thinks I ought to be out there in the sun working, with Talbot standing over me like I belonged in the chain gang. Well, he's got another thought coming! [*Stubbornly*] I'm a Norwood— not a field-hand nigger.

CORA.   You means you ain't workin' no mo'?   135

ROBERT.   [*Flaring*] No, I'm not going to work in the fields. What did he send me away to school for—just to come back here and be his servant, or pick his hills of cotton?

CORA.   He sent you away to de school because *I* asked him and begged him, and got down on my knees to him, that's why. [*Quietly*] And now I just wants to make you see some sense, if you can. I knows, honey, you reads in de books and de papers, and you knows a lot more'n I do. But, chile, you's in Georgy—and I don't see how it is you don't know where you's at. This ain't up North—and even up yonder where we hears it's so fine, yo' sister has to pass for white to get along good.

ROBERT.   [*Bitterly*] I know it.

CORA.   She ain't workin' in no hotel kitchen like de Colonel thinks. She's in a office typewriting. And Sallie's studyin' de typewriter, too, at de school, but yo' pappy don't know it. I knows we ain't s'posed to study nothin' but cookin' and hard workin' here in Georgy. That's all I ever done, or knowed about. I been workin' on this very place all ma life—even 'fore I come to live in this Big House. When de Colonel's wife died, I come here, and borned you chilluns. And de Colonel's been real good to me in his way. Let you all sleep in this house with me when you was little, and sent you all off to school when you growed up. Ain't no white man in this county done that with his cullud chilluns before, far as I can know. But you—Robert, be awful, awful careful! When de Colonel comes back, in a few minutes, he wants to talk to you. Talk right to him, boy. Talk like you was colored, 'cause you ain't white.

ROBERT.   [*Angrily*] And I'm not black either. Look at me, mama. [*Rising and   140 throwing up his arms*] Don't I look like my father? Ain't I as light as he is? Ain't my eyes gray like his eyes are? [*The noise of a car is heard outside*] Ain't this our house?

CORA.   That's him now. [*Agitated*] Hurry, chile, and let's get out of this room. Come on through yonder to the kitchen. [*She starts toward the door left.*] And I'll tell him you're here.

ROBERT.   I don't want to run into the kitchen. Isn't this our house? [*As CORA crosses hurriedly left, ROBERT goes toward the front door*] The Ford is parked out in front, anyway.

CORA.   [*At the door left to the rear of the house*] Robert! Robert! [*As ROBERT nears the front door, COLONEL NORWOOD enters, almost runs into the boy, stops at the threshold and stares unbelievingly at his son. CORA backs up against the door left.*]

NORWOOD.   Get out of here! [*He points toward the door to rear of the house where CORA is standing*].

ROBERT.   [*Half-smiling*] Didn't you want to talk to me?   145

NORWOOD.   Get out of here!

ROBERT.   Not that way. [*The COLONEL raises his cane to strike the boy. CORA screams. BERT draws himself up to his full height, taller than the old man and looking very much like him, pale and proud. The man and the boy face each other. NORWOOD does not strike.*]

NORWOOD.   [*In a hoarse whisper*] Get out of here. [*His hand is trembling as he points.*]

CORA.   Robert! Come on, son, come on! Oh, my God, come on. [*Opening the door left*]

ROBERT.   Not that way, ma. [*ROBERT walks proudly out the front door. NORWOOD, in   150 an impotent rage, crosses the room to a small cabinet right, opens it nervously with a key from his pocket, takes out a pistol, and starts toward the front door. CORA overtakes him, seizes his arm, stops him.*]

CORA.   He's our son, Tom. [*She sinks slowly to her knees, holding his body.*]
Remember, he's our son.

Curtain

ACT II

Scene 1

TIME.   *After supper. Sunset.*
SETTING.   *The same.*
ACTION.   *As the curtain rises, the stage is empty. Through the windows the late afternoon
sun makes two bright paths toward the footlights.* SAM, *carrying a tray bearing a whiskey bottle
and a bowl of ice, enters left and crosses toward the library. He stoops at the door right, listens a
moment, knocks, then opens the door and goes in. In a moment* SAM *returns. As he leaves the
library, he is heard replying to a request of* NORWOOD'S.

SAM.   Yes, sah, Colonel! Sho' will, sah! Right away, sah! Yes, sah, I'll tell him. [*He
closes the door and crosses the stage muttering to himself.*] Six o'clock. Most nigh that now.
Better tell Cora to get that boy right in here. Can't nobody else do notiñ' with that fool
Bert but Cora. [*He exits left. Can be heard calling*] Cora! You, Cora . . .

[*Again the stage is empty. Off stage, outside, the bark of a dog is heard, the sound of Negroes
singing down the road, the cry of a child. The breeze moves the shadows of leaves and tree limbs
across the sunlit paths from the windows. The door left opens and* CORA *enters, followed by*
ROBERT.]

CORA.   [*Softly to* ROBERT *behind her in the dining room*] It's all right, son. He ain't
come out yet, but it's nearly six, and that's when he said he wanted you, but I was afraid
maybe you was gonna be late. I sent for you to come up here to de house and eat supper
with me in de kitchen. Where'd you eat yo' vittuals at, chile?
ROBERT.   Down at Willie's house, ma. After the old man tried to hit me you still
want me to hang around and eat up here?
CORA.   I wanted you to be here on time, honey, that's all. [*She is very nervous.*] I
kinder likes to have you eat with me sometimes, too, but you ain't et up here more'n
once this summer. But this evenin' I just wanted you to be here when de Colonel sent
word for you, 'cause we's done had enough trouble today.
ROBERT.   He's not here on time, himself, is he?   5
CORA.   He's in de library. Sam couldn't get him to eat no supper tonight, and I
ain't seen him a-tall.
ROBERT.   Maybe he wants to see me in the library, then.
CORA.   You know he don't 'low no colored folks in there 'mongst his books and
things 'cept Sam. Some o' his white friends goes in there, but none o' us.
ROBERT.   Maybe he wants to see *me* in there, though.
CORA.   Can't you never talk sense, Robert? This ain't no time for foolin' and   10
jokin'. Nearly thirty years in this house and I ain't never been in there myself, not once,
'mongst de Colonel's papers. [*The clock strikes six.*] Stand over yonder and wait till he
comes out. I's gwine on upstairs now, so's he can talk to you. And don't aggravate him no
mo' for' God's sake. Agree to whatever he say. I's scared fo' you, chile, de way you been
actin', and de fool tricks you done today, and de trouble about de post office besides.

Don't aggravate him. Fo' yo' sake, honey, 'cause I loves you—and fo' all de po' colored folks on this place what has such a hard time when his humors get on him—agree to whatever he say, will you Bert?

ROBERT.   All right, ma. [*Voice rising*] But he better not start to hit me again.

CORA.   Shs-ss-s! He'll hear you. He's right in there.

ROBERT.   [*Sullenly*] This was the day I ought to have started back to school—like my sister. I stayed my summer out here, didn't I? Why didn't he keep his promise to me? You said if I came home I could go back to college again.

CORA.   Shs-ss-s! He'll be here now. Don't say nothin', chile, I's done all I could.

ROBERT.   All right, ma.

CORA.   [*Approaching the stairs*] I'll be in ma room, honey, where I can hear you when you goes out. I'll come down to de back door and see you 'fore you goes back to de shack. Don't aggravate him, chile.

[*She ascends the stairs. The boy sits down sullenly, left, and stares at the door opposite from which his father must enter. The clock strikes the quarter after six. The shadows of the window curtains have lengthened on the carpet. The sunshine has deepened to a pale orange, and the light paths grow less distinct across the floor. The boy sits up straight in his chair. He looks at the library door. It opens. NORWOOD enters. He is bent and pale. He looks across the room and sees the boy. Suddenly he straightens up. The old commanding look comes into his face. He strides directly across the room toward his son. The boy, half afraid, half defiant, yet sure of himself, rises. Now that ROBERT is standing, the white man turns, goes back to a chair near the table, right, and seats himself. He takes out a cigar, cuts off the end and lights it, and in a voice of mixed condescension and contempt, he speaks to his son. ROBERT remains standing near the chair.*]

NORWOOD.   I don't want to have to beat you another time as I did when you were a child. The next time I might not be able to control myself. I might kill you if I touched you again. I been runnin' this plantation for thirty-five years, and I never had to beat a Nigra as old as you are. I never had to beat one of Cora's children either—but you. The rest of 'em had **sense** 'nough to keep out of my sight, and to speak to me like they should . . . I don't have any trouble with my colored folks. Never have trouble. They do what I say, or what Mr. Talbot says, and that's all there is to it, I give 'em a chance. If they turn in their crops they get paid. If they're workin' for wages, they get paid. If they want to spend their money on licker, or buy an old car, or fix up their cabins, they can. Do what they choose long as they know their places and it don't hinder their work. And to Cora's young ones I give all the chances any colored folks ever had in these parts. More'n many a white child's had. I sent you all off to school. Let Bertha go on up North when she got grown and educated. Intend to let Sallie do the same. Gave your brother William that house he's living in when he got married, pay him for his work, help him out if he needs it. None of my darkies suffer. Sent you to college. Would have kept on, would have sent you back today, but I don't intend to pay for no darky, or white boy either if I had one, that acts the way you've been acting. And certainly for no black fool. Now I want to know what's wrong with you? I don't usually talk about what I'm going to do with anybody on this place. It's my habit to tell people *what to do*, not to discuss it with 'em. But I want to know what's the matter with you—whether you're crazy or not. In that case, you'll have to be locked up. And if you aren't, you'll have to change your ways a damn sight or it won't be safe for you here, and you know it—venting your impudence on white women, parking the car in front of my door, driving like mad through the Junction, and going, everywhere, just as you please. Now, I'm going to let you talk to me, but I want you to talk right.

ROBERT.   [*Still standing*] What do you mean, "talk right"?

NORWOOD.   I mean talk like a nigger should to a white man.

ROBERT.   Oh! But I'm not a nigger, Colonel Tom. I'm your son.   20

NORWOOD.   [*Testily*] You're Cora's boy.

ROBERT.   Women don't have children by themselves.

NORWOOD.   Nigger women don't know the fathers. You're a bastard.

[*ROBERT clenches his fist. NORWOOD turns toward the drawer where the pistol is, takes it out, and lays it on the table. The wind blows the lace curtains at the windows, and sweeps the shadows of falling leaves across the paths of sunlight on the floor.*]

ROBERT.   I've heard that before. I've heard it from Negroes, and I've heard it from white folks. Now I hear it from you. [*Slowly*] You're talking about my mother.

NORWOOD.   I'm talking about Cora, yes. Her children are bastards.   25

ROBERT.   [*Quickly*] And you're their father. [*Angrily*] How come I look like you, if you're not my father?

NORWOOD.   Don't shout at me, boy. I can hear you. [*Half-smiling*] How come your skin is yellow and your elbows rusty? How come they threw you out of the post office today for talking to a white woman? How come you're the crazy young buck you are?

ROBERT.   They had no right to throw me out. I asked for my money back when I saw the broken tubes. Just as you had no right to raise that cane today when I was standing at the door of this house where *you* live, while *I* have to sleep in a shack down the road with the field hands. [*Slowly*] But my mother sleeps with you.

NORWOOD.   You don't like it?

ROBERT.   No, I don't like it.   30

NORWOOD.   What can you do about it?

ROBERT.   [*After a pause*] I'd like to kill all the white men in the world.

NORWOOD.   [*Starting*] Niggers like you are hung to trees.

ROBERT.   I'm not a nigger.

NORWOOD.   You don't like your own race? [*ROBERT is silent*] Yet you don't like   35
white folks either?

ROBERT.   [*Defiantly*] You think I ought to?

NORWOOD.   You evidently don't like me.

ROBERT.   [*Boyishly*] I used to like you, when I first knew you were my father, when I was a little kid, before that time you beat me under the feet of your horses. [*Slowly*] I liked you until then.

NORWOOD.   [*A little pleased*] So you did, heh? [*Fingering his pistol*] A pickaninny calling me "papa." I should've broken your young neck for that first time. I should've broken your head for you today, too—since I didn't then.

ROBERT.   [*Laughing scornfully*] You should've broken my head?   40

NORWOOD.   Should've gotten rid of you before this. But you was Cora's child. I tried to help you. [*Aggrieved*] I treated you decent, schooled you. Paid for it. But tonight you'll get the hell off this place and stay off. Get the hell out of this county. [*Suddenly furious*] Get out of this state. Don't let me lay eyes on you again. Get out of here now. Talbot and the storekeeper are coming up here this evening to talk cotton with me. I'll tell Talbot to *see* that you go. That's all. [*NORWOOD motions toward the door, left.*] Tell Sam to come in here when you go out. Tell him to make a light here.

ROBERT.   [*Impudently*] *Ring* for Sam—I'm not going through the kitchen. [*He starts toward the front door*] I'm not your servant. You're not going to tell me what to do.

You're not going to have Talbot run me off the place like a field hand you don't want to use any more.

NORWOOD. [*Springing between his son and the front door, pistol in hand*] You black bastard! [*ROBERT goes toward him calmly, grasps his father's arm and twists it until the gun falls to the floor. The older man bends backward in startled fury and pain.*] Don't you dare put your . . .

ROBERT. [*Laughing*] Why don't you shoot, papa? [*Louder*] Why don't you shoot?

NORWOOD. [*Gasping as he struggles, fighting back*] . . . black . . . hands . . . on . . .   45
you . . .

ROBERT. [*Hysterically, as he takes his father by the throat*] Why don't you shoot, papa? [*NORWOOD's hands claw the air helplessly. ROBERT chokes the struggling white man until his body grows limp*] Why don't you shoot! [*Laughing*] Why don't you shoot? Huh? Why?

[*CORA appears at the top of the stairs, hearing the commotion. She screams.*]

CORA. Oh, my God! [*She rushes down. ROBERT drops the body of his father at her feet in a path of flame from the setting sun. CORA starts and stares in horror.*]

ROBERT. [*Wildly*] Why didn't he shoot, mama? He didn't want *me* to live. Why didn't he shoot? [*Laughing*] He was the boss. Telling me what to do. Why didn't he shoot, then? He was the white man.

CORA. [*Falling on the body*] Colonel Tom! Colonel Tom! Tom! Tom! [*Gazes across the corpse at her son*] He's yo' father, Bert.

ROBERT. He's dead. The white man's dead. My father's dead. [*Laughing*] I'm   50
living.

CORA. Tom! Tom! Tom!

ROBERT. Niggers are living. He's dead. [*Picks up the pistol*] This is what he wanted to kill me with, but he's dead. I can use it now. Use it on all the white men in the world, because they'll be coming looking for me now. [*Stuffs the pistol into his shirt*] They'll want me now.

CORA. [*Rising and running toward her boy*] Quick, chile, out that way, [*Pointing toward the front door*] so they won't see you in de kitchen. Make for de swamp, honey. Cross de fields fo' de swamp. Go de crick way. In runnin' water, dogs can't smell no tracks. Hurry, chile!

ROBERT. Yes, mama. I can go out the front way now, easy. But if I see they gonna get me before I can reach the swamp, I'm coming back here, mama, and [*Proudly*] let them take me out of my father's house—if they can. [*Pats the gun under his shirt*] They're not going to string me up to some roadside tree for the crackers to laugh at.

CORA. [*Moaning aloud*] Oh, O-o-o! Hurry! Hurry, chile!   55

ROBERT. I'm going, ma. [*He opens the door. The sunset streams in like a river of blood*]

CORA. Run, chile!

ROBERT. Not out of my father's house. [*He exits slowly, tall and straight against the sun.*]

CORA. Fo' God's sake, hurry, chile! [*Glancing down the road*] Lawd have mercy! There's Talbot and de storekeeper in de drive. They sees my boy! [*Moaning*] They sees ma boy. [*Relieved*] But thank God, they's passin' him! [*CORA backs up against the wall in the vestibule. She stands as if petrified as TALBOT and the STOREKEEPER enter.*]

TALBOT. Hello, Cora. What's the matter with you? Where's that damn fool boy o'   60
your'n goin', coming out the front door like he owned the house? What's the matter with you, woman? Can't you talk? Can't you talk? Where's Norwood? Let's have some

light in this dark place. [*He reaches behind the door and turns on the lights.* CORA *remains backed up against the wall, looking out into the twilight, watching* ROBERT *as he goes across the field*] Good God, Jim! Look at this! [*The* TWO WHITE MEN *stop in horror before the sight of* NORWOOD's *body on the floor.*]

STOREKEEPER.   He's blue in the face. [*Bends over the body*] That nigger we saw walking out the door! [*Rising excitedly*] That nigger bastard of Cora's . . . [*Stooping over the body again*] Why the Colonel's dead!

TALBOT.   That nigger! [*Rushes toward the door*] He's running toward the swamp now . . . We'll get him . . . Telephone town—there, in the library. Telephone the sheriff. Get men, white men, after that nigger.

[*The* STOREKEEPER *rushes into the library. He can be heard talking excitedly on the phone.*]

STOREKEEPER.   Sheriff! Sheriff! Is this the sheriff? I'm calling from Norwood's plantation. That nigger, Bert, has just killed Norwood—and run, headed for the swamp. Notify the gas station at the crossroads! Tell the boys at the sawmill to head him off at the creek. Warn everybody to be on the lookout. Call your deputies! Yes! Spread a dragnet. Get out the dogs. Meanwhile we'll start after him. [*He slams the phone down and comes back into the room.*] Cora, where's Norwood's car? In the barn? [CORA *does not answer.*]

TALBOT.   Talk, you black bitch!

[*She remains silent.* TALBOT *runs, yelling and talking, out into the yard, followed by the* STOREKEEPER. *Sounds of excited shouting outside, and the roar of a motor rushing down the drive. In the sky the twilight deepens into early night.* CORA *stands looking into the darkness.*]

CORA.   My boy can't get to de swamp now. They's telephoned the white folks   65
down that way. So he'll come back home now. Maybe he'll turn into de crick and follow de branch home directly. [*Protectively*] But they shan't get him. I'll make a place for to hide him. I'll make a place upstairs down under de floor, under ma bed. In a minute ma boy'll be runnin' from de white folks with their hounds and their ropes and their guns and everything they uses to kill po' colored folks with. [*Distressed*] Ma boy'll be out there runnin. [*Turning to the body on the floor*] Colonel Tom, you hear me? Our boy, out there runnin'. [*Fiercely*] *You* said he was ma boy—*ma* bastard boy. I heard you . . . but he's yours too . . . but yonder in de dark runnin'—runnin' from yo' people, from white people. [*Pleadingly*] Why don't you get up and stop 'em? He's *your* boy. His eyes is gray—like your eyes. He's tall like you's tall. He's proud like you's proud. And he's runnin'—runnin' from po' white trash what ain't worth de little finger o' nobody what's got your blood in 'em, Tom. [*Demandingly*] Why don't you get up from there and stop 'em, Colonel Tom? What's that you say? He ain't your chile? He's ma bastard chile? My yellow bastard chile? [*Proudly*] Yes, he's mine. But don't call him that. Don't you touch him. Don't you put your white hands on him. You's beat him enough, and cussed him enough. Don't you touch him now. He *is* ma boy and no white folks gonna touch him now. That's finished. I'm gonna make a place for him upstairs under ma bed. [*Backs away from the body toward the stairs*] He's ma chile. Don't you come in ma bedroom while he's up there. Don't you come to my bed no mo'. I calls you to help me now, and you just lays there. I calls you for to wake up, and you just lays there. Whenever you called me, in de night, I woke up. When you called for me to love, I always reached out ma arms fo' you. I borned you five chilluns and now one of 'em is out yonder in de dark runnin' from yo' people. Our youngest boy out yonder in de dark runnin'. [*Accusingly*] He's runnin' from you, too. You said he warn't your'n—he's just Cora's po' little yellow bastard. But he *is* your'n, Colonel Tom. [*Sadly*] And he's runnin' from you. You are out yonder in de dark,

[*Points toward the door*] runnin' our chile, with de hounds and de gun in yo' hand, and Talbot's followin' 'hind you with a rope to hang Robert with. [*Confidently*] I been sleepin' with you too long, Colonel Tom, not to know that this ain't you layin' down there with yo' eyes shut on de floor. You can't fool me—you ain't never been so still like this before—you's out yonder runnin' ma boy through de fields in de dark, runnin' ma poor little helpless Bert through de fields in de dark to lynch him . . . Damn you, Colonel Norwood! [*Backing slowly up the stairs, staring at the rigid body below her*] Damn you, Thomas Norwood! God damn you!

Curtain

Scene 2

TIME.   One hour later. Night.
SETTING.   The same.
ACTION.   As the curtain rises, the UNDERTAKER *is talking to* SAM *at the outer door. All through this act the approaching cries of the man hunt are heard.*

UNDERTAKER.   Reckon there won't be no orders to bring his corpse back out here, Sam. None of us ain't seen Talbot or Mr. Higgins, but I'm sure they'll be having the funeral in town. The coroner told us to bring the body into the Junction. Ain't nothin' but niggers left out here now.

SAM.   [*Very frightened*] Yes, sah! Yes, sah! You's right, sah! Nothin' but us niggers, sah!

UNDERTAKER.   The Colonel didn't have no relatives far as you know, did he, Sam?

SAM.   No, sah. Ain't had none. No, sah! You's right, sah!

UNDERTAKER.   Well, you got everything o' his locked up around here, ain't you?   5
Too bad there ain't no white folks about to look after the Colonel's stuff, but every white man that's able to walk's out with the posse. They'll have that young nigger swingin' before ten.

SAM.   [*Trembling*] Yes, sah, yes, sah! I 'spects so. Yes, sah!

UNDERTAKER.   Say, where's that woman the Colonel's been living with—where's that black housekeeper, Cora, that murderin's bastard's mother?

SAM.   She here, sah! She's up in her room.

UNDERTAKER.   [*Curiously*] I'd like to see how she looks. Get her down here. Say, how about a little drink before we start that ride back to town, for me and my partner out there with the body?

SAM.   Cora got de keys to all de licker, sah!   10

UNDERTAKER.   Well, get her down here then, double quick! [SAM *goes up the stairs.* The UNDERTAKER *leans in the front doorway talking to his partner outside in the wagon*] Bad business, a white man having saucy nigger children on his hands, and his black woman living in his own house.

VOICE OUTSIDE.   Damn right, Charlie.

UNDERTAKER.   Norwood didn't have a gang o' yellow gals, though, like Higgins and some o' these other big bugs. Just this one bitch far's I know, livin' with him damn near like a wife. Didn't even have much company out here. And they tell me ain't been a white woman stayed here overnight since his wife died when I was a baby. [SAM's *shuffle is heard on the stairs*] Here comes a drink, I reckon, boy. You needn't get down off the ambulance. I'll have Sam bring it out there to you. [SAM *descends followed by* CORA *who comes down the stairs. She says nothing. The* UNDERTAKER *looks up grinning at* CORA] Well, so you're the Cora that's got these educated nigger children? Hum-m! Well, I guess you'll see one of 'em swinging full of bullet holes when you wake up in the morning. They'll probably hang him to that tree down here by the Colonel's gate—'cause they tell me he strutted right out the front gate past that tree after the murder. Or maybe they'll burn him. How'd you like to see him swinging there roasted in the morning when you wake up, girlie?

CORA.   [*Calmly*] Is that all you wanted to say to me?

UNDERTAKER.   Don't get smart! Maybe you think there's nobody to boss you now. 15
We gonna have a little drink before we go. Get out a bottle of rye.

CORA.   I takes ma orders from Colonel Norwood, sir.

UNDERTAKER.   Well, you'll take no more orders from him. He's dead out there in my wagon—so get along and get the bottle.

CORA.   He's out yonder with de mob, not in your wagon.

UNDERTAKER.   I tell you he's in my wagon!

CORA.   He's out there with de mob. 20

UNDERTAKER.   God damn! [*To his partner outside*] I believe this black woman's gone crazy in here. [*To* CORA] Get the keys out for that licker, and be quick about it! [CORA *does not move.* SAM *looks from one to the other, frightened.*]

VOICE OUTSIDE.   Aw, to hell with the licker, Charlie. Come on, let's start back to town. We want to get in on some of that excitement, too. They should've found that nigger by now—and I want to see 'em drag him out here.

UNDERTAKER.   All right, Jim. [*To* CORA *and* SAM] Don't you all go to bed until you see that bonfire. You niggers are getting besides yourselves around Polk County. We'll burn a few more of you if you don't be careful. [*He exits, and the noise of the dead-wagon going down the road is heard.*]

SAM.   Oh, Lawd, hab mercy on me! I prays, Lawd hab mercy! O, ma Lawd, ma Lawd, ma Lawd! Cora, is you a fool? *Is* you a fool? Why didn't you give de mens de licker, riled as these white folks is? In ma old age is I gonna be burnt by de crackers? Lawd, is I sinned? Lawd, what has I done? [*Suddenly stops moaning and becomes schemingly calm*] I don't have to stay here tonight, does I? I done locked up de Colonel's library, and he can't be wantin' nothin'. No, ma Lawd, he won't want nothin' now. He's with Jesus—or with de devil, one. [*To* CORA] I's gwine on away from here. Sam's gwine in town to his chilluns' house, and I ain't gwine by no road either. I gwine through de holler where I don't have to pass no white folks.

CORA.   Yes, Samuel, you go on. De Colonel can get his own drinks when he comes 25
back tonight.

SAM.   [*Bucking his eyes in astonishment at* CORA] Lawd God Jesus!

[*He bolts out of the room as fast as his old legs will carry him.* CORA *comes down stairs, looks for a long moment out into the darkness, then closes the front door and draws the blinds. She looks down at the spot where the* COLONEL's *body lay.*]

CORA.   All de colored folks are runnin' from you tonight. Po' Colonel Tom, you too old now to be out with de mob. You got no business goin', but you had to go, I reckon. I 'members that time they hung Luke Jordon, you sent yo' dogs out to hunt him. The next day you killed all de dogs. You were kinder softhearted. Said you didn't like that kind of sport. Told me in bed one night you could hear them dogs howlin' in yo' sleep. But de time they burnt de courthouse when that po' little cullud boy was locked up in it cause they said he hugged a white girl, you was with 'em again. Said you had to go help 'em. Now you's out chasin' ma boy. [*As she stands at the window, she sees a passing figure.*] There goes yo' other woman, Colonel Tom, Livonia is runnin' from you too, now. She would've wanted you last night. Been wantin' you again ever since she got old and fat and you stopped layin' with her and put her in the kitchen to cook. Don't think I don't know, Colonel Tom. Don't think I don't remember them nights when you used to sleep in that cabin down by de spring. I knew 'Vonia was there with you. I ain't no fool, Colonel Tom. But she ain't bore you no chilluns. I'm de one that bore 'em. [*Musing*] White mens, and colored womens, and little bastard chilluns—that's de old way of de South—but it's ending now. Three of your yellow brothers yo' father had by Aunt Sallie Deal—what had to come and do your laundry to make her livin'—you got colored relatives scattered all over this county. Them de ways o' de South—mixtries, mixtries. [*WILLIAM enters left, silently, as his mother talks. She is sitting in a chair now. Without looking up*] Is that you, William?

WILLIAM.   Yes, ma, it's me.

CORA.   Is you runnin' from him, too?

WILLIAM.   [*Hesitatingly*] Well, ma, you see . . . don't you think kinder . . . well, I   30
reckon I ought to take Libby and ma babies on down to de church house with Reverend Martin and them, or else get 'long to town if I can hitch up them mules. They's scared to be out here, my wife and her ma. All de folks done gone from de houses down yonder by de branch, and you can hear de hounds a bayin' off yonder by de swamp, and cars is tearin' up that road, and de white folks is yellin' and hollerin' and carryin' on some-thin' terrible over toward de brook. I done told Robert 'bout his foolishness. They's gonna hang him sure. Don't you think you better be comin' with us, ma. That is, do you want to? 'Course we can go by ourselves, and maybe you wants to stay here and take care o' de big house. I don't want to leave you, ma, but I . . . I . . .

CORA.   Yo' brother'll be back, son, then I won't be by myself.

WILLIAM.   [*Bewildered by his mothers sureness*] I thought Bert went . . . I thought he run . . . I thought . . .

CORA.   No, honey. He went, but they ain't gonna get him out there. I sees him comin' back here now, to be with me. I's gwine to guard him 'till he can get away.

WILLIAM.   Then de white folks'll come here, too.

CORA.   Yes, de Colonel'll come back here sure. [*The deep baying of the hounds is   35
heard at a distance through the night.*] Colonel Tom will come after his son.

WILLIAM.   My God, ma! Come with us to town.

CORA.   Go on, William, go on! Don't wait for them to get back. You never was much like neither one o' them—neither de Colonel or Bert—you's mo' like de field hands. Too much o' ma blood in you, I guess. You never liked Bert much, neither, and you always was afraid of de Colonel. Go on, son, and hide yo' wife and her ma and your chilluns. Ain't nothin' gonna hurt you. You never did go against nobody. Neither did I, till tonight. Tried to live right and not hurt a soul, white or colored. [*Addressing space*] I tried to live right, Lord. [*Angrily*] Tried to live right, Lord. [*Throws out her arms resent-fully as if to say, "and this is what you give me."*] What's de matter, Lawd, you ain't with me?

[*The hounds are heard howling again.*]

WILLIAM.   I'm gone, ma. [*He exits fearfully as his mother talks.*]

CORA.   [*Bending over the spot on the floor where the COLONEL has lain. She calls.*] Colonel Tom! Colonel Tom! Colonel Tom! Look! Bertha and Sallie and William and Bert, all your chilluns, runnin' from you, and you layin' on de floor there, dead! [*Pointing*] Out yonder with the mob, dead. And when you come home, upstairs in my bed on top of my body, dead. [*Goes to the window, returns, sits down, and begins to speak as if remembering a far-off dream.*] Colonel Thomas Norwood! I'm just poor Cora Lewis, Colonel Norwood. Little black Cora Lewis, Colonel Norwood. I'm just fifteen years old. Thirty years ago, you put your hands on me to feel my breasts, and you say, "You a pretty little piece of flesh, ain't you? Black and sweet, ain't you?" And I lift up ma face, and you pull me to you, and we laid down under the trees that night, and I wonder if your wife'll know when you go back up the road into the big house. And I wonder if my mama'll know it, when I go back to our cabin. Mama said she nursed you when you was a baby, just like she nursed me. And I loved you in the dark, down there under that tree by de gate, afraid of you and proud of you, feelin' your gray eyes lookin' at me in de dark. Then I cried and cried and told ma mother about it, but she didn't take it hard like I thought she'd take it. She said fine white mens like de young Colonel always took good care o' their colored womens. She said it was better than marryin' some black field hand and workin' all your life in de cotton and cane. Better even than havin' a job like ma had, takin' care o' de white chilluns. Takin' care o' you, Colonel Tom. [*As Cora speaks the sound of the approaching mob gradually grows louder and louder. Auto horns, the howling of dogs, the far-off shouts of men, full of malignant force and power, increase in volume.*] And I was happy because I liked you, 'cause you was tall and proud, 'cause you said I was sweet to you and called me purty. And when yo' wife died—de Mrs. Norwood [*Scornfully*] that never bore you any chilluns, the pale beautiful Mrs. Norwood that was like a slender pine tree in de winter frost . . . I knowed you wanted me. I was full with child by you then— William, it was—our first boy. And ma mammy said, go up there and keep de house for Colonel Tom, sweep de floors and make de beds, and by and by, you won't have to sweep de floors and make no beds. And what ma mammy said was right. It all come true. Sam and Rusus and 'Vonia and Lucy did de waitin' on you and me, and de washin' and de cleanin' and de cookin'. And all I did was a little sewin' now and then, and a little pre-servin' in de summer and a little makin' of pies and sweet cakes and things you like to eat on Christmas. And de years went by. And I was always ready for you when you come to me in de night. And we had them chilluns, your chilluns and mine, Tom Norwood, all of 'em! William, born dark like me, dumb like me, and then Baby John what died; then Bertha, white and smart like you; and then Bert with your eyes and your ways and your temper, and mighty nigh your color; then Sallie, nearly white, too, and smart, and purty. But Bert was yo' chile! He was always yo' child . . . Good-looking, and kind, and head-strong, and strange, and stubborn, and proud like you, and de one I could love most 'cause he needed de most lovin'. And he wanted to call you "papa," and I tried to teach him no, but he did it anyhow and [*Sternly*] you beat him, Colonel Thomas Norwood. And he growed up with de beatin' in his heart and your eyes in his head, and your ways, and your pride. And this summer he looked like you that time I first knowed you down by de road under them trees, young and fiery and proud. There was no touchin' Bert, just like there was no touchin' you. I could only love him, like I loved you. I could only love him. But I couldn't talk to him, because he hated you. He had your ways—and you beat him! After you beat that chile, then you died, Colonel Norwood. You died here in this house, and you been living dead a long time. You lived dead. [*Her voice rises above the nearing sounds of the mob.*] And when I said this evenin', "Get up! Why don't you help me?" You'd done been dead a long time—a long time before you laid down on this floor, here, with the breath choked out o' you—and Bert standin' over you living, living, living. That's why you hated him. And you want to kill him. Always, you wanted to kill him. Out there with de hounds and de torches and de cars and de guns, you want to kill ma boy. But you won't kill him! He's comin' home first. He's comin' home to me. He's comin' home! [*Outside the noise is tremendous now, the lights of autos flash on the window curtains, there are shouts and cries. CORA sits, tense, in the middle of the room.*] He's comin' home!

A MAN'S VOICE.   [*Outside*] He's somewhere on this lot. 40

ANOTHER VOICE.   Don't shoot, men. We want to get him alive.

VOICE.   Close in on him. He must be in them bushes by the house.

FIRST VOICE.   Porch! Porch! Porch! There he is yonder—running to the door!

[*Suddenly shots are heard. The door bursts open and ROBERT enters, firing back into the darkness. The shots are returned by the mob, breaking the windows. Flares, lights, voices, curses, screams.*]

VOICES.   Nigger! Nigger! Nigger! Get the nigger!

[*CORA rushes toward the door and bolts it after her son's entrance.*]

CORA.   [*Leaning against the door*] I was waiting for you, honey. Yo' hiding place is 45
all ready, upstairs, under ma bed, under de floor. I sawed a place there fo' you. They can't find you there. Hurry—before yo' father comes.

ROBERT.   [*Panting*] No time to hide, ma. They're at the door now. They'll be coming up the back way, too. [*Sounds of knocking and the breaking of glass*] They'll be coming in the windows. They'll be coming in everywhere. And only one bullet left, ma. It's for me.

CORA.   Yes, it's fo' you, chile. Save it. Go upstairs in mama's room. Lay on ma bed and rest.

ROBERT.   [*Going slowly toward the stairs with the pistol in his hand*] Goodnight, ma. I'm awful tired of running, ma. They been chasing me for hours.

CORA.   Goodnight, son.

[*CORA follows him to the foot of the steps. The door begins to give at the forcing of the mob. As ROBERT disappears above, it bursts open. A great crowd of white men pour into the room with guns, ropes, clubs, flashlights, and knives. CORA turns on the stairs, facing them quietly. TALBOT, the leader of the mob, stops.*]

TALBOT.   Be careful, men. He's armed. [*To CORA*] Where is that yellow bastard of 50
yours—upstairs?

CORA.   Yes, he's going to sleep. Be quiet, you all. Wait. [*She bars the way with outspread arms.*]

TALBOT.   [*Harshly*] Wait, hell! Come on, boys, let's go. [*A single shot is heard upstairs.*] What's that?

CORA.   [*Calmly*] My boy . . . is gone . . . to sleep!

[*TALBOT and some of the men rush up the stairway, CORA makes a final gesture of love toward the room above. Yelling and shouting, through all the doors and windows, a great crowd pours into the room. The roar of the mob fills the house, the whole night, the whole world. Suddenly TALBOT returns at the top of the steps and a hush falls over the crowd.*]

TALBOT.   Too late, men. We're just a little too late.

[*A sigh of disappointment rises from the mob. TALBOT comes down the stairs, walks up to CORA and slaps her once across the face. She does not move. It is as though no human hand can touch her again.*]

Curtain

QUESTIONS

Act I

1. Throughout the act—and the play—why are the children of Colonel Norwood and Cora referred to as just Cora's children?
2. Why does the Colonel deny permission for Sallie's bags to be carried through the front door?
3. Throughout the act, what do we learn about Robert's attitudes toward his circumstances on the plantation? What do the Colonel and Higgins say about his attitude? Once Robert appears, what does he himself say about his situation?
4. What does the Colonel say about Sallie's ambition to start a nearby school? What does he advise her to do instead?
5. Who is Talbot? What does he represent? Why does he not appear until late in the second act?
6. What does Higgins report about how Robert has behaved in town? What does he tell Colonel Norwood to do about it?
7. As expressed in speech 61, what is Higgins's attitude toward black women? What does this attitude disclose about his character?
8. Describe the effect on both Robert and Colonel Norwood of the childhood incident when Robert called the Colonel "papa."
9. What has the Colonel decided to do about Robert? What are Cora's fears not only for Robert but for others?

Act II, Scene 1

10. What are the issues in the confrontation between Robert and Colonel Norwood?
11. What is Robert's dilemma (speech 35)? What has the Colonel now determined to do about Robert?
12. What is Robert's response to the Colonel's display of the gun, and his threat to use it?
13. What do Talbot and the storekeeper do once they learn that Colonel Norwood is dead? What chance does Robert have to escape?
14. Why does Cora speak so extensively over the Colonel's body?

Act II, Scene 2

15. Why are the undertaker and his companion introduced at this point? What are they like?
16. According to Cora (speech 27), what was the nature of the old "ways" of the south?
17. What is the purpose of Cora's second extensive monologue (speech 39)?
18. What finally happens to Robert? Why does Talbot slap Cora at the end?

GENERAL QUESTIONS

1. Describe *Mulatto* as a realistic play. Why is it important that the play contain many details about the plantation and the customs of the country?

2. What is the symbolism of the front door? The incident at the post office in town? Driving the Ford fast?

3. Describe Colonel Norwood. What characteristics of a southern plantation owner does he exhibit? What is shown about him by his having sent Robert and Sallie away to school? What does Cora say about him before and after he is dead?

4. Describe the character of Robert. What are his dominant traits? How politic is he in dealing with his circumstances? To what extent does he bring about his own destruction?

5. Describe Cora. What has her life been like? To what degree has she sacrificed her individuality to stay with Colonel Norwood? How does she try to protect her children? In her two major lengthy speeches, what seems to be happening to her?

6. In light of the historical time when the play was written and produced, could there have been any other outcome?

BETTY KELLER, *TEA PARTY*

Betty Keller has brought a wide variety of experience to her work for the theater, including such unlikely jobs as insurance adjuster, farmer, photographer's assistant, and prison matron. She served as a teacher for many theatrical workshops in Vancouver, including four years with Playhouse Holiday. She taught drama and theater at the Windsor Secondary School in North Vancouver until 1974, the year she published *Improvisations in Creative Drama,* the collection of short plays and sketches from which *Tea Party* is selected. She also taught at Simon Fraser University and the University of British Columbia. She was the  founder/producer of the western Canadian writers festival and workshop program, *The Festival of the Written Arts,* from 1983 to 1994. In addition to her work in drama she has written biographical and historical works, including *Pauline: A Biography of E. Pauline Johnson* (1982); *Black Wolf: A Life of Ernest Thompson Seton* (1984); *On the Shady Side: Vancouver 1886–1914* (1986); *Sea Silver: Salmon Farming on the West Coast* (1996); and *Bright Seas and Pioneer Spirits* (1996).

Brief as *Tea Party* is, it illustrates the power of drama to depict character and situation and to convey emotion. The main characters are two lonely elderly sisters who have outlived their friends and relatives and have no one except the people who occasionally come to their house to perform various services, such as delivering the paper and reading the meters. The sketch presents their plight deftly and succinctly, touching with great tenderness on the pathos of their loneliness.

Tea Party is too short to present difficult choices for the characters, and hence they hardly get the opportunity to go through the responses and changes that are found in full-length plays. Both Alma and Hester are individualized, however, as they carry on a minor controversy about names and dates from their long-vanished past. Beyond this, in Alma's last speech, which ends the dramatic sketch, one might find a hint of the awareness and recognition that we expect of round, developed characters. Even though the paperboy is not a speaking part, his unkindness to the sisters is clearly shown, and in this way Keller dramatizes the poignant situation of persons whom life has passed by. It is difficult to find a play that conveys so much of life and feeling in so short a span of time and action.

BETTY KELLER   (b. 1930)

Tea Party _____ *1974*

CHARACTERS

> Alma Evans: *seventy-five years old, small and spare framed. Her clothing is simple but not outdated, her grey hair cut short and neat. She walks with the aid of a cane, although she would not be classed as a cripple.*
>
> Hester Evans: *seventy-nine years old. There is little to distinguish her physically from her sister, except perhaps a face a little more pinched and pain-worn. She sits in a wheelchair; but although her legs may be crippled, her mind certainly is not.*
>
> The Boy: *in his early teens, seen only fleetingly.*

SCENE. *The sitting room of the Evans sisters' home. The door to the street is on the rear wall Upstage Left,° a large window faces the street Upstage Center. On the right wall is the door to the kitchen; on the left, a door to the remainder of the house. Downstage Left is an easy chair, Upstage Right a sofa, Downstage Right a tea trolley. The room is crowded with the knickknacks gathered by its inhabitants in three-quarters of a century of living.*

[*At rise,* ALMA *is positioning* HESTER'S *wheelchair Upstage Left.* ALMA'S *cane is on* HESTER'S *lap.*]

> HESTER.   That's it.

[ALMA *takes her cane from* HESTER. *They both survey the room.*]

> ALMA.   I think I'll sit on the sofa . . . at the far end.
> HESTER.   Yes. That will be cosy. Then he can sit on this end between us.

[ALMA *sits on the Downstage Right end of the sofa. They both study the effect.*]

> ALMA.   But then he's too close to the door, Hester!

[HESTER *nods, absorbed in the problem.*]

> ALMA.   [*Moving to the Upstage Left end of sofa.*] Then I'd better sit here.   5

Upstage Left: To visualize stage locations, assume that the stage directions are described from the viewpoint of an actor facing the audience. Thus "Right" is actually to the left of the audience, and "Left" is right. "Downstage" refers to the front of the stage, while "Upstage" is the back. The terms *down* and *up* were established at a time when stages were tilted toward the audience, so that spectators at floor level could have as complete a view as possible of the entire stage.

HESTER.   But now he's too far away from me, Alma.

[*ALMA stands; both of them study the room again.*]

ALMA.   But if I push the tea trolley in front of you, he'll have to come to you, won't he?

HESTER.   Oh, all right, Alma. You're sure it's today?

ALMA.   [*Pushing the tea trolley laden with cups and napkins, etc. to HESTER.*] The first Thursday of the month.

HESTER.   You haven't forgotten the chocolate biscuits?°   10

ALMA.   No dear, they're on the plate. I'll bring them in with the tea. [*Goes to the window, peering up the street to the Right.*]

HESTER.   And cocoa?

ALMA.   I remembered.

HESTER.   You didn't remember for Charlie's visit.

ALMA.   Charlie drinks tea, Hester. I didn't make cocoa for him because he drinks   15
tea.

HESTER.   Oh. He didn't stay last time anyway.

ALMA.   It was a busy day. . . .

HESTER.   Rushing in and out like that. I was going to tell him about father and the *Bainbridge* . . . and he didn't stay.

ALMA.   What about the *Bainbridge?*

HESTER.   Her maiden voyage out of Liverpool . . . when father was gone three   20
months and we thought he'd gone down with her.

ALMA.   That wasn't the *Bainbridge.*

HESTER.   Yes, it was. It was the *Bainbridge.* I remember standing on the dock in the snow when she finally came in. That was the year I'd begun first form, and I could spell out the letters on her side.

ALMA.   It was her sister ship, the *Heddingham.*

HESTER.   The *Bainbridge.* You were too young to remember. Let's see, the year was . . .

ALMA.   Mother often told the story. It was the *Heddingham* and her engine broke   25
down off Cape Wrath beyond the Hebrides.

HESTER.   It was 1902 and you were just four years old.

ALMA.   The *Heddingham*, and she limped into port on January the fifth.

HESTER.   January the fourth just after nine in the morning, and we stood in the snow and watched the *Bainbridge* nudge the pier, and I cried and the tears froze on my cheeks.

ALMA.   The *Heddingham.*

HESTER.   Alma, mother didn't cry, you know. I don't think she ever cried. My   30
memory of names and places is sharp so that I don't confuse them as some others I could mention, but sometimes I can't remember things like how people reacted. But I remember that day. There were tears frozen on my cheeks but mother didn't cry.

ALMA.   [*Nodding.*] She said he didn't offer a word of explanation. Just marched home beside her.

HESTER.   [*Smiling.*] He never did say much. . . . Is he coming yet?

ALMA.   No, can't be much longer though. Almost half past four.

10 *chocolate biscuits:* chocolate cookies.

HESTER.   Perhaps you'd better bring in the tea. Then it will seem natural.

ALMA.   Yes dear, I know. [*Exits out door Upstage Right.*] Everything's ready.   35

HESTER.   What will you talk about?

ALMA.   [*Re-entering with the teapot*] I thought perhaps . . . [*Carefully putting down the teapot.*] . . . perhaps brother George!

HESTER.   And the torpedo? No, Alma, he's not old enough for that story!

ALMA.   He's old enough to know about courage. I thought I'd show him the medal, too. [*She goes to the window, peers both ways worriedly, then carries on towards the kitchen.*]

HESTER.   Not yet? He's late to-night. You're sure it's today?   40

ALMA.   He'll come. It's the first Thursday. [*Exit.*]

HESTER.   You have his money?

ALMA.   [*Returning with the plate of biscuits.*] I've got a twenty dollar bill, Hester.

HESTER.   Alma!

ALMA.   Well, we haven't used that one on him. It was Dennis, the last one, who   45
always had change. We could get two visits this way, Hester.

HESTER.   Maybe Dennis warned him to carry change for a twenty.

ALMA.   It seemed worth a try. [*Goes to the window again.*] Are you going to tell him about the *Heddingham*?

HESTER.   The *Bainbridge*. Maybe . . . or maybe I'll tell him about the day the Great War ended. Remember, Alma, all the noise, the paper streamers . . .

ALMA.   And father sitting silent in his chair.

HESTER.   It wasn't the same for him with George gone. Is he coming yet?   50

ALMA.   No dear, maybe he's stopped to talk somewhere. [*Looking to the right.*] . . . No . . . no, there he is, on the Davis' porch now!

HESTER.   I'll pour then. You get the cocoa, Alma.

ALMA.   [*Going out.*] It's all ready, I just have to add hot water.

HESTER.   Don't forget the marshmallows!

ALMA.   [*Reappearing*] Oh, Hester, what if he comes in and just sits down closest to   55
the door? He'll never stay!

HESTER.   You'll have to prod him along. For goodness sakes, Alma, get his cocoa!

[*ALMA disappears.*]

HESTER.   He must be nearly here. He doesn't go to the Leschynskis, and the Blackburns don't get home till after six.

ALMA.   [*Returning with the cocoa.*] Here we are! Just in . . .

[*The BOY passes the window. There is a slapping sound as the newspaper lands on the porch.*]

[*ALMA and HESTER look at the door and wait, hoping to hear a knock, but they both know the truth. Finally, ALMA goes to the door, opens it and looks down at the newspaper.*]

ALMA.   He's gone on by.

HESTER.   You must have had the day wrong.   60

ALMA.   No, he collected at the Davis'.

HESTER.   [*After a long pause.*] He couldn't have forgotten us.

ALMA.   [*Still holding the cocoa, she turns from the door.*] He's collecting at the Kerighan's now. [*She closes the door and stands forlornly.*]

HESTER.   Well, don't stand there with that cocoa! You look silly. [*ALMA brings the cocoa to the tea trolley.*] Here's your tea. [ALMA *takes the cup, sits on the Upstage Left end of the sofa. There is a long silence.*]

    HESTER.   I think I'll save that story for the meter man.   65

    ALMA.   The *Heddingham?*

    HESTER.   The *Bainbridge.*

    ALMA.   [*After a pause.*] They don't read the meters for two more weeks.

SLOW BLACKOUT

QUESTIONS

1.   What is the play's major conflict? The minor conflict?

2.   Why do the two sisters discuss their seating arrangements for the paperboy? How do we learn that they have made these arrangements before?

3.   What does Alma's plan for the twenty-dollar bill show about her? What does the discussion about both the money and the paperboys indicate about their own self-awareness?

4.   How does controversy about the names *Bainbridge* and *Heddingham* help you understand the two sisters?

GENERAL QUESTIONS

1.   How does Keller's description of the sets aid you in understanding the action? The normal tasks of the women? From the setting of this play, what are your conclusions about the relationship of objects and spatial arrangements to the action and development of drama?

2.   Consider the women particularly with regard to their age. In the light of their health and their isolation, how does *Tea Party* present the circumstances of the aged? How can the play be construed as a sociological/political argument, with the elderly as the focus?

EUGENE O'NEILL, *BEFORE BREAKFAST*

Eugene O'Neill is one of America's great play-wrights. He wrote more than forty plays and won three Pulitzer Prizes. He is still the only American dramatist to have received the Nobel Prize for literature (1936).

O'Neill was born in New York, the son of a well-known actor, and was educated sporadically as his parents traveled from city to city on theatrical tours. Eventually he studied at Princeton, but he left to go to work, first in a mail-order house and then in Honduras, where he engaged in prospecting. He then began a brief career as a seaman, traveling on both sides of the Atlantic. He contracted tuberculosis in about 1912, and while in a sanitarium he began to write plays. Upon release he studied playwriting at Harvard, but by 1916 he had left to try his luck as a playwright with the Provincetown Players, the same company that Susan Glaspell had helped found and where she began her writing career. It was in 1916, the same year that Glaspell wrote *Trifles,* that the Provincetown Players produced O'Neill's first drama, *Bound East for Cardiff.*

O'Neill maintained a close connection with the Provincetown Players for several years, providing them with ten one-act plays between 1916 and 1920. Among these were *Thirst* (1916), *Before Breakfast* (1916), *Fog* ((1917), *The Long Voyage Home* (1917), *Ile* (1917), and *The Rope* (1917). His later (and longer) works include *The Emperor Jones* (1920), *Anna Christie* (1921), *Desire Under the Elms* (1924), *Strange Interlude* (1928), *Mourning Becomes Electra* (1931), and *The Iceman Cometh* (1946). O'Neill also wrote an autobiographical play, *Long Day's Journey into Night* (1936), that at his request was withheld until after his death. Staged on Broadway in 1956, it received the Pulitzer Prize in drama (O'Neill's third Pulitzer); it was later made into a film starring Katherine Hepburn.

Before Breakfast, though one of O'Neill's earliest plays, shows his characteristic control of point of view, conflict, character, and setting. The play was first staged in December 1916 by the Provincetown Players in New York City's Greenwich Village (where Christopher Street, the address of the Rowlands' apartment, is located). The play contains little action, and yet it is charged with conflict. The plot is simple and straightforward—a wife onstage berates her offstage husband for twenty minutes. The conflict between them is long-standing and bitter, and it is resolved in the play's horrifying conclusion.

Above all, *Before Breakfast* illustrates O'Neill's skillful control over the dramatic point of view. By giving Mrs. Rowland every word spoken on the stage, O'Neill causes the audience to understand everything as it is filtered through her mind. Indeed, the play is a bravura piece for a gifted actress. Because Mrs. Rowland dominates the stage so completely, it is tempting to see her character as one of constantly nagging spitefulness. It is to O'Neill's credit, however, that she is not without basic strength, and that her bitterness is not without cause. Alfred, the unseen and unheard offstage husband, has contributed to their estranged relationship.

Of particular note in indicating the impasse that the characters have reached are O'Neill's extensive stage directions describing the setting. We learn that the Rowlands' flat is in Greenwich Village, the traditional New York home of artists, poets, and actors. On the one hand, therefore, the flat suggests Alfred's artistic aspirations, but on the other, the poverty of the surroundings indicates the sad truth that such dreams cannot be sustained unless someone pays the rent.

The language of Mrs. Rowland, the only speaking character in the play, indicates both her lack of education and her intense dissatisfaction. Phrases such as "I got," "like I was," "liable" for "likely," and "sewing my fingers off" suggest that her knowledge of language has not been derived from education and study. Her speech also suggests the social gulf that originally separated her from

Alfred, a gulf that they tried to bridge in their marriage but which now has opened up irretrievably. A number of other phrases embody the taunts that Mrs. Rowland directs at Alfred ("pawn, pawn, pawn," "like a man," "a fine life," "in trouble," etc.).

EUGENE O'NEILL   (1888–1953)

Before Breakfast ————————————————————————————— *1916*

CHARACTERS

>   Mrs. Rowland, *the wife*
>   Mr. Alfred Rowland, *the husband*

SCENE. *A small room serving both as kitchen and dining room in a flat on Christopher Street, New York City. In the rear, to the right, a door leading to the outer hallway. On the left of the doorway, a sink, and a two-burner gas stove. Over the stove, and extending to the left wall, a wooden closet for dishes, etc. On the left, two windows looking out on a fire escape where several potted plants are dying of neglect. Before the windows, a table covered with oilcloth. Two cane-bottomed chairs are placed by the table. Another stands against the wall to the right of door in rear. In the right wall, rear, a doorway leading into a bedroom. Farther forward, different articles of a man's and a woman's clothing are hung on pegs. A clothes line is strung from the left corner, rear, to the right wall, forward.*

It is about eight-thirty in the morning of a fine, sunshiny day in the early fall.

Mrs. Rowland enters from the bedroom, yawning, her hands still busy putting the finishing touches on a slovenly toilet by sticking hairpins into her hair which is bunched up in a drab-colored mass on top of her round head. She is of medium height and inclined to a shapeless stoutness, accentuated by her formless blue dress, shabby and worn. Her face is characterless, with small regular features and eyes of a nondescript blue. There is a pinched expression about her eyes and nose and her weak, spiteful mouth. She is in her early twenties but looks much older.

She comes to the middle of the room and yawns, stretching her arms to their full length. Her drowsy eyes stare about the room with the irritated look of one to whom a long sleep has not been a long rest. She goes wearily to the clothes hanging on the right and takes an apron from a hook. She ties it about her waist, giving vent to an exasperated "damn" when the knot fails to obey her clumsy fingers. Finally gets it tied and goes slowly to the gas stove and lights one burner. She fills the coffee pot at the sink and sets it over the flame. Then slumps down into a chair by the table and puts a hand over her forehead as if she were suffering from headache. Suddenly her face brightens as though she had remembered something, and she casts a quick glance at the dish closet; then looks sharply at the bedroom door and listens intently for a moment or so.

MRS. ROWLAND.   [*In a low voice.*] Alfred! Alfred! [*There is no answer from the next room and she continues suspiciously in a louder tone.*] You needn't pretend you're asleep. [*There is no reply to this from the bedroom, and, reassured, she gets up from her chair and tiptoes cautiously to the dish closet. She slowly opens one door, taking great care to make no noise, and slides out, from their hiding place behind the dishes, a bottle of Gordon gin and a glass. In doing so she disturbs the top dish, which rattles a little. At this sound she starts guiltily and looks with sulky defiance at the doorway to the next room.*]

[*Her voice trembling.*] Alfred!

[*After a pause, during which she listens for any sound, she takes the glass and pours out a large drink and gulps it down; then hastily returns the bottle and glass to their hiding place. She closes the closet door with the same care as she had opened it, and, heaving a great sigh of relief, sinks down into her chair again. The large dose of alcohol she has taken has an almost immediate effect. Her features become more animated, she seems to gather energy, and she looks at the bedroom door with a hard, vindictive smile on her lips. Her eyes glance quickly about the room and are fixed on a man's coat and vest which hang from a hook at right. She moves stealthily over to the open doorway and stands there, out of sight of anyone inside, listening for any movement.*]

[*Calling in a half-whisper.*] Alfred!

[*Again there is no reply. With a swift movement she takes the coat and vest from the hook and returns with them to her chair. She sits down and takes the various articles out of each pocket but quickly puts them back again. At last, in the inside pocket of the vest, she finds a letter.*]

[*Looking at the handwriting—slowly to herself.*] Hmm! I knew it.

[*She opens the letter and reads it. At first her expression is one of hatred and rage, but as she goes on to the end it changes to one of triumphant malignity. She remains in deep thought for a moment, staring before her, the letter in her hands, a cruel smile on her lips. Then she puts the letter back in the pocket of the vest, and still careful not to awaken the sleeper, hangs the clothes up again on the same hook, and goes to the bedroom door and looks in.*]

[*In a loud, shrill voice.*] Alfred! [*Still louder.*] Alfred! [*There is a muffled, yawning groan from the next room.*] Don't you think it's about time you got up? Do you want to stay in bed all day? [*Turning around and coming back to her chair.*] Not that I've got any doubts about your being lazy enough to stay in bed forever. [*She sits down and looks out of the window, irritably.*] Goodness knows what time it is. We haven't even got any way of telling the time since you pawned your watch like a fool. The last valuable thing we had, and you knew it. It's been nothing but pawn, pawn, pawn, with you—anything to put off getting a job, anything to get out of going to work like a man. [*She taps the floor with her foot nervously, biting her lips.*]

[*After a short pause.*] Alfred! Get up, do you hear me? I want to make that bed before I go out. I'm sick of having this place in a continual muss on your account. [*With a certain vindictive satisfaction.*] Not that we'll be here long unless you manage to get some money some place. Heaven knows I do my part—and more—going out to sew every day while you play the gentleman and loaf around bar rooms with that good-for-nothing lot of artists from the Square.°

[*A short pause during which she plays nervously with a cup and saucer on the table.*]

And where are you going to get money, I'd like to know? The rent's due this week and you know what the landlord is. He won't let us stay a minute over our time. You say you *can't* get a job. That's a lie and you know it. You never even look for one. All you do is moon around all day writing silly poetry and stories that no one will buy—and no wonder they won't. I notice I can always get a position, such as it is; and it's only that which keeps us from starving to death.

[*Gets up and goes over to the stove—looks into the coffee pot to see if the water is boiling; then comes back and sits down again.*]

5

---

6 *Square:* Washington Square, at the center of Greenwich Village.

You'll have to get money to-day some place. I can't do it all, and I won't do it all. You've got to come to your senses. You've got to beg, borrow, or steal it somewheres. [*With a contemptuous laugh.*] But where, I'd like to know? You're too proud to beg, and you've borrowed the limit, and you haven't the nerve to steal.

[*After a pause—getting up angrily.*] Aren't you up yet, for heaven's sake? It's just like you to go to sleep again, or pretend to. [*She goes to the bedroom door and looks in.*] Oh, you are up. Well, it's about time. You needn't look at me like that. Your airs don't fool me a bit any more. I know you too well—better than you think I do—you and your goings-on. [*Turning away from the door—meaningly.*] I know a lot of things, my dear. Never mind what I know, now. I'll tell you before I go, you needn't worry. [*She comes to the middle of the room and stands there, frowning.*]

[*Irritably.*] Hmm! I suppose I might as well get breakfast ready—not that there's anything much to get. [*Questioningly.*] Unless you have some money? [*She pauses for an answer from the next room which does not come.*] Foolish question! [*She gives a short, hard laugh.*] I ought to know you better than that by this time. When you left here in such a huff last night I knew what would happen. You can't be trusted for a second. A nice condition you came home in! The fight we had was only an excuse for you to make a beast of yourself. What was the use pawning your watch if all you wanted with the money was to waste it in buying drink? 10

[*Goes over to the dish closet and takes out plates, cups, etc., while she is talking.*]

Hurry up! It don't take long to get breakfast these days, thanks to you. All we got this morning is bread and butter and coffee; and you wouldn't even have that if it wasn't for me sewing my fingers off. [*She slams the loaf of bread on the table with a bang.*]

The bread's stale. I hope you'll like it. *You* don't deserve any better, but I don't see why *I* should suffer.

[*Going over to the stove.*] The coffee'll be ready in a minute, and you needn't expect me to wait for you.

[*Suddenly with great anger.*] What on earth are you doing all this time? [*She goes over to the door and looks in.*] Well, you're *almost* dressed at any rate. I expected to find you back in bed. That'd be just like you. How awful you look this morning! For heaven's sake, shave! You're disgusting! You look like a tramp. No wonder no one will give you a job. I don't blame them—when you don't even look halfway decent. [*She goes to the stove.*] There's plenty of hot water right here. You've got no excuse. [*Gets a bowl and pours some of the water from the coffee pot into it.*] Here.

[*He reaches his hand into the room for it. It is a sensitive hand with slender fingers. It trembles and some of the water spills on the floor.*]

[*Tauntingly.*] Look at your hand tremble! You'd better give up drinking. You can't 15 stand it. It's just your kind that get the D.T.'s. *That would be* the last straw! [*Looking down at the floor.*] Look at the mess you've made of this floor—cigarette butts and ashes all over the place. Why can't you put them on a plate? No, you wouldn't be considerate enough to do that. You never think of me. You don't have to sweep the room and that's all you care about.

[*Takes the broom and commences to sweep viciously, raising a cloud of dust. From the inner room comes the sound of a razor being stropped.*]°

15.1 *stropped:* Alfred is using a leather strap to sharpen a straight razor, the kind barbers still use, with a very sharp steel blade that is hinged to a handle.

[*Sweeping.*] Hurry up! It must be nearly time for me to go. If I'm late I'm liable to lose my position, and then I couldn't support you any longer. [*As an afterthought she adds sarcastically.*] And then you'd have to go to work or something dreadful like that. [*Sweeping under the table.*] What I want to know is whether you're going to look for a job to-day or not. You know your family won't help us any more. They've had enough of you, too. [*After a moment's silent sweeping.*] I'm about sick of all this life. I've a good notion to go home, if I wasn't too proud to let them know what a failure you've been—you, the millionaire Rowland's only son, the Harvard graduate, the poet, the catch of the town— Huh! [*With bitterness.*] There wouldn't be many of them now envy my catch if they knew the truth. What has our marriage been, I'd like to know? Even before your *millionaire* father died owing every one in the world money, you certainly never wasted any of your time on your wife. I suppose you thought I'd ought to be glad you were *honorable* enough to marry me—after getting me into trouble. You were ashamed of me with your fine friends because my father's only a grocer, that's what you were. At least he's honest, which is more than any one could say about yours. [*She is sweeping steadily toward the door. Leans on her broom for a moment.*]

You hoped every one'd think you'd been forced to marry me, and pity you, didn't you? You didn't hesitate much about telling me you loved me, and making me believe your lies, before it happened, did you? You made me think you didn't want your father to buy me off as he tried to do. I know better now. I haven't lived with you all this time for nothing. [*Somberly.*] It's lucky the poor thing was born dead, after all. What a father you'd have been!

[*Is silent, brooding moodily for a moment—then she continues with a sort of savage joy.*]

But I'm not the only one who's got you to thank for being unhappy. There's one other, at least, and *she* can't hope to marry you now. [*She puts her head into the next room.*] How about Helen? [*She starts back from the doorway, half frightened.*]

Don't look at me that way! Yes, I read her letter. What about it? I got a right to. I'm your wife. And I know all there is to know, so don't lie. You needn't stare at me so. You can't bully me with your superior airs any longer. Only for me you'd be going without breakfast this very morning. [*She sets the broom back in the corner—whiningly.*] You never did have any gratitude for what I've done. [*She comes to the stove and puts the coffee into the pot.*] The coffee's ready. I'm not going to wait for you. [*She sits down in her chair again.*]

[*After a pause—puts her hand to her head—fretfully.*] My head aches so this morning. It's a shame I've got to go to work in a stuffy room all day in my condition. And I wouldn't if you were half a man. By rights I ought to be lying on my back instead of you. You know how sick I've been this last year; and yet you object when I take a little something to keep up my spirits. You even didn't want me to take that tonic I got at the drug store. [*With a hard laugh.*] I know you'd be glad to have me dead and out of your way; then you'd be free to run after all these silly girls that think you're such a wonderful, misunderstood person—this Helen and the others. [*There is a sharp exclamation of pain from the next room.*]

[*With satisfaction.*] There! I knew you'd cut yourself. It'll be a lesson to you. You know you oughtn't to be running around nights drinking with your nerves in such an awful shape. [*She goes to the door and looks in.*]

What makes you so pale? What are you staring at yourself in the mirror that way for? For goodness sake, wipe that blood off your face! [*With a shudder.*] It's horrible. [*In relieved tones.*] There, that's better. I never could stand the sight of blood. [*She shrinks

20

back from the door a little.] You better give up trying and go to a barber shop. Your hand shakes dreadfully. Why do you stare at me like that? [*She turns away from the door.*] Are you still mad at me about that letter? [*Defiantly.*] Well, I had a right to read it. I'm your wife. [*She comes to the chair and sits down again. After a pause.*]

I knew all the time you were running around with someone. Your lame excuses about spending the time at the library didn't fool me. Who is this Helen, anyway? One of those artists? Or does she write poetry, too? Her letter sounds that way. I'll bet she told you your things were the best ever, and you believed her, like a fool. Is she young and pretty? I was young and pretty, too, when you fooled me with your fine, poetic talk; but life with you would soon wear anyone down. What I've been through!

[*Goes over and takes the coffee off the stove.*] Breakfast is ready. [*With a contemptuous glance.*] Breakfast! [*Pours out a cup of coffee for herself and puts the pot on the table.*] Your coffee'll be cold. What are you doing—still shaving, for heaven's sake? You'd better give it up. One of these mornings you'll give yourself a serious cut. [*She cuts off bread and butters it. During the following speeches she eats and sips her coffee.*]

I'll have to run as soon as I've finished eating. One of us has got to work. [*Angrily.*] Are you going to look for a job to-day or aren't you? I should think some of your fine friends would help you, if they really think you're so much. But I guess they just like to hear you talk. [*Sits in silence for a moment.*]   25

I'm sorry for this Helen, whoever she is. Haven't you got any feelings for other people? What will her family say? I see she mentions them in her letter. What is she going to do—have the child—or go to one of those doctors? That's a nice thing, I must say. Where can she get the money? Is she rich? [*She waits for some answer to this volley of questions.*]

Hmm! You won't tell me anything about her, will you? Much I care. Come to think of it, I'm not so sorry for her after all. She knew what she was doing. She isn't any schoolgirl, like I was, from the looks of her letter. Does she know you're married? Of course, she must. All your friends know about your unhappy marriage. I know they pity you, but they don't know my side of it. They'd talk different if they did.

[*Too busy eating to go on for a second or so.*]

This Helen must be a fine one, if she knew you were married. What does she expect, then? That I'll divorce you and let her marry you? Does she think I'm crazy enough for that—after all you've made me go through? I guess not! And you can't get a divorce from me and you know it. No one can say *I've* ever done anything wrong. [*Drinks the last of her cup of coffee.*]

She deserves to suffer, that's all I can say. I'll tell you what I think; I think your Helen is no better than a common street-walker, that's what I think. [*There is a stifled groan of pain from the next room.*]

Did you cut yourself again? Serves you right. [*Gets up and takes off her apron.*] Well,   30
I've got to run along. [*Peevishly.*] This is a fine life for me to be leading! I won't stand for your loafing any longer. [*Something catches her ear and she pauses and listens intently.*] There! You've overturned the water all over everything. Don't say you haven't. I can hear it dripping on the floor. [*A vague expression of fear comes over her face.*] Alfred! Why don't you answer me?

[*She moves slowly toward the room. There is the noise of a chair being overturned and something crashes heavily to the floor. She stands, trembling with fright.*]

Alfred! Alfred! Answer me! What is it you knocked over? Are you still drunk?
[*Unable to stand the tension a second longer she rushes to the door of the bedroom.*]
Alfred!

[*She stands in the doorway looking down at the floor of the inner room, transfixed with horror. Then she shrieks wildly and runs to the other door, unlocks it and frenziedly pulls it open, and runs shrieking madly into the outer hallway.*]

[*The curtain falls.*]

QUESTIONS

1. What does the setting tell you about the Rowlands?

2. How is Mrs. Rowland described in the opening stage directions? How does O'Neill use adjectives to shape your initial response to her? How does the rest of the play sustain or alter this image?

3. How does Mrs. Rowland speak to Alfred? What does she complain about? What does she accuse Alfred of being and doing?

4. What happened during Mrs. Rowland's premarital affair with Alfred? Why didn't she let Alfred's father "buy her off"?

5. Where is the play's crisis? Which character comes to a crisis? What leads you to conclude that the character and play have reached a crisis?

6. Mrs. Rowland precipitates the climax by discussing Alfred's affair. What do we learn about Helen? What pushes Alfred over the edge?

GENERAL QUESTIONS

1. How does the setting define the characters, their relationship, and their life? What details of setting are most significant?

2. Is Mrs. Rowland flat or round? Static or dynamic? Individualized or stereotyped? Why does she have no first name?

3. Why is Alfred Rowland kept off stage (except for his hand) and given no dialogue? How does this affect the play?

4. Alfred is presented from his wife's point of view. How accurate is this portrait? To what degree does Alfred justify his wife's accusations?

5. Why does O'Neill present the history of Alfred's family and his relationship with Mrs. Rowland out of chronological order? What is the effect of this method of presentation?

WRITING ABOUT THE ELEMENTS OF DRAMA

Although some aspects of drama, such as lighting and stage movement, are purely theatrical, drama shares a number of elements with fiction and poetry. The planning and the writing processes for essays about drama are therefore similar to those used for essays on the other genres. As you plan, select a play and an appropriate element or series of elements. It would be inappropriate, for example, to attempt an essay about character development in *Tea Party* (pp. 872–75) because this play is too short to probe the two characters deeply.

Once you select the play, choose a focus, which will be your central idea. For example, you might argue that a character is flat, static, nonrealistic, or symbolic of good or evil. Or, to assert relationships among elements, you might claim that a play's meaning is shaped and emphasized through setting or through conflict.

Topics for Discovering Ideas

PLOT, ACTION, CONFLICT.   (See also Chapter 3.) In planning an essay on plot or structure, demonstrate how actions and conflicts unfold. In addition, link this concern to other dramatic elements, such as tone or theme. In general, this topic breaks down into three areas—conflict, plot, and structure. For conflict, determine what the conflicts are, which one is central, and how it is resolved. What kind of conflict is it? Does it suggest any general behavioral patterns? For plot, determine the separate stages of development. What is the climax? The dénouement? How are they anticipated or foreshadowed? In examining plot structures and patterns, determine whether the play has a sub-plot or second plot. If so, how is it related to the main plot? Is a significant pattern of action repeated? If so, what is the effect? To what extent do these parallel or repetitive patterns influence theme and meaning? How do they control your responses?

CHARACTERS.   (See also Chapter 4.) Focus on a significant figure and formulate a central idea about his or her personality, function, or meaning. Is the character round or flat? Static or dynamic? Individualized or stereotyped? Realistic or nonrealistic? Symbolic? How is the character described in the stage directions? By other characters? By himself or herself? What does he or she do, think, say? What is the character's attitude toward the environment? The action? Other characters? Himself or herself? To what extent does he or she articulate and/or embody key ideas in the play?

POINT OF VIEW AND PERSPECTIVE.   (See also Chapter 5.) In many plays, such as *Hamlet, Before Breakfast,* and *The Glass Menagerie,* the playwright presents the action from the perspective of an individual character. The audience therefore sees things as this character sees the same things, influences them, and is influenced by them. When you deal with such a technique, consider how the perspective affects the play's structure and meaning. Why is this point of view useful or striking? What does it suggest about character? Theme? To what extent does your reaction to the play correspond with or diverge from this perspective?

Another feature of perspective is that characters may speak directly to the audience, in a *soliloquy,* or indirectly, in a *monologue.* In dealing with these perspectives, consider whether you sympathize with the character doing the speaking. What information does the character convey? What is he or she trying to prove? What is the tone of the speech? What do these devices contribute to your response? Generally, what does the perspective contribute to your understanding of the play?

SETTING, SETS, AND PROPS.   (See also Chapter 6.) Normally, you will not write about setting and properties in isolation; such an essay would simply produce a detailed description of the setting(s) and objects. Instead, a discussion of setting in drama should be linked to another element, such as character, mood, or meaning. Such an essay will demonstrate the ways in which setting(s) and objects help establish the time, place, characters, lifestyle, values, or ideas.

When dealing with a single setting, pay close attention to the opening stage directions and any other directions or dialogue that describe the environment or objects. In plays with multiple settings, you will normally select one or two for examination. Ask yourself whether the setting is realistic or nonrealistic and to what extent it may be symbolic. What details and objects are specified? What do these tell you about the time, the place, and the characters and their way of life and values? To what extent does the setting contribute to the play's tone, atmosphere, impact, and meaning?

DICTION, IMAGERY, AND STYLE.   (See also Chapters 7, 12, and 13.) As with setting, try to connect the devices of language to some other element such as tone, character, or meaning. Investigate the play's levels of diction and types of dialect, jargon, slang, or clichés. To what extent do these techniques define the characters and support or undercut their ideas? What connotative words or phrases are repeated? Which are spoken at particularly significant moments? What striking or consistent threads of imagery, metaphor, tone, or meaning do you find? How do all these aspects of language shape your reaction?

TONE AND ATMOSPHERE.   (See also Chapters 7 and 15.) Try to deal with *how* the tone is established and *what* impact it has on the play's meaning. Seek those devices the playwright employs to control your attitudes toward individual characters, situations, and outcomes. Look for clues in stage directions, diction, imagery, rhetorical devices, tempo, and context. Is tone articulated directly? Or indirectly, through irony? Also try to establish the presence of dramatic irony: To what extent do you (as a reader or spectator) know more than many of the onstage characters?

SYMBOLISM AND ALLEGORY.   (See also Chapters 8 and 18.) Try to determine the characters, objects, settings, situations, actions, words or phrases, and/or costumes that seem to be symbolic. What do they symbolize, and how do you know that they are symbolic? Are they cultural or contextual? Is the symbolism extensive and consistent enough to form an allegorical system? If so, what are the two levels of meaning addressed by the allegory? To what extent does the symbolism or allegory shape the play's meaning and your responses to it?

THEME.   (See also Chapter 9.) The questions and areas of concern listed above should help you in discussing theme. Try to connect theme with various other aspects of the play such as character, conflict, action, setting, language, or symbolism. What key ideas does the play explore, and what aspects of the play convey these ideas most emphatically? In dealing with each topic and question, isolate the elements and devices that have the strongest impact on meaning.

REFERRING TO PLAYS AND PARTS OF PLAYS

Underline (or *italicize*) the titles of plays as you would a book title. In referring to speeches, assume that your reader may have a text different from yours. Therefore provide the information necessary for finding the exact location, regardless of text.

In the body of the essay, for a play with act, scene, and line or speech numbers, refer to *Act* (roman numeral), *scene* (Arabic numeral), and *line* or *speech* number (Arabic numeral). For clarity, spell out these words: *Act II, scene 3, line 24,* or *Act IV, scene 1, speech 4.*

In direct quotations, however, including block quotations (set apart from your own writing), write the numbers in parentheses following the quotation: (*III, 1.33*) or (*III.1, speech 4*). When no word precedes the last number, it is understood to refer to a line; for clarity, it is best to spell out that you are referring to a speech number.

When a play is divided into acts but not scenes, or if the play contains only one act, spell out the details completely. Thus, in a play like *Death of a Salesman,* which contains two acts and an epilogue, you may refer to *Act I, speech 348* or *Epilogue, speech 5,* both in your text and in block quotations. If the play contains only numbered scenes, like *The Glass Menagerie,* spell things out similarly: *scene 1, speech 29.* When referring to a one-act play like *The Bear,* use the speech or line number: *speech 265.*

For stage directions, use the line or speech number immediately preceding the direction, and abbreviate *stage direction* as S.D.: *scene I, speech 16 S.D.* Your reader will then know that you are referring to the stage direction following speech 16 in scene 1. If there are stage directions at the opening of the play before the speeches begin (as in *The Glass Menagerie* and *Before Breakfast*), use a zero and then a decimal point followed by an Arabic numeral to refer to the paragraph of directions. Thus *0.3 S.D.* refers to the third paragraph of directions at the play's beginning.

For prefaces, scene directions, and casts of characters, such as the "Production Notes" of *The Glass Menagerie,* use the title and then the paragraph number: *In the "Production Notes," Williams describes* The Glass Menagerie *as a "memory play" (paragraph 1).*

For scene directions at the beginning of acts or scenes, the most specific style spells out the circumstances: *The scene directions for Act III of* A Dollhouse *describe the Torvalds' living room after the Christmas party.*

For the cast of characters, the same principle applies. Spell out what you mean, such as *the cast of characters, the Characters list,* or the *Dramatis Personae.* The important thing about referring to parts of plays is that you be clear and exact. The guidance offered here will cover most situations, but complications and exceptions will occur. When they do, always ask your instructor for help.

Strategies for Organizing Ideas

For an essay on drama, you might choose from a number of strategies. If you are writing about loneliness and frustration in Keller's *Tea Party*, for example, you might select a number of objects or occurrences as the launching point for your discussion. Some of these might be the tea trolley and the sofa, the bringing in of the cocoa, or the paperboy's rapid movement past the window. In discussing the crimes of Claudius in *Hamlet*, you might choose (1) the testimony of the Ghost to Hamlet, (2) Claudius's reaction to the Players' scene, (3) his speech as he is praying, and (4) his poisoning of the cup, to show how these actions convincingly establish his villainy. For such essays, you might devote separate paragraphs to each element, or you might use two or more paragraphs for each element as you develop your ideas further.

Similar strategies can be found for every possible type of essay on drama. In dealing with character in Glaspell's *Trifles*, for example, you might claim that a number of symbolic props help to establish and reinforce the character of Minnie Wright or the ideas about marriage conveyed in the play. You might then use separate paragraphs to discuss these related symbols, such as Minnie's clothes, her dead canary, and her unfinished quilt. Similarly, in writing about language in plays like Chekhov's *The Bear* or O'Neill's *Before Breakfast*, you would establish how the particular play connects qualities of speech to revelations about topics such as character and idea. Thus, in *The Bear*, Smirnov's constant use of exclamations, shouts, and profanity, at least until shortly before the play's end, establish his irascibility.

SAMPLE STUDENT ESSAY

O'Neill's Use of Negative Descriptions and Stage Directions in *Before Breakfast*° as a Means of Revealing Character

[1] In the one-act play *Before Breakfast,* Eugene O'Neill dramatizes the suicidal crisis and climax of a worsening husband-wife relationship. The story is clear. Mrs. Rowland, when still a young girl, was naive and opportunistic. She seduced and then married Alfred Rowland, who was the heir of his father's millions. Her resulting pregnancy ended in stillbirth. As if this were not enough, Alfred's father died not a millionaire, but a pauper. During the years of these disappointments, Mrs. Rowland has lost whatever pleasantness she once possessed and has descended into a state of personal neglect, alcoholism, and selfishness.* To bring out these traits early in the play, O'Neill relies on negative descriptions and stage directions.†

[2] The descriptions of Mrs. Rowland's personal neglect emphasize her loss of self-esteem. The directions indicate that she has allowed her figure to become "a

° See pp. 877–82 for this play.
* Central idea.
† Thesis sentence.

shapeless stoutness," and that she has piled her hair into a "drab-colored mass." This neglect of her physical person is capped off, according to O'Neill's description, by her blue dress, which is "shabby and worn" and "formless" (0.1, S.D.). Clearly, the shabbiness and excessive wear may result from poverty and thus [2] show little about her character, but the formlessness of the dress indicates a characteristic lack of concern about appearance, also shown by her stoutness and her hair. This slovenliness shows how she wants to appear in public, because she is dressed and ready to go to work for the day. O'Neill's negative descriptions thus define her lack of self-respect.

Similarly uncomplimentary, O'Neill's directions about her sneakiness reveal her dependence on alcohol. A serious sign of distress, even though it might also be funny onstage, is the direction indicating that she takes out a bottle of gin that she keeps hidden in a "dish closet" (speech 1, S.D). With this stage direction O'Neill symbolizes the weakest trait of the secret drinker, which he also shows in the direction that Mrs. Rowland brightens up once she has taken a stiff jolt of gin:

[3]

> The large dose of alcohol she has taken has an almost immediate effect. Her features become more animated, she seems to gather energy, and she looks at the bedroom with a hard, vindictive smile on her lips. (speech 1, S.D.)

It is safe to assume that these stage directions, on the morning of the play's action, would also have applied to her behavior on many previous mornings. In short, O'Neill is telling us that Mrs. Rowland is a secret alcoholic.

The furtiveness of her drinking also shows up in her search of Alfred's clothing, which also shows her selfishness and bitterness. When she methodically empties his pockets and uncovers the letter that we soon learn is from his mistress, the stage directions show that she unhesitatingly reads the letter. Then O'Neill directs the actress to form "a cruel smile on her lips" as she thinks about [4] what to do with this new information (speech 34, S.D.). As with the drinking, we see Mrs. Rowland rifling through Alfred's things only this once, but the action suggests that this secretive prying is a regular feature of her life. However, it is her discovery on *this* morning--before breakfast--that is the key to the action, because her extensive monologue against her husband, which constitutes most of the play, allows her to vent all her hatred by reproaching him about his lack of work, his neglect of her, the time he spends with friends, and his love affair.

While O'Neill uses these stage directions and descriptions to convey Mrs. Rowland's unpleasantness, he provides balance in her speeches and additional actions. He makes her a master of harangue, but there is nothing either in the directions or in her speeches to indicate that she wants to drive Alfred to suicide. Indeed, her horror at his suicide is genuine--just as it concludes [5] the play with an incredible shock. In addition, on the positive side, her speeches show that despite her alcoholism and anger she is actually functioning in the outside world--as a seamstress--and that it is she who provides the meager money on which the couple is living (speech 6). In addition, she is working despite the fact that she has been feeling ill for a period of time (speech 20). She also has enough concern for Alfred to bring him hot water for shaving (speech 14, S.D.).

[6]   It is clear that O'Neill wants us to conclude that if Mrs. Rowland were a supportive person, Alfred might not be the nervous alcoholic who cuts his throat in the bathroom. However, the play does not make clear that he ever could have been better, even with the maximum support of a perfect wife. Certainly, Mrs. Rowland is not supportive. The stage directions and speeches show that she is limited by her weakness and bitterness. With such defects of character, she has unquestionably never given Alfred any support at all, and probably never could. Everything that O'Neill tells us about her indicates that she is petty and selfish, and that she originally married Alfred expecting to receive and not to give.

[7]   As things stand at the beginning of the play, then, Alfred is at the brink of despair, and Mrs. Rowland's bitter and reproachful speeches drive him to self-destruction. Despite all the malice that O'Neill attributes to her character through the stage descriptions and directions, however, it is not possible to say that she is the sole cause of Alfred's suicide. O'Neill shows that Mrs. Rowland is an unpleasant, spiteful, and messy whiner, but it is not possible to reach any conclusions beyond this characterization.

Commentary on the Essay

This essay shows how dramatic conventions can be considered in reference to the analysis of character. Although the essay refers briefly to Mrs. Rowland's speeches, it stresses those descriptions and directions that O'Neill designs specifically for the actress performing the role. The essay thus indicates one way to discuss a play, as distinguished from a story or poem.

The introductory paragraph contains enough of the story about Mrs. Rowland and her husband to help the reader make sense of the subsequent material about the stage directions and descriptions. Throughout the essay, paragraph transitions are effected by words such as *similarly, also, while,* and *then.*

Paragraph 2, the first of the body, deals with O'Neill's stage directions concerning Mrs. Rowland's slovenly appearance and lack of personal care. Paragraphs 3 and 4 are concerned with directions about her behavior—first her drinking and then her search of Alfred's clothing. Paragraph 5 briefly attempts to consider how O'Neill uses Mrs. Rowland's speeches and other actions to balance the totally negative portrait he builds up through the negative stage directions.

Paragraphs 6 and 7 close the essay. Paragraph 6 considers how the stage directions lead no further than the conclusion that the Rowlands' marriage is a terrible one. Paragraph 7 continues the argument of paragraph 6, with the additional thought that O'Neill's stage directions do not justify concluding that Mrs. Rowland's spiteful character is the cause of her husband's suicide.

SPECIAL WRITING TOPICS FOR CONSIDERING THE ELEMENTS OF DRAMA

1.   *Tea Party* might be considered sentimental, on the grounds that the two elderly characters are presented to evoke sympathy and anguish, not to resemble the

lives of real persons. Write an essay defending the play against this judgment, being sure to make references to Keller's portrayal of character.

2. *Before Breakfast* is set in an apartment in Greenwich Village in lower Manhattan around 1916. It was performed in Greenwich Village in December 1916. Write an essay that deals with the following questions:

   a. What do you make of this convergence of settings—artistic and realistic?

   b. What did O'Neill assume about his original audience's reaction to the setting?

3. Write an essay that considers the following questions. Is Glaspell's *Trifles* about crime? Rural life? Marriage? The roles of rural and frontier women? The way men regard women? The way in which anger that is bottled up must eventually explode? Write an essay detailing your response, using specific details from the play to support your argument. To what degree is the situation in the play realistic? If it were to be presented as a play about a similar murder in the 1980s and 1990s (there have been a number of them), what freedom would the women have to explore the kitchen?

4. Read the story "A Jury of Her Peers" (Chapter 4, p. 166), which Glaspell wrote a year after *Trifles*. Write an essay comparing and contrasting the story and the play (see Chapter 29). You might wish to concentrate, for example, on the openings of the two works, the descriptions of the women's reactions, and the quantity of detail used in the play and in the story. On the basis of your essay, contrast the characteristics of drama and of fiction.

5. Describe Hughes's symbolism in *Mulatto*. How does the symbolism bring out the black-white differences in the play? Which locations, objects, and actions are symbolic, and what do they symbolize? In what ways are the symbols realistic? If they were not realistic, would they be successful as symbols?

6. Write an essay on one of the following topics. Before you begin writing, consult Chapter 27 for a description of how to proceed.

   a. A feminist analysis of *Trifles*.

   b. A psychological consideration of Mrs. Rowland in *Before Breakfast*.

   c. The two sisters as archetypal old people in *Tea Party*.

7. On the basis of the plays included in this chapter, write an essay dealing with the characteristics of the dramatic form. Consider topics such as dialogue, monologue, soliloquy, action, vocal ranges, staging, comparative lengths of plays, pauses in speech, stage directions, laughter, seriousness, and the means by which the dramatists engage the audience in characters and situations.

8. Using the catalogue in your library, look up the category *Drama—Criticism*, or *Drama—History and Criticism*, whichever title your library uses. You will find there a number of categories, such as the relationship of drama to (a) elements, (b) history, (c) origin, (d) philosophy, (e) production, (f) religion, (g) stagecraft, and (h) themes. Develop a short bibliography on one of these topics and take out two or three of the relevant books. Describe them briefly, and explain—and criticize if possible—the principal ideas in one of the chapters.

23

The Tragic Vision: Affirmation Through Loss

Tragedy is drama in which a major character undergoes a loss but also achieves illumination or a new perspective. It is considered the most elevated literary form because it concentrates affirmatively on the religious and cosmic implications of its major character's misfortunes. In ancient Greece, it began as a key element in Athenian religious festivals during the decades before Athens became a major military, economic, and cultural power during the fifth century B.C.E.

Tragedy, however, was not religious in a sectarian sense. It did not dramatize religious doctrines and did not present a consistent religious view. To the Athenians, religion connected the past with the present and with the gods, and through this connection it served to enrich individuals, society, and the state.

Originally, tragedy in Athens was associated with the worship of a specific god—Dionysus, one of the twelve principal Athenian deities who, it was thought, transformed human personality and freed people from care and grief. To elevate this god in the eyes of his fellow Athenians, the Athenian tyrant Peisistratus (ruled 560–527 B.C.E.) added Dionysus worship to the annual religious festivals that the Athenians held for their gods.[1]

---

[1] Ancient religion is difficult for us to understand because of our completely different religious traditions and the passage of 2,500 years of history. In its origins, Greek religion was local in nature—a by-product of the comparative isolation of the various Greek city-states. Collective public worship of a centralized god within centrally located religious buildings—like the churches, temples, and mosques we know today—did not then exist. Instead, the Greeks believed in many gods with varying powers and interests who could travel invisibly and at will from place to place within their dominions. Consequently the Greeks erected many separate local shrines and sanctuaries, which were considered holy to particular gods and where people might place offerings and say prayers. Large temples built in important city-states like Athens and Corinth were dedicated to gods, such as Zeus, Athena, and Apollo, that important citizens especially revered. Even then, the temples were not designed for mass worship, but rather were considered resident sanctuaries for the gods themselves. Therefore, the major space in the temples was a holy of holies reserved only for the god. To make public this essentially private worship, the Greek city-states held religious

THE ORIGINS OF TRAGEDY

Tragedy: The Earliest Dramatic Form

From the standpoint of drama, the most significant of these Dionysiac festivals were the *Lenaia* and the *Great* or *City Dionysia*. The Lenaia was a short celebration held in January (the Greek month *Gamelion*), and the City Dionysia was a week-long event in March–April (*Elaphebolion*, the month of stags). In the sixth century B.C.E., ceremonies held during the festival of the City Dionysia began to include tragedy, although not in the form that has been transmitted to us. The philosopher and critic Aristotle (384–322 B.C.E.), writing almost two hundred years after the form appeared, claimed that the first tragedies developed from a choral ode called a **dithyramb**—an ode or song that was sung or chanted and also danced by large choruses at the festivals.[2] According to Aristotle, the first tragedies were choral improvisations originating with "the authors of the Dithyramb" (*Poetics* IV.12, p. 19).

The Heroic Subjects of Tragedy

From Aristotle's claim, we may conclude that tragedy soon took on the characteristics and conventions that elevated it. For subject matter, writers turned to well-known myths about the heroes and demigods of the prehistoric period between the vanished age of bronze and the living age of iron. The myths described individual adventures and achievements, including epic explorations and battles that had taken place principally during the time of the Trojan War. Like the stories in the Hebrew Scriptures, the Greek myths illustrated divine-human relationships and also served as examples or models of heroic behavior. With very few exceptions, these myths became the fixed tragic subject matter. Indeed, Aristotle called them the "received legends" that by his time had become the "usual subjects of tragedy" (*Poetics* IX.8, p. 37).

The mythical heroes—many of whom were objects of cult worship—were kings, queens, princes, and princesses. They engaged in conflicts; they suffered; and, often, they died. Though great they were nevertheless human, and a common critical judgment is that they were dominated by *hubris* or *hybris* (arrogant pride, insolence, contemptuous violence), which was manifested in destructive actions such as deceit, subterfuge, lying, betrayal, revenge, murder,

---

festivals such as the Athenian celebrations of Dionysus and Athena. In short, the gods who became prominent and were widely worshiped in ancient Greece achieved their status because of the political power of their principal worshipers.

[2] S. H. Butcher, *Aristotle's Theory of Poetry and Fine Art*, 4th ed. (New York: Dover, 1951), p. 19 (VI.12). All parenthetical references to Aristotle are from this edition. The origin of the word *dithyramb* is obscure. Some ancient etymologists claimed that the word was derived from the legendary "double birth" of Dionysus. This derivation is based on the idea that *dithyramb* is a compound (*dis*, "two," and *thyra*, "door") referring to the myth that Zeus removed Dionysus from the womb of his mother, Semele, and then placed the fetus within his thigh. When Zeus removed Dionysus, the god had "come through the door" of birth twice. This derivation, however, has been disputed. For a description of the origin of comedy during the festivals for Dionysus, see pp. 1065–67.

suicide, patricide, infanticide, and self-mutilation. By truthfully demonstrating the faults of these heroes along with their greatness, the writers of tragedy also invoked philosophical and religious issues that provide meaning and value in the face of misfortune and suffering.

The Word Tragedy *and Its Elevation in Meaning*

One of the puzzles of tragedy is the word itself, which combines the Greek words *tragos* ("goat") and *oide* ("ode" or "song")—a "goat ode" or "goat song." This meaning raises the question of how so unlikely a word is linked to the tragic form. One oft-repeated answer is that the word was first applied to choral ceremonials performed at the ritual sacrifice of a goat. Another is that the word described a choral competition in which a goat was the prize.

A more persuasive recent answer is that the word *tragedy* stemmed from the word *tragoidoi*, or "billy goat singers," which was applied pejoratively to the young men (*ephebes*) in the choruses.[3] The ephebes were military trainees between the ages of eighteen and twenty; those trainees who were best at close-order drill were selected as choral members because the dramatic choruses required precision movements. Because they were young, however, they were still likened to goats.[4] Indeed, at first tragedy was apparently not called *tragodia* (tragedy) at all, but rather *tragoidoi*, as though the chorus members were more important than the words they spoke. This explanation is consistent with the improvisatory origins of tragedy that Aristotle describes: In the decades following its beginnings, the genre grew in importance, quality, and stature, and its name underwent the accompanying elevation that it still possesses.

The Evolution of Tragedy from a Choral Form to a Dramatic Form

Because the surviving Athenian plays are dominated by acting parts, modern readers sometimes conclude that the chorus parts needlessly interrupt the main action. It may be surprising to recognize that in the beginning there were no individual actors at all, only choruses. The introduction of actors—and their eventual domination—was one of the improvisations that Aristotle associates with the evolution of tragedy. At some point in the performance of a choral ode, the chorus leader delivered lines introducing and linking the choral speeches. Because of this special function, the new speaker (called a *hypocrites*, which became the word for actor) was soon separated and distinguished from the chorus.

---

[3] For this argument, see John J. Winkler, "The Ephebes' Song: *Tragodia* and *Polis*," in John J. Winkler and Froma I. Zeitlin, eds., *Nothing to Do with Dionysos? Athenian Drama in Its Social Context* (Princeton: Princeton UP, 1990), pp. 20–62. For a discussion of the military nature of the ancient Greek city-state, see Paul Rahe, "The Martial Republics of Classical Greece," *The Wilson Quarterly*, vol. 17, no. 1 (Winter 1993): 58–70.

[4] There is nothing unusual about this comparison. In modern English, for example, a common slang word for a child is "kid," the standard word for a young goat and also other young animals.

The next essential step was *impersonation*, or the assuming of a role. The *hypocrites* would represent a hero, and the chorus would represent groups such as townspeople, worshipers, youths, or elders. With the commencement of such role playing, genuine drama had begun. According to tradition, the first *hypocrites* or actor—and therefore the acknowledged founder of the acting profession—was the writer and choral leader Thespis, in about 536–533 B.C.E., during the time of Peisistratus.

THE ORIGIN OF TRAGEDY, A SUMMARY

In Athens during the sixth century B.C.E., tragedy originated during the *City Dionysia*, one of the major Athenian religious festivals held to celebrate Dionysus, a liberating god and one of the twelve major gods. As a genre, tragedy first featured improvisations upon a type of choral ode called a *dithyramb*. It then evolved, as Aristotle says, "by slow degrees" (*Poetics*, IV.12, p. 19), developing new elements as they seemed appropriate and necessary.

One of the vital new elements was an emphasis on the death or misfortune of a major character.* This emphasis resulted *not* from a preconceived theoretical design, however, but rather from the reality of suffering in the lives of the heroic subjects. As writers of tragedy developed the cosmic and religious implications of such adversity, they in effect offered philosophic, religious, moral, and civic benefits, and therefore the simple attendance at the performance of a tragedy came to be regarded as a religious experience.

Because tragedy was originally linked to the choral dithyrambs, it is important to stress that *tragedy, and therefore drama, began as a form for choruses, not for actors.* Even after actors became dominant in the plays, the chorus was important enough for Aristotle to state that "the chorus should be regarded as one of the actors" (XVIII.7, p. 69).

---

* Although the tragic protagonist often dies at the play's end, the extant Athenian tragedies do not follow this pattern rigidly. It is true that the major figures suffer, and sometimes they die, but often they escape punishment, and they may even receive divine pardon.

THE ANCIENT COMPETITIONS IN TRAGEDY

Once Thespis set the pattern of action between actor and chorus, the writing of tragedies as a competition within the Dionysiac festivals became institutionalized.

The Tragic Dramatists and Their Work

Early each summer, a number of dramatists vied for the honor of having their plays performed at the next City Dionysia, to be held the following spring. They prepared three tragedies (a **trilogy**)[5] together with a **satyr play** (a boisterous burlesque) and submitted the four works to the Eponymous

---

[5] In the earliest dramas, the trilogies shared a common subject, as seen in the *Oresteia* of Aeschylus, which is a cycle of three plays on the subject of the house of Agamemnon. But by the time of Sophocles and Euripides, connected trilogies were no longer required. Sophocles's *Oedipus the King* and *Oedipus at Colonus*, for example, were submitted at widely different times.

Archon (the man for whom the year was named), one of the city's two magistrates. The three best submissions were approved ("given a chorus") for performance at the festival. On the last day of the festival, after the performances were over, the archon awarded a prize to the tragic playwright voted best for that year; there was also a prize for the best writer of a comedy. The winner's prize was not money, but rather a crown of ivy and the glory of triumph.

The Three Great Athenian Tragic Playwrights

To gain the honor of victory during the centuries of the competitions, many playwrights wrote many hundreds, probably thousands, of plays. Most of these have long since vanished because the writers were insignificant and also because there were no more than a few copies of each play, all handwritten on perishable papyrus scrolls.

A small number of works by three tragic playwrights, however, have survived. These dramatists are **Aeschylus** (525–456 B.C.E.), who added a second actor; **Sophocles** (ca. 496–406/5 B.C.E.), who added a third actor, created scene design, and increased the chorus from twelve to fifteen; and **Euripides** (ca. 484–406 B.C.E.). Although these three playwrights did not win prizes every time they entered the competitions, a consensus grew that they were the best, and by the middle of the fourth century B.C.E., their works were elevated to the status of classics. Although tragedies had originally been intended for only one performance, at the festival in which they competed, an exception was made for these three dramatists, whose tragedies were then performed repeatedly both in Athens and elsewhere in the Greek-speaking world.

The combined output of the three classic playwrights was slightly more than three hundred plays, of which three-fourths were tragedies and one-fourth were satyr plays. As many as eight hundred years after the end of the fifth century B.C.E., these plays, together with many other Greek tragedies, satyr plays, and comedies, were available to readers who could afford to buy copies or commission scribes to copy them.[6] However, with the increasing dominance of Christianity the plays fell into neglect because they were considered pagan and also because vellum or parchment, which made up the pages of the books (*codices*) that replaced papyrus scrolls, was enormously expensive and was reserved for Christian works. Most of the unique and priceless copies of Athenian plays were subsequently destroyed or thrown away.

The Preservation of Plays
by the Three Great Athenian Dramatists

The Greek dramatic tradition might have vanished entirely had it not been for the efforts of Byzantine scholars during the ninth century C.E., when

---

[6] In the third century B.C.E., a complete and definitive hand-copied set of Greek plays was held in the Ptolemaic Library of Alexandria, but at some point all the holdings were lost or destroyed, along with the library building itself. In modern Alexandria, not even the location of the ancient library is known.

Constantinople became the center of a revival of interest in classical Greek language and literature. A primary characteristic of this revival was the copying and preservation of important texts—including those of the three major Greek playwrights. We may conclude that the scholars copied as many of the major plays as they could locate and that they tried to secure their copies safely in monastery libraries.

However, security could not be maintained during those years. Fire, neglect, time, political destabilization, and pillage (such as the sack of Constantinople by Crusaders in 1204) took an enormous toll on the Byzantine manuscript collections. Even so, seven tragedies by Aeschylus, seven by Sophocles, and ten by Euripides somehow were saved from destruction.[7] Additionally, in the fourteenth century, a scholar named Demetrius Triclinius made a lucky find of scrolls containing nine more plays by Euripides (part of what was once a complete set), bringing the total of Euripidean plays to nineteen. Therefore, of all the many thousands of plays written by the Greek tragic playwrights, thirty-three still survive intact; these plays make up the complete Greek tragedies as we know them.[8]

There is, however, just a little more: Many ancient writers often quoted brief passages from plays that were not otherwise preserved, and these portions therefore still exist. Moreover, collectors living in ancient Egypt owned many copies of the plays, and not everything from these collections was lost. In recent centuries, papyrus and vellum fragments—some quite extensive—have been recovered by archaeologists from such unlikely locations as ancient Egyptian rubbish heaps, tombs, and the linings of coffins.

ARISTOTLE AND THE NATURE OF TRAGEDY

Because Aristotle's *Poetics* (*Peri Poietikes*), the first section of his major critical work, survives intact from antiquity, he is in effect the Western world's first critic and aesthetician. From him later critics derived the various "rules" of tragic composition. He also wrote a second part of the *Poetics* concerning comedy. This second work is lost, but enough fragments and summaries survive to

---

[7] Many standard reference works contain the assertion that these twenty-four plays were selected by an unnamed Byzantine schoolmaster for use in the Byzantine schools, and that this anthology was widely adopted and exclusively used thereafter. This claim would explain why the anthologized plays were preserved while unanthologized plays were lost. L. D. Reynolds and N. G. Wilson, in their authoritative *Scribes and Scholars: A Guide to the Transmission of Greek and Latin Literature*, 3rd ed. (Oxford UP, 1991), question this hypothesis. They point out that there is no historical record that such an anthology was ever made, that modern scholars are in truth ignorant "of the origin of the selection," and that therefore "it is perhaps best to abandon the idea that a conscious act of selection by an individual was a primary factor in determining the survival of texts" (p. 54).

[8] The survival of Greek drama was threatened until the first printed editions were published at the beginning of the sixteenth century.

permit a partial hypothetical reconstruction.[9] Aristotle also considered aspects of literature in parts of other philosophical works, principally the *Ethics* and the *Politics.* In addition he, along with his students, assembled a complete catalogue of Greek tragedy from its beginnings to his own time (the *Didaskaliae*). He was therefore able to base his criticism on virtually the entire body of Greek tragedy, including written copies of many plays that he had never seen performed. No one before or since has had more firsthand knowledge of Greek tragedy. His criticism is therefore especially valuable because it rests not only on his acute powers of observation, but also on his unique and encyclopedic knowledge.

As we have seen, Aristotle states that tragedy grew out of improvisations related to dithyrambic choral odes. He adds that once tragedy reached its "natural" or ideal form it stopped evolving (*Poetics* IV.12, p. 19). His criticism is designed to explain the ideal characteristics: Throughout the *Poetics* he stresses concepts of exactitude, proportion, appropriateness, and control. His famous definition of tragedy is in accord with these concepts. In the sixth chapter of the *Poetics*, he claims that tragedy is "an imitation of an action that is serious, complete, and of a certain magnitude; in language embellished with each kind of artistic ornament, the several kinds being found in separate parts of the play; in the form of action, not of narrative; through pity and fear effecting the proper purgation of these emotions" (VI.2, p. 23).

Aristotle's Concept of Catharsis

The last part of this definition—that purgation or **catharsis** is the end or goal of tragedy—crystallizes the earlier parts. In Aristotle's view, tragedy arouses the painful emotions of pity and fear (*eleos* and *phobos*), and, through the experience of the drama, brings about a "proper purgation" or purification of these emotions. Originally, the word *catharsis* was a medical term, and therefore many interpreters argue that tragedy produces a therapeutic effect through an actual purging or "vomiting" of emotions, a sympathetic release of feelings that produces emotional relief and encourages psychological health. In other words, tragedy heals.

A complementary view is that tragic catharsis has a larger public and moral purpose. In this sense, Aristotle's description of tragedy is an implicit argument defending literature itself against the strong disapproval of his teacher, Plato.[10] Both master and pupil accepted the premise that human beings behave thoughtlessly and stupidly as a result of uncontrolled emotion. While in the grip of emotion, people cannot be virtuous and can do no good for others because they make bad decisions that produce bad personal, social, political, military, and moral results. Consequently, if individual temperance and public justice are to prevail, there is a universal need to moderate and regulate the emotions.

---

[9] See Richard Janko, trans., *Aristotle, Poetics I with the Tractatus Coislinianus, A Hypothetical Reconstruction of Poetics II, the Fragments of the On Poets* (Indianapolis: Hackett, 1987), pp. 47–55.

[10] See Janko, especially pp. xvi–xx, and Butcher's discussion on pp. 245–51 of *Aristotle's Theory of Poetry and Fine Art.*

Because Plato states that the emotionalism of literature is untrue, undignified, and also unreasonable, he denies that literature can address this need.

But in the *Poetics* and in relevant parts of other works, Aristotle shows that tragedy indeed addresses this need, and does so through the effect of catharsis. By arousing the powerful feelings of pity and fear, tragedy trains or shapes the emotions so that people become *habituated* to measuring, shaping, and channeling their feelings—controlling them, and not being controlled by them. Through catharsis, people are led to the development of an emotional *mean*, a condition of poise and balance among emotional forces, and they achieve this state harmlessly because in the artistic context of tragedy they are immune to the damage that they may do in actual life. Tragedy therefore assists in the development of moral virtue, for people who have experienced the emotional catharsis or regulation of tragedy will be led to love and hate correctly, to direct their loyalties correctly, and also to make correct decisions and take correct actions, both for themselves and, more significantly, for the public.

It is important to stress that Aristotle states that catharsis is also brought about by other literary genres, especially comedy and epic, and also by music. In other words, artistic works have in common that they cleanse or purify the emotions. It is through the continuous and renewed shaping and regulating of feelings—catharsis—that tragedy, and literature broadly, encourages moral virtue and thereby on both philosophical and religious grounds is necessary and defensible.

The Structure of the Tragic Plot

In light of the concept of catharsis, Aristotle's description of the formal aspects and characteristics of tragedy can be seen as an outline of the ways in which these characteristics first arouse the emotions and then regulate and shape them.

A REPRESENTATION OF AN ACTION. Aristotle concedes that tragedy is not true in the sense that actual history is true. He therefore stresses that a tragic plot (*muthos*) is not an exact imitation or duplication of life, but rather a **representation** (*mimesis*). The concept of representation acknowledges both the moral role of the writer and also the artistic freedom needed to create works conducive to the proper responses. A tragic plot therefore consists of a self-contained and concentrated single action. Anything outside this action, such as unrelated incidents in the life of the major character, is not to be contained in the play. The action of *Oedipus the King*, for example, is focused on Oedipus's determination as king of Thebes to free his city from the pestilence that is destroying it. Although other aspects of his life are introduced in the play's dialogue because they are relevant to the action, they are reported rather than dramatized. Only those incidents integral to the action are included in the play.

REVERSAL, RECOGNITION, AND SUFFERING. Aristotle's discussion of the three major elements of tragic plot is particularly significant. The elements all appear near the conclusion of a tragic play because they are necessary and probable results of the early elements of exposition and complication. First is the "**reversal of the situation**" (*peripeteia*) from apparent good to bad, or a "change [usually also a surprise] by which the action veers round to its opposite," as in *Oedipus the King*, where the outcome is the reverse of what Oedipus intends and expects (XI.1, p. 41). Even if the outcome is unhappy—especially if it is unhappy—it is "the right ending" (XIII.6, p. 47) because it is the most tragic; that is, it evokes the greatest degree of pity and fear.

Second is "a change from ignorance to knowledge, producing love or hate between the persons destined by the poet for good or bad fortune." Aristotle calls this change *anagnorisis* or **recognition** (XI.2, p. 41). In the best and most powerful tragedies, according to him, the reversal and the recognition occur together and create surprise. Aristotle considers recognition to be the discovery of the true identity and involvement of persons, the establishment of guilt or innocence, and the revelation of previously unknown details, for "it is upon such situations that the issues of good or bad fortune will depend" (XI.4, p. 41). One might add that recognition is of major importance because ideally, upon discovering the truth, the protagonist acknowledges errors and accepts responsibility. In *Oedipus the King*, for example, Oedipus ultimately recognizes the truth of his own guilt even though during most of the play he has been trying to evade it. He then becomes the agent of his own punishment. Because such recognition illustrates that human beings have the strength to preserve their integrity even in the depths of adversity, it is one of the elements making tragedy the highest of all literary forms.

Aristotle describes the third part of plot as a "scene of suffering" (*pathos*), which he defines as "a destructive or painful action, such as death on the stage, bodily agony, wounds, and the like" (XI.6, p. 43). He stresses that the destructive or painful action (not necessarily death) should be caused by "those who are near or dear to one another" (XIV.4, pp. 49–50). That is, violence should occur within a royal household or family rather than against a hostile foe. Because the trust, love, and protectiveness that one hopes for in a family is replaced by treachery, hate, and mayhem, the suffering of the tragic protagonist is one of the major ways in which tragedy arouses fear and pity.

Seriousness, Completeness, and Artistic Balance

The first part of Aristotle's definition, asserting that a tragedy is "serious, complete, and of a certain magnitude" can be seen as a vital aspect of his analysis of how tragedy shapes responses. The term **serious,** or *noble* or *elevated*, concerns the play's tone and level of life, in contrast with the boisterousness and ribaldry of Athenian comedies. While comedy represents human character as less serious than it is, tragedy shows it as more serious (II.4, p. 13). Seriousness is also a consequence of the political and cosmological dimensions of the issues with which the heroic characters are engaged. By **complete,** we understand that a tragedy must be shaped and perfected into a logical and finished whole.

Beginning, middle, and end must be so perfectly placed that changing or removing any part would spoil the work's integrity (VII.2, 3, p. 31). By stating that a tragedy should be of a "certain" or proportional **magnitude,** Aristotle refers to a balance of length and subject matter. The play should be short enough to "be easily embraced by the memory" and long enough to "admit of a change . . . from good fortune to bad" (VII.5–7, p. 33). In other words, everything is artistically balanced; nothing superfluous is included, and nothing essential is omitted.

Diction and Song

For modern readers, Aristotle's description of tragic structure is more easily understood than his discussion of tragic language. His statement about tragic poetry—that it is the "mere metrical arrangement of the words" (VI.4, p. 25)—is clear as far as it goes, for the plays themselves show that the tragic playwrights used poetic forms deliberately and exactly. These characteristics, however, do not survive translation into modern English. As for *song* (*melos*), Aristotle's claim that it is "a term whose sense everyone understands" (VI.4, p. 25) is not illuminating. What is therefore significant about his discussion of verse and song is his statement that the "several kinds of artistic ornament are to be found in separate parts of the play" (VI.2, p. 23). That is, where verse is appropriate, the tragic playwrights include poetry as a means of elevating the drama; where music and song are appropriate, they include these to increase beauty and intensify the drama. As with the other aspects of tragedy, therefore, placement, balance, and appropriateness are the most fitting standards of judgment.

The Tragic Hero

Aristotle's description of the tragic protagonist or hero, though not included in his definition of tragedy, is integral to the concept of catharsis and therefore to his description of tragedy. As with the other parts of his analysis, he demonstrates the exact effects and limits of the topic—the perfected balance of form necessary to bring about proper tragic responses. To this end, he states that we, as normally imperfect human beings, are able to sympathize with a "highly renowned and prosperous" protagonist because that protagonist is also imperfect—a person who exists between extremes, just "like ourselves" (XIII.2, p. 45). The misfortunes of this noble protagonist are caused not by "vice" or "depravity" but rather by "some great error or frailty" (XIII.4, p. 47). Aristotle's word for such shortcomings is *hamartia,* which is often translated as **tragic flaw,** and it is this flaw that makes the protagonist human—neither a saint nor a villain. If the protagonist were a saint (one who is "eminently good and just"), his or her suffering would be undeserved and unfair, and our pity would be overwhelmed by indignation and anger—not a proper tragic reaction. Nor could we pity a villain in adversity and pain, for we would judge the suffering to be deserved, and our primary response would then be satisfaction—also not a proper reaction. Therefore, an ideal tragedy is fine-tuned to control our emotions exactly, producing horror and fear because the suffering protagonist is a person like ourselves, and pity because the suffering far exceeds what the protagonist deserves.

ARISTOTLE'S VIEW OF TRAGEDY, A SUMMARY

Aristotle's definition of tragedy hinges on his idea that tragedy, as a dramatic form, is designed to evoke powerful emotions and thereby, through catharsis, to serve both a salutary and ethical purpose. The tragic incidents and plot must be artistically constructed to produce the "essential tragic effect" (VI.12, p. 27). Therefore Aristotle stresses that plot and incidents, arranged for this effect, form the end or goal—the "chief thing of all"—of tragedy (VI.10, p. 27).

IRONY IN TRAGEDY

Implicit in the excessiveness of tragic suffering is the idea that the universe is mysterious and often unfair, and that unseen but powerful forces—fate, fortune, circumstances, and the gods—directly intervene in human life. Ancient Athenian belief was that the gods give rewards or punishments to suit their own purposes, which mortals cannot understand, bring about, or prevent. For example, in *Prometheus Bound* (attributed to Aeschylus), the god Hephaestus binds Prometheus to a rock in the Scythian Mountains as punishment for having given fire and technology to humankind. (A good deed produces suffering.) Conversely, in *Medea,* Euripides shows that the god Apollo permits Medea to escape after killing her own children. (An evil deed produces reward.)

Situational and Cosmic Irony

These examples illustrate the pervasiveness of situational and cosmic irony in tragedy. Characters are thrust into situations that are caused by others or that they themselves unwittingly cause. When they try to act responsibly and nobly to relieve their situations, their actions do not produce the expected results—this is consistent with Aristotle's idea of reversal—and usually things come out badly. For example, Oedipus brings suffering on himself just when he succeeds—and *because* he succeeds—in rescuing his city. Whether on the personal or cosmic level, therefore, there is no escape—no way to evade responsibility, and no way to change the universal laws that cast human beings in such situations. Such irony is not confined to ancient tragedies. Shakespeare's tragic hero Hamlet speaks about the "divinity that shapes our ends," thus expressing the unpredictability of hopes, plans, and achievements, and also the wisdom of resignation. In *Death of a Salesman,* Arthur Miller's hero, Willy Loman, is gripped not so much by divine power as by time, the agent of destruction being the inexorable force of economic circumstances.

The Tragic Dilemma and Free Will

These ironies are related to what is called the **tragic dilemma**—a situation that forces the tragic protagonist to make a difficult choice. The tragic dilemma has also been called a "lose-lose" situation. Thus, Oedipus cannot shirk his duty as king of Thebes because that would be ruinous. He therefore tries to eliminate his city's affliction, but that course also is ruinous. In other words, the choices posed in a tragic dilemma seemingly permit freedom of will, but the consequences of any choice demonstrate the inescapable fact that powerful forces baffle even the most reasonable and noble intentions.

Dramatic Irony

It is from a perspective of something like divinity that we as readers or spectators perceive the action of tragedies. We are like the gods because we always know more than the characters. Such dramatic irony permits us, for example, to know what Oedipus does not know: In defensive rage, he killed his real father, and he himself is therefore his city's bane. Similar dramatic irony can be found in Shakespeare's *Hamlet*, for we realize that Claudius murdered Hamlet's father while Hamlet himself has only unconfirmable suspicions of this truth.

THE ANCIENT ATHENIAN AUDIENCE AND THEATER

Athenian audiences of the fifth century B.C.E., predominantly men but also a small number of women and slaves, took their theater seriously. Indeed, as young men many citizens had taken active parts in the parades and choruses. Admission was charged for those able to pay, but subsidies allowed poorer people to attend as well. Rich Athenians, as a duty (*liturgeia*) to the state, underwrote the costs of the productions—except for the three professional actors who were paid by the government. Each wealthy man, for his contribution, was known as a *choragos,* or choral sponsor. To gain public recognition, the choragos sometimes performed as the leader of the chorus.

The Origin of Theater in the Athenian Marketplace

In the beginning, tragic performances were given specially designated space in the Athenian *agora,* or marketplace. In the center of the performing area was an altar dedicated to Dionysus, around which the choruses danced and chanted. Wooden risers were set up for the spectators.

The Athenian Theater of Dionysus

By the early fifth century B.C.E., a half-circular outdoor theater (*theatron,* or "place for seeing") was created out of the hill at the southern base of the Acropolis in the area sacred to Dionysus. All later performances of tragedies were held at this **Theater of Dionysus,** which held as many as fourteen thousand people (the comic dramatist Aristophanes indicated that thirteen thousand were in attendance at one of his plays). In the earliest days of the Theater, most spectators sat on the sloping ground, but eventually wooden and then

Ancient theater at Epidauros, Greece. Gian Berto Vanni/Art Resource, New York, NY.

stone benches were constructed in the rising semicircle, with more elegant seating for dignitaries in front. Although the Theater was outdoors, the acoustics were sufficiently good to permit audiences to hear both the chorus and the actors, provided that they remained reasonably quiet during performances.

THE ORCHESTRA.   Centered at the base of the hill—the focus of attention— was a round area modeled on the one that had been used in the agora. This was the *orchestra* or "dancing place," which was about sixty-five feet in diameter. Here, each chorus sang its odes and performed its dance movements to the rhythm of a double-piped flute (*aulos*), an instrument that was also used to mark the step in military drill. In the center was a permanent altar.

THE SKENE AND ITS USE.   Behind the *orchestra* was a building for actors, costumes, and props called the *skene* ("tent"), from which is derived our modern word *scene*. Originally a tent or hut, the *skene* was later made of wood and decorated to provide backdrops for the various plays. At its center a double door for entrances and exits opened out to the *orchestra*. Through this door a large platform (*ekkyklyma*) could be rolled out to show interior scenes. Some theater historians argue that there was a wooden platform (*proskenion* or proscenium) in front of the *skene* to elevate the actors and set them off from the chorus. There was no curtain.

The roof of the *skene* was sometimes used as a place of action (as in Aeschylus's *Agamemnon*). A *mechane* (may-KAH-nay), or crane, was also located there so that actors playing gods could be swung up, down, and around as a mark of divine power. It was this crane that gave rise to the Latin phrase ***deus ex machina*** ("a god out of the machine"), a term that refers to an artificial and/or illogical action or device introduced at a play's end to bring otherwise impossible conflicts to a satisfactory solution.

PERFORMANCE AREAS. The performing space for the actors was mainly in front of the *skene*. The space for the chorus was the entire *orchestra*. The chorus entered the *orchestra*—and left it at the end of the play—along the aisles between the retaining wall of the hillside seats and the front of the *skene*. Each of these lateral walkways was known as a *parados* ("way in"), the name also given to the chorus's entry scene. The actors often used the *skene* for entrances and exits, but they were also free to use either of the walkways.

THE HISTORY AND APPEARANCE OF THE THEATER. In the centuries after it was built, the Theater of Dionysus was remodeled and restored a number of times. Aeschylus' trilogy the *Oresteia* was performed in 458 B.C.E., for example, not long after a renovation. The ruins existing on the south slope of the Acropolis today are not those of the theater known by Sophocles, but rather those of a Roman restoration. A better sense of how the Theater looked during the time of Sophocles can be gained from the Theater of Epidaurus, which has been preserved in excellent condition and which even in antiquity was considered one of the best Greek theaters.

TRAGIC ACTORS AND THEIR COSTUMES

The task of the three competing playwrights who had been "given a chorus" by the archon to stage their works during the City Dionysia (and later during the Lenaia) was to plan, choreograph, and direct the productions, usually with the aid of professionals. By performance time, the dramatists would already have spent many months preparing the three assigned actors and fifteen choristers. They also would have directed rehearsals for a small number of auxiliary chorus members and other silent extras in roles such as servants and soldiers.

Costumes

All these participants needed costumes. The chorus members were lightly clad, for ease of movement, and were apparently barefoot. The main actors wore the identifying costumes of tragedy, namely, sleeved robes, boots, and masks. Their robes were heavily decorated and embroidered. Their calf-high leather boots, called *kothornoi* or, in English, **buskins,** were like the elegant boots worn by the patron god Dionysus in painting and statuary. During the following centuries, the buskins became elevator shoes that made the tragic actors taller, in keeping with their heroic stature.

Masks

A vital aspect of ancient tragic costuming was the use of conventionalized masks made of plaster and linen. Up to twenty-eight different kinds of masks were available for the tragic productions. Each mask portrayed a distinct facial type and expression (e.g., king, queen, young woman, old man).

View of a modern production of Sophocles' *Oedipus at Colonus* at the Theater of Epidauros (see also p. 902). Note the size of the orchestra, the formation and gestures of the chorus (fifteen members, in masks, together with the choral leader), the central altar, the reconstructed *skene,* and the single actor on the proscenium. Dimitrios Harissiadis/Benaki Museum, Athens, Greece, Photographic Archive.

The choristers wore identical masks for their group roles. Apparently the masks covered the entire head, except for openings for seeing, breathing, and speaking. They also contained a high headdress and, when necessary, a beard.

The masks, along with costume changes, gave the actors great versatility. Each actor could assume a number of different roles simply by entering the *skene,* changing mask and costume, and reentering as a new character. Thus, in *Oedipus the King* a single actor could represent the seer Tiresias and later reappear as the Messenger. The masks even made it possible for two actors, or even all three, to perform as the same character in separate parts of the play if the need arose.

PERFORMANCE AND THE FORMAL ORGANIZATION OF GREEK TRAGEDY

On performance days, the competing playwrights staged their plays from morning to afternoon, first the tragedies, then the satyr plays (and after these, comedies by other writers). Because plays were performed with a minimum of scenery and props, dramatists used dialogue to establish times and locations. Each tragedy was performed in the order of the formally designated sections that modern editors have marked in the printed texts. It is therefore possible to describe the production of a play in terms of these structural divisions.

PROLOGUE.   The first scene was the **prologue,** which contained the exposition. There was considerable variety in the performance of the prologue.

Sometimes it was given by a single actor, speaking as either a mortal or a god. In *Oedipus the King*, Sophocles used all three actors for the prologue (Oedipus, the Priest, and Creon), speaking to themselves and also to the extras acting as the Theban populace.

PARADOS.   The next unit was the *parados*, or the entry of the chorus into the *orchestra*, where they remained until the play's end. Because the chorus needed to project their voices to spectators in the top seats, they both sang and chanted their lines. They also moved rhythmically in a number of stanzaic *strophes* (turns), *antistrophes* (counterturns), and *epodes* (units following the songs). These dance movements, regulated by the rhythm of the flute as in military drill, were done in straight-line formations of five or three, but we do not know whether the chorus stopped or continued moving when delivering their lines. After the *parados*, the choristers would necessarily have knelt or sat at attention, in this way focusing on the activities of the actors and, when necessary, responding as a group (see photo, p. 904).

EPISODES AND STASIMONS.   With the chorus as a model audience, the drama itself consisted of four full sections or acting units. The major part of each section was the **episode.** Each episode featured the actors, who presented both action and speech, including swift one-line interchanges known as **stichomythy.**

When the episode ended, the actors withdrew.[11] The following second part of the acting section was called a *stasimon* (plural *stasima*), performed by the chorus exclusively in the *orchestra*. Like the *parados*, the *stasima* required dance movements, along with the chanting and singing of strophes, antistrophes, and epodes. The topics concerned the play's developing action, although over time the *stasima* became more general and therefore less integral to the play.

EXODOS.   When the last of the four episode-*stasimon* sections had been completed, the *exodos* (literally, "a way out"), or the final section, commenced. It contained the resolution of the drama, the exit of the actors, and the last pronouncements, dance movements, and exit of the chorus.

THE EVOLUTION OF THE FORMAL STRUCTURE.   We know little about tragic structure at the very beginning of the form, but Athenian tragedies of the fifth century B.C.E. evolved to follow the pattern just described. Aeschylus, the earliest of the Athenian writers of tragedy, lengthened the episodes, thus emphasizing the actors and minimizing the chorus (*Poetics* IV.13, p. 19). Sophocles made the chorus even less important. Euripides, Sophocles's younger contemporary, concentrated on the episodes, making the chorus almost incidental. In later centuries, dramatists dropped the choral sections completely, establishing a precedent for the five-act structure adopted by Roman dramatists and later by Renaissance dramatists.

---

[11] For example, at the end of the first episode, Oedipus goes into the *skene*—the palace—while a servant leads Tiresias off along the *parados*, thus indicating that he is leaving Thebes entirely.

SOPHOCLES, *OEDIPUS THE KING*

Sophocles was born between 500 and 494 B.C.E. into an affluent Athenian family. He began acting and singing early, and he served as a choral leader in the celebrations for the defeat of the Persians at Marathon in 480 B.C.E. In 468 he won highest festival honors for the first play he submitted for competition, *Triptolemos.* He wrote at least 120 plays, approximately 90 of them tragedies, and he won the prize a record 24 times. He was also an active citizen. He was twice elected general of his tribe, and he served as a priest in the cult of Asclepius, the god of healing. Because of his dramatic and public achievements, he was venerated during his lifetime, and after his death in 406–405 B.C.E., a cult was established in his honor.

When *Oedipus the King* was first performed between 430 and 425 B.C.E., most of the audience would have known the general outlines of the story inasmuch as it was one of the "received legends" of tragedy: the antagonism of the gods Hephaestus and Hera toward Cadmus of Thebes (of whom Oedipus was a descendant); the prophecy that the Theban king Laius would be killed by his own son; the exposure of the newly born Oedipus on a mountainside; his rescue by a well-meaning shepherd; his youth spent as the adopted son of King Polybus and Queen Merope of Corinth; his trip to Delphi to learn his origins; his impetuous murder of Laius (a stranger to him); his solution of the Sphinx's riddle; his ascension as king of Thebes and his marriage to Queen Jocasta, his mother; his reign as king; the plague that afflicted Thebes; his attempts at restoration; and Jocasta's suicide when the truth of Oedipus's past was revealed.

Although these details were commonly known, there was disagreement about the outcome of Oedipus's life. One version told that he remarried, had four children with his new wife, reigned long and successfully, died in battle, and was finally worshiped as a hero. Sophocles, however, dramatizes a version—either borrowed or of his own creation—that tells of Oedipus's self-imposed punishment.

As we have said, Aristotle prized *Oedipus the King* so highly that he used it to illustrate many of his principles of tragedy. Of particular interest is that the play embodies the so-called **three unities,** which are implicit in the *Poetics* although Aristotle does not stress them. Sophocles creates *unity of place* by using the front of the royal palace of Thebes as the location for the entire action. He creates *unity of action* by dramatizing only those activities leading to Oedipus's recognition of the true scourge of the city. Finally, he creates *unity of time* because the stage or action time coincides with real-life time. In fact, the play's time is considerably shorter than the "single revolution of the sun" that Aristotle recommends as the proper period for a complete tragic action (V.4, p. 23).

Above all, *Oedipus the King* meets Aristotle's requirements for one of the very best plays because of the skill with which Sophocles makes Oedipus's recognition of his guilt coincide exactly with the disastrous reversal of his fortunes (XI.2, p. 41).

SOPHOCLES   (ca. 496–406 B.C.E.)

Oedipus the King ————————————————————————*430–425* B.C.E.

Translated by Thomas Gould

CHARACTERS

> Oedipus,° *The King of Thebes*
> Priest of Zeus, *Leader of the Suppliants*
> Creon, *Oedipus's Brother-in-law*
> Chorus, *a Group of Theban Elders*
> Choragos, *Spokesman of the Chorus*
> Tiresias, *a blind Seer or Prophet*
> Jocasta, *The Queen of Thebes*
> Messenger, *from Corinth, once a Shepherd*
> Herdsman, *once a Servant of Laius*
> Second Messenger, *a Servant of Oedipus*

MUTES

> Suppliants, *Thebans seeking Oedipus's help*
> Attendants, *for the Royal Family*
> Servants, *to lead Tiresias and Oedipus*
> Antigone, *Daughter of Oedipus and Jocasta*
> Ismene, *Daughter of Oedipus and Jocasta*

[*The action takes place during the day in front of the royal palace in Thebes. There are two altars (left and right) on the Proscenium and several steps leading down to the Orchestra. As the play opens, Thebans of various ages who have come to beg Oedipus for help are sitting on these steps and in part of the Orchestra. These suppliants are holding branches of laurel or olive which have strips of wool°wrapped around them. Oedipus enters from the palace (the central door of the Skene).*]

PROLOGUE

OEDIPUS.   My children, ancient Cadmus'° newest care,
> why have you hurried to those seats, your boughs
> wound with the emblems of the suppliant?
> The city is weighed down with fragrant smoke,
> with hymns to the Healer° and the cries of mourners.   5

Oedipus: The name means "swollen foot." It refers to the mutilation of Oedipus's feet by his father, Laius, before the infant was sent to Mount Cithaeron to be put to death by exposure. 0.1 S.D. *wool:* Branches wrapped with wool are traditional symbols of prayer or supplication. 1 *Cadmus:* Oedipus's great-great-grandfather (although he does not know this) and the founder of Thebes.   5 *Healer:* Apollo, god of prophecy, light, healing, justice, purification, and destruction.

I thought it wrong, my sons, to hear your words
through emissaries, and have come out myself,
I, Oedipus, a name that all men know.

[*OEDIPUS addresses the PRIEST.*]

Old man—for it is fitting that you speak
for all—what is your mood as you entreat me,   10
fear or trust? You may be confident
that I'll do anything. How hard of heart
if an appeal like this did not rouse my pity!
PRIEST.   You, Oedipus, who hold the power here,
you see our several ages, we who sit   15
before your altars—some not strong enough
to take long flight, some heavy in old age,
the priests, as I of Zeus,° and from our youths
a chosen band. The rest sit with their windings
in the markets, at the twin shrines of Pallas,°   20
and the prophetic embers of Ismēnos.°
Our city, as you see yourself, is tossed
too much, and can no longer lift its head
above the troughs of billows red with death.
It dies in the fruitful flowers of the soil,   25
it dies in its pastured herds, and in its women's
barren pangs. And the fire-bearing god°
has swooped upon the city, hateful plague,
and he has left the house of Cadmus empty.
Black Hades° is made rich with moans and weeping.   30
Not judging you an equal of the gods,
do I and the children sit here at your hearth,
but as the first of men, in troubled times
and in encounters with divinities.
You came to Cadmus' city and unbound   35
the tax we had to pay to the harsh singer,°
did it without a helpful word from us,
with no instruction; with a god's assistance
you raised up our life, so we believe.

---

18 *Zeus:* father and king of the gods.   20 *Pallas:* Athena, goddess of wisdom, arts, crafts, and war.   21 *Ismēnos:* a reference to the temple of Apollo near the river Ismenos in Thebes. Prophecies were made here by "reading" the ashes of the altar fires.   27 *fire-bearing god:* contagious fever viewed as a god.   30 *Black Hades:* refers to both the underworld, where the spirits of the dead go, and the god of the underworld.   36 *harsh singer:* the Sphinx, a monster with a woman's head, a lion's body, and wings. The "tax" that Oedipus freed Thebes from was the destruction of all the young men who failed to solve the Sphinx's riddle and were subsequently devoured. The Sphinx always asked the same riddle: "What goes on four legs in the morning, two legs at noon, and three legs in the evening, and yet is weakest when supported by the largest number of feet?" Oedipus discovered the correct answer—man, who crawls in infancy, walks in his prime, and uses a stick in old age—and thus ended the Sphinx's reign of terror. The Sphinx destroyed herself when Oedipus answered the riddle. Oedipus's reward for freeing Thebes of the Sphinx was the throne and the hand of the recently widowed Jocasta.

Again now Oedipus, our greatest power, 40
we plead with you, as suppliants, all of us,
to find us strength, whether from a god's response,
or learned in some way from another man.
I know that the experienced among men
give counsels that will prosper best of all. 45
Noblest of men, lift up our land again!
Think also of yourself; since now the land
calls you its Savior for your zeal of old,
oh let us never look back at your rule
as men helped up only to fall again! 50
Do not stumble! Put our land on firm feet!
The bird of omen was auspicious then,
when you brought that luck; be that same man again!
The power is yours; if you will rule our country,
rule over men, not in an empty land. 55
A towered city or a ship is nothing
if desolate and no man lives within.

OEDIPUS.   Pitiable children, oh I know, I know
the yearnings that have brought you. Yes, I know
that you are sick. And yet, though you are sick, 60
there is not one of you so sick as I.
For your affliction comes to each alone,
for him and no one else, but my soul mourns
for me and for you, too, and for the city.
You do not waken me as from a sleep, 65
for I have wept, bitterly and long,
tried many paths in the wanderings of thought,
and the single cure I found by careful search
I've acted on: I sent Menoeceus' son,
Creon, brother of my wife, to the Pythian 70
halls of Phoebus,° so that I might learn
what I must do or say to save this city.
Already, when I think what day this is,
I wonder anxiously what he is doing.
Too long, more than is right, he's been away. 75
But when he comes, then I shall be a traitor
if I do not do all that the god reveals.

PRIEST.   Welcome words! But look, those men have signaled
that it is Creon who is now approaching!

OEDIPUS.   Lord Apollo! May he bring Savior Luck, 80
a Luck as brilliant as his eyes are now!

PRIEST.   His news is happy, it appears. He comes,
forehead crowned with thickly berried laurel.°

OEDIPUS.   We'll know, for he is near enough to hear us.

[*Enter* CREON *along one of the Parados.*]

70–71 *Pythian . . . Phoebus:* the temple of Phoebus Apollo's oracle or prophet at Delphi.
83 *laurel:* Creon is wearing a garland of laurel leaves, sacred to Apollo.

Lord, brother in marriage, son of Menoeceus!   85
What is the god's pronouncement that you bring?
CREON.   It's good. For even troubles, if they chance
to turn out well, I always count as lucky.
OEDIPUS.   But what was the response? You seem to say
I'm not to fear—but not to take heart either.   90
CREON.   If you will hear me with these men present,
I'm ready to report—or go inside.

[*CREON moves up the steps toward the palace.*]

OEDIPUS.   Speak out to all! The grief that burdens me
concerns these men more than it does my life.
CREON.   Then I shall tell you what I heard from the god.   95
The task Lord Phoebus sets for us is clear:
drive out pollution sheltered in our land,
and do not shelter what is incurable.
OEDIPUS.   What is our trouble? How shall we cleanse ourselves?
CREON.   We must banish or murder to free ourselves   100
from a murder that blows storms through the city.
OEDIPUS.   What man's bad luck does he accuse in this?
CREON.   My Lord, a king named Laius ruled our land
before you came to steer the city straight.
OEDIPUS.   I know. So I was told—I never saw him.   105
CREON.   Since he was murdered, you must raise your hand
against the men who killed him with their hands.
OEDIPUS.   Where are they now? And how can we ever find
the track of ancient guilt now hard to read?
CREON.   In our own land, he said. What we pursue,   110
that can be caught; but not what we neglect.
OEDIPUS.   Was Laius home, or in the countryside—
or was he murdered in some foreign land?
CREON.   He left to see a sacred rite, he said;
He left, but never came home from his journey.   115
OEDIPUS.   Did none of his party see it and report—
someone we might profitably question?
CREON.   They were all killed but one, who fled in fear,
and he could tell us only one clear fact.
OEDIPUS.   What fact? One thing could lead us on to more   120
if we could get a small start on our hope.
CREON.   He said that bandits chanced on them and killed him—
with the force of many hands, not one alone.
OEDIPUS.   How could a bandit dare so great an act—
unless this was a plot paid off from here!   125
CREON.   We thought of that, but when Laius was killed,
we had no one to help us in our troubles.
OEDIPUS.   It was your very kingship that was killed!
What kind of trouble blocked you from a search?
CREON.   The subtle-singing Sphinx asked us to turn   130
from the obscure to what lay at our feet.

OEDIPUS. Then I shall begin again and make it plain.
    It was quite worthy of Phoebus, and worthy of you,
    to turn our thoughts back to the murdered man,
    and right that you should see me join the battle   135
    for justice to our land and to the god.
    Not on behalf of any distant kinships,
    it's for myself I will dispel this stain.
    Whoever murdered him may also wish
    to punish me—and with the selfsame hand.   140
    In helping him I also serve myself.
    Now quickly, children: up from the altar steps,
    and raise the branches of the suppliant!
    Let someone go and summon Cadmus' people:
    say I'll do anything.

                 [*Exit an* ATTENDANT *along one of the Parados.*]

             Our luck will prosper   145
    if the god is with us, or we have already fallen.
PRIEST. Rise, my children; that for which we came,
    he has himself proclaimed he will accomplish.
    May Phoebus, who announced this, also come
    as Savior and reliever from the plague.   150

[*Exit* OEDIPUS *and* CREON *into the Palace. The* PRIEST *and the* SUPPLIANTS *exit left
    and right along the Parados. After a brief pause, the* CHORUS *(including the*
                  CHORAGOS) *enters the Orchestra from the Parados.*]

PARADOS

Strophe 1°

CHORUS. Voice from Zeus,° sweetly spoken, what are you
    that have arrived from golden
    Pytho° to our shining
    Thebes? I am on the rack, terror
        shakes my soul.
    Delian Healer,° summoned by "iē!"   155
    I await in holy dread what obligation, something new
    or something back once more with the revolving years,
        you'll bring about for me.
    Oh tell me, child of golden Hope,   160
        deathless Response!

151, 162 *Strophe, Antistrophe:* These stanzaic units refer to movements, counter-movements, and
gestures that the Chorus performed while singing or chanting in the orchestra. See p. 905.
151 *Voice from Zeus:* a reference to Apollo's prophecy. Zeus taught Apollo how to prophesy.
153 *Pytho:* Delphi.   156 *Delian Healer:* Apollo.

Antistrophe 1°

I appeal to you first, daughter of Zeus,
    deathless Athena,
    and to your sister who protects this land,
    Artemis,° whose famous throne is the whole circle   165
    of the marketplace,
and Phoebus, who shoots from afar: iō!
    Three-fold defenders against death, appear!
    If ever in the past, to stop blind ruin
        sent against the city,   170
you banished utterly the fires of suffering,
        come now again!

Strophe 2

Ah! Ah! Unnumbered are the miseries
I bear. The plague claims all
our comrades. Nor has thought found yet a spear   175
by which a man shall be protected. What our glorious
earth gives birth to does not grow. Without a birth
from cries of labor
        do the women rise.
One person after another   180
        you may see, like flying birds,
faster than indomitable fire, sped
to the shore of the god that is the sunset.°

Antistrophe 2

And with their deaths unnumbered dies the city.
Her children lie unpitied on the ground,   185
spreading death, unmourned.
Meanwhile young wives, and gray-haired mothers with them,
on the shores of the altars, from this side and that,
suppliants from mournful trouble,
        cry out their grief.   190
A hymn to the Healer shines,
        the flute a mourner's voice.
Against which, golden goddess, daughter of Zeus,
        send lovely Strength.

Strophe 3

Cause raging Ares°—who,   195
        armed now with no shield of bronze,
burns me, coming on amid loud cries—

165 *Artemis:* goddess of virginity, childbirth, and hunting.   183 *god . . . sunset:* Hades, god of
the underworld.   195 *Ares:* god of war and destruction.

to turn his back and run from my land,
with a fair wind behind, to the great
    hall of Amphitritē,°   200
or to the anchorage that welcomes no one,
Thrace's troubled sea!
If night lets something get away at last,
    it comes by day.
Fire-bearing god   205
    you who dispense the might of lightning,
Zeus! Father! Destroy him with your thunderbolt!

[*Enter* OEDIPUS *from the palace.*]

Antistrophe 3

Lycēan Lord!° From your looped
    bowstring, twisted gold,
I wish indomitable missiles might be scattered   210
and stand forward, our protectors; also fire-bearing
radiance of Artemis, with which
    she darts across the Lycian mountains.
I call the god whose head is bound in gold,
with whom this country shares its name,   215
Bacchus,° wine-flushed, summoned by "euoi!,"
    Maenads' comrade,
to approach ablaze
    with gleaming . . . . . .
pine, opposed to that god-hated god.   220

EPISODE 1

OEDIPUS.   I hear your prayer. Submit to what I say
    and to the labors that the plague demands
    and you'll get help and a relief from evils.
    I'll make the proclamation, though a stranger
    to the report and to the deed. Alone,   225
    had I no key, I would soon lose the track.
    Since it was only later that I joined you,
    to all the sons of Cadmus I say this:
    whoever has clear knowledge of the man
    who murdered Laius, son of Labdacus,   230
    I command him to reveal it all to me—
    nor fear if, to remove the charge, he must
    accuse himself: his fate will not be cruel—
    he will depart unstumbling into exile.
    But if you know another, or a stranger,   235
    to be the one whose hand is guilty, speak:

200 *Amphitritē:* the Atlantic Ocean.   208 *Lycēan Lord:* Apollo.   216 *Bacchus:* Dionysus, god

I shall reward you and remember you.
But if you keep your peace because of fear,
and shield yourself or kin from my command,
hear you what I shall do in that event: 240
I charge all in this land where I have throne
and power, shut out that man—no matter who—
both from your shelter and all spoken words,
nor in your prayers or sacrifices make
him partner, nor allot him lustral° water.   245
All men shall drive him from their homes: for he
is the pollution that the god-sent Pythian
response has only now revealed to me.
In this way I ally myself in war
with the divinity and the deceased.°   250
And this curse, too, against the one who did it,
whether alone in secrecy, or with others:
may he wear out his life unblest and evil!
I pray this, too: if he is at my hearth
and in my home, and I have knowledge of him,   255
may the curse pronounced on others come to me.
All this I lay to you to execute,
for my sake, for the god's, and for this land
now ruined, barren, abandoned by the gods.
Even if no god had driven you to it,   260
you ought not to have left this stain uncleansed,
the murdered man a nobleman, a king!
You should have looked! But now, since, as it happens,
It's I who have the power that he had once,
and have his bed, and a wife who shares our seed,   265
and common bond had we had common children
(had not his hope of offspring had back luck—
but as it happened, luck lunged at his head);
because of this, as if for my own father,
I'll fight for him, I'll leave no means untried,   270
to catch the one who did it with his hand,
for the son of Labdacus, of Polydorus,
of Cadmus before him, and of Agēnor.°
This prayer against all those who disobey:
the gods send out no harvest from their soil,   275
nor children from their wives. Oh, let them die
victims of this plague, or of something worse.
Yet for the rest of us, people of Cadmus,
we the obedient, may Justice, our ally,
and all the gods, be always on our side!   280

CHORAGOS.   I speak because I feel the grip of your curse:
      the killer is not I. Nor can I point

of fertility and wine.
245 *lustral:* purifying.   250 *the deceased:* Laius.   272–73 *son . . . Agēnor:* refers to Laius by

to him. The one who set us to this search,
Phoebus, should also name the guilty man.

OEDIPUS.   Quite right, but to compel unwilling gods—   285
no man has ever had that kind of power.

CHORAGOS.   May I suggest to you a second way?

OEDIPUS.   A second or a third—pass over nothing!

CHORAGOS.   I know of no one who sees more of what
Lord Phoebus sees than Lord Tiresias.   290
My Lord, one might learn brilliantly from him.

OEDIPUS.   Nor is this something I have been slow to do.
At Creon's word I sent an escort—twice now!
I am astonished that he has not come.

CHORAGOS.   The old account is useless. It told us nothing.   295

OEDIPUS.   But tell it to me. I'll scrutinize all stories.

CHORAGOS.   He is said to have been killed by travelers.

OEDIPUS.   I have heard, but the one who did it no one sees.

CHORAGOS.   If there is any fear in him at all,
he won't stay here once he has heard that curse.   300

OEDIPUS.   He won't fear words: he had no fear when he did it.

[Enter TIRESIAS from the right, led by a SERVANT and two of Oedipus's ATTENDANTS.]

CHORAGOS.   Look there! There is the man who will convict him!
It's the god's prophet they are leading here,
one gifted with the truth as no one else.

OEDIPUS.   Tiresias, master of all omens—   305
public and secret, in the sky and on the earth—
your mind, if not your eyes, sees how the city
lives with a plague, against which Thebes can find
no Saviour or protector, Lord, but you.
For Phoebus, as the attendants surely told you,   310
returned this answer to us: liberation
from the disease would never come unless
we learned without a doubt who murdered Laius—
put them to death, or sent them into exile.
Do not begrudge us what you may learn from birds   315
or any other prophet's path you know!
Care for yourself, the city, care for me,
care for the whole pollution of the dead!
We're in your hands. To do all that he can
to help another is man's noblest labor.   320

TIRESIAS.   How terrible to understand and get
no profit from the knowledge! I knew this,
but I forgot, or I had never come.

OEDIPUS.   What's this? You've come with very little zeal.

TIRESIAS.   Let me go home! If you will listen to me,   325
You will endure your troubles better—and I mine.

OEDIPUS.   A strange request, not very kind to the land
that cared for you—to hold back this oracle!

TIRESIAS.   I see your understanding comes to you
    inopportunely. So that won't happen to me . . .   330
OEDIPUS.   Oh, by the gods, if you understand about this,
    don't turn away! We're on our knees to you.
TIRESIAS.   None of you understands! I'll never bring
    my grief to light—I will not speak of yours.
OEDIPUS.   You know and won't declare it! Is your purpose   335
    to betray us and to destroy this land?
TIRESIAS.   I will grieve neither of us. Stop this futile
    cross-examination. I'll tell you nothing!
OEDIPUS.   Nothing? You vile traitor! You could provoke
    a stone to anger! You still refuse to tell?   340
    Can nothing soften you, nothing convince you?
TIRESIAS.   You blamed anger in me—you haven't seen.
    Can nothing soften you, nothing convince you?
OEDIPUS.   Who wouldn't fill with anger, listening
    to words like yours which now disgrace this city?   345
TIRESIAS.   It will come, even if my silence hides it.
OEDIPUS.   If it will come, then why won't you declare it?
TIRESIAS.   I'd rather say no more. Now if you wish,
    respond to that with all your fiercest anger!
OEDIPUS.   Now I am angry enough to come right out   350
    with this conjecture: you, I think, helped plot
    the deed; you did it—even if your hand
    cannot have struck the blow. If you could see,
    I should have said the deed was yours alone.
TIRESIAS.   Is that right! Then I charge you to abide   355
    by the decree you have announced: from this day
    say no word to either these or me,
    for you are the vile polluter of this land!
OEDIPUS.   Aren't you appalled to let a charge like that
    come bounding forth? How will you get away?   360
TIRESIAS.   You cannot catch me. I have the strength of truth.
OEDIPUS.   Who taught you this? Not your prophetic craft!
TIRESIAS.   You did. You made me say it. I didn't want to.
OEDIPUS.   Say what? Repeat it so I'll understand.
TIRESIAS.   I made no sense? Or are you trying me?   365
OEDIPUS.   No sense I understood. Say it again!
TIRESIAS.   I say you are the murderer you seek.
OEDIPUS.   Again that horror! You'll wish you hadn't said that.
TIRESIAS.   Shall I say more, and raise your anger higher?
OEDIPUS.   Anything you like! Your words are powerless.   370
TIRESIAS.   You live, unknowing, with those nearest to you
    in the greatest shame. You do not see the evil.
OEDIPUS.   You won't go on like that and never pay!
TIRESIAS.   I can if there is any strength in truth.
OEDIPUS.   In truth, but not in you! You have no strength,   375
    blind in your ears, your reason, and your eyes.

TIRESIAS.   Unhappy man! Those jeers you hurl at me
    before long all these men will hurl at you.
OEDIPUS.   You are the child of endless night; it's not
    for me or anyone who sees to hurt you.   380
TIRESIAS.   It's not my fate to be struck down by you.
    Apollo is enough. That's his concern.
OEDIPUS.   Are these inventions Creon's or your own?
TIRESIAS.   No, your affliction is yourself, not Creon.
OEDIPUS.   Oh success!—in wealth, kingship, artistry,   385
    in any life that wins much admiration—
    the envious ill will stored up for you!
    to get at my command, a gift I did not
    seek, which the city put into my hands,
    my loyal Creon, colleague from the start,   390
    longs to sneak up in secret and dethrone me.
    So he's suborned this fortuneteller—schemer!
    deceitful beggar-priest!—who has good eyes
    for gains alone, though in his craft he's blind.
    Where were your prophet's powers ever proved?   395
    Why, when the dog who chanted verse° was here,
    did you not speak and liberate this city?
    Her riddle wasn't for a man chancing by
    to interpret; prophetic art was needed,
    but you had none, it seems—learned from birds   400
    or from a god. I came along, yes I,
    Oedipus the ignorant, and stopped her—
    by using thought, not augury from birds.
    And it is I whom you may wish to banish,
    so you'll be close to the Creontian throne.   405
    You—and the plot's concocter—will drive out
    pollution to your grief: you look quite old
    or you would be the victim of that plot!
CHORAGOS.   It seems to us that this man's words were said
    in anger, Oedipus, and yours as well.   410
    Insight, not angry words, is what we need,
    the best solution to the god's response.
TIRESIAS.   You are the king, and yet I am your equal
    in my right to speak. In that I too am Lord,
    for I belong to Loxias,° not you.   415
    I am not Creon's man. He's nothing to me.
    Hear this, since you have thrown my blindness at me:
    Your eyes can't see the evil to which you've come,
    nor where you live, nor who is in your house.
    Do you know your parents? Now knowing, you are   420
    their enemy, in the underworld and here.
    A mother's and a father's double-lashing

396 *dog . . . verse:* the Sphinx.   415 *Loxias:* Apollo.

terrible-footed curse will soon drive you out.
Now you can see, then you will stare into darkness.
What place will not be harbor to your cry,   425
or what Cithaeron° not reverberate
when you have heard the bride-song in your palace
to which you sailed? Fair wind to evil harbor!
Nor do you see how many other woes
will level you to yourself and to your children.   430
So, at my message, and at Creon, too,
splatter muck! There will never be a man
ground into wretchedness as you will be.

OEDIPUS.   Am I to listen to such things from him!
May you be damned! Get out of here at once!   435
Go! Leave my palace! Turn around and go!

[*TIRESIAS begins to move away from OEDIPUS.*]

TIRESIAS.   I wouldn't have come had you not sent for me.
OEDIPUS.   I did not know you'd talk stupidity,
or I wouldn't have rushed to bring you to my house.
TIRESIAS.   Stupid I seem to you, yet to your parents   440
who gave you natural birth I seemed quite shrewd.
OEDIPUS.   Who? Wait! Who is the one who gave me birth?
TIRESIAS.   This day will give you birth,° and ruin too.
OEDIPUS.   What murky, riddling things you always say!
TIRESIAS.   Don't you surpass us all at finding out?   445
OEDIPUS.   You sneer at what you'll find has brought me greatness.
TIRESIAS.   And that's the very luck that ruined you.
OEDIPUS.   I wouldn't care, just so I saved the city.
TIRESIAS.   In that case I shall go. Boy, lead the way!
OEDIPUS.   Yes, let him lead you off. Here, underfoot,   450
you irk me. Gone, you'll cause no further pain.
TIRESIAS.   I'll go when I have said what I was sent for.
Your face won't scare me. You can't ruin me.
I say to you, the man whom you have looked for
as you pronounced your curses, your decrees   455
on the bloody death of Laius—he is here!
A seeming stranger, he shall be shown to be
a Theban born, though he'll take no delight
in that solution. Blind, who once could see,
a beggar who was rich, through foreign lands   460
he'll go and point before him with a stick.
To his beloved children, he'll be shown
a father who is also brother; to the one
who bore him, son and husband; to his father,
his seed-fellow and killer. Go in   465
and think this out; and if you find I've lied,
say then I have no prophet's understanding!

426 *Cithaeron:* reference to the mountain on which Oedipus was to be exposed as an infant.
443 *give you birth:* that is, identify your parents.

[*Exit* TIRESIAS, *led by a* SERVANT. OEDIPUS *exits into the palace with his* ATTENDANTS.]

STASIMON 1

Strophe 1

CHORUS.   Who is the man of whom the inspired
           rock of Delphi° said
       he has committed the unspeakable   470
           with blood-stained hands?
   Time for him to ply a foot
   mightier than those of the horses
           of the storm in his escape;
   upon him mounts and plunges the weaponed   475
   son of Zeus,° with fire and thunderbolts,
   and in his train the dreaded goddesses
   of Death, who never miss.

Antistrophe 1

   The message has just blazed,
           gleaming from the snows   480
   of Mount Parnassus: we must track
           everywhere the unseen man.
   He wanders, hidden by wild
   forests, up through caves
           and rocks, like a bull,   485
   anxious, with an anxious foot, forlorn.
   He puts away from him the mantic° words come from earth's
   navel,° at its center, yet these live
   forever and still hover round him.

Strophe 2

   Terribly he troubles me,   490
           the skilled interpreter of birds!°
   I can't assent, nor speak against him.
       Both paths are closed to me.
   I hover on the wings of doubt,
           not seeing what is here nor what's to come.   495
   What quarrel started in the house of Labdacus°
   or in the house of Polybus,°
           either ever in the past
           or now, I never
   heard, so that . . . with this fact for my touchstone   500

469 *rock of Delphi:* Apollo's oracle at Delphi.   476 *son of Zeus:* Apollo.   487 *mantic:* prophetic.
487–88 *earth's navel:* Delphi.   491 *interpreter of birds:* Tiresias. The Chorus is troubled by his accusations.   496 *house of Labdacus:* the line of Laius.   497 *Polybus:* Oedipus's foster father.

I could attack the public
　　fame of Oedipus, by the side of the Labdaceans
an ally, against the dark assassination.

Antistrophe 2

No, Zeus and Apollo
　　understand and know things   505
mortal; but that another man
　　can do more as a prophet than I can—
for that there is no certain test,
　　though, skill to skill,
one man might overtake another.   510
No, never, not until
　　I see the charges proved,
when someone blames him shall I nod assent.
For once, as we all saw, the winged maiden° came
against him: he was seen then to be skilled,   515
　　proved, by that touchstone, dear to the people. So,
never will my mind convict him of the evil.

EPISODE 2

[*Enter* CREON *from the right door of the skene and speaks to the* CHORUS.]

CREON.　　Citizens, I hear that a fearful charge
　　is made against me by King Oedipus!
　　I had to come. If, in this crisis,   520
　　he thinks that he has suffered injury
　　from anything that I have said or done,
　　I have no appetite for a long life—
　　bearing a blame like that! It's no slight blow
　　the punishment I'd take from what he said: 525
　　it's the ultimate hurt to be called traitor
　　by the city, by you, by my own people!
CHORAGOS.　　The thing that forced that accusation out
　　could have been anger, not the power of thought.
CREON.　　But who persuaded him that thoughts of mine   530
　　had led the prophet into telling lies?
CHORAGOS.　　I do not know the thought behind his words.
CREON.　　But did he look straight at you? Was his mind right
　　when he said that I was guilty of this charge?
CHORAGOS.　　I have no eyes to see what rulers do.   535
　　But here he comes himself out of the house.

[*Enter* OEDIPUS *from the palace.*]

OEDIPUS.　　What? You here? And can you really have
　　the face and daring to approach my house

514 *winged maiden:* the Sphinx.

when you're exposed as its master's murderer
and caught, too, as the robber of my kingship?   540
Did you see cowardice in me, by the gods,
or foolishness, when you began this plot?
Did you suppose that I would not detect
your stealthy moves, or that I'd not fight back?
It's your attempt that's folly, isn't it—   545
tracking without followers or connections,
kingship which is caught with wealth and numbers?
CREON.   Now wait! Give me as long to answer back!
Judge me for yourself when you have heard me!
OEDIPUS.   You're eloquent, but I'd be slow to learn   550
from you, now that I've seen your malice toward me.
CREON.   That I deny. Hear what I have to say.
OEDIPUS.   Don't you deny it! You are the traitor here!
CREON.   If you consider mindless willfulness
a prized possession, you are not thinking sense.   555
OEDIPUS.   If you think you can wrong a relative
and get off free, you are not thinking sense.
CREON.   Perfectly just, I won't say no. And yet
what is this injury you say I did you?
OEDIPUS.   Did you persuade me, yes or no, to send   560
someone to bring that solemn prophet here?
CREON.   And I still hold to the advice I gave.
OEDIPUS.   How many years ago did your King Laius . . .
CREON.   Laius! Do what? Now I don't understand.
OEDIPUS.   Vanish—victim of a murderous violence?   565
CREON.   That is a long count back into the past.
OEDIPUS.   Well, was this seer then practicing his art?
CREON.   Yes, skilled and honored just as he is today.
OEDIPUS.   Did he, back then, ever refer to me?
CREON.   He did not do so in my presence ever.   570
OEDIPUS.   You did inquire into the murder then.
CREON.   We had to, surely, though we discovered nothing.
OEDIPUS.   But the "skilled" one did not say this then? Why not?
CREON.   I never talk when I am ignorant.
OEDIPUS.   But you're not ignorant of your own part.   575
CREON.   What do you mean? I'll tell you if I know.
OEDIPUS.   Just this: if he had not conferred with you
he'd not have told about my murdering Laius.
CREON.   If he said that, you are the one who knows.
But now it's fair that you should answer me.   580
OEDIPUS.   Ask on! You won't convict me as the killer.
CREON.   Well then, answer. My sister is your wife?
OEDIPUS.   Now there's a statement that I can't deny.
CREON.   You two have equal power in this country?
OEDIPUS.   She gets from me whatever she desires.   585
CREON.   And I'm a third? The three of us are equals?
OEDIPUS.   That's where you're treacherous to your kinship!

CREON.   But think about this rationally, as I do.
　　　First look at this: do you think anyone
　　　prefers the anxieties of being king   590
　　　to untroubled sleep—if he has equal power?
　　　I'm not the kind of man who falls in love
　　　with kingship. I am content with a king's power.
　　　And so would any man who's wise and prudent.
　　　I get all things from you, with no distress;   595
　　　as king I would have onerous duties, too.
　　　How could the kingship bring me more delight
　　　than this untroubled power and influence?
　　　I'm not misguided yet to such a point
　　　that profitable honors aren't enough.   600
　　　As it is, all wish me well and all salute;
　　　those begging you for something have me summoned,
　　　for their success depends on that alone.
　　　Why should I lose all this to become king?
　　　A prudent mind is never traitorous.   605
　　　Treason's a thought I'm not enamored of;
　　　nor could I join a man who acted so.
　　　In proof of this, first go yourself to Pytho°
　　　and ask if I brought back the true response.
　　　Then, if you find I plotted with that portent   610
　　　reader,° don't have me put to death by your vote
　　　only—I'll vote myself for my conviction.
　　　Don't let an unsupported thought convict me!
　　　It's not right mindlessly to take the bad
　　　for good or to suppose the good are traitors.   615
　　　Rejecting a relation who is loyal
　　　is like rejecting life, our greatest love.
　　　In time you'll know securely without stumbling,
　　　for time alone can prove a just man just,
　　　though you can know a bad man in a day.   620
CHORAGOS.   Well said, to one who's anxious not to fall.
　　　Swift thinkers, Lord, are never safe from stumbling.
OEDIPUS.   But when a swift and secret plotter moves
　　　against me, I must make swift counterplot.
　　　If I lie quiet and await his move,   625
　　　he'll have achieved his aims and I'll have missed.
CREON.   You surely cannot mean you want me exiled!
OEDIPUS.   Not exiled, no. Your death is what I want!
CREON.   If you would first define what envy is . . .
OEDIPUS.   Are you still stubborn! Still disobedient?   630
CREON.   I see you cannot think!
OEDIPUS.   For me I can.
CREON.   You should for me as well!

608 *Pytho:* Delphi.   610–11 *portent reader:* Apollo's oracle or prophet.

OEDIPUS.   But you're a traitor!

CREON.   What if you're wrong?

OEDIPUS.   Authority must be maintained.

CREON.   Not if the ruler's evil.

OEDIPUS.   Hear that, Thebes!

CREON.   It is my city too, not yours alone!   635

CHORAGOS.   Please don't, my Lords! Ah, just in time, I see
    Jocasta there, coming from the palace.
    With her help you must settle your quarrel.

[*Enter JOCASTA from the Palace.*]

JOCASTA.   Wretched men! What has provoked this ill-
    advised dispute? Have you no sense of shame,   640
    with Thebes so sick, to stir up private troubles?
    Now go inside! And Creon, you go home!
    Don't make a general anguish out of nothing!

CREON.   My sister, Oedipus your husband here
    sees fit to do one of two hideous things: 645
    to have me banished from the land—or killed!

OEDIPUS.   That's right: I caught him, Lady, plotting harm
    against my person—with a malignant science.

CREON.   May my life fail, may I die cursed, if I
    did any of the things you said I did!   650

JOCASTA.   Believe his words, for the god's sake, Oedipus,
    in deference above all to his oath
    to the gods. Also for me, and for these men!

KOMMOS°

Strophe 1

CHORUS.   Consent, with will and mind,
    my king, I beg of you!   655

OEDIPUS.   What do you wish me to surrender?

CHORUS.   Show deference to him who was not feeble in time past
    and is now great in the power of his oath!

OEDIPUS.   Do you know what you're asking?

CHORUS.   Yes.

OEDIPUS.   Tell me then.

CHORUS.   Never to cast into dishonored guilt, with an unproved   660
    assumption, a kinsman who has bound himself by curse.

OEDIPUS.   Now you must understand, when you ask this,
    you ask my death or banishment from the land.

Strophe 2

CHORUS.   No, by the god who is the foremost of all gods,
    the Sun! No! Godless,   665

Kommos: a dirge or lament sung by the Chorus and one or more of the chief characters.

friendless, whatever death is worst of all,
let that be my destruction, if this
        thought ever moved me!
But my ill-fated soul
        this dying land   670
wears out—the more if to these older troubles
she adds new troubles from the two of you!

OEDIPUS.   Then let him go, though it must mean my death,
or else disgrace and exile from the land.
My pity is moved by your words, not by his—   675
he'll only have my hate, wherever he goes.

CREON.   You're sullen as you yield; you'll be depressed
when you've passed through this anger. Natures like yours
are hardest on themselves. That's as it should be.

OEDIPUS.   Then won't you go and let me be?

CREON.   I'll go.   680
Though you're unreasonable, they know I'm righteous.

[*Exit CREON.*]

Antistrophe 1

CHORUS.   Why are you waiting, Lady?
Conduct him back into the palace!

JOCASTA.   I will, when I have heard what chanced.   685

CHORUS.   Conjectures—words alone, and nothing based on thought.
But even an injustice can devour a man.

JOCASTA.   Did the words come from both sides?

CHORUS.   Yes.

JOCASTA. What was said?

CHORUS.   To me it seems enough! enough! the land already troubled,   690
that this should rest where it has stopped.

OEDIPUS.   See what you've come to in your honest thought,
in seeking to relax and blunt my heart?

Antistrophe 2

CHORUS.   I have not said this only once, my Lord.
That I had lost my sanity,   695
        without a path in thinking—
be sure this would be clear
        if I put you away
who, when my cherished land
        wandered crazed   700
with suffering, brought her back on course.
Now, too, be a lucky helmsman!

JOCASTA.   Please, for the god's sake, Lord, explain to me
the reason why you have conceived this wrath?

OEDIPUS.   I honor you, not them,° and I'll explain   705
to you how Creon has conspired against me.

705 *them:* the Chorus.

JOCASTA.   All right, if that will explain how the quarrel started.
OEDIPUS.   He says I am the murderer of Laius!
JOCASTA.   Did he claim knowledge or that someone told him?
OEDIPUS.   Here's what he did: he sent that vicious seer   710
    so he could keep his own mouth innocent.
JOCASTA.   Ah then, absolve yourself of what he charges!
    Listen to this and you'll agree, no mortal
    is ever given skill in prophecy.
    I'll prove this quickly with one incident.   715
    It was foretold to Laius—I shall not say
    by Phoebus himself, but by his ministers—
    that when his fate arrived he would be killed
    by a son who would be born to him and me.
    And yet, so it is told, foreign robbers   720
    murdered him, at a place where three roads meet.
    As for the child I bore him, not three days passed
    before he yoked the ball-joints of its feet,°
    then cast it, by others' hands, on a trackless mountain.
    That time Apollo did not make our child   725
    a patricide, or bring about what Laius
    feared, that he be killed by his own son.
    That's how prophetic words determined things!
    Forget them. The things a god must track
    he will himself painlessly reveal.   730
OEDIPUS.   Just now, as I was listening to you, Lady,
    what a profound distraction seized my mind!
JOCASTA.   What made you turn around so anxiously?
OEDIPUS.   I thought you said that Laius was attacked
    and butchered at a place where three roads meet.   735
JOCASTA.   That is the story, and it is told so still.
OEDIPUS.   Where is the place where this was done to him?
JOCASTA.   The land's called Phocis, where a two-forked road
    comes in from Delphi and from Daulia.
OEDIPUS.   And how much time has passed since these events?   740
JOCASTA.   Just prior to your presentation here
    as king this news was published to the city.
OEDIPUS.   Oh, Zeus, what have you willed to do to me?
JOCASTA.   Oedipus, what makes your heart so heavy?
OEDIPUS.   No, tell me first of Laius' appearance,   745
    what peak of youthful vigor he had reached.
JOCASTA.   A tall man, showing his first growth of white.
    He had a figure not unlike your own.
OEDIPUS.   Alas! It seems that in my ignorance
    I laid those fearful curses on myself.   750
JOCASTA.   What is it, Lord? I flinch to see your face.
OEDIPUS.   I'm dreadfully afraid the prophet sees.
    But I'll know better with one more detail.

723 *ball-joints of its feet:* the ankles.

JOCASTA.   I'm frightened too. But ask: I'll answer you.
OEDIPUS.   Was his retinue small, or did he travel   755
    with a great troop, as would befit a prince?
JOCASTA.   There were just five in all, one a herald.
    There was a carriage, too, bearing Laius.
OEDIPUS.   Alas! Now I see it! But who was it,
    Lady, who told you what you know about this?   760
JOCASTA.   A servant who alone was saved unharmed.
OEDIPUS.   By chance, could he be now in the palace?
JOCASTA.   No, he is not. When he returned and saw
    you had the power of the murdered Laius,
    he touched my hand and begged me formally   765
    to send him to the fields and to the pastures,
    so he'd be out of sight, far from the city.
    I did. Although a slave, he well deserved
    to win this favor, and indeed far more.
OEDIPUS.   Let's have him called back in immediately.   770
JOCASTA.   That can be done, but why do you desire it?
OEDIPUS.   I fear, Lady, I have already said
    too much. That's why I wish to see him now.
JOCASTA.   Then he shall come; but it is right somehow
    that I, too, Lord, should know what troubles you.   775
OEDIPUS.   I've gone so deep into the things I feared
    I'll tell you everything. Who has a right
    greater than yours, while I cross through this chance?
    Polybus of Corinth was my father,
    my mother was the Dorian Meropē.   780
    I was first citizen, until this chance
    attacked me—striking enough, to be sure,
    but not worth all the gravity I gave it.
    This: at a feast a man who'd drunk too much
    denied, at the wine, I was my father's son.   785
    I was depressed and all that day I barely
    held it in. Next day I put the question
    to my mother and father. They were enraged
    at the man who'd let this fiction fly at me.
    I was much cheered by them. And yet it kept   790
    grinding into me. His words kept coming back.
    Without my mother's or my father's knowledge
    I went to Pytho. But Phoebus sent me away
    dishonoring my demand. Instead, other
    wretched horrors he flashed forth in speech.   795
    He said that I would be my mother's lover,
    show offspring to mankind they could not look at,
    and be his murderer whose seed I am.°
    When I heard this, and ever since, I gauged
    the way to Corinth by the stars alone,   800

798 *be . . . am:* that is, murder my father.

running to a place where I would never see
the disgrace in the oracle's words come true.
But I soon came to the exact location
where, as you tell of it, the king was killed.
Lady, here is the truth. As I went on,   805
when I was just approaching those three roads,
a herald and a man like him you spoke of
came on, riding a carriage drawn by colts.
Both the man out front and the old man himself°
tried violently to force me off the road.   810
The driver, when he tried to push me off,
I struck in anger. The old man saw this, watched
me approach, then leaned out and lunged down
with twin prongs° at the middle of my head!
He got more than he gave. Abruptly—struck   815
once by the staff in this my hand—he tumbled
out, head first, from the middle of the carriage.
And then I killed them all. But if there is
a kinship between Laius and this stranger,
who is more wretched than the man you see?   820
Who was there born more hated by the gods?
For neither citizen nor foreigner
may take me in his home or speak to me.
No, they must drive me off. And it is I
who have pronounced these curses on myself!   825
I stain the dead man's bed with these my hands,
by which he died. Is not my nature vile?
Unclean?—if I am banished and even
in exile I may not see my own parents,
or set foot in my homeland, or else be yoked   830
in marriage to my mother, and kill my father,
Polybus, who raised me and gave me birth?
If someone judged a cruel divinity
did this to me, would he not speak the truth?
You pure and awful gods, may I not ever   835
see that day, may I be swept away
from men before I see so great and so
calamitous a stain fixed on my person!
CHORAGOS.   These things seem fearful to us, Lord, and yet,
until you hear it from the witness, keep hope!   840
OEDIPUS.   That is the single hope that's left to me,
to wait for him, that herdsman—until he comes.
JOCASTA.   When he appears, what are you eager for?
OEDIPUS.   Just this: if his account agrees with yours
then I shall have escaped this misery.   845
JOCASTA.   But what was it that struck you in my story?

809 *old man himself:* Laius.   813–14 *lunged . . . prongs:* Laius strikes Oedipus with a two-pronged horse goad or whip.

OEDIPUS.   You said he spoke of robbers as the ones
    who killed him. Now: if he continues still
    to speak of many, then I could not have killed him.
    One man and many men just do not jibe.   850
    But if he says one belted man, the doubt
    is gone. The balance tips toward me. I did it.
JOCASTA.   No! He told it as I told you. Be certain.
    He can't reject that and reverse himself.
    The city heard these things, not I alone.   855
    But even if he swerves from what he said,
    he'll never show that Laius' murder, Lord,
    occurred just as predicted. For Loxias
    expressly said my son was doomed to kill him.
    The boy—poor boy—he never had a chance   860
    to cut him down, for he was cut down first.
    Never again, just for some oracle
    will I shoot frightened glances right and left.
OEDIPUS.   That's full of sense. Nonetheless, send a man
    to bring that farm hand here. Will you do it?   865
JOCASTA.   I'll send one right away. But let's go in.
    Would I do anything against your wishes?

        [*Exit OEDIPUS and JOCASTA through the central door into the palace.*]

STASIMON 2

Strophe 1

CHORUS.   May there accompany me
    the fate to keep a reverential purity in what I say,
    in all I do, for which the laws have been set forth   870
    and walk on high, born to traverse the brightest,
    highest upper air; Olympus° only
    is their father, nor was it
    mortal nature
    that fathered them, and never will   875
    oblivion lull them into sleep;
    the god in them is great and never ages.

Antistrophe 1

    The will to violate, seed of the tyrant,
    if it has drunk mindlessly of wealth and power,
    without a sense of time or true advantage,   880
    mounts to a peak, then
    plunges to an abrupt . . . destiny,
    where the useful foot

---

872 *Olympus:* Mount Olympus, home of the gods, treated as a god.

is of no use. But the kind
of struggling that is good for the city   885
I ask the god never to abolish.
The god is my protector: never will I give that up.

Strophe 2

But if a man proceeds disdainfully
    in deeds of hand or word
and has no fear of Justice   890
    or reverence for shrines of the divinities
(may a bad fate catch him
    for his luckless wantonness!),
if he'll not gain what he gains with justice
and deny himself what is unholy,   895
or if he clings, in foolishness, to the untouchable
(what man, finally, in such an action, will have strength
enough to fend off passion's arrows from his soul?),
if, I say, this kind of
    deed is held in honor—   900
why should I join the sacred dance?

Antistrophe 2

No longer shall I visit and revere
    Earth's navel,° the untouchable,
nor visit Abae's° temple,
    or Olympia,°   905
if the prophecies are not matched by events
    for all the world to point to.
No, you who hold the power, if you are rightly called
Zeus the king of all, let this matter not escape you
and your ever-deathless rule,   910
for the prophecies to Laius fade . . .
and men already disregard them;
nor is Apollo anywhere
    glorified with honors.
Religion slips away.   915

EPISODE 3

[*Enter* JOCASTA *from the palace carrying a branch wound with wool and a jar of incense. She is attended by two women.*]

JOCASTA.   Lords of the realm, the thought has come to me
    to visit shrines of the divinities
    with suppliant's branch in hand and fragrant smoke.

903 *Earth's navel:* Delphi.   904 *Abae:* a town in Phocis where there was another oracle of Apollo.   905 *Olympia:* site of the oracle of Zeus.

For Oedipus excites his soul too much
with alarms of all kinds. He will not judge   920
the present by the past, like a man of sense.
He's at the mercy of all terror-mongers.

[*JOCASTA approaches the altar on the right and kneels.*]

Since I can do no good by counseling,
Apollo the Lycēan!—you are the closest—
I come a suppliant, with these my vows,   925
for a cleansing that will not pollute him.
For when we see him shaken we are all
afraid, like people looking at their helmsman.

[*Enter a MESSENGER along one of the Parados. He sees JOCASTA at the altar and then addresses
the CHORUS.*]

MESSENGER.   I would be pleased if you would help me, stranger.
    Where is the palace of King Oedipus?   930
    Or tell me where he is himself, if you know.
CHORUS.   This is his house, stranger. He is within.
    This is his wife and mother of his children.
MESSENGER.   May she and her family find prosperity,
    if, as you say, her marriage is fulfilled.   935
JOCASTA.   You also, stranger, for you deserve as much
    for your gracious words. But tell me why you've come.
    What do you wish? Or what have you to tell us?
MESSENGER.   Good news, my Lady, both for your house and
        husband.
JOCASTA.   What is your news? And who has sent you to us?   940
MESSENGER.   I come from Corinth. When you have heard my
        news
    you will rejoice, I'm sure—and grieve perhaps.
JOCASTA.   What is it? How can it have this double power?
MESSENGER.   They will establish him their king, so say
    the people of the land of Isthmia.°   945
JOCASTA.   But is old Polybus not still in power?
MESSENGER.   He's not, for death has clasped him in the tomb.
JOCASTA.   What's this? Has Oedipus' father died?
MESSENGER.   If I have lied then I deserve to die.
JOCASTA.   Attendant! Go quickly to your master,   950
    and tell him this.

[*Exit an ATTENDANT into the palace.*]

Oracles of the gods!
Where are you now? The man whom Oedipus
fled long ago, for fear that he should kill him—
he's been destroyed by chance and not by him!

---

945 *land of Isthmia:* Corinth, which is on an isthmus.

[*Enter* OEDIPUS *from the palace.*]

OEDIPUS.   Darling Jocasta, my beloved wife,   955
        Why have you called me from the palace?
JOCASTA.   First hear what this man has to say. Then see
        what the god's grave oracle has come to now!
OEDIPUS.   Where is he from? What is this news he brings me?
JOCASTA.   From Corinth. He brings news about your father: 960
        that Polybus is no more! that he is dead!
OEDIPUS.   What's this, old man? I want to hear you say it.
MESSENGER.   If this is what must first be clarified,
        please be assured that he is dead and gone.
OEDIPUS.   By treachery or by the touch of sickness?   965
MESSENGER.   Light pressures tip agéd frames into their sleep.
OEDIPUS.   You mean the poor man died of some disease.
MESSENGER.   And of the length of years that he had tallied.
OEDIPUS.   Aha! Then why should we look to Pytho's vapors,°
        or to the birds that scream above our heads?°   970
        If we could really take those things for guides,
        I would have killed my father. But he's dead!
        He is beneath the earth, and here am I,
        who never touched a spear. Unless he died
        of longing for me and I "killed" him that way!   975
        No, in this case, Polybus, by dying, took
        the worthless oracle to Hades with him.
JOCASTA.   And wasn't I telling you that just now?
OEDIPUS.   You were indeed. I was misled by fear.
JOCASTA.   You should not care about this anymore.   980
OEDIPUS.   I must care. I must stay clear of my mother's bed.
JOCASTA.   What's there for man to fear? The realm of chance
        prevails. True foresight isn't possible.
        His life is best who lives without a plan.
        This marriage with your mother—don't fear it.   985
        How many times have men in dreams, too, slept
        with their own mothers! Those who believe such things
        mean nothing endure their lives most easily.
OEDIPUS.   A fine, bold speech, and you are right, perhaps,
        except that my mother is still living,   990
        so I must fear her, however well you argue.
JOCASTA.   And yet your father's tomb is a great eye.
OEDIPUS.   Illuminating, yes. But I still fear the living.
MESSENGER.   Who is the woman who inspires this fear?
OEDIPUS.   Meropē, Polybus' wife, old man.   995
MESSENGER.   And what is there about her that alarms you?
OEDIPUS.   An oracle, god-sent and fearful, stranger.
MESSENGER.   Is it permitted that another know?

---

969 *Pytho's vapors:* the prophecies of the oracle at Delphi.   970 *birds . . . heads:* the prophecies
derived from interpreting the flights of birds.

OEDIPUS.   It is. Loxias once said to me
　　I must have intercourse with my own mother   1000
　　and take my father's blood with these my hands.
　　So I have long lived far away from Corinth.
　　This has indeed brought much good luck, and yet,
　　to see one's parents' eyes is happiest.
MESSENGER.   Was it for this that you have lived in exile?   1005
OEDIPUS.   So I'd not be my father's killer, sir.
MESSENGER.   Had I not better free you from this fear,
　　my Lord? That's why I came—to do you service.
OEDIPUS.   Indeed, what a reward you'd get for that!
MESSENGER.   Indeed, this is the main point of my trip,   1010
　　to be rewarded when you get back home.
OEDIPUS.   I'll never rejoin the givers of my seed!°
MESSENGER.   My son, clearly you don't know what you're doing.
OEDIPUS.   But how is that, old man? For the gods' sake, tell me!
MESSENGER.   If it's because of them you won't go home.   1015
OEDIPUS.   I fear that Phoebus will have told the truth.
MESSENGER.   Pollution from the ones who gave you seed?
OEDIPUS.   That is the thing, old man, I always fear.
MESSENGER.   Your fear is groundless. Understand that.
OEDIPUS.   Groundless? Not if I was born their son.   1020
MESSENGER.   But Polybus is not related to you.
OEDIPUS.   Do you mean Polybus was not my father?
MESSENGER.   No more than I. We're both the same to you.
OEDIPUS.   Same? One who begot me and one who didn't?
MESSENGER.   He didn't beget you any more than I did.   1025
OEDIPUS.   But then, why did he say I was his son?
MESSENGER.   He got you as a gift from my own hands.
OEDIPUS.   He loved me so, though from another's hands?
MESSENGER.   His former childlessness persuaded him.
OEDIPUS.   But had you bought me, or begotten me?   1030
MESSENGER.   Found you. In the forest hallows of Cithaeron.
OEDIPUS.   What were you doing traveling in that region?
MESSENGER.   I was in charge of flocks which grazed those mountains.
OEDIPUS.   A wanderer who worked the flocks for hire?
MESSENGER.   Ah, but that day I was your savior, son.   1035
OEDIPUS.   From what? What was my trouble when you took me?
MESSENGER.   The ball-joints of your feet might testify.
OEDIPUS.   What's that? What makes you name that ancient trouble?
MESSENGER.   Your feet were pierced and I am your rescuer.
OEDIPUS.   A fearful rebuke those tokens left for me!   1040
MESSENGER.   That was the chance that names you who you are.
OEDIPUS.   By the gods, did my mother or my father do this?
MESSENGER.   That I don't know. He might who gave you to me.
OEDIPUS.   From someone else? You didn't chance on me?
MESSENGER.   Another shepherd handed you to me.   1045

1012 *givers of my seed:* that is, my parents. Oedipus still thinks Meropē and Polybus are his parents.

OEDIPUS.   Who was he? Do you know? Will you explain!
MESSENGER.   They called him one of the men of—was it Laius?
OEDIPUS.   The one who once was king here long ago?
MESSENGER.   That is the one! The man was shepherd to him.
OEDIPUS.   And is he still alive so I can see him?   1050
MESSENGER.   But you who live here ought to know that best.
OEDIPUS.   Does any one of you now present know
    about the shepherd whom this man has named?
    Have you seen him in town or in the fields? Speak out!
    The time has come for the discovery!   1055
CHORAGOS.   The man he speaks of, I believe, is the same
    as the field hand you have already asked to see.
    But it's Jocasta who would know this best.
OEDIPUS.   Lady, do you remember the man we just
    now sent for—is that the man he speaks of?   1060
JOCASTA.   What? The man he spoke of? Pay no attention!
    His words are not worth thinking about. It's nothing.
OEDIPUS.   With clues like this within my grasp, give up?
    Fail to solve the mystery of my birth?
JOCASTA.   For the love of the gods, and if you love your life,   1065
    give up this search! My sickness is enough.
OEDIPUS.   Come! Though my mothers for three generations
    were in slavery, you'd not be lowborn!
JOCASTA.   No, listen to me! Please! Don't do this thing!
OEDIPUS.   I will not listen; I will search out the truth.   1070
JOCASTA.   My thinking is for you—it would be best.
OEDIPUS.   This "best" of yours is starting to annoy me.
JOCASTA.   Doomed man! Never find out who you are!
OEDIPUS.   Will someone go and bring that shepherd here?
    Leave her to glory in her wealthy birth!   1075
JOCASTA.   Man of misery! No other name
    shall I address you by, ever again.

[*Exit JOCASTA into the palace after a long pause.*]

CHORAGOS.   Why has your lady left, Oedipus,
    hurled by a savage grief? I am afraid
    disaster will come bursting from this silence.   1080
OEDIPUS.   Let it burst forth! However low this seed
    of mine may be, yet I desire to see it.
    She, perhaps—she has a woman's pride—
    is mortified by my base origins.
    But I who count myself the child of Chance,   1085
    the giver of good, shall never know dishonor.
    She is my mother,° and the months my brothers
    who first marked out my lowness, then my greatness.
    I shall not prove untrue to such a nature
    by giving up the search for my own birth.   1090

1087 *She . . . mother:* Chance is my mother.

STASIMON 3

Strophe

CHORUS.   If I have mantic power
    and excellence in thought,
    by Olympus,
        you shall not, Cithaeron, at tomorrow's
    full moon,   1095
    fail to hear us celebrate you as the countryman
    of Oedipus, his nurse and mother,
    or fail to be the subject of our dance,
        since you have given pleasure
    to our king.   1100
    Phoebus, whom we summon by "iē!,"
    may this be pleasing to you!

Antistrophe

    Who was your mother, son?
    which of the long-lived nymphs
    after lying with Pan,°   1105
        the mountain roaming . . . Or was it a bride
    of Loxias?°
    For dear to him are all the upland pastures.
    Or was it Mount Cyllēnē's lord,°
    or the Bacchic god,°   1110
        dweller of the mountain peaks,
    who received you as a joyous find
    from one of the nymphs of Helicon,
    the favorite sharers of his sport?

EPISODE 4

OEDIPUS.   If someone like myself, who never met him,   1115
    may calculate—elders, I think I see
    the very herdsman we've been waiting for.
    His many years would fit that man's age,
    and those who bring him on, if I am right,
    are my own men. And yet, in real knowledge,   1120
    you can outstrip me, surely: you've seen him.

[*Enter the old* HERDSMAN *escorted by two of Oedipus's* ATTENDANTS. *At first, the* HERDSMAN *will
not look at* OEDIPUS.]

CHORAGOS.   I know him, yes, a man of the house of Laius,
    a trusty herdsman if he ever had one.

1105 *Pan:* god of shepherds and woodlands, half man and half goat.   1107 *Loxias:* Apollo.
1109 *Mount Cyllēnē's lord:* Hermes, messenger of the gods.   1110 *Bacchic god:* Dionysus.

OEDIPUS.   I ask you first, the stranger come from Corinth:
    is this the man you spoke of?
MESSENGER.   That's he you see.   1125
OEDIPUS.   Then you, old man. First look at me! Now answer:
    did you belong to Laius' household once?
HERDSMAN.   I did. Not a purchased slave but raised in the palace.
OEDIPUS.   How have you spent your life? What is your work?
HERDSMAN.   Most of my life now I have tended sheep.   1130
OEDIPUS.   Where is the usual place you stay with them?
HERDSMAN.   On Mount Cithaeron. Or in that district.
OEDIPUS.   Do you recall observing this man there?
HERDSMAN.   Doing what? Which is the man you mean?
OEDIPUS.   This man right here. Have you had dealings with him?   1135
HERDSMAN.   I can't say right away. I don't remember.
MESSENGER.   No wonder, master. I'll bring clear memory
    to his ignorance. I'm absolutely sure
    he can recall it, the district was Cithaeron,
    he with a double flock, and I, with one,   1140
    lived close to him, for three entire seasons,
    six months long, from spring right to Arcturus.°
    Then for the winter I'd drive mine to my fold,
    and he'd drive his to Laius' pen again.
    Did any of the things I say take place?   1145
HERDSMAN.   You speak the truth, though it's from long ago.
MESSENGER.   Do you remember giving me, back then,
    a boy I was to care for as my own?
HERDSMAN.   What are you saying? Why do you ask me that?
MESSENGER.   There, sir, is the man who was that boy!   1150
HERDSMAN.   Damn you! Shut your mouth! Keep your silence!
OEDIPUS.   Stop! Don't you rebuke his words.
    Your words ask for rebuke far more than his.
HERDSMAN.   But what have I done wrong, most royal master?
OEDIPUS.   Not telling of the boy of whom he asked.   1155
HERDSMAN.   He's ignorant and blundering toward ruin.
OEDIPUS.   Tell it willingly—or under torture.
HERDSMAN.   Oh god! Don't—I am old—don't torture me!
OEDIPUS.   Here! Someone put his hands behind his back!
HERDSMAN.   But why? What else would you find out, poor man?   1160
OEDIPUS.   Did you give him the child he asks about?
HERDSMAN.   I did. I wish that I had died that day!
OEDIPUS.   You'll come to that if you don't speak the truth.
HERDSMAN.   It's if I speak that I shall be destroyed.
OEDIPUS.   I think this fellow struggles for delay.   1165
HERDSMAN.   No, no! I said already that I gave him.
OEDIPUS.   From your own home, or got from someone else?

1142 *from spring right to Arcturus:* That is, from spring to early fall, when the summer star Arcturus
(in the constellation Boötes) is no longer visible in the early evening sky. It does not rise at night
again until the following spring.

HERDSMAN.   Not from my own. I got him from another.
OEDIPUS.   Which of these citizens? What sort of house?
HERDSMAN.   Don't—by the gods!—don't, master, ask me more!   1170
OEDIPUS.   It means your death if I must ask again.
HERDSMAN.   One of the children of the house of Laius.
OEDIPUS.   A slave—or born into the family?
HERDSMAN.   I have come to the dreaded thing, and I shall say it.
OEDIPUS.   And I to hearing it, but hear I must.   1175
HERDSMAN.   He was reported to have been—his son.
    Your lady in the house could tell you best.
OEDIPUS.   Because she gave him to you?
HERDSMAN.   Yes, my lord.
OEDIPUS.   What was her purpose?
HERDSMAN.   I was to kill the boy.
OEDIPUS.   The child she bore?
HERDSMAN.   She dreaded prophecies.   1180
OEDIPUS.   What were they?
HERDSMAN.   The word was that he'd kill his parents.
OEDIPUS.   Then why did you give him up to this old man?
HERDSMAN.   In pity, master—so he would take him home,
    to another land. But what he did was save him
    for this supreme disaster. If you are the one   1185
    he speaks of—know your evil birth and fate!
OEDIPUS.   Ah! All of it was destined to be true!
    Oh light, now may I look my last upon you,
    shown monstrous in my birth, in marriage monstrous,
    a murderer monstrous in those I killed.   1190

[*Exit OEDIPUS, running into the palace.*]

STASIMON 4

Strophe 1

CHORUS.   Oh generations of mortal men,
    while you are living, I will
        appraise your lives at zero!
    What man
    comes closer to seizing lasting blessedness   1195
    than merely to seize its semblance,
    and after living in this semblance, to plunge?
    With your example before us,
    with your destiny, yours,
        suffering Oedipus, no mortal   1200
    can I judge fortunate.

Antistrophe 1

For he,° outranging everybody,
    shot his arrow° and became the lord

1202 *he:* Oedipus.   1203 *shot his arrow:* took his chances; made a guess at the Sphinx's riddle.

of wide prosperity and blessedness,
oh Zeus, after destroying   1205
the virgin with the crooked talons,°
singer of oracles; and against death,
in my land, he arose a tower of defense.
From which time you were called my king
and granted privileges supreme—in mighty   1210
Thebes the ruling lord.

Strophe 2

But now—whose story is more sorrowful than yours?
Who is more intimate with fierce calamities,
with labors, now that your life is altered?
Alas, my Oedipus, whom all men know: 1215
one great harbor°—
one alone sufficed for you,
as son and father,
when you tumbled,° plowman° of the woman's chamber.
How, how could your paternal   1220
     furrows, wretched man,
endure you silently so long.

Antistrophe 2

Time, all-seeing, surprised you living an unwilled life
and sits from of old in judgment on the marriage, not a marriage,
where the begetter is the begot as well.   1225
Ah, son of Laius . . . ,
would that—oh, would that
I had never seen you!
I wail, my scream climbing beyond itself
from my whole power of voice. To say it straight: 1230
     from you I got new breath—
but I also lulled my eye to sleep.°

EXODOS

[Enter the SECOND MESSENGER from the palace.]

SECOND MESSENGER.   You who are first among the citizens,
     what deeds you are about to hear and see!
     What grief you'll carry, if, true to your birth,   1235
     you still respect the house of Labdacus!
     Neither the Ister nor the Phasis river

1206 *virgin . . . talons:* the Sphinx.   1216 *one great harbor:* metaphorical allusion to Jocasta's
body.   1219 *tumbled:* were born and had sex.   *plowman:* Plowing is used here as a sexual
metaphor.   1232 *I . . . sleep:* I failed to see the corruption you brought.

could purify this house, such suffering
does it conceal, or soon must bring to light—
willed this time, not unwilled. Griefs hurt worst   1240
which we perceive to be self-chosen ones.
CHORAGOS.   They were sufficient, the things we knew before,
to make us grieve. What can you add to those?
SECOND MESSENGER.   The thing that's quickest said and quickest heard:
our own, our royal one, Jocasta's dead.   1245
CHORAGOS.   Unhappy queen! What was responsible?
SECOND MESSENGER.   Herself. The bitterest of these events
is not for you, you were not there to see,
but yet, exactly as I can recall it,
you'll hear what happened to that wretched lady.   1250
She came in anger through the outer hall,
and then she ran straight to her marriage bed,
tearing her hair with the fingers of both hands.
Then, slamming shut the doors when she was in,
she called to Laius, dead so many years,   1255
remembering the ancient seed which caused
his death, leaving the mother to the son
to breed again an ill-born progeny.
She mourned the bed where she, alas, bred double—
husband by husband, children by her child.   1260
From this point on I don't know how she died,
for Oedipus then burst in with a cry,
and did not let us watch her final evil.
Our eyes were fixed on him. Wildly he ran
to each of us, asking for his spear   1265
and for his wife—no wife: where he might find
the double mother-field, his and his children's.
He raved, and some divinity then showed him—
for none of us did so who stood close by.
With a dreadful shout—as if some guide were leading—   1270
he lunged through the double doors; he bent the hollow
bolts from the sockets, burst into the room,
and there we saw her, hanging from above,
entangled in some twisted hanging strands.
He saw, was stricken, and with a wild roar   1275
ripped down the dangling noose. When she, poor woman,
lay on the ground, there came a fearful sight:
he snatched the pins of worked gold from her dress,
with which her clothes were fastened: these he raised
and struck into the ball-joints of his eyes.°   1280
He shouted that they would no longer see
the evils he had suffered or had done,
see in the dark those he should not have seen,
and know no more those he once sought to know.

1280 *ball-joints of his eyes:* his eyeballs. Oedipus blinds himself in both eyes at the same time.

While chanting this, not once but many times   1285
he raised his hand and struck into his eyes.
Blood from his wounded eyes poured down his chin,
not freed in moistening drops, but all at once
a stormy rain of black blood burst like hail.
These evils, coupling them, making them one,   1290
have broken loose upon both man and wife.
The old prosperity that they had once
was true prosperity, and yet today,
mourning, ruin, death, disgrace, and every
evil you could name—not one is absent.   1295
CHORAGOS.   Has he allowed himself some peace from all this grief?
SECOND MESSENGER.   He shouts that someone slide the bolts and show
to all the Cadmeians the patricide,
his mother's—I can't say it, it's unholy—
so he can cast himself out of the land,   1300
not stay and curse his house by his own curse.
He lacks the strength, though, and he needs a guide,
for his is a sickness that's too great to bear.
Now you yourself will see: the bolts of the doors
are opening. You are about to see   1305
a vision even one who hates must pity.

[*Enter the blinded* OEDIPUS *from the palace, led in by a household* SERVANT.]

CHORAGOS.   This suffering sends terror through men's eyes,
terrible beyond any suffering
my eyes have touched. Oh man of pain,
what madness reached you? Which god from far off,   1310
surpassing in range his longest spring,
struck hard against your god-abandoned fate?
Oh man of pain,
I cannot look upon you—though there's so much
I would ask you, so much to hear,   1315
so much that holds my eyes—
so awesome the convulsions you send through me.
OEDIPUS.   Ah! Ah! I am a man of misery.
Where am I carried? Pity me! Where
is my voice scattered abroad on wings?   1320
Divinity, where has your lunge transported me?
CHORAGOS.   To something horrible, not to be heard or seen.

KOMMOS

Strophe 1

OEDIPUS.   Oh, my cloud
of darkness, abominable, unspeakable as it attacks me,
not to be turned away, brought by an evil wind!   1325

Alas!
Again alas! Both enter me at once:
the sting of the prongs,° the memory of evils!
CHORUS.   I do not marvel that in these afflictions
you carry double griefs and double evils.   1330

Antistrophe 1

OEDIPUS.   Ah, friend,
so you at least are there, resolute servant!
Still with a heart to care for me, the blind man.
Oh! Oh!
I know that you are there. I recognize   1335
even inside my darkness, that voice of yours.
CHORUS.   Doer of horror, how did you bear to quench
your vision? What divinity raised your hand?

Strophe 2

OEDIPUS.   It was Apollo there, Apollo, friends,
who brought my sorrows, vile sorrows to their perfection,   1340
these evils that were done to me.
But the one who struck them with his hand,
that one was none but I, in wretchedness.
For why was I to see
when nothing I could see would bring me joy?   1345
CHORUS.   Yes, that is how it was.
OEDIPUS.   What could I see, indeed,
or what enjoy—what greeting
is there I could hear with pleasure, friends?
Conduct me out of the land   1350
as quickly as you can!
Conduct me out, my friends,
the man utterly ruined,
supremely cursed,
the man who is by gods   1355
the most detested of all men!
CHORUS.   Wretched in disaster and in knowledge:
oh, I could wish you'd never come to know!

Antistrophe 2

OEDIPUS.   May he be destroyed, whoever freed the savage shackles
from my feet when I'd been sent to the wild pasture,   1360
whoever rescued me from murder
and became my savior—
a bitter gift:

1328 *prongs:* refers to both the whip that Laius used and the two gold pins Oedipus used to blind himself.

if I had died then,
I'd not have been such grief to self and kin.   1365
CHORUS.   I also would have had it so.
OEDIPUS.   I'd not have returned to be my father's
    murderer; I'd not be called by men
    my mother's bridegroom.
Now I'm without a god,   1370
    child of a polluted parent,
fellow progenitor with him
    who gave me birth in misery.
If there's an evil that
    surpasses evils, that   1375
has fallen to the lot of Oedipus.
CHORAGOS.   How can I say that you have counseled well?
    Better not to be than live a blind man.
OEDIPUS.   That this was not the best thing I could do—
    don't tell me that, or advise me any more!   1380
    Should I descend to Hades and endure
    to see my father with these eyes? Or see
    my poor unhappy mother? For I have done,
    to both of these, things too great for hanging.
    Or is the sight of children to be yearned for,   1385
    to see new shoots that sprouted as these did?
    Never, never with these eyes of mine!
    Nor city, nor tower, nor holy images
    of the divinities! For I, all-wretched,
    most nobly raised—as no one else in Thebes—   1390
    deprived myself of these when I ordained
    that all expel the impious one—god-shown
    to be polluted, and the dead king's son!°
    Once I exposed this great stain upon me,
    could I have looked on these with steady eyes?   1395
    No! No! And if there were a way to block
    the source of hearing in my ears, I'd gladly
    have locked up my pitiable body,
    so I'd be blind and deaf. Evils shut out—
    that way my mind could live in sweetness.   1400
    Alas, Cithaeron,° why did you receive me?
    Or when you had me, not killed me instantly?
    I'd not have had to show my birth to mankind.
    Polybus, Corinth, halls—ancestral,
    they told me—how beautiful was your ward,   1405
    a scar that held back festering disease!
    Evil my nature, evil my origin.
    You, three roads, and you, secret ravine,

1391–1393 *I . . . son:* Oedipus refers to his own curse against the murderer as well as his sins of patricide and incest.   1401 *Cithaeron:* the mountain on which the infant Oedipus was exposed.

you oak grove, narrow place of those three paths
that drank my blood° from these my hands, from him   1410
who fathered me, do you remember still
the things I did to you? When I'd come here,
what I then did once more? Oh marriages! Marriages!
You gave us life and when you'd planted us
you sent the same seed up, and then revealed   1415
fathers, brothers, sons, and kinsman's blood,
and brides, and wives, and mothers, all the most
atrocious things that happen to mankind!
One should not name what never should have been.
Somewhere out there, then, quickly, by the gods,   1420
cover me up, or murder me, or throw me
to the ocean where you will never see me more!

[*OEDIPUS moves toward the CHORUS and they back away from him.*]

Come! Don't shrink to touch this wretched man!
Believe me, do not be frightened! I alone
of all mankind can carry these afflictions.   1425

[*Enter CREON from the palace with ATTENDANTS.*]

CHORAGOS.   Tell Creon what you wish for. Just when we need him
    he's here. He can act, he can advise you.
    He's now the land's sole guardian in your place.
OEDIPUS.   Ah! Are there words that I can speak to him?
    What ground for trust can I present? It's proved   1430
    that I was false to him in everything.
CREON.   I have not come to mock you, Oedipus,
    nor to reproach you for your former falseness.
    You men, if you have no respect for sons
    of mortals, let your awe for the all-feeding   1435
    flames of lordly Hēlius° prevent
    your showing unconcealed so great a stain,
    abhorred by earth and sacred rain and light.
    Escort him quickly back into the house!
    If blood kin only see and hear their own   1440
    afflictions, we'll have no impious defilement.
OEDIPUS.   By the gods, you've freed me from one terrible fear,
    so nobly meeting my unworthiness:
    grant me something—not for me; for you!
CREON.   What do you want that you should beg me so?   1445
OEDIPUS.   To drive me from the land at once, to a place
    where there will be no man to speak to me!
CREON.   I would have done just that—had I not wished
    to ask first of the god what I should do.
OEDIPUS.   His answer was revealed in full—that I,   1450
    the patricide, unholy, be destroyed.

1410 *my blood:* that is, the blood of my father, Laius.   1436 *Hēlius:* the sun.

CREON.   He said that, but our need is so extreme,
    it's best to have sure knowledge what must be done.
OEDIPUS.   You'll ask about a wretched man like me?
CREON.   Is it not time you put your trust in the god?   1455
OEDIPUS.   But I bid you as well, and shall entreat you.
    Give her who is within what burial
    you will—you'll give your own her proper rites;
    but me—do not condemn my fathers' land
    to have me dwelling here while I'm alive,   1460
    but let me live on mountains—on Cithaeron
    famed as mine, for my mother and my father,
    while they yet lived, made it my destined tomb,
    and I'll be killed by those who wished my ruin!
    And yet I know: no sickness will destroy me,   1465
    nothing will: I'd never have been saved
    when left to die unless for some dread evil.
    Then let my fate continue where it will!
    As for my children, Creon, take no pains
    for my sons—they're men and they will never lack   1470
    the means to live, wherever they may be—
    but my two wretched, pitiable girls,
    who never ate but at my table, never
    were without me—everything that I
    would touch, they'd always have a share of it—   1475
    please care for them! Above all, let me touch
    them with my hands and weep aloud my woes!
    Please, my Lord!
    Please, noble heart! Touching with my hands,
    I'd think I held them as when I could see.   1480

[*Enter* ANTIGONE *and* ISMENE *from the palace with* ATTENDANTS.]

    What's this?
    Oh gods! Do I hear, somewhere, my two dear ones
    sobbing? Has Creon really pitied me
    and sent to me my dearest ones, my children?
    Is that it?   1485
CREON.   Yes, I prepared this for you, for I knew
    you'd feel this joy, as you have always done.
OEDIPUS.   Good fortune, then, and, for your care, be guarded
    far better by divinity than I was!
    Where are you, children? Come to me! Come here   1490
    to these my hands, hands of your brother, hands
    of him who gave you seed, hands that made
    these once bright eyes to see now in this fashion.

[OEDIPUS *embraces his daughters.*]

    He, children, seeing nothing, knowing nothing,
    he fathered you where his own seed was plowed.   1495
    I weep for you as well, though I can't see you,

imagining your bitter life to come,
the life you will be forced by men to live.
What gatherings of townsmen will you join,
what festivals, without returning home   1500
in tears instead of watching holy rites?
And when you've reached the time for marrying,
where, children, is the man who'll run the risk
of taking on himself the infamy
that will wound you as it did my parents?   1505
What evil is not here? Your father killed
his father, plowed the one who gave him birth,
and from the place where he was sown, from there
he got you, from the place he too was born.
These are the wounds: then who will marry you?   1510
No man, my children. No, it's clear that you
must wither in dry barrenness, unmarried.

[*Oedipus addresses Creon.*]

Son of Menoeceus! You are the only father
left to them—we two who gave them seed
are both destroyed: watch that they don't become   1515
poor, wanderers, unmarried—they are your kin.
Let not my ruin be their ruin, too!
No, pity them! You see how young they are,
bereft of everyone, except for you.
Consent, kind heart, and touch me with your hand!   1520

[*Creon grasps Oedipus's right hand.*]

You, children, if you had reached an age of sense,
I would have counseled much. Now, pray you may live
always where it's allowed, finding a life
better than his was, who gave you seed.

CREON.   Stop this now. Quiet your weeping. Move away, into the house.   1525
OEDIPUS.   Bitter words, but I obey them.
CREON.   There's an end to all things.
OEDIPUS.   I have first this request.
CREON.   I will hear it.
OEDIPUS.   Banish me from my homeland.
CREON.   You must ask that of the god.
OEDIPUS.   But I am the gods' most hated man!
CREON.   Then you will soon get what you want.
OEDIPUS.   Do you consent?
CREON.   I never promise when, as now, I'm ignorant. 1530
OEDIPUS.   Then lead me in.
CREON.   Come. But let your hold fall from your children.
OEDIPUS.   Do not take them from me, ever!
CREON.   Do not wish to keep all of the
power. You had power, but that power did not follow you through life.

[OEDIPUS'S *daughters are taken from him and led into the palace by* ATTENDANTS. OEDIPUS *is led into the palace by a* SERVANT. CREON *and the other* ATTENDANTS *follow. Only the* CHORUS *remains.*]

CHORUS.   People of Thebes, my country, see: here is that Oedipus—
    he who "knew" the famous riddle, and attained the highest power,   1535
    whom all citizens admired, even envying his luck!
    See the billows of wild troubles which he has entered now!
    Here is the truth of each man's life: we must wait, and see his end,
    scrutinize his dying day, and refuse to call him happy
    till he has crossed the border of his life without pain.   1540

[*Exit the* CHORUS *along each of the Parados.*]

QUESTIONS

Prologue and Parados

1.   What is the situation in Thebes as the play begins? Why does Oedipus want to find Laius's murderer?

Episode 1 and Stasimon 1

2.   How does Oedipus react to Tiresias's refusal to speak? How is this reaction characteristic of Oedipus? What other instances of this sort of behavior can you find in Oedipus's story?
3.   When Tiresias does speak, he answers the central question of the play and tells the truth. Why doesn't Oedipus recognize this as the truth?

Episode 2 and Stasimon 2

4.   What does Oedipus accuse Creon of doing? How does Creon defend himself? Do you find Creon's defense convincing? Why?
5.   What is Jocasta's attitude toward oracles and prophecy? Why does she have this attitude? How does it contrast with the attitude of the chorus?
6.   At what point in the play does Oedipus begin to suspect that he killed Laius? What details make him begin to suspect himself?

Episode 3 and Stasimon 3

7.   What news does the messenger from Corinth bring? Why does this news seem to be good at first? How is this situation reversed?

Episode 4 and Stasimon 4

8.   What do you make of the coincidence that the same herdsman (1) saved the infant Oedipus from death, (2) was with Laius at the place where three roads meet and was the lone survivor of the attack, and (3) will now be the agent to destroy Oedipus?
9.   What moral does the chorus see in Oedipus's life?

Exodos

10. Why does Oedipus blind himself? What is the significance of the instruments that he uses to blind himself?

11. Who or what does Oedipus blame for his tragic life and destruction?

GENERAL QUESTIONS

1. In *Oedipus*, the peripeteia, anagnorisis, and catastrophe all occur at the same moment. When is this moment? Who is most severely affected by it?

2. Sophocles tells the events of Oedipus's life out of chronological order. Put all the events of his life in chronological order and consider how you might dramatize them. Why does Sophocles's ordering of these events produce an effective play?

3. Each episode of the play introduces new conflicts: Oedipus against the plague, against Tiresias, against Creon. What is the central conflict of the play? Why is it central?

4. All the violent acts of this play—the suicide of Jocasta and the blinding of Oedipus—occur offstage and are reported rather than shown. What are the advantages and disadvantages of dealing with violence this way?

5. Discuss the use of coincidences in the play. How do you react to them? Do they seem convincing or forced, given the plot of the play?

6. Explore the ways in which Sophocles employs dramatic irony, with reference to three specific examples.

7. Consider that *Oedipus* is a tragedy of both the individual and the state. What do you think will happen to Thebes after Oedipus is exiled?

8. Discuss the functions of the chorus and the Choragos. What do the choral odes contribute to the play?

9. Early in the play Oedipus begins a search for a murderer. How does the object of his search change as the play progresses? Why does it change?

THE REBIRTH AND DEVELOPMENT OF DRAMA IN THE CENTURIES BEFORE SHAKESPEARE

As the Roman Empire in western Europe disintegrated in the fifth century C.E., many of its institutions, including the theater, disintegrated with it. In the next five centuries, often called the Dark Ages, Europe fell into feudalism, characterized by political decentralization and social fragmentation. The intellectuals of the period, most of them clergy, were creating Christian theology and establishing the growing church while abandoning the memories and records of the past, of which drama was a major element. As far as we know, there were no public theaters, no patrons able to support public performances, no popular audiences with the money to pay for admission, no official permission by secular and religious authorities to perform plays, and no practicing dramatists—in short, there was no organized theater. It is hard to believe, however, that the human need for stories and fantasies did not remain, expressed in tales and songs passed on from parents to children and community to community throughout these dark centuries.

Medieval Religious Drama

During the tenth century—five centuries after the breakup of the western Roman Empire—the clergy started to elaborate on the dramatic appeal of the mass. It was then that dramatic **tropes** (short didactic presentations performed in conjunction with the mass, either with or without musical accompaniment) developed as a teaching tool in the churches. The earliest tropes were written to dramatize the background story of the Easter rituals. As time went on, the church also developed special Christmas ceremonies such as those for the Three Wise Men, the Shepherds, and the ranting Herod. These ceremonies became regular parts of Easter and Christmas rituals for hundreds of years.

CORPUS CHRISTI PLAYS.   Growing out of this tradition, a full-blown religious and civic drama developed in the fourteenth century in Europe, just as the drama of ancient Athens had developed out of religious festivals for the god Dionysus in the sixth century B.C.E.[12] The major expression of the new religious drama came during the celebration of Corpus Christi Day ("body of Christ" day), a celebration of the doctrine of transubstantiation (i.e., during mass, the Eucharistic bread and wine were said to become transformed miraculously into the real body and blood of Christ). Corpus Christi Day was observed on a Thursday sixty days after Easter.

Corpus Christi Day featured local processions devoted to the worship of the Eucharist, and in this way it brought religious celebration into the streets and before the public. Because the feast occurred at the end of the liturgical year, it coincided with the beginning of good weather. The winter and spring rains abated, daylight hours lengthened, short trips from country villages to nearby towns became possible, and people could spend an entire day outside and still be comfortable.

THE CRAFT GUILDS, OR MYSTERIES.   Facilitating the development of drama was the growth of medieval trade or craft guilds. The guilds controlled the various practices and standards of their trades as well as the prices and general conditions governing their work. Naturally, guild leaders ("masters") wanted to boost the prestige of their towns and their own wealth and power. They therefore welcomed an annual religious celebration that would attract customers and patrons.

THE DEVELOPMENT OF ENGLISH AS THE MAJOR LANGUAGE OF ENGLAND.   A further influence on the drama was the increasing importance of the English language

[12] See p. 890.

at this time. During the two centuries following the Norman conquest in 1066, the ruling and intellectual languages of England had been French and Latin. By the fourteenth century, however, things were changing: English had been enriched with huge numbers of French words and was reasserting its role as the major language of England. More and more, the governing classes were committed to England—having a centuries-long tradition there—and used English as the language of intellectual and political discourse. Native writers began looking with increased favor on English as a literary language. A new literature in English—including drama—was ripe for development.

BIBLICAL STORIES AS THE BASIS OF THE CORPUS CHRISTI PLAYS.   In the Middle Ages the Bible, with its accompanying church interpretations and traditions, was viewed not only as religious truth about God's revelation to humankind, but also as historical truth. Knowledge of the major biblical stories was therefore considered essential for practicing Christians. But most people at the time were illiterate and could not read the Bible themselves. They knew biblical texts only from passages delivered during church services, or from the depictions of Bible stories brilliantly depicted in stained glass windows or in the sculptures that decorated both the interiors and exteriors of the churches. The dramatization of religious stories during the Corpus Christi feasts thus became an important method of biblical and theological instruction.

THE CORPUS CHRISTI CYCLES, OR MYSTERY PLAYS.[13]   The goal of the plays was to create a complete sequence or **cycle** of plays dramatizing the divine history of the world from the Creation to Judgment Day. As the Corpus Christi feasts grew in importance, the plays became a highlight of town life in the early summer. By the fifteenth century as many as forty towns had their own cycles. Some were large and elaborate; some—probably those performed in the smaller towns— were modest. Often the performances took place not only on Corpus Christi Thursday but also on Friday and Saturday, thus creating an extensive religious and secular celebration. Although the texts of most of these cycles have been lost, cycles from four towns have been preserved. These cycles, named after the towns that presented them, contain more than 150 plays.

PARTICIPANTS IN THE CYCLES.   Although there were as yet no professional acting companies like the one that Shakespeare joined in the late sixteenth century, the annual staging of the Corpus Christi plays required large numbers of participants. In the Wakefield cycle, for example, there are 243 separate speaking parts. Other cycles had comparable needs. Although many townspeople likely volunteered for small parts, the leading roles were taken by local people who performed yearly and were paid for their services. Some of these same actors, along with the volunteers, also assumed minor roles. Because of this doubling of roles, the total number of performers needed for the entire cycle was reduced. But the number was still surprisingly high.

---

[13] The word *mystery* was derived from the sponsoring *masters* of the guilds. The phrase *mystery plays* should not be taken to imply that the plays were mysterious or suspenseful.

For a full production of a Corpus Christi cycle there were an extremely large number of additional people working as managers, directors, prompters, and stagehands, to say nothing of the need for horses and wagons along with the drivers to control them. The planning by the local guilds was complex and challenging indeed. But the result was a vital, durable, instructive, and exciting drama.

Other Religious Dramas

In the course of time, additional types of religious dramas were developed. One of these was the **miracle play**, a devotional dramatization of the lives of saints. In addition, the **morality play** was developed as a genre instructing the faithful in the proper way to lead a devotional life. The most famous of these, in about 1500, was *Everyman*, which even today retains a good deal of interest and power.

RENAISSANCE DRAMA AND SHAKESPEARE'S THEATER

In the early phase of the English Renaissance, then, there was a flourishing native tradition of theater. The bridge from religious drama to the drama of the Renaissance was created in a number of ways. Of great importance was the growth of traveling dramatic companies, who performed their plays in local innyards—square or quadrangular spaces surrounded by the rooms of the inn. In addition, plays were performed at court, in the great rooms of aristocratic houses, in the law courts, and at universities.

Aside from the performing tradition, the immediate influence on the creation of a new drama was the development of a taste for dramatic topics drawn from nonreligious sources. The earliest of such plays in the sixteenth century was the so-called **Tudor interlude,** named after the monarchs of the Tudor family who ruled England from 1485 to 1603. *Interlude* is a misnomer, for the plays were often quite long, one of them lasting an entire day. The interludes, supported by the nobility, were short tragedies, comedies, or historical plays that were performed by both professional actors and students. They sometimes featured abstract and allegorical characters and provided opportunities for both music and farcical action.

After the middle of the sixteenth century the revival of ancient drama and culture came increasingly to the fore. The dominating influence was the Roman dramatist Seneca (4 B.C.E.–65 C.E.), eight of whose tragedies, derived from Greek tragedy, had survived from antiquity. A vital quality of the Senecan tragedies was that they were bloody, and thus they gave a classical precedent for the revenge and murder that were to be featured in the Elizabethan drama. Seneca became important not so much because he had written great works but rather because he had written in Latin. He could therefore be readily understood by a generation of new dramatists who had been schooled in Roman history, culture, and literature.

The front exterior of the newly reconstructed *Shakespeare's Globe* theater in Southwark, London (with some scaffolding still in place). This theater duplicates the original Globe known by Shakespeare and his audiences. Plans for reconstruction were based on contemporary drawings and archaeological discoveries at the original site. Rebuilding was carried out in accord with authentic Elizabethan materials and methods; note the thatched roof, the half-timbering, the windows, and the building's many sides. Regular performances began here on August 21, 1996.

Elizabethan Dramatists and Shakespeare

The first group of these Elizabethan playwrights included Christopher Marlowe, Thomas Kyd, Robert Greene, George Peele, Thomas Lodge, and John Lyly. These were the men whose plays William Shakespeare watched and acted in when he first arrived in London from Stratford-upon-Avon early in the 1590s. By 1594 Shakespeare had joined the Lord Chamberlain's Men, the most popular of the London acting companies. He rose swiftly as both an actor and a dramatist, and by 1599 he had become an active partner with the Lord Chamberlain's Men in a venture to construct a new theater, the Globe, within a stone's throw of the earlier theater, the Rose. It was at the Globe that Shakespeare's greatest plays (including *Hamlet*) were first produced.

Shakespeare's Theater, the Globe (1599–1612)

Compared with the massive Greek outdoor theaters, the Globe was small. Some theater historians have calculated that it could have held as many as 2,000 to 3,000 people, although this estimate seems excessive, for half that number would have made an extremely large audience.

SIZE AND SHAPE OF THE GLOBE.   Recent archaeological excavations of the site of the Globe, together with a complete reconstruction based on the knowledge newly gained, show that it was a twenty-sided building. For practical purposes it was round—as it is shown in a contemporary drawing—and its outer diameter was approximately a hundred feet. From above, it would have resembled a ring, or, as Shakespeare called the type in *Henry V*, a "wooden O." Its central yard was open to the sky, a detail that it had appropriated from the confined areas of the inns. The thrust stage, covered by a roof, was built thirty feet into the yard at the building's south side.

ACTING AREAS.   This thrust stage was close to five feet high—probably lower in front (*downstage*) and higher in back (*upstage*). The area below the stage was called the *hell*. At center stage there was a trapdoor to the hell that was used for the entrances and exits of devils, monsters, and ghosts. Downstage there were two columns holding up the protective roof. Called the *heavens*, the ceiling of the roof was decorated, and a hut on the roof itself contained machinery used to lower and raise actors taking the roles of witches, fairies, and deities. Behind the upstage area, which could be curtained off for interior scenes, there was a *tiring house* and storage area where actors changed their costumes and waited for their cues. Two or three doors opened out from the tiring house to the stage. On the second level above the stage was a gallery for spectators, musicians, and actors (as in the balcony scene in Shakespeare's *Romeo and Juliet*).

PLACES FOR THE AUDIENCE.   The admission price permitted spectators into the ground area. Those who remained there stood during the entire performance and crowded as close as they could to the stage. These people were patronizingly called the *groundlings*. For additional charges, spectators could sit in one of the three seating levels within the roofed galleries (part of the "O"). Those who could afford it paid still another charge for seats directly on the stage—a custom that continued in English theaters until the time of David Garrick in the eighteenth century.

PRODUCTION AND STAGE CONVENTIONS.   Just as in the Athenian theater, there was no artificial lighting, and performances therefore took place in the afternoon. The plays were performed rapidly, without intermissions or indications of act and scene changes except for occasional rhymed couplets. With no curtain and no scenery, shifts in scene were indicated by the exits and entrances of the actors. This type of scene division produced swift changes in time and place and made for great fluidity and fast pacing.

The conditions of performance and the physical shape of the theater produced a number of theatrical conventions. The two columns supporting the stage roof, for example, were versatile. Sometimes they represented trees or the sides of buildings, and conventionally they were used as places of concealment and for eavesdropping. Time, place, and circumstances of weather were established through dialogue, as in the first scene of *Hamlet* when Horatio speaks of "the morn, in russet mantle clad" (line 166), or in *As You Like It*, when Rosalind says, "This is the forest of Arden" (Act II, scene 4, line 15).

The Globe's relatively small size and its thrust stage made for intimate performances. There was little separation of the audience and the actors, unlike the case with the *orchestra* in Greek theaters that widened the distance between actors and spectators or the proscenium and curtain found in many modern theaters. Consequently, there was much interaction between actors and spectators. The closeness of spectators to the stage led to two unique stage conventions. One of these, the **aside,** permits a character to make brief remarks directly to the audience or to another character without the rest of the characters hearing the words. In the other, the **soliloquy,** a character alone onstage speaks his or her thoughts or plans directly to the audience. For example, in Hamlet's second soliloquy, he criticizes his emotional detachment from his father's murder and explains how he plans to test Claudius's guilt (Act II, scene 2, lines 524–580). We should realize that actors using these conventions spoke directly to members of the audience who were sitting next to the action. These spectators almost literally became additional members of the cast.

ACTING CONVENTIONS AND COSTUMES.   The actors in Shakespeare's day were legally bound to the company of which they were members. Without the protection of the company, they were considered as "rogues and vagabonds." They were always male, with adolescent boys performing the women's roles because women were excluded from the stage. The actors used no masks. Instead, they developed conventional expressions and gestures that would seem to us, today, excessively stylized. The acting conventions sometimes seemed excessive to Shakespeare, too, as is indicated by Hamlet's instructions to the traveling actors. He tells them not to "saw the air too much with your hand" and not to "tear a passion to tatters, to very rags" (Act III, scene 2, lines 4, 9).

The actors wore elaborate costumes to demonstrate the nature and status of the characters. Thus kings always wore robes and crowns, and they carried orbs and scepters. A fool (a type of comic and ironic commentator) wore a multicolored or *motley* costume, and clowns and "mechanicals" wore the common clothing of the humble classes. Ragged clothing indicated a reduction in circumstances, as in *King Lear*, and Ophelia's description of Hamlet's disordered clothing in the second act of *Hamlet* indicates the prince's disturbed mental condition (scene 1, lines 74–81). Whenever characters took on a disguise, as in *As You Like It*, this disguise was impenetrable to the other characters.

CURRENT RECONSTRUCTION OF THE GLOBE.   Shakespeare's Globe burned in 1612, and the rebuilt Globe was torn down by the Puritans under Oliver Cromwell in 1644. From then on the site was variously occupied by tenements, breweries, other buildings, and a road. In the late 1980s, however, archaeological excavations took place at the sites of both the Globe and the nearby Rose theaters, and the subsequent discoveries have provided exciting new information about theaters and theatergoing in Shakespeare's day. A reconstruction of the Globe was undertaken and is now complete—not at the original location but close by; the original site could not be used because it is preempted by a protected building and a vital street leading to Southwark Bridge. Theatergoers in London are now able to attend performances of Shakespeare's plays in this new theater under conditions almost identical to those that Shakespeare's audiences and acting company knew.[14]

WILLIAM SHAKESPEARE, *HAMLET*

Shakespeare was born in 1564 in Stratford-upon-Avon, in western England. He attended the Stratford grammar school, married in 1582, and had three children. He left his family and moved to London sometime between 1585 and 1592. During this period he became a professional actor and began writing plays and poems. Because the London theaters were closed during the plague years 1592 to 1594, he apparently worked at other jobs, about which we know nothing. By 1595, however, he was recognized as a major writer of comedies and tragedies. He soon became a member of the Lord Chamberlain's Men, the leading theatrical company, and, as we have seen, he became a shareholder in the new Globe Theatre in 1599. Because he realized good returns from the business venture and also from his plays, he became moderately wealthy. He stopped writing for the stage in 1611, having written a total of thirty-seven plays, of which eleven were tragedies. He spent his retirement years in Stratford. He died in 1616 and is buried next to the altar of Stratford's Trinity Church, beneath a bust and an inscribed gravestone.

When the Lord Chamberlain's Men first staged *Hamlet* in 1600 or 1601 at the Globe, it was not the first time that the story had been dramatized on the London stage. There is evidence that a play based on the Hamlet story, now lost, had been performed before 1589. Therefore, at least some of the theatergoers might have known the story.

Even if none of them knew it, however, they would have known the tradition of **revenge tragedy.** The Elizabethans had been introduced to the drama of vengeance through the English translations of Seneca's tragedies during the 1570s and early 1580s. Another important precedent was Thomas Kyd's *Spanish Tragedy* (ca. 1587), which was the first English play in the revenge tradition and

---

[14] A current e-mail address for further information about the Globe Theatre is globe@uga.cc.uga.edu.

which featured a hero who commits suicide. The genre featured a number of conventions. The major ones were a ghost who calls for vengeance and a revenger who pretends to be insane at least part of the time. Above all, the tradition required that the revenger would also die, no matter how good the person or how just the cause.

Although Elizabethan audiences were prepared for *Hamlet* by the revenge formula, they could have anticipated neither a protagonist of Hamlet's likeableness and complexity nor a play of such profundity. The earlier revengers were flat characters with a single fixation on getting even through personal vengeance. Hamlet, however, is acutely aware of the political and moral corruption of the Danish court, and he reflects on the fallen state of humanity. Experiencing despair and guilt, he even contemplates suicide. He learns from his experiences and meditations, discovering that he must look beyond reason and philosophy for ways of coping with the world. He also develops patience and learns to trust in Providence, the "divinity that shapes our ends" (Act V, scene 2, line 10).

The play itself demonstrates the far-reaching effects of evil, which branches inexorably outward from Claudius's initial act of murder. The evil ensnares innocent and guilty alike. Hamlet, the avenger, becomes the direct and indirect cause of deaths, and as a result, he also becomes an object of revenge. By the play's end, all the major and two of the minor characters are dead: Polonius, Ophelia, Rosencrantz, Guildenstern, Gertrude, Claudius, Laertes, and, finally, Hamlet himself. The play's crowning irony is that Hamlet does not complete his vengeance because of the murder of his father, King Hamlet; rather, he kills Claudius immediately upon learning that the king has murdered Gertrude, his mother.

In the centuries since Shakespeare wrote *Hamlet*, the play has remained among the most popular, most moving, and most effective plays in the world. It has been translated into scores of languages. Major actors from Shakespeare's day to ours—including Richard Burbage, the first Hamlet, and Mel Gibson and Kenneth Branagh, the most recent—have starred in the role. Beyond the play's stage popularity, *Hamlet* has become one of the central documents of Western civilization. Somehow, we all know about Hamlet, and we know passages like "to be or not to be," "the play's the thing," and "The undiscovered country, from whose bourn / No traveler returns" even if we have never read the play or seen a live or filmed performance.

WILLIAM SHAKESPEARE   (1564–1616)

The Tragedy of Hamlet, Prince of Denmark _____ *ca. 1600*

Edited by Alice Griffin°

Professor Griffin's text for *Hamlet* was the Second Quarto (edition) published in 1604, with modifications based on the First Folio, published in 1623. Stage directions in those editions are printed here without brackets; added stage directions are printed within brackets. We have edited Griffin's notes for this text.

CHARACTERS

Claudius, *King of Denmark*
Hamlet, *Son to the former, and nephew to the present King*
Polonius, *Lord Chamberlain*
Horatio, *Friend to Hamlet*
Laertes, *Son to Polonius*
Valtemand
Cornelius
Rosencrantz } *Courtiers*
Guildenstern
Osric
A Gentleman
A Priest
Marcellus
Barnardo } *Officers*
Francisco, *a Soldier*
Reynaldo, *Servant to Polonius*
Players
Two Clowns, *gravediggers*
Fortinbras, *Prince of Norway*
A Norwegian Captain
English Ambassadors
Gertrude, *Queen of Denmark, mother to Hamlet*
Ophelia, *Daughter to Polonius*
Ghost of Hamlet's Father
Lords, Ladies, Officers, Soldiers, Sailors, Messengers, Attendants

[*SCENE: Elsinore*]

ACT 1

Scene 1. *[A platform on the battlements of the castle]*

Enter BARNARDO *and* FRANCISCO, *two Sentinels.*

BARNARDO.   Who's there?
FRANCISCO.   Nay, answer me. Stand and unfold° yourself.
BARNARDO.   Long live the king.
FRANCISCO.   Barnardo?
BARNARDO.   He.   5
FRANCISCO.   You come most carefully upon your hour.
BARNARDO.   'Tis now struck twelve, get thee to bed Francisco.
FRANCISCO.   For this relief much thanks, 'tis bitter cold,
    And I am sick at heart.
BARNARDO.   Have you had quiet guard?
FRANCISCO.   Not a mouse stirring.   10

2 *unfold:* reveal.

BARNARDO.   Well, good night:
    If you do meet Horatio and Marcellus,
    The rivals° of my watch, bid them make haste.

Enter HORATIO and MARCELLUS.

FRANCISCO.   I think I hear them. Stand ho, who is there?
HORATIO.   Friends to this ground.
MARCELLUS.   And liegemen° to the Dane.°   15
FRANCISCO.   Give you good night.
MARCELLUS.   O, farewell honest soldier,
    Who hath relieved you?
FRANCISCO.   Barnardo hath my place;
    Give you good night.   *Exit FRANCISCO.*
MARCELLUS.   Holla, Barnardo!
BARNARDO.   Say,
    What, is Horatio there?
HORATIO.   A piece of him.
BARNARDO.   Welcome Horatio, welcome good Marcellus.   20
HORATIO.   What, has this thing appeared again tonight?
BARNARDO.   I have seen nothing.
MARCELLUS.   Horatio says 'tis but our fantasy,°
    And will not let belief take hold of him,
    Touching this dreaded sight twice seen of us,   25
    Therefore I have entreated him along
    With us to watch the minutes of this night,
    That if again this apparition come,
    He may approve° our eyes and speak to it.
HORATIO.   Tush, tush, 'twill not appear.
BARNARDO.   Sit down awhile,   30
    And let us once again assail your ears,
    That are so fortified against our story,
    What we have two nights seen.
HORATIO.   Well, sit we down,
    And let us hear Barnardo speak of this.   35
BARNARDO.   Last night of all,
    When yon same star that's westward from the pole°
    Had made his course t'illume that part of heaven
    Where now it burns, Marcellus and myself,
    The bell then beating one—

Enter GHOST.

MARCELLUS.   Peace, break thee off, look where it comes again.   40
BARNARDO.   In the same figure like the king that's dead.
MARCELLUS.   Thou art a scholar, speak to it Horatio.
BARNARDO.   Looks a' not like the king? mark it Horatio.
HORATIO.   Most like, it harrows me with fear and wonder.
BARNARDO.   It would be spoke to.

13 *rivals:* partners.   15 *liegemen:* subjects.   *Dane:* King of Denmark.   23 *fantasy:* imagination.   29 *approve:* prove reliable.   36 *pole:* North Star.

MARCELLUS.   Question it Horatio.   45
HORATIO.   What art thou that usurp'st° this time of night,
    Together with that fair and warlike form,
    In which the majesty of buried Denmark°
    Did sometimes° march? by heaven I charge thee speak.
MARCELLUS.   It is offended.
BARNARDO.   See, it stalks away.   50
HORATIO.   Stay, speak, speak, I charge thee speak.   *Exit* GHOST.
MARCELLUS.   'Tis gone and will not answer.
BARNARDO.   How now Horatio, you tremble and look pale,
    Is not this something more than fantasy?
    What think you on't?   55
HORATIO.   Before my God I might not this believe,
    Without the sensible and true avouch°
    Of mine own eyes.
MARCELLUS.   Is it not like the king?
HORATIO.   As thou art to thyself.
    Such was the very armour he had on,   60
    When he the ambitious Norway° combated:
    So frowned he once, when in an angry parle°
    He smote the sledded Polacks° on the ice.
    'Tis strange.
MARCELLUS.   Thus twice before, and jump° at this dead hour,   65
    With martial stalk hath he gone by our watch.
HORATIO.   In what particular thought to work, I know not,
    But in the gross and scope° of mine opinion,
    This bodes some strange eruption to our state.
MARCELLUS.   Good now sit down, and tell me he that knows,   70
    Why this same strict and most observant watch
    So nightly toils the subject° of the land,
    And why such daily cast of brazen cannon
    And foreign mart,° for implements of war,
    Why such impress° of shipwrights, whose sore° task   75
    Does not divide the Sunday from the week,
    What might be toward° that this sweaty haste
    Doth make the night joint-labourer with the day,
    Who is't that can inform me?
HORATIO.   That can I.
    At least the whisper goes so; our last king,   80
    Whose image even but now appeared to us,
    Was as you know by Fortinbras of Norway,
    Thereto pricked on by a most emulate° pride,
    Dared to the combat; in which our valiant Hamlet

---

46 *usurp'st:* wrongfully occupy (both the time and the shape of the dead king).   48 *buried*
Denmark: the buried King of Denmark.   49 *sometimes:* formerly.   57 *Sensible . . . avouch:*
assurance of the truth of the senses.   61 *Norway:* King of Norway.   62 *parle:* parley, verbal
battle.   63 *sledded Polacks:* Poles on sleds.   65 *jump:* just.   68 *gross and scope:* general view.
72 *toils the subject:* makes the subjects toil.   74 *mart:* trade.   75 *impress:* conscription.
sore: difficult.   77 *toward:* forthcoming.   83 *emulate:* rivaling

(For so this side of our known world esteemed him)   85
Did slay this Fortinbras, who by a sealed compact,°
Well ratified by law and heraldy,°
Did forfeit (with his life) all those his lands
Which he stood seized° of, to the conqueror:
Against the which a moiety competent°   90
Was gagèd° by our King, which had returned
To the inheritance of Fortinbras,
Had he been vanquisher; as by the same co-mart,°
And carriage of the article designed,°
His fell to Hamlet; now sir, young Fortinbras,   95
Of unimprovèd mettle° hot and full,
Hath in the skirts° of Norway here and there
Sharked up° a list of lawless resolutes°
For food and diet to some enterprise
That hath a stomach° in't, which is no other,   100
As it doth well appear unto our state,
But to recover of us by strong hand
And terms compulsatory, those foresaid lands
So by his father lost; and this I take it,
Is the main motive of our preparations,   105
The source of this our watch, and the chief head°
Of this post-haste and romage° in the land.
BARNARDO.   I think it be no other, but e'en so;
    Well may it sort° that this portentous figure
    Comes armèd through our watch so like the king   110
    That was and is the question of these wars.
HORATIO.   A mote it is to trouble the mind's eye:
    In the most high and palmy° state of Rome,
    A little ere the mightest Julius fell,
    The graves stood tenantless, and the sheeted dead   115
    Did squeak and gibber in the Roman streets,
    As stars with trains of fire,° and dews of blood,
    Disasters° in the sun; and the moist star,°
    Upon whose influence Neptune's empire stands,
    Was sick almost to doomsday with eclipse.   120
    And even the like precurse° of feared events,
    As harbingers preceding still° the fates
    And prologue to the omen° coming on,
    Have heaven and earth together demonstrated
    Unto our climatures° and countrymen.   125

---

86 *compact:* treaty.   87 *law and heraldy:* heraldic law regulating combats.   89 *seized:* possessed.
90 *moiety competent:* equal amount.   91 *gagèd:* pledged.   93 *co-mart:* joint bargain.   94 *carriage . . . designed:* intent of the treaty drawn up.   96 *unimprovèd mettle:* untested (1) metal (2)
spirit.   97 *skirts:* outskirts.   98 *Sharked up:* gathered up indiscriminately (as a shark preys).
lawless resolutes: determined outlaws.   100 *stomach:* show of courage.   106 *head:* fountainhead.
107 *romage:* bustle (rummage).   109 *sort:* turn out.   113 *palmy:* triumphant.   117 *stars . . .
fire:* meteors.   118 *Disasters:* unfavorable portents.   *moist star:* moon.   121 *precurse:* portent.   122 *still:* always.   123 *omen:* disaster.   125 *climatures:* regions.

Enter GHOST.

But soft, behold, lo where it comes again.
I'll cross° it though it blast me: *Spreads his arms.*
                          stay illusion,
If thou hast any sound or use of voice,
Speak to me.
If there be any good thing to be done   130
That may to thee do ease, and grace° to me,
Speak to me.
If thou art privy° to thy country's fate
Which happily° foreknowing may avoid,
O speak: 135
Or if thou hast uphoarded in thy life
Extorted treasure in the womb of earth,
For which they say you spirits oft walk in death,

                                                      The cock crows.

Speak of it, stay and speak. Stop it Marcellus.
MARCELLUS.   Shall I strike at it with my partisan?°   140
HORATIO.   Do, if it will not stand
BARNARDO.   'Tis here.
HORATIO.   'Tis here.
MARCELLUS.   'Tis gone.   *Exit* GHOST.
We do it wrong being so majestical,
To offer it the show of violence,
For it is as the air, invulnerable,   145
And our vain blows malicious mockery.°
BARNARDO.   It was about to speak when the cock crew.°
HORATIO.   And then it started like a guilty thing,
Upon a fearful summons; I have heard,
The cock that is the trumpet to the morn,   150
Doth with his lofty and shrill-sounding throat
Awake the god of day, and at his warning
Whether in sea or fire, in earth or air,°
Th'extravagant and erring° spirit hies°
To his confine, and of the truth herein   155
This present object made probation.°
MARCELLUS.   It faded on the crowing of the cock.
Some say that ever 'gainst° that season comes
Wherein our Saviour's birth is celebrated
This bird of dawning singeth all night long,   160
And then they say no spirit dare stir abroad,

127 *cross:* (1) cross its path (2) spread my arms to make a cross of my body (to ward against evil).   131 *grace:* (1) honor (2) blessedness.   133 *art privy:* know secretly of.   134 *happily:* perhaps.   140 *partisan:* spear.   146 *malicious mockery:* mockery because they only imitate harm.   147 *cock crew:* (traditional signal for ghosts to return to their confines).   153 *sea . . . air:* the four elements (inhabited by spirits, each indigenous to a particular element).   154 *extravagant and erring:* going beyond its bounds (vagrant) and wandering.   *hies:* hastens.   156 *made probation:* gave proof.   158 *'gainst:* just before.

The nights are wholesome,° then no planets strike,°
No fairy takes,° nor witch hath power to charm,
So hallowed, and so gracious is that time.
HORATIO.   So have I heard and do in part believe it.   165
But look, the morn in russet° mantle clad
Walks o'er the dew of yon high eastward hill:
Break we our watch up and by my advice
Let us impart what we have seen tonight
Unto young Hamlet, for upon my life   170
This spirit dumb to us, will speak to him:
Do you consent we shall acquaint him with it,
As needful in our loves,° fitting our duty?
MARCELLUS.   Let's do't I pray, and I this morning know
Where we shall find him most convenient.   *Exeunt.*°   175

Scene 2. *[A room of state in the castle]*

Flourish.° Enter CLAUDIUS *King of Denmark,* GERTRUDE *the Queen,* [*members of the*] *Council: as*
POLONIUS; *and his son* LAERTES, HAMLET, [VALTEMAND *and* CORNELIUS] *cum aliis.*°

KING.   Though yet of Hamlet our dear brother's death
The memory be green, and that it us befitted
To bear our hearts in grief, and our whole kingdom
To be contracted in one brow of woe,
Yet so far hath discretion fought with nature,°   5
That we° with wisest sorrow think on him
Together with remembrance of ourselves:°
Therefore our sometime° sister,° now our queen,
Th'imperial jointress° to this warlike state,
Have we as 'twere with a defeated joy,   10
With an auspicious, and a dropping eye,°
With mirth in funeral, and with dirge in marriage,
In equal scale weighing delight and dole,
Taken to wife: nor have we herein barred
Your better wisdoms,° which have freely gone   15
With this affair along—for all, our thanks.
Now follows that you know, young Fortinbras,
Holding a weak supposal of our worth,°
Or thinking by our late dear brother's death
Our state to be disjoint and out of frame,°   20
Colleaguèd° with this dream of his advantage,°

---

162 *wholesome:* healthy (night air was considered unhealthy).   *strike:* exert evil influence.   163 *takes:* bewitches.   166 *russet:* reddish.   173 *needful . . . loves:* urged by our
friendship.   175 S.D.: *Exeunt:* all exit.   0.1 S.D.: *Flourish:* fanfare of trumpets.   *cum aliis:*
with others.   5 *nature:* natural impulse (of grief).   6 *we:* royal plural. The King speaks not
only for himself, but for his entire government.   7 *remembrance of ourselves:* reminder of our
duties.   8 *sometime:* former.   *sister:* sister-in-law.   9 *jointress:* widow who inherits the
estate.   11 *auspicious . . . eye:* one eye happy, the other tearful.   14–15 *barred . . . wisdoms:*
failed to seek and abide by your good advice.   18 *weak . . . worth:* low opinion of my ability in
office.   20 *out of frame:* tottering.   21 *Colleaguèd:* supported.   *advantage:* superiority.

He hath not failed to pester us with message
Importing the surrender of those lands
Lost by his father, with all bands° of law,
To our most valiant brother—so much for him: 25
Now for ourself, and for this time of meeting,
Thus much the business is. We have here writ
To Norway, uncle of young Fortinbras—
Who impotent and bed-rid scarcely hears
Of this his nephew's purpose—to suppress 30
His further gait° herein, in that the levies,
The lists, and full proportions are all made
Out of his subject:° and we here dispatch
You good Cornelius, and you Valtemand,
For bearers of this greeting to old Norway, 35
Giving to you no further personal power
To business with the king, more than the scope
Of these delated° articles allow:
Farewell, and let your haste commend your duty.°
CORNELIUS, VALTEMAND. In that, and all things, will we show our duty. 40
KING. We doubt it nothing, heartily farewell.

Exeunt VALTEMAND *and* CORNELIUS.

And now Laertes what's the news with you?
You told us of some suit, what is't Laertes?
You cannot speak of reason to the Dane
And lose your voice;° what wouldst thou beg Laertes, 45
That shall not be my offer, not thy asking?°
The head is not more native° to the heart,
The hand more instrumental to the mouth,
Than is the throne of Denmark to thy father.
What wouldst thou have Laertes?
LAERTES.   My dread lord, 50
Your leave and favour° to return to France,
From whence, though willingly I came to Denmark,
To show my duty in your coronation,
Yet now I must confess, that duty done,
My thoughts and wishes bend again toward France, 55
And bow them to your gracious leave and pardon.°
KING. Have you your father's leave? What says Polonius?
POLONIUS. He hath my lord wrung from me my slow leave
By laboursome petition, and at last
Upon his will I sealed my hard consent.° 60
I do beseech you give him leave to go.

---

24 *bands:* bonds. 31 *gait:* progress. 31–33 *levies . . . subject:* Taxes, conscriptions, and supplies are all obtained from his subjects. 38 *delated:* accusing. 39 *haste . . . duty:* prompt
departure signify your respect. 45 *lose your voice:* speak in vain. 46 *offer . . . asking:* grant
even before requested. 47 *native:* related. 51 *leave and favour:* kind permission. 56 *pardon:* allowance. 60 *Upon . . . consent:* (1) At his request, I gave my grudging
consent. (2) On the soft sealing wax of his (legal) will, I stamped my approval.

KING.   Take thy fair hour Laertes, time be thine,
    And thy best graces spend it at thy will.
    But now my cousin° Hamlet, and my son—
HAMLET.   [*Aside.*] A little more than kin,° and less than kind.°   65
KING.   How is it that the clouds still hang on you?
HAMLET.   Not so my lord, I am too much in the sun.°
QUEEN.   Good Hamlet cast they nighted colour° off
    And let thine eye look like a friend on Denmark,°
    Do not for ever with they vailèd° lids   70
    Seek for thy noble father in the dust,
    Thou know'st 'tis common, all that lives must die,
    Passing through nature to eternity.
HAMLET.   Ay madam, it is common.°
QUEEN.   If it be,   75
    Why seems it so particular with thee?
HAMLET.   Seems, madam? nay it is, I know not "seems."
    'Tis not alone my inky cloak good mother,
    Nor customary suits of solemn black,
    Nor windy suspiration of forced breath,   80
    No, nor the fruitful river in the eye,°
    Nor the dejected haviour° of the visage,
    Together with all forms, moods, shapes of grief,
    That can denote me truly: these indeed seem,
    For they are actions that a man might play,°
    But I have that within which passes show,   85
    These but the trappings and the suits of woe.°
KING.   'Tis sweet and commendable in your nature Hamlet,
    To give these mourning duties to your father:
    But you must know your father lost a father,
    That father lost, lost his, and the survivor bound   90
    In filial obligation for some term
    To do obsequious sorrow:° but to persever
    In obstinate condolement,° is a course
    Of impious stubbornness, 'tis unmanly grief,
    It shows a will most incorrect to heaven,   95
    A heart unfortified, a mind impatient,
    An understanding simple and unschooled:
    For what we know must be, and is as common
    As any the most vulgar thing to sense,°

64 *cousin:* kinsman (used for relatives outside the immediate family).   65 *more than kin:* too much of a kinsman, being both uncle and stepfather.   *less than kind:* (1) unkind because of being a kin (proverbial) and taking the throne from the former king's son (2) unnatural (as it was considered incest to marry the wife of one's dead brother).   67 *in the sun:* (1) in presence of the king (often associated metaphorically with the sun) (2) proverbial: "out of heaven's blessing into the warm sun" (3) of a "son."   68 *nighted colour:* black.   69 *Denmark:* the King of Denmark.   70 *vailèd:* downcast.   74 *common:* (1) general (2) vulgar.   79–80 *windy . . . eye:* (hyperbole used to describe exaggerated sighs and tears).   81 *haviour:* behavior.   84 *play:* act.   86 *trappings . . . woe:* outward, superficial costumes of mourning.   92 *do obsequious sorrow:* express sorrow befitting obsequies or funerals.   93 *condolement:* grief.   99 *As any . . . sense:* as the most ordinary thing the senses can perceive.

Why should we in our peevish opposition   100
Take it to heart? Fie, 'tis a fault to heaven,
A fault against the dead, a fault to nature,
To reason most absurd, whose common theme
Is death of fathers, and who still° hath cried
From the first corse,° till he that died today,   105
"This must be so." We pray you throw to earth
This unprevailing° woe, and think of us
As of a father, for let the world take note
You are the most immediate° to our throne,
And with no less nobility of love   110
Than that which dearest father bears his son,
Do I impart toward you. For your intent
In going back to school in Wittenberg,
It is most retrograde° to our desire,
And we beseech you, bend you° to remain   115
Here in the cheer and comfort of our eye,
Our chiefest courtier, cousin, and our son.
QUEEN.   Let not thy mother lose her prayers Hamlet,
     I pray thee stay with us, go not to Wittenberg.
HAMLET.   I shall in all my best obey you madam.   120
KING.   Why 'tis a loving and a fair reply,
     Be as ourself in Denmark. Madam come,
     This gentle and unforced accord of Hamlet
     Sits smiling to my heart, in grace whereof,
     No jocund health that Denmark drinks today,   125
     But the great cannon to the clouds shall tell,
     And the king's rouse° the heaven shall bruit° again,
     Re-speaking earthly thunder; come away.

Flourish, Exeunt all but HAMLET.

HAMLET.   O that this too too sullied° flesh would melt,
     Thaw and resolve itself into a dew,   130
     Or that the Everlasting had not fixed
     His canon° 'gainst self-slaughter. O God, God,
     How weary, stale, flat, and unprofitable
     Seems to me all the uses of this world!
     Fie on't, ah fie, 'tis an unweeded garden   135
     That grows to seed, things rank° and gross in nature
     Possess it merely.° That it should come to this,
     But two months dead, nay not so much, not two,
     So excellent a king, that was to this

---

104 *still:* always.   105 *corse:* corpse (of Abel, also, ironically, the first fratricide).   107 *unprevailing:* useless.   109 *most immediate:* next in succession (though Danish kings were elected by the council, an Elizabethan audience might feel that Hamlet, not Claudius, should be king).   114 *retrograde:* movement (of planets) in a reverse direction.   115 *beseech . . . you:* hope you will be inclined.   127 *rouse:* toast that empties the wine cup.   *bruit:* sound.   129 *sullied:* tainted.   132 *canon:* divine edict.   136 *rank:* (1) luxuriant, excessive (2) bad-smelling.   137 *merely:* entirely.

Hyperion° to a satyr,° so loving to my mother,   140
That he might not beteem° the winds of heaven
Visit her face too roughly—heaven and earth,
Must I remember? why, she would hang on him
As if increase of appetite had grown
By what it fed on,° and yet within a month—   145
Let me not think on't: Frailty, thy name is woman—
A little month or ere those shoes were old
With which she followed my poor father's body
Like Niobe° all tears, why she, even she—
O God, a beast that wants° discourse of reason   150
Would have mourned longer—married with my uncle,
My father's brother, but no more like my father
Than I to Hercules: within a month,
Ere yet the salt of most unrighteous° tears
Had left the flushing° in her gallèd° eyes,   155
She married. O most wicked speed, to post°
With such dexterity to incestuous° sheets:
It is not, nor it cannot come to good,
But break my heart, for I must hold my tongue.

Enter HORATIO, MARCELLUS *and* BARNARDO.

HORATIO.   Hail to your lordship.
HAMLET.   I am glad to see you well;   160
    Horatio, or I do forget my self.
HORATIO.   The same my lord, and your poor servant ever.
HAMLET.   Sir my good friend, I'll change° that name with you:
    And what make you from Wittenberg, Horatio?
    Marcellus.   165
MARCELLUS.   My good lord.
HAMLET.   I am very glad to see you: good even, sir.
    But what in faith make you from Wittenberg?
HORATIO.   A truant disposition, good my lord.
HAMLET.   I would not hear your enemy say so,   170
    Nor shall you do mine ear that violence
    To make it truster of your own report
    Against yourself. I know you are no truant,
    But what is your affair in Elsinore?
    We'll teach you to drink deep ere you depart.   175
HORATIO.   My Lord, I came to see your father's funeral.
HAMLET.   I prithee do not mock me, fellow student,
    I think it was to see my mother's wedding.

---

140 *Hyperion:* god of the sun.   *satyr:* part-goat, part-man woodland deity (noted for
lust).   141 *beteem:* allow.   144–145 *As if . . . on:* as if the more she fed, the more her
appetite increased.   149 *Niobe:* (who boasted of her children before Leto and was punished by
their destruction; Zeus changed the weeping mother to a stone dropping continual tears).   150
wants: lacks.   154 *unrighteous:* (because untrue).   155 *flushing:* redness.   *gallèd:* rubbed
sore.   156 *post:* rush.   157 *incestuous:* (the church forbade marriage to one's brother's
widow).   163 *change:* exchange (and be called your friend).

HORATIO.   Indeed my lord it followed hard upon.
HAMLET.   Thrift, thrift, Horatio, the funeral baked meats°   180
    Did coldly° furnish forth the marriage tables.
    Would I had met my dearest° foe in heaven
    Or ever I had seen that day Horatio.
    My father, methinks I see my father.
HORATIO.   Where my lord?
HAMLET.   In my mind's eye Horatio.   185
HORATIO.   I saw him once, a' was a goodly° king.
HAMLET.   A' was a man, take him for all in all,
    I shall not look upon his like again.
HORATIO.   My lord, I think I saw him yesternight.
HAMLET.   Saw? Who?   190
HORATIO.   My lord, the king your father.
HAMLET.   The king my father?
HORATIO.   Season your admiration° for a while
    With an attent ear till I may deliver
    Upon the witness of these gentlemen
    This marvel to you.
HAMLET.   For God's love let me hear!   195
HORATIO.   Two nights together had these gentlemen,
    Marcellus and Barnardo, on their watch
    In the dead waste and middle of the night,
    Been thus encountered. A figure like your father
    Armed at point exactly, cap-a-pe,°   200
    Appears before them, and with solemn march,
    Goes slow and stately by them; thrice he walked
    By their oppressed° and fear-surprisèd eyes
    Within his truncheon's° length, whilst they distilled°
    Almost to jelly with the act of fear,   205
    Stand dumb and speak not to him; this to me
    In dreadful secrecy° impart they did,
    And I with them the third night kept the watch,
    Where as they had delivered, both in time,
    Form of the thing, each word made true and good,   210
    The apparition comes: I knew your father,
    These hands are not more like.
HAMLET.   But where was this?
MARCELLUS.   My lord upon the platform where we watch.
HAMLET.   Did you not speak to it?
HORATIO.   My lord I did,
    But answer made it none, yet once methought   215
    It lifted up it° head, and did address
    Itself to motion° like as it would speak:

180 *funeral baked meats:* food prepared for the funeral.   181 *coldly:* when cold.   182 *dearest:*
direst.   186 *goodly:* handsome.   192 *Season your admiration:* control your wonder.   200
at point . . . cap-a-pe: in every detail, head to foot.   203 *oppressed:* overcome by horror.   204
truncheon: staff (of office).   *distilled:* dissolved.   207 *in dreadful secrecy:* as a dread
secret.   216 *it:* its.   216–217 *address . . . motion:* start to move.

> But even then the morning cock crew loud,
> And at the sound it shrunk in haste away
> And vanished from our sight.

HAMLET.   'Tis very strange.   220

HORATIO.   As I do live my honoured lord 'tis true,
> And we did think it writ down in our duty
> To let you know of it.

HAMLET.   Indeed indeed sirs, but this troubles me.
> Hold you the watch tonight?

ALL.   We do my lord.   225

HAMLET.   Armed say you?

ALL.   Armed my lord.

HAMLET.   From top to toe?

ALL.   My lord from head to foot.

HAMLET.   Then saw you not his face.

HORATIO.   O yes my lord, he wore his beaver° up.   230

HAMLET.   What, looked he frowningly?

HORATIO.   A countenance more in sorrow than in anger.

HAMLET.   Pale, or red?

HORATIO.   Nay, very pale.

HAMLET.   And fixed his eyes upon you?

HORATIO.   Most constantly.

HAMLET.   I would I had been there.   235

HORATIO.   It would have much amazed you.

HAMLET.   Very like, very like, stayed it long?

HORATIO.   While one with moderate haste might tell° a hundred.

MARCELLUS, BARNARDO.   Longer, longer.

HORATIO.   Not when I saw't.

HAMLET.   His beard was grizzled,° no?   240

HORATIO.   It was as I have seen it in his life,
> A sable silvered.°

HAMLET.   I will watch tonight;
> Perchance 'twill walk again.

HORATIO.   I warr'nt it will.

HAMLET.   If it assume my noble father's person,
> I'll speak to it though hell itself should gape   245
> And bid me hold my peace;° I pray you all
> If you have hitherto concealed this sight
> Let it be tenable° in your silence still,
> And whatsoever else shall hap tonight,
> Give it an understanding but no tongue.   250
> I will requite your loves, so fare you well:
> Upon the platform 'twixt eleven and twelve
> I'll visit you.

ALL.   Our duty to your honour.

---

230 *beaver:* visor.   238 *tell:* count.   240 *grizzled:* grey.   242 *A sable silvered:* black flecked with grey.   245–246 *though hell . . . peace:* despite the risk of hell (for speaking to a demon) warning me to be silent.   248 *tenable:* held, kept.

HAMLET.   Your loves, as mine to you:° farewell.   *Exeunt.*
  My father's spirit (in arms) all is not well,   255
  I doubt° some foul play, would the night were come;
  Till then sit still my soul, foul deeds will rise,
  Though all the earth o'erwhelm them, to men's eyes.   *Exit.*

Scene 3. *[Polonius's chambers]*

Enter LAERTES *and* OPHELIA *his sister.*

LAERTES.   My necessaries are embarked, farewell,
  And sister, as the winds give benefit
  And convoy° is assistant, do not sleep
  But let me hear from you.
OPHELIA.   Do you doubt that?
LAERTES.   For Hamlet, and the trifling of his favour,   5
  Hold it a fashion, and a toy in blood,°
  A violet in the youth of primy nature,°
  Forward,° not permanent, sweet, not lasting,
  The perfume and suppliance of° a minute,
  No more.
OPHELIA.   No more but so?
LAERTES.   Think it no more.   10
  For nature crescent° does not grow alone
  In thews and bulk,° but as this temple waxes°
  The inward service of the mind and soul
  Grows wide withal.° Perhaps he loves you now,
  And now no soil nor cautel° doth besmirch   15
  The virtue of his will:° but you must fear,
  His greatness weighed,° his will is not his own,
  For he himself is subject to his birth:
  He may not as unvalued persons° do,
  Carve° for himself, for on his choice depends   20
  The sanctity and health of this whole state,
  And therefore must his choice be circumscribed
  Unto the voice and yielding° of that body
  Whereof he is the head. Then if he says he loves you,
  It fits your wisdom so far to believe it   25
  As he in his particular act and place
  May give his saying deed,° which is no further
  Than the main voice of Denmark goes withal.
  Then weigh what loss your honour may sustain

---

254 *Your loves . . . you:* offer your friendship (rather than duty) in exchange for mine.   256 *doubt:*
fear.   3 *convoy:* conveyance.   6 *toy in blood:* whim of the passions.   7 *youth of primy nature:*
early spring.   8 *Forward:* premature.   9 *suppliance of:* supplying diversion for.   11 *nature
crescent:* man as he grows.   12 *thews and bulk:* sinews and body.   *temple waxes:* body grows
(1 Cor. 6:19).   14 *withal:* at the same time.   15 *cautel:* deceit.   16 *will:* desire.   17
weighed: considered.   19 *unvalued persons:* common people.   20 *Carve:* choose (as does the
one who carves the food).   23 *voice and yielding:* approving vote.   26–27 *in his . . . deed:* limited by personal responsibilities and rank, may perform what he promises.

If with too credent° ear you list° his songs,   30
Or lose your heart, or your chaste treasure open
To his unmast'red importunity.°
Fear it Ophelia, fear it my dear sister,
And keep you in the rear of your affection,
Out of the shot and danger of desire.   35
The chariest° maid is prodigal enough
If she unmask her beauty to the moon.
Virtue itself 'scapes not calumnious strokes.
The canker galls the infants° of the spring
Too oft before their buttons° be disclosed,   40
And in the morn and liquid dew of youth
Contagious blastments° are most imminent.
Be wary then, best safety lies in fear,
Youth to itself rebels,° though none else near.

OPHELIA.   I shall the effect° of this good lesson keep   45
As watchman to my heart: but good my brother,
Do not as some ungracious° pastors do,
Show me the steep and thorny way to heaven,
Whiles like a puffed and reckless libertine
Himself the primrose path of dalliance treads,   50
And recks not his own rede.°

Enter POLONIUS.

LAERTES.   O fear me not,°
I stay too long, but here my father comes:
A double blessing is a double grace,
Occasion smiles upon a second leave.°
POLONIUS.   Yet here Laertes? aboard, aboard for shame,   55
The wind sits in the shoulder of your sail,
And you are stayed for: there, my blessing with thee,
And these few precepts in thy memory
Look thou character.° Give thy thoughts no tongue,
Nor any unproportioned thought his act: 60
Be thou familiar, but by no means vulgar:°
Those friends thou hast, and their adoption tried,°
Grapple them unto thy soul with hoops of steel,
But do not dull° thy palm with entertainment
Of each new-hatched unfledged° comrade. Beware   65
Of entrance to a quarrel, but being in,
Bear't that th'opposèd may beware of thee.
Give every man thy ear, but few thy voice:

30 *credent:* credulous.   *list:* listen to.   31–32 *your chaste . . . importunity:* lose your virginity
to his uncontrolled persistence.   36 *chariest:* most cautious.   39 *canker . . . infants:* canker-
worm or caterpillar harms the young plants.   40 *buttons:* buds.   42 *blastments:*
blights.   44 *to itself rebels:* lusts by nature.   45 *effect:* moral.   47 *ungracious:* lacking God's
grace.   51 *recks . . . rede:* does not follow his own advice.   *fear me not:* Don't worry about
me.   54 *Occasion . . . leave:* opportunity favors a second leave-taking.   59 *character:* write,
impress, imprint.   61 *vulgar:* indiscriminately friendly.   62 *adoption tried:* loyalty
proved.   64 *dull:* get calluses on.   65 *new-hatched unfledged:* new and untested.

Take each man's censure,° but reserve thy judgment.
Costly thy habit° as thy purse can buy,   70
But not expressed in fancy;° rich, not gaudy,
For the apparel oft proclaims the man,
And they in France of the best rank and station,
Are of a most select and generous chief° in that:
Neither a borrower nor a lender be,   75
For loan oft loses both itself and friend,
And borrowing dulls the edge of husbandry;°
This above all, to thine own self be true
And it must follow as the night the day,
Thou canst not then be false to any man.   80
Farewell, my blessing season° this in thee.

LAERTES.   Most humbly do I take my leave my lord.
POLONIUS.   The time invites you, go, your servants tend.°
LAERTES.   Farewell Ophelia, and remember well
What I have said to you.
OPHELIA.   'Tis in my memory locked,   85
And you yourself shall keep the key of it.
LAERTES.   Farewell.   *Exit* LAERTES.
POLONIUS.   What is't Ophelia he hath said to you?
OPHELIA.   So please you, something touching the Lord Hamlet.
POLONIUS.   Marry,° well bethought: 90
'Tis told me he hath very oft of late
Given private time to you, and you yourself
Have of your audience been most free and bounteous.
If it be so, as so 'tis put on me,
And that in way of caution, I must tell you,   95
You do not understand yourself so clearly
As it behooves my daughter, and your honour.
What is between you? give me up the truth.
OPHELIA.   He hath my lord of late made many tenders°
Of his affection to me.   100
POLONIUS.   Affection, puh, you speak like a green girl
Unsifted° in such perilous circumstance.
Do you believe his tenders as you call them?
OPHELIA.   I do not know my lord what I should think.
POLONIUS.   Marry, I will teach you; think yourself a baby   105
That you have ta'en these tenders° for true pay
Which are not sterling.° Tender yourself more dearly,°
Or (not to crack the wind of the poor phrase,
Running it thus°) you'll tender me a fool.°

---

69 *censure:* opinion.   70 *habit:* clothing.   71 *expressed in fancy:* so fantastic as to be
ridiculous.   74 *select . . . chief:* judicious and noble eminence.   77 *husbandry:* thrift.   81
season: bring to maturity.   83 *tend:* attend, wait.   90 *Marry:* (a mild oath, from "By the Virgin
Mary").   99 *tenders:* offers (see lines 106–109).   102 *Unsifted:* untested.   106 *tenders:* offers
(of money).   107 *sterling:* genuine (currency).   *Tender . . . dearly:* hold yourself at a higher
value.   108–109 *crack . . . thus:* make the phrase lose its breath.   109 *tender . . . fool:* (1) make
me look foolish (2) present me with a baby.

OPHELIA.   My lord he hath importuned me with love   110
    In honourable fashion.
POLONIUS.   Ay, fashion you may call it, go to, go to.
OPHELIA.   And hath given countenance° to his speech, my lord,
    With almost all the holy vows of heaven.
POLONIUS.   Ay, springes° to catch woodcocks.° I do know   115
    When the blood burns, how prodigal the soul
    Lends the tongue vows: these blazes daughter,
    Giving more light than heat, extinct in both,
    Even in their promise, as it is a-making,°
    You must not take for fire. From this time   120
    Be something scanter of your maiden presence,
    Set your entreatments at a higher rate
    Than a command to parle;° for Lord Hamlet,
    Believe so much in him that he is young,
    And with a larger tether may he walk   125
    Than may be given you: in few° Ophelia,
    Do not believe his vows, for they are brokers°
    Not of that dye which their investments° show,
    But mere implorators° of unholy suits,
    Breathing° like sanctified and pious bonds,°   130
    The better to beguile. This is for all,
    I would not in plain terms from this time forth
    Have you so slander any moment leisure
    As to give words or talk with the Lord Hamlet.
    Look to't I charge you, come your ways.°   135
OPHELIA.   I shall obey, my lord.   *[Exeunt.]*

Scene 4. *[The platform on the battlements]*

Enter HAMLET, HORATIO and MARCELLUS.

HAMLET.   The air bites shrewdly,° it is very cold.
HORATIO.   It is a nipping and an eager° air.
HAMLET.   What hour now?
HORATIO.   I think it lacks of twelve.
MARCELLUS.   No, it is struck.
HORATIO.   Indeed? I heard it not: it then draws near the season,°   5
    Wherein the spirit held his wont to walk.

A flourish of trumpets, and two pieces [of ordnance] go off.

    What does this mean my lord?

---

113 *countenance:* confirmation.   115 *springes:* snares.   *woodcocks:* snipelike birds (believed to
be stupid and therefore easily trapped).   118–119 *extinct . . . a-making:* losing both appearance,
because of brevity, and substance, because of broken promises.   122–123 *Set . . . parle:* Don't
rush to negotiate a surrender as soon as the besieger asks for a discussion of terms.   126 *few:*
short.   127 *brokers:* (1) business agents (2) procurers.   128 *investments:* (1) business ventures (2) clothing.   129 *implorators:* solicitors.   130 *Breathing:* speaking softly.   *bonds:*
pledges.   135 *come your ways:* come along.   1 *shrewdly:* piercingly.   2 *eager:* sharp.   5
season: time, period.

HAMLET. The king doth wake° tonight and takes his rouse,°
    Keeps wassail° and the swagg'ring up-spring° reels:
    And as he drains his draughts of Rhenish° down,   10
    The kettle-drum and trumpet thus bray out
    The triumph of his pledge.°
HORATIO.   Is it a custom?
HAMLET. Ay marry is't,
    But to my mind, though I am native here
    And to the manner born,° it is a custom   15
    More honoured in the breach than the observance.°
    This heavy-headed revel east and west
    Makes us traduced and taxed of° other nations:
    They clepe° us drunkards, and with swinish phrase
    Soil our addition,° and indeed it takes   20
    From our achievements, though performed at height,°
    The pith and marrow of our attribute.°
    So oft it chances in particular men,
    That for some vicious mole of nature° in them,
    As in their birth, wherein they are not guilty   25
    (Since nature cannot choose his origin),
    By the o'ergrowth of some complexion,°
    Oft breaking down the pales° and forts of reason,
    Or by some habit, that too much o'er-leavens°
    The form of plausive° manners—that these men,   30
    Carrying I say the stamp of one defect,
    Being nature's livery,° or fortune's star,°
    His virtues else be they as pure as grace,
    As infinite as man may undergo,
    Shall in the general censure° take corruption   35
    From that particular fault: the dram of evil
    Doth all the noble substance of a doubt,
    To his own scandal.°

Enter GHOST.

HORATIO.   Look my lord, it comes.
HAMLET. Angels and ministers of grace defend us:
    Be thou a spirit of health, or goblin damned,°   40

8 *wake:* stay awake.   *rouse:* drinks that empty the cup.   9 *Keeps wassail:* holds drinking
bouts.   *up-spring:* a vigorous German dance.   10 *Rhenish:* Rhine wine.   12 *triumph . . .
pledge:* victory of emptying the cup with one draught.   15 *to . . . born:* accustomed to the practice since birth.   16 *More . . . observance:* better to break than to observe.   18 *traduced and
taxed of:* defamed and taken to task by.   19 *clepe:* call.   19–20 *with swinish . . . addition:* blemish our reputation by comparing us to swine.   21 *at height:* to the maximum.   22 *attribute:*
reputation.   24 *mole of nature:* natural blemish.   27 *o'er growth . . . complexion:* overbal-
ance of one of the body's four humors or fluids believed to determine temperament.   28 *pales:*
defensive enclosures.   29 *too much o'er-leavens:* excessively modifies (like too much leaven in
bread).   30 *plausive:* pleasing.   32 *nature's livery:* marked by nature.   *fortune's star:* destined by chance.   35 *general censure:* public opinion.   36–38 *the dram . . . scandal:* the minute
quantity of evil casts doubt upon his noble nature, to his shame.   40 *spirit . . . damned:* true
ghost or demon from hell.

Bring with thee airs from heaven, or blasts from hell,
Be thy intents wicked, or charitable,
Thou com'st in such a questionable° shape,
That I will speak to thee. I'll call thee Hamlet,
King, father, royal Dane. O answer me,   45
Let me not burst in ignorance, but tell
Why thy canonized° bones hearsèd° in death
Have burst their cerements°? why the sepulchre,
Wherein we saw thee quietly interred
Hath oped his ponderous and marble jaws,   50
To cast thee up again? What may this mean
That thou, dead corse, again in complete steel
Revisits thus the glimpses of the moon,
Making night hideous, and we fools of nature°
So horridly to shake our disposition   55
With thoughts beyond the reaches of our souls,
Say why is this? wherefore? what should we do?   *GHOST beckons HAMLET.*
HORATIO.   It beckons you to go away with it,
    As if it some impartment did desire°
    To you alone.
MARCELLUS.   Look with what courteous action   60
    It waves you to a more removèd ground,
    But do not go with it.
HORATIO.   No, by no means.
HAMLET.   It will not speak, then I will follow it.
HORATIO.   Do not my lord.
HAMLET.   Why what should be the fear?
    I do not set my life at a pin's fee,°   65
    And for my soul, what can it do to that
    Being a thing immortal as itself;
    It waves me forth again, I'll follow it.
HORATIO.   What if it tempt you toward the flood my lord,
    Or to the dreadful summit of the cliff   70
    That beetles o'er° his base into the sea,
    And there assume some other horrible form
    Which might deprive your sovereignty of reason,°
    And draw you into madness? think of it,
    The very place puts toys of desperation,°   75
    Without more motive, into every brain
    That looks so many fathoms to the sea
    And hears it roar beneath.
HAMLET.   It waves me still:
    Go on, I'll follow thee.

---

43 *questionable:* question-raising.   47 *canonized:* buried in accordance with church
edict.   *hearsèd:* entombed.   48 *cerements:* waxed cloth wrappings.   54 *fools of nature:*
mocked by our natural limitations when faced with the supernatural.   59 *some . . . desire:* desired
to impart something.   65 *fee:* value.   71 *beetles o'er:* overhangs.   73 *deprive . . . reason:*
dethrone your reason from its sovereignty.   75 *toys of desperation:* desperate whims.

MARCELLUS.   You shall not go my lord.
HAMLET.   Hold off your hands.   80
HORATIO.   Be ruled, you shall not go.
HAMLET.   My fate cries out,
    And makes each petty artire° in this body
    As hardy as the Nemean lion's° nerve;°
    Still am I called, unhand me gentlemen,
    By heaven I'll make a ghost of him that lets° me: 85
    I say away; go on, I'll follow thee.   *Exeunt* GHOST *and* HAMLET.
HORATIO.   He waxes desperate° with imagination.
MARCELLUS.   Let's follow, 'tis not fit thus to obey him.
HORATIO.   Have after—to what issue will this come?
MARCELLUS.   Something is rotten in the state of Denmark.   90
HORATIO.   Heaven will direct it.
MARCELLUS.   Nay, let's follow him.   *Exeunt.*

Scene 5. *[Another part of the platform]*

Enter GHOST *and* HAMLET.

HAMLET.   Whither wilt thou lead me? Speak, I'll go no further.
GHOST.   Mark me.
HAMLET.   I will.
GHOST.   My hour is almost come
    When I to sulphurous and tormenting flames
    Must render up myself.
HAMLET.   Alas poor ghost.
GHOST.   Pity me not, but lend thy serious hearing   5
    To what I shall unfold.
HAMLET.   Speak, I am bound° to hear.
GHOST.   So art thou to revenge, when thou shalt hear.
HAMLET.   What?
GHOST.   I am thy father's spirit,
    Doomed for a certain term to walk the night,   10
    And for the day confined to fast in fires,
    Till the foul crimes done in my days of nature°
    Are burnt and purged away: but that I am forbid
    To tell the secrets of my prison-house,
    I could a tale unfold whose lightest word   15
    Would harrow up thy soul, freeze thy young blood,
    Make thy two eyes like stars start from their spheres,°
    Thy knotted and combinèd locks to part,
    And each particular hair to stand an° end,
    Like quills upon the fretful porpentine:°   20

---

82 *artire:* ligament.   83 *Nemean lion:* (killed by Hercules as one of his twelve labors).   *nerve:*
sinew.   85 *lets:* prevents.   87 *waxes desperate:* grows frantic.   6 *bound:* obliged by
duty.   12 *crimes . . . nature:* sins committed during my life on earth.   17 *spheres:* (1) orbits
(according to Ptolemy, each planet was confined to a sphere revolving around the earth)
(2) sockets.   19 *an:* on.   20 *fretful porpentine:* angry porcupine.

But this eternal blazon° must not be
To ears of flesh and blood; list, list, O list:
If though didst ever thy dear father love—
HAMLET.   O God!
GHOST.   Revenge his foul and most unnatural murder.   25
HAMLET.   Murder?
GHOST.   Murder most foul, as in the best it is,
  But this most foul, strange and unnatural.
HAMLET.   Haste me to know't, that I with wings as swift
  As meditation or the thoughts of love,   30
  May sweep to my revenge.
GHOST.   I find thee apt,°
  And duller shouldst thou be than the fat° weed
  That rots itself in ease on Lethe wharf,°
  Wouldst thou not stir in this; now Hamlet hear,
  'Tis given out, that sleeping in my orchard,°   35
  A serpent stung me, so the whole ear of Denmark
  Is by a forgèd process° of my death
  Rankly abused:° but know thou noble youth,
  The serpent that did sting thy father's life
  Now wears his crown.
HAMLET.   O my prophetic soul!   40
  My uncle?
GHOST.   Ay, that incestuous, that adulterate° beast,
  With witchcraft of his wit, with traitorous gifts,
  O wicked wit and gifts, that have the power
  So to seduce; won to his shameful lust   45
  The will of my most seeming-virtuous queen;
  O Hamlet, what a falling-off was there,
  From me whose love was of that dignity
  That it went hand in hand, even with the vow
  I made to her in marriage, and to decline   50
  Upon° a wretch whose natural gifts were poor
  To° those of mine;
  But virtue, as it never will be moved,
  Though lewdness court it in a shape of heaven,°
  So lust, though to a radiant angle linked,   55
  Will sate itself in a celestial bed
  And prey on garbage.
  But soft, methinks I scent the morning air,
  Brief let me be; sleeping within my orchard,
  My custom always of the afternoon,   60
  Upon my secure° hour thy uncle stole

---

21 *eternal blazon:* revelation about eternity.   31 *apt:* ready.   32 *fat:* slimy.   33 *Lethe wharf:*
the banks of Lethe (river in Hades from which spirits drank to forget their past lives).   35
orchard: garden.   37   *process:* account.   38   *abused:* deceived.   42   *adulterate:*
adulterous.   50–51 *decline Upon:* descend to.   52 *To:* compared to.   54 *shape of heaven:*
angelic appearance.   61 *secure:* unsuspecting.

With juice of cursèd hebona° in a vial,
And in the porches of my ears did pour
The leperous° distilment, whose effect
Holds such an enmity with blood of man,   65
That swift as quicksilver it courses through
The natural gates and alleys of the body,
And with a sudden vigour it doth posset°
And curd, like eager° droppings into milk,
The thin and wholesome° blood; so did it mine,   70
And a most instant tetter° barked about°
Most lazar°-like with vile and loathsome crust
All my smooth body.
Thus was I sleeping by a brother's hand,
Of life, of crown, of queen at once dispatched,   75
Cut off even in the blossoms of my sin,
Unhouseled, disappointed, unaneled,°
No reck'ning° made, but sent to my account°
With all my imperfections on my head;
O horrible, O horrible, most horrible!   80
If thou hast nature in thee bear it not,
Let not the royal bed of Denmark be
A couch for luxury° and damnèd incest.
But howsoever thou pursues this act,
Taint not thy mind, nor let thy soul contrive   85
Against thy mother aught;° leave her to heaven,
And to those thorns that in her bosom lodge
To prick and sting her. Fare thee well at once,
The glow-worm shows the matin° to be near
And 'gins to pale this uneffectual fire:°   90
Adieu, adieu, adieu, remember me.   *Exit.*
HAMLET.   O all you host of heaven! O earth! what else?
And shall I couple° hell? O fie! Hold, hold my heart,
And you my sinews, grow not instant old,
But bear me stiffly up; remember thee?   95
Ay thou poor ghost, whiles memory holds a seat
In this distracted globe.° Remember thee?
Yea, from the table° of my memory
I'll wipe away all trivial fond° records,
All saws of books,° all forms, all pressures° past   100

---

62 *hebona:* poisonous sap of the ebony or henbane.   64 *leperous:* leprosy-causing.   68 *posset:*
curdle.   69 *eager:* sour.   70 *wholesome:* healthy.   71 *tetter:* skin eruption.   *barked about:*
covered (like bark on a tree).   72 *lazar:* leper.   77 *Unhouseled . . . unaneled:* without final
sacrament, unprepared (without confession) and lacking extreme unction (anointing).   78
reck'ning: (1) accounting (2) payment of my bill (3) confession and absolution.   *account:* judgment.   83 *luxury:* lust.   86 *aught:* anything.   89 *matin:* dawn.   90 *'gins . . . fire:* his
light becomes ineffective, made pale by day.   93 *couple:* engage in a contest against.   97 *distracted globe:* (his head).   98 *table:* tablet, "table-book."   99 *fond:* foolish.   100 *saws of
books:* maxims (sayings) copied from books.   *forms, pressures:* ideas, impressions.

That youth and observation copied there,
And thy commandment all alone shall live
Within the book and volume of my brain,
Unmixed with baser matter, yes by heaven:
O most pernicious woman!   105
O villain, villain, smiling damnèd villain!
My tables,° meet° it is I set it down
That one may smile, and smile, and be a villain,
At least I am sure it may be so in Denmark.
So uncle, there you are: now to my word,°   110
It is 'Adieu, adieu, remember me.'
I have sworn't.

Enter HORATIO and MARCELLUS.

HORATIO.   My lord, my lord!
MARCELLUS.   Lord Hamlet!
HORATIO.   Heaven secure° him.
HAMLET.   So be it.
MARCELLUS.   Illo, ho, ho, my lord!   115
HAMLET.   Hillo, ho, ho, boy, come° bird, come.
MARCELLUS.   How is't my noble lord?
HORATIO.   What news my lord?
HAMLET.   O, wonderful!
HORATIO.   Good my lord, tell it.
HAMLET.   No, you will reveal it.
HORATIO.   Not I my lord, by heaven.
MARCELLUS.   Nor I my lord.   120
HAMLET.   How say you then, would heart of man once think it?
    But you'll be secret?
BOTH.   Ay, by heaven, my lord.
HAMLET.   There's ne'er a villain dwelling in all Denmark
    But he's an arrant° knave.
HORATIO.   There needs no ghost my lord, come from the grave   125
    To tell us this.
HAMLET.   Why right, you are in the right,
    And so without more circumstance° at all
    I hold it fit that we shake hands and part,
    You, as your business and desire shall point you,
    For every man hath business and desire   130
    Such as it is, and for my own poor part,
    Look you, I will go pray.
HORATIO.   These are but wild and whirling words my lord.
HAMLET.   I am sorry they offend you, heartily,
    Yes faith, heartily.
HORATIO.   There's no offence my lord.   135

---

107 *tables:* See note for line 98.   *meet:* fitting.   110 *word:* motto (to guide my actions).   113
secure: protect.   116 *Hillo . . . come:* falconer's cry with which Hamlet replies to their calls.   124
arrant: thoroughgoing.   127 *circumstance:* ceremony.

HAMLET.   Yes by Saint Patrick, but there is Horatio,
　　And much offence too: touching this vision here,
　　It is an honest° ghost, that let me tell you:
　　For your desire to know what is between us,
　　O'ermaster't as you may. And now good friends,　　　　　　　　　　140
　　As you are friends, scholars, and soldiers,
　　Give me one poor request.
HORATIO.   What is't, my lord? we will.
HAMLET.   Never make known what you have seen tonight.
BOTH.   My lord we will not.
HAMLET.　　　　　　　　　　Nay, but swear't.
HORATIO.　　　　　　　　　　　　In faith　　　　　　　　　　　　145
　　My lord, not I.
MARCELLUS.　　　　Nor I my lord, in faith.
HAMLET.   Upon my sword.
MARCELLUS.　　　　　　　　We have sworn my lord already.
HAMLET.   Indeed, upon my sword,° indeed.
GHOST.   Swear.　　　　　　　　　　　　　*Ghost cries under the stage.*
HAMLET.   Ha, ha, boy, say'st thou so, art thou there, truepenny°?　　　150
　　Come on, you hear this fellow in the cellarage,
　　Consent to swear.
HORATIO.　　　　　　Propose the oath my lord.
HAMLET.   Never to speak of this that you have seen.
　　Swear by my sword.
GHOST.   [*Beneath.*] Swear.　　　　　　　　　　　　　　　　　155
HAMLET.   Hic et ubique?° then we'll shift our ground:
　　Come hither gentlemen,
　　And lay your hands again upon my sword,
　　Swear by my sword
　　Never to speak of this that you have heard.　　　　　　　　　160
GHOST.   [*Beneath.*] Swear by his sword.
HAMLET.   Well said old mole, canst work i'th' earth so fast?
　　A worthy pioner°—once more remove,° good friends.
HORATIO.   O day and night, but this is wondrous strange.
HAMLET.   And therefore as a stranger give it welcome.　　　　　165
　　There are more things in heaven and earth Horatio,
　　Than are dreamt of in your philosophy.
　　But come,
　　Here as before, never so help you mercy,
　　How strange or odd some'er I bear myself,　　　　　　　　170
　　(As I perchance hereafter shall think meet
　　To put an antic disposition on°)
　　That you at such times seeing me, never shall
　　With arms encumbered° thus, or this head-shake,
　　Or by pronouncing of some doubtful phrase,　　　　　　　175

138 *honest:* true (not a devil in disguise).　　**148** *sword:* (the cross-shaped hilt).　　**150** *truepenny:* old pal.　　**156** *Hic et ubique:* here and everywhere.　　**163** *pioner:* digger (army trencher).　　*remove:* move elsewhere.　　**172** *put . . . on:* assume a mad or grotesque behavior.　　**174** *encumbered:* folded.

As "Well, well, we know," or "We could and if we would,"
Or "If we list° to speak," or "There be and if they might,"
Or such ambiguous giving out, to note
That you know aught of me; this do swear,
So grace and mercy at your need help you.   180
GHOST.   [*Beneath*.] Swear.   [*They swear.*]
HAMLET.   Rest, rest, perturbed spirit: so gentlemen,
    With all my love I do commend me to you,°
    And what so poor a man as Hamlet is,
    May do t'express his love and friending to you   185
    God willing shall not lack: let us go in together,
    And still° your fingers on your lips I pray.
    The time is out of joint: O cursèd spite,
    That ever I was born to set it right.
    Nay come, let's go together.   *Exeunt.*   190

ACT 2

Scene 1. *[Polonius's chambers]*

Enter old POLONIUS *with his man* REYNALDO.

POLONIUS.   Give him this money, and these notes Reynaldo.
REYNALDO.   I will my lord.
POLONIUS.   You shall do marvellous° wisely, good Reynaldo,
    Before you visit him, to make inquire
    Of his behaviour.
REYNALDO.   My lord, I did intend it.   5
POLONIUS.   Marry, well said, very well said; look you sir,
    Inquire me first what Danskers° are in Paris,
    And how, and who, what means, and where they keep,°
    What company, at what expense, and finding
    By this encompassment° and drift of question   10
    That they do know my son, come you more nearer
    Than your particular demands° will touch it,
    Take you as 'twere some distant knowledge of him,
    As thus, "I know his father, and his friends,
    And in part him"—do you mark this, Reynaldo?   15
REYNALDO.   Ay, very well my lord.
POLONIUS.   'And in part him, but,' you may say, 'not well,
    But if't be he I mean, he's very wild,
    Addicted so and so;' and there put on him
    What forgeries° you please, marry none so rank°   20
    As may dishonour him, take heed of that,

---

177 *list:* please.   183 *commend . . . you:* put myself in your hands.   187 *still:* always.   3
marvellous: wonderfully.   7 *Danskers:* Danes.   8 *keep:* lodge.   10 *encompassment:* roundabout way.   12 *particular demands:* specific questions.   20 *forgeries:* inventions.   *rank:*
excessive.

But sir, such wanton, wild, and usual slips,
As are companions noted and most known
To youth and liberty.
REYNALDO.   As gaming my lord.
POLONIUS.   Ay, or drinking, fencing, swearing,   25
Quarrelling, drabbing°—you may go so far.
REYNALDO.   My lord, that would dishonour him.
POLONIUS.   Faith no, as you may season it in the charge.°
You must not put another scandal on him,
That he is open to incontinency,°   30
That's not my meaning, but breathe his faults so quaintly°
That they may seem the taints of° liberty,
The flash and outbreak of a fiery mind,
A savageness in unreclaimèd blood,°
Of general assault.°
REYNALDO.   But my good lord—   35
POLONIUS.   Wherefore° should you do this?
REYNALDO.   Ay my lord,
I would know that.
POLONIUS.   Marry sir, here's my drift,
And I believe it is a fetch of warrant:°
You laying these slight sullies on my son,
As 'twere a thing a little soiled i'th' working,°   40
Mark you, your party in converse, him you would sound,
Having ever seen° in the prenominate crimes°
The youth you breathe of guilty, be assured
He closes with you in this consequence,°
"Good sir," or so, or "friend," or "gentleman,"   45
According to the phrase, or the addition°
Of man and country.
REYNALDO.   Very good my lord.
POLONIUS.   And then sir, does a'° this, a' does, what was I
about to say?
By the mass I was about to say something,
Where did I leave?
REYNALDO.   At "closes in the consequence,"   50
At "friend, or so, and gentleman."
POLONIUS.   At "closes in the consequence," ay marry,
He closes thus, "I know the gentleman,
I saw him yesterday, or th'other day,
Or then, or then, with such or such, and as you say,   55
There was a' gaming, there o'ertook in's rouse,°

---

26 *drabbing:* whoring.   28 *season . . . charge:* temper the charge as you make it.   30 *inconti-*
nency: uncontrolled lechery.   31 *quaintly:* delicately.   32 *taints of:* blemishes due to.   34
unreclaimèd blood: unbridled passion.   35 *general assault:* attacking all (young men).   36 *Where-*
fore: why.   38 *fetch of warrant:* trick guaranteed to succeed.   40 *working:* handling.   42
Having ever seen: if he has ever seen.   *prenominate crimes:* aforenamed sins.   44 *closes . . .*
consequence: comes to terms with you as follows.   46 *addition:* title, form of address.
48 *'a:* he.   56 *o'ertook in's rouse:* overcome by drunkenness.

There falling out at tennis," or perchance
"I saw him enter such a house of sale,"
Videlicet,° a brothel, or so forth. See you now,
Your bait of falsehood takes this carp of truth,   60
And thus do we of wisdom, and of reach,°
With windlasses,° and with assays of bias,°
By indirections find directions out:
So by my former lecture and advice
Shall you my son; you have me, have you not?   65
REYNALDO.   My lord I have.
POLONIUS.   God bye ye, fare ye well.
REYNALDO.   Good my lord.
POLONIUS.   Observe his inclination in yourself.°
REYNALDO.   I shall my lord.
POLONIUS.   And let him ply° his music.
REYNALDO.   Well my lord.   70
POLONIUS.   Farewell.

Exit REYNALDO.

Enter OPHELIA.

How now Ophelia, what's the matter?
OPHELIA.   O my lord, my lord, I have been so affrighted.
POLONIUS.   With what, i'th'name of God?
OPHELIA.   My lord, as I was sewing in my closet,°
Lord Hamlet with his doublet all unbraced,°   75
No hat upon his head, his stockings fouled,
Ungart'red, and down-gyvèd° to his ankle,
Pale as his shirt, his knees knocking each other,
And with a look so piteous in purport°
As if he had been loosèd out of hell   80
To speak of horrors, he comes before me.
POLONIUS.   Mad for thy love?
OPHELIA.   My lord I do not know,
But truly I do fear it.
POLONIUS.   What said he?
OPHELIA.   He took me by the wrist, and held me hard,
Then goes he to the length of all his arm,°   85
And with his other hand thus o'er his brow,
He falls to such perusal of my face
As° a' would draw it; long stayed he so,
At last, a little shaking of mine arm,
And thrice his head thus waving up and down,   90
He raised a sigh so piteous and profound
As it did seem to shatter all his bulk,°

59 *Videlicet:* namely.   61 *reach:* far-reaching knowledge.   62 *windlasses:* roundabout
approaches.   *assays of bias:* indirect attempts.   68 *in yourself:* personally.   70 *ply:* practice.   74 *closet:* private room.   75 *doublet all unbraced:* jacket all unfastened.   77 *down-
gyvèd:* down around his ankles (like prisoners' fetters or gyves).   79 *purport:* expression.   85
goes . . . arm: holds me at arm's length.   88 *As:* as if.   92 *bulk:* body.

And end his being; that done, he lets me go,
And with his head over his shoulder turned
He seemed to find his way without his eyes,   95
For out adoors he went without their helps,
And to the last bended their light on me.
POLONIUS.   Come, go with me, I will go seek the king,
This is the very ecstasy° of love,
Whose violent property fordoes itself,°   100
And leads the will to desperate undertakings
As oft as any passion under heaven
That does afflict our natures: I am sorry.
What, have you given him any hard words of late?
OPHELIA.   No my good lord, but as you did command   105
I did repel his letters, and denied
His access to me.
POLONIUS.   That hath made him mad.
I am sorry that with better heed and judgment
I had not quoted° him. I feared he did but trifle
And meant to wrack° thee, but beshrew my jealousy:°   110
By heaven it is as proper to our age
To cast beyond ourselves in our opinions,°
As it is common for the younger sort
To lack discretion; come, go we to the king,
This must be known, which being kept close, might move   115
More grief to hide, than hate to utter love.°   [*Exeunt.*]

Scene 2. [*A room in the Castle*]

Flourish. Enter KING *and* QUEEN, ROSENCRANTZ *and* GUILDENSTERN, *cum aliis.*

KING.   Welcome dear Rosencrantz and Guildenstern.
Moreover° that we much did long to see you,
The need we have to use you did provoke
Our hasty sending. Something have you heard
Of Hamlet's transformation—so call it.   5
Sith° nor th'exterior nor the inward man
Resembles that it was. What it should be,
More than his father's death, that thus hath put him
So much from th'understanding of himself,
I cannot dream of: I entreat you both,   10
That being of so young days° brought up with him,
And sith so neighboured to his youth and haviour,
That you vouchsafe your rest° here in our court
Some little time, so by your companies

99 *ecstasy:* madness.   100 *Whose . . . itself:* that, by its violent nature, destroys the lover.   109
quoted: observed.   110 *wrack:* ruin.   *beshrew my jealousy:* curse my suspicion.   111–112
proper . . . opinions: natural for old people to read more into something than is actually
there.   115–116 *being kept . . . love:* if kept secret, might cause more grief than if we risked the
king's displeasure.   2 *Moreover:* in addition to the fact.   6 *Sith:* since.   11 *of . . . days:*
from your early days.   13 *vouchsafe your rest:* agree to stay.

To draw him on to pleasures, and to gather   15
So much as from occasion you may glean,
Whether aught to us unknown afflicts him thus,
That opened° lies within our remedy.

QUEEN.   Good gentlemen, he hath much talked of you,
And sure I am, two men there are not living   20
To whom he more adheres. If it will please you
To show us so much gentry° and good will,
As to expend your time with us awhile,
For the supply and profit of our hope,
Your visitation shall receive such thanks   25
As fits a king's remembrance.

ROSENCRANTZ.   Both your majesties
Might by the sovereign power you have of us,
Put your dread pleasures more into command
Than to entreaty.

GUILDENSTERN.   But we both obey,
And here give up ourselves in the full bent,°   30
To lay our service freely at your feet
To be commanded.

KING.   Thanks Rosencrantz, and gentle Guildenstern.

QUEEN.   Thanks Guildenstern, and gentle Rosencrantz.
And I beseech you instantly to visit   35
My too much changèd son. Go some of you
And bring these gentlemen where Hamlet is.

GUILDENSTERN.   Heavens make our presence and our practices°
Pleasant and helpful to him.

QUEEN.   Ay, amen.

Exeunt ROSENCRANTZ *and* GUILDENSTERN.

Enter POLONIUS.

POLONIUS.   Th'ambassadors from Norway my good lord,   40
Are joyfully returned.

KING.   Thou still° hast been the father of good news.

POLONIUS.   Have I, my lord? Assure you, my good liege,
I hold my duty as I hold my soul,
Both to my God and to my gracious king;   45
And I do think, or else this brain of mine
Hunts not the trail of policy° so sure
As it hath used to do, that I have found
The very cause of Hamlet's lunacy.

KING.   O speak of that, that do I long to hear.   50

POLONIUS.   Give first admittance to th' ambassadors,
My news shall be the fruit° to that great feast.

---

18 *opened:* discovered.   22 *gentry:* courtesy.   30 *in the full bent:* to the utmost (in archery,
bending the bow).   38 *practices:* (1) actions (2) plots.   42 *still:* always.   47 *policy:* (1) politics (2) plots.   52 *fruit:* dessert.

KING.   Thyself do grace to them, and bring them in.   [*Exit POLONIUS.*]
    He tells me my dear Gertrude, he hath found
    The head and source of all your son's distemper.   55
QUEEN.   I doubt° it is no other but the main,
    His father's death and our o'erhasty marriage.
KING.   Well, we shall sift him.

Enter POLONIUS, VALTEMAND, and CORNELIUS.

                    Welcome, my good friends.
    Say Valtemand, what from our brother Norway?
VALTEMAND.   Most fair return of greetings and desires;   60
    Upon our first,° he sent out to suppress
    His nephew's levies, which to him appeared
    To be a preparation 'gainst the Polack,
    But better looked into, he truly found
    It was against your highness, whereat grieved   65
    That so his sickness, age, and impotence
    Was falsely borne in hand,° sends out arrests
    On Fortinbras, which he in brief obeys,
    Receives rebuke from Norway, and in fine,°
    Makes vow before his uncle never more   70
    To give th'assay° of arms against your majesty:
    Whereon old Norway, overcome with joy,
    Gives him threescore thousand crowns in annual fee,
    And his commission to employ those soldiers
    So levied (as before) against the Polack,   75
    With an entreaty herein further shown,
    That it might please you to give quiet pass°
    Through your dominions for this enterprise,
    On such regards of safety and allowance
    As therein are set down.   [*Giving a paper.*]
KING.   It likes° us well,   80
    And at our more considered time,° we'll read,
    Answer, and think upon this business:
    Meantime, we thank you for your well-took labour,
    Go to your rest, at night we'll feast together.
    Most welcome home.   *Exeunt AMBASSADORS.*
POLONIUS.   This business is well ended.   85
    My liege and madam, to expostulate°
    What majesty should be, what duty is,
    Why day is day, night night, and time is time.
    Were nothing but to waste night, day, and time.
    Therefore since brevity is the soul of wit,°   90
    And tediousness the limbs and outward flourishes,°

---

56 *doubt:* suspect.   61 *first:* first presentation.   67 *borne in hand:* deceived.   69 *fine:* finishing.   71 *assay:* test.   77 *pass:* passage.   80 *likes:* pleases.   81 *at . . . time:* when time is available for consideration.   86 *expostulate:* discuss.   90 *wit:* understanding.   91 *tediousness . . . flourishes:* embellishments and flourishes cause tedium.

I will be brief. Your noble son is mad:
Mad call I it, for to define true madness,
What is't but to be nothing else but mad?
But let that go.
QUEEN.   More matter, with less art.   95
POLONIUS.   Madam, I swear I use no art at all:
That he is mad 'tis true: 'tis true, 'tis pity,
And pity 'tis 'tis true: a foolish figure,°
But farewell it, for I will use no art.
Mad let us grant him then, and now remains   100
That we find out the cause of this effect,
Or rather say, the cause of this defect,
For this effect defective comes by cause:
Thus it remains, and the remainder thus.
Perpend.°   105
I have a daughter, have while she is mine,
Who in her duty and obedience, mark,
Hath given me this, now gather and surmise.
[*Reads.*] "To the celestial, and my soul's idol, the most
beautified° Ophelia,"—   110
That's an ill phrase, a vile phrase, "beautified" is a vile
phrase, but you shall hear. Thus: [*Reads.*]
        "In her excellent white bosom, these," &c.—
QUEEN.   Came this from Hamlet to her?
POLONIUS.   Good madam stay awhile, I will be faithful.   [*Reads.*]   115
        "Doubt thou the stars are fire,
            Doubt that the sun doth move,°
        Doubt° truth to be a liar,
            But never doubt I love.
O dear Ophelia, I am ill at these numbers, I have not   120
art to reckon° my groans, but that I love thee best, O
most best, believe it. Adieu.
        Thine evermore, most dear lady, whilst
            this machine° is to° him, Hamlet."
This in obedience hath my daughter shown me,   125
And more above hath his solicitings,
As they fell out by time, by means, and place,
All given to mine ear.
KING.   But how hath she
    Received his love?
POLONIUS.   What do you think of me?
KING.   As of a man faithful and honourable.   130
POLONIUS.   I would fain prove so. But what might you think
        When I had seen this hot love on the wing,
        As I perceived it (I must tell you that)

---

98 *figure:* rhetorical figure.   105 *Perpend:* consider.   110 *beautified:* beautiful.   117 *move:*
(as it was believed to do, around the earth).   118 *Doubt:* suspect.   121 *reckon:* express in
meter.   124 *machine:* body.   *to:* attached to.

Before my daughter told me, what might you,
Or my dear majesty your queen here think,   135
If I had played the desk or table-book,°
Or given my heart a winking° mute and dumb,
Or looked upon this love with idle° sight,
What might you think? No, I went round to work,
And my young mistress this I did bespeak,   140
"Lord Hamlet is a prince out of thy star,°
This must not be:" and then I prescripts° gave her
That she should lock herself from his resort,°
Admit no messengers, receive no tokens:
Which done, she took the fruits of my advice,   145
And he repellèd, a short tale to make,
Fell into a sadness, then into a fast,
Thence to a watch,° thence into a weakness,
Thence to a lightness,° and by this declension,
Into the madness wherein now he raves,   150
And all we mourn for.
KING.   Do you think 'tis this?
QUEEN.   It may be very like.
POLONIUS.   Hath there been such a time, I would fain know that,
    That I have positively said "'Tis so,"
    When it proved otherwise?
KING.   Not that I know.   155
POLONIUS.   Take this, from this, if this be otherwise;

[*Points to his head and shoulder.*]

    If circumstances lead me, I will find
    Where truth is hid, though it were hid indeed
    Within the center.
KING.   How may we try° it further?
POLONIUS.   You know sometimes he walks four hours together   160
    Here in the lobby.
QUEEN.   So he does indeed.
POLONIUS.   At such a time, I'll loose° my daughter to him.
    Be you and I behind an arras° then,
    Mark the encounter: if he love her not,
    And be not from his reason fall'n thereon,   165
    Let me be no assistant for a state,°
    But keep a farm and carters.
KING.   We will try it.

Enter HAMLET reading on a book.

QUEEN.   But look where sadly the poor wretch comes reading.

136 *played . . . book:* kept it concealed as in a desk or personal notebook.   137 *given . . . winking:*
had my heart shut its eyes to the matter.   138 *idle:* unseeing.   141 *out . . . star:* out of your
sphere (above you in station).   142 *prescripts:* orders.   143 *resort:* company.   148 *watch:*
sleeplessness.   149 *lightness:* lightheadedness.   159 *try:* test.   162 *loose:* (1) release (2)
turn loose.   163 *arras:* hanging tapestry.   166 *assistant . . . state:* state official.

POLONIUS.   Away, I do beseech you both away,
I'll board him presently,° O give me leave.   *Exeunt* KING *and* QUEEN.   170
How does my good Lord Hamlet?

HAMLET.   Well, God-a-mercy.

POLONIUS.   Do you know me, my lord?

HAMLET.   Excellent well, you are a fishmonger.°

POLONIUS.   Not I my lord.   175

HAMLET.   Then I would you were so honest a man.

POLONIUS.   Honest, my lord?

HAMLET.   Ay sir, to be honest as this world goes, is to be one
man picked out of ten thousand.

POLONIUS.   That's very true, my lord.   180

HAMLET.   For if the sun breed maggots° in a dead dog, being a good
kissing carrion°—have you a daughter?

POLONIUS.   I have my lord.

HAMLET.   Let her not walk i'th'sun:° conception° is a blessing, but as
your daughter may conceive, friend look to'it.   185

POLONIUS.   [*Aside.*] How say you by that? Still harping on my daughter,
yet he knew me not at first, a' said I was a fishmonger.
A' is far gone, far gone, and truly in my youth, I suffered
much extremity for love, very near this. I'll speak to him
again. What do you read my lord?   190

HAMLET.   Words, words, words.

POLONIUS.   What is the matter my lord?

HAMLET.   Between who?

POLONIUS.   I mean the matter° that you read, my lord.

HAMLET.   Slanders sir; for the satirical rogue says here, that old men   195
have grey beards, that their faces are wrinkled, their eyes
purging thick amber and plum-tree gum,° and that they
have a plentiful lack of wit, together with most weak
hams. All which sir, though I most powerfully and
potently believe, yet I hold it not honesty° to have it thus set   200
down, for yourself sir shall grow old as I am: if like a crab
you could go backward.

POLONIUS.   [*Aside.*] Though this be madness, yet there is method
in't.
Will you walk out of the air° my lord?   205

HAMLET.   Into my grave.

POLONIUS.   [*Aside.*] Indeed that's out of the air; how pregnant°
sometimes his replies are, a happiness° that often

---

170 *board him presently:* approach him immediately.   174 *fishmonger:* (1) fish dealer (2)
pimp.   181 *breed maggots:* (in the belief that the rays of the sun caused maggots to breed in
dead flesh).   182 *kissing carrion:* piece of flesh for kissing.   184 *Let . . . sun:* (1) (proverbial: "out of God's blessing, into the warm sun") (2) because the sun is a breeder (3) don't let her
go near me (with a pun on "sun" and "son").   *conception:* (1) understanding (2) pregnancy.
194 *matter:* (1) content (Polonius's meaning) (2) cause of a quarrel (Hamlet's
interpretation).   197–198 *purging . . . gum:* exuding a viscous yellowish discharge.   200 *honesty:* decency.   205 *out . . . air:* (in the belief that fresh air was bad for the sick).   207 *pregnant:* full of meaning.   208 *happiness:* aptness.

madness hits on, which reason and sanity could not so
prosperously° be delivered of. I will leave him, and   210
suddenly contrive the means of meeting between him
and my daughter. My honourable lord, I will most
humbly take leave of you.

HAMLET.   You cannot sir take from me anything that I will more
willingly part withal: except my life, except my life,   215
except my life.

POLONIUS.   Fare you well my lord.

HAMLET.   These tedious old fools.

Enter ROSENCRANTZ and GUILDENSTERN.

POLONIUS.   You go to seek the Lord Hamlet, there he is.

ROSENCRANTZ.   [*To POLONIUS.*] God save you sir.   [*Exit POLONIUS.*]   220

GUILDENSTERN.   My honoured lord.

ROSENCRANTZ.   My most dear lord.

HAMLET.   My excellent good friends, how dost thou Guildenstern?
Ah Rosencrantz, good lads, how do you both?

ROSENCRANTZ.   As the indifferent° children of the earth.   225

GUILDENSTERN.   Happy, in that we are not over-happy:
On Fortune's cap we are not the very button.°

HAMLET.   Nor the soles of her shoe?

ROSENCRANTZ.   Neither my lord.

HAMLET.   Then you live about her waist, or in the middle of her   230
favours?

GUILDENSTERN.   Faith, her privates° we.

HAMLET.   In the secret parts of Fortune? O most true, she is a
strumpet.° What news?

ROSENCRANTZ.   None my lord, but that the world's grown honest.   235

HAMLET.   Then is doomsday near: but your news is not true. Let me
question more in particular: what have you my good
friends, deserved at the hands of Fortune, that she sends
you to prison hither?

GUILDENSTERN.   Prison, my lord?   240

HAMLET.   Denmark's a prison.

ROSENCRANTZ.   Then is the world one.

HAMLET.   A goodly one, in which there are many confines, wards,°
and dungeons; Denmark being one o'th'worst.

ROSENCRANTZ.   We think not so my lord.   245

HAMLET.   Why then 'tis none to you; for there is nothing either good
or bad, but thinking makes it so: to me it is a prison.

ROSENCRANTZ.   Why then your ambition makes it one: 'tis too narrow for
your mind.

HAMLET.   O God, I could be bounded in a nutshell, and count   250
myself a king of infinite space; were it not that I have bad
dreams.

---

210 *prosperously:* successfully.   225 *indifferent:* ordinary.   227 *on Fortune's . . . button:* we are not
at the height of our fortunes.   232 *privates:* (1) intimate friends (2) private parts.   234 *strum-*
pet: inconstant woman, giving favor to many.   243 *wards:* cells.

GUILDENSTERN.   Which dreams indeed are ambition: for the very substance
of the ambitious, is merely the shadow of a dream.
HAMLET.   A dream itself is but a shadow.   255
ROSENCRANTZ.   Truly, and I hold ambition of so airy and light a quality,
that it is but a shadow's shadow.
HAMLET.   Then are our beggars bodies, and our monarchs and
outstretched heroes the beggars' shadows:° shall we to th'
court? for by my fay,° I cannot reason.   260
BOTH.   We'll wait upon° you.
HAMLET.   No such matter. I will not sort° you with the rest of my
servants: for to speak to you like an honest man, I am most
dreadfully attended. But in the beaten way of friendship,
what make you at Elsinore?   265
ROSENCRANTZ.   To visit you my lord, no other occasion.
HAMLET.   Beggar that I am, I am even poor in thanks, but I thank
you, and sure dear friends, my thanks are too dear a
halfpenny:° were you not sent for? is it your own inclining?
is it a free° visitation? come, come, deal justly with me,   270
come, come, nay speak.
GUILDENSTERN.   What should we say my lord?
HAMLET.   Anything but to th'purpose: you were sent for, and there
is a kind of confession in your looks, which your modesties
have not craft enough to colour: I know the good king and   275
queen have sent for you.
ROSENCRANTZ.   To what end my lord?
HAMLET.   That you must teach me: but let me conjure° you, by the
rights of our fellowship, by the consonancy of our youth,°
by the obligation of our ever-preserved love, and by what   280
more dear a better proposer can charge you withal,° be
even and direct with me whether you were sent for or no.
ROSENCRANTZ.   [*Aside to Guildenstern.*] What say you?
HAMLET.   Nay then, I have an eye of° you: If you love me,
hold not off.   285
GUILDENSTERN.   My lord, we were sent for.
HAMLET.   I will tell you why, so shall my anticipation prevent° your
discovery,° and your secrecy to the king and queen moult
no feather.° I have of late, but wherefore I know not, lost all
my mirth, forgone all custom of exercises: and indeed it   290
goes so heavily with my disposition, that this goodly
frame the earth, seems to me a sterile promontory, this
most excellent canopy the air, look you, this brave°
o'erhanging firmament, this majestical roof fretted° with

258–259 *Then are . . . shadows:* then beggars are the true substance and ambitious kings and heroes
the elongated shadows of beggars' bodies (for only a real substance can cast a shadow).
260 *fay:* faith.   261 *wait upon:* attend.   262 *sort:* class.   268–269 *too dear a halfpenny:*
worth not even a halfpenny (as I have no influence).   270 *free:* voluntary.   278 *conjure:*
appeal to.   279 *consonancy . . . youth:* agreement in our ages.   281 *withal:* with.   284 *of:*
on.   287 *prevent:* forestall.   288 *discovery:* disclosure.   288–289 *moult no feather:* change in
no way.   293 *brave:* splendid.   294 *fretted:* ornamented with fretwork.

golden fire,° why it appeareth nothing to me but a foul and   295
pestilent congregation of vapours.° What a piece of work is
a man! How noble in reason, how infinite in faculties,° in
form and moving, how express° and admirable in action,
how like an angel in apprehension, how like a god: the
beauty of the world; the paragon of animals; and yet to   300
me, what is this quintessence of dust? Man delights not
me, no, nor woman neither, though by your smiling, you
seem to say so.

ROSENCRANTZ.   My lord, there was no such stuff in my thoughts.

HAMLET.   Why did ye laugh then, when I said 'man delights not me'?   305

ROSENCRANTZ.   To think, my lord, if you delight not in man, what lenten
entertainment° the players shall receive from you: we coted°
them on the way, and hither are they coming to offer you
service.

HAMLET.   He that plays the king shall be welcome, his majesty shall   310
have tribute of me, the adventurous knight° shall use his
foil and target,° the lover shall not sigh gratis,° the humorous
man° shall end his part in peace,° the clown shall make
those laugh whose lungs are tickle o'th'sere,° and the lady
shall say her mind freely: or the blank verse shall halt° for't.   315
What players are they?

ROSENCRANTZ.   Even those you were wont to take such delight in, the
tragedians of the city.

HAMLET.   How chances it they travel? Their residence° both in
reputation and profit was better both ways.   320

ROSENCRANTZ.   I think their inhibition comes by the means of the late
innovation.°

HAMLET.   Do they hold the same estimation they did when I was in
the city; are they so followed?

ROSENCRANTZ.   No indeed are they not.   325

HAMLET.   How comes it? Do they grow rusty?

ROSENCRANTZ.   Nay, their endeavour keeps in the wonted pace; but there
is sir an aery° of children, like eyases,° that cry out on the
top of question,° and are most tyrannically° clapped for't:
these are now the fashion, and so berattle° the common   330

295 *golden fire:* stars.   296 *pestilent . . . vapours:* (clouds were believed to carry contagion).
297 *faculties:* physical powers.   298 *express:* well framed.   306–307 *lenten entertainment:* meager
treatment.   307 *coted:* passed.   311 *adventurous knight:* knight errant (a popular stage character).   312 *foil and target:* sword blunted for stage fighting, and small shield.   312 *gratis:*
(without applause).   312–313 *humorous man:* eccentric character with a dominant trait, caused by
an excess of one of the four humors, or bodily fluids.   313 *in peace:* without interruption.
314 *tickle o'th'sere:* attuned to respond to laughter, as the finely adjusted gunlock responds to the
touch of the trigger (fr. hunting).   315 *halt:* limp (if she adds her own opinions and spoils the
meter).   319 *residence:* i.e., in a city theatre.   321–322 *inhibition . . . innovation:* i.e., they were
forced out of town by a more popular theatrical fashion. The following speeches allude to the "War
of the Theatres" (1601–1602) between the child and adult acting companies.   328 *aery:*
nest.   *eyases:* young hawks.   328–329 *that cry . . . question:* whose shrill voices can be heard
above all others.   329 *tyrannically:* strongly.   330 *berattle:* berate.   330–331 *common stages:*
public playhouses (the children's companies performed in private theatres).

stages° (so they call them) that many wearing rapiers° are
afraid of goose-quills,° and dare scarce come thither.
HAMLET.   What, are they children? Who maintains 'em? How are
they escoted°? Will they pursue the quality no longer than
they can sing°? Will they not say afterwards if they should   335
grow themselves to common players (as it is most like, if
their means are not better) their writers do them wrong, to
make them exclaim against their own succession°?
ROSENCRANTZ.   Faith, there has been much to-do on both sides: and the
nation holds it no sin to tarre° them to controversy. There   340
was for a while, no money bid for argument,° unless the
poet and the player went to cuffs in the question.°
HAMLET.   Is't possible?
GUILDENSTERN.   O there has been much throwing about of brains.
HAMLET.   Do the boys carry it away°?   345
ROSENCRANTZ.   Ay, that they do my lord, Hercules and his load too.°
HAMLET.   It is not very strange, for my uncle is king of Denmark,
and those that would make mows° at him while my father
lived, give twenty, forty, fifty, a hundred ducats apiece
for his picture in little.° 'Sblood,° there is something in this   350
more than natural, if philosophy° could find it out.

A flourish for the Players.

GUILDENSTERN.   There are the players.
HAMLET.   Gentlemen, you are welcome to Elsinore: your hands,
come then, th'appurtenance° of welcome is fashion and
ceremony; let me comply with you in this garb,° lest my   355
extent° to the players, which I tell you must show fairly
outwards, should more appear like entertainment than
yours.° You are welcome: but my uncle-father, and aunt-
mother, are deceived.
GUILDENSTERN.   In what my dear lord?   360
HAMLET.   I am but mad north-north-west; when the wind is southerly,
I know a hawk from a handsaw.°

Enter POLONIUS.

POLONIUS.   Well be with you, gentlemen.

---

331 *wearing rapiers:* (worn by gentlemen).   332 *goose-quills:* pens (of satirical dramatists who wrote
for the children).   334 *escoted:* supported.   334–335 *pursue . . . sing:* continue acting only until
their voices change.   338 *succession:* inheritance.   340 *tarre:* provoke.   341 *bid for
argument:* paid for the plot of a proposed play.   342 *went . . . question:* came to blows on the subject.   345 *carry it away:* carry off the prize.   346 *Hercules . . . too:* (Shakespeare's own company at the Globe Theatre, whose sign was Hercules carrying the globe of the world).
348 *mows:* mouths, grimaces.   350 *little:* a miniature.   *'Sblood:* by God's blood.   351 *philosophy:* science.   354 *appurtenance:* accessory.   355 *comply . . . garb:* observe the formalities
with you in this style.   356 *extent:* i.e., of welcome.   357–358 *should . . . yours:* should appear
more hospitable than yours.   362 *I know . . . handsaw:* I can tell the difference between two
things that are unlike ("hawk" = (1) bird of prey (2) mattock, pickaxe; "handsaw" = (1) hernshaw
or heron bird (2) small saw).

HAMLET.   Hark you Guildenstern, and you too, at each ear a hearer:
that great baby you see there is not yet out of his swaddling   365
clouts.°
ROSENCRANTZ.   Happily° he is the second time come to them, for they say
an old man is twice a child.
HAMLET.   I will prophesy, he comes to tell me of the players, mark
it.—You say right sir, a Monday morning, 'twas then   370
indeed.
POLONIUS.   My lord, I have news to tell you.
HAMLET.   My lord, I have news to tell you. When Roscius° was an
actor in Rome—
POLONIUS.   The actors are come hither, my lord.   375
HAMLET.   Buz, buz.°
POLONIUS.   Upon my honour.
HAMLET.   Then came each actor on his ass—
POLONIUS.   The best actors in the world, either for tragedy, comedy,
history, pastoral, pastoral-comical, historical-pastoral,   380
tragical-historical, tragical-comical-historical-pastoral,
scene individable,° or poem unlimited.° Seneca cannot be
too heavy, nor Plautus° too light for the law of writ, and the
liberty:° these are the only men.
HAMLET.   O Jephthah,° judge of Israel, what a treasure hadst thou.   385
POLONIUS.   What a treasure had he, my lord?
HAMLET.   Why
'One fair daughter and no more,
    The which he lovèd passing° well.'
POLONIUS.   [*Aside.*] Still on my daughter.   390
HAMLET.   Am I not i'th' right, old Jephthah?
POLONIUS.   If you call me Jephthah my lord, I have a daughter that I
love passing well.
HAMLET.   Nay, that follows not.
POLONIUS.   What follows then, my lord?   395
HAMLET.   Why
    "As by lot, God wot,"
and then you know
    "It came to pass, as most like° it was:"
the first row° of the pious chanson will show you more, for   400
look where my abridgement° comes.

Enter four or five PLAYERS.

You are welcome masters, welcome all. I am glad to see
thee well: welcome, good friends. O my old friend, why

365–366 *swaddling clouts:* strips of cloth binding a newborn baby.   367 *Happily:* perhaps.   373
Roscius: famous Roman actor.   376 *Buz, buz:* (contemptuous).   382 *scene individable:* play
observing the unities (time, place, action).   *poem unlimited:* play ignoring the unities.   382–383 *Seneca, Plautus:* Roman writers of tragedy and comedy, respectively.   383–384
law . . . liberty: "rules" regarding the unities and those exercising freedom from the unities.   385
Jephthah: (who was forced to sacrifice his only daughter because of a rash promise: Judges
11:29–39).   389 *passing:* surpassingly.   399 *like:* likely.   400 *row:* stanza.   401 *abridge-
ment:* (the players who will cut short my song).

thy face is valanced° since I saw thee last, com'st thou to
beard me in Denmark? What, my young lady° and   405
mistress? by'r lady, your ladyship is nearer to heaven than
when I saw you last, by the altitude of a chopine.° Pray
God your voice, like a piece of uncurrent° gold, be not
cracked within the ring.° Masters, you are all welcome:
we'll e'en to't like French falconers, fly at any thing we see:°   410
we'll have a speech straight. Come give us a taste of your
quality: come, a passionate speech.

1. PLAYER.   What speech, my good lord?

HAMLET.   I heard thee speak me a speech once, but it was never
acted, or if it was, not above once, for the play I remember   415
pleased not the million, 'twas caviary to the general,° but it
was (as I received it, and others, whose judgments in such
matters cried in the top of mine°) an excellent play, well
digested in the scenes, set down with as much modesty as
cunning.° I remember one said there were no sallets° in the   420
lines, to make the matter savoury, nor no matter in the
phrase that might indict the author of° affection, but called
it an honest method, as wholesome as sweet, and by very
much more handsome than fine:° one speech in't I chiefly
loved, 'twas Aeneas' tale to Dido, and thereabout of it   425
especially where he speaks of Priam's slaughter.° If it live in
your memory begin at this line, let me see, let me see:
      "The rugged Pyrrhus,° like th'Hyrcanian beast"°—
'tis not so: it begins with Pyrrhus—
      "The rugged Pyrrhus, he whose sable° arms,   430
Black as his purpose, did the night resemble
When he lay couched in th'ominous horse,°
Hath now this dread and black complexion smeared
With heraldy more dismal: head to foot
Now is he total gules,° horridly tricked°   435
With blood of fathers, mothers, daughters, sons,
Baked and impasted° with the parching° streets,
That lend a tyrannous and damnèd light
To their lord's murder. Roasted in wrath and fire,
And thus o'er-sizèd° with coagulate gore,   440
With eyes like carbuncles,° the hellish Pyrrhus

---

404 *valanced:* fringed with a beard.   405 *lady:* boy playing women's role.   407 *chopine:* thick-
soled shoe.   408 *uncurrent:* not legal tender.   409 *ring:* (1) ring enclosing the design on a
gold coin (to crack it within the ring [to steal the gold] made it "uncurrent") (2) sound.
410 *fly . . . see:* undertake any difficulty.   416 *caviary . . . general:* like caviar, too rich for the
general public.   418 *cried . . . mine:* spoke with more authority than mine.   419–420 *modesty
as cunning:* moderation as skill.   420 *sallets:* spicy bits.   422 *indict . . . of:* charge . . .
with.   424 *handsome than fine:* dignified than finely wrought.   426 *Priam's slaughter:* the
murder of the King of Troy (as told in the Aeneid).   428 *Pyrrhus:* son of
Achilles.   *Hyrcanian beast:* tiger noted for fierceness.   430 *sable:* black.   432 *horse:* the
hollow wooden horse used by the Greeks to enter Troy.   435 *gules:* red.   *horridly tricked:*
horribly decorated.   437 *impasted:* coagulated.   *parching:* (because the city was on
fire).   440 *o'er-sizèd:* covered over.   441 *carbuncles:* red gems.

Old grandsire Priam seeks;"
So proceed you.
POLONIUS.   'Fore God, my lord, well spoken, with good accent and
    good discretion.°   445
1. PLAYER.   "Anon he finds him,
    Striking too short at Greeks, his antique° sword,
    Rebellious to his arm, lies where it falls,
    Repugnant to command;° unequal matched,
    Pyrrhus at Priam drives, in rage strikes wide,   450
    But with the whiff and wind of his fell° sword,
    Th'unnerved father falls: then senseless Ilium,°
    Seeming to feel this blow, with flaming top
    Stoops to his base; and with a hideous crash
    Takes prisoner Pyrrhus' ear. For lo, his sword   455
    Which was declining on the milky head
    Of reverend Priam, seemed i'th'air to stick;
    So as a painted° tyrant Pyrrhus stood,
    And like a neutral to his will and matter,°
    Did nothing: 460
    But as we often see, against° some storm,
    A silence in the heavens, the rack° stand still,
    The bold winds speechless, and the orb° below
    As hush as death, anon the dreadful thunder
    Doth rend the region, so after Pyrrhus' pause,   465
    A rousèd vengeance sets him new awork,
    And never did the Cyclops'° hammers fall
    On Mars's armour, forged for proof eterne,°
    With less remorse than Pyrrhus' bleeding sword
    Now falls on Priam.   470
    Out, out, thou strumpet Fortune: all you gods,
    In general synod° take away her power,
    Break all the spokes and fellies from her wheel,°
    And bowl the round nave° down the hill of heaven
    As low as to the fiends."°   475
POLONIUS.   This is too long.
HAMLET.   It shall to the barber's with your beard; prithee say on: he's
    for a jig, or a tale of bawdry, or he sleeps. Say on, come to
    Hecuba.
1. PLAYER.   "But who, ah woe, had seen the mobled° queen—"   480
HAMLET.   "The mobled queen"?
POLONIUS.   That's good, "mobled queen" is good.

---

445 *discretion:* interpretation.   447 *antique:* ancient.   449 *Repugnant to command:* refusing
to obey its commander.   451 *fell:* savage.   452 *senseless Ilium:* unfeeling Troy.   458
painted: pictured.   459 *like . . . matter:* unmoved by either his purpose or its achievement.
461 *against:* before.   462 *rack:* clouds.   463 *orb:* earth.   467 *Cyclops:* workmen of Vulcan,
armorer of the gods.   468 *for proof eterne:* to be eternally invincible.   472 *synod:*
assembly.   473 *fellies . . . wheel:* curved pieces of the rim of the wheel that fortune turns, representing a man's fortunes.   474 *nave:* hub.   475 *fiends:* i.e., of hell.   480 *mobled:* muffled
in a scarf.

1. PLAYER.   "Run barefoot up and down, threat'ning the flames
　　　With bissom rheum,° a clout° upon that head
　　　Where late the diadem stood, and for a robe,　　　　　　　　485
　　　About her lank and all o'er-teemèd° loins,
　　　A blanket in the alarm of fear caught up—
　　　Who this had seen, with tongue in venom steeped,
　　　'Gainst Fortune's state° would treason have pronounced;
　　　But if the gods themselves did see her then,　　　　　　　　490
　　　When she saw Pyrrhus make malicious sport
　　　In mincing with his sword her husband's limbs,
　　　The instant burst of clamour that she made,
　　　Unless things mortal move them not at all,
　　　Would have made milch° the burning eyes of heaven,　　　495
　　　And passion in the gods."
POLONIUS.   Look whe'r° he has not turned° his colour, and has tears in's
　　　eyes, prithee no more.
HAMLET.   'Tis well, I'll have thee speak out the rest of this soon.
　　　Good my lord, will you see the players well bestowed;° do　　　500
　　　you hear, let them be well used, for they are the abstract°
　　　and brief chronicles° of the time; after your death you were
　　　better have a bad epitaph than their ill report while you
　　　live.
POLONIUS.   My lord, I will use them according to their desert.°　　　505
HAMLET.   God's bodkin° man, much better. Use every man after° his
　　　desert, and who shall 'scape whipping? Use them after
　　　you own honour and dignity: the less they deserve, the
　　　more merit is in your bounty. Take them in.
POLONIUS.   Come sirs.　　　　　　　　　　*Exeunt POLONIUS and PLAYERS.*　510
HAMLET.   Follow him friends, we'll hear a play tomorrow; [*Stops the
　　　First Player.*] dost thou hear me, old friend, can you play
　　　The Murder of Gonzago?
1. PLAYER.   Ay my lord.
HAMLET.   We'll ha't tomorrow night. You could for a need° study a　　515
　　　speech of some dozen or sixteen lines, which I would set
　　　down and insert in't, could you not?
1. PLAYER.   Ay my lord.
HAMLET.   Very well, follow that lord, and look you mock him not.

　　　　　　　　　　　　　　　　　　　　　　[*Exit FIRST PLAYER.*]

　　　[*To Rosencrantz and Guildenstern.*] My good friends, I'll　　　520
　　　leave you till night, you are welcome to Elsinore.
ROSENCRANTZ.   Good my lord.　　　　[*Exeunt ROSENCRANTZ and GUILDENSTERN.*]
HAMLET.   Ay so, God bye to you, now I am alone.
　　　O what a rogue and peasant slave am I.

484 *bissom rheum:* binding tears.　　*clout:* cloth.　　486 *o'erteemed:* worn out by excessive childbearing.　　489 *state:* reign.　　495 *milch:* milky, moist.　　497 *whe'r:* whether.　　*turned:*
changed.　　500 *bestowed:* lodged.　　501 *abstract:* summary (noun).　　502 *brief chronicles:* history in brief.　　505 *desert:* merit.　　506 *God's bodkin:* God's little body, the communion wafer
(an oath).　　*after:* according to.　　515 *for a need:* if necessary.

Is it not monstrous that this player here,   525
But in a fiction, in a dream of passion,°
Could force his soul so to his own conceit°
That from her working all his visage wanned,°
Tears in his eyes, distraction in his aspect,
A broken voice, and his whole function° suiting   530
With forms° to his conceit; and all for nothing,
For Hecuba!
What's Hecuba to him, or he to Hecuba,
That he should weep for her? what would he do,
Had he the motive and the cue for passion   535
That I have? he would drown the stage with tears,
And cleave the general ear° with horrid speech,
Make mad the guilty and appal the free,°
Confound° the ignorant, and amaze indeed
The very faculties of eyes and ears; yet I,   540
A dull and muddy-mettled° rascal, peak°
Like John-a-dreams,° unpregnant of° my cause,
And can say nothing; no, not for a king,
Upon whose property and most dear life,
A damned defeat was made: am I a coward?   545
Who calls me villain, breaks my pate° across,
Plucks off my beard° and blows it in my face,
Tweaks me by the nose, gives me the lie i'th'throat
As deep as to the lungs,° who does me this?
Ha, 'swounds,° I should take it; for it cannot be   550
But I am pigeon-livered,° and lack gall
To make oppression bitter, or ere this
I should ha' fatted all the region kites°
With this slave's offal: bloody, bawdy villain,
Remorseless, treacherous, lecherous, kindless° villain! 555
O vengeance!
Why what an ass am I, this is most brave,°
That I, the son of a dear father murdered,
Prompted to my revenge by heaven and hell,
Must like a whore unpack my heart with words,   560
And fall a-cursing like a very drab,°
A scullion,° fie upon't, foh.
About, my brains; hum, I have heard,
That guilty creatures sitting at a play,

---

526 *dream of passion:* portrayal of emotion.   527 *conceit:* imagination.   528 *wanned:* grew pale.   530 *function:* bearing.   531 *With forms:* in appearance.   537 *general ear:* ears of all in the audience.   538 *free:* innocent.   539 *Confound:* confuse.   541 *muddy-mettled:* dull-spirited.   *peak:* pine, mope.   542 *John-a-dreams:* a daydreaming fellow.   *unpregnant of:* unstirred by.   546 *pate:* head.   547 *Plucks . . . beard:* (a way of giving insult).   548–549 *gives . . . lungs:* insults me by calling me a liar of the worst kind (the lungs being deeper than the throat).   550 *'swounds:* God's wounds.   551 *pigeon-livered:* meek and uncourageous.   553 *region kites:* vultures of the upper air.   555 *kindless:* unnatural.   557 *brave:* fine.   561 *drab:* whore.   562 *scullion:* kitchen wench.

Have by the very cunning of the scene   565
Been struck so to the soul, that presently°
They have proclaimed their malefactions:
For murder, though it have no tongue, will speak
With most miraculous organ: I'll have these players
Play something like the murder of my father   570
Before mine uncle, I'll observe his looks,
I'll tent° him to the quick, if a' do blench°
I know my course. The spirit that I have seen
May be a devil, and the devil hath power
T'assume a pleasing shape, yea, and perhaps   575
Out of my weakness, and my melancholy,
As he is very potent with such spirits,
Abuses me to damn me; I'll have grounds
More relative than this: the play's the thing
Wherein I'll catch the conscience of the king.   *Exit.*

[ACT 3]

Scene 1. *[A room in the castle]*

Enter KING, QUEEN, POLONIUS, OPHELIA, ROSENCRANTZ, GUILDENSTERN, and LORDS.

KING.   And can you by no drift of conference°
   Get from him why he puts on this confusion,°
   Grating so harshly all his days of quiet
   With turbulent and dangerous lunacy?
ROSENCRANTZ.   He does confess he feels himself distracted,   5
   But from what cause, a' will by no means speak.
GUILDENSTERN.   Nor do we find him forward to be sounded,°
   But with a crafty madness keeps aloof
   When we would bring him on to some confession
   Of his true state.
QUEEN.   Did he receive you well?   10
ROSENCRANTZ.   Most like a gentleman.
GUILDENSTERN.   But with much forcing of his disposition.°
ROSENCRANTZ.   Niggard of question,° but of our demands
   Most free in his reply.
QUEEN.   Did you assay° him
   To any pastime?   15
ROSENCRANTZ.   Madam, it so fell out that certain players
   We o'er-raught° on the way: of these we told him,
   And there did seem in him a kind of joy

---

566 *presently:* immediately.   572 *tent:* probe.   *blench:* flinch.   1 *drift of conference:* turn of conversation.   2 *puts . . . confusion:* seems so distracted ("puts on" indicates the king's private suspicion that Hamlet is playing mad).   7 *forward . . . sounded:* disposed to be sounded out.   12 *forcing . . . disposition:* forcing himself to be so.   13 *Niggard of question:* unwilling to talk.   14 *assay:* tempt.   17 *o'er-raught:* overtook.

To hear of it: they are here about the court,
And as I think, they have already order   20
This night to play before him.
POLONIUS.   'Tis most true,
And he beseeched me to entreat your majesties
To hear and see the matter.°
KING.   With all my heart, and it doth much content me
To hear him so inclined.   25
Good gentlemen, give him a further edge,°
And drive his purpose into these delights.
ROSENCRANTZ.   We shall my lord.   *Exeunt ROSENCRANTZ and GUILDENSTERN.*
KING.   Sweet Gertrude, leave us too,
For we have closely° sent for Hamlet hither,
That he, as 'twere by accident, may here   30
Affront° Ophelia;
Her father and myself, lawful espials,°
Will so bestow° ourselves, that seeing unseen,
We may of their encounter frankly° judge,
And gather by him as he is behaved,   35
If't be th'affliction of his love or no
That thus he suffers for.
QUEEN.   I shall obey you.
And for your part Ophelia, I do wish
That your good beauties be the happy cause
Of Hamlet's wildness, so shall I hope your virtues   40
Will bring him to his wonted° way again,
To both your honours.
OPHELIA.   Madam, I wish it may.   [*Exit QUEEN.*]
POLONIUS.   Ophelia, walk you here—Gracious,° so please you,
We will bestow° ourselves—read on this book,°
That show of such an exercise° may colour°   45
Your loneliness; we are oft to blame in this,
'Tis too much proved,° that with devotion's visage
And pious action, we do sugar o'er
The devil himself.
KING.   [*Aside.*] O 'tis too true,°
How smart a lash that speech doth give my conscience.   50
The harlot's cheek, beautied with plast'ring art,
Is not more ugly to° the thing that helps it,
Than is my deed to my most painted word:°
O heavy burden!

---

23 *matter:* i.e., of the play.   26 *give . . . edge:* encourage his keen interest.   29 *closely:*
secretly.   31 *Affront:* meet face to face with.   32 *espials:* spies.   33, 44 *bestow:*
place.   34 *frankly:* freely.   41 *wonted:* customary.   43 *Gracious:* i.e., Your Grace.   44
book: (of prayer).   45 *exercise:* religious exercise.   *colour:* make plausible.   47 *'Tis . . .*
proved: it is all too apparent.   49 *'tis too true:* (the king's first indication that he is guilty).   52
to: compared to.   51–53 *harlot's cheek . . . word:* just as the harlot's cheek is even uglier by contrast to the makeup that tries to beautify it, so my deed is uglier by contrast to the hypocritical
words under which I hide it.

POLONIUS.   I hear him coming, let's withdraw my lord.   *Exeunt.*   55

Enter HAMLET.

HAMLET.   To be, or not to be, that is the question,
  Whether 'tis nobler in the mind° to suffer
  The slings and arrows of outrageous fortune,
  Or to take arms against a sea of troubles,
  And by opposing, end them: to die, to sleep,   60
  No more; and by a sleep, to say we end
  The heart-ache, and the thousand natural shocks
  That flesh is heir to; 'tis a consummation
  Devoutly to be wished. To die, to sleep,
  To sleep, perchance to dream, ay there's the rub,°   65
  For in that sleep of death what dreams may come
  When we have shuffled off this mortal coil°
  Must give us pause—there's the respect°
  That makes calamity of so long life:°
  For who would bear the whips and scorns of time,   70
  Th'oppressor's wrong, the proud man's contumely,°
  The pangs of disprized love, the law's delay,°
  The insolence of office,° and the spurns
  That patient merit of th'unworthy takes,
  When he himself might his quietus° make   75
  With a bare bodkin;° who would fardels° bear,
  To grunt and sweat under a weary life,
  But that the dread of something after death,
  The undiscovered° country, from whose bourn°
  No traveller returns, puzzles the will,   80
  And makes us rather bear those ills we have,
  Than fly to others that we know not of.
  Thus conscience does make cowards of us all,
  And thus the native hue° of resolution
  Is sicklied o'er with the pale cast of thought,   85
  And enterprises of great pitch° and moment,°
  With this regard° their currents turn awry,°
  And lose the name of action. Soft you now,
  The fair Ophelia—Nymph, in thy orisons°
  Be all my sins remembered.
OPHELIA.   Good my lord,   90
  How does your honour for this many a day°?

---

57 *nobler in the mind:* best, according to "sovereign" reason.   65 *rub:* obstacle.   67 *mortal coil:* (1) turmoil of mortal life (2) coil of flesh encircling the body.   68 *respect:* consideration.   69 *makes calamity of so long life:* makes living long a calamity.   71 *contumely:* contempt.   72 *law's delay:* longevity of lawsuits.   73 *office:* officials.   75 *quietus:* settlement of his debt.   76 *bare bodkin:* mere dagger.   *fardels:* burdens.   79 *undiscovered:* unknown, unexplored.   *bourn:* boundary.   84 *native hue:* natural complexion.   86 *pitch:* height, excellence.   *moment:* importance.   87 *regard:* consideration.   *their currents turn awry:* change their course.   89 *orisons:* prayers (referring to her prayer book).   91 *this . . . day:* all these days.

HAMLET.   I humbly thank you: well, well, well.

OPHELIA.   My lord, I have remembrances of yours
  That I have longèd long to re-deliver,
  I pray you now receive them.

HAMLET.   No, not I,   95
  I never gave you aught.

OPHELIA.   My honoured lord, you know right well you did,
  And with them words of so sweet breath° composed
  As made the things more rich: their perfume lost,
  Take these again, for to the noble mind   100
  Rich gifts wax° poor when givers prove unkind.
  There my lord.

HAMLET.   Ha, ha, are you honest°?

OPHELIA.   My lord.

HAMLET.   Are you fair°?   105

OPHELIA.   What means your lordship?

HAMLET.   That if you be honest and fair, your honesty should admit
  no discourse to your beauty.°

OPHELIA.   Could beauty my lord, have better commerce than with
  honesty?   110

HAMLET.   Ay truly, for the power of beauty will sooner transform
  honesty° from what it is to a bawd,° than the force of
  honesty can translate beauty into his likeness. This was
  sometime° a paradox, but now the time gives it proof. I did
  love you once.   115

OPHELIA.   Indeed my lord, you made me believe so.

HAMLET.   You should not have believed me, for virtue cannot so
  inoculate our old stock, but we shall relish of it.° I loved
  you not.

OPHELIA.   I was the more deceived.   120

HAMLET.   Get thee to a nunnery,° why wouldst thou be a breeder of
  sinners? I am myself indifferent honest,° but yet I could
  accuse me of such things, that it were better my mother
  had not borne me: I am very proud, revengeful, ambitious,
  with more offences at my beck,° than I have thoughts   125
  to put them in, imagination to give them shape, or time to
  act them in: what should such fellows as I do, crawling
  between earth and heaven? we are arrant° knaves all,
  believe none of us, go thy ways to a nunnery. Where's
  your father?   130

OPHELIA.   At home my lord.

98 *breath:* speech.   101 *wax:* grow.   103 *honest:* (1) chaste (2) truthful.   105 *fair:* (1)
beautiful (2) honorable.   107–108 *admit . . . beauty:* (1) not allow communication with your
beauty (2) not allow your beauty to be used as a trap (Hamlet may have overheard the
Polonius–Claudius plot or spotted their movement behind the arras).   112 *honesty:*
chastity.   *bawd:* procurer, pimp.   114 *sometime:* once.   118 *inoculate . . . it:* change our
sinful nature (as a tree is grafted to improve it) but we will keep our old taste (as will the fruit of
the grafted tree).   121 *nunnery:* (1) cloister (2) slang for "brothel" (cf. "bawd" above).   122
indifferent honest: reasonably virtuous.   125 *beck:* beckoning.   128 *arrant:* absolute.

HAMLET.   Let the doors be shut upon him, that he may play the fool
no where but in's own house. Farewell.

OPHELIA.   O help him, you sweet heavens.

HAMLET.   If thou dost marry, I'll give thee this plague° for thy dowry: 135
be thou as chaste as ice, as pure as snow, thou shalt not
escape calumny; get thee to a nunnery, go, farewell. Or if
thou wilt needs marry, marry a fool, for wise men know
well enough what monsters° you make of them: to a nunnery
go, and quickly too, farewell.   140

OPHELIA.   O heavenly powers, restore him.

HAMLET.   I have heard of your paintings too, well enough. God hath
given you one face, and you make yourselves another: you
jig,° you amble, and you lisp,° you nick-name God's
creatures, and make your wantonness your ignorance;° go to,   145
I'll no more on't, it hath made me mad. I say we will have
no moe° marriage. Those that are married already, all but
one shall live, the rest shall keep as they are: to a nunnery,
go.   *Exit* HAMLET.

OPHELIA.   O what a noble mind is here o'erthrown!   150
The courtier's, soldier's, scholar's, eye, tongue, sword,
Th'expectancy and rose° of the fair state,
The glass° of fashion, and the mould of form,°
Th'observed of all observers, quite quite down,
And I of ladies most deject and wretched,   155
That sucked the honey of his music vows,
Now see that noble and most sovereign° reason
Like sweet bells jangled, out of tune and harsh,
That unmatched form and feature° of blown° youth
Blasted with ecstasy.° O woe is me,   160
T'have seen what I have seen, see what I see.

Enter KING *and* POLONIUS.

KING.   Love? his affections° do not that way tend,
Nor what he spake, though it lacked form a little,
Was not like madness. There's something in his soul
O'er which his melancholy sits on brood,   165
And I do doubt,° the hatch and the disclose°
Will be some danger; which for to prevent,
I have in quick determination
Thus set it down: he shall with speed to England,
For the demand of our neglected° tribute: 170

---

135 *plague:* curse.   139 *monsters:* horned cuckolds (men whose wives were unfaithful).   144
jig: walk in a mincing way.   *lisp:* put on affected speech.   145 *make your . . . ignorance:*
excuse your caprices as being due to ignorance.   147 *moe:* more.   152 *expectancy and rose:*
fair hope.   153 *glass:* mirror.   *mould of form:* model of manners.   157 *sovereign:* (because
it should rule).   159 *feature:* external appearance.   159 *blown:* flowering.   160 *Blasted
with ecstasy:* blighted by madness.   162 *affections:* emotions, afflictions.   166 *doubt:*
fear.   165–166 *on brood . . . hatch . . . disclose:* (metaphor of a hen sitting on eggs).   170
neglected: (being unpaid).

Haply° the seas, and countries different,
With variable° objects, shall expel
This something°-settled matter in his heart,
Whereon his brains still beating puts him thus
From fashion of himself.° What think you on't?   175
POLONIUS.   It shall do well. But yet do I believe
The origin and commencement of his grief
Sprung from neglected° love. How now Ophelia?
You need not tell us what Lord Hamlet said,
We heard it all. My lord, do as you please,   180
But if you hold it fit, after the play,
Let his queen-mother all alone entreat him
To show his grief, let her be round° with him,
And I'll be placed (so please you) in the ear
Of° all their conference. If she find° him not,   185
To England send him: or confine him where
Your wisdom best shall think.
KING.   It shall be so,
Madness in great ones must not unwatched go.   *Exeunt.*

Scene 2. *[A hall in the castle]*

Enter HAMLET and three of the PLAYERS.

HAMLET.   Speak the speech° I pray you as I pronounced it to you,
trippingly on the tongue, but if you mouth it° as many of
your players do, I had as lief the town-crier spoke my
lines. Nor do not saw the air too much with your hand
thus, but use all gently, for in the very torrent, tempest,   5
and as I may say, whirlwind of your passion, you must
acquire and beget° a temperance that may give it smoothness.
O it offends me to the soul, to hear a robustious°
periwig-pated° fellow tear a passion to tatters, to very rags,
to split the ears of the groundlings,° who for the most part   10
are capable of° nothing but inexplicable dumb shows° and
noise: I would have such a fellow whipped for o'erdoing
Termagant:° it out-herods Herod,° pray you avoid it.
1. PLAYER.   I warrant you honour.
HAMLET.   Be not too tame neither, but let your own discretion be   15
your tutor, suit the action to the word, the word to the

---

171 *Haply:* perhaps.   172 *variable:* varied.   173 *something-:* somewhat-.   175 *fashion of himself:* his usual self.   178 *neglected:* unrequited.   183 *round:* direct.   184–185 *in the ear Of:* so as to overhear.   185 *find:* find out.   1 *the speech:* i.e., that Hamlet has inserted.   2 *mouth it:* deliver it slowly and overdramatically.   7 *acquire and beget:* achieve for yourself and instill in other actors.   8 *robustious:* boisterous.   9 *periwig-pated:* wig-wearing.   10 *groundlings:* audience who paid least and stood on the ground floor.   11 *capable of:* able to understand.   13 *dumb shows:* pantomimed synopses of the action to follow (as below).   13 *Termagant:* violent, ranting character in the guild or mystery plays.   *out-herods Herod:* outdoes even Herod, King of Judea (who commanded the slaughter of the innocents and who was a ranting tyrant in the mystery plays).

action, with this special observance, that you o'erstep not
the modesty° of nature: for any thing so o'erdone, is from°
the purpose of playing, whose end both at the first, and
now, was and is, to hold as 'twere the mirror up to nature,   20
to show virtue her own feature, scorn° her own image, and
the very age and body of the time his form and pressure.°
Now this overdone, or come tardy off,° though it make the
unskilful° laugh, cannot but make the judicious grieve, the
censure of the which one,° must in your allowance°   25
o'erweigh a whole theatre of others. O there be players
that I have seen play, and heard others praise, and that
highly (not to speak it profanely) that neither having
th'accent of Christians, nor the gait of Christian, pagan,
nor man, have so strutted and bellowed, that I have   30
thought some of nature's journeymen° had made men, and
not made them well, they imitated humanity so
abominably.

1. PLAYER.   I hope we have reformed that indifferently° with us, sir.

HAMLET.   O reform it altogether, and let those that play your clowns   35
speak no more than is set down for them,° for there be of
them that will themselves laugh, to set on some quantity
of barren° spectators to laugh too, though in the meantime,
some necessary question° of the play be then to be considered:
that's villainous, and shows a most pitiful ambition   40
in the fool that uses it. Go make you ready.   *Exeunt PLAYERS.*

Enter POLONIUS, ROSENCRANTZ, and GUILDENSTERN.

How now my lord, will the king hear this piece of work?

POLONIUS.   And the queen too, and that presently.

HAMLET.   Bid the players make haste.   *Exit POLONIUS.*
Will you two help to hasten them?   45

ROSENCRANTZ.   Ay my lord.   *Exeunt they two.*

HAMLET.   What ho, Horatio!

Enter HORATIO.

HORATIO.   Here sweet lord, at your service.

HAMLET.   Horatio, thou art e'en as just° a man
As e'er my conversation coped withal.°   50

HORATIO.   O my dear lord.

HAMLET.   Nay, do not think I flatter,
For what advancement may I hope from thee,

---

18 *modesty:* moderation.   *from:* away from.   21 *scorn:* that which should be scorned.
22 *age . . . pressure:* shape of the times in its accurate impression.   23 *come tardy off:* understated,
underdone.   24 *unskilful:* unsophisticated.   25 *one:* the judicious.   *allowance:* estimation.   31 *journeymen:* artisans working for others and not yet masters of their trades.
34 *indifferently:* reasonably well.   36 *speak no more . . . them:* stick to their lines.   38 *barren:*
witless.   39 *question:* dialogue.   49 *just:* well balanced.   50 *coped withal:* had to do with.

That no revenue hast but thy good spirits
To feed and clothe thee? Why should the poor be flattered?
No, let the candied° tongue lick° absurd pomp,   55
And crook the pregnant° hinges of the knee
Where thrift may follow fawning.° Dost thou hear,
Since my dear soul was mistress of her choice,
And could of men distinguish her election,°
Sh'hath sealed° thee for herself, for thou hast been   60
As one in suff'ring all that suffers nothing,
A man that Fortune's buffets° and rewards
Hast ta'en with equal thanks; and blest are those
Whose blood° and judgment are so well co-mingled,
That they are not a pipe for Fortune's finger   65
To sound what stop° she please:° give me that man
That is not passion's slave, and I will wear him
In my heart's core, ay in my heart of heart,
As I do thee. Something too much of this.
There is a play tonight before the king,   70
One scene of it comes near the circumstance
Which I have told thee of my father's death.
I prithee when thou seest that act afoot,
Even with the very comment° of thy soul
Observe my uncle: if his occulted° guilt   75
Do not itself unkennel° in one speech,
It is a damnèd ghost° that we have seen,
And my imaginations are as foul
As Vulcan's stithy;° give him heedful note,
For I mine eyes will rivet to his face,   80
And after we will both our judgments join
In censure of his seeming.°
HORATIO.   Well my lord,
If a' steal aught the whilst this play is playing,
And 'scape detecting, I will pay° the theft.   *Sound a flourish.*
HAMLET.   They are coming to the play. I must be idle,°   85
Get you a place.

Enter Trumpets and Kettledrums, KING, QUEEN, POLONIUS, OPHELIA, ROSENCRANTZ, GUILD-
ENSTERN, and other LORDS attendant, with his GUARD carrying torches. Danish March.

KING.   How fares° our cousin Hamlet?

55–57 *candied . . . fawning:* (metaphor of a dog licking and fawning for candy).   55 *candied:* flattering.   *lick:* pay court to.   56–57 *crook . . . fawning:* obsequiously kneel when personal profit
may ensue.   56 *pregnant:* quick in motion.   59 *election:* choice.   60 *sealed:*
confirmed.   62 *buffets:* blows.   64 *blood:* passions.   66 *sound . . . please:* play whatever tune
she likes.   *stop:* finger hole in wind instrument for varying the sound.   74 *very comment:*
acutest observation.   75 *occulted:* hidden.   76 *unkennel:* force from hiding.   77 *damnèd
ghost:* devil (not the ghost of my father).   79 *Vulcan's stithy:* the forge of the blacksmith of the
gods.   82 *censure . . . seeming:* (1) judgment of his appearance (2) disapproval of his pretending.   84 *pay:* i.e., for.   85 *be idle:* act mad.   87 *fares:* does, but Hamlet takes it to mean
"eats" or "dines."

HAMLET.   Excellent i'faith, of the chameleon's dish: I eat the air,°
    promise-crammed, you cannot feed capons so.°

KING.   I have nothing with° this answer Hamlet, these words are   90
    not mine.°

HAMLET.   No, nor mine now. [*To Polonius.*] My lord, you played
    once i'th'university you say?

POLONIUS.   That did I my lord, and was accounted a good actor.

HAMLET.   What did you enact?   95

POLONIUS.   I did enact Julius Caesar, I was killed i'th'Capitol, Brutus
    killed me.

HAMLET.   It was a brute part of him to kill so capital a calf there. Be
    the players ready?

ROSENCRANTZ.   Ay my lord, they stay upon your patience.°   100

QUEEN.   Come hither my dear Hamlet, sit by me.

HAMLET.   No, good mother, here's metal more attractive.°

POLONIUS.   [*To the King.*] O ho, do you mark that?

HAMLET.   Lady, shall I lie in your lap?

OPHELIA.   No my lord.   105

HAMLET.   I mean, my head upon your lap?

OPHELIA.   Ay my lord.

HAMLET.   Do you think I meant country° matters?

OPHELIA.   I think nothing my lord.

HAMLET.   That's a fair thought to lie between maids' legs.   110

OPHELIA.   What is, my lord?

HAMLET.   Nothing.

OPHELIA.   You are merry my lord.

HAMLET.   Who, I?

OPHELIA.   Ay my lord.   115

HAMLET.   O God, your only jig-maker: what should a man do but be
    merry, for look you how cheerfully my mother looks, and
    my father died within's two hours.

OPHELIA.   Nay, 'tis twice two months my lord.

HAMLET.   So long? Nay then let the devil wear black, for I'll have a   120
    suit of sables;° O heavens, die two months ago, and not
    forgotten yet? Then there's hope a great man's memory
    may outlive his life half a year, but by'r lady° a' must build
    churches then, or else shall a' suffer not thinking on,° with
    the hobby-horse,° whose epitaph is "For O, for O, the   125
    hobby-horse is forgot."

---

88 *eat the air:* the chamelion supposedly ate air, but Hamlet also puns on "heir."   89 *you cannot . . .
so:* (1) even a capon cannot feed on air and your promises (2) like a capon stuffed with food before
being killed, I am stuffed (fed up) with your promises.   90 *nothing with:* nothing to do
with.   91 *not mine:* not in answer to my question.   100 *stay . . . patience:* await your permission.   102 *metal more attractive:* (1) iron more magnetic (2) stuff ("mettle") more
beautiful.   108 *country:* rustic, sexual (with a pun on a slang word for the female sexual
organ).   121 *sables:* (1) rich fur (2) black mourning garb.   123 *by'r lady:* by Our Lady (the
Virgin Mary).   124 *not thinking on:* being forgotten.   125 *hobby-horse:* (1) character in the
May games (2) slang for "prostitute."

*The trumpets sound. The Dumb Show° follows. Enter a King and a Queen, very lovingly, the Queen embracing him, and he her. She kneels and makes show of protestation unto him. He takes her up, and declines his head upon her neck. He lies him down upon a bank of flowers; she seeing him asleep leaves him: anon comes in another man, takes off his crown, kisses it, pours poison in the sleeper's ears, and leaves him: the Queen returns, finds the King dead, and makes passionate action. The poisoner with some three or four mutes° comes in again, seeming to condole with her. The dead body is carried away. The poisoner wooes the Queen with gifts: she seems harsh and unwilling awhile, but in the end accepts his love.
Exeunt.*

OPHELIA.   What means this, my lord?
HAMLET.   Marry, this is miching mallecho,° it means mischief.
OPHELIA.   Belike this show imports the argument° of the play.

Enter PROLOGUE.

HAMLET.   We shall know by this fellow: the players cannot keep   130
    counsel,° they'll tell all.
OPHELIA.   Will a' tell us what this show meant?
HAMLET.   Ay, or any show that you will show him. Be not you
    ashamed to show, he'll not shame to tell you what it
    means.   135
OPHELIA.   You are naught,° you are naught, I'll mark the play.
PROLOGUE.   For us and for our tragedy,
    Here stooping to your clemency,
    We beg your hearing patiently.   *[Exit.]*
HAMLET.   Is this a prologue, or the posy° of a ring?   140
OPHELIA.   'Tis brief, my lord.
HAMLET.   As woman's love.

Enter Player KING and QUEEN.

PLAYER KING.   Full thirty times hath Phoebus' cart° gone round
    Neptune's salt wash,° and Tellus' orbèd ground,°
    And thirty dozen moons with borrowed sheen   145
    About the world have times twelve thirties been,
    Since love our hearts, and Hymen° did our hands
    Unite commutual,° in most sacred bands.
PLAYER QUEEN.   So many journeys may the sun and moon
    Make us again count o'er ere love be done,   150
    But woe is me, you are so sick of late,
    So far from cheer, and from your former state,
    That I distrust you:° yet though I distrust,
    Discomfort you, my lord, it nothing must.
    For women fear too much, even as they love,   155

126 S.D.: *Dumb Show:* pantomimed synopsis of the action to follow.   126 S.D.: *mutes:* actors without speaking parts.   128 *miching mallecho:* skulking mischief.   129 *imports the argument:* signifies the plot.   131 *counsel:* a secret.   136 *naught:* naughty, lewd.   140 *posy:* motto (engraved in a ring).   143 *Phoebus' cart:* chariot of the sun.   144 *wash:* sea.   *Tellus' . . . ground:* the earth (Tellus was a Roman earth goddess).   147 *Hymen:* Roman god of marriage.   148 *commutual:* mutually.   153 *distrust you:* am worried about you.

And women's fear and love hold quantity,°
In neither aught, or in extremity:°
Now what my love is, proof° hath made you know,
And as my love is sized, my fear is so.
Where love is great, the littlest doubts are fear,   160
Where little fears grow great, great love grows there.
PLAYER KING.   Faith, I must leave thee love, and shortly too,
   My operant° powers their functions leave° to do,
   And thou shalt live in this fair world behind,
   Honoured, beloved, and haply° one as kind   165
   For husband shalt thou—
PLAYER QUEEN.   O confound the rest:
   Such love must needs be treason in my breast.
   In second husband let me be accurst,
   None wed the second, but who killed the first.
HAMLET.   [*Aside.*] That's wormwood,° wormwood.   170
PLAYER QUEEN.   The instances° that second marriage move°
   Are base respects of thrift,° but none of love.
   A second time I kill my husband dead,
   When second husband kisses me in bed.
PLAYER KING.   I do believe you think what now you speak,   175
   But what we do determine, oft we break:
   Purpose is but the slave to memory,
   Of violent birth but poor validity:°
   Which now like fruit unripe sticks on the tree,
   But fall unshaken when they mellow be.   180
   Most necessary 'tis that we forget
   To pay ourselves what to ourselves is debt:°
   What to ourselves in passion we propose,
   The passion ending, doth the purpose lose.
   The violence of either grief or joy   185
   Their own enactures° with themselves destroy:
   Where joy most revels, grief doth most lament;
   Grief joys, joy grieves, on slender accident.
   This world is not for aye,° nor 'tis not strange
   That even our loves should with our fortunes change: 190
   For 'tis a question left us yet to prove,
   Whether love lead fortune, or else fortune love.°
   The great man down, you mark his favourite flies,
   The poor advanced, makes friends of enemies:
   And hitherto doth love on fortune tend,   195
   For who not needs, shall never lack a friend,
   And who in want a hollow friend doth try,

---

156 *quantity:* proportion.   157 *In neither . . . extremity:* their love and fear are either absent or
excessive.   158 *proof:* experience.   163 *operant:* vital.   *leave:* cease.   165 *haply:* perhaps.   170 *wormwood:* bitter (like the herb).   171 *instances:* causes.   *move:* moti-
vate.   172 *respects of thrift:* consideration of profit.   178 *validity:* strength.   181–182
Most . . . debt: we are easy creditors to ourselves and forget our former promises (debts).   186
enactures: fulfillments.   189 *aye:* ever.   192 *fortune love:* fortune lead love.

Directly seasons him° his enemy.
But orderly to end where I begun,
Our wills and fates do so contrary run,   200
That our devices still° are overthrown,
Our thoughts are ours, their ends none of our own.
So think thou wilt no second husband wed,
But die thy thoughts when thy first lord is dead.
PLAYER QUEEN.   Nor earth to me give food, nor heaven light,   205
 Sport and repose lock from me day and night,
 To desperation turn my trust and hope,
 An anchor's° cheer in prison be my scope,
 Each opposite that blanks° the face of joy,
 Meet what I would have well, and it destroy,   210
 Both here and hence° pursue me lasting strife,
 If once a widow, ever I be wife.
HAMLET.   If she should break it now.
PLAYER KING.   'Tis deeply sworn: sweet, leave me here awhile,
 My spirits grow dull, and fain° I would beguile   215
 The tedious day with sleep.   *Sleeps.*
PLAYER QUEEN.   Sleep rock thy brain.
 And never come mischance between us twain.   *Exit.*
HAMLET.   Madam, how like you this play?
QUEEN.   The lady doth protest too much methinks.
HAMLET.   O but she'll keep her word.   220
KING.   Have you heard the argument°? Is there no offence in't?
HAMLET.   No, no, they do but jest, poison in jest, no offence
 i'th'world.
KING.   What do you call the play?
HAMLET.   The Mouse-trap. Marry, how? Tropically:° this play is the   225
 image of a murder done in Vienna: Gonzago is the duke's
 name, his wife Baptista, you shall see anon, 'tis a knavish
 piece of work, but what of that? Your majesty, and we
 that have free° souls, it touches us not: let the galled jade
 winch,° our withers are unwrung.°   230

Enter LUCIANUS.

 This is one Lucianus, nephew to the king.
OPHELIA.   You are as good as a chorus,° my lord.
HAMLET.   I could interpret between you and your love, if I could see
 the puppets dallying.
OPHELIA.   You are keen my lord, you are keen.°   235
HAMLET.   It would cost you a groaning to take off mine edge.

---

198 *seasons him:* causes him to become.   201 *devices still:* plans always.   208 *anchor's:* hermit's.   209 *opposite that blanks:* contrary event that pales.   211 *here and hence:* in this world and the next.   215 *fain:* gladly.   221 *argument:* plot.   225 *Tropically:* figuratively.   229 *free:* innocent.   229–230 *galled jade winch:* chafed old horse wince (from its sores).   230 *withers are unwrung:* (1) shoulders are unchafed (2) consciences are clear. 232 *chorus:* actor who introduced the action.   235 *keen:* (1) sharp (Ophelia's meaning) (2) sexually excited (Hamlet's interpretation).

OPHELIA.   Still better and worse.°

HAMLET.   So you mistake° your husbands. Begin, murderer. Pox,°
    leave thy damnable faces° and begin. Come, the croaking
    raven doth bellow for revenge.   240

LUCIANUS.   Thoughts black, hands apt, drugs fit, and time agreeing,
    Confederate season, else no creature seeing,°
    Thou mixture rank, of midnight weeds collected,
    With Hecate's° ban° thrice blasted, thrice infected,
    Thy natural magic, and dire property,   245
    On wholesome° life usurps immediately.   *Pours the poison in his ears.*

HAMLET.   A' poisons him i'th'garden for's estate, his name's Gonzago,
    the story is extant, and written in very choice
    Italian, you shall see anon how the murderer gets the love
    of Gonzago's wife.   250

OPHELIA.   The king rises.

HAMLET.   What, frighted with false fire°?

QUEEN.   How fares my lord?

POLONIUS.   Give o'er the play.

KING.   Give me some light. Away!   255

ALL.   Lights, lights, lights!   *Exeunt all but* HAMLET *and* HORATIO.

HAMLET.   Why, let the stricken deer go weep,
        The hart ungallèd° play,°
    For some must watch while some must sleep,
        Thus runs the world away.   260
    Would not this° sir, and a forest of feathers,° if the rest of my
    fortunes turn Turk with° me, with two Provincial roses° on
    my razed° shoes, get me a fellowship° in a cry° of players?

HORATIO.   Half a share.°

HAMLET.   A whole one, I.   265
    For thou dost know, O Damon° dear,
        This realm dismantled was
    Of Jove° himself, and now reigns here
        A very very—pajock.°

HORATIO.   You might have rhymed.°   270

HAMLET.   O good Horatio, I'll take the ghost's word for a thousand
    pound. Didst perceive?

HORATIO.   Very well my lord.

---

237 *better and worse:* better wit but a worse meaning, with a pun on "better" and "bitter."   238 *mistake:* mis-take.   *Pox:* a plague on it.   239 *faces:* exaggerated facial expressions. 242 *Confederate . . . seeing:* no one seeing me except time, my confederate.   244 *Hecate:* goddess of witchcraft.   *ban:* evil spell.   246 *wholesome:* healthy.   252 *false fire:* discharge of blanks (not gunpowder).   257–258 *deer . . . play:* (the belief that a wounded deer wept, abandoned by the others).   258 *ungallèd:* unhurt.   261 *this:* i.e., sample (of my theatrical talent).   *feathers:* plumes (worn by actors).   262 *turn Turk with:* cruelly turn against.   *Provincial roses:* rosettes named for Provins, France.   263 *razed:* slashed, decorated with cutouts.   *fellowship:* partnership.   *cry:* pack, troupe.   264 *share:* divisions of profits among members of a theatrical production company.   266 *Damon:* legendary ideal friend to Pythias.   268 *Jove:* (Hamlet's father).   269 *pajock:* peacock (associated with lechery).   270 *rhymed:* (used "ass" instead of "pajock").

HAMLET.   Upon the talk of the poisoning?

HORATIO.   I did very well note him.   275

Enter ROSENCRANTZ and GUILDENSTERN.

HAMLET.   Ah ha, come, some music. Come, the recorders.°
  For if the king like not the comedy,
  Why then belike he likes it not, perdy.°
  Come, some music.

GUILDENSTERN.   Good my lord, vouchsafe me a word with you.   280

HAMLET.   Sir, a whole history.

GUILDENSTERN.   The king, sir—

HAMLET.   Ay sir, what of him?

GUILDENSTERN.   Is in his retirement, marvellous distempered.

HAMLET.   With drink sir?   285

GUILDENSTERN.   No my lord, with choler.°

HAMLET.   Your wisdom should show itself more richer to signify
  this to the doctor: for, for me to put him to his purgation,°
  would perhaps plunge him into more choler.

GUILDENSTERN.   Good my lord, put your discourse into some frame,° and   290
  start not so wildly from my affair.

HAMLET.   I am tame sir, pronounce.

GUILDENSTERN.   The queen your mother, in most great affliction of spirit,
  hath sent me to you.

HAMLET.   You are welcome.   295

GUILDENSTERN.   Nay good my lord, this courtesy is not of the right breed.°
  If it shall please you to make me a wholesome° answer, I
  will do your mother's commandment: if not, your pardon°
  and my return shall be the end of my business.

HAMLET.   Sir I cannot.   300

ROSENCRANTZ.   What, my lord?

HAMLET.   Make you a wholesome answer: my wit's diseased. But
  sir, such answer as I can make, you shall command, or
  rather as you say, my mother: therefore no more, but to
  the matter. My mother you say.   305

ROSENCRANTZ.   Then thus she says, your behaviour hath struck her into
  amazement and admiration.°

HAMLET.   O wonderful son that can so 'stonish a mother. But is there
  no sequel at the heels of this mother's admiration? Impart.

ROSENCRANTZ.   She desires to speak with you in her closet°   310
  ere you go to bed.

HAMLET.   We shall obey, were she ten times our mother. Have you
  any further trade with us?

ROSENCRANTZ.   My lord, you once did love me.

---

276 *recorders:* soft-toned woodwind instruments, similar to flutes.   278 *perdy:* by God (*par dieu*).   286 *choler:* anger.   288 *purgation:* (1) purging of excessive bile (2) judicial investigations (3) purgatory.   290 *frame:* order.   296 *breed:* (1) species (2) manners.   297 *wholesome:* reasonable.   298 *pardon:* permission to depart.   307 *admiration:* wonder.   310 *closet:* private room, bedroom.

HAMLET.   And do still, by these pickers and stealers.°   315
ROSENCRANTZ.   Good my lord, what is your cause of distemper? You do
    surely bar the door upon your own liberty, if you deny
    your griefs to your friend.°
HAMLET.   Sir, I lack advancement.
ROSENCRANTZ.   How can that be, when you have the voice° of the king   320
    himself for your succession in Denmark?
HAMLET.   Ay sir, but 'while the grass grows'°—the proverb is
    something musty.°

Enter the PLAYERS with recorders.

    O the recorders, let me see one. To withdraw° with you,
    why do you go about to recover the wind of me,° as if you   325
    would drive me into a toil°?
GUILDENSTERN.   O my lord, if my duty be too bold, my love is too
    unmannerly.°
HAMLET.   I do not well understand that. Will you play
    upon this pipe°?   330
GUILDENSTERN.   My lord I cannot.
HAMLET.   I pray you.
GUILDENSTERN.   Believe me. I cannot.
HAMLET.   I do beseech you.
GUILDENSTERN.   I know no touch of it° my lord.   335
HAMLET.   It is as easy as lying; govern these ventages° with your
    fingers and thumb, give it breath with your mouth, and it
    will discourse most eloquent music. Look you, these are
    the stops.
GUILDENSTERN.   But these cannot I command to any utt'rance of harmony,   340
    I have not the skill.
HAMLET.   Why look you now how unworthy a thing you make of
    me: you would play upon me, you would seem to know
    my stops, you would pluck out the heart of my mystery,
    you would sound me from my lowest note to the top of my   345
    compass:° and there is much music, excellent voice in this
    little organ,° yet cannot you make it speak. 'Sblood, do you
    think I am easier to be played on than a pipe? Call me what
    instrument you will, though you can fret° me, you cannot
    play upon me.   350

Enter POLONIUS.

    God bless you sir.

315 *pickers and stealers:* hands (from the prayer, "Keep my hands from picking and stealing").
317–318 *deny . . . friend:* refuse to let your friend know the cause of your suffering.   320 *voice:*
vote.   322 *while . . . grows:* (the proverb ends: "the horse starves").   323 *something musty:*
somewhat too old and trite (to finish).   324 *withdraw:* speak privately.   325 *recover . . . me:*
drive me toward the wind, as with a prey, to avoid its scenting the hunter.   326 *toil:* snare.
327–328 *is too unmannerly:* makes me forget my good manners.   330 *pipe:* recorder.
335 *know . . . it:* have no skill at fingering it.   336 *ventages:* holes, stops.   346 *compass:*
range.   347 *organ:* musical instrument.   349 *fret:* (1) irritate (2) play an instrument that
has "frets" or bars to guide the fingering.

POLONIUS.　My lord, the queen would speak with you, and presently.

HAMLET.　Do you see yonder cloud that's almost in shape of a camel?

POLONIUS.　By th'mass and 'tis, like a camel indeed.

HAMLET.　Methinks it is like a weasel.　　　　　　　　　　　　　　　　355

POLONIUS.　It is backed like a weasel.

HAMLET.　Or like a whale?

POLONIUS.　Very like a whale.

HAMLET.　Then I will come to my mother by and by.°

　　　[*Aside.*] They fool me to the top of my bent.°　　　　　　　360

　　　I will come by and by.

POLONIUS.　I will say so.　　　　　　　　　　　　　　　　　　*Exit.*

HAMLET.　"By and by" is easily said.

　　　Leave me, friends.　　　　　　　　　　　[*Exeunt all but* HAMLET.]

　　　'Tis now the very witching time of night.　　　　　　　　365

　　　When churchyards yawn,° and hell itself breathes out

　　　Contagion° to this world: now could I drink hot blood,

　　　And do such bitter business as the day

　　　Would quake to look on: soft, now to my mother—

　　　O heart, lose not thy nature,° let not ever　　　　　　　370

　　　The soul of Nero° enter this firm bosom,

　　　Let me be cruel, not unnatural.

　　　I will speak daggers to her, but use none:

　　　My tongue and soul in this be hypocrites,°

　　　How in my words somever she be shent,°　　　　　　　　375

　　　To give them seals,° never my soul consent.　　　　　　*Exit.*

Scene 3. [*A room in the castle*]

Enter KING, ROSENCRANTZ, *and* GUILDENSTERN.

KING.　I like him not, nor stands it safe with us

　　　To let his madness range. Therefore prepare you,

　　　I your commission will forthwith dispatch,°

　　　And he to England shall along with you:

　　　The terms of our estate° may not endure　　　　　　　　5

　　　Hazard so near's° as doth hourly grow

　　　Out of his brows.°

GUILDENSTERN.　　　We will ourselves provide:°

　　　Most holy and religious fear it is

　　　To keep those many many bodies safe

　　　That live and feed upon your majesty.　　　　　　　　10

ROSENCRANTZ.　The single and peculiar° life is bound

　　　With all the strength and armour of the mind

---

359 *by and by:* very soon.　　　360 *fool me . . . bent:* force me to play the fool to my utmost.
366 *churchyards yawn:* graves open.　　367 *Contagion:* (1) evil (2) diseases.　　　370 *nature:* natural affection.　　371 *Nero:* (who killed his mother).　　374 *My tongue . . . hypocrites:* I will speak cruelly but intend no harm.　　375 *shent:* chastised.　　376 *give them seals:* confirm them with action (as a legal "deed" is confirmed with a "seal").　　3 *forthwith dispatch:* immediately have prepared.　　5 *terms . . . estate:* circumstances of my royal office.　　6 *near's:* near us.　　7 *brows:* effronteries.　　*provide:* prepare.　　11 *peculiar:* individual.

To keep itself from noyance,° but much more
That spirit, upon whose weal° depends and rests
The lives of many; the cess° of majesty   15
Dies not alone, but like a gulf° doth draw
What's near it, with it. O 'tis a massy wheel
Fixed on the summit of the highest mount,
To whose huge spokes, ten thousand lesser things
Are mortised° and adjoined, which when it falls,   20
Each small annexment, petty consequence,
Attends° the boist'rous ruin. Never alone
Did the king sigh, but with a general groan.

KING.   Arm° you I pray you, to this speedy voyage,
For we will fetters put about this fear,   25
Which now goes too free-footed.

ROSENCRANTZ.   We will haste us.

                               Exeunt [ROSENCRANTZ *and* GUILDENSTERN.]

Enter POLONIUS.

POLONIUS.   My lord, he's going to his mother's closet:
Behind the arras I'll convey myself
To hear the process.° I'll warrant she'll tax him home,
And as you said, and wisely was it said,   30
'Tis meet° that some more audience than a mother,
Since nature makes them partial, should o'erhear
The speech of vantage;° fare you well my liege,°
I'll call upon you ere you go to bed,
And tell you what I know.

KING.   Thanks, dear my lord.   *Exit* [POLONIUS.]   35
O my offence is rank, it smells to heaven,
It hath the primal eldest curse° upon't,
A brother's murder. Pray can I not,
Though inclination be as sharp as will:°
My stronger guilt defeats my strong intent,   40
And like a man to double business bound,
I stand in pause where I shall first begin,
And both neglect; what if this cursèd hand
Were thicker than itself with brother's blood,
Is there not rain enough in the sweet heavens   45
To wash it white as snow? Whereto serves mercy
But to confront the visage of offence°?
And what's in prayer but this two-fold force,
To be forestallèd° ere we come to fall,
Or pardoned being down? Then I'll look up,   50

---

13 *noyance:* harm.   14 *weal:* well-being.   15 *cess:* cessation, death.   16 *gulf:* whirl-
pool.   20 *mortised:* securely fitted.   22 *Attends:* accompanies.   24 *Arm:* prepare.   29
the process: what proceeds.   31 *meet:* fitting.   33 *of vantage:* from an advantageous
position.   *liege:* lord.   37 *primal . . . curse:* curse of Cain.   39 *inclination . . . will:* my desire
to pray is as strong as my determination to do so.   47 *confront . . . offence:* plead in man's behalf
against sin (at the Last Judgment).   49 *forestallèd:* prevented.

My fault is past. But O what form of prayer
Can serve my turn? "Forgive me my foul murder":
That cannot be, since I am still possessed
Of those effects° for which I did the murder:
My crown, mine own ambition, and my queen.   55
May one be pardoned and retain th'offence?
In the corrupted currents of this world,
Offence's gilded hand may shove by justice,
And oft 'tis seen the wicked prize itself
Buys out the law;° but 'tis not so above,   60
There is no shuffling,° there the action lies
In his true nature,° and we ourselves compelled
Even to the teeth and forehead of our faults°
To give in evidence. What then? What rests°?
Try what repentance can. What can it not?   65
Yet what can it, when one can not repent?
O wretched state? O bosom black as death!
O limèd soul, that struggling to be free,
Art more engaged;° help, angels, make assay:°
Bow stubborn knees, and heart with strings of steel,   70
Be soft as sinews of the new-born babe,
All may be well.   [*He kneels.*]

Enter HAMLET.

HAMLET.   Now might I do it pat,° now a' is a-praying,
      And now I'll do't, [*Draws his sword.*] and so a' goes to heaven,
      And so am I revenged: that would be scanned:°   75
      A villain kills my father, and for that,
      I his sole son, do this same villain send
      To heaven.
      Why, this is hire and salary, not revenge.
      A' took my father grossly,° full of bread,°   80
      With all his crimes° broad blown,° as flush° as May,
      And how his audit° stands who knows save heaven,
      But in our circumstance and course of thought,
      'Tis heavy° with him: and am I then revenged
      To take him in the purging of his soul,   85
      when he is fit and seasoned° for his passage?
      No.   [*Sheathes his sword.*]
      Up sword, and know thou a more horrid hent,°

54 *effects:* results.   59–60 *wicked . . . law:* fruits of the crime bribe the judge.   61 *shuffling:*
evasion.   61–62 *action . . . nature:* (1) deed is seen in its true nature (2) legal action is sustained
according to the truth.   63 *to the teeth . . . faults:* meeting our sins face to face.   64 *rests:*
remains.   68–69 *limèd . . . engaged:* like a bird caught in lime (a sticky substance spread on twigs
as a snare), the soul in its struggle to clear itself only becomes more entangled.   69 *make assay:*
I'll make an attempt.   73 *pat:* opportunely.   75 *would be scanned:* needs closer examination.   80 *grossly:* unpurified (by final rites).   *bread:* self-indulgence.   81 *crimes:*
sins.   *broad blown:* in full flower.   *flush:* lusty.   82 *audit:* account.   84 *heavy:* grievous.   86 *seasoned:* ready (prepared).   88 *horrid hent:* horrible opportunity ("hint") for
seizure ("hent") by me.

When he is drunk asleep, or in his rage,
Or in th'incestuous pleasure of his bed,   90
At game, a-swearing, or about some act
That has no relish° of salvation in't,
Then trip him that his heels may kick at heaven,
And that his soul may be as damned and black
As hell whereto it goes; my mother stays,   95
This physic° but prolongs thy sickly days.   *Exit.*
KING.   [*Rises.*] My words fly up, my thoughts remain below,
    Words without thoughts never to heaven go.   *Exit.*

Scene 4. [*The queen's closet*]

Enter QUEEN *and* POLONIUS.

POLONIUS.   A' will come straight, look you lay home° to him,
    Tell him his pranks have been too broad° to bear with,
    And that your grace hath screened and stood between
    Much heat° and him. I'll silence me° even here:
    Pray you be round with him.   5
HAMLET.   [*Within.*] Mother, mother, mother.
QUEEN.   I'll war'nt you,
    Fear me not. Withdraw, I hear him coming. [POLONIUS *hides behind the arras.*]

Enter HAMLET.

HAMLET.   Now mother, what's the matter?
QUEEN.   Hamlet, thou hast thy father much offended.
HAMLET.   Mother, you have my father much offended.   10
QUEEN.   Come, come, you answer with an idle° tongue.
HAMLET.   Go, go, you question with a wicked tongue.
QUEEN.   Why, how now Hamlet?
HAMLET.   What's the matter now?
QUEEN.   Have you forgot me?
HAMLET.   No by the rood,° not so,
    You are the queen, your husband's brother's wife,   15
    And would it were not so, you are my mother.
QUEEN.   Nay, then I'll set those to you that can speak.°
HAMLET.   Come, come, and sit you down, you shall not budge,
    You go not till I set you up a glass°
    Where you may see the inmost part of you.   20
QUEEN.   What wilt thou do? Thou wilt not murder me?
    Help, help, ho!
POLONIUS.   [*Behind the arras.*] What ho! help, help, help!
HAMLET.   How now, a rat? dead for a ducat,° dead.

                   Kills POLONIUS [*through the arras.*]

92 *relish:* taste.   96 *physic:* (1) medicine (2) purgation of your soul by prayer.   1 *lay home:*
thrust home; speak sharply.   2 *broad:* unrestrained.   4 *heat:* anger.   *silence me:* hide in
silence.   11 *idle:* foolish.   14 *rood:* cross.   17 *speak:* i.e., to you as you should be spoken
to.   19 *glass:* looking glass.   23 *for a ducat:* I wager a ducat (an Italian gold coin).

POLONIUS.   O I am slain!

QUEEN.   O me, what hast thou done?

HAMLET.   Nay I know not,   25
    Is it the king?

QUEEN.   O what a rash and bloody deed is this!

HAMLET.   A bloody deed, almost as bad, good mother,
    As kill a king, and marry with his brother.

QUEEN.   As kill a king?

HAMLET.   Ay lady, it was my word.   30
    [*To Polonius.*] Thou wretched, rash, intruding fool, farewell,
    I took thee for thy better,° take thy fortune,
    Thou find'st to be too busy is some danger.
    [*To the Queen.*] Leave wringing of your hands, peace, sit you down,
    And let me wring your heart, for so I shall   35
    If it be made of penetrable stuff,
    If damnèd custom° have not brazed° it so,
    That it be proof° and bulwark against sense.°

QUEEN.   What have I done, that thou dar'st wag thy tongue
    In noise so rude against me?

HAMLET.   Such an act   40
    That blurs the grace and blush of modesty,
    Calls virtue hypocrite, takes off the rose°
    From the fair forehead of an innocent love
    And sets a blister there,° makes marriage vows
    As false as dicers' oaths, O such a deed,   45
    As from the body of contraction° plucks
    The very soul, and sweet religion makes
    A rhapsody° of words; heaven's face does glow,°
    Yea this solidity and compound mass°
    With heated visage, as against the doom,°   50
    Is thought-sick at the act.

QUEEN.   Ay me, what act,
    That roars so loud, and thunders in the index°?

HAMLET.   Look here upon this picture, and on this,
    The counterfeit presentment° of two brothers:
    See what a grace was seated on this brow,   55
    Hyperion's° curls, the front° of Jove himself,
    An eye like Mars, to threaten and command,
    A station° like the herald Mercury,
    New-lighted on a heaven-kissing hill,
    A combination and a form indeed,   60
    Where every god did seem to set his seal

---

32 *thy better:* the king.   37 *custom:* habit.   *brazed:* brass-plated (brazened).   38 *proof:* armor.   *sense:* sensibility.   42 *rose:* (symbol of perfection and innocence).   44 *blister there:* (whores were punished by being branded on the forehead).   46 *body of contraction:* marriage contract.   48 *rhapsody:* (meaningless) mixture.   *glow:* blush.   49 *solidity . . . mass:* solid earth, compounded of the four elements.   50 *against the doom:* expecting Judgment Day.   52 *index:* (1) table of contents (2) prologue.   54 *counterfeit presentment:* painted likeness.   56 *Hyperion:* Greek sun god.   *front:* forehead.   58 *station:* bearing.

To give the world assurance of a man.
This was your husband. Look you now what follows.
Here is your husband, like a mildewed ear,°
Blasting° his wholesome brother. Have you eyes?   65
Could you on this fair mountain leave to feed,°
And batten° on this moor? Ha! Have you eyes?
You cannot call it love, for at your age
The hey-day in the blood° is tame, it's humble,
And waits upon the judgment, and what judgment   70
Would step from this to this? Sense° sure you have
Else could you not have motion,° but sure that sense
Is apoplexed,° for madness would not err,
Nor sense to ecstasy was ne'er so thralled°
But it reserved some quantity of choice   75
To serve in such a difference.° What devil was't
That thus hath cozened you at hoodman-blind°?
Eyes without feeling, feeling without sight,
Ears without hands or eyes, smelling sans all,°
Or but a sickly part of one true sense   80
Could not so mope:° O shame, where is thy blush?
Rebellious hell,
If thou canst mutine in a matron's bones,
To flaming youth let virtue be as wax
And melt in her own fire. Proclaim no shame   85
When the compulsive° ardour gives the charge,°
Since frost itself as actively doth burn,
And reason panders will.°
QUEEN.   O Hamlet, speak no more,
Thou turn'st my eyes into my very soul,
And there I see such black and grainèd° spots   90
As will not leave their tinct.°
HAMLET.   Nay, but to live
In the rank sweat of an enseamèd° bed,
Stewed in corruption, honeying, and making love
Over the nasty sty.
QUEEN.   O speak to me no more,
These words like daggers enter in mine ears,   95
No more, sweet Hamlet.
HAMLET.   A murderer and a villain,
A slave that is not twentieth part the tithe°

---

64 *ear:* i.e., of grain.   65 *Blasting:* blighting.   66 *leave to feed:* leave off feeding.   67 *batten:* gorge yourself.   69 *hey-day in the blood:* youthful passion.   71 *Sense:* perception by the senses.   72 *motion:* impulse.   73 *apoplexed:* paralyzed.   74 *sense . . . thralled:* sensibility was never so enslaved by madness.   76 *in . . . difference:* where the difference was so great.   77 *cozened . . . blind:* cheated you at blindman's bluff.   79 *sans all:* without the other senses.   81 *so mope:* be so dull.   86 *compulsive:* compelling.   *gives the charge:* attacks.   88 *panders will:* pimps for lust.   90 *grainèd:* dyed in grain, unfading.   91 *leave their tinct:* lose their color.   92 *enseamèd:* greasy.   97 *tithe:* one-tenth part.

Of your precedent lord, a vice° of kings,
A cutpurse° of the empire and the rule,
That from a shelf the precious diadem stole   100
And put it in his pocket.

QUEEN.   No more.

HAMLET.   A king of shreds and patches—

Enter the GHOST in his night-gown.°

Save me and hover o'er me with your wings,
You heavenly guards. What would your gracious figure?

QUEEN.   Alas, he's mad.   105

HAMLET.   Do you not come your tardy son to chide,
That lapsed in time and passion° lets go by
Th'important acting of your dread command?
O say!

GHOST.   Do not forget: this visitation   110
Is but to whet thy almost blunted purpose.
But look, amazement on thy mother sits,
O step between her and her fighting soul,
Conceit° in weakest bodies strongest works,
Speak to her Hamlet.

HAMLET.   How is it with you lady?   115

QUEEN.   Alas, how is't with you,
That you do bend your eye on vacancy,°
And with th'incorporal° air do hold discourse?
Forth at your eyes your spirits° wildly peep,
And as the sleeping soldiers in th'alarm,   120
Your bedded° hairs, like life in excrements,°
Start up and stand an° end. O gentle son,
Upon the heat and flame of thy distemper
sprinkle cool patience. Whereon do you look?

HAMLET.   On him, on him, look you how pale he glares,   125
His form and cause conjoined, preaching to stones,
Would make them capable.° Do not look upon me,
Lest with this piteous action you convert
My stern effects,° then what I have to do
Will want° true colour,° tears perchance for blood.   130

QUEEN.   To whom do you speak this?

HAMLET.   Do you see nothing there?

QUEEN.   Nothing at all, yet all that is I see.

HAMLET.   Nor did you nothing hear?

---

98 *vice:* buffoon (like the character of Vice in the morality plays).   99 *cutpurse:* pick-
pocket.   102.1 S.D.: *night-gown:* dressing gown.   107 *lapsed . . . passion:* having let time
elapse and passion cool.   114 *Conceit:* imagination.   117 *vacancy:* (she cannot see the
ghost).   118 *incorporal:* bodiless.   119 *spirits:* vital forces.   121 *bedded:* lying flat.   *excrements:* outgrowths (of the body).   122 *an:* on.   127 *capable:* i.e., of feeling pity.   128–129
convert . . . effects: transform my outward signs of sternness.   130 *want:* lack.   *colour:* (1)
complexion (2) motivation.

QUEEN.   No, nothing but ourselves.
HAMLET.   Why look you there, look how it steals away,
    My father in his habit as he lived,°   135
    Look where he goes, even now out at the portal.   *Exit* [*GHOST.*]
QUEEN.   This is the very coinage of your brain,
    This bodiless creation ecstasy
    Is very cunning in.°
HAMLET.   Ecstasy?
    My pulse as yours doth temperately keep time,   140
    And makes as healthful music. It is not madness
    That I have uttered; bring me to the test
    And I the matter will re-word, which madness
    Would gambol° from. Mother, for love of grace,
    Lay not that flattering unction° to your soul,   145
    That not your trespass but my madness speaks,
    It will but skin and film the ulcerous place,
    Whiles rank corruption mining° all within,
    Infects unseen. Confess yourself to heaven,
    Repent what's past, avoid what is to come,   150
    And do not spread the compost° on the weeds
    To make them ranker. Forgive me this my virtue,°
    For in the fatness° of these pursy° times
    Virtue itself of vice must pardon beg,
    Yea curb and woo° for leave to do him° good.   155
QUEEN.   O Hamlet, thou hast cleft my heart in twain.
HAMLET.   O throw away the worser part of it,
   And live the purer with the other half.
    Good night, but go not to my uncle's bed,
    Assume° a virtue if you have it not.   160
    That monster custom, who all sense doth eat
    Of habits evil,° is angel yet in this,
    That to the use° of actions fair and good,
    He likewise gives a frock or livery
    That aptly° is put on. Refrain tonight,   165
    And that shall lend a kind of easiness
    To the next abstinence, the next more easy:
    For use° almost can change the stamp° of nature,
    And either . . . the° devil, or throw him out
    With wondrous potency: once more good night,   170
    And when you are desirous to be blessed,
    I'll blessing beg of you. For this same lord,°

---

135 *habit . . . lived:* clothing he wore when alive.   138–139 *bodiless . . . cunning in:* madness
(ecstasy) is very skillful in causing an affected person to hallucinate.   144 *gambol:* leap.
145 *unction:* salve.   148 *mining:* undermining.   151 *compost:* manure.   152 *virtue:*
sermon on virtue.   153 *fatness:* grossness.   *pursy:* flabby.   155 *curb and woo:* bow and
plead.   *him:* vice.   160 *Assume:* put on the guise of.   161–162 *all sense . . . evil:* confuses
the sense of right and wrong in a habitué.   163 *use:* habit.   165 *aptly:* readily.   168 *use:*
habit.   *stamp:* form.   169 *either . . . the:* (word omitted, for which "tame," "curls," and "quell"
have been suggested).   172 *lord:* Polonius.

I do repent; but heaven hath pleased it so
To punish me with this, and this with me,
That I must be their scourge and minister.°   175
I will bestow° him and will answer well°
The death I gave him; so again good night.
I must be cruel only to be kind;
This bad begins, and worse remains behind.°
One word more, good lady.
QUEEN.   What shall I do?   180
HAMLET.   Not this by no means that I bid you do:
Let the bloat° king tempt you again to bed,
Pinch wanton on your cheek, call you his mouse,
And let him for a pair of reechy° kisses,
Or paddling in your neck with his damned fingers,   185
Make you to ravel° all this matter out
That I essentially am not in madness,
But mad in craft. 'Twere good you let him know,
For who that's but a queen, fair, sober, wise,
Would from a paddock, from a bat, a gib,°   190
Such dear concernings hide? who would do so?
No, in despite of sense and secrecy,
Unpeg the basket on the house's top,
Let the birds fly, and like the famous ape,
To try conclusions° in the basket creep,   195
And break your own neck down.°
QUEEN.   Be thou assured, if words be made of breath,
And breath of life, I have no life to breathe
What thou hast said to me.
HAMLET.   I must to England, you know that.
QUEEN.   Alack,   200
I had forgot: 'tis so concluded on.
HAMLET.   There's letters sealed, and my two school-fellows,
Whom I will trust as I will adders fanged,
They bear the mandate, they must sweep my way
And marshal me to knavery:° let it work,   205
For 'tis the sport to have the enginer°
Hoist with his own petar,° and't shall go hard
But I will delve one yard below their mines,
And blow them at the moon: O 'tis most sweet

175 *their . . . minister:* heaven's punishment and agent of retribution.   176 *bestow:* stow
away.   *answer well:* assume full responsibility for.   179 *bad . . . behind:* is a bad beginning to a
worse end to come.   182 *bloat:* bloated with dissipation.   184 *reechy:* filthy.   186 *ravel:*
unravel.   190 *paddock, bat, gib:* toad, bat, tomcat ("familiars" or demons in animal shape that
attend on witches).   193–196 *Unpeg . . . down:* (the story refers to an ape that climbs to the
top of a house and opens a basket of birds; when the birds fly away, the ape crawls into the basket,
tries to fly, and breaks his neck. The point is that if she gives away Hamlet's secret, she harms herself).   195 *try conclusions:* experiment.   204–205 *sweep . . . knavery:* (like the marshal who
went before a royal procession, clearing the way, so Rosencrantz and Guildenstern clear Hamlet's
path to some unknown evil).   206 *enginer:* maker of war engines.   207 *Hoist . . . petar:* blown
up by his own bomb.

When in one line two crafts directly meet.°   210
This man shall set me packing,°
I'll lug the guts into the neighbour room;
Mother good night indeed. This counsellor
Is now most still, most secret, and most grave,
Who was in life a foolish prating knave.   215
Come sir, to draw toward an end with you.
Good night mother.   *Exit* HAMLET *tugging in* POLONIUS.

[ACT 4]

Scene 1. *[A room in the castle]*

Enter KING *and* QUEEN *with* ROSENCRANTZ *and* GUILDENSTERN.

KING.   There's matter in these sighs, these profound heaves,
     You must translate, 'tis fit we understand them.
     Where is your son?
QUEEN.   Bestow this place on us° a little while.

                         Exeunt ROSENCRANTZ *and* GUILDENSTERN.

     Ah mine own lord, what have I seen tonight!   5
KING.   What, Gertrude? How does Hamlet?
QUEEN.   Mad as the sea and wind when both contend
     Which is the mightier, in his lawless fit,
     Behind the arras hearing something stir,
     Whips out his rapier, cries "A rat, a rat,"   10
     And in this brainish apprehension° kills
     The unseen good old man.
KING.   O heavy deed!
     It had been so with us° had we been there:
     His liberty is full of threats to all,
     To you yourself, to us, to every one.   15
     Alas, how shall this bloody deed be answered?
     It will be laid to us,° whose providence°
     Should have kept short,° restrained, and out of haunt°
     This mad young man; but so much was our love,
     We would not understand what was most fit,   20
     But like the owner of a foul disease,
     To keep it from divulging,° let it feed
     Even on the pith of life: where is he gone?

210 *in one . . . meet:* the digger of the mine and the digger of the countermine meet halfway in
their tunnels.   211 *packing:* (1) i.e., my bags (2) rushing away (3) plotting.   4 *Bestow . . .*
us: leave us.   11 *brainish apprehension:* insane delusion.   13 *us:* me (royal plural).
17 *laid to us:* blamed on me.   *providence:* foresight.   18 *short:* tethered by a short
leash.   *out of haunt:* away from others.   22 *divulging:* being divulged.

QUEEN.   To draw apart the body he hath killed,
    O'er whom his very madness, like some ore   25
    Among a mineral of metals base,°
    Shows itself pure: a' weeps for what is done.
KING.   O Gertrude, come away:
    The sun no sooner shall the mountains touch,
    But we will ship him hence and this vile deed   30
    We must with all our majesty and skill
    Both countenance° and excuse. Ho Guildenstern!

Enter ROSENCRANTZ and GUILDENSTERN.

    Friends both, go join you with some further aid;
    Hamlet in madness hath Polonius slain,
    And from his mother's closet hath he dragged him.   35
    Go seek him out, speak fair, and bring the body
    Into the chapel; I pray you haste in this.   *[Exeunt Gentlemen.]*
    Come Gertrude, we'll call up our wisest friends,
    And let them know both what we mean to do
    And what's untimely done: [so haply slander,]   40
    Whose whisper o'er the world's diameter,
    As level° as the cannon to his blank°
    Transports his° poisoned shot, may miss our name,
    And hit the woundless° air. O come away,
    My soul is full of discord and dismay.   *Exeunt.*   45

Scene 2. *[Another room in the castle]*

Enter HAMLET.

HAMLET.   Safely stowed.
    Gentlemen within: Hamlet, Lord Hamlet!
    But soft, what noise, who calls on Hamlet?
    O here they come.

Enter ROSENCRANTZ and GUILDENSTERN.

ROSENCRANTZ.   What have you done my lord with the dead body?
HAMLET.   Compounded it with dust whereto 'tis kin.   5
ROSENCRANTZ.   Tell us where 'tis that we may take it thence,
    And bear it to the chapel.
HAMLET.   Do not believe it.
ROSENCRANTZ.   Believe what?
HAMLET.   That I can keep your counsel° and not mine own.° Besides,   10
    to be demanded of° a sponge, what replication° should be
    made by the son of a king?

25–26 *ore . . . base:* pure ore (such as gold) in a mine of base metal.   32 *countenance:*
defend.   42 *As level:* with a straight aim.   *blank:* while bull's-eye at the target's center.   43
his: slander's.   44 *woundless:* invulnerable.   10 *counsel:* (1) advice (2) secret.   *keep . . .*
own: follow your advice and not keep my own secret.   11 *demanded of:* questioned by.   *repli-*
cation: reply to a charge.

ROSENCRANTZ.   Take you me for a sponge, my lord?

HAMLET.   Ay sir, that soaks up the king's countenance,° his rewards,
his authorities. But such officers do the king best service in   15
the end; he keeps them like an apple in the corner of his
jaw, first mouthed to be last swallowed: when he needs
what you have gleaned, it is but squeezing you, and
sponge, you shall be dry again.

ROSENCRANTZ.   I understand you not my lord.   20

HAMLET.   I am glad of it: a knavish speech sleeps in° a foolish ear.

ROSENCRANTZ.   My lord, you must tell us where the body is, and go with
us to the king.

HAMLET.   The body is with the king, but the king° is not with the
body. The king is a thing—   25

GUILDENSTERN.   A thing my lord?

HAMLET.   Of nothing, bring me to him. Hide fox, and all after.°   *Exeunt.*

Scene 3. [Another room in the castle.]

Enter KING and two or three.

KING.   I have sent to seek him, and to find the body:
How dangerous is it that this man goes loose,
Yet must not we put the strong law on him,
He's loved of the distracted multitude,°
Who like not in° their judgment, but their eyes,   5
And where 'tis so, th'offender's scourge° is weighed
But never the offence: to bear all° smooth and even,
This sudden sending him away must seem
Deliberate pause:° diseases desperate grown,
By desperate appliance° are relieved,   10
Or not at all.

Enter ROSENCRANTZ and all the rest.

How now, what hath befallen?

ROSENCRANTZ.   Where the dead body is bestowed my lord,
We cannot get from him.

KING.   But where is he?

ROSENCRANTZ.   Without, my lord, guarded,° to know your pleasure.

KING.   Bring him before us.

ROSENCRANTZ.   Ho, bring in the lord.   15

Enter HAMLET (guarded) and GUILDENSTERN.

KING.   Now Hamlet, where's Polonius?

HAMLET.   At supper.

KING.   At supper? where?

14 *countenance:* favor.   21 *sleeps in:* means nothing to.   24 *king . . . king:* Hamlet's father . . .
Claudius.   27 *Hide fox . . . after:* (cry in a children's game, like hide-and-seek).   4 *distracted
multitude:* confused mob.   5 *in:* according to.   6 *scourge:* punishment.   7 *bear all:* carry
out everything.   9 *Deliberate pause:* considered delay.   10 *appliance:* remedy.   14 *guarded:*
(Hamlet is under guard until he boards the ship).

HAMLET.   Not where he eats, but where a' is eaten: a certain
    convocation of politic° worms are e'en° at him. Your worm is your   20
    only emperor for diet, we fat all creatures else to fat us,
    and we fat ourselves for maggots. Your fat king and your
    lean beggar is but variable service,° two dishes but to one
    table, that's the end.
KING.   Alas, alas.   25
HAMLET.   A man may fish with the worm that hath eat of a king, and
    eat of the fish that hath fed of that worm.
KING.   What dost thou mean by this?
HAMLET.   Nothing but to show you how a king may go a progress°
    through the guts of a beggar.   30
KING.   Where is Polonius?
HAMLET.   In heaven, send thither to see. If your messenger find him
    not there, seek him i'th'other place yourself: but if indeed
    you find him not within this month, you shall nose him as
    you go up the stairs into the lobby.   35
KING.   [*To Attendants.*] Go seek him there.
HAMLET.   A' will stay till you come.   [*Exeunt.*]
KING.   Hamlet, this deed, for thine especial safety—
    Which we do tender,° as we dearly grieve
    For that which thou hast done—must send thee hence
    With fiery quickness. Therefore prepare thyself,   40
    The bark is ready, and the wind at help,°
    Th'associates tend,° and every thing is bent
    For England.
HAMLET.   For England.
KING.   Ay Hamlet.
HAMLET.   Good.
KING.   So is it if thou knew'st our purposes.   45
HAMLET.   I see a cherub° that sees them: but come, for England.
    Farewell dear mother.
KING.   Thy loving father, Hamlet.
HAMLET.   My mother: father and mother is man and wife, man and
    wife is one flesh, and so my mother: come, for England.   *Exit.*   50
KING.   [*To ROSENCRANTZ and GUILDENSTERN.*]
    Follow him at foot,° tempt him with speed aboard,
    Delay it not, I'll have him hence tonight.
    Away, for every thing is sealed and done
    That else leans on° th'affair, pray you make haste.   [*Exeunt.*]
    And England,° if my love thou hold'st at aught°—   55
    As my great power thereof may give thee sense,
    Since yet thy cicatrice° looks raw and red

---

20 *politic:* (1) statesmanlike (2) crafty.   *e'en:* even now.   23 *variable service:* different types
of food.   29 *go a progress:* make a splendid royal journey from one part of the country
to another.   39 *tender:* cherish.   42 *at help:* helpful.   43 *tend:* wait.   46 *cherub:* (considered the watchmen of heaven).   51 *at foot:* at his heels.   54 *leans on:* relates to.
55 *England:* King of England.   *my love . . . aught:* you place any value on my favor.   57 *cica-
trice:* scar.

After the Danish sword, and thy free awe
Pays homage° to us—thou mayst not coldly set°
Our sovereign process,° which imports at full   60
By letters congruing° to that effect,
The present° death of Hamlet. Do it England,
For like the hectic° in my blood he rages,
And thou must cure me; till I know 'tis done,
Howe'er my haps,° my joys were ne'er begun.   *Exit.*   65

Scene 4. [A plain in Denmark]

Enter FORTINBRAS with his army over the stage.

FORTINBRAS.   Go captain, from me greet the Danish king,
    Tell him that by his license, Fortinbras
    Craves the conveyance° of a promised march
    Over his kingdom. You know the rendezvous:
    If that his majesty would aught with us,   5
    We shall express our duty in his eye,°
    And let him know so.
CAPTAIN.   I will do't, my lord.
FORTINBRAS.   Go softly° on.   *Exit.*

Enter HAMLET, ROSENCRANTZ, [GUILDENSTERN,] etc.

HAMLET.   Good sir whose powers° are these?
CAPTAIN.   They are of Norway sir.   10
HAMLET.   How purposed sir I pray you?
CAPTAIN.   Against some part of Poland.
HAMLET.   Who commands them sir?
CAPTAIN.   The nephew to old Norway, Fortinbras.
HAMLET.   Goes it against the main° of Poland sir,   15
    Or for some frontier?
CAPTAIN.   Truly to speak, and with no addition,
    We go to gain a little patch of ground
    That hath in it no profit but the name.°
    To pay five ducats, five, I would not farm it;   20
    Nor will it yield to Norway or the Pole
    A ranker° rate, should it be sold in fee.°
HAMLET.   Why then the Polack never will defend it.
CAPTAIN.   Yes, it is already garrisoned.
HAMLET.   Two thousand souls, and twenty thousand ducats   25
    Will not debate the question of° this straw:°
    This is th'imposthume of much wealth and peace,°

58–59 *free . . . homage:* awe which you, though free, still show by paying homage.   59 *coldly set:*
lightly estimate.   60 *process:* command.   61 *congruing:* agreeing.   62 *present:* immediate.   63 *hectic:* fever.   65 *haps:* fortunes.   3 *conveyance of:* escort for.   6 *in his eye:* face
to face.   8 *softly:* slowly.   9 *powers:* troops.   15 *main:* body.   19 *name:* glory.   22
ranker: higher (as annual interest on the total).   *in fee:* outright.   26 *debate . . . of:* settle the
dispute over.   *straw:* triviality.   27 *imposthume . . . peace:* swelling discontent (inner abscess)
resulting from too much wealth and peace.

That inward breaks, and shows no cause without
Why the man dies. I humbly thank you sir.
CAPTAIN.   God bye you sir.   [*Exit.*]
ROSENCRANTZ.   Will't please you go my lord?   30
HAMLET.   I'll be with you straight, go a little before.

                                        [*Exeunt all but* HAMLET.]

How all occasions do inform against me,
And spur my dull revenge. What is a man
If his chief good and market° of his time
Be but to sleep and feed? a beast, no more: 35
Sure he that made us with such large discourse,°
Looking before and after,° gave us not
That capability and god-like reason
To fust° in us unused. Now whether it be
Bestial oblivion,° or some craven° scruple   40
Of thinking too precisely on th'event°—
A thought which quartered hath but one part wisdom,
And ever three parts coward—I do not know
Why yet I live to say "This thing's to do,"
Sith I have cause, and will, and strength, and means   45
To do't; examples gross° as earth exhort me:
Witness this army of such mass and charge,°
Led by a delicate and tender° prince,
Whose spirit with divine ambition puffed,
Makes mouths° at the invisible event,°   50
Exposing what is mortal, and unsure,
To all that fortune, death, and danger dare,
Even for an egg-shell. Rightly to be great,
Is not to stir without great argument,
But greatly to find quarrel in a straw   55
When honour's at the stake.° How stand I then
That have a father killed, a mother stained,
Excitements° of my reason, and my blood,
And let all sleep, while to my shame I see
The imminent death of twenty thousand men,   60
That for a fantasy and trick° of fame
Go to their graves like beds, fight for a plot
Whereon the numbers cannot try the cause,°
Which is not tomb enough and continent°
To hide the slain. O from this time forth,   65
My thoughts be bloody, or be nothing worth.   *Exit.*

34 *market:* profit.   36 *discourse:* power of reasoning.   37 *Looking . . . after:* seeing causes and
effects.   39 *fust:* grow moldy.   40 *Bestial oblivion:* forgetfulness, as a beast forgets its
parents.   *craven:* cowardly.   41 *event:* outcome.   46 *gross:* obvious.   47 *charge:*
expense.   48 *delicate and tender:* gentle and young.   50 *mouths:* faces.   *event:*
outcome.   53–56 *Rightly . . . stake:* the truly great do not fight without just cause ("argument"),
but it is nobly ("greatly") done to fight even for a trifle if honor is at stake.   58 *Excitements:* incentives.   61 *fantasy and trick:* illusion and trifle.   63 *Whereon . . . cause:* too small to accommodate all the troops fighting for it.   64 *continent:* container.

Scene 5. *[A room in the castle]*

Enter QUEEN, HORATIO *and a* GENTLEMAN.

QUEEN.   I will not speak with her.
GENTLEMAN.   She is importunate, indeed distract,°
    Her mood will needs be° pitied.
QUEEN.   What would she have?
GENTLEMAN.   She speaks much of her father, says she hears
    There's tricks i'th'world, and hems,° and beats her heart,   5
    Spurns enviously at straws,° speaks things in doubt°
    That carry but half sense: her speech is nothing,
    Yet the unshapèd use of it doth move
    The hearers to collection;° they aim° at it,
    And botch° the words up fit to their own thoughts,   10
    Which as her winks, and nods, and gestures yield them,
    Indeed would make one think there might be thought,
    Though nothing sure, yet much unhappily.
HORATIO.   'Twere good she were spoken with, for she may strew
    Dangerous conjectures in ill-breeding minds.   15
QUEEN.   Let her come in.   *Exit* GENTLEMAN.
    [*Aside.*] To my sick soul, as sin's true nature is,°
    Each toy° seems prologue to some great amiss,°
    So full of artless jealousy° is guilt,
    It spills itself, in fearing to be spilt.   20

Enter OPHELIA, *distracted.*°

OPHELIA.   Where is the beauteous majesty of Denmark?
QUEEN.   How now Ophelia?
OPHELIA.   [*Sings.*] How should I your true love know
          From another one?
          By his cockle hat and staff,°   25
          And his sandal shoon.°
QUEEN.   Alas sweet lady, what imports this song?
OPHELIA.   Say you? nay, pray you mark.
    [*Sings.*] He is dead and gone, lady,
          He is dead and gone,   30
       At his head a grass-green turf,
         At his heels a stone.
      O ho.
QUEEN.   Nay but Ophelia—
OPHELIA   Pray you mark.
    [*Sings.*] White his shroud as the mountain snow—

Enter KING.

2 *distract:* insane.   3 *will needs be:* needs to be.   5 *hems:* coughs.   6 *Spurns . . . straws:* reacts maliciously to trifles.   *in doubt:* ambiguous.   9 *collection:* inference.   *aim:* guess.   10 *botch:* patch.   17 *as sin's . . . is:* as is natural for the guilty.   18 *toy:* trifle.   *amiss:* disaster.   19 *artless jealousy:* uncontrollable suspicion.   20 S.D.: *distracted:* insane.   25 *cockle hat and staff:* (marks of the pilgrim, the cockle shell symbolizing his journey to the shrine of St. James; the pilgrim was a common metaphor for the lover).   26 *shoon:* shoes.

QUEEN.   Alas, look here my lord.   35
OPHELIA.   [*Sings.*] Larded° all with sweet flowers,
                Which bewept to the ground did not go,
                With true-love showers.
KING.   How do you, pretty lady?
OPHELIA.   Well, God 'ild° you. They say the owl was a baker's   40
        daughter.° Lord, we know what we are, but know not what
        we may be. God be at your table.°
KING.   Conceit° upon her father.
OPHELIA.   Pray you let's have no words of this, but when they ask
        you what it means, say you this: 45

            [*Sings.*] Tomorrow is Saint Valentine's day,
                All in the morning betime,°
            And I a maid at your window
                To be your Valentine.
            Then up he rose, and donned his clo'es,   50
                And dupped° the chamber door,
            Let in the maid, that out a maid,
                Never departed more.
KING.   Pretty Ophelia.
OPHELIA.   Indeed, la, without an oath I'll make an end on't.   55

            [*Sings.*] By Gis° and by Saint Charity,
                Alack and fie for shame,
            Young men will do't, if they come to't,
                By Cock° they are to blame.
            Quoth she, Before you tumbled me,   60
                You promised me to wed.

    (He answers)
            So would I ha' done, by yonder sun,
                An° thou hadst not come to my bed.
KING.   How long hath she been thus?   65
OPHELIA.   I hope all will be well. We must be patient, but I cannot
        choose but weep to think they would lay him i'th'cold
        ground. My brother shall know of it, and so I thank you
        for your good counsel. Come, my coach: good night
        ladies, good night. Sweet ladies, good night, good night.   [*Exit* OPHELIA.]   70
KING.   Follow her close, give her good watch I pray you.   [*Exit* HORATIO.]
        O this is the poison of deep grief, it springs
        All from her father's death, and now behold:
        O Gertrude, Gertrude,
        When sorrows come, they come not single spies,   75
        But in battalions: first her father slain,

---

36 *Larded:* trimmed.   40 *God 'ild:* God yield (reward).   40–41 *owl . . . daughter:* (in a medieval legend, a baker's daughter was turned into an owl because she gave Jesus short weight on a loaf of bread).   42 *God . . . table:* (a blessing at dinner).   43 *Conceit:* thinking.   47 *betime:* early (because the first woman a man saw on Valentine's Day would be his true love).   51 *dupped:* opened.   56 *Gis:* contraction of "Jesus."   59 *Cock:* (vulgarization of "God" in oaths). 64 *An:* if.

Next, your son gone, and he most violent author
Of his own just remove, the people muddied,°
Thick and unwholesome in their thoughts and whispers
For good Polonius' death: and we have done but greenly°   80
In hugger-mugger° to inter him: poor Ophelia
Divided from herself and her fair judgment,
Without the which we are pictures or mere beasts,
Last, and as much containing° as all these,
Her brother is in secret come from France,   85
Feeds on his wonder,° keeps himself in clouds,°
And wants not buzzers° to infect his ear
With pestilent speeches of his father's death,
Wherein necessity, of matter beggared,
Will nothing stick our person to arraign°   90
In ear and ear:° O my dear Gertrude, this
Like to a murdering-piece° in many places
Gives me superfluous death.   *A noise within.*

QUEEN.   Alack, what noise is this?
KING.   Attend!   *Enter a* MESSENGER.
Where are my Switzers°? Let them guard the door.   95
What is the matter?
MESSENGER.   Save yourself, my lord.
The ocean, overpeering of his list,°
Eats not the flats° with more impiteous haste
Than young Laertes in a riotous head°
O'erbears your officers: the rabble call him lord,   100
And as the world were now but to begin,
Antiquity forgot, custom not known,
The ratifiers and props of every word,
They cry "Choose we, Laertes shall be king!"
Caps, hands, and tongues applaud it to the clouds,   105
"Laertes shall be king, Laertes king!"   *A noise within.*
QUEEN.   How cheerfully on the false trail they cry.
O this is counter,° you false Danish dogs.
KING.   The doors are broke.

Enter LAERTES *with others.*

LAERTES.   Where is this king? Sirs, stand you all without.°   110
DANES.   No, let's come in.
LAERTES.   I pray you give me leave.°
DANES.   We will, we will.   [*They retire.*]

78 *muddied:* stirred up.   80 *done but greenly:* acted like amateurs.   81 *hugger-mugger:* secret haste.   84 *containing:* i.e., cause for sorrow.   86 *Feeds . . . wonder:* sustains himself by wondering about his father's death.   *clouds:* gloom, obscurity.   87 *wants not buzzers:* lacks not whispering gossips.   89–90 *Wherein . . . arraign:* in which the tellers, lacking facts, will not hesitate to accuse me.   91 *In ear and ear:* whispering from one ear to another.   92 *murdering-piece:* small cannon shooting shrapnel, to inflict numerous wounds.   95 *Switzers:* Swiss guards.   97 *overpeering . . . list:* rising above its usual limits.   98 *flats:* lowlands.   99 *head:* armed force.   108 *counter:* following the scent backward.   110 *without:* outside.   111 *leave:* i.e., to enter alone.

LAERTES.   I thank you, keep the door. O thou vile king,
  Give me my father.
QUEEN.   Calmly, good Laertes.
LAERTES.   That drop of blood that's calm proclaims me bastard,   115
  Cries cuckold° to my father, brands° the harlot
  Even here between the chaste unsmirchèd brows
  Of my true mother.
KING.   What is the cause Laertes,
  That thy rebellion looks so giant-like?
  Let him go Gertrude, do not fear° our person,   120
  There's such divinity° doth hedge a king,
  That treason can but peep to° what it would,
  Acts little of his° will. Tell me Laertes,
  Why thou art this incensed. Let him go Gertrude.
  Speak man.   125
LAERTES.   Where is my father?
KING.   Dead.
QUEEN.   But not by him.
KING.   Let him demand his fill.
LAERTES.   How came he dead? I'll not be juggled with.
  To hell allegiance, vows to the blackest devil,
  Conscience and grace, to the profoundest pit.   130
  I dare damnation: to this point I stand,
  That both the worlds I give to negligence,°
  Let come what comes, only I'll be revenged
  Most throughly for my father.
KING.   Who shall stay you?
LAERTES.   My will, not all the world's:°   135
  And for my means, I'll husband° them so well,
  They shall go far with little.
KING.   Good Laertes,
  If you desire to know the certainty
  Of your dear father, is't writ in your revenge
  That swoopstake,° you will draw both friend and foe,   140
  Winner and loser?
LAERTES.   None but his enemies.
KING.   Will you know them then?
LAERTES.   To his good friends thus wide I'll ope my arms,
  And like the kind life-rend'ring pelican,°
  Repast them with my blood.
KING.   Why now you speak   145
  Like a good child, and a true gentleman.
  That I am guiltless of your father's death,

---

116 *cuckold:* betrayed husband.   *brands:* (so harlots were punished).   120 *fear:* i.e.,
for.   121 *divinity:* divine protection.   122 *peep to:* strain to see.   123 *his:* treason's.
132 *both . . . negligence:* I care nothing for this world or the next.   135 *world's:* i.e., will.
136 *husband:* economize.   140 *swoopstake:* sweeping in all the stakes in a game, both of winner
and loser.   144 *pelican:* (the mother pelican was believed to nourish her young with blood
pecked from her own breast).

And am most sensibly° in grief for it,
It shall as level° to your judgment 'pear
As day does to your eye.   150

[*A noise within.*]

[*Crowd shouts.*] Let her come in.
LAERTES.   How now, what noise is that?

Enter OPHELIA.

O heat, dry up my brains, tears seven time salt,
Burn out the sense and virtue° of mine eye!
By heaven, thy madness shall be paid with weight,°
Till our scale turn the beam,° O rose of May,   155
Dear maid, kind sister, sweet Ophelia:
O heavens, is't possible a young maid's wits
Should be as mortal as an old man's life?
Nature is fine in love, and where 'tis fine,
It sends some previous instance of itself   160
after the thing it loves.°

OPHELIA.   [*Sings.*] They bore him barefaced on the bier,
                          Hey non nonny, nonny, hey nonny:
                          And in his grave rained many a tear—
                     Fare you well my dove.   165

LAERTES.   Hadst thou thy wits, and didst persuade revenge,
It could not move thus.

OPHELIA.   You must sing "adown adown," and you call him adown-a.
O how the wheel becomes it.° It is the false steward that
stole his master's daughter.   170

LAERTES.   This nothing's more than matter.°

OPHELIA.   There's rosemary,° that's for remembrance, pray you love
remember: and there is pansies, that's for thoughts.

LAERTES.   A document° in madness, thoughts and remembrance
fitted.°   175

OPHELIA.   There's fennel for you, and columbines.° There's rue° for
you, and here's some for me, we may call it herb of grace°
o'Sundays: O, you must wear your rue with a difference.°
There's a daisy,° I would give you some violets,° but they
withered all when my father died: they say a' made a good   180
end;
                [*Sings.*] For bonny sweet Robin is all my joy.

148 *sensibly:* feelingly.   149 *level:* plain.   153 *sense and virtue:* feeling and power.   154 *with weight:* with equal weight.   155 *turn the beam:* outweigh the other side.   159–161 *Nature . . . loves:* filial love that is so refined and pure sends some precious token (her wits) after the beloved dead.   169 *wheel becomes it:* refrain ("adown") suits the subject (Polonius's fall).   171 *more than matter:* more eloquent than sane speech.   172 *There's rosemary:* (given to Laertes; she may be distributing imaginary or real flowers).   174 *document:* lesson.   *thoughts . . . fitted:* thoughts of revenge matched with remembrance of Polonius.   176 *fennel, columbines:* (given to the king, symbolizing flattery and ingratitude).   *rue:* (given to the queen, symbolizing sorrow or repentance).   177 *herb of grace:* (because it symbolizes repentance).   178 *with a difference:* for a different reason (Ophelia's is for sorrow and the queen's for repentance).   179 *daisy:* (symbolizing dissembling).   *violets:* (symbolizing faithfulness).

LAERTES.   Thought and affliction, passion, hell itself,
    She turns to favour and to prettiness.
OPHELIA.   [*Sings.*] And will a' not come again,   185
               And will a' not come again?
                   No, no, he is dead,
                   Go to thy death-bed,
               He never will come again.
               His beard was as white as snow,   190
               All flaxen was his poll,°
                   He is gone, he is gone,
                   And we cast away moan,
               God ha' mercy on his soul.
    And of all Christian souls, I pray God. God bye you.   195

                                        Exit OPHELIA.

LAERTES.   Do you see this, O God?
KING.   Laertes, I must commune with your grief,
    Or you deny me right: go but apart,
    Make choice of whom your wisest friends you will,
    And they shall hear and judge 'twixt you and me;   200
    If by direct or by collateral° hand
    They find us touched,° we will our kingdom give,
    Our crown, our life, and all that we call ours
    To you in satisfaction; but if not,
    Be you content to lend your patience to us,   205
    And we shall jointly labour with your soul
    To give it due content.
LAERTES.   Let this be so.
    His means of death, his obscure funeral,
    No trophy,° sword, nor hatchment° o'er his bones,
    No noble rite, nor formal ostentation,°   210
    Cry° to be heard as 'twere from heaven to earth,
    That I must call't in question.
KING.   So you shall,
    And where th'offence is, let the great axe fall.
    I pray you go with me.   *[Exeunt.]*

Scene 6. *[Another room in the castle]*

Enter HORATIO and others.

HORATIO.   What are they that would speak with me?
GENTLEMAN.   Seafaring men sir, they say they have letters for you.
HORATIO.   Let them come in.   *[Exit ATTENDANT.]*
    I do not know from what part of the world
    I should be greeted, if not from Lord Hamlet.   5

---

191 *flaxen . . . poll:* white was his head.   201 *collateral:* indirect.   202 *touched:* tainted with
guilt.   209 *trophy:* memorial.   *hatchment:* tablet displaying coat of arms.   210 *ostentation:*
ceremony.   211 *Cry:* cry out.

Enter SAILORS.

SAILOR.   God bless you sir.

HORATIO.   Let him bless thee too.

SAILOR.   A' shall sir, an't please him. There's a letter for you sir, it
came from th'ambassador that was bound for England, if
your name be Horatio, as I am let to know it is.   10

HORATIO.   [*Reads the letter.*] "Horatio, when thou shalt have
overlooked° this, give these fellows some means to the king,
they have letters for him. Ere we were two days old at sea,
a pirate of very warlike appointment° gave us chase.
Finding ourselves too slow of sail, we put on a compelled   15
valour, and in the grapple° I boarded them. On the instant
they got clear of our ship, so I alone became their prisoner.
They have dealt with me like thieves of mercy,° but they
knew what they did. I am to do a good turn for them. Let
the king have the letters I have sent, and repair° thou to me   20
with as much speed as thou wouldst fly death. I have
words to speak in thine ear will make thee dumb, yet are
they much too light for the bore° of the matter. These good
fellows will bring thee where I am. Rosencrantz and
Guildenstern hold their course for England. Of them I   25
have much to tell thee. Farewell.

                              He that thou knowest thine, Hamlet."

Come, I will give you way° for these your letters,
And do't the speedier that you may direct me
To him from whom you brought them.   *Exeunt.*   30

Scene 7. *[Another room in the castle]*

Enter KING and LAERTES.

KING.   Now must your conscience my acquittance seal,°
And you must put me in your heart for friend,
Sith you have heard and with a knowing ear,
That he which hath your noble father slain
Pursued my life.

LAERTES.   It well appears: but tell me   5
Why you proceeded not against these feats
So crimeful and so capital in nature,
As by your safety, greatness, wisdom, all things else,
You mainly were stirred up.°

KING.   O for two special reasons,
Which may to you perhaps seem much unsinewed,°   10
But yet to me they're strong. The queen his mother
Lives almost by his looks, and for myself,

---

12 *overlooked:* read over.   14 *appointment:* equipment.   16 *in the grapple:* when the pirate
ship hooked onto ours.   18 *of mercy:* merciful.   20 *repair:* come.   23 *bore:* size,
caliber.   28 *way:* access (to the king).   1 *my acquittance seal:* confirm my acquittal.
9 *mainly . . . up:* were strongly urged.   10 *much unsinewed:* very weak.

My virtue or my plague, be it either which,
She's so conjunctive° to my life and soul,
That as the star moves not but in his sphere,°   15
I could not but by her. The other motive,
Why to a public count° I might not go,
Is the great love the general gender° bear him,
Who dipping all his faults in their affection,
Would like the spring that turneth wood to stone,°   20
Convert his gyves to graces,° so that my arrows,
Too slightly timbered° for so loud a wind,
Would have reverted to my bow again,
And not where I had aimed them.

LAERTES.   And so have I a noble father lost,   25
A sister driven into desperate terms,°
Whose worth, if praises may go back° again,
Stood challenger on mount of all the age
For her perfections.° But my revenge will come.

KING.   Break not your sleeps for that, you must not think   30
That we are made of stuff so flat and dull,
That we can let our beard be shook with danger,
And think it pastime. You shortly shall hear more,
I loved your father, and we love ourself,
And that I hope will teach you to imagine—   35

Enter a MESSENGER *with letters.*

How now. What news?
MESSENGER.   Letters my lord, from Hamlet.
These to your majesty, this to the queen.
KING.   From Hamlet? Who brought them?
MESSENGER.   Sailors my lord they say, I saw them not:
They were given me by Claudio, he received them   40
Of him that brought them.
KING.   Laertes you shall hear them:
Leave us.   *Exit [*MESSENGER*]*
[*Reads*] "High and mighty, you shall know I am set naked° on
your kingdom. Tomorrow shall I beg leave to see your kingly
eyes, when I shall, first asking your pardon° thereunto,   45
recount the occasion of my sudden and more strange return.
                                          Hamlet."
What should this mean? Are all the rest come back?
Or is it some abuse,° and no such thing?

---

14 *conjunctive:* closely allied.   15 *in his sphere:* (referring to the Ptolemaic belief that each planet,
fixed in its own sphere, revolved around the earth).   17 *count:* accounting.   18 *general gender:*
common people.   20 *the spring . . . stone:* (the baths of King's Newnham in Warwickshire were
described as being able to turn wood into stone because of their high concentrations of
lime).   21 *Convert . . . graces:* regard his fetters (had he been imprisoned) as honors.
22 *slightly timbered:* light-shafted.   26 *desperate terms:* madness.   27 *go back:* i.e., before her
madness.   28–29 *challenger . . . perfections:* like a challenger on horseback, ready to defend against
the world her claim to perfection.   43 *naked:* without resources.   45 *pardon:*
permission.   49 *abuse:* deception.

LAERTES.   Know you the hand?

KING.   'Tis Hamlet's character.° "Naked,"   50
    And in a postscript here he says "alone."
    Can you devise° me?

LAERTES.   I am lost in it my lord, but let him come,
    It warms the very sickness in my heart
    That I shall live and tell him to his teeth,   55
    "Thus didest thou."

KING.   If it be so Laertes—
    As how should it be so? how otherwise?—
    Will you be ruled by me?

LAERTES.   Ay my lord,
    So you will not o'errule me to a peace.

KING.   To thine own peace: if he be now returned,   60
    As checking at° his voyage, and that he means
    No more to undertake it, I will work him
    To an exploit, now ripe in my device,°
    Under the which he shall not choose but fall:
    And for his death no wind of blame shall breathe,   65
    But even his mother shall uncharge the practice,°
    And call it accident.

LAERTES.   My lord, I will be ruled,
    The rather if you could devise it so
    That I might be the organ.°

KING.   It falls right.
    You have been talked of since your travel much,   70
    And that in Hamlet's hearing, for a quality
    Wherein they say you shine: your sum of parts°
    Did not together pluck such envy from him
    As did that one, and that in my regard
    Of the unworthiest siege.°

LAERTES.   What part is that my lord?   75

KING.   A very riband° in the cap of youth,
    Yet needful too, for youth no less becomes°
    The light and careless livery° that it wears,
    Than settled age his sables° and his weeds°
    Importing health and graveness; two months since,°   80
    Here was a gentleman of Normandy—
    I have seen myself, and served against the French,
    And they can° well on horseback—but this gallant
    Had witchcraft in't, he grew unto his seat,
    And to such wondrous doing brought his horse,   85

---

50 *character:* handwriting.   52 *devise me:* explain it.   61 *checking at:* altering the course of (when the falcon forsakes one quarry for another).   63 *ripe in my device:* already planned by me.   66 *uncharge the practice:* acquit the plot (of treachery).   69 *organ:* instrument.   72 *your sum of parts:* all your accomplishments.   75 *siege:* rank.   76 *riband:* decoration.   77 *becomes:* befits.   78 *livery:* clothing (denoting rank or occupation).   79 *sables:* fur-trimmed gowns.   *weeds:* garments.   80 *since:* ago.   83 *can:* can do.

As had he been incorpsed and demi-natured°
   With the brave beast. So far he topped my thought,
   That I in forgery of° shapes and tricks
   Come short of what he did.
LAERTES.   A Norman was't?
KING.   A Norman.   90
LAERTES.   Upon my life, Lamord.
KING.   The very same.
LAERTES.   I know him well, he is the brooch° indeed
   And gem of all the nation.
KING.   He made confession° of you,
   And gave you such a masterly report   95
   For art and exercise in your defence,
   And for your rapier most especial,
   That he cried out 'twould be a sight indeed
   If one could match you; the scrimers° of their nation
   He swore had neither motion, guard, nor eye,   100
   If you opposed them; sir this report of his
   Did Hamlet so envenom° with his envy,
   That he could nothing do but wish and beg
   Your sudden coming o'er to play with him.
   Now out of this—
LAERTES.   What out of this, my lord?   105
KING.   Laertes, was your father dear to you?
   Or are you like the painting of a sorrow,
   A face without a heart?
LAERTES.   Why ask you this?
KING.   Not that I think you did not love your father,
   But that I know love is begun by time,   110
   And that I see in passages of proof,°
   Time qualifies° the spark and fire of it:
   There lives within the very flame of love
   A kind of wick or snuff that will abate it,°
   And nothing is at a like goodness still,°   115
   For goodness growing to a plurisy,°
   Dies in his own too-much. That we would do
   We should do when we would: for this "would"° changes,
   And hath abatements and delays as many
   As there are tongues, are hands, are accidents,   120
   And then this "should"° is like a spendthrift sigh,
   That hurts by easing;° but to the quick° of th'ulcer:

---

86 *incorpsed . . . natured:* made into one body, sharing half its nature.   88 *in forgery of:* imagining.   92 *brooch:* ornament.   94 *confession:* report.   99 *scrimers:* fencers.   102 *envenom:* poison.   111 *passages of proof:* examples drawn from experience.   112 *qualifies:* weakens.   114 *snuff . . . it:* charred end of the wick that will diminish the flame.   115 *still:* always.   116 *plurisy:* excess.   118 *"would":* will to act.   121*"should":* reminder of one's duty.   121–122 *spendthrift . . . easing:* A sigh which, though giving temporary relief, wastes life, as each sigh draws a drop of blood away from the heart (a common Elizabethan belief). 122 *quick:* most sensitive spot.

Hamlet comes back, what would you undertake
To show yourself in deed your father's son
More than in words?
LAERTES.   To cut his throat i'th'church.   125
KING.   No place indeed should murder sanctuarize,°
    Revenge should have no bounds: but good Laertes,
    Will you do this, keep close within your chamber:
    Hamlet returned shall know you are come home,
    We'll put on° those shall praise your excellence,   130
    And set a double varnish on the fame
    The Frenchman gave you, bring you in fine° together,
    And wager on your heads; he being remiss,°
    Most generous, and free from all contriving,
    Will not peruse the foils, so that with ease,   135
    Or with a little shuffling, you may choose
    A sword unbated,° and in a pass of practice°
    Requite him for your father.
LAERTES.   I will do't,
    And for the purpose, I'll anoint my sword.
    I bought an unction° of a mountebank°   140
    So mortal,° that but dip a knife in it,
    Where it draws blood, no cataplasm° so rare,
    Collected from all simples° that have virtue°
    Under the moon,° can save the thing from death
    That is but scratched withal: I'll touch my point   145
    With this contagion, that if I gall° him slightly,
    It may be death.
KING.   Let's further think of this,
    Weigh what convenience both of time and means
    May fit us to our shape;° if this should fail,
    And that our drift° look through° our bad performance,   150
    'Twere better not assayed; therefore this project
    Should have a back or second that might hold
    If this did blast in proof;° soft, let me see,
    We'll make a solemn wager on your cunnings°—
    I ha't: 155
    When in your motion you are hot and dry,
    As make your bouts more violent to that end,
    And that he calls for drink, I'll have prepared him
    A chalice for the nonce,° whereon but sipping,
    If he by chance escape your venomed stuck,°   160

126 *murder sanctuarize:* give sanctuary to murder.   130 *put on:* incite.   132 *in fine:*
finally.   133 *remiss:* easy-going.   137 *unbated:* not blunted (the edges and points were
blunted for fencing).   *pass of practice:* (1) match for exercise (2) treacherous thrust.
140 *unction:* ointment.   *mountebank:* quack doctor, medicine man.   141 *mortal:*
deadly.   142 *cataplasm:* poultice.   143 *simples:* herbs.   *virtue:* power (of healing).
144 *Under the moon:* (when herbs were supposed to be collected to be most effective).   146
gall: scratch.   149 *shape:* plan.   150 *drift:* aim.   *look through:* be exposed by.   153 *blast
in proof:* fail when tested (as a bursting cannon).   154 *cunnings:* skills.   159 *nonce:*
occasion.   160 *stuck:* thrust.

Our purpose may hold there; but stay, what noise?

Enter QUEEN.

How, sweet queen?

QUEEN.   One woe doth tread upon another's heel,
So fast they follow; your sister's drowned, Laertes.

LAERTES.   Drowned! O where?   165

QUEEN.   There is a willow grows aslant a brook,
That shows his hoar° leaves in the glassy stream,
There with fantastic garlands did she make
Of crow-flowers,° nettles, daisies, and long purples,°
That liberal° shepherds give a grosser name,   170
But our cold° maids do dead men's fingers call them.
There on the pendent boughs her coronet weeds°
Clamb'ring to hang, an envious sliver° broke,
When down her weedy trophies and herself
Fell in the weeping brook: her clothes spread wide,   175
And mermaid-like awhile they bore her up,
Which time she chanted snatches of old tunes,
As one incapable of° her own distress,
Or like a creature native and indued
Unto° that element: but long it could not be   180
Till that her garments, heavy with their drink,
Pulled the poor wretch from her melodious lay
To muddy death.

LAERTES.   Alas, then she is drowned?

QUEEN.   Drowned, drowned.

LAERTES.   Too much of water hast thou, poor Ophelia,   185
And therefore I forbid my tears; but yet
It is our trick, nature her custom holds,
Let shame say what it will; when these° are gone,
The woman will be out.° Adieu my lord,
I have a speech o' fire that fain would blaze,   190
But that this folly douts it.°   *Exit.*

KING.   Let's follow, Gertrude,
How much I had to do to calm his rage;
Now fear I this will give it start again,
Therefore let's follow.   *Exeunt.*

[ACT 5]

Scene 1. *[A churchyard]*

Enter two CLOWNS.°

---

167 *hoar:* grey (on the underside).   169 *crow-flowers:* buttercups.   *long purples:* spike-like early orchid.   170 *liberal:* libertine.   171 *cold:* chaste.   172 *coronet weeds:* garland of weeds.   173 *envious sliver:* malicious branch.   178 *incapable of:* unable to understand.   179–180 *indued Unto:* endowed by nature to exist in.   188 *these:* i.e., tears.   189 *woman . . . out:* womanly habits will be out of me.   191 *folly douts it:* tears put it out.   0.2 S.D.: *Clowns:* rustics.

1. CLOWN.   Is she to be buried in Christian burial,° when she wilfully
seeks her own salvation?°
2. CLOWN.   I tell thee she is, therefore make her grave straight.° The
crowner hath sat on her,° and finds it Christian burial.
1. CLOWN.   How can that be, unless she drowned herself in her own   5
defence?°
2. CLOWN.   Why, 'tis found so.
1. CLOWN.   It must be "se offendendo,"° it cannot be else: for here lies
the point: if I drown myself wittingly, it argues an act,
and an act hath three branches, it is to act, to do, and to   10
perform; argal,° she drowned herself wittingly.
2. CLOWN.   Nay, but hear you, goodman delver.
1. CLOWN.   Give me leave: here lies the water, good. Here stands the
man, good. If the man go to this water and drown himself,
it is, will he nill he,° he goes, mark you that. But if the   15
water come to him, and drown him, he drowns not
himself. Argal, he that is not guilty of his own death, shortens not his own
life.
2. CLOWN.   But is this law?
1. CLOWN.   Ay marry is't, crowner's quest° law.   20
2. CLOWN.   Will you ha' the truth on't? If this had not been a
gentlewoman, she would have been buried out o'Christian
burial.
1. CLOWN.   Why there thou say'st, and the more pity that great folk
should have countenance° in this world to drown or hang   25
themselves more than their even-Christen.° Come, my
spade; there is no ancient gentlemen but gardeners,
ditchers and grave-makers; they hold up Adam's profession.
2. CLOWN.   Was he a gentleman?
1. CLOWN.   A' was the first that ever bore arms.°   30
2. CLOWN.   Why, he had none.
1. CLOWN.   What, art a heathen? How dost thou understand the
Scripture? The Scripture says Adam digged; could he dig
without arms? I'll put another question to thee; if thou
answerest me not to the purpose, confess thyself—   35
2. CLOWN.   Go to.
1. CLOWN.   What is he that builds stronger than either the mason, the
shipwright, or the carpenter?
2. CLOWN.   The gallows-maker, for that frame outlives a thousand
tenants.   40

1 *Christian burial:* consecrated ground within a churchyard (where suicides were not allowed
burial).   2 *salvation:* i.e., "damnation." The gravediggers make a number of such "mistakes,"
later termed "malapropisms."   3 *straight:* straightaway, at once.   4 *crowner . . . her:* coroner
has ruled on her case.   5–6 *her own defence:* (as self-defense justifies homicide, so may it justify
suicide).   8 *"se offendendo":* (he means "*se defendendo*," in self-defense).   11 *argal:* (corruption of "ergo" = therefore).   15 *will he nill he:* will he or will he not (willy nilly).   20 *quest:*
inquest.   25 *countenance:* privilege.   26 *even-Christen:* fellow Christian.   30 *arms:* (with a
pun on "coat of arms").

1. CLOWN.   I like thy wit well in good faith, the gallows does well, but
how does it well? It does well to those that do ill. Now
thou dost ill to say the gallows is built stronger than the
church. Argal, the gallows may do well to thee.° To't
again, come.   45
2. CLOWN.   'Who builds stronger than a mason, a shipwright, or a
carpenter?'
1. CLOWN.   Ay, tell me that, and unyoke.°
2. CLOWN.   Marry, now I can tell.
1. CLOWN.   To't.   50
2. CLOWN.   Mass,° I cannot tell.
1. CLOWN.   Cudgel thy brains no more about it, for your dull ass will
not mend his pace with beating, and when you are asked
this question next, say "a grave-maker:" the houses he
makes last till doomsday. Go get thee to Yaughan,° and   55
fetch me a stoup° of liquor.   [*Exit 2. CLOWN.*]

Enter HAMLET and HORATIO afar off.

1. CLOWN.   (*Sings.*) In youth when I did love, did love,
                              Methought it was very sweet,
                    To contract oh the time for a° my behove,°
                    O methought there a was nothing a meet.°   60
HAMLET.   Has this fellow no feeling of his business, that a'sings in
grave-making?
HORATIO.   Custom hath made it in him a property of easiness.°
HAMLET.   'Tis e'en so, the hand of little employment hath the
daintier sense.°   65
1. CLOWN.   (*Sings.*) But age with his stealing steps
                              Hath clawed me in his clutch,
                    And hath shipped me intil° the land,
                              As if I had never been such.   [*Throws up a skull.*]
HAMLET.   That skull had a tongue in it, and could sing once: how the   70
knave jowls° it to the ground, as if'twere Cain's jaw-bone,°
that did the first murder. This might be the pate of a
politician, which this ass now o'erreaches;° one that
would circumvent° God, might it not?
HORATIO.   It might my lord.   75
HAMLET.   Or of a courtier, which could say "Good morrow sweet
lord, how dost thou good lord?" This might be my lord
such-a-one, that praised my lord such-a-one's horse, when
a'meant to beg it, might it not?

---

44 *to thee:* i.e., by hanging you.   48 *unyoke:* unharness (your wits, after this exertion).   51 *Mass:*
by the mass.   55 *Yaughan:* probably a local innkeeper.   56 *stoup:* stein, drinking mug.   59
oh, a: (he grunts as he works).   *behove:* benefit.   60 *meet:* suitable.   63 *Custom . . . easiness:*
being accustomed to it has made him indifferent.   65 *daintier sense:* finer sensibility (being uncal-
loused).   68 *intil:* into.   71 *jowls:* casts (with obvious pun).   *Cain's jaw-bone:* the jawbone of
an ass with which Cain murdered Abel.   73 *o'erreaches:* (1) reaches over (2) gets the better
of.   74 *would circumvent:* tried to outwit.

HORATIO.   It might my lord.   80
HAMLET.   Why e'en so, and now my Lady Worm's, chopless,° and
   knocked about the mazzard° with a sexton's spade; here's
   fine revolution an° we had the trick° to see't. Did these
   bones cost no more the breeding, but to play at loggets°
   with them? Mine ache to think on't.   85
1. CLOWN.   (*Sings.*) A pick-axe and a spade, a spade,
                           For and a shrouding sheet,
                           O a pit of clay for to be made
                           For such a guest is meet.°   [*Throws up another skull.*]
HAMLET.   There's another: why may not that be the skull of a   90
   lawyer? Where be his quiddities° now, his quillets,° his
   cases, his tenures,° and his tricks? Why does he suffer this
   rude knave now to knock him about the sconce° with a
   dirty shovel, and will not tell him of his action of battery?
   Hum, this fellow might be in's time a great buyer of land,   95
   with his statutes,° his recognizances,° his fines,° his double
   vouchers,° his recoveries:° is this the fine° of his fines, and
   the recovery° of his recoveries, to have his fine pate full of
   fine dirt? Will his vouchers vouch him no more of his
   purchases, and double ones too, than the length and   100
   breadth of a pair of indentures?° The very conveyances° of
   his lands will scarcely lie in this box,° and must th'inheritor°
   himself have no more, ha?
HORATIO.   Not a jot more my lord.
HAMLET.   Is not parchment made of sheep-skins?   105
HORATIO.   Ay my lord, and of calves'-skins too.
HAMLET.   They are sheep and calves which seek out assurance° in
   that. I will speak to this fellow. Whose grave's this, sirrah?
1. CLOWN.   Mine sir:
                  [*Sings.*] O a pit of clay for to be made   110
                           For such a guest is meet.
HAMLET.   I think it be thine indeed, for thou liest in't.
1. CLOWN.   You lie out on't° sir, and therefore 'tis not yours; for my
   part I do not lie in't, and yet it is mine.
HAMLET.   Thous dost lie in't, to be in't and say it is thine: 'tis for the   115
   dead, not for the quick,° therefore thou liest.
1. CLOWN.   'Tis a quick lie sir, 'twill away again from me to you.
HAMLET.   What man dost thou dig it for?

---

81 *chopless:* lacking the lower jaw.   82 *mazzard:* head.   83 *an:* if.   *trick:* knack.   84
loggets: game in which small pieces of wood were thrown at fixed stakes.   89 *meet:* fitting.   91
quiddities: subtle definition.   *quillets:* minute distinctions.   92 *tenures:* property holdings.   93 *sconce:* head.   96 *statutes:* mortgages.   *recognizances:* promissory bonds.   96–97
fines, recoveries: legal processes for transferring real estate.   97 *vouchers:* persons who vouched for
a title to real estate.   *fine:* end.   98 *recovery:* attainment.   100–101 *length . . . indentures:*
contracts in duplicate, which spread out, would just cover his grave.   101 *conveyances:*
deeds.   102 *box:* the grave.   *inheritor:* owner.   107 *assurance:* (1) security (2) transfer of
land.   113 *on:* of.   116 *quick:* living.

1. CLOWN.   For no man sir.

HAMLET.   What woman then?   120

1. CLOWN.   For none neither.

HAMLET.   Who is to be buried in't?

1. CLOWN.   One that was a woman sir, but rest her soul she's dead.

HAMLET.   How absolute° the knave is, we must speak by the card,° or
      equivocation° will undo us. By the lord, Horatio, this   125
      three years I have took note of it, the age is grown so
      picked,° that the toe of the peasant comes so near the heel of
      the courtier, he galls his kibe.° How long hast thou been
      grave-maker?

1. CLOWN.   Of all the days i'th'year I came to't that day that our last   130
      king Hamlet overcame Fortinbras.

HAMLET.   How long is that since?

1. CLOWN.   Cannot you tell that? Every fool can tell that. It was the very
      day that young Hamlet was born: he that is mad and
      sent into England.   135

HAMLET.   Ay marry, why was he sent into England?

1. CLOWN.   Why because a' was mad: a' shall recover his wits there, or
      if a' do not, 'tis no great matter there.

HAMLET.   Why?

1. CLOWN.   'Twill not be seen in him there, there the men are as mad   140
      as he.

HAMLET.   How came he mad?

1. CLOWN.   Very strangely they say.

HAMLET.   How strangely?

1. CLOWN.   Faith, e'en with losing his wits.   145

HAMLET.   Upon what ground?

1. CLOWN.   Why here in Denmark: I have been sexton here man and
      boy thirty years.

HAMLET.   How long will a man lie i'th'earth ere he rot?

1. CLOWN.   Faith, if a' be not rotten before a' die, as we have many   150
      pocky° corses nowadays that will scarce hold the laying in,
      a' will last you some eight year, or nine year. A tanner will
      last you nine year.

HAMLET.   Why he more than another?

1. CLOWN.   Why sir, his hide is so tanned with his trade, that a' will   155
      keep out water a great while; and your water is a sore°
      decayer of your whoreson dead body. Here's a skull now:
      this skull hath lain you i'th'earth three-and-twenty years.

HAMLET.   Whose was it?

1. CLOWN.   A whoreson mad fellow's it was, whose do you think it   160
      was?

HAMLET.   Nay, I know not.

---

124 *absolute:* precise.   *by the card:* exactly to the point (card on which compass points are
marked).   125 *equivocation:* ambiguity.   127 *picked:* fastidious ("picky").   128 *galls his kibe:*
chafes the sore on the courtier's heel.   151 *pocky:* rotten (with venereal disease).   156 *sore:*
grievous.

1. CLOWN.   A pestilence on him for a mad rogue, a' poured a flagon of
    Rhenish° on my head once; this same skull sir, was sir,
    Yorick's skull, the king's jester.   165
HAMLET.   This?
1. CLOWN.   E'en that.
HAMLET.   Let me see. [*Takes the skull.*] Alas poor Yorick, I knew him
    Horatio, a fellow of infinite jest, of most excellent fancy,°
    he hath borne me on his back a thousand times: and now   170
    how abhorred in my imagination it is: my gorge rises at it.
    Here hung those lips that I have kissed I know not how
    oft. Where be your gibes now? your gambols, your songs,
    your flashes of merriment, that were wont to set the table
    on a roar?° not one now to mock your own grinning? quite   175
    chop-fallen?° Now get you to my lady's chamber, and tell
    her, let her paint an inch thick, to this favour° she must
    come. Make her laugh at that. Prithee Horatio, tell me one
    thing.
HORATIO.   What's that, my lord?   180
HAMLET.   Dost thou think Alexander looked o' this fashion
    i'th'earth?
HORATIO.   E'en so.
HAMLET.   And smelt so? pah.   [*Puts down the skull.*]
HORATIO.   E'en so my lord.   185
HAMLET.   To what base uses we may return, Horatio. Why may not
    imagination trace the noble dust of Alexander, til a'find it
    stopping a bung-hole?°
HORATIO.   'Twere to consider too curiously,° to consider so.
HAMLET.   No faith, not a jot, but to follow him thither with modesty°   190
    enough, and likelihood to lead it; as thus: Alexander died,
    Alexander was buried, Alexander returneth to dust, the
    dust is earth, of earth we make loam,° and why of that loam
    whereto he was converted, might they not stop a
    beer-barrel?   195
        Imperious Caesar, dead and turned to clay,
        Might stop a hole to keep the wind away.
        O that that earth which kept the world in awe,
        Should patch a wall t'expel the winter's flaw.°
    But soft, but soft awhile, here comes the king,   200
    The queen, the courtiers.

Enter KING, QUEEN, LAERTES, *[Doctor of Divinity], and a coffin, with Lords attendant.*

                    Who is this they follow?
        And with such maimèd° rites? This doth betoken
        The corse they follow did with desp'rate hand

---

164 *Rhenish:* Rhine wine.   169 *fancy:* imagination.   175 *on a roar:* roaring with
laughter.   176 *chop-fallen:* (1) lacking a lower jaw (2) dejected, "down in the mouth."   177
favour: appearance.   188 *bung-hole:* hole in a cask.   189 *curiously:* minutely.   190 *modesty:* moderation.   193 *loam:* a clay mixture used as plaster.   199 *flaw:* windy gusts.   202
maimèd: abbreviated.

Fordo it° own life; 'twas of some estate.°
Couch° we awhile, and mark.   [*They retire.*]   205
HAMLET.   That is Laertes,
    A very noble youth: mark.
LAERTES.   What ceremony else?
DOCTOR.   Her obsequies have been as far enlarged
    As we have warranty: her death was doubtful,°   210
    And but that great command o'ersways the order,
    She should in ground unsanctified have lodged
    Til the last trumpet: for charitable prayers,
    Shards,° flints and pebbles should be thrown on her:
    Yet here she is allowed her virgin crants,°   215
    Her maiden strewments,° and the bringing home
    Of° bell and burial.
LAERTES.   Must there no more be done?
DOCTOR.   No more be done:
    We should profane the service of the dead,
    To sing sage requiem° and such rest to her   220
    As to peace-parted souls.
LAERTES.   Lay her i'th'earth,
    And from her fair and unpolluted flesh
    May violets spring: I tell thee churlish priest,
    A minist'ring angel shall my sister be,
    When thou liest howling.
HAMLET.   What, the fair Ophelia?   225
QUEEN.   [*Scattering flowers.*] Sweets to the sweet, farewell.
    I hoped thou shouldst have been my Hamlet's wife:
    I thought thy bride-bed to have decked, sweet maid,
    And not have strewed thy grave.
LAERTES.   O treble woe
    Fall ten times treble on that cursèd head   230
    Whose wicked deed thy most ingenious sense°
    Deprived thee of. Hold off the earth awhile,
    Till I have caught her once more in mine arms;   *Leaps in the grave.*
    Now pile your dust upon the quick° and dead,
    Till of this flat a mountain you have made   235
    T'o'ertop old Pelion,° or the skyish head
    Of blue Olympus.
HAMLET.   [*Comes forward.*] What is he whose grief
    Bears such an emphasis? whose phrase of sorrow
    Conjures the wand'ring stars,° and makes them stand
    Like wonder-wounded hearers? This is I,   240
    Hamlet the Dane.   *HAMLET leaps in after LAERTES.*

204 *Fordo it:* destroy its.   *estate:* social rank.   205 *Couch:* hide.   210 *doubtful:* suspicious.   214 *Shards:* bits of broken pottery.   215 *crants:* garland.   216 *strewments:* flowers
strewn on the grave.   216–217 *bringing home Of:* laying to rest with.   220 *sage requiem:* solemn
dirge.   231 *sense:* mind.   234 *quick:* live.   236 *Pelion:* mountain (on which the Titans
placed Mt. Ossa, to scale Mt. Olympus and reach the gods).   239 *Conjures . . . stars:* casts a spell
over the planets.

LAERTES.   [*Grapples with him.*] The devil take thy soul.

HAMLET.   Thou pray'st not well,
  I prithee take thy fingers from my throat,
  For though I am not splenitive° and rash,
  Yet have I in me something dangerous,   245
  Which let thy wiseness fear; hold off thy hand.

KING.   Pluck them asunder.

QUEEN.   Hamlet, Hamlet!

ALL.   Gentlemen!

HORATIO.   Good my lord, be quiet.

        [*Attendants part them, and they come out of the grave.*]

HAMLET.   Why, I will fight with him upon this theme
  Until my eyelids will no longer wag.   250

QUEEN.   O my son, what theme?

HAMLET.   I loved Ophelia, forty thousand brothers
  Could not with all their quantity of love
  Make up my sum. What wilt thou do for her?

KING.   O he is mad, Laertes.   255

QUEEN.   For love of God, forbear° him.

HAMLET.   'Swounds,° show me what thou't do:
  Woo't° weep? woo't fight? woo't fast? woo't tear thyself?
  Woo't drink up eisel?° eat a crocodile?°
  I'll do't. Dost thou come here to whine?   260
  To outface me with leaping in her grave?
  Be buried quick with her, and so will I.
  And if thou prate of mountains, let them throw
  Millions of acres on us, till our ground,
  Singeing his pate against the burning zone,°   265
  Make Ossa° like a wart. Nay, an thou'lt mouth,
  I'll rant as well as thou.

QUEEN.   This is mere° madness,
  And thus awhile the fit will work on him:
  Anon as patient as the female dove
  When that her golden couplets° are disclosed,   270
  His silence will sit drooping.

HAMLET.   Hear you sir,
  What is the reason that you use me thus?
  I loved you ever; but it is no matter.
  Let Hercules himself do what he may,
  The cat will mew, and dog will have his day.   *Exit HAMLET.*   275

KING.   I pray thee good Horatio, wait upon him.   [*HORATIO* follows.]

    [*Aside to Laertes.*] Strengthen your patience in our last night's speech,

---

244 *spenitive:* quick-tempered (anger was thought to originate in the spleen).   256 *forbear:*
be patient with.   257 *'Swounds:* corruption of "God's wounds."   258 *Woo't:* wilt
thou.   259 *eisel:* vinegar (thought to reduce anger and encourage melancholy).   *crocodile:*
(associated with hypocritical tears).   265 *burning zone:* sun's sphere.   266 *Ossa:* (see above,
line 236 n.).   267 *mere:* absolute.   270 *golden couplets:* fuzzy yellow twin fledglings.

We'll put the matter to the present push°—
Good Gertrude, set some watch over your son—
This grave shall have a living monument:°   280
An hour of quiet shortly shall we see,
Till then, in patience our proceeding be.   *Exeunt.*

Scene 2. *[A hall in the castle]*

Enter HAMLET and HORATIO.

HAMLET. So much for this sir, now shall you see the other;
  You do remember all the circumstance.
HORATIO. Remember it my lord!
HAMLET. Sir, in my heart there was a kind of fighting
  That would not let me sleep; methought I lay   5
  Worse than the mutines in the bilboes.° Rashly—
  And praised be rashness for it: let us know,
  Our indiscretion sometimes serves us well
  When our deep plots do pall,° and that should learn us
  There's a divinity that shapes our ends,   10
  Rough-hew them how we will—
HORATIO.   That is most certain.
HAMLET. Up from my cabin,
  My sea-gown° scarfed about me, in the dark
  Groped I to find out them, had my desire,
  Fingered° their packet, and in fine° withdrew   15
  To mine own room again, making so bold,
  My fears forgetting manners, to unseal
  Their grand commission; where I found, Horatio—
  Ah royal knavery—an exact command,
  Larded° with many several sorts of reasons,   20
  Importing Denmark's health, and England's too,
  With ho, such bugs and goblins in my life,°
  That on the supervise,° no leisure bated,°
  No, not to stay° the grinding of the axe,
  My head should be struck off.
HORATIO.   Is't possible?   25
HAMLET. Here's the commission, read it at more leisure.
  But wilt thou hear now how I did proceed?
HORATIO. I beseech you.
HAMLET. Being thus be-netted round with villainies,
  Ere I could make a prologue to my brains,   30
  They had begun the play.° I sat me down,

---

278 *present push:* immediate test.   280 *living monument:* (1) lasting tombstone (2) living sacrifice (Hamlet) to memorialize it.   6 *mutines . . . bilboes:* mutineers in shackles.   9 *pall:* fail.   13 *sea-gown:* short-sleeved knee-length gown worn by seamen.   15 *Fingered:* got my fingers on.   *in fine:* to finish.   20 *Larded:* embellished.   22 *bugs . . . life:* imaginary evils attributed to me, like imaginary goblins ("bugs") meant to frighten children.   23 *supervise:* looking over (the commission).   *leisure bated:* delay excepted.   24 *stay:* await.   30–31 *Ere . . . play:* Before I could outline the action in my mind, my brains started to play their part.

Devised a new commission, wrote it fair°—
I once did hold it, as our statists° do,
A baseness° to write fair, and laboured much
How to forget that learning, but sir now   35
It did me yeoman's° service: wilt thou know
Th'effect of what I wrote?
HORATIO.   Ay, good my lord.
HAMLET.   An earnest conjuration° from the king,
   As England was his faithful tributary,
   As love between them like the palm might flourish,   40
   As peace should still her wheaten garland wear
   And stand a comma° 'tween their amities,
   And many such like "as'es"° of great charge,°
   That on the view and know of these contents,
   Without debatement further, more or less,   45
   He should those bearers put to sudden death,
   Not shriving° time allowed.
HORATIO.   How was this sealed?
HAMLET.   Why even in that was heaven ordinant,°
   I had my father's signet° in my purse,
   Which was the model° of that Danish seal: 50
   Folded the writ up in the form of th'other,
   Subscribed° it, gave't th'impression,° placed it safely,
   The changeling° never known: now the next day
   Was our sea-fight, and what to this was sequent
   Thou knowest already.   55
HORATIO.   So Guildenstern and Rosencrantz go to't.
HAMLET.   Why man, they did make love to this employment,°
   They are not near my conscience, their defeat
   Does by their own insinuation° grow:
   'Tis dangerous when the baser nature comes   60
   Between the pass° and fell° incensed points
   Of mighty opposites.
HORATIO.   Why, what a king is this!
HAMLET.   Does it not, think thee, stand me now upon°—
   He that hath killed my king, and whored my mother,
   Popped in between th'election° and my hopes,   65
   Thrown out his angle° for my proper° life,
   And with such cozenage°—is't not perfect conscience

---

32 *wrote it fair:* wrote a finished (neat) copy, a "fair copy."   33 *statists:* statesmen.   34 *baseness:*
mark of humble status.   36 *yeoman's:* (in the sense of "faithful").   38 *conjuration:* entreaty (he
parodies the rhetoric of such documents).   42 *comma:* connection.   43 *as'es:* (1) the "as"
clauses in the commission (2) asses.   *charge:* (1) weight (in the clauses) (2) burdens (on the
asses).   47 *shriving:* confession and absolution.   48 *was heaven ordinant:* it was divinely
ordained.   49 *signet:* seal.   50 *model:* replica.   52 *Subscribed:* signed.   *impression:* i.e., of
the seal.   53 *changeling:* substitute (baby imp left when an infant was spirited away).   57 *did . . .
employment:* asked for it.   59 *insinuation:* intrusion.   61 *pass:* thrust.   *fell:* fierce.   63
stand . . . upon: become incumbent upon me now.   65 *election:* (the Danish king was so
chosen).   66 *angle:* fishing hook.   *proper:* very own.   67 *cozenage:* deception.

To quit° him with this arm? And is't not to be damned,
To let this canker of our nature° come
In further evil?   70
HORATIO.   It must be shortly known to him from England
What is the issue of the business there.
HAMLET.   It will be short, the interim is mine,
And a man's life's no more than to say "One."°
But I am very sorry good Horatio,   75
That to Laertes I forgot myself;
For by the image of my cause, I see
The portraiture of his;° I'll court his favours:
But sure the bravery° of his grief did put me
Into a towering passion.
HORATIO.   Peace, who comes here?   80

Enter young OSRIC.

OSRIC.   Your lordship is right welcome back to Denmark.
HAMLET.   I humbly thank you sir. [*Aside to Horatio.*] Dost know this
water-fly?
HORATIO.   No my good lord.
HAMLET.   Thy state is the more gracious,° for 'tis a vice to know him: 85
he hath much land, and fertile: let a beast be lord of beasts,
and his crib shall stand at the king's mess;° 'tis a chough,°
but as I say, spacious in the possession of dirt.
OSRIC.   Sweet lord, if your lordship were at leisure, I should
impart a thing to you from his majesty.   90
HAMLET.   I will receive it sir, with all diligence of spirit; put your
bonnet° to his right use, 'tis for the head.
OSRIC.   I thank your lordship, it is very hot.
HAMLET.   No, believe me, 'tis very cold, the wind is northerly.
OSRIC.   It is indifferent° cold my lord indeed.   95
HAMLET.   But yet methinks it is very sultry and hot for my
complexion.°
OSRIC.   Exceedingly, my lord, it is very sultry, as 'twere, I cannot
tell how: but my lord, his majesty bade me signify to you
that a' has laid a great wager on your head. Sir, this is the   100
matter—
HAMLET.   [*Moves him to put on his hat.*] I beseech you remember—
OSRIC.   Nay good my lord, for mine ease,° in good faith. Sir, here
is newly come to court Laertes, believe me, an absolute
gentleman, full of most excellent differences,° of very soft   105
society, and great showing: indeed to speak feelingly of

68 *quit:* repay, requite.   69 *canker of our nature:* cancer of humanity.   74 *to say "One":* to
score one hit in fencing.   77–78 *by the image . . . his:* in the depiction of my situation, I see the
reflection of his.   79 *bravery:* ostentation.   85 *gracious:* favorable.   86–87 *let a beast . . .
mess:* An ass who owns enough property can eat with the king.   87 *chough:* chattering bird,
jackdaw.   92 *bonnet:* hat.   95 *indifferent:* reasonably.   97 *complexion:* temperament.   103 *for mine ease:* for my own comfort.   105 *differences:* accomplishments.

him, he is the card° or calendar of gentry: for you shall find
in him the continent of what part a gentleman would see.°

HAMLET.   Sir, his definement° suffers no perdition° in you, though I
know to divide him inventorially would dozy°   110
th'arithmetic of memory, and yet but yaw neither, in
respect of his quick sail,° but in the verity of extolment,° I
take him to be a soul of great article,° and his infusion° of
such dearth and rareness, as to make true diction of him,
his semblable° is his mirror, and who else would trace° him,   115
his umbrage,° nothing more.°

OSRIC.   Your lordship speaks most infallibly of him.

HAMLET.   The concernancy° sir? why do we wrap the gentleman in
our more rawer breath?°

OSRIC.   Sir?   120

HORATIO.   Is't not possible to understand in another tongue?° You
will do't sir, really.

HAMLET.   What imports the nomination° of this gentleman?

OSRIC.   Of Laertes?

HORATIO.   His purse is empty already, all's golden words are spent.   125

HAMLET.   Of him, sir.

OSRIC.   I know you are not ignorant—

HAMLET.   I would you did sir, yet in faith if you did, it would not
much approve me.° Well, sir.

OSRIC.   You are not ignorant of what excellence Laertes is—   130

HAMLET.   I dare not confess that, lest I should compare with him in
excellence, but to know a man well were to know himself.°

OSRIC.   I mean sir for his weapon, but in the imputation° laid on
him by them in his meed,° he's unfellowed.°

HAMLET.   What's his weapon?   135

OSRIC.   Rapier and dagger.

HAMLET.   That's two of his weapons—but well.

OSRIC.   The king sir, hath wagered with him six Barbary horses,
against which he has impawned,° as I take it, six French
rapiers and poniards,° with their assigns,° as girdle, hangers,°   140
and so. Three of the carriages° in faith are very dear to

---

107 *card:* shipman's compass card.   108 *continent . . . see:* (continuing the marine metaphor)
(1) geographical continent (2) all the qualities a gentleman would look for.   109–116 *Sir . . .
more:* (Hamlet outdoes Osric in affected speech).   109 *definement:* description.   *perdition:*
loss.   110 *dozy:* dizzy.   111–112 *yaw . . . sail:* (1) moving in an unsteady course (as another
boat would do, trying to catch up with Laertes' "quick sail") (2) staggering to one trying to list his
accomplishments.   112 *in . . . extolment:* to praise him truthfully.   113 *article:* scope.   *infu-
sion:* essence.   114–116 *as to make . . . more:* to describe him truly I would have to employ his
mirror to depict his only equal—himself, and who would follow him is only a shadow.   115 *sem-
blable:* equal.   *trace:* (1) describe (2) follow.   116 *umbrage:* shadow.   118 *concernancy:* relevance.   119 *rawer breath:* crude speech.   121 *Is't not . . . tongue:* Cannot Osric understand
his own way of speaking when used by another?   123 *nomination:* naming.   128–129 *if you
did . . . me:* If you found me to be "not ignorant," it would prove little (as you are no judge of ignorance).   132 *to know . . . himself:* to know a man well, one must first know oneself.   133 *impu-
tation:* repute.   134 *meed:* worth.   *unfellowed:* unequaled.   139 *impawned:* staked.
140 *poniards:* daggers.   *assigns:* accessories.   *girdle, hangers:* belt, straps attached thereto,
from which swords were hung.   141 *carriages:* hangers.

fancy,° very responsive to the hilts, most delicate carriages,
and of very liberal conceit.°

HAMLET.   What call you the carriages?

HORATIO.   I knew you must be edified by the margent° ere you had   145
done.

OSRIC.   The carriages sir, are the hangers.

HAMLET.   The phrase would be more germane to the matter, if we
could carry a cannon by our sides: I would it might be
hangers till then, but on: six Barbary horses against six   150
French swords, their assigns, and three liberal-conceited
carriages—that's the French bet against the Danish. Why
is this all "impawned" as you call it?

OSRIC.   The king sir, hath laid sir, that in a dozen passes between
yourself and him, he shall not exceed you three hits°; he   155
hath laid on twelve for nine, and it would come to
immediate trial, if your lordship would vouchsafe the
answer.°

HAMLET.   How if I answer no?

OSRIC.   I mean my lord, the opposition of your person in trial.   160

HAMLET.   Sir, I will walk here in the hall; if it please his majesty, it is
the breathing time° of day with me; let the foils be brought,
the gentleman willing, and the king hold his purpose, I
will win for him an I can, if not, I will gain nothing but my
shame and the odd hits.   165

OSRIC.   Shall I re-deliver you° e'en so?

HAMLET.   To this effect sir, after what flourish your nature will.°

OSRIC.   I commend° my duty to your lordship.

HAMLET.   Yours, yours.   *[Exit OSRIC.]*

He does well to commend it himself, there are no tongues   170
else for's turn.°

HORATIO.   This lapwing° runs away with the shell on his head.

HAMLET.   A' did comply° sir, with his dug° before a' sucked it: thus
has he—and many more of the same bevy that I know the
drossy° age dotes on—only got the tune of the time, and   175
out of an habit of encounter,° a kind of yeasty collection,°
which carries them through and through the most fond
and winnowed° opinions; and do but blow them to their
trial, and bubbles are out.°

141–142 *dear to fancy:* rare in design.   143 *liberal conceit:* elaborate conception.   145 *margent:* marginal note.   154–155 *laid . . . three hits:* wagered that in twelve bouts Laertes must win three more than Hamlet.   158 *answer:* acceptance of the challenge (Hamlet interprets as "reply").   163 *breathing time:* exercise period.   166 *re-deliver you:* take back your answer. 167 *after . . . will:* embellished as you wish.   168 *commend:* offer (Hamlet interprets as "praise").   170–171 *no tongues . . . turn:* no others who would.   172 *lapwing:* (reported to be so precocious that it ran as soon as hatched).   173 *comply:* observe the formalities of courtesy.   *dug:* mother's breast.   175 *drossy:* frivolous.   176 *habit of encounter:* habitual association (with others as frivolous).   *yeasty collection:* frothy assortment of phrases.   177–178 *fond and winnowed:* trivial and considered.   178–179 *blow . . . out:* blow on them to test them and they are gone.

Enter a LORD.

LORD.   My lord, his majesty commended him to you by young   180
    Osric, who brings back to him that you attend him in
    the hall. He sends to know if your pleasure hold to play
    with Laertes, or that you will take longer time.
HAMLET.   I am constant to my purposes, they follow the king's
    pleasure, if his fitness speaks,° mine is ready: now or   185
    whensoever, provided I be so able as now.
LORD.   The king, and queen, and all are coming down.
HAMLET.   In happy time.
LORD.   The queen desires you to use some gentle entertainment°
    to Laertes, before you fall to play.   190
HAMLET.   She well instructs me.   [*Exit* LORD.]
HORATIO.   You will lose this wager, my lord.
HAMLET.   I do not think so, since we went into France, I have been in
    continual practice, I shall win at the odds; but thou
    wouldst not think how ill all's here about my heart: but it   195
    is no matter.
HORATIO.   Nay good my lord—
HAMLET.   It is but a foolery, but it is such a kind of gaingiving° as
    would perhaps trouble a woman.
HORATIO.   If your mind dislike any thing, obey it. I will forestall their   200
    repair° hither, and say you are not fit.
HAMLET.   Not a whit, we defy augury;° there is a special providence
    in the fall of a sparrow.° If it be now, 'tis not to come:
    if it be not to come, it will be now; if it be not now,
    yet it will come—the readiness is all. Since no man has   205
    aught of what he leaves, what is't to leave betimes?° let
    be.

A table prepared. Trumpets, Drums, and officers with cushions. Enter KING, QUEEN, *and all the*
state, [OSRIC], *foils daggers, and* LAERTES.

KING.   Come Hamlet, come and take this hand from me.
    [*Puts Laertes' hand into Hamlet's.*]
HAMLET.   Give me your pardon sir, I have done you wrong,
    But pardon't as you are a gentleman.   210
    This presence knows, and you must needs have heard,
    How I am punished with a sore distraction.°
    What I have done
    That might your nature, honour, and exception°
    Roughly awake, I here proclaim was madness: 215
    Was't Hamlet wronged Laertes? never Hamlet.
    If Hamlet from himself be ta'en away,

---

185 *his fitness speaks:* it agrees with his convenience.   189 *gentle entertainment:* friendly treatment.   198 *gaingiving:* misgiving.   201 *repair:* coming.   202 *augury:* omens.   202–203
special . . . sparrow: ("Are not two sparrows sold for a farthing? and one of them shall not fall on
the ground without your Father": Matthew 10:29).   206 *betimes:* early (before one's
time).   212 *sore distraction:* grievous madness.   214 *exception:* disapproval.

And when he's not himself, does wrong Laertes,
Then Hamlet does it not, Hamlet denies it:
Who does it then? his madness. If't be so, 220
Hamlet is of the faction that is wronged,
His madness is poor Hamlet's enemy.
Sir, in this audience,
Let my disclaiming from a purposed evil,
Free me so far in your most generous thoughts, 225
That I have shot my arrow o'er the house
And hurt my brother.°
LAERTES.   I am satisfied in nature,
Whose motive in this case should stir me most
To my revenge, but in my terms of honour
I stand aloof, and will no reconcilement, 230
Till by some elder masters of known honour
I have a voice and precedent° of peace
To keep my name ungored:° but till that time,
I do receive your offered love, like love,
And will not wrong it.
HAMLET.   I embrace it freely, 235
And will this brother's wager frankly° play.
Give us the foils: come on.
LAERTES.   Come, one for me.
HAMLET.   I'll be your foil° Laertes, in mine ignorance
Your skill shall like a star i'th' darkest night
Stick fiery off° indeed. 240
LAERTES.   You mock me sir.
HAMLET. No, by this hand.
KING.   Give them the foils young Osric. Cousin° Hamlet,
You know the wager.
HAMLET.   Very well my lord.
Your grace has laid the odds o'th'weaker side.
KING.   I do not fear it, I have seen you both, 245
But since he is bettered,° we have therefore odds.
LAERTES.   This is too heavy: let me see another.°
HAMLET.   This likes° me well, these foils have all a° length?
OSRIC.   Ay my good lord.   *Prepare to play.*
KING.   Set me the stoups° of wine upon that table: 250
If Hamlet give the first or second hit,
Or quit in answer of° the third exchange,
Let all the battlements their ordnance fire.

226–227 *That I have . . . brother:* (that it was accidental).   232 *voice and precedent:* opinion based
on precedent.   233 *name ungored:* reputation uninjured. Laertes says that he cannot accept
Hamlet's apology formally until he is assured that his acceptance will not harm his honor or
damage his reputation.   236 *frankly:* freely.   238 *foil:* (1) the blunted sword with which they
fence (2) leaf of metal set under a jewel to make it shine more brilliantly.   240 *Stick fiery off:*
show in shining contrast.   242 *Cousin:* kinsman.   246 *bettered:* either (a) judged to be better,
or (b) better trained.   247 *another:* (the unbated and poisoned sword).   248 *likes:*
pleases.   *all a:* all the same.   250 *stoups:* goblets.   252 *quit in answer of:* score a draw in.

The king shall drink to Hamlet's better breath,
And in the cup an union° shall he throw,   255
Richer than that which four successive kings
In Denmark's crown have worn: give me the cups,
And let the kettle° to the trumpet speak,
The trumpet to the cannoneer without,
The cannons to the heavens, the heaven to earth,   260
"Now the king drinks to Hamlet." Come begin.
And you the judges bear a wary eye.   *Trumpets the while.*

HAMLET.   Come on sir.
LAERTES.   Come my lord.   *They play.*
HAMLET.   One.
LAERTES.   No.
HAMLET.   Judgment.
OSRIC.   A hit, a very palpable hit.

> *Flourish. Drum, trumpets and shot. A piece° goes off.*

LAERTES.   Well, again.
KING.   Stay, give me drink. Hamlet, this pearl is thine.   265
    Here's to thy health: give him the cup.
HAMLET.   I'll play this bout first, set it by a while.
    Come.   *[They play.]*
            Another hit. What say you?
LAERTES.   A touch, a touch, I do confess't.
KING.   Our son shall win.
QUEEN.   He's fat° and scant of breath.   270
    Here Hamlet, take my napkin,° rub thy brows.   *[She takes HAMLET's cup.]*
    The queen carouses° to thy fortune, Hamlet.
HAMLET.   Good madam.
KING.   Gertrude, do not drink.
QUEEN.   I will my lord, I pray you pardon me.
KING.   [*Aside.*] It is the poisoned cup, it is too late.   275
HAMLET.   I dare not drink yet madam: by and by.
QUEEN.   Come, let me wipe thy face.
LAERTES.   [*To the King.*] My lord, I'll hit him now.
KING.   I do not think't.
LAERTES.   [*Aside.*] And yet 'tis almost 'gainst my conscience.
HAMLET.   Come for the third Laertes, you do but dally,   280
    I pray you pass° with your best violence,
    I am afeard you make a wanton of me.°
LAERTES.   Say you so? Come on.   *Play.*
OSRIC.   Nothing neither way   *[They break off.]*
LAERTES.   Have at you now.°   *[Wounds Hamlet.]*

---

255 *union:* large pearl.   258 *kettle:* kettledrum.   264.1 S.D.: *piece:* i.e., a cannon.   270 *fat:* sweating (sweat was thought to be melted body fat).   271 *napkin:* handkerchief.   272 *carouses:* drinks.   281 *pass:* thrust.   282 *make a wanton of me:* are indulging me like a spoiled child.   285 *Have . . . now:* (the bout is over when Laertes attacks Hamlet and catches him off guard).

In scuffling they change rapiers.

KING.	Part them, they are incensed.	285

HAMLET.   Nay, come again.   [*The* QUEEN *falls.*]

OSRIC.   Look to the queen there, ho!

[HAMLET *wounds* LAERTES.]

HORATIO.   They bleed on both side. How is it, my lord?

OSRIC.   How is't, Laertes?

LAERTES.   Why as a woodcock° to my own springe,° Osric,
    I am justly killed with mine own treachery.   290

HAMLET.   How does the queen?

KING.   She sounds° to see them bleed.

QUEEN.   No, no, the drink, the drink, O my dear Hamlet,
    The drink, the drink, I am poisoned.   [*Dies.*]

HAMLET.   O villainy! ho! let the door be locked,
    Treachery, seek it out!   295

LAERTES.   It is here Hamlet. Hamlet, thou art slain,
    No medicine in the world can do thee good,
    In thee there is not half an hour of life,
    The treacherous instrument is in thy hand,
    Unbated° and envenomed. The foul practice°   300
    Hath turned itself on me, lo, here I lie
    Never to rise again: thy mother's poisoned:
    I can no more: the king, the king's to blame.

HAMLET.   The point envenomed too:
    Then venom, to thy work.   *Hurts the* KING. 305

ALL.   Treason! treason!

KING.   O yet defend me friends, I am but hurt.°

HAMLET.   Here, thou incestuous, murderous, damnèd Dane,
    Drink off this potion: is thy union here?
    Follow my mother.   *King dies.*   310

LAERTES.   He is justly served,
    It is a poison tempered° by himself:
    Exchange forgiveness with me, noble Hamlet,
    Mine and my father's death come not upon thee,°
    Nor thine on me.   *Dies.*

HAMLET.   Heaven make thee free° of it, I follow thee.   315
    I am dead, Horatio; wretched queen, adieu.
    You that look pale, and tremble at this chance,
    That are but mutes,° or audience to this act,
    Had I but time, as this fell sergeant° Death
    Is strict in his arrest, O I could tell you—   320
    But let it be; Horatio, I am dead,

---

289 *woodcock:* snipe-like bird (believed to be foolish and therefore easily trapped).   *springe:*
trap.   291 *sounds:* swoons.   300 *Unbated:* not blunted.   *practice:* plot.   307 *but hurt:*
only wounded.   311 *tempered:* mixed.   313 *come . . . thee:* are not to be blamed on
you.   315 *free:* guiltless.   318 *mutes:* actors without speaking parts.   319 *fell sergeant:* cruel
sheriff's officer.

Thou livest, report me and my cause aright
To the unsatisfied.°
HORATIO.   Never believe it;
I am more an antique Roman° than a Dane:
Here's yet some liquor left.
HAMLET.   As thou'rt a man,   325
Give me the cup, let go, by heaven I'll ha't.
O God, Horatio, what a wounded name,
Things standing thus unknown, shall live behind me.
If thou didst ever hold me in thy heart,
Absènt thee from felicity awhile,   330
And in this harsh world draw thy breath in pain
To tell my story.   *A march afar off, and shot within.*
                    What warlike noise is this?
OSRIC.   Young Fortinbras with conquest come from Poland,
To th'ambassadors of England gives
This warlike volley.
HAMLET.   O I die Horatio,   335
The potent poison quite o'er-crows° my spirit,
I cannot live to hear the news from England,
But I do prophesy th'election° lights
On Fortinbras, he has my dying voice,°
So tell him, with th'occurrents more and less°   340
Which have solicited°—the rest is silence.   *Dies.*
HORATIO.   Now cracks a noble heart: good night sweet prince,
And flights of angels sing thee to thy rest.
Why does the drum come hither?

Enter FORTINBRAS *and English Ambassadors, with drum, colours, and attendants.*

FORTINBRAS.   Where is this sight?
HORATIO.   What is it you would see?   345
If aught of woe, or wonder, cease your search.
FORTINBRAS.   This quarry cries on havoc.° O proud death,
What feast is toward° in thine eternal cell,
That thou so many princes at a shot
So bloodily hast struck?   350
AMBASSADOR.   The sight is dismal,
And our affairs from England come too late;
The ears° are senseless that should give us hearing,
To tell him his commandment is fulfilled,
That Rosencrantz and Guildenstern are dead:
Where should we have our thanks?
HORATIO.   Not from his mouth,   355
Had it th'ability of life to thank you;

323 *unsatisfied:* uninformed.   324 *antique Roman:* ancient Roman (who considered suicide honorable).   336 *o'er-crows:* overpowers, conquers.   338 *election:* (for king of Denmark).   339 *voice:* vote.   340 *occurrents more and less:* events great and small.   341 *solicited:* incited me.   347 *quarry . . . havoc:* heap of dead bodies proclaims slaughter done here.
348 *toward:* in preparation.   352 *ears:* (of Claudius).

He never gave commandment for their death;
But since so jump° upon this bloody question,
You from the Polack wars, and you from England
Are here arrived, give order that these bodies   360
High on a stage be placèd to the view,
And let me speak to th'yet unknowing world
How these things came about; so shall you hear
Of carnal, bloody and unnatural acts,
Of accidental judgments, casual° slaughters,   365
Of deaths put on° by cunning and forced cause,°
And in this upshot, purposes mistook,
Fall'n on th'inventors' heads:° all this can I
Truly deliver.
FORTINBRAS.   Let us haste to hear it,
And call the noblest to the audience.   370
For me, with sorrow I embrace my fortune;
I have some rights of memory° in this kingdom,
Which now to claim my vantage° doth invite me.
HORATIO.   Of that I shall have also cause to speak,
And from his mouth whose voice will draw on more:°   375
But let this same° be presently performed,
Even while men's minds are wild,° lest more mischance
On° plots and errors happen.
FORTINBRAS.   Let four captains
Bear Hamlet like a soldier to the stage,
For he was likely, had he been put on,°   380
To have proved most royal; and for his passage,°
The soldiers' music and the rite of war
Speak loudly for him:
Take up the bodies, such a sight as this,
Becomes the field, but here shows much amiss.   385
Go bid the soldiers shoot.

Exeunt marching: after the which a peal of ordnance are shot off.

QUESTIONS

Act I

1. Discuss the various ways in which the first scene of *Hamlet* shows you that something is wrong in Denmark.

2. What impression does Claudius make in scene 2? Is he a rational man? A good administrator? A competent ruler? A loving husband and uncle?

3. What does Hamlet reveal about his own mental state in his first soliloquy?

358 *jump:* opportunely.   365 *casual:* unpremeditated.   366 *put on:* prompted by.   *forced cause:* being forced to act in self-defense.   367–368 *purposes . . . heads:* plots gone wrong and destroying their inventors.   372 *of memory:* remembered.   373 *vantage:* advantageous position.   375 *draw on more:* influence more (votes).   376 *this same:* this telling of the story.   377 *wild:* upset.   378 *On:* on top of.   380 *put on:* i.e., put on the throne. 381 *passage:* i.e., to the next world.

4. What attitude toward Ophelia's relationship with Hamlet do Laertes and Polonius share? What do they want Ophelia to do? Why?

5. What does the ghost tell Hamlet? What does the ghost want Hamlet to do and not to do? Why does Hamlet need proof that the ghost's words are true?

Act II

6. What does Polonius think is the cause of Hamlet's madness? What do Polonius's diagnosis and his handling of the situation show us about him?

7. What does Hamlet accuse himself of in the soliloquy that begins "O what a rogue and peasant slave am I" (Act II, scene 2, lines 524–580)? To what extent is his self-accusation justified?

Act III

8. How do you react to Hamlet's treatment of Ophelia in the first scene of Act III? What evidence might indicate that Hamlet knows that Claudius and Polonius are watching and listening to everything that occurs?

9. Hamlet sets up the performance of "The Murder of Gonzago"—the play-within-a-play—to test Claudius's guilt. What is the relationship between the events of this play-within-a-play and the events of *Hamlet*?

10. How does Claudius react to "The Murder of Gonzago"? What does this reaction tell Hamlet? Why do you suppose Claudius does not react to the dumb show presented at the beginning of the play-within-a-play?

11. What is Hamlet's reason for not killing Claudius at prayer?

12. How does Hamlet treat his mother during their confrontation in her closet? Is Hamlet's behavior overly nasty or justified? Why does the ghost reappear during this confrontation?

13. What crimes or sins does Hamlet accuse Gertrude of committing?

Act IV

14. Do you think Laertes's desire to avenge his father's murder is any more or less justified than Hamlet's desire?

15. How does Claudius plan to use Laertes's desire for revenge to manipulate him? To what extent does Laertes unwittingly allow himself to be used by Claudius?

Act V

16. The conversation between the two clowns (gravediggers) and between Hamlet and the first clown is seen as comic relief—a humorous episode designed to ease tension. Why is comic relief appropriate at this point?

17. How does this scene of comic relief reflect and broaden the play's themes?

18. Why does Hamlet describe Osric as a "water-fly"? How does Shakespeare use Osric's language and behavior to characterize him?

19. Discuss the lessons that Hamlet tells Horatio he has learned about life. How does this understanding change Hamlet? Why is it ironic?

20. How is Gertrude killed? Hamlet? Laertes? Claudius? Why does Hamlet insist that Horatio not commit suicide?

GENERAL QUESTIONS

1. Describe the character of Claudius. Do you consider him purely evil or merely a flawed human being? Why? To what degree can you justify calling this play "The Tragedy of Claudius, King of Denmark"?

2. Characterize Horatio. Why does Hamlet admire and trust him? How is he different from Polonius or Rosencrantz and Guildenstern?

3. Describe Rosencrantz and Guildenstern. Are they round or flat? How does Claudius use them? Why do they cooperate with Claudius? How does Hamlet arrange their deaths? To what extent can this action be justified?

4. Evaluate Polonius's character. Is he a wise counselor? A fool? Sincere? Self-serving? Hypocritical? What are his motives? How is he like Rosencrantz and Guildenstern? How is his death like their deaths?

5. *Hamlet* is full of conflicts that oppose people to other people, to society, and to themselves. List all the conflicts you can find in the play. Decide which of these is the central conflict, and explain your choice.

6. What is the crisis of *Hamlet*? When does it occur? Whom does it affect? What is the catastrophe? The resolution?

7. In Act IV, Claudius notes that "sorrows come . . . in battalions." By the end of the play these sorrows include the deaths of Polonius, Rosencrantz, Guildenstern, Ophelia, Laertes, Gertrude, Claudius, and Hamlet. To what degree can Claudius be held responsible for all the sorrows of the play? Which sorrows are primarily Hamlet's responsibility?

8. Is *Hamlet* a tragedy of the state as well as a tragedy of the individual? In what condition is Denmark at the beginning of the play? Is the condition of Denmark better or worse at the end?

WRITING ABOUT TRAGEDY

As you plan and write an essay about tragedy, keep in mind all the elements of drama. A full discussion of traditional approaches to these elements—plot, character, point of view, setting, language, tone, symbol, and theme—is found in Chapter 22. Review this material before you begin your essay.

Although the basic elements remain consistent in tragedy, the form requires a few special considerations. In planning to write about plot and conflict, you might explore the crisis or climax—that point at which the downfall becomes inevitable. Similarly, you might consider the degree to which the conflicts shape or accelerate the tragic action. With character, pay special attention to the tragic protagonist and the major antagonists: What is the connection between the protagonist's strengths and weaknesses? To what extent does the protagonist bring on or cooperate with his or her own destruction? What key characteristics and behavior patterns ensure both the protagonist's heroic stature and fall? In dealing with tone, consider the degree to which the play is ironic. Do you know more about what is going on than the protagonist? Than most of the characters? If so, how does your knowledge affect your understanding of the play?

Along with these considerations, all the traditional elements of drama can provide fruitful essays about tragic drama. Here, however, our emphasis is to be the examination of a problem that arises in the course of a play—a difficult or even baffling question about a play's action, characters, structure, language, and so on. Of course, this type of essay can also be used to write about prose fiction, poetry, or any other type of drama such as comedy or farce. Our emphasis, however, will be on tragedy—specifically *Hamlet*—to demonstrate how problem solving can generate effective essays.

AN ESSAY ABOUT A PROBLEM

A **problem** is any question that you cannot answer easily and correctly about a body of material that you know. The question "Who is the major character in *Hamlet?*" is not a problem, because the obvious answer is Hamlet. Let us, however, ask another question: "Why is it *correct* to say that Hamlet is the major character?" This question is not as easy as the first, and for this reason it is a problem. It requires that we think about our answer, even though we do not need to search very far. Hamlet is the title character. He is involved in most of the actions of the play. He is so much the center of our liking and concern that his death causes sadness and regret. To "solve" this problem has required a set of responses, all of which provide answers to the question "why?"

More complex, however, and more typical of most problems, are questions like these: "Why does Hamlet talk of suicide in his first soliloquy?" "Why does he treat Ophelia so coarsely in the 'nunnery' scene?" "Why does he delay in avenging his father's death?" Essays on a problem are normally concerned with such questions, because they require a good deal of thought, together with a number of interpretations knitted together into a whole essay. More broadly, dealing with problems is one of the major tasks of the intellectual, scientific, social, and political disciplines. Being able to advance and then explain solutions is therefore one of the most important techniques that you can acquire.

Strategies for Developing an Essay about a Problem

Your first purpose is to convince your reader that your solution is a good one. This you do by making sound conclusions from supporting evidence. In nonscientific subjects like literature you rarely find absolute proofs, so your conclusions will not be *proved* in the way you prove triangles congruent in geometry. But your organization, your use of facts from the text, your interpretations, and your application of general or specific knowledge should all make your conclusions convincing. Thus your basic strategy is *persuasion.*

1. *Demonstrate that conditions for a solution are fulfilled.* This type of development is the most basic in writing—namely, illustration. You first explain that

certain conditions need to exist for your solution to be plausible. Your central idea—really a brief answer to the question—is that the conditions do indeed exist. Your development is to show how the conditions can be found in the work.

Suppose that you are writing on the problem of why Hamlet delays revenge against Claudius. Suppose also that you make the point that Hamlet delays because he is never sure that Claudius is guilty. This is your "solution" to the problem. In your essay you support your answer by challenging the credibility of the information Hamlet receives about the crime (i.e., the two visits from the Ghost and Claudius's distress at the play within the play). Once you have "attacked" these sources of data on the grounds that they are unreliable, you have succeeded because your solution is consistent with the details of the play.

2. *Analyze words in the phrasing of the problem.* Your object in this approach is to clarify important words in the statement of the problem, and then to decide how applicable they are. This kind of attention to words, in fact, might give you enough material for all or part of your essay. Thus, an essay on the problem of Hamlet's delay might focus in part on a treatment of the word *delay*: What, really, does *delay* mean? For Hamlet, is there a difference between delay that is reasonable and delay that is unreasonable? Does Hamlet delay unreasonably? Is his delay the result of a psychological fault? Would speedy revenge be more or less reasonable than the delay? By the time you have answered such pointed questions, you will also have sufficient material for your full essay.

3. *Refer to literary conventions or expectations.* With this strategy, the argument is to establish that the problem can be solved by reference to the literary mode or conventions of a work, or to the limitations of the work itself. In other words, what appears to be a problem is really no more than a normal characteristic. A problem about the artificiality of the choruses in *Oedipus the King*, for example, might be resolved by reference to the fact that choruses were a normal feature of Greek drama. In a similar manner, the knowledge that delay is a convention of all revenge tragedy might provide a key to the problem of Hamlet's apparent procrastination. Similarly, a question about the differing functions of Tom in *The Glass Menagerie* (pp. 1289–1338) can be explained by the free use that Tennessee Williams makes of nonrealistic stage conventions.

4. *Argue against possible objections.* With this strategy, you raise your own objections and then argue against them. Called **procatalepsis** or **anticipation,** this approach helps you sharpen your arguments, because *anticipating* and dealing with objections forces you to make analyses and use facts that you might otherwise overlook. Although procatalepsis can be used point by point throughout your essay, you may find it most useful at the end.

The situation to imagine is that someone is raising objections to your solution to the problem. It is then your task to show that the objections (1) are not accurate or valid, (2) are not strong or convincing, or (3) are based on unusual rather than usual conditions (on an exception and not the rule). Here are some examples of these approaches:

1. *The objection is not accurate or valid.* You reject this objection by showing that either the interpretation or the conclusions are wrong and also by emphasizing that the evidence supports your solution.

    Although Hamlet's delay is reasonable, the claim might be made that his duty is to kill Claudius in revenge immediately after the Ghost's accusations. This claim is not persuasive because it assumes that Hamlet knows everything the audience knows. The audience accepts the Ghost's word that Claudius is guilty, but Hamlet has no certain reasons to believe the Ghost. Would it not seem insane for Hamlet to kill Claudius, who reigns legally, and then to claim he did it because of the Ghost's words? The argument for speedy revenge is not good because it is based on an incorrect view of Hamlet's situation.

2. *The objection is not strong or convincing.* You *concede* that the objection has some truth or validity, but you then try to show that it is weak and that your own solution is stronger.

    One might claim that Claudius's distress at the play within the play is evidence for his guilt and that therefore Hamlet should carry out his revenge right away. This argument has merit, and Hamlet's speech after Claudius has fled the scene ("I'll take the Ghost's word for a thousand pound") shows that the "conscience of the king" has been caught. But the king's guilty behavior is not a strong cause for killing him. Hamlet could justifiably ask for an investigation of his father's death on these grounds, but he could not justify a revenge killing. Claudius could not be convicted in any court on the testimony that he was disturbed at seeing "The Murder of Gonzago." Even after the play within the play, the reasons for delay are stronger than for action.

3. *The objection depends on unusual rather than usual conditions.* You reject the objection on the grounds that it could be valid only if normal conditions were suspended. The objection depends on an exception, not a rule.

    The case for quick action is simple: Hamlet should kill Claudius right after seeing the Ghost (I.3), or else after seeing the king's reaction to the stage murder of Gonzago (III.2), or else after seeing the Ghost again (III.4). Redress under these circumstances, goes the argument, must be both personal and extralegal. This argument wrongly assumes that due process does not exist in the Denmark of Hamlet and Claudius. Nothing in the play indicates that the Danes, even though they carouse a bit, do not value legality and the rules of evidence. Thus Hamlet cannot rush out to kill Claudius, because he knows that the king has not had anything close to due process. The argument for quick action is poor because it rests on an exception being made from civilized law.

Remember that writing an essay on a problem requires you to argue a position: Either there is a solution or there is not. To develop your position requires that you show the steps to your conclusion. Your general thematic form is thus (1) to describe the conditions that need to be met for the solution you propose, and then (2) to demonstrate that these conditions exist. If you assert that there is no solution, then your form would be the same for the first part, but your second part—the development—would show that these conditions have *not* been met.

In developing your response, use one or more of the strategies described in this chapter. These are, again, (1) to demonstrate that conditions for a solution are fulfilled, (2) to analyze the words in the phrasing of the problem, (3) to refer to literary conventions or expectations, and (4) to argue against possible objections. You might combine these. Thus, if we assume that your argument is that Hamlet's delay is reasonable, you might first consider the word *delay* (strategy 2). Then you might use strategy 1 to explain the reasons for Hamlet's delay. Finally, to answer objections to your argument, you might show that he acts promptly when he believes he is justified (strategy 4). Whatever your topic, the important thing is to use the method or methods that best help you make a good argument for your solution.

In your conclusion, try to affirm the validity of your solution in view of the supporting evidence. You might do this by reemphasizing your strongest points, or you might simply present a brief summary. Or you might think of your argument as still continuing and thus use the strategy of procatalepsis to raise and answer possible objections to your solution, as in the last paragraph of the sample student essay that follows.

SAMPLE STUDENT ESSAY

The Problem of Hamlet's Apparent Delay°

[1] For hundreds of years, readers and spectators of Shakespeare's *Hamlet* have been puzzled by the prince's apparent failure to kill Claudius quickly. Early in the play, the Ghost calls on his son to "Revenge his foul and most unnatural murder" (Act I, scene 5, line 25). Hamlet, however, delays his vengeance until the end of the play. Why does he not act sooner? The answer is that there is no unjustified delay and that in fact Hamlet acts as quickly as possible.* This becomes evident when we examine the conventions of revenge tragedy, the actual "call to revenge," and the steps that Hamlet takes to achieve vengeance.†

[2] Revenge tragedy conventionally requires that vengeance be delayed until the closing moments of the play. Given this limitation, Shakespeare must justify the wide gap of time between the call to revenge in Act I and the killing of Claudius in Act V. We find such justification in the unreliability of the ghost's initial accusation, Hamlet's need for additional evidence, and the events that occur after this evidence is obtained.

[3] The Ghost's accusations and demands are straightforward: he accuses his brother of murdering him, and he calls on his son for vengeance. Shakespeare is careful, however, to establish that this testimony may be doubtful. Horatio questions the Ghost's truthfulness and motives, and he warns Hamlet that the spirit might "assume some other horrible form / Which might deprive your

° See pp. 955–1055 for this play.
* Central idea.
† Thesis sentence.

sovereignty of reason, / And draw you into madness" (Act I, scene 4, lines 72–74). Hamlet himself expresses doubt about the ghost:

> The spirit that I have seen
> May be a devil, and the devil hath power
> T'assume a pleasing shape, yea, and perhaps
> Out of my weakness, and my melancholy,
> As he is very potent with such spirits,
> Abuses me to damn me; I'll have grounds
> More relative than this.   (II.2, 573–79)

The prince thus cannot act simply on the unsupported word of the ghost; he needs more evidence.

[4]

There is no delay at this point in the play, because Hamlet quickly begins developing a plan of action. Immediately after speaking with the Ghost, he decides to cover himself under an "antic disposition" while he gathers information. He swears his companions to silence and warns them not to react knowingly if he should seem to behave strangely or insanely (Act I, scene 5, lines 169–79). His idea is that this pose will make him less suspect and make others less careful.

Once Hamlet has begun his plan, he takes advantage of every opportunity to carry out his vengeance. When the players come to Elsinore, he adroitly plans to test Claudius by making him publicly view a play, *The Mousetrap,* which shows a murder just like Claudius's murder of Hamlet's father. Hamlet states that Claudius's appearance will give him the clue he needs to confirm the Ghost's information:

> I'll observe his looks,
> I'll tent him to the quick, if a' do blench
> I know my course.   (II.2, 571–73)

[5]

Once the king breaks up the performance in great agitation, which Hamlet correctly interprets as an admission of guilt, Hamlet declares confidence in the Ghost ("I'll take the ghost's word for a thousand pound" [Act III, scene 2, lines 271–72]). Moreover, he is psychologically ready to act against the king, for he asserts that he could "drink hot blood, / And do such bitter business as the day / Would quake to look on" (Act III, scene 2, lines 367–69). Without doubt, Hamlet is only a prayer away from stabbing Claudius, for when he sees the king kneeling, his opportunity has merged with his desire and also with his promise to the Ghost. He tells the audience, "Now might I do it pat, now a' is a-praying, / And now I'll do't" (Act III, scene 3, lines 73–74).

[6]

But he does not "do't," and for this reason he is open to the claim that he cannot act. Again, however, Shakespeare carefully justifies this hesitation. The prince does not want to send Claudius's soul to heaven by killing him at prayer. Rather, he wants the revenge to match Claudius's treacherous murder of old King Hamlet, who died without the chance to pray and repent:

> Up sword, and know thou a more horrid hent,
> When he is drunk asleep, or in his rage,
> Or in th'incestuous pleasure of his bed,

> At game, a-swearing, or about some act
> That has no relish of salvation in't,
> Then trip him that his heels may kick at heaven,
> And that his soul may be as damned and black
> As hell whereto it goes.   (III.3, 88–95)

This deferral is in keeping with the code of personal blood vengeance, whereby the revenge must match or exceed the original crime. There is no question of Hamlet's incapacity to act, because his putting up his sword is totally reasonable and justifiable.

[7]
From this point on, Hamlet acts or reacts to every situation as the opportunity presents itself. After he kills Polonius, Claudius initiates a counterplot to send Hamlet off to England and execution. Clearly, Hamlet's chances to kill the king are thus reduced to zero. It is not until Act V that Hamlet gets back to Denmark, after having decisively thwarted Claudius's murderous instructions by turning them against Rosencrantz and Guildenstern. He makes it clear to Horatio, however, that he will take the earliest opportunity, and that "the readiness is all" (Act V, scene 2, line 205). Once the rigged fencing match is under way, the opportunity finally comes. Claudius, Hamlet learns, has not only killed his father, but has poisoned his mother, and he himself is about to die from Laertes's poisoned sword. Upon such certain information, Hamlet immediately kills Claudius. When the revenge is complete, the Ghost, who began the cry for vengeance, is nowhere to be heard or seen, and four bodies lie on the stage.

[8]
Thus, we see that the problem of Hamlet's delay—and the vengeance does take four acts to carry out—is really not a problem. The prince acts in accordance with the code of revenge as quickly as circumstances permlt. Although the text of the play supports this solution, critics might still argue that procrastination is an issue because Hamlet twice accuses himself of delay. This objection does not take into consideration that Hamlet's perception of time and action is distorted by his eagerness for vengeance. From Hamlet's subjective point of view, any break in activity is delay. From our objective viewpoint, however, delay is not a true issue.

Commentary on the Essay

The structure of the essay illustrates strategy 1 (p. 1058). Paragraph 2, however, makes brief use of strategy 3 in its reference to the conventions of revenge tragedy. In both paragraphs 6 and 8, the argument is carried on by use of procatalepsis, or strategy 4, whereby a counterargument is raised and then answered.

The introductory paragraph raises the problem of Hamlet's apparent delay and offers a brief statement of the solution (the central idea). This plan is developed in paragraphs 2–7 in exactly the same order in which the issues are raised in the introduction. Paragraph 2 deals with the conventions of revenge tragedy, and paragraph 3 takes up the issue of the Ghost's reliability. Paragraphs 4 and 5 deal with Hamlet's attempts to corroborate the ghost's accusations, and paragraphs 6 and 7 consider the subsequent action. Note that each paragraph in the argument grows naturally out of the one that precedes it, just as all the paragraphs are linked to the introductory paragraph.

The concluding paragraph asserts that the original problem is solved; the paragraph then summarizes the steps of the solution. It also continues the argument by raising and then dealing with a possible objection.

SPECIAL WRITING TOPICS FOR CONSIDERING TRAGEDY

1. Much has been made of the contrast in *Oedipus the King* between seeing and blindness. Write an essay that considers this contrast as it is related to the character of Oedipus. How are blindness and seeing reversed, with regard to his understanding about the curse on the city, his attempts to ferret out the guilty ones, his awakening perceptions of his own responsibility and guilt, and his self-blinding? How can Tiresias be compared and contrasted with Oedipus?

2. Develop an argument for one of these assertions:

   a. Oedipus's fall is the result of fate, predestination, and the gods, and it would happen despite his character.

   b. Oedipus's fall is the result only of his character and has nothing to do with fate or the gods.

3. Write an essay considering the degree to which Gertrude and Ophelia in *Hamlet* justify Hamlet's assertion "Frailty, thy name is woman" (in Act I, scene 2, line 146). Questions you might take into account concern the status of these women, their power to exert their own individuality and to make their own decisions, Gertrude as a royal queen and Ophelia as an aristocratic daughter, their capacity to undergo the pain of bereavement, Hamlet's own feelings about the death of his father, and so on. To what degree should issues concerning these women be subjected to a feminist critical analysis? (See Chapter 27.)

4. Hamlet, Laertes, and Fortinbras are all young men whose fathers have been killed and who set out to avenge these deaths. Their courses of action, however, are different. In an essay, consider these three as typical or archetypal sons. What characteristics do they share? What, in turn, makes them individual and distinct? Compare and contrast how each character deals with his father's death. Which approach seems most reasonable to you? Most emotional? Most effective? For additional directions about comparison-contrast, consult Chapter 29.

5. Considering *Oedipus the King* and *Hamlet,* write an essay defining and explaining tragedy. Include references to the nature of the tragic protagonists, the situations they face, their solutions to their problems, their responses to the consequences of their actions, and their worthiness of character. Be sure to compare and contrast the actions and speeches of the characters in the plays as evidence.

6. Use your library to locate books on tragedy. Some general topics might be *ancient and modern tragedy, definitions, emotions, heroes, passions, problems,* and *questions.* You might also wish to locate specific books on Aristotle and tragedy, or else books on *Oedipus the King* and *Hamlet.* Write a brief report on one of the books, being careful to consider topics such as the author's definitions of tragedy and the author's application of the topic to various specific plays. Try also to consider the completeness of the author's presentation of material and the persuasiveness of the author's arguments.

24

The Comic Vision: Restoring the Balance

Comedy as we know it arose in ancient Greece, just as tragedy did.[1] In effect, therefore, comedy is the fraternal twin of tragedy. Many comedies are filled with tragic potential, and many tragedies contain potentially comic plots. Indeed, tragedy can be seen as an abortive or incomplete comedy in which affairs go wrong, and comedy can be considered a tragedy in which the truth is discovered (or covered up), the hero saves the day, the villain is overcome, and equilibrium and balance are restored. The major differences are that tragedy moves toward despair or death, while comedy moves toward success, happiness, and marriage. Tragic diction is elevated and heroic; comic diction can be elevated too, but often it is common or colloquial, and although it is frequently witty, it is also often witless and bawdy. The primary difference is that the mask of tragedy grieves and weeps, but the mask of comedy laughs and smiles.

THE ORIGINS OF COMEDY

In the *Poetics,* Aristotle states that he knows less about the origin of Athenian comedy than of tragedy because at first comedy was not taken as seriously as tragedy (V.2, p. 21). He does say, however, that comedy, like tragedy, developed as an improvisatory form (IV.12, p. 19). Most comic improvisations were an outgrowth of "phallic songs," which were bacchanalian processions that took place during the *Lenaia,* the religious festival held in January–February each year in *Gamelion,* the month of weddings, just following the winter solstice.

The word *comedy* is consistent with this explanation, for as "a *komos* song" its Greek meaning is a "song of revels" or "songs sung by merrymakers." The revels, like the tragedies, were religious in ways that the Greeks appreciated, though

[1] For a more detailed discussion of how drama developed as part of the ancient Athenian religious festivals, see Chapter 23, pp. 890–93.

they seem secular to us today. During parades or processions at the *Lenaia,* the merrymakers expressed their joy boisterously, traded bawdy and obscene remarks with spectators, lampooned public persons, wore ceremonial phalluses, and dressed in paunchy costumes suggesting feasting, fatness, fertility, and fun. We may conclude that these *komos* processions were encouraged officially in the belief and hope that human ceremonies would encourage divine favor and bring about prosperity and happiness. As the form developing out of such processions, comedy began with many of these characteristics and has retained them to the present day. If one briefly may generalize about subsequent comedies—even those that are cold sober rather than boisterous—it is clear that love, marriage, and ritualized celebrations of a happy future are usually major concerns.

Comedy Competitions

Tragedy originated in Athens, but the same does not appear to be true of comedy. Rather, comedy coexisted in the areas surrounding Greece called *Magna Graecia* ("Greater Greece"). Aristotle himself admitted that it was "late" when comic performances were separated from the phallic songs (V.2, p. 21); that is, comedy followed tragedy by many years. The earliest certain date for the existence of Athenian comedy is 486 B.C.E., when a state-sponsored comedy competition was won by a writer named Chionides. Although these earliest comedies apparently consisted of little more than loosely connected lampoons, they were highly enough regarded to justify regular competitions. Comedies were scheduled on each day of the festivals, following the tragedies and satyr plays.

According to Aristotle, the first writer to transform comedy by creating a thematic plot development was Crates, who won the first of his three prizes in about the mid-fifth century B.C.E.(V.3, p. 21). It was at this time that comedies became popular enough to justify an additional state comedy competition, which was instituted in about 440 B.C.E. For the remainder of the century, writers of comedy as well as tragedy tried to win prizes for their new plays at both the *Lenaia* and the City Dionysia.

GREEK OLD COMEDY.   The comedies of the fifth century B.C.E., called **Old Comedy** or **Old Attic Comedy** by later historians, followed intricate structural patterns and displayed complex poetic conventions. Nevertheless, they bore the marks of their origins in the bacchanalian *komos* processions. The actors (three or four men) and the chorus (twenty-four) each dressed in a distortingly padded costume, wore a character-defining mask, and displayed a ceremonial phallus. The role of the chorus usually dictated the comedy's title (e.g., *The Frogs, The Wasps*). Customarily, the plot was fantastic and impossible, and the dialogue was farcical and bawdy. In the tradition of satires and tirades associated with the phallic songs and with early comedy, the comic dramatists freely lashed public persons (usually but not always without legal reprisal).

Although the most successful comedy writer of the fifth century B.C.E. was Magnes (flourished 475–450 B.C.E.), who won eleven times, the only writer whose works survive is Aristophanes (ca. 450–388 B.C.E.), who won four times. His work constitutes our principal firsthand knowledge of Greek Old Comedy. He wrote at least thirty-two comedies. Fortunately, eleven have survived, along with fragments of some of his other plays. His plots and actions are outrageous, his characters are funny, and his language is satirical, bawdy, and biting.

MIDDLE COMEDY.   Aristophanes lived into the next period of Greek comedy, called **Middle Comedy.** Except for his plays *Ecclesiazusae* (ca. 391 B.C.E.) and *Plutus* (388 B.C.E.), which presaged Middle Comedy, all the Middle Comedy plays are lost, although there are many extant fragments. Middle Comedy eliminated some of the complex patterns of Old Comedy and treated less narrowly Athenian and more broadly international topics. Political criticism was abandoned, and character types such as the braggart soldier were introduced. The role of the chorus was diminished or eliminated (as with tragedy), and the exaggerated costumes were eliminated.

NEW COMEDY.   By the end of the fourth century B.C.E., Middle Comedy was replaced by **New Comedy.** The most important of the New Comedy dramatists was Menander (342–292 B.C.E.), who was heralded in ancient times as the greatest comic writer of them all. Everyone knows quotations from Menander, such as "calling a spade a spade" and "the gods first make mad those they intend to destroy." St. Paul quotes him in 1 Corinthians 15:33 ("Bad company ruins good morals"), but after the fifth century C.E., Menander's plays were lost. In the last hundred years, however, many Menandrian manuscripts have been discovered, mostly in the sands of Egypt. We now have Menander's *Dyscolus* (*The Grouch*) in its entirety and near-complete versions of his other comedies, together with numerous fragments and passages. In total, the titles of close to one hundred of his plays are known. His comedies, which are romantic rather than satirical, employ such stock characters as young lovers, stubborn fathers, clever slaves, and long-separated relatives.

Roman Comedy

After the time of Menander, Greek power in the Mediterranean waned and was replaced by the might of Rome. In the third century B.C.E. Roman comedy began and flourished, largely through the translation and adaptation of Greek New Comedies. The significant Roman writers were Plautus (ca. 254–184 B.C.E.), with twenty surviving comedies, and Terence (ca. 186–159 B.C.E.), all of whose six comedies exist. Briefly, the comedies of Plautus are brisk, while those of Terence are more restrained. The central issue in most of the Roman comedies is the overcoming of a **blocking agent,** or obstruction to true love, that could be almost anyone or anything—a rival lover, an angry father, a family feud, an old law, a previously arranged marriage, or differences in social class. The pattern of action, traditionally called the **plot of intrigue,** stems from the subterfuges that young lovers undertake to overcome the blocking agent, so that the outcome frequently heralds the victory of youth over age and the passing of control from one generation to the next.

COMEDY FROM ROMAN TIMES TO THE RENAISSANCE

By the time the Roman Empire was established in 29 B.C.E., the writing of comedy had virtually disappeared because Roman dramatic creativity had been preempted by pantomime entertainments and public spectacles, principally gladiatorial combat. Comedy thus accompanied tragedy into fifteen hundred years of obscurity—a period when the empire rose and fell, the dark ages descended, and the medieval period flourished. Although many comic and farcical scenes were included in the medieval mystery cycles of late medieval times,[2] comedy as a form was not reestablished until the Renaissance.

Once reintroduced, comedy grew rapidly. By 1500 the six plays of Terence were achieving recognition, followed by the twenty surviving plays of Plautus. When English dramatists began writing comedies, they followed Roman conventions. The English plays of the mid-sixteenth century contained five acts and observed the unities of time, place, and action, thus following the rules and justifying the claim that they were "regular." Character types from the Roman comedies, such as the intriguing couple, the fussing father, and the bragging soldier, initially predominated. Soon, more specifically English types appeared, anticipating the roisterers in Shakespeare's *Henry IV* plays and the "mechanicals" in *A Midsummer Night's Dream*. By the end of the sixteenth century, when Shakespeare had completed many of his comedies, English comedy was in full bloom. It has commonly been observed that the comedy was Latin in structure but English in character.

When the sixteenth century began, the chief obstacle to a wide public assimilation of drama had been the absence of institutionalized theaters. London authorities, maintaining that playgoing was a sinful public nuisance, banned theaters within the city itself. Theater builders therefore had to locate them outside the London city limits. For example, the Rose and the Globe theaters, where Shakespeare saw his plays produced from the mid-1590s to 1611, were built in Southwark across the Thames. We should realize that most people in Shakespeare's audiences got to the theater by walking over London Bridge or by being ferried across the river, and they returned home the same way.

COMIC PATTERNS, CHARACTERS, AND LANGUAGE

Dictionaries sometimes give *funny* as a synonym for *comic*, but the two terms are not the same. Words like *funny*, *amusing*, or *humorous* define our emotional

---

[2] For a description of the medieval mystery or Corpus Christi plays, see Chapter 23, pp. 947–48.

conditioning to incidents, and our reactions always depend on context. We usually think it is funny to see an actor in a slapstick routine being struck with a paddle, whereas if we leave the theater and see a person being beaten with a similar object, such as a baseball bat, we are repelled and horrified. The *context* makes the difference.

The Comic Pattern

Comic, the adjective derived from *comedy,* describes the pattern or context that conditions our responses. *Comic* means that a literary work or set of situations conforms to the patterns and characteristics of comedy. Within these patterns, we are conditioned to perceive most dialogue and action—even serious problems and dangerous situations—as being amusing. At heart, therefore, comedy and the term *comic* suggest a pattern of action, including funny situations and language, that we perceive as solvable and correctable. The pattern grows out of character or situation, and it leads to a resolution that satisfies us.

COMIC PROBLEMS.   The problems with which comedies begin can be individual or social. They can involve thwarted love, eccentric behavior, corruption in high places, or a combination of other difficulties. As the comedies move from exposition to complication, the problems usually get much worse. In comedy, complication is often fueled by confusion, misunderstanding, mistakes in identity, errors in judgment, excessive or unreasonable behavior, and coincidences that stretch our credulity.

THE COMIC CLIMAX.   The climax of a comedy occurs when these confusions reach a peak, misunderstanding is dominant, pressure is at a high point, choices must be made, and solutions must be found. The catastrophe—the changing or turning point—frequently introduces a sudden revelation in which a key fact, identity, or event is explained to characters and audience at the same time.

THE COMIC DÉNOUEMENT.   In most comedies, the events of the dénouement resolve the initial problems and allow for the comic resolution, which involves setting things right at every level of action. Individual lives are thereby straightened out, people at odds with each other are reconciled, new families are formed through marriage, and a healthy social order is reestablished.

COMIC EDUCATION AND CHANGE.   Two key features of the comic pattern are *education* and *change*. In many comedies, at least some of the characters learn something about themselves, their society, or the way to love and live. Their education makes it possible for them to improve, and, by implication, for the world also to improve. In other comedies, however, particularly those that touch on major social and political problems, the *audience* is educated, and the playwright hopes that change will occur in the world as well as on the stage.

Comic Characters

Characters in comedy are far more limited than in tragedy because comedies usually deal with representative types or groups rather than with individuals of heroic stature. In comedy, we rarely find characters with the depth or individuality of Hamlet or Oedipus. Instead, comedy gives us stock characters who represent classes, types, and generations. In Shakespeare's *A Midsummer Night's Dream,* for instance, most of the characters are representative and stock figures. Egeus is a conventional indignant father. Similarly, Hermia and Lysander (along with Helena and Demetrius) are typical young lovers.

Comic Language

As in other types of literature, comic dramatists use language to delineate character, to establish tone and mood, and to express ideas and feelings. In comedy, however, language is also one of the most important vehicles for humor. Some comedies are characterized by elegant and witty language, others by puns and bawdy jokes. Both kinds of language are seen in *A Midsummer Night's Dream,* where characters are either masters of language or are mastered by it. The courtly characters (e.g., Theseus, Hippolyta, the young lovers) often speak in clear and sometimes incisive poetic lines, and the "hempen homespun" characters, principally Bottom, bungle through their speeches with many inadvertent puns and misuses of words. Both types of characters are amusing; we smile a knowing smile with the wits and laugh out loud at the bunglers.

TYPES OF COMEDY

Differences in comic style, content, and intent that have evolved over the centuries make it possible to divide comedy into various types. The broadest of these divisions, based on both style and content, separates all comic literature into *high comedy* and *low comedy*.

High Comedy

Ideally, high comedy (a term coined by George Meredith in 1877 in *The Idea of Comedy*) is witty, graceful, and sophisticated. The complications and problems grow out of character rather than situation, and the appeal is to the intellect.

ROMANTIC COMEDY.   One of the major kinds of high comedy is **romantic comedy,** which views action and character from the standpoint of earnest young lovers like Hermia and Lysander in *A Midsummer Night's Dream.* Ultimately derived from Roman comedy, this kind of play is built on a plot of intrigue featuring lovers who try to overcome opposition (like Egeus) to achieve a successful union. The aim of such plays is amusement and entertainment rather than ridicule and reform. Although vice and folly may be exposed in romantic comedy, especially in the antagonists blocking the young lovers, the dominant impulse is toleration and amused indulgence.

COMEDY OF MANNERS.   Related to romantic comedy is the **comedy of manners,** an important type from the seventeenth century to our own times. The comedy of manners examines and satirizes attitudes and customs in the light of high intellectual and moral standards. The dialogue is witty and sophisticated, and characters are often measured according to their linguistic and intellectual powers. The love plots are serious and real, even though they share with romantic comedy the need to create intrigues to overcome blocking forces. The realism and seriousness in some of the manners comedies written in Restoration England (1660–1700) in fact are so great that one might consider them not only as plays of manners but also of social and personal problems.

SATIRIC COMEDY.   Midway between high and low comedy is **satiric comedy,** which is designed to ridicule vices and follies. The playwright of satiric comedy assumes the perspective of a rational and moderate observer measuring human life against a moderate norm that can be represented by high and serious characters. The audience is invited to share this viewpoint as they, along with the dramatist, heap scorn upon the vicious and laugh loudly at the eccentric and the foolish.

Low Comedy

In low comedy emphasis is on funny remarks and outrageous circumstances; complications develop from situation and plot rather than from character. Plays of this type are by definition full of physical humor and stage business—a character rounds his forefinger and thumb to imitate a wall, through which other characters speak; an irascible man constantly breaks furniture; a character disguised as a doctor takes a father's pulse to determine his daughter's condition.

FARCE.   The quintessential type of low comedy is **farce** (a word derived from the Latin word *farsus,* meaning "stuffed"). A farce is an outlandish physical comedy overflowing with silly characters, improbable happenings, wild clowning, extravagant language, and bawdy jokes.

COMMEDIA DELL'ARTE.   A unique kind of farce is the ***commedia dell'arte,*** which developed among traveling companies in Italy and France in the sixteenth and seventeenth centuries. The broadly humorous characters of *commedia dell'arte* recurred from play to play with consistent names and characteristics.

The action usually involved a plot of intrigue. The lovers were *Inamorato* and *Inamorata*, who were aided by Inamorata's clever servant, the *soubrette*, to overcome *Pantaloon*, the old man. The servant characters were *Harlequin* (who was invisible) and *Columbine* (his sweetheart, also invisible), who were joined in highjinks by *Pierrot* (a clown lover) and *Scaramouche* (the soldier). Other stock characters, most of whom were derived from Greek New Comedy by way of Roman comedy, have in turn become constant features of much subsequent comedy.

SLAPSTICK.   With characters of low comedy, of course, there is much tomfoolery and improvisation—the major qualities of the extreme form of farce, **slapstick,** which is named after the double paddles ("slap sticks") that made loud cracking noises when actors in the *commedia dell'arte* used them to whack each other. Slapstick depends heavily on exaggerated poses and facial expressions. In slapstick there is constant onstage business with objects like paddles, pies, pails, paint, paste, or toilet paper, along with wild and improbable actions such as squirming, hiding, tripping, stumbling, tumbling, falling, and flopping.

Other Kinds of Comedy

Other types of modern and contemporary comedy include **ironic comedy, realistic comedy,** and **comedy of the absurd.** All of these usually shun the happy endings of traditional comedy. Often, the blocking agents are successful, the protagonists are defeated, and the initial problem—either a realistic or an absurdist dilemma—remains unresolved. Such comedies, which began to appear in the late nineteenth century, illustrate the complexities and absurdities of modern life and the funny but futile efforts that people make when coming to grips with existence.

Many of the types of comedy just discussed still flourish. Romantic comedies, comedies of manners, and farces can be found on innumerable stages and movie screens. They revolve about a central situation that might be quite ordinary (Will Art get along with a visiting lodge member? Will Sue get accepted by schoolmates at her new school? Will Jim get a date for the prom?). Such situations find their ways into the many *sitcoms* (*situation comedies*) that occupy primetime television programs.

In view of the variety of comedy, it is most important to recognize that comedy is rarely a pure and discrete form. High comedies might include crude physical humor, especially with characters to be disapproved. Low comedies can sometimes contain wit and elegance. Satiric comedies might deal with successful young lovers. Romantic comedies can mock the vices and follies of weird and eccentric characters. Farce and slapstick can contain satire on social values and conventions.

WILLIAM SHAKESPEARE, *A MIDSUMMER NIGHT'S DREAM*

A Midsummer Night's Dream was written early in Shakespeare's career, in 1594 or 1595.[3] It is a romantic comedy dramatizing the idea that "the course of true love never did run smooth." This central line of action, which owes much to Roman comedy, involves blocked love, a journey of circumvention and education that takes the lovers from the world of laws and problems into an imaginary world of chaos and transformations, and an ultimate victory back in the world of daylight and order.

The subject of *A Midsummer Night's Dream* is love. Shakespeare skillfully interweaves this topic in the play's four separate plots, four groups of characters, and four styles of language. Each plot explores the nature of love, the madness of irrational love, and the harmony needed for regenerative love.

In the *overplot*—the action that establishes the time for the play—the relationship is between the rulers, Theseus and Hippolyta, who have undergone a change from irrational war to rational peace. As such, they represent the dynastic continuity of the state, the order of the daylight world of Athens, and the rigor of the law. These characters are the rulers, and they speak predominantly in blank verse (unrhymed iambic pentameter; see p. 620).

The two connected *middle plots* concern the adventures of the four lovers and the actions of Oberon and Titania. The four lovers, embodying the most passionate and insistent phase of love, are from the middle class, and they speak mainly in rhymed couplets (see p. 620). During their long night in the woods of illusion conjured by Oberon and his servant, Puck, their adventures drive them toward rationality, and they recognize and accept the need for faithfulness and constancy.

The parallel middle love plot involves the conflict between Oberon and Titania, the king and queen of the fairies, because of their infatuations for a "changeling" child. To cure Titania's infatuation, Oberon humbles her, and she then reacknowledges his superiority—the proper attitude of a wife, according to Elizabethan males. Oberon and Titania, of course, are supernatural forces. Although they and the other fairies speak in both blank verse and rhymed couplets, the fairies are the only singing characters, and also the only characters to speak in iambic tetrameter.

The examination of love in the *subplot* occurs partly in Titania's relationship with Bottom—the most hilarious instance of love madness in the play—and partly in the play-within-a-play about Pyramus and Thisby. This absurd and funny tragedy echoes the central plot of *A Midsummer Night's Dream* and demonstrates, again, the pitfalls and unpredictability of love. It also emphasizes the happy and harmonious marriages and rapprochements that occur in both the overplot and the middle plots.

---

[3] See Chapter 23, pp. 949–54, for a description of Shakespeare's theater and career as a dramatist.

While *A Midsummer Night's Dream* is chiefly about love, it is equally concerned with the complicated relationship of perception, imagination, passion, art, and illusion. In Act V Theseus asserts that "The lunatic, the lover, and the poet" are alike because they all try to make reality conform with their own imaginations and desires (scene 1, lines 7–22). It would seem that chaos would therefore be the normal state, but, as Hippolyta concludes in response to Theseus, order and certainty somehow prevail, "howsoever" extraordinary and almost miraculous this result may seem (lines 23–27). The movement of the play is governed by these ideas that, along with the brilliant language and comic actions, are directly attributable to the genius of Shakespeare.

WILLIAM SHAKESPEARE   (1564–1616)

A Midsummer Night's Dream ————————————— *1600 (ca. 1594)*

Edited by Alice Griffin°

THE NAMES OF THE ACTORS

Theseus, *Duke of Athens*
Egeus, *father of Hermia*
Lysander, *beloved of Hermia*
Demetrius, *in love with Hermia, favoured by Egeus*
Philostrate, *Master of the Revels to Theseus*
Peter Quince, *a carpenter* (*Prologue*)*
Nick Bottom, *a weaver* (*Pyramus*)*
Francis Flute, *a bellows-mender* (*Thisby*)*
Tom Snout, *a tinker* (*Wall*)*
Snug, *a joiner* (*Lion*)*
Robin Starveling, *a tailor* (*Moonshine*)*
Hippolyta, *Queen of the Amazons, betrothed to Theseus*
Hermia, *daughter of Egeus, in love with Lysander*
Helena, *in love with Demetrius*
Oberon, *King of the Fairies*
Titania, *Queen of the Fairies*
Puck, *or* Robin Goodfellow
Peaseblossom ⎫
Cobweb ⎬ *Fairies*
Moth ⎪
Mustardseed ⎭

Other Fairies attending Oberon and Titania. Attendants on Theseus and Hippolyta.

Scene: *Athens, and a wood nearby*

Professor Griffin's text for *A Midsummer Night's Dream* is the First Quarto (edition) published in 1600, with modifications based on the Quarto edition of 1619 and the First Folio, published in 1623. Stage directions in those editions are printed here without brackets; added stage directions are printed within brackets. We have edited Griffin's notes for this text.   *Characters who play in the interlude.

ACT 1

[*Scene 1. Athens. The palace of Theseus*]

Enter THESEUS, HIPPOLYTA,° [PHILOSTRATE,] *with others.*

THESEUS. Now fair Hippolyta, our nuptial hour
　　Draws on apace: four happy days bring in
　　Another moon: but O, methinks how slow
　　This old moon wanes! she lingers° my desires,
　　Like to a stepdame or a dowager,°　　　　　　　　　　　　　　　5
　　Long withering out° a young man's revenue.
HIPPOLYTA. Four days will quickly steep themselves in night:
　　Four nights will quickly dream away the time:
　　And then the moon, like to a silver bow
　　New-bent in heaven, shall behold the night　　　　　　　　　10
　　Of our solemnities.
THESEUS.　　　　　　　Go Philostrate,
　　Stir up the Athenian youth to merriments,
　　Awake the pert° and nimble spirit of mirth,
　　Turn melancholy forth to funerals:
　　The pale companion° is not for our pomp.　　　[*Exit* PHILOSTRATE.]　15
　　Hippolyta, I wooed thee with my sword,
　　And won thy love doing thee injuries;
　　But I will wed thee in another key,
　　With pomp, with triumph,° and with revelling.

Enter EGEUS *and his daughter* HERMIA, LYSANDER *and* DEMETRIUS.

EGEUS. Happy be Theseus, our renownèd duke.　　　　　　　　20
THESEUS. Thanks good Egeus:° what's the news with thee?
EGEUS. Full of vexation come I, with complaint
　　Against my child, my daughter Hermia.
　　Stand forth Demetrius. My noble lord,
　　This man hath my consent to marry her.　　　　　　　　　　25
　　Stand forth Lysander. And my gracious duke,
　　This man hath bewitched the bosom of my child.
　　Thou, thou Lysander, thou hast given her rhymes,
　　And interchanged love tokens with my child:
　　Thou hast by moonlight at her window sung,　　　　　　　30
　　With feigning voice, verses of feigning° love,
　　And stol'n the impression of her fantasy°

0.3 S.D.: *Theseus, Hippolyta:* In Greek legend, Theseus captured the Amazon Queen Hippolyta and brought her to Athens where they were married.　　4 *lingers:* delays the fulfillment of.　　5 *dowager:* a widow supported by her dead husband's heirs.　　6 *withering out:* (1) depleting (2) growing withered.　　13 *pert:* lively.　　15 *companion:* fellow (contemptuous).　　19 *triumph:* public festival.　　21 *Egeus:* (trisyllabic).　　31 *feigning:* (1) deceptive (2) desirous ("faining").　　32 *stol'n . . . fantasy:* stealthily imprinted your image upon her fancy.

With bracelets of thy hair, rings, gauds,° conceits,°
Knacks,° trifles, nosegays, sweetmeats—messengers
Of strong prevailment in unhardened youth.   35
With cunning hast thou filched my daughter's heart,
Turned her obedience, which is due to me,
To stubborn harshness. And my gracious duke,
Be it so° she will not here before your grace
Consent to marry with Demetrius,   40
I beg the ancient privilege of Athens:
As she is mine, I may dispose of her:
    Which shall be, either to this gentleman,
    Or to her death, according to our law
    Immediately° provided in that case.   45
THESEUS. What say you, Hermia? Be advised, fair maid.
To you your father should be as a god:
One that composed your beauties: yea and one
To whom you are but as a form in wax
By him imprinted, and within his power   50
To leave the figure, or disfigure it:
Demetrius is a worthy gentleman.
HERMIA. So is Lysander.
THESEUS   In himself he is:
But in this kind, wanting your father's voice,°
The other must be held the worthier.   55
HERMIA. I would my father looked but with my eyes.
THESEUS. Rather your eyes must with his judgment look.
HERMIA. I do entreat your grace to pardon me.
I know not by what power I am made bold,
Nor how it may concern my modesty,   60
In such a presence, here to plead my thoughts:
But I beseech your grace that I may know
The worst that may befall me in this case,
If I refuse to wed Demetrius.
THESEUS. Either to die the death, or to abjure   65
For ever the society of men.
Therefore fair Hermia, question your desires,
Know of your youth,° examine well your blood,°
Whether, if you yield not to your father's choice,
You can endure the livery° of a nun,   70
For aye° to be in shady cloister mewed,°
To live a barren sister all your life,
Chanting faint hymns to the cold fruitless moon.°
Thrice blessèd they that master so their blood,
To undergo such maiden pilgrimage: 75

33 *gauds:* trinkets.   *conceits:* either (a) love poetry, or (b) love tokens.   34 *Knacks:* knick-knacks.   39 *Be it so:* if it be that.   45 *Immediately:* precisely.   54 *in . . . voice:* in this respect, lacking your father's approval.   68 *Know . . . youth:* ask yourself as a young person.   68 *blood:* passions.   70 *livery:* habit.   71 *aye:* ever.   *mewed:* shut up.   73 *moon:* (the moon goddess Diana represented unmarried chastity).

But earthlier happy° is the rose distilled,°
Than that which, withering on the virgin thorn,
Grows, lives, and dies, in single blessedness.
HERMIA.   So will I grow, so live, so die my lord,
Ere I will yield my virgin patent° up   80
Unto his lordship, whose unwishèd yoke
My soul consents not to give sovereignty.
THESEUS.   Take time to pause, and by the next moon,
The sealing day betwixt my love and me,
For everlasting bond of fellowship,   85
Upon that day either prepare to die
For disobedience to your father's will,
Or else to wed Demetrius, as he would,
Or on Diana's altar to protest°
For aye, austerity and single life.   90
DEMETRIUS.   Relent, sweet Hermia, and Lysander, yield
Thy crazèd° title to my certain right.
LYSANDER.   You have her father's love, Demetrius:
Let me have Hermia's: do you marry him.
EGEUS.   Scornful Lysander, true, he hath my love: 95
And what is mine, my love shall render him.
And she is mine, and all my right of her
I do estate° unto Demetrius.
LYSANDER.   I am, my lord, as well derived° as he,
As well possessed:° my love is more than his: 100
My fortunes every way as fairly ranked
(If not with vantage) as° Demetrius':
And, which is more than all these boasts can be,
I am beloved of beauteous Hermia.
Why should not I then prosecute my right?   105
Demetrius, I'll avouch it to his head,°
Made love to Nedar's daughter, Helena,
And won her soul: and she, sweet lady, dotes,
Devoutly dotes, dotes in idolatry,
Upon this spotted° and inconstant man.   110
THESEUS.   I must confess that I have heard so much,
And with Demetrius thought to have spoke thereof:
But being over-full of self-affairs,
My mind did lose it. But Demetrius come,
And come Egeus, you shall go with me: 115
I have some private schooling for you both.
For you fair Hermia, look you arm yourself,
To fit your fancies to your father's will;

---

76 *earthlier happy:* more happy on earth.   *distilled:* i.e., into perfume (thus its essence is passed
on, as to a child).   80 *patent:* privilege.   89 *protest:* vow.   92 *crazèd:* flawed.   98 *estate:*
transfer.   99 *well derived:* well born.   100 *well possessed:* wealthy.   102 *with vantage, as:*
better, than.   106 *avouch . . . head:* prove it to his face.   110 *spotted:* stained (by betrayal of
Helena).

Or else the law of Athens yields you up
(Which by no means we may extenuate)   120
To death or to a vow of single life.
Come my Hippolyta, what cheer my love?
Demetrius and Egeus, go along:
I must employ you in some business
Against° our nuptial, and confer with you   125
Of something nearly° that concerns yourselves.
EGEUS.   With duty and desire we follow you.

                              Exeunt.° Manent° LYSANDER and HERMIA.

LYSANDER.   How now my love? Why is your cheek so pale?
    How chance the roses there do fade so fast?
HERMIA.   Belike° for want of rain, which I could well   130
    Beteem° them from the tempest of my eyes,
LYSANDER.   Ay me, for aught that I could ever read,
    Could ever hear by tale or history,
    The course of true love never did run smooth;
    But either it was different in blood—   135
HERMIA.   O cross! too high° to be enthralled to low.°
LYSANDER.   Or else misgraffèd° in respect of years—
HERMIA.   O spite! too old to be engaged to young.
LYSANDER.   Or else it stood upon the choice of friends—
HERMIA.   O hell! to choose love by another's eyes.   140
LYSANDER.   Or if there were a sympathy in choice,
    War, death, or sickness did lay siege to it;
    Making it momentany° as a sound,
    Swift as a shadow, short as any dream,
    Brief as the lightning in the collied° night,   145
    That, in a spleen,° unfolds both heaven and earth;
    And ere a man hath power to say "Behold,"
    The jaws of darkness do devour it up:
    So quick bright things come to confusion.
HERMIA.   If then true lovers have been ever crossed,°   150
    It stands as an edict in destiny:
    Then let us teach our trial patience,°
    Because it is a customary cross,
    As due to love as thoughts and dreams and sighs,
    Wishes and tears; poor Fancy's° followers.   155
LYSANDER.   A good persuasion: therefore hear me, Hermia:
    I have a widow aunt, a dowager,
    Of great revenue, and she hath no child:

---

125 *Against:* in preparation for.   126 *nearly:* closely.   127 S.D.: *Exeunt:* they exit.   *Manent:*
they remain.   130 *Belike:* likely.   131 *Beteem:* (1) pour out on (2) allow.   136 *high:* high-
born.   *enthralled to low:* made a slave to one of low birth.   137 *misgraffèd:* badly
joined.   143 *momentany:* momentary.   145 *collied:* black as coal.   146 *in a spleen:* impul-
sively, in a sudden outburst.   150 *ever crossed:* evermore thwarted.   152 *teach . . . patience:*
teach ourselves to be patient.   155 *Fancy:* love (sometimes infatuation).

From Athens is her house remote seven leagues,
And she respects° me as her only son: 160
There gentle Hermia, may I marry thee,
And to that place the sharp Athenian law
Cannot pursue us. If thou lov'st me then,
Steal forth thy father's house tomorrow night:
And in the wood, a league without the town,   165
Where I did meet thee once with Helena
To do observance to a morn of May,°
There will I stay° for thee.
HERMIA.   My good Lysander,
I swear to thee, by Cupid's strongest bow,
By his best arrow, with the golden head,°   170
By the simplicity of Venus' doves,
By that which knitteth souls and prospers loves,
And by that fire which burned the Carthage queen,
When the false Troyan° under sail was seen,
By all the vows that ever men have broke,   175
(In number more than ever women spoke)
In that same place thou has appointed me,
Tomorrow truly will I meet with thee.
LYSANDER.   Keep promise love: look, here comes Helena.

Enter HELENA.

HERMIA.   God speed fair Helena: whither away?   180
HELENA.   Call you me fair? That fair again unsay.
Demetrius loves your fair:° O happy fair!
Your eyes are lodestars,° and your tongue's sweet air°
More tuneable than lark to shepherd's ear,
When wheat is green, when hawthorn buds appear.   185
Sickness is catching: O were favour° so,
Yours would I catch, fair Hermia, ere I go,
My ear should catch your voice,° my eye your eye,°
My tongue should catch your tongue's sweet melody.
Were the world mine, Demetrius being bated,°   190
The rest I'ld give to be to you translated.°
O teach me how you look, and with what art
You sway the motion of Demetrius' heart.
HERMIA.   I frown upon him; yet he loves me still.
HELENA.   O that your frowns would teach my smiles such skill.   195
HERMIA.   I give him curses; yet he gives me love.
HELENA.   O that my prayers could such affection move.
HERMIA.   The more I hate, the more he follows me.

---

160 *respects:* regards.   167 *do . . . May:* celebrate May Day.   168 *stay:* wait.   170 *golden head:* (The arrow with the gold head causes love).   173–174 *Carthage Queen . . . false Troyan:* Dido, who burned herself to death on a funeral pyre when Trojan Aeneas deserted her.   182 *your fair:* i.e., beauty.   183 *lodestars:* guiding stars.   *air:* music.   186 *favour:* appearance.   188 *My ear . . . voice:* my ear should catch the tone of your voice.   *my eye your eye:* my eye should catch the way you glance.   190 *bated:* subtracted, excepted.   191 *translated:* transformed.

HELENA.   The more I love, the more he hateth me.
HERMIA.   His folly, Helena, is no fault of mine.   200
HELENA.   None but your beauty; would that fault were mine.
HERMIA.   Take comfort: he no more shall see my face:
    Lysander and myself will fly this place.
    Before the time I did Lysander see,
    Seemed Athens as a paradise to me: 205
    O then, what graces in my love do dwell,
    That he hath turned a heaven unto a hell!
LYSANDER.   Helen, to you our minds we will unfold:
    Tomorrow night, when Phoebe° doth behold
    Her silver visage in the wat'ry glass,°   210
    Decking with liquid pearl the bladed grass
    (A time that lovers' flights doth still° conceal)
    Through Athens gates have we devised to steal.
HERMIA.   And in the wood, where often you and I
    Upon faint primrose beds were wont to lie,   215
    Emptying our bosoms of their counsel° sweet,
    There my Lysander and myself shall meet,
    And thence from Athens turn away our eyes,
    To see new friends and stranger companies.°
    Farewell, sweet playfellow: pray thou for us: 220
    And good luck grant thee thy Demetrius.
    Keep word Lysander: we must starve our sight
    From lovers' food,° till morrow deep midnight.
LYSANDER.   I will my Hermia.   *Exit* HERMIA.
           Helena adieu:
    As you on him, Demetrius dote on you.°   *Exit* LYSANDER.   225
HELENA.   How happy some, o'er other some, can be!
    Through Athens I am thought as fair as she.
    But what of that? Demetrius thinks not so:
    He will not know what all but he do know.
    And as he errs, doting on Hermia's eyes,   230
    So I, admiring of his qualities.
    Things base and vile, holding no quantity.°
    Love can transpose to form and dignity.
    Love looks not with the eyes, but with the mind:
    And therefore is winged Cupid painted blind.   235
    Nor hath Love's mind of any judgment taste:
    Wings, and no eyes, figure° unheedy haste.
    And therefore is Love said to be a child:
    Because in choice he is so oft beguiled.
    As waggish boys in game themselves forswear: 240
    So the boy Love is perjured everywhere.

---

209 *Phoebe:* Diana, the moon.   210 *wat'ry glass:* mirror of the water.   212 *still:* always.   216
counsel: secrets.   219 *stranger companies:* the companionship of strangers.   223 *lovers' food:*
the sight of the loved one.   225 *As . . . you:* As you dote on Demetrius, so may Demetrius also
dote on you.   232 *holding no quantity:* out of proportion.   237 *figure:* symbolize.

For ere Demetrius looked on Hermia's eyne,°
He hailed down oaths that he was only mine.
And when this hail some heat from Hermia felt,
So he dissolved, and show'rs of oaths did melt.   245
I will go tell him of fair Hermia's flight:
Then to the wood will he tomorrow night
Pursue her: and for this intelligence,°
If I have thanks, it is a dear expense:°
But herein mean I to enrich my pain,   250
To have his sight° thither and back again.   *Exit.*

[*Scene 2. Quince's house*]

Enter QUINCE *the Carpenter; and* SNUG *the Joiner; and* BOTTOM *the Weaver; and* FLUTE *the Bellows-mender; and* SNOUT *the Tinker; and* STARVELING *the Tailor.*°

QUINCE.   Is all our company here?
BOTTOM.   You were the best to call them generally,° man by man,
    according to the scrip.
QUINCE.   Here is the scroll of every man's name which is thought
    fit, through all Athens, to play in our interlude° before   5
    the duke and the duchess, on his wedding-day at night.
BOTTOM.   First good Peter Quince, say what the play treats on,
    then read the names of the actors: and so grow to a point.
QUINCE.   Marry,° our play is "The most lamentable comedy, and
    most cruel death of Pyramus and Thisby."   10
BOTTOM.   A very good piece of work I assure you, and a merry. Now
    good Peter Quince, call forth your actors by the scroll.
    Masters, spread yourselves.
QUINCE.   Answer as I call you. Nick Bottom the weaver?
BOTTOM.   Ready: name what part I am for, and proceed.   15
QUINCE.   You, Nick Bottom, are set down for Pyramus.
BOTTOM.   What is Pyramus? A lover, or a tyrant?
QUINCE.   A lover that kills himself, most gallant, for love.
BOTTOM.   That will ask some tears in the true performing of it. If I
    do it, let the audience look to their eyes: I will move   20
    storms: I will condole° in some measure. To the rest—
    yet my chief humour° is for a tyrant. I could play Ercles°
    rarely, or a part to tear a cat in, to make all split.°

---

242 *eyne:* eyes.   248 *intelligence:* information.   249 *dear expense:* costly outlay (on Demetrius' part).   250–251 *But . . . sight:* but I will be rewarded just by the sight of him.   0.2 S.D.: the low characters' names describe their work: *Quince:* quoins, wooden wedges used in building.   *Snug:* fitting snugly, suiting a joiner of furniture.   *Bottom:* bobbin or core on which yarn is wound.   *Flute:* mender of fluted church organs and bellows.   *Snout:* spout (of the kettles he mends).   *Starveling:* (tailors being traditionally thin).   2 *generally:* Bottom often uses the wrong word; here he means the opposite: "severally, one-by-one."   5 *interlude:* short play.   9 *Marry:* indeed (mild oath, corruption of "by the Virgin Mary").   21 *condole:* lament.   22 *humour:* inclination.   *Ercles:* Hercules (typified by ranting).   23 *tear . . . split:* (terms for ranting and raging on the stage).

> The raging rocks
> And shivering shocks,   25
> Shall break the locks
>   Of prison gates,
> And Phibbus' car°
> Shall shine from far,
> And make and mar   30
>   The foolish Fates.

This was lofty. Now name the rest of the players. This is
Ercles' vein, a tyrant's vein: a lover is more condoling.

QUINCE.   Francis Flute, the bellows-mender?

FLUTE.   Here Peter Quince.   35

QUINCE.   Flute, you must take Thisby on you.

FLUTE.   What is Thisby? A wand'ring knight?

QUINCE.   It is the lady that Pyramus must love.

FLUTE.   Nay faith, let not me play a woman: I have a beard
    coming.   40

QUINCE.   That's all one:° you shall play it in a mask, and you may
    speak as small° as you will.

BOTTOM.   And° I may hide my face, let me play Thisby too: I'll speak
    in a monstrous little voice; "Thisne, Thisne," "Ah
    Pyramus, my lover dear, thy Thisby dear, and lady   45
    dear."

QUINCE.   No, no, you must play Pyramus: and Flute, you Thisby.

BOTTOM.   Well, proceed.

QUINCE.   Robin Starveling, the tailor?

STARVELING.   Here Peter Quince.   50

QUINCE.   Robin Starveling, you must play Thisby's mother. Tom
    Snout, the tinker?

SNOUT.   Here Peter Quince.

QUINCE.   You, Pyramus' father; myself, Thisby's father; Snug the
    joiner, you the lion's part: and I hope here is a play   55
    fitted.°

SNUG.   Have you the lion's part written? Pray you, if it be, give
    it me: for I am slow of study.

QUINCE.   You may do it extempore: for it is nothing but roaring.

BOTTOM.   Let me play the lion too. I will roar, that° I will do any   60
    man's heart good to hear me. I will roar, that I will make
    the duke say "Let him roar again: let him roar again."

QUINCE.   And you should do it too terribly, you would fright the
    duchess and the ladies, that they would shriek: and
    that were enough to hang us all.   65

ALL.   That would hang us, every mother's son.

---

28 *Phibbus' car:* Phoebus Apollo's chariot.   41 *That's all one:* never mind.   42 *small:*
softly.   43 *And:* if.   56 *fitted:* cast.   60 *that:* so that.

BOTTOM.   I grant you, friends, if you should fright the ladies out of
their wits, they would have no more discretion but to
hang us: but I will aggravate° my voice so, that I will roar
you as gently as any sucking dove: I will roar you and   70
'twere° any nightingale.

QUINCE.   You can play no part but Pyramus: for Pyramus is a
sweet-faced man; a proper° man as one shall see in a
summer's day; a most lovely gentleman-like man: therefore
you must needs play Pyramus.   75

BOTTOM.   Well: I will undertake it. What beard were I best to play
it in?

QUINCE.   Why, what you will.

BOTTOM.   I will discharge it in either your straw-colour beard, your
orange-tawny beard, your purple-in-grain° beard, or your   80
French-crown-colour° beard, your perfit yellow.

QUINCE.   Some of your French crowns° have no hair at all; and
then you will play barefaced. But masters here are your
parts, and I am to entreat you, request you, and desire
you, to con° them by tomorrow night: and meet me in the   85
palace wood, a mile without the town, by moonlight;
there will we rehearse: for if we meet in the city, we
shall be dogged with company, and our devices° known.
In the meantime, I will draw a bill of properties,° such
as our play wants. I pray you fail me not.   90

BOTTOM.   We will meet, and there we may rehearse most obscenely°
and courageously. Take pain, be perfit: adieu.

QUINCE.   At the duke's oak we meet.

BOTTOM.   Enough: hold, or cut bow-strings.°   *Exeunt.*

ACT 2

[*Scene 1. A wood near Athens*]

Enter a FAIRY *at one door, and* ROBIN GOODFELLOW [*Puck*] *at another.*

PUCK.   How now spirit, whither wander you?

FAIRY.   Over hill, over dale,
       Thorough bush, thorough brier,
   Over park, over pale,°
       Thorough flood, thorough fire:
   I do wander everywhere,   5
   Swifter than the moon's sphere:

---

69 *aggravate:* (he means "moderate").   70–71 *and 'twere:* as if it were.   73 *proper:* handsome.   80 *purple-in-grain:* dyed permanently purple.   81 *French-crown-colour:* golden, like
French crowns (gold coins).   82 *French crowns:* bald heads believed to be caused by syphilis,
the "French" disease.   85 *con:* learn by heart.   88 *devices:* plans.   89 *bill of properties:* list
of stage props.   91 *obscenely:* (he may mean "fittingly" or "obscurely").   94 *hold, or cut bow-
strings:* (meaning uncertain, but equivalent to "fish, or cut bait").   4 *pale:* enclosure.

And I serve the Fairy Queen,
To dew ° her orbs° upon the green.
The cowslips° tall her pensioners° be,   10
In their gold coats, spots you see:
Those be rubies, fairy favours:°
In those freckles live their savours.°
I must go seek some dewdrops here,
And hang a pearl in every cowslip's ear.   15
Farewell thou lob° of spirits: I'll be gone,
Our queen and all her elves come here anon.

PUCK.   The king doth keep his revels here tonight.
Take heed the queen come not within his sight.
For Oberon is passing fell° and wrath,   20
Because that she, as her attendant, hath
A lovely boy, stol'n from an Indian king:
She never had so sweet a changeling.°
And jealous Oberon would have the child
Knight of his train, to trace° the forests wild.   25
But she, perforce,° withholds the lovèd boy,
Crowns him with flowers, and makes him all her joy.
And now, they never meet in grove or green,
By fountain clear, or spangled starlight sheen,
But they do square,° that all their elves for fear   30
Creep into acorn cups, and hide them there.

FAIRY.   Either I mistake your shape and making quite,
Or else you are that shrewd and knavish sprite
Called Robin Goodfellow. Are not you he
That frights the maidens of the villagery,   35
Skim milk,° and sometimes labour in the quern,°
And bootless° make the breathless housewife churn,
And sometime make the drink to bear no barm,°
Mislead night-wanderers, laughing at their harm?
Those that Hobgoblin call you, and sweet Puck,   40
You do their work, and they shall have good luck.
Are not you he?

PUCK.   Thou speakest aright;
I am that merry wanderer of the night.
I jest to Oberon, and make him smile,
When I a fat and bean-fed horse beguile,   45
Neighing in likeness of a filly foal;
And sometime lurk I in a gossip's° bowl,
In very likeness of a roasted crab,°

---

9 *dew:* bedew.   *orbs:* fairy rings (circles of high grass).   10 *cowslips:* primroses.   *pension-ers:* royal bodyguards.   12 *favours:* gifts.   13 *savours:* perfumes.   16 *lob:* lout, lubber.   20 *passing fell:* surpassingly fierce.   23 *changeling:* creature exchanged by fairies for a stolen baby (among the fairies, the stolen child).   25 *trace:* traverse.   26 *perforce:* by force.   30 *square:* quarrel.   36 *Skim milk:* steals the cream off the milk.   *quern:* handmill for grinding grain.   37 *bootless:* without result.   38 *barm:* foamy head (therefore the drink was flat).   47 *gossip's:* old woman's.   48 *crab:* crabapple (often put into ale).

And when she drinks, against her lips I bob,
And on her withered dewlap° pour the ale.   50
The wisest aunt, telling the saddest tale,
Sometime for three-foot stool mistaketh me:
Then slip I from her bum, down topples she,
And "tailor"° cries, and falls into a cough;
And then the whole quire° hold their hips and laugh,   55
And waxen° in their mirth, and neeze,° and swear
A merrier hour was never wasted° there.
But room° fairy: here comes Oberon.
FAIRY.   And here, my mistress. Would that he were gone.

Enter [OBERON] the King Of Fairies, at one door with his TRAIN, and the QUEEN [TITANIA], at another, with hers.

OBERON.   Ill met by moonlight, proud Titania.   60
QUEEN.   What, jealous Oberon? Fairy, skip hence.
    I have forsworn his bed and company.
OBERON.   Tarry, rash wanton.° Am not I thy lord?
QUEEN.   Then I must be thy lady: but I know
    When thou hast stol'n away from fairyland,   65
    And in the shape of Corin° sat all day,
    Playing on pipes of corn,° and versing love
    To amorous Phillida.° Why art thou here
    Come from the farthest steep of India?
    But that, forsooth, the bouncing Amazon,°   70
    Your buskined° mistress and your warrior love,
    To Theseus must be wedded; and you come,
    To give their bed joy and prosperity.
OBERON.   How canst thou thus, for shame, Titania,
    Glance at my credit with° Hippolyta,   75
    Knowing I know thy love to Theseus?
    Didst thou not lead him through the glimmering night,
    From Perigenia, whom he ravishèd?
    And make him with fair Aegles break his faith,
    With Ariadne, and Antiopa°?   80
QUEEN.   These are the forgeries of jealousy:
    And never, since the middle summer's spring,°
    Met we on hill, in dale, forest, or mead,
    By pavèd° fountain, or by rushy brook,
    Or in the beachèd margent° of the sea,   85

50 *dewlap:* loose skin hanging about the throat.   54 *"tailor":* (variously explained: perhaps the squatting position of the tailor, or "tailard"—one with a tail).   55 *quire:* choir, group.   56 *waxen:* increase.   *neeze:* sneeze.   57 *wasted:* spent.   58 *room:* make room.   63 *Tarry, rash wanton:* wait, headstrong one.   66–68 *Corin, Phillida:* (traditional names in pastoral literature for a shepherd and his loved one, respectively).   67 *corn:* wheat straws.   70 *Amazon:* Hippolyta.   71 *buskined:* wearing boots.   75 *Glance . . . credit with:* hint at my favors from.   78–80 *Perigenia . . . Antiopa:* women that Theseus supposedly loved and deserted.   82 *middle . . . spring:* beginning of midsummer.   84 *pavèd:* with a pebbly bottom.   85 *margent:* margin, shore.

To dance our ringlets to the whistling wind,
But with thy brawls thou hast disturbed our sport.
Therefore the winds, piping to us in vain,
As in revenge, have sucked up from the sea
Contagious° fogs: which falling in the land,   90
Hath every pelting° river made so proud,
That they have overborne their continents.°
The ox hath therefore stretched his yoke in vain,
The ploughman lost his sweat, and the green corn°
Hath rotted, ere his youth attained a beard:°   95
The fold° stands empty in the drownèd field,
And crows are fatted with the murrion° flock.
The nine men's morris° is filled up with mud:
And the quaint mazes° in the wanton green,°
For lack of tread, are undistinguishable.   100
The human mortals want° their winter here,
No night is now with hymn or carol blest;
Therefore the moon, the governess of floods,
Pale in her anger, washes all the air,
That rheumatic diseases do abound.   105
And thorough this distemperature,° we see
The seasons alter: hoary-headed frosts
Fall in the fresh lap of the crimson rose,
And on old Hiems'° thin and icy crown,
An odorous chaplet° of sweet summer buds   110
Is, as in mockery, set. The spring, the summer,
The childing° autumn, angry winter change
Their wonted liveries:° and the mazèd° world,
By their increase, now knows not which is which:
And this same progeny of evils comes   115
From our debate, from our dissension:
We are their parents and original.°
OBERON.   Do you amend it then: it lies in you.
Why should Titania cross her Oberon?
I do but beg a little changeling boy,   120
To be my henchman.°
QUEEN.   Set your heart at rest.
The fairy land buys not the child of me.
His mother was a vot'ress° of my order:

88–117 *Therefore . . . original:* (the disturbance in nature reflects the discord between Oberon and
Titania).   90 *Contagious:* spreading pestilence.   91 *pelting:* paltry.   92 *overborne their continents:* overflown the banks which contain them.   94 *corn:* grain.   95 *beard:* the tassels on
ripened grain.   96 *fold:* enclosure for livestock.   97 *murrion:* dead from murrain, a cattle disease.   98 *nine men's morris:* game played on squares cut in the grass on which stones or disks are
moved.   99 *quaint mazes:* intricate paths.   *wanton green:* luxuriant grass.   101 *want:*
lack.   106 *distemperature:* upset in nature.   109 *Hiems:* god of winter.   110 *odorous
chaplet:* sweet-smelling wreath.   112 *childing:* fruitful.   113 *wonted liveries:* accustomed
dress.   *mazèd:* amazed.   121 *henchman:* attendant.   123 *vot'ress:* vowed and devoted
follower.

And in the spicèd Indian air, by night,
Full often hath she gossiped by my side.   125
And sat with me on Neptune's yellow sands,
Marking th' embarkèd traders° on the flood:
When we have laughed to see the sails conceive,
And grow big-bellied with the wanton° wind:
Which she, with pretty and with swimming gait,   130
Following (her womb then rich with my young squire)
Would imitate, and sail upon the land,
To fetch me trifles, and return again,
As from a voyage, rich with merchandise.
But she, being mortal, of that boy did die,   135
And for her sake, do I rear up her boy:
And for her sake, I will not part with him.
OBERON.   How long within this wood intend you stay?
QUEEN.   Perchance till after Theseus' wedding day.
If you will patiently dance in our round,°   140
And see our moonlight revels, go with us:
If not, shun me, and I will spare° your haunts.
OBERON.   Give me that boy, and I will go with thee.
QUEEN.   Not for thy fairy kingdom. Fairies away
We shall chide downright, if I longer stay.   145

Exeunt [*Titania and her Train.*]

OBERON.   Well, go thy way. Thou shalt not from this grove,
Till I torment thee for this injury.
My gentle Puck come hither: thou rememb'rest,
Since° once I sat upon a promontory,
And heard a mermaid, on a dolphin's back,   150
Uttering such dulcet and harmonious breath,
That the rude° sea grew civil° at her song,
And certain stars shot madly from their spheres,
To hear the sea-maid's music.
PUCK.   I remember.
OBERON.   That very time, I saw (but thou couldst not)   155
Flying between the cold moon and the earth,
Cupid, all armed: a certain aim he took
At a fair Vestal,° thronèd by the west,
And loosed his love-shaft smartly from his bow,
As it should pierce a hundred thousand hearts: 160
But I might see young Cupid's fiery shaft
Quenched in the chaste beams of the wat'ry moon:
And the imperial vot'ress° passèd on,
In maiden meditation, fancy-free.°

127 *traders:* merchant ships.   129 *wanton:* sportive.   140 *round:* round dance.   142 *spare:*
shun.   149 *Since:* when.   152 *rude:* rough.   *civil:* calm.   158 *Vestal:* virgin, probable
reference to Queen Elizabeth.   162 *imperial vot'ress:* royal devotee (Queen Elizabeth) of
Diana.   164 *fancy-free:* free from love.

Yet marked I where the bolt° of Cupid fell.   165
It fell upon a little western flower;
Before, milk-white; now purple with love's wound,
And maidens call it love-in-idleness.°
Fetch me that flow'r: the herb I showed thee once.
The juice of it, on sleeping eyelids laid,   170
Will make or man or woman madly dote
Upon the next live creature that it sees.
Fetch me this herb, and be thou here again
Ere the leviathan° can swim a league.

PUCK.   I'll put a girdle round about the earth,   175
In forty minutes.   [*Exit.*]

OBERON.   Having once this juice,
I'll watch Titania when she is asleep,
And drop the liquor of it in her eyes:
The next thing then she waking looks upon,
(Be it on lion, bear, or wolf, or bull,   180
On meddling monkey, or on busy° ape)
She shall pursue it, with the soul of love.
And ere I take this charm from off her sight
(As I can take it with another herb)
I'll make her render up her page to me.   185
But who comes here? I am invisible,
And I will overhear their conference.

Enter DEMETRIUS, HELENA following him.

DEMETRIUS.   I love thee not: therefore pursue me not.
Where is Lysander and fair Hermia?
The one I'll slay: the other slayeth me.   190
Thou told'st me they were stol'n unto this wood:
And here am I, and wood° within this wood:
Because I cannot meet my Hermia.
Hence, get thee gone, and follow me no more.

HELENA.   You draw me, you hard-hearted adamant:°   195
But yet you draw not iron, for my heart
Is true as steel. Leave you your power to draw,
And I shall have no power to follow you.

DEMETRIUS.   Do I entice you? Do I speak you fair°?
Or rather do I not in plainest truth   200
Tell you I do not, nor I cannot love you?

HELENA.   And even for that, do I love you the more:
I am your spaniel: and Demetrius,
The more you beat me, I will fawn on you.
Use me but as your spaniel: spurn me, strike me,   205
Neglect me, lose me: only give me leave,

---

165 *bolt:* arrow.   168 *love-in-idleness:* pansy.   174 *leviathan:* whale.   181 *busy:* mischievous.   192 *wood:* crazy.   195 *adamant:* (1) magnet (2) impenetrably hard lodestone.   199
you fair: to you in a kindly way.

Unworthy as I am, to follow you.
What worser place can I beg in your love
(And yet a place of high respect with me)
Than to be usèd as you use your dog.   210
DEMETRIUS.   Tempt not too much the hatred of my spirit,
For I am sick, when I do look on thee.
HELENA.   And I am sick, when I look not on you.
DEMETRIUS.   You do impeach° your modesty too much,
To leave the city and commit yourself   215
Into the hands of one that loves you not,
To trust the opportunity of night,
And the ill counsel of a desert° place,
With the rich worth of your virginity.
HELENA.   Your virtue is my privilege:° for that°   220
It is not night, when I do see your face,
Therefore I think I am not in the night.
Nor doth this wood lack worlds of company,
For you, in my respect,° are all the world.
Then how can it be said I am alone,   225
When all the world is here to look on me?
DEMETRIUS.   I'll run from thee and hide me in the brakes,°
And leave thee to the mercy of wild beasts.
HELENA.   The wildest hath not such a heart as you.
Run when you will: the story shall be changed;   230
Apollo flies, and Daphne° holds the chase:
The dove pursues the griffin:° the mild hind°
Makes speed to catch the tiger. Bootless° speed,
When cowardice pursues, and valour flies.
DEMETRIUS.   I will not stay° thy questions. Let me go: 235
Or if thou follow me, do not believe
But I shall do thee mischief in the wood.   [*Exit* DEMETRIUS.]
HELENA.   Ay, in the temple, in the town, the field,
You do me mischief. Fie Demetrius,
Your wrongs do set a scandal on my sex: 240
We cannot fight for love, as men may do:
We should be wooed, and were not made to woo.
I'll follow thee and make a heaven of hell,
To die upon the hand I love so well.   *Exit.*
OBERON.   Fare thee well nymph. Ere he do leave this grove,   245
Thou shalt fly him, and he shall seek thy love.

Enter PUCK.

Hast thou the flower there? Welcome wanderer.

---

214 *impeach:* discredit.   218 *desert:* deserted.   220 *Your . . . privilege:* your attraction is my
excuse (for coming).   *for that:* because.   224 *respect:* regard.   227 *brakes:* thickets.   231
Apollo . . . Daphne: (in Ovid, Apollo pursues Daphne, who turns into a laurel tree).   232 *griffin:*
legendary beast with the head of an eagle and the body of a lion.   *hind:* doe.   233 *Bootless:*
useless.   235 *stay:* wait for.

PUCK.   Ay, there it is.
OBERON.   I pray thee give it me.
    I know a bank where the wild thyme blows,
    Where oxlips and the nodding violet grows,   250
    Quite over-canopied with luscious woodbine,
    With sweet musk-roses, and with eglantine:
    There sleeps Titania, sometime of the night,
    Lulled in these flowers, with dances and delight:
    And there the snake throws° her enamelled skin,   255
    Weed° wide enough to wrap a fairy in.
    And with the juice of this, I'll streak her eyes,
    And make her full of hateful fantasies.
    Take thou some of it, and seek through this grove:
    A sweet Athenian lady is in love   260
    With a disdainful youth: anoint his eyes.
    But do it when the next thing he espies
    May be the lady. Thou shalt know the man
    By the Athenian garments he hath on.
    Effect it with some care, that he may prove   265
    More fond° on her, than she upon her love:
    And look thou meet me ere the first cock crow.
PUCK.   Fear not my lord: your servant shall do so.   *Exeunt.*

[Scene 2. Another part of the wood]

Enter TITANIA Queen of Fairies with her train.

QUEEN.   Come, now a roundel° and a fairy song:
    Then, for the third part of a minute, hence—
    Some to kill cankers in the musk-rose buds,
    Some war with reremice° for their leathren wings,
    To make my small elves coats, and some keep back   5
    The clamorous owl, that nightly hoots and wonders
    At our quaint° spirits. Sing me now asleep:
    Then to your offices,° and let me rest.

Fairies sing.

    You spotted snakes with double° tongue,
      Thorny hedgehogs be not seen,   10
    Newts and blind-worms° do no wrong,
      Come not near our Fairy Queen.

      Philomele,° with melody,
      Sing in our sweet lullaby,
    Lulla, lulla, lullaby, lulla, lulla, lullaby.   15

---

255 *throws:* casts off.   256 *weed:* garment.   266 *fond:* doting, madly in love.   1 *roundel:*
dance in a ring.   4 *reremice:* bats.   7 *quaint:* dainty.   8 *offices:* duties.   9 *double:*
forked.   11 *blind-worms:* legless lizards.   13 *Philomele:* the nightingale.

Never harm,
Nor spell, nor charm,
Come our lovely lady nigh.
So good night, with lullaby.
1. FAIRY.   Weaving spiders come not here: 20
Hence you long-legged spinners, hence:
Beetles black approach not near:
Worm nor snail do no offence.
Philomele, with melody, &c.   *She sleeps.*
2. FAIRY.   Hence away: now all is well: 25
One aloof stand sentinel.   [*Exeunt fairies.*]

Enter OBERON [*and applies the flower juice to* TITANIA'S *eyelids.*]

OBERON.   What thou seest, when thou dost wake,
Do it for thy true love take:
Love and languish for his sake.
Be it ounce,° or cat, or bear,   30
Pard,° or boar with bristled hair,
In thy eye that shall appear,
When thou wak'st, it is thy dear:
Wake when some vile thing is near.   [*Exit.*]

Enter LYSANDER *and* HERMIA.

LYSANDER.   Fair love, you faint with wand'ring in the wood: 35
And to speak troth° I have forgot our way.
We'll rest us Hermia, if you think it good,
And tarry for the comfort of the day.
HERMIA.   Be't so Lysander: find you out a bed:
For I upon this bank will rest my head.   40
LYSANDER.   One turf shall serve as pillow for us both,
One heart, one bed, two bosoms, and one troth.°
HERMIA.   Nay good Lysander: for my sake, my dear,
Lie further off yet; do not lie so near.
LYSANDER.   O take the sense, sweet, of my innocence:°   45
Love takes the meaning in love's conference.°
I mean that my heart unto yours is knit,
So that but one heart we can make of it:
Two bosoms interchainèd with an oath,
So then two bosoms and a single troth.   50
Then by your side no bed-room me deny:
For lying so, Hermia, I do not lie.
HERMIA.   Lysander riddles very prettily.
Now much beshrew° my manners and my pride,
If Hermia meant to say Lysander lied.   55

30 *ounce:* lynx.   31 *Pard:* leopard.   36 *troth:* truth.   42 *troth:* true love.   45 *take . . . innocence:* understand the innocence of my remark.   46 *Love . . . conference:* love enables lovers to understand each other when they converse.   54 *beshrew:* curse.

But gentle friend, for love and courtesy,
Lie further off, in human modesty:
Such separation as may well be said
Becomes a virtuous bachelor and a maid,
So far be distant, and good night sweet friend: 60
Thy love ne'er alter till thy sweet life end.
LYSANDER.   Amen, amen, to that fair prayer say I,
And then end life, when I end loyalty.
Here is my bed: sleep give thee all his rest.
HERMIA.   With half that wish, the wisher's eyes be pressed.°   65

                                                            They sleep.

Enter PUCK.

PUCK.   Through the forest have I gone,
But Athenian found I none,
On whose eyes I might approve°
This flower's force in stirring love.
Night and silence. Who is here?   70
Weeds° of Athens he doth wear:
This is he (my master said)
Despisèd the Athenian maid:
And here the maiden, sleeping sound,
On the dank and dirty ground.   75
Pretty soul, she durst not lie
Near this lack-love, this kill-courtesy.
Churl, upon thy eyes I throw
All the power this charm doth owe:°
When thou wak'st, let love forbid   80
Sleep his seat on thy eyelid.°
So awake when I am gone:
For I must now to Oberon.   *Exit.*

Enter DEMETRIUS *and* HELENA *running.*

HELENA.   Stay, thou kill me, sweet Demetrius.
DEMETRIUS.   I charge thee hence, and do not haunt me thus.   85
HELENA.   O, wilt thou darkling° leave me? Do not so.
DEMETRIUS.   Stay on thy peril: I alone will go.   *Exit* DEMETRIUS.
HELENA.   O, I am out of breath in this fond° chase:
The more my prayer, the lesser is my grace.°
Happy is Hermia, wheresoe'er she lies: 90
For she hath blessèd and attractive eyes.
How came her eyes so bright? Not with salt tears:
If so, my eyes are oft'ner washed than hers.

---

65 *pressed:* i.e., by sleep.   68 *approve:* test   71 *Weeds:* garments.   79 *owe:* own.   80–81
forbid . . . eyelid: make you sleepless (with love).   86 *darkling:* in the dark.   88 *fond:* foolishly doting.   89 *my grace:* favor shown to me.

No, no: I am as ugly as a bear:
For beasts that meet me run away for fear.   95
Therefore no marvel, though Demetrius
Do as a monster, fly my presence thus.
What wicked and dissembling glass° of mine,
Made me compare with Hermia's sphery eyne°!
But who is here? Lysander, on the ground?   100
Dead, or asleep? I see no blood, no wound.
Lysander, if you live, good sir awake.
LYSANDER.   [*Wakes.*] And run through fire, I will for thy sweet sake.
Transparent° Helena, nature shows art,
That through thy bosom, makes me see thy heart.   105
Where is Demetrius? O how fit a word
Is that vile name to perish on my sword!
HELENA.   Do not say so, Lysander, say not so.
What though he love your Hermia? Lord, what though?
Yet Hermia still loves you: then be content.   110
LYSANDER.   Content with Hermia? No: I do repent
The tedious minutes I with her have spent.
Not Hermia, but Helena I love.
Who will not change a raven for a dove?
The will of man is by his reason swayed:°   115
And reason says you are the worthier maid.
Things growing are not ripe until their season:
So I, being young, till now ripe° not to reason.
And touching now the point° of human skill,°
Reason becomes the marshal to my will,   120
And leads me to your eyes; where I o'erlook
Love's stories, written in love's richest book.
HELENA.   Wherefore° was I to this keen mockery born?
When at your hands did I deserve this scorn?
Is't not enough, is't not enough, young man,   125
That I did never, no, nor never can,
Deserve a sweet look from Demetrius' eye,
But you must flout° my insufficiency?
Good troth you do me wrong, good sooth you do,
In such disdainful manner me to woo.   130
But fare you well: perforce I must confess,
I thought you lord of more true gentleness.°
O, that a lady, of one man refused,
Should of another, therefore be abused!   *Exit.*
LYSANDER.   She sees not Hermia. Hermia, sleep thou there,   135
And never mayst thou come Lysander near.
For, as a surfeit of the sweetest things
The deepest loathing to the stomach brings:

98 *glass:* looking glass.   99 *sphery eyne:* starry eyes.   104 *Transparent:* radiant.   115
swayed: ruled.   118 *ripe:* mature.   119 *point:* peak.   *skill:* knowledge.   123 *Wherefore:*
why.   128 *flout:* mock.   132 *lord . . . gentleness:* more of a gentleman.

Or as the heresies that men do leave,
Are hated most of those they did deceive: 140
So thou, my surfeit and my heresy,
Of all be hated; but the most, of me:
And all my powers, address your love and might,
To honour Helen, and to be her knight.

                                                                    Exit.

HERMIA.   [*Wakes.*] Help me Lysander, help me: do thy best   145
To pluck this crawling serpent from my breast.
Ay me, for pity. What a dream was here?
Lysander, look how I do quake with fear.
Methought a serpent eat my heart away,
And you sat smiling at his cruel prey.°   150
Lysander: what, removed? Lysander, lord!
What, out of hearing, gone? No sound, no word?
Alack, where are you? Speak, and if you hear:
Speak, of° all loves. I swoon almost with fear.
No? Then I well perceive you are not nigh: 155
Either death, or you, I'll find immediately.   *Exit.*

ACT 3

[*Scene 1. The wood*]

Enter the CLOWNS [*QUINCE, SNUG, BOTTOM, FLUTE, SNOUT, and STARVELING.*]

BOTTOM.   Are we all met?
QUINCE.   Pat, pat: and here's a marvellous convenient place for
    our rehearsal. This green plot shall be our stage, this
    hawthorn brake° our tiring-house,° and we will do it in
    action, as we will do it before the duke.   5
BOTTOM.   Peter Quince?
QUINCE.   What sayest thou, bully° Bottom?
BOTTOM.   There are things in this Comedy of Pyramus and Thisby
    that will never please. First, Pyramus must draw a sword
    to kill himself; which the ladies cannot abide. How   10
    answer you that?
SNOUT.   By'r lakin,° a parlous° fear.
STARVELING.   I believe we must leave the killing out, when all is done.
BOTTOM.   Not a whit: I have a device to make all well. Write me
    a prologue, and let the prologue seem to say, we will   15
    do no harm with our swords, and that Pyramus is not
    killed indeed: and for the more better assurance, tell
    them that I Pyramus am not Pyramus, but Bottom the
    weaver: this will put them out of fear.

---

150 *prey:* preying.   154 *of:* for the sake of.   4 *brake:* thicket.   *tiring-house:* dressing room.   7 *bully:* "old pal."   12 *By'r lakin:* mild oath, "by Our Lady."   *parlous:* awful,
perilous.

QUINCE.   Well, we will have such a prologue, and it shall be   20
  written in eight and six.°
BOTTOM.   No, make it two more: let it be written in eight and
  eight.
SNOUT.   Will not the ladies be afeared of the lion?
STARVELING.   I fear it, I promise you.   25
BOTTOM.   Masters, you ought to consider with yourselves, to bring
  in (God shield us) a lion among ladies, is a most dreadful
  thing. For there is not a more fearful wild-fowl than
  your lion living: and we ought to look to't.
SNOUT.   Therefore another prologue must tell he is not a lion.   30
BOTTOM.   Nay, you must name his name, and half his face must be
  seen through the lion's neck, and he himself must speak
  through, saying thus, or to the same defect:° "Ladies,"
  or "Fair ladies—I would wish you," or "I would request
  you," or "I would entreat you, not to fear,   35
  not to tremble: my life for yours. If you think I come
  hither as a lion, it were pity of my life. No, I am no
  such thing: I am a man as other men are." And there
  indeed let him name his name, and tell them plainly he
  is Snug the joiner.   40
QUINCE.   Well, it shall be so, but there is two hard things: that is,
  to bring the moonlight into a chamber: for you know,
  Pyramus and Thisby meet by moonlight.
SNOUT.   Doth the moon shine that night we play our play?
BOTTOM.   A calendar, a calendar: look in the almanac: find out   45
  moonshine, find out moonshine.
QUINCE.   Yes, it doth shine that night.
BOTTOM.   Why then may you leave a casement of the great
  chamber window, where we play, open; and the moon may
  shine in at the casement.   50
QUINCE.   Ay, or else one must come in with a bush of thorns° and
  a lantern, and say he comes to disfigure,° or to present,
  the person of Moonshine. Then, there is another thing;
  we must have a wall in the great chamber: for Pyramus
  and Thisby, says the story, did talk through the chink   55
  of a wall.
SNOUT.   You can never bring in a wall. What say you, Bottom?
BOTTOM.   Some man or other must present wall: and let him have
  some plaster, or some loam, or some rough-cast° about
  him, to signify wall; and let him hold his fingers thus: 60
  and through that cranny, shall Pyramus and Thisby whisper.
QUINCE.   If that may be, then all is well. Come, sit down every
  mother's son, and rehearse your parts. Pyramus, you

---

21 *eight and six:* alternate lines of eight and six syllables (the ballad meter).   33 *defect:* (he means "effect").   51 *bush of thorns:* bundle of firewood (the man in the moon was supposed to have been placed there as a punishment for gathering wood on Sundays).   52 *disfigure:* (he means "figure," symbolize).   59 *rough-cast:* coarse plaster of lime and gravel.

begin: when you have spoken your speech, enter into that
  brake, and so every one according to his cue.   65

Enter PUCK.

PUCK.   What hempen homespuns° have we swagg'ring here,
  So near the cradle of the Fairy Queen?
  What, a play toward°? I'll be an auditor,
  An actor too perhaps, if I see cause.
QUINCE.   Speak Pyramus. Thisby stand forth.   70
PYRAMUS.   Thisby, the flowers of odious savours sweet—
QUINCE.   "Odorous, odorous."
PYRAMUS.   —odours savours sweet,
  So hath thy breath, my dearest Thisby dear.
  But hark, a voice: stay thou but here awhile,   75
  And by and by I will to thee appear.   *Exit PYRAMUS.*
PUCK.   A stranger Pyramus than e'er played here.   [*Exit.*]
THISBY.   Must I speak now?
QUINCE.   Ay marry must you. For you must understand he goes
  but to see a noise that he heard, and is to come again.   80
THISBY.   Most radiant Pyramus, most lily-white of hue,
    Of colour like the red rose, on triumphant brier,
  Most brisky juvenal,° and eke most lovely Jew,°
    As true as truest horse, that yet would never tire,
  I'll meet thee Pyramus, at Ninny's tomb.   85
QUINCE.   "Ninus' tomb,"° man: why, you must not speak that yet.
  That you answer to Pyramus. You speak all your part
  at once, cues and all. Pyramus, enter; your cue is past:
  it is "never tire."
THISBY.   O—As true as truest horse, that yet would never tire.   90

Enter PYRAMUS with the ass-head [followed by PUCK].

PYRAMUS.   If I were fair, Thisby, I were only thine.
QUINCE.   O monstrous! O strange! We are haunted. Pray masters,
  fly masters. Help!   *The clowns all exeunt.*
PUCK.   I'll follow you: I'll lead you about a round,°
    Through bog, through bush, through brake, through brier.   95
  Sometime a horse I'll be, sometime a hound,
    A hog, a headless bear, sometime a fire,
  And neigh, and bark, and grunt, and roar, and burn,
  Like horse, hound, hog, bear, fire, at every turn.   *Exit.*
BOTTOM.   Why do they run away? This is a knavery of them to   100
  make me afeared.

Enter SNOUT.

---

66 *hempen homespuns:* wearers of clothing spun at home from hemp.   68 *toward:* in preparation.   83 *brisky juvenal:* lively youth.   *Jew:* diminutive of either "juvenal" or "jewel."   86
Ninus' tomb: (tomb of the founder of Nineveh, and meeting place of the lovers in Ovid's version of
the Pyramus story).   94 *about a round:* in circles, like a round dance (round about).

SNOUT.   O Bottom, thou art changed. What do I see on thee?

BOTTOM.   What do you see? You see an ass-head of your own, do
you?   [*Exit SNOUT.*]

Enter QUINCE.

QUINCE.   Bless thee Bottom, bless thee. Thou art translated.°   *Exit.*   105

BOTTOM.   I see their knavery. This is to make an ass of me, to
fright me if they could: but I will not stir from this
place, do what they can. I will walk up and down here,
and will sing that they shall hear I am not afraid.
    [*Sings.*] The woosel° cock, so black of hue,   110
        With orange tawny bill,
        The throstle,° with his note so true,
        The wren, with little quill.°

TITANIA.   What angel wakes me from my flow'ry bed?

BOTTOM.   [*Sings.*] The finch, the sparrow, and the lark,   115
        The plain-song° cuckoo gray:
        Whose note full many a man doth mark,
        And dares not answer, nay.
For indeed, who would set his wit to° so foolish a bird?
Who would give a bird the lie,° though he cry "cuckoo"°   120
never so°?

TITANIA.   I pray thee, gentle mortal, sing again.
Mine ear is much enamoured of thy note:
So is mine eye enthrallèd to thy shape,
And thy fair virtue's force (perforce°) doth move me,   125
On the first view to say, to swear, I love thee.

BOTTOM.   Methinks mistress, you should have little reason for
that. And yet, to say the truth, reason and love keep
little company together now-a-days. The more the pity,
That some honest neighbours will not make them friends.   130
Nay, I can gleek° upon occasion.

TITANIA.   Thou art as wise as thou art beautiful.

BOTTOM.   Not so neither: but if I had wit enough to get out of
this wood, I have enough to serve mine own turn.

TITANIA.   Out of this wood do not desire to go: 135
Thou shalt remain here, whether thou wilt or no.
I am a spirit of no common rate:°
The summer still doth tend upon my state,°
And I do love thee: therefore go with me.
I'll give thee fairies to attend on thee: 140
And they shall fetch thee jewels from the deep,
And sing, while thou on pressèd flowers dost sleep:

105 *translated:* transformed.   110 *woosel:* ousel, blackbird.   112 *throstle:* thrush.   113
quill: piping note.   116 *plain-song:* sounding a simple unvaried note.   119 *set . . . to:* match
his wit against.   120 *Who . . . lie:* who could call a bird a liar.   *"cuckoo":* (which sounded like
"cuckold" = a deceived husband).   121 *never so:* i.e., often.   125 *perforce:* by force.   131
gleek: joke satirically.   137 *rate:* rank, value   138 *still . . . state:* always serves as an attendant
in my royal train.

And I will purge thy mortal grossness so,
That thou shalt like an airy spirit go.
Peaseblossom, Cobweb, Moth,° and Mustardseed!   145

Enter four FAIRIES.

PEASEBLOSSOM.   Ready.
COBWEB.   And I.
MOTH.   And I.
MUSTARDSEED.   And I.
ALL.   Where shall we go?
TITANIA.   Be kind and courteous to this gentleman,
    Hop in his walks and gambol° in his eyes,
    Feed him with apricocks° and dewberries,°   150
    With purple grapes, green figs, and mulberries.
    The honey-bags steal from the humblebees,°
    And for night-tapers, crop° their waxen thighs,
    And light them at the fiery glow-worm's eyes,
    To have my love to bed and to arise: 155
    And pluck the wings from painted butterflies,
    To fan the moonbeams from his sleeping eyes.
    Nod to him elves, and do him courtesies.
PEASEBLOSSOM.   Hail, mortal.
COBWEB.   Hail.   160
MOTH.   Hail.
MUSTARDSEED.   Hail.
BOTTOM.   I cry your worships mercy,° heartily: I beseech your
    worship's name.
COBWEB.   Cobweb.   165
BOTTOM.   I shall desire you of more acquaintance, good Master
    Cobweb: if I cut my finger,° I shall make bold with you.
    Your name, honest gentleman?
PEASEBLOSSOM.   Peaseblossom.
BOTTOM.   I pray you commend me° to Mistress Squash,° your mother,   170
    and to Master Peascod,° your father. Good Master Peaseblossom,
    I shall desire you of more acquaintance, too.
    Your name I beseech you sir?
MUSTARDSEED.   Mustardseed.
BOTTOM.   Good Master Mustardseed, I know your patience well.   175
    That same cowardly giant-like ox beef hath devoured
    many a gentleman of your house. I promise you, your
    kindred hath made my eyes water ere now. I desire you
    of more acquaintance, good Master Mustardseed.
TITANIA.   Come wait upon him: lead him to my bower.   180
            The moon methinks looks with a wat'ry eye:

---

145 *Moth:* mote (so pronounced), tiny speck.   149 *gambol in:* caper before.   150 *apricocks:*
apricots.   *dewberries:* blackberries.   152 *humblebees:* bumblebees.   153 *crop:* clip.   163
I . . . mercy: I respectfully beg your pardons.   167 *cut my finger:* (cobwebs were used to stop
bleeding).   170 *commend me:* offer my respects.   *Squash:* unripe peapod.   171 *Peascod:*
ripe peapod.

And when she weeps, weeps every little flower,
Lamenting some enforcèd° chastity.
Tie up my lover's tongue, bring him silently. *Exeunt.*

[*Scene 2. Another part of the wood*]

*Enter [*OBERON,*] King of Fairies, solus.°*

OBERON. I wonder if Titania be awaked;
Then what it was that next came in her eye,
Which she must dote on in extremity.

Enter PUCK.

Here comes my messenger. How now, mad spirit?
What night-rule° now about this haunted grove? 5
PUCK. My mistress with a monster is in love.
Near to her close and consecrated bower,
While she was in her dull° and sleeping hour,
A crew of patches,° rude mechanicals,°
That work for bread upon Athenian stalls,° 10
Were met together to rehearse a play,
Intended for great Theseus' nuptial day:
The shallowest thickskin of that barren sort,°
Who Pyramus presented in their sport,
Forsook his scene and entered in a brake: 15
When I did him at this advantage take,
An ass's nole° I fixèd on his head.
Anon° his Thisby must be answerèd,
And forth my mimic° comes. When they him spy,
As wild geese, that the creeping fowler° eye, 20
Or russet-pated choughs,° many in sort,°
Rising and cawing at the gun's report,
Sever themselves and madly sweep the sky,
So at his sight away his fellows fly:
And at our stamp, here o'er and o'er one falls: 25
He murder cries, and help from Athens calls.
Their sense thus weak, lost with their fears thus strong,
Made senseless things begin to do them wrong.
For briers and thorns at their apparel snatch:
Some° sleeves, some hats; from yielders, all things catch.° 30
I led them on in this distracted° fear,
And left sweet Pyramus translated there:
When in that moment (so it came to pass)
Titania waked, and straightway loved an ass.

---

183 *enforcèd:* violated.   S.D.: *solus:* alone.   5 *night-rule:* diversion ("misrule") in the
night.   8 *dull:* drowsy.   9 *patches:* fools.   *mechanicals:* workers.   10 *stalls:* shops.   13
barren sort: stupid crew.   17 *nole:* head, noodle.   18 *Anon:* presently.   19 *mimic:*
actor.   20 *fowler:* hunter of fowl.   21 *russet-pated choughs:* grey-headed jackdaws.   *sort:* a
flock.   30 *Some:* ie., snatch.   *from yielders . . . catch:* (everything joins in to harm the
weak).   31 *distracted:* maddened.

OBERON.   This falls out better than I could devise.   35
    But has thou yet latched° the Athenian's eyes
    With the love-juice, as I did bid thee do?
PUCK.   I took him sleeping (that is finished too)
    And the Athenian woman by his side;
    That when he waked, of force° she must be eyed.   40

Enter DEMETRIUS *and* HERMIA.

OBERON.   Stand close:° this is the same Athenian.
PUCK.   This is the woman: but not this the man.
DEMETRIUS.   O why rebuke you him that loves you so?
    Lay breath so bitter on your bitter foe.
HERMIA.   Now I but chide: but I should use thee worse,   45
    For thou, I fear, hast given me cause to curse.
    If thou hast slain Lysander in his sleep,
    Being o'er shoes in blood, plunge in the deep,
    And kill me too.
    The sun was not so true unto the day,   50
    As he to me. Would he have stolen away
    From sleeping Hermia? I'll believe as soon
    This whole° earth may be bored,° and that the moon
    May through the center creep, and so displease
    Her brother's noontide with th' Antipodes.°   55
    It cannot be but thou hast murdered him.
    So should a murderer look; so dead,° so grim.
DEMETRIUS.   So should the murdered look, and so should I,
    Pierced through the heart with your stern cruelty.
    Yet you, the murderer, look as bright, as clear,   60
    As yonder Venus in her glimmering sphere.°
HERMIA.   What's this to my Lysander? Where is he?
    Ah good Demetrius, wilt thou give him me?
DEMETRIUS.   I had rather give his carcass to my hounds.
HERMIA.   Out dog, out cur! Thou driv'st me past the bounds   65
    Of maiden's patience. Hast thou slain him then?
    Henceforth be never numbered among men.
    O, once tell true: tell true, even for my sake:
    Durst thou have looked upon him, being awake?
    And hast thou killed him sleeping? O brave touch°!   70
    Could not a worm,° an adder, do so much?
    An adder did it: for with doubler tongue°
    Than thine, thou serpent, never adder stung.

---

36 *latched:* moistened.   40 *of force:* by necessity.   41 *close:* hidden.   53 *whole:* solid.   *be bored:* have a hole bored through it.   55 *Her brother's . . . Antipodes:* the noon of her brother sun, by appearing among the Antipodes (the people on the other side of the earth).   57 *dead:* deadly.   61 *sphere:* (in the Ptolemaic system, each planet moved in its own sphere around the earth).   70 *brave touch:* splendid stroke (ironic).   71 *worm:* snake.   72 *doubler tongue:* (1) tongue more forked (2) more deceitful speech.

DEMETRIUS. You spend your passion on a misprised mood:°
    I am not guilty of Lysander's blood: 75
    Nor is he dead, for aught that I can tell.
HERMIA. I pray thee, tell me then that he is well.
DEMETRIUS. And if I could, what should I get therefore?
HERMIA. A privilege never to see me more:
    And from thy hated presence part I so: 80
    See me no more, whether he be dead or no.   *Exit.*
DEMETRIUS. There is no following her in this fierce vein.
    Here therefore for a while I will remain.
    So sorrow's heaviness doth heavier grow
    For debt that bankrout sleep doth sorrow owe:° 85
    Which now in some slight measure it will pay,
    If for his tender° here I make some stay.°   *Lies down.*
OBERON. What hast thou done? Thou hast mistaken quite,
    And laid the love-juice on some true-love's sight.
    Of thy misprision° must perforce° ensue 90
    Some true love turned, and not a false turned true.
PUCK. Then fate o'errules, that one man holding troth,
    A million fail, confounding° oath on oath.°
OBERON. About the wood, go swifter than the wind,
    And Helena of Athens look thou find. 95
    All fancy-sick° she is, and pale of cheer,°
    With sighs of love, that costs the fresh blood dear.
    By some illusion see thou bring her here:
    I'll charm his eyes against she do appear.°
PUCK. I go, I go, look how I go. 100
    Swifter than arrow from the Tartar's bow.°   *Exit.*
OBERON. Flower of this purple dye,
    Hit with Cupid's archery,
    Sink in apple of his eye:
    When his love he doth espy, 105
    Let her shine as gloriously
    As the Venus of the sky.
    When thou wak'st, if she be by,
    Beg of her for remedy.

Enter PUCK.

PUCK. Captain of our fairy band, 110
    Helena is here at hand,
    And the youth, mistook by me,
    Pleading for a lover's fee.°

---

74 *on . . . mood:* in mistaken anger.   85 *For debt . . . owe:* because sleep cannot pay the debt of repose he owes the man who is kept awake by sorrow.   87 *tender:* offer.   *stay:* pause.   90 *misprision:* mistake.   *perforce:* of necessity.   93 *confounding:* destroying.   *oath on oath:* one oath after another.   96 *fancy-sick:* lovesick.   *cheer:* face.   99 *against . . . appear:* in preparation for her appearance.   101 *Tartar's bow:* (the Tartars, who used powerful Oriental bows, were famed as archers).   113 *fee:* reward.

115

> Shall we their fond pageant° see?
> Lord, what fools these mortals be!

OBERON.   Stand aside. The noise they make
> Will cause Demetrius to awake.

PUCK.   Then will two at once woo one:
> That must needs be sport alone.°
> And those things do best please me   120
> That befall prepost'rously.

Enter LYSANDER *and* HELENA.

LYSANDER.   Why should you think that I should woo in scorn?
> Scorn and derision never come in tears.
> Look when I vow, I weep: and vows so born,
> In their nativity all truth appears.°   125
> How can these things in me seem scorn to you,
> Bearing the badge° of faith to prove them true?

HELENA.   You do advance your cunning more and more.
> When truth kills truth,° O devilish-holy fray!
> These vows are Hermia's. Will you give her o'er?   130
> Weigh oath with oath, and you will nothing weigh.
> Your vows to her and me, put in two scales,
> Will even weigh: and both as light as tales.

LYSANDER.   I had no judgment, when to her I swore.

HELENA.   Nor none, in my mind, now you give her o'er.   135

LYSANDER.   Demetrius loves her: and he loves not you.

DEMETRIUS.   (*Awakes.*) O Helen, goddess, nymph, perfect, divine,
> To what, my love, shall I compare thine eyne!
> Crystal is muddy. O, how ripe in show,
> Thy lips, those kissing cherries, tempting grow!   140
> That pure congealèd white, high Taurus'° snow,
> Fanned with the eastern wind, turns to a crow,
> When thou hold'st up thy hand. O let me kiss
> This princess of pure white,° this seal of bliss.

HELENA.   O spite! O hell! I see you all are bent   145
> To set against me, for your merriment.
> If you were civil,° and knew courtesy,
> You would not do me thus much injury.
> Can you not hate me, as I know you do,
> But you must join in souls° to mock me too?   150
> If you were men, as men you are in show,
> You would not use a gentle lady so;
> To vow, and swear, and superpraise my parts,°
> When I am sure you hate me with your hearts.
> You both are rivals, and love Hermia: 155

---

114 *fond pageant:* foolish spectacle.   119 *alone:* unique.   124–125 *vows . . . appears:* vows born in weeping must be true ones.   127 *badge:* (1) outward signs (2) family crest.   129 *truth kills truth:* former true love is killed by vows of present true love.   141 *Taurus:* mountain range in Asia Minor.   144 *princess . . . white:* sovereign example of whiteness (her hand).   147 *civil:* well behaved.   150 *join in souls:* agree in spirit.   153 *parts:* qualities.

And now both rivals, to mock Helena.
A trim° exploit, a manly enterprise,
To conjure tears up in a poor maid's eyes
With your derision. None of noble sort
Would so offend a virgin, and extort°   160
A poor soul's patience, all to make you sport.

LYSANDER.   You are unkind, Demetrius: be not so.
For you love Hermia: this you know I know.
And here, with all good will, with all my heart,
In Hermia's love I yield you up my part: 165
And yours of Helena to be bequeath,
Whom I do love, and will do to my death.

HELENA.   Never did mockers waste more idle breath.

DEMETRIUS.   Lysander, keep thy Hermia: I will none.°
If e'er I loved her, all that love is gone.   170
My heart to her but as guest-wise sojourned:°
And now to Helen is it home returned,
There to remain.

LYSANDER.   Helen, it is not so.

DEMETRIUS.   Disparage not the faith thou dost not know,
Lest to thy peril thou aby it dear.°   175
Look where thy love comes: yonder is thy dear.

Enter HERMIA.

HERMIA.   Dark night, that from the eye his function takes,
The ear more quick of apprehension makes.
Wherein it doth impair the seeing sense,
It pays the hearing double recompense.   180
Thou art not by mine eye, Lysander, found:
Mine ear, I thank it, brought me to thy sound.
But why unkindly didst thou leave me so?

LYSANDER.   Why should he stay, whom love doth press to go?

HERMIA.   What love could press Lysander from my side?   185

LYSANDER.   Lysander's love, that would not let him bide—
Fair Helena: who more engilds the night
Than all your fiery oes and eyes of light.°
Why seek'st thou me? Could not this make thee know,
The hate I bare thee made me leave thee so?   190

HERMIA.   You speak not as you think: it cannot be.

HELENA.   Lo: She is one of this confederacy.
Now I perceive they have conjoined all three,
To fashion this false sport in spite of° me.
Injurious° Hermia, most ungrateful maid,   195
Have you conspired, have you with these contrived
To bait° me with this foul derision?

---

157 *trim:* fine (ironic).   160 *extort:* wring.   169 *none:* have none of her.   171 *to her . . .*
sojourned: visited her only as a guest.   175 *aby it dear:* buy it at a high price.   188 *oes . . .*
light: stars.   194 *in spite of:* to spite.   195 *Injurious:* insulting.   197 *bait:* attack.

Is all the counsel° that we two have shared,
The sisters' vows, the hours that we have spent,
When we have chid the hasty-footed time   200
For parting us; O, is all forgot?
All schooldays' friendship, childhood innocence?
We Hermia, like two artificial° gods,
Have with our needles created both one flower,
Both on one sampler,° sitting on one cushion,   205
Both warbling of one song, both in one key;
As if our hands, our sides, voices, and minds
Had been incorporate.° So we grew together,
Like to a double cherry, seeming parted,
But yet an union in partition,   210
Two lovely berries moulded on one stem:
So with two seeming bodies, but one heart,
Two of the first, like coats in heraldry,
Due but to one, and crownèd with one crest.°
And will you rent° our ancient love asunder,   215
To join with men in scorning your poor friend?
It is not friendly, 'tis not maidenly.
Our sex, as well as I, may chide you for it;
Though I alone do feel the injury.
HERMIA.   I am amazèd at your passionate words: 220
    I scorn you not. It seems that you scorn me.
HELENA.   Have you not set Lysander, as in scorn,
    To follow me, and praise my eyes and face?
    And made your other love, Demetrius
    (Who even but now did spurn° me with his foot)   225
    To call me goddess, nymph, divine, and rare,
    Precious, celestial? Wherefore speaks he this
    To her he hates? And wherefore doth Lysander
    Deny your love, so rich within his soul,
    And tender° me (forsooth) affection,   230
    But by your setting on, by your consent?
    What though I be not so in grace° as you,
    So hung upon with love, so fortunate,
    But miserable most, to love unloved?
    This you should pity, rather than despise.   235
HERMIA.   I understand not what you mean by this.
HELENA.   Ay, do. Persèver, counterfeit sad° looks:
    Make mouths upon° me when I turn my back:
    Wink each at other, hold the sweet jest up.
    This sport well carried, shall be chronicled.°   240
    If you have any pity, grace, or manners,

198 *counsel:* secrets.   203 *artificial:* skilled in art.   205 *sampler:* work of embroidery.   208
incorporate: in one body.   213–214 *Two . . . crest:* (the two bodies being) like double coats of
arms joined under one crest (with one heart).   215 *rent:* rend, tear.   225 *spurn:* kick.
230 *tender:* offer.   232 *in grace:* favored.   237 *sad:* serious.   238 *mouths upon:* faces at.
240 *chronicled:* written down in the history books.

You would not make me such an argument.°
But fare ye well: 'tis partly my own fault:
Which death or absence soon shall remedy.

LYSANDER. Stay, gentle Helena: hear my excuse,   245
  My love, my life, my soul, fair Helena.

HELENA. O excellent!

HERMIA.   Sweet, do not scorn her so.

DEMETRIUS. If she cannot entreat,° I can compel.

LYSANDER. Thou canst compel no more than she entreat.
  Thy threats have no more strength than her weak prayers.   250
  Helen, I love thee, by my life I do:
  I swear by that which I will lose for thee,
  To prove° him false that says I love thee not.

DEMETRIUS. I say I love thee more than he can do.

LYSANDER. If thou say so, withdraw, and prove° it too.   255

DEMETRIUS. Quick, Come.

HERMIA.   Lysander, whereto tends all this?

LYSANDER. Away, you Ethiope.°

DEMETRIUS.   No, no, sir,
  Seem to break loose: take on as you would follow;
  But yet come not.° You are a tame man, go.

LYSANDER. Hang off,° thou cat, thou burr: vile thing, let loose;   260
  Or I will shake thee from me like a serpent.

HERMIA. Why are you grown so rude? What change is this,
  Sweet love?

LYSANDER.   Thy love? Out, tawny Tartar, out:
  Out, loathèd med'cine: O hated potion, hence!

HERMIA. Do you not jest?

HELENA.   Yes sooth: and so do you.   265

LYSANDER. Demetrius, I will keep my word° with thee.

DEMETRIUS. I would I had your bond.° For I perceive
  A weak bond holds you. I'll not trust your word.

LYSANDER. What? Should I hurt her, strike her, kill her dead?
  Although I hate her, I'll not harm her so.   270

HERMIA. What? Can you do me greater harm than hate?
  Hate me, wherefore°? O me, what news,° my love?
  Am not I Hermia? Are not you Lysander?
  I am as fair now, as I was erewhile.°
  Since night, you loved me; yet since night, you left me.   275
  Why then, you left me—O, the gods forbid—
  In earnest, shall I say?

LYSANDER   Ay, by my life:
  And never did desire to see thee more.

---

242 *argument:* subject (of your mockery).   248 *entreat:* sway you by entreaty.   253, 255 *prove:*
i.e., by a duel.   257 *Ethiope:* (because she is a brunette).   258–259 *Seem . . . not:* You only seem
to break loose from Hermia and pretend to follow me to a duel, but you actually hold back.   260
Hang off: let go.   266 *keep my word:* i.e., to duel.   267 *bond:* written agreement.   272 *where-*
fore: why.   *what news:* what's the matter.   274 *erewhile:* a short while ago.

Therefore be out of hope, of question, of doubt:
Be certain: nothing truer: 'tis no jest   280
That I do hate thee, and love Helena.

HERMIA.   O me, you juggler,° you canker blossom,°
You thief of love: what, have you come by night,
And stol'n my love's heart from him?

HELENA.   Fine, i' faith.
Have you no modesty, no maiden shame,   285
No touch of bashfulness? What, will you tear
Impatient answers from my gentle tongue?
Fie, fie, you counterfeit, you puppet,° you.

HERMIA.   Puppet? Why so—ay, that way goes the game.
Now I perceive that she hath made compare   290
Between our statures, she hath urged her height,
And with her personage, her tall personage,
Her height (forsooth) she hath prevailed with him.
And are you grown so high in his esteem,
Because I am so dwarfish and so low?   295
How low am I, thou painted maypole? Speak:
How low am I? I am not yet so low,
But that my nails can reach unto thine eyes.

HELENA.   I pray you, though you mock me, gentlemen,
Let her not hurt me. I was never curst:°   300
I have no gift at all in shrewishness:
I am a right maid for my cowardice:°
Let her not strike me. You perhaps may think,
Because she is something lower than myself,
That I can match her.

HERMIA.   Lower? Hark again.   305

HELENA.   Good Hermia, do not be so bitter with me,
I evermore did love you Hermia.
Did ever keep your counsels, never wronged you;
Save that in love unto Demetrius,
I told him of your stealth unto this wood.   310
He followed you: for love I followed him.
But he hath chid me hence, and threatened me
To strike me, spurn me, nay to kill me too;
And now, so° you will let me quiet go,
To Athens will I bear my folly back,   315
And follow you no further. Let me go.
You see how simple and how fond° I am.

HERMIA.   Why, get you gone. Who is't that hinders you?

HELENA.   A foolish heart, that I leave here behind.

HERMIA.   What, with Lysander?

---

282 *juggler:* deceiver.   *canker blossom:* worm that causes canker in blossoms.   288 *puppet:*
(Hermia is short and Helena tall).   300 *curst:* bad-tempered.   302 *right . . . cowardice:* true
woman in being cowardly.   314 *so:* if.   317 *fond:* foolish.

HELENA.   With Demetrius.   320
LYSANDER.   Be not afraid: she shall not harm thee Helena.
DEMETRIUS.   No sir: she shall not, though you take her part.
HELENA.   O when she's angry, she is keen and shrewd.°
    She was a vixen when she went to school:
    And though she be but little, she is fierce.   325
HERMIA.   "Little" again? Nothing but "low" and "little"?
    Why will you suffer her to flout° me thus?
    Let me come to her.
LYSANDER.   Get you gone, you dwarf;
    You minimus,° of hind'ring knot-grass° made;   330
    You bead, you acorn.
DEMETRIUS.   You are too officious
    In her behalf that scorns your services.
    Let her alone: speak not of Helena,
    Take not her part. For if thou dost intend°
    Never so little show of love to her,
    Thou shalt aby it.°
LYSANDER.   Now she holds me not: 335
    Now follow, if thou dar'st, to try whose right,
    Of thine or mine, is most in Helena.°
DEMETRIUS.   Follow? Nay, I'll go with thee, cheek by jowl.

                                        Exeunt LYSANDER *and* DEMETRIUS.

HERMIA.   You, mistress, all this coil is long of° you.
    Nay, go not back.
HELENA.   I will not trust you, I,   340
    Nor longer stay in your curst company
    Your hands than mine are quicker for a fray:
    My legs are longer though, to run away.   [*Exit.*]
HERMIA.   I am amazed,° and know not what to say.   *Exit.*
OBERON.   This is thy negligence: still thou mistak'st,   345
    Or else commit'st thy knaveries wilfully.
PUCK.   Believe me, king of shadows, I mistook.
    Did not you tell me I should know the man
    By the Athenian garments he had on?
    And so far blameless proves my enterprise,   350
    That I have 'nointed an Athenian's eyes:
    And so far am I glad it so did sort,°
    As this their jangling I esteem a sport.
OBERON.   Thou seest these lovers seek a place to fight;
    Hie therefore Robin, overcast the night,   355
    The starry welkin° cover thou anon

---

323 *keen and shrewd:* sharp and malicious.   327 *flout:* mock.   329 *minimus:* smallest of creatures.   *knot-grass:* weed believed to stunt the growth if eaten.   333 *intend:* extend.   335
aby it: buy it dearly.   336–337 *try . . . Helena:* prove by fighting which of us has most right to
Helena.   339 *coil is long of:* turmoil is because of.   344 *amazed:* confused.   352 *sort:* turn
out.   356 *welkin:* sky.

With drooping fog as black as Acheron,°
And lead these testy° rivals so astray,
As° one come not within another's way.
Like to Lysander sometime frame thy tongue: 360
Then stir Demetrius up with bitter wrong:°
And sometime rail thou like Demetrius:
And from each other look thou lead them thus;
Till o'er their brows death-counterfeiting sleep
With leaden legs and batty wings doth creep: 365
Then crush this herb into Lysander's eye;
Whose liquor hath this virtuous° property,
To take from thence all error with his might,
And make his eyeballs roll with wonted° sight.
When they next wake, all this derision°   370
Shall seem a dream, and fruitless vision,
And back to Athens shall the lovers wend,
With league whose date° till death shall never end.
Whiles I in this affair do thee employ,
I'll to my queen and beg her Indian boy: 375
And then I will her charmèd eye release
From monster's view, and all things shall be peace.

PUCK.   My fairy lord, this must be done with haste,
For night's swift dragons cut the clouds full fast:
And yonder shines Aurora's harbinger,°   380
At whose approach, ghosts wand'ring here and there,
Troop home to churchyards: damnèd spirits all,
That in crossways° and floods° have burial,
Already to their wormy beds are gone:
For fear lest day should look their shames upon,   385
They wilfully themselves exile from light,
And must for aye consort° with black-browed night.

OBERON.   But we are spirits of another sort.
I with the morning's love have oft made sport,°
And like a forester, the groves may tread   390
Even till the eastern gate all fiery red,
Opening on Neptune, with fair blessèd beams,
Turns into yellow gold his salt green streams.
But notwithstanding, haste, make no delay:
We may effect this business yet ere day.   [*Exit.*]   395

PUCK.   Up and down, up and down,
        I will lead them up and down.

---

357 *Acheron:* one of the four rivers in the underworld.   358 *testy:* irritable.   359 *As:* so
that.   361 *wrong:* insult.   367 *virtuous:* potent.   369 *wonted:* (previously) accustomed.   370 *derision:* laughable interlude.   373 *date:* term.   380 *Aurora's harbinger:* the
morning star heralding Aurora, the dawn.   383 *crossways:* crossroads, where suicides were
buried.   *floods:* those who drowned.   387 *aye consort:* ever associate.   389 *morning's . . .
sport:* hunted with Cephalus (beloved of Aurora and himself devoted to his wife Procris, whom
he killed by accident; "sport" also = "amorous dalliance," and "love" = Aurora's love for
Oberon).

I am feared in field and town.
Goblin, lead them up and down.
 Here comes one.   400

Enter LYSANDER.

LYSANDER. Where art thou, proud Demetrius? Speak thou now.
PUCK. Here villain, drawn° and ready. Where art thou?
LYSANDER. I will be with thee straight.
PUCK.   Follow me then
 To plainer° ground.   [*Exit LYSANDER.*]

Enter DEMETRIUS.

DEMETRIUS.   Lysander, speak again.
 Thou runaway, thou coward, art thou fled?   405
 Speak: in some bush? Where dost thou hide thy head?
PUCK. Thou coward, art thou bragging to the stars,
 Telling the bushes that thou look'st for wars,
 And wilt not come? Come recreant,° come thou child,
 I'll whip thee with a rod. He is defiled   410
 That draws a sword on thee.
DEMETRIUS.   Yea, art thou there?
PUCK. Follow my voice: we'll try no manhood° here.   *Exeunt.*

[*Enter LYSANDER.*]

LYSANDER. He goes before me and still dares me on:
 When I come where he calls, then he is gone
 The villain is much lighter-heeled than I;   415
 I followed fast: but faster he did fly,
 That fallen am I in dark uneven way,
 And here will rest me. (*Lie down.*) Come thou gentle day,
 For if but once thou show me thy grey light.
 I'll find Demetrius and revenge this spite.   [*Sleeps.*] 420

Enter PUCK and DEMETRIUS.

PUCK. Ho, ho, ho! Coward, why com'st thou not?
DEMETRIUS. Abide° me, if thou dar'st, for well I wot°
 Thou run'st before me, shifting every place,
 And dar'st not stand, nor look me in the face.
 Where art thou now?
PUCK.   Come hither: I am here.   425
DEMETRIUS. Nay then thou mock'st me. Thou shalt buy this dear,°
 If ever I thy face by daylight see.
 Now go thy way. Faintness constraineth me
 To measure out my length on this cold bed.
 By day's approach look to be visited.   [*Lies down and sleeps.*] 430

---

402 *drawn:* with sword drawn.   404 *plainer:* more level.   409 *recreant:* oath-breaker,
coward.   412 *try no manhood:* test no valor.   422 *Abide:* wait for.   *wot:* know.   426 *buy
this dear:* pay dearly for this.

Enter HELENA.

HELENA.   O weary night, O long and tedious night,
  Abate° thy hours; shine comforts° from the east,
  That I may back to Athens by daylight,
  From these that my poor company detest:
  And sleep, that sometimes shuts up sorrow's eye.   435
  Steal me awhile from mine own company.   *Sleeps.*
PUCK.   Yet but three? Come one more,
  Two of both kinds makes up four.
  Here she comes, curst° and sad.
  Cupid is a knavish lad,   440
  Thus to make poor females mad.

Enter HERMIA.

HERMIA.   Never so weary, never so in woe,
   Bedabbled with the dew, and torn with briers:
    I can no further crawl, no further go:
    My legs can keep no pace with my desires.   445
    Here will I rest me till the break of day.
    Heavens shield Lysander, if they mean a fray.   *[Lies down and sleeps.]*
PUCK.   On the ground,
  Sleep sound:
  I'll apply   450
  To your eye,
 Gentle lover, remedy.   *[Squeezes the love-juice on* LYSANDER'S *eyelids.]*
  When thou wak'st,
  Thou tak'st
  True delight   455
  In the sight
 Of thy former lady's eye:
 And the country proverb known,
 That every man should take his own,
 In your waking shall be shown.   460
  Jack shall have Jill:
  Naught shall go ill:
 The man shall have his mare again, and all shall be well.

         [Exit PUCK. *The lovers remain asleep on stage.]*

ACT 4

[Scene 1. The wood]

Enter [TITANIA] QUEEN OF FAIRIES, *and* [BOTTOM] THE CLOWN, *and* FAIRIES, *and the* KING
[OBERON] *behind them* [unseen].

432 *Abate:* shorten. *shine comforts:* may comforts shine. 439 *curst:* cross.

TITANIA. Come sit thee down upon this flow'ry bed,
      While I thy amiable° cheeks do coy,°
      And stick musk-roses in thy sleek smooth head,
      And kiss thy fair large ears, my gentle joy.

BOTTOM. Where's Peaseblossom?   5

PEASEBLOSSOM. Ready.

BOTTOM. Scratch my head, Peaseblossom. Where's Mounsieur
    Cobweb?

COBWEB. Ready.

BOTTOM. Mounsieur Cobweb, good mounsieur, get you your weapons   10
    in your hand, and kill me a red-hipped humblebee on
    the top of a thistle: and good mounsieur, bring me the
    honey-bag. Do not fret yourself too much in the action,
    mounsieur: and good mounsieur have a care the honey-
    bag break not, I would be loath to have you overflowen   15
    with a honey bag, signior. Where's Mounsieur
    Mustardseed?

MUSTARDSEED. Ready.

BOTTOM. Give me your neaf,° Mounsieur Mustardseed. Pray you
    leave your curtsy,° good mounsieur.   20

MUSTARDSEED. What's your will?

BOTTOM. Nothing, good mounsieur, but to help Cavalery° Cobweb
    to scratch. I must to the barber's mounsieur, for
    methinks I am marvellous hairy about the face. And I am
    such a tender ass, if my hair do but tickle me, I must   25
    scratch.

TITANIA. What, will thou hear some music, my sweet love?

BOTTOM. I have a reasonable good ear in music. Let's have the tongs°
    and the bones.°

TITANIA. Or say, sweet love, what thou desirest to eat.   30

BOTTOM. Truly, a peck of provender. I could munch your good
    dry oats. Methinks I have a great desire to a bottle° of hay.
    Good hay, sweet hay, hath no fellow.

TITANIA. I have a venturous fairy that shall seek
    The squirrel's hoard, and fetch thee new nuts.   35

BOTTOM. I had rather have a handful or two of dried pease. But
    I pray you, let none of your people stir me: I have an
    exposition of° sleep come upon me.

TITANIA. Sleep thou, and I will wind thee in my arms.
    Fairies, be gone, and be all ways° away.   *[Exeunt FAIRIES.]*   40
    So doth the woodbine the sweet honeysuckle
    Gently entwist: the female ivy so
    Enrings the barky fingers of the elm.
    O how I love thee! how I dote on thee!   *[They sleep.]*

2 *amiable:* lovely.   *coy:* caress.   19 *neaf:* fist.   20 *leave your curtsy:* either (a) stop bowing,
or (b) replace your hat.   22 *Cavalery:* (he means "cavalier").   29 *tongs:* crude music made
by striking tongs with a piece of metal.   *bones:* pieces of bone held between the fingers and
clapped together rhythmically.   32 *bottle:* bundle.   38 *exposition of:* (he means "disposition
to").   40 *all ways:* in every direction.

Enter ROBIN GOODFELLOW [*PUCK.*]

OBERON.   [*Advances.*] Welcome good Robin. Seest thou this sweet sight?   45
    Her dotage now I do begin to pity.
    For meeting her of late behind the wood,
    Seeking sweet favours° for this hateful fool,
    I did upbraid her and fall out with her.
    For she his hairy temples then had rounded   50
    With coronet of fresh and fragrant flowers
    And that same dew which sometime° on the buds
    Was wont to° swell like round and orient° pearls,
    Stood now within the pretty flowerets' eyes,
    Like tears that did their own disgrace bewail.   55
    When I had at my pleasure taunted her,
    And she in mild terms begged my patience,
    I then did ask of her her changeling child:
    Which straight she gave me, and her fairy sent
    To bear him to my bower in fairy land.   60
    And now I have the boy, I will undo
    This hateful imperfection of her eyes.
    And gentle Puck, take this transformèd scalp
    From off the head of this Athenian swain;
    That he awaking when the other do,   65
    May all to Athens back again repair,°
    And think no more of this night's accidents,°
    But as the fierce vexation of a dream.
    But first I will release the Fairy Queen.
        Be as thou wast wont to be: 70
        See, as thou wast wont to see.
        Dian's bud o'er Cupid's flower°
        Hath such force and blessèd power.
    Now my Titania, wake you, my sweet queen.
TITANIA.   My Oberon, what visions have I seen!   75
    Methought I was enamoured of an ass.
OBERON.   There lies your love.
TITANIA.   How came these things to pass?
    O, how mine eyes do loathe his visage now!
OBERON.   Silence awhile Robin, take off this head:
    Titania, music call, and strike more dead   80
    Than common sleep of all these five the sense.°
TITANIA.   Music, ho music! such as charmeth sleep.
PUCK.   Now, when thou wak'st, with thine own fools' eyes peep.

---

48 *favours:* bouquets as love tokens.   52 *sometime:* formerly.   53 *Was wont to:* used to.
orient: (where the most beautiful pearls came from).   66 *repair:* return.   67 *accidents:* incidents.   72 *Dian's bud . . . flower:* (Diana's bud counteracts the effects of love-in-idleness, the
pansy).   80–81 *strike . . . sense:* Make these five (the lovers and Bottom) sleep more
soundly.

OBERON. Sound music: *Music still.°*
      come my queen, take hands with me,
And rock the ground whereon these sleepers be. *[Dance.]* 85
Now thou and I are new in amity,
And will tomorrow midnight solemnly
Dance in Duke Theseus' house triumphantly,°
And bless it to all fair prosperity.
There shall the pairs of faithful lovers be 90
Wedded, with Theseus, all in jollity.

PUCK. Fairy King, attend and mark:
      I do hear the morning lark.

OBERON. Then my queen, in silence sad,°
      Trip we after the night's shade: 95
We the globe can compass soon,
Swifter than the wand'ring moon.

TITANIA. Come my lord, and in our flight,
Tell me how it came this night,
That I sleeping here was found, 100
With these mortals on the ground. *Exeunt.*

Wind° horns. Enter THESEUS, HIPPOLYTA, EGEUS *and all his train.*

THESEUS. Go one of you, find out the forester:
For now our observation° is performed.
And since we have the vaward° of the day,
My love shall hear the music of my hounds. 105
Uncouple° in the western valley, let them go:
Dispatch I say, and find the forester. *[Exit an* ATTENDANT.*]*
We will, fair queen, up to the mountain's top,
And mark the musical confusion
Of hounds and echo in conjunction. 110

HIPPOLYTA. I was with Hercules and Cadmus° once,
When in a wood of Crete they bayed the bear,°
With hounds of Sparta:° never did I hear
Such gallant chiding. For besides the groves,
The skies, the fountains, every region near 115
Seemed all one mutual cry. I never heard
So musical a discord, such sweet thunder.

THESEUS. My hounds are bred out of the Spartan kind:
So flewed, so sanded:° and their heads are hung
With ears that sweep away the morning dew, 120
Crook-kneed, and dewlapped° like Thessalian bulls:

84.1 S.D.: *still:* continuously.　　88 *triumphantly:* in celebration.　　94 *sad:* serious.　　101.1 S.D.: *wind:* blow, sound.　　103 *observation:* observance of the May Day rites.　　104 *vaward:* vanguard, earliest part.　　106 *Uncouple:* unleash (the dogs).　　111 *Cadmus:* mythical builder of Thebes.　　112 *bayed the bear:* brought the bear to bay, to its last stand.　　113 *hounds of Sparta:* (a breed famous for their swiftness and quick scent).　　119 *flewed, so sanded:* with hanging cheeks, so sand-colored.　　121 *dewlapped:* with skin hanging from the chin.

Slow in pursuit; but matched in mouth like bells,
Each under each.° A cry° more tuneable
Was never holloa'd to, nor cheered with horn,
In Crete, in Sparta, nor in Thessaly.   125
Judge when you hear. But soft.° What nymphs are these?
EGEUS.   My lord, this is my daughter here asleep,
And this Lysander, this Demetrius is,
This Helena, old Nedar's Helena.
I wonder of their being here together.   130
THESEUS.   No doubt they rose up early to observe
The rite of May: and hearing our intent,
Came here in grace° of our solemnity.
But speak Egeus, is not this the day
That Hermia should give answer of her choice?   135
EGEUS.   It is, my lord.
THESEUS.   Go bid the huntsmen wake them with their horns.

Shout within: wind horns. They all start up.

Good morrow, friends. Saint Valentine is past.
Begin these wood-birds but to couple now?°
LYSANDER.   Pardon, my lord.   [*They kneel.*]
THESEUS.   I pray you all, stand up.   140
I know you two are rival enemies.
How comes this gentle concord in the world,
That hatred is so far from jealousy,°
To sleep by hate° and fear no enmity?
LYSANDER.   My lord, I shall reply amazedly,   145
Half sleep, half waking. But as yet, I swear,
I cannot truly say how I came here.
But as I think—for truly would I speak,
And now I do bethink me, so it is—
I came with Hermia hither. Our intent   150
Was to be gone from Athens, where we might,
Without° the peril of the Athenian law—
EGEUS.   Enough, enough, my lord: you have enough.
I beg the law, the law upon his head:
They would have stol'n away, they would, Demetrius,   155
Thereby to have defeated you and me:
You of your wife, and me of my consent:
Of my consent that she should be your wife.
DEMETRIUS.   My lord, fair Helen told me of their stealth,
Of this their purpose hither, to this wood,   160
And I in fury hither followed them;
Fair Helena in fancy° following me.

122–23 *matched . . . each:* with each voice matched for harmony with the next in pitch, like bells in a chime.   123 *cry:* pack of dogs.   126 *soft:* wait.   133 *grace:* honor.   138–139 *Saint . . . now:* (birds traditionally chose their mates on St. Valentine's Day).   143 *jealousy:* suspicion.   144 *hate:* one it hates.   152 *Without:* beyond.   162 *in fancy:* out of doting love.

But my good lord, I wot not by what power
(But by some power it is) my love to Hermia,
Melted as the snow, seems to me now   165
As the remembrance of an idle gaud,°
Which in my childhood I did dote upon:
And all the faith, the virtue of my heart,
The object and the pleasure of mine eye,
Is only Helena. To her, my lord,   170
Was I betrothed ere I saw Hermia:
But like a sickness,° did I loathe this food.
But as in health, come° to my natural taste,
Now I do wish it, love it, long for it.
And will for evermore be true to it.   175
THESEUS.   Fair lovers, you are fortunately met.
Of this discourse we more will hear anon.
Egeus, I will overbear your will:
For in the temple, by and by,° with us,
These couples shall eternally be knit.   180
And for the morning now is something worn,°
Our purposed hunting shall be set aside.
Away with us to Athens. Three and three,
We'll hold a feast in great solemnity.
Come Hippolyta.   185

Exeunt DUKE [HIPPOLYTA, EGEUS] and LORDS.

DEMETRIUS.   These things seem small and undistinguishable,
Like far-off mountains turnèd into clouds.
HERMIA.   Methinks I see these things with parted° eye,
When everything seems double.
HELENA.   So methinks:
And I have found Demetrius, like a jewel,   190
Mine own, and not mine own.°
DEMETRIUS.   Are you sure
That we are awake? It seems to me,
That yet we sleep, we dream. Do not you think
The duke was here, and bid us follow him?
HERMIA.   Yea, and my father.
HELENA.   And Hippolyta.   195
LYSANDER.   And he did bid us follow to the temple.
DEMETRIUS.   Why then, we are awake: let's follow him,
And by the way let us recount our dreams.   *Exeunt Lovers.*
BOTTOM.   (*Wakes.*) When my cue comes, call me, and I will answer.
My next is "Most fair Pyramus." Hey ho. Peter Quince?   200
Flute the bellows-mender? Snout the tinker? Starveling?

---

166 *idle gaud:* trifling toy.   172 *sickness:* sick person.   173 *come:* i.e., back.   179 *by and by:* immediately.   181 *something worn:* somewhat worn on.   188 *parted:* divided (each eye seeing a separate image).   190–191 *like . . . own:* like a person who finds a jewel: the finder is the owner, but insecurely so.

God's my life! Stol'n hence, and left me asleep? I have
had a most rare vision. I have had a dream, past the wit
of man to say what dream it was. Man is but an ass, if he
go about° to expound this dream. Methought I was—   205
there is no man can tell what. Methought I was, and
methought I had—but man is but a patched fool,° if he
will offer to say what methought I had. The eye of man
hath not heard, the ear of man hath not seen, man's hand is
not able to taste, his tongue to conceive, nor his   210
heart to report, what my dream was. I will get Peter
Quince to write a ballad of this dream: it shall be called
Bottom's Dream; because it hath no bottom: and I
will sing it in the latter end of our play, before the duke.
Peradventure, to make it the more gracious, I shall sing   215
it at her° death.   *Exit.*

[*Scene 2. Athens, Quince's house*]

Enter QUINCE, FLUTE, SNOUT, *and* STARVELING.

QUINCE.   Have you sent to Bottom's house? Is he come home yet?
STARVELING.   He cannot be heard of. Out of doubt he is transported.°
FLUTE.   If he come not, then the play is marred. It goes not forward,
    doth it?
QUINCE.   It is not possible. You have not a man in all Athens able   5
    to discharge° Pyramus but he.
FLUTE.   No, he hath simply the best wit of any handicraft man in Athens.
QUINCE.   Yea, and the best person too, and he is a very paramour
    for a sweet voice.
FLUTE.   You must say "paragon." A paramour is (God bless us)   10
    a thing of naught.°

Enter SNUG THE JOINER.

SNUG.   Masters, the duke is coming from the temple, and there
    is two or three lords and ladies more married. If our
    sport had gone forward, we had all been made men.°
FLUTE.   O sweet bully Bottom. Thus hath he lost sixpence a day°   15
    during his life: he could not have 'scaped sixpence a day.
    And the duke had not given him sixpence a day for playing
    Pyramus, I'll be hanged. He would have deserved it.
    Sixpence a day in Pyramus, or nothing.

Enter BOTTOM.

BOTTOM.   Where are these lads? Where are these hearts?   20
QUINCE.   Bottom! O most courageous° day! O most happy hour!

---

205 *go about:* attempt.   207 *patched fool:* fool dressed in motley.   216 *her:* Thisby's.   2
transported: carried away (by spirits).   6 *discharge:* portray.   11 *of naught:* wicked,
naughty.   14 *made men:* men made rich.   15 *sixpence a day:* i.e., as a pension   21 *courageous:* (he may mean "auspicious").

BOTTOM.   Masters, I am to discourse wonders: but ask me not what.
For if I tell you, I am not true Athenian. I will tell you
everything, right as it fell out.
QUINCE.   Let us hear, sweet Bottom.   25
BOTTOM.   Not a word of me. All that I will tell you is, that the
duke hath dined. Get your apparel together, good
strings to your beards, new ribbands to your pumps, meet
presently° at the palace, every man look o'er his part: for
the short and the long is, our play is preferred.° In any   30
case, let Thisby have clean linen: and let not him that
plays the lion pare his nails, for they shall hang out for
the lion's claws. And most dear actors, eat no onions nor
garlic, for we are to utter sweet breath: and I do not
doubt but to hear them say it is a sweet comedy. No more   35
words: away, go away.   *Exeunt.*

ACT 5

[*Scene 1. The palace of Theseus*]

Enter THESEUS, HIPPOLYTA, *and* PHILOSTRATE, *and his* LORDS.

HIPPOLYTA.   'Tis strange, my Theseus, that these lovers speak of.
THESEUS.   More strange than true. I never may believe
These antick° fables, nor these fairy toys.°
Lovers and madmen have such seething brains,
Such shaping fantasies,° that apprehend   5
More than cool reason ever comprehends.
The lunatic, the lover, and the poet,
Are of imagination all compact.°
One sees more devils than vast hell can hold:
That is the madman. The lover, all as frantic,   10
Sees Helen's beauty in a brow of Egypt.°
The poet's eye, in a fine frenzy rolling,
Doth glance from heaven to earth, from earth to heaven.
And as imagination bodies forth
The forms of things unknown, the poet's pen   15
Turns them to shapes, and gives to airy nothing,
A local habitation and a name.
Such tricks hath strong imagination,
That if it would but apprehend some joy,
It comprehends° some bringer of that joy.   20
Or in the night, imagining some fear,
How easy is a bush supposed a bear.

29 *presently:* immediately.   30 *preferred:* recommended (for presentation).   3 *antick:* fantastic.   *fairy toys:* trivial fairy stories.   5 *fantasies:* imaginations.   8 *of . . . compact:* totally
composed of imagination.   11 *a brow of Egypt:* the swarthy face of a gypsy (believed to come
from Egypt).   20 *comprehends:* includes.

HIPPOLYTA.   But all the story of the night told over,
And all their minds transfigured so together,
More witnesseth than fancy's images,°   25
And grows to something of great constancy:°
But howsoever, strange and admirable.°

Enter LOVERS: LYSANDER, DEMETRIUS, HERMIA, and HELENA.

THESEUS.   Here come the lovers, full of joy and mirth.
Joy, gentle friends, joy and fresh days of love
Accompany your hearts.
LYSANDER.   More° than to us   30
Wait in your royal walks, your board, your bed.
THESEUS.   Come now, what masques,° what dances shall we have,
To wear away this long age of three hours
Between our after-supper° and bed-time?
Where is our usual manager of mirth?   35
What revels are in hand? Is there no play,
To ease the anguish of a torturing hour?
Call Philostrate.
PHILOSTRATE.   Here, mighty Theseus.
THESEUS.   Say, what abridgment° have you for this evening?
What masque,° what music? How shall we beguile   40
The lazy time, if not with some delight?
PHILOSTRATE.   There is a brief° how many sports are ripe:°
Make choice of which your highness will see first.

[*Gives a paper.*]

THESEUS.   "The battle with the Centaurs, to be sung
By an Athenian eunuch to the harp."   45
We'll none of that. That have I told my love
In glory of my kinsman Hercules.
"The riot of the tipsy Bacchanals,
Tearing the Thracian singer in their rage."°
That is an old device: and it was played   50
When I from Thebes came last a conqueror.
"The thrice three Muses mourning for the death
Of Learning, late deceased in beggary."
That is some satire keen and critical,
Not sorting with° a nuptial ceremony.   55
"A tedious brief scene of young Pyramus
And his love Thisby; very tragical mirth."
Merry and tragical? Tedious and brief?

---

25 *More . . . images:* testifies that it is more than just imagination.   26 *constancy:* certainty.   27 *admirable:* to be wondered at.   30 *More:* even more (joy and love).   32, 40 *masques:* lavish courtly entertainments combining song and dance.   34 *after-supper:* late supper.   39 *abridgment:* either (a) diversion to make the hours seem shorter or (b) short entertainment.   42 *brief:* list.   *ripe:* ready.   48–49 *riot . . . rage:* (The singer Orpheus of Thrace was torn limb from limb by the Maenads, frenzied female priests of Bacchus).   55 *sorting with:* befitting.

That is hot ice and wondrous strange snow.
How shall we find the concord of this discord?   60
PHILOSTRATE.   A play there is, my lord, some ten words long,
   Which is as brief as I have known a play:
   But by ten words, my lord, it is too long,
   Which makes it tedious: for in all the play
   There is not one word apt, one player fitted.°   65
   And tragical, my noble lord, it is:
   For Pyramus therein doth kill himself.
   Which when I saw rehearsed, I must confess,
   Made mine eyes water; but more merry tears
   The passion of loud laughter never shed.   70
THESEUS.   What are they that do play it?
PHILOSTRATE.   Hard-handed men, that work in Athens here,
   Which never laboured in their minds till now:
   And now have toiled their unbreathed° memories
   With this same play, against° your nuptial.   75
THESEUS.   And we will hear it.
PHILOSTRATE.   No, my noble lord,
   It is not for you. I have heard it over,
   And it is nothing, nothing in the world;
   Unless you can find sport in their intents,
   Extremely stretched and conned° with cruel pain.   80
   To do your service.
THESEUS.   I will hear that play.
   For never anything can be amiss,
   When simpleness and duty tender° it.
   Go bring them in, and take your places, ladies.   [*Exit* PHILOSTRATE.]
HIPPOLYTA.   I love not to see wretchedness o'ercharged,°   85
   And duty in his service perishing.
THESEUS.   Why, gentle sweet, you shall see no such thing.
HIPPOLYTA.   He says they can do nothing in this kind.°
THESEUS.   The kinder we, to give them thanks for nothing.
   Our sport shall be to take what they mistake.   90
   And what poor duty cannot do, noble respect
   Takes it in might, not merit.°
   Where I have come, great clerks° have purposèd
   To greet me with premeditated welcomes;
   Where I have seen them shiver and look pale,   95
   Make periods in the midst of sentences,
   Throttle° their practised accent in their fears,
   And in conclusion dumbly have broke off,
   Not paying me a welcome. Trust me, sweet,
   Out of this silence yet I picked a welcome: 100

65 *fitted:* (well) cast.   74 *unbreathed:* unpracticed, unexercised.   75 *against:* in preparation
for.   80 *stretched and conned:* strained and memorized.   83 *tender:* offer.   85 *wretchedness
o'ercharged:* poor fellows taxing themselves too much.   88 *in this kind:* of this sort.   91–92
noble . . . merit: a noble nature considers the sincerity of effort rather than the skill of execution.   93 *clerks:* scholars.   97 *Throttle:* choke on.

And in the modesty of fearful duty°
I read as much as from the rattling tongue
Of saucy and audacious eloquence.
Love, therefore, and tongue-tied simplicity,
In° least, speak most, to my capacity.°   105

[*Enter* PHILOSTRATE.]

PHILOSTRATE.   So please your grace, the Prologue is addressed.°
THESEUS.   Let him approach.

Flourish trumpets. Enter the PROLOGUE [*QUINCE*].

PROLOGUE.   If we offend, it is with our good will.
    That you should think, we come not to offend,
But with good will. To show our simple skill,   110
    That is the true beginning of our end.
Consider then, we come but in despite.°
    We do not come, as minding to content you,
Our true intent is. All for your delight,
    We are not here. That you should here repent you,   115
The actors are at hand: and by their show,
    You shall know all, that you are like to know.°
THESEUS.   This fellow doth not stand upon points.°
LYSANDER.   He hath rid his prologue like a rough colt: he knows
    not the stop.° A good moral my lord: it is not enough   120
    to speak; but to speak true.
HIPPOLYTA.   Indeed he hath played on his prologue like a child on a
    recorder:° a sound, but not in government.°
THESEUS.   His speech was like a tangled chain: nothing impaired, but
    all disordered. Who is next?   125

Enter PYRAMUS *and* THISBY, WALL, MOONSHINE, *and* LION.

PROLOGUE.   Gentles, perchance you wonder at this show,
    But wonder on, till truth make all things plain.
This man is Pyramus, if you would know:
    This beauteous lady, Thisby is certain.
This man, with lime and rough-cast,° doth present   130
    Wall, that vile wall which did these lovers sunder:
And through Wall's chink, poor souls, they are content
    To whisper. At the which, let no man wonder.
This man, with lantern, dog, and bush of thorn,
    Presenteth Moonshine. For if you will know,   135
By moonshine did these lovers think no scorn
    To meet at Ninus' tomb, there, there to woo:

---

101 *fearful duty:* subjects whose devotions gave them stage fright.   105 *In:* i.e., saying.   *capacity:* way of thinking.   106 *addressed:* ready.   108–117 *If . . . know:* (Quince's blunders in punctuation exactly reverse the meaning).   112 *despite:* malice.   118 *stand upon points:* (1) pay attention to punctuation (2) bother about the niceties (of expression).   120 *stop:* (1) halt (2) period.   123 *recorder:* flutelike wind instrument.   *in government:* well managed.   130 *rough-cast:* rough plaster made of lime and gravel.

This grisly beast (which Lion hight° by name)
The trusty Thisby, coming first by night,
Did scare away, or rather did affright: 140
And as she fled, her mantle she did fall:°
    Which Lion vile with bloody mouth did stain.
Anon comes Pyramus, sweet youth and tall,°
    And finds his trusty Thisby's mantle slain:
Whereat, with blade, with bloody blameful blade, 145
    He bravely broached° his boiling bloody breast.
And Thisby, tarrying in mulberry shade,
    His dagger drew, and died. For all the rest,
Let Lion, Moonshine, Wall, and lovers twain.
    At large° discourse, while here they do remain. 150
THESEUS.   I wonder if the lion be to speak.
DEMETRIUS.   No wonder, my lord: one lion may, when many asses do.

Exeunt [PROLOGUE, PYRAMUS,] LION, THISBY, MOONSHINE.

WALL.   In this same interlude° it doth befall
    That I, one Snout by name, present a wall:
    And such a wall, as I would have you think, 155
    That had in it a crannied hole or chink:
    Through which the lovers, Pyramus and Thisby,
    Did whisper often, very secretly.
    This loam, this rough-cast, and this stone doth show
    That I am that same wall: the truth is so. 160
    And this the cranny is, right and sinister,°
    Through which the fearful lovers are to whisper.
THESEUS.   Would you desire lime and hair to speak better?
DEMETRIUS.   It is the wittiest° partition° that ever I heard discourse,
    my lord. 165

Enter PYRAMUS.

THESEUS.   Pyramus draws near the wall: silence.
PYRAMUS.   O grim-looked night, O night with hue so black,
        O night, which ever art when day is not:
        O night, O night, alack, alack, alack,
        I fear my Thisby's promise is forgot. 170
    And thou O wall, O sweet, O lovely wall,
        That stand'st between her father's ground and mine,
    Thou wall, O wall, O sweet and lovely wall,
        Show me thy chink, to blink through with mine eyne.°

[*WALL holds up his fingers.*]

---

138 *hight:* is called.   141 *fall:* let fall.   143 *tall:* brave.   146 *broached:* opened (Shakespeare
parodies the overuse of alliteration in the earlier bombastic Elizabethan plays).   150 *At large:*
in full.   153 *interlude:* short play.   161 *right and sinister:* from right to left (he probably uses
the fingers of his right and left hands to form the cranny).   1164 *wittiest:* most intelligent.   *partition:* (1) wall (2) section of a learned book or speech.   174 *eyne:* eyes.

Thanks, courteous wall. Jove shield thee well for this.   175
   But what see I? No Thisby do I see.
O wicked wall, through whom I see no bliss,
   Cursed by thy stones for thus deceiving me.

THESEUS.   The wall methinks being sensible,° should curse again.°

PYRAMUS.   No in truth sir, he should not. "Deceiving me" is   180
Thisby's cue: she is to enter now, and I am to spy her
through the wall. You shall see it will fall pat° as I told you:
yonder she comes.

Enter THISBY.

THISBY.   O wall, full often hast thou heard my moans,
   For parting my fair Pyramus and me.   185
My cherry lips have often kissed thy stones;
   Thy stones with lime and hair knit up in thee.

PYRAMUS.   I see a voice: now will I to the chink,
   To spy and I can hear my Thisby's face.
Thisby?   190

THISBY.   My love thou art, my love I think.

PYRAMUS.   Think what thou wilt, I am thy lover's grace:
   And, like Limander,° am I trusty still.

THISBY.   And I like Helen,° till the Fates me kill.

PYRAMUS.   Not Shafalus to Procrus,° was so true.   195

THISBY.   As Shafalus to Procrus, I to you.

PYRAMUS.   O kiss me through the hole of this vile wall.

THISBY.   I kiss the wall's hole, not your lips at all.

PYRAMUS.   Wilt thou at Ninny's° tomb meet me straightway?

THISBY.   Tide° life, tide death, I come without delay.   200

                                    [*Exeunt* PYRAMUS *and* THISBY.]

WALL.   Thus have I, Wall, my part dischargèd so;
   And being done, thus Wall away doth go.   *Exit.*

THESEUS.   Now is the mural° down between the two neighbours.

DEMETRIUS.   No remedy my lord, when walls are so wilful to hear
without warning.°   205

HIPPOLYTA.   This is the silliest stuff that ever I heard.

THESEUS.   The best in this kind are but shadows:° and the worst are
no worse, if imagination amend them.

HIPPOLYTA.   It must be your imagination then, and not theirs.

THESEUS.   If we imagine no worse of them than they of themselves,   210
they may pass for excellent men. Here come two noble
beasts in, a man and a lion.

---

179 *sensible:* capable of feelings and perception.   *again:* back.   182 *pat:* exactly.   193
Limander: (he means "Leander").   194 *Helen:* (he means "Hero").   195 *Shafalus to Procrus:*
(he means "Cephalus" and "Procis" [see Act III, scene 2, 389 n.]).   199 *Ninny:* fool (he means
"Ninus").   200 *Tide:* come, betide.   203 *mural:* wall.   205 *without warning:* either (a)
without warning the parents or (b) unexpectedly.   207 *in . . . shadows:* of this sort are only
plays (or only actors).

Enter LION and MOONSHINE.

LION.   You ladies, you, whose gentle hearts do fear
  The smallest monstrous mouse that creeps on floor,
 May now perchance both quake and tremble here.   215
  When lion rough in wildest rage doth roar.
 Then know that I, as Snug the joiner am
 A lion fell,° nor else no lion's dam:°
 For if I should as lion come in strife
 Into this place, 'twere pity on my life.   220
THESEUS.   A very gentle beast, and of a good conscience.
DEMETRIUS.   The very best at a beast,° my lord, that e'er I saw.
LYSANDER.   This lion is a very fox for his valour.
THESEUS.   True: and a goose for his discretion.
DEMETRIUS.   Not so my lord: for his valour cannot carry his discretion, 225
 and the fox carries the goose.
THESEUS.   His discretion, I am sure, cannot carry his valour: for the
 goose carries not the fox. It is well: leave it to his discretion,
 and let us listen to the moon.
MOONSHINE.   This lanthorn° doth the hornèd moon present— 230
DEMETRIUS.   He should have worn the horns on his head.°
THESEUS.   He is no crescent, and his horns are invisible within the
 circumference.
MOONSHINE.   This lanthorn doth the hornèd moon present,
 Myself, the man i' th' moon do seem to be.   235
THESEUS.   This is the greatest error of all the rest; the man should
 be put into the lanthorn. How is it else the man i' th'
 moon?
DEMETRIUS.   He dares not come there for the candle; for you see, it
 is already in snuff.°   240
HIPPOLYTA.   I am aweary of this moon. Would he would change.
THESEUS.   It appears, by his small light of discretion, that he is in
 the wane: but yet in courtesy, in all reason, we must stay°
 the time.
LYSANDER.   Proceed, Moon.   245
MOONSHINE.   All that I have to say, is to tell you that the lanthorn is
 the moon, I the man i' th' moon, this thornbush my
 thornbush, and this dog my dog.
DEMETRIUS.   Why, all these should be in the lanthorn: for all these are
 in the moon. But silence: here comes Thisby. 250

Enter THISBY.

THISBY.   This is old Ninny's tomb. Where is my love?
LION.   Oh!
            The LION roars. THISBY runs off.

---

218 *fell:* fierce. *nor . . . dam:* and not a lioness. 222 *best, beast:* (pronounced similarly). 230 *lanthorn:* lantern (once made of horn). 230–231 *hornèd . . . head:* (referring
to the cuckold or deceived husband, who supposedly grew horns). 240 *in snuff:* (1) in need of
snuffing (having a long, burnt-out wick or snuff) (2) in a temper. 243 *stay:* await.

DEMETRIUS.   Well roared, Lion.

THESEUS.   Well run, Thisby.

HIPPOLYTA.   Well shone, Moon. Truly, the moon shines with a good   255
grace.

[*The* LION *shakes* THISBY'S *mantle.*]

THESEUS.   Well moused,° Lion.

DEMETRIUS.   And then came Pyramus.

Enter PYRAMUS. [*Exit* LION.]

LYSANDER.   And so the lion vanished.

PYRAMUS.   Sweet moon, I thank thee for thy sunny beams,   260
  I thank thee, moon, for shining now so bright.
  For by thy gracious, golden, glittering gleams,
   I trust to take of truest Thisby sight.
    But stay: O spite!
    But mark, poor knight,   265
    What dreadful dole° is here?
     Eyes, do you see!
     How can it be!
    O dainty duck, O dear!
     Thy mantle good,   270
     What, stained with blood?
    Approach, ye Furies° fell:
     O Fates!° come, come:
     Cut thread and thrum.°
    Quail,° crush, conclude, and quell.°   275

THESEUS.   This passion, and the death of a dear friend, would go
near to make a man look sad.

HIPPOLYTA.   Beshrew° my heart, but I pity the man.

PYRAMUS.   O wherefore Nature, didst thou lions frame?
  Since lion vile hath here deflowered my dear.   280
  Which is—no, no—which was the fairest dame
   That lived, that loved, that liked, that looked with cheer.
  Come tears, confound:
   Out sword, and wound
  The pap° of Pyramus: 285
   Ay, that left pap,
   Where heart doth hop.   [*Stabs himself.*]
  Thus die, I, thus, thus, thus.
   Now am I dead,
   Now am I fled,   290
  My soul is in the sky.

---

257 *moused:* shaken, as a cat shakes a mouse. 266 *dole:* grief. 272 *Furies:* classical spirits
of the underworld who avenged murder. 273 *Fates:* three sisters who spun the thread of
human destiny, which at will was cut with a shears. 274 *thrum:* fringelike end of the warp in
weaving. 275 *Quail:* subdue. *quell:* kill. 278 *Beshrew:* curse (meant lightly). 285
pap: breast.

Tongue lose thy light,
Moon° take thy flight,   [*Exit* MOONSHINE.]
Now die, die, die, die, die.   [*Dies.*]
DEMETRIUS.   No die,° but an ace° for him. For he is but one.   295
LYSANDER.   Less than an ace, man. For he is dead, he is nothing.
THESEUS.   With the help of a surgeon, he might yet recover, and
prove an ass.
HIPPOLYTA.   How chance Moonshine is gone before Thisby comes
back and finds her lover?   300

Enter THISBY.

THESEUS.   She will find him by starlight. Here she comes, and her
passion ends the play.
HIPPOLYTA.   Methinks she should not use a long one for such a
Pyramus: I hope she will be brief.
DEMETRIUS.   A mote will turn the balance, which Pyramus, which   305
Thisby, is the better: he for a man. God warr'nt° us;
she for a woman, God bless us.
LYSANDER.   She hath spied him already with those sweet eyes.
DEMETRIUS.   And thus she means,° videlicet°—
THISBY.   Asleep my love?   310
                What, dead, my dove?
            O Pyramus, arise,
                Speak, speak. Quite dumb?
                Dead, dead? A tomb
            Must cover thy sweet eyes.   315
                These lily lips,
                This cherry nose,
            These yellow cowslip° cheeks,
                Are gone, are gone:
                Lovers, make moan: 320
            His eyes were green as leeks.
                O Sisters Three,°
                Come, come to me,
            With hands as pale as milk,
                Lay them in gore,   325
                Since you have shore
            With shears his thread of silk.
                Tongue, not a word:
                Come trusty sword,
            Come blade, my breast imbrue°   [*Stabs herself.*]   330
                And farewell friends:
                Thus Thisby ends:
            Adieu, adieu, adieu.   [*Dies.*]

292–293 *Tongue . . . Moon:* (he reverses the two subjects).   295 *die:* (singular of "dice").   *ace:*
a throw of one at dice.   306 *warr'nt:* warrant, protect.   309 *means:* laments.   *videlicet:*
namely.   318 *cowslip:* yellow primrose.   322 *Sisters Three:* the Fates.   330 *imbrue:* stain
with gore.

THESEUS.   Moonshine and Lion are left to bury the dead.
DEMETRIUS.   Ay, and Wall too.   335
BOTTOM.   [*Starts up*] No, I assure you, the wall is down that parted
    their fathers. Will it please you to see the Epilogue, or
    to hear a Bergomask° dance between two of our company?
THESEUS.   No epilogue, I pray you; for your play needs no excuse.
    Never excuse: for when the players are all dead, there   340
    need none to be blamed. Marry, if he that writ it had
    played Pyramus and hanged himself in Thisby's garter,
    it would have been a fine tragedy: and so it is truly, and
    very notably discharged. But come, your Bergomask:
    let your Epilogue alone.   [*A dance.*]   345
    The iron tongue° of midnight hath told° twelve.
    Lovers, to bed, 'tis almost fairy time.°
    I fear we shall outsleep the coming morn,
    As much as we this night have overwatched.
    This palpable gross° play hath well beguiled   350
    The heavy gait of night. Sweet friends, to bed.
    A fortnight hold we this solemnity,
    In nightly revels, and new jollity.   *Exeunt.*

Enter PUCK [with a broom].

PUCK.   Now the hungry lion roars,
       And the wolf behowls the moon;   355
    Whilst the heavy° ploughman snores,
       All with weary task fordone.°
    Now the wasted brands° do glow,
    Whilst the screech-owl, screeching loud,
       Puts the wretch that lies in woe°   360
    In remembrance of a shroud.
       Now it is the time of night,
    That the graves, all gaping wide,
       Every one lets forth his sprite,°
    In the church-way paths to glide.   365
       And we fairies, that do run
    By the triple Hecate's° team,°
       From the presence of the sun,
Following darkness like a dream,
       Now are frolic:° not a mouse   370
    Shall disturb this hallowed house.

---

338 *Bergomask:* exaggerated country dance.   346 *iron tongue:* i.e., of the bell.   *told:*
counted, tolled.   347 *fairy time:* (from midnight to daybreak).   350 *palpable gross:* obvious
and crude.   356 *heavy:* sleepy.   357 *fordone:* worn out, "done in."   358 *wasted brands:*
burnt logs.   360 *wretch . . . woe:* sick person.   364 *sprite:* spirit, ghost.   367 *triple Hecate:*
the moon goddess, identified as Cynthia in heaven, Diana on earth, and Hecate in hell.   *team:*
dragons that pull the chariot of the night moon.   370 *frolic:* frolicsome.

I am sent with broom before,
To sweep the dust° behind° the door.

Enter KING and QUEEN OF FAIRIES, with all their train.

OBERON.   Through the house give glimmering light,
      By the dead and drowsy fire,   375
    Every elf and fairy sprite,
      Hop as light as bird from brier,
    And this ditty after me,
    Sing, and dance it trippingly.
TITANIA.   First rehearse your song by rote,   380
To each word a warbling note.
Hand in hand, with fairy grace,
Will we sing and bless this place.   *[Song and dance.]*
OBERON.   Now, until the break of day,
Through this house each fairy stray.   385
To the best bride-bed will we,
Which by us shall blessèd be:
And the issue° there create,°
Ever shall be fortunate:
So shall all the couples three   390
Ever true in loving be:
And the blots of Nature's hand°
Shall not in their issue° stand.
Never mole, harelip, nor scar,
Nor mark prodigious,° such as are   395
Despisèd in nativity,
Shall upon their children be.
With this field-dew consecrate.
Every fairy take his gait,°
And each several° chamber bless,   400
Through this palace, with sweet peace;
And the owner of its blest,
Ever shall in safety rest.
Trip away: make no stay: *Exeunt [all but PUCK].* 405
Meet me all by break of day.
PUCK.   If we shadows have offended,
Think but this, and all is mended,
That you have but slumbered here,
While these visions did appear.
And this weak and idle° theme,   410
No more yielding but° a dream,
Gentles, do not reprehend.

---

373 *To sweep the dust:* (Puck often helped with household chores).   *behind:* from
behind.   388, 393 *issue:* children.   388 *create:* created.   392 *blots . . . hand:* birth defects.
395 *mark prodigious:* unnatural birthmark.   399 *take his gait:* proceed.   400 *several:* separate.   410 *idle:* foolish.   411 *No . . . but:* yielding nothing more than.

If you pardon, we will mend.°
And as I am an honest Puck,
If we have unearnèd luck,   415
Now to scape the serpent's tongue,°
We will make amends, ere long:
Else the Puck a liar call.
So, good night unto you all.
Give me your hands,° if we be friends;   420
And Robin shall restore amends.°   [*Exit.*]

QUESTIONS

Act I

1. Describe the relationship between Theseus and Hippolyta. What does each of them represent? How does Shakespeare show us that they have different attitudes toward their marriage?

2. Characterize Hermia and Lysander. What blocks their relationship? How do they plan to circumvent these obstructions?

3. What are Helena's feelings about herself? About Hermia? About Demetrius? How might you account for her self-image?

4. Why have the mechanicals gathered at Quince's house? How does Shakespeare show us that Bottom is eager, ill-educated, energetic, and funny?

Act II

5. What is Puck's job? What do you find out about his personality, habits, and pastimes in his first conversation?

6. Why are Titania and Oberon fighting with each other, and what are the specific consequences of their conflict?

7. What does Oberon plan to do to Titania? Why? What is "love-in-idleness"? What power does it have? What does it symbolize?

8. Why are Demetrius and Helena in the woods? What does Oberon decide to do to them? What error occurs? What happens to Lysander when Helena awakens him?

Act III

9. How and why does Puck change Bottom? How is this transformation appropriate? What happens when Bottom awakens Titania? Why?

10. What does Oberon decide to do when he realizes that Puck has made a mistake? What is Puck's attitude toward the confusion he has created?

---

413 *mend:* improve.   416 *serpent's tongue:* hissing of the audience.   420 *hands:* applause.
421 *restore amends:* do better in the future.

11. What happens when Helena awakens Demetrius? How does this situation reverse the one that began the play? Explain Helena's reaction to the behavior of Demetrius and Lysander.

12. What real dangers (tragic potential) do the lovers face in Act III? How do Oberon and Puck deal with these dangers? What is their plan? How successful is it?

Act IV

13. Why does Oberon cure Titania of her infatuation with Bottom? How does the relationship between Oberon and Titania change? How is this change symbolized? Why is it significant?

14. How are the relationships among the four lovers straightened out? How does each explain his or her feelings? What does Theseus decide about the couples? Why is this significant?

15. What momentous event occurs offstage and is briefly reported in Act IV, scene 2?

Act V

16. Describe Pyramus and Thisby. What blocks their relationship? How do they plan to circumvent these obstructions? What happens to them?

17. What is the significance of the fairy masque (a combination of poetry, music, dance, and drama) that ends the play?

18. What does Puck's epilogue suggest about you as a reader or spectator? How does it reinforce the connections among dreaming, imagination, illusion, and drama?

GENERAL QUESTIONS

1. To what extent are the characters in this play conventional and representative types? What is the effect of Shakespeare's style of characterization?

2. Are any of the characters symbolic? If so, what do they symbolize? How does such symbolism reinforce the themes of the play?

3. How does Shakespeare employ language, imagery, and poetic form to define the characters in this play and differentiate among the various groups of characters?

4. To what extent do the two settings—city and woods—structure the play? Where does exposition occur? Complication and catastrophe? The comic resolution? How complete is the resolution? Why is the round-trip journey from one setting to the other necessary for the lovers? The rulers? The "hempen homespuns"?

5. What are the similarities or parallels in plot and theme between *A Midsummer Night's Dream* and "Pyramus and Thisby"? To what degree are they versions of the same play with different endings? Why do you think Shakespeare included the play-within-the-play in *A Midsummer Night's Dream*?

6. In the first soliloquy of the play, Helena discusses love. What kind of love is she talking about? What are its qualities and characteristics? How far do the relationships in the play bear out her ideas about love?

7. How well do the mechanicals understand the nature of dramatic illusion? What sorts of production problems concern them? How do they solve these?

8. What ideas about drama and the ways in which audiences respond to it does *A Midsummer Night's Dream* explore?

9. Compare the play-within-a-play in *A Midsummer Night's Dream* to the one in Act III of *Hamlet*. How are the internal plays and situations similar? Different? What parallels do you see in the connections between each play-within-a-play and the larger play in which each occurs?

COMEDY AFTER SHAKESPEARE

The subject of comedy in the centuries from Shakespeare to the present is vast. In all the major European countries, and eventually in the United States, there were many comic dramatists. Some of them were successful in their time but are neglected today, such as Eugène Scribe in France, and some, such as Anton Chekhov in Russia, are known not only for their comedy but also for other works (such as Chekhov's tragi-comedies and stories).

The acknowledged master of comedy in the years following Shakespeare was Molière, the pen name of Jean Baptiste Poquelin (1622–1673). He wrote twenty-nine comedies, ranging from broad farce to satirical comedies of manners. Generally he drew his plots from Roman comedy, Italian *commedia dell'arte*, and French farce, all of which schooled him in comic character, tempo, and situation. He elevated comedy to the seriousness of tragedy, as in his satiric comedies *The Ridiculous Dilettantes* (*Les Précieuses Ridicules*, 1659), *The Misanthrope* (1666), *The Miser* (1668), and *Tartuffe* (1669). His plays advocate a balance or norm of behavior, and from this standpoint they mock and expose greed, snobbery, personal rigidity, religious posturing, and professional hypocrisy.

This is not to say that comedy was not flourishing in other nations. In England in the seventeenth century, dramatists such as William Wycherley (1640–1716) and William Congreve (1670–1729) created a sophisticated type of drama, in the comedy-of-manners tradition, that is termed "Restoration comedy" because it developed after King Charles II was reestablished on the English throne in 1660. The Restoration comedies combined and contrasted elegant and boisterous manners, and they often dealt with serious social and sexual problems. In the first part of the eighteenth century dramatists created "sentimental" drama. Sentimental comedies showed individuals who verge on behavioral excesses but who eventually conform to morality because their goodness of heart overcomes their personal interests, feelings, and self-indulgence— hence the term "sentimental."

The first half of the eighteenth century saw the popularity of other forms such as the musical play and the burlesque play. The musical play was first known as **ballad opera,** and later it was called **comic opera** and **musical comedy.** The characteristic of the musical play was the combination of spoken dialogue and brief songs. The first such play was *The Beggar's Opera* (1728) by John Gay (1685–1732).[1] *The Beggar's Opera* was also a burlesque that satirized the Italian operas so popular in the early eighteenth century. Henry Fielding (1707–1754), known for his later novels, wrote the best of English burlesque plays, *Tom Thumb* (1730, 1731), and, in addition, he wrote at least nine ballad operas in the manner of *The Beggar's Opera.* Also unique to Fielding's comic writing were a number of five-act plays dealing with serious social situations. The comic opera reached its high point in the nineteenth century with the Savoy Operas of William Gilbert (1836–1911) and Arthur Sullivan (1842–1900). The Gilbert and Sullivan operas, such as *H.M.S. Pinafore* (1878) and *The Mikado* (1885), are regularly performed today by both professionals and amateurs. In the United States during the twentieth century, the musical comedy form became a major force, as with the plays of Richard Rodgers (1902–1979) and Oscar Hammerstein II (1895–1960), and Alan Jay Lerner (1918–1986) and Frederick Loewe (1901–1987).

At the turn of the nineteenth century the major comic dramatists in addition to Chekhov were Oscar Wilde (1854–1900) and George Bernard Shaw (1856–1950), all of whose plays are still regularly revived and well attended. The twentieth century marked the appearance of numbers of important comic dramatists, including many, like Eugene O'Neill and Tennessee Williams, who are better known for more serious plays (see pp. 877 and 1289). A number of writers divided their time between theater and film, as with George Kaufman (1889–1961), whose *The Man Who Came to Dinner* (1939) was successful both on stage and on the screen. For a time, Kaufman also wrote film scripts for some of the early film comedies of the Marx Brothers. Many other comic playwrights experimented with comedy. Such a writer is Arthur Kopit (b. 1937), whose *Oh Dad, Poor Dad, Mamma's Hung You in the Closet and I'm Feelin' so Sad* (1961) created a great stir when it was first performed. Of particular note is the development of the "Theater of the Absurd." Some significant plays in this tradition are *Waiting for Godot* (1953) by Samuel Beckett (1906–1989), *Rhinocéros* (1960), by Jean Genet (1910–1986), and *The Homecoming* (1960) by Harold Pinter (b. 1930).

It is fair to say that comedy today is characterized by great variety. All the types described earlier are being written (see pp. 1070–72). Serious plays may contain comic and farcical elements. Comic and farcical plays may introduce serious sequences and also may contain strong elements of satire. Satirical plays may contain songs to complement the onstage action and also to divert and entertain. It is clear that writers at the end of the twentieth century were combining the various comic forms that were brought into prominence by writers since the time of Shakespeare.

---

[1] See p. 522 for a song from *The Beggar's Opera.*

ANTON CHEKHOV, *THE BEAR*

Anton Chekhov was born in Taganrog in southern Russia in 1860, the son of a merchant and grandson of a serf. He entered medical school in Moscow in 1879, graduating in 1884. While a student he was also obligated to help support his family, and he turned to writing stories, jokes, and potboilers for pay under a variety of pen names, one of which was "The Doctor Without Patients." *The Bear* belongs to the end of this early period, ten years before Chekhov's association with the Moscow Art Theater at the end of the century.

Chekhov minimized *The Bear*, referring to it as a "joke" and a "vaudeville"—both words suggesting a farcical work with little form or substance. Nevertheless the play was greatly acclaimed and financially successful, to the author's amazement and delight. Three months after its first performance in 1888, he likened *The Bear* to a "milk cow" ("cash cow") because, to his happiness, it earned him a steady income.

The Bear is a farce, a dramatic form designed preeminently to evoke laughter, and it therefore contains extravagant language and boisterous and sudden action. But there is also an underlying seriousness that sustains the humor. In their way, both Smirnov and Mrs. Popov have been failures; they could conceivably sink into lives of depression and futility, and both are walking a very fine wire as the play begins. Chekhov makes clear that Mrs. Popov is filled with resentment at her unfaithful and now dead husband, and also that she is chafing under her self-imposed resolution to lead a life of mourning and self-denial in his memory. Smirnov is having difficulty with creditors, and he admits that his relationships with the many women he has known have ended unhappily. He is therefore both cynical and angry.

The climax of the play is the improbable and preposterous challenge that Smirnov offers Mrs. Popov, resolved by the equally sudden and preposterous outcome. Despite the improbabilities of the play, however, the actions are not impossible because they manifest the true internal needs of the main characters. Chekhov's friend Leo Tolstoy, who criticized some of Chekhov's late plays, laughed heartily at *The Bear*, and countless audiences and readers since then have joined him in laughter.

ANTON CHEKHOV (1860–1904)

The Bear, A Joke in One Act _____ *1900*

CAST OF CHARACTERS

Mrs. Popov. *A widow of seven months, Mrs. Popov is small and pretty, with dimples. She is a landowner. At the start of the play, she is pining away in memory of her dead husband.*

Grigory Stepanovich Smirnov. *Easily angered and loud, Smirnov is older. He is a landowner, too, and a man of substance.*

Luka. *Luka is Mrs. Popov's footman (a servant whose main tasks were to wait table and attend the carriages, in addition to general duties). He is old enough to feel secure in telling Mrs. Popov what he thinks.*

Gardener, Coachman, Workmen, *who enter at the end.*

SCENE. *The drawing room of MRS. POPOV's country home.*

[*MRS. POPOV, in deep mourning, does not remove her eyes from a photograph.*]

LUKA.   It isn't right, madam . . . you're only destroying yourself. . . . The chambermaid and the cook have gone off berry picking; every living being is rejoicing; even the cat knows how to be content, walking around the yard catching birds, and you sit in your room all day as if it were a convent, and you don't take pleasure in anything. Yes, really! Almost a year has passed since you've gone out of the house!

MRS. POPOV.   And I shall never go out. . . . What for? My life is already ended. *He* lies in his grave; I have buried myself in these four walls . . . we are both dead.

LUKA.   There you go again! Your husband is dead, that's as it was meant to be, it's the will of God, may he rest in peace. . . . You've done your mourning and that will do. You can't go on weeping and mourning forever. My wife died when her time came, too. . . . Well? I grieved, I wept for a month, and that was enough for her; the old lady wasn't worth a second more. [*Sighs.*] You've forgotten all your neighbors. You don't go anywhere or accept any calls. We live, so to speak, like spiders. We never see the light. The mice have eaten my uniform. It isn't as if there weren't any nice neighbors—the district is full of them . . . there's a regiment stationed at Riblov, such officers—they're like candy—you'll never get your fill of them! And in the barracks, never a Friday goes by without a dance; and, if you please, the military band plays music every day. . . . Yes, madam, my dear lady: you're young, beautiful, in the full bloom of youth—if only you took a little pleasure in life . . . beauty doesn't last forever, you know! In ten years' time, you'll be wanting to wave your fanny in front of the officers—and it will be too late.

MRS. POPOV.   [*Determined.*] I must ask you never to talk to me like that! You know that when Mr. Popov died, life lost all its salt for me. It may seem to you that I am alive, but that's only conjecture! I vowed to wear mourning to my grave and not to see the light of day. . . . Do you hear me? May his departed spirit see how much I love him. . . . Yes, I know, it's no mystery to you that he was often mean to me, cruel . . . and even unfaithful, but I shall remain true to the grave and show him I know how to love. There, beyond the grave, he will see me as I was before his death. . . .

LUKA.   Instead of talking like that, you should be taking a walk in the garden or   5
have Toby or Giant harnessed and go visit some of the neighbors . . .

MRS. POPOV.   Ai! [*She weeps.*]

LUKA.   Madam! Dear lady! What's the matter with you! Christ be with you!

MRS. POPOV.   Oh, how he loved Toby! He always used to ride on him to visit the Korchagins or the Vlasovs. How wonderfully he rode! How graceful he was when he pulled at the reins with all his strength! Do you remember? Toby, Toby! Tell them to give him an extra bag of oats today.

LUKA.   Yes, madam.

[*Sound of loud ringing.*]

MRS. POPOV.   [*Shudders.*] Who's that? Tell them I'm not at home!   10

LUKA.   Of course, madam. [*He exits.*]

MRS. POPOV.   [*Alone. Looks at the photograph.*] You will see, Nicholai, how much I can love and forgive . . . my love will die only when I do, when my poor heart stops beating. [*Laughing through her tears.*] Have you no shame? I'm a good girl, a virtuous little wife. I've locked myself in and I'll be true to you to the grave, and you . . . aren't you ashamed, you chubby cheeks? You deceived me, you made scenes, for weeks on end you left me alone . . .

LUKA.   [*Enters, alarmed.*] Madam, somebody is asking for you. He wants to see you. . . .

MRS. POPOV.   But didn't you tell them that since the death of my husband, I don't see anybody?

LUKA.   I did, but he didn't want to listen; he spoke about some very important   15
business.

MRS. POPOV.   I am *not at home!*

LUKA.   That's what I told him . . . but . . . the devil . . . he cursed and pushed past me right into the room . . . he's in the dining room right now.

MRS. POPOV.   [*Losing her temper.*] Very well, let him come in . . . such manners! [*LUKA goes out.*] How difficult these people are! What does he want from me? Why should he disturb my peace? [*Sighs.*] But it's obvious I'll have to go live in a convent. . . . [*Thoughtfully.*] Yes, a convent. . . .

SMIRNOV.   [*Enters while speaking to LUKA.*] You idiot, you talk too much. . . . Ass! [*Sees MRS. POPOV and changes to dignified speech.*] Madam, may I introduce myself: retired lieutenant of the artillery and landowner, Grigory Stepanovich Smirnov! I feel the necessity of troubling you about a highly important matter. . . .

MRS. POPOV.   [*Refusing her hand.*] What do you want?   20

SMIRNOV.   Your late husband, whom I had the pleasure of knowing, has remained in my debt for two twelve-hundred-ruble notes. Since I must pay the interest at the agricultural bank tomorrow, I have come to ask you, madam, to pay me the money today.

MRS. POPOV.   One thousand two hundred. . . . And why was my husband in debt to you?

SMIRNOV.   He used to buy oats from me.

MRS. POPOV.   [*Sighing, to LUKA.*] So, Luka, don't you forget to tell them to give Toby an extra bag of oats.

[*LUKA goes out.*]

[*To SMIRNOV.*] If Nikolai, my husband, was in debt to you, then it goes without saying that I'll pay; but please excuse me today. I haven't any spare cash. The day after tomorrow, my steward will be back from town and I will give him instructions to pay you what is owed; until then I cannot comply with your wishes. . . . Besides, today is the anniversary—exactly seven months ago my husband died, and I'm in such a mood that I'm not quite disposed to occupy myself with money matters.

SMIRNOV.   And I'm in such a mood that if I don't pay the interest tomorrow, I'll   25
be owing so much that my troubles will drown me. They'll take away my estate!

MRS. POPOV.   You'll receive your money the day after tomorrow.

SMIRNOV.   I don't want the money the day after tomorrow. I want it today.

MRS. POPOV.   You must excuse me. I can't pay you today.

SMIRNOV.   And I can't wait until after tomorrow.

MRS. POPOV.   What can I do, if I don't have it now?   30

SMIRNOV.   You mean to say you can't pay?

MRS. POPOV.   I can't pay. . . .

SMIRNOV.   Hm! Is that your last word?

MRS. POPOV.   That is my last word.

SMIRNOV.   Positively the last?   35

MRS. POPOV.   Positively.

SMIRNOV.   Thank you very much. We'll make a note of that. [*Shrugs his shoulders.*] And people want me to be calm and collected! Just now, on the way here, I met a tax officer and he asked me: why are you always so angry, Grigory Stepanovich? Goodness' sake, how can I be anything but angry? I need money desperately . . . I rode out yesterday early in the morning, at daybreak, and went to see all my debtors; and if only one of them had paid his debt . . . I was dog-tired, spent the night God knows where—a Jewish tavern beside a barrel of vodka. . . . Finally I got here, fifty miles from home, hoping to be paid, and you treat me to a "mood." How can I help being angry?

MRS. POPOV.   It seems to me that I clearly said: My steward will return from the country and then you will be paid.

SMIRNOV.   I didn't come to your steward, but to you! What the hell, if you'll pardon the expression, would I do with your steward?

MRS. POPOV.   Excuse me, my dear sir, I am not accustomed to such profane   40
expressions nor to such a tone. I'm not listening to you any more. [*Goes out quickly.*]

SMIRNOV.   [*Alone.*] Well, how do you like that? "A mood." . . . "Husband died seven months ago"! Must I pay the interest or mustn't I? I ask you: Must I pay, or must I not? So, your husband's dead, and you're in a mood and all that finicky stuff . . . and your steward's away somewhere; may he drop dead. What do you want me to do? Do you think I can fly away from my creditors in a balloon or something? Or should I run and bash my head against the wall? I go to Gruzdev—and he's not at home; Yaroshevich is hiding, with Kuritsin it's a quarrel to the death and I almost throw him out the window; Mazutov has diarrhea, and this one is in a "mood." Not one of these swine wants to pay me! And all because I'm too nice to them! I'm a sniveling idiot, I'm spineless, I'm an old lady! I'm too delicate with them! So, just you wait! You'll find out what I'm like! I won't let you play around with me, you devils! I'll stay and stick it out until she pays. Rrr! . . . How furious I am today, how furious! I'm shaking inside from rage and I can hardly catch my breath. . . . Damn it! My God, I even feel sick! [*He shouts.*] Hey, you!

LUKA.   [*Enters.*] What do you want?

SMIRNOV.   Give me some beer or some water! [*LUKA exits.*] What logic is there in this! A man needs money desperately, it's like a noose around his neck—and she won't pay because, you see, she's not disposed to occupy herself with money matters! . . . That's the logic of a woman! That's why I never did like and do not like to talk to women. I'd rather sit on a keg of gunpowder than talk to a woman. Brr! . . . I even have goose pimples, this broad has put me in such a rage! All I have to do is see one of those spoiled bitches from a distance, and I get so angry it gives me a cramp in the leg. I just want to shout for help.

LUKA.   [*Entering with water.*] Madam is sick and won't see anyone.

SMIRNOV.   Get out! [*LUKA goes.*] Sick and won't see anyone! No need to see me . . .   45
I'll stay and sit here until you give me the money. You can stay sick for a week, and I'll stay for a week . . . if you're sick for a year, I'll stay a year. . . . I'll get my own back, dear lady! You can't impress me with your widow's weeds and your dimpled cheeks . . . we know all about those dimples! [*Shouts through the window.*] Semyon, unharness the horses! We're not going away quite yet! I'm staying here! Tell them in the stable to give the horses some oats! You brute, you let the horse on the left side get all tangled up in

the reins again! [*Teasing.*] "Never mind" . . . I'll give you a never mind! [*Goes away from the window.*] Shit! The heat is unbearable and nobody pays up. I slept badly last night and on top of everything else this broad in mourning is "in a mood" . . . my head aches . . . [*Drinks, and grimaces.*] Shit! This is water! What I need is a drink! [*Shouts.*] Hey, you!

LUKA.   [*Enters.*] What is it?

SMIRNOV.   Give me a glass of vodka. [*LUKA goes out.*] Oaf! [*Sits down and examines himself.*] Nobody would say I was looking well! Dusty all over, boots dirty, unwashed, unkept, straw on my waistcoat. . . . The dear lady probably took me for a robber. [*Yawns.*] It's not very polite to present myself in a drawing room looking like this; oh well, who cares? . . . I'm not here as a visitor but as a creditor, and there's no official costume for creditors. . . .

LUKA.   [*Enters with vodka.*] You're taking liberties, my good man. . . .

SMIRNOV.   [*Angrily.*] What?

LUKA.   I . . . nothing . . . I only . . .   50

SMIRNOV.   Who are you talking to? Shut up!

LUKA.   [*Aside.*] The devil sent this leech. An ill wind brought him. . . . [*LUKA goes out.*]

SMIRNOV.   Oh how furious I am! I'm so mad I could crush the whole world into a powder! I even feel faint! [*Shouts.*] Hey, you!

MRS. POPOV.   [*Enters, eyes downcast.*] My dear sir, in my solitude, I have long ago grown unaccustomed to the masculine voice and I cannot bear shouting. I must request you not to disturb my peace and quiet!

SMIRNOV.   Pay me my money and I'll go.   55

MRS. POPOV.   I told you in plain language: I haven't any spare cash now; wait until the day after tomorrow.

SMIRNOV.   And I also told you respectfully, in plain language: I don't need the money the day after tomorrow, but today. If you don't pay me today, then tomorrow I'll have to hang myself.

MRS. POPOV.   But what can I do if I don't have the money? You're so strange!

SMIRNOV.   Then you won't pay me now? No?

MRS. POPOV.   I can't. . . .   60

SMIRNOV.   In that case, I can stay here and wait until you pay. . . . [*Sits down.*] You'll pay the day after tomorrow? Excellent! In that case I'll stay here until the day after tomorrow. I'll sit here all that time . . . [*Jumps up.*] I ask you: Have I got to pay the interest tomorrow, or not? Or do you think I'm joking?

MRS. POPOV.   My dear sir, I ask you not to shout! This isn't a stable!

SMIRNOV.   I wasn't asking you about a stable but about this: Do I have to pay the interest tomorrow or not?

MRS. POPOV.   You don't know how to behave in the company of a lady!

SMIRNOV.   No, I don't know how to behave in the company of a lady!   65

MRS. POPOV.   No, you don't! You are an ill-bred, rude man! Respectable people don't talk to a woman like that!

SMIRNOV.   Ach, it's astonishing! How would you like me to talk to you? In French, perhaps? [*Lisps in anger.*] *Madame, je vous prie°* . . . how happy I am that you're not paying me the money. . . . Ah, pardon, I've made you uneasy! Such lovely weather we're having today! And you look so becoming in your mourning dress. [*Bows and scrapes.*]

Madame, je vous prie: I beg you, Madam.

MRS. POPOV. That's rude and not very clever!

SMIRNOV. [*Teasing.*] Rude and not very clever! I don't know how to behave in the company of ladies. Madam, in my time I've seen far more women than you've seen sparrows. Three times I've fought duels over women; I've jilted twelve women, nine have jilted me! Yes! There was a time when I played the fool; I became sentimental over women, used honeyed words, fawned on them, bowed and scraped. . . . I loved, suffered, sighed at the moon; I became limp, melted, shivered . . . I loved passionately, madly, every which way, devil take me, I chattered away like a magpie about the emancipation of women, ran through half my fortune as a result of my tender feelings; but now, if you will excuse me, I'm on to your ways! I've had enough! Dark eyes, passionate eyes, ruby lips, dimpled cheeks; the moon, whispers, bated breath—for all that I wouldn't give a good goddamn. Present company excepted, of course, but all women, young and old alike, are affected clowns, gossips, hateful, consummate liars to the marrow of their bones, vain, trivial, ruthless, outrageously illogical, and as far as this is concerned [*taps on his forehead.*], well, excuse my frankness, any sparrow could give pointers to a philosopher in petticoats! Look at one of those romantic creatures: muslin, ethereal demigoddess, a thousand raptures, and you look into her soul—a common crocodile! [*Grips the back of a chair; the chair cracks and breaks.*] But the most revolting part of it all is that this crocodile imagines that she has, above everything, her own privilege, a monopoly on tender feelings. The hell with it—you can hang me upside down by that nail if a woman is capable of loving anything besides a lapdog. All she can do when she's in love is slobber! While the man suffers and sacrifices, all her love is expressed in playing with her skirt and trying to lead him around firmly by the nose. You have the misfortune of being a woman, you know yourself what the nature of a woman is like. Tell me honestly: Have you ever in your life seen a woman who is sincere, faithful, and constant? You never have! Only old and ugly ladies are faithful and constant! You're more liable to meet a horned cat or a white woodcock than a faithful woman!

MRS. POPOV. Pardon me, but in your opinion, who is faithful and constant in love? The man?   70

SMIRNOV. Yes, the man!

MRS. POPOV. The man! [*Malicious laugh.*] Men are faithful and constant in love! That's news! [*Heatedly.*] What right have you to say that? Men are faithful and constant! For that matter, as far as I know, of all the men I have known and now know, my late husband was the best. . . . I loved him passionately, with all my being, as only a young intellectual woman can love; I gave him my youth, my happiness, my life, my fortune; he was my life's breath; I worshipped him as if I were a heathen, and . . . and, what good did it do—this best of men himself deceived me shamelessly at every step of the way. After his death, I found his desk full of love letters; and when he was alive—it's terrible to remember—he used to leave me alone for weeks at a time, and before my eyes he flirted with other women and deceived me. He squandered my money, made a mockery of my feelings . . . and, in spite of all that, I loved him and was true to him . . . and besides, now that he is dead, I am still faithful and constant. I have shut myself up in these four walls forever and I won't remove these widow's weeds until my dying day. . . .

SMIRNOV. [*Laughs contemptuously.*] Widow's weeds! . . . I don't know what you take me for! As if I didn't know why you wear that black outfit and bury yourself in these four walls! Well, well! It's no secret, so romantic! When some fool of a poet passes by this country house, he'll look up at your window and think: "Here lives the mysterious Tamara, who, for the love of her husband, buried herself in these four walls." We know these tricks!

MRS. POPOV.   [*Flaring.*] What? How dare you say that to me?

SMIRNOV.   You may have buried yourself alive, but you haven't forgotten to   75
powder yourself!

MRS. POPOV.   How dare you use such expressions with me?

SMIRNOV.   Please don't shout. I'm not your steward! You must allow me to call a
spade a spade. I'm not a woman and I'm used to saying what's on my mind! Don't you
shout at me!

MRS. POPOV.   I'm not shouting, you are! Please leave me in peace!

SMIRNOV.   Pay me my money and I'll go.

MRS. POPOV.   I won't give you any money!   80

SMIRNOV.   Yes, you will.

MRS. POPOV.   To spite you, I won't pay you anything. You can leave me in peace!

SMIRNOV.   I don't have the pleasure of being either your husband or your fiancé,
so please don't make scenes! [*Sits down.*] I don't like it.

MRS. POPOV.   [*Choking with rage.*] You're sitting down?

SMIRNOV.   Yes, I am.   85

MRS. POPOV.   I ask you to get out!

SMIRNOV.   Give me my money . . . [*Aside.*] Oh, I'm so furious! Furious!

MRS. POPOV.   I don't want to talk to impudent people! Get out of here! [*Pause.*]
You're not going? No?

SMIRNOV.   No.

MRS. POPOV.   No?   90

SMIRNOV.   No!

MRS. POPOV.   We'll see about that. [*Rings.*]

[*LUKA enters.*]

Luka, show the gentleman out!

LUKA.   [*Goes up to SMIRNOV.*] Sir, will you please leave, as you have been asked. You
mustn't . . .

SMIRNOV.   [*Jumping up.*] Shut up! Who do you think you're talking to? I'll make
mincemeat out of you!

LUKA.   [*His hand to his heart.*] Oh my God! Saints above! [*Falls into chair.*] Oh,   95
I feel ill! I can't catch my breath!

MRS. POPOV.   Where's Dasha? Dasha! [*She shouts.*] Dasha! Pelagea! Dasha! [*She
rings.*]

LUKA.   Oh! They've all gone berry picking . . . there's nobody at home . . . I'm ill!
Water!

MRS. POPOV.   Will you please get out!

SMIRNOV.   Will you please be more polite?

MRS. POPOV.   [*Clenches her fist and stamps her feet.*] You're nothing but a crude bear!   100
A brute! A monster!

SMIRNOV.   What? What did you say?

MRS. POPOV.   I said that you were a bear, a monster!

SMIRNOV.   [*Advancing toward her.*] Excuse me, but what right do you have to
insult me?

MRS. POPOV.   Yes, I am insulting you . . . so what? Do you think I'm afraid of you?

SMIRNOV.   And do you think just because you're one of those romantic creations,   105
that you have the right to insult me with impunity? Yes? I challenge you!

LUKA.   Lord in Heaven! Saints above! . . . Water!

SMIRNOV.   Pistols!

MRS. POPOV.   Do you think just because you have big fists and you can bellow like a bull, that I'm afraid of you? You're such a bully!

SMIRNOV.   I challenge you! I'm not going to let anybody insult me, and I don't care if you are a woman, a delicate creature!

MRS. POPOV.   [*Trying to get a word in edgewise.*] Bear! Bear! Bear!   110

SMIRNOV.   It's about time we got rid of the prejudice that only men must pay for their insults! Devil take it, if women want to be equal, they should behave as equals! Let's fight!

MRS. POPOV.   You want to fight! By all means!

SMIRNOV.   This minute!

MRS. POPOV.   This minute! My husband had some pistols . . . I'll go and get them right away. [*Goes out hurriedly and then returns.*] What pleasure I'll have putting a bullet through that thick head of yours! The hell with you! [*She goes out.*]

SMIRNOV.   I'll shoot her down like a chicken! I'm not a little boy or a sentimental   115
puppy. I don't care if she is delicate and fragile.

LUKA.   Kind sir! Holy father! [*kneels.*] Have pity on a poor old man and go away from here! You've frightened her to death and now you're going to shoot her?

SMIRNOV.   [*Not listening to him.*] If she fights, then it means she believes in equality of rights and emancipation of women. Here the sexes are equal! I'll shoot her like a chicken! But what a woman! [*Imitates her.*] "The hell with you! . . . I'll put a bullet through that thick head of yours! . . . " What a woman! How she blushed, her eyes shone . . . she accepted my challenge! To tell the truth, it was the first time in my life I've seen a woman like that. . . .

LUKA.   Dear sir, please go away! I'll pray to God on your behalf as long as I live!

SMIRNOV.   That's a woman for you! A woman like that I can understand! A real woman! Not a sour-faced nincompoop but fiery, gunpowder! Fireworks! I'm even sorry to have to kill her!

LUKA.   [*Weeps.*] Dear sir . . . go away!   120

SMIRNOV.   I positively like her! Positively! Even though she has dimpled cheeks, I like her! I'm almost ready to forget about the debt. . . . My fury has diminished. Wonderful woman!

MRS. POPOV.   [*Enters with pistols.*] Here they are, the pistols. Before we fight, you must show me how to fire. . . . I've never had a pistol in my hands before . . .

LUKA.   Oh dear Lord, for pity's sake. . . . I'll go and find the gardener and the coachman. . . . What did we do to deserve such trouble? [*Exit.*]

SMIRNOV.   [*Examining the pistols.*] You see, there are several sorts of pistols . . . there are special dueling pistols, the Mortimer with primers. Then there are Smith and Wesson revolvers, triple action with extractors . . . excellent pistols! . . . they cost a minimum of ninety rubles a pair. . . . You must hold the revolver like this . . . [*Aside.*] What eyes, what eyes! A woman to set you on fire!

MRS. POPOV.   Like this?   125

SMIRNOV.   Yes, like this . . . then you cock the pistol . . . take aim . . . put your head back a little . . . stretch your arm out all the way . . . that's right . . . then with this finger press on this little piece of goods . . . and that's all there is to do . . . but the most important thing is not to get excited and aim without hurrying . . . try to keep your arm from shaking.

MRS. POPOV.   Good . . . it's not comfortable to shoot indoors. Let's go into the garden.

SMIRNOV.   Let's go. But I'm giving you advance notice that I'm going to fire into the air.

MRS. POPOV.   That's the last straw! Why?

SMIRNOV.   Why? . . . Why . . . because it's my business, that's why.   130

MRS. POPOV.   Are you afraid? Yes? Aahhh! No, sir. You're not going to get out of it that easily! Be so good as to follow me! I will not rest until I've put a hole through your forehead . . . that forehead I hate so much! Are you afraid?

SMIRNOV.   Yes, I'm afraid.

MRS. POPOV.   You're lying! Why don't you want to fight?

SMIRNOV.   Because . . . because you . . . because I like you.

MRS. POPOV.   [*Laughs angrily.*] He likes me! He dares say that he likes me! [*Points*   135
to the door.] Out!

SMIRNOV.   [*Loads the revolver in silence, takes cap and goes; at the door, stops for half a minute while they look at each other in silence; then he approaches MRS. POPOV hesitantly.*] Listen. . . . Are you still angry? I'm extremely irritated, but, do you understand me, how can I express it . . . the fact is, that, you see, strictly speaking . . . [*He shouts.*] Is it my fault, really, for liking you? [*Grabs the back of a chair, which cracks and breaks.*] Why the hell do you have such fragile furniture! I like you! Do you understand? I . . . I'm almost in love with you!

MRS. POPOV.   Get away from me—I hate you!

SMIRNOV.   God, what a woman! I've never in my life seen anything like her! I'm lost! I'm done for! I'm caught like a mouse in a trap!

MRS. POPOV.   Stand back or I'll shoot!

SMIRNOV.   Shoot! You could never understand what happiness it would be to die   140
under the gaze of those wonderful eyes, to be shot by a revolver which was held by those little velvet hands. . . . I've gone out of my mind! Think about it and decide right away, because if I leave here, then we'll never see each other again! Decide . . . I'm a nobleman, a respectable gentleman, of good family. I have an income of ten thousand a year. . . . I can put a bullet through a coin tossed in the air . . . I have some fine horses. . . . Will you be my wife?

MRS. POPOV.   [*Indignantly brandishes her revolver.*] Let's fight! I challenge you!

SMIRNOV.   I'm out of my mind . . . I don't understand anything . . . [*Shouts.*] Hey, you, water!

MRS. POPOV.   [*Shouts.*] Let's fight!

SMIRNOV.   I've gone out of my mind. I'm in love like a boy, like an idiot! [*He grabs her hand, she screams with pain.*] I love you! [*Kneels.*] I love you as I've never loved before! I've jilted twelve women, nine women have jilted me, but I've never loved one of them as I love you. . . . I'm weak, I'm a limp rag. . . . I'm on my knees like a fool, offering you my hand. . . . Shame, shame! I haven't been in love for five years, I vowed I wouldn't; and suddenly I'm in love, like a fish out of water. I'm offering my hand in marriage. Yes or no? You don't want to? You don't need to! [*Gets up and quickly goes to the door.*]

MRS. POPOV.   Wait!   145

SMIRNOV.   [*Stops.*] Well?

MRS. POPOV.   Nothing . . . you can go . . . go away . . . wait. . . . No, get out, get out! I hate you! But—don't go! Oh, if you only knew how furious I am, how angry! [*Throws revolver on table.*] My fingers are swollen from that nasty thing. . . . [*Tears her hand-kerchief furiously.*] What are you waiting for? Get out!

SMIRNOV.   Farewell!

MRS. POPOV. Yes, yes, go away! [*Shouts.*] Where are you going? Stop. . . . Oh, go away! Oh, how furious I am! Don't come near me! Don't come near me!

SMIRNOV. [*Approaching her.*] How angry I am with myself! I'm in love like a student. I've been on my knees. . . . It gives me the shivers. [*Rudely.*] I love you! A lot of good it will do me to fall in love with you! Tomorrow I've got to pay the interest, begin the mowing of the hay. [*Puts his arm around her waist.*] I'll never forgive myself for this. . . . 150

MRS. POPOV. Get away from me! Get your hands away! I . . . hate you! I . . . challenge you!

[*Prolonged kiss, LUKA enters with an ax, the GARDENER with a rake, the COACHMAN with a pitchfork, and WORKMEN with cudgels.*]

LUKA. [*Catches sight of the pair kissing.*] Lord in heaven! [*Pause.*]

MRS. POPOV. [*Lowering her eyes.*] Luka, tell them in the stable not to give Toby any oats today.

CURTAIN

QUESTIONS

1. What was Mrs. Popov's life like with her late husband? What did she learn about him after his death? How has this knowledge affected her?

2. Who is Smirnov? What is he like, and how do you know? Why does he say what he does about women?

3. Why is Luka important? How do his responses highlight the emotions developing between Smirnov and Mrs. Popov?

4. What causes Mrs. Popov to call Smirnov a bear, a brute, a monster? What is his immediate response?

5. Why is Toby significant? How does he symbolize Mrs. Popov's shifting emotions?

GENERAL QUESTIONS

1. Where did you laugh in the play? Analyze those moments and try to determine the causes of your laughter.

2. From this play, what conclusions can you draw about farce as a dramatic form? Consider the breaking chairs, the shouting, the challenge, the attitude of Smirnov about being shot, the shifting of feelings, etc.

3. How does Chekhov's presentation of Smirnov and Mrs. Popov make their reversal of feelings seem normal and logical, although sudden, unexpected, and surprising?

4. What are the major ideas or themes in *The Bear*? Consider vows made by the living to the dead, the difficulty of keeping resolutions, the nature of powerful emotions, the need to maintain conventions and expectations, etc.

BETH HENLEY, *AM I BLUE*

Brought up in Mississippi, Beth Henley attended Southern Methodist University, where in her sophomore year she wrote *Am I Blue*, which was first produced in December 1981. She attended acting school in Illinois and went to Hollywood to take up a career as a movie actress. However, at the same time she continued to work on new plays, and it is as a writer that she has been successful. Her most notable achievement is her "southern Gothic" play *Crimes of the Heart* (first titled *Crimes of Passion*), for which she won the Great American Play contest in 1978 and the Pulitzer Prize for Drama in 1981. She

also wrote *The Wake of Jamey Foster* (1983), *The Lucky Spot* (1987), *The Debutante Ball* (1991), and *Abundance* (1991). The year 1992 saw the publication of four collected plays (*Beth Henley: Four Plays*), including *The Miss Firecracker Contest*, a two-act play written in 1979 and first performed in 1984. In addition, she has also seen some of her shorter scripts produced as television plays. *Crimes of the Heart* was made into a successful film in 1986, starring Diane Keaton, Jessica Lange, Sam Shepard, and Sissy Spacek.

In many of her plays, Henley's comedic manner develops out of the eccentricity or "kookiness" of her main female characters. The comic *donnée* is that an unusual or even disturbed action is accepted as a normal event that begins a course of dramatic action. A character in one of Henley's television plays, for example, inadvertently sets a house on fire, but the outcome turns out to be fortunate because of a rewarding home insurance policy. In *Crimes of the Heart*, one of the characters, after a failed suicide attempt, explains herself by saying that she has been having "a bad day." Even in the serious play *Abundance*, the two main female characters begin their twenty-five-year-long friendship after they have come west in the 1860s to become mail-order brides of men they have never seen. Ashbe of *Am I Blue* is an early original in the pattern, with her liking for hot Kool-Aid and colored marshmallows, her habit of stealing ashtrays and then donating them to a fellow tenant, and her dabbling in voodoo.

Although *Am I Blue* is an amusing play, it deals with serious problems: the difficulties of adjustment to adulthood, misconceptions about social roles, unfulfilled dreams, general aimlessness and indecisiveness, and the attempt to develop individuality. The larger political and historical context of the year of the supposed events of the play, 1968, is mentioned by neither Ashbe nor John Polk, but one might connect their difficulties with some of the disturbances of that year, particularly the assassinations of Robert Kennedy and Martin Luther King, Jr.; the frustrating and seemingly endless war in Vietnam; and the many antiwar demonstrations and riots, especially during the Democratic National Convention in Chicago in the summer. Henley is particular in dating the action of *Am I Blue* on the night of November 11, 1968—in other words, after all these disturbing and destabilizing events had taken place, and also less than a week after the election that made Richard Nixon president. One might also note the irony that November 11 had before 1954 been called "Armistice Day" (now Veterans Day)—a holiday dedicated to peace and stability.

    Am I Blue thus reflects the disturbances and disruptions of the late 1960s, even though it focuses on the individual concerns and problems of John Polk and Ashbe. Ashbe's father is an alcoholic who is absent when she needs him, and her mother has deserted the home entirely. John Polk is facing a difficult choice about his future career, and he is also trying to stay afloat in the swim of fraternity life. Unable to succeed in either situation, he seeks strength in rum instead of calling on his own inner resources. Nothing earthshaking is claimed for either John Polk or Ashbe at the play's end, but they both succeed in developing a degree of recognition—rejecting conventional behaviors and discovering their own capacities for friendship and dignity.

BETH HENLEY (b. 1952)

Am I Blue° _____ *(1973) 1982*

CHARACTERS

    John Polk Richards, *seventeen*
    Ashbe Williams, *sixteen*
    Hilda, *a waitress, thirty-five*
    Street People: Barker, Whore, Bum, Clareece

[*SCENE: A bar, the street, the living room of a run-down apartment.*]

[*TIME: Fall 1968.*]

The scene opens on a street in the New Orleans French Quarter on a rainy, blue bourbon night. Various people—a WHORE, BUM, STREET BARKER, CLAREECE—appear and disappear along the street. The scene then focuses on a bar where a piano is heard from the back room playing softly and indistinctly "Am I Blue?" The lights go up on JOHN POLK, who sits alone at a table. He is seventeen, a bit overweight and awkward. He wears nice clothes, perhaps a navy sweater with large white monograms. His navy raincoat is slung over an empty chair. While drinking John Polk concentrates on the red and black card that he holds in his hand. As soon as the scene is established, ASHBE enters from the street. She is sixteen, wears a flowered plastic raincoat, a white plastic rain cap, red galoshes, a butterfly barrette, and jeweled cat-eye glasses. She is carrying a bag full of stolen goods. Her hair is very curly. Ashbe makes her way cautiously to John Polk's table. As he sees her coming, he puts the card into his pocket. She sits in the empty chair and pulls his raincoat over her head.

    ASHBE.   Excuse me . . . do you mind if I sit here please?
    JOHN POLK.   [*Looks up at her—then down into his glass.*] What are you doing hiding under my raincoat? You're getting it all wet.
    ASHBE.   Well, I'm very sorry, but after all it is a raincoat. [*He tries to pull off coat.*] It was rude of me I know, but look I just don't want them to recognize me.

AM I BLUE: first produced in New York City by the Circle Repertory Company.

JOHN POLK.   [*Looking about.*] Who to recognize you?   5

ASHBE.   Well, I stole these two ashtrays from the Screw Inn, ya know right down the street. [*She pulls out two glass commercial ashtrays from her white plastic bag.*] Anyway, I'm scared the manager saw me. They'll be after me I'm afraid.

JOHN POLK.   Well, they should be. Look, do you mind giving me back my raincoat? I don't want to be found protecting any thief.

ASHBE.   [*Coming out from under coat.*] Thief—would you call Robin Hood a thief?

JOHN POLK.   Christ.

ASHBE.   [*Back under coat.*] No, you wouldn't. He was valiant—all the time stealing from the rich and giving to the poor.

JOHN POLK.   But your case isn't exactly the same, is it? You're stealing from some   10 crummy little bar and keeping the ashtrays for yourself. Now give me back my coat.

ASHBE.   [*Throws coat at him.*] Sure, take your old coat. I suppose I should have explained—about Miss Marcey. [*Silence.*] Miss Marcey, this cute old lady with a little hump in her back. I always see her in her sun hat and blue print dress. Miss Marcey lives in the apartment building next to ours. I leave all the stolen goods, as gifts on her front steps.

JOHN POLK.   Are you one of those kleptomaniacs? [*He starts checking his wallet.*]

ASHBE.   You mean when people all the time steal and they can't help it?

JOHN POLK.   Yeah.   15

ASHBE.   Oh, no. I'm not a bit careless. Take my job tonight, my very first night job, if you want to know. Anyway, I've been planning it for two months, trying to decipher which bar most deserved to be stolen from. I finally decided on the Screw Inn. Mainly because of the way they're so mean to Mr. Groves. He works at the magazine rack at Diver's Drugstore and is really very sweet, but he has a drinking problem. I don't think that's fair to be mean to people simply because they have a drinking problem—and, well, anyway, you see I'm not just stealing for personal gain. I mean, I don't even smoke.

JOHN POLK.   Yeah, well, most infants don't, but then again, most infants don't hang around bars.

ASHBE.   I don't see why not, Toulouse Lautrec did.

JOHN POLK.   They'd throw me out.

ASHBE.   Oh, they throw me out too, but I don't accept defeat. [*Slowly moves into him.*] Why it's the very same with my pickpocketing.

[*JOHN POLK sneers, turns away.*]

ASHBE.   It's a very hard act to master. Why every time I've done it, I've been   20 caught.

JOHN POLK.   That's all I need, is to have some slum kid tell me how good it is to steal. Everyone knows it's not.

ASHBE.   [*About his drink.*] That looks good. What is it?

JOHN POLK.   Hey, would you mind leaving me alone—I just wanted to be alone.

ASHBE.   Okay. I'm sorry. How about if I'm quiet?

[*JOHN POLK shrugs. He sips drink, looks around, catches her eye, she smiles and sighs.*]

ASHBE.   I was just looking at your pin. What fraternity are you in?   25

JOHN POLK.   S.A.E.

ASHBE.   Is it a good fraternity?

JOHN POLK.   Sure, it's the greatest.

ASHBE.   I bet you have lots of friends.

JOHN POLK.   Tons.   30

ASHBE.   Are you being serious?

JOHN POLK.   Yes.

ASHBE.   Hmm. Do they have parties and all that?

JOHN POLK.   Yeah, lots of parties, booze, honking horns, it's exactly what you would expect.

ASHBE.   I wouldn't expect anything. Why did you join?   35

JOHN POLK.   I don't know. Well, my brother . . . I guess it was my brother . . . he told me how great it was, how the fraternity was supposed to get you dates, make you study, solve all your problems.

ASHBE.   Gee, does it?

JOHN POLK.   Doesn't help you study.

ASHBE.   How about dates? Do they get you a lot of dates?

JOHN POLK.   Some.   40

ASHBE.   What were the girls like?

JOHN POLK.   I don't know—they were like girls.

ASHBE.   Did you have a good time?

JOHN POLK.   I had a pretty good time.

ASHBE.   Did you make love to any of them?   45

JOHN POLK.   [*To self.*] Oh, Christ . . .

ASHBE.   I'm sorry . . . I just figured that's why you had the appointment with the whore . . . cause you didn't have anyone else . . . to make love to.

JOHN POLK.   How did you know I had the, ah, the appointment?

ASHBE.   I saw you put the red card in your pocket when I came up. Those red cards are pretty familiar around here. The house is only about a block or so away. It's one of the best though, really very plush. Only two murders and a knifing in its whole history. Do you go there often?

JOHN POLK.   Yeah, I like to give myself a treat.   50

ASHBE.   Who do you have?

JOHN POLK.   What do you mean?

ASHBE.   I mean which girl. [*JOHN POLK gazes into his drink.*] Look, I just thought I might know her is all.

JOHN POLK.   Know her, ah, how would you know her?

ASHBE.   Well, some of the girls from my high school go there to work when they   55
get out.

JOHN POLK.   G.G., her name is G.G.

ASHBE.   G.G. . . . Hmm, well, how does she look?

JOHN POLK.   I don't know.

ASHBE.   Oh, you've never been with her before?

JOHN POLK.   No.   60

ASHBE.   [*Confidentially.*] Are you one of those kinds that likes a lot of variety?

JOHN POLK.   Variety? Sure, I guess I like variety.

ASHBE.   Oh, yes, now I remember.

JOHN POLK.   What?

ASHBE.   G.G., that's just her working name. Her real name is Myrtle Reims, she's   65
Kay Reims' older sister. Kay is in my grade at school.

JOHN POLK.   Myrtle? Her name is Myrtle?

ASHBE.   I never liked the name either.

JOHN POLK.   Myrtle, oh, Christ. Is she pretty?

ASHBE.   [*Matter of fact.*] Pretty, no she's not real pretty.

JOHN POLK.   What does she look like?   70

ASHBE.   Let's see . . . she's, ah, well, Myrtle had acne and there are a few scars left. It's not bad. I think they sort of give her character. Her hair's red, only I don't think it's really red. It sort of fizzles out all over her head. She's got a pretty good figure . . . big top . . . but the rest of her is kind of skinny.

JOHN POLK.   I wonder if she has a good personality.

ASHBE.   Well, she was a senior when I was a freshman; so I never really knew her. I remember she used to paint her fingernails lots of different colors . . . pink, orange, purple. I don't know, but she kind of scares me. About the only time I ever saw her true personality was around a year ago. I was over at Kay's making a health poster for school. Anyway, Myrtle comes busting in, screaming about how she can't find her spangled bra anywhere. Kay and I just sat on the floor cutting pictures of food out of magazines while she was storming about slamming drawers and swearing. Finally, she found it. It was pretty garish—red with black and gold sequined G's on each cup. That's how I remember the name—G.G.

[*As Ashbe illustrates the placement of the G's she spots Hilda, the waitress, approaching. Ashbe pulls the raincoat over her head and hides on the floor. Hilda enters through the beaded curtains spilling her tray. Hilda is a woman of few words.*]

HILDA.   Shit, damn curtain. Nuther drink?

JOHN POLK.   Mam?   75

HILDA.   [*Points to drink.*] Vodka coke?

JOHN POLK.   No, thank you. I'm not quite finished yet.

HILDA.   Napkins clean.

[*ASHBE pulls her bag off the table. HILDA looks at ASHBE then to JOHN POLK. She walks around the table, as ASHBE is crawling along the floor to escape. ASHBE runs into HILDA's toes.*]

ASHBE.   Are those real gold?

HILDA.   You again. Out.   80

ASHBE.   She wants me to leave. Why should a paying customer leave? [*Back to* HILDA.] Now I'll have a mint julip and easy on the mint.

HILDA.   This pre-teen with you?

JOHN POLK.   Well, I . . . No . . . I . . .

HILDA.   I.D.'s.

ASHBE.   Certainly, I always try to cooperate with the management.   85

HILDA.   [*Looking at JOHN POLK's I.D.*] I.D., 11-12-50. Date: 11-11-68.

JOHN POLK.   Yes, but . . . well, 11-12 is less than two hours away.

HILDA.   Back in two hours.

ASHBE.   I seem to have left my identification in my gold lamé bag.

HILDA.   Well, boo-hoo. [*Motions for ASHBE to leave with a minimum of effort. She goes   90 back to table.*] No tip.

ASHBE.   You didn't tip her?

JOHN POLK.   I figured the drinks were so expensive . . . I just didn't . . .

HILDA.   No tip!

JOHN POLK.   Look, Miss, I'm sorry. [*Going through his pockets.*] Here would you like a . . . a nickel . . . wait, wait, here's a quarter.

HILDA.   Just move ass, sonny. You too, Barbie.   95

ASHBE.   Ugh, I hate public rudeness. I'm sure I'll refrain from ever coming here again.

HILDA. Think I'll go in the back room and cry.

[*Ashbe and John Polk exit. Hilda picks up tray and exits through the curtain, tripping again.*]

HILDA. Shit. Damn curtain.

[*ASHBE and JOHN POLK are now standing outside under the awning of the bar.*]

ASHBE. Gee, I didn't know it was your birthday tomorrow. Happy birthday! Don't be mad. I thought you were at least twenty or twenty-one, really.
JOHN POLK. It's o.k. Forget it.   100

[*As they begin walking, various blues are heard coming from the nearby bars.*]

ASHBE. It's raining.
JOHN POLK. I know.
ASHBE. Are you going over to the house now?
JOHN POLK. No, not till twelve.
ASHBE. Yeah, the red and black cards—they mean all night. Midnight till   105
morning.

[*At this point a street BARKER beckons the couple into his establishment. Perhaps he is accompanied by a WHORE.*]

BARKER. Hey mister, bring your baby on in, buy her a few drinks, maybe tonight
ya get lucky.
ASHBE. Keep walking.
JOHN POLK. What's wrong with the place?
ASHBE. The drinks are watery rot gut, and the show girls are boys . . .
BARKER. Up yours, punk!   110
JOHN POLK. [*Who has now sat down on a street bench.*] Look, just tell me where a
cheap bar is. I've got to stay drunk, but I don't have much money left.
ASHBE. Yikes, there aren't too many cheap bars around here, and a lot of them
check I.D.'s.
JOHN POLK. Well, do you know of any that don't?
ASHBE. No, not for sure.
JOHN POLK. Oh, God, I need to get drunk.   115
ASHBE. Aren't you?
JOHN POLK. Some, but I'm losing ground fast.

[*By this time a BUM who has been traveling drunkenly down the street falls near the couple and begins throwing up.*]

ASHBE. Oh, I know! You can come to my apartment. It's just down the block. We
keep one bottle of rum around. I'll serve you a grand drink, three or four if you like.
JOHN POLK. [*Fretfully.*] No, thanks.
ASHBE. But look, we're getting all wet.   120
JOHN POLK. Sober too, wet and sober.
ASHBE. Oh, come on! Rain's blurring my glasses.
JOHN POLK. Well, how about your parents? What would they say?
ASHBE. Daddy's out of town and Mama lives in Atlanta; so I'm sure they won't
mind. I think we have some cute little marshmallows. [*Pulling on him.*] Won't you really
come?

JOHN POLK.   You've probably got some gang of muggers waiting to kill me. Oh, all   125
right . . . what the hell, let's go.

ASHBE.   Hurrah! Come on. It's this way. [*She starts across the stage, stops, and picks up
an old hat.*] Hey, look at this hat. Isn't it something! Here, wear it to keep off the rain.

JOHN POLK.   [*Throwing hat back onto street.*] No, thanks, you don't know who's worn
it before.

ASHBE.   [*Picking hat back up.*] That makes it all the more exciting. Maybe it was a
butcher's who slaughtered his wife or a silver pirate with a black bird on his throat. Who
do you guess?

JOHN POLK.   I don't know. Anyway what's the good of guessing? I mean you'll
never really know.

ASHBE.   [*Trying the hat on.*] Yeah, probably not.   130

[*At this point ASHBE and JOHN POLK reach the front door.*]

ASHBE.   Here we are.

[*ASHBE begins fumbling for her key. CLAREECE, a teeny-bopper, walks up to JOHN POLK.*]

CLAREECE.   Hey, man, got any spare change?

JOHN POLK.   [*Looking through his pockets.*] Let me see . . . I . . .

ASHBE.   [*Coming up between them, giving CLAREECE a shove.*] Beat it, Clareece. He's
my company.

CLAREECE.   [*Walks away and sneers.*] Oh, shove it, Frizzels.   135

ASHBE.   A lot of jerks live around here. Come on in. [*She opens the door. Lights go up
on the living room of a run-down apartment in a run-down apartment house. Besides being merely
run-down the room is a malicious pig sty with colors, paper hats, paper dolls, masks, torn up stuffed
animals, dead flowers and leaves, dress-up clothes, etc., thrown all about.*] My bones are cold. Do
you want a towel to dry off?

JOHN POLK.   Yes, thank you.

ASHBE.   [*She picks up a towel off the floor and tosses it to him.*] Here. [*He begins drying
off, as she takes off her rain things; then she begins raking things off the sofa.*] Please do sit down.
[*He sits.*] I'm sorry the place is disheveled, but my father's been out of town. I always try
to pick up and all before he gets in. Of course, he's pretty used to messes. My mother
never was too good at keeping things clean.

JOHN POLK.   When's he coming back?

ASHBE.   Sunday, I believe. Oh, I've been meaning to say . . .   140

JOHN POLK.   What?

ASHBE.   My name's Ashbe Williams.

JOHN POLK.   Ashbe?

ASHBE.   Yeah, Ashbe.

JOHN POLK.   My name's John Polk Richards.   145

ASHBE.   John Polk? They call you John Polk?

JOHN POLK.   It's family.

ASHBE.   [*Putting on socks.*] These are my favorite socks, the red furry ones. Well,
here's some books and magazines to look at while I fix you something to drink. What do
you want in your rum?

JOHN POLK.   Coke's fine.

ASHBE.   I'll see if we have any. I think I'll take some hot Kool-Aid myself.   150

[*She exits to the kitchen.*]

JOHN POLK.   Hot Kool-Aid?

ASHBE.   It's just Kool-Aid that's been heated, like hot chocolate or hot tea.

JOHN POLK.   Sounds great.

ASHBE.   Well, I'm used to it. You get so much for your dime, it makes it worth your while. I don't buy presweetened, of course, it's better to sugar your own.

JOHN POLK.   I remember once I threw up a lot of grape Kool-Aid when I was a   155
kid. I've hated it ever since. Hey, would you check on the time?

ASHBE.   [*She enters carrying a tray with several bottles of food coloring, a bottle of rum, and a huge glass.*] I'm sorry we don't have Coke. I wonder if rum and Kool-Aid is good? Oh, we don't have a clock either.

[*She pours a large amount of rum into the large glass.*]

JOHN POLK.   I'll just have it with water then.

ASHBE.   [*She finds an almost empty glass of water somewhere in the room and dumps it in with the rum.*] Would you like food coloring in the water? It makes a drink all the more aesthetic. Of course, some people don't care for aesthetics.

JOHN POLK.   No, thank you, just plain water.

ASHBE.   Are you sure? The taste is entirely the same. I put it in all my water.   160

JOHN POLK.   Well . . .

ASHBE.   What color do you want?

JOHN POLK.   I don't know.

ASHBE.   What's your favorite color?

JOHN POLK.   Blue, I guess.   165

[*She puts a few blue drops into the glass. As she has nothing to stir with, she blows into the glass turning the water blue.*]

JOHN POLK.   Thanks.

ASHBE.   [*Exits. She screams from kitchen.*] Come on, say come on, cat, eat your fresh, good milk.

JOHN POLK.   You have a cat?

ASHBE.   [*off.*] No.

JOHN POLK.   Oh.   170

ASHBE.   [*She enters carrying a tray with a cup of hot Kool-Aid and Cheerios and colored marshmallows.*] Here are some Cheerios and some cute, little, colored marshmallows to eat with your drink.

JOHN POLK.   Thanks.

ASHBE.   I one time smashed all the big white marshmallows in the plastic bag at the grocery store.

JOHN POLK.   Why did you do that?

ASHBE.   I was angry. Do you like ceramics?   175

JOHN POLK.   Yes.

ASHBE.   My mother makes them. It's sort of her hobby. She is very talented.

JOHN POLK.   My mother never does anything. Well, I guess she can shuffle the bridge deck okay.

ASHBE.   Actually, my mother is a dancer. She teaches at a school in Atlanta. She's really very talented.

JOHN POLK.   [*Indicates ceramics.*] She must be to do all these.   180

ASHBE.   Well, Madeline, my older sister, did the blue one. Madeline gets to live with Mama.

JOHN POLK.   And you live with your father.

ASHBE.   Yeah, but I get to go visit them sometimes.

JOHN POLK.   You do ceramics too?

ASHBE.   No, I never learned . . . but I have this great potholder set. [*Gets up to   185
show him.*] See, I make lots of multicolored potholders and send them to Mama and
Madeline. I also make paper hats. [*Gets material to show him.*] I guess they're more creative, but making potholders is more relaxing. Here, would you like to make a hat?

JOHN POLK.   I don't know, I'm a little drunk.

ASHBE.   It's not hard a bit. [*Hands him material.*] Just draw a real pretty design on
the paper. It really doesn't have to be pretty, just whatever you want.

JOHN POLK.   It's kind of you to give my creative drives such freedom.

ASHBE.   Ha, ha, ha, I'll work on my potholder set a bit.

JOHN POLK.   What time is it? I've really got to check on the time.   190

ASHBE.   I know. I'll call the time operator.

[*She goes to the phone.*]

JOHN POLK.   How do you get along without a clock?

ASHBE.   Well, I've been late for school a lot. Daddy has a watch. It's 11:03.

JOHN POLK.   I've got a while yet. [*Ashbe twirls back to her chair, drops, and sighs.*] Are
you a dancer, too?

ASHBE.   [*Delighted.*] I can't dance a bit, really. I practice a lot is all, at home in the   195
afternoon. I imagine you go to a lot of dances.

JOHN POLK.   Not really, I'm a terrible dancer. I usually get bored or drunk.

ASHBE.   You probably drink too much.

JOHN POLK.   No, it's just since I've come to college. All you do there is drink more
beer and write more papers.

ASHBE.   What are you studying for to be?

JOHN POLK.   I don't know.   200

ASHBE.   Why don't you become a rancher?

JOHN POLK.   Dad wants me to help run his soybean farm.

ASHBE.   Soybean farm. Yikes, that's really something. Where is it?

JOHN POLK.   Well, I live in the Delta, Hollybluff, Mississippi. Anyway, Dad feels I
should go to business school first; you know, so I'll become, well, management-minded.
Pass the blue.

ASHBE.   Is that what you really want to do?   205

JOHN POLK.   I don't know. It would probably be as good as anything else I could
do. Dad makes good money. He can take vacations whenever he wants. Sure it'll be a ball.

ASHBE.   I'd hate to have to be management-minded. [*John Polk shrugs.*] I don't
mean to hurt your feelings, but I would really hate to be a management mind. [*She starts
walking on her knees, twisting her fists in front of her eyes, and making clicking sounds as a management mind would make.*]

JOHN POLK.   Cut it out. Just forget it. The farm could burn down, and I wouldn't
even have to think about it.

ASHBE.   [*After a pause.*] Well, what do you want to talk about?

JOHN POLK.   I don't know.   210

ASHBE.   When was the last dance you went to?

JOHN POLK.   Dances. That's a great subject. Let's see, oh, I don't really remember—it was probably some blind date. God, I hate dates.

ASHBE. Why?

JOHN POLK. Well, they always say that they don't want popcorn, and they wind up eating all of yours.

ASHBE. You mean, you hate dates just because they eat your popcorn? Don't you think that's kind of stingy? 215

JOHN POLK. It's the principle of the thing. Why can't they just say, yes, I'd like some popcorn when you ask them. But, no, they're always so damn coy.

ASHBE. I'd tell my date if I wanted popcorn. I'm not that immature.

JOHN POLK. Anyway, it's not only the popcorn. It's a lot of little things. I've finished coloring. What do I do now?

ASHBE. Now you have to fold it. Here . . . like this. [*She explains the process with relish.*] Say, that's really something.

JOHN POLK. It's kind of funny looking. [*Putting the hat on.*] Yeah, I like it, but you could never wear it anywhere. 220

ASHBE. Well, like what anyway?

JOHN POLK. Huh?

ASHBE. The things dates do to you that you don't like, the little things.

JOHN POLK. Oh, well, just the way they wear those false eyelashes and put their hand on your knee when you're trying to parallel park, and keep on giggling and going off to the bathroom with their girl friends. It's obvious they don't want to go out with me. They just want to go out so that they can wear their new clothes and won't have to sit on their ass in the dormitory. They never want to go out with me. I can never even talk to them.

ASHBE. Well, you can talk to me, and I'm a girl. 225

JOHN POLK. Well, I'm really kind of drunk, and you're a stranger . . . well, I probably wouldn't be able to talk to you tomorrow. That makes a difference.

ASHBE. Maybe it does. [*A bit of a pause and then extremely pleased by the idea she says.*] You know we're alike because I don't like dances either.

JOHN POLK. I thought you said you practiced . . . in the afternoons.

ASHBE. Well, I like dancing. I just don't like dances. At least not like . . . well, not like the one our school was having tonight . . . they're so corny.

JOHN POLK. Yeah, most dances are. 230

ASHBE. All they serve is potato chips and fruit punch, and then this stupid baby band plays and everybody dances around thinking they're so hot. I frankly wouldn't dance there. I would prefer to wait till I am invited to an exclusive ball. It doesn't really matter which ball, just one where they have huge, golden chandeliers and silver fountains, and serve delicacies of all sorts and bubble blue champagne. I'll arrive in a pink silk cape. [*Laughing.*] I want to dance in pink!

JOHN POLK. You're mixed up. You're probably one of those people that live in a fantasy world.

ASHBE. I do not. I accept reality as well as anyone. Anyway, you can talk to me, remember. I know what you mean by the kind of girls it's hard to talk to. There are girls a lot that way in the small clique at my school. Really tacky and mean. They expect everyone to be as stylish as they are, and they won't even speak to you in the hall. I don't mind if they don't speak to me, but I really love the orphans, and it hurts my feelings when they are so mean to them.

JOHN POLK. What do you mean—they're mean to the "orpheens"? [*Giggles to himself at the wordplay.*]

ASHBE.   Oh, well, they sometimes snicker at the orphans' dresses. The orphans   235
usually have hand-me-down, drab, ugly dresses. Once Shelly Maxwell wouldn't let Glinda
borrow her pencil, even though she had two. It hurt her feelings.

JOHN POLK.   Are you best friends with these orphans?

ASHBE.   I hardly know them at all. They're really shy. I just like them a lot. They're
the reason I put spells on the girls in the clique.

JOHN POLK.   Spells, what do you mean, witch spells?

ASHBE.   Witch spells? Not really, mostly just voodoo.

JOHN POLK.   Are you kidding? Do you really do voodoo?   240

ASHBE.   Sure, here I'll show you my doll. [*Goes to get doll, comes back with straw
voodoo doll. Her air as she returns is one of frightening mystery.*] I know a lot about the subject.
Cora, she used to wash dishes in the Moonlight Cafe, told me all about voodoo. She's a
real expert on the subject, went to all the meetings and everything. Once she caused a
man's throat to rot away and turn almost totally black. She's moved to Chicago now.

JOHN POLK.   It doesn't really work. Does it?

ASHBE.   Well, not always. The thing about voodoo is that both parties have to
believe in it for it to work.

JOHN POLK.   Do the girls in school believe in it?

ASHBE.   Not really, I don't think. That's where my main problem comes in. I have   245
to make the clique believe in it, yet I have to be very subtle. Mainly, I give reports in
English class or Speech.

JOHN POLK.   Reports?

ASHBE.   On voodoo.

JOHN POLK.   That's really kind of sick, you know.

ASHBE.   Not really. I don't cast spells that'll do any real harm. Mainly, just the
kind of thing to make them think . . . to keep them on their toes. [*Blue-drink intoxication
begins to take over and JOHN POLK begins laughing.*] What's so funny?

JOHN POLK.   Nothing. I was just thinking what a mean little person you are.   250

ASHBE.   Mean! I'm not mean a bit.

JOHN POLK.   Yes, you are mean . . . [*Picking up color.*] . . . and green too.

ASHBE.   Green?

JOHN POLK.   Yes, green with envy of those other girls; so you play all those mean
little tricks.

ASHBE.   Envious of those other girls, that stupid, close-minded little clique!   255

JOHN POLK.   Green as this marshmallow. [*Eats marshmallow.*]

ASHBE.   You think I want to be in some group . . . a sheep like you? A little sheep
like you that does everything when he's supposed to do it!

JOHN POLK.   Me a sheep . . . I do what I want!

ASHBE.   Ha! I've known you for an hour and already I see you for the sheep you
are!

JOHN POLK.   Don't take your green meanness out on me.   260

ASHBE.   Not only are you a sheep, you are a NORMAL sheep. Give me back my
colors! [*Begins snatching colors away.*]

JOHN POLK.   [*Pushing colors at her.*] Green and mean! Green and mean! Green
and mean!

ASHBE.   [*Throwing marshmallows at him.*] That's the reason you're in a fraternity
and the reason you're going to manage your mind. And dates . . . you go out on dates
merely because it's expected of you even though you have a terrible time. That's the

reason you go to the whorehouse to prove you're a normal man. Well, you're much too normal for me.

JOHN POLK.   Infant bitch. You think you're really cute.

ASHBE.   That really wasn't food coloring in your drink, it was poison! [*She laughs,*   265
he picks up his coat to go, and she stops throwing marshmallows at him.] Are you going? I was only kidding. For Christ sake, it wasn't really poison. Come on, don't go. Can't you take a little friendly criticism?

JOHN POLK.   Look, did you have to bother me tonight? I had enough problems without . . .

[*Phone rings. Both look at phone, it rings for the third time. He stands undecided.*]

ASHBE.   Look, wait, we'll make it up. [*She goes to answer phone.*] Hello . . . Daddy. How are you? . . . I'm fine . . . Dad, you sound funny . . . What? . . . Come on, Daddy, you know she's not here. [*Pause.*] Look, I told you I wouldn't call anymore. You've got her number in Atlanta. [*Pause, as she sinks to the floor.*] Why have you started again? . . . Don't say that. I can tell it. I can. Hey, I have to go to bed now, I don't want to talk anymore, okay? [*Hangs up phone, then softly to self.*] Goddamnit.

JOHN POLK.   [*He has heard the conversation and is taking off his coat.*] Hey, Ashbe . . . [*She looks at him blankly, her mind far away.*] You want to talk?

ASHBE.   No. [*Slight pause.*] Why don't you look at my shell collection? I have this special shell collection. [*She shows him collection.*]

JOHN POLK.   They're beautiful, I've never seen colors like this. [*ASHBE is silent, he   270
continues to himself.*] I used to go to Biloxi° a lot when I was a kid . . . One time my brother and I, we camped out on the beach. The sky was purple. I remember it was really purple. We ate pork and beans out of a can. I'd always kinda wanted to do that. Every night for about a week after I got home, I dreamt about these waves foaming over my head and face. It was funny. Did you find these shells or buy them?

ASHBE.   Some I found, some I bought. I've been trying to decipher their meaning. Here, listen, do you hear that?

JOHN POLK.   Yes.

ASHBE.   That's the soul of the sea. [*She listens.*] I'm pretty sure it's the soul of the sea. Just imagine when I decipher the language. I'll know all the secrets of the world.

JOHN POLK.   Yeah, probably you will. [*Looking into the shell.*] You know, you were right.

ASHBE.   What do you mean?   275

JOHN POLK.   About me, you were right. I am a sheep, a normal one. I've been trying to get out of it, but now I'm as big a sheep as ever.

ASHBE.   Oh, it doesn't matter. You're company. It was rude of me to say.

JOHN POLK.   No, because it was true. I really didn't want to go into a fraternity, I didn't even want to go to college, and I sure as hell don't want to go back to Hollybluff and work the soybean farm till I'm eighty.

ASHBE.   I still say you could work on a ranch.

JOHN POLK.   I don't know. I wanted to be a minister or something good, but I   280
don't even know if I believe in God.

ASHBE.   Yeah.

270 *Biloxi:* city in southern Mississippi, on the Gulf of Mexico.

JOHN POLK.   I never used to worry about being a failure. Now I think about it all the time. It's just I need to do something that's . . . fulfilling.

ASHBE.   Fulfilling, yes, I see what you mean. Well, how about college? Isn't it fulfilling? I mean, you take all those wonderful classes, and you have all your very good friends.

JOHN POLK.   Friends, yeah, I have some friends.

ASHBE.   What do you mean?   285

JOHN POLK.   Nothing . . . well, I do mean something. What the hell, let me try to explain. You see it was my "friends," the fraternity guys that set me up with G.G., excuse me, Myrtle, as a gift for my eighteenth birthday.

ASHBE.   You mean, you didn't want the appointment?

JOHN POLK.   No, I didn't want it. Hey, ah, where did my blue drink go?

ASHBE.   [*As she hands him the drink.*] They probably thought you really wanted to go.

JOHN POLK.   Yeah, I'm sure they gave a damn what I wanted. They never even   290
asked me. Hell, I would have told them a handkerchief, a pair of argyle socks, but, no, they have to get me a whore just because it's a cool-ass thing to do. They make me sick. I couldn't even stay at the party they gave. All the sweaty T-shirts, and moron sex stories . . . I just couldn't take it.

ASHBE.   Is that why you were at the Blue Angel so early?

JOHN POLK.   Yeah, I needed to get drunk, but not with them. They're such creeps.

ASHBE.   Gosh, so you really don't want to go to Myrtle's?

JOHN POLK.   No, I guess not.

ASHBE.   Then are you going?   295

JOHN POLK.   [*Pause.*] Yes.

ASHBE.   That's wrong. You shouldn't go just to please them.

JOHN POLK.   Oh, that's not the point anymore, maybe at first it was, but it's not anymore. Now I have go for myself . . . to prove to myself that I'm not afraid.

ASHBE.   Afraid? [*Slowly, as she begins to grasp his meaning.*] You mean, you've never slept with a girl before?

JOHN POLK.   Well, I've never been in love.   300

ASHBE.   [*In amazement.*] You're a virgin?

JOHN POLK.   Oh, God.

ASHBE.   No, don't feel bad, I am too.

JOHN POLK.   I thought I should be in love . . .

ASHBE.   Well, you're certainly not in love with Myrtle. I mean, you haven't even   305
met her.

JOHN POLK.   I know, but, God, I thought maybe I'd never fall in love. What then? You should experience everything . . . shouldn't you? Oh, what's it matter, everything's so screwed.

ASHBE.   Screwed? Yeah, I guess it is. I mean, I always thought it would be fun to have a lot of friends who gave parties and go to dances all dressed up. Like the dance tonight . . . it might have been fun.

JOHN POLK.   Well, why didn't you go?

ASHBE.   I don't know. I'm not sure it would have been fun. Anyway, you can't go . . . alone.

JOHN POLK.   Oh, you need a date?   310

ASHBE.   Yeah, or something.

JOHN POLK.   Say, Ashbe, ya wanna dance here?

ASHBE.   No, I think we'd better discuss your dilemma.

JOHN POLK.   What dilemma?

ASHBE.   Myrtle. It doesn't seem right you should . . .   315

JOHN POLK.   Let's forget Myrtle for now. I've got a while yet. Here have some more of this blue-moon drink.

ASHBE.   You're only trying to escape through artificial means.

JOHN POLK.   Yeah, you got it. Now come on. Would you like to dance? Hey, you said you liked to dance.

ASHBE.   You're being ridiculous.

JOHN POLK.   [*Winking at her.*] Dance?   320

ASHBE.   John Polk, I just thought . . .

JOHN POLK.   Hmm?

ASHBE.   How to solve your problem . . .

JOHN POLK.   Well . . .

ASHBE.   Make love to me!   325

JOHN POLK.   What?!

ASHBE.   It all seems logical to me. It would prove you weren't scared, and you wouldn't be doing it just to impress others.

JOHN POLK.   Look, I . . . I mean, I hardly know you . . .

ASHBE.   But we've talked. It's better this way, really. I won't be so apt to point out your mistakes.

JOHN POLK.   I'd feel great, stripping a twelve-year-old of her virginity.   330

ASHBE.   I'm sixteen! Anyway, I'd be stripping you of yours just as well. I'll go put on some Tiger Claw perfume. [*She runs out.*]

JOHN POLK.   Hey, come back! Tiger Claw perfume, Christ.

ASHBE.   [*Entering.*] I think one should have different scents for different moods.

JOHN POLK.   Hey, stop spraying that! You know I'm not going to . . . well, you'd get neurotic, or pregnant, or some damn thing. Stop spraying, will you!

ASHBE.   Pregnant? You really think I could get pregnant?   335

JOHN POLK.   Sure, it'd be a delightful possibility.

ASHBE.   It really wouldn't be bad. Maybe I would get to go to Tokyo for an abortion. I've never been to the Orient.

JOHN POLK.   Sure getting cut on is always a real treat.

ASHBE.   Anyway, I might just want to have my dear baby. I could move to Atlanta with Mama and Madeline. It'd be wonderful fun. Why I could take him to the supermarket, put him in one of those little baby seats to stroll him about. I'd buy peach baby food and feed it to him with a tiny golden spoon. Why I could take colored pictures of him and send them to you through the mail. Come on . . . [*Starts putting pillows onto the couch.*] Well, I guess you should kiss me for a start. It's only etiquette, everyone begins with it.

JOHN POLK.   I don't think I could even kiss you with a clear conscience. I mean,   340
you're so small with those little cat-eye glasses and curly hair . . . I couldn't even kiss you.

ASHBE.   You couldn't even kiss me? I can't help it if I have to wear glasses. I got the prettiest ones I could find.

JOHN POLK.   Your glasses are fine. Let's forget it, okay?

ASHBE.   I know, my lips are too purple, but if I eat carrots, the dye'll come off and they'll be orange.

JOHN POLK.   I didn't say anything about your lips being too purple.

ASHBE.   Well, what is it? You're just plain chicken, I suppose . . .   345

JOHN POLK.   Sure, right, I'm chicken, totally chicken. Let's forget it. I don't know how, but, somehow, this is probably all my fault.

ASHBE.   You're darn right it's all your fault! I want to have my dear baby or at least get to Japan. I'm so sick of school I could smash every marshmallow in sight! [*She starts smashing.*] Go on to your skinny pimple whore. I hope the skinny whore laughs in your face, which she probably will because you have an easy face to laugh in.

JOHN POLK.   You're absolutely right, she'll probably hoot and howl her damn fizzle red head off. Maybe you can wait outside the door and hear her, give you lots of pleasure, you sadistic, little thief.

ASHBE.   Thief! Was Robin Hood . . . Oh, what's wrong with this world? I just wasn't made for it, is all. I've probably been put in the wrong world, I can see that now.

JOHN POLK.   You're fine in this world.   350

ASHBE.   Sure, everyone just views me as an undesirable lump.

JOHN POLK.   Who?

ASHBE.   You, for one.

JOHN POLK.   [*Pause.*] You mean because I wouldn't make love to you?

ASHBE.   It seems clear to me.   355

JOHN POLK.   But you're wrong, you know.

ASHBE.   [*To self, softly.*] Don't pity me.

JOHN POLK.   The reason I wouldn't wasn't that . . . it's just that . . . well, I like you too much to.

ASHBE.   You like me?

JOHN POLK.   Undesirable lump, Jesus. Your cheeks they're . . . they're . . .   360

ASHBE.   My cheeks? They're what?

JOHN POLK.   They're rosy.

ASHBE.   My cheeks are rosy?

JOHN POLK.   Yeah, your cheeks, they're really rosy.

ASHBE.   Well, they're natural, you know. Say, would you like to dance?   365

JOHN POLK.   Yes.

ASHBE.   I'll turn on the radio. [*She turns on radio. Ethel Waters is heard singing "Honey in the Honeycomb." ASHBE begins snapping her fingers.*] Yikes, let's jazz it out.

[*They dance.*]

JOHN POLK.   Hey, I'm not good or anything . . .

ASHBE.   John Polk.

JOHN POLK.   Yeah?   370

ASHBE.   Baby, I think you dance fine!

[*They dance on, laughing, saying what they want till end of song. Then a radio announcer comes on and says the 12:00 news will be in five minutes. Billie Holiday, or Terry Pierce, begins singing, "Am I Blue?"*]

JOHN POLK.   Dance?

ASHBE.   News in five minutes.

JOHN POLK.   Yeah.

ASHBE.   That means five minutes till midnight.   375

JOHN POLK.   Yeah, I know.

ASHBE.   Then you're not . . .

JOHN POLK.   Ashbe, I've never danced all night. Wouldn't it be something to . . . to dance all night and watch the rats come out of the gutter?

ASHBE.   Rats?

JOHN POLK.   Don't they come out at night? I hear New Orleans has lots of rats.   380

ASHBE.   Yeah, yeah, it's got lots of rats.

JOHN POLK.   Then let's dance all night and wait for them to come out.

ASHBE.   All right . . . but, but how about our feet?

JOHN POLK.   Feet?

ASHBE.   They'll hurt.   385

JOHN POLK.   Yeah.

ASHBE.   [*Smiling.*] Okay, then let's dance.

[*He takes her hand, and they dance as lights black out and the music soars and continues to play.*]

End.

QUESTIONS

1.   What do Ashbe's actions at the start tell you about her (such as hiding under the coat, stealing and giving the stolen things away, crawling away from the waitress)? What is disclosed by her speeches?

2.   Describe the circumstances of Ashbe and her family. To what degree can her character and behavior be explained by these circumstances?

3.   What is Ashbe's intention in her description of G.G., or Myrtle? What does her description tell you about her? What do you learn about her from her description of the only sort of dance she would like to go to (speech 231)?

4.   What personal, occupational, and social difficulties is John Polk experiencing? Why is he trying to stay drunk before going to G.G.? What are his reactions to fraternity life and to the family business?

5.   Explain the effects of the arguments between Ashbe and John Polk. How does their occasionally taunting each other influence their developing relationship?

6.   Why does John Polk not take up Ashbe's invitation to make love? How does this refusal suggest the development of his character? Of Ashbe's character? What may be inferred by their concluding decision to dance the night away?

GENERAL QUESTIONS

1.   What is the plot of *Am I Blue?* Who is the protagonist (or protagonists)? Who or what is the antagonist? How is the plot resolved?

2.   Describe and analyze the verbal comedy of the play, such as the "two murders and a knifing" (speech 49), Ashbe's description of Myrtle (speeches 71–73), and the inquiry about what to mix with rum (speech 148).

3.   What is appealing (or not appealing) about Ashbe and John Polk? To what extent are you to consider them as realistic persons? How might they be seen as symbols, and what might they symbolize?

4.   What are the major themes or ideas of the play? To what extent does the comic mode obscure these ideas? To what extent does it bring them out?

5.   What is the effect of the setting in the New Orleans French Quarter and the characters to be found there? What is shown about Ashbe and John Polk by

their brief interactions with the characters in the bar, especially Hilda, and on the street?

WRITING ABOUT COMEDY

For an essay about comedy, you can choose most of the conventional topics, such as *plot, conflict, character, point of view, setting, style, tone, symbolism,* or *theme.* You might choose one of these, or two or more—for example, how language and action define character, how character and symbol convey meaning, or how setting can influence comic structure.

Planning and prewriting strategies for each of these conventional elements are discussed at some length in Chapter 22 (pp. 883–85) and in other chapters on prose fiction and poetry. As you develop your essay, you will find it helpful to look at these suggestions.

For the most part, planning and writing about specific features of comedy are much like addressing the same topics in other forms of drama, short stories, and poetry. However, a few areas of consideration—such as plot, character, and language—are especially significant in comic drama and can be handled in a distinctive fashion.

Questions for Discovering Ideas

PLOT, CONFLICT, STRUCTURE.   What problems, adversities, or abnormal situations are in place at the comedy's opening? How is this initial situation complicated? Do the complications spring mainly from character or from situation? If from character, what aspects of behavior or personality create the problems? If from situation, what dilemmas or troubles plague the characters? What kinds of complications dominate—misunderstandings, disagreements, mistakes in identity, situational problems, or emotional entanglements? How important is coincidence?

What problems and complications occur early? Who is the comic protagonist (or protagonists), and what is the protagonist's goal (money, success, marriage, land, freedom)? How is the protagonist blocked (fathers, rivals, laws, customs, his or her own personality)? How threatening is the obstruction? What plans are hatched to overcome the blocking agents? Are the plans sensible or silly? Who initiates and executes the plans? To what extent do plans succeed (or fail)—because of chance and good luck or because of skillful planning and manipulation?

Describe the conflicts. Which conflict is central, and whom do the conflicts involve? Do they result from personality clashes or from situations? To what degree are they related to blocking activities? How does the action reach the crisis, and which characters are involved? What choices, decisions, plans, or conclusions become necessary? What events or revelations (of character, emotion, background) produce the catastrophe, and how do these affect characters, circumstances, and relationships?

In the comic resolution, to what extent are loose ends tied up and lives straightened out? Is reasonable order restored and regeneration assured or implied? Is the resolution satisfying? Disturbing? Does it leave you happy or thoughtful, or both? Are you amused by farce, pleased by romance, or disturbed by satire? If there is to be a marriage, whom will it bring together? What will the marriage settle, or whom will it divide? Most important, how can you account for your responses to the resolution and the play as a whole? How do they reflect the general aims of comedy?

CHARACTER. Which characters are realistic, conventional, round, flat, changing, standing still? Who is the protagonist or lover, the antagonist or blocking agent? Which characters seem excessive, eccentric, or irrational? What is the nature of their excesses? To what extent do the excesses define the characters? How do you respond to the excessive or exaggerated characters? Does the comedy provide a "cure" for the excesses? In other words, do the characters learn and change? If so, why and how? If not, why not?

From what classes are the characters derived? What class characteristics do you find? Who are the stock or stereotyped characters, and what is their significance to the protagonist? How does the playwright invigorate the characters? Who is the choric figure or *raisonneur,* if there is one? Who is the confidant? Which character or characters can be considered foils?

LANGUAGE. Does the language consist of witty turns of phrase, confusions, puns, misunderstandings, or a mixture? Which characters are masters of language, and which are mastered by it? Do characters use the same type of language and level of diction consistently? To what extent does language expose a character's self-interest or hypocrisy? If the language is witty and sparkling, what devices make it work effectively? If it is garbled and filled with misunderstandings, what types of errors does the playwright put into the characters' mouths? How does the language shape your response to characters, to ideas, and to the play as a whole?

Strategies for Organizing Ideas

To develop a central idea, isolate the feature you wish to explore and consider how it affects the shape and impact of the play. For *A Midsummer Night's Dream,* for example, you might focus on Puck's character and function. You might also develop a link between Puck's conventional role as a tricky servant with his love of mischief and the chaos he creates. Remember that it is difficult to develop essays from sentences like "Puck is a comic character" or "*The Bear* contains dramatic satire." A more focused assertion that also reveals your thematic development is necessary, such as "Puck, modeled on the tricky servant of Roman comedy, causes most of the play's confusion," or "*The Bear* satirizes the sentimentality of bereavement on the grounds that it ignores the need for getting on with life."

Organize your essay by grouping related types of details together (such as observations about characters, actions, direct statements, and specific words), and choose your own order of presentation. In writing about Puck as a tricky servant and creator of chaos, for example, you might present only one kind of detail—such as direct statements—and introduce these not in their order in the play but rather as they contribute to your analysis of Puck's character.

More often than not, your supporting details will represent a variety of types of evidence—dramatic dialogue and action, individual soliloquies, special properties (such as a love potion or a disguise), or the failure or development of various plans. For example, you might support an assertion about Puck by referring to his reputation, actions, and attitudes as though each of these is equally important. Other possible strategies are to demonstrate how the topics are related according to cause and effect, to build the topics from the least to the most significant, and to trace how a common idea or image provides unity. Whatever your method of development, be sure to validate your arguments with supporting details.

A summary of key points will make your conclusion useful and effective. In addition, you can show how your conclusions in the body of the essay bear upon larger aspects of the play's meaning.

SAMPLE STUDENT ESSAY

Setting as Symbol and Comic Structure in
A Midsummer Night's Dream°

[1]   Shakespeare's *A Midsummer Night's Dream* might superficially be considered light and inconsequential. The changes of mind undergone by the two sets of lovers, the placing of an ass's head on one of the characters, the presence of unrealistic fairies, the acting of a silly sketch--all seem far-fetched. But the play is real. It dramatizes the accidental and arbitrary origins of love, even though it considers this serious subject in the good-natured medium of comedy.* To bring out both message and merriment, Shakespeare uses two settings--the city of Athens and the nearby forest. The play's comic structure is governed by the movements between the order and the chaos that these two locations represent.†

[2]   At the play's beginning, Athens is presented as a world of daylight, order, and law. In this setting, Duke Theseus has absolute authority, fathers are always right, and the law permits Egeus to "dispose" of Hermia "either to this gentleman [Demetrius],/Or to her death" (Act I, scene 1, lines 43–44). The city is also the place for the exposition and the beginning of complications. Here, we meet the

° See pp. 1074–1128 for this play.
* Central idea.
† Thesis sentence.

various groups of characters (except the fairies), and we learn about the initial problem--namely that the relationship between Hermia and Lysander is blocked by a raging father, a rival suitor, and an old law. To flee and then to overcome these obstructions, Lysander asks Hermia to meet him in the woods. Her agreement begins a journey from Athens to the forest that ultimately includes everyone in the play--the four lovers, Egeus, the city rulers, and the "mechanicals."

[3]   The play's second setting, the woods outside Athens, is the kingdom of Oberon and Titania, the king and queen of the fairies. It is a world of darkness, moonlight, chaos, madness, and dreams, a world that symbolizes the power of imagination and passion. The disorder in this world has many sources, including Oberon's jealousy, Titania's infatuation, and Puck's delight in mischief. When the lovers and the mechanicals enter this setting, they also become disordered and chaotic.

[4]   The woods are the setting for complication, crisis, and catastrophe. Confusion dominates the action here. Puck disrupts the mechanicals' rehearsal and transforms Bottom into an ass-headed monster. More important, the passions of the lovers are rearranged and rearranged again by Oberon and Puck through the magic of "love-in-idleness," a flower that symbolizes love's irrational but overwhelming power. Although the first two adjustments of the lovers' feelings are done to help, each has the effect of raising the levels of complication and disorder. Puck gleefully observes that his actions are the cause of the play's confusions:

> those things do best please me
> That befall prepost'rously. (III.2, 120–121)

Puck is right; his first application of love-in-idleness causes Lysander to fall wildly in love with Helena, and his second does the same to Demetrius.

[5]   The crisis and dénouement of the main plot also occur in the woods. A crisis occurs when the two lovers challenge each other and the women attack each other. At this point, complication is at a peak, and the fairies must develop a plan to resolve the threats. Puck therefore misleads the lovers to end their potential duel, and he adjusts their emotions one more time. The dénouement--the revelation of the newly restored emotions--occurs the next morning at the edge of the woods, in the presence of Egeus, Theseus, and Hippolyta. Thus, it ends the confusing relationships occurring in the forest and begins the regularity of relationships in the orderly world of city and society.

[6]   Resolution--the marriages and the mechanicals' production of "Pyramus and Thisby"--occurs in the first setting, the city, which represents law and order. But the journey to the second setting has had a significant effect on the urban world both for Theseus and for the lovers. The law has been softened, Egeus overruled, the young lovers allowed to marry as they like, and lives set right. In the end, this second setting has also become the dream world of night and the supernatural, and the fairy dance and blessings closing the play only emphasize the harmony and the regenerative implications of the comic resolutions.

[7]   Setting, symbolism, and comic pattern thus combine in *A Midsummer Night's Dream* to produce an intricately plotted structure. Each element reinforces the others, bringing the play toward completion though time after time there seems to be no way out. The marvel of the play is that the two settings represent,

realistically, two opposed states of being, and, dramatically, two distinct stages of comic structure. The journey *out of* Athens, *into* the woods, and then *back to* the city is also a journey *from* exposition and adversity, *through* complication, crisis, and catastrophe, *to* comic resolution.

Commentary on the Essay

This essay deals with three elements of *A Midsummer Night's Dream:* setting, symbol, and comic structure. It demonstrates the way a number of different topics can be combined in a single essay. Consequently, the essay is organized to reflect the journey from the city to the woods and then back to the city.

The body of the essay takes up the settings, their symbolic meaning, and the relationship between setting and structure. Paragraph 2 deals with Athens both as a world of law and order and as the setting for exposition and the beginnings of complication. The supporting details include circumstance, actions, and dialogue.

Paragraphs 3–5 deal with the middle of the journey and of the play. Paragraph 3 discusses the symbolic implications of the forest setting, and paragraphs 4 and 5 take up the connection between the setting and comic structure, specifically complication, crisis, and catastrophe. Again, the supporting details in these paragraphs are a mixture of actions, circumstances, and direct quotations.

Paragraph 6 deals briefly with the return to the city, linking this setting with the play's comic resolution. The concluding paragraph returns to the idea about how *A Midsummer Night's Dream* connects setting, symbol, and comic pattern.

SPECIAL WRITING TOPICS FOR CONSIDERING COMEDY

1. Write an essay describing Shakespeare's comic technique in *A Midsummer Night's Dream.* Consider these questions: Is the basic situation serious? How does Shakespeare keep it comic? How does the boisterousness of the low characters influence your perceptions of the lovers and the courtly characters? Would the play be as interesting without Bottom and his crowd, and without the fairies and their involvement? How does the comic outcome depend on the boisterousness and colorfulness provided by the players and the fairies? For research on Shakespeare as a comic dramatist, you might wish to consult Henry B. Charlton's classic study *Shakespeare's Comedies* (rpt. 1972) and/or a more recent book by Michael Mangan, *A Preface to Shakespeare's Comedies* (1996).

2. Write an essay that analyzes the relationship of situation to comedy in *Am I Blue.* How do the eccentricity of the characters and the improbability of their circumstances produce amusement? When you finish the play, do you believe that you have been seriously engaged? Simply entertained? Explain. For comparison with other Henley plays, you might wish to take out Beth Henley's *Beth Henley: Four Plays* (1992) from your college library.

3. *The Bear* is one of Chekhov's most popular plays. Read another Chekhov play (for example, *The Cherry Orchard, The Seagull, Three Sisters, Uncle Vanya*) and compare it to *The Bear* (characters with characters, dialogue with dialogue,

situations with situations, and so on). In light of your comparison, write an essay in which you explain and justify the continued popularity of *The Bear*.

4. Treat the lovers in *A Midsummer Night's Dream* and *The Bear* as types or archetypes (see Chapter 27). What is their situation? What problems block the fulfillment of their love? How serious are these problems? What actions and ruses do they plan to make things right? How are the pairs of lovers in the two plays similar? Different?

5. Write a comic scene of your own between two people, perhaps between a boy and a girl, as in *Am I Blue*, or between a father and daughter, as in *A Midsummer Night's Dream*, or between a person under a spell and a person in normal touch with reality, also as in *A Midsummer Night's Dream*. When you've finished, write a short essay explaining the principles on which you've written your scene, such as the reasons for your choice of material, your use of jokes (if any), straightforward dialogue, anger, outrage, amused responses, and so on.

6. Write an essay about the nature of comedy, using *A Midsummer Night's Dream*, *Am I Blue*, and *The Bear* as material. Deal with issues like the following: How can comic material be defined? Does the happy outcome of a serious action qualify a play as a comedy, or should no action be serious ? When does a play stop being comic and start being tragic? Are jokes necessary? Is farcical action necessary? Where are the edges between comedy and farce, on the one hand, and comedy and tragedy on the other? For a research component for this topic, you might wish to introduce materials from books by Wylie Sypher (1956, rpt. 1982, an edition of two classic essays on the comic), G. S. Amur (1963), Robert Corrigan (1965), Robert B. Heilman (1978), T. G. A. Nelson (1990), Athene Seyler (1990), Frances Teague (1994), and Janet Suzman (1995).

25

Plays for Additional Study

HENRIK IBSEN, *A DOLLHOUSE*

The Norwegian playwright Henrik Johan Ibsen (1828–1906) is the acknowledged originator—the "father"—of modern drama. He deserves this recognition because of his pioneering selections of challenging and sometime shocking private and public issues. Today there are few restrictions on dramatists except success at the box office. Plays may range freely on almost any subject, such as the drug culture, sexual perversity, the right to commit suicide, the problems of real-estate dealers, the life of a go-go dancer, violence, family dissension, homosexuality, and the Vietnam war. If one includes film as drama, there is virtually no limit to the topics that dramatists can explore. It is well to stress that dramatists have not always been this free, and that Ibsen was in the forefront of the struggle for free dramatic expression. A brief consideration of some of his major dramatic topics shows his originality and daring: the blinding and crippling effects of congenital syphilis, a woman's renunciation of a traditional protective marriage, suicide, the manipulations of people seeking personal benefits, the sacrifices of pursuing truth, the rejection of a child by a parent, and the abandonment of personal happiness in favor of professional interests.

Ibsen's Life and Early Work

From Ibsen's beginnings, there was little to indicate how important he was to become. He was born in Skien (*shee-en*), Norway, a small town just seventy miles southwest of the capital, Christiana (now Oslo). Although his parents had been prosperous, they went bankrupt when he was only seven, and afterward the family struggled against poverty. When Ibsen was fifteen he was apprenticed to a pharmacist, and he seemed headed for a career in this profession even though he hated it. By 1849, however, when he wrote *Catiline*, his first play in verse, it was clear that the theater was to be his life. Largely through the efforts of the famous violinist Ole Bull, a new National Theater had been established in Bergen, and Ibsen was appointed its director. He stayed in Bergen for six years and then went to Christiana, where for the next five years he tried to fashion a genuine Norwegian national theater. His attempts proved fruitless, for the theater went bankrupt in 1862. After writing *The Pretenders* in 1864, he secured enough governmental travel money to enable him to leave Norway. For the next twenty-seven years he lived in Germany and Italy in what has been called a "self-imposed" exile.

Although this first part of Ibsen's theatrical career was devoted to many practical matters—production, management, directing, and finances—he was also constantly writing. His early plays were in verse and were mainly nationalist and romantic, as a few representative titles suggest: *Lady Inger of Oestraat* (1855), *The Feast of Solhaug* (1856), *Olaf Liljekrans* (1857). In his first ten years in Germany and Italy he finished four plays. The best known of these is *Peer Gynt* (1867), a fantasy play about a historical Norwegian hero, Peer Gynt, who is saved from spiritual emptiness by the love of the patient heroine Solveig. Today, *Peer Gynt* is best known because of the incidental music written for it by Norway's major composer, Edvard Grieg (1843–1907). Ibsen asked Grieg to compose the music for the initial performances in 1876. Grieg's response was enthusiastic and creative, and the result is enjoyed today by millions. Ibsen also supplied the poem for which Grieg composed one of his loveliest songs, "A Swan."

Ibsen's Prose "Problem" Plays

During the years when Ibsen was fighting poverty and establishing his career in the theater, Europe was undergoing great political and intellectual changes. Throughout the nineteenth century, Ibsen's home country, Norway, was trying to release itself from the domination of neighboring Sweden and to establish its own territorial and national integrity. In Ibsen's twentieth year, 1848, the "February Uprising" in Paris resulted in the deposition of the French king and the establishment of a new French republic. This same year also saw the publication of the *Communist Manifesto* of Karl Marx (1818–1883). In 1864, the year Ibsen left Norway, Marx's first socialist International was held in London. In addition, during the time Ibsen lived in Italy and Germany, both countries were going through the tenuous political processes of becoming true nation-states. In short, change was everywhere.

Ibsen also was changing and growing as a thinker and dramatist, driven by the idea that a forward and creative drama could bring about deeper and more permanent changes than could be effected by soldiers and politicians. Toward this end he developed the realistic *problem play*. Such a play posited a major personal, social, professional, or political problem that occasioned the play's dramatic conflicts and tensions. Each problem was timely, topical, and realistic, as were the characters, places, situations, and outcomes. In this vein Ibsen wrote the twelve prose plays on which his reputation rests: *The Pillars of Society* (1877), *A Dollhouse* (1879), *Ghosts* (1881), *An Enemy of the People* (1882), *The Wild Duck* (1884), *Rosmersholm* (1886), *The Lady from the Sea* (1888), *Hedda Gabler* (1890), *The Master Builder* (1892), *Little Eyolf* (1894), *John Gabriel Borkman* (1896), and *When We Dead Awaken* (1899). He finished the first eight of these plays while living in Germany and Italy, the last four after returning to Norway in 1891.

In these major plays Ibsen dramatizes human beings breaking free from restrictions and inhibitions and trying to establish their individuality and freedom—freedom of self, inquiry, pursuit of truth, artistic dedication, and, above all, the freedom of love. In attempting to achieve these goals, Ibsen's dramatic characters find internal opposition in self-interest, self-indulgence, and self-denial, and external opposition in the personal and political influences and manipulations of others. Because the plays are designed to be realistic, Ibsen's characters fall short of their goals. At best they achieve a respite in their combat, as in *An Enemy of the People*, or begin a quest in new directions, as in *A Dollhouse*. They always make great sacrifices, sometimes losing life itself, as in *Hedda Gabler* and *John Gabriel Borkman*.

A Dollhouse: *One of Ibsen's Realistic Problem Plays*

A Dollhouse (*Et Dukkehjem*, 1879)[1] is representative of Ibsen's realistic drama. Its scenes are realistic, including appropriate furniture, a piano, a Christmas tree, carpeting, and wall engravings. Its characters are realistically confronting overwhelming personal, marital, and economic problems. Realism extends also to the technique of presentation, particularly the exposition about the root causes of the problems that come to a head in the play itself. As *A Dollhouse* unfolds, we learn that years earlier, Nora Helmer had extended herself beyond her means to save Torvald from a near-fatal illness. We also learn that there had been an earlier relationship between Krogstad and Christine Linde.

IBSEN'S SYMBOLISM.   *A Dollhouse* is representative of Ibsen's realism, but it is also replete with contextual symbolism, like the major plays which came before and after it. At the end of the late play *John Gabriel Borkman*, for example, the major character freezes to death, an occurrence symbolic of what he had done to himself much earlier by denying love. In reference to *A Dollhouse*, the title

---

[1]Ibsen's title *Et Dukkehjem* literally means the home (*hjem*) of a doll or puppet (*dukke*). *A Doll's House*, the traditional and most common English title of the play, is not an accurate rendering of *dukkehjem*, and, in addition, it is misleading because of some of the connotations of our word *doll*. Recent translators have used *A Doll House* as the title, but this form is not in regular use. Our English word for a toy house for dolls is listed in collegiate dictionaries as *dollhouse*, a one-word compound. *A Dollhouse* is therefore preferable to the other two titles because it accurately renders *Et Dukkehjem*, and it is also the form accepted in current dictionaries.

itself symbolizes the dependent and dehumanized role of the wife within traditional middle-class marriages. (The Norwegian-Danish word for *doll* [*dukke*] may also mean "puppet" or "marionette.") In addition, the entire nation of Norway (cold, legal, male) is contrasted symbolically with Italy (warm, emotional, female). Ironically, the break in the Helmers' marriage is symbolically aligned with events that occur or have occurred in both locations. Other symbols in *A Dollhouse* are the Christmas tree, the children's presents, the death of Dr. Rank, and the mailbox.

Ibsen and the "Well-Made Play"

The plot and structure of *A Dollhouse* show Ibsen's use of the conventions of the **well-made play** (*la pièce bien faite*), a form developed and popularized in nineteenth-century France by Eugène Scribe (1791–1861) and Victorien Sardou (1831–1908). Ibsen was familiar with well-made plays, having directed many of them himself at Bergen and Christiana (Oslo). The well-made play follows a rigid and efficient structure in which the drama begins at the story's climax. Usually the plot is built on a secret known by the audience and perhaps one or two of the characters. The well-made play thus begins in suspense and offers a pattern of increasing tension produced through exposition and the timely arrivals of new characters (like Krogstad) and threatening news or props like the disclosure of Nora's earlier financial transactions. In the course of action of the well-made play, the fortunes of the protagonist go from a low point, through a *peripeteia* or reversal (Aristotle's concept), to a high point at which the protagonist confronts and defeats the villain.

Although Ibsen makes use of many of the structural elements of the well-made play, he varies and departs from the pattern to suit his realistic purposes. Thus in *A Dollhouse* his variation is that Nora's confrontation with Krogstad, who is the apparent villain, does not lead to a satisfactory resolution, but rather precipitates the more significant albeit intractable confrontation with her husband. In *A Dollhouse*, just as in many other Ibsen plays, there is not a traditionally well-made victorious outcome; rather there are provisional outcomes—adjustments—in keeping with the realistic concept that as life goes on, problems continue.

Ibsen's Timeliness and Dramatic Power

Ibsen's focus on real-life issues has given his plays continued timeliness and strength. *A Dollhouse*, for example, is almost prophetic in its portrayal of the helpless position of married women in the nineteenth century. Most notably, a woman could not borrow funds without a man's cosignature, and Nora had been forced to violate the law to obtain the money to restore her husband's health. The mailbox, to which Torvald has the only key, symbolizes this limitation, and the ultimate disclosure of the box's contents, rather than freeing Nora and Torvald, highlights her dependency. Today's feminism has stressed the issues of female freedom and equality, together with many other issues vital to women, but the need for feminine individuality and independence has not been more originally and forcefully dramatized than in *A Dollhouse.*

HENRIK IBSEN   (1828–1906)

A Dollhouse (Et Dukkehjem) ————————————————————— *1879*

Translated by R. Farquharson Sharp

CHARACTERS

> Torvald Helmer, *a lawyer and bank manager*
> Nora, *his wife*
> Doctor Rank
> Mrs. Christine Linde
> Nils Krogstad, *a lawyer and bank clerk*
> Ivar, Bob, *and* Emmy, the Helmers' *three young children*
> Anne, *their nurse*
> Helen, *a housemaid*
> A Porter

> *The action takes place in* HELMER'S *apartment.*

ACT 1

SCENE. *A room furnished comfortably and tastefully, but not extravagantly. At the back, a door to the right leads to the entrance hall, another to the left leads to* HELMER'S *study. Between the doors stands a piano. In the middle of the left-hand wall is a door, and beyond it a window. Near the window are a round table, armchairs and a small sofa. In the right-hand wall, at the farther end, another door; and on the same side, nearer the footlights, a stove, two easy chairs and a rocking-chair; between the stove and the door, a small table. Engravings on the walls; a cabinet with china and other small objects; a small book-case with well-bound books. The floors are carpeted, and a fire burns in the stove. It is winter.*

> *A bell rings in the hall; shortly afterwards the door is heard to open. Enter* NORA, *humming a tune and in high spirits. She is in outdoor dress and carries a number of parcels; these she lays on the table to the right. She leaves the outer door open after her, and through it is seen a* PORTER *who is carrying a Christmas Tree and a basket, which he gives to the* MAID *who has opened the door.*

NORA.   Hide the Christmas Tree carefully, Helen. Be sure the children do not see it till this evening, when it is dressed. [*to the* PORTER, *taking out her purse.*] How much?

PORTER.   Sixpence.

NORA.   There is a shilling. No, keep the change. [*The* PORTER *thanks her, and goes out.* NORA *shuts the door. She is laughing to herself, as she takes off her hat and coat. She takes a packet of macaroons from her pocket and eats one or two; then goes cautiously to her husband's door and listens.*] Yes, he is in.

[*Still humming, she goes to the table on the right.*]

HELMER. [*calls out from his room*] Is that my little lark twittering out there?

NORA. [*busy opening some of the parcels*] Yes, it is! 5

HELMER. Is my little squirrel bustling about?

NORA. Yes!

HELMER. When did my squirrel come home?

NORA. Just now. [*puts the bag of macaroons into her pocket and wipes her mouth.*] Come in here, Torvald, and see what I have bought.

HELMER. Don't disturb me. [*A little later, he opens the door and looks into the room, pen* 10 *in hand.*] Bought, did you say? All these things? Has my little spendthrift been wasting money again?

NORA. Yes, but, Torvald, this year we really can let ourselves go a little. This is the first Christmas that we have not needed to economise.

HELMER. Still, you know, we can't spend money recklessly.

NORA. Yes, Torvald, we may be a wee bit more reckless now, mayn't we? Just a tiny wee bit! You are going to have a big salary and earn lots and lots of money.

HELMER. Yes, after the New Year; but then it will be a whole quarter before the salary is due.

NORA. Pooh! we can borrow till then. 15

HELMER. Nora! [*goes up to her and takes her playfully by the ear.*] The same little featherhead! Suppose, now, that I borrowed fifty pounds to-day, and you spent it all in the Christmas week, and then on New Year's Eve a slate fell on my head and killed me, and—

NORA. [*putting her hands over his mouth*] Oh! don't say such horrid things.

HELMER. Still, suppose that happened—what then?

NORA. If that were to happen, I don't suppose I should care whether I owed money or not.

HELMER. Yes, but what about the people who had lent it? 20

NORA. They? Who would bother about them? I should not know who they were.

HELMER. That is like a woman! But seriously, Nora, you know what I think about that. No debt, no borrowing. There can be no freedom or beauty about a home life that depends on borrowing and debt. We two have kept bravely on the straight road so far, and we will go on the same way for the short time longer that there need be any struggle.

NORA. [*moving towards the stove*] As you please, Torvald.

HELMER. [*following her*] Come, come, my little skylark must not droop her wings. What is this! Is my little squirrel out of temper? [*taking out his purse.*] Nora, what do you think I have got here?

NORA. [*turning around quickly*] Money! 25

HELMER. There you are. [*gives her some money*] Do you think I don't know what a lot is wanted for housekeeping at Christmas-time?

NORA. [*counting*] Ten shillings—a pound—two pounds! Thank you, thank you, Torvald; that will keep me going for a long time.

HELMER. Indeed it must.

NORA. Yes, yes, it will. But come here and let me show you what I have bought. And all so cheap! Look, here is a new suit for Ivar, and a sword; and a horse and a trumpet for Bob; and a doll and dolly's bedstead for Emmy—they are very plain, but anyway she will soon break them in pieces. And here are dress-lengths and handkerchiefs for the maids; old Anne ought really to have something better.

HELMER. And what is in this parcel? 30

NORA. [*crying out*] No, no! you mustn't see that till this evening.

HELMER.   Very well. But now tell me, you extravagant little person, what would you like for yourself?

NORA.   For myself? Oh, I am sure I don't want anything.

HELMER.   Yes, but you must. Tell me something reasonable that you would particularly like to have.

NORA.   No, I really can't think of anything—unless, Torvald—   35

HELMER.   Well?

NORA.   [*playing with his coat buttons, and without raising her eyes to his*] If you really want to give me something, you might—you might—

HELMER.   Well, out with it!

NORA.   [*speaking quickly*] You might give me money, Torvald. Only just as much as you can afford; and then one of these days I will buy something with it.

HELMER.   But, Nora—   40

NORA.   Oh, do! dear Torvald; please, please do! Then I will wrap it up in beautiful gilt paper and hang it on the Christmas Tree. Wouldn't that be fun?

HELMER.   What are little people called that are always wasting money?

NORA.   Spendthrifts—I know. Let us do as you suggest, Torvald, and then I shall have time to think what I am most in want of. That is a very sensible plan, isn't it?

HELMER.   [*smiling*] Indeed it is—that is to say, if you were really to save out of the money I give you, and then really buy something for yourself. But if you spend it all on the housekeeping and any number of unnecessary things, then I merely have to pay up again.

NORA.   Oh but, Torvald—   45

HELMER.   You can't deny it, my dear little Nora. [*puts his arm round her waist*] It's a sweet little spendthrift, but she uses up a deal of money. One would hardly believe how expensive such little persons are!

NORA.   It's a shame to say that. I do really save all I can.

HELMER.   [*laughing*] That's very true—all you can. But you can't save anything!

NORA.   [*smiling quietly and happily*] You haven't any idea how many expenses we skylarks and squirrels have, Torvald.

HELMER.   You are an odd little soul. Very like your father. You always find some   50
new way of wheedling money out of me, and, as soon as you have got it, it seems to melt in your hands. You never know where it has gone. Still, one must take you as you are. It is in the blood; for indeed it is true that you can inherit these things, Nora.

NORA.   Ah, I wish I had inherited many of papa's qualities.

HELMER.   And I would not wish you to be anything but just what you are, my sweet little skylark. But, do you know, it strikes me that you are looking rather—what shall I say—rather uneasy to-day?

NORA.   Do I?

HELMER.   You do, really. Look straight at me.

NORA.   [*looks at him*] Well?   55

HELMER.   [*wagging his finger at her*] Hasn't Miss Sweet-Tooth been breaking rules in town to-day?

NORA.   No; what makes you think that?

HELMER.   Hasn't she paid a visit to the confectioner's?

NORA.   No, I assure you, Torvald—

HELMER.   Not been nibbling sweets?   60

NORA.   No, certainly not.

HELMER.   Not even taken a bite at a macaroon or two?

NORA.   No, Torvald, I assure you really—

HELMER.   There, there, of course I was only joking.

NORA.   [*going to the table on the right*] I should not think of going against your   65
wishes.

HELMER.   No, I am sure of that! besides, you gave me your word—[*going up to
her*] Keep your little Christmas secrets to yourself, my darling. They will all be revealed tonight when the Christmas Tree is lit, no doubt.

NORA.   Did you remember to invite Doctor Rank?

HELMER.   No. But there is no need; as a matter of course he will come to dinner
with us. However, I will ask him when he comes in this morning. I have ordered some
good wine. Nora, you can't think how I am looking forward to this evening.

NORA.   So am I! And how the children will enjoy themselves, Torvald!

HELMER.   It is splendid to feel that one has a perfectly safe appointment, and a   70
big enough income. It's delightful to think of, isn't it?

NORA.   It's wonderful!

HELMER.   Do you remember last Christmas? For a full three weeks beforehand
you shut yourself up every evening till long after midnight, making ornaments for the
Christmas Tree and all the other fine things that were to be a surprise to us. It was the
dullest three weeks I ever spent!

NORA.   I didn't find it dull.

HELMER.   [*smiling*] But there was precious little result, Nora.

NORA.   Oh, you shouldn't tease me about that again. How could I help the cat's   75
going in and tearing everything to pieces?

HELMER.   Of course you couldn't, poor little girl. You had the best of intentions
to please us all, and that's the main thing. But it is a good thing that our hard times are
over.

NORA.   Yes, it is really wonderful.

HELMER.   This time I needn't sit here and be dull all alone, and you needn't ruin
your dear eyes and your pretty little hands—

NORA.   [*clapping her hands*] No, Torvald, I needn't any longer, need I! It's wonderfully lovely to hear you say so! [*taking his arm*] Now I will tell you how I have been thinking we ought to arrange things, Torvald. As soon as Christmas is over—[*A bell rings in the
hall.*] There's the bell. [*She tidies the room a little.*] There's someone at the door. What a
nuisance!

HELMER.   If it is a caller, remember I am not at home.   80

MAID.   [*in the doorway*] A lady to see you, ma'am—a stranger.

NORA.   Ask her to come in.

MAID.   [*to HELMER*] The doctor came at the same time, sir.

HELMER.   Did he go straight into my room?

MAID.   Yes sir.   85

[*HELMER goes into his room. The MAID ushers in MRS. LINDE, who is in travelling dress, and
shuts the door.*]

MRS. LINDE.   [*in a dejected and timid voice*] How do you do, Nora?

NORA.   [*doubtfully*] How do you do—

MRS. LINDE.   You don't recognise me, I suppose.

NORA.   No, I don't know—yes, to be sure, I seem to—[*suddenly*] Yes! Christine! Is it really you?

MRS. LINDE.   Yes, it is I.   90

NORA.   Christine! To think of my not recognising you! And yet how could I—[*in a gentle voice*] How you have altered, Christine!

MRS. LINDE.   Yes, I have indeed. In nine, ten long years—

NORA.   Is it so long since we met? I suppose it is. The last eight years have been a happy time for me, I can tell you. And so now you have come into the town, and have taken this long journey in winter—that was plucky of you.

MRS. LINDE.   I arrived by steamer this morning.

NORA.   To have some fun at Christmas-time, of course. How delightful! We will   95
have such fun together! But take off your things. You are not cold, I hope. [*helps her*] Now we will sit down by the stove, and be cosy. No, take this arm-chair; I will sit here in the rocking-chair. [*takes her hands*] Now you look like your old self again; it was only the first moment—You are a little paler, Christine, and perhaps a little thinner.

MRS. LINDE.   And much, much older, Nora.

NORA.   Perhaps a little older; very, very little; certainly not much. [*stops suddenly and speaks seriously*] What a thoughtless creature I am, chattering away like this. My poor, dear Christine, do forgive me.

MRS. LINDE.   What do you mean, Nora?

NORA.   [*gently*] Poor Christine, you are a widow.

MRS. LINDE.   Yes; it is three years ago now.   100

NORA.   Yes, I knew; I saw it in the papers. I assure you, Christine, I meant ever so often to write to you at the time, but I always put it off and something always prevented me.

MRS. LINDE.   I quite understand, dear.

NORA.   It was very bad of me, Christine. Poor thing, how you must have suffered. And he left you nothing?

MRS. LINDE.   No.

NORA.   And no children?   105

MRS. LINDE.   No.

NORA.   Nothing at all, then?

MRS. LINDE.   Not even any sorrow or grief to live upon.

NORA.   [*looking incredulously at her*] But, Christine, is that possible?

MRS. LINDE.   [*smiles sadly and strokes her hair*] It sometimes happens, Nora.   110

NORA.   So you are quite alone. How dreadfully sad that must be. I have three lovely children. You can't see them just now, for they are out with their nurse. But now you must tell me all about it.

MRS. LINDE.   No, no; I want to hear you.

NORA.   No, you must begin. I mustn't be selfish to-day; to-day I must only think of your affairs. But there is one thing I must tell you. Do you know we have just had a great piece of good luck?

MRS. LINDE.   No, what is it?

NORA.   Just fancy, my husband has been made manager of the Bank!   115

MRS. LINDE.   Your husband? What good luck!

NORA.   Yes, tremendous! A barrister's profession is such an uncertain thing, especially if he won't undertake unsavoury cases; and naturally Torvald has never been willing to do that, and I quite agree with him. You may imagine how pleased we are! He is to take up his work in the Bank at the New Year, and then he will have a big salary and lots of commissions. For the future we can live quite differently—we can do just as we like. I feel so relieved and so happy, Christine! It will be splendid to have heaps of money and not need to have any anxiety, won't it?

MRS. LINDE.   Yes, anyhow I think it would be delightful to have what one needs.

NORA.   No, not only what one needs, but heaps and heaps of money.

MRS. LINDE.   [*smiling*] Nora, Nora haven't you learnt sense yet? In our schooldays   120
you were a great spendthrift.

NORA.   [*laughing*] Yes, that is what Torvald says now. [*wags her finger at her*] But "Nora, Nora" is not so silly as you think. We have not been in a position for me to waste money. We have both had to work.

MRS. LINDE.   You too?

NORA.   Yes; odds and ends, needlework, crochet-work, embroidery, and that kind of thing. [*dropping her voice*] And other things as well. You know Torvald left his office when we were married? There was no prospect of promotion there, and he had to try and earn more than before. But during the first year he overworked himself dreadfully. You see, he had to make money every way he could, and he worked early and late; but he couldn't stand it, and fell dreadfully ill, and the doctors said it was necessary for him to go south.

MRS. LINDE.   You spent a whole year in Italy didn't you?

NORA.   Yes. It was no easy matter to get away, I can tell you. It was just after Ivar   125
was born; but naturally we had to go. It was a wonderfully beautiful journey, and it saved Torvald's life. But it cost a tremendous lot of money, Christine.

MRS. LINDE.   So I should think.

NORA.   It cost about two hundred and fifty pounds. That's a lot, isn't it?

MRS. LINDE.   Yes, and in emergencies like that it is lucky to have the money.

NORA.   I ought to tell you that we had it from papa.

MRS. LINDE.   Oh, I see. It was just about that time that he died, wasn't it?   130

NORA.   Yes; and, just think of it, I couldn't go and nurse him. I was expecting little Ivar's birth every day and I had my poor sick Torvald to look after. My dear, kind father—I never saw him again, Christine. That was the saddest time I have known since our marriage.

MRS. LINDE.   I know how fond you were of him. And then you went off to Italy?

NORA.   Yes; you see we had money then, and the doctors insisted on our going, so we started a month later.

MRS. LINDE.   And your husband came back quite well?

NORA.   As sound as a bell!   135

MRS. LINDE.   But—the doctor?

NORA.   What doctor?

MRS. LINDE.   I thought your maid said the gentleman who arrived here just as I did was the doctor?

NORA.   Yes, that was Doctor Rank, but he doesn't come here professionally. He is our greatest friend, and comes in at least once every day. No, Torvald has not had an hour's illness since then, and our children are strong and healthy and so am I. [*jumps up and claps her hands*] Christine! Christine! it's good to be alive and happy!—But how horrid of me; I am talking of nothing but my own affairs. [*Sits on a stool near her, and rests her arms on her knees*] You mustn't be angry with me. Tell me, is it really true that you did not love your husband? Why did you marry him?

MRS. LINDE.   My mother was alive then, and was bedridden and helpless, and I   140
had to provide for my two younger brothers; so I did not think I was justified in refusing his offer.

NORA.   No, perhaps you were quite right. He was rich at that time, then?

MRS. LINDE.   I believe he was quite well off. But his business was a precarious one; and, when he died, it all went to pieces and there was nothing left.

NORA.   And then?—

MRS. LINDE.   Well, I had to turn my hand to anything I could find—first a small shop, then a small school, and so on. The last three years have seemed like one long working-day, with no rest. Now it is at an end, Nora. My poor mother needs me no more, for she is gone; and the boys do not need me either; they have got situations and can shift for themselves.

NORA.   What a relief you must feel it—   145

MRS. LINDE.   No, indeed; I only feel my life unspeakably empty. No one to live for any more. [*gets up restlessly*] That was why I could not stand the life in my little back-water any longer. I hope it may be easier here to find something which will busy me and occupy my thoughts. If only I could have the good luck to get some regular work—office work of some kind—

NORA.   But, Christine, that is so frightfully tiring, and you look tired out now. You had far better go away to some watering-place.

MRS. LINDE.   [*walking to the window*] I have no father to give me money for a journey, Nora.

NORA.   [*rising*] Oh, don't be angry with me.

MRS. LINDE.   [*going up to her*] It is you that must not be angry with me, dear. The   150 worst of a position like mine is that it makes one so bitter. No one to work for, and yet obliged to be always on the look-out for chances. One must live, and so one becomes selfish. When you told me of the happy turn your fortunes have taken—you will hardly believe it—I was delighted not so much on your account as on my own.

NORA.   How do you mean?—Oh, I understand. You mean that perhaps Torvald could get you something to do.

MRS. LINDE.   Yes, that was what I was thinking of.

NORA.   He must, Christine. Just leave it to me; I will broach the subject very cleverly—I will think of something that will please him very much. It will make me so happy to be of some use to you.

MRS. LINDE.   How kind you are, Nora, to be so anxious to help me! It is doubly kind in you, for you know so little of the burdens and troubles of life.

NORA.   I—? I know so little of them?   155

MRS. LINDE.   [*smiling*] My dear! Small household cares and that sort of thing!— You are a child, Nora.

NORA.   [*tosses her head and crosses the stage*] You ought not to be so superior.

MRS. LINDE.   No?

NORA.   You are just like the others. They all think that I am incapable of anything really serious—

MRS. LINDE.   Come, come—   160

NORA.   —that I have gone through nothing in this world of cares.

MRS. LINDE.   But, my dear Nora, you have just told me all your troubles.

NORA.   Pooh!—those were trifles. [*lowering her voice*] I have not told you the important thing.

MRS. LINDE.   The important thing? What do you mean?

NORA.   You look down upon me altogether, Christine—but you ought not to. You   165 are proud, aren't you, of having worked so hard and so long for your mother?

MRS. LINDE.   Indeed, I don't look down on any one. But it is true that I am both proud and glad to think that I was privileged to make the end of my mother's life almost free from care.

NORA.   And you are proud to think of what you have done for your brothers.

MRS. LINDE.   I think I have the right to be.

NORA.   I think so, too. But now, listen to this; I too have something to be proud of and glad of.

MRS. LINDE.   I have no doubt you have. But what do you refer to?   170

NORA.   Speak low. Suppose Torvald were to hear! He mustn't on any account—no one in the world must know, Christine, except you.

MRS. LINDE.   But what is it?

NORA.   Come here. [*pulls her down on the sofa beside her*] Now I will show you that I too have something to be proud and glad of. It was I who saved Torvald's life.

MRS. LINDE.   "Saved"? How?

NORA.   I told you about our trip to Italy. Torvald would never have recovered if   175
he had not gone there—

MRS. LINDE.   Yes, but your father gave you the necessary funds.

NORA.   [*smiling*] Yes, that is what Torvald and all the others think, but—

MRS. LINDE.   But—

NORA.   Papa didn't give us a shilling. It was I who procured the money.

MR. LINDE.   You? All that large sum?   180

NORA.   Two hundred and fifty pounds. What do you think of that?

MRS. LINDE.   But, Nora, how could you possibly do it? Did you win a prize in the Lottery?

NORA.   [*contemptuously*] In the Lottery? There would have been no credit in that.

MRS. LINDE.   But where did you get it from, then?

NORA.   [*humming and smiling with an air of mystery*] Hm, hm! Aha!   185

MRS. LINDE.   Because you couldn't have borrowed it.

NORA.   Couldn't I? Why not?

MRS. LINDE.   No, a wife cannot borrow without her husband's consent.

NORA.   [*tossing her head*] Oh, if it is a wife who has any head for business—a wife who has the wit to be a little bit clever—

MRS. LINDE.   I don't understand it at all, Nora.   190

NORA.   There is no need you should. I never said I had borrowed the money. I may have got it some other way. [*lies back on the sofa*] Perhaps I got it from some other admirer. When anyone is as attractive as I am—

MRS. LINDE.   You are a mad creature.

NORA.   Now, you know you're full of curiosity, Christine.

MRS. LINDE.   Listen to me, Nora dear. Haven't you been a little bit imprudent?

NORA.   [*sits up straight*] Is it imprudent to save your husband's life?   195

MRS. LINDE.   It seems to me imprudent, without his knowledge, to—

NORA.   But it was absolutely necessary that he should not know! My goodness, can't you understand that? It was necessary he should have no idea what a dangerous condition he was in. It was to me that the doctors came and said that his life was in danger, and that the only thing to save him was to live in the south. Do you suppose I didn't try, first of all, to get what I wanted as if it were for myself? I told him how much I should love to travel abroad like other young wives; I tried tears and entreaties with him; I told him that he ought to remember the condition I was in, and that he ought to be kind and indulgent to me; I even hinted that he might raise a loan. That nearly made him angry, Christine. He said I was thoughtless, and that it was his duty as my husband not to indulge me in my whims and caprices—as I believe he called them. Very well I thought, you must be saved—and that was how I came to devise a way out of the difficulty—

MRS. LINDE.   And did your husband never get to know from your father that the money had not come from him?

NORA.   No, never. Papa died just at that time. I had meant to let him into the secret and beg him never to reveal it. But he was so ill then—alas, there never was any need to tell him.

MRS. LINDE.   And since then have you never told your secret to your husband?   200

NORA.   Good Heavens, no! How could you think so? A man who has such strong opinions about these things! And besides, how painful and humiliating it would be for Torvald, with his manly independence, to know that he owed me anything! It would upset our mutual relations altogether; our beautiful happy home would no longer be what it is now.

MRS. LINDE.   Do you mean never to tell him about it?

NORA.   [*meditatively, and with a half smile*] Yes—some day, perhaps, after many years, when I am no longer as nice-looking as I am now. Don't laugh at me! I mean of course, when Torvald is no longer as devoted to me as he is now; when my dancing and dressing-up and reciting have palled on him; then it may be a good thing to have something in reserve—[*breaking off*] What nonsense! That time will never come. Now, what do you think of my great secret, Christine? Do you still think I am of no use? I can tell you, too, that this affair has caused me a lot of worry. It has been by no means easy for me to meet my engagements punctually. I may tell you that there is something that is called, in business, quarterly interest, and another thing called payment in instalments, and it is always so dreadfully difficult to manage them. I have had to save a little here and there, where I could, you understand. I have not been able to put aside much from my house-keeping money, for Torvald must have a good table. I couldn't let my children be shabbily dressed; I have felt obliged to use up all he gave me for them, the sweet little darlings!

MRS. LINDE.   So it has all had to come out of your own necessaries of life, poor Nora?

NORA.   Of course. Besides, I was the one responsible for it. Whenever Torvald   205
has given me the money for new dresses and such things, I have never spent more than half of it; I have always bought the simplest and cheapest things. Thank Heaven, any clothes look well on me, and so Torvald has never noticed it. But it was often very hard on me, Christine—because it is delightful to be really well dressed, isn't it?

MRS. LINDE.   Quite so.

NORA.   Well, then I have found other ways of earning money. Last winter I was lucky enough to get a lot of copying to do; so I locked myself up and sat writing every evening until quite late at night. Many a time I was desperately tired; but all the same it was a tremendous pleasure to sit there working and earning money. It was like being a man.

MRS. LINDE.   How much have you been able to pay off in that way?

NORA.   I can't tell you exactly. You see, it is very difficult to keep an account of a business matter of that kind. I only know that I have paid every penny that I could scrape together. Many a time I was at my wits' end. [*smiles*] Then I used to sit here and imagine that a rich old gentleman had fallen in love with me—

MRS. LINDE.   What! Who was it?   210

NORA.   Be quiet!—that he had died; and that when his will was opened it contained, written in big letters, the instruction: "The lovely Mrs. Nora Helmer is to have all I possess paid over to her at once in cash."

MRS. LINDE.   But, my dear Nora—who could the man be?

NORA.   Good gracious, can't you understand? There was no old gentleman at all; it was only something that I used to sit here and imagine, when I couldn't think of any way of procuring money. But it's all the same now; the tiresome old person can stay where he is, as far as I am concerned; I don't care about him or his will either, for I am free from care now. [*jumps up*] My goodness, it's delightful to think of, Christine! Free from care! To be able to be free from care, quite free from care; to be able to play and romp with the children; to be able to keep the house beautifully and have everything just as Torvald likes it! And, think of it, soon the spring will come and the big blue sky! Perhaps we shall be able to take a little trip—perhaps I shall see the sea again! Oh, it's a wonderful thing to be alive and be happy. [*A bell is heard in the hall.*]

MRS. LINDE.   [*rising*] There is the bell; perhaps I had better go.

NORA.   No, don't go; no one will come in here; it is sure to be for Torvald.   215

SERVANT.   [*at the hall door*] Excuse me, ma'am—there is a gentleman to see the master, and as the doctor is with him—

NORA.   Who is it?

KROGSTAD.   [*at the door*] It is I, Mrs. Helmer. [*MRS. LINDE starts, trembles, and turns to the window.*]

NORA.   [*takes a step towards him, and speaks in a strained, low voice*] You? What is it? What do you want to see my husband about?

KROGSTAD.   Bank business—in a way. I have a small post in the Bank, and I hear   220 your husband is to be our chief now—

NORA.   Then it is—

KROGSTAD.   Nothing but dry business matters, Mrs. Helmer; absolutely nothing else.

NORA.   Be so good as to go into the study, then. [*She bows indifferently to him and shuts the door into the hall; then comes back and makes up the fire in the stove.*]

MRS. LINDE.   Nora—who was that man?

NORA.   A lawyer, of the name of Krogstad.   225

MRS. LINDE.   Then it really was he.

NORA.   Do you know the man?

MRS. LINDE.   I used to—many years ago. At one time he was a solicitor's clerk in our town.

NORA.   Yes, he was.

MRS. LINDE.   He is greatly altered.   230

NORA.   He made a very unhappy marriage.

MRS. LINDE.   He is a widower now, isn't he?

NORA.   With several children. There now, it is burning up.

[*Shuts the door of the stove and moves the rocking-chair aside.*]

MRS. LINDE.   They say he carries on various kinds of business.

NORA.   Really! Perhaps he does; I don't know anything about it. But don't let us   235 think of business; it is so tiresome.

DOCTOR RANK.   [*comes out of HELMER's study. Before he shuts the door he calls to him.*] No, my dear fellow, I won't disturb you; I would rather go into your wife for a little while. [*shuts the door and sees MRS. LINDE*] I beg your pardon; I am afraid I am disturbing you too.

NORA.   No, not at all. [*introducing him*] Doctor Rank, Mrs. Linde.

RANK.   I have often heard Mrs. Linde's name mentioned here. I think I passed you on the stairs when I arrived, Mrs. Linde?

MRS. LINDE.   Yes, I go up very slowly; I can't manage stairs well.

RANK.   Ah! some slight internal weakness?   240

MRS. LINDE.   No, the fact is I have been overworking myself.

RANK.   Nothing more than that? Then I suppose you have come to town to amuse yourself with our entertainments?

MRS. LINDE.   I have come to look for work.

RANK.   Is that a good cure for overwork?

MRS. LINDE.   One must live, Doctor Rank.   245

RANK.   Yes, the general opinion seems to be that it is necessary.

NORA.   Look here, Doctor Rank—you know you want to live.

RANK.   Certainly. However wretched I may feel, I want to prolong the agony as long as possible. All my patients are like that. And so are those who are morally diseased; one of them, and a bad case too, is at this very moment with Helmer—

MRS. LINDE.   [*sadly*] Ah!

NORA.   Whom do you mean?   250

RANK.   A lawyer of the name of Krogstad, a fellow you don't know at all. He suffers from a diseased moral character, Mrs. Helmer; but even he began talking of its being highly important that he should live.

NORA.   Did he? What did he want to speak to Torvald about?

RANK.   I have no idea; I only heard that it was something about the Bank.

NORA.   I didn't know this—what's his name—Krogstad had anything to do with the Bank.

RANK.   Yes, he has some sort of appointment there. [*to MRS. LINDE*] I don't know   255
whether you find also in your part of the world that there are certain people who go zealously snuffing about to smell out moral corruption, and, as soon as they have found some, put the person concerned into some lucrative position where they can keep their eye on him. Healthy natures are left out in the cold.

MRS. LINDE.   Still I think the sick are those who most need taking care of.

RANK.   [*shrugging his shoulders*] Yes, there you are. That is the sentiment that is turning Society into a sickhouse.

[*NORA, who has been absorbed in her thoughts, breaks out into smothered laughter and claps her hands.*]

RANK.   Why do you laugh at that? Have you any notion what Society really is?

NORA.   What do I care about tiresome Society? I am laughing at something quite different, something extremely amusing. Tell me, Doctor Rank, are all the people who are employed in the Bank dependent on Torvald now?

RANK.   Is that what you find so extremely amusing?   260

NORA.   [*smiling and humming*] That's my affair! [*walking about the room*] It's perfectly glorious to think that we have—that Torvald has so much power over so many people. [*takes the packet from her pocket*] Doctor Rank, what do you say to a macaroon?

RANK.   What, macaroons? I thought they were forbidden here.

NORA.   Yes, but these are some Christine gave me.

MRS. LINDE.   What! I?—

NORA.   Oh, well, don't be alarmed! You couldn't know that Torvald had forbid-   265
den them. I must tell you that he is afraid they will spoil my teeth. But, bah!—once in a

way— That's so, isn't it, Doctor Rank? By your leave? [*puts a macaroon into his mouth*] You must have one too, Christine. And I shall have one, just a little one—or at most two. [*walking about*] I am tremendously happy. There is just one thing in the world now that I should dearly love to do.

RANK.   Well, what is that?

NORA.   It's something I should dearly love to say, if Torvald could hear me.

RANK.   Well, why can't you say it?

NORA.   No, I daren't; it's so shocking.

MRS. LINDE.   Shocking?   270

RANK.   Well, I should not advise you to say it. Still, with us you might. What is it you would so much like to say if Torvald could hear you?

NORA.   I should just love to say—Well, I'm damned!

RANK.   Are you mad?

MRS. LINDE.   Nora, dear—!

RANK.   Say it, here he is!   275

NORA.   [*hiding the packet*] Hush! Hush! Hush!

[*HELMER comes out of his room, with his coat over his arm and his hat in his hands.*]

NORA.   Well, Torvald dear, have you got rid of him?

HELMER.   Yes, he has just gone.

NORA.   Let me introduce you—this is Christine, who has come to town.

HELMER.   Christine—? Excuse me, but I don't know—   280

NORA.   Mrs. Linde, dear; Christine Linde.

HELMER.   Of course. A school friend of my wife's, I presume?

MRS. LINDE.   Yes, we have known each other since then.

NORA.   And just think, she has taken a long journey in order to see you.

HELMER.   What do you mean?   285

MRS. LINDE.   No, really, I—

NORA.   Christine is tremendously clever at book-keeping, and she is frightfully anxious to work under some clever man, so as to perfect herself—

HELMER.   Very sensible, Mrs. Linde.

NORA.   And when she heard you had been appointed manager of the Bank—the news was telegraphed, you know—she travelled here as quick as she could. Torvald, I am sure you will be able to do something for Christine, for my sake, won't you?

HELMER.   Well, it is not altogether impossible. I presume you are a widow, Mrs.   290
Linde?

MRS. LINDE.   Yes.

HELMER.   And have had some experience of book-keeping?

MRS. LINDE.   Yes, a fair amount.

HELMER.   Ah! well, it's very likely I may be able to find something for you—

NORA.   [*clapping her hands*]What did I tell you? What did I tell you?   295

HELMER.   You have just come at a fortunate moment, Mrs. Linde.

MRS. LINDE.   How am I to thank you?

HELMER.   There is no need. [*puts on his coat*] But to-day you must excuse me—

RANK.   Wait a minute; I will come with you.

[*Brings his fur coat from the hall and warms it at the fire.*]

NORA.   Don't be long away, Torvald dear.   300

HELMER.   About an hour, not more.

NORA.   Are you going too, Christine?

MRS. LINDE.   [*putting on her cloak*] Yes, I must go and look for a room.

HELMER.   Oh, well then, we can walk down the street together.

NORA.   [*helping her*] What a pity it is we are so short of space here: I am afraid it is   305
impossible for us—

MRS. LINDE.   Please don't think of it! Good-bye, Nora dear, and many thanks.

NORA.   Good-bye for the present. Of course you will come back this evening. And
you too, Dr. Rank. What do you say? If you are well enough? Oh, you must be! Wrap
yourself up well.

[*They go to the door all talking together. Children's voices are heard on the staircase.*]

NORA.   There they are. There they are! [*She runs to open the door. The* NURSE *comes
in with the children.*] Come in! Come in! [*stoops and kisses them*] Oh, you sweet blessings!
Look at them, Christine! Aren't they darlings?

RANK.   Don't let us stand here in the draught.

HELMER.   Come along, Mrs. Linde; the place will only be bearable for a mother   310
now!

[RANK, HELMER *and* MRS. LINDE *go downstairs. The* NURSE *comes forward with the children;*
NORA *shuts the hall door.*]

NORA.   How fresh and well you look! Such red cheeks!—like apples and roses.
[*The children all talk at once while she speaks to them.*] Have you had great fun? That's splendid! What, you pulled both Emmy and Bob along on the sledge?—both at once?—that
was good. You are a clever boy, Ivar. Let me take her for a little, Anne. My sweet little
baby doll! [*takes the baby from the* MAID *and dances it up and down*] Yes, yes, mother will
dance with Bob too. What! Have you been snowballing? I wish I had been there too! No,
no, I will take their things off, Anne; please let me do it, it is such fun. Go in now, you
look half frozen. There is some coffee for you on the stove.

[*The* NURSE *goes into the room on the left.* NORA *takes off the children's things and throws them
about, while they all talk to her at once.*]

NORA.   Really! Did a big dog run after you? But it didn't bite you? No, dogs don't
bite nice little dolly children. You mustn't look at the parcels, Ivar. What are they? Ah, I
daresay you would like to know. No, no—it's something nasty! Come, let us have a game!
What shall we play at? Hide and Seek? Yes, we'll play Hide and Seek. Bob shall hide first.
Must I hide? Very well, I'll hide first.

[*She and the children laugh and shout, and romp in and out of the room; at last* NORA *hides
under the table, the children rush in and look for her, but do not see her; they hear her smothered
laughter, run to the table, lift up the cloth and find her. Shouts of laughter. She crawls forward
and pretends to frighten them. Fresh laughter. Meanwhile there has been a knock at the hall door,
but none of them has noticed it. The door is half opened, and* KROGSTAD *appears. He waits a
little; the game goes on.*]

KROGSTAD.   Excuse me, Mrs. Helmer.

NORA.   [*with a stifled cry, turns round and gets up on to her knees*] Ah! what do you
want?

KROGSTAD.   Excuse me, the outer door was ajar; I suppose someone forgot to   315
shut it.

NORA. [*rising*] My husband is out, Mr. Krogstad.

KROGSTAD. I know that.

NORA. What do you want here, then?

KROGSTAD. A word with you.

NORA. With me?—[*to the children, gently*] Go in to nurse. What? No, the strange   320
man won't do mother any harm. When he has gone we will have another game. [*She
takes the children into the room on the left, and shuts the door after them.*] You want to speak
to me?

KROGSTAD. Yes, I do.

NORA. To-day? It is not the first of the month yet.

KROGSTAD. No, it is Christmas Eve, and it will depend on yourself what sort of a
Christmas you will spend.

NORA. What do you want? To-day it is absolutely impossible for me—

KROGSTAD. We won't talk about that till later on. This is something different. I   325
presume you can give me a moment?

NORA. Yes—yes, I can—although—

KROGSTAD. Good. I was in Olsen's Restaurant and saw your husband going down
the street—

NORA. Yes?

KROGSTAD. With a lady.

NORA. What then?   330

KROGSTAD. May I make so bold as to ask if it was a Mrs. Linde?

NORA. It was.

KROGSTAD. Just arrived in town?

NORA. Yes, to-day.

KROGSTAD. She is a great friend of yours, isn't she?   335

NORA. She is. But I don't see—

KROGSTAD. I knew her too, once upon a time.

NORA. I am aware of that.

KROGSTAD. Are you? So you know all about it; I thought as much. Then I can ask
you, without beating about the bush—is Mrs. Linde to have an appointment in the
Bank?

NORA. What right have you to question me, Mr. Krogstad?—You, one of my hus-   340
band's subordinates! But since you ask, you shall know. Yes, Mrs. Linde *is* to have an
appointment. And it was I who pleaded her cause, Mr. Krogstad, let me tell you that.

KROGSTAD. I was right in what I thought, then.

NORA. [*walking up and down the stage*] Sometimes one has a tiny little bit of influence, I should hope. Because one is a woman, it does not necessarily follow that—.
When anyone is in a subordinate position, Mr. Krogstad, they should really be careful to
avoid offending anyone who—who—

KROGSTAD. Who has influence?

NORA. Exactly.

KROGSTAD. [*changing his tone*] Mrs. Helmer, you will be so good as to use your   345
influence on my behalf.

NORA. What? What do you mean?

KROGSTAD. You will be so kind as to see that I am allowed to keep my subordinate
position in the Bank.

NORA. What do you mean by that? Who proposes to take your post away from
you?

KROGSTAD.   Oh, there is no necessity to keep up the pretence of ignorance. I can quite understand that your friend is not very anxious to expose herself to the chance of rubbing shoulders with me; and I quite understand, too, whom I have to thank for being turned out.

NORA.   But I assure you—   350

KROGSTAD.   Very likely; but, to come to the point, the time has come when I should advise you to use your influence to prevent that.

NORA.   But, Mr. Krogstad, I *have* no influence.

KROGSTAD.   Haven't you? I thought you said yourself just now—

NORA.   Naturally I did not mean you to put that construction on it. I! What should make you think I have any influence of that kind with my husband?

KROGSTAD.   Oh, I have known your husband from our student days. I don't sup-   355
pose he is any more unassailable than other husbands.

NORA.   If you speak slightingly of my husband, I shall turn you out of the house.

KROGSTAD.   You are bold, Mrs. Helmer.

NORA.   I am not afraid of you any longer. As soon as the New Year comes, I shall in a very short time be free of the whole thing.

KROGSTAD.   [*controlling himself*] Listen to me, Mrs. Helmer. If necessary, I am pre-pared to fight for my small post in the Bank as if I were fighting for my life.

NORA.   So it seems.   360

KROGSTAD.   It is not only for the sake of the money; indeed, that weighs least with me in the matter. There is another reason—well, I may as well tell you. My position is this. I daresay you know, like everybody else, that once, many years ago, I was guilty of an indiscretion.

NORA.   I think I have heard something of the kind.

KROGSTAD.   The matter never came into court; but every way seemed to be closed to me after that. So I took to the business that you know of. I had to do something; and, honestly, I don't think I've been one of the worst. But now I must cut myself free from all that. My sons are growing up; for their sake I must try and win back as much respect as I can in the town. This post in the Bank was like the first step up for me—and now your husband is going to kick me downstairs again into the mud.

NORA.   But you must believe me, Mr. Krogstad; it is not in my power to help you at all.

KROGSTAD.   Then it is because you haven't the will; but I have means to compel   365
you.

NORA.   You don't mean that you will tell my husband that I owe you money?

KROGSTAD.   Hm!—suppose I were to tell him?

NORA.   It would be perfectly infamous of you. [*Sobbing*] To think of his learning my secret, which has been my joy and pride, in such an ugly, clumsy way—that he should learn it from you! And it would put me in a horribly disagreeable position—

KROGSTAD.   Only disagreeable?

NORA.   [*impetuously*] Well, do it, then!—and it will be the worse for you. My hus-   370
band will see for himself what a blackguard you are, and you certainly won't keep your post then.

KROGSTAD.   I asked you if it was only a disagreeable scene at home that you were afraid of?

NORA.   If my husband does get to know of it, of course he will at once pay you what is still owing, and we shall have nothing more to do with you.

KROGSTAD.   [*coming a step nearer*] Listen to me, Mrs. Helmer. Either you have a very bad memory or you know very little of business. I shall be obliged to remind you of a few details.

NORA.   What do you mean?

KROGSTAD.   When your husband was ill, you came to me to borrow two hundred   375
and fifty pounds.

NORA.   I didn't know any one else to go to.

KROGSTAD.   I promised to get you that amount—

NORA.   Yes, and you did so.

KROGSTAD.   I promised to get you that amount, on certain conditions. Your mind was so taken up with your husband's illness, and you were so anxious to get the money for your journey, that you seem to have paid no attention to the conditions of our bargain. Therefore it will not be amiss if I remind you of them. Now, I promised to get the money on the security of a bond which I drew up.

NORA.   Yes, and which I signed.   380

KROGSTAD.   Good. But below your signature there were a few lines constituting your father a surety for the money; those lines your father should have signed.

NORA.   Should? He did sign them.

KROGSTAD.   I had left the date blank; that is to say your father should himself have inserted the date on which he signed the paper. Do you remember that?

NORA.   Yes, I think I remember—

KROGSTAD.   Then I gave you the bond to send by post to your father. Is that not   385
so?

NORA.   Yes.

KROGSTAD.   And you naturally did so at once, because five or six days afterwards you brought me the bond with your father's signature. And then I gave you the money.

NORA.   Well, haven't I been paying it off regularly?

KROGSTAD.   Fairly so, yes. But—to come back to the matter in hand—that must have been a very trying time for you, Mrs. Helmer?

NORA.   It was, indeed.   390

KROGSTAD.   Your father was very ill, wasn't he?

NORA.   He was very near his end.

KROGSTAD.   And died soon afterwards?

NORA.   Yes.

KROGSTAD.   Tell me, Mrs. Helmer, can you by any chance remember what day   395
your father died?—on what day of the month, I mean.

NORA.   Papa died on the 29th of September.

KROGSTAD.   That is correct; I have ascertained it for myself. And, as that is so, there is a discrepancy [*taking a paper from his pocket*] which I cannot account for.

NORA.   What discrepancy? I don't know—

KROGSTAD.   The discrepancy consists, Mrs. Helmer, in the fact that your father signed this bond three days after his death.

NORA.   What do you mean? I don't understand—   400

KROGSTAD.   Your father died on the 29th of September. But, look here; your father has dated his signature the 2nd of October. It is a discrepancy, isn't it? [*NORA is silent.*] Can you explain it to me? [*NORA is still silent.*] It is a remarkable thing, too, that the words "2nd of October," as well as the year, are not written in your father's handwriting but in one that I think I know. Well, of course it can be explained; your father may have forgotten to date his signature, and someone else may have dated it haphazard before they knew of his death. There is no harm in that. It all depends on the signature of the name; and *that* is genuine, I suppose, Mrs. Helmer? It was your father himself who signed his name here?

NORA.   [*after a short pause, throws her head up and looks defiantly at him*] No, it was not. It was I that wrote papa's name.

KROGSTAD.   Are you aware that is a dangerous confession?

NORA.   In what way? You shall have your money soon.

KROGSTAD.   Let me ask you a question; why did you not send the paper to your   405 father?

NORA.   It was impossible; papa was so ill. If I had asked him for his signature, I should have had to tell him what the money was to be used for; and when he was so ill himself I couldn't tell him that my husband's life was in danger—it was impossible.

KROGSTAD.   It would have been better for you if you had given up your trip abroad.

NORA.   No, that was impossible. That trip was to save my husband's life; I couldn't give that up.

KROGSTAD.   But did it never occur to you that you were committing a fraud on me?

NORA.   I couldn't take that into account; I didn't trouble myself about you at all.   410 I couldn't bear you, because you put so many heartless difficulties in my way, although you knew what a dangerous condition my husband was in.

KROGSTAD.   Mrs. Helmer, you evidently do not realise clearly what it is that you have been guilty of. But I can assure you that my one false step, which lost me all my reputation, was nothing more or nothing worse than what you have done.

NORA.   You? Do you ask me to believe that you were brave enough to run a risk to save your wife's life?

KROGSTAD.   The law cares nothing about motives.

NORA.   Then it must be a very foolish law.

KROGSTAD.   Foolish or not, it is the law by which you will be judged, if I produce   415 this paper in court.

NORA.   I don't believe it. Is a daughter not to be allowed to spare her dying father anxiety and care? Is a wife not to be allowed to save her husband's life? I don't know much about law; but I am certain that there must be laws permitting such things as that. Have you no knowledge of such laws—you who are a lawyer? You must be a very poor lawyer, Mr. Krogstad.

KROGSTAD.   Maybe. But matters of business—such business as you and I have had together—do you think I don't understand that? Very well. Do as you please. But let me tell you this—if I lose my position a second time, you shall lose yours with me.

[*He bows, and goes out through the hall.*]

NORA.   [*appears buried in thought for a short time, then tosses her head*] Nonsense! Trying to frighten me like that!—I am not so silly as he thinks. [*begins to busy herself putting the children's things in order*] And yet—? No, it's impossible! I did it for love's sake.

THE CHILDREN.   [*in the doorway on the left*] Mother, the stranger man has gone out through the gate.

NORA.   Yes, dears, I know. But, don't tell anyone about the stranger man. Do you   420 hear? Not even papa.

CHILDREN.   No, mother; but will you come and play again?

NORA.   No, no—not now.

CHILDREN.   But, mother, you promised us.

NORA.   Yes, but I can't now. Run away in; I have such a lot to do. Run away in, my sweet little darlings. [*She gets them into the room by degrees and shuts the door on them; then sits down on the sofa, takes up a piece of needlework and sews a few stitches, but soon stops.*] No! [*throws down the work, gets up, goes to the hall door and calls out*] Helen! bring the Tree in. [*goes to the table on the left, opens a drawer, and stops again*] No, no! it is quite impossible!

MAID.   [*coming in with the Tree*] Where shall I put it, ma'am?   425

NORA.   Here, in the middle of the floor.

MAID.   Shall I get you anything else?

NORA.   No, thank you. I have all I want.   [*Exit* MAID.]

NORA.   [*begins dressing the tree*] A candle here—and flowers here—. The horrible man! It's all nonsense—there's nothing wrong. The Tree shall be splendid! I will do everything I can think of to please you, Torvald!—I will sing for you, dance for you— [*HELMER comes in with some papers under his arm*] Oh! are you back already?

HELMER.   Yes. Has anyone been here?   430

NORA.   Here? No.

HELMER.   That is strange. I saw Krogstad going out of the gate.

NORA.   Did you? Oh yes, I forgot, Krogstad was here for a moment.

HELMER.   Nora, I can see from your manner that he has been here begging you to say a good word for him.

NORA.   Yes.   435

HELMER.   And you were to appear to do it of your own accord; you were to conceal from me the fact of his having been here; didn't he beg that of you too?

NORA.   Yes, Torvald, but—

HELMER.   Nora, Nora, and you would be a party to that sort of thing? To have any talk with a man like that, and give him any sort of promise? And to tell me a lie into the bargain?

NORA.   A lie—?

HELMER.   Didn't you tell me no one had been here? [*shakes his finger at her*] My   440
little song-bird must never do that again. A song-bird must have a clean beak to chirp with—no false notes! [*puts his arm round her waist*] That is so, isn't it? Yes, I am sure it is. [*lets her go*] We will say no more about it. [*sits down by the stove*] How warm and snug it is here!

[*Turns over his papers.*]

NORA.   [*after a short pause, during which she busies herself with the Christmas Tree*] Torvald!

HELMER.   Yes.

NORA.   I am looking forward tremendously to the fancy dress ball at the Stenborgs' the day after to-morrow.

HELMER.   And I am tremendously curious to see what you are going to surprise me with.

NORA.   It was very silly of me to want to do that.   445

HELMER.   What do you mean?

NORA.   I can't hit upon anything that will do; everything I think of seems so silly and insignificant.

HELMER.   Does my little Nora acknowledge that at last?

NORA.   [*standing behind his chair with her arms on the back of it*] Are you very busy, Torvald?

HELMER.   Well—   450

NORA.   What are all those papers?

HELMER.   Bank business.

NORA.   Already?

HELMER.   I have got authority from the retiring manager to undertake the necessary changes in the staff and in the rearrangement of the work; and I must make use of the Christmas week for that, so as to have everything in order for the new year.

NORA.   Then that was why this poor Krogstad—   455

HELMER.   Hm!

NORA.   [*leans against the back of his chair and strokes his hair*] If you hadn't been so busy I should have asked you a tremendously big favour, Torvald.

HELMER.   What is that? Tell me.

NORA.   There is no one has such good taste as you. And I do so want to look nice at the fancy-dress ball. Torvald, couldn't you take me in hand and decide what I shall go as, and what sort of a dress I shall wear?

HELMER.   Aha! so my obstinate little woman is obliged to get someone to come to   460
her rescue?

NORA.   Yes, Torvald, I can't get along a bit without your help.

HELMER.   Very well, I will think it over, we shall manage to hit upon something.

NORA.   That *is* nice of you. [*goes to the Christmas Tree. A short pause.*] How pretty the red flowers look—. But, tell me, was it really something very bad that this Krogstad was guilty of?

HELMER.   He forged someone's name. Have you any idea what that means?

NORA.   Isn't it possible that he was driven to do it by necessity?   465

HELMER.   Yes; or, as in so many cases, by imprudence. I am not so heartless as to condemn a man altogether because of a single false step of that kind.

NORA.   No you wouldn't, would you, Torvald?

HELMER.   Many a man has been able to retrieve his character, if he has openly confessed his fault and taken his punishment.

NORA.   Punishment—?

HELMER.   But Krogstad did nothing of that sort; he got himself out of it by a cun-   470
ning trick, and that is why he has gone under altogether.

NORA.   But do you think it would—?

HELMER.   Just think how a guilty man like that has to lie and play the hypocrite with everyone, how he has to wear a mask in the presence of those near and dear to him, even before his own wife and children. And about the children—that is the most terrible part of it all, Nora.

NORA.   How?

HELMER.   Because such an atmosphere of lies infects and poisons the whole life of a home. Each breath the children take in such a house is full of the germs of evil.

NORA.   [*coming nearer him*] Are you sure of that?   475

HELMER.   My dear, I have often seen it in the course of my life as a lawyer. Almost everyone who has gone to the bad early in life has had a deceitful mother.

NORA.   Why do you only say—mother?

HELMER.   It seems most commonly to be the mother's influence, though naturally a bad father's would have the same result. Every lawyer is familiar with the fact.

This Krogstad, now, has been persistently poisoning his own children with lies and dissimulation; that is why I say he has lost all moral character. [*holds out his hands to her*] That is why my sweet little Nora must promise me not to plead his cause. Give me your hand on it. Come, come, what is this? Give me your hand. There now, that's settled. I assure you it would be quite impossible for me to work with him; I literally feel physically ill when I am in the company of such people.

NORA.   [*takes her hand out of his and goes to the opposite side of the Christmas Tree*] How hot it is in here; and I have such a lot to do.

HELMER.   [*getting up and putting his papers in order*] Yes, and I must try and read   480
through some of these before dinner; and I must think about your costume, too. And it is just possible I may have something ready in gold paper to hang up on the Tree. [*Puts his hand on her head.*] My precious little singing-bird!

[*He goes into his room and shuts the door after him.*]

NORA.   [*after a pause, whispers*] No, no—it isn't true. It's impossible; it must be impossible.

[*The NURSE opens the door on the left.*]

NURSE.   The little ones are begging so hard to be allowed to come in to mamma.
NORA.   No, no, no! Don't let them come in to me! You stay with them, Anne.
NURSE.   Very well, ma'am.

[*Shuts the door.*]

NORA.   [*pale with terror*] Deprave my little children? Poison my home? [*a short   485
pause. Then she tosses her head.*] It's not true. It can't possibly be true.

ACT 2

THE SAME SCENE. *The Christmas Tree is in the corner by the piano, stripped of its ornaments and with burnt-down candle-ends on its dishevelled branches. NORA'S cloak and hat are lying on the sofa. She is alone in the room, walking about uneasily. She stops by the sofa and takes up her cloak.*

NORA.   [*drops the cloak*] Someone is coming now! [*goes to the door and listens*] No—it is no one. Of course, no one will come to-day, Christmas Day—nor tomorrow either. But, perhaps—[*opens the door and looks out*] No, nothing in the letter-box; it is quite empty. [*comes forward*] What rubbish! of course he can't be in earnest about it. Such a thing couldn't happen; it is impossible—I have three little children.

[*Enter the NURSE from the room on the left, carrying a big cardboard box.*]

NURSE.   At last I have found the box with the fancy dress.
NORA.   Thanks; put it on the table.
NURSE.   [*doing so*] But it is very much in want of mending.
NORA.   I should like to tear it into a hundred thousand pieces.   5
NURSE.   What an idea! It can easily be put in order—just a little patience.
NORA.   Yes, I will go and get Mrs. Linde to come and help me with it.
NURSE.   What, out again? In this horrible weather? You will catch cold, ma'am, and make yourself ill.
NORA.   Well, worse than that might happen. How are the children?

NURSE.   The poor little souls are playing with their Christmas presents, but—   10
NORA.   Do they ask much for me?
NURSE.   You see, they are so accustomed to have their mamma with them.
NORA.   Yes, but, nurse, I shall not be able to be so much with them now as I was
before.
NURSE.   Oh well, young children easily get accustomed to anything.
NORA.   Do you think so? Do you think they would forget their mother if she went   15
away altogether?
NURSE.   Good heavens!—went away altogether?
NORA.   Nurse, I want you to tell me something I have often wondered about—
how could you have the heart to put your own child out among strangers?
NURSE.   I was obliged to, if I wanted to be little Nora's nurse.
NORA.   Yes, but how could you be willing to do it?
NURSE.   What, when I was going to get such a good place by it? A poor girl who   20
has got into trouble should be glad to. Besides, that wicked man didn't do a single thing
for me.
NORA.   But I suppose your daughter has quite forgotten you.
NURSE.   No, indeed she hasn't. She wrote to me when she was confirmed, and
when she was married.
NORA.   [*putting her arms round her neck*] Dear old Anne, you were a good mother
to me when I was little.
NURSE.   Little Nora, poor dear, had no other mother but me.
NORA.   And if my little ones had no other mother, I am sure you would—What   25
nonsense I am talking! [*opens the box*] Go in to them. Now I must—. You will see to-
morrow how charming I shall look.
NURSE.   I am sure there will be no one at the ball so charming as you, ma'am.

[*Goes into the room on the left.*]

NORA.   [*begins to unpack the box, but soon pushes it away from her*] If only I dared go
out. If only no one would come. If only I could be sure nothing would happen here in
the meantime. Stuff and nonsense! No one will come. Only I mustn't think about it. I
will brush my muff. What, lovely gloves! Out of my thoughts, out of my thoughts! One,
two, three, four, five, six—[*screams.*] Ah! there is someone coming—

[*Makes a movement towards the door, but stands irresolute.*]

[*Enter MRS. LINDE from the hall, where she has taken off her cloak and hat.*]

NORA.   Oh, it's you, Christine. There is no one else out there, is there? How good
of you to come!
MRS. LINDE.   I heard you were up asking for me.
NORA.   Yes, I was passing by. As a matter of fact, it is something you could help me   30
with. Let us sit down here on the sofa. Look here. To-morrow evening there is to be a
fancy-dress ball at the Stenborgs', who live about us; and Torvald wants me to go as a
Neapolitan fisher-girl, and dance the Tarantella that I learnt at Capri.
MRS. LINDE.   I see; you are going to keep up the character.
NORA.   Yes, Torvald wants me to. Look, here is the dress; Torvald had it made
for me there, but now it is all so torn, and I haven't any idea—
MRS. LINDE.   We will easily put that right. It is only some of the trimming come
unsewn here and there. Needle and thread? Now then, that's all we want.

NORA.   It *is* nice of you.

MRS. LINDE.   [*sewing*] So you are going to be dressed up to-morrow, Nora. I will   35
tell you what—I shall come in for a moment and see you in your fine feathers. But I
have completely forgotten to thank you for a delightful evening yesterday.

NORA.   [*gets up, and crosses the stages*] Well I don't think yesterday was a pleasant as
usual. You ought to have come to town a little earlier, Christine. Certainly Torvald does
understand how to make a house dainty and attractive.

MRS. LINDE.   And so do you, it seems to me; you are not your father's daughter
for nothing. But tell me, is Doctor Rank always as depressed as he was yesterday?

NORA.   No; yesterday it was very noticeable. I must tell you that he suffers from a
very dangerous disease. He has consumption of the spine, poor creature. His father was
a horrible man who committed all sorts of excesses; and that is why his son was sickly
from childhood, do you understand?

MRS. LINDE.   [*dropping her sewing*] But, my dearest Nora, how do you know anything about such things?

NORA.   [*walking about*] Pooh! When you have three children, you get visits now   40
and then from—from married women, who know something of medical matters, and
they talk about one thing and another.

MRS. LINDE.   [*goes on sewing. A short silence*] Does Doctor Rank come here every
day?

NORA.   Every day regularly. He is Torvald's most intimate friend, and a great
friend of mine too. He is just like one of the family.

MRS. LINDE.   But tell me this—is he perfectly sincere? I mean, isn't he the kind of
man that is very anxious to make himself agreeable?

NORA.   Not in the least. What makes you think that?

MRS. LINDE.   When you introduced him to me yesterday, he declared he had   45
often heard my name mentioned in this house; but afterwards I noticed that your husband hadn't the slightest idea who I was. So how could Doctor Rank—?

NORA.   That is quite right, Christine. Torvald is so absurdly fond of me that he
wants me absolutely to himself, as he says. At first he used to seem almost jealous if I
mentioned any of the dear folk at home, so naturally I gave up doing so. But I often talk
about such things with Doctor Rank, because he likes hearing about them.

MRS. LINDE.   Listen to me, Nora. You are still very like a child in many things,
and I am older than you in many ways and have a little more experience. Let me tell
you this—you ought to make an end of it with Doctor Rank.

NORA.   What ought I to make an end of?

MRS. LINDE.   Of two things, I think. Yesterday you talked some nonsense about a
rich admirer who was to leave you money—

NORA.   An admirer who doesn't exist, unfortunately! But what then?   50

MRS. LINDE.   Is Doctor Rank a man of means?

NORA.   Yes, he is.

MRS. LINDE.   And has no one to provide for?

NORA.   No, no one; but—

MRS. LINDE.   And comes here every day?   55

NORA.   Yes, I told you so.

MRS. LINDE.   But how can this well-bred man be so tactless?

NORA.   I don't understand you at all.

MRS. LINDE.   Don't prevaricate, Nora. Do you suppose I don't guess who lent you
the two hundred and fifty pounds?

NORA.   Are you out of your senses? How can you think of such a thing! A friend   60
of ours, who comes here every day! Do you realise what a horribly painful position that
would be?

MRS. LINDE.   Then it really isn't he?

NORA.   No, certainly not. It would never have entered into my head for a
moment. Besides, he had no money to lend then; he came into his money afterwards.

MRS. LINDE.   Well, I think that was lucky for you, my dear Nora.

NORA.   No, it would never have come into my head to ask Doctor Rank. Although
I am quite sure that if I had asked him—

MRS. LINDE.   But of course you won't.   65

NORA.   Of course not. I have no reason to think it could possibly be necessary.
But I am quite sure that if I told Doctor Rank—

MRS. LINDE.   Behind your husband's back?

NORA.   I must make an end of it with the other one, and that will be behind his
back too. I *must* make an end of it with him.

MRS. LINDE.   Yes, that is what I told you yesterday, but—

NORA.   [*walking up and down*] A man can put a thing like that straight much   70
easier than a woman—

MRS. LINDE.   One's husband, yes.

NORA.   Nonsense! [*standing still*] When you pay off a debt you get your bond
back, don't you?

MRS. LINDE.   Yes, as a matter of course.

NORA.   And can tear it into a hundred thousand pieces, and burn it up—the
nasty dirty paper!

MRS. LINDE.   [*looks hard at her, lays down her sewing and gets up slowly*] Nora, you are   75
concealing something from me.

NORA.   Do I look as if I were?

MRS. LINDE.   Something has happened to you since yesterday morning. Nora,
what is it?

NORA.   [*going nearer to her*] Christine! [*listens*] Hush! there's Torvald come home.
Do you mind going in to the children for the present? Torvald can't bear to see dress-
making going on. Let Anne help you.

MRS. LINDE.   [*gathering some of the things together*] Certainly—but I am not going
away from here till we have had it out with one another.

[*She goes into the room on the left, as* HELMER *comes in from the hall.*]

NORA.   [*going up to* HELMER] I have wanted you so much, Torvald dear.   80

HELMER.   Was that the dressmaker?

NORA.   No, it was Christine; she is helping me to put my dress in order. You will
see I shall look quite smart.

HELMER.   Wasn't that a happy thought of mine, now?

NORA.   Splendid! But don't you think it is nice of me, too, to do as you wish?

HELMER.   Nice?—because you do as your husband wishes? Well, well, you little   85
rogue, I am sure you did not mean it in that way. But I am not going to disturb you; you
will want to be trying on your dress, I expect.

NORA.   I suppose you are going to work.

HELMER.   Yes. [*shows her a bundle of papers*] Look at that. I have just been into the
bank. [*Turns to go into his room.*]

NORA. Torvald.

HELMER. Yes.

NORA. If your little squirrel were to ask you for something very, very prettily—? 90

HELMER. What then?

NORA. Would you do it?

HELMER. I should like to hear what it is, first.

NORA. Your squirrel would run about and do all her tricks if you would be nice, and do what she wants.

HELMER. Speak plainly. 95

NORA. Your skylark would chirp about in every room, with her song rising and falling—

HELMER. Well, my skylark does that anyhow.

NORA. I would play the fairy and dance for you in the moonlight, Torvald.

HELMER. Nora—you surely don't mean that request you made of me this morning?

NORA. [*going near him*] Yes, Torvald, I beg you so earnestly— 100

HELMER. Have you really the courage to open up that question again?

NORA. Yes, dear, you *must* do as I ask; you *must* let Krogstad keep his post in the Bank.

HELMER. My dear Nora, it is his post that I have arranged Mrs. Linde shall have.

NORA. Yes, you have been awfully kind about that; but you could just as well dismiss some other clerk instead of Krogstad.

HELMER. This is simply incredible obstinacy! Because you chose to give him a 105
thoughtless promise that you would speak for him, I am expected to—

NORA. That isn't the reason, Torvald. It is for your own sake. This fellow writes in the most scurrilous newspapers; you have told me so yourself. He can do you an unspeakable amount of harm. I am frightened to death of him—

HELMER. Ah, I understand; it is recollections of the past that scare you.

NORA. What do you mean?

HELMER. Naturally you are thinking of your father.

NORA. Yes—yes, of course. Just recall to your mind what these malicious crea- 110
tures wrote in the papers about papa, and how horribly they slandered him. I believe they would have procured his dismissal if the Department had not sent you over to inquire into it, and if you had not been so kindly disposed and helpful to him.

HELMER. My little Nora, there is an important difference between your father and me. Your father's reputation as a public official was not above suspicion. Mine is, and I hope it will continue to be so, as long as I hold my office.

NORA. You never can tell what mischief these men may contrive. We ought to be so well off, so snug and happy here in our peaceful home, and have no cares—you and I and the children, Torvald! That is why I beg you so earnestly—

HELMER. And it is just by interceding for him that you make it impossible for me to keep him. It is already known at the Bank that I mean to dismiss Krogstad. Is it to get about now that the new manager has changed his mind at his wife's bidding—

NORA. And what if it did?

HELMER. Of course!—if only this obstinate little person can get her way! Do you 115
suppose I am going to make myself ridiculous before my whole staff, to let people think that I am a man to be swayed by all sorts of outside influence? I should very soon feel the

consequences of it, I can tell you! And besides, there is one thing that makes it quite impossible for me to have Krogstad in the Bank as long as I am manager.

NORA.   Whatever is that?

HELMER.   His moral failings I might perhaps have overlooked, if necessary—

NORA.   Yes, you could—couldn't you?

HELMER.   And I hear he is a good worker, too. But I knew him when we were boys. It was one of those rash friendships that so often prove an incubus in after life. I may as well tell you plainly, we were once on very intimate terms with one another. But this tactless fellow lays no restraint on himself when other people are present. On the contrary, he thinks it gives him the right to adopt a familiar tone with me, and every minute it is "I say, Helmer, old fellow!" and that sort of thing. I assure you it is extremely painful for me. He would make my position in the Bank intolerable.

NORA.   Torvald, I don't believe you mean that.   120

HELMER.   Don't you? Why not?

NORA.   Because it is such a narrow-minded way of looking at things.

HELMER.   What are you saying? Narrow-minded? Do you think I am narrow-minded?

NORA.   No, just the opposite, dear—and it is exactly for that reason.

HELMER.   It's the same thing. You say my point of view is narrow-minded, so I   125
must be so too. Narrow-minded! Very well—I must put an end to this. [*Goes to the hall-door and calls.*] Helen!

NORA.   What are you going to do?

HELMER.   [*looking among his papers*] Settle it. [*Enter MAID.*] Look here; take this letter and go downstairs with it at once. Find a messenger and tell him to deliver it, and be quick. The address is on it, and here is the money.

Maid.   Very well, sir.

[*Exits with the letter.*]

HELMER.   [*putting his papers together*] Now then, little Miss Obstinate.

NORA.   [*breathlessly*] Torvald—what was that letter?   130

HELMER.   Krogstad's dismissal.

NORA.   Call her back, Torvald! There is still time. Oh Torvald, call her back! Do it for my sake—for your own sake—for the children's sake! Do you hear me, Torvald? Call her back!! You don't know what that letter can bring upon us.

HELMER.   It's too late.

NORA.   Yes, it's too late.

HELMER.   My dear Nora, I can forgive the anxiety you are in, although really it is   135
an insult to me. It is, indeed. Isn't it an insult to think that I should be afraid of a starving quill-driver's vengeance? But I forgive you nevertheless, because it is such eloquent witness to your great love for me. [*takes her in his arms*] And that is as it should be, my own darling Nora. Come what will, you may be sure I shall have both courage and strength if they be needed. You will see I am man enough to take everything upon myself.

NORA.   [*in a horror-stricken voice*] What do you mean by that?

HELMER.   Everything, I say—

NORA.   [*recovering herself*] You will never have to do that.

HELMER.   That's right. Well, we will share it, Nora, as man and wife should. That is how it shall be. [*caressing her*] Are you content now? There! there!—not these frightened dove's eyes! The whole thing is only the wildest fancy!—Now, you must go and play through the Tarantella and practise with your tambourine. I shall go into the inner office and shut the door, and I shall hear nothing; you can make as much noise as you please. [*turns back at the door*] And when Rank comes, tell him where he will find me.

[*Nods to her, takes his papers and goes into his room, and shuts the door after him*]

NORA.   [*bewildered with anxiety, stands as if rooted to the spot, and whispers*] He is   140
capable of doing it. He will do it. He will do it in spite of everything.—No, not that! Never, never! Anything rather than that! Oh, for some help, some way out of it! [*The door-bell rings.*] Doctor Rank! Anything rather than that—anything, whatever it is!

[*She puts her hands over her face, pulls herself together, goes to the door and opens it. RANK is standing without, hanging up his coat. During the following dialogue it begins to grow dark.*]

NORA.   Good-day, Doctor Rank. I knew your ring. But you mustn't go in to Torvald now; I think he is busy with something.
RANK.   And you?
NORA.   [*brings him in and shuts the door after him*] Oh, you know very well I always have time for you.
RANK.   Thank you. I shall make use of as much of it as I can.
NORA.   What do you mean by that? As much of it as you can?   145
RANK.   Well, does that alarm you?
NORA.   It was such a strange way of putting it. Is anything likely to happen?
RANK.   Nothing but what I have long been prepared for. But I certainly didn't expect it to happen so soon.
NORA.   [*gripping him by the arm*] What have you found out? Doctor Rank, you must tell me.
RANK.   [*sitting down by the stove*] It is all up with me. And it can't be helped.   150
NORA.   [*with a sigh of relief*] Is it about yourself?
RANK.   Who else? It is no use lying to one's self. I am the most wretched of all my patients, Mrs. Helmer. Lately I have been taking stock of my internal economy. Bankrupt! Probably within a month I shall lie rotting in the churchyard.
NORA.   What an ugly thing to say!
RANK.   The thing itself is cursedly ugly, and the worst of it is that I shall have to face so much more that is ugly before that. I shall only make one more examination of myself; when I have done that, I shall know pretty certainly when it will be that the horrors of dissolution will begin. There is something I want to tell you. Helmer's refined nature gives him an unconquerable disgust at everything that is ugly; I won't have him in my sick-room.
NORA.   Oh, but, Doctor Rank—   155
RANK.   I won't have him there. Not on any account. I bar my door to him. As soon as I am quite certain that the worst has come, I shall send you my card with a black cross on it, and then you will know that the loathsome end has begun.
NORA.   You are quite absurd to-day. And I wanted you so much to be in a really good humour.
RANK.   With death stalking beside me?—To have to pay this penalty for another man's sin! Is there any justice in that? And in every single family, in one way or another, some such inexorable retribution is being exacted—
NORA.   [*putting her hands over her ears*] Rubbish! Do talk of something cheerful.

RANK.   Oh, it's a mere laughing matter, the whole thing. My poor innocent spine   160
has to suffer for my father's youthful amusements.

NORA.   [*sitting at the table on the left*] I suppose you mean that he was too partial to
asparagus and pâté de foie gras, don't you.

RANK.   Yes, and to truffles.

NORA.   Truffles, yes. And oysters too, I suppose?

RANK.   Oysters, of course, that goes without saying.

NORA.   And heaps of port and champagne. It is sad that all these nice things   165
should take their revenge on our bones.

RANK.   Especially that they should revenge themselves on the unlucky bones of
those who have not had the satisfaction of enjoying them.

NORA.   Yes, that's the saddest part of it all.

RANK.   [*with a searching look at her*] Hm!—

NORA.   [*after a short pause*] Why did you smile?

RANK.   No, it was you that laughed.

NORA.   No, it was you that smiled, Doctor Rank!   170

RANK.   [*rising*] You are a greater rascal than I thought.

NORA.   I am in a silly mood to-day.

RANK.   So it seems.

NORA.   [*putting her hands on his shoulders*] Dear, dear Doctor Rank, death mustn't   175
take you away from Torvald and me.

RANK.   It is a loss you would easily recover from. Those who are gone are soon
forgotten.

NORA.   [*looking at him anxiously*] Do you believe that?

RANK.   People form new ties, and then—

NORA.   Who will form new ties?

RANK.   Both you and Helmer, when I am gone. You yourself are already on the   180
high road to it, I think. What did that Mrs. Linde want here last night?

NORA.   Oho!—you don't mean to say you are jealous of poor Christine?

RANK.   Yes, I am. She will be my successor in this house. When I am done for, this
woman will—

NORA.   Hush! don't speak so loud. She is in that room.

RANK.   To-day again. There, you see.

NORA.   She has only come to sew my dress for me. Bless my soul, how unreason-   185
able you are! [*sits down on the sofa*] Be nice now, Doctor Rank, and tomorrow you will
see how beautifully I shall dance, and you can imagine I am doing it all for you—and for
Torvald too, of course. [*takes various things out of the box*] Doctor Rank, come and sit down
here, and I will show you something.

RANK.   [*sitting down*] What is it?

NORA.   Just look at those!

RANK.   Silk stockings.

NORA.   Flesh-coloured. Aren't they lovely? It is so dark here now, but tomorrow—. No, no, no! you must only look at the feet. Oh well, you may have leave to
look at the legs too.

RANK.   Hm!—   190

NORA.   Why are you looking so critical? Don't you think they will fit me?

RANK.   I have no means of forming an opinion about that.

NORA.   [*looks at him for a moment*] For shame! [*hits him lightly on the ear with the
stockings*] That's to punish you. [*folds them up again*]

RANK. And what other nice things am I to be allowed to see?

NORA. Not a single thing more, for being so naughty. [*She looks among the things,* 195
humming to herself.]

RANK. [*after a short silence*] When I am sitting here, talking to you as intimately as
this, I cannot imagine for a moment what would have become of me if I had never come
into this house.

NORA. [*smiling*] I believe you do feel thoroughly at home with us.

RANK. [*in a lower voice, looking straight in front of him*] And to be obliged to leave it
all—

NORA. Nonsense, you are not going to leave it.

RANK. [*as before*] And not be able to leave behind one the slightest token of one's 200
gratitude, scarcely even a fleeting regret—nothing but an empty place which the first
comer can fill as well as any other.

NORA. And if I asked you now for a—? No!

RANK. For what?

NORA. For a big proof of your friendship—

RANK. Yes, yes!

NORA. I mean a tremendously big favour— 205

RANK. Would you really make me so happy for once?

NORA. Ah, but you don't know what it is yet.

RANK. No—but tell me.

NORA. I really can't, Doctor Rank. It is something out of all reason; it means
advice, and help, and a favour—

RANK. The bigger a thing it is the better. I can't conceive what it is you mean. 210
Do tell me. Haven't I your confidence?

NORA. More than anyone else. I know you are my truest and best friend, and so
I will tell you what it is. Well, Doctor Rank, it is something you must help me to prevent.
You know how devotedly, how inexpressibly deeply Torvald loves me; he would never
for a moment hesitate to give his life for me.

RANK. [*leaning towards her*] Nora—do you think he is the only one—?

NORA. [*with a slight start*] The only one—?

RANK. The only one who would gladly give his life for your sake.

NORA. [*sadly*] Is that it? 215

RANK. I was determined you should know it before I went away, and there will
never be a better opportunity than this. Now you know it, Nora. And now you know, too,
that you can trust me as you would trust no one else.

NORA. [*rises, deliberately and quietly*] Let me pass.

RANK. [*makes room for her to pass him, but sits still*] Nora!

NORA. [*at the hall door*] Helen, bring in the lamp. [*goes over to the stove*] Dear
Doctor Rank, that was really horrid of you.

RANK. To have loved you as much as anyone else does? Was that horrid? 220

NORA. No, but to go and tell me so. There was really no need—

RANK. What do you mean? Did you know—? [*MAID enters with lamp, puts it down
on the table, and goes out.*] Nora—Mrs. Helmer—tell me, had you any idea of this?

NORA. Oh, how do I know whether I had or whether I hadn't? I really can't tell
you— To think you could be so clumsy, Doctor Rank! We were getting on so nicely.

RANK. Well, at all events you know now that you can command me, body and
soul. So won't you speak out?

NORA. [*looking at him*] After what happened? 225

RANK.   I beg you to let me know what it is.

NORA.   I can't tell you anything now.

RANK.   Yes, yes. You mustn't punish me in that way. Let me have permission to do for you whatever a man may do.

NORA.   You can do nothing for me now. Besides, I really don't need any help at all. You will find that the whole thing is merely fancy on my part. It really is so—of course it is! [*Sits down in the rocking-chair, and looks at him with a smile*] You are a nice sort of man, Doctor Rank!—don't you feel ashamed of yourself, now the lamp has come?

RANK.   Not a bit. But perhaps I had better go—for ever?   230

NORA.   No, indeed, you shall not. Of course you must come here just as before. You know very well Torvald can't do without you.

RANK.   Yes, but you?

NORA.   Oh, I am always tremendously pleased when you come.

RANK.   It is just that, that put me on the wrong track. You are a riddle to me. I have often thought that you would almost as soon be in my company as in Helmer's.

NORA.   Yes—you see there are some people one loves best, and others whom one   235
would almost always rather have as companions.

RANK.   Yes, there is something in that.

NORA.   When I was at home, of course I loved papa best. But I always thought it tremendous fun if I could steal down into the maid's room, because they never moralised at all, and talked to each other about such entertaining things.

RANK.   I see—it is *their* place I have taken.

NORA.   [*jumping up and going to him*] Oh, dear, nice Doctor Rank, I never meant that at all. But surely you can understand that being with Torvald is a little like being with papa—

[*Enter MAID from the hall*]

MAID.   If you please, ma'am. [*whispers and hands her a card*]   240

NORA.   [*glancing at the card*] Oh! [*puts it in her pocket*]

RANK.   Is there anything wrong?

NORA.   No, no, not in the least. It is only something—it is my new dress—

RANK.   What? Your dress is lying there.

NORA.   Oh, yes, that one; but this is another. I ordered it. Torvald mustn't know   245
about it—

RANK.   Oho! Then that was the great secret.

NORA.   Of course. Just go in to him; he is sitting in the inner room. Keep him as long as—

RANK.   Make your mind easy; I won't let him escape. [*goes into HELMER'S room*]

NORA.   [*to the MAID*] And he is standing waiting in the kitchen?

MAID.   Yes; he came up the back stairs.   250

NORA.   But didn't you tell him no one was in?

MAID.   Yes, but it was no good.

NORA.   He won't go away?

MAID.   No; he says he won't until he has seen you, ma'am.

NORA.   Well, let him come in—but quietly. Helen, you mustn't say anything about   255
it to anyone. It is a surprise for my husband.

MAID.   Yes, ma'am, I quite understand. [*Exit.*]

NORA.   This dreadful thing is going to happen! It will happen in spite of me! No, no, no, it can't happen—it shan't happen!

[*She bolts the door of* HELMER'S *room. The* MAID *opens the hall door for* KROGSTAD *and shuts it after him. He is wearing a fur coat, high boots and a fur cap.*]

NORA.   [*advancing towards him*] Speak low—my husband is at home.

KROGSTAD.   No matter about that.

NORA.   What do you want of me?   260

KROGSTAD.   An explanation of something.

NORA.   Make haste then. What is it?

KROGSTAD.   You know, I suppose, that I have got my dismissal.

NORA.   I couldn't prevent it, Mr. Krogstad. I fought as hard as I could on your side, but it was no good.

KROGSTAD.   Does your husband love you so little, then? He knows that what I can   265
expose you to, and yet he ventures—

NORA.   How can you suppose that he has any knowledge of the sort?

KROGSTAD.   I didn't suppose so at all. It would not be the least like our dear Torvald Helmer to show so much courage—

NORA.   Mr. Krogstad, a little respect for my husband, please.

KROGSTAD.   Certainly—all the respect he deserves. But since you have kept the matter so carefully to yourself, I make bold to suppose that you have a little clearer idea, than you had yesterday, of what it actually is that you have done?

NORA.   More than you could ever teach me.   270

KROGSTAD.   Yes, such a bad lawyer as I am.

NORA.   What is it you want of me?

KROGSTAD.   Only to see how you were, Mrs. Helmer. I have been thinking about you all day long. A mere cashier, a quill-driver, a—well, a man like me—even he has a little of what is called feeling, you know.

NORA.   Show it, then; think of my little children.

KROGSTAD.   Have you and your husband thought of mine? But never mind about   275
that. I only wanted to tell you that you need not take this matter too seriously. In the first place there will be no accusation made on my part.

NORA.   No, of course not; I was sure of that.

KROGSTAD.   The whole thing can be arranged amicably; there is no reason why anyone should know anything about it. It will remain a secret between us three.

NORA.   My husband must never get to know anything about it.

KROGSTAD.   How will you be able to prevent it? Am I to understand that you can pay the balance that is owing?

NORA.   No, not just at present.   280

KROGSTAD.   Or perhaps that you have some expedient for raising the money soon?

NORA.   No expedient that I mean to make use of.

KROGSTAD.   Well, in any case, it would have been of no use to you now. If you stood there with ever so much money in your hand, I would never part with your bond.

NORA.   Tell me what purpose you mean to put it to.

KROGSTAD.   I shall only preserve it—keep it in my possession. No one who is not   285
concerned in the matter shall have the slightest hint of it. So that if the thought of it has driven you to any desperate resolution—

NORA.   It has.

KROGSTAD.   If you had it in your mind to run away from your home—

NORA.   I had.

KROGSTAD.   Or even something worse—

NORA.   How could you know that?   290

KROGSTAD.   Give up the idea.

NORA.   How did you know I had thought of *that*?

KROGSTAD.   Most of us think of that at first. I did, too—but I hadn't the courage.

NORA.   [*faintly*] No more had I.

KROGSTAD.   [*in a tone of relief*] No, that's it, isn't it—you hadn't the courage   295
either?

NORA.   No, I haven't—I haven't.

KROGSTAD.   Besides, it would have been a great piece of folly. Once the first storm
at home is over—. I have a letter for your husband in my pocket.

NORA.   Telling him everything?

KROGSTAD.   In as lenient a manner as I possibly could.

NORA.   [*quickly*] He mustn't get the letter. Tear it up. I will find some means of   300
getting money.

KROGSTAD.   Excuse me, Mrs. Helmer, but I think I told you just now—

NORA.   I am not speaking of what I owe you. Tell me what sum you are asking
my husband for, and I will get the money.

KROGSTAD.   I am not asking your husband for a penny.

NORA.   What do you want, then?

KROGSTAD.   I will tell you. I want to rehabilitate myself, Mrs. Helmer; I want to   305
get on; and in that your husband must help me. For the last year and a half I have not
had a hand in anything dishonourable, and all that time I have been struggling in most
restricted circumstances. I was content to work my way up step by step. Now I am turned
out, and I am not going to be satisfied with merely being taken into favour again. I want
to get on, I tell you. I want to get into the Bank again, in a higher position. Your husband
must make a place for me—

NORA.   That he will never do!

KROGSTAD.   He will; I know him; he dare not protest. And as soon as I am in there
again with him, then you will see! Within a year I shall be the manager's right hand. It
will be Nils Krogstad and not Torvald Helmer who manages the Bank.

NORA.   That's a thing you will never see!

KROGSTAD.   Do you mean that you will—?

NORA.   I have courage enough for it now.   310

KROGSTAD.   Oh, you can't frighten me. A fine, spoilt lady like you—

NORA.   You will see, you will see.

KROGSTAD.   Under the ice, perhaps? Down into the cold, coal-black water? And
then, in the spring, to float up to the surface, all horrible and unrecognisable, with your
hair fallen out—

NORA.   You can't frighten me.

KROGSTAD.   Nor you me. People don't do such things, Mrs. Helmer. Besides, what   31
use would it be? I should have him completely in my power all the same.

NORA.   Afterwards? When I am no longer—

KROGSTAD.   Have you forgotten that it is I who have the keeping of your reputation? [*NORA stands speechlessly looking at him.*] Well, now, I have warned you. Do not do
anything foolish. When Helmer has had my letter, I shall expect a message from him.

And be sure you remember that it is your husband himself who has forced me into such ways as this again. I will never forgive him for that. Good-bye, Mrs. Helmer.

[*Exit through the hall*]

NORA. [*goes to the hall door, opens it slightly and listens*] He is going. He is not putting the letter in the box. Oh no, no! that's impossible! [*opens the door by degrees*] What is that? He is standing outside. He is not going downstairs. Is he hesitating? Can he—

[*A letter drops into the box; then* KROGSTAD's *footsteps are heard, till they die away as he goes downstairs.* NORA *utters a stifled cry and runs across the room to the table by the sofa. A short pause.*]

NORA.   In the letter-box. [*steals across to the hall door*] There it lies—Torvald, Torvald, there is no hope for us now!

[*MRS. LINDE comes in from the room on the left, carrying the dress.*]

MRS. LINDE.   There, I can't see anything more to mend now. Would you like to try   320
it on—?
NORA.   [*in a hoarse whisper*] Christine, come here.
MRS. LINDE.   [*throwing the dress down on the sofa*] What is the matter with you? You look so agitated!
NORA.   Come here. Do you see that letter? There, look—you can see it through the glass in the letter-box.
MRS. LINDE.   Yes, I see it.
NORA.   That letter is from Krogstad.   325
MRS. LINDE.   Nora—it was Krogstad who lent you the money!
NORA.   Yes, and now Torvald will know all about it.
MRS. LINDE.   Believe me, Nora, that's the best thing for both of you.
NORA.   You don't know all. I forged a name.
MRS. LINDE.   Good heavens—!   330
NORA.   I only want to say this to you, Christine—you must be my witness.
MRS. LINDE.   Your witness? What do you mean? What am I to—?
NORA.   If I should go out of my mind—and it might easily happen—
MRS. LINDE.   Nora!
NORA.   Or if anything else should happen to me—anything, for instance, that   335
might prevent my being here—
MRS. LINDE.   Nora! Nora! you are quite out of your mind.
NORA.   And if it should happen that there were someone who wanted to take all the responsibility, all the blame, you understand—
MRS. LINDE.   Yes, yes—but how can you suppose—?
NORA.   Then you must be my witness, that it is not true, Christine. I am not out of my mind at all; I am in my right senses now, and I tell you no one else has known anything about it; I, and I alone, did the whole thing. Remember that.
MRS. LINDE.   I will, indeed. But I don't understand all this.   340
NORA.   How should you understand it? A wonderful thing is going to happen.
MRS. LINDE.   A wonderful thing?
NORA.   Yes, a wonderful thing!—But it is so terrible, Christine; it *mustn't* happen, not for all the world.
MRS. LINDE.   I will go at once and see Krogstad.
NORA.   Don't go to him; he will do you some harm.   345
MRS. LINDE.   There was a time when he would gladly do anything for my sake.

NORA.   He?

MRS. LINDE.   Where does he live?

NORA.   How should I know—? Yes [*feeling in her pocket*] here is his card. But the letter, the letter—!

HELMER.   [*calls from his room, knocking at the door*] Nora!   350

NORA.   [*cries out anxiously*] Oh, what's that? What do you want?

HELMER.   Don't be so frightened. We are not coming in; you have locked the door. Are you trying on your dress?

NORA.   Yes, that's it. I look so nice, Torvald.

MRS. LINDE.   [*who has read the card*] I see he lives at the corner here.

NORA.   Yes, but it's no use. It is hopeless. The letter is lying there in the box.   355

MRS. LINDE.   And your husband keeps the key?

NORA.   Yes, always.

MRS. LINDE.   Krogstad must ask for his letter back unread, he must find some pretence—

NORA.   But it is just at this time that Torvald generally—

MRS. LINDE.   You must delay him. Go in to him in the meantime. I will come back   360 as soon as I can.

[*She goes out hurriedly through the hall door.*]

NORA.   [*goes to HELMER's door, opens it and peeps in*] Torvald!

HELMER.   [*from the inner room*] Well? May I venture at last to come into my own room again? Come along, Rank, now you will see— [*halting in the doorway*] But what is this?

NORA.   What is what, dear?

HELMER.   Rank led me to expect a splendid transformation.

RANK.   [*in the doorway*] I understood so, but evidently I was mistaken.   365

NORA.   Yes, nobody is to have the chance of admiring me in my dress until tomorrow.

HELMER.   But, my dear Nora, you look so worn out. Have you been practising too much?

NORA.   No, I have not practised at all.

HELMER.   But you will need to—

NORA.   Yes, indeed I shall, Torvald. But I can't get on a bit without you to help   370 me; I have absolutely forgotten the whole thing.

HELMER.   Oh, we will soon work it up again.

NORA.   Yes, help me, Torvald. Promise that you will! I am so nervous about it—all the people—. You must give yourself up to me entirely this evening. Not the tiniest bit of business—you mustn't even take a pen in your hand. Will you promise, Torvald dear?

HELMER.   I promise. This evening I will be wholly and absolutely at your service, you helpless little mortal. Ah, by the way, first of all I will just—

[*Goes towards the hall door*]

NORA.   What are you going to do there?

HELMER.   Only see if any letters have come.   37

NORA.   No, no! don't do that, Torvald!

HELMER.   Why not?

NORA.   Torvald, please don't. There is nothing there.

HELMER.   Well, let me look. [*Turns to go to the letter-box. NORA, at the piano, plays the first bars of the Tarantella. HELMER stops in the doorway.*] Aha!

NORA.   I can't dance to-morrow if I don't practise with you.   380

HELMER.   [*going up to her*] Are you really so afraid of it, dear.

NORA.   Yes, so dreadfully afraid of it. Let me practise at once; there is time now, before we go to dinner. Sit down and play for me, Torvald dear; criticise me, and correct me as you play.

HELMER.   With great pleasure, if you wish me to.

[*Sits down at the piano.*]

NORA.   [*takes out of the box a tambourine and a long variegated shawl. She hastily drapes the shawl round her. Then she springs to the front of the stage and calls out.*] Now play for me! I am going to dance!

[*HELMER plays and NORA dances. RANK stands by the piano behind HELMER and looks on.*]

HELMER.   [*as he plays*] Slower, slower!   385

NORA.   I can't do it any other way.

HELMER.   Not so violently, Nora!

NORA.   This is the way.

HELMER.   [*stops playing*] No, no—that is not a bit right.

NORA.   [*laughing and swinging the tambourine*] Didn't I tell you so?   390

RANK.   Let me play for her.

HELMER.   [*getting up*] Yes, do. I can correct her better then.

[*RANK sits down at the piano and plays. NORA dances more and more wildly. HELMER has taken up a position beside the stove, and during her dance gives her frequent instructions. She does not seem to hear him; her hair comes down and falls over her shoulders; she pays no attention to it, but goes on dancing. Enter MRS. LINDE.*]

MRS. LINDE.   [*standing as if spell-bound in the doorway*] Oh!—

NORA.   [*as she dances*] Such fun, Christine!

HELMER.   My dear darling Nora, you are dancing as if your life depended on it.   395

NORA.   So it does.

HELMER.   Stop, Rank; this is sheer madness. Stop, I tell you! [*RANK stops playing, and NORA suddenly stands still. HELMER goes up to her.*] I could never have believed it. You have forgotten everything I taught you.

NORA.   [*throwing away the tambourine*] There, you see.

HELMER.   You will want a lot of coaching.

NORA.   Yes, you see how much I need it. You must coach me up to the last   400
minute. Promise me that, Torvald!

HELMER.   You can depend on me.

NORA.   You must not think of anything but me, either to-day or to-morrow; you mustn't open a single letter—not even open the letter-box—

HELMER.   Ah, you are still afraid of that fellow—

NORA.   Yes, indeed I am.

HELMER.   Nora, I can tell from your looks that there is a letter from him lying   405
there.

NORA.   I don't know; I think there is; but you must not read anything of that kind now. Nothing horrid must come between us till this is all over.

RANK.   [*whispers to HELMER*] You mustn't contradict her.

HELMER.   [*taking her in his arms*] The child shall have her way. But to-morrow night, after you have danced—

NORA.   Then you will be free.

[*MAID appears in the doorway to the right.*]

MAID.   Dinner is served, ma'am.   410

NORA.   We will have champagne, Helen.

MAID.   Very good, ma'am.   [*Exit.*]

HELMER.   Hullo!—are we going to have a banquet?

NORA.   Yes, a champagne banquet till the small hours. [*calls out*] And a few macaroons, Helen—lots, just for once!

HELMER.   Come, come, don't be so wild and nervous. Be my own little skylark,   415
as you used.

NORA.   Yes, dear, I will. But go in now and you too, Doctor Rank. Christine, you must help me to do up my hair.

RANK.   [*whispers to HELMER as they go out*] I suppose there is nothing—she is not expecting anything?

HELMER.   Far from it, my dear fellow; it is simply nothing more than this childish nervousness I was telling you of.

[*They go into the right-hand room.*]

NORA.   Well!

MRS. LINDE.   Gone out of town.   420

NORA.   I could tell from your face.

MRS. LINDE.   He is coming home to-morrow evening. I wrote a note for him.

NORA.   You should have let it alone; you must prevent nothing. After all, it is splendid to be waiting for a wonderful thing to happen.

MRS. LINDE.   What is it that you are waiting for?

NORA.   Oh, you wouldn't understand. Go in to them, I will come in a moment.   425
[*MRS. LINDE goes into the dining-room. NORA stands still for a little while, as if to compose herself. Then she looks at her watch.*] Five o'clock. Seven hours till midnight; and then four-and twenty hours till the next midnight. Then the Tarantella will be over. Twenty-four and seven? Thirty-one hours to live.

HELMER.   [*from the doorway on the right*] Where's my little skylark?

NORA.   [*going to him with her arms outstretched*] Here she is!

ACT 3

THE SAME SCENE. *The table has been placed in the middle of the stage, with chairs round it. A lamp is burning on the table. The door into the hall stands open. Dance music is heard in the room above. MRS. LINDE is sitting at the table idly turning over the leaves of a book; she tries to read, but does not seem able to collect her thoughts. Every now and then she listens intently for a sound at the outer door.*

MRS. LINDE.   [*looking at her watch*] Not yet—and the time is nearly up. If only he does not—. [*listens again*] Ah, there he is. [*Goes into the hall and opens the outer door carefully. Light footsteps are heard on the stairs. She whispers.*] Come in. There is no one here.

KROGSTAD.   [*in the doorway*] I found a note from you at home. What does this mean?

MRS. LINDE.   It is absolutely necessary that I should have a talk with you.

KROGSTAD.   Really? And is it absolutely necessary that it should be here?

MRS. LINDE.   It is impossible where I live; there is no private entrance to my   5
rooms. Come in; we are quite alone. The maid is asleep, and the Helmers are at the dance upstairs.

KROGSTAD.   [*coming into the room*] Are the Helmers really at a dance to-night?

MRS. LINDE.   Yes, why not?

KROGSTAD.   Certainly—why not?

MRS. LINDE.   Now, Nils, let us have a talk.

KROGSTAD.   Can we two have anything to talk about?   10

MRS. LINDE.   We have a great deal to talk about.

KROGSTAD.   I shouldn't have thought so.

MRS. LINDE.   No, you have never properly understood me.

KROGSTAD.   Was there anything else to understand except what was obvious to all the world—a heartless woman jilts a man when a more lucrative chance turns up?

MRS. LINDE.   Do you believe I am as absolutely heartless as all that? And do you   15
believe that I did it with a light heart?

KROGSTAD.   Didn't you?

MRS. LINDE.   Nils, did you really think that?

KROGSTAD.   If it were as you say, why did you write to me as you did at the time?

MRS. LINDE.   I could do nothing else. As I had to break with you, it was my duty also to put an end to all that you felt for me.

KROGSTAD.   [*wringing his hands*] So that was it. and all this—only for the sake of   20
money!

MRS. LINDE.   You must not forget that I had a helpless mother and two little brothers. We couldn't wait for you, Nils; your prospects seemed hopeless then.

KROGSTAD.   That may be so, but you had no right to throw me over for any one else's sake.

MRS. LINDE.   Indeed I don't know. Many a time did I ask myself if I had the right to do it.

KROGSTAD.   [*more gently*] When I lost you, it was as if all the solid ground went from under my feet. Look at me now—I am a shipwrecked man clinging to a bit of wreckage.

MRS. LINDE.   But help may be near.   25

KROGSTAD.   It *was* near; but then you came and stood in my way.

MRS. LINDE.   Unintentionally, Nils. It was only to-day that I learnt it was your place I was going to take in the Bank.

KROGSTAD.   I believe you, if you say so. But now that you know it, are you not going to give it up to me?

MRS. LINDE.   No, because that would not benefit you in the least.

KROGSTAD.   Oh, benefit, benefit—I would have done it whether or no.   30

MRS. LINDE.   I have learnt to act prudently. Life, and hard, bitter necessity have taught me that.

KROGSTAD.   And life has taught me not to believe in fine speeches.

MRS. LINDE.   Then life has taught you something very reasonable. But deeds you must believe in?

KROGSTAD.   What do you mean by that?

MRS. LINDE.   You said you were like a shipwrecked man clinging to some wreckage.   35
KROGSTAD.   I had good reason to say so.
MRS. LINDE.   Well, I am like a shipwrecked woman clinging to some wreckage—no one to mourn for, no one to care for.
KROGSTAD.   It was your own choice.
MRS. LINDE.   There was no other choice—then.
KROGSTAD.   Well, what now?   40
MRS. LINDE.   Nils, how would it be if we two shipwrecked people could join forces?
KROGSTAD.   What are you saying?
MRS. LINDE.   Two on the same piece of wreckage would stand a better chance than each on their own.
KROGSTAD.   Christine!
MRS. LINDE.   What do you suppose brought me to town?   45
KROGSTAD.   Do you mean that you gave me a thought?
MRS. LINDE.   I could not endure life without work. All my life, as long as I can remember, I have worked, and it has been my greatest and only pleasure. But now I am quite alone in the world—my life is so dreadfully empty and I feel so forsaken. There is not the least pleasure in working for one's self. Nils, give me someone and something to work for.
KROGSTAD.   I don't trust that. It is nothing but a woman's overstrained sense of generosity that prompts you to make such an offer of yourself.
MRS. LINDE.   Have you ever noticed anything of the sort in me?
KROGSTAD.   Could you really do it? Tell me—do you know all about my past life?   50
MRS. LINDE.   Yes.
KROGSTAD.   And do you know what they think of me here?
MRS. LINDE.   You seemed to me to imply that with me you might have been quite another man.
KROGSTAD.   I am certain of it.
MRS. LINDE.   Is it too late now?   55
KROGSTAD.   Christine, are you saying this deliberately? Yes, I am sure you are. I see it in your face. Have you really the courage, then—?
MRS. LINDE.   I want to be a mother to someone, and your children need a mother. We two need each other. Nils, I have faith in your real character—I can dare anything together with you.
KROGSTAD.   [*grasps her hands*] Thanks, thanks, Christine! Now I shall find a way to clear myself in the eyes of the world. Ah, but I forgot—
MRS. LINDE.   [*listening*] Hush! The Tarantella! Go, go!
KROGSTAD.   Why? What is it?   60
MRS. LINDE.   Do you hear them up there? When that is over, we may expect them back.
KROGSTAD.   Yes, yes—I will go. But it is all no use. Of course you are not aware what steps I have taken in the matter of the Helmers.
MRS. LINDE.   Yes. I know all about that.
KROGSTAD.   And in spite of that have you the courage to—?
MRS. LINDE.   I understand very well to what lengths a man like you might be   65
driven by despair.
KROGSTAD.   If I could only undo what I have done!
MRS. LINDE.   You can. Your letter is lying in the letter-box now.

KROGSTAD.   Are you sure of that?

MRS. LINDE.   Quite sure, but—

KROGSTAD.   [*with a searching look at her*] Is that what it all means?—that you want to   70
save your friend at any cost? Tell me frankly. Is that it?

MRS. LINDE.   Nils, a woman who has once sold herself for another's sake, doesn't
do it a second time.

KROGSTAD.   I will ask for my letter back.

MRS. LINDE.   No, no.

KROGSTAD.   Yes, of course I will. I will wait here till Helmer comes; I will tell him
he must give me my letter back—that it only concerns my dismissal—that he is not to
read it—

MRS. LINDE.   No, Nils, you must not recall your letter.   75

KROGSTAD.   But, tell me, wasn't it for that very purpose that you asked me to meet
you here?

MRS. LINDE.   In my first moment of fright, it was. But twenty-four hours have
elapsed since then, and in that time I have witnessed incredible things in this house.
Helmer must know all about it. This unhappy secret must be disclosed; they must have a
complete understanding between them, which is impossible with all this concealment
and falsehood going on.

KROGSTAD.   Very well, if you will take the responsibility. But there is one thing I
can do in any case, and I shall do it at once.

MRS. LINDE.   [*listening*] You must be quick and go! The dance is over; we are not
safe a moment longer.

KROGSTAD.   I will wait for you below.   80

MRS. LINDE.   Yes, do. You must see me back to my door.

KROGSTAD.   I have never had such an amazing piece of good fortune in my life.

[*Goes out through the outer door. The door between the room and the hall remains open.*]

MRS. LINDE.   [*tidying up the room and laying her hat and cloak ready*] What a difference! what a difference! Someone to work for and live for—a home to bring comfort
into. That I will do, indeed. I wish they would be quick and come— [*listens*] Ah, there
they are now. I must put on my things.

[*Takes up her hat and cloak. HELMER'S and NORA'S voices are heard outside; a key is turned,
and HELMER brings NORA almost by force into the hall. She is in an Italian costume with a large
black shawl round her; he is in evening dress and a black domino which is flying open.*]

NORA.   [*hanging back in the doorway, and struggling with him*] No, no, no!—don't
take me in. I want to go upstairs again; I don't want to leave so early.

HELMER.   But, my dearest Nora—   85

NORA.   Please, Torvald dear—please, *please*—only an hour more.

HELMER.   Not a single minute, my sweet Nora. You know that was our agreement.
Come along into the room; you are catching cold standing there.

[*He brings her gently into the room, in spite of her resistance.*]

MRS. LINDE.   Good evening.

NORA.   Christine!

HELMER.   You here, so late, Mrs. Linde?   90

MRS. LINDE.   Yes, you must excuse me; I was so anxious to see Nora in her dress.

NORA.   Have you been sitting here waiting for me?

MRS. LINDE.   Yes, unfortunately I came too late, you had already gone upstairs; and I thought I couldn't go away without having seen you.

HELMER.   [*taking off NORA's shawl*] Yes, take a good look at her. I think she is worth looking at. Isn't she charming, Mrs. Linde?

MRS. LINDE.   Yes, indeed she is.   95

HELMER.   Doesn't she look remarkably pretty? Everyone thought so at the dance. But she is terribly self-willed, this sweet little person. What are we to do with her? You will hardly believe that I had almost to bring her away by force.

NORA.   Torvald, you will repent not having let me stay, even if it were only for half an hour.

HELMER.   Listen to her, Mrs. Linde! She had danced her Tarantella, and it had been a tremendous success, as it deserved—although possibly the performance was a trifle too realistic—a little more so, I mean, than was strictly compatible with the limitations of art. But never mind about that! The chief thing is, she had made a success— she had made a tremendous success. Do you think I was going to let her remain there after that, and spoil the effect? No indeed! I took my charming little Capri maiden— my capricious little Capri maiden, I should say—on my arm; took one quick turn round the room; a curtsey on either side, and, as they say in novels, the beautiful apparition disappeared. An exit ought always to be effective, Mrs. Linde; but that is what I cannot make Nora understand. Pooh! this room is hot. [*throws his domino on a chair and opens the door of his room*] Hullo! it's all dark in here. Oh, of course—excuse me—.

[*He goes in and lights some candles.*]

NORA.   [*in a hurried and breathless whisper*] Well?

MRS. LINDE.   [*in a low voice*] I have had a talk with him.   100

NORA.   Yes, and—

MRS. LINDE.   Nora, you must tell your husband all about it.

NORA.   [*in an expressionless voice*] I knew it.

MRS. LINDE.   You have nothing to be afraid of as far as Krogstad is concerned; but you must tell him.

NORA.   I won't tell him.   105

MRS. LINDE.   Then the letter will.

NORA.   Thank you, Christine. Now I know what I must do. Hush—!

HELMER.   [*coming in again*] Well, Mrs. Linde, have you admired her?

MRS. LINDE.   Yes, and now I will say good-night.

HELMER.   What already? Is this yours, this knitting?   110

MRS. LINDE.   [*taking it*] Yes, thank you, I had very nearly forgotten it.

HELMER.   So you knit?

MRS. LINDE.   Of course.

HELMER.   Do you know, you ought to embroider.

MRS. LINDE.   Really? Why?   115

HELMER.   Yes, it's far more becoming. Let me show you. You hold the embroidery thus in your left hand, and use the needle with the right—like this—with a long, easy sweep. Do you see?

MRS. LINDE.   Yes, perhaps—

HELMER.   But in the case of knitting—that can never be anything but ungraceful; look here—the arms close together, the knitting-needles going up and down—it has a sort of Chinese effect—. That was really excellent champagne they gave us.

MRS. LINDE.   Well,—good-night, Nora, and don't be self-willed any more.

HELMER. That's right, Mrs. Linde. 120

MRS. LINDE. Good-night, Mr. Helmer.

HELMER. [*accompanying her to the door*] Good-night, good-night. I hope you will get home all right. I should be very happy to—but you haven't any great distance to go. Good-night, good-night. [*She goes out; he shuts the door after her, and comes in again.*] Ah!— at last we have got rid of her. She is a frightful bore, that woman.

NORA. Aren't you very tired, Torvald?

HELMER. No, not in the least.

NORA. Nor sleepy? 125

HELMER. Not a bit. On the contrary, I feel extraordinarily lively. And you?—you really look both tired and sleepy.

NORA. Yes, I am very tired. I want to go to sleep at once.

HELMER. There, you see it was quite right of me not to let you stay there any longer.

NORA. Everything you do is quite right, Torvald.

HELMER. [*kissing her on the forehead*] Now my little skylark is speaking reasonably. 130 Did you notice what good spirits Rank was in this evening?

NORA. Really? Was he? I didn't speak to him at all.

HELMER. And I very little, but I have not for a long time seen him in such good form. [*looks for a while at her and then goes nearer to her*] It is delightful to be at home by ourselves again, to be all alone with you—you fascinating, charming little darling!

NORA. Don't look at me like that, Torvald.

HELMER. Why shouldn't I look at my dearest treasure?—at all the beauty that is mine, all my very own?

NORA. [*going to the other side of the table*] You mustn't say things like that to me 135 to-night.

HELMER. [*following her*] You have still got the Tarantella in your blood, I see. And it makes you more captivating than ever. Listen—the guests are beginning to go now. [*in a lower voice*] Nora—soon the whole house will be quiet.

NORA. Yes, I hope so.

HELMER. Yes, my own darling Nora. Do you know, when I am out at a party with you like this, why I speak so little to you, keep away from you, and only send a stolen glance in your direction now and then?—do you know why I do that? It is because I make believe to myself that we are secretly in love, and you are my secretly promised bride, and that no one suspects there is anything between us.

NORA. Yes, yes—I know very well your thoughts are with me all the time.

HELMER. And when we are leaving, and I am putting the shawl over your beau- 140 tiful young shoulders—on your lovely neck—then I imagine that you are my young bride and that we have just come from the wedding, and I am bringing you for the first time into our home—to be alone with you for the first time—quite alone with my shy little darling! All this evening I have longed for nothing but you. When I watched the seductive figures of the Tarantella, my blood was on fire; I could endure it no longer, and that was why I brought you down so early—

NORA. Go away, Torvald! You must let me go. I won't—

HELMER. What's that? You're joking, my little Nora! You won't—you won't? Am I not your husband—?

[*A knock is heard at the outer door.*]

NORA. [*starting*] Did you hear—?

HELMER.   [*going into the hall*] Who is it?

RANK.   [*outside*] It is I. May I come in for a moment?   145

HELMER.   [*in a fretful whisper*] Oh, what does he want now? [*aloud*] Wait a minute!
[*unlocks the door*] Come, that's kind of you not to pass by our door.

RANK.   I thought I heard your voice, and felt as if I should like to look in. [*with a
swift glance round*] Ah, yes!—these dear familiar rooms. You are very happy and cosy in
here, you two.

HELMER.   It seems to me that you looked after yourself pretty well upstairs too.

RANK.   Excellently. Why shouldn't I? Why shouldn't one enjoy everything in this
world?—at any rate as much as one can, and as long as one can. The wine was capital—

HELMER.   Especially the champagne.   150

RANK.   So you noticed that too? It is almost incredible how much I managed to
put away!

NORA.   Torvald drank a great deal of champagne tonight, too.

RANK.   Did he?

NORA.   Yes, and he is always in such good spirits afterwards.

RANK.   Well, why should one not enjoy a merry evening after a well-spent day?   155

HELMER.   Well spent? I am afraid I can't take credit for that.

RANK.   [*clapping him on the back*] But I can, you know!

NORA.   Doctor Rank, you must have been occupied with some scientific investigation to-day.

RANK.   Exactly.

HELMER.   Just listen!—little Nora talking about scientific investigations!   160

NORA.   And may I congratulate you on the result?

RANK.   Indeed you may.

NORA.   Was it favourable, then?

RANK.   The best possible, for both doctor and patient—certainty.

NORA.   [*quickly and searchingly*] Certainty?   165

RANK.   Absolute certainty. So wasn't I entitled to make a merry evening of it
after that?

NORA.   Yes, you certainly were, Doctor Rank.

HELMER.   I think so too, so long as you don't have to pay for it in the morning.

RANK.   Oh well, one can't have anything in this life without paying for it.

NORA.   Doctor Rank—are you fond of fancy-dress balls?   170

RANK.   Yes, if there is a fine lot of pretty costumes.

NORA.   Tell me—what shall we two wear at the next?

HELMER.   Little featherbrain!—are you thinking of the next already?

RANK.   We two? Yes, I can tell you. You shall go as a good fairy—

HELMER.   Yes, but what do you suggest as an appropriate costume for that?   175

RANK.   Let your wife go dressed just as she is in everyday life.

HELMER.   That was really very prettily turned. But can't you tell us what you
will be?

RANK.   Yes, my dear friend, I have quite made up my mind about that.

HELMER.   Well?

RANK.   At the next fancy dress ball I shall be invisible.   180

HELMER.   That's a good joke!

RANK.   There is a big black hat—have you never heard of hats that make you
invisible? If you put one on, no one can see you.

HELMER. [*suppressing a smile*] Yes, you are quite right.

RANK. But I am clean forgetting what I came for. Helmer, give me a cigar—one of the dark Havanas.

HELMER. With the greatest pleasure. [*offers him his case*]

RANK. [*takes a cigar and cuts off the end*] Thanks.

NORA. [*striking a match*] Let me give you a light.

RANK. Thank you. [*She holds the match for him to light his cigar.*] And now good-bye!

HELMER. Good-bye, good-bye, dear old man!

NORA. Sleep well, Doctor Rank.

RANK. Thank you for that wish.

NORA. Wish me the same.

RANK. You? Well, if you want me to sleep well! And thanks for the light.

[*He nods to them both and goes out.*]

HELMER. [*in a subdued voice*] He has drunk more than he ought.

NORA. [*absently*] Maybe. [*HELMER takes a bunch of keys out of his pocket and goes into the hall.*] Torvald! what are you going to do there?

HELMER. Empty the letter-box; it is quite full; there will be no room to put the newspaper in to-morrow morning.

NORA. Are you going to work to-night?

HELMER. You know quite well I'm not. What is this? Some one has been at the lock.

NORA. At the lock—?

HELMER. Yes, someone has. What can it mean? I should never have thought the maid—. Here is a broken hairpin. Nora, it is one of yours.

NORA. [*quickly*] Then it must have been the children—

HELMER. Then you must get them out of those ways. There, at last I have got it open. [*Takes out the contents of the letter-box, and calls to the kitchen.*] Helen!— Helen, put out the light over the front door. [*Goes back into the room and shuts the door into the hall. He holds out his hand full of letters.*] Look at that—look what a heap of them there are. [*turning them over*] What on earth is that?

NORA. [*at the window*] The letter—No! Torvald, no!

HELMER. Two cards—of Rank's.

NORA. Of Doctor Rank's?

HELMER. [*looking at them*] Doctor Rank. They were on the top. He must have put them in when he went out.

NORA. Is there anything written on them?

HELMER. There is a black cross over the name. Look there—what an uncomfortable idea! It looks as if he were announcing his own death.

NORA. It is just what he is doing.

HELMER. What? Do you know anything about it? Has he said anything to you?

NORA. Yes. He told me that when the cards came it would be his leave-taking from us. He means to shut himself up and die.

HELMER. My poor old friend. Certainly I knew we should not have him very long with us. But so soon! And so he hides himself away like a wounded animal.

NORA. If it has to happen, it is best it should be without a word—don't you think so, Torvald?

HELMER.   [*walking up and down*] He had so grown into our lives. I can't think of him as having gone out of them. He, with his sufferings and his loneliness, was like a cloudy background to our sunlit happiness. Well, perhaps it is best so. For him, anyway. [*standing still*] And perhaps for us too, Nora. We two are thrown quite upon each other now. [*puts his arms round her*] My darling wife, I don't feel as if I could hold you tight enough. Do you know, Nora, I have often wished that you might be threatened by some great danger, so that I might risk my life's blood, and everything, for your sake.

NORA.   [*disengages herself, and says firmly and decidedly*] Now you must read your   215
letters, Torvald.

HELMER.   No, no; not to-night. I want to be with you, my darling wife.

NORA.   With the thought of your friend's death—

HELMER.   You are right, it has affected us both. Something ugly has come between us—the thought of the horrors of death. We must try and rid our minds of that. Until then—we will each go to our own room.

NORA.   [*hanging on his neck*] Good-night, Torvald—Good-night!

HELMER.   [*kissing her on the forehead*]. Good-night, my little singing-bird. Sleep   220
sound, Nora. Now I will read my letters through.

[*He takes his letters and goes into his room, shutting the door after him.*]

NORA.   [*gropes distractedly about, seizes* HELMER'S *domino, throws it round her, while she says in quick, hoarse, spasmodic whispers*] Never to see him again. Never! Never! [*puts her shawl over her head*] Never to see my children again either—never again. Never! Never!— Ah! the icy, black water—the unfathomable depths—If only it were over! He has got it now—now he is reading it. Good-by, Torvald and my children!

[*She is about to rush out through the hall, when* HELMER *opens his door hurriedly and stands with an open letter in his hand.*]

HELMER.   Nora!

NORA.   Ah!—

HELMER.   What is this? Do you know what is in this letter?

NORA.   Yes, I know. Let me go! Let me get out!   225

HELMER.   [*holding her back*] Where are you going?

NORA.   [*trying to get free*] You shan't save me, Torvald!

HELMER.   [*reeling*] True? Is this true, that I read here? Horrible! No, no—it is impossible that it can be true.

NORA.   It is true. I have loved you above everything else in the world.

HELMER.   Oh, don't let us have any silly excuses.   230

NORA.   [*taking a step towards him*] Torvald—!

HELMER.   Miserable creature—what have you done?

NORA.   Let me go. You shall not suffer for my sake. You shall not take it upon yourself.

HELMER.   No tragedy airs, please. [*locks the hall door*] Here you shall stay and give me an explanation. Do you understand what you have done? Answer me! Do you under-stand what you have done?

NORA.   [*looks steadily at him and says with a growing look of coldness in her face*] Yes,   235
now I am beginning to understand thoroughly.

HELMER.   [*walking about the room*] What a horrible awakening! All these eight years—she who was my joy and pride—a hypocrite, a liar—worse, worse—a criminal! The unutterable ugliness of it all! For shame! For shame! [NORA *is silent and looks steadily at him. He stops in front of her.*] I ought to have suspected that something of the sort would happen. I ought to have foreseen it. All your father's want of principle—be silent!—all your father's want of principle has come out in you. No religion, no morality, no sense of duty—. How I am punished for having winked at what he did! I did it for your sake, and this is how you repay me.

NORA.   Yes, that's just it.

HELMER.   Now you have destroyed all my happiness. You have ruined all my future. It is horrible to think of! I am in the power of an unscrupulous man; he can do what he likes with me, ask anything he likes of me, give me any orders he pleases—I dare not refuse. And I must sink to such miserable depths because of a thoughtless woman!

NORA.   When I am out of the way, you will be free.

HELMER.   No fine speeches, please. Your father had always plenty of those ready, too. What good would it be to me if you were out of the way, as you say? Not the slightest. He can make the affair known everywhere; and if he does, I may be falsely suspected of having been a party to your criminal action. Very likely people will think I was behind it all—that it was I who prompted you! And I have to thank you for all this—you whom I have cherished during the whole of our married life. Do you understand now what it is you have done for me? 240

NORA.   [*coldly and quietly*] Yes.

HELMER.   It is so incredible that I can't take it in. But we must come to some understanding. Take off that shawl. Take it off, I tell you. I must try and appease him some way or another. The matter must be hushed up at any cost. And as for you and me, it must appear as if everything between us were just as before—but naturally only in the eyes of the world. You will still remain in my house, that is a matter of course. But I shall not allow you to bring up the children; I dare not trust them to you. To think that I should be obliged to say so to one whom I have loved so dearly, and whom I still—. No, that is all over. From this moment happiness is not the question; all that concerns us is to save the remains, the fragments, the appearance—

[*A ring is heard at the front-door bell.*]

HELMER.   [*with a start*] What is that? So late! Can the worst—? Can he—? Hide yourself, Nora. Say you are ill.

[NORA *stands motionless.* HELMER *goes and unlocks the hall door.*]

MAID.   [*half-dressed, comes to the door*] A letter for the mistress.

HELMER.   Give it to me. [*takes the letter, and shuts the door*] Yes, it is from him. You shall not have it; I will read it myself. 245

NORA.   Yes, read it.

HELMER.   [*standing by the lamp*] I scarcely have the courage to do it. It may mean ruin for both of us. No, I must know. [*tears open the letter, runs his eye over a few lines, looks at a paper enclosed and gives a shout of joy*] Nora! [*She looks at him questioningly.*] Nora!—No, I must read it once again—. Yes, it is true! I am saved! Nora, I am saved!

NORA.   And I?

HELMER.   You too, of course; we are both saved, both you and I. Look, he sends you your bond back. He says he regrets and repents—that a happy change in his life— never mind what he says! We are saved, Nora! No one can do anything to you. Oh, Nora, Nora!—no, first I must destroy these hateful things. Let me see—. [*takes a look at the bond*] No, no, I won't look at it. The whole thing shall be nothing but a bad dream to

me. [*tears up the bond and both letters, throws them all into the stove, and watches them burn*]
There—now it doesn't exist any longer. He says that since Christmas Eve you—. These
must have been three dreadful days for you, Nora.

NORA.   I have fought a hard fight these three days.   250

HELMER.   And suffered agonies, and seen no way out but—. No, we won't call
any of the horrors to mind. We will only shout with joy, and keep saying "It's all over! It's
all over!" Listen to me, Nora. You don't seem to realise that it is all over. What is this?—
such a cold, set face! My poor little Nora, I quite understand; you don't feel as if you
could believe that I have forgiven you. But it is true, Nora, I swear it; I have forgiven you
everything. I know that what you did, you did out of love for me.

NORA.   That is true.

HELMER.   You have loved me as a wife ought to love her husband. Only you had
not sufficient knowledge to judge of the means you used. But do you suppose you are
any the less dear to me, because you don't understand how to act on your own responsibility? No, no; only lean on me; I will advise you and direct you. I should not be a man
if this womanly helplessness did not just give you a double attractiveness in my eyes. You
must not think any more about the hard things I said in my first moment of consterna-
tion, when I thought everything was going to overwhelm me. I have forgiven you, Nora;
I swear to you I have forgiven you.

NORA.   Thank you for your forgiveness.

[*She goes out through the door to the right.*]

HELMER.   No, don't go—. [*looks in*] What are you doing in there?   255

NORA.   [*from within*] Taking off my fancy dress.

HELMER.   [*standing at the open door*] Yes, do. Try and calm yourself, and make your
mind easy again, my frightened little singing-bird. Be at rest, and feel secure; I have
broad wings to shelter you under. [*walks up and down by the door*] How warm and cosy
our home is, Nora. Here is shelter for you; here I will protect you like a hunted dove
that I have saved from a hawk's claws. I will bring peace to your poor beating heart. It will
come, little by little, Nora, believe me. Tomorrow morning you will look upon it all quite
differently; soon everything will be just as it was before. Very soon you won't need me to
assure you that I have forgiven you; you will yourself feel the certainty that I have done
so. Can you suppose I should ever think of such a thing as repudiating you, or even
reproaching you? You have no idea what a true man's heart is like, Nora. There is something so indescribably sweet and satisfying, to a man, in the knowledge that he has forgiven his wife—forgiven her freely, and with all his heart. It seems as if that had made
her, as it were, doubly his own; he has given her a new life, so to speak; and she has in a
way become both wife and child to him. So you shall be for me after this, my little scared,
helpless darling. Have no anxiety about anything, Nora; only be frank and open with
me, and I will serve as will and conscience both to you—. What is this? Not gone to bed?
Have you changed your things?

NORA.   [*in everyday dress*] Yes, Torvald, I have changed my things now.

HELMER.   But what for?—so late as this.   260

NORA.   I shall not sleep to-night.

HELMER.   But, my dear Nora—

NORA.   [*looking at her watch*] It is not so very late. Sit down here, Torvald. You and
I have much to say to one another.

[*She sits down at one side of the table.*]

HELMER.   Nora—what is this?—this cold, set face?

NORA.   Sit down. It will take some time; I have a lot to talk over with you.

HELMER.   [*sits down at the opposite side of the table*] You alarm me, Nora!—and I 265
don't understand you.

NORA.   No, that is just it. You don't understand me, and I have never understood
you either—before to-night. No, you mustn't interrupt me. You must simply listen to
what I say. Torvald, this is a settling of accounts.

HELMER.   What do you mean by that?

NORA.   [*after a short silence*] Isn't there one thing that strikes you as strange in our
sitting here like this?

HELMER.   What is that?

NORA.   We have been married now eight years. Does it not occur to you that this 270
is the first time we two, you and I, husband and wife, have had a serious conversation?

HELMER.   What do you mean by serious?

NORA.   In all these eight years—longer than that—from the very beginning of
our acquaintance, we have never exchanged a word on any serious subject.

HELMER.   Was it likely that I would be continually and for ever telling you about
worries that you could not help me to bear?

NORA.   I am not speaking about business matters. I say that we have never sat
down in earnest together to try and get at the bottom of anything.

HELMER.   But, dearest Nora, would it have been any good to you? 275

NORA.   That is just it; you have never understood me. I have been greatly
wronged, Torvald—first by papa and then by you.

HELMER.   What! By us two—by us two, who have loved you better than anyone
else in the world?

NORA.   [*shaking her head*] You have never loved me. You have only thought it
pleasant to be in love with me.

HELMER.   Nora, what do I hear you saying?

NORA.   It is perfectly true, Torvald. When I was at home with papa, he told me his 280
opinion about everything, and so I had the same opinions; and if I differed from him I
concealed the fact, because he would not have liked it. He called me his doll-child, and
he played with me just as I used to play with my dolls. And when I came to live with
you—

HELMER.   What sort of an expression is that to use about our marriage?

NORA.   [*undisturbed*] I mean that I was simply transferred from papa's hands into
yours. You arranged everything according to your own taste, and so I got the same tastes
as you—or else I pretended to, I am really not quite sure which—I think sometimes the
one and sometimes the other. When I look back on it, it seems to me as if I had been
living here like a poor woman—just from hand to mouth. I have existed merely to perform tricks for you, Torvald. But you would have it so. You and papa have committed a
great sin against me. It is your fault that I have made nothing of my life.

HELMER.   How unreasonable and how ungrateful you are, Nora! Have you not
been happy here?

NORA.   No, I have never been happy. I thought I was, but it has never really been
so.

HELMER.   Not—not happy! 285

NORA.   No, only merry. And you have always been so kind to me. But our home
has been nothing but a playroom. I have been your doll-wife, just as at home I was papa's
doll-child; and here the children have been my dolls. I thought it great fun when you

played with me, just as they thought it great fun when I played with them. That is what our marriage has been, Torvald.

HELMER.   There is some truth in what you say—exaggerated and strained as your view of it is. But for the future it shall be different. Playtime shall be over, and lesson-time shall begin.

NORA.   Whose lessons? Mine, or the children's?

HELMER.   Both yours and the children's, my darling Nora.

NORA.   Alas, Torvald, you are not the man to educate me into being a proper   290 wife for you.

HELMER.   And you can say that!

NORA.   And I—how am I fitted to bring up the children?

HELMER.   Nora!

NORA.   Didn't you say so yourself a little while ago—that you dare not trust me to bring them up?

HELMER.   In a moment of anger! Why do you pay any heed to that?   295

NORA.   Indeed, you were perfectly right. I am not fit for the task. There is another task I must undertake first. I must try and educate myself—you are not the man to help me in that. I must do that for myself. And that is why I am going to leave you now.

HELMER.   [*springing up*] What do you say?

NORA.   I must stand quite alone, if I am to understand myself and everything about me. It is for that reason that I cannot remain with you any longer.

HELMER.   Nora! Nora!

NORA.   I am going away from here now, at once. I am sure Christine will take me   300 in for the night—

HELMER.   You are out of your mind! I won't allow it! I forbid you!

NORA.   It is no use forbidding me anything any longer. I will take with me what belongs to myself. I will take nothing from you, either now or later.

HELMER.   What sort of madness is this!

NORA.   To-morrow I shall go home—I mean, to my old home. It will be easiest for me to find something to do there.

HELMER.   You blind, foolish woman!   305

NORA.   I must try and get some sense, Torvald.

HELMER.   To desert your home, your husband and your children! And you don't consider what people will say!

NORA.   I cannot consider that at all. I only know that it is necessary for me.

HELMER.   It's shocking. This is how you would neglect your most sacred duties.

NORA.   What do you consider my most sacred duties?   310

HELMER.   Do I need to tell you that? Are they not your duties to your husband and your children?

NORA.   I have other duties just as sacred.

HELMER.   That you have not. What duties could those be?

NORA.   Duties to myself.

HELMER.   Before all else, you are a wife and a mother.   315

NORA.   I don't believe that any longer. I believe that before all else I am a reasonable human being, just as you are—or, at all events, that I must try and become one. I know quite well, Torvald, that most people would think you right, and that views of that kind are to be found in books; but I can no longer content myself with what most people say, or with what is found in books. I must think over things for myself and get to understand them.

HELMER.   Can you not understand your place in your own home? Have you not a reliable guide in such matters as that?—have you no religion?

NORA.   I am afraid, Torvald, I do not exactly know what religion is.

HELMER.   What are you saying?

NORA.   I know nothing but what the clergyman said when I went to be con-   320
firmed. He told us that religion was this, and that, and the other. When I am away from all this, and am alone, I will look into that matter too. I will see if what the clergyman said is true, or at all events if it is true for me.

HELMER.   This is unheard of in a girl of your age! But if religion cannot lead you aright, let me try and awaken your conscience. I suppose you have some moral sense? Or—answer me—am I to think you have none?

NORA.   I assure you, Torvald, that is not an easy question to answer. I really don't know. The thing perplexes me altogether. I only know that you and I look at it in quite a different light. I am learning, too, that the law is quite another thing from what I supposed; but I find it impossible to convince myself that the law is right. According to it a woman has no right to spare her old dying father, or to save her husband's life. I can't believe that.

HELMER.   You talk like a child. You don't understand the conditions of the world in which you live.

NORA.   No, I don't. But now I am going to try. I am going to see if I can make out   325
who is right, the world or I.

HELMER.   You are ill, Nora; you are delirious; I almost think you are out of your mind.

NORA.   I have never felt my mind so clear and certain as to-night.

HELMER.   And is it with a clear and certain mind that you forsake your husband and your children?

NORA.   Yes, it is.

HELMER.   Then there is only one possible explanation.

NORA.   What is that?   330

HELMER.   You do not love me any more.

NORA.   No, that is just it.

HELMER.   Nora!—and you can say that?

NORA.   It gives me great pain, Torvald, for you have always been so kind to me, but I cannot help it. I do not love you any more.

HELMER.   [*regaining his composure*] Is that a clear and certain conviction too?   335

NORA.   Yes, absolutely clear and certain. That is the reason why I will not stay here any longer.

HELMER.   And can you tell me what I have done to forfeit your love?

NORA.   Yes, indeed I can. It was to-night, when the wonderful thing did not happen; then I saw you were not the man I had thought you.

HELMER.   Explain yourself better—I don't understand you.

NORA.   I have waited so patiently for eight years; for, goodness knows, I knew   340
very well that wonderful things don't happen every day. Then this horrible misfortune came upon me; and then I felt quite certain that the wonderful thing was going to happen at last. When Krogstad's letter was lying out there, never for a moment did I imagine that you would consent to accept this man's conditions. I was so absolutely

certain that you would say to him: Publish the thing to the whole world. And when that was done—

HELMER. Yes, what then?—when I had exposed my wife to shame and disgrace?

NORA. When that was done, I was so absolutely certain, you would come forward and take everything upon yourself, and say: I am the guilty one.

HELMER. Nora—!

NORA. You mean that I would never have accepted such a sacrifice on your part? No, of course not. But what would my assurances have been worth against yours? That was the wonderful thing which I hoped for and feared; and it was to prevent that, that I wanted to kill myself.

HELMER. I would gladly work night and day for you, Nora—bear sorrow and want   345
for your sake. But no man would sacrifice his honour for the one he loves.

NORA. It is a thing hundreds of thousands of women have done.

HELMER. Oh, you think and talk like a heedless child.

NORA. Maybe. But you neither think nor talk like the man I could bind myself to. As soon as your fear was over—and it was not fear for what threatened me, but for what might happen to you—when the whole thing was past, as far as you were concerned it was exactly as if nothing at all had happened. Exactly as before, I was your little skylark, your doll, which you would in future treat with doubly gentle care, because it was so brittle and fragile. [*getting up*] Torvald—it was then it dawned upon me that for eight years I had been living here with a strange man, and had borne him three children—. Oh, I can't bear to think of it! I could tear myself into little bits!

HELMER. [*sadly*] I see, I see. An Abyss has opened between us—there is no denying it. But, Nora, would it not be possible to fill it up?

NORA. As I am now, I am no wife for you.   350

HELMER. I have it in me to become a different man.

NORA. Perhaps—if your doll is taken away from you.

HELMER. But to part!—to part from you! No, no, Nora, I can't understand that idea.

NORA. [*going out to the right*] That makes it all the more certain that it must be done.

[*She comes back with her cloak and hat and a small bag which she puts on a chair by the table.*]

HELMER. Nora, Nora, not now! Wait till to-morrow.   355

NORA. [*putting on her cloak*] I cannot spend the night in a strange man's room.

HELMER. But can't we live here like brother and sister—?

NORA. [*putting on her hat*] You know very well that would not last long. [*puts the shawl round her*] Good-bye, Torvald. I won't see the little ones. I know they are in better hands than mine. As I am now, I can be of no use to them.

HELMER. But some day, Nora—some day?

NORA. How can I tell? I have no idea what is going to become of me.   360

HELMER. But you are my wife, whatever becomes of you.

NORA. Listen, Torvald. I have heard that when a wife deserts her husband's house, as I am doing now, he is legally freed from all obligations towards her. In any case I set you free from all your obligations. You are not to feel yourself bound in the slightest way, any more than I shall. There must be perfect freedom on both sides. See here is your ring back. Give me mine.

HELMER. That too?

NORA. That too.

HELMER.   Here it is.   365

NORA.   That's right. Now it is all over. I have put the keys here. The maids know all about everything in the house—better than I do. To-morrow, after I have left her, Christine will come here and pack up my own things that I brought with me from home. I will have them sent after me.

HELMER.   All over! All over!—Nora, shall you never think of me again?

NORA.   I know I shall often think of you and the children and this house.

HELMER.   May I write to you, Nora?

NORA.   No—never. You must not do that.   370

HELMER.   But at least let me send you—

NORA.   Nothing—nothing—

HELMER.   Let me help you if you are in want.

NORA.   No. I can receive nothing from a stranger.

HELMER.   Nora—can I never be anything more than a stranger to you?   375

NORA.   [*taking her bag*] Ah, Torvald, the most wonderful thing of all would have to happen.

HELMER.   Tell me what that would be!

NORA.   Both you and I would have to be so changed that—. Oh, Torvald, I don't believe any longer in wonderful things happening.

HELMER.   But I will believe in it. Tell me? So changed that—?

NORA.   That our life together would be a real wedlock. Good-bye.   380

[*She goes out through the hall.*]

HELMER.   [*sinks down on a chair at the door and buries his face in his hands*] Nora! Nora! [*looks round, and rises*] Empty. She is gone. [*A hope flashes across his mind.*] The most wonderful thing of all—?

[*The sound of a door slamming is heard from below.*]

QUESTIONS

Act I

1. What does the opening stage direction reveal about the Helmer family? About the time of year?

2. Explain the ways Nora and Torvald behave toward each other.

3. What does Torvald's refusal to consider borrowing and debt tell you about him (speech 22)? Where else in the play are these characteristics important?

4. What have the Helmer finances been like in the past? How is their situation about to change?

5. How are Mrs. Linde and Nora alike? Different? Why is it ironic that Nora helps Christine get a job at the bank? How will this affect Krogstad? Nora?

6. How does Ibsen show that Krogstad is a threat when he first appears?

7. Why should Nora's scene with her children in Act I not be cut in production? What does it show about Nora and the household?

8. What is Nora's secret "crime"? What is the explanation and justification for it? At the end of the act, what new problems does she face?

Act II

9. What is symbolized by the stripped Christmas tree?

10. What is implied about Nora's self perceptions when she calls herself "your little squirrel" and "your skylark"?

11. After sending Krogstad's dismissal, Torvald tells Nora that "You will see I am man enough to take everything upon myself" (speech 135). How does this speech conform to Nora's hopes? How is it ironic?

12. Why does Nora flirt with Dr. Rank? How and why does he distress her?

13. Why does Nora dance the Tarantella so wildly?

14. What is the "wonderful thing" that Nora is waiting for?

Act III

15. Explain Christine's past rejection of Krogstad. Why will she accept him now? How will their union differ from the Helmers' marriage?

16. What does Christine decide to do about Krogstad's letter? Why?

17. Explain the reactions of Torvald and Nora to the death of Dr. Rank.

18. Describe Torvald's reaction to Krogstad's first letter. How does Nora respond to Torvald? How do you respond to him? Why?

19. Explain what Nora learns about Torvald, herself, her marriage, and her identity as a woman as a result of Torvald's responses. Why does she decide to leave?

GENERAL QUESTIONS

1. Which elements and aspects of *A Dollhouse* are most and least realistic? Explain.

2. Consider Ibsen's symbolism, with reference to Dr. Rank, macaroons, the Christmas tree, the presents, the locked mailbox, the dance, Nora's black shawl, her change of clothing in Act III, and the door slam at the play's close.

3. Is Nora a victim of circumstances or a villain who brings about problems? What is Ibsen's view? What is yours? Why?

4. Describe the "role-playing" in the Helmer marriage. Does any evidence suggest that Nora knows she is playing a role? What degree of self-awareness, if any, characterizes Torvald's role-playing?

5. When Nora asks Torvald to restore Krogstad's job, Torvald refuses on the ground that he should not give in to his wife's pressure (Act II, speech 113). Later, he claims that their marriage is destroyed, but that they should keep up the appearance of marital stability (Act III, speech 242). In the light of such statements, describe Torvald's character. What concerns him most about life and marriage?

6. A major theme in the play is that weakness and corruption are passed from generation to generation. Examine this theme in connection with Krogstad and his sons, Nora and her children, Nora and her father, and Dr. Rank.

7. Discuss the ideas about individual growth, marriage, and social convention in the play. How are these ideas developed and related? Which character most closely embodies Ibsen's ideas?

8. Write an essay about any or all of the following questions:

   a. Is *A Dollhouse* a comedy, a tragedy, or something in between?

   b. How do the play's characters change for the better (or worse)?

   c. How negative, or affirmative, is the conclusion? Why?

ARTHUR MILLER, *DEATH OF A SALESMAN*

Because of his large number of important dramas, Miller can justly be considered a dominant modern American playwright. He was born in New York in 1915 and educated at the University of Michigan, where he won a prize for a play he had written as an undergraduate. After graduation he wrote with the Federal Theater Project (part of President Roosevelt's New Deal). When that project lost funding he began writing radio plays, a novel, and, during World War II, an account of military training. He then wrote a play, *The Man Who Had All the Luck*, which met little success on Broadway in 1944. After the war he quickly catapulted into fame as a dramatist with *All My Sons* (1947), *Death of a Salesman* (1949), *An Enemy of the People* (1951, an adaptation of Ibsen's play), *The Crucible* (1953), and *A View from the Bridge* (1955). Many of these combine his interests in family relationships and sociopolitical issues. For instance, *All My Sons* explores the relationship between Joe Keller, an industrialist and war profiteer who had allowed faulty engines to be installed in U.S. military aircraft, and his son Chris, an army pilot returning home from World War II. The play investigates Joe Keller's guilt and his emerging realization that the airmen who died because of his defective engines were "all" his sons. Another of Miller's most important plays, *The Crucible*, reflects the suspicions and unfounded accusations rampant in the McCarthy era early in the 1950s.

Miller's later work includes the screenplay *The Misfits* (1961), the last film in which Marilyn Monroe, who was then his wife, starred, and the plays *After the Fall* (1964), *Incident at Vichy* (1964), *The Price* (1968), *Fame* (1970), *The Reason Why* (1972), *The Creation of the World and Other Business* (1972), *The Archbishop's Ceiling* (1976), *The American Clock* (1980), *Playing for Time* (1985), *I Can't Remember Anything* (1987), *Clara* (1987), a filmscript titled *Everybody Wins* (1990), and *Broken Glass* (1994). In 1996 *The Crucible* was revised and presented as a successful film with Daniel Day-Lewis and Winona Ryder.

Death of a Salesman, which opened on Broadway on February 10, 1949, is similar to both *Oedipus the King* and the traditional *well-made play* (see p. 1167). Miller's play dramatizes the end of a much longer story. The stage action in the present (in Acts I and II) covers about twenty-four hours, from Monday evening to Tuesday evening. The story, however, covers much of Willy Loman's life, and his memories of past events constantly impose themselves on the present. One of the play's central conflicts stems from a secret known only to Willy and his son Biff, a secret that is unrevealed until near the play's end. Such secrets, having a profound significance in the action, are a feature of the traditional well-made play.

In writing a tragedy about the struggle and failure of Willy Loman (i.e., a "low man," an ordinary man), Miller effectively redefines the nature of tragedy in our modern period of democracy and belief in the significance of common people. In a *New York Times* essay published shortly after the Broadway opening, Miller argues that "the common man is as apt a subject for tragedy in its highest sense as kings were."[2] He asserts that tragedy springs from the individual's quest for a proper place in the world and from his or her readiness "to lay down . . . life, if need be, to secure . . . [a] sense of personal dignity." Willy is flawed: He is self-deluded, deceitful, unfaithful, and weak; he denies the truth when he is confronted with it. But Miller links Willy's defects with the quest for dignity: "the flaw or crack in the character is really . . . his inherent unwillingness to remain passive in the face of what he conceives to be a challenge to his dignity, his image of his rightful status." It is with great justice that Linda asserts to her sons that attention must be paid to a such a person. In this sense, Miller meets the challenge of creating a modern character worthy of tragic elevation.

Accordingly, *Death of a Salesman* is developed around the character of Willy Loman. At first, Miller wanted to call the play "The Inside of His Head," and his initial vision was of "an enormous face the height of the proscenium arch that would appear and open up, and we would see the inside of a man's head."[3] The play contains two types of time and action: real and remembered. Present events are enacted and described realistically, but such action often triggers Willy's memory of the past, which is always with him, shaping the way he reacts to the present. Sometimes past events can even occur simultaneously with present action, as in Act I when Willy speaks with his dead brother, whom he is remembering, at the same time as he is playing cards with Charley. At other times, past events take over the play completely, although Willy still continues to exist in the present.

Like the acting of past events, the setting of *Death of a Salesman* is symbolic and nonrealistic. The play demonstrates the degree to which Miller relies on developments in the physical theater that took place between Shakespeare's day and our own. Miller adapts both the concepts of the picture-frame proscenium

---

[2] "Tragedy and the Common Man," *New York Times*, February 27, 1949, sec. 2, p. 1.

[3] Arthur Miller, "Introduction to the Collected Plays," *Arthur Miller's Collected Plays* (New York: Viking, 1957), p. 23.

stage and the apron stage. Thus the Loman house—set on the proscenium stage—is a framework with three rooms (or acting areas) on three levels: the kitchen, the sons' bedroom, and Willy's bedroom. The forestage and apron are used for all scenes away from the house and for "memory" scenes. The house is hemmed in by apartment houses and lit with an "angry glow of orange," thus suggesting that Willy's present existence is urbanized and claustrophobic. When memory takes over, however, the apartment houses disappear (a technique of lighting), and the orange glow gives way to pastoral colors and the shadows of leaves—the setting for dreams about past times and hopes.

Death of a Salesman is very much about dreams, illusions, and self-deception. Dreams pervade Willy's thoughts, conversation, family, and house, and the staging allows fluid transitions between current action and memory. Willy's central illusion is the American dream of success and wealth through the merchandizing of the self. This dream is embodied in a series of smaller dreams (illusions, lies) that Willy has created out of hope and then tried to bequeath to his sons. But reality destroys these dreams. Willy's expectation of a New York City job and a salary, for example, founders on the reality of his disastrous encounter with his preoccupied and unsympathetic boss. Only Linda escapes the tyranny of dreams. While she serves and supports Willy completely, she remains firmly planted in the reality of house payments, insurance premiums, and Willy's need for dignity and attention as his world falls apart.

At the end of the play, we are left with a number of questions about the degree to which Willy recognizes and understands the illusory nature of his dreams and his self-image. He does understand that he has run out of lies and has nothing left to sell. He also understands—according to Miller—his alienation from true values:

> Had Willy been unaware of his separation from values that endure he would have died contentedly while polishing his car. . . . But he was agonized by his awareness of being in a false position, so constantly haunted by the hollowness of all he had placed his faith in, so aware, in short, that he must somehow be filled with his spirit or fly apart, that he staked his life on the ultimate assertion.[4]

Yet at the end of the play, Willy is still in the grip of delusion. He imagines that his insurance money will make Biff "magnificent," and he dreams that his funeral will be massive. Both visions are delusions, for Biff has already abandoned the business world, and the funeral is attended by only five people. In the Requiem scene, Biff states that Willy's dreams were illusory: "He had all the wrong dreams. All, all wrong" (speech 16). Only the character ironically named Happy retains his own unreconstructed version of Willy's dream: "He had a good dream. It's the only dream you can have—to come out number-one man" (speech 25). Miller leaves it to the audience to evaluate the truth and validity of each character's assertions.

[4] *Ibid.*, pp. 34–35.

ARTHUR MILLER   (b. 1915)

Death of a Salesman ———————————————————————— *1949*

CHARACTERS

> Willy Loman
> Linda, *his wife*
> Biff ⎫
> Happy ⎭ *his sons*
> Uncle Ben
> Charley
> Bernard
> The Woman
> Howard Wagner
> Jenny
> Stanley
> Miss Forsythe
> Letta

The action takes place in WILLY LOMAN'*s house and yard and in various places he visits in the New York and Boston of today.*

ACT 1

A melody is heard, played upon a flute. It is small and fine, telling of grass and trees and the horizon. The curtain rises.

Before us is the Salesman's house. We are aware of towering, angular shapes behind it, surrounding it on all sides. Only the blue light of the sky falls upon the house and forestage; the surrounding area shows an angry glow of orange. As more light appears, we see a solid vault of apartment houses around the small, fragile-seeming home. An air of the dream clings to the place, a dream rising out of reality. The kitchen at center seems actual enough, for there is a kitchen table with three chairs, and a refrigerator. But no other fixtures are seen. At the back of the kitchen there is a draped entrance, which leads to the living-room. To the right of the kitchen, on a level raised two feet, is a bedroom furnished only with a brass bedstead and a straight chair. On a shelf over the bed a silver athletic trophy stands. A window opens onto the apartment house at the side.

Behind the kitchen, on a level raised six and a half feet, is the boys' bedroom, at present barely visible. Two beds are dimly seen, and at the back of the room a dormer window. (This bedroom is above the unseen living-room.) At the left a stairway curves up to it from the kitchen.

The entire setting is wholly or, in some places, partially transparent. The roof-line of the house is one-dimensional; under and over it we see the apartment buildings. Before the house lies an apron, curving beyond the forestage into the orchestra. This forward area serves as the back yard as well as the locale of all WILLY'*s imaginings and of his city scenes. Whenever the action is in the present the actors observe the imaginary wall-lines, entering the house only through its door at the left. But in the scenes of the past these boundaries are broken, and characters enter or leave a room by stepping "through" a wall onto the forestage.*

[*From the right,* WILLY LOMAN, *The Salesman, enters, carrying two large sample cases. The flute plays on. He hears but is not aware of it. He is past sixty years of age, dressed quietly. Even as he crosses the stage to the doorway of the house, his exhaustion is apparent. He unlocks the door, comes into the kitchen, and thankfully lets his burden down, feeling the soreness of his palms. A word-sigh escapes his lips—it might be "Oh, boy, oh, boy." He closes the door, then carries his cases out into the living-room, through the draped kitchen doorway.*]

[LINDA, *his wife, has stirred in her bed at the right. She gets out and puts on a robe, listening. Most often jovial, she has developed an iron repression of her exceptions to* WILLY'S *behavior—she more than loves him, she admires him, as though his mercurial nature, his temper, his massive dreams and little cruelties, served her only as sharp reminders of the turbulent longings within him, longings which she shares but lacks the temperament to utter and follow to their end.*]

LINDA.   [*hearing* WILLY *outside the bedroom, calls with some trepidation*] Willy!

WILLY.   It's all right. I came back.

LINDA.   Why? What happened? [*slight pause*] Did something happen, Willy?

WILLY.   No, nothing happened.

LINDA.   You didn't smash the car, did you?   5

WILLY.   [*with casual irritation*] I said nothing happened. Didn't you hear me?

LINDA.   Don't you feel well?

WILLY.   I'm tired to the death. [*The flute has faded away. He sits on the bed beside her, a little numb.*] I couldn't make it. I just couldn't make it, Linda.

LINDA.   [*very carefully, delicately*] Where were you all day? You look terrible.

WILLY.   I got as far as a little above Yonkers.° I stopped for a cup of coffee. Maybe   10
it was the coffee.

LINDA.   What?

WILLY.   [*after a pause*] I suddenly couldn't drive any more. The car kept going off onto the shoulder, y'know?

LINDA.   [*helpfully*] Oh. Maybe it was the steering again. I don't think Angelo knows the Studebaker.

WILLY.   No, it's me, it's me. Suddenly I realize I'm goin' sixty miles an hour and I don't remember the last five minutes. I'm—I can't seem to—keep my mind to it.

LINDA.   Maybe it's your glasses. You never went for your new glasses.   15

WILLY.   No, I see everything. I came back ten miles an hour. It took me nearly four hours from Yonkers.

LINDA.   [*resigned*] Well, you'll just have to take a rest, Willy, you can't continue this way.

WILLY.   I just got back from Florida.

LINDA.   But you didn't rest your mind. Your mind is overactive, and the mind is what counts, dear.

WILLY.   I'll start out in the morning. Maybe I'll feel better in the morning. [*She is   20
taking off his shoes.*] These goddam arch supports are killing me.

LINDA.   Take an aspirin. Should I get you an aspirin? It'll soothe you.

WILLY.   [*with wonder*] I was driving along, you understand? And I was fine. I was even observing the scenery. You can imagine, me looking at scenery, on the road every week of my life. But it's so beautiful up there, Linda, the trees are so thick, and the sun is warm. I opened the windshield and just let the warm air bathe over me. And then all of a sudden I'm goin' off the road! I'm tellin' ya, I absolutely forgot I was driving. If I'd've gone the other way over the white line I might've killed some-body. So I went on again—and five minutes later I'm dreamin' again, and I nearly—

10 *Yonkers:* Yonkers is immediately north of New York City, touching the city limits of the Bronx. Because Willy lives in Brooklyn, to the south, he got no more than thirty or thirty-five miles from home.

[*He presses two fingers against his eyes.*] I have such thoughts, I have such strange thoughts.

LINDA.   Willy, dear. Talk to them again. There's no reason why you can't work in New York.

WILLY.   They don't need me in New York. I'm the New England man. I'm vital in New England.

LINDA.   But you're sixty years old. They can't expect you to keep traveling every   25 week.

WILLY.   I'll have to send a wire to Portland. I'm supposed to see Brown and Morrison tomorrow morning at ten o'clock to show the line. Goddammit, I could sell them! [*He starts putting on his jacket.*]

LINDA.   [*taking the jacket from him*] Why don't you go down to the place tomorrow and tell Howard you've simply got to work in New York? You're too accommodating, dear.

WILLY.   If old man Wagner was alive I'd a been in charge of New York now! That man was a prince, he was a masterful man. But that boy of his, that Howard, he don't appreciate. When I went north the first time, the Wagner Company didn't know where New England was!

LINDA.   Why don't you tell those things to Howard, dear?

WILLY.   [*encouraged*] I will, I definitely will. Is there any cheese?   30

LINDA.   I'll make you a sandwich.

WILLY.   No, go to sleep. I'll take some milk. I'll be up right away. The boys in?

LINDA.   They're sleeping. Happy took Biff on a date tonight.

WILLY.   [*interested*] That so?

LINDA.   It was so nice to see them shaving together, one behind the other,   35 in the bathroom. And going out together. You notice? The whole house smells of shaving lotion.

WILLY.   Figure it out. Work a lifetime to pay off a house. You finally own it, and there's nobody to live in it.

LINDA.   Well, dear, life is a casting off. It's always that way.

WILLY.   No, no, some people—some people accomplish something. Did Biff say anything after I went this morning?

LINDA.   You shouldn't have criticized him, Willy, especially after he just got off the train. You mustn't lose your temper with him.

WILLY.   When the hell did I lose my temper? I simply asked him if he was   40 making any money. Is that a criticism?

LINDA.   But, dear, how could he make any money?

WILLY.   [*worried and angered*] There's such an undercurrent in him. He became a moody man. Did he apologize when I left this morning?

LINDA.   He was crestfallen, Willy. You know how he admires you. I think if he finds himself, then you'll both be happier and not fight any more.

WILLY.   How can he find himself on a farm? Is that a life? A farmhand? In the beginning, when he was young, I thought, well, a young man, it's good for him to tramp around, take a lot of different jobs. But it's more than ten years now and he has yet to make thirty-five dollars a week!

LINDA.   He's finding himself, Willy.   45

WILLY.   Not finding yourself at the age of thirty-four is a disgrace!

LINDA.   Shh!

WILLY.   The trouble is he's lazy, goddammit!

LINDA.   Willy, please!

WILLY.   Biff is a lazy bum!   50

LINDA.   They're sleeping. Get something to eat. Go on down.

WILLY.   Why did he come home? I would like to know what brought him home.

LINDA.   I don't know. I think he's still lost, Willy. I think he's very lost.

WILLY.   Biff Loman is lost. In the greatest country in the world a young man with such—personal attractiveness, gets lost. And such a hard worker. There's one thing about Biff—he's not lazy.

LINDA.   Never.   55

WILLY.   [*with pity and resolve*] I'll see him in the morning; I'll have a nice talk with him. I'll get him a job selling. He could be big in no time. My God! Remember how they used to follow him around in high school? When he smiled at one of them their faces lit up. When he walked down the street . . . [*He loses himself in reminiscences.*]

LINDA.   [*trying to bring him out of it*] Willy, dear, I got a new kind of American-type cheese today. It's whipped.

WILLY.   Why do you get American when I like Swiss?

LINDA.   I just thought you'd like a change—

WILLY.   I don't want a change! I want Swiss cheese. Why am I always being   60
contradicted?

LINDA.   [*with a covering laugh*] I thought it would be a surprise.

WILLY.   Why don't you open a window in here, for God's sake?

LINDA.   [*with infinite patience*] They're all open dear.

WILLY.   The way they boxed us in here. Bricks and windows, windows and bricks.

LINDA.   We should've bought the land next door.   65

WILLY.   The street is lined with cars. There's not a breath of fresh air in the neighborhood. The grass don't grow any more, you can't raise a carrot in the back yard. They should've had a law against apartment houses. Remember those two beautiful elm trees out there? When I and Biff hung the swing between them?

LINDA.   Yeah, like being a million miles from the city.

WILLY.   They should've arrested the builder for cutting those down. They massacred the neighborhood. [*lost*] More and more I think of those days, Linda. This time of year it was lilac and wisteria. And then the peonies would come out, and the daffodils. What fragrance in this room!

LINDA.   Well, after all, people had to move somewhere.

WILLY.   No, there's more people now.   70

LINDA.   I don't think there's more people. I think—

WILLY.   There's more people! That's what's ruining this country! Population is getting out of control. The competition is maddening! Smell the stink from that apartment house! And another one on the other side . . . How can they whip cheese?

[*On WILLY's last line, BIFF and HAPPY raise themselves up in their beds, listening.*]

LINDA.   Go down, try it. And be quiet.

WILLY.   [*turning to LINDA, guiltily*] You're not worried about me, are you, sweetheart?

BIFF.   What's the matter?   75

HAPPY.   Listen!

LINDA.   You've got too much on the ball to worry about.

WILLY.   You're my foundation and my support, Linda.

LINDA.   Just try to relax, dear. You make mountains out of molehills.

WILLY.   I won't fight with him any more. If he wants to go back to Texas, let   80
him go.

LINDA.   He'll find his way.

WILLY.   Sure. Certain men just don't get started till later in life. Like Thomas Edison, I think. Or B. F. Goodrich.° One of them was deaf. [*He starts for the bedroom doorway.*] I'll put my money on Biff.

LINDA.   And Willy—if it's warm Sunday we'll drive in the country. And we'll open the windshield, and take lunch.

WILLY.   No, the windshields don't open on the new cars.

LINDA.   But you opened it today.   85

WILLY.   Me? I didn't. [*He stops.*] Now isn't that peculiar! Isn't that a remarkable— [*He breaks off in amazement and fright as the flute is heard distantly.*]

LINDA.   What, darling?

WILLY.   That is the most remarkable thing.

LINDA.   What, dear?

WILLY.   I was thinking of the Chevvy. [*slight pause*] Nineteen twenty-eight . . . when   90 I had that red Chevvy— [*Breaks off.*] That funny? I coulda sworn I was driving that Chevvy today.

LINDA.   Well, that's nothing. Something must've reminded you.

WILLY.   Remarkable. Ts. Remember those days? The way Biff used to simonize that car? The dealer refused to believe there was eighty thousand miles on it. [*He shakes his head.*] Heh! [*to Linda*] Close your eyes, I'll be right up. [*He walks out of the bedroom.*]

HAPPY.   [*to BIFF*] Jesus, maybe he smashed up the car again!

LINDA.   [*calling after WILLY*] Be careful on the stairs, dear! The cheese is on the middle shelf! [*She turns, goes over to the bed, takes his jacket, and goes out of the bedroom.*]

[*Light has risen on the boys' room. Unseen, WILLY is heard talking to himself, "Eighty thousand miles," and a little laugh. BIFF gets out of bed, comes downstage a bit, and stands attentively. BIFF is two years older than his brother HAPPY, well built, but in these days bears a worn air and seems less self-assured. He has succeeded less, and his dreams are stronger and less acceptable than HAPPY's. HAPPY is tall, powerfully made. Sexuality is like a visible color on him, or a scent that many women have discovered. He, like his brother, is lost, but in a different way, for he has never allowed himself to turn his face toward defeat and is thus more confused and hard-skinned, although seemingly more content.*]

HAPPY.   [*getting out of bed*] He's going to get his license taken away if he   95 keeps that up. I'm getting nervous about him, y'know, Biff?

BIFF.   His eyes are going.

HAPPY.   No, I've driven with him. He sees all right. He just doesn't keep his mind on it. I drove into the city with him last week. He stops at a green light and then it turns red and he goes. [*He laughs.*]

BIFF.   Maybe he's color-blind.

HAPPY.   Pop? Why he's got the finest eye for color in the business. You know that.

BIFF.   [*sitting down on his bed*] I'm going to sleep.   100

HAPPY.   You're not still sour on Dad, are you, Biff?

BIFF.   He's all right, I guess.

WILLY.   [*underneath them, in the living-room*] Yes, sir, eighty thousand miles—eighty-two thousand!

82 *Thomas Edison, B. F. Goodrich:* Thomas A. Edison (1847–1931) was an American inventor who developed the electric light and the phonograph. Benjamin Franklin Goodrich (1841–1888) founded the B. F. Goodrich Rubber and Tire Company. It was Edison who suffered from deafness.

BIFF.   You smoking?

HAPPY.   [*holding out a pack of cigarettes*] Want one?   105

BIFF.   [*taking a cigarette*] I can never sleep when I smell it.

WILLY.   What a simonizing job, heh!

HAPPY.   [*with deep sentiment*] Funny, Biff y'know? Us sleeping in here again? The old beds. [*He pats his bed affectionately.*] All the talk that went across those two beds, huh? Our whole lives.

BIFF.   Yeah. Lotta dreams and plans.

HAPPY.   [*with a deep and masculine laugh*] About five hundred women would like to   110 know what was said in this room.

[*They share a soft laugh.*]

BIFF.   Remember that big Betsy something—what the hell was her name—over on Bushwick Avenue?

HAPPY.   [*combing his hair*] With the collie dog!

BIFF.   That's the one. I got you in there, remember?

HAPPY.   Yeah, that was my first time—I think. Boy, there was a pig! [*They laugh, almost crudely.*] You taught me everything I know about women. Don't forget that.

BIFF.   I bet you forgot how bashful you used to be. Especially with girls.   115

HAPPY.   Oh, I still am, Biff.

BIFF.   Oh, go on.

HAPPY.   I just control it, that's all. I think I got less bashful and you got more so. What happened, Biff? Where's the old humor, the old confidence? [*He shakes BIFF's knee. BIFF gets up and moves restlessly about the room.*] What's the matter?

BIFF.   Why does Dad mock me all the time?

HAPPY.   He's not mocking you, he—   120

BIFF.   Everything I say there's a twist of mockery on his face. I can't get near him.

HAPPY.   He just wants you to make good, that's all. I wanted to talk to you about Dad for a long time, Biff. Something's—happening to him. He—talks to himself.

BIFF.   I noticed that this morning. But he always mumbled.

HAPPY.   But not so noticeable. It got so embarrassing I sent him to Florida. And you know something? Most of the time he's talking to you.

BIFF.   What's he say about me?   125

HAPPY.   I can't make it out.

BIFF.   What's he say about me?

HAPPY.   I think the fact that you're not settled, that you're still kind of up in the air . . .

BIFF.   There's one or two other things depressing him, Happy.

HAPPY.   What do you mean?   130

BIFF.   Never mind. Just don't lay it all to me.

HAPPY.   But I think if you just got started—I mean—is there any future for you out there?

BIFF.   I tell ya, Hap, I don't know what the future is. I don't know—what I'm supposed to want.

HAPPY.   What do you mean?

BIFF.   Well, I spent six or seven years after high school trying to work myself up.   135 Shipping clerk, salesman, business of one kind or another. And it's a measly manner of existence. To get on that subway on the hot mornings in summer. To devote your whole life to keeping stock, or making phone calls, or selling or buying. To suffer fifty weeks of the year for the sake of a two-week vacation, when all you really desire is to be outdoors, with your shirt off. And always to have to get ahead of the next fella. And still—that's how you build a future.

HAPPY.   Well, you really enjoy it on a farm? Are you content out there?

BIFF.   [*with rising agitation*] Hap, I've had twenty or thirty different kinds of jobs since I left home before the war, and it always turns out the same. I just realized it lately. In Nebraska when I herded cattle, and the Dakotas, and Arizona, and now in Texas. It's why I came home now, I guess, because I realized it. This farm I work on, it's spring there now, see? And they've got about fifteen new colts. There's nothing more inspiring or—beautiful than the sight of a mare and a new colt. And it's cool there now, see? Texas is cool now, and it's spring. And whenever spring comes to where I am, I suddenly get the feeling, my God, I'm not gettin' anywhere! What the hell am I doing, playing around with horses, twenty-eight dollars a week! I'm thirty-four years old, I oughta be makin' my future. That's when I come running home. And now, I get here, and I don't know what to do with myself. [*after a pause*] I've always made a point of not wasting my life, and everytime I come back here I know that all I've done is to waste my life.

HAPPY.   You're a poet, you know that, Biff? You're a—you're an idealist!

BIFF.   No, I'm mixed up very bad. Maybe I oughta get married. Maybe I oughta get stuck into something. Maybe that's my trouble. I'm like a boy. I'm not married, I'm not in business, I just—I'm like a boy. Are you content, Hap? You're a success, aren't you? Are you content?

HAPPY.   Hell, no!   140

BIFF.   Why? You're making money, aren't you?

HAPPY.   [*moving about with energy, expressiveness*] All I can do now is wait for the merchandise manager to die. And suppose I get to be merchandise manager? He's a good friend of mine, and he just built a terrific estate on Long Island. And he lived there about two months and sold it, and now he's building another one. He can't enjoy it once it's finished. And I know that's just what I would do. I don't know what the hell I'm workin' for. Sometimes I sit in my apartment—all alone. And I think of the rent I'm paying. And it's crazy. But then, it's what I always wanted. My own apartment, a car, and plenty of women. And still, goddammit, I'm lonely.

BIFF.   [*with enthusiasm*] Listen, why don't you come out West with me?

HAPPY.   You and I, heh?

BIFF.   Sure, maybe we could buy a ranch. Raise cattle, use our muscles. Men   145
built like we are should be working out in the open.

HAPPY.   [*avidly*] The Loman Brothers, heh?

BIFF.   [*with vast affection*] Sure, we'd be known all over the counties!

HAPPY.   [*enthralled*] That's what I dream about, Biff. Sometimes I want to just rip my clothes off in the middle of the store and outbox that goddam merchandise manager. I mean I can outbox, outrun, and outlift anybody in that store, and I have to take orders from those common, petty sons-of-bitches till I can't stand it any more.

BIFF.   I'm tellin' you, kid, if you were with me I'd be happy out there.

HAPPY.   [*enthused*] See, Biff, everybody around me is so false that I'm constantly   150
lowering my ideals . . .

BIFF.   Baby, together we'd stand up for one another, we'd have someone to trust.

HAPPY.   If I were around you—

BIFF.   Hap, the trouble is we weren't brought up to grub for money. I don't know how to do it.

HAPPY.   Neither can I!

BIFF.   Then let's go!   155

HAPPY.   The only thing is—what can you make out there?

BIFF.   But look at your friend. Builds an estate and then hasn't the peace of mind to live in it.

HAPPY.   Yeah, but when he walks into the store the waves part in front of him. That's fifty-two thousand dollars a year coming through the revolving door, and I got more in my pinky finger than he's got in his head.

BIFF.   Yeah, but you just said—

HAPPY.   I gotta show some of those pompous, self-important executives over   160
there that Hap Loman can make the grade. I want to walk into the store the way he walks in. Then I'll go with you, Biff. We'll be together yet, I swear. But take those two we had tonight. Now weren't they gorgeous creatures?

BIFF.   Yeah, yeah, most gorgeous I've had in years.

HAPPY.   I get that any time I want, Biff. Whenever I feel disgusted. The only trouble is, it gets like bowling or something. I just keep knockin' them over and it doesn't mean anything. You still run around a lot?

BIFF.   Naa. I'd like to find a girl—steady, somebody with substance.

HAPPY.   That's what I long for.

BIFF.   Go on! You'd never come home.   165

HAPPY.   I would! Somebody with character, with resistance! Like Mom, y'know? You're gonna call me a bastard when I tell you this. That girl Charlotte I was with tonight is engaged to be married in five weeks. [*He tries on his new hat.*]

BIFF.   No kiddin'!

HAPPY.   Sure, the guy's in line for the vice-presidency of the store. I don't know what gets into me, maybe I just have an overdeveloped sense of competition or something, but I went and ruined her, and furthermore I can't get rid of her. And he's the third executive I've done that to. Isn't that a crummy characteristic? And to top it all, I go to their weddings! [*Indignantly, but laughing*] Like I'm not supposed to take bribes. Manufacturers offer me a hundred-dollar bill now and then to throw an order their way. You know how honest I am, but it's like this girl, see. I hate myself for it. Because I don't want the girl, and, still, I take it and—I love it!

BIFF.   Let's go to sleep.

HAPPY.   I guess we didn't settle anything, heh?   170

BIFF.   I just got one idea that I think I'm going to try.

HAPPY.   What's that?

BIFF.   Remember Bill Oliver?

HAPPY.   Sure, Oliver is very big now. You want to work for him again?

BIFF.   No, but when I quit he said something to me. He put his arm on my   175
shoulder and he said, "Biff, if you ever need anything, come to me."

HAPPY.   I remember that. That sounds good.

BIFF.   I think I'll go to see him. If I could get ten thousand or even seven or eight thousand dollars I could buy a beautiful ranch.

HAPPY.   I bet he'd back you. 'Cause he thought highly of you, Biff. I mean, they all do. You're well liked, Biff. That's why I say to come back here, and we both have the apartment. And I'm tellin' you, Biff, any babe you want . . .

BIFF.   No, with a ranch I could do the work I like and still be something. I just wonder though. I wonder if Oliver still thinks I stole that carton of basketballs.

HAPPY.   Oh, he probably forgot that long ago. It's almost ten years. You're too   180
sensitive. Anyway, he didn't really fire you.

BIFF.   Well, I think he was going to. I think that's why I quit. I was never sure whether he knew or not. I know he thought the world of me, though. I was the only one he'd let lock up the place.

WILLY.   [*below*] You gonna wash the engine, Biff?

HAPPY.   Shh!

[*BIFF looks at HAPPY, who is gazing down, listening. WILLY is mumbling in the parlor.*]

HAPPY.   You hear that?

[*They listen. WILLY laughs warmly.*]

BIFF.   [*growing angry*] Doesn't he know Mom can hear that?   185

WILLY.   Don't get your sweater dirty, Biff!

[*A look of pain crosses BIFF's face.*]

HAPPY.   Isn't that terrible! Don't leave again, will you? You'll find a job here. You gotta stick around. I don't know what to do about him, it's getting embarrassing.

WILLY.   What a simonizing job!

BIFF.   Mom's hearing that!

WILLY.   No kiddin', Biff, you got a date? Wonderful!   190

HAPPY.   Go on to sleep. But talk to him in the morning, will you?

BIFF.   [*reluctantly getting into bed*] With her in the house. Brother!

HAPPY.   [*getting into bed*] I wish you'd have a good talk with him.

[*The light on their room begins to fade.*]

BIFF.   [*to himself in bed*] That selfish, stupid . . .

HAPPY.   Sh . . . Sleep, Biff.   195

[*Their light is out. Well before they have finished speaking, WILLY's form is dimly seen below in the darkened kitchen. He opens the refrigerator, searches in there, and takes out a bottle of milk. The apartment houses are fading out, and the entire house and surroundings become covered with leaves. Music insinuates itself as the leaves appear.*]

WILLY.   Just wanna be careful with those girls, Biff, that's all. Don't make any promises. No promises of any kind. Because a girl, y'know, they always believe what you tell 'em, and you're very young, Biff, you're too young to be talking seriously to girls.

[*Light rises on the kitchen. WILLY, talking, shuts the refrigerator door and comes downstage to the kitchen table. He pours milk into a glass. He is totally immersed in himself, smiling faintly.*]

WILLY.   Too young entirely, Biff. You want to watch your schooling first. Then when you're all set, there'll be plenty of girls for a boy like you. [*He smiles broadly at a kitchen chair.*] That so? The girls pay for you? [*He laughs.*] Boy, you must really be makin' a hit.

[*WILLY is gradually addressing—physically—a point offstage, speaking through the wall of the kitchen, and his voice has been rising in volume to that of a normal conversation.*]

WILLY.   I been wondering why you polish the car so careful. Ha! Don't leave the hubcaps, boys. Get the chamois to the hubcaps. Happy, use newspaper on the windows, it's the easiest thing. Show him how to do it, Biff! You see, Happy? Pad it up, use it like a pad. That's it, that's it, good work. You're doin' all right, Hap. [*He pauses, then nods in approbation for a few seconds, then looks upward.*] Biff, first thing we gotta do when we get time is clip that big branch over the house. Afraid it's gonna fall in a storm and hit the roof. Tell you what. We get a rope and sling her around, and then we climb up there with a couple of saws and take her down. Soon as you finish the car, boys, I wanna see ya. I got a surprise for you, boys.

BIFF.   [*offstage*] Whatta ya got, Dad?

WILLY.   No, you finish first. Never leave a job till you're finished—remember   200
that. [*looking toward the "big trees"*] Biff, up in Albany I saw a beautiful hammock. I think I'll buy it next trip, and we'll hang it right between those two elms. Wouldn't that be something? Just swingin' there under those branches. Boy, that would be . . .

[*YOUNG BIFF and YOUNG HAPPY appear from the direction WILLY was addressing. HAPPY carries rags and a pail of water. BIFF, wearing a sweater with a block "S," carries a football.*]

BIFF.   [*pointing in the direction of the car offstage*] How's that, Pop, professional?

WILLY.   Terrific. Terrific job, boys. Good work, Biff.

HAPPY.   Where's the surprise, Pop?

WILLY.   In the back seat of the car.

HAPPY.   Boy! [*He runs off.*]   205

BIFF.   What is it, Dad? Tell me, what'd you buy?

WILLY.   [*laughing, cuffs him*] Never mind, something I want you to have.

BIFF.   [*turns and starts off*] What is it, Hap?

HAPPY.   [*offstage*] It's a punching bag!

BIFF.   Oh, Pop!   210

WILLY.   It's got Gene Tunney's° signature on it!

[*HAPPY runs onstage with a punching bag.*]

BIFF.   Gee, how'd you know we wanted a punching bag?

WILLY.   Well, it's the finest thing for the timing.

HAPPY.   [*lies down on his back and pedals with his feet*] I'm losing weight, you notice, Pop?

WILLY.   [*to HAPPY*] Jumping rope is good too.   215

BIFF.   Did you see the new football I got?

WILLY.   [*examining the ball*] Where'd you get a new ball?

BIFF.   The coach told me to practice my passing.

WILLY.   That so? And he gave you the ball, heh?

BIFF.   Well, I borrowed it from the locker room. [*He laughs confidentially.*]   220

WILLY.   [*laughing with him at the theft*] I want you to return that.

HAPPY.   I told you he wouldn't like it!

BIFF.   [*angrily*] Well, I'm bringing it back!

WILLY.   [*stopping the incipient argument, to HAPPY*] Sure, he's gotta practice with a regulation ball, doesn't he? [*to BIFF*] Coach'll probably congratulate you on your initiative!

BIFF.   Oh, he keeps congratulating my initiative all the time, Pop.   225

WILLY.   That's because he likes you. If somebody else took that ball there'd be an uproar. So what's the report, boys, what's the report?

BIFF.   Where'd you go this time, Dad? Gee we were lonesome for you.

WILLY.   [*pleased, puts an arm around each boy and they come down to the apron*] Lonesome, heh?

BIFF.   Missed you every minute.

---

211 *Gene Tunney:* James Joseph Tunney, a boxer who won the heavyweight championship from Jack Dempsey in 1926 and retired undefeated in 1928.

WILLY.   Don't say? Tell you a secret, boys. Don't breathe it to a soul. Someday I'll   230
have my own business, and I'll never have to leave home any more.

HAPPY.   Like Uncle Charley, heh?

WILLY.   Bigger than Uncle Charley! Because Charley is not—liked. He's liked,
but he's not—well liked.

BIFF.   Where'd you go this time, Dad?

WILLY.   Well, I got on the road, and I went north to Providence. Met the Mayor.

BIFF.   The Mayor of Providence!   235

WILLY.   He was sitting in the hotel lobby.

BIFF.   What'd he say?

WILLY.   He said, "Morning!" And I said, "You got a fine city here, Mayor." And
then he had coffee with me. And then I went to Waterbury. Waterbury is a fine city. Big
clock city, the famous Waterbury clock. Sold a nice bill there. And then Boston—Boston
is the cradle of the Revolution. A fine city. And a couple of other towns in Mass., and on
to Portland and Bangor and straight home!

BIFF.   Gee, I'd love to go with you sometime, Dad.

WILLY.   Soon as summer comes.   240

HAPPY.   Promise?

WILLY.   You and Hap and I, and I'll show you all the towns. America is full
of beautiful towns and fine, upstanding people. And they know me, boys, they know
me up and down New England. The finest people. And when I bring you fellas up,
there'll be open sesame for all of us, 'cause one thing, boys: I have friends. I can park
my car in any street in New England, and the cops protect it like their own. This
summer, heh?

BIFF and HAPPY.   [*together*] Yeah! You bet!

WILLY.   We'll take our bathing suits.

HAPPY.   We'll carry your bags, Pop!   245

WILLY.   Oh, won't that be something! Me comin' into the Boston stores with you
boys carryin' my bags. What a sensation!

[*BIFF is prancing around, practicing passing the ball.*]

WILLY.   You nervous, Biff, about the game?

BIFF.   Not if you're gonna be there.

WILLY.   What do they say about you in school, now that they made you captain?

HAPPY.   There's a crowd of girls behind him everytime the classes change.   250

BIFF.   [*taking WILLY's hand*] This Saturday, Pop, this Saturday—just for you, I'm
going to break through for a touchdown.

HAPPY.   You're supposed to pass.

BIFF.   I'm takin' one play for Pop. You watch me, Pop, and when I take off my
helmet, that means I'm breakin' out. Then you watch me crash through that line!

WILLY.   [*kisses BIFF*] Oh, wait'll I tell this in Boston!

[*BERNARD enters in knickers. He is younger than BIFF, earnest and loyal, a worried boy.*]

BERNARD.   Biff, where are you? You're supposed to study with me today.   255

WILLY.   Hey, looka Bernard. What're you lookin' so anemic about, Bernard?

BERNARD.   He's gotta study, Uncle Willy. He's got Regents° next week.

HAPPY.   [*tauntingly, spinning BERNARD around*] Let's box, Bernard!

---

257 *Regents:* A statewide high school proficiency examination administered in New York State.

BERNARD. Biff! [*He gets away from HAPPY.*] Listen, Biff, I heard Mr. Birnbaum say that if you don't start studyin' math he's gonna flunk you, and you won't graduate. I heard him!

WILLY. You better study with him, Biff. Go ahead now.   260

BERNARD. I heard him!

BIFF. Oh, Pop, you didn't see my sneakers! [*He holds up a foot for WILLY to look at.*]

WILLY. Hey, that's a beautiful job of printing!

BERNARD. [*wiping his glasses*] Just because he printed University of Virginia on his sneakers doesn't mean they've got to graduate him, Uncle Willy!

WILLY. [*angrily*] What're you talking about? With scholarships to three uni-   265
versities they're gonna flunk him?

BERNARD. But I heard Mr. Birnbaum say—

WILLY. Don't be a pest, Bernard! [*to his boys*] What an anemic!

BERNARD. Okay, I'm waiting for you in my house, Biff.

[*BERNARD goes off. The LOMANS laugh.*]

WILLY. Bernard is not well liked, is he?

BIFF. He's liked, but he's not well liked.   270

HAPPY. That's right, Pop.

WILLY. That's just what I mean. Bernard can get the best marks in school, y'un-
derstand, but when he gets out in the business world, y'understand, you are going to be five times ahead of him. That's why I thank Almighty God you're both built like Adonises. Because the man who makes an appearance in the business world, the man who creates personal interest, is the man who gets ahead. Be liked and you will never want. You take me, for instance. I never have to wait in line to see a buyer. "Willy Loman is here!" That's all they have to know, and I go right through.

BIFF. Did you knock them dead, Pop?

WILLY. Knocked 'em cold in Providence, slaughtered 'em in Boston.

HAPPY. [*on his back, pedaling again*] I'm losing weight, you notice, Pop?   275

[*LINDA enters, as of old, a ribbon in her hair, carrying a basket of washing.*]

LINDA. [*with youthful energy*] Hello, dear!

WILLY. Sweetheart!

LINDA. How'd the Chevvy run?

WILLY. Chevrolet, Linda, is the greatest car ever built. [*to the boys*] Since when do you let your mother carry wash up the stairs?

BIFF. Grab hold there, boy!   280

HAPPY. Where to, Mom?

LINDA. Hang them up on the line. And you better go down to your friends, Biff. The cellar is full of boys. They don't know what to do with themselves.

BIFF. Ah, when Pop comes home they can wait!

WILLY. [*laughs appreciatively*] You better go down and tell them what to do, Biff.

BIFF. I think I'll have them sweep out the furnace room.   285

WILLY. Good work, Biff.

BIFF. [*goes through wall-line of kitchen to doorway at back and calls down*] Fellas! Everybody sweep out the furnace room! I'll be right down!

VOICES. All right! Okay, Biff.

BIFF. George and Sam and Frank, come out back! We're hangin' up the wash! Come on, Hap, on the double! [*He and HAPPY carry out the basket.*]

LINDA.   The way they obey him!   290

WILLY.   Well, that's training, the training. I'm tellin' you, I was sellin' thousands and thousands, but I had to come home.

LINDA.   Oh, the whole block'll be at that game. Did you sell anything?

WILLY.   I did five hundred gross in Providence and seven hundred gross in Boston.

LINDA.   No! Wait a minute, I've got a pencil. [*She pulls pencil and paper out of her apron pocket.*] That makes your commission . . . Two hundred—my God! Two hundred and twelve dollars!

WILLY.   Well, I didn't figure it yet, but . . .   295

LINDA.   How much did you do?

WILLY.   Well, I—I did—about a hundred and eighty gross in Providence. Well, no—it came to—roughly two hundred gross on the whole trip.

LINDA.   [*without hesitation*] Two hundred gross. That's . . . [*She figures.*]

WILLY.   The trouble was that three of the stores were half closed for inventory in Boston. Otherwise I woulda broke records.

LINDA.   Well, it makes seventy dollars and some pennies. That's very good.   300

WILLY.   What do we owe?

LINDA.   Well, on the first there's sixteen dollars on the refrigerator—

WILLY.   Why sixteen?

LINDA.   Well, the fan belt broke, so it was a dollar eighty.

WILLY.   But it's brand new.   305

LINDA.   Well, the man said that's the way it is. Till they work themselves in, y'know.

[*They move through the wall-line into the kitchen.*]

WILLY.   I hope we didn't get stuck on that machine.

LINDA.   They got the biggest ads of any of them!

WILLY.   I know, it's a fine machine. What else?

LINDA.   Well, there's nine-sixty for the washing machine. And for the vacuum   310
cleaner there's three and a half due on the fifteenth. Then the roof, you got twenty-one dollars remaining.

WILLY.   It don't leak, does it?

LINDA.   No, they did a wonderful job. Then you owe Frank for the carburetor.

WILLY.   I'm not going to pay that man! That goddam Chevrolet, they ought to prohibit the manufacture of that car!

LINDA.   Well, you owe him three and a half. And odds and ends, comes to around a hundred and twenty dollars by the fifteenth.

WILLY.   A hundred and twenty dollars! My God, if business don't pick up   315
I don't know what I'm gonna do!

LINDA.   Well, next week you'll do better.

WILLY.   Oh, I'll knock 'em dead next week. I'll go to Hartford. I'm very well liked in Hartford. You know, the trouble is, Linda, people don't seem to take to me.

[*They move onto the forestage.*]

LINDA.   Oh, don't be foolish.

WILLY.   I know it when I walk in. They seem to laugh at me.

LINDA.   Why? Why would they laugh at you? Don't talk that way, Willy.   320

[*WILLY moves to the edge of the stage. LINDA goes into the kitchen and starts to darn stockings.*]

WILLY.   I don't know the reason for it, but they just pass me by. I'm not noticed.

LINDA.   But you're doing wonderful, dear. You're making seventy to a hundred dollars a week.

WILLY.   But I gotta be at it ten, twelve hours a day. Other men—I don't know—they do it easier. I don't know why—I can't stop myself—I talk too much. A man oughta come in with a few words. One thing about Charley. He's a man of few words, and they respect him.

LINDA.   You don't talk too much, you're just lively.

WILLY.   [*smiling*] Well, I figure, what the hell, life is short, a couple of jokes.   325
[*to himself*] I joke too much! [*The smile goes.*]

LINDA.   Why? You're—

WILLY.   I'm fat. I'm very—foolish to look at, Linda. I didn't tell you, but Christmas time I happened to be calling on F. H. Stewarts, and a salesman I know, as I was going in to see the buyer I heard him say something about—walrus. And I—I cracked him right across the face. I won't take that. I simply will not take that. But they do laugh at me. I know that.

LINDA.   Darling . . .

WILLY.   I gotta overcome it. I know I gotta overcome it. I'm not dressing to advantage, maybe.

LINDA.   Willy, darling, you're the handsomest man in the world—   330

WILLY.   Oh, no, Linda.

LINDA.   To me you are. [*slight pause*] The handsomest.

[*From the darkness is heard the laughter of a woman. WILLY doesn't turn to it, but it continues through LINDA's lines.*]

LINDA.   And the boys, Willy. Few men are idolized by their children the way you are.

[*Music is heard as behind a scrim, to the left of the house, THE WOMAN, dimly seen, is dressing.*]

WILLY.   [*with great feeling*] You're the best there is, Linda, you're a pal, you know that? On the road—on the road I want to grab you sometimes and just kiss the life outa you.

[*The laughter is loud now, and he moves into a brightening area at the left, where THE WOMAN has come from behind the scrim and is standing, putting on her hat, looking into a "mirror" and laughing.*]

WILLY.   Cause I get so lonely—especially when business is bad and there's   335
nobody to talk to. I get the feeling that I'll never sell anything again, that I won't make a living for you, or a business, a business for the boys. [*He talks through THE WOMAN's subsiding laughter; THE WOMAN primps at the "mirror."*] There's so much I want to make for—

THE WOMAN.   Me? You didn't make me, Willy. I picked you.

WILLY.   [*pleased*] You picked me?

THE WOMAN.   [*who is quite proper-looking, WILLY's age*] I did. I've been sitting at that desk watching all the salesmen go by, day in, day out. But you've got such a sense of humor, and we do have such a good time together, don't we?

WILLY.   Sure, sure. [*He takes her in his arms.*] Why do you have to go now?

THE WOMAN.   It's two o'clock . . .   340

WILLY.   No, come on in! [*He pulls her.*]

THE WOMAN.   . . . my sisters'll be scandalized. When'll you be back?

WILLY.   Oh, two weeks about. Will you come up again?

THE WOMAN.   Sure thing. You do make me laugh. It's good for me. [*She squeezes his arm, kisses him.*] And I think you're a wonderful man.

WILLY.   You picked me, heh?   345

THE WOMAN.   Sure. Because you're so sweet. And such a kidder.

WILLY.   Well, I'll see you next time I'm in Boston.

THE WOMAN.   I'll put you right through to the buyers.

WILLY.   [*slapping her bottom*] Right. Well, bottoms up!

THE WOMAN.   [*slaps him gently and laughs*] You just kill me, Willy. [*He suddenly*   350 *grabs her and kisses her roughly.*] You kill me. And thanks for the stockings. I love a lot of stockings. Well, good night.

WILLY.   Good night. And keep your pores open!

THE WOMAN.   Oh, Willy!

[*THE WOMAN bursts out laughing, and LINDA's laughter blends in. THE WOMAN disappears into the dark. Now the area at the kitchen table brightens. LINDA is sitting where she was at the kitchen table, but now is mending a pair of her silk stockings.*]

LINDA.   You are, Willy. The handsomest man. You've got no reason to feel that—

WILLY.   [*coming out of THE WOMAN's dimming area and going over to LINDA*] I'll make it all up to you, Linda, I'll—

LINDA.   There's nothing to make up, dear. You're doing fine, better than—   355

WILLY.   [*noticing her mending*] What's that?

LINDA.   Just mending my stockings. They're so expensive—

WILLY.   [*angrily, taking them from her*] I won't have you mending stockings in this house! Now throw them out!

[*LINDA puts the stockings in her pocket.*]

BERNARD.   [*entering on the run*] Where is he? If he doesn't study!

WILLY.   [*moving to the forestage, with great agitation*] You'll give him the   360 answers!

BERNARD.   I do, but I can't on a Regents! That's a state exam! They're liable to arrest me!

WILLY.   Where is he? I'll whip him, I'll whip him!

LINDA.   And he'd better give back that football, Willy, it's not nice.

WILLY.   Biff! Where is he? Why is he taking everything?

LINDA.   He's too rough with the girls, Willy. All the mothers are afraid of   365 him!

WILLY.   I'll whip him!

BERNARD.   He's driving the car without a license!

[*THE WOMAN's laugh is heard.*]

WILLY.   Shut up!

LINDA.   All the mothers—

WILLY.   Shut up!   370

BERNARD.   [*backing quietly away and out*] Mr. Birnbaum says he's stuck up.

WILLY.   Get outa here!

BERNARD.   If he doesn't buckle down he'll flunk math! [*He goes off.*]

LINDA.   He's right, Willy, you've gotta—

WILLY.   [*exploding at her*] There's nothing the matter with him! You want   37 him to be a worm like Bernard? He's got spirit, personality . . .

[*As he speaks, LINDA, almost in tears, exits into the living-room. WILLY is alone in the kitchen, wilting and staring. The leaves are gone. It is night again, and the apartment houses look down from behind.*]

WILLY.   Loaded with it. Loaded! What is he stealing? He's giving it back, isn't he? Why is he stealing? What did I tell him? I never in my life told him anything but decent things.

[*HAPPY in pajamas has come down the stairs; WILLY suddenly becomes aware of HAPPY's presence.*]

HAPPY.   Let's go now, come on.
WILLY.   [*sitting down at the kitchen table*] Huh! Why did she have to wax the floors herself? Everytime she waxes the floors she keels over. She knows that!
HAPPY.   Shh! Take it easy. What brought you back tonight?
WILLY.   I got an awful scare. Nearly hit a kid in Yonkers. God! Why didn't   380
I go to Alaska with my brother Ben that time! Ben! That man was a genius, that man was success incarnate! What a mistake! He begged me to go.
HAPPY.   Well, there's no use in—
WILLY.   You guys! There was a man started with the clothes on his back and ended up with diamond mines!
HAPPY.   Boy, someday I'd like to know how he did it.
WILLY.   What's the mystery? The man knew what he wanted and went out and got it! Walked into a jungle, and comes out, the age of twenty-one, and he's rich! The world is an oyster, but you don't crack it open on a mattress!
HAPPY.   Pop, I told you I'm gonna retire you for life.   385
WILLY.   You'll retire me for life on seventy goddam dollars a week? And your women and your car and your apartment, and you'll retire me for life! Christ's sake, I couldn't get past Yonkers today! Where are you guys, where are you? The woods are burning! I can't drive a car!

[*CHARLEY has appeared in the doorway. He is a large man, slow of speech, laconic, immovable. In all he says, despite what he says, there is pity, and now, trepidation. He has a robe over pajamas, slippers on his feet. He enters the kitchen.*]

CHARLEY.   Everything all right?
HAPPY.   Yeah, Charley, everything's . . .
WILLY.   What's the matter?
CHARLEY.   I heard some noise. I thought something happened. Can't we do   390
something about the walls? You sneeze in here, and in my house hats blow off.
HAPPY.   Let's go to bed, Dad. Come on.

[*CHARLEY signals to HAPPY to go.*]

WILLY.   You go ahead, I'm not tired at the moment.
HAPPY.   [*to WILLY*] Take it easy, huh? [*He exits.*]
WILLY.   What're you doin' up?
CHARLEY.   [*sitting down at the kitchen table opposite WILLY*] Couldn't sleep good.   395
I had a heartburn.
WILLY.   Well, you don't know how to eat.
CHARLEY.   I eat with my mouth.
WILLY.   No, you're ignorant. You gotta know about vitamins and things like that.
CHARLEY.   Come on, let's shoot. Tire you out a little.

WILLY.   [*hesitantly*] All right. You got cards?   400

CHARLEY.   [*taking a deck from his pocket*] Yeah, I got them. Someplace. What is it with those vitamins?

WILLY.   [*dealing*] They build up your bones. Chemistry.

CHARLEY.   Yeah, but there's no bones in a heartburn.

WILLY.   What are you talkin' about? Do you know the first thing about it?

CHARLEY.   Don't get insulted.   405

WILLY.   Don't talk about something you don't know anything about.

[*They are playing. Pause.*]

CHARLEY.   What're you doin' home?

WILLY.   A little trouble with the car.

CHARLEY.   Oh. [*Pause*] I'd like to take a trip to California.

WILLY.   Don't say.   410

CHARLEY.   You want a job?

WILLY.   I got a job, I told you that. [*after a slight pause*] What the hell are you offering me a job for?

CHARLEY.   Don't get insulted.

WILLY.   Don't insult me.

CHARLEY.   I don't see no sense in it. You don't have to go on this way.   415

WILLY.   I got a good job. [*slight pause*] What do you keep comin' in for?

CHARLEY.   You want me to go?

WILLY.   [*after a pause, withering*] I can't understand it. He's going back to Texas again. What the hell is that?

CHARLEY.   Let him go.

WILLY.   I got nothin' to give him, Charley, I'm clean, I'm clean.   420

CHARLEY.   He won't starve. None a them starve. Forget about him.

WILLY.   Then what have I got to remember?

CHARLEY.   You take it too hard. To hell with it. When a deposit bottle is broken you don't get your nickel back.

WILLY.   That's easy enough for you to say.

CHARLEY.   That ain't easy for me to say.   425

WILLY.   Did you see the ceiling I put up in the living-room?

CHARLEY.   Yeah, that's a piece of work. To put up a ceiling is a mystery to me. How do you do it?

WILLY.   What's the difference?

CHARLEY.   Well, talk about it.

WILLY.   You gonna put up a ceiling?   430

CHARLEY.   How could I put up a ceiling?

WILLY.   Then what the hell are you bothering me for?

CHARLEY.   You're insulted again.

WILLY.   A man who can't handle tools is not a man. You're disgusting.

CHARLEY.   Don't call me disgusting, Willy.   435

[*UNCLE BEN, carrying a valise and an umbrella, enters the forestage from around the right corner of the house. He is a stolid man, in his sixties, with a mustache and an authoritative air. He is utterly certain of his destiny, and there is an aura of far places about him. He enters exactly as WILLY speaks.*]

WILLY.   I'm getting awfully tired, Ben.

[*BEN's music is heard. BEN looks around at everything.*]

CHARLEY.   Good, keep playing; you'll sleep better. Did you call me Ben?

[*BEN looks at his watch.*]

WILLY.   That's funny. For a second there you reminded me of my brother Ben.

BEN.   I only have a few minutes. [*He strolls, inspecting the place. WILLY and CHARLEY continue playing.*]

CHARLEY.   You never heard from him again, heh? Since that time?   440

WILLY.   Didn't Linda tell you? Couple of weeks ago we got a letter from his wife in Africa. He died.

CHARLEY.   That so.

BEN.   [*chuckling*] So this is Brooklyn, eh?

CHARLEY.   Maybe you're in for some of his money.

WILLY.   Naa, he had seven sons. There's just one opportunity I had with   445
that man . . .

BEN.   I must make a train, William. There are several properties I'm looking at in Alaska.

WILLY.   Sure, sure! If I'd gone with him to Alaska that time, everything would've been totally different.

CHARLEY.   Go on, you'd froze to death up there.

WILLY.   What're you talking about?

BEN.   Opportunity is tremendous in Alaska, William. Surprised you're not   450
up there.

WILLY.   Sure, tremendous.

CHARLEY.   Heh?

WILLY.   There was the only man I ever met who knew the answers.

CHARLEY.   Who?

BEN.   How are you all?   455

WILLY.   [*taking a pot, smiling*] Fine, fine.

CHARLEY.   Pretty sharp tonight.

BEN.   Is Mother living with you?

WILLY.   No, she died a long time ago.

CHARLEY.   Who?   460

BEN.   That's too bad. Fine specimen of a lady, Mother.

WILLY.   [*to CHARLEY*] Heh?

BEN.   I'd hoped to see the old girl.

CHARLEY.   Who died?

BEN.   Heard anything from Father, have you?   465

WILLY.   [*unnerved*] What do you mean, who died?

CHARLEY.   [*taking a pot*] What're you talkin' about?

BEN.   [*looking at his watch*] William, it's half-past eight!

WILLY.   [*As though to dispel his confusion he angrily stops CHARLEY's hand.*] That's my build!

CHARLEY.   I put the ace—   470

WILLY.   If you don't know how to play the game I'm not gonna throw my money away on you!

CHARLEY.   [*rising*] It was my ace, for God's sake!

WILLY.   I'm through, I'm through!

BEN.   When did Mother die?

WILLY.   Long ago. Since the beginning you never knew how to play cards.   475

CHARLEY.   [*picks up the cards and goes to the door*] All right! Next time I'll bring a deck with five aces.

WILLY.   I don't play that kind of game!

CHARLEY.   [*turning to him*] You ought to be ashamed of yourself!

WILLY.   Yeah?

CHARLEY.   Yeah! [*He goes out.*]   480

WILLY.   [*slamming the door after him*] Ignoramus!

BEN.   [*as WILLY comes toward him through the wall-line of the kitchen*] So you're William.

WILLY.   [*shaking BEN's hand*] Ben! I've been waiting for you so long! What's the answer? How did you do it?

BEN.   Oh, there's a story in that.

[*LINDA enters the forestage, as of old, carrying the wash basket.*]

LINDA.   Is this Ben?   485

BEN.   [*gallantly*] How do you do, my dear.

LINDA.   Where've you been all these years? Willy's always wondered why you—

WILLY.   [*pulling BEN away from her impatiently*] Where is Dad? Didn't you follow him? How did you get started?

BEN.   Well, I don't know how much you remember.

WILLY.   Well, I was just a baby, of course, only three or four years old—   490

BEN.   Three years and eleven months.

WILLY.   What a memory, Ben!

BEN.   I have many enterprises, William, and I have never kept books.

WILLY.   I remember I was sitting under the wagon in—was it Nebraska?

BEN.   It was South Dakota, and I gave you a bunch of wild flowers.   495

WILLY.   I remember you walking away down some open road.

BEN.   [*laughing*] I was going to find Father in Alaska.

WILLY.   Where is he?

BEN.   At that age I had a very faulty view of geography, William. I discovered after a few days that I was heading due south, so instead of Alaska, I ended up in Africa.

LINDA.   Africa!   500

WILLY.   The Gold Coast!

BEN.   Principally diamond mines.

LINDA.   Diamond mines!

BEN.   Yes, my dear. But I've only a few minutes—

WILLY.   No! Boys! Boys! [*YOUNG BIFF and HAPPY appear.*] Listen to this. This   505
is your Uncle Ben, a great man! Tell my boys, Ben!

BEN.   Why, boys, when I was seventeen I walked into the jungle, and when I was twenty-one I walked out. [*He laughs.*] And by God I was rich.

WILLY.   [*to the boys*] You see what I been talking about? The greatest things can happen!

BEN.   [*glancing at his watch*] I have an appointment in Ketchikan Tuesday week.

WILLY.   No, Ben. Please tell about Dad. I want my boys to hear. I want them to know the kind of stock they spring from. All I remember is a man with a big beard, and I was in Mamma's lap, sitting around a fire, and some kind of high music.

BEN.   His flute. He played the flute.   510
WILLY.   Sure, the flute, that's right!

[*New music is heard, a high, rollicking tune.*]

BEN.   Father was a very great and a very wild-hearted man. We would start in
Boston, and he'd toss the whole family into the wagon, and then he'd drive the team
right across the country; through Ohio, and Indiana, Michigan, Illinois, and all the
Western states. And we'd stop in the towns and sell the flutes that he'd made on the way.
Great inventor, Father. With one gadget he made more in a week than a man like you
could make in a lifetime.
WILLY.   That's just the way I'm bringing them up, Ben—rugged, well liked, all-
around.
BEN.   Yeah? [*to BIFF*] Hit that, boy—hard as you can. [*He pounds his stomach.*]
BIFF.   Oh, no, sir!   515
BEN.   [*taking boxing stance*] Come on, get to me! [*He laughs.*]
BIFF.   Okay! [*He cocks his fists and starts in.*]
WILLY.   Go to it, Biff! Go ahead, show him!
LINDA.   [*to WILLY*] Why must he fight, dear?
BEN.   [*sparring with BIFF*] Good boy! Good boy!   520
WILLY.   How's that, Ben, heh?
HAPPY.   Give him the left, Biff!
LINDA.   Why are you fighting?
BEN.   Good boy! [*suddenly comes in, trips BIFF, and stands over him, the point of his
umbrella poised over BIFF's eye.*]
LINDA.   Look out, Biff!   525
BIFF.   Gee!
BEN.   [*patting BIFF's knee*] Never fight fair with a stranger, boy. You'll never get out
of the jungle that way. [*taking LINDA's hand and bowing*] It was an honor and a pleasure to
meet you, Linda.
LINDA.   [*withdrawing her hand coldly, frightened*] Have a nice—trip.
BEN.   [*to WILLY*] And good luck with your—what do you do?
WILLY.   Selling.   530
BEN.   Yes. Well . . . [*He raises his hand in farewell to all.*]
WILLY.   No, Ben, I don't want you to think . . . [*He takes BEN's arm to show him.*]
It's Brooklyn, I know, but we hunt too.
BEN.   Really, now.
WILLY.   Oh, sure, there's snakes and rabbits and—that's why I moved out here.
Why, Biff can fell any one of these trees in no time! Boys! Go right over to where they're
building the apartment house and get some sand. We're gonna rebuild the entire front
stoop right now! Watch this, Ben!
BIFF.   Yes, sir! On the double, Hap!   535
HAPPY.   [*as he and BIFF run off*] I lost weight, Pop, you notice?

[*CHARLEY enters in knickers, even before the boys are gone.*]

CHARLEY.   Listen, if they steal any more from that building the watchman'll put
the cops on them!
LINDA.   [*to WILLY*] Don't let Biff . . .

[*BEN laughs lustily.*]

WILLY.   You shoulda seen the lumber they brought home last week. At least a dozen six-by-tens worth all kinds a money.

CHARLEY.   Listen, if that watchman—   540

WILLY.   I gave them hell, understand. But I got a couple of fearless characters there.

CHARLEY.   Willy, the jails are full of fearless characters.

BEN.   [*clapping WILLY on the back, with a laugh at CHARLEY*] And the stock exchange, friend!

WILLY.   [*joining in BEN's laughter*] Where are the rest of your pants?

CHARLEY.   My wife bought them.   545

WILLY.   Now all you need is a golf club and you can go upstairs and go to sleep. [*to BEN*] Great athlete! Between him and his son Bernard they can't hammer a nail!

BERNARD.   [*rushing in*] The watchman's chasing Biff!

WILLY.   [*angrily*] Shut up! He's not stealing anything!

LINDA.   [*alarmed, hurrying off left*] Where is he? Biff, dear! [*She exits.*]

WILLY.   [*moving toward the left, away from BEN*] There's nothing wrong. What's   550
the matter with you?

BEN.   Nervy boy. Good!

WILLY.   [*laughing*] Oh, nerves of iron, that Biff!

CHARLEY.   Don't know what it is. My New England man comes back and he's bleedin', they murdered him up there.

WILLY.   It's contacts, Charley, I got important contacts!

CHARLEY.   [*sarcastically*] Glad to hear it, Willy. Come in later, we'll shoot a   555
little casino. I'll take some of your Portland money. [*He laughs at WILLY and exits.*]

WILLY.   [*turning to BEN*] Business is bad, it's murderous. But not for me, of course.

BEN.   I'll stop by on my way back to Africa.

WILLY.   [*longingly.*] Can't you stay a few days? You're just what I need, Ben, because I—I have a fine position here, but I—well, Dad left when I was such a baby and I never had a chance to talk to him and I still feel—kind of temporary about myself.

BEN.   I'll be late for my train.

[*They are at opposite ends of the stage.*]

WILLY.   Ben, my boys—can't we talk? They'd go into the jaws of hell for me, see,   560
but I—

BEN.   William, you're being first-rate with your boys. Outstanding, manly chaps!

WILLY.   [*hanging on to his words*] Oh, Ben, that's good to hear! Because sometimes I'm afraid that I'm not teaching them the right kind of—Ben, how should I teach them?

BEN.   [*giving great weight to each word, and with a certain vicious audacity*] William, when I walked into the jungle, I was seventeen. When I walked out I was twenty-one. And, by God, I was rich! [*He goes off into darkness around the right corner of the house.*]

WILLY.   . . . was rich! That's just the spirit I want to imbue them with! To walk into a jungle! I was right! I was right! I was right!

[*BEN is gone, but WILLY is still speaking to him as LINDA, in her nightgown and robe, enters the kitchen, glances around for WILLY, then goes to the door of the house, looks out and sees him. Comes down to his left. He looks at her.*]

LINDA.   Willy, dear? Willy?   565
WILLY.   I was right!
LINDA.   Did you have some cheese? [*He can't answer.*] It's very late, darling. Come
to bed, heh?
WILLY.   [*looking straight up*] Gotta break your neck to see a star in this yard.
LINDA.   You coming in?
WILLY.   Whatever happened to that diamond watch fob? Remember? When Ben   570
came from Africa that time? Didn't he give me a watch fob with a diamond in it?
LINDA.   You pawned it, dear. Twelve, thirteen years ago. For Biff's radio corre-
spondence course.
WILLY.   Gee, that was a beautiful thing. I'll take a walk.
LINDA.   But you're in your slippers.
WILLY.   [*starting to go around the house at the left*] I was right! I was! [*Half to* LINDA, *as*   575
he goes, shaking his head] What a man! There was a man worth talking to. I was right!
LINDA.   [*calling after* WILLY] But in your slippers, Willy!

[*WILLY is almost gone when* BIFF, *in his pajamas, comes down the stairs and enters the kitchen.*]

BIFF.   What is he doing out there?
LINDA.   Sh!
BIFF.   God Almighty, Mom, how long has he been doing this?
LINDA.   Don't, he'll hear you.   580
BIFF.   What the hell is the matter with him?
LINDA.   It'll pass by morning.
BIFF.   Shouldn't we do anything?
LINDA.   Oh, my dear, you should do a lot of things, but there's nothing to do, so
go to sleep.

[*HAPPY comes down the stairs and sits on the steps.*]

HAPPY.   I never heard him so loud, Mom.   585
LINDA.   Well, come around more often; you'll hear him. [*She sits down at the
table and mends the lining of* WILLY'S *jacket.*]
BIFF.   Why didn't you ever write me about this, Mom?
LINDA.   How would I write to you? For over three months you had no address.
BIFF.   I was on the move. But you know I thought of you all the time. You know
that, don't you, pal?
LINDA.   I know, dear, I know. But he likes to have a letter. Just to know that there's
still a possibility for better things.
BIFF.   He's not like this all the time, is he?   590
LINDA.   It's when you come home he's always the worst.
BIFF.   When I come home?
LINDA.   When you write you're coming, he's all smiles, and talks about the future,
and—he's just wonderful. And then the closer you seem to come, the more shaky he
gets, and then, by the time you get here, he's arguing, and he seems angry at you. I think
it's just that maybe he can't bring himself to—to open up to you. Why are you so hateful
to each other? Why is that?
BIFF.   [*evasively*] I'm not hateful, Mom.
LINDA.   But you no sooner come in the door than you're fighting!   595
BIFF.   I don't know why. I mean to change. I'm tryin', Mom, you understand?

LINDA.   Are you home to stay now?

BIFF.   I don't know. I want to look around, see what's doin'.

LINDA.   Biff, you can't look around all your life, can you?

BIFF.   I just can't take hold, Mom. I can't take hold of some kind of a life.   600

LINDA.   Biff, a man is not a bird, to come and go with the springtime.

BIFF.   Your hair . . . [*He touches her hair.*] Your hair got so gray.

LINDA.   Oh, it's been gray since you were in high school. I just stopped dyeing it, that's all.

BIFF.   Dye it again, will ya? I don't want my pal looking old. [*He smiles.*]

LINDA.   You're such a boy! You think you can go away for a year and . . .   605
You've got to get it into your head now that one day you'll knock on this door and there'll be strange people here—

BIFF.   What are you talking about? You're not even sixty, Mom.

LINDA.   But what about your father?

BIFF.   [*lamely*] Well, I meant him, too.

HAPPY.   He admires Pop.

LINDA.   Biff, dear, if you don't have any feeling for him, then you can't have any   610
feeling for me.

BIFF.   Sure I can, Mom.

LINDA.   No. You can't just come to see me, because I love him. [*with a threat, but only a threat, of tears*] He's the dearest man in the world to me, and I won't have anyone making him feel unwanted and low and blue. You've got to make up your mind now, darling, there's no leeway any more. Either he's your father and you pay him that respect, or else you're not to come here. I know he's not easy to get along with—nobody knows that better than me—but . . .

WILLY.   [*from the left, with a laugh*] Hey, hey, Biffo!

BIFF.   [*starting to go out after WILLY*] What the hell is the matter with him? [*HAPPY stops him.*]

LINDA.   Don't—don't go near him!   615

BIFF.   Stop making excuses for him! He always, always wiped the floor with you. Never had an ounce of respect for you.

HAPPY.   He's always had respect for—

BIFF.   What the hell do you know about it?

HAPPY.   [*surlily*] Just don't call him crazy!

BIFF.   He's got no character—Charley wouldn't do this. Not in his own   620
house—spewing out that vomit from his mind.

HAPPY.   Charley never had to cope with what he's got to.

BIFF.   People are worse off than Willy Loman. Believe me, I've seen them!

LINDA.   Then make Charley your father, Biff. You can't do that, can you? I don't say he's a great man. Willy Loman never made a lot of money. His name was never in the paper. He's not the finest character that ever lived. But he's a human being, and a terrible thing is happening to him. So attention must be paid. He's not to be allowed to fall into his grave like an old dog. Attention, attention must be finally paid to such a person. You called him crazy—

BIFF.   I didn't mean—

LINDA.   No, a lot of people think he's lost his—balance. But you don't have   625
to be very smart to know what his trouble is. The man is exhausted.

HAPPY.   Sure!

LINDA.   A small man can be just as exhausted as a great man. He works for a company thirty-six years this March, opens up unheard-of-territories to their trademark, and now in his old age they take his salary away.

HAPPY.   [*indignantly*] I didn't know that, Mom.

LINDA.   You never asked, my dear! Now that you get your spending money someplace else you don't trouble your mind with him.

HAPPY.   But I gave you money last—   630

LINDA.   Christmas time, fifty dollars! To fix the hot water it cost ninety-seven fifty! For five weeks he's been on straight commission,° like a beginner, an unknown!

BIFF.   Those ungrateful bastards!

LINDA.   Are they any worse than his sons? When he brought them business, when he was young, they were glad to see him. But now his old friends, the old buyers that loved him so and always found some order to hand him in a pinch—they're all dead, retired. He used to be able to make six, seven calls a day in Boston. Now he takes his valises out of the car and puts them back and takes them out again and he's exhausted. Instead of walking he talks now. He drives seven hundred miles, and when he gets there no one knows him any more, no one welcomes him. And what goes through a man's mind, driving seven hundred miles home without having earned a cent? Why shouldn't he talk to himself? Why? When he has to go to Charley and borrow fifty dollars a week and pretend to me that it's his pay? How long can that go on? How long? You see what I'm sitting here and waiting for? And you tell me he has no character? The man who never worked a day but for your benefit? When does he get the medal for that? Is this his reward—to turn around at the age of sixty-three and find his sons, who he loved better than his life, one a philandering bum—

HAPPY.   Mom!

LINDA.   That's all you are, my baby! [*To BIFF*] And you! What happened to   635
the love you had for him? You were such pals! How you used to talk to him on the phone every night! How lonely he was till he could come home to you!

BIFF.   All right, Mom. I'll live here in my room, and I'll get a job. I'll keep away from him, that's all.

LINDA.   No, Biff. You can't stay here and fight all the time.

BIFF.   He threw me out of this house, remember that.

LINDA.   Why did he do that? I never knew why.

BIFF.   Because I know he's a fake and he doesn't like anybody around who knows!   640

LINDA.   Why a fake? In what way? What do you mean?

BIFF.   Just don't lay it all at my feet. It's between me and him—that's all I have to say. I'll chip in from now on. He'll settle for half my pay check. He'll be all right. I'm going to bed. [*He starts for the stairs.*]

LINDA.   He won't be all right.

BIFF.   [*turning on the stairs, furiously*] I hate this city and I'll stay here. Now what do you want?

LINDA.   He's dying, Biff.   645

[*HAPPY turns quickly to her, shocked.*]

BIFF.   [*after a pause*] Why is he dying?

---

631 *straight commission:* refers to the fact that Willy is receiving no salary, only a commission (percentage) on the sales he makes.

LINDA.   He's been trying to kill himself.

BIFF.   [*with great horror*] How?

LINDA.   I live from day to day.

BIFF.   What're you talking about?   650

LINDA.   Remember I wrote you that he smashed up the car again? In February?

BIFF.   Well?

LINDA.   The insurance inspector came. He said that they have evidence. That all these accidents in the last year—weren't—weren't—accidents.

HAPPY.   How can they tell that? That's a lie.

LINDA.   It seems there's a woman . . . [*She takes a breath as*]   655

} BIFF.   [*sharply but contained*] What woman?

LINDA.   [*simultaneously*] . . . and this woman . . .

LINDA.   What?

BIFF.   Nothing. Go ahead.

LINDA.   What did you say?   660

BIFF.   Nothing. I just said what woman?

HAPPY.   What about her?

LINDA.   Well, it seems she was walking down the road and saw his car. She says that he wasn't driving fast at all, and that he didn't skid. She says he came to that little bridge, and then deliberately smashed into the railing, and it was only the shallowness of the water that saved him.

BIFF.   Oh, no, he probably just fell asleep again.

LINDA.   I don't think he fell asleep.   665

BIFF.   Why not?

LINDA.   Last month . . . [*with great difficulty*] Oh, boys, it's so hard to say a thing like this! He's just a big stupid man to you, but I tell you there's more good in him than in many other people. [*She chokes, wipes her eyes.*] I was looking for a fuse. The lights blew out, and I went down the cellar. And behind the fuse box—it happened to fall out—was a length of rubber pipe—just short.

HAPPY.   No kidding?

LINDA.   There's a little attachment on the end of it. I knew right away. And sure enough, on the bottom of the water heater there's a new little nipple on the gas pipe.

HAPPY.   [*angrily*] That—jerk.   670

BIFF.   Did you have it taken off?

LINDA.   I'm—I'm ashamed to. How can I mention it to him? Every day I go down and take away that little rubber pipe. But, when he comes home, I put it back where it was. How can I insult him that way? I don't know what to do. I live from day to day, boys. I tell you, I know every thought in his mind. It sounds so old-fashioned and silly, but I tell you he put his whole life into you and you've turned your backs on him. [*She is bent over in the chair, weeping, her face in her hands.*] Biff, I swear to God! Biff, his life is in your hands!

HAPPY.   [*to BIFF*] How do you like that damned fool!

BIFF.   [*kissing her*] All right, pal, all right. It's all settled now. I've been remiss. I know that, Mom. But now I'll stay, and I swear to you, I'll apply myself. [*kneeling in front of her, in a fever of self-reproach*] It's just—you see, Mom, I don't fit in business. Not that I won't try. I'll try, and I'll make good.

HAPPY.   Sure you will. The trouble with you in business was you never tried   675
to please people.

BIFF.   I know, I—

HAPPY.   Like when you worked for Harrison's. Bob Harrison said you were tops, and then you go and do some damn fool thing like whistling whole songs in the elevator like a comedian.

BIFF.   [*against HAPPY*] So what? I like to whistle sometimes.

HAPPY.   You don't raise a guy to a responsible job who whistles in the elevator!

LINDA.   Well, don't argue about it now.   680

HAPPY.   Like when you'd go off and swim in the middle of the day instead of taking the line around.

BIFF.   [*his resentment rising*] Well, don't you run off? You take off sometimes, don't you? On a nice summer day?

HAPPY.   Yeah, but I cover myself!

LINDA.   Boys!

HAPPY.   If I'm going to take a fade the boss can call any number where I'm sup-   685
posed to be and they'll swear to him that I just left. I'll tell you something that I hate to say, Biff, but in the business world some of them think you're crazy.

BIFF.   [*angered*] Screw the business world!

HAPPY.   All right, screw it! Great, but cover yourself!

LINDA.   Hap, Hap!

BIFF.   I don't care what they think! They've laughed at Dad for years, and you know why? Because we don't belong in this nuthouse of a city! We should be mixing cement on some open plain, or—or carpenters. A carpenter is allowed to whistle!

[*WILLY walks in from the entrance of the house, at left.*]

WILLY.   Even your grandfather was better than a carpenter. [*pause. They watch*   690
him.] You never grew up. Bernard does not whistle in the elevator, I assure you.

BIFF.   [*as though to laugh WILLY out of it*] Yeah, but you do, Pop.

WILLY.   I never in my life whistled in an elevator! And who in the business world thinks I'm crazy?

BIFF.   I didn't mean it like that, Pop. Now don't make a whole thing out of it, will ya?

WILLY.   Go back to the West! Be a carpenter, a cowboy, enjoy yourself!

LINDA.   Willy, he was just saying—   695

WILLY.   I heard what he said!

HAPPY.   [*trying to quiet WILLY*] Hey, Pop, come on now . . .

WILLY.   [*continuing over HAPPY's line*] They laugh at me, heh? Go to Filene's, go to the Hub, go to Slattery's,° Boston. Call out the name Willy Loman and see what happens! Big shot!

BIFF.   All right, Pop.

WILLY.   Big!   700

BIFF.   All right!

WILLY.   Why do you always insult me?

BIFF.   I didn't say a word. [*to LINDA*] Did I say a word?

LINDA.   He didn't say anything, Willy.

WILLY.   [*going to the doorway of the living room*] All right, good night, good   705
night.

LINDA.   Willy, dear, he just decided . . .

698 *Filene's, the Hub, Slattery's:* department stores in New England.

WILLY.   [*to BIFF*] If you get tired hanging around tomorrow, paint the ceiling I put up in the living-room.

BIFF.   I'm leaving early tomorrow.

HAPPY.   He's going to see Bill Oliver, Pop.

WILLY.   [*interestedly*] Oliver? For what?   710

BIFF.   [*with reserve, but trying, trying*] He always said he'd stake me. I'd like to go into business, so maybe I can take him up on it.

LINDA.   Isn't that wonderful?

WILLY.   Don't interrupt. What's wonderful about it? There's fifty men in the City of New York who'd stake him. [*to BIFF*] Sporting goods?

BIFF.   I guess so. I know something about it and—

WILLY.   He knows something about it! You know sporting goods better than   715
Spalding, for God's sake! How much is he giving you?

BIFF.   I don't know. I didn't even see him yet, but—

WILLY.   Then what're you talkin' about?

BIFF.   [*getting angry*] Well, all I said was I'm gonna see him, that's all!

WILLY.   [*turning away*] Ah, you're counting your chickens again.

BIFF.   [*starting left for the stairs*] Oh, Jesus, I'm going to sleep!   720

WILLY.   [*calling after him*] Don't curse in this house!

BIFF.   [*turning*] Since when did you get so clean?

HAPPY.   [*trying to stop them*] Wait a . . .

WILLY.   Don't use that language to me! I won't have it!

HAPPY.   [*grabbing BIFF, shouts*] Wait a minute! I got an idea. I got a feasible idea.   725
Come here, Biff, let's talk this over now, let's talk some sense here. When I was down in Florida last time, I thought of a great idea to sell sporting goods. It just came back to me. You and I, Biff—we have a line, the Loman Line. We train a couple of weeks, and put on a couple of exhibitions, see?

WILLY.   That's an idea!

HAPPY.   Wait! We form two basketball teams, see? Two waterpolo teams. We play each other. It's a million dollars' worth of publicity. Two brothers, see? The Loman Brothers. Displays in the Royal Palms—all the hotels. And banners over the ring and the basketball court: "Loman Brothers." Baby, we could sell sporting goods!

WILLY.   That is a one-million-dollar idea!

LINDA.   Marvelous!

BIFF.   I'm in great shape as far as that's concerned.   730

HAPPY.   And the beauty of it is, Biff, it wouldn't be like a business. We'd be out playin' ball again . . .

BIFF.   [*enthused*] Yeah, that's . . .

WILLY.   Million-dollar . . .

HAPPY.   And you wouldn't get fed up with it, Biff. It'd be the family again. There'd be the old honor, and comradeship, and if you wanted to go off for a swim or somethin'—well, you'd do it! Without some smart cooky gettin' up ahead of you!

WILLY.   Lick the world! You guys together could absolutely lick the civilized world.   735

BIFF.   I'll see Oliver tomorrow. Hap, if we could work that out . . .

LINDA.   Maybe things are beginning to—

WILLY.   [*wildly enthused, to LINDA*] Stop interrupting! [*to BIFF*] But don't wear sport jacket and slacks when you see Oliver.

BIFF.   No, I'll—

WILLY.   A business suit, and talk as little as possible, and don't crack any jokes.   740
BIFF.   He did like me. Always liked me.
LINDA.   He loved you!
WILLY.   [*to LINDA*] Will you stop! [*to BIFF*] Walk in very serious. You are not apply-
ing for a boy's job. Money is to pass. Be quiet, fine, and serious. Everybody likes a kidder,
but nobody lends him money.
HAPPY.   I'll try to get some myself, Biff. I'm sure I can.
WILLY.   I see great things for you kids. I think your troubles are over. But   745
remember, start big and you'll end big. Ask for fifteen. How much you gonna ask for?
BIFF.   Gee, I don't know—
WILLY.   And don't say "Gee." "Gee" is a boy's word. A man walking in for fifteen
thousand dollars does not say "Gee!"
BIFF.   Ten, I think, would be top though.
WILLY.   Don't be so modest. You always started too low. Walk in with a big laugh.
Don't look worried. Start off with a couple of your good stories to lighten things up. It's
not what you say, it's how you say it—because personality always wins the day.
LINDA.   Oliver always thought the highest of him—   750
WILLY.   Will you let me talk?
BIFF.   Don't yell at her, Pop, will ya?
WILLY.   [*angrily*] I was talking, wasn't I?
BIFF.   I don't like you yelling at her all the time, and I'm tellin' you, that's all.
WILLY.   What're you, takin' over this house?   755
LINDA.   Willy—
WILLY.   [*turning on her*] Don't take his side all the time, godammit!
BIFF.   [*furiously*] Stop yelling at her!
WILLY.   [*suddenly pulling on his cheek, beaten down, guilt ridden*] Give my best to Bill
Oliver—he may remember me.

[*He exits through the living-room doorway.*]

LINDA.   [*her voice subdued*] What'd you have to start that for? [*BIFF turns away.*]   760
You see how sweet he was as soon as you talked hopefully? [*She goes over to BIFF.*] Come up
and say good night to him. Don't let him go to bed that way.
HAPPY.   Come on, Biff, let's buck him up.
LINDA.   Please, dear. Just say good night. It takes so little to make him happy.
Come. [*She goes through the living-room doorway, calling upstairs from within the living-room.*]
Your pajamas are hanging in the bathroom, Willy!
HAPPY.   [*looking toward where LINDA went out*] What a woman! They broke the mold
when they made her. You know that, Biff?
BIFF.   He's off salary. My God, working on commission!   765
HAPPY.   Well, let's face it: he's no hot-shot selling man. Except that some-
times, you have to admit, he's a sweet personality.
BIFF.   [*deciding*] Lend me ten bucks, will ya? I want to buy some new ties.
HAPPY.   I'll take you to a place I know. Beautiful stuff. Wear one of my striped
shirts tomorrow.
BIFF.   She got gray. Mom got awful old. Gee, I'm gonna go in to Oliver tomor-
row and knock him for a—
HAPPY.   Come on up. Tell that to Dad. Let's give him a whirl. Come on.   770
BIFF.   [*steamed up*] You know, with ten thousand bucks, boy!

HAPPY.   [*as they go into the living-room*] That's the talk, Biff, that's the first time I've heard the old confidence out of you! [*from within the living-room, fading off*] You're gonna live with me, kid, and any babe you want just say the word . . . [*The last lines are hardly heard. They are mounting the stairs to their parents' bedroom.*]

LINDA.   [*entering her bedroom and addressing WILLY, who is in the bathroom. She is straightening the bed for him.*] Can you do anything about the shower? It drips.

WILLY.   [*from the bathroom*] All of a sudden everything falls to pieces! Goddam plumbing, oughta be sued, those people. I hardly finished putting it in and the thing . . . [*His words rumble off.*]

LINDA.   I'm just wondering if Oliver will remember him. You think he might?   775

WILLY.   [*coming out of the bathroom in his pajamas*] Remember him? What's the matter with you, you crazy? If he'd've stayed with Oliver he'd be on top by now! Wait'll Oliver gets a look at him. You don't know the average caliber any more. The average young man today—[*He is getting into bed*]—is got a caliber of zero. Greatest thing in the world for him was to bum around.

[*BIFF and HAPPY enter the bedroom. Slight pause.*]

WILLY.   [*stops short, looking at BIFF*] Glad to hear it, boy.

HAPPY.   He wanted to say good night to you, sport.

WILLY.   [*to BIFF*] Yeah. Knock him dead, boy. What'd you want to tell me?

BIFF.   Just take it easy, Pop. Good night. [*He turns to go.*]   780

WILLY.   [*unable to resist*] And if anything falls off the desk while you're talking to him—like a package or something—don't you pick it up. They have office boys for that.

LINDA.   I'll make a big breakfast—

WILLY.   Will you let me finish? [*to BIFF*] Tell him you were in the business in the West. Not farm work.

BIFF.   All right, Dad.

LINDA.   I think everything—   785

WILLY.   [*going right through her speech*] And don't undersell yourself. No less than fifteen thousand dollars.

BIFF.   [*unable to bear him*] Okay. Good night, Mom. [*He starts moving.*]

WILLY.   Because you got a greatness in you, Biff, remember that. You got all kinds a greatness . . . [*He lies back, exhausted.*]

[*BIFF walks out.*]

LINDA.   [*calling after BIFF*] Sleep well, darling!

HAPPY.   I'm gonna get married, Mom. I wanted to tell you.   790

LINDA.   Go to sleep, dear.

HAPPY.   [*going*] I just wanted to tell you.

WILLY.   Keep up the good work. [*HAPPY exits.*] God . . . remember that Ebbets Field° game? The championship of the city?

LINDA.   Just rest. Should I sing to you?

WILLY.   Yeah. Sing to me. [*LINDA hums a soft lullaby.*] When that team came out—   795 he was the tallest, remember?

LINDA.   Oh, yes. And in gold.

---

792 *Ebbets Field:* the baseball stadium of the Brooklyn Dodgers before they moved to Los Angeles in 1958. Biff had played there in a city championship football game. See II.210.

[*BIFF enters the darkened kitchen, takes a cigarette, and leaves the house. He comes downstage into a golden pool of light. He smokes, staring at the night.*]

WILLY.   Like a young god. Hercules—something like that. And the sun, the sun all around him. Remember how he waved to me? Right up from the field, with the representatives of three colleges standing by? And the buyers I brought, and the cheers when he came out—Loman, Loman, Loman! God Almighty, he'll be great yet. A star like that, magnificent, can never really fade away!

[*The light on* WILLY *is fading. The gas heater begins to glow through the kitchen wall, near the stairs, a blue flame beneath red coils.*]

LINDA.   [*timidly*] Willy dear, what has he got against you?
WILLY.   I'm so tired. Don't talk any more.

[*BIFF slowly returns to the kitchen. He stops, stares toward the heater.*]

LINDA.   Will you ask Howard to let you work in New York?   800
WILLY.   First thing in the morning. Everything'll be all right.

[*BIFF reaches behind the heater and draws out a length of rubber tubing. He is horrified and turns his head toward* WILLY'S *room, still dimly lit, from which the strains of* LINDA'S *desperate but monotonous humming rise.*]

WILLY.   [*staring through the window into the moonlight*] Gee, look at the moon moving between the buildings!

[*BIFF wraps the tubing around his hand and quickly goes up the stairs.*]

ACT 2

[*Music is heard, gay and bright. The curtain rises as the music fades away.* WILLY, *in shirt sleeves, is sitting at the kitchen table, sipping coffee, his hat in his lap.* LINDA *is filling his cup when she can.*]

WILLY.   Wonderful coffee. Meal in itself.
LINDA.   Can I make you some eggs?
WILLY.   No. Take a breath.
LINDA.   You look so rested, dear.
WILLY.   I slept like a dead one. First time in months. Imagine, sleeping till ten on   5
a Tuesday morning. Boys left nice and early, heh?
LINDA.   They were out of here by eight o'clock.
WILLY.   Good work!
LINDA.   It was so thrilling to see them leaving together. I can't get over the shaving lotion in this house!
WILLY.   [*smiling*] Mmm—
LINDA.   Biff was very changed this morning. His whole attitude seemed to   10
be hopeful. He couldn't wait to get downtown to see Oliver.
WILLY.   He's heading for a change. There's no question, there simply are certain men that take longer to get—solidified. How did he dress?
LINDA.   His blue suit. He's so handsome in that suit. He could be a—anything in that suit!

[WILLY *gets up from the table.* LINDA *holds his jacket for him.*]

WILLY.   There's no question, no question at all. Gee, on the way home tonight I'd like to buy some seeds.

LINDA.   [*laughing*] That'd be wonderful. But not enough sun gets back there. Nothing'll grow any more.

WILLY.   You wait, kid, before it's all over we're gonna get a little place out   15 in the country, and I'll raise some vegetables, a couple of chickens . . .

LINDA.   You'll do it yet, dear.

[*WILLY walks out of his jacket, LINDA follows him.*]

WILLY.   And they'll get married, and come for a weekend. I'd build a little guest house. 'Cause I got so many fine tools, all I'd need would be a little lumber and some peace of mind.

LINDA.   [*joyfully*] I sewed the lining . . .

WILLY.   I could build two guest houses, so they'd both come. Did he decide how much he's going to ask Oliver for?

LINDA.   [*getting him into the jacket*] He didn't mention it, but I imagine ten   20 or fifteen thousand. You going to talk to Howard today?

WILLY.   Yeah. I'll put it to him straight and simple. He'll just have to take me off the road.

LINDA.   And Willy, don't forget to ask for a little advance, because we've got the insurance premium. It's the grace period now.

WILLY.   That's a hundred . . . ?

LINDA.   A hundred and eight, sixty-eight. Because we're a little short again.

WILLY.   Why are we short?   25

LINDA.   Well, you had the motor job on the car . . .

WILLY.   That goddam Studebaker!

LINDA.   And you got one more payment on the refrigerator . . .

WILLY.   But it just broke again!

LINDA.   Well, it's old, dear.   30

WILLY.   I told you we should've bought a well-advertised machine. Charley bought a General Electric and it's twenty years old and it's still good, that son-of-a-bitch.

LINDA.   But, Willy—

WILLY.   Whoever heard of a Hastings refrigerator? Once in my life I would like to own something outright before it's broken! I'm always in a race with the junkyard! I just finished paying for the car and it's on its last legs. The refrigerator consumes belts like a goddam maniac. They time those things. They time them so when you finally paid for them, they're used up.

LINDA.   [*buttoning up his jacket as he unbuttons it*] All told, about two hundred dollars would carry us, dear. But that includes the last payment on the mortgage. After this payment, Willy, the house belongs to us.

WILLY.   It's twenty-five years!   35

LINDA.   Biff was nine years old when we bought it.

WILLY.   Well, that's a great thing. To weather a twenty-five year mortgage is—

LINDA.   It's an accomplishment.

WILLY.   All the cement, the lumber, the reconstruction I put in this house! There ain't a crack to be found in it any more.

LINDA.   Well, it served its purpose.   40

WILLY.   What purpose? Some stranger'll come along, move in, and that's that. If only Biff would take this house, and raise a family . . . [*He starts to go.*] Good-by, I'm late.

LINDA.   [*suddenly remembering*] Oh, I forgot! You're supposed to meet them for dinner.

WILLY.   Me?

LINDA.   At Frank's Chop House on Forty-eighth near Sixth Avenue.

WILLY.   Is that so! How about you?   45

LINDA.   No, just the three of you. They're gonna blow you to a big meal!

WILLY.   Don't say! Who thought of that?

LINDA.   Biff came to me this morning, Willy, and he said, "Tell Dad, we want to blow him to a big meal." Be there six o'clock. You and your two boys are going to have dinner.

WILLY.   Gee whiz! That's really somethin'. I'm gonna knock Howard for a loop, kid. I'll get an advance, and I'll come home with a New York job. Goddammit, now I'm gonna do it!

LINDA.   Oh, that's the spirit, Willy!   50

WILLY.   I will never get behind a wheel the rest of my life!

LINDA.   It's changing, Willy, I can feel it changing!

WILLY.   Beyond a question. G'by, I'm late. [*He starts to go again.*]

LINDA.   [*calling after him as she runs to the kitchen table for a handkerchief*] You got your glasses?

WILLY.   [*feels for them, then comes back in*] Yeah, yeah, got my glasses.   55

LINDA.   [*giving him the handkerchief*] And a handkerchief.

WILLY.   Yeah, handkerchief.

LINDA.   And your saccharine?

WILLY.   Yeah, my saccharine.

LINDA.   Be careful on the subway stairs.   60

[*She kisses him, and a silk stocking is seen hanging from her hand. WILLY notices it.*]

WILLY.   Will you stop mending stockings? At least while I'm in the house. It gets me nervous. I can't tell you. Please.

[*LINDA hides the stocking in her hand as she follows WILLY across the forestage in front of the house.*]

LINDA.   Remember, Frank's Chop House.

WILLY.   [*passing the apron*] Maybe beets would grow out there.

LINDA.   [*laughing*] But you tried so many times.

WILLY.   Yeah. Well, don't work hard today. [*He disappears around the right corner of*   65
the house.]

LINDA.   Be careful!

[*As WILLY vanishes, LINDA waves to him. Suddenly the phone rings. She runs across the stage and into the kitchen and lifts it.*]

LINDA.   Hello? Oh, Biff! I'm so glad you called, I just . . . Yes, sure, I just told him. Yes, he'll be there for dinner at six o'clock, I didn't forget. Listen, I was just dying to tell you. You know that little rubber pipe I told you about? That he connected to the gas heater? I finally decided to go down the cellar this morning and take it away and destroy it. But it's gone! Imagine? He took it away himself, it isn't there! [*She listens.*] When? Oh, then you took it. Oh—nothing, it's just that I'd hoped he'd taken it away himself. Oh, I'm not worried, darling, because this morning he left in such high spirits, it was like the old days! I'm not afraid any more. Did Mr. Oliver see you? . . . Well, you wait there then. And make a nice impression on him, darling. Just don't perspire too much before you see him. And have a nice time with Dad. He may have big news too! . . . That's right, a New York job. And be sweet to him tonight, dear. Be loving to him. Because he's only a little boat looking for a harbor. [*She is trembling with sorrow and joy.*] Oh, that's wonderful, Biff, you'll save his life. Thanks, darling. Just put your arm around him when he comes into the restaurant. Give him a smile. That's the boy . . . Good-by, dear . . . You got your comb? . . . That's fine. Good-by, Biff dear.

[*In the middle of her speech,* HOWARD WAGNER, *thirty-six, wheels in a small typewriter table on which is a wire-recording machine and proceeds to plug it in. This is on the left forestage. Light slowly fades on* LINDA *as it rises on* HOWARD. HOWARD *is intent on threading the machine and only glances over his shoulder as* WILLY *appears.*]

> WILLY.   Pst! Pst!
> HOWARD.   Hello, Willy, come in.
> WILLY.   Like to have a little talk with you, Howard.   70
> HOWARD.   Sorry to keep you waiting. I'll be with you in a minute.
> WILLY.   What's that, Howard?
> HOWARD.   Didn't you ever see one of these? Wire recorder.
> WILLY.   Oh. Can we talk a minute?
> HOWARD.   Records things. Just got delivery yesterday. Been driving me crazy, the   75
> most terrific machine I ever saw in my life. I was up all night with it.
> WILLY.   What do you do with it?
> HOWARD.   I bought it for dictation, but you can do anything with it. Listen to this. I
> had it home last night. Listen to what I picked up. The first one is my daughter. Get this.
> [*He flicks the switch and "Roll out the Barrel" is heard being whistled.*] Listen to that kid whistle.
> WILLY.   That is lifelike, isn't it?
> HOWARD.   Seven years old. Get that tone.
> WILLY.   Ts, ts. Like to ask a little favor if you . . .   80

[*The whistling breaks off, and the voice of* HOWARD'S DAUGHTER *is heard.*]

> HIS DAUGHTER.   "Now you, Daddy."
> HOWARD.   She's crazy for me! [*Again the same song is whistled.*] That's me! Ha! [*He
> winks.*]
> WILLY.   You're very good!

[*The whistling breaks off again. The machine runs silent for a moment.*]

> HOWARD.   Sh! Get this now, this is my son.
> HIS SON.   "The capital of Alabama is Montgomery; the capital of Arizona is   85
> Phoenix; the capital of Arkansas is Little Rock; the capital of California is Sacramento
> . . ." [*and on, and on*]
> HOWARD.   [*holding up five fingers*] Five years old, Willy!
> WILLY.   He'll make an announcer some day!
> HIS SON.   [*continuing*] "The capital . . ."
> HOWARD.   Get that—alphabetical order! [*The machine breaks off suddenly.*] Wait a
> minute. The maid kicked the plug out.
> WILLY.   It certainly is a—   90
> HOWARD.   Sh, for God's sake!
> HIS SON.   "It's nine o'clock, Bulova watch time. So I have to go to sleep."
> WILLY.   That really is—

HOWARD.   Wait a minute! The next is my wife.

[*They wait.*]

HOWARD'S VOICE.   "Go on, say something." [*pause*] "Well, you gonna talk?"   95
HIS WIFE.   "I can't think of anything."
HOWARD'S VOICE.   "Well, talk—it's turning."
HIS WIFE.   [*shyly, beaten*] "Hello." [*Silence*] "Oh, Howard, I can't talk into this . . ."
HOWARD.   [*snapping the machine off*] That was my wife.
WILLY.   That is a wonderful machine. Can we—   100
HOWARD.   I tell you, Willy, I'm gonna take my camera, and my bandsaw, and all my hobbies, and out they go. This is the most fascinating relaxation I ever found.
WILLY.   I think I'll get one myself.
HOWARD.   Sure, they're only a hundred and a half. You can't do without it. Supposing you wanna hear Jack Benny,° see? But you can't be at home at that hour. So you tell the maid to turn the radio on when Jack Benny comes on, and this automatically goes on with the radio . . .
WILLY.   And when you come home you . . .
HOWARD.   You can come home twelve o'clock, one o'clock, any time you like,   105
and you get yourself a Coke and sit yourself down, throw the switch, and there's Jack Benny's program in the middle of the night!
WILLY.   I'm definitely going to get one. Because lots of time I'm on the road, and I think to myself, what I must be missing on the radio!
HOWARD.   Don't you have a radio in the car?
WILLY.   Well, yeah, but who ever thinks of turning it on?
HOWARD.   Say, aren't you supposed to be in Boston?
WILLY.   That's what I want to talk to you about, Howard. You got a minute?   110

[*He draws a chair in from the wing.*]

HOWARD.   What happened? What're you doing here?
WILLY.   Well . . .
HOWARD.   You didn't crack up again, did you?
WILLY.   Oh, no. No . . .
HOWARD.   Geez, you had me worried there for a minute. What's the trouble?   115
WILLY.   Well, tell you the truth, Howard, I've come to the decision that I'd rather not travel any more.
HOWARD.   Not travel! Well, what'll you do?
WILLY.   Remember, Christmas time, when you had the party here? You said you'd try to think of some spot for me here in town.
HOWARD.   With us?
WILLY.   Well, sure.   120
HOWARD.   Oh, yeah, yeah. I remember. Well, I couldn't think of anything for you, Willy.
WILLY.   I tell ya, Howard. The kids are all grown up, y'know. I don't need much any more. If I could take home—well, sixty-five dollars a week, I could swing it.
HOWARD.   Yeah, but Willy, see I—

---

103 *Jack Benny:* (1894–1974), vaudeville, radio, television, and movie comedian.

WILLY.   I tell ya why, Howard. Speaking frankly and between the two of us, y'know—I'm just a little tired.

HOWARD.   Oh, I could understand that, Willy. But you're a road man, Willy, and we do a road business. We've only got a half-dozen salesmen on the floor here.

WILLY.   God knows, Howard, I never asked a favor of any man. But I was with the firm when your father used to carry you up here in his arms.

HOWARD.   I know that, Willy, but—

WILLY.   Your father came to me the day you were born and asked me what I thought of the name of Howard, may he rest in peace.

HOWARD.   I appreciate that, Willy, but there just is no spot here for you. If I had a spot I'd slam you right in, but I just don't have a single solitary spot.

[*He looks for his lighter. WILLY has picked it up and gives it to him. Pause.*]

WILLY.   [*with increasing anger*] Howard, all I need to set my table is fifty dollars a week.

HOWARD.   But where am I going to put you, kid?

WILLY.   Look, it isn't a question of whether I can sell merchandise, is it?

HOWARD.   No, but it's a business, kid, and everybody's gotta pull his own weight.

WILLY.   [*desperately*] Just let me tell you a story, Howard—

HOWARD.   'Cause you gotta admit, business is business.

WILLY.   [*angrily*] Business in definitely business, but just listen for a minute. You don't understand this. When I was a boy—eighteen, nineteen—I was already on the road. And there was a question in my mind as to whether selling had a future for me. Because in those days I had a yearning to go to Alaska. See, there were three gold strikes in one month in Alaska, and I felt like going out. Just for the ride, you might say.

HOWARD.   [*barely interested*] Don't say.

WILLY.   Oh, yeah, my father lived many years in Alaska. He was an adventurous man. We've got quite a little streak of self-reliance in our family. I thought I'd go out with my older brother and try to locate him, and maybe settle in the North with the old man. And I was almost decided to go, when I met a salesman in the Parker House.° His name was Dave Singleman. And he was eighty-four years old, and he'd drummed merchandise in thirty-one states. And old Dave, he'd go up to his room, y'understand, put on his green velvet slippers—I'll never forget—and pick up his phone and call the buyers, and without ever leaving his room, at the age of eighty-four, he made his living. And when I saw that, I realized that selling was the greatest career a man could want. 'Cause what could be more satisfying than to be able to go, at the age of eighty-four, into twenty or thirty different cities, and pick up a phone, and be remembered and loved and helped by so many different people? Do you know? when he died—and by the way he died the death of a salesman, in his green velvet slippers in the smoker of the New York, New Haven and Hartford, going into Boston—when he died, hundreds of salesmen and buyers were at his funeral. Things were sad on a lotta trains for months after that. [*He stands up. HOWARD has not looked at him.*] In those days there was personality in it, Howard. There was respect, and comradeship, and gratitude in it. Today, it's all cut and dried, and there's no chance for bringing friendship to bear—or personality. You see what I mean? They don't know me any more.

HOWARD.   [*moving away, to the right*] That's just the thing, Willy.

WILLY.   If I had forty dollars a week—that's all I'd need. Forty dollars, Howard.

138 *Parker House:* a hotel in Boston.

HOWARD.   Kid, I can't take blood from a stone, I—

WILLY.   [*desperation is on him now*] Howard, the year Al Smith° was nominated, your father came to me and—

HOWARD.   [*starting to go off*] I've got to see some people, kid.

WILLY.   [*stopping him*] I'm talking about your father! There were promises made across this desk! You mustn't tell me you've got people to see—I put thirty-four years into this firm, Howard, and now I can't pay my insurance! You can't eat the orange and throw the peel away—a man is not a piece of fruit! [*after a pause*] Now pay attention. Your father—in 1928 I had a big year. I averaged a hundred and seventy dollars a week in commissions.

HOWARD.   [*impatiently*] Now, Willy, you never averaged—   145

WILLY.   [*banging his hand on the desk*] I averaged a hundred and seventy dollars a week in the year of 1928! And your father came to me—or rather, I was in the office here—it was right over this desk—and he put his hand on my shoulder—

HOWARD.   [*getting up*] You'll have to excuse me, Willy, I gotta see some people. Pull yourself together. [*going out*] I'll be back in a little while.

[*On* HOWARD'S *exit, the light on his chair grows very bright and strange.*]

WILLY.   Pull myself together! What the hell did I say to him? My God, I was yelling at him! How could I! [WILLY *breaks off, staring at the light, which occupies the chair, animating it. He approaches this chair, standing across the desk from it.*] Frank, Frank, don't you remember what you told me that time? How you put your hand on my shoulder, and Frank . . . [*He leans on the desk and as he speaks the dead man's name he accidentally switches on the recorder, and instantly*]

HOWARD'S SON.   ". . . of New York is Albany. The capital of Ohio is Cincinnati, the capital of Rhode Island is . . ." [*The recitation continues.*]

WILLY.   [*leaping away with fright, shouting*] Ha! Howard! Howard! Howard!   150

HOWARD.   [*rushing in*] What happened?

WILLY.   [*pointing at the machine, which continues nasally, childishly, with the capital cities*] Shut it off! Shut it off!

HOWARD.   [*pulling the plug out*] Look, Willy . . .

WILLY.   [*pressing his hands to his eyes*] I gotta get myself some coffee. I'll get some coffee . . .

[WILLY *starts to walk out.* HOWARD *stops him.*]

HOWARD.   [*rolling up the cord*] Willy, look . . .   155

WILLY.   I'll go to Boston.

HOWARD.   Willy, you can't go to Boston for us.

WILLY.   Why can't I go?

HOWARD.   I don't want you to represent us. I've been meaning° to tell you for a long time now.

WILLY.   Howard, are you firing me?   160

HOWARD.   I think you need a good long rest, Willy.

WILLY.   Howard—

HOWARD.   And when you feel better, come back, and we'll see if we can work something out.

142 *Al Smith:* Alfred E. Smith was governor of New York State (1919–1921, 1923–1929) and the Democratic presidential candidate defeated by Herbert Hoover in 1928.

WILLY.   But I gotta earn money, Howard. I'm in no position to—

HOWARD.   Where are your sons? Why don't your sons give you a hand?   165

WILLY.   They're working on a very big deal.

HOWARD.   This is no time for false pride, Willy. You go to your sons and you tell them that you're tired. You've got two great boys, haven't you?

WILLY.   Oh, no question, no question, but in the meantime . . .

HOWARD.   Then that's that, heh?

WILLY.   All right, I'll go to Boston tomorrow.   170

HOWARD.   No, no.

WILLY.   I can't throw myself on my sons. I'm not a cripple!

HOWARD.   Look, kid, I'm busy this morning.

WILLY.   [*grasping HOWARD's arm*] Howard, you've got to let me go to Boston!

HOWARD.   [*hard, keeping himself under control*] I've got a line of people to see   175
this morning. Sit down, take five minutes, and pull yourself together, and then go home, will ya? I need the office, Willy. [*He starts to go, turns, remembering the recorder, starts to push off the table holding the recorder.*] Oh, yeah. Whenever you can this week, stop by and drop off the samples. You'll feel better, Willy, and then come back and we'll talk. Pull yourself together, kid, there's people outside.

[*HOWARD exits, pushing the table off left. WILLY stares into space, exhausted. Now the music is heard—BEN's music—first distantly, then closer. As WILLY speaks, BEN enters from the right. He carries valise and umbrella.*]

WILLY.   Oh, Ben, how did you do it? What is the answer? Did you wind up the Alaska deal already?

BEN.   Doesn't take much time if you know what you're doing. Just a short business trip. Boarding ship in an hour. Wanted to say good-by.

WILLY.   Ben, I've got to talk to you.

BEN.   [*glancing at his watch*] Haven't much time, William.

WILLY.   [*crossing the apron to BEN*] Ben, nothing's working out. I don't know   180
what to do.

BEN.   Now, look here, William. I've bought timberland in Alaska and I need a man to look after things for me.

WILLY.   God, timberland! Me and my boys in those grand outdoors!

BEN.   You've a new continent at your doorstep, William. Get out of these cities, they're full of talk and time payments and courts of law. Screw on your fists and you can fight for a fortune up there.

WILLY.   Yes, yes! Linda, Linda!

[*LINDA enters as of old, with the wash.*]

LINDA.   Oh, you're back?   185

BEN.   I haven't much time.

WILLY.   No, wait! Linda, he's got a proposition for me in Alaska.

LINDA.   But you've got—[*to BEN*] He's got a beautiful job here.

WILLY.   But in Alaska, kid, I could—

LINDA.   You're doing well enough, Willy!   190

BEN.   [*to LINDA*] Enough for what, my dear?

LINDA.   [*frightened of BEN and angry at him*] Don't say those things to him! Enough to be happy right here, right now. [*to WILLY, while BEN laughs*] Why must everybody conquer the world? You're well liked, and the boys love you, and someday—[*to BEN*]—why old man Wagner told him just the other day that if he keeps it up he'll be a member of the firm, didn't he, Willy?

WILLY.   Sure, sure. I am building something with this firm, Ben, and if a man is building something he must be on the right track, mustn't he?

BEN.   What are you building? Lay your hand on it. Where is it?

WILLY.   [*hesitantly*] That's true, Linda, there's nothing.   195

LINDA.   Why? [*to BEN*] There's a man eighty-four years old—

WILLY.   That's right, Ben, that's right. When I look at that man I say, what is there to worry about?

BEN.   Bah!

WILLY.   It's true, Ben. All he has to do is go into any city, pick up the phone, and he's making his living and you know why?

BEN.   [*picking up his valise*] I've got to go.   200

WILLY.   [*holding BEN back*] Look at this boy!

[*BIFF, in his high school sweater, enters carrying suitcase. HAPPY carries BIFF'S shoulder guards, gold helmet, and football pants.*]

WILLY.   Without a penny to his name, three great universities are begging for him, and from there the sky's the limit, because it's not what you do, Ben. It's who you know and the smile on your face! It's contacts, Ben, contacts! The whole wealth of Alaska passes over the lunch table at the Commodore Hotel,° and that's the wonder, the wonder of this country, that a man can end with diamonds here on the basis of being liked! [*He turns to BIFF*] And that's why when you get out on that field today it's important. Because thousands of people will be rooting for you and loving you. [*to BEN, who has again begun to leave*] And Ben! when he walks into a business office his name will sound out like a bell and all the doors will open to him! I've seen it, Ben, I've seen it a thousand times! You can't feel it with your hand like timber, but it's there!

BEN.   Good-by, William.

WILLY.   Ben, am I right? Don't you think I'm right? I value your advice.

BEN.   There's a new continent at your doorstep, William. You could walk out rich.   205 Rich! [*He is gone.*]

WILLY.   We'll do it here, Ben! You hear me? We're gonna do it here!

[*YOUNG BERNARD rushes in. The gay music of the Boys is heard.*]

BERNARD.   Oh, gee, I was afraid you left already!

WILLY.   Why? What time is it?

BERNARD.   It's half-past one!

WILLY.   Well, come on, everybody! Ebbets Field next stop! Where's the pennants?   210
[*He rushes through the wall-line of the kitchen and out into the dining-room.*]

LINDA.   [*to BIFF*] Did you pack fresh underwear?

BIFF.   [*who has been limbering up*] I want to go!

BERNARD.   Biff, I'm carrying your helmet, ain't I?

HAPPY.   No, I'm carrying the helmet.

BERNARD.   Oh, Biff, you promised me.   215

HAPPY.   I'm carrying the helmet.

BERNARD.   How am I going to get in the locker room?

202 *Commodore Hotel:* a large hotel in New York City.

LINDA.   Let him carry the shoulder guards. [*She puts her coat and hat on in the kitchen.*]

BERNARD.   Can I, Biff? 'Cause I told everybody I'm going to be in the locker room.

HAPPY.   In Ebbets Field it's the clubhouse.   220

BERNARD.   I meant the clubhouse. Biff!

HAPPY.   Biff!

BIFF.   [*grandly, after a slight pause.*] Let him carry the shoulder guards.

HAPPY.   [*as he gives BERNARD the shoulder guards*] Stay close to us now.

[*WILLY rushes in with the pennants.*]

WILLY.   [*handing them out*] Everybody wave when Biff comes out on the field.   225
[*HAPPY and BERNARD run off.*] You set now, boy?

[*The music has died away.*]

BIFF.   Ready to go, Pop. Every muscle is ready.

WILLY.   [*at the edge of the apron*] You realize what this means?

BIFF.   That's right, Pop.

WILLY.   [*feeling BIFF's muscles*] You're comin' home this afternoon captain of the All-Scholastic Championship Team of the City of New York.

BIFF.   I got it, Pop. And remember, pal, when I take off my helmet, that touch-   230
down is for you.

WILLY.   Let's go! [*He is starting out, with his arm around BIFF, when CHARLEY enters, as of old, in knickers.*] I got no room for you, Charley.

CHARLEY.   Room? For what?

WILLY.   In the car.

CHARLEY.   You goin' for a ride? I wanted to shoot some casino.

WILLY.   [*furiously*] Casino! [*incredulously*] Don't you realize what today is?   235

LINDA.   Oh, he knows, Willy. He's just kidding you.

WILLY.   That's nothing to kid about!

CHARLEY.   No, Linda, what's goin' on?

LINDA.   He's playing in Ebbets Field.

CHARLEY.   Baseball in this weather?   240

WILLY.   Don't talk to him. Come on, come on! [*He is pushing them out.*]

CHARLEY.   Wait a minute, didn't you hear the news?

WILLY.   What?

CHARLEY.   Don't you listen to the radio? Ebbets Field just blew up.

WILLY.   You go to hell! [*CHARLEY laughs. Pushing them out.*] Come on, come   245
on! We're late.

CHARLEY.   [*as they go*] Knock a homer, Biff, knock a homer!

WILLY.   [*the last to leave, turning to CHARLEY*] I don't think that was funny, Charley. This is the greatest day of his life.

CHARLEY.   Willy, when are you going to grow up?

WILLY.   Yeah, heh? When this game is over, Charley, you'll be laughing out the other side of your face. They'll be calling him another Red Grange.° Twenty-five thousand a year.

249 *Red Grange:* Harold Edward Grange (1903–1991), all-America halfback (1923–1925) at the University of Illinois.

CHARLEY. [*kidding*] Is that so? 250
WILLY. Yeah, that's so.
CHARLEY. Well, then, I'm sorry, Willy. But tell me something.
WILLY. What?
CHARLEY. Who is Red Grange?
WILLY. Put up your hands. Goddam you, put up your hands! 255

[*CHARLEY, chuckling, shakes his head and walks away, around the left corner of the stage. WILLY follows him. The music rises to a mocking frenzy.*]

WILLY. Who the hell do you think you are, better than everybody else? You don't know everything, you big, ignorant, stupid. . . . Put up your hands!

[*Light rises, on the right side of the forestage, on a small table in the reception room of CHARLEY's office. Traffic sounds are heard. BERNARD, now mature, sits whistling to himself. A pair of tennis rackets and an overnight bag are on the floor beside him.*]

WILLY. [*offstage*] What are you walking away for? Don't walk away! If you're going to say something say it to my face! I know you laugh at me behind my back. You'll laugh out of the other side of your goddam face after this game. Touchdown! Touchdown! Eighty thousand people! Touchdown. Right between the goal posts.

[*BERNARD is a quiet, earnest, but self-assured young man. WILLY's voice is coming from right upstage now. BERNARD lowers his feet off the table and listens. JENNY, his father's secretary, enters.*]

JENNY. [*distressed*] Say, Bernard, will you go out in the hall?
BERNARD. What is that noise? Who is it?
JENNY. Mr. Loman. He just got off the elevator. 260
BERNARD. [*getting up*] Who's he arguing with?
JENNY. Nobody. There's nobody with him. I can't deal with him any more, and your father gets all upset everytime he comes. I've got a lot of typing to do, and your father's waiting to sign it. Will you see him?
WILLY. [*entering*] Touchdown! Touch—[*He sees JENNY.*] Jenny, Jenny, good to see you. How're ya? Workin'? Or still honest?
JENNY. Fine. How've you been feeling?
WILLY. Not much any more, Jenny. Ha, ha! [*He is surprised to see the rackets.*] 265
BERNARD. Hello, Uncle Willy.
WILLY. [*almost shocked*] Bernard! Well, look who's here! [*He comes quickly, guiltily, to BERNARD and warmly shakes his hand.*]
BERNARD. How are you? Good to see you.
WILLY. What are you doing here?
BERNARD. Oh, just stopped off to see Pop. Get off my feet till my train leaves. I'm 270
going to Washington in a few minutes.
WILLY. Is he in?
BERNARD. Yes, he's in his office with the accountants. Sit down.
WILLY. [*sitting down*] What're you going to do in Washington?
BERNARD. Oh, just a case I've got there, Willy.
WILLY. That so? [*Indicating the rackets*] You going to play tennis there? 275
BERNARD. I'm staying with a friend who's got a court.
WILLY. Don't say. His own tennis court. Must be fine people, I bet.
BERNARD. They are, very nice. Dad tells me Biff's in town.
WILLY. [*with a big smile*] Yeah, Biff's in. Working on a very big deal, Bernard.

BERNARD.   What's Biff doing?   280

WILLY.   Well, he's been doing very big things in the West. But he decided to establish himself here. Very big. We're having dinner. Did I hear your wife had a boy?

BERNARD.   That's right. Our second.

WILLY.   Two boys! What do you know!

BERNARD.   What kind of a deal has Biff got?

WILLY.   Well, Bill Oliver—very big sporting-goods man—he wants Biff very   285
badly. Called him in from the West. Long distance, carte blanche, special deliveries. Your
friends have their own private tennis court?

BERNARD.   You still with the old firm, Willy?

WILLY.   [*after a pause*] I'm—I'm overjoyed to see how you made the grade,
Bernard, overjoyed. It's an encouraging thing to see a young man really—really—Looks
very good for Biff—very—[*He breaks off, then*] Bernard—[*He is so full of emotion, he breaks
off again.*]

BERNARD.   What is it, Willy?

WILLY.   [*small and alone*] What—what's the secret?

BERNARD.   What secret?   290

WILLY.   How—how did you? Why didn't he ever catch on?

BERNARD.   I wouldn't know that, Willy.

WILLY.   [*confidentially, desperately*] You were his friend, his boyhood friend. There's
something I don't understand about it. His life ended after that Ebbets Field game.
From the age of seventeen nothing good ever happened to him.

BERNARD.   He never trained himself for anything.

WILLY.   But he did, he did. After high school he took so many correspondence   295
courses. Radio mechanics; television; God knows what, and never made the slightest mark.

BERNARD.   [*taking off his glasses*] Willy, do you want to talk candidly?

WILLY.   [*rising, faces BERNARD*] I regard you as a very brilliant man, Bernard. I value
your advice.

BERNARD.   Oh, the hell with the advice, Willy. I couldn't advise you. There's just
one thing I've always wanted to ask you. When he was supposed to graduate, and the
math teacher flunked him—

WILLY.   Oh, that son-of-a-bitch ruined his life.

BERNARD.   Yeah, but, Willy, all he had to do was go to summer school and make   30
up that subject.

WILLY.   That's right, that's right.

BERNARD.   Did you tell him not to go to summer school?

WILLY.   Me? I begged him to go. I ordered him to go!

BERNARD.   Then why wouldn't he go?

WILLY.   Why? Why! Bernard, that question has been trailing me like a ghost   3C
for the last fifteen years. He flunked the subject, and laid down and died like a hammer
hit him!

BERNARD.   Take it easy, kid.

WILLY.   Let me talk to you—I got nobody to talk to. Bernard, Bernard, was it my
fault? Y'see? It keeps going around in my mind, maybe I did something to him. I got
nothing to give him.

BERNARD.   Don't take it so hard.

WILLY.   Why did he lay down? What is the story there? You were his friend!

BERNARD.   Willy, I remember, it was June, and our grades came out. And he'd   310
flunked math.

WILLY.   That son-of-a-bitch!

BERNARD.   No, it wasn't right then. Biff just got very angry, I remember, and he
was ready to enroll in summer school.

WILLY.   [*surprised*] He was?

BERNARD.   He wasn't beaten by it at all. But then, Willy, he disappeared from the
block for almost a month. And I got the idea that he'd gone up to New England to see
you. Did he have a talk with you then?

[*WILLY stares in silence.*]

BERNARD.   Willy?   315

WILLY.   [*with a strong edge of resentment in his voice*] Yeah, he came to Boston. What
about it?

BERNARD.   Well, just that when he came back—I'll never forget this, it always mys-
tifies me. Because I'd thought so well of Biff, even though he'd always taken advantage
of me. I loved him, Willy, y'know? And he came back after that month and took his
sneakers—remember the sneakers with "University of Virginia" printed on them? He
was so proud of those, wore them every day. And he took them down in the cellar, and
burned them up in the furnace. We had a fist fight. It lasted at least half an hour. Just the
two of us, punching each other down the cellar, and crying right through it. I've often
thought of how strange it was that I knew he'd given up his life. What happened in
Boston, Willy?

[*WILLY looks at him as at an intruder.*]

BERNARD.   I just bring it up because you asked me.

WILLY.   [*angrily*] Nothing. What do you mean, "What happened?" What's that got
to do with anything?

BERNARD.   Well, don't get sore.   320

WILLY.   What are you trying to do, blame it on me? If a boy lays down is that my
fault?

BERNARD.   Now, Willy, don't get—

WILLY.   Well, don't—don't talk to me that way! What does that mean, "What
happened?"

[*CHARLEY enters. He is in his vest, and he carries a bottle of bourbon.*]

CHARLEY.   Hey, you're going to miss that train. [*He waves the bottle.*]

BERNARD.   Yeah, I'm going. [*He takes the bottle.*] Thanks, Pop. [*He picks up*   325
his rackets and bag.] Good-by, Willy, and don't worry about it. You know, "If at first you
don't succeed . . ."

WILLY.   Yes, I believe in that.

BERNARD.   But sometimes, Willy, it's better for a man just to walk away.

WILLY.   Walk away?

BERNARD.   That's right.

WILLY.   But if you can't walk away?   330

BERNARD.   [*after a slight pause*] I guess that's when it's tough. [*extending his hand*]
Good-by, Willy.

WILLY.   [*shaking BERNARD'S hand*] Good-by, boy.

CHARLEY.   [*an arm on* BERNARD'S *shoulder*] How do you like this kid? Gonna argue a
case in front of the Supreme Court.
BERNARD.   [*protesting*] Pop!
WILLY.   [*genuinely shocked, pained, and happy*] No! The Supreme Court!   335
BERNARD.   I gotta run. 'By, Dad!
CHARLEY.   Knock 'em dead, Bernard!

[BERNARD *goes off.*]

WILLY.   [*as* CHARLEY *takes out his wallet*] The Supreme Court! And he didn't even
mention it!
CHARLEY.   [*counting out money on the desk*] He don't have to—he's gonna do it.
WILLY.   And you never told him what to do, did you? You never took any   340
interest in him.
CHARLEY.   My salvation is that I never took any interest in anything. There's some
money—fifty dollars. I got an accountant inside.
WILLY.   Charley, look . . . [*with difficulty*] I got my insurance to pay. If you can
manage it—I need a hundred and ten dollars.

[CHARLEY *doesn't reply for a moment; merely stops moving.*]

WILLY.   I'd draw it from my bank but Linda would know, and I . . .
CHARLEY.   Sit down, Willy.
WILLY.   [*moving toward the chair*] I'm keeping an account of everything,   345
remember. I'll pay every penny back. [*He sits.*]
CHARLEY.   Now listen to me, Willy . . .
WILLY.   I want you to know I appreciate . . .
CHARLEY.   [*sitting down on the table*] Willy, what're you doin'? What the hell is goin'
on in your head?
WILLY.   Why? I'm simply . . .
CHARLEY.   I offered you a job. You can make fifty dollars a week. And I won't send   350
you on the road.
WILLY.   I've got a job.
CHARLEY.   Without pay? What kind of job is a job without pay? [*He rises.*] Now,
look, kid, enough is enough. I'm no genius but I know when I'm being insulted.
WILLY.   Insulted!
CHARLEY.   Why don't you want to work for me?
WILLY.   What's the matter with you? I've got a job.   355
CHARLEY.   Then what're you walkin' in here every week for?
WILLY.   [*getting up*] Well, if you don't want me to walk in here—
CHARLEY.   I am offering you a job.
WILLY.   I don't want your goddam job!
CHARLEY.   When the hell are you going to grow up?   360
WILLY.   [*furiously*] You big ignoramus, if you say that to me again I'll rap you one!
I don't care how big you are! [*He's ready to fight.*]

[*Pause.*]

CHARLEY.   [*kindly, going to him*] How much do you need, Willy?
WILLY.   Charley, I'm strapped. I'm strapped. I don't know what to do. I was just
fired.

CHARLEY. Howard fired you?

WILLY. That snotnose. Imagine that? I named him. I named him Howard. 365

CHARLEY. Willy, when're you gonna realize that them things don't mean anything? You named him Howard, but you can't sell that. The only thing you got in this world is what you can sell. And the funny thing is that you're a salesman, and you don't know that.

WILLY. I've tried to think otherwise, I guess. I always felt that if a man was impressive, and well liked, that nothing—

CHARLEY. Why must everybody like you? Who liked J. P. Morgan?° Was he impressive? In a Turkish bath he'd look like a butcher. But with his pockets on he was very well liked. Now listen, Willy, I know you don't like me, and nobody can say I'm in love with you, but I'll give you a job because—just for the hell of it, put it that way. Now what do you say?

WILLY. I—I just can't work for you, Charley.

CHARLEY. What're you, jealous of me? 370

WILLY. I can't work for you, that's all, don't ask me why.

CHARLEY. [*angered, takes out more bills*] You been jealous of me all your life, you damned fool! Here, pay your insurance. [*He puts the money in WILLY'S hand.*]

WILLY. I'm keeping strict accounts.

CHARLEY. I've got some work to do. Take care of yourself. And pay your insurance.

WILLY. [*moving to the right*] Funny, y'know? After all the highways, and the 375
trains, and the appointments, and the years, you end up worth more dead than alive.

CHARLEY. Willy, nobody's worth nothin' dead. [*after a slight pause*] Did you hear what I said?

[*WILLY stands still, dreaming.*]

CHARLEY. Willy!

WILLY. Apologize to Bernard for me when you see him. I didn't mean to argue with him. He's a fine boy. They're all fine boys, and they'll end up big—all of them. Someday they'll all play tennis together. Wish me luck, Charley. He saw Bill Oliver today.

CHARLEY. Good luck.

WILLY. [*on the verge of tears*] Charley, you're the only friend I got. Isn't that a 380
remarkable thing? [*He goes out.*]

CHARLEY. Jesus!

[*CHARLEY stares after him a moment and follows. All light blacks out. Suddenly raucous music is heard, and a red glow rises behind the screen at right. STANLEY, a young waiter, appears, carrying a table, followed by HAPPY, who is carrying two chairs.*]

STANLEY. [*putting the table down*] That's all right, Mr. Loman. I can handle it myself. [*He turns and takes the chairs from HAPPY and places them at the table.*]

HAPPY. [*glancing around.*] Oh, this is better.

STANLEY. Sure, in the front there you're in the middle of all kinds a noise. Whenever you got a party, Mr. Loman, you just tell me and I'll put you back here.

---

368 *J. P. Morgan:* John Pierpont Morgan (1837–1913) was the founder of U.S. Steel and the head of a gigantic family fortune that was enlarged by his son, John Pierpont Morgan (1867–1943). Charley is probably referring to the son.

Y' know, there's a lotta people they don't like it private, because when they go out they like to see a lotta action around them because they're sick and tired to stay in the house by theirself. But I know you, you ain't from Hackensack.° You know what I mean?

HAPPY. [*sitting down*] So how's it coming, Stanley? 385

STANLEY. Ah, it's a dog's life. I only wish during the war they'd a took me in the Army. I coulda been dead by now.

HAPPY. My brother's back, Stanley.

STANLEY. Oh, he come back, heh? From the Far West.

HAPPY. Yeah, big cattle man, my brother, so treat him right. And my father's coming too.

STANLEY. Oh, your father too! 390

HAPPY. You got a couple of nice lobsters?

STANLEY. Hundred per cent, big.

HAPPY. I want them with claws.

STANLEY. Don't worry. I don't give you no mice. [*HAPPY laughs.*] How about some wine? It'll put a head on the meal.

HAPPY. No. You remember, Stanley, that recipe I brought you from overseas? 395
With the champagne in it?

STANLEY. Oh, yeah, sure. I still got it tacked up yet in the kitchen. But that'll have to cost a buck apiece anyways.

HAPPY. That's all right.

STANLEY. What'd you, hit a number or somethin'?

HAPPY. No, it's a little celebration. My brother is—I think he pulled off a big deal today. I think we're going into business together.

STANLEY. Great! That's the best for you. Because a family business, you know what 400
I mean?—that's the best.

HAPPY. That's what I think.

STANLEY. 'Cause what's the difference? Somebody steals? It's in the family. Know what I mean? [*sotto voce°*] Like this bartender here. The boss is goin' crazy what kinda leak he's got in the cash register. You put it in but it don't come out.

HAPPY. [*raising his head*] Sh!

STANLEY. What?

HAPPY. You notice I wasn't lookin' right or left, was I? 405

STANLEY. No.

HAPPY. And my eyes are closed.

STANLEY. So what's the—?

HAPPY. Strudel's comin'.

STANLEY. [*catching on, looks around*] Ah, no, there's no— 410

[*He breaks off as a furred, lavishly dressed GIRL enters and sits at the next table. Both follow her with their eyes.*]

STANLEY. Geez, how'd ya know?

HAPPY. I got radar or something. [*staring directly at her profile*] Ooooooooo . . . Stanley.

STANLEY. I think that's for you, Mr. Loman.

---

384 *Hackensack:* a city in northeastern New Jersey; Stanley uses the name as a reference to unsophisticated visitors to New York City.
402 *sotto voce:* spoken in an undertone or "stage" whisper.

HAPPY.   Look at that mouth. Oh God. And the binoculars.

STANLEY.   Geez, you got a life, Mr. Loman.   415

HAPPY.   Wait on her.

STANLEY.   [*going to the GIRL's table*] Would you like a menu, ma'am?

GIRL.   I'm expecting someone, but I'd like a—

HAPPY.   Why don't you bring her—excuse me, miss, do you mind? I sell champagne, and I'd like you to try my brand. Bring her a champagne, Stanley.

GIRL.   That's awfully nice of you.   420

HAPPY.   Don't mention it. It's all company money. [*He laughs.*]

GIRL.   That's a charming product to be selling, isn't it?

HAPPY.   Oh, gets to be like everything else. Selling is selling, y'know.

GIRL.   I suppose.

HAPPY.   You don't happen to sell, do you?   425

GIRL.   No, I don't sell.

HAPPY.   Would you object to a compliment from a stranger? You ought to be on a magazine cover.

GIRL.   [*looking at him a little archly*] I have been.

[*STANLEY comes in with a glass of champagne.*]

HAPPY.   What'd I say before, Stanley? You see? She's a cover girl.

STANLEY.   Oh, I could see, I could see.   430

HAPPY.   [*to the GIRL*] What magazine?

GIRL.   Oh, a lot of them. [*She takes the drink.*] Thank you.

HAPPY.   You know what they say in France, don't you? "Champagne is the drink of the complexion"—Hya, Biff!

[*BIFF has entered and sits with HAPPY.*]

BIFF.   Hello, kid. Sorry I'm late.

HAPPY.   I just got here. Uh, Miss—?   435

GIRL.   Forsythe.

HAPPY.   Miss Forsythe, this is my brother.

BIFF.   Is Dad here?

HAPPY.   His name if Biff. You might've heard of him. Great football player.

GIRL.   Really? What team?   440

HAPPY.   Are you familiar with football?

GIRL.   No. I'm afraid I'm not.

HAPPY.   Biff is quarterback with the New York Giants.

GIRL.   Well, that is nice, isn't it? [*She drinks.*]

HAPPY.   Good health.   445

GIRL.   I'm happy to meet you.

HAPPY.   That's my name. Hap. It's really Harold, but at West Point they called me Happy.

GIRL.   [*now really impressed*] Oh, I see. How do you do? [*She turns her profile.*]

BIFF.   Isn't Dad coming?

HAPPY.   You want her?   450

BIFF.   Oh, I could never make that.

HAPPY.   I remember the time that idea would never come into your head. Where's the old confidence, Biff?

BIFF.   I just saw Oliver—

HAPPY.   Wait a minute. I've got to see that old confidence again. Do you want her? She's on call.

BIFF.   Oh, no. [*He turns to look at the GIRL.*]   455

HAPPY.   I'm telling you. Watch this. [*turning to the GIRL*] Honey? [*She turns to him.*] Are you busy?

GIRL.   Well, I am . . . but I could make a phone call.

HAPPY.   Do that, will you, honey? And see if you can get a friend. We'll be here for a while. Biff is one of the greatest football players in the country.

GIRL.   [*standing up*] Well, I'm certainly happy to meet you.

HAPPY.   Come back soon.   460

GIRL.   I'll try.

HAPPY.   Don't try, honey, try hard.

[*The GIRL exits. STANLEY follows, shaking his head in bewildered admiration.*]

HAPPY.   Isn't that a shame now? A beautiful girl like that? That's why I can't get married. There's not a good woman in a thousand. New York is loaded with them, kid!

BIFF.   Hap, look—

HAPPY.   I told you she was on call!   465

BIFF.   [*strangely unnerved*] Cut it out, will ya? I want to say something to you.

HAPPY.   Did you see Oliver?

BIFF.   I saw him all right. Now look, I want to tell Dad a couple of things and I want you to help me.

HAPPY.   What? Is he going to back you?

BIFF.   Are you crazy? You're out of your goddam head, you know that?   470

HAPPY.   Why? What happened?

BIFF.   [*breathlessly*] I did a terrible thing today, Hap. It's been the strangest day I ever went through. I'm all numb, I swear.

HAPPY.   You mean he wouldn't see you?

BIFF.   Well, I waited six hours for him, see? All day. Kept sending my name in. Even tried to date his secretary so she'd get me to him, but no soap.

HAPPY.   Because you're not showin' the old confidence, Biff. He remembered   475
you, didn't he?

BIFF.   [*stopping HAPPY with a gesture*] Finally, about five o'clock, he comes out. Didn't remember who I was or anything. I felt like such an idiot, Hap.

HAPPY.   Did you tell him my Florida idea?

BIFF.   He walked away. I saw him for one minute. I got so mad I could've torn the walls down! How the hell did I ever get the idea I was a salesman there? I even believed myself that I'd been a salesman for him! And then he gave me one look and— I realized what a ridiculous lie my whole life has been! We've been talking in a dream for fifteen years. I was a shipping clerk.

HAPPY.   What'd you do?

BIFF.   [*with great tension and wonder*] Well, he left, see. And the secretary   48
went out. I was all alone in the waiting-room. I don't know what came over me, Hap. The next thing I know I'm in his office—paneled walls, everything. I can't explain it. I—Hap, I took his fountain pen.

HAPPY.   Geez, did he catch you?

BIFF.   I ran out. I ran down all eleven flights. I ran and ran and ran.

HAPPY.   That was an awful dumb—what'd you do that for?

BIFF. [*agonized*] I don't know, I just—wanted to take something. I don't know. You gotta help me, Hap, I'm gonna tell Pop.

HAPPY.   You crazy? What for?   485

BIFF.   Hap, he's got to understand that I'm not the man somebody lends that kind of money to. He thinks I've been spiting him all these years and it's eating him up.

HAPPY.   That's just it. You tell him something nice.

BIFF.   I can't.

HAPPY.   Say you got a lunch date with Oliver tomorrow.

BIFF.   So what do I do tomorrow?   490

HAPPY.   You leave the house tomorrow and come back at night and say Oliver is thinking it over. And he thinks it over for a couple of weeks, and gradually it fades away and nobody's the worse.

BIFF.   But it'll go on forever!

HAPPY.   Dad is never so happy as when he's looking forward to something!

[*WILLY enters.*]

HAPPY.   Hello, scout!

WILLY.   Gee, I haven't been here in years!   495

[*STANLEY has followed WILLY in and sets a chair for him. STANLEY starts off but HAPPY stops him.*]

HAPPY.   Stanley!

[*STANLEY stands by, waiting for an order.*]

BIFF.   [*going to WILLY with guilt, as to an invalid*] Sit down, Pop. You want a drink?

WILLY.   Sure, I don't mind.

BIFF.   Let's get a load on.

WILLY.   You look worried.   500

BIFF.   N-no. [*to STANLEY*] Scotch all around. Make it doubles.

STANLEY.   Doubles, right. [*He goes.*]

WILLY.   You had a couple already, didn't you?

BIFF.   Just a couple, yeah.

WILLY.   Well, what happened, boy? [*nodding affirmatively, with a smile*] Every-   505
thing go all right?

BIFF.   [*takes a breath, then reaches out and grasps WILLY's hand*] Pal . . . [*He is smiling bravely, and WILLY is smiling too.*] I had an experience today.

HAPPY.   Terrific, Pop.

WILLY.   That so? What happened?

BIFF.   [*high, slightly alcoholic, above the earth*] I'm going to tell you everything from first to last. It's been a strange day. [*Silence. He looks around, composes himself as best he can, but his breath keeps breaking the rhythm of his voice.*] I had to wait quite a while for him, and—

WILLY.   Oliver?   510

BIFF.   Yeah, Oliver. All day, as a matter of cold fact. And a lot of—instances—facts, Pop, facts about my life came back to me. Who was it, Pop? Who ever said I was a sales-man with Oliver?

WILLY.   Well, you were.

BIFF.   No, Dad, I was a shipping clerk.

WILLY.   But you were practically—

BIFF.   [*with determination*] Dad, I don't know who said it first, but I was never   515
a salesman for Bill Oliver.

WILLY.   What're you talking about?

BIFF.   Let's hold on to the facts tonight, Pop. We're not going to get anywhere
bullin' around. I was a shipping clerk.

WILLY.   [*angrily*] All right, now listen to me—

BIFF.   Why don't you let me finish?

WILLY.   I'm not interested in stories about the past or any crap of that kind   520
because the woods are burning, boys, you understand? There's a big blaze going on all
around. I was fired today.

BIFF.   [*shocked*] How could you be?

WILLY.   I was fired, and I'm looking for a little good news to tell your mother,
because the woman has waited and the woman has suffered. The gist of it is that I
haven't got a story left in my head, Biff. So don't give me a lecture about facts and
aspects. I am not interested. Now what've you got to say to me?

[*STANLEY enters with three drinks. They wait until he leaves.*]

WILLY.   Did you see Oliver?

BIFF.   Jesus, Dad!

WILLY.   You mean you didn't go up there?   525

HAPPY.   Sure he went up there.

BIFF.   I did. I—saw him. How could they fire you?

WILLY.   [*on the edge of his chair*] What kind of a welcome did he give you?

BIFF.   He won't even let you work on commission?

WILLY.   I'm out! [*driving*] So tell me, he gave you a warm welcome?   530

HAPPY.   Sure, Pop, sure!

BIFF.   [*driven*] Well, it was kind of—

WILLY.   I was wondering if he'd remember you. [*to HAPPY*] Imagine, man
doesn't see him for ten, twelve years and gives him that kind of a welcome!

HAPPY.   Damn right!

BIFF.   [*trying to return to the offensive*] Pop, look—   535

WILLY.   You know why he remembered you, don't you? Because you impressed
him in those days.

BIFF.   Let's talk quietly and get this down to the facts, huh?

WILLY.   [*as though BIFF had been interrupting*] Well, what happened? It's great news,
Biff. Did he take you into his office or'd you talk in the waiting-room?

BIFF.   Well, he came in, see, and—

WILLY.   [*with a big smile*] What'd he say? Betcha he threw his arm around you.   540

BIFF.   Well, he kinda—

WILLY.   He's a fine man. [*to HAPPY*] Very hard man to see, y'know.

HAPPY.   [*agreeing*] Oh, I know.

WILLY.   [*to BIFF*] Is that where you had the drinks?

BIFF.   Yeah, he gave me a couple of—no, no!   545

HAPPY.   [*cutting in*] He told him my Florida idea.

WILLY.   Don't interrupt. [*to BIFF*] How'd he react to the Florida idea?

BIFF.   Dad, will you give me a minute to explain?

WILLY.   I've been waiting for you to explain since I sat down here! What happened? He took you into his office and what?

BIFF.   Well—I talked. And—and he listened, see.   550

WILLY.   Famous for the way he listens, y'know. What was his answer?

BIFF.   His answer was—[*He breaks off, suddenly angry.*] Dad, you're not letting me tell you what I want to tell you!

WILLY.   [*accusing, angered*] You didn't see him, did you?

BIFF.   I did see him!

WILLY.   What'd you insult him or something? You insulted him, didn't you?   555

BIFF.   Listen, will you let me out of it, will you just let me out of it!

HAPPY.   What the hell!

WILLY.   Tell me what happened!

BIFF.   [*to HAPPY*] I can't talk to him!

[*A single trumpet note jars the ear. The light of green leaves stains the house, which holds the air of night and a dream. YOUNG BERNARD enters and knocks on the door of the house.*]

YOUNG BERNARD.   [*frantically*] Mrs. Loman, Mrs. Loman!   560

HAPPY.   Tell him what happened!

BIFF.   [*to HAPPY*] Shut up and leave me alone!

WILLY.   No, no! You had to go and flunk math!

BIFF.   What math? What're you talking about?

YOUNG BERNARD.   Mrs. Loman, Mrs. Loman!   565

[*LINDA appears in the house, as of old.*]

WILLY.   [*wildly*] Math, math, math!

BIFF.   Take it easy, Pop!

YOUNG BERNARD.   Mrs. Loman!

WILLY.   [*furiously*] If you hadn't flunked you'd've been set by now!

BIFF.   Now, look, I'm gonna tell you what happened, and you're going to   570
listen to me.

YOUNG BERNARD.   Mrs. Loman!

BIFF.   I waited six hours—

HAPPY.   What the hell are you saying?

BIFF.   I kept sending in my name but he wouldn't see me. So finally he . . .

[*He continues unheard as light fades low on the restaurant.*]

YOUNG BERNARD.   Biff flunked math!   575

LINDA.   No!

YOUNG BERNARD.   Birnbaum flunked him! They won't graduate him!

LINDA.   But they have to. He's gotta go to the university. Where is he? Biff! Biff!

YOUNG BERNARD.   No, he left. He went to Grand Central.

LINDA.   Grand—You mean he went to Boston!   580

YOUNG BERNARD.   Is Uncle Willy in Boston?

LINDA.   Oh, maybe Willy can talk to the teacher. Oh, the poor, poor boy!

[*Light on house area snaps out.*]

BIFF.   [*at the table, now audible, holding up a gold fountain pen*] . . . so I'm washed up with Oliver, you understand? Are you listening to me?

WILLY.   [*at a loss*] Yeah, sure. If you hadn't flunked—

BIFF.   Flunked what? What're you talking about?   585

WILLY.   Don't blame everything on me! I didn't flunk math—you did! What pen?

HAPPY.   That was awful dumb, Biff, a pen like that is worth—

WILLY.   [*seeing the pen for the first time*] You took Oliver's pen?

BIFF.   [*weakening*] Dad, I just explained it to you.

WILLY.   You stole Bill Oliver's fountain pen!   590

BIFF.   I didn't exactly steal it! That's just what I've been explaining to you!

HAPPY.   He had it in his hand and just then Oliver walked in, so he got nervous and stuck it in his pocket!

WILLY.   My God, Biff!

BIFF.   I never intended to do it, Dad!

OPERATOR'S VOICE.   Standish Arms, good evening!   595

WILLY.   [*shouting*] I'm not in my room!

BIFF.   [*frightened*] Dad, what's the matter? [*He and HAPPY stand up.*]

OPERATOR.   Ringing Mr. Loman for you!

WILLY.   I'm not there, stop it!

BIFF.   [*horrified, gets down on one knee before WILLY*] Dad, I'll make good, I'll   600
make good. [*WILLY tries to get to his feet. BIFF holds him down.*] Sit down now.

WILLY.   No, you're no good, you're no good for anything.

BIFF.   I am, Dad, I'll find something else, you understand? Now don't worry about anything. [*He holds up WILLY's face.*] Talk to me, Dad.

OPERATOR.   Mr. Loman does not answer. Shall I page him?

WILLY.   [*attempting to stand, as though to rush and silence the OPERATOR*] No, no, no!

HAPPY.   He'll strike something, Pop.   605

WILLY.   No, no . . .

BIFF.   [*desperately, standing over WILLY*] Pop, listen! Listen to me! I'm telling you something good. Oliver talked to his partner about the Florida idea, you listening? He— he talked to his partner, and he came to me . . . I'm going to be all right, you hear? Dad, listen to me, he said it was just a question of the amount!

WILLY.   Then you . . . got it?

HAPPY.   He's gonna be terrific, Pop!

WILLY.   [*trying to stand*] Then you got it, haven't you? You got it! You got it!   610

BIFF.   [*agonized, holds WILLY down*] No, no. Look, Pop. I'm supposed to have lunch with them tomorrow. I'm just telling you this so you'll know that I can still make an impression, Pop. And I'll make good somewhere, but I can't go tomorrow, see?

WILLY.   Why not? You simply—

BIFF.   But the pen, Pop!

WILLY.   You give it to him and tell him it was an oversight!

HAPPY.   Sure, have lunch tomorrow!   615

BIFF.   I can't say that—

WILLY.   You were doing a crossword puzzle and accidentally used his pen!

BIFF.   Listen, kid, I took those balls years ago, now I walk in with his fountain pen? That clinches it, don't you see? I can't face him like that! I'll try elsewhere.

PAGE'S VOICE.   Paging Mr. Loman!

WILLY.   Don't you want to be anything?   620

BIFF.   Pop, how can I go back?

WILLY.   You don't want to be anything, is that what's behind it?

BIFF.   [*now angry at WILLY for not crediting his sympathy*] Don't take it that way! You think it was easy walking into that office after what I'd done to him? A team of horses couldn't have dragged me back to Bill Oliver!

WILLY.   Then why'd you go?

BIFF. Why did I go? Why did I go? Look at you! Look at what's become   625
of you!

[*Off left,* THE WOMAN *laughs.*]

WILLY. Biff, you're going to go to that lunch tomorrow, or—
BIFF. I can't go. I've got no appointment!
HAPPY. Biff, for . . . !
WILLY. Are you spiting me?
BIFF. Don't take it that way! Goddammit!   630
WILLY. [*strikes* BIFF *and falters away from the table*] You rotten little louse! Are you
spiting me?
THE WOMAN. Someone's at the door, Willy!
BIFF. I'm no good, can't you see what I am?
HAPPY. [*separating them*] Hey, you're in a restaurant! Now cut it out, both of you!
[*The girls enter.*] Hello, girls, sit down.

[THE WOMAN *laughs, off left.*]

MISS FORSYTHE. I guess we might as well. This is Letta.   635
THE WOMAN. Willy, are you going to wake up?
BIFF. [*ignoring* WILLY] How're ya, miss, sit down. What do you drink?
MISS FORSYTHE. Letta might not be able to stay long.
LETTA. I gotta get up very early tomorrow. I got jury duty. I'm so excited! Were
you fellows ever on a jury?
BIFF. No, but I been in front of them! [*The girls laugh.*] This is my father.   640
LETTA. Isn't he cute? Sit down with us, Pop.
HAPPY. Sit him down, Biff!
BIFF. [*going to him*] Come on, slugger, drink us under the table. To hell with it!
Come on, sit down, pal.

[*On* BIFF'S *last insistence,* WILLY *is about to sit.*]

THE WOMAN. [*now urgently*] Willy, are you going to answer the door!

[THE WOMAN'S *call pulls* WILLY *back. He starts right, befuddled.*]

BIFF. Hey, where are you going?   645
WILLY. Open the door.
BIFF. The door?
WILLY. The washroom . . . the door . . . where's the door?
BIFF. [*leading* WILLY *to the left*] Just go straight down.

[WILLY *moves left.*]

THE WOMAN. Willy, Willy, are you going to get up, get up, get up, get up?   650

[WILLY *exits left.*]

LETTA. I think it's sweet you bring your daddy along.
MISS FORSYTHE. Oh, he isn't really your father!
BIFF. [*at left, turning to her resentfully*] Miss Forsythe, you've just seen a prince walk
by. A fine, troubled prince. A hard-working, unappreciated prince. A pal, you under-
stand? A good companion. Always for his boys.
LETTA. That's so sweet.

HAPPY.   Well, girls, what's the program? We're wasting time. Come on, Biff.   655
Gather round. Where would you like to go?

BIFF.   Why don't you do something for him?

HAPPY.   Me!

BIFF.   Don't you give a damn for him, Hap?

HAPPY.   What're you talking about? I'm the one who—

BIFF.   I sense it, you don't give a good goddam about him. [*He takes the rolled-up*   660
hose from his pocket and puts it on the table in front of HAPPY.] Look what I found in the cellar,
for Christ's sake. How can you bear to let it go on?

HAPPY.   Me? Who goes away? Who runs off and—

BIFF.   Yeah, but he doesn't mean anything to you. You could help him—I can't!
Don't you understand what I'm talking about? He's going to kill himself, don't you know
that?

HAPPY.   Don't I know it! Me!

BIFF.   Hap, help him! Jesus . . . help him . . . Help me, help me, I can't bear to
look at his face! [*Ready to weep, he hurries out, up right.*]

HAPPY.   [*staring after him*] Where are you going?   665

MISS FORSYTHE.   What's he so mad about?

HAPPY.   Come on, girls, we'll catch up with him.

MISS FORSYTHE.   [*as HAPPY pushes her out*] Say, I don't like that temper of his!

HAPPY.   He's just a little overstrung, he'll be all right!

WILLY.   [*off left, as THE WOMAN laughs*] Don't answer! Don't answer!   670

LETTA.   Don't you want to tell your father—

HAPPY.   No, that's not my father. He's just a guy. Come on, we'll catch Biff, and,
honey, we're going to paint this town! Stanley, where's the check! Hey, Stanley!

[*They exit. STANLEY looks toward left.*]

STANLEY.   [*calling to HAPPY indignantly*] Mr. Loman! Mr. Loman!

[*STANLEY picks up a chair and follows them off. Knocking is heard off left. THE WOMAN enters,*
laughing. WILLY follows her. She is in a black slip; he is buttoning his shirt. Raw, sensuous
music accompanies their speech.]

WILLY.   Will you stop laughing? Will you stop?

THE WOMAN.   Aren't you going to answer the door? He'll wake the whole   675
hotel.

WILLY.   I'm not expecting anybody.

THE WOMAN.   Whyn't you have another drink, honey, and stop being so damn
self-centered?

WILLY.   I'm so lonely.

THE WOMAN.   You know you ruined me, Willy? From now on, whenever you come
to the office, I'll see that you go right through to the buyers. No waiting at my desk any
more, Willy. You ruined me.

WILLY.   That's nice of you to say that.   680

THE WOMAN.   Gee, you are self-centered! Why so sad? You are the saddest, self-
centeredest soul I ever did see-saw. [*She laughs. He kisses her.*] Come on inside, drummer
boy. It's silly to be dressing in the middle of the night. [*As knocking is heard*] Aren't you
going to answer the door?

WILLY.   They're knocking on the wrong door.

THE WOMAN.   But I felt the knocking! And he heard us talking in here. Maybe the hotel's on fire!

WILLY.   [*his terror rising*] It's a mistake.

THE WOMAN.   Then tell him to go away!   685

WILLY.   There's nobody there.

THE WOMAN.   It's getting on my nerves, Willy. There's somebody standing out there and it's getting on my nerves!

WILLY.   [*pushing her away from him*] All right, stay in the bathroom here, and don't come out. I think there's a law in Massachusetts about it, so don't come out. It may be that new room clerk. He looked very mean. So don't come out. It's a mistake, there's no fire.

[*The knocking is heard again. He takes a few steps away from her, and she vanishes into the wing. The light follows him, and now he is facing YOUNG BIFF, who carries a suitcase. BIFF steps toward him. The music is gone.*]

BIFF.   Why didn't you answer?

WILLY.   Biff! What are you doing in Boston?   690

BIFF.   Why didn't you answer? I've been knocking for five minutes, I called you on the phone—

WILLY.   I just heard you. I was in the bathroom and had the door shut. Did anything happen home?

BIFF.   Dad—I let you down.

WILLY.   What do you mean?

BIFF.   Dad . . .   695

WILLY.   Biffo, what's this about? [*putting his arm around BIFF*] Come on, let's go downstairs and get you a malted.

BIFF.   Dad, I flunked math.

WILLY.   Not for the term?

BIFF.   The term. I haven't got enough credits to graduate.

WILLY.   You mean to say Bernard wouldn't give you the answers?   700

BIFF.   He did, he tried, but I only got a sixty-one.

WILLY.   And they wouldn't give you four points?

BIFF.   Birnbaum refused absolutely. I begged him, Pop, but he won't give me those points. You gotta talk to him before they close the school. Because if he saw the kind of man you are, and you just talked to him in your way, I'm sure he'd come through for me. The class came right before practice, see, and I didn't go enough. Would you talk to him? He'd like you, Pop. You know the way you could talk.

WILLY.   You're on. We'll drive right back.

BIFF.   Oh, Dad, good work! I'm sure he'll change it for you!   705

WILLY.   Go downstairs and tell the clerk I'm checkin' out. Go right down.

BIFF.   Yes, sir! See, the reason he hates me, Pop—one day he was late for class so I got up at the blackboard and imitated him. I crossed my eyes and talked with a lithp.

WILLY.   [*laughing*] You did? The kids like it?

BIFF.   They nearly died laughing!

WILLY.   Yeah? What'd you do?   710

BIFF.   The thquare root of thixthy twee is . . . [*WILLY bursts out laughing; BIFF joins him.*] And in the middle of it he walked in!

[*WILLY laughs and THE WOMAN joins in offstage.*]

WILLY. [*without hesitation*] Hurry downstairs and—
BIFF. Somebody in there?
WILLY. No, that was next door.

[*THE WOMAN laughs offstage.*]

BIFF. Somebody got in your bathroom!   715
WILLY. No, it's the next room, there's a party—
THE WOMAN. [*enters, laughing. She lisps this.*] Can I come in? There's something in
the bathtub, Willy, and it's moving!

[*WILLY looks at BIFF, who is staring open-mouthed and horrified at THE WOMAN.*]

WILLY. Ah—you better go back to your room. They must be finished painting by
now. They're painting her room so I let her take a shower here. Go back, go
back . . . [*He pushes her.*]
THE WOMAN. [*resisting*] But I've got to get dressed, Willy, I can't—
WILLY. Get out of here! Go back, go back . . . [*suddenly striving for the ordinary*]   720
This is Miss Francis, Biff, she's a buyer. They're painting her room. Go back, Miss
Francis, go back . . .
THE WOMAN. But my clothes, I can't go out naked in the hall!
WILLY. [*pushing her offstage*] Get outa here! Go back, go back!

[*BIFF slowly sits down on his suitcase as the argument continues offstage.*]

THE WOMAN. Where's my stockings? You promised me stockings, Willy!
WILLY. I have no stockings here!
THE WOMAN. You had two boxes of size nine sheers for me, and I want them!   725
WILLY. Here, for God's sake, will you get outa here!
THE WOMAN. [*enters holding a box of stockings*] I just hope there's nobody in the
hall. That's all I hope. [*To BIFF*] Are you football or baseball?
BIFF. Football.
THE WOMAN. [*angry, humiliated*] That's me too. G'night. [*she snatches her clothes
from WILLY, and walks out.*]
WILLY. [*after a pause*] Well, better get going. I want to get to the school first thing   730
in the morning. Get my suits out of the closet. I'll get my valise. [*BIFF doesn't move.*]
What's the matter? [*BIFF remains motionless, tears falling*] She's a buyer. Buys for J. H.
Simmons. She lives down the hall—they're painting. You don't imagine—[*He breaks off.
After a pause*] Now listen, pal, she's just a buyer. She sees merchandise in her room and
they have to keep it looking just so . . . [*Pause. Assuming command*] All right, get my suits.
[*BIFF doesn't move.*] Now stop crying and do as I say. I gave you an order. Biff, I gave you
an order! Is that what you do when I give you an order? How dare you cry! [*putting his
arm around BIFF*] Now look, Biff, when you grow up you'll understand about these things.
You mustn't—you mustn't overemphasize a thing like this. I'll see Birnbaum first thing
in the morning.
BIFF. Never mind.
WILLY. [*getting down beside BIFF*] Never mind! He's going to give you those points.
I'll see to it.
BIFF. He wouldn't listen to you.
WILLY. He certainly will listen to me. You need those points for the U. of
Virginia.
BIFF. I'm not going there.   735

WILLY.   Heh? If I can't get him to change that mark you'll make it up in summer school. You've got all summer to—

BIFF.   [*his weeping breaking from him*] Dad . . .

WILLY.   [*infected by it*] Oh, my boy . . .

BIFF.   Dad . . .

WILLY.   She's nothing to me, Biff. I was lonely, I was terribly lonely.   740

BIFF.   You—you gave her Mama's stockings! [*His tears break through and he rises to go.*]

WILLY.   [*grabbing for BIFF*] I gave you an order!

BIFF.   Don't touch me, you—liar!

WILLY.   Apologize for that!

BIFF.   You fake! You phony little fake! [*Overcome, he turns quickly and weeping*   745
fully goes out with his suitcase. WILLY is left on the floor on his knees.]

WILLY.   I gave you an order! Biff, come back here or I'll beat you! Come back here! I'll whip you!

[*STANLEY comes quickly in from the right and stands in front of WILLY.*]

WILLY.   [*shouts at STANLEY*] I gave you an order . . .

STANLEY.   Hey, let's pick it up, pick it up, Mr. Loman. [*He helps WILLY to his feet.*] Your boys left with the chippies. They said they'll see you home.

[*A SECOND WAITER watches some distance away.*]

WILLY.   But we were supposed to have dinner together.

[*Music is heard, WILLY'S theme.*]

STANLEY.   Can you make it?   750

WILLY.   I'll—sure, I can make it. [*suddenly concerned about his clothes*] Do I—I look all right?

STANLEY.   Sure, you look all right. [*He flicks a speck off WILLY's lapel.*]

WILLY.   Here—here's a dollar.

STANLEY.   Oh, your son paid me. It's all right.

WILLY.   [*putting it in STANLEY's hand*] No, take it. You're a good boy.   755

STANLEY.   Oh, no, you don't have to . . .

WILLY.   Here—here's some more, I don't need it any more. [*after a slight pause*] Tell me—is there a seed store in the neighborhood?

STANLEY.   Seeds? You mean like to plant?

[*As WILLY turns, STANLEY slips the money back into his jacket pocket.*]

WILLY.   Yes. Carrots, peas . . .

STANLEY.   Well, there's hardware stores on Sixth Avenue, but it may be too   760
late now.

WILLY.   [*anxiously*] Oh, I'd better hurry. I've got to get some seeds. [*He starts off to the right.*] I've got to get some seeds, right away. Nothing's planted. I don't have a thing in the ground.

[*WILLY hurries out as the light goes down. STANLEY moves over to the right after him, watches him off. The other waiter has been staring at WILLY.*]

STANLEY.   [*to the WAITER*] Well, whatta you looking at?

[*The WAITER picks up the chairs and moves off right. STANLEY takes the table and follows him. The light fades on this area. There is a long pause, the sound of the flute coming over. The light gradually rises on the kitchen, which is empty. HAPPY appears at the door of the house, followed by BIFF. HAPPY is carrying a large bunch of long-stemmed roses. He enters the kitchen, looks around for LINDA. Not seeing her, he turns to BIFF, who is just outside the house door, and makes a gesture with his hands, indicating "Not here, I guess." He looks into the living-room and freezes. Inside, LINDA, unseen, is seated, WILLY'S coat on her lap. She rises ominously and quietly and moves toward HAPPY, who backs up into the kitchen, afraid.*]

HAPPY.   Hey, what're you doing up? [*LINDA says nothing but moves toward him implacably.*] Where's Pop? [*He keeps backing to the right, and now LINDA is in full view in the doorway to the living-room.*] Is he sleeping?

LINDA.   Where were you?

HAPPY.   [*trying to laugh it off*] We met two girls, Mom, very fine types. Here,   765
we brought you some flowers. [*offering them to her*] Put them in your room, Ma.

[*She knocks them to the floor at BIFF's feet. He has now come inside and closed the door behind him. She stares at BIFF, silent.*]

HAPPY.   Now what'd you do that for? Mom, I want you to have some flowers—

LINDA.   [*cutting HAPPY off, violently to BIFF*] Don't you care whether he lives or dies?

HAPPY.   [*going to the stairs*] Come upstairs, Biff.

BIFF.   [*with a flare of disgust, to HAPPY*] Go away from me! [*to LINDA*] What do you mean, lives or dies? Nobody's dying around here, pal.

LINDA.   Get out of my sight! Get out of here!   770

BIFF.   I wanna see the boss.

LINDA.   You're not going near him!

BIFF.   Where is he? [*He moves into the living-room and LINDA follows.*]

LINDA.   [*shouting after BIFF*] You invite him for dinner. He looks forward to it all day—[*BIFF appears in his parents' bedroom, looks around, and exits.*]—and then you desert him there. There's no stranger you'd do that to!

HAPPY.   Why? He had a swell time with us. Listen, when I—[*LINDA comes back into*   775
the kitchen.]—desert him I hope I don't outlive the day!

LINDA.   Get out of here!

HAPPY.   Now look, Mom . . .

LINDA.   Did you have to go to women tonight? You and your lousy rotten whores!

[*BIFF re-enters the kitchen.*]

HAPPY.   Mom, all we did was follow Biff around trying to cheer him up! [*to BIFF*] Boy, what a night you gave me!

LINDA.   Get out of here, both of you, and don't come back! I don't want you tor-   780
menting him any more. Go on now, get your things together! [*to BIFF*] You can sleep in his apartment. [*She starts to pick up the flowers and stops herself.*] Pick up this stuff, I'm not your maid any more. Pick it up, you bum, you!

[*HAPPY turns his back to her in refusal. BIFF slowly moves over and gets down on his knees, picking up the flowers.*]

LINDA.   You're a pair of animals! Not one, not another living soul would have had the cruelty to walk out on that man in a restaurant!

BIFF.   [*not looking at her*] Is that what he said?

LINDA.   He didn't have to say anything. He was so humiliated he nearly limped when he came in.

HAPPY.   But, Mom, he had a great time with us—

BIFF.   [*cutting him off violently*] Shut up!   785

[*Without another word, HAPPY goes upstairs.*]

LINDA.   You! You didn't even go in to see if he was all right!

BIFF.   [*still on the floor in front of LINDA, the flowers in his hand; with self-loathing*] No. Didn't. Didn't do a damned thing. How do you like that, heh? Left him babbling in a toilet.

LINDA.   You louse. You . . .

BIFF.   Now you hit it on the nose! [*He gets up, throws the flowers in the wastebasket.*] The scum of the earth, and you're looking at him!

LINDA.   Get out of here!   790

BIFF.   I gotta talk to the boss, Mom. Where is he?

LINDA.   You're not going near him. Get out of this house!

BIFF.   [*with absolute assurance, determination*] No. We're gonna have an abrupt conversation, him and me.

LINDA.   You're not talking to him!

[*Hammering is heard from outside the house, off right. BIFF turns toward the noise.*]

LINDA.   [*suddenly pleading*] Will you please leave him alone?   795

BIFF.   What's he doing out there?

LINDA.   He's planting the garden!

BIFF.   [*quietly*] Now? Oh, my God!

[*BIFF moves outside, LINDA following. The light dies down on them and comes up on the center of the apron as WILLY walks into it. He is carrying a flashlight, a hoe, and a handful of seed packets. He raps the top of the hoe sharply to fix it firmly, and then moves to the left, measuring off the distance with his foot. He holds the flashlight to look at the seed packets, reading off the instructions. He is in the blue of night.*]

WILLY.   Carrots . . . quarter-inch apart. Rows . . . one-foot rows. [*He measures it off.*] One foot. [*He puts down a package and measures off.*] Beets. [*He puts down another package and measures again.*] Lettuce. [*He reads the package, puts it down.*] One foot—[*He breaks off as BEN appears at the right and moves slowly down to him.*] What a proposition, ts, ts. Terrific, terrific. 'Cause she's suffered, Ben, the woman has suffered. You understand me? A man can't go out the way he came in, Ben, a man has got to add up to something. You can't, you can't—[*BEN moves toward him as though to interrupt.*] You gotta consider, now. Don't answer so quick. Remember, it's a guaranteed twenty-thousand-dollar proposition. Now look, Ben, I want you to go through the ins and outs of this thing with me. I've got nobody to talk to, Ben, and the woman has suffered, you hear me?

BEN.   [*standing still, considering*] What's the proposition?   800

WILLY.   It's twenty thousand dollars on the barrelhead. Guaranteed, gilt-edged, you understand?

BEN.   You don't want to make a fool of yourself. They might not honor the policy.

WILLY.   How can they dare refuse? Didn't I work like a coolie to meet every premium on the nose? And now they don't pay off? Impossible!

BEN.   It's called a cowardly thing, William.

WILLY.   Why? Does it take more guts to stand here the rest of my life ringing up   805
a zero?

BEN.   [*yielding*] That's a point, William. [*He moves, thinking, turns.*] And twenty
thousand—that *is* something one can feel with the hand, it is there.

WILLY.   [*now assured, with rising power*] Oh, Ben, that's the whole beauty of it! I see
it like a diamond, shining in the dark, hard and rough, that I can pick up and touch in
my hand. Not like—like an appointment! This would not be another damned-fool
appointment, Ben, and it changes all the aspects. Because he thinks I'm nothing, see,
and so he spites me. But the funeral—[*straightening up*] Ben, that funeral will be massive!
They'll come from Maine, Massachusetts, Vermont, New Hampshire! All the old-timers
with the strange license plates—that boy will be thunder-struck, Ben, because he never
realized—I am known! Rhode Island, New York, New Jersey—I am known, Ben, and he'll
see it with his eyes once and for all. He'll see what I am, Ben! He's in for a shock, that boy!

BEN.   [*coming down to the edge of the garden*] He'll call you a coward.

WILLY.   [*suddenly fearful*] No, that would be terrible.

BEN.   Yes. And a damned fool.   810

WILLY.   No, no, he mustn't, I won't have that! [*He is broken and desperate.*]

BEN.   He'll hate you, William.

[*The gay music of the Boys is heard.*]

WILLY.   Oh, Ben, how do we get back to all the great times? Used to be so full of
light, and comradeship, the sleigh-riding in winter, and the ruddiness on his cheeks.
And always some kind of good news coming up, always something nice coming up
ahead. And never even let me carry the valises in the house, and simonizing, simonizing
that little red car! Why, why can't I give him something and not have him hate me?

BEN.   Let me think about it. [*He glances at his watch.*] I still have a little time.
Remarkable proposition, but you've got to be sure you're not making a fool of yourself.

[*BEN drifts upstage and goes out of sight. BIFF comes down from the left.*]

WILLY.   [*suddenly conscious of BIFF, turns and looks up at him, then begins picking*   815
up the packages of seeds in confusion] Where the hell is that seed? [*Indignantly*] You can't see
nothing out here! They boxed in the whole goddam neighborhood!

BIFF.   There are people all around here. Don't you realize that?

WILLY.   I'm busy. Don't bother me.

BIFF.   [*taking the hoe from WILLY*] I'm saying good-by to you, Pop. [*WILLY looks at*
him, silent, unable to move.] I'm not coming back any more.

WILLY.   You're not going to see Oliver tomorrow?

BIFF.   I've got no appointment, Dad.   820

WILLY.   He put his arm around you, and you've got no appointment?

BIFF.   Pop, get this now, will you? Everytime I've left it's been a fight that sent me
out of here. Today I realized something about myself and I tried to explain it to you and
I—I think I'm just not smart enough to make any sense out of it for you. To hell with
whose fault it is or anything like that. [*He takes WILLY's arm.*] Let's just wrap it up, heh?
Come on in, we'll tell Mom. [*He gently tries to pull WILLY to left.*]

WILLY.   [*frozen, immobile, with guilt in his voice*] No, I don't want to see her.

BIFF.   Come on! [*He pulls again, and WILLY tries to pull away.*]

WILLY.   [*highly nervous*] No, no, I don't want to see her.   825

BIFF.   [*tries to look into WILLY's face, as if to find the answer there*] Why don't you want
to see her?

WILLY.   [*more harshly now*] Don't bother me, will you?

BIFF.   What do you mean, you don't want to see her? You don't want them calling you yellow, do you? This isn't your fault; it's me, I'm a bum. Now come inside! [*WILLY strains to get away.*] Did you hear what I said to you?

[*WILLY pulls away and quickly goes by himself into the house. BIFF follows.*]

LINDA.   [*to WILLY*] Did you plant, dear?

BIFF.   [*at the door, to LINDA*] All right, we had it out. I'm going and I'm not writing   830
any more.

LINDA.   [*going to WILLY in the kitchen*] I think that's the best way, dear. 'Cause there's no use drawing it out, you'll just never get along.

[*WILLY doesn't respond.*]

BIFF.   People ask where I am and what I'm doing, you don't know, and you don't care. That way it'll be off your mind and you can start brightening up again. All right? That clears it, doesn't it? [*WILLY is silent, and BIFF goes to him.*] You gonna wish me luck, scout? [*He extends his hand.*] What do you say?

LINDA.   Shake his hand, Willy.

WILLY.   [*turning to her, seething with hurt*] There's no necessity to mention the pen at all, y'know.

BIFF.   [*gently*] I've got no appointment, Dad.   835

WILLY.   [*erupting fiercely*] He put his arm around . . . ?

BIFF.   Dad, you're never going to see what I am, so what's the use of arguing? If I strike oil I'll send you a check. Meantime forget I'm alive.

WILLY.   [*to LINDA*] Spite, see?

BIFF.   Shake hands, Dad.

WILLY.   Not my hand.   840

BIFF.   I was hoping not to go this way.

WILLY.   Well, this is the way you're going. Good-by.

[*BIFF looks at him a moment, then turns sharply and goes to the stairs.*]

WILLY.   [*stops him with*] May you rot in hell if you leave this house!

BIFF.   [*turning*] Exactly what is it that you want from me?

WILLY.   I want you to know, on the train, in the mountains, in the valleys,   845
wherever you go, that you cut down your life for spite!

BIFF.   No, no.

WILLY.   Spite, spite, is the word of your undoing! And when you're down and out, remember what did it. When you're rotting somewhere beside the railroad tracks, remember, and don't you dare blame it on me!

BIFF.   I'm not blaming it on you!

WILLY.   I won't take the rap for this, you hear?

[*HAPPY comes down the stairs and stands on the bottom step, watching.*]

BIFF.   That's just what I'm telling you!   850

WILLY.   [*sinking into a chair at the table, with full accusation*] You're trying to put a knife in me—don't think I don't know what you're doing!

BIFF.   All right, phony! Then let's lay it on the line. [*He whips the rubber tube out of his pocket and puts it on the table.*]

HAPPY.   You crazy—

LINDA. Biff! [*She moves to grab the hose, but* BIFF *holds it down with his hand.*]

BIFF. Leave it here! Don't move it! 855

WILLY. [*not looking at it*] What is that?

BIFF. You know goddam well what that is.

WILLY. [*caged, wanting to escape*] I never saw that.

BIFF. You saw it. The mice didn't bring it into the cellar! What is this supposed to do, make a hero out of you? This supposed to make me sorry for you?

WILLY. Never heard of it. 860

BIFF. There'll be no pity for you, you hear it? No pity!

WILLY. [*to* LINDA] You hear the spite!

BIFF. No, you're going to hear the truth—what you are and what I am!

LINDA. Stop it!

WILLY. Spite! 865

HAPPY. [*coming down toward* BIFF] You cut it now!

BIFF. [*to* HAPPY] The man don't know who we are! The man is gonna know! [*to* WILLY] We never told the truth for ten minutes in this house!

HAPPY. We always told the truth!

BIFF. [*turning on him*] You big blow, are you the assistant buyer? You're one of the two assistants to the assistant, aren't you?

HAPPY. Well, I'm practically— 870

BIFF. You're practically full of it! We all are! And I'm through with it. [*to* WILLY] Now hear this, Willy, this is me.

WILLY. I know you!

BIFF. You know why I had no address for three months? I stole a suit in Kansas City and I was in jail. [*to* LINDA, *who is sobbing*] Stop crying. I'm through with it.

[LINDA *turns from them, her hands covering her face.*]

WILLY. I suppose that's my fault!

BIFF. I stole myself out of every good job since high school! 875

WILLY. And whose fault is that?

BIFF. And I never got anywhere because you blew me so full of hot air I could never stand taking orders from anybody! That's whose fault it is!

WILLY. I hear that!

LINDA. Don't, Biff!

BIFF. It's goddam time you heard that! I had to be boss big shot in two weeks, 880 and I'm through with it!

WILLY. Then hang yourself! For spite, hang yourself!

BIFF. No! Nobody's hanging himself, Willy! I ran down eleven flights with a pen in my hand today. And suddenly I stopped, you hear me? And in the middle of that office building, do you hear this? I stopped in the middle of that building and I saw—the sky. I saw the things that I love in this world. The work and the food and time to sit and smoke. And I looked at the pen and said to myself, what the hell am I grabbing this for? Why am I trying to become what I don't want to be? What am I doing in an office, making a contemptuous, begging fool of myself, when all I want is out there, waiting for me the minute I say I know who I am! Why can't I say that, Willy?

[*He tries to make* WILLY *face him, but* WILLY *pulls away and moves to the left.*]

WILLY. [*with hatred, threateningly.*] The door of your life is wide open!

BIFF. Pop! I'm a dime a dozen, and so are you!

WILLY. [*turning on him now in an uncontrolled outburst*] I am not a dime a   885
dozen! I am Willy Loman, and you are Biff Loman!

[*BIFF starts for WILLY, but is blocked by HAPPY. In his fury, BIFF seems on the verge of attacking his father.*]

BIFF. I am not a leader of men, Willy, and neither are you. You were never any-thing but a hard-working drummer who landed in the ash can like all the rest of them! I'm one dollar an hour, Willy! I tried seven states and couldn't raise it. A buck an hour! Do you gather my meaning? I'm not bringing home any prizes any more, and you're going to stop waiting for me to bring them home!

WILLY. [*directly to BIFF*] You vengeful, spiteful mutt!

[*BIFF breaks from HAPPY. WILLY, in fright, starts up the stairs. BIFF grabs him.*]

BIFF. [*at the peak of his fury*] Pop I'm nothing! I'm nothing, Pop. Can't you under-stand that? There's no spite in it any more. I'm just what I am, that's all.

[*BIFF's fury has spent itself, and he breaks down, sobbing, holding on to WILLY, who dumbly fumbles for BIFF's face.*]

WILLY. [*astonished*] What're you doing? What're you doing? [*to LINDA*] Why is he crying?

BIFF. [*crying, broken*] Will you let me go, for Christ's sake? Will you take that   890
phony dream and burn it before something happens? [*Struggling to contain himself, he pulls away and moves to the stairs.*] I'll go in the morning. Put him—put him to bed. [*Exhausted, BIFF moves up the stairs to his room.*]

WILLY. [*after a long pause, astonished, elevated*] Isn't that—isn't that remarkable? Biff—he likes me!

LINDA. He loves you, Willy!

HAPPY. [*deeply moved*] Always did, Pop.

WILLY. Oh, Biff! [*staring wildly*] He cried! Cried to me. [*He is choking with his love, and now cries out his promise.*] That boy—that boy is going to be magnificent!

[*BEN appears in the light just outside the kitchen.*]

BEN. Yes, outstanding, with twenty thousand behind him.   895

LINDA. [*sensing the racing of his mind, fearfully, carefully*] Now come to bed, Willy. It's all settled now.

WILLY. [*finding it difficult not to rush out of the house*] Yes, we'll sleep. Come on. Go to sleep, Hap.

BEN. And it does take a great kind of a man to crack the jungle.

[*In accents of dread, BEN's idyllic music starts up.*]

HAPPY. [*his arm around LINDA*] I'm getting married, Pop, don't forget it. I'm changing everything. I'm gonna run that department before the year is up. You'll see, Mom. [*He kisses her.*]

BEN. The jungle is dark but full of diamonds, Willy.   900

[*WILLY turns, moves, listening to BEN.*]

LINDA. Be good. You're both good boys, just act that way, that's all.

HAPPY. 'Night, Pop. [*He goes upstairs.*]

LINDA.   [*to* WILLY] Come, dear.

BEN.   [*with greater force*] One must go in to fetch a diamond out.

WILLY.   [*to* LINDA, *as he moves slowly along the edge of the kitchen, toward the   905
door*] I just want to get settled down, Linda. Let me sit alone for a little.

LINDA.   [*almost uttering her fear*] I want you upstairs.

WILLY.   [*taking her in his arms*] In a few minutes, Linda. I couldn't sleep right now.
Go on, you look awful tired. [*He kisses her.*]

BEN.   Not like an appointment at all. A diamond is rough and hard to the touch.

WILLY.   Go on now. I'll be right up.

LINDA.   I think this is the only way, Willy.   910

WILLY.   Sure, it's the best thing.

BEN.   Best thing!

WILLY.   The only way. Everything is gonna be—go on, kid, get to bed. You look so
tired.

LINDA.   Come right up.

WILLY.   Two minutes.   915

[LINDA *goes into the living-room, then reappears in her bedroom.* WILLY *moves just outside the
kitchen door.*]

WILLY.   Loves me. [*wonderingly*] Always loved me. Isn't that a remarkable thing?
Ben, he'll worship me for it!

BEN.   [*with promise*] It's dark there, but full of diamonds.

WILLY.   Can you imagine that magnificence with twenty thousand dollars in his
pocket?

LINDA.   [*calling from her room*] Willy! Come up!

WILLY.   [*calling into the kitchen*] Yes! Yes. Coming! It's very smart, you realize that,   920
don't you, sweetheart? Even Ben sees it. I gotta go, baby. 'By! 'By! [*going over to* BEN,
almost dancing] Imagine? When the mail comes he'll be ahead of Bernard again!

BEN.   A perfect proposition all around.

WILLY.   Did you see how he cried to me? Oh, if I could kiss him, Ben!

BEN.   Time, William, time!

WILLY.   Oh, Ben, I always knew one way or another we were gonna make it, Biff
and I!

BEN.   [*looking at his watch*] The boat. We'll be late. [*He moves slowly off into the   925
darkness.*]

WILLY.   [*elegiacally, turning to the house*] Now when you kick off, boy, I want a
seventy-yard boot, and get right down the field under the ball, and when you hit, hit low
and hit hard, because it's important, boy. [*He swings around and faces the audience.*]
There's all kinds of important people in the stands, and the first thing you
know . . . [*suddenly realizing he is alone*] Ben! Ben, where do I . . . ? [*He makes a sudden
movement of search.*] Ben, how do I . . . ?

LINDA.   [*calling*] Willy, you coming up?

WILLY.   [*uttering a gasp of fear, whirling about as if to quiet her*] Sh! [*He turns around as
if to find his way; sounds, faces, voices, seem to be swarming in upon him and he flicks at them,
crying*] Sh! Sh! [*Suddenly music, faint and high, stops him. It rises in intensity, almost to an
unbearable scream. He goes up and down on his toes, and rushes off around the house.*] Shhh!

LINDA.   Willy?

[*There is no answer. LINDA waits. BIFF gets up off his bed. He is still in his clothes. HAPPY sits up. BIFF stands listening.*]

LINDA. [*with real fear*] Willy, answer me! Willy!   930

[*There is the sound of a car starting and moving away at full speed.*]

LINDA. No!
BIFF. [*rushing down the stairs*] Pop!

[*As the car speeds off, the music crashes down in a frenzy of sound, which becomes the soft pulsation of a single cello string. BIFF slowly returns to his bedroom. He and HAPPY gravely don their jackets. LINDA slowly walks out of her room. The music has developed into a dead march. The leaves of day are appearing over everything. CHARLEY and BERNARD somberly dressed, appear and knock on the kitchen door. BIFF and HAPPY slowly descend the stairs to the kitchen as CHARLEY and BERNARD enter. All stop a moment when LINDA, in clothes of mourning, bearing a little bunch of roses, comes through the draped doorway into the kitchen. She goes to CHARLEY and takes his arm. Now all move toward the audience, through the wall-line of the kitchen. At the limit of the apron, LINDA lays down the flowers, kneels, and sits back on her heels. All stare down at the grave.*]

REQUIEM

CHARLEY. It's getting dark, Linda.

[*LINDA doesn't react. She stares at the grave.*]

BIFF. How about it, Mom? Better get some rest, heh? They'll be closing the gate soon.

[*LINDA makes no move. Pause.*]

HAPPY. [*deeply angered*] He had no right to do that. There was no necessity for it. We would've helped him.
CHARLEY. [*grunting*] Hmmm.
BIFF. Come along, Mom.   5
LINDA. Why didn't anybody come?
CHARLEY. It was a very nice funeral.
LINDA. But where are all the people he knew? Maybe they blame him.
CHARLEY. Naa. It's a rough world, Linda. They wouldn't blame him.
LINDA. I can't understand it. At this time especially. First time in thirty-five years   10
we were just about free and clear. He only needed a little salary. He was even finished with the dentist.
CHARLEY. No man only needs a little salary.
LINDA. I can't understand it.
BIFF. There were a lot of nice days. When he'd come home from a trip; or on Sundays, making the stoop; finishing the cellar; putting on the new porch; when he built the extra bathroom; and put up the garage. You know something, Charley, there's more of him in that front stoop than in all the sales he ever made.
CHARLEY. Yeah. He was a happy man with a batch of cement.
LINDA. He was so wonderful with his hands.   15

BIFF.   He had all the wrong dreams. All, all, wrong.

HAPPY.   [*almost ready to fight BIFF*] Don't say that!

BIFF.   He never knew who he was.

CHARLEY.   [*stopping HAPPY's movement and reply. To BIFF*] Nobody dast blame this man. You don't understand. Willy was a salesman. And for a salesman, there is no rock bottom to the life. He don't put a bolt to a nut, he don't tell you the law or give you medicine. He's a man way out there in the blue, riding on a smile and a shoeshine. And when they start not smiling back—that's an earthquake. And then you get yourself a couple of spots on your hat, and you're finished. Nobody dast blame this man. A salesman is got to dream, boy. It comes with the territory.

BIFF.   Charley, the man didn't know who he was.   20

HAPPY.   [*infuriated*] Don't say that!

BIFF.   Why don't you come with me, Happy?

HAPPY.   I'm not licked that easily. I'm staying right in this city, and I'm gonna beat this racket! [*He looks at BIFF, his chin set.*] The Loman Brothers!

BIFF.   I know who I am, kid.

HAPPY.   All right, boy. I'm gonna show you and everybody else that Willy Loman   25
did not die in vain. He had a good dream. It's the only dream you can have—to come out number-one man. He fought it out here, and this is where I'm gonna win it for him.

BIFF.   [*with a hopeless glance at HAPPY, bends toward his mother*] Let's go, Mom.

LINDA.   I'll be with you in a minute. Go on, Charley. [*He hesitates.*] I want to, just for a minute. I never had a chance to say good-by.

[*CHARLEY moves away, followed by HAPPY. BIFF remains a slight distance up and left of LINDA. She sits there, summoning herself. The flute begins, not far away, playing behind her speech.*]

LINDA.   Forgive me, dear. I can't cry. I don't know what it is, but I can't cry. I don't understand it. Why did you ever do that? Help me, Willy, I can't cry. It seems to me that you're just on another trip. I keep expecting you. Willy, dear, I can't cry. Why did you do it? I search and search and I search, and I can't understand it, Willy. I made the last payment on the house today. Today, dear. And there'll be nobody home. [*A sob rises in her throat.*] We're free and clear. [*sobbing more fully, released*] We're free. [*BIFF comes slowly toward her.*] We're free . . . We're free . . .

[*BIFF lifts her to her feet and moves out up right with her in his arms. LINDA sobs quietly. BERNARD and CHARLEY come together and follow them, followed by HAPPY. Only the music of the flute is left on the darkening stage as over the house the hard towers of the apartment buildings rise into sharp focus, and*]

The curtain falls.]

QUESTIONS

Act I

1.   What do you learn about Willy from the first stage direction?

2.   What instances of stealing are in the play? Why do Biff and Happy steal? Where did they learn about stealing? How is stealing related to salesmanship?

3.   In Act I Willy claims that "I never in my life told him [Biff] anything but decent things." Is this assertion true? What does it show you about Willy?

Act II and Requiem

4. What does Willy's difficulty with machines—especially his car, the refrigerator, and Howard's wire recorder—suggest about him? To what extent are these machines symbolic?

5. When Willy sees Bernard in Charley's office, he asks, "What—what's the secret?" What secret is he asking about? Does such a secret exist?

6. In Act II Willy buys seeds and tries to plant a garden at night. Why is Willy so disturbed that "nothing's planted" and "I don't have a thing in the ground"? What do this garden and having "things in the ground" mean to Willy?

7. In Act II, speech 867, Biff claims that "we never told the truth for ten minutes in this house!" What does he mean? To what extent is he right?

8. Linda's last line in the play—"We're free . . . we're free"—seems to refer to the house mortgage. In what other ways, however, might you take it?

GENERAL QUESTIONS

1. How does Miller use lighting, the set, blocking, and music to differentiate between action in the present and "memory" action?

2. The stage directions are full of information that cannot be played. In describing Happy, for example, Miller notes that "sexuality is like a color on him." What is the function of such stage directions?

3. How is Willy's suicide foreshadowed throughout the play? To what extent does this foreshadowing create tension?

4. Which characters are "real" and which are "hallucinations" that spring from Willy's memory? What are the major differences between these two groups?

5. Which characters are symbolic and what do they symbolize?

6. Describe the character of Willy Loman. What are his good qualities? In what ways does he have heroic stature? What are his bad qualities? To what extent is his "fall" the result of his flaws, and to what extent is it caused by circumstances beyond his control?

7. How is the relationship between Charley and Bernard different from the one between Willy and his sons? Why is this difference important?

8. Discuss Linda's character and role. In what ways is she supportive of Willy? In what ways does she encourage his deceptions and self-delusions?

9. What sort of person is Happy? What has he inherited from Willy? How is he a debasement of Willy? To what degree is he successful or happy?

10. Willy claims that success in business is based not on "what you do" but on "who you know and the smile on your face! It's contacts. . . . a man can end up with diamonds on the basis of being well liked." How does the play support or reject this assertion?

11. Most of Willy's memories—Ben's visit, Boston, the football game—are from 1928. Why does Willy's memory return to 1928? Why is the contrast between 1928 and the present significant for Willy and for the play as a whole?

TENNESSEE WILLIAMS, *THE GLASS MENAGERIE*

Tennessee Williams (1911–1983) grew up in Mississippi and Missouri, and many of his plays reflect the attitudes and customs that he encountered in his early years. Until he was eight, his family lived in genteel poverty, mostly in Mississippi. In 1919 the family moved to a lower-class neighborhood in St. Louis. Williams, who was sickly and bookish, tried to escape from poverty and family conflicts by writing and going to the movies. One of his few companions during those years was his shy and withdrawn sister, Rose.

He entered the University of Missouri in 1931, but the Depression and family poverty forced him to drop out and go to work in a shoe warehouse. After two years of this work, he suffered a nervous collapse, but he finally finished college at the University of Iowa. He then began wandering the country, doing odd jobs and also writing. His first full-length play, *Battle of Angels*, was produced in 1940 but was unsuccessful. He continued to write, however, and was able to get *The Glass Menagerie* staged in 1945. The critical and popular success of this play marked the beginning of many good years in the theater. Along with Arthur Miller, during the 1940s and 1950s Williams dominated the American stage, going on to write many one-act plays and more than fifteen full-length dramas (many of which became successful films), including *A Streetcar Named Desire* (1947, Pulitzer Prize), *The Rose Tattoo* (1951), *Cat on a Hot Tin Roof* (1955, Pulitzer Prize), *Suddenly Last Summer* (1958), and *The Night of the Iguana* (1961).

The Glass Menagerie, written in 1944 and produced with favorable reviews in Chicago and New York in 1945, is a highly autobiographical play that explores the family dynamics, delusions, and personalities of the Wingfields. Williams originally developed his ideas for the play in a short story called "Portrait of a Girl in Glass" and then in a screenplay for Metro-Goldwyn-Mayer titled "The Gentleman Caller." In these treatments as well as in *The Glass Menagerie*, Laura Wingfield is modeled after his sister, Rose Williams. The least competent member of the family, she is crippled by her own insecurity and her mother's expectations. At every opportunity, Laura withdraws into a world of glass figurines and old phonograph records left by her father when he abandoned the family. Amanda Wingfield is patterned after Williams's mother. She valiantly tries to hold the family together and provide for Laura's future, but her perspectives are skewed by her romanticized memories of a gracious southern past of plantations, formal dances, and "gentleman callers." Tom, a figure based on the playwright himself, is desperate to escape the trap of his impoverished family. He seeks to emulate the long-missing father and move out of the drab Wingfield apartment into adventure and experience.

The play offers a fascinating mixture of realistic and nonrealistic dramatic techniques. The realistic elements are the characters (excluding Tom when he narrates) and the language. This is especially true of Amanda's language, in which Williams skillfully recreates the diction and cadences characteristic of the deep south. As he points out in his production notes and stage directions, the play's structure and staging are nonrealistic. Williams employs various devices nonrealistically, including the narrator, music, lighting, and screen projections, to underscore the emotions of his characters and to explore ideas about family and personality.

One of Williams's most effective nonrealistic techniques in *The Glass Menagerie* is its structure as "a memory play," and therefore its illustration of how a first-person narrator can be used in a drama. The characters and the action are not real and they do not exist in the present. Rather, they represent Tom's memories and feelings about events that occurred approximately five years earlier, when America was in the grip of the Great Depression, when the Spanish Civil War had resulted in the imposition of a fascist dictatorship in Spain, and when World War II was beginning in Europe. As the narrator, Tom exists at the time of the action (1944), but the events he introduces are occurring in about 1939. When Tom becomes a character in the Wingfield household, he is the Tom of this earlier period, quite distinct from his identity as the present narrator. Thus, the action in the apartment is not strictly a realistic recreation of life. Instead, even though the actions and characters seem realistic, they are exaggerated and reshaped as Tom remembers them and regrets them.

TENNESSEE WILLIAMS   (1911–1983)

The Glass Menagerie _____ 1945

THE CHARACTERS

Amanda Wingfield (*the mother*)

A little woman of great but confused vitality clinging frantically to another time and place. Her characterization must be carefully created, not copied from type. She is not paranoiac, but her life is paranoia. There is much to admire in Amanda, and as much to love and pity as there is to laugh at. Certainly she has endurance and a kind of heroism, and though her foolishness makes her unwittingly cruel at times, there is tenderness in her slight person.

Laura Wingfield (*her daughter*)

Amanda, having failed to establish contact with reality, continues to live vitally in her illusions, but Laura's situation is even graver. A childhood illness has left her crippled, one leg slightly shorter than the other, and held in a brace. This defect need not be more than suggested on the stage. Stemming from this, Laura's separation increases till she is like a piece of her own glass collection, too exquisitely fragile to move from the shelf.

Tom Wingfield (*her son*)
And the narrator of the play. A poet with a job in a warehouse. His nature is not remorseless, but to escape from a trap he has to act without pity.

Jim O'Connor (*the gentleman caller*)
A nice, ordinary, young man.

PRODUCTION NOTES
Being a "memory play," *The Glass Menagerie* can be presented with unusual freedom of convention. Because of its considerably delicate or tenuous material, atmospheric touches and subtleties of direction play a particularly important part. Expressionism and all other unconventional techniques in drama have only one valid aim, and that is a closer approach to truth. When a play employs unconventional techniques, it is not, or certainly shouldn't be, trying to escape its responsibility of dealing with reality, or interpreting experience, but is actually or should be attempting to find a closer approach, a more penetrating and vivid expression of things as they are. The straight realistic play with its genuine Frigidaire and authentic ice-cubes, its characters who speak exactly as its audience speaks, corresponds to the academic landscape and has the same virtue of a photographic likeness. Everyone should know nowadays the unimportance of the photographic in art: that truth, life, or reality is an organic thing which the poetic imagination can represent or suggest, in essence, only through transformation, through changing into other forms than those which were merely present in appearance.

These remarks are not meant as a preface only to this particular play. They have to do with a conception of a new, plastic theatre which must take the place of the exhausted theatre of realistic conventions if the theatre is to resume vitality as a part of our culture.

THE SCREEN DEVICE: There is *only one important difference between the original and the acting version of the play* and that is the *omission* in the latter of the device that I tentatively included in my *original* script. This device was the use of a screen on which were projected magic-lantern slides bearing images or titles. I do not regret the omission of this device from the original Broadway production. The extraordinary power of Miss Taylor's° performance made it suitable to have the utmost simplicity in the physical production. But I think it may be interesting to some readers to see how this device was conceived. So I am putting it into the published manuscript. These images and legends, projected from behind, were cast on a section of wall between the front-room and dining-room areas, which should be indistinguishable from the rest when not in use.

The purpose of this will probably be apparent. It is to give accent to certain values in each scene. Each scene contains a particular point (or several) which is structurally the most important. In an episodic play, such as this, the basic structure or narrative line may be obscured from the audience; the effect may seem fragmentary rather than architectural. This may not be the fault of the play so much as a lack of attention in the audience. The legend or image upon the screen will strengthen the effect of what is merely allusion in the writing and allow the primary point to be made more simply and lightly than if the entire responsibility were on the spoken lines. Aside from this structural value, I think the screen will have a definite emotional appeal, less definable but just as important. An imaginative producer or director may invent many other uses for this

Miss Taylor's: The role of Amanda was first played by the American actress Laurette Taylor (1884–1946).

device than those indicated in the present script. In fact the possibilities of the device seem much larger to me than the instance of this play can possibly utilize.

THE MUSIC: Another extra-literary accent in this play is provided by the use of music. A single recurring tune, "The Glass Menagerie,"° is used to give emotional emphasis to suitable passages. This tune is like circus music, not when you are on the grounds or in the immediate vicinity of the parade, but when you are at some distance and very likely thinking of something else. It seems under those circumstances to continue almost interminably and it weaves in and out of your preoccupied consciousness; then it is the lightest, most delicate music in the world and perhaps the saddest. It expresses the surface vivacity of life with the underlying strain of immutable and inexpressible sorrow. When you look at a piece of delicately spun glass you think of two things: how beautiful it is and how easily it can be broken. Both of those ideas should be woven into the recurring tune, which dips in and out of the play as if it were carried on a wind that changes. It serves as a thread of connection and allusion between the narrator with his separate point in time and space and the subject of his story. Between each episode it returns as reference to the emotion, nostalgia, which is the first condition of the play. It is primarily Laura's music and therefore comes out most clearly when the play focuses upon her and the lovely fragility of glass which is her image.

THE LIGHTING: The lighting in the play is not realistic. In keeping with the atmosphere of memory, the stage is dim. Shafts of light are focused on selected areas or actors, sometimes in contradistinction to what is the apparent center. For instance, in the quarrel scene between Tom and Amanda, in which Laura has no active part, the clearest pool of light is on her figure. This is also true of the supper scene, when her silent figure on the sofa should remain the visual center. The light upon Laura should be distinct from the others, having a peculiar pristine clarity such as light used in early religious portraits of female saints or madonnas. A certain correspondence to light in religious paintings, such as El Greco's,° where the figures are radiant in atmosphere that is relatively dusky, could be effectively used throughout the play. (It will also permit a more effective use of the screen.) A free, imaginative use of light can be of enormous value in giving a mobile, plastic quality to plays of a more or less static nature.

Tennessee Williams

Scene 1

The Wingfield apartment is in the rear of the building, one of those vast hive-like conglomerations of cellular living-units that flower as warty growths in overcrowded urban centers of lower middle-class population and are symptomatic of the impulse of this largest and fundamentally enslaved section of American society to avoid fluidity and differentiation and to exist and function as one interfused mass of automatism.

The apartment faces an alley and is entered by a fire escape, a structure whose name is a touch of accidental poetic truth, for all of these huge buildings are always burning with the slow and implacable fires of human desperation. The fire escape is part of what we see—that is, the landing of it and steps descending from it.

"The Glass Menagerie": Original music, including this recurrent theme, was composed for the play by Paul Bowles.   *El Greco:* Greek painter (ca. 1548–1614) who lived in Spain; typical paintings have elongated and distorted figures and extremely vivid foreground lighting set against a murky background.

The scene is memory and is therefore nonrealistic. Memory takes a lot of poetic license. It omits some details; others are exaggerated, according to the emotional value of the articles it touches, for memory is seated predominantly in the heart. The interior is therefore rather dim and poetic.

At the rise of the curtain, the audience is faced with the dark, grim rear wall of the Wingfield tenement. This building is flanked on both sides by dark, narrow alleys which run into murky canyons of tangled clotheslines, garbage cans, and the sinister latticework of neighboring fire escapes. It is up and down these side alleys that exterior entrances and exits are made during the play. At the end of TOM's opening commentary, the dark tenement wall slowly becomes transparent° and reveals the interior of the ground-floor Wingfield apartment.

Nearest the audience is the living room, which also serves as a sleeping room for LAURA, the sofa unfolding to make her bed. Just beyond, separated from the living room by a wide arch or second proscenium with transparent faded portieres° (or second curtain), is the dining room. In an old-fashioned whatnot° in the living room are seen scores of transparent glass animals. A blown-up photograph of the father hangs on the wall of the living room, to the left of the archway. It is the face of a very handsome young man in a doughboy's° First World War cap. He is gallantly smiling, ineluctably smiling, as if to say "I will be smiling forever."

Also hanging on the wall, near the photograph, are a typewriter keyboard chart and a Gregg shorthand diagram. An upright typewriter on a small table stands beneath the charts.

The audience hears and sees the opening scene in the dining room through both the transparent fourth wall of the building and the transparent gauze portieres of the dining-room arch. It is during this revealing scene that the fourth wall slowly ascends, out of sight. This transparent exterior wall is not brought down again until the very end of the play, during TOM's final speech.

The narrator is an undisguised convention of the play. He takes whatever license with dramatic convention is convenient to his purposes.

TOM enters, dressed as a merchant sailor, and strolls across to the fire escape. There he stops and lights a cigarette. He addresses the audience.

TOM.   Yes, I have tricks in my pocket, I have things up my sleeve. But I am the opposite of a stage magician. He gives you illusion that has the appearance of truth. I give you truth in the pleasant disguise of illusion.

To begin with, I turn back time. I reverse it to that quaint period, the thirties, when the huge middle class of America was matriculating in a school for the blind. Their eyes had failed them, or they had failed their eyes, and so they were having their fingers pressed forcibly down on the fiery Braille alphabet of a dissolving economy.

In Spain there was revolution. Here there was only shouting and confusion. In Spain there was Guernica.° Here there were disturbances of labor, sometimes pretty violent, in otherwise peaceful cities such as Chicago, Cleveland, Saint Louis . . . This is the social background of the play.

[*Music begins to play.*]

The play is memory. Being a memory play, it is dimly lighted, it is sentimental, it is not realistic. In memory everything seems to happen to music. That explains the fiddle in the wings.

---

transparent: The wall is painted on a scrim, a transparent curtain that is opaque when lit from the front and transparent when lit from behind.   *portieres:* curtains hung in a doorway; in production, these may also be painted on a scrim.   *whatnot:* a small set of shelves for ornaments. *doughboy:* popular name for an American infantryman during World War I.   *Guernica:* a Basque town that was destroyed in 1937 by German planes fighting on General Franco's side during the Spanish Civil War. The huge mural *Guernica*, painted by Pablo Picasso, depicts the horror of that bombardment.

I am the narrator of the play, and also a character in it. The other characters are my mother, Amanda, my sister, Laura, and a gentleman caller who appears in the final scenes. He is the most realistic character in the play, being an emissary from a world of reality that we were somehow set apart from. But since I have a poet's weakness for symbols, I am using this character also as a symbol; he is the long-delayed but always expected something that we live for.

There is a fifth character in the play who doesn't appear except in this larger-than-life-size photograph over the mantel. This is our father who left us a long time ago. He was a telephone man who fell in love with long distances; he gave up his job with the telephone company and skipped the light fantastic out of town . . .

The last we heard of him was a picture postcard from Mazatlan, on the Pacific coast of Mexico, containing a message of two words: "Hello—Goodbye!" and no address.

I think the rest of the play will explain itself. . . .

[*AMANDA's voice becomes audible through the portieres.*]

[*Legend on screen:* "Où sont les neiges."°]

TOM divides the portieres and enters the dining room. AMANDA and LAURA are seated at a drop-leaf table. Eating is indicated by gestures without food or utensils. AMANDA faces the audience. TOM and LAURA are seated profile. The interior has lit up softly and through the scrim we see AMANDA and LAURA seated at the table.]

AMANDA.   [*calling*] Tom?

TOM.   Yes, Mother.

AMANDA.   We can't say grace until you come to the table!

TOM.   Coming, Mother. [*He bows slightly and withdraws, reappearing a few moments later in his place at the table.*]

AMANDA.   [*to her son*] Honey, don't *push* with your *fingers*. If you have to push with   5
something, the thing to push with is a crust of bread. And chew—chew! Animals have secretions in their stomachs which enable them to digest food without mastication, but human beings are supposed to chew their food before they swallow it down. Eat food leisurely, son, and really enjoy it. A well-cooked meal has lots of delicate flavors that have to be held in the mouth for appreciation. So chew your food and give your salivary glands a chance to function!

[*TOM deliberately lays his imaginary fork down and pushes his chair back from the table.*]

TOM.   I haven't enjoyed one bite of this dinner because of your constant directions on how to eat it. It's you that make me rush through meals with your hawklike attention to every bite I take. Sickening—spoils my appetite—all this discussion of—animals' secretion—salivary glands—mastication!

AMANDA.   [*lightly*] Temperament like a Metropolitan star.°

[*TOM rises and walks toward the living room.*]

You're not excused from the table.

TOM.   I'm getting a cigarette.

AMANDA.   You smoke too much.   10

---

1 S.D.: *"Où sont les neiges":* "Where are the snows (of yesteryear)," refrain from "The Ballade of Dead Ladies" by the French poet François Villon (ca. 1431–1463).   8 *Metropolitan star:* the Metropolitan Opera in New York City; opera stars are traditionally considered to be highly temperamental.

[*LAURA rises.*]

> LAURA.   I'll bring in the blanc mange.°

[*TOM remains standing with his cigarette by the portieres.*]

> AMANDA.   [*rising*] No, sister, no, sister°—you be the lady this time and I'll be the darky.
> LAURA.   I'm already up.
> AMANDA.   Resume your seat, little sister—I want you to stay fresh and pretty—for gentlemen callers!
> LAURA.   [*sitting down*] I'm not expecting any gentlemen callers.   15
> AMANDA.   [*crossing out to the kitchenette, airily*] Sometimes they come when they are least expected! Why, I remember one Sunday afternoon in Blue Mountain°—

[*She enters the kitchenette.*]

> TOM.   I know what's coming!
> LAURA.   Yes. But let her tell it.
> TOM.   Again?
> LAURA.   She loves to tell it.   20

[*AMANDA returns with a bowl of dessert.*]

> AMANDA.   One Sunday afternoon in Blue Mountain—your mother received—*seventeen!*—gentlemen callers! Why, sometimes there weren't chairs enough to accommodate them all. We had to send the nigger over to bring in folding chairs from the parish house.
> TOM.   [*remaining at the portieres*] How did you entertain those gentlemen callers?
> AMANDA.   I understood the art of conversation!
> TOM.   I bet you could talk.
> AMANDA.   Girls in those days *knew* how to talk, I can tell you.   25
> TOM.   Yes?

[*Image on screen: AMANDA as a girl on a porch, greeting callers.*]

> AMANDA.   They knew how to entertain their gentlemen callers. It wasn't enough for a girl to be possessed of a pretty face and a graceful figure—although I wasn't slighted in either respect. She also needed to have a nimble wit and a tongue to meet all occasions.
> TOM.   What did you talk about?
> AMANDA.   Things of importance going on in the world! Never anything coarse or common or vulgar.

[*She addresses TOM as though he were seated in the vacant chair at the table though he remains by the portieres. He plays this scene as though reading from a script.°*]

---

11 *blanc mange:* a bland molded pudding or custard.   12 *sister:* In the south of Amanda's youth, the oldest daughter in a family was frequently called "sister" by her parents and siblings.   16 *Blue Mountain:* a town in northern Mississippi modeled after Clarksdale, where Williams spent much of his youth. The area is at the northern edge of the Mississippi Delta, a large fertile plain that supports numerous plantations. This is the recollected world of Amanda's youth—plantations, wealth, servants, and gentlemen callers who were the sons of cotton planters.   29.1 *script:* Here Tom becomes both a character in the play and the stage manager.

My callers were gentleman—all! Among my callers were some of the most prominent young planters of the Mississippi Delta—planters and sons of planters!

[*TOM motions for music and a spot of light on* AMANDA. *Her eyes lift, her face glows, her voice becomes rich and elegiac.*

[*Screen legend:* "Où sont les neiges d'antan?"°]

There was young Champ Laughlin who later became vice-president of the Delta Planters Bank. Hadley Stevenson who was drowned in Moon Lake and left his widow one hundred and fifty thousand in Government bonds. There were the Cutrere brothers, Wesley and Bates. Bates was one of my bright particular beaux! He got in a quarrel with that wild Wainwright boy. They shot it out on the floor of Moon Lake Casino. Bates was shot through the stomach. Died in the ambulance on his way to Memphis. His widow was also well provided-for, came into eight or ten thousand acres, that's all. She married him on the rebound—never loved her—carried my picture on him the night he died! And there was that boy that every girl in the Delta had set her cap for! That beautiful, brilliant young Fitzhugh boy from Greene County!

TOM.   What did he leave his widow?   30

AMANDA.   He never married! Gracious, you talk as though all of my old admirers had turned up their toes to the daisies!

TOM.   Isn't this the first you've mentioned that still survives?

AMANDA.   That Fitzhugh boy went North and made a fortune—came to be known as the Wolf of Wall Street! He had the Midas touch,° whatever he touched turned to gold! And I could have been Mrs. Duncan J. Fitzhugh, mind you! But—I picked your *father!*

LAURA.   [*rising*] Mother, let me clear the table.

AMANDA.   No, dear, you go in front and study your typewriter chart. Or practice   35
your shorthand a little. Stay fresh and pretty!—It's almost time for our gentlemen callers to start arriving. [*She flounces girlishly toward the kitchenette.*] How many do you suppose we're going to entertain this afternoon?

[*TOM throws down the paper and jumps up with a groan.*]

LAURA.   [*alone in the dining room*] I don't believe we're going to receive any, Mother.

AMANDA.   [*reappearing airily*] What? No one?—not one? You must be joking!

[*LAURA nervously echoes her laugh. She slips in a fugitive manner through the half-open portieres and draws them gently behind her. A shaft of very clear light is thrown on her face against the faded tapestry of the curtains. Faintly the music of "The Glass Menagerie" is heard as she continues lightly:*]

Not one gentleman caller? It can't be true! There must be a flood, there must have been a tornado!

LAURA.   It isn't a flood, it's not a tornado, Mother. I'm just not popular like you were in Blue Mountain. . . .

29.2 *"Où sont les neiges d'antan?":* Where are the snows of yesteryear? See p. 1293.   33 *Midas touch:* In Greek mythology, King Midas was given the power to turn everything he touched into gold.

[*Tom utters another groan. Laura glances at him with a faint, apologetic smile. Her voice catches a little:*]

Mother's afraid I'm going to be an old maid.

[*The scene dims out with the "Glass Menagerie" music.*]

Scene 2

On the dark stage the screen is lighted with the image of blue roses. Gradually Laura's figure becomes apparent and the screen goes out. The music subsides.

Laura *is seated in the delicate ivory chair at the small clawfoot table. She wears a dress of soft violet material for a kimono—her hair is tied back from her forehead with a ribbon. She is washing and polishing her collection of glass.* Amanda *appears on the fire escape steps. At the sound of her ascent,* Laura *catches her breath, thrusts the bowl of ornaments away, and seats herself stiffly before the diagram of the typewriter keyboard as though it held her spellbound. Something has happened to* Amanda*. It is written in her face as she climbs to the landing: a look that is grim and hopeless and a little absurd. She has on one of those cheap or imitation velvety-looking cloth coats with imitation fur collar. Her hat is five or six years old, one of those dreadful cloche hats that were worn in the late Twenties, and she is clutching an enormous black patent-leather pocketbook with nickel clasps and initials. This is her full-dress outfit, the one she usually wears to the D.A.R.° Before entering she looks through the door. She purses her lips, opens her eyes very wide, rolls them upward and shakes her head. Then she slowly lets herself in the door. Seeing her mother's expression,* Laura *touches her lips with a nervous gesture.*

LAURA.   Hello, Mother, I was—[*She makes a nervous gesture toward the chart on the wall.* Amanda *leans against the shut door and stares at* Laura *with a martyred look.*]

AMANDA.   Deception? Deception? [*She slowly removes her hat and gloves, continuing the sweet suffering stare. She lets the hat and gloves fall on the floor—a bit of acting.*]

LAURA.   [*shakily*] How was the D.A.R. meeting?

[Amanda *slowly opens her purse and removes a dainty white handkerchief which she shakes out delicately and delicately touches to her lips and nostrils.*]

Didn't you go to the D.A.R. meeting, Mother?

AMANDA.   [*faintly, almost inaudibly*] —No.—No. [*then more forcibly:*] I did not have the strength—to go to the D.A.R. In fact, I did not have the courage! I wanted to find a hole in the ground and hide myself in it forever! [*She crosses slowly to the wall and removes the diagram of the typewriter keyboard. She holds it in front of her for a second, staring at it sweetly and sorrowfully—then bites her lips and tears it in two pieces.*]

LAURA.   [*faintly*] Why did you do that, Mother?   5

[Amanda *repeats the same procedure with the chart of the Gregg Alphabet.*]

Why are you—

AMANDA.   Why? Why? How old are you, Laura?

LAURA.   Mother, you know my age.

AMANDA.   I thought you were an adult; it seems that I was mistaken. [*She crosses slowly to the sofa and sinks down and stares at* Laura*.*]

0.2 *D.A.R.:* Daughters of the American Revolution, a patriotic women's organization (founded in 1890) open only to women whose ancestors aided the American Revolution.

LAURA.   Please don't stare at me, Mother.

[*AMANDA closes her eyes and lowers her head. There is a ten-second pause.*]

AMANDA.   What are we going to do, what is going to become of us, what is the   10
future?

[*There is another pause.*]

LAURA.   Has something happened, Mother?

[*AMANDA draws a long breath, takes out the handkerchief again, goes through the dabbing process.*]

Mother, has—something happened?

AMANDA.   I'll be all right in a minute, I'm just bewildered—[*She hesitates.*]—by
life. . . .

LAURA.   Mother, I wish that you would tell me what's happened!

AMANDA.   As you know, I was supposed to be inducted into my office at the D.A.R.
this afternoon.

[*Screen image: A swarm of typewriters.*]

But I stopped off at Rubicam's Business College to speak to your teachers about
your having a cold and ask them what progress they thought you were making down
there.

LAURA.   Oh. . . .   15

AMANDA.   I went to the typing instructor and introduced myself as your mother.
She didn't know who you were.

"Wingfield," she said, "We don't have any such student enrolled at the school!"

I assured her she did, that you had been going to classes since early in January.

"I wonder," she said, "if you could be talking about that terribly shy little girl who
dropped out of school after only a few days' attendance?"

"No," I said, "Laura, my daughter, has been going to school every day for the past
six weeks!"

"Excuse me," she said. She took the attendance book out and there was your
name, unmistakably printed, and all the dates you were absent until they decided that
you had dropped out of school.

I still said, "No, there must have been some mistake! There must have been some
mix-up in the records!"

And she said, "No—I remember her perfectly now. Her hands shook so that she
couldn't hit the right keys! The first time we gave a speed test, she broke down completely—was sick at the stomach and almost had to be carried into the wash room! After
that morning she never showed up any more. We phoned the house but never got any
answer"—While I was working at Famous-Barr,° I suppose, demonstrating those—

[*She indicates a brassiere with her hands.*]

Oh! I felt so weak I could barely keep on my feet! I had to sit down while they got me a
glass of water! Fifty dollars' tuition, all of our plans—my hopes and ambitions for you—
just gone up the spout, just gone up the spout like that.

16.8 *Famous-Barr:* a department store in St. Louis.

[*Laura draws a long breath and gets awkwardly to her feet. She crosses to the Victrola and winds it up.*°]

What are you doing?

    Laura.   Oh! [*She releases the handle and returns to her seat.*]

    Amanda.   Laura, where have you been going when you've gone out pretending that you were going to business college?

    Laura.   I've just been going out walking.

    Amanda.   That's not true.   20

    Laura.   It is. I just went walking.

    Amanda.   Walking? Walking? In winter? Deliberately courting pneumonia in that light coat? Where did you walk to, Laura?

    Laura.   All sorts of places—mostly in the park.

    Amanda.   Even after you'd started catching that cold?

    Laura.   It was the lesser of two evils, Mother.   25

[*Screen image: Winter scene in a park.*]

I couldn't go back there. I—threw up—on the floor!

    Amanda.   From half past seven till after five every day you mean to tell me you walked around the park, because you wanted to make me think that you were still going to Rubicam's Business College?

    Laura.   It wasn't as bad as it sounds. I went inside places to get warmed up.

    Amanda.   Inside where?

    Laura.   I went in the art museum and the bird houses at the Zoo. I visited the penguins every day! Sometimes I did without lunch and went to the movies. Lately I've been spending most of my afternoons in the Jewel Box, that big glass house where they raise the tropical flowers.

    Amanda.   You did all this to deceive me, just for deception? [*Laura looks down.*]   30
Why?

    Laura.   Mother, when you're disappointed, you get that awful suffering look on your face, like the picture of Jesus' mother in the museum!

    Amanda.   Hush!

    Laura.   I couldn't face it.

[*There is a pause. A whisper of strings is heard. Legend on screen: "The Crust of Humility."*]

    Amanda.   [*hopelessly fingering the huge pocketbook*] So what are we going to do the rest of our lives? Stay home and watch the parades go by? Amuse ourselves with the glass menagerie, darling? Eternally play those worn-out phonograph records your father left as a painful reminder of him? We won't have a business career—we've given that up because it gave us nervous indigestion! [*She laughs wearily.*] What is there left but dependency all our lives? I know so well what becomes of unmarried women who aren't prepared to occupy a position. I've seen such pitiful cases in the South—barely tolerated spinsters living upon the grudging patronage of sister's husband or brother's wife!—stuck away in some little mousetrap of a room—encouraged by one in-law to visit another—little birdlike women without any nest—eating the crust of humility all their life!

16.11, S.D., *winds it up:* Laura is using a spring-powered (rather than electric) phonograph that has to be rewound frequently.

Is that the future that we've mapped out for ourselves? I swear it's the only alternative I can think of! [*She pauses.*] It isn't a very pleasant alternative, is it? [*She pauses again.*] Of course—some girls *do marry.*

[*LAURA twists her hands nervously.*]

Haven't you ever liked some boy?

LAURA.   Yes. I liked one once. [*She rises.*] I came across his picture a while ago.   35
AMANDA.   [*with some interest*] He gave you his picture?
LAURA.   No, it's in the yearbook.
AMANDA.   [*disappointed*] Oh—a high school boy.

[*Screen image: JIM as the high school hero bearing a silver cup.*]

LAURA.   Yes. His name was Jim. [*She lifts the heavy annual from the claw-foot table.*] Here he is in *The Pirates of Penzance.*°
AMANDA.   [*absently*] The what?   40
LAURA.   The operetta the senior class put on. He had a wonderful voice and we sat across the aisle from each other Mondays, Wednesdays and Fridays in the Aud. Here he is with the silver cup for debating! See his grin?
AMANDA.   [*absently*] He must have had a jolly disposition.
LAURA.   He used to call me—Blue Roses.

[*Screen image: Blue roses.*]

AMANDA.   Why did he call you such a name as that?
LAURA.   When I had that attack of pleurosis—he asked me what was the matter   45
when I came back. I said pleurosis—he thought that I said Blue Roses! So that's what he always called me after that. Whenever he saw me, he'd holler, "Hello, Blue Roses!" I didn't care for the girl that he went out with. Emily Meisenbach. Emily was the best-dressed girl at Soldan. She never struck me, though, as being sincere . . . It says in the Personal Section—they're engaged. That's—six years ago! They must be married by now.
AMANDA.   Girls that aren't cut out for business careers usually wind up married to some nice man. [*She gets up with a spark of revival.*] Sister, that's what you'll do!

[*LAURA utters a startled, doubtful laugh. She reaches quickly for a piece of glass.*]

LAURA.   But, Mother—
AMANDA.   Yes? [*She goes over to the photograph.*]
LAURA.   [*in a tone of frightened apology*] I'm—crippled!
AMANDA.   Nonsense! Laura, I've told you never, never to use that word.   50
Why, you're not crippled, you just have a little defect—hardly noticeable, even! When people have some slight disadvantage like that, they cultivate other things to make up for it—develop charm—and vivacity—and—*charm*! That's all you have to do! [*She turns again to the photograph.*] One thing your father had *plenty of*—was *charm*!

[*The scene fades out with music.*]

---

39 *The Pirates of Penzance:* a comic light opera (1879) by Gilbert and Sullivan.

Scene 3

[Legend on screen: "After the fiasco—"

TOM *speaks from the fire escape landing.]*

TOM. After the fiasco at Rubicam's Business College, the idea of getting a gentleman caller for Laura began to play a more and more important part in Mother's calculations. It became an obsession. Like some archetype of the universal unconscious, the image of the gentleman caller haunted our small apartment. . . .

[Screen image: A young man at the door of a house with flowers.]

An evening at home rarely passed without some allusion to this image, this specter, this hope. . . . Even when he wasn't mentioned, his presence hung in Mother's preoccupied look and in my sister's frightened, apologetic manner—hung like a sentence passed upon the Wingfields!

Mother was a woman of action as well as words. She began to take logical steps in the planned direction. Late that winter and in the early spring—realizing that extra money would be needed to properly feather the nest and plume the bird—she conducted a vigorous campaign on the telephone, roping in subscribers to one of those magazines for matrons called *The Homemaker's Companion,* the type of journal that features the serialized sublimations of ladies of letters who think in terms of delicate cuplike breasts, slim, tapering waists, rich, creamy thighs, eyes like wood smoke in autumn, fingers that soothe and caress like strains of music, bodies as powerful as Etruscan sculpture.

[Screen image: The cover of a glamor magazine.

AMANDA *enters with the telephone on a long extension cord. She is spotlighted in the dim stage.]*

AMANDA. Ida Scott? This is Amanda Wingfield! We *missed* you at the D.A.R. last Monday! I said to myself: She's probably suffering with that sinus condition! How is that sinus condition?

Horrors! Heaven have mercy!—You're a Christian martyr, yes, that's what you are, a Christian martyr!

Well, I just now happened to notice that your subscription to the *Companion's* about to expire! Yes, it expires with the next issue, honey!—just when that wonderful new serial by Bessie Mae Hopper is getting off to such an exciting start. Oh, honey, it's something that you can't miss! You remember how *Gone with the Wind°* took everybody by storm? You simply couldn't go out if you hadn't read it. All everybody *talked* was Scarlett O'Hara. Well, this is a book that critics already compare to *Gone with the Wind.* It's the *Gone with the Wind* of the post-World-War generation!—What?—Burning?—Oh, honey, don't let them burn, go take a look in the oven and I'll hold the wire! Heavens— I think she's hung up!

[The scene dims out.]

[Legend on screen: "You think I'm in love with Continental Shoemakers?"]

2.3 *Gone with the Wind:* popular novel (1936) by Margaret Mitchell (1900–1949), set in the south before, during, and after the Civil War. Scarlett O'Hara was the heroine. The "storm" was perhaps caused as much by the film (1939) as by the novel.

[*Before the lights come up again, the violent voices of* TOM *and* AMANDA *are heard. They are quarreling behind the portieres. In front of them stands* LAURA *with clenched hands and panicky expression. A clear pool of light is on her figure throughout this scene.*]

TOM.   What in Christ's name am I—
AMANDA.   [*shrilly*] Don't you use that—   5
TOM.   —supposed to do!
AMANDA.   —expression! Not in my—
TOM.   Ohhh!
AMANDA.   —presence! Have you gone out of your senses?
TOM.   I have, that's true, *driven* out!
AMANDA.   What is the matter with you, you—big—big—IDIOT!   10
TOM.   Look!—I've got *no thing*, no single thing—
AMANDA.   Lower your voice!
TOM.   —in my life here that I can call my OWN! Everything is—
AMANDA.   Stop that shouting!
TOM.   Yesterday you confiscated my books! You had the nerve to—   15
AMANDA.   I took that horrible novel back to the library—yes! That hideous book
by that insane Mr. Lawrence.°

[*TOM laughs wildly.*]

I cannot control the output of diseased minds or people who cater to them—

[*TOM laughs still more wildly.*]

BUT I WON'T ALLOW SUCH FILTH BROUGHT INTO MY HOUSE! No, no, no, no, no!
TOM.   House, house! Who pays rent on it, who makes a slave of himself to—
AMANDA.   [*fairly screeching*] Don't you DARE to—
TOM.   No, no, *I* mustn't say things! *I've* got to just—
AMANDA.   Let me tell you—   20
TOM.   I don't want to hear any more!

[*He tears the portieres open. The dining-room area is lit with turgid smoky red glow. Now we see* AMANDA; *her hair is in metal curlers and she is wearing a very old bathrobe, much too large for her slight figure, a relic of the faithless Mr. Wingfield. The upright typewriter now stands on the dropleaf table, along with a wild disarray of manuscripts. The quarrel was probably precipitated by* AMANDA'S *interruption of* TOM'S *creative labor. A chair lies overthrown on the floor. Their gesticulating shadows are cast on the ceiling by the fiery glow.*]

AMANDA.   You *will* hear more, you—
TOM.   No, I won't hear more, I'm going out!
AMANDA.   You come right back in—
TOM.   Out, out, out! Because I'm—   25
AMANDA.   Come back here, Tom Wingfield! I'm not through talking to you!
TOM.   Oh, go—
LAURA.   [*desperately*]—Tom!
AMANDA.   You're going to listen, and no more insolence from you! I'm at the end
of my patience!

16 *Lawrence:* D. H. Lawrence (1885–1930), English poet and fiction writer, popularly known as an advocate of passion and sexuality. See "The Horse Dealer's Daughter," p. 372.

[*He comes back toward her.*]

TOM. What do you think I'm at? Aren't I supposed to have any patience to reach   30
the end of, Mother? I know, I know. It seems unimportant to you, what I'm *doing*—what
I *want* to do—having a little *difference* between them! You don't think that—

AMANDA. I think you've been doing things that you're ashamed of. That's why
you act like this. I don't believe that you go every night to the movies. Nobody goes to
the movies night after night. Nobody in their right minds goes to the movies as often as
you pretend to. People don't go to the movies at nearly midnight, and movies don't let
out at two A.M. Come in stumbling. Muttering to yourself like a maniac! You get three
hours' sleep and then go to work. Oh, I can picture the way you're doing down there.
Moping, doping, because you're in no condition.

TOM. [*wildly*] No, I'm in no condition!

AMANDA. What right have you got to jeopardize your job? Jeopardize the security of us all? How do you think we'd manage if you were—

TOM. Listen! You think I'm crazy about the *warehouse*? [*He bends fiercely toward
her slight figure.*] You think I'm in love with the Continental Shoemakers? You think I
want to spend fifty-five *years* down there in that—*celotex interior!* with—*fluorescent—tubes!*
Look! I'd rather somebody picked up a crowbar and battered out my brains—than go
back mornings! I *go!* Every time you come in yelling that God damn "*Rise and Shine!*"
"*Rise and Shine!*" I say to myself, "How *lucky dead* people are!" But I get up. I *go!* For sixty-
five dollars a month I give up all that I dream of doing and being *ever!* And you say self—
self's all I ever think of. Why, listen, if self is what I thought of, Mother, I'd be where he
is—GONE! [*He points to his father's picture.*] As far as the system of transportation reaches!
[*He starts past her. She grabs his arm.*] Don't grab at me, Mother!

AMANDA. Where are you going?   35

TOM. I'm going to the *movies!*

AMANDA. I don't believe that lie!

[*TOM crouches toward her, overtowering her tiny figure. She backs away, gasping.*]

TOM. I'm going to opium dens! Yes, opium dens, dens of vice and criminals'
hangouts, Mother. I've joined the Hogan Gang,° I'm a hired assassin, I carry a tommy
gun in a violin case! I run a string of cat houses in the Valley! They call me Killer, Killer
Wingfield, I'm leading a double-life, a simple, honest warehouse worker by day, by night
a dynamic *czar* of the *underworld, Mother*. I go to gambling casinos, I spin away fortunes
on the roulette table! I wear a patch over one eye and a false mustache, sometimes I put
on green whiskers. On those occasions they call me—*El Diablo!*° Oh, I could tell you
many things to make you sleepless! My enemies plan to dynamite this place. They're
going to blow us all sky-high some night! I'll be glad, very happy, and so will you! You'll
go up, up on a broomstick, over Blue Mountain with seventeen gentlemen callers! You
ugly—babbling old—*witch*. . . .

[*He goes through a series of violent, clumsy movements, seizing his overcoat, lunging to the door,
pulling it fiercely open. The women watch him, aghast. His arm catches in the sleeve of the coat
as he struggles to pull it on. For a moment he is pinioned by the bulky garment. With an outraged
groan he tears the coat off again, splitting the shoulder of it, and hurls it across the room. It
strikes against the shelf of LAURA's glass collection, and there is a tinkle of shattering glass. LAURA
cries out as if wounded.*]

38 *Hogan Gang:* one of the major criminal organizations in St. Louis in the 1930s.   *El Diablo:*
the devil.

Music.

Screen legend: "The Glass Menagerie."]

LAURA.   [*shrilly*] My glass!—menagerie. . . . [*She covers her face and turns away.*]

[*But* AMANDA *is still stunned and stupefied by the "ugly witch" so that she barely notices this occurrence. Now she recovers her speech.*]

AMANDA.   [*in an awful voice*] I won't speak to you—until you apologize!   40

[*She crosses through the portieres and draws them together behind her.* TOM *is left with* LAURA. LAURA *clings weakly to the mantel with her face averted.* TOM *stares at her stupidly for a moment. Then he crosses to the shelf. He drops awkwardly on his knees to collect the fallen glass, glancing at* LAURA *as if he would speak but couldn't.*]

"The Glass Menagerie" music steals in as the scene dims out.]

Scene 4

The interior of the apartment is dark. There is a faint light in the alley. A deep-voiced bell in a church is tolling the hour of five.

TOM appears at the top of the alley. After each solemn boom of the bell in the tower, he shakes a little noisemaker or rattle as if to express the tiny spasm of man in contrast to the sustained power and dignity of the Almighty. This and the unsteadiness of his advance make it evident that he has been drinking. As he climbs the few steps to the fire escape landing light steals up inside. LAURA *appears in the front room in a nightdress. She notices that* TOM's *bed is empty.* TOM *fishes in his pockets for his door key, removing a motley assortment of articles in the search, including a shower of movie ticket stubs and an empty bottle. At last he finds the key, but just as he is about to insert it, it slips from his fingers. He strikes a match and crouches below the door.*

TOM.   [*bitterly*] One crack—and it falls through!

[LAURA *opens the door.*]

LAURA.   Tom! Tom, what are you doing?
TOM.   Looking for a door key.
LAURA.   Where have you been all this time?
TOM.   I have been to the movies.   5
LAURA.   All this time at the movies?
TOM.   There was a very long program. There was a Garbo° picture and a Mickey Mouse and a travelogue and a newsreel and a preview of coming attractions. And there was an organ solo and a collection for the Milk Fund—simultaneously—which ended up in a terrible fight between a fat lady and an usher!
LAURA.   [*innocently*] Did you have to stay through everything?
TOM.   Of course! And, oh I forgot! There was a big stage show! The headliner on this stage show was Malvolio° the Magician. He performed wonderful tricks, many of them, such as pouring water back and forth between pitchers. First it turned to wine and then it turned to beer and then it turned to whisky. I know it was whisky it finally

---

7 *Garbo:* Greta Garbo (1905–1990), Swedish star of American silent and early sound films.
9 *Malvolio:* the name, borrowed from a puritanical character in Shakespeare's *Twelfth Night*, means "malevolence" or "ill-will."

turned into because he needed somebody to come up out of the audience to help him, and I came up—both shows! It was Kentucky Straight Bourbon. A very generous fellow, he gave souvenirs. [*He pulls from his back pocket a shimmering rainbow-colored scarf.*] He gave me this. This is his magic scarf. You can have it, Laura. You wave it over a canary cage and you get a bowl of goldfish. You wave it over the goldfish bowl and they fly away canaries. . . . But the wonderfullest trick of all was the coffin trick. We nailed him into a coffin and he got out of the coffin without removing one nail. [*He has come inside.*] There is a trick that would come in handy for me—get me out of this two-by-four situation! [*He flops onto the bed and starts removing his shoes.*]

    LAURA.   Tom—shhh!   10

    TOM.   What're you shushing me for?

    LAURA.   You'll wake up Mother.

    TOM.   Goody, goody! Pay 'er back for all those "Rise an' Shines." [*He lies down, groaning.*] You know it don't take much intelligence to get yourself into a nailed-up coffin, Laura. But who in hell ever got himself out of one without removing one nail?

[*As if in answer, the father's grinning photograph lights up. The scene dims out.*]

[*Immediately following, the church bell is heard striking six. At the sixth stroke the alarm clock goes off in* AMANDA'S *room, and after a few moments we hear her calling: "Rise and Shine! Rise and Shine! Laura, go tell your brother to rise and shine!"*]

    TOM.   [*sitting up slowly*] I'll rise—but I won't shine.

[*The light increases.*]

    AMANDA.   Laura, tell your brother his coffee is ready.   15

[*LAURA *slips into the front room.*]

    LAURA.   Tom!—It's nearly seven. Don't make Mother nervous.

[*He stares at her stupidly.*]

[*Beseechingly.*] Tom, speak to Mother this morning. Make up with her, apologize, speak to her!

    TOM.   She won't to me. It's her that started not speaking.

    LAURA.   If you just say you're sorry she'll start speaking.   20

    TOM.   Her not speaking—is that such a tragedy?

    LAURA.   Please—please!

    AMANDA.   [*calling from the kitchenette*] Laura, are you going to do what I asked you to do, or do I have to get dressed and go out myself?

    LAURA.   Going, going—soon as I get on my coat!

[*She pulls on a shapeless felt hat with a nervous, jerky movement, pleadingly glancing at* TOM. *She rushes awkwardly for her coat. The coat is one of* AMANDA'S, *inaccurately made-over, the sleeves too short for* LAURA.]

Butter and what else?

    AMANDA.   [*entering from the kitchenette*] Just butter. Tell them to charge it.

    LAURA.   Mother, they make such faces when I do that.

    AMANDA.   Sticks and stones can break our bones, but the expression on Mr.   25
Garfinkel's face won't harm us! Tell your brother his coffee is getting cold.

LAURA.   [*at the door*] Do what I asked you, will you, will you, Tom?

[*He looks sullenly away.*]

AMANDA.   Laura, go now or just don't go at all!
LAURA.   [*rushing out*] Going—going!

[*A second later she cries out. TOM springs up and crosses to the door. TOM opens the door.*]

TOM.   Laura?
LAURA.   I'm all right. I slipped, but I'm all right.   30
AMANDA.   [*peering anxiously after her*] If anyone breaks a leg on those fire-escape steps, the landlord ought to be sued for every cent he possesses! [*She shuts the door. Now she remembers she isn't speaking to TOM and returns to the other room.*]

[*As TOM comes listlessly for his coffee, she turns her back to him and stands rigidly facing the window on the gloomy gray vault of the areaway. Its light on her face with its aged but childish features is cruelly sharp, satirical as a Daumier print.°*]

The music of "Ave Maria"° is heard softly.

TOM glances sheepishly but sullenly at her averted figure and slumps at the table. The coffee is scalding hot; he sips it and gasps and spits it back in the cup. At his gasp, AMANDA catches her breath and half turns. Then she catches herself and turns back to the window. TOM blows on his coffee, glancing sidewise at his mother. She clears her throat. TOM clears his. He starts to rise, sinks back down again, scratches his head, clears his throat again. AMANDA coughs. TOM raises his cup in both hands to blow on it, his eyes staring over the rim of it at his mother for several moments. Then he slowly sets the cup down and awkwardly and hesitantly rises from the chair.]

TOM.   [*hoarsely*] Mother. I—I apologize, Mother.

[*AMANDA draws a quick, shuddering breath. Her face works grotesquely. She breaks into childlike tears.*]

I'm sorry for what I said, for everything that I said, I didn't mean it.
AMANDA.   [*sobbingly*] My devotion has made me a witch and so I make myself hateful to my children!
TOM.   *No*, you *don't*.
AMANDA.   I worry so much, don't sleep, it makes me nervous!   35
TOM.   [*gently*] I understand that.
AMANDA.   I've had to put up a solitary battle all these years. But you're my right-hand bower!° Don't fall down, don't fail!
TOM.   [*gently*] I try, Mother.
AMANDA.   [*with great enthusiasm*] Try and you will *succeed!* [*The notion makes her breathless.*] Why, you—you're just *full* of natural endowments! Both of my children—they're *unusual* children! Don't you think I know it? I'm so—*proud!* Happy and—feel I've—so much to be thankful for but—promise me one thing, son!
TOM.   What, Mother?   40
AMANDA.   Promise, son, you'll—never be a drunkard!

31.2 *Daumier print:* Honoré Daumier (1808–1879), French painter and engraver whose prints frequently satirized his society.   31.3 *"Ave Maria":* a Roman Catholic prayer to the Virgin Mary; the musical setting called for here is by Franz Schubert (1797–1828).   37 *right-hand bower,* or *right bower:* the Jack of trump in the card game *500*, the second-highest card (below the joker).

TOM. [*turns to her grinning*] I will never be a drunkard, Mother.

AMANDA. That's what frightened me so, that you'd be drinking! Eat a bowl of Purina!

TOM. Just coffee, Mother.

AMANDA. Shredded wheat biscuit? 45

TOM. No. No, Mother, just coffee.

AMANDA. You can't put in a day's work on an empty stomach. You've got ten minutes—don't gulp! Drinking too-hot liquids makes cancer of the stomach. . . . Put cream in.

TOM. No, thank you.

AMANDA. To cool it.

TOM. No! No, thank you, I want it black. 50

AMANDA. I know, but it's not good for you. We have to do all that we can to build ourselves up. In these trying times we live in, all that we have to cling to is—each other. . . . That's why it's so important to—Tom, I—I sent out your sister so I could discuss something with you. If you hadn't spoken I would have spoken to you. [*She sits down.*]

TOM. [*gently*] What is it, Mother, that you want to discuss?

AMANDA. *Laura!*

[*TOM puts his cup down slowly.*]

[*Legend on screen "Laura." Music: "The Glass Menagerie."*]

TOM. —Oh.—Laura . . .

AMANDA. [*touching his sleeve*] You know how Laura is. So quiet but—still water 55 runs deep! She notices things and I think she—broods about them.

[*TOM looks up.*]

A few days ago I came in and she was crying.

TOM. What about?

AMANDA. You.

TOM. Me?

AMANDA. She has an idea that you're not happy here.

TOM. What gave her that idea? 60

AMANDA. What gives her any idea? However, you do act strangely. I—I'm not criticizing, understand *that!* I know your ambitions do not lie in the warehouse, that like everybody in the whole wide world—you've had to—make sacrifices, but—Tom—Tom—life's not easy, it calls for—Spartan endurance! There's so many things in my heart that I cannot describe to you! I've never told you but I—*loved* your father. . . .

TOM. [*gently*] I know that, Mother.

AMANDA. And you—when I see you taking after his ways! Staying out late—and—well, you *had* been drinking the night you were in that—terrifying condition! Laura says that you hate the apartment and that you go out nights to get away from it! Is that true, Tom?

TOM. No. You say there's so much in your heart that you can't describe to me. That's true of me, too. There's so much in my heart that I can't describe to *you!* So let's respect each other's—

AMANDA. But, why—*why,* Tom—are you always so *restless?* Where do you *go to,* 65 nights?

TOM.   I—go to the movies.

AMANDA.   Why do you go to the movies so much, Tom?

TOM.   I go to the movies because—I like adventure. Adventure is something I don't have much of at work, so I go to the movies.

AMANDA.   But, Tom, you go to the movies *entirely* too *much!*

TOM.   I like a lot of adventure.   70

[*AMANDA looks baffled, then hurt. As the familiar inquisition resumes, TOM becomes hard and impatient again. AMANDA slips back into her querulous attitude toward him.*

Image on screen: A sailing vessel with Jolly Roger.°]

AMANDA.   Most young men find adventure in their careers.

TOM.   Then most young men are not employed in a warehouse.

AMANDA.   The world is full of young men employed in warehouses and offices and factories.

TOM.   Do all of them find adventure in their careers?

AMANDA.   They do or they do without it! Not everybody has a craze for adventure.   75

TOM.   Man is by instinct a lover, a hunter, a fighter, and none of those instincts are given much play at the warehouse!

AMANDA.   Man is by instinct! Don't quote instinct to me! Instinct is something that people have got away from! It belongs to animals! Christian adults don't want it!

TOM.   What do Christian adults want, then, Mother?

AMANDA.   Superior things! Things of the mind and the spirit! Only animals have to satisfy instincts! Surely your aims are somewhat higher than theirs! Than monkeys— pigs—

TOM.   I reckon they're not.   80

AMANDA.   You're joking. However, that isn't what I wanted to discuss.

TOM.   [*rising*] I haven't much time.

AMANDA.   [*pushing his shoulders*] Sit down.

TOM.   You want me to punch in red° at the warehouse, Mother?

AMANDA.   You have five minutes. I want to talk about Laura.   85

[*Screen legend: "Plans and Provisions."*]

TOM.   All right! What about Laura?

AMANDA.   We have to be making some plans and provisions for her. She's older than you, two years, and nothing has happened. She just drifts along doing nothing. It frightens me terribly how she just drifts along.

TOM.   I guess she's the type that people call home girls.

AMANDA.   There's no such type, and if there is, it's a pity! That is unless the home is hers, with a husband!

TOM.   What?   90

AMANDA.   Oh, I can see the handwriting on the wall as plain as I see the nose in front of my face! It's terrifying! More and more you remind me of your father! He was out all hours without explanation! —Then *left! Goodbye!* And me with the bag to hold. I saw that letter you got from the Merchant Marine. I know what you're dreaming of. I'm

---

70.3 *Jolly Roger:* the traditional flag of a pirate ship—a skull and crossbones on a field of black.
84 *punch in red:* arrive late for work; the time clock stamps late arrival times in red on the time card.

not standing here blindfolded. [*She pauses.*] Very well, then. Then *do* it! But not till there's somebody to take your place.

TOM.   What do you mean?

AMANDA.   I mean that as soon as Laura has got somebody to take care of her, married, a home of her own, independent—why, then you'll be free to go wherever you please, on land, on sea, whichever way the wind blows you! But until that time you've got to look out for your sister. I don't say me because I'm old and don't matter! I say for your sister because she's young and dependent.

I put her in business college—a dismal failure! Frightened her so it made her sick at the stomach. I took her over to the Young People's League at the church. Another fiasco. She spoke to nobody, nobody spoke to her. Now all she does is fool with those pieces of glass and play those worn-out records. What kind of a life is that for a girl to lead?

TOM.   What can I do about it?

AMANDA.   Overcome selfishness! Self, self, self is all that you ever think of!   95

[*TOM springs up and crosses to get his coat. It is ugly and bulky. He pulls on a cap with earmuffs.*]

Where is your muffler? Put your wool muffler on!

[*He snatches it angrily from the closet, tosses it around his neck and pulls both ends tight.*]

Tom! I haven't said what I had in mind to ask you.

TOM.   I'm too late to—

AMANDA.   [*catching his arm—very importunately; then shyly*] Down at the warehouse, aren't there some—nice young men?

TOM.   No!

AMANDA.   There *must* be—some . . .

TOM.   Mother— [*He gestures.*]   100

AMANDA.   Find out one that's clean-living—doesn't drink and ask him out for sister!

TOM.   What?

AMANDA.   For *sister!* To *meet!* Get *acquainted!*

TOM.   [*stamping to the door*] Oh, my *go-osh!*

AMANDA.   Will you? [*He opens the door. She says, imploringly:*] Will you?   105

[*He starts down the fire escape.*]

Will you? *Will* you, dear?

TOM.   [*calling back*] Yes!

[*AMANDA closes the door hesitantly and with a troubled but faintly hopeful expression.*

Screen image: The cover of a glamor magazine.

The spotlight picks up AMANDA on the phone.]

AMANDA.   Ella Cartwright? This is Amanda Wingfield! How are you honey? How is that kidney condition?

[*There is a five-second pause.*]

Horrors!

[*There is another pause.*]

You're a Christian martyr, yes, honey, that's what you are, a Christian martyr! Well, I just now happened to notice in my little red book that your subscription to the *Companion* has just run out! I knew that you wouldn't want to miss out on the wonderful serial starting in this new issue. It's by Bessie Mae Hopper, the first thing she's written since *Honeymoon for Three*. Wasn't that a strange and interesting story? Well, this one is even lovelier, I believe. It has a sophisticated, society background. It's all about the horsey set on Long Island!

[*The light fades out.*]

Scene 5

[*Legend on the screen: "Annunciation."*]

> *Music is heard as the light slowly comes on.*
> *It is early dusk of a spring evening. Supper has just been finished in the Wingfield apartment.* AMANDA *and* LAURA, *in light-colored dresses, are removing dishes from the table in the dining room, which is shadowy, their movements formalized almost as a dance or ritual, their moving forms as pale and silent as moths.* TOM, *in white shirt and trousers, rises from the table and crosses toward the fire escape.*]

AMANDA. [*as he passes her*] Son, will you do me a favor?
TOM. What?
AMANDA. Comb your hair! You look so pretty when your hair is combed!

[TOM *slouches on the sofa with the evening paper. Its enormous headline reads: "Franco Triumphs."°*]

There is only one respect in which I would like you to emulate your father.
TOM. What respect is that?
AMANDA. The care he always took of his appearance. He never allowed himself to   5
look untidy.

[*He throws down the paper and crosses to the fire escape.*]

Where are you going?
TOM. I'm going out to smoke.
AMANDA. You smoke too much. A pack a day at fifteen cents a pack. How much would that amount to in a month? Thirty times fifteen is how much, Tom? Figure it out and you will be astounded at what you could save. Enough to give you a night-school course in accounting at Washington U.°! Just think what a wonderful thing that would be for you, son!

[TOM *is unmoved by the thought.*]

TOM. I'd rather smoke. [*He steps out on the landing, letting the screen door slam.*]
AMANDA. [*sharply*] I know! That's the tragedy of it. . . . [*Alone, she turns to look at her husband's picture.*]

3.1 *"Franco Triumphs"*: Francisco Franco (1892–1975), dictator of Spain from 1939 until his death, was the general of the victorious Falangist armies in the Spanish Civil War (1936–1939).
7 *Washington U:* Washington University, a liberal arts school in St. Louis.

[*Dance music: "The World Is Waiting for the Sunrise!"*°]

TOM.   [*to the audience*] Across the alley from us was the Paradise Dance Hall. On   10
evenings in spring the windows and doors were open and the music came outdoors.
Sometimes the lights were turned out except for a large glass sphere that hung from
the ceiling. It would turn slowly about and filter the dusk with delicate rainbow colors.
Then the orchestra played a waltz or a tango, something that had a slow and sensuous
rhythm. Couples would come outside, to the relative privacy of the alley. You could see
them kissing behind ash pits and telephone poles. This was the compensation for lives
that passed like mine, without any change or adventure. Adventure and change were
imminent in this year. They were waiting around the corner for all these kids.
Suspended in the mist over Berchtesgaden,° caught in the folds of Chamberlain's
umbrella. In Spain there was Guernica! But here there was only hot swing music and
liquor, dance halls, bars, and movies, and sex that hung in the gloom like a chandelier
and flooded the world with brief, deceptive rainbows. . . . All the world was waiting for
bombardments!

[*AMANDA turns from the picture and comes outside.*]

AMANDA.   [*sighing*] A fire escape landing's a poor excuse for a porch. [*She spreads
a newspaper on a step and sits down, gracefully and demurely as if she were settling into a swing on
a Mississippi veranda.*] What are you looking at?
      TOM.   The moon.
      AMANDA.   Is there a moon this evening?
      TOM.   It's rising over Garfinkel's Delicatessen.
      AMANDA.   So it is! A little silver slipper of a moon. Have you made a wish on it   15
yet?
      TOM.   Um-hum.
      AMANDA.   What did you wish for?
      TOM.   That's a secret.
      AMANDA.   A secret, huh? Well, I won't tell mine either. I will be just as mysterious
as you.
      TOM.   I bet I can guess what yours is.   20
      AMANDA.   Is my head so transparent?
      TOM.   You're not a sphinx.°
      AMANDA.   No, I don't have secrets. I'll tell you what I wished for on the moon.
Success and happiness for my precious children! I wish for that whenever there's a
moon, and when there isn't a moon, I wish for it, too.
      TOM.   I thought perhaps you wished for a gentleman caller.
      AMANDA.   Why do you say that?   25
      TOM.   Don't you remember asking me to fetch one?

9.1 *"The World . . . Sunrise"*: popular song written in 1919 by Eugene Lockhart and Ernest Seitz.
10 *Berchtesgaden . . . Guernica:* The three names mentioned are all foreshadowings of World War II.
Berchtesgaden, a resort in the Bavarian Alps, was Adolf Hitler's favorite residence. Neville
Chamberlain was the British prime minister who signed the Munich Pact with Hitler in 1938,
allowing Nazi Germany to occupy parts of Czechoslovakia. Chamberlain, who always carried an
umbrella, declared that he had ensured "peace in our time." The bombardment of Guernica
during the Spanish Civil War made the name of the town synonymous with the horrors of war,
and especially with the killing of civilian women and children.   22 *sphinx:* a mythological
monster with the head of a woman and body of a lion, famous for her riddles.

AMANDA.   I remember suggesting that it would be nice for your sister if you brought home some nice young man from the warehouse. I think that I've made that suggestion more than once.

TOM.   Yes, you have made it repeatedly.

AMANDA.   Well?

TOM.   We are going to have one.   30

AMANDA.   *What?*

TOM.   A gentleman caller!

[*The annunciation is celebrated with music.*

AMANDA *rises.*

Image on screen: A caller with a bouquet.]

AMANDA.   You mean you have asked some nice young man to come over?

TOM.   Yep. I've asked him to dinner.

AMANDA.   You really did?   35

TOM.   I did!

AMANDA.   You did, and did he—*accept?*

TOM.   He did!

AMANDA.   Well, well—well, well! That's—lovely!

TOM.   I thought that you would be pleased.   40

AMANDA.   It's definite then?

TOM.   Very definite.

AMANDA.   Soon?

TOM.   Very soon.

AMANDA.   For heaven's sake, stop putting on and tell me some things, will you?   45

TOM.   What things do you want me to tell you?

AMANDA.   *Naturally* I would like to know when he's *coming!*

TOM.   He's coming tomorrow.

AMANDA.   *Tomorrow?*

TOM.   Yep. Tomorrow.   50

AMANDA.   But, Tom!

TOM.   Yes, Mother?

AMANDA.   Tomorrow gives me no time!

TOM.   Time for what?

AMANDA.   Preparations! Why didn't you phone me at once, as soon as you asked   55
him, the minute that he accepted? Then, don't you see, I could have been getting ready!

TOM.   You don't have to make any fuss.

AMANDA.   Oh, Tom, Tom, Tom, of course I have to make a fuss! I want things nice,
not sloppy! Not thrown together. I'll certainly have to do some fast thinking, won't I?

TOM.   I don't see why you have to think at all.

AMANDA.   You just don't know. We can't have a gentleman caller in a pigsty! All
my wedding silver has to be polished, the monogrammed table linen ought to be laundered! The windows have to be washed and fresh curtains put up. And how about
clothes? We have to *wear* something, don't we?

TOM.   Mother, this boy is no one to make a fuss over!   60

AMANDA.   Do you realize he's the first young man we've introduced to your sister?
It's terrible, disgraceful that poor little sister has never received a single gentleman
caller! Tom, come inside! [*She opens the screen door.*]

TOM.   What for?

AMANDA.   I want to ask you some things.

TOM.   If you're going to make such a fuss, I'll call it off, I'll tell him not to come!

AMANDA.   You certainly won't do anything of the kind. Nothing offends people   65
worse than broken engagements. It simply means I'll have to work like a Turk! We won't
be brilliant, but we will pass inspection. Come on inside.

[*TOM follows her inside, groaning.*]

Sit down.

TOM.   Any particular place you would like me to sit?

AMANDA.   Thank heavens I've got that new sofa! I'm also making payments on a
floor lamp I'll have sent out! And put the chintz covers on, they'll brighten things up! Of
course I'd hoped to have these walls re-papered. . . . What is the young man's name?

TOM.   His name is O'Connor.

AMANDA.   That, of course, means fish°—tomorrow is Friday! I'll have that salmon
loaf—with Durkee's dressing! What does he do? He works at the warehouse?

TOM.   Of course! How else would I—   70

AMANDA.   Tom, he—doesn't drink?

TOM.   Why do you ask me that?

AMANDA.   Your father *did!*

TOM.   Don't get started on that!

AMANDA.   He *does* drink, then?   75

TOM.   Not that I know of!

AMANDA.   Make sure, be certain! The last thing I want for my daughter's a boy
who drinks!

TOM.   Aren't you being a little bit premature? Mr. O'Connor has not yet
appeared on the scene!

AMANDA.   But will tomorrow. To meet your sister, and what do I know about his
character? Nothing! Old maids are better off than wives of drunkards!

TOM.   Oh, my God!   80

AMANDA.   Be still!

TOM.   [*leaning forward to whisper*] Lots of fellows meet girls whom they don't
marry!

AMANDA.   Oh, talk sensibly, Tom—and don't be sarcastic! [*She has gotten a
hairbrush.*]

TOM.   What are you doing?

AMANDA.   I'm brushing that cowlick down! [*She attacks his hair with the brush.*]   85
What is this young man's position at the warehouse?

TOM.   [*submitting grimly to the brush and the interrogation*] This young man's position is that of a shipping clerk, Mother.

AMANDA.   Sounds to me like a fairly responsible job, the sort of job *you* would be
in if you just had more *get-up.* What is his salary? Have you any idea?

TOM.   I would judge it to be approximately eighty-five dollars a month.

AMANDA.   Well—not princely, but—

TOM.   Twenty more than I make.   90

69 *fish:* Amanda assumes that O'Connor is Catholic. Until the 1960s, Roman Catholics were
required by the church to abstain from meat on Fridays.

AMANDA. Yes, how well I know! But for a family man, eighty-five dollars a month is not much more than you can just get by on. . . .

TOM. Yes, but Mr. O'Connor is not a family man.

AMANDA. He might be, mightn't he? Some time in the future?

TOM. I see. Plans and provisions.

AMANDA. You are the only young man that I know of who ignores the fact that   95
the future becomes the present, the present the past, and the past turns into everlasting regret if you don't plan for it!

TOM. I will think that over and see what I can make of it.

AMANDA. Don't be supercilious with your mother! Tell me some more about this—what do you call him?

TOM. James D. O'Connor. The D. is for Delaney.

AMANDA. Irish on *both* sides! *Gracious!* And he doesn't drink?

TOM. Shall I call him up and ask him right this minute?   100

AMANDA. The only way to find out about those things is to make discreet inquiries at the proper moment. When I was a girl in Blue Mountain and it was suspected that a young man drank, the girl whose attentions he had been receiving, if any girl *was*, would sometimes speak to the minister of his church, or rather her father would if her father was living, and sort of feel him out on the young man's character. That is the way such things are discreetly handled to keep a young woman from making a tragic mistake!

TOM. Then how did you happen to make a tragic mistake?

AMANDA. That innocent look of your father's had everyone fooled! He *smiled*— the world was *enchanted!* No girl can do worse than put herself at the mercy of a handsome appearance! I hope that Mr. O'Connor is not too good-looking.

TOM. No, he's not too good-looking. He's covered with freckles and hasn't too much of a nose.

AMANDA. He's not right-down homely, though?   105

TOM. Not right-down homely. Just medium homely, I'd say.

AMANDA. Character's what to look for in a man.

TOM. That's what I've always said, Mother.

AMANDA. You've never said anything of the kind and I suspect you would never give it a thought.

TOM. Don't be so suspicious of me.   110

AMANDA. At least I hope he's the type that's up and coming.

TOM. I think he really goes in for self-improvement.

AMANDA. What reason have you to think so?

TOM. He goes to night school.

AMANDA. [*beaming*] Splendid! What does he do, I mean study?   115

TOM. Radio engineering and public speaking!

AMANDA. Then he has visions of being advanced in the world! Any young man who studies public speaking is aiming to have an executive job some day! And radio engineering? A thing for the future! Both of these facts are very illuminating. Those are the sort of things that a mother should know concerning any young man who comes to call on her daughter. Seriously or—not.

TOM. One little warning. He doesn't know about Laura. I didn't let on that we had dark ulterior motives. I just said, why don't you come and have dinner with us? He said okay and that was the whole conversation.

AMANDA.   I bet it was! You're eloquent as an oyster. However, he'll know about Laura when he gets here. When he sees how lovely and sweet and pretty she is, he'll thank his lucky stars he was asked to dinner.

TOM.   Mother, you mustn't expect too much of Laura.   120

AMANDA.   What do you mean?

TOM.   Laura seems all those things to you and me because she's ours and we love her. We don't even notice she's crippled any more.

AMANDA.   Don't say crippled! You know that I never allow that word to be used!

TOM.   But face facts, Mother. She is and—that's not all—

AMANDA.   What do you mean "not all"?   125

TOM.   Laura is very different from other girls.

AMANDA.   I think the difference is all to her advantage.

TOM.   Not quite all—in the eyes of others—strangers—she's terribly shy and lives in a world of her own and those things make her seem a little peculiar to people outside the house.

AMANDA.   Don't say peculiar.

TOM.   Face the facts. She is.   130

[*The dance hall music changes to a tango that has a minor and somewhat ominous tone.*]

AMANDA.   In what way is she peculiar—may I ask?

TOM.   [*gently*] She lives in a world of her own—a world of little glass ornaments, Mother. . . .

[*He gets up.* AMANDA *remains holding the brush, looking at him, troubled.*]

She plays old phonograph records and—that's about all—[*He glances at himself in the mirror and crosses to the door.*]

AMANDA.   [*sharply*] Where are you going?

TOM.   I'm going to the movies. [*He goes out the screen door.*]

AMANDA.   Not to the movies, every night to the movies! [*She follows quickly to the*   135 *screen door.*] I don't believe you always go to the movies!

[*He is gone.* AMANDA *looks worriedly after him for a moment. Then vitality and optimism return and she turns from the door, crossing to the portieres.*]

Laura! Laura!

[LAURA *answers from the kitchenette.*]

LAURA.   Yes, Mother.

AMANDA.   Let those dishes go and come in front!

[LAURA *appears with a dish towel.* AMANDA *speaks to her gaily.*]

Laura, come here and make a wish on the moon!

[*Screen image: The Moon.*]

LAURA.   [*entering*] Moon—moon?

AMANDA.   A little silver slipper of a moon. Look over your left shoulder, Laura, and make a wish!

[LAURA *looks faintly puzzled as if called out of sleep.* AMANDA *seizes her shoulders and turns her at an angle by the door.*]

Now! Now, darling, *wish!*

LAURA.   What shall I wish for, Mother?   140

    AMANDA.   [*her voice trembling and her eyes suddenly filling with tears*] Happiness! Good fortune!

[*The sound of the violin rises and the stage dims out.*]

Scene 6

[*The light comes up on the fire escape landing. Tom is leaning against the grill, smoking. Screen image: The high school hero.*]

TOM.   And so the following evening I brought Jim home to dinner. I had known Jim slightly in high school. In high school Jim was a hero. He had tremendous Irish good nature and vitality with the scrubbed and polished look of white chinaware. He seemed to move in a continual spotlight. He was a star in basketball, captain of the debating club, president of the senior class and the glee club and he sang the male lead in the annual light operas. He was always running or bounding, never just walking. He seemed always at the point of defeating the law of gravity. He was shooting with such velocity through his adolescence that you would logically expect him to arrive at nothing short of the White House by the time he was thirty. But Jim apparently ran into more interference after his graduation from Soldan. His speed had definitely slowed. Six years after he left high school he was holding a job that wasn't much better than mine.

[*Screen image: The Clerk.*]

He was the only one at the warehouse with whom I was on friendly terms. I was valuable to him as someone who could remember his former glory, who had seen him win basketball games and the silver cup in debating. He knew of my secret practice of retiring to a cabinet of the washroom to work on poems when business was slack in the warehouse. He called me Shakespeare. And while the other boys in the warehouse regarded me with suspicious hostility, Jim took a humorous attitude toward me. Gradually his attitude affected the others, their hostility wore off and they also began to smile at me as people smile at an oddly fashioned dog who trots across their path at some distance.

    I knew that Jim and Laura had known each other at Soldan, and I had heard Laura speak admiringly of his voice. I didn't know if Jim remembered her or not. In high school Laura had been as unobtrusive as Jim had been astonishing. If he did remember Laura, it was not as my sister, for when I asked him to dinner, he grinned and said, "You know, Shakespeare, I never thought of you as having folks!"

    He was about to discover that I did. . . .

[*Legend on screen: "The accent of a coming foot."*]

[*The light dims out on Tom and comes up in the Wingfield living room—a delicate lemony light. It is about five on a Friday evening of late spring which comes "scattering poems in the sky."*

    AMANDA *has worked like a Turk in preparation for the gentleman caller. The results are astonishing. The new floor lamp with its rose silk shade is in place, a colored paper lantern conceals the broken light fixture in the ceiling, new billowing white curtains are at the windows, chintz covers are on the chairs and sofa, a pair of new sofa pillows make their initial appearance. Open boxes and tissue paper are scattered on the floor.*

LAURA stands in the middle of the room with lifted arms while AMANDA crouches before her, adjusting the hem of a new dress, devout and ritualistic. The dress is colored and designed by memory. The arrangement of LAURA's hair is changed; it is softer and more becoming. A fragile, unearthly prettiness has come out in LAURA: she is like a piece of translucent glass touched by light, given a momentary radiance, not actual, not lasting.]

AMANDA.   [*impatiently*] Why are you trembling?
LAURA.   Mother, you've made me so nervous!
AMANDA.   How have I made you nervous?
LAURA.   By all this fuss! You make it seem so important!
AMANDA.   I don't understand you, Laura. You couldn't be satisfied with just sit-   5
ting home, and yet whenever I try to arrange something for you, you seem to resist it.
[*She gets up.*] Now take a look at yourself. No, wait! Wait just a moment—I have an idea!
LAURA.   What is it now?

[*AMANDA produces two powder puffs which she wraps in handkerchiefs and stuffs in LAURA's bosom.*]

LAURA.   Mother, what are you doing?
AMANDA.   They call them "Gay Deceivers"!   10
LAURA.   I won't wear them!
AMANDA.   You will!
LAURA.   Why should I?
AMANDA.   Because, to be painfully honest, your chest is flat.
LAURA.   You make it seem like we were setting a trap.   15
AMANDA.   All pretty girls are a trap, a pretty trap, and men expect them to be.

[*Legend on screen: "A pretty trap."*]

Now look at yourself, young lady. This is the prettiest you will ever be! [*She stands back to admire LAURA.*] I've got to fix myself now! You're going to be surprised by your mother's appearance!

[*AMANDA crosses through the portieres, humming gaily. LAURA moves slowly to the long mirror and stares solemnly at herself. A wind blows the white curtains inward in a slow, graceful motion and with a faint, sorrowful sighing.*]

AMANDA.   [*from somewhere behind the portieres*] It isn't dark enough yet.

[*LAURA turns slowly before the mirror with a troubled look.*

Legend on screen: "This is my sister: Celebrate her with strings!" Music plays.]

AMANDA.   [*laughing, still not visible*] I'm going to show you something. I'm going to make a spectacular appearance!
LAURA.   What is it, Mother?
AMANDA.   Possess your soul in patience—you will see! Something I've resurrected from that old trunk! Styles haven't changed so terribly much after all. . . . [*She parts the portieres.*] Now just look at your mother! [*She wears a girlish frock of yellowed voile with a blue silk sash. She carries a bunch of jonquils—the legend of her youth is nearly revived. Now she speaks feverishly:*] This is the dress in which I led the cotillion. Won the cakewalk twice at Sunset

Hill, wore one Spring to the Governor's Ball in Jackson!° See how I sashayed around the ballroom, Laura? [*She raises her skirt and does a mincing step around the room.*] I wore it on Sundays for my gentlemen callers! I had it on the day I met your father. . . . I had malaria fever all that Spring. The change of climate from East Tennessee to the Delta— weakened resistance. I had a little temperature all the time—not enough to be serious— just enough to make me restless and giddy! Invitations poured in—parties all over the Delta! "Stay in bed," said Mother, "you have a fever!"—but I just wouldn't. I took quinine° but kept on going, going! Evenings, dances! Afternoons, long, long rides! Picnics—lovely! So lovely, that country in May—all lacy with dogwood, literally flooded with jonquils! That was the spring I had the craze for jonquils. Jonquils became an absolute obsession. Mother said, "Honey, there's no more room for jonquils." And still I kept on bringing in more jonquils. Whenever, wherever I saw them, I'd say, "Stop! Stop! I see jonquils!" I made the young men help me gather the jonquils! It was a joke, Amanda and her jonquils. Finally there were no more vases to hold them, every available space was filled with jonquils. No vases to hold them? All right, I'll hold them myself! And then I—[*She stops in front of the picture. Music plays.*] met your father! Malaria fever and jonquils and then—this—boy. . . . [*She switches on the rose-colored lamp.*] I hope they get here before it starts to rain. [*She crosses the room and places the jonquils in a bowl on the table.*] I gave your brother a little extra change so he and Mr. O'Connor could take the service car home.

LAURA.   [*with an altered look*] What did you say his name was?   20
AMANDA.   O'Connor.
LAURA.   What is his first name?
AMANDA.   I don't remember. Oh, yes, I do. It was—Jim.

[*LAURA sways slightly and catches hold of a chair.*

Legend on screen: "Not Jim!"]

LAURA.   [*faintly*] Not—Jim!
AMANDA.   Yes, that was it, it was Jim! I've never known a Jim that wasn't nice!   25

[*The music becomes ominous.*]

LAURA.   Are you sure his name is Jim O'Connor?
AMANDA.   Yes. Why?
LAURA.   Is he the one that Tom used to know in high school?
AMANDA.   He didn't say so. I think he just got to know him at the warehouse.
LAURA.   There was a Jim O'Connor we both knew in high school—[*Then, with*   30
effort.] If that is the one that Tom is bringing to dinner—you'll have to excuse me, I won't come to the table.
AMANDA.   What sort of nonsense is this?
LAURA.   You asked me once if I'd ever liked a boy. Don't you remember I showed you this boy's picture?
AMANDA.   You mean the boy you showed me in the yearbook?
LAURA.   Yes, that boy.

---

19 *Jackson:* capital of Mississippi. Amanda refers to the social events of her youth. A cotillion is a formal ball, often given for debutantes. The cakewalk is a strutting dance step.   *quinine:* long used as a standard drug to control malaria.

AMANDA.   Laura, Laura, were you in love with that boy?   35

LAURA.   I don't know, Mother. All I know is I couldn't sit at the table if it was him!

AMANDA.   It won't be him! It isn't the least bit likely. But whether it is or not, you will come to the table. You will not be excused.

LAURA.   I'll have to be, Mother.

AMANDA.   I don't intend to humor your silliness, Laura. I've had too much from you and your brother, both! So just sit down and compose yourself till they come. Tom has forgotten his key so you'll have to let them in, when they arrive.

LAURA.   [*panicky*] Oh, Mother—*you* answer the door!   40

AMANDA.   [*lightly*] I'll be in the kitchen—busy!

LAURA.   Oh, Mother, please answer the door, don't make me do it!

AMANDA.   [*crossing into the kitchenette*] I've got to fix the dressing for the salmon. Fuss, fuss—silliness!—over a gentleman caller!

[*The door swings shut, LAURA is left alone.*

Legend on screen: "Terror!"

She utters a low moan and turns off the lamp—sits stiffly on the edge of the sofa, knotting her fingers together.

Legend on screen: "The Opening of a Door!"

TOM *and* JIM *appear on the fire escape steps and climb to the landing. Hearing their approach,* LAURA *rises with a panicky gesture. She retreats to the portieres. The doorbell rings.* LAURA *catches her breath and touches her throat. Low drums sound.*]

AMANDA.   [*calling*] Laura, sweetheart! The door!

[*LAURA stares at it without moving.*]

JIM.   I think we just beat the rain.   45

TOM.   Uh-huh. [*He rings again, nervously.* JIM *whistles and fishes for a cigarette.*]

AMANDA.   [*very, very gaily*] Laura, that is your brother and Mr. O'Connor! Will you let them in, darling?

[*LAURA crosses toward the kitchenette door.*]

LAURA.   [*breathlessly*] Mother—you go to the door!

[*AMANDA steps out of the kitchenette and stares furiously at* LAURA. *She points imperiously at the door.*]

LAURA.   Please, please!

AMANDA.   [*in a fierce whisper*] What is the matter with you, you silly thing?   50

LAURA.   [*desperately*] Please, you answer it, *please!*

AMANDA.   I told you I wasn't going to humor you, Laura. Why have you chosen this moment to lose your mind?

LAURA.   Please, please, please, you go!

AMANDA.   You'll have to go to the door because I can't.

LAURA.   [*despairingly*] I can't either!   55

AMANDA.   *Why?*

LAURA.   I'm *sick!*

AMANDA.   I'm sick, too—of your nonsense! Why can't you and your brother be normal people? Fantastic whims and behavior!

[*TOM gives a long ring.*]

Preposterous goings on! Can you give me one reason—[*She calls out lyrically.*] Coming! Just one second!—why you should be afraid to open a door? Now you answer it, Laura!

    LAURA.   Oh, oh, oh . . . [*She returns through the portieres, darts to the Victrola, winds it frantically and turns it on.*]

    AMANDA.   Laura Wingfield, you march right to that door!   60

    LAURA.   *Yes—yes, Mother!*

[*A faraway, scratchy rendition of "Dardanella"° softens the air and gives her strength to move through it. She slips to the door and draws it cautiously open. TOM enters with the caller, JIM O'CONNOR.*]

    TOM.   Laura, this is Jim. Jim, this is my sister, Laura.

    JIM.   [*stepping inside*] I didn't know that Shakespeare had a sister!

    LAURA.   [*retreating, stiff and trembling, from the door*] How—how do you do?

    JIM.   [*heartily, extending his hand*] Okay!   65

[*LAURA touches it hesitantly with hers.*]

    JIM.   Your hand's *cold*, Laura!

    LAURA.   Yes, well—I've been playing the Victrola. . . .

    JIM.   Must have been playing classical music on it! You ought to play a little hot swing music to warm you up!

    LAURA.   Excuse me—I haven't finished playing the Victrola. . . . [*She turns awkwardly and hurries into the front room. She pauses a second by the Victrola. Then she catches her breath and darts through the portieres like a frightened deer.*]

    JIM.   [*grinning*] What was the matter?   70

    TOM.   Oh—with Laura? Laura is—terribly shy.

    JIM.   Shy, huh? It's unusual to meet a shy girl nowadays. I don't believe you ever mentioned you had a sister.

    TOM.   Well, now you know. I have one. Here is the *Post Dispatch.*° You want a piece of it?

    JIM.   Uh-huh.

    TOM.   What piece? The comics?   75

    JIM.   Sports! [*He glances at it.*] Ole Dizzy Dean° is on his bad behavior.

    TOM.   [*uninterested*] Yeah? [*He lights a cigarette and goes over to the fire-escape door.*]

    JIM.   Where are *you* going?

    TOM.   I'm going out on the terrace.

    JIM.   [*going after him*] You know, Shakespeare—I'm going to sell you a bill of   80
goods!

    TOM.   What goods?

    JIM.   A course I'm taking.

    TOM.   Huh?

    JIM.   In public speaking! You and me, we're not the warehouse type.

61.2 *"Dardanella":* a popular song and dance tune written in 1919 by Fred Fisher, Felix Bernard, and Johnny S. Black.   **73** *Post Dispatch:* The *St. Louis Post Dispatch,* a newspaper.   **76** *Dizzy Dean:* Jerome Herman (or Jay Hanna) Dean (1911–1974), outstanding pitcher with the St. Louis Cardinals (1932–1938).

TOM.   Thanks—that's good news. But what has public speaking got to do with it?   85
JIM.   It fits you for—executive positions!
TOM.   Awww.
JIM.   I tell you it's done a helluva lot for me.

[*Image on screen: Executive at his desk.*]

TOM.   In what respect?
JIM.   In every! Ask yourself what is the difference between you an' me and men in   90
the office down front? Brains?—No!—Ability?—No! Then what? Just one little thing—
TOM.   What is that one little thing?
JIM.   Primarily it amounts to—social poise! Being able to square up to people and
hold your own on any social level!
AMANDA.   [*from the kitchenette*] Tom?
TOM.   Yes, Mother?
AMANDA.   Is that you and Mr. O'Connor?   95
TOM.   Yes, Mother.
AMANDA.   Well, you just make yourselves comfortable in there.
TOM.   Yes, Mother.
AMANDA.   Ask Mr. O'Connor if he would like to wash his hands.
JIM.   Aw, no—no—thank you—I took care of that at the warehouse. Tom—   100
TOM.   Yes?
JIM.   Mr. Mendoza was speaking to me about you.
TOM.   Favorably?
JIM.   What do you think?
TOM.   Well—   105
JIM.   You're going to be out of a job if you don't wake up.
TOM.   I am waking up—
JIM.   You show no signs.
TOM.   The signs are interior.

[*Image on screen: The sailing vessel with the Jolly Roger again.*]

TOM.   I'm planning to change. [*He leans over the fire escape rail, speaking with quiet*   110
exhilaration. The incandescent marquees and signs of the first-run movie houses light his face from
across the alley. He looks like a voyager.] I'm right at the point of committing myself to a
future that doesn't include the warehouse and Mr. Mendoza or even a night-school
course in public speaking.
JIM.   What are you gassing about?
TOM.   I'm tired of the movies.
JIM.   Movies!
TOM.   Yes, movies! Look at them—[*a wave toward the marvels of Grand Avenue*] All
of those glamorous people—having adventures—hogging it all, gobbling the whole
thing up! You know what happens? People go to the *movies* instead of *moving!* Hollywood
characters are supposed to have all the adventures for everybody in America, while
everybody in America sits in a dark room and watches them have them! Yes, until there's
a war. That's when adventure becomes available to the masses! *Everyone's* dish, not only
Gable's!° Then the people in the dark room come out of the dark room to have some

---

114 *Gable:* Clark Gable (1901–1960), popular American screen actor and matinee idol from the
1930s to his death.

adventures themselves—goody, goody! It's our turn now, to go to the South Sea Island—to make a safari—to be exotic, far-off! But I'm not patient. I don't want to wait till then. I'm tired of the *movies* and I am *about* to *move!*

JIM. [*incredulously*] Move?   115
TOM. Yes.
JIM. When?
TOM. Soon!
JIM. Where? Where?

[*The music seems to answer the question, while* TOM *thinks it over. He searches in his pockets.*]

TOM. I'm starting to boil inside. I know I seem dreamy, but inside—well, I'm   120
boiling! Whenever I pick up a shoe, I shudder a little thinking how short life is and what
I am doing! Whatever that means, I know it doesn't mean shoes—except as something to
wear on a traveler's feet! [*He finds what he has been searching for in his pockets and holds out
a paper to JIM.*] Look—
JIM. What?
TOM. I'm a member.
JIM. [*reading*] The Union of Merchant Seamen.
TOM. I paid my dues this month, instead of the light bill.
JIM. You will regret it when they turn off the lights.   125
TOM. I won't be here.
JIM. How about your mother?
TOM. I'm like my father. The bastard son of a bastard! Did you notice how he's
grinning in his picture in there? And he's been absent going on sixteen years!
JIM. You're just talking, you drip. How does your mother feel about it?
TOM. Shhh! Here comes Mother! Mother is not acquainted with my plans!   130
AMANDA. [*coming through the portieres*] Where are you all?
TOM. On the terrace, Mother.

[*They start inside. She advances to them.* TOM *is distinctly shocked at her appearance. Even* JIM
*blinks a little. He is making his first contact with the girlish Southern vivacity and in spite of the
night-school course in public speaking is somewhat thrown off the beam by the unexpected outlay
of social charm. Certain responses are attempted by* JIM *but are swept aside by* AMANDA's *gay
laughter and chatter.* TOM *is embarrassed but after the first shock* JIM *reacts very warmly. He
grins and chuckles, is altogether won over.*

Image on screen: AMANDA *as a girl.*]

AMANDA. [*coyly smiling, shaking her girlish ringlets*] Well, well, well, so this is Mr.
O'Connor. Introductions entirely unnecessary. I've heard so much about you from my
boy. I finally said to him, Tom—good gracious!—why don't you bring this paragon to
supper? I'd like to meet this nice young man at the warehouse!—instead of just hearing him sing your praises so much! I don't know why my son is so stand-offish—that's not
Southern behavior!

Let's sit down and—I think we could stand a little more air in here! Tom, leave the
door open. I felt a nice fresh breeze a moment ago. Where has it gone to? Mmm, so
warm already! And not quite summer, even. We're going to burn up when summer really
gets started. However, we're having—we're having a very light supper. I think light things
are better fo' this time of year. The same as light clothes are. Light clothes an' light food
are what warm weather calls fo'. You know our blood gets so thick during th' winter—it

takes a while fo' us to *adjust* ourselves!—when the season changes . . . It's come so quick this year. I wasn't prepared. All of sudden—heavens! Already summer! I ran to the trunk an' pulled out this light dress—terribly old! Historical almost! But feels so good—so good an' co-ol, y'know. . . .

TOM.   Mother—

AMANDA.   Yes, honey?   135

TOM.   How about—supper?

AMANDA.   Honey, you go ask Sister if supper is ready! You know that Sister is in full charge of supper! Tell her you hungry boys are waiting for it. [*To Jim.*] Have you met Laura?

JIM.   She—

AMANDA.   Let you in? Oh, good, you've met already! It's rare for a girl as sweet an' pretty as Laura to be domestic! But Laura is, thank heavens, not only pretty but also very domestic. I'm not at all. I never was a bit. I never could make a thing but angel-food cake. Well, in the South we had so many servants. Gone, gone, gone. All vestige of gracious living! Gone completely! I wasn't prepared for what the future brought me. All of my gentlemen callers were sons of planters and so of course I assumed that I would be married to one and raise my family on a large piece of land with plenty of servants. But man proposes—and woman accepts the proposal! to vary that old, old saying a little but—I married no planter! I married a man who worked for the telephone company! That gallantly smiling gentleman over there! [*She points to the picture.*] A telephone man who—fell in love with long-distance! Now he travels and I don't even know where! But what am I going on for about my—tribulations? Tell me yours—I hope you don't have any! Tom?

TOM.   [*returning*] Yes, Mother?   140

AMANDA.   Is supper nearly ready?

TOM.   It looks to me like supper is on the table.

AMANDA.   Let me look—[*She rises prettily and looks through the portieres.*] Oh lovely! But where is Sister?

TOM.   Laura is not feeling well and she says that she thinks she'd better not come to the table.

AMANDA.   What? Nonsense! Laura? Oh, Laura!

LAURA.   [*from the kitchenette, faintly*] Yes, Mother.   145

AMANDA.   You really must come to the table. We won't be seated until you come to the table! Come in, Mr. O'Connor. You sit over there and I'll. . . . Laura? Laura Wingfield! You're keeping us waiting, honey! We can't say grace until you come to the table!

[*The kitchenette door is pushed weakly open and LAURA comes in. She is obviously quite faint, her lips trembling, her eyes wide and staring. She moves unsteadily toward the table.*]

Screen legend: "Terror!"

Outside a summer storm is coming on abruptly. The white curtains billow inward at the windows and there is a sorrowful murmur from the deep blue dusk.

LAURA suddenly stumbles; she catches at a chair with a faint moan.]

TOM.   Laura!

AMANDA.   Laura!

[*There is a clap of thunder.*

Screen legend: "Ah!"]

[*despairingly*] Why, Laura, you *are* ill, darling! Tom, help your sister into the living room, dear! Sit in the living room, Laura—rest on the sofa. Well! [*To JIM as TOM helps his sister to the sofa in the living room.*] Standing over the hot stove made her ill! I told her that it was just too warm this evening, but—

[*TOM comes back to the table.*]

Is Laura all right now?

    TOM.   Yes.

    AMANDA.   What is that? Rain? A nice cool rain has come up! [*She gives JIM a frightened look.*] I think we may—have grace—now . . . [*TOM looks at her stupidly.*] Tom, honey—you say grace!

    TOM.   Oh . . . "For these and all thy mercies—"

[*They bow their heads, AMANDA stealing a nervous glance at JIM. In the living room LAURA, stretched on the sofa, clenches her hand to her lips, to hold back a shuddering sob.*]

God's Holy Name be praised—

[*The scene dims out.*]

Scene 7

    [*It is half an hour later. Dinner is just being finished in the dining room, LAURA is still huddled upon the sofa, her feet drawn under her, her head resting on a pale blue pillow, her eyes wide and mysteriously watchful. The new floor lamp with its shade of rose-colored silk gives a soft, becoming light to her face, bringing out the fragile, unearthly prettiness which usually escapes attention. From outside there is a steady murmur of rain, but it is slackening and soon stops; the air outside becomes pale and luminous as the moon breaks through the clouds. A moment after the curtain rises, the lights in both rooms flicker and go out.*]

    JIM.   Hey, there, Mr. Light Bulb!

[*AMANDA laughs nervously.*

Legend on screen: "Suspension of a public service."]

    AMANDA.   Where was Moses when the lights went out? Ha-ha. Do you know the answer to that one, Mr. O'Connor?

    JIM.   No, Ma'am, what's the answer?

    AMANDA.   In the dark!

[*JIM laughs appreciatively.*]

    Everybody sit still. I'll light the candles. Isn't it lucky we have them on the table? Where's a match? Which of you gentlemen can provide a match?

    JIM.   Here.

    AMANDA.   Thank you, Sir.

    JIM.   Not at all, Ma'am!

    AMANDA.   [*as she lights the candles*] I guess the fuse has burnt out. Mr. O'Connor, can you tell a burnt-out fuse? I know I can't and Tom is a total loss when it comes to

mechanics. [*They rise from the table and go into the kitchenette, from where their voices are heard.*]
Oh, be careful you don't bump into something. We don't want our gentleman caller to
break his neck. Now wouldn't that be a fine howdy-do?

JIM.   Ha-ha! Where is the fuse-box?

AMANDA.   Right here next to the stove. Can you see anything?   10

JIM.   Just a minute.

AMANDA.   Isn't electricity a mysterious thing? Wasn't it Benjamin Franklin who
tied a key to a kite? We live in such a mysterious universe, don't we? Some people say that
science clears up all the mysteries for us. In my opinion it only creates more! Have you
found it yet?

JIM.   No, Ma'am. All these fuses look okay to me.

AMANDA.   Tom!

TOM.   Yes, Mother?   15

AMANDA.   That light bill I gave you several days ago. That one I told you we got
the notices about?

[*Legend on screen: "Ha!"*]

TOM.   Oh—yeah.

AMANDA.   You didn't neglect to pay it by any chance?

TOM.   Why, I—

AMANDA.   Didn't! I might have known it!   20

JIM.   Shakespeare probably wrote a poem on that light bill, Mrs. Wingfield.

AMANDA.   I might have known better than to trust him with it! There's such a
high price for negligence in this world!

JIM.   Maybe the poem will win a ten-dollar prize.

AMANDA.   We'll just have to spend the remainder of the evening in the nineteenth century, before Mr. Edison made the Mazda lamp!°

JIM.   Candlelight is my favorite kind of light.   25

AMANDA.   That shows you're romantic! But that's no excuse for Tom. Well, we
got through dinner. Very considerate of them to let us get through dinner before they
plunged us into everlasting darkness, wasn't it, Mr. O'Connor?

JIM.   Ha-ha!

AMANDA.   Tom, as a penalty for your carelessness you can help me with the
dishes.

JIM.   Let me give you a hand.

AMANDA.   Indeed you will not!   30

JIM.   I ought to be good for something.

AMANDA.   Good for something? [*Her tone is rhapsodic.*] *You?* Why, Mr. O'Connor,
nobody, *nobody's* given me this much entertainment in years—as you have!

JIM.   Aw, now, Mrs. Wingfield!

AMANDA.   I'm not exaggerating, not one bit! But Sister is all by her lonesome.
You go keep her company in the parlor! I'll give you this lovely old candelabrum that
used to be on the altar at the Church of the Heavenly Rest. It was melted a little out of
shape when the church burnt down. Lightning struck it one spring. Gypsy Jones was
holding a revival at the time and he intimated that the church was destroyed because
the Episcopalians gave card parties.

---

24 *Mazda lamp:* Thomas A. Edison (1847–1931) developed the first practical incandescent lamp in
1879.

JIM. Ha-ha. 35
AMANDA. And how about you coaxing Sister to drink a little wine? I think it would be good for her! Can you carry both at once?
JIM. Sure. I'm Superman!
AMANDA. Now, Thomas, get into this apron!

[*JIM comes into the dining room, carrying the candelabrum, its candles lighted, in one hand and a glass of wine in the other. The door of the kitchenette swings closed on AMANDA's gay laughter; the flickering light approaches the portieres. LAURA sits up nervously as JIM enters. She can hardly speak from the almost intolerable strain of being alone with a stranger.*]

Screen legend: "I don't suppose you remember me at all!"

At first, before JIM's warmth overcomes her paralyzing shyness, LAURA's voice is thin and breathless, as though she had just run up a steep flight of stairs. JIM's attitude is gently humorous. While the incident is apparently unimportant, it is to LAURA the climax of her secret life.]

JIM. Hello there, Laura.
LAURA. [*faintly*] Hello. 40

[*She clears her throat.*]

JIM. How are you feeling now? Better?
LAURA. Yes. Yes, thank you.
JIM. This is for you. A little dandelion wine. [*He extends the glass toward her with extravagant gallantry.*]
LAURA. Thank you.
JIM. Drink it—but don't get drunk! 45

[*He laughs heartily. LAURA takes the glass uncertainly; she laughs shyly.*]

Where shall I set the candles?
LAURA. Oh—oh, anywhere . . .
JIM. How about here on the floor? Any objections?
LAURA. No.
JIM. I'll spread a newspaper under to catch the drippings. I like to sit on the floor. Mind if I do?
LAURA. Oh, no. 50
JIM. Give me a pillow?
LAURA. What?
JIM. A pillow!
LAURA. Oh . . . [*She hands him one quickly.*]
JIM. How about you? Don't you like to sit on the floor? 55
LAURA. Oh—yes.
JIM. Why don't you, then?
LAURA. I—will.
JIM. Take a pillow!

[*Laura does. She sits on the floor on the other side of the candelabrum. JIM crosses his legs and smiles engagingly at her.*] I can't hardly see you sitting way over there.

LAURA. I can—see you. 60
JIM. I know, but that's not fair, I'm in the limelight.

[*LAURA moves her pillow closer.*]

Good! Now I can see you! Comfortable?

    LAURA.   Yes.

    JIM.   So am I. Comfortable as a cow! Will you have some gum?

    LAURA.   No, thank you.

    JIM.   I think that I will indulge, with your permission. [*He musingly unwraps a stick*   65
of gum and holds it up.] Think of the fortune made by the guy that invented the first piece
of chewing gum. Amazing, huh? The Wrigley Building° is one of the sights of Chicago—
I saw it when I went up to the Century of Progress.° Did you take in the Century of
Progress?

    LAURA.   No, I didn't.

    JIM.   Well, it was quite a wonderful exposition. What impressed me most was the
Hall of Science. Gives you an idea of what the future will be in America, even more wonderful than the present time is! [*There is a pause. JIM smiles at her.*] Your brother tells me
you're shy. Is that right—Laura?

    LAURA.   I—don't know.

    JIM.   I judge you to be an old-fashioned type of girl. Well, I think that's a pretty
good type to be. Hope you don't think I'm being too personal—do you?

    LAURA.   [*Hastily, out of embarrassment*] I believe I *will* take a piece of gum, if you—   70
don't mind. [*clearing her throat*] Mr. O'Connor, have you—kept up with your singing?

    JIM.   Singing? Me?

    LAURA.   Yes. I remember what a beautiful voice you had.

    JIM.   When did you hear me sing?

[*LAURA does not answer, and in the long pause which follows a man's voice is heard singing
offstage.*]

    VOICE:

        O blow, ye winds, heigh-ho,

        A-roving I will go!

          I'm off to my love

          With a boxing glove—

        Ten thousand miles away!

    JIM.   You say you've heard me sing?   7

    LAURA.   Oh, Yes! Yes, very often . . . I—don't suppose—you remember me—
at all?

    JIM.   [*smiling doubtfully*] You know I have an idea I've seen you before. I had that
idea soon as you opened the door. It seemed almost like I was about to remember your
name. But the name that I started to call you—wasn't a name! And so I stopped myself
before I said it.

    LAURA.   Wasn't it—Blue Roses?

    JIM.   [*springing up, grinning*] Blue Roses! My gosh, yes—Blue Roses! That's what I
had on my tongue when you opened the door! Isn't it funny what tricks your memory
plays? I didn't connect you with high school somehow or other. But that's where it was; it
was high school. I didn't even know you were Shakespeare's sister! Gosh, I'm sorry.

    LAURA.   I didn't expect you to. You—barely knew me!   8

    JIM.   But we did have a speaking acquaintance, huh?

65 *Wrigley Building:* Finished in 1924, this was one of the first skyscrapers in the United States.
Century of Progress: a world's fair held in Chicago (1933–1934) to celebrate the city's centennial.

LAURA.   Yes, we—spoke to each other.
JIM.   When did you recognize me?
LAURA.   Oh, right away!
JIM.   Soon as I came in the door?   85
LAURA.   When I heard your name I thought it was probably you. I knew that Tom used to know you a little in high school. So when you came in the door—well, then I was—sure.
JIM.   Why didn't you *say* something, then?
LAURA.   [*breathlessly*] I didn't know what to say, I was—too surprised!
JIM.   For goodness' sakes! You know, this sure is funny!
LAURA.   Yes! Yes, isn't it, though . . .   90
JIM.   Didn't we have a class in something together?
LAURA.   Yes, we did.
JIM.   What class was that?
LAURA.   It was—singing—chorus!
JIM.   Aw!   95
LAURA.   I sat across the aisle from you in the Aud.
JIM.   Aw!
LAURA.   Mondays, Wednesdays, and Fridays.
JIM.   Now I remember—you always came in late.
LAURA.   Yes, it was so hard for me, getting upstairs. I had that brace on my leg—   100
it clumped so loud!
JIM.   I never heard any clumping.
LAURA.   [*wincing at the recollection*] To me it sounded like—thunder!
JIM.   Well, well, well, I never even noticed.
LAURA.   And everybody was seated before I came in. I had to walk in front of all those people. My seat was in the back row. I had to go clumping all the way up the aisle with everyone watching!
JIM.   You shouldn't have been self-conscious.   105
LAURA.   I know, but I was. It was always such a relief when the singing started.
JIM.   Aw, yes, I've placed you now! I used to call you Blue Roses. How was it that I got started calling you that?
LAURA.   I was out of school a little while with pleurosis. When I came back you asked me what was the matter. I said I had pleurosis—you thought that I said *Blue Roses*. That's what you always called me after that!
JIM.   I hope you didn't mind.
LAURA.   Oh, no—I liked it. You see, I wasn't acquainted with many—people. . . .   110
JIM.   As I remember you sort of stuck by yourself.
LAURA.   I—I—never have had much luck at—making friends.
JIM.   I don't see why you wouldn't.
LAURA.   Well, I—started out badly.
JIM.   You mean being—   115
LAURA.   Yes, it sort of—stood between me—
JIM.   You shouldn't have let it!
LAURA.   I know, but it did, and—
JIM.   You were shy with people!
LAURA.   I tried not to be but never could—   120
JIM.   Overcome it?
LAURA.   No, I—I never could!

JIM. I guess being shy is something you have to work out of kind of gradually.

LAURA. [*sorrowfully*] Yes—I guess it—

JIM. Takes time! 125

LAURA. Yes—

JIM. People are not so dreadful when you know them. That's what you have to remember! And everybody has problems, not just you, but practically everybody has got some problems. You think of yourself as having the only problems, as being the only one who is disappointed. But just look around you and you will see lots of people as disappointed as you are. For instance, I hoped when I was going to high school that I would be further along at this time, six years later, than I am now. You remember that wonderful write-up I had in *The Torch?*

LAURA. Yes! [*She rises and crosses to the table.*]

JIM. It said I was bound to succeed in anything I went into!

[*LAURA returns with the high school yearbook.*]

Holy Jeez! *The Torch!*

[*He accepts it reverently. They smile across the book with mutual wonder. LAURA crouches beside him and they begin to turn the pages. LAURA's shyness is dissolving in his warmth.*]

LAURA. Here you are in *The Pirates of Penzance!* 130

JIM. [*wistfully*] I sang the baritone lead in that operetta.

LAURA. [*raptly*] So—*beautifully!*

JIM. [*protesting*] Aw—

LAURA. Yes, yes—beautifully—beautifully!

JIM. You heard me? 135

LAURA. All three times!

JIM. No!

LAURA. Yes!

JIM. All three performances?

LAURA. [*looking down*] Yes. 140

JIM. Why?

LAURA. I—wanted to ask you to—autograph my program. [*She takes the program from the back of the yearbook and shows it to him.*]

JIM. Why didn't you ask me to?

LAURA. You were always surrounded by your own friends so much that I never had a chance to.

JIM. You should have just— 145

LAURA. Well, I—thought you might think I was—

JIM. Thought I might think you was—what?

LAURA. Oh—

JIM. [*with reflective relish*] I was beleaguered by females in those days.

LAURA. You were terribly popular! 150

JIM. Yeah—

LAURA. You had such a—friendly way—

JIM. I was spoiled in high school.

LAURA. Everybody—liked you!

JIM. Including you? 155

LAURA. I—yes, I—did, too— [*She gently closes the book in her lap.*]

JIM. Well, well, well! Give me that program, Laura.

[*She hands it to him. He signs it with a flourish.*]

There you are—better late than never!

    LAURA.   Oh, I—what a—surprise!

    JIM.   My signature isn't worth very much right now. But some day—maybe—it will increase in value! Being disappointed is one thing and being discouraged is something else. I am disappointed but I am not discouraged. I'm twenty-three years old. How old are you?

    LAURA.   I'll be twenty-four in June.   160

    JIM.   That's not old age!

    LAURA.   No, but—

    JIM.   You finished high school?

    LAURA.   [*with difficulty*] I didn't go back.

    JIM.   You mean you dropped out?   165

    LAURA.   I made bad grades in my final examinations. [*She rises and replaces the book and the program on the table. Her voice is strained.*] How is—Emily Meisenbach getting along?

    JIM.   Oh, that kraut-head!

    LAURA.   Why do you call her that?

    JIM.   That's what she was.

    LAURA.   You're not still—going with her?   170

    JIM.   I never see her.

    LAURA.   It was in the "Personal" section that you were—engaged!

    JIM.   I know, but I wasn't impressed by that—propaganda!

    LAURA.   It wasn't—the truth?

    JIM.   Only in Emily's optimistic opinion!   175

    LAURA.   Oh—

[*Legend: "What have you done since high school?"*

JIM lights a cigarette and leans indolently back on his elbows smiling at LAURA with a warmth and charm which lights her inwardly with altar candles. She remains by the table, picks up a piece from the glass menagerie collection, and turns it in her hands to cover her tumult.]

    JIM.   [*after several reflective puffs on his cigarette*] What have you done since high school?

[*She seems not to hear him.*]

    Huh?

[*LAURA looks up.*]

I said what have you done since high school, Laura?

    LAURA.   Nothing much.

    JIM.   You must have been doing something these six long years.

    LAURA.   Yes.   180

    JIM.   Well, then, such as what?

    LAURA.   I took a business course at business college—

    JIM.   How did that work out?

    LAURA.   Well, not very—well—I had to drop out, it gave me—indigestion—

[*JIM laughs gently.*]

JIM. What are you doing now? 185

LAURA. I don't do anything—much. Oh, please don't think I sit around doing nothing! My glass collection takes up a good deal of time. Glass is something you have to take good care of.

JIM. What did you say—about glass?

LAURA. Collection I said—I have one—[*She clears her throat and turns away again, acutely shy.*]

JIM. [*abruptly*] You know what I judge to be the trouble with you? Inferiority complex! Know what that is? That's what they call it when someone low-rates himself! I understand it because I had it too. Although my case was not so aggravated as yours seems to be. I had it until I took up public speaking, developed my voice, and learned that I had an aptitude for science. Before that time I never thought of myself as being outstanding in any way whatsoever! Now I've never made a regular study of it, but I have a friend who says I can analyze people better than doctors that make a profession of it. I don't claim that to be necessarily true, but I can sure guess a person's psychology. Laura! [*He takes out his gum.*] Excuse me, Laura. I always take it out when the flavor is gone. I'll use this scrap of paper to wrap it in. I know how it is to get it stuck on a shoe. [*He wraps the gum in paper and puts it in his pocket.*] Yep—that's what I judge to be your principal trouble. A lack of confidence in yourself as a person. You don't have the proper amount of faith in yourself. I'm basing that fact on a number of your remarks and also on certain observations I've made. For instance that clumping you thought was so awful in high school. You say that you even dreaded to walk into class. You see what you did? You dropped out of school, you gave up an education because of a clump, which as far as I know was practically nonexistent! A little physical defect is what you have. Hardly noticeable even! Magnified thousands of times by imagination! You know what my strong advice to you is? Think of yourself as *superior* in some way!

LAURA. In what way would I think? 190

JIM. Why, man alive, Laura! Just look about you a little. What do you see? A world full of common people! All of 'em born and all of 'em going to die! Which of them has one-tenth of your good points! Or mine! Or anyone else's, as far as that goes—gosh! Everybody excels in some one thing. Some in many! [*He unconsciously glances at himself in the mirror.*] All you've got to do is discover in *what!* Take me, for instance. [*He adjusts his tie at the mirror.*] My interest happens to lie in electro-dynamics. I'm taking a course in radio engineering at night school, Laura, on top of a fairly responsible job at the warehouse. I'm taking that course and studying public speaking.

LAURA. Ohhhh.

JIM. Because I believe in the future of television! [*turning his back to her*] I wish to be ready to go up right along with it. Therefore I'm planning to get in on the ground floor. In fact I've already made the right connections and all that remains is for the industry itself to get under way! Full steam—[*His eyes are starry.*] Knowledge—Zzzzzp! Money—Zzzzzp!—Power! That's the cycle democracy is built on!

[*His attitude is convincingly dynamic. LAURA stares at him, even her shyness eclipsed in her absolute wonder. He suddenly grins.*]

I guess you think I think a lot of myself!

LAURA. No—o-o-o, I—

JIM. Now how about you? Isn't there something you take more interest in than anything else? 195

LAURA. Well, I do—as I said—have my—glass collection—

[*A peal of girlish laughter rings from the kitchenette.*]

JIM.   I'm not right sure I know what you're talking about. What kind of glass is it?

LAURA.   Little articles of it, they're ornaments mostly! Most of them are little animals made out of glass, the tiniest little animals in the world. Mother calls them a glass
menagerie! Here's an example of one, if you'd like to see it! This one is one of the
oldest. It's nearly thirteen.

[*Music: "The Glass Menagerie."*

He stretches out his hand.]

Oh, be careful—if you breathe, it breaks!

JIM.   I'd better not take it. I'm pretty clumsy with things.

LAURA.   Go, on, I trust you with him! [*She places the piece in his palm.*] There now—   200
you're holding him gently! Hold him over the light, he loves the light! You see how the
light shines through him?

JIM.   It sure does shine!

LAURA.   I shouldn't be partial, but he is my favorite one.

JIM.   What kind of a thing is this one supposed to be?

LAURA.   Haven't you noticed the single horn on his forehead?   205

JIM.   A unicorn, huh?

LAURA.   Mmmm-hmmm!

JIM.   Unicorns—aren't they extinct in the modern world?

LAURA.   I know!

JIM.   Poor little fellow, he must feel sort of lonesome.

LAURA.   [*smiling*] Well, if he does, he doesn't complain about it. He stays on a   210
shelf with some horses that don't have horns and all of them seem to get along nicely
together.

JIM.   How do you know?

LAURA.   [*lightly*] I haven't heard any arguments among them!

JIM.   [*grinning*] No arguments, huh? Well, that's a pretty good sign! Where shall I
set him?

LAURA.   Put him on the table. They all like a change of scenery once in a while!

JIM.   Well, well, well, well—[*He places the glass piece on the table, then raises his arms*   215
and stretches.] Look how big my shadow is when I stretch!

LAURA.   Oh, oh, yes—it stretches across the ceiling!

JIM.   [*crossing to the door*] I think it's stopped raining. [*He opens the fire-escape door*
and the background music changes to a dance tune.] Where does the music come from?

LAURA.   From the Paradise Dance Hall across the alley.

JIM.   How about cutting the rug a little, Miss Wingfield?

LAURA.   Oh, I—   220

JIM.   Or is your program filled up? Let me have a look at it. [*He grasps an imaginary card.*] Why, every dance is taken! I'll just have to scratch some out.

[*Waltz music: "La Golondrina"°*]

Ahh, a waltz! [*He executes some sweeping turns by himself, then holds his arms toward*
LAURA.]

220.2 *"La Golondrina":* a popular Mexican song (1883) written by Narciso Seradell (1843–1910).

LAURA.   [*breathlessly*] I—can't dance.

JIM.   There you go, that inferiority stuff!

LAURA.   I've never danced in my life!

JIM.   Come on, try!   225

LAURA.   Oh, but I'd step on you!

JIM.   I'm not made out of glass.

LAURA.   How—how—how do we start?

JIM.   Just leave it to me. You hold your arms out a little.

LAURA.   Like this?   230

JIM.   [*taking her in his arms*] A little bit higher. Right. Now don't tighten up, that's the main thing about it—relax.

LAURA.   [*laughing breathlessly*] It's hard not to.

JIM.   Okay.

LAURA.   I'm afraid you can't budge me.

JIM.   What do you bet I can't? [*He swings her into motion.*]   235

LAURA.   Goodness, yes, you can!

JIM.   Let yourself go, now, Laura, just let yourself go.

LAURA.   I'm—

JIM.   Come on!

LAURA.   —trying!   240

JIM.   Not so stiff—easy does it!

LAURA.   I know but I'm—

JIM.   Loosen th' backbone! There now, that's a lot better.

LAURA.   Am I?

JIM.   Lots, lots better! [*He moves her about the room in a clumsy waltz.*]   245

LAURA.   Oh, my!

JIM.   Ha-ha!

LAURA.   Oh, my goodness!

JIM.   Ha-ha-ha!

[*They suddenly bump into the table, and the glass piece on it falls to the floor. JIM stops the dance.*]

What did we hit?

LAURA.   Table.   250

JIM.   Did something fall off it? I think—

LAURA.   Yes.

JIM.   I hope that it wasn't the little glass horse with the horn!

LAURA.   Yes. [*She stoops to pick it up.*]

JIM.   Aw, aw, aw. Is it broken?   255

LAURA.   Now it is just like all the other horses.

JIM.   It's lost its—

LAURA.   Horn! It doesn't matter. Maybe it's a blessing in disguise.

JIM.   You'll never forgive me. I bet that that was your favorite piece of glass.

LAURA.   I don't have favorites much. It's no tragedy, Freckles. Glass breaks so   260
easily. No matter how careful you are. The traffic jars the shelves and things fall off them.

JIM.   Still I'm awfully sorry that I was the cause.

LAURA.   [*smiling*] I'll just imagine he had an operation. The horn was removed to make him feel less—freakish!

[*They both laugh.*]

Now he will feel more at home with the other horses, the ones that don't have horns. . . .

JIM.   Ha-ha, that's very funny! [*Suddenly he is serious.*] I'm glad to see that you have a sense of humor. You know—you're—well—very different! Surprisingly different from anyone else I know! [*His voice becomes soft and hesitant with a genuine feeling.*] Do you mind me telling you that?

[*LAURA is abashed beyond speech.*]

I mean it in a nice way—

[*LAURA nods shyly, looking away.*]

You make me feel sort of—I don't know how to put it! I'm usually pretty good at express-ing things, but—this is something that I don't know how to say!

[*LAURA touches her throat and clears it—turns the broken unicorn in her hands. His voice becomes softer.*]

Has anyone ever told you that you were pretty?

[*There is a pause, and the music rises slightly. LAURA looks up slowly, with wonder, and shakes her head.*]

Well, you are! In a very different way from anyone else. And all the nicer because of the difference, too.

[*His voice becomes low and husky. LAURA turns away, nearly faint with the novelty of her emotions.*]

I wish that you were my sister. I'd teach you to have some confidence in yourself. The different people are not like other people, but being different is nothing to be ashamed of. Because other people are not such wonderful people. They're one hun-dred times one thousand. You're one times one! They walk all over the earth. You just stay here. They're common as—weeds, but—you—well, you're—*Blue Roses!*

[*Image on screen: Blue Roses.*

The music changes.]

LAURA.   But blue is wrong for—roses. . . .
JIM.   It's right for you! You're—pretty!   265
LAURA.   In what respect am I pretty?
JIM.   In all respects—believe me! Your eyes—your hair—are pretty! Your hands are pretty! [*He catches hold of her hand.*] You think I'm making this up because I'm invited to dinner and have to be nice. Oh, I could do that! I could put on an act for you, Laura, and say lots of things without being very sincere. But this time I am. I'm talking to you sincerely. I happened to notice you had this inferiority complex that keeps you from feeling comfortable with people. Somebody needs to build your confidence up and make you proud instead of shy and turning away and—blushing. Somebody—ought to—*kiss* you, Laura!

[*His hand slips slowly up her arm to her shoulder as the music swells tumultuously. He suddenly turns about and kisses her on the lips. When he releases her,* LAURA *sinks on the sofa with a bright, dazed look.* JIM *backs away and fishes in his pocket for a cigarette.*

Legend on screen: "A souvenir."]

Stumblejohn!

[*He lights the cigarette, avoiding her look. There is a peal of girlish laughter from* AMANDA *in the kitchenette.* LAURA *slowly raises and opens her hand. It still contains the little broken glass animal. She looks at it with a tender, bewildered expression.*]

Stumblejohn! I shouldn't have done that—that was way off the beam. You don't smoke, do you?

[*She looks up, smiling, not hearing the question. He sits beside her rather gingerly. She looks at him speechlessly—waiting. He coughs decorously and moves a little further aside as he considers the situation and senses her feelings, dimly, with perturbation. He speaks gently.*]

Would you—care for a mint?

[*She doesn't seem to hear him but her look grows brighter even.*]

Peppermint? Life Saver? My pocket's a regular drugstore—wherever I go. . . . [*He pops a mint in his mouth. Then he gulps and decides to make a clean breast of it. He speaks slowly and gingerly.*] Laura, you know, if I had a sister like you, I'd do the same thing as Tom. I'd bring out fellows and—introduce her to them. The right type of boys—of a type to—appreciate her. Only—well—he made a mistake about me. Maybe I've got no call to be saying this. That may not have been the idea in having me over. But what if it was? There's nothing wrong about that. The only trouble is that in my case—I'm not in a situation to—do the right thing. I can't take down your number and say I'll phone. I can't call up next week and—ask for a date. I thought I had better explain the situation in case you—misunderstood it and—I hurt your feelings. . . .

[*There is a pause. Slowly, very slowly,* LAURA'S *look changes, her eyes returning slowly from his to the glass figure in her palm.* AMANDA *utters another gay laugh in the kitchenette.*]

    LAURA.   [*faintly*] You—won't—call again?

    JIM.   No, Laura, I can't. [*He rises from the sofa.*] As I was just explaining, I've—got strings on me, Laura, I've—been going steady! I go out all the time with a girl named Betty. She's a home-girl like you, and Catholic, and Irish, and in a great many ways we—get along fine. I met her last summer on a moonlight boat trip up the river to Alton,° on the *Majestic.* Well—right away from the start it was—love!

[*Legend: Love!*]

LAURA *sways slightly forward and grips the arm of the sofa. He fails to notice, now enrapt in his own comfortable being.*]

Being in love has made a new man of me!

[*Leaning stiffly forward, clutching the arm of the sofa,* LAURA *struggles visibly with her storm. But* JIM *is oblivious; she is a long way off.*]

269.1 *Alton:* a city in Illinois about twenty miles north of St. Louis on the Mississippi River.

The power of love is really pretty tremendous! Love is something that—changes the whole world, Laura!

[*The storm abates a little and* LAURA *leans back. He notices her again.*]

It happened that Betty's aunt took sick, she got a wire and had to go to Centralia.° So Tom—when he asked me to dinner—I naturally just accepted the invitation, not knowing that you—that he—that I—[*He stops awkwardly.*] Huh—I'm a stumblejohn!

[*He flops back on the sofa. The holy candles on the altar of* LAURA'*s face have been snuffed out. There is a look of almost infinite desolation.* JIM *glances at her uneasily.*]

I wish that you would—say something.

[*She bites her lip which was trembling and then bravely smiles. She opens her hand again on the broken glass figure. Then she gently takes his hand and raises it level with her own. She carefully places the unicorn in the palm of his hand, then pushes his fingers closed upon it.*]

What are you—doing that for? You want me to have him? Laura?

[*She nods.*]

What for?

    LAURA.   A—souvenir. . . .   270

[*She rises unsteadily and crouches beside the Victrola to wind it up.*

Legend on screen: "Things have a way of turning out so badly!" Or image: "Gentleman caller waving goodbye—gaily."

At this moment AMANDA *rushes brightly back into the living room. She bears a pitcher of fruit punch in an old-fashioned cut-glass pitcher, and a plate of macaroons. The plate has a gold border and poppies painted on it.*]

    AMANDA.   Well, well, well! Isn't the air delightful after the shower? I've made you children a little liquid refreshment. [*She turns gaily to* JIM.] Jim, do you know that song about lemonade?
    "Lemonade, lemonade
    Made in the shade and stirred with a spade—
    Good enough for any old maid!"
    JIM.   [*uneasily*] Ha-ha! No—I never heard it.
    AMANDA.   Why, Laura! You look so serious!
    JIM.   We were having a serious conversation.
    AMANDA.   Good! Now you're better acquainted!   275
    JIM.   [*uncertainly*] Ha-ha! Yes.
    AMANDA.   You modern young people are much more serious-minded than my generation. I was so gay as a girl!
    JIM.   You haven't changed, Mrs. Wingfield.
    AMANDA.   Tonight I'm rejuvenated! The gaiety of the occasion, Mr. O'Connor!
[*She tosses her head with a peal of laughter, spilling some lemonade.*] Oooo! I'm baptizing myself!
    JIM.   Here—let me—   280

269.8 *Centralia:* a city in Illinois about sixty miles east of St. Louis.

AMANDA. [*setting the pitcher down*] There now. I discovered we had some maraschino cherries. I dumped them in, juice and all!

JIM. You shouldn't have gone to that trouble, Mrs. Wingfield.

AMANDA. Trouble, trouble? Why, it was loads of fun! Didn't you hear me cutting up in the kitchen? I bet your ears were burning! I told Tom how outdone with him I was for keeping you to himself so long a time! He should have brought you over much, much sooner! Well, now that you've found your way, I want you to be a very frequent caller! Not just occasional but all the time. Oh, we're going to have a lot of gay times together! I see them coming! Mmm, just breathe that air! So fresh, and the moon's so pretty! I'll skip back out—I know where my place is when young folks are having a— serious conversation!

JIM. Oh, don't go out, Mrs. Wingfield. The fact of the matter is I've got to be going.

AMANDA. Going, now? You're joking! Why, it's only the shank of the evening,° 285 Mr. O'Connor!

JIM. Well, you know how it is.

AMANDA. You mean you're a young workingman and have to keep working-men's hours. We'll let you off early tonight. But only on the condition that next time you stay later. What's the best night for you? Isn't Saturday night the best night for you workingmen?

JIM. I have a couple of time-clocks to punch, Mrs. Wingfield. One at morning, another one at night!

AMANDA. My, but you *are* ambitious! You work at night, too?

JIM. No, Ma'am, not work but—Betty!   290

[*He crosses deliberately to pick up his hat. The band at the Paradise Dance Hall goes into a tender waltz.*]

AMANDA. Betty? Betty? Who's—Betty!

[*There is an ominous cracking sound in the sky.*]

JIM. Oh, just a girl. The girl I go steady with!

[*He smiles charmingly. The sky falls.*

Legend: "The Sky Falls."]

AMANDA. [*a long-drawn exhalation*] Ohhh . . . Is it a serious romance, Mr. O'Connor?

JIM. We're going to be married the second Sunday in June.

AMANDA. Ohhh—how nice! Tom didn't mention that you were engaged to be   295 married.

JIM. The cat's not out of the bag at the warehouse yet. You know how they are. They call you Romeo and stuff like that. [*He stops at the oval mirror to put on his hat. He carefully shapes the brim and the crown to give a discreetly dashing effect.*] It's been a wonderful evening, Mrs. Wingfield. I guess this is what they mean by Southern hospitality.

AMANDA. It really wasn't anything at all.

---

285 *shank of the evening:* still early, the best part of the evening.

JIM.   I hope it don't seem like I'm rushing off. But I promised Betty I'd pick her up at the Wabash depot, an' by the time I get my jalopy down there her train'll be in. Some women are pretty upset if you keep 'em waiting.

AMANDA.   Yes, I know—the tyranny of women! [*She extends her hand.*] Goodbye, Mr. O'Connor. I wish you luck—and happiness—and success! All three of them, and so does Laura! Don't you, Laura?

LAURA.   Yes!   300

JIM.   [*taking LAURA's hand*] Goodbye, Laura. I'm certainly going to treasure that souvenir. And don't you forget the good advice I gave you. [*He raises his voice to a cheery shout.*] So long, Shakespeare! Thanks again, ladies. Good night!

[*He grins and ducks jauntily out. Still bravely grimacing, AMANDA closes the door on the gentleman caller. Then she turns back to the room with a puzzled expression. She and LAURA don't dare to face each other. LAURA crouches beside the Victrola to wind it.*]

AMANDA.   [*faintly*] Things have a way of turning out so badly. I don't believe that I would play the Victrola. Well, well—well! Our gentleman caller was engaged to be married? [*She raises her voice.*] Tom!

TOM.   [*from the kitchenette*] Yes, Mother?

AMANDA.   Come in here a minute. I want to tell you something awfully funny.

TOM.   [*entering with a macaroon and a glass of the lemonade*] Has the gentleman   305
caller gotten away already?

AMANDA.   The gentleman caller has made an early departure. What a wonderful joke you played on us!

TOM.   How do you mean?

AMANDA.   You didn't mention that he was engaged to be married.

TOM.   Jim? Engaged?

AMANDA.   That's what he just informed us.   310

TOM.   I'll be jiggered! I didn't know about that.

AMANDA.   That seems very peculiar.

TOM.   What's peculiar about it?

AMANDA.   Didn't you call him your best friend down at the warehouse?

TOM.   He is, but how did I know?   315

AMANDA.   It seems extremely peculiar that you wouldn't know your best friend was going to be married!

TOM.   The warehouse is where I work, not where I know things about people!

AMANDA.   You don't know things anywhere! You live in a dream; you manufacture illusions!

[*He crosses to the door.*]

Where are you going?

TOM.   I'm going to the movies.

AMANDA.   That's right, now that you've had us make such fools of ourselves. The   320
effort, the preparations, all the expense! The new floor lamp, the rug, the clothes for Laura! All for what? To entertain some other girl's fiancé! Go to the movies, go! Don't think about us, a mother deserted, an unmarried sister who's crippled and has no job! Don't let anything interfere with your selfish pleasure! Just go, go, go—to the movies!

TOM.   All right, I will! The more you shout about my selfishness to me the quicker I'll go, and I won't go to the movies!

AMANDA.   Go, then! Go to the moon—you selfish dreamer!

[*TOM smashes his glass on the floor. He plunges out on the fire escape, slamming the door. LAURA screams in fright. The dance-hall music becomes louder. TOM stands on the fire escape, gripping the rail. The moon breaks through the storm clouds, illuminating his face.*

Legend on screen: "And so goodbye . . ."

TOM's closing speech is timed with what is happening inside the house. We see, as though through soundproof glass, that AMANDA appears to be making a comforting speech to LAURA, who is huddled upon the sofa. Now that we cannot hear the mother's speech, her silliness is gone and she has dignity and tragic beauty. LAURA's hair hides her face until, at the end of the speech, she lifts her head to smile at her mother. AMANDA's gestures are slow and graceful, almost dancelike, as she comforts her daughter. At the end of her speech she glances a moment at the father's picture— then withdraws through the portieres. At the close of TOM's speech, LAURA blows out the candles, ending the play.]

TOM.   I didn't go to the moon, I went much further—for time is the longest distance between two places. Not long after that I was fired for writing a poem on the lid of a shoe-box. I left Saint Louis. I descended the steps of this fire escape for a last time and followed, from then on, in my father's footsteps, attempting to find in motion what was lost in space. I traveled around a great deal. The cities swept about me like dead leaves, leaves that were brightly colored but torn away from the branches. I would have stopped, but I was pursued by something. It always came upon me unawares, taking me altogether by surprise. Perhaps it was a familiar bit of music. Perhaps it was only a piece of transparent glass. Perhaps I am walking along a street at night, in some strange city, before I have found companions. I pass the lighted window of a shop where perfume is sold. The window is filled with pieces of colored glass, tiny transparent bottles in delicate colors, like bits of a shattered rainbow. Then all at once my sister touches my shoulder. I turn around and look into her eyes. Oh, Laura, Laura, I tried to leave you behind me, but I am more faithful than I intended to be! I reach for a cigarette, I cross the street, I run into the movies or a bar, I buy a drink, I speak to the nearest stranger—anything that can blow your candles out!

[*LAURA bends over the candles.*]

For nowadays the world is lit by lightning! Blow out your candles, Laura—and so goodbye. . . .

[*She blows the candles out.*]

QUESTIONS

1.   What does the setting described in the opening stage direction tell you about the Wingfields? Consider especially the adjectives and the symbolism of the alley and the fire escape.

2.   Who is the "fifth character" in the play, and how is his presence established? In what ways is Tom a parallel to this character?

3.   What does Amanda reveal about her past in scene 1? How does Williams reveal that Amanda often dwells in the past?

4.   What happened to Laura at Rubicam's Business College? How can you account for her behavior? What plan of Amanda's did she upset?

5. What new plan for Laura's future does Amanda begin to develop in scene 2? Why is the plan impracticable? Why is the image of Jim introduced here?

6. Summarize the argument between Tom and Amanda in scene 3. What does Amanda assert about Tom? What does he claim about his life? Why is Laura spotlighted throughout the argument?

7. What sort of agreement does Amanda try to reach with Tom about Laura in scene 4?

8. How do Amanda and Laura react to the news of a gentleman caller? Describe Laura's feelings toward Jim during the conversation and the dancing in scene 7. Describe how he changes after the kiss.

9. Explain the symbolism of the unicorn (both whole and broken). Why does Laura give it to Jim as a souvenir?

10. What is Tom's situation at the end? To what degree has he achieved his dreams of escape and adventure?

11. Describe Amanda's and Laura's concluding situations. Why does Laura blow out the candles? What is the future for these women?

GENERAL QUESTIONS

1. Explain the most striking nonrealistic aspects of the play. What do these contribute to the play's meaning and impact? Which aspect is the most effective? Why?

2. Which characters in the play change significantly? To what extent do the characters succeed or fail? How do they try to escape the realities they face?

3. Consider Tom as character and narrator. Explain why his language changes as he shifts between narrator and character. What does the character dream about and strive for? What does the narrator learn about these dreams and strivings?

4. Explain why Laura cannot deal with reality. What does her glass menagerie symbolize?

5. Williams says that there is much to admire, pity, and laugh at in Amanda. What aspects of her character are admirable? Pitiable? Laughable? Which reaction is dominant for you at the close of the play? Why?

6. Tom calls Jim the play's "most realistic character." In what ways is Jim realistic? How are his dreams and goals more (or less) realistic than Tom's?

7. At the opening, Tom (as narrator) mentions the "social background," and he remarks on it throughout. Discuss how this background relates to the play, especially the events occurring in Europe.

8. Discuss the play's religious allusion and imagery, especially Malvolio the Magician, the "Ave Maria," the "Annunciation," the Paradise Dance Hall, and Laura's candles. How do these references affect the play's level of reality?

SPECIAL
WRITING
TOPICS
ABOUT

LITERATURE

26

Writing and Documenting the Research Essay

Broadly, **research** is the act of systematic investigation, examination, and experimentation. It is the basic tool of intellectual inquiry for anyone engaged in any discipline—physics, chemistry, biology, psychology, anthropology, history, and literature, to name just a few disciplines. With research, our understanding and our civilization grow; without it, they die.

The beginning assumption of doing research is that the researcher is exploring new areas of knowledge. With each assignment the researcher acquires not only the knowledge gained from the particular task, but also the skills needed to undertake further research and thereby to gain further knowledge. Some research tasks are elementary, such as using a dictionary to discover the meaning of a word and thereby aiding the understanding of an important passage. More involved research uses an array of resources: encyclopedias, biographies, introductions, critical studies, bibliographies, and histories. When you begin a research task you usually have little or no knowledge about your topic, but with such resources it is possible to acquire a good deal of expert knowledge in a relatively short time.

While research is the animating spark of all disciplines, our topic here is **literary research**—the systematic use of primary and secondary sources in studying a literary problem. In doing literary research, you consult not only individual works themselves (*primary sources*) but many other works that shed light on them and interpret them (*secondary sources*). Typical research tasks are to learn important facts about a work and about the period in which it was written; to learn about the lives, careers, and other works of authors; to discover and apply the comments and judgments of modern or earlier critics; to learn details that help explain the meaning of works; and to learn about critical and artistic taste.

SELECTING A TOPIC

In most instances, your instructor assigns a research essay on a specific topic. Sometimes, however, the choice of a topic is left entirely up to you. For such assignments, it is helpful to know the types of research essays you might find most congenial. Here are some possibilities:

1. *A particular work.* You might treat character (for example, "The Character of Bottom in *A Midsummer Night's Dream*" or "The Question of Whether Willie Loman is a Hero or Antihero in *Death of a Salesman*") or tone, ideas, form, problems, and the like. A research paper on a single work is similar to an essay on the same work, except that the research paper takes into account more views and facts than those you are likely to have without the research.

2. *A particular author.* This essay is about an idea or some facet of style, imagery, setting, or tone of the author, tracing the origins and development of the topic through a number of different stories, poems, or plays. An example is "The Idea of the True Self as Developed by Frost in His Poetry before 1920." This type of essay is suitable if you are writing on a poet whose works are short, though a topic like "Shakespeare's Idea of the Relationships between Men and Women as Dramatized in *A Midsummer Night's Dream* and *Hamlet*" is also possible.

3. *Comparison and contrast* (see Chapter 29). There are two types:

    a. *An idea or quality common to two or more authors.* Here you show points of similarity or contrast, or else show how one author's work may criticize another's. A possible subject is "The Theme of Ineffectuality in Eliot, Steinbeck, and Williams" or "Hughes's Antidiscrimination Poems in the Context of Twentieth-Century Race Relations."

    b. *Different critical views of a particular work or body of works.* Sometimes much is to be gained from an examination of differing critical opinions on topics like "The Meaning of Shirley Jackson's 'The Lottery,'" "Various Interpretations of Gray's *Elegy*," or "The Question of Hamlet's Hesitation." Such a study would attempt to determine the critical opinion and taste to which a work did or did not appeal, and it might also aim at conclusions about whether the work was in the advance or rear guard of its time.

4. *The influence of an idea, author, philosophy, political situation, or artistic movement on specific works of an author or authors.* An essay on influences can be specific and to the point, as in "Details of 1960s Military Life in Vietnam in O'Brien's 'The Things They Carried,'" or else it can be more abstract and critical, as in "The Influence of Attitudes toward the Vietnam War on the Narration of O'Brien's 'The Things They Carried.'"

5. *The origin of a particular work or type of work.* Such an essay might examine an author's biography to discover the germination and development of a work—for example, "'The Loons' as an Aspect of Laurence's Life in Rural Canada." Another way of discovering origins might be to relate a work to a particular type or tradition: "*Hamlet* as Revenge Tragedy," or "Sophocles's *Oedipus the King* and Its Origins in the Conventions of Ancient Athenian Drama."

If you consider these types, an idea of what to write may come to you. Perhaps you have particularly liked one author or several authors. If so, you might start to think along the lines of types 1, 2, and 3. If you are interested in influences or in origins, then types 4 or 5 may suit you better.

If you still cannot decide on a topic after rereading the works you have liked, then you should carry your search for a topic into your school library. Look up your author or authors in the computer or card catalogue. Your first goal should be to find a relatively recent book-length critical study published by a university press. Look for a title indicating that the book is a general one dealing with the author's major works rather than just one work. Study those chapters relevant to the work or works you have chosen. Most writers of critical studies describe their purpose and plan in their introductions or first chapters, so begin with the first part of the book. If there is no separate chapter on the primary text, use the index and go to the relevant pages. Reading in this way will give you enough knowledge about the issues and ideas raised by the work to enable you to select a promising topic. Once you make your decision, you are ready to develop a working bibliography.

SETTING UP A BIBLIOGRAPHY

The best way to develop a working bibliography of books and articles is to begin with major critical studies of the writer or writers. Again, go to the catalogue and find books that have been published by university presses. These books usually contain comprehensive bibliographies. Be careful to read the chapters on your primary work or works and to look for the footnotes or endnotes, for often you can save time if you record the names of books and articles listed in these notes. Then refer to the bibliographies included at the ends of the books, and select likely looking titles. Now, look at the dates of publication of the critical books. Let us suppose that you have been looking at three, published in 1963, 1987, and 1995. The chances are that the bibliography in a book published in 1995 will be complete up through about 1994, for the writer will usually have completed the manuscript at least a year before the book was published. What you should do then is to gather a bibliography of works published since 1994; you can safely assume that writers of critical works will have done the selecting for you of important works published before that time.

Bibliographical Guides

Fortunately for students doing literary research, the Modern Language Association (MLA) of America has been providing a complete bibliography of literary studies for years, not only in English and American literatures but in the literatures of many foreign languages. This is the *MLA International Bibliography of Books and Articles on the Modern Languages and Literatures* (*MLA Bibliography*). The *MLA Bibliography* started achieving completeness in the late 1950s. By 1969 the project had grown so large that it was published in many parts, which are bound together in library editions. University and college libraries have sets of these bibliographies on open shelves or tables. Recently, they have become available on CD-ROM.

There are many other bibliographies useful for students doing literary research, such as the *Essay and General Literature Index,* the *International Index,* and various specific indexes. For most undergraduate and many graduate purposes, however, the *MLA Bibliography* is more than adequate. Remember that as you progress in your reading, the notes and bibliographies in the works you consult also will constitute an unfolding bibliography. For the sample research essay in this chapter, for example, a number of entries were discovered not from the bibliographies, but from the reference lists in critical works.

The *MLA Bibliography* is conveniently organized by period and author. If your author is Gwendolyn Brooks, for example, look her up in *Volume I: British and Irish, Commonwealth, English, Caribbean, and American Literatures,* where you will also find references to authors such as Shakespeare, Wordsworth, and Munro. You will find most books and articles listed under the author's last name. In the *MLA Bibliography,* journal references are abbreviated, but a lengthy list explaining abbreviations appears at the beginning of the volume. Using the *MLA Bibliography,* begin with the most recent one and then go backward to your stopping point. Be sure to get the complete information, especially volume numbers and years of publication, for each article and book. You are now ready to find your sources and to take notes.

ONLINE LIBRARY SERVICES

Today, most libraries have their own computerized catalogues. In addition, many libraries are connected with a vast array of local, national, and even international libraries, so that by using various online services, you can extend your research far beyond the capacities of your own library. You can even use your own personal computer to gain access to the catalogues of large research libraries, provided that you have a modem, the right computer program, the correct entry information, the willingness and ability to follow the program codes, and patience and persistence. By using various "search engines" to gain access to sites on the World Wide Web, you can also discover special topics directly related to your subject—organizations devoted to making awards, for example, or clubs or other organizations that have been established in the home cities of particular authors, or works on topics inspired by such authors.

The ease with which you can gain access to the various libraries through a computer search is variable. Some library catalogues are friendly while others require a certain amount of trial and error.[1] In many cases you cannot determine exactly how to find what you are looking for without practice, for the

---

[1] Libraries generally encourage access to their resources, however, so proper entry instructions are often attached to computer terminals, particularly for internal use. When you are hooked into catalogues of distant libraries, you will find that the computer screen itself contains easily followed instructions about what you need to do to continue your search.

words some libraries use to categorize holdings are not immediately apparent. In all cases, practice with the various systems is essential, for you cannot expect to get the most out of an electronic search the first time you try.

After you have gained access, you can ask for books by specific authors, or for books about particular topics. If your author is Shakespeare, for example, you can ask for specific titles of his works or for books about him. A recent search for critical and interpretive works about Shakespeare in a large urban university library produced a list of 577 titles with accompanying bibliographical information. The same library listed 167 works dealing specifically with *Hamlet*. Another large library produced 2,412 titles on the criticism and interpretation of Shakespeare (not just in English, but also in other languages). Once you have such materials on your screen, you can select and list only the titles that you think will be most useful to you.

Such a list comprises a fairly comprehensive search bibliography, which you can use when you physically enter the library to begin collecting and using materials. A major convenience is that many associated libraries, such as state colleges and urban public libraries, have pooled their resources. Thus, if you use the services of a network of nearby county libraries, you can go to another library to use materials that are not accessible at your own college or branch. If distances are great, however, and your own library does not have a book that you think is important to your project, you can ask a librarian to get the book for you through the Interlibrary Loan Service. Usually, with time, the libraries will accommodate as many of your needs as they can.

IMPORTANT CONSIDERATIONS
ABOUT COMPUTER-AIDED RESEARCH

You must always keep in mind that online catalogues can give you only what has been entered into them. If one library classifies a work under "criticism and interpretation" and another classifies it under "characters," a search of "criticism and interpretation" at the first library will find the work but a search at the second will not. Sometimes the inclusion of an author's life dates immediately following the name will throw off your search. Typographic errors in the system will cause additional search problems, although many search programs attempt to forestall such difficulties by providing "nearby" entries to enable you to determine whether incorrectly entered topics can actually prove fruitful for your further examination. Also, if you use online services, be careful to determine the year when the computerization began. Many libraries have a recent commencement date—1978, for example, or 1985. For completeness, therefore, you would need assistance in finding catalogue entries for items published before these years.

Just a few years ago, the broadness of scope that electronic searches provide for most undergraduate students doing research assignments was not possible; today, it is a commonplace. Even with the astounding possibilities of electronic resources, however, it is still necessary to take out actual books and articles—and read them and take notes on them—before you can begin and complete a research essay. The electronic services can help you locate materials, but they cannot do your reading, note taking, and writing. All that is still up to you, as it always has been.

TAKING NOTES AND PARAPHRASING MATERIAL

There are many ways of taking notes, but the consensus is that the best method is to use note cards. If you have never used cards before, you might profit from consulting any one of a number of handbooks and special workbooks on research.[2] The principal advantage of cards is that they can be classified; numbered and renumbered; shuffled; tried out in one place, rejected, and then used in another place (or thrown away); and arranged in order when you start to write.

Taking Notes

WRITE THE SOURCE ON EACH CARD.   As you take notes, write the source of your information on each card. This may seem bothersome, but it is easier than going back to the library to locate the correct source after you have begun your essay. You can save time if you take the complete data on one card—a "master card" for that source—and then create an abbreviation for the separate note cards you take from the source. Here is an example, which also includes the location where the reference was originally found (e.g., card catalogue, computer search, bibliography in a book, the *MLA Bibliography*, etc.). Observe that the author's last name goes first.

```
Donovan, Josephine, ed.                          PN
     Feminist Literary Criticism: Explorations   98
     in Theory. Lexington: The University        W64
     Press of Kentucky, 1975.                    F4

DONOVAN

Card Catalogue, "Women"
```

If you take many notes from this book, the name *Donovan* will serve as identification. Be sure not to lose your complete master cards because you will need them when you prepare your list of works cited. If possible, record the complete bibliographical data in a computer file.

RECORD THE PAGE NUMBER FOR EACH NOTE.   It would be hard to guess how much exasperation has been caused by the failure to record page numbers in notes. Be sure to get the page number down first, *before* you begin to take your note, and, to be doubly sure, write the page number again at the end of your

---

[2] See, for example, Melinda G. Kramer, Glenn Leggett, and C. David Mead, *Prentice Hall Handbook for Writers*, 12th ed. (Englewood Cliffs: Prentice Hall, 1995), 501–05.

note. If the detail goes from one page to the next in your source, record the exact spot where the page changes, as in this example:

> **Heilbrun and Stimson, in DONOVAN, pp. 63–64**
>
> [63] After the raising of the feminist consciousness it is necessary to develop / [64] "the growth of moral perception" through anger and the correction of social inequality.

The reason for such care is that you may wish to use only a part of a note you have taken, and when there are two pages you will need to be accurate in locating what goes where.

RECORD ONLY ONE FACT OR OPINION ON A CARD.   Record only one major element on each card—one quotation, one paraphrase, one observation—*never two or more*. You might be tempted to fill up the entire card with many separate but unrelated details, but such a try at economy often gets you in trouble because you might want to use some of the details in other places. If you have only one entry per card, you will avoid such problems and also retain the freedom you need.

USE QUOTATION MARKS FOR ALL QUOTED MATERIAL.   In taking notes it is extremely important to distinguish copied material from your own words. *Always put quotation marks around every direct quotation you copy verbatim from a source.* Make the quotation marks immediately, before you forget, so that you will always know that the words of your notes within quotation marks are the words of another writer.

Often, as you take a note, you can use some of your own words and some of the words from your source. In cases like this you should be even more cautious. Put quotation marks around *every word* that you take directly from the source, even if your note looks like a picket fence. Later, when you begin writing your paper, your memory of what is yours and not yours will be dim, and if you use another's words in your own essay without proper acknowledgment, you are risking the charge of plagiarism. Most of the time, plagiarism is caused not by deliberate deception but rather by sloppy note taking.

Paraphrasing

When you take notes, it is best to paraphrase the sources. A paraphrase is a restatement in your own words, and because of this it is actually a first step in the writing of the essay. Chapter 2 (pp. 85–91) explains in full how to write a précis or abridgment. If you work on this technique, you will be well prepared to paraphrase for your research paper.

A big problem in paraphrasing is to capture the idea in the source without duplicating the words. The best way is to read and reread the passage you are noting. Turn over the book or journal and write out the idea *in your own words* as accurately as you can. Once you have this note, compare it with the original and make corrections to improve your thought and emphasis. Add a short quotation if you believe it is needed, but be sure to use quotation marks. If your paraphrase is too close to the original, *throw out the note and try again.* This effort is worthwhile because often you can transfer all or some of your note directly to the appropriate place in your research paper.

To see the problems of paraphrasing, let us look at a paragraph of criticism and then see how a student doing research might take notes on it. The paragraph is by Maynard Mack, from an essay titled "The World of Hamlet," originally published in *The Yale Review* 41 (1952) and reprinted in *Twentieth Century Interpretations of Hamlet,* ed. David Bevington (Englewood Cliffs: Prentice Hall, 1968), p. 57.

> The powerful sense of mortality in *Hamlet* is conveyed to us, I think, in three ways. First, there is the play's emphasis on human weakness, the instability of human purpose, the subjection of humanity to fortune—all that we might call the aspect of failure in man. Hamlet opens this theme in Act I, when he describes how from that single blemish, perhaps not even the victim's fault, a man's whole character may take corruption. Claudius dwells on it again, to an extent that goes far beyond the needs of the occasion, while engaged in seducing Laertes to step behind the arras of a seemer's world and dispose of Hamlet by a trick. Time qualifies everything, Claudius says, including love, including purpose. As for love—it has a "plurisy" in it and dies of its own too much. As for purpose—"That we would do, We should do when we would, for the 'would' changes. And hath abatements and delays as many As there are tongues, are hands, are accidents; And then this 'should' is like a spendthrift's sigh, That hurts by easing." The player-king, in his long speeches to his queen in the play within the play, sets the matter in a still darker light. She means these protestations of undying love, he knows, but our purposes depend on our memory, and our memory fades fast. Or else, he suggests, we propose something to ourselves in a condition of strong feeling, but then the feeling goes, and with it the resolve. Or else our fortunes change, he adds, and with these our loves: "The great man down, you mark his favorite flies." The subjection of human aims to fortune is a reiterated theme in *Hamlet,* as subsequently in *Lear.* Fortune is the harlot goddess in whose secret parts men like Rosencrantz and Guildenstern live and thrive; the strumpet who threw down Troy and Hecuba and Priam; the outrageous foe whose slings and arrows a man of principle must suffer or seek release in suicide. Horatio suffers them with composure: he is one of the blessed few "Whose blood and judgment are so well co-mingled That there are not a pipe for fortune's finger To sound what stop she please." For Hamlet the task is of a greater difficulty.

Because taking notes forces a shortening of this or any criticism, it also requires you to discriminate, judge, interpret, and select; good note taking is not easy.

There are some things to guide you, however, when you go through the many sources you uncover.

THINK OF THE PURPOSE OF YOUR RESEARCH.   You may not know exactly what you are "fishing for" when you start to take notes, for you cannot prejudge what your essay will contain. Research is a form of discovery. But soon you will notice subjects and issues that your sources constantly explore. If you can accept one of these as your major topic, or focus of interest, you may use that as your guide in all further note taking.

For example, suppose you are taking notes on critical works about *Hamlet*, and after a certain amount of reading you have decided to focus on "Shakespeare's Tragic Views in *Hamlet*." This decision would prompt you to take a note when you come to Mack's thought about mortality and death in the passage quoted above. In this instance, the following note would suffice:

Mack, in Bevington, 57   Death and
                                                                          Mortality

Mack cites three ways in which <u>Hamlet</u> stresses death and mortality. The
first (57) is an emphasis on human shortcomings and "weakness." Corruption,
loss of memory and enthusiasm, bad luck, misery—all suit the sense of the
closeness of death to life.   57

Let us now suppose that you want a fuller note, in the expectation that you need not just the topic but also some of Mack's detail. Such a note might look like this:

Mack, in Bevington, 57   Death and
                                                                          Mortality

The first of Mack's "three ways" in which a "powerful sense of mortality" is
shown in <u>Hamlet</u> is the illustration of human "weakness," "instability," and
helplessness before fate. In support, Mack refers to Hamlet's early speech on
a single fault leading to "corruption," also to Claudius's speech (in the scene
persuading Laertes to trick Hamlet). The player-king also talks about his
queen's forgetfulness and therefore inconstancy by default. As slaves to
fortune, Rosencrantz and Guildenstern are examples. Horatio is not a slave,
however. Hamlet's case is by far the worst of all.   57

In an actual essay, any part of this note would be useful. The words are almost all the note taker's own, and the few quotations are within quotation marks.

Note that Mack, the critic, is properly recognized as the source of the criticism, so that you could adapt the note easily when you are doing your writing. The key here is that your taking of notes should be guided by your developing plan for your essay.

Note taking is part of your thinking and composing process. You cannot predict whether you will be able to use each of your notes, and you will therefore exclude many notes when you write your essay. You will always find, however, that taking notes is easier once you have determined your purpose.

GIVE EACH NOTE A TITLE.   To help plan and develop the various parts of your essay, write a title for each of your notes in the upper right corner of the card, as in the examples in this chapter. *This practice is a form of outlining that will help you immeasurably when you write your essay.* Let us assume that you have chosen to study the importance of the Ghost in the play (the topic of the sample research essay on p. 1362). As you delve into your sources, you discover that there are conflicting views about how the Ghost should be understood. Here is a note about one of the questionable qualities of this character:

Prosser, 133, 134   **Negative, Devilish**

   133 When describing his pain and suffering as a dead spirit, the Ghost is not specific but emphasizes the horror. He should, if a good spirit, try to use his suffering to urge repentance and salvation for Hamlet. 134 This emphasis is a sign that he is closer in nature to a devil than to a soul earning its way to redemption.

Notice that the title classifies the topic of the note. If you use such classifications while taking notes, a number of like-titled cards could form the substance of a section in your essay about the negative qualities of the Ghost in *Hamlet*. In addition, once you decide that "Negative, Devilish" is one of the topics you plan to explore, the topic itself will guide you in further study and note taking.

RECORD YOUR OWN THOUGHTS.   As you take your notes, you will be getting good thoughts of your own. Do not push these aside in your mind, on the chance of remembering them later, but write them down immediately. Often you may notice a detail that your source does not mention, or you may get a hint for an idea that the critic does not develop. Often, too, you may get thoughts that can serve as "bridges" between details in your notes or as introductions or concluding observations. Be sure to title your comment and also to mark it as your own thought. Here is such a note, which is related to the importance of the Ghost in the structure of *Hamlet*:

My Own   Structure

    Shakespeare does a superb job with the Ghost. His characterization shows many qualities of a living human being, and the Ghost is fully integrated in the play's structure.

Observe that some of the ideas and language from this note are used in paragraphs 9 and 10 of the sample research essay (pp. 1365–66).

    SORT YOUR CARDS INTO GROUPS.   If you do a careful and thorough job of taking notes, your essay will have been forming in your mind already. The titles of your cards will suggest areas to be developed as you do your planning and initial drafting. Once you have assembled a stack of note cards derived from a reasonable number of sources (your instructor may have assigned a minimum number), you can sort them into groups according to the topics and titles. For the sample research essay, after some shuffling and retitling, the cards were assembled in the following groups:

1. Importance in the play's action
2. Importance in the play's themes
3. Condition as a spirit
   a. Good signs
   b. Negative, devilish signs
4. Human traits
5. Importance in the play's structure
6. Effect on other characters

If you look at the major sections of the sample research essay, you will see that the topics are closely adapted from these groups of cards. In other words, *the arrangement of the cards is an effective means of outlining and organizing a research essay.*

    ARRANGE THE CARDS IN EACH GROUP.   There is still much to do with each group of cards. You cannot use the details as they fall randomly in your stack. You need to decide which notes are relevant. You might also need to retitle some cards and use them elsewhere. Those that remain will have to be arranged in a clear and logical order to be used in the essay.

    Once you have your cards in order, you can write whatever comments or transitions are needed to move from detail to detail. Write this material directly on the cards, and be sure to use pencils or inks of different color, so that you can distinguish later between the original note and what you add now. Here is an example of such a "developed" note card:

Campbell, 127   Negative, Devilish

Shakespeare's Ghost reflects the general uncertainty at the time about how ghosts were to be interpreted.   127

This may be the best way to answer the questions about the Ghost's ambiguous nature. Moreover, Shakespeare may have been trying to be more lifelike than consistent with his Ghost.

By adding such commentary to your note cards, you will facilitate the actual writing of your first draft. In many instances, the note and the comment can be moved directly into the paper with minor adjustments (material from this note and comment appears in paragraph 5 of the sample research essay).

BE CREATIVE AND ORIGINAL.   You will not always transfer your notes directly into your essay. The major trap to avoid in a research paper is that your use of sources can become an end in itself and therefore a shortcut for your own thinking and writing. Often, students make the mistake of introducing details the way a master of ceremonies introduces performers in a variety show. This is unfortunate because it is the *student* whose essay will be judged, even though the sources, like the performers, do all the work. Thus, it is important to be creative and original in a research essay and to do your own thinking and writing, even though you are relying heavily on your sources. Here are four ways in which research essays may be original:

1. *Selection.* In each major section of your essay you will include many details from your sources. To be creative you should select different but related details and avoid overlapping or repetition. The essay will be judged on the basis of the thoroughness with which you make your point with different details (which in turn will represent the completeness of your research). Even though you are relying on published materials and cannot be original on that score, your selection can be original because you bring *these* materials together for the first time, and because you emphasize some details and minimize others. Inevitably, your assemblage of details from your sources will be unique and therefore original.

2. *Development.* Your arrangement of your various points is an obvious area of originality: One detail seems naturally to precede another, and certain conclusions

stem from certain details. As you present the details, conclusions, and arguments from your sources, you can also add an original stamp by introducing supporting details different from those in the source material. You can also add your own emphasis to particular points—an emphasis that you do not find in your sources.

Naturally, the words that you use will be original. Your topic sentences, for example, will all be your own. As you introduce details and conclusions, you will need to write "bridges" to get yourself from point to point. These may be introductory remarks or transitions. In other words, as you write, you are not just stringing your notes together—you are actively tying thoughts together in a variety of creative ways. Your success in these efforts will constitute your greatest originality.

3. *Explanation of controversial views.* Closely related to your selection is that in your research you may have found conflicting or differing views on a topic. If you make a point to describe and distinguish these views, and explain the reasons for the differences, you are presenting material originally. To see how differing views can be handled, see paragraphs 4 and 5 of the sample research essay on page 1363.

4. *Creation of your own insights and positions.* There are three possibilities here, all related to how well you have learned the primary texts on which your research in secondary sources is based:

   a. *Your own interpretations and ideas.* An important part of taking notes is to make your own points *precisely when they occur to you.* Often you can expand these as truly original parts of your essay. Your originality does not need to be extensive; it may consist of no more than a single insight. Here is such a card, which was written during the research on the ghost in *Hamlet:*

My Own   **Introductory**

   The Ghost is minor in the action but major in the play he is seen twice in scene 1, but this scene is really all about him. (Also about his appearances before the play opens.) In scene 4 of Act 1 he comes again and leads Hamlet off to scene 5—the biggest for him as an acting and speaking character. He speaks after this only from under the stage, and then a small appearance (but important) in 3.4, and that's all. He is dominant because he set everything in motion and therefore his presence is felt everywhere in the play.

The originality here is built around the idea of the small role but dominant significance of the Ghost. The discovery is not unusual or startling, but it nevertheless represents original thought about *Hamlet.* When modified and adapted (and put into full sentences with proper punctuation), the material of the card supplies much of the opening paragraph of the sample essay. You can see that the development of a "My Own" note card is important for a research essay.

   b. *Gaps in the sources.* As you read your secondary sources you may realize that an obvious conclusion is not made, or that a certain detail is not stressed. Here is an area for you to develop on your own. Your conclusion may involve a particular interpretation or major point of comparison, or it may rest on a particularly important but underemphasized word or fact. In the sample research essay, for example, the writer discusses the idea that the Ghost's commands make it impossible for Hamlet to solve problems through negotiation—the way he might have chosen as prince and student. The commands force him instead into a plan requiring murder. Most critics observe that Hamlet's life is changed because of the Ghost but have not stressed this aspect of the change. Given such a critical "vacuum" (assuming that you cannot read all the articles about some of your topics, where your discovery may already have been published a number of times), it is right to begin filling it with your own insights. A great deal of scholarship is created in this way.

c. *Disputes with the sources.* Your sources may present certain arguments that you wish to dispute. As you develop your disagreement, you will be arguing originally, for you will be using details in a different way from that of the critic or critics whom you are disputing, and your conclusions will be your own. This area of originality is similar to the laying out of controversial critical views, except that you furnish one of the opposing views yourself. The approach is limited because it is difficult to find many substantive points of interpretation on which there are not already clearly delineated opposing views. Paragraph 5 of the sample research essay shows a small point of disagreement (about whether Shakespeare was concerned with consistency in presenting the Ghost's spirit nature), but one that is nevertheless original.

DOCUMENTING YOUR WORK

It is essential to acknowledge—to *document*—all sources from which you have *quoted or paraphrased* factual and interpretive information. If you do not give due acknowledgment, you run the risk of being challenged for presenting other people's work as your own. This is plagiarism. As the means of documentation, there are many reference systems, some using parenthetical references and others using footnotes or endnotes. Whatever system is used, documentation almost always includes a carefully prepared list of works cited or bibliography.

We will first discuss the list of works cited and then review the two major reference systems for use in a research paper. Parenthetical references, preferred by the Modern Language Association (MLA) since 1984, are described in Joseph Gibaldi, *MLA Handbook for Writers of Research Papers*, 4th ed., 1995. Footnotes or endnotes, recommended by the MLA before 1984, are still widely required.

List of Works Cited (Bibliography)

The key to any reference system is a carefully prepared list of works cited that is included at the end of the essay. "Works Cited" means exactly that; the list should contain just those books and articles which you have actually *used* in your essay. If, however, your instructor requires that you use footnotes or endnotes, you can extend your concluding list to be a complete bibliography both of works cited and also of works consulted but not actually used. *Always, always, always, follow your instructor's directions.*

The list of works cited should include the following information, in each entry, in the form indicated. If you are using a word processor with the capacity to make italics, you may italicize book and article titles, but be sure to notify your instructor in advance.

FOR A BOOK

1. The author's name, last name first, followed by first name and middle name or initial, period.
2. Title, underlined (or italicized), period.
3. City of publication (not state or nation), colon; publisher (easily recognized abbreviations or key words may be used unless they seem awkward or strange; see the *MLA Handbook*, 218–20), comma; year of publication, period.

FOR AN ARTICLE

1. The author's name, last name first, followed by first name and middle name or initial, period.
2. Title of article in quotation marks, period.
3. Name of journal or periodical, underlined or italicized, followed by volume number in Arabic (*not* Roman) numbers with no punctuation, followed by the year of publication within parentheses, colon. For a daily paper or weekly magazine, omit the parentheses and cite the date in the British style followed by a colon (day, month, year; i.e., 29 Feb. 1988:). Inclusive page numbers, period (without any preceding "p." or "pp.").

The list of works cited should be arranged alphabetically by author, with unsigned articles being listed by title. Bibliographical lists are begun at the left margin, with subsequent lines in hanging indention, so that the key locating word—usually the author's last name—can be easily seen. The many unpredictable and complex combinations, including ways to describe works of art, musical or other performances, and films, are detailed extensively in the *MLA Handbook* (104–82). Here are two model entries:

BOOK: Alpers, Antony. <u>The Life of Katherine Mansfield, A Biography</u>. New York: Viking, 1980.

ARTICLE: Hankin, Cheryl. "Fantasy and the Sense of an Ending in the Work of Katherine Mansfield." <u>Modern Fiction Studies</u> 24 (1978): 465–74.

Parenthetical References to the List of Works Cited

Within the text of your research essay, refer *parenthetically* to the list of works cited. This parenthetical reference system is recommended in the *MLA Handbook* (183–205), and its principle is to provide documentation without asking readers to interrupt their reading to find footnotes or endnotes. Readers wanting to see the complete reference can easily find it in your list of works cited. With this system, you insert the author's last name and the relevant page number or numbers into the body of your essay. If the author's name is mentioned in the discussion, only the page number or numbers are given in parentheses. Here are two examples:

> Alexander Pope believed in the idea that the universe is a whole, a totally unified body, which provides a "viable benevolent system for the salvation of everyone who does good" (Kallich 24).

> Martin Kallich draws attention to Alexander Pope's belief in the idea that the universe is a whole, a totally unified body, which provides a "viable benevolent system for the salvation of everyone who does good" (24).

Footnotes and Endnotes

The most formal system of documentation still widely used is that of *footnotes* (references at the bottom of each page) or *endnotes* (references listed numerically at the end of the essay). If your instructor wants you to use one of these formats, do the following: Make a note the first time you quote or refer to a source, with the details ordered as outlined below.

FOR A BOOK

1. The author's name, first name or initials first, followed by middle name or initial, then last name, comma.
2. The title, underlined or italicized for a book, no punctuation. If you are referring to a work in a collection (article, story, poem), use quotation marks for that, but underline the title of the book. (Use a comma after the title if an editor, translator, or edition number follows.)
3. The name of the editor or translator, if relevant. Abbreviate "editor" or "edited by" as *ed.*, "editors" as *eds.* Use *trans.* for "translator" or "translated by."
4. The edition (if indicated), abbreviated thus: *2nd ed., 3rd ed.*, and so on.
5. The publication facts, in parentheses, without any preceding or following punctuation, in the following order:
   a. City (but *not* the state or nation) of publication, colon.
   b. Publisher (clear abbreviations are acceptable and desirable), comma.
   c. Year of publication, comma.
6. The page number(s) with no *p.* or *pp.*, for example, 65, 6–10, 15–19, 295–307, 311–16. If you are referring to longer works, such as novels or longer stories that have division or chapter numbers, include these numbers for readers who may be using an edition different from yours.

FOR AN ARTICLE

1. The author, first name or initials first, followed by middle name or initial, then last name, comma.
2. The title of the article, in quotation marks, comma.
3. The name of the journal, underlined or italicized, no punctuation.

4. The volume number, in Arabic letters, no punctuation.

5. The year of publication in parentheses, colon. For newspaper and journal articles, omit the parentheses, and include day, month, and year (in the British style—i.e., 21 May 1996), colon.

6. The page number(s) with no *p.* or *pp.*, for example, 65, 6–10, 34–36, 98–102, 345–47.

For later notes to the same work, use the last name of the author as the reference unless you are referring to two or more works by the same author. Thus, if you refer to only one work by, say, Langston Hughes, the name "Hughes" will be enough for all later references. Should you be referring to other works by Hughes, however, you will also need to make a short reference to the specific works to distinguish them, such as "Hughes, 'Mulatto'" and "Hughes, 'Let America Be America Again.'"

Footnotes are placed at the bottom of each page, and endnotes are included in separate page(s) at the end of the essay. The first lines of both footnotes and endnotes should be paragraph indented, and continuing lines should be flush with the left margin. Both endnote and footnote numbers are positioned slightly above the line (as superior numbers) like this: [12]. Generally, you may single-space footnotes and endnotes, and leave a space between them. Additionally, today's computer programs have specially designed and consecutively numbered footnote formats. These are generally acceptable, but be sure to make the proper agreements with your instructor. For more detailed coverage of footnoting practices, see the *MLA Handbook*, 242–56.

SAMPLE FOOTNOTES. In the examples below, book titles and periodicals are shown <u>underlined</u>, as they would be in a typewritten or carefully handwritten essay.

[1] Blanche H. Gelfant, <u>Women Writing in America: Voices in Collage</u> (Hanover: UP of New England, for Dartmouth College, 1984), 110.

[2] Günter Grass, "Losses," <u>Granta</u> 42 (Winter 1992): 99.

[3] John O'Meara, "<u>Hamlet</u> and the Fortunes of Sorrowful Imagination: A Reexamination of the Genesis and Fate of the Ghost," <u>Cahiers Élisabéthains</u> 35 (1989), 21.

[4] Grass 104.

[5] Gelfant 141.

[6] O'Meara 17.

As a principle, you do not need to repeat in a note any material you have already mentioned in your own discourse. For example, if you recognize the author and title of your source, then the note should give no more than the data about publication. Here is an example:

In <u>The Fiction of Katherine Mansfield</u>, Marvin Magalaner points out that Mansfield was as skillful in the development of epiphanies (that is, the use of highly significant though perhaps unobtrusive actions or statements to reveal the depths of a particular character) as James Joyce himself, the "inventor" of the technique.[9]

[9] (Carbondale: Southern Illinois UP, 1971) 130.

Other Reference Systems

Other reference systems and style manuals have been adopted by various disciplines (e.g., mathematics, medicine, psychology) to serve their own particular needs. If you receive no instructions from your instructors in other courses, you can adapt the systems described here. If you need to use the documentation methods of other fields, however, use the MLA Handbook, 256–61, particularly 260-61, for guidance about what style manual to select.

Some Final Advice

As long as all you want from a reference is the page number of a quotation or paraphrase, the parenthetical system described briefly here—and detailed fully in the *MLA Handbook*—is the most suitable and convenient one you can use. However, you may wish to use footnotes or endnotes if you need to add more details, provide additional explanations, or refer your readers to other materials that you are not using.

Whatever method you follow, *you must always acknowledge sources properly*. Remember that whenever you begin to write and make references, you might forget a number of specific details about documentation, and you will certainly discover that you have many questions. Be sure then to ask your instructor, who is your final authority.

STRATEGIES FOR ORGANIZING IDEAS

In your research essay you may wish to expand your introduction more than usual because of the need to relate the problem of research to your topic. You may wish to bring in relevant historical or biographical information (see, for example, the introduction of the sample research essay on pp. 1362–63). You may also wish to summarize critical opinion or describe critical problems about your topic. The idea is to lead your reader into your topic by providing interesting and significant materials that you have found.

Because of the greater length of most research essays, some instructors require a topic outline, which is in effect a brief table of contents. This pattern is observed in the sample research essay. *Because the inclusion of an outline is a matter of instructor's choice, be sure you understand whether your instructor requires it.*

As you write the body and conclusion of your research essay, your development will be governed by your choice of topic. Consult the relevant chapters in this book about what to include for whatever approach or approaches you select (setting, idea, point of view, character, tone, or any other).

In length, the research essay may be anywhere from five to fifteen or more pages, depending on your instructor's assignment. Obviously, an essay on a single work will be shorter than one based on several. If you narrow the scope of your topic, as suggested in the approaches described at the beginning of this chapter, you can readily keep your essay within the assigned length. The following sample research essay, for example, illustrates the first approach (p. 1344) by being limited to only one character in one play. Were you to write on characters in a number of other plays by Shakespeare (the second approach), you could limit your total number of pages by stressing comparative treatments and by avoiding excessive detail about problems pertaining to only one work.

Although you limit your topic yourself in consultation with your instructor, you may encounter problems because you will be dealing not with one source alone but with many. Naturally the sources will provide you with details and also with many of your ideas. The problem is to handle the many strands without piling on too many details, and also without being led into digressions. It is important therefore to keep your central idea foremost; the constant stressing of your central idea will help you both to select relevant materials and to reject irrelevant ones.

It bears reemphasis that you need to distinguish between *your own work* and the *sources* you are using. Your readers will assume that everything you write is your own unless you indicate otherwise. Therefore, when blending your words with the ideas from sources, be clear about proper acknowledgments. Most commonly, if you are simply presenting details and facts, you can write straightforwardly and let parenthetical references suffice as your authority, as in the following sentence from the sample research essay:

> Thus he is most emphatic that Hamlet should not kill her along with Claudius (Fisch 80), and he also voices concern about the reputation and future of Denmark (Gottschalk, "Scanning" 165).

Although the words belong to the writer of the essay, the parenthetical references clearly indicate that the sentence is based on the two sources.

If you are using an interpretation unique to a particular writer, or if you are relying on a significant quotation from your source, you should make your acknowledgment as an essential part of your discussion, as in this sentence:

> A. C. Bradley (126) suggests that these speeches indicate Shakespeare's master touch in the development of the Ghost's character.

Here the idea of the critic is singled out for special acknowledgment. If you indicate your sources in this way, no confusion can possibly arise about how you have used your sources.

SAMPLE STUDENT RESEARCH ESSAY

The Ghost in *Hamlet*

Outline

I.   Introduction
    A.   The Importance of the Ghost in *Hamlet*
    B.   The Ghost's Influence on the Play's Themes
II.   The Ghost as a Spirit
III. The Ghost's Character
IV.   The Ghost's Importance in the Structure of the Play
V.   The Ghost's Effect
VI.   Conclusion

I. Introduction

    A. The Importance of the Ghost in *Hamlet*

[1]

Even though the Ghost of old Hamlet is present in only a few scenes of *Hamlet*, he is a dominating presence.* He appears twice in the first scene, and this entire scene itself is about the meaning of these and earlier appearances. He enters again in the fourth scene of the first act, when he beckons to Hamlet and leads him offstage, in this way providing an early illustration of Hamlet's courage (Edgar 257). In the fifth scene of Act I he finally speaks, explaining how his brother Claudius murdered him and urging his son, Hamlet, to kill Claudius in retribution. The Ghost's appeal for revenge causes the rest of the play's action, and it is no exaggeration to say, with Bert O. States, that he "haunts the play as a principle" (95). After some words which the Ghost speaks from underground (i.e., under the stage), he does not enter again until the fourth scene of Act III, in the queen's closet or bedroom, when he reveals himself to Hamlet--but not to Gertrude--to reproach the prince for not having yet killed Claudius. The Ghost is not present at the play's end, but the actions he sets in motion are concluded there, and hence his effect remains dominant.

    B. The Ghost's Influence on the Play's Themes

[2]

Not only is the Ghost dominant over actions; he is also directly linked to many of the play's themes. William Kerrigan calls the Ghost a "nightmind" who introduces the mental darkness of evil that dominates the play (42). In addition to darkness, as Jean Paris says, the Ghost also intensifies the play's "interior suffering" (85). This suffering is brought out in Hamlet's anguished soliloquies and also in the pain of Ophelia and Laertes (and even that of Claudius himself). Another theme is shown by the Ghost's commands to Hamlet--that of responsibility, whether personal, political, or conjugal (McFarland 15). Hamlet of course does not rush right out to kill Claudius, despite the Ghost's urgings, and hence the Ghost is indirectly responsible for the theme of hesitation--this great "Sphinx of modern Literature"--which has become one of the weaknesses cited most frequently about Hamlet's character (Jones 22). The Ghost's scary presence also

---

* Central idea.

poses questions about the power of superstition, terror, and fear (Campbell 211). Beyond these, deeply within the psychological realm, the Ghost has been cited as a "confirmation" of the influence of "psychic residues in governing and shaping human life" (McFarland 34), not to mention the significance of the Oedipus complex in the development of Hamlet's character.

[3]
Because the Ghost is so important, one hardly needs to justify studying him. His importance can be traced in his spirit nature, his influence on the play's structure, and his effect upon Hamlet and therefore indirectly on all the major characters.†

II. The Ghost as a Spirit

[4]
The Ghost is an apparition of questionable status. When Hamlet first sees the Ghost, he raises a question about whether the vision is "a spirit of health, or goblin damned" (I.4, 40). Horatio adds that Hamlet is "desperate with imagination" (I.4, 87), thus casting doubt upon the Ghost's reality even though he is seen by everyone on stage. When speaking with Hamlet, the Ghost is vague about his out-of-earth location, complaining that he is suffering hellish fires but intimating that he will do so only until his earthly sins are purged away. In the meanwhile, he says, he is able to walk the earth for a certain time, presumably only at night (but is his visit in III.4 made in the daytime?). Surprising at it might seem, this detail about where ghosts spend their time reflects Renaissance religious controversies. Dramatizing a ghost returning from purgatory might have been interpreted as a ratification of Catholic doctrine, and so it was apparently safest for Protestant writers like Shakespeare to show a ghost only of a person who was "freshly dead or on the point of death" (O'Meara 15) but to make the details vague.

[5]
The status and existence of ghosts therefore reflects uncertainties during the Elizabethan period. Lily Campbell offers a number of ways in which Elizabethans dealt with these uncertainties. First, James I of England (when still James VI of Scotland), in writing about departed spirits, emphasized that the devil himself could choose the shape of loved ones in order to deceive living persons and lead them to hell. It is this danger that Hamlet specifically describes. Second, as already mentioned, Elizabethan Catholic teaching held it possible for souls in purgatory to return to earth for a time to communicate with the living. Third, scientifically oriented thinkers interpreted ghostly appearances as a sign of madness or deep melancholia (121), or what O'Meara calls "sorrowful imagination" (19). There were apparently a number of "tests" that might have enabled people to determine whether ghosts were authentic, and not creations of the devil or products of a sick imagination. Most of these required that the spirit in question be good and comforting (Campbell 123).

[6]
The Ghost of King Hamlet both passes and fails these tests. He is not totally bad (Campbell 126), but he urges Hamlet to commit murder, something that no ghost trying to reach heaven would ever do (Prosser 136; McFarland 36). Although the Ghost describes the pain of a soul in purgatory, he does so to create fear, not to urge Hamlet to seek salvation. Thus he indicates that he is more like the devil than a soul earning its way to redemption (Prosser 133–34; Frye 22). Another sign suggesting the Ghost's devilishness is that he withholds

† Thesis sentence.

his appearance from Gertrude when he shows himself to Hamlet in Act III, scene 4 (Campbell 124; Prosser 200). Hamlet creates his own test of the Ghost by getting the touring actors to perform *The Murder of Gonzago*. Once he sees the king's disturbance at the play, he concludes that the Ghost is real and not just a "figment of his melancholy imagination" (Harrison 883). However, perhaps the best answer to the conflicting signs about the Ghost is provided by Lily Campbell, who suggests that the ambiguity is a reflection of the general uncertainty about ghosts among Shakespeare's contemporaries (127). In other words, there was no unanimity about the nature and purposes of ghosts at the time Shakespeare wrote, and Shakespeare, if he was even concerned about theological issues of ghostly consistency, was reflecting common understanding and attitudes.

III. The Ghost's Character

[7]   Uncertainty aside, the Ghost is probably Shakespeare's rendering of what he thought a ghost would be like. He inherited a tradition of noisy, bloodthirsty ghosts from his sources--what Harold Fisch calls a "Senecan ghost" (91). There was also a tradition of the "hungry ghost," spirits who prowled about the earth "searching for the life they were deprived of" (Austin 93). In this tradition, Shakespeare's Ghost is bloodthirsty, although ironically not as bloodthirsty as Hamlet himself (Gottschalk 166). The Ghost is also surrounded by awe and horror (DeLuca 147) and is frightening, both to the soldiers at the beginning of the play and also to Hamlet in Act III, scene 4 (Charney, *Style* 167–168). In addition, his speeches are designed to evoke grief, fear, and despair (Prosser 135). This effect also refers to readers and viewers; a famous example is James Boswell's testimony that Dr. Johnson, when young, was "terrified" when he read "the speech of the ghost when alone" (52). It would seem that horror is the main effect that Shakespeare was trying to create with the Ghost.

[8]   The Ghost is certainly bloodthirsty, but he has at least some redeeming qualities (Alexander 30). He is toned down from a ghost in an earlier play, perhaps one of the sources Shakespeare used for *Hamlet*, which was described by Shakespeare's contemporary Thomas Lodge (1558–1625). Lodge talked about "ye ghost which cried so miserally [pitifully, sorrowfully] at ye theator . . . *Hamlet, reuenge*" (sic). Like this vengeful ghost, Shakespeare's Ghost is preoccupied with vengeance (Allman 243), but as a former king he is concerned about his country, and as a former loving husband he is also considerate of Hamlet's mother, Gertrude. Thus he is most emphatic that Hamlet should treat her kindly and help her (Fisch 80; Kerrigan 54), and he also voices concern about the reputation and future of Denmark (Gottschalk 165). Paul Gottschalk draws attention to this redeeming dimension as an indication that the Ghost is concerned with "restoration" as well as "retaliation" (166), a view not shared by Norman Austin, who calls the Ghost "the spirit of ruin" (105).

[9]   Indeed, the Ghost has many qualities of a living human being. For example, he is witty, as Maurice Charney observes about the following interchange between the Ghost and Hamlet just at the beginning of the revelation speeches in Act I, scene 5, lines 6–7:

HAMLET.   Speak, I am bound to hear.
GHOST.   So art thou to revenge, when thou shalt hear.

In other words, even though the Ghost may have come "with . . . airs from heaven, or blasts from hell" (I.4, 41), he is still mentally alert enough to make a pun out of Hamlet's word "bound" (Charney, *Style*, 118). To this quickness can be added his shrewd ability to judge his son's character. He knows that Hamlet may neglect duty, and hence his last words in Act I, scene 5 are "remember me," and his first words in III.4 are "Do not forget." A. C. Bradley suggests that these speeches indicate Shakespeare's master touch in the development of the Ghost's character (126).

[10] The Ghost also shows other human traits. He feels strong remorse about his lifelong crimes and "imperfections" for which his sudden death did not give him time to atone. It is this awareness that has made him bitter and vengeful. Also, he has a sense of appropriateness that extends to what he wears. Thus, at the beginning he appears on the parapets dressed in full armor. This battle uniform is in keeping with the location, and also with his vengeful mission urging Hamlet to kill Claudius (Aldus 54). The armor is intimidating, a means of enforcing the idea that the Ghost in death has become a "spirit of hatred" (Austin 99). By contrast, in the closet scene he wears a dressing gown ("in his habit as he lived," III.4, 135), as though he is prepared for ordinary palace activities of both business and leisure (Charney, *Style* 26).

IV. The Ghost's Importance in the Structure of the Play

[11] Shakespeare's great strength as a dramatist is shown not only in his giving the Ghost such a round, full character, but also in his integrating the Ghost fully within the play's structure. According to Peter Alexander, the Ghost is "indispensable" in the plot as the source of communication to set things in motion (29). He is also a director and organizer as well as an informer--a figure who keeps the action moving until there is no stopping it (Aldus 100). A careful study of his speeches shows that he is a manipulator, playing upon his son's emotions to make him see that his role is to carry out the necessary revenge. In addition, the Ghost is persistent, because his return to Hamlet in Act III, scene 4 "to whet thy almost blunted purpose" (line 111) is the mark of a manager who gets nervous and then intervenes when he sees his directions being neglected by the one entrusted to carry them out.

[12] The Ghost is also significant as a part of some of the other major structures of the play. During the imagined period when the events at Elsinore are taking place, there is a national mobilization going on in preparation for war against Norway (Alexander 34). Structurally, the beginning and ending of *Hamlet* are marked by the fear of war and the political takeover by "Young Fortinbras" of Norway. As if the kingship were not already destabilized by King Hamlet's death, the Ghost urges Hamlet to further his country's destabilization by seeking vengeance against Claudius. It is therefore ironic that the Ghost in death is bringing about the fall of the kingdom he courageously defended in life.

[13] There is an additional major structure involving the Ghost. Maurice Charney observes that the Ghost is significant in the "symmetrical" poison plots in the play (*Style*, 39). The first of these plots, the poisoning of King Hamlet, is described by the Ghost himself in Act I, scene 5. The poisoning of the player king in Act III, scene 2 is a reenactment of the first murder, and it occurs in approximately the middle of the action. The final poisonings--of Gertrude,

Laertes, Claudius, and finally Hamlet himself--occur in Act V, scene 2, the play's last scene. These actions have value as a set of symbolic frames that measure the deterioration of the play's major characters.

V. The Ghost's Effect

[14] Beyond the Ghost's practical and structural importance in the action, he has profound psychological influence, mainly negative, on the characters. Roy Walker describes him as a "prologue" to the "omen" of Hamlet himself, who is the agent of the "dread purpose" of vengeance (220). Because Hamlet is already suffering depression and melancholia, this murderous mission opens the wounds of his vulnerability (Campbell 127-28). Literally, Hamlet must give up everything he has ever learned, even "the movement of existence itself," so that he can carry out the Ghost's commandment (McFarland 32-33). In an invasive, overpowering manner, Hamlet's melancholy influences his love for Ophelia, his possible friendship with Laertes, and his relationship with his mother (Kott 49; Kirsch 31). No one escapes. The effect is like waves radiating outwardly, with the Ghost at the center as a relentless, destructive force.

[15] These effects occur because, almost literally, Hamlet himself cannot escape (Allman 218). In Act I, scene 5, the Ghost, who has gone underground, follows him and hears his conversations with Horatio and the guards--a symbolic representation of the Ghost's pervasive power. He therefore represents "dimensions of reality" beyond what we see on the stage, a mysterious world "elsewhere" that dominates the very souls of living persons (Charney, "Asides" 127). As a result of this ever-present force, which as far as Hamlet is concerned might become visible at any moment, Hamlet is denied the healing that might normally occur after the death of a parent (Kirsch 26). The steady pressure toward vengeance disrupts any movement to mental health and creates what Kirsch calls a "pathology of depression" (26) that inhibits Hamlet's actions (Bradley 123), causes his Oedipal preoccupation with the sexuality of his parents (Kirsch 22), and brings about his desire for the oblivion that suicide might bring (Kirsch 27).

[16] It is, finally, this power over his son that gives the Ghost the greatest influence in the play. Once the Ghost has appeared, Hamlet can never be the same. He loses the dignity and composure that he has assumed as his right as a prince of Denmark and as a student in quest of knowledge (McFarland 38). The Ghost's commands make it impossible for Hamlet to solve problems through negotiation--the way he might have chosen as prince and student. The commands force him instead into a plan requiring murder. What could be more normal than hesitation under such circumstances? Despite all his reflection, however, finally the web of vengeance woven by the Ghost closes in on all those caught in it, and the consequence is that Hamlet becomes not only a murderer but a victim (Allman 254). There is no solution but the final one--real death, which is the literal conclusion of the symbolic death represented by the Ghost when he first appears on the Elsinore battlements.

VI. Conclusion

[17] The Ghost is real in terms of the play's action and structure. He is seen by the characters on the stage, and when he speaks we hear him. He is made round and full by Shakespeare, and his motivation is direct and clear, even

though the signs of his status as a spirit are presented ambiguously. But the Ghost is more. He has been made a Ghost by the greed and envy of Claudius, and in this respect he becomes in the play either a conscious or an unwitting agent of the "unseen Fates or forces" of his own doom (Walker 220). What he brings is the unavoidable horror that seems somehow to be just beneath the surface of good, moral people, waiting for the chance to reach out and destroy. Once the forces are released, there is no holding them, and the tragedy of *Hamlet* is that there is no way to win against these odds.

Works Cited

Aldus, P. J. Mousetrap: Structure and Meaning in Hamlet. Toronto: U of Toronto P, 1977.

Alexander, Peter. Hamlet: Father and Son. Oxford: Clarendon, 1955.

Allman, Eileen Jorge. Player-King and Adversary. Baton Rouge: Louisiana State UP, 1980.

Austin, Norman. "Hamlet's Hungry Ghost." Shenandoah 37.1 (1987): 78–105.

Boswell, James. Boswell's Life of Johnson. 1952. London: Oxford UP, 1957.

Bradley, A. C. Shakespearean Tragedy. 1904. London: Macmillan, 1950.

Campbell, Lily B. Shakespeare's Tragic Heroes: Slaves of Passion. New York: Barnes & Noble, 1959.

Charney, Maurice. "Asides, Soliloquies, and Offstage Speech in Hamlet." Shakespeare and the Sense of Performance: Essays in the Tradition of Performance Criticism in Honor of Bernard Beckerman, Ed. Marvin and Ruth Thompson. Newark: U of Delaware P, 1989. 116–31.

—. Style in Hamlet. Princeton: Princeton UP, 1969.

DeLuca, Diana Macintyre. "The Movements of the Ghost in Hamlet." Shakespeare Quarterly 24 (1973): 147–54.

Edgar, Irving I. Shakespeare, Medicine and Psychiatry. New York, Philosophical Library, 1970.

Fisch, Harold. Hamlet and the Word. New York: Ungar, 1971.

Frye, Roland Mushat. The Renaissance Hamlet: Issues and Responses in 1600. Princeton: Princeton UP, 1984.

Gottschalk, Paul. "Hamlet and the Scanning of Revenge." Shakespeare Quarterly 24 (1973): 155–70.

Harrison, G. B., ed. Shakespeare: The Complete Works. 1948. New York: Harcourt, 1968.

Jones, Ernest. Hamlet and Oedipus. 1949. New York: Doubleday, 1954.

Kerrigan, William. Hamlet's Perfection. Baltimore: Johns Hopkins UP, 1994.

Kirsch, Arthur. "Hamlet's Grief." ELH 48 (1981): 17–36.

Kott, Jan. Shakespeare, Our Contemporary. Trans. Boleslaw Taborski. 1967. London: Methuen, 1970.

McFarland, Thomas. Tragic Meanings in Shakespeare. New York: Random House, 1966.

O'Meara, John. "Hamlet and the Fortunes of Sorrowful Imagination: A Re-examination of the Genesis and Fate of the Ghost." Cahiers Élisabéthains 35 (1989): 15–25.

Paris, Jean. Shakespeare. Trans. Richard Seaver. New York: Grove, 1960.

Prosser, Eleanor. Hamlet and Revenge. 2nd ed. Stanford: Stanford UP, 1971.

States, Bert O. Hamlet and the Concept of Character. Baltimore: Johns Hopkins UP, 1992.

Walker, Roy. "Hamlet: the Opening Scene." Shakespeare: Modern Essays in Criticism. Ed. Leonard F. Dean. New York: Oxford UP, 1961.

Commentary on the Essay

This sample research essay illustrates an assignment requiring about twenty-five sources and about 2,500 words. The sources were located through an examination of library catalogues, the *MLA Bibliography*, library bookshelves, and the bibliographies in some of the listed books. They represent the range of materials available in a college library with a selective, not exhaustive, set of holdings. Two of the sources (Austin and O'Meara) were obtained through the interlibrary loan service.

The writing itself is developed from the sources listed. Originality (see pp. 1354–56) is provided by the structure and development of the essay, additional observations not existing in the sources, and transitions. The topic outline is placed appropriately at the beginning—a pattern you may follow unless your instructor asks for a more detailed outline, or, perhaps, for no outline at all.

Because the essay is concerned with only one work—and one subject about that work—it demonstrates the first approach to a problem in research as outlined on page 1344. The essay is eclectic, introducing discussions of ideas, character, style, and structure. These four topics fulfill the goal of covering the ground thoroughly, within the confines of the assignment. A shorter research assignment might deal with no more than, say, the Ghost's character, ignoring the other topics in the sample research essay. On the other hand, a longer essay might deal further with the philosophical and theological meanings of ghosts during the Elizabethan period, or a more detailed study of all the traits of the Ghost's character, and so on.

The central idea of the sample research essay is stressed in paragraph 1, along with an assertion that the Ghost is a major influence in the play, together with a concession that the Ghost is only a minor character in the action. The research for this paragraph is derived primarily from a close reading of the play itself. Paragraph 2, continuing the exploration of the central idea, demonstrates that the Ghost figures in the major themes of *Hamlet*. Paragraph 3 is mainly functional, being used as the location of the thesis sentence.

Part II, containing paragraphs 4 through 6, deals with the Ghost's status as a spirit. Part III, with four paragraphs (7–10), is concerned with the Ghost's human rather than spiritual characteristics. Part IV, with paragraphs 11–13, deals with the significance of the Ghost in four of the major structures that dominate the play. Part V, with three paragraphs, considers the Ghost's negative and inexorable influence over the major figures of *Hamlet,* the emphasis being the character of Hamlet as the transferring agent of the Ghost's destructive revenge. The concluding paragraph (17) sums up the essay with the final idea of how the Ghost affects the tragic nature of *Hamlet.*

The list of works cited is the basis of all parenthetical references in the essay, in accordance with the *MLA Handbook for Writers of Research Papers,* 4th ed. Using these references, an interested reader can consult the sources for a more detailed development of the ideas in the sample essay. The works cited can also serve as a springboard for expanded research.

27

Critical Approaches Important in the Study of Literature

A number of critical theories or approaches for understanding and interpreting literature are available to critics and students alike. Many of these have been developed during the twentieth century to create a discipline of literary studies comparable with disciplines in the natural and social sciences. Literary critics have often borrowed liberally from other disciplines (e.g., history, psychology, anthropology) but have primarily aimed at developing literature as study in its own right.

At the heart of the various critical approaches are many fundamental questions: What is literature? What does it do? Is its concern only to tell stories, or is it to express emotions? Is it private? Public? How does it get its ideas across? What more does it do than express ideas? How valuable was literature in the past, and how valuable is it now? What can it contribute to intellectual, artistic, and social history? To what degree is literature an art, as opposed to an instrument for imparting knowledge? How is literature used, and how and why is it misused? What theoretical and technical expertise may be invoked to enhance literary studies?

Questions such as these indicate that criticism is concerned not only with reading and interpreting stories, poems, and plays, but also with establishing theoretical understanding. Because of such extensive aims, you will understand that a full explanation and illustration of the approaches would fill the pages of a long book. The following descriptions are therefore intended as no more than brief introductions. Bear in mind that in the hands of skilled critics, the approaches are so subtle, sophisticated, and complex that they are not only critical stances but also philosophies.

Although the various approaches provide widely divergent ways to study literature and literary problems, they reflect major tendencies rather than absolute straitjacketing. Not every approach is appropriate for every work, nor are the approaches always mutually exclusive. Even the most devoted practitioners of the methods do not pursue them rigidly. In addition, some of the approaches are more "user-friendly" for certain types of discovery than others. To a degree at least, most critics therefore utilize methods that technically belong to one or more of the other approaches. A critic stressing the topical/historical approach, for example, might introduce the close study of a work that is associated with the method of the New Criticism. Similarly, a psychoanalytical critic might include details about archetypes. In short, a great deal of criticism is *pragmatic* or *eclectic* rather than rigid.

The approaches to be considered here are these: moral/intellectual; topical/historical; New Critical/formalist; structuralist; feminist; economic determinist/Marxist; psychological/psychoanalytic; archetypal/symbolic/mythic; deconstructionist; and reader-response criticism.

The object of learning about these approaches, like everything in this book, is to help you develop your own reading and writing. Accordingly, following each of the descriptions there is a brief paragraph showing how Hawthorne's story "Young Goodman Brown" (p. 324) might be considered in the light of the particular approach. The paragraph following the discussion of structuralism, for example, shows how the structuralist approach can be applied to Goodman Brown and his story, and so also with the feminist approach, the economic determinist approach, and the others. Whenever you are doing your own writing about literature, you are free to use the various approaches as part or all of your assignment, as you believe the approach may help you.

MORAL/INTELLECTUAL

The moral/intellectual approach is concerned with content and values (see Chapter 9). The approach is as old as literature itself, for literature is a traditional mode of imparting morality, philosophy, and religion. The concern in moral/intellectual criticism is not only to discover meaning but also to determine whether works of literature are both *true* and *significant*.

To study literature from the moral/intellectual perspective is therefore to determine whether a work conveys a lesson or a message, and whether it can help readers lead better lives and improve their understanding of the world: What ideas does the work contain? How strongly does the work bring forth its ideas? What application do the ideas have to the work's characters and situations? How may they be evaluated intellectually? Morally? Discussions based on such questions do not imply that literature is primarily a medium of moral and intellectual exhortation. Ideally, moral/intellectual criticism should differ from sermonizing to the degree that readers should always be left with their own decisions about whether they wish to assimilate the content of a work and about whether this content is personally or morally acceptable.

Sophisticated critics have sometimes demeaned the moral/intellectual approach on the grounds that "message hunting" reduces a work's artistic value by treating it like a sermon or political speech; but the approach will be valuable as long as readers expect literature to be applicable to their own lives.

EXAMPLE

"Young Goodman Brown" raises the issue of how an institution designed for human elevation, such as the religious system of colonial Salem, can be so ruinous. Does the failure result from the system itself or from the people who misunderstand it? Is what is true of religion as practiced by Brown also true of social and political institutions? Should any religious or political philosophy be given greater credence than good will and mutual trust? One of the major virtues of "Young Goodman Brown" is that it provokes questions like these but at the same time provides a number of satisfying answers. A particularly important one is that religious and moral beliefs should not be used to justify the condemnation of others. Another important answer is that attacks made from the refuge of a religion or group, such as Brown's puritanical judgment, is dangerous because it enables the judge to condemn without thought and without personal responsibility.

TOPICAL/HISTORICAL

This traditional approach stresses the relationship of literature to its historical period, and for this reason it has had a long life. Although much literature may be applicable to many places and times, much of it also directly reflects the intellectual and social worlds of the authors. When was the work written? What were the circumstances that produced it? What major issues does it deal with? How does it fit into the author's career? Keats's poem "On First Looking into Chapman's Homer," for example, is his excited response to his reading of one of the major literary works of Western civilization. Owen's "Dulce et Decorum Est" is an ironic response, in light of the brutality of twentieth-century warfare, to the idea that war is heroic and glorious.

The topical/historical approach investigates relationships of this sort, including the elucidation of words and concepts that today's readers may not immediately understand. Obviously, the approach requires the assistance of footnotes, dictionaries, library catalogues, histories, and handbooks.

A common criticism of the topical/historical approach is that in the extreme it deals with background knowledge rather than with literature itself. It is possible, for example, for a topical/historical critic to describe a writer's life, the period of the writer's work, and the social and intellectual ideas of the time—all without ever considering the meaning, importance, and value of the work itself.

A reaction against such an unconnected use of historical details is the so-called "New Historicism." This approach justifies the introduction of historical knowledge by integrating it with the understanding of particular texts. Modern readers cannot understand Dryden's "Song for St. Cecilia's Day," for example, without first learning about a number of details and concepts that Dryden took for granted, such as the seventeenth-century explanations of cosmic origins and the image of God as a maker and shaper of universal order. Because the introduction of such historical material is designed to facilitate the reading of the poem—and also the reading of other literature of the period—the New Historicism thus represents an integration of knowledge and interpretation.

EXAMPLE

"Young Goodman Brown" is an allegorical story by Nathaniel Hawthorne (1804–1864), a New England writer who probed deeply into the relationships between religion and guilt. His ancestors had been involved in religious persecutions, including the Salem witch trials, and he, living 150 years afterward, wanted to analyze the weaknesses and uncertainties of the sin-dominated religion of the earlier period, a tradition of which he was a resentful heir. Not surprisingly, therefore, "Young Goodman Brown" takes place in Puritan colonial Salem, and Hawthorne's implied judgments are those of a severe critic of how the harsh old religion destroyed personal and family relationships. Although the immediate concerns of the story belong to a vanished age, Hawthorne's treatment is still valuable because it is still timely.

NEW CRITICAL/FORMALIST

The New Criticism began in the 1930s and 1940s and has since been a dominant force in twentieth-century literary studies. To the degree that New Criticism focuses upon literary texts as formal works of art, it departs from the traditional topical/historical approach. The objection raised by the New Critics is that as topical/historical critics consider literary history, they evade direct contact with actual texts.

The inspiration for the formalist or New Critical approach was the French practice of *explication de texte*, a method that emphasizes detailed examination and explanation. The New Criticism is at its most brilliant in the formal analysis of smaller units such as entire poems and short passages. For the analysis of larger structures, the New Criticism also utilizes a number of techniques that form the basis for the chapters in this book. Discussions of point of view, tone, plot, character, and structure, for example, are formal ways of looking at literature that are derived from the New Criticism.

The aim of the formalist study of literature is to provide readers not only with the means of explaining the content of works (What, specifically, does a work say?) but also with the insights needed for evaluating the artistic quality of individual works and writers (How well is it said?). A major aspect of New Critical thought is that content and form—including all ideas, ambiguities, subtleties, and even apparent contradictions—were originally within the conscious or subconscious control of the author. There are no accidents. It does not necessarily follow, however, that today's critic is able to define the author's intentions exactly, for such intentions require knowledge of biographical details that are irretrievably lost. Each literary work therefore takes on its own existence and identity, and the critic's work is to discover a reading or readings that explain the facts of the text. Note that the New Critic does not claim infallible interpretations and does not exclude the validity of multiple readings of the same work.

Dissenters from the New Criticism have noted a tendency by New Critics to ignore relevant knowledge that history and biography can bring to literary studies. In addition, the approach has been subject to the charge that stressing the explication of texts alone fails to deal with literary value and appreciation. In other words, the formalist critic, in explaining the meaning of literature, sometimes neglects the reasons for which readers find literature stimulating and valuable.

EXAMPLE

A major aspect of Hawthorne's "Young Goodman Brown" is that the details are so vague and dreamlike that many readers are uncertain about what is happening. The action is a nighttime walk by the protagonist, Young Goodman Brown, into a deep forest where he encounters a mysterious satanic ritual that leaves him bitter and misanthropic. This much seems clear, but the precise nature of Brown's experience is not clear, nor is the identity of the stranger (father, village elder, devil) who accompanies Brown as he begins his walk. At the story's end Hawthorne's narrator states that the whole episode may have been no more than a dream or nightmare. Yet when morning comes, Brown walks back into town as though returning from an overnight trip, and he recoils in horror from his fellow villagers, including his wife Faith (paragraph 70). Could his attitude result from nothing more than a nightmare?

Even at the story's end these uncertainties remain. For this reason one may conclude that Hawthorne deliberately creates the uncertainties to reveal how persons like Brown build defensive walls of judgment around themselves. The story thus implies that the real source of Brown's anger is as vague as his nocturnal walk, but he doesn't understand it in this way. Because Brown's vision and judgment are absolute, he rejects everyone around him, even if the cost is a life of bitter suspicion and spiritual isolation.

STRUCTURALIST

The principle of structuralism stems from the attempt to find relationships and connections among elements that appear to be separate and discrete. Just as physical science reveals unifying universal principles of matter such as gravity and the forces of electromagnetism (and is constantly searching for a "unified field theory"), structuralism attempts to discover the forms unifying all literatures. Thus a structural description of Maupassant's "The Necklace" stresses that the main character, Mathilde, is an *active* protagonist who undergoes a *test* (or series of tests) and emerges with a victory, though not the kind she had originally hoped for. The same might be said of Phoenix in Welty's "A Worn Path." If this same kind of structural view is applied to Bierce's "An Occurrence at Owl Creek Bridge," the protagonist is defeated in the test. Generally, the structural approach applies such patterns to other works of literature to determine that some protagonists are active or submissive, that they pass or fail their tests, or that they succeed or fail at other encounters. The key is that many apparently unrelated works reveal many common patterns or contain similar structures with important variations.

The structural approach is important because it enables critics to discuss works from widely separate cultures and historical periods. In this respect, critics have followed the leads of modern anthropologists, most notably Claude Lévi-Strauss (1908–1990). Along such lines, critics have undertaken the serious examination of folk and fairy tales. Some of the groundbreaking structuralist criticism, for example, was devoted to the structural principles underlying folktales of Russia. The method also bridges popular and serious literature, making little distinction between the two insofar as the description of the structures is concerned. Indeed, structuralism furnishes an ideal approach for comparative literature, and the method also enables critics to consolidate genres such as modern romances, detective tales, soap operas, and film.

Like the New Criticism, structuralism aims at comprehensiveness of description, and many critics would insist that the two are complementary and not separate. A distinction is that the New Criticism is at its best in dealing with smaller units of literature, whereas structuralism is best in the analysis of narratives and therefore larger units such as novels, myths, and stories. Because structuralism shows how fiction is organized into various typical situations, the approach merges with the *archetypal* approach, and at times it is difficult to find any distinctions between structuralism and archetypalism.

Structuralism, however, deals not just with narrative structures but also with structures of any type, wherever they occur. For example, structuralism makes great use of linguistics. Modern linguistic scholars have determined that there is a difference between "deep structures" and "surface structures" in language. A structuralist analysis of style, therefore, emphasizes how writers utilize such structures. The structuralist interpretation of language also perceives distinguishing types or "grammars" of language that are recurrent in various types of literature. Suppose, for example, that you encounter opening passages like the following:

> Once upon a time a young prince fell in love with a young princess. He decided to tell her of his love, and early one morning he left his castle on his white charger, riding toward her castle home high in the mountains.

> Early that morning, Alan had found himself thinking about Anne. He had believed her when she said she loved him, but his feelings about her were not certain, and his thinking had left him still unsure.

The words of these two passages create different and distinct frames of reference. One is a fairy tale, the other the internalized reflection of feeling. The passages therefore demonstrate how language itself fits into predetermined patterns or structures. Similar uses of language structures can be associated with other types of literature.

EXAMPLE

Young Goodman Brown is a hero who is passive, not active. He is a *witness*, a *receiver* rather than a *doer*. His only action—taking his trip in the forest—occurs at the story's beginning. After that point, he no longer acts but instead is acted upon, and what he sees puts his life's beliefs to a test. Of course, many protagonists undergo similar testing (such as rescuing victims and slaying particularly terrible dragons), and they emerge triumphant. Not so with Goodman Brown. He is a responder who allows himself to be victimized by his own perceptions—or misperceptions. Despite all his previous experiences with his wife and with the good people of his village, he generalizes too hastily. He lets the single disillusioning experience of his nightmare govern his entire outlook on others, and thus he fails his test and turns his entire life into failure.

FEMINIST

The feminist approach holds that most of our literature presents a masculine-patriarchal view in which the role of women is negated or at best minimized. As an adjunct of the feminist movement in politics, the feminist critique of literature seeks to raise consciousness about the importance and unique nature of women in literature.

Specifically, the feminist view attempts (1) to show that writers of traditional literature have ignored women and have also transmitted misguided and prejudiced views of them, (2) to stimulate the creation of a critical milieu that reflects a balanced view of the nature and value of women, (3) to recover the works of women writers of past times and to encourage the publication of present women writers so that the literary canon can be expanded to recognize women as thinkers and artists, and (4) to urge transformations in the language to eliminate inequities and inequalities that result from linguistic distortions.

In form, the feminist perspective seeks to evaluate various literary works from the standpoint of the presentation of women. For works such as "The Necklace" (story), "Patterns" (poem), and *The Bear* (play), a feminist critique focuses on how such works treat women and also on either the shortcomings or enlightenment of the author as a result of this treatment: How important are the female characters, how individual in their own right? Are they credited with their own existence and their own character? In their relationships with men, how are they treated? Are they given equal status? Ignored? Patronized? Demeaned? Pedestalized? How much interest do the male characters exhibit about women's concerns?

EXAMPLE

At the beginning of "Young Goodman Brown," Brown's wife, Faith, is only peripheral. In the traditional patriarchal spirit of wife-as-adjunct, she asks her husband to stay at home and take his journey at another time. Hawthorne does not give her the intelligence or dignity, however, to let her explain her concern (or might he not have been interested in what she had to say?), and she therefore remains in the background with her pink hair ribbon as her distinguishing characteristic. During the mid-forest satanic ritual she appears again and is given power, but only the power to cause her husband to go astray. Once she is led in as a novice in the practice of demonism, her husband falls right in step. Unfortunately, by following her, Brown can conveniently excuse himself from guilt by claiming that "she" had made him do it, just as Eve "made" Adam eat the apple (Genesis 3:16–17). Hawthorne's attention to the male hero, in other words, permits him to distort the female's role.

ECONOMIC DETERMINIST/MARXIST

The concept of cultural and economic determinism is one of the major political ideas of the last century. Karl Marx (1818–1883) emphasized that the primary influence on life was economic, and he saw society as an opposition between the capitalist and working classes. The literature that emerged from this kind of analysis features individuals in the grips of the class struggle. Often called "proletarian literature," it emphasizes persons of the lower class—the poor and oppressed who spend their lives in endless drudgery and misery, and whose attempts to rise above their disadvantages usually result in renewed suppression.

Marx's political ideas were never widely accepted in the United States and have faded still more after the political breakup of the Soviet Union, but the idea of economic determinism (and the related term Social Darwinism) is still credible. As a result, much literature can be judged from an economic perspective: What is the economic status of the characters? What happens to them as a result of this status? How do they fare against economic and political odds? What other conditions stemming from their class does the writer emphasize (e.g., poor education, poor nutrition, poor health care, inadequate opportunity)? To what extent does the work fail by overlooking the economic, social, and political implications of its material? In what other ways does economic determinism affect the work? How should readers consider the story in today's developed or underdeveloped world? Seemingly, the specimen work "Young Goodman Brown" has no economic implications, but an economically oriented discussion might take the following turns:

EXAMPLE

"Young Goodman Brown" is a fine story just as it is. It deals with the false values instilled by the skewed acceptance of sin-dominated religion, but it overlooks the economic implications of this situation. One suspects that the real story in the little world of Goodman Brown's Salem should be about survival and the disruption that an alienated member of society can produce. After Brown's condemnation and distrust of others forces him into his own shell of sick imagination, Hawthorne does not consider how such a disaffected character would injure the economic and public life of the town. Consider this, just for a moment: Why would the people from whom Brown recoils in disgust want to deal with him in business or personal matters? In town meetings, would they want to follow his opinions on crucial issues of public concern and investment? Would his preoccupation with sin and damnation make him anything more than a horror in his domestic life? Would his wife, Faith, be able to discuss household management with him, or how to take care of the children? All these questions of course are pointed toward another story—a story that Hawthorne did not write. They also indicate the shortcomings of Hawthorne's approach, because it is clear that the major result of Young Goodman Brown's selfish preoccupation with evil would be a serious disruption of the economic and political affairs of his small community.

PSYCHOLOGICAL/PSYCHOANALYTIC

The scientific study of the mind is a product of psychodynamic theory as established by Sigmund Freud (1856–1939) and of the psychoanalytic method practiced by his followers. Psychoanalysis provided a new key to the understanding of character by claiming that behavior is caused by hidden and unconscious motives. It was greeted as a virtual revelation, and not surprisingly it had a profound effect on twentieth-century literature.

In addition, its popularity produced a psychological/psychoanalytic approach to criticism.[1] Some critics use the approach to explain fictional characters, as in the landmark interpretation by Freud and Ernest Jones that Shakespeare's Hamlet suffers from an Oedipus complex. Still other critics use it as a way of analyzing authors and the artistic process. For example, John Livingston Lowes's *The Road to Xanadu* presents a detailed examination of the mind, reading, and neuroses of Coleridge, the author of "Kubla Khan" (p. 503).

Critics using the psychoanalytic approach treat literature somewhat like information about patients in therapy. In the work itself, what are the obvious and hidden motives that cause a character's behavior and speech? How much background (*e.g.*, repressed childhood trauma, adolescent memories) does the author reveal about a character? How purposeful is this information with regard to the character's psychological condition? How much is important in analyzing and understanding the character?

In the consideration of authors, critics utilizing the psychoanalytic model consider questions like these: What particular life experiences explain characteristic subjects or preoccupations? Was the author's life happy? Miserable? Upsetting? Solitary? Social? Can the death of someone in the author's family be associated with melancholy situations in that author's work? (All eleven brothers and sisters of the English poet Thomas Gray, for example, died before

[1] See also Chapter 4, "Characters: The People in Fiction."

reaching adulthood. Gray was the only one to survive. In his poetry, Gray often deals with death, and he is therefore considered one of the "Graveyard School" of eighteenth-century poets. A psychoanalytical critic might make much of this connection.)

EXAMPLE

At the end of "Young Goodman Brown," Hawthorne's major character is no longer capable of normal existence. His nightmare should be read as a symbol of what in reality would have been lifelong mental subjection to the type of puritanical religion that emphasizes sin and guilt. Such preoccupation with sin is no hindrance to psychological health if the preoccupied people are convinced that God forgives them and grants them mercy. In their dealings with others, they remain healthy as long as they believe that other people have the same sincere trust in divine forgiveness. If their own faith is weak and uncertain, however, and they cannot believe in forgiveness, then they are likely to project their own guilt—really a form of personal terror—onto others. They remain conscious of their own sins, but they find it easy to claim that others are sinful—even those who are spiritually spotless, and even their own family, who should be dearest to them. When this process of projection occurs, such people have created the rationale of condemning others because of their own guilt. The cost they pay is a life of gloom, a fate that Hawthorne designates for Goodman Brown after the nightmare about demons in human form.

ARCHETYPAL/SYMBOLIC/MYTHIC

The archetypal approach, derived from the work of the Swiss psychoanalyst Carl Jung (1875–1961), presupposes that human life is built up out of patterns, or *archetypes* ("first molds" or "first patterns"), that are similar throughout various cultures and historical times.[2] The approach is similar to the structuralist analysis of literature, for both approaches stress the connections that may be discovered in literature written in different times and in vastly different locations in the world.

In literary evaluation, the archetypal approach is used to support the claim that the very best literature is grounded in archetypal patterns. The archetypal critic therefore looks for archetypes such as God's creation of human beings, the sacrifice of a hero, or the search for paradise. How does an individual story, poem, or play fit into any of the archetypal patterns? What truths does this correlation provide (particularly truths that cross historical, national, and cultural lines)? How closely does the work fit the archetype? What variations can be seen? What meaning or meanings do the connections have?

The most tenuous aspect of archetypal criticism is Jung's assertion that the recurring patterns provide evidence for a "universal human consciousness"

---

[2] Symbolism and myths are also considered in Chapters 8, 18, and 19.

that all of us, by virtue of our humanity, still retain in our minds and in our very blood.

Not all critics accept the hypothesis of a universal human consciousness, but they nevertheless consider the approach important for comparisons and contrasts (see Chapter 29). Many human situations, such as adolescence, dawning love, the search for success, the reconciliation with one's mother and father, and the encroachment of age and death, are similar in structure and can be analyzed as archetypes. For example, the following situations can be seen as a pattern or archetype of initiation: A young man discovers the power of literature and understanding ("On first Looking into Chapman's Homer"); a man determines the importance of truth and fidelity amidst uncertainty ("Dover Beach"); a man and woman fall in love despite their wishes to remain independent (*The Bear*); a woman gains strength and integrity because of previously unrealized inner resources ("The Necklace"). The archetypal approach encourages the analysis of variations on the same theme, as in Glaspell's *Trifles*, when the two women develop their impromptu cover-up of the crime (one sort of initiation) and also begin to assert their freedom of thought and action independent of their husbands (another sort of initiation).

EXAMPLE

In the sense that Young Goodman Brown undergoes a change from psychological normality to rigidity, the story is a reverse archetype of the initiation ritual. According to the archetype of successful initiation, initiates seek to demonstrate their worthiness to become full-fledged members of society. Telemachus in Homer's *Odyssey*, for example, is a young man who in the course of the epic goes through the initiation rituals of travel, discussion, and battle. But in "Young Goodman Brown" we see initiation in reverse, for just as there is an archetype of successful initiation, Brown's initiation leads him into failure. In the private areas of life on which happiness depends, he falls short. He sees evil in his fellow villagers, condemns his own minister, and shrinks even from his own family. His life is one of despair and gloom. His suspicions are those of a Puritan of long ago, but the timeliness of Hawthorne's story is that the archetype of misunderstanding and condemnation has not changed. Today's headlines of misery and war are produced by the same kind of intolerance that is exhibited by Goodman Brown.

DECONSTRUCTIONIST

The *deconstructionist* approach—which deconstructionists explain not as an approach but rather as a performance—was developed by the French critic Jacques Derrida (b. 1930). In the 1970s and 1980s it became a major but also controversial mode of criticism. As a literary theory, deconstructionism produces a type of analysis that stresses ambiguity and contradiction.

A major principle of deconstructionism is that Western thought has been *logocentric;* that is, Western philosophers have based their ideas on the assumption that central truth is knowable and entire (this view is incorrect, according to a deconstructionist). The deconstructionist view is instead that there is no central truth because circumstances and time, which are changeable and sometimes arbitrary, govern the world of the intellect. This analysis leads to the declaration "All interpretation is misinterpretation." That is, literary works cannot be encapsulated as organically unified entireties, and therefore there is not *one correct interpretation* but only *interpretations,* each one possessing its own validity.

In "deconstructing" a work, therefore, the deconstructionist critic raises questions about what other critics have claimed about the work: Is a poem accepted as a model of classicism? Then it also exhibits qualities of romanticism. Is a story about a young Native American's flight from school commonly taken as a criticism of modern urban life? Then it may also be taken as a story of the failure of youth. In carrying out such criticism, deconstructionist critics place heavy emphasis on the ideas contained in words such as *ambivalence, discrepancy, enigma, uncertainty, delusion, indecision,* and *lack of resolution,* among others.

The deconstructionist attack on "correct," "privileged," or "accepted" readings is also related to the principle that language, and therefore literature, is unstable. "Linguistic instability" means that the full understanding of words is never exact because there is a never-ending *play* between the words in a text and their many shades of meaning, including possible future meanings. That is, the words do not remain constant and produce a definite meaning, but instead call forth the possibility of "infinite substitutions" of meaning. Each work of literature is therefore ambiguous and uncertain because its full meaning is constantly *deferred.* This infinite play or semantic tension renders language unstable and makes correct or accepted readings impossible.

It is fair to state that deconstructionism, among all the literary theories, has received intense criticism that has sometimes bordered on discrediting the theory entirely. A number of critics find that the position is elusive and vague. They grant that literary works are often ambiguous, uncertain, and apparently contradictory, but explain that the cause of these conditions is not linguistic instability but rather authorial intention. They also point out that the deconstructionist linguistic analysis is derivative and misunderstood, and that it does not support deconstructionist assertions about linguistic instability. Critics also draw attention to the contradiction that deconstructionism cannot follow its major premise about there being no "privileged readings" because it must recognize the privileged readings in order to invalidate or "subvert" them.

EXAMPLE

There are many uncertainties in the details of "Young Goodman Brown." If one starts with the stranger on the path, one might conclude that he could be Brown's father, because he recognizes Brown immediately and speaks to him jovially. On the other hand, the stranger could be the devil (he is recognized as such by Goody Cloyse) because of his wriggling walking stick. After disappearing, the stranger also takes on the characteristics of an omniscient cult leader and seer, because at the satanic celebration he knows all the secret sins committed by

Brown's neighbors and the community of greater New England. Additionally, he might represent a perverted conscience whose aim is to mislead and befuddle people by steering them into the holier-than-thou judgmentalism that Brown adopts. This method would be truly diabolical—to use religion in order to bring people to their own damnation. That the stranger is an evil force is therefore clear, but the pathways of his evil are not as clear. He seems to work his mission of damnation by reaching souls like that of Goodman Brown through means ordinarily attributed to conscience. If the stranger represents a satanic conscience, what are we to suppose that Hawthorne is asserting about what is considered real conscience?

READER-RESPONSE[3]

The theory of reader-response is rooted in *phenomenology*, a branch of philosophy that deals with "the understanding of how things appear." The phenomenological idea of knowledge is that reality is to be found *not* in the external world itself but rather in the mental *perception* of externals. That is, all that we human beings can know—actual *knowledge*—is our collective and personal understanding of the world and our conclusions about it.

As a consequence of the phenomenological concept, reader-response theory holds that the reader is a necessary third party in the author-text-reader relationship that constitutes the literary work. The work, in other words, is not fully created until readers make a *transaction* with it by assimilating it and *actualizing* it in the light of their own knowledge and experience. The representative questions of the theory are these: What does this work mean to me, in my present intellectual and moral makeup? What particular aspects of my life can help me understand and appreciate the work? How can the work improve my understanding and widen my insights? How can my increasing understanding help me understand the work more deeply? The theory is that the free interchange or transaction that such questions bring about leads toward interest and growth so that readers can assimilate literary works and accept them as part of their lives.

As an initial way of reading, the reader-response method may be personal and anecdotal. In addition, by stressing response rather than interpretation, one of the leading exponents of the method (Stanley Fish) has raised the extreme question about whether texts, by themselves, have objective identity. These aspects have been cited as both a shortcoming and an inconsequentiality of the method.

It is therefore important to stress that the reader-response theory is *open*. It permits beginning readers to bring their own personal reactions to literature, but it also aims to increase the discipline and skills of readers. The more that

---

[3] See *Responding to Literature: Likes and Dislikes* in Chapter 1, pp. 38–45.

readers bring to literature through their interests and disciplined studies, the more "competent" and comprehensive their responses will be. With cumulative experience, the disciplined reader will habitually adjust to new works and respond to them with increasing skill. If the works require special knowledge in fields such as art, politics, science, philosophy, religion, or morality, then competent readers will seek out such knowledge and utilize it in developing their responses. Also, because students experience many similar intellectual and cultural disciplines, it is logical to conclude that responses will tend not to diverge but rather to coalesce; agreements result not from personal but from cultural similarities. The reader-response theory, then, can and should be an avenue toward informed and detailed understanding of literature, but the initial emphasis is the *transaction* between readers and literary works.

EXAMPLE

"Young Goodman Brown" is worrisome because it shows so disturbingly that good intentions may cause harmful results. I think that a person with too high a set of expectations is ripe for disillusionment, just as Goodman Brown is. When people don't measure up to this person's standard of perfection, they can be thrown aside as though they are worthless. They may be good, but their past mistakes make it impossible for the person with high expectations to endure them. I have seen this situation occur among some of my friends and acquaintances, particularly in romantic relationships. Goodman Brown makes the same kind of misjudgment, expecting perfection and turning sour when he learns about flaws. It is not that he is not a good man, because he is shown at the start as a person of belief and stability. He uncritically accepts his nightmare revelation that everyone else is evil, however (including his parents), and he finally distrusts everyone because of this baseless suspicion. He cannot look at his neighbors without avoiding them like an "anathema," and he turns away from his own wife "without a greeting" (paragraph 70). Brown's problem is that he equates being human with being unworthy. By such a distorted standard of judgment all of us fail, and that is what makes the story so disturbing.

28

Taking Examinations
on Literature

Succeeding on a literature examination is largely a result of intelligent and skill-ful preparation. Preparing means (1) studying the material assigned, in con-junction with the comments made in class by your instructor and by fellow students in discussion; (2) developing and reinforcing your own thoughts; (3) anticipating exam questions by creating and answering your own practice ques-tions; and (4) understanding the precise function of the test in your education.

First, realize that the test is not designed either to trap you or to hold down your grade. The grade you receive is a reflection of your achievement in the course. If your grades are low, you can improve them by studying coher-ently and systematically. Those students who can easily do satisfactory work might do superior work if they improved their method of preparation. From whatever level you begin, you can increase your achievement by improving your method of study.

Your instructor has three major concerns in evaluating your tests (assuming the correct use of English): (1) to assess the extent of your command over the subject material of the course (How good is your retention?); (2) to assess how well you are able to think about the material (How well are you educating your-self?); and (3) to assess how well you respond to a question or deal with an issue.

ANSWER THE QUESTIONS ASKED

Many elements go into writing good answers on tests, but responsiveness is the most important. A major cause of low exam grades is that students really do not *answer* the questions asked. Does that seem surprising? The problem is that some students do no more than retell a story or restate an argument; they never con-front the issues in the question. This common problem has been treated throughout this book. Therefore, if you are asked, "Why does . . . ," be sure to emphasize the *why,* and use the *does* only to exemplify the *why.* If the question is about *organization,* focus on organization. If a *problem* has been raised, deal with the problem. In short, always *respond directly* to the question or instruction. Compare the following two answers to the same question:

Question: How is the setting of Bierce's "An Occurrence at Owl Creek Bridge" important in the story's development?

A

The setting of Bierce's "An Occurrence at Owl Creek Bridge" is a major element in the development of the story. The first scene is on a railroad bridge in northern Alabama, and the action is that a man, Peyton Farquhar, is about to be hanged. He is a Southerner who has been surrounded and captured by Union soldiers. They are ready to string him up and they have the guns and power, so he cannot escape. He is so scared that the sound of his own watch sounds loudly and slowly like a cannon. He also thinks about how he might free himself, once he is hanged, by freeing his hands and throwing off the noose that will be choking and killing him. The scene shifts to the week before, at Farquhar's plantation. A Union spy deceives Farquhar, thereby tempting him to try to sabotage the Union efforts to keep the railroad open. Because the spy tells Farquhar about the punishment, the reader assumes that Farquhar had tried the sabotage, was caught, and now is going to be hanged. The third scene is also at the bridge, but it is about what Farquhar sees and thinks in his own mind: He imagines that he has been hanged and then escapes. He thinks he falls into the creek, frees himself from the ropes, and makes it to shore, from which he makes the long walk home. His final thoughts are of his wife coming out of the house to meet him, with everything looking beautiful in the morning sunshine. Then we find out that all this was just in his mind, because we are back on the bridge, from which Farquhar is swinging, hanged, dead, with a broken neck.

B

The setting of Bierce's "An Occurrence at Owl Creek Bridge" is a major element in the development of the story. The railroad bridge in northern Alabama, from which the doomed Peyton Farquhar will be hanged, is a frame for the story. The bridge, which begins as the real-life bridge in the first scene, becomes the bridge that the dying man imagines in the third. In between there is a brief scene at Farquhar's home, which took place a week before. The setting thus marks the progression of Farquhar's dying vision. He begins to distort and slow down reality—at the real bridge— when he realizes that there is no escape. The first indication of this distortion is that his watch seems to be ticking as slowly as a blacksmith's hammer. Once he is dropped from the bridge to be hanged, his perceptions slow down time so much that he imagines his complete escape before his death: falling into the water, freeing himself, being shot at, getting to shore, walking through a darkening forest, and returning home in beautiful morning sunshine. The final sentence brutally restores the real setting of the railroad bridge and makes clear that Farquhar is actually dead despite his imaginings. In all respects, therefore, the setting is essential to the story's development.

While column *A* begins well and introduces important details of the story's setting, it does not address the question because it does not show how the details figure into the story's development. On the other hand, column *B* focuses directly on the connection between the locations and the changes in the protagonist's perceptions. Because of this emphasis, *B* is shorter than *A*; with the focus directly on the issue, there is no need for irrelevant narrative details. Thus, *A* is unresponsive and unnecessarily long, while *B* is responsive and includes details only if they exemplify the major points.

PREPARATION

Your challenge is how best to prepare yourself to have a knowledgeable and ready mind at examination time. If you simply cram facts into your head for the examination in the hope that you can adjust to the questions, you will likely flounder. You need a systematic approach.

Read and Reread

Above all, keep in mind that your preparation should begin as soon as the course begins, not on the night before the exam. Complete each assignment by the date it is due, for you will understand the classroom discussion only if you know the material (see also the guides for study in Chapter 1, pp. 11–14). Then, about a week before the exam, review each assignment, preferably rereading everything completely. With this preparation, your study on the night before the exam will be fruitful and might be viewed as a climax of preparation, not the entire preparation.

Construct Your Own Questions: Go on the Attack

To prepare yourself fully for an exam, read *actively*, not passively. Read with a goal, and *go on the attack* by anticipating test conditions—creating and answering your own practice questions. Don't waste time trying to guess the questions you think your instructor might ask. That might happen (and wouldn't you be happy if it did?), but do not turn your study into a game of chance. Instead, arrange the subject matter by asking yourself questions that help you get things straight.

How can you construct your own questions? It is not as hard as you might think. Your instructor may have announced certain topics or ideas to be tested on the exam, and you might develop questions from these, or you might apply general questions to the specifics of your assignments, as in the following examples:

1. *About a character and the interactions of characters* (see also Chapter 4). What is *A* like? How does *A* grow or change in the work? What does *A* learn or not learn that brings about the conclusion? To what degree does *A* represent a type or an idea?

How does *B* influence *A*? Does a change in *C* bring about any corresponding change in *A*?

2. *About technical and structural questions.* These may be broad, covering everything from point of view (Chapter 5) to prosody and rhyme (Chapter 16). The best guide here is to study those technical aspects that have been discussed in class, for it is unlikely that you will be asked to go beyond the levels expected in classroom discussion.

3. *About events or situations.* What relationship does episode *A* have to situation *B*? Does *C*'s thinking about situation *D* have any influence on the outcome of event *E*?

4. *About a problem* (see also Chapter 23, pp. 1058–61). Why is character *A* or situation *X* this way and not that way? Is the conclusion justified by the ideas and events leading up to it?

Convert Your Notes to Questions

One of the best ways to construct questions is to adapt your classroom notes because notes are the fullest record you have about your instructor's views. As you work with your notes, refer to passages from the text that were studied by the class or stressed by your instructor. If there is time, memorize as many important phrases or lines as you can; plan to incorporate these into your answers as evidence to support the points you make. Remember that it is useful to work not only with main ideas from your notes, but also with matters such as style, imagery, and organization.

Obviously, you cannot make questions from all your notes, and you will therefore need to select from those that seem most important. As an example, here is a short note from a classroom discussion of *Hamlet:* "In a major respect, a study in how private problems get public, how a court conspiracy can produce disastrous consequences." Notice how you can devise practice questions from this note:

1. In what ways is *Hamlet* not only about private problems but also about public ones?
2. Why should the consequences of Claudius's murder of Hamlet's father be considered disastrous?

The principle shown here is that exam questions should never be asked just about *what* but should rather get into the issues of *why*. Observe that the first question therefore adapts the words *in what ways* to the phrasing of the note. For the second, the word *why* has been adapted. Either question forces pointed study, and neither asks you merely to describe events. Question 1 requires you to consider the wider political effects of Hamlet's hostility toward Claudius, including Hamlet's murder of Polonius and the subsequent madness of Ophelia. Question 2, with its emphasis on disaster, leads you to consider not only the ruination of the hopes and lives of those in the play but also the importance of young Fortinbras and the eventual establishment of Norwegian control over Denmark after Claudius and Hamlet are gone. If you spent fifteen or twenty minutes writing practice answers to these questions, you could be confident in taking an examination on the material, for it is likely that you could adapt your study answers to any exam question about the personal and political implications of Claudius's murder of his brother.

Work with Questions Even When Time Is Short

Whatever your subject, spend as much study time as possible making and answering your own questions. Remember also to work with your own remarks and the ideas you develop in the journal entries you make when doing your regular assignments (see Chapter 1, pp. 11–14). Many of these will give you additional ideas for your own questions, which you may practice along with the questions you develop from your notes.

Obviously, with limited study time, you will not be able to create your own questions and answers indefinitely. Even so, don't neglect asking and answering your own questions. If time is too short for full practice answers, write out the main heads, or topics, of an answer. When the press of time (or the need for sleep) no longer permits you to make even such a brief outline answer, keep thinking of questions and their answers on the way to the exam. *Never read passively or unresponsively, but always read with a creative, question-and-answer goal.* Think of studying as a prewriting experience.

The time you spend in this way will be valuable, for as you practice, you will develop control and therefore confidence. Often those who have difficulty with tests, or claim a phobia about them, prepare passively rather than actively. Your instructor's test questions compel responsiveness, thought, organization, and knowledgeable writing; but a passively prepared student is not ready for this challenge and therefore writes answers that are unresponsive and filled with summary. The grade for such a performance is low, and the student's fear of tests is reinforced. The best way to break such long-standing patterns of fear or uncertainty is active, creative study.

Study with a Classmate

Often the thoughts of another person can help you understand the material to be tested. Find a fellow student with whom you can work comfortably but also productively, for both of you together can help each other individually. In view of the need for steady preparation throughout a course, regular discussions about the material are a good idea. You might also make your joint study systematic by setting aside a specific evening or afternoon for work sessions. Working with someone else can be stimulating and rewarding. Make the effort.

TWO BASIC TYPES OF QUESTIONS ABOUT LITERATURE

Generally, there are two types of questions on literature exams. Keep them in mind as you prepare. The first type is *factual*, or *mainly objective*, and the second is *general, comprehensive, broad,* or *mainly subjective.* Except for multiple-choice questions, very few questions are purely objective in a literature course.

Factual Questions

MULTIPLE-CHOICE. These questions are mainly factual. Your instructor will most likely use them for short quizzes, usually on days when an assignment is due, to make sure that you are keeping up with the reading. Multiple-choice questions test your knowledge of facts and your ingenuity in perceiving subtleties of phrasing. On a literature exam, however, this type of question is rare.

IDENTIFICATION. These questions are more interesting and challenging because they require you both to know details and also to develop thoughts about them. This type of question will frequently be used as a check on the depth and scope of your reading. In fact, an entire exam could be composed of only identification questions, each demanding perhaps five minutes to write. Here are some typical examples of what you might be asked to identify:

1. *A character.* To identify a character, it is necessary to describe briefly the character's position, main activity, and significance. Let us assume that Montresor is the character to be identified. Our answer should state that he is the narrator of "The Cask of Amontillado" (position) who invites Fortunato into his wine vaults on the pretext of testing the quality of some new Amontillado wine (main activity). He is therefore the major cause of the action, and he embodies one of the story's themes, that the desire for revenge makes human beings diabolically cruel (significance). Under the category of "significance," of course, you might develop as many ideas as you have time for, but the short example here is a general model for most examinations.

2. *Incidents or situations.* To identify an incident (for example, "A woman mourns the death of her husband"), first give the location (Mrs. Popov in Chekhov's play *The Bear*), and then try to demonstrate its significance in the work. That is, in *The Bear* Mrs. Popov is mourning the death of her husband, and in the course of the play Chekhov uses her feelings to show amusingly that life with real emotion is stronger than duty to the dead.

3. *Things, places, and dates.* Your instructor may ask you to identify a hair ribbon (Hawthorne's "Young Goodman Brown") or a beach (Arnold's "Dover Beach"), or the dates of Welty's "A Worn Path" (1941) or Lowell's "Patterns" (1916). For dates, you may be given a leeway of five or ten years. What is important about a date is not so much exactness as historical and intellectual perspective. The date of "Patterns," for example, was the third year of World War I, and the poem consequently reflects a reaction against the protracted and senseless loss of life in war (even though details of the poem itself suggest an eighteenth-century war). To claim "World War I" as the date of the poem would likely be acceptable as an answer if it happens that you cannot remember the exact date.

4.   *Quotations.* You should remember enough of the text to identify a passage taken from it, or at least to make an informed guess. Generally, you should (1) locate the quotation, if you remember it, or else describe the probable location; (2) show the ways in which the quotation is typical of the content and style of the work you have read; and (3) describe the importance of the passage. If you suffer a momentary lapse of memory, write a reasoned and careful explanation of your guess. Even if your guess is wrong, the knowledge and cogency of your explanation should give you points.

TECHNICAL AND ANALYTICAL QUESTIONS AND PROBLEMS.   In a scale of ascending importance, the third and most difficult type of factual question relates to those matters with which this book has been concerned: technique, analysis, and problems. You might be asked to discuss the *setting, images, point of view,* or *important idea* of a work; you might be asked about the *tone* of a story or poem; or you might be asked to *explicate* a poem that may or may not be duplicated for your benefit (if it is not duplicated, woe to students who have not studied their assignments). Questions like these assume that you have technical knowledge, and they also ask you to examine the text within the limitations imposed by the terms.

Obviously, technical questions occur more frequently in advanced courses than in elementary ones, and the questions become more subtle as the courses become more advanced. Instructors of elementary courses may ask about ideas and problems but will likely not use many of the others unless they state their intentions to do so in advance, or unless technical terms have been studied in class.

Questions of this type are fairly long, perhaps allowing from fifteen to twenty-five minutes for each. If you have two or more of these questions, try to space your time sensibly; do not devote eighty percent of your time to one question and leave only twenty percent for the rest.

Basis of Judging Factual Questions

IDENTIFICATION QUESTIONS.   In all factual questions, your instructor is testing (1) your factual command and (2) your quickness in relating a part to the whole. Thus, suppose you are identifying the incident "a man kills a canary." It is correct to say that Susan Glaspell's play *Trifles* is the location of the incident, that the murdered farmer John Wright was the killer, and that the canary belonged to his wife. Knowledge of these details clearly establishes that you know the facts. But a strong answer must go further. Even in the brief time you have for short answers, you should always connect the facts to (1) major causation in the work, (2) an important idea or ideas, (3) the development of the work, and (4) for a quotation, the style. Time is short and you must be selective, but if you can make your answer move from facts to significance, you will always fashion superior responses. Along these lines, let us look at an answer identifying the action from *Trifles* (and also, of course, from "A Jury of Her Peers"):

The action is from Glaspell's *Trifles*. The man who kills the bird is John Wright, and the owner is Mrs. Wright. The killing is important because it is shown as the final indignity in Mrs. Wright's desperate life, and it prompts her to strangle Wright in his sleep. It is thus the cause not only of the murder but also of the investigation bringing the officers and their wives onstage. In fact, the wringing of the bird's neck makes the play possible because it is the wives who discover the dead bird, and this discovery is the means by which Glaspell highlights them as the major characters in the play. Because the husband's brutal act shows how bleak the life of Mrs. Wright actually was, it dramatizes the lonely plight of women in a male-dominated way of life like that on the Wright farm. The discovery also raises the issue of legality and morality, because the two wives decide to conceal the evidence, therefore protecting Mrs. Wright from conviction and punishment.

Any of the points in this answer could be developed as a separate essay, but the paragraph is successful as a short answer because it goes beyond fact to deal with significance. Clearly, such answers are possible at the time of an exam only if you have devoted considerable thought to the various exam works beforehand. The more thinking and practicing you do before an exam, the better your answers will be. Remember this advice as an axiom: *You cannot write superior answers if you do not think extensively before the exam.* By studying well beforehand, you will be able to reduce surprise to an absolute minimum.

LONGER FACTUAL QUESTIONS.   More extended factual questions also require more thoroughly developed organization. Remember that for these questions your knowledge of essay writing is important, for the quality of your composition will determine a major share of your instructor's evaluation of your answers. It is therefore best to take several minutes to gather your thoughts together before you begin to write, because *a ten-minute planned answer is preferable to a twenty-five-minute unplanned answer.* You do not need to write every possible fact on each particular question. Of greater importance is the use to which you put the facts you know and the organization of your answer. Use a sheet of scratch paper to jot down the facts you remember and your ideas about them in relation to the question. Then put them together, phrase a thesis sentence, and use your facts to exemplify and support your thesis.

It is always necessary to begin your answer pointedly, using key words or phrases from the question or direction if possible, so that your answer will have thematic shape. You should never begin an answer with "Because" and then go on from there without referring again to the question. To be most responsive during the short time available for an exam, you should use the question as your guide for your answer. Let us suppose that you have the following question on your test: "How does Glaspell use details in *Trifles* to reveal the character of Minnie Wright?" The most common way to go astray on such a question—and the easiest thing to do also—is to concentrate on Mrs. Wright's character rather than on how Glaspell uses detail to bring out her character. The word *how* makes a vast difference in the nature of the final answer, and hence a good method on the exam is to duplicate key phrases in the question to ensure that you make your major points clear. Here is an opening sentence that uses the key words and phrases (italicized here) from the question to direct thought and provide focus:

> Glaspell *uses details* of setting, marital relationships, and personal habits *to reveal the character of Mrs. Wright* as a person of great but unfulfilled potential whom anger has finally overcome.

Because this sentence repeats the key phrases from the question and also because it promises to show *how* the details are to be focused on the character, it suggests that the answer to follow will be responsive.

General or Comprehensive Questions

General or comprehensive questions are particularly important on final examinations, when your instructor is testing your total comprehension of the course material. Considerable time is usually allowed for answering this type of question, which can be phrased in a number of ways:

1. A *direct question* asking about philosophy, underlying attitudes, main ideas, characteristics of style, backgrounds, and so on. Here are some possible questions in this category:

    What use do _____, _____, and _____ make of the topic of _____?

    Define and characterize the short story as a genre of literature.

    Explain the use of dialogue by Hawthorne, Welty, and Maupassant.

    Contrast the technique of point of view as used by _____, _____, and _____.

2. A *"comment" question*, often based on an extensive quotation, borrowed from a critic or written by your instructor for the occasion, asking about a broad class of writers, a literary movement, or the like. Your instructor may ask you to treat this question broadly (taking in many writers) or else to apply the quotation to a specific writer.

3. A *"suppose" question*, such as "What advice might Minnie Wright of *Trifles* give the speakers of Lowell's 'Patterns' and Keats's 'Bright Star'?" or "What might the speaker of Rossetti's poem 'Echo' say if she learned that her dead lover was Goodman Brown of Hawthorne's 'Young Goodman Brown'?" Although "suppose" questions might seem whimsical at first sight, they have a serious design and should prompt original and radical thinking. The first question, for example, should cause a test writer to bring out, from Minnie Wright's perspective, that the love of both speakers was or is potential, not actual. She would likely sympathize with the speaker's loss in "Patterns," but she might also say the lost married life might not have been as totally happy as the speaker assumes. For the speaker of "Bright Star," a male, Mrs. Wright might say that the steadfast love sought by him should also be linked to kindness and toleration as well as passion.

Although "suppose" questions (and answers) are speculative, the need to respond to them requires a detailed consideration of the works involved, and in this respect the "suppose" question is a salutary means of learning. It is of course difficult to prepare for a "suppose" question, which you can therefore regard as a test not only of your knowledge but also of your inventiveness and ingenuity.

Basis of Judging General Questions

When answering broad, general questions, you are dealing with an unstructured situation, and you not only must supply an *answer* but—equally important—you must also create a *structure* within which your answer can have meaning. You might say that you make up your own specific question out of the original general question. If you were asked to consider the role of women as seen in works by Lowell, Welty, and Glaspell, for example, you would do well to structure the question by focusing a number of clearly defined topics. A possible way to begin answering such a question might be this:

> Lowell, Welty, and Glaspell present a view of female resilience by demonstrating inner control, power of adaptation, and endurance.

With this sort of focus you would be able to proceed point by point, introducing supporting data as you form your answer.

As a general rule, the best method for answering a comprehensive question is comparison-contrast (see also Chapter 29). The reason is that in dealing with, say, a general question on Rossetti, Chekhov, and Keats, it is too easy to write *three* separate essays rather than *one*. Thus, you should try to create a topic such as "The treatment of real or idealized love" or "The difficulties in male-female relationships," and then develop your answer point by point rather than writer by writer. By creating your answer in this way, you can bring in references to each or all of the writers as they become relevant to your main idea. If you were to treat each writer separately, your comprehensive answer would lose focus and effectiveness, and it would be needlessly repetitive.

Remember that in judging your response to a general question, your instructor is interested in seeing (1) how effectively you perceive and explain the significant issues in the question, (2) how intelligently and clearly you organize your answer, and (3) how persuasively you use materials from the work as supporting evidence.

Bear in mind that in answering comprehensive questions, you don't have complete freedom. What you have is the freedom to create your own structure. The underlying idea of the comprehensive, general question is that you possess special knowledge and insights that cannot be discovered by more factual questions. You must therefore formulate your own responses to the material and introduce evidence that reflects your own insights and command of information.

Two final words: Good luck.

29

Comparison-Contrast and Extended Comparison-Contrast: Learning by Seeing Literary Works Together

A comparison-contrast essay is used to compare and contrast different authors, or two or more works by the same author; different drafts of the same work; or characters, incidents, techniques, and ideas in the same work or in different works. The virtue of comparison-contrast is that it enables the study of works in perspective. No matter what works you consider together, the method helps you isolate and highlight individual characteristics, for the quickest way to get at the essence of one thing is to compare it with another. Similarities are brought out by comparison; differences, by contrast. In other words, you can enhance your understanding of what a thing *is* by using comparison-contrast to determine what it *is not*.

For example, our understanding of Shakespeare's Sonnet 30, "When to the Sessions of Sweet Silent Thought" (p. 533), may be enhanced if we compare it with Christina Rossetti's poem "Echo" (p. 614). Both poems treat personal recollections of past experiences, told by a speaker to a listener who is not intended to be the reader. Both also refer to persons, now dead, with whom the speakers were closely involved. In these respects, the poems are comparable.

In addition to these similarities, there are important differences. Shakespeare's speaker numbers the dead persons as friends whom he laments generally, while Rossetti refers specifically to one person with whom the speaker was in love. Rossetti's topic is the sorrow of dead love, the irrevocability of the past, and the present loneliness of the speaker. Shakespeare includes the references to dead friends as a way of accounting for present sorrows, but then his speaker turns to the present and asserts that thinking about the "dear friend" being addressed enables him to restore past "losses" and end all "sorrows." In Rossetti's poem, there is no reconciliation of past and present; instead the speaker focuses entirely upon the sadness of the present moment. Though both poems are retrospective, Shakespeare's poem looks toward the present, and Rossetti's looks to the past. These differences show how the poems may be contrasted.

GUIDELINES FOR THE COMPARISON-CONTRAST METHOD

The preceding example, although brief, shows how the comparison-contrast method makes it possible to identify leading similarities and distinguishing differences in two works. Frequently you can overcome difficulty with one work by comparing and contrasting it with another work on a comparable subject. A few guidelines will help direct your efforts in writing comparison-contrast essays.

Clarify Your Intention

When planning a comparison-contrast essay, first decide on your goal, for you can use the method in a number of ways. One objective may be the *equal and mutual illumination of two (or more) works*. For example, an essay comparing Welty's "A Worn Path" with Hawthorne's "Young Goodman Brown" might be designed to (1) compare ideas, characters, or methods in these stories equally, without stressing or favoring either. You might also (2) emphasize "Young Goodman Brown," and therefore you would use "A Worn Path" as material for highlighting Hawthorne's story. Or, instead, you could (3) show your liking of one story at the expense of another, or (4) emphasize a method or idea that you think is especially noteworthy or appropriate.

A first task is therefore to decide what to emphasize. The sample student essay on pages 1400–1402 gives "equal time" to both works being considered, without claiming the superiority of either. Unless you have a different rhetorical goal, this essay is a suitable model for most comparisons.

Find Common Grounds for Comparison

The second stage in prewriting for a comparison-contrast essay is to select a common ground for discussion. It is pointless to compare dissimilar things, for the resulting conclusions will not have much value. Instead, compare like with like: idea with idea, characterization with characterization, imagery with imagery, point of view with point of view, tone with tone, problem with problem. Nothing much can be learned from a comparison of Welty's view of courage and Chekhov's view of love; but a comparison of the relationship of love to stability and courage in Chekhov and Welty suggests common ground, with the promise of important ideas to be developed through the examination of similarities and differences.

In seeking common ground, you will need to be inventive and creative. For instance, if you compare Maupassant's "The Necklace" and Chekhov's *The*

Bear, these two works at first seem dissimilar. Yet common ground can be discovered, such as the treatment of self-deceit, the effects of chance on human affairs, and the author's views of women. Although other works may seem even more dissimilar than these, it is usually possible to find a common ground for comparison and contrast. Much of your success in an essay of this type depends on your finding a workable basis—a common denominator—for comparison.

Integrate the Bases of Comparison

Let us assume that you have decided on your rhetorical purpose and on the basis or bases of your comparison. You have done your reading and taken notes, and you have a rough idea of what to say. The remaining problem is the treatment of your material.

One method is to make your points first about one work and then about the other. Unfortunately, such a comparison makes your paper seem like two separate lumps. ("Work 1" takes up one half of your paper, and "Work 2" takes up the other half.) Also, the method involves repetition because you must repeat many points when you treat the second subject.

A *better method* therefore is to treat the major aspects of your main idea and to refer to the two (or more) works as they support your arguments. Thus you refer constantly to *both* works, sometimes within the same sentence, and remind your reader of the point of your discussion. There are reasons for the superiority of this method: (1) You do not repeat your points needlessly, for you develop them as you raise them. (2) By constantly referring to the two works, you make your points without requiring a reader with a poor memory to reread previous sections.

As a model, here is a paragraph on "Natural References as a Basis of Comparison in Frost's 'Desert Places' and Shakespeare's Sonnet 73 ('That Time of Year Thou Mayst in Me Behold')."[1] The virtue of the paragraph is that it uses material from both poems simultaneously (as nearly as the time sequence of sentences allows) as the substance for the development of the ideas:

(1) Both writers link their ideas to events occurring in the natural world. (2) Night as a parallel with death is common to both poems, with Frost speaking about it in his first line and Shakespeare introducing it in his seventh. (3) Along with night, Frost emphasizes the onset of winter and snow as a time of death and desolation. (4) With this natural description, Frost also symbolically refers to empty, secret, dead places in the inner spirit—crannies of the soul where bleak winter snowfalls correspond to selfishness and indifference. (5) By contrast, Shakespeare uses the fall season, with yellowing and dropping of leaves and migrating birds, to stress the closeness of real death and therefore the need to love fully during the time remaining. (6) Both poems therefore share a sense of gloom, because both present death as inevitable and final, just like the emptiness of winter. (7) Because Shakespeare's sonnet is addressed to a listener who is also a loved one, however, it is more outgoing than the more introspective poem of

[1] These poems are on pp. 631 and 597.

Frost. (8) Frost turns the snow, the night, and the emptiness of the universe inwardly in order to show the speaker's inner bleakness, and by extension, the bleakness of many human spirits. (9) Shakespeare instead uses the bleakness of seasons, night, and dying fires to state the need for loving "well." (10) The poems thus use common and similar references for different purposes and effects.

The paragraph links Shakespeare's references to nature with those of Frost. Five sentences speak of both authors together; three speak of Frost alone, and two of Shakespeare alone, but all the sentences are unified topically. This interweaving of references indicates that the writer has learned both poems well enough to think of them at the same time, and it also enables the writing to be more pointed and succinct than if the works were separately treated.

You can learn from this example: If you develop your essay by putting your two subjects constantly together, you will write economically and pointedly (not only for essays but also for tests). Beyond that, if you digest the material as successfully as this method indicates, you demonstrate that you are fulfilling a major educational goal—the assimilation and *use* of material. Too often, because you learn things separately (in separate works and courses, at separate times), you tend also to compartmentalize them. Instead, you should always try to relate them, to *synthesize* them. Comparison and contrast help in this process of putting together, of seeing things not as fragments but as parts of wholes.

Avoid the "Tennis-Ball" Method

As you make your comparison, do not confuse an interlocking method with a "tennis-ball" method, in which you bounce your subject back and forth constantly and repetitively, almost as though you were hitting observations back and forth over a net. The tennis-ball method is shown in the following example from a comparison of the characters Mathilde (Maupassant's "The Necklace") and Mrs. Popov (Chekhov's *The Bear*)[2]:

> Mathilde is a young married woman; Mrs. Popov is also young but a widow. Mathilde has at least some kind of social life, even though she doesn't have more than one friend; but Mrs. Popov chooses to lead a life of solitude. Mathilde's daydreams about wealth are responsible for her misfortune, and Mrs. Popov's dedication to the memory of her husband could ruin her also. Mathilde is therefore made unhappy because of her own shortcomings, but Mrs. Popov is rescued despite her shortcomings. In Mathilde's case the focus is on adversity not only causing trouble but also strengthening character. Similarly, in Mrs. Popov's case the focus is on a strong person realizing her strength regardless of her conscious decision to weaken herself.

Imagine the effect of an entire essay written in this boring "1, 2, 1, 2, 1, 2" order. Aside from the repetition and unvaried patterning of subjects, the tennis-ball method does not permit much illustrative development. You should not feel so

[2] These works are on pp. 3 and 1132.

constrained that you cannot take two or more sentences to develop a point about one writer or subject before you include comparative references to another. If you remember to interlock the two subjects of comparison, however, as in the paragraph about Frost and Shakespeare, your method will give you the freedom to develop your topics fully.

THE EXTENDED COMPARISON-CONTRAST ESSAY

For a longer essay about a number of works—such as a limited research paper, a comprehensive exam question, or the sort of extended essay required at the end of a semester—comparison-contrast is an essential method. You may wish to compare the works on the basis of elements such as ideas, plot, structure, character, metaphor, point of view, or setting. Because of the larger number of works, however, you will need to modify the way in which you employ the comparison-contrast method. Suppose that you are dealing with not just two works but six, seven, or more. You need first to find a common ground to use as your central, unifying idea, just as you do for a comparison of only two works. Once you establish the common ground, you can classify or group your works on the basis of the similarities and differences they exemplify with regard to the topic. The idea is to get two *groups* for comparison, not just two works.

Let us assume that three or four works treat a topic in one way, but two or three do it in another (e.g., either criticism or praise of wealth and trade, the joys or sorrows of love, or the enthusiasm or disillusionment of youth). In writing about these works, you might treat the topic itself in a straightforward comparison-contrast method but use details from the works within the groupings as your material for illustration and argument.

To make your essay as specific as possible, it is best to stress only a small number of works with each of your subpoints. Once you have established these points in detail, there is no need to go into similar detail with all the other works you are studying. Instead, you may refer to the other works briefly, your purpose being to strengthen your points without creating more and more examples. Once you go to another subpoint, you may use different works for illustration so that by the end of your essay you will have given due attention to each work in your assignment. In this way—by treating many works in small comparative groups—you can keep your essay reasonably brief, for there is no need for unproductive detail.

For illustration, the sample student essay on pages 1403–1405 shows how this grouping may be done. In the first part of the body of this essay, six works are used comparatively to show how private needs conflict with social, public demands. The next part shows how three works can be compared and contrasted on the basis of how they treat the topic of public concerns as expressed through law.

**THE USE OF REFERENCES IN A LONGER
COMPARISON-CONTRAST ESSAY**

For the longer comparison-contrast essay you may find a problem in making references to many different works. Generally you do not need to repeat full references. For example, if you refer to Phoenix of Welty's "A Worn Path" or to Montresor of Poe's "The Cask of Amontillado," you should make the full references only once and then refer later just to the character, story, or author, according to your needs.

When you quote lines or passages or when you cite actions or characters in special ways, you should use parenthetical line, speech, or paragraph references. Be guided by the following principle: If you make a specific reference that you think your reader might want to examine in more detail, supply the line, speech, or paragraph number. If you refer to minor details that might easily be unnoticed or forgotten, also supply the appropriate number. (For more details about how to handle references to plays, see pp. 885–86.)

WRITING A COMPARISON-CONTRAST ESSAY

When you start to plan your essay, you must first narrow and simplify your subject so that you can handle it conveniently. Should your subject be a comparison of Amy Lowell and Wilfred Owen (as in the sample student essay on pp. 1400–1402), choose one or two of each poet's poems on the same or a similar topic and write your essay about these.

Once you have found an organizing principle, along with the relevant works, begin to refine and focus the direction of your essay. As you study each work, note common or contrasting elements and use these to form your central idea. At the same time, you can select the most illustrative works and classify them according to your topic, such as war, love, work, faithfulness, or self-analysis.

Strategies for Organizing Ideas

Begin by stating the works, authors, characters, or ideas that you are considering; then show how you have narrowed the topic. Your central idea should briefly highlight the principal grounds of comparison and contrast, such as that both works treat a common topic, exhibit a similar idea, use a similar form, or develop an identical attitude, and also that major or minor differences help make the works unique. You may also assert that one work is superior to the other, if you wish to make this judgment and defend it.

The body of your essay is governed by the works and your basis of comparison (ideas and essays, depictions of character, uses of setting, qualities of style, uses of point of view, and so on). For a comparison-contrast treatment on such a basis, your goal should be to shed light on both (or more) of the works you are treating. For example, you might examine a number of stories written in the first-person point of view (see Chapter 5). An essay on this topic might compare the ways each author uses the point of view to achieve similar or distinct effects; or you might compare a group of poems that employ similar images, symbols, or ironic methods. Sometimes, the process can be as simple as identifying female or male protagonists and comparing the ways in which their characters are developed. Another approach is to compare the *subjects*, as opposed to the *idea*. You might identify works dealing with general subjects such as love, death, youth, race, or war. Such groupings provide a basis for excellent comparisons and contrasts.

As you develop your essay, remember to keep comparison-contrast foremost. That is, your discussions of point of view, metaphorical language, or whatever should not so much explain these topics *as topics* but rather explore *similarities and differences* of the works you are comparing. If your topic is an idea, for example, you need to explain the idea, but only enough to establish points of similarity or difference. As you develop such an essay, you might illustrate your arguments by referring to related uses of elements such as setting, characterization, rhythm or rhyme, symbolism, point of view, or metaphor. When you introduce these new subjects, you will be on target as long as you use them comparatively.

In concluding you may reflect on other ideas or techniques in the works you have compared, make observations about similar qualities, or summarize briefly the grounds of your comparison. If there is a point that you have considered especially important, you might stress that point again in your conclusion. Also, your comparison might have led you to conclude that one work—or group of works—is superior to another. Stressing that point again would make an effective conclusion.

SAMPLE STUDENT ESSAY
(TWO WORKS)

The Treatment of Responses to War in Amy Lowell's
"Patterns" and Wilfred Owen's "Anthem for Doomed Youth"°

[1]

"Patterns" and "Anthem for Doomed Youth" are both powerful and unique condemnations of war.* Owen's short poem speaks broadly and generally about the ugliness of war and also about large groups of sorrowful people; Lowell's longer poem focuses upon the personal grief of just one person. In a sense, Lowell's poem begins where Owen's ends, a fact that accounts for both the similarities and differences between the two works. The antiwar themes may be compared on the basis of their subjects, their lengths, their concreteness, and their use of a common metaphor.†

° See pp. 777 and 497 for these poems.
* Central idea.
† Thesis sentence.

[2] "Anthem for Doomed Youth" attacks war more directly than "Patterns." Owen's opening line, "What passing-bells for those who die as cattle?," suggests that in war human beings are depersonalized before they are slaughtered, like so much meat, while his observations about the "monstrous" guns and the "shrill, demented" shells unambiguously condemn the horrors of war. By contrast, in "Patterns" warfare is far away, on another continent, intruding only when the messenger delivers the letter stating that the speaker's fiancé has been killed (lines 63–64). A comparable situation governs the last six lines of Owen's poem, quietly describing how those at home respond to the news that their loved ones have died in war. Thus the antiwar focus in "Patterns" is the contrast between the calm, peaceful life of the speaker's garden and the anguish of her responses; in "Anthem for Doomed Youth" the stress is more the external horrors of war that bring about the need for ceremonies honoring the dead.

[3] Another difference is that Owen's poem is less than one-seventh as long as Lowell's. "Patterns" is an interior monologue or meditation of 107 lines, but it could not be shorter and still be convincing. In the poem the speaker thinks of the past and contemplates her future loneliness. Her final outburst, "Christ! What are patterns for?," could make no sense if she did not explain her situation as extensively as she does. On the other hand, "Anthem for Doomed Youth" is brief--a fourteen-line sonnet--because it is more general and less personal than "Patterns." Although Owen's speaker shows great sympathy, he or she views the sorrows of others distantly, unlike Lowell, who goes right into the mind and spirit of the grieving woman. Owen's use, in his last six lines, of phrases such as "tenderness of patient minds" and "drawing-down of blinds" is a powerful representation of deep grief. He gives no further detail even though thousands of individual stories might be told. In contrast, Lowell tells one of these stories as she focuses on her solitary speaker's lost hopes and dreams. Thus the contrasting lengths of the poems are governed by each poet's treatment of the topic.

[4] Despite these differences of approach and length, both poems are similarly concrete and real. Owen moves from the real scenes and sounds of far-off battlefields to the homes of the many soldiers who have been killed in battle, but Lowell's scene is a single place--the garden of her speaker's estate. The speaker walks on real gravel along garden paths that contain daffodils, squills, a fountain, and a lime tree. She thinks of her clothing and her ribboned shoes, and also of her fiancé's boots, sword hilts, and buttons. The images in Owen's poem are equally real but are not associated with individuals as in "Patterns." Thus Owen's images are those of cattle, bells, rifle shots, shells, bugles, candles, and window blinds. While both poems reflect reality, Owen's details are more general and public; Lowell's are more personal and intimate.

[5] Along with this concreteness, the poems share a major metaphor: that cultural patterns both control and frustrate human wishes and hopes. In "Patterns" this metaphor is shown in warfare itself (line 106), which is the supremely destructive political structure, or pattern. Further examples of the metaphor are found in details about clothing (particularly the speaker's stiff, confining gown in lines 5, 18, 21, 73, and 101, and also the lover's military boots in lines 46 and 49); the orderly, formal garden paths in which the speaker is walking (lines 1, 93); her restraint at hearing about her lover's death; and her courtesy, despite her grief, in ordering refreshment for the messenger (line 69). Within

[5]
such rigid patterns, her hopes for happiness have vanished, along with the sensuous spontaneity symbolized by her lover's plans to make love with her on a "shady seat" in the garden (lines 85–89). The metaphor of the constricting pattern is also seen in "Anthem for Doomed Youth," except that in this poem the pattern is the funeral, not love or marriage. Owen's speaker contrasts the calm, peaceful tolling of "passing-bells" (line 1) with the frightening sounds of war represented by the "monstrous anger of the guns," "the stuttering rifles' rapid rattle," and "the demented choirs of wailing shells" (lines 2–8). Thus, while Lowell uses the metaphor to reveal the irony of hope and desire being destroyed by war, Owen uses it to reveal the irony of war's negation of peaceful ceremonies.

[6]
    Though the poems, in these ways, share topics and some aspects of treatment, they are distinct and individual. "Patterns" is visual and kinesthetic, whereas "Anthem for Doomed Youth" is auditory. Both poems conclude on powerfully emotional although different notes. Owen's poem dwells on the pathos and sadness that war brings to many unnamed people, and Lowell's expresses the most intimate thoughts of a solitary woman in the agony of sorrow. Although neither poem attacks the usual platitudes and justifications for war (the needs to mobilize, to sacrifice, to achieve peace through fighting, and so on), the attack is there by implication, for both poems make their appeal by stressing how war destroys the relationships that make life worth living. For this reason, despite their differences, both "Patterns" and "Anthem for Doomed Youth" are parallel antiwar poems, and both are strong expressions of feeling.

Commentary on the Essay

    This sample student essay shows how approximately equal attention can be given to the two works being studied. Words stressing similarity are *common, share, equally, parallel, both, similar,* and *also.* Contrasts are stressed by *while, whereas, different, dissimilar, contrast, although,* and *except.* Transitions from paragraph to paragraph are not different in this type of essay from those in other essays. Thus, the phrases *despite, along with this,* and *in these ways,* which are used here, could be used anywhere for the same transitional purpose.

    The central idea—that the poems mutually condemn war—is brought out in the introductory paragraph, together with the supporting idea that the poems blend into each other because both show responses to news of battle casualties.

    Paragraph 2, the first in the body, discusses how each poem brings out its attack on warfare. Paragraph 3 explains the differing lengths of the poems as a function of differences in perspective. Because Owen's sonnet views war and its effects at a distance, it is brief; but Lowell's interior monologue views death intimately, needing more detail and greater length.

    Paragraph 4, on the topic of concreteness and reality, shows that the two works can receive equal attention without the bouncing of the tennis-ball method. Three of the sentences in this paragraph (3, 4, and 6) are devoted exclusively to details in one poem or the other; but sentences 1, 2, 5, and 7 refer to both works, stressing points of broad or specific comparison. The scheme demonstrates that the two works are, in effect, interlocked within the paragraph.

Paragraph 5, the last in the body, considers the similar and dissimilar ways in which the poems treat the common metaphor of cultural patterns.

The final paragraph summarizes the central idea, and it also stresses the ways in which both poems, while similar, are distinct and unique.

SAMPLE STUDENT ESSAY
(EXTENDED COMPARISON-CONTRAST)

Literary Treatments of the Conflicts
between Private and Public Life

[1]
The conflict between private or personal life, on the one hand, and public or civic and national life, on the other, is a topic common to many literary works.* Authors show that individuals try to maintain their personal lives and commitments even though they are tested and stressed by public and external forces. Ideally, individuals should have the freedom to follow their own wishes independently of the outside world. It is a fact, however, that living itself causes people to venture into the public world and therefore to encounter conflicts. Getting married, following a profession, observing the natural world, looking at a person's possessions, taking a walk--all these draw people into the public world in which rules, regulations, and laws override private wishes. To greater and lesser degrees, such conflicts can be traced in Arnold's "Dover Beach," Bierce's "An Occurrence at Owl Creek Bridge," Chekhov's *The Bear*, Glaspell's *Trifles*, Hardy's "Channel Firing," Hawthorne's "Young Goodman Brown," Keats's "Bright Star," Layton's "Rhine Boat Trip," Lowell's "Patterns," Shakespeare's Sonnet 73 ("That Time of Year"), Welty's "A Worn Path," and Wordsworth's "Lines Written in Early Spring." In these works, conflicts are shown between interests of individuals and those of the social, legal, and military public.†

[2]
One of the major private-public conflicts is created by the way in which characters respond to social conventions and expectations. In Chekhov's *The Bear*, for example, Mrs. Popov has virtually given up her personal life to memorialize her dead husband. She wears black, stays in her house for a whole year, and swears eternal fidelity; and she does all this to show her public role as a grieving widow. Fortunately for her, Smirnov arrives on the scene and excites her enough to make her give up this deadly pose. Not as fortunate is Hawthorne's Goodman Brown in "Young Goodman Brown." Brown's obligation is much less public and also more philosophical than that of Mrs. Popov because his religiously inspired vision of the power of evil creates an impenetrable gloom in him. Mrs. Popov readily gives up her pose because of the prospect of immediate life and vitality, but Brown's fidelity to his distrustful vision locks him into a fear of evil from which not even his own faithful wife can shake him. The two characters therefore go in entirely different directions--one toward personal fulfillment, the other toward personal destruction.

* Central idea.
† Thesis sentence.

[3]   Of particular note is that philosophical or religious difficulties such as those of Goodman Brown may force a crisis in an individual life. In Arnold's "Dover Beach," for example, the speaker expresses regret about the loss of religious faith and uncertainty that encroaches on civilization the way the surf beats on Dover Beach. This situation might make a person dreary and depressed, just like Goodman Brown. Arnold's speaker, however, in the lines "Ah, love, let us be true / To one another," finds power in personal fidelity and commitment (lines 29–30). In other words, the public world of "human misery" and the diminishing "Sea of Faith" is beyond control, and therefore all that is left is personal commitment. This is not to say that "Young Goodman Brown," as a story, is negative, for Hawthorne clearly implies that a positive personal life lies in the denial of Brown's type of choice and in the acceptance of choices like those made by Mrs. Popov and Arnold's speaker.

[4]   To deny or to ignore the public world is a possible option that, under some circumstances, may be chosen. To a degree, for example, "Dover Beach" reflects a conscious decision to ignore the philosophic and religious uncertainty that the speaker finds in the intellectual and public world. Even more independent of such a public world, Shakespeare's "That Time of Year" and Keats's "Bright Star" bring out their ideas as reflections on purely personal situations. Shakespeare's speaker deals with the love between himself and the listener, while Keats's speaker, addressing a distant star, considers his need for steadfastness in his relationship with his "fair love." Beyond the absolute focus on personal matters in these two sonnets, Phoenix Jackson of Welty's "A Worn Path" seems totally outside the public world as she walks to town to attend to the needs of her invalid grandson. Despite the hopelessness of her poverty and her advancing age, her strength is her personal duty to her grandson. Even so, however, she depends on the public charity she receives in the medical building, and she therefore lives in the public world although she shows great difficulty in adjusting to it in the medical building (paragraphs 70-82).

[5]   The complexity of the conflicts between private and public life is brought out in the way in which public structures secure their power through law and legality. With immense power, the law sometimes seems to be an arbitrary form of public judgment that disregards personal needs and circumstances. This idea is brought out on the most personal level in Glaspell's *Trifles*, in which the two major characters, both women, are urgently faced with the conflict between their personal identification with the accused woman, Minnie Wright, and their public obligation to the law. One of the women, Mrs. Peters, is reminded that she is "married to the law" (speech 142); but she and Mrs. Hale suppress the evidence that they know would condemn Minnie, even though technically--by law, that is-- their knowledge is public property. Their resolution of the conflict therefore involves the rejection of public demands in favor of personal concerns.

[6]   The legal conflict may also be treated more generally and philosophically. For example, Wordsworth deals with the morality--or immorality--of the conflict in "Lines Written in Early Spring," when he says, "Have I not reason to lament / What man has made of man?" (lines 23–24). In its most extreme form, which Wordsworth does no more than touch, is legalized suppression and persecution. Layton's "Rhine Boat Trip" deals with this extremity. In this poem Layton condemns the Nazi exterminations of "Jewish mothers" and "murdered

rabbis" during the Holocaust. Ironically, the exterminations were carried out legally; it has commonly been observed that the Nazis created laws to justify all their atrocities.

[7]   It is works about warfare that especially highlight how irreconcilable the conflicts between personal and public concerns may become. A comic but nevertheless real instance is dramatized by Thomas Hardy in "Channel Firing." In this poem, set in a church graveyard, the skeleton of "Parson Thirdly" views "gunnery practice out at sea" (line 10) as evidence that his "forty year" dedication to serving his church was meaningless. His conclusion is that he would have been better off ignoring his public role and instead sticking "to pipes and beer." Although Thirdly is disillusioned, he has not been touched personally by warfare as much as the speaker of Lowell's "Patterns." Her fiancé, she learns, has been killed fighting abroad; and his death leads her to doubt the external "patterns" that destroy one's personal plans for life (line 107). Unlike both these characters, who are deeply affected by warfare, Peyton Farquhar, the main character in Bierce's story "An Occurrence at Owl Creek Bridge," is actually killed by his commitment to a public concern--that of the South in the Civil War. As in "Channel Firing" and "Patterns," his situation shows the absolute power of the public world over the private.

[8]   The works examined generally show that, under ideal conditions, the private world should be supreme. They also demonstrate that in many ways the public world intrudes upon the private with a wide range of effects, from making people behave foolishly to destroying them utterly. Naturally, the tone of the works is shaped by the degree of seriousness of the conflict. Chekhov's *The Bear* is good-humored and farcical, because the characters overcome the social roles in which they are cast. More sober are works such as "Dover Beach" and "Young Goodman Brown," in which characters are either overcome by public commitments or deliberately turn their backs on them. In the highest range of seriousness are works such as "Rhine Boat Trip," "Patterns," and "An Occurrence at Owl Creek Bridge," in which the individual is crushed by irresistible public forces. The works compared and contrasted here show these varied and powerful conflicts between personal interests and public demands.

Commentary on the Essay

This essay, combining for discussion all three of the genres, is visualized as an assignment at the end of a unit of study. The expectation prompting the assignment is that a fairly large number of literary works can be profitably compared on the basis of a unifying subject, idea, or technique. For this sample, the works—seven poems, three stories, and two plays—are compared and contrasted on the common topic of private-public conflicts. It is obviously impossible to discuss all the works in detail in every paragraph. The essay is therefore designed to demonstrate that a writer can introduce a large number of works in a straightforward comparison-contrast method without a need for a detailed comparison of each work with every other work on each of the major subtopics (social, legal, military).

Thus, the first section, consisting of paragraphs 2–4, treats six of the works. In paragraph 2, however, only two works are discussed, and in paragraph 3 one of these works is carried over for comparison with only one additional work. Paragraph 4 springs out of the second, utilizing one of the works discussed there and then bringing out comparisons with three additional works.

The same technique is used in the rest of the essay. Paragraph 5 introduces only one work; paragraph 6 introduces two additional works; and paragraph 7 introduces three works for comparison and contrast. Each of the twelve works is then eventually discussed at least once in terms of how it contributes to the major topic. One might note that the essay concentrates on a relatively small number of the works, such as Chekhov's *The Bear* and Hawthorne's "Young Goodman Brown," but that as newer topics are introduced, the essay goes on to works that are more closely connected to these topics.

The technique of extended comparison-contrast used in this way shows how the various works may be defined and distinguished in relation to the common idea. Paragraph 8 concludes the essay, summarizing these distinctions by suggesting a continuous line along which each of the works may be placed.

Even so, the treatment of so many texts might easily cause crowding and confusion. The division of the major topic into subtopics, as noted, is an important means of trying to make the essay easy to follow. An additional means is the introduction of transitional phrases and words such as *one of the major conflicts, like those, to choose,* and *also.*

Clearly, an extended comparison-contrast essay cannot present a full treatment of each of the works. The works are unique, and there are many elements that would not yield to the comparison-contrast method. In "Channel Firing," for example, there are ideas that human beings need eternal rest and not eternal life, that God is amused by—or indifferent to—human affairs, that religious duty may be futile, and that war itself is the supreme form of cruelty. To introduce the poem into this comparison-contrast structure requires introducing the character of Parson Thirdly (paragraph 7), who has experienced the private-public conflict directly. This consideration therefore links Hardy's poem to the other works. So it is with the other works, each of which could be the subject of analysis from a number of separate standpoints. The effect of the comparison of all the works collectively, however, is the enhanced understanding of each of the works separately. To achieve such an understanding and to explain it are the major goals of the extended comparison-contrast method.

SPECIAL WRITING TOPICS FOR COMPARISON AND CONTRAST

1. The use of the speaker in Arnold's "Dover Beach" and Wordsworth's "Lines Written in Early Spring."

2. The description of fidelity to love in Keats's "Bright Star" and Shakespeare's Sonnet 73 ("That Time of Year"), Arnold's "Dover Beach," or Lowell's "Patterns."

3. The view of women in Chekhov's *The Bear* and Welty's "A Worn Path," or in Glaspell's *Trifles* and Rossetti's "Echo."

4. The use of descriptive scenery in Wordsworth's "Lines Written in Early Spring" and Lowell's "Patterns," or in Poe's "The Cask of Amontillado" and Bierce's "An Occurrence at Owl Creek Bridge."

5. Symbols of disapproval in Arnold's "Dover Beach" and Frost's "Desert Places."

6. Any of the foregoing topics applied to a number of separate works.

Appendix
Brief Biographies
of the Poets in Part III

Brian W. Aldiss (b. 1925) • Aldiss is best known as a writer of science fiction, but he has also written novels, dramas, reviews, and considerable poetry. He was educated in English private schools, and during World War II he served in the far east (Burma, Sumatra). After the war he worked for a time as a bookseller in Oxford, when he also began writing. His first published work was *The Brightfount Diaries* (1955), after which his output flourished. Among his many works are the companion novels *Frankenstein Unbound* (1973) and *Dracula Unbound* (1991). One of his poetry collections is *Homelife with Cats* (1992). He was the recipient of the British Science Fiction Award in 1972, and is a founding trustee of World Science Fiction (1982).

Maya Angelou (b. 1928) • Born in St. Louis, Angelou acted and sang before becoming a writer. She is known as much for her fiction as for her poetry, and has also written plays. She achieved recognition with *I Know Why the Caged Bird Sings* (1970). *Just Give Me a Cool Drink of Water 'fore I Die* appeared in 1971, and she has published regularly since. Her national importance was recognized when she was chosen to read her poetry at the inauguration of President Bill Clinton in January, 1993. Recently she has spoken and sung on a number of public television productions.

Matthew Arnold (1822–1888) • One of the major Victorian poets, Arnold was brought up among books and learning, and eventually (1857) became Professor of Poetry at Oxford. In his Oxford lectures he described a loss of security and religious faith, and hence he stressed the need to recover absolutes—which to him was the major "function of criticism at the present time." "Dover Beach" is, along with "The Scholar Gypsy" and "Stanzas from the Grande Chartreuse," among his best-known poems.

Margaret Atwood (b. 1939) • For a brief biography, see p. 275.

W. H. Auden (Wystan Hugh Auden, 1907–1973) • Auden was born in England, but moved to the United States after the Spanish Civil War and then lived here permanently. A Marxist in his youth, he became a devout Christian in later years. He wrote prolifically, including collaborations with the dramatist Christopher Isherwood and the poet Louis MacNeice. Another notable collaboration is the libretto for Igor Stravinsky's opera *The Rake's Progress* (1951). He edited the *Oxford Book of Light Verse* (1938).

Imamu Amiri Baraka (LeRoi Jones, b. 1934) • Born in New Jersey, LeRoi Jones attended Rutgers, Howard, and Columbia Universities, and also the New School. After serving in the Air Force, he adopted the name Imamu Amiri Baraka. As a practical outgrowth of his devotion to African-American causes, he founded a community center—"Spirit House"—for African Americans in Newark, New Jersey. Among his many works are *Four Black Revolutionary Plays* (1969), and *African Revolution* (1973). His *Selected Poetry* appeared in 1979.

Marvin Bell (b. 1937) ▪ Originally from New York, Bell teaches at the University of Iowa and has taught in Australia and Yugoslavia. He has published a number of poetry collections, the most recent being *Drawn by Stones, by Earth, by Things that Have Been in the Fire* (1984), *New and Selected Poems* (1987), *The Iris of Creation* (1990), and *The Book of the Dead Man* (1994). "Things We Dreamt We Died For" appeared in *A Probable Volume of Dreams* (1969).

Earle Birney (b. 1904) ▪ One of the major modern Canadian writers, Birney was born in Calgary, Alberta. He is editor of *Twentieth Century Canadian Poetry* (1953). In 1975 his collected poetry was issued by McClelland and Stewart of Canada. By 1985 he had published more than twelve collections of poetry, in addition to his stories and plays.

Elizabeth Bishop (1911–1979) ▪ Bishop was brought up by an aunt in Worcester, Massachusetts. She attended private schools and Vassar. During much of her life she lived in Brazil. She taught for a time at the University of Washington and then at Harvard. Her first collection of poems was *North and South* (1946), which she expanded in 1955 as *North and South—A Cold Spring*, for which she received the Pulitzer Prize in Poetry in 1956.

William Blake (1757–1827) ▪ Blake was apprenticed to an engraver in London at the age of fourteen. Throughout his career he published his poems with his own engravings, and these original editions are now invaluable collector's items. Blake was a revolutionary at heart who thought that humanity would flower if institutions were eliminated or at least redirected. *Songs of Experience,* from which "London" is taken, is a collection of poems on this theme, published in 1794, five years after the outbreak of the French Revolution. In this same year he published *Songs of Innocence,* from which "The Lamb" is taken.

Arna Bontemps (1902–1973) ▪ Born in Louisiana, Bontemps by profession was a librarian (at Fisk University). In addition to poetry, he published a number of novels and works of children's fiction. *One Hundred Years of Negro Freedom* (1961), is a widely heralded historical work.

Anne Bradstreet (1612–1672) ▪ Bradstreet was born in England. She married early and came to the American colonies when she was eighteen. Her career was that of wife and mother, and she bore eight children. Nevertheless she managed to write poems regularly, and kept them together in manuscript. In 1650 her brother-in-law had them published in London without her knowledge, and she was therefore unable to make corrections (see lines 3–6 of "The Author to Her Book"). The volume, entitled *The Tenth Muse,* was the first poetic publication in England by anyone living in colonial America. A second and corrected edition was considered in about 1666, and "The Author to Her Book" was composed in this expectation, but the new edition did not appear until six years after her death.

Joseph Brodsky (Iosif Alexandrovich Brodsky, 1940–1996) ▪ Brodsky, a native Russian, came to the United States after he was exiled in 1972 for what was then considered subversion of the Russian government (i.e., he declared that people should be free). As a new American he attempted to become a poet of English. Usually, however, he wrote in Russian and then translated his verse into English himself or with the aid of others. Professionally, he served as a poet in residence at a number of schools from Michigan to Massachusetts. His greatest recognition came with his receiving a MacArthur Foundation Fellowship and with his being named American Poet Laureate in 1991. His verse is collected in *To Urania: Selected Poems 1965–1985* (1988). His posthumous collection of poems, *So Forth*, was published in 1996.

Gwendolyn Brooks (b. 1917) • Brooks was born in Chicago, where she has spent most of her life. Winner of the Pulitzer Prize for Poetry in 1950 (for *Annie Allen*, 1949), she is concerned with race in both her fictional and poetic works. "We Real Cool" exemplified this emphasis. In 1967 she began directing her work toward African-American readers, and has been involved in publishing a number of her poems in pamphlet form, of which *Primer for Blacks* (1980) is one.

Elizabeth Barrett Browning (1806–1861) • Elizabeth Barrett suffered a crippling spinal injury when still a girl in England. She was a recognized poet when she married Robert Browning in 1846. Because of her condition and the English climate, the Brownings moved to Italy, where they remained until Elizabeth's death. During her lifetime, her reputation as a poet eclipsed Robert's. Her *Cry of the Children* (1843) was an early poetic protest against the industrial exploitation of children. In 1850 she published *Sonnets from the Portuguese*, which she presented as a gift to her husband.

Robert Browning (1812–1889) • In his twenties and early thirties, Browning wrote a number of versified plays for the stage, but these were unsuccessful, and he did not achieve fame in his native England until he was well into his fifties. Because of his experience with drama, he found his poetic voice within the medium of the dramatic monologue, which he perfected to a high degree. Both "My Last Duchess" and "Soliloquy of the Spanish Cloister" appeared in his *Dramatic Lyrics* of 1842, exactly during the time when he was also writing his plays.

Robert Burns (1759–1796) • The best known and loved poet of Scotland, Burns gave up farming and taught himself to read and write English, French, and Latin. He published his first volume, *Scots Poems Chiefly in the Scottish Dialect*, in 1786. His use of the down-to-earth idiom of Scots peasants, together with joyous irreverence and frank lustiness, made him instantly famous.

George Gordon, Lord Byron (1788–1824) • One of the major English Romantic poets, Byron created the so-called "Byronic hero," a driven and solitary figure who is misunderstood by his fellow human beings. He published his semi-autobiographical poem "Childe Harolde's Pilgrimage" in 1811. In 1815 he published *Hebrew Melodies*, in which "The Destruction of Sennacherib" appeared. That year, he left England and never returned. He continued writing poetry as he traveled, including the 16,000-line unfinished poem *Don Juan*. He died at Missolonghi, in Greece, while fighting for Greek independence.

Amy Clampitt (1920–1994) • Clampitt was a native of Iowa, receiving her education at Grinnell College and later at Columbia University. For many years she worked in the publishing field and also for the National Audubon Society. Although she wrote poetry during most of her lifetime, she was not published until she was in her 60s, her first volume being *The Kingfisher* (1983). During the remainder of her life she published regular volumes of poems, completing *What the Light was Like* (1985), *Archaic Figure* (1987), and *Westward* (1990). In 1994, the last year of her life, she published her final collection, *A Silence Opens*.

Lucille Clifton (b. 1936) • Clifton was born and educated in New York. Her productivity as a writer began in the 1970s, and has been strong ever since. One of her earliest poetry collections was *An Ordinary Woman* (1974). Recently she published *Next: New*

Poems (1987), and *Good Woman: Poems and a Memoir, 1969–1980* (1987). In addition to her poetry, she has written a number of stories and poems for children, such as *All Us Come Cross the Water* (1973).

Leonard Cohen (b. 1934) • Cohen is a native of Montreal, and he received his education at McGill University and also at Columbia. He traveled widely, spending years in Greece, England, New York, and California. He began writing poetry early. His first collections were *Let Us Compare Mythologies* (1956) and *The Spice Box of Earth* (1961). He also published two extremely successful novels, *The Favorite Game* (1963) and *Beautiful Losers* (1966). Today he is best known for his featured television concerts and also for the many record albums and compact disc collections of his songs and music. Among the most recent of these are *The Future* (1992) and *Cohen Live* (1994).

Samuel Taylor Coleridge (1772–1834) • Coleridge was born in Devon, in southern England, and studied at Cambridge University but did not earn a degree. After a short stint as a soldier he fell into dire financial straits, from which he was rescued by the Wedgewood brothers (of ceramic fame), who provided him with an annuity so that he could devote himself to poetry. Wordsworth and he together published the *Lyrical Ballads* of 1798, a collection which is the benchmark of the English Romantic Movement. Coleridge contributed "The Rime of the Ancient Mariner," his most famous poem, and also "Kubla Khan." After 1802 he wrote little poetry, but his *Biographia Literaria* of 1817 is one of the major works of literary criticism of the early nineteenth century.

Billy Collins (b. 1941) • A native of New York, Collins received degrees at Holy Cross and the University of California at Riverside. He lives in New York and is a Professor of English at Lehman College. Among his collections of poetry are *The Apple that Astonished Paris* (1989), which includes "Schoolsville," *Questions About Angels* (1991), a winner in the National Poetry Series competition, and *The Art of Drowning* (1995).

Stephen Crane (1871–1900) • For a brief biography, see p. 97.

Richard Crashaw (1612–1649) • Crashaw left England when the English Civil War was beginning in 1642, and spent the remainder of his life in Italy. He is best known as a religious and devotional poet, although he also wrote on so conventional a topic as "Wishes to His Supposed Mistress." In 1646 he published *Steps to the Temple*, which contained "On Our Crucified Lord." Other works (with Latin titles) were *A Book of Holy Epigrams* (1634), and the posthumous *Poems to Our God* (1652).

Countée Cullen (1903–1946) • Poet, novelist, and writer of children's books, Cullen studied at New York University and Harvard, and became one of the leading figures in the Harlem Renaissance of the 1920s. Because he used an acute accent in spelling his first name, his friends gave him the nickname "Tay." He was a pioneer in dealing with the conditions and aspirations of African Americans. His earliest book of poems was *Color* (1925), which included "Yet Do I Marvel." Among his later collections were *The Ballad of the Brown Girl* (1927) and *The Black Christ and Other Poems* (1929).

e. e. cummings (1894–1962) • cummings studied at Harvard, receiving a Master's degree there. During World War I, he served in the Ambulance Corps in France, and, as a result of false charges of treason, was imprisoned—an experience he wrote about in his first work, *The Enormous Room* (1922). He began publishing poetry shortly thereafter, and continued doing so throughout his life. His collected poetry, consisting of more than a thousand poems, was published in 1992.

James Dickey (1923–1997) • Dickey was a native of Georgia. He served in World War II, and afterwards spent a number of years writing advertising copy. After 1969 he became a full-time writer and teacher. During the 1980s he published three volumes of poetry. Usually his poems are narratives which touch on violence and tragedy. "The Performance," for example, demonstrates, on the one hand, the violence that characterizes Dickey's well-received novel *Deliverance* (1970), and on the other, the courageousness of a man insisting on his individuality and rights even against the greatest odds. One of his late novels was *To the White Sea*, published in 1993.

Emily Dickinson • For a brief biography, see pp. 711–18.

John Donne (ca. 1572–1631) • Donne was born into a Roman Catholic family at a time when the Protestant reign of Elizabeth I was firmly established. In 1591 he enrolled at Lincoln's Inn in London to study science, philosophy, law, languages, and literature. In order to rise in English aristocratic circles, he changed his religion to Anglicanism. His hopes were ended in 1601, however, because of his elopement with Ann More, whose uncle accused him of a clandestine marriage (then a crime if the woman was an heiress) and had him jailed. Although the marriage was recognized in 1602, Donne could not regain political favor, and he and Ann struggled until he took a Doctorate of Divinity in 1616 (Ann died in 1617). He found favor and rose quickly to become Dean of St. Paul's Cathedral in London, where his sermons were well attended by the "nobility and gentry." He became widely known, publishing more than 130 of the sermons he delivered during his decade as Dean. His poems, both religious and love poems, were not published during his lifetime, but were circulated only privately in manuscript. They were first published two years after his death. For two centuries he was neglected, but in the twentieth century he earned recognition as one of the greatest of English poets.

Michael Drayton (1563–1631) • Like his friend Shakespeare, Drayton was a native of Warwickshire. He became educated while serving in an aristocratic household. He was a versatile poet, writing not only sonnets but topographic poetry (*England's Heroical Epistles,* 1599), epic (*Nymphidia,* 1627), and satire (*The Owl,* 1604), in addition to popular ballads, myths, and scriptural paraphrases. "Since There's No Help" appeared in his sonnet sequence *Idea, the Shepherd's Garland.*

John Dryden (1631–1700) • Poet Laureate from 1668 to 1688, Dryden was one of the foremost English poets and dramatists of the seventeenth century. His major poetic achievement was to fine-tune the heroic or neo-classic couplet, which he used for "To the Memory of Mr. Oldham." Nevertheless, he used blank verse for his best play, *All For Love* (1677), which deals with the same material as Acts IV and V of Shakespeare's *Antony and Cleopatra.* In 1688 he lost his official positions because he had been a supporter of the deposed James II. During the last twelve years of his life, therefore, he was forced to support himself mainly with translations, providing his contemporaries with poetic versions of Virgil, Ovid, Juvenal, and Chaucer.

Paul Laurence Dunbar (1872–1906) • Dunbar was born in Ohio, the son of former slaves. During his brief life he rose to prominence as a poet, dramatist, and novelist. His first two collections of poems, *Oak and Ivy* (1893) and *Majors and Minors* (1895), in which "Sympathy" appeared, were favorably reviewed by William Dean Howells. His collected poems were published posthumously in 1913.

Richard Eberhart (b. 1904) • Eberhart, the recipient of many awards, including the Pulitzer Prize in Poetry in 1966, was born in Minnesota and received his higher education at Dartmouth and Cambridge. His many works include *Collected Poems* of 1930 and 1976. In 1982 the governor of New Hampshire, Eberhart's home, proclaimed a "Richard Eberhart Day" in his honor.

T. S. Eliot (1888–1965) • Born in Missouri, Thomas Stearns Eliot moved to England in 1914 and became a British citizen in 1927. With *The Waste Land* in 1922, he electrified the literary world because of his poetic use of colloquial speech and frank subject matter. Though he is considered a hyper-serious poet, his lighter side is shown in *Old Possum's Book of Practical Cats* (1939). These poems achieved popular fame in 1981 in the Broadway musical *Cats,* which was still running in early 1998.

Edward Field (b. 1924) • A native of Brooklyn, Field studied at New York University, and also, for a time, studied method acting at the Moscow Art Theatre. "Icarus" is taken from his first collection of poems, *Stand Up, Friend, with Me* (1963). Another of his collections is *Stars in My Eyes* (1979). In 1990 he edited *Head of a Sad Angel,* stories by Alfred Chester, with an introduction by Gore Vidal.

Carolyn Forché (b. 1950) • Forché is a native of Detroit. After her first volume of poems in the Yale Younger Poets series (*Gathering the Tribes* [1976]) she spent two years in El Salvador as a journalist for Amnesty International. In 1982 she translated Claribel Alegria's *Flowers for the Volcano* in an English-Spanish edition. Her next volume of poetry was *The Country Between Us* in 1982, which includes "Because One Is Always Forgotten." In 1993 she published *Against Forgetting: Twentieth-Century Poetry of Witness,* an anthology of poems protesting against repression and genocide.

Robert Frost (1874–1963) • For a brief biography, see pp. 728–30.

John Gay (1685–1732) • English poet and playwright John Gay was born and educated in Devon. As a young boy he was apprenticed to a silk mercer, but freed himself to become a writer in London. For a time in the late 1720s, he was a gentleman-in-waiting to the young Duke of Cumberland, for whom he wrote his *Fables,* which were among the most popular poems in the eighteenth century. His most famous play is *The Beggar's Opera* (1728), which at a stroke created *ballad opera*—a form featuring spoken dialogue and songs sung to popular music. "Let Us Take the Road" is from this play, and the music is the March in the opera *Rinaldo* (1711) by Georg Friderich Handel.

Allen Ginsberg (1926–1997) • One of the major voices of the "beat generation" of the fifties and sixties, Ginsberg was born in New Jersey and lived in San Francisco for a time. For many years he was a Distinguished Professor at Brooklyn College. His landmark poetry collection was *Howl and Other Poems* (1956), which occasioned a court case when certain persons sued, unsuccessfully, to suppress it on the grounds of obscenity. Ironically, his collection of 1973, *The Fall of America: Poems of These States,* received a National Book Award. Among his later publications were *Cosmopolitan Greetings: Poems 1986–1992* (1994) and a four-CD/Cassette Box set entitled *Holy Soul Jelly Roll: Poems and Songs 1949–1993* (available from Rhino Word Beat [1-800-432-0020]).

Nikki Giovanni (Yolande Cornelia Giovanni, Jr., b. 1943) • Giovanni, a poet whose reputation has coincided with the development of African-American consciousness and pride, was born in Tennessee. She has written poems for children, and has also published interviews with James Baldwin and Alice Walker. Among her collections of poetry are *Black Feeling, Black Talk* (1968), *Black Judgment* (1968), and *Cotton Candy on a Rainy Day* (1978). Recent works are *Those Who Ride the Night Winds* (1983) and *Sacred Cows— and Other Edibles* (1988).

Jorie Graham (b. 1951) • Graham is a person of international credentials. She is a native of New York but was brought up in Italy, studied in Paris, and received a degree in film from New York University. Later she studied writing at the University of Iowa, where she is now on the faculty. Her poetry is thoughtful—some would say difficult—reflective, and challenging. Among her collections are *The End of Beauty* (1987), *Region of Unlikeness* (1991), *Materialism* (1993), and *The Dream of the Unified Field* (1995).

Robert Graves (1895–1985) • Graves fought in the British Army in World War I and was badly wounded. His early autobiographical memoir, *Good-Bye to All That* (1929), deals in part with his war experiences. He became famous in the 1970s, when the BBC and PBS dramatized his historical novels about the life and times of Roman Emperor Claudius. His studies of mythology, *The White Goddess* (1947) and *The Greek Myths* (1955), explained the meaning of ancient religion to a generation of students.

Thomas Gray (1716–1771) • Gray was Professor of History at Cambridge University. His poetic output was small, but nevertheless in 1757 he was offered the honor of Poet Laureate, which he refused. The "Elegy Written in a Country Churchyard" has been called one of the most often quoted poems of the English language. Another of Gray's frequently quoted poems is the "Ode on a Distant Prospect of Eton College," which concludes with the familiar lines "Where ignorance is bliss / 'Tis folly to be wise."

Marilyn Hacker (b. 1942) • Hacker, a native of New York City, has been the recipient of a National Book Award (1975) and a Guggenheim Fellowship. Her collections of poems include *Presentation Piece* (1974), *Separations* (1976), *Taking Notice* (1980), which includes "Sonnet Ending with a Film Subtitle," and *Selected Poems* (1994). The year 1990 saw the publication of the collection *Going Back to the River,* and in the same year she included new and selected poems in *The Hang-Glider's Daughter.* In 1989 the composer Dennis Riley set five of her poems to music for soprano and chamber ensemble. In 1995 she was awarded the Lenore Marshall Poetry Prize for her eighth book of poems, *Winter Numbers* (1994).

Donald Hall (b. 1928) • Hall was born in Connecticut. In addition to his devotion to poetry, he is a literary and art critic, a collector of literary anecdotes, and a student of baseball. He has published a number of poetry collections, including *The Alligator Bride* (1969), *Kicking the Leaves* (1978), *The Happy Man* (1986), and *The Old Life* (1996). His *The One Day* was the winning poetry collection of the National Book Critics Circle Award in 1988.

Daniel Halpern (b. 1945) • Halpern was born and raised in New York, and is currently a Professor in the graduate writing program of Columbia University. He has lived on both the east and west coasts, and also has a residence in Morocco. He has produced seven volumes of poetry, including *Traveling on Credit, Seasonal Rights,* and *Foreign Neon* (1991), and he has also done work in editing and translating. Uniquely interesting about him is that he has co-authored a cookbook, *The Good Food: Soups, Stews, and Pastas* (1985). He has also written a tourist's guide to the "Essential Restaurants of Italy" (1990).

H. S. Hamod (b. 1936) • Sam Hamod is a Lebanese American who was born in Indiana. He received a Ph.D. from the Writer's Workshop of the University of Iowa, and is currently director of the National Communications Institute in Washington, D.C. He has published eight books of poetry, including *Dying with the Wrong Name* (1980), from which "Leaves" is selected.

Thomas Hardy (1840–1928) • Hardy was born in Dorsetshire, in southwest England, which he called "Wessex" in his novels and poems. He began a career as an architect, but gave it up to become a novelist. In 1898, after he had published more than a dozen novels, including *Tess of the D'Urbervilles, The Return of the Native,* and *Jude the Obscure,* he gave up novels and devoted himself to poetry. Before his death in 1928, he had published eight volumes of verse, which were collected and published posthumously in 1931.

Joy Harjo (b. 1951) • Harjo, who is Creek, Cherokee, and French, was born in Oklahoma. She received her B.A. from the University of New Mexico and her M.F.A. at the University of Iowa, and has taught at a number of schools, including Arizona State University. In 1991 she received the Josephine Miles Award for excellence in literature. Among her poetry collections are *The Last Song* (1975), *What Moon Drove Me to This?* (1980), and *She Had Some Horses* (1983).

Frances E. W. Harper (1825–1911) ▪ Although Harper was a native of Maryland, a slave state in 1825, she was born free. She insured her continued freedom by eventually moving to the free state of Pennsylvania. Before the Civil War she lectured extensively against slavery and supported the Underground Railway. Early collections of her work were *Forest Leaves* (1845), *Eventide* (1854), and *Poems on Miscellaneous Subjects* (1854), the last containing a preface by William Lloyd Garrison. Her novel, *Iola Leroy, or Shadows Uplifted* (1892), was well received, and was included as part of a collection of fiction by African-American writers. One of her better known poetry collections is *Atlanta Offering: Poems* (1895). In 1970 and 1988 her reputation as a poet was permanently secured with the publication of complete editions of her poems.

Michael S. Harper (b. 1938) ▪ Born in Brooklyn, the American poet Michael S. Harper should not be confused with the English writer Michael Harper. Harper has held distinguished visiting professorships at Carlton College and at Colgate, and has received both a Guggenheim Fellowship and an NEA Creative Writing Award. He currently teaches at Brown University. Some of his collections of poems are *Dear John, Dear Coltrane* (1970, 1985), *Images of Kin* (1977), *Nightmare Begins Responsibility* (1975), *Healing Songs for the Inner Ear* (1984), and *Honorable Amendments* (1995). "Called" is from *Nightmare Begins Responsibility*.

Robert Hass (b. 1941) ▪ A native of California, Hass is one of America's most distinguished poets. He was educated at Stanford. He taught at St. Mary's College and then became Poet Resident at the University of California at Berkeley. His first collection of poems, *Field Guide* (1973), received the Yale Series of Younger Poets Award. Among his many later collections are *Praise* (1979), *Twentieth Century Pleasures* (1984), *Human Wishes* (1989), and *Sun Under Wood* (1996). In 1995 he was made United States poet laureate.

Robert Hayden (1913–1980) ▪ Born in Detroit and educated at the University of Michigan, Hayden became a Professor of English at both Fisk and Michigan. His earliest collection of poems was *Heart-Shape in the Dust* (1940). He received a special prize for *A Ballad of Remembrance* at the World Festival of Negro Arts held in Senegal in 1962. His *Words in the Mourning Time* (1970) included laments for the assassinated leaders Martin Luther King and Robert Kennedy, together with poems opposing the Vietnamese war.

Seamus Heaney (b. 1939) ▪ Heaney lives in Northern Ireland, which for many decades has been beset with Protestant-Catholic strife. Although the tensions of this situation have permeated some of his work, he has written broadly on many topics, as can be inferred from "The Otter," which is taken from his 1979 collection *Field Work*. Among Heaney's other collections of verse are *Wintering Out* (1972), *Seamus Heaney: Selected Peoms, 1966–1987* (1990), and *The Spirit Level* (1996). He has received many awards and distinctions, the major one being the Nobel Prize for literature in 1995.

George Herbert (1593–1633) ▪ Herbert, whose brother was an English lord, became a priest in 1630 after a career in governmental service. He died in 1633, leaving his poems to a friend, Nicholas Ferrar, who had them printed in 1633 as *The Temple*. The intricacy of Herbert's thought, illustrated in poems like "The Pulley" and "The Collar," has caused later critics to classify him as a "metaphysical" poet. In the twentieth century a large number of church-music composers have set many of his lyrics as choral anthems.

Robert Herrick (1591–1674) ▪ Herrick attended Cambridge, and became an Anglican priest in 1627. During the English Civil War he remained loyal to King Charles I, for which he was removed from service in 1647, but he resumed his duties after the Restoration of Charles II in 1660. His major collection of poems was *Hesperides*, published in 1648. A number of persons expressed disapproval because of his frank subject matter, but, as he said, though his muse was jocund, his spirit was chaste. "To the Virgins, to Make Much of Time" is one of the better known poems in the *carpe diem* tradition.

William Heyen (b. 1940) • Heyen's father came to America from Germany in 1928. Two uncles who remained in Germany joined the Nazi party and were killed in combat when serving in the German army in World War II. Heyen's concern with the Holocaust is thus a complex product of his ethnic ties and his anguish over Nazi atrocities. "The Hair: Jacob Korman's Story" was published in *Erika: Poems of the Holocaust* (1984). Among his volumes of poems are *The City Parables* (1980), *Pterodactyl Rose: Poems of Ecology*, and *Ribbons: The Gulf War*. A collection of his poems titled *The Host: Selected Poems, 1965–1990* was published in 1994. This collection is also available in cassette form.

A. D. Hope (Alec Derwent Hope, b. 1907) • Hope is a native Australian whose lyrics have been praised for their traditionalism, their satire, and for their search for redemption in love, literature, and art. Collections are *Collected Poems, 1930–1970* (1972), *Antechinus: Poems 1975–1980* (1981), and *Selected Poems* (1992). A play, *Ladies from the Sea*, appeared in 1987.

Gerard Manley Hopkins (1844–1889) • Hopkins was an English poet gifted not only in poetry but also in music and art. At the age of twenty-two he converted to Roman Catholicism and became a Jesuit priest. Although he published the long poem *The Wreck of the Deutschland* in 1875, the poems linking his devotion to Nature, on which his reputation now rests, were not published until early in the twentieth century. Hopkins used the term "sprung rhythm" for his metrical system (see Glossary).

A. E. Housman (1859–1936) • Housman was a professor of Classics at Cambridge University. He created one major book of verse, *A Shropshire Lad* (1896), a collection of poems stressing the brevity and fragility of youth and love. His major scholarly pursuit was a study of the ancient Latin writer Manilius, whose works he edited. His *More Poems* was published posthumously, and his *Complete Poems* was published in 1956.

Langston Hughes (1902–1967) • See pp. 845–48 for a short biography.

Randall Jarrell (1914–1965) • Jarrell was born in Tennessee. He received his B.A. and M.A. degrees from Vanderbilt University. He wrote poetry, criticism, a novel, and children's fiction. His 1945 collection of poems, *Little Friend, Little Friend*, which includes "The Death of the Ball Turret Gunner," resulted from his service in the Army Air Corps during World War II. He published a number of other verse collections, including *Selected Poems* (1955) and *The Woman at the Washington Zoo* (1960).

Robinson Jeffers (1887–1962) • Jeffers was born in Pittsburgh and spent most of his life in California. He used negative and often brutal subject matter in his poetry, for example fratricide in *Give Your Heart to the Hawks* (1933), betrayal in *Dear Judas, and Other Poems* (1929), and infidelity in *Thurso's Landing, and Other Poems* (1932). His adaptation of Euripides' *Medea* (1947), starring Judith Anderson in the title role, won him wide national recognition. "The Answer" and "The Purse-Seine" appeared in his *Selected Poetry* (1938).

Ben Jonson (1573–1637) • Jonson was raised in the household of his stepfather, a bricklayer, and young Ben began his working life in that trade. He was able to free himself to attend the Westminster School, where he began acquiring his immense store of knowledge. After brief service as a soldier, he embarked upon a career as a poet and playwright. After Shakespeare retired in 1611, Jonson was, in effect, the major practicing dramatist in England. In 1616 he published his non-dramatic poems, *Epigrams* and *The Forrest*. He became England's first Poet Laureate in 1619.

Donald Justice (b. 1925) • Born in Florida, Justice received his B. A. from the University of Miami (1945). He received his Ph.D. from the University of Iowa, and became a member of the faculty there. His collections of poetry include *The Summer Anniversaries* (1959), *Departures* (1973), and *Selected Poems* (1979), for which he was awarded the Pulitzer Prize in 1980, *The Sunset Maker* (1987), and *New and Selected Poems* (1995). A generous selection of his work has been included in the recent publication, *A Donald Justice Reader.*

John Keats (1795–1821) • Keats is one of the major English Romantic poets. Both his parents died when he was still a child, and at the age of fifteen he was apprenticed to an apothecary-surgeon. In 1816 he received his license to practice medicine, but almost immediately he gave up that career in order to become a full-time poet. In the following five years he created a magnificent body of poetry. Mortally afflicted with tuberculosis, he went to Rome, where he took rooms in the building adjoining the Spanish Steps. He died in Rome at the age of 26, and is buried in the English Cemetery near the Pyramid of Sestus Sextus.

X. J. Kennedy (Joseph Charles Kennedy, b. 1929) • Kennedy is a New Jersey native. He received an M.A. from Columbia, and a *Certificat* from the University of Paris (1956). His first book of verse was *Nude Descending a Staircase* (1961), and since then he has published eight major poetry collections. "Old Men Pitching Horseshoes" is from *Cross Ties* (1985), which received the *Los Angeles Times* Book Award for Poetry in 1985. "John While Swimming" is selected from the 1986 "juvenile" collection entitled *Brats.*

Jane Kenyon (1947–1995) • Kenyon was a long-time resident of New Hampshire. She received fellowships from the National Endowment for the Arts and also from the Guggenheim Foundation. Collections of her poetry are *Room to Room* (1978), *The Boat of Quiet Hours* (1986), *Let Evening Come* (1990), and *Constance* (1993). *Otherwise: New and Selected Poems* (1996) is a posthumous collection. Along with her husband, Donald Hall, she is the subject of a video interview by Bill Moyers for the *Films for the Humanities and Sciences* series (1994).

Etheridge Knight (1931–1991) • Knight was born in Mississippi and educated himself in various jails and prisons. He was convicted of robbery and was sent to the Indiana State Prison (1960–1966). When there he was visited by Dudley Randall, who persuaded him that his salvation lay in the development of his power to write. One of the products was the set of haiku included here, which were included in his first book, *Poems from Prison.* Knight went on to write and teach at the University of Pittsburgh. His collection *Belly Song and Other Poems* was published in 1973, and earned him a nomination for both the Pulitzer Prize and a National Book Award.

Maxine Kumin (Maxine Winokur Kumin, b. 1925) • Kumin was born in Philadelphia and now lives in New Hampshire. She received B.A. and M.A. degrees at Radcliffe. In addition to her many volumes of poetry she has written novels, stories, children's books (two in collaboration with Anne Sexton), and essays. Her fourth collection of poetry, *Up Country: Poems of New England* (1972) received the 1973 Pulitzer Prize. *Our Ground Time Here Will Be Brief* appeared in 1982. Recently she has published a new collection, *Connecting the Dots* (1996).

Irving Layton (b. 1912) • Since 1945 Layton, one of Canada's major poets, has published more than fifty books. A comprehensive selection of his poems, *A Wild Peculiar Joy: Selected Poems 1945–1982*, was published in 1983. *The Love Poems of Irving Layton* and *Dance with Desire: Love Poems* were published in 1984 and 1986. In 1982 and 1983 he was one of those nominated for the Nobel Prize in Literature.

Li-Young Lee (b. 1957) • Lee is a native of Indonesia and is acknowledged as a powerful voice among Asian Americans. He was the recipient of grants from the National Endowment for the Arts and from the Guggenheim Foundation. His major collections thus far are *Rose Poems* (1986) and *The City in Which I Love You* (1990), which was the Lamont Poetry Selection for 1990. In 1995 he published *The Winged Seed: A Remembrance*, an autobiographical memoir.

Denise Levertov (b. 1923) • Levertov is a native of England whose parents were Welsh and Jewish. She was educated at home and served as a nurse in World War II. After the war she married an American and left England to live in the United States. She began publishing poems in her twenties. Since her first poetry collection *The Double Image*, which appeared in 1946, she has published at least two collections each decade. In the 1970s she published four. Her collections have ranged from personal topics to deeply political ones, particularly *Light Up the Cave* (1981), which contains a number of poems on the Vietnam War. Recent poetry collections are *The Double Image* (1991), *Evening Train* (1992), and *Sands of the Well* (1996). In 1995 the Academy of American Poets awarded her the 1995 Academy Fellowship.

Philip Levine (b. 1928) • Levine's parents were Russian Jewish immigrants who settled in Detroit. He was educated there, and for higher education went to Wayne University (now Wayne State University) and also the University of Iowa. For a long time he took industrial jobs, living in a number of cities before he became a Professor at Fresno State in California. He is noted for his use of plain language and straightforward, simple syntax, in keeping with his pronounced sympathies for ordinary, working-class people. He has published many collections of poetry, including *They Feed, They Lion* (1972), *The Names of the Lost* (1976), *One for the Rose* (1981), *A Walk with Tom Jefferson* (1988), *What Work Is Like* (1991), *The Simple Truth* (1994), and *New Selected Poems* (1995). He has been honored with the American Book Award, the National Book Award, and the Pulitzer Prize for *The Simple Truth*.

Alan P. Lightman (b. 1948) • Lightman, a faculty member of the Massachusetts Institute of Technology, is a native of Tennessee. He received degrees from Princeton and the California Institute of Technology. He is well known for his scientific writings, such as *Great Ideas in Physics* and *Time for the Stars*. He has also written fiction. His recent novel *Good Benito* (1994), for example, describes the life and tribulations of a young scientist.

Audre Lorde (1934–1992) • Lorde was a New Yorker whose parents were from Jamaica. She was educated at the National University of Mexico, Hunter College, and Columbia. Recent poetry collections are *Chosen Poems Old and New* (1982), *Our Dead Behind Us* (1986), *Undersong* (1992), and *The Marvelous Arithmetics of Distance: Poems 1987–1992* (1993).

Richard Lovelace (1618–ca. 1657) • One of the best-known "Cavalier" poets of the early seventeenth century, Lovelace served King Charles I in the Civil Wars and was twice imprisoned by the Parliament side. Stripped of his wealth, he died obscurely and in poverty. A collection of his poems was published posthumously, and his collected works were published in 1925.

Amy Lowell (1874–1925) • Lowell was a proponent of the "Imagist" school of poetry early in the twentieth century. Her earliest collection of poems was *A Dome of Many-Colored Glass* (1912). Later collections were *Sword Blades and Poppy Seed* (1914) and *Legends* (1921). "Patterns" appeared in her collection *Men, Women, and Ghosts* (1916).

Archibald MacLeish (1892–1982) • A native of Illinois, MacLeish graduated from Yale and had a varied public career during the years when he was also writing poetry. He received a Pulitzer Prize three times, twice for his poetry (1932, for *Conquistador*, and

1952, for *Collected Poems, 1917–1952*). In 1944 and 1945 he served President Franklin D. Roosevelt as an Assistant Secretary of State. Among his many poetry collections are *Songs for a Summer Day* (1915), *Songs for Eve* (1954), and *New and Collected Poems 1917–1976* (1976). "Ars Poetica" appeared in *Streets of the Moon* (1926).

Christopher Marlowe (1564–1593) • Marlowe is known as the major English dramatist before Shakespeare (*Tamberlaine the Great, Dr. Faustus, The Jew of Malta, Edward II*), and he may have collaborated with Shakespeare in some of Shakespeare's earliest plays. Marlowe's unfinished poem *Hero and Leander* was completed by George Chapman and published in 1598. "Come Live with Me and Be My Love" was first published in 1599 in *The Passionate Pilgrim*, and was republished with Sir Walter Raleigh's accompanying poem in *England's Helicon* in 1600. A definitive edition of Marlowe's poems appeared in 1968.

Andrew Marvell (1621–1678) • Marvell, one of the major Metaphysical poets of the seventeenth century, was active during the unsettled period of the English Civil Wars of 1642–1649, the Commonwealth, and the Protectorate of Oliver Cromwell. The Restoration of King Charles II (1660) ushered in a period of relative calm in Marvell's life. During his long career, which he began as a tutor in an aristocratic household, he assisted Milton (who served as Latin Secretary for the English Commonwealth), and he also was a Member of Parliament. His poems were not published until three years after his death. A modern edition of his *Poems and Letters* was published in 1971.

John Masefield (1878–1967) • The English poet John Masefield, though not an academic, was a compulsive reader and writer. His youth was spent as a merchant seaman and worker at odd jobs in the United States. Eventually he published fifty volumes of poems, together with many plays and novels, and he became Poet Laureate of England in 1930. His two best-known poems are "I Must Go Down to the Sea Again," included in *Salt-Water Ballads* (1902), and "Cargoes," which appeared in *Ballads and Poems* (1910).

Gwendolyn MacEwen (1941-1987) • A major Canadian voice in poetry as well as the short story and the novel, MacEwen treats subjects such as birth, the passing of time, death, and the importance of the spiritual. From her first collection of poems in 1963 (*The Rising Sun*), she published regularly until her death in 1987. Some of her later collections are *Magic Animals* (1974), *Earthlight* (1982), and *Afterworlds* (1987).

Claude McKay (1890–1948) • McKay, one of the important voices in the Harlem Renaissance of the 1920s, was born in Jamaica, immigrated to the United States in 1912, and settled in Harlem in 1914. He wrote a number of novels, including *Home to Harlem* (1928), and short stories, published in *Gingertown* (1932). His poems were collected in *Songs of Jamaica* (1911), *Spring in New Hampshire and other Poems* (1920), and *Harlem Shadows* (1922), where we find "In Bondage" and "The White City."

W. S. Merwin (William Stanley Merwin, b. 1927) • Merwin was born in New York and raised in New Jersey and Pennsylvania. He currently lives in Hawaii. He published *Selected Translations 1948–1968* in 1968 and was distinguished by a PEN translation prize for this work. In 1988 he published two collections of poems: *The Rain in the Trees* and *Selected Poems*. In 1996 he published *The Vixen*, a collection of poems about people and life in the southern part of France. Also in 1996 he published *Flower & Hand: Poems 1977–1983*. He received the Pulitzer Prize in Poetry for *The Carriers of Ladders* (1970). "Odysseus" appeared in one of his early collections, *The Drunk in the Furnace* (1960).

Edna St. Vincent Millay (1892–1950) • Known as a free spirit at Vassar, Millay matured quickly, receiving the Pulitzer Prize for Poetry—the first woman to do so—for *The Harp Weaver and Other Poems* (1923), which contained "What Lips My Lips Have Kissed." Her maturing concerns were reflected in *Make Bright the Arrows* (1940) and especially *The*

Murder of Lidice (1942), which she wrote for radio presentation after the Nazi extermination of that Czech village. She published her *Collected Sonnets* in 1941. *Edna St. Vincent Millay: Collected Poems*, a centenary edition, was published in 1993.

John Milton (1608–1674) • Milton is acknowledged as one of the greatest English poets. His fame rests largely on the epic poem *Paradise Lost*, which he wrote in 1667, long after he became blind. He led a varied career, and wrote extensively in both verse and prose, including many Latin poems. His most important political position was as Latin Secretary to Oliver Cromwell during the Interregnum (1649–1660). Latin at that time was the language of diplomacy, and a good Latinist like Milton was essential. Milton's *Poems* was published in 1645, and he issued a second edition in 1673.

Marianne Moore (1887–1972) • A native of Missouri, Moore graduated from Bryn Mawr. Her first poetry collection, *Poems*, was published without her knowledge in 1921. Later she published *Selected Poems* (1935), *Nevertheless* (1944), and *Collected Poems* (1951), for which she received a Pulitzer Prize. In 1967 she put together all the poems on which she wished her reputation to rest, and published the collection as *Complete Poems*.

Carol Muske (b. 1945) • Muske was born in St. Paul, Minnesota. She lives in California with her husband, the actor David Dukes, and teaches writing at the University of Southern California. She has received a Guggenheim Fellowship and also a fellowship from the Ingram Merrill Foundation. An early collection of her poems is *Applause*, and her first novel is *Dear Digby*. Her second novel, *Saving St. Germ*, was published in 1993. *The American Poetry Review* featured seven poems from a new collection, *Red Trousseau*, in the July/August, 1991, issue, and *Red Trousseau* was published in 1993.

Ogden Nash (1902–1971) • Nash is most closely associated with *The New Yorker*, which he served as an editor for many years. His verse is characterized by wit, humor, and satire, with an emphasis on original and funny rhymes and rhythms. Students of music may remember his voice on a 1950s recording of Camille Saint-Saens's *Carnival of the Animals*. His many poetry collections include *Free Wheeling* (1931), *The Bad Parents' Garden of Verse* (1936), *You Can't Get There from Here* (1957), *Everyone But Thee and Me* (1962), and *Bed Riddance* (1970).

Jim Northrup (b. 1943) • Northrup is a Chippewa Indian and lives with his family on the Fond du Lac Reservation in Minnesota. He has published a number of stories, and his poems have been published mainly in magazines and journals. His major poetry collection, which also contains stories, is *Walking the Rez Road* (1993). He writes a syndicated column and also works as an artist.

Frank O'Hara (1926–1966) • Both a poet and a playwright, O'Hara was a native of Baltimore but spent much of his life in New York City, where he worked for the Museum of Modern Art. In a freak accident in the summer of 1966, he was walking on a beach and was struck and killed by a dune buggy. During his short life he published a large number of poetry collections, including *A City, Winter, and Other Poems* (1952), *Meditations in an Emergency* (1957), from which "Poem" is taken, and *Love Poems* (1965). Posthumous collections are *In Memory of My Feelings: A Selection of Poems* (1967) and *The Collected Poems of Frank O'Hara* (1971).

Sharon Olds (b. 1942) • Born in San Francisco, Olds received her Ph.D. from Columbia in 1972, and has taught at New York University, Sarah Lawrence, Brandeis, and Columbia. In a recent informal survey among members of the Academy of American Poets, she was named most often as their favorite contemporary American poet. Her early poetry collections are *Satan Says* (1980) and *The Dead and the Living* (1984), which contains "35/10." Recent collections are *The Gold Cell* (1987), *The Father* (1992), and *The Wellspring* (1996).

Mary Oliver (b. 1935) • A native of Cleveland, Oliver took her higher education at Ohio State University and Vassar College. She is a longtime resident of Provincetown, Massachusetts, and is on the faculty of Bennington College. Her poetry collections have been regular and numerous, including *No Voyage and Other Poems* (1963), *Sleeping in the Forest* (1978), *American Primitive* (1983), *New and Selected Poems* (1992), *White Pine: Poems and Prose Poems* (1994), *Blue Pastures* (1995), and *West Wind* (1997). She is also the author of *A Poetry Handbook* (1994). She received the National Book Award and the Shelley Memorial Award, and in 1984 was honored with the Pulitzer Prize for Poetry for *American Primitive.*

Michael Ondaatje (b. 1943) • Ondaatje was born in Ceylon (now Sri Lanka), and was educated in Ceylon, England, and Canada. He lives in Toronto, where he teaches. He is best known for his novel *The English Patient* (1992), which was made into a movie (1996) which received a number of best-picture awards and also won nine Oscars at the 1997 Academy Awards ceremony. Before this overwhelming success, Ondaatje had written plays and had also directed films. The interest he has in film is also shown in "Watching the Late Movies with Skyler." Among his ten volumes of poetry are *There's a Trick with a Knife I'm Learning to Do* (1979) and *The Cinnamon Peeler* (1991).

Simon Ortiz (b. 1941) • Ortiz, of the Acoma Pueblo Indian Nation, was born in New Mexico. He attended the Universities of New Mexico and Iowa. His first volume of poetry was *Naked in the Wind* (1971). In 1991 he published the collection *After and Before the Lightning. Woven Stone*, a three-in-one volume of poems containing a memoir, appeared in 1992. His best-known collection of stories is *Howbah Indians* (1978).

Wilfred Owen (1893–1918) • A native of Shropshire, England, Owen became a British Army officer and was killed in France in 1918, just a week before the Armistice. He published only four poems in his lifetime, but after his death Siegfried Sassoon issued a collection of twenty-four poems (1920). Benjamin Britten used a number of Owen's poems, including "Anthem for Doomed Youth," as texts for his *War Requiem* (1962). The popular band "10,000 Maniacs" recorded a version of both "Anthem for Doomed Youth" and "Dulce et Decorum Est" on their album *Hope Chest* (Elektra 9-60962-2).

P. K. Page (Patricia Kathleen Page Irwin, b. 1916) • Versatile as artist, fiction writer, and poet, Page was born in England and came to Canada with her parents in 1919. After completing school she did work in business, research, and radio. She married a diplomat, W. A. Irwin, who at various times served as Canadian ambassador to Australia, Brazil, and Mexico. One of her earliest works, a novel titled *The Sun and the Moon* (1944), was published under the pen-name "Judith Cape." Her earliest collection of poetry was *As Ten as Twenty* (1946). Among her many later collections are *The Metal and the Flower* (1954), *Evening Dance of the Grey Flies* (1981), *The Glass Air* (1985), and *A Flask of Sea Water* (1989).

Dorothy Parker (1893–1967) • Parker became legendary because of her many witty "one-liners" and also because of her often caustic book and drama reviews for *The New Yorker* in the period between the World Wars. Her first volume of poetry was *Enough Rope* (1926), which included "Resumé." "Penelope" was included in her comprehensive collection *Not So Deep as a Well* (1936). She wrote many short stories, and served as a correspondent during the Spanish Civil War in the late 1930s.

Linda Pastan (b. 1932) • Pastan was born in New York. She received a B.A. from Radcliffe and an M.A. from Brandeis. Among her eight volumes of verse are *A Perfect Circle of Sun* (1971), *Setting the Table* (1980), *Waiting for My Life* (1981), *PM/AM: New and Selected Poems* (1983), and *A Fraction of Darkness* (1985).

Marge Piercy (b. 1936) • A native of Detroit, Piercy received her B.A. from the University of Michigan (1957) and M.A. from Northwestern (1958). She now lives in

Cape Cod. Among her novels are *Braided Lives* (1980) and *Fly Away Home* (1984). The first of her many poetry collections was *Breaking Camp* (1968). Others are *The Moon Is Always Female* (1980), in which "Will We Work Together" appeared, *Circles on the Water: Selected Poems* (1982), including "A Work of Artifice" and "The Secretary Chant," and *Available Light* (1988), which includes "Wellfleet Sabbath." Recently she published a new collection of poems, *What Are Big Girls Made Of?* (1996).

Sylvia Plath (1932–1963) • One of the most confessional of poets, Plath was born in Massachusetts. After graduating from Smith College in 1955 she received a Fulbright Scholarship to England. She spent 1955–1956 in Cambridge, where she married Ted Hughes (now Poet Laureate). The following years brought overpowering emotional distress, and she took her life in 1963. Her poetry during these final years reflects the personal anguish that led to her suicide. Plath's *The Collected Poems* (1981) was awarded the 1982 Pulitzer Prize in Poetry.

Edgar Allan Poe (1809–1849) • See p. 258 for a brief biography.

Katha Pollitt (b. 1949) • A native of New York, Pollitt received her B.A. at Radcliffe. She has been an editor for the weekly magazine *The Nation* for many years, and serves as an associate faculty member of the Bennington Writing Seminars Program. She has also achieved wide recognition as an essayist. Her first book of poems was *Antarctic Traveler* (1982).

Alexander Pope (1688–1744) • Pope is the eminent eighteenth-century English poet, the acknowledged master of the neo-classic couplet. A childhood accident deformed his spine and retarded his physical growth, but it did not hinder his poetic gifts. Because his family was Roman Catholic, he was not sent to school but was educated at home. By age 23 he had completed *An Essay on Criticism* (1711), the leading English work of criticism in poetic form. After 1725 he devoted himself principally to writing satire, producing *The Dunciad* (1728, rev. 1743), the *Moral Essays* (1731–35), *An Epistle to Dr. Arbuthnot* (1735), and other satiric works, including the *Epilogues to the Satires* in dialogue form (1738). One of his life's plans was to publish a major philosophic work in poetry, but the only part he completed was the *Essay on Man* (1734).

Ezra Pound (1885–1972) • A native of Idaho, Pound was educated at the University of Pennsylvania and spent most of his life in Europe. He was the leading exponent of poetic "Imagism" (see Amy Lowell). During World War II he broadcast pro-Axis propaganda from Rome. After the war he was prosecuted for this, but was exonerated on the grounds of insanity. Pound is as much known for his influence on other poets as for his own poetry (T. S. Eliot acknowledged him as "the better maker" in the dedication to *The Waste Land*). He published many poetry collections, such as *Exultations* (1909), *Canzoni* (1911), and *Cathay* (1915), which contained his versions of Chinese poems (see p. 790). His major work was the *Cantos*, which he worked on throughout his life after publishing the first portion in 1925.

Al Purdy (Alfred Wellington Purdy, b. 1918) • Purdy was born in Ontario and spent considerable time as a factory worker, not coming to poetry until he was in his forties with his first collection, *Poems for all the Annettes* (1962; 1968). Since then he has published regularly, including *The Cariboo Horses* (1965), *The Stone Bird* (1981), *Piling Blood* (1984), and *Collected Poems* (1986).

Sir Walter Raleigh (ca. 1552–1618) • Raleigh was a courtier, explorer, and adventurer who alternately pleased and displeased Queen Elizabeth I. During the reign of James I he was imprisoned for thirteen years in the Tower of London. He was released to go on an expedition to South America, which proved disastrous. In 1618 he was executed for treason. Like many aristocrats he wrote extensively but circulated his poetry mostly in manuscript, with rare exceptions such as "The Nymph's Reply to the Shepherd." His collected poems were edited and published in 1951.

Dudley Randall (b. 1914) • A native of Washington, D. C., Randall spent five years working in the foundry at the Ford River Rouge plant in Michigan. He became a librarian after that, and went on to the position of head librarian. In 1965 he founded the Broadside Press, an important and valuable publisher for African-American writers. One of the first poems from the press was "Ballad of Birmingham," which had earlier (1963) been set to music and made popular by the folk singer Jerry Moore. Randall's major poetry collections are *More to Remember: Poems of Four Decades* (1971) and *A Litany of Friends: New and Selected Poems* (1981).

John Crowe Ransom (1888–1974) • Along with Robert Penn Warren, Alan Tate, and Cleanth Brooks, Ransom was one of the important exponents of the New Criticism (see Chapter 27, p. 1373). He founded the *Kenyon Review* and edited it for twenty years. His major poetry collections are *Chills and Fever* (1924), *Two Gentlemen in Bonds* (1927), and *Selected Poems* (1945, revised in 1963 and 1969).

Henry Reed (1914–1986) • Reed was English and received a degree from the University of Birmingham. He became best known in England for his translations and radio dramas. His major book of poems was *A Map of Verona* (1946), which contains "Naming of Parts." His radio plays were published in *The Streets of Pompeii* (1971, five plays in verse), and *Hilda Tablet and Others* (1971, four comedies in prose).

Adrienne Rich (b. 1929) • Rich is a native of Baltimore. She was educated at Radcliffe, studying writing with Robert Lowell. In 1986 she became a professor at Stanford. Her first collection of poetry, *A Change of World* (1951) received the Yale Series of Younger Poets award. Since then she has published collections regularly, and is acknowledged today as one of America's foremost poets. An advocate of women's rights and also of Lesbian rights, she is a major confessional poet, as may be inferred from the titles of two of her many collections: *Snapshots of a Daughter-in-Law* (1963) and *An Atlas of the Difficult World* (1991). She was offered the National Book Award for Poetry in 1974, but to show her unity with women she refused to accept for herself, accepting jointly with Audre Lorde "in the name of all women."

Edwin Arlington Robinson (1869–1935) • Robinson began his career inauspiciously with various jobs in New York City. The publication of *The Children of the Night* (1897) and *Captain Craig* (1902) impressed President Theodore Roosevelt, who arranged a position for him as clerk in the New York Customs House. After the publication of *The Town Down the River* in 1910, he was able to support himself with his poetry. "Tilbury Town," where many of his poetic characters reside, is modeled on Gardiner, Maine, the town where he grew up. He is particularly notable because he received the first Pulitzer Prize for poetry ever to be awarded (1922). He received the prize twice more, in 1924 and 1928.

Theodore Roethke (1908–1963) • Roethke was born in Saginaw, Michigan, where his father operated a greenhouse. His first collection of poems was *The Lost Son* (1948), which included "My Papa's Waltz." He achieved wide recognition before his death in 1963. In addition to distinguishing himself, he also taught other poets, numbering James Wright among his students at the University of Washington.

Christina Rossetti (1830–1894) • English-born Christina Rossetti's religious lyrics and ballads have made her a favorite with composers such as Gustav Holst and John Rutter. Painters of the Pre-Raphaelite Brotherhood, of whom her brother Dante Gabriel Rossetti was a leading figure, frequently called upon her to pose for their paintings. Ill health forced her to forsake a career as a governess, and after 1874 she became a virtual invalid. Some of her poetry collections are *Goblin Market and Other Poems* (1862), *The Prince's Progress and Other Poems* (1866), and *A Pageant and Other Poems* (1872). A modern edition of her *Complete Poems* was published in 1979.

Muriel Rukeyser (1913–1980) ▪ A *poète engagée*, Rukeyser was arrested in Alabama in the 1930s for demonstrating in favor of the Scottsboro Nine. Later, she wrote on behalf of an imprisoned Korean poet in *The Gates* (1976). She published many collections, including *Theory of Flight* (1935), *Beast in View* (1944), *Body of Waking* (1958), and *Collected Poems* (1979).

Sonia Sanchez (b. 1934) ▪ Sanchez was born in Alabama. She received a B.A. from Hunter College in 1955, and for a time after that she worked for the Congress of Racial Equality. Her major teaching position was at Temple University. Early volumes of poetry were *Homecoming* (1969) and *We a BaddDDD People* (1970). More recently she published *homegirls & handgrenades* (1984) and *Under a Soprano Sky* (1987).

Carl Sandburg (1878–1967) ▪ It is fair to say that Sandburg "knocked around" a good deal in his youth before working his way through Knox (then Lombard) College in Galesburg, Illinois, his home town. He published a volume of poetry in 1904, but did not gain recognition until 1914, when *Poetry* printed some of his poems. Later he published *Chicago Poems* (1916), *Smoke and Steel* (1920), *Selected Poems* (1926), and *Good Morning, America* (1928). He received the Pulitzer Prize in History (1939) for his biography of Abraham Lincoln, and the Pulitzer Prize in Poetry (1951) for his *Complete Poems* of 1950.

May Sarton (Eleanor May Sarton, 1912–1995) ▪ Sarton was born in Belgium and at the age of four came to the United States with her parents. Eventually she taught at both Harvard University and Wellesley College. Her first poetry volume appeared in 1937, when she was twenty-five (*Encounter in April*), and she published regularly after that, her final volume (*Coming into Eighty*), appearing in 1994, the year before her death. Her *Collected Poems, 1930–1970*, was published in 1974. An anthology of her work in all literary genres was edited by Bradford Daziel and published in 1991 as *Sarton Selected.*

Siegfried Sassoon (1886–1967) ▪ Sassoon served as an officer in World War I, was wounded twice, and was awarded two medals for bravery (one of which he threw away). He is most widely recognized for his anti-war collections *The Old Huntsman* (1917) and *Counter-Attack and Other Poems* (1918), which contains "Dreamers." Neither of these books was well received. Later, Sassoon turned to spiritual subjects, as shown in *Vigils* (1935) and *Sequences* (1956). His *Collected Poems* was published in 1961.

Virginia Scott (b. 1937) ▪ Canadian born, Scott received her degrees at Boston University and Wisconsin. She created, edited, and managed the Sunbury Press, a small press, and received a national award for this work in 1980. She has published poetry widely in journals. Her collected poems appear in *The Witness Box* (1985) and *Toward Appomatox* (1992). She has taught at Lehman College for many years, and is currently preparing a new collection of poems and also doing research into the work of Canadian poet Alden Nolan.

Alan Seeger (1886–1916) ▪ Seeger was born in New York and was educated at Harvard. When World War I began he joined the French Foreign Legion. He was killed in the Battle of the Somme in 1916. His war poems were published in *Collected Poems* (1916).

Anne Sexton (1928–1974) ▪ Massachusetts born, Sexton is one of the more personal confessional poets. *To Bedlam and Part Way Back* (1960), for example, developed out of a nervous breakdown, and her posthumous *The Awful Rowing Toward God* (1975) describes some of the feelings leading to her suicide in 1974. Her collection *Live or Die* (1966) was awarded the Pulitzer Prize in Poetry for 1967.

William Shakespeare (1564–1616) • For a brief biography, see pp. 953–54.

Karl Shapiro (b. 1913) • Baltimore born, Shapiro has lived in Nebraska and California. He was recognized early in his distinguished career as a poet and critic—his *V-Letter and Other Poems* (1944) receiving the 1945 Pulitzer Prize. Among his many poetry collections are *Essay on Rime* (1945), *Poems of a Jew* (1958), *Selected Poems* (1968), and *Selected Poems: 1940–1977* (1978). He edited *Poetry* magazine for five years, and *Prairie Schooner* for ten.

Percy Bysshe Shelley (1792–1822) • Shelley is one of the major English Romantic poets. He was a quintessential revolutionary, and suffered expulsion from Oxford as a result of an early pamphlet entitled *The Necessity of Atheism*. He married before he was twenty but within three years left his wife and went to Italy with Mary Godwin (1797–1851), the author of *Frankenstein*. The two were married in 1816. Throughout these years Shelley was writing his best-known short poems. He was working on his long philosophic poem *The Triumph of Life* in 1922 when he was drowned during a storm at sea. There are many excellent modern editions of his works, including the Houghton-Mifflin Cambridge edition and the Oxford edition.

Leslie Marmon Silko (b. 1948) • A Native American, Leslie Marmon Silko was brought up in Laguna Pueblo, New Mexico. She has taught at the University of Arizona and also at the University of New Mexico, and she has been honored with a MacArthur Foundation Fellowship. The topic in most of her works is the tradition of the Navajo People, which she treats with great love and understanding, as in "Where Mountain Lion Lay Down with Deer" (p. 799), which connects the individual with the past, the land, and Nature.

Dave Smith (b. 1942) • Smith, a native of Virginia, earned his B.A. from the University of Virginia in 1965, and for a time taught high school, including the coaching of football. He received his Ph.D. at Ohio University in 1976. He now teaches at the University of Utah in Salt Lake City. Some of his collections are *Bull Island* (1970), *Goshawk, Antelope* (1979), and *The Roundhouse Voice: Poems 1970–1985* (1985). "Bluejays" is from *Homage to Edgar Allan Poe* (1981).

Stevie Smith (Florence Margaret Smith, 1902–1971) • Smith was a native of Hull, in Yorkshire. During her life she worked in publishing, and in addition she became well known as a radio personality because of her many poetry readings for the BBC. Some of her poetry collections were *A Good Time Was Had by All* (1937) and *Not Waving but Drowning* (1957). Posthumous collections of her work are *Scorpion and Other Poems* (1972) and *Collected Poems* (1975).

W. D. Snodgrass (b. 1926) • Snodgrass is a native of Pennsylvania. He received his B.A. from the University of Iowa, and also did graduate study there. He taught at Wayne State University in Detroit (1959–1967), and was there when he published *Heart's Needle*, for which he received the 1960 Pulitzer Prize in Poetry. Among his other collections are *Gallows Songs of Christian Morgenstern* (1967), *After Experience* (1968), *If Birds Build with Your Hair* (1979), *Each in His Season* (1993), and *The Fuehrer Bunker: The Complete Cycle* (1995).

Cathy Song (b. 1955) • A native of Honolulu, Cathy Song received her B.A. at Wellesley College and her M.A. from Boston University. She lives and teaches in Hawaii. Her first volume of verse was *Picture Bride* (1983), for which she received both the Yale Series of Younger Poets Award and a National Book Critics Circle Award. Her collection *School Figures* was published in 1994.

Gary Soto (b. 1952) • Soto is a native of Fresno, California, and was educated in California. Since 1980 he has taught at Berkeley. Because of his native city he has sometimes been grouped with a "Fresno" school of poets. His first poetry collection was *The Elements of San Joaquin* (1977). Later collections are *The Tale of Sunlight* (1978), *Where Sparrows Work Hard* (1981), *Black Hair* (1985), and *New and Selected Poems* (1995). Soto is a prolific writer with many different interests. His book *Baseball in April* (1990), for example, was named a "Best Book for Young Adults" in 1990.

Stephen Spender (1909–1995) • Spender, along with W. H. Auden, Christopher Isherwood, and Louis MacNeice, was one of the poets known as the "Oxford Poets" because they all attended Oxford in the late twenties and early thirties. After leaving Oxford, Spender lived for a time in Germany. He believed firmly in the need for poets to be politically engaged, and he joined the Communist Party for a few weeks in the 1930s although he later renounced this affiliation (in *The God that Failed* [1950]). Along with editing journals and writing many prose works, he, with John Lehmann, wrote a five-act poetic play *Trial of a Judge*, based on circumstances in Germany at the time of Hitler. Spender's first poems were collected in a small book entitled *Twenty Poems* in 1930. Later collections were *Poems of Dedication* (1947), *Edge of Being: Poems* (1949), and *Collected Poems 1928–1953* (1955). He was knighted in 1962.

William E. Stafford (1914–1993) • Stafford, who published more than two dozen volumes of verse, was born in Kansas. He received his Ph.D. from Iowa State in 1955. In 1975 he was named Poet Laureate of Oregon, and at his death in 1993 he was a Professor Emeritus at Lewis and Clark College. For *Traveling through the Dark* (1962), his second volume of poetry, he won the National Book Award for Poetry in 1963. Among his many poetry collections are *Wyoming* (1985), and *An Oregon Message* (1987). With Marvin Bell, he published *Segues* in 1983. *Down in My Heart* (1994) in his autobiography of the years he spent in an internment camp for conscientious objectors in World War II.

Maura Stanton (b. 1946) • Stanton was born in Illinois. She took her B.A. at the University of Minnesota (1969) and her M.F.A. at the University of Iowa (1971). Since 1982 she has taught at the University of Indiana. Her major collections of poems are *Snow on Snow* (1975), which includes "The Conjurer," *Cries of Swimmers* (1984), and *The Country I Come From* (1988). Her major novel is *Molly Companion* (1977).

Gerald Stern (b. 1925) • Stern was born in Pittsburgh and became a faculty member of the University of Iowa's Writer's Workshop. He was honored by three grants from the NEA and by a Guggenheim Fellowship. His *Lucky Life* (1977), which contains "Burying an Animal," received the Lamont Prize in Poetry in 1977. Most recently he published *Leaving Another Kingdom: Selected Poems* (1990), *Bread Without Sugar* (1992), and *Odd Mercy* (1995).

Wallace Stevens (1879–1955) • Stevens spent his professional life in business rather than academia. He wrote most of his poems after the age of fifty, but he included "The Emperor of Ice-Cream" and "Disillusionment of Ten O'Clock," both earlier poems, in the first edition of *Harmonium* in 1923. Some of his poetic collections are a second version of *Harmonium* (1931), and also *The Auroras of Autumn* (1950) and *Collected Poems* (1954).

Mark Strand (b. 1934) • Strand was born in Canada, on Prince Edward Island. He studied at Antioch, Yale, and the University of Iowa. He is currently a Professor at the University of Utah. He has been honored with a MacArthur Foundation Fellowship, and in 1990 he was named American Poet Laureate. One of his recent collections of poems is *The Continuous Life* (1990). "The Remains," which was first published in *The New Yorker* in 1969, was also published in *Selected Poems* (1980).

May Swenson, (1919–1989) • Swenson was born in Utah and was of Swedish ancestry. She experimented constantly in her poetry, not only in content but also in form, as is shown in her work with shaped verse. Her *Iconographs* (1970) was a collection of formed poetry. The formed poem "Women" was included in her collection *New and Selected Things Taking Place* (1978). She also did translations from Swedish, as represented by *Windows and Stones* (1972).

James Tate (b. 1943) ▪ Tate was born in Kansas City, earning degrees from the Universities of Kansas and Iowa. He now is a Professor of English at the University of Massachusetts. Since his first collection, *The Lost Pilot*, published when he was only 23, he has published a dozen volumes of verse. "The Blue Booby" is selected from *The Oblivion Ha-Ha* (1970), his second major collection. More recent works include *Viper Jazz* (1976), *Riven Doggeries* (1979), *Reckoner* (1986), *Distances from Loved Ones* (1990) and *Selected Poems* (1991), for which he received the Pulitzer Prize for Poetry in 1992. In 1994 he received the National Book Award for his new collection *Worshipful Company of Fletchers*, and in 1995 he was awarded the Tanning Prize—the largest annual literary prize in the United States—for achievement as a poet.

Alfred, Lord Tennyson (1809–1892) ▪ One of the most popular of the Victorian poets, Tennyson became Poet Laureate in 1850. His earliest verse was published in collaboration with his brother, *Poems by Two Brothers* (1727). Some of his other collections were *Poems* (1842), *Locksley Hall* (1842), *The Princess* (1847), *Maud, and Other Poems* (1855) and *Idylls of the King* (1857–1891). He wrote *In Memoriam*, in which the well known phrase "nature red in tooth and claw" appears, from 1833 to 1850. A collected and annotated edition of his poetry was published in 1969, but there are also many other useful editions.

Dylan Thomas (1914–1953) ▪ A native of Wales, Thomas published his first collection, *Eighteen Poems*, in 1934. After World War II he became immensely popular in America as a speaker and lecturer because of the incantatory power with which he read his own poems. Fortunately, many of his readings survive on records available in college libraries. Thomas's *Collected Poems 1934–1952* was published in 1952 and was a commercial success. *The Poems of Dylan Thomas*, a definitive edition, was published in 1971. In the 1980s, the musician John Cale set "Do Not Go Gentle" to music as part of his *Falklands Suite* (found on Cale's *Words for the Dying*, Opal/Warner Bros. 9-26024-2).

Jean Toomer (1894–1967) ▪ Toomer was born in Washington, D.C., studied at five colleges, and eventually settled in the African-American community in Sparta, Georgia. An important voice in the Harlem Renaissance, Toomer published his only book, *Cane*, a grouping of stories, poems, and a play, in 1923. A collection of his works may be found in *The Wayward and the Seeking* (1980).

Peter Ulisse (b. 1944) ▪ Ulisse currently lives in Connecticut, where he chairs the Humanities Department of Housatonic Community Technical College. He has written many poetry reviews for *Small Pond of Literature* and has served as editor of the *Connecticut River Review*. His first major poetry collection was *Vietnam Voices* (1990). In 1995 he published *Memory Is an Illusive State*, which includes "Odyssey: 20 Years Later."

Judith Viorst (b. 1931) ▪ Viorst is a native of New Jersey and received her degrees from Rutgers and the Washington Psychoanalytic Institute. She is known for her wry humor. Her first major volume was *It's Hard to Be Hip over Thirty and Other Tragedies of Married Life* in 1968. Her *Necessary Losses* (1986) is a collection of poems and anecdotes. She also writes children's fiction.

Shelly Wagner (b. ca. 1948) ▪ Wagner received her B.A. from Old Dominion University, after which she worked as an interior designer and social worker. Her younger son Andrew drowned in 1984, and it was five years later that she began her cycle of elegiac poems, *The Andrew Poems*, including "Boxes," which was published in 1994. Before this she had published poetry in publications like *American Poetry Review* and *Poetry East*. With her husband, she lives in Norfolk, Virginia.

David Wagoner (b. 1926) • Wagoner was born in Ohio and studied at Pennsylvania State University and the University of Indiana. In 1954 he began teaching at the University of Washington, where he was a colleague, and later an editor, of Theodore Roethke. He has been extremely productive both as poet and novelist. A few of his many poetry collections are *Dry Sun, Dry Wind* (1953), *Staying Alive* (1966), *Collected Poems* (1976), *Landfall* (1981), *Through the Forest: New and Selected Poems* (1987), and *Walt Whitman Bathing* (1996).

Alice Walker (b. 1944) • For a brief biography, see p. 72.

Edmund Waller (1606–1687) • Waller, whom Dryden constantly praised for the quality and originality of his poetic couplets, was a Royalist during the English Civil Wars of 1642–1649, and for his efforts was forced into exile. He returned in 1651 after swearing loyalty to Oliver Cromwell. After the Restoration, he supported King Charles II. His major collections of poetry were *Poems* (1645) and *Divine Poems* (1685).

Robert Penn Warren (1905–1989) • Three-time winner of the Pulitzer Prize (1947, 1957, 1978), and the first American Poet Laureate (1985), Warren was one of the leaders of the New Criticism (see Chapter 27), and was also a leading exponent of Southern literature and culture. With Cleanth Brooks, his *Understanding Poetry, Understanding Drama,* and *Understanding Fiction* series of textbooks taught the techniques of New Criticism to a generation of graduate and undergraduate students. His novel *All the King's Men* (1946) was made into a prize winning motion picture in 1950. During his teaching career he taught at the University of Minnesota and then at Yale. Some of his poetry collections are *Thirty-Six Poems* (1935), *Promises* (1957), and *New and Selected Poems* (1985).

Charles H. Webb (b. 1952) • Webb is a native of Pennsylvania but grew up in Texas. He received degrees at Rice University, the University of Washington, and the University of Southern California. He now teaches at California State University at Long Beach. Recent poetry collections are *Everyday Outrages* (1989) and *A Webb for All Seasons* (1992). He has also published a novel, *The Wilderness Effect* (1982). Interestingly, before he took up teaching as a profession he had spent a decade as a rock guitarist and singer.

Phyllis Webb (b. 1927) • Webb is a native of British Columbia. She was educated at the University of British Columbia and also at McGill University. During her career she worked with the Canadian Broadcasting Company both as a program planner and a producer; she has also taught in various Canadian colleges and universities as a guest lecturer and professor. A major concern in her poetry has been the problem of maintaining personal integrity amid a world of "hate and broken things," to quote from one of her poems in *Trio* (1954). One of her interests has been to experiment with a form of Persian poetry, the *ghazal*, which consists of five couplets. Among her poetry collections are *Wilson's Bowl* (1980), *The Vision Tree* (1982), and *Water and Light: Ghazals and Anti Ghazals* (1984).

Bruce Weigl (b. 1949) • Weigl, who teaches at Penn State, was born in Ohio. He took his B.A. at Oberlin (1974), and his Ph.D. at the University of Utah (1979). His poetry collections include *Like a Sack Full of Old Quarrels* (1976), *Executioner* (1977), *A Romance* (1979), *The Monkey Wars* (1984), *Song of Napalm* (1988), *What Saves Us* (1992), and *Sweet Lorain* (1996).

Phillis Wheatley (ca. 1753–1784) • Wheatley was born in Africa. She was captured by slave traders and sold to John Wheatley, a Boston merchant, who treated her virtually as a daughter and saw to it that she was educated. When she published her *Poems on Various Subjects, Religious and Moral* (1773), however, the temper of the times made it necessary to include prefaces by Massachusetts men verifying that she was qualified to write poetry, and that she had indeed written the poems in the collection. Although she wrote a second volume of poetry, she could not find a publisher for it during her lifetime. Her collected works were published in 1988.

Walt Whitman (1819–1892) • Whitman, who became a legend during his lifetime, is one of America's major poets. He was born in New York, and lived with his family in both Long Island and Brooklyn. At various times he worked as a printer, teacher, reporter, and government bureaucrat. In addition, he served as a nurse during the Civil War. His major work was *Leaves of Grass*, which he first published as a collection of twelve poems in 1855, and to which he added as time went on. Many editions were published in his lifetime, the last one in 1892. *Drum Taps*, poems based on his Civil War experiences, was published in 1865; a second edition contained "When Lilacs Last in the Dooryard Bloom'd," his poem on the death of Lincoln.

Cornelius Whur (1782–1853) • Whur was a Methodist minister in Suffolk, England. In 1837 he published a poetry collection, *Village Musings on Moral and Religious Subjects*, which included "The First-Rate Wife." In his obituary notice he was recognized not only as a "distinguished" poet but also as a gardener.

Richard Wilbur (b. 1921) • Wilbur was born in New York. He has published a number of poetry collections, including *New and Collected Poems* (1988), for which he was awarded the Pulitzer Prize in Poetry. In 1988 he was distinguished as the second American Poet Laureate (the first being Robert Penn Warren). One of his early collections was *Advice to a Prophet and Other Poems* (1961), and "The Sirens" appeared in *Ceremony and Other Poems* (1950).

C. K. Williams (Charles Kenneth Williams, b. 1936) • Williams is a native of New Jersey who graduated from Bucknell and the University of Pennsylvania. He taught at a number of schools and colleges, and has taken up permanent residence in France. He has become particularly known for discursively long lines in the manner of Walt Whitman. Among his many volumes of poems are *Tar* (1983) and *Flesh and Blood* (1987), for which he was awarded the 1987 National Book Critics Circle Award, *Poems, 1963–1983* (1988), and *A Dream of the Mind* (1992). "Dimensions" is taken from *Lies*, his collection of 1969.

William Carlos Williams (1883–1963) • Williams spent his career as a practicing pediatrician, but he early became friendly with Ezra Pound and Hilda Doolittle (H. D.). He developed a second career as a writer, producing poems, plays, stories, novels, and essays. He published poems throughout his life, beginning with *Poems* (1913) and *Tempers* (1913), and ending with *Pictures from Brueghel* (1963), for which he was posthumously awarded the Pulitzer Prize.

David Wojahn (b. 1953) • Wojahn is a native of Minnesota who received degrees from the Universities of Minnesota and Arizona. He teaches at the University of Arkansas, where he is also poetry editor of the journal *Crazy Horse*. His first volume of verse was *Icehouse Lights* (1981), which was distinguished by the Yale Series of Younger Poets Award. More recently he published *Mystery Train* (1990), which contains "It's Only Rock and Roll, But I Like It," and *Late Empire* (1994).

William Wordsworth (1770–1850) • Along with Coleridge, Wordsworth was the first of the English "Romantic" poets. In 1798 the two men published *Lyrical Ballads*, a collection of poems which emphasize the importance of imagination in revealing the significance of events in the lives of people. One of Wordsworth's major ideas is that poetry grows from "emotions recollected in tranquillity," and also that poetic diction should consist of everyday language that the poet chooses as a result of looking steadily at the poetic subject. Throughout much of his adult life Wordsworth wrote and revised his long poem, *The Prelude*, which was intended to show how the mysterious "wisdom and spirit of the universe" reached him through his imagination and brought out his power as a poet. He became English Poet Laureate in 1843.

James Wright (1927–1980) • Wright was born in Martins Ferry, Ohio, and received his Ph.D. at the University of Washington, where he was a student of Theodore Roethke. In 1966 he began teaching at Hunter College, and remained there until his death in 1980. His first poetry collection, *The Green Wall*, appeared in 1957, and after that he published collections regularly, receiving the 1972 Pulitzer Prize in Poetry for his *Collected Poems* (1971). *This Journey* was published posthumously in 1982, and *Above the River: The Complete Poems* appeared in 1990.

Sir Thomas Wyatt (ca. 1503–1542) • Wyatt was a courtier in the service of King Henry VIII. He is credited with introducing the sonnet form into English as a result of his translations of the sonnets of the Italian sonneteer Petrarch. He circulated his poems in manuscript, although a number of them were anthologized after his death in *The Court of Venus* (1542) and *Seven Penitential Psalms* (1549). Modern editions of his poems were published in 1969, 1975, and 1978.

William Butler Yeats (1865–1939) • The foremost Irish poet of the twentieth century, Yeats was instrumental in the founding of the Abbey Theatre in Dublin in 1899. An unorthodox thinker, he developed his poems out of his vast reading and his special interest in spiritualism. He published many volumes of poems, including *The Green Helmet* (1910), *The Wild Swans at Coole* (1917), *The Winding Stair* (1929), and *The Collected Poems* (1932). He was awarded the Nobel Prize for Literature in 1923.

Paul Zimmer (b. 1934) • Zimmer, whose sister is the science-fiction writer Marion Zimmer Bradley, was born in Canton, Ohio, and received his B.A. from Kent State. He has managed bookstores and university presses, at the present time serving at the University of Iowa Press. Among his many volumes of poems are *A Seed on the Wind* (1960), *The Ribs of Death* (1967), *Family Reunion* (1983), and *Big Blue Train* (1993). His "Zimmer" poems are collected in *The Zimmer Poems* (1976), *Earthbound Zimmer* (1983), *The American Zimmer* (1984), and *The Great Bird of Love* (1989).

Glossary
of Literary Terms

This glossary presents brief definitions of terms boldfaced in the text. Page references indicate where readers may find additional detail and illustration, together with discussions about how the concepts can be utilized in studying literature and, ultimately, in writing about literature.

Abstract diction Language describing qualities that are rarefied and theoretical (e.g., "good," "interesting," "neat," and so on); distinguished from *concrete diction.* 271, 469

Absurd, Comedy of See *Comedy of the Absurd.*

Accentual rhythm See *Sprung rhythm.*

Actions or **incidents** The events or occurrences in a work. 54, 60, 821, 883

Allegory A complete *narrative* that may also be applied to a parallel set of external situations that may be political, moral, religious, or philosophical. 59, 60, 318–62, 884

Alliteration The repetition of identical consonant sounds (most often the sounds beginning words) in close proximity (e.g., "pensive poets," "grown grey"). 573, 580

Allusion Unacknowledged references and quotations. Authors assume that readers will recognize the original sources, and relate their meaning to the new context. 322–23, 661

Amphibrach A three-syllable poetic *foot* consisting of a light, heavy, and light stress. 577

Amphimacer or **Cretic** A three-syllable *foot* consisting of a heavy, light, and heavy stress. 577

Anagnorisis or **recognition** Aristotle's term describing the point in a play, usually the *climax,* when a character experiences understanding. 898

Analytical sentence outline A scheme or plan for an essay, arranged according to topics (A, B, C, etc.) and with the topics expressed in sentences. 24–25

Analyzed rhyme See *Inexact rhyme.*

Anapest A three-syllable *foot* consisting of two light stresses climaxed by a heavy stress. 576

Anaphora ("to carry again or **repeat")** The repetition of the same word or phrase throughout a work or a section of a work. The effect is to lend weight and emphasis. 520, 710

Ancillary characters Characters who set off or highlight the protagonist and who provide insight into the action. The *foil, choric figure,* and *raisonneur* are all ancillary characters. 821

Antagonist The person, idea, force, or general set of circumstances opposing the *protagonist,* an essential element of *plot.* 54, 136, 820

Anticipation See *Procatalepsis.*

Antimetabole See *Chiasmus.*

Antithesis A rhetorical device of opposition, in which one idea or word is established, and then the opposite idea or word is expressed, as in "I *burn* and *freeze*" and "I *love* and *hate.*" 473, 620

Apostrophe The addressing of a discourse to a real or imagined person who is not present; also, a speech to an abstraction. 520

Apron or **thrust stage** A stage that projects into the auditorium area, thus increasing the space for action; a characteristic feature of Elizabethan theaters and many recent ones. 826

Archetypal / Symbolic / Mythic critical approach An interpretive approach explaining literature in terms of archetypal patterns (e.g., God's creation of human beings, the sacrifice of a hero, or the search for paradise). 1379

Archetype A character, action, or situation that is a prototype or pattern of human life generally; a situation that occurs over and over again in literature, such as a quest, an initiation, or an attempt to overcome evil. Many *myths* are archetypes. 691

Arena stage or **theater in the round** A theater arrangement, often outdoors, in which the audience totally surrounds the stage, with all actors entering and exiting along the same aisles used by the audience. 826

Argument The development of an idea, including the introduction of a hypothesis or major idea, supporting details, and logical conclusions. 27

Aside A short speech delivered by a character to another character or to the audience, the convention being that the other characters on stage cannot hear it; the speaker usually reveals his or her thoughts or plans. 952

Assonance The repetition of identical vowel sounds in different words in close proximity, as in the d*ee*p gr*ee*n s*ea*. 573, 579

Atmosphere or **mood** The emotional aura invoked by a work. 58, 243, 824, 884

Audience or **intended reader** (1) The people attending a theatrical production. (2) The intended group of readers for whom a writer writes. 828

Auditory images References to sounds. 497

Authorial voice The *voice* or *speaker* used by authors when seemingly speaking for themselves. The use of the term makes it possible to discuss a narration or presentation without identifying the ideas absolutely with those of the author. See also *Speaker, Point of view,* and *Third-person point of view.* 57, 199

Bacchius or **Bacchic** A three-syllable *foot* consisting of a light stress followed by two heavy stresses, as in "a new song." 577

Ballad, ballad measure   A narrative poem composed of *quatrains* in which lines of iambic tetrameter alternate with iambic trimeter, rhyming X-A-X-A. 452, 585, 622

Ballad opera   An eighteenth-century comic drama, originated by John Gay's *The Beggar's Opera* in 1728, featuring lyrics set to existing tunes. 1131

Beast fable   A fable featuring animals with human characteristics. 321

Beat or **Accent**   The heavy stresses or accents in lines of poetry. The number of beats in a line usually dictates the meter of the line (five beats in a pentameter line, etc.). 573

Blank verse   Unrhymed iambic pentameter. 619–20

Blocking   In the performance of a play, the grouping and movement of characters on stage. 826

Blocking agent   A person, circumstance, or attitude that obstructs the union of lovers. 1067

Box set   In the modern theater, a realistic setting of a single room from which the "fourth wall" is missing, so that the stage resembles a three-dimensional picture. 826

Brainstorming   The exploration, discovery, and development of details to be used in a composition. 15–19

Breve   A mark in the shape of a bowl-like half circle (˘) to indicate a light stress or unaccented syllable. 574

Business or **stage business**   The gestures, expressions, and general activity (beyond blocking) of actors on stage. Usually, business is designed to create laughter. It is often spontaneous. 826

Buskins   Elegantly laced boots (*kothorni* or *cothurni*) worn by the actors in ancient Greek tragedy. Eventually the buskins became elevator shoes to stress the royal status of actors by making them tall. 903

Cacophony   Meaning "bad sound," *cacophony* refers to words combining sharp or harsh sounds. 581

Cadence group   A coherent word group spoken as a single rhythmical unit, such as a noun phrase ("our sacred honor") or prepositional phrase ("of parting day"). 578

Caesura, caesurae   The pause(s) separating phrases within lines of poetry, an important aspect of poetic *rhythm*. 576–79, 715

Catastrophe   The "turning downward" of the dramatic plot, the fourth stage in the structure after the climax. The dénouement of a play, in which things are explained and put into place. 823

Catharsis (purgation)   Aristotle's concept that tragedy, by arousing pity and fear (*eleos* and *phobos*), regularizes and shapes the emotions, and that therefore tragedy is essential in civilized society. 896

Central idea   (1) The thesis or main idea of an essay. (2) The theme of a literary work. 19–21, 28–31

Character   An extended verbal representation of a human being, the inner self that determines thought, speech, and behavior. 53, 60, 134–93, 820–21, 883

Chiasmus or **antimetabole**   A rhetorical pattern in which words and ideas are repeated in the sequence A-B-B-A, as in "I *sing* of *love* and *love* to *sing*." 474

Choragos or **choregus**   The sponsor or financial backer of a classical Greek dramatic production. Often the *choragos* was honored by serving as the leader (*koryphaios*) of the chorus. 901

Choric figure   A character who remains detached from the action and who provides commentary. See also *Raisonneur.* 821

Chorus In ancient Athenian drama, the chorus was composed of fifteen young men who chanted in unison and performed dance movements to a flute accompaniment. 891–93, 904

Chronology ("logic of time") The sequence of events in a work, with emphasis upon the complex intertwining of cause and effect. 54, 821

Cliché rhymes Trite and widely used rhymes, such as *moon* and *June* or *trees* and *breeze.* 582

Climax (Greek for *ladder*) The high point of *conflict* and tension preceding the resolution of a drama or story; the point of decision, of inevitability and no return. The climax is sometimes merged with the *crisis* in the consideration of dramatic and narrative structure. 95, 823

Closed-form poetry Poetry written in specific and traditional patterns produced through rhyme, meter, line-length, and line groupings. 619–25

Comedy A literary genre which like tragedy originated in the Dionysiac festivals of ancient Athens. Derived from the Greek "komos" songs or "songs of merry-makers," the first comedies were wildly boisterous. Subsequently comedies became more subdued and realistic. In typical comedies today, confusions and doubts are resolved satisfactorily if not happily, and usually comedies are characterized by smiles and laughter. 1065–1163

Comedy of the Absurd A modern form of comedy dramatizing the apparent pointlessness, ambiguity, uncertainty, and absurdity of existence. 1072

Comedy of manners A form of comedy, usually regular (five acts or three acts), in which attitudes and customs are examined and satirized in the light of high intellectual and moral standards. The dialogue is witty and sophisticated, and characters are often measured according to

their linguistic and intellectual powers. 1071

Comic opera An outgrowth of eighteenth-century ballad operas (*q.v.*), but different from them in having music specially composed for the lyrics. 1131

Commedia dell'arte Broadly humorous farce developed in sixteenth-century Italy, featuring stock characters, stock situations, and much improvised dialogue. 1071

Commentary, analysis, or **interpretation** Passages of explanation and reflection about the meaning of actions, thoughts, dialogue, historical movements, and so on. 59–60

Commentator See *Raisonneur.*

Common ground of assent Those interests, concerns, and assumptions that the writer assumes in common with readers so that an effective and persuasive tone may be maintained. 547

Common measure A closed poetic quatrain, rhyming A-B-A-B, in which lines of iambic tetrameter alternate with iambic trimeter. See also *Ballad measure.* 623

Comparison-contrast A technique of analyzing two or more works in order to determine similarities and differences in topic, treatment, and quality. 1394–1407

Complete The second aspect of Aristotle's definition of tragedy, emphasizing the logic and wholeness of the play. 898

Complication A stage of narrative and dramatic structure in which the major *conflicts* are brought out; the *rising action* of a *drama.* 94, 823

Concrete diction Words that describe exact and particular conditions or qualities, such as *cold, sweet,* and *creamy* in reference to an ice-cream sundae. These words are *concrete,* while the application of *good* or *neat* to the sundae are *abstract*. See also *Abstract diction*. 56, 271, 469

Concrete poetry Poetry depicting visual shapes in addition to ideas and emotions. 628

Conflict The opposition between two characters, between large groups of people, or between *protagonists* and larger forces such as natural objects, ideas, modes of behavior, public opinion, and the like. Conflict may also be internal and psychological, involving choices facing a *protagonist*. It is the essence of *plot*. 54, 92, 821, 883

Connotation The meanings that words suggest beyond their bare dictionary definitions. 272, 474

Consonant segments Consonant sounds; sounds produced as a result of the touching or close proximity of the tongue or the lips in relation to the teeth or palate (e.g., *m, n, p, f, sh, ch*); contrasted with *vowel segments*. 580

Contextual symbol A symbol which is derived not from common historical, cultural, or religious materials, but which is rather developed within the context of an individual work. See also *Cultural symbol*. 319–20, 658

Convention An accepted feature of a genre, such as the point of view in a story, the form of a poem (e.g., sonnet, ode), the competence or brilliance of the detective in detective fiction, the impenetrability of disguise and concealment in a Shakespearean play, or the chorus in Greek drama. 17

Corpus Christi play A type of medieval drama that enacts events from the Bible, such as the killing of Abel by Cain, the problems of Noah, the anger of Herod, and so on. The word is derived from the religious festival of *Corpus Christi* ("Christ's body"), held in the spring of each year. Also called *mystery plays*. 947–49, 830

Cosmic irony (irony of fate) *Situational irony* that is connected to a pessimistic or fatalistic view of life. 900

Costumes The clothes worn by actors, designed to indicate historical periods, social status, economic levels, etc. 828

Cothurni See *Buskins*.

Couplet Two successive rhyming lines. 620

Cretic See *Amphimacer*.

Crisis The point of uncertainty and tension—the *turning point*—that results from the *conflicts* and difficulties brought about through the complications of the *plot*. The crisis leads to the *climax*—that is, to the decision made by the protagonist to resolve the conflict. Sometimes the *crisis* and the *climax* are considered as two elements of the same stage of plot development. 94–95, 823

Cultural (universal) symbol A symbol recognized and shared as a result of a common social and cultural heritage. See also *Contextual symbol*. 59, 319, 658

Cycle (1) A group of closely related works. (2) In medieval religious drama, the complete set of plays performed during the Corpus Christi festival, from the creation of the world to the resurrection. As many as forty or fifty plays could make up the cycle. See also *Corpus Christi play*. 948

Dactyl A three-syllable *foot* consisting of a heavy stress followed by two lights, such as *notable* and *parable*. 576

Dactylic or **triple rhyme** Rhyming *dactyls*. 582–83

Deconstructionist critical approach An interpretive literary approach that rejects absolute interpretations and stresses ambiguities and contradictions. 1380

Decorum The convention or expectation that words and subjects should be exactly appropriate—high or formal words for serious subjects (e.g., epic poems, tragedy), and low or informal words for low subjects (e.g., limericks, farce). 472

Denotation   The standard dictionary meaning of a word. 272, 474

Dénouement (untying) or **resolution** The final stage of *plot* development, in which mysteries are explained, characters find their destinies, and the work is completed. Usually the dénouement is done as speedily as possible, for it occurs after all conflicts are ended. 95, 823

Description   The exposition of scenes, actions, attitudes, and feelings. 58

Device   A rhetorical figure or strategy. 17

***Deus ex machina* (A god out of the machine. *Theos apo mechanes* in Greek)**   In ancient Greek drama, the entrance of a god to unravel the problems in a play. Today, the phrase *deus ex machina* refers to the artificial and illogical solution of problems. 902

Dialect   The speech of a particular region or social group, usually characterized by unique words, expressions, and pronunciation. When a dialect becomes widespread in government, business, education, and literature, it is claimed as the standard of the particular language. 470

Dialogue   The speeches of two or more characters in a story, play, or poem. 58, 60, 820

Diction   Word choice, types of words, and the level of language. 269, 468–93, 823, 884

Diction, formal or **high**   Proper, elevated, elaborate, and often polysyllabic language. 269, 270–71, 470

Diction, informal or **low**   Relaxed, conversational, and familiar language, utilizing contractions and elisions, and sometimes employing slang and grammatical mistakes. 269, 270–71, 470

Diction, neutral or **middle**   Correct language characterized by directness and simplicity. 269–70, 470

Digraph   Two alphabetical letters spelling one sound, as in *digraph*, where <ph> spells the / f / sound, *stick*, where <ck> spells the / k / sound, and *thumb*, where <mb> spells the / m / sound. 573

Dilemma   Two choices facing a protagonist, usually in a tragic situation, with either choice being unacceptable or damaging; a cause of both internal and external conflict. 93, 900

Dimeter   A line of two metrical feet. 574

Dionysia   The religious festivals of ancient Athens held to celebrate the god Dionysius. Both tragedy and comedy developed as major features of these festivals. 829, 891

Dipody, dipodic foot, or **syzygy**   The submergence of two normal *feet*, usually iambs or trochees, under a stronger beat, so that a "galloping" or "rollicking" rhythm results. 577

Director   The person in charge of guiding and instructing all persons involved in a dramatic production. 826

Dithyramb   An ancient Athenian poetic form sung by choruses during the earliest Dionysiac festivals. The first tragedies originated from the dithyrambs. 829, 891

***Donnée* (French for "given")**   The given action or set of assumptions on which a work of literature is based. 52–53

Double entendre ("double meaning")   Deliberate ambiguity, often sexual and usually humorous. 273

Double rhyme   See *Trochaic rhyme*.

Double plot   Two different but related lines of action, often in a play. 822

Drama   An individual play; also plays considered as a group; one of the three major *genres* of literature. 2, 819

Dramatic convention   See *Convention*.

Dramatic irony   A special kind of *situational irony* in which a character perceives his or her plight in a limited way while the audience and one or more of the other characters understand it entirely. 59, 550, 825, 901

Dramatic (objective) point of view   A third-person *narration* reporting speech and action, but excluding commentary on the actions and thoughts of the characters. 57, 199

Dying rhyme   See *Falling rhyme*.

Dynamic character   A character who undergoes adaptation, change, or growth, unlike a *static character*, who remains constant. In a *short story*, there is usually only one dynamic character, whereas in a *novel* there may be many. 134, 820

Echoic words   Words echoing the actions they describe, such as *buzz, bump*, and *slap*; important in the device of *onomatopoeia*. 580

Economic Determinist / Marxist critical approach   An interpretive approach based on the theories of Karl Marx (1818–1883), stressing that literature is to be judged from an economic perspective. 1377

Enclosing method   See *Framing method*.

End-stopped line   A line ending in a full pause, usually indicated with a period or semi-colon. 578

English (Shakespearean) sonnet   A fourteen-line poem, in iambic pentameter, composed of three quatrains and a couplet, rhyming A-B-A-B, C-D-C-D, E-F-E-F, G-G. 622

Enjambement or **run-on line**   A line having no end punctuation but running over to the next line. 578

Epic   A long narrative poem elevating character, speech, and action. 2, 49

Episodia or **episode**   An acting scene or section of Greek tragedy. Divisions separating the episodes were called *stasima*, or sections for the chorus. 60, 905

Euphony   Meaning "good sound," *euphony* refers to word groups containing consonants that permit an easy and pleasant flow of spoken sound; opposite of *cacophony*. 581

Exact rhyme   Rhyming words in which both the vowel and consonant sounds rhyme; also called *perfect rhyme*. It is important to note that rhymes result from *sound* rather than spelling; words do not have to be spelled the same way or look alike to rhyme. (Thus *break, take, ache*, and *opaque* are rhyming words.) 581

Exodos   The final episode in a Greek tragedy, occurring after the last choral ode. 905

Explication   A complete and detailed analysis of a work of literature, often word-by-word and line-by-line. 463–66

Exposition   The stage of dramatic or narrative structure which introduces all things necessary for the development of the *plot*. 94–822

Eye rhyme   Words which seem to rhyme because parts of them are spelled identically but pronounced differently (e.g., *bear, fear; fury, bury; stove, shove; wonder, yonder*). 582–584

Fable   A brief *story* illustrating a moral truth, most often associated with the ancient Greek writer Aesop. 50, 321

Falling action   See *Catastrophe*.

Falling rhyme   Trochaic rhymes, such as *dying* and *crying*, and also dactylic rhymes, such as *flattery* and *battery*. 583

Fantasy   The creation of events that are dreamlike or fantastic, departing from ordinary understanding of reality because of apparently illogical location, movement, causation, and chronology. 52

Farce   A word derived from the Latin word *farsus,* meaning "stuffed," farce is an outlandish physical comedy overflowing with silly characters, improbable happenings, wild clowning, extravagant language, and bawdy jokes. 831, 1071

Feminine rhyme   See *Falling rhyme.*

Feminist critical approach   An interpretive approach designed to raise consciousness about the importance and unique nature of women in literature. 1376

Fiction   *Narratives* based in the imagination of the author, not in literal, reportorial facts; one of the three major *genres* of literature. 2–3, 49–91

Figurative language   Words and expressions that conform to a particular pattern or form, such as *metaphor, simile,* and *parallelism.* 2, 366, 516

First-person point of view   The use of an "I," or first-person, *speaker* or *narrator* who tells about things that he/she has seen, done, spoken, heard, thought, and also learned about in other ways. 56, 59–60, 197, 201

Flashback   A method of *narration* in which past events are introduced into a present action. 96

Flat character   A character, usually minor, who is not individual, but rather useful and structural, static and unchanging; distinguished from *round character.* 136, 821

Foil   A character designed to highlight qualities of a major character. 821

Foot   Measured combinations of heavy and light *stresses,* such as the iamb, which contains a light and a heavy stress. 574

Form, poetic   The various shapes and organizational modes of poetry. 619–56

Formalist critical approach   See *New Critical / Formalist critical approach.*

Formal substitution   See *Substitution.*

Framing (enclosing) method   The same features of topic or setting used at both the beginning and ending of a work so as to "frame" or "enclose" the work. 242

Free verse   Poetry based on the natural rhythms of phrases and normal pauses, not metrical feet. 625

Freewriting   See *Brainstorming.*

Freytag Pyramid   A diagram showing how the five stages of dramatic plot structure go up and down like the sides of a pyramid. 822

General language   Words referring to broad classes of persons, objects, or phenomena; distinguished from *specific language.* 271, 469

Genre   A type of literature, such as *fiction* and *poetry*; also a type of work, such as detective fiction, epic poetry, tragedy, etc. 2–5

Graph, Graphics (spelling)   Writing or spelling; the appearance of words on a page, as opposed to their actual sounds. 573

Gustatory images   References to impressions of taste. 498

Haiku   A poetic form derived from Japanese, traditionally containing three lines of 5, 7, and 5 syllables. 2, 623

Half rhyme   See *Inexact rhyme.*

Hamartia   The error or frailty that causes the downfall of a tragic protagonist. 899

Heavy-stress rhyme   A *rhyme,* such as rhyming iambs or anapests, ending with a strong stress. 573, 582

Heptameter or **the septenary**   A line consisting of seven metrical *feet.* 574

Hero, heroine The major male and female *protagonists* in a narrative or drama; the terms are often used to describe leading characters in adventures and romances. 136

Heroic couplet Also called the *neoclassic couplet.* Two successive rhyming lines of iambic pentameter; the second line is usually end-stopped. Couplets written between 1660 and 1800 are often called "heroic" regardless of their topic matter. 620

Hexameter A line consisting of six metrical *feet.* 574

High comedy Elegant comedies characterized by wit and sophistication, in which the complications grow out of character; also, a *comedy of manners.* 1070

Historical critical approach See *Topical / Historical critical approach.*

Hovering accent See *Spondee.*

Hubris (also *hybris*) Meaning "insolence, contemptuous violence," or pride; *hubris* defines the attitude/attitudes that lead tragic figures to commit their offenses. 891

Humor A quality of merriment, laughter, good spirits, and fun; also, the capacity to cause laughter, etc. 274

Hymn A religious song, consisting of one and usually many more replicating rhythmical stanzas. 623

Hyperbole A rhetorical figure in which emphasis is achieved through exaggeration. 273, 523

Iamb A two-syllable *foot* consisting of a light stress followed by a heavy stress (e.g., *the winds*). 574–75

Iambic pentameter A line consisting of five iambic *feet.* 574–75, 619–20

Idea A concept, thought, opinion, or belief; in literature, a unifying, centralizing conception or *theme.* 55, 60, 363–93

Identical rhyme The use of the same words in rhyming positions, such as *veil* and *veil,* or *stone* and *stone.* 582, 584, 715

Idiom Usage that produces unique words and phrases within regions, classes, or groups; e.g., standing *on* line or *in* line; carrying a *pail* or a *bucket;* drinking *pop* or *soda.* Also, the habits and structures of particular languages. 470

Image, Imagery Images are references that trigger the mind to fuse together memories of sights (*visual*), sounds (*auditory*), tastes (*gustatory*), smells (*olfactory*), and sensations of touch (*tactile*). "Image" refers to a single mental creation. "Imagery" refers to images throughout a work or throughout the works of a writer or group of writers. Images may be *literal* (descriptive and pictorial) and *metaphorical* (figurative and suggestive). 2, 494–515, 823, 884

Imaginative literature Literature based in the imagination of the writer, usually *fiction, poetry,* and *drama.* 2–3

Imitation The theory that literature is derived from life and is an imaginative duplication of experience; closely connected to *realism* and *verisimilitude.* 52

Imperfect foot A metrical *foot* consisting of a single syllable, either heavily or lightly stressed. 576

Incidents See *Actions.*

Inexact rhyme Rhymes that are created out of words with similar but not identical sounds. In most of these instances, either the vowel segments are different while the consonants are the same, or vice versa. This type of rhyme is variously called *slant rhyme, near rhyme, half rhyme, off rhyme, analyzed rhyme,* or *suspended rhyme.* 583

Internal rhyme The occurrence of rhyming words within a single line of verse. 583

Intrigue plot The dramatic rendering of how a young woman and her lover foil the blocking mechanisms of a parent or guardian, often aided by a maidservant or *soubrette*. 1067

Invention   The process of discovering and determining materials to be included in a composition, whether an essay or an imaginative work; a vital phase of *prewriting*. 52

Ironic comedy   A form of comedy in which characters seem to be in the grips of uncontrollable, cosmic forces. The dominant tone is therefore ironic. 1072

Irony   Broadly, a means of indirection. Language that states the opposite of what is intended is *verbal irony*. The placement of characters in a state of ignorance is *dramatic irony*, while an emphasis on powerlessness is *situational irony*. 59, 60, 273, 548, 900

Italian or **Petrarchan sonnet**   An iambic pentameter poem of fourteen lines, divided between the first eight lines (the *octave*) and the last six (the *sestet*). 622

Jargon   Words and phrases characteristic of a particular profession, trade, or pursuit such as medicine, sociology, football, or the military. 471

Journal   A notebook or word-processor file for recording observations, here, about reading. 11–14, 16–17

Kinesthetic images   Words describing human or animal motion and activity. 498

Kinetic images   Words describing general motion. 498

Kothorni   See *Buskins*.

Lighting   The general word describing the many types, positions, directions, and intensities of artificial lights used in the theater. 827–28

Limited or **limited-omniscient point of view**   A third-person narration in which the actions and thoughts of the protagonist are the focus of attention. 200

Literature   Written or oral compositions that tell stories, dramatize situations, express emotions, and analyze and advocate ideas. Literature is designed to engage readers emotionally as well as intellectually, with the major genres being *fiction, poetry, drama*, and *nonfiction prose*, and with many separate sub-forms. 1–3, *passim*

Low comedy   Crude, violent, and physical comedies and farces, characterized by sight gags, bawdy jokes, and outrageous situations. 1071

Lyric   A short poem written in a repeating stanzaic form, often designed to be set to music; a *song*. 623

Magnitude   The third aspect of Aristotle's definition of tragedy, emphasizing that a play should be neither too long nor too short, so that artistic balance and proportion may be maintained. 899

Main plot   The central and major line of causation and action in a literary work. 822

Major mover   A major participant in a work's action, who either causes things to happen or who is the subject of major events. If the first-person narrator is also a major mover, such as the *protagonist*, that fact gives first-hand authenticity to the narration. 202

Makeup   The materials, such as cosmetics, wigs, and padding, applied to an actor to change appearance for a specific role, such as a youth, an aged person, or a hunchback. 828

Marxist critical approach   See *Economic determinist / Marxist critical approach*.

Masculine rhyme   See *Rising rhyme*.

Masks   Masks were worn by ancient Athenian actors to illustrate and define the dramatic characters, such as youths, aged men, women, warriors, etc. 903

Mechanics of verse See *Prosody.*

Melodrama A sentimental dramatic form with an artificially happy ending. 831

Metaphor (the "carrying out of a change") *Figurative language* that describes something as though it actually were something else, thereby enhancing understanding and insight. 17, 58, 516

Metaphorical language See *Figurative language.*

Meter The number of *feet* within a line of traditional verse, such as *iambic pentameter* referring to a line containing five *iambs.* 574

Metonymy A rhetorical figure in which one thing is used as a substitute for another with which it is closely identified. 521

Metrical foot See *Foot.*

Metrics See *Prosody.*

Middle Comedy The Greek comedies written in the first two-thirds of the fourth Century B.C.E. Middle Comedy lessened or eliminated the chorus, and did away with the exaggerated costumes of the Old Comedy. No Middle Comedies survive from antiquity. 1067

Mimesis See *Representation.*

Miracle play A medieval play dramatizing a miracle or miracles performed by a saint. An outgrowth of the earlier medieval *Corpus Christi* play (q.v.). 949

Monologue A long speech spoken by a single character to himself or herself, to the audience, or to an off-stage character. 820

Monometer A line consisting of one metrical foot. 574

Mood See *Atmosphere.*

Moral / Intellectual critical approach An approach to the interpretation of literature that is concerned primarily with content and values. 1371

Morality play A type of medieval and early Renaissance play that dramatizes the way to live a pious life. 830, 949

Multiple plot A work in which two or more stories are both contrasted and woven together, as in *A Midsummer Night's Dream.* 822

Musical comedy A modern prose play integrated with lyrics set to specially composed music. 1131

Music of poetry Broadly, the rhythms, sounds, and rhymes of poetry. See *Prosody.*

Muthos See *Plot.*

Mystery plays See *Corpus Christi play.*

Myth, mythology, mythos A *myth* is a story that deals with the relationships of gods to humanity , or with battles among heroes. A myth may also be a set of beliefs or assumptions among societies. *Mythology* refers collectively to all the stories and beliefs, either of a single group or number of groups. A system of beliefs and religious or historical doctrine is a *mythos.* 2, 322, 688–710

Mythical reader See *Audience.*

Mythic critical approach See *Archetypal / Symbolic / Mythic critical approach.*

Mythopoeic The propensity to create myths and to live in terms of them. 689

Narration, narrative fiction The relating or recounting of a sequence of events or actions. While a *narration* may be reportorial and historical, *narrative fiction* is primarily creative and imaginative. 2, 49, 56, 60

Narrative fiction See *Prose fiction.*

Narrator See *Speaker.*

Near rhyme   See *Inexact rhyme.*

Neoclassic couplet   See *Heroic couplet.*

New comedy   The Greek comedy that developed at the end of the fourth century B.C.E., stressing wit, romanticism, and twists of plot. 1067

New Critical / Formalist critical approach An approach to the interpretation of literature based on the French practice of *explication de texte*, stressing the form and details of literary works. 1373

Nonfiction prose   A *genre* consisting of essays, articles, and books that are concerned with real as opposed to fictional things; one of the major *genres* of literature. 2–3

Nonrealistic drama   Dreamlike, fantastic, symbolic, and otherwise artificial plays that make no attempt to present an imitation of everyday reality. 827

Novel   A long work of prose fiction. 2, 51

Objective point of view   See *Dramatic point of view.*

Octameter   A line of eight metrical feet. 574

Octave   The first eight lines of an Italian sonnet, unified by rhythm, rhyme, and topic. 622

Ode   A stanzaic poetic form (usually long, to contrast it with the *song*) with varying line lengths and sometimes intricate *rhyme* schemes. 623

Off rhyme   See *Inexact rhyme.*

Old comedy (Old Attic Comedy)   The Athenian comedies of the fifth century B.C.E., featuring song, dance, ribaldry, satire, and invective. 1067

Olfactory imagery   Images referring to smell. 498

Omniscient point of view   A *third-person narrative* in which the *speaker* or *narrator*, with no apparent limitations, may describe intentions, actions, reactions, locations, and speeches of any or all of the characters, and may also describe their innermost thoughts (when necessary). 57, 200

Onomatopoeia   A blending of consonant and vowel sounds designed to imitate or suggest the activity being described. 580

Open-form poetry   Poems that avoid traditional structural patterns, such as rhyme or meter, in favor of other methods of organization. 619, 625–27

Orchestra (theaters)   (1) In ancient Greek theaters, the *orchestra*, or dancing place, was the central circle where the chorus performed. (2) As applied to theaters, and not symphonic groups, the word now refers to the ground floor or first-floor where the audience sits. 902

Organic unity   Derived from Aristotle, the concept of organic unity refers to the interdependence of all elements of a work, including character, actions, speeches, descriptions, thoughts, and observations. 54

Overstatement   See *Hyperbole.*

Parable   A short *allegory* designed to illustrate a religious truth, most often associated with Jesus as recorded in the Gospels. 2, 50, 322

Parados   (1) A *parados* was either of the two aisles on each side of the orchestra in ancient Greek theaters, along which the performers could enter or exit. (2) The entry and first lyrical ode of the chorus in Greek tragedy, after the prologue. 905

Paradox   A rhetorical figure embodying a contradiction that is nevertheless true. 519

Parallelism   A rhetorical structure in which the same grammatical forms are repeated. 473, 620

Paranomasia See *Pun*.

Paraphrase A brief restatement, in one's own words, of all or part of a literary work; a *précis*. 416

Pathos The "scene of suffering" in tragedy, which Aristotle defines as "a destructive or painful action, such as death on the stage, bodily agony, wounds, and the like." 898

Pentameter A line of five metrical *feet*. 574

Perfect rhyme See *Exact rhyme*.

Performance A production of a play, either for an evening or for an extended period, comprising acting, movement, lighting, sound effects, staging and scenery, ticket sales, and the accommodation of the audience. 825

Peripeteia or **reversal** Aristotle's term for a sudden reversal, when the action of a work, particularly a play, veers around quickly to its opposite. 898

Persona (Latin for **"mask"** [*prosopon* in Greek.]) The narrator or speaker of a story or poem. See also *Speaker*. 57, 194

Personification A rhetorical figure in which human characteristics are attributed to nonhuman things or abstractions. 521

Petrarchan sonnet See *Italian sonnet*.

Phonetic, phonetics The actual pronunciation of sounds, as distinguished from spelling or *graphics*. 573

Plausibility See *Verisimilitude*.

Play See *Drama*.

Plot The plan or groundwork for a story, with the actions resulting from believable and authentic human responses to a *conflict*. It is causation, conflict, response, opposition, and interaction that make a *plot* out of a series of

actions. Aristotle's word for plot is *muthos*. 54, 60, 92–129, 821, 883, 897

Poem, poet, poetry A variable literary genre which is, foremost, characterized by the rhythmical qualities of language. While poems may be short (including *epigrams* and *haiku* of just a few lines) or long (*epics* of thousands of lines), the essence of poetry is compression, economy, and force, in contrast with the expansiveness of prose. There is no bar to the topics that poets may consider, and poems may range from the personal and lyric to the public and discursive. A *poem* is one poetic work. A *poet* is a person who writes poems. *Poetry* may refer to the poems of one writer, to poems of a number of writers, to all poems generally, or to the aesthetics of poetry considered as an art. 2, 445, Chapters 11–21

Point of view The *speaker, voice, narrator,* or *persona* of a work; the position from which details are perceived and related; a centralizing mind or intelligence; not to be confused with *opinion* or *belief*. 56–58, 194–239, 883

Point-of-view character The central figure or *protagonist* in a *limited-point-of-view narration*, the character about whom events turn, the focus of attention in the narration. 200

Postulate or **premise** The assumption on which a work of literature is based, such as a level of absolute, literal reality, or as a dreamlike, fanciful set of events. See also *Donnée*. 52–53

Précis A shortening, or cutting down, of a narrative into its essential parts—a synopsis, abridgment, paraphrase, condensation, or epitome. 85–90

Private symbol See *Contextual symbol*.

Probability or **plausibility** The standard that literature should be about what is probable, common, normal, and usual. 139

Problem   A question or issue about the interpretation or understanding of a work. 1058–63

Problem play   A type of play dealing with a problem, whether personal, social, political, environmental, or religious. 832, 1165

Procatalepsis or **anticipation**   A rhetorical strategy whereby the writer raises an objection and then answers it; the idea is to strengthen an argument by dealing with possible objections before a dissenter can raise them. 1059

Producer   The person in charge of practical matters connected with a stage production, such as securing finances, arranging for theater use, furnishing materials, renting or making costumes and properties, guaranteeing payments, and so on. 826

Prologue   In Greek tragedy, the introductory action and speeches before the *parados*, or first entry of the chorus. 904

Props or **properties**   The objects, furniture, and the like used on stage during a play. 827, 884

Proscenium, proscenium stage   (1) See *proskenion*. (2) An arch that frames a *box set (q.v.)* and holds the curtain, thus creating the invisible fourth wall through which the audience sees the action of the play. 826

Prose fiction   Imaginative prose narratives (short stories and novels) that focus on one or a few characters who undergo a change or development as they interact with other characters and deal with their problems. 2–3, Chapters 2–10

Prose poem   A short work, written in prose, but employing the methods of verse, such as imagery, for poetic ends. 626

Proskenion   A raised stage built in front of the *skene* in ancient Greek theaters to separate the actors from the chorus and make them more prominent. 826

Prosody   The sounds and rhythms of poetry. 572–618

Protagonist   The central character and focus of interest in a *narrative* or *drama*. 54, 60, 136, 820

Psychological / Psychoanalytic critical approach   An interpretive literary approach stressing how psychology may be used in the explanation of both authors and literary works. 1378

Public mythology   See *Universal mythology*.

Pun, or **paranomasia**   A witty word-play which reveals that words with different meanings have similar or even identical sounds. 522

Purgation   See *Catharsis*.

Pyrrhic   A metrical *foot* consisting of two unaccented syllables. 575

Quatrain   (1) A four-line stanza or poetic unit. (2) In an *English* or *Shakespearean* sonnet, a group of four lines united by rhyme. 585, 621

Raisonneur   A character who remains detached from the action and provides reasoned commentary; a choric character. 821

Reader-Response critical approach   An interpretive approach based in the proposition that literary works are not fully created until readers make *transactions* with them by *actualizing* them in the light of their own knowledge and experience. 1382

Realism or **verisimilitude**   The use of true, lifelike, or probable situations and concerns. Also, the theory underlying the use of reality in literature. 52, 242

Realistic comedy   See *Ironic comedy*.

Realistic setting A setting designed to resemble places that actually exist or that might exist. The settings of Ibsen's *A Dollhouse* are realistic. 827

Recognition See *Anagnorisis.*

Repetition See *Anaphora.*

Representation The Aristotelian concept of *mimesis*; namely, that drama (tragedy) represents rather than duplicates history. 897

Representative character A *flat character* with the qualities of all other members of a group (i.e., clerks, cowboys, detectives, etc.); a *stereotype.* 137

Research, literary The systematic use of primary and secondary sources for assistance in studying a literary problem. 1343–69

Resolution See *Dénouement.*

Response A reader's intellectual and emotional reactions to a literary work. 38–45

Revenge tragedy A popular type of English Renaissance drama, developed by Thomas Kyd, in which a person is called upon (often by a ghost) to avenge the murder of a loved one. Shakespeare's *Hamlet* is in the tradition of revenge tragedy. 953

Reversal See *Peripeteia.*

Revision Rewriting and improving a piece of writing. 26–37

Rhetorical figure See *Figurative language.*

Rhetorical substitution See *Substitution.*

Rhyme The repetition of identical concluding syllables in different words, most often at the ends of lines. 573, 581–85

Rhyme scheme The pattern of rhyme, usually indicated by assigning a letter of the alphabet to each rhyming sound. 584

Rhythm The varying speed, intensity, elevation, pitch, loudness, and expressiveness of speech, especially poetry. 573–79

Rising action The action in a play before the climax. 823

Rising rhyme Rhymes produced with one-syllable words, like *sky* and *fly,* or with multisyllabic words in which the accent falls on the last syllable, such as *decline* and *confine.* 582

Romance (1) Lengthy Spanish and French stories of the sixteenth and seventeenth centuries. (2) Modern formulaic stories describing the growth of an enthusiastic love relationship. 2, 51

Romantic comedy Sympathetic comedy that presents the adventures of young lovers trying to overcome opposition and achieve a successful union. 1070

Round character A character who profits from experience and undergoes a change or development; usually but not necessarily the *protagonist.* 136, 820–21

Run-on line See *Enjambement.*

Satire An attack on human follies or vices (negative), as measured against a normative religious, moral, or social standard (positive). 550–51

Satiric comedy A form of comedy designed to correct social and individual behavior by ridiculing human vices and follies. 1071

Satyr play A comic and burlesque play submitted by the ancient Athenian tragic dramatists along with their trilogies of tragedies. On each day of tragic performances, the satyr play was performed after the three tragedies. See also *Trilogy.* 893

Scansion The act of determining the prevailing *rhythm* of a poem. 573

Scene (1) In a play, a part or division (of an act, as in *Hamlet,* or entire play, as in

Death of a Salesman) in which there is a unity of subject, setting, and (often) actors. (2) In a film, a unit of continuous action in one location. 827

Scenery   The artificial environment created on stage to produce the illusion of a specific or generalized place and time. 827

Second-person point of view   A *narration* in which a second-person listener ("you") is the *protagonist* and the speaker is someone with knowledge the protagonist does not possess or understand about his or her own actions (e.g., doctor, parent, rejected lover, etc.). 198, 202

Segment   The smallest meaningful unit of sound, such as the *l, uh,* and *v* sounds making up the word "love." Segments are to be distinguished from spellings. 572

Septenary   See *Heptameter.*

Seriousness   The first aspect of Aristotle's definition of tragedy, defining human character at its most elevated and significant. 898

Sestet   (1) A six-line stanza or unit of poetry. (2) The last six lines of an *Italian* sonnet. 622

Sets   The physical objects used in a theatrical production. 884, 827

Setting   The natural, manufactured, and cultural environment in which characters live and move, including all the artifacts they use in their lives. 240–67, 450

Shakespearean sonnet   See *English sonnet.*

Shaped verse   Poetry written so that the lines or words of the poem form a recognizable shape, such as a pair of wings or a geometrical figure. 627

Short story   A compact, concentrated work of narrative fiction that may also contain description, dialogue, and commentary. Poe used the term "brief prose tale" for the short story, and emphasized that it should create a major, unified impact. 2, 51, Chapters 2–10

Sight rhyme   See *Eye rhyme.*

Simile   A figure of comparison, using "like" with nouns and "as" with clauses, as in "the trees were bent by the wind *like actors bowing after a performance.*" 17, 517

Situational irony   A type of *irony* emphasizing that human beings are enmeshed in forces beyond their comprehension and control. 59–60, 548–50, 825, 900

Skene   In ancient Greek theaters, the *skene* ("tent," "hut") was a building in front of the orchestra which contained front and side doors from which actors could make entrances and exits. It served a variety of purposes, including the storage of costumes and props. 902

Slang   Informal and substandard vocabulary. Some slang is a permanent part of the language (e.g., phrases like "I'll be damned," "Go jump in the lake," and our many four-letter words). Other slang is spontaneous, rising within a group (jargon), and often then being replaced when new slang emerges. 471

Slant rhyme   A *near rhyme,* in which the concluding consonant sounds are identical, but not the vowels, such as "should" and "food," "slim" and "ham." 582, 584

Slapstick comedy   A type of low farce in which the humor depends almost entirely on physical actions and sight gags. 1072

Social drama   A type of problem play that deals with current social issues and the place of individuals in society. 832

Soliloquy   A speech made by a character, alone on stage, directly to the audience, the convention being that the character is revealing thoughts and feelings. A soliloquy is to be distinguished from an *aside,* which is made to the audience (or confidentially to another character) when other characters are present. 952

Song A lyric poem with a number of repeating stanzas, written to be set to music. 623

Sonnet A poem of fourteen lines in iambic pentameter. 619

Sound The phonetics of language, collectively and separately considered. See also *Prosody*. 2, 573

Speaker The *narrator* of a story or poem, the *point of view*, often an independent character who is completely imagined and consistently maintained by the author. In addition to narrating the essential events of the work (justifying status as the *narrator*), the speaker may also introduce other aspects of his or her knowledge, and may interject judgments and opinions. Often the character of the speaker is of as much interest as the *actions* or *incidents*. 57, 194

Specific language Words referring to objects or conditions that may be perceived or imagined; distinguished from *general language*. 56, 271, 469

Speeches See *Dialogue*.

Spondee A two-syllable foot consisting of successive, equally heavy accents (e.g., *slow time, men's eyes*). 575

Sprung or **accentual rhythm** A method of accenting, developed by Gerard Manley Hopkins, in which major stresses are "sprung" from the poetic line. 577

Stage business See *Business*.

Stage convention See *Convention*.

Stage directions A playwright's instructions concerning lighting, scenery, blocking, tone of voice, action, entrances and exits, and the like. 820

Stanza A group of poetic lines corresponding to paragraphs in prose; the

meters and rhymes are usually repeating or systematic. 585, 619

Stasima (**singular** *stasimon*) Choral odes separating the episodes in Greek tragedies. 905

Static character A character who undergoes no change; contrasted with a *dynamic character*. 136, 821

Stereotype A character who is so ordinary and unoriginal that he/she seems to have been cast in a mold; a *representative* character. 137, 821

Stichomythy In Greek tragedies, dialogue consisting of one-line and half-line speeches designed for rapid delivery. 905

Stock character A *flat character* in a standard role with standard *traits*, such as the irate police captain, the bored hotel clerk, etc.; a stereotype. 136, 821

Story A narrative, usually fictional, centering on a major character, and rendering a complete action. 50–52

Stress The emphasis given to a syllable, either strong or light. See also *Beat*. 574

Strong-stress rhythm See *Heavy-stress rhythm*.

Structuralist critical approach An interpretive approach attempting to find relationships and connections among elements that appear to be separate and discrete. 1374

Structure The arrangement and placement of materials in a work. 54–55, 60, 94–133, 822–24

Style The manipulation of language, the placement of words in the service of content. 56, 268–317, 823, 884

Subject The topic that a literary work addresses, such as love, marriage, war, and death. 825

Subplot A secondary line of action in a literary work that often comments directly or obliquely on the main plot. See also *Multiple plot*. 822

Substitution   *Formal substitution* is the use of an actual variant foot within a line, such as an anapest being used in place of an iamb. *Rhetorical substitution* is the manipulation of the *caesura* to create the effect of a series of differing feet. 577–79

Suspended rhyme   See *Inexact rhyme*.

Syllable   A separately pronounced part of a word (e.g., the *eat* and *ing* parts of "eating") or, in some cases, a complete word (e.g., *the, when, flounced*). 573

Symbol, symbolism   A specific word, idea, or object that may stand for ideas, values, persons, or ways of life. 58-60, 243, 318-62, 657-87, 821, 884

Symbolic   critical   approach   See *Archetypal / Symbolic / Mythic critical approach*.

Synecdoche   A rhetorical figure in which a part stands for a whole, or a whole for a part. 521

Synesthesia   A rhetorical figure uniting or fusing separate sensations or feelings; the description of one type of perception or thought with words that are appropriate to another. 522

Syntax   Word order and sentence structure. A mark of style is a writer's syntactical patterning (regular patterns and variations), depending on the rhetorical needs of the literary work. 472

Syzygy   See *Dipody*.

Tactile imagery   Images of touch and feeling. 498

Tenor (figurative language)   The sense, or meaning, of a *metaphor, symbol,* or other rhetorical figure. See *Vehicle*. 519

Tercet   A three-line unit or stanza of poetry, often rhyming A-A-A or A-B-A. 621

Terza rima   A three-line stanza form with the pattern A-B-A, B-C-B, etc. 621

Tetrameter   A line consisting of four metrical *feet*. 574

Theater of Dionysus   The ancient Athenian outdoor theater where Greek drama began. 901

Theater in the round   See *Arena stage*.

Theme   (1) The major or central idea of a work. (2) An essay, a short composition developing an interpretation or advancing an argument. (3) The main point or idea that a writer of an essay asserts and illustrates. 55, 60, 364, 450, 825, 885

Thesis statement or **thesis sentence**   An introductory sentence which names the topics to be developed in the body of an essay. 21–22

Third-person point of view   A third-person method of *narration* (i.e., *she, he, it, they, them,* etc.), in which the *speaker* or *narrator* is not a part of the story, as with the *first-person point of view*. Because the third-person speaker may exhibit great knowledge and understanding, together with other qualities of character, he or she is often virtually identified with the author, but this identification is not easily decided. See also *Authorial voice, Omniscient point of view*. 199, 202

Third-person objective point of view   See *Dramatic point of view*.

Thrust stage   See *Apron stage*.

Tiring house   An enclosed area in an Elizabethan theater in which actors changed costumes and awaited their cues, and in which stage properties were kept. 951

Tone   The techniques and modes of presentation that reveal or create attitudes. 59, 268–317, 543–71, 824, 885

Topic sentence   The sentence determining the subject matter of a paragraph. 22–24

Topical / Historical critical approach An interpretive approach that stresses the relationship of literature to its historical period. 1372

Traditional poetry See *Closed-form poetry.*

Tragedy A drama or other literary work that recounts the fall of an individual who, while undergoing suffering, deals responsibly with the situations and dilemmas that he or she faces, and who thus demonstrates the value of human effort. 829, 890–1064

Tragicomedy A literary work—drama or story—containing a mixture of tragic and comic elements. 831

Trait, traits A typical mode of behavior; the study of major traits provides a guide to the description of *character.* 135

Tragic flaw See *Hamartia.*

Trilogy A group of three literary works, usually related or unified. For the ancient Athenian Dionysiac festivals, each competing dramatist submitted a *trilogy* (three tragedies), together with a *satyr play.* 893

Trimeter A line consisting of three metrical *feet.* 574

Triple rhyme See *Dactylic rhyme.*

Triplet See *Tercet.*

Trochaic (double) rhyme Rhyming trochees such as *flower* and *shower.* 582–83

Trochee, trochaic A two-syllable *foot* consisting of a heavy followed by a light stress. 575

Trope A short dramatic dialogue inserted into the Church mass during the early middle ages. 947

Tudor interlude Comedies, tragedies, or historical plays performed by both professional actors and students during the reigns of Henry VII and Henry VIII (i.e., the first half of the sixteenth century). They sometimes featured abstract and allegorical characters and provided opportunities for both music and farcical action. 949

Understatement The deliberate underplaying or undervaluing of a thing to create emphasis. 273, 523

Unit set A series of platforms, rooms, stairs, and exits that form the locations for all of a play's actions. A unit set enables scenes to change rapidly, without the drawing of a curtain and the placement of new sets. 827

Unities The concept, related to *verisimilitude,* that literary works should comprise a single major action, take place in as little time as possible, and be confined to a single location (*action, time,* and *place*). During the Renaissance some critics considered the unities to be essential aspects of *regular drama.* Later critics considered the unity of action important, but minimized the unities of place and time. 906

Universal (public) mythology Widely known mythic systems that have been well established over a long period of time, such as Greco-Roman mythology and Germanic mythology. 691

Universal symbol See *Cultural symbols.*

Value, values The expression of an idea or ideas that concurrently asserts their importance and desirability as goals, standards, and ideals. 364

Vehicle The image or reference of a rhetorical figure, such as a *metaphor* or *simile*; it is the vehicle that carries or embodies the *tenor* (q.v.). 519

Verbal irony Language stressing the importance of an idea by stating the opposite of what is meant. 59, 273, 550, 825

Verisimilitude ("like truth") or realism A characteristic whereby the setting, circumstances, characters, dialogue, actions, and outcomes in a work are designed to seem true, lifelike, real, plausible, and probable. 52, 139, 242

Versification   See *Prosody.*

Villanelle   A closed poetic form of nineteen lines, composed of five triplets and a concluding quatrain. The form requires that whole lines be repeated in a specific order and that only two rhyming sounds occur throughout. 621

Virgule   A slashmark (/) used in scansion to mark the boundaries of poetic feet. 574

Visual image   Language describing visible objects. 496

Visual poetry   Poetry that draws much of its power from the appearance of the verse on the page. See also *Concrete verse* and *Shaped verse.* 627

Voice   See *Speaker.*

Vowel rhyme   The use of any vowels in rhyming positions, as in *day* and *sky*, or *key* and *play.* 584

Well-made play (*la pièce bien faite*)   A form developed and popularized in nineteenth-century France by Eugène Scribe (1791–1861) and Victorien Sardou (1831–1908). Typically, the well-made play is built on both secrets and the timely arrivals of new characters and threats. The protagonist overcomes adversity and ultimately overcomes it. Ibsen's *A Dollhouse* exhibits many characteristics of a well-made play. 1167

Credits

Text

Brian W. Aldiss. "flight 063" by Brian Aldiss from *Asimov's Science Fiction*. Copyright (c) 1994. Reprinted by permission.

A. R. Ammons. "80 Proof" copyright (c) 1964 by A.R. Ammons, from *Diversifications* by A. R. Ammons. Reprinted by permission of W. W. Norton & Company, Inc.

Maya Angelou. "My Arkansas" from *And I Still Rise* by Maya Angelou. Copyright (c) 1978 by Maya Angelou. Reprinted by permission of Random House, Inc.

Margaret Atwood. "Rape Fantasies" from the short story collection *Dancing Girls* by Margaret Atwood (c) 1977 Simon & Schuster. Reprinted with permission of the author and McClelland & Stewart, Inc., Toronto, The Canadian Publishers.

Margaret Atwood. "Siren Song" from *You Are Happy, Selected Poems 1965–1975*. Copyright (c) 1976 by Margaret Atwood. Reprinted by permission of Houghton Mifflin Co., and Oxford University Press, Canada. All rights reserved.

Margaret Atwood. "Variation on The Word Sleep" from *Selected Poems II: Poems Selected and New 1976–1986* by Margaret Atwood. Copyright (c) 1987 by Margaret Atwood. Reprinted by permission of Houghton Mifflin Company and Oxford University Press, Canada. All rights reserved.

W. H. Auden. "The Unkown Citizen" from *W. H. Auden: Collected Poems* by W. H. Auden, edited by Edward Mendelson. Copyright 1940 and renewed 1968 by W. H. Auden. Reprinted by permission of Random House, Inc.

Amiri Baraka. "Ka'Ba" from *Black Magic Poetry* by Amiri Baraka. Copyright (c) 1969. Reprinted by permission.

Marvin Bell. "Things We Dreamt We Died For" reprinted from *New and Selected Poems* by Marvin Bell, Atheneum, copyright (c) 1987 by Marvin Bell. Reprinted by permission of the author.

Earle Birney. From *Collected Poems of Earle Birney* by Earle Birney. Used by permission of McClelland & Stewart, Inc., Toronto, The Canadian Publishers.

Elizabeth Bishop. "Rain Towards Morning" from *The Complete Poems 1927–1979* by Elizabeth Bishop.Copyright (c) 1979, 1983 by Alice Helen Methfessel. Reprinted by permission of Farrar, Straus & Giroux, Inc.

Elizabeth Bishop. "The Fish" from *The Complete Poems 1927–1979* by Elizabeth Bishop. Copyright (c) 1979, 1983 by Alice Helen Methfessel. Reprinted by permission of Farrar, Straus & Giroux.

Arna Bontemps. "A Black Man Talks of Reaping" by Arna Bontemps from *Personal* by Arna Bontemps.Copyright (c) 1963 by Arna Bontemps. Reprinted by permission of Harold Ober Associates Incorporated.

Joseph Brodsky. "In Memory of My Father: Australia" from *So Forth* by Joseph Brodsky. Copyright (c) 1995 by The Estate of Joseph Brodsky. Reprinted by permission of Farrar, Straus & Giroux, Inc.

Gwendolyn Brooks. "Primer for Blacks" by Gwendolyn Brooks. Reprinted by permission.

Photographs

Chapter 2: page 61, Broadway Books; p. 72, AP/Wide World Photos; p. 79, Nancy Crampton.

Chapter 3: page 97, Corbis-Bettmann; p. 115, AP/Wide World Photos.

Chapter 4: page 140, Culver Pictures, Inc.; p. 154, Corbis-Bettmann; p. 180, Robert Foothorap/ Amy Tan.

Chapter 5: page 203, Culver Pictures, Inc.; p. 209, Erich Hartmann/Magnum Photos, Inc.; p. 215, Corbis-Bettmann;
p. 219, Nancy Crampton; p. 224, Leonda Finke; p. 229, UPI/Corbis-Bettmann.

Chapter 6: page 244, Missouri Historical Society; p. 246, Monika Hilleary/Henry Holt & Company, Inc.; p. 255, Julius Ozick/Alfred A. Knopf, Inc.; p. 258, Corbis-Bettmann.

Chapter 7: page 275, UPI/Corbis-Bettmann; p. 281, UPI/Corbis-Bettmann; p. 287, Tyler Hodgins/McClelland & Stewart, Inc.; p. 299, Jerry Bauer/Alfred A. Knopf, Inc.; p. 306, G. Paul Bishop/Alfred A. Knopf, Inc.

Chapter 8: page 324, Corbis-Bettmann; p. 347, UPI/Corbis-Bettmann; p. 354, Arvind Garg/Globe Photos, Inc.

Chapter 9: page 368, Corbis-Bettmann; p. 372, Corbis-Bettmann; p. 383, Gil Ihrig/Irene Zabytko.

Chapter 10: page 394, Gray Little/Henry Holt & Company, Inc.; p. 400, Marion Ellinger/Vintage Books; p. 408, Culver Pictures, Inc.; p. 419, David Laurence; p. 426, Corbis-Bettmann; p. 436, UPI/Corbis-Bettmann.

Chapter 17: page 649, Foto Marburg/Art Resource.

Chapter 19: page 705, Foto Marburg/Art Resource.

Chapter 20: page 713, Corbis-Bettmann; p. 729, Herbert H. Lamson Library, Plymouth State College, Plymouth, New Hampshire.

Chapter 22: page 833, AP/Wide World Photos; p. 845, UPI/Corbis-Bettmann; p. 871, Betty C. Keller; p. 875, UPI/Corbis-Bettmann.

Chapter 23: page 902, Gian Berto Vanni/Art Resource, NY; p. 904, Dimitrios Harissiadis/Benaki Museum, Athens, Photographic Archive; p. 906, Alinari/Art Resource, NY; p. 950, Richard Kalina; p. 953, Stock Montage, Inc./Historical Pictures Collection.

Chapter 24: page 1132, Corbis-Bettmann; p. 1142, William Morris Agency, Inc.

Chapter 25: page 1164, Corbis-Bettmann; p. 1219, AP/Wide World Photos; p. 1288, Friedman-Abeles Collection, New York Public Library at Lincoln Center.

Index of Authors, Titles, and First Lines

Author's names are printed in **bold** type, titles in *italic* type, and first lines in Roman type.

Afterword: Appendix II
English on the Internet:
Documenting Your Electronic Sources

This appendix provides general information for making electronic source citations, and therefore is intended to augment the section entitled "Documenting Your Work" in Chapter 32 of the text. For general information on citation recommendations by the Modern Language Association (MLA), see Joseph Gibaldi, MLA Handbook for Writers of Research Papers, 4th ed. (New York: MLA, 1995; briefly summarized on pages 1812-16 of the text). Because the available methods of obtaining electronic information are developing so rapidly, the printed style manuals have had difficulty keeping up with the changes. If you do a web search looking for information on these styles, chances are the information you discover will vary from site to site. Therefore, you need to know the basics which are required for the citation of your sources. When citing electronic sources, it is vital to type every letter, number, symbol, and space accurately. Recovery systems are unforgiving, and mistakes or omissions of any sort make it impossible to retrieve your source. Electronic sources are often transitory (and therefore unreliable), so printing a copy of any sources you plan to cite will make your citations both accurate and complete.

The style recommended by the MLA places angle brackets (< >) before and after Internet addresses and Uniform Resource Locators (URLs). If you see brackets around an address you want to use, do not use them as part of the address when you are seeking retrieval. Also, since a number of word-processing programs now support the use of italics, you can use either italics or underlines when needed. Each letter and symbol must be clearly identifiable, and italics may sometimes be ambiguous, so the use of underlines is generally more specific. {Angle brackets are not used currently in the system recommended by the American Psychological Association (APA); also, the APA prefers italics in the citation of addresses, whereas the MLA prefers the use of underlines. }

MLA Style Guidelines

The MLA has authorized guidelines for the citation of electronic sources. Many of these overlap with the MLA recommendations for printed sources, but to avoid ambiguity a number of recommendations bear repetition. Web sources are documented in basically the same style as printed sources. According to the MLA Web site,{Source: Modern Language Association (MLA), <http://www.mla.org/main.stl.htm> } the following items need to be included if they are available:

1. The name of the author, editor, compiler, or translator of the source (if available and relevant), reversed for alphabetizing [i.e., last name first], and followed by an abbreviation, such as ed., if appropriate.

2. The title of a poem, short story, article, or similar short work within a scholarly project, database, or periodical (in quotation marks); or title of a posting to a discussion list or forum (taken from the subject line and enclosed by quotation marks), followed by the description Online Posting.
3. The title of a book (underlined).
4. The name of the editor, compiler, or translator of the text (if relevant and if not cited earlier), preceded by the appropriate abbreviation, such as Ed.
5. Publication information for any printed version of the source.
6. The title of the scholarly project, database, periodical, or professional or personal site (underlined); or, for a professional or personal site with no title, a description such as Home Page.
7. The name of the editor of the scholarly project or database (if available).
8. The version number of the source (if not part of the title), or, for a journal, the volume number, issue number, or other identifying number.
9. The date of electronic publication, of the latest update, or of posting.
10. For a posting to a discussion list or forum, the name of the list or forum.
11. The number range or total number of pages, paragraphs, or other sections, if they are numbered.
12. The name of any institution or organization sponsoring or associated with the Web site.
13. The date when the researcher accessed the source.
14. The electronic address, or Uniform Resource Locator, of the source (in angle brackets [<>]).